MANAGERIAL STRATEGY

ETHICS TODAY

DIGITAL UPDATE

GLOBAL INSIGHT

BUSINESS LAW

TEXT AND CASES

Fourteenth Edition

Kenneth W. Clarkson

The University of Miami

Roger LeRoy Miller

Institute for University Studies
Arlington, Texas

Frank B. Cross

Herbert D. Kelleher
Centennial Professor in Business Law
University of Texas at Austin

Australia • Brazil • Mexico • Singapore • United Kingdom • United States

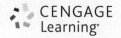

Business Law
TEXT AND CASES

Fourteenth Edition

Kenneth W. Clarkson
Roger LeRoy Miller
Frank B. Cross

**Vice President for Social Science
and Qualitative Business:** *Erin Joyner*

Product Director: *Jason Fremder*

Senior Product Manager: *Vicky True-Baker*

Managing Content Developer:
Suzanne Wilder

Content Developer: *Sarah Huber*

Product Assistant: *Christian Wood*

Marketing Director: *Kristen Hurd*

Marketing Manager: *Katie Jergens*

Marketing Coordinator: *Casey Binder*

Production Director: *Sharon Smith*

Senior Content Project Manager:
Ann Borman

Digital Content Specialist: *Charles Nichols*

Manufacturing Planner: *Kevin Kluck*

Senior Inventory Analyst: *Terina Bradley*

Senior IP Director: *Julie Geagan-Chavez*

IP Analyst: *Jennifer Nonenmacher*

IP Project Manager: *Reba Frederics*

Senior Art Director: *Michelle Kunkler*

Interior and Cover Designer:
Harasymczuk Design

Design Elements:
linen texture: Lisa-Blue/iStockphoto;
justice scales: imagedb.com/Shutterstock;
gavel: koosen/Shutterstock; media
network: solarseven/Shutterstock; building
windows: Nneirda/Shutterstock; puzzle
icon: Shebeko/Shutterstock; spotlight:
Ivan Lord/Shutterstock; ethics scale:
Lightspring/Shutterstock; magnifying
glass icon: sergign/Shutterstock; globe:
mj007/Shutterstock; compass: Taddeus/
Shutterstock; Insight Global globe:
evantravels/Shutterstock

> For product information and technology assistance, contact us at
> **Cengage Learning Customer & Sales Support,**
> **1-800-354-9706**
> For permission to use material from this text or product,
> submit all requests online at
> **www.cengage.com/permissions.**
> Further permissions questions can be emailed to
> **permissionrequest@cengage.com.**

Library of Congress Control Number: 2016952073

Student Edition ISBN: 978-1-305-96725-0

Cengage Learning
20 Channel Center Street
Boston, MA 02210
USA

Cengage Learning is a leading provider of customized learning solutions with employees residing in nearly 40 different countries and sales in more than 125 countries around the world. Find your local representative at **www.cengage.com.**

Cengage Learning products are represented in Canada by Nelson Education, Ltd.

To learn more about Cengage Learning Solutions, visit **www.cengage.com.**

Purchase any of our products at your local college store or at our preferred online store **www.cengagebrain.com.**

Printed in Canada
Print Number: 01   Print Year: 2016

Brief Contents

Contents

Concept Summaries

Exhibits

Preface

The study of business law and the legal environment of business has universal applicability. A student entering any field of business must have at least a passing understanding of business law in order to function in the real world. *Business Law,* Fourteenth Edition, provides the information that students need in an interesting and contemporary way.

Additionally, students preparing for a career in accounting, government and political science, economics, and even medicine can use much of the information they learn in a business law and legal environment course. In fact, every individual throughout his or her lifetime can benefit from knowledge of contracts, real property law, landlord-tenant relationships, and other business law topics. Consequently, we have fashioned this text as a useful "tool for living" for all of your students (including those taking the CPA exam).

For the Fourteenth Edition, we have spent a great deal of effort making this best-selling text more modern, exciting, and visually appealing than ever before. We have added more than forty new features, ninety-two new cases, and twenty-four new exhibits. The text also contains nearly two hundred new highlighted and numbered *Cases in Point* and *Examples,* and more than a hundred new case problems. Special pedagogical elements within the text focus on legal, ethical, global, and corporate issues while addressing core curriculum requirements.

Highlights of the Fourteenth Edition

Instructors have come to rely on the coverage, accuracy, and applicability of *Business Law.* To make sure that our text engages your students, solidifies their understanding of legal concepts, and provides the best teaching tools available, we now offer the following.

A Variety of New and Exciting Features

The Fourteenth Edition of *Business Law* is filled with many new features specifically designed to cover current legal topics of high interest. There are forty-one features in this edition, thirty-eight of which are new.

Each feature is related to a topic discussed in the text and ends with *Critical Thinking* or *Business Questions.* **Suggested answers to all the *Critical Thinking* and *Business Questions* are included in the *Solutions Manual for this text.***

1. ***Ethics Today*** These features focus on the ethical aspects of a topic discussed in the text to emphasize that ethics is an integral part of a business law course. Examples include:
   - *Stare Decisis* versus Spiderman (Chapter 1)
   - Forced Arbitration: Right or Wrong? (Chapter 15)
   - When Imported Beer Really Isn't Imported (Chapter 24)
   - Should There Be More Relief for Student Loan Defaults? (Chapter 31)
   - Is It Fair to Classify Uber and Lyft Drivers as Independent Contractors? (Chapter 32)

2. ***Global Insight*** These features illustrate how other nations deal with specific legal concepts to give students a sense of the global legal environment. Subjects include:
   - Islamic Law and *Respondeat Superior* (Chapter 33)
   - Does Cloud Computing Have a Nationality? (Chapter 39)
   - Anti-Bribery Charges Take Their Toll on U.S. and Foreign Corporations (Chapter 40)

3. **NEW *Digital Update*** These features are designed to examine cutting-edge cyberlaw topics, such as the following:
   - Using Social Media for Service of Process (Chapter 3)
   - Should Employees Have a "Right of Disconnecting"? (Chapter 5)
   - Revenge Porn and Invasion of Privacy (Chapter 6)
   - Monitoring Employees' Social Media—Right or Wrong? (Chapter 9)
   - Hiring Discrimination Based on Social Media Posts (Chapter 35)

4. ***Managerial Strategy*** These features emphasize the management aspects of business law and the legal environment. Topics include:
   - Should You Consent to Have Your Business Case Decided by a U.S. Magistrate Judge? (Chapter 2)
   - Marriage Equality and the Constitution (Chapter 4)

- When Is a Warning Legally Bulletproof? (Chapter 7)
- The Criminalization of American Business (Chapter 10)
- Commercial Use of Drones (Chapter 21)
- The SEC's New CEO Pay-Ratio Disclosure Rule (Chapter 42)

Entire Chapter on Internet Law, Social Media, And Privacy

For the Fourteenth Edition, we include a whole chapter (Chapter 9) on *Internet Law, Social Media, and Privacy.* Social media have entered the mainstream and become a part of everyday life for many businesspersons. In this special chapter, we give particular emphasis to the legal issues surrounding the Internet, social media, and privacy. We also recognize this trend throughout the text by incorporating the Internet and social media as they relate to the topics under discussion.

New Coverage of Topics on the Revised 2017 CPA Exam

In 2016, the American Institute of CPAs (AICPA) issued its final report on "Maintaining the Relevance of the Uniform CPA Exam." In addition to more focus on critical thinking, authentic applications, and problem solving, the content of the exam will change to an extent.

The Fourteenth Edition of *Business Law* incorporates information on the new topics on the CPA exam, specifically addressing the following:

- Agency law (worker classification and duties of principals and agents)
- Employment law (Affordable Care Act)
- Business organizations (corporate governance issues, including Sarbanes-Oxley compliance and criminal liability for organizations and management)

In addition, the Fourteenth Edition continues to cover topics that are essential to new CPAs who are working with sophisticated business clients, regardless of whether the CPA exam covers these topics. We recognize that today's business leaders must often think "outside the box" when making business decisions. For this reason, we strongly emphasize business and critical thinking elements throughout the text. We have carefully chosen cases, features, and problems that are relevant to business operations. Almost all of the features and cases conclude with some type of critical thinking

question. For those teaching future CPAs, this is consistent with the new CPA exam's focus on higher-order skills, such as critical thinking and problem solving.

Highlighted and Numbered *Examples* and *Case in Point* Illustrations

Many instructors use cases and examples to illustrate how the law applies to business. Students understand legal concepts better in the context of their real-world application. Therefore, for this edition of *Business Law,* we have expanded the number of highlighted numbered *Examples* and *Cases in Point* in every chapter. We have added 137 new *Cases in Point* and 52 new *Examples.*

Examples illustrate how the law applies in a specific situation. *Cases in Point* present the facts and issues of an actual case and then describe the court's decision and rationale. These two features are uniquely designed and consecutively numbered throughout each chapter for easy reference. The *Examples* and *Cases in Point* are integrated throughout the text to help students better understand how courts apply legal principles in the real world.

New Unit-Ending *Application and Ethics* Features

For the Fourteenth Edition, we have created an entirely new feature that concludes each of the ten units in the text. Each of these *Application and Ethics* features provides additional analysis on a topic related to that unit and explores its ethics ramifications. Each of the features ends with two questions—a *Critical Thinking* and an *Ethics Question.* Some topics covered by these features include the following:

- The Biggest Data Breach of All Time (Unit 2)
- Fantasy Sports—Legal Gambling? (Unit 3)
- Virtual Currency—Is It Safe? (Unit 5)
- Health Insurance and Small Business (Unit 7)

Suggested answers to the questions in *Application and Ethics* features are included in the *Solutions Manual* for this text.

New Cases and Case Problems

For the Fourteenth Edition of *Business Law,* we have added 92 new cases and 111 new case problems, most from 2016 and 2015. The new cases and problems have been carefully selected to illustrate important points of law and to be of high interest to students and instructors.

We have made it a point to find recent cases that enhance learning and are relatively easy to understand.

1. **Spotlight Cases and Classic Cases.** Certain cases and case problems that are exceptionally good teaching cases are labeled as *Spotlight Cases* and *Spotlight Case Problems*. Examples include *Spotlight on Amazon, Spotlight on Beer Labels, Spotlight on Gucci, Spotlight on Nike,* and *Spotlight on the Seattle Mariners*. Instructors will find these *Spotlight Cases* useful to illustrate the legal concepts under discussion, and students will enjoy studying the cases because they involve interesting and memorable facts. Other cases have been chosen as *Classic Cases* because they establish a legal precedent in a particular area of law.

2. **Critical Thinking Section.** Each case concludes with a *Critical Thinking* section, which normally includes two questions. The questions may address *Legal Environment, E-Commerce, Economic, Environmental, Ethical, Global, Political,* or *Technological* issues, or they may ask *What If the Facts Were Different?* Each *Classic Case* has a section titled *Impact of This Case on Today's Law* and one *Critical Thinking* question.

3. **Longer Excerpts for Case Analysis.** We have also included one longer case excerpt in every chapter—labeled *Case Analysis*—followed by three *Legal Reasoning Questions*. The questions are designed to guide students' analysis of the case and build their legal reasoning skills. These *Case Analysis* cases may be used for case-briefing assignments and are also tied to the *Special Case Analysis* questions found in every unit of the text (one per unit).

Suggested answers to all case-ending questions and case problems are included in the *Solutions Manual* for this text.

Business Case Problem with Sample Answer in Each Chapter

In response to those instructors who would like students to have sample answers available for some of the questions and case problems, we include a *Business Case Problem* with *Sample Answer* in each chapter. The *Business Case Problem with Sample Answer* is based on an actual case, and students can find a sample answer at the end of the text. **Suggested answers to the *Business Case Problems with Sample Answers* are provided in Appendix E at the end of the text and in the *Solutions Manual* for this text.**

New Exhibits and Concept Summaries

For this edition, we have spent considerable effort reworking and redesigning all of the exhibits and concept summaries in the text to achieve better clarity and more visual appeal. In addition, we have added twenty-four new exhibits and four new concept summaries.

Special Case Analysis Questions

For one chapter in every unit of the text, we provide a *Special Case Analysis* question that is based on the *Case Analysis* excerpt in that chapter. These special questions appear in the *Business Case Problems* at the ends of selected chapters.

The *Special Case Analysis* questions are designed to build students' analytical skills. They test students' ability to perform IRAC (Issue, Rule, Application, and Conclusion) case analysis. Students must identify the legal issue presented in the chapter's *Case Analysis Case,* understand the rule of law, determine how the rule applies to the facts of the case, and describe the court's conclusion. Instructors can assign these questions as homework or use them in class to elicit student participation and teach case analysis. **Suggested answers to the *Special Case Analysis* questions can be found in the *Solutions Manual* for this text.**

Reviewing Features in Every Chapter

In the Fourteenth Edition of *Business Law,* we continue to offer a *Reviewing* feature at the end of every chapter to help solidify students' understanding of the chapter materials. Each *Reviewing* feature presents a hypothetical scenario and then asks a series of questions that require students to identify the issues and apply the legal concepts discussed in the chapter.

These features are designed to help students review the chapter topics in a simple and interesting way and see how the legal principles discussed in the chapter affect the world in which they live. An instructor can use these features as the basis for in-class discussion or encourage students to use them for self-study prior to completing homework assignments. **Suggested answers to the questions posed in the *Reviewing* features can be found in the *Solutions Manual* for this text.**

Two *Issue Spotters*

At the conclusion of each chapter, we have included a special section with two *Issue Spotters* related to the chapter's topics. These questions facilitate student learning and review of the chapter materials. **Suggested answers to the *Issue Spotters* in every chapter are provided in Appendix D at the end of the text and in the *Solutions Manual* for this text.**

Legal Reasoning Group Activities

For instructors who want their students to engage in group projects, each chapter of the Fourteenth Edition includes a special *Legal Reasoning Group Activity.* Each activity begins by describing a business scenario and then poses several specific questions pertaining to the scenario. Each question is to be answered by a different group of students based on the information in the chapter. These projects may be used in class to spur discussion or as homework assignments. **Suggested answers to the *Legal Reasoning Group Activities* are included in the *Solutions Manual* for this text.**

Supplements/Digital Learning Systems

Business Law, Fourteenth Edition, provides a comprehensive supplements package designed to make the tasks of teaching and learning more enjoyable and efficient. The following supplements and exciting new digital products are offered in conjunction with the text.

MindTap

MindTap for *Business Law,* Fourteenth Edition, is a fully online, highly personalized learning experience built upon Cengage Learning content. MindTap combines student learning tools—such as readings, multimedia, activities, and assessments from CengageNOW—into a singular Learning Path that intuitively guides students through their course.

Instructors can personalize the experience by customizing authoritative Cengage Learning content and learning tools. MindTap offers instructors the ability to add their own content in the Learning Path with apps that integrate into the MindTap framework seamlessly with Learning Management Systems (LMS).

MindTap includes:

- **An Interactive book with Whiteboard Videos and Interactive Cases.**
- **Automatically graded homework** with the following consistent question types:

- **Worksheets**—Interactive Worksheets prepare students for class by ensuring reading and comprehension.
- **Video Activities**—Real-world video exercises make business law engaging and relevant.
- **Brief Hypotheticals**—These applications provide students practice in spotting the issue and applying the law in the context of a short, factual scenario.
- **Case Problem Analyses**—These promote deeper critical thinking and legal reasoning by guiding students step-by-step through a case problem and then adding in a critical thinking section based on "What If the Facts Were Different?" These now include a third section, a writing component, which requires students to demonstrate their ability to forecast the legal implications of real-world business scenarios.
- **Personalized Student Plan with multimedia study tools and videos.**
- **New Adaptive Test Prep** helps students study for exams.
- **Test Bank.**
- **Reporting and Assessment options.**

By using the MindTap system, students can complete the assignments online and can receive instant feedback on their answers. Instructors can utilize MindTap to upload their course syllabi, create and customize homework assignments, and keep track of their students' progress. By hiding, rearranging, or adding content, instructors control what students see and when they see it to match the Learning Path to their course syllabus exactly. Instructors can also communicate with their students about assignments and due dates, and create reports summarizing the data for an individual student or for the whole class.

Cengage Learning Testing Powered by Cognero

Cengage Learning Testing Powered by Cognero is a flexible, online system that allows you to do the following:

- Author, edit, and manage *Test Bank* content from multiple Cengage Learning solutions.
- Create multiple test versions in an instant.
- Deliver tests from your LMS, your classroom, or wherever you want.

Start Right Away! *Cengage Learning Testing Powered by Cognero* works on any operating system or browser.

- No special installs or downloads are needed.
- Create tests from school, home, the coffee shop—anywhere with Internet access.

What Will You Find?

- *Simplicity at every step.* A desktop-inspired interface features drop-down menus and familiar intuitive tools that take you through content creation and management with ease.
- *Full-featured test generator.* Create ideal assessments with your choice of fifteen question types—including true/false, multiple choice, opinion scale/Likert, and essay). Multi-language support, an equation editor, and unlimited metadata help ensure your tests are complete and compliant.
- *Cross-compatible capability.* Import and export content to and from other systems.

Instructor's Companion Web Site

The Web site for the Fourteenth Edition of *Business Law* can be found by going to www.cengagebrain.com and entering ISBN 9781305967250. The Instructor's Companion Web Site contains the following supplements:

- ***Instructor's Manual.*** Includes sections entitled "Additional Cases Addressing This Issue" at the end of selected case synopses.
- ***Solutions Manual.*** Provides answers to all questions presented in the text, including the questions in each case and feature, the *Issue Spotters,* the *Business Scenarios* and *Case Problems,* and the unit-ending features.
- ***Test Bank.*** A comprehensive test bank that contains multiple-choice, true/false, and short essay questions.
- ***Case-Problem Cases.***
- ***Case Printouts.***
- ***PowerPoint Slides.***
- ***Lecture Outlines.***

Complete Series of *Business Law* Texts

We also want instructors to know that there is now an entire family of derivative texts based on the *Business Law*

materials for instructors wishing to customize the text for their purposes. (See www.cengagebrain.com or your local sales representative for more information on the entire series of *Business Law* texts.) The series includes:

- ***Business Law: Text and Cases: The First Course*** Includes the first twenty-four chapters of *Business Law,* plus four chapters on agency and employment and four chapters on business organizations.
- ***Business Law: Text and Cases: The First Course—Summarized Case Edition*** Includes the same chapters as *The First Course* (above), except that the cases are presented in a summarized format and do not contain excerpts from the court's decision.
- ***Business Law: Text and Cases: An Accelerated Course*** Includes a total of nineteen chapters, seven of which combine materials from two chapters in *Business Law.* This text provides a brief version of the core content suitable for a one-semester course.
- ***Business Law: Text and Cases: Commercial Law for Accountants*** This exciting text is tailor-made for those entering the field of accounting and includes topics from *Business Law* that accountants need to know. The text focuses on the basics of business law for accountants—including subjects on the revised 2017 CPA exam. It has a strong emphasis on business organizations, securities law and corporate governance, agency and employment, sales and lease contracts, creditors' rights and bankruptcy, professional liability, government regulation, and property.

For Users of the Thirteenth Edition

First of all, we want to thank you for helping make *Business Law* the best-selling business law text in America today. Second, we want to make you aware of the numerous additions and changes that we have made in this edition—many in response to comments from reviewers.

Every chapter of the Fourteenth Edition has been revised as necessary to incorporate new developments in the law or to streamline the presentations. Other major changes and additions for this edition include the following:

- Chapter 4 (Business and the Constitution)—The chapter has been revised and updated to be more business oriented. It has two new cases, four new *Cases in Point,* a new exhibit, and three new case problems. A *Managerial Strategy* feature on marriage equality and the constitution discusses United States Supreme Court decisions on this issue.

- Chapter 5 (Business Ethics)—This chapter contains two new cases, two new *Issue Spotters,* three new *Cases in Point* (including a case involving Tom Brady's suspension from the NFL as a result of "deflategate"), and three new case problems. The chapter includes a section on business ethics and social media, and discusses stakeholders and corporate social responsibility. The chapter also provides step-by-step guidance on making ethical business decisions and includes materials on global business ethics. A new *Digital Update* feature examines whether employees should have the right to disconnect from their electronic devices after work hours.

- Chapter 8 (Intellectual Property Rights)—The materials on intellectual property rights have been thoroughly revised and updated to reflect the most current laws and trends. The 2016 case involves the Hustler Club and a trademark infringement claim between brothers. A *Digital Update* feature examines the problem of patent trolls. There are eleven new *Cases in Point,* including cases involving FedEx's color and logo, Google's digitalization of books, and how the Sherlock Holmes copyright fell into the public domain.

- Chapter 9 (Internet Law, Social Media, and Privacy)—This chapter, which was new to the last edition and covers legal issues that are unique to the Internet, has been thoroughly revised and updated for the Fourteenth Edition. It includes a new section on cyberstalking, two new cases, and a new *Digital Update* feature on whether employers can monitor employees' social media use.

- Chapter 10 (Criminal Law and Cyber Crime)—This chapter includes three new cases, five new *Cases in Point,* three new examples, and four new case problems. A new *Managerial Strategy* feature discusses the criminalization of American business.

- Chapters 11 through 19 (the Contracts and E-Contracts unit)—In this unit, we have added fifteen new cases (including a *Spotlight Case* and several *Case Analysis* cases), twenty-four new *Cases in Point,* nine new *Examples,* and nineteen new case problems. We have also added new exhibits, graphic concept summaries, numbered lists, a new

Reviewing feature, and a new *Managerial Strategy* on the commercial use of drones. These updates clarify and enhance our already superb contract law coverage.

- Chapters 20 through 23 (the first three chapters in the Domestic and International Sales and Lease Contracts unit)—We have streamlined and simplified our coverage of the Uniform Commercial Code and added six new cases (including a 2016 *Spotlight Case*). We have added fifteen new *Cases in Point* and five new *Examples* in these chapters to increase student comprehension. New exhibits, new business scenarios, and many new case problems have also been added.

- Chapter 24 (International and Space Law)—The last chapter in the unit on Domestic and International Sales and Lease Contracts has been expanded to include a new section on space law—international and domestic. All three cases presented are new to this edition, including a *Spotlight Case* on a United States Supreme Court decision concerning the Alien Tort Claims Act. The chapter also now covers the Trans-Pacific Partnership (TPP) and includes an *Ethics Today* feature on the domestic brewing of imported beer brands.

- Chapter 28 (Banking in the Digital Age)—We have updated this entire chapter to reflect the realities of banking in today's digital world. All three cases are new and recent. There are three new *Cases in Point,* a new *Issue Spotter,* and three new case problems. A new *Digital Update* feature explains how electronic payment systems are reducing the use of checks.

- Chapters 29 through 31 (the Creditors' Rights and Bankruptcy unit)—This unit has been revised to be more up to date and comprehensible. Each chapter in the unit has two new cases and a new feature. We have also streamlined the materials to focus on those concepts that students need to know. We have added new exhibits, concept summaries, key terms, *Examples,* and *Cases in Point* to better clarify concepts. Chapter 30 (Secured Transactions) was substantially reworked to clarify the general principles and exceptions. Chapter 31 (Bankruptcy Law) includes updated dollar amounts of various provisions of the Bankruptcy Code, six new *Cases in Point,* and an *Ethics Today* feature on whether there should be more relief for student loan debt.

- Chapter 32 (Agency Formation and Duties) and Chapter 33 (Agency Liability and Termination)—These two chapters have been updated to reflect the realities of the gig economy in which many people are working as independent contractors. A new *Ethics Today* feature continues that emphasis with a discussion of whether Uber and Lyft drivers should be considered employees rather than independent contractors. There is also a new *Global Insight* feature in Chapter 33 concerning Islamic law and *respondeat superior.* In addition, new *Examples, Cases in Point,* and case problems have been added to help students comprehend the important issues and liability in agency relationships.

- Chapter 34 (Employment, Immigration, and Labor Law) and Chapter 35 (Employment Discrimination)—These two chapters covering employment law have been thoroughly updated to include discussions of legal issues facing employers today. Chapter 34 has three new cases, three new *Cases in Point,* three new *Examples* (including one involving wage claims of Oakland Raiders cheerleaders), and three new case problems. We have added two new features—an *Ethics Today* on whether employees should receive paid bathroom breaks and a *Managerial Strategy* on union organizing using company e-mail systems. Chapter 35 has a new section discussing discrimination based on military status and new coverage of same-sex discrimination and discrimination against transgender persons. All three cases are new. There are seven new *Cases in Point,* five new *Examples,* a new exhibit, and three new case problems. A *Digital Update* feature discusses hiring discrimination based on social media posts. We discuss relevant United States Supreme Court decisions affecting employment issues throughout both chapters.

- Chapters 36 through 42 (the Business Organizations unit)—This unit has been revised and updated to improve flow and clarity. We provide more practical information and recent examples.

We start with small business forms, go on to partnerships, and then cover limited liability companies. We discuss corporations in Chapters 39 through 42. There are thirteen new cases in this unit and nineteen new *Cases in Point.* Five of the six chapters in the unit include new features. For instance, in Chapter 39, a *Global Insight* feature examines whether cloud computing has a nationality. We also discuss crowdfunding and venture capital in that chapter. We have added new exhibits and key terms throughout this unit as well. In the chapter on securities law (Chapter 42), we have updated the materials on Regulation A offerings because the cap went from 5 million to 50 million in 2015. We also discuss how to deal with the SEC's new CEO pay-ratio rule in a *Managerial Strategy* feature.

- Chapter 43 through 47 (the Government Regulation unit)—This unit has been streamlined, updated, and simplified. There are eleven new cases and four new features. Chapter 44 (Consumer Law) and Chapter 46 (Antitrust Law) include all new cases, and both have been significantly updated with new coverage, *Examples,* and *Cases in Point.* A *Digital Update* in Chapter 44 deals with "native" ads on the Internet, and a *Digital Update* in Chapter 46 discusses the European Union's antitrust complaint against Google.

- Chapter 48 (Personal Property and Bailments) and Chapter 49 (Real Property and Landlord-Tenant Law)—We have rearranged the materials in the property chapters somewhat and now cover fixtures in the real property chapter. Each chapter includes two new cases as well as a *Classic Case* or *Spotlight Case.* There are six new *Examples,* seven new *Cases in Point,* two new exhibits, and seven new case problems in these two chapters. Both chapters also include new features (an *Ethics Today* and a *Digital Update*).

Acknowledgments for Previous Editions

Since we began this project many years ago, a sizable number of business law professors and others have helped us in revising the book, including the following:

Jeffrey E. Allen
University of Miami

Judith Anshin
Sacramento City College

Thomas M. Apke
California State University, Fullerton

Raymond August
Washington State University

William Auslen
San Francisco City College

Mary B. Bader
Moorhead State University

Frank Bagan
County College of Morris

John J. Balek
Morton College, Illinois

Michael G. Barth
University of Phoenix

David L. Baumer
North Carolina State University

Barbara E. Behr
Bloomsburg University of Pennsylvania

Robert B. Bennett, Jr.
Butler University

Robert C. Bird
University of Connecticut

Heidi Boerstler
University of Colorado at Denver

Maria Kathleen Boss
California State University, Los Angeles

Lawrence J. Bradley
University of Notre Dame

Dean Bredeson
University of Texas at Austin

Kylar William Broadus, Esq.
Lincoln University in Missouri

Doug Brown
Montana State University

Kristi K. Brown
University of Texas at Austin

Elizabeth K. Brunn, Esq.
University of Baltimore; University of Maryland University College

William J. Burke
University of Massachusetts, Lowell

Kenneth Burns
University of Miami

Daniel R. Cahoy
Pennsylvania State University

Rita Cain
University of Missouri—Kansas City

Jeanne A. Calderon
New York University

Joseph E. Cantrell
DeAnza College, California

Donald Cantwell
University of Texas at Arlington

Arthur J. Casey
San Jose State University, College of Business, Organization and Management

Thomas D. Cavenagh
North Central College—Naperville, Illinois

Robert Chatov
State University of New York, Buffalo

Corey Ciocchetti
University of Denver

Nanette C. Clinch
San Jose State University, California

Robert J. Cox
Salt Lake Community College

Thomas Crane
University of Miami

Angela Crossin
Purdue University, Calumet

Kenneth S. Culott
University of Texas at Austin

Larry R. Curtis
Iowa State University

Richard Dalebout
Brigham Young University

William H. Daughtrey, Jr.
Virginia Commonwealth University

Michael DeAngelis
University of Rhode Island

James Doering
University of Wisconsin, Green Bay

John V. Dowdy
University of Texas at Arlington

Michele A. Dunkerley
University of Texas at Austin

Julia M. Dunlap, Esq.
University of California, San Diego

Paul Dusseault
Herkimer Community College (SUNY)

Maria Elena Ellison
Florida Atlantic University

Nena Ellison
Florida Atlantic University

O. E. Elmore
Texas A&M University

Robert J. Enders
California State Polytechnic University, Pomona

Michael Engber
Ball State University

David A. Escamilla
University of Texas at Austin

Denise M. Farag
Linfield College

James S. Fargason
Louisiana State University

Frank S. Forbes
University of Nebraska at Omaha

Joe W. Fowler
Oklahoma State University

Stanley G. Freeman
University of South Carolina

Joan Gabel
Florida State University

Christ Gaetanos
State University of New York, Fredonia

Chester S. Galloway
Auburn University

Bob Garrett
American River College, California

Gary L. Giese
University of Colorado at Denver

Thomas Gossman
Western Michigan University

John D. Grigsby
Pennsylvania College of Technology

Dr. J. Keaton Grubbs
Stephen F. Austin State University

Patrick O. Gudridge
University of Miami School of Law

Paul Guymon
William Rainey Harper College

Jacqueline Hagerott
Franklin University

James M. Haine
University of Wisconsin, Stevens Point

Gerard Halpern
University of Arkansas

Christopher L. Hamilton
Golden West College, California

JoAnn W. Hammer
University of Texas at Austin

Charles Hartman
Wright State University, Ohio

Richard A. Hausler
University of Miami School of Law

Harry E. Hicks
Butler University, Indianapolis

Janine S. Hiller
Virginia Polytechnic Institute and State University

Rebecca L. Hillyer
Chemeketa Community College

E. Clayton Hipp, Jr.
Clemson University

Anthony H. Holliday, Jr.
Howard University

Telford Hollman
University of Northern Iowa

June A. Horrigan
California State University, Sacramento

John P. Huggard
North Carolina State University

Terry Hutchins
Pembroke State University, North Carolina

Robert Jesperson
University of Houston

Debra M. Johnson
Montana State University—Billings

Bryce J. Jones
Northeast Missouri State University

Margaret Jones
Southwest Missouri State College

Peter A. Karl III
SUNY Institute of Technology at Utica

Jack E. Karns
East Carolina University

Anne E. Kastle
Edmonds Community College

Tamra Kempf
University of Miami

Judith Kenney
University of Miami

Barbara Kincaid
Southern Methodist University

Carey Kirk
University of Northern Iowa

Nancy P. Klintworth
University of Central Florida

Kurtis P. Klumb
University of Wisconsin at Milwaukee

Kathleen M. Knutson
College of St. Catherine, St. Paul, Minnesota

Lisa Quinn Knych
Syracuse University, Whitman School of Management

Peter Kwiatkowski, Esq.
Baldwin Wallace University

Meg Costello Lambert
Oakland Community College— Auburn Hills Campus

Vonda M. Laughlin
Carson-Newman College

M. Alan Lawson
Mt. San Antonio College

Leslie E. Lenn
St. Edwards University

Susan Liebeler
Loyola University

Robert B. Long
Oakland Community College

Stuart MacDonald
University of Central Oklahoma

Thomas E. Maher
California State University, Fullerton

Sal Marchionna
Triton College, Illinois

Gene A. Marsh
University of Alabama

Michael Martin, J.D., M.B.A., LL.M.
University of Northern Colorado, Monfort College of Business

Karen Kay Matson
University of Texas at Austin

Woodrow J. Maxwell
Hudson Valley Community College, New York

Bruce E. May
University of South Dakota

Diane May
Winona State University, Minnesota

Gail McCracken
University of Michigan, Dearborn

John W. McGee
Southwest Texas State University

Cotton Meagher
University of Nevada at Las Vegas

Christopher Meakin
University of Texas at Austin

Roger E. Meiners
University of Texas at Arlington

Gerald S. Meisel
Bergen Community College, New Jersey

Jennifer Merton, J.D.
University of Massachusetts at Amherst

Richard Mills
Cypress College

David Minars
City University of New York, Brooklyn

Leo Moersen
The George Washington University

Alan Moggio
Illinois Central College

Violet E. Molnar
Riverside City College

James E. Moon
Meyer, Johnson & Moon, Minneapolis

Melinda Ann Mora
University of Texas at Austin

Bob Morgan
Eastern Michigan University

Barry S. Morinaka
Baker College—Michigan

Melanie Morris
Raritan Valley Community College

Joan Ann Mrava
Los Angeles Southwest College

Dwight D. Murphey
Wichita State University

Daniel E. Murray
University of Miami School of Law

Paula C. Murray
University of Texas

Gregory J. Naples
Marquette University

George A. Nation III
Lehigh University

Caleb L. Nichols
Western Connecticut State University

John M. Norwood
University of Arkansas

Jamie O'Brien
University of Notre Dame

Dr. Kelly E. O'Donnell, J.C.D
*California Lutheran University,
Thousand Oaks, California*

Michael J. O'Hara
University of Nebraska at Omaha

Rick F. Orsinger
College of DuPage, Illinois

Daniel J. O'Shea
Hillsborough Community College

Thomas L. Palmer
Northern Arizona University

Charles M. Patten
University of Wisconsin, Oshkosh

Patricia Pattison
Texas State University, San Marcos

Peyton J. Paxson
University of Texas at Austin

Carlton Perkins
Texas Southern University

Darren A. Prum
The Florida State University

Ralph L. Quinones
University of Wisconsin, Oshkosh

Carol D. Rasnic
Virginia Commonwealth University

Marvin H. Robertson
Harding University

Bert K. Robinson
Kennesaw State University

Norberto Ruiz
Chabot College

Gary K. Sambol
Rutgers State University

Rudy Sandoval
University of Texas, San Antonio

Sidney S. Sappington
York College of Pennsylvania

Martha Sartoris
North Hennepin Community College

Barbara P. Scheller
Temple University

S. Alan Schlact
Kennesaw State University, Georgia

Lorne H. Seidman
University of Nevada at Las Vegas

Ira Selkowitz
University of Colorado at Denver

Roscoe B. Shain
Austin Peay University

Bennett D. Shulman
Lansing Community College, Michigan

S. Jay Sklar
Temple University

Dana Blair Smith
University of Texas at Austin

Michael Smydra
Oakland Community College—Royal Oak

Arthur Southwick
University of Michigan

Sylvia A. Spade
University of Texas at Austin

John A. Sparks
Grove City College, Pennsylvania

Robert D. Sprague
University of Wyoming

Elisabeth Sperow
*California Polytechnic University, San
Luis Obispo*

Brenda Steuer
North Harris College, Houston

Craig Stilwell
Michigan State University

Irwin Stotsky
University of Miami School of Law

Larry Strate
University of Nevada at Las Vegas

Charles R. B. Stowe
Sam Houston State University

Raymond Mason Taylor
North Carolina State University

Thomas F. Taylor
Campbell University

Ray Teske
University of Texas at San Antonio

H. Allan Tolbert
Central Texas College

Jesse C. Trentadue
University of North Dakota

Edwin Tucker
University of Connecticut

Gary Victor
Eastern Michigan University

William H. Volz
Wayne State University

David Vyncke
Scott Community College, Iowa

William H. Walker,
*Indiana University–Purdue University,
Fort Wayne*

Diana Walsh
County College of Morris

Robert J. Walter
University of Texas at El Paso

Gary Watson
California State University, Los Angeles

Katherine Hannan Wears, J.D.
Clarkson University School of Business

John L. Weimer
Nicholls State University, Louisiana

Marshall Wilkerson
University of Texas at Austin

Melanie Stallings Williams
California State University—Northridge

Arthur D. Wolfe
Michigan State University

Elizabeth A. Wolfe
University of Texas at Austin

Daniel R. Wrentmore
Santa Barbara City College

Eric D. Yordy
Northern Arizona University

Norman Gregory Young
*California State Polytechnic University,
Pomona*

Ronald C. Young
*Kalamazoo Valley Community College,
Michigan*

Bob Zaffram
*Erie Community College, Buffalo,
New York*

As in all past editions, we owe a debt of extreme gratitude to the numerous individuals who worked directly with us or at Cengage Learning. In particular, we wish to thank Vicky True-Baker, senior product manager; Jason Fremder, product director; Suzanne Wilder, managing content developer; Sarah Huber, content developer; and Ann Borman, senior content project manager. We also thank Katie Jergens in marketing and Michelle Kunkler, art director. We are indebted as well to the staff at Lachina, our compositor, for accurately generating pages for this text and making it possible for us to meet our ambitious printing schedule.

We especially wish to thank Katherine Marie Silsbee for her management of the entire project, as well as for the application of her superb research and editorial skills. We also wish to thank William Eric Hollowell, who co-authored the *Instructor's Manual* and the *Test Bank,* for his excellent research efforts. We were fortunate enough to have the copyediting of Beverly Peavler and the proofreading services of Jeanne Yost. We are grateful for the efforts of Vickie Reierson and Roxanna Lee for their proofreading and other assistance, which helped to ensure an error-free text. Finally, we thank Suzanne Jasin of K & M Consulting for her many special efforts on this project.

Through the years, we have enjoyed an ongoing correspondence with many of you who have found points on which you wish to comment. We continue to welcome all comments and promise to respond promptly. By incorporating your ideas, we can continue to write a business law text that is best for you and best for your students.

K.S.C.
R.L.M.
F.B.C.

To Philip,

*You are just like
your wine cellar—
aging very well.*

R.L.M.

To my parents and sisters.

F.B.C.

The Legal Environment of Business

CHAPTER 1

Law and Legal Reasoning

One of the most important functions of law in any society is to provide stability, predictability, and continuity so that people can know how to order their affairs. If any society is to survive, its citizens must be able to determine what is legally right and legally wrong. They must know what sanctions will be imposed on them if they commit wrongful acts. If they suffer harm as a result of others' wrongful acts, they must know how they can seek compensation. By setting forth the rights, obligations, and privileges of citizens, the law enables individuals to go about their business with confidence and a certain degree of predictability.

Although law has various definitions, they all are based on the general observation that **law** consists of *enforceable rules governing relationships among individuals and between individuals and their society.* These "enforceable rules" may consist of unwritten principles of behavior established by a nomadic tribe. They may be set forth in a law code, such as the Code of Hammurabi in ancient Babylon (c. 1780 B.C.E.) or the law code of one of today's European nations. They may consist of written laws and court decisions created by modern legislative and judicial bodies, as in the United States. Regardless of how such rules are created, they all have one thing in common: they establish rights, duties, and privileges that are consistent with the values and beliefs of their society or its ruling group.

In this introductory chapter, we first look at an important question for any student reading this text: How does the legal environment affect business decision making? We next describe the major sources of American law, the common law tradition, and some basic schools of legal thought. We conclude the chapter with sections offering practical guidance on several topics, including how to find the sources of law discussed in this chapter (and referred to throughout the text) and how to read and understand court opinions.

1–1 Business Activities and the Legal Environment

Laws and government regulations affect almost all business activities—from hiring and firing decisions to workplace safety, the manufacturing and marketing of products, business financing, and more. To make good business decisions, a basic knowledge of the laws and regulations governing these activities is beneficial—if not essential.

Realize also that in today's business world, a knowledge of "black-letter" law and what conduct can lead to legal **liability** is not enough. Businesspersons must develop critical thinking and legal reasoning skills so that they can evaluate how various laws might apply to a given situation and determine the best course of action. Businesspersons are also expected to make ethical decisions. Thus, the study of business law necessarily involves an ethical dimension.

1–1a Many Different Laws May Affect a Single Business Decision

As you will note, each chapter in this text covers specific areas of the law and shows how the legal rules in each area affect business activities. Although compartmentalizing the law in this fashion promotes conceptual clarity, it does not indicate the extent to which a number of different laws may apply to just one decision. Exhibit 1–1 illustrates the various areas of the law that may influence business decision making.

■ **EXAMPLE 1.1** When Mark Zuckerberg started Facebook as a Harvard student, he probably did not imagine all the legal challenges his company would face as a result of his business decisions.

- Shortly after Facebook was launched, others claimed that Zuckerberg had stolen their ideas for a social networking site. Their claims involved alleged theft of intellectual property, fraudulent misrepresentation, and

EXHIBIT 1–1 Areas of the Law That Can Affect Business Decision Making

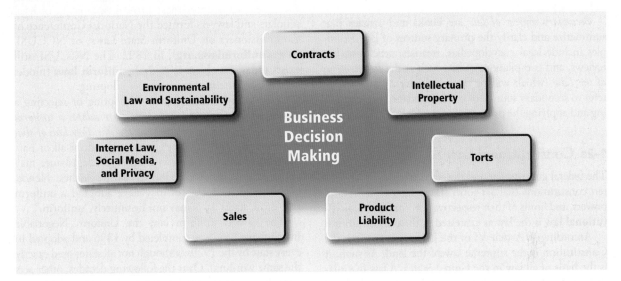

violations of partnership law and securities law. Facebook ultimately paid $65 million to settle those claims out of court.

- Facebook has been sued repeatedly for violating users' privacy (and federal laws) by tracking their Web site usage and by scanning private messages for purposes of data mining and user profiling. A class-action suit filed in Europe alleges that Facebook's data-use policies violate the law of the European Union. Facebook might have to pay millions in damages in this case.
- Facebook's business decisions have also come under scrutiny by federal regulators, such as the Federal Trade Commission (FTC). The company settled a complaint filed by the FTC alleging that Facebook had failed to keep "friends" lists and other user information private. ∎

1–1b Ethics and Business Decision Making

Merely knowing the areas of law that may affect a business decision is not sufficient in today's business world. Today, business decision makers need to consider not just whether a decision is legal, but also whether it is ethical.

Ethics generally is defined as the principles governing what constitutes right or wrong behavior. Often, as in several of the claims against Facebook discussed above, disputes arise in business because one party feels that he or she has been treated unfairly. Thus, the underlying reason for bringing some lawsuits is a breach of ethical duties (such as when a partner or employee attempts to secretly take advantage of a business opportunity).

Throughout this text, you will learn about the relationship between the law and ethics, as well as about some of the types of ethical questions that arise in business. For instance, all of the new unit-ending *Unit Application and Ethics* features include an *Ethical Connection* section that explores the ethical dimensions of a topic treated within the unit. We have also included *Ethical Questions* for each unit, as well as within the critical thinking sections of many of the cases presented in this text. *Ethics Today* features, which focus on ethical considerations in today's business climate, appear in selected chapters, including this chapter. *A Question of Ethics* case problem is included at the end of every chapter to introduce you to the ethical aspects of specific cases involving real-life situations.

1–2 Sources of American Law

American law has numerous sources. Often, these sources of law are classified as either primary or secondary.

Primary sources of law, or sources that establish the law, include the following:

1. The U.S. Constitution and the constitutions of the various states.
2. Statutory law—including laws passed by Congress, state legislatures, or local governing bodies.
3. Regulations created by administrative agencies, such as the Federal Trade Commission.
4. Case law and common law doctrines.

We describe each of these important sources of law in the following pages.

Secondary sources of law are books and articles that summarize and clarify the primary sources of law. Examples include legal encyclopedias, treatises, articles in law reviews, and compilations of law, such as the *Restatements of the Law* (which will be discussed later). Courts often refer to secondary sources of law for guidance in interpreting and applying the primary sources of law discussed here.

1–2a Constitutional Law

The federal government and the states have separate written constitutions that set forth the general organization, powers, and limits of their respective governments. **Constitutional law** is the law as expressed in these constitutions.

According to Article VI of the U.S. Constitution, the Constitution is the supreme law of the land. As such, it is the basis of all law in the United States. A law in violation of the Constitution, if challenged, will be declared unconstitutional and will not be enforced, no matter what its source. Because of its importance in the American legal system, we present the complete text of the U.S. Constitution in Appendix B.

The Tenth Amendment to the U.S. Constitution reserves to the states all powers not granted to the federal government. Each state in the union has its own constitution. Unless it conflicts with the U.S. Constitution or a federal law, a state constitution is supreme within the state's borders.

1–2b Statutory Law

Laws enacted by legislative bodies at any level of government, such as statutes passed by Congress or by state legislatures, make up the body of law known as **statutory law.** When a legislature passes a statute, that statute ultimately is included in the federal code of laws or the relevant state code of laws.

Statutory law also includes local **ordinances**—regulations passed by municipal or county governing units to deal with matters not covered by federal or state law. Ordinances commonly have to do with city or county land use (zoning ordinances), building and safety codes, and other matters affecting the local community.

A federal statute, of course, applies to all states. A state statute, in contrast, applies only within the state's borders. State laws thus may vary from state to state. No federal statute may violate the U.S. Constitution, and no state statute or local ordinance may violate the U.S. Constitution or the relevant state constitution.

Uniform Laws During the 1800s, the differences among state laws frequently created difficulties for businesspersons conducting trade and commerce among the states. To counter these problems, a group of legal scholars and lawyers formed the National Conference of Commissioners on Uniform State Laws, or NCCUSL (**www.uniformlaws.org**), in 1892. The NCCUSL still exists today. Its object is to draft **uniform laws** (model statutes) for the states to consider adopting.

Each state has the option of adopting or rejecting a uniform law. *Only if a state legislature adopts a uniform law does that law become part of the statutory law of that state.* Note that a state legislature may adopt all or part of a uniform law as it is written, or the legislature may rewrite the law however the legislature wishes. Hence, even though many states may have adopted a uniform law, those states' laws may not be entirely "uniform."

The earliest uniform law, the Uniform Negotiable Instruments Law, was completed by 1896 and adopted in every state by the 1920s (although not all states used exactly the same wording). Over the following decades, other acts were drawn up in a similar manner. In all, more than two hundred uniform acts have been issued by the NCCUSL since its inception. The most ambitious uniform act of all, however, was the Uniform Commercial Code.

The Uniform Commercial Code One of the most important uniform acts is the Uniform Commercial Code (UCC), which was created through the joint efforts of the NCCUSL and the American Law Institute.[1] The UCC was first issued in 1952 and has been adopted in all fifty states,[2] the District of Columbia, and the Virgin Islands.

The UCC facilitates commerce among the states by providing a uniform, yet flexible, set of rules governing commercial transactions. Because of its importance in the area of commercial law, we cite the UCC frequently in this text. We also present the full UCC in Appendix C. From time to time, the NCCUSL revises the articles contained in the UCC and submits the revised versions to the states for adoption.

1–2c Administrative Law

Another important source of American law is **administrative law,** which consists of the rules, orders, and decisions of administrative agencies. An **administrative agency** is a federal, state, or local government agency established to perform a specific function. Administrative law and procedures constitute a dominant element in the regulatory environment of business.

---

1. This institute was formed in the 1920s and consists of practicing attorneys, legal scholars, and judges.
2. Louisiana has not adopted Articles 2 and 2A (covering contracts for the sale and lease of goods), however.

Rules issued by various administrative agencies now affect almost every aspect of a business's operations. Regulations govern a business's capital structure and financing, its hiring and firing procedures, its relations with employees and unions, and the way it manufactures and markets its products. Regulations enacted to protect the environment also often play a significant role in business operations.

Federal Agencies At the national level, the cabinet departments of the executive branch include numerous **executive agencies.** The U.S. Food and Drug Administration, for instance, is an agency within the U.S. Department of Health and Human Services. Executive agencies are subject to the authority of the president, who has the power to appoint and remove their officers.

There are also major **independent regulatory agencies** at the federal level, such as the Federal Trade Commission, the Securities and Exchange Commission, and the Federal Communications Commission. The president's power is less pronounced in regard to independent agencies, whose officers serve for fixed terms and cannot be removed without just cause.

State and Local Agencies There are administrative agencies at the state and local levels as well. Commonly, a state agency (such as a state pollution-control agency) is created as a parallel to a federal agency (such as the Environmental Protection Agency). Just as federal statutes take precedence over conflicting state statutes, federal agency regulations take precedence over conflicting state regulations.

1–2d Case Law and Common Law Doctrines

The rules of law announced in court decisions constitute another basic source of American law. These rules include interpretations of constitutional provisions, of statutes enacted by legislatures, and of regulations created by administrative agencies.

Today, this body of judge-made law is referred to as **case law.** Case law—the doctrines and principles announced in cases—governs all areas not covered by statutory law or administrative law and is part of our common law tradition. We look at the origins and characteristics of the common law tradition in some detail in the pages that follow.

See Concept Summary 1.1 for a review of the sources of American law.

Concept Summary 1.1

Sources of American Law

Constitutional Law	• Law as expressed in the U.S. Constitution or state constitutions. • The U.S. Constitution is the supreme law of the land. • State constitutions are supreme within state borders to the extent that they do not conflict with the U.S. Constitution.
Statutory Law	• Statutes (including uniform laws) and ordinances enacted by federal, state, and local legislatures. • Federal statutes may not violate the U.S. Constitution. • State statutes and local ordinances may not violate the U.S. Constitution or the relevant state constitution.
Administrative Law	• The rules, orders, and decisions of federal, state, and local administrative agencies.
Case Law and Common Law Doctrines	• Judge-made law, including interpretations of constitutional provisions, of statutes enacted by legislatures, and of regulations created by administrative agencies.

1–3 The Common Law Tradition

Because of our colonial heritage, much of American law is based on the English legal system. Knowledge of this tradition is crucial to understanding our legal system today because judges in the United States still apply common law principles when deciding cases.

1–3a Early English Courts

After the Normans conquered England in 1066, William the Conqueror and his successors began the process of unifying the country under their rule. One of the means they used to do this was the establishment of the king's courts, or *curiae regis*.

Before the Norman Conquest, disputes had been settled according to the local legal customs and traditions in various regions of the country. The king's courts sought to establish a uniform set of customs for the country as a whole. What evolved in these courts was the beginning of the **common law**—a body of general rules that applied throughout the entire English realm. Eventually, the common law tradition became part of the heritage of all nations that were once British colonies, including the United States.

Courts of Law and Remedies at Law The early English king's courts could grant only very limited kinds of **remedies** (the legal means to enforce a right or redress a wrong). If one person wronged another in some way, the king's courts could award as compensation one or more of the following: (1) land, (2) items of value, or (3) money.

The courts that awarded this compensation became known as **courts of law,** and the three remedies were called **remedies at law.** (Today, the remedy at law normally takes the form of monetary **damages**—an amount given to a party whose legal interests have been injured.) This system made the procedure for settling disputes more uniform. When a complaining party wanted a remedy other than economic compensation, however, the courts of law could do nothing, so "no remedy, no right."

Courts of Equity When individuals could not obtain an adequate remedy in a court of law, they petitioned the king for relief. Most of these petitions were decided by an adviser to the king, called a *chancellor,* who had the power to grant new and unique remedies. Eventually, formal chancery courts, or **courts of equity,** were established. *Equity* is a branch of law—founded on notions of justice and fair dealing—that seeks to supply a remedy when no adequate remedy at law is available.

Remedies in Equity The remedies granted by the equity courts became known as **remedies in equity,** or equitable remedies. These remedies include specific performance, injunction, and rescission. *Specific performance* involves ordering a party to perform an agreement as promised. An *injunction* is an order to a party to cease engaging in a specific activity or to undo some wrong or injury. *Rescission* is the cancellation of a contractual obligation. We will discuss these and other equitable remedies in more detail in later chapters.

As a general rule, today's courts, like the early English courts, will not grant equitable remedies unless the remedy at law—monetary damages—is inadequate. ■ **EXAMPLE 1.2** Ted forms a contract (a legally binding agreement) to purchase a parcel of land that he thinks will be perfect for his future home. The seller **breaches** (fails to fulfill) this agreement. Ted could sue the seller for the return of any deposits or down payment he might have made on the land, but this is not the remedy he really wants. What Ted wants is to have a court order the seller to perform the contract. In other words, Ted will seek the equitable remedy of specific performance because monetary damages are inadequate in this situation. ■

Equitable Maxims In fashioning appropriate remedies, judges often were (and continue to be) guided by so-called **equitable maxims**—propositions or general statements of equitable rules. Exhibit 1–2 lists some important equitable maxims.

The last maxim listed in the exhibit—"Equity aids the vigilant, not those who rest on their rights"—merits special attention. It has become known as the equitable doctrine of **laches** (a term derived from the Latin *laxus*, meaning "lax" or "negligent"), and it can be used as a defense. A **defense** is an argument raised by the **defendant** (the party being sued) indicating why the **plaintiff** (the suing party) should not obtain the remedy sought. (Note that in equity proceedings, the party bringing a lawsuit is called the **petitioner,** and the party being sued is referred to as the **respondent.**)

The doctrine of laches arose to encourage people to bring lawsuits while the evidence was fresh. What constitutes a reasonable time, of course, varies according to the circumstances of the case. Time periods for different types of cases are now usually fixed by **statutes of limitations.** After the time allowed under a statute of limitations has expired, no action (lawsuit) can be brought, no matter how strong the case was originally.

EXHIBIT 1–2 Equitable Maxims

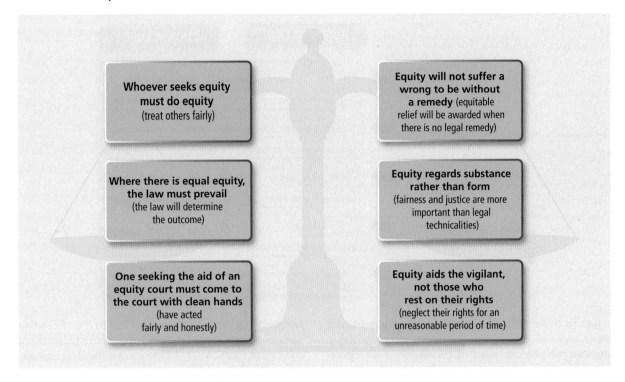

Whoever seeks equity must do equity (treat others fairly)

Where there is equal equity, the law must prevail (the law will determine the outcome)

One seeking the aid of an equity court must come to the court with clean hands (have acted fairly and honestly)

Equity will not suffer a wrong to be without a remedy (equitable relief will be awarded when there is no legal remedy)

Equity regards substance rather than form (fairness and justice are more important than legal technicalities)

Equity aids the vigilant, not those who rest on their rights (neglect their rights for an unreasonable period of time)

1–3b Legal and Equitable Remedies Today

The establishment of courts of equity in medieval England resulted in two distinct court systems: courts of law and courts of equity. The courts had different sets of judges and granted different types of remedies. During the nineteenth century, however, most states in the United States adopted rules of procedure that resulted in the combining of courts of law and equity. A party now may request both legal and equitable remedies in the same action, and the trial court judge may grant either or both forms of relief.

The distinction between legal and equitable remedies remains relevant to students of business law, however, because these remedies differ. To seek the proper remedy for a wrong, you must know what remedies are available. Additionally, certain vestiges of the procedures used when there were separate courts of law and equity still exist. For instance, a party has the right to demand a jury trial in an action at law, but not in an action in equity. Exhibit 1–3 summarizes the procedural differences (applicable in most states) between an action at law and an action in equity.

1–3c The Doctrine of *Stare Decisis*

One of the unique features of the common law is that it is *judge-made* law. The body of principles and doctrines that form the common law emerged over time as judges decided legal controversies.

Case Precedents and Case Reporters When possible, judges attempted to be consistent and to base their decisions on the principles suggested by earlier cases. They sought to decide similar cases in a similar way, and they considered new cases with care because they knew that their decisions would make new law. Each interpretation became part of the law on the subject and thus served as a legal **precedent.** A precedent is a decision that furnishes an example or authority for deciding subsequent cases involving identical or similar legal principles or facts.

In the early years of the common law, there was no single place or publication where court opinions, or written decisions, could be found. By the fourteenth century, portions of the most important decisions from each year were being gathered together and recorded in *Year Books*, which became useful references for lawyers and judges. In the

EXHIBIT 1–3 Procedural Differences between Actions at Law and Actions in Equity

		ACTION AT LAW	ACTION IN EQUITY
PROCEDURE	**Initiation of lawsuit**	By filing a complaint	By filing a petition
	Parties	Plaintiff and defendant	Petitioner and respondent
	Decision	By jury or judge	By judge (no jury)
	Result	Judgment	Decree
	Remedy	Monetary damages	Injunction, specific performance, or rescission

sixteenth century, the *Year Books* were discontinued, and other forms of case publication became available. Today, cases are published, or "reported," in volumes called **reporters,** or *reports*—and are also posted online. We describe today's case reporting system in detail later in this chapter.

Stare Decisis and the Common Law Tradition

The practice of deciding new cases with reference to former decisions, or precedents, became a cornerstone of the English and American judicial systems. The practice formed a doctrine known as ***stare decisis*,**[3] a Latin phrase meaning "to stand on decided cases."

Under the doctrine of *stare decisis*, judges are obligated to follow the precedents established within their jurisdictions. The term *jurisdiction* refers to a geographic area in which a court or courts have the power to apply the law. Once a court has set forth a principle of law as being applicable to a certain set of facts, that court must apply the principle in future cases involving similar facts. Courts of lower rank (within the same jurisdiction) must do likewise. Thus, *stare decisis* has two aspects:

1. A court should not overturn its own precedents unless there is a compelling reason to do so.
2. Decisions made by a higher court are binding on lower courts.

Controlling Precedents Precedents that must be followed within a jurisdiction are called *controlling*

precedents. Controlling precedents are a type of binding authority. A **binding authority** is any source of law that a court must follow when deciding a case. Binding authorities include constitutions, statutes, and regulations that govern the issue being decided, as well as court decisions that are controlling precedents within the jurisdiction. United States Supreme Court case decisions, no matter how old, remain controlling until they are overruled by a subsequent decision of the Supreme Court or changed by further legislation or a constitutional amendment.

Stare Decisis and Legal Stability The doctrine of *stare decisis* helps the courts to be more efficient because, if other courts have analyzed a similar case, their legal reasoning and opinions can serve as guides. *Stare decisis* also makes the law more stable and predictable. If the law on a subject is well settled, someone bringing a case can usually rely on the court to rule based on what the law has been in the past. See this chapter's *Ethics Today* feature for a discussion of how courts often defer to case precedent even when they disagree with the reasoning in the case.

Although courts are obligated to follow precedents, sometimes a court will depart from the rule of precedent if it decides that the precedent should no longer be followed. If a court decides that a ruling precedent is simply incorrect or that technological or social changes have rendered the precedent inapplicable, the court might rule contrary to the precedent. Cases that overturn precedent often receive a great deal of publicity.

■ **CASE IN POINT 1.3** The United States Supreme Court expressly overturned precedent in the case of

---

3. Pronounced *ster-ay* dih-*si*-ses.

ETHICS TODAY	*Stare Decisis* versus Spider-Man

Supreme Court Justice Elena Kagan, in a recent decision involving Marvel Comics' Spider-Man, ruled that, "What we can decide, we can undecide. But *stare decisis* teaches that we should exercise that authority sparingly." Citing a Spider-Man comic book, she went on to say that "in this world, with great power there must also come—great responsibility."[a] In its decision in the case—*Kimble v. Marvel Entertainment, LLC*—the Supreme Court applied *stare decisis* and ruled against Stephen Kimble, the creator of a toy related to the Spider-Man figure.[b]

Can a Patent Involving Spider-Man Last Super Long?

A patent is an exclusive right granted to the creator of an invention. Under U.S. law, patent owners generally possess that right for twenty years. Patent holders can license the use of their patents as they see fit during that period. In other words, they can allow others (called *licensees*) to use their invention in return for a fee (called *royalties*).

More than fifty years ago, the Supreme Court ruled in its *Brulotte* decision that a licensee cannot be forced to pay royalties to a patent holder after the patent has expired.[c] So if a licensee signs a contract to continue to pay royalties after the patent has expired, the contract is invalid and thus unenforceable.

At issue in the *Kimble* case was a contract signed between Marvel Entertainment and Kimble, who had invented a toy made up of a glove equipped with a valve and a canister of pressurized foam. The patented toy allowed people to shoot fake webs intended to look like Spider-Man's. In 1990, Kimble tried to cut a deal with Marvel Entertainment concerning his toy, but he was unsuccessful. Then Marvel started selling its own version of the toy.

When Kimble sued Marvel for patent infringement, he won. The result was a settlement that involved a licensing agreement between Kimble and Marvel with a lump-sum payment plus a royalty to Kimble of 3 percent of all sales of the toy. The agreement did not specify an end date for royalty payments to Kimble, and Marvel later sued to have the payments stop after the patent expired, consistent with the Court's earlier *Brulotte* decision.

A majority of the Supreme Court justices agreed with Marvel. As Justice Kagan said in the opinion, "Patents endow their holders with certain super powers, but only for a limited time." The court further noted that the fifty-year-old *Brulotte* decision was perhaps based on what today is an outmoded understanding of economics. That decision, according to some, may even hinder competition and innovation. But "respecting *stare decisis* means sticking to some wrong decisions."

The Ethical Side

In a dissenting opinion, Supreme Court Justice Samuel A. Alito, Jr., said, "The decision interferes with the ability of parties to negotiate licensing agreements that reflect the true value of a patent, and it disrupts contractual expectations. *Stare decisis* does not require us to retain this baseless and damaging precedent. . . . *Stare decisis* is important to the rule of law, but so are correct judicial decisions."

In other words, *stare decisis* holds that courts should adhere to precedent in order to promote predictability and consistency. But in the business world, shouldn't parties to contracts be able to, for example, allow a patent licensee to make smaller royalty payments that exceed the life of the patent? Isn't that a way to reduce the yearly costs to the licensee? After all, the licensee may be cash-strapped in its initial use of the patent. Shouldn't the parties to a contract be the ones to decide how long the contract should last?

Critical Thinking *When is the Supreme Court justified in* not *following the doctrine of* stare decisis?

---

a. "Spider-Man," Amazing Fantasy No. 15 (1962), p. 13.
b. 576 U.S. ___, 135 S.Ct. 2401, 192 L.Ed.2d 463 (2015).
c. *Brulotte v. Thys Co.*, 379 U.S. 29, 85 S.Ct. 176 (1964).

Brown v. Board of Education of Topeka.[4] The Court concluded that separate educational facilities for whites and blacks, which it had previously upheld as constitutional,[5] were inherently unequal. The Supreme Court's departure from precedent in this case received a tremendous amount of publicity as people began to realize the ramifications of this change in the law. ∎

Note that a lower court will sometimes avoid applying a precedent set by a higher court in its jurisdiction by

---

4. 347 U.S. 483, 74 S.Ct. 686, 98 L.Ed. 873 (1954).
5. See *Plessy v. Ferguson*, 163 U.S. 537, 16 S.Ct. 1138, 41 L.Ed. 256 (1896).

distinguishing the two cases based on their facts. When this happens, the lower court's ruling stands unless it is appealed to a higher court and that court overturns the decision.

When There Is No Precedent Occasionally, courts must decide cases for which no precedents exist, called *cases of first impression*. For instance, as you will read throughout this text, the Internet and certain other technologies have presented many new and challenging issues for the courts to decide.

■ **EXAMPLE 1.4** Google Glass is a Bluetooth-enabled, hands-free, wearable computer. A person using Google Glass can take photos and videos, surf the Internet, and do other things through voice commands. Many people expressed concerns about this new technology. Privacy advocates claimed that it is much easier to secretly film or photograph others with wearable video technology than with a camera or a smartphone. Indeed, numerous bars and restaurants, among others, banned the use of Google Glass to protect their patrons' privacy. Police officers were concerned about driver safety. A California woman was ticketed for wearing Google Glass while driving. But the court dismissed this case of first impression because it was not clear whether the device had been in operation at the time of the offense. ■

In deciding cases of first impression, courts often look at **persuasive authorities**—legal authorities that a court may consult for guidance but that are not binding on the court. A court may consider precedents from other jurisdictions, for instance, although those precedents are not binding. A court may also consider legal principles and policies underlying previous court decisions or existing statutes. Additionally, a court might look at issues of fairness, social values and customs, and public policy (governmental policy based on widely held societal values). Today, federal courts can also look at unpublished opinions (those not intended for publication in a printed legal reporter) as sources of persuasive authority.[6]

1–3d *Stare Decisis* and Legal Reasoning

In deciding what law applies to a given dispute and then applying that law to the facts or circumstances of the case, judges rely on the process of **legal reasoning.** Through the use of legal reasoning, judges harmonize their decisions with those that have been made before, as the doctrine of *stare decisis* requires.

Students of business law and the legal environment also engage in legal reasoning. For instance, you may be asked to provide answers for some of the case problems

that appear at the end of every chapter in this text. Each problem describes the facts of a particular dispute and the legal question at issue. If you are assigned a case problem, you will be asked to determine how a court would answer that question, and why. In other words, you will need to give legal reasons for whatever conclusion you reach.[7] We look next at the basic steps involved in legal reasoning and then describe some forms of reasoning commonly used by the courts in making their decisions.

Basic Steps in Legal Reasoning At times, the legal arguments set forth in court opinions are relatively simple and brief. At other times, the arguments are complex and lengthy. Regardless of the length of a legal argument, however, the basic steps of the legal reasoning process remain the same. These steps, which you can also follow when analyzing cases and case problems, form what is commonly referred to as the *IRAC method* of legal reasoning. IRAC is an acronym formed from the first letters of the words *Issue, Rule, Application*, and *Conclusion*. To apply the IRAC method, you ask the following questions:

1. **Issue**—*What are the key facts and issues?* Suppose that a plaintiff comes before the court claiming *assault* (words or acts that wrongfully and intentionally make another person fearful of immediate physical harm). The plaintiff claims that the defendant threatened her while she was sleeping. Although the plaintiff was unaware that she was being threatened, her roommate heard the defendant make the threat. The legal issue is whether the defendant's action constitutes the tort of assault, given that the plaintiff was unaware of that action at the time it occurred. (A tort is a wrongful act. As you will see later, torts fall under the governance of civil law rather than criminal law.)

2. **Rule**—*What rule of law applies to the case?* A rule of law may be a rule stated by the courts in previous decisions, a state or federal statute, or a state or federal administrative agency regulation. In our hypothetical case, the plaintiff **alleges** (claims) that the defendant committed a tort. Therefore, the applicable law is the common law of torts—specifically, tort law governing assault. Case precedents involving similar facts and issues thus would be relevant. Often, more than one rule of law will be applicable to a case.

3. **Application**—*How does the rule of law apply to the particular facts and circumstances of this case?* This step is often the most difficult because each case presents a unique set of facts, circumstances, and parties.

---

6. See Rule 32.1 of the Federal Rules of Appellate Procedure.

7. See Appendix A for further instructions on how to analyze case problems.

Although cases may be similar, no two cases are ever identical in all respects. Normally, judges (and lawyers and law students) try to find **cases on point**—previously decided cases that are as similar as possible to the one under consideration.

4. **Conclusion**—*What conclusion should be drawn?* This step normally presents few problems. Usually, the conclusion is evident if the previous three steps have been followed carefully.

There Is No One "Right" Answer Many people believe that there is one "right" answer to every legal question. In most legal controversies, however, there is no single correct result. Good arguments can usually be made to support either side of a legal controversy. Quite often, a case does not involve a "good" person suing a "bad" person. In many cases, both parties have acted in good faith in some measure or in bad faith to some degree. Additionally, each judge has her or his own personal beliefs and philosophy. At least to some extent, these personal factors shape the legal reasoning process. In short, the outcome of a particular lawsuit before a court cannot be predicted with certainty.

1–3e The Common Law Today

Today, the common law derived from judicial decisions continues to be applied throughout the United States. Common law doctrines and principles, however, govern only areas *not* covered by statutory or administrative law. In a dispute concerning a particular employment practice, for instance, if a statute regulates that practice, the statute will apply rather than the common law doctrine that applied before the statute was enacted. The common law tradition and its application are reviewed in Concept Summary 1.2.

Courts Interpret Statutes Even in areas governed by statutory law, judge-made law continues to be important because there is a significant interplay between statutory law and the common law. For instance, many statutes essentially codify existing common law rules, and regulations issued by various administrative agencies usually are based, at least in part, on common law principles. Additionally, the courts, in interpreting statutory law, often rely on the common law as a guide to what the legislators intended. Frequently, the applicability of a newly enacted statute does not become clear until a body of case law develops to clarify how, when, and to whom the statute applies.

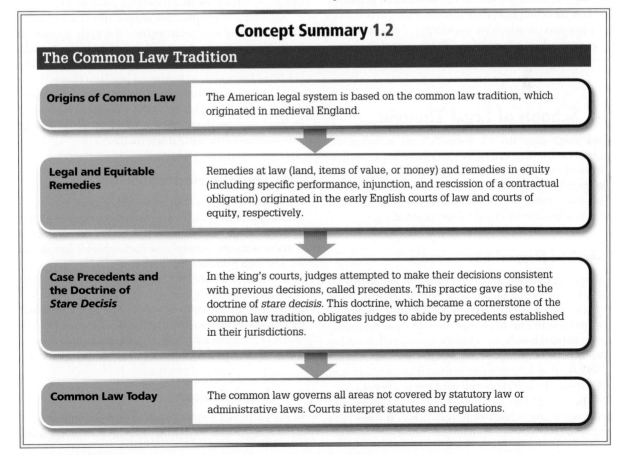

Concept Summary 1.2

The Common Law Tradition

Origins of Common Law	The American legal system is based on the common law tradition, which originated in medieval England.
Legal and Equitable Remedies	Remedies at law (land, items of value, or money) and remedies in equity (including specific performance, injunction, and rescission of a contractual obligation) originated in the early English courts of law and courts of equity, respectively.
Case Precedents and the Doctrine of *Stare Decisis*	In the king's courts, judges attempted to make their decisions consistent with previous decisions, called precedents. This practice gave rise to the doctrine of *stare decisis*. This doctrine, which became a cornerstone of the common law tradition, obligates judges to abide by precedents established in their jurisdictions.
Common Law Today	The common law governs all areas not covered by statutory law or administrative laws. Courts interpret statutes and regulations.

Clearly, a judge's function is not to *make* the laws—that is the function of the legislative branch of government—but to interpret and apply them. From a practical point of view, however, the courts play a significant role in defining the laws enacted by legislative bodies, which tend to be expressed in general terms. Judges thus have some flexibility in interpreting and applying the law. It is because of this flexibility that different courts can, and often do, arrive at different conclusions in cases that involve nearly identical issues, facts, and applicable laws.

Restatements of the Law Clarify and Illustrate the Common Law The American Law Institute (ALI) has published compilations of the common law called *Restatements of the Law*, which generally summarize the common law rules followed by most states. There are *Restatements of the Law* in the areas of contracts, torts, agency, trusts, property, restitution, security, judgments, and conflict of laws. The *Restatements,* like other secondary sources of law, do not in themselves have the force of law, but they are an important source of legal analysis and opinion. Hence, judges often rely on them in making decisions.

Many of the *Restatements* are now in their second, third, or fourth editions. We refer to the *Restatements* frequently in subsequent chapters of this text, indicating in parentheses the edition to which we are referring. For instance, we refer to the third edition of the *Restatement of the Law of Contracts* as simply the *Restatement (Third) of Contracts*.

1–4 Schools of Legal Thought

How judges apply the law to specific cases, including disputes relating to the business world, depends in part on their philosophical approaches to law. Thus, the study of law, or **jurisprudence,** involves learning about different schools of legal thought and how the approaches to law characteristic of each school can affect judicial decision making.

1–4a The Natural Law School

An age-old question about the nature of law has to do with the finality of a nation's laws. What if a particular law is deemed to be a "bad" law by a substantial number of the nation's citizens? Must they obey that law? According to the **natural law** theory, a higher, or universal, law exists that applies to all human beings. Each written law should reflect the principles inherent in natural law. If it does not, then it loses its legitimacy and need not be obeyed.

The natural law tradition is one of the oldest and most significant schools of jurisprudence. It dates back to the days of the Greek philosopher Aristotle (384–322

B.C.E.), who distinguished between natural law and the laws governing a particular nation. According to Aristotle, natural law applies universally to all humankind.

The notion that people have "natural rights" stems from the natural law tradition. Those who claim that a specific foreign government is depriving certain citizens of their human rights, for instance, are implicitly appealing to a higher law that has universal applicability.

The question of the universality of basic human rights also comes into play in the context of international business operations. U.S. companies that have operations abroad often hire foreign workers as employees. Should the same laws that protect U.S. employees apply to these foreign employees? This question is rooted implicitly in a concept of universal rights that has its origins in the natural law tradition.

1–4b The Positivist School

Positive law, or national law, is the written law of a given society at a particular time. In contrast to natural law, it applies only to the citizens of that nation or society. Those who adhere to **legal positivism** believe that there can be no higher law than a nation's positive law.

According to the positivist school, there are no "natural rights." Rather, human rights exist solely because of laws. If the laws are not enforced, anarchy will result. Thus, whether a law is "bad" or "good" is irrelevant. The law is the law and must be obeyed until it is changed—in an orderly manner through a legitimate lawmaking process. A judge who takes this view will probably be more inclined to defer to an existing law than would a judge who adheres to the natural law tradition.

1–4c The Historical School

The **historical school** of legal thought emphasizes the evolutionary process of law by concentrating on the origin and history of the legal system. This school looks to the past to discover what the principles of contemporary law should be. The legal doctrines that have withstood the passage of time—those that have worked in the past—are deemed best suited for shaping present laws. Hence, law derives its legitimacy and authority from adhering to the standards that historical development has shown to be workable. Followers of the historical school are more likely than those of other schools to strictly follow decisions made in past cases.

1–4d Legal Realism

In the 1920s and 1930s, a number of jurists and scholars, known as *legal realists*, rebelled against the historical approach to law. **Legal realism** is based on the idea that law is just one of many institutions in society and that it is shaped by social forces and needs. Because the law is a human enterprise, this school reasons that judges should take social and economic realities into account when deciding cases.

Legal realists also believe that the law can never be applied with total uniformity. Given that judges are human beings with unique personalities, value systems, and intellects, different judges will obviously bring different reasoning processes to the same case. Female judges, for instance, might be more inclined than male judges to consider whether a decision might have a negative impact on the employment of women or minorities.

Legal realism strongly influenced the growth of what is sometimes called the **sociological school,** which views law as a tool for promoting justice in society. In the 1960s, for instance, the justices of the United States Supreme Court helped advance the civil rights movement by upholding long-neglected laws calling for equal treatment for all Americans, including African Americans and other minorities. Generally, jurists who adhere to this philosophy of law are more likely to depart from past decisions than are jurists who adhere to other schools of legal thought.

Concept Summary 1.3 reviews the schools of jurisprudential thought.

1–5 Classifications of Law

The law may be broken down according to several classification systems. One system, for instance, divides law into substantive law and procedural law. **Substantive law** consists of all laws that define, describe, regulate, and create legal rights and obligations. **Procedural law** consists of all laws that outline the methods of enforcing the rights established by substantive law.

Note that many statutes contain both substantive and procedural provisions. ■ **EXAMPLE 1.5** A state law that provides employees with the right to *workers' compensation benefits* for on-the-job injuries is a substantive law because it creates legal rights. Procedural laws establish the method by which an employee must notify the employer about an on-the-job injury, prove the injury, and periodically submit additional proof to continue receiving workers' compensation benefits. ■

Other classification systems divide law into federal law and state law, private law (dealing with relationships between private entities) and public law (addressing the relationship between persons and their governments), and national law and international law. Here we look at still another classification system, which divides law into

Concept Summary 1.3

Schools of Jurisprudential Thought

Natural Law School	One of the oldest and most significant schools of legal thought. Those who believe in natural law hold that there is a universal law applicable to all human beings.
Positivist School	A school of legal thought centered on the assumption that there is no law higher than the laws created by the government.
Historical School	A school of legal thought that stresses the evolutionary nature of law and looks to doctrines that have withstood the passage of time for guidance in shaping present laws.
Legal Realism	A school of legal thought that advocates a less abstract and more realistic and pragmatic approach to the law and takes into account customary practices and the circumstances surrounding the particular transaction.

civil law and criminal law. We also explain what is meant by the term *cyberlaw*.

1–5a Civil Law and Criminal Law

Civil law spells out the rights and duties that exist between persons and between persons and their governments, as well as the relief available when a person's rights are violated. Typically, in a civil case, a private party sues another private party who has failed to comply with a duty. (Note that the government can also sue a party for a civil law violation.) Much of the law that we discuss in this text is civil law, including contract law and tort law.

Criminal law, in contrast, is concerned with wrongs committed *against the public as a whole*. Criminal acts are defined and prohibited by local, state, or federal government statutes. Criminal defendants are thus prosecuted by public officials, such as a district attorney (D.A.), on behalf of the state, not by their victims or other private parties. Some statutes, such as those protecting the environment or investors, have both civil and criminal provisions.

1–5b Cyberlaw

The use of the Internet to conduct business has led to new types of legal issues. In response, courts have had to adapt traditional laws to situations that are unique to our age. Additionally, legislatures at both the federal and the state levels have created laws to deal specifically with such issues.

Frequently, people use the term **cyberlaw** to refer to the emerging body of law that governs transactions conducted via the Internet. Cyberlaw is not really a classification of law, though, nor is it a new *type* of law. Rather, it is an informal term used to refer to both new laws and modifications of traditional laws that relate to the online environment. Throughout this book, you will read how the law in a given area is evolving to govern specific legal issues that arise in the online context.

1–6 How to Find Primary Sources of Law

This text includes numerous references, or *citations*, to primary sources of law—federal and state statutes, the U.S. Constitution and state constitutions, regulations issued by administrative agencies, and court cases. A **citation** identifies the publication in which a legal authority—such as a statute or a court decision or other source—can be found. In this section, we explain how you can use citations to find primary sources of law. Note

that in addition to being published in sets of books, as described next, most federal and state laws and case decisions are available online.

1–6a Finding Statutory and Administrative Law

When Congress passes laws, they are collected in a publication titled *United States Statutes at Large*. When state legislatures pass laws, they are collected in similar state publications. Most frequently, however, laws are referred to in their codified form—that is, the form in which they appear in the federal and state codes. In these codes, laws are compiled by subject.

United States Code The *United States Code* (U.S.C.) arranges all existing federal laws by broad subject. Each of the fifty-two subjects is given a title and a title number. For instance, laws relating to commerce and trade are collected in Title 15, "Commerce and Trade." Each title is subdivided by sections. A citation to the U.S.C. includes both title and section numbers. Thus, a reference to "15 U.S.C. Section 1" means that the statute can be found in Section 1 of Title 15. ("Section" may be designated by the symbol §, and "Sections," by §§.)

In addition to the print publication, the federal government provides a searchable online database at **www .gpo.gov**. It includes the *United States Code,* the U.S. Constitution, and many other federal resources. (Click on "Libraries" and then "Core Documents of Our Democracy" to find these resources.)

Commercial publications of federal laws and regulations are also available. For instance, Thomson Reuters publishes the *United States Code Annotated* (U.S.C.A.). The U.S.C.A. contains the official text of the U.S.C., plus notes (annotations) on court decisions that interpret and apply specific sections of the statutes. The U.S.C.A. also includes additional research aids, such as cross-references to related statutes, historical notes, and library references. A citation to the U.S.C.A. is similar to a citation to the U.S.C.: "15 U.S.C.A. Section 1."

State Codes State codes follow the U.S.C. pattern of arranging law by subject. They may be called codes, revisions, compilations, consolidations, general statutes, or statutes, depending on the preferences of the states.

In some codes, subjects are designated by number. In others, they are designated by name. ■ **EXAMPLE 1.6** "13 Pennsylvania Consolidated Statutes Section 1101" means that the statute can be found in Title 13, Section 1101, of the Pennsylvania code. "California Commercial Code Section 1101" means that the statute can be found under the subject heading "Commercial Code" of the California code in Section 1101. Abbreviations are often used. For example, "13 Pennsylvania Consolidated Statutes Section 1101" is abbreviated "13 Pa. C.S. § 1101," and "California Commercial Code Section 1101" is abbreviated "Cal. Com. Code § 1101." ■

Administrative Rules Rules and regulations adopted by federal administrative agencies are initially published in the *Federal Register,* a daily publication of the U.S. government. Later, they are incorporated into the *Code of Federal Regulations* (C.F.R.). The C.F.R. is available online on the government database (**www.gpo.gov**).

Like the U.S.C., the C.F.R. is divided into titles. Rules within each title are assigned section numbers. A full citation to the C.F.R. includes title and section numbers. ■ **EXAMPLE 1.7** A reference to "17 C.F.R. Section 230.504" means that the rule can be found in Section 230.504 of Title 17. ■

1–6b Finding Case Law

Before discussing the case reporting system, we need to look briefly at the court system. There are two types of courts in the United States, federal courts and state courts. Both systems consist of several levels, or tiers, of courts. *Trial courts,* in which evidence is presented and testimony given, are on the bottom tier. Decisions from a trial court can be appealed to a higher court, which commonly is an intermediate *court of appeals,* or *appellate court.* Decisions from these intermediate courts of appeals may be appealed to an even higher court, such as a state supreme court or the United States Supreme Court.

State Court Decisions Most state trial court decisions are not published in books (except in New York and a few other states, which publish selected trial court opinions). Decisions from state trial courts are typically filed in the office of the clerk of the court, where the decisions are available for public inspection. (Increasingly, they can be found online as well.)

Written decisions of the appellate, or reviewing, courts, however, are published and distributed (in print and online). As you will note, most of the state court cases presented in this textbook are from state appellate courts. The reported appellate decisions are published in volumes called *reports* or *reporters,* which are numbered consecutively. State appellate court decisions are found in the state reporters of that particular state. Official reports are published by the state, whereas unofficial reports are published by nongovernment entities.

Regional Reporters. State court opinions appear in regional units of the West's National Reporter System, published by Thomson Reuters. Most lawyers and libraries have these reporters because they report cases more quickly and are distributed more widely than the state-published reporters. In fact, many states have eliminated their own reporters in favor of the National Reporter System.

The National Reporter System divides the states into the following geographic areas: *Atlantic* (A., A.2d, or A.3d), *North Eastern* (N.E. or N.E.2d), *North Western* (N.W. or N.W.2d), *Pacific* (P., P.2d, or P.3d), *South Eastern* (S.E. or S.E.2d), *South Western* (S.W., S.W.2d, or S.W.3d), and *Southern* (So., So.2d, or So.3d). (The *2d* and *3d* in the preceding abbreviations refer to *Second Series* and *Third Series*, respectively.) The states included in each of these regional divisions are indicated in Exhibit 1–4, which illustrates the National Reporter System.

Case Citations. After appellate decisions have been published, they are normally referred to (cited) by the name of the case and the volume, name, and page number of the reporter(s) in which the opinion can be found. The citation first lists the state's official reporter (if different from the National Reporter System), then the National Reporter, and then any other selected reporter. (Citing a reporter by volume number, name, and page number, in that order, is common to all citations. The year that the decision was issued is often included at the end in parentheses.) When more than one reporter is cited for the same case, each reference is called a *parallel citation.*

Note that some states have adopted a "public domain citation system" that uses a somewhat different format for the citation. For instance, in Wisconsin, a Wisconsin Supreme Court decision might be designated "2016 WI 40," meaning that the case was decided in the year 2016 by the Wisconsin Supreme Court and was the fortieth decision issued by that court during that year. Parallel citations to the *Wisconsin Reports* and the *North Western Reporter* are still included after the public domain citation.

■ **EXAMPLE 1.8** Consider the following case citation: *Summerhill, LLC v. City of Meridan,* 162 Conn.App. 469, 131 A.3d. 1225 (2016). We see that the opinion in this case can be found in Volume 162 of the official *Connecticut Appellate Court Reports*, on page 469. The parallel citation is to Volume 131 of the *Atlantic Reporter, Third Series*, page 1225. ■

When we present opinions in this text, in addition to the reporter, we give the name of the court hearing the case and the year of the court's decision. Sample citations to state court decisions are explained in Exhibit 1–5.

EXHIBIT 1–4 National Reporter System—Regional/Federal

Regional Reporters	Coverage Beginning	Coverage
Atlantic Reporter (A., A.2d, or A.3d)	1885	Connecticut, Delaware, District of Columbia, Maine, Maryland, New Hampshire, New Jersey, Pennsylvania, Rhode Island, and Vermont.
North Eastern Reporter (N.E. or N.E.2d)	1885	Illinois, Indiana, Massachusetts, New York, and Ohio.
North Western Reporter (N.W. or N.W.2d)	1879	Iowa, Michigan, Minnesota, Nebraska, North Dakota, South Dakota, and Wisconsin.
Pacific Reporter (P., P.2d, or P.3d)	1883	Alaska, Arizona, California, Colorado, Hawaii, Idaho, Kansas, Montana, Nevada, New Mexico, Oklahoma, Oregon, Utah, Washington, and Wyoming.
South Eastern Reporter (S.E. or S.E.2d)	1887	Georgia, North Carolina, South Carolina, Virginia, and West Virginia.
South Western Reporter (S.W., S.W.2d, or S.W.3d)	1886	Arkansas, Kentucky, Missouri, Tennessee, and Texas.
Southern Reporter (So., So.2d, or So.3d)	1887	Alabama, Florida, Louisiana, and Mississippi.

Federal Reporters		
Federal Reporter (F., F.2d, or F.3d)	1880	U.S. Circuit Courts from 1880 to 1912; U.S. Commerce Court from 1911 to 1913; U.S. District Courts from 1880 to 1932; U.S. Court of Claims (now called U.S. Court of Federal Claims) from 1929 to 1932 and since 1960; U.S. Courts of Appeals since 1891; U.S. Court of Customs and Patent Appeals since 1929; U.S. Emergency Court of Appeals since 1943.
Federal Supplement (F.Supp., F.Supp.2d, or F.Supp.3d)	1932	U.S. Court of Claims from 1932 to 1960; U.S. District Courts since 1932; U.S. Customs Court since 1956.
Federal Rules Decisions (F.R.D.)	1939	U.S. District Courts involving the Federal Rules of Civil Procedure since 1939 and Federal Rules of Criminal Procedure since 1946.
Supreme Court Reporter (S.Ct.)	1882	United States Supreme Court since the October term of 1882.
Bankruptcy Reporter (Bankr.)	1980	Bankruptcy decisions of U.S. Bankruptcy Courts, U.S. District Courts, U.S. Courts of Appeals, and the United States Supreme Court.
Military Justice Reporter (M.J.)	1978	U.S. Court of Military Appeals and Courts of Military Review for the Army, Navy, Air Force, and Coast Guard.

NATIONAL REPORTER SYSTEM MAP

EXHIBIT 1–5 How to Read Citations

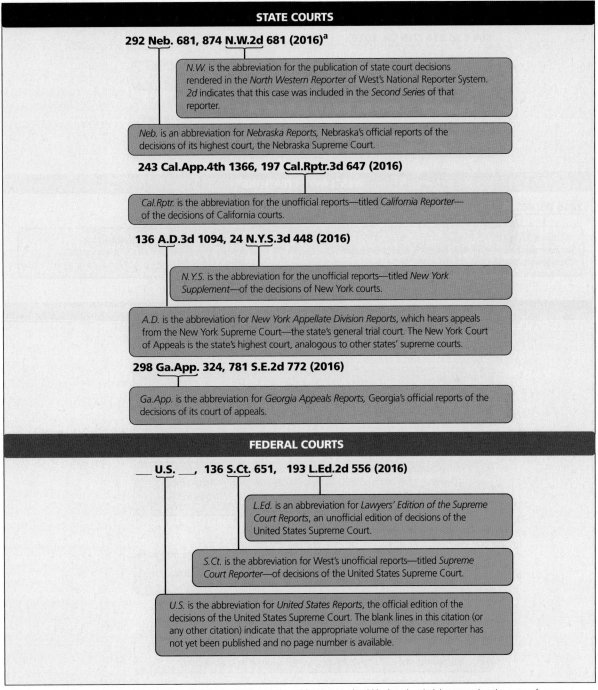

Continued

---

a. The case names have been deleted from these citations to emphasize the publications. It should be kept in mind, however, that the name of a case is as important as the specific page numbers in the volumes in which it is found. If a citation is incorrect, the correct citation may be found in a publication's index of case names. In addition to providing a check on errors in citations, the date of a case is important because the value of a recent case as an authority is likely to be greater than that of older cases from the same court.

EXHIBIT 1–5   How to Read Citations—Continued

FEDERAL COURTS (Continued)

809 F.3d 376 (7th Cir. 2016)

7th Cir. is an abbreviation denoting that this case was decided in the U.S. Court of Appeals for the Seventh Circuit.

___ F.Supp.3d ___ 2016 WL 466132 (E.D.Cal. 2016)

E.D.Cal. is an abbreviation indicating that the U.S. District Court for the Eastern District of California decided this case.

WESTLAW® CITATIONS[b]

2016 WL 66334

WL is an abbreviation for Westlaw. The number 2016 is the year of the document that can be found with this citation in the Westlaw database. The number 66334 is a number assigned to a specific document. A higher number indicates that a document was added to the Westlaw database later in the year.

STATUTORY AND OTHER CITATIONS

18 U.S.C. Section 1961(1)(A)

U.S.C. denotes *United States Code*, the codification of *United States Statutes at Large*. The number 18 refers to the statute's U.S.C. title number and 1961 to its section number within that title. The number 1 in parentheses refers to a subsection within the section, and the letter A in parentheses to a subsection within the subsection.

UCC 2–206(1)(b)

UCC is an abbreviation for *Uniform Commercial Code*. The first number 2 is a reference to an article of the UCC, and 206 to a section within that article. The number 1 in parentheses refers to a subsection within the section, and the letter b in parentheses to a subsection within the subsection.

Restatement (Third) of Torts, Section 6

Restatement (Third) of Torts refers to the third edition of the American Law Institute's *Restatement of the Law of Torts*. The number 6 refers to a specific section.

17 C.F.R. Section 230.505

C.F.R. is an abbreviation for *Code of Federal Regulations*, a compilation of federal administrative regulations. The number 17 designates the regulation's title number, and 230.505 designates a specific section within that title.

b. Many court decisions that are not yet published or that are not intended for publication can be accessed through Westlaw, an online legal database.

Federal Court Decisions Federal district (trial) court decisions are published unofficially in the *Federal Supplement* (F.Supp. or F.Supp.2d), and opinions from the circuit courts of appeals (reviewing courts) are reported unofficially in the *Federal Reporter* (F., F.2d, or F.3d). Cases concerning federal bankruptcy law are published unofficially in the *Bankruptcy Reporter* (Bankr. or B.R.).

The official edition of the United States Supreme Court decisions is the *United States Reports* (U.S.), which is published by the federal government. Unofficial editions of Supreme Court cases include the *Supreme Court Reporter* (S.Ct.) and the *Lawyers' Edition of the Supreme Court Reports* (L.Ed. or L.Ed.2d). Sample citations for federal court decisions are also listed and explained in Exhibit 1–5.

Unpublished Opinions Many court opinions that are not yet published or that are not intended for publication can be accessed through Thomson Reuters Westlaw® (abbreviated in citations as "WL"), an online legal database. When no citation to a published reporter is available for cases cited in this text, we give the WL citation (such as 2016 WL 145734, which means it was case number 145734 decided in the year 2016). In addition, federal appellate court decisions that are designated as unpublished may appear in the *Federal Appendix* (Fed. Appx.) of the National Reporter System.

Old Case Law On a few occasions, this text cites opinions from old, classic cases dating to the nineteenth century or earlier. Some of these are from the English courts. The citations to these cases may not conform to the descriptions just presented because the reporters in which they were originally published were often known by the names of the persons who compiled the reporters.

1–7 How to Read and Understand Case Law

The decisions made by the courts establish the boundaries of the law as it applies to almost all business relationships. It thus is essential that businesspersons know how to read and understand case law.

The cases that we present in this text have been condensed from the full text of the courts' opinions and are presented in a special format. In approximately two-thirds of the cases (including the cases designated as *Classic* and *Spotlight*), we have summarized the background and facts, as well as the court's decision and remedy, in our own words. In those cases, we have included only selected excerpts from the court's opinion ("In the Language of the Court"). In the remaining one-third of the cases (labeled "Case Analysis"), we have provided a longer excerpt from the court's opinion without summarizing the background and facts or decision and remedy.

The following sections provide useful insights into how to read and understand case law.

1–7a Case Titles and Terminology

The title of a case, such as *Adams v. Jones*, indicates the names of the parties to the lawsuit. The *v.* in the case title stands for *versus*, which means "against." In the trial court, Adams was the plaintiff—the person who filed the suit. Jones was the defendant.

If the case is appealed, however, the appellate court will sometimes place the name of the party appealing the decision first, so the case may be called *Jones v. Adams* if Jones appealed. Because some appellate courts retain the trial court order of names, it is often impossible to distinguish the plaintiff from the defendant in the title of a reported appellate court decision. You must carefully read the facts of each case to identify the parties.

The following terms, phrases, and abbreviations are frequently encountered in court opinions and legal publications.

Parties to Lawsuits The party initiating a lawsuit is referred to as the *plaintiff* or *petitioner*, depending on the nature of the action. The party against whom a lawsuit is brought is the *defendant* or *respondent*. Lawsuits frequently involve more than one plaintiff and/or defendant.

When a case is appealed from the original court or jurisdiction to another court or jurisdiction, the party appealing the case is called the **appellant.** The **appellee** is the party against whom the appeal is taken. (In some appellate courts, the party appealing a case is referred to as the *petitioner*, and the party against whom the suit is brought or appealed is called the *respondent*.)

Judges and Justices The terms *judge* and *justice* are usually synonymous and represent two designations given to judges in various courts. All members of the United States Supreme Court, for instance, are referred to as justices. Justice is the formal title often given to judges of appellate courts, although this is not always true. In New York, a justice is a judge of the trial court (called the Supreme Court), and a member of the Court of Appeals (the state's highest court) is called a judge.

The term *justice* is commonly abbreviated to J., and *justices*, to JJ. A United States Supreme Court case might refer to Justice Sotomayor as Sotomayor, J., or to Chief Justice Roberts as Roberts, C.J.

Decisions and Opinions Most decisions reached by reviewing, or appellate, courts are explained in written **opinions.** The opinion contains the court's reasons for its decision, the rules of law that apply, and the judgment. You may encounter several types of opinions as you read appellate cases, including the following:

- When all the judges (or justices) agree, a *unanimous opinion* is written for the entire court.
- When there is not unanimous agreement, a **majority opinion** is generally written. It outlines the views of the majority of the judges deciding the case.
- A judge who agrees (concurs) with the majority opinion as to the result but not as to the legal reasoning often writes a **concurring opinion.** In it, the judge sets out the reasoning that he or she considers correct.
- A **dissenting opinion** presents the views of one or more judges who disagree with the majority view.
- Sometimes, no single position is fully supported by a majority of the judges deciding a case. In this situation, we may have a **plurality opinion.** This is the opinion that has the support of the largest number of judges, but the group in agreement is less than a majority.
- Finally, a court occasionally issues a ***per curiam* opinion** (*per curiam* is Latin for "of the court"), which does not indicate which judge wrote the opinion.

1–7b Sample Court Case

To illustrate the various elements contained in a court opinion, we present an annotated court opinion in Exhibit 1–6. The opinion is from an actual case that the United States Court of Appeals for the Eleventh Circuit decided in 2016.

Background of the Case In December 1955, on a bus in Montgomery, Alabama, Rosa Parks refused to give up her seat to a white man in violation of the city's segregation law. This "courageous act" sparked the modern civil rights movement. Parks's role in "the most significant social movement in the history of the United States" has been chronicled in books and movies, and featured on mementoes, some of which are offered for sale by Target Corp. The Rosa and Raymond Parks Institute for Self Development is a Michigan firm that owns the right to use Parks's name and likeness for commercial purposes. The Institute filed a suit in a federal district court against Target, alleging misappropriation in violation of the Institute's right of publicity. The court dismissed the complaint. The Institute appealed to the U.S. Court of Appeals for the Eleventh Circuit, arguing that Target's sales of books, movies, and other items that depict or discuss Rosa Parks and the modern civil rights movement violated Michigan law.

Editorial Practice You will note that triple asterisks (* * *) and quadruple asterisks (* * * *) frequently appear in the opinion. The triple asterisks indicate that we have deleted a few words or sentences from the opinion for the sake of readability or brevity. Quadruple asterisks mean that an entire paragraph (or more) has been omitted.

Additionally, when the opinion cites another case or legal source, the citation to the case or source has been omitted, again for the sake of readability and brevity. These editorial practices are continued in the other court opinions presented in this book. In addition, whenever we present a court opinion that includes a term or phrase that may not be readily understandable, a bracketed definition or paraphrase has been added.

Briefing Cases Knowing how to read and understand court opinions and the legal reasoning used by the courts is an essential step in undertaking accurate legal research. A further step is "briefing," or summarizing, the case.

Legal researchers routinely brief cases by reducing the texts of the opinions to their essential elements. Generally, when you brief a case, you first summarize the background and facts of the case, as the authors have done for most of the cases presented in this text. You then indicate the issue (or issues) before the court. An important element in the case brief is, of course, the court's decision on the issue and the legal reasoning used by the court in reaching that decision.

Detailed instructions on how to brief a case are given in Appendix A, which also includes a briefed version of the sample court case presented in Exhibit 1–6.

EXHIBIT 1–6 A Sample Court Case

This section contains the citation—the name of the case, the name of the court that heard the case, the year of the decision, and reporters in which the court's opinion can be found.	**Rosa and Raymond Parks Institute for Self Development v. Target Corporation** United States Court of Appeals, Eleventh Circuit, 812 F.3d 824 (2016).
This line provides the name of the judge (or justice) who authored the court's opinion.	*ROSENBAUM*, Circuit Judge: * * * *
In December 1955, on a bus in Montgomery, Alabama, Parks refused to give up her seat to a white man in violation of the city's segregation law.	[Rosa] **Parks's courageous act** inspired the Montgomery Bus Boycott and served as the **impetus** for the **modern Civil Rights Movement,** transforming the nation.
An *impetus* is a stimulus or a spark.	In response to Parks's arrest, for 381 days, 42,000 African–Americans boycotted Montgomery buses, until the United States Supreme Court held the Montgomery segregation law unconstitutional and ordered desegregation of the buses.
The *modern civil rights movement* (1954–1964) included mass demonstrations in which participants sought equality in public and private life at national, state, and local levels, as well as an end to state and local segregation and discrimination in schools, in the workplace and at the polls. The movement culminated in the enactment of two federal Civil Rights acts in 1957 and 1964.	Parks's refusal to **cede** ground in the face of continued injustice has made her among the most revered heroines of our national story; her role in American history cannot be over-emphasized. Indeed, the United States Congress * * * has credited Parks with "igniting the most significant social movement in the history of the United States."
To *cede* is to yield or surrender.	So it is not surprising that authors would write about Parks's story and artists would celebrate it with their works. The commemoration and dissemination of Parks's journey continues to entrench and embolden our pursuit of justice. And it is in the general public interest to relentlessly preserve, spotlight, and recount the story
A *right of publicity* is a person's right to the use of his or her name and likeness for a commercial purpose.	of Rosa Parks and the Civil Rights Movement—even when that interest allegedly conflicts with an individual **right of publicity.**
The court divides the opinion into three sections. The first section summarizes the factual background of the case.	**I.** The Rosa and Raymond Parks Institute for Self Development (the "Institute") is a Michigan * * * corporation that owns the name and likeness of the late Rosa Parks * * * .

Continued

EXHIBIT 1–6   A Sample Court Case—Continued

Target Corporation ("Target"), a national retail corporation headquartered in Minneapolis, Minnesota, operates more than 1,800 retail stores across the United States.

Target offered [for sale] seven books about Parks * * * , the * * * movie *The Rosa Parks Story,* and a * * * plaque that included * * * a picture of Parks.

* * * *

Misappropriation is the use of a person's name or likeness without his or her consent for a commercial purpose. This is commonly referred to as a violation of the individual's right of publicity.

* * * The Institute filed the underlying complaint in [a federal district court]. The Institute alleged claims for * * * **misappropriation** * * * for Target's sales of all items using the name and likeness of Rosa Parks.

Generally, the Institute complained that * * * Target had unfairly and "without the Institute's prior knowledge, or consent, used Parks's name, likeness, and image to sell products * * * for Target's own commercial advantage." * * * The district court dismissed the complaint, and this appeal followed.

The second major section of the opinion responds to the plaintiff's appeal.

II.

Substantive law is law that defines the rights and duties of persons with respect to each other. A federal court exercising jurisdiction based on diversity of citizenship—as in this case, where the two corporate parties are "citizens" of different states—applies the substantive law of the state in which the court sits (except in cases governed by federal law or the United States Constitution).

* * * In this case we apply * * * the **substantive law** of Michigan.

* * * *

Michigan's common-law right of publicity is founded upon the interest of the individual in the exclusive use of his own identity, in so far as it is represented by his name or likeness, and in so far as the use may be of benefit to him or to others. This * * * privacy right guards against the appropriation of the commercial value of a person's identity by using without consent the person's name, likeness, or other ***indicia***

Indicia is a synonym for indications or signs.

of identity for the purpose of trade.

Privacy rights, however, are not absolute. * * * Individual rights must yield to the

Qualified privilege gives someone a limited right to act contrary to another person's right without the other person's having legal recourse for the act.

qualified privilege to communicate on matters of public interest.

* * * *

In this context, *bona fide* means sincerely and honestly.

* * * The privilege attaches to matters of general public interest and extends to all communications made ***bona fide*** upon any subject matter where the party

EXHIBIT 1–6 A Sample Court Case—Continued

communicating has an interest or a [legal, moral, or social] duty to a person having a corresponding interest or duty.

* * * *

Of course, it is beyond dispute that Rosa Parks is a figure of great historical significance and the Civil Rights Movement a matter of legitimate and important public interest. And it is **uncontested** that * * * the * * * books * * * and the movie are all *bona fide* works * * * discussing Parks and her role in the Civil Rights Movement.

> Here, *uncontested* can mean unchallenged or accepted, as well as evident or obvious.

Similarly, the plaque depicts images and mentions dates and statements related to Parks and the Civil Rights Movement, in an effort to convey a message concerning Parks, her courage, and the results of her strength. Indeed, all of the works in question communicate information, express opinions, recite grievances, and protest claimed abuses on behalf of a movement whose existence and objectives continue to be of the highest public interest and concern.

* * * *

* * * The Institute has not articulated any argument as to why Michigan's qualified privilege for matters of public concern would not apply to these works, in light of the conspicuous historical importance of Rosa Parks. Nor can we conceive of any.

* * * Indeed, it is difficult to conceive of a discussion of the Civil Rights Movement without reference to Parks and her role in it. And Michigan law does not make discussion of these topics of public concern contingent on paying a fee. As a result, [the] books, the movie, and the plaque find protection in Michigan's qualified privilege protecting matters of public interest.

> In the third major section of the opinion, the court states its decision.

[III.]

In short, the district court did not err in dismissing the Institute's complaint. The district court's order is **AFFIRMED.**

> To *affirm* is to validate, to give legal force to.

Reviewing: Law and Legal Reasoning

Suppose that the California legislature passes a law that severely restricts carbon dioxide emissions from automobiles in that state. A group of automobile manufacturers files suit against the state of California to prevent the enforcement of the law. The automakers claim that a federal law already sets fuel economy standards nationwide and that fuel economy standards are essentially the same as carbon dioxide emission standards. According to the automobile manufacturers, it is unfair to allow California to impose more stringent regulations than those set by the federal law. Using the information presented in the chapter, answer the following questions.

1. Who are the parties (the plaintiffs and the defendant) in this lawsuit?
2. Are the plaintiffs seeking a legal remedy or an equitable remedy?
3. What is the primary source of the law that is at issue here?
4. Where would you look to find the relevant California and federal laws?

Debate This . . . *Under the doctrine of* stare decisis, *courts are obligated to follow the precedents established in their jurisdiction unless there is a compelling reason not to. Should U.S. courts continue to adhere to this common law principle, given that our government now regulates so many areas by statute?*

Terms and Concepts

administrative agency 4	defendant 6	*per curiam* opinion 20
administrative law 4	defense 6	petitioner 6
allege 10	dissenting opinion 20	plaintiff 6
appellant 19	equitable maxims 6	plurality opinion 20
appellee 19	executive agency 5	precedent 7
binding authority 8	historical school 12	procedural law 13
breach 6	independent regulatory agency 5	remedy 6
case law 5	jurisprudence 12	remedy at law 6
case on point 11	laches 6	remedy in equity 6
citation 14	law 2	reporter 8
civil law 14	legal positivism 12	respondent 6
common law 6	legal realism 13	sociological school 13
concurring opinion 20	legal reasoning 10	*stare decisis* 8
constitutional law 4	liability 2	statute of limitations 6
court of equity 6	majority opinion 20	statutory law 4
court of law 6	natural law 12	substantive law 13
criminal law 14	opinion 20	uniform law 4
cyberlaw 14	ordinance 4	
damages 6	persuasive authority 10	

Issue Spotters

1. Under what circumstances might a judge rely on case law to determine the intent and purpose of a statute? (See *Sources of American Law.*)

2. After World War II, several Nazis were convicted of "crimes against humanity" by an international court. Assuming that these convicted war criminals had not disobeyed any law of their country and had merely been following their government's orders, what law had they violated? Explain. (See *Schools of Legal Thought.*)

- **Check your answers to the Issue Spotters against the answers provided in Appendix D at the end of this text.**

Business Scenarios

1–1. Binding versus Persuasive Authority. A county court in Illinois is deciding a case involving an issue that has never been addressed before in that state's courts. The Iowa Supreme Court, however, recently decided a case involving a very similar fact pattern. Is the Illinois court obligated to follow the Iowa Supreme Court's decision on the issue? If the United States Supreme Court had decided a similar case, would that decision be binding on the Illinois court? Explain. (See *The Common Law Tradition*.)

1–2. Sources of Law. This chapter discussed a number of sources of American law. Which source of law takes priority in the following situations, and why? (See *Sources of American Law*.)

(a) A federal statute conflicts with the U.S. Constitution.

(b) A federal statute conflicts with a state constitutional provision.

(c) A state statute conflicts with the common law of that state.

(d) A state constitutional amendment conflicts with the U.S. Constitution.

1–3. Stare Decisis. In this chapter, we stated that the doctrine of *stare decisis* "became a cornerstone of the English and American judicial systems." What does *stare decisis* mean, and why has this doctrine been so fundamental to the development of our legal tradition? (See *The Common Law Tradition*.)

Business Case Problems

1–4. Spotlight on AOL—Common Law. AOL, LLC, mistakenly made public the personal information of 650,000 of its members. The members filed a suit, alleging violations of California law. AOL asked the court to dismiss the suit on the basis of a "forum-selection clause" in its member agreement that designates Virginia courts as the place where member disputes will be tried. Under a decision of the United States Supreme Court, a forum-selection clause is unenforceable "if enforcement would contravene a strong public policy of the forum in which suit is brought." California courts have declared in other cases that the AOL clause contravenes a strong public policy. If the court applies the doctrine of *stare decisis*, will it dismiss the suit? Explain. [*Doe 1 v. AOL LLC*, 552 F.3d 1077 (9th Cir. 2009)] (See *The Common Law Tradition*.)

1–5. Business Case Problem with Sample Answer—Reading Citations. Assume that you want to read the entire court opinion in the case of *Equal Employment Opportunity Commission v. Autozone, Inc.*, 809 F.3d 916 (7th Cir. 2016). Refer to the subsection entitled "Finding Case Law" in this chapter, and then explain specifically where you would find the court's opinion. (See *How to Find Primary Sources of Law*.)

• **For a sample answer to Problem 1–5, go to Appendix E at the end of this text.**

1–6. A Question of Ethics—The Common Law Tradition. *On July 5, 1884, Dudley, Stephens, and Brooks—* *"all able-bodied English seamen"—and a teenage English boy were cast adrift in a lifeboat following a storm at sea. They had no water with them in the boat, and all they had for sustenance were two one-pound tins of turnips. On July 24, Dudley proposed that one of the four in the lifeboat be sacrificed to save the others. Stephens agreed with Dudley, but Brooks refused to consent—and the boy was never asked for his opinion. On July 25, Dudley killed the boy, and the three men then fed on the boy's body and blood. Four days later, a passing vessel rescued the men. They were taken to England and tried for the murder of the boy. If the men had not fed on the boy's body, they would probably have died of starvation within the four-day period. The boy, who was in a much weaker condition, would likely have died before the rest.* [Regina v. Dudley and Stephens, 14 Q.B.D. *(Queen's Bench Division, England) 273 (1884)*] (See *The Common Law Tradition*.)

(a) The basic question in this case is whether the survivors should be subject to penalties under English criminal law, given the men's unusual circumstances. Were the defendants' actions necessary but unethical? Explain your reasoning. What ethical issues might be involved here?

(b) Should judges ever have the power to look beyond the written "letter of the law" in making their decisions? Why or why not?

Legal Reasoning Group Activity

1–7. Court Opinions. Read through the subsection in this chapter entitled "Decisions and Opinions." (See *How to Read and Understand Case Law*.)

(a) One group will explain the difference between a concurring opinion and a majority opinion.

(b) Another group will outline the difference between a concurring opinion and a dissenting opinion.

(c) A third group will explain why judges and justices write concurring and dissenting opinions, given that these opinions will not affect the outcome of the case at hand, which has already been decided by majority vote.

CHAPTER 2

Courts and Alternative Dispute Resolution

The United States has fifty-two court systems—one for each of the fifty states, one for the District of Columbia, and a federal system. Keep in mind that the federal courts are not superior to the state courts. They are simply an independent system of courts, which derives its authority from Article III, Section 2, of the U.S. Constitution. By the power given to it under the U.S. Constitution, Congress has extended the federal court system to U.S. territories such as Guam, Puerto Rico, and the Virgin Islands.[1]

As we shall see, the United States Supreme Court is the final controlling voice over all of these fifty-two systems, at least when questions of federal law are involved. The Supreme Court's decisions—whether on free speech and social media, health-care subsidies, environmental regulation, or same-sex marriage—represent the last word in the most controversial legal debates in our society. Nevertheless, many of the legal issues that arise in our daily lives, such as the use of social media by courts, employers, and law enforcement, have not yet come before the nation's highest court. The lower courts usually resolve

such pressing matters, making these courts equally important in our legal system.

Although an understanding of our nation's court systems is beneficial for anyone, it is particularly crucial for businesspersons, who will likely face a lawsuit at some time during their careers. Anyone involved in business should be familiar with the basic requirements that must be met before a party can bring a lawsuit before a particular court.

---

1. In Guam and the Virgin Islands, territorial courts serve as both federal courts and state courts. In Puerto Rico, they serve only as federal courts.

2–1 The Judiciary's Role in American Government

The body of American law includes the federal and state constitutions, statutes passed by legislative bodies, administrative law, and the case decisions and legal principles that form the common law. These laws would be meaningless, however, without the courts to interpret and apply them. The essential role of the judiciary—the courts—in the American governmental system is to interpret the laws and apply them to specific situations.

2–1a Judicial Review

As the branch of government entrusted with interpreting the laws, the judiciary can decide, among other things, whether the laws or actions of the other two branches are constitutional. The process for making such a determination is known as **judicial review.** The power of judicial review enables the judicial branch to act as a check on the other two branches of government, in line with the

system of checks and balances established by the U.S. Constitution.[2]

2–1b The Origins of Judicial Review in the United States

The power of judicial review is not mentioned in the U.S. Constitution (although many constitutional scholars believe that the founders intended the judiciary to have this power). The United States Supreme Court explicitly established this power in 1803 in the case *Marbury v. Madison.*[3] In that decision, the Court stated, "It is emphatically the province [authority] and duty of the Judicial Department to say what the law is. . . . If two laws conflict with each other, the courts must decide

---

2. In a broad sense, judicial review occurs whenever a court "reviews" a case or legal proceeding—as when an appellate court reviews a lower court's decision. When discussing the judiciary's role in American government, however, the term *judicial review* refers to the power of the judiciary to decide whether the actions of the other two branches of government violate the U.S. Constitution.

3. 5 U.S. (1 Cranch) 137, 2 L.Ed. 60 (1803).

on the operation of each. . . . [I]f both [a] law and the Constitution apply to a particular case, . . . the Court must determine which of these conflicting rules governs the case. This is of the very essence of judicial duty." Since the *Marbury v. Madison* decision, the power of judicial review has remained unchallenged. Today, this power is exercised by both federal and state courts.

2–2 Basic Judicial Requirements

Before a lawsuit can be brought before a court, certain requirements must be met. These requirements relate to jurisdiction, venue, and standing to sue. We examine each of these important concepts here.

2–2a Jurisdiction

In Latin, *juris* means "law," and *diction* means "to speak." Thus, "the power to speak the law" is the literal meaning of the term **jurisdiction.** Before any court can hear a case, it must have jurisdiction over the person (or company) against whom the suit is brought (the defendant) or over the property involved in the suit. The court must also have jurisdiction over the subject matter of the dispute.

Jurisdiction over Persons or Property Generally, a particular court can exercise *in personam* **jurisdiction** (personal jurisdiction) over any person or business that resides in a certain geographic area. A state trial court, for instance, normally has jurisdictional authority over residents (including businesses) of a particular area of the state, such as a county or district. A state's highest court (often called the state supreme court[4]) has jurisdictional authority over all residents within the state.

A court can also exercise jurisdiction over property that is located within its boundaries. This kind of jurisdiction is known as *in rem* **jurisdiction**, or "jurisdiction over the thing." ■ **EXAMPLE 2.1** A dispute arises over the ownership of a boat in dry dock in Fort Lauderdale, Florida. The boat is owned by an Ohio resident, over whom a Florida court normally cannot exercise personal jurisdiction. The other party to the dispute is a resident of Nebraska. In this situation, a lawsuit concerning the boat could be brought in a Florida state court on the basis of the court's *in rem* jurisdiction. ■

Long Arm Statutes and Minimum Contacts. Under the authority of a state **long arm statute,** a court can exercise personal jurisdiction over certain out-of-state defendants based on activities that took place within the state. Before a court can exercise jurisdiction, though, it must be demonstrated that the defendant had sufficient contacts, or *minimum contacts*, with the state to justify the jurisdiction.[5]

Generally, the minimum-contacts requirement means that the defendant must have sufficient connection to the state for the judge to conclude that it is fair for the state to exercise power over the defendant. For instance, if an out-of-state defendant caused an automobile accident within the state or breached a contract formed there, a court will usually find that minimum contacts exist to exercise jurisdiction over that defendant. Similarly, a state may exercise personal jurisdiction over a nonresident defendant that is sued for selling defective goods within the state.

■ **CASE IN POINT 2.2** An Xbox game system caught fire in Bonnie Broquet's home in Texas and caused substantial personal injuries. Broquet filed a lawsuit in a Texas court against Ji-Haw Industrial Company, a nonresident company that made the Xbox components. Broquet alleged that Ji-Haw's components were defective and had caused the fire. Ji-Haw argued that the Texas court lacked jurisdiction over it, but a state appellate court held that the Texas long arm statute authorized the exercise of jurisdiction over the out-of-state defendant.[6] ■

Corporate Contacts. Because corporations are considered legal persons, courts use the same principles to determine whether it is fair to exercise jurisdiction over a corporation. A corporation normally is subject to personal jurisdiction in the state in which it is incorporated, has its principal office, and/or is doing business.

Courts apply the minimum-contacts test to determine if they can exercise jurisdiction over out-of-state corporations. The minimum-contacts requirement is usually met if the corporation advertises or sells its products within the state, or places its goods into the "stream of commerce" with the intent that the goods be sold in the state. ■ **EXAMPLE 2.3** A business is incorporated under the laws of Maine but has a branch office and manufacturing plant in Georgia. The corporation also advertises and sells its products in Georgia. These activities would likely constitute sufficient contacts with the state of

---

4. As will be discussed shortly, a state's highest court is often referred to as the state supreme court, but there are exceptions. For instance, in New York the supreme court is a trial court.

5. The minimum-contacts standard was first established in *International Shoe Co. v. State of Washington,* 326 U.S. 310, 66 S.Ct. 154, 90 L.Ed. 95 (1945).

6. *Ji-Haw Industrial Co. v. Broquet,* 2008 WL 441822 (Tex.App.—San Antonio 2008).

Georgia to allow a Georgia court to exercise jurisdiction over the corporation. ■

Some corporations do not sell or advertise their products in the general marketplace. Determining what constitutes minimum contacts in these situations can be more difficult. ■ **CASE IN POINT 2.4** Independence Plating Corporation is a New Jersey corporation that provides metal-coating services. Its only office and all of its personnel are located in New Jersey, and it does not advertise out of state. Independence had a long-standing business relationship with Southern Prestige Industries, Inc., a North Carolina company. Eventually, Southern Prestige filed suit in North Carolina against Independence for defective workmanship. Independence argued that North Carolina did not have jurisdiction over it, but the court held that Independence had sufficient minimum contacts with the state to justify jurisdiction. The two parties had exchanged thirty-two separate purchase orders in a period of less than twelve months.[7] ■

Jurisdiction over Subject Matter Subject-matter jurisdiction refers to the limitations on the types of cases a court can hear. Certain courts are empowered to hear certain kinds of disputes. In both the federal and the state court systems, there are courts of general (unlimited) jurisdiction and courts of limited jurisdiction.

A *court of general jurisdiction* can decide cases involving a broad array of issues. An example of a court of general jurisdiction is a state trial court or a federal district court.

In contrast, a *court of limited jurisdiction* can hear only specific types of cases. An example of a state court of limited jurisdiction is a probate court. **Probate courts** are state courts that handle only the disposition of a person's assets and obligations after that person's death, including issues relating to the custody and guardianship of children. An example of a federal court of limited subject-matter jurisdiction is a bankruptcy court. **Bankruptcy courts** handle only bankruptcy proceedings, which are governed by federal bankruptcy law.

A court's jurisdiction over subject matter is usually defined in the statute or constitution that created the court. In both the federal and the state court systems, a court's subject-matter jurisdiction can be limited by any of the following:

1. The subject of the lawsuit.
2. The sum in controversy.

3. Whether the case involves a felony (a serious type of crime) or a misdemeanor (a less serious type of crime).
4. Whether the proceeding is a trial or an appeal.

Original and Appellate Jurisdiction The distinction between courts of original jurisdiction and courts of appellate jurisdiction normally lies in whether the case is being heard for the first time. Courts having original jurisdiction are courts of the first instance, or trial courts. These are courts in which lawsuits begin, trials take place, and evidence is presented. In the federal court system, the *district courts* are trial courts. In the various state court systems, the trial courts are known by various names, as will be discussed shortly.

The key point here is that any court having original jurisdiction normally serves as a trial court. Courts having appellate jurisdiction act as reviewing, or appellate, courts. In general, cases can be brought before appellate courts only on appeal from an order or a judgment of a trial court or other lower courts.

Jurisdiction of the Federal Courts Because the federal government is a government of limited powers, the jurisdiction of the federal courts is limited. Federal courts have subject-matter jurisdiction in two situations: when a federal question is involved and when there is diversity of citizenship.

Federal Questions. Article III of the U.S. Constitution establishes the boundaries of federal judicial power. Section 2 of Article III states that "the judicial Power shall extend to all Cases, in Law and Equity, arising under this Constitution, the Laws of the United States, and Treaties made, or which shall be made, under their Authority."

In effect, this clause means that whenever a plaintiff's cause of action is based, at least in part, on the U.S. Constitution, a treaty, or a federal law, a **federal question** arises. Any lawsuit involving a federal question, such as a person's rights under the U.S. Constitution, can originate in a federal court. Note that in a case based on a federal question, a federal court will apply federal law.

Diversity of Citizenship. Federal district courts can also exercise original jurisdiction over cases involving **diversity of citizenship.** The most common type of diversity jurisdiction[8] requires *both* of the following:

---

7. *Southern Prestige Industries, Inc. v. Independence Plating Corp.*, 690 S.E.2d 768 (N.C. 2010).

8. Diversity jurisdiction also exists in cases between (1) a foreign country and citizens of a state or of different states and (2) citizens of a state and citizens or subjects of a foreign country. Cases based on these types of diversity jurisdiction occur infrequently.

1. The plaintiff and defendant must be residents of different states.
2. The dollar amount in controversy must exceed $75,000.

For purposes of diversity jurisdiction, a corporation is a citizen of both the state in which it is incorporated and the state in which its principal place of business is located.

A case involving diversity of citizenship can be filed in the appropriate federal district court. (If the case starts in a state court, it can sometimes be transferred, or "removed," to a federal court.) A large percentage of the cases filed in federal courts each year are based on diversity of citizenship. As noted before, a federal court will apply federal law in cases involving federal questions.

In a case based on diversity of citizenship, in contrast, a federal court will apply the relevant state law (which is often the law of the state in which the court sits).

The following case focused on whether diversity jurisdiction existed. A boat owner was severely burned when his boat exploded after being overfilled with fuel at a marina in the U.S. Virgin Islands. The owner filed a suit in a federal district court against the marina and sought a jury trial. The defendant argued that a plaintiff in an admiralty, or maritime, case (a case based on something that happened at sea) does not have a right to a jury trial unless the court has diversity jurisdiction. The defendant claimed that because both parties were citizens of the Virgin Islands, the court had no such jurisdiction.

Case Analysis 2.1

Mala v. Crown Bay Marina, Inc.

United States Court of Appeals, Third Circuit, 704 F.3d 239 (2013).

In the Language of the Court
SMITH, Circuit Judge.
    * * * *

Kelley Mala is a citizen of the United States Virgin Islands. * * * He went for a cruise in his powerboat near St. Thomas, Virgin Islands. When his boat ran low on gas, he entered Crown Bay Marina to refuel. Mala tied the boat to one of Crown Bay's eight fueling stations and began filling his tank with an automatic gas pump. Before walking to the cash register to buy oil, Mala asked a Crown Bay attendant to watch his boat.

By the time Mala returned, the boat's tank was overflowing and fuel was spilling into the boat and into the water. The attendant manually shut off the pump and acknowledged that the pump had been malfunctioning in recent days. Mala began cleaning up the fuel, and at some point, the attendant provided soap and water. Mala eventually departed the marina, but as he did so, the engine caught fire and exploded. Mala was thrown into the water and was severely burned. His boat was unsalvageable.

* * * Mala sued Crown Bay in the District Court of the Virgin Islands.

Mala's * * * complaint asserted * * * that Crown Bay negligently maintained its gas pump. [Negligence is the failure to exercise the standard of care that a reasonable person would exercise in similar circumstances. Negligence can form the basis for a legal claim.] The complaint also alleged that the District Court had admiralty and diversity jurisdiction over the case, and it requested a jury trial.
    * * * *

* * * Crown Bay filed a motion to strike Mala's jury demand. Crown Bay argued that plaintiffs generally do not have a jury-trial right in admiralty cases—only when the court also has diversity jurisdiction. And Crown Bay asserted that the parties were not diverse in this case * * * . In response to this motion, the District Court ruled that both Mala and Crown Bay were citizens of the Virgin Islands. The court therefore struck Mala's jury demand, but nevertheless opted to empanel an advisory jury. [The court could accept or reject the advisory jury's verdict.]

* * * At the end of the trial, the advisory jury returned a verdict of $460,000 for Mala—$400,000 for pain and suffering and $60,000 in compensatory

damages. It concluded that Mala was 25 percent at fault and that Crown Bay was 75 percent at fault. The District Court ultimately rejected the verdict and entered judgment for Crown Bay.
    * * * *

This appeal followed.
    * * * *

Mala * * * argues that the District Court improperly refused to conduct a jury trial. This claim ultimately depends on whether the District Court had diversity jurisdiction.

The Seventh Amendment [to the U.S. Constitution] creates a right to civil jury trials in federal court: "In Suits at common law * * * the right of trial by jury shall be preserved." Admiralty suits are not "Suits at common law," which means that when a district court has only admiralty jurisdiction the plaintiff does not have a jury-trial right. But [a federal statute] allows plaintiffs to pursue state claims in admiralty cases as long as the district court also has diversity jurisdiction. In such cases [the statute] preserves whatever jury-trial right exists with respect to the underlying state claims.

Case 2.1 Continues

Mala argues that the District Court had both admiralty and diversity jurisdiction. As a preliminary matter, the court certainly had admiralty jurisdiction. The alleged tort occurred on navigable water and bore a substantial connection to maritime activity.

The grounds for diversity jurisdiction are less certain. *District courts have jurisdiction only if the parties are completely diverse. This means that no plaintiff may have the same state or territorial citizenship as any defendant.* The parties agree that Mala was a citizen of the Virgin Islands. [Emphasis added.]

Unfortunately for Mala, the District Court concluded that Crown Bay also was a citizen of the Virgin Islands. Mala rejects this conclusion.

Mala bears the burden of proving that the District Court had diversity jurisdiction. Mala failed to meet that burden because he did not offer evidence that Crown Bay was anything other than a citizen of the Virgin Islands. Mala contends that Crown Bay admitted to being a citizen of Florida, but Crown Bay actually denied Mala's allegation.

Absent evidence that the parties were diverse, we are left with Mala's allegations. *Allegations are insufficient at trial. And they are especially insufficient on appeal*, where we review the District Court's underlying factual findings for clear error. Under this standard, we will not reverse unless we are left with the definite and firm conviction that Crown Bay was in fact a citizen of Florida. Mala has not presented any credible evidence that Crown Bay was a citizen of Florida—much less evidence that would leave us with the requisite firm conviction. [Emphasis added.]

* * * Accordingly, the parties were not diverse and Mala does not have a jury-trial right.

* * * *

* * * For these reasons we will affirm the District Court's judgment.

Legal Reasoning Questions

1. What is "diversity of citizenship"?

2. How does the presence—or lack—of diversity of citizenship affect a lawsuit?

3. What did the court conclude with respect to the parties' diversity of citizenship in this case?

Exclusive versus Concurrent Jurisdiction When both federal and state courts have the power to hear a case, as is true in lawsuits involving diversity of citizenship, **concurrent jurisdiction** exists. When cases can be tried only in federal courts or only in state courts, **exclusive jurisdiction** exists.

Federal courts have exclusive jurisdiction in cases involving federal crimes, bankruptcy, most patent and copyright claims, suits against the United States, and some areas of admiralty law. State courts also have exclusive jurisdiction over certain subjects—for instance, divorce and adoption.

When concurrent jurisdiction exists, a party may choose to bring a suit in either a federal court or a state court. Many factors can affect a party's decision to litigate in a federal versus a state court. Examples include the availability of different remedies, the distance to the respective courthouses, or the experience or reputation of a particular judge.

For instance, if the dispute involves a trade secret, a party might conclude that a federal court—which has exclusive jurisdiction over copyrights and patents—would have more expertise in the matter. In contrast, a plaintiff might choose to litigate in a state court if the court has a reputation for awarding substantial amounts of damages or if the judge is perceived as being pro-plaintiff. The concepts of exclusive and concurrent jurisdiction are illustrated in Exhibit 2–1.

Jurisdiction in Cyberspace The Internet's capacity to bypass political and geographic boundaries undercuts the traditional basis on which courts assert personal jurisdiction. As discussed, for a court to compel a defendant to come before it, the defendant must have a sufficient connection—that is, minimum contacts—with the state. When a defendant's only contacts with the state are through a Web site, however, it can be difficult to determine whether these contacts are sufficient for a court to exercise jurisdiction.

The "Sliding-Scale" Standard. The courts have developed a "sliding-scale" standard to determine when they can exercise personal jurisdiction over an out-of-state defendant based on the defendant's Web activities. The sliding-scale standard identifies three types of Internet business contacts and outlines the following rules for jurisdiction:

1. When the defendant conducts substantial business over the Internet (such as contracts and sales), jurisdiction is proper.

2. When there is some interactivity through a Web site, jurisdiction may be proper, depending on the

EXHIBIT 2–1 Exclusive and Concurrent Jurisdiction

Exclusive Federal Jurisdiction
(cases involving federal crimes, federal antitrust law, bankruptcy, patents, copyrights, trademarks, suits against the United States, some areas of admiralty law, and certain other matters speci ed in federal statutes)

Concurrent Jurisdiction
(most cases involving federal questions, diversity-of-citizenship cases)

Exclusive State Jurisdiction
(cases involving all matters not subject to federal jurisdiction—for example, divorce and adoption cases)

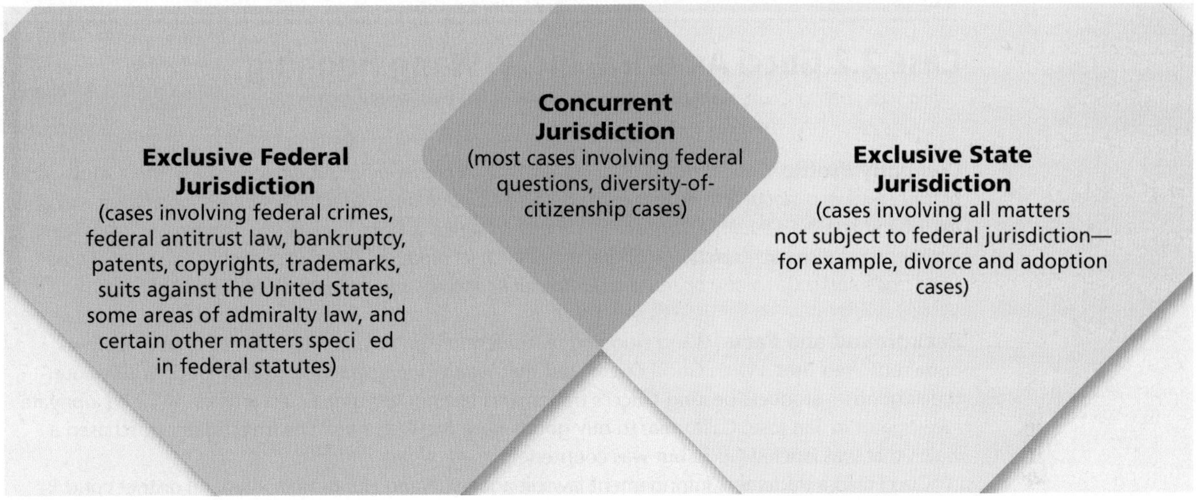

circumstances. Even a single contact can satisfy the minimum-contacts requirement in certain situations.

3. When a defendant merely engages in passive advertising on the Web, jurisdiction is never proper.[9] An Internet communication is typically considered passive if people have to voluntarily access it to read the message and active if it is sent to specific individuals.

■ **CASE IN POINT 2.5** Samantha Guffey lives in Oklahoma. She placed a winning bid on eBay for a used 2009 Volvo XC90 from Motorcars of Nashville, Inc. (MNI), a Tennessee corporation. Before she won the auction, she spoke with Otto Ostonakulov at the dealership. Later, Ostonakulov sent the necessary paperwork to Guffey in Oklahoma. She signed and returned it by mail, and he arranged for MNI to ship the Volvo to Oklahoma.

When the car was delivered to Guffey, she discovered it was not in the condition advertised. She filed a lawsuit in Oklahoma against MNI and Ostonakulov, alleging fraud and a violation of state consumer protection laws. Guffey's complaint alleged that the defendants were active "power sellers" on eBay, averaging twelve to twenty-five cars for sale every day. The sellers claimed that the Oklahoma court lacked jurisdiction over them, and a trial court dismissed the complaint. Guffey appealed. The reviewing court found that Oklahoma had jurisdiction because the sellers' "use of eBay to make multiple sales is systemic and appears to be a

core part of their business." They had negotiated with Guffey directly to sell her a vehicle in Oklahoma and had regularly used eBay to sell vehicles to remote parties in the past.[10] ■

International Jurisdictional Issues. Because the Internet is international in scope, it obviously raises international jurisdictional issues. The world's courts seem to be developing a standard that echoes the requirement of minimum contacts applied by the U.S. courts.

Most courts are indicating that minimum contacts—doing business within the jurisdiction, for instance—are enough to compel a defendant to appear and that a physical presence in the country is not necessary. The effect of this standard is that a business firm has to comply with the laws in any jurisdiction in which it targets customers for its products. This situation is complicated by the fact that many countries' laws on particular issues—free speech, for instance—are very different from U.S. laws.

The following case illustrates how federal courts apply a sliding-scale standard to determine if they can exercise jurisdiction over a foreign defendant whose only contact with the United States is through a Web site.

---

9. For a leading case on this issue, see *Zippo Manufacturing Co. v. Zippo Dot Com, Inc.*, 952 F.Supp. 1119 (W.D.Pa. 1997).

10. *Guffey v. Ostonakulov*, 2014 OK 6, 321 P.3d 971 (Ok.Sup. 2014). Note that a single sale on eBay does not necessarily form the basis for jurisdiction. Jurisdiction depends on whether the seller regularly uses eBay as a means for doing business with remote buyers. See *Hinners v. Robey*, 336 S.W.3d 891 (Ky.Sup. 2008).

Spotlight on Gucci

Case 2.2 Gucci America, Inc. v. Wang Huoqing
United States District Court, Northern District of California, 2011 WL 30972 (2011).

Company Profile *Gucci America, Inc., a New York corporation headquartered in New York City, is part of Gucci Group, a global fashion firm with offices in China, France, Great Britain, Italy, and Japan. Gucci makes and sells high-quality luxury goods, including footwear, belts, sunglasses, handbags, wallets, jewelry, fragrances, and children's clothing. In connection with its products, Gucci uses twenty-one federally registered trademarks. Gucci also operates a number of boutiques, some of which are located in California.*

Background and Facts Wang Huoqing, a resident of the People's Republic of China, operates numerous Web sites. When Gucci discovered that Wang Huoqing's Web sites offered for sale counterfeit goods—products bearing Gucci's trademarks but not genuine Gucci articles—it hired a private investigator in San Jose, California, to buy goods from the Web sites. The investigator purchased a wallet that was labeled Gucci but was counterfeit.

Gucci filed a trademark infringement lawsuit against Wang Huoqing in a federal district court in California seeking damages and an injunction to prevent further infringement. Wang Huoqing was notified of the lawsuit via e-mail but did not appear in court. Gucci asked the court to enter a default judgment—that is, a judgment entered when the defendant fails to appear. First, however, the court had to determine whether it had personal jurisdiction over Wang Huoqing based on the Internet sales.

In the Language of the Court
Joseph C. *SPERO*, United States Magistrate Judge.

* * * *

* * * Under California's long-arm statute, federal courts in California may exercise jurisdiction to the extent permitted by the Due Process Clause of the Constitution. The Due Process Clause allows federal courts to exercise jurisdiction where * * * the defendant has had sufficient minimum contacts with the forum to subject him or her to the specific jurisdiction of the court. The courts apply a three-part test to determine whether specific jurisdiction exists:

> (1) The nonresident defendant must do some act or consummate some transaction with the forum or perform some act by which he purposefully avails himself of the privilege of conducting activities in the forum, thereby invoking the benefits and protections of its laws; (2) the claim must be one which arises out of or results from the defendant's forum-related activities; and (3) exercise of jurisdiction must be reasonable.

* * * *

In order to satisfy the first prong of the test for specific jurisdiction, a defendant must have either purposefully availed itself of the privilege of conducting business activities within the forum or purposefully directed activities toward the forum. *Purposeful availment typically consists of action taking place in the forum that invokes the benefits and protections of the laws of the forum, such as executing or performing a contract within the forum.* To show purposeful availment, a plaintiff must show that the defendant "engage[d] in some form of affirmative conduct allowing or promoting the transaction of business within the forum state." [Emphasis added.]

"In the Internet context, the Ninth Circuit utilizes a sliding scale analysis under which 'passive' websites do not create sufficient contacts to establish purposeful availment, whereas interactive websites may create sufficient contacts, depending on how interactive the website is." * * * *Personal jurisdiction is appropriate where an entity is conducting business over the Internet and has offered for sale and sold its products to forum [California] residents.* [Emphasis added.]

Here, the allegations and evidence presented by Plaintiffs in support of the Motion are sufficient to show purposeful availment on the part of Defendant Wang Huoqing. Plaintiffs have alleged that Defendant operates "fully interactive Internet websites operating under the Subject Domain Names" and have presented evidence in the form of copies of web pages showing that the websites are, in fact, interactive.

Case 2.2 Continued

* * * Additionally, Plaintiffs allege Defendant is conducting counterfeiting and infringing activities within this Judicial District and has advertised and sold his counterfeit goods in the State of California. * * * Plaintiffs have also presented evidence of one actual sale within this district, made by investigator Robert Holmes from the website bag2do.cn.* * * Finally, Plaintiffs have presented evidence that Defendant Wang Huoqing owns or controls the twenty-eight websites listed in the Motion for Default Judgment. * * * Such commercial activity in the forum amounts to purposeful availment of the privilege of conducting activities within the forum, thus invoking the benefits and protections of its laws. Accordingly, the Court concludes that Defendant's contacts with California are sufficient to show purposeful availment.

Decision and Remedy   *The U.S. District Court for the Northern District of California held that it had personal jurisdiction over the foreign defendant, Wang Huoqing. The court entered a default judgment against Wang Huoqing and granted Gucci an injunction.*

Critical Thinking
- **What If the Facts Were Different?**   *Suppose that Gucci had not presented evidence that Wang Huoqing had made one actual sale through his Web site to a resident of the court's district (the private investigator). Would the court still have found that it had personal jurisdiction over Wang Huoqing? Why or why not?*
- **Legal Environment**   *Is it relevant to the analysis of jurisdiction that Gucci America's principal place of business is in New York rather than California? Explain.*

Minimum Contacts and Smartphones. The widespread use of cellular phones, particularly smartphones, also complicates the determination of personal jurisdiction. People use their smartphones while traveling to make purchases, negotiate business deals, enter contracts, and download applications (apps). If a person traveling in another state (or nation) uses a smartphone to form a contract, does that forum have jurisdiction over the person? Is the party that creates an app subject to jurisdiction anywhere the app is downloaded or used? Because an app differs from a Web page, what degree of interactivity is required for apps to confer jurisdiction in the sliding-scale analysis? The courts will be addressing these questions in coming years and adapting traditional notions of jurisdiction to ever-changing technology.

Concept Summary 2.1 reviews the various types of jurisdiction, including jurisdiction in cyberspace.

2–2b Venue

Jurisdiction has to do with whether a court has authority to hear a case involving specific persons, property, or subject matter. **Venue**[11] is concerned with the most appropriate location for a trial. For instance, two state courts (or two federal courts) may have the authority to exercise jurisdiction over a case. Nonetheless, it may be

more appropriate or convenient to hear the case in one court than in the other.

The concept of venue reflects the policy that a court trying a case should be in the geographic neighborhood (usually the county) where the incident occurred or where the parties reside. Venue in a civil case typically is where the defendant resides or does business, whereas venue in a criminal case normally is where the crime occurred.

In some cases, pretrial publicity or other factors may require a change of venue to another community, especially in criminal cases in which the defendant's right to a fair and impartial jury has been impaired. Note, though, that venue has lost some significance in today's world because of the Internet and 24/7 news reporting. Courts now rarely grant requests for a change of venue. Because everyone has instant access to all information about a purported crime, courts reason that no community is more or less informed or prejudiced for or against a defendant.

2–2c Standing to Sue

Before a party can bring a lawsuit to court, that party must have **standing to sue,** or a sufficient stake in a matter to justify seeking relief through the court system. Standing means that the party that filed the action in court has a legally protected interest at stake in the litigation. At times, a person can have standing to sue on behalf of another person, such as a minor (child) or a mentally incompetent person.

---

11. Pronounced *ven*-yoo.

Concept Summary 2.1

Jurisdiction

Personal
Exists when a defendant:
- Is located in the court's territorial boundaries.
- Qualifies under state long arm statutes.
- Is a corporation doing business within the state.
- Advertises, sells, or places goods into commerce within the state.

Property
- Exists when the property that is subject to a lawsuit is located within the court's territorial boundaries.

Subject Matter
Limits the court's jurisdictional authority to particular types of cases.
- *General jurisdiction*—Exists when a court can hear cases involving a broad array of issues.
- *Limited jurisdiction*—Exists when a court is limited to a specific subject matter, such as probate or divorce.

Original
- Exists with courts that have the authority to hear a case for the first time (trial courts, district courts).

Appellate
- Exists with courts of appeal and review. Generally, appellate courts do not have original jurisdiction.

Federal
A federal court can exercise jurisdiction:
- When the plaintiff's cause of action involves a federal question (is based at least in part on the U.S. Constitution, a treaty, or a federal law).
- In cases between citizens of different states (or cases involving U.S. citizens and foreign countries or their citizens) when the amount in controversy exceeds $75,000 (diversity-of-citizenship jurisdiction).

Concurrent
- Exists when both federal and state courts have authority to hear the same case.

Exclusive
- Exists when only state courts or only federal courts have authority to hear a case.

Cyberspace
- The courts have developed a sliding-scale standard to use in determining when jurisdiction over a Web site owner or operator in another state is proper.

Standing can be broken down into three elements:

1. *Harm.* The party bringing the action must have suffered harm—an invasion of a legally protected interest—or must face imminent harm. The controversy must be real and substantial rather than hypothetical.

2. *Causation.* There must be a causal connection between the conduct complained of and the injury.

3. *Remedy.* It must be likely, as opposed to merely speculative, that a favorable court decision will remedy the injury suffered.

■ **CASE IN POINT 2.6** Harold Wagner obtained a loan through M.S.T. Mortgage Group to buy a house in Texas. After the sale, M.S.T. transferred its interest in the loan to another lender, which, in turn, assigned it to another lender (a common practice in the mortgage industry). Eventually, when Wagner failed to make the loan payments, CitiMortgage, Inc., notified him that it was going to foreclose on the property and sell the house.

Wagner filed a lawsuit, claiming that the lenders had improperly assigned the mortgage loan. In 2014, a federal district court ruled that Wagner lacked standing to contest the assignment. Under Texas law, only the parties directly involved in an assignment can challenge its validity. In this case, the assignment was between two lenders and did not directly involve Wagner.[12] ■

_____

12. *Wagner v. CitiMortgage, Inc.*, 995 F.Supp.2d 621 (N.D.Tex. 2014).

2-3 The State and Federal Court Systems

Each state has its own court system. Additionally, there is a system of federal courts. The right-hand side of Exhibit 2–2 illustrates the basic organizational framework characteristic of the court systems in many states. The exhibit also shows how the federal court system is structured. We turn now to an examination of these court systems, beginning with the state courts.

2-3a The State Court Systems

No two state court systems are exactly the same. Typically, though, a state court system includes several levels, or tiers, of courts, as shown in Exhibit 2–2. State courts may include (1) trial courts of limited jurisdiction, (2) trial courts of general jurisdiction, (3) appellate courts (intermediate appellate courts), and (4) the state's highest court (often called the state supreme court).

Generally, any person who is a party to a lawsuit has the opportunity to plead the case before a trial court and then, if he or she loses, before at least one level of appellate court. If the case involves a federal statute or a federal constitutional issue, the decision of the state supreme court may be further appealed to the United States Supreme Court. Note that lawsuits can take years to resolve through the courts, especially since many states have experienced large cuts in court funding in recent years. In fact, the United States Supreme Court decided a

EXHIBIT 2–2 The State and Federal Court Systems

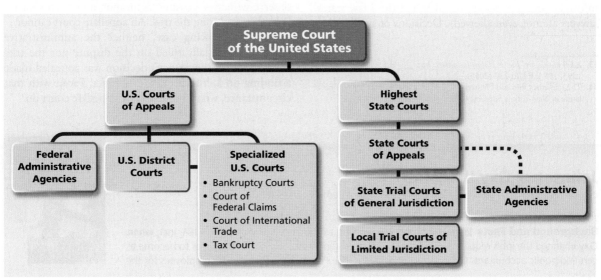

case in 2015 involving a trademark dispute that had been in the courts for more than sixteen years.[13]

The states use various methods to select judges for their courts. Usually, voters elect judges, but in some states judges are appointed. For instance, in Iowa, the governor appoints judges, and then the general population decides whether to confirm their appointment in the next general election. The states usually specify the number of years that judges will serve.

Trial Courts   Trial courts are exactly what their name implies—courts in which trials are held and testimony is taken. State trial courts have either general or limited jurisdiction, as defined earlier.

General Jurisdiction.   Trial courts that have general jurisdiction as to subject matter may be called county, district, superior, or circuit courts.[14] State trial courts of general jurisdiction have jurisdiction over a wide variety of subjects, including both civil disputes and criminal prosecutions. In some states, trial courts of general jurisdiction may hear appeals from courts of limited jurisdiction.

Limited Jurisdiction.   Courts of limited jurisdiction as to subject matter are generally inferior trial courts or minor judiciary courts. Limited jurisdiction courts might include local municipal courts (which could include separate traffic courts and drug courts) and domestic relations courts (which handle divorce and child-custody disputes).

Small claims courts are inferior trial courts that hear only civil cases involving claims of less than a certain amount, such as $5,000 (the amount varies from state to state). Procedures in small claims courts are generally informal, and lawyers are not required (in a few states, lawyers are not even allowed). Decisions of small claims

courts and municipal courts may sometimes be appealed to a state trial court of general jurisdiction.

A few states have also established Islamic law courts, which are courts of limited jurisdiction that serve the American Muslim community. These courts decide cases with reference to the *sharia*, a system of law used in most Islamic countries that is derived from the Qur'an and the sayings and doings of Muhammad and his followers.

Appellate, or Reviewing, Courts   Every state has at least one court of appeals (appellate court, or reviewing court), which may be an intermediate appellate court or the state's highest court. About three-fourths of the states have intermediate appellate courts.

Generally, courts of appeals do not conduct new trials, in which evidence is submitted to the court and witnesses are examined. Rather, an appellate court panel of three or more judges reviews the record of the case on appeal, which includes a transcript of the trial proceedings. The appellate court hears arguments from attorneys and determines whether the trial court committed an error.

Reviewing courts focus on questions of law, not questions of fact. A **question of fact** deals with what really happened in regard to the dispute being tried—such as whether a party actually burned a flag. A **question of law** concerns the application or interpretation of the law—such as whether flag-burning is a form of speech protected by the First Amendment to the U.S. Constitution. Only a judge, not a jury, can rule on questions of law.

Appellate courts normally defer (give significant weight) to the trial court's findings on questions of fact because the trial court judge and jury were in a better position to evaluate testimony. The trial court judge and jury can directly observe witnesses' gestures, demeanor, and other nonverbal behavior during the trial. An appellate court cannot.

In the following case, neither the administrative agency that initially ruled on the dispute nor the trial court to which the agency's decision was appealed made a finding on a crucial question of fact. Faced with that circumstance, what should a state appellate court do?

---

13. *B&B Hardware, Inc. v. Hargis Industries, Inc.*, ___ U.S. ___, 135 S.Ct. 1293, 191 L.Ed.2d 222 (2015).
14. The name in Ohio and Pennsylvania is Court of Common Pleas. The name in New York is Supreme Court, Trial Division.

Case 2.3

Johnson v. Oxy USA, Inc.

Court of Appeals of Texas, Houston—14th District, __ S.W.3d __ , 2016 WL 93559 (2016).

Background and Facts   Jennifer Johnson was working as a finance analyst for Oxy USA, Inc., when Oxy changed the job's requirements. To meet the new standards, Johnson took courses to become a certified public accountant. Oxy's "Educational Assistance Policy" was to reimburse employees for the cost of such courses. Johnson further agreed that Oxy could withhold the reimbursed amount from her final paycheck if she quit Oxy within a year. When she resigned less than a year later, Oxy withheld that amount from her last check. Johnson filed a claim for the amount with the Texas Workforce Commission (TWC). The TWC ruled that she was not entitled to the unpaid wages. She filed a suit in a Texas state court against Oxy, alleging breach of contract. The court affirmed the TWC's ruling. Johnson appealed.

Case 2.3 Continued

In the Language of the Court

Ken WISE, Justice

* * * *

* * * The trial court * * * held that Johnson's [claim for breach of contract was] barred by *res judicata* ["a matter judged"]. In a court of law, a claimant typically cannot pursue one remedy to an unfavorable outcome and then seek the same remedy in another proceeding before the same or a different tribunal. Res judicata *bars the relitigation of claims that have been finally adjudicated or that could have been litigated in the prior action.* [Emphasis added.]

Johnson argues that *res judicata* does not apply here because the TWC did not render a final judgment on the merits of her claim that Oxy misinterpreted its Educational Assistance Policy. Specifically, Johnson claims she was "denied the right of full adjudication of her claim because the TWC refused to consider her arguments at the administrative level as beyond its jurisdiction." To support this contention, Johnson points to the following excerpt from the * * * decision:

> * * * The TWC does not interpret contracts between employers and employee but only enforces the Texas Payday Law [the Texas state law that governs the timing of employees' paychecks]. * * * The question of whether the employer properly interpreted their policy on reimbursed educational expenses versus a business expense is a question for a different forum.

According to Johnson, this language shows that the TWC refused to consider the merits of the issue she raised as "beyond its reach." In contrast, the defendants contend that Johnson's claims are barred by *res judicata* because they are based on claims previously decided by the TWC.

* * * *

In Johnson's case, however, the TWC did not decide the key question of fact in dispute—whether Oxy violated its own Educational Assistance Policy when it withheld Johnson's final wages as reimbursement for the CPA courses. In fact, the TWC explicitly refused to do so, stating that the agency "does not interpret contracts between employers and employee." * * * Because this question goes to the heart of Johnson's breach of contract * * * claim, we hold that *res judicata* does not bar [that] claim. [Emphasis added.]

The defendants argue that because Johnson seeks to recover the same wages in this suit as she did in her claim with the TWC, *res judicata* must bar her common law cause of action. However, * * * *res judicata* would only bar a claim if TWC's order is considered final. * * * Here, the order in Johnson's case made no such findings with regard to the Educational Assistance Policy. The order expressly declined to address that issue. Therefore, * * * *res judicata* will not bar Johnson's breach of contract * * * claim.

Decision and Remedy *A state intermediate appellate court reversed the lower court's decision. "The TWC did not decide the key question of fact in dispute—whether Oxy violated its own Educational Assistance Policy when it withheld Johnson's final wages. In fact, the TWC explicitly refused to do so, stating that the agency 'does not interpret contracts between employers and employee.'" The appellate court remanded the case for a trial on the merits.*

Critical Thinking

- **Legal Environment** *Who can decide questions of fact? Who can rule on questions of law? Why?*
- **Global** *In some cases, a court may be asked to determine and interpret the law of a foreign country. Some states consider the issue of what the law of a foreign country requires to be a question of fact. Federal rules of procedure provide that this issue is a question of law. Which position seems more appropriate? Why?*

Highest State Courts The highest appellate court in a state is usually called the supreme court but may be designated by some other name. For instance, in both New York and Maryland, the highest state court is called the Court of Appeals. The highest state court in Maine and Massachusetts is the Supreme Judicial Court. In West Virginia, it is the Supreme Court of Appeals.

The decisions of each state's highest court on all questions of state law are final. Only when issues of federal law are involved can the United States Supreme Court overrule a decision made by a state's highest court. ■ **EXAMPLE 2.7** A city enacts an ordinance that prohibits citizens from engaging in door-to-door advocacy without first registering with the mayor's office and receiving a permit. A religious group then sues the city, arguing that the law violates the freedoms of speech and religion guaranteed by the First Amendment. If the state supreme court upholds the law, the group could appeal the decision to the United States Supreme Court, because a constitutional (federal) issue is involved. ■

2–3b The Federal Court System

The federal court system is basically a three-tiered model consisting of (1) U.S. district courts (trial courts of general jurisdiction) and various courts of limited

---

MANAGERIAL STRATEGY

Should You Consent to Have Your Business Case Decided by a U.S. Magistrate Judge?

You have a strong case in a contract dispute with one of your business's suppliers. The supplier is located in another state. Your attorney did everything necessary to obtain your "day in court." The court in question is a federal district court. But you have just found out that your case may not be heard for several years—or even longer. Your attorney tells you that the case can be heard in just a few months if you consent to place it in the hands of a U.S. magistrate judge.[a] Should you consent?

A Short History of U.S. Magistrate Judges

Congress authorized the creation of a new federal judicial officer, the U.S. magistrate, in 1968 to help reduce delays in the U.S. district courts.[b] These junior federal officers were to conduct a wide range of judicial proceedings as set out by statute and as assigned by the district judges under whom they served. In 1979, Congress gave U.S. magistrates consent jurisdiction, which authorized them to conduct all civil trials as long as the parties consent.[c] Currently, magistrate judges dispose of over one million civil and criminal district court matters, which include motions and hearings.

The Selection and Quality of Magistrate Judges

As mentioned, federal district judges are nominated by the president, confirmed by the Senate, and appointed for life. In contrast, U.S. magistrate judges are selected by federal district court judges based on the recommenda-

tions of a merit screening committee. They serve an eight-year term (which can be renewed).

By statute, magistrate judges must be chosen through a merit selection process. Applicants are interviewed by a screening committee of lawyers and others from the district in which the position will be filled.[d] Political party affiliation plays no part in the process.

A variety of experienced attorneys, administrative law judges, state court judges, and others apply for magistrate judge positions. A typical opening receives about a hundred applicants. The merit selection panel selects the five most qualified, who are then voted on by federal district court judges.

Because the selection process for a magistrate judge is not the same as for a district judge, some critics have expressed concerns about the quality of magistrate judges. Some groups, such as People for the American Way, are not in favor of allowing magistrate judges the power to decide cases. These critics believe that because of their limited terms, they are not completely immune from outside pressure.

Business Questions

1. *If you were facing an especially complex legal dispute—one involving many facets and several different types of law—would you consent to allowing a U.S. magistrate judge to decide the case? Why or why not?*

2. *If you had to decide whether to allow a U.S. magistrate judge to hear your case, what information might you ask your attorney to provide concerning that individual?*

a. 28 U.S.C. Sec 636(c); *Roell v. Withrow*, 538 U.S. 580, 123 S.Ct. 1698, 155 L.Ed.2d 775 (2003).
b. Federal Magistrates Act, 82 Stat. 1107, October 17, 1968.
c. U.S.C. Section 636(c)(1).

d. 28 U.S.C. Section 631(b)(5).

jurisdiction, (2) U.S. courts of appeals (intermediate courts of appeals), and (3) the United States Supreme Court.

Unlike state court judges, who are usually elected, federal court judges—including the justices of the Supreme Court—are appointed by the president of the United States, subject to confirmation by the U.S. Senate. Federal judges receive lifetime appointments under Article III of the U.S. Constitution, which states that federal judges "hold their offices during good Behaviour." In the entire history of the United States, only seven federal judges have been removed from office through impeachment proceedings.

Certain federal court officers are not chosen in the way just described. This chapter's *Managerial Strategy* feature describes how U.S. magistrate judges are selected.

U.S. District Courts At the federal level, the equivalent of a state trial court of general jurisdiction is the district court. U.S. district courts have original jurisdiction in matters involving a federal question and concurrent jurisdiction with state courts when diversity jurisdiction exists. Federal cases typically originate in district courts. There are other federal courts with original, but special (or limited), jurisdiction, such as the federal bankruptcy courts and tax courts.

Every state has at least one federal district court. The number of judicial districts can vary over time, primarily owing to population changes and corresponding changes in caseloads. Today, there are ninety-four federal judicial districts. Exhibit 2–3 shows the boundaries of both the U.S. district courts and the U.S. courts of appeals.

U.S. Courts of Appeals In the federal court system, there are thirteen U.S. courts of appeals—referred to as U.S. circuit courts of appeals. Twelve of these courts (including the Court of Appeals for the D.C. Circuit) hear appeals from the federal district courts located within their respective judicial circuits (shown in Exhibit 2–3).[15]

---

15. Historically, judges were required to "ride the circuit" and hear appeals in different courts around the country, which is how the name "circuit court" came about.

EXHIBIT 2–3 Geographic Boundaries of the U.S. Courts of Appeals and U.S. District Courts

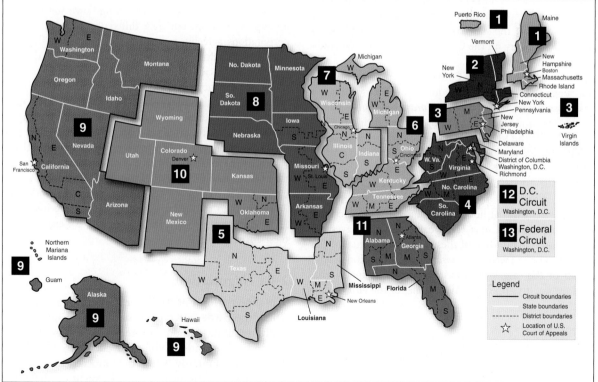

Source: Administrative Office of the United States Courts.

The Court of Appeals for the Thirteenth Circuit, called the Federal Circuit, has national appellate jurisdiction over certain types of cases, including those involving patent law and those in which the U.S. government is a defendant.

The decisions of a circuit court of appeals are binding on all courts within the circuit court's jurisdiction. These decisions are final in most cases, but appeal to the United States Supreme Court is possible.

The United States Supreme Court The highest level of the three-tiered federal court system is the United States Supreme Court. According to the U.S. Constitution, there is only one national Supreme Court. All other courts in the federal system are considered "inferior." Congress is empowered to create inferior courts as it deems necessary. The inferior courts that Congress has created include the second tier in our model—the U.S. circuit courts of appeals—as well as the district courts and the various federal courts of limited, or specialized, jurisdiction.

The United States Supreme Court consists of nine justices. Although the Supreme Court has original, or trial, jurisdiction in rare instances (set forth in Article III, Sections 1 and 2), most of its work is as an appeals court. The Supreme Court can review any case decided by any of the federal courts of appeals. It also has appellate authority over cases involving federal questions that have been decided in the state courts. The Supreme Court is the final authority on the Constitution and federal law.

Appeals to the Supreme Court. To bring a case before the Supreme Court, a party requests the Court to issue a writ of *certiorari*.[16] A **writ of *certiorari*** is an order issued by the Supreme Court to a lower court requiring the latter to send it the record of the case for review. The Court will not issue a writ unless at least four of the nine justices approve of it. This is called the **rule of four.**

Whether the Court will issue a writ of *certiorari* is entirely within its discretion, and most petitions for writs are denied. (Although thousands of cases are filed with the Supreme Court each year, it hears, on average, fewer than one hundred of these cases.)[17] A denial of the request to issue a writ of *certiorari* is not a decision on the merits of the case, nor does it indicate agreement with the lower court's opinion. Also, denial of the writ has no

value as a precedent. Denial simply means that the lower court's decision remains the law in that jurisdiction.

Petitions Granted by the Court. Typically, the Court grants petitions when cases raise important constitutional questions or when the lower courts have issued conflicting decisions on a significant issue. The justices, however, never explain their reasons for hearing certain cases and not others, so it is difficult to predict which type of case the Court might select.

Concept Summary 2.2 reviews the courts in the federal and state court systems.

2–4 Alternative Dispute Resolution

Litigation—the process of resolving a dispute through the court system—is expensive and time consuming. Litigating even the simplest complaint is costly, and because of the backlog of cases pending in many courts, several years may pass before a case is actually tried. For these and other reasons, more and more businesspersons are turning to **alternative dispute resolution (ADR)** as a means of settling their disputes.

The great advantage of ADR is its flexibility. Methods of ADR range from the parties sitting down together and attempting to work out their differences to multinational corporations agreeing to resolve a dispute through a formal hearing before a panel of experts. Normally, the parties themselves can control how they will attempt to settle their dispute. They can decide what procedures will be used, whether a neutral third party will be present or make a decision, and whether that decision will be legally binding or nonbinding. ADR also offers more privacy than court proceedings and allows disputes to be resolved relatively quickly.

Today, more than 90 percent of civil lawsuits are settled before trial using some form of ADR. Indeed, most states either require or encourage parties to undertake ADR prior to trial. Many federal courts have instituted ADR programs as well. In this section, we examine the basic forms of ADR.

2–4a Negotiation

The simplest form of ADR is **negotiation,** a process in which the parties attempt to settle their dispute informally, with or without attorneys to represent them. Attorneys frequently advise their clients to negotiate a settlement voluntarily before they proceed to trial. Parties may even try to negotiate a settlement during a trial or after the trial but before an appeal.

---

16. Pronounced sur-shee-uh-*rah*-ree.
17. From the mid-1950s through the early 1990s, the Supreme Court reviewed more cases per year than it has since then. In the Court's 1982–1983 term, for example, the Court issued written opinions in 151 cases. In contrast, during the Court's 2015–2016 term, the Court issued written opinions in only 81 cases.

Concept Summary 2.2

Types of Courts

Trial Courts	Trial courts are courts of original jurisdiction in which actions are initiated. • *State courts* —Courts of general jurisdiction can hear any case that has not been specifically designated for another court. Courts of limited jurisdiction include, among others, domestic relations courts, probate courts, municipal courts, and small claims courts. • *Federal courts* —The federal district court is the equivalent of the state trial court. Federal courts of limited jurisdiction include the bankruptcy courts and others shown in Exhibit 2–2.
Intermediate Appellate Courts	Courts of appeals are reviewing courts. Generally, appellate courts do not have original jurisdiction. • About three-fourths of the states have intermediate appellate courts. • In the federal court system, the U.S. circuit courts of appeals are the intermediate appellate courts.
Supreme Courts	The highest state court is that state's supreme court, although it may be called by some other name. • Appeal from state supreme courts to the United States Supreme Court is possible only if a federal question is involved. • The United States Supreme Court is the highest court in the federal court system and the final authority on the Constitution and federal law.

Negotiation traditionally involves just the parties themselves and (typically) their attorneys. The attorneys, though, are advocates—they are obligated to put their clients' interests first.

2–4b Mediation

In **mediation,** a neutral third party acts as a mediator and works with both sides in the dispute to facilitate a resolution. The mediator, who need not be a lawyer, usually charges a fee for his or her services (which can be split between the parties). States that require parties to undergo ADR before trial often offer mediation as one of the ADR options or (as in Florida) the only option.

During mediation, the mediator normally talks with the parties separately as well as jointly, emphasizes their points of agreement, and helps them to evaluate their options. Although the mediator may propose a solution (called a mediator's proposal), he or she does not make a decision resolving the matter.

One of the biggest advantages of mediation is that it is less adversarial than litigation. In mediation, the mediator takes an active role and attempts to bring the parties together so that they can come to a mutually satisfactory resolution. The mediation process tends to reduce the antagonism between the disputants, allowing them to resume their former relationship while minimizing hostility. For this reason, mediation is often the preferred form of ADR for disputes between business partners, employers and employees, or other parties involved in long-term relationships.

2–4c Arbitration

A more formal method of ADR is **arbitration,** in which an arbitrator (a neutral third party or a panel of experts) hears a dispute and imposes a resolution on the parties. Arbitration differs from other forms of ADR in that the third party hearing the dispute makes a decision for the parties. Exhibit 2–4 outlines the basic differences among the three traditional forms of ADR.

Usually, the parties in arbitration agree that the third party's decision will be *legally binding*, although the parties can also agree to *nonbinding* arbitration. In nonbinding arbitration, the parties can go forward with a lawsuit if they do not agree with the arbitrator's decision. Arbitration that is mandated by the courts often is not binding on the parties.

In some respects, formal arbitration resembles a trial, although usually the procedural rules are much less restrictive than those governing litigation. In a typical arbitration, the parties present opening arguments and ask for specific remedies. Both sides present evidence and may call and examine witnesses. The arbitrator then renders a decision.

The Arbitrator's Decision The arbitrator's decision is called an **award.** It is usually the final word on the matter. Although the parties may appeal an arbitrator's decision, a court's review of the decision will be much more restricted in scope than an appellate court's review of a trial court's decision. The general view is that because the parties were free to frame the issues and set the powers of the arbitrator at the outset, they cannot complain about the results. A court will set aside an award only in the event of one of the following:

1. The arbitrator's conduct or "bad faith" substantially prejudiced the rights of one of the parties.
2. The award violates an established public policy.
3. The arbitrator exceeded her or his powers—that is, arbitrated issues that the parties did not agree to submit to arbitration.

Arbitration Clauses Almost any commercial matter can be submitted to arbitration. Frequently, parties include an **arbitration clause** in a contract specifying that any dispute arising under the contract will be resolved through arbitration rather than through the court system. Parties can also agree to arbitrate a dispute *after* it arises.

Arbitration Statutes Most states have statutes (often based, in part, on the Uniform Arbitration Act) under which arbitration clauses will be enforced. Some state statutes compel arbitration of certain types of disputes, such as those involving public employees.

At the federal level, the Federal Arbitration Act (FAA), enacted in 1925, enforces arbitration clauses in contracts involving maritime activity and interstate commerce. As you will see in later chapters, the courts have defined *interstate commerce* broadly, and so arbitration

EXHIBIT 2–4   Basic Differences in the Traditional Forms of ADR

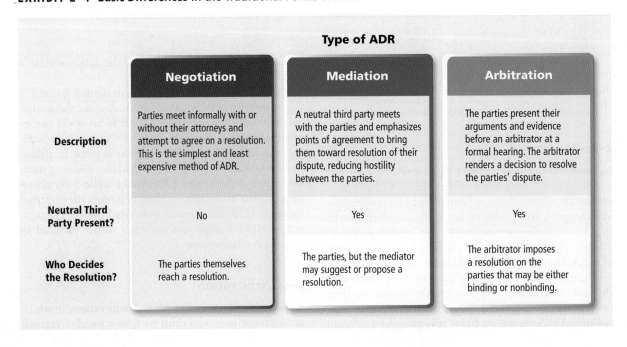

	Type of ADR		
	Negotiation	**Mediation**	**Arbitration**
Description	Parties meet informally with or without their attorneys and attempt to agree on a resolution. This is the simplest and least expensive method of ADR.	A neutral third party meets with the parties and emphasizes points of agreement to bring them toward resolution of their dispute, reducing hostility between the parties.	The parties present their arguments and evidence before an arbitrator at a formal hearing. The arbitrator renders a decision to resolve the parties' dispute.
Neutral Third Party Present?	No	Yes	Yes
Who Decides the Resolution?	The parties themselves reach a resolution.	The parties, but the mediator may suggest or propose a resolution.	The arbitrator imposes a resolution on the parties that may be either binding or nonbinding.

agreements involving transactions only slightly connected to the flow of interstate commerce may fall under the FAA. The FAA established a national policy favoring arbitration that the United States Supreme Court has continued to reinforce.[18]

■ **CASE IN POINT 2.8** Cleveland Construction, Inc. (CCI), was the general contractor on a project to build a grocery store in Houston, Texas. CCI hired Levco Construction, Inc., as a subcontractor. Their contract included an arbitration provision stating that any disputes would be resolved by arbitration in Ohio. When a dispute arose between the parties, Levco filed a suit against CCI in a Texas state court. CCI sought to compel arbitration in Ohio under the Federal Arbitration Act (FAA), but a Texas statute allows a party to void a contractual provision that requires arbitration outside Texas. Ultimately, a Texas appellate court held that the FAA preempted (took priority over) the state law. CCI could compel arbitration in Ohio.[19] ■

The Issue of Arbitrability

The terms of an arbitration agreement can limit the types of disputes that the parties agree to arbitrate. Disputes can arise, however, when the parties do not specify limits or when the parties disagree on whether a particular matter is covered by their arbitration agreement.

When one party files a lawsuit to compel arbitration, it is up to the court to resolve the issue of *arbitrability*. That is, the court must decide whether the matter is one that must be resolved through arbitration. If the court finds that the subject matter in controversy is covered by the agreement to arbitrate, then it may compel arbitration.

Usually, a court will allow a claim to be arbitrated if the court finds that the relevant statute (the state arbitration statute or the FAA) does not exclude such claims. No party, however, will be ordered to submit a particular dispute to arbitration unless the court is convinced that the party has consented to do so. Additionally, the courts will not compel arbitration if it is clear that the arbitration rules and procedures are inherently unfair to one of the parties.

Mandatory Arbitration in the Employment Context

A significant question for businesspersons has concerned mandatory arbitration clauses in employment contracts. Many employees claim they are at a disadvantage when they are forced, as a condition of being hired,

to agree to arbitrate all disputes and thus waive their rights under statutes designed to protect employees.

The United States Supreme Court, however, has held that mandatory arbitration clauses in employment contracts are generally enforceable. ■ **CASE IN POINT 2.9** In a landmark decision, *Gilmer v. Interstate Johnson Lane Corp.*,[20] the Supreme Court held that a claim brought under a federal statute prohibiting age discrimination could be subject to arbitration. The Court concluded that the employee had waived his right to sue when he agreed, as part of a required application to be a securities representative, to arbitrate "any dispute, claim, or controversy" relating to his employment. ■

Since the *Gilmer* decision, some courts have refused to enforce one-sided arbitration clauses.[21] Nevertheless, the policy favoring enforcement of mandatory arbitration agreements in employment contracts remains strong.

■ **CASE IN POINT 2.10** Stephanie Cruise was hired by Kroger Co. to work in its deli. Her job application had included a clause requiring arbitration of "employment-related disputes." When Cruise was fired four years later, she filed a lawsuit claiming that Kroger had violated a number of laws prohibiting employment discrimination. Kroger filed a motion to compel arbitration. A state appellate court concluded that the arbitration clause in the employment application established that the parties had agreed to arbitrate their "employment-related disputes." Cruise's claims fell within the meaning of that agreement, and therefore she was required to arbitrate.[22] ■

2–4d Other Types of ADR

The three forms of ADR just discussed are the oldest and traditionally the most commonly used forms. In addition, a variety of newer types of ADR have emerged, including those described here.

1. In **early neutral case evaluation,** the parties select a neutral third party (generally an expert in the subject matter of the dispute) and explain their respective positions to that person. The case evaluator assesses the strengths and weaknesses of each party's claims.

2. In a **mini-trial,** each party's attorney briefly argues the party's case before the other party and a panel of representatives from each side who have the authority to settle the dispute. Typically, a neutral third party (usually an expert in the area being disputed) acts as

---

18. See, for example, *AT&T Mobility LLC v. Concepcion*, 563 U.S. 333, 131 S.Ct. 1740, 179 L.Ed.2d 742 (2010).

19. *Cleveland Construction, Inc. v. Levco Construction, Inc.*, 359 S.W.3d 843 (Tex.App. 2012).

20. 500 U.S. 20, 111 S.Ct. 1647, 114 L.Ed.2d 26 (1991).

21. See, for example, *Mohamed v. Uber Technologies, Inc.*, 2015 WL 3749716 (N.D.Cal. 2015); *Macias v. Excel Building Services, LLC*, 767 F.Supp.2d 1002 (N.D.Cal. 2011).

22. *Cruise v. Kroger Co.*, 233 Cal.App.4th 390, 183 Cal.Rptr.3d 17 (2015).

an adviser. If the parties fail to reach an agreement, the adviser renders an opinion as to how a court would likely decide the issue.

3. Numerous federal courts hold **summary jury trials,** in which the parties present their arguments and evidence and the jury renders a verdict. The jury's verdict is not binding, but it does act as a guide to both sides in reaching an agreement during the mandatory negotiations that immediately follow the trial.

4. Other alternatives being employed by the courts include summary proceedings, which dispense with some formal court procedures, and the appointment of special masters to assist judges in deciding complex issues.

2–4e Providers of ADR Services

ADR services are provided by both government agencies and private organizations. A major provider of ADR services is the American Arbitration Association (AAA), which handles more than 200,000 claims a year in its numerous offices worldwide. Most of the largest U.S. law firms are members of this nonprofit association.

Cases brought before the AAA are heard by an expert or a panel of experts in the area relating to the dispute and are usually settled quickly. Generally, about half of the panel members are lawyers. To cover its costs, the AAA charges a fee, paid by the party filing the claim. In addition, each party to the dispute pays a specified amount for each hearing day, as well as a special additional fee in cases involving personal injuries or property loss.

Hundreds of for-profit firms around the country also provide dispute-resolution services. Typically, these firms hire retired judges to conduct arbitration hearings or otherwise assist parties in settling their disputes. The judges follow procedures similar to those of the federal courts and use similar rules. Usually, each party to the dispute pays a filing fee and a designated fee for a hearing session or conference.

2–4f Online Dispute Resolution

An increasing number of companies and organizations are offering dispute-resolution services using the Internet. The settlement of disputes in these forums is known as **online dispute resolution (ODR).** The disputes resolved have most commonly involved rights to domain names (Web site addresses) or the quality of goods sold via the Internet, including goods sold through Internet auction sites.

Rules being developed in online forums may ultimately become a code of conduct for everyone who does business in cyberspace. Most online forums do not automatically apply the law of any specific jurisdiction. Instead, results are often based on general, universal legal principles. As with most offline methods of dispute resolution, any party may appeal to a court at any time.

ODR may be best for resolving small- to medium-sized business liability claims, which may not be worth the expense of litigation or traditional ADR methods. In addition, some cities use ODR as a means of resolving claims against them. ■ **EXAMPLE 2.11** New York City uses Cybersettle.com to resolve auto accident, sidewalk, and other personal-injury claims made against the city. Parties with complaints submit their demands, and the city submits its offers confidentially online. If an offer exceeds a demand, the claimant keeps half the difference as a bonus, plus the original claim. ■

2–5 International Dispute Resolution

Businesspersons who engage in international business transactions normally take special precautions to protect themselves in the event that a party with whom they are dealing in another country breaches an agreement. Often, parties to international contracts include special clauses in their contracts providing for how disputes arising under the contracts will be resolved. Sometimes, international treaties (formal agreements among several nations) even require parties to arbitrate any disputes.

2–5a Forum-Selection and Choice-of-Law Clauses

Parties to international transactions often include forum-selection and choice-of-law clauses in their contracts. These clauses designate the jurisdiction (court or country) where any dispute arising under the contract will be litigated and which nation's law will be applied.

When an international contract does not include such clauses, any legal proceedings arising under the contract will be more complex and attended by much more uncertainty. For instance, litigation may take place in two or more countries, with each country applying its own national law to the particular transactions.

Furthermore, even if a plaintiff wins a favorable judgment in a lawsuit litigated in the plaintiff's country, the defendant's country could refuse to enforce the court's judgment. The judgment may be enforced in the defendant's country for reasons of courtesy. The United States, for instance, will generally enforce a foreign court's decision if it is consistent with U.S. national law and policy. Other nations, however, may not be as accommodating as the United States, and the plaintiff may be left empty-handed.

2–5b Arbitration Clauses

International contracts also often include arbitration clauses that require a neutral third party to decide any contract disputes. Many of the institutions that offer arbitration, such as the International Chamber of Commerce or the Hong Kong International Arbitration Centre, have formulated model clauses for parties to use. In international arbitration proceedings, the third party may be a neutral entity, a panel of individuals representing both parties' interests, or some other group or organization.

The United Nations Convention on the Recognition and Enforcement of Foreign Arbitral Awards[23] has been implemented in more than 145 countries, including the United States. This convention assists in the enforcement of arbitration clauses, as do provisions in specific treaties among nations. The American Arbitration Association provides arbitration services for international as well as domestic disputes.

---

23. June 10, 1958, 21 U.S.T. 2517, T.I.A.S. No. 6997 (the "New York Convention").

Reviewing: Courts and Alternative Dispute Resolution

Stan Garner resides in Illinois and promotes boxing matches for SuperSports, Inc., an Illinois corporation. Garner created the concept of "Ages" promotion—a three-fight series of boxing matches pitting an older fighter (George Foreman) against a younger fighter. The concept had titles for each of the three fights, including "Battle of the Ages." Garner contacted Foreman and his manager, who both reside in Texas, to sell the idea, and they arranged a meeting in Las Vegas, Nevada. During negotiations, Foreman's manager signed a nondisclosure agreement prohibiting him from disclosing Garner's promotional concepts unless the parties signed a contract. Nevertheless, after negotiations fell through, Foreman used Garner's "Battle of the Ages" concept to promote a subsequent fight. Garner filed a suit against Foreman and his manager in a federal district court located in Illinois, alleging breach of contract. Using the information presented in the chapter, answer the following questions.

1. On what basis might the federal district court in Illinois exercise jurisdiction in this case?
2. Does the federal district court have original or appellate jurisdiction?
3. Suppose that Garner had filed his action in an Illinois state court. Could an Illinois state court have exercised personal jurisdiction over Foreman or his manager? Why or why not?
4. Now suppose that Garner had filed his action in a Nevada state court. Would that court have had personal jurisdiction over Foreman or his manager? Explain.

Debate This . . .   *In this age of the Internet, when people communicate via e-mail, texts, tweets, Facebook, and Skype, is the concept of jurisdiction losing its meaning?*

Terms and Concepts

alternative dispute resolution (ADR) 40	federal question 28	online dispute resolution (ODR) 44
arbitration 41	*in personam* jurisdiction 27	probate court 28
arbitration clause 42	*in rem* jurisdiction 27	question of fact 36
award 42	judicial review 26	question of law 36
bankruptcy court 28	jurisdiction 27	rule of four 40
concurrent jurisdiction 30	litigation 40	small claims court 36
diversity of citizenship 28	long arm statute 27	standing to sue 33
early neutral case evaluation 43	mediation 41	summary jury trial 44
exclusive jurisdiction 30	mini-trial 43	venue 33
	negotiation 40	writ of *certiorari* 40

Issue Spotters

1. Sue uses her smartphone to purchase a video security system for her architectural firm from Tipton, Inc., a company located in a different state. The system arrives a month after the projected delivery date, is of poor quality, and does not function as advertised. Sue files a suit against Tipton in a state court. Does the court in Sue's state have jurisdiction over Tipton? What factors will the court consider in determining jurisdiction? (See *Basic Judicial Requirements*.)

2. The state in which Sue resides requires that her dispute with Tipton be submitted to mediation or nonbinding arbitration. If the dispute is not resolved, or if either party disagrees with the decision of the mediator or arbitrator, will a court hear the case? Explain. (See *Alternative Dispute Resolution*.)

• **Check your answers to the Issue Spotters against the answers provided in Appendix D at the end of this text.**

Business Scenarios

2–1. Standing. Jack and Maggie Turton bought a house in Jefferson County, Idaho, located directly across the street from a gravel pit. A few years later, the county converted the pit to a landfill. The landfill accepted many kinds of trash that cause harm to the environment, including major appliances, animal carcasses, containers with hazardous content warnings, leaking car batteries, and waste oil. The Turtons complained to the county, but the county did nothing. The Turtons then filed a lawsuit against the county alleging violations of federal environmental laws pertaining to groundwater contamination and other pollution. Do the Turtons have standing to sue? Why or why not? (See *Basic Judicial Requirements*.)

Business Case Problems

2–2. Venue. Brandy Austin used powdered infant formula manufactured by Nestlé USA, Inc., to feed her infant daughter. Austin claimed that a can of the formula was contaminated with *Enterobacter sakazakii* bacteria, causing severe injury to the infant. The bacteria can cause infections of the bloodstream and central nervous system—in particular, meningitis (inflammation of the tissue surrounding the brain or spinal cord). Austin filed an action against Nestlé in Hennepin County District Court in Minnesota. Nestlé argued for a change of venue because the alleged harm had occurred in South Carolina. Austin is a South Carolina resident and had given birth to her daughter in that state. Should the case be transferred to a South Carolina venue? Why or why not? [*Austin v. Nestlé USA, Inc.*, 677 F.Supp.2d 1134 (D.Minn. 2009)] (See *Basic Judicial Requirements*.)

2–3. Arbitration. PRM Energy Systems owned patents licensed to Primenergy to use in the United States. Their contract stated that "all disputes" would be settled by arbitration. Kobe Steel of Japan was interested in using the technology represented by PRM's patents. Primenergy agreed to let Kobe use the technology in Japan without telling PRM. When PRM learned about the secret deal, the firm filed a suit against Primenergy for fraud and theft. Does this dispute go to arbitration or to trial? Why? [*PRM Energy Systems v. Primenergy*, 592 F.3d 830 (8th Cir. 2010)] (See *Alternative Dispute Resolution*.)

2–4. Spotlight on the National Football League—Arbitration. Bruce Matthews played football for the Tennessee Titans. As part of his contract, he agreed to submit any dispute to arbitration. He also agreed that Tennessee law would determine all matters related to workers' compensation. After Matthews retired, he filed a workers' compensation claim in California. The arbitrator ruled that Matthews could pursue his claim in California but only under Tennessee law. Should this award be set aside? Explain. [*National Football League Players Association v. National Football League Management Council*, 2011 WL 1137334 (S.D.Cal. 2011)] (See *Alternative Dispute Resolution*.)

2–5. Minimum Contacts. Seal Polymer Industries sold two freight containers of latex gloves to Med-Express, Inc., a company based in North Carolina. When Med-Express failed to pay the $104,000 owed for the gloves, Seal Polymer sued in an Illinois court and obtained a judgment against Med-Express. Med-Express argued that it did not have minimum contacts with Illinois because it was incorporated under North Carolina law and had its principal place of business in North Carolina. Therefore, the Illinois judgment based on personal jurisdiction was invalid. Was this argument alone sufficient to prevent the Illinois judgment from being collected against Med-Express in North Carolina? Why or why not? [*Seal Polymer Industries v. Med-Express, Inc.*, 725 S.E.2d 5 (N.C.App. 2012)] (See *Basic Judicial Requirements*.)

2–6. Arbitration. Horton Automatics and the Industrial Division of the Communications Workers of America, the union that represented Horton's workers, negotiated a collective bargaining agreement. If an employee's discharge for a workplace-rule violation was submitted to arbitration, the agreement limited the arbitrator to determining whether the rule was reasonable and whether the employee had violated it. When Horton discharged employee Ruben de la Garza, the union appealed to arbitration. The arbitrator found that de la Garza had violated a reasonable safety rule, but "was not totally convinced" that Horton should have treated the violation more seriously than other rule violations. The arbitrator ordered de la Garza reinstated. Can a court set aside this order? Explain. [*Horton Automatics v. The Industrial Division of the Communications Workers of America, AFL-CIO*, 2013 WL 59204 (5th Cir. 2013)] (See *Alternative Dispute Resolution*.)

2–7. Business Case Problem with Sample Answer— Corporate Contacts. LG Electronics, Inc., a South Korean company, and nineteen other foreign companies participated in the global market for cathode ray tube (CRT) products. CRTs were integrated as components in consumer goods, including television sets, and were sold for many years in high volume in the United States, including the state of Washington. The state filed a suit in a Washington state court against LG and the others, alleging a conspiracy to raise prices and set production levels in the market for CRTs in violation of a state consumer protection statute. The defendants filed a motion to dismiss the suit for lack of personal jurisdiction. Should this motion be granted? Explain. [*State of Washington v. LG Electronics, Inc.*, 341 P.3d 346 (Wash. App., Div. 1 2015)] (See *Basic Judicial Requirements*.)

- **For a sample answer to Problem 2–7, go to Appendix E at the end of this text.**

2–8. Appellate, or Reviewing, Courts. Angelica Westbrook was employed as a collector for Franklin Collection Service, Inc. During a collection call, Westbrook told a debtor that a $15 processing fee was an "interest" charge. This violated company policy. Westbrook was fired. She filed a claim for unemployment benefits, which the Mississippi Department of Employment Security (MDES) approved. Franklin objected. At an MDES hearing, a Franklin supervisor testified that she had heard Westbrook make the false statement, although she admitted that there had been no similar incidents with Westbrook. Westbrook denied making the statement, but added that if she had said it, she did not remember it. The agency found that Franklin's reason for terminating Westbrook did not amount to the misconduct required to disqualify her for benefits and upheld the approval. Franklin appealed to a state intermediate appellate court. Is the court likely to uphold the agency's findings of fact? Explain. [*Franklin Collection Service, Inc. v. Mississippi Department of Employment Security*, 184 So.3d 330 (Miss.App. 2016)] (See *The State and Federal Court Systems*.)

2–9. A Question of Ethics—Agreement to Arbitrate. *Nellie Lumpkin, who suffered from various illnesses, including dementia, was admitted to the Picayune Convalescent Center, a nursing home. Because of her mental condition, her daughter, Beverly McDaniel, filled out the admissions paperwork and signed the admissions agreement. It included a clause requiring parties to submit to arbitration any disputes that arose. After Lumpkin left the center two years later, she sued, through her husband, for negligent treatment and malpractice during her stay. The center moved to force the matter to arbitration. The trial court held that the arbitration agreement was not enforceable. The center appealed. [Covenant Health & Rehabilitation of Picayune, LP v. Lumpkin, 23 So.3d 1092 (Miss.App. 2009)]* (See *Alternative Dispute Resolution*.)

(a) Should a dispute involving medical malpractice be forced into arbitration? This is a claim of negligent care, not a breach of a commercial contract. Is it ethical for medical facilities to impose such a requirement? Is there really any bargaining over such terms? Discuss fully.

(b) Should a person with limited mental capacity be held to an arbitration clause agreed to by the next of kin who signed on behalf of that person? Why or why not?

Legal Reasoning Group Activity

2–10. Access to Courts. Assume that a statute in your state requires that all civil lawsuits involving damages of less than $50,000 be arbitrated. Such a case can be tried in court only if a party is dissatisfied with the arbitrator's decision. The statute also provides that if a trial does not result in an improvement of more than 10 percent in the position of the party who demanded the trial, that party must pay the entire cost of the arbitration proceeding. (See *Alternative Dispute Resolution*.)

(a) One group will argue that the state statute violates litigants' rights of access to the courts and trial by jury.

(b) Another group will argue that the statute does not violate litigants' right of access to the courts.

(c) A third group will evaluate how the determination on right of access would be changed if the statute was part of a pilot program that affected only a few judicial districts in the state.

CHAPTER 3

Court Procedures

Amerian and English courts follow the *adversarial system of
justice*. Although parties are
allowed to represent themselves in
court (called *pro se* representation),[1]

most parties to lawsuits hire attorneys
to represent them. Each lawyer acts as
his or her client's advocate. Each lawyer presents his or her client's version
of the facts in such a way as to convince the judge (or the judge and jury,
in a jury trial) that this version is correct. Most of the judicial procedures

that you will read about are rooted
in the adversarial framework of the
American legal system.

---

1. This right was definitively established in
   Faretta v. California, 422 U.S. 806, 95 S.Ct.
   2525, 45 L.Ed.2d 562 (1975).

3–1 Procedural Rules

The parties to a lawsuit must comply with the procedural
rules of the court in which the lawsuit is filed. Although
people often think that substantive law determines the
outcome of a case, procedural law can have a significant
impact on a person's ability to pursue a legal claim. Procedural rules provide a framework for every dispute and
specify what must be done at each stage of the litigation
process.

Procedural rules are complex, and they vary from
court to court and from state to state. There is a set of
federal rules of procedure as well as various sets of rules for
state courts. Additionally, the applicable procedures will
depend on whether the case is a civil or criminal proceeding. All civil trials held in federal district courts are governed by the **Federal Rules of Civil Procedure (FRCP).**[2]

3–1a Stages of Litigation

Broadly speaking, the litigation process has three phases:
pretrial, trial, and posttrial. Each phase involves specific procedures, as discussed throughout this chapter.
Although civil lawsuits may vary greatly in terms of complexity, cost, and detail, they typically progress through
the stages charted in Exhibit 3–1.

---

2. The United States Supreme Court has authority to establish these rules,
   as spelled out in 28 U.S.C. Sections 2071–2077. Generally, though, the
   federal judiciary appoints committees that make recommendations to the
   Supreme Court. The Court then publishes any proposed changes in the
   rules and allows for public comment before finalizing the rules.

To illustrate the procedures involved in a civil lawsuit,
we will use a simple hypothetical case. The case arose
from an automobile accident, which occurred when a
car driven by Antonio Carvello, a resident of New Jersey, collided with a car driven by Jill Kirby, a resident of
New York. The accident took place at an intersection in
New York City. Kirby suffered personal injuries, which
caused her to incur medical and hospital expenses as well
as lost wages for four months. In all, she calculated that
the cost to her of the accident was $500,000.[3] Carvello
and Kirby have been unable to agree on a settlement, and
Kirby now must decide whether to sue Carvello for the
$500,000 compensation she feels she deserves.

3–1b Hire an Attorney

As mentioned, rules of procedure often affect the outcome of a dispute—a fact that highlights the importance
of obtaining the advice of counsel. The first step taken
by almost anyone contemplating a lawsuit is to seek the
guidance of a licensed attorney.

In the hypothetical Kirby-Carvello case, assume that
Kirby consults with a lawyer. The attorney will advise
her regarding what she can expect in a lawsuit, her probability of success at trial, and the procedures that will be
involved. If more than one court would have jurisdiction
over the matter, the attorney will also discuss the advantages and disadvantages of filing in a particular court. In
addition, the attorney will indicate how long it will take

---

3. For simplicity, we are ignoring damages for pain and suffering and for permanent disabilities, which plaintiffs in personal-injury cases often seek.

EXHIBIT 3–1 Stages in a Typical Lawsuit

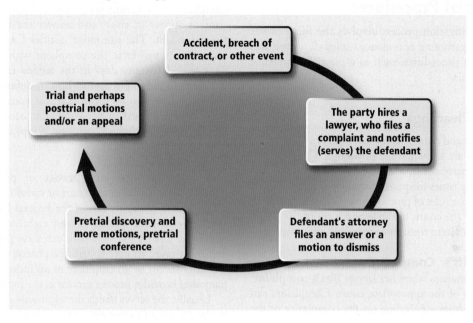

to resolve the dispute through litigation in a particular court and provide an estimate of the costs involved.

The attorney will also inform Kirby of the legal fees that she will have to pay in an attempt to collect damages from the defendant, Carvello. Attorneys base their fees on such factors as the difficulty of the matter at issue, the attorney's experience and skill, and the amount of time involved. In the United States, legal fees range from $200 to $700 per hour or even higher (the average fee is between $200 and $450 per hour). The client normally must also pay various expenses related to the case (called "out-of-pocket" costs), such as court filing fees, travel expenses, and the costs of expert witnesses and investigators.

Types of Attorneys' Fees For a particular legal matter, an attorney may charge one type of fee or a combination of several types.

1. *Fixed fees* may be charged for the performance of such services as drafting a simple will.
2. *Hourly fees* may be charged for matters that will involve an indeterminate period of time. The amount of time required to bring a case to trial, for instance, probably cannot be precisely estimated in advance.
3. *Contingency fees* are fixed as a percentage (usually 33 percent) of a client's recovery in certain types of lawsuits, such as a personal-injury lawsuit.[4] If the

lawsuit is unsuccessful, the attorney receives no fee, but the client will have to reimburse the attorney for all out-of-pocket costs incurred.

Because Kirby's claim involves a personal injury, her lawyer will likely take the case on a contingency-fee basis. In some cases, the winning party may be able to recover at least some portion of her or his attorneys' fees from the losing party.

Settlement Considerations Once an attorney has been retained, the attorney is required to pursue a resolution of the matter on the client's behalf. Nevertheless, the amount of resources an attorney will spend on a given case is affected by the time and funds the client wishes to devote to the process.

If the client is willing to pay for a lengthy trial and one or more appeals, the attorney may pursue those actions. Often, however, after learning of the substantial costs that litigation entails, a client may decide to pursue a settlement of the claim. Attempts to settle the case may be ongoing throughout the litigation process.

Another important consideration in deciding whether to pursue litigation is the defendant's ability to pay the damages sought. Even if Kirby is awarded damages, it may be difficult to enforce the court's judgment if the amount exceeds the limits of Carvello's automobile insurance policy. (We will discuss the problems involved in enforcing a judgment later in this chapter.)

---

4. Contingency-fee arrangements are typically prohibited in criminal cases, divorce cases, and cases involving the distribution of assets after death.

3–2 Pretrial Procedures

The pretrial litigation process involves the filing of the *pleadings*, the gathering of evidence (called *discovery*), and possibly other procedures, such as a pretrial conference and jury selection.

3–2a The Pleadings

The *complaint* and *answer* (and other legal documents discussed below) are known as the **pleadings.** The pleadings inform each party of the other's claims, reveal the facts, and specify the issues (disputed questions) involved in the case. Because the rules of procedure vary depending on the jurisdiction of the court, the style and form of the pleadings may be different from those shown in this chapter.

The Plaintiff's Complaint Kirby's action against Carvello commences when her lawyer files a **complaint**[5] with the clerk of the appropriate court. Complaints can be lengthy or brief, depending on the complexity of the case and the rules of the jurisdiction. The complaint contains statements or allegations concerning the following:

1. *Jurisdiction.* Facts showing that the particular court has subject-matter and personal jurisdiction.
2. *Legal theory.* The facts establishing the plaintiff's claim and basis for relief.
3. *Remedy.* The remedy (such as an amount of damages) that the plaintiff is seeking.

Exhibit 3–2 illustrates how a complaint in the Kirby-Carvello case might appear. The complaint asserts facts indicating that the federal district court has subject-matter jurisdiction because of diversity of citizenship. It then gives a brief statement of the facts of the accident and alleges that Carvello negligently drove his vehicle through a red light, striking Kirby's car. The complaint alleges that Carvello's actions caused Kirby serious personal injury and property damage. The complaint goes on to state that Kirby is seeking $500,000 in damages. (In some state civil actions, the plaintiff need not specify the amount of damages sought.)

Service of Process. Before the court can exercise personal jurisdiction over the defendant (Carvello)—in effect, before the lawsuit can begin—the court must have proof that the defendant was notified of the lawsuit. Formally notifying the defendant of a lawsuit is called **service of process.**

The plaintiff must deliver, or serve, a copy of the complaint and a **summons** (a notice requiring the defendant to appear in court and answer the complaint) to the defendant. The summons notifies Carvello that he must file an answer to the complaint within a specified time period (twenty days in the federal courts) or suffer a default judgment against him. A **default judgment** in Kirby's favor would mean that she would be awarded the damages alleged in her complaint because Carvello failed to respond to the allegations. A typical summons is shown in Exhibit 3–3.

Method of Service. How service of process occurs depends on the rules of the court or jurisdiction in which the lawsuit is brought. Under the Federal Rules of Civil Procedure, anyone who is at least eighteen years of age and is not a party to the lawsuit can serve process in federal court cases. In state courts, the process server is often a county sheriff or an employee of an independent company that provides process service in the local area.

Usually, the server hands the summons and complaint to the defendant personally or leaves it at the defendant's residence or place of business. In some states, process can be served by mail if the defendant consents (accepts service). When the defendant cannot be reached, special rules provide for alternative means of service, such as publishing a notice in the local newspaper.

In some situations, courts allow service of process via e-mail, as long as it is reasonably calculated to provide notice and an opportunity to respond. Today, some judges have even allowed defendants to be served legal documents via social media, as discussed in this chapter's *Digital Update* feature.

In cases involving corporate defendants, the summons and complaint may be served on an officer or on a *registered agent* (representative) of the corporation. The name of a corporation's registered agent can usually be obtained from the secretary of state's office in the state where the company incorporated its business (and, frequently, from the secretary of state's office in any state where the corporation does business).

Waiver of Formal Service of Process. In many instances, the defendant is already aware that a lawsuit is being filed and is willing to waive (give up) her or his right to be served personally. The Federal Rules of Civil Procedure (FRCP) and many states' rules allow defendants to waive formal service of process, provided that certain procedures are followed.

In the Kirby case, for example, Kirby's attorney could mail to defendant Carvello a copy of the complaint, along with "Waiver of Service of Summons" forms for

---

5. Sometimes, the document filed with the court is called a *petition* or a *declaration* instead of a complaint.

EXHIBIT 3-2 A Typical Complaint

```
                 IN THE UNITED STATES DISTRICT COURT
              FOR THE SOUTHERN DISTRICT OF NEW YORK


                                              CIVIL NO. 9-1047

   JILL KIRBY

                         Plaintiff,

   v.                                         COMPLAINT

   ANTONIO CARVELLO

                         Defendant.
```

The plaintiff brings this cause of action against the defendant, alleging as follows:

1. This action is between the plaintiff, who is a resident of the State of New York, and the defendant, who is a resident of the State of New Jersey. There is diversity of citizenship between the parties.
2. The amount in controversy, exclusive of interest and costs, exceeds the sum of $75,000.
3. On September 10th, 2017, the plaintiff, Jill Kirby, was exercising good driving habits and reasonable care in driving her car through the intersection of Boardwalk and Pennsylvania Avenue, New York City, New York, when the defendant, Antonio Carvello, negligently drove his vehicle through a red light at the intersection and collided with the plaintiff's vehicle.
4. As a result of the collision, the plaintiff suffered severe physical injury, which prevented her from working, and property damage to her car.

WHEREFORE, the plaintiff demands judgment against the defendant for the sum of $500,000 plus interest at the maximum legal rate and the costs of this action.

By ___*Joseph Roe*___

Joseph Roe
Attorney for Plaintiff
100 Main Street
New York, New York

1/3/18

Carvello to sign. If Carvello signs and returns the forms within thirty days, formal service of process is waived.

Moreover, under the FRCP, defendants who agree to waive formal service of process receive additional time to respond to the complaint (sixty days, instead of twenty days). Some states provide similar incentives to encourage defendants to waive formal service of process and thereby reduce associated costs and foster cooperation between the parties.

The Defendant's Response Typically, the defendant's response to the complaint takes the form of an **answer.** In an answer, the defendant either admits or denies each of the allegations in the plaintiff's complaint and may also set forth defenses to those allegations.

Under the federal rules, any allegations that are not denied by the defendant will be deemed by the court to have been admitted. If Carvello admits to all of Kirby's allegations in his answer, a judgment will be entered for

EXHIBIT 3–3 A Typical Summons

```
                    UNITED STATES DISTRICT COURT
              FOR THE SOUTHERN DISTRICT OF NEW YORK

                                      CIVIL ACTION, FILE NO. 9-1047

   JILL KIRBY

                    Plaintiff,

   v.                                         SUMMONS

   ANTONIO CARVELLO

                    Defendant.


   To the above-named Defendant:

   You are hereby summoned and required to serve upon Joseph Roe,
   plaintiff's attorney, whose address is 100 Main Street, New York, NY, an
   answer to the complaint which is herewith served upon you, within 20 days
   after service of this summons upon you, exclusive of the day of service.
   If you fail to do so, judgment by default will be taken against you for
   the relief demanded in the complaint.


   C. H. Hynek                          January 3, 2018
   ───────────────────                  ─────────────────────
   CLERK                                DATE


   John Dolan
   ───────────────────
   BY DEPUTY CLERK
```

Kirby. If Carvello denies Kirby's allegations, the matter will proceed further.

Affirmative Defenses. Carvello can also admit the truth of Kirby's complaint but raise new facts to show that he should not be held liable for Kirby's damages. This is called raising an **affirmative defense.**

Defendants in both civil and criminal cases can raise affirmative defenses. For example, Carvello could assert Kirby's own negligence as a defense by alleging that Kirby was driving negligently at the time of the accident. In some states, a plaintiff's contributory negligence operates as a complete defense. In most states, however, the plaintiff's own negligence constitutes only a partial defense.

Counterclaims. Carvello could also deny Kirby's allegations and set forth his own claim that the accident occurred as a result of Kirby's negligence and therefore she owes Carvello for damage to his car. This is appropriately called a **counterclaim.** If Carvello files a counterclaim, Kirby will have to submit an answer to the counterclaim.

3–2b Dismissals and Judgments before Trial

Many actions for which pleadings have been filed never come to trial. The parties may, for instance, negotiate a settlement of the dispute at any stage of the litigation process. There are also numerous procedural avenues for disposing of a case without a trial. Many of them involve one or the other party's attempts to get the case dismissed through the use of various motions.

A **motion** is a procedural request submitted to the court by an attorney on behalf of her or his client. When a motion is filed with the court, the filing party must also send to, or personally serve, the opposing party a *notice of*

Using Social Media for Service of Process

Historically, when process servers failed to reach a defendant at home, they attempted to serve process at the defendant's workplace, by mail, and by publication. In our digital age, does publication via social media qualify as legitimate service of process?

Can You Serve a Divorce Summons Through a Private Message on a Facebook Account?

Facebook has well over 1.6 billion active users per month. Assume that a man has a Facebook account and so does his spouse. He has moved out and is intentionally avoiding service of a divorce summons. Even a private investigator has not been able to deliver that summons. What to do? According to a New York state court ruling, the lawyer for the woman can serve the divorce summons through a private message from her Facebook account. "The past decade has . . . seen the advent and ascendancy of social media. . . . Thus, it would appear that the next frontier in the developing law of the service of process over the Internet is the use of social media sites as forums through which a summons can be delivered."[a]

An Increasing Use of Social Media for Service of Process

More and more courts are allowing service of process via Facebook and other social media. One New York City family court judge ruled that a divorced man could

serve his ex-wife through her active Facebook account. She had moved out of the house and provided no forwarding address. A Dallas district judge authorized service of process via social media, and other judges in that state have agreed with the ruling. A bill pending in the Texas state legislature would allow service via social media whenever a plaintiff can authenticate the social media account. Other states are considering similar legislation.

Not All Courts Agree, Though

In spite of these examples, the courts have not uniformly approved of using social media to serve process. In one federal district court case, the court pointed out the relative simplicity of creating a fake Facebook account and the court's resulting inability to verify the true owner of that account.[b] In another case, involving the Federal Trade Commission (FTC), the court did allow service of process via Facebook, but noted that "if the FTC were proposing to serve the defendants only by means of Facebook, as opposed to using Facebook as a supplemental means of service, a substantial question would arise whether that service comports with due process."[c]

Critical Thinking *In our connected world, is there any way a defendant could avoid service of process via social media?*

a. *Baido v. Blood-Dzraqu*, 48 Misc.3d 309, 5 N.Y.S.3d 709 (2015).
b. *Fortunato v. Chase Bank USA*, 2011 WL 5574884 (S.D.N.Y. 2011) and 2012 WL 2086950 (S.D.N.Y. 2012).
c. *FTC v. PCCare247, Inc.*, 2013 WL 841037 (S.D.N.Y. 2013).

motion. The notice of motion informs the opposing party that the motion has been filed. **Pretrial motions** include the motion to dismiss, the motion for judgment on the pleadings, and the motion for summary judgment, as well as the other motions listed in Exhibit 3–4.

Motion to Dismiss Either party can file a **motion to dismiss** asking the court to dismiss the case for the reasons stated in the motion. Normally, though, it is the defendant who requests dismissal.

A defendant can file a motion to dismiss if the plaintiff's complaint fails to state a claim for which relief (a remedy) can be granted. Such a motion asserts that even if the facts alleged in the complaint are true, they

do not give rise to any legal claim against the defendant. For example, if the allegations in Kirby's complaint do not constitute negligence on Carvello's part, Carvello can move to dismiss the case for failure to state a claim. Defendant Carvello could also file a motion to dismiss on the grounds that he was not properly served, that the court lacked jurisdiction, or that the venue was improper.

If the judge grants the motion to dismiss, the plaintiff generally is given time to file an amended complaint. If the judge denies the motion, the suit will go forward, and the defendant must then file an answer. Note that if Carvello wishes to discontinue the suit because, for example, an out-of-court settlement has been reached, he can likewise move for dismissal. The

EXHIBIT 3–4 Pretrial Motions

Motion to Dismiss	A motion (normally filed by the defendant) that asks the court to dismiss the case for a specified reason, such as lack of personal jurisdiction or failure to state a claim
Motion to Strike	A defendant's motion asking the court to strike (delete or remove) certain paragraphs from the complaint to better clarify the issues in dispute
Motion to Make More Definite or Certain	A motion by the defendant when the complaint is vague that asks the court to compel the plaintiff to clarify the cause of action
Motion for Judgment on the Pleadings	A motion by either party asking the court to enter judgment in his or her favor based on the pleadings because there are no facts in dispute
Motion to Compel Discovery	A motion asking the court to force the nonmoving party to comply with a discovery request
Motion for Summary Judgment	A motion asking the court to enter a judgment in his or her favor without a trial

court can also dismiss a case on its own motion. In the following case, one party filed a complaint against two others, alleging a breach of contract. The defendants filed a motion to dismiss on the ground that the venue was improper. The court denied the motion, and the defendants appealed.

Case Analysis 3.1

Espresso Disposition Corp. 1 v. Santana Sales & Marketing Group, Inc.
Florida Court of Appeal, Third District, 105 So.3d 592 (2013).

In the Language of the Court
CORTIÑAS, J. [Judge]
* * * *

Espresso Disposition Corporation 1 and Rowland Coffee Roasters, Inc. (collectively "Appellants") seek review of the trial court's order denying their motions to dismiss [Santana Sales & Marketing Group, Inc.'s ("Appellee's")]

third amended complaint. Appellants claim that the trial court erred in denying their motions to dismiss because the plain and unambiguous language in the parties' * * * agreement contains a mandatory forum selection clause [a provision in a contract designating the court, jurisdiction, or tribunal that will decide any disputes arising under the contract]

requiring that all lawsuits brought under the agreement shall be in Illinois.

Espresso Disposition Corporation 1 and Santana and Associates entered into the * * * agreement in 2002. The agreement provides for a mandatory forum selection clause in paragraph 8. The provision states:

The venue with respect to any action pertaining to this Agreement shall be the State of Illinois. The laws of the State of Illinois shall govern the application and interpretation of this Agreement.

However, Appellee filed a lawsuit against Appellants alleging a breach of the agreement in Miami–Dade County, Florida. In fact, Appellee filed four subsequent complaints—an initial complaint, amended complaint, second amended complaint, and third amended complaint—after each and every previous pleading's dismissal was based upon venue as provided for in the agreement's mandatory forum selection clause. Appellee's third amended complaint alleges the forum selection clause was a mistake that was made at the time the agreement was drafted. Additionally, Appellee attached an affidavit [a sworn statement] which states that, in drafting the agreement, Appellee * * * copied a form version of an agreement between different parties, and by mistake, forgot to change the venue provision from Illinois to Florida. In response, Appellants filed their motions to dismiss the third amended complaint, which the trial court denied.

Florida appellate courts interpret a contractual forum selection clause under a *de novo* standard of review. [The courts review the issue anew, as if the lower courts had not ruled on the issue.] Likewise, as the trial court's order denying appellant's motion to dismiss is based on the interpretation of the contractual forum selection clause, this court's standard of review is *de novo*. Therefore, the narrow issue before this court is whether the * * *

agreement provides for a mandatory forum selection clause that is enforceable under Florida law.

Florida courts have long recognized that forum selection clauses such as the one at issue here are presumptively valid. *This is because forum selection clauses provide a degree of certainty to business contracts by obviating [preventing] jurisdictional struggles and by allowing parties to tailor the dispute resolution mechanism to their particular situation. Moreover, forum selection clauses reduce litigation over venue, thereby conserving judicial resources, reducing business expenses, and lowering consumer prices.* [Emphasis added.]

Because Florida law presumes that forum selection clauses are valid and enforceable, the party seeking to avoid enforcement of such a clause must establish that enforcement would be unjust or unreasonable. Under Florida law, the clause is only considered unjust or unreasonable if the party seeking avoidance establishes that enforcement would result in no forum at all. There is absolutely no set of facts that Appellee could plead and prove to demonstrate that Illinois state courts do not exist. Illinois became the twenty-first state in 1818, and has since established an extensive system of state trial and appellate courts. Clearly, Appellee failed to establish that enforcement would be unreasonable since the designated forum—Illinois—does not result in Appellee's having "no forum at all."

Further, as we have said on a number of occasions, if a forum selection clause unambiguously mandates that litigation be subject to an agreed upon forum, then it is error for the trial court to ignore the clause. Generally, the clause

is mandatory where the plain language used by the parties indicates exclusivity. Importantly, if the forum selection clause states or clearly indicates that any litigation must or shall be initiated in a specified forum, then it is mandatory. Here, the agreement's plain language provides that the venue for any action relating to a controversy under the agreement * * * "shall be the State of Illinois." The clear language unequivocally renders the forum selection clause mandatory.

Appellee would have us create an exception to our jurisprudence on mandatory forum selection clauses based on their error in cutting and pasting the clause from another agreement. Of course, the origin of "cutting and pasting" comes from the traditional practice of manuscript-editing whereby writers used to cut paragraphs from a page with editing scissors, that had blades long enough to cut an 8½ inch-wide page, and then physically pasted them onto another page. Today, the cut, copy, and paste functions contained in word processing software render unnecessary the use of scissors or glue. However, what has not been eliminated is the need to actually read and analyze the text being pasted, especially where it is to have legal significance. Thus, in reviewing the mandatory selection clause which Appellant seeks to enforce, we apply the legal maxim "be careful what you ask for" and enforce the pasted forum.

Accordingly, we reverse [the] trial court's denial of the motions to dismiss Appellee's third amended complaint on the basis of improper venue, and remand for entry of an order of dismissal.

Legal Reasoning Questions

1. Compare and contrast a motion to dismiss with other pretrial motions. Identify their chief differences.
2. Why did the appellants in this case file a motion to dismiss?
3. What is the effect of granting a motion to dismiss?

Motion for Judgment on the Pleadings At the close of the pleadings, either party may make a **motion for judgment on the pleadings.** This motion asks the court to decide the issue solely on the pleadings without proceeding to trial.

The judge will grant the motion only when there is no dispute over the facts of the case and the sole issue to be resolved is a question of law. For example, in the Kirby-Carvello case, if Carvello had admitted to all of Kirby's allegations in his answer and had raised no affirmative defenses, Kirby could file a motion for judgment on the pleadings.

In deciding a motion for judgment on the pleadings, the judge may consider only the evidence contained in the pleadings. In contrast, in a motion for summary judgment, discussed next, the court may consider evidence outside the pleadings, such as sworn statements and other materials that would be admissible as evidence at trial.

Motion for Summary Judgment Either party can file a **motion for summary judgment,** which asks the court to grant a judgment in that party's favor without a trial. The motion can be made before or during the trial. As with a motion for judgment on the pleadings, a court will grant a motion for summary judgment only if no facts are in dispute and the only question is how the law applies to the facts. In determining whether no facts are in contention, the court considers the evidence in the light most favorable to the other party.

To support a motion for summary judgment, a party can submit evidence obtained at any point before the trial that refutes the other party's factual claim. The evidence may consist of **affidavits** (sworn statements by parties or witnesses) or copies of documents, such as contracts, e-mails, and letters obtained through the course of discovery (discussed next).

Of course, the evidence must be *admissible* evidence—that is, evidence that the court would allow to be presented during the trial. As mentioned, the use of additional evidence is one feature that distinguishes the motion for summary judgment from the motion to dismiss and the motion for judgment on the pleadings.

On appeal of a court's grant or denial of a motion for summary judgment, the appellate court engages in *de novo* review—that is, it applies the same standard that the trial court applied. In the following case, an appellate court took a fresh look at the evidence that had been presented with a motion for summary judgment granted by the lower court.

Case 3.2

Lewis v. Twenty-First Century Bean Processing

United States Court of Appeals, Tenth Circuit, __ F.3d __, 2016 WL 66334 (2016).

Background and Facts Twenty-First Century Bean Processing hired Anthony Lewis, a forty-seven-year-old African American male, for a warehouse position, subject to a thirty-day probationary period. At the end of the period, Twenty-First Century evaluated Lewis's performance to determine whether he would remain an employee. The employer decided not to retain Lewis, who then filed a suit in a federal district court against Twenty-First Century. Lewis alleged discrimination on the basis of race and age in violation of Title VII of the Civil Rights Act and the Age Discrimination in Employment Act. Twenty-First Century filed a motion for summary judgment. As evidence, the employer presented proof concerning Lewis's job performance during the probationary period. The court granted the motion. Lewis appealed.

In the Language of the Court

Robert E. *BACHARACH*, Circuit Judge.

* * * *

When a plaintiff alleges discrimination but offers no direct evidence of discrimination, the plaintiff bears the initial burden to establish a prima facie *case of discrimination.* [This requires a showing that (1) the plaintiff is a member of a protected class—a person defined by certain criteria, including race or age; (2) the plaintiff applied and was qualified for the job at issue; (3) the plaintiff was rejected by the employer; and (4) the employer filled the position with someone not in a protected class.] *If a plaintiff* *establishes a* prima facie *case, the burden shifts to the defendant to articulate a * * * nondiscriminatory reason for its actions.* If the defendant satisfies that burden, the employee would bear the burden to prove the defendant's actions were discriminatory, which the employee could do by showing defendant's proffered reason is a pretext for illegal discrimination. [Emphasis added.]

* * * *

Mr. Lewis alleges age discrimination under the Age Discrimination in Employment Act. * * * Mr. Lewis had not presented any direct evidence of discrimination [and] the court determined that Mr. Lewis had not established a *prima facie* case because he had failed to provide evidence that his work was satisfactory. In our view, that conclusion was proper. Therefore, we affirm the district court's grant of summary judgment to Twenty-First Century on the age discrimination claim.

* * * *

Mr. Lewis also alleges race discrimination under Title VII of the Civil Rights Act. Again finding no direct evidence of discrimination, * * * the court assumed without deciding that Mr. Lewis had established a *prima facie* case of race discrimination. Thus, the burden shifted to Twenty-First Century to show a nondiscriminatory reason for terminating Mr. Lewis.

As evidence of a non-discriminatory purpose, Twenty-First Century pointed out that Mr. Lewis had missed too many work days, slept at work, used his personal cellphone at work, and reacted argumentatively when warned about his cellphone usage. After finding that any one of these policy violations could serve as a nondiscriminatory reason for the firing, the court placed the burden on Mr. Lewis to show * * * that Twenty-First Century's explanation was pretextual [not legitimate]. The district court concluded that Mr. Lewis was unable to meet this burden, and we agree.

Decision and Remedy *The U.S. Court of Appeals for the Tenth Circuit affirmed the lower court's summary judgment. Of the twenty-five work days in the probationary period, Lewis was absent for four days, found sleeping twice, and seen several times texting and talking on his personal phone. When informed that this use of a phone was against company policy, Lewis argued with his superior.*

Critical Thinking
- **Legal Environment** *Should motions for summary judgment and other pretrial motions be abolished so that all lawsuits proceed to trial? Why or why not?*
- **What If the Facts Were Different?** *Suppose that at this stage of the litigation, Twenty-First Century had not been able to provide evidence in support of its asserted reason for Lewis's firing. What would have been the result? Why?*

3–2c Discovery

Before a trial begins, the parties can use a number of procedural devices to obtain information and gather evidence about the case. Kirby, for example, will want to know how fast Carvello was driving. She will also want to learn whether he had been drinking, was under the influence of medication, and was wearing corrective lenses if required by law to do so while driving.

The process of obtaining information from the opposing party or from witnesses prior to trial is known as **discovery.** Discovery includes gaining access to witnesses, documents, records, and other types of evidence.

In federal courts, the parties are required to make initial disclosures of relevant evidence to the opposing party. A court can impose sanctions on a party who fails to respond to discovery requests.

Discovery prevents surprises at trial by giving both parties access to evidence that might otherwise be hidden. This allows the litigants to learn as much as they can about what to expect at a trial before they reach the courtroom. Discovery also serves to narrow the issues so that trial time is spent on the main questions in the case. The following case shows how vital discovery can be to the outcome of litigation.

Brothers v. Winstead

Supreme Court of Mississippi, 129 So.3d 906 (2014).

Background and Facts   Phillips Brothers, LP (limited partnership), Harry Simmons, and Ray Winstead were the owners of Kilby Brake Fisheries, LLC (limited liability company), a catfish farm in Mississippi. For nearly eight years, Winstead operated a hatchery for the firm. During this time, the hatchery had only two profitable years. Consequently, Winstead was fired. He filed a suit in a Mississippi state court against Kilby Brake and its other owners, alleging a "freeze-out." (A freeze-out occurs when a majority of the owners of a firm exclude other owners from certain benefits of participating in the firm.)

The defendants filed a counterclaim of theft. To support this claim, the defendants asked the court to allow them to obtain documents from Winstead regarding his finances, particularly income from his Winstead Cattle Company. The court refused this request. A jury awarded Winstead more than $1.7 million, and the defendants appealed.

In the Language of the Court

WALLER, Chief Justice for the Court.

* * * *

During discovery, Winstead produced his tax returns from 2006 to 2009, which showed substantial income as coming from the Winstead Cattle Company. The only other income listed on Winstead's tax returns was from Kilby Brake * * * . Winstead had also produced [other documents showing income] from a fish farmer named Scott Kiker, which did not appear on his tax returns. [The documents supposedly involved income from sales of cattle.] Kilby Brake's theory was the entries for "cattle" represented income from sales of Kilby Brake fish Winstead was brokering and thus, it sought to compel [discovery] of all of the Winstead Cattle Company's financial records. Winstead [testified] in his deposition and again at trial that the Winstead Cattle Company did no actual business, and it was simply his hunting camp. The trial court denied Kilby Brake's motion to compel discovery into Winstead's finances.

* * * [Winstead was questioned about the forms he] had produced in discovery showing income from Kiker. Winstead testified that he would often act as a middle man if he knew of a farmer who was in need of fish and another who had fish for sale, taking a commission for brokering the deal.

* * * *

* * * Kiker testified that he had received a load of fish from Kilby Brake [but that] there was no paperwork on the transaction [and] that he sold this load of fish, gave Winstead a commission and did not pay Kilby Brake for the sales.

*From the evidence noted above, we find the trial court's refusal to allow both discovery into the finances of Winstead and questions concerning Winstead Cattle Company on his tax return prevented Kilby Brake and the jury from finding out whether Winstead was selling fish from Kilby Brake and disguising it on his income tax returns * * * .* Importantly, the decisions by the trial court denied Kilby Brake the ability to present its case as to what happened to the fish. The record shows there were years in which Winstead received substantial income from brokering fish sales, almost $20,000 in one year. He [testified] that Winstead Cattle Company did no business and was simply his hunting camp, yet it made significant amounts of money. [Emphasis added.]

Decision and Remedy   *The Mississippi Supreme Court reversed the lower court's decision to deny discovery of information concerning Winstead's outside finances, especially regarding income from Winstead Cattle Company. The state supreme court remanded the case for a new trial.*

Critical Thinking

- **Ethical**   *Does Winstead have an ethical duty to comply with the defendants' discovery request? Discuss.*
- **Legal Environment**   *Did the defendants have a legitimate basis to make a discovery request for information regarding Winstead's outside income? Explain.*

Discovery Rules The FRCP and similar state rules set forth the guidelines for discovery activity. Generally, discovery is allowed regarding any matter that is relevant to the claim or defense of any party. Discovery rules also attempt to protect witnesses and parties from undue harassment, and to prevent privileged or confidential material from being disclosed. Only information that is relevant to the case at hand—or likely to lead to the discovery of relevant information—is discoverable.

If a discovery request involves privileged or confidential business information, a court can deny the request and can limit the scope of discovery in a number of ways. For instance, a court can require the party to submit the materials to the judge in a sealed envelope so that the judge can decide if they should be disclosed to the opposing party.

Depositions Discovery can involve the use of depositions. A **deposition** is sworn testimony by a party to the lawsuit or by any witness, recorded by an authorized court official. The person deposed gives testimony and answers questions asked by the attorneys from both sides. The questions and answers are recorded, sworn to, and signed. These answers, of course, will help the attorneys prepare their cases.

Depositions also give attorneys the opportunity to ask immediate follow-up questions and to evaluate how their witnesses will conduct themselves at trial. In addition, depositions can be employed in court to **impeach** (challenge the credibility of) a party or a witness who changes his or her testimony at the trial. Finally, a deposition can be used as testimony if the witness is not available at trial.

Interrogatories Discovery can also involve **interrogatories**—written questions for which written answers are prepared and then signed under oath. The main difference between interrogatories and written depositions is that interrogatories are directed to a party to the lawsuit (the plaintiff or the defendant), not to a witness. The party usually has thirty days to prepare answers.

The party's attorney often drafts the answers to interrogatories in a manner calculated to give away as little information as possible. Whereas depositions elicit candid answers not prepared in advance, interrogatories are designed to obtain accurate information about specific topics, such as how many contracts were signed and when. The scope of interrogatories is also broader because parties are obligated to answer questions, even if that means disclosing information from their records and files. As with discovery requests, a court can impose sanctions on a party who fails to answer interrogatories.

■ **CASE IN POINT 3.1** Ronald J. Hass (doing business as Valley Corp. and R. J. Hass Corp.) was a contractor who built a home for Ty and Karen Levine. Probuilders Specialty Insurance Co. provided commercial liability insurance for the contractor. Later, when the Levines sued Hass and his company for shoddy and incomplete work, Hass blamed the subcontractors. Probuilders provided Hass with legal representation, but the Levines won a judgment for more than $2 million. Then Probuilders sued Hass and his company, claiming that he had made misrepresentations to them regarding the facts of the case and seeking to avoid paying the judgment. Hass filed a counterclaim against Probuilders.

A dispute arose between Probuilders and Hass concerning discovery. Hass refused to respond fully to interrogatories and other discovery requests, and refused to give a deposition. Probuilders filed a motion to compel, and the court ordered Hass to respond to the discovery requests. Although Probuilders sent letters specifying what was needed, Hass continued to be evasive. The court imposed sanctions on Hass more than once. Ultimately, the court found that Hass had acted willfully and in bad faith, and recommended that his answers and counterclaim against Probuilders be dismissed.[6] ■

Requests for Admissions One party can serve the other party with a written request for an admission of the truth of matters relating to the trial. Any fact admitted under such a request is conclusively established as true for the trial. For example, Kirby can ask Carvello to admit that his driver's license was suspended at the time of the accident. A request for admission shortens the trial because the parties will not have to spend time proving facts on which they already agree.

Requests for Documents, Objects, and Entry upon Land A party can gain access to documents and other items not in her or his possession in order to inspect and examine them. Carvello, for example, can gain permission to inspect and copy Kirby's car repair bills. Likewise, a party can gain "entry upon land" to inspect the premises.

Requests for Examinations When the physical or mental condition of one party is in question, the opposing party can ask the court to order a physical or mental examination by an independent examiner. If the court agrees to make the order, the opposing party can obtain the results of the examination. Note that the court will

---

6. *Probuilders Specialty Insurance Co. v. Valley Corp.*, 2012 WL 6045753 (N.D.Cal. 2012).

make such an order only when the need for the information outweighs the right to privacy of the person to be examined.

Electronic Discovery Any relevant material, including information stored electronically, can be the object of a discovery request. The federal rules and most state rules (as well as court decisions) specifically allow individuals to obtain discovery of electronic "data compilations." Electronic evidence, or **e-evidence,** consists of all computer-generated or electronically recorded information, such as e-mail, voice mail, tweets, blogs, social media posts, spreadsheets, documents, and other data stored electronically.

E-evidence can reveal significant facts that are not discoverable by other means. Computers, smartphones, cameras, and other devices automatically record certain information about files—such as who created the file and when, and who accessed, modified, or transmitted it—on their hard drives. This information is called **metadata,** which can be thought of as "data about data." Metadata can be obtained only from the file in its electronic format—not from printed-out versions.

■ **EXAMPLE 3.2** In 2012, John McAfee, the programmer responsible for creating McAfee antivirus software, was wanted for questioning in the murder of his neighbor in Belize. McAfee left Belize and was on the run from police, but he allowed a journalist to come with him and photograph him. When the journalist posted photos of McAfee online, some metadata were attached to a photo. The police used the metadata to pinpoint the latitude and longitude of the image and subsequently arrested McAfee in Guatemala. ■

E-Discovery Procedures. The Federal Rules of Civil Procedure deal specifically with the preservation, retrieval, and production of electronic data. Although traditional interrogatories and depositions are still used to find out whether e-evidence exists, a party usually must hire an expert to retrieve the evidence in its electronic format. The expert uses software to reconstruct e-mail, text, and other exchanges to establish who knew what and when they knew it. The expert can even recover computer files that the user thought had been deleted.

Advantages and Disadvantages. Electronic discovery has significant advantages over paper discovery. Electronic versions of documents, e-mail, and text messages can provide useful—and often quite damaging—information about how a particular matter progressed over several weeks or months. E-discovery can uncover the proverbial smoking gun that will win the lawsuit. But it is also time consuming and expensive, especially when lawsuits involve large firms with multiple offices. Indeed, many firms are finding it difficult to fulfill their duty to preserve electronic evidence from a vast number of sources.

A party that fails to preserve e-evidence may find itself at such a disadvantage that it will settle a dispute rather than continue litigation. ■ **CASE IN POINT 3.3** Advanced Micro Devices, Inc. (AMD), sued Intel Corporation, one of the world's largest microprocessor suppliers, for violating antitrust laws. Immediately after the lawsuit was filed, Intel began collecting and preserving the electronic evidence on its servers and instructed its employees to retain documents and e-mails related to competition with AMD. Nevertheless, many employees saved only copies of the e-mails that they had received and not e-mails that they had sent. In addition, Intel did not stop its automatic e-mail deletion system, causing other information to be lost. In the end, although Intel produced data equivalent to "somewhere in the neighborhood of a pile 137 miles high" in paper, its failure to preserve e-discovery led it to settle the dispute.[7] ■

3–2d Pretrial Conference

After discovery has taken place and before the trial begins, the attorneys may meet with the trial judge in a **pretrial conference,** or hearing. Usually, the conference consists of an informal discussion between the judge and the opposing attorneys after discovery has taken place. The purpose is to explore the possibility of a settlement without trial and, if this is not possible, to identify the matters in dispute and to plan the course of the trial. In particular, the parties may attempt to establish ground rules to restrict the number of expert witnesses or discuss the admissibility or costs of certain types of evidence.

3–2e The Right to a Jury Trial

The Seventh Amendment to the U.S. Constitution guarantees the right to a jury trial for cases at law in *federal* courts when the amount in controversy exceeds $20. Most states have similar guarantees in their own constitutions (although the threshold dollar amount is higher than $20).

The right to a trial by jury need not be exercised, and many cases are tried without a jury. In most states and in federal courts, one of the parties must request a jury, or the judge presumes the parties waive this right. If there

---

7. *In re Intel Corp. Microprocessor Antitrust Litigation,* 2008 WL 2310288 (D.Del. 2008).

is no jury, the judge determines the truth of the facts alleged in the case.

3–2f Jury Selection

Before a jury trial commences, a panel of jurors must be selected. Although some types of trials require twelve-person juries, most civil matters can be heard by six-person juries. The jury selection process is known as **voir dire.**[8] In most jurisdictions, attorneys for the plaintiff and the defendant ask prospective jurors oral questions to determine whether they are biased or have any connection with a party to the action or with a prospective witness. In some jurisdictions, the judge may do all or part of the questioning based on written questions submitted by counsel for the parties.

During *voir dire,* a party may challenge a certain number of prospective jurors *peremptorily*—that is, ask that an individual not be sworn in as a juror without providing any reason. Alternatively, a party may challenge a prospective juror *for cause*—that is, provide a reason why an individual should not be sworn in as a juror. If the judge grants the challenge, the individual is asked to step down. A prospective juror, however, may not be excluded by the use of discriminatory challenges, such as those based on racial criteria or gender.

See Concept Summary 3.1 for a review of pretrial procedures.

3–3 The Trial

Various rules and procedures govern the trial phase of the litigation process. There are rules governing what kind of evidence will or will not be admitted during the trial, as well as specific procedures that the participants in the lawsuit must follow. For instance, a trial judge may instruct jurors not to communicate with anyone about the case or order reporters not to use social media to comment on the case while in the courtroom.

3–3a Opening Statements

At the beginning of the trial, both attorneys are allowed to make **opening statements** setting forth the facts that they expect to prove during the trial. The opening statement provides an opportunity for each lawyer to give a

brief version of the facts and the supporting evidence that will be used during the trial. Then the plaintiff's case is presented. In our hypothetical case, Kirby's lawyer would introduce evidence (relevant documents, exhibits, and the testimony of witnesses) to support Kirby's position.

3–3b Rules of Evidence

Whether evidence will be admitted in court is determined by the **rules of evidence.** These are a series of rules that the courts have created to ensure that any evidence presented during a trial is fair and reliable. The Federal Rules of Evidence govern the admissibility of evidence in federal courts.

Evidence Must Be Relevant to the Issues Evidence will not be admitted in court unless it is relevant to the matter in question. **Relevant evidence** is evidence that tends to prove or disprove a fact in question or to establish the degree of probability of a fact or action. For instance, evidence that the defendant was in another person's home when the victim was shot would be relevant, because it would tend to prove that the defendant was not the shooter.

Hearsay Evidence Is Not Admissible Generally, hearsay is not admissible as evidence. **Hearsay** is testimony someone gives in court about a statement made by someone else who was not under oath at the time of the statement. Literally, it is what someone heard someone else say. If a witness in the Kirby-Carvello case testified in court concerning what he or she heard another observer say about the accident, for example, that testimony would be hearsay. Admitting hearsay into evidence carries many risks because, even though it may be relevant, there is no way to test its reliability.

3–3c Examination of Witnesses and Potential Motions

Because Kirby is the plaintiff, she has the burden of proving that her allegations are true. Her attorney begins the presentation of Kirby's case by calling the first witness for the plaintiff and examining, or questioning, the witness. (For both attorneys, the types of questions and the manner of asking them are governed by the rules of evidence.) This questioning is called **direct examination.**

After Kirby's attorney is finished, the witness is subject to **cross-examination** by Carvello's attorney. Then Kirby's attorney has another opportunity to question the witness in *redirect examination,* and Carvello's

---

8. Pronounced *vwahr deehr.* These verbs, based on Old French, mean "to speak the truth." In legal language, the phrase refers to the process of questioning jurors to learn about their backgrounds, attitudes, and similar attributes.

Concept Summary 3.1

Pretrial Procedures

The Pleadings

- *The plaintiff's complaint*—The plaintiff's statement of the cause of action and the parties involved, filed with the court by the plaintiff's attorney. After the filing, the defendant is notified of the suit through service of process.
- *The defendant's response*—The defendant's response to the plaintiff's complaint may take the form of an answer, in which the defendant admits or denies the plaintiff's allegations. The defendant may also raise an affirmative defense and/or assert a counterclaim.

Pretrial Motions

- *Motion to dismiss*—See Exhibit 3–4.
- *Motion for judgment* on the pleadings—May be made by either party and will be granted only if no facts are in dispute and only questions of law are at issue.
- *Motion for summary judgment*—See Exhibit 3–4.

Discovery

The process of gathering evidence concerning the case, which may involve the following:
- *Depositions* (sworn testimony by either party or any witness).
- *Interrogatories* (in which parties to the action write answers to questions with the aid of their attorneys).
- Requests for admissions, documents, examinations, or other information relating to the case.
- Requests for electronically recorded information, such as e-mail, text messages, voice mail, and other data.

Pretrial Conference

- A pretrial hearing, at the request of either party or the court, to identify the matters in dispute after discovery has taken place and to explore the possibility of settling the dispute without a trial. If no settlement is possible, the parties plan the course of the trial.

Jury Selection

- In a jury trial, the selection of members of the jury from a pool of prospective jurors. During a process known as *voir dire*, the attorneys for both sides may challenge prospective jurors either for cause or peremptorily (for no cause).

attorney may follow the redirect examination with a *recross-examination*. When both attorneys have finished with the first witness, Kirby's attorney calls the succeeding witnesses in the plaintiff's case. Each witness is subject to examination by the attorneys in the manner just described.

Expert Witnesses As part of their cases, both the plaintiff and the defendant may present testimony from one or more expert witnesses, such as forensic scientists, physicians, and psychologists. An *expert witness* is a person who, by virtue of education, training, skill, or experience, has scientific, technical, or other specialized knowledge in a particular area beyond that of an average person. In Kirby's case, her attorney might hire an accident reconstruction specialist to establish Carvello's negligence or a physician to testify to the extent of Kirby's injuries.

Normally, witnesses can testify only about the facts of a case—that is, what they personally observed. When witnesses are qualified as experts in a particular field, however, they can offer their opinions and conclusions about the evidence in that field. Because numerous experts are available for hire and expert testimony is powerful and effective with juries, there is tremendous potential for abuse. Therefore, judges act as gatekeepers to ensure that the experts are qualified. If a party believes that the opponent's expert witness is not a qualified expert in the relevant field, that party can make a motion to prevent the witness from testifying.[9]

■ **CASE IN POINT 3.4** Yvette Downey bought a children's bedroom set from Bob's Discount Furniture Holdings, Inc. She later discovered that it was infested with bed bugs, which had spread throughout her home. Downey spoke with Edward Gordinier, a licensed and experienced exterminator, who identified the bedroom set as the source of the problem. Although Bob's retrieved the bedroom set and refunded the purchase price, it refused to pay for the costs of extermination or any other damages. Downey sued.

Before the trial, Downey's attorney named Gordinier as a witness but did not submit a written report describing his anticipated testimony or specifying his qualifications. The defendants filed a motion to prevent his testimony. The district court refused to allow Gordinier to testify, but that decision was reversed on appeal. The appellate court concluded that Gordinier was not the type of expert who regularly was hired by plaintiffs to testify in court, in which case a report would have been required. Gordinier was simply an expert on bugs, and he was allowed to give his opinion on the infestation.[10] ■

Possible Motion and Judgment At the conclusion of the plaintiff's case, the defendant's attorney may ask the judge to direct a verdict for the defendant on the ground that the plaintiff has presented no evidence to support her or his claim. This is called a **motion for a judgment as a matter of law** (or a **motion for a directed verdict** in state courts). In considering the motion, the judge looks at the evidence in the light most favorable to the plaintiff and grants the motion only if there is insufficient evidence to raise an issue of fact. (Motions for directed verdicts at this stage of a trial are seldom granted.)

Defendant's Evidence The defendant's attorney then presents the evidence and witnesses for the defendant's case. Witnesses are called and examined by the defendant's attorney. The plaintiff's attorney has the right to cross-examine them, and there may be a redirect examination and possibly a recross-examination.

At the end of the defendant's case, either attorney can move for a directed verdict. Again, the test is whether the jury can, through any reasonable interpretation of the evidence, find for the party against whom the motion has been made. After the defendant's attorney has finished introducing evidence, the plaintiff's attorney can present a **rebuttal** by offering additional evidence that refutes the defendant's case. The defendant's attorney can, in turn, refute that evidence in a **rejoinder.**

3–3d Closing Arguments, Jury Instructions, and Verdict

After both sides have rested their cases, each attorney presents a **closing argument.** In the closing argument, each attorney summarizes the facts and evidence presented during the trial and indicates why the facts and evidence support his or her client's claim. In addition to generally urging a verdict in favor of the client, the closing argument typically reveals the shortcomings of the points made by the opposing party during the trial.

Jury Instructions Attorneys usually present closing arguments whether or not the trial was heard by a jury. If it was a jury trial, the attorneys will have met with the judge before the closing arguments to determine how the jury will be instructed on the law. The attorneys can refer to these instructions in their closing arguments. After closing arguments are completed, the judge instructs the jury in the law that applies to the case (these instructions are often called *charges*). The jury then retires to the jury room to deliberate a verdict.

Juries are instructed on the standard of proof they must apply to the case. In most civil cases, the standard of proof is a *preponderance of the evidence.*[11] In other words, the plaintiff (Kirby in our hypothetical case) need only show that her factual claim is more likely to be true than the defendant's. (In a criminal trial, the prosecution has a higher standard of proof to meet—it must prove its case *beyond a reasonable doubt.*)

---

9. See Edward J. Imwinkelried, *The Methods of Attacking Scientific Evidence,* 5th ed. (2014).

10. *Downey v. Bob's Discount Furniture Holdings, Inc.,* 633 F.3d 1 (1st Cir. 2011).

11. Note that some civil claims must be proved by "clear and convincing evidence," meaning that the evidence must show that the truth of the party's claim is *highly* probable. This standard is often applied in situations that present a particular danger of deception, such as allegations of fraud.

Verdict Once the jury has reached a decision, it issues a **verdict** in favor of one party. The verdict specifies the jury's factual findings. In some cases, the jury also decides on the amount of the *award* (the compensation to be paid to the prevailing party). After the announcement of the verdict, which marks the end of the trial itself, the jurors are dismissed.

See Concept Summary 3.2 for a review of trial procedures.

3–4 Posttrial Motions

After the jury has rendered its verdict, either party may make a posttrial motion. The prevailing party usually requests that the court enter a judgment in accordance with the verdict. The nonprevailing party frequently files one of the motions discussed next.

3–4a Motion for a New Trial

At the end of the trial, the losing party may make a motion to set aside the adverse verdict and any judgment and to hold a new trial. After looking at all the evidence, the judge will grant the **motion for a new trial** only if she or he believes that the jury was in error and that it is not appropriate to grant judgment for the other side.

Usually, a new trial is granted only when the jury verdict is obviously the result of a misapplication of the law or a misunderstanding of the evidence presented at trial. A new trial can also be granted on the grounds of newly discovered evidence, misconduct by the participants during the trial (such as when a juror has made prejudicial and inflammatory remarks), or an error by the judge.

3–4b Motion for Judgment *N.O.V.*

If Kirby wins and if Carvello's attorney has previously moved for a judgment as a matter of law, then Carvello's

---

Concept Summary 3.2

Trial Procedure

Opening Statements	• Each party's attorney is allowed to present an opening statement indicating what the attorney will attempt to prove during the course of the trial.
Examination of Witnesses	• Plaintiff's introduction and direct examination of witnesses, cross-examination by defendant's attorney, possible redirect examination by plaintiff's attorney, and possible recross-examination by defendant's attorney. • Both the plaintiff and the defendant may present testimony from one or more expert witnesses. • At the close of the plaintiff's case, the defendant may make a motion for a directed verdict (or for judgment as a matter of law). If granted by the court, this motion will end the trial before the defendant presents witnesses. • Defendant's introduction and direct examination of witnesses, cross-examination by plaintiff's attorney, possible redirect examination by defendant's attorney, and possible recross-examination by plaintiff's attorney. • Possible rebuttal of defendant's argument by plaintiff's attorney, who presents more evidence. • Possible rejoinder by defendant's attorney to meet that evidence.
Closing Arguments, Jury Instructions, and Verdict	• Each party's attorney argues in favor of a verdict for his or her client. • The judge instructs (or charges) the jury as to how the law applies to the issue, and the jury retires to deliberate. • When the jury renders its verdict, the trial comes to an end.

attorney can make a second motion for a judgment as a matter of law (the terminology used in federal courts). State courts may use different terms for these motions.

In many state courts, if the defendant's attorney moved earlier for a directed verdict, he or she may now make a **motion for judgment *n.o.v.***—from the Latin *non obstante veredicto*, meaning "notwithstanding the verdict." Such a motion will be granted only if the jury's verdict was unreasonable and erroneous.

If the judge grants the motion, then the jury's verdict will be set aside, and a judgment will be entered in favor of the opposing party (Carvello). If the motion is denied, Carvello may then appeal the case. (Kirby may also appeal the case, even though she won at trial. She might appeal, for example, if she received a smaller monetary award than she had sought.)

3–5 The Appeal

Either party may appeal not only the jury's verdict but also the judge's ruling on any pretrial or posttrial motion. Many of the appellate court cases that appear in this text involve appeals of motions for summary judgment or other motions that were denied by trial court judges.

Note that a party must have legitimate grounds to file an appeal (some legal error) and that few trial court decisions are reversed on appeal. Moreover, the expenses associated with an appeal can be considerable.

3–5a Filing the Appeal

If Carvello decides to appeal the verdict in Kirby's favor, then his attorney must file a *notice of appeal* with the clerk of the trial court within a prescribed period of time. Carvello then becomes the *appellant* or *petitioner*. The clerk of the trial court sends to the reviewing court (usually an intermediate court of appeals) the *record on appeal*. The record contains all the pleadings, motions, and other documents filed with the court and a complete written transcript of the proceedings, including testimony, arguments, jury instructions, and judicial rulings.

Carvello's attorney will file an appellate **brief** with the reviewing court. The brief is a formal legal document outlining the facts and issues of the case, the judge's rulings or jury's findings that should be reversed or modified, the applicable law, and arguments on Carvello's behalf (citing applicable statutes and relevant cases as precedents). The attorney for the *appellee* (Kirby, in our hypothetical case) usually files an answering brief. Carvello's attorney can file a reply, although it is not required. The reviewing court then considers the case.

3–5b Appellate Review

A court of appeals does not hear any evidence. Rather, it reviews the record for errors of law. Its decision concerning a case is based on the record on appeal and the briefs and arguments. The attorneys present oral arguments, after which the case is taken under advisement. The court then issues a written opinion. In general, appellate courts do not reverse findings of fact unless the findings are unsupported or contradicted by the evidence.

An appellate court has the following options after reviewing a case:

1. The court can *affirm* the trial court's decision. (Most decisions are affirmed.)
2. The court can *reverse* the trial court's judgment if it concludes that the trial court erred or that the jury did not receive proper instructions.
3. The appellate court can *remand* (send back) the case to the trial court for further proceedings consistent with its opinion on the matter.
4. The court might also affirm or reverse a decision *in part*. For example, the court might affirm the jury's finding that Carvello was negligent but remand the case for further proceedings on another issue (such as the extent of Kirby's damages).
5. An appellate court can also *modify* a lower court's decision. If the appellate court decides that the jury awarded an excessive amount in damages, for example, the court might reduce the award to a more appropriate, or fairer, amount.

3–5c Higher Appellate Courts

If the reviewing court is an intermediate appellate court, the losing party may decide to appeal the decision to the state's highest court, usually called its supreme court. Although the losing party has a right to ask (petition) a higher court to review the case, the party does not have a right to have the case heard by the higher appellate court. Appellate courts normally have discretionary power and can accept or reject an appeal. Like the United States Supreme Court, state supreme courts generally deny most petitions for appeal.

If the petition for review is granted, new briefs must be filed before the state supreme court, and the attorneys may be allowed or requested to present oral arguments. Like the intermediate appellate courts, the state supreme court can reverse or affirm the lower appellate court's decision or remand the case. At this point, the case typically has reached its end (unless a federal question is at issue and one of the parties has legitimate grounds to seek review by a federal appellate court).

Concept Summary 3.3 reviews the options that the parties may pursue after the trial.

3-6 Enforcing the Judgment

The uncertainties of the litigation process are compounded by the lack of guarantees that any judgment will be enforceable. Even if the jury awards Kirby the full amount of damages requested ($500,000), for example, Carvello's auto insurance coverage might have lapsed. If so, the company would not pay any of the damages. Alternatively, Carvello's insurance policy might be limited to $250,000, meaning that Carvello personally would have to pay the remaining $250,000.

3-6a Requesting Court Assistance in Collecting the Judgment

If the defendant does not have the funds available to pay the judgment, the plaintiff can go back to the court and request that the court issue a writ of execution. A **writ**

of execution is an order directing the sheriff to seize and sell the defendant's nonexempt assets, or property (certain assets are exempted by law from creditors' actions). The proceeds of the sale are then used to pay the damages owed, and any excess proceeds are returned to the defendant. Alternatively, the nonexempt property itself could be transferred to the plaintiff in lieu of an outright payment. (Creditors' remedies, discussed elsewhere in this text, may also be available.)

3-6b Availability of Assets

The problem of collecting a judgment is less pronounced when a party is seeking to satisfy a judgment against a defendant with substantial assets that can be easily located, such as a major corporation. Usually, one of the factors considered by the plaintiff and his or her attorney before a lawsuit is initiated is whether the defendant has sufficient assets to cover the amount of damages sought. In addition, during the discovery process, attorneys routinely seek information about the location of the defendant's assets that might potentially be used to satisfy a judgment.

Concept Summary 3.3

Posttrial Options

Posttrial Motions	• *Motion for a new trial*—If the judge believes that the jury was in error but is not convinced that the losing party should have won, the motion normally is granted. It can also be granted on the basis of newly discovered evidence, misconduct by the participants during the trial, or error by the judge. • *Motion for judgment n.o.v.* ("*notwithstanding the verdict*")—The party making the motion must have filed a motion for a directed verdict at the close of the presentation of evidence during the trial. The motion will be granted if the judge is convinced that the jury was in error.
The Appeal	Either party can appeal the trial court's judgment to an appropriate court of appeals. • *Filing the appeal*—The appealing party must file a notice of appeal with the clerk of the trial court, who forwards the record on appeal to the appellate court. Attorneys file appellate briefs. • *Appellate review*—The appellate court does not hear evidence but bases its opinion, which it issues in writing, on the record on appeal and the attorneys' briefs and oral arguments. The court may affirm or reverse all (or part) of the trial court's judgment and/or remand the case for further proceedings consistent with its opinion. Most decisions are affirmed on appeal. • *Further review*—In some cases, further review may be sought from a higher appellate court, such as a state supreme court. If a federal question is involved, the case may ultimately be appealed to the United States Supreme Court.

Reviewing: Court Procedures

Ronald Metzgar placed his fifteen-month-old son, Matthew, awake and healthy, in his playpen. Ronald left the room for five minutes and on his return found Matthew lifeless. A toy block had lodged in the boy's throat, causing him to choke to death. Ronald called 911, but efforts to revive Matthew were to no avail. There was no warning of a choking hazard on the box containing the block. Matthew's parents hired an attorney and sued Playskool, Inc., the manufacturer of the block, alleging that the manufacturer had been negligent in failing to warn of the block's hazard. Playskool filed a motion for summary judgment, arguing that the danger of a young child's choking on a small block was obvious. Using the information presented in the chapter, answer the following questions.

1. Suppose that the attorney the Metzgars hired agreed to represent them on a contingency-fee basis. What does that mean?
2. How would the Metzgars' attorney likely have served process (the summons and complaint) on Playskool, Inc.?
3. Should Playskool's request for summary judgment be granted? Why or why not?
4. Suppose that the judge denied Playskool's motion and the case proceeded to trial. After hearing all the evidence, the jury found in favor of the defendant. What options do the plaintiffs have at this point if they are not satisfied with the verdict?

Debate This … *Some consumer advocates argue that attorneys' high contingency fees—sometimes reaching 40 percent—unfairly deprive winning plaintiffs of too much of their awards. Should the government cap contingency fees at, say, 20 percent of the award? Why or why not?*

Terms and Concepts

affidavit 56
affirmative defense 52
answer 51
brief 65
closing argument 63
complaint 50
counterclaim 52
cross-examination 61
default judgment 50
deposition 59
direct examination 61
discovery 57
e-evidence 60
Federal Rules of Civil Procedure
  (FRCP) 48

hearsay 61
impeach 59
interrogatories 59
metadata 60
motion 52
motion for a directed verdict 63
motion for a judgment as a matter
  of law 63
motion for a new trial 64
motion for judgment *n.o.v.* 65
motion for judgment on the
  pleadings 56
motion for summary judgment 56
motion to dismiss 53
opening statement 61

pleadings 50
pretrial conference 60
pretrial motion 53
rebuttal 63
rejoinder 63
relevant evidence 61
rules of evidence 61
service of process 50
summons 50
verdict 64
voir dire 61
writ of execution 66

Issue Spotters

1. At the trial, after Sue calls her witnesses, offers her evidence, and otherwise presents her side of the case, Tom has at least two choices between courses of actions. Tom can call his first witness. What else might he do? (See *The Trial.*)

2. After the trial, the judge issues a judgment that includes a grant of relief for Sue, but the relief is less than Sue wanted. Neither Sue nor Tom is satisfied with this result. Who can appeal to a higher court? (See *The Appeal.*)

• **Check your answers to the Issue Spotters against the answers provided in Appendix D at the end of this text.**

Business Scenarios

3–1. Discovery Rules. In the past, the rules of discovery were very restrictive, and trials often turned on elements of surprise. For example, a plaintiff would not necessarily know until the trial what the defendant's defense was going to be. In the last several decades, however, new rules of discovery have substantially changed this situation. Now each attorney can access practically all of the evidence that the other side intends to present at trial, with the exception of certain information—namely, the opposing attorney's work product. Work product is not a precise concept. Basically, it includes all of the attorney's thoughts on the case. Can you see any reason why such information should not be made available to the opposing attorney? Discuss fully. (See *Pretrial Procedures.*)

3–2. Motions. When and for what purpose is each of the following motions made? Which of them would be appropriate if a defendant claimed that the only issue between the parties was a question of law and that the law was favorable to the defendant's position? (See *Pretrial Procedures.*)

(a) A motion for judgment on the pleadings.

(b) A motion for a directed verdict.

(c) A motion for summary judgment.

(d) A motion for judgment *n.o.v.*

3–3. Motion for a New Trial. Washoe Medical Center, Inc., admitted Shirley Swisher for the treatment of a fractured pelvis. During her stay, Swisher suffered a fatal fall from her hospital bed. Gerald Parodi, the administrator of her estate, and others filed an action against Washoe seeking damages for the alleged lack of care in treating Swisher. During *voir dire*, when the plaintiffs' attorney returned a few minutes late from a break, the trial judge led the prospective jurors in a standing ovation. The judge joked with one of the prospective jurors, whom he had known in college, about his fitness to serve as a judge and personally endorsed another prospective juror's business. After the trial, the jury returned a verdict in favor of Washoe. The plaintiffs moved for a new trial, but the judge denied the motion. The plaintiffs then appealed, arguing that the tone set by the judge during *voir dire* prejudiced their right to a fair trial. Should the appellate court agree? Why or why not? (See *Posttrial Motions.*)

3–4. Discovery. Advance Technology Consultants, Inc. (ATC), contracted with RoadTrac, LLC, to provide software and client software systems for the products of global positioning satellite (GPS) technology being developed by RoadTrac. RoadTrac agreed to provide ATC with hardware with which ATC's software would interface. Problems soon arose, however. ATC claimed that RoadTrac's hardware was defective, making it difficult to develop the software. RoadTrac contended that its hardware was fully functional and that ATC had simply failed to provide supporting software.

ATC told RoadTrac that it considered their contract terminated. RoadTrac filed a suit in a Georgia state court against ATC alleging breach of contract. During discovery, RoadTrac requested ATC's customer lists and marketing procedures. ATC objected to providing this information because RoadTrac and ATC had become competitors in the GPS industry. Should a party to a lawsuit have to hand over its confidential business secrets as part of a discovery request? Why or why not? What limitations might a court consider imposing before requiring ATC to produce this material? (See *Pretrial Procedures.*)

Business Case Problems

3–5. Jury Misconduct. Michelle Fleshner worked for Pepose Vision Institute (PVI), a surgical practice. She was fired after she provided information to the U.S. Department of Labor about PVI's overtime pay policy. She sued for wrongful termination, and the jury awarded her $125,000. After the trial, a juror told PVI's attorneys that another juror had made anti-Semitic statements during jury deliberations. The comments concerned a witness who testified on PVI's behalf. According to the juror, the other juror said, about the witness: "She is a Jewish witch." "She is a penny-pinching Jew." "She was such a cheap Jew that she did not want to pay Plaintiff unemployment compensation." Another juror confirmed the remarks. PVI filed a motion for a new trial on the basis of juror misconduct. The trial judge held that the comments had not prevented a fair trial from occurring. PVI appealed. Do you think such comments are sufficient to require a new trial, or must a juror's bias be discovered during *voir dire* for it to matter? Explain. [*Fleshner v. Pepose Vision Institute*, 304 S.W.3d 81 (Mo. 2010)] (See *The Trial.*)

3–6. Service of Process. Dr. Kevin Bardwell owns Northfield Urgent Care, LLC, a Minnesota medical clinic. Northfield ordered flu vaccine from Clint Pharmaceuticals, a licensed distributer of flu vaccine located in Tennessee. The parties signed a credit agreement that specified that any disputes would be litigated in the Tennessee state courts. When Northfield failed to pay what it owed for the vaccine, Clint Pharmaceuticals filed a lawsuit in Tennessee and served process on the clinic via registered mail to Dr. Bardwell, the registered agent of Northfield.

Bardwell's wife, who worked as a receptionist at the clinic and handled inquiries on the clinic's Facebook site, signed for the letter. Bardwell did not appear on the trial date, however, and the Tennessee court entered a default judgment against Northfield. When Clint Pharmaceuticals attempted to collect on the judgment in Minnesota, Bardwell claimed that the judgment was unenforceable. He asserted that he had not been properly served because his wife was not a registered agent. Should the Minnesota court invalidate the Tennessee judgment? Was service of process proper when it was mailed to the defendant medical clinic and the wife of the physician who owned the clinic opened the letter? Explain. [*Clint Pharmaceuticals v. Northfield Urgent Care, LLC*, 2012 WL 3792546 (Minn.App. 2012).] (See *Pretrial Procedures*.)

3–7. Business Case Problem with Sample Answer—Discovery.

 Jessica Lester died from injuries suffered in an auto accident caused by the driver of a truck owned by Allied Concrete Co. Jessica's widower, Isaiah, filed a suit against Allied for damages. The defendant requested copies of all of Isaiah's Facebook photos and other postings. Before responding, Isaiah "cleaned up" his Facebook page. Allied suspected that some items had been deleted, including a photo of Isaiah holding a beer can while wearing a T-shirt that declared "I [heart] hot-moms." Can this material be recovered? If so, how? What effect might Isaiah's "postings" have on the result in this case? Discuss. [*Allied Concrete Co. v. Lester*, 736 S.E.2d 699 (2013)] (See *Pretrial Procedures*.)

• For a sample answer to Problem 3–7, go to Appendix E at the end of this text.

3–8. Motion for Summary Judgment.

Rebecca Nichols drove a truck for Tri-National Logistics, Inc. (TNI). On a delivery trip, Nichols's fellow driver, James Paris, made unwelcome sexual advances. Paris continued to make advances during a subsequent mandatory layover. Nichols reported this behavior to their employer. TNI nevertheless left her with Paris in Pharr, Texas, for another seven days with no alternative form of transportation before sending a driver to pick her up. She filed a suit in a federal district court against TNI, alleging discrimination on the basis of sex in violation of Title VII of the Civil Rights Act. Disputed facts included whether Nichols subjectively felt abused by Paris and whether their employer was aware of his conduct and failed to take appropriate action.

Could TNI successfully file a motion for summary judgment at this point? Explain. [*Nichols v. Tri-National Logistics, Inc,* 809 F.3d 981 (8th Cir. 2016)] (See *Pretrial Procedures*.)

3–9. A Question of Ethics—Service of Process.

 Narnia Investments, Ltd., filed a suit in a Texas state court against several defendants, including Harvestons Securities, Inc., a securities dealer. (Securities are investments that include stocks and bonds.) Harvestons is registered with the state of Texas. Thus, a party may serve a summons and a copy of a complaint on Harvestons by serving the Texas Securities Commissioner. In this case, the return of service indicated that process had been served on the commissioner "by delivering to JoAnn Kocerek defendant, in person, a true copy of this [summons] together with the accompanying copy(ies) of the [complaint]."

Harvestons did not file an answer, and Narnia obtained a default judgment against the defendant for $365,000, plus attorneys' fees and interest. Five months after this judgment, Harvestons filed a motion for a new trial, which the court denied. Harvestons appealed to a state intermediate appellate court, claiming that it had not been served in strict compliance with the rules governing service of process. [Harvestons Securities, Inc. v. Narnia Investments, Ltd., *218 S.W.3d 126 (Tex.App.—Houston 2007)*] (See *Pretrial Procedures*.)

(a) Harvestons asserted that Narnia's service was invalid, in part, because "the return of service states that process was delivered to 'JoAnn Kocerek'" and did not show that she "had the authority to accept process on behalf of Harvestons or the Texas Securities Commissioner." Should such a detail, if it is required, be strictly construed and applied? Should it apply in this case? Explain.

(b) Who is responsible for ensuring that service of process is accomplished properly? Was it accomplished properly in this case? Why or why not?

Legal Reasoning Group Activity

3–10. Court Procedures.

Bento Cuisine is a lunch-cart business. It occupies a street corner in Texarkana, a city that straddles the border of Arkansas and Texas. Across the street— and across the state line, which runs down the middle of the street—is Rico's Tacos. The two businesses compete for customers. Recently, Bento has begun to suspect that Rico's is engaging in competitive behavior that is illegal. Bento's manager overheard several of Rico's employees discussing these competitive tactics while on a break at a nearby Starbucks. Bento files a lawsuit against Rico's in a federal court based on diversity jurisdiction. (See *Pretrial Procedures*.)

(a) The first group will discuss whether Rico's could file a motion claiming that the federal court lacks jurisdiction over this dispute.

(b) The second group will assume that the case goes to trial. Bento's manager believes that Bento's has both the law and the facts on its side. Nevertheless, at the end of the trial, the jury decides against Bento, and the judge issues a ruling in favor of Rico's. If Bento is unwilling to accept this result, what are its options?

(c) As discussed in this chapter, hearsay is literally what a witness says he or she heard another person say. A third group will decide whether Bento's manager can testify about what he heard some of Rico's employees say to one another while at a coffee shop. This group will also discuss what makes the admissibility of hearsay evidence potentially unethical.

CHAPTER 4

Business and the Constitution

aws that govern business have their origin in the lawmaking authority granted by the U.S. Constitution, which is the supreme law in this country.[1] Neither Congress nor any state may pass a law that is in conflict with the Constitution.

Constitutional disputes frequently come before the courts. For instance, numerous states challenged the Obama administration's Affordable Care Act on constitutional grounds. The United States Supreme Court decided in 2012 that the provisions of this law, which required most Americans to have health insurance by 2014, did not exceed the constitutional authority of the federal government. The Court's decision in the matter continues to have a significant impact on the business environment.

1. See Appendix B for the full text of the U.S. Constitution.

4-1 The Constitutional Powers of Government

Following the Revolutionary War, the states adopted the Articles of Confederation. The Articles created a *confederal form of government* in which the states had the authority to govern themselves and the national government could exercise only limited powers. Problems soon arose because the nation was facing an economic crisis and state laws interfered with the free flow of commerce. A national convention was called, and the delegates drafted the U.S. Constitution. This document, after its ratification by the states in 1789, became the basis for an entirely new form of government.

4-1a A Federal Form of Government

The new government created by the U.S. Constitution reflected a series of compromises made by the convention delegates on various issues. Some delegates wanted sovereign power to remain with the states. Others wanted the national government alone to exercise sovereign power. The end result was a compromise—a **federal form of government** in which the national government and the states *share* sovereign power.

Federal Powers The Constitution sets forth specific powers that can be exercised by the national (federal) government. It further provides that the national government has the implied power to undertake actions necessary to carry out its expressly designated powers (or *enumerated powers*). All other powers are expressly "reserved" to the states under the Tenth Amendment to the U.S. Constitution.

Regulatory Powers of the States As part of their inherent **sovereignty** (power to govern themselves), state governments have the authority to regulate certain affairs within their borders. As mentioned, this authority stems, in part, from the Tenth Amendment, which reserves all powers not delegated to the national government to the states or to the people.

State regulatory powers are often referred to as **police powers.** The term encompasses more than just the enforcement of criminal laws. Police powers also give state governments broad rights to regulate private activities to protect or promote the public order, health, safety, morals, and general welfare. Fire and building codes, antidiscrimination laws, parking regulations, zoning restrictions, licensing requirements, and thousands of other state statutes have been enacted pursuant to states' police powers. Local governments, such as cities, also exercise police powers.[2] Generally, state laws enacted

2. Local governments derive their authority to regulate their communities from the state, because they are creatures of the state. In other words, they cannot come into existence unless authorized by the state to do so.

pursuant to a state's police powers carry a strong presumption of validity.

4–1b Relations among the States

The U.S. Constitution also includes provisions concerning relations among the states in our federal system. Particularly important are the *privileges and immunities clause* and the *full faith and credit clause.*

The Privileges and Immunities Clause Article IV, Section 2, of the Constitution provides that the "Citizens of each State shall be entitled to all Privileges and Immunities of Citizens in the several States." This clause is often referred to as the interstate **privileges and immunities clause.**[3] It prevents a state from imposing unreasonable burdens on citizens of another state—particularly with regard to means of livelihood or doing business.

When a citizen of one state engages in basic and essential activities in another state (the "foreign state"), the foreign state must have a *substantial reason* for treating the nonresident differently than its own residents. Basic activities include transferring property, seeking employment, and accessing the court system. The foreign state must also establish that its reason for the discrimination is *substantially related* to the state's ultimate purpose in adopting the legislation or regulating the activity.[4]

The Full Faith and Credit Clause Article IV, Section 1, of the U.S. Constitution provides that "Full Faith and Credit shall be given in each State to the public Acts, Records, and judicial Proceedings of every other State." This clause, which is referred to as the **full faith and credit clause,** applies only to civil matters. It ensures that rights established under deeds, wills, contracts, and similar instruments in one state will be honored by other states. It also ensures that any judicial decision with respect to such property rights will be honored and enforced in all states.

The legal issues raised by same-sex marriage involve, among other things, the full faith and credit clause, because that clause requires each state to honor marriage decrees issued by another state. See this chapter's *Managerial Strategy* feature for a discussion of marriage equality laws.

The full faith and credit clause has contributed to the unity of American citizens because it protects their legal rights as they move about from state to state. It also protects the rights of those to whom they owe obligations, such as persons who have been awarded monetary damages by courts. The ability to enforce such rights is extremely important for the conduct of business in a country with a very mobile citizenry.

4–1c The Separation of Powers

To make it more difficult for the national government to use its power arbitrarily, the Constitution provided for three branches of government. The legislative branch makes the laws, the executive branch enforces the laws, and the judicial branch interprets the laws. Each branch performs a separate function, and no branch may exercise the authority of another branch.

Additionally, a system of **checks and balances** allows each branch to limit the actions of the other two branches, thus preventing any one branch from exercising too much power. Some examples of these checks and balances include the following:

1. The legislative branch (Congress) can enact a law, but the executive branch (the president) has the constitutional authority to veto that law.
2. The executive branch is responsible for foreign affairs, but treaties with foreign governments require the advice and consent of the Senate.
3. Congress determines the jurisdiction of the federal courts, and the president appoints federal judges, with the advice and consent of the Senate. The judicial branch has the power to hold actions of the other two branches unconstitutional.[5]

4–1d The Commerce Clause

To prevent states from establishing laws and regulations that would interfere with trade and commerce among the states, the Constitution expressly delegated to the national government the power to regulate interstate commerce. Article I, Section 8, of the U.S. Constitution explicitly permits Congress "[t]o regulate Commerce with foreign Nations, and among the several States, and with the Indian Tribes." This clause, referred to as the **commerce clause,** has had a greater impact on business than any other provision in the Constitution. The commerce clause provides the basis for the national government's extensive regulation of state and even local affairs.

---

3. Interpretations of this clause commonly use the terms *privilege* and *immunity* synonymously. Generally, the terms refer to certain rights, benefits, or advantages enjoyed by individuals.
4. This test was first announced in *Supreme Court of New Hampshire v. Piper,* 470 U.S. 274, 105 S.Ct. 1272, 84 L.Ed.2d 205 (1985). For another example, see *Lee v. Miner,* 369 F.Supp.2d 527 (D.Del. 2005).

5. The power of judicial review was established by the United States Supreme Court in *Marbury v. Madison,* 5 U.S. (1 Cranch) 137, 2 L.Ed. 60 (1803).

Marriage Equality and the Constitution

The debate over same-sex marriage has been raging across the country for years. The legal issues raised by marriage equality involve privacy rights and equal protection. Although marriage equality may not appear at first glance to be business related, it is an important legal issue for managers. Companies like Barilla Pasta, Chick-fil-A, Exxon Mobil, and Target Corporation have lost significant business for purportedly supporting anti-gay organizations and legislation.

The Definition of Marriage

Before 1996, federal law did not define marriage, and the U.S. government recognized any marriage that was recognized by a state. Then Congress passed the Defense of Marriage Act (DOMA), which explicitly defined marriage as a union of one man and one woman. DOMA was later challenged, and a number of federal courts found it to be unconstitutional in the context of bankruptcy, public employee benefits, and estate taxes. In 2013, the United States Supreme Court struck down part of DOMA as unconstitutional.[a] Today, once again, no federal law defines marriage.

Bans on Same-Sex Marriage Eliminated by the Supreme Court

During this period, federal courts became increasingly likely to invalidate state bans on same-sex marriage. In 2013, a federal district court held that Utah's same-sex marriage ban was unconstitutional.[b] In 2014, federal

district courts in Arkansas, Mississippi, and Oklahoma struck down state same-sex marriage bans.[c] Moreover, public sentiment on the issue had shifted, and more states recognized the rights of same-sex couples. By 2015, thirty-seven states, as well as the District of Columbia, had legalized same-sex marriage.

In 2015, the United States Supreme Court determined that the remaining state-level prohibitions on same-sex marriage were unconstitutional. In a landmark decision, the Court ruled that the Fourteenth Amendment requires individual states to (1) issue marriage licenses to same-sex couples and (2) recognize same-sex marriages performed in other states.[d]

The landmark Supreme Court decision requiring all states to recognize same-sex marriage means that businesses must make adjustments. Company policies need to be revised to specify how same-sex partners will be treated in terms of family and medical leave, health-insurance coverage, pensions, and other benefits.

Business Questions

1. Can a business manager's religious beliefs legally factor into the business's hiring and treatment of same-sex partners? Why or why not?

2. Must business owners in all states provide the same benefits to employees in a same-sex union as they do to heterosexual couples?

a. *Windsor v. United States,* ___ U.S. ___, 133 S.Ct. 2675, 186 L.Ed.2d 808 (2013).
b. *Kitchen v. Herbert,* 961 F.Supp.2d 1181 (D.Utah 2013).
c. *Campaign for Southern Equality v. Bryant,* 64 F.Supp.3d 906 (S.D. Miss. 2014); *Jernigan v. Crane,* 64 F.Supp.3d 1260 (E.D.Ark. 2014); and *Bishop v. U.S. ex rel. Holder,* 962 F.Supp.2d 1252 (N.D. Okla. 2014).
d. *Obergefell v. Hodges,* ___ U.S. ___, 135 S.Ct. 2584, 192 L.Ed.2d 609 (2015).

Initially, the courts interpreted the commerce clause to apply only to commerce between the states (*interstate* commerce) and not commerce within the states (*intrastate* commerce). That changed in 1824, however, when the United States Supreme Court decided the landmark case of *Gibbons v. Ogden.*[6] The Court held that commerce within the states could also be regulated by the national government as long as the commerce *substantially affected* commerce involving more than one state.

The Expansion of National Powers under the Commerce Clause
As the nation grew and faced

new kinds of problems, the commerce clause became a vehicle for the additional expansion of the national government's regulatory powers. Even activities that seemed purely local in nature came under the regulatory reach of the national government if those activities were deemed to substantially affect interstate commerce. In 1942, the Supreme Court held that wheat production by an individual farmer intended wholly for consumption on his own farm was subject to federal regulation.[7]

The following *Classic Case* involved a challenge to the scope of the national government's constitutional authority to regulate local activities.

6. 22 U.S. (9 Wheat.) 1, 6 L.Ed. 23 (1824).

7. *Wickard v. Filburn,* 317 U.S. 111, 63 S.Ct. 82, 87 L.Ed. 122 (1942).

Classic Case **4.1**

Heart of Atlanta Motel v. United States

Supreme Court of the United States, 379 U.S. 241, 85 S.Ct. 348, 13 L.Ed.2d 258 (1964).

Background and Facts   In the 1950s, the United States Supreme Court ruled that racial segregation imposed by the states in school systems and other public facilities violated the Constitution. Privately owned facilities were not affected until Congress passed the Civil Rights Act of 1964, which prohibited racial discrimination in "establishments affecting interstate commerce."

The owner of the Heart of Atlanta Motel, in violation of the Civil Rights Act of 1964, refused to rent rooms to African Americans. The motel owner brought an action in a federal district court to have the Civil Rights Act declared unconstitutional on the ground that Congress had exceeded its constitutional authority to regulate commerce by enacting the statute.

The owner argued that his motel was not engaged in interstate commerce but was "of a purely local character." The motel, however, was accessible to state and interstate highways. The owner advertised nationally, maintained billboards throughout the state, and accepted convention trade from outside the state (75 percent of the guests were residents of other states).

The district court ruled that the act did not violate the Constitution and enjoined (prohibited) the owner from discriminating on the basis of race. The motel owner appealed. The case ultimately went to the United States Supreme Court.

In the Language of the Court

Mr. Justice *CLARKE* delivered the opinion of the Court.

 * * * *

While the Act as adopted carried no congressional findings, the record of its passage through each house is replete with evidence of the burdens that discrimination by race or color places upon interstate commerce * * * . This testimony included the fact that our people have become increasingly mobile with millions of all races traveling from State to State; that Negroes in particular have been the subject of discrimination in transient accommodations, having to travel great distances to secure the same; that often they have been unable to obtain accommodations and have had to call upon friends to put them up overnight. * * * These exclusionary practices were found to be nationwide, the Under Secretary of Commerce testifying that there is "no question that this discrimination in the North still exists to a large degree" and in the West and Midwest as well * * * . This testimony indicated a qualitative as well as quantitative effect on interstate travel by Negroes. The former was the obvious impairment of the Negro traveler's pleasure and convenience that resulted when he continually was uncertain of finding lodging. As for the latter, there was evidence that this uncertainty stemming from racial discrimination had the effect of discouraging travel on the part of a substantial portion of the Negro community * * * . We shall not burden this opinion with further details since the voluminous testimony presents overwhelming evidence that discrimination by hotels and motels impedes interstate travel.

 * * * *

It is said that the operation of the motel here is of a purely local character. But, assuming this to be true, "if it is interstate commerce that feels the pinch, it does not matter how local the operation that applies the squeeze." * * * *Thus the power of Congress to promote interstate commerce also includes the power to regulate the local incidents thereof, including local activities in both the States of origin and destination, which might have a substantial and harmful effect upon that commerce.* [Emphasis added.]

Decision and Remedy   *The United States Supreme Court upheld the constitutionality of the Civil Rights Act of 1964. The power of Congress to regulate interstate commerce permitted the enactment of legislation that could halt local discriminatory practices.*

Impact of This Case on Today's Law   *If the United States Supreme Court had invalidated the Civil Rights Act of 1964, the legal landscape of the United States would be much different today. The act prohibits discrimination based on race, color, national origin, religion, or gender in all "public accommodations," including hotels and restaurants.*

Case 4.1 Continues

Case 4.1 Continued

The act also prohibits discrimination in employment based on these criteria. Although state laws now prohibit many of these forms of discrimination as well, the protections available vary from state to state—and it is not certain whether such laws would have been passed had the outcome in this case been different.

Critical Thinking

- **What If the Facts Were Different?** *If this case had involved a small, private retail business that did not advertise nationally, would the result have been the same? Why or why not?*

The Commerce Clause Today Today, at least theoretically, the power over commerce authorizes the national government to regulate almost every commercial enterprise in the United States. The breadth of the commerce clause permits the national government to legislate in areas in which Congress has not explicitly been granted power. Only occasionally has the Supreme Court curbed the national government's regulatory authority under the commerce clause.[8]

The Supreme Court has, for instance, allowed the federal government to regulate noncommercial activities relating to medical marijuana that take place wholly within a state's borders. **■ CASE IN POINT 4.1** More than half the states, including California, have adopted laws that legalize marijuana for medical purposes (and a handful of states now permit the recreational use of marijuana). Marijuana possession, however, is illegal under the federal Controlled Substances Act (CSA).[9] After the federal government seized the marijuana that two seriously ill California women were using on the advice of their physicians, the women filed a lawsuit. They argued that it was unconstitutional for the federal statute to prohibit them from using marijuana for medical purposes that were legal within the state.

The Supreme Court, though, held that Congress has the authority to prohibit the *intrastate* possession and noncommercial cultivation of marijuana as part of a larger regulatory scheme (the CSA).[10] In other words, the federal government may still prosecute individuals for possession of marijuana regardless of whether they reside in a state that allows the medical or recreational use of marijuana. **■**

The "Dormant" Commerce Clause The Supreme Court has interpreted the commerce clause to mean that the national government has the *exclusive* authority to regulate commerce that substantially affects trade and commerce among the states. This express grant of authority to the national government is often referred to as the "positive" aspect of the commerce clause. But this positive aspect also implies a negative aspect—that the states do *not* have the authority to regulate interstate commerce. This negative aspect of the commerce clause is often referred to as the "dormant" (implied) commerce clause.

The dormant commerce clause comes into play when state regulations affect interstate commerce. In this situation, the courts weigh the state's interest in regulating a certain matter against the burden that the state's regulation places on interstate commerce. Because courts balance the interests involved, it is difficult to predict the outcome in a particular case. State laws that alter conditions of competition to favor in-state interests over out-of-state competitors in a market (such as wineries or construction workers) are usually invalidated, however.[11]

■ CASE IN POINT 4.2 Maryland imposed personal income taxes on its residents at the state level and the county level. Maryland residents who paid income tax in another state were allowed a credit against the *state* portion of their Maryland taxes, but not the *county* portion. Several Maryland residents who had earned profits in and paid taxes to other states but had not received a credit against their county tax liability sued. They claimed that Maryland's system discriminated against intrastate commerce because those who earned income in other states paid more taxes than residents whose only income came from within Maryland. When the case reached the United States Supreme Court in 2015, the

---

8. See, for example, *United States v. Morrison*, 529 U.S. 598, 120 S.Ct. 1740, 146 L.Ed.2d 658 (2000), holding that the federal Violence Against Women Act violated Congress's commerce clause authority.

9. 21 U.S.C. Sections 801 *et seq.*

10. *Gonzales v. Raich*, 545 U.S. 1, 125 S.Ct. 2195, 162 L.Ed.2d 1 (2005).

11. See *Family Winemakers of California v. Jenkins*, 592 F.3d 1 (1st Cir. 2010); and *Tri-M Group, LLC v. Sharp*, 638 F.3d 406 (3d Cir. 2011).

Court held that Maryland's personal income tax scheme violated the dormant commerce clause.[12] ■

4–1e The Supremacy Clause and Federal Preemption

Article VI of the U.S. Constitution, commonly referred to as the **supremacy clause,** provides that the Constitution, laws, and treaties of the United States are "the supreme Law of the Land." When there is a direct conflict between a federal law and a state law, the state law is rendered invalid. Because some powers are *concurrent* (shared by the federal government and the states), however, it is necessary to determine which law governs in a particular circumstance.

Preemption When Congress chooses to act exclusively in a concurrent area, **preemption** occurs. In this circumstance, a valid federal statute or regulation will take precedence over a conflicting state or local law or regulation on the same general subject.

Congressional Intent Often, it is not clear whether Congress, in passing a law, intended to preempt an entire subject area. In these situations, the courts determine whether Congress intended to exercise exclusive power.

No single factor is decisive as to whether a court will find preemption. Generally, though, congressional intent to preempt will be found if a federal law regulating an activity is so pervasive, comprehensive, or detailed that the states have little or no room to regulate in that area. Also, when a federal statute creates an agency to enforce the law, matters that may come within the agency's jurisdiction will likely preempt state laws.

■ **CASE IN POINT 4.3**   A man who alleged that he had been injured by a faulty medical device (a balloon catheter that was inserted into his artery following a heart attack) sued the manufacturer. The case ultimately came before the United States Supreme Court. The Court noted that the relevant federal law (the Medical Device Amendments of 1976) had included a preemption provision. Furthermore, the device had passed the U.S. Food and Drug Administration's rigorous premarket approval process. Therefore, the Court ruled that the federal regulation of medical devices preempted the man's state law claims.[13] ■

4–1f The Taxing and Spending Powers

Article I, Section 8, of the U.S. Constitution provides that Congress has the "Power to lay and collect Taxes, Duties, Imposts, and Excises." Section 8 further requires uniformity in taxation among the states, and thus Congress may not tax some states while exempting others.

In the distant past, if Congress attempted to regulate indirectly, by taxation, an area over which it had no authority, the courts would invalidate the tax. Today, however, if a tax measure is reasonable, it generally is held to be within the national taxing power. Moreover, the expansive interpretation of the commerce clause almost always provides a basis for sustaining a federal tax.

Article I, Section 8, also gives Congress its spending power—the power "to pay the Debts and provide for the common Defence and general Welfare of the United States." Congress can spend revenues not only to carry out its expressed powers but also to promote any objective it deems worthwhile, so long as it does not violate the Bill of Rights. The spending power necessarily involves policy choices, with which taxpayers (and politicians) may disagree.

4–2 Business and the Bill of Rights

The importance of a written declaration of the rights of individuals caused the first Congress of the United States to submit twelve amendments to the U.S. Constitution to the states for approval. Ten of these amendments, known as the **Bill of Rights,** were adopted in 1791 and embody a series of protections for the individual against various types of interference by the federal government.[14]

The protections guaranteed by these ten amendments are summarized in Exhibit 4–1.[15] Some of these constitutional protections apply to business entities as well as individuals. For example, corporations exist as separate legal entities, or *legal persons,* and enjoy many of the same rights and privileges as *natural persons* do.

---

12. *Comptroller of Treasury of Maryland v. Wynne,* ___ U.S. ___, 135 S.Ct. 1787, 191 L.Ed.2d 813 (2015).

13. *Riegel v. Medtronic, Inc.,* 552 U.S. 312, 128 S.Ct. 999, 169 L.Ed.2d 892 (2008).

---

14. Another of these proposed amendments was ratified more than two hundred years later (in 1992) and became the Twenty-seventh Amendment to the Constitution. See Appendix B.

15. See the Constitution in Appendix B for the complete text of each amendment.

EXHIBIT 4–1 Protections Guaranteed by the Bill of Rights

First Amendment:	Guarantees the freedoms of religion, speech, and the press and the rights to assemble peaceably and to petition the government.
Second Amendment:	States that the right of the people to keep and bear arms shall not be infringed.
Third Amendment:	Prohibits, in peacetime, the lodging of soldiers in any house without the owner's consent.
Fourth Amendment:	Prohibits unreasonable searches and seizures of persons or property.
Fifth Amendment:	Guarantees the rights to *indictment* (formal accusation) by a grand jury, to due process of law, and to fair payment when private property is taken for public use. The Fifth Amendment also prohibits compulsory self-incrimination and double jeopardy (trial for the same crime twice).
Sixth Amendment:	Guarantees the accused in a criminal case the right to a speedy and public trial by an impartial jury and with counsel. The accused has the right to cross-examine witnesses against him or her and to solicit testimony from witnesses in his or her favor.
Seventh Amendment:	Guarantees the right to a trial by jury in a civil case involving at least twenty dollars.
Eighth Amendment:	Prohibits excessive bail and fines, as well as cruel and unusual punishment.
Ninth Amendment:	Establishes that the people have rights in addition to those specified in the Constitution.
Tenth Amendment:	Establishes that those powers neither delegated to the federal government nor denied to the states are reserved to the states and to the people.

4–2a Limits on Federal and State Governmental Actions

As originally intended, the Bill of Rights limited only the powers of the national government. Over time, however, the United States Supreme Court "incorporated" most of these rights into the protections against state actions afforded by the Fourteenth Amendment to the Constitution.

The Fourteenth Amendment The Fourteenth Amendment, passed in 1868 after the Civil War, provides, in part, that "[n]o State shall . . . deprive any person of life, liberty, or property, without due process of law." Starting in 1925, the Supreme Court began to define various rights and liberties guaranteed in the U.S. Constitution as constituting "due process of law," which was required of state governments under that amendment.

Today, most of the rights and liberties set forth in the Bill of Rights apply to state governments as well as the national government. In other words, neither the federal government nor state governments can deprive persons of those rights and liberties.

Judicial Interpretation The rights secured by the Bill of Rights are not absolute. Many of the rights guaranteed by the first ten amendments are set forth in very general terms. The Second Amendment states that people have a right to keep and bear arms, but it does not describe the extent of this right. As the Supreme Court has noted, this right does not mean that people can "keep and carry any weapon whatsoever in any manner whatsoever and for whatever purpose."[16] Legislatures can prohibit the carrying of concealed weapons or certain types of weapons, such as machine guns.

Ultimately, the United States Supreme Court, as the final interpreter of the Constitution, gives meaning to these rights and determines their boundaries. Changing public views on controversial topics, such as privacy in an era of terrorist threats or the rights of gay men and lesbians, can affect the way the Supreme Court decides a case.

4–2b Freedom of Speech

A democratic form of government cannot survive unless people can freely voice their political opinions and criticize government actions or policies. Freedom of speech,

---

16. *District of Columbia v. Heller*, 554 U.S. 570, 128 S.Ct. 2783, 171 L.Ed.2d 637 (2008).

particularly political speech, is thus a prized right, and traditionally the courts have protected this right to the fullest extent possible.

Symbolic speech—gestures, movements, articles of clothing, and other forms of expressive conduct—is also given substantial protection by the courts. The Supreme Court has held that the burning of the American flag as part of a peaceful protest is a constitutionally protected form of expression.[17] Similarly, wearing a T-shirt with a photo of a presidential candidate is a constitutionally protected form of expression. ■ **EXAMPLE 4.4** As a form of expression, Nate has gang signs tattooed on his torso, arms, neck, and legs. If a reasonable person would interpret this conduct as conveying a message, then it might be a protected form of symbolic speech. ■

Reasonable Restrictions A balance must be struck between a government's obligation to protect its citizens and those citizens' exercise of their rights. Expression—oral, written, or symbolized by conduct—is therefore subject to reasonable restrictions. Reasonableness is analyzed on a case-by-case basis.

Content-Neutral Laws. Laws that regulate the time, manner, and place, but not the content, of speech receive less scrutiny by the courts than do laws that restrict the content of expression. If a restriction imposed by the government is content neutral, then a court may allow it. To be content neutral, the restriction must be aimed at combatting some societal problem, such as crime or drug abuse, and not be aimed at suppressing the expressive conduct or its message.

Courts have often protected nude dancing as a form of symbolic expression but typically allow content-neutral laws that ban all public nudity. ■ **CASE IN POINT 4.5** Ria Ora was charged with dancing nude at an annual "anti-Christmas" protest in Harvard Square in Cambridge, Massachusetts, under a statute banning public displays of open and gross lewdness. Ora argued that the statute was overbroad and unconstitutional, and a trial court agreed. On appeal, however, a state appellate court upheld the statute as constitutional in situations in which there was an unsuspecting or unwilling audience.[18] ■

Laws That Restrict the Content of Speech. Any law that regulates the content of expression must serve a compelling state interest and must be narrowly written to achieve that interest. Under the **compelling government**

interest test, the government's interest is balanced against the individual's constitutional right to free expression. For the statute to be valid, there must be a compelling government interest that can be furthered only by the law in question.

The United States Supreme Court has held that schools may restrict students' speech at school events. ■ **CASE IN POINT 4.6** Some high school students held up a banner saying "Bong Hits 4 Jesus" at an off-campus but school-sanctioned event. The Supreme Court ruled that the school did not violate the students' free speech rights when school officials confiscated the banner and suspended the students for ten days. Because the banner could reasonably be interpreted as promoting drugs, the Court concluded that the school's actions were justified. Several justices disagreed, however, noting that the majority's holding creates an exception that will allow schools to censor any student speech that mentions drugs.[19] ■

Corporate Political Speech Political speech by corporations also falls within the protection of the First Amendment. Many years ago, the United States Supreme Court struck down as unconstitutional a Massachusetts statute that prohibited corporations from making political contributions or expenditures that individuals were permitted to make.[20] The Court has also held that a law forbidding a corporation from including inserts with its bills to express its views on controversial issues violates the First Amendment.[21]

Corporate political speech continues to be given significant protection under the First Amendment. ■ **CASE IN POINT 4.7** In *Citizens United v. Federal Election Commission,*[22] the Supreme Court issued a landmark decision that overturned a twenty-year-old precedent on campaign financing. The case involved Citizens United, a nonprofit corporation that runs a *political action committee* (an organization that registers with the government and campaigns for or against political candidates).

Citizens United had produced a film called *Hillary: The Movie* that was critical of Hillary Clinton, who was seeking the Democratic nomination for presidential candidate. Campaign-finance law restricted Citizens United from broadcasting the movie. The Court ruled that these

17. *Texas v. Johnson,* 491 U.S. 397, 109 S.Ct. 2533, 105 L.Ed.2d 342 (1989).
18. *Commonwealth v. Ora,* 451 Mass. 125, 883 N.E.2d 1217 (2008).
19. *Morse v. Frederick,* 551 U.S. 393, 127 S.Ct. 2618, 168 L.Ed.2d 290 (2007).
20. *First National Bank of Boston v. Bellotti,* 435 U.S. 765, 98 S.Ct. 1407, 55 L.Ed.2d 707 (1978).
21. *Consolidated Edison Co. v. Public Service Commission,* 447 U.S. 530, 100 S.Ct. 2326, 65 L.Ed.2d 319 (1980).
22. 558 U.S. 310, 130 S.Ct. 876, 175 L.Ed.2d 753 (2010).

restrictions were unconstitutional and that the First Amendment prevents limits from being placed on independent political expenditures by corporations. ■

Commercial Speech The courts also give substantial protection to *commercial speech,* which consists of communications—primarily advertising and marketing—made by business firms that involve only their commercial interests. The protection given to commercial speech under the First Amendment is less extensive than that afforded to noncommercial speech, however.

A state may restrict certain kinds of advertising, for instance, in the interest of preventing consumers from being misled. States also have a legitimate interest in roadside beautification and therefore may impose restraints on billboard advertising. ■ **EXAMPLE 4.8** Café Erotica, a nude dancing establishment, sues the state after being denied a permit to erect a billboard along an interstate highway in Florida. Because the law directly advances a substantial government interest in highway beautification and safety, a court will likely find that it is not an unconstitutional restraint on commercial speech. ■

Generally, a restriction on commercial speech will be considered valid as long as it meets three criteria:

1. It must seek to implement a substantial government interest.
2. It must directly advance that interest.
3. It must go no further than necessary to accomplish its objective.

At issue in the following case was whether a government agency had unconstitutionally restricted commercial speech when it prohibited the inclusion of a certain illustration on beer labels.

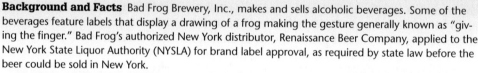

Spotlight on Beer Labels

Case 4.2 Bad Frog Brewery, Inc. v. New York State Liquor Authority
United States Court of Appeals, Second Circuit, 134 F.3d 87 (1998).

Background and Facts Bad Frog Brewery, Inc., makes and sells alcoholic beverages. Some of the beverages feature labels that display a drawing of a frog making the gesture generally known as "giving the finger." Bad Frog's authorized New York distributor, Renaissance Beer Company, applied to the New York State Liquor Authority (NYSLA) for brand label approval, as required by state law before the beer could be sold in New York.

The NYSLA denied the application, in part, because "the label could appear in grocery and convenience stores, with obvious exposure on the shelf to children of tender age." Bad Frog filed a suit in a federal district court against the NYSLA, asking for, among other things, an injunction against the denial of the application. The court granted summary judgment in favor of the NYSLA. Bad Frog appealed to the U.S. Court of Appeals for the Second Circuit.

In the Language of the Court
Jon O. *NEWMAN,* Circuit Judge:
* * * *

* * * To support its asserted power to ban Bad Frog's labels [NYSLA advances] * * * the State's interest in "protecting children from vulgar and profane advertising" * * * .

[This interest is] substantial * * * . *States have a compelling interest in protecting the physical and psychological wellbeing of minors* * * * . [Emphasis added.]
* * * *

* * * NYSLA endeavors to advance the state interest in preventing exposure of children to vulgar displays by taking only the limited step of barring such displays from the labels of alcoholic beverages. *In view of the wide currency of vulgar displays throughout contemporary society, including comic books targeted directly at children, barring such displays from labels for alcoholic beverages cannot realistically be expected to reduce children's exposure to such displays to any significant degree.* [Emphasis added.]

* * * If New York decides to make a substantial effort to insulate children from vulgar displays in some significant sphere of activity, at least with respect to materials likely to be seen by children, NYSLA's label prohibition might well be found to make a justifiable contribution to the material

Case 4.2 Continued

advancement of such an effort, but its currently isolated response to the perceived problem, applicable only to labels on a product that children cannot purchase, does not suffice. * * * A state must demonstrate that its commercial speech limitation is part of a substantial effort to advance a valid state interest, not merely the removal of a few grains of offensive sand from a beach of vulgarity.

* * * *

* * * Even if we were to assume that the state materially advances its asserted interest by shielding children from viewing the Bad Frog labels, it is plainly excessive to prohibit the labels from all use, including placement on bottles displayed in bars and taverns where parental supervision of children is to be expected. Moreover, to whatever extent NYSLA is concerned that children will be harmfully exposed to the Bad Frog labels when wandering without parental supervision around grocery and convenience stores where beer is sold, that concern could be less intrusively dealt with by placing restrictions on the permissible locations where the appellant's products may be displayed within such stores.

Decision and Remedy *The U.S. Court of Appeals for the Second Circuit reversed the judgment of the district court and remanded the case for the entry of a judgment in favor of Bad Frog. The NYSLA's ban on the use of the labels lacked a "reasonable fit" with the state's interest in shielding minors from vulgarity. In addition, the NYSLA had not adequately considered alternatives to the ban.*

Critical Thinking
- **What If the Facts Were Different?** *If Bad Frog had sought to use the offensive label to market toys instead of beer, would the court's ruling likely have been the same? Why or why not?*
- **Legal Environment** *Whose interests are advanced by the banning of certain types of advertising?*

Unprotected Speech The United States Supreme Court has made it clear that certain types of speech will not be protected under the First Amendment. Unprotected speech includes fighting words, or words that are likely to incite others to respond violently. It also includes speech that harms the good reputation of another, or defamatory speech. In addition, speech that violates criminal laws (threatening speech or possession of child pornography, for instance) is not constitutionally protected.

Threatening Speech. Note that in the case of threatening speech, the speaker must have posed a "true threat"— that is, must have meant to communicate a serious intent to commit an unlawful, violent act against a particular person or group. ■ **CASE IN POINT 4.9** After Anthony Elonis's wife, Tara, left him and took their two children, Elonis was upset and experienced problems at work. A coworker filed five sexual harassment reports against him. When Elonis posted a photograph of himself in a Halloween costume holding a toy knife to the coworker's neck, he was fired from his job. Elonis then began posting violent statements on his Facebook page, mostly focusing on his former wife and talking about killing her.

Elonis continued to post statements about killing his wife and eventually was arrested and prosecuted for his online posts. Elonis was convicted by a jury of violating a statute and ordered to serve time in prison. He appealed

to the United States Supreme Court, which held that it is not enough that a reasonable person might view the defendant's Facebook posts as threats. Elonis must have intended to issue threats or known that his statements would be viewed as threats to be convicted of a crime. The Court reversed Elonis's conviction and remanded the case back to the lower court to determine if there was sufficient evidence of intent.[23] ■

Obscene Speech. The First Amendment, as interpreted by the Supreme Court, also does not protect obscene speech. Numerous state and federal statutes make it a crime to disseminate and possess obscene materials, including child pornography. Objectively defining obscene speech has proved difficult, however. It is even more difficult to prohibit the dissemination of obscenity and pornography online.

Most of Congress's attempts to pass legislation protecting minors from pornographic materials on the Internet have been struck down on First Amendment grounds when challenged in court. One exception is a law that requires public schools and libraries to install **filtering software** on computers to keep children from accessing adult content.[24] Such software is designed to

---

23. *Elonis v. United States,* ___ U.S. ___, 135 S.Ct. 2001, 192 L.Ed.2d 1 (2015).

24. Children's Internet Protection Act (CIPA), 17 U.S.C. Sections 1701–1741.

prevent persons from viewing certain Web sites based on a site's Internet address or its **meta tags,** or key words. The Supreme Court held that the act does not unconstitutionally burden free speech because it is flexible and libraries can disable the filters for any patrons who ask.[25]

Another exception is a law that makes it a crime to intentionally distribute *virtual child pornography*—which uses computer-generated images, not actual people—without indicating that it is computer-generated.[26] In a case challenging the law's constitutionality, the Supreme Court held that the statute is valid because it does not prohibit a substantial amount of protected speech.[27] Nevertheless, because of the difficulties of policing the Internet, as well as the constitutional complexities of prohibiting obscenity through legislation, online obscenity remains a legal issue.

4–2c Freedom of Religion

The First Amendment states that the government may neither establish any religion nor prohibit the free exercise of religious practices. The first part of this constitutional provision is referred to as the **establishment clause,** and the second part is known as the **free exercise clause**. Government action, both federal and state, must be consistent with this constitutional mandate.

The Establishment Clause The establishment clause prohibits the government from establishing a state-sponsored religion, as well as from passing laws that promote (aid or endorse) religion or show a preference for one religion over another. Although the establishment clause involves the separation of church and state, it does not require a complete separation.

Applicable Standard. Establishment clause cases often involve such issues as the legality of allowing or requiring school prayers, using state-issued vouchers to pay tuition at religious schools, and teaching creation theories versus evolution. Federal or state laws that do not promote or place a significant burden on religion are constitutional even if they have some impact on religion. For a government law or policy to be constitutional, it must not have the primary effect of promoting or inhibiting religion.

Religious Displays. Religious displays on public property have often been challenged as violating the establishment clause, and the United States Supreme Court has

ruled on a number of such cases. Generally, the Court has focused on the proximity of the religious display (such as a Christian Christmas symbol) to nonreligious symbols (such as reindeer and candy canes) or symbols from different religions (such as a menorah, a nine-branched candelabrum used in celebrating Hanukkah).

The Supreme Court took a slightly different approach when it held that public displays having historical, as well as religious, significance do not necessarily violate the establishment clause.[28] Still, historical significance must be carefully weighed against religious elements in establishment clause cases.

■ **CASE IN POINT 4.10** Mount Soledad is a prominent hill near San Diego. There has been a forty-foot cross on top of Mount Soledad since 1913. In the 1990s, a war memorial with six walls listing the names of veterans was constructed next to the cross. The site was privately owned until 2006, when Congress authorized the property's transfer to the federal government "to preserve a historically significant war memorial."

Steve Trunk and the Jewish War Veterans filed lawsuits claiming that the cross violated the establishment clause because it endorsed the Christian religion. A federal appellate court agreed, finding that the primary effect of the memorial as a whole sent a strong message of endorsement of Christianity and exclusion of non-Christian veterans. The court noted that although not all cross displays at war memorials violate the establishment clause, the cross in this case physically dominated the site. Additionally, it was originally dedicated to religious purposes, had a long history of religious use, and was the only portion visible to drivers on the freeway below.[29] ■

The Free Exercise Clause The free exercise clause guarantees that people can hold any religious beliefs they want or can hold no religious beliefs. The constitutional guarantee of personal freedom restricts only the actions of the government, however, and not those of individuals or private businesses.

Restrictions Must Be Necessary. The government must have a compelling state interest for restricting the free exercise of religion, and the restriction must be the only way to further that interest. ■ **CASE IN POINT 4.11** Gregory Holt, an inmate in an Arkansas state prison, was a devout Muslim who wished to grow a beard in accord with his religious beliefs. The Arkansas Department of

---

25. *United States v. American Library Association*, 539 U.S. 194, 123 S.Ct. 2297, 156 L.Ed.2d 221 (2003).

26. The Prosecutorial Remedies and Other Tools to End the Exploitation of Children Today Act (Protect Act), 18 U.S.C. Section 2252A(a)(5)(B).

27. *United States v. Williams*, 553 U.S. 285, 128 S.Ct. 1830, 170 L.Ed.2d 650 (2008).

28. *Van Orden v. Perry*, 545 U.S. 677, 125 S.Ct. 2854, 162 L.Ed.2d 607 (2005). The Court held that a six-foot-tall monument of the Ten Commandments on the Texas state capitol grounds did not violate the establishment clause because the Ten Commandments have historical significance.

29. *Trunk v. City of San Diego*, 629 F.3d 1099 (9th Cir. 2011).

Correction prohibited inmates from growing beards (except for medical reasons). Holt asked for an exemption to grow a half-inch beard on religious grounds, and prison officials denied his request. Holt filed a suit in a federal district court against Ray Hobbs, the director of the department, and others.

A federal statute prohibits the government from taking any action that substantially burdens the religious exercise of an institutionalized person unless the action constitutes the least restrictive means of furthering a compelling governmental interest. The defendants argued that beards compromise prison safety—a compelling government interest—because contraband can be hidden in them and because an inmate can quickly shave his beard to disguise his identity.

The district court dismissed Holt's suit, and the dismissal was affirmed on appeal. Holt then appealed to the United States Supreme Court. The Court noted that "an item of contraband would have to be very small indeed to be concealed by a 1/2–inch beard." Moreover, the Court reasoned that the department could satisfy its security concerns by simply searching the beard, the way it already searches prisoners' hair and clothing. The Court concluded that the department's grooming policy, which prevented Holt from growing a half-inch beard, violated his right to exercise his religious beliefs.[30] ∎

Restrictions Must Not Be a Substantial Burden. To comply with the free exercise clause, a government action must not place a substantial burden on religious practices. A burden is substantial if it pressures an individual to modify his or her behavior and to violate his or her beliefs.

At issue in the following case was whether forcing a state prison inmate to choose between daily nutrition and a religious practice is a substantial burden.

---

30. *Holt v. Hobbs*, ___ U.S. ___, 135 S.Ct. 853, 190 L.Ed.2d 747 (2015).

Case Analysis 4.3

Thompson v. Holm
United States Court of Appeals, Seventh Circuit, 809 F.3d 376 (2016).

In the Language of the Court
ROVNER, Circuit Judge.
Michael Thompson, a Muslim inmate incarcerated at Waupun Correctional Institution in Wisconsin, sued members of the prison staff for violating his right under the First Amendment to exercise his religion freely. The violation occurred, Thompson says, when for two days prison staff prevented him from fasting properly during Ramadan.

* * * A central religious practice of the Islamic faith is a sunrise-to-sunset fast during the month of Ramadan. The prison normally accommodates this practice by providing Ramadan "meal bags" at sunset to each Muslim prisoner listed as eligible. The prison's chaplain determines eligibility. Each Ramadan meal bag contains two meals: the post-sunset dinner and the next morning's pre-sunrise breakfast. A prisoner who eats at the prison cafeteria during Ramadan forfeits his right to the meal bags for the rest of the month-long fast. Thompson, a practicing Muslim, began fasting for Ramadan after sunrise on August 11—the first day of Ramadan. He received his daily meal bags until August 21, about one-third into the month.

* * * Thompson says that shortly before August 21, as he was on his way back to his cell, Randall Lashock, a prison guard, handed him a meal bag. When Thompson arrived at his cell, he found that a guard had already left a meal bag for him there. Thompson could not leave his cell to return the extra bag without risking a conduct violation, so he left one of the two bags unopened for Lashock to retrieve. Lashock asserts that when he later retrieved that extra meal bag from Thompson's cell, he found Thompson eating from both bags.

Thompson received no meal bags on August 21 and 22. Lashock was supposed to deliver the Ramadan meal bags to every prisoner on the eligibility list. But on those two days, Lashock brought Thompson nothing, even though * * * he remained on the list. Receiving no meals, and learning from [prison guards] Bruce Bleich and Matthew Larson when he complained to them that he would have to go to the cafeteria if he wanted to eat, Thompson felt pressure to break his fast by going to the cafeteria. But he knew that under the prison's policy he could not do that without forfeiting meal bags for the rest of the month-long fast. He also had hunger pangs and felt tired and unwell. Because of his hunger, exhaustion, and anxiety, he missed one of his morning prayers and did not properly experience Ramadan, which is meant to be a time of peace and focus.

* * * *

While he was receiving no meal bags, Thompson asked other prison officials to explain why Lashock was not bringing him food * * * . Bleich and Larson told him that Captain William Holm had ordered his name removed from the list because he had stolen a meal bag; they too refused to bring him any meals. But Holm * * * did not remove Thompson from the list and had no authority to do so; only the chaplain could do that.

* * * On August 23, Thompson received a Ramadan meal bag at sunset

Case 4.3 Continues

and continued to receive a bag each day until the end of Ramadan.

Thompson [filed a suit in a federal district court against] Lashock, Holm, Bleich, and Larson * * * for violating his First Amendment rights, and the defendants moved for summary judgment. * * * They argued the lack of meal bags for two days did not substantially burden Thompson's free-exercise rights.

Thompson responded that the defendants unlawfully withheld his meal bags. * * * By forcing him to choose between adequate nutrition and a central tenet of his religion, the defendants substantially burdened his free-exercise rights.

[The court] granted the defendants' motion for summary judgment. The judge ruled that receiving no meal bags for just two days was not a substantial burden on Thompson's free-exercise rights because he kept fasting, praying, and reading the Koran.

On appeal Thompson challenges the entry of summary judgment.

We begin our analysis by asking whether the denial of meal bags substantially burdened Thompson's free exercise rights. The answer is yes. *Without the meal bags, Thompson was forced to choose between foregoing adequate nutrition or violating a central tenet of his religion. Facing that choice for "only" two days was not, as defendants argue, a "de minimis" [minimal] burden.* Not only did Thompson receive no proper meal for 55 hours, leaving him weak and tired, he did not know if he would ever be put back on the Ramadan list and get regular food. This uncertainty put pressure on him to resign himself to the cafeteria; the anxiety left him unable to practice Ramadan properly. [Emphasis added.]

* * * *

We next consider whether Thompson produced sufficient evidence that all the defendants were personally involved in imposing this burden. Once again, the answer is yes. We consider the defendants individually, beginning with

Lashock. He was responsible for delivering the meal bags to all inmates on the eligibility list. Yet he personally denied them to Thompson for two days even though * * * Thompson remained on the list. As to Holm, * * * Holm lied about whether he had removed Thompson from the meal list. Finally, as to Bleich and Larson, they also bear responsibility for depriving Thompson of his food. By (falsely) telling Thompson that Holm had removed him from the religious meal list, refusing to bring him any meals, and warning him to go to the cafeteria if he wanted to eat, * * * they were involved in a joint effort to pressure Thompson to break his fast.

* * * *

Accordingly, we VACATE the judgment. This case is REMANDED for further proceedings consistent with this order.

Legal Reasoning Questions

1. What is the standard for determining whether a restriction on a religious practice is constitutional under the First Amendment?
2. How did that standard apply to the prison guards' conduct in this case?
3. Were all of the guards personally involved in the alleged violation of the First Amendment? Explain.

Public Welfare Exception. When religious *practices* work against public policy and the public welfare, the government can act. For instance, the government can require that a child receive certain types of vaccinations or medical treatment if his or her life is in danger—regardless of the child's or parent's religious beliefs. When public safety is an issue, an individual's religious beliefs often have to give way to the government's interest in protecting the public.

■ **EXAMPLE 4.12** A woman of the Muslim faith may choose not to appear in public without a scarf, known as a *hijab,* over her head. Nevertheless, due to public safety concerns, many courts today do not allow the wearing of any headgear (hats or scarves) in courtrooms. ■

4–2d Searches and Seizures

The Fourth Amendment protects the "right of the people to be secure in their persons, houses, papers, and effects."

Before searching or seizing private property, law enforcement officers must usually obtain a **search warrant**—an order from a judge or other public official authorizing the search or seizure. Because of the strong government interest in protecting the public, however, a warrant normally is not required for seizures of spoiled or contaminated food. Nor are warrants required for searches of businesses in such highly regulated industries as liquor, guns, and strip mining.

To obtain a search warrant, law enforcement officers must convince a judge that they have reasonable grounds, or **probable cause,** to believe a search will reveal evidence of a specific illegality. To establish probable cause, the officers must have trustworthy evidence that would convince a reasonable person that the proposed search or seizure is more likely justified than not.

■ **CASE IN POINT 4.13** Citlalli Flores was driving across the border into the United States from Tijuana, Mexico, when a border protection officer became suspicious because she was acting nervous and looking around inside her car.

On further inspection, the officer found thirty-six pounds of marijuana hidden in the car's quarter panels. Flores claimed that she had not known about the marijuana.

Flores was arrested for importing marijuana into the United States. She then made two jail-recorded phone calls in which she asked her cousin to delete whatever he felt needed to be removed from Flores's Facebook page. The government got a warrant to search Flores's Facebook messages, where they found references to her "carrying" or "bringing" marijuana into the United States that day. Flores's Facebook posts were later used as evidence against her at trial, and she was convicted.

On appeal, the court held that the phone calls had given the officers probable cause to support a warrant to search Flores's social networking site for incriminating statements. Her conviction was affirmed.[31] ■

4–2e Self-Incrimination

The Fifth Amendment guarantees that no person "shall be compelled in any criminal case to be a witness against himself." Thus, in any court proceeding, an accused person cannot be forced to give testimony that might subject him or her to any criminal prosecution. The guarantee applies to both federal and state proceedings because the due process clause of the Fourteenth Amendment (discussed shortly) extends the protection to state courts.

The Fifth Amendment's guarantee against self-incrimination extends only to natural persons. Neither corporations nor partnerships receive Fifth Amendment protection. When a partnership is required to produce business records, it must therefore do so even if the information provided incriminates the individual partners of the firm. In contrast, sole proprietors and sole practitioners (those who individually own their businesses) cannot be compelled to produce their business records. These individuals have full protection against self-incrimination because they function in only one capacity, and there is no separate business entity.

4–3 Due Process and Equal Protection

Other constitutional guarantees of great significance to Americans are mandated by the *due process clauses* of the Fifth and Fourteenth Amendments and the *equal protection clause* of the Fourteenth Amendment.

4–3a Due Process

Both the Fifth and Fourteenth Amendments provide that no person shall be deprived "of life, liberty, or property, without due process of law." The **due process clause** of these constitutional amendments has two aspects—procedural and substantive. Note that the due process clause applies to "legal persons" (that is, corporations), as well as to individuals.

Procedural Due Process *Procedural* due process requires that any government decision to take life, liberty, or property must be made equitably. In other words, the government must give a person proper notice and an opportunity to be heard. Fair procedures must be used in determining whether a person will be subjected to punishment or have some burden imposed on her or him.

Fair procedure has been interpreted as requiring that the person have at least an opportunity to object to a proposed action before an impartial, neutral decision maker (who need not be a judge). ■ **EXAMPLE 4.14** Doyle Burns, a nursing student in Kansas, poses for a photograph standing next to a placenta used as a lab specimen. Although she quickly deletes the photo from her library, it ends up on Facebook. When the director of nursing sees the photo, Burns is expelled. She sues for reinstatement and wins. The school violated Burns's due process rights by expelling her from the nursing program for taking a photo without giving her an opportunity to present her side to school authorities. ■

Substantive Due Process *Substantive* due process focuses on the content of legislation rather than the fairness of procedures. Substantive due process limits what the government may do in its legislative and executive capacities. Legislation must be fair and reasonable in content and must further a legitimate governmental objective.

If a law or other governmental action limits a fundamental right, the state must have a legitimate and compelling interest to justify its action. Fundamental rights include interstate travel, privacy, voting, marriage and family, and all First Amendment rights. Thus, for instance, a state must have a substantial reason for taking any action that infringes on a person's free speech rights.

In situations not involving fundamental rights, a law or action does not violate substantive due process if it rationally relates to any legitimate government purpose. It is almost impossible for a law or action to fail the "rationality" test. Under this test, almost any business regulation will be upheld as reasonable.

---

31. *United States v. Flores*, 830 F.3d 1028 (9th Cir. 2015).

4–3b Equal Protection

Under the Fourteenth Amendment, a state may not "deny to any person within its jurisdiction the equal protection of the laws." The United States Supreme Court has interpreted the due process clause of the Fifth Amendment to make the **equal protection clause** applicable to the federal government as well. Equal protection means that the government cannot enact laws that treat similarly situated individuals differently.

Equal protection, like substantive due process, relates to the substance of a law or other governmental action. When a law or action limits the liberty of *all* persons, it may violate substantive due process. When a law or action limits the liberty of *some* persons but not others, it may violate the equal protection clause. ■ **EXAMPLE 4.15** If a law prohibits all advertising on the sides of trucks, it raises a substantive due process question. If the law makes an exception to allow truck owners to advertise their own businesses, it raises an equal protection issue. ■

In an equal protection inquiry, when a law or action distinguishes between or among individuals, the basis for the distinction—that is, the classification—is examined. Depending on the classification, the courts apply different levels of scrutiny, or "tests," to determine whether the law or action violates the equal protection clause. The courts use one of three standards: strict scrutiny, intermediate scrutiny, or the "rational basis" test.

Strict Scrutiny If a law or action prohibits or inhibits some persons from exercising a fundamental right, the law or action will be subject to "strict scrutiny" by the courts. Under this standard, the classification must be necessary to promote a *compelling state interest.*

Compelling state interests include remedying past unconstitutional or illegal discrimination but do not include correcting the general effects of "society's discrimination." ■ **EXAMPLE 4.16** For a city to give preference to minority applicants in awarding construction contracts, it normally must identify past unconstitutional or illegal discrimination against minority construction firms. Because the policy is based on suspect traits (race and national origin), it will violate the equal protection clause *unless* it is necessary to promote a compelling state interest. ■ Generally, few laws or actions survive strict-scrutiny analysis by the courts.

Intermediate Scrutiny Another standard, that of *intermediate scrutiny,* is applied in cases involving discrimination based on gender or legitimacy (children born out of wedlock). Laws using these classifications must be *substantially related to important government*

objectives. ■ **EXAMPLE 4.17** An important government objective is preventing illegitimate teenage pregnancies. Males and females are not similarly situated in this regard because only females can become pregnant. Therefore, a law that punishes men but not women for statutory rape will be upheld even though it treats men and women unequally. ■

The state also has an important objective in establishing time limits (called *statutes of limitation*) for how long after an event a particular type of action can be brought. Nevertheless, the limitation period must be substantially related to the important objective of preventing fraudulent or outdated claims. ■ **EXAMPLE 4.18** A state law requires illegitimate children to bring paternity suits within six years of their births in order to seek support from their fathers. A court will strike down this law if legitimate children are allowed to seek support from their parents at any time. Distinguishing between support claims on the basis of legitimacy is not related to the important government objective of preventing fraudulent or outdated claims. ■

The "Rational Basis" Test In matters of economic or social welfare, a classification will be considered valid if there is any conceivable *rational basis* on which the classification might relate to a legitimate government interest. It is almost impossible for a law or action to fail the rational basis test.

■ **CASE IN POINT 4.19** A Kentucky statute prohibits businesses that sell substantial amounts of staple groceries or gasoline from applying for a license to sell wine and liquor. A local grocer (Maxwell's Pic-Pac) filed a lawsuit against the state, alleging that the statute and the regulation were unconstitutional under the equal protection clause. The court applied the rational basis test and ruled that the statute and regulation were rationally related to a legitimate government interest in reducing access to products with high alcohol content.

The court cited the problems caused by alcohol, including drunk driving, and noted that the state's interest in limiting access to such products extends to the general public. Grocery stores and gas stations pose a greater risk of exposing members of the public to alcohol. For these and other reasons, the state can restrict these places from selling wine and liquor.[32] ■

4–4 Privacy Rights

The U.S. Constitution does not explicitly mention a general right to privacy. In a 1928 Supreme Court case,

---

32. *Maxwell's Pic-Pac, Inc. v. Dehner,* 739 F.3d 936 (6th Cir. 2014).

Olmstead v. United States,[33] Justice Louis Brandeis stated in his dissent that the right to privacy is "the most comprehensive of rights and the right most valued by civilized men." The majority of the justices at that time, however, did not agree with Brandeis.

It was not until the 1960s that the Supreme Court endorsed the view that the Constitution protects individual privacy rights. In a landmark 1965 case, *Griswold v. Connecticut,*[34] the Supreme Court held that a constitutional right to privacy was implied by the First, Third, Fourth, Fifth, and Ninth Amendments.

Today, privacy rights receive protection under various federal statutes as well the U.S. Constitution. State constitutions and statutes also secure individuals' privacy rights, often to a significant degree. Privacy rights are also protected to an extent under tort law, consumer law, and employment law.

4–4a Federal Privacy Legislation

In the last several decades, Congress has enacted a number of statutes that protect the privacy of individuals in various areas of concern. Most of these statutes deal with personal information collected by governments or private businesses.

In the 1960s, Americans were sufficiently alarmed by the accumulation of personal information in government files that they pressured Congress to pass laws permitting individuals to access their files. Congress responded by passing the Freedom of Information Act, which allows any person to request copies of any information on her or him contained in federal government files. Congress later enacted the Privacy Act, which also gives persons the right to access such information.

In the 1990s, responding to the growing need to protect the privacy of individuals' health records—particularly computerized records—Congress passed the Health Insurance Portability and Accountability Act (HIPAA).[35] This act defines and limits the circumstances in which an individual's "protected health information" may be used or disclosed by health-care providers, health-care plans, and others. These and other major federal laws protecting privacy rights are listed and briefly described in Exhibit 4–2.

33. 277 U.S. 438, 48 S.Ct. 564, 72 L.Ed. 944 (1928).
34. 381 U.S. 479, 85 S.Ct. 1678, 14 L.Ed.2d 510 (1965).
35. HIPAA was enacted as Pub. L. No. 104-191 (1996) and is codified in 29 U.S.C.A. Sections 1181 *et seq.*

EXHIBIT 4–2   Federal Legislation Relating to Privacy

Freedom of Information Act (1966)	Provides that individuals have a right to obtain access to information about them collected in government files.
Privacy Act (1974)	Protects the privacy of individuals about whom the federal government has information. Regulates agencies' use and disclosure of data, and gives individuals access to and a means to correct inaccuracies.
Electronic Communications Privacy Act (1986)	Prohibits the interception of information communicated by electronic means.
Health Insurance Portability and Accountability Act (1996)	Requires health-care providers and health-care plans to inform patients of their privacy rights and of how their personal medical information may be used. States that medical records may not be used for purposes unrelated to health care or disclosed without permission.
Financial Services Modernization Act (Gramm-Leach-Bliley Act) (1999)	Prohibits the disclosure of nonpublic personal information about a consumer to an unaffiliated third party unless strict disclosure and opt-out requirements are met.

4–4b The USA Patriot Act and the USA Freedom Act

The USA Patriot Act was passed by Congress in the wake of the terrorist attacks of September 11, 2001.[36] The Patriot Act has given government officials increased authority to monitor Internet activities (such as e-mail and Web site visits) and to gain access to personal financial information and student information. Law enforcement officials can track the telephone and e-mail communications of one party to find out the identity of the other party or parties. Privacy advocates argue that this law adversely affects the constitutional rights of all Americans, and it has been widely criticized in the media.

While the bulk of the Patriot Act is permanent law, its most controversial surveillance provisions had to be reauthorized every four years and expired in June 2015. Most of the expired provisions were restored by the USA Freedom Act, which extends surveillance authority through 2019.[37] The Freedom Act did amend a portion of the Patriot Act in an attempt to stop the National Security Agency (NSA) from collecting mass phone data. (Note, however, that the act still allows the data to be collected by private phone companies, and the NSA can obtain data about targeted individuals through these companies.)

---

36. The Uniting and Strengthening America by Providing Appropriate Tools Required to Intercept and Obstruct Terrorism Act of 2001, also known as the USA Patriot Act, was enacted as Pub. L. No. 107-56 (2001) and last reauthorized by Pub. L. No. 112-114 (2011).

37. The full title of this statute is Uniting and Strengthening America by Fulfilling Rights and Ending Eavesdropping, Dragnet-collection and Online Monitoring, H.R. 3361.

Reviewing: Business and the Constitution

A state legislature enacted a statute that required any motorcycle operator or passenger on the state's highways to wear a protective helmet. Jim Alderman, a licensed motorcycle operator, sued the state to block enforcement of the law. Alderman asserted that the statute violated the equal protection clause because it placed requirements on motorcyclists that were not imposed on other motorists. Using the information presented in the chapter, answer the following questions.

1. Why does this statute raise equal protection issues instead of substantive due process concerns?
2. What are the three levels of scrutiny that the courts use in determining whether a law violates the equal protection clause?
3. Which standard of scrutiny, or test, would apply to this situation? Why?
4. Applying this standard, is the helmet statute constitutional? Why or why not?

Debate This . . . *Legislation aimed at "protecting people from themselves" concerns the individual as well as the public in general. Protective helmet laws are just one example of such legislation. Should individuals be allowed to engage in unsafe activities if they choose to do so?*

Terms and Concepts

Bill of Rights 75	federal form of government 70	privileges and immunities clause 71
checks and balances 71	filtering software 79	probable cause 82
commerce clause 71	free exercise clause 80	search warrant 82
compelling government interest 77	full faith and credit clause 71	sovereignty 70
due process clause 83	meta tag 80	supremacy clause 75
equal protection clause 84	police powers 70	symbolic speech 77
establishment clause 80	preemption 75	

Issue Spotters

1. Can a state, in the interest of energy conservation, ban all advertising by power utilities if conservation could be accomplished by less restrictive means? Why or why not? (See *Business and the Bill of Rights*.)

2. Suppose that a state imposes a higher tax on out-of-state companies doing business in the state than it imposes on in-state companies. Is this a violation of equal protection if the only reason for the tax is to protect the local firms from out-of-state competition? Explain. (See *The Constitutional Powers of Government*.)

- Check your answers to the Issue Spotters against the answers provided in Appendix D at the end of this text.

Business Scenarios

4–1. Commerce Clause. A Georgia state law requires the use of contoured rear-fender mudguards on trucks and trailers operating within Georgia state lines. The statute further makes it illegal for trucks and trailers to use straight mudguards. In approximately thirty-five other states, straight mudguards are legal. Moreover, in Florida, straight mudguards are explicitly required by law. There is some evidence suggesting that contoured mudguards might be a little safer than straight mudguards. Discuss whether this Georgia statute violates any constitutional provisions. (See *The Constitutional Powers of Government*.)

4–2. Equal Protection. With the objectives of preventing crime, maintaining property values, and preserving the quality of urban life, New York City enacted an ordinance to regulate the locations of adult entertainment establishments. The ordinance expressly applied to female, but not male, topless entertainment. Adele Buzzetti owned the Cozy Cabin, a New York City cabaret that featured female topless dancers. Buzzetti and an anonymous dancer filed a suit in a federal district court against the city, asking the court to block the enforcement of the ordinance. The plaintiffs argued, in part, that the ordinance violated the equal protection clause. Under the equal protection clause, what standard applies to the court's consideration of this ordinance? Under this test, how should the court rule? Why? (See *Due Process and Equal Protection*.)

Business Case Problems

4–3. Spotlight on Plagiarism—Due Process. The Russ College of Engineering and Technology of Ohio University announced in a press conference that it had found "rampant and flagrant plagiarism" in the theses of mechanical engineering graduate students. Faculty singled out for "ignoring their ethical responsibilities" included Jay Gunasekera, chair of the department. Gunasekera was prohibited from advising students. He filed a suit against Dennis Irwin, the dean of Russ College, for violating his due process rights. What does due process require in these circumstances? Why? [*Gunasekera v. Irwin*, 551 F.3d 461 (6th Cir. 2009)] (See *Due Process and Equal Protection*.)

4–4. Business Case Problem with Sample Answer— The Dormant Commerce Clause. In 2001, Puerto Rico enacted a law that requires specific labels on cement sold in Puerto Rico and imposes fines for any violations of these requirements. The law prohibits the sale or distribution of cement manufactured outside Puerto Rico that does not carry a required label warning that the cement may not be used in government-financed construction projects. Antilles Cement Corp., a Puerto Rican firm that imports foreign cement, filed a complaint in federal court, claiming that this law violated the dormant commerce clause. (The dormant commerce clause doctrine applies not only to commerce among the states and U.S. territories, but also to international commerce.) Did the 2001 Puerto Rican law violate the dormant commerce clause? Why or why not? [*Antilles Cement Corp. v. Fortuno*, 670 F.3d 310 (1st Cir. 2012)] (See *The Constitutional Powers of Government*.)

- For a sample answer to Problem 4–4, go to Appendix E at the end of this text.

4–5. Freedom of Speech. Mark Wooden sent an e-mail to an alderwoman for the city of St. Louis. Attached was a nineteen-minute audio file that compared her to the biblical character Jezebel. The audio said she was a "bitch in the Sixth Ward," spending too much time with the rich and powerful and too little time with the poor. In a menacing, maniacal tone, Wooden said that he was "dusting off a sawed-off shotgun," called himself a "domestic terrorist," and referred to the assassination of President John Kennedy, the murder of federal judge John Roll, and the shooting of Representative Gabrielle Giffords. Feeling threatened, the alderwoman called the police. Wooden was convicted of harassment under a state criminal statute. Was this conviction unconstitutional under the First Amendment? Discuss. [*State of Missouri v. Wooden*, 388 S.W.3d 522 (Mo. 2013)] (See *Business and the Bill of Rights*.)

4–6. Equal Protection. Abbott Laboratories licensed SmithKline Beecham Corp. to market an Abbott human immunodeficiency virus (HIV) drug in conjunction with one of SmithKline's drugs. Abbott then increased the price of its drug fourfold, forcing SmithKline to increase its prices and thereby driving business to Abbott's own combination drug. SmithKline filed a suit in a federal district court against Abbott. During jury selection, Abbott struck the only self-identified gay person among the potential jurors. (The pricing of HIV drugs is of considerable concern in the gay community.) Could the equal protection clause be applied to prohibit discrimination based on sexual orientation in jury selection? Discuss. [*SmithKline Beecham Corp. v. Abbott Laboratories,* 740 F.3d 471 (9th Cir. 2014)] (See *Due Process and Equal Protection.*)

4–7. Procedural Due Process. Robert Brown applied for admission to the University of Kansas School of Law. Brown answered "no" to questions on the application asking if he had a criminal history and acknowledged that a false answer constituted "cause for . . . dismissal." In fact, Brown had criminal convictions for domestic battery and driving under the influence. He was accepted for admission to the school. When school officials discovered his history, however, he was notified of their intent to dismiss him and given an opportunity to respond in writing. He demanded a hearing. The officials refused to grant Brown a hearing and then expelled him. Did the school's actions deny Brown due process? Discuss. [*Brown v. University of Kansas,* 599 Fed.Appx. 833 (10th Cir. 2015)] (See *Due Process and Equal Protection.*)

4–8. The Commerce Clause. Regency Transportation, Inc., operates a freight business throughout the eastern United States. Regency maintains its corporate headquarters, four warehouses, and a maintenance facility and terminal location for repairing and storing vehicles in Massachusetts. All of the vehicles in Regency's fleet were bought in other states. Massachusetts imposes a use tax on all taxpayers subject to its jurisdiction, including those that do business in interstate commerce, as Regency does. When Massachusetts imposed the tax on the purchase price of each tractor and trailer in Regency's fleet, the trucking firm challenged the assessment as discriminatory under the commerce clause. What is the chief consideration under the commerce clause when a state law affects interstate commerce?

Is Massachusetts's use tax valid? Explain. [*Regency Transportation, Inc. v. Commissioner of Revenue,* 473 Mass. 459, 42 N.E.3d 1133 (2016)] (See *The Constitutional Powers of Government.*)

4–9. A Question of Ethics—Defamation. *Aric Toll owns and manages the Balboa Island Village Inn, a restaurant and bar in Newport Beach, California. Anne Lemen lives across from the inn. Lemen complained to the authorities about the inn's customers, whom she called "drunks" and "whores." She referred to Aric's wife as "Madam Whore" and told neighbors that the owners were involved in illegal drugs and prostitution. Lemen told Ewa Cook, a bartender at the Inn, that Cook "worked for Satan." She repeated her statements to potential customers, and the inn's sales dropped more than 20 percent. The inn filed a suit against Lemen.* [*Balboa Island Village Inn, Inc. v. Lemen, 40 Cal.4th 1141, 156 P.3d 339 (2007)*] (See *Business and the Bill of Rights.*)

(a) Are Lemen's statements about the inn's owners, customers, and activities protected by the U.S. Constitution? Should such statements be protected? In whose favor should the court rule? Why?

(b) Did Lemen behave unethically in the circumstances of this case? Explain.

4–10. Special Case Analysis—Freedom of Religion. Go to Case Analysis 4.3, *Thompson v. Holm.* Read the excerpt, and answer the following questions.

(a) **Issue:** The focus in this case was on an allegation of the violation of which clause of the U.S. Constitution, and by what means?

(b) **Rule of Law:** What is required to establish that this clause has been violated?

(c) **Applying the Rule of Law:** How did the court determine whether the claim of a violation was supported in this case?

(d) **Conclusion:** What did the federal appellate court conclude with respect to the plaintiff's claim, and what did the court order as the next step in the case?

Legal Reasoning Group Activity

4–11. Free Speech and Equal Protection. For many years, New York City has had to deal with the vandalism and defacement of public property caused by unauthorized graffiti. In an effort to stop the damage, the city banned the sale of aerosol spray-paint cans and broad-tipped indelible markers to persons under twenty-one years of age. The new rules also prohibited people from possessing these items on property other than their own. Within a year, five people under age twenty-one were cited for violations of these regulations, and 871 individuals were arrested for actually making graffiti.

Lindsey Vincenty and other artists wished to create graffiti on legal surfaces, such as canvas, wood, and clothing. Unable to buy supplies in the city or to carry them into the city from elsewhere, Vincenty and others filed a lawsuit on behalf of themselves and other young artists against Michael

Bloomberg, the city's mayor, and others. The plaintiffs claimed that, among other things, the new rules violated their right to freedom of speech.

(a) One group will argue in favor of the plaintiffs and provide several reasons why the court should hold that the city's new rules violate the plaintiffs' freedom of speech. (See *Business and the Bill of Rights.*)

(b) Another group will develop a counterargument that outlines the reasons why the new rules do not violate free speech rights. (See *Business and the Bill of Rights.*)

(c) A third group will argue that the city's ban violates the equal protection clause because it applies only to persons under age twenty-one. (See *Due Process and Equal Protection.*)

CHAPTER 5

Business Ethics

One of the most complex issues businesspersons and corporations face is ethics. It is not as well defined as the law, and yet it can have substantial impacts on a firm's finances and reputation, especially when the firm is involved in a well-publicized scandal. Some scandals arise from activities that are legal, but are ethically questionable. Other scandals arise from conduct that is both illegal and unethical.

Consider, for example, Volkswagen's corporate executives, who were accused of cheating on the pollution emissions tests of millions of vehicles that were sold in the United States. Volkswagen admitted in 2015 that it had installed "defeat device" software in its diesel models. The software detected when the car was being tested and changed its performance to improve the test outcome. As a result, the diesel cars showed low emissions—a feature that made the cars more attractive to today's consumers. Ultimately, millions of Volkswagen vehicles were recalled, and the company suffered its first quarterly loss in fifteen years.

5–1 Business Ethics

At the most basic level, the study of **ethics** is the study of what constitutes right or wrong behavior. It is a branch of philosophy focusing on morality and the way moral principles are derived and implemented. Ethics has to do with the fairness, justness, rightness, or wrongness of an action.

The study of **business ethics** typically looks at the decisions businesses make or have to make and whether those decisions are right or wrong. It has to do with how businesspersons apply moral and ethical principles in making their decisions. Those who study business ethics also evaluate what duties and responsibilities exist or should exist for businesses.

In this book, we include an *Application and Ethics* feature at the end of each unit to expand on the concepts of business ethics discussed in that unit. We also cover ethical issues in *Ethics Today* features that appear in a number of chapters.

5–1a Why Is Studying Business Ethics Important?

Over the last hundred years, the public perception of the corporation has changed from an entity that primarily generates revenues for its owners to an entity that participates in society as a corporate citizen. Originally, the only goal or duty of a corporation was to maximize profits. Although many people today may view this idea as greedy or inhumane, the rationale for the profit-maximization theory is still valid.

Profit Maximization In theory, if all firms strictly adhere to the goal of profit maximization, resources flow to where they are most highly valued by society. Corporations can focus on their strengths, and other entities that are better suited to deal with social problems and perform charitable acts can specialize in those activities. The government, through taxes and other financial allocations, can shift resources to those other entities to perform public services. Thus, in an ideal world, profit maximization leads to the most efficient allocation of scarce resources.

The Rise of Corporate Citizenship Over the years, as resources purportedly were not sufficiently reallocated to cover the costs of social needs, many people became dissatisfied with the profit-maximization theory. Investors and others began to look beyond profits and dividends and to consider the **triple bottom line**—a corporation's profits, its impact on people, and its impact on the planet. Magazines and Web sites began to rank companies based on their environmental impacts and their ethical decisions. The corporation came to be viewed as a "citizen" that was expected to participate in bettering communities and society.

Even so, many still believe that corporations are fundamentally profit-making entities that should have no responsibility other than profit maximization.

5–1b The Importance of Ethics in Making Business Decisions

Whether one believes in profit maximization or corporate citizenship, ethics is important in making business decisions. When making decisions, a business should evaluate:

1. The legal implications of each decision.
2. The public relations impact.
3. The safety risks for consumers and employees.
4. The financial implications.

This four-part analysis will assist the firm in making decisions that not only maximize profits but also reflect good corporate citizenship.

Long-Run Profit Maximization In attempting to maximize profits, corporate executives and employees have to distinguish between *short-run* and *long-run* profit maximization. In the short run, a company may increase its profits by continuing to sell a product even though it knows that the product is defective. In the long run, though, because of lawsuits, large settlements, and bad publicity, such unethical conduct will cause profits to suffer. Thus, business ethics is consistent only with long-run profit maximization. An overemphasis on short-term profit maximization is the most common reason that ethical problems occur in business.

■ **CASE IN POINT 5.1** When the powerful narcotic painkiller OxyContin was first marketed, its manufacturer, Purdue Pharma, claimed that it was unlikely to lead to drug addiction or abuse. Internal company documents later showed that the company's executives knew that OxyContin could be addictive, but kept this risk a secret to boost sales and maximize short-term profits.

Subsequently, Purdue Pharma and three former executives pleaded guilty to criminal charges that they had misled regulators, patients, and physicians about Oxy-Contin's risks of addiction. Purdue Pharma agreed to pay $600 million in fines and other payments. The three former executives agreed to pay $34.5 million in fines and were barred from federal health programs for a period of fifteen years. Thus, the company's focus on maximizing profits in the short run led to unethical conduct that hurt profits in the long run.[1] ■

The Internet Can Ruin Reputations In the past, negative information or opinions about a company might remain hidden. Now, however, cyberspace provides a forum where disgruntled employees, unhappy consumers, or special interest groups can post derogatory remarks. Thus, the Internet has increased the potential for a major corporation (or other business) to suffer damage to its reputation or loss of profits through negative publicity.

Wal-Mart and Nike in particular have been frequent targets for advocacy groups that believe those corporations exploit their workers. Although some of these assertions may be unfounded or exaggerated, the courts generally have refused to consider them *defamatory* (a tort giving rise to a civil lawsuit). Most courts regard online attacks as expressions of opinion protected by the First Amendment. Even so, corporations often incur considerable expense in running marketing campaigns to thwart bad publicity and may even face legal costs if the allegations lead to litigation.

Image Is Everything The study of business ethics is concerned with the purposes of a business and how that business achieves those purposes. Thus, business ethics is concerned not only with the image of the business, but also with the impact that the business has on the environment, customers, suppliers, employees, and the global economy.

Unethical corporate decision making can negatively affect suppliers, consumers, the community, and society as a whole. It can also have a negative impact on the reputation of the company and the individuals who run that company. Hence, an in-depth understanding of business ethics is important to the long-run viability of any corporation today.

5–1c The Relationship of Law and Ethics

Because the law does not codify all ethical requirements, compliance with the law is not always sufficient to determine "right" behavior. Laws have to be general enough to apply in a variety of circumstances. Laws are broad in their purpose and their scope. They prohibit or require certain actions to avoid significant harm to society.

When two competing companies secretly agree to set prices on products, for instance, society suffers harm—typically, the companies will charge higher prices than they could if they continued to compete. This harm inflicted on consumers has negative consequences for the economy, and so colluding to set prices is an illegal activity. Similarly, when a company is preparing to issue stock, the law requires certain disclosures to potential investors. This requirement is meant to prevent harms that come

---

1. *United States v. Purdue Frederick Co.*, 495 F.Supp.2d 569 (W.D.Va. 2007).

with uninformed investing. Such harms occurred in the 1920s and may have contributed to the stock market crash and the Great Depression.

Moral Minimum Compliance with the law is sometimes called the **moral minimum.** If people and entities merely comply with the law, they are acting at the lowest ethical level society will tolerate. The study of ethics goes beyond those legal requirements to evaluate what is right for society. The following case illustrates some consequences of a businessperson's failure to meet the moral minimum.

Case 5.1

Scott v. Carpanzano

United States Court of Appeals, Fifth Circuit, 556 Fed.Appx. 288 (2014).

Background and Facts Rick Scott deposited $2 million into an escrow account maintained by a company owned by Salvatore Carpanzano. Immediately after the deposit was made, in violation of the escrow agreement, the funds were withdrawn. When Scott was unable to recover his money, he filed a suit against Salvatore Carpanzano and others, including Salvatore's daughter Carmela Carpanzano. In the complaint, Scott made no allegations of acts or knowledge on Carmela's part.

Salvatore failed to cooperate with discovery and did not respond to attempts to contact him by certified mail, regular mail, or e-mail. Salvatore also refused to make an appearance in the court and did not finalize a settlement negotiated between the parties' attorneys. Carmela denied that she was involved in her father's business or the Scott transaction. The court found that the defendants had intentionally failed to respond to the litigation and issued a judgment for more than $6 million in Scott's favor. The defendants appealed to the U.S. Court of Appeals for the Fifth Circuit.

In the Language of the Court
PER CURIAM [By the Whole Court].
* * * *

A willful default is an *intentional failure to respond to litigation.* The district court found that [the] Defendants willfully defaulted based on evidence that the Defendants were aware of the proceedings against them and that [their] attorneys were specifically instructed not to enter an appearance [participate] in this case. [Emphasis added.]

The evidence substantially supports the district court's finding as to Mr. Carpanzano. First, Mr. Carpanzano's first attorney withdrew [from the case] because Mr. Carpanzano failed to cooperate with the discovery process and refused to appear as requested and ordered. Second, * * * Mr. Carpanzano instructed his second set of attorneys to negotiate settlement of this matter but not to enter an appearance in the district court. Significantly, Mr. Carpanzano never denies this allegation. Third, * * * Mr. Carpanzano and his attorneys were well aware that the case was proceeding toward default and * * * were in communication with each other during this time. Fourth, * * * once final execution of settlement papers was at hand, Mr. Carpanzano also ceased communication with his second set of attorneys and did not finalize the settlement. Finally, other than ambiguously suggesting that a health condition (unsupported by any evidence of what the condition was) and absence from the country (unsupported by any evidence that electronic communication was not possible from that country) prevented him from defending this action, Mr. Carpanzano offers no real reason why he did not answer the * * * complaint.
* * * *

By contrast, the record does not support the district court's finding that * * * Ms. [Carmela] Carpanzano also willfully defaulted.

* * * Ms. Carpanzano repeatedly indicated that [she was] relying on Mr. Carpanzano * * * to make sure [her] interests were protected. Nothing in the record contradicts this assertion. While [her] reliance on Mr. Carpanzano acting with the attorneys he retained may have been negligent, it does not amount to an intentional failure to respond to litigation.

Case 5.1 Continues

* * * *

* * * [Furthermore] the * * * complaint * * * contains no factual allegations of acts or omissions on the part of Ms. Carpanzano. It does not allege that she ever was in contact with Scott, that she was in control of the * * * escrow account, or that she wrongfully transferred any funds out of the account. Nor does it allege any intent or knowledge on the part of Ms. Carpanzano * * *. Indeed, an examination of the complaint reveals that there is not a sufficient basis in the pleadings for the judgment * * * entered against Ms. Carpanzano.

The defenses presented by Ms. Carpanzano to the district court assert that she had no knowledge of the details of her father's business transactions, she did not personally enter into any contracts with Scott or seek to defraud him, and * * * she had limited involvement in the facts of this case.

* * * *

* * * Even if Scott were able to prove the entirety of the * * * complaint, we fail to see how it would justify a judgment * * * against Ms. Carpanzano.

Decision and Remedy *The U.S. Court of Appeals for the Fifth Circuit affirmed the judgment against Salvatore, but reversed the decision against Carmela. Scott had made no allegations of acts on Carmela's part.*

Critical Thinking
- **Ethical** *Are Salvatore's actions likely to affect his business's ability to profit in the long run? Discuss.*
- **Legal Environment** *Did Carmela Carpanzano meet the minimum acceptable standard for ethical business behavior? Explain.*

Ethical Requirements The study of ethics goes beyond legal requirements to evaluate what is right for society. Businesspersons thus must remember that an action that is legal is not necessarily ethical. For instance, a company's refusal to negotiate liability claims for alleged injuries because of a faulty product is legal. But it may not be ethical if the reason the business refuses to negotiate is to increase the injured party's legal costs and force the person to drop a legitimate claim.

Private Company Codes of Ethics Most companies attempt to link ethics and law through the creation of internal codes of ethics. Company codes are not law. Instead, they are rules that the company sets forth that it can also enforce (by terminating an employee who does not follow them, for instance). Codes of conduct typically outline the company's policies on particular issues and indicate how employees are expected to act.

■ **EXAMPLE 5.2** Google's code of conduct starts with the motto "Don't be evil." The code then makes general statements about how Google promotes integrity, mutual respect, and the highest standard of ethical business conduct. Google's code also provides specific rules on a number of issues, such as privacy, drugs and alcohol, conflicts of interest, co-worker relationships, and confidentiality.

It even has a dog policy. The company takes a stand against employment discrimination that goes further than the law requires—it prohibits discrimination based on sexual orientation, gender identity or expression, and veteran status. ■

Industry Ethical Codes Numerous industries have also developed their own codes of ethics. The American Institute of Certified Public Accountants (AICPA) has a comprehensive Code of Professional Conduct for the ethical practice of accounting. The American Bar Association has model rules of professional conduct for attorneys, and the American Nurses Association has a code of ethics that applies to nurses. These codes can give guidance to decision makers facing ethical questions.

Violation of an industry code may result in discipline of an employee or sanctions against a company from the industry organization. Remember, though, that these internal codes are not laws, so their effectiveness is determined by the commitment of the industry or company leadership to enforcing the codes.

■ **CASE IN POINT 5.3** National Football League (NFL) rules require footballs to be inflated to a minimum air pressure (pounds per square inch, or psi) as measured by the referees. This rule gained attention when the New

England Patriots played the Indianapolis Colts for the American Football Conference championship in early 2015. After Tom Brady, the Patriots quarterback, threw a pass that was intercepted, officials became suspicious that the football was underinflated. The game continued after NFL officials verified the psi in all the footballs, and the Patriots won.

Nevertheless, allegations continued that Brady and the Patriots had deflated balls during the game—a controversy popularly known as "deflategate." The NFL performed an investigation, and after arbitration, the league announced that Brady would be suspended for four games. Brady appealed, and a federal district court vacated the arbitrator's decision to suspend, but a federal appellate court reinstated Brady's suspension in 2016. The reviewing court held that the arbitrator had grounds to suspend Brady for being generally aware that the team had intentionally released air from the game balls.[2] ■

"Gray Areas" in the Law Because it is often highly subjective and subject to change over time without any sort of formal process, ethics is less certain than law. But the law can also be uncertain. Numerous "gray areas" in the law make it difficult to predict with certainty how a court will apply a given law to a particular action. In addition, laws frequently change.

5–2 Business Ethics and Social Media

Most young people may think of social media— Facebook, Flickr, Instagram, Tumblr, Twitter, Pinterest, Google+, LinkedIn, VR, and the like—as simply ways to communicate rapidly. Businesses, though, often face ethical issues with respect to these same social media platforms.

5–2a Hiring Procedures

In the past, to learn about a prospective employee, an employer would ask the candidate's former employers for references. Today, employers are likely to also conduct Internet searches to discover what job candidates have posted on their Facebook pages, blogs, and tweets.

On the one hand, job candidates may be judged by what they post on social media. On the other hand,

though, they may be judged because they *do not* participate in social media. Given that the vast majority of younger people do use social media, some employers have decided that the failure to do so raises a red flag. In either case, many people believe that judging a job candidate based on what she or he does outside the work environment is unethical.

5–2b The Use of Social Media to Discuss Work-Related Issues

Because so many Americans use social media daily, they often discuss work-related issues there. Numerous companies have strict guidelines about what is appropriate and inappropriate for employees to say when making posts on their own or others' social media accounts. A number of companies have fired employees for such activities as criticizing other employees or managers through social media outlets. Until recently, such disciplinary measures were considered ethical and legal.

Responsibility of Employers Today, in contrast, a ruling by the National Labor Relations Board (NLRB—the federal agency that investigates unfair labor practices) has changed the legality of such actions. ■ **EXAMPLE 5.4** At one time, Costco's social media policy specified that its employees should not make statements that would damage the company, harm another person's reputation, or violate the company's policies. Employees who violated these rules were subject to discipline and could be fired.

The NLRB ruled that Costco's social media policy violated federal labor law, which protects employees' right to engage in "concerted activities." Employees can freely associate with each other and have conversations about common workplace issues without employer interference. This right extends to social media posts. Therefore, an employer cannot broadly prohibit its employees from criticizing the company or co-workers, supervisors, or managers via social media. ■

Responsibility of Employees While most of the discussion in this chapter concerns the ethics of business management, employee ethics is also an important issue. For instance, is it ethical for employees to make negative posts in social media about other employees or, more commonly, about managers? After all, negative comments about managers reflect badly on those managers, who often are reluctant to respond via social media to such criticism. Disgruntled employees may exaggerate the negative qualities of managers whom they do not like.

---

2. *National Football League Management Council v. National Football League Players Association*, 820 F.3d 527 (2d Cir. 2016).

Some may consider the decision by the National Labor Relations Board outlined in *Example 5.4* to be too lenient toward employees and too stringent toward management. There is likely to be an ongoing debate about how to balance employees' right to free expression against employers' right to prevent the spreading of inaccurate negative statements across the Internet.

5–3 Ethical Principles and Philosophies

As Dean Krehmeyer, executive director of the Business Roundtable's Institute for Corporate Ethics, once said, "Evidence strongly suggests being ethical—doing the right thing—pays." Even if ethics "pays," though, instilling ethical business decision making into the fabric of a business organization is no small task.

How do business decision makers decide whether a given action is the "right" one for their firms? What ethical standards should be applied? Broadly speaking, **ethical reasoning**—the application of morals and ethics to a situation—applies to businesses just as it does to individuals. As businesses make decisions, they must analyze their alternatives in a variety of ways, one of which is the ethical implications of each alternative.

Generally, the study of ethics is divided into two major categories—duty-based ethics and outcome-based ethics. **Duty-based ethics** is rooted in the idea that every person has certain duties to others, including both humans and the planet. **Outcome-based ethics** focuses on the impacts of a decision on society or on key *stakeholders.*

5–3a Duty-Based Ethics

Duty-based ethics focuses on the obligations of the corporation. It deals with standards for behavior that traditionally were derived from revealed truths, religious authorities, or philosophical reasoning. These standards involve concepts of right and wrong, duties owed, and rights to be protected. Corporations today often describe these values or duties in their mission statements or strategic plans. Some companies base their statements on a nonreligious rationale, while others derive their values from religious doctrine.

Religious Ethical Principles Nearly every religion has principles or beliefs about how one should treat others. In the Judeo-Christian tradition, which is the dominant religious tradition in the United States, the Ten Commandments of the Old Testament establish these fundamental rules for moral action. The principles of the Muslim faith are set out in the Qur'an, and Hindus find their principles in the four Vedas.

Religious rules generally are absolute with respect to the behavior of their adherents. ■ **EXAMPLE 5.5** The commandment "Thou shalt not steal" is an absolute mandate for a person who believes that the Ten Commandments reflect revealed truth. Even a benevolent motive for stealing (such as Robin Hood's) cannot justify the act because the act itself is inherently immoral and thus wrong. ■

For businesses, religious principles can be a unifying force for employees or a rallying point to increase employee motivation. They can also present problems, however, because different owners, suppliers, employees, and customers may have different religious backgrounds. Taking an action based on religious principles, especially when those principles address socially or politically controversial topics, can lead to negative publicity and even to protests or boycotts.

Principles of Rights Another view of duty-based ethics focuses on basic rights. The principle that human beings have certain fundamental rights (to life, freedom, and the pursuit of happiness, for example) is deeply embedded in Western culture.

Those who adhere to this **principle of rights,** or "rights theory," believe that a key factor in determining whether a business decision is ethical is how that decision affects the rights of others. These others include the firm's owners, its employees, the consumers of its products or services, its suppliers, the community in which it does business, and society as a whole.

Conflicting Rights. A potential dilemma for those who support rights theory is that they may disagree on which rights are most important. When considering all those affected by a business decision to downsize a firm, for example, how much weight should be given to employees relative to shareholders? Which employees should be laid off first—those with the highest salaries or those who have worked there for less time (and have less seniority)? How should the firm weigh the rights of customers relative to the community, or employees relative to society as a whole?

Resolving Conflicts. In general, rights theorists believe that whichever right is stronger in a particular circumstance takes precedence. ■ **EXAMPLE 5.6** Murray

Chemical Corporation has to decide whether to keep a chemical plant in Utah open, thereby saving the jobs of a hundred and fifty workers, or shut it down. Closing the plant will avoid contaminating a river with pollutants that might endanger the health of tens of thousands of people. In this situation, a rights theorist can easily choose which group to favor because the value of the right to health and well-being is obviously stronger than the basic right to work. Not all choices are so clear-cut, however. ■

Kantian Ethical Principles Duty-based ethical standards may also be derived solely from philosophical reasoning. The German philosopher Immanuel Kant (1724–1804) identified some general guiding principles for moral behavior based on what he thought to be the fundamental nature of human beings. Kant believed that human beings are qualitatively different from other physical objects and are endowed with moral integrity and the capacity to reason and conduct their affairs rationally.

People Are Not a Means to an End. Based on this view of human beings, Kant said that when people are treated merely as a means to an end, they are being treated as the equivalent of objects and are being denied their basic humanity. For instance, a manager who treats subordinates as mere profit-making tools is less likely to retain motivated and loyal employees than a manager who respects employees. Management research has shown that, in fact, employees who feel empowered to share their thoughts, opinions, and solutions to problems are happier and more productive.

Categorical Imperative. When a business makes unethical decisions, it often rationalizes its action by saying that the company is "just one small part" of the problem or that its decision has had "only a small impact." A central theme in Kantian ethics is that individuals should evaluate their actions in light of the consequences that would follow if everyone in society acted in the same way. This **categorical imperative** can be applied to any action.
　　■ **EXAMPLE 5.7** CHS Fertilizer is deciding whether to invest in expensive equipment that will decrease profits but will also reduce pollution from its factories. If CHS has adopted Kant's categorical imperative, the decision makers will consider the consequences if every company invested in the equipment (or if no company did so). If the result would make the world a better place (less polluted), CHS's decision would be clear. ■

5–3b Outcome-Based Ethics: Utilitarianism

In contrast to duty-based ethics, outcome-based ethics focuses on the consequences of an action, not on the nature of the action itself or on any set of preestablished moral values or religious beliefs. Outcome-based ethics looks at the impacts of a decision in an attempt to maximize benefits and minimize harms.

The premier philosophical theory for outcome-based decision making is **utilitarianism,** a philosophical theory developed by Jeremy Bentham (1748–1832) and modified by John Stuart Mill (1806–1873)—both British philosophers. "The greatest good for the greatest number" is a paraphrase of the major premise of the utilitarian approach to ethics.

Cost-Benefit Analysis Under a utilitarian model of ethics, an action is morally correct, or "right," when, among the people it affects, it produces the greatest amount of good for the greatest number or creates the least amount of harm for the fewest people. When an action affects the majority adversely, it is morally wrong. Applying the utilitarian theory thus requires the following steps:

1. A determination of which individuals will be affected by the action in question.
2. A **cost-benefit analysis,** which involves an assessment of the negative and positive effects of alternative actions on these individuals.
3. A choice among alternative actions that will produce maximum societal utility (the greatest positive net benefits for the greatest number of individuals).

Thus, if expanding a factory would provide hundreds of jobs but generate pollution that could endanger the lives of thousands of people, a utilitarian analysis would find that saving the lives of thousands creates greater good than providing jobs for hundreds.

Problems with the Utilitarian Approach There are problems with a strict utilitarian analysis. In some situations, an action that produces the greatest good for the most people may not seem to be the most ethical. ■ **EXAMPLE 5.8** Phazim Company is producing a drug that will cure a disease in 85 percent of patients, but the other 15 percent will experience agonizing side effects and a horrible, painful death. A quick utilitarian analysis would suggest that the drug should be produced and marketed because the majority of patients will benefit. Many people, however, have significant concerns about manufacturing a drug that will cause such harm to anyone. ■

5–3c Corporate Social Responsibility

In pairing duty-based concepts with outcome-based concepts, strategists and theorists developed the idea of the corporate citizen. **Corporate social responsibility (CSR)** combines a commitment to good citizenship with a commitment to making ethical decisions, improving society, and minimizing environmental impact.

CSR is a relatively new concept in the history of business, but a concept that becomes more important every year. Although CSR is not imposed on corporations by law, it does involve a commitment to self-regulation in a way that attends to the text and intent of the law as well as to ethical norms and global standards. A survey of U.S. executives undertaken by the Boston College Center for Corporate Citizenship found that more than 70 percent of those polled agreed that corporate citizenship must be treated as a priority. More than 60 percent said that good corporate citizenship added to their companies' profits.

CSR can be a successful strategy for companies, but corporate decision makers must not lose track of the two descriptors in the title: *corporate* and *social.* The company must link the responsibility of citizenship with the strategy and key principles of the business. Incorporating both the social and the corporate components of CSR and making ethical decisions can help companies grow and prosper. CSR is most successful when a company undertakes activities that are significant and related to its business operations.

The Social Aspects of CSR Because business controls so much of the wealth and power in this country, business has a responsibility to use that wealth and power in socially beneficial ways. Thus, the social aspect requires that corporations demonstrate that they are promoting goals that society deems worthwhile and are moving toward solutions to social problems. Companies may be judged on how much they donate to social causes, as well as how they conduct their operations with respect to employment discrimination, human rights, environmental concerns, and similar issues.

Some corporations publish annual social responsibility reports, which may also be called corporate sustainability (referring to the capacity to endure) or citizenship reports. ■ **EXAMPLE 5.9** The software company Symantec Corporation issues corporate responsibility reports to demonstrate its focus on critical environmental, social, and governance issues. In its 2014 report, Symantec pointed out that 88 percent of facilities it owns or leases on a long-term basis are certified as environmentally friendly by the LEED program. LEED stands for Leadership in Energy and Environmental Design. Certification requires the achievement of high standards for energy efficiency, material usage in construction, and other environmental qualities. ■

The Corporate Aspects of CSR Arguably, any socially responsible activity will benefit a corporation. A corporation may see an increase in goodwill from the local community for creating a park, for instance. A corporation that is viewed as a good citizen may see an increase in sales.

At times, the benefit may not be immediate. Constructing a new plant that meets the high LEED standards may cost more initially. Nevertheless, over the life of the building, the savings in maintenance and utilities may more than make up for the extra cost of construction.

Surveys of college students about to enter the job market confirm that young people are looking for socially responsible employers. Socially responsible activities may thus cost a corporation now, but may lead to more impressive and more committed employees. Corporations that engage in meaningful social activities retain workers longer, particularly younger ones.

■ **EXAMPLE 5.10** Pacific Gas and Electric (PG&E) in California sends its employees out on Earth Day to help clean and restore state parks. PG&E also provides free solar panels for new Habitat for Humanity homes and donates food to the needy. LinkedIn employees participate in an "InDay" every month to donate time and resources to the community. Zappos donates large amounts of its goods to charities and pays its employees for time off if they are volunteering. ■

Stakeholders One view of CSR stresses that corporations have a duty not just to shareholders, but also to other groups affected by corporate decisions—called **stakeholders.** The rationale for this "stakeholder view" is that, in some circumstances, one or more of these other groups may have a greater stake in company decisions than the shareholders do.

Under this approach, a corporation considers the impact of its decisions on its employees, customers, creditors, suppliers, and the community in which it operates. Stakeholders could also include advocacy groups such as environmental groups and animal rights groups. To avoid making a decision that may be perceived as unethical and result in negative publicity or protests, a corporation should consider the impact of its decision on the stakeholders.

The most difficult aspect of the stakeholder analysis is determining which group's interests should receive greater weight if the interests conflict. For instance, companies that are struggling financially sometimes lay off workers to reduce labor costs. But in recent years, some corporations have given greater weight to employees' interests and have found ways to avoid slashing their workforces. Companies finding alternatives to layoffs included Dell (extended unpaid holidays), Cisco Systems (four-day end-of-year shutdowns), Motorola (salary cuts), and Honda (voluntary unpaid vacation time).

5-4 Making Ethical Business Decisions

Even if officers, directors, and others in a company want to make ethical decisions, it is not always clear what is ethical in a given situation. Thinking beyond things that are easily measured, such as profits, can be challenging. Although profit projections are not always accurate, they are more objective than considering the personal impacts of decisions on employees, shareholders, customers, and the community. But this subjective component of decision making potentially has a great potential influence on a company's profits.

Companies once considered leaders in their industry, such as Enron and the worldwide accounting firm Arthur Andersen, were brought down by the unethical behavior of a few. A two-hundred-year-old British investment banking firm, Barings Bank, was destroyed by the actions of one employee and a few of his friends. Clearly, ensuring that all employees get on the ethical business decision-making "bandwagon" is crucial in today's fast-paced world.

Individuals entering the global corporate community, even in entry-level positions, must be prepared to make hard decisions. Sometimes, there is no "good" answer to the questions that arise. Therefore, it is important to have tools to help in the decision-making process and to create a framework for organizing those tools. Business decisions can be complex and may involve legal concerns, financial questions, possibly health and safety concerns, and ethical components.

5-4a A Systematic Approach

Organizing the ethical concerns and issues and approaching them systematically can help a businessperson eliminate various alternatives and identify the strengths and weaknesses of the remaining alternatives. Ethics consultant Leonard H. Bucklin of Corporate-Ethics.US™ has devised a procedure that he calls Business Process Pragmatism™. It involves five steps:

Step 1: Inquiry. First, the decision maker must understand the problem. This step involves identifying the parties involved (the stakeholders) and collecting the relevant facts. Once the ethical problem or problems are clarified, the decision maker lists any relevant legal and ethical principles that will guide the decision.

Step 2: Discussion. In this step, the decision maker lists possible actions. The ultimate goals for the decision are determined, and each option is evaluated using the laws and ethical principles listed in Step 1.

Step 3: Decision. In this step, those participating in the decision making work together to craft a consensus decision or consensus plan of action for the corporation.

Step 4: Justification. In this step, the decision maker articulates the reasons for the proposed action or series of actions. Generally, these reasons should come from the analysis done in Step 3. This step essentially results in documentation to be shared with stakeholders explaining why the proposal is an ethical solution to the problem.

Step 5: Evaluation. This final step occurs once the decision has been made and implemented. The solution should be analyzed to determine if it was effective. The results of this evaluation may be used in making future decisions.

5-4b The Importance of Ethical Leadership

Talking about ethical business decision making is meaningless if management does not set standards. Furthermore, managers must apply the same standards to themselves as they do to the company's employees. See this chapter's *Digital Update* feature for a discussion of an ethical dilemma that has arisen from the increased use of digital technology by employees after work hours.

Attitude of Top Management One of the most important ways to create and maintain an ethical

DIGITAL UPDATE   Should Employees Have a "Right of Disconnecting"?

Almost all jobs today involve digital technology, whether it be e-mail, Internet access, or smartphone use. Most employees, when interviewed, say that digital technology increases their productivity and flexibility.

The downside is what some call an "electronic leash"—meaning that employees are constantly connected and end up working when they are not "at work." Over one-third of full-time workers, for example, say that they frequently check e-mails outside normal working hours.

Do Workers Have the Right to Disconnect?

Because the boundaries between being "at work" and being "at leisure" can be so hazy, some labor unions in other countries have attempted to pass rules that allow employees to disconnect from e-mail and other work-related digital communication during nonworking hours. For instance, a French labor union representing high-tech workers signed an agreement with a large business association recognizing a "right of disconnecting." In Germany, Volkswagen and BMW no longer forward e-mail to staff from company servers after the end of the workday. Other German firms have declared that workers are not expected to check e-mail on weekends and holidays. The government is considering legislating such restrictions nationwide.

The Thorny Issue of Overtime and the Fair Labor Standards Act

Payment for overtime work is strictly regulated under the Fair Labor Standards Act (FLSA). According to the United States Supreme Court, in this context, *work* is "physical or mental exertion (whether burdensome or not) controlled or required by the employer and pursued necessarily for the benefit of the employer and his business."[a]

This definition was extended to off-duty work if such work is an "integral and indispensible part of [employees'] activities."[b]

Today's modern digital connectivity raises issues about the definition of *work*. Employees at several major companies, including Black & Decker, T-Mobile, and Verizon, have sued for unpaid overtime related to smartphone use. In another case, a police sergeant has sued the city of Chicago, claiming that he should have been paid overtime for hours spent using his personal digital assistant (PDA).[c] The police department issues PDAs to officers and requires them to respond to work-related text messages, e-mails, and voice mails not only while on duty, but also while off duty. Off-duty responses are not compensated by the city.

Not All Employees Demand the "Right to Disconnect"

According to a recent Gallup poll, 79 percent of full-time employees had either strongly positive or somewhat positive views of using computers, e-mail, tablets, and smartphones to work remotely outside of normal business hours. According to the same poll, 17 percent of them report "better overall lives" because of constant online connectivity with their work. Finally, working remotely after business hours apparently does not necessarily result in additional work-related stress.

Critical Thinking *From an ethical point of view, is there any difference between calling subordinates during off hours for work-related questions and sending them e-mails or text messages?*

---

a. *Tennessee Coal, Iron & R. Co. v. Muscoda Local No. 123*, 321 U.S. 590, 64 S.Ct. 698, 8 L.Ed. 949 (1944). Although Congress later passed a statute that superseded the holding in this case, the statute gave the courts broad authority to interpret the FLSA's definition of *work*. 29 U.S.C. Section 251(a). See *Integrity Staffing Solutions, Inc. v. Busk*, ___ U.S. ___, 135 S.Ct. 513, 190 L.Ed.2d 410 (2014).

b. *Steiner v. Mitchell*, 350 U.S. 247, 76 S.Ct. 330, 100 L.Ed. 267 (1956).
c. *Allen v. City of Chicago*, 2014 WL 5461856 (N.D.Ill. 2014).

---

workplace is for top management to demonstrate its commitment to ethical decision making. A manager who is not totally committed to an ethical workplace rarely succeeds in creating one. Management's behavior, more than anything else, sets the ethical tone of a firm. Employees take their cues from management.

Managers have found that discharging even one employee for ethical reasons has a tremendous impact as a deterrent to unethical behavior in the workplace. This is true even if the company has a written code of ethics. If management does not enforce the company code, the code is essentially nonexistent.

The administration of a university may have had a similar concept in mind in the following case when it applied the school's professionalism standard to a student who had engaged in serious misconduct.

Al-Dabagh v. Case Western Reserve University

United States Court of Appeals, Sixth Circuit, 777 F.3d 355 (2015).

Background and Facts The curriculum at Case Western Reserve University School of Medicine identifies nine "core competencies." At the top of the list is professionalism, which includes "ethical, honest, responsible and reliable behavior." The university's Committee on Students determines whether a student has met the professionalism requirements.

Amir Al-Dabagh enrolled at the school and did well academically. But he sexually harassed fellow students, often asked an instructor not to mark him late for class, received complaints from hospital staff about his demeanor, and was convicted of driving while intoxicated. The Committee on Students unanimously refused to certify him for graduation and dismissed him from the university.

He filed a suit in a federal district court against Case Western, alleging a breach of good faith and fair dealing. The court ordered the school to issue a diploma. Case Western appealed.

In the Language of the Court

SUTTON, Circuit Judge.

* * * *

* * * Case Western's student handbook * * * makes clear that the only thing standing between Al-Dabagh and a diploma is the Committee on Students' finding that he lacks professionalism. Unhappily for Al-Dabagh, that is an academic judgment. And *we can no more substitute our personal views for the Committee's when it comes to an academic judgment than the Committee can substitute its views for ours when it comes to a judicial decision.* [Emphasis added.]

* * * *

* * * *The Committee's professionalism determination is an academic judgment. That conclusion all but resolves this case. We may overturn the Committee only if it substantially departed from accepted academic norms when it refused to approve Al-Dabagh for graduation.* And given Al-Dabagh's track record—one member of the Committee does not recall encountering another student with Al-Dabagh's "repeated professionalism issues" in his quarter century of experience—we cannot see how it did. [Emphasis added.]

To the contrary, Al-Dabagh insists: The Committee's decision was a "punitive disciplinary measure" that had nothing to do with academics. * * * His argument fails to wrestle with the prominent place of professionalism in the university's academic curriculum—which itself is an academic decision courts may not lightly disturb.

Even if professionalism is an academic criterion, Al-Dabagh persists that the university defined it too broadly. As he sees it, the only professional lapses that matter are the ones linked to academic performance. That is not how we see it or for that matter how the medical school sees it. That many professionalism-related cases involve classroom incidents does not establish that only classroom incidents are relevant to the professionalism inquiry * * * . Our own standards indicate that professionalism does not end at the courtroom door. Why should hospitals operate any differently? As for the danger that an expansive view of professionalism might forgive, or provide a cloak for, arbitrary or discriminatory behavior, we see no such problem here. Nothing in the record suggests that the university had impermissible motives or acted in bad faith in this instance. And nothing in our deferential standard prevents us from invalidating genuinely objectionable actions when they occur.

Decision and Remedy *The U.S. Court of Appeals for the Sixth Circuit reversed the lower court's order to issue a diploma to Al-Dabagh. The federal appellate court found nothing to indicate that Case Western had "impermissible motives," acted in bad faith, or dealt unfairly with Al-Dabagh.*

Critical Thinking

- **What If the Facts Were Different?** *Suppose that Case Western had tolerated Al-Dabagh's conduct and awarded him a diploma. What impact might that had on other students at the school? Why?*

Behavior of Owners and Managers Certain types of behavior on the part of managers and owners contribute to unethical behavior among employees. Managers who set unrealistic production or sales goals increase the probability that employees will act unethically. If a sales quota can be met only through high-pressure, unethical sales tactics, employees will try to act "in the best interest of the company" and will continue to behave unethically. A manager who looks the other way when she or he knows about an employee's unethical behavior also sets an example—one indicating that ethical transgressions will be accepted.

Business owners and managers sometimes take more active roles in fostering unethical and illegal conduct. This sort of misbehavior can have negative consequences for the owners and managers and their business. Not only can a court sanction them, but it can also issue an injunction that prevents them from engaging in similar patterns of conduct in the future.

■ **CASE IN POINT 5.11** John Robert Johnson, Jr., took a truck that needed repair along with its fifteen-ton trailer to Bubba Shaffer, doing business as Shaffer's Auto and Diesel Repair, LLC. The truck was supposedly fixed, and Johnson paid the bill, but the truck continued to leak oil and water. Johnson returned the truck to Shaffer, who again claimed to have fixed the problem. Johnson paid the second bill. The problems with the truck continued, however, so Johnson returned the truck and trailer to Shaffer a third time.

Johnson was given a verbal estimate of $1,000 for the repairs, but Shaffer ultimately sent an invoice for $5,863. Johnson offered to settle for $2,480, the amount of the initial estimate ($1,000), plus the costs of parts and shipping. Shaffer refused the offer and would not return Johnson's truck or trailer until full payment was made. Shaffer retained possession for almost four years and also charged Johnson a storage fee of $50 a day and 18 percent interest on the $5,863. Johnson sued for unfair trade practices and won. The court awarded him $3,500 in damages plus attorneys' fees and awarded Shaffer $1,000 (the amount of his estimate).[3] ■

The following case further demonstrates the types of situations that can occur when management demonstrates a lack of concern about ethics.

3. *Johnson Construction Co. v. Shaffer,* 87 So.3d 203 (La.App. 2012).

Case Analysis 5.3

Moseley v. Pepco Energy Services, Inc.

United States District Court, District of New Jersey, 2011 WL 1584166 (2011).

In the Language of the Court
Joseph H. *RODRIGUEZ*, District Judge.

* * * Plaintiff Moseley is an employee of Defendant Pepco Energy Services, Inc. ("PES"). He has been employed by PES or its corporate predecessors for over twenty-five years. PES, a subsidiary of Defendant Pepco Holdings, Inc. ("PHI"), provides deregulated energy and energy-related services for residential, small business, and large commercial customers.

* * * *

In 1998, Thomas Herzog held the position of Vice President of CTS. * * * In or around 2002, CTS merged with Potomic Electric Power Company, Inc., and each company became a subsidiary of PHI. Following the merger, according to Plaintiff, he continued to work for PHI, still as Maintenance Manager at Midtown Thermal, until December 31, 2009.

* * * *

Following the 2002 merger with PHI, employees were required to complete an annual ethics survey. By March of 2007, Plaintiff and two co-workers had discussed their respective observations of Herzog's conduct, which they deemed questionable and possibly unethical. Specifically, they felt that Herzog improperly used company assets and improperly hired immediate family members and friends who did not appear on the payroll. The three decided to disclose this information on PHI's annual "Ethics Survey."

The three planned to reveal that Herzog employed his daughter, Laurie, as his secretary in the summer of 2005 and the beginning of 2006 without posting the position first and in violation of PHI's anti-nepotism policy.

* * * *

Next, Herzog hired his girlfriend's daughter as his secretary after his daughter had gone back to school. Plaintiff believed this was in violation of Company policy because the position again was not posted. Herzog also hired his son as a project manager, again through a third party independent contractor, Walter Ratai. Plaintiff thought this was wrong because (1) Herzog circumvented the Company's hiring process, (2) it violated Company policy, and (3) Herzog's son was being paid $75.00/hr, which was more than Plaintiff was making. * * *

Case 5.3 Continued

In addition, Plaintiff had learned that Herzog was improperly using the Company's Eagles' tickets for personal use. Finally, Herzog had leased a new SUV with Company funds, but which was not approved by the Company.

* * * *

[After the surveys were completed, an] investigation ensued. Following the investigation, effective on or about May 10, 2007, Herzog was escorted out of the building. * * * On March 8, 2008, Plaintiff received his annual performance evaluation * * * ; for the first time in twenty-three years, Plaintiff's performance review was negative. Plaintiff feels that this negative performance review was a further act of retaliation for his disclosure of Herzog's conduct.

* * * *

On or about June 11, 2008 the Plant/Operations Manager position was posted * * * . Plaintiff applied for the position, but it was offered to [another person]. Plaintiff alleges that he "was not promoted to the position of Plant/Operations Manager despite his experience performing the job for the previous two and a half years, qualifications for same and seniority, as a direct and proximate result of his prior complaints and/or disclosures regarding the Herzog illegal conduct and activities."

* * * *

The New Jersey Legislature enacted the Conscientious Employee Protection Act (CEPA) to "protect and encourage employees to report illegal or unethical workplace activities." * * * CEPA prohibits a New Jersey employer from taking "retaliatory action" against an employee who objects to "any activity, policy or practice which the employee reasonably believes" is in violation of applicable law. * * * "To prevail on a claim under

this provision, a plaintiff must establish that: (1) he reasonably believed that [the complained-of] conduct was violating a law or rule or regulation promulgated pursuant to law; (2) he objected to the conduct; (3) an adverse employment action was taken against him; and (4) a causal connection exists between the whistleblowing activity and the adverse employment action.

* * * *

The first element of the prima facie case [a case sufficient to be sent to the jury] under CEPA is that the Plaintiff reasonably believed that the complained-of conduct (1) was violating a "law, rule, or regulation promulgated pursuant to law, including any violation involving deception of, or misrepresentation to, any shareholder, investor, client, patient, customer, employee, former employee, retiree or pensioner of the employer or any governmental entity"; or "(2) is fraudulent or criminal, including any activity, policy or practice of deception or misrepresentation which the employee reasonably believes may defraud any shareholder, investor, client, patient, customer, employee, former employee, retiree or pensioner of the employer or any governmental entity."

Although Defendants have argued that Plaintiff merely disclosed a violation of Company policy, Moseley has testified that in March 2007, he reported what he believed to be "unethical conduct, misappropriation of company funds, and theft" by his direct supervisor. * * * *Moreover, a plaintiff need not demonstrate that there was a violation of the law or fraud, but instead that he "reasonably believed" that to be the case.* The facts in this case support an objectively reasonable belief that a violation of law or

fraudulent conduct was being committed by Plaintiff's supervisor. [Emphasis added.]

Regarding the causal connection between Plaintiff's whistleblowing activity and the negative adverse employment actions taken against him, Plaintiff stresses that he was employed by the Defendants for twenty-five years without a negative employment evaluation or any form of discipline until immediately after he disclosed the wrongful conduct of his supervisor. Not only did Plaintiff then receive a negative performance evaluation, but the posted position of Plant Manager was given to [another], despite [the other's] alleged past negative history and despite that Plaintiff asserts he had been acting in that job for over two years. Plaintiff contends that this is sufficient evidence of pretext.

The Court is unable to find as a matter of law that Defendants' inferences prevail or that a jury could not reasonably adopt a contrary inference of retaliation. There are questions of fact as to how much the individuals responsible for Plaintiff's negative performance evaluations knew about Plaintiff's complaints. "[A] finding of the required causal connection may be based solely on circumstantial evidence that the person ultimately responsible for an adverse employment action was aware of an employee's whistle-blowing activity." Because jurors may infer a causal connection from the surrounding circumstances, as well as temporal proximity, the Court will not grant summary judgment. [Emphasis added.]

* * * *

IT IS ORDERED on this 26th day of April, 2011 that Defendants' motion for summary judgment is hereby DENIED.

Legal Reasoning Questions

1. Using duty-based ethical principles, what facts or circumstances in this case would lead Moseley to disclose Herzog's behavior?

2. Using outcome-based ethical principles, what issues would Moseley have to analyze in making the decision to report Herzog's behavior? What would be the risks to Moseley? The benefits?

3. Under the Business Process Pragmatism™ steps, what alternatives might Moseley have had in this situation?

The Sarbanes-Oxley Act Congress enacted the Sarbanes-Oxley Act[4] to help reduce corporate fraud and unethical management decisions. The act requires companies to set up confidential systems so that employees and others can "raise red flags" about suspected illegal or unethical auditing and accounting practices.

Some companies have implemented online reporting systems to accomplish this goal. In one such system, employees can click on an on-screen icon that anonymously links them with NAVEX Global, an organization based in Oregon. Through NAVEX Global, employees can report suspicious accounting practices, sexual harassment, and other possibly unethical behavior. NAVEX, in turn, alerts management personnel or the audit committee at the designated company to the possible problem.

5–5 Global Business Ethics

Just as different religions have different moral codes, different countries, regions, and even states have different ethical expectations and priorities. Some of these differences are based in religious values, whereas others are cultural in nature. Such differences make it even more difficult to determine what is ethical in a particular situation. For instance, in certain countries the consumption of alcohol is forbidden for religious reasons. It would be considered unethical for a U.S. business to produce alcohol in those countries and employ local workers to assist in alcohol production.

International transactions often involve issues related to employment and financing. Congress has addressed some of these issues, not eliminating the ethical components but clarifying some of the conflicts between the ethics of the United States and the ethics of other nations. For instance, the Civil Rights Act and the Foreign Corrupt Practices Act have clarified the U.S. ethical position on employment issues and bribery in foreign nations. (Other nations, including Mexico, have also enacted laws that prohibit bribery.)

5–5a Monitoring the Employment Practices of Foreign Suppliers

Many businesses contract with companies in developing nations to produce goods, such as shoes and clothing, because the wage rates in those nations are significantly lower than those in the United States. But what if one of those contractors hires women and children at below-minimum-wage rates or requires its employees to work long hours in a workplace full of health hazards? What if the company's supervisors routinely engage in workplace conduct that is offensive to women? What if plants located abroad routinely violate labor and environmental standards?

■ **EXAMPLE 5.12** Pegatron Corporation, a company based in China, manufactures and supplies parts to Apple, Inc., for iPads and other Apple products. After an explosion at a Pegatron factory in Shanghai, allegations surfaced that the conditions at the factory violated labor and environmental standards. Similar allegations were made about other Apple suppliers.

Apple started to evaluate practices at companies in its supply chain and to communicate its ethics policies to them. Its audits revealed numerous violations. Apple released a list of its suppliers for the first time and issued a lengthy "Supplier Responsibility Report" detailing supplier practices. Numerous facilities had withheld worker pay as a disciplinary measure. Some had falsified pay records and forced workers to use machines without safeguards. Others had engaged in unsafe environmental practices, such as dumping wastewater on neighboring farms. Apple terminated its relationship with one supplier and turned over its findings to the Fair Labor Association for further inquiry. ■

Given today's global communications network, few companies can assume that their actions in other nations will go unnoticed by "corporate watch" groups that discover and publicize unethical corporate behavior. As a result, U.S. businesses today usually take steps to avoid such adverse publicity—either by refusing to deal with certain suppliers or by arranging to monitor their suppliers' workplaces to make sure that the employees are not being mistreated.

5–5b The Foreign Corrupt Practices Act

Another ethical problem in international business dealings has to do with the legitimacy of certain side payments to government officials. In the United States, the majority of contracts are formed within the private sector. In many foreign countries, however, government officials make the decisions on most major construction and manufacturing contracts because of extensive government regulation and control over trade and industry.

Side payments to government officials in exchange for favorable business contracts are not unusual in such countries, nor have they been considered unethical. In the past, U.S. corporations doing business in these nations largely followed the dictum "When in Rome, do as the Romans do."

In the 1970s, however, the U.S. media uncovered a number of business scandals involving large side

---

4. 15 U.S.C. Sections 7201 *et seq.*

payments by U.S. corporations to foreign representatives for the purpose of securing advantageous international trade contracts. In response to this unethical behavior, Congress passed the Foreign Corrupt Practices Act[5] (FCPA), which prohibits U.S. businesspersons from bribing foreign officials to secure beneficial contracts.

Prohibition against the Bribery of Foreign Officials   The first part of the FCPA applies to all U.S. companies and their directors, officers, shareholders, employees, and agents. This part prohibits the bribery of most officials of foreign governments if the purpose of the payment is to motivate the official to act in his or her official capacity to provide business opportunities.

The FCPA does not prohibit payments made to minor officials whose duties are ministerial. A ministerial action is a routine activity, such as the processing of paperwork, with little or no discretion involved in the action. These payments are often referred to as "grease," or facilitating payments. They are meant to accelerate the performance of administrative services that might otherwise be carried out at a slow pace. Thus, for instance, if a firm makes a payment to a minor official to speed up an import licensing process, the firm has not violated the FCPA.

Generally, the act, as amended, permits payments to foreign officials if such payments are lawful within the foreign country. Payments to private foreign companies or other third parties are permissible—unless the U.S. firm knows that the payments will be passed on to a foreign government in violation of the FCPA. The U.S. Department of Justice also uses the FCPA to prosecute foreign companies suspected of bribing officials outside the United States.

Accounting Requirements   In the past, bribes were often concealed in corporate financial records. Thus, the second part of the FCPA is directed toward accountants.

All companies must keep detailed records that "accurately and fairly" reflect their financial activities. Their accounting systems must provide "reasonable assurance" that all transactions entered into by the companies are accounted for and legal. These requirements assist in detecting illegal bribes. The FCPA prohibits any person from making false statements to accountants or false entries in any record or account.

■ **CASE IN POINT 5.13**   Noble Corporation, an international provider of offshore drilling services and equipment, was operating some drilling rigs offshore in Nigeria. Mark Jackson and James Ruehlen were officers at Noble. The U.S. government accused Noble of bribing Nigerian government officials and charged Jackson and Ruehlen individually with violating the FCPA's accounting provisions. Jackson and Ruehlen allegedly assisted in the bribery because they repeatedly allowed allegedly illegal payments to be posted on Noble's books as legitimate operating expenses.[6] ■

Penalties for Violations   The FCPA provides that business firms that violate the act may be fined up to $2 million. Individual officers or directors who violate the FCPA may be fined up to $100,000 (the fine cannot be paid by the company) and may be imprisoned for up to five years. These statutory amounts can be significantly increased under the Alternative Fines Act[7] (up to twice the amount of any gain that the defendant obtained by making the corrupt payment).

Today, the U.S. government is actively seeking out violators and has around 150 FCPA investigations going on at any given time. In recent years, a high percentage of the total fines imposed by the Department of Justice have come from FCPA cases.

---

5. 15 U.S.C. Sections 78dd-1 *et seq.*

6. *S.E.C. v. Jackson*, 908 F.Supp.2d 834 (S.D.Tex—Houston Div. 2012).
7. 18 U.S.C. Section 3571.

Reviewing: Business Ethics

James Stilton is the chief executive officer (CEO) of RightLiving, Inc., a company that buys life insurance policies at a discount from terminally ill persons and sells the policies to investors. RightLiving pays the terminally ill patients a percentage of the future death benefit (usually 65 percent) and then sells the policies to investors for 85 percent of the value of the future benefit. The patients receive the cash to use for medical and other expenses. The investors are "guaranteed" a positive return on their investment, and RightLiving profits on the difference between the purchase and sale prices. Stilton is aware that some sick patients might obtain insurance policies through fraud (by not revealing the illness on the insurance application). Insurance companies that discover this will cancel the policy and refuse to pay.

Continues

Stilton believes that most of the policies he has purchased are legitimate, but he knows that some probably are not. Using the information presented in this chapter, answer the following questions.

1. Would a person who adheres to the principle of rights consider it ethical for Stilton not to disclose the potential risk of cancellation to investors? Why or why not?
2. Using Immanuel Kant's categorical imperative, are the actions of RightLiving, Inc., ethical? Why or why not?
3. Under utilitarianism, are Stilton's actions ethical? Why or why not? What difference does it make if most of the policies are legitimate?
4. Using the Business Process Pragmatism™ steps discussed in this chapter, discuss the decision process Stilton should use in deciding whether to disclose the risk of fraudulent policies to potential investors.

> **Debate This** . . .   *Executives in large corporations are ultimately rewarded if their companies do well, particularly as evidenced by rising stock prices. Consequently, should we let those who run corporations decide what level of negative side effects of their goods or services is "acceptable"?*

Terms and Concepts

business ethics 89	duty-based ethics 94	principle of rights 94
categorical imperative 95	ethical reasoning 94	stakeholders 96
corporate social responsibility (CSR) 96	ethics 89	triple bottom line 89
cost-benefit analysis 95	moral minimum 91	utilitarianism 95
	outcome-based ethics 94	

Issue Spotters

1. Acme Corporation decides to respond to what it sees as a moral obligation to correct for past discrimination by adjusting pay differences among its employees. Does this raise an ethical conflict between Acme and its employees? Between Acme and its shareholders? Explain your answers. (See *Making Ethical Business Decisions.*)

2. Delta Tools, Inc., markets a product that under some circumstances is capable of seriously injuring consumers. Does Delta have an ethical duty to remove this product from the market, even if the injuries result only from misuse? Why or why not? (See *Making Ethical Business Decisions.*)

• **Check your answers to the Issue Spotters against the answers provided in Appendix D at the end of this text.**

Business Scenarios

5–1. Business Ethics. Jason Trevor owns a commercial bakery in Blakely, Georgia, that produces a variety of goods sold in grocery stores. Trevor is required by law to perform internal tests on food produced at his plant to check for contamination. On three occasions, the tests of food products containing peanut butter were positive for salmonella contamination. Trevor was not required to report the results to U.S. Food and Drug Administration officials, however, so he did not. Instead, Trevor instructed his employees to simply repeat the tests until the results were negative. Meanwhile, the products that had originally tested positive for salmonella were eventually shipped out to retailers.

Five people who ate Trevor's baked goods that year became seriously ill, and one person died from a salmonella infection. Even though Trevor's conduct was legal, was it unethical for him to sell goods that had once tested positive for salmonella? Why or why not? (See *Business Ethics.*)

Business Case Problems

5–2. Spotlight on Pfizer, Inc.—Corporate Social Responsibility. Methamphetamine (meth) is an addictive

drug made chiefly in small toxic labs (STLs) in homes, tents, barns, or hotel rooms. The manufacturing process is dangerous and often results in explosions, burns, and toxic fumes. Government entities spend time and resources to find and destroy STLs, imprison meth dealers and users, treat addicts, and provide services for affected families. Meth cannot be made without ingredients that are also used in cold and allergy medications. Arkansas has one of the highest numbers of STLs in the United States. To recoup the costs of fighting the meth epidemic, twenty counties in Arkansas filed a suit against Pfizer, Inc., which makes cold and allergy medications. What is Pfizer's ethical responsibility here, and to whom is it owed? Why? [*Ashley County, Arkansas v. Pfizer, Inc.,* 552 F.3d 659 (8th Cir. 2009)] (See *Ethical Principles and Philosophies.*)

5–3. Business Case Problem with Sample Answer— Online Privacy. Facebook, Inc., launched a program called

"Beacon" that automatically updated the profiles of users on Facebook's social networking site when those users had any activity on Beacon "partner" sites. For example, one partner site was Blockbuster.com. When a user rented or purchased a movie through Blockbuster.com, the user's Facebook profile would be updated to share the purchase. The Beacon program was set up as a default setting, so users never consented to the program, but they could opt out. What are the ethical implications of an opt-in program versus an opt-out program in social media? [*Lane v. Facebook, Inc.,* 696 F.3d 811 (9th Cir. 2011)] (See *Business Ethics and Social Media.*)

- **For a sample answer to Problem 5–3, go to Appendix E at the end of this text.**

5–4. Business Ethics on a Global Scale. After the fall of the Soviet Union, the new government of Azerbaijan began converting certain state-controlled industries to private ownership. Ownership in these companies could be purchased through a voucher program. Frederic Bourke, Jr., and Viktor Kozeny wanted to purchase the Azerbaijani oil company, SOCAR, but it was unclear whether the Azerbaijani president would allow SOCAR to be put up for sale. Kozeny met with one of the vice presidents of SOCAR (who was also the son of the president of Azerbaijan) and other Azerbaijani leaders to discuss the sale of SOCAR. To obtain their cooperation, Kozeny set up a series of parent and subsidiary companies through which the Azerbaijani leaders would eventually receive two-thirds of the SOCAR profits without ever investing any of their own funds. In return, the Azerbaijani leaders would attempt to use their influence to convince the president to put SOCAR up for sale. Assume that Bourke and Kozeny are operating out of a U.S. company. Discuss the ethics of this scheme, both in terms of the Foreign Corrupt Practices Act

(FCPA) and as a general ethical issue. What duties did Kozeny have under the FCPA? [*United States v. Kozeny,* 667 F.3d 122 (2d Cir. 2011)] (See *Making Ethical Business Decisions.*)

5–5. Business Ethics. Mark Ramun worked as a manager for Allied Erecting and Dismantling Co., where he had a tense relationship with his father, who was Allied's president. After more than ten years, Mark left Allied, taking 15,000 pages of Allied's documents on DVDs and CDs, which constituted trade secrets. Later, he joined Genesis Equipment & Manufacturing, Inc., a competitor. Genesis soon developed a piece of equipment that incorporated elements of Allied equipment. How might business ethics have been violated in these circumstances? Discuss. [*Allied Erecting and Dismantling Co. v. Genesis Equipment & Manufacturing, Inc.,* 511 Fed.Appx. 398 (6th Cir. 2013)] (See *Business Ethics.*)

5–6. Business Ethics. Stephen Glass made himself infamous as a dishonest journalist by fabricating material for more than forty articles for *The New Republic* magazine and other publications. He also fabricated supporting materials to delude *The New Republic*'s fact checkers. At the time, he was a law student at Georgetown University. Once suspicions were aroused, Glass tried to avoid detection. Later, Glass applied for admission to the California bar. The California Supreme Court denied his application, citing "numerous instances of dishonesty and disingenuousness" during his "rehabilitation" following the exposure of his misdeeds. How do these circumstances underscore the importance of ethics? Discuss. [*In re Glass,* 58 Cal.4th 500, 316 P.3d 1199 (2014)] (See *Business Ethics.*)

5–7. Business Ethics. Operating out of an apartment in Secane, Pennsylvania, Hratch Ilanjian convinced Vicken Setrakian, the president of Kenset Corp., that he was an international businessman who could help Kenset turn around its business in the Middle East. At Ilanjian's insistence, Setrakian provided confidential business documents. Claiming that they had an agreement, Ilanjian demanded full, immediate payment and threatened to disclose the confidential information to a Kenset supplier if payment was not forthcoming. Kenset denied that they had a contract and filed a suit in a federal district court against Ilanjian, seeking return of the documents. During discovery, Ilanjian was uncooperative. Who behaved unethically in these circumstances? Explain. [*Kenset Corp. v. Ilanjian,* 600 Fed.Appx. 827 (3rd Cir. 2015)] (See *Business Ethics.*)

5–8. Business Ethics. Priscilla Dickman worked as a medical technologist at the University of Connecticut Health Center. Dickman's supervisor received complaints that she was getting nonbusiness-related phone calls and was absent from her work area when she should have been working. Based on e-mails and other documents found on Dickman's work computer, the state investigated her for violations of state law. She was convicted of conducting "personal business for financial gain on state time utilizing state resources." Separate criminal investigations resulted in convictions for forgery and filing an unrelated fraudulent insurance claim. She "retired" from her job and filed a claim with the state of Connecticut against the health center, alleging that her former employer had initiated the investigations to harass her and force her to quit. For lack of "credible evidence or legal support," the claim was dismissed. Which of these acts, if any, were unethical? Why? [*Dickman v. University of Connecticut Health Center,* 162 Conn.App. 441, __ A.3d __ (2016)] (See *Business Ethics.*)

5–9. A Question of Ethics—Consumer Rights. *Best Buy,*

a national electronics retailer, offered a credit card that allowed users to earn "reward points" that could be redeemed for discounts on Best Buy goods. After reading a newspaper advertisement for the card, Gary Davis applied for, and was given, a credit card. As part of the application process, he visited a Web page containing Frequently Asked Questions as well as terms and conditions for the card. He clicked on a button affirming that he understood the terms and conditions. When Davis received his card, it came with seven brochures about the card and the reward point program. As he read the brochures, he discovered that a $59 annual fee would be charged for the card. Davis went back to the Web pages he had visited and found a statement that the card "may" have an annual fee. Davis sued, claiming that the company did not adequately disclose the fee. *[Davis v. HSBC Bank Nevada, N.A., 691 F.3d 1152 (9th Cir. 2012)]* (See *Business Ethics.*)

(a) Online applications frequently have click-on buttons or check boxes for consumers to acknowledge that they have read and understand the terms and conditions of applications or purchases. Often, the terms and conditions are so long that they cannot all be seen on one screen and users must scroll to view the entire document. Is it unethical for companies to put terms and conditions, especially terms that may cost the consumer, in an electronic document that is too long to read on one screen? Why or why not? Does this differ from having a consumer sign a hard-copy document with terms and conditions printed on it? Why or why not?

(b) The Truth-in-Lending Act requires that credit terms be clearly and conspicuously disclosed in application materials. Assuming that the Best Buy credit-card materials had sufficient legal disclosures, discuss the ethical aspects of businesses strictly following the language of the law as opposed to following the intent of the law.

Legal Reasoning Group Activity

5–10. Global Business Ethics. Pfizer, Inc., developed a new antibiotic called Trovan (trovafloxacinmesylate). Tests showed that in animals Trovan had life-threatening side effects, including joint disease, abnormal cartilage growth, liver damage, and a degenerative bone condition. Several years later, an epidemic of bacterial meningitis swept across Nigeria. Pfizer sent three U.S. physicians to test Trovan on children who were patients in Nigeria's Infectious Disease Hospital. Pfizer did not obtain the patients' consent, alert them to the risks, or tell them that Médecins Sans Frontières (Doctors without Borders) was providing an effective conventional treatment at the same site. Eleven children died in the experiment, and others were left blind, deaf, paralyzed, or brain damaged. Rabi Abdullahi and other Nigerian children filed a suit in a U.S. federal court against Pfizer, alleging a violation of a customary international law norm prohibiting involuntary medical experimentation on humans. (See *Global Business Ethics.*)

(a) One group should use the principles of ethical reasoning discussed in this chapter to develop three arguments that Pfizer's conduct was a violation of ethical standards.

(b) A second group should take a pro-Pfizer position and argue that the company did not violate any ethical standards (and counter the first group).

(c) A third group should come up with proposals for what Pfizer might have done differently to avert the consequences.

"Arbitration, No Class Actions"

It is nearly impossible to apply for credit, obtain phone or Internet service, or buy goods online without agreeing to submit any claim arising from the deal to arbitration. This is also true with respect to employment—job applicants are generally informed by a potential employer that "any controversy or claim arising out of or relating to this employment application shall be settled by arbitration."[1]

By including arbitration clauses in consumer and employment contracts, businesses can prevent customers and employees from getting their day in court. Claims removed from consideration by the courts in favor of arbitration have involved theft, fraud, sexual harassment, employment discrimination, and other serious issues.

Class Action

A *class action* is a suit in which a large number of plaintiffs file a complaint as a group. A class action can increase the efficiency of the legal process and lower the costs to the parties. It can be an important method by which plaintiffs with similar claims seek relief. More importantly, a class action may be the best means by which the costs of wrongdoing can be imposed on a wrongdoer.

Best Means to Stop a Bad Practice In some circumstances, a class-action suit may be the only practical method for a group of individuals to stop an allegedly harmful business practice. For example, suppose a business pads all of its customers' bills with an unexpected fee—adding up to millions in profit for the business. An individual customer may find it too costly to bring suit against the business or even to engage in arbitration to contest the charge. But a number of customers together could afford to fight the charge.

Groundless Claims and High Fees "Arbitration, No Class Actions," states the terms of use for Budget Rent a Car System, Inc.[2] Everyone who rents a car from Budget must agree to these terms. Businesses, such as Budget, assert that class-action suits are fomented by lawyers, who make millions of dollars in fees. Businesses claim that they have no choice but to settle such claims, even those that are groundless. Arbitration, they argue, can prevent these consequences.

Arbitration

Arbitration is a method of alternative dispute resolution in which a dispute is submitted to a third party (an arbitrator), who listens to the parties, reviews the evidence, and renders a decision. Arbitration clauses can be mandatory or voluntary. A dispute that is subject to mandatory

Continues

---

1. American Arbitration Association, *Drafting Dispute Resolution Clauses: A Practical Guide*, https://www.adr.org/aaa/ShowPDF?doc=ADRSTG_002540 (Nov. 6, 2015).
2. Budget Rent a Car System, Inc., *Terms of Use*, http://www.budget.com /budgetWeb/html/en/customer/termsofuse.html (Nov. 6, 2015).

arbitration must be resolved through arbitration. The parties give up their right to sue in court, participate in a class action, or appeal the arbitration decision.

Professional and Unbiased Businesses argue that class-action suits are unnecessary because individuals can more easily resolve their complaints through arbitration. With arbitration, disputes can be resolved quickly without complicated procedures, the limits of judicial rules, or the time constraints of a crowded court's schedule.

Proponents of arbitration also contend that arbitrators can act professionally and without bias. The American Arbitration Association and JAMS, the two largest arbitration firms, claim to ensure a professional and unbiased process. These organizations require an arbitrator to disclose any conflict of interest before taking a case, for instance.

Biased and Unprofessional Opponents of arbitration emphasize that a party's right to appeal an arbitrator's handling of a case and its outcome is limited. Questions about a witness's testimony, a party's handling of the evidence, an arbitrator's potential conflict of interest, and many other issues are not grounds for appeal to a court.

Arbitrators often depend for their business on a company against whom a customer or employee may have a grievance. An arbitrator may handle many cases involving the same company and may therefore consider the company his or her client. For this reason, critics argue that an arbitrator is more likely to rule in favor of the business, regardless of the merits of a claim against it.

What Do the Courts Say?

Most plaintiffs who are blocked from pursuing their claim as a group drop their case. Furthermore, in four out of five class actions filed between 2014 and 2016, judges remanded the disputes to arbitration. During the same period, only about five hundred consumers went to arbitration over a dispute of $2,500 or less. Among those contesting a credit card or loan fee, two-thirds received no award of money in arbitration.

In other words, individual consumers whose only recourse against a company is arbitration do not normally prevail in their claims. Despite this history, recent decisions by the United States Supreme Court upheld the use of arbitration clauses in consumer and merchant contracts to prohibit class-action suits.

Class Actions Interfere with Arbitration Vincent and Liza Concepcion, along with other consumers, filed a class action in a California state court against AT&T Mobility LLC, alleging that the company had promised them a free phone if they agreed to service but actually charged them $30.22 for the phone. AT&T responded that a class-action ban in an arbitration clause in the customers' contracts barred the suit. The court ruled that the ban was unconscionable.

AT&T appealed to the United States Supreme Court, which reasoned that "requiring the availability of class-wide arbitration interferes with fundamental attributes of arbitration." The main purpose of the federal law that applied in this case—the Federal Arbitration Act—"is to ensure the enforcement of arbitration agreements according to their terms." This conclusion relegated *state* law on this issue, including California's ruling, to the sidelines.[3]

---

3. *AT&T Mobility LLC v. Concepcion*, 563 U.S. 333, 131 S.Ct. 1740, 179 L.Ed.2d 742 (2011).

Arbitration Clauses Trump Class Actions Meanwhile, Alan Carlson, the owner of the restaurant Italian Colors, pursued a suit against American Express Company over the fee that the company assessed merchants to process American Express credit-card charges. Carlson argued that a class-action ban in an arbitration clause in the company's merchant contract prevented merchants from exercising their *federal* right to fight a monopoly. None of the merchants could afford to fight the charge individually.

On appeal, the Supreme Court ruled in favor of American Express. The Court stated that federal antitrust "laws do not guarantee an affordable procedural path to the vindication of every claim."[4] Under this decision, an arbitration clause can outlaw a class action even if it is the only realistic, practical way to bring a case.

More recently, the U.S. Court of Appeals for the Fifth Circuit concluded that employers who require prospective employees to sign mandatory arbitration agreements do not violate the National Labor Relations Act.[5]

Ethical Connection

Some persons would contend that a business's principal ethical obligation is to make a profit for its owners. Others might propose that a business take a number of stakeholders' perspectives into account when deciding on a course of action. Still others might insist that a business has a responsibility to act chiefly in the best interests of society. And there may be some who would impose a different ethical standard—religious, philosophical, or political.

Whichever standard is applied, a business has an interest in staying in business. Sometimes, a class action may be based on a groundless claim and brought for the sole purpose of generating a fee for the lawyer who brings it. There is no ethical requirement for a business to exhaust its assets to litigate or settle such a case.

Other times, though, a class action may be the best means of curbing a bad business practice. In that circumstance, engaging in harmful conduct and then cutting off an important means of redress for those harmed by the conduct cannot be seen as ethical.

Ethics Question *Is it unethical for a business to include an arbitration clause with a class-action ban in its contracts with customers, employees, and other businesses? Discuss.*

Critical Thinking *Many businesses include opt-out provisions in their arbitration clauses, but few consumers and employees take advantage of them. Why?*

---

4. *American Express Co. v. Italian Colors Restaurant*, 570 U.S. 333, 133 S.Ct. 2304, 186 L.Ed.2d 417 (2013).
5. *Murphy Oil USA, Inc. v. National Labor Relations Board*, 808 F.3d 1013 (5th Cir. 2015).

Torts and Crimes

BUSINESS LAW

CLARKSON · MILLER · CROSS

CHAPTER 6

Tort Law

Part of doing business today—and, indeed, part of everyday life—is the risk of being involved in a lawsuit. The list of circumstances in which businesspersons can be sued is long and varied. A customer who is injured by a security guard at a business establishment, for instance, may sue the business owner, claiming that the security guard's conduct was intentionally wrongful. A person who slips and falls at a retail store may sue the company for negligence.

Any time that one party's allegedly wrongful conduct causes injury to another, an action may arise under the law of *torts* (the word *tort* is French for "wrong"). Through tort law, society compensates those who have suffered injuries as a result of the wrongful conduct of others. Many of the lawsuits brought by or against business firms are based on various tort theories.

6–1 The Basis of Tort Law

Two notions serve as the basis of all **torts:** wrongs and compensation. Tort law is designed to compensate those who have suffered a loss or injury due to another person's wrongful act. In a tort action, one person or group brings a lawsuit against another person or group to obtain compensation (monetary damages) or other relief for the harm suffered.

6–1a The Purpose of Tort Law

Generally, the purpose of tort law is to provide remedies for the violation of various *protected interests.* Society recognizes an interest in personal physical safety. Thus, tort law provides remedies for acts that cause physical injury or that interfere with physical security and freedom of movement. Society also recognizes an interest in protecting property, and tort law provides remedies for acts that cause destruction of or damage to property.

6–1b Damages Available in Tort Actions

Because the purpose of tort law is to compensate the injured party for the damage suffered, you need to have an understanding of the types of damages that plaintiffs seek in tort actions. Note that legal usage distinguishes between the terms *damage* and *damages. Damage* refers to harm or injury to persons or property, while **damages** refers to monetary compensation for such harm or injury.

Compensatory Damages A plaintiff is awarded **compensatory damages** to compensate or reimburse the plaintiff for actual losses. Thus, the goal is to make the plaintiff whole and put her or him in the same position that she or he would have been in had the tort not occurred. Compensatory damages awards are often broken down into *special damages* and *general damages.*

Special damages compensate the plaintiff for quantifiable monetary losses, such as medical expenses and lost wages and benefits (now and in the future). Special damages might also be awarded to compensate for extra costs, the loss of irreplaceable items, and the costs of repairing or replacing damaged property.

■ **CASE IN POINT 6.1** Seaway Marine Transport operates the *Enterprise,* a large cargo ship, which has twenty-two hatches for storing coal. When the *Enterprise* positioned itself to receive a load of coal on the shores of Lake Erie, in Ohio, it struck a land-based coal-loading machine operated by Bessemer & Lake Erie Railroad Company. A federal court found Seaway liable and awarded $522,000 in special damages to compensate Bessemer for the cost of repairing the damage to the loading boom.[1] ■

General damages compensate individuals (not companies) for the nonmonetary aspects of the harm suffered, such as pain and suffering. A court might award general damages for physical or emotional pain and suffering, loss of companionship, loss of consortium (losing

---

1. *Bessemer & Lake Erie Railroad Co. v. Seaway Marine Transport,* 357 F.3d 596 (6th Cir. 2010).

the emotional and physical benefits of a spousal relationship), disfigurement, loss of reputation, or loss or impairment of mental or physical capacity.

Punitive Damages Occasionally, the courts also award **punitive damages** in tort cases to punish the wrongdoer and deter others from similar wrongdoing. Punitive damages are appropriate only when the defendant's conduct was particularly egregious (flagrant) or reprehensible (blameworthy).

Usually, this means that punitive damages are available in *intentional* tort actions and only rarely in negligence lawsuits (negligence actions will be discussed later in this chapter). They may be awarded, however, in suits involving *gross negligence*. Gross negligence can be defined as an intentional failure to perform a manifest duty in reckless disregard of the consequences of such a failure for the life or property of another.

Courts exercise great restraint in granting punitive damages to plaintiffs in tort actions because punitive damages are subject to limitations under the due process clause of the U.S. Constitution. The United States Supreme Court has held that to the extent that an award of punitive damages is grossly excessive, it furthers no legitimate purpose and violates due process requirements.[2] Consequently, an appellate court will sometimes reduce the amount of punitive damages awarded to a plaintiff on the ground that it is excessive and thereby violates the due process clause.

Legislative Caps on Damages State laws may limit the amount of damages—both punitive and general—that can be awarded to the plaintiff. More than half of the states have placed caps ranging from $250,000 to $750,000 on noneconomic general damages (such as for pain and suffering), especially in medical malpractice suits. More than thirty states have limited punitive damages, with some imposing outright bans.

6–1c Classification of Torts

There are two broad classifications of torts: *intentional torts* and *unintentional torts* (torts involving negligence). The classification of a particular tort depends largely on how the tort occurs (intentionally or negligently) and the surrounding circumstances. Intentional torts result from the intentional violation of person or property (fault plus intent). Negligence results from the breach of a duty to act reasonably (fault without intent).

---

2. *State Farm Mutual Automobile Insurance Co. v. Campbell*, 538 U.S. 408, 123 S.Ct. 1513, 155 L.Ed.2d 585 (2003).

6–1d Defenses

Even if a plaintiff proves all the elements of a tort, the defendant can raise a number of legally recognized *defenses* (reasons why the plaintiff should not obtain damages). A successful defense releases the defendant from partial or full liability for the tortious act.

The defenses available may vary depending on the specific tort involved. A common defense to intentional torts against persons, for instance, is *consent*. When a person consents to the act that damages her or him, there is generally no liability. The most widely used defense in negligence actions is *comparative negligence*.

In addition, most states have a *statute of limitations* that establishes the time limit (often two years from the date of discovering the harm) within which a particular type of lawsuit can be filed. After that time period has run, the plaintiff can no longer file a claim.

6–2 Intentional Torts against Persons

An **intentional tort,** as the term implies, requires intent. The **tortfeasor** (the one committing the tort) must intend to commit an act, the consequences of which interfere with another's personal or business interests in a way not permitted by law. An evil or harmful motive is not required—in fact, the person committing the action may even have a beneficial motive for doing what turns out to be a tortious act.

In tort law, *intent* means only that the person intended the consequences of his or her act or knew with substantial certainty that specific consequences would result from the act. The law generally assumes that individuals intend the *normal* consequences of their actions. Thus, forcefully pushing another—even if done in jest—is an intentional tort (if injury results), because the object of a strong push can ordinarily be expected to fall down.

In addition, intent can be transferred when a defendant intends to harm one individual, but unintentionally harms a second person. This is called **transferred intent.** ■ **EXAMPLE 6.2** Alex swings a bat intending to hit Blake but misses and hits Carson instead. Carson can sue Alex for the tort of battery (discussed shortly) because Alex's intent to harm Blake can be transferred to Carson. ■

6–2a Assault

An **assault** is any intentional and unexcused threat of immediate harmful or offensive contact—words or acts that create a reasonably believable threat. An assault can occur even if there is no actual contact with the plaintiff, provided that the defendant's conduct creates a reasonable apprehension of imminent harm in the plaintiff. Tort law aims to protect individuals from having to expect harmful or offensive contact.

6–2b Battery

If the act that created the apprehension is *completed* and results in harm to the plaintiff, it is a **battery**—an unexcused and harmful or offensive physical contact *intentionally* performed. ■ **EXAMPLE 6.3** Ivan threatens Jean with a gun and then shoots her. The pointing of the gun at Jean is an assault. The firing of the gun (if the bullet hits Jean) is a battery. ■

The contact can be harmful, or it can be merely offensive (such as an unwelcome kiss). Physical injury need not occur. The contact can involve any part of the body or anything attached to it—for instance, a hat, a purse, or a jacket. The contact can be made by the defendant or by some force set in motion by the defendant, such as a rock thrown by the defendant. Whether the contact is offensive is determined by the *reasonable person standard.*[3]

If the plaintiff shows that there was contact, and the jury (or judge, if there is no jury) agrees that the contact was offensive, then the plaintiff has a right to compensation. A plaintiff may be compensated for the emotional harm or loss of reputation resulting from a battery, as well as for physical harm. A defendant may assert self-defense or defense of others in an attempt to justify his or her conduct.

6–2c False Imprisonment

False imprisonment is the intentional confinement or restraint of another person's activities without justification. False imprisonment interferes with the freedom to move without restraint. The confinement can be accomplished through the use of physical barriers, physical restraint, or threats of physical force. Moral pressure does not constitute false imprisonment. It is essential that the person being restrained does not wish to be restrained. (The plaintiff's consent to the restraint bars any liability.)

Businesspersons often face suits for false imprisonment after they have attempted to confine a suspected shoplifter for questioning. Under the "privilege to detain" granted to merchants in most states, a merchant can use *reasonable force* to detain or delay persons suspected of shoplifting and hold them for the police. Although laws pertaining to this privilege vary from state to state, generally any detention must be conducted in a *reasonable* manner and for only a *reasonable* length of time. Undue force or unreasonable detention can lead to liability for the business.

Cities and counties may also face lawsuits for false imprisonment if they detain individuals without reason. ■ **CASE IN POINT 6.4** Police arrested Adetokunbo Shoyoye for riding the subway without a ticket and for a theft that had been committed by someone who had stolen his identity. A court ordered him to be released, but a county employee mistakenly confused Shoyoye's paperwork with that of another person who was scheduled to be sent to state prison. As a result, instead of being released, Shoyoye was held in county jail for more than two weeks. Shoyoye later sued the county for false imprisonment and won.[4] ■

6–2d Intentional Infliction of Emotional Distress

The tort of *intentional infliction of emotional distress* involves an intentional act that amounts to extreme and outrageous conduct resulting in severe emotional distress to another. To be **actionable** (capable of serving as the ground for a lawsuit), the act must be extreme and outrageous to the point that it exceeds the bounds of decency accepted by society.

Outrageous Conduct Courts in most jurisdictions are wary of emotional distress claims and confine them to situations involving truly outrageous behavior. Generally, repeated annoyances (such as those experienced by a person who is being stalked), coupled with threats, are enough. Acts that cause indignity or annoyance alone usually are not sufficient.

■ **EXAMPLE 6.5** A father attacks a man who has had consensual sexual relations with the father's nineteen-year-old daughter. The father handcuffs the man to a steel pole and threatens to kill him unless he leaves town immediately. The father's conduct may be sufficiently extreme and outrageous to be actionable as an intentional infliction of emotional distress. ■

Limited by the First Amendment When the outrageous conduct consists of speech about a public figure,

---

3. The *reasonable person standard* is an "objective" test of how a reasonable person would have acted under the same circumstances. See "The Duty of Care and Its Breach" later in this chapter.

4. *Shoyoye v. County of Los Angeles,* 203 Cal.App.4th 947, 137 Cal.Rptr.3d 839 (2012).

the First Amendment's guarantee of freedom of speech also limits emotional distress claims.

■ **CASE IN POINT 6.6** *Hustler* magazine once printed a false advertisement that showed a picture of the late Reverend Jerry Falwell and described him as having lost his virginity to his mother in an outhouse while he was drunk. Falwell sued the magazine for intentional infliction of emotional distress and won, but the United States Supreme Court overturned the decision. The Court held that parodies of public figures are protected under the First Amendment from intentional infliction of emotional distress claims. (The Court uses the same standards that apply to public figures in defamation lawsuits, discussed next.)[5] ■

6–2e Defamation

The freedom of speech guaranteed by the First Amendment is not absolute. The courts are required to balance the vital guarantee of free speech against other pervasive and strong social interests, including society's interest in preventing and redressing attacks on reputation.

Defamation of character involves wrongfully hurting a person's good reputation. The law imposes a general duty on all persons to refrain from making false, defamatory *statements of fact* about others. Breaching this duty in writing or other permanent form (such as a digital recording) involves the tort of **libel.** Breaching this duty orally involves the tort of **slander.** The tort of defamation also arises when a false statement of fact is made about a person's product, business, or legal ownership rights to property.

Establishing defamation involves proving the following elements:

1. The defendant made a false statement of fact.
2. The statement was understood as being about the plaintiff and tended to harm the plaintiff's reputation.
3. The statement was published to at least one person other than the plaintiff.
4. If the plaintiff is a public figure, she or he must also prove *actual malice,* discussed later in the chapter.

The following case involved the application of free speech guarantees to online reviews of professional services.

---

5. *Hustler Magazine, Inc. v. Falwell*, 485 U.S. 46, 108 S.Ct. 876, 99 L.Ed.2d 41 (1988). For another example of how the courts protect parody, see *Busch v. Viacom International, Inc.*, 477 F.Supp.2d 764 (N.D.Tex. 2007), involving a false endorsement of televangelist Pat Robertson's diet shake.

Case Analysis 6.1

Blake v. Giustibelli

District Court of Appeal of Florida, Fourth District, 182 So.3d 881, 41 Fla.L.Weekly D122 (2016).

In the Language of the Court

CIKLIN, C.J. [Chief Judge]

* * * *

[Ann-Marie] Giustibelli represented Copia Blake in a dissolution of marriage proceeding brought against Peter Birzon. After a breakdown in the attorney-client relationship between Giustibelli and her client[,] Blake, and oddly, Birzon as well, took to the Internet to post defamatory reviews of Giustibelli. In response, Giustibelli brought suit [in a Florida state court against Blake and Birzon], pleading a count for libel.

Blake's and Birzon's posted Internet reviews contained the following statements:

This lawyer represented me in my divorce. She was combative and explosive and took my divorce to a level of anger which caused major suffering of my minor children. She insisted I was an emotionally abused wife who couldn't make rational decisions which caused my case to drag on in the system for a year and a half so her FEES would continue to multiply!! She misrepresented her fees with regards to the contract I initially signed. The contract she submitted to the courts for her fees were 4 times her original quote and pages of the original had been exchanged to support her claims, only the signature page was the same. Shame on me that I did not have an original copy, but like an idiot * * * I trusted my lawyer. Don't mistake sincerity for honesty because I assure you, that in this attorney's case, they are NOT the same thing. She absolutely perpetuates the horrible image of attorneys who are only out for the money and themselves. Although I know this isn't the case and there are some very good honest lawyers out there, Mrs. Giustibelli is simply not one of the "good ones." Horrible horrible experience. Use anyone else, it would have to be a better result.

* * * *

No integrity. Will say one thing and do another. Her fees outweigh the truth. Altered her charges to 4 times the original quote with no explanation. Do not use her. Don't mistake sincerity for honesty. In her case, they're not at all the same. Will literally lie to your face if it means more money for her. Get someone else.

Case 6.1 Continues

*** Anyone else would do a superior effort for you.

****

I accepted an initial VERY fair offer from my ex. Mrs. Giustibelli convinced me to "crush" him and that I could have permanent etc. Spent over a year (and 4 times her original estimate) to arrive at the same place we started at. Caused unnecessary chaos and fear with my kids, convinced me that my ex cheated (which he didn't), that he was hiding money (which he wasn't), and was mad at ME when I realized her fee circus had gone on long enough and finally said "stop." Altered her fee structures, actually replaced original documents with others to support her charges and generally gave the kind of poor service you only hear about. I'm not a disgruntled

ex-wife. I'm just the foolish person who believes that a person's word should be backed by integrity. Not even remotely true in this case. I've had 2 prior attorneys and never ever have I seen ego and monies be so blatantly out of control.

Both Blake and Birzon admitted to posting the reviews on various Internet sites. The evidence showed that Blake had agreed to pay her attorney the amount reflected on the written retainer agreement—$300 an hour. Blake and Birzon both admitted at trial that Giustibelli had not charged Blake four times more than what was quoted in the agreement. The court entered judgment in favor of Giustibelli and awarded punitive damages of $350,000.

On appeal, Blake and Birzon argue that their Internet reviews constituted

statements of opinion and thus were protected by the First Amendment and not actionable as defamation. We disagree. *An action for libel will lie for a false and unprivileged publication by letter, or otherwise, which exposes a person to distrust, hatred, contempt, ridicule or obloquy [censure or disgrace] or which causes such person to be avoided, or which has a tendency to injure such person in their office, occupation, business or employment.* [Emphasis added.]

Here, all the reviews contained allegations that Giustibelli lied to Blake regarding the attorney's fee. Two of the reviews contained the allegation that Giustibelli falsified a contract. These are factual allegations, and the evidence showed they were false.

****

Affirmed.

Legal Reasoning Questions

1. What is the standard for the protection of free speech guaranteed by the First Amendment?

2. How did this standard apply to the statements posted online by Blake and Birzon?

3. The First Amendment normally protects statements of opinion, and this can be an effective defense against a charge of defamation. Does it seem reasonable to disregard this defense, however, if *any* assertion of fact within a statement of opinion is false? Explain.

Statement-of-Fact Requirement Often at issue in defamation lawsuits (including online defamation) is whether the defendant made a statement of fact or a *statement of opinion*. Statements of opinion normally are not actionable, because they are protected under the First Amendment.

In other words, making a negative statement about another person is not defamation unless the statement is false and represents something as a fact rather than a personal opinion. ■ **EXAMPLE 6.7** The statement "Lane cheats on his taxes," if false, can lead to liability for defamation. The statement "Lane is a jerk" cannot constitute defamation because it is clearly an opinion. ■

The Publication Requirement The basis of the tort of defamation is the publication of a statement or statements that hold an individual up to contempt, ridicule, or

hatred. *Publication* here means that the defamatory statements are communicated (either intentionally or accidentally) to persons other than the defamed party.

The courts have generally held that even dictating a letter to a secretary constitutes publication, although the publication may be privileged (a concept that will be explained shortly). Moreover, if a third party merely overhears defamatory statements by chance, the courts usually hold that this also constitutes publication. Defamatory statements made via the Internet are actionable as well. Note also that any individual who repeats or republishes defamatory statements normally is liable even if that person reveals the source of the statements.

■ **CASE IN POINT 6.8** Eddy Ramirez, a meat cutter at Costco Wholesale Corporation, was involved in a workplace incident with a coworker, and Costco gave him a notice of suspension. After an investigation in which coworkers were interviewed, Costco fired Ramirez. Ramirez sued, claiming that the suspension notice was defamatory. The court ruled in Costco's favor. Ramirez could not establish defamation, because he had not shown that the suspension notice was published to any third parties. Costco did nothing beyond what was necessary to investigate the events that led to Ramirez's termination.[6] ∎

Damages for Libel Once a defendant's liability for libel is established, general damages are presumed as a matter of law. General damages are designed to compensate the plaintiff for nonspecific harms such as disgrace or dishonor in the eyes of the community, humiliation, injured reputation, and emotional distress—harms that are difficult to measure. In other words, to recover damages, the plaintiff need not prove that he or she was actually harmed in any specific way as a result of the libelous statement.

Damages for Slander In contrast to cases alleging libel, in a case alleging slander, the plaintiff must prove *special damages* to establish the defendant's liability. The plaintiff must show that the slanderous statement caused her or him to suffer actual economic or monetary losses.

Unless this initial hurdle of proving special damages is overcome, a plaintiff alleging slander normally cannot go forward with the suit and recover any damages. This requirement is imposed in slander cases because oral statements have a temporary quality. In contrast, a libelous (written) statement has the quality of permanence and can be circulated widely, especially through tweets and blogs. Also, libel usually results from some degree of deliberation by the author.

Slander *Per Se* Exceptions to the burden of proving special damages in cases alleging slander are made for certain types of slanderous statements. If a false statement constitutes "slander *per se*," it is actionable with no proof of special damages required. In most states, the following four types of declarations are considered to be slander *per se:*

1. A statement that another has a "loathsome" disease (such as a sexually transmitted disease).
2. A statement that another has committed improprieties while engaging in a profession or trade.
3. A statement that another has committed or has been imprisoned for a serious crime.

4. A statement that a person is unchaste or has engaged in serious sexual misconduct. (This usually applies only to unmarried persons and sometimes only to women.)

Defenses to Defamation Truth is normally an absolute defense against a defamation charge. In other words, if a defendant in a defamation case can prove that the allegedly defamatory statements of fact were true, normally no tort has been committed.

∎ **CASE IN POINT 6.9** David McKee, a neurologist, went to examine a patient who had been transferred from the intensive care unit (ICU) to a private room. In the room were family members of the patient, including his son. The patient's son later made the following post on a "rate your doctor" Web site: "[Dr. McKee] seemed upset that my father had been moved [into a private room]. Never having met my father or his family, Dr. McKee said 'When you weren't in ICU, I had to spend time finding out if you transferred or died.' When we gaped at him, he said 'Well, 44 percent of hemorrhagic strokes die within 30 days. I guess this is the better option.'"

McKee filed suit for defamation but lost. The court found that all the statements made by the son were essentially true, and truth is a complete defense to a defamation action.[7] ∎ In other words, true statements are not actionable no matter how disparaging. Even the presence of minor inaccuracies of expression or detail does not render basically true statements false.

Other defenses to defamation may exist if the speech is privileged or if it concerns a public figure. We discuss these defenses next. Note that the majority of defamation actions are filed in state courts, and state laws differ somewhat in the defenses they allow.

Privileged Communications. In some circumstances, a person will not be liable for defamatory statements because she or he enjoys a **privilege,** or immunity. Privileged communications are of two types: absolute and qualified.[8] Only in judicial proceedings and certain government proceedings is an *absolute privilege* granted. Thus, statements made by attorneys and judges in the courtroom during a trial are absolutely privileged, as are statements made by government officials during legislative debate.

---

6. *Ramirez v. Costco Wholesale Corp.,* 2014 WL 2696737 (Ct.Sup.Ct. 2014).

7. *McKee v. Laurion,* 825 N.W.2d 725 (Minn.Sup. 2013).
8. Note that the term *privileged communication* in this context is not the same as privileged communication between a professional, such as an attorney, and his or her client.

In other situations, a person will not be liable for defamatory statements because he or she has a *qualified, or conditional, privilege.* An employer's statements in written evaluations of employees, for instance, are protected by a qualified privilege. Generally, if the statements are made in good faith and the publication is limited to those who have a legitimate interest in the communication, the statements fall within the area of qualified privilege.

■ **EXAMPLE 6.10** Jorge has worked at Google for five years and is being considered for a management position. His supervisor, Lydia, writes a memo about Jorge's performance to those evaluating him for the position. The memo contains certain negative statements, which Lydia honestly believes are true. If Lydia limits the disclosure of the memo to company representatives, her statements will likely be protected by a qualified privilege. ■

Public Figures. Politicians, entertainers, professional athletes, and others in the public eye are considered **public figures.** Public figures are regarded as "fair game." False and defamatory statements about public figures that are published in the media will not constitute defamation unless the statements are made with **actual malice.**[9] To be made with actual malice, a statement must be made *with either knowledge of its falsity or a reckless disregard of the truth.*

Statements made about public figures, especially when they are communicated via a public medium, usually relate to matters of general interest. They are made about people who substantially affect all of us. Furthermore, public figures generally have some access to a public medium for answering belittling falsehoods about themselves. For these reasons, public figures have a greater burden of proof in defamation cases—to show actual malice—than do private individuals.

■ **CASE IN POINT 6.11** *In Touch* magazine published a story about a former call girl who claimed to have slept with legendary soccer player David Beckham more than once. Beckham sued *In Touch* magazine for libel, seeking $25 million in damages. He said that he had never met the woman, had not cheated on his wife with her, and had not paid her for sex. After months of litigation, a federal district court dismissed the case because Beckham could not show that the magazine had acted with actual malice. Whether or not the statements in the article were accurate, there was no evidence that the defendants had made the statements with knowledge of their falsity or reckless disregard for the truth.[10] ■

---

9. *New York Times Co. v. Sullivan,* 376 U.S. 254, 84 S.Ct. 710, 11 L.Ed.2d 686 (1964).

10. *Beckham v. Bauer Pub. Co., L.P.,* 2011 WL 977570 (2011).

6–2f Invasion of Privacy

A person has a right to solitude and freedom from prying public eyes—in other words, to privacy. The courts have held that certain amendments to the U.S. Constitution imply a right to privacy. Some state constitutions explicitly provide for privacy rights, as do a number of federal and state statutes.

Tort law also safeguards these rights through the tort of *invasion of privacy.* Generally, to sue successfully for an invasion of privacy, a person must have a reasonable expectation of privacy, and the invasion must be highly offensive. (See this chapter's *Digital Update* feature for a discussion of how invasion of privacy claims can arise when someone posts pictures or videos taken with digital devices.)

Invasion of Privacy under the Common Law

The following four acts qualify as an invasion of privacy under the common law:

1. *Intrusion into an individual's affairs or seclusion.* Invading someone's home or searching someone's briefcase or laptop without authorization is an invasion of privacy. This tort has been held to extend to eavesdropping by wiretap, unauthorized scanning of a bank account, compulsory blood testing, and window peeping. ■ **EXAMPLE 6.12** A female sports reporter for ESPN is digitally videoed while naked through the peephole in the door of her hotel room. She will probably win a lawsuit against the man who took the video and posted it on the Internet. ■

2. *False light.* Publication of information that places a person in a false light is also an invasion of privacy. For instance, writing a story that attributes to a person ideas and opinions not held by that person is an invasion of privacy. (Publishing such a story could involve the tort of defamation as well.) ■ **EXAMPLE 6.13** An Iowa newspaper prints an article saying that nineteen-year-old Yassine Alam is part of the terrorist organization Islamic State of Iraq (ISIL). Next to the article is a photo of Yassine's brother, Salaheddin. Salaheddin can sue the paper for putting him in a false light by using his photo. If the report is not true, and Yassine is not involved with ISIL, Yassine can sue the paper for defamation. ■

3. *Public disclosure of private facts.* This type of invasion of privacy occurs when a person publicly discloses private facts about an individual that an ordinary person would find objectionable or embarrassing. A newspaper account of a private citizen's sex life or financial affairs could be an actionable invasion of

DIGITAL UPDATE   Revenge Porn and Invasion of Privacy

Nearly every digital device today takes photos and videos at virtually no cost. Software allows the recording of conversations via Skype. Many couples immortalize their "private moments" using such digital devices. One partner may take a racy selfie and send it as an attachment to a text message to the other partner, for example.

Occasionally, after a couple breaks off their relationship, one of them seeks a type of digital revenge. The result, called revenge porn, has been defined in the Cyber Civil Rights Initiative as "the online distribution of sexually explicit images of a non-consenting individual with the intent to humiliate that person."

Until relatively recently, few states had criminal statutes that covered revenge porn. Therefore, victims have sued on the basis of (1) invasion of privacy, (2) public disclosure of private facts, and (3) intentional infliction of emotional distress.

It Is More Than Just Pictures and Videos

Perhaps the worst form of revenge porn occurs when the perpetrator provides detailed information about the victim. Such information may include the victim's name, Facebook page, address, and phone number, as well as the victim's workplace and children's names. This information, along with the sexually explicit photos and videos, are posted on hosting Web sites. Many such Web sites have been shut down, as was the case with IsAnybodyDown? and Texxxan.com. But others are still active, usually with offshore servers and foreign domain name owners.

The Injurious Results of Revenge Porn

Of course, victims of revenge porn suffer extreme embarrassment. They may also have their reputations ruined. Some have lost their jobs. Others have been unable to obtain jobs because employers have seen their pictures online. A number of victims have been stalked in the physical world and harassed online and offline. When attempts to have offending photos removed from Web sites have failed, victims have changed their phone numbers and sometimes their names.

A Class-Action Lawsuit

Hollie Toups, along with twenty-two other female plaintiffs, sued the domain name registrar and Web hosting company GoDaddy in a Texas court. Although GoDaddy did not create the defamatory and offensive material at issue, GoDaddy knew of the content and did not remove it. The plaintiffs asserted causes of action "for intentional infliction of emotional distress," among other claims.

Additionally, the plaintiffs argued that "by its knowing participation in these unlawful activities, GoDaddy has also committed the intentional Texas tort of invasion of privacy . . . as well as intrusion on Plaintiffs' right to seclusion, the public disclosure of their private facts, [and] the wrongful appropriation of their names and likenesses. . . ." GoDaddy sought to dismiss the case, and an appeals court eventually granted the motion to dismiss.[a]

Another Texas woman had better luck. The woman's ex-boyfriend had uploaded videos of her to YouTube and other sites. At the time she made the complaint, revenge porn was not a crime in Texas. Nevertheless, in a jury trial in 2014, she won a $500,000 award. Since then, a handful of states have made revenge porn a crime. In 2015, a California man, Kevin Bollaert, was convicted for creating a revenge porn Web site and sentenced to serve eighteen years in prison.

Critical Thinking *Should domain name hosting companies be liable for revenge porn?*

a. *GoDaddy.com, LLC. v. Toups*, 429 S.W.3d 752 (Tex.App.—Beaumont 2014).

privacy. This is so even if the information revealed is true, because it should not be a matter of public concern.

4. *Appropriation of identity.* Using a person's name, picture, likeness, or other identifiable characteristic for commercial purposes without permission is also an invasion of privacy. An individual's right to privacy normally includes the right to the exclusive use of her or his identity. ■ **EXAMPLE 6.14** An advertising agency asks a singer with a distinctive voice and stage presence to take part in a marketing campaign for a new automobile. The singer rejects the offer. If the

agency then uses someone who imitates the singer's voice and dance moves in the ad, it will be actionable as an appropriation of identity. ■

Appropriation Statutes Most states today have codified the common law tort of appropriation of identity in statutes that establish the distinct tort of appropriation, or right of publicity. States differ as to the degree of likeness that is required to impose liability for appropriation, however.

Some courts have held that even when an animated character in a video or a video game is made to look like an actual person, there are not enough similarities to constitute appropriation. ■ **CASE IN POINT 6.15** Robert Burck is a street entertainer in New York City who has become famous as "The Naked Cowboy." Burck performs wearing only a white cowboy hat, white cowboy boots, and white underwear. He carries a guitar strategically placed to give the illusion of nudity. Burck sued Mars, Inc., the maker of M&Ms candy, over a video it showed on billboards in Times Square that depicted a blue M&M dressed exactly like The Naked Cowboy. The court, however, held that the use of Burck's signature costume did not amount to appropriation.[11] ■

---
11. *Burck v. Mars, Inc.*, 571 F.Supp.2d 446 (S.D.N.Y. 2008).

6–2g Fraudulent Misrepresentation

A misrepresentation leads another to believe in a condition that is different from the condition that actually exists. Although persons sometimes make misrepresentations accidentally because they are unaware of the existing facts, the tort of **fraudulent misrepresentation (fraud),** involves *intentional* deceit for personal gain. The tort includes several elements:

1. A misrepresentation of material facts or conditions with knowledge that they are false or with reckless disregard for the truth.
2. An intent to induce another party to rely on the misrepresentation.
3. A justifiable reliance on the misrepresentation by the deceived party.
4. Damages suffered as a result of that reliance.
5. A causal connection between the misrepresentation and the injury suffered.

For fraud to occur, more than mere **puffery,** or *seller's talk,* must be involved. Fraud exists only when a person represents as a fact something he or she knows is untrue. For instance, it is fraud to claim that the roof of a building does not leak when one knows that it does. Facts are objectively ascertainable, whereas seller's talk (such as "I am the best accountant in town") is not, because the use of the word *best* is subjective.

In the following case, the court considered each of the elements of fraud.

Case 6.2

Revell v. Guido

New York Supreme Court, Appellate Division, Third Department, 124 A.D.3d 1006, 2 N.Y.S.3d 252 (2015).

Background and Facts Joseph Guido bought a parcel of land in Stillwater, New York, that contained nine rental houses. The houses shared a waste disposal system that was defective. Guido had a new septic system installed. When town officials discovered sewage on the property, Guido had the system partially replaced. Prospective buyers, including Danny Revell, were given a property information sheet that stated, "Septic system totally new—each field totally replaced." In response to a questionnaire from the buyers' bank, Guido denied any knowledge of environmental problems.

A month after the buyers bought the houses, the septic system failed and required substantial repairs. The lender foreclosed on the property. The buyers filed a suit in a New York state court against Guido and his firm, Real Property Solutions, LLC, alleging fraud. A jury found fraud and awarded damages. The court issued a judgment in the plaintiffs' favor. The defendants appealed.

In the Language of the Court

EGAN, Jr., J: [Judge:]
* * * *

To prevail upon their cause of action for fraud, plaintiffs were required to establish that defendants, with the intent to deceive, misrepresented or omitted a material fact that they knew to be false and that plaintiffs,

Case 6.2 Continued

in turn, justifiably relied upon such misrepresentation or omission, thereby incurring damages. As to the misrepresentation element, plaintiffs point to the statement made on the property information sheet * * *, as well as Guido's responses to certain of the inquiries contained on the environmental questionnaire. In this regard, the record reflects that the [replacement] septic system * * * was not "totally new," as it retained the original pump house structure and, more to the point, utilized the holding tanks that originally were part of the system * * *. There also is no question that Guido provided false answers to various inquiries posed on the environmental questionnaire. For example, Guido disavowed any knowledge of "governmental notification relating to past or recurrent violations of environmental laws with respect to the property * * *"—despite having been advised by the Town of Stillwater * * * that partially treated sewage was discovered on the property. [Emphasis added.]

As to the intent element, * * * given the arguably cavalier [offhand] manner in which Guido completed the environmental questionnaire, as well as his extensive knowledge regarding the * * * problems with the original septic system * * *, the jury could properly find that Guido made the cited misrepresentations with the intent to deceive plaintiffs.

With respect to the issue of justifiable reliance, Revell * * * conducted a visual inspection of the property prior to making an offer and did not observe any conditions indicative of a problem with the septic system. * * * If a septic system was represented to be "totally new" and a visual inspection of the property did not reveal any red flags, [that is,] boggy areas, odors or liquids bubbling up to the surface, one would assume that the system was working properly. * * * The jury [could] find that plaintiffs' reliance upon the representation contained in the property information sheet was reasonable.

* * * *

Nor are we persuaded that plaintiffs failed to tender sufficient admissible proof to substantiate the damages awarded by the jury. During the trial, the parties stipulated to the admission into evidence of a binder containing, among other things, an abundance of receipts, invoices, billing statements and canceled checks detailing plaintiffs' expenditures related to the subject property—and plaintiffs' forensic accountant, in turn, utilized such documents to arrive at a damages figure. * * * We are satisfied that plaintiffs tendered sufficient admissible proof to sustain the damages awarded by the jury.

Decision and Remedy   *The state intermediate appellate court affirmed the lower court's judgment in the plaintiffs' favor. The facts of the case and the plaintiffs' proof met all of the requirements for establishing fraud.*

Critical Thinking

- **Legal Environment**   *Financing for the purchase of the property was conditioned on the bank's review of Guido's answers to the environmental questionnaire. How could the court conclude that the plaintiffs justifiably relied on misrepresentations made to the bank? Explain.*
- **What If the Facts Were Different?**   *If a visual inspection of the property had revealed "boggy areas, odors or liquids bubbling up to the surface" indicating that the septic system was not working properly, would the outcome of this case have been different?*

Statement of Fact versus Opinion   Normally, the tort of fraudulent misrepresentation occurs only when there is reliance on a *statement of fact*. Sometimes, however, reliance on a *statement of opinion* may involve the tort of fraudulent misrepresentation if the individual making the statement of opinion has superior knowledge of the subject matter. For instance, when a lawyer makes a statement of opinion about the law in a state in which the lawyer is licensed to practice, a court might treat it as a statement of fact.

Negligent Misrepresentation   Sometimes, a tort action can arise from misrepresentations that are made negligently rather than intentionally. The key difference between intentional and negligent misrepresentation is whether the person making the misrepresentation had actual knowledge of its falsity. Negligent misrepresentation requires only that the person making the statement or omission did not have a reasonable basis for believing its truthfulness.

Liability for negligent misrepresentation usually arises when the defendant who made the misrepresentation owed a duty of care to the plaintiff to supply correct information. (We discuss the duty of care in more detail later in the chapter.) Statements or omissions made by attorneys and accountants to their clients, for instance, can lead to liability for negligent misrepresentation.

6–2h Abusive or Frivolous Litigation

Tort law recognizes that people have a right not to be sued without a legally just and proper reason, and therefore it protects individuals from the misuse of litigation. Torts related to abusive litigation include malicious prosecution and abuse of process. If a party initiates a lawsuit out of malice and without a legitimate legal reason, and ends up losing the suit, that party can be sued for *malicious prosecution*. *Abuse of process* can apply to any person using a legal process against another in an improper manner or to accomplish a purpose for which the process was not designed.

The key difference between the torts of abuse of process and malicious prosecution is the level of proof. Unlike malicious prosecution, abuse of process is not limited to prior litigation and does not require the plaintiff to prove malice. It can be based on the wrongful use of subpoenas, court orders to attach or seize real property, or other types of formal legal process.

Concept Summary 6.1 reviews intentional torts against persons.

Concept Summary 6.1

Intentional Torts against Persons

Assault and Battery	Any unexcused and intentional act that causes another person to be apprehensive of immediate harm is an assault. An assault resulting in physical contact is a battery.
False Imprisonment	An intentional confinement or restraint of another person's movement without justification.
Intentional Infliction of Emotional Distress	An intentional act that amounts to extreme and outrageous conduct resulting in severe emotional distress to another.
Defamation (Libel or Slander)	A false statement of fact, not made under privilege, that is communicated to a third person and that causes damage to a person's reputation. For public figures, the plaintiff must also prove that the statement was made with actual malice.
Invasion of Privacy	Publishing or otherwise making known or using information relating to a person's private life and affairs, with which the public has no legitimate concern, without that person's permission or approval.
Fraudulent Misrepresentation (Fraud)	A false representation made by one party, through misstatement of facts or through conduct, with the intention of deceiving another and on which the other reasonably relies to his or her detriment.
Abusive or Frivolous Litigation	The filing of a lawsuit without legitimate grounds and with malice. Alternatively, the use of a legal process in an improper manner.

6-2i Wrongful Interference

The torts known as *business torts* generally involve wrongful interference with another's business rights. Public policy favors free competition, and these torts protect against tortious interference with legitimate business. Business torts involving wrongful interference generally fall into two categories: interference with a contractual relationship and interference with a business relationship.

Wrongful Interference with a Contractual Relationship Three elements are necessary for wrongful interference with a contractual relationship to occur:

1. A valid, enforceable contract must exist between two parties.
2. A third party must know that this contract exists.
3. This third party must *intentionally induce* a party to the contract to breach the contract.

■ **CASE IN POINT 6.16** A landmark case in this area involved an opera singer, Joanna Wagner, who was under contract to sing for a man named Lumley for a specified period of years. A man named Gye, who knew of this contract, nonetheless "enticed" Wagner to refuse to carry out the agreement, and Wagner began to sing for Gye. Gye's action constituted a tort because it interfered with the contractual relationship between Wagner and Lumley. (Wagner's refusal to carry out the agreement also entitled Lumley to sue Wagner for breach of contract.)[12] ■

The body of tort law relating to wrongful interference with a contractual relationship has increased greatly in recent years. In principle, any lawful contract can be the basis for an action of this type. The contract could be between a firm and its employees or a firm and its customers. Sometimes, a competitor of a firm lures away one of the firm's key employees. In this situation, the original employer can recover damages from the competitor only if it can be shown that the competitor knew of the contract's existence and intentionally induced the breach.

Wrongful Interference with a Business Relationship Businesspersons devise countless schemes to attract customers. They are prohibited, however, from unreasonably interfering with another's business in their attempts to gain a greater share of the market.

There is a difference between *competitive practices* and *predatory behavior*—actions undertaken with the intention of unlawfully driving competitors completely out of the market. Attempting to attract customers in general is a legitimate business practice, whereas specifically

targeting the customers of a competitor is more likely to be predatory. A plaintiff claiming predatory behavior must show that the defendant used predatory methods to intentionally harm an established business relationship or gain a prospective economic advantage.

■ **EXAMPLE 6.17** A shopping mall contains two athletic shoe stores: Joe's and Ultimate Sport. Joe's cannot station an employee at the entrance of Ultimate Sport's to divert customers to Joe's by telling them that Joe's will beat Ultimate Sport's prices. This type of activity constitutes the tort of wrongful interference with a business relationship, which is commonly considered to be an unfair trade practice. If this activity were permitted, Joe's would reap the benefits of Ultimate Sport's advertising. ■

Defenses to Wrongful Interference A person will not be liable for the tort of wrongful interference with a contractual or business relationship if it can be shown that the interference was justified or permissible. Bona fide competitive behavior—such as marketing and advertising strategies—is a permissible interference even if it results in the breaking of a contract.

■ **EXAMPLE 6.18** Taylor Meats advertises so effectively that it induces Sam's Restaurant to break its contract with Burke's Meat Company. In that situation, Burke's Meat Company will be unable to recover against Taylor Meats on a wrongful interference theory. The public policy that favors free competition through advertising outweighs any possible instability that such competitive activity might cause in contractual relations. ■

6–3 Intentional Torts against Property

Intentional torts against property include trespass to land, trespass to personal property, conversion, and disparagement of property. These torts are wrongful actions that interfere with individuals' legally recognized rights with regard to their land or personal property.

The law distinguishes real property from personal property. *Real property* is land and things permanently attached to the land, such as a house. *Personal property* consists of all other items, including cash and securities (such as stocks and bonds).

6–3a Trespass to Land

A **trespass to land** occurs when a person, without permission, does any of the following:

---

12. *Lumley v. Gye*, 118 Eng.Rep. 749 (1853).

1. Enters onto, above, or below the surface of land that is owned by another.
2. Causes anything to enter onto land owned by another.
3. Remains on land owned by another or permits anything to remain on it.

Actual harm to the land is not an essential element of this tort, because the tort is designed to protect the right of an owner to exclusive possession.

Common types of trespass to land include walking or driving on another's land, shooting a gun over another's land, and throwing rocks at a building that belongs to someone else. Another common form of trespass involves constructing a building so that part of it extends onto an adjoining landowner's property.

Establishing Trespass Before a person can be a trespasser, the real property owner (or another person in actual and exclusive possession of the property, such as a renter) must establish that person as a trespasser. For instance, "posted" trespass signs expressly establish as a trespasser a person who ignores these signs and enters onto the property. A guest in your home is not a trespasser, unless he or she has been asked to leave and refuses. Any person who enters onto another's property to commit an illegal act (such as a thief entering a lumberyard at night to steal lumber) is impliedly a trespasser, with or without posted signs.

Liability for Harm At common law, a trespasser is liable for any damage caused to the property and generally cannot hold the owner liable for injuries that the trespasser sustains on the premises. This common law rule is being modified in many jurisdictions, however, in favor of a *reasonable duty of care* rule that varies depending on the status of the parties.

For instance, a landowner may have a duty to post a notice that guard dogs patrol the property. Also, if young children are attracted to the property by some object, such a swimming pool or a sand pile, and are injured, the landowner may be held liable (under the *attractive nuisance doctrine*). Still, an owner can normally use reasonable force to remove a trespasser from the premises or detain the trespasser for a reasonable time without liability for damages.

Defenses against Trespass to Land One defense to a claim of trespass is to show that the trespass was warranted, such as when a trespasser enters a building to assist someone in danger. Another defense exists when the trespasser can show that she or he had a *license* to come onto the land.

A **licensee** is one who is invited (or allowed to enter) onto the property of another for the licensee's benefit. A person who enters another's property to read an electric meter, for example, is a licensee. When you purchase a ticket to attend a movie or sporting event, you are licensed to go onto the property of another to view that movie or event.

Note that licenses to enter onto another's property are *revocable* by the property owner. If a property owner asks an electric meter reader to leave and she or he refuses to do so, the meter reader at that point becomes a trespasser.

6–3b Trespass to Personal Property

Whenever any individual wrongfully takes or harms the personal property of another or otherwise interferes with the lawful owner's possession and enjoyment of personal property, **trespass to personal property** occurs. This tort may also be called *trespass to chattels* or *trespass to personalty.*[13] In this context, harm means not only destruction of the property, but also anything that diminishes its value, condition, or quality.

Trespass to personal property involves intentional meddling with a possessory interest (one arising from possession), including barring an owner's access to personal property. ■ **EXAMPLE 6.19** Kelly takes Ryan's business law book as a practical joke and hides it so that Ryan is unable to find it for several days before the final examination. Here, Kelly has engaged in a trespass to personal property (and also *conversion,* the tort discussed next). ■

If it can be shown that trespass to personal property was warranted, then a complete defense exists. Most states, for instance, allow automobile repair shops to hold a customer's car (under what is called an *artisan's lien*) when the customer refuses to pay for repairs already completed.

6–3c Conversion

Any act that deprives an owner of personal property or of the use of that property without the owner's permission and without just cause can constitute **conversion.** Even the taking of electronic records and data may form the basis of a conversion claim. Often, when conversion occurs, a trespass to personal property also occurs. The original taking of the personal property from the owner was a trespass. Wrongfully retaining the property is conversion.

---

13. Pronounced *per-sun-ul-tee.*

Failure to Return Goods   Conversion is the civil side of crimes related to theft, but it is not limited to theft. Even when the rightful owner consented to the initial taking of the property, so no theft or trespass occurred, a failure to return the property may still be conversion.   ■ **EXAMPLE 6.20**   Chen borrows Mark's iPad mini to use while traveling home from school for the holidays. When Chen returns to school, Mark asks for his iPad back, but Chen says that he gave it to his little brother for Christmas. In this situation, Mark can sue Chen for conversion, and Chen will have to either return the iPad or pay damages equal to its replacement value. ■

Intention   Conversion can occur even when a person mistakenly believed that she or he was entitled to the goods. In other words, good intentions are not a defense against conversion. Someone who buys stolen goods, for instance, may be sued for conversion even if he or she did not know the goods were stolen. If the true owner of the goods sues the buyer, the buyer must either return the property to the owner or pay the owner the full value of the property.

Conversion can also occur from an employee's unauthorized use of a credit card.   ■ **CASE IN POINT 6.21**   Nicholas Mora worked for Welco Electronics, Inc., but had also established his own company, AQM Supplies. Mora used Welco's credit card without permission and deposited more than $375,000 into AQM's account, which he then transferred to his personal account. Welco sued. A California court held that Mora was liable for conversion. The court reasoned that when Mora misappropriated Welco's credit card and used it, he took part of Welco's credit balance with the credit-card company.[14] ■

6-3d Disparagement of Property

Disparagement of property occurs when economically injurious falsehoods are made about another's product or property rather than about another's reputation (as in the tort of defamation). *Disparagement of property* is a general term for torts that can be more specifically referred to as *slander of quality* or *slander of title.*

Slander of Quality   The publication of false information about another's product, alleging that it is not what its seller claims, constitutes the tort of **slander of quality,** or **trade libel.** To establish trade libel, the plaintiff must prove that the improper publication caused a third

person to refrain from dealing with the plaintiff and that the plaintiff sustained economic damages (such as lost profits) as a result.

An improper publication may be both a slander of quality and a defamation of character. For instance, a statement that disparages the quality of a product may also, by implication, disparage the character of a person who would sell such a product.

Slander of Title   When a publication falsely denies or casts doubt on another's legal ownership of property, resulting in financial loss to the property's owner, the tort of **slander of title** occurs. Usually, this is an intentional tort in which someone knowingly publishes an untrue statement about another's ownership of certain property with the intent of discouraging a third person from dealing with the person slandered. For instance, it would be difficult for a car dealer to attract customers after competitors published a notice that the dealer's stock consisted of stolen automobiles.

See Concept Summary 6.2 for a review of intentional torts against property.

6-4 Unintentional Torts—Negligence

The tort of **negligence** occurs when someone suffers injury because of another's failure to live up to a required *duty of care.* In contrast to intentional torts, in torts involving negligence, the tortfeasor neither wishes to bring about the consequences of the act nor believes that they will occur. The person's conduct merely creates a risk of such consequences. If no risk is created, there is no negligence.

Moreover, the risk must be foreseeable. In other words, it must be such that a reasonable person engaging in the same activity would anticipate the risk and guard against it. In determining what is reasonable conduct, courts consider the nature of the possible harm.

Many of the actions giving rise to the intentional torts discussed earlier in the chapter constitute negligence if the element of intent is missing (or cannot be proved).   ■ **EXAMPLE 6.22**   Juan walks up to Maya and intentionally shoves her. Maya falls and breaks her arm as a result. In this situation, Juan is liable for the intentional tort of battery. If Juan carelessly bumps into Maya, however, and she falls and breaks her arm as a result, Juan's action constitutes negligence. In either situation, Juan has committed a tort. ■

---

14. *Welco Electronics, Inc. v. Mora,* 223 Cal.App.4th 202, 166 Cal.Rptr.3d 877 (2014).

Concept Summary 6.2

Intentional Torts against Property

Trespass to Land	The invasion of another's real property without consent or privilege. Once a person is expressly or impliedly established as a trespasser, the property owner has specific rights, which may include the right to detain or remove the trespasser.
Trespass to Personal Property	The intentional interference with an owner's right to use, possess, or enjoy his or her personal property without the owner's consent.
Conversion	The wrongful possession or use of another person's personal property without just cause.
Disparagement of Property	Any economically injurious falsehood that is made about another's product or property; an inclusive term for the torts of *slander of quality* and *slander of title*.

To succeed in a negligence action, the plaintiff must prove each of the following:

1. *Duty.* The defendant owed a duty of care to the plaintiff.
2. *Breach.* The defendant breached that duty.
3. *Causation.* The defendant's breach caused the plaintiff's injury.
4. *Damages.* The plaintiff suffered a legally recognizable injury.

6-4a The Duty of Care and Its Breach

Central to the tort of negligence is the concept of a **duty of care.** The basic principle underlying the duty of care is that people are free to act as they please so long as their actions do not infringe on the interests of others. When someone fails to comply with the duty to exercise reasonable care, a potentially tortious act may have been committed.

Failure to live up to a standard of care may be an act (accidentally setting fire to a building) or an omission (neglecting to put out a campfire). It may be a careless act or a carefully performed but nevertheless dangerous act that results in injury. In determining whether the duty of care has been breached, courts consider several factors:

1. The nature of the act (whether it is outrageous or commonplace).
2. The manner in which the act was performed (cautiously versus heedlessly).
3. The nature of the injury (whether it is serious or slight).

Creating even a very slight risk of a dangerous explosion might be unreasonable, whereas creating a distinct possibility of someone's burning his or her fingers on a stove might be reasonable.

The Reasonable Person Standard Tort law measures duty by the **reasonable person standard.** In determining whether a duty of care has been breached, the courts ask how a reasonable person would have acted in the same circumstances. The reasonable person standard is said to be objective. It is not necessarily how a particular person *would* act. It is society's judgment of how an ordinarily prudent person *should* act. If the so-called reasonable person existed, he or she would be careful, conscientious, even tempered, and honest.

The degree of care to be exercised varies, depending on the defendant's occupation or profession, her or his relationship with the plaintiff, and other factors. Generally, whether an action constitutes a breach of the duty of care is determined on a case-by-case basis. The outcome depends on how the judge (or jury) decides that a reasonable person in the position of the defendant would have acted in the particular circumstances of the case.

Note that the courts frequently use the reasonable person standard in other areas of law as well as in negligence cases. Indeed, the principle that individuals are required to exercise a reasonable standard of care in their activities is a pervasive concept in business law.

The Duty of Landowners Landowners are expected to exercise reasonable care to protect individuals coming onto their property from harm. In some jurisdictions, landowners may even have a duty to protect trespassers against certain risks. Landowners who rent or lease premises to tenants are expected to exercise reasonable care to ensure that the tenants and their guests are not harmed in common areas, such as stairways, entryways, and laundry rooms.

The Duty to Warn Business Invitees of Risks. Retailers and other business operators who explicitly or implicitly invite persons to come onto their premises have a duty to exercise reasonable care to protect these **business invitees.** The duty normally requires storeowners to warn business invitees of foreseeable risks, such as construction zones or wet floors, about which the owners knew or *should have known.*

■ **EXAMPLE 6.23** Liz enters Kwan's neighborhood market, slips on a wet floor, and sustains injuries as a result. If there was no sign or other warning that the floor was wet at the time Liz slipped, the owner, Kwan, would be liable for damages. A court would hold that Kwan was negligent because he failed to exercise a reasonable degree of care to protect customers against foreseeable risks about which he knew or should have known. That a patron might slip on the wet floor and be injured was a foreseeable risk, and Kwan should have taken care to avoid this risk or warn the customer of it. ■

A business owner also has a duty to discover and remove any hidden dangers that might injure a customer or other invitee. Hidden dangers might include uneven surfaces or defects in the pavement of a parking lot or a walkway, or merchandise that has fallen off shelves in a store.

Obvious Risks Provide an Exception. Some risks are so obvious that an owner need not warn of them. For instance, a business owner does not need to warn customers to open a door before attempting to walk through it. Other risks, however, even though they may seem obvious

to a business owner, may not be so in the eyes of another, such as a child. In addition, even if a risk is obvious, a business owner is not necessarily excused from the duty to protect customers from foreseeable harm from that risk.

■ **CASE IN POINT 6.24** Giorgio's Grill is a restaurant in Florida that becomes a nightclub after hours. At those times, traditionally, as the manager of Giorgio's knew, the staff and customers throw paper napkins into the air as the music plays. The napkins land on the floor, but no one picks them up. One night, Jane Izquierdo went to Giorgio's. Although she had been to the club on prior occasions and knew about the napkin-throwing tradition, she slipped and fell, breaking her leg. She sued Giorgio's for negligence, but lost at trial because a jury found that the risk of slipping on the napkins was obvious. A state appellate court reversed, however, holding that the obviousness of a risk does not discharge a business owner's duty to its invitees to maintain the premises in a safe condition.[15] ■

The Duty of Professionals Persons who possess superior knowledge, skill, or training are held to a higher standard of care than others. Professionals—including physicians, dentists, architects, engineers, accountants, and lawyers, among others—are required to have a standard minimum level of special knowledge and ability. In determining what constitutes reasonable care in the case of professionals, the law takes their training and expertise into account. Thus, an accountant's conduct is judged not by the reasonable person standard, but by the reasonable accountant standard.

If a professional violates his or her duty of care toward a client, the client may bring a suit against the professional, alleging **malpractice,** which is essentially professional negligence. For instance, a patient might sue a physician for *medical malpractice.* A client might sue an attorney for *legal malpractice.*

6–4b Causation

Another element necessary to a negligence action is *causation.* If a person breaches a duty of care and someone suffers injury, the person's act must have caused the harm for it to constitute the tort of negligence.

Courts Ask Two Questions In deciding whether the requirement of causation is met, the court must address two questions:

---

15. *Izquierdo v. Gyroscope, Inc.,* 946 So.2d 115 (Fla.App. 2007).

1. *Is there causation in fact?* Did the injury occur because of the defendant's act, or would it have occurred anyway? If the injury would not have occurred without the defendant's act, then there is causation in fact.

   Causation in fact usually can be determined by use of the *but for* test: "but for" the wrongful act, the injury would not have occurred. This test seeks to determine whether there was a cause-and-effect relationship between the act and the injury suffered. In theory, causation in fact is limitless. One could claim, for example, that "but for" the creation of the world, a particular injury would not have occurred. Thus, as a practical matter, the law has to establish limits, and it does so through the concept of proximate cause.

2. *Was the act the proximate, or legal, cause of the injury?* **Proximate cause,** or *legal cause,* exists when the connection between an act and an injury is strong enough to justify imposing liability. Proximate cause asks whether the injuries sustained were foreseeable or were too remotely connected to the incident to trigger liability. Judges use proximate cause to limit the scope of the defendant's liability to a subset of the total number of potential plaintiffs that might have been harmed by the defendant's actions.

   ■ **EXAMPLE 6.25** Ackerman carelessly leaves a campfire burning. The fire not only burns down the forest but also sets off an explosion in a nearby chemical plant that spills chemicals into a river, killing all the fish for twenty miles downstream and ruining the economy of a tourist resort. Should Ackerman be liable to the resort owners? To the tourists whose vacations were ruined? These are questions of proximate cause that a court must decide. ■

Both of these causation questions must be answered in the affirmative for liability in tort to arise. If there is causation in fact but a court decides that the defendant's action is not the proximate cause of the plaintiff's injury, the causation requirement has not been met. Therefore, the defendant normally will not be liable to the plaintiff.

Foreseeability Questions of proximate cause are linked to the concept of foreseeability because it would be unfair to impose liability on a defendant unless the defendant's actions created a foreseeable risk of injury. Generally, if the victim or the consequences of a harm done were unforeseeable, there is no proximate cause.

Probably the most cited case on the concept of foreseeability and proximate cause is the *Palsgraf* case, which established foreseeability as the test for proximate cause. ■ **CASE IN POINT 6.26** Helen Palsgraf was waiting for a train on a station platform. A man carrying a package was rushing to catch a train that was moving away from a platform across

the tracks from Palsgraf. As the man attempted to jump aboard the moving train, he seemed unsteady and about to fall. A railroad guard on the car reached forward to grab him, and another guard on the platform pushed him from behind to help him board the train.

In the process, the man's package, which (unknown to the railroad guards) contained fireworks, fell on the railroad tracks and exploded. There was nothing about the package to indicate its contents. The repercussions of the explosion caused weighing scales at the other end of the train platform to fall on Palsgraf, causing injuries for which she sued the railroad company. At the trial, the jury found that the railroad guards had been negligent in their conduct. The railroad company appealed. New York's highest state court held that the railroad company was not liable to Palsgraf. The railroad had not been negligent toward her, because injury to her was not foreseeable.[16] ■

6–4c The Injury Requirement and Damages

For tort liability to arise, the plaintiff must have suffered a *legally recognizable* injury. To recover damages, the plaintiff must have suffered some loss, harm, wrong, or invasion of a protected interest. Essentially, the purpose of tort law is to compensate for legally recognized harms and injuries resulting from wrongful acts. If no harm or injury results from a given negligent action, there is nothing to compensate, and no tort exists.

For instance, if you carelessly bump into a passerby, who stumbles and falls as a result, you may be liable in tort if the passerby is injured in the fall. If the person is unharmed, however, there normally can be no lawsuit for damages, because no injury was suffered.

Compensatory damages are the norm in negligence cases. A court will award punitive damages only if the defendant's conduct was grossly negligent, reflecting an intentional failure to perform a duty with reckless disregard of the consequences to others.

6–4d Good Samaritan Statutes

Most states now have what are called **Good Samaritan statutes.**[17] Under these statutes, someone who is aided voluntarily by another cannot turn around and sue the "Good Samaritan" for negligence. These laws were passed largely to protect physicians and medical personnel who

---

16. *Palsgraf v. Long Island Railroad Co.,* 248 N.Y. 339, 162 N.E. 99 (1928).

17. These laws derive their name from the Good Samaritan story in the Bible. In the story, a traveler who had been robbed and beaten lay along the roadside, ignored by those passing by. Eventually, a man from the region of Samaria (the "Good Samaritan") stopped to render assistance to the injured person.

volunteer their services in emergency situations to those in need, such as individuals hurt in car accidents.

6–4e Dram Shop Acts

Many states have also passed **dram shop acts,**[18] under which a bar's owner or bartender may be held liable for injuries caused by a person who became intoxicated while drinking at the bar. The owner or bartender may also be held responsible for continuing to serve a person who was already intoxicated.

Some states' statutes also impose liability on *social hosts* (persons hosting parties) for injuries caused by guests who became intoxicated at the hosts' homes. Under these statutes, it is unnecessary to prove that the bar owner, bartender, or social host was negligent. ■ **EXAMPLE 6.27** Jane hosts a Super Bowl party at which Brett, a minor, sneaks alcoholic drinks. Jane is potentially liable for damages resulting from Brett's drunk driving after the party. ■

6–5 Defenses to Negligence

Defendants often defend against negligence claims by asserting that the plaintiffs have failed to prove

---

18. Historically, a dram was a small unit of liquid, and distilled spirits (strong alcoholic liquor) were sold in drams. Thus, a dram shop was a place where liquor was sold in drams.

the existence of one or more of the required elements for negligence. Additionally, there are three basic *affirmative* defenses in negligence cases (defenses that a defendant can use to avoid liability even if the facts are as the plaintiff states): *assumption of risk, superseding cause,* and *contributory and comparative negligence.*

6–5a Assumption of Risk

A plaintiff who voluntarily enters into a risky situation, knowing the risk involved, will not be allowed to recover. This is the defense of **assumption of risk,** which requires two elements:

1. Knowledge of the risk.
2. Voluntary assumption of the risk.

The defense of assumption of risk is frequently asserted when the plaintiff was injured during a recreational activity that involves known risk, such as skiing or skydiving. (Courts do not apply the assumption of risk doctrine in emergency situations.)

Assumption of risk can apply not only to participants in sporting events, but also to spectators and bystanders who are injured while attending those events. In the following *Spotlight Case,* the issue was whether a spectator at a baseball game voluntarily assumed the risk of being hit by an errant ball thrown while the players were warming up before the game.

Spotlight on the Seattle Mariners

Case 6.3 Taylor v. Baseball Club of Seattle, LP

Court of Appeals of Washington, 132 Wash.App. 32, 130 P.3d 835 (2006).

Background and Facts Delinda Taylor went to a Seattle Mariners baseball game at Safeco Field with her boyfriend and her two minor sons. Their seats were four rows up from the field along the right field foul line. They arrived more than an hour before the game so that they could see the players warm up and get their autographs. When she walked in, Taylor saw that a Mariners pitcher, Freddy Garcia, was throwing a ball back and forth with José Mesa right in front of their seats.

As Taylor stood in front of her seat, she looked away from the field, and a ball thrown by Mesa got past Garcia and struck her in the face, causing serious injuries. Taylor sued the Mariners for the allegedly negligent warm-up throw. The Mariners filed a motion for summary judgment in which they argued that Taylor, a longtime Mariners fan, was familiar with baseball and the inherent risk of balls entering the stands. Thus, the motion asserted, Taylor had assumed the risk of her injury. The trial court granted the motion and dismissed Taylor's case. Taylor appealed.

In the Language of the Court
DWYER, J. [Judge]
* * * *

* * * For many decades, courts have required baseball stadiums to screen some seats—generally those behind home plate—to provide protection to spectators who choose it.

Case 6.3 Continues

Case 6.3 Continued

A sport spectator's assumption of risk and a defendant sports team's duty of care are accordingly discerned under the doctrine of primary assumption of risk. * * * "Implied *primary* assumption of risk arises where a plaintiff has impliedly consented (often in advance of any negligence by defendant) to relieve defendant of a duty to plaintiff regarding specific *known* and appreciated risks."

* * * *

Under this implied primary assumption of risk, defendant must show that plaintiff had full subjective understanding of the specific risk, both its nature and presence, and that he or she voluntarily chose to encounter the risk.

* * * It is undisputed that the warm-up is part of the sport, that spectators such as Taylor purposely attend that portion of the event, and that the Mariners permit ticket-holders to view the warm-up.

* * * We find the fact that Taylor was injured during warm-up is not legally significant because that portion of the event is necessarily incident to the game.

* * * *

Here, there is no evidence that the circumstances leading to Taylor's injury constituted an unusual danger. It is undisputed that it is the normal, every-day practice at all levels of baseball for pitchers to warm up in the manner that led to this incident. *The risk of injuries such as Taylor's are within the normal comprehension of a spectator who is familiar with the game.* Indeed, the possibility of an errant ball entering the stands is part of the game's attraction for many spectators. [Emphasis added.]

* * * The record contains substantial evidence regarding Taylor's familiarity with the game. She attended many of her sons' baseball games, she witnessed balls entering the stands, she had watched Mariners' games both at the Kingdome and on television, and she knew that there was no screen protecting her seats, which were close to the field. In fact, as she walked to her seat she saw the players warming up and was excited about being in an unscreened area where her party might get autographs from the players and catch balls.

Decision and Remedy   *The state intermediate appellate court affirmed the lower court's judgment. As a spectator who chose to sit in an unprotected area of seats, Taylor voluntarily undertook the risk associated with being hit by an errant baseball thrown during the warm-up before the game.*

Critical Thinking

- **What If the Facts Were Different?**   *Would the result in this case have been different if it had been Taylor's minor son, rather than Taylor herself, who had been struck by the ball? Should courts apply the doctrine of assumption of risk to children? Discuss.*
- **Legal Environment**   *What is the basis underlying the defense of assumption of risk? How does that basis support the court's decision in this case?*

6–5b Superseding Cause

An unforeseeable intervening event may break the causal connection between a wrongful act and an injury to another. If so, the intervening event acts as a **superseding cause**—that is, it relieves the defendant of liability for injuries caused by the intervening event.

■ **EXAMPLE 6.28**   While riding his bicycle, Derrick negligently runs into Julie, who is walking on the sidewalk. As a result of the impact, Julie falls and fractures her hip. While she is waiting for help to arrive, a small aircraft crashes nearby and explodes, and some of the fiery debris hits her, causing her to sustain severe burns. Derrick will be liable for the damages related to Julie's fractured hip, because the risk of injuring her with his bicycle was foreseeable. Normally, though, Derrick will not be liable for the burns caused by the plane crash, because he could not have foreseen the risk that a plane would crash nearby and injure Julie. ■

6–5c Contributory Negligence

All individuals are expected to exercise a reasonable degree of care in looking out for themselves. In the past, under the common law doctrine of **contributory negligence,** a plaintiff who was also negligent (who failed to exercise a reasonable degree of care) could not recover anything from the defendant. Under this rule, no matter how insignificant the plaintiff's negligence was relative to the defendant's negligence, the plaintiff would be precluded from recovering any damages. Today, only a few jurisdictions still follow this doctrine.

6–5d Comparative Negligence

In most states, the doctrine of contributory negligence has been replaced by a **comparative negligence** standard. Under this standard, both the plaintiff's and the defendant's negligence are computed, and the liability for damages is distributed accordingly.

Some jurisdictions have adopted a "pure" form of comparative negligence that allows the plaintiff to recover, even if the extent of his or her fault is greater than that of the defendant. Under pure comparative negligence, if the plaintiff was 80 percent at fault and the defendant 20 percent at fault, the plaintiff can recover 20 percent of his or her damages.

Many states' comparative negligence statutes, however, contain a "50 percent" rule that prevents the plaintiff from recovering any damages if she or he was more than 50 percent at fault. Under this rule, a plaintiff who was 35 percent at fault can recover 65 percent of his or her damages, but a plaintiff who was 65 percent (more than 50 percent) at fault can recover nothing.

Reviewing: Tort Law

Elaine Sweeney went to Ragged Mountain Ski Resort in New Hampshire with a friend. Elaine went snow tubing down a run designed exclusively for snow tubers. There were no Ragged Mountain employees present in the snow-tube area to instruct Elaine on the proper use of a snow tube. On her fourth run down the trail, Elaine crossed over the center line between snow-tube lanes, collided with another snow tuber, and was injured. Elaine filed a negligence action against Ragged Mountain seeking compensation for the injuries that she sustained. Two years earlier, the New Hampshire state legislature had enacted a statute that prohibited a person who participates in the sport of skiing from suing a ski-area operator for injuries caused by the risks inherent in skiing. Using the information presented in the chapter, answer the following questions.

1. What defense will Ragged Mountain probably assert?
2. The central question in this case is whether the state statute establishing that skiers assume the risks inherent in the sport bars Elaine's suit. What would your decision be on this issue? Why?
3. Suppose that the court concludes that the statute applies only to skiing and not to snow tubing. Will Elaine's lawsuit be successful? Explain.
4. Now suppose that the jury concludes that Elaine was partly at fault for the accident. Under what theory might her damages be reduced in proportion to the degree to which her actions contributed to the accident and her resulting injuries?

Debate This . . . *Each time a state legislature enacts a law that applies the assumption of risk doctrine to a particular sport, participants in that sport suffer.*

Terms and Concepts

actionable 114	contributory negligence 130	general damages 112
actual malice 118	conversion 124	Good Samaritan statute 128
assault 113	damages 112	intentional tort 113
assumption of risk 129	defamation 115	libel 115
battery 114	disparagement of property 125	licensee 124
business invitee 127	dram shop act 129	malpractice 127
causation in fact 128	duty of care 126	negligence 125
comparative negligence 131	fraudulent misrepresentation	privilege 117
compensatory damages 112	(fraud) 120	proximate cause 128

Issue Spotters

1. Jana leaves her truck's motor running while she enters a Kwik-Pik Store. The truck's transmission engages, and the vehicle crashes into a gas pump, starting a fire that spreads to a warehouse on the next block. The warehouse collapses, causing its billboard to fall and injure Lou, a bystander. Can Lou recover from Jana? Why or why not? (See *Unintentional Torts—Negligence*.)

2. A water pipe bursts, flooding a Metal Fabrication Company utility room and tripping the circuit breakers on a panel in the room. Metal Fabrication contacts Nouri, a licensed electrician with five years' experience, to check the damage and turn the breakers back on. Without testing for short circuits, which Nouri knows that he should do, he tries to switch on a breaker. He is electrocuted, and his wife sues Metal Fabrication for damages, alleging negligence. What might the firm successfully claim in defense? (See *Defenses to Negligence*.)

• **Check your answers to the Issue Spotters against the answers provided in Appendix D at the end of this text.**

Business Scenarios

6–1. Defamation. Richard is an employee of the Dun Construction Corp. While delivering materials to a construction site, he carelessly backs Dun's truck into a passenger vehicle driven by Green. This is Richard's second accident in six months. When the company owner, Dun, learns of this latest accident, a heated discussion ensues, and Dun fires Richard. Dun is so angry that he immediately writes a letter to the union of which Richard is a member and to all other construction companies in the community, stating that Richard is the "worst driver in the city" and that "anyone who hires him is asking for legal liability." Richard files a suit against Dun, alleging libel on the basis of the statements made in the letters. Discuss the results. (See *Intentional Torts against Persons*.)

6–2. Liability to Business Invitees. Kim went to Ling's Market to pick up a few items for dinner. It was a stormy day, and the wind had blown water through the market's door each time it opened. As Kim entered through the door, she slipped and fell in the rainwater that had accumulated on the floor. The manager knew of the weather conditions but had not posted any sign to warn customers of the water hazard. Kim injured her back as a result of the fall and sued Ling's for damages. Can Ling's be held liable for negligence? Discuss. (See *Unintentional Torts—Negligence*.)

Business Case Problems

6–3. Spotlight on Intentional Torts—Defamation.

Sharon Yeagle was an assistant to the vice president of student affairs at Virginia Polytechnic Institute and State University (Virginia Tech). As part of her duties, Yeagle helped students participate in the Governor's Fellows Program. The *Collegiate Times,* Virginia Tech's student newspaper, published an article about the university's success in placing students in the program. The article's text surrounded a block quotation attributed to Yeagle with the phrase "Director of Butt Licking" under her name. Yeagle sued the *Collegiate Times* for defamation. She argued that the phrase implied the commission of sodomy and was therefore actionable. What is *Collegiate Times* defense to this claim? [*Yeagle v. Collegiate Times,* 497 S.E.2d 136 (Va. 1998)] (See *Intentional Torts against Persons*.)

6–4. Intentional Infliction of Emotional Distress. While living in her home country of Tanzania, Sophia Kiwanuka signed an employment contract with Anne Margareth Bakilana, a Tanzanian living in Washington, D.C. Kiwanuka traveled to the United States to work as a babysitter and maid in Bakilana's house. When Kiwanuka arrived, Bakilana confiscated her passport, held her in isolation, and forced her to work long hours under threat of having her deported. Kiwanuka worked seven days a week without breaks and was subjected to regular verbal and psychological abuse by Bakilana. Kiwanuka filed a complaint against Bakilana for intentional infliction of emotional distress, among other claims. Bakilana argued that Kiwanuka's complaint should be dismissed because the allegations were insufficient to show outrageous intentional conduct that resulted in severe emotional distress.

If you were the judge, in whose favor would you rule? Why? [*Kiwanuka v. Bakilana*, 844 F.Supp.2d 107 (D.D.C. 2012)] (See *Intentional Torts against Persons*.)

6–5. Business Case Problem with Sample Answer—Negligence.

 At the Weatherford Hotel in Flagstaff, Arizona, in Room 59, a balcony extends across thirty inches of the room's only window, leaving a twelve-inch gap with a three-story drop to the concrete below. A sign prohibits smoking in the room but invites guests to "step onto the balcony" to smoke. Toni Lucario was a guest in Room 59 when she climbed out of the window and fell to her death. Patrick McMurtry, her estate's personal representative, filed a suit against the Weatherford. Did the hotel breach a duty of care to Locario? What might the Weatherford assert in its defense? Explain. [*McMurtry v. Weatherford Hotel, Inc.*, 231 Ariz. 244, 293 P.3d 520 (2013)] (See *Unintentional Torts—Negligence*.)

- For a sample answer to Problem 6–5, go to Appendix E at the end of this text.

6–6. Negligence.
Ronald Rawls and Zabian Bailey were in an auto accident in Bridgeport, Connecticut. Bailey rear-ended Rawls at a stoplight. Evidence showed it was more likely than not that Bailey failed to apply his brakes in time to avoid the collision, failed to turn his vehicle to avoid the collision, failed to keep his vehicle under control, and was inattentive to his surroundings. Rawls filed a suit in a Connecticut state court against his insurance company, Progressive Northern Insurance Co., to obtain benefits under an underinsured motorist clause, alleging that Bailey had been negligent. Could Rawls collect? Discuss. [*Rawls v. Progressive Northern Insurance Co.*, 310 Conn. 768, 83 A.3d 576 (2014)] (See *Unintentional Torts—Negligence*.)

6–7. Negligence.
Charles Robison, an employee of West Star Transportation, Inc., was ordered to cover an unevenly loaded flatbed trailer with a 150-pound tarpaulin (a waterproof cloth). The load included uncrated equipment and pallet crates of different heights, about thirteen feet off the ground at its highest point. While standing on the load, manipulating the tarpaulin without safety equipment or assistance, Robison fell and sustained a traumatic head injury. He filed a suit against West Star to recover for his injury. Was West Star "negligent in failing to provide a reasonably safe place to work," as Robison claimed? Explain. [*West Star Transportation, Inc. v. Robison*, 457 S.W.3d 178 (Tex.App.—Amarillo 2015)] (See *Unintentional Torts—Negligence*.)

6–8. Negligence.
DSC Industrial Supply and Road Rider Supply are located in North Kitsap Business Park in Seattle, Washington. Both firms are owned by Paul and Suzanne Marshall. The Marshalls had outstanding commercial loans from Frontier Bank. The bank dispatched one of its employees, Suzette Gould, to North Kitsap to "spread Christmas cheer" to the Marshalls as an expression of appreciation for their business. Approaching the entry to Road Rider, Gould tripped over a concrete "wheel stop" and fell, suffering a broken arm and a dislocated elbow. The stop was not clearly visible, it had not been painted a contrasting color, and it was not marked with a sign. Gould had not been aware of the stop before she tripped over it. Is North Kitsap liable to Gould for negligence? Explain. [*Gould v. North Kitsap Business Park Management, LLC*, 2016 WL 236455 (2016)] (See *Unintentional Torts—Negligence*.)

6–9. A Question of Ethics—Wrongful Interference.
 White Plains Coat & Apron Co. is a New York–based linen rental business. Cintas Corp. is a competitor. White Plains had five-year exclusive contracts with some of its customers. As a result of Cintas's soliciting of business, dozens of White Plains' customers breached their contracts and entered into rental agreements with Cintas. White Plains filed a suit against Cintas, alleging wrongful interference. [White Plains Coat & Apron Co. v. Cintas Corp., *8 N.Y.3d 422, 867 N.E.2d 381 (2007)*] (See *Intentional Torts against Persons*.)

(a) What are the two important policy interests at odds in wrongful interference cases? Which of these interests should be accorded priority?

(b) The U.S. Court of Appeals for the Second Circuit asked the New York Court of Appeals to answer a question: Is a general interest in soliciting business for profit a sufficient defense to a claim of wrongful interference with a contractual relationship? What do you think? Why?

Legal Reasoning Group Activity

6–10. Negligence.
Donald and Gloria Bowden hosted a cookout at their home in South Carolina, inviting mostly business acquaintances. Justin Parks, who was nineteen years old, attended the party. Alcoholic beverages were available to all of the guests, even those who, like Parks, were between the ages of eighteen and twenty-one. Parks consumed alcohol at the party and left with other guests. One of these guests detained Parks at the guest's home to give Parks time to "sober up." Parks then drove himself from this guest's home and was killed in a one-car accident. At the time of death, he had a blood alcohol content of 0.291 percent, which exceeded the state's limit for driving a motor vehicle. Linda Marcum, Parks's mother, filed a suit in a South Carolina state court against the Bowdens and others, alleging that they were negligent. (See *Unintentional Torts—Negligence*.)

(a) The first group will present arguments in favor of holding the social hosts liable in this situation.

(b) The second group will formulate arguments against holding the social hosts liable based on principles in this chapter.

(c) The third group will determine the reasons why some courts do not treat social hosts the same as parents who serve alcoholic beverages to their underage children.

CHAPTER 7

Strict Liability and Product Liability

In this chapter, we look at a category of tort called **strict liability,** or *liability without fault.* Under the doctrine of strict liability, a person who engages in certain activities can be held responsible for any harm that results to others, even if the person used the utmost care.

We then look at an area of tort law of particular importance to businesspersons—product liability. The manufacturers and sellers of products may incur **product liability** when product defects cause injury or property damage to consumers, users, or bystanders.

Although multimillion-dollar product liability claims often involve big automakers, pharmaceutical companies, or tobacco companies, many businesses face potential liability. For instance, a number of product liability lawsuits have been filed claiming that energy drinks like Monster, Red Bull, and Rockstar have serious adverse effects—especially on young people. A man who swallowed a bone fragment while eating sued McDonald's in 2015 for allegedly defective chicken McNuggets.

Product liability lawsuits also reach across international borders. Takata

Corporation, a global company that supplies seat belts, airbags, and other automobile safety systems, is being sued by hundreds of plaintiffs in the United States. Takata manufactured allegedly defective airbags, which violently exploded and ejected metal debris, resulting in injuries and deaths.[1] Takata has already paid a $70 million penalty to the National Highway Safety Administration for failing to promptly disclose defects in its airbags, millions of which have now been recalled.

---

1. *In re Takata Airbag Products Liability Litigation,* 84 F.Supp.3d 1371 (2015).

7-1 Strict Liability

The modern concept of strict liability traces its origins, in part, to an English case decided in 1868. ■ **CASE IN POINT 7.1** In the coal-mining area of Lancashire, England, the Rylands, who were mill owners, had constructed a reservoir on their land. Water from the reservoir broke through a filled-in shaft of an abandoned coal mine nearby and flooded the connecting passageways in an active coal mine owned by Fletcher.

Fletcher sued the Rylands, and the court held that the defendants (the Rylands) were liable, even though the circumstances did not fit within existing tort liability theories. The court held that a "person who for his own purposes brings on his land and collects and keeps there anything likely to do mischief if it escapes . . . is *prima facie*[2] answerable for all the damage which is the natural consequence of its escape."[3] ■

---

2. *Prima facie* is Latin for "at first sight." Legally, it refers to a fact that is presumed to be true unless contradicted by evidence.
3. *Rylands v. Fletcher,* 3 L.R.–E & I App. [Law Reports, English & Irish Appeal Cases] (H.L. [House of Lords] 1868).

British courts liberally applied the doctrine that emerged from the case. Initially, though, few U.S. courts accepted the doctrine, presumably because the courts were worried about its effect on the expansion of American business. Today, however, the doctrine of strict liability is the norm rather than the exception.

7-1a Abnormally Dangerous Activities

Strict liability for damages proximately caused by an abnormally dangerous, or ultrahazardous, activity is one application of strict liability. Courts apply the doctrine of strict liability in these situations because of the extreme risk of the activity. Abnormally dangerous activities are those that involve a high risk of serious harm to persons or property that cannot be completely guarded against by the exercise of reasonable care.

Activities such as blasting or storing explosives qualify as abnormally dangerous, for instance. Even if blasting with dynamite is performed with all reasonable care, there is still a risk of injury. Considering the potential for harm, it seems reasonable to ask the person engaged in the activity to pay for injuries caused by that activity. Although there is no fault, there is still responsibility because of the dangerous nature of the undertaking.

Similarly, persons who keep wild animals are strictly liable for any harm inflicted by the animals. The basis for applying strict liability is that wild animals, should they escape from confinement, pose a serious risk of harm to people in the vicinity. Even an owner of domestic animals (such as dogs or horses) may be strictly liable for harm caused by those animals if the owner knew, or should have known, that the animals were dangerous or had a propensity to harm others.

7–1b Application of Strict Liability to Product Liability

A significant application of strict liability is in the area of product liability—liability of manufacturers and sellers for harmful or defective products. Liability here is a matter of social policy and is based on two factors:

1. The manufacturer can better bear the cost of injury because it can spread the cost throughout society by increasing the prices of its goods.
2. The manufacturer is making a profit from its activities and therefore should bear the cost of injury as an operating expense.

We discuss product liability in detail next. Strict liability is also applied in certain types of *bailments* (a bailment exists when goods are transferred temporarily into the care of another).

7–2 Product Liability

Those who make, sell, or lease goods can be held liable for physical harm or property damage caused by those goods to a consumer, user, or bystander. This is called *product liability.* Product liability may be based on the theories of negligence, misrepresentation, strict liability, and warranties. Multiple theories of liability can be, and often are, asserted in the same case. We look here at product liability based on negligence and on misrepresentation.

7–2a Based on Negligence

Negligence is the failure to exercise the degree of care that a reasonable, prudent person would have exercised under the circumstances. If a manufacturer fails to exercise "due care" to make a product safe, a person who is injured by the product may sue the manufacturer for negligence.

Due Care Must Be Exercised Manufacturers must use due care in all of the following areas:

1. Designing the product.
2. Selecting the materials.
3. Using the appropriate production process.
4. Assembling and testing the product.
5. Placing adequate warnings on the label to inform the user of dangers of which an ordinary person might not be aware.
6. Inspecting and testing any purchased components used in the product.

Privity of Contract Not Required A product liability action based on negligence does not require *privity of contract* between the injured plaintiff and the defendant-manufacturer. **Privity of contract** refers to the relationship that exists between the parties to a contract. Privity is the reason that normally only the parties to a contract can enforce that contract.

In the context of product liability law, though, privity is not required. A person who is injured by a defective product may bring a negligence suit even though he or she was not the one who actually purchased the product—and thus is not in privity. A manufacturer, seller, or lessor is liable for failure to exercise due care to *any person* who sustains an injury proximately caused by a negligently made (defective) product.

A 1916 landmark decision established this exception to the privity requirement. ■ **CASE IN POINT 7.2** Donald MacPherson suffered injuries while riding in a Buick automobile that suddenly collapsed because one of the wheels was made of defective wood. The spokes crumbled into fragments, throwing MacPherson out of the vehicle and injuring him.

MacPherson had purchased the car from a Buick dealer, but he brought a lawsuit against the manufacturer, Buick Motor Company, alleging negligence. Buick itself had not made the wheel but had bought it from another manufacturer. There was evidence, though, that the defects could have been discovered by a reasonable inspection by Buick and that no such inspection had taken place. The primary issue was whether Buick owed a duty of care to anyone except the immediate purchaser of the car—that is, the Buick dealer. Although Buick itself had not manufactured the wheel, New York's highest state court held that Buick had a duty to inspect the wheels and that Buick "was responsible for the finished product." Therefore, Buick was liable to MacPherson for the injuries he sustained. [4] ■

---

4. *MacPherson v. Buick Motor Co.,* 217 N.Y. 382, 111 N.E. 1050 (1916).

"Cause in Fact" and Proximate Cause In a product liability suit based on negligence, as in any action alleging that the defendant was negligent, the plaintiff must show that the defendant's conduct was the "cause in fact" of an injury. "Cause in fact" requires showing that "but for" the defendant's action, the injury would not have occurred.

It must also be determined that the defendant's act was the *proximate cause* of the injury. This determination focuses on the foreseeability of the consequences of the act and whether the defendant should be held legally responsible. For proximate cause to become a relevant issue, however, a plaintiff first must establish cause in fact. The cause of a serious accident was at issue in the following case.

Case Analysis 7.1

Schwarck v. Arctic Cat, Inc.
Court of Appeals of Michigan, __ Mich.App. __, 2016 WL 191992 (2016).

In the Language of the Court
PER CURIAM. [By the Whole Court]
* * * *

* * * Karen Schwarck * * * was operating an Arctic Cat [660 snowmobile] near Mackinac Island's Grand Hotel [in Michigan] with her sister, Edith Bonno, as passenger. The sisters met their demise when the Arctic Cat went, in reverse, backward through a wooden fence and over the West Bluff of the Island.

[Donald Schwarck and Joshua Bonno] the spouses of decedents, as their personal representatives, filed this action [in a Michigan state court] against defendant Arctic Cat [the manufacturer of the 660]. Plaintiffs alleged that the Arctic Cat 660 was negligently designed * * * without a backup alarm that operated throughout all the reverse travel positions and as a result proximately caused decedents' injuries.

Defendant filed a motion for summary [judgment]. Defendant denied the existence of a "silent reverse zone," but argued that even if such a zone existed, it was not a cause of the accident because the alarm was intended as a warning to bystanders and not as an indicator of shift position for operators.
* * * *

* * * The court issued its decision and order in favor of defendant. [The plaintiffs appealed.]
* * * *

There is no dispute that on the day of the accident decedent Schwarck was driving the Arctic Cat 660 * * * and that she attempted to execute a three-point

or K-turn * * * . To make the turn decedent Schwarck had to turn left to face north, stop, reverse south, stop, and then complete the turn to drive east.
* * * Plaintiffs argue that after decedent Schwarck reversed, she stopped a second time and shifted forward, and not hearing the reverse alarm, believed she was in forward, and accelerated. As a result, the craft went in reverse through the fence and off the bluff.

The trial court determined that there were no material questions of fact on * * * the operability of the reverse alarm. * * * It was undisputed that an inspection of the Arctic Cat post-accident showed the reverse alarm to be operable.
* * * *

* * * [But] the court's conclusion that the reverse alarm was working at the time of the accident does not determine whether its operational process constituted a product defect. Plaintiffs' claim was that the reverse alarm was defective because it did not sound during the entire time the vehicle was in reverse. Plaintiffs' causation theory was that the Arctic Cat's reverse alarm caused decedent Schwarck to be confused about whether she was in forward or reverse gear and that the confusion led to the accident that caused decedents' deaths.

[Plaintiffs' expert John Frackelton, an accident reconstructionist and snowmobile mechanic,] observed that the shift lever traveled from full reverse to full forward in a distance of four inches. Frackelton's testing revealed that when the lever was shifted all the way down

and pressed against the reverse buffer switch, the switch sounded a chime and the snowmobile was in full reverse mode. Frackelton experimented with the lever, shifting it up toward forward gear, an inch at a time. For the next two inches of shift travel forward, the reverse alarm did not sound, but the snowmobile was still in reverse. Frackelton observed that it was only in the last or fourth inch of shift travel that the snowmobile was in full forward.

* * * Frackelton observed that the transition from full reverse to full forward was smooth and accomplished with little pressure. He opined that an operator could "become accustomed to the highly repeatable return performance." On two occasions, however, Frackelton pushed the gearshift forward and the Arctic Cat did not return to forward gear as expected.

* * * Frackelton's opinion * * * creates a material question of fact as to whether the alarm failed to sound at all times when the gear was in reverse. Defendant argues that the alarm served its intended purpose which is to notify bystanders and not operators that the snowmobile is in reverse and that it was unreasonable for decedent Schwarck to rely on the alarm to determine the gear of the snowmobile. *The fact that the manufacturer's intended purpose for the alarm was to warn third-parties is not dispositive of the issue of whether decedent Schwarck relied on the alarm to*

Case 7.1 Continued

determine her gear or whether that reliance was reasonable or a foreseeable misuse of the alarm and snowmobile. Decedent Schwarck is assumed to have acted with due care for her own safety. Her widower averred that, based upon his observations, decedent Schwarck had a practice and routine of relying upon the sounding of the alarm as a signal that she was in reverse. Evidence from Frackelton's test runs also demonstrate that despite manual control of the shift lever, the lever could stop just short of the forward position and prevent the snowmobile from going into drive. [Emphasis added.]

Reasonable minds could differ as to whether a reverse alarm that does not sound throughout the reverse trajectory or only operates in a partial manner is defective.

* * * *

Legal cause becomes a relevant issue after cause in fact has been established. * * * *To establish legal cause, the plaintiff* *must show that it was foreseeable that the defendant's conduct may create a risk of harm to the victim, and * * * that the result of that conduct and intervening causes were foreseeable.* * * * It is foreseeable that an operator of the Arctic Cat may rely on the sound of the reverse alarm to indicate when the snowmobile is no longer in reverse and experience unexpected travel backward because the alarm does not sound during the entire reverse gear. It is further foreseeable that unanticipated reverse travel may cause a risk of harm to the operator. * * * Frackelton's tests regarding speed velocity without aggressive throttle demonstrate how the Arctic Cat can travel almost thirty feet in just 5.4 seconds. Not only can an operator of the Arctic Cat find him or herself unexpectedly travelling in reverse, but also doing so quickly. Plaintiffs' other expert [Lila Laux, a psychologist and engineer] testified * * * that time is * * * required for the operator to determine how to respond to the unexpected stimuli, to engage the brake, and for the brake to activate. [Emphasis added.]

A jury could infer that traveling backward when one thought he or she would go forward is an unexpected stimulus. It is also a reasonable inference, from the opinions of both plaintiffs' experts, that it was foreseeable that the operator would be surprised by the rearward motion. Given the evidence, reasonable minds may differ as to whether decedent Schwarck did not or could not correct the snowmobile's rearward direction in the time allotted.

Based on the whole record, there is evidence that warrants submission of this case to a jury to determine whether the reverse alarm was defective and whether that defect caused decedent Schwarck and Bonno's deaths.

* * * *

[The trial court's judgment is] vacated and remanded for proceedings consistent with this opinion.

Legal Reasoning Questions

1. According to the plaintiffs, what was the product defect at the center of this case? According to the defendant, why was this not a defect?

2. How did the plaintiffs use evidence to support their claim?

3. Why did the court conclude that this case should be submitted to a jury? Explain.

7–2b Misrepresentation

When a user or consumer is injured as a result of a manufacturer's or seller's fraudulent misrepresentation, the basis of liability may be the tort of fraud. In this situation, the misrepresentation must have been made knowingly or with reckless disregard for the facts. The intentional mislabeling of packaged cosmetics, for instance, or the intentional concealment of a product's defects would constitute fraudulent misrepresentation.

In addition, the misrepresentation must be of a material fact, and the seller must have intended to induce the buyer's reliance on the misrepresentation. Misrepresentation on a label or advertisement is enough to show an intent to induce the reliance of anyone who may use the product. In addition, the buyer must have relied on the misrepresentation.

7–3 Strict Product Liability

As mentioned earlier, under the doctrine of strict liability, people may be liable for the results of their acts regardless of their intentions or their exercise of reasonable care. In addition, liability does not depend on privity of contract. Thus, the injured party does not have to be the buyer, as required under contract warranty theories. In the 1960s, courts applied the doctrine of strict liability in several landmark cases involving manufactured goods, and it has since become a common method of holding manufacturers liable.

7–3a Strict Product Liability and Public Policy

The law imposes strict product liability as a matter of public policy. This public policy rests on a threefold assumption:

1. Consumers should be protected against unsafe products.
2. Manufacturers and distributors should not escape liability for faulty products simply because they are not in privity of contract with the ultimate user of those products.
3. Manufacturers and distributors can better bear the costs associated with injuries caused by their products, because they can ultimately pass the costs on to all consumers in the form of higher prices.

Development of the Doctrine California was the first state to impose strict product liability in tort on manufacturers. ■ **CASE IN POINT 7.3** William Greenman

was injured when his Shopsmith combination power tool threw off a piece of wood that struck him in the head. He sued the manufacturer, claiming that he had followed the product's instructions and the product must be defective. In a landmark decision, *Greenman v. Yuba Power Products, Inc.,*[5] the California Supreme Court set out the reason for applying tort law rather than contract law (including laws governing warranties) in cases involving consumers who were injured by defective products.

According to the *Greenman* court, the "purpose of such liability is to [e]nsure that the costs of injuries resulting from defective products are borne by the manufacturers . . . rather than by the injured persons who are powerless to protect themselves." ■ Today, the majority of states recognize strict product liability, although some state courts limit its application to situations involving personal injuries (rather than property damage).

Stated Public Policy Public policy may be expressed in a statute or in the common law. Sometimes, public policy may be revealed in a court's interpretation of a statute, as in the following case.

---

5. 59 Cal.2d 57, 377 P.2d 897, 27 Cal.Rptr. 697 (1962).

Spotlight on Injuries from Vaccines

Case 7.2 Bruesewitz v. Wyeth, LLC
Supreme Court of the United States, 562 U.S. 223, 131 S.Ct. 1068, 179 L.Ed.2d 1 (2011).

Company Profile *Wyeth, LLC—a subsidiary of Pfizer, Inc.—is an international pharmaceutical and health-care company with its corporate headquarters in Madison, New Jersey. Wyeth develops, makes, and markets medical therapies, clinical programs, nutritional supplements, prescription drugs, and other health-care products, including over-the-counter medications. Wyeth was incorporated in 1926. In 1994, the company bought Lederle Laboratories. Since 1948, Lederle had been making the diphtheria, tetanus, and pertussis (DTP) vaccine for children.*

Background and Facts When Hannah Bruesewitz was six months old, her pediatrician administered a dose of the DTP vaccine according to the Centers for Disease Control's recommended childhood immunization schedule. Within twenty-four hours, Hannah began to experience seizures. She suffered more than one hundred seizures during the next month. Her doctors diagnosed her with "residual seizure disorder" and "developmental delay."

Hannah's parents, Russell and Robalee Bruesewitz, filed a claim for relief in the U.S. Court of Federal Claims under the National Childhood Vaccine Injury Act (NCVIA). The NCVIA had set up a no-fault compensation program for persons injured by vaccines. The claim was denied. The Bruesewitzes then filed a suit in a state court against Wyeth, LLC, the maker of the vaccine, alleging strict product liability. The suit was moved to a federal district court. The court held that the claim was preempted by the NCVIA, which includes provisions protecting manufacturers from liability for "a vaccine's unavoidable, adverse side effects." The U.S. Court of Appeals for the Third Circuit affirmed the district court's judgment. The Bruesewitzes appealed to the United States Supreme Court.

Case 7.2 Continued

In the Language of the Court

Justice *SCALIA* delivered the opinion of the Court.

* * * *

In the 1970's and 1980's vaccines became, one might say, victims of their own success. They had been so effective in preventing infectious diseases that the public became much less alarmed at the threat of those diseases, and much more concerned with the risk of injury from the vaccines themselves.

Much of the concern centered around vaccines against * * * DTP, which were blamed for children's disabilities * * * . This led to a massive increase in vaccine-related tort litigation. * * * This destabilized the DTP vaccine market, causing two of the three domestic manufacturers to withdraw.

* * * *

To stabilize the vaccine market and facilitate compensation, Congress enacted the NCVIA in 1986. The Act establishes a no-fault compensation program designed to work faster and with greater ease than the civil tort system. A person injured by a vaccine, or his legal guardian, may file a petition for compensation in the United States Court of Federal Claims.

* * * *

Successful claimants receive compensation for medical, rehabilitation, counseling, special education, and vocational training expenses; diminished earning capacity; pain and suffering; and $250,000 for vaccine-related deaths. Attorney's fees are provided * * * . These awards are paid out of a fund created by a * * * tax on each vaccine dose.

The *quid pro quo* [something done in exchange] for this, designed to stabilize the vaccine market, was the provision of significant tort-liability protections for vaccine manufacturers. * * * *Manufacturers are generally immunized from liability * * * if they have complied with all regulatory requirements* * * * . * * * *And most relevant to the present case, the Act expressly eliminates liability for a vaccine's unavoidable, adverse side effects.* [Emphasis added.]

* * * *

The Act's structural *quid pro quo* leads to the * * * conclusion: The vaccine manufacturers fund from their sales an informal, efficient compensation program for vaccine injuries; in exchange they avoid costly tort litigation.

Decision and Remedy *The United States Supreme Court affirmed the lower court's judgment. The NCVIA preempted the Bruesewitzes' claim against Wyeth for compensation for the injury to their daughter caused by the DTP vaccine's side effects. The Court found that the NCVIA's compensation program strikes a balance between paying victims harmed by vaccines and protecting the vaccine industry from collapsing under the costs of tort liability.*

Critical Thinking
- **Economic** *What is the public policy expressed by the provisions of the NCVIA?*
- **Political** *If the public wants to change the policy outlined in this case, which branch of the government—and at what level—should be lobbied to make the change? Explain.*

7-3b The Requirements for Strict Product Liability

After the *Restatement (Second) of Torts* was issued in 1964, Section 402A became a widely accepted statement of how the doctrine of strict liability should be applied to sellers of goods (including manufacturers, processors, assemblers, packagers, bottlers, wholesalers, distributors, retailers, and lessors). The bases for an action in strict liability that are set forth in Section 402A can be summarized as a set of six requirements.

1. The product must be in a *defective condition* when the defendant sells it.

2. The defendant must normally be engaged in the *business of selling* (or otherwise distributing) that product.

3. The product must be *unreasonably dangerous* to the user or consumer because of its defective condition (in most states).

4. The plaintiff must incur *physical harm* to self or property by use or consumption of the product.

5. The defective condition must be the *proximate cause* of the injury or damage.
6. The *goods must not have been substantially changed* from the time the product was sold to the time the injury was sustained.

Depending on the jurisdiction, if these requirements are met, a manufacturer's liability to an injured party can be almost unlimited.

Proving a Defective Condition Under these requirements, in any action against a manufacturer, seller, or lessor, the plaintiff need not show why or in what manner the product became defective. The plaintiff does, however, have to prove that the product was defective at the time it left the hands of the seller or lessor. The plaintiff must also show that this defective condition made the product "unreasonably dangerous" to the user or consumer.

Unless evidence can be presented to support the conclusion that the product was defective when it was sold or leased, the plaintiff will not succeed. If the product was delivered in a safe condition and subsequent mishandling made it harmful to the user, the seller or lessor normally is not strictly liable.

Unreasonably Dangerous Products The *Restatement* recognizes that many products cannot be made entirely safe for all uses. Thus, sellers or lessors are liable only for products that are *unreasonably* dangerous. A court could consider a product so defective as to be an **unreasonably dangerous product** in either of the following situations:

1. The product was dangerous beyond the expectation of the ordinary consumer.
2. A less dangerous alternative was *economically* feasible for the manufacturer, but the manufacturer failed to produce it.

As will be discussed next, a product may be unreasonably dangerous due to the manufacturing process, the design, or the warning.

7–3c Product Defects

The *Restatement (Third) of Torts: Products Liability* defines the three types of product defects that have traditionally been recognized in product liability law—manufacturing defects, design defects, and inadequate warnings.

Manufacturing Defects According to Section 2(a) of the *Restatement (Third) of Torts,* a product "contains a manufacturing defect when the product departs from

its intended design even though all possible care was exercised in the preparation and marketing of the product." Basically, a manufacturing defect is a departure from a product unit's design specifications that results in products that are physically flawed, damaged, or incorrectly assembled. A glass bottle that is made too thin and explodes in a consumer's face is an example of a product with a manufacturing defect.

Quality Control. Usually, manufacturing defects occur when a manufacturer fails to assemble, test, or check the quality of a product adequately. Liability is imposed on the manufacturer (and on the wholesaler and retailer) regardless of whether the manufacturer's quality control efforts were "reasonable." The idea behind holding defendants strictly liable for manufacturing defects is to encourage greater investment in product safety and stringent quality control standards.

Expert Testimony. Cases involving allegations of a manufacturing defect are often decided based on the opinions and testimony of experts. ■ **CASE IN POINT 7.4** Kevin Schmude purchased an eight-foot stepladder and used it to install radio-frequency shielding in a hospital room. While Schmude was standing on the ladder, it collapsed, and he was seriously injured. He filed a lawsuit against the ladder's maker, Tricam Industries, Inc., based on a manufacturing defect.

Experts testified that the preexisting holes in the ladder's top cap did not properly line up with the holes in the rear right rail and backing plate. As a result of the misalignment, the rear legs of the ladder were not securely fastened in place, causing the ladder to fail. A jury concluded that this manufacturing defect made the ladder unreasonably dangerous and awarded Schmude more than $677,000 in damages.[6] ■

Design Defects Unlike a product with a manufacturing defect, a product with a design defect is made in conformity with the manufacturer's design specifications. Nevertheless, the product results in injury to the user because the design itself was faulty. A product "is defective in design when the foreseeable risks of harm posed by the product could have been reduced or avoided by the adoption of a reasonable alternative design by the seller or other distributor, or a predecessor in the commercial chain of distribution, and the omission of the alternative design renders the product not reasonably safe."[7]

---

6. *Schmude v. Tricam Industries, Inc.*, 550 F.Supp.2d 846 (E.D.Wis. 2008).
7. *Restatement (Third) of Torts: Products Liability*, Section 2(b).

Test for Design Defects. To successfully assert a design defect, a plaintiff has to show that:

1. A reasonable alternative design was available.
2. As a result of the defendant's failure to adopt the alternative design, the product was not reasonably safe.

In other words, a manufacturer or other defendant is liable only when the harm was reasonably preventable.

Factors to Be Considered. According to the *Restatement,* a court can consider a broad range of factors in deciding claims of design defects. These include the magnitude and probability of the foreseeable risks, as well as the relative advantages and disadvantages of the product as it was designed and as it could have been designed.

Risk-Utility Analysis. Most courts engage in a risk-utility analysis to determine whether the risk of harm from the product as designed outweighs its utility to the user and to the public. ■ **CASE IN POINT 7.5** Benjamin Riley, the county sheriff, was driving his Ford F-150 pickup truck near Ehrhardt, South Carolina, when it collided with another vehicle. The impact caused Riley's truck to leave the road and roll over. The driver's door of the truck opened in the collision, and Riley was ejected and killed.

Riley's widow, Laura, as the representative of his estate, filed a product liability suit against Ford Motor Company. She alleged that the design of the door-latch system of the truck allowed the door to open in the collision. A state court awarded the estate $900,000 in damages "because of the stature of Riley and what he's done in life, what he's contributed to his family."

Ford appealed, but the court found that a reasonable alternative design was available for the door-latch system. Evidence showed that Ford was aware of the safety problems presented by the current system (a rod-linkage system). After conducting a risk-utility analysis of a different system (a cable-linkage system), Ford had concluded that the alternative system was feasible and perhaps superior. The state's highest court affirmed the damages award.[8] ■

Consumer-Expectation Test. Other courts apply the consumer-expectation test to determine whether a product's design was defective. Under this test, a product is unreasonably dangerous when it fails to perform in the manner that would reasonably be expected by an ordinary consumer.

■ **CASE IN POINT 7.6** A representative from Wilson Sporting Goods Company gave Edwin Hickox an umpire's mask that was designed to be safer than other such masks. The mask had a newly designed throat guard that angled forward instead of extending straight down. Hickox was wearing the mask while working as an umpire at a game when he was struck by a ball and injured. He suffered a concussion and damage to his inner ear, which caused permanent hearing loss.

Hickox and his wife sued Wilson for product liability based on a defective design and won. Wilson appealed. The reviewing court affirmed the jury's verdict. The design was defective because "an ordinary consumer would have expected the mask to perform more safely than it did." The evidence presented to the jury had shown that Wilson's mask was more dangerous than comparable masks sold at the time.[9] ■

Inadequate Warnings A product may also be deemed defective because of inadequate instructions or warnings. A product will be considered defective "when the foreseeable risks of harm posed by the product could have been reduced or avoided by the provision of reasonable instructions or warnings by the seller or other distributor . . . and the omission of the instructions or warnings renders the product not reasonably safe."[10] Generally, a seller must also warn consumers of the harm that can result from the *foreseeable misuse* of its product.

Content of Warnings. Important factors for a court to consider include the risks of a product, the "content and comprehensibility" and "intensity of expression" of warnings and instructions, and the "characteristics of expected user groups."[11] Courts apply a "reasonableness" test to determine if the warnings adequately alert consumers to the product's risks. For instance, children will likely respond readily to bright, bold, simple warning labels, whereas educated adults might need more detailed information. For more on tips on making sure a product's warnings are adequate, see this chapter's *Managerial Strategy* feature.

■ **CASE IN POINT 7.7** Jeffrey Johnson went to an emergency room for an episode of atrial fibrillation, a heart rhythm disorder. Dr. David Hahn used a defibrillator manufactured by Medtronic, Inc., to deliver electric shocks to Johnson's heart. The defibrillator had synchronous and asynchronous modes, and it reverted to the

8. *Riley v. Ford Motor Co.,* 414 S.C. 185, 777 S.E.2d 824 (2015).

9. *Wilson Sporting Goods Co. v. Hickox,* 59 A.3d 1267 (D.C.App. 2013).
10. *Restatement (Third) of Torts: Products Liability,* Section 2(c).
11. *Restatement (Third) of Torts: Products Liability,* Section 2, Comment h.

MANAGERIAL STRATEGY

When Is a Warning Legally Bulletproof?

A company can sell a perfectly manufactured and designed product, yet still face product liability lawsuits for failure to provide appropriate warnings. According to the *Restatement (Third) of Torts,* a product may be deemed defective because of inadequate instructions or warnings when the foreseeable risks of harm posed by the product could have been reduced by reasonable warnings offered by the seller or other distributor.

Manufacturers and distributors have a duty to warn users of any hidden dangers of their products. Additionally, they have a duty to instruct users in how to use the product to avoid any dangers. Warnings generally must be clear and specific. They must also be conspicuous.

When No Warning Is Required

Not all products have to provide warnings. People are expected to know that knives can cut fingers, for example, so a seller need not place a bright orange label on each knife sold reminding consumers of this danger. Most household products are generally safe when used as intended.

In a New Jersey case, an appeals court reviewed a product liability case against the manufacturer of a Razor A–type kick scooter. A ten-year-old boy was injured when he fell and struck his face on the scooter's handlebars. The padded end caps on the handlebars had deteriorated, and the boy's mother had thrown them away, exposing the metal ends.

The boy and his mother sued, claiming that the manufacturer was required to provide a warning to prevent injuries of this type. The appellate court noted, however, that the plaintiffs were not able to claim that the Razor A was defective. "Lacking evidence that Razor A's end-cap design was defective, plaintiffs cannot show that Razor A had a duty to warn of such a defect, and

therefore cannot make out their failure to warn claim."[a]

Warnings on Medications

In a case involving a prescription medication, a woman suffered neurological disorders after taking a generic drug to treat her gastroesophageal reflux disease. Part of her complaint asserted strict liability for failure to warn. The plaintiff claimed that the manufacturer had not updated its label to indicate that usage should not exceed twelve weeks. The reviewing court reasoned that "The adequacy of the instructions . . . made no difference to the outcome . . . because [the plaintiff alleges that her prescribing physician] did not read those materials." [b]

In contrast, in a 2014 Pennsylvania case, a family was awarded over $10 million in a lawsuit against Johnson & Johnson for defective warnings on bottles of children's Motrin. A three-year-old girl suffered burns over 84 percent of her skin, experienced brain damage, and went blind after suffering a reaction to the drug. The drug did have a specific warning label that instructed consumers to stop taking the medication and contact a physician in the event of an allergic reaction. Nonetheless, Johnson & Johnson was found liable for failing to warn about the known risk of severe side effects.[c]

Business Questions

1. *To protect themselves, manufacturers have been forced to include lengthy safety warnings for their products. What might be the downside of such warnings?*

2. *Does a manufacturer have to create safety warnings for every product? Why or why not?*

a. *Vann v. Toys R Us,* 2014 WL3537937 (N.J.Sup. A.D. 2014).
b. *Brinkley v. Pfizer, Inc.,* 772 F.3d 1133 (8th Cir. 2014).
c. *Maya v. Johnson and Johnson,* 97 A.3d 1203, 2014 PA Super. 152 (2014).

---

asynchronous mode after each use. Hahn intended to deliver synchronized shocks, which would have required him to select the synchronous mode for each shock. But Hahn did not read the device's instructions, which Medtronic had provided both in a manual and on the device itself. As a result, the physician delivered one synchronized shock, followed by twelve asynchronous shocks that endangered Johnson's life.

Johnson and his wife filed a product liability suit against Medtronic, asserting that Medtronic had provided

inadequate warnings about the defibrillator and that the device had a design defect. A Missouri appellate court held that the Johnsons could not pursue a claim based on the inadequacy of Medtronic's warnings, but they could pursue a claim alleging a design defect. The court reasoned that, in some cases, "a manufacturer may be held liable where it chooses to warn of the danger . . . rather than preclude the danger by design."[12] ■

---

12. *Johnson v. Medtronic, Inc.,* 365 S.W.3d 226 (Mo.App. 2012).

Obvious Risks. There is no duty to warn about risks that are obvious or commonly known. Warnings about such risks do not add to the safety of a product and could even detract from it by making other warnings seem less significant. As will be discussed later in the chapter, the obviousness of a risk and a user's decision to proceed in the face of that risk may be a defense in a product liability suit based on an inadequate warning.

■ **EXAMPLE 7.8** Sixteen-year-old Lana White attempts to do a back flip on a trampoline and fails. She is paralyzed as a result. There are nine warning labels affixed to the trampoline, an instruction manual with safety warnings, and a placard at the entrance advising users not to do flips. If White sues the manufacturer for inadequate warnings in this situation, she is likely to lose. The warning labels are probably sufficient to make the risks obvious and insulate the manufacturer from liability for her injuries. ■

Risks that may seem obvious to some users, though, will not be obvious to all users, especially when the users are likely to be children. A young child may not be able to read or understand warning labels or comprehend the risk of certain activities. To avoid liability, the manufacturer would have to prove that the warnings it provided were adequate to make the risk of injury obvious to a young child.[13]

State Laws and Constitutionality. An action alleging that a product is defective due to an inadequate label can be based on state law, but that law must not violate the U.S. Constitution. ■ **CASE IN POINT 7.9** California once enacted a law imposing restrictions and a labeling requirement on the sale or rental of "violent video games" to minors. Although the video game industry had adopted a voluntary rating system for games, the legislators deemed those labels inadequate.

The Video Software Dealers Association and the Entertainment Software Association immediately filed a suit in federal court to invalidate the law, and the law was struck down. The state appealed to the United States Supreme Court. The Court found that the definition of a violent video game in California's law was unconstitutionally vague and violated the First Amendment's guarantee of freedom of speech.[14] ■

7–3d Market-Share Liability

Ordinarily, in all product liability claims, a plaintiff must prove that the defective product that caused his or her injury was the product of a specific defendant. In a few situations, however, courts have dropped this requirement when plaintiffs could not prove which of many distributors of a harmful product supplied the particular product that caused the injuries. Under a theory of **market-share liability,** a court can hold each manufacturer responsible for a percentage of the plaintiff's damages that is equal to the percentage of its market share.

■ **CASE IN POINT 7.10** Suffolk County Water Authority (SCWA) is a municipal water supplier in New York. SCWA discovered the presence of a toxic chemical—perchlorethylene (PCE), which is used by dry cleaners and others—in its local water. SCWA filed a product liability lawsuit against Dow Chemical Corporation and other companies that manufactured and distributed PCE. Dow filed a motion to dismiss the case for failure to state a claim, since SCWA could not identify each defendant whose allegedly defective product caused the water contamination.

A state trial court refused to dismiss the action, holding that SCWA's allegations were sufficient to invoke market-share liability. Under market-share liability, the burden of identification shifts to defendants if the plaintiff establishes a *prima facie* case on every element of the claim except identification of the specific defendant. (A *prima facie* case is one in which the plaintiff has presented sufficient evidence for the claim to go forward.)[15] ■

Many jurisdictions do not recognize the market-share theory of liability because they believe that it deviates too significantly from traditional legal principles. Jurisdictions that do recognize market-share liability apply it only when it is difficult to determine which company made a particular product.

7–3e Other Applications of Strict Product Liability

Almost all courts extend the strict liability of manufacturers and other sellers to injured bystanders. Thus, if a defective forklift that will not go into reverse injures a passerby, that individual can sue the manufacturer for product liability (and possibly also sue the forklift operator for negligence).

Strict product liability also applies to suppliers of component parts. ■ **EXAMPLE 7.11** Toyota buys brake pads from a subcontractor and puts them in Corollas without changing their composition. If those pads are defective, both the supplier of the brake pads and Toyota will be held strictly liable for the injuries caused by the defects. ■

13. See, for example, *Bunch v. Hoffinger Industries, Inc.*,123 Cal.App.4th 1278, 20 Cal.Rptr.3d 780 (2004).
14. *Video Software Dealers Association v. Schwarzenegger*, 556 F.3d 950 (9th Cir. 2009); *Brown v. Entertainment Merchants Association*, ___ U.S. ___, 131 S.Ct. 2729, 180 L.Ed.2d 708 (2011).
15. *Suffolk County Water Authority v. Dow Chemical Co.*, 44 Misc.3d 569, 987 N.Y.S.2d 819 (N.Y.Sup. 2014).

7-4 Defenses to Product Liability

Defendants in product liability suits can raise a number of defenses. One defense, of course, is to show that there is no basis for the plaintiff's claim. Thus, for instance, in an action based on negligence, If a defendant can show that the plaintiff has *not* met the requirements for such an action (such as causation), then generally the defendant will not be liable.

Similarly, in a case involving strict product liability, a defendant can claim that the plaintiff failed to meet one of the requirements. For instance, if the defendant shows that the goods were altered after they were sold, normally the defendant will not be held liable.

In the following case, a product's safety switch had been disabled before the plaintiff used the product.

Case 7.3

VeRost v. Mitsubishi Caterpillar Forklift America, Inc.

New York Supreme Court, Appellate Division, Fourth Department, 124 A.D.3d 1219, 1 N.Y.S.3d 589 (2015).

Background and Facts   Drew VeRost was employed at a manufacturing facility in Buffalo, New York, owned by Nuttall Gear, LLC. While operating a forklift at Nuttall's facility, VeRost climbed out of the seat and attempted to engage a lever on the vehicle. As he stood on the front of the forklift and reached for the lever with his hand, he inadvertently stepped on the vehicle's gearshift. The activated gears caused part of the forklift to move backward, injuring him. He filed a suit in a New York state court against the forklift's maker, Mitsubishi Caterpillar Forklift America, Inc., and others, asserting claims in product liability.

The defendants established that the vehicle had been manufactured with a safety switch that would have prevented the accident had it not been disabled after delivery to Nuttall. The court issued a summary judgment in the defendants' favor. VeRost appealed.

In the Language of the Court

MEMORANDUM:

　　* * * *

The forklift in question was manufactured by defendant Mitsubishi Caterpillar Forklift America, Inc. (MCFA), and sold new to Nuttall Gear by defendants Buffalo Lift Trucks, Inc. (Buffalo Lift) and Mullen Industrial Handling Corp. (Mullen). The forklift as manufactured was equipped with a seat safety switch that would render the forklift inoperable if the operator was not in the driver's seat. At the time of the accident, however, someone had intentionally disabled the safety switch by installing a "jumper wire" under the seat of the forklift. As a result, the forklift still had power when the operator was not in the driver's seat. Of the 10 forklifts owned by Nuttall Gear, seven had "jumper wires" installed that disabled the safety switches.

The complaint asserts causes of action against MCFA, Buffalo Lift and Mullen sounding in strict products liability, alleging, *inter alia* ["among other things"], that the forklift was defectively designed and that those defendants failed to provide adequate "warnings for the safe operation, maintenance repair and servicing of the forklift." * * * Following discovery, the * * * defendants * * * each moved for summary judgment dismissing the complaint against them, contending that the forklift was safe when it was manufactured and delivered to Nuttall Gear, and that it was thereafter rendered unsafe by a third party who deactivated the safety switch. * * * [The] Supreme Court [of New York] granted the motions and dismissed the complaint in its entirety, and this appeal ensued.

We conclude that the court properly granted the motions of the * * * defendants. * * * *A manufacturer, who has designed and produced a safe product, will not be liable for injuries resulting from substantial alterations or modifications of the product by a third party which render the product defective or otherwise unsafe.* Here, the * * * defendants established as a matter of law that the forklift was not defectively designed by establishing that, when it was manufactured and delivered to Nuttall Gear, it had a safety switch that would have prevented plaintiff's accident, and a third party thereafter made a substantial modification to the forklift by disabling the safety switch. [Emphasis added.]

Case 7.3 Continued

Decision and Remedy *The state intermediate appellate court affirmed the lower court's judgment in Mitsubishi's favor. To succeed in an action based on product liability, the goods at issue must not have been substantially changed from the time the product was sold to the time the injury was sustained. VeRost could not meet this requirement.*

Critical Thinking

- **Legal Environment** *Could VeRost succeed in an action against Nuttall, alleging that the company's failure to maintain the forklift in a safe condition constituted negligence? Discuss.*

7–4a Preemption

A defense that has been successfully raised by defendants in recent years is preemption—that government regulations preempt claims for product liability (see *Spotlight Case* 7.2). An injured party may not be able to sue the manufacturer of defective products that are subject to comprehensive federal regulatory schemes.

■ **CASE IN POINT 7.12** Medical devices are subject to extensive government regulation and undergo a rigorous premarket approval process. The United States Supreme Court decided in *Riegel v. Medtronic, Inc.,* that a man who was injured by an approved medical device (a balloon catheter) could not sue its maker for product liability. The Court reasoned that Congress had created a comprehensive scheme of federal safety oversight for medical devices. The U.S. Food and Drug Administration is required to review the design, labeling, and manufacturing of medical devices before they are marketed to make sure that they are safe and effective. Because premarket approval is a "rigorous process," it preempts all common law claims challenging the safety or effectiveness of a medical device that has been approved.[16] ■

Since the *Medtronic* decision, some courts have extended the preemption defense to other product liability actions. Other courts have been unwilling to deny an injured party relief simply because the federal government was supposed to ensure a product's safety.[17] Even the United States Supreme Court refused to extend the preemption defense to preclude a drug maker's liability in one subsequent case.[18]

7–4b Assumption of Risk

Assumption of risk can sometimes be used as a defense in a product liability action. To establish assumption of risk, the defendant must show the following:

1. The plaintiff knew and appreciated the risk created by the product defect.
2. The plaintiff voluntarily assumed the risk—by express agreement or by words or conduct—even though it was unreasonable to do so.

Some states do not allow the defense of assumption of risk in strict product liability claims, however. ■ **CASE IN POINT 7.13** When Savannah Boles became a customer of Executive Tans, she signed a contract. One part of the contract stated that signers used the company's tanning booths at their own risk. It also released the manufacturer and others from liability for any injuries.

Later, Boles's fingers were partially amputated when they came into contact with a tanning booth's fan. Boles sued the manufacturer for strict product liability. The Colorado Supreme Court held that assumption of risk was not applicable because strict product liability is driven by public-policy considerations. The theory focuses on the nature of the product rather than the conduct of either the manufacturer or the person injured.[19] ■

7–4c Product Misuse

Similar to the defense of voluntary assumption of risk is that of **product misuse,** which occurs when a product is used for a purpose for which it was not intended. The courts have severely limited this defense, however, and it is now recognized as a defense *only when the particular use was not foreseeable.* If the misuse is reasonably foreseeable, the seller must take measures to guard against it.

---

16. *Riegel v. Medtronic, Inc.,* 552 U.S. 312, 128 S.Ct. 999, 169 L.Ed.2d 892 (2008).

17. See, for example, *McGuan v. Endovascular Technologies, Inc.,* 182 Cal. App.4th 974, 106 Cal.Rptr.3d 277 (2010), and *Paduano v. American Honda Motor Co.,* 169 Cal.App.4th 1453, 88 Cal.Rptr.3d 90 (2009).

18. *Wyeth v. Levine,* 555 U.S. 555, 129 S.Ct. 1187, 173 L.Ed.2d 51 (2009).

19. *Boles v. Sun Ergoline, Inc.,* 223 P.3d 724 (Col.Sup.Ct. 2010).

■ **CASE IN POINT 7.14** David Stults developed bronchiolitis obliterans ("popcorn lung") from consuming multiple bags of microwave popcorn daily for several years. When Stults filed a lawsuit against the popcorn manufacturers, they asked the court for a summary judgment in their favor. The court denied the defendants' motion and found that a manufacturer has a duty to warn of dangers associated with reasonably foreseeable misuses of a product. If it is foreseeable that a person might consume several bags of microwave popcorn a day, then the manufacturer might have to warn users about the potential health risks associated with doing so.[20] ■

7–4d Comparative Negligence (Fault)

Comparative negligence, or fault, can also affect strict liability claims. Today, courts in many jurisdictions consider the negligent or intentional actions of both the plaintiff and the defendant when apportioning liability and damages. A defendant may be able to limit some of its liability if it can show that the plaintiff's misuse of the product contributed to his or her injuries.

When proved, comparative negligence differs from other defenses in that it does not completely absolve the defendant of liability. It can, however, reduce the total amount of damages that will be awarded to the plaintiff. Note that some jurisdictions allow only intentional conduct to affect a plaintiff's recovery, whereas other states allow ordinary negligence to be used as a defense to product liability.

7–4e Commonly Known Dangers

The dangers associated with certain products (such as matches and sharp knives) are so commonly known that, as mentioned, manufacturers need not warn users of those dangers. If a defendant succeeds in convincing the court that a plaintiff's injury resulted from a *commonly known danger,* the defendant will not be liable.

■ **CASE IN POINT 7.15** In a classic example from 1957, Marguerite Jamieson was injured when an elastic exercise rope slipped off her foot and struck her in the eye, causing a detachment of the retina. Jamieson claimed that the manufacturer should be liable because it had failed to warn users that the exerciser might slip off a foot in such a manner.

The court stated that to hold the manufacturer liable in these circumstances "would go beyond the reasonable dictates of justice in fixing the liabilities of manufacturers." After all, stated the court, "almost every physical object can be inherently dangerous or potentially dangerous in a sense. . . . A manufacturer cannot manufacture a knife that will not cut or a hammer that will not mash a thumb or a stove that will not burn a finger. The law does not require [manufacturers] to warn of such common dangers."[21] ■

7–4f Knowledgeable User

A related defense is the *knowledgeable user* defense. If a particular danger (such as electrical shock) is or should be commonly known by particular users of a product (such as electricians), the manufacturer need not warn these users of the danger.

■ **CASE IN POINT 7.16** The parents of teenagers who had become overweight and developed health problems filed a product liability suit against McDonald's. The plaintiffs claimed that the fast-food chain had failed to warn customers of the adverse health effects of eating its food. The court rejected this claim, however, based on the knowledgeable user defense.

The court found that it is well known that the food at McDonald's contains high levels of cholesterol, fat, salt, and sugar and is therefore unhealthful. The court stated: "If consumers know (or reasonably should know) the potential ill health effects of eating at McDonald's, they cannot blame McDonald's if they, nonetheless, choose to satiate their appetite with a surfeit [excess] of supersized McDonald's products."[22] ■

7–4g Statutes of Limitations and Repose

Statutes of limitations restrict the time within which an action may be brought. The statute of limitations for product liability cases varies according to state law. Usually, the injured party must bring a product liability claim within two to four years. Often, the running of the prescribed period is **tolled** (that is, suspended) until the party suffering an injury has discovered it or should have discovered it.

To ensure that sellers and manufacturers will not be left vulnerable to lawsuits indefinitely, many states have passed **statutes of repose,** which place *outer* time limits on product liability actions. For instance, a statute of repose may require that claims be brought within twelve years from the date of sale or manufacture of the defective product. If the plaintiff does not bring an action before the prescribed period expires, the seller cannot be held liable.

Concept Summary 7.1 reviews the possible defenses in product liability actions.

---

20. *Stults v. International Flavors and Fragrances, Inc.,* 31 F.Supp.3d 1015 (N.D. Iowa 2014).

21. *Jamieson v. Woodward & Lothrop,* 247 F.2d 23 (D.C.Cir. 1957).
22. *Pelman v. McDonald's Corp.,* 237 F.Supp.2d 512 (S.D.N.Y. 2003).

Concept Summary 7.1

Defenses to Product Liability

Preemption	If the product is subject to comprehensive federal safety regulations
Assumption of Risk	When the user or consumer knew the risk and voluntarily assumed it
Product Misuse	If the consumer misused the product in an unforeseeable way
Comparative Negligence	Apportions liability if the defendant was also negligent
Commonly Known Dangers	If the product was commonly known to be dangerous
Knowledgeable User	If the particular danger is commonly known by particular users of the product
Statutory Time Periods	If the statute of limitations or statute of repose period has expired

Reviewing: Strict Liability and Product Liability

Shalene Kolchek bought a Great Lakes Spa from Val Porter, a dealer who was selling spas at the state fair. Kolchek signed an installment contract. Porter then handed her the manufacturer's paperwork and arranged for the spa to be delivered and installed for her. Three months later, Kolchek left her six-year-old daughter, Litisha, alone in the spa. While exploring the spa's hydromassage jets, Litisha stuck her index finger into one of the jet holes and was unable to remove her finger from the jet.

Litisha yanked hard, injuring her finger, then panicked and screamed for help. Kolchek was unable to remove Litisha's finger, and the local police and rescue team were called to assist. After a three-hour operation that included draining the spa, sawing out a section of the spa's plastic molding, and slicing the jet casing, Litisha's finger was freed. Following this procedure, the spa was no longer functional. Litisha was taken to the local emergency room, where she was told that a bone in her finger was broken in two places. Using the information presented in the chapter, answer the following questions.

1. Under which theories of product liability can Kolchek sue Porter to recover for Litisha's injuries?
2. Would privity of contract be required for Kolchek to succeed in a product liability action against Great Lakes? Explain.
3. For an action in strict product liability against Great Lakes, what six requirements must Kolchek meet?
4. What defenses to product liability might Porter or Great Lakes be able to assert?

Debate This . . . *All liability suits against tobacco companies for lung cancer should be thrown out of court now and forever.*

Terms and Concepts

market-share liability 143	product misuse 145	tolling 146
privity of contract 135	statute of repose 146	unreasonably dangerous
product liability 134	strict liability 134	product 140

Issue Spotters

1. Rim Corporation makes tire rims that it sells to Superior Vehicles, Inc., which installs them on cars. One set of rims is defective, which an inspection would reveal. Superior does not inspect the rims. The car with the defective rims is sold to Town Auto Sales, which sells the car to Uri. Soon, the car is in an accident caused by the defective rims, and Uri is injured. Is Superior Vehicles liable? Explain your answer. (See *Strict Product Liability*.)

2. Bensing Company manufactures generic drugs for the treatment of heart disease. A federal law requires generic drug makers to use labels that are identical to the labels on brand-name versions of the drugs. Hunter Rothfus purchased Bensing's generic drugs in Ohio and wants to sue Bensing for defective labeling based on its failure to comply with Ohio state common law (rather than the federal labeling requirements). What defense might Bensing assert to avoid liability under state law? (See *Defenses to Product Liability*.)

• Check your answers to the Issue Spotters against the answers provided in Appendix D at the end of this text.

Business Scenarios

7–1. Strict Liability. Danny and Marion Klein were injured when part of a fireworks display went astray and exploded near them. They sued Pyrodyne Corp., the pyrotechnic company that was hired to set up and discharge the fireworks. The Kleins alleged, among other things, that the company should be strictly liable for damages caused by the fireworks display. Will the court agree with the Kleins? What factors will the court consider in making its decision? Discuss fully. (See *Strict Liability*.)

7–2. Product Liability. Jason Clark, an experienced hunter, bought a paintball gun. Clark practiced with the gun and knew how to screw in the carbon dioxide cartridge, pump the gun, and use its safety and trigger. Although Clark was aware that he could purchase protective eyewear, he chose not to buy it.

Clark had taken gun safety courses and understood that it was "common sense" not to shoot anyone in the face. Clark's friend, Chris Wright, also owned a paintball gun and was similarly familiar with the gun's use and its risks.

Clark, Wright, and their friends played a game that involved shooting paintballs at cars whose occupants also had the guns. One night, while Clark and Wright were cruising with their guns, Wright shot at Clark's car, but hit Clark in the eye. Clark filed a product liability lawsuit against the manufacturer of Wright's paintball gun to recover for the injury. Clark claimed that the gun was defectively designed. During the trial, Wright testified that his gun "never malfunctioned." In whose favor should the court rule? Why? (See *Product Liability*.)

Business Case Problems

7–3. Design Defects. Yun Tung Chow tried to unclog a floor drain in the kitchen of the restaurant where he worked. He used a drain cleaner called Lewis Red Devil Lye that contained crystalline sodium hydroxide. The product label said to wear eye protection, to put one tablespoon of lye directly into the drain, and to keep one's face away from the drain because there could be dangerous backsplash.

Without eye protection, Chow mixed three tablespoons of lye in a can and poured that mixture down the drain while bending over it. Liquid splashed back into his face, causing injury. He brought a product liability suit based on inadequate warnings and design defect. The trial court granted summary judgment to the manufacturer, and Chow appealed. An expert for Chow stated that the product was defective because it had a tendency to backsplash. Is that a convincing argument? Why or why not? [*Yun Tung Chow v. Reckitt & Coleman, Inc.,* 69 A.D.3d 413, 891 N.Y.S.2d 402 (N.Y.A.D. 1 Dept. 2010)] (See *Strict Product Liability*.)

7–4. Strict Product Liability. David Dobrovolny bought a new Ford F-350 pickup truck. A year later, the truck spontaneously caught fire in Dobrovolny's driveway. The truck was destroyed, but no other property was damaged, and no one was injured. Dobrovolny filed a suit in a Nebraska state court against Ford Motor Co. on a theory of strict product liability to recover the cost of the truck. Nebraska limits the application of strict product liability to situations involving personal injuries. Is Dobrovolny's claim likely to succeed? Why or why not? Is there another basis for liability on which he might recover? Explain. [*Dobrovolny v. Ford Motor Co.,* 281 Neb. 86, 793 N.W.2d 445 (2011)] (See *Strict Product Liability*.)

7–5. Product Misuse. Five-year-old Cheyenne Stark was riding in the backseat of her parents' Ford Taurus. Cheyenne was not sitting in a booster seat. Instead, she was using a seatbelt designed by Ford, but was wearing the shoulder belt behind her back. The car was involved in a collision. As a result, Cheyenne suffered a spinal cord injury and was paralyzed from the waist down. The family filed a suit against Ford Motor Co., alleging that the seatbelt was defectively designed. Could Ford successfully claim that Cheyenne had misused the seatbelt? Why or why not? [*Stark v. Ford Motor Co.,* 365 N.C. 468, 723 S.E.2d 753 (2012)] (See *Defenses to Product Liability.*)

7–6. Business Case Problem with Sample Answer— Product Liability. While driving on Interstate 40 in North Carolina, Carroll Jett became distracted by a texting system in the cab of his tractor-trailer truck. He smashed into several vehicles that were slowed or stopped in front of him, injuring Barbara and Michael Durkee and others. The injured motorists filed a suit in a federal district court against Geologic Solutions, Inc., the maker of the texting system, alleging product liability. Was the accident caused by Jett's inattention or the texting device? Should a manufacturer be required to design a product that is incapable of distracting a driver? Discuss. [*Durkee v. Geologic Solutions, Inc.,* 2013 WL 14717 (4th Cir. 2013)] (See *Product Liability.*)

- **For a sample answer to Problem 7–6, go to Appendix E at the end of this text.**

7–7. Strict Product Liability. Medicis Pharmaceutical Corp. makes Solodyn, a prescription oral antibiotic. Medicis warns physicians that "autoimmune syndromes, including drug-induced lupus-like syndrome," may be associated with use of the drug. Amanda Watts had chronic acne. Her physician prescribed Solodyn. Information included with the drug did not mention the risk of autoimmune disorders, and Watts was not otherwise advised of it. She was prescribed the drug twice, each time for twenty weeks. Later, she experienced debilitating joint pain and, after being hospitalized, was diagnosed with lupus. On what basis could Watts recover from Medicis in an action grounded in product liability? Explain. [*Watts v. Medicis Pharmaceutical Corp.,* 236 Ariz. 511, 342 P.3d 847 (2015)] (See *Strict Product Liability.*)

7–8. Strict Product Liability. Duval Ford, LLC, sold a new Ford F-250 pick-up truck to David Sweat. Before taking delivery, Sweat ordered a lift kit to be installed on the truck by a Duval subcontractor. Sweat also replaced the tires and modified the suspension system to increase the towing capacity. Later, through Burkins Chevrolet, Sweat sold the truck to

Shaun Lesnick. Sweat had had no problems with the truck's steering or suspension, but Lesnick did. He had the steering repaired and made additional changes, including installing a steering stabilizer and replacing the tires. Two months later, Lesnick was driving the truck when the steering and suspension suddenly failed, and the truck flipped over, causing Lesnick severe injuries. Could Lesnick successfully claim that Duval and Burkins had failed to warn him of the risk of a lifted truck? Explain. [*Lesnick v. Duval Ford, LLC,* 41 Fla.L.Weekly D281, __ So.3d __ (Fla.Dist.Ct.App., 1 Dist. 2016)] (See *Strict Product Liability.*)

7–9. A Question of Ethics—Dangerous Products. *Susan* *Calles lived with her four daughters—Amanda, age eleven; Victoria, age five; and Jenna and Jillian, age three. In March 1998, Calles bought an Aim N Flame utility lighter, which she stored on the top shelf of her kitchen cabinet. A trigger can ignite the Aim N Flame after an "ON/OFF" switch is slid to the "on" position. On the night of March 31, Calles and Victoria left to get videos. Jenna and Jillian were in bed, and Amanda was watching television. Calles returned to find fire trucks and emergency vehicles around her home. Robert Finn, a fire investigator, determined that Jenna had started a fire using the lighter. Jillian suffered smoke inhalation, was hospitalized, and died on April 21. Calles filed a suit in an Illinois state court against Scripto-Tokai Corp., which distributed the Aim N Flame, and others. In her suit, which was grounded, in part, in strict liability claims, Calles alleged that the lighter was an "unreasonably dangerous product." Scripto filed a motion for summary judgment. [Calles v. Scripto-Tokai Corp., 224 Ill.2d 247, 864 N.E.2d 249, 309 Ill. Dec. 383 (2007)] (See Strict Product Liability.)*

(a) A product is "unreasonably dangerous" when it is dangerous beyond the expectation of the ordinary consumer. Whose expectation—Calles's or Jenna's—applies? Does the lighter pass this test? Explain.

(b) Calles presented evidence as to the likelihood and seriousness of injury from lighters that do not have child-safety devices. Scripto argued that the Aim N Flame is an alternative source of fire and is safer than a match. Calles admitted that she knew the dangers presented by lighters in the hands of children. Scripto admitted that it had been a defendant in several suits for injuries under similar circumstances. How should the court rule? Why?

Legal Reasoning Group Activity

7–10. Product Liability. Bret D'Auguste was an experienced skier when he rented equipment to ski at Hunter Mountain Ski Bowl in New York. When D'Auguste entered an extremely difficult trail, he noticed immediately that the surface consisted of ice with almost no snow. He tried to exit the steeply declining trail by making a sharp right turn, but in the attempt, his left ski snapped off. D'Auguste lost his balance, fell, and slid down the mountain, striking his face and head against a fence along the trail. According to a report by a rental shop employee, one of the bindings on D'Auguste's skis had a "cracked heel housing." D'Auguste filed a lawsuit

against the bindings' manufacturer on a theory of strict product liability. The manufacturer filed a motion for summary judgment. (See *Product Liability.*)

(a) The first group will take the position of the manufacturer and develop an argument for why the court should *grant* the summary judgment motion and dismiss the strict product liability claim.

(b) The second group will take the position of D'Auguste and formulate a basis for why the court should *deny* the motion and allow the strict product liability claim.

CHAPTER 8

Intellectual Property Rights

Intellectual **property** is any property that results from intellectual, creative processes—the products of an individual's mind. Although it is an abstract term for an abstract concept, intellectual property is nonetheless familiar to almost everyone. The apps for your iPhone, iPad, or Samsung Galaxy, the movies you see, and the music you listen to are all forms of intellectual property.

More than two hundred years ago, the framers of the U.S. Constitution recognized the importance of protecting creative works in Article I, Section 8. Statutory protection of these rights began in the 1940s and continues to evolve to meet the needs of modern society. In today's global economy, however, protecting intellectual property in one country is no longer sufficient. The United States is participating in various international agreements to secure ownership rights in intellectual property in other countries.

Whether locally or globally, businesspersons have a vital need to protect their rights in intellectual property, which may be more valuable than their physical property, such as machines and buildings. Consider, for instance, the importance of intellectual property rights to technology companies, such as Apple, Inc., and Samsung. These two companies have been involved in patent litigation over the designs of their smartphones for several years.

8–1 Trademarks and Related Property

A **trademark** is a distinctive mark, motto, device, or implement that a manufacturer stamps, prints, or otherwise affixes to the goods it produces so that they can be identified on the market and their origins made known. In other words, a trademark is a source indicator. At common law, the person who used a symbol or mark to identify a business or product was protected in the use of that trademark. Clearly, by using another's trademark, a business could lead consumers to believe that its goods were made by the other business. The law seeks to avoid this kind of confusion.

In the following classic case, the defendants argued that the Coca-Cola trademark was entitled to no protection under the law because the term did not accurately represent the product.

The Coca-Cola Co. v. The Koke Co. of America

Supreme Court of the United States, 254 U.S. 143, 41 S.Ct. 113, 65 L.Ed.189 (1920).

Company Profile *John Pemberton, an Atlanta pharmacist, invented a caramel-colored, carbonated soft drink in 1886. His bookkeeper, Frank Robinson, named the beverage Coca-Cola after two of the ingredients, coca leaves and kola nuts. Asa Candler bought the Coca-Cola Company in 1891, and within seven years, he had made the soft drink available throughout the United States, as well as in parts of Canada and Mexico. Candler continued to sell Coke aggressively and to open up new markets, reaching Europe before 1910. In doing so, however, he attracted numerous competitors, some of which tried to capitalize directly on the Coke name.*

Case 8.1 Continued

Background and Facts The Coca-Cola Company sought to enjoin (prevent) the Koke Company of America and other beverage companies from, among other things, using the word *Koke* for their products. The Koke Company of America and other beverage companies contended that the Coca-Cola trademark was a fraudulent representation and that Coca-Cola was therefore not entitled to any help from the courts. The Koke Company and the other defendants alleged that the Coca-Cola Company, by its use of the Coca-Cola name, represented that the beverage contained cocaine (from coca leaves), which it no longer did. The trial court granted the injunction against the Koke Company, but the appellate court reversed the lower court's ruling. Coca-Cola then appealed to the United States Supreme Court.

In the Language of the Court

Mr. Justice *HOLMES* delivered the opinion of the Court.

* * * *

* * * Before 1900 the beginning of [Coca-Cola's] good will was more or less helped by the presence of cocaine, a drug that, like alcohol or caffeine or opium, may be described as a deadly poison or as a valuable [pharmaceutical item, depending on the speaker's purposes]. The amount seems to have been very small,[a] but it may have been enough to begin a bad habit and after the Food and Drug Act of June 30, 1906, if not earlier, long before this suit was brought, it was eliminated from the plaintiff's compound.

* * * Since 1900 the sales have increased at a very great rate corresponding to a like increase in advertising. The name now characterizes a beverage to be had at almost any soda fountain. It means a single thing coming from a single source, and well known to the community. It hardly would be too much to say that the drink characterizes the name as much as the name the drink. In other words *Coca-Cola probably means to most persons the plaintiff's familiar product to be had everywhere rather than a compound of particular substances.* * * * Before this suit was brought the plaintiff had advertised to the public that it must not expect and would not find cocaine, and had eliminated everything tending to suggest cocaine effects except the name and the picture of [coca] leaves and nuts, which probably conveyed little or nothing to most who saw it. It appears to us that it would be going too far to deny the plaintiff relief against a palpable [readily evident] fraud because possibly here and there an ignorant person might call for the drink with the hope for incipient cocaine intoxication. The plaintiff's position must be judged by the facts as they were when the suit was begun, not by the facts of a different condition and an earlier time. [Emphasis added.]

Decision and Remedy *The district court's injunction was allowed to stand. The competing beverage companies were enjoined from calling their products Koke.*

Impact of This Case on Today's Law *In this early case, the United States Supreme Court made it clear that trademarks and trade names (and nicknames for those marks and names, such as the nickname "Coke" for "Coca-Cola") that are in common use receive protection under the common law. This holding is significant historically because it is the predecessor to the federal statute later passed to protect trademark rights—the Lanham Act of 1946. In many ways, this act represented a codification of common law principles governing trademarks.*

Critical Thinking

- **What If the Facts Were Different?** *Suppose that Coca-Cola had been trying to make the public believe that its product contained cocaine. Would the result in this case likely have been different? Why or why not?*

---

a. In reality, until 1903 the amount of active cocaine in each bottle of Coke was equivalent to one "line" of cocaine.

8–1a Statutory Protection of Trademarks

Statutory protection of trademarks and related property is provided at the federal level by the Lanham Act of 1946.[1] The Lanham Act was enacted, in part, to protect manufacturers from losing business to rival companies that used confusingly similar trademarks. The act incorporates the common law of trademarks and provides remedies for owners of trademarks who wish to enforce their claims in federal court. Many states also have trademark statutes.

Trademark Dilution In 1995, Congress amended the Lanham Act by passing the Federal Trademark Dilution Act,[2] which allowed trademark owners to bring suits in federal court for trademark **dilution.** In 2006, Congress further amended the law on trademark dilution by passing the Trademark Dilution Revision Act (TDRA).[3]

Under the TDRA, to state a claim for trademark dilution, a plaintiff must prove the following:

1. The plaintiff owns a famous mark that is distinctive.
2. The defendant has begun using a mark in commerce that allegedly is diluting the famous mark.
3. The similarity between the defendant's mark and the famous mark gives rise to an *association* between the marks.
4. The association is likely to impair the distinctiveness of the famous mark or harm its reputation.

Trademark dilution laws protect "distinctive" or "famous" trademarks (such as Rolls Royce, McDonald's, Starbucks, and Apple) from certain unauthorized uses. Such a mark is protected even when the use is on noncompeting goods or is unlikely to cause confusion. More than half of the states have also enacted trademark dilution laws.

Marks Need Not Be Identical Note that a famous mark may be diluted by the use of an *identical* mark or by the use of a *similar* mark.[4] A similar mark is more likely to lessen the value of a famous mark when the companies using the marks provide related goods or compete against each other in the same market.

■ **CASE IN POINT 8.1** Samantha Lundberg opened a business called "Sambuck's Coffeehouse," in Astoria, Oregon, even though she knew that "Starbucks" was one of the largest coffee chains in the nation. Starbucks Corporation filed a dilution lawsuit, and a federal court ruled that use of the "Sambuck's" mark constituted trademark dilution because it created confusion for consumers. Not only was there a "high degree" of similarity between the marks, but also both companies provided coffee-related services and marketed their services through "stand-alone" retail stores. Therefore, the use of the similar mark (Sambuck's) reduced the value of the famous mark (Starbucks).[5] ■

8–1b Trademark Registration

Trademarks may be registered with the state or with the federal government. To register for protection under federal trademark law, a person must file an application with the U.S. Patent and Trademark Office in Washington, D.C. Under current law, a mark can be registered (1) if it is currently in commerce or (2) if the applicant intends to put it into commerce within six months.

In special circumstances, the six-month period can be extended by thirty months. Thus, the applicant would have a total of three years from the date of notice of trademark approval to make use of the mark and file the required use statement. Registration is postponed until the mark is actually used. During this waiting period, any applicant can legally protect his or her trademark against a third party who previously has neither used the mark nor filed an application for it.

Registration is renewable between the fifth and sixth years after the initial registration and every ten years thereafter (every twenty years for those trademarks registered before 1990).

8–1c Trademark Infringement

Registration of a trademark with the U.S. Patent and Trademark Office gives notice on a nationwide basis that the trademark belongs exclusively to the registrant. The registrant is also allowed to use the symbol ® to indicate that the mark has been registered. Whenever that trademark is copied to a substantial degree or used in its entirety by another, intentionally or unintentionally, the trademark has been *infringed* (used without authorization).

When a trademark has been infringed, the owner of the mark has a cause of action against the infringer. To succeed in a trademark infringement action, the owner must show that the defendant's use of the mark created a likelihood of confusion about the origin of the defendant's goods or services. The owner need not prove that

---

1. 15 U.S.C. Sections 1051–1128.
2. 15 U.S.C. Section 1125.
3. Pub. L. No. 103-312, 120 Stat. 1730 (2006).
4. See *Louis Vuitton Malletier S.A. v. Haute Diggity Dog, LLC,* 507 F.3d 252 (4th Cir. 2007); and *Moseley v. V Secret Catalogue, Inc.,* 537 U.S. 418, 123 S.Ct. 1115, 155 L.Ed.2d 1 (2003).
5. *Starbucks Corp. v. Lundberg,* 2005 WL 3183858 (D.Or. 2005).

the infringer acted intentionally or that the trademark was registered (although registration does provide proof of the date of inception of the trademark's use).

The most commonly granted remedy for trademark infringement is an *injunction* to prevent further infringement. Under the Lanham Act, a trademark owner that successfully proves infringement can recover actual damages, plus the profits that the infringer wrongfully

received from the unauthorized use of the mark. A court can also order the destruction of any goods bearing the unauthorized trademark. In some situations, the trademark owner may also be able to recover attorneys' fees.

At the center of the following case was an injunction granted in an earlier dispute between two brothers prohibiting one of them from using trademarks owned by the other, including a mark featuring their shared last name.

Case 8.2

LFP IP, LLC v. Hustler Cincinnati, Inc.

United States Court of Appeals, Sixth Circuit, 810 F.3d 424 (2016).

Background and Facts Brothers Jimmy and Larry Flynt owned "The Hustler Club," a bar and nightclub in Cincinnati, Ohio. Larry opened Hustler clubs in other Ohio cities. Within a few years, he also began publishing *Hustler,* a sexually explicit magazine. Larry formed LFP IP, Inc., and other corporations to conduct his enterprises. Many of them used the trademarks "HUSTLER" and "LARRY FLYNT," which LFP owned. Jimmy opened his own store, Hustler Cincinnati, and paid LFP licensing fees to use the "HUSTLER" mark.

When the store stopped paying the fees, LFP filed a suit in a federal district court against the store's corporate owner, alleging trademark infringement. The court issued an injunction prohibiting Jimmy from using the "HUSTLER" mark. Later, he opened a store called "FLYNT Sexy Gifts." LFP claimed that this name was likely to cause confusion with the "LARRY FLYNT" mark. The court modified the injunction to limit Jimmy's use of the "Flynt" name without "Jimmy." Jimmy appealed.

In the Language of the Court
SUTTON, Circuit Judge.
* * * *

Courts * * * may exercise their sound judicial discretion to modify an injunction if the circumstances, whether of law or fact, obtaining at the time of its issuance have changed, or new ones have since arisen.

* * * The [district] court * * * applied the traditional test for trademark infringement under federal law, asking whether (1) Larry and his companies owned the LARRY FLYNT trademark, (2) Jimmy used the mark in commerce, and (3) the use was likely to cause confusion. The court found all three elements satisfied * * * . Because the original injunction was tailored to prevent trademark infringement by [Jimmy] and because Jimmy had committed new violations, the district court acted appropriately when it modified its initial grant of relief to cover Jimmy's conduct at the [new] outlet.

The district court's modified injunction was also suitably tailored to the changed circumstances. Balancing the competing interests of Larry and Jimmy, the court permitted Jimmy to use his full name while protecting Larry's interest in the LARRY FLYNT trademark.
* * * *

Jimmy * * * takes issue with some of the factual findings that the district court used to justify the modified injunction.

But none of the district court's factual findings is clearly erroneous. * * * Larry * * * presented evidence that he used the mark in connection with a wide range of adult entertainment products, including the kinds of products sold at Jimmy's store. Because *product use * * * marks the salient [most noticeable] indicator of ownership in trademark-infringement actions*, the district court reasonably found that Larry * * * owned the LARRY FLYNT trademark with respect to retail goods. The court also reasonably found that Larry began using the mark on adult entertainment products before Jimmy did. * * * And * * * Larry's company * * * continued to use that mark in commerce. [Emphasis added.]

In claiming an absence of evidence of consumer confusion, Jimmy missteps. Some of the evidence comes from Jimmy himself. When asked about instances where a consumer has been confused, in terms of whether or not Jimmy was the owner of the store, Jimmy responded, "I have experienced the

Case 8.2 Continues

confusion in the names, you know. Jimmy and Larry Flynt, in this market area, is somewhat synonymous with Hustler or with Flynt. You're not going to get around that."

Decision and Remedy *The U.S. Court of Appeals for the Sixth Circuit affirmed the lower court's modification of the injunction. The injunction was initially tailored to prevent Jimmy's infringement of his brother's marks. When Jimmy committed a new violation by opening "FLYNT Sexy Gifts," the district court acted appropriately in modifying the injunction to cover this conduct.*

Critical Thinking
- **E-Commerce** *Could Jimmy use his last name—the name that he shares with his brother—as a domain name? Why or why not?*
- **What If the Facts Were Different?** *Suppose that Jimmy had used the marks at the center of this case on an entirely different line of goods, not adult entertainment products. Would the result have been the same? Explain.*

8–1d Distinctiveness of the Mark

A trademark must be sufficiently distinctive to enable consumers to identify the manufacturer of the goods easily and to distinguish between those goods and competing products.

Strong Marks Fanciful, arbitrary, or suggestive trademarks are generally considered to be the most distinctive (strongest) trademarks. These marks receive automatic protection because they serve to identify a particular product's source, as opposed to describing the product itself.

Fanciful and Arbitrary Trademarks. Fanciful trademarks use invented words, such as "Xerox" for one manufacturer's copiers and "Google" for a search engine. Arbitrary trademarks use common words in an uncommon way that is not descriptive of the product, such as "Dutch Boy" as a name for paint.

Even a single letter used in a particular style can be an arbitrary trademark. ■ **CASE IN POINT 8.2** Sports entertainment company ESPN sued Quiksilver, Inc., a maker of youth-oriented clothing, alleging trademark infringement. ESPN claimed that Quiksilver's clothing used the stylized "X" mark that ESPN uses in connection with the "X Games" ("extreme" sports competitions).

Quiksilver filed counterclaims for trademark infringement and dilution, arguing that it had a long history of using the stylized X on its products. ESPN had created the X Games in the mid-1990s, and Quiksilver had been using the X mark since 1994. ESPN asked the court to dismiss Quiksilver's counterclaims, but the court refused, holding that the X on Quiksilver's clothing is clearly an arbitrary mark. The court found that the two Xs are "similar enough that a consumer might well confuse them." Therefore, Quicksilver could continue its claim for trademark infringement.[6] ■

Suggestive Trademarks. Suggestive trademarks indicate something about a product's nature, quality, or characteristics, without describing the product directly. These marks require imagination on the part of the consumer to identify the characteristic.

"Dairy Queen," for instance, suggests an association between its products and milk, but it does not directly describe ice cream. "Blu-ray" is a suggestive mark that is associated with the high-quality, high-definition video contained on a particular type of optical data storage disc. Although blue-violet lasers are used to read blu-ray discs, the term *blu-ray* does not directly describe the disc.

Secondary Meaning Descriptive terms, geographic terms, and personal names are not inherently distinctive and do not receive protection under the law until they acquire a secondary meaning. A secondary meaning may arise when customers begin to associate a specific term or phrase (such as *London Fog*) with specific trademarked items (coats with "London Fog" labels) made by a particular company.

Whether a secondary meaning becomes attached to a name usually depends on how extensively the product is advertised, the market for the product, the number of sales, and other factors. ■ **CASE IN POINT 8.3** Unity Health Plans Insurance Corporation has been a health maintenance organization (HMO) insurer in Wisconsin since 1955. In 2013, another health-care provider, Iowa

---

6. *ESPN, Inc. v. Quiksilver, Inc.*, 586 F.Supp.2d 219 (S.D.N.Y. 2008).

Health System, began rebranding itself (changing its name and marketing) as UnityPoint Health. When the company expanded into Wisconsin, where Unity Health already had an established presence, Unity Health filed a trademark infringement suit in federal court.

The court found that Unity Health was a descriptive mark, and thus not inherently distinctive. But the court also held that the Unity Health mark had acquired a secondary meaning, largely because it had been used for so long and so exclusively by one health insurer in Wisconsin. It made no difference to the court that only one part of the mark (Unity) was common to both trademarks. To allow Iowa Health Systems to use the mark UnityPoint Health in Wisconsin would likely create confusion for consumers. Therefore, the court issued an injunction and blocked Iowa Health from using the trademark Unity-Point Health.[7] ■

Once a secondary meaning is attached to a term or name, a trademark is considered distinctive and is protected. Even a color can qualify for trademark protection, as did the color schemes used by some state university sports teams, including Ohio State University and Louisiana State University.[8]

■ **CASE IN POINT 8.4** Federal Express Corporation (FedEx) provides transportation and delivery services worldwide using the logo FedEx in a specific color combination. FedEx sued a competitor, JetEx Management Services, Inc., for using the same color combination and a similar name and logo. JetEx also mimicked FedEx's trademarked slogan ("The World on Time" for FedEx, and "Keeping the World on Time" for JetEx). FedEx alleged trademark infringement and dilution, among other claims. A federal district court in New York granted a permanent injunction to block JetEx from using the infringing mark in FedEx colors.[9] ■

Generic Terms Generic terms that refer to an entire class of products, such as *bicycle* and *computer,* receive no protection, even if they acquire secondary meanings. A particularly thorny problem arises when a trademark acquires generic use. For instance, *aspirin* and *thermos* were originally the names of trademarked products, but today the words are used generically. Other trademarks that have acquired generic use are *escalator, trampoline, raisin bran, dry ice, lanolin, linoleum, nylon,* and *cornflakes.*

A trademark does not become generic simply because it is commonly used, however. ■ **CASE IN POINT 8.5** In 2014, David Elliot and Chris Gillespie sought to register numerous domain names, including "googledisney.com" and "googlenewstvs.com." (A *domain name* is part of an Internet address, such as "cengage.com.") They were unable to register the names because all of them used the word *google,* a trademark of Google, Inc.

Elliot and Gillespie brought an action in federal court to have the Google trademark cancelled because it had become a generic term. They argued that because most people now use *google* as a verb ("to google") when referring to searching the Internet with any search engine (not just Google), the term should no longer be protected. The court held that even if people do use the word *google* as a verb, it is still a protected trademark if consumers associate the noun with one company. The court concluded that "the primary significance of the word *google* to a majority of the public who utilize Internet search engines is a designation of the Google search engine."[10] ■

8–1e Service, Certification, and Collective Marks

A **service mark** is essentially a trademark that is used to distinguish the *services* (rather than the products) of one person or company from those of another. For instance, each airline has a particular mark or symbol associated with its name. Titles and character names used in radio and television are frequently registered as service marks.

Other marks protected by law include certification marks and collective marks. A **certification mark** is used by one or more persons, other than the owner, to certify the region, materials, mode of manufacture, quality, or other characteristic of specific goods or services. Certification marks include "Good Housekeeping Seal of Approval" and "UL Tested."

When used by members of a cooperative, association, or other organization, a certification mark is referred to as a **collective mark.** ■ **EXAMPLE 8.6** Collective marks appear at the ends of motion picture credits to indicate the various associations and organizations that participated in the making of the films. The union marks found on the tags of certain products are also collective marks. ■

8–1f Trade Dress

The term **trade dress** refers to the image and overall appearance of a product. Trade dress is a broad concept

---

7. *Unity Health Plans Insurance Co. v. Iowa Health System,* 995 F.Supp.2d 874 (W.D.Wis. 2014).

8. *Board of Supervisors of Louisiana State University v. Smack Apparel Co.,* 438 F.Supp.2d 653 (E.D.La. 2006). See also *Abraham v. Alpha Chi Omega,* 781 F.Supp.2d 396 (N.D.Tex. 2011).

9. *Federal Express Corp. v. JetEx Management Services, Inc.,* 2014 WL 4628983 (E.D.N.Y. 2014).

10. *Elliot v. Google,* 45 F.Supp.3d 1156 (D.Ariz. 2014).

and can include either all or part of the total image or overall impression created by a product or its packaging.

■ **EXAMPLE 8.7** The distinctive decor, menu, layout, and style of service of a particular restaurant may be regarded as trade dress. Trade dress can also include the layout and appearance of a catalogue, the use of a lighthouse as part of the design of a golf hole, the fish shape of a cracker, or the G-shaped design of a Gucci watch. ■

Basically, trade dress is subject to the same protection as trademarks. In cases involving trade dress infringement, as in trademark infringement cases, a major consideration is whether consumers are likely to be confused by the allegedly infringing use.

8–1g Counterfeit Goods

Counterfeit goods copy or otherwise imitate trademarked goods, but they are not the genuine trademarked goods. The importation of goods that bear counterfeit (fake) trademarks poses a growing problem for U.S. businesses, consumers, and law enforcement. In addition to the negative financial effects on legitimate businesses, certain counterfeit goods, such as pharmaceuticals and nutritional supplements, can present serious public health risks.

The Stop Counterfeiting in Manufactured Goods Act The Stop Counterfeiting in Manufactured Goods Act[11] (SCMGA) was enacted to combat counterfeit goods. The act makes it a crime to traffic intentionally in or attempt to traffic in counterfeit goods or services, or to knowingly use a counterfeit mark on or in connection with goods or services.

Before this act, the law did not prohibit the creation or shipment of counterfeit labels that were not attached to any product. Therefore, counterfeiters would make labels and packaging bearing another's trademark, ship the labels to another location, and then affix them to an inferior product to deceive buyers. The SCMGA closed this loophole by making it a crime to knowingly traffic in counterfeit labels, stickers, packaging, and the like, regardless of whether the items are attached to any goods.

Penalties for Counterfeiting Persons found guilty of violating the SCMGA may be fined up to $2 million or imprisoned for up to ten years (or more if they are repeat offenders). If a court finds that the statute was violated, it must order the defendant to forfeit the counterfeit products (which are then destroyed), as well as any property

used in the commission of the crime. The defendant must also pay restitution to the trademark holder or victim in an amount equal to the victim's actual loss.

■ **CASE IN POINT 8.8** Charles Anthony Jones pleaded guilty to trafficking of counterfeit prescription erectile dysfunction drugs. The court sentenced Jones to thirty-seven months in prison and ordered him to pay $633,019 in restitution. Jones appealed, arguing that the amount awarded was more than the pharmaceutical companies' actual losses. The court agreed. The pharmaceutical companies were entitled only to their lost net profits rather than the retail price of the genuine drugs.[12] ■

Combating Foreign Counterfeiters Although Congress has enacted statutes against counterfeit goods, the United States cannot prosecute foreign counterfeiters because our national laws do not apply to them. One effective tool that U.S. officials have used to combat online sales of counterfeit goods is to obtain a court order to close down the domain names of Web sites that sell such goods. For instance, U.S. agents have shut down hundreds of domain names on the Monday after Thanksgiving ("Cyber Monday"). Shutting down the Web sites, particularly on key shopping days, prevents some counterfeit goods from entering the United States. Europol, an international organization, has also used this tactic.

8–1h Trade Names

Trademarks apply to *products.* A **trade name** indicates part or all of a business's name, whether the business is a sole proprietorship, a partnership, or a corporation. Generally, a trade name is directly related to a business and its goodwill.

A trade name may be protected as a trademark if the trade name is also the name of the company's trademarked product—for example, Coca-Cola. Unless it is also used as a trademark or service mark, a trade name cannot be registered with the federal government. Trade names are protected under the common law, but only if they are unusual or fancifully used. The word *Safeway,* for example, was sufficiently fanciful to obtain protection as a trade name for a grocery chain.

8–1i Licensing

One way to avoid litigation and still make use of another's trademark or other form of intellectual property is to obtain a license to do so. A **license** in this context is an agreement, or contract, permitting the use of a

---

11. Pub. L. No. 109-181 (2006), which amended 18 U.S.C. Sections 2318–2320.

12. *United States v. Jones,* 616 Fed.Appx. 726 (5th Cir. 2015).

trademark, copyright, patent, or trade secret for certain purposes. The party that owns the intellectual property rights and issues the license is the *licensor,* and the party obtaining the license is the *licensee.* The licensee generally pays fees, or *royalties,* for the privilege of using the intellectual property.

A license grants only the rights expressly described in the license agreement. A licensor might, for example, allow the licensee to use the trademark as part of its company or domain name, but not otherwise use the mark on any products or services. Disputes frequently arise over licensing agreements, particularly when the license involves Internet uses.

■ **CASE IN POINT 8.9**   George V Restauration S.A. and others owned and operated the Buddha Bar Paris, a restaurant with an Asian theme in Paris, France. One of the owners allowed Little Rest Twelve, Inc., to use the Buddha Bar trademark and its associated concept in New York City under the name *Buddha Bar NYC.* Little Rest paid royalties for its use of the Buddha Bar mark and advertised Buddha Bar NYC's affiliation with Buddha Bar Paris. This connection was also noted on its Web site and in the media.

When a dispute arose, the owners of Buddha Bar Paris withdrew their permission for Buddha Bar NYC's use of their mark, but Little Rest continued to use it. The owners of the mark filed a suit in a New York state court against Little Rest. The court granted an injunction to prevent Little Rest from using the mark.[13] ■

8–2 Patents

A **patent** is a grant from the government that gives an inventor the exclusive right to make, use, or sell his or her invention for a period of twenty years. Patents for designs, as opposed to those for inventions, are given for a fourteen-year period. The applicant must demonstrate to the satisfaction of the U.S. Patent and Trademark Office that the invention, discovery, process, or design is novel, useful, and not obvious in light of current technology.

Until recently, U.S. patent law differed from the laws of many other countries because the first person to invent a product obtained the patent rights rather than the first person to file for a patent. It was often difficult to prove who invented an item first, however, which prompted Congress to change the system in 2011 by passing the

America Invents Act.[14] Now the first person to file an application for a patent on a product or process will receive patent protection. In addition, the new law established a nine-month limit for challenging a patent on any ground.

The period of patent protection begins on the date the patent application is filed, rather than when the patent is issued, which may sometimes be years later. After the patent period ends (either fourteen or twenty years later), the product or process enters the public domain, and anyone can make, sell, or use the invention without paying the patent holder.

8–2a Searchable Patent Databases

A significant development relating to patents is the availability online of the world's patent databases. The Web site of the U.S. Patent and Trademark Office (www.uspto.gov) provides searchable databases covering U.S. patents granted since 1976. The Web site of the European Patent Office (www.epo.org) provides online access to 50 million patent documents in more than seventy nations through a searchable network of databases.

Businesses use these searchable databases in many ways. Companies may conduct patent searches to list or inventory their patents, which are valuable assets. Patent searches may also be conducted to study trends and patterns in a specific technology or to gather information about competitors in the industry.

8–2b What Is Patentable?

Under federal law, "[w]hoever invents or discovers any new and useful process, machine, manufacture, or composition of matter, or any new and useful improvement thereof, may obtain a patent therefor, subject to the conditions and requirements of this title."[15] Thus, to be patentable, the applicant must prove that the invention, discovery, process, or design is *novel, useful,* and *not obvious* in light of current technology.

In sum, almost anything is patentable, except the laws of nature, natural phenomena, and abstract ideas (including algorithms[16]). Even artistic methods and works of art, certain business processes, and the structures of storylines

---

13. *George V Restauration S.A. v. Little Rest Twelve, Inc.,* 58 A.D.3d 428, 871 N.Y.S.2d 65 (2009).

14. The full title of this law is the Leahy-Smith America Invents Act, Pub. L. No. 112-29 (2011), which amended 35 U.S.C. Sections 1, 41, and 321.

15. 35 U.S.C. Section 101.

16. An *algorithm* is a step-by-step procedure, formula, or set of instructions for accomplishing a specific task. An example is the set of rules used by a search engine to rank the listings contained within its index in response to a query.

are patentable, provided that they are novel and not obvious.[17]

Plants that are reproduced asexually (by means other than from seed), such as hybrid or genetically engineered plants, are patentable in the United States, as are genetically engineered (or cloned) microorganisms and animals. ■ **CASE IN POINT 8.10** Monsanto, Inc., sells its patented genetically modified (GM) seeds to farmers to help them achieve higher yields from crops using fewer pesticides. It requires farmers who buy GM seeds to sign licensing agreements promising to plant the seeds for only one crop and to pay a technology fee for each acre planted. To ensure compliance, Monsanto has many full-time employees whose job is to investigate and prosecute farmers who use the GM seeds illegally. Monsanto has filed nearly 150 lawsuits against farmers in the United States and has been awarded more than $15 million in damages (not including out-of-court settlement amounts).[18] ■

8–2c Patent Infringement

If a firm makes, uses, or sells another's patented design, product, or process without the patent owner's permission, that firm commits the tort of patent infringement. Patent infringement may occur even though the patent owner has not put the patented product into commerce. Patent infringement may also occur even though not all features or parts of a product are copied. (To infringe the patent on a process, however, all steps or their equivalent must be copied.) To read about an important issue in patent infringement today, see this chapter's *Digital Update* feature.

Patent Infringement Lawsuits and High-Tech Companies Obviously, companies that specialize in developing new technology stand to lose significant profits if someone "makes, uses, or sells" devices that incorporate their patented inventions. Because these firms are the holders of numerous patents, they are frequently involved in patent infringement lawsuits (as well as other types of intellectual property disputes).

■ **CASE IN POINT 8.11** Apple sued Samsung in federal court alleging that Samsung's Galaxy smartphones and tablets that use Google's HTC Android operating system infringe on Apple's patents. Apple has design patents that cover its devices' graphical user interface (the display of icons on the home screen), shell, and screen and button design. Apple has also patented the way information is displayed on iPhones and other devices, the way windows pop open, and the way information is scaled and rotated.

A jury found that Samsung had willfully infringed five of Apple's patents and awarded damages. The parties appealed. A judge later reduced the amount of damages awarded on the patent claims, but litigation between the two companies has continued. In 2015, a federal appellate court held that elements of the physical design of these two manufacturers' mobile devices and their on-screen icons were functional and thus not protected under the Lanham Act. A product feature is functional and not protected as trade dress if it is essential to the article's use or purpose or affects the cost or quality of the article.[19] ■

Patent Infringement and Foreign Sales Many companies that make and sell electronics and computer software and hardware are based in foreign nations (for instance, Samsung Electronics Company is a Korean firm). Foreign firms can apply for and obtain U.S. patent protection on items that they sell within the United States. Similarly, U.S. firms can obtain protection in foreign nations where they sell goods.

In the United States, the Supreme Court has narrowly construed patent infringement as it applies to exported software, however. As a general rule, under U.S. law, no patent infringement occurs when a patented product is made and sold in another country. ■ **CASE IN POINT 8.12** AT&T Corporation holds a patent on a device used to digitally encode, compress, and process recorded speech. AT&T brought an infringement case against Microsoft Corporation, which admitted that its Windows operating system incorporated software code that infringed on AT&T's patent.

The United States Supreme Court held that Microsoft was liable only for infringement in the United States and not for the Windows-based computers produced in foreign locations. The Court reasoned that Microsoft had not "supplied" the software for the computers but had only electronically transmitted a master copy, which the foreign manufacturers copied and loaded onto the computers.[20] ■

---

17. For a United States Supreme Court case discussing the obviousness requirement, see *KSR International Co. v. Teleflex, Inc.*, 550 U.S. 398, 127 S.Ct. 1727, 167 L.Ed.2d 705 (2007).

18. See, for example, *Monsanto Co. v. Bowman*, 657 F.3d 1341 (Fed.Cir. 2011); and *Monsanto Co. v. Scruggs*, 2009 WL 1228318 (Fed.Cir. 2009).

19. *Apple, Inc. v. Samsung Electronics Co.*, 926 F.Supp.2d 1110 (N.D.Cal. 2013); 786 F.3d 983 (Fed. Cir. 2015).

20. *Microsoft Corp. v. AT&T Corp.*, 550 U.S. 437, 127 S.Ct. 1746, 167 L.Ed.2d 737 (2007).

DIGITAL UPDATE   The Problem of Patent Trolls

In recent years, a huge number of patent infringement lawsuits have been filed against software and technology firms. Many patent cases involve companies defending real innovations, but some lawsuits are "shakedowns" by patent trolls.

Patent trolls—more formally called nonpracticing entities (NPEs) or patent assertion entities (PAEs)—are firms that do not make or sell products or services but are in the business of patent litigation. These firms buy patents and then try to enforce them against companies that *do* sell products or services, demanding licensing fees and threatening infringement lawsuits. Patent trolls usually target online businesses.

"I'm Going to Sue You Unless You Pay Me to Go Away"

Patent trolls literally bank on the fact that when threatened with infringement suits, most companies would rather pay to settle than engage in costly litigation, even if they believe they could win.

Consider an example. Soverain Software, LLC, sued dozens of online retailers, including Amazon, Avon, Home Depot, Macy's, Nordstrom, Kohl's, RadioShack, The Gap, and Victoria's Secret. Soverain claimed that it owned patents that covered nearly any use of online shopping-cart technology and that all these retailers had infringed on its patents. Amazon paid millions to settle with Soverain, as did most of the other defendants.

Interestingly, one online retailer, Newegg, Inc., refused to pay Soverain and ultimately won in court. In 2013, a federal appellate court held that the shopping-cart patent claim was invalid on the ground of obviousness because the technology for it had already existed before Soverain obtained its patent.[a]

The Role of Software Patents

The patent troll problem is concentrated in software patents, which often include descriptions of what the software does rather than the computer code involved. Many software patents are vaguely worded and overly broad. In the United States, both the patent system and the courts have had difficulty evaluating and protecting such patents.

As a result, nearly any business that uses basic technology can be a target of patent trolls. In fact, *more than 60 percent of all new patent cases* are filed by patent trolls. The firms most commonly targeted by patent trolls are large technology companies, including AT&T, Google, Apple, Samsung, Amazon, and Verizon. In one recent year, "AT&T was sued for patent infringement by patent trolls 54 times—more than once a week."[b]

Critical Thinking *Some argue that the best way to stop patent trolls from taking advantage of the system would be to eliminate software patents completely and pass a law that makes software unpatentable. Would this be fair to software and technology companies? Why or why not?*

a. *Soverain Software, LLC v. Newegg, Inc.*, 728 F.3d 1332 (Fed. Cir. 2013), *cert.* denied, 134 S.Ct. 910 (2014).
b. Roger Parloff, "Taking on the Patent Trolls," *Fortune*, February 27, 2014.

8–2d Remedies for Patent Infringement

If a patent is infringed, the patent holder may sue for relief in federal court. The patent holder can seek an injunction against the infringer and can also request damages for royalties and lost profits. In some cases, the court may grant the winning party reimbursement for attorneys' fees and costs. If the court determines that the infringement was willful, the court can triple the amount of damages awarded (treble damages).

In the past, permanent injunctions were routinely granted to prevent future infringement. Today, however, according to the United States Supreme Court, a patent holder must prove that it has suffered irreparable injury and that the public interest would not be *disserved* by a permanent injunction.[21] Thus, courts have discretion to decide what is equitable in the circumstances and to consider what is in the public interest rather than just the interests of the parties.

■ **CASE IN POINT 8.13** Cordance Corporation developed some of the technology and software that automates Internet communications. Cordance sued Amazon.com, Inc., for patent infringement, claiming that Amazon's one-click purchasing interface infringed on one of Cordance's patents. After a jury found Amazon guilty of infringement, Cordance requested the court to issue a permanent injunction against Amazon's infringement or,

21. *eBay, Inc. v. MercExchange, LLC*, 547 U.S. 388, 126 S.Ct. 1837, 164 L.Ed.2d 641 (2006).

alternatively, to order Amazon to pay Cordance an ongoing royalty.

The court refused to issue a permanent injunction because Cordance had not proved that it would otherwise suffer irreparable harm. Cordance and Amazon were not direct competitors in the relevant market. Cordance had never sold or licensed the technology infringed by Amazon's one-click purchasing interface and had presented no market data or evidence to show how the infringement negatively affected Cordance. The court also refused to impose an ongoing royalty on Amazon.[22] ■

8–3 Copyrights

A **copyright** is an intangible property right granted by federal statute to the author or originator of a literary or artistic production of a specified type. The Copyright Act of 1976,[23] as amended, governs copyrights. Works created after January 1, 1978, are automatically given statutory copyright protection for the life of the author plus 70 years. For copyrights owned by publishing houses, the copyright expires 95 years from the date of publication or 120 years from the date of creation, whichever comes first. For works by more than one author, the copyright expires 70 years after the death of the last surviving author.[24]

When copyright protection ends, works enter into the *public domain*. Intellectual property, such as songs and other published works, that have entered into the public domain belong to everyone and are not protected by copyright or patent laws.

■ **CASE IN POINT 8.14** The popular character Sherlock Holmes originated in stories written by Arthur Conan Doyle and published from 1887 through 1927. Over the years, elements of the characters and stories created by Doyle have appeared in books, movies, and television series, including *Elementary* on CBS and *Sherlock* on BBC.

Before 2013, those who wished to use the copyrighted Sherlock material had to pay a licensing fee to Doyle's estate. Then, in 2013, the editors of a book of Holmes-related stories filed a lawsuit in federal court claiming that the basic Sherlock Holmes story elements introduced before 1923 should no longer be protected. The court agreed and ruled that these elements have entered the public domain—that is, the copyright has expired, and they can be used without permission.[25] ■

8–3a Registration

Copyrights can be registered with the U.S. Copyright Office (www.copyright.gov) in Washington, D.C. Registration is not required, however. A copyright owner no longer needs to place the symbol © or the term *Copr.* or *Copyright* on the work to have the work protected against infringement. Chances are that if somebody created it, somebody owns it.

Generally, copyright owners are protected against the following:

1. Reproduction of the work.
2. Development of derivative works.
3. Distribution of the work.
4. Public display of the work.

8–3b What Is Protected Expression?

Works that are copyrightable include books, records, films, artworks, architectural plans, menus, music videos, product packaging, and computer software. To be protected, a work must be "fixed in a durable medium" from which it can be perceived, reproduced, or communicated. As noted, protection is automatic, and registration is not required.

Section 102 of the Copyright Act explicitly states that it protects original works that fall into one of the following categories:

1. Literary works (including newspaper and magazine articles, computer and training manuals, catalogues, brochures, and print advertisements).
2. Musical works and accompanying words (including advertising jingles).
3. Dramatic works and accompanying music.
4. Pantomimes and choreographic works (including ballets and other forms of dance).
5. Pictorial, graphic, and sculptural works (including cartoons, maps, posters, statues, and even stuffed animals).
6. Motion pictures and other audiovisual works (including multimedia works).
7. Sound recordings.
8. Architectural works.

---

22. *Cordance Corp. v. Amazon.com, Inc.*, 730 F.Supp.2d 333 (D.Del. 2010).
23. 17 U.S.C. Sections 101 *et seq.*
24. These time periods reflect the extensions of the length of copyright protection enacted by Congress in the Copyright Term Extension Act of 1998, 17 U.S.C. Section 302. The United States Supreme Court upheld the constitutionality of the act in 2003. See *Eldred v. Ashcroft*, 537 U.S. 186, 123 S.Ct. 769, 154 L.Ed.2d 683 (2003).

25. *Klinger v. Conan Doyle Estate, Ltd.*, 988 F.Supp.2d 879 (N.D.Ill. 2013).

Section 102 Exclusions Generally, anything that is not an original expression will not qualify for copyright protection. Facts widely known to the public are not copyrightable. Page numbers are not copyrightable because they follow a sequence known to everyone. Mathematical calculations are not copyrightable.

Furthermore, it is not possible to copyright an *idea.* Section 102 of the Copyright Act specifically excludes copyright protection for any "idea, procedure, process, system, method of operation, concept, principle, or discovery, regardless of the form in which it is described, explained, illustrated, or embodied." Thus, anyone can freely use the underlying ideas or principles embodied in a work.

What is copyrightable is the particular way in which an idea is *expressed.* Whenever an idea and an expression are inseparable, the expression cannot be copyrighted. An idea and its expression, then, must be separable to be copyrightable. Thus, for the design of a useful item to be copyrightable, the way it looks must be separate from its utilitarian (functional) purpose.

■ **CASE IN POINT 8.15** Inhale, Inc., registered a copyright on a hookah—a device for smoking tobacco by filtering the smoke through water held in a container at the base. Starbuzz Tobacco, Inc., sold hookahs with water containers shaped exactly like the Inhale containers.

Inhale filed a suit in a federal district court against Starbuzz for copyright infringement. The court determined that the shape of the water container on Inhale's hookahs was not copyrightable. The U.S. Court of Appeals for the Ninth Circuit affirmed the judgment. "The shape of a container is not independent of the container's utilitarian function—to hold the contents within its shape—because the shape accomplishes the function."[26] ■

---

26. *Inhale, Inc. v. Starbuzz Tobacco, Inc.,* 755 F.3d 1038 (2014).

Compilations of Facts Unlike ideas, *compilations* of facts are copyrightable. Under Section 103 of the Copyright Act, a compilation is "a work formed by the collection and assembling of preexisting materials or data that are selected, coordinated, or arranged in such a way that the resulting work as a whole constitutes an original work of authorship."

The key requirement in the copyrightability of a compilation is originality. If the facts are selected, coordinated, or arranged in an original way, they can qualify for copyright protection. Therefore, the White Pages of a telephone directory do not qualify for copyright protection, because they simply list alphabetically names and telephone numbers. The Yellow Pages of a directory can be copyrightable, provided the information is selected, coordinated, or arranged in an original way. Similarly, a compilation of information about yachts listed for sale has qualified for copyright protection.[27]

8–3c Copyright Infringement

Whenever the form or expression of an idea is copied, an infringement of copyright has occurred. The reproduction does not have to be exactly the same as the original, nor does it have to reproduce the original in its entirety. If a substantial part of the original is reproduced, the copyright has been infringed.

In the following case, rapper Curtis Jackson—better known as "50 Cent"—was the defendant in a suit that claimed his album *Before I Self-Destruct,* and the film of the same name, infringed the copyright of Shadrach Winstead's book *The Preacher's Son—But the Streets Turned Me into a Gangster.*

---

27. *BUC International Corp. v. International Yacht Council, Ltd.,* 489 F.3d 1129 (11th Cir. 2007).

Case Analysis 8.3

Winstead v. Jackson
United States Court of Appeals, Third Circuit, 509 Fed.Appx. 139 (2013).

In the Language of the Court
PER CURIAM. [By the Whole Court]
* * * *

* * * Winstead filed his * * * complaint in the United States District Court for the District of New Jersey, claiming that Jackson's album/CD and film derived their contents from, and infringed the copyright of, his book.
* * * *

* * * The District Court dismissed Winstead's * * * complaint * * *, concluding that Jackson * * * did not improperly copy protected aspects of Winstead's book.
* * * *

Winstead appeals.
* * * *

Here, it is not disputed that Winstead is the owner of the copyrighted

property * * *. However, *not all copying is copyright infringement, so even if actual copying is proven, the court must decide, by comparing the allegedly infringing work with the original work, whether the copying was unlawful. Copying may be proved inferentially by showing that the allegedly infringing work is substantially similar to the copyrighted*

Case 8.3 Continues

Case 8.3 Continued

work. A court compares the allegedly infringing work with the original work, and considers whether a "lay-observer" would believe that the copying was of protectable aspects of the copyrighted work. The inquiry involves distinguishing between the author's expression and the idea or theme that he or she seeks to convey or explore, because the former is protected and the latter is not. The court must determine whether the allegedly infringing work is similar because it appropriates the unique expressions of the original work, or merely because it contains elements that would be expected when two works express the same idea or explore the same theme. [Emphasis added.]

* * * A lay observer would not believe that Jackson's album/CD and film copied protectable aspects of Winstead's book. Jackson's album/CD is comprised of 16 individual songs, which explore drug-dealing, guns and money, vengeance, and other similar clichés of hip hop gangsterism. Jackson's fictional film is the story of a young man who turns to violence when his mother is killed in a drive-by shooting. The young man takes revenge by killing the man who killed his mother, and then gets rich by becoming an "enforcer" for a powerful criminal. He takes up with a woman who eventually betrays him, and is shot to death by her boyfriend, who has just been released from prison. The movie ends with his younger brother vowing to seek vengeance. Winstead's book purports to be autobiographical and tells the story of a young man whose beloved father was a Bishop in the church. The protagonist was angry as a child because his stepmother abused him, but he found acceptance and self-esteem on the streets of Newark because he was physically

powerful. He earned money robbing and beating people, went to jail, returned to crime upon his release, and then made even more money. The protagonist discusses his time at Rahway State Prison in great and compelling detail. The story ends when the protagonist learns that his father has passed away; he conveys his belief that this tragedy has led to his redemption, and he hopes that others might learn from his mistakes.

* * * Although Winstead's book and Jackson's works share similar themes and setting, the story of an angry and wronged protagonist who turns to a life of violence and crime has long been a part of the public domain [and is therefore not protected by copyright law]. Winstead argues * * * that a protagonist asking for God's help when his father dies, cutting drugs with mixing agents to maximize profits, and complaining about relatives who are addicts and steal the product, are protectable, but these things are not unique. To the extent that Jackson's works contain these elements, they are to be expected when two works express the same idea about "the streets" or explore the same theme. Winstead argues that not every protagonist whose story concerns guns, drugs, and violence in an urban setting winds up in prison or loses a parent, but this argument only serves to illustrate an important difference between his book and Jackson's film. Jackson's protagonist never spends any time in prison, whereas Winstead's protagonist devotes a considerable part of his story to his incarcerations.

In addition, Winstead's book and Jackson's works are different with respect to character, plot, mood, and sequence of events. Winstead's protagonist embarks on a life of crime at a very young age, but is redeemed by the death of his beloved

father. Jackson's protagonist turns to crime when he is much older and only after his mother is murdered. He winds up dead at a young age, unredeemed. Winstead's book is hopeful; Jackson's film is characterized * * * by moral apathy. It is true that both works involve the loss of a parent and the protagonist's recognition of the parent's importance in his life, but nowhere does Jackson appropriate anything unique about Winstead's expression of this generic topic.

Winstead contends that direct phrases from his book appear in Jackson's film. * * * He emphasizes these phrases: "Yo, where is my money at," "I would never have done no shit like that to you," "my father, my strength was gone," "he was everything to me," and "I did not know what to do," but, like the phrases "putting the work in," "get the dope, cut the dope," "let's keep it popping," and "the strong take from the weak but the smart take from everybody," they are either common in general or common with respect to hip hop culture, and do not enjoy copyright protection. The average person reading or listening to these phrases in the context of an overall story or song would not regard them as unique and protectable. Moreover, words and short phrases do not enjoy copyright protection. The similarity between Winstead's book and the lyrics to Jackson's songs on the album/CD is even more tenuous. "Stretching the dope" and "bloodshot red eyes" are common phrases that do not enjoy copyright protection. A side-by-side comparison of Winstead's book and the lyrics from Jackson's album/CD do not support a claim of copyright infringement.

For the foregoing reasons, we will affirm the order of the District Court dismissing [Winstead's] complaint.

Legal Reasoning Questions

1. Which expressions of an original work are protected by copyright law?

2. Is all copying copyright infringement? If not, what is the test for determining whether a creative work has been unlawfully copied?

3. How did the court in this case determine whether the defendant's work infringed on the plaintiff's copyright?

Remedies for Copyright Infringement Those who infringe copyrights may be liable for damages or criminal penalties. These range from actual damages or statutory damages, imposed at the court's discretion, to criminal proceedings for willful violations.

Actual damages are based on the harm caused to the copyright holder by the infringement, while statutory damages, not to exceed $150,000, are provided for under the Copyright Act. Criminal proceedings may result in fines and/or imprisonment. A court can also issue a permanent injunction against a defendant when the court deems it necessary to prevent future copyright infringement.

■ **CASE IN POINT 8.16** Rusty Carroll operated an online term paper business, R2C2, Inc., that offered up to 300,000 research papers for sale at nine Web sites. Individuals whose work was posted on these Web sites without their permission filed a lawsuit against Carroll for copyright infringement. Because Carroll had repeatedly failed to comply with court orders regarding discovery, the court found that the copyright infringement was likely to continue unless an injunction was issued. The court therefore issued a permanent injunction prohibiting Carroll and R2C2 from selling any term paper without sworn documentary evidence that the paper's author had given permission.[28] ■

The "Fair Use" Exception An exception to liability for copyright infringement is made under the "fair use" doctrine. In certain circumstances, a person or organization can reproduce copyrighted material without paying royalties. Section 107 of the Copyright Act provides as follows:

> [T]he fair use of a copyrighted work, including such use by reproduction in copies or phonorecords or by any other means specified by [Section 106 of the Copyright Act], for purposes such as criticism, comment, news reporting, teaching (including multiple copies for classroom use), scholarship, or research, is not an infringement of copyright. In determining whether the use made of a work in any particular case is a fair use the factors to be considered shall include—
>
> (1) the purpose and character of the use, including whether such use is of a commercial nature or is for nonprofit educational purposes;
> (2) the nature of the copyrighted work;
> (3) the amount and substantiality of the portion used in relation to the copyrighted work as a whole; and
> (4) the effect of the use upon the potential market for or value of the copyrighted work.

What Is Fair Use? Because these guidelines are very broad, the courts determine whether a particular use is fair on a case-by-case basis. Thus, anyone who reproduces copyrighted material may be committing a violation. In determining whether a use is fair, courts have often considered the fourth factor to be the most important.

■ **CASE IN POINT 8.17** A number of research universities, in partnership with Google, Inc., agreed to digitize books from their libraries and create a repository for them. Eighty member institutions (including many colleges and universities) contributed more than ten million works into the HathiTrust Digital Library. Some authors complained that this book scanning violated their rights and sued the HathiTrust and several associated entities for copyright infringement.

The court, however, sided with the defendants and held that making digital copies for the purposes of online search was a fair use. The library's searchable database enabled researchers to find terms of interest in the digital volumes—but not to read the volumes online. Therefore, the court concluded that the digitization did not provide a substitute that damaged the market for the original works.[29] ■

The First Sale Doctrine Section 109(a) of the Copyright Act provides that the owner of a particular item that is copyrighted can, without the authority of the copyright owner, sell or otherwise dispose of it. This rule is known as the first sale doctrine.

Under this doctrine, once a copyright owner sells or gives away a particular copy of a work, the copyright owner no longer has the right to control the distribution of that copy. Thus, for instance, a person who buys a copyrighted book can sell it to someone else. The first sale doctrine also applies to a person who receives promotional CDs, such as a music critic or radio programmer.[30]

■ **CASE IN POINT 8.18** Supap Kirtsaeng, a citizen of Thailand, was a graduate student at the University of Southern California. He enlisted friends and family in Thailand to buy copies of textbooks there and ship them to him in the United States. Kirtsaeng resold the textbooks on eBay, where he eventually made about $100,000.

John Wiley & Sons, Inc., had printed eight of those textbooks in Asia. Wiley sued Kirtsaeng in federal district court for copyright infringement. Kirtsaeng argued that Section 109(a) of the Copyright Act allows the first purchaser-owner of a book to sell it without the copyright owner's permission. The trial court held in favor of Wiley, and that decision was affirmed on appeal. Kirtsaeng then appealed to the United States Supreme Court, which ruled

---

28. *Weidner v. Carroll,* 2010 WL 310310 (S.D.Ill. 2010).

29. *Authors Guild, Inc., v. HathiTrust,* 755 F.3d 87 (2d Cir. 2014).
30. See, for example, *UMG Recordings, Inc. v. Augusto,* 628 F.3d 1175 (9th Cir. 2011).

in Kirtsaeng's favor. The first sale doctrine applies even to goods purchased abroad and resold in the United States.[31] ■

8–3d Copyright Protection for Software

The Computer Software Copyright Act amended the Copyright Act to include computer programs in the list of creative works protected by federal copyright law.[32] Generally, copyright protection extends to those parts of a computer program that can be read by humans, such as the "high-level" language of a source code. Protection also extends to the binary-language object code, which is readable only by the computer, and to such elements as the overall structure, sequence, and organization of a program.

Not all aspects of software are protected, however. Courts typically have not extended copyright protection to the "look and feel"—the general appearance, command structure, video images, menus, windows, and other screen displays—of computer programs. (Note that copying the "look and feel" of another's product may be a violation of trade dress or trademark laws, however.) Sometimes it can be difficult for courts to decide which particular aspects of software are protected.

■ **CASE IN POINT 8.19** Oracle America, Inc., is a software company that owns numerous application programming interfaces, or API packages. Oracle grants licenses to others to use these API packages to write applications in the Java programming language. Java is open and free for anyone to use, but using it requires an interface. When Google began using some of Oracle's API packages to run Java on its Android mobile devices, Oracle sued for copyright infringement. Google argued that the software packages were command structure and, as such, not protected under copyright law. Ultimately, a federal appellate court concluded that the API packages were source code and were entitled to copyright protection.[33] ■

8–4 Trade Secrets

The law of trade secrets protects some business processes and information that are not, or cannot be, patented, copyrighted, or trademarked. A **trade secret** is basically information of commercial value, such as customer lists, plans, and research and development. Trade secrets may also include pricing information, marketing methods, production techniques, and generally anything that makes an individual company unique and that would have value to a competitor.

Unlike copyright and trademark protection, protection of trade secrets extends to both ideas and their expression. For this reason, and because there are no registration or filing requirements for trade secrets, trade secret protection may be well suited for software.

Of course, a company's trade secrets must be disclosed to some persons, particularly to key employees. Businesses generally attempt to protect their trade secrets by having all employees who use a protected process or information agree in their contracts, or in confidentiality agreements, never to divulge it.

8–4a State and Federal Law on Trade Secrets

Under Section 757 of the *Restatement of Torts,* those who disclose or use another's trade secret, without authorization, are liable to that other party if either of the following is true:

1. They discovered the secret by improper means.
2. Their disclosure or use constitutes a breach of a duty owed to the other party.

Stealing confidential business data by industrial espionage, such as by tapping into a competitor's computer, is a theft of trade secrets without any contractual violation and is actionable in itself.

Trade secrets have long been protected under the common law. Today, nearly every state has enacted trade secret laws based on the Uniform Trade Secrets Act.[34] Additionally, the Economic Espionage Act[35] makes the theft of trade secrets a federal crime.

8–4b Trade Secrets in Cyberspace

Computer technology is undercutting many business firms' ability to protect their confidential information, including trade secrets. For example, a dishonest employee could e-mail trade secrets in a company's computer to a competitor or a future employer. If e-mail is not an option, the employee might walk out with the information on a flash drive.

Misusing a company's social media account is yet another way in which employees may appropriate trade secrets. ■ **CASE IN POINT 8.20** Noah Kravitz worked for a company called PhoneDog for four years as a product reviewer and video blogger. PhoneDog provided him with the Twitter account "@PhoneDog_Noah." Kravitz's popularity grew, and he had approximately 17,000

---

31. *Kirtsaeng v. John Wiley & Sons, Inc.*, ___ U.S. ___, 133 S.Ct. 1351, 185 L.Ed.2d 392 (2013).

32. Pub. L. No. 96-517 (1980), amending 17 U.S.C. Sections 101, 117.

33. *Oracle America, Inc. v. Google Inc.*, 750 F.3d 1339 (Fed.Cir. 2014).

34. The Uniform Trade Secrets Act, as drafted by the National Conference of Commissioners on Uniform State Laws (NCCUSL), can be found at uniformlaws.org.

35. 18 U.S.C. Sections 1831–1839.

followers by the time he quit. PhoneDog requested that Kravitz stop using the Twitter account. Although Kravitz changed his handle to "@noahkravitz," he continued to use the account. PhoneDog subsequently sued Kravitz for misappropriation of trade secrets, among other things. Kravitz moved for a dismissal, but the court found that the complaint adequately stated a cause of action for misappropriation of trade secrets and allowed the suit to continue.[36] ∎

Exhibit 8–1 outlines trade secrets and other forms of intellectual property discussed in this chapter.

36. *PhoneDog v. Kravitz*, 2011 WL 5415612 (N.D.Cal. 2011). See also *Mintel Learning Technology, Inc. v. Ambrow Education Holding Ltd.*, 2012 WL 762126 (N.D.Cal. 2012).

EXHIBIT 8–1 Forms of Intellectual Property

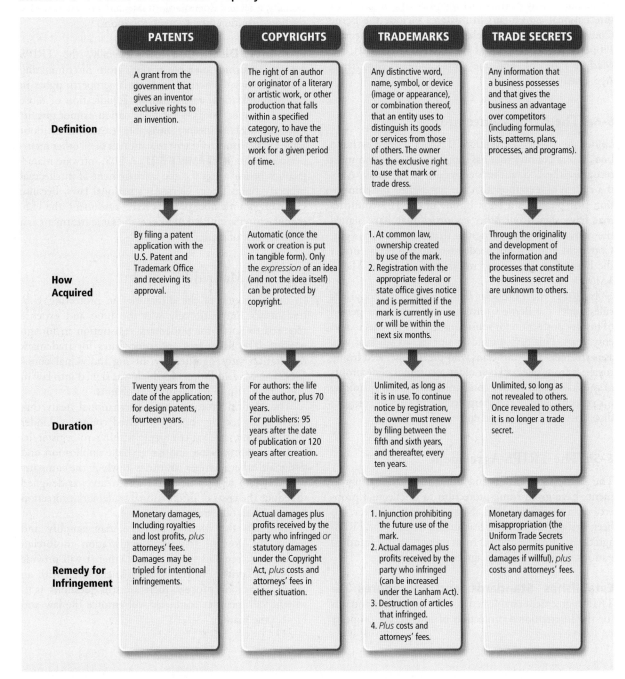

	PATENTS	COPYRIGHTS	TRADEMARKS	TRADE SECRETS
Definition	A grant from the government that gives an inventor exclusive rights to an invention.	The right of an author or originator of a literary or artistic work, or other production that falls within a specified category, to have the exclusive use of that work for a given period of time.	Any distinctive word, name, symbol, or device (image or appearance), or combination thereof, that an entity uses to distinguish its goods or services from those of others. The owner has the exclusive right to use that mark or trade dress.	Any information that a business possesses and that gives the business an advantage over competitors (including formulas, lists, patterns, plans, processes, and programs).
How Acquired	By filing a patent application with the U.S. Patent and Trademark Office and receiving its approval.	Automatic (once the work or creation is put in tangible form). Only the *expression* of an idea (and not the idea itself) can be protected by copyright.	1. At common law, ownership created by use of the mark. 2. Registration with the appropriate federal or state office gives notice and is permitted if the mark is currently in use or will be within the next six months.	Through the originality and development of the information and processes that constitute the business secret and are unknown to others.
Duration	Twenty years from the date of the application; for design patents, fourteen years.	For authors: the life of the author, plus 70 years. For publishers: 95 years after the date of publication or 120 years after creation.	Unlimited, as long as it is in use. To continue notice by registration, the owner must renew by filing between the fifth and sixth years, and thereafter, every ten years.	Unlimited, so long as not revealed to others. Once revealed to others, it is no longer a trade secret.
Remedy for Infringement	Monetary damages, Including royalties and lost profits, *plus* attorneys' fees. Damages may be tripled for intentional infringements.	Actual damages plus profits received by the party who infringed *or* statutory damages under the Copyright Act, *plus* costs and attorneys' fees in either situation.	1. Injunction prohibiting the future use of the mark. 2. Actual damages plus profits received by the party who infringed (can be increased under the Lanham Act). 3. Destruction of articles that infringed. 4. *Plus* costs and attorneys' fees.	Monetary damages for misappropriation (the Uniform Trade Secrets Act also permits punitive damages if willful), *plus* costs and attorneys' fees.

8–5 International Protection for Intellectual Property

For many years, the United States has been a party to various international agreements relating to intellectual property rights. For instance, the Paris Convention of 1883, to which almost 180 countries are signatory, allows parties in one country to file for patent and trademark protection in any of the other member countries. Other international agreements in this area include the Berne Convention, the Trade-Related Aspects of Intellectual Property Rights (known as the TRIPS agreement), the Madrid Protocol, and the Anti-Counterfeiting Trade Agreement.

8–5a The Berne Convention

Under the Berne Convention, if a U.S. citizen writes a book, every country that has signed the convention must recognize the U.S. author's copyright in the book. Also, if a citizen of a country that has not signed the convention first publishes a book in one of the 169 countries that have signed, all other countries that have signed the convention must recognize that author's copyright. Copyright notice is not needed to gain protection under the Berne Convention for works published after March 1, 1989.

In 2011, the European Union altered its copyright rules under the Berne Convention to extend the period of royalty protection for musicians from fifty years to seventy years. This decision aids major record labels as well as performers and musicians who previously faced losing royalties from sales of their older recordings. The profits of musicians and record companies have been shrinking for years because of the sharp decline in sales of compact discs and the rise in illegal downloads.

8–5b The TRIPS Agreement

The Berne Convention and other international agreements have given some protection to intellectual property on a worldwide level. None of them, however, has been as significant and far reaching in scope as the TRIPS agreement. Representatives from more than one hundred nations signed the TRIPS agreement in 1994.

Establishes Standards and Procedures The TRIPS agreement established, for the first time, standards for the international protection of intellectual property

rights, including patents, trademarks, and copyrights for movies, computer programs, books, and music. Each member country of the World Trade Organization must include in its domestic laws broad intellectual property rights and effective remedies (including civil and criminal penalties) for violations of those rights.

Each member nation must also ensure that legal procedures are available for parties who wish to bring actions for infringement of intellectual property rights. Additionally, a related document established a mechanism for settling disputes among member nations.

Prohibits Discrimination Generally, the TRIPS agreement forbids member nations from discriminating against foreign owners of intellectual property rights in the administration, regulation, or adjudication of those rights. In other words, a member nation cannot give its own nationals (citizens) favorable treatment without offering the same treatment to nationals of all other member countries. ■ **EXAMPLE 8.21** A U.S. software manufacturer brings a suit for the infringement of intellectual property rights under Germany's national laws. Because Germany is a member of the TRIPS agreement, the U.S. manufacturer is entitled to receive the same treatment as a German manufacturer. ■

8–5c The Madrid Protocol

In the past, one of the difficulties in protecting U.S. trademarks internationally was the time and expense required to apply for trademark registration in foreign nations. The filing fees and procedures for trademark registration vary significantly among individual countries. The Madrid Protocol, which was signed into law in 2003, may help to resolve these problems.

The Madrid Protocol is an international treaty that has been signed by about a hundred countries. Under its provisions, a U.S. company wishing to register its trademark abroad can submit a single application and designate other member countries in which the company would like to register its mark. The treaty was designed to reduce the costs of international trademark protection by more than 60 percent.

Although the Madrid Protocol may simplify and reduce the cost of trademark registration in foreign countries, it remains to be seen whether it will provide significant benefits to trademark owners. Even with an easier registration process, there are still questions as to whether all member countries will enforce the law and protect the mark.

8–5d The Anti-Counterfeiting Trade Agreement

In 2011, Australia, Canada, Japan, Korea, Morocco, New Zealand, Singapore, and the United States signed the Anti-Counterfeiting Trade Agreement (ACTA), an international treaty to combat global counterfeiting and piracy. Other nations have since signed the agreement.

Goals and Provisions The goals of the treaty are to increase international cooperation, facilitate the best law enforcement practices, and provide a legal framework to combat counterfeiting. ACTA applies not only to counterfeit physical goods, such as medications, but also to pirated copyrighted works being distributed via the Internet. The idea is to create a new standard of enforcement for intellectual property rights that goes beyond the TRIPS agreement and encourages international cooperation and information sharing among signatory countries.

Border Searches Under ACTA, member nations are required to establish border measures that allow officials, on their own initiative, to search commercial shipments of imports and exports for counterfeit goods. The treaty neither requires nor prohibits random border searches of electronic devices, such as laptops, tablet devices, and smartphones, for infringing content.

If border authorities reasonably believe that any goods in transit are counterfeit, the treaty allows them to keep the suspect goods unless the owner proves that the items are authentic and noninfringing. The treaty allows member nations, in accordance with their own laws, to order online service providers to furnish information about suspected trademark and copyright infringers, including their identities.

Reviewing: Intellectual Property Rights

Two computer science majors, Trent and Xavier, have an idea for a new video game, which they propose to call Hallowed. They form a business and begin developing their idea. Several months later, Trent and Xavier run into a problem with their design and consult a friend, Brad, who is an expert in designing computer source codes. After the software is completed but before Hallowed is marketed, a video game called Halo 2 is released for both the Xbox and the Playstation systems. Halo 2 uses source codes similar to those of Hallowed and imitates Hallowed's overall look and feel, although not all the features are alike. Using the information presented in the chapter, answer the following questions.

1. Would the name *Hallowed* receive protection as a trademark or as trade dress? Explain.
2. If Trent and Xavier had obtained a patent on Hallowed, would the release of Halo 2 have infringed on their patent? Why or why not?
3. Based only on the facts described above, could Trent and Xavier sue the makers of Halo 2 for copyright infringement? Why or why not?
4. Suppose that Trent and Xavier discover that Brad took the idea of Hallowed and sold it to the company that produced Halo 2. Which type of intellectual property issue does this raise?

Debate This . . . *Congress has amended copyright law several times so that copyright holders now have protection for many decades. Was Congress right in extending these copyright time periods?*

Terms and Concepts

certification mark 155	intellectual property 150	trade dress 155
collective mark 155	license 156	trade name 156
copyright 160	patent 157	trade secret 164
dilution 152	service mark 155	trademark 150

Issue Spotters

1. Roslyn, a food buyer for Organic Cornucopia Food Company, decides to go into business for herself as Roslyn's Kitchen. She contacts Organic's suppliers, offering to buy their entire harvest for the next year. She also contacts Organic's customers, offering to sell her products at prices lower than Organic's prices. Has Roslyn violated any of the intellectual property rights discussed in this chapter? Explain. (See *Trade Secrets*.)

2. Global Products develops, patents, and markets software. World Copies, Inc., sells Global's software without the maker's permission. Is this patent infringement? If so, how might Global save the cost of suing World for infringement and at the same time profit from World's sales? (See *Patents*.)

- **Check your answers to the Issue Spotters against the answers provided in Appendix D at the end of this text.**

Business Scenarios

8–1. Fair Use. Professor Wise is teaching a summer seminar in business torts at State University. Several times during the course, he makes copies of relevant sections from business law texts and distributes them to his students. Wise does not realize that the daughter of one of the textbook authors is a member of his seminar. She tells her father about Wise's copying activities, which have taken place without her father's or his publisher's permission. Her father sues Wise for copyright infringement. Wise claims protection under the fair use doctrine. Who will prevail? Explain. (See *Copyrights*.)

8–2. Patent Infringement. John and Andrew Doney invented a hard-bearing device for balancing rotors. Although they obtained a patent for their invention from the U.S. Patent and Trademark Office, it was never used as an automobile wheel balancer. Some time later, Exetron Corp. produced an automobile wheel balancer that used a hard-bearing device with a support plate similar to that of the Doneys' device. Given that the Doneys had not used their device for automobile wheel balancing, does Exetron's use of a similar device infringe on the Doneys' patent? Why or why not? (See *Patents*.)

Business Case Problems

8–3. Spotlight on Macy's—Copyright Infringement.

United Fabrics International, Inc., bought a fabric design from an Italian designer and registered a copyright to it with the U.S. Copyright Office. When Macy's, Inc., began selling garments with a similar design, United filed a copyright infringement suit against Macy's. Macy's argued that United did not own a valid copyright to the design and so could not claim infringement. Does United have to prove that the copyright is valid to establish infringement? Explain. [*United Fabrics International, Inc. v. C&J Wear, Inc.,* 630 F.3d 1255 (9th Cir. 2011)] (See *Copyrights*.)

8–4. Theft of Trade Secrets. Hanjuan Jin, a citizen of China, worked as a software engineer for Motorola for many years in a division that created proprietary standards for cellular communications. Contrary to Motorola's policies, Jin also secretly began working as a consultant for Lemko Corp., as well as with Sun Kaisens, a Chinese software company, and with the Chinese military. She started corresponding with Sun Kaisens's management about a possible full-time job in China. Jin took several medical leaves of absence from Motorola to return to Beijing and work with Sun Kaisens and the military.

After one of these medical leaves, Jin returned to Motorola. Over a period of several days, Jin accessed and downloaded thousands of documents on her personal laptop and on pen drives. When, later, she attempted to board a flight to China from Chicago, she was randomly searched by U.S. Customs

and Border Protection officials at the airport. U.S. officials discovered the downloaded Motorola documents. Are there any circumstances under which Jin could avoid being prosecuted for theft of trade secrets? If so, what are these circumstances? Discuss fully. [*United States v. Hanjuan Jin,* 833 F.Supp.2d 977 (N.D.Ill. 2012)] (See *Trade Secrets*.)

8–5. Copyright Infringement. SilverEdge Systems Software hired Catherine Conrad to perform a singing telegram. SilverEdge arranged for James Bendewald to record Conrad's performance of her copyrighted song to post on its Web site. Conrad agreed to wear a microphone to assist in the recording, told Bendewald what to film, and asked for an additional fee only if SilverEdge used the video for a commercial purpose. Later, the company chose to post a video of a different performer's singing telegram instead. Conrad filed a suit in a federal district court against SilverEdge and Bendewald for copyright infringement. Are the defendants liable? Explain. [*Conrad v. Bendewald,* 500 Fed.Appx. 526 (7th Cir. 2013)] (See *Copyrights*.)

8–6. Business Case Problem with Sample Answer—Patents. The U.S. Patent and Trademark Office (PTO)

denied Raymond Gianelli's application for a patent for a "Rowing Machine"—an exercise machine on which a user *pulls* on handles to perform a rowing motion against a selected resistance. The PTO considered the device obvious in light of a previously patented "Chest Press Apparatus for Exercising

Regions of the Upper Body"—an exercise machine on which a user *pushes* on handles to overcome a selected resistance. On what ground might this result be reversed on appeal? Discuss. [*In re Gianelli,* 739 F.3d 1375 (Fed. Cir. 2014)] (See *Patents.*)

- **For a sample answer to Problem 8–6, go to Appendix E at the end of this text.**

8–7. Patents. Rodney Klassen was employed by the U.S. Department of Agriculture (USDA). Without the USDA's authorization, Klassen gave Jim Ludy, a grape grower, plant material for two unreleased varieties of grapes. For almost two years, most of Ludy's plantings bore no usable fruit, none of the grapes were sold, and no plant material was given to any other person. The plantings were visible from publicly accessible roads, but none of the vines were labeled, and the variety could not be identified by simply viewing the vines. Under patent law, an applicant may not obtain a patent for an invention that is in public use for more than one year before the date of the application. Could the USDA successfully apply for patents on the two varieties given to Ludy? Explain. [*Delano Farms Co. v. California Table Grape Commission,* 778 F.3d 1243 (Fed. Cir. 2015)] (See *Patents.*)

8–8. Copyright. Savant Homes, Inc., is a custom home designer and builder. Using what it called the "Anders Plan," Savant built a model house in Windsor, Colorado. This was a ranch house with two bedrooms on one side and a master suite on the other, separated by a combined family room, dining room, and kitchen. Ron and Tammie Wagner toured the Savant house. The same month, the Wagners hired builder Douglas Collins and his firm, Douglas Consulting, LLC, to build a house for them in Windsor. After it was built, Savant filed a suit in a federal district court against Collins for copyright infringement, alleging that the builder had copied the Anders Plan in the design and construction of the Wagner house. Collins showed that the Anders Plan consisted of standard elements and standard arrangements of elements. In these circumstances, has infringement occurred? Explain.

[*Savant Homes, Inc. v. Collins,* 809 F.3d 1133 (10th Cir. 2016)] (See *Copyrights.*)

8–9. A Question of Ethics—Copyright Infringement.

 Custom Copies, Inc., prepares and sells coursepacks, which contain compilations of readings for college courses. A teacher selects the readings and delivers a syllabus to the copy shop, which obtains the materials from a library, copies them, and binds the copies. Blackwell Publishing, Inc., which owns the copyright to some of the materials, filed a suit, alleging copyright infringement. Custom Copies filed a motion to dismiss for failure to state a claim. [*Blackwell Publishing, Inc. v. Custom Copies, Inc., 2006 WL 1529503 (N.D.Fla. 2006)*] (See *Copyrights.*)

(a) Custom Copies argued, in part, that creating and selling did not "distribute" the coursepacks. Does a copy shop violate copyright law if it only copies materials for coursepacks? Does the copying fall under the "fair use" exception? Should the court grant the defendant's motion? Why or why not?

(b) What is the potential impact of copying and selling a book or journal without the permission of, and the payment of royalties or a fee to, the copyright owner? Explain.

8–10. Special Case Analysis—Copyright Infringement. Go to Case Analysis 8.3, *Winstead v. Jackson.* Read the excerpt, and answer the following questions. (See *Copyrights.*)

(a) Issue: This case focused on an allegation of copyright infringement involving what parties and which creative works?

(b) Rule of Law: What is the test for determining whether a creative work infringes the copyright of another work?

(c) Applying the Rule of Law: How did the court determine whether the claim of copyright infringement was supported in this case?

(d) Conclusion: Was the defendant liable for copyright infringement? Why or why not?

Legal Reasoning Group Activity

8–11. Patents. After years of research, your company develops a product that might revolutionize the green (environmentally conscious) building industry. The product is made from relatively inexpensive and widely available materials combined in a unique way that can substantially lower the heating and cooling costs of residential and commercial buildings. The company has registered the trademark it intends to use on the product and has filed a patent application with the U.S. Patent and Trademark Office. (See *Patents.*)

(a) One group should provide three reasons why this product does or does not qualify for patent protection.

(b) Another group should develop a four-step procedure for how your company can best protect its intellectual property rights (trademark, trade secret, and patent) and prevent domestic and foreign competitors from producing counterfeit goods or cheap knockoffs.

(c) Another group should list and explain three ways your company can utilize licensing.

CHAPTER 9

Internet Law, Social Media, and Privacy

The Internet has changed our lives and our laws. Technology has put the world at our fingertips and now allows even the smallest business to reach customers around the globe. At the same time, the Internet presents a variety of challenges for the law.

Courts are often in uncharted waters when deciding disputes that involve the Internet, social media, and online privacy. Judges may have no common law precedents to rely on

when resolving a case. Long-standing principles of justice may be inapplicable. New rules are evolving, but often not as quickly as technology.

For instance, Facebook is confronting lawsuits over its facial recognition software, which scans the faces in uploaded photos and identifies them in other photos across the site. As a result of this technology, Facebook has collected and stored a huge amount of facial recognition data—data that some users claim violates

their privacy. The situation has been complicated by DeepFace, a sophisticated new technology developed by Facebook that can recognize faces almost as well as humans. In fact, Facebook has already agreed not to use the facial recognition software in Europe due to privacy complaints. In the United States, however, privacy rights generally hinge on whether the person has a reasonable expectation of privacy, which might be lacking in photos posted online.

9–1 Internet Law

A number of laws specifically address issues that arise only on the Internet. Three such issues are unsolicited e-mail, domain names, and cybersquatting, as we discuss here. We also discuss how the law is dealing with problems of trademark infringement and dilution online.

9–1a Spam

Businesses and individuals alike are targets of **spam.**[1] Spam is the unsolicited "junk e-mail" that floods virtual mailboxes with advertisements, solicitations, and other messages. Considered relatively harmless in the early days of the Internet, by 2017 spam accounted for roughly 75 percent of all e-mails.

State Regulation of Spam In an attempt to combat spam, thirty-seven states have enacted laws that prohibit or regulate its use. Many state laws that regulate spam require the senders of e-mail ads to instruct the recipients on how they can "opt out" of further e-mail ads from the

same sources. For instance, in some states, an unsolicited e-mail must include a toll-free phone number or return e-mail address that the recipient can use to ask the sender to send no more unsolicited e-mails.

The Federal CAN-SPAM Act In 2003, Congress enacted the Controlling the Assault of Non-Solicited Pornography and Marketing (CAN-SPAM) Act.[2] The legislation applies to any "commercial electronic mail messages" that are sent to promote a commercial product or service. Significantly, the statute preempts state antispam laws except for those provisions in state laws that prohibit false and deceptive e-mailing practices.

Generally, the act permits the sending of unsolicited commercial e-mail but prohibits certain types of spamming activities. Prohibited activities include the use of a false return address and the use of false, misleading, or deceptive information when sending e-mail. The statute also prohibits the use of "dictionary attacks"—sending messages to randomly generated e-mail addresses—and the "harvesting" of e-mail addresses from Web sites through the use of specialized software.

■ **EXAMPLE 9.1** Sanford Wallace, known as the "Spam King," is considered to be one of the world's most prolific

---

1. The term *spam* is said to come from the lyrics of a Monty Python song that repeats the word *spam* over and over.

2. 15 U.S.C. Sections 7701 *et seq.*

spammers. He has operated several businesses over the years that used *botnets* (automated spamming networks) to send out hundreds of millions of unwanted e-mails. Wallace also infected computers with spyware and then sold consumers the software to fix it. He infiltrated Facebook accounts to spam 27 million of its users. He has been sued by the Federal Trade Commission, Facebook, and MySpace, and ordered to pay millions of dollars in fines. The Federal Bureau of Investigation ultimately arrested Wallace and brought criminal charges. In 2015, he pleaded guilty to fraud, spam, and violating a court order not to access Facebook. ■

Arresting prolific spammers, however, has done little to curb spam, which continues to flow at a rate of 70 billion messages per day. In effect, this means that the federal CAN-SPAM act has done little or nothing to reduce the amount of spam.

The U.S. Safe Web Act After the CAN-SPAM Act prohibited false and deceptive e-mails originating in the United States, spamming from servers located in other nations increased. These cross-border spammers generally were able to escape detection and legal sanctions because the Federal Trade Commission (FTC) lacked the authority to investigate foreign spamming.

Congress sought to rectify the situation by enacting the U.S. Safe Web Act (also known as the Undertaking Spam, Spyware, and Fraud Enforcement with Enforcers Beyond Borders Act).[3] The act allows the FTC to cooperate and share information with foreign agencies in investigating and prosecuting those involved in spamming, spyware, and various Internet frauds and deceptions.

The Safe Web Act also provides a "safe harbor" for **Internet service providers (ISPs)**—that is, organizations that provide access to the Internet. The safe harbor gives ISPs immunity from liability for supplying information to the FTC concerning possible unfair or deceptive conduct in foreign jurisdictions.

9–1b Domain Names

As e-commerce expanded worldwide, one issue that emerged involved the rights of a trademark owner to use the mark as part of a domain name. A **domain name** is part of an Internet address, such as "cengage.com."

Structure of Domain Names Every domain name ends with a top-level domain (TLD), which is the part of the name to the right of the period. The TLD often indicates the type of entity that operates the site. For instance, *com* is an abbreviation for *commercial*, and *edu* is short for *education*.

The second-level domain (SLD)—the part of the name to the left of the period—is chosen by the business entity or individual registering the domain name. Competition for SLDs among firms with similar names and products has led to numerous disputes. By using an identical or similar domain name, parties have attempted to profit from a competitor's **goodwill** (the nontangible value of a business).

Distribution System The Internet Corporation for Assigned Names and Numbers (ICANN), a nonprofit corporation, oversees the distribution of domain names and operates an online arbitration system. Due to numerous complaints, ICANN recently overhauled the domain name distribution system.

In 2012, ICANN started selling new generic top-level domain names (gTLDs) for an initial price of $185,000 plus an annual fee of $25,000. Whereas TLDs were limited to only a few terms (such as *com, net,* and *org*), gTLDs can take any form. By 2017, many companies and corporations had acquired gTLDs based on their brands, such as *aol, bmw, canon, target,* and *walmart.* Some companies have numerous gTLDs. Google's gTLDs, for instance, include *android, bing, chrome, gmail, goog,* and *YouTube.*

Because gTLDs have greatly increased the potential number of domain names, domain name registrars have proliferated. Registrar companies charge a fee to businesses and individuals to register new names and to renew annual registrations (often through automated software). Many of these companies also buy and sell expired domain names.

9–1c Cybersquatting

One of the goals of the new gTLD system was to address the problem of *cybersquatting.* **Cybersquatting** occurs when a person registers a domain name that is the same as, or confusingly similar to, the trademark of another and then offers to sell the domain name back to the trademark owner.

■ **CASE IN POINT 9.2** Apple, Inc., has repeatedly sued cybersquatters that registered domain names similar to its products, such as iphone4s.com and ipods.com. Apple won a judgment in litigation at the World Intellectual Property Organization against a company that was squatting on the domain name iPhone6s.com.[4] ■

---

3. Pub. L. No. 109-455, 120 Stat. 3372 (2006), codified in various sections of 15 U.S.C. and 12 U.S.C. Section 3412.

4. WIPO Case No. D2012-0951.

Anticybersquatting Legislation Because cybersquatting has led to so much litigation, Congress enacted the Anticybersquatting Consumer Protection Act (ACPA),[5] which amended the Lanham Act—the federal law protecting trademarks. The ACPA makes cybersquatting illegal when both of the following are true:

1. The domain name is identical or confusingly similar to the trademark of another.
2. The one registering, trafficking in, or using the domain name has a "bad faith intent" to profit from that trademark.

Despite the ACPA, cybersquatting continues to present a problem for businesses.

Frequent Changes in Domain Name Ownership Facilitates Cybersquatting All domain name registrars are supposed to relay information about their transactions to ICANN and other companies that keep a master list of domain names, but this does not always occur. The speed at which domain names change hands and the difficulty in tracking mass automated registrations have created an environment in which cybersquatting can flourish.

■ **CASE IN POINT 9.3** OnNet USA, Inc., owns the English-language rights to 9Dragons, a game with a martial arts theme, and operates a Web site for its promotion. When a party known as "Warv0x" began to operate a pirated version of the game at Play9D.com, OnNet filed an action under the ACPA in a federal court. OnNet was unable to obtain contact information for the owner of Play9D.com through its Australian domain name registrar, however, and thus could not complete service of process. Therefore, the federal court allowed OnNet to serve the defendant by publishing a notice of the suit in a newspaper in Gold Coast, Australia.[6] ■

Typosquatting Typosquatting is registering a name that is a misspelling of a popular brand, such as googl. com or appple.com. Because many Internet users are not perfect typists, Web pages using these misspelled names receive a lot of traffic. More traffic generally means increased profit (advertisers often pay Web sites based on the number of unique visits, or hits).

Typosquatting may sometimes fall beyond the reach of the ACPA. If the misspelling is significant, the trademark owner may have difficulty proving that the name is identical or confusingly similar to the trademark of another, as the ACPA requires.

Typosquatting adds costs for businesses seeking to protect their domain name rights. Companies must attempt to register not only legitimate variations of their domain names but also potential misspellings. Large corporations may have to register thousands of domain names across the globe just to protect their basic brands and trademarks.

Applicability and Sanctions of the ACPA The ACPA applies to all domain name registrations of trademarks. Successful plaintiffs in suits brought under the act can collect actual damages and profits, or they can elect to receive statutory damages ranging from $1,000 to $100,000.

Although some companies have been successful suing under the ACPA, there are roadblocks to pursuing such lawsuits. Some domain name registrars offer privacy services that hide the true owners of Web sites, making it difficult for trademark owners to identify cybersquatters. Thus, before bringing a suit, a trademark owner has to ask the court for a subpoena to discover the identity of the owner of the infringing Web site. Because of the high costs of court proceedings, discovery, and even arbitration, many disputes over cybersquatting are settled out of court.

To facilitate dispute resolution, ICANN now offers the Uniform Rapid Suspension (URS) system. URS allows trademark holders with clear-cut infringement claims to obtain rapid relief. ■ **EXAMPLE 9.4** In the first dispute filed involving gTLDs, IBM filed a complaint with URS against an individual who registered the domain names IBM.guru and IBM.ventures in February 2014. A week later, the URS panel decided in IBM's favor and suspended the two domain names. ■

9–1d Meta Tags

Meta tags are key words that give Internet browsers specific information about a Web page. Meta tags can be used to increase the likelihood that a site will be included in search engine results, even if the site has nothing to do with the key words. In effect, one site can appropriate the key words of other sites with more frequent hits so that the appropriating site will appear in the same search engine results as the more popular sites.

Using another's trademark in a meta tag without the owner's permission normally constitutes trademark infringement. Some uses of another's trademark as a meta tag may be permissible, however, if the use is reasonably

---

5. 15 U.S.C. Section 1129.
6. *OnNet USA, Inc. v. Play9D.com*, 2013 WL 120319 (N.D.Cal. 2013).

necessary and does not suggest that the owner authorized or sponsored the use.

■ **CASE IN POINT 9.5** Farzad and Lisa Tabari are auto brokers—the personal shoppers of the automotive world. They contact authorized dealers, solicit bids, and arrange for customers to buy from the dealer offering the best combination of location, availability, and price. The Tabaris offered this service at the Web sites buy-a-lexus.com and buyorleaselexus.com.

Toyota Motor Sales U.S.A., Inc., the exclusive distributor of Lexus vehicles and the owner of the Lexus mark, objected to the Tabaris' practices. The Tabaris removed Toyota's photographs and logo from their site and added a disclaimer in large type at the top, but they refused to give up their domain names. Toyota sued for infringement. The court forced the Tabaris to stop using any "domain name, service mark, trademark, trade name,

meta tag or other commercial indication of origin that includes the mark LEXUS."[7] ■

9–1e Trademark Dilution in the Online World

Trademark *dilution* occurs when a trademark is used, without authorization, in a way that diminishes the distinctive quality of the mark. Unlike trademark infringement, a claim of dilution does not require proof that consumers are likely to be confused by a connection between the unauthorized use and the mark. For this reason, the products involved need not be similar, as the following *Spotlight Case* illustrates.

---

7. *Toyota Motor Sales, U.S.A., Inc. v. Tabari*, 610 F.3d 171 (9th Cir. 2011).

Spotlight on Internet Porn

Case 9.1 Hasbro, Inc. v. Internet Entertainment Group, Ltd.
United States District Court, Western District of Washington, 1996 WL 84853 (1996).

Background and Facts In 1949, Hasbro, Inc.—then known as the Milton Bradley Company—published its first version of Candy Land, a children's board game. Hasbro is the owner of the trademark "Candy Land," which has been registered with the U.S. Patent and Trademark Office since 1951. Over the years, Hasbro has produced several versions of the game, including Candy Land puzzles, a travel version, a computer game, and a handheld electronic version. In the mid-1990s, Brian Cartmell and his employer, the Internet Entertainment Group, Ltd., used the term *candyland.com* as a domain name for a sexually explicit Internet site. Anyone who performed an online search using the word *candyland* was directed to this adult Web site. Hasbro filed a trademark dilution claim in a federal court, seeking a permanent injunction to prevent the defendants from using the Candy Land trademark.

In the Language of the Court
DWYER, U.S. District Judge
　＊ ＊ ＊ ＊

2. Hasbro has demonstrated a probability of proving that defendants Internet Entertainment Group, Ltd., Brian Cartmell and Internet Entertainment Group, Inc. (collectively referred to as "defendants") have been diluting the value of Hasbro's CANDY LAND mark by using the name CANDYLAND to identify a sexually explicit Internet site, and by using the name string "candyland.com" as an Internet domain name which, when typed into an Internet-connected computer, provides Internet users with access to that site.
　＊ ＊ ＊ ＊

4. Hasbro has shown that defendants' use of the CANDY LAND name and the domain name candyland.com in connection with their Internet site is causing irreparable injury to Hasbro.

5. *The probable harm to Hasbro from defendants' conduct outweighs any inconvenience that defendants will experience if they are required to stop using the CANDYLAND name.* [Emphasis added.]
　＊ ＊ ＊ ＊

THEREFORE, IT IS HEREBY ORDERED that Hasbro's motion for preliminary injunction is granted.

Decision and Remedy *The federal district court granted Hasbro an injunction against the defendants, agreeing that the domain name* candyland *was "causing irreparable injury to Hasbro." The judge ordered the defendants to immediately remove all content from the* candyland.com *Web site and to stop using the Candy Land mark.*

Critical Thinking

• **Economic** *How can companies protect themselves from others who create Web sites that have similar domain names, and what limits each company's ability to be fully protected?*

• **What If the Facts Were Different?** *Suppose that the site using* candyland.com *had not been sexually explicit but had sold candy. Would the result have been the same? Explain.*

9–1f Licensing

A company may permit another party to use a trademark (or other intellectual property) under a license. A licensor might grant a license allowing its trademark to be used as part of a domain name, for instance.

Another type of license involves the use of a product such as software. This sort of licensing is ubiquitous in the online world. When you download an application on your smartphone, tablet, or other mobile device, for instance, you are typically entering into a license agreement. You are obtaining only a *license* to use that app and not ownership rights in it. Apps published on Google Play, for instance, may use its licensing service to prompt users to agree to a license at the time of installation and use.

Licensing agreements frequently include restrictions that prohibit licensees from sharing the file and using it to create similar software applications. The license may also limit the use of the application to a specific device or give permission to the user for a certain time period.

9–2 Copyrights in Digital Information

Copyright law is probably the most important form of intellectual property protection on the Internet. This is because much of the material on the Internet (including software and database information) is copyrighted, and in order to transfer that material online, it must be "copied." Generally, whenever a party downloads software or music into a computer's random access memory, or RAM, without authorization, a copyright is infringed.

Initially, criminal penalties for copyright violations could be imposed only if unauthorized copies were exchanged for financial gain. Then, Congress amended the law and extended criminal liability for the piracy of copyrighted materials to persons who exchange unauthorized copies of copyrighted works without realizing a profit.

9–2a Digital Millennium Copyright Act

In 1998, Congress enacted the Digital Millennium Copyright Act (DMCA).[8] The DMCA gave significant protection to owners of copyrights in digital information. Among other things, the act established civil and criminal penalties for anyone who circumvents (bypasses) encryption software or other technological antipiracy protection. Also prohibited are the manufacture, import, sale, and distribution of devices or services for circumvention.

Allows Fair Use The DMCA provides for exceptions to fit the needs of libraries, scientists, universities, and others. In general, the law does not restrict the "fair use" of circumvention methods for educational and other noncommercial purposes. For instance, circumvention is allowed to test computer security, to conduct encryption research, to protect personal privacy, and to enable parents to monitor their children's use of the Internet. The exceptions are to be reconsidered every three years.

One federal appellate court extended the situations in which the fair use doctrine applies. ■ **CASE IN POINT 9.6** Stephanie Lenz posted a short video on YouTube of her toddler son dancing with the Prince song "Let's Go Crazy" playing in the background. Universal Music Group (UMG) sent YouTube a take-down notice that stated that the video violated copyright law under the DMCA. YouTube removed the "dancing baby" video and

---

8. 17 U.S.C. Sections 512, 1201–1205, 1301–1332; and 28 U.S.C. Section 4001.

notified Lenz of the allegations of copyright infringement, warning her that repeated incidents of infringement could lead it to delete her account.

Lenz filed a lawsuit against UMG claiming that accusing her of infringement constituted a material misrepresentation (fraud) because UMG knew that Lenz's video was a fair use of the song. The district court held that UMG should have considered the fair use doctrine before sending the take-down notice. UMG appealed, and the U.S. Court of Appeals for the Ninth Circuit affirmed. Lenz was allowed to pursue nominal damages from UMG for sending the notice without considering whether her use was fair.[9] ■

Limits Liability of Internet Service Providers

The DMCA also limits the liability of Internet service providers (ISPs). Under the act, an ISP is not liable for copyright infringement by its customer *unless* the ISP is aware of the subscriber's violation. An ISP may be held liable only if it fails to take action to shut down the subscriber after learning of the violation. A copyright holder must act promptly, however, by pursuing a claim in court, or the subscriber has the right to be restored to online access.

9–2b File-Sharing Technology

Soon after the Internet became popular, a few enterprising programmers created software to compress large data files, particularly those associated with music. The best-known compression and decompression system is MP3, which enables music fans to download songs or entire CDs onto their computers or onto portable listening devices, such as smartphones and tablets. The MP3 system also made it possible for music fans to access other fans' files by engaging in file-sharing via the Internet.

Methods of File-Sharing File-sharing is accomplished through **peer-to-peer (P2P) networking.** The concept is simple. Rather than going through a central Web server, P2P networking uses numerous personal computers (PCs) that are connected to the Internet. Individuals on the same network can access files stored on one another's PCs through a **distributed network.** Parts of the network may be distributed all over the country or the world, which offers an unlimited number of uses. Persons scattered throughout the country or the world can work together on the same project by using file-sharing programs.

A newer method of sharing files via the Internet is **cloud computing,** which is essentially a subscription-based or pay-per-use service that extends a computer's software or storage capabilities. Cloud computing can deliver a single application through a browser to multiple users. Alternatively, cloud computing might be a utility program to pool resources and provide data storage and virtual servers that can be accessed on demand. Amazon, Facebook, Google, IBM, and Sun Microsystems are using and developing more cloud computing services.

Sharing Stored Music and Movies When file-sharing is used to download others' stored music files, copyright issues arise. Recording artists and their labels stand to lose large amounts of royalties and revenues if relatively few digital downloads or CDs are purchased and then made available on distributed networks. Anyone can get the music for free on these networks, which has prompted recording companies to pursue individuals for file-sharing copyrighted works.

■ **CASE IN POINT 9.7** Maverick Recording Company and other recording companies sued Whitney Harper in federal court for copyright infringement. Harper had used a file-sharing program to download a number of copyrighted songs from the Internet and had then shared the audio files with others via a P2P network. The plaintiffs sought $750 per infringed work—the minimum amount of statutory damages available under the Copyright Act.

Harper claimed that she was an "innocent" infringer because she was unaware that her actions constituted copyright infringement. Under the act, innocent infringement can result in a reduced penalty. The court, however, noted that a copyright notice appeared on all the songs that Harper had downloaded. She therefore could not assert the innocent infringer defense, and the court ordered her to pay damages of $750 per infringed work.[10] ■

Pirated Movies and Television File-sharing also creates problems for the motion picture and television industries, which lose significant amounts of revenue annually as a result of piracy. Numerous Web sites offer software that facilitates the illegal copying of movies and television programs. BitTorrent, for instance, is a P2P protocol that enables users to download and transfer high-quality files from the Internet. Popcorn Time is a BitTorrent site that offers streaming services that enable users to watch pirated movies and television shows without downloading them.

---

9. *Lenz v. Universal Music Group,* 801 F.3d 1126 (9th Cir. 2015).

10. *Maverick Recording Co. v. Harper,* 598 F.3d 193 (2010).

9–3 Social Media

Social media provide a means by which people can create, share, and exchange ideas and comments via the Internet. Social networking sites, such as Facebook, Google+, LinkedIn, Pinterest, and Tumblr, have become ubiquitous. Studies show that Internet users spend more time on social networks than at any other sites. The amount of time people spend accessing social networks on their smartphones and other mobile devices has been increasing every year (by nearly 30 percent in 2016 alone).

■ **EXAMPLE 9.8** Facebook has more than 1.6 billion active monthly users. Individuals use Facebook to maintain social contacts, update friends on events, and distribute images to others. Facebook members often share common interests based on their school, location, or recreational affiliation, such as a sports team. ■

9–3a Legal Issues

The emergence of Facebook and other social networking sites has created a number of legal and ethical issues for businesses. For instance, a firm's rights in valuable intellectual property may be infringed if users post trademarked images or copyrighted materials on these sites without permission. Various aspects of the legal process may involve the content of social media, as discussed next. Employers' social media policies may also be at issue.

Impact on Litigation Social media posts now are routinely included in discovery in litigation because they can provide damaging information that establishes a person's intent or what she or he knew at a particular time. Like e-mail, posts on social networks can be the smoking gun that leads to liability.

Tweets and other social media posts can also be used to reduce damages awards. ■ **EXAMPLE 9.9** Jill Daniels sued for injuries she sustained in a car accident, claiming that her injuries made it impossible for her to continue working as a hairstylist. The jury initially determined that her damages were $237,000, but when the jurors saw tweets and photographs of Daniels partying in New Orleans and vacationing on the beach, they reduced the final award to $142,000. ■

Impact on Settlement Agreements Social media posts have been used to invalidate settlement agreements that contain confidentiality clauses. ■ **CASE IN POINT 9.10** Patrick Snay was the headmaster of Gulliver Preparatory School in Florida. When Gulliver did not renew Snay's employment contract, Snay sued the school for age discrimination. During mediation, Snay agreed to settle the case for $80,000 and signed a confidentiality clause that required him and his wife not to disclose the "terms and existence" of the agreement. Nevertheless, Snay and his wife told their daughter, Dana, that the dispute had been settled and that they were happy with the results.

Dana, a college student, had recently graduated from Gulliver and, according to Snay, had suffered retaliation at the school. Dana posted a Facebook comment that said "Mama and Papa Snay won the case against Gulliver. Gulliver is now officially paying for my vacation to Europe this summer. SUCK IT." The comment went out to 1,200 of Dana's Facebook friends, many of whom were Gulliver students, and school officials soon learned of it. The school immediately notified Snay that he had breached the confidentiality clause and refused to pay the settlement amount. Ultimately, a state intermediate appellate court held that Snay had breached the confidentiality clause and therefore could not enforce the settlement agreement.[11] ■

Criminal Investigations Law enforcement uses social media to detect and prosecute criminals. A surprising number of criminals boast about their illegal activities on social media. ■ **EXAMPLE 9.11** A nineteen-year-old posts a message on Facebook bragging about how drunk he was on New Year's Eve and apologizing to the owner of the parked car that he hit. The next day, police officers arrest him for drunk driving and leaving the scene of an accident. ■

Some police departments now authorize officers to go undercover on social media sites. ■ **EXAMPLE 9.12** As part of Operation Crew Cut, New York Police Department (NYPD) officers routinely pretend to be young women in order to "friend" suspects on Facebook. Using these fake identities, officers are able to avoid the social media site's privacy settings and gain valuable information about illegal activities. ■

Administrative Agency Investigations Federal regulators also use social media posts in their investigations into illegal activities. ■ **EXAMPLE 9.13** Reed Hastings, the top executive of Netflix, stated on Facebook that Netflix subscribers had watched a billion hours of video the previous month. As a result, Netflix's stock price rose, which prompted a federal agency investigation. Under securities laws, such a statement is considered to be material information to investors. Thus, it must be disclosed to

---

11. *Gulliver Schools, Inc. v. Snay*, 137 So.3d 1045 (Fla.App. 2014).

all investors, not just a select group, such as those who had access to Hastings's Facebook post.

The agency ultimately concluded that it could not hold Hastings responsible for any wrongdoing because the agency's policy on social media use was not clear. The agency then issued new guidelines that allow companies to disclose material information through social media if investors have been notified in advance. ■

In addition, an administrative law judge can base her or his decision on the content of social media posts. ■ **CASE IN POINT 9.14** Jennifer O'Brien was a tenured teacher at a public school in New Jersey when she posted two messages on her Facebook page. "I'm not a teacher—I'm a warden for future criminals!" and "They had a scared straight program in school—why couldn't I bring first graders?" Not surprisingly, outraged parents protested. The deputy superintendent of schools filed a complaint against O'Brien with the state's commissioner of education, charging her with conduct unbecoming a teacher.

After a hearing, an administrative law judge (ALJ) ordered that O'Brien be removed from her teaching position. O'Brien appealed to a state court, claiming that her Facebook postings were protected by the First Amendment and could not be used by the school district to discipline or discharge her. The court found that O'Brien had failed to establish that her Facebook postings were protected speech and that the seriousness of O'Brien's conduct warranted removal from her position.[12] ■

Employers' Social Media Policies Many large corporations have established specific guidelines on using social media in the workplace. Employees who use social media in a way that violates their employer's stated policies may be disciplined or fired from their jobs. Courts and administrative agencies usually uphold an employer's right to terminate a person based on his or her violation of a social media policy.

■ **CASE IN POINT 9.15** Virginia Rodriquez worked for Wal-Mart Stores, Inc., for almost twenty years and had been promoted to management. Then she was disciplined for violating the company's policies by having a fellow employee use Rodriquez's password to alter the price of an item that she purchased. Under Wal-Mart's rules, another violation within a year would mean termination.

Nine months later, on Facebook, Rodriquez publicly chastised employees under her supervision for calling in sick to go to a party. The posting violated Wal-Mart's "Social Media Policy," which was "to avoid public comment that adversely affects employees." Wal-Mart

terminated Rodriquez. She filed a lawsuit, alleging discrimination, but the court issued a summary judgment in Wal-Mart's favor.[13] ■

9–3b The Electronic Communications Privacy Act

The Electronic Communications Privacy Act (ECPA)[14] amended federal wiretapping law to cover electronic forms of communications. Although Congress enacted the ECPA many years before social media networks existed, it nevertheless applies to communications through social media.

The ECPA prohibits the intentional interception of any wire, oral, or electronic communication. It also prohibits the intentional disclosure or use of the information obtained by the interception.

Exclusions Excluded from the ECPA's coverage are any electronic communications through devices that an employer provides for its employee to use "in the ordinary course of its business." Consequently, if a company provides the electronic device (cell phone, laptop, tablet) to the employee for ordinary business use, the company is not prohibited from intercepting business communications made on it. This "business-extension exception" permits employers to monitor employees' electronic communications made in the ordinary course of business. It does not, however, permit employers to monitor employees' personal communications.

Another exception to the ECPA allows an employer to avoid liability under the act if the employees consent to having their electronic communications monitored by the employer.

Stored Communications Part of the ECPA is known as the Stored Communications Act (SCA).[15] The SCA prohibits intentional and unauthorized access to *stored* electronic communications and sets forth criminal and civil sanctions for violators. A person can violate the SCA by intentionally accessing a stored electronic communication. The SCA also prevents "providers" of communication services (such as cell phone companies and social media networks) from divulging private communications to certain entities and individuals.

■ **CASE IN POINT 9.16** Two restaurant employees, Brian Pietrylo and Doreen Marino, were fired after their manager uncovered their password-protected MySpace group. The group's communications, stored on MySpace's

---

12. *In re O'Brien*, 2013 WL 132508 (N.J. Sup. 2013).

13. *Rodriquez v. Wal-Mart Stores, Inc.*, 2013 WL 102674 (N.D.Tex. 2013).
14. 18 U.S.C. Sections 2510–2521.
15. 18 U.S.C. Sections 2701–2711.

Web site, contained sexual remarks about customers and management, as well as comments about illegal drug use and violent behavior. One employee said the group's purpose was to "vent about any BS we deal with out of work without any outside eyes spying on us."

The restaurant learned about the private MySpace group when a hostess showed it to a manager who requested access. The hostess was not explicitly threatened with termination but feared she would lose her job if she did not comply.

After they were fired, Pietrylo and Marino filed a lawsuit against the restaurant. They claimed that their former employer had gained unauthorized access to their MySpace group communications in violation of the SCA. The court allowed the employees' SCA claim, and the jury awarded them $17,003 in compensatory and punitive damages.[16] ■

9–3c Protection of Social Media Passwords

In recent years, employees and applicants for jobs or colleges have sometimes been asked to divulge their social media passwords. An employer or school may look at an individual's Facebook or other account to see if it includes controversial postings such as racially discriminatory remarks or photos of drug parties. Such postings can have a negative effect on a person's prospects even if they were made years earlier or are taken out of context.

By 2017, about half of the states had enacted legislation to protect individuals from having to disclose their social media passwords. Each state's law is slightly different. Some states, such as Michigan, prohibit employers from taking adverse action against an employee or job applicant based on what the person has posted online. Michigan's law also applies to e-mail and cloud storage accounts.

Legislation will not completely prevent employers and others from taking actions against a person based on his or her social network postings, though. Management and human resources personnel are unlikely to admit that they looked at someone's Facebook page and that it influenced their decision. They may not even have to admit to looking at the Facebook page if they use private browsing, which enables people to keep their Web browsing activities confidential. How, then, would a rejected job applicant be able to prove that she or he was rejected because the employer accessed social media postings? See this chapter's *Digital Update* feature for a discussion of employer monitoring of social media.

---

16. *Pietrylo v. Hillstone Restaurant Group*, 2009 WL 3128420 (D.N.J. 2009).

9–3d Company-wide Social Media Networks

Many companies, including Dell, Inc., and Nikon Instruments, form their own internal social media networks. Software companies offer a variety of systems, including Salesforce.com's Chatter, Microsoft's Yammer, and Cisco Systems' WebEx Social. Posts on these internal networks, or *intranets,* are quite different from the typical posts on Facebook, LinkedIn, and Twitter. Employees use these intranets to exchange messages about topics related to their work, such as deals that are closing, new products, production flaws, how a team is solving a problem, and the details of customer orders. Thus, the tone is businesslike.

Protection of Trade Secrets An important advantage to using an internal system for employee communications is that the company can better protect its trade secrets. The company usually decides which employees can see particular intranet files and which employees will belong to each specific "social" group within the company. Companies providing internal social media networks often keep the resulting data on their own servers in secure "clouds."

Other Advantages Internal social media systems also offer additional benefits. They provide real-time information about important issues, such as production glitches. Additionally, posts can include tips on how to best sell new products or deal with difficult customers, as well as information about competitors' products and services. Another major benefit is a significant reduction in e-mail. Rather than wasting fellow employees' time reading mass e-mailings, workers can post messages or collaborate on presentations via the company's social network.

9–4 Online Defamation

Cyber torts are torts that arise from online conduct. One of the most prevalent cyber torts is online defamation. Defamation is wrongfully hurting a person's reputation by communicating false statements about that person to others. Because the Internet enables individuals to communicate with large numbers of people simultaneously (via a blog or tweet, for instance), online defamation has become a problem in today's legal environment.

■ **EXAMPLE 9.17** Singer-songwriter Courtney Love was sued for defamation based on remarks she posted

DIGITAL UPDATE — Monitoring Employees' Social Media—Right or Wrong?

Just about everyone seems to be using some form of social media. That, of course, includes employees. Increasingly, employees' social media use is being monitored by their employers. Sometimes, employees are even being fired over their social media posts.

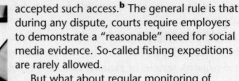

Monitoring of Employees' Social Media Use

Employers have monitored their employees' Internet use for years. According to Gartner, Inc., an information technology advisory company, employers are now using the same technology to examine workers' social media use.

Companies have a number of concerns about how their employees use social media. For one thing, they may worry about security problems, such as employees' posting unauthorized videos of company activities. In addition, they do not wish to have their clients discussed on employees' social media posts. Finally, some companies are concerned that certain posts may violate the law. For instance, if hospital employees discuss patients, they not only are disregarding hospital regulations, but also are violating the federal Health Insurance Portability and Accountability Act (HIPAA).[a]

Restrictions on Access to Employees' Social Media Records

In disputes over discrimination, hostile work environment, and other employment situations, employers typically seek access to certain employees' complete social media records. The courts have not uniformly accepted such access.[b] The general rule is that during any dispute, courts require employers to demonstrate a "reasonable" need for social media evidence. So-called fishing expeditions are rarely allowed.

But what about regular monitoring of employee online behavior? As long as an employee has no expectation of privacy on the social media site and is not part of a protected class, courts will side with employers. After all, social media posts are public, even when privacy settings are enabled. Note, though, that whenever employer monitoring involves obtaining information about religious affiliation, sexual orientation, or pregnancies, litigation may ensue.

The rule of thumb is that the more personal the information about any employee, the more problematic social media monitoring becomes. As one expert in the field stated, "Recent cases teach that when a company decides to monitor employee behavior online, uncertainty takes over."[c]

Critical Thinking *Some companies use internal social media networks for work-related employee communications. Would the same legal rules that apply to monitoring public social media platforms, such as Twitter and Facebook, also apply to company-provided social media platforms?*

a. Pub. L. No. 104-191 (1996); 29 U.S.C. Sections 1181 *et seq.*

b. *Ogden v. All-State Career School*, 299 F.R.D. 446 (2014). See also *Appler v. Mead Johnson & Co., LLC*, 2015 WL 5615038, and *In re Milo's Kitchen Dog Treats Consol*, 307 F.R.D. 177 (2015).

c. Rodney Satterwhite, "'Friend' or Foe? Balancing the Litigation Risks of Monitoring Employees' Social Media Profiles at Various Stages of Employment," 2014 WL 5465794 (2014).

---

about fashion designer Dawn Simorangkir on Twitter. Love claimed that her statements were statements of opinion (rather than statements of fact, as required) and therefore were not actionable as defamation. Nevertheless, Love ended up paying $430,000 to settle the case out of court. ∎

9–4a Identifying the Author of Online Defamation

An initial issue raised by online defamation is simply discovering who is committing it. In the real world,

identifying the author of a defamatory remark generally is an easy matter. It is more difficult if a business firm discovers that defamatory statements about its policies and products are being posted in an online forum, because the postings are anonymous. Therefore, a threshold barrier to anyone who seeks to bring an action for online defamation is discovering the identity of the person who posted the defamatory message.

An Internet service provider (ISP) can disclose personal information about its customers only when ordered to do so by a court. Consequently, businesses and individuals are increasingly bringing lawsuits against "John Does" (John Doe, Jane Doe, and the like are fictitious names used in lawsuits when the identity of a party is not known or when a party wishes to conceal his or her name for privacy reasons). Then, using the authority of the courts, the plaintiffs can obtain from the ISPs the identity of the persons responsible for the defamatory messages.

■ **CASE IN POINT 9.18**   Seven users of Yelp, Inc.— a social networking Web site for consumer reviews— posted negative reviews of Hadeed Carpet Cleaning, Inc., in Alexandria, Virginia. Hadeed brought a defamation suit against the "John Doe" reviewers in a Virginia state court, claiming that because these individuals were not actual customers, their comments were false and defamatory. Yelp failed to comply with a court order to reveal the users' identities and was held in contempt.

Yelp appealed, claiming that releasing the identities would violate the defendants' First Amendment right to free speech. A state intermediate appellate court affirmed the lower court's judgment, noting that Hadeed could not move forward with its defamation lawsuit unless it knew the identities of the defendants. Revealing the identities of Yelp reviewers was not a violation of their First Amendment rights.[17] ■

9–4b Liability of Internet Service Providers

Recall that under tort law those who repeat or otherwise republish a defamatory statement are normally subject to liability. Thus, newspapers, magazines, and television and radio stations are subject to liability for defamatory content that they publish or broadcast, even though the content was prepared or created by others. Applying this rule to cyberspace, however, raises an important issue: Should ISPs be regarded as publishers and therefore be held liable for defamatory messages that are posted by their users?

General Rule   The Communications Decency Act (CDA) states that "[n]o provider or user of an interactive computer service shall be treated as the publisher or speaker of any information provided by another information content provider."[18] Thus, under the CDA, ISPs usually are treated differently from publishers in print and other media and are not liable for publishing defamatory statements that come from a third party.

Exceptions   Although the courts generally have construed the CDA as providing a broad shield to protect ISPs from liability for third party content, some courts have started establishing limits to this immunity. ■ **CASE IN POINT 9.19**   Roommate.com, LLC, operates an online roommate-matching Web site that helps individuals find roommates based on their descriptions of themselves and their roommate preferences. Users respond to a series of online questions, choosing from answers in drop-down and select-a-box menus.

Some of the questions asked users to disclose their sex, family status, and sexual orientation—which is not permitted under the federal Fair Housing Act. When a nonprofit housing organization sued Roommate.com, the company claimed it was immune from liability under the CDA. A federal appellate court disagreed and ruled that Roommate.com was not immune from liability. By creating the Web site and the questionnaire and answer choices, Roommate.com prompted users to express discriminatory preferences and matched users based on these preferences in violation of federal law.[19] ■

9–5 Other Actions Involving Online Posts

Online conduct can give rise to a wide variety of legal actions. E-mails, tweets, posts, and every sort of online communication can form the basis for almost any type of tort. For example, in addition to defamation, suits relating to online conduct may involve allegations of wrongful interference or infliction of emotional distress.

Besides actions grounded in the common law, online conduct may give rise to a cause of action directed expressly at online communications by a statute. In the following case, the court was asked to issue an injunction to prohibit speech that was alleged to constitute *cyberstalking*. The applicable statute defined this term to require, in part, "substantial emotional distress."

---

17. *Yelp, Inc. v. Hadeed Carpet Cleaning, Inc.*, 62 Va.App. 678, 752 S.E.2d 554 (2014).
18. 47 U.S.C. Section 230.

19. *Fair Housing Council of San Fernando Valley v. Roommate.com, LLC*, 666 F.3d 1216 (9th Cir. 2012).

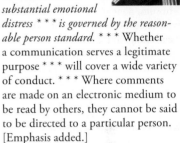

Case Analysis 9.2

David v. Textor

District Court of Appeal of Florida, Fourth District, 41 Fla.L.Weekly D131, __ So.3d __ (2016).

In the Language of the Court

WARNER, J. [Judge].

* * * *

[Alkiviades] David and [John] Textor both have companies which produce holograms used in the music industry. * * * Shortly before the Billboard Music Awards show, it was announced that Textor's company, Pulse Entertainment, would show a Michael Jackson hologram performance. Immediately thereafter, David's company, Hologram USA, Inc., * * * filed suit for patent infringement against Pulse in the U.S. District Court in Nevada * * * . Pulse countered by filing a business tort suit against David in California.

[One month later,] Textor filed a petition [in a Florida state court against David under Florida Statutes] Sections 784.046 and 784.0485, which concern cyberstalking.

The alleged acts of cyberstalking were (1) a * * * text from David to Textor, demanding that Textor give credit to David's company at the Billboard Awards show for the hologram, for which David would drop his patent infringement suit; otherwise, he threatened to increase damages in that suit and stated, "You will be ruined I promise you"; (2) an e-mail from David to business associates (other than Textor) that he had more information about Textor that would be released soon, but not specifying what that information was; (3) an online article from July 2014 on Entrepreneur.com, in which David was quoted as saying that he "would have killed [Textor] if he could"; and (4) articles about Textor that David posted and reposted in various online outlets.

* * * *

The trial court [issued an injunction] prohibiting David from communicating with Textor or posting any information about him online, and ordering that

he remove any materials he already had posted.

David * * * moved to dissolve the * * * injunction. * * * The court denied the motion to dissolve and amended its order to prohibit David from communicating with Textor either through electronic means, in person, or through third parties. The amended order also provided:

> Respondent David shall immediately cease and desist from sending any text messages, e-mails, posting any tweets (including the re-tweeting or forwarding), posting any images or other forms of communication directed at John Textor without a legitimate purpose. Threats or warnings of physical or emotional harm or attempts to extort Textor or any entity associated with Textor by Respondent David, personally or through his agents, directed to John Textor, directly or by other means, are prohibited.

From this order, David appeals.

David claims that none of the allegations in the petition constitute cyberstalking, but are merely heated rhetoric over a business dispute. Further, he claims that the injunction constitutes a prior restraint on speech, which violates the First Amendment.

[Florida Statutes] Section 784.0485 allows an injunction against * * * cyberstalking. * * * Section 784.048 defines * * * cyberstalking:

> * * * "Cyberstalk" means to engage in a course of conduct to communicate, or to cause to be communicated, words, images, or language by or through the use of electronic mail or electronic communication, directed at a specific person, causing substantial emotional distress to that person and serving no legitimate purpose.

Whether a communication causes substantial emotional distress * * * is governed by the reasonable person standard. * * * Whether a communication serves a legitimate purpose * * * will cover a wide variety of conduct. * * * Where comments are made on an electronic medium to be read by others, they cannot be said to be directed to a particular person. [Emphasis added.]

In this case, Textor alleged that two communications came directly from David to him, both of which were demands that Textor drop his lawsuit. In neither of them did David make any threat to Textor's safety. From the full e-mail, David's threats that Textor would be "sorry" if he didn't settle must be taken in the context of the lawsuit and its potential cost to Textor. Because of the existence of the various lawsuits and the heated controversy over the hologram patents, these e-mails had a legitimate purpose in trying to get Textor to drop what David considered a spurious lawsuit. Moreover, nothing in the e-mails should have caused substantial emotional distress to Textor, himself a sophisticated businessman. Indeed, that they did not is reflected in Textor's refusal to settle or adhere to their terms.

The postings online are also not communications which would cause substantial emotional distress. Most of them are simply re-tweets of articles or headlines involving Textor. That they may be embarrassing to Textor is not at all the same as causing him substantial emotional distress sufficient to obtain an injunction.

Even the alleged physical threat made by David in an online interview, that David would have killed Textor if he could have, would not cause a reasonable person substantial emotional distress.

Case 9.2 Continues

Case 9.2 Continued

In the online article the author stated that "David joked" when stating that he would have killed Textor. Spoken to a journalist for publication, it hardly amounts to an actual and credible threat of violence to Textor.

In sum, none of the allegations in Textor's petition show acts constituting cyberstalking, in that a reasonable person would not suffer substantial emotional distress over them. Those communications made directly to Textor served a legitimate purpose.

An injunction in this case would also violate [the freedom of speech under the U.S. Constitution's First Amendment. An] injunction directed to speech is a classic example of prior restraint on speech triggering First Amendment concerns. * * * *Prior restraints on speech and publication are the most serious and the least tolerable infringement on First Amendment rights.* [Florida Statutes] Section 784.048 itself recognizes the First Amendment rights of individuals by concluding that a "course of conduct" for

purposes of the statute does not include protected speech. [Emphasis added.]

Here, the online postings simply provide information, gleaned from other sources, regarding Textor and the many lawsuits against him. The injunction prevents not only communications *to* Textor, but also communications *about* Textor. Such prohibition by prior restraint violates the Constitution.

For the foregoing reasons, we reverse the * * * injunction and remand with directions to dismiss the petition.

Legal Reasoning Questions

1. How is *cyberstalking* defined by the statute in this case, and what conduct by the defendant allegedly fit this definition?

2. What standard determines whether certain conduct meets the requirements of the cyberstalking statute? What law or legal principle limits an injunction that is directed at speech?

3. Why did the court in this case "reverse the . . . injunction and remand with directions to dismiss the petition"? Explain.

9–6 Privacy

Facebook, Google, and Yahoo have all been accused of violating users' privacy rights. The right to privacy is guaranteed by the Bill of Rights, and some state constitutions. To maintain a suit for the invasion of privacy, though, a person must have a reasonable expectation of privacy in the particular situation.

9–6a Reasonable Expectation of Privacy

People clearly have a reasonable expectation of privacy when they enter their personal banking or credit-card information online. They also have a reasonable expectation that online companies will follow their own privacy policies. But it is probably not reasonable to expect privacy in statements made on Twitter—or photos posted on Twitter, Flickr, or Instagram, for that matter.

Sometimes, to be sure, people mistakenly believe that they are making statements or posting photos in a private forum. ■ **EXAMPLE 9.20** Randi Zuckerberg, the older sister of Mark Zuckerberg (the founder of Facebook), used a mobile app called "Poke" to post a "private" photo on Facebook of their family gathering during the holidays. Poke allows the sender to decide how long the photo can be seen by others. Facebook allows users to configure their privacy settings to limit access to photos, which Randi thought she had done. Nonetheless, the photo showed up in the Facebook feed of Callie Schweitzer, who then put it on Twitter, where it eventually "went viral." Schweitzer apologized and removed the photo, but it had already gone public for the world to see. ■

In the following case, the court considered whether a Facebook user's expectation of privacy in photos that she posted on the site was reasonable.

Case 9.3

Nucci v. Target Corp.

District Court of Appeal of Florida, Fourth District, 162 So.3d 146 (2015).

Background and Facts Maria Nucci filed a suit in a Florida state court against Target Corporation, alleging that she suffered an injury when she slipped and fell on a "foreign substance" on the floor of a Target store. Target filed a motion to compel an inspection of Nucci's Facebook profile, which

Case 9.3 Continued

included 1,249 photos. Target argued that it was entitled to view the profile because Nucci's lawsuit put her physical and mental condition at issue.

Nucci responded that her Facebook page's privacy setting prevented the general public from having access to it. She claimed that she had a reasonable expectation of privacy in the profile and that Target's access would invade that privacy right. The court issued an order to compel discovery of certain photos, including some on Nucci's Facebook page, that were relevant to her physical and mental condition before and following the alleged injury. Nucci petitioned a state intermediate appellate court for relief from the order.

In the Language of the Court

GROSS, J. [Judge]
* * * *

In a personal injury case * * * , *the fact-finder is required to examine the quality of the plaintiff's life before and after the accident to determine the extent of the loss.* From testimony alone, it is often difficult for the fact-finder to grasp what a plaintiff's life was like prior to an accident. It would take a great novelist, a Tolstoy, a Dickens, or a Hemingway, to use words to summarize the totality of a prior life. If a photograph is worth a thousand words, *there is no better portrayal of what an individual's life was like than those photographs the individual has chosen to share through social media before the occurrence of an accident causing injury.* Such photographs are the equivalent of a "day in the life" slide show produced by the plaintiff before the existence of any motive to manipulate reality. [Emphasis added.]
* * * *

The Florida Constitution expressly protects an individual's right to privacy. * * * The right to privacy in the Florida Constitution ensures that individuals are able to determine for themselves when, how and to what extent information about them is communicated to others.

Before the right to privacy attaches, there must exist a legitimate expectation of privacy. * * *

* * * Social networking sites, such as Facebook, are free websites where an individual creates a "profile" which functions as a personal Web page and may include, at the user's discretion, numerous photos and a vast array of personal information including age, employment, education, religious and political views and various recreational interests. Once a user joins a social networking site, he or she can use the site to search for "friends" and create linkages to others based on similar interests.
* * * *

* * * *Generally, the photographs posted on a social networking site are neither privileged nor protected by any right of privacy, regardless of any privacy settings that the user may have established.* Such posted photographs are unlike medical records or communications with one's attorney, where disclosure is confined to narrow, confidential relationships. Facebook itself does not guarantee privacy. By creating a Facebook account, a user acknowledges that her personal information would be shared with others. Indeed, that is the very nature and purpose of these social networking sites else they would cease to exist. [Emphasis added.]

* * * The expectation that such information is private, in the traditional sense of the word, is not a reasonable one.

Decision and Remedy   *The state intermediate appellate denied Nucci's petition for relief from the order to compel discovery of her Facebook photos. The court concluded that "the photographs sought were reasonably calculated to lead to the discovery of admissible evidence, and Nucci's privacy interest in them was minimal."*

Critical Thinking

- **What If the Facts Were Different?**   *Suppose that Target had asked for a much broader range of Facebook material that concerned not just Nucci's physical and mental condition at the time of her alleged injury but also her personal relationships with her family, romantic partners, and significant others. Would the result have been the same? Discuss.*
- **Ethical**   *Would a court also allow Target discovery of Facebook photos that were posted by Nucci's friends and family? Why or why not?*

9–6b Data Collection and Cookies

Whenever a consumer purchases items online from a retailer, such as Amazon.com or Best Buy, the retailer collects information about the consumer. **Cookies** are invisible files that computers, smartphones, and other mobile devices create to track a user's Web browsing activities. Cookies provide detailed information to marketers about an individual's behavior and preferences, which is then used to personalize online services.

Over time, a retailer can amass considerable data about a person's shopping habits. Does collecting this information violate a consumer's right to privacy? Should retailers be able to pass on the data they have collected to their affiliates? Should they be able to use the information to predict what a consumer might want and then create online "coupons" customized to fit the person's buying history?

■ **EXAMPLE 9.21** Facebook, Inc., once used a targeted advertising technique called "Sponsored Stories." An ad would display a Facebook friend's name and profile picture, along with a statement that the friend "likes" the company sponsoring the advertisement. A group of plaintiffs filed suit, claiming that Facebook had used their pictures for advertising without their permission. When a federal court refused to dismiss the case, Facebook agreed to settle. ■

9–6c Internet Companies' Privacy Policies

The Federal Trade Commission (FTC) investigates consumer complaints of privacy violations. The FTC has forced many companies, including Google, Facebook, Twitter, and MySpace, to enter a consent decree that gives the FTC broad power to review their privacy and data practices. It can then sue companies that violate the terms of the decree.

■ **EXAMPLE 9.22** In 2012, Google settled a suit brought by the FTC alleging that it had misused data from Apple's Safari users. Google allegedly had used cookies to trick the Safari browser on iPhones and iPads so that Google could monitor users who had blocked such tracking. This violated the company's consent decree with the FTC. Google agreed to pay $22.5 million to settle the suit without admitting liability. ■

Facebook has faced a number of complaints about its privacy policy and has changed its policy several times to satisfy its critics and ward off potential government investigations. Other companies, including mobile app developers, have also changed their privacy policies to provide more information to consumers. Consequently, it is frequently the companies, rather than courts or legislatures, that are defining the privacy rights of their online users.

Reviewing: Internet Law, Social Media, and Privacy

While he was in high school, Joel Gibb downloaded numerous songs to his smartphone from an unlicensed file-sharing service. He used portions of the copyrighted songs when he recorded his own band and posted videos on YouTube and Facebook. Gibb also used BitTorrent to download several movies from the Internet. Now he has applied to Boston University. The admissions office has requested access to his Facebook password, and he has complied. Using the information presented in the chapter, answer the following questions.

1. What laws, if any, did Gibb violate by downloading the music and videos from the Internet?
2. Was Gibb's use of portions of copyrighted songs in his own music illegal? Explain.
3. Can individuals legally post copyrighted content on their Facebook pages? Why or why not?
4. Did Boston University violate any laws when it asked Joel to provide his Facebook password? Explain.

Debate This . . . *Internet service providers should be subject to the same defamation laws as newspapers, magazines, and television and radio stations.*

Terms and Concepts

cloud computing 175	distributed network 175	peer-to-peer (P2P) networking 175
cookie 184	domain name 171	social media 176
cybersquatting 171	goodwill 171	spam 170
cyber tort 178	Internet service provider (ISP) 171	typosquatting 172

Issue Spotters

1. Karl self-publishes a cookbook titled *Hole Foods*, in which he sets out recipes for donuts, Bundt cakes, tortellini, and other foods with holes. To publicize the book, Karl designs the Web site holefoods.com. Karl appropriates the key words of other cooking and cookbook sites with more frequent hits so that holefoods.com will appear in the same search engine results as the more popular sites. Has Karl done anything wrong? Explain. (See *Internet Law.*)

2. Eagle Corporation began marketing software in 2007 under the mark "Eagle." In 2017, Eagle.com, Inc., a different company selling different products, begins to use *eagle* as part of its URL and registers it as a domain name. Can Eagle Corporation stop this use of *eagle*? If so, what must the company show? (See *Internet Law.*)

- **Check your answers to the Issue Spotters against the answers provided in Appendix D at the end of this text.**

Business Scenarios

9–1. Internet Service Providers. CyberConnect, Inc., is an Internet service provider (ISP). Pepper is a CyberConnect subscriber. Market Reach, Inc., is an online advertising company. Using sophisticated software, Market Reach directs its ads to those users most likely to be interested in a particular product. When Pepper receives one of the ads, she objects to the content. Further, she claims that CyberConnect should pay damages for "publishing" the ad. Is the ISP regarded as a publisher and therefore liable for the content of Market Reach's ad? Why or why not? (See *Online Defamation.*)

9–2. Privacy. SeeYou, Inc., is an online social network. SeeYou's members develop personalized profiles to interact and share information—photos, videos, stories, activity updates, and other items—with other members. Members post the information that they want to share and decide with whom they want to share it. SeeYou launched a program to allow members to share with others what they do elsewhere online. For example, if a member rents a movie through Netflix, SeeYou will broadcast that information to everyone in the member's online network. How can SeeYou avoid complaints that this program violates its members' privacy? (See *Privacy.*)

Business Case Problems

9–3. Business Case Problem with Sample Answer— Privacy. Using special software, South Dakota law enforcement officers found a person who appeared to possess child pornography at a specific Internet address. The officers subpoenaed Midcontinent Communications, the service that assigned the address, for the personal information of its subscriber. With this information, the officers obtained a search warrant for the residence of John Rolfe, where they found a laptop that contained child pornography. Rolfe argued that the subpoenas violated his "expectation of privacy." Did Rolfe have a privacy interest in the information obtained by the subpoenas issued to Midcontinent? Discuss. [*State of South Dakota v. Rolfe*, 825 N.W.2d 901 (S.Dak. 2013)] (See *Privacy.*)

- **For a sample answer to Problem 9–3, go to Appendix E at the end of this text.**

9–4. File-Sharing. Dartmouth College professor M. Eric Johnson, in collaboration with Tiversa, Inc., a company that monitors peer-to-peer networks to provide security services, wrote an article titled "Data Hemorrhages in the Health-Care Sector." In preparing the article, Johnson and Tiversa searched the networks for data that could be used to commit medical or financial identity theft. They found a document that contained the Social Security numbers, insurance information, and treatment codes for patients of LabMD, Inc. Tiversa notified LabMD of the find in order to solicit its business. Instead of hiring Tiversa, however, LabMD filed a suit in a federal district court against the company, alleging trespass, conversion, and violations of federal statutes. What do these facts indicate about the security of private information? Explain. How should the court rule? [*LabMD, Inc. v. Tiversa, Inc.,* 2013 WL 425983 (11th Cir. 2013)] (See *Copyrights in Digital Information.*)

9–5. Social Media. Mohammad Omar Aly Hassan and nine others were indicted in a federal district court on charges of conspiring to advance violent jihad (holy war against enemies of Islam) and other offenses related to terrorism. The evidence at Hassan's trial included postings he made on Facebook concerning his adherence to violent jihadist ideology. Convicted, Hassan appealed, contending that the Facebook items had not been properly authenticated (established as his own comments). How might the government show the connection between postings on Facebook and those who post them? Discuss. [*United States v. Hassan,* 742 F.3d 104 (4th Cir. 2014)] (See *Social Media.*)

9–6. Social Media. Kenneth Wheeler was angry at certain police officers in Grand Junction, Colorado, because of a driving-under-the-influence arrest that he viewed as unjust. While in Italy, Wheeler posted a statement to his Facebook page urging his "religious followers" to "kill cops, drown them in the blood of their children, hunt them down and kill their entire bloodlines" and provided names. Later, Wheeler added a post to "commit a massacre in the

Stepping Stones preschool and day care, just walk in and kill everybody." Could a reasonable person conclude that Wheeler's posts were true threats? How might law enforcement officers use Wheeler's posts? Explain. [*United States v. Wheeler,* 776 F.3d 736 (10th Cir. 2015)] (See *Social Media.*)

9–7. Social Media. Irvin Smith was charged in a Georgia state court with burglary and theft. Before the trial, during the selection of the jury, the state prosecutor asked the prospective jurors whether they knew Smith. No one responded affirmatively. Jurors were chosen and sworn in, without objection. After the trial, during deliberations, the jurors indicated to the court that they were deadlocked. The court charged them to try again. Meanwhile, the prosecutor learned that "Juror 4" appeared as a friend on the defendant's Facebook page and filed a motion to dismiss her. The court replaced Juror 4 with an alternate. Was this an appropriate action, or was it an "abuse of discretion"? Should the court have admitted evidence that Facebook friends do not always actually know each other? Discuss. [*Smith v. State of Georgia,* 335 Ga.App. 497, 782 S.E.2d 305 (2016)] (See *Social Media.*)

9–8. A Question of Ethics—Criminal Investigations.

 After the unauthorized release and posting of classified U.S. government documents to WikiLeaks.org, allegedly involving Bradley Manning, a U.S. Army private first class, the U.S. government began a criminal investigation. The government obtained a court order to require Twitter, Inc., to turn over subscriber information and communications to and from the e-mail addresses of Birgitta Jonsdottir and others. The court sealed the order and the other documents in the case, reasoning that "there exists no right to public notice of all the types of documents filed in a . . . case." Jonsdottir and the others appealed this decision. [In re Application of the United States of America for an Order Pursuant to 18 U.S.C. Section 2703(d), 707 F.3d 283 (4th Cir. 2013)] (See *Social Media.*)

(a) Why would the government want to "seal" the documents of an investigation? Why would the individuals under investigation want those documents to be "unsealed"? What factors should be considered in striking a balance between these competing interests?

(b) How does law enforcement use social media to detect and prosecute criminals? Is this use of social media an unethical invasion of individuals' privacy? Discuss.

Legal Reasoning Group Activity

9–9. File-Sharing. James, Chang, and Sixta are roommates. They are music fans and frequently listen to the same artists and songs. They regularly exchange MP3 music files that contain songs from their favorite artists. (See *Copyrights in Digital Information.*)

(a) One group of students will decide whether the fact that the roommates are transferring files among themselves for

no monetary benefit precludes them from being subject to copyright law.

(b) The second group will consider an additional fact. Each roommate regularly buys CDs and rips (copies) them to his or her hard drive. Then the roommate gives the CDs to the other roommates to do the same.

CHAPTER 10

Criminal Law and Cyber Crime

C riminal law is an important part of the legal environment of business. Society imposes a variety of sanctions to protect businesses from harm so that they can compete and flourish. These sanctions include damages for various types of tortious conduct, damages for breach of contract, and various equitable remedies. Additional sanctions are imposed under criminal law. Many statutes regulating business provide for criminal as well as civil penalties.

In this chapter, after explaining some essential differences between criminal law and civil law, we look at how crimes are classified and at the elements that must be present for criminal liability to exist. We then examine the various categories of crimes, the defenses that can be raised to avoid criminal liability, and the rules of criminal procedure.

We conclude the chapter with a discussion of crimes that occur in cyberspace, which are often called *cyber crimes*. Cyber attacks are becoming all too common—even e-mail and data of government agencies and of former U.S. presidents have been hacked.

10–1 Civil Law and Criminal Law

Civil law pertains to the duties that exist between persons or between persons and their governments. Criminal law, in contrast, has to do with crime. A **crime** can be defined as a wrong against society set forth in a statute and punishable by a fine and/or imprisonment—or, in some cases, death.

Because crimes are *offenses against society as a whole,* they are prosecuted by a public official, such as a district attorney (D.A.) or an attorney general (A.G.), not by the victims. Once a crime has been reported, the D.A.'s office decides whether to file criminal charges and to what extent to pursue the prosecution or carry out additional investigation.

10–1a Key Differences between Civil Law and Criminal Law

Because the state has extensive resources at its disposal when prosecuting criminal cases, there are numerous procedural safeguards to protect the rights of defendants. We look here at one of these safeguards—the higher burden of proof that applies in a criminal case—as well as the harsher sanctions for criminal acts compared with those for civil wrongs. Exhibit 10–1 summarizes these and other key differences between civil law and criminal law.

Burden of Proof In a civil case, the plaintiff usually must prove his or her case by a *preponderance of the evidence.* Under this standard, the plaintiff must convince the court that based on the evidence presented by both parties, it is more likely than not that the plaintiff's allegation is true.

In a criminal case, in contrast, the government must prove its case **beyond a reasonable doubt.** If the jury views the evidence in the case as reasonably permitting either a guilty or a not guilty verdict, then the jury's verdict must be not guilty. In other words, the government (prosecutor) must prove beyond a reasonable doubt that the defendant has committed every essential element of the offense with which she or he is charged.

Note also that in a criminal case, the jury's verdict normally must be unanimous—agreed to by all members of the jury—to convict the defendant.[1] (In a civil trial by jury, in contrast, typically only three-fourths of the jurors need to agree.)

---

1. A few states allow jury verdicts that are not unanimous. Arizona, for example, allows six of eight jurors to reach a verdict in criminal cases. Louisiana and Oregon have also relaxed the requirement of unanimous jury verdicts.

EXHIBIT 10–1 Key Differences between Civil Law and Criminal Law

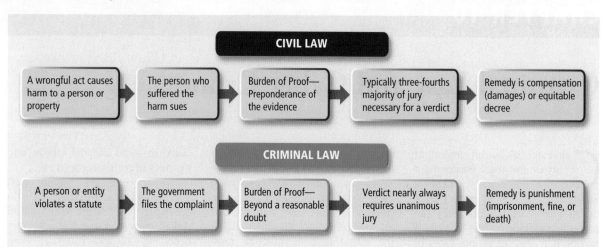

Criminal Sanctions The sanctions imposed on criminal wrongdoers are normally harsher than those applied in civil cases. Remember that the purpose of tort law is to enable a person harmed by a wrongful act to obtain compensation from the wrongdoer, rather than to punish the wrongdoer. In contrast, criminal sanctions are designed to punish those who commit crimes and to deter others from committing similar acts in the future.

Criminal sanctions include fines as well as the much stiffer penalty of the loss of one's liberty by incarceration in a jail or prison. Most criminal sanctions also involve probation and sometimes require performance of community service, completion of an educational or treatment program, or payment of restitution. The harshest criminal sanction is, of course, the death penalty.

10–1b Civil Liability for Criminal Acts

Some torts, such as assault and battery, provide a basis for a criminal prosecution as well as a civil action in tort. ■ **EXAMPLE 10.1** Jonas is walking down the street, minding his own business, when a person attacks him. In the ensuing struggle, the attacker stabs Jonas several times, seriously injuring him. A police officer restrains and arrests the assailant. In this situation, the attacker may be subject both to criminal prosecution by the state and to a tort lawsuit brought by Jonas to obtain compensation for his injuries. ■

Exhibit 10–2 illustrates how the same wrongful act can result in both a civil (tort) action and a criminal action against the wrongdoer.

10–1c Classification of Crimes

Depending on their degree of seriousness, crimes are classified as felonies or misdemeanors. **Felonies** are serious crimes punishable by death or by imprisonment for more than one year.[2] Many states also define different degrees of felony offenses and vary the punishment according to the degree.[3] For instance, most jurisdictions punish a burglary that involves forced entry into a home at night more harshly than a burglary that involves breaking into a nonresidential building during the day.

Misdemeanors are less serious crimes, punishable by a fine or by confinement for up to a year. **Petty offenses** are minor violations, such as jaywalking or violations of building codes, considered to be a subset of misdemeanors. Even for petty offenses, however, a guilty party can be put in jail for a few days, fined, or both, depending on state or local law. Whether a crime is a felony or a misdemeanor can determine in which court the case is tried and, in some states, whether the defendant has a right to a jury trial.

---

2. Federal law and most state laws use this definition, but there is some variation among states as to the length of imprisonment associated with a felony conviction.

3. Note that the Model Penal Code is not a uniform code and each state has developed its own set of laws governing criminal acts. Thus, types of crimes and prescribed punishments may differ from one jurisdiction to another.

EXHIBIT 10–2 Civil (Tort) Lawsuit and Criminal Prosecution for the Same Act

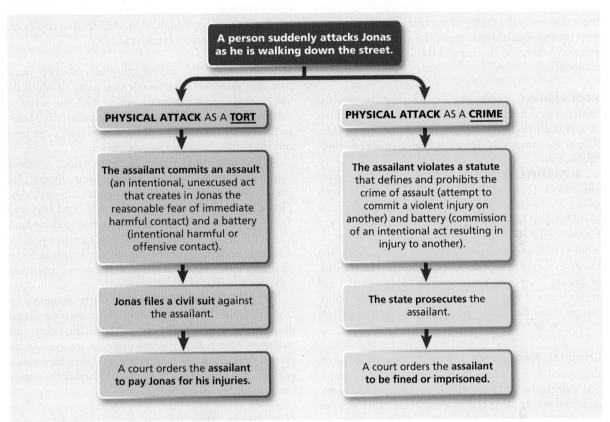

10-2 Criminal Liability

The following two elements normally must exist *simultaneously* for a person to be convicted of a crime:

1. The performance of a prohibited act *(actus reus)*.
2. A specified state of mind, or intent, on the part of the actor *(mens rea)*.

10-2a The Criminal Act

Every criminal statute prohibits certain behavior. Most crimes require an act of *commission*—that is, a person must *do* something in order to be accused of a crime. In criminal law, a prohibited act is referred to as the **actus reus,**[4] or guilty act. In some instances, an act of omission can be a crime, but only when a person has a legal duty to perform the omitted act, such as filing a tax return.

The guilty act requirement is based on one of the premises of criminal law—that a person should be punished for harm done to society. For a crime to exist, the guilty act must thus cause some harm to a person or to property. Thinking about killing someone or about stealing a car may be morally wrong, but the thoughts do no harm until they are translated into action.

Of course, a person can be punished for *attempting* murder or robbery, but normally only if he or she has taken substantial steps toward the criminal objective. Additionally, the person must have specifically intended to commit the crime to be convicted of an attempt.

10-2b State of Mind

Mens rea,[5] or wrongful mental state, also is typically required to establish criminal liability. The required mental state, or intent, is indicated in the applicable statute or law. Murder, for instance, involves the guilty act of

---

4. Pronounced *ak*-tuhs *ray*-uhs.

5. Pronounced *mehns ray*-uh.

killing another human being, and the guilty mental state is the desire, or intent, to take another's life. For theft, the guilty act is the taking of another person's property. The mental state involves both the awareness that the property belongs to another and the desire to deprive the owner of it.

Recklessness A court can also find that the required mental state is present when a defendant's acts are reckless or criminally negligent. A defendant is *criminally reckless* if he or she consciously disregards a substantial and unjustifiable risk.

■ **EXAMPLE 10.2** A fourteen-year-old New Jersey girl posts a Facebook message saying that she is going to launch a terrorist attack on her high school and asking if anyone wants to help. The police arrest the girl for the crime of making a terrorist threat. The statute requires the intent to commit an act of violence with "the intent to terrorize" or "in reckless disregard of the risk of causing" terror or inconvenience. Although the girl argues that she had no intent to cause harm, the police can prosecute her under the "reckless disregard" part of the statute. ■

Criminal Negligence *Criminal negligence* involves the mental state in which the defendant takes an unjustified, substantial, and foreseeable risk that results in harm. A defendant can be negligent even if she or he was not actually aware of the risk but *should have been aware* of it.[6]

A homicide is classified as *involuntary manslaughter* when it results from an act of criminal negligence and there is no intent to kill. ■ **EXAMPLE 10.3** Dr. Conrad Murray, the personal physician of pop star Michael Jackson, was convicted of involuntary manslaughter for prescribing the drug that led to Jackson's sudden death. Murray had given Jackson propofol, a powerful anesthetic normally used in surgery, as a sleep aid on the night of his death, even though he knew that Jackson had already taken other sedatives. ■

Strict Liability and Overcriminalization An increasing number of laws and regulations impose criminal sanctions for strict liability crimes. Strict liability crimes are offenses that do not require a wrongful mental state to establish criminal liability.

Proponents of strict liability criminal laws argue that they are necessary to protect the public and the environment. Critics say laws that criminalize conduct without requiring intent have led to *overcriminalization*. They argue that when the requirement of intent is removed,

people are more likely to commit crimes unknowingly—and perhaps even innocently. When an honest mistake can lead to a criminal conviction, the idea that crimes are a wrong against society is undermined.

Federal Crimes. The federal criminal code lists more than four thousand criminal offenses, many of which do not require a specific mental state. In addition, many of these rules do not require intent. See this chapter's *Managerial Strategy* feature for a discussion of how these laws and rules affect American businesspersons.

■ **EXAMPLE 10.4** Eddie Leroy Anderson, a retired logger and former science teacher, went digging for arrowheads with his son near a campground in Idaho. They did not realize that they were on federal land and that it is a felony to remove artifacts from federal land without a permit. Although the crime carries a penalty of as much as two years in prison, the father and son pleaded guilty, and each received a sentence of probation and a $1,500 fine. ■

Strict liability crimes are particularly common in environmental laws, laws aimed at combating illegal drugs, and other laws affecting public health, safety, and welfare. Under federal law, for instance, tenants can be evicted from public housing if one of their relatives or a guest used illegal drugs—regardless of whether the tenant knew about the drug activity.

State Crimes. Many states have also enacted laws that punish behavior as criminal without the need to show criminal intent. ■ **EXAMPLE 10.5** In Arizona, a hunter who shoots an elk outside the area specified by the hunting permit has committed a crime. The hunter can be convicted of the crime regardless of her or his intent or knowledge of the law. ■

10–2c Corporate Criminal Liability

A corporation is a legal entity created under the laws of a state. At one time, it was thought that a corporation could not incur criminal liability because, although a corporation is a legal person, it can act only through its agents (corporate directors, officers, and employees). Therefore, the corporate entity itself could not "intend" to commit a crime. Over time, this view has changed. Obviously, corporations cannot be imprisoned, but they can be fined or denied certain legal privileges (such as necessary licenses).

Liability of the Corporate Entity Today, corporations normally are liable for the crimes committed by their agents and employees within the course and scope of

---

6. Model Penal Code Section 2.02(2)(d).

The Criminalization of American Business

What do Bank of America, Citigroup, JPMorgan Chase, and Goldman Sachs have in common? All paid hefty fines for purportedly misleading investors about mortgage-backed securities. In fact, these companies paid the government a total of $50 billion in fines. The payments were made in lieu of criminal prosecutions.

In 2014, FedEx Corporation was indicted for purportedly illegally shipping prescription drugs ordered through Web sites. FedEx has chosen to proceed to trial in the U.S. District Court for the Northern District of California in San Francisco.[d] Many companies, however, choose to reach settlement agreements with the government rather than fight criminal indictments.

Today, several hundred thousand federal rules that apply to businesses carry some form of criminal penalty. That is in addition to more than four thousand federal laws, many of which carry criminal sanctions for their violation. From 2000 to the beginning of 2017, about 2,200 corporations either were convicted or pleaded guilty to violating federal statutes or rules.

Criminal Convictions

The first successful criminal conviction in a federal court against a company—the New York Central and Hudson River Railroad—was upheld by the Supreme Court in 1909 (the violation: cutting prices).[a] Many other successful convictions followed.

One landmark case developed the *aggregation test,* now called the Doctrine of Collective Knowledge.[b] This test aggregates the omissions and acts of two or more persons in a corporation, thereby constructing an *actus reus* and a *mens rea* out of the conduct and knowledge of several individuals.

Not all government attempts at applying criminal law to corporations survive. In 2013, for example, Sentinel Offender Services, LLC, prevailed on appeal. There was no actual evidence to show that the company had acted with specific intent to commit theft by deception.[c]

Many Pay Substantial Fines in Lieu of Prosecution

More than three hundred corporations reached so-called non-prosecution agreements with the government from 2000 to the beginning of 2017. These agreements typically involve multimillion- or multibillion-dollar fines. This number does not include fines paid to the Environmental Protection Agency or to the Fish and Wildlife Service.

According to law professors Margaret Lemos and Max Minzner, "Public enforcers often seek large monetary awards for self-interested reasons divorced from the public interest and deterrents. The incentives are strongest when enforcement agencies are permitted to retain all or some of the proceeds of enforcement."[e]

Business Questions

1. *Why might a corporation's managers agree to pay a large fine rather than to be indicted and proceed to trial?*

2. *How does a manager determine the optimal amount of legal research to undertake to prevent her or his company from violating the many thousands of federal regulations?*

a. *New York Central and Hudson River Railroad v. United States,* 212 U.S. 481, 29 S.Ct. 304, 53 L.Ed 613 (1909).
b. *United States v. Bank of New England,* 821 F.2d 844 (1st Cir. 1987).
c. *McGee v. Sentinel Offender Services, LLC,* 719 F.3d 1236 (11th Cir. 2013).

d. *United States v. FedEx Corp.,* Case No. CR14-380 Northern District, California, July 17, 2014.
e. Margaret Lemos and Max Minzner, "For-Profit Public Enforcement," *Harvard Law Review 127,* January 17, 2014.

their employment.[7] For liability to be imposed, the prosecutor generally must show that the corporation could have prevented the act or that a supervisor authorized or had knowledge of the act. In addition, corporations can be criminally liable for failing to perform specific duties imposed by law (such as duties under environmental laws or securities laws).

■ **CASE IN POINT 10.6** A prostitution ring, the Gold Club, was operating out of some motels in West Virginia. A motel manager, who was also a corporate officer, gave discounted rates to Gold Club prostitutes, and they paid him in cash. The corporation received a portion of the

7. See Model Penal Code Section 2.07.

funds generated by the Gold Club's illegal operations. A jury found that the corporation was criminally liable because a supervisor within the corporation—the motel manager—had knowledge of the prostitution activities and the corporation had allowed it to continue.[8] ∎

Liability of Corporate Officers and Directors Corporate directors and officers are personally liable for the crimes they commit, regardless of whether the crimes were committed for their private benefit or on the corporation's behalf. Additionally, corporate directors and officers may be held liable for the actions of employees under their supervision. Under the *responsible corporate officer* doctrine, a court may impose criminal liability on a corporate officer who participated in, directed, or merely knew about a given criminal violation.

∎ **CASE IN POINT 10.7** Austin DeCoster owned and controlled Quality Egg, LLC, an egg production and processing company with facilities across Iowa. His son Peter DeCoster was the chief operating officer. Due to unsanitary conditions in some of its facilities, Quality shipped and sold eggs that contained salmonella bacteria, which sickened thousands of people across the United States.

The federal government prosecuted the DeCosters under the responsible corporate officer doctrine, in part, for Quality's failure to comply with regulations on egg production facilities. The DeCosters ultimately pleaded guilty to violating three criminal statutes. But when they were ordered to serve three months in jail, the DeCosters challenged the sentence as unconstitutional. The court held that the sentence of incarceration was appropriate because the evidence suggested that the defendants knew about the unsanitary conditions in their processing plants.[9] ∎

10–3 Types of Crimes

Federal, state, and local laws provide for the classification and punishment of hundreds of thousands of different criminal acts. Generally, though, criminal acts fall into five broad categories: violent crime (crimes against persons), property crime, public order crime, white-collar crime, and organized crime. In addition, when crimes are committed in cyberspace rather the physical world, we often refer to them as cyber crimes.

10–3a Violent Crime

Certain crimes are called *violent crimes,* or crimes against persons, because they cause others to suffer harm or death. Murder is a violent crime. So is sexual assault, or rape. **Robbery**—defined as the taking of money, personal property, or any other article of value from a person by means of force or fear—is also a violent crime. Typically, states have more severe penalties for *aggravated robbery*—robbery with the use of a deadly weapon.

Assault and battery, which were discussed in the context of tort law, are also classified as violent crimes. ∎ **EXAMPLE 10.8** Former rap star Flavor Flav (whose real name is William Drayton) was arrested in Las Vegas on assault and battery charges. During an argument with his fiancée, Drayton allegedly threw her to the ground and then grabbed two kitchen knives and chased her son. ∎

Each violent crime is further classified by degree, depending on the circumstances surrounding the criminal act. These circumstances include the intent of the person committing the crime and whether a weapon was used. For crimes other than murder, the level of pain and suffering experienced by the victim is also a factor.

10–3b Property Crime

The most common type of criminal activity is property crime, in which the goal of the offender is some form of economic gain or the damaging of property. Robbery is a form of property crime, as well as a violent crime, because the offender seeks to gain the property of another.

Burglary Traditionally, **burglary** was defined as breaking and entering the dwelling of another at night with the intent to commit a felony. This definition was aimed at protecting an individual's home and its occupants.

Most state statutes have eliminated some of the requirements found in the common law definition. The time of day at which the breaking and entering occurs, for instance, is usually immaterial. State statutes frequently omit the element of breaking, and some states do not require that the building be a dwelling. When a deadly weapon is used in a burglary, the perpetrator can be charged with *aggravated burglary* and punished more severely.

The defendant in the following case challenged whether the evidence presented by the state was sufficient to support his conviction for burglary.

---

8. As a result of the convictions, the motel manager was sentenced to fifteen months in prison, and the corporation was ordered to forfeit the motel property. *United States v. Singh,* 518 F.3d 236 (4th Cir. 2008).

9. *United States v. Quality Egg, LLC,* 99 F.Supp.3d 920 (N.D. Iowa 2015).

State of Minnesota v. Smith

Court of Appeals of Minnesota, 2015 WL 303643 (2015).

Background and Facts Over a Labor Day weekend in Rochester, Minnesota, two homes and the Rochester Tennis Center, a business, were burglarized. One day later, at the nearby Bell Tower Inn, cleaning personnel found a garbage bag in the room of Albert Smith. The bag contained a passport that belonged to the owner of one of the burglarized homes and documents that belonged to the business.

Police officers arrested Smith. They found a Sentry safe stolen in one of the burglaries in Smith's room. A search of a bag in his possession revealed other stolen items, as well as burglary tools. Smith claimed that he had bought some of the items from a man named Mali and had bought other items on Craigslist. He said that he had found the documents from the tennis center in a dumpster. Convicted of burglary in a Minnesota state court, Smith appealed.

In the Language of the Court

CHUTICH, Judge.

* * * *

* * * Both burglarized homes and the burglarized business were within a few blocks of the hotel where Smith stayed over the Labor Day weekend, and each burglary occurred during the holiday weekend. In fact, two of the burglaries occurred in the morning and early evening of September 3. On the morning of September 4, only hours after two of the burglaries occurred, Smith possessed property stolen in each of the three burglaries. Some of the items found in Smith's possession were worthless to anyone but their owners, including a passport, a birth certificate, and property documents. In addition, the hotel manager saw Smith carrying the stolen Sentry safe into the hotel during the relevant time frame and identified the safe found in Smith's room as the Sentry safe. When the police confronted Smith in the hotel, he was carrying a bag that contained numerous stolen electronics and burglary tools, including a flashlight and gloves.

* * * Smith possessed property reported as stolen from both homes and the business, and the nature of several of the items he possessed suggested that they came directly from the burglaries. * * * The assortment of items found in Smith's possession, from the electronics to the financially worthless documents, as well as gloves and a flashlight, illustrate Smith's guilt of each of the burglaries. The mishmash of items found in defendant's possession looks like the raw loot that a thief quickly grabbed and made off with. Moreover, *the brief time that passed between the burglaries and the discovery of the stolen items in Smith's possession, along with the close proximity of the hotel to the burglarized homes and tennis center, are consistent with the findings that Smith was the thief.* [Emphasis added.]

Smith contends that a reasonable inference can be drawn from his alternate explanation of the events that is inconsistent with finding him guilty of the burglaries, namely that he obtained the valuable stolen items from Mali or from Craigslist, while he found the tennis club's records in a dumpster. The [trial] court, however, did not find Smith's testimony credible, determining that Smith "demonstrated a flexible approach to the truth—a looseness with the facts, in which the incriminatory truth is conceded only when and to the extent it is inescapable." Further, we consider it improbable, considering the timing and locations of the break-ins, that Smith came into possession of stolen items from a September 3 burglary by way of Mali, while finding additional stolen items from another September 3 burglary that same evening by fortuitously finding them in a dumpster. * * * The only rational hypothesis that can be drawn from the proved circumstances is that Smith committed the burglaries.

Decision and Remedy *A state intermediate appellate court affirmed Smith's conviction for burglary. The appellate court concluded that the circumstances "are consistent with guilt and inconsistent with any rational hypothesis except that of guilt."*

Critical Thinking

- **Social** *Who is in the best position to evaluate the credibility of the evidence and the witnesses in a case? Why?*

Larceny Under the common law, the crime of **larceny** involved the unlawful taking and carrying away of someone else's personal property with the intent to permanently deprive the owner of possession. Put simply, larceny is stealing, or theft. Whereas robbery involves force or fear, larceny does not. Therefore, picking pockets is larceny, not robbery. Similarly, an employee taking company products and supplies home for personal use without permission is committing larceny.

Most states have expanded the definition of property that is subject to larceny statutes. Stealing computer programs may constitute larceny even though the "property" is not physical (see the discussion of computer crime later in this chapter). The theft of natural gas, Internet access, or television cable service can also constitute larceny.

Obtaining Goods by False Pretenses Obtaining goods by means of false pretenses is a form of theft that involves trickery or fraud, such as using someone else's credit-card number without permission to purchase an iPad. Statutes dealing with such illegal activities vary widely from state to state. They often apply not only to property, but also to services and cash.

■ **CASE IN POINT 10.9** While Matthew Steffes was incarcerated, he started a scheme to make free collect calls from prison. (A *collect call* is a telephone call in which the calling party places a call at the called party's expense.) Steffes had his friends and family members set up new phone number accounts by giving false information to AT&T. This information included fictitious business names, as well as personal identifying information stolen from a health-care clinic. Once a new phone number was working, Steffes made unlimited collect calls to it without paying the bill until AT&T eventually shut down the account. For nearly two years, Steffes used sixty fraudulently obtained phone numbers to make hundreds of collect calls. The loss to AT&T was more than $28,000.

Steffes was convicted in a state court of theft by fraud of property in excess of $10,000. He appealed, arguing that he had not made false representations to AT&T. The Wisconsin Supreme Court affirmed his conviction. The court held that Steffes had made false representations to AT&T by providing fictitious business names and stolen personal identifying information to the phone company. He made these false representations so that he could make phone calls without paying for them, which deprived the company of its "property"—meaning its electricity.[10] ■

---

10. *State of Wisconsin v. Steffes*, 347 Wis.2d 683, 832 N.W.2d 101 (2013).

Theft Sometimes, state statutes consolidate the crime of obtaining goods by false pretenses with other property offenses, such as larceny and embezzlement (discussed shortly), into a single crime called simply "theft." Under such a statute, it is not necessary for a defendant to be charged specifically with larceny or obtaining goods by false pretenses. *Petty theft* is the theft of a small quantity of cash or low-value goods. *Grand theft* is the theft of a larger amount of cash or higher-value property.

Receiving Stolen Goods It is a crime to receive goods that a person knows or should have known were stolen or illegally obtained. To be convicted, the recipient of such goods need not know the true identity of the owner or the thief, and need not have paid for the goods. All that is necessary is that the recipient knows or should know that the goods are stolen, which implies an intent to deprive the true owner of those goods.

Arson The willful and malicious burning of a building (or, in some states, a vehicle or other item of personal property) is the crime of **arson.** At common law, arson applied only to burning down another person's house. The law was designed to protect human life. Today, arson statutes have been extended to cover the destruction of any building, regardless of ownership, by fire or explosion.

Every state has a special statute that covers the act of burning a building for the purpose of collecting insurance. (Of course, the insurer need not pay the claim when insurance fraud is proved.)

Forgery The fraudulent making or altering of any writing (including an electronic record) in a way that changes the legal rights and liabilities of another is **forgery.** ■ **EXAMPLE 10.10** Without authorization, Severson signs Bennett's name to the back of a check made out to Bennett and attempts to cash it. Severson is committing forgery. ■ Forgery also includes changing trademarks, falsifying public records, counterfeiting, and altering a legal document.

10–3c Public Order Crime

Historically, societies have always outlawed activities that are considered contrary to public values and morals. Today, the most common public order crimes include public drunkenness, prostitution, gambling, and illegal drug use. These crimes are sometimes referred to as *victimless crimes* because they normally harm only the offender. From a broader perspective, however, they are deemed detrimental to society as a whole because they may create an environment that gives rise to property and violent crimes.

■ EXAMPLE 10.11 A flight attendant observes a man and woman engaging in sex acts while on a flight to Las Vegas. A criminal complaint is filed, and the two defendants plead guilty in federal court to misdemeanor disorderly conduct. ■

10–3d White-Collar Crime

Crimes occurring in the business context are popularly referred to as *white-collar crimes,* although this is not an official legal term. Ordinarily, **white-collar crime** involves an illegal act or series of acts committed by an individual or business entity using some nonviolent means to obtain a personal or business advantage.

Usually, this kind of crime takes place in the course of a legitimate business occupation. Corporate crimes fall into this category. Certain property crimes, such as larceny and forgery, may also be white-collar crimes if they occur within the business context. The crimes discussed next normally occur only in the business context.

Embezzlement When a person who is entrusted with another person's property fraudulently appropriates it, **embezzlement** occurs. Embezzlement is not larceny, because the wrongdoer does not *physically* take the property from another's possession, and it is not robbery, because no force or fear is used.

Typically, embezzlement is carried out by an employee who steals funds a small amount at a time over a long period. Banks are particularly prone to this problem, but embezzlement can occur in any firm. In a number of businesses, corporate officers or accountants have fraudulently converted funds for their own benefit and then "fixed" the books to cover up their crimes.

Embezzlement occurs whether the embezzler takes the funds directly from the victim or from a third person. If the financial officer of a large corporation pockets checks from third parties that were given to her to deposit into the corporate account, she is embezzling.

The intent to return embezzled property—or its actual return—is not a defense to the crime of embezzlement, as the following *Spotlight Case* illustrates.

Spotlight on White-Collar Crime

Case 10.2 People v. Sisuphan
Court of Appeal of California, First District, 181 Cal.App.4th 800, 104 Cal.Rptr.3d 654 (2010).

Background and Facts Lou Sisuphan was the director of finance at a Toyota dealership. His responsibilities included managing the financing contracts for vehicle sales and working with lenders to obtain payments. Sisuphan complained repeatedly to management about the performance and attitude of one of the finance managers, Ian McClelland. The general manager, Michael Christian, would not terminate McClelland "because he brought a lot of money into the dealership."

One day, McClelland accepted $22,600 in cash and two checks totaling $7,275.51 from a customer in payment for a car. McClelland placed the cash, the checks, and a copy of the receipt in a large envelope. As he tried to drop the envelope into the safe through a mechanism at its top, the envelope became stuck. While McClelland went for assistance, Sisuphan wiggled the envelope free and kept it. On McClelland's return, Sisuphan told him that the envelope had dropped into the safe. When the payment turned up missing, Christian told all the managers he would not bring criminal charges if the payment was returned within twenty-four hours.

After the twenty-four-hour period had lapsed, Sisuphan told Christian that he had taken the envelope, and he returned the cash and checks to Christian. Sisuphan claimed that he had no intention of stealing the payment but had taken it to get McClelland fired. Christian fired Sisuphan the next day, and the district attorney later charged Sisuphan with embezzlement.

After a jury trial, Sisuphan was found guilty. Sisuphan appealed, arguing that the trial court had erred by excluding evidence that he had returned the payment. The trial court had concluded that the evidence was not relevant because return of the property is not a defense to embezzlement.

Case 10.2 Continues

Case 10.2 Continued

In the Language of the Court

JENKINS, J. [Judge]
* * * *

Fraudulent intent is an essential element of embezzlement. Although restoration of the property is not a defense, evidence of repayment may be relevant to the extent it shows that a defendant's intent at the time of the taking was not fraudulent. Such evidence is admissible "only when [a] defendant shows a relevant and probative [confirming] link in his subsequent actions from which it might be inferred his original intent was innocent." The question before us, therefore, is whether evidence that Sisuphan returned the money reasonably tends to prove he lacked the requisite intent at the time of the taking. [Emphasis added.]

Section 508 [of the California Penal Code], which sets out the offense of which Sisuphan was convicted, provides: "Every clerk, agent, or servant of any person who fraudulently appropriates to his own use, or secretes with a fraudulent intent to appropriate to his own use, any property of another which has come into his control or care by virtue of his employment * * * is guilty of embezzlement." Sisuphan denies he ever intended "to use the [money] to financially better himself, even temporarily" and contends the evidence he sought to introduce showed "he returned the [money] without having appropriated it to his own use in any way." He argues that this evidence negates fraudulent intent because it supports his claim that he took the money to get McClelland fired and acted "to help his company by drawing attention to the inadequacy and incompetency of an employee." We reject these contentions.

In determining whether Sisuphan's intent was fraudulent at the time of the taking, the issue is not whether he intended to spend the money, but whether he intended to use it for a purpose other than that for which the dealership entrusted it to him. *The offense of embezzlement contemplates a principal's entrustment of property to an agent for certain purposes and the agent's breach of that trust by acting outside his authority in his use of the property.* * * * Sisuphan's undisputed purpose—to get McClelland fired—was beyond the scope of his responsibility and therefore outside the trust afforded him by the dealership. Accordingly, even if the proffered [submitted] evidence shows he took the money for this purpose, it does not tend to prove he lacked fraudulent intent, and the trial court properly excluded this evidence. [Emphasis added.]

Decision and Remedy *The California appellate court affirmed the trial court's decision. The fact that Sisuphan had returned the payment was irrelevant. He was guilty of embezzlement.*

Critical Thinking

- **Legal Environment** *Why was Sisuphan convicted of embezzlement instead of larceny? What is the difference between these two crimes?*
- **Ethical** *Given that Sisuphan returned the cash, was it fair of the dealership's general manager to terminate Sisuphan's employment? Why or why not?*

Mail and Wire Fraud Among the most potent weapons against white-collar criminals are the federal laws that prohibit mail fraud[11] and wire fraud.[12] These laws make it a federal crime to devise any scheme that uses U.S. mail, commercial carriers (FedEx, UPS), or wire (telegraph, telephone, television, the Internet, e-mail) with the intent to defraud the public. These laws are often applied when persons send out advertisements or e-mails with the intent to fraudulently obtain cash or property by false pretenses.

■ **CASE IN POINT 10.12** Cisco Systems, Inc., offers a warranty program to authorized resellers of Cisco parts.

Iheanyi Frank Chinasa and Robert Kendrick Chambliss devised a scheme to intentionally defraud Cisco with respect to this program and to obtain replacement parts to which they were not entitled. The two men planned and used specific language in numerous e-mails and Internet service requests that they sent to Cisco to convince Cisco to ship them new parts via commercial carriers. Ultimately, Chinasa and Chambliss were convicted of mail and wire fraud and of conspiracy to commit mail and wire fraud.[13] ■

---

11. The Mail Fraud Act, 18 U.S.C. Sections 1341–1342.
12. 18 U.S.C. Section 1343.

13. *United States v. Chinasa*, 789 F.Supp.2d 691 (E.D.Va. 2011). See also *United States v. Lyons*, 569 F.3d 995 (9th Cir. 2009).

The maximum penalty under these statutes is substantial. Persons convicted of mail, wire, and Internet fraud may be imprisoned for up to twenty years and/or fined. If the violation affects a financial institution or involves fraud in connection with emergency disaster-relief funds, the violator may be fined up to $1 million, imprisoned for up to thirty years, or both.

Bribery The crime of bribery involves offering to give something of value to a person in an attempt to influence that person in a way that serves a private interest. Three types of bribery are considered crimes: bribery of public officials, commercial bribery, and bribery of foreign officials.

The bribe itself can be anything the recipient considers to be valuable, but the defendant must have intended it as a bribe. Realize that the *crime of bribery occurs when the bribe is offered*—it is not required that the bribe be accepted. *Accepting a bribe* is a separate crime.

Commercial bribery involves corrupt dealings between private persons or businesses. Typically, people make commercial bribes to obtain proprietary information, cover up an inferior product, or secure new business. Industrial espionage sometimes involves commercial bribes. ■ **EXAMPLE 10.13** Kent Peterson works at the firm of Jacoby & Meyers. He offers to pay Laurel, an employee in a competing firm, to give him that firm's trade secrets and pricing schedules. Peterson has committed commercial bribery. ■ So-called kickbacks, or payoffs for special favors or services, are a form of commercial bribery in some situations.

Bankruptcy Fraud Federal bankruptcy law allows individuals and businesses to be relieved of oppressive debt through bankruptcy proceedings. Numerous white-collar crimes may be committed during the many phases of a bankruptcy action. A creditor may file a false claim against the debtor, which is a crime. Also, a debtor may fraudulently transfer assets to favored parties before or after the bankruptcy is filed. For instance, a company-owned automobile may be "sold" at a bargain price to a trusted friend or relative. Closely related to the crime of fraudulent transfer of property is the crime of fraudulent concealment of property, such as the hiding of gold coins.

Insider Trading An individual who obtains "inside information" about the plans of a publicly listed corporation can often make stock-trading profits by purchasing or selling corporate securities based on this information. *Insider trading* is a violation of securities law. Basically, a person who possesses inside information and has a duty not to disclose it to outsiders may not trade on that information. A person may not profit from the purchase or sale of securities based on inside information until the information is made available to the public.

Theft of Trade Secrets and Other Intellectual Property The Economic Espionage Act[14] makes the theft of trade secrets a federal crime. The act also makes it a federal crime to buy or possess another person's trade secrets, knowing that the trade secrets were stolen or otherwise acquired without the owner's authorization.

Violations of the Economic Espionage Act can result in steep penalties: imprisonment for up to ten years and a fine of up to $500,000. A corporation or other organization can be fined up to $5 million. Additionally, any property acquired as a result of the violation, such as airplanes and automobiles, is subject to criminal forfeiture, or seizure by the government. Similarly, any property used in the commission of the violation is subject to forfeiture.

10–3e Organized Crime

White-collar crime takes place within the confines of the legitimate business world. *Organized crime,* in contrast, operates *illegitimately* by, among other things, providing illegal goods and services. Traditionally, organized crime has been involved in gambling, prostitution, illegal narcotics, counterfeiting, and loan sharking (lending funds at higher-than-legal interest rates), along with more recent ventures into credit-card scams and cyber crime.

Money Laundering The profits from organized crime and illegal activities amount to billions of dollars a year. These profits come from illegal drug transactions and, to a lesser extent, from racketeering, prostitution, and gambling. Under federal law, banks, savings and loan associations, and other financial institutions are required to report currency transactions involving more than $10,000. Consequently, those who engage in illegal activities face difficulties in depositing their cash profits from illegal transactions.

As an alternative to storing the cash from illegal transactions in a safe-deposit box, wrongdoers and racketeers often launder "dirty" money through legitimate businesses to make it "clean." **Money laundering** is engaging in financial transactions to conceal the identity, source, or destination of illegally gained funds. ■ **EXAMPLE 10.14** Leo Harris, a successful drug dealer, becomes a partner with a restaurateur. Little by little, the restaurant shows increasing profits. As a partner

---

14. 18 U.S.C. Sections 1831–1839.

in the restaurant, Harris is able to report the "profits" of the restaurant as legitimate income on which he pays federal and state taxes. He can then spend those funds without worrying that his lifestyle may exceed the level possible with his reported income. ■

Racketeering To curb the entry of organized crime into the legitimate business world, Congress enacted the Racketeer Influenced and Corrupt Organizations Act (RICO).[15] The statute makes it a federal crime to:

1. Use income obtained from racketeering activity to purchase any interest in an enterprise.
2. Acquire or maintain an interest in an enterprise through racketeering activity.
3. Conduct or participate in the affairs of an enterprise through racketeering activity.
4. Conspire to do any of the preceding activities.

Broad Application of RICO. The broad language of RICO has allowed it to be applied in cases that have little or nothing to do with organized crime. RICO incorporates by reference twenty-six separate types of federal crimes and nine types of state felonies.[16] If a person commits two of these offenses, he or she is guilty of "racketeering activity."

Under the criminal provisions of RICO, any individual found guilty is subject to a fine of up to $25,000 per violation, imprisonment for up to twenty years, or both. Additionally, any assets (property or cash) that were acquired as a result of the illegal activity or that were "involved in" or an "instrumentality of" the activity are subject to government forfeiture.

Civil Liability. In the event of a RICO violation, the government can seek not only criminal penalties but also civil penalties. The government can, for instance, seek the divestiture of a defendant's interest in a business or the dissolution of the business. (Divestiture refers to the taking of possession—or forfeiture—of the defendant's interest and its subsequent sale.)

Moreover, in some cases, the statute allows private individuals to sue violators and potentially recover three times their actual losses (treble damages), plus attorneys' fees, for business injuries caused by a RICO violation. This is perhaps the most controversial aspect of RICO and one that continues to cause debate in the nation's federal courts. The prospect of receiving treble damages in

civil RICO lawsuits has given plaintiffs a financial incentive to pursue businesses and employers for violations.

See Concept Summary 10.1 for a review of the different types of crimes.

10–4 Defenses to Criminal Liability

Persons charged with crimes may be relieved of criminal liability if they can show that their criminal actions were justified under the circumstances. In certain situations, the law may also allow a person to be excused from criminal liability because she or he lacks the required mental state. We look at several defenses to criminal liability here.

Note that procedural violations (such as obtaining evidence without a valid search warrant) may also operate as defenses. Evidence obtained in violation of a defendant's constitutional rights may not be admitted in court. If the evidence is suppressed, then there may be no basis for prosecuting the defendant.

10–4a Justifiable Use of Force

Probably the best-known defense to criminal liability is **self-defense.** Other situations, however, also justify the use of force: the defense of one's dwelling, the defense of other property, and the prevention of a crime. In all of these situations, it is important to distinguish between deadly and nondeadly force. *Deadly force* is likely to result in death or serious bodily harm. *Nondeadly force* is force that reasonably appears necessary to prevent the imminent use of criminal force.

Generally speaking, people can use the amount of nondeadly force that seems necessary to protect themselves, their dwellings, or other property, or to prevent the commission of a crime. Deadly force can be used in self-defense only when the defender *reasonably believes* that imminent death or grievous bodily harm will otherwise result. In addition, normally the attacker must be using unlawful force, and the defender must not have initiated or provoked the attack.

Many states are expanding the situations in which the use of deadly force can be justified. Florida, for instance, allows the use of deadly force to prevent the commission of a "forcible felony," including robbery, carjacking, and sexual battery.

10–4b Necessity

Sometimes, criminal defendants can be relieved of liability by showing **necessity**—that a criminal act was

---

15. 18 U.S.C. Sections 1961–1968.
16. See 18 U.S.C. Section 1961(1)(A). The crimes listed in this section include murder, kidnapping, gambling, arson, robbery, bribery, extortion, money laundering, securities fraud, counterfeiting, dealing in obscene matter, dealing in controlled substances (illegal drugs), and a number of others.

Concept Summary 10.1

Types of Crimes

Violent Crime	Crimes that cause others to suffer harm or death, such as murder, assault and battery, and robbery.
Property Crime	Crimes in which the goal of the offender is some form of economic gain or the damaging of property. Property crime includes theft-related offenses such as burglary, larceny, and forgery.
Public Order Crime	Crimes that are contrary to public values and morals, such as public drunkenness and prostitution.
White-Collar Crime	An illegal act or series of acts committed by an individual or business entity using some nonviolent means to obtain a personal or business advantage. These crimes are usually committed in the course of a legitimate occupation. Examples include embezzlement, bribery, and fraud.
Organized Crime	Crime conducted by groups operating illegitimately to provide illegal goods and services, such as narcotics. Organized crime may also include money laundering and racketeering.

necessary to prevent an even greater harm. ■ **EXAMPLE 10.15** Jake Trevor is a convicted felon and, as such, is legally prohibited from possessing a firearm. While he and his wife are in a convenience store, a man draws a gun, points it at the cashier, and demands all the cash in the register. Afraid that the man will start shooting, Trevor grabs the gun and holds onto it until police arrive. In this situation, if Trevor is charged with possession of a firearm, he can assert the defense of necessity. ■

10–4c Insanity

A person who suffers from a mental illness may be incapable of the state of mind required to commit a crime. Thus, insanity may be a defense to a criminal charge. Note that an insanity defense does not enable a person to avoid imprisonment. It simply means that if the defendant successfully proves insanity, she or he will be placed in a mental institution.

■ **EXAMPLE 10.16** James Holmes opened fire with an automatic weapon in a crowded Colorado movie theater during a screening of *The Dark Knight Rises,* killing twelve people and injuring seventy. Holmes had been a graduate student but had suffered from mental health problems and had left school. Before the incident, he had no criminal history. Holmes's attorneys asserted the defense of insanity to try to avoid a possible death sentence. Although a jury ultimately rejected the defense and convicted Holmes of multiple counts of murder in 2015, he was sentenced to life in prison rather than death. If the insanity defense had been successful, Holmes would have been confined to a mental institution, not a prison. ■

Model Penal Code The courts have had difficulty deciding what the test for legal insanity should be. Federal courts and some states use the substantial-capacity test set forth in the Model Penal Code:

A person is not responsible for criminal conduct if at the time of such conduct as a result of mental disease or defect he or she lacks substantial capacity either to appreciate the wrongfulness of his [or her] conduct or to conform his [or her] conduct to the requirements of the law.

M'Naghten and Other Tests Some states use the *M'Naghten* test.[17] Under this test, a person is not responsible if, at the time of the offense, he or she did not know the nature and quality of the act or did not know that the act was wrong. Other states use the irresistible-impulse test. A person operating under an irresistible impulse may know an act is wrong but cannot refrain from doing it.

Under any of these tests, proving insanity is extremely difficult. For this reason, the insanity defense is rarely used and usually is not successful. Four states have abolished the insanity defense.

10-4d Mistake

Everyone has heard the saying "Ignorance of the law is no excuse." Ordinarily, ignorance of the law or a mistaken idea about what the law requires is not a valid defense. A *mistake of fact,* however, as opposed to a *mistake of law,* can normally excuse criminal responsibility if it negates the mental state necessary to commit a crime.

■ **EXAMPLE 10.17** Oliver Wheaton mistakenly walks off with Julie Tyson's briefcase. If Wheaton genuinely thought that the case was his, there is no theft. Theft requires knowledge that the property belongs to another. (If Wheaton's act causes Tyson to incur damages, however, she may sue him in a civil tort action for trespass to personal property or conversion.) ■

10-4e Duress

Duress exists when the *wrongful threat* of one person induces another person to perform an act that he or she would not otherwise have performed. In such a situation, duress is said to negate the mental state necessary to commit a crime because the defendant was forced or compelled to commit the act.

Duress can be used as a defense to most crimes except murder. Both the definition of duress and the types of crimes that it can excuse vary among the states, however. Generally, to successfully assert duress as a defense, the defendant must reasonably have believed that he or she was in immediate danger, and the jury (or judge) must conclude that the defendant's belief was reasonable.

10-4f Entrapment

Entrapment is a defense designed to prevent police officers or other government agents from enticing persons

to commit crimes in order to later prosecute them for those crimes. In the typical entrapment case, an undercover agent *suggests* that a crime be committed and somehow pressures or induces an individual to commit it. The agent then arrests the individual for the crime.

For entrapment to be considered a defense, both the suggestion and the inducement must take place. The defense is not intended to prevent law enforcement agents from setting a trap for an unwary criminal. Rather, its purpose is to prevent them from pushing the individual into a criminal act. The crucial issue is whether the person who committed a crime was predisposed to commit the illegal act or did so only because the agent induced it.

10-4g Statute of Limitations

With some exceptions, such as the crime of murder, statutes of limitations apply to crimes just as they do to civil wrongs. In other words, the government must initiate criminal prosecution within a certain number of years. If a criminal action is brought after the statutory time period has expired, the accused person can raise the statute of limitations as a defense.

The running of the time period in a statute of limitations may be *tolled*—that is, suspended or stopped temporarily—if the defendant is a minor or is not in the jurisdiction. When the defendant reaches the age of majority or returns to the jurisdiction, the statutory time period begins to run again.

10-4h Immunity

Accused persons are understandably reluctant to give information if it will be used to prosecute them, and they cannot be forced to do so. The privilege against **self-incrimination** is guaranteed by a clause in the Fifth Amendment to the U.S. Constitution. The clause reads "nor shall [any person] be compelled in any criminal case to be a witness against himself."

When the state wishes to obtain information from a person accused of a crime, the state can grant *immunity* from prosecution. Alternatively, the state can agree to prosecute the accused for a less serious offense in exchange for the information. Once immunity is given, the person has an absolute privilege against self-incrimination and therefore can no longer refuse to testify on Fifth Amendment grounds.

Often, a grant of immunity from prosecution for a serious crime is part of the **plea bargaining** between the defending and prosecuting attorneys. The defendant

---

17. A rule derived from *M'Naghten's* Case, 8 Eng.Rep. 718 (1843).

may be convicted of a lesser offense, while the state uses the defendant's testimony to prosecute accomplices for serious crimes carrying heavy penalties.

10–5 Criminal Procedures

Criminal law brings the force of the state, with all of its resources, to bear against the individual. Criminal procedures are designed to protect the constitutional rights of individuals and to prevent the arbitrary use of power on the part of the government.

The U.S. Constitution provides specific safeguards for those accused of crimes. The United States Supreme Court has ruled that most of these safeguards apply not only in federal court but also in state courts by virtue of the due process clause of the Fourteenth Amendment. These protections include the following:

1. The Fourth Amendment protection from unreasonable searches and seizures.
2. The Fourth Amendment requirement that no warrant for a search or an arrest be issued without probable cause.
3. The Fifth Amendment requirement that no one be deprived of "life, liberty, or property without due process of law."
4. The Fifth Amendment prohibition against **double jeopardy** (trying someone twice for the same criminal offense).[18]
5. The Fifth Amendment requirement that no person be required to be a witness against (incriminate) himself or herself.
6. The Sixth Amendment guarantees of a speedy trial, a trial by jury, a public trial, the right to confront witnesses, and the right to a lawyer at various stages in some proceedings.
7. The Eighth Amendment prohibitions against excessive bail and fines and against cruel and unusual punishment.

10–5a Fourth Amendment Protections

The Fourth Amendment protects the "right of the people to be secure in their persons, houses, papers, and effects." Before searching or seizing private property, normally law enforcement officers must obtain a **search warrant**—an order from a judge or other public official authorizing the search or seizure.

Advances in technology allow the authorities to track phone calls and vehicle movements with greater ease and precision. The use of such technology can constitute a search within the meaning of the Fourth Amendment. ■ **CASE IN POINT 10.18** Antoine Jones owned and operated a nightclub in the District of Columbia. Government agents suspected that he was also trafficking in narcotics. As part of their investigation, agents obtained a warrant to attach a global positioning system (GPS) device to Jones's wife's car, which Jones regularly used. The warrant authorized installation in the District of Columbia within ten days, but agents installed the device on the eleventh day in Maryland.

The agents then tracked the vehicle's movement for about a month, eventually arresting Jones for possession and intent to distribute cocaine. Jones was convicted. He appealed, arguing that the government did not have a valid warrant for the GPS tracking. The United States Supreme Court held that the attachment of a GPS tracking device to a suspect's vehicle does constitute a Fourth Amendment search. The Court did not rule on whether the search in this case was unreasonable, however, and allowed Jones's conviction to stand.[19] ■

Probable Cause To obtain a search warrant, law enforcement officers must convince a judge that they have reasonable grounds, or **probable cause,** to believe a search will reveal a specific illegality. Probable cause requires the officers to have trustworthy evidence that would convince a reasonable person that the proposed search or seizure is more likely justified than not.

■ **CASE IN POINT 10.19** Based on a tip that Oscar Gutierrez was involved in drug trafficking, law enforcement officers went to his home with a drug-sniffing dog. The dog alerted officers to the scent of narcotics at the home's front door. Officers knocked for fifteen minutes, but no one answered. Eventually, they entered and secured the men inside the home. They then obtained a search warrant based on the dog's positive alert. Officers found eleven pounds of methamphetamine in the search, and Gutierrez was convicted.

On appeal, a court held that the search was permissible because the evidence of the drug-sniffing dog's positive alert for the presence of drugs established probable cause for the warrant.[20] The court noted that a recent

---

18. The prohibition against double jeopardy does not preclude the crime victim from bringing a *civil* suit against that same person to recover damages, however. Additionally, a state's prosecution of a crime will not prevent a separate federal prosecution of the same crime, and vice versa.

19. *United States v. Jones,* __ U.S. __, 132 S.Ct. 945, 181 L.Ed.2d 911 (2012).
20. *United States v. Gutierrez,* 760 F.3d 750 (7th Cir. 2014).

United States Supreme Court decision would have prohibited the search. In that decision, the Court held that
police officers cannot bring drug-sniffing dogs onto the
front porch of a person's home without a warrant.[21] But
the officers' conduct in this case had occurred before the
Supreme Court's decision, so the officers could reasonably rely on the sniff evidence. ■

Scope of Warrant The Fourth Amendment prohibits general warrants. It requires a specific description of
what is to be searched or seized. General searches through
a person's belongings are impermissible. The search cannot extend beyond what is described in the warrant. Nevertheless, if a warrant is issued for a person's residence,
items in that residence may be searched even if they do
not belong to that individual.

Reasonable Expectation of Privacy The Fourth
Amendment protects only against searches that violate
a person's *reasonable expectation of privacy*. A reasonable
expectation of privacy exists if (1) the individual actually
expects privacy and (2) the person's expectation is one that
society as a whole would consider legitimate.

■ **CASE IN POINT 10.20** Angela Marcum was the drug
court coordinator responsible for collecting money for
the District Court of Pittsburg County, Oklahoma. She
was romantically involved with James Miller, an assistant district attorney. The state charged Marcum with
obstructing an investigation of suspected embezzlement
and offered in evidence text messages sent and received
by her and Miller. The state had obtained a search warrant and collected the records of the messages from U.S.
Cellular, Miller's phone company.

Marcum filed a motion to suppress the messages,
which the court granted. The state appealed. A state
intermediate appellate court reversed the lower court's
judgment. Marcum had no reasonable expectation of
privacy in U.S. Cellular's records of her text messages in
Miller's account. "Once the messages were both transmitted and received, the expectation of privacy was
lost."[22] ■

10–5b The Exclusionary Rule

Under what is known as the **exclusionary rule,** any evidence obtained in violation of the constitutional rights
spelled out in the Fourth, Fifth, and Sixth Amendments
generally is not admissible at trial. All evidence derived

from the illegally obtained evidence is known as the
"fruit of the poisonous tree," and it normally must also
be excluded from the trial proceedings. For instance, if a
confession is obtained after an illegal arrest, the arrest is
the "poisonous tree," and the confession, if "tainted" by
the arrest, is the "fruit."

The purpose of the exclusionary rule is to deter police
from conducting warrantless searches and engaging
in other misconduct. The rule can sometimes lead to
injustice, however. If evidence of a defendant's guilt was
obtained improperly (without a valid search warrant, for
instance), it normally cannot be used against the defendant in court.

10–5c The *Miranda* Rule

In *Miranda v. Arizona,*[23] a landmark case decided in 1966,
the United States Supreme Court established the rule
that individuals who are arrested must be informed of
certain constitutional rights. Suspects must be informed
of their Fifth Amendment right to remain silent and their
Sixth Amendment right to counsel. If the arresting officers fail to inform a criminal suspect of these constitutional rights, any statements the suspect makes normally
will not be admissible in court.

Although the Supreme Court's decision in the
Miranda case was controversial, it has survived several
attempts by Congress to overrule it. Over time, however,
the Supreme Court has made a number of exceptions to
the *Miranda* ruling.

For instance, the Court has recognized a "public safety"
exception that allows certain statements to be admitted
even if the defendant was not given *Miranda* warnings.
A defendant's statements that reveal the location of a
weapon would be admissible under this exception.

Additionally, a suspect must unequivocally and assert-
ively ask to exercise her or his right to counsel in order to
stop police questioning. Saying "Maybe I should talk to
a lawyer" during an interrogation after being taken into
custody is not enough.

10–5d Criminal Process

A criminal prosecution differs significantly from a civil
case in several respects. These differences reflect the desire
to safeguard the rights of the individual against the state.
Exhibit 10–3 summarizes the major steps in processing a
criminal case, several of which we discuss here.

---

21. *Florida v. Jardines,* 569 U.S. 1, 133 S.Ct. 1409, 185 L.Ed.2d 495
(2013).
22. *State of Oklahoma v. Marcum,* 319 P.3d 681 (2014).

23. 384 U.S. 436, 86 S.Ct. 1602, 16 L.Ed.2d 694 (1966).

EXHIBIT 10–3 Major Procedural Steps in a Criminal Case

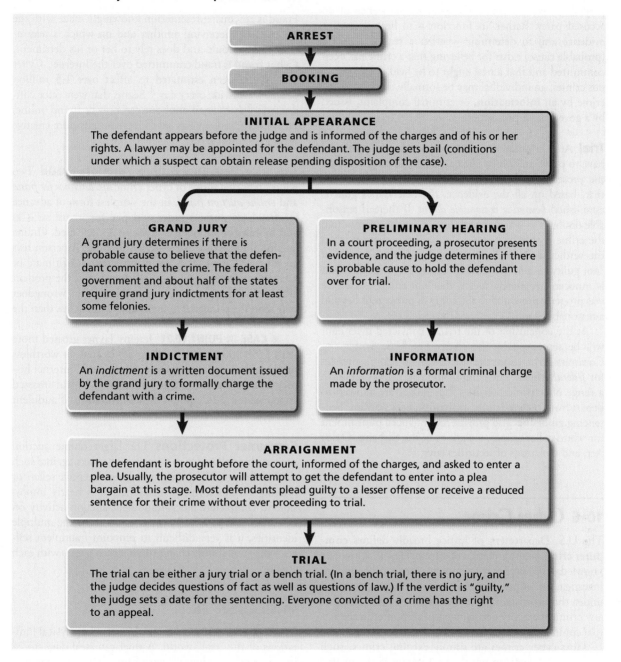

Arrest Before a warrant for arrest can be issued, there must be probable cause to believe that the individual in question has committed a crime. Note that probable cause involves a substantial likelihood that the person has committed a crime, not just a possibility. Arrests can be made without a warrant if there is no time to obtain one,

but the action of the arresting officer is still judged by the standard of probable cause.

Indictment or Information Individuals must be formally charged with having committed specific crimes before they can be brought to trial. If issued by a grand jury, such a charge is called an **indictment.**[24] A **grand jury** does not determine the guilt or innocence of an accused party. Rather, its function is to hear the state's evidence and to determine whether a reasonable basis (probable cause) exists for believing that a crime has been committed and that a trial ought to be held. For less serious crimes, an individual may be formally charged with a crime by an **information,** or criminal complaint, issued by a government prosecutor.

Trial At a criminal trial, the accused person does not have to prove anything. The entire burden of proof is on the prosecutor (the state). The prosecution must show that, based on all the evidence, the defendant's guilt is established *beyond a reasonable doubt.* If there is reasonable doubt as to whether a criminal defendant committed the crime with which she or he has been charged, then the verdict must be "not guilty." Returning a verdict of "not guilty" is not the same as stating that the defendant is innocent. It merely means that not enough evidence was properly presented to the court to prove guilt beyond a reasonable doubt.

At the conclusion of the trial, a convicted defendant will be sentenced by the court. The U.S. Sentencing Commission performs the task of standardizing sentences for *federal* crimes. The commission's guidelines establish a range of possible penalties, but judges are allowed to depart from the guidelines if circumstances warrant. Sentencing guidelines also provide for enhanced punishment for white-collar crimes, violations of the Sarbanes-Oxley Act, and violations of securities laws.[25]

10–6 Cyber Crime

The U.S. Department of Justice broadly defines **computer crime** as any violation of criminal law that involves knowledge of computer technology for its perpetration, investigation, or prosecution. Many computer crimes fall under the broad label of **cyber crime,** which describes any criminal activity occurring via a computer in the virtual community of the Internet.

Most cyber crimes are simply existing crimes, such as fraud and theft, in which the Internet is the instrument of wrongdoing. Here, we look at several types of activities that constitute cyber crimes against persons or property.

10–6a Cyber Fraud

Fraud is any misrepresentation knowingly made with the intention of deceiving another and on which a reasonable person would and does rely to her or his detriment. **Cyber fraud** is fraud committed over the Internet. Cyber scams have been estimated to affect over 1.5 million people worldwide every day.[26] Scams that were once conducted solely by mail or phone can now be found online, and new technology has led to increasingly more creative ways to commit fraud.

Advance Fee and Online Auction Fraud Two widely reported forms of cyber crime are *advance fee fraud* and *online auction fraud.* In the simplest form of advance fee fraud, consumers order and pay for items, such as automobiles or antiques, that are never delivered. Online auction fraud is also fairly straightforward. A person lists an expensive item for auction, on either a legitimate or a fake auction site, and then refuses to send the product after receiving payment. Or, as a variation, the wrongdoer may send the purchaser an item that is worth less than the one offered in the auction.

■ **CASE IN POINT 10.21** Jeremy Jaynes grossed more than $750,000 per week selling nonexistent or worthless products such as "penny stock pickers" and "Internet history erasers." By the time he was arrested, he had amassed an estimated $24 million from his various fraudulent schemes.[27] ■

Consumer Protections The larger online auction sites, such as eBay, try to protect consumers against such schemes by providing warnings about deceptive sellers or offering various forms of insurance. It is nearly impossible to completely block fraudulent auction activity on the Internet, however. Because users can assume multiple identities, it is very difficult to pinpoint fraudulent sellers—they will simply change their screen names with each auction.

10–6b Cyber Theft

In cyberspace, thieves are not subject to the physical limitations of the "real" world. A thief can steal data stored in a networked computer with Internet access from anywhere on the globe. Only the speed of the connection and the thief's computer equipment limit the quantity of data that can be stolen.

---

24. Pronounced in-*dyte*-ment.
25. The sentencing guidelines were amended in 2003, as required under the Sarbanes-Oxley Act of 2002, to impose stiffer penalties for corporate securities fraud.

26. *2013 Norton Report* (Mountain View, Calif.: Symantec, 2014), pg. 8.
27. *Jaynes v. Commonwealth of Virginia*, 276 Va. 443, 666 S.E.2d 303 (2008).

Identity Theft Not surprisingly, there has been a marked increase in identity theft in recent years. **Identity theft** occurs when the wrongdoer steals a form of identification—such as a name, date of birth, or Social Security number—and uses the information to access the victim's financial resources. According to the federal government, about 7 percent of Americans have been victims of identity theft.

More than half of identity thefts involve the misappropriation of an existing credit-card account. In most situations, the legitimate holders of credit cards are not held responsible for the costs of purchases made with a stolen number. The loss is born by the businesses and banks.

The Internet has provided relatively easy access to private data that includes credit-card numbers and more. Frequent Web surfers surrender a wealth of information about themselves. Web sites use "cookies" to collect data on those who visit their sites and make purchases. Often, sites store information such as the consumer's name, e-mail address, and credit-card number. Identity thieves may be able to steal this information by fooling a Web site into thinking that they are the true account holders.

In addition, people often enter important personal information, such as their birthdays, hometowns, or employers, on social media sites. Identity thieves can use such information to convince a third party to reveal someone's Social Security or bank account number.

Identity theft can be committed in the course of pursuing other criminal objectives. In the following case, for example, the defendant was charged with identity theft in connection with the filing of five thousand false income tax returns to obtain refunds. He challenged his conviction on these charges and sought a new trial.

Case Analysis 10.3

United States v. Warner

United States Court of Appeals, Eleventh Circuit, 2016 WL 403166 (2016).

In the Language of the Court

PER CURIAM [By the Whole Court]:
* * * *

A [federal district court] jury convicted Mauricio Warner on all 50 counts of an indictment that charged him with obtaining individuals' identities and using such identities to file over 5,000 false income tax returns resulting in millions of dollars in refunds that were deposited in bank accounts Warner controlled. [The court sentenced Warner to prison for a total of 240 months.] He now appeals his convictions. He seeks the vacation of his convictions and a new trial on the grounds that the District Court abused its discretion (1) in refusing to permit a polygraph examiner to testify to the results of a polygraph examination he administered to Warner; (2) admitting into evidence government Exhibits 500 and 500A, spreadsheets of fraudulently submitted tax returns, as business records; and (3) permitting each juror to have a copy of the indictment throughout trial.
* * * *

A district court's decision to admit or exclude expert testimony under Federal Rule of Evidence 702 is reviewed for abuse of discretion, which is the standard we apply in reviewing evidentiary rulings in general. *A district court abuses its discretion when it applies the wrong law, follows the wrong procedure, bases its decision on clearly erroneous facts, or commits a clear error in judgment.* [Emphasis added.]

Federal Rule of Evidence 702 provides that an expert witness may testify in the form of an opinion if the expert's specialized knowledge will assist the trier of fact to understand the evidence or to determine a fact at issue.

The results of a polygraph examination are not inadmissible *per se.* The trial judge in the exercise of discretion may admit the results of such examination to impeach or corroborate witness testimony.

The District Court did not abuse its discretion in concluding that the polygraph examination was inadmissible under Rule 702. The question posed by the examiner addressed an issue that was to be decided by the jury, that is, whether Warner knowingly filed tax returns without the individuals' authority or knowing that they were not entitled to the refund requested. Since Warner took the stand and answered the same questions, the jury was capable of determining his credibility without the aid of an expert.
* * * *

Federal Rule of Evidence 1006 authorizes the admission into evidence of a summary of voluminous business records but only where the originals or duplicates of those originals are available for examination or copying by the other party.

The business record exception to the hearsay rule under Federal Rule of Evidence 803(6) states, in relevant part, that a record will be admitted if:

(A) the record was made at or near the time by—or from information transmitted by—someone with knowledge;

Case 10.3 Continues

Case 10.3 Continued

(B) the record was kept in the course of a regularly conducted activity of a business, organization, occupation, or calling, whether or not for profit;

(C) making the record was a regular practice of that activity;

(D) all these conditions are shown by the testimony of the custodian or another qualified witness * * *;

(E) the opponent does not show that the source of information or the method of circumstances of preparation indicate a lack of trustworthiness.

Rule 803(6) requires that both the underlying records and the report summarizing those records be prepared and maintained for business purposes in the ordinary course of business and not for purposes of litigation. * * * *The touchstone of admissibility under Rule 803(6) is reliability, and a trial judge has broad discretion to determine the admissibility of such evidence.* [Emphasis added.]

Computer-generated business records are admissible under the following circumstances: (1) the records must be kept pursuant to some routine procedure designed to assure their accuracy, (2) they must be created for motives that would tend to assure accuracy (preparation for litigation, for example, is not such a motive), and (3) they must not themselves be mere accumulations of hearsay or uninformed opinion.

* * * A typed summary of handwritten business records created solely for litigation [is] inadmissible hearsay evidence. [This is] distinguishable from * * * records [that consist of] electronically stored information and the summary [is] simply a printout of that information.

* * * *

* * * Airline check-in and reservation records and flight manifests that [are] kept in the ordinary course of business and printed at the government's request [for a trial are admissible]. Computer data compiled and presented in computer printouts prepared specifically for trial is admissible under Rule 803(6), even though the printouts themselves are not kept in the ordinary course of business.

We find no abuse of discretion in admitting government Exhibits 500 and 500A under Rule 803(6). Although the spreadsheets were formatted to be easier to understand and printed for litigation, the underlying records were kept in the ordinary course of business and the data was not modified or combined when entered into the spreadsheet.

* * * *

The decision to provide the jury with a copy of an indictment is committed to the district court's sound discretion.

As a general rule, a trial court may, in the exercise of discretion, allow the indictment to be taken into the jury room. Likewise, a court may provide the jury copies of the indictment before trial, provided that the court gives specific instructions that the indictment is not evidence.

There was no abuse of discretion here. The court specifically instructed the jurors on two separate occasions that the indictment was not evidence or proof of any guilt. Even if the court's lack of contemporaneous instructions was error, it was harmless.

For the foregoing reasons, Warner's convictions are

AFFIRMED.

Legal Reasoning Questions

1. What three reasons did the defendant assert to support a request for a new trial?

2. What standard applies to an appellate court's consideration of a contention that a trial court's evidentiary ruling was in error?

3. What were the appellate court's conclusions with respect to the trial court's rulings in this case? What reasons support these conclusions?

Password Theft The more personal information a cyber criminal obtains, the easier it is for him or her to find a victim's online user name at a particular Web site. Once the online user name has been compromised, it is easier to steal the victim's password, which is often the last line of defense to financial information.

Numerous software programs aid identity thieves in illegally obtaining passwords. A technique called *keystroke logging,* for instance, relies on software that embeds itself in a victim's computer and records every keystroke made on that computer. User names and passwords are then recorded and sold to the highest bidder. Internet users should also be wary of any links contained within e-mails sent from unknown sources. These links can sometimes be used to illegally obtain personal information.

Phishing A form of identity theft known as **phishing** has added a different wrinkle to the practice. In a phishing attack, the perpetrator "fishes" for financial data and passwords from consumers by posing as a legitimate business, such as a bank or credit-card company. The "phisher" sends an e-mail asking the recipient to update or confirm vital information. Often, the e-mail includes a threat that an account or some other service will be discontinued if the information is not provided. Once the unsuspecting individual enters the information, the phisher can sell it or use it to masquerade as that person or to drain his or her bank or credit account.

■ **EXAMPLE 10.22** Customers of Wells Fargo Bank received official-looking e-mails telling them to type in personal information in an online form to complete a mandatory installation of a new Internet security certificate. But the Web site was bogus. When people filled out the forms, their computers were infected and funneled their data to a computer server. The cyber criminals then sold the data. ■ Phishing scams have also spread to text messaging and social networking sites.

10–6c Hacking

A **hacker** is someone who uses one computer to break into another. The danger posed by hackers has increased significantly because of **botnets,** or networks of computers that have been appropriated by hackers without the knowledge of their owners. A hacker may secretly install a program on thousands, even millions, of personal computer "robots," or "bots." The program, in turn, allows the hacker to forward transmissions to an even larger number of systems.

■ **EXAMPLE 10.23** Almost as soon as Apple, Inc., introduced a new mobile-payment system in late 2014, cyber thieves began hacking into the company's smartphones and tablets to make purchases with stolen credit-card numbers. At about the same time, cyber criminals were stealing the credit-card data of at least 60 million Home Depot customers and illegally accessing the financial information of 76 million JPMorgan Chase clients. In 2015, hackers stole the personal information of 19.7 million individuals from the U.S. Office of Personnel Management's background-investigation databases.

It has also been demonstrated that hackers can take over the dashboard computer systems that control cars— General Motors' OnStar system, for example. This risk of takeover extends to numerous wireless-enabled medical devices in use today, such as pacemakers, insulin pumps, and neurostimulators. A criminal could hack someone's car or pacemaker with the intent of causing the person harm. ■

Malware Botnets are one of the latest forms of **malware,** a term that refers to any program that is harmful to a computer or, by extension, a computer user. Malware can be programmed to perform a number of functions, such as prompting host computers to continually "crash" and reboot or otherwise infecting the systems.

One type of malware is a **worm**—a software program that is capable of reproducing itself as it spreads from one computer to the next. The Conflicker worm, for instance, spread to more than a million personal computers around the world within a three-week period. It was transmitted to some computers through the use of Facebook and Twitter.

A **virus,** another form of malware, is also able to reproduce itself, but must be attached to an "infested" host file to travel from one computer network to another. For instance, hackers are now capable of corrupting banner ads that use Adobe's Flash Player. When an Internet user clicks on the banner ad, a virus is installed.

■ **EXAMPLE 10.24** During the 2013 holiday season, a group of Eastern European hackers managed to gain access to Target's computer system. Once "inside," these hackers infected the in-store devices that Target customers use to swipe their credit and debit cards with "memory scraper" malware nicknamed Kaptoxa. Over the course of several weeks, the malware was used to steal the credit- and debit-card data of as many as 40 million Target customers. Personal data such as passwords, phone numbers, and addresses were stolen from at least 70 million more customers. Some experts estimate that the incident resulted in billions of dollars in losses to consumers, their banks, and others. ■

Service-Based Hacking Today, many companies offer "software as a service." Instead of buying software to install on a computer, the user connects to Web-based software. The user can then write e-mails, edit spreadsheets, or perform other tasks using his or her Web browser.

Cyber criminals have adapted this distribution method to provide "crimeware as a service." A would-be thief no longer has to be a computer hacker to create a botnet or steal banking information and credit-card numbers. He or she can rent the online services of cyber criminals to do the work for a small price. Fake security software (also known as scareware) is a common example. The thief can even target individual groups, such as U.S. physicians or British attorneys.

Cyberterrorism Cyberterrorists, as well as hackers, may target businesses. The goals of a hacking operation might include a wholesale theft of data, such as a merchant's customer files, or the monitoring of a computer to discover a business firm's plans and transactions. A cyberterrorist might also want to insert false codes or data. For instance, the processing control system of a food manufacturer could be changed to alter the levels of ingredients so that consumers of the food would become ill.

A cyberterrorist attack on a major financial institution, such as the New York Stock Exchange or a large bank, could leave securities or money markets in flux. Such an attack could seriously affect U.S. citizens, business operations, and national security.

10–6d Prosecuting Cyber Crime

Cyber crime has raised new issues in the investigation of crimes and the prosecution of offenders. Determining the "location" of a cyber crime and identifying a criminal in cyberspace present significant challenges for law enforcement.

Jurisdiction and Identification Challenges A threshold issue is, of course, jurisdiction. Each state and nation has jurisdiction, or authority, over crimes committed within its boundaries. But geographic boundaries simply do not apply in cyberspace. A person who commits an act against a business in California, where the act is a cyber crime, might never have set foot in California. Instead, the perpetrator might reside in another state, or even another nation, where the act may not be a crime. Indeed, many cyber crimes emanate from Russia and China.

Identifying the wrongdoer can also be difficult. Cyber criminals do not leave physical traces, such as fingerprints or DNA samples, as evidence of their crimes. Even electronic "footprints" can be hard to find and follow. For instance, cyber criminals may employ software such as Tor to mask their IP addresses (codes that identify individual computers) and the IP addresses of those with whom they communicate. Law enforcement has to hire computer forensic experts to bypass the software and track down the criminal. For these reasons, laws written to protect physical property are often difficult to apply in cyberspace.

The Computer Fraud and Abuse Act Perhaps the most significant federal statute specifically addressing cyber crime is the Counterfeit Access Device and Computer Fraud and Abuse Act.[28] This act is commonly known as the Computer Fraud and Abuse Act (CFAA).

Among other things, the CFAA provides that a person who accesses a computer online, without authority, to obtain classified, restricted, or protected data (or attempts to do so) is subject to criminal prosecution. Such data could include financial and credit records, medical records, legal files, military and national security files, and other confidential information. The data can be located in government or private computers. The crime has two elements: accessing a computer without authority and taking data.

The theft is a felony if it is committed for a commercial purpose or for private financial gain, or if the value of the stolen data (or computer time) exceeds $5,000. Penalties include fines and imprisonment for up to twenty years. A person who violates the CFAA can also be sued in a civil action for damages.

---

28. 18 U.S.C. Section 1030.

Reviewing: Criminal Law and Cyber Crime

Edward Hanousek worked for Pacific & Arctic Railway and Navigation Company (P&A) as a roadmaster of the White Pass & Yukon Railroad in Alaska. Hanousek was responsible "for every detail of the safe and efficient maintenance and construction of track, structures and marine facilities of the entire railroad," including special projects. One project was a rock quarry, known as "6-mile," above the Skagway River. Next to the quarry, and just beneath the surface, ran a high-pressure oil pipeline owned by Pacific & Arctic Pipeline, Inc., P&A's sister company. When the quarry's backhoe operator punctured the pipeline, an estimated 1,000 to 5,000 gallons of oil were discharged into the river. Hanousek was charged with negligently discharging a harmful quantity of oil into a navigable water of the United States in violation of the criminal provisions of the Clean Water Act (CWA). Using the information presented in the chapter, answer the following questions.

1. Did Hanousek have the required mental state *(mens rea)* to be convicted of a crime? Why or why not?
2. Which theory discussed in the chapter would enable a court to hold Hanousek criminally liable for violating the statute if he participated in, directed, or merely knew about the specific violation?
3. Could the backhoe operator who punctured the pipeline also be charged with a crime in this situation? Explain.
4. Suppose that at trial, Hanousek argued that he should not be convicted because he was not aware of the requirements of the CWA. Would this defense be successful? Why or why not?

Debate This . . . *Because of overcriminalization, particularly by the federal government, Americans may be breaking the law regularly without knowing it. Should Congress rescind many of the more than four thousand federal crimes now on the books?*

Terms and Concepts

actus reus 189	beyond a reasonable doubt 187	burglary 192
arson 194	botnet 207	computer crime 204

crime 187
cyber crime 204
cyber fraud 204
double jeopardy 201
duress 200
embezzlement 195
entrapment 200
exclusionary rule 202
felony 188
forgery 194
grand jury 204

hacker 207
identity theft 205
indictment 204
information 204
larceny 194
malware 207
mens rea 189
misdemeanor 188
money laundering 197
necessity 198
petty offense 188

phishing 206
plea bargaining 200
probable cause 201
robbery 192
search warrant 201
self-defense 198
self-incrimination 200
virus 207
white-collar crime 195
worm 207

Issue Spotters

1. Dana takes her roommate's credit card without permission, intending to charge expenses that she incurs on a vacation. Her first stop is a gas station, where she uses the card to pay for gas. With respect to the gas station, has she committed a crime? If so, what is it? (See *Types of Crimes.*)

2. Without permission, Ben downloads consumer credit files from a computer belonging to Consumer Credit Agency. He then sells the data to Dawn. Has Ben committed a crime? If so, what is it? (See *Cyber Crime.*)

• **Check your answers to the Issue Spotters against the answers provided in Appendix D at the end of this text.**

Business Scenarios

10–1. Types of Cyber Crimes. The following situations are similar, but each represents a variation of a particular crime. Identify the crime and point out the differences in the variations. (See *Cyber Crime.*)

(a) Chen, posing fraudulently as Diamond Credit Card Co., sends an e-mail to Emily, stating that the company has observed suspicious activity in her account and has frozen the account. The e-mail asks her to reregister her credit-card number and password to reopen the account.

(b) Claiming falsely to be Big Buy Retail Finance Co., Conner sends an e-mail to Dino, asking him to confirm or update his personal security information to prevent his Big Buy account from being discontinued.

(c) Felicia posts her résumé on GotWork.com, an online job-posting site, seeking a position in business and managerial finance and accounting. Hayden, who misrepresents himself as an employment officer with International Bank & Commerce Corp., sends her an e-mail asking for more personal information.

10–2. Cyber Scam. Kayla, a student at Learnwell University, owes $20,000 in unpaid tuition. If Kayla does not pay the tuition, Learnwell will not allow her to graduate. To obtain the funds to pay the debt, she sends e-mails to people that she does not personally know asking for financial help to send Milo, her disabled child, to a special school. In reality, Kayla has no children. Is this a crime? If so, which one? (See *Cyber Crime.*)

Business Case Problems

10–3. Credit-Card Theft. Jacqueline Barden was shopping for school clothes with her children when her purse and automobile were taken. In Barden's purse were her car keys, credit and debit cards, and the children's Social Security cards and birth certificates, which were needed for enrollment at school. Immediately after the purse and car were stolen, Rebecca Mary Turner attempted to use Barden's credit card at a local Exxon gas station, but the card was declined. The gas station attendant recognized Turner because she had previously written bad checks and used credit cards that did not belong to her.

Turner was later arrested while attempting to use one of Barden's checks to pay for merchandise at a Wal-Mart—where the clerk also recognized Turner from prior criminal activity. Turner claimed that she had not stolen Barden's purse or car. Instead, she said that a friend had told her he had some checks and credit cards and asked her to try using them at Wal-Mart. Turner was convicted at trial. She appealed, claiming that there was insufficient evidence that she committed credit- and debit-card theft. Was the evidence sufficient to uphold her conviction? Why or why not? [*Turner v. State of Arkansas,* 2012 Ark.App. 150 (2012)] (See *Types of Crimes.*)

**10–4. Business Case Problem with Sample Answer—
Criftinal Liability.** During the morning rush hour, David

Green threw bottles and plates from a twenty-
sixth-floor hotel balcony overlooking Seventh
Avenue in New York City. A video of the incident
also showed him doing cartwheels while holding a
beer bottle and sprinting toward the balcony while holding a
glass steadily in his hand. When he saw police on the street
below and on the roof of the building across the street, he suspended his antics but resumed tossing objects off the balcony
after the police left. He later admitted that he could recall what
he had done, but claimed to have been intoxicated and said his
only purpose was to amuse himself and his friends. Did Green
have the mental state required to establish criminal liability?
Discuss. [*State of New York v. Green,* 104 A.D.3d 126, 958
N.Y.S.2d 138 (1 Dept. 2013)] (See *Criminal Liability.*)

- **For a sample answer to Problem 10–4, go to Appendix E at
the end of this text.**

10–5. White-Collar Crime. Matthew Simpson and others
created and operated a series of corporate entities to defraud
telecommunications companies, creditors, credit reporting
agencies, and others. Through these entities, Simpson and his
confederates used routing codes and spoofing services to make
long-distance calls appear to be local. They stole other firms'
network capacity and diverted payments to themselves. They
leased goods and services without paying for them. To hide
their association with their corporate entities and with each
other, they used false identities, addresses, and credit histories,
and issued false bills, invoices, financial statements, and credit
references. Did these acts constitute mail and wire fraud? Discuss. [*United States v. Simpson,* 741 F.3d 539 (5th Cir. 2014)]
(See *Types of Crimes.*)

10–6. Defenses to Criminal Liability. George Castro told
Ambrosio Medrano that a bribe to a certain corrupt Los Angeles
County official would buy a contract with the county hospitals.
To share in the deal, Medrano recruited Gustavo Buenrostro. In
turn, Buenrostro contacted his friend James Barta, the owner of
Sav–Rx, which provides prescription benefit management services. Barta was asked to pay a "finder's fee" to Castro. He did
not pay, even after frequent e-mails and calls with deadlines and
ultimatums delivered over a period of months. Eventually, Barta
wrote Castro a Sav–Rx check for $6,500, saying that it was to
help his friend Buenrostro. Castro was an FBI agent, and the
county official and contract were fictional. Barta was charged
with conspiracy to commit bribery. At trial, the government
conceded that Barta was not predisposed to commit the crime.

Could he be absolved of the charge on a defense of entrapment?
Explain. [*United States v. Barta,* 776 F.3d 931 (7th Cir. 2015)]
(See *Defenses to Criminal Liability.*)

10–7. Criminal Procedures. Federal officers obtained a
warrant to arrest Kateena Norman on charges of credit-card
fraud and identity theft. Evidence of the crime included videos, photos, and a fingerprint on a fraudulent check. A previous search of Norman's house had uncovered credit cards, new
merchandise, and identifying information for other persons.
An Internet account registered to the address had been used to
apply for fraudulent credit cards, and a fraudulently obtained
rental car was parked on the property. As the officers arrested
Norman outside her house, they saw another woman and a
caged pit bull inside. They further believed that Norman's boyfriend, who had a criminal record and was also suspected of
identify theft, could be there. In less than a minute, the officers
searched only those areas within the house in which a person
could hide. Would it be reasonable to admit evidence revealed
in this "protective sweep" during Norman's trial on the arrest
charges? Discuss. [*United States v. Norman,* __ F.3d __, 2016
WL 324949 (11th Cir. 2016)] (See *Criminal Procedures.*)

10–8. A Question of Ethics—Criminal Process. *Gary*

*Peters fraudulently told an undocumented immi-
grant that Peters could help him obtain lawful status.
Peters said that he knew immigration officials and
asked for money to aid in the process. The victim paid
Peters at least $25,000 in wire transfers and checks. Peters had
others call the victim, falsely represent that they were agents with
the U.S. Department of Homeland Security, and induce continued payments. He threatened to contact authorities to detain or
deport the victim and his wife. Peters was convicted of wire fraud
in a federal district court.* [United States v. Peters, *597
Fed.Appx. 1033 (11th Cir. 2015)]* (See *Criminal Procedures.*)

(a) Peters had previously committed theft and fraud. The
court stated, "This is the person he is. He steals from his
relatives. He steals from his business partner. He steals
from immigrants. He steals from anybody he comes into
contact with." What does Peters's conduct indicate about
his ethics?

(b) Peters's attorney argued that his client's criminal history
was partially due to "difficult personal times" caused by
divorce, illness, and job loss. Despite this claim, Peters was
sentenced to forty-eight months imprisonment, which
exceeded the federal sentencing guidelines but was less
than the statutory maximum of twenty years. Was this
sentence too harsh? Was it too lenient? Discuss.

Legal Reasoning Group Activity

10–9. Cyber Crime. Cyber crime costs consumers millions
of dollars per year, and it costs businesses, including banks and
other credit-card issuers, even more. Nonetheless, when cyber
criminals are caught and convicted, they are rarely ordered to
pay restitution or sentenced to long prison terms. (See *Cyber
Crime.*)

(a) One group should argue that stiffer sentences would
reduce the amount of cyber crime.

(b) A second group should determine how businesspersons
can best protect themselves from cyber crime and avoid
the associated costs.

The Biggest Data Breach of All Time

For almost ten years, a group of hackers in Russia and Ukraine attacked the computer systems of U.S. companies, including 7-Eleven, Inc., JetBlue Airways Corporation, and J.C. Penney Company. The systems of firms based in other countries, including Visa Jordan and French retailer Carrefour SA, came under attack as well. The hackers stole more than 160 million credit- and debit-card numbers and breached 800,000 bank accounts.[1] Among incidents of unauthorized access to company systems—not leaks of information from within—this was the biggest data breach of all time.

Businesses collect, process, and store confidential information on computer systems and transmit that data across networks to other computer systems. Data compromised by hackers affects all of these systems, and us as individuals, in ways that range from inconvenient to devastating. As the number of users and networks increases, the opportunities for breaches multiply.

Data Breaches

A *data breach* is an event in which sensitive, protected, or confidential data are copied, transmitted, viewed, stolen, or used by an individual unauthorized to do so. The data may include individuals' personal health information or personal identity information, such as birth dates and addresses, or a company's intellectual property, including patents, copyrights, and trade secrets.

Most breaches reported in the media involve individuals' private information, such as credit-card numbers. Loss of a business's data often goes unreported, unless there is a potential for harm to private individuals, because the publicity can do more damage to the business than the loss of the data.

How Do They Do It? Hackers break into computer systems by exploiting vulnerabilities in software code. A hacker may spend days, weeks, or longer setting up a position within the system, creating escape routes, and stealing information. Data may be stolen through phishing or spoofing, or with the help of malware.

Users of a system themselves may unwittingly facilitate attacks by downloading files or software, opening e-mail attachments, clicking on ads, or visiting fraudulent sites. In fact, individuals within an organization may cause as many as 37 percent of all data breaches.

Why Do They Do It? Normally, the focus of a hacker's attack is to steal data and sell the information.[2] With stolen personal information obtained from a hacker, a criminal can buy goods, empty bank accounts, or obtain funds in a number of ways. Intellectual property theft is a leading cause of financial losses to businesses. Hackers often steal trade secrets and other intellectual property for competing businesses.

Cyber Security

Cyber security consists of steps that can be taken to protect computers, networks, software, and confidential data from unauthorized access, alteration, or destruction. As the number and

Continues

---

1. A total loss for all of the victims has not been determined, but three of the companies estimate their combined loss to be more than $300 million.
2. The hackers who committed the biggest data breach of all time sold U.S. citizens' stolen credit-card numbers for ten dollars apiece.

sophistication of attacks increases, ongoing attention to security is required to protect sensitive business and personal information.

Prevent Attacks Being vigilant in protecting information is an important way to prevent attacks. A business can encrypt data, install firewalls, and train employees to take appropriate steps to guard customers' personal information and company trade secrets.

Notify Authorities and Victims If an attack does occur, a business should respond appropriately. Forty-seven states, the District of Columbia, Guam, Puerto Rico, and the Virgin Islands require businesses (and other entities) to notify individuals of data breaches involving their personal information.[3] Businesses should also notify the appropriate authorities.

A breached business may offer to cover the cost of credit monitoring and identity-theft protection for those whose personal information was stolen. In any event, individuals who are the victims of identity theft should inform their banks of the theft, place fraud alerts on their credit files, and review their credit reports.

Prosecute Hackers Hackers who can be identified can be charged with computer crimes. That happened to the hackers who committed the biggest data breach of all time, described at the beginning of this feature. Five defendants were charged in a federal district court with unauthorized access of protected computers, wire fraud, and conspiracy to commit those crimes.[4] In 2015, one of the five, Vladimir Drinkman, pleaded guilty. Drinkman and two of the others, Alexandr Kalinin and Mikhail Rytikov, were charged in connection with other data breaches as well.

Recover Losses Traditional insurance policies for businesses typically exclude the risk of a data breach. *Cyber security insurance* is designed to protect against losses from a variety of online incidents, including data breaches. The protection may cover costs arising from the destruction or theft of data, hacking, or denial of service attacks, as well as any related liability for privacy violations. Some policies limit coverage to $100 million.

Avoid Sanctions Earlier, we mentioned the importance of protecting data by preventing attacks. Attack prevention can have the added benefit of helping the business to avoid government sanctions.

A lack of security that allows hackers to steal customers' personal data from a business's computer system can be the ground for a suit by the Federal Trade Commission (FTC). The business may be liable for any resulting fraudulent charges to the customers' accounts. The FTC may also impose a fine and oversee the company's data protection for up to twenty years.

"A company does not act equitably when it publishes a privacy policy to attract customers who are concerned about data privacy, fails to make good on that promise by investing inadequate resources in cybersecurity, exposes its unsuspecting customers to substantial financial injury, and retains the profits of their business."[5]

---

3. See, for example, California Civil Code Sections 1798.29 and 1798.80 *et seq.*

4. These charges represent violations of the Computer Fraud and Abuse Act, 18 U.S.C. Section 1030; the Mail Fraud Act, 18 U.S.C. Sections 1343 and 1349; and 18 U.S.C. Section 371 ("Conspiracy to Commit Offense or to Defraud the United States").

5. *Federal Trade Commission v. Wyndham Worldwide Corp.*, 799 F.3d 236 (3d Cir. 2015).

Ethical Connection

Does a business have an ethical duty to prevent potential harm to its customers' credit that may result from a data breach? Some courts have held that consumers whose data have been stolen from a business's computer system can base a suit against the business on injuries consisting of lost time and money.[6]

The idea is that consumers whose data are stolen must spend time and money to resolve fraudulent charges and to protect against future identity theft and fraud. These individuals, after all, trusted the business with their information. They must now cancel or replace credit or debit cards and monitor credit reports even if actual fraud has not yet occurred.

As mentioned earlier, a business may offer credit monitoring and identity-theft protection after a breach. This offer indicates that the business recognizes a continuing risk of harm from the breach. It also supports the existence of an ethical duty on the part of the business to prevent this harm.

Ethics Question *What is the extent of a business's ethical obligation to protect the personal information of its customers and employees? Discuss.*

Critical Thinking *Most likely, hackers will always exist, attempting to breach computer systems using the most up-to-date technology. What can businesses do to prevent breaches to their systems?*

---

6. See, for example, *Remijas v. Neiman Marcus Group, LLC,* 794 F.3d 688 (7th Cir. 2015). Some courts disagree—for example, see *Reilly v. Ceridian Corp.*, 664 F.3d 38 (3d Cir. 2011).

Unit Three

Contracts and E-Contracts

CHAPTER 11

Nature and Terminology

ontract law deals with, among other things, the formation and keeping of promises. A **promise** is a declaration by a person (the *promisor*) to do or not to do a certain act. As a result, the person to whom the promise is made (the *promisee*) has a right to expect or demand that something either will or will not happen in the future.

Like other types of law, contract law reflects our social values, interests, and expectations at a given point in time. It shows, for instance, to what extent our society allows people to make promises or commitments that are legally binding. It distinguishes between promises that create only *moral* obligations (such as a promise to take a friend to lunch) and promises that are legally binding (such as a promise to pay for items ordered online).

Contract law also demonstrates which excuses our society accepts for breaking certain types of promises. In addition, it indicates which promises are considered to be contrary to public policy—against the interests of society as a whole—and therefore legally invalid. When the person making a promise is a child or is mentally incompetent, for instance, a question will arise as to whether the promise should be enforced. Resolving such questions is the essence of contract law.

11–1 An Overview of Contract Law

Before we look at the numerous rules that courts use to determine whether a particular promise will be enforced, it is necessary to understand some fundamental concepts of contract law. In this section, we describe the sources and general function of contract law and introduce the objective theory of contracts.

11–1a Sources of Contract Law

The common law governs all contracts except when it has been modified or replaced by statutory law, such as the Uniform Commercial Code (UCC), or by administrative agency regulations. Contracts relating to services, real estate, employment, and insurance, for instance, generally are governed by the common law of contracts.

Contracts for the sale and lease of goods, however, are governed by the UCC—to the extent that the UCC has modified general contract law. In the discussion of general contract law that follows, we indicate in footnotes the areas in which the UCC has significantly altered common law contract principles.

11–1b The Function of Contract Law

No aspect of modern life is entirely free of contractual relationships. You acquire rights and obligations, for example, when you borrow funds, buy or lease a house, obtain insurance, and purchase goods or services. Contract law is designed to provide stability and predictability, as well as certainty, for both buyers and sellers in the marketplace.

Contract law assures the parties to private agreements that the promises they make will be enforceable. Clearly, many promises are kept because the parties involved feel a moral obligation to keep them or because keeping a promise is in their mutual self-interest. The **promisor** (the person making the promise) and the **promisee** (the person to whom the promise is made) may also decide to honor their agreement for other reasons. In business agreements, the rules of contract law are often followed to avoid potential disputes.

By supplying procedures for enforcing private contractual agreements, contract law provides an essential condition for the existence of a market economy. Without a legal framework of reasonably assured expectations within which to make long-run plans, businesspersons would be able to rely only on the good faith of others.

Duty and good faith are usually sufficient to obtain compliance with a promise. When price changes or adverse economic factors make contract compliance costly, however, these elements may not be enough. Contract law is necessary to ensure compliance with a promise or to entitle the innocent party to some form of relief.

11–1c The Definition of a Contract

A **contract** is "a promise or a set of promises for the breach of which the law gives a remedy, or the performance of which the law in some way recognizes as a duty."[1] Put simply, a contract is an agreement that can be enforced in court. It is formed by two or more parties who agree to perform or to refrain from performing some act now or in the future.

Generally, contract disputes arise when there is a promise of future performance. If the contractual promise is not fulfilled, the party who made it is subject to the sanctions of a court. That party may be required to pay damages for failing to perform the contractual promise. In a few instances, the party may be required to perform the promised act.

11–1d The Objective Theory of Contracts

In determining whether a contract has been formed, the element of intent is of prime importance. In contract law, intent is determined by what is called the **objective theory of contracts,** not by the personal or subjective intent, or belief, of a party.

The theory is that a party's intention to enter into a legally binding agreement, or contract, is judged by outward, objective facts. The facts are as interpreted by a *reasonable* person, rather than by the party's own secret, subjective intentions. Objective facts may include:

1. What the party said when entering into the contract.
2. How the party acted or appeared (intent may be manifested by conduct as well as by oral or written words).
3. The circumstances surrounding the transaction.

■ **CASE IN POINT 11.1** Pan Handle Realty, LLC, built a luxury home in Westport, Connecticut. Robert Olins signed a lease for the property and gave Pan Handle a check for the amount of the annual rent—$138,000. Olins planned to move into the home on January 28, but on January 27, Olins's bank informed Pan Handle that payment had been stopped on the rental check. Olins then told Pan Handle that he was "unable to pursue any further interest in the property."

When Pan Handle was not able to find a new tenant, it filed a lawsuit in a Connecticut state court against Olins, alleging that he had breached the lease. Olins argued that when he signed the lease, he did not intend to be bound by it. The court ruled in Pan Handle's favor and awarded $138,000 in damages, plus $8,000 for utilities, interest, and attorneys' fees. The decision was affirmed on appeal. The objective fact, as supported by the evidence, was that the parties intended to be bound by the lease when they signed it. The fact that Olins had a change of heart after signing the contract was irrelevant.[2] ■

11–2 Elements of a Contract

The many topics that will be discussed in the following chapters on contract law require an understanding of the basic elements of a valid contract and the way in which a contract is created. It is also necessary to understand the types of circumstances in which even legally valid contracts will not be enforced.

11–2a Requirements of a Valid Contract

The following list briefly describes the four requirements that must be met before a valid contract exists. If any of these elements is lacking, no contract will have been formed. (Each requirement will be explained more fully in subsequent chapters.)

1. *Agreement.* An agreement to form a contract includes an *offer* and an *acceptance.* One party must offer to enter into a legal agreement, and another party must accept the terms of the offer.
2. *Consideration.* Any promises made by the parties to the contract must be supported by legally sufficient and bargained-for *consideration* (something of value received or promised, such as money, to convince a person to make a deal).
3. *Contractual capacity.* Both parties entering into the contract must have the contractual *capacity* to do so. The law must recognize them as possessing characteristics that qualify them as competent parties.
4. *Legality.* The contract's purpose must be to accomplish some goal that is legal and not against public policy.

---

1. *Restatement (Second) of Contracts,* Section 1. *Restatements of the Law* are scholarly books that restate the existing common law principles distilled from court opinions as sets of rules on particular topics. Courts often refer to the *Restatements* for guidance. The *Restatement* dealing with contracts will be referred to throughout the material on contract law. *Second* in the title indicates that this *Restatement* is in its second edition. A third edition is being drafted.

2. *Pan Handle Realty, LLC v. Olins,* 140 Conn.App. 556, 59 A.3d 842 (2013).

An agreement to form a contract can modify the terms of a previous contract. When a dispute concerns whether this occurred, the offer and acceptance of both agreements can be reviewed to determine their effect. As in every case involving a contract, the parties' *subjective* beliefs with respect to the terms are irrelevant, particularly in the absence of any evidence to support those beliefs. At issue in the following case was the effect of an offer and acceptance on a previous agreement between a university and an associate professor.

Case Analysis 11.1

Weston v. Cornell University

New York Supreme Court, Appellate Division, Third Department, 136 A.D.3d 1094, 24 N.Y.S.3d 448 (2016).

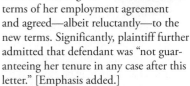

In the Language of the Court

ROSE, J. [Judge]

* * * *

Defendant [Cornell University in Ithaca, New York] appointed plaintiff [Leslie Weston] to an associate professorship in 1998 for an initial term of five years. The 1998 offer letter described the position as being "with tenure," but it stated that, although no problems were anticipated, the offer of tenure would have to be confirmed by defendant's review process shortly after plaintiff's arrival on campus. For a variety of reasons, plaintiff delayed her tenure submission for five years and, when she finally submitted it, she was not awarded tenure. In 2003, defendant gave plaintiff a two-year extension of her appointment, this time as an "associate professor without tenure," to allow her an opportunity to improve and resubmit her tenure package. Plaintiff resubmitted her request for tenure in 2005, but it was again denied, resulting in her eventual termination. Plaintiff then commenced this action [in a New York state court] seeking * * * to recover for breach of contract. * * * Following the completion of discovery, defendant moved for summary judgment dismissing the complaint * * * . The Supreme Court [a New York state trial court] denied that portion of the motion seeking dismissal of the breach of contract claim. Defendant now appeals.

Contrary to defendant's argument, Supreme Court properly found that issues of fact exist as to whether defendant's 1998 offer letter reflects an intent to assure plaintiff that she would be granted tenure. * * * The terms of the letter are ambiguous. Accordingly, Supreme Court properly relied upon extrinsic evidence to determine the parties' intent.[a] Based upon the affidavit of the then-chair of defendant's department who hired plaintiff and wrote the 1998 offer letter, as well as correspondence from the dean and associate dean of the college in which plaintiff's department was located, Supreme Court appropriately declined to award summary judgment to defendant with respect to the 1998 offer of tenure.

However, we must agree with defendant's alternative argument that the terms of its original offer were materially modified by plaintiff's acceptance of its 2003 offer to extend her appointment. *Defendant's 2003 letter offering to extend her appointment unambiguously replaced the "with tenure" language contained in the 1998 offer letter by restating her job title as "associate professor without tenure."* Defendant also points to plaintiff's deposition testimony, in which she explicitly acknowledged that she

---

a. *Extrinsic evidence*, which is evidence outside the contract itself, will be discussed later in this chapter.

understood the 2003 letter to be a modification of the original terms of her employment agreement and agreed—albeit reluctantly—to the new terms. Significantly, plaintiff further admitted that defendant was "not guaranteeing her tenure in any case after this letter." [Emphasis added.]

In response to this *prima facie* showing by defendant, plaintiff contends that, regardless of what she agreed to in 2003, her oft-repeated assertions of her belief that defendant still owed her tenure based upon the original letter suffice to preclude summary judgment. Aside from plaintiff's own opinions on the matter, however, there is nothing in the record to indicate that any alleged guarantee of tenure remained beyond the date of the 2003 letter. Accordingly, we find that plaintiff's subjective beliefs and unsupported arguments regarding the 2003 modification of her employment agreement are insufficient to raise triable issues of fact to defeat defendant's motion for summary judgment dismissing the breach of contract cause of action.

ORDERED that the order is modified * * * by reversing so much thereof as partially denied defendant's motion for summary judgment; said motion granted in its entirety and breach of contract cause of action dismissed.

Legal Reasoning Questions

1. What did the plaintiff seek in this action? What was the legal ground for her claim? What was her principal contention regarding the offers and acceptances at the center of this case?

2. Why did the trial court deny the defendant's motion for summary judgment to dismiss the plaintiff's claim?

3. Why did the appellate court modify the trial court's denial of the defendant's motion?

11–2b Defenses to the Enforceability of a Contract

Even if all of the requirements listed above are satisfied, a contract may be unenforceable if the following requirements are not met. These requirements typically are raised as *defenses* to the enforceability of an otherwise valid contract.

1. *Voluntary consent.* The consent of both parties must be voluntary. For instance, if a contract was formed as a result of fraud, undue influence, mistake, or duress, the contract may not be enforceable.
2. *Form.* The contract must be in whatever form the law requires. Some contracts must be in writing to be enforceable.

11–3 Types of Contracts

There are many types of contracts. They are categorized based on legal distinctions as to their formation, performance, and enforceability.

11–3a Contract Formation

Contracts can be classified according to how and when they are formed. Exhibit 11–1 shows three such classifications, and the following subsections explain them in greater detail.

Bilateral versus Unilateral Contracts Every contract involves at least two parties. The **offeror** is the party making the offer. The **offeree** is the party to whom the offer is made. Whether the contract is classified as *bilateral* or *unilateral* depends on what the offeree must do to accept the offer and bind the offeror to a contract.

Bilateral Contracts. If the offeree can accept simply by promising to perform, the contract is a **bilateral contract.** Hence, a bilateral contract is a "promise for a promise." No performance, such as payment of funds or delivery of goods, need take place for a bilateral contract to be formed. The contract comes into existence at the moment the promises are exchanged.

■ **EXAMPLE 11.2** Jacob offers to buy Ann's smartphone for $200. Jacob tells Ann that he will give her the $200 for the smartphone next Friday, when he gets paid. Ann accepts Jacob's offer and promises to give him the smartphone when he pays her on Friday. Jacob and Ann have formed a bilateral contract. ■

Unilateral Contracts. If the offer is phrased so that the offeree can accept the offer only by completing the contract performance, the contract is a **unilateral contract.** Hence, a unilateral contract is a "promise for an act." In other words, a unilateral contract is formed not at the moment when promises are exchanged but at the moment when the contract is *performed.*

■ **EXAMPLE 11.3** Reese says to Celia, "If you drive my car from New York to Los Angeles, I'll give you $1,000." Only on Celia's completion of the act—bringing the car to Los Angeles—does she fully accept Reese's offer to pay $1,000. If she chooses not to accept the offer to drive the car to Los Angeles, there are no legal consequences. ■

Contests, Lotteries, and Prizes. Contests, lotteries, and other competitions involving prizes are examples of offers

EXHIBIT 11–1 Classifications Based on Contract Formation

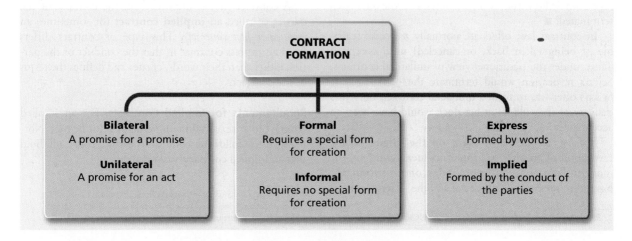

CONTRACT FORMATION		
Bilateral A promise for a promise	**Formal** Requires a special form for creation	**Express** Formed by words
Unilateral A promise for an act	**Informal** Requires no special form for creation	**Implied** Formed by the conduct of the parties

to form unilateral contracts. If a person complies with the rules of the contest—such as by submitting the right lottery number at the right place and time—a unilateral contract is formed. The organization offering the prize is then bound to a contract to perform as promised in the offer. If the person fails to comply with the contest rules, however, no binding contract is formed.

■ **CASE IN POINT 11.4** John Rogalski entered a poker tournament sponsored by Little Poker League (LPL) that lasted several months. During the final event, all contestants signed an agreement that said LPL would pay the tournament winner's entry fee and travel expenses to the World Series of Poker (WSOP). The agreement also stated that if the winner did not attend the WSOP, he or she would relinquish the WSOP seat and return the expense money to LPL.

Rogalski won and accepted $2,500 for travel-related expenses from the sponsor, but he did not attend the WSOP. He then filed a suit for $10,000 against LPL, arguing that it had advertised that the winner could choose to receive the cash value of the prizes ($12,500) instead of going to the WSOP. Rogalski claimed that he had accepted LPL's offer by participating in the tournament. The court rejected this argument and found in favor of LPL. The contract was formed when Rogalski signed the WSOP agreement. Under the contest rules as stated in that agreement, Rogalski had to return the $2,500 to LPL.[3] ■

Revocation of Offers for Unilateral Contracts. A problem arises in unilateral contracts when the promisor attempts to *revoke* (cancel) the offer after the promisee has begun performance but before the act has been completed. ■ **EXAMPLE 11.5** Seiko offers to buy Jin's sailboat, moored in San Francisco, on delivery of the boat to Seiko's dock in Newport Beach, three hundred miles south of San Francisco. Jin rigs the boat and sets sail. Shortly before his arrival at Newport Beach, Jin receives a message from Seiko withdrawing her offer. Has the offer been terminated? ■

In contract law, offers are normally *revocable* (capable of being taken back, or canceled) until accepted. Thus, under the traditional view of unilateral contracts, Seiko's revocation would terminate the offer. Because Seiko's offer was to form a unilateral contract, only Jin's delivery of the sailboat at her dock would have been an acceptance.

Because of the harsh effect on the offeree of the revocation of an offer to form a unilateral contract, the modern-day view is different. Today, once performance has been *substantially* undertaken, the offeror cannot

revoke the offer. Thus, in *Example 11.5*, even though Jin has not yet accepted the offer by complete performance, Seiko is normally prohibited from revoking it. Jin can deliver the boat and bind Seiko to the contract.

Formal versus Informal Contracts Another classification system divides contracts into formal contracts and informal contracts. **Formal contracts** are contracts that require a special form or method of creation (formation) to be enforceable.[4] One example is *negotiable instruments,* which include checks, drafts, promissory notes, bills of exchange, and certificates of deposit. Negotiable instruments are formal contracts because, under the Uniform Commercial Code (UCC), a special form and language are required to create them.

Letters of credit, which are frequently used in international sales contracts, are another type of formal contract. Letters of credit are agreements to pay contingent on the purchaser's receipt of invoices and *bills of lading* (documents evidencing receipt of, and title to, goods shipped).

Informal contracts (also called *simple contracts*) include all other contracts. No special form is required (except for certain types of contracts that must be in writing), as the contracts are usually based on their substance rather than their form. Typically, businesspersons put their contracts in writing (including electronic records) to ensure that there is some proof of a contract's existence should disputes arise.

Express versus Implied Contracts Contracts may also be categorized as *express* or *implied.* In an **express contract,** the terms of the agreement are fully and explicitly stated in words, oral or written. A signed lease for an apartment or a house is an express written contract. If one classmate calls another on the phone and agrees to buy her textbooks from last semester for $200, an express oral contract has been made.

A contract that is implied from the conduct of the parties is called an **implied contract** (or sometimes an *implied-in-fact contract*). This type of contract differs from an express contract in that the conduct of the parties, rather than their words, creates and defines the terms of the contract.

Requirements for Implied Contracts. For an implied contract to arise, certain requirements must be met. Normally, if the following conditions exist, a court will hold that an implied contract was formed:

---

3. *Rogalski v. Little Poker League, LLC,* 2011 Wl 589636 (Minn.App. 2011).

4. See *Restatement (Second) of Contracts,* Section 6, which explains that formal contracts include (1) contracts under seal, (2) recognizances, (3) negotiable instruments, and (4) letters of credit.

1. The plaintiff furnished some service or property.
2. The plaintiff expected to be paid for that service or property, and the defendant knew or should have known that payment was expected.
3. The defendant had a chance to reject the services or property and did not.

■ **EXAMPLE 11.6** Alex, a small-business owner, needs an accountant to complete his tax return. He drops by a local accountant's office, explains his situation to the accountant, and learns what fees she charges. The next day, he returns and gives the receptionist all of the necessary documents to complete his return. Then he walks out without saying anything further to the accountant. In this situation, Alex has entered into an implied contract to pay the accountant the usual fees for her services. The contract is implied because of Alex's conduct and hers. She expects to be paid for completing the tax return, and by bringing in the records she will need to do the job, Alex has implied an intent to pay her. ■

Mixed Contracts with Express and Implied Terms.
Note that a contract may be a mixture of an express contract and an implied contract. In other words, a contract may contain some express terms and some implied terms. During the construction of a home, for instance, the homeowner often asks the builder to make changes in the original specifications.

■ **CASE IN POINT 11.7** Lamar Hopkins hired Uhrhahn Construction & Design, Inc., for several projects in building his home. For each project, the parties signed a written contract that was based on a cost estimate and specifications and that required changes to the agreement to be in writing. While the work was in progress, however, Hopkins repeatedly asked Uhrhahn to deviate from the contract specifications, which Uhrhahn did. None of these requests was made in writing.

One day, Hopkins asked Uhrhahn to use Durisol blocks instead of the cinder blocks specified in the original contract, indicating that the cost would be the same. Uhrhahn used the Durisol blocks but demanded extra payment when it became clear that the Durisol blocks were more complicated to install. Although Hopkins had paid for the other deviations from the contract that he had orally requested, he refused to pay Uhrhahn for the substitution of the Durisol blocks. Uhrhahn sued for breach of contract. The court found that Hopkins, through his conduct, had waived the provision requiring written contract modification and created an implied contract to pay the extra cost of installing the Durisol blocks.[5] ■

Among other implied terms, all contracts include an implied covenant of good faith and fair dealing. This implied term requires the parties to perform in accord with the contract and the parties' reasonable expectations under it. In the following case, the plaintiff claimed that the defendant had breached both the express terms of the parties' contract and the implied covenant of good faith and fair dealing.

5. *Uhrhahn Construction & Design, Inc. v. Hopkins*, 179 P.3d 808 (Utah App. 2008).

Case 11.2

Vukanovich v. Kine
Court of Appeals of Oregon, 268 Or.App. 623, 342 P.3d 1075 (2015).

Background and Facts Mark Vukanovich and Larry Kine agreed under a "Letter of Understanding" to work together to buy a certain parcel of real property in Eugene, Oregon, from Umpqua Bank. They expressly agreed to develop the property and to split the cost and profits equally. Vukanovich shared confidential financial information with Kine that he would not otherwise have shared. The bank agreed to accept $1.6 million for the property, and a closing date was set. Kine then said that he no longer wanted to pursue the deal with Vukanovich or to buy the property. The closing did not occur.

A month later, without Vukanovich's knowledge, Kine made a new offer to buy the property. At about the same time, Vukanovich made his own new offer. The bank accepted Kine's offer. Vukanovich filed a suit in an Oregon state court against Kine, alleging breach of contract. The jury returned a verdict in favor of Vukanovich, awarding him $686,000 on the breach of contract claim and other damages, but the court entered a judgment in favor of Kine. Vukanovich appealed.

In the Language of the Court
LAGESEN, J. [Judge]
　　* * * *

Case 11.2 Continues

Case 11.2 Continued

*** *Plaintiff's claim for breach of contract was predicated [based] on the theory that defendant breached both the express terms of the parties' "Letter of Understanding" and the implied covenant of good faith and fair dealing, damaging plaintiff by cutting plaintiff * * * out of an ownership interest in the property and the profits generated by the property.* [Emphasis added.]

*** Based on the evidence presented at trial, the jury could permissibly find that plaintiff and defendant entered into a contract to buy the property together and that defendant breached the express terms of that contract when, after the bank accepted the parties' joint offer to purchase the property * * *, defendant refused to close on the purchase and subsequently repudiated [renounced] the contract, even though defendant had the capacity to close the agreed upon * * * purchase of the property. The jury also could permissibly find that defendant lied to plaintiff about the reasons for not closing the * * * purchase of the property from the bank and used confidential information provided by plaintiff to develop a more lucrative plan for the property that cut out plaintiff, thereby breaching the implied covenant of good faith and fair dealing. Finally, the jury could find that defendant's breaches damaged plaintiff—that, but for those breaches, the * * * purchase would have been completed, and plaintiff would have been a part owner of the property and would have been entitled to a share of the profits that the property was expected to earn.

*** Defendant argues that * * * after the agreement was undisputedly terminated * * *, both plaintiff and defendant made separate attempts to purchase the property. Defendant contends that his efforts to purchase the property after the contract was terminated could not constitute a breach of the parties' contract because, at that point in time, both parties understood that the agreement was over and were engaging in similar conduct.

The problem with defendant's argument is that plaintiff ultimately did not predicate his breach of contract claim on defendant's conduct of purchasing the property separately from plaintiff. Although the complaint identified defendant's separate purchase of the property as "among" the breaches committed by defendant, plaintiff's focus at trial * * * was on * * * defendant's refusal to complete the purchase of the property with plaintiff, his surreptitious [secret] use of the information that plaintiff had provided him to devise a more favorable transaction for himself * * *, and his lies to plaintiff about his reasons for not closing the deal. It is the evidence of that conduct, not the evidence of defendant's conduct following the termination of the contract, that permits the finding that defendant breached the parties' contract, damaging plaintiff by causing the planned * * * purchase of the property to fail.

Decision and Remedy *A state intermediate appellate court reinstated the jury verdict. The court ruled that there was sufficient evidence to permit the jury to find that Kine had "breached both the express terms of the parties' Letter of Understanding and the implied covenant of good faith and fair dealing."*

Critical Thinking

- **Economic** *What did the amount of the jury's award of $686,000 in damages represent? Explain.*

11–3b Contract Performance

Contracts are also classified according to the degree to which they have been performed. A contract that has been fully performed on both sides is called an **executed contract.** A contract that has not been fully performed by the parties is called an **executory contract.** If one party has fully performed but the other has not, the contract is said to be executed on the one side and executory on the other, but the contract is still classified as executory.

■ **EXAMPLE 11.8** Jackson, Inc., agreed to buy ten tons of coal from the Northern Coal Company. Northern delivered the coal to Jackson's steel mill, where it is being burned. At this point, the contract is executed on the part of Northern and executory on Jackson's part. After Jackson pays Northern, the contract will be executed on both sides. ■

11–3c Contract Enforceability

A **valid contract** has the elements necessary to entitle at least one of the parties to enforce it in court. Those elements, as mentioned earlier, consist of (1) an agreement (offer and acceptance), (2) supported by legally sufficient consideration, (3) made by parties who have the legal capacity to enter into the contract, and (4) a legal purpose.

As you can see in Exhibit 11–2, valid contracts may be enforceable, voidable, or unenforceable. Additionally, a contract may be referred to as a *void contract*. We look next at the meaning of the terms *voidable, unenforceable,* and *void* in relation to contract enforceability.

Voidable Contracts A **voidable contract** is a valid contract but one that can be avoided at the option of one or both of the parties. The party having the option can elect either to avoid any duty to perform or to *ratify* (make valid) the contract. If the contract is avoided, both parties are released from it. If it is ratified, both parties must fully perform their respective legal obligations.

For instance, contracts made by minors generally are voidable at the option of the minor (with certain exceptions). Contracts made by mentally incompetent persons and intoxicated persons may also be voidable. Additionally, contracts entered into under fraudulent conditions are voidable at the option of the defrauded party. Contracts entered into under legally defined duress or undue influence are also voidable.

Unenforceable Contracts An **unenforceable contract** is one that cannot be enforced because of certain legal defenses against it. It is not unenforceable because a party failed to satisfy a legal requirement of the contract. Rather, it is a valid contract rendered unenforceable by some statute or law. For instance, certain contracts must be in writing, and if they are not, they will not be enforceable except in certain exceptional circumstances.

Void Contracts A **void contract** is no contract at all. The terms *void* and *contract* are contradictory. None of the parties have any legal obligations if a contract is void. A contract can be void because one of the parties was determined by a court to be mentally incompetent, for instance, or because the purpose of the contract was illegal.

To review the various types of contracts, see Concept Summary 11.1.

11–4 Quasi Contracts

Express contracts and implied contracts are actual or true contracts formed by the words or actions of the parties. **Quasi contracts,** or contracts *implied in law,* are not actual contracts. Rather, they are fictional contracts that courts can impose on the parties "as if" the parties had entered into an actual contract. (The word *quasi* is Latin for "as if.")

Quasi contracts are equitable rather than legal contracts. Usually, they are imposed to avoid the *unjust enrichment* of one party at the expense of another. The doctrine of unjust enrichment is based on the theory that individuals should not be allowed to profit or enrich themselves inequitably at the expense of others.

EXHIBIT 11–2 Enforceable, Voidable, Unenforceable, and Void Contracts

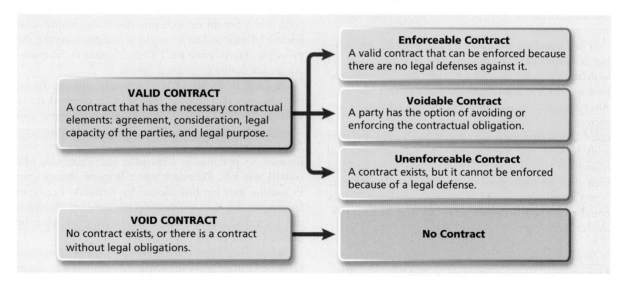

VALID CONTRACT
A contract that has the necessary contractual elements: agreement, consideration, legal capacity of the parties, and legal purpose.

Enforceable Contract
A valid contract that can be enforced because there are no legal defenses against it.

Voidable Contract
A party has the option of avoiding or enforcing the contractual obligation.

Unenforceable Contract
A contract exists, but it cannot be enforced because of a legal defense.

VOID CONTRACT
No contract exists, or there is a contract without legal obligations.

No Contract

Concept Summary 11.1

Types of Contracts

Formation	• *Bilateral*—A promise for a promise. • *Unilateral*—A promise for an act—that is, acceptance is the completed performance of the act. • *Formal*—Requires a special form for creation. • *Informal*—Requires no special form for creation. • *Express*—Formed by words, such as oral, written, or a combination. • *Implied*—Formed by the conduct of the parties.
Performance	• *Executed*—A fully performed contract. • *Executory*—A contract not fully performed.
Enforceability	• *Valid*—The contract has the necessary contractual elements: agreement (offer and acceptance), consideration, legal capacity of the parties, and legal purpose. • *Voidable*—One party has the option of avoiding or enforcing the contractual obligation. • *Unenforceable*—A contract exists, but it cannot be enforced because of a legal defense. • *Void*—No contract exists, or there is a contract without legal obligations.

■ **CASE IN POINT 11.9** Seawest Services Association operated a water distribution system that served homes inside a housing development (full members) and some homes located outside the subdivision (limited members). Both full and limited members paid water bills and assessments for work performed on the water system when necessary.

The Copenhavers purchased a home outside the housing development. They did not have an express contract with Seawest, but they paid water bills for eight years and paid one $3,950 assessment for water system upgrades. After a dispute arose, the Copenhavers refused to pay their water bills and assessments. Seawest sued. The court found that the Copenhavers had a quasi contract with Seawest and were liable. The Copenhavers had enjoyed the benefits of Seawest's water services and had even paid for them prior to their dispute. In addition, "the Copenhavers would be unjustly enriched if they could retain benefits provided by Seawest without paying for them."[6] ■

11–4a Limitations on Quasi-Contractual Recovery

Although quasi contracts exist to prevent unjust enrichment, the party obtaining the enrichment is not held liable in some situations. In general, a party who has conferred a benefit on someone else unnecessarily or as a result of misconduct or negligence cannot invoke the principle of quasi contract. The enrichment in those situations will not be considered "unjust."

■ **CASE IN POINT 11.10** Michael Plambeck owned two chiropractic clinics in Kentucky that treated many patients injured in car accidents, including some who were customers of State Farm Automobile Insurance Company. All of the clinics' treating chiropractors were licensed to practice in Kentucky, but Plambeck (the owner) was not. Plambeck was a licensed chiropractor in another state but had allowed his Kentucky license to lapse because he was not treating any patients. Plambeck did not realize that Kentucky state law required him to be licensed as the owner of the clinics.

When State Farm discovered that Plambeck was not licensed in Kentucky, it filed a suit against the clinics

---

6. *Seawest Services Association v. Copenhaver*, 166 Wash.App. 1006 (2012).

seeking to recover payments it had made on behalf of its customers. The trial court awarded State Farm $577,124 in damages for unjust enrichment, but the appellate court reversed. The court reasoned that State Farm had a legal duty to pay for the chiropractic treatment of its customers and could not avoid paying for the services because the clinics' owner was not licensed. The payments did not constitute unjust enrichment, because the patients had, in fact, received treatment by licensed chiropractors.[7] ■

11–4b When an Actual Contract Exists

The doctrine of quasi contract generally cannot be used when there is an *actual contract* that covers the matter in controversy. A remedy already exists if a party is unjustly enriched as a result of a breach of contract: the non-breaching party can sue the breaching party for breach of contract.

■ **EXAMPLE 11.11** Fung contracts with Cameron to deliver a furnace to a building owned by Grant. Fung delivers the furnace, but Cameron never pays Fung. Grant has been unjustly enriched in this situation, to be sure. Fung, however, cannot recover from Grant in quasi contract, because Fung had an actual contract with Cameron. Fung already has a remedy—he can sue for breach of contract to recover the price of the furnace from Cameron. The court does not need to impose a quasi contract in this situation to achieve justice. ■

---

7. *State Farm Automobile Insurance Co. v. Newburg Chiropractic, P.S.C.*, 741 F.3d 661 (6th Cir. 2013).

11–5 Interpretation of Contracts

Sometimes, parties agree that a contract has been formed but disagree on its meaning or legal effect. One reason this may happen is that one of the parties is not familiar with the legal terminology used in the contract. To an extent, *plain language* laws (enacted by the federal government and a majority of the states) have helped to avoid this difficulty. Sometimes, though, a dispute may arise over the meaning of a contract simply because the rights or obligations under the contract are not expressed clearly—no matter how "plain" the language used.

In this section, we look at some common law rules of contract interpretation. These rules, which have evolved over time, provide the courts with guidelines for deciding disputes over how contract terms or provisions should be interpreted. Exhibit 11–3 provides a brief graphic summary of how these rules are applied.

11–5a The Plain Meaning Rule

When a contract's writing is clear and unequivocal, a court will enforce it according to its obvious terms. The meaning of the terms must be determined from the *face of the instrument*—from the written document alone. This is sometimes referred to as the *plain meaning rule*. The words—and their plain, ordinary meaning—determine the intent of the parties at the time that they entered into the contract. A court is bound to give effect to the contract according to this intent.

EXHIBIT 11–3 Rules of Contract Interpretation

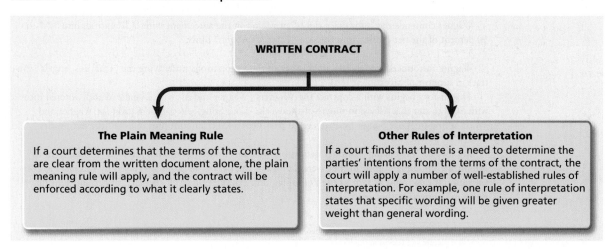

WRITTEN CONTRACT

The Plain Meaning Rule
If a court determines that the terms of the contract are clear from the written document alone, the plain meaning rule will apply, and the contract will be enforced according to what it clearly states.

Other Rules of Interpretation
If a court finds that there is a need to determine the parties' intentions from the terms of the contract, the court will apply a number of well-established rules of interpretation. For example, one rule of interpretation states that specific wording will be given greater weight than general wording.

Ambiguity A court will consider a contract to be unclear, or ambiguous, in the following situations:

1. When the intent of the parties cannot be determined from the contract's language.
2. When the contract lacks a provision on a disputed term.
3. When a term is susceptible to more than one interpretation.
4. When there is uncertainty about a provision.

Extrinsic Evidence If a contract term is ambiguous, a court may interpret the ambiguity against the party who drafted the term. The court may also consider *extrinsic evidence* when a term is ambiguous. **Extrinsic evidence** is any evidence not contained in the document itself—such as the testimony of parties and witnesses, additional agreements or communications, or other relevant information.

The admissibility of extrinsic evidence can significantly affect the court's interpretation of ambiguous contractual provisions and thus the outcome of litigation. When a contract is clear and unambiguous, a court cannot consider extrinsic evidence. The following case illustrates these points.

Spotlight on Columbia Pictures

Case 11.3 Wagner v. Columbia Pictures Industries, Inc.
California Court of Appeal, Second District, 146 Cal.App.4th 586, 52 Cal.Rptr.3d 898 (2007).

Background and Facts Actor Robert Wagner entered into an agreement with Spelling-Goldberg Productions (SGP) "relating to *Charlie's Angels* (herein called the 'series')." The contract entitled Wagner to 50 percent of the net profits that SGP received from broadcasting the series and from all ancillary, music, and subsidiary rights in connection with the series. SGP hired Ivan Goff and Ben Roberts to write the series, under a contract subject to the Writers Guild of America Minimum Basic Agreement (MBA).[a] The MBA stipulates that the writer of a television show retains the right to make and market films based on the material, subject to the producer's right to buy this right if the writer decides to sell it within five years.

The first *Charlie's Angels* episode aired in 1976. In 1982, SGP sold its rights to the series to Columbia Pictures Industries, Inc. Thirteen years later, Columbia bought the movie rights to the material from Goff's and Roberts's heirs. In 2000 and 2003, Columbia produced and distributed two *Charlie's Angels* films. Wagner filed a suit in a California state court against Columbia, claiming a share of the profits from the films. The court granted Columbia's motion for summary judgment. Wagner appealed to a state intermediate appellate court.

In the Language of the Court
JOHNSON, Acting P.J. [Presiding Judge]
    * * * *

Wagner contends the "subsidiary rights" provision in the agreement with SGP entitles him * * * to 50 percent of the net profits from the two "Charlie's Angels" films.
    * * * *

Wagner introduced evidence of the history of the negotiations underlying the "Charlie's Angels" contract in support of his [contention].

This history begins with a contract the Wagners [Wagner and his wife, Natalie Wood] entered into with SGP to star in a television movie-of-the-week, "Love Song." As compensation for Wagner and Wood acting in "Love Song," SGP agreed to pay them a fixed amount plus one-half the net profits * * * .
    * * * *

In the * * * "Love Song" contract net profits were not limited to monies received "for the right to exhibit the Photoplay." Instead they were defined as the net of "all monies received by Producer as consideration for the right to exhibit the Photoplay, and exploitation of all ancillary, music and subsidiary rights in connection therewith."
    * * * *

---

a. The Writers Guild of America is an association of screen and television writers that negotiates industry-wide agreements with motion picture and television producers.

Case 11.3 Continued

Wagner's argument is simple and straightforward. The net profits provision in the "Love Song" agreement was intended to give the Wagners a one-half share in the net profits received by SGP "from all sources" without limitation as to source or time. The "Charlie's Angels" agreement was based on the "Love Song" agreement and defines net profits in identical language. Therefore, the "Charlie's Angels" agreement should also be interpreted as providing the Wagners with a 50 percent share in SGP's income "from all sources" without limitation as to source or time. Since Columbia admits it stands in SGP's shoes with respect to SGP's obligations under the "Charlie's Angels" agreement, Columbia is obligated to pay Wagner * * * 50 percent of the net profits derived from the "Charlie's Angels" movies.
* * * *

The problem with Wagner's extrinsic evidence is that it does not explain the ["Charlie's Angels"] contract language, it contradicts it. *Under the parol evidence rule,*[b] *extrinsic evidence is not admissible to contradict express terms in a written contract or to explain what the agreement was. The agreement is the writing itself. Parol evidence cannot be admitted to show intention independent of an unambiguous written instrument.* [Emphasis added.]

Even if the Wagners and SGP intended the Wagners would share in the net profits "from any and all sources" they did not say so in their contract. What they said in their contract was the Wagners would share in "all monies actually received by Producer, as consideration for the right to exhibit photoplays of the series, and from the exploitation of all ancillary, music and subsidiary rights in connection therewith." For a right to be "subsidiary" or "ancillary," meaning supplementary or subordinate, there must be a primary right to which it relates. The only primary right mentioned in the contract is "the right to exhibit photoplays of the series." Thus the Wagners were entitled to share in the profits from the exploitation of the movie rights to "Charlie's Angels" if those rights were exploited by Columbia as ancillary or subsidiary rights of its primary "right to exhibit photoplays of the series" but not if those rights were acquired by Columbia independently from its right to exhibit photoplays.

Decision and Remedy *The state intermediate appellate court affirmed the lower court's summary judgment in favor of Columbia. The contract "unambiguously" stated the conditions under which the parties were to share the films' profits, and those conditions had not occurred.*

Critical Thinking
- **What If the Facts Were Different?** *How might the result in this case have been different if the court had admitted Wagner's evidence of the* Love Song *contract?*
- **Legal Environment** *Under what circumstances would Wagner have been entitled to a share of the profits from the* Charlie's Angels *movies even though the evidence of the* Love Song *contract was irrelevant?*

---

b. The *parol evidence rule* prohibits the parties from introducing in court evidence of an oral agreement that contradicts the written terms of a contract.

11–5b Other Rules of Interpretation

Generally, a court will interpret the language to give effect to the parties' intent as *expressed in their contract*. This is the primary purpose of the rules of interpretation—to determine the parties' intent from the language used in their agreement and to give effect to that intent. A court normally will not make or remake a contract, nor will it interpret the language according to what the parties *claim* their intent was when they made it.

Rules the Courts Use The courts use the following rules in interpreting contractual terms:

1. As far as possible, a reasonable, lawful, and effective meaning will be given to all of a contract's terms.
2. A contract will be interpreted as a whole. Individual, specific clauses will be considered subordinate to the contract's general intent. All writings that are a part of the same transaction will be interpreted together.
3. Terms that were the subject of separate negotiation will be given greater consideration than standardized terms and terms that were not negotiated separately.
4. A word will be given its ordinary, commonly accepted meaning, and a technical word or term will be given its technical meaning, unless the parties clearly intended something else.

5. Specific and exact wording will be given greater consideration than general language.
6. Written or typewritten terms will prevail over preprinted ones.
7. Because a contract should be drafted in clear and unambiguous language, a party who uses ambiguous expressions is held to be responsible for the ambiguities. Thus, when the language has more than one meaning, it will be interpreted against the party who drafted the contract.
8. Evidence of *usage of trade, course of dealing,* and *course of performance* may be admitted to clarify the meaning of an ambiguously worded contract. (We will define and discuss these terms in a later chapter.)

Express Terms Usually Given the Most Weight

Express terms (terms expressly stated in the contract) are given the greatest weight, followed by course of performance, course of dealing, and custom and usage of trade—in that order. When considering custom and usage, a court will look at the trade customs and usage common to the particular business or industry and to the locale in which the contract was made or is to be performed.

■ **CASE IN POINT 11.12**   Jessica Robbins bought a house in Tennessee. U.S. Bank financed the purchase, and Tennessee Farmers Mutual Insurance Company issued the homeowner's insurance policy. The policy included a clause that promised payment to the bank for losses unless the loss was due to an "increase in hazard" about which the bank knew but did not tell the insurer. When Robbins fell behind on her mortgage payments, the bank started foreclosure proceedings. No one told the insurer. Robbins filed for bankruptcy, which postponed foreclosure.

Meanwhile, the house was destroyed in a fire. The bank filed a claim under the policy, but the insurer refused to pay because it had not been told by the bank of an "increase in hazard"—the foreclosure. The bank then filed a lawsuit. The court found that the plain meaning of the words "increase in hazard" in the policy referred to physical conditions on the property that posed a risk, not to events such as foreclosure. Thus, the bank was not required to notify the insurer under the terms of the policy, and the lack of notice did not invalidate the coverage.[8] ■

---

8. *U.S. Bank, N.A. v. Tennessee Farmers Mutual Insurance Co.,* 277 S.W.3d 381 (Tenn.Sup.Ct. 2009).

Reviewing: Nature and Terminology

Mitsui Bank hired Ross Duncan as a branch manager in one of its Southern California locations. At that time, Duncan received an employee handbook informing him that Mitsui would review his performance and salary level annually. In 2016, Mitsui decided to create a new lending program to help financially troubled businesses stay afloat. It hired Duncan to be the credit development officer (CDO) and gave him a written compensation plan. Duncan's compensation was to be based on the program's success and involved a bonus and commissions based on the volume of new loans and sales. The written plan also stated, "This compensation plan will be reviewed and potentially amended after one year and will be subject to such review and amendment annually thereafter."

Duncan's efforts as CDO were successful, and the program he developed grew to represent 25 percent of Mitsui's business in 2016 and 40 percent in 2017. Nevertheless, Mitsui refused to give Duncan a raise in 2016. Mitsui also amended his compensation plan to significantly reduce his compensation and to change his performance evaluation schedule to every six months. When he had still not received a raise by 2018, Duncan resigned as CDO and filed a lawsuit alleging breach of contract. Using the information presented in the chapter, answer the following questions.

1. What are the four requirements of a valid contract?
2. Did Duncan have a valid contract with Mitsui for employment as CDO? If so, was it a bilateral or a unilateral contract?
3. What are the requirements of an implied contract?
4. Can Duncan establish an implied contract based on the employment manual or the written compensation plan? Why or why not?

Debate This . . .   *Companies should be able to make or break employment contracts whenever and however they wish.*

Terms and Concepts

Issue Spotters

1. Dyna tells Ed that she will pay him $1,000 to set fire to her store so that she can collect under a fire insurance policy. Ed sets fire to the store, but Dyna refuses to pay. Can Ed recover? Why or why not? (See *Elements of a Contract*.)

2. Alison receives a notice of property taxes due from a local tax collector. The notice is for tax on Jerry's property, but Alison believes that the tax is on her property and pays it. Can Alison recover from Jerry the amount that she paid? Why or why not? (See *Quasi Contracts*.)

• **Check your answers to the Issue Spotters against the answers provided in Appendix D at the end of this text.**

Business Scenarios

11–1. Unilateral Contract. Rocky Mountain Races, Inc., sponsors the "Pioneer Trail Ultramarathon," with an advertised first prize of $10,000. The rules require the competitors to run 100 miles from the floor of Blackwater Canyon to the top of Pinnacle Mountain. The rules also provide that Rocky reserves the right to change the terms of the race at any time. Monica enters the race and is declared the winner. Rocky offers her a prize of $1,000 instead of $10,000. Did Rocky and Monica have a contract? Explain. (See *Types of Contracts*.)

11–2. Implied Contract. Janine was hospitalized with severe abdominal pain and placed in an intensive care unit. Her doctor told the hospital personnel to order around-the-clock nursing care for Janine. At the hospital's request, a nursing services firm, Nursing Services Unlimited, provided two weeks of in-hospital care and, after Janine was sent home, an additional two weeks of at-home care. During the at-home period of care, Janine was fully aware that she was receiving the benefit of the nursing services. Nursing Services later billed Janine $4,000 for the nursing care, but Janine refused to pay on the ground that she had never contracted for the services, either orally or in writing. In view of the fact that no express contract was ever formed, can Nursing Services recover the $4,000 from Janine? If so, under what legal theory? Discuss. (See *Types of Contracts*.)

Business Case Problems

11–3. Spotlight on Taco Bell—Implied Contract.

Thomas Rinks and Joseph Shields developed Psycho Chihuahua, a caricature of a Chihuahua dog with a "do-not-back-down" attitude. They promoted and marketed the character through their company, Wrench, L.L.C. Ed Alfaro and Rudy Pollak, representatives of Taco Bell Corp., learned of Psycho Chihuahua and met with Rinks and Shields to talk about using the character as a Taco Bell "icon." Wrench sent artwork, merchandise, and marketing ideas to Alfaro, who promoted the character within Taco Bell. Alfaro asked Wrench to propose terms for Taco Bell's use of Psycho Chihuahua. Taco Bell did not accept Wrench's terms, but Alfaro continued to promote the character within the company.

Meanwhile, Taco Bell hired a new advertising agency, which proposed an advertising campaign involving a Chihuahua. When Alfaro learned of this proposal, he sent the Psycho Chihuahua materials to the agency. Taco Bell made a Chihuahua the focus of its marketing but paid nothing to Wrench. Wrench filed a suit against Taco Bell in a federal court claiming that it had an implied contract with Taco Bell and that Taco Bell breached that contract. Do these facts satisfy the requirements for an implied contract? Why or why not? [*Wrench, L.L.C. v. Taco Bell Corp.*, 256 F.3d 446 (6th Cir. 2001), *cert.* denied, 534 U.S. 1114, 122 S.Ct. 921, 151 L.Ed.2d 805 (2002)] (See *Types of Contracts*.)

11–4. Business Case Problem with Sample Answer— Quasi Contract. Robert Gutkowski, a sports marketing

expert, met numerous times with George Steinbrenner, the owner of the New York Yankees, to discuss the Yankees Entertainment and Sports Network (YES). Gutkowski was paid as a consultant. Later, he filed a suit, seeking an ownership share in YES. There was no written contract for the share, but he claimed that there were discussions about his being a part owner. Does Gutkowski have a valid claim for payment? Discuss. [*Gutkowski v. Steinbrenner,* 680 F.Supp.2d 602 (S.D.N.Y. 2010)] (See *Quasi Contracts.*)

- **For a sample answer to Problem 11–4, go to Appendix E at the end of this text.**

11–5. Quasi Contract. Kim Panenka asked to borrow $4,750 from her sister, Kris, to make a mortgage payment. Kris deposited a check for that amount into Kim's bank account. Hours later, Kim asked to borrow another $1,100. Kris took a cash advance on her credit card and deposited this amount into Kim's account. When Kim did not repay the amounts, Kris filed a suit, arguing that she had "loaned" Kim the money. Can the court impose a contract between the sisters? Explain. [*Panenka v. Panenka,* 331 Wis.2d 731, 795 N.W.2d 493 (2011)] (See *Quasi Contracts.*)

11–6. Implied Contracts. Ralph Ramsey insured his car with Allstate Insurance Co. He also owned a house on which he maintained a homeowner's insurance policy with Allstate. Bank of America had a mortgage on the house and paid the insurance premiums on the homeowner's policy from Ralph's account. After Ralph died, Allstate canceled the car insurance. Ralph's son Douglas inherited the house. The bank continued to pay the premiums on the homeowner's policy, but from Douglas's account, and Allstate continued to renew the insurance. When a fire destroyed the house, Allstate denied coverage, however, claiming that the policy was still in Ralph's name. Douglas filed a suit in a federal district court against the insurer. Was Allstate liable under the homeowner's policy? Explain. [*Ramsey v. Allstate Insurance Co.,* 514 Fed.Appx. 554 (6th Cir. 2013)] (See *Types of Contracts.*)

11–7. Quasi Contracts. Lawrence M. Clarke, Inc., was the general contractor for construction of a portion of a sanitary sewer system in Billings, Michigan. Clarke accepted Kim Draeger's proposal to do the work for a certain price. Draeger arranged with two subcontractors to work on the project. The work provided by Draeger and the subcontractors proved unsatisfactory. All of the work fell under Draeger's contract with Clarke. Clarke filed a suit in a Michigan state court against Draeger, seeking to recover damages on a theory of quasi contract. The court awarded Clarke $900,000 in damages on that theory. A state intermediate appellate court reversed this award. Why? [*Lawrence M. Clarke, Inc. v. Draeger,* 2015 WL 205182 (Mich.App. 2015)] (See *Quasi Contracts.*)

11–8. Interpretation of Contracts. Lehman Brothers, Inc. (LBI), wrote a letter to Mary Ortegón offering her employment as LBI's "Business Chief Administrative Officer in Its Fixed Income Division." The offer included a salary of $150,000 per year and an annual "minimum bonus" of $350,000. The letter stated that the bonus would be paid unless Ortegón resigned or was terminated for certain causes. In other words, the bonus was not a "signing" bonus—it was clearly tied to her performance on the job. Ortegón accepted the offer. Before she started work, however, LBI rescinded it. Later, LBI filed for bankruptcy in a federal court. Ortegón filed a claim with the court for the amount of the bonus on the ground that LBI had breached its contract with her by not paying it. Can extrinsic evidence be admitted to interpret the meaning of the bonus term? Explain. [*Ortegón v. Giddens,* __ F.3d __, 2016 WL 125268 (2d Cir. 2016)] (See *Interpretation of Contracts.*)

11–9. A Question of Ethics—Unilateral Contracts.
 *International Business Machines Corp. (IBM) hired Niels Jensen in 2000 as a software sales representative. According to the brochure on IBM's "Sales Incentive Plan" (SIP), "the more you sell, the more earnings for you." But "the SIP program does not constitute a promise by IBM. IBM reserves the right to modify the program at any time." Jensen was given a "quota letter" that said he would be paid $75,000 as a base salary and, if he attained his quota, an additional $75,000 as incentive pay. Jensen closed a deal worth more than $24 million to IBM. When IBM paid him less than $500,000 as a commission, Jensen filed a suit. He argued that the SIP was a unilateral offer that became a binding contract when he closed the sale. [*Jensen v. International Business Machines Corp., 454 F.3d 382 (4th Cir. 2006)]* (See *Types of Contracts.*)

(a) Would it be fair to the employer for the court to hold that the SIP brochure and the quota letter created a unilateral contract if IBM did not *intend* to create such a contract? Would it be fair to the employee to hold that *no* contract was created? Explain.

(b) The "Sales Incentives" section of IBM's brochure included a clause providing that "management will decide if an adjustment to the payment is appropriate" when an employee closes a large transaction. Does this affect your answers to the questions above? From an ethical perspective, would it be fair to hold that a contract exists despite these statements? Why or why not?

Legal Reasoning Group Activity

11–10. Contracts. Review the basic requirements for a valid contract listed at the beginning of this chapter. Now consider the relationship created when a student enrolls in a college or university. (See *Elements of a Contract.*)

(a) One group should analyze and discuss whether a contract has been formed between the student and the college or university.

(b) A second group should assume that there is a contract and explain whether it is bilateral or unilateral.

Agreement in Traditional and E-Contracts

ontract law developed over time to meet society's need to know with certainty what kinds of promises, or contracts, will be enforced and the point at which a valid and binding contract is formed. For a contract to be considered valid and enforceable, four basic requirements—agreement, consideration, contractual capacity, and legality—must be met. In this chapter, we look closely at the first of these requirements, *agreement*.

Agreement is required to form a contract, whether it is formed in the traditional way (on paper) or online.

In today's world, many contracts are formed via the Internet. We discuss online offers and acceptances and examine some laws that have been created to apply to electronic contracts, or *e-contracts*, in the latter part of this chapter.

12–1 Agreement

An essential element for contract formation is **agreement**—the parties must agree on the terms of the contract and manifest to each other their *mutual assent* (agreement) to the same bargain. Ordinarily, agreement is evidenced by two events: an *offer* and an *acceptance*. One party offers a certain bargain to another party, who then accepts that bargain.

An agreement does not necessarily have to be in writing. Both parties, however, must manifest their assent, or voluntary consent, to the same bargain. Once an agreement is reached, if the other elements of a contract (consideration, capacity, and legality—discussed in subsequent chapters) are present, a valid contract is formed. Generally, the contract creates enforceable rights and duties between the parties.

Because words often fail to convey the precise meaning intended, the law of contracts generally adheres to the *objective theory of contracts*. Under this theory, a party's words and conduct are held to mean whatever a reasonable person in the offeree's position would think they meant.

12–1a Requirements of the Offer

An **offer** is a promise or commitment to do or refrain from doing some specified action in the future. The party making an offer is called the *offeror*, and the party to whom the offer is made is called the *offeree*. Under the common law, three elements are necessary for an offer to be effective:

1. The offeror must have a serious intention to become bound by the offer.
2. The terms of the offer must be reasonably certain, or definite, so that the parties and the court can ascertain the terms of the contract.
3. The offer must be communicated to the offeree.

Once an effective offer has been made, the offeree's acceptance of that offer creates a legally binding contract (providing the other essential elements for a valid and enforceable contract are present).

Intention The first requirement for an effective offer is a serious intent on the part of the offeror. Serious intent is not determined by the subjective intentions, beliefs, and assumptions of the offeror. Rather, it is determined by what a reasonable person in the offeree's position would conclude that the offeror's words and actions meant. Offers made in obvious anger, jest, or undue excitement do not meet the serious-and-objective-intent test. A reasonable person would realize that such offers were not made seriously. Because these offers are not effective, an offeree's acceptance does not create an agreement.

■ **EXAMPLE 12.1** Linda and Dena ride to school each day in Dena's new automobile, which has a market value of $20,000. One cold morning, they get into the car, but the car will not start. Dena yells in anger, "I'll sell this car to anyone for $500!" Linda drops $500 on Dena's lap. A reasonable person—taking into consideration Dena's frustration and the obvious difference in value between the market price of the car and the proposed purchase price—would realize that Dena's offer was not made with serious and objective intent. No agreement is formed. ■

In the classic case presented next, the court considered whether an offer made "after a few drinks" met the serious-and-objective-intent requirement.

Classic Case 12.1

Lucy v. Zehmer

Supreme Court of Appeals of Virginia, 196 Va. 493, 84 S.E.2d 516 (1954).

Background and Facts   W. O. Lucy, the plaintiff, filed a suit against A. H. and Ida Zehmer, the defendants, to compel the Zehmers to transfer title of their property, known as the Ferguson Farm, to the Lucys (W. O. and his wife) for $50,000, as the Zehmers had allegedly agreed to do. Lucy had known A. H. Zehmer for fifteen or twenty years and for the last eight years or so had been anxious to buy the Ferguson Farm from him. One night, Lucy stopped to visit the Zehmers in the combination restaurant, filling station, and motor court they operated. While there, Lucy tried to buy the Ferguson Farm once again. This time he tried a new approach. According to the trial court transcript, Lucy said to Zehmer, "I bet you wouldn't take $50,000 for that place." Zehmer replied, "Yes, I would too; you wouldn't give fifty." Throughout the evening, the conversation returned to the sale of the Ferguson Farm for $50,000. All the while, the men continued to drink whiskey and engage in light conversation.

Eventually, Lucy enticed Zehmer to write up an agreement to the effect that the Zehmers would sell the Ferguson Farm to Lucy for $50,000 complete. Later, Lucy sued Zehmer to compel him to go through with the sale. Zehmer argued that he had been drunk and that the offer had been made in jest and hence was unenforceable. The trial court agreed with Zehmer, and Lucy appealed.

In the Language of the Court
BUCHANAN, J. [Justice] delivered the opinion of the court.
* * * *

In his testimony, Zehmer claimed that he "was high as a Georgia pine," and that the transaction "was just a bunch of two doggoned drunks bluffing to see who could talk the biggest and say the most." That claim is inconsistent with his attempt to testify in great detail as to what was said and what was done.
* * * *

The appearance of the contract, the fact that it was under discussion for forty minutes or more before it was signed; Lucy's objection to the first draft because it was written in the singular, and he wanted Mrs. Zehmer to sign it also; the rewriting to meet that objection and the signing by Mrs. Zehmer; the discussion of what was to be included in the sale, the provision for the examination of the title, the completeness of the instrument that was executed, the taking possession of it by Lucy with no request or suggestion by either of the defendants that he give it back, are facts which furnish persuasive evidence that the execution of the contract was a serious business transaction rather than a casual, jesting matter as defendants now contend.
* * * *

In the field of contracts, as generally elsewhere, *we must look to the outward expression of a person as manifesting his intention rather than to his secret and unexpressed intention.* The law imputes to a person an intention corresponding to the reasonable meaning of his words and acts. [Emphasis added.]
* * * *

Whether the writing signed by the defendants and now sought to be enforced by the complainants was the result of a serious offer by Lucy and a serious acceptance by the defendants, or was a serious offer by Lucy and an acceptance in secret jest by the defendants, in either event it constituted a binding contract of sale between the parties.

Case 12.1 Continued

Decision and Remedy *The Supreme Court of Appeals of Virginia determined that the writing was an enforceable contract and reversed the ruling of the lower court. The Zehmers were required by court order to follow through with the sale of the Ferguson Farm to the Lucys.*

Impact of This Case on Today's Law *This is a classic case in contract law because it illustrates so clearly the objective theory of contracts with respect to determining whether a serious offer was intended. Today, the courts continue to apply the objective theory of contracts and routinely cite* Lucy v. Zehmer *as a significant precedent in this area.*

Critical Thinking
- **What If the Facts Were Different?** *Suppose that the day after Lucy signed the purchase agreement, he decided that he did not want the farm after all, and Zehmer sued Lucy to perform the contract. Would this change in the facts alter the court's decision that Lucy and Zehmer had created an enforceable contract? Why or why not?*

Situations in Which Intent May Be Lacking

The concept of intention can be further clarified by looking at statements that are *not* offers and situations in which the parties' intent to be bound might be questionable.

1. *Expressions of opinion.* An expression of opinion is not an offer. It does not indicate an intention to enter into a binding agreement.
2. *Statements of future intent.* A statement of an intention to do something in the future (such as "I plan to sell my Verizon stock") is not an offer.
3. *Preliminary negotiations.* A request or invitation to negotiate is not an offer. It only expresses a willingness to discuss the possibility of entering into a contract. Statements such as "Will you sell your farm?" or "I wouldn't sell my car for less than $8,000" are examples.
4. *Invitations to bid.* When a government entity or private firm needs to have construction work done, contractors are invited to submit bids. The invitation to submit bids is not an offer. The bids that contractors submit are offers, however, and the government entity or private firm can bind the contractor by accepting the bid.
5. *Advertisements and price lists.* In general, representations made in advertisements and price lists are treated not as offers to contract but as invitations to negotiate.[1]
6. *Live and online auctions.* In a live auction, a seller "offers" goods for sale through an auctioneer, but this is not an offer to form a contract. Rather, it is an invitation asking bidders to submit offers. In the context of an auction, a bidder is the offeror, and the auctioneer is the offeree. The offer is accepted when the auctioneer strikes the hammer.

The most familiar type of auction today takes place online through Web sites like eBay and eBid. "Offers" to sell an item on these sites generally are treated as invitations to negotiate. Unlike live auctions, online auctions are automated. Buyers can enter incremental bids on an item (without approving each price increase) up to a specified amount or without a limit.

Agreements to Agree. Traditionally, agreements to agree—that is, agreements to agree to the material terms of a contract at some future date—were not considered to be binding contracts. The modern view, however, is that agreements to agree may be enforceable agreements (contracts) if it is clear that the parties intended to be bound by the agreements. In other words, under the modern view the emphasis is on the parties' intent rather than on form.

■ **CASE IN POINT 12.2** After a person was injured and nearly drowned on a water ride at one of its amusement parks, Six Flags, Inc., filed a lawsuit against the manufacturer that had designed the ride. The defendant manufacturer claimed that the parties did not have a binding contract but had only engaged in preliminary negotiations that were never formalized in a construction contract.

The court, however, held that the evidence was sufficient to show an intent to be bound. The evidence included a faxed document specifying the details of the water ride, along with the parties' subsequent actions (having begun construction and written notes on the faxed document). The manufacturer was required to provide insurance for the water ride at Six Flags. In addition, its insurer was required to defend Six Flags in the personal-injury lawsuit that arose out of the incident.[2] ■

---
1. *Restatement (Second) of Contracts*, Section 26, Comment b.

2. *Six Flags, Inc. v. Steadfast Insurance Co.*, 474 F.Supp.2d 201 (D.Mass. 2007).

Preliminary Agreements. Increasingly, the courts are holding that a preliminary agreement constitutes a binding contract if the parties have agreed on all essential terms and no disputed issues remain to be resolved. In contrast, if the parties agree on certain major terms but leave other terms open for further negotiation, a preliminary agreement is not binding. The parties are bound only in the sense that they have committed themselves to negotiate the undecided terms in good faith in an effort to reach a final agreement.

In the following *Spotlight Case,* a dispute arose over an agreement to settle a case during the trial. One party claimed that the agreement, which was formed via e-mail, was binding. The other party claimed that the e-mail exchange was merely an agreement to work out the terms of a settlement in the future. Can an exchange of e-mails create a complete and unambiguous agreement?

Spotlight on Amazon.com

Case 12.2 Basis Technology Corp. v. Amazon.com, Inc.

Appeals Court of Massachusetts, 71 Mass.App.Ct. 29, 878 N.E.2d 952 (2008).

Background and Facts Basis Technology Corporation created software and provided technical services for a Japanese-language Web site belonging to Amazon.com, Inc. The agreement between the two companies allowed for separately negotiated contracts for additional services that Basis might provide to Amazon. At the end of 1999, Basis and Amazon entered into stock-purchase agreements. Later, Basis sued Amazon for various claims involving these securities and for failure to pay for services performed by Basis that were not included in the original agreement. During the trial, the two parties appeared to reach an agreement to settle out of court via a series of e-mail exchanges outlining the settlement. When Amazon reneged, Basis served a motion to enforce the proposed settlement. The trial judge entered a judgment against Amazon, which appealed.

In the Language of the Court

SIKORA, J. [Judge]

* * * *

* * * On the evening of March 23, after the third day of evidence and after settlement discussions, Basis counsel sent an e-mail with the following text to Amazon counsel:

> [Amazon counsel]—This e-mail confirms the essential business terms of the settlement between our respective clients * * *. Basis and Amazon agree that they promptly will take all reasonable steps to memorialize in a written agreement, to be signed by individuals authorized by each party, the terms set forth below, as well as such other terms that are reasonably necessary to make these terms effective.
>
> * * * *
>
> [Amazon counsel], please contact me first thing tomorrow morning if this e-mail does not accurately summarize the settlement terms reached earlier this evening.
> See you tomorrow morning when we report this matter settled to the Court.

At 7:26 A.M. on March 24, Amazon counsel sent an e-mail with a one-word reply: "correct." Later in the morning, in open court and on the record, both counsel reported the result of a settlement without specification of the terms.

On March 25, Amazon's counsel sent a facsimile of the first draft of a settlement agreement to Basis's counsel. The draft comported with all the terms of the e-mail exchange, and added some implementing and boilerplate [standard contract provisions] terms.

* * * *

[Within a few days, though,] the parties were deadlocked. On April 21, Basis served its motion to enforce the settlement agreement. Amazon opposed. * * * The motion and opposition presented the issues whether the e-mail terms were sufficiently complete and definite to form an agreement and whether Amazon had intended to be bound by them.

* * * *

We examine the text of the terms for the incompleteness and indefiniteness charged by Amazon. *Provisions are not ambiguous simply because the parties have developed different interpretations of them.* [Emphasis added.]

Case 12.2 Continued   * * * *

We must interpret the document as a whole. In the preface to the enumerated terms, Basis counsel stated that the "e-mail confirms the essential business terms of the settlement between our respective clients," and that the parties "agree that they promptly will take all reasonable steps to memorialize" those terms. Amazon counsel concisely responded, "correct." Thus the "essential business terms" were resolved. The parties were proceeding to "memorialize" or record the settlement terms, not to create them.

* * * *

To ascertain intent, a court considers the words used by the parties, the agreement taken as a whole, and surrounding facts and circumstances. The essential circumstance of this disputed agreement is that it concluded a trial.

* * * As the trial judge explained in her memorandum of decision, she "terminated" the trial; she did not suspend it for exploratory negotiations. She did so in reliance upon the parties' report of an accomplished agreement for the settlement of their dispute.

* * * *

In sum, the deliberateness and the gravity attributable to a report of a settlement, especially during the progress of a trial, weigh heavily as circumstantial evidence of the intention of a party such as Amazon to be bound by its communication to the opposing party and to the court.

Decision and Remedy *The Appeals Court of Massachusetts affirmed the trial court's finding that Amazon intended to be bound by the terms of the March 23 e-mail. That e-mail constituted a complete and unambiguous statement of the parties' desire to be bound by the settlement terms.*

Critical Thinking
- **What If the Facts Were Different?** *Assume that, instead of exchanging e-mails, the attorneys for both sides had agreed by telephone to all of the terms actually included in their e-mail exchanges. Would the court have ruled differently? Why or why not?*
- **Legal Environment** *What does the result in this case suggest that a businessperson should do before agreeing to a settlement of a legal dispute?*

Definiteness of Terms The second requirement for an effective offer involves the definiteness of its terms. An offer must have reasonably definite terms so that a court can determine if a breach has occurred and give an appropriate remedy.[3] The specific terms required depend, of course, on the type of contract. Generally, a contract must include the following terms, either expressed in the contract or capable of being reasonably inferred from it:

1. The identification of the parties.
2. The identification of the object or subject matter of the contract (also the quantity, when appropriate), including the work to be performed, with specific identification of such items as goods, services, and land.
3. The consideration to be paid.
4. The time of payment, delivery, or performance.

An offer may invite an acceptance to be worded in such specific terms that the contract is made definite. ■**EXAMPLE 12.3** Nintendo of America, Inc., contacts your Play 2 Win Games store and offers to sell "from one to twenty-five Nintendo 3DS.XL gaming systems for $75 each. State number desired in acceptance." You agree to buy twenty systems. Because the quantity is specified in the acceptance, the terms are definite, and the contract is enforceable. ■

When the parties have clearly manifested their intent to form a contract, courts sometimes are willing to supply a missing term in a contract, especially a sales contract.[4] But a court will not rewrite a contract if the parties' expression of intent is too vague or uncertain to be given any precise meaning.

Communication The third requirement for an effective offer is communication—the offer must be communicated to the offeree. Ordinarily, one cannot agree to a bargain without knowing that it exists. ■ **CASE IN POINT 12.4** Adwoa Gyabaah was hit by a bus owned by Rivlab Transportation Corporation. Gyabaah filed a suit in a New York state court against the bus company. Rivlab's

---

3. *Restatement (Second) of Contracts*, Section 33.

4. See UCC 2–204. Article 2 of the UCC modifies general contract law by requiring *less* specificity, or definiteness of terms, in sales and lease contracts.

insurer offered to tender the company's policy limit of $1 million in full settlement of Gyabaah's claims. On the advice of her attorney, Jeffrey Aronsky, Gyabaah signed a release (a contract forfeiting the right to pursue a legal claim) to obtain the settlement funds.

The release, however, was not sent to Rivlab or its insurer, National Casualty. Moreover, Gyabaah claimed that she had not decided whether to settle. Two months later, Gyabaah changed lawyers and changed her mind about signing the release. Her former attorney, Aronsky, filed a motion to enforce the release so that he could obtain his fees from the settlement funds. The court denied the motion, and Aronsky appealed. The reviewing court held that there was no binding settlement agreement. The release was never delivered to Rivlab or its insurer nor was acceptance of the settlement offer otherwise communicated to them.[5] ■

12–1b Termination of the Offer

The communication of an effective offer to an offeree gives the offeree the power to transform the offer into a binding, legal obligation (a contract) by an acceptance. This power of acceptance does not continue forever, though. It can be terminated either by action of the parties or by operation of law.

Termination by Action of the Parties An offer can be terminated by action of the parties in any of three ways: by revocation, by rejection, or by counteroffer.

Revocation. The offeror's act of revoking, or withdrawing, an offer is known as **revocation**. Unless an offer is irrevocable, the offeror usually can revoke the offer, as long as the revocation is communicated to the offeree before the offeree accepts. Revocation may be accomplished by either of the following:

1. Express repudiation of the offer (such as "I withdraw my previous offer of October 17").
2. Performance of acts that are inconsistent with the existence of the offer and are made known to the offeree (for instance, selling the offered property to another person in the offeree's presence).

In most states, a revocation becomes effective when the offeree or the offeree's *agent* (a person acting on behalf of the offeree) actually receives it. Therefore, a revocation sent via FedEx on April 1 and delivered at the offeree's residence or place of business on April 3 becomes effective on April 3. An offer made to the general public can

be revoked in the same manner in which it was originally communicated. For instance, an offer made on specific Web sites or in particular newspapers can be revoked on the same Web sites or in the same newspapers.

Irrevocable Offers. Although most offers are revocable, some can be made irrevocable—that is, they cannot be revoked. One form of irrevocable offer is an **option contract.** An option contract is created when an offeror promises to hold an offer open for a specified period of time in return for a payment (consideration) given by the offeree. An option contract takes away the offeror's power to revoke the offer for the period of time specified in the option.

Option contracts are frequently used in conjunction with the sale or lease of real estate. ■ **EXAMPLE 12.5** Tyler agrees to lease a house from Jackson, the property owner. The lease contract includes a clause stating that Tyler is paying an additional $15,000 for an option to purchase the property within a specified period of time. If Tyler decides not to purchase the house after the specified period has lapsed, he loses the $15,000, and Jackson is free to sell the property to another buyer. ■

Rejection. If the offeree rejects the offer—by words or by conduct—the offer is terminated. Any subsequent attempt by the offeree to accept will be construed as a new offer, giving the original offeror (now the offeree) the power of acceptance.

Like a revocation, a rejection of an offer is effective only when it is actually received by the offeror or the offeror's agent. ■ **EXAMPLE 12.6** Goldfinch Farms offers to sell specialty Maitake mushrooms to a Japanese buyer, Kinoko Foods. If Kinoko rejects the offer by sending a letter via U.S. mail, the rejection will not be effective (and the offer will not be terminated) until Goldfinch receives the letter. ■

Merely inquiring about the "firmness" of an offer does not constitute rejection. ■ **EXAMPLE 12.7** Raymond offers to buy Francie's digital pen for $100. She responds, "Is that your best offer?" A reasonable person would conclude that Francie has not rejected the offer but has merely made an inquiry. Francie could still accept and bind Raymond to the $100 price. ■

Counteroffer. A **counteroffer** is a rejection of the original offer and the simultaneous making of a new offer. ■ **EXAMPLE 12.8** Burke offers to sell his home to Lang for $270,000. Lang responds, "Your price is too high. I'll offer to purchase your house for $250,000." Lang's response is a counteroffer because it rejects Burke's offer to sell at $270,000 and creates a new offer by Lang to purchase the home for $250,000. ■

At common law, the **mirror image rule** requires the offeree's acceptance to match the offeror's offer exactly—to

---

5. *Gyabaah v. Rivlab Transportation Corp.*, 102 A.D.3d 451, 958 N.Y.S.2d 109 (N.Y.A.D. 2013).

mirror the offer. Any change in, or addition to, the terms of the original offer automatically terminates that offer and substitutes the counteroffer. The counteroffer, of course, need not be accepted, but if the original offeror does accept the terms of the counteroffer, a valid contract is created.[6]

Termination by Operation of Law The power of the offeree to transform the offer into a binding, legal obligation can be terminated by operation of law through the occurrence of any of the following events:

1. Lapse of time.
2. Destruction of the specific subject matter of the offer.
3. Death or incompetence of the offeror or the offeree.
4. Supervening illegality of the proposed contract. (A statute or court decision that makes an offer illegal automatically terminates the offer.)

Lapse of Time. An offer terminates automatically by law when the period of time *specified in the offer* has passed. If the offer states that it will be left open until a particular date, then the offer will terminate at midnight on that day. If the offer states that it will be open for a number of days, this time period normally begins to run when the offeree *receives* the offer (not when it is formed or sent).

If the offer does not specify a time for acceptance, the offer terminates at the end of a *reasonable* period of time. What constitutes a reasonable period of time depends on the subject matter of the contract, business and market conditions, and other relevant circumstances. An offer to sell farm produce, for instance, will terminate sooner than

an offer to sell farm equipment. Farm produce is perishable and is also subject to greater fluctuations in market value.

Destruction, Death, or Incompetence. An offer is automatically terminated if the specific subject matter of the offer (such as a smartphone or a house) is destroyed before the offer is accepted.[7] Notice of the destruction is not required for the offer to terminate.

An offeree's power of acceptance is also terminated when the offeror or offeree dies or is legally incapacitated—*unless the offer is irrevocable.* ■**EXAMPLE 12.9** Sybil Maven offers to sell commercial property to Westside Investment for $2 million. In June, Westside pays Maven $5,000 in exchange for her agreement to hold the offer open for ten months (forming an option contract). If Maven dies in July, her offer is not terminated, because it is irrevocable. Westside can purchase the property from Maven's estate at any time within the ten-month period. ■

In contrast, a revocable offer is personal to both parties and cannot pass to the heirs, guardian, or the estate of either party. This rule applies whether or not the other party had notice of the death or incompetence.

Supervening Illegality. A statute or court decision that makes an offer illegal automatically terminates the offer.[8] ■**EXAMPLE 12.10** Lee offers to lend Kim $10,000 at an annual interest rate of 15 percent. Before Kim can accept the offer, a law is enacted that prohibits interest rates higher than 8 percent. Lee's offer is automatically terminated. (If the statute is enacted after Kim accepts the offer, a valid contract is formed, but the contract may still be unenforceable.) ■

Concept Summary 12.1 reviews the ways in which an offer can be terminated.

---

6. The mirror image rule has been greatly modified in regard to sales contracts. Section 2–207 of the UCC provides that a contract is formed if the offeree makes a definite expression of acceptance (such as signing a form in the appropriate location), even though the terms of the acceptance modify or add to the terms of the original offer.

7. *Restatement (Second) of Contracts*, Section 36.
8. *Restatement (Second) of Contracts*, Section 36.

Concept Summary 12.1

Methods by Which an Offer Can Be Terminated

By Action of the Parties	• Revocation • Rejection • Counteroffer
By Operation of Law	• Lapse of time • Destruction of the subject matter • Death or incompetence of the offeror or offeree • Supervening illegality

12–1c Acceptance

Acceptance is a voluntary act by the offeree that shows assent (agreement) to the terms of an offer. The offeree's act may consist of words or conduct. The acceptance must be unequivocal and must be communicated to the offeror.

Generally, only the person to whom the offer is made or that person's agent can accept the offer and create a binding contract. (See this chapter's *Digital Update* feature for a discussion of how parties can sometimes inadvertently accept a contract via e-mail or instant messages.)

DIGITAL UPDATE   Can Your E-Mails or Instant Messages Create a Valid Contract?

Instant messaging and e-mailing are among the most common forms of informal communication. Not surprisingly, parties considering an agreement often exchange offers and counteroffers via e-mail (and, to a lesser extent, instant messaging). The parties may believe that these informal electronic exchanges are for negotiation purposes only. But such communications can lead to the formation of valid contracts.

E-Mails and Settlements

After automobile accidents, the parties' attorneys sometimes exchange e-mails as part of the negotiation process. For instance, John Forcelli, who was injured in an automobile accident, sued the owner of the vehicle, Gelco Corporation. While the suit was pending, Gelco's insurance company's representative orally offered Forcelli a $230,000 settlement, which Forcelli accepted. The representative then sent an e-mail confirming the terms of the settlement, and Forcelli signed a notarized release.

A few days later, however, a New York trial court (unaware of the settlement) granted Gelco's motion for summary judgment and dismissed Forcelli's claims. Gelco then tried to rescind the settlement, claiming that the e-mail did not constitute a binding written settlement agreement. The trial court ruled against Gelco, and an appeal followed. The reviewing court affirmed. The e-mail contained all the necessary elements of contract.[a]

"Accidental" Contracts via E-Mails

When a series of e-mails signal intent to be bound, a contract may be formed, even though some language in the e-mails may be careless or accidental. What matters is whether a court determines that it is reasonable for the receiving party to believe that there is an agreement.

Indeed, e-mail contracting has become so common that only unusually strange circumstances will cause a court to reject such contracts.[b] Furthermore, under the Uniform Electronic Transactions Act (UETA), a contract "may not be denied legal effect solely because an electronic record was used in its formation." Most states have adopted this act, at least in part. (The UETA is discussed later in this chapter.)

Instant Messaging Can Create Valid Contract Modifications

Like e-mail exchanges, instant messaging conversations between individuals in the process of negotiations can result in the formation (or modification) of a contract. One case involved an online marketing service, CX Digital Media, Inc., which provides clients with advertising referrals from its network of affiliates.

CX Digital charges a fee for its services based on the number of referrals. One of its clients was Smoking Everywhere, Inc., a seller of electronic cigarettes. While the two companies were negotiating a change in contract terms via instant messaging, the issue of the maximum number of referrals per day came up. A CX Digital employee sent an instant message to a Smoking Everywhere executive asking about the maximum number. The executive responded, "NO LIMIT," and CX Digital's employee replied, "Awesome!"

After that, CX Digital referred a higher volume of sales leads than it had previously. Smoking Everywhere refused to pay for these additional referrals, claiming that the instant messaging chat did not constitute an enforceable modification of the initial contract. At trial, CX Digital prevailed. Smoking Everywhere had to pay more than $1 million for the additional sales leads.[c]

Critical Thinking *How can a company structure e-mail negotiations to avoid "accidentally" forming a contract?*

b. See, for example, *Beastie Boys v. Monster Energy Co.*, 983 F.Supp.2d 338 (S.D.N.Y. 2013).
c. *CX Digital Media, Inc. v. Smoking Everywhere, Inc.*, 2011 WL 1102782 (S.D.Fla. 2011).

a. *Forcelli v. Gelco Corporation*, 109 A.D.3d 244, 972 N.Y.S.2d 570 (2013).

Unequivocal Acceptance To exercise the power of acceptance effectively, the offeree must accept unequivocally. This is the *mirror image rule* previously discussed. An acceptance may be unequivocal even though the offeree expresses dissatisfaction with the contract. For instance, "I accept the offer, but can you give me a better price?" or "I accept, but please send a written contract" is an effective acceptance. (Notice how important each word is!)

An acceptance cannot impose new conditions or change the terms of the original offer. If it does, the acceptance may be considered a counteroffer, which is a rejection of the original offer. For instance, the statement "I accept the offer but only if I can pay on ninety days' credit" is a counteroffer and not an unequivocal acceptance.

Note that even when the additional terms are construed as a counteroffer, the other party can accept the terms by words or by conduct. ■ **CASE IN POINT 12.11** Lagrange Development is a nonprofit corporation in Ohio that acquires and rehabilitates real property. Sonja Brown presented Lagrange with a written offer to buy a particular house for $79,900. Lagrange's executive director, Terry Glazer, penciled in modifications to the offer—an increased purchase price of $84,200 and a later date for acceptance. Glazer initialed the changes and signed the document.

Brown initialed the date change but not the price increase, and did not sign the revised document. Nevertheless, Brown went through with the sale and received ownership of the property. When a dispute later arose as to the purchase price, a court found that Glazer's modification of the terms had constituted a counteroffer, which Brown had accepted by performance. Therefore, the contract was enforceable for the modified price of $84,200.[9] ■

Silence as Acceptance Ordinarily, silence cannot constitute acceptance, even if the offeror states, "By your silence and inaction, you will be deemed to have accepted this offer." An offeree should not be obligated to act affirmatively to reject an offer when no consideration (nothing of value) has passed to the offeree to impose such a duty.

In some instances, however, the offeree does have a duty to speak, and her or his silence or inaction will operate as an acceptance. Silence can constitute an acceptance when the offeree has had prior dealings with the offeror. ■ **EXAMPLE 12.12** Marabel's restaurant routinely receives shipments of produce from a certain supplier. That supplier notifies Marabel's that it is raising its prices because its crops were damaged by a late freeze. If the restaurant does not respond in any way, the silence may operate as an acceptance, and the supplier will be justified in continuing regular shipments. ■

Communication of Acceptance Whether the offeror must be notified of the acceptance depends on the nature of the contract. In a unilateral contract, the full performance of some act is called for. Acceptance is usually evident, and notification is therefore unnecessary (unless the law requires it or the offeror asks for it). In a bilateral contract, in contrast, communication of acceptance is necessary, because acceptance is in the form of a promise. The bilateral contract is formed when the promise is made rather than when the act is performed.

■ **CASE IN POINT 12.13** Powerhouse Custom Homes, Inc., owed $95,260.42 to 84 Lumber Company under a credit agreement. When Powerhouse failed to pay, 84 Lumber filed a suit to collect. During mediation, the parties agreed to a deadline for objections to whatever agreement they might reach. If there were no objections, the agreement would be binding.

Powerhouse then offered to pay less than the amount owed, but 84 Lumber did not respond. Powerhouse later argued that 84 Lumber had accepted the offer by not objecting to it within the deadline. The court ruled in 84 Lumber's favor for the entire amount of the debt. To form a contract, an offer must be accepted unequivocally. Powerhouse made an offer, but 84 Lumber did not communicate acceptance. Therefore, the parties did not reach an agreement on settlement.[10] ■

At issue in the following case was the validity and enforceability of a waiver of liability on the back page of a gym's membership agreement. In this case, the court had to determine whether the circumstances indicated that the offeree's acceptance of the agreement was unequivocal and clearly communicated.

---

9. *Brown v. Lagrange Development Corp.*, 2015 WL 223877 (Ohio App. 2015).

10. *Powerhouse Custom Homes, Inc. v. 84 Lumber Co.*, 307 Ga.App. 605, 705 S.E.2d 704 (2011).

Hinkal v. Pardoe

Superior Court of Pennsylvania, 2016 PA Super 11, 133 A.3d 738 (2016).

In the Language of the Court

Opinion by STABILE, J. [Judge]

* * * *

[Melinda Hinkal filed a suit in a Pennsylvania state court against personal trainer Gavin Pardoe and Gold's Gym, Inc., alleging that] she sustained a serious neck injury while using a piece of exercise equipment under * * * Pardoe's direction [at Gold's Gym. Hinkal] alleges that she suffered a rupture of the C5 disc in her neck requiring two separate surgeries. [Gold's and Pardoe] filed a Motion for Summary Judgment [asserting] that as a member of Gold's Gym [Hinkal] signed * * * a Membership Agreement [that] contains legally valid "waiver of liability" provisions, which in turn, bar [her] claims.

The trial court concluded that the waiver language set forth in Gold's Membership Agreement was valid and enforceable.

[Hinkal] filed a timely appeal to this [state intermediate appellate] Court.

* * * *

* * * Appellant [Hinkal] questions whether the waiver on the back page of her membership agreement is valid and enforceable. The language on the back page of the agreement reads in pertinent part as follows:

WAIVER OF LIABILITY; ASSUMPTION OF RISK: Member acknowledges that the use of Gold's Gym's facilities, equipment, services and programs involves an inherent risk of personal injury to Member. * * * Member voluntarily agrees to assume all risks of personal injury to Member * * * and waives any and all claims or actions that Member may have against Gold's Gym * * * and any * * * employees * * * for * * * injuries arising from

use of any exercise equipment * * * in supervised or unsupervised activities.

The Gold's Gym Membership Agreement signed by Appellant further instructs:

Do not sign this Agreement until you have read both sides. The terms on each side of this form are a part of this Agreement. * * * By signing this Agreement, Member acknowledges that This Agreement is a contract that will become legally binding upon its acceptance.

The signature line follows immediately and the words "Notice: See other side for important information" appear in bold typeface below the signature line.

* * * *

* * * Appellant * * * asserts that her claim is not barred by the "exclusion clause" on the back of the membership agreement. * * * Appellant contends the waiver is invalid because the waiver language appeared on the back of the agreement, she never read or was told to read the back of the agreement, and the clause was not "brought home" to her in a way that could suggest she was aware of the clause and its contents. However, * * * Appellant admitted she did not read the agreement prior to signing it. * * * Her failure to read her agreement does not render it either invalid or unenforceable. *The law of Pennsylvania is clear. One who is about to sign a contract has a duty to read that contract first.* * * * It is well established that, in the absence of fraud, the failure to read a contract before signing it is an unavailing excuse or defense and cannot justify an avoidance, modification or nullification of the contract. [Emphasis added.]

[To support her claim, Appellant cites *Beck-Hummel v. Ski Shawnee, Inc.*,

a previous case before this court, but] the signed Gold's Gym membership agreement cannot be compared in any way to the unread and unsigned disclaimer on a ski facility ticket in [*Beck-Hummel.*]

* * * *

* * * In [*Beck-Hummel,*] the release provision was contained on the face of an entry ticket purchased for use of a ski facility. The ticket did not require a signature or an express acknowledgment that its terms were read and accepted before using the facility. Nothing about the ticket ensured that a purchaser would be aware of its release provision. The purchasers were mere recipients of the document. In short, there was not sufficient evidence to find conclusively that there was a meeting of the minds that part of the consideration for use of the facility was acceptance of a release provision. In stark contrast, here there is a written, signed and acknowledged agreement between the parties.

* * * *

Here, without reading it, Appellant signed the membership agreement, which included an unambiguous directive not to sign before reading both sides, a clear pronouncement that the terms on both sides of the form are part of the agreement, and a straightforward statement that the agreement constitutes the entire agreement between the parties. * * * We find no genuine issue as to any material fact or any error in the lower court's determination that the waiver was valid and enforceable. Appellant is not entitled to relief based on [this] issue.

* * * *

Order affirmed.

Legal Reasoning Questions

1. What indicated that the terms in the agreement at issue in this case were accepted?

2. What were the appellant's arguments in support of her claim? Which of those contentions did the court imply was irrelevant? Why?

3. How did the court distinguish its conclusion in this case from its decision in *Beck-Hummel*?

Mode and Timeliness of Acceptance In bilateral contracts, acceptance must be timely. The general rule is that acceptance in a bilateral contract is timely if it is made before the offer is terminated. Problems may arise, though, when the parties involved are not dealing face to face. In such situations, the offeree should use an authorized mode of communication.

The Mailbox Rule. Acceptance takes effect, thus completing formation of the contract, at the time the offeree sends or delivers the communication via the mode expressly or impliedly authorized by the offeror. This is the so-called **mailbox rule,** also called the *deposited acceptance rule,* which the majority of courts follow. Under this rule, if the authorized mode of communication is the mail, then an acceptance becomes valid when it is dispatched (placed in the control of the U.S. Postal Service)—*not* when it is received by the offeror. (Note, however, that if the offer stipulates when acceptance will be effective, then the offer will not be effective until the time specified.)

The mailbox rule does not apply to instantaneous forms of communication, such as when the parties are dealing face to face, by telephone, by fax, and (usually) by e-mail. Under the Uniform Electronic Transactions Act, e-mail is considered sent when it either leaves the control of the sender or is received by the recipient. This rule takes the place of the mailbox rule when the parties have agreed to conduct transactions electronically and allows an e-mail acceptance to become effective when sent.

Authorized Means of Acceptance. A means of communicating acceptance can be expressly authorized by the offeror or impliedly authorized by the facts and circumstances of the situation.[11] An acceptance sent by means not expressly or impliedly authorized normally is not effective until it is received by the offeror.

When an offeror specifies how acceptance should be made (for instance, by overnight delivery), *express authorization* is said to exist. The contract is not formed unless the offeree uses that specified mode of acceptance. Moreover, both offeror and offeree are bound in contract the moment this means of acceptance is employed. ■ **EXAMPLE 12.14** Motorola Mobility, Inc., offers to sell 144 Atrix 4G smartphones and 72 Lapdocks to Call Me Plus phone stores. The offer states that Call Me Plus must accept the offer via FedEx overnight delivery. The acceptance is effective (and a binding contract is formed) the moment that Call Me Plus gives the overnight envelope containing the acceptance to the FedEx driver. ■

If the offeror does not expressly authorize a certain mode of acceptance, then acceptance can be made by *any reasonable means.*[12] Courts look at the prevailing business usages and the surrounding circumstances to determine whether the mode of acceptance used was reasonable.

Usually, the offeror's choice of a particular means in making the offer implies that the offeree can use the *same or a faster means* for acceptance. Thus, if the offer is made via Priority U.S. mail, it would be reasonable to accept the offer via Priority mail or by a faster method, such as overnight delivery.

Substitute Method of Acceptance. Sometimes, the offeror authorizes a particular method of acceptance, but the offeree accepts by a different means. In that situation, the acceptance may still be effective if the substituted method serves the same purpose as the authorized means.

Acceptance by a substitute method is not effective on dispatch, however. No contract will be formed until the acceptance is received by the offeror. ■ **EXAMPLE 12.15** Bennion's offer specifies acceptance via FedEx overnight delivery, but the offeree accepts instead by overnight delivery from UPS. The substitute method of acceptance will still be effective, but not until the offeror (Bennion) receives it from UPS. ■

12–2 Agreement in E-Contracts

Numerous contracts are formed online. Electronic contracts, or **e-contracts,** must meet the same basic requirements (agreement, consideration, contractual capacity, and legality) as paper contracts. Disputes concerning e-contracts, however, tend to center on contract terms and whether the parties voluntarily agreed to those terms.

Online contracts may be formed not only for the sale of goods and services but also for *licensing.* The "sale" of software generally involves a license, or a right to use the software, rather than the passage of title (ownership rights) from the seller to the buyer. ■ **EXAMPLE 12.16** Lauren wants to obtain software that will allow her to work on spreadsheets on her smartphone. She goes online and purchases GridMagic. During the transaction, she clicks on several on-screen "I agree" boxes to indicate her understanding that she is purchasing only the right to use the software, not ownership rights. After she agrees to these terms (the licensing agreement), she can download the software. ■

As you read through the following subsections, you will see that we typically refer to the offeror and the

---

11. *Restatement (Second) of Contracts,* Section 30, provides that an offer invites acceptance "by any medium reasonable in the circumstances," unless the offer specifies the means of acceptance.

12. *Restatement (Second) of Contracts,* Section 30. This is also the rule under UCC 2–206(1)(a).

offeree as a *seller* and a *buyer*. Keep in mind, though, that in many online transactions these parties would be more accurately described as a *licensor* and a *licensee*.

12–2a Online Offers

Sellers doing business via the Internet can protect themselves against contract disputes and legal liability by creating offers that clearly spell out the terms that will govern their transactions if the offers are accepted. All important terms should be conspicuous and easy to view.

Displaying the Offer The seller's Web site should include a hypertext link to a page containing the full contract so that potential buyers are made aware of the terms to which they are assenting. The contract generally must be displayed online in a readable format, such as a twelve-point typeface. All provisions should be reasonably clear.

Provisions to Include An important point to keep in mind is that the offeror (the seller) controls the offer and thus the resulting contract. The seller should therefore anticipate the terms he or she wants to include in a contract and provide for them in the offer. In some instances, a standardized contract form may suffice.

At a minimum, an online offer should include the following provisions:

1. *Acceptance of terms.* A clause that clearly indicates what constitutes the buyer's agreement to the terms of the offer, such as a box containing the words "I accept" that the buyer can click.
2. *Payment.* A provision specifying how payment for the goods (including any applicable taxes) must be made.
3. *Return policy.* A statement of the seller's refund and return policies.
4. *Disclaimer.* Disclaimers of liability for certain uses of the goods. For instance, an online seller of business forms may add a disclaimer that the seller does not accept responsibility for the buyer's reliance on the forms rather than on an attorney's advice.
5. *Limitation on remedies.* A provision specifying the remedies available to the buyer if the goods are found to be defective or if the contract is otherwise breached. Any limitation of remedies should be clearly spelled out.
6. *Privacy policy.* A statement indicating how the seller will use the information gathered about the buyer.
7. *Dispute resolution.* Provisions relating to dispute settlement, which we examine more closely in the following section.

Dispute-Settlement Provisions Online offers frequently include provisions relating to dispute settlement. For instance, an offer might include an arbitration clause specifying that any dispute arising under the contract will be arbitrated in a designated forum. The parties might also select the forum and the law that will govern any disputes.

Forum-Selection Clause. Many online contracts contain a **forum-selection clause** indicating the forum, or location (such as a court or jurisdiction), in which contract disputes will be resolved. Significant jurisdictional issues may arise when parties are at a great distance, as they often are when they form contracts via the Internet. A forum-selection clause will help to avert future jurisdictional problems and also help to ensure that the seller will not be required to appear in court in a distant state.

■ **CASE IN POINT 12.17** Scott Rosendahl enrolled in an online college, Ashford University. He claimed that the school's adviser had told him that Ashford offered one of the cheapest undergraduate degree programs in the country. In fact, it did not. Rosendahl later sued the school, claiming that it had violated unfair competition laws and false advertising laws and had engaged in fraud and negligent misrepresentation.

The university argued that its enrollment agreement clearly contained a requirement that all disputes be arbitrated. Rosendahl, like other students, had electronically assented to this agreement when he enrolled. Ashford presented the online application forms to the court, and the court dismissed Rosendahl's lawsuit. Rosendahl had agreed to arbitrate any disputes he had with Ashford.[13] ■

Choice-of-Law Clause. Some online contracts may also include a *choice-of-law clause,* specifying that any contract dispute will be settled according to the law of a particular jurisdiction, such as a state or country. Choice-of-law clauses are particularly common in international contracts, but they may also appear in e-contracts to specify which state's laws will govern in the United States.

12–2b Online Acceptances

The *Restatement (Second) of Contracts,* which is a compilation of common law contract principles, states that parties may agree to a contract "by written or spoken words or by other action or by failure to act."[14] The Uniform Commercial Code (UCC), which governs sales contracts, has a similar provision. Section 2–204 of the UCC states

---

13. *Rosendahl v. Bridgepoint Education, Inc.*, 2012 WL 667049 (S.D.Cal. 2012).
14. *Restatement (Second) of Contracts*, Section 19.

that any contract for the sale of goods "may be made in any manner sufficient to show agreement, including conduct by both parties which recognizes the existence of such a contract." The courts have used these provisions in determining what constitutes an online acceptance.

Click-On Agreements The courts have concluded that the act of clicking on a box labeled "I accept" or "I agree" can indicate acceptance of an online offer. The agreement resulting from such an acceptance is often called a **click-on agreement** (sometimes referred to as a *click-on license* or *click-wrap agreement*). Exhibit 12–1 shows a portion of a typical click-on agreement that accompanies a software package.

Generally, the law does not require that the parties have read all of the terms in a contract for it to be effective. Therefore, clicking on a box that states "I agree" to certain terms can be enough. The terms may be contained on a Web site through which the buyer is obtaining goods or services. They may also appear on a screen when software is downloaded from the Internet.

■ **CASE IN POINT 12.18** The "Terms of Use" that govern Facebook users' accounts include a forum-selection clause that provides for the resolution of all disputes in a court in Santa Clara County, California. To sign up for a Facebook account, a person must click on a box indicating that he or she has agreed to this term.

Mustafa Fteja was an active user of facebook.com when his account was disabled. He sued Facebook in a federal court in New York, claiming that it had disabled his Facebook page without justification and for discriminatory reasons. Facebook filed a motion to transfer the case to California under the forum-selection clause. The court found that the clause in Facebook's online contract was binding and transferred the case. When Fteja clicked on the button to accept the contract terms, he agreed to resolve all disputes with Facebook in Santa Clara County, California.[15] ■

Shrink-Wrap Agreements With a **shrink-wrap agreement** (or *shrink-wrap license*), the terms are expressed inside the box in which the goods are packaged. (The term *shrink-wrap* refers to the plastic that covers the box.) Usually, the party who opens the box is told that she or he agrees to the terms by keeping whatever is in the box. Similarly, when a purchaser opens a software package, he or she agrees to abide by the terms of the limited license agreement.

■ **EXAMPLE 12.19** Ava orders a new iMac from Big Ed's Electronics, which ships it to her. Along with the iMac, the box contains an agreement setting forth the terms of the sale, including what remedies are available.

---

15. *Fteja v. Facebook, Inc.*, 841 F.Supp.2d 829 (S.D.N.Y. 2012).

EXHIBIT 12–1 A Click-On Agreement Sample

This exhibit illustrates an online offer to form a contract. To accept the offer, the user simply scrolls down the page and clicks on the "Accept and Install" button.

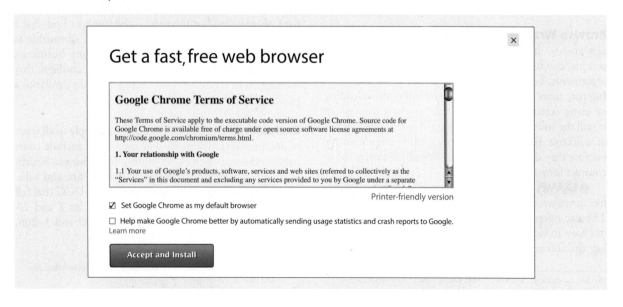

The document also states that Ava's retention of the iMac for longer than thirty days will be construed as an acceptance of the terms. ∎

In most instances, a shrink-wrap agreement is not between a retailer and a buyer, but is between the manufacturer of the hardware or software and the ultimate buyer-user of the product. The terms generally concern warranties, remedies, and other issues associated with the use of the product.

Shrink-Wrap Agreements and Enforceable Contract Terms. In some cases, the courts have enforced the terms of shrink-wrap agreements in the same way as the terms of other contracts. These courts have reasoned that by including the terms with the product, the seller proposed a contract. The buyer could accept this contract by using the product after having an opportunity to read the terms. Thus, a buyer's failure to object to terms contained within a shrink-wrapped software package may constitute an acceptance of the terms by conduct.

Shrink-Wrap Terms That May Not Be Enforced. Sometimes, however, the courts have refused to enforce certain terms included in shrink-wrap agreements because the buyer did not expressly consent to them. An important factor is when the parties formed their contract.

If a buyer orders a product over the telephone, for instance, and is not informed of an arbitration clause or a forum-selection clause at that time, the buyer clearly has not expressly agreed to these terms. If the buyer discovers the clauses *after* the parties have entered into a contract, a court may conclude that those terms were proposals for additional terms and were not part of the contract.

Browse-Wrap Terms Like the terms of click-on agreements, **browse-wrap terms** can occur in transactions conducted over the Internet. Unlike click-on agreements, however, browse-wrap terms do not require Internet users to assent to the terms before downloading or using certain software. In other words, a person can install the software without clicking "I agree" to the terms of a license. Browse-wrap terms are often unenforceable because they do not satisfy the agreement requirement of contract formation.[16]

∎ **EXAMPLE 12.20** BrowseNet Corporation provides free downloadable "QuickLoad" software on its Web site. The site refers to a license agreement but the user does not have to view it or agree to its terms before downloading the software. One of the license terms requires all disputes to be submitted to arbitration in California. If a user sues BrowseNet in Washington State, the arbitration clause might not be enforceable, because users were not required to indicate their assent to the agreement. ∎

12–2c Federal Law on E-Signatures and E-Documents

An **e-signature** has been defined as "an electronic sound, symbol, or process attached to or logically associated with a record and executed or adopted by a person with the intent to sign the record."[17] In 2000, Congress enacted the Electronic Signatures in Global and National Commerce Act (E-SIGN Act).[18]

The E-SIGN Act provides that no contract, record, or signature may be "denied legal effect" solely because it is in electronic form. In other words, under this law, an electronic signature is as valid as a signature on paper, and an e-document can be as enforceable as a paper one. For an e-signature to be enforceable, however, the contracting parties must have agreed to use electronic signatures. For an electronic document to be valid, it must be in a form that can be retained and accurately reproduced.

E-Signature Technologies Electronic documents can be signed in a number of ways. E-signature technologies include encrypted digital signatures, names intended as signatures at the end of e-mail messages, and clicks on a Web page if the clicks include some means of identification.

Note that although courts do not question that documents can be signed electronically under the E-SIGN Act, some courts will question the validity of the signatures themselves. For instance, a court might find that a typed name at the bottom of e-mail is not admissible as the person's signature. For this reason, many businesses use special software, such as DocuSign or EchoSign, that is designed to create an e-signature that looks similar to a person's handwritten signature.

Exclusions The E-SIGN Act does not apply to all types of documents. Documents that are exempt include court papers, divorce decrees, evictions, foreclosures, health-insurance terminations, prenuptial agreements, and wills. Also, the only agreements governed by the UCC that fall under this law are those covered by Articles 2 and 2A (sales and lease contracts) and UCC 1–107 and 1–206.

---

16. See, for example, *Waldman v. New Chapter, Inc.*, 714 F.Supp.2d 398 (2010).

17. This definition is from the Uniform Electronic Transactions Act, discussed later in this chapter.

18. 15 U.S.C. Sections 7001 *et seq.*

Despite these limitations, the E-SIGN Act has significantly expanded online contracting.

12–2d Partnering Agreements

One way that online sellers and buyers can prevent disputes over signatures in their e-contracts, as well as disputes over the terms and conditions of those contracts, is to form partnering agreements. In a **partnering agreement,** a seller and a buyer who frequently do business with each other agree in advance on the terms and conditions that will apply to all transactions subsequently conducted electronically. The partnering agreement can also establish special access and identification codes to be used by the parties when transacting business electronically.

A partnering agreement reduces the likelihood that contract disputes will arise because the parties have agreed in advance to the terms and conditions that will accompany each sale. Furthermore, if a dispute does arise, a court or arbitration forum will be able to refer to the partnering agreement when determining the parties' intent.

12–3 The Uniform Electronic Transactions Act

The National Conference of Commissioners on Uniform State Laws and the American Law Institute promulgated the Uniform Electronic Transactions Act (UETA) in 1999. The UETA has been adopted, at least in part, by forty-eight states, resulting in more uniformity among state laws governing electronic transactions. Among other things, the UETA declares that a signature may not be denied legal effect or enforceability solely because it is in electronic form.

The primary purpose of the UETA is to remove barriers to e-commerce by giving the same legal effect to electronic records and signatures as is given to paper documents and signatures. As mentioned, the UETA broadly defines an *e-signature* as "an electronic sound, symbol, or process attached to or logically associated with a record and executed or adopted by a person with the intent to sign the record."[19] A **record** is "information that is inscribed on a tangible medium or that is stored in an electronic or other medium and is retrievable in perceivable [visual] form."[20]

12–3a The Scope and Applicability of the UETA

The UETA does not create new rules for electronic contracts. Rather, it establishes that records, signatures, and contracts may not be denied enforceability solely due to their electronic form.

The UETA does not apply to all writings and signatures. It covers only electronic records and electronic signatures *relating to a transaction.* A *transaction* is defined as an interaction between two or more people relating to business, commercial, or governmental activities.[21] The act specifically does not apply to wills or testamentary trusts or to transactions governed by the UCC (other than those covered by Articles 2 and 2A).[22] In addition, the provisions of the UETA allow the states to exclude its application to other areas of law.

12–3b The Federal E-SIGN Act and the UETA

Earlier, we discussed the provisions of the federal E-SIGN Act. Congress passed the E-SIGN Act in 2000, a year after the UETA was presented to the states for adoption. Thus, a significant issue was to what extent the federal E-SIGN Act preempted the UETA as adopted by the states.

The E-SIGN Act[23] explicitly provides that if a state has enacted the uniform version of the UETA, that law is not preempted by the E-SIGN Act. In other words, if the state has enacted the UETA without modification, state law will govern. The problem is that many states have enacted nonuniform (modified) versions of the UETA, usually to exclude other areas of state law from the UETA's terms. The E-SIGN Act specifies that those exclusions will be preempted to the extent that they are inconsistent with the E-SIGN Act's provisions.

The E-SIGN Act explicitly allows the states to enact alternative requirements for the use of electronic records or electronic signatures. Generally, however, the requirements must be consistent with the provisions of the E-SIGN Act, and the state must not give greater legal status or effect to one specific type of technology. Additionally, state laws that include alternative requirements, if enacted after the adoption of the E-SIGN Act, must specifically refer to the E-SIGN Act. The relationship between the UETA and the E-SIGN Act is illustrated in Exhibit 12–2.

---

19. UETA 102(8).
20. UETA 102(15).

21. UETA 2(12) and 3.
22. UETA 3(b).
23. 15 U.S.C. Section 7002(2)(A)(i).

EXHIBIT 12–2 The E-SIGN Act and the UETA

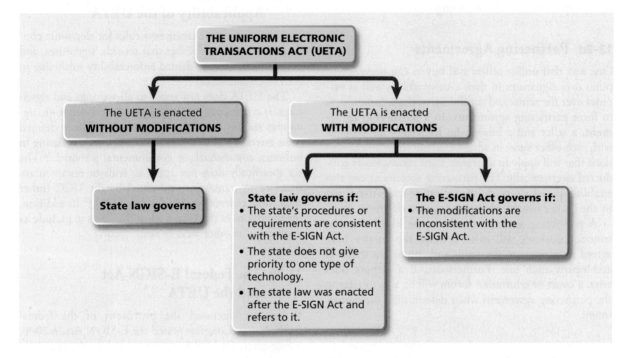

12–3c Highlights of the UETA

The UETA does not apply to a transaction unless each of the parties has previously agreed to conduct transactions by electronic means. The agreement may be explicit, or it may be implied by the conduct of the parties and the surrounding circumstances.[24] It may sometimes be reasonable to infer that a person who gives out a business card with an e-mail address on it has consented to transact business electronically, for instance. Agreement may also be inferred from an e-mail or even a verbal communication between the parties.

A person who has agreed to an electronic transaction can withdraw his or her consent and refuse to conduct further business electronically. In addition, the parties can agree to opt out of all or some of the terms of the UETA. If they do not do so, then the UETA terms will govern their electronic transactions.

Attribution of Signatures Under the UETA, if an electronic record or signature is the act of a particular person, the record or signature may be attributed to that person. If a person types her or his name at the bottom of an e-mail purchase order, for instance, that name qualifies as

a "signature." The signature is therefore attributed to the person whose name appears on the purchase order.

The UETA does not contain any express provisions about what constitutes fraud or whether an agent is authorized to enter into a contract. Under the UETA, other state laws control if any issues relating to agency, authority, forgery, or contract formation arise. If existing state law requires a document to be notarized, the UETA provides that this requirement is satisfied by the electronic signature of a notary public or other person authorized to verify signatures.

The Effect of Errors The UETA encourages, but does not require, the use of security procedures (such as encryption) to verify changes to electronic documents and to correct errors.

The parties themselves may agree to use a security procedure. If they do, and if one party does not follow the procedure and thus fails to detect an error, the party that followed procedure can legally avoid the effect of the error. When the parties have not agreed to use a security procedure, then other state laws (including contract law governing mistakes) will determine the effect of the error.

To avoid the effect of errors, a party must promptly notify the other party of the error and of her or his intent

---

24. UETA 5(b), and Comment 4B.

not to be bound by the error. In addition, the party must take reasonable steps to return any benefit received. Parties cannot avoid a transaction if they have benefited.

Timing An electronic record is considered *sent* when it is properly directed to the intended recipient in a form readable by the recipient's computer system. Once the electronic record leaves the control of the sender or comes under the control of the recipient, the UETA deems it to have been sent. An electronic record is considered *received* when it enters the recipient's processing system in a readable form—*even if no individual is aware of its receipt.*

12–4 International Treaties Affecting E-Contracts

Much of the e-commerce conducted on a worldwide basis involves buyers and sellers from the United States.

The preeminence of U.S. law in this area is likely to be challenged in the future, however, as Internet use continues to expand worldwide. Already, several international organizations have created their own regulations for global Internet transactions.

The United Nations Convention on the Use of Electronic Communications in International Contracts improves commercial certainty by determining an Internet user's location for legal purposes. The convention also establishes standards for creating functional equivalence between electronic communications and paper documents. In addition, it provides that e-signatures will be treated as the equivalent of signatures on paper documents.

Another treaty relevant to e-contracts is the Hague Convention on the Choice of Court Agreements. Although it does not specifically mention e-commerce, this convention provides more certainty regarding jurisdiction and recognition of judgments by other nations' courts, thereby facilitating both offline and online transactions.

Reviewing: Agreement in Traditional and E-Contracts

Shane Durbin wanted to have a recording studio custom-built in his home. He sent invitations to a number of local contractors to submit bids on the project. Rory Amstel submitted the lowest bid, which was $20,000 less than any of the other bids Durbin received. Durbin called Amstel to ascertain the type and quality of the materials that were included in the bid and to find out if he could substitute a superior brand of acoustic tiles for the same bid price. Amstel said he would have to check into the price difference. The parties also discussed a possible start date for construction.

Two weeks later, Durbin changed his mind and decided not to go forward with his plan to build a recording studio. Amstel filed a suit against Durbin for breach of contract. Using the information presented in the chapter, answer the following questions.

1. Did Amstel's bid meet the requirements of an offer? Explain.
2. Was there an acceptance of the offer? Why or why not?
3. Suppose that the court determines that the parties did not reach an agreement. Further suppose that Amstel, in anticipation of building Durbin's studio, had purchased materials and refused other jobs so that he would have time in his schedule for Durbin's project. Under what theory discussed in the chapter might Amstel attempt to recover these costs?
4. How is an offer terminated? Assuming that Durbin did not inform Amstel that he was rejecting the offer, was the offer terminated at any time described here? Explain.

Debate This . . .   *The terms and conditions in click-on agreements are so long and detailed that no one ever reads the agreements. Therefore, the act of clicking on "I agree" is not really an acceptance.*

Terms and Concepts

acceptance 238	browse-wrap terms 244	counteroffer 236
agreement 231	click-on agreement 243	e-contract 241

Issue Spotters

1. Fidelity Corporation offers to hire Ron to replace Monica, who has given Fidelity a month's notice of intent to quit. Fidelity gives Ron a week to decide whether to accept. Two days later, Monica decides not to quit and signs an employment contract with Fidelity for another year. The next day, Monica tells Ron of the new contract. Ron immediately faxes a formal letter of acceptance to Fidelity. Do Fidelity and Ron have a contract? Why or why not? (See *Agreement*.)

2. Applied Products, Inc., does business with Beltway Distributors, Inc., online. Under the Uniform Electronic Transactions Act, what determines the effect of the electronic documents evidencing the parties' deal? Is a party's "signature" necessary? Explain. (See *The Uniform Electronic Transactions Act*.)

• **Check your answers to the Issue Spotters against the answers provided in Appendix D at the end of this text.**

Business Scenarios

12–1. Agreement. Ball e-mails Sullivan and inquires how much Sullivan is asking for a specific forty-acre tract of land Sullivan owns. Sullivan responds, "I will not take less than $60,000 for the forty-acre tract as specified." Ball immediately sends Sullivan a fax stating, "I accept your offer for $60,000 for the forty-acre tract as specified." Discuss whether Ball can hold Sullivan to a contract for the sale of the land. (See *Agreement*.)

12–2. Offer and Acceptance. Schmidt, the owner of a small business, has a large piece of used farm equipment for sale. He offers to sell the equipment to Barry for $10,000. Discuss the legal effects of the following events on the offer: (See *Agreement*.)

(a) Schmidt dies prior to Barry's acceptance, and at the time he accepts, Barry is unaware of Schmidt's death.

(b) The night before Barry accepts, fire destroys the equipment.

(c) Barry pays $100 for a thirty-day option to purchase the equipment. During this period, Schmidt dies, and later Barry accepts the offer, knowing of Schmidt's death.

(d) Barry pays $100 for a thirty-day option to purchase the equipment. During this period, Barry dies, and Barry's estate accepts Schmidt's offer within the stipulated time period.

Business Case Problems

12–3. Spotlight on Crime Stoppers—Communication.

The Baton Rouge Crime Stoppers (BCS) offered a reward for information about the "South Louisiana Serial Killer." The information was to be provided via a hot line. Dianne Alexander had survived an attack by a person suspected of being the killer. She identified a suspect in a police photo lineup and later sought to collect the reward. BCS refused to pay because she had not provided information to them via the hot line. Had Alexander complied with the terms of the offer? Explain. [*Alexander v. Lafayette Crime Stoppers, Inc.*, 38 So.3d 282 (La. App. 3 Dist. 2010) (See *Agreement*.)

12–4. Business Case Problem with Sample Answer—Online Acceptances. Heather Reasonover opted to try

Internet service from Clearwire Corp. Clearwire sent her a confirmation e-mail and a modem. When Reasonover plugged in the modem, an "I accept terms" box appeared. Without clicking on the box, Reasonover quit the page. She had not seen Clearwire's "Terms of Service," accessible only through its Web

site. Although the e-mail she received and the printed materials included with the model included URLs to the company's Web site, neither URL gave direct access to the "Terms of Service." A clause in the "Terms of Service" required subscribers to submit any dispute to arbitration. Is Reasonover bound to this clause? Why or why not? [*Kwan v. Clearwire Corp.*, 2012 WL 32380 (W.D.Wash. 2012)] (See *Agreement in E-Contracts*.)

• **For a sample answer to Problem 12–4, go to Appendix E at the end of this text.**

12–5. Acceptance. Judy Olsen, Kristy Johnston, and their mother, Joyce Johnston, owned seventy-eight acres of real property on Eagle Creek in Meagher County, Montana. When Joyce died, she left her interest in the property to Kristy. Kristy wrote to Judy, offering to buy Judy's interest or to sell her own interest to Judy. The letter said to "please respond to Bruce Townsend." In a letter to Kristy—not to Bruce—Judy accepted Kristy's offer to sell her interest. By that time, however, Kristy had made the same offer to sell her interest to their brother, Dave, and he had accepted. Did Judy and Kristy have an enforceable, binding contract? Or did Kristy's offer specifying one exclusive mode of acceptance mean that Judy's reply was not effective? Discuss. [*Olsen v. Johnston,* 368 Mont. 347, 301 P.3d 791 (2013)] (See *Agreement.*)

12–6. Agreement. Amy Kemper was seriously injured when her motorcycle was struck by a vehicle driven by Christopher Brown. Kemper's attorney wrote to Statewide Claims Services, the administrator for Brown's insurer, asking for "all the insurance money that Mr. Brown had under his insurance policy." In exchange, the letter indicated that Kemper would sign a "limited release" on Brown's liability, provided that it did not include any language requiring her to reimburse Brown or his insurance company for any of their incurred costs. Statewide then sent a check and release form to Kemper, but the release demanded that Kemper "place money in an escrow account in regards to any and all liens pending." Kemper refused the demand, claiming that Statewide's response was a counteroffer rather than an unequivocal acceptance of the settlement offer. Did Statewide and Kemper have an enforceable agreement? Discuss. [*Kemper v. Brown,* 325 Ga.App. 806, 754 S.E.2d 141 (2014)] (See *Agreement.*)

12–7. Requirements of the Offer. Technical Consumer Products, Inc. (TCP), makes and distributes energy-efficient lighting products. Emily Bahr was TCP's district sales manager in Minnesota, North Dakota, and South Dakota when the company announced the details of a bonus plan. A district sales manager who achieved 100 percent year-over-year sales growth and a 42 percent gross margin would earn 200 percent of his or her base salary as a bonus. TCP retained absolute discretion to modify the plan. Bahr's base salary was $42,500. Her final sales results for the year showed 113 percent year-over-year sales growth and a 42 percent gross margin. She anticipated a bonus of $85,945, but TCP could not afford to pay the bonuses as planned, and Bahr received only $34,229. In response to Bahr's claim for breach of contract, TCP argued that the bonus plan was too indefinite to be an offer. Is TCP correct? Explain. [*Bahr v. Technical Consumer Products, Inc.,* 601 Fed.Appx. 359 (6th Cir. 2015)] (See *Agreement.*)

12–8. Acceptance. Altisource Portfolio Solutions, Inc., is a global corporation that provides real property owners with a variety of services, including property preservation—repairs, debris removal, and so on. Lucas Contracting, Inc., is a small trade contractor in Carrollton, Ohio. On behalf of Altisource, Berghorst Enterprises, LLC, hired Lucas to perform preservation work on certain foreclosed properties in eastern Ohio.

When Berghorst did not pay for the work, Lucas filed a suit in an Ohio state court against Altisource. Before the trial, Lucas e-mailed the terms of a settlement. The same day, Altisource e-mailed a response that did not challenge or contradict Lucas's proposal and indicated agreement to it. Two days later, however, Altisource forwarded a settlement document that contained additional terms. Which proposal most likely satisfies the element of agreement to establish a contract? Explain. [*Lucas Contracting, Inc. v. Altisource Portfolio Solutions, Inc.,* __ Ohio App.3d __, 2016-Ohio-474, __ N.E.2d __ (2016)] (See *Agreement.*)

12–9. A Question of Ethics—E-Contract Disputes.
 Dewayne Hubbert, Elden Craft, Chris Grout, and Rhonda Byington bought computers from Dell Corp. through its Web site. Before buying, Hubbert and the others configured their own computers. To make a purchase, each buyer completed forms on five Web pages. On each page, Dell's "Terms and Conditions of Sale" were accessible by clicking on a blue hyperlink. A statement on three of the pages read, "All sales are subject to Dell's Term[s] and Conditions of Sale," but a buyer was not required to click an assent to the terms to complete a purchase. The terms were also printed on the backs of the invoices and on separate documents contained in the shipping boxes with the computers. Among those terms was a "Binding Arbitration" clause.

The computers contained Pentium 4 microprocessors, which Dell advertised as the fastest, most powerful Intel Pentium processors then available. In 2002, Hubbert and the others filed a suit in an Illinois state court against Dell, alleging that this marketing was false, misleading, and deceptive. The plaintiffs claimed that the Pentium 4 microprocessor was slower and less powerful, and provided poorer performance, than either a Pentium III or an AMD Athlon, and at a greater cost. Dell asked the court to compel arbitration. [*Hubbert v. Dell Corp., 359 Ill.App.3d 976, 835 N.E.2d 113, 296 Ill.Dec. 258 (5 Dist. 2005)]* (See *Agreement in E-Contracts.*)

(a) Should the court enforce the arbitration clause in this case? If you were the judge, how would you rule on this issue?

(b) Do you think shrink-wrap, click-on, and browse-wrap terms impose too great a burden on purchasers? Why or why not?

(c) An ongoing complaint about shrink-wrap, click-on, and browse-wrap terms is that sellers (often large corporations) draft them and buyers (typically individual consumers) do not read them. Should purchasers be bound in contract by terms that they have not even read? Why or why not?

Legal Reasoning Group Activity

12–10. E-Contracts. To download a specific application (app) to your smartphone or tablet device, usually you have to check a box indicating that you agree to the company's terms and conditions. Most individuals do so without ever reading those terms and conditions. Print out a specific set of terms and conditions from a downloaded app to use in this assignment. (See *Agreement in E-Contracts.*)

(a) One group will determine which of these terms and conditions are favorable to the company.

(b) Another group will determine which of these terms and conditions conceivably will be favorable to the individual.

(c) A third group will determine which terms and conditions, on net, favor the company too much.

CHAPTER 13

Consideration

The fact that a promise has been made does not mean the promise can or will be enforced. Under Roman law, a promise was not enforceable without a *causa*—that is, a reason for making the promise that was also deemed to be a sufficient reason for enforcing it.

Under the common law, a primary basis for the enforcement of promises is consideration. **Consideration** usually is defined as the value given in return for a promise (in a bilateral contract) or in return for a performance (in a unilateral contract). It is the inducement, price, or motive that causes a party to enter into an agreement.

As long as consideration is present, the courts generally do not interfere with contracts based on the amount of consideration paid. It is up to the contracting parties to determine how much their bargain is worth.

13–1 Elements of Consideration

Often, consideration is broken down into two parts: (1) something of *legally sufficient value* must be given in exchange for the promise, and (2) there must be a *bargained-for* exchange.

13–1a Legally Sufficient Value

To be legally sufficient, consideration must be something of value in the eyes of the law. The "something of legally sufficient value" may consist of the following:

1. A promise to do something that one has no prior legal duty to do.
2. The performance of an action that one is otherwise not obligated to undertake.
3. The refraining from an action that one has a legal right to undertake (called a **forbearance**).

Consideration in bilateral contracts normally consists of a promise in return for a promise. In a contract for the sale of goods, for instance, the seller promises to ship specific goods to the buyer, and the buyer promises to pay for those goods. Each of these promises constitutes consideration for the contract.

In contrast, unilateral contracts involve a promise in return for a performance (an action). ■ **EXAMPLE 13.1** Anita says to her neighbor, "When you finish painting the garage, I will pay you $800." Anita's neighbor paints the garage. The act of painting the garage is the consideration that creates Anita's contractual obligation to pay her neighbor $800. ■ Exhibit 13–1 illustrates how consideration differs by types of contracts.

What if, in return for a promise to pay, a person refrains from pursuing harmful habits (a forbearance), such as the use of tobacco and alcohol? Does such forbearance constitute legally sufficient consideration? This was the issue before the court in the following classic case concerning consideration.

Classic Case 13.1

Hamer v. Sidway

Court of Appeals of New York, Second Division, 124 N.Y. 538, 27 N.E. 256 (1891).

Background and Facts William E. Story, Sr., was the uncle of William E. Story II. In the presence of family members and others, the uncle promised to pay his nephew $5,000 ($76,000 in today's dollars) if he would refrain from drinking, using tobacco, swearing, and playing cards or billiards for

Case 13.1 Continued

money until he reached the age of twenty-one. (Note that in 1869, when this contract was formed, it was legal in New York to drink and play cards for money before the age of twenty-one.)

The nephew agreed and fully performed his part of the bargain. When he reached the age of twenty-one, he wrote and told his uncle that he had kept his part of the agreement and was therefore entitled to $5,000. The uncle wrote a letter back indicating that he was pleased with his nephew's performance and saying "you shall have five thousand dollars, as I promised you." The uncle also said that the $5,000 was in the bank and that the nephew could "consider this money on interest." The nephew left the $5,000 in the care of his uncle, where it would earn interest under the terms and conditions of the letter.

The uncle died about twelve years later without having paid his nephew any part of the $5,000 and interest. The executor of the uncle's estate (Sidway, the defendant in this action) claimed that there had been no valid consideration for the promise. Sidway refused to pay the $5,000 (plus interest) to Hamer, a third party to whom the nephew had transferred his rights in the note. The court reviewed the case to determine whether the nephew had given valid consideration under the law.

In the Language of the Court

PARKER, J. [Justice]

* * * *

* * * Courts will not ask whether the thing which forms the consideration does in fact benefit the promisee or a third party, or is of any substantial value to any one. It is enough that something is promised, done, forborne, or suffered by the party to whom the promise is made as consideration for the promise made to him. *In general a waiver of any legal right at the request of another party is a sufficient consideration for a promise.* Any damage, or suspension, or forbearance of a right will be sufficient to sustain a promise. * * * Now, applying this rule to the facts before us, the promisee used tobacco, occasionally drank liquor, and he had a legal right to do so. That right he abandoned for a period of years upon the strength of the promise of the testator [his uncle] that for such forbearance he would give him $5,000. We need not speculate on the effort which may have been required to give up the use of those stimulants. It is sufficient that he restricted his lawful freedom of action within certain prescribed limits upon the faith of his uncle's agreement * * *. [Emphasis added.]

Decision and Remedy *The court ruled that the nephew had provided legally sufficient consideration by giving up smoking, drinking, swearing, and playing cards or billiards for money until he reached the age of twenty-one. Therefore, he was entitled to the funds.*

Impact of This Case on Today's Law *Although this case was decided more than a century ago, the principles enunciated by the court remain applicable to contracts formed today, including online contracts. For a contract to be valid and binding, consideration must be given, and that consideration must be something of legally sufficient value.*

Critical Thinking
- **What If the Facts Were Different?** *If the nephew had not had a legal right to engage in the behavior that he agreed to forgo, would the result in this case have been different? Explain.*

13–1b Bargained-for Exchange

The second element of consideration is that it must provide the basis for the bargain struck between the contracting parties. That is, the item of value must be given or promised by the promisor (offeror) in return for the promisee's promise, performance, or promise of performance.

This element of bargained-for exchange distinguishes contracts from gifts. ■ **EXAMPLE 13.2** Sheng-Li says to his son, "In consideration of the fact that you are not as wealthy as your brothers, I will pay you $5,000." The fact that the word *consideration* is used does not, by itself, mean that consideration has been given. Indeed, Sheng-Li's promise is not enforceable, because the son does not have to do anything in order to receive the $5,000 promised. Because the son does not need to give Sheng-Li something of legal value in return for his promise, there is no bargained-for exchange. Rather, Sheng-Li has simply stated his motive for giving his son a gift. ■

EXHIBIT 13-1 Consideration in Bilateral and Unilateral Contracts

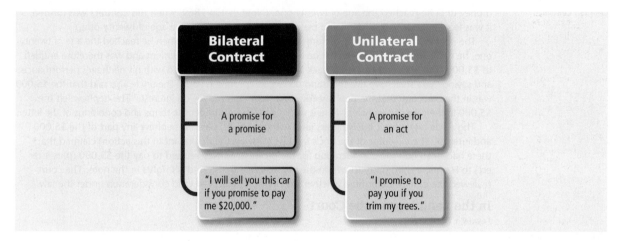

Sometimes, employers offer to cover the costs of employment-related education for their employees. The employees may then be required to repay their employers for all or a portion of the costs. At the center of the dispute in the following case was an agreement signed by an employee to reimburse his employer for educational costs. The question was whether the agreement met the requirement of a bargained-for exchange.

Case Analysis 13.2

USS–POSCO Industries v. Case

California Court of Appeal, First District, Division 1, 244 Cal.App.4th 197, 197 Cal.Rptr.3d 791 (2016).

In the Language of the Court

BANKE, J. [Judge]

* * * *

[USS–POSCO Industries (UPI) in Pittsburg, California,] hired [Floyd] Case in 2007. He initially worked as an entry-level Laborer and Side Trim Operator. As a condition of employment, Case joined Local 1440 of the United Steelworkers of America.

UPI faced a shortage of skilled Maintenance Technical Electrical (MTE) workers. To address this, UPI, after consultation with Local 1440, decided to implement a Learner Program. Thus, in June 2008, the company and Local 1440 entered into a Memorandum of Understanding (MOU) stating UPI would train up to 10 current employees, while continuing to pay their wages and benefits, in an effort to qualify them as MTEs. UPI and the union recognized "that, due to the strong demand

for Maintenance Technician Electrical [workers] the Company needs to retain successful candidates as employees for a reasonable period of time in order to recoup its substantial $46,000 investment in their training." UPI and the union therefore agreed UPI "may require candidates in the Learner Program to sign [a] Reimbursement Agreement that would require reimbursement for a portion of the training should a candidate voluntarily terminate employment within 30 months of completion of the Learner Program."

The Learner Program required 135 weeks of instruction, 90 weeks of on the job training and 45 weeks of classroom work (partially courses at a local community college, partially other courses). The goal was to complete training within 162 weeks, or just over three years. If a participant successfully completed the program and then passed UPI's MTE test,

he or she would be assigned to an MTE vacancy.

The MTE position and Learner Program aligned with Case's desire to work as an engineer. Case understood joining the Learner Program was voluntary. He also understood he did not need to go through the Learner Program or a similar formal educational program to obtain an MTE position. * * * A prospect could simply take and pass UPI's MTE test. However, Case did not attempt the test prior to participating in the Learner Program because he did not think he had the knowledge to pass. He was also unsure if he would pass if he undertook a self-study program. In any case, the Learner Program allowed him to get trained during the workday instead of after hours, and it would lead to higher pay. Accordingly, he applied for the program and was one of [the] selected participants.

Case 13.2 Continued

Case was informed of the reimbursement obligation during a training session for prospective participants. A presentation slide entitled "Repayment Agreement" told prospects they would "sign an agreement to reimburse a portion of their training cost should they voluntarily terminate employment within 30 months of program completion." The slide, consistent with the MOU, indicated the obligation would be "$46,000 prorated over 30 months."

Case was subsequently presented with a written reimbursement agreement and signed it without objection. Under that one-page agreement, Case acknowledged UPI would pay his "wages, benefits and training expenses" while he was in the Learner Program, but there would be no guarantee participation in the program would insure promotion, transfer, or continued employment with UPI. He further agreed that if he was fired for cause or voluntarily left UPI within 30 months after completing the program, he would, absent a compelling hardship such as a serious injury or family death, refund $30,000 of the expense of his training, less $1,000 per month of subsequent service at UPI.

Two months after completing the Learner Program and obtaining an MTE position, Case left UPI for Lawrence Livermore National Laboratory to work as a high voltage electrician.

* * * *

When Case refused to reimburse UPI, the company filed the instant lawsuit [in a California state court] alleging breach of contract * * * . UPI sought damages of $28,000—that is, $1,000 per month that remained in Case's 30-month earn-back period.

Case, in turn, filed a cross-complaint. [He] alleged the [reimbursement] agreement was unlawful because * * * it lacked consideration.

UPI subsequently moved for summary judgment on its complaint and Case's cross-complaint, asserting the reimbursement agreement was valid.

The trial court granted UPI's motion, and the parties thereafter stipulated to a judgment in favor of UPI in the amount of $28,000 plus prejudgment interest and costs. [The court also awarded UPI attorneys' fees of $80,000.]

[Case appealed the judgment to a state intermediate appellate court.]

Case maintains the reimbursement agreement * * * lacked consideration because UPI had no obligation to keep Case employed and, thus, no obligation to provide education, which Case views as "the only possible consideration listed in the Reimbursement Agreement."

Case's view of the bargained-for exchange is too constrained.

On entering the program, Case held a new position of Learner, which meant he would remain on UPI's payroll while *additionally* getting classroom and on-the-job training, the costs of which UPI would front. While Case was not guaranteed a promotion, transfer, or continued employment, exactly the same had been true with respect to his previous position. The exchange, frankly, is obvious: Case got continued wages and fronted education costs, and UPI got Case's agreement to repay those costs if he both completed the training and left the company before it could benefit from the investment. *That either Case or UPI could have terminated the agreement by ending the employment relationship at some point during the educational program does not render illusory the parties' bargained-for exchange*—or require us to ignore the substantial benefits Case obtained every day he spent on the payroll receiving advanced training with no upfront cost and potentially no cost at all to him. [Emphasis added.]

* * * *

The summary judgment in favor of UPI is affirmed.

Legal Reasoning Questions

1. What did Case view as "the only possible consideration" for his agreement to reimburse UPI for some of the cost of his employment-related education?

2. How did the court interpret Case's view of "the only possible consideration"? Why?

3. If UPI had simply offered to pay its employees' wages and training expenses during their participation in a program of instruction "subject entirely and exclusively to UPI's approval," would the element of bargained-for exchange have been met? Explain.

13–1c Adequacy of Consideration

Adequacy of consideration involves how much consideration is given. Essentially, adequacy of consideration concerns the fairness of the bargain.

The General Rule On the surface, when the items exchanged are of unequal value, fairness would appear to be an issue. Normally, however, a court will not question the adequacy of consideration based solely on the comparative value of the things exchanged.

In other words, the determination of whether consideration exists does not depend on a comparison of the values of the things exchanged. Something need not be of direct economic or financial value to be considered legally sufficient consideration. In many situations, the exchange of promises and potential benefits is deemed to be sufficient consideration.

Under the doctrine of freedom of contract, courts leave it up to the parties to decide what something is worth, and parties are usually free to bargain as they wish. If people could sue merely because they had entered into an unwise contract, the courts would be overloaded with frivolous suits.

When Voluntary Consent May Be Lacking

When there is a large disparity in the amount or value of the consideration exchanged, it may raise a red flag for a court to look more closely at the bargain. Shockingly inadequate consideration can indicate that fraud, duress, or undue influence was involved. ■ **EXAMPLE 13.3** Spencer pays $500 for an iPhone 7 that he later discovers is a fake (counterfeit). Because the device is not authentic, he could claim that there was no valid contract because of inadequate consideration and fraud. ■

Disparity in the consideration exchanged may also cause a judge to question whether the contract is so one sided that it is *unconscionable*.[1] For instance, an experienced appliance dealer induces a consumer to sign a contract written in complicated legal language. If the contract requires the consumer to pay twice the market value of the appliance, the disparity in value may indicate that the sale involved undue influence or fraud. A judge would thus want to make sure that the person voluntarily entered into this agreement.[2]

Concept Summary 13.1 provides a review of the main aspects of consideration.

---

1. Pronounced un-*kon*-shun-uh-bul.
2. For an example of an unconscionable home loan contract, see *Orcilla v. Big Sur, Inc.,* 244 Cal.App.4th 982, 198 Cal.Rptr.3d 715 (2016).

13–2 Agreements That Lack Consideration

Sometimes, one of the parties (or both parties) to an agreement may think that consideration has been exchanged when in fact it has not. Here, we look at some situations in which the parties' promises or actions do not qualify as contractual consideration.

13–2a Preexisting Duty

Under most circumstances, a promise to do what one already has a legal duty to do does not constitute legally sufficient consideration. The preexisting legal duty may be imposed by law or may arise out of a previous contract. A sheriff, for instance, has a duty to investigate crime and to arrest criminals. Hence, a sheriff cannot collect a reward for providing information leading to the capture of a criminal.

Likewise, if a party is already bound by contract to perform a certain duty, that duty cannot serve as consideration for a second contract. ■ **EXAMPLE 13.4** Ajax Contractors begins construction on a seven-story office building and after three months demands an extra $75,000 on its contract. If the extra $75,000 is not paid, the contractor will stop working. The owner of the land, finding no one else to complete the construction, agrees to pay the extra $75,000. The agreement is unenforceable because it is not supported by legally sufficient consideration. Ajax Contractors had a preexisting contractual duty to complete the building. ■

Concept Summary 13.1

Consideration

Elements of Consideration	Consideration is the value given in exchange for a promise that is necessary to form a contract. Consideration is often broken down into two elements: • *Legal value*—Something of legally sufficient value must be given in exchange for a promise. This may consist of a promise, a performance, or a forbearance. • *Bargained-for exchange*—There must be a bargained-for exchange.
Adequacy of Consideration	• Adequacy of consideration relates to how much consideration is given and whether a fair bargain was reached. • Courts will inquire into the adequacy of consideration (if the consideration is legally sufficient) only when fraud, undue influence, duress, or the lack of a bargained-for exchange may be involved.

Unforeseen Difficulties The rule regarding preexisting duty is meant to prevent extortion and the so-called holdup game. Nonetheless, if, during performance of a contract, extraordinary difficulties arise that were totally unforeseen at the time the contract was formed, a court may allow an exception to the rule. The key is whether the court finds that the modification is fair and equitable in view of circumstances not anticipated by the parties when the contract was made.[3]

Suppose that in *Example 13.4*, Ajax Contractors had asked for the extra $75,000 because it encountered a rock formation that no one knew existed. If the landowner agrees to pay the extra $75,000 to excavate the rock and the court finds that it is fair to do so, Ajax Contractors can enforce the agreement. If rock formations are common in the area, however, the court may determine that the contractor should have known of the risk. In that situation, the court may choose to apply the preexisting duty rule and prevent Ajax Contractors from obtaining the extra $75,000.

Rescission and New Contract The law recognizes that two parties can mutually agree to rescind, or cancel, their contract, at least to the extent that it is *executory* (still to be carried out). **Rescission**[4] is the unmaking of a contract so as to return the parties to the positions they occupied before the contract was made.

Sometimes, parties rescind a contract and make a new contract at the same time. When this occurs, it is often difficult to determine whether there was consideration for the new contract, or whether the parties had a preexisting duty under the previous contract. If a court finds there was a preexisting duty, then the new contract will be invalid because there was no consideration.

13–2b Past Consideration

Promises made in return for actions or events that have already taken place are unenforceable. These promises lack consideration in that the element of bargained-for exchange is missing. In short, you can bargain for something to take place now or in the future but not for something that has already taken place. Therefore, **past consideration** is no consideration.

■ **CASE IN POINT 13.5** Jamil Blackmon became friends with Allen Iverson when Iverson was a high school student who showed tremendous promise as an athlete. One evening, Blackmon suggested that Iverson use "The Answer" as a nickname in the summer league basketball tournaments. Blackmon said that Iverson would be "The Answer" to all of the National Basketball Association's woes. Later that night, Iverson said that he would give Blackmon 25 percent of any proceeds from the merchandising of products that used "The Answer" as a logo or a slogan. Because Iverson's promise was made in return for past consideration, it was unenforceable. In effect, Iverson stated his intention to give Blackmon a gift.[5] ■

In a variety of situations, an employer will often ask an employee to sign a *noncompete agreement,* also called a *covenant not to compete.* Under such an agreement, the employee agrees not to compete with the employer for a certain period of time after the employment relationship ends. When a current employee is required to sign a noncompete agreement, his or her employment is not sufficient consideration for the agreement, because the individual is already employed. To be valid, the agreement requires new consideration.

13–2c Illusory Promises

If the terms of the contract express such uncertainty of performance that the promisor has not definitely promised to do anything, the promise is said to be *illusory*—without consideration and unenforceable. A promise is illusory when it fails to bind the promisor.

■ **EXAMPLE 13.6** The president of Tuscan Corporation says to her employees, "If profits continue to be high, everyone will get a 10 percent bonus at the end of the year—if management agrees." This is an *illusory promise,* or no promise at all, because performance depends solely on the discretion of management. There is no bargained-for consideration. The statement indicates only that management may or may not do something in the future. Therefore, even though the employees work hard and profits remain high, the company is not obligated to pay the bonus now or later. ■

Option-to-Cancel Clauses Sometimes, option-to-cancel clauses in contracts present problems in regard to consideration. When the promisor has the option to cancel the contract before performance has begun, the promise is illusory.

■ **EXAMPLE 13.7** Abe contracts to hire Chris for one year at $5,000 per month, reserving the right to cancel the contract at any time. On close examination of these words, you can see that Abe has not actually agreed to hire Chris, as Abe could cancel without liability before Chris started performance. This contract is therefore illusory.

---

3. *Restatement (Second) of Contracts*, Section 73.
4. Pronounced reh-*sih*-zhen.

5. *Blackmon v. Iverson,* 324 F.Supp.2d 602 (E.D.Pa. 2003).

But if Abe instead reserves the right to cancel the contract at any time *after* Chris has begun performance by giving Chris *thirty days' notice,* the promise is not illusory. Abe, by saying that he will give Chris thirty days' notice, is relinquishing the opportunity (legal right) to hire someone else instead of Chris for a thirty-day period. If Chris works for one month and Abe then gives him thirty days' notice, Chris has an enforceable claim for two months' salary ($10,000). ∎

Exhibit 13–2 illustrates some common situations in which promises or actions do not constitute contractual consideration.

Requirements and Output Contracts Problems with consideration may also arise in other types of contracts because of uncertainty of performance. Uncertain performance is characteristic of requirements and output contracts, for instance. In a *requirements contract,* a buyer and a seller agree that the buyer will purchase from the seller all of the goods of a designated type that the buyer needs, or requires. In an *output contract,* the buyer and seller agree that the buyer will purchase from the seller all of what the seller produces, or the seller's output. These types of contracts will be discussed further in a later chapter.

13–3 Settlement of Claims

Businesspersons and others often enter into contracts to settle legal claims. It is important to understand the nature of consideration given in these kinds of settlement agreements, or contracts. A claim may be settled through an *accord and satisfaction,* a *release,* or a *covenant not to sue.*

13–3a Accord and Satisfaction

In an **accord and satisfaction,** a debtor offers to pay, and a creditor accepts, a lesser amount than the creditor originally claimed was owed. The *accord* is the agreement. In the accord, one party undertakes to give or perform, and the other to accept, in satisfaction of a claim, something other than that on which the parties originally agreed. *Satisfaction* is the performance (usually payment) that takes place after the accord is executed.

A basic rule is that there can be no satisfaction unless there is first an accord. In addition, for accord and satisfaction to occur, the amount of the debt *must be in dispute.*

Liquidated Debts If a debt is *liquidated,* accord and satisfaction cannot take place. A **liquidated debt** is one whose amount has been ascertained, fixed, agreed on, settled, or exactly determined.

■ **EXAMPLE 13.8** Barbara Kwan signs an installment loan contract with her bank. In the contract, Kwan agrees to pay a set rate of interest on a specified amount of borrowed funds at monthly intervals for two years. Because both parties know the precise amount of the total obligation, it is a liquidated debt. ∎

In the majority of states, a creditor's acceptance of a lesser sum than the entire amount of a liquidated debt is *not* satisfaction, and the balance of the debt is still legally owed. The reason for this rule is that the debtor has given no consideration to satisfy the obligation of paying the balance to the creditor. The debtor had a preexisting legal

---

EXHIBIT 13–2 Examples of Agreements That Lack Consideration

PREEXISTING DUTY	PAST CONSIDERATION	ILLUSORY PROMISES
When a person already has a legal duty to perform an action, there is no legally sufficient consideration.	When a person makes a promise in return for actions or events that have already taken place, there is no consideration.	When a person expresses contract terms with such uncertainty that the terms are not definite, the promise is illusory.
Example: A firefighter cannot receive a cash reward from a business owner for putting out a fire in a downtown commercial district. As a city employee, the firefighter had a duty to extinguish the fire.	*Example:* A real estate agent sold a friend's house without charging a commission, and in return, the friend promises to give the agent $1,000. The friend's promise is simply an intention to give a gift.	*Example:* A storeowner promises a $500 bonus to each employee who works Christmas Day, as long as the owner feels that they did their jobs well. The owner's promise is just a statement of something she may or may not do in the future.

obligation to pay the entire debt. (Of course, even with liquidated debts, creditors often do negotiate debt settlement agreements with debtors for a lesser amount than was originally owed. Creditors sometimes even forgive, or write off, a liquidated debt as uncollectable.)

Unliquidated Debts An **unliquidated debt** is the opposite of a liquidated debt. The amount of the debt is *not* settled, fixed, agreed on, ascertained, or determined, and reasonable persons may differ over the amount owed. In these circumstances, acceptance of a lesser sum operates as satisfaction, or discharge, of the debt because there is valid consideration. The parties give up a legal right to contest the amount in dispute.

13–3b Release

A **release** is a contract in which one party forfeits the right to pursue a legal claim against the other party. It bars any further recovery beyond the terms stated in the release.

A release will generally be binding if it meets the following requirements:

1. The agreement is made in good faith (honestly).
2. The release contract is in a signed writing (required in many states).
3. The contract is accompanied by consideration.[6]

---

6. Under the Uniform Commercial Code (UCC), a written, signed waiver or renunciation by an aggrieved party discharges any further liability for a breach, even without consideration.

Clearly, an individual is better off knowing the extent of his or her injuries or damages before signing a release. ■ **EXAMPLE 13.9** Lupe's car is damaged in an automobile accident caused by Dexter's negligence. Dexter offers to give her $3,000 if she will release him from further liability resulting from the accident. Lupe agrees and signs the release.

If Lupe later discovers that it will cost $4,200 to repair her car, she normally cannot recover the additional amount from Dexter. Lupe is limited to the $3,000 specified in the release. Lupe and Dexter voluntarily agreed to the terms in the release, which was in a signed writing, and sufficient consideration was present. The consideration was the legal right Lupe forfeited to sue to recover damages, should they be more than $3,000, in exchange for Dexter's promise to give her $3,000. ■

13–3c Covenant Not to Sue

Unlike a release, a **covenant not to sue** does not always bar further recovery. The parties simply substitute a contractual obligation for some other type of legal action based on a valid claim. Suppose that, in *Example 13.9*, Lupe agrees with Dexter not to sue for damages in a tort action if he will pay for the damage to her car. If Dexter fails to pay for the repairs, Lupe can bring an action against him for breach of contract.

As the following case illustrates, a covenant not to sue can form the basis for a dismissal of the claims of either party to the covenant.

Spotlight on Nike

Case 13.3 Already, LLC v. Nike, Inc.

Supreme Court of the United States, __ U.S. __, 133 S.Ct. 721, 184 L.Ed.2d 553 (2013).

Background and Facts Nike, Inc., designs, makes, and sells athletic footwear, including a line of shoes known as "Air Force 1." Already, LLC, also designs and markets athletic footwear, including the "Sugar" and "Soulja Boy" lines. Nike filed a suit in a federal district court against Already, alleging that Soulja Boys and Sugars infringed the Air Force 1 trademark. Already filed a counterclaim, contending that the Air Force 1 trademark was invalid. While the suit was pending, Nike issued a covenant not to sue. Nike promised not to raise any trademark claims against Already or any affiliated entity based on Already's existing footwear designs or any future Already designs that constituted a "colorable imitation" of Already's current products. Nike then filed a motion to dismiss its own claims and to dismiss Already's counterclaim. Already opposed the dismissal of its counterclaim, but the court granted Nike's motion. The U.S. Court of Appeals for the Second Circuit affirmed. Already appealed to the United States Supreme Court.

In the Language of the Court

Chief Justice *ROBERTS* delivered the opinion of the Court.
* * * *

Case 13.3 Continues

Case 13.3 Continued

* * * A defendant cannot automatically moot a case simply by ending its unlawful conduct once sued. [A matter is *moot* if it involves no actual controversy for the court to decide, and federal courts will dismiss moot cases.] Otherwise, a defendant could engage in unlawful conduct, stop when sued to have the case declared moot, then pick up where he left off, repeating this cycle until he achieves all his unlawful ends. Given this concern, * * * *a defendant claiming that its voluntary compliance moots a case bears the formidable burden of showing that it is absolutely clear the allegedly wrongful behavior could not reasonably be expected to recur.* [This is the voluntary cessation test. Emphasis added.]

* * * *

We begin our analysis with the terms of the covenant:

[Nike] unconditionally and irrevocably covenants to refrain from making *any* claim(s) or demand(s) * * * against Already or *any* of its * * * related business entities * * * [including] distributors * * * and employees of such entities and *all* customers * * * on account of any *possible* cause of action based on or involving trademark infringement * * * relating to the NIKE Mark based on the appearance of *any* of Already's current and/or previous footwear product designs, and *any* colorable imitations thereof, regardless of whether that footwear is produced * * * or otherwise used in commerce.

The breadth of this covenant suffices to meet the burden imposed by the voluntary cessation test.

In addition, Nike originally argued that the Sugars and Soulja Boys infringed its trademark; in other words, Nike believed those shoes were "colorable imitations" of the Air Force 1s. Nike's covenant now allows Already to produce all of its existing footwear designs—including the Sugar and Soulja Boy—and any "colorable imitation" of those designs. * * * It is hard to imagine a scenario that would potentially infringe Nike's trademark and yet not fall under the covenant. Nike, having taken the position in court that there is no prospect of such a shoe, would be hard pressed to assert the contrary down the road. If such a shoe exists, the parties have not pointed to it, there is no evidence that Already has dreamt of it, and we cannot conceive of it. It sits, as far as we can tell, on a shelf between Dorothy's ruby slippers and Perseus's winged sandals.

* * * *

* * * Given the covenant's broad language, and given that Already has asserted no concrete plans to engage in conduct not covered by the covenant, we can conclude the case is moot because the challenged conduct cannot reasonably be expected to recur.

Decision and Remedy *The United States Supreme Court affirmed the judgment of the lower court. Under the covenant not to sue, Nike could not file a claim for trademark infringement against Already, and Already could not assert that Nike's trademark was invalid.*

Critical Thinking
- **Economic** *Why would any party agree to a covenant not to sue?*
- **Legal Environment** *Which types of contracts are similar to covenants not to sue? Explain.*

See Concept Summary 13.2 to review the methods of settling claims.

13–4 Exceptions to the Consideration Requirement

There are some exceptions to the rule that only promises supported by consideration are enforceable. The following types of promises may be enforced despite the lack of consideration:

1. Promises that induce detrimental reliance, under the doctrine of *promissory estoppel.*
2. Promises to pay debts that are barred by a statute of limitations.
3. Promises to make charitable contributions.

13–4a Promissory Estoppel

Sometimes, individuals rely on promises to their detriment, and their reliance may form a basis for a court to infer contract rights and duties. Under the doctrine of **promissory estoppel** (also called *detrimental reliance*), a person who

Concept Summary 13.2

Settlement of Claims

Accord and Satisfaction	An *accord* is an agreement in which a debtor offers to pay a lesser amount than the creditor claims is owed. *Satisfaction* takes place when the accord is executed.
Release	An agreement in which, for consideration, a party forfeits the right to seek further recovery beyond the terms specified in the release.
Covenant Not to Sue	An agreement not to sue on a present, valid claim.

has reasonably and substantially relied on the promise of another may be able to obtain some measure of recovery.

Promissory estoppel is applied in a wide variety of contexts in which a promise is otherwise unenforceable, such as when a promise is made *without consideration.* Under this doctrine, a court may enforce an otherwise unenforceable promise to avoid the injustice that would otherwise result.

Requirements to Establish Promissory Estoppel For the promissory estoppel doctrine to be applied, the following elements are required:

1. There must be a clear and definite promise.
2. The promisor should have expected that the promisee would rely on the promise.
3. The promisee reasonably relied on the promise by acting or refraining from some act.
4. The promisee's reliance was definite and resulted in substantial detriment.
5. Enforcement of the promise is necessary to avoid injustice.

If these requirements are met, a promise may be enforced even though it is not supported by consideration.[7] In essence, the promisor will be **estopped** (prevented) from asserting the lack of consideration as a defense.

Promissory estoppel is similar in some ways to the doctrine of quasi contract. In both situations, a court, acting in the interests of equity, imposes contract obligations on the parties to prevent unfairness even though no actual contract exists. The difference is that with

quasi contract, no promise was made at all. In contrast, with promissory estoppel, an unenforceable promise was made and relied on but not performed.

Application of the Doctrine Promissory estoppel was originally applied to situations involving promises of gifts and of donations to charities. Later, courts began to apply the doctrine to avoid inequity or hardship in other situations, including business transactions, some employment relationships, and even disputes among family members.

■ **CASE IN POINT 13.10** Jeffrey and Kathryn Dow owned 125 acres of land in Corinth, Maine. The Dows regarded the land as their children's heritage, and the subject of the children's living on the land was often discussed within the family. With the Dows' permission, their daughter Teresa installed a mobile home and built a garage on the land. After Teresa married Jarrod Harvey, the Dows agreed to finance the construction of a house on the land for the couple. When Jarrod died in a motorcycle accident, however, Teresa financed the house with his life insurance proceeds. The construction cost about $200,000. Her father, Jeffrey, performed a substantial amount of carpentry and other work on the house.

Teresa then asked her parents for a deed to the property so that she could obtain a mortgage. They refused. Teresa sued her parents for promissory estoppel. Maine's highest court ruled in favor of Teresa's promissory estoppel claim. The court reasoned that the Dows' support and encouragement of their daughter's construction of a house on the land "conclusively demonstrated" their intent to transfer. For years, they had made general promises to convey the land to their children, including Teresa.

---

7. *Restatement (Second) of Contracts*, Section 90.

Teresa had reasonably relied on their promise in financing construction of a house to her detriment ($200,000). The court concluded that enforcing the promise was the only way to avoid injustice in this situation.[8] ■

13–4b Promises to Pay Debts Barred by a Statute of Limitations

Statutes of limitations in all states require a creditor to sue within a specified period to recover a debt. If the creditor fails to sue in time, recovery of the debt is barred by the statute of limitations.

A debtor who promises to pay a previous debt even though recovery is barred by the statute of limitations makes an enforceable promise. *The promise needs no consideration.* (Some states, however, require that it be in writing.) In effect, the promise extends the limitations period, and the creditor can sue to recover the entire debt or at least the amount promised. The promise can be implied if the debtor acknowledges the barred debt by making a partial payment.

---

8. *Harvey v. Dow*, 2011 ME 4, 11 A.3d 303 (2011).

13–4c Charitable Subscriptions

A charitable subscription is a promise to make a donation to a religious, educational, or charitable institution. Traditionally, such promises were unenforceable because they are not supported by legally sufficient consideration. A gift, after all, is the opposite of bargained-for consideration. The modern view, however, is to make exceptions to the general rule by applying the doctrine of promissory estoppel.

■ **EXAMPLE 13.11** A church solicits and receives pledges (commitments to contribute funds) from church members to erect a new church building. On the basis of these pledges, the church purchases land, hires architects, and makes other contracts that change its position. Because of the church's detrimental reliance, a court may enforce the pledges under the theory of promissory estoppel. Alternatively, a court may find consideration in the fact that each promise was made in reliance on the other promises of support or that the church trustees, by accepting the subscriptions, impliedly promised to complete the proposed undertaking. ■

Reviewing: Consideration

John operates a motorcycle repair shop from his home but finds that his business is limited by the small size of his garage. Driving by a neighbor's property, he notices a for-sale sign on a large, metal-sided garage. John contacts the neighbor and offers to buy the building, hoping that it can be dismantled and moved to his own property.

The neighbor accepts John's payment and makes a generous offer in return. If John will help him dismantle the garage, which will take a substantial amount of time, he will help John reassemble it after it has been transported to John's property. They agree to have the entire job completed within two weeks.

John spends every day for a week working with his neighbor to disassemble the building. In his rush to acquire a larger workspace, he turns down several lucrative repair jobs. Once the disassembled building has been moved to John's property, however, the neighbor refuses to help John reassemble it as he originally promised. Using the information presented in the chapter, answer the following questions.

1. Are the basic elements of consideration present in the neighbor's promise to help John reassemble the garage? Why or why not?
2. Suppose that the neighbor starts to help John but then realizes that putting the building back together will take much more work than dismantling it. Under which principle discussed in the chapter might the neighbor be allowed to ask for additional compensation?
3. What if John's neighbor made his promise to help reassemble the garage at the time he and John were moving it? Suppose he said, "Since you helped me take it down, I will help you put it back up." Would John be able to enforce this promise? Why or why not?
4. Under what doctrine discussed in the chapter might John seek to recover the profits he lost when he turned down repair jobs for one week?

Debate This . . . *Courts should not be able to rule on the adequacy of consideration. A deal is a deal.*

Terms and Concepts

accord and satisfaction 256
consideration 250
covenant not to sue 257
estopped 259

forbearance 250
liquidated debt 256
past consideration 255
promissory estoppel 258

release 257
rescission 255
unliquidated debt 257

Issue Spotters

1. In September, Sharyn agrees to work for Totem Productions, Inc., at $500 a week for a year beginning January 1. In October, Sharyn is offered the same work at $600 a week by Umber Shows, Ltd. When Sharyn tells Totem about the other offer, a Totem representative tears up their contract and agrees that Sharyn will be paid $575. Is the new contract binding? Explain. (See *Agreements That Lack Consideration.*)

2. Before Maria starts her first year of college, Fred promises to give her $5,000 when she graduates. She goes to

college, borrowing and spending far more than $5,000. At the beginning of the spring semester of her senior year, she reminds Fred of the promise. Fred sends her a note that says, "I revoke the promise." Is Fred's promise binding? Explain. (See *Exceptions to the Consideration Requirement.*)

• **Check your answers to the Issue Spotters against the answers provided in Appendix D at the end of this text.**

Business Scenarios

13–1. Preexisting Duty. Tabor is a buyer of file cabinets manufactured by Martin. Martin's contract with Tabor calls for delivery of fifty file cabinets at $40 per cabinet in five equal installments. After delivery of two installments (twenty cabinets), Martin informs Tabor that because of inflation, Martin is losing money. Martin will promise to deliver the remaining thirty cabinets only if Tabor will pay $50 per cabinet. Tabor agrees in writing to do so. Discuss whether Martin can legally collect the additional $100 on delivery to Tabor of the next installment of ten cabinets. (See *Agreements That Lack Consideration.*)

13–2. Consideration. Daniel, a recent college graduate, is on his way home for the Christmas holidays from his new job. He is caught in a snowstorm and is taken in by an elderly couple, who provide him with food and shelter. After the snowplows have cleared the road, Daniel proceeds home. Daniel's

father, Fred, is most appreciative of the elderly couple's action and promises to pay them $500. The elderly couple, in need of funds, accept Fred's offer. Then, because of a dispute between Daniel and Fred, Fred refuses to pay the elderly couple the $500. Discuss whether the couple can hold Fred liable in contract for the services rendered to Daniel. (See *Agreements That Lack Consideration.*)

13–3. Accord and Satisfaction. Merrick grows and sells blueberries. Maine Wild Blueberry Co. agreed to buy all of Merrick's crop under a contract that left the price unliquidated. Merrick delivered the berries, but a dispute arose over the price. Maine Wild sent Merrick a check with a letter stating that the check was the "final settlement." Merrick cashed the check but filed a suit for breach of contract, claiming that he was owed more. What will the court likely decide in this case? Why? (See *Settlement of Claims.*)

Business Case Problems

13–4. Rescission. Farrokh and Scheherezade Sharabianlou signed a purchase agreement to buy a building owned by Berenstein Associates for $2 million. They deposited $115,000 toward the purchase. Before the deal closed, an environmental assessment of the property indicated the presence of chemicals used in dry cleaning. This substantially reduced the property's value. Do the Sharabianlous have a good argument for the return of their deposit and rescission of the contract Explain your answer. [*Sharabianlou v. Karp*, 181 Cal.App.4th 1133, 105 Cal.Rptr.3d 300 (1st Dist. 2010)] (See *Agreements That Lack Consideration.*)

13–5. Statute of Limitations. Leonard Kranzler loaned Lewis Saltzman $100,000. Saltzman made fifteen payments on the loan, but this did not repay the entire amount. More than ten years after the date of the loan, but less than two years after the date of the last payment, Kranzler filed a suit against Saltzman to recover the outstanding balance. Saltzman claimed that the suit was barred by a ten-year statute of limitations. Does Kranzler need to prove a new promise with new consideration to collect the unpaid debt? Explain. [*Kranzler v. Saltzman*, 407 Ill.App.3d 24, 942 N.E.2d 722, 347 Ill.Dec. 519 (1 Dist. 2011)] (See *Exceptions to the Consideration Requirement.*)

13–6. Spotlight on Kansas City Chiefs—Consideration. On Brenda Sniezek's first day of work for the Kansas City Chiefs Football Club, she signed a document that purported to compel arbitration of any disputes that she might have with the Chiefs. In the document, Sniezek agreed to comply at all times with and be bound by the constitution and bylaws of the National Football League (NFL). She agreed to refer all disputes to the NFL Commissioner for a binding decision. On the Commissioner's decision, she agreed to release the Chiefs and others from any related claims. Nowhere in the document did the Chiefs agree to do anything. Was there consideration for the arbitration provision? Explain. [*Sniezek v. Kansas City Chiefs Football Club*, 402 S.W.3d 580 (Mo.App. W.D. 2013)] (See *Elements of Consideration*.)

13–7. Business Case Problem with Sample Answer—Consideration. Citynet, LLC, established an employee incentive plan "to enable the Company to attract and retain experienced individuals." The plan provided that a participant who left Citynet's employment was entitled to "cash out" his or her entire vested balance. (When an employee's rights to a particular benefit become *vested*, they belong to that employee and cannot be taken away. The vested balance refers to the part of an account that goes with the employee if he or she leaves the company.) When Citynet employee Ray Toney terminated his employment, he asked to redeem his vested balance, which amounted to $87,000.48. Citynet refused, citing a provision of the plan that limited redemptions to no more than 20 percent annually. Toney filed a suit in a West Virginia state court against Citynet, alleging breach of contract. Citynet argued that the plan was not a contract but a discretionary bonus over which Citynet had sole discretion. Was the plan a contract? If so, what was the consideration? [*Citynet, LLC v. Toney*, 235 W.Va. 79, 772 S.E.2d 36 (2015)] (See *Elements of Consideration*.)

• For a sample answer to Problem 13–7, go to Appendix E at the end of this text.

13–8. Agreements That Lack Consideration. Arkansas-Missouri Forest Products, LLC (Ark-Mo), sells supplies to make wood pallets. Blue Chip Manufacturing (BCM) makes pallets. Mark Garnett, an owner of Ark-Mo, and Stuart Lerner, an owner of BCM, went into business together. Garnett and Lerner agreed that Ark-Mo would have a 30-percent ownership interest in their future projects. When Lerner formed Blue Chip Recycling, LLC (BCR), to manage a pallet repair facility in California, however, he allocated only a 5-percent interest to Ark-Mo. Garnett objected. In a "Telephone Deal," Lerner then promised Garnett that Ark-Mo would receive a 30-percent interest in their future projects in the Midwest, and Garnett agreed to forgo an ownership interest in BCR. But when Blue Chip III, LLC (BC III), was formed to operate a repair facility in the Midwest, Lerner told Garnett that he "was not getting anything." Ark-Mo filed a suit in a Missouri state court against Lerner, alleging breach of contract. Was there consideration to support the Telephone Deal? Explain. [*Arkansas-Missouri Forest Products, LLC v. Lerner*, __ S.W.3d __, 2016 WL 234889 (Mo.App. E.D. 2016)] (See *Agreements That Lack Consideration*.)

13–9. A Question of Ethics—Promissory Estoppel. *Claudia Aceves borrowed from U.S. Bank to buy a home. Two years later, she could no longer afford the monthly payments. The bank notified her that it planned to foreclose on her home. (Foreclosure is a process that allows a lender to repossess and sell the property that secures a loan.) Aceves filed for bankruptcy. The bank offered to modify Aceves's mortgage if she would forgo bankruptcy. She agreed. Once she withdrew the filing, however, the bank foreclosed.* [Aceves v. U.S. Bank, N.A., *192 Cal.App.4th 218, 120 Cal.Rptr.3d 507 (2 Dist. 2011)] (See *Exceptions to the Consideration Requirement*.)

(a) Could Aceves succeed on a claim of promissory estoppel? Why or why not?

(b) Did Aceves or U.S. Bank behave unethically? Discuss.

Legal Reasoning Group Activity

13–10. Preexisting Duty. Melissa Faraj owns a lot and wants to build a house according to a particular set of plans and specifications. She solicits bids from building contractors and receives three bids: one from Carlton for $160,000, one from Feldberg for $158,000, and one from Siegel for $153,000. She accepts Siegel's bid. One month after beginning construction of the house, Siegel contacts Faraj and tells her that because of inflation and a recent price hike for materials, his costs have gone up. He says he will not finish the house unless Faraj agrees to pay an extra $13,000. Faraj reluctantly agrees to pay the additional sum. (See *Agreements That Lack Consideration*.)

(a) One group will discuss whether a contractor can ever raise the price of completing construction because of inflation and the rising cost of materials.

(b) A second group will assume that after the house is finished, Faraj refuses to pay the extra $13,000. The group will decide whether Faraj is legally required to pay this additional amount.

(c) A third group will discuss the types of extraordinary difficulties that could arise during construction that would justify a contractor's charging more than the original bid.

CHAPTER 14

Capacity and Legality

The first two requirements for a valid contract are agreement and consideration. This chapter examines the third and fourth requirements—*contractual capacity* and *legality.* The parties to the contract must have **contractual capacity**—the legal ability to enter into a contractual relationship. Courts generally presume the existence of contractual capacity, but in some situations, as when a person is very young or mentally incompetent, capacity may be lacking or questionable. Similarly, contracts calling for the performance of an illegal act are illegal and thus void—they are not contracts at all.

14–1 Contractual Capacity

Historically, the law has given special protection to those who bargain with the inexperience of youth and those who lack the degree of mental competence required by law. A person who has been determined by a court to be mentally incompetent, for instance, cannot form a legally binding contract with another party. In other situations, a party may have the capacity to enter into a valid contract but also have the right to avoid liability under it. Minors—or *infants,* as they are commonly referred to in legal terminology—usually are not legally bound by contracts. In this section, we look at the effect of youth, intoxication, and mental incompetence on contractual capacity.

14–1a Minors

Today, in almost all states, the **age of majority** (when a person is no longer a minor) for contractual purposes is eighteen years.[1] In addition, some states provide for the termination of minority on marriage.

Minority status may also be terminated by a minor's **emancipation,** which occurs when a child's parent or legal guardian relinquishes the legal right to exercise control over the child. Normally, minors who leave home to support themselves are considered emancipated. Several jurisdictions permit minors themselves to petition a court for emancipation. For business purposes, a minor may petition a court to be treated as an adult.

The general rule is that a minor can enter into any contract that an adult can, except contracts prohibited by law for minors (such as contracts to purchase tobacco or alcoholic beverages). A contract entered into by a minor, however, is voidable at the option of that minor, subject to certain exceptions. To exercise the option to avoid a contract, a minor need only manifest (clearly show) an intention not to be bound by it. The minor "avoids" the contract by disaffirming it.

Disaffirmance The legal avoidance, or setting aside, of a contractual obligation is referred to as **disaffirmance.** To disaffirm, a minor must express his or her intent, through words or conduct, not to be bound to the contract. The minor must disaffirm the entire contract, not merely a portion of it. For instance, the minor cannot decide to keep part of the goods purchased under a contract and return the remaining goods.

■ **CASE IN POINT 14.1** Fifteen-year-old Morgan Kelly was a cadet in her high school's Navy Junior Reserve Officer Training Corps. As part of the program, she visited a U.S. Marine Corps training facility. To enter the camp, she was required to sign a waiver that exempted the Marines from all liability for any injuries arising from her visit.

While participating in activities on the camp's confidence-building course, Kelly fell from the "Slide for Life" and suffered serious injuries. She filed a suit to recover her medical costs. The Marines asserted that she had signed their waiver of liability. Kelly claimed that she had disaffirmed the waiver when she filed suit. The court ruled in Kelly's favor. Liability waivers are generally

---

1. The age of majority may still be twenty-one for other purposes, such as the purchase and consumption of alcohol.

enforceable contracts, but a minor can avoid a contract by disaffirming it.[2] ■

Note that an adult who enters into a contract with a minor cannot avoid his or her contractual duties on the ground that the minor can do so. Unless the minor exercises the option to disaffirm the contract, the adult party normally is bound by it. On disaffirming a contract, a minor normally can recover any property that he or she transferred to the adult as consideration, even if the property is in the possession of a third party.[3]

The question in the following case was whether a minor had effectively disaffirmed an agreement to arbitrate with her employer.

---

2. *Kelly v. United States*, 809 F.Supp.2d 429 (E.D.N.C. 2011).

3. Section 2–403(1) of the Uniform Commercial Code (UCC) allows an exception if the third party is a "good faith purchaser for value."

Case 14.1

PAK Foods Houston, LLC v. Garcia

Court of Appeals of Texas, Houston (14th District), 433 S.W.3d 171 (2014).

Background and Facts S.L., a female sixteen-year-old minor, worked at a KFC Restaurant operated by PAK Foods Houston, LLC. PAK Foods' policy was to resolve any dispute with an employee through arbitration. At the employer's request, S.L. signed an acknowledgment of this policy. S.L. was injured on the job and subsequently terminated her employment. S.L.'s mother, Marissa Garcia, filed a suit on S.L.'s behalf in a Texas state court against PAK Foods to recover the medical expenses for the injury. PAK Foods filed a motion to compel arbitration. The court denied the motion. "To the extent any agreement to arbitrate existed between S.L. and PAK Foods Houston, LLC, S.L. voided such agreement by filing this suit." PAK Foods appealed.

In the Language of the Court

Martha Hill *JAMISON*, Justice.

* * * *

* * * It is undisputed S.L. was a 16-year-old minor when the arbitration agreement was executed and she remained a minor during her employment by PAK Foods, including at the time of her injury. In Texas, the age of majority is 18 years.

It has long been the law in Texas that a contract executed by a minor is not void, but it is voidable by the minor. * * * [A minor's contracts] may be either disaffirmed by the minor or ratified after the minor reaches majority. This means that the minor may set aside the entire contract at her option. [Emphasis added.]

Appellees assert that S.L. elected to void any agreement to arbitrate by filing the underlying suit.

* * * *

PAK Foods argues that * * * S.L. was an at-will employee and did not execute an employment contract. PAK Foods also notes that S.L. did not notify PAK Foods prior to filing suit that she was voiding the arbitration agreement. These distinctions do not alter the settled law that a minor may void a contract at her election. The arbitration agreement is a contract with a minor, S.L., who had the option to disaffirm the contract.

While appellees assert that S.L. voided the agreement by filing suit, the mere filing of suit may not necessarily disaffirm an arbitration agreement. A party may file suit but later determine arbitration is appropriate. Here, appellees' original petition does not expressly disaffirm an agreement to arbitrate; the petition is silent about arbitration. However, appellees' response filed in opposition to the motion to compel arbitration is a definitive disaffirmance of any agreement to arbitrate. The response states in relevant part:

> S.L. was a minor at the time of her employment. * * * Contracts such as this Arbitration Agreement are voidable at her instance, and may be disaffirmed or repudiated by her or her guardian, * * * . Thus as S.L.'s disaffirmance of the Arbitration agreement has manifestly occurred with her termination of employment and election to file suit, she cannot be bound by the terms of the Arbitration Agreement.

S.L. was still a minor when she objected to arbitration and elected to void the contract. The record contains sufficient evidence of her election to support the trial court's fact finding. The trial court also did not abuse its discretion in concluding as a matter of law that S.L.'s action voided the contract.

Case 14.1 Continued

Decision and Remedy *A state intermediate appellate court affirmed the decision of the lower court. A minor may disaffirm a contract at his or her option. S.L. opted to disaffirm the agreement to arbitrate by terminating her employment and filing the lawsuit.*

Critical Thinking

- **Legal Environment** *Could PAK Foods successfully contend that S.L.'s minority does not bar enforcement of the arbitration agreement because medical expenses are necessaries[a]? Discuss.*
- **Ethical** *Is it fair that a minor can work for an employer yet not be bound by a contract with the employer? Why or why not?*

---

a. *Necessaries* are basic needs, such as food, clothing, shelter, and medical services. As you will read shortly, minors can disaffirm contracts for necessaries but remain liable for the value of goods or services.

Disaffirmance within a Reasonable Time. A contract can ordinarily be disaffirmed at any time during minority or for a reasonable period after the minor reaches the age of majority.[4] What constitutes a "reasonable" time may vary, depending on the jurisdiction and to what extent the contract has been performed.

Minors' Obligations on Disaffirmance. Although all states' laws permit minors to disaffirm contracts, states differ on the extent of a minor's obligations on disaffirmance. Courts in most states hold that the minor need only return the goods (or other consideration) subject to the contract, provided the goods are in the minor's possession or control. Even if the minor returns damaged goods, the minor often is entitled to disaffirm the contract and obtain a full refund of the purchase price.

A growing number of states place an additional duty of restitution on the minor to restore the adult party to the position she or he held before the contract was made. These courts may hold a minor responsible for damage, ordinary wear and tear, and depreciation of goods that the minor used prior to disaffirmance.

■ **EXAMPLE 14.2** Sixteen-year-old Paul Dodson buys a pickup truck from a used-car dealer. The truck develops mechanical problems nine months later, but Dodson continues to drive it until it stops running. Then Dodson disaffirms the contract and attempts to return the truck to the dealer for a full refund. Dodson lives in a state that imposes a duty of restitution on minors. Therefore, he can disaffirm the contract but will not be entitled to a full refund of the purchase price. Dodson can only recover the fair market value of the truck in its current condition. ■

Exceptions to a Minor's Right to Disaffirm
State courts and legislatures have carved out several exceptions to the minor's right to disaffirm. For public-policy reasons, some contracts, such as marriage contracts and contracts to enlist in the armed services, cannot be avoided.

In addition, although ordinarily minors can disaffirm contracts even when they have misrepresented their age, a growing number of states have enacted laws to prohibit disaffirmance in such situations. Other states prohibit disaffirmance by minors who misrepresented their age while engaged in business as an adult.

Finally, a minor who enters into a contract for necessaries may disaffirm the contract but remains liable for the reasonable value of the goods. **Necessaries** are basic needs, such as food, clothing, shelter, and medical services. What is a necessary for one minor, however, may be a luxury for another, depending on the minors' customary living standard. Contracts for necessaries are enforceable only to the level of value needed to maintain the minor's standard of living.

Ratification In contract law, **ratification** is the act of accepting and giving legal force to an obligation that previously was not enforceable. A minor who has reached the age of majority can ratify a contract expressly or impliedly.

Express ratification takes place when the individual, on reaching the age of majority, states orally or in writing that he or she intends to be bound by the contract. *Implied* ratification takes place when the minor, on reaching the age of majority, indicates an intent to abide by the contract.

■ **EXAMPLE 14.3** Lin enters into a contract to sell her laptop to Andrew, a minor. If, on reaching the age of majority, Andrew e-mails Lin stating that he still agrees to buy the laptop, he has *expressly* ratified the contract. If, instead, Andrew takes possession of the

---

4. In some states, a minor who enters into a contract for the sale of land cannot disaffirm the contract until she or he reaches the age of majority.

laptop as a minor and continues to use it well after reaching the age of majority, he has *impliedly* ratified the contract. ∎

If a minor fails to disaffirm a contract within a reasonable time after reaching the age of majority, then the court must determine whether the conduct constitutes ratification or disaffirmance. Typically, courts presume that executed contracts (fully performed contracts) are ratified and that executory contracts (contracts not yet fully performed by both parties) are disaffirmed.

Parents' Liability As a general rule, parents are not liable for contracts made by minor children acting on their own, except contracts for necessaries, which parents are legally required to provide. As a consequence, businesses ordinarily require parents to cosign any contract made with a minor. The parents then become personally obligated under the contract to perform the conditions of the contract, even if their child avoids liability.

Concept Summary 14.1 reviews the rules relating to contracts by minors.

14–1b Intoxication

Intoxication is a condition in which a person's normal capacity to act or think is inhibited by alcohol or some other drug. A contract entered into by an intoxicated person can be either voidable or valid (and thus enforceable).

If the person was sufficiently intoxicated to lack mental capacity, then the agreement may be voidable even if the intoxication was purely voluntary. If, despite intoxication, the person understood the legal consequences of the agreement, the contract will be enforceable.

Courts look at objective indications of the intoxicated person's condition to determine if he or she possessed or lacked the required capacity. It is difficult to prove that a person's judgment was so severely impaired that he or she could not comprehend the legal consequences of entering into a contract. Therefore, courts rarely permit contracts to be avoided due to intoxication.

Disaffirmance If a contract is voidable because one party was intoxicated, that person has the option of disaffirming it while intoxicated and for a reasonable time after becoming sober. The person claiming intoxication typically must be able to return all consideration received unless the contract involved necessaries. Contracts for necessaries are voidable, but the intoxicated person is liable in quasi contract for the reasonable value of the consideration received.

Ratification An intoxicated person, after becoming sober, may ratify a contract expressly or impliedly, just as a minor may do on reaching majority. Implied ratification occurs when a person enters into a contract while intoxicated and fails to disaffirm the contract within a *reasonable*

Concept Summary 14.1

Contracts by Minors

The General Rule	• Contracts entered into by minors are *voidable* at the option of the minor.
Rules of Disaffirmance	• A minor may disaffirm the contract at any time while still a minor and within a reasonable time after reaching the age of majority. • Most states do not require restitution.
Exceptions to Basic Rules of Disaffirmance	• *Misrepresentation of age (or fraud)*—In many jurisdictions, misrepresentation of age prohibits the right of disaffirmance. • *Necessaries*—Minors remain liable for the reasonable value of necessaries (goods and services). • *Ratification*—After reaching the age of majority, a person can ratify a contract that he or she formed as a minor, thereby becoming fully liable for it.

Concept Summary 14.2

Contracts by Intoxicated Persons

The General Rules	• If a person was sufficiently intoxicated to lack the mental capacity to comprehend the legal consequences of entering into the contract, the contract may be *voidable* at the option of the intoxicated person. • If, despite intoxication, the person understood these legal consequences, the contract will be enforceable.
Rules of Disaffirmance	• An intoxicated person may disaffirm the contract at any time while intoxicated and for a reasonable time after becoming sober but must make full restitution. • Contracts for necessaries are voidable, but the intoxicated person is liable for the reasonable value of the goods or services.
Ratification	• After becoming sober, a person can ratify a contract that she or he formed while intoxicated, thereby becoming fully liable for it.

time after becoming sober. Acts or conduct inconsistent with an intent to disaffirm—such as the continued use of property purchased under a voidable contract—will also ratify the contract.

See Concept Summary 14.2 for a review of the rules relating to contracts by intoxicated persons.

14–1c Mental Incompetence

Contracts made by mentally incompetent persons can be void, voidable, or valid. We look here at the circumstances that determine when each of these classifications applies.

When the Contract Will Be Void If a court has previously determined that a person is mentally incompetent, any contract made by that person is void—no contract exists. On determining that someone is mentally incompetent, the court appoints a guardian to represent the individual. Only the guardian can enter into binding legal obligations on behalf of the mentally incompetent person.

When the Contract Will Be Voidable If a court has not previously judged a person to be mentally incompetent but the person was incompetent at the time the contract was formed, the contract may be voidable. The

contract is voidable if the person did not know he or she was entering into the contract or lacked the mental capacity to comprehend its nature, purpose, and consequences. In such situations, the contract is voidable (or can be ratified) at the option of the mentally incompetent person but not at the option of the other party.

■ **EXAMPLE 14.4** Larry agrees to sell his stock in Google, Inc., to Sergey for substantially less than its market value. At the time of the deal, Larry is confused about the purpose and details of the transaction, but he has not been declared incompetent. Nonetheless, if a court finds that Larry did not understand the nature and consequences of the contract due to a lack of mental capacity, he can avoid the sale. ■

When the Contract Will Be Valid A contract entered into by a mentally ill person (not previously declared incompetent) may be valid if the person had capacity *at the time the contract was formed*. Some people who are incompetent due to age or illness have *lucid intervals*—periods during which their intelligence, judgment, and will are temporarily restored. During such intervals, they will be considered to have legal capacity to enter into contracts.

See Concept Summary 14.3 for a review of the rules relating to contracts entered into by mentally incompetent persons.

Concept Summary 14.3

Contracts by Mentally Incompetent Persons

When the Contract Will Be Void	If a court has declared a person to be mentally incompetent and has appointed a legal guardian, any contract made by that person is void from the outset.
When the Contract Will Be Voidable	If a court has *not* declared a person mentally incompetent, but that person lacked the capacity to comprehend the subject matter, nature, and consequences of the agreement, then the contract is voidable at that person's option.
When the Contract Will Be Valid	If a court has *not* declared a person mentally incompetent and that person was able to understand the nature and effect of the contract at the time it was formed, then the contract is valid and enforceable.

14–2 Legality

For a contract to be valid and enforceable, it must be formed for a legal purpose. A contract to do something that is prohibited by federal or state statutory law is illegal and, as such, void from the outset and thus unenforceable. Additionally, a contract to commit a tortious act (such as an agreement to engage in defamation or fraud) is contrary to public policy and therefore illegal and unenforceable.

14–2a Contracts Contrary to Statute

Statutes often set forth rules specifying what may be included in contracts and what is prohibited. We now examine several ways in which contracts may be contrary to statute and thus illegal.

Contracts to Commit a Crime Any contract to commit a crime is in violation of a statute. Thus, a contract to sell illegal drugs in violation of criminal laws is unenforceable, as is a contract to hide a corporation's violation of securities laws or environmental regulations.

Sometimes, the object or performance of a contract is rendered illegal by a statute *after* the parties entered into the contract. In that situation, the contract is considered to be discharged (terminated) by law.

Usury Almost every state has a statute that sets the maximum rate of interest that can be charged for different types of transactions, including ordinary loans. A lender who makes a loan at an interest rate above the lawful maximum commits **usury.**

Although usurious contracts are illegal, most states simply limit the interest that the lender may collect on the contract to the lawful maximum interest rate in that state. In a few states, the lender can recover the principal amount of the loan but no interest. In addition, states can make exceptions to facilitate business transactions. For instance, many states exempt corporate loans from the usury laws, and nearly all states allow higher-interest-rate loans for borrowers who could not otherwise obtain loans.

Gambling Gambling is the creation of risk for the purpose of assuming it. Any scheme that involves the distribution of property by chance among persons who have paid valuable consideration for the opportunity (chance) to receive the property is gambling.

Traditionally, the states deemed gambling contracts illegal and thus void. Today, many states allow (and regulate) certain forms of gambling, such as horse racing, video poker machines, and charity-sponsored bingo. In addition, nearly all states allow state-operated lotteries and gambling on Native American reservations. Even in states that permit certain types of gambling, though, courts often find that gambling contracts are illegal.

■ **CASE IN POINT 14.5** Video poker machines are legal in Louisiana, but their use requires the approval of the state video gaming commission. Gaming Venture, Inc., did not obtain this approval before agreeing with

Tastee Restaurant Corporation to install poker machines in some of its restaurants. For this reason, when Tastee allegedly reneged on the deal by refusing to install the machines, a state court held that their agreement was an illegal gambling contract and therefore void.[5] ■

Licensing Statutes   All states require members of certain professions—including physicians, lawyers, real estate brokers, accountants, architects, electricians, and stockbrokers—to have licenses. Some licenses are obtained only after extensive schooling and examinations, which indicate to the public that a special skill has been acquired. Others require only that the applicant be of good moral character and pay a fee.

Whether a contract with an unlicensed person is legal and enforceable depends on the purpose of the licensing statute. If the statute's purpose is to protect the public from unauthorized practitioners (such as unlicensed attorneys and electricians), then a contract involving an unlicensed practitioner is generally illegal and unenforceable. If the statute's purpose is merely to raise government revenues, however, a court may enforce the contract and fine the unlicensed person.

---

5. *Gaming Venture, Inc. v. Tastee Restaurant Corp.*, 996 So.2d 515 (La.App. 5 Cir. 2008).

■ **CASE IN POINT 14.6**   The United Arab Emirates (UAE) held a competition for the design of a new embassy in Washington, D.C. Elena Sturdza—an architect licensed in Maryland but not in the District of Columbia—won. Sturdza and the UAE exchanged proposals, but the UAE stopped communicating with her before the parties had signed a contract. Later, Sturdza learned that the UAE had contracted with a District of Columbia architect to use another design. She filed a suit against the UAE for breach of contract.

Sturdza argued that the licensing statute should not apply to architects who submit plans in international architectural design competitions. The court held, however, that licensing requirements are necessary to ensure the safety of those who work in and visit buildings in the District of Columbia, as well as the safety of neighboring buildings. Because Sturdza was not a licensed architect in the District of Columbia, she could not recover on a contract to perform architectural services there.[6] ■

The following case involved a contract for the construction of an assisted living facility to be sanctioned by the state of Tennessee. On the project's completion, the facility was constructively delivered and accepted. At no time, however, was the party acting as the contractor licensed by the state to perform that function.

---

6. *Sturdza v. United Arab Emirates*, 11 A.3d 251 (D.C.App. 2011).

Case 14.2

McNatt v. Vestal

Court of Appeals of Tennessee, __ S.W.3d __, 2016 WL 659847 (2016).

Background and Facts   Cecil McNatt contracted with Jane Vestal to build Henderson Villa, an assisted living facility, in Henderson, Tennessee, for $1.4 million. Three days later, McNatt formed a joint venture with M. S. Burton Construction Company to build two assisted living facilities, including Henderson Villa. Burton was licensed under the state's Contractors Licensing Act. McNatt was not. During the construction of Henderson Villa, McNatt remained onsite, selecting, supervising, and paying the subcontractors.

Following completion of the project, Vestal refused to pay the balance owed on the contract. McNatt filed a suit in a Tennessee state court against Vestal to collect. She filed a counterclaim, alleging breach of contract for his lack of a contractor's license. The court dismissed her claim and awarded him $96,280.11 in damages. Vestal appealed.

In the Language of the Court

Kenny *ARMSTRONG*, J. [Judge]

* * * *

Under Tennessee Code Annotated Section 62–6–103(a), it is "unlawful for any person, firm or corporation to engage in, or offer to engage in, contracting * * * unless the person, firm or corporation has been duly licensed under this part." "Contracting" is defined as when "any person or entity * * * offers to construct * * * or in any manner assume charge of the construction * * * for any building * * * for

Case 14.2 Continues

Case 14.2 Continued

which the total cost is twenty-five thousand dollars ($25,000) or more." "Any contractor * * * who is in violation of this part * * * shall not be permitted to recover any damages in any court other than actual documented expenses that can be shown by clear and convincing proof."

* * * *

The contract between McNatt and Vestal required payment in excess of $25,000. * * * *Merely offering to construct the assisted living facility constitutes contracting work, and the duties that McNatt performed under the contract fall within the definition of contracting work as well. Here, McNatt was not licensed at the time he made his offer to Vestal or at any time during the construction project.* [Emphasis added.]

* * * Tennessee Code Annotated Section 62–6–115 allows that entities engaged in a partnership may perform contracting work as long as one of the partners holds a contracting license.

* * * It is undisputed that McNatt and Burton Construction executed their agreement after McNatt executed his agreement with Vestal. * * * Because McNatt began performing contracting services before associating with Burton Construction, the subsequent association with Burton Construction does not cure his unlicensed contracting activity. We, therefore, conclude that the trial court erred in finding that McNatt did not violate the Contractors Licensing Act.

* * * *

At trial, [McNatt] presented an itemized list of costs [that] included architect fees, appraisal fees, interest paid on construction loans, application fees for licensure, charter fees, attorney's fees, insurance costs, payments to engineers, the costs of blueprints, gasoline, and an administrative fee. Upon review of the record, we conclude that the majority of these costs are supported by clear and convincing evidence. However, we conclude that the awards for [the] administrative duties and the costs of gas are not supported by clear and convincing evidence.

* * * *

* * * In subtracting these costs from the total costs presented at trial, we conclude that there is clear and convincing evidence to support an award of only $72,952.03.

Decision and Remedy *A state intermediate appellate court reversed the lower court's finding that McNatt had not violated the state Contractors Licensing Act and reduced the amount of his award. The appellate court affirmed the judgment as modified and remanded the case for further proceedings.*

Critical Thinking

- **Legal Environment** *In Tennessee, at common law, unlicensed contractors had no right to recover anything on their contracts. The Contractors Licensing Act changed this rule to permit unlicensed contractors to recover documented expenses proved by clear and convincing evidence. Why?*
- **What If the Facts Were Different?** *Suppose that McNatt had held a valid contractor's license when he entered into the contract with Vestal but that the license had expired while he was overseeing the construction of Henderson Villa. Would the result in that case have been different? Explain.*

14–2b Contracts Contrary to Public Policy

Although contracts involve private parties, some are not enforceable because of the negative impact they would have on society. These contracts are said to be *contrary to public policy.* Examples include a contract to commit an immoral act, such as selling a child, and a contract that prohibits marriage. Business contracts that may be against public policy include contracts in restraint of trade and unconscionable contracts or clauses.

Contracts in Restraint of Trade The United States has a strong public policy favoring competition in the economy. Thus, contracts in restraint of trade (anticompetitive agreements) generally are unenforceable because they are contrary to public policy. Typically, such contracts also violate one or more federal or state antitrust statutes.[7]

An exception is recognized when the restraint is reasonable and is contained in an ancillary (secondary or subordinate) clause in a contract. Such restraints often are included in contracts for the sale of an ongoing business and for employment contracts.

---

7. Federal statutes include the Sherman Antitrust Act, the Clayton Act, and the Federal Trade Commission Act.

Covenants Not to Compete and the Sale of an Ongoing Business.

Many contracts involve a type of restraint called a **covenant not to compete,** or a restrictive covenant (promise). A covenant not to compete may be created when a merchant who sells a store agrees not to open a new store in a certain geographic area surrounding the old business. Such an agreement enables the seller to sell, and the purchaser to buy, the goodwill and reputation of an ongoing business without having to worry that the seller will open a competing business a block away. Provided the restrictive covenant is reasonable and is an ancillary part of the sale of an ongoing business, it is enforceable.

Covenants Not to Compete in Employment Contracts.

Sometimes, agreements not to compete (also referred to as *noncompete agreements*) are included in employment contracts. People in middle- or upper-level management positions commonly agree not to work for competitors or not to start competing businesses for a specified period of time after termination of employment.

Noncompete agreements are legal in most states so long as the specified period of time (of restraint) is not excessive in duration and the geographic restriction is reasonable. What constitutes a reasonable time period may be shorter in the online environment than in conventional employment contracts. Because the geographical restrictions apply worldwide, the time restrictions may be shorter.

A restraint that is found to be overly broad will not be enforced. ■ **CASE IN POINT 14.7** An insurance firm in New York City, Brown & Brown, Inc., hired Theresa Johnson to perform actuarial analysis. On her first day of work, Johnson was asked to sign a nonsolicitation covenant. The covenant prohibited her from soliciting or servicing any of Brown's clients for two years after the termination of her employment.

Less than five years later, when Johnson's employment with Brown was terminated, she went to work for Lawley Benefits Group, LLC. Brown sued to enforce the covenant. A state appellate court ruled that the covenant was overly broad and unenforceable. It attempted to restrict Johnson from working for any of Brown's clients, without regard to whether she had had a relationship with those clients.[8] ■

Enforcement Issues.

The laws governing the enforceability of covenants not to compete vary significantly from state to state. California prohibits the enforcement of covenants not to compete altogether. In some states, including Texas, such a covenant will not be enforced unless the employee has received some benefit in return for signing the noncompete agreement. This is true even if the covenant is reasonable as to time and area. If the employee receives no benefit, the covenant will be deemed void.

Occasionally, depending on the jurisdiction, courts will *reform* covenants not to compete. If a covenant is found to be unreasonable in time or geographic area, the court may convert the terms into reasonable ones and then enforce the reformed covenant. Such court actions present a problem, though, in that the judge implicitly becomes a party to the contract. Consequently, courts usually resort to contract **reformation** only when necessary to prevent undue burdens or hardships.

Unconscionable Contracts or Clauses

A court ordinarily does not look at the fairness or equity of a contract (or inquire into the adequacy of consideration). Persons are assumed to be reasonably intelligent, and the courts will not come to their aid just because they have made unwise or foolish bargains.

In certain circumstances, however, bargains are so oppressive that the courts relieve innocent parties of part or all of their duties. Such bargains are deemed **unconscionable**[9] because they are so unscrupulous or grossly unfair as to be "void of conscience." A contract can be unconscionable on either procedural or substantive grounds, as illustrated in Exhibit 14–1. The Uniform Commercial Code (UCC) incorporates the concept of unconscionability in its provisions regarding the sale and lease of goods.[10]

Procedural Unconscionability.

Procedural unconscionability often involves inconspicuous print, unintelligible language ("legalese"), or the lack of an opportunity to read the contract or ask questions about its meaning. This type of unconscionability typically arises when a party's lack of knowledge or understanding of the contract terms deprived him or her of any meaningful choice.

Procedural unconscionability can also occur when there is such disparity in bargaining power between the two parties that the weaker party's consent is not voluntary. This type of situation often involves an *adhesion* contract, which is a contract written exclusively by one party and presented to the other on a take-it-or-leave-it basis.[11] In other words, the party to whom the contract is presented (usually a buyer or borrower) has no opportunity to negotiate its terms.

---

8. *Brown & Brown, Inc. v. Johnson,* 115 A.D.3d 52, 980 N.Y.S.2d 631 (2014).

9. Pronounced un-*kon*-shun-uh-bul.

10. See UCC 2–302 and 2A–719.

11. For a classic case involving an adhesion contract, see *Henningsen v. Bloomfield Motors, Inc.,* 32 N.J. 358, 161 A.2d 69 (1960).

EXHIBIT 14–1   Unconscionability

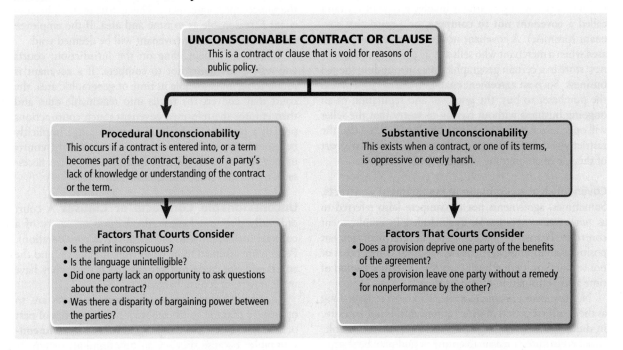

UNCONSCIONABLE CONTRACT OR CLAUSE
This is a contract or clause that is void for reasons of public policy.

Procedural Unconscionability
This occurs if a contract is entered into, or a term becomes part of the contract, because of a party's lack of knowledge or understanding of the contract or the term.

Factors That Courts Consider
• Is the print inconspicuous?
• Is the language unintelligible?
• Did one party lack an opportunity to ask questions about the contract?
• Was there a disparity of bargaining power between the parties?

Substantive Unconscionability
This exists when a contract, or one of its terms, is oppressive or overly harsh.

Factors That Courts Consider
• Does a provision deprive one party of the benefits of the agreement?
• Does a provision leave one party without a remedy for nonperformance by the other?

Not all adhesion contracts are unconscionable, only those that unreasonably favor the drafter. ■ **CASE IN POINT 14.8** Tiffany Brinkley committed to take six real estate investment training sessions at a cost of $4,195. She paid $850 and signed a retail installment contract promising to pay monthly payments on the balance to Monterey Financial Services. The contract contained an arbitration agreement. When a dispute arose, Brinkley stopped making payments and filed a lawsuit against Monterey in a California state court.

Monterey filed a motion to arbitrate, which the trial court granted. Brinkley appealed. She argued that the arbitration clause was procedurally unconscionable because it was part of an adhesion contract. The court, though, found that the arbitration clause was enforceable and dismissed the lawsuit. The court held that the "purported lack of meaningful choice did not render the arbitration provision in retail installment contract procedurally unconscionable."[12] ■

Substantive Unconscionability. *Substantive* unconscionability occurs when contracts, or portions of contracts, are oppressive or overly harsh. Courts generally focus on

provisions that deprive one party of the benefits of the agreement or leave that party without a remedy for nonperformance by the other.

Substantive unconscionability can arise in a wide variety of business contexts. For instance, a contract clause that gives the business entity unconstrained access to the courts but requires the other party to arbitrate any dispute with the firm may be unconscionable.

Exculpatory Clauses Often closely related to the concept of unconscionability are **exculpatory clauses,** which release a party from liability in the event of monetary or physical injury *no matter who is at fault.* Indeed, courts sometimes refuse to enforce such clauses on the ground that they are unconscionable.

Often Violate Public Policy. Most courts view exculpatory clauses with disfavor. Exculpatory clauses found in rental agreements for commercial property are frequently held to be contrary to public policy, and such clauses are almost always unenforceable in residential property leases. Courts also usually hold that exculpatory clauses are against public policy in the employment context. Thus, employers frequently cannot enforce exculpatory clauses in contracts with employees or independent contractors to avoid liability for work-related injuries.

---

12. *Brinkley v. Monterey Financial Services, Inc.,* 242 Cal.App.4th 314, 196 Cal.Rptr.3d 1 (2015). See also *Louisiana Extended Care Centers, LLC v. Bindon,* 180 So.3d 791 (2015).

■ **CASE IN POINT 14.9** Crum Motor Sales entered into an agreement with Martin County Coal Corporation to service Martin Coal's pickup trucks and light-duty vehicles. The parties agreed that when vehicles needed service, Crum Motor would pick up the vehicles from Martin Coal's mining site, repair them, and then bring them back. Martin Coal required Crum Motor to sign an indemnification agreement (exculpatory clause) for all injuries sustained on the mining site and to have insurance coverage.

A few years later, Philip Crum (an employee of Crum Motor) was driving on a road on the mining site when a falling boulder crushed the cab of his pickup. He was seriously injured and spent the rest of the year in a hospital and rehabilitation facility. Philip Crum and Crum Motor sued Martin Coal for negligence in maintaining the road and the site. Martin Coal counterclaimed, arguing that it was not liable under the indemnification agreement.

Crum Motor's insurance provider (Universal Underwriters) declined to represent the company in the lawsuit. Eventually, Martin Coal settled with Philip Crum and Crum Motor for $3.65 million and filed a suit against Universal Underwriters for that same amount. The court held that the indemnification agreement between Crum Motor and Martin Coal was against public policy and void. Therefore, Martin Coal was responsible for paying the settlement, not Crum Motor's insurance provider.[13] ■

When Courts Will Enforce Exculpatory Clauses. Courts do enforce exculpatory clauses if they are reasonable, do not violate public policy, and do not protect parties from liability for intentional misconduct. The language used must not be ambiguous, and the parties must have been in relatively equal bargaining positions.

Businesses such as health clubs, racetracks, amusement parks, skiing facilities, horse-rental operations, golf-cart concessions, and skydiving organizations frequently use exculpatory clauses to limit their liability for patrons' injuries. Because these services are not essential, the companies offering them have no relative advantage in bargaining strength, and anyone contracting for their services does so voluntarily. Courts also may enforce reasonable exculpatory clauses in loan documents, real estate contracts, and trust agreements. See this chapter's *Managerial Strategy* feature for more about exculpatory clauses that will not be considered unconscionable.

In the following case, the court considered whether an exculpatory clause that released "any Event sponsors and their agents and employees" from liability for future negligence was ambiguous.

---

13. *Martin County Coal Corp. v. Universal Underwriters Ins. Co.*, 727 F.3d 589 (6th Cir. 2013).

Case Analysis 14.3

Holmes v. Multimedia KSDK, Inc.
Missouri Court of Appeals, Eastern District, Division Two, 395 S.W.3d 557 (2013).

In the Language of the Court
Kathianne *KNAUP CRANE*, Presiding Judge.
* * * *

* * * On or about May 12, 2009, plaintiff Colleen M. Holmes signed and dated an Entry Form for the 2009 Susan G. Komen Race for the Cure (the Event) to be held on Saturday, June 13, 2009 [in St. Louis, Missouri]. The one-page entry form contained a section titled, "RACE WAIVER AND RELEASE." This section contained the following language:

* * * I understand that my consent to these provisions is given in consideration for being permitted to participate in this Event. I further understand that I may be removed from this competition if I do not follow all the rules of this Event. I am a voluntary participant in this Event, and in good physical condition. I know that this Event is a potentially hazardous activity and I hereby voluntarily assume full and complete responsibility for, and the risk of, any injury or accident that may occur during my participation in this Event or while on the premises of this Event. I * * * hereby release and hold harmless and covenant not to file suit against The Susan G. Komen Breast Cancer Foundation, Inc., * * * D/B/A Susan G. Komen for the Cure, The St. Louis Affiliate of The Susan G. Komen Breast Cancer Foundation * * *, their Affiliates and any affiliated Individuals, any Event sponsors and their agents and employees, and all other persons or entities associated with this Event (collectively, the "Releasees") for any injury or damages I might suffer in connection with my participation in this Event or while on the premises of this Event. This release applies to any and all loss, liability, or claims I may have arising out of my participation in this Event, including but not limited to, personal injury or damage suffered by me or others, whether such losses, liabilities, or claims be caused by falls, contact with and/or the actions of other participants, contact with fixed or non-fixed

Case 14.3 Continues

objects, contact with animals, conditions of the premises of the Event, negligence of the Releasees, risks not known to me or not reasonably foreseeable at this time, or otherwise.

On June 1, 2009, defendant Multimedia KSDK, Inc. (KSDK) executed a Race Sponsorship Agreement with the St. Louis Affiliate of the Event. This agreement governed the terms of KSDK's sponsorship of the Event in 2009. KSDK, as an Event sponsor, agreed to, and did, broadcast the Event. Defendants Lynn Beall and Michael Shipley, KSDK employees, were involved in arranging the live coverage.

On February 23, 2011, Mrs. Holmes and her husband, Rick W. Holmes (collectively, plaintiffs) filed a lawsuit in the Circuit Court of the City of St. Louis. Plaintiffs alleged that while Mrs. Holmes was a participant in the Event, she was caused to trip and fall over an audiovisual box, and she sustained injuries. Plaintiffs alleged that the audio-visual box was owned and operated by KSDK and was placed on the ground without barricades or warnings in a high pedestrian traffic area.

The circuit court entered summary judgment in defendants' favor on the grounds that plaintiffs' claims were barred by the language of the release, the release was not ambiguous, and the release applied to defendants. Plaintiffs appeal.

* * * *

[The plaintiffs] on appeal claim the release is ambiguous. Whether a release is ambiguous is a question of law. Interpretation of a release or settlement agreement is governed by the same principles as any other contract. * * * *Contract terms are ambiguous only if the language*

may be given more than one reasonable interpretation. Simply because parties disagree over the meaning of a contract does not mean that it is ambiguous. [Emphasis added.]

* * * *

* * * Plaintiffs assert that the trial court erred in entering summary judgment because the release was ambiguous in that it did not clearly and explicitly set forth the individuals and entities it purported to release from liability. We disagree.

The release described the individuals and entities to be released in the following language:

> The St. Louis Affiliate of Susan G. Komen for the Cure, their affiliates, and any affiliated individuals, any Event sponsors and their agents and employees, and all other persons or entities associated with this Event.

Plaintiffs argue that the * * * language is ambiguous because it does not specifically name the individuals and entities being released. They contend that such specificity is required in a prospective release.

We have routinely held that the word "any" when used with a class in a release is all-inclusive, it excludes nothing, and it is not ambiguous. * * * *A release that releases claims against "any and all persons" is unambiguous and enforceable to bar claims against third parties who were not parties to the release, and it is not necessary that the release identify those persons by name or otherwise.* Thus, * * * the release of "any Event sponsors" unambiguously releases all Event sponsors without exclusion, and it is not necessary that each sponsor be named. [Emphasis added.]

However, plaintiffs argue that this reasoning does not apply to the use of "any" with classes of persons in a prospective release for future acts of negligence because courts require more specificity in a prospective release. We disagree.

Public policy disfavors but *does not prohibit* releases of future negligence. * * * To be enforceable in Missouri, exculpatory clauses must contain clear, unambiguous, unmistakable, and conspicuous language in order to release a party from his or her own future negligence. The exculpatory language must effectively notify a party that he or she is releasing the other party from claims arising from the other party's own negligence. * * * The words "negligence" or "fault" or their equivalents must be used conspicuously so that a clear and unmistakable waiver and shifting of risk occurs. There must be no doubt that a reasonable person agreeing to an exculpatory clause actually understands what future claims he or she is waiving.

* * * *

* * * [It is] not required that for a release of liability for future negligence to be effective, it must identify every individual sought to be released by name.

The release of "any Event sponsors and their agents and employees" from liability for future negligence clearly releases all Event sponsors and their agents and employees without exclusion. It is not ambiguous because it does not name each individual Event sponsor it purported to release from liability.

* * * *

The judgment of the trial court is affirmed.

Legal Reasoning Questions

1. When do courts enforce exculpatory clauses?

2. What are the specific requirements for an exculpatory clause to be enforceable in Missouri?

3. Was the exculpatory clause at issue in this case enforceable? Why or why not?

Creating Liability Waivers That Are Not Unconscionable

Blanket liability waivers that absolve a business from virtually every event, even those caused by the business's own negligence, are usually unenforceable because they are unconscionable. Exculpatory waivers are common, nonetheless. We observe such waivers in gym memberships, on ski lift tickets, on admissions tickets to sporting events, and in simple contracts for the use of campgrounds.

Typically, courts view liability waivers as voluntarily bargained for whether or not they have been read. Thus, a waiver included in the fine print on the back of an admission ticket or on an entry sign to a stadium may be upheld. In general, if such waivers are unambiguous and conspicuous, the assumption is that patrons have had a chance to read them and have accepted their terms.

Activities with Inherent Risks

Cases challenging liability waivers have been brought against skydiving operations, skiing operations, bobsledding operations, white-water rafting companies, and health clubs. For example, in *Bergin v. Wild Mountain, Inc.,*[a] an appellate court in Minnesota upheld a ski resort's liability waiver.

In that case, the plaintiff hit a snowmaking mound, which was "an inherent risk of skiing." Before the accident, the plaintiff had stated that he knew "that an inherent risk of serious injury in downhill skiing was hitting snowmaking mounds." Furthermore, he had not rejected the season pass that contained the

resort's exculpatory clause. Thus, the ski resort prevailed.

Overly Broad Waivers

While most liability waivers have survived legal challenges, some have not. In *Bagley v. Mt. Bachelor, Inc.,*[b] the Supreme Court of Oregon ruled against a ski resort's "very broad" liability waiver. The case involved an eighteen-year-old, Myles Bagley, who was paralyzed from the waist down after a snowboarding accident at Mt. Bachelor ski resort. The season pass that Bagley signed included a liability waiver. The waiver stated that the signer agreed not to sue the resort for injury even if "caused by negligence."

Bagley argued that the resort had created a dangerous condition because of the way it had set up a particular ski jump. He sued for $21.5 million and eventually won the right to go forward with his lawsuit. The Oregon Supreme Court found that, for various reasons, enforcement of the release would have been unconscionable. "Because the release is unenforceable, genuine issues of fact exist that preclude summary judgment in defendant's favor."

Business Questions

1. *If you are running a business, why would you opt to include overly broad waivers in your contracts with customers?*
2. *Under what circumstances would you, as a business owner, choose to aggressively defend your business against a customer's liability lawsuit?*

a. 2014 WL 996788 (Minn.App. 2014).

b. 356 Or. 543, 340 P.3d 27 (2014).

Discriminatory Contracts Contracts in which a party promises to discriminate on the basis of race, color, national origin, religion, gender, age, or disability are contrary to both statute and public policy. They are also unenforceable.[14] For instance, if a property owner promises in a contract not to sell the property to a member of a particular race, the contract is unenforceable. The public policy underlying these prohibitions is very strong, and the courts are quick to invalidate discriminatory contracts.

Exhibit 14–2 illustrates the types of contracts that may be illegal because they are contrary to statute or public policy.

---

14. The major federal statute prohibiting discrimination is the Civil Rights Act of 1964, 42 U.S.C. Sections 2000e–2000e-17.

14–2c Effect of Illegality

In general, an illegal contract is void—that is, the contract is deemed never to have existed, and the courts will not aid either party. In most illegal contracts, both parties are considered to be equally at fault—*in pari delicto.*[15] If the contract is executory (not yet fulfilled), neither party can enforce it. If it has been executed, neither party can recover damages.

Usually, the courts are not concerned if one wrongdoer in an illegal contract is unjustly enriched at the expense of the other. The main reason for this hands-off attitude is the belief that a plaintiff who has broken the law by entering into an illegal bargain should not be allowed to obtain help from the courts. Another justification is the

---

15. Pronounced in-*pah*-ree deh-*lick*-tow.

EXHIBIT 14–2   Contract Legality

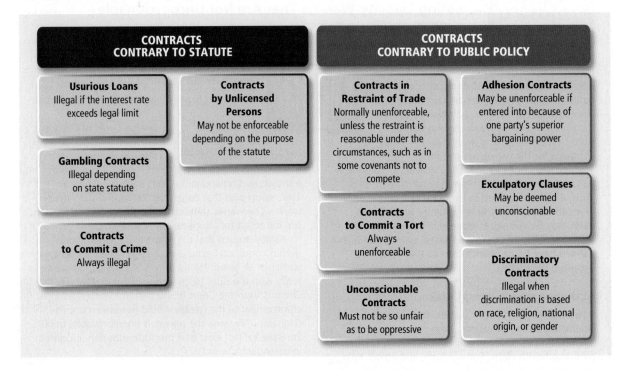

hoped-for deterrent effect. A plaintiff who suffers a loss because of an illegal bargain will presumably be deterred from entering into similar illegal bargains in the future.

There are, however, exceptions to the general rule that neither party to an illegal bargain can sue for breach and neither party can recover for performance rendered. We look at these exceptions next.

Justifiable Ignorance of the Facts Sometimes, one of the parties to a contract has no reason to know that the contract is illegal and thus is relatively innocent. That party can often recover any benefits conferred in a partially executed contract. In this situation, the courts will not enforce the contract but will allow the parties to return to their original positions.

Sometimes, a court may permit an innocent party who has fully performed under the contract to enforce the contract against the guilty party. ■ **EXAMPLE 14.10** A trucking company contracts with Gillespie to carry crates filled with goods to a specific destination for the normal fee of $5,000. The trucker delivers the crates and later finds out that they contained illegal goods. Although the law specifies that the shipment, use, and sale of the goods were illegal, the trucker, being an innocent party, can still legally collect the $5,000 from Gillespie. ■

Members of Protected Classes When a statute is clearly designed to protect a certain class of people, a member of that class can enforce a contract in violation of the statute even though the other party cannot. ■ **EXAMPLE 14.11** Statutes prohibit certain employees (such as flight attendants and pilots) from working more than a certain number of hours per month. An employee who is required to work more than the maximum can recover for those extra hours of service. ■

Other examples of statutes designed to protect a particular class of people are state statutes that regulate the sale of insurance. If an insurance company violates a statute when selling insurance, the purchaser can still enforce the policy and recover from the insurer.

Withdrawal from an Illegal Agreement If the illegal part of a bargain has not yet been performed, the party rendering performance can withdraw from the contract and recover the performance or its value. ■ **EXAMPLE 14.12** Sam and Jim decide to wager (illegally) on the outcome of a boxing match. Each deposits cash with a stakeholder, who agrees to pay the winner of the bet. At this point, each party has performed part of the agreement. Before payment occurs, either party is entitled to withdraw from the bargain by giving notice of repudiation to the stakeholder. ■

Contract Illegal through Fraud, Duress, or Undue Influence Often, one party to an illegal contract is more at fault than the other. When one party uses fraud, duress, or undue influence to induce another party to enter into an illegal bargain, the second party will be allowed to recover for the performance or its value.

Severable, or Divisible, Contracts A contract that is *severable,* or divisible, consists of distinct parts that can be performed separately, with separate consideration provided for each part. With an *indivisible* contract, in contrast, complete performance by each party is essential, even if the contract contains a number of seemingly separate provisions.

If a contract is divisible into legal and illegal portions, a court may enforce the legal portion but not the illegal one, so long as the illegal portion does not affect the essence of the bargain. This approach is consistent with the courts' basic policy of enforcing the legal intentions of the contracting parties whenever possible.

■ **EXAMPLE 14.13** Cole signs an employment contract that includes an overly broad and thus illegal covenant not to compete. In that situation, a court might allow the employment contract to be enforceable but reform the unreasonably broad covenant by converting its terms into reasonable ones. Alternatively, the court could declare the covenant illegal (and thus void) and enforce the remaining employment terms. ■

A contract clause stating that the parties intend the contract terms to be enforced to "the fullest extent possible" indicates that the parties regard their contract as divisible. In the event of a dispute, the parties intend that the court will strike out the illegal terms and enforce the rest.

Reviewing: Capacity and Legality

Renee Beaver started racing go-karts competitively in 2016, when she was fourteen. Many of the races required her to sign an exculpatory clause to participate, which she or her parents regularly signed. In 2018, right before her sixteenth birthday, Renee participated in the annual Elkhart Grand Prix, a series of races in Elkhart, Indiana. During the event in which she drove, a piece of foam padding used as a course barrier was torn from its base and ended up on the track. A portion of the padding struck Beaver in the head, and another portion was thrown into oncoming traffic, causing a multikart collision during which she sustained severe injuries. Beaver filed an action against the race organizers for negligence. The race organizers could not locate the exculpatory clause that Beaver had supposedly signed. The organizers argued that she must have signed one to enter the race, but even if she had not signed one, her actions showed her intent to be bound by its terms. Using the information presented in the chapter, answer the following questions.

1. Did Beaver have the contractual capacity to enter a contract with an exculpatory clause? Why or why not?
2. Assuming that Beaver did, in fact, sign the exculpatory clause, did she later disaffirm or ratify the contract? Explain.
3. Now assume that Beaver stated that she was eighteen years old at the time she signed the exculpatory clause. How might this affect her ability to disaffirm or ratify the contract?
4. If Beaver did not actually sign the exculpatory clause, could a court conclude that she impliedly accepted its terms by participating in the race? Why or why not?

Debate This . . . *After agreeing to an exculpatory clause or purchasing some item, minors often seek to avoid the contracts. Today's minors are far from naïve and should not be allowed to avoid their contractual obligations.*

Terms and Concepts

age of majority 263	emancipation 263	reformation 271
contractual capacity 263	exculpatory clause 272	unconscionable 271
covenant not to compete 271	necessaries 265	usury 268
disaffirmance 263	ratification 265	

Issue Spotters

1. Joan, who is sixteen years old, moves out of her parents' home and signs a one-year lease for an apartment at Kenwood Apartments. Joan's parents tell her that she can return to live with them at any time. Unable to pay the rent, Joan moves back to her parents' home two months later. Can Kenwood enforce the lease against Joan? Why or why not? (See *Contractual Capacity*.)

2. Sun Airlines, Inc., prints on its tickets that it is not liable for any injury to a passenger caused by the airline's negligence. If the cause of an accident is found to be the airline's negligence, can it use the clause as a defense to liability? Why or why not? (See *Legality*.)

• **Check your answers to the Issue Spotters against the answers provided in Appendix D at the end of this text.**

Business Scenarios

14–1. Covenants Not to Compete. A famous New York City hotel, Hotel Lux, is noted for its food as well as its luxury accommodations. Hotel Lux contracts with a famous chef, Chef Perlee, to become its head chef at $30,000 per month. The contract states that should Perlee leave the employment of Hotel Lux for any reason, he will not work as a chef for any hotel or restaurant in New York, New Jersey, or Pennsylvania for a period of one year. During the first six months of the contract, Hotel Lux heavily advertises Perlee as its head chef, and business at the hotel is excellent. Then a dispute arises between the hotel's management and Perlee, and Perlee terminates his employment. One month later, he is hired by a famous New Jersey restaurant just across the New York state line. Hotel Lux learns of Perlee's employment through a large advertisement in a New York City newspaper. It seeks to enjoin (prevent) Perlee from working in that restaurant as a chef for one year. Discuss how successful Hotel Lux will be in its action. (See *Legality*.)

14–2. Capacity. Joanne is a seventy-five-year-old widow who survives on her husband's small pension. Joanne has become increasingly forgetful, and her family worries that she may have Alzheimer's disease (a brain disorder that seriously affects a person's ability to carry out daily activities). No physician has diagnosed her, however, and no court has ruled on her legal competence. One day while she is out shopping, Joanne stops by a store that is having a sale on pianos and enters into a fifteen-year installment contract to buy a grand piano. When the piano arrives the next day, Joanne seems confused and repeatedly asks the delivery person why a piano is being delivered. Joanne claims that she does not recall buying a piano. Explain whether this contract is void, voidable, or valid. Can Joanne avoid her contractual obligation to buy the piano? If so, how? (See *Contractual Capacity*.)

Business Case Problems

14–3. Business Case Problem with Sample Answer—Unconscionable Contracts or Clauses. Geographic Expeditions, Inc. (GeoEx), which guided climbs up Mount Kilimanjaro, required climbers to sign a release to participate in an expedition. The form mandated the arbitration of any dispute in San Francisco and limited damages to the cost of the trip. GeoEx told climbers that the terms were nonnegotiable and were the same as terms imposed by other travel firms. Jason Lhotka died on a GeoEx climb. His mother filed a suit against GeoEx. GeoEx sought arbitration. Was the arbitration clause unconscionable? Why or why not? [*Lhotka v. Geographic Expeditions, Inc.*, 181 Cal.App.4th 816, 104 Cal.Rptr.3d 844 (1 Dist. 2010)] (See *Legality*.)

• **For a sample answer to Problem 14–3, go to Appendix E at the end of this text.**

14–4. Mental Incompetence. Dorothy Drury suffered from dementia and chronic confusion. When she became unable to manage her own affairs, including decisions about medical and financial matters, her son Eddie arranged for her

move to an assisted living facility. During admission, she signed a residency agreement, which included an arbitration clause. After she sustained injuries in a fall at the facility, a suit was filed to recover damages. The facility asked the court to compel arbitration. Was Dorothy bound to the residency agreement? Discuss. [*Drury v. Assisted Living Concepts, Inc.*, 245 Or.App. 217, 262 P.3d 1162 (2011)] (See *Contractual Capacity*.)

14–5. Licensing Statutes. PEMS Co. International, Inc., agreed to find a buyer for Rupp Industries, Inc., for a commission of 2 percent of the purchase price, which was to be paid by the buyer. Using PEMS's services, an investment group bought Rupp for $20 million and changed its name to Temp-Air, Inc. PEMS asked Temp-Air to pay a commission on the sale. Temp-Air refused, arguing that PEMS had acted as a broker in the deal without a license. The applicable statute defines a broker as any person who deals with the sale of a business. If this statute was intended to protect the public, can PEMS collect its commission? Explain. [*PEMS Co. International, Inc. v. Temp-Air, Inc.*, 2011 WL 69098 (Minn.App. 2011)] (See *Legality*.)

14–6. Minors. D.V.G. (a minor) was injured in a one-car auto accident in Hoover, Alabama. The vehicle was covered by an insurance policy issued by Nationwide Mutual Insurance Co. Stan Brobston, D.V.G.'s attorney, accepted Nationwide's offer of $50,000 on D.V.G.'s behalf. Before the settlement could be submitted to an Alabama state court for approval, D.V.G. died from injuries received in a second, unrelated auto accident. Nationwide argued that it was not bound to the settlement, because a minor lacks the capacity to contract and so cannot enter into a binding settlement without court approval. Should Nationwide be bound to the settlement? Why or why not? [*Nationwide Mutual Insurance Co. v. Wood,* 121 So.3d 982 (Ala. 2013)] (See *Contractual Capacity.*)

14–7. Adhesion Contracts. David Desgro hired Paul Pack to inspect a house that Desgro wanted to buy. Pack had Desgro sign a standard-form contract that included a twelve-month limit for claims based on the agreement. Pack reported that the house had no major problems, but after Desgro bought it, he discovered issues with the plumbing, insulation, heat pump, and floor support. Thirteen months after the inspection, Desgro filed a suit in a Tennessee state court against Pack. Was Desgro's complaint filed too late, or was the contract's twelve-month limit unenforceable? Discuss. [*Desgro v. Pack,* 2013 WL 84899 (Tenn.App. 2013)] (See *Legality.*)

14–8. Legality. Sue Ann Apolinar hired a guide through Arkansas Valley Adventures, LLC, for a rafting excursion on the Arkansas River. At the outfitter's office, Apolinar signed a release that detailed potential hazards and risks, including "overturning," "unpredictable currents," "obstacles" in the water, and "drowning." The release clearly stated that her signature discharged Arkansas Valley from liability for all claims arising in connection with the trip. On the river, while attempting to maneuver around a rapid, the raft capsized. The current swept Apolinar into a logjam where, despite efforts to save her, she drowned. Her son, Jesus Espinoza, Jr., filed a suit in a federal district court against the rafting company, alleging negligence. What are the arguments for and against enforcing the release that Apolinar signed? Discuss. [*Espinoza v. Arkansas Valley Adventures, LLC,* 809 F.3d 1150 (10th Cir. 2016)] (See *Legality.*)

14–9. A Question of Ethics—Covenants Not to Compete. Brendan Coleman created and marketed Clinex, a software billing program. Later, Retina Consultants, P.C., a medical practice, hired Coleman as a software engineer. Together, they modified the Clinex program to create Clinex-RE. Coleman signed an agreement to the effect that he owned Clinex, Retina owned Clinex-RE, and he would not market Clinex in competition with Clinex-RE. After Coleman quit Retina, he withdrew funds from a Retina bank account and marketed both forms of the software to other medical practices. At trial, the court entered a judgment enjoining (preventing) Coleman from marketing the software that was in competition with the software he had developed for Retina Consultants. The court also obligated Coleman to return the funds taken from the company's bank account. Coleman appealed. [*Coleman v. Retina Consultants, P.C., 286 Ga. 317, 687 S.E.2d 457 (2009)]* (See *Legality.*)

(a) Should the court uphold the noncompete clause? If so, why? If not, why not?

(b) Should the court require Coleman to return the funds he withdrew from the company's accounts? Discuss fully.

(c) Did Coleman's behavior after he left the company influence the court's decision? Explain your answer.

Legal Reasoning Group Activity

14–10. Covenants Not to Compete. Assume that you are part of a group of executives at a large software corporation. The company is considering whether to incorporate covenants not to compete into its employment contracts. You know that there are some issues with the enforceability of these covenants, and you want to make an informed decision. (See *Legality.*)

(a) One group should make a list of what interests are served by enforcing covenants not to compete.

(b) A second group should create a list of what interests are served by refusing to enforce covenants not to compete.

(c) A third group is to consider whether a court should reform (and then enforce) a covenant not to compete that it determines is illegal. The group should create an argument for and an argument against reformation.

CHAPTER 15

Mistakes, Fraud, and Voluntary Consent

An otherwise valid contract may still be unenforceable if the parties have not genuinely agreed to its terms. A lack of *voluntary consent* (assent) can be used as a defense to the contract's enforceability.

Voluntary consent may be lacking because of a mistake, misrepresentation, undue influence, or duress—in other words, because there is no true "meeting of the minds." Generally, a party who demonstrates that he or she did not truly agree to the terms of a contract has a choice. That party can choose either to carry out the contract or to rescind (cancel) it and thus avoid the entire transaction. In this chapter, we examine the kinds of factors that may indicate a lack of voluntary consent.

15–1 Mistakes

We all make mistakes, so it is not surprising that mistakes are made when contracts are formed. In certain circumstances, contract law allows a contract to be avoided on the basis of mistake.

It is important to distinguish between *mistakes of fact* and *mistakes of value or quality*. Only a mistake of fact makes a contract voidable. Also, the mistake must involve some *material fact*—a fact that a reasonable person would consider important when determining his or her course of action.

Mistakes of fact occur in two forms—*bilateral* and *unilateral*. A unilateral mistake is made by only *one* of the parties. A bilateral, or mutual, mistake is made by *both* of the contracting parties. We look next at these two types of mistakes and illustrate them graphically in Exhibit 15–1.

15–1a Unilateral Mistakes of Fact

A **unilateral mistake** is made by only one of the parties. In general, a unilateral mistake does not give the mistaken party any right to relief from the contract. Normally, the contract is enforceable.

■ **EXAMPLE 15.1** Elena intends to sell her jet ski for $2,500. When she learns that Chin is interested in buying a used jet ski, she sends him an e-mail offering to sell the jet ski to him. When typing the e-mail, however, she mistakenly keys in the price of $1,500. Chin immediately sends Elena an e-mail reply accepting her offer. Even though Elena intended to sell her personal jet ski for $2,500, she has made a unilateral mistake and is bound by the contract to sell it to Chin for $1,500. ■

This general rule has at least two exceptions.[1] The contract may not be enforceable if:

1. The *other* party to the contract knows or should have known that a mistake of fact was made.
2. The error was due to a *substantial* mathematical mistake in addition, subtraction, division, or multiplication and was made inadvertently and without gross (extreme) negligence. If, for instance, a contractor's bid was significantly low because he or she made a mistake in addition when totaling the estimated costs, any contract resulting from the bid normally may be rescinded.

Of course, in both situations, the mistake must still involve some material fact.

15–1b Bilateral (Mutual) Mistakes of Fact

A **bilateral mistake** is a "mutual misunderstanding concerning a basic assumption on which the contract was made."[2] Note that, as with unilateral mistakes, the mistake must be about a material fact.

---

1. The *Restatement (Second) of Contracts*, Section 153, liberalizes the general rule to take into account the modern trend of allowing avoidance even though only one party has been mistaken.
2. *Restatement (Second) of Contracts*, Section 152.

EXHIBIT 15–1 Mistakes of Fact

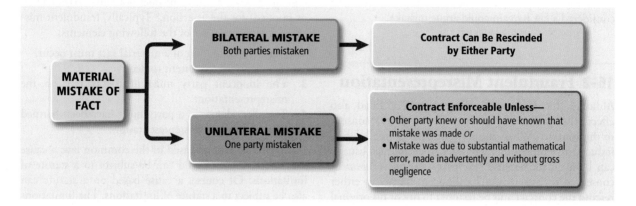

Either Party Can Rescind the Contract When both parties are mistaken about the same material fact, the contract can be rescinded by either party. ■ **CASE IN POINT 15.2** Coleman Holdings LP bought a parcel of real estate subject to setback restrictions imposed in a document entitled "Partial Release of Restrictions" that effectively precluded building a structure on the property. Lance and Joanne Eklund offered to buy the parcel from Coleman, intending to combine it with an adjacent parcel and build a home. Coleman gave the Eklunds a title report that referred to the "Partial Release of Restrictions," but they were not given a copy of the release.

Mistakenly believing that the document released restrictions on the property, the Eklunds did not investigate further. Meanwhile, Coleman also mistakenly believed that the setback restrictions had been removed. After buying the property and discovering the restrictions, the Eklunds filed a suit in a Nevada state court against Coleman, seeking rescission of the sale. The court ordered the deal rescinded. The Nevada Supreme Court affirmed the order. "The parties made a mutual mistake in their mutual belief that the parcel had no setback restrictions."[3] ■

When the Parties Reasonably Interpret a Term Differently A word or term in a contract may be subject to more than one reasonable interpretation. If the parties to the contract attach materially different meanings to the term, a court may allow the contract to be rescinded because there has been no true "meeting of the minds."

■ **CASE IN POINT 15.3** L&H Construction Company contracted with Circle Redmont, Inc., to make a cast-iron staircase and a glass flooring system. Redmont's original proposal was to "engineer, fabricate, and install" the staircase and flooring system, but installation was later dropped from the deal as a cost-cutting measure. The final contract stated that payment was due on "Supervision of Installation," although "install" appeared elsewhere in the contract. L&H insisted that installation was included and sued Redmont. The court found that the word *install* in the phrase "engineer, fabricate, and install" was the result of a mutual mistake. Both parties understood that Redmont would only supervise the installation, not perform it. Therefore, Redmont was not required to install the staircase and flooring.[4] ■

15–1c Mistakes of Value

If a mistake concerns the future market value or quality of the object of the contract, the mistake is one of *value,* and the contract normally is enforceable. ■ **EXAMPLE 15.4** Sung buys a violin from Bev for $250. Although the violin is very old, neither party believes that it is valuable. Later, however, an antiques dealer informs the parties that the violin is rare and worth thousands of dollars. Here, both parties were mistaken, but the mistake is a mistake of *value* rather than a mistake of *fact.* Because mistakes of value do not warrant contract rescission, Bev cannot rescind the contract. ■

The reason that mistakes of value do not affect the enforceability of contracts is that value is variable. Depending on the time, place, and other circumstances, the same item may be worth considerably different amounts. When parties form a contract, their agreement establishes the value of the object of their transaction—for the moment. Each party is considered to have assumed the risk that the value will change in the future or prove

---

3. *Coleman Holdings Limited Partnership v. Eklund,* 2015 WL 428567 (Nev. Sup.Ct. 2015).

4. *L&H Construction Co. v. Circle Redmont, Inc.,* 55 So.3d 630 (Fla.App. 2011).

to be different from what he or she thought. Without this rule, almost any party who did not receive what she or he considered a fair bargain could argue mistake.

15–2 Fraudulent Misrepresentation

Although fraud is a tort, the presence of fraud also affects the authenticity of the innocent party's consent to the contract. When an innocent party is fraudulently induced to enter into a contract, the contract usually can be avoided, because that party has not *voluntarily* consented to its terms.[5] The innocent party can either rescind the contract and be restored to her or his original position or enforce the contract and seek damages for any harms resulting from the fraud.

Generally, fraudulent misrepresentation refers only to misrepresentation that is consciously false and is intended to mislead another. The person making the fraudulent

misrepresentation knows or believes that the assertion is false or knows that she or he does not have a basis (stated or implied) for the assertion.[6] Typically, fraudulent misrepresentation consists of the following elements:

1. A misrepresentation of a material fact must occur.
2. There must be an intent to deceive.
3. The innocent party must justifiably rely on the misrepresentation.
4. To collect damages, a party must have been harmed as a result of the misrepresentation.

Like other actions based in the common law, a cause of action based on fraud can be subject to a statute of limitations. Of course, a cause based on a statute can also be subject to a statute of limitations. The limitations periods governing these actions may be different. In the following case, the issue was which limit to apply to a specific fraud claim—the three-year limit that applied to certain statute-based actions or the six-year limit that applied to common law actions.

---

5. *Restatement (Second) of Contracts*, Sections 163 and 164.

6. *Restatement (Second) of Contracts*, Section 162.

Schneiderman v. Trump Entrepreneur Initiative, LLC

New York Supreme Court, Appellate Division, First Department, 137 A.D.3d 409, 26 N.Y.S.3d 66 (2016).

Background and Facts   Donald Trump and Michael Sexton formed Trump University, LLC—later known as Trump Entrepreneur Initiative, LLC (TEI)—to sell courses in real estate investing. To attract students, Trump made a promotional video. In it, he said, "We're going to have professors that are absolutely terrific—terrific people, terrific brains, successful, the best. . . . All people that are hand-picked by me."

New York Attorney General Eric Schneiderman brought a proceeding in a New York state court against TEI, Trump, and Sexton, alleging that they had operated an illegal educational institution between 2005 and 2011. The attorney general sought an injunction, damages, penalties, and restitution under a state statute that provided for these remedies in cases of "persistent fraud." TEI was charged with intentionally misleading more than 5,000 students, including over 600 New York residents, into paying as much as $35,000 each to participate in its programs. Among other things, according to the attorney general, Trump did not handpick the instructors as he claimed.

The court dismissed the claim on the ground that it exceeded a three-year limit imposed on all statutory causes of action. The court also held that the specific statute did not provide the state with an independent cause of action for fraud. The attorney general appealed.

In the Language of the Court

MAZZARELLI, J.P. [Justice Presiding], *RENWICK, SAXE, MOSKOWITZ*, J.J. [Justices]
* * * *

* * * [New York] Executive Law Section 63(12) states, in relevant part:

Whenever any person shall engage in repeated fraudulent or illegal acts or otherwise demonstrate persistent fraud or illegality in the carrying on, conducting or transaction of business, the attorney general may apply * * * to the supreme court of the state of New York * * * for an order enjoining the continuance of such business activity or of any fraudulent or illegal acts and directing restitution and damages * * * and the court may award [such] relief * * * as it may deem proper.

Case 15.1 Continued   * * * *

[In its ruling, the lower court cited *People v. Charles Schwab & Co., Inc.,* 109 A.D.3d 445, 971 N.Y.S.2d 267 (1 Dept. 2013).] In *Charles Schwab,* the Attorney General had brought an enforcement action asserting claims under Section 63(12) * * * . The court dismissed the Section 63(12) claim.

On appeal to this Court, * * * we found that the court had properly dismissed that claim, stating that the section does not create independent claims, but merely authorizes the Attorney General to seek injunctive and other relief * * * in cases involving persistent fraud.

Although the holding of *Charles Schwab* purported to be based on the [New York] Court of Appeals' ruling in *State v. Cortelle Corp.,* 38 N.Y.2d 83, 378 N.Y.S.2d 654, 341 N.E.2d 223 (1975), *Cortelle* does not, in fact, hold that the Attorney General cannot bring a standalone cause of action for fraud under Executive Law Section 63(12).

* * * *

In *Cortelle,* the Court of Appeals [found] that * * * causes of action [under Section 63(12)] addressing * * * allegedly fraudulent practices did not rely on liabilities, penalties, or forfeitures created or imposed by statute. *Specifically, Section 63(12) did not make unlawful the alleged fraudulent practices, but only provided standing in the Attorney General to seek redress and additional remedies for recognized wrongs which pre-existed the statute.* [Emphasis added.]

* * * *

* * * Other New York courts addressing that issue * * * have generally allowed for independent causes of action for fraud under Section 63(12).

* * * *

Thus, *Charles Schwab* does not comport with prevailing authority.

* * * Hence, we hold that the Attorney General is, in fact, authorized to bring a cause of action for fraud under Section 63(12).

Decision and Remedy   *A state intermediate appellate court reversed the lower court's dismissal of the fraud claim, holding that the three-year limit on statutory causes of action did not apply. Because material issues of fact still existed as to that claim, however, the court remanded the case for further proceedings.*

Critical Thinking

- **Legal Environment**   *The statute at the center of this case provides for remedies that may not be available at common law. Why would those additional remedies be sought, and when would they most likely be awarded?*
- **What If the Facts Were Different?**   *Suppose that Trump University, or Trump Entrepreneur Initiative, had offered courses in real estate investing only online. Would the result in this case have been different? Explain.*

15–2a Misrepresentation Has Occurred

The first element of proving fraud is to show that misrepresentation of a material fact has occurred. This misrepresentation can occur by words or actions. For instance, the statement "This sculpture was created by Michelangelo" is a misrepresentation of fact if another artist sculpted the statue. Similarly, if a customer asks to see only paintings by Jasper Johns and the gallery owner immediately leads the customer to paintings that were not done by Johns, the owner's actions can be a misrepresentation.

Misrepresentation by Conduct   Misrepresentation also occurs when a party takes specific action to conceal a fact that is material to the contract.[7] Therefore, if a seller,

by her or his actions, prevents a buyer from learning of some fact that is material to the contract, such behavior constitutes misrepresentation by conduct.

■ **CASE IN POINT 15.5**   Actor Tom Selleck contracted to purchase a horse named Zorro for his daughter from Dolores Cuenca. Cuenca acted as though Zorro were fit to ride in competitions, when in reality the horse was unfit for this use because of a medical condition. Selleck filed a lawsuit against Cuenca for wrongfully concealing the horse's condition and won. A jury awarded Selleck more than $187,000 for Cuenca's misrepresentation by conduct.[8] ■

Statements of Opinion   Statements of opinion and representations of future facts (predictions) generally are

---

7. *Restatement (Second) of Contracts,* Section 160.

8. *Selleck v. Cuenca,* Case No. GIN056909, North County of San Diego, California, decided September 9, 2009.

not subject to claims of fraud. Statements such as "This land will be worth twice as much next year" and "This car will last for years and years" are statements of opinion, not fact. A fact is objective and verifiable, whereas an opinion is usually subject to debate. Contracting parties should know the difference and should not rely on statements of opinion.

Here, as in other areas of contract law, every person is expected to exercise care and judgment when entering into contracts. The law will not come to the aid of one who simply makes an unwise bargain. Nevertheless, in certain situations, such as when a naïve purchaser relies on an opinion from an expert, the innocent party may be entitled to rescission or reformation. (*Reformation* occurs when a court alters the terms of a contract to prevent undue hardships or burdens.)

■ **CASE IN POINT 15.6** In a classic case, an instructor at an Arthur Murray dance school told Audrey Vokes, a widow without family, that she had the potential to become an accomplished dancer. The instructor sold her 2,302 hours of dancing lessons for a total amount of $31,090.45 (equivalent to $146,000 in 2018). When it became clear to Vokes that she did not, in fact, have the potential to be an excellent dancer, she sued the school for fraudulent misrepresentation. The court held that because the dance school had superior knowledge about dance potential, the instructor's statements could be considered statements of fact rather than opinion.[9] ■

Misrepresentation of Law Misrepresentation of law *ordinarily* does not entitle a party to relief from a contract. ■ **EXAMPLE 15.7** Camara has a parcel of property that she is trying to sell to Pike. Camara knows that a local ordinance prohibits the construction of anything higher than three stories on the property. Nonetheless, she tells Pike, "You can build a condominium a hundred stories high on this land if you want to." Pike buys the land and later discovers that Camara's statement was false. Normally, Pike cannot avoid the contract, because people are assumed to know local zoning laws. ■

Exceptions to this rule occur when the misrepresenting party is in a profession that is known to require greater knowledge of the law than the average citizen possesses. For instance, if Camara, in *Example 15.7*, had been a lawyer or a real estate broker, her willful misrepresentation of the area's zoning laws probably would have constituted fraud.

Misrepresentation by Silence Ordinarily, neither party to a contract has a duty to come forward and disclose facts. Therefore, courts typically do not set aside contracts because a party did not volunteer pertinent

information. ■ **EXAMPLE 15.8** Jim is selling a car that has been in an accident and has been repaired. He does not need to volunteer this information to a potential buyer. If, however, the purchaser asks Jim if the car has had extensive bodywork and he lies, he has committed a fraudulent misrepresentation. ■

In general, if a seller knows of a serious potential problem that the buyer cannot reasonably be expected to discover, the seller may have a duty to speak. Usually, the seller must disclose only **latent defects**—that is, defects that could not readily be ascertained. Because a buyer of a house could easily discover the presence of termites through an inspection, for instance, termites may not qualify as a latent defect. Also, when the parties are in a *fiduciary relationship*—one of trust, such as partners, physician and patient, or attorney and client—they have a duty to disclose material facts. Failure to do so may constitute fraud.

15–2b Intent to Deceive

The second element of fraud is knowledge on the part of the misrepresenting party that facts have been falsely represented. This element, normally called ***scienter***,[10] or "guilty knowledge," signifies that there was an *intent to deceive*.

Scienter clearly exists if a party knows that a fact is not as stated. ■ **EXAMPLE 15.9** Richard Wright applies for a position as a business law professor two weeks after his release from prison. On his résumé, he lies and says that he was a corporate president for fourteen years and taught business law at another college. After he is hired, his probation officer alerts the school to Wright's criminal history. The school immediately fires him. If Wright sues the school for breach of his employment contract, he is unlikely to succeed. Because Wright clearly exhibited an intent to deceive the college by not disclosing his history, the school can rescind his employment contract without incurring liability. ■

Scienter also exists if a party makes a statement that he or she believes is not true or makes a statement recklessly, without regard to whether it is true or false. Finally, this element is met if a party says or implies that a statement is made on some basis, such as personal knowledge or personal investigation, when it is not.

Innocent Misrepresentation What if a person makes a statement that she or he believes to be true but that actually misrepresents material facts? In this situation, the person is guilty only of an **innocent misrepresentation,** not of fraud. When an innocent misrepresentation occurs, the aggrieved party can rescind the contract but usually cannot seek damages.

---

9. *Vokes v. Arthur Murray, Inc.*, 212 So.2d 906 (Fla.App. 1968).

10. Pronounced sy-*en*-ter.

■ **EXAMPLE 15.10** Parris tells Roberta that a tract of land contains 250 acres. Parris is mistaken—the tract contains only 215 acres—but Parris had no knowledge of the mistake. Roberta relies on the statement and contracts to buy the land. Even though the misrepresentation is innocent, Roberta can avoid the contract if the misrepresentation is material. ■

Negligent Misrepresentation Sometimes, a party makes a misrepresentation through carelessness, believing the statement is true, which can constitute **negligent misrepresentation.** Negligent misrepresentation occurs if the party does not exercise reasonable care in uncovering or disclosing facts, or use the skill and competence required by his or her business or profession.

■ **EXAMPLE 15.11** Kirk, an operator of a weight scale, certifies the weight of Sneed's commodity. If Kirk knows that the scale's accuracy has not been checked for more than three years, his action may constitute negligent misrepresentation. ■

In almost all states, such negligent misrepresentation is equal to *scienter,* or knowingly making a misrepresentation. In effect, negligent misrepresentation is treated as fraudulent misrepresentation, even though the misrepresentation was not purposeful. In negligent misrepresentation, culpable ignorance of the truth supplies the intention to mislead, even if the defendant can claim, "I didn't know."

15–2c Justifiable Reliance on the Misrepresentation

The third element of fraud is reasonably *justifiable reliance* on the misrepresentation of fact. The deceived party must have a justifiable reason for relying on the misrepresentation. Also, the misrepresentation must be an important factor (but not necessarily the sole factor) in inducing the deceived party to enter into the contract. Reliance is not justified if the innocent party knows the true facts or relies on obviously extravagant statements (such as, "this pickup truck will get fifty miles to the gallon").

■ **EXAMPLE 15.12** Meese, a securities broker, offers to sell BIM stock to Packer. Meese assures Packer that BIM shares are blue chip securities—that is, they are stable, have limited risk, and yield a good return on investment over time. In reality, Meese knows nothing about the quality of BIM stock and does not believe the truth of what he is saying. Thus, Meese's statement is an intentional misrepresentation of a material fact. If Packer is induced by Meese's statement to enter into a contract to buy the stock, he probably can avoid the contract. Packer justifiably relied on his broker's misrepresentation of material fact. ■

The same rule applies to defects in property sold. If the defects would be obvious on inspection, the buyer cannot justifiably rely on the seller's representations. If the defects are hidden or latent, as previously discussed, the buyer is justified in relying on the seller's statements.

In the following case, the receiver for a car wash assured the buyer that the property would be "appropriately winterized," but it was not. Was the buyer justified in relying on the seller's representations? (A *receiver,* also called a *trustee,* is an independent, impartial party appointed by a bankruptcy court to manage property in bankruptcy and dispose of it in an orderly manner for the benefit of the creditors.)

Case Analysis 15.2

Cronkelton v. Guaranteed Construction Services, LLC

Court of Appeals of Ohio, Third District, 988 N.E.2d 656, 2013-Ohio-328 (2013).

In the Language of the Court
PRESTON, P.J. [Presiding Judge]
* * * *

The case before this Court stems from a real estate transaction for a foreclosed car wash in Bellefontaine, Ohio. [A court had appointed Patrick Shivley to be a receiver for the protection of the property, which was offered for sale by Huntington Bank. Clifford] Cronkelton filed a complaint against appellants [Guaranteed Construction Services, LLC, and Shivley] in the Logan County

Court of Common Pleas following his purchase of the car wash. Cronkelton asserted * * * fraud.
* * * *

* * * The trial court held a jury trial on the fraud claim. The jury returned a verdict for Cronkelton.

* * * The trial court filed its judgment entry recording the jury's verdict for Cronkelton and awarding Cronkelton $43,671 in compensatory damages, $66,000 in punitive damages, and $30,000 for attorney fees. [Guaranteed Construction

Services and Shivley filed an appeal.]
* * * *

* * * [At the trial] Cronkelton testified that he first inspected the foreclosed car wash at the end of November 2009. At that time, Cronkelton tested the equipment and knew that some of the pieces of equipment were fully functioning and some were not. * * * Shortly thereafter, Cronkelton called Shivley to discuss the winterization of the property. Cronkelton testified:

Case 15.2 Continues

Case 15.2 Continued

So I called him, said, hey, it's going to freeze here this week. * * * It's supposed to get down to like ten degrees, have you got it winterized, you know. If it's not winterized, I'm not interested in the property. If it freezes, I'm not interested in the property at all. And he guaranteed me. He said, no, it will be taken care of. We don't have a problem. That's my job as receiver. I'll take care of it.

After the phone call, Shivley sent Cronkelton an e-mail dated December 7, 2009 that stated:

As per our phone conversation Guaranteed [Construction Services] will winterize the Car Wash with the anticipation of reopening the wash in the near future. Within this Winterization we will put antifreeze and secure floor heating as well as blow water out of all lines in self serve bays as well as empty tanks, etc. We will leave the heat on at a minimal level in the pump room. * * * We will complete all of this on Wednesday, December 9, 2009.

[Guaranteed Construction Services hired Strayer Company to winterize the property. But on December 10, Strayer's owner sent a memo to Guaranteed Construction Services and Shivley stating that the building was not designed to be winterized and that the only way to avoid problems was to leave the heat on. Shivley knew Huntington Bank had shut off the heat because the property was not generating income. In March 2010, Shivley informed Huntington of damage to the property as a result of freezing. Shivley did not share any of this information with Cronkelton.]

Cronkelton testified that they closed on the property in June and he received the keys at that time. Cronkelton testified that he immediately went to the property:

I opened the door, and the huge canisters that I was telling you about were all busted. The tops had been exploded off the top of them. * * * You could see pipes that were busted * * * . So it was clear at that time that this whole thing had froze up, and the extent of the damage could not even be, you know, detailed at that point.

* * * *

* * * Appellants argue Cronkelton unjustifiably relied on Shivley's statements about the car wash's condition because Cronkelton had the opportunity to inspect the property prior to closing.

* * * *

* * * Whether or not reliance on a material misrepresentation was justified under the facts of a case is a question for the trier of fact. Consequently, we must determine whether the jury's decision is supported by competent, credible evidence.

In the present case, it is undisputed that the damage caused by freezing was open and obvious upon inspection, that Cronkelton did inspect the property in November 2009, and that he could have inspected the property again before signing the purchase agreement. Cronkelton testified regarding why he did not inspect the property after November 2009:

* * * [Shivley] wrote me this e-mail, guaranteed me it was taken care of in detail what he was going to do, so I had no reason. And because * * * he was appointed by the Court, I don't know how much more I could have done to know that I could trust him.

* * * The jury found that Cronkelton had reasonably relied on Shivley's representations.

The jury's finding was supported by competent, credible evidence. * * * *When determining whether reliance is justifiable, courts consider the various circumstances involved, such as the nature of the transaction, the form and materiality of the transaction, the form and materiality of the representation, the relationship of the parties, the respective intelligence, experience, age, and mental and physical condition of the parties, and their respective knowledge and means of knowledge.* [Emphasis added.]

Cronkelton relied on representations made by Shivley * * * . As a receiver, Shivley had a fiduciary duty to the assets under his control. Under the circumstances of this case, Cronkelton had a reasonable basis to believe that Shivley, who was acting as an arm of the court, would take the promised steps to winterize the property.

* * * *

* * * We affirm the judgment of the trial court.

Legal Reasoning Questions

1. In evaluating a claim of fraud, what factors does a court consider in determining whether reliance was justifiable?

2. In this case, what did the jury find with respect to the plaintiff's claim of reliance? What was the appellate court's opinion of this finding?

3. Did Shivley's misrepresentations rise to the level of fraud? Explain.

15–2d Injury to the Innocent Party

Most courts do not require a showing of injury when the action is to rescind the contract. These courts hold that because rescission returns the parties to the positions they held before the contract was made, a showing of injury to the innocent party is unnecessary.

In contrast, to recover damages caused by fraud, proof of harm is universally required. The measure of damages is ordinarily equal to the property's value had it been delivered as represented, less the actual price paid for the property. (Additionally, because fraud actions necessarily involve wrongful conduct, courts may also sometimes award punitive damages, which are not ordinarily available in contract actions.)

In the following case, a real estate investor claimed that a seller's failure to disclose material facts about the property affected its value. The court had to determine not only if the seller's conduct constituted fraud, but also whether the fraud had caused harm to the property value.

Case 15.3

Fazio v. Cypress/GR Houston I, LP

Court of Appeals of Texas, First District, 403 S.W.3d 390 (2013).

Background and Facts Peter Fazio began talks with Cypress/GR Houston I, LP, to buy retail property whose main tenant was a Garden Ridge store. In performing a background investigation, Fazio and his agents became concerned about Garden Ridge's financial health. Nevertheless, after being assured that Garden Ridge had a positive financial outlook, Fazio sent Cypress a letter of intent to buy the property for $7.67 million "[b]ased on the currently reported absolute net income of $805,040.00." Cypress then agreed to provide all information in its possession, but it failed to disclose the following:

1. A consultant for Garden Ridge had recently requested a $240,000 reduction in the annual rent as part of a restructuring of the company's real estate leases.
2. Cypress's bank was so concerned about Garden Ridge's financial health that it had required a personal guaranty of the property's loan.

The parties entered into a purchase agreement, but Garden Ridge went into bankruptcy shortly after the deal closed. Fazio, along with other members of his family, sued Cypress for fraud after he was forced to sell the property three years later for only $3.75 million. A jury found in Fazio's favor. Although the jury agreed that Cypress had failed to disclose a material fact, however, it determined that Fazio was not entitled to any damages. The jury concluded that the fraud had not negatively affected the value of the property at the time it was sold to Fazio. Thus, no damages had been proximately caused by the fraud. The trial court entered a judgment notwithstanding the verdict in favor of Cypress, and Fazio appealed.

In the Language of the Court

Jane *BLAND*, Justice.

In this suit arising from the sale of land, we examine the appropriate measure of damages for a sale obtained through fraudulent inducement. A jury concluded that the seller of the land had failed to disclose material information to the buyer about the financial state of a commercial tenant who leased the land. But the jury further concluded that the buyers suffered nothing in damages proximately caused by the fraud, measured at the time of the sale, and it awarded no damages * * * . The trial court entered a take-nothing judgment [a judgment in which the plaintiff will receive no damages or other relief] in favor of the seller.
* * * *

The Fazios appeal the trial court's judgment against them on their claim for fraudulent inducement, contending that the trial court erred in disregarding the jury's * * * findings in their favor.
* * * *

There are two measures of direct damages in a fraud case: out-of-pocket and benefit-of-the-bargain. Out-of-pocket damages measure the difference between the amount the buyer paid and the value of the property the buyer received. Benefit-of-the-bargain damages measure the difference between the value of the property as represented and the actual value of the property. Both measures are determined at the time of the sale induced by the fraud. [Emphasis added.]

Losses that arise after the time of sale may be recoverable as consequential damages in appropriate cases. Consequential damages must be foreseeable and directly traceable to the misrepresentation and result from it. * * * Consequential damages must be explicitly premised on findings that the losses were foreseeable and directly traceable to the misrepresentation.

Case 15.3 Continues

Case 15.3 Continued

* * * *

* * * [The jury was] instructed * * * to determine the difference between the fraud-induced price that the Fazios paid for the property and the actual value of the property they received when they purchased it. * * * The question correctly focused the jury on the time of the sale, *because direct damages for fraud, including out-of-pocket damages, are properly measured at the time of the sale induced by the fraud—in this case, when the purchase agreement was executed—and not at some future time.* The jury responded that such damages were $0. It found other sorts of incidental and consequential damage to be $0 as well. [Emphasis added.]

* * * *

* * * The trial court properly * * * accorded judgment based on the jury's zero damages finding.

Decision and Remedy *A state intermediate appellate court affirmed the trial court's judgment based on the jury's finding. Fazio was not entitled to damages, because the misrepresentation (fraud) had not negatively affected the property's value at the time Fazio purchased the property.*

Critical Thinking
* **Ethical** *Was Cypress's conduct unethical? Why or why not?*
* **Social** *What does the decision in this case suggest to sellers of commercial real estate and others who engage in business negotiations?*

15–3 Undue Influence

Undue influence arises from relationships in which one party can greatly influence another party, thus overcoming that party's free will. A contract entered into under excessive or undue influence lacks voluntary consent and is therefore voidable.[11]

15–3a One Party Dominates the Other

In various types of relationships, one party may have the opportunity to dominate and unfairly influence another party. Minors and elderly people, for instance, are often under the influence of guardians (persons who are legally responsible for them). If a guardian induces a young or elderly ward (a person whom the guardian looks after) to enter into a contract that benefits the guardian, the guardian may have exerted undue influence. Undue influence can arise from a number of fiduciary relationships, such as physician-patient, parent-child, husband-wife, or guardian-ward situations.

The essential feature of undue influence is that the party being taken advantage of does not, in reality, exercise free will in entering into a contract. It is not enough that a person is elderly or suffers from some physical or mental impairment. There must be clear and convincing evidence that the person did not act out of her or his free will.[12] Similarly, the existence of a fiduciary relationship alone is insufficient to prove undue influence.[13]

15–3b Presumption of Undue Influence in Certain Situations

When the dominant party in a fiduciary relationship benefits from that relationship, a presumption of undue influence arises. The dominant party must exercise the utmost good faith in dealing with the other party. When a contract enriches the dominant party, the court will often *presume* that the contract was made under undue influence.

■ **EXAMPLE 15.13** Erik is the guardian for Kinsley, his ward. Erik is the dominant party in this relationship. On Kinsley's behalf, he enters into a contract from which he benefits financially. If Kinsley challenges the contract, the court will likely presume that the guardian has taken advantage of his ward. To rebut (refute) this presumption, Erik has to show that he made full disclosure to Kinsley and that consideration was present. He must also show that Kinsley received, if available, independent and competent advice before completing the transaction. Unless the presumption can be rebutted, the contract will be rescinded. ■

---

11. *Restatement (Second) of Contracts*, Section 177.

12. See, for example, *Ayers v. Shaffer*, 286 Va. 212, 748 S.E.2d 83 (2013).
13. See, for example, *Sleepy Hollow Ranch LLC v. Robinson*, 373 S.W.3d 485 (Mo.App. 2012).

15–4 Duress

Agreement to the terms of a contract is not voluntary if one of the parties is *forced* into the agreement. The use of threats to force a party to enter into a contract constitutes **duress.** Similarly, the use of blackmail or extortion to induce consent to a contract is duress. Duress is both a defense to the enforcement of a contract and a ground for the rescission of a contract.

15–4a The Threatened Act Must Be Wrongful or Illegal

To establish duress, there must be proof of a threat to do something that the threatening party has no right to do. Generally, for duress to occur, the threatened act must be wrongful or illegal. It also must render the person who is threatened incapable of exercising free will. A threat to exercise a legal right, such as the right to sue someone, ordinarily does not constitute duress.

■ **EXAMPLE 15.14** Joan accidentally drives into Olin's car at a stoplight. Joan has no automobile insurance, but she has substantial assets. At the scene, Olin claims to have suffered whiplash and tells Joan that he will agree not to file a lawsuit against her if she pays him $5,000. Joan initially refuses, but Olin says, "If you don't pay me $5,000 right now, I'm going to sue you for $25,000." Joan then gives Olin a check for $5,000 to avoid the lawsuit. The next day, Joan stops payment on the check. When Olin later sues to enforce their oral settlement agreement for $5,000, Joan claims duress as a defense to its enforcement. In this situation, because Olin had a right to sue Joan, his threat to sue her does not constitute duress. A court normally would not consider the threat of a civil suit to be duress. ■

15–4b Economic Duress

Economic need generally is not sufficient to constitute duress, even when one party exacts a very high price for an item that the other party needs. If the party exacting the price also creates the need, however, *economic duress* may be found.[14]

■ **EXAMPLE 15.15** The Internal Revenue Service (IRS) assesses a large tax and penalty against Weller. Weller retains Eyman, the accountant who prepared the tax returns on which the assessment was based, to challenge the assessment. Two days before the deadline for filing a reply with the IRS, Eyman declines to represent Weller unless he signs a very expensive contingency-fee agreement for the services.

In this situation, a court might find that the agreement is unenforceable because of economic duress. Eyman threatened only to withdraw his services, something that he was legally entitled to do. However, he delayed the withdrawal until two days before the IRS deadline. It would have been impossible at that late date to obtain adequate representation elsewhere. Therefore, Weller can argue that he was forced either to sign the contract or to lose his right to challenge the IRS assessment. ■

15–5 Adhesion Contracts and Unconscionability

Sometimes, the terms of a contract are dictated by a party with overwhelming bargaining power. The signer must agree to those terms or go without the commodity or service in question. In these situations, questions concerning voluntary consent may arise. (Many such contracts include arbitration provisions, as discussed in this chapter's *Ethics Today* feature.)

Adhesion contracts are written *exclusively* by one party and presented to the other party on a take-it-or-leave-it basis. These contracts often use standard forms, which give the adhering party no opportunity to negotiate the contract terms.

15–5a Standard-Form Contracts

Standard-form contracts often contain fine-print provisions that shift a risk ordinarily borne by one party to the other. A variety of businesses use such contracts. Life insurance policies, residential leases, loan agreements, and employment agency contracts are often standard-form contracts. To avoid enforcement of the contract or of a particular clause, the plaintiff normally must show that the contract or particular term is *unconscionable.*

■ **CASE IN POINT 15.16** Gregory and Stephanie Smith bought a house in Summerville, South Carolina, that was built by D. R. Horton, Inc. The standard purchase agreement they signed included a "Warranties and Dispute Resolution Section" that contained an arbitration clause and limited Horton's liability. After the Smiths moved in, they found extensive defects in the home. The Smiths

---

14. For a decision discussing the requirements for establishing economic duress, see *Cate Street Capital, Inc. v. DG Whitefield, LLC,* 2014 WL 8382756 (N.H.Super. 2014).

filed a lawsuit against Horton and numerous subcontractors for negligence, breach of contract, breach of warranties, and unfair trade practices.

Horton moved to compel arbitration, but the trial court denied the motion, holding that the arbitration clause was unconscionable. Horton appealed. The reviewing court affirmed the lower court's decision. The standard-form contract's "Warranties and Dispute Resolution Section" required binding arbitration of certain disputes and included "an entire host of attempted waivers of important legal remedies." Therefore, the court found that it was oppressive, unconscionable, and unenforceable. The Smiths could sue Horton and its subcontractors for the alleged defects.[15] ∎

---

15. *Smith v. D.R. Horton, Inc.,* 403 S.C. 10, 742 S.E.2d 37 (2013).

15–5b Unconscionability and the Courts

Technically, unconscionability under Section 2–302 of the Uniform Commercial Code (UCC) applies only to contracts for the sale of goods. Many courts, however, have broadened the concept and applied it in other situations.

It is important to note here that the UCC gives courts a great degree of discretion to invalidate or strike down a contract or clause as being unconscionable. As a result, some states have *not* adopted Section 2–302 of the UCC. In those states, the legislature and the courts prefer to rely on traditional notions of fraud, undue influence, and duress.

See Concept Summary 15.1 for a review of the factors that may indicate a lack of voluntary consent.

Concept Summary 15.1

Factors That May Indicate a Lack of Voluntary Consent

Mistakes	• *Bilateral (mutual) mistake*—If both parties are mistaken about a material fact, either party can avoid the contract. If the mistake relates to the value or quality of the subject matter, either party can enforce the contract. • *Unilateral mistake*—Generally, the mistaken party is bound by the contract, unless the other party knows or should have known of the mistake, or the mistake is an inadvertent mathematical error that is committed without gross negligence.
Fraudulent Misrepresentation	• A misrepresentation of a material fact has occurred. • There has been an intent to deceive. • The innocent party has justifiably relied on the misrepresentation. • To collect damages, a party must have been harmed as a result of the misrepresentation.
Undue Influence and Duress	• *Undue influence*—Arises from special relationships, in which one party's free will has been overcome by the undue influence of another. Usually, the contract is voidable. • *Duress*—Defined as the use of threats to force a party to enter into a contract out of fear; for example, the threat of violence or economic pressure. The party forced to enter into the contract can rescind the contract.
Adhesion Contracts and Unconscionability	• Concerns one-sided bargains in which one party has substantially superior bargaining power and can dictate the terms of a contract. • Unconscionability can occur in standard-form contracts and take-it-or-leave-it (adhesion) contracts.

ETHICS TODAY

Forced Arbitration: Right or Wrong?

Knowingly or not, many consumers sign contracts that include arbitration clauses. Such clauses require that dissatisfied consumers submit to arbitration, rather than pursue litigation through the court system. Not surprisingly, there is a growing movement in protest of arbitration clauses of this kind, which some believe are unfair to consumers.

Governing Arbitration Law

For the most part, federal law encourages arbitration through the Federal Arbitration Act (FAA).[a] Generally, federal courts have ruled in favor of contracts with arbitration clauses if those clauses provide a meaningful way for consumers to seek redress for alleged harms.

Over the past few years, the United States Supreme Court has held that the FAA preempts state courts' interpretations of arbitration clauses. For instance, in *AT&T Mobility, LLC v. Concepcion*,[b] the Court ruled that federal law preempts state laws that bar enforcement of arbitration clauses prohibiting class-action suits. Later, in *DIRECTV, Inc. v. Imburgia*,[c] the Court again upheld an arbitration clause, citing the *Concepcion* case. The Court stated that the FAA "is the law of the United States, and [the] *Concepcion* [case] is an authoritative interpretation of the act." The Court stated that "the judges of every

State must follow it" because of the supremacy clause of the U.S. Constitution.

Federal Attempts to Circumvent the Supreme Court's Decisions

Even within the federal government, certain entities wish to reduce the use of arbitration clauses in consumer contracts. In the fall of 2015, the Consumer Financial Protection Bureau announced that it would seek to implement new rules barring contracts from substituting private arbitration for class-action litigation. Such rules would apply to checking accounts, credit cards, and other financial products. If that federal agency is successful, it will undoubtedly face litigation that will go to the Supreme Court.

Why Arbitration Is So Prevalent

Many corporations favor arbitration clauses in consumer contracts because arbitration is less expensive than litigation. Arbitration is certainly the preferred remedy for disputes involving relatively small sums—disputes over cell phone contracts, for instance. While individuals may feel that they are at a disadvantage if they are forced to go to arbitration, for the economy as a whole, there are benefits. In particular, according to some estimates, the rate of growth in liability costs has fallen relative to the growth in the economy since 2003. Ultimately, consumers on average pay lower costs for products and services when corporations spend less on litigation.

Critical Thinking *What might happen if arbitration clauses were prohibited in all consumer contracts?*

---

a. 9 U.S.C. Sections 1 *et seq.*
b. 563 U.S. 333, 131 S.Ct. 1740, 179 L.Ed.2d 742 (2011). See also *American Express Co. v. Italian Colors Restaurant*, ___ U.S. ___, 133 S.Ct. 2304, 186 L.Ed.2d 417 (2013).
c. ___ U.S. ___, 135 S.Ct. 1547, 191 L.Ed.2d 636 (2015).

Reviewing: Mistakes, Fraud, and Voluntary Consent

Chelene had been a caregiver for Marta's eighty-year-old mother, Janis, for nine years. Shortly before Janis passed away, Chelene convinced her to buy Chelene's house for Marta. The elderly woman died before the papers were signed, however. Four months later, Marta used her inheritance to buy Chelene's house without having it inspected. The house was built in the 1950s, and Chelene said it was in "perfect condition." Nevertheless, one year after the purchase, the basement started leaking. Marta had the paneling removed from the basement walls and discovered that the walls were bowed inward and cracked. Marta then had a civil engineer inspect the basement walls, and he found that the cracks had been caulked and painted over before the paneling was installed. He concluded that the "wall failure" had existed "for at least thirty years" and that the basement walls were "structurally unsound." Using the information presented in the chapter, answer the following questions.

Continues

1. Can Marta avoid the contract on the ground that both parties made a mistake about the condition of the house? Explain.
2. Can Marta sue Chelene for fraudulent misrepresentation? Why or why not? What element or elements might be lacking?
3. Now assume that Chelene knew that the basement walls were cracked and bowed and that she had hired someone to install paneling before she offered to sell the house. Did she have a duty to disclose this defect to Marta? Could a court find that Chelene's silence in this situation constituted misrepresentation? Explain.
4. Can Marta obtain rescission of the contract based on undue influence? If the sale to Janis had been completed before her death, could Janis have obtained rescission based on undue influence? Explain.

Debate This . . . *The concept of* caveat emptor *("let the buyer beware") should be applied to all sales, including those of real property.*

Terms and Concepts

adhesion contract 289	latent defect 284	unilateral mistake 280
bilateral mistake 280	negligent misrepresentation 285	voluntary consent 280
duress 289	*scienter* 284	
innocent misrepresentation 284	undue influence 288	

Issue Spotters

1. In selling a house, Matt tells Ann that the wiring, fixtures, and appliances are of a certain quality. Matt knows nothing about the quality, but it is not as specified. Ann buys the house. On learning the true quality, Ann confronts Matt. He says he wasn't trying to fool her, he was only trying to make a sale. Can she rescind the deal? Why or why not? (See *Fraudulent Misrepresentation*.)

2. Elle, an accountant, certifies several audit reports for Flite Corporation, her client, knowing that Flite intends to use the reports to obtain loans from Good Credit Company (GCC). Elle believes that the reports are true and does not intend to deceive GCC, but she does not check the reports before certifying them. Can Elle be held liable to GCC? Why or why not? (See *Fraudulent Misrepresentation*.)

- **Check your answers to the Issue Spotters against the answers provided in Appendix D at the end of this text.**

Business Scenarios

15–1. Undue Influence. Juan is an elderly man who lives with his nephew, Samuel. Juan is totally dependent on Samuel's support. Samuel tells Juan that unless he transfers a tract of land he owns to Samuel for a price 35 percent below its market value, Samuel will no longer support and take care of him. Juan enters into the contract. Discuss fully whether Juan can set aside this contract. (See *Undue Influence*.)

15–2. Fraudulent Misrepresentation. Grano owns a forty-room motel on Highway 100. Tanner is interested in purchasing the motel. During the course of negotiations, Grano tells Tanner that the motel netted $30,000 during the previous year and that it will net at least $45,000 the next year. The motel books, which Grano turns over to Tanner before the purchase, clearly show that Grano's motel netted only $15,000 the previous year. Also, Grano fails to tell Tanner that a bypass to Highway 100 is being planned that will redirect most traffic away from the front of the motel. Tanner purchases the motel. During the first year under Tanner's operation, the motel nets only $18,000. At this time, Tanner learns of the motel's previous low profits and the planned bypass. Tanner wants Grano to return the purchase price. Discuss fully Tanner's probable success in getting his funds back. (See *Fraudulent Misrepresentation*.)

15–3. Voluntary Consent. Discuss whether either of the following contracts will be unenforceable on the ground that voluntary consent is lacking:

(a) Simmons finds a stone in his pasture that he believes to be quartz. Jenson, who also believes that the stone is quartz, contracts to purchase it for $10. Just before delivery, the stone is discovered to be a diamond worth $1,000. (See *Mistakes.*)

(b) Jacoby's barn is burned to the ground. He accuses Goldman's son of arson and threatens to have the prosecutor bring a criminal action unless Goldman agrees to pay him $5,000. Goldman agrees to pay. (See *Duress.*)

Business Case Problems

15–4. Fraudulent Misrepresentation. Ricky and Sherry Wilcox hired Esprit Log and Timber Frame Homes to build a log house, which the Wilcoxes intended to sell. They paid Esprit $125,260 for materials and services. They eventually sold the home for $1,620,000 but sued Esprit due to construction delays. The logs were supposed to arrive at the construction site precut and predrilled, but that did not happen. It took five extra months to build the house while the logs were cut and drilled one by one. The Wilcoxes claimed that the interest they paid on a loan for the extra construction time cost them about $200,000. The jury agreed and awarded them that much in damages, plus $250,000 in punitive damages and $20,000 in attorneys' fees. Esprit appealed, claiming that the evidence did not support the verdict because the Wilcoxes had sold the house for a good price. Is Esprit's argument credible? Why or why not? How should the court rule? [*Esprit Log and Timber Frame Homes, Inc. v. Wilcox,* 302 Ga.App. 550, 691 S.E.2d 344 (2010)] (See *Fraudulent Misrepresentation.*)

15–5. Fraudulent Misrepresentation. Charter One Bank owned a fifteen-story commercial building. A fire inspector told Charter that the building's drinking-water and fire-suppression systems were linked, which violated building codes. Without disclosing this information, Charter sold the building to Northpoint Properties, Inc. Northpoint spent $280,000 to repair the water and fire-suppression systems and filed a suit against Charter One. Is the seller liable for not disclosing the building's defects? Discuss. [*Northpoint Properties, Inc. v. Charter One Bank,* 2011-Ohio-2512 (Ohio App. 8 Dist. 2011)] (See *Fraudulent Misrepresentation.*)

15–6. Standard-Form Contracts. David Desgro hired Paul Pack to inspect a house that Desgro wanted to buy. Pack had Desgro sign a standard-form contract that included a twelve-month limit for claims based on the agreement. Pack reported that the house had no major problems, but after Desgro bought it, he discovered issues with the plumbing, insulation, heat pump, and floor support. Thirteen months after the inspection, Desgro filed a suit in a Tennessee state court against Pack. Was Desgro's complaint filed too late, or was the contract's twelve-month limit unenforceable? Discuss. [*Desgro v. Pack,* 2013 WL 84899 (Tenn.App. 2013)] (See *Adhesion Contracts and Unconscionability.*)

15–7. Business Case Problem with Sample Answer— Fraudulent Misrepresentation. Joy Pervis and Brenda Pauley worked together as talent agents in Georgia. When Pervis "discovered" actress Dakota Fanning, Pervis sent Fanning's audition tape to Cindy Osbrink, a talent agent in California. Osbrink agreed to represent Fanning in California and to pay 3 percent of Osbrink's commissions to Pervis and Pauley, who agreed to split the payments equally. Six years later, Pervis told Pauley that their agreement with Osbrink had expired and there would be no more payments. Nevertheless, Pervis continued to receive payments from Osbrink. Each time Pauley asked about commissions, however, Pervis replied that she was not receiving any. Do these facts evidence fraud? Explain. [*In re Pervis,* 512 Bankr. 348 (N.D.Ga. 2014)] (See *Fraudulent Misrepresentation.*)

- **For a sample answer to Problem 15–7, go to Appendix E at the end of this text.**

15–8. Fraudulent Misrepresentation. Vianna Stibal owns and operates the ThetaHealing Institute of Knowledge (THInK) in Idaho Falls, Idaho. ThetaHealing is Stibal's "self-discovered" healing method. In her book *Go Up and Seek God,* Stibal stated that she had been diagnosed with cancer and had cured herself using ThetaHealing. But Stibal's representation that she cured herself of cancer was false, and she knew it—her medical records did not confirm a cancer diagnosis. Believing Stibal's claim, Kara Alexander traveled from New York to Idaho to pay for, and attend, classes in ThetaHealing from Stibal. Later, Alexander began to question the validity of her THInK degree. What are the elements of a cause of action for fraudulent misrepresentation? Do the facts in this situation meet these requirements? Discuss. [*Alexander v. Stibal,* 160 Idaho 10, 368 P.3d 630 (2016)] (See *Fraudulent Misrepresentation.*)

15–9. A Question of Ethics—Mistake. *On behalf of BRJM, LLC, Nicolas Kepple offered Howard Engelsen $210,000 for a parcel of land known as lot five on the north side of Barnes Road in Stonington, Connecticut. Engelsen's company, Output Systems, Inc., owned the land. Engelsen had the lot surveyed and obtained an appraisal. The appraiser determined that the property was 3.0 acres in size. It thus could not be subdivided because it did not* *meet the town's minimum legal requirement of 3.7 acres for sub-division. The appraiser then valued the property at $277,000. Engelsen responded to Kepple's offer of $210,000 with a counter-offer of $230,000, which Kepple accepted. On May 3, 2002, the parties signed a contract. When Engelsen refused to go through with the deal, BRJM filed a suit in a Connecticut state court against Output, seeking specific performance and other relief. The defendant asserted the defense of mutual mistake on at least two grounds. [BRJM, LLC v. Output Systems, Inc., 100 Conn. App. 153, 917 A.2d 605 (2007)]* (See *Mistakes.*)

(a) In the counteroffer, Engelsen asked Kepple to remove from their contract a clause requiring written confirmation of the availability of a "free split," which meant that the property could be subdivided without the town's prior approval. Kepple agreed. After signing the contract, Kepple learned that the property was *not* entitled to a free split. Would this circumstance qualify as a mistake on which the defendant could avoid the contract? Discuss.

(b) After signing the contract, Engelsen obtained a second appraisal that established the size of lot five as 3.71 acres, which meant that it could be subdivided, and valued the property at $490,000. Can the defendant avoid the contract on the basis of a mistake in the first appraisal? Explain.

Legal Reasoning Group Activity

15–10. Fraudulent Misrepresentation. Radiah Givens was involved romantically with Joseph Rosenzweig. She moved into an apartment on which he made the down payment. She signed the mortgage, but he made the payments and paid household expenses. They later married. She had their marriage annulled, however, when she learned that he was married to someone else. Rosenzweig then filed a suit against her to collect on the mortgage. (See *Fraudulent Misrepresentation.*)

(a) The first group should decide whether Rosenzweig committed fraud.

(b) The second group should evaluate whether Rosenzweig's conduct was deceitful, and if so, whether his deceitfulness should affect the decision in this case.

(c) The third group should consider how fraud is related to ethics. Can a contracting party act ethically and still commit fraud? How?

CHAPTER 16

The Writing Requirement in Our Digital World

contract that is otherwise valid may still be unenforceable if it is not in the proper form. Certain types of contracts are required to be in writing or evidenced by a memorandum or an electronic record. An agreement subject to the writing requirement does not necessarily have to be written on paper. An exchange of e-mails that evidences the parties' contract can be sufficient, provided that they are "signed," or agreed to, by the party against whom enforcement is sought.

In this chapter, we examine the kinds of contracts that require a writing and some exceptions to the writing requirement. We also discuss the *parol evidence rule,* which courts follow when determining whether evidence that is extraneous, or external, to written contracts may be admissible at trial.

16–1 The Statute of Frauds

Every state has a statute that stipulates what types of contracts must be in writing. We refer to such a statute as the **Statute of Frauds.** The origins of these statutes can be traced to early English law.

16–1a Origins of the Statute

At early common law, parties to a contract were not allowed to testify if a dispute arose. This led to the practice of hiring third party witnesses. As early as the seventeenth century, the English recognized that this practice created many problems and enacted a statute to help deal with them.

The statute, passed by the English Parliament in 1677, was known as "An Act for the Prevention of Frauds and Perjuries." The act established that certain types of contracts, to be enforceable, had to be evidenced by a writing and signed by the party against whom enforcement was sought. The primary purpose of the statute was to ensure that, for certain types of contracts, there was reliable evidence of the contracts and their terms.

16–1b State Legislation

Today, although each state has a statute modeled after the English act, the statutes vary slightly from state to state. All states require certain types of contracts to be in writing or evidenced by a written memorandum or an electronic record. In addition, the party or parties against whom enforcement is sought must have signed the contract, unless certain exceptions apply (as discussed later in this chapter). Recall that in the context of electronic communications, a party's name typed at the bottom of an e-mail can qualify as a signature.

The actual name of the Statute of Frauds is misleading because the statute does not apply to fraud. Rather, it denies enforceability to certain contracts that do not comply with its writing requirements. The primary purpose of the statute is to prevent harm to innocent parties by requiring written evidence of agreements concerning important transactions. A contract that is oral when it is required to be in writing is normally voidable by a party who later does not wish to follow through with the agreement.

16–2 Contracts That Require a Writing

The following types of contracts are generally required to be in writing or evidenced by a written memorandum or electronic record:

1. Contracts involving interests in land.
2. Contracts that cannot *by their terms* be performed within one year from the day after the date of formation.

3. Collateral, or secondary, contracts, such as promises to answer for the debt or duty of another and promises by the administrator or executor of an estate to pay a debt of the estate personally—that is, out of her or his own pocket.

4. Promises made in consideration of marriage.

5. Under the Uniform Commercial Code (UCC), contracts for the sale of goods priced at $500 or more.

16–2a Contracts Involving Interests in Land

A contract calling for the sale of land is not enforceable unless it is in writing or evidenced by a written memorandum. Land is *real property* and includes all physical objects that are permanently attached to the soil, such as buildings, fences, trees, and the soil itself.

The Statute of Frauds operates as a *defense* to the enforcement of an oral contract for the sale of land. ■ **EXAMPLE 16.1** Skylar contracts orally to sell his property in Fair Oaks to Beth. If he later decides not to sell, under most circumstances, Beth cannot enforce the contract. ■

The Statute of Frauds also requires written evidence of contracts for the transfer of other interests in land, such as mortgage agreements and leases. Similarly, an agreement that includes an option to purchase real property must be in writing for the option to be enforced.

Generally, for a land sale contract to be enforceable under the Statute of Frauds, the contract must describe the property being transferred with sufficient certainty for it to be identified. ■ **CASE IN POINT 16.2** Talat Solaiman and Sabina Chowdhury agreed to buy a convenience store and gas station owned by Mohammad Salim for $975,000 and gave Salim a $25,000 security deposit. They signed a handwritten contract, which was later typed up, but the contract described the property only by its street address (199 Upper Riverdale Road, Jonesboro, GA 30236).

When Solaiman and Chowdhury decided not to go through with the deal, Salim kept their deposit and filed a breach of contract lawsuit. The court held that the parties' purchase agreement was unenforceable because it did not sufficiently describe the real property to be purchased. To comply with the Statute of Frauds, "a contract must describe the property . . . with the same degree of certainty as that required in a deed conveying realty." Therefore, the contract was void, and Salim had to return the buyers' security deposit.[1] ■

The issue in the following case was whether a contract for a sale of land sufficiently identified the property and the sellers.

---

1. *Salim v. Solaiman*, 302 Ga.App. 607, 691 S.E.2d 389 (2010).

Sloop v. Kiker

Court of Appeals of Arkansas, Division III, 2016 Ark. App. 125 (2016).

In the Language of the Court

Cliff HOOFMAN, Judge

* * * *

[Russell and Sally] Kiker * * * own a house on 134.5 acres in Newton County [Arkansas]. On January 26, 2012, [Mona] Sloop contracted to purchase the house and the land for $850,000. The contract contained the following down-payment provision:

The *nonrefundable down payment shall be $350,000,* due upon execution of this contract by both parties * * * . Time is of the essence in satisfying the terms of this contract. In the event closing does not occur on or before August 31, 2013, this contract shall be null and void, the down payment

shall be retained by Seller. Buyer, if then occupying the property shall vacate the property * * * .

Sloop made the $350,000 down payment on January 26, 2012. That same day, the parties executed two additional documents: a warranty deed and a lease/caretaker agreement. The deed recited that the Kikers * * * conveyed the property to Sloop * * * . It further contained a full metes-and-bounds description of the property, which the contract had described only by street address. The lease/caretaker agreement essentially allowed Sloop to live on the property as a tenant until the $500,000 balance due was paid, subject to an August 31, 2013 deadline. Sloop assumed occupancy of

the property in the summer of 2012.

* * * As the August 31, 2013 deadline approached, [Sloop] informed the Kikers that she would * * * not be able to pay the balance by that date.

* * * On or about September 6, 2013, the Kikers served Sloop with a notice to vacate the premises. The notice stated that the lease/caretaker agreement had expired and that Sloop had missed the August 31, 2013 deadline to pay the balance due on the property, requiring her to forfeit her $350,000 nonrefundable down payment.

Sloop refused to vacate the property, and the Kikers filed suit against her in

Case 16.1 Continued

Newton County Circuit Court. Their complaint sought an order removing Sloop from the property and a declaration that they were entitled to retain the $350,000 down payment. Sloop voluntarily abandoned the property a month after the complaint was filed, but she filed a counterclaim asking that the Kikers return her $350,000 down payment.

The Kikers moved for summary judgment, arguing that the real-estate contract unambiguously provided that the $350,000 down payment was nonrefundable, given that Sloop had failed to pay the balance due by August 31, 2013. Sloop responded that * * * the parties' contract violated the Statute of Frauds because it lacked a sufficient property description and failed to identify the sellers.

After a hearing, the circuit court entered an order granting the Kikers' motion for summary judgment * * *

on the ground that any uncertainties in the real-estate contract were cured by the warranty deed—a clear reference to Sloop's Statute-of-Frauds argument. Sloop now appeals from the summary-judgment order.

* * * *

* * * Sloop argues that the circuit court erred in determining that the parties' real-estate contract satisfied the Statute of Frauds. We see no error on this point.

The Statute of Frauds provides that a contract for the sale of land must be in writing to be enforceable. Additionally, the contract must contain certain essential information, such as the terms and conditions of the sale, the price to be paid, the time for payment, and a description of the property. [Emphasis added.]

Sloop contends that the contract in this case was deficient because it did not name the Kikers * * * as sellers of the

property and did not contain a sufficient description of the property. However, as noted by the circuit court, the warranty deed that the parties executed on the same day as the real-estate contract named the Kikers * * * as grantors and provided a formal, legal description of the property. Generally, instruments executed at the same time by the same parties, for the same purpose, and in the course of the same transaction, are, in the eyes of the law, one instrument and will be read and construed together. Moreover, if a contract furnishes a means by which realty can be identified—a key to the property's location—the Statute of Frauds is satisfied. Here, the contract's designation of the premises by street address met this requirement.

* * * *

Affirmed.

Legal Reasoning Questions

1. Why does the Statute of Frauds require that a contract for a sale of land contain a sufficient description of the property?
2. How did the court construe the deed and the contract in this case—as one instrument or as separate documents? Why?
3. What effect did the court's construction of the deed and the contract have on the outcome in this case? Explain.

16–2b The One-Year Rule

A contract that cannot, *by its own terms,* be performed within one year *from the day after* the contract is formed must be in writing to be enforceable.[2] The reason for this rule is that the parties' memory of their contract's terms is not likely to be reliable for longer than a year. Disputes are unlikely to occur until some time after the contracts are made, and if the terms have not been put into writing, resolving such disputes is difficult.

Time Period Starts the Day after the Contract Is Formed The one-year period begins to run *the day after the contract is made.* ■ **EXAMPLE 16.3** Superior University forms a contract with Kimi San stating that San will teach three courses in history during the coming academic year (September 15 through June 15). If the contract is formed in March, it must be in writing to be

enforceable—because it cannot be performed within one year. If the contract is not formed until July, however, it does not have to be in writing to be enforceable—because it can be performed within one year. ■

Must Be Objectively Impossible to Perform within One Year The test for determining whether an oral contract is enforceable under the one-year rule is whether performance is *possible* within one year. It does not matter whether the agreement is *likely* to be performed during that period.

When performance of a contract is objectively impossible during the one-year period, the contract must be in writing (or a record) to be enforceable. ■ **EXAMPLE 16.4** A contract to provide five crops of tomatoes to be grown on a specific farm in Illinois would be objectively impossible to perform within one year. No farmer in Illinois can grow five crops of tomatoes in a single year. ■

If performance is possible within one year under the contract's terms, the contract does not fall under the

---

2. *Restatement (Second) of Contracts,* Section 130.

Statute of Frauds and need not be in writing. ■ **EXAMPLE 16.5** Janine enters into a contract to create a carving of President Barack Obama's face on a mountainside, similar to the carvings of other presidents' faces on Mount Rushmore. It is technically possible—although not very likely—that the contract could be performed within one year. (Mount Rushmore took over fourteen years to complete.) Therefore, Janine's contract need not be in writing to be enforceable. ■

Exhibit 16–1 graphically illustrates the one-year rule.

16–2c Collateral Promises

A **collateral promise,** or secondary promise, is one that is ancillary (subsidiary) to a principal transaction or primary contractual relationship. In other words, a collateral promise is one made by a third party to assume the debts or obligations of a primary party to a contract if that party does not perform. Any collateral promise of this nature falls under the Statute of Frauds and therefore must be in writing to be enforceable.

Primary versus Secondary Obligations To understand this concept, it is important to distinguish between primary and secondary promises and obligations. A promise to pay another person's debt (or other obligation) that is *not conditioned on the person's failure to pay (or perform)* is a primary obligation. A promise to pay another's debt *only if that party fails to pay* is a secondary obligation. A contract in which a party assumes a primary obligation normally does not need to be in writing to

be enforceable, whereas a contract assuming a secondary obligation does.

■ **EXAMPLE 16.6** Connor tells Leanne Lu, an orthodontist, that he will pay for the services provided for Connor's niece, Allison. Because Connor has assumed direct financial responsibility for his niece's debt, this is a primary obligation and need not be in writing to be enforceable. In contrast, if Connor commits to paying Allison's orthodontist bill only if her mother does not, it is a secondary obligation. In that situation, Lu must have a signed writing or record proving that Connor assumed this secondary obligation for it to be enforced. ■

Exhibit 16–2 illustrates the concept of a collateral promise.

An Exception—The "Main Purpose" Rule An oral promise to answer for the debt of another is covered by the Statute of Frauds *unless* the guarantor's main purpose in incurring a secondary obligation is to secure a personal benefit. This type of contract need not be in writing.[3] The assumption is that a court can infer from the circumstances of a particular case whether the "leading objective" of the guarantor was to secure a personal benefit. In this situation, the guarantor is, in effect, answering for (guaranteeing) her or his own debt.

■ **EXAMPLE 16.7** Carlie Braswell contracts with Winsom Manufacturing Company to have some machines custom-made for her factory. She promises Newform Supply, Winsom's supplier, that if Newform continues to

---

3. *Restatement (Second) of Contracts,* Section 116.

EXHIBIT 16–1 The One-Year Rule

Under the Statute of Frauds, contracts that by their terms are impossible to perform within one year from the day after the date of contract formation must be in writing to be enforceable. Put another way, if it is at all possible to perform an oral contract within one year from the day after the contract is made, the contract will fall outside the Statute of Frauds and be enforceable.

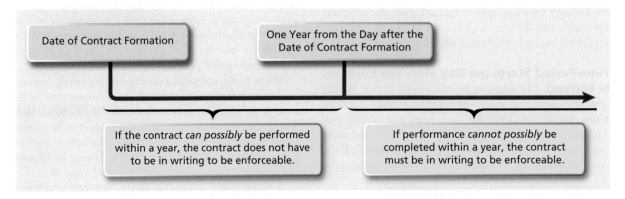

Date of Contract Formation

One Year from the Day after the Date of Contract Formation

If the contract *can possibly* be performed within a year, the contract does not have to be in writing to be enforceable.

If performance *cannot possibly* be completed within a year, the contract must be in writing to be enforceable.

EXHIBIT 16–2 Collateral Promises

A collateral (secondary) promise is one made by a third party (C, in this exhibit) to a creditor (B, in this exhibit) to pay the debt of another (A, in this exhibit), who is primarily obligated to pay the debt. Under the Statute of Frauds, collateral promises must be in writing to be enforceable.

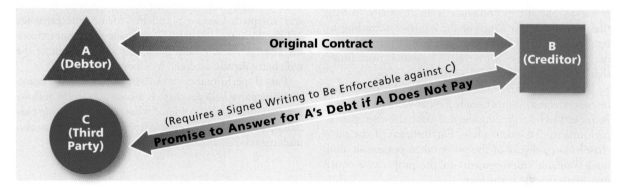

deliver the materials to Winsom for the production of the custom-made machines, she will guarantee payment. This promise need not be in writing, even though the effect may be to pay the debt of another. This is because Braswell's main purpose in forming the contract is to secure a benefit for herself. ■

Another typical application of the main purpose rule occurs when one creditor guarantees a debtor's debt to another creditor to forestall litigation. A creditor might do this to allow the debtor to remain in business long enough to generate profits sufficient to pay *both* creditors. In this situation, the guaranty does not need to be in writing to be enforceable.

16–2d Promises Made in Consideration of Marriage

A unilateral promise to make a monetary payment or to give property in consideration of a promise to marry must be in writing. In other words, if a mother promises to pay a man $20,000 if he marries her daughter, that promise must be in writing to be enforceable. ■ **EXAMPLE 16.8** Evan promises to buy Celeste a condo in Maui if she marries him. Celeste would need written evidence of Evan's promise to enforce it. ■

The same rule applies to **prenuptial agreements**— agreements made before marriage that define each partner's ownership rights in the other partner's property. Prenuptial agreements must be in writing to be enforceable. ■ **EXAMPLE 16.9** Before marrying country singer Keith Urban, actress Nicole Kidman entered into a prenuptial agreement with him. Kidman agreed that

if the couple divorced, she would pay Urban $640,000 for every year they had been married, unless Urban had started to use drugs again. In that event, he would receive nothing. ■

16–2e Contracts for the Sale of Goods

The Uniform Commercial Code (UCC) includes Statute of Frauds provisions that require written evidence or an electronic record of a contract for the sale of goods priced at $500 or more. (This low threshold amount may be increased in the future.)

A writing that will satisfy the UCC requirement need only state the quantity term (6,000 boxes of cotton gauze, for instance). The contract will not be enforceable for any quantity greater than that set forth in the writing.

Other agreed-on terms can be omitted or stated imprecisely in the writing, as long as they adequately reflect both parties' intentions. A written memorandum or series of communications evidencing a contract will suffice, provided that the writing is signed by the party against whom enforcement is sought. The writing normally need not designate the buyer or the seller, the terms of payment, or the price.

16–3 Exceptions to the Writing Requirement

Exceptions to the writing requirement are made in certain circumstances. We describe those situations here.

16–3a Partial Performance

When a contract has been partially performed and the parties cannot be returned to their positions prior to the contract's formation, a court may grant *specific performance*. Specific performance is an equitable remedy that requires performance of the contract according to its precise terms. Courts may sometimes grant specific performance of an oral contract. The parties must prove that an oral contract existed, of course.

In cases involving oral contracts for the transfer of interests in land, courts usually look at whether justice is better served by enforcing the oral contract when partial performance has taken place. For instance, if the purchaser has paid part of the price, taken possession, and made valuable improvements to the property, a court may grant specific performance.

In some states, mere reliance on certain types of oral contracts is enough to remove them from the Statute of Frauds.[4] Under the UCC, an oral contract for the sale of goods is enforceable to the extent that a seller accepts payment or a buyer accepts delivery of the goods.[5] ■ **EXAMPLE 16.10** Cooper orders twenty chairs from an online seller. After ten chairs have been delivered and accepted, Cooper repudiates (denies the existence of) the contract. In that situation, the seller can enforce the contract (and obtain payment) to the extent of the ten chairs already accepted by Cooper. ■

Partial performance is an unmistakable indication that one party believes there is a contract. In the following case, the court considered whether, by accepting partial performance, the other party indicated that it also understood that a contract was in effect.

---

4. *Restatement (Second) of Contracts*, Section 129.
5. UCC 2–201(3)(c).

Case 16.2

NYKCool A.B.[a] v. Pacific Fruit, Inc.
United States Court of Appeals, Second Circuit, 507 Fed.Appx. 83 (2013).

Company Profile *NYKCool A.B., based in Stockholm, Sweden, provides maritime transportation for hire. It is a subsidiary of NYKReefers Limited, which operates as a subsidiary of Nippon Yusen Kabushiki Kaisha, one of the world's largest shipping companies. NYKCool has a fleet of more than fifty ships and has offices in Argentina, Brazil, Chile, Ecuador, Japan, New Zealand, South Africa, the United Kingdom, and the United States. NYKCool focuses on transporting perishables, especially fruit. To reduce the number of empty containers, the firm disperses its large fleet around the globe in cost-efficient patterns and carries other cargoes on its vessels' return trips.*

Background and Facts Pacific Fruit, Inc., exports cargo from Ecuador. NYKCool and Pacific entered into a written contract with a two-year duration, under which NYKCool agreed to transport weekly shipments of bananas from Ecuador to California and Japan. At the end of the period, the parties agreed to extend the deal. Due to a disagreement over one of the terms, a new contract was never signed, but the parties' trade continued.

After nearly four more years of performance between 2005 and 2008, a dispute arose over unused cargo capacity and unpaid freight charges. An arbitration panel of the Society of Maritime Arbitrators found that Pacific Fruit was liable to NYKCool for $8,787,157 for breach of contract. NYKCool filed a petition in a federal district court to confirm the award. Pacific Fruit appealed the judgment in NYKCool's favor, contending that the arbitration panel "manifestly disregarded" the law when it concluded that the parties had an enforceable contract.

In the Language of the Court
Robert A. *KATZMANN*, Barrington D. *PARKER* and Richard C. *WESLEY*, Circuit Judges.
    * * * *

On appeal, Pacific Fruit first contends that the arbitration panel manifestly disregarded the New York contract law by concluding that Pacific Fruit * * * entered into an oral contract with NYKCool, under which NYKCool agreed to transport weekly shipments of [Pacific Fruit's] bananas from Ecuador

---

a. The initials *A.B.* stand for *Aktiebolag*, which is the Swedish term for "limited company."

Case 16.2 Continued

to California and Japan for the period between 2005 and 2008. In order to vacate an arbitration award for manifest disregard of the law, a court must conclude that the arbitrator knew of the relevant legal principle, appreciated that this principle controlled the outcome of the disputed issue, and nonetheless willfully flouted the governing law by refusing to apply it. This rigorous standard ensures that awards are vacated on grounds of manifest disregard only in those exceedingly rare instances where some egregious [shocking] impropriety on the part of the arbitrator is apparent. As such, the standard essentially bars review of whether an arbitrator misconstrued a contract.

Here, we detect no manifest disregard of the law in the arbitration panel's conclusion that the parties had entered into a binding oral contract for the period between 2005 and 2008. In particular, we agree with the panel's conclusion that *the parties' substantial partial performance on the contract weighs strongly in favor of contract formation.* It is undisputed that in 2005 and 2006 NYKCool transported 30 million boxes of cargo for [Pacific Fruit] on over 100 voyages, for which it received $70 million dollars in payments even though there was no written contract in place. Moreover, *the parties' behavior during 2005 and 2006 strongly suggests that they believed themselves subject to a binding agreement.* Notably, the parties engaged in extensive renegotiation of the terms of the contract when [Pacific Fruit] began facing difficulties meeting its cargo commitments. In these circumstances, the panel cannot be said to have engaged in egregious impropriety in concluding that the parties intended to enter a binding oral agreement. [Emphasis added.]

* * * *

For the foregoing reasons, the Order of the district court confirming the arbitration award is hereby AFFIRMED.

Decision and Remedy *The U.S. Court of Appeals for the Second Circuit affirmed the judgment of the lower court. The appellate court reasoned that "the parties' substantial partial performance on the contract weighs strongly in favor of contract formation."*

Critical Thinking
- **Legal Environment** *What circumstance in this case demonstrates most strongly that Pacific did not truly believe that it did not have a contract with NYKCool? Explain.*
- **Economic** *How can a carrier avoid losses under a contract that obligates it only to transport cargo one way and not on the return voyage?*

16–3b Admissions

If a party against whom enforcement of an oral contract is sought "admits" under oath that a contract for sale was made, the contract will be enforceable.[6] The party's admission can occur at any stage of the court proceedings, such as during a deposition or other discovery, pleadings, or testimony.

If a party admits a contract subject to the UCC, the contract is enforceable, but only to the extent of the quantity admitted.[7] ■ **EXAMPLE 16.11** Rachel, the president of Bistro Corporation, admits under oath that an oral agreement was made with Commercial Kitchens, Inc., to buy certain equipment for $10,000. A court will enforce the agreement only to the extent admitted ($10,000),

even if Commercial Kitchens claims that the agreement involved $20,000 worth of equipment. ■

16–3c Promissory Estoppel

An oral contract that would otherwise be unenforceable under the Statute of Frauds may be enforced in some states under the doctrine of promissory estoppel. Recall that if a person justifiably relies on another's promise to his or her detriment, a court may *estop* (prevent) the promisor from denying that a contract exists. Section 139 of the *Restatement (Second) of Contracts* provides that in these circumstances, an oral promise can be enforceable notwithstanding the Statute of Frauds.

For the promise to be enforceable, the promisee must have justifiably relied on it to her or his detriment, and the reliance must have been foreseeable to the person making the promise. In addition, there must be no way

---

6. *Restatement (Second) of Contracts*, Section 133.
7. UCC 2–201(3)(b).

to avoid injustice except to enforce the promise. (Note the similarities between promissory estoppel and the doctrine of partial performance discussed previously. Both require reasonable reliance and operate to estop a party from claiming that no contract exists.)

16–3d Special Exceptions under the UCC

Special exceptions to the writing requirement apply to sales contracts. Oral contracts for customized goods may be enforced in certain circumstances. Another exception has to do with oral contracts *between merchants* that have been confirmed in a written memorandum. We will examine these exceptions in more detail when we discuss the UCC's Statute of Frauds provisions in a later chapter.

Exhibit 16–3 graphically summarizes the types of contracts that fall under the Statute of Frauds and the various exceptions that apply.

16–4 Sufficiency of the Writing

A written contract will satisfy the writing requirement, as will a written memorandum or an electronic record that evidences the agreement and is signed by the party against whom enforcement is sought. The signature need not be placed at the end of the document but can be anywhere in the writing. A signature can consist of a typed name or even just initials.

16–4a What Constitutes a Writing?

A writing can consist of any order confirmation, invoice, sales slip, check, fax, or e-mail—or such items in combination. The written contract need not consist of a single document in order to constitute an enforceable contract. One document may incorporate another document by expressly referring to it. Several documents may form a single contract if they are physically attached, such as by staple, paper clip, or glue. Several documents may form a single contract even if they are only placed in the same envelope.

■ **EXAMPLE 16.12** Simpson orally agrees to sell some land next to a shopping mall to Terro Properties. Simpson gives Terro an unsigned memo that contains a legal description of the property, and Terro gives Simpson an unsigned first draft of their real estate contract. Simpson sends Terro a signed letter that refers to the memo and to the first and final drafts of the contract. Terro sends Simpson an unsigned copy of the final draft of the contract with a signed check stapled to it. Together, the documents can constitute a writing sufficient to satisfy the writing requirement and bind both parties to the terms of the contract. ■

EXHIBIT 16–3 Business Contracts and the Writing Requirement

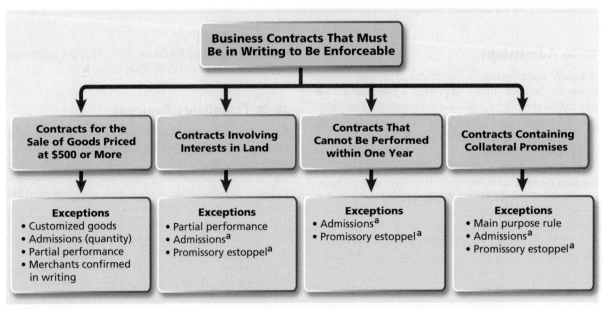

a. Some states follow Section 133 (on admissions) and Section 139 (on promissory estoppel) of the *Restatement (Second) of Contracts.*

16–4b What Must Be Contained in the Writing?

A memorandum or note evidencing an oral contract need only contain the essential terms of the contract, not every term. There must, of course, also be some indication that the parties voluntarily agreed to the terms. As mentioned, under the UCC, a writing evidencing a contract for the sale of goods need only state the quantity and be signed by the party against whom enforcement is sought.

Under most state laws, the writing must also name the parties and identify the subject matter, the consideration, and the essential terms with reasonable certainty. In addition, contracts for the sale of land often are required to state the price and describe the property with sufficient clarity to allow them to be determined without reference to outside sources.

Note that because only the party against whom enforcement is sought must have signed the writing, a contract may be enforceable by one of its parties but not by the other. For instance, if a person borrows funds to purchase a home but does not sign a loan contract, the lender cannot enforce the contract but the borrower probably can.[8]

16–5 The Parol Evidence Rule

Sometimes, a written contract does not include—or contradicts—an oral understanding reached by the parties before or at the time of contracting. For instance, a landlord might tell a person who agrees to rent an apartment that cats are allowed, whereas the lease contract clearly states that no pets are permitted. In deciding such disputes, the courts look to a common law rule called the *parol evidence rule*

Under the **parol evidence rule,** if a court finds that a written contract represents the complete and final statement of the parties' agreement, it will not allow either party to present parol evidence. *Parol evidence* is testimony or other evidence of communications between the parties that is not contained in the contract itself. A party normally *cannot* present any evidence of the following if that evidence contradicts or varies the terms of the written contract:

1. Negotiations prior to contract formation.
2. Agreements prior to contract formation.

3. Oral agreements contemporaneous with (at the same time as) contract formation.[9]

16–5a Exceptions to the Parol Evidence Rule

Because of the rigidity of the parol evidence rule, the courts have created the following exceptions:

1. *Contracts subsequently modified.* Evidence of any subsequent modification (oral or written) of a written contract can be introduced in court. Oral modifications may not be enforceable under the Statute of Frauds, however (for instance, a modification that increases the price of the goods being sold to more than $500). Also, oral modifications will not be enforceable if the original contract provides that any modification must be in writing.[10]
2. *Voidable or void contracts.* Oral evidence can be introduced in all cases to show that the contract was voidable or void (for example, induced by mistake, fraud, or misrepresentation). The reason is simple: if deception led one of the parties to agree to the terms of a written contract, oral evidence attesting to the fraud should not be excluded. Courts frown on bad faith and are quick to allow such evidence when it establishes fraud.
3. *Contracts containing ambiguous terms.* When the terms of a written contract are ambiguous and require interpretation, evidence is admissible to show the meaning of the terms. ■ **CASE IN POINT 16.13** Pamela Watkins bought a home from Sandra Schexnider. Their agreement stated that Watkins would make payments on the mortgage until the note was paid in full, when "the house" would become hers. The agreement also stipulated that she would pay for insurance on "the property." The home was destroyed in a hurricane, and the insurance proceeds paid off the mortgage. Watkins claimed that she owned the land, but Schexnider argued that she had sold only the house. The court found that because "the house" term in the contract was ambiguous, parol evidence was admissible. The court also concluded that the parties had intended to transfer ownership of both the house and the land, and ordered that title to the property be transferred to Watkins.[11] ■
4. *Incomplete contracts.* When the written contract is incomplete in that it lacks one or more of the essential terms, the courts allow additional evidence to "fill in the gaps."

---

8. See, for example, *Beneficial Homeowner Service Corp. v. Steele,* 30 Misc.3d 1208(A), 958 N.Y.S.2d 644 (2011).

9. *Restatement (Second) of Contracts,* Section 213.
10. UCC 2–209(2), (3).
11. *Watkins v. Schexnider,* 31 So.3d 609 (La.App. 3 Cir. 2010).

5. *Prior dealing, course of performance, or usage of trade.* Under the UCC, evidence can be introduced to explain or supplement a written contract by showing a prior dealing, course of performance, or usage of trade.[12] This is because when buyers and sellers deal with each other over extended periods of time, certain customary practices develop. These practices are often overlooked in writing the contract, so courts allow the introduction of evidence to show how the parties have acted in the past. Usage of trade—practices and customs generally followed in a particular industry—can also shed light on the meaning of certain contract provisions. Thus, evidence of trade usage may be admissible. We will discuss these terms in further detail later in the context of sales contracts.

6. *Contracts subject to an orally agreed-on condition precedent.* Sometimes the parties agree that a condition must be fulfilled before a party is required to perform the contract. This is called a *condition precedent.* If the parties have orally agreed on a condition precedent that does not conflict with the terms of their written agreement, a court may allow parol evidence to prove the oral condition. The parol evidence rule does not apply here because the existence of the entire written contract is subject to an orally agreed-on condition. Proof of the condition does not alter or modify the written terms but affects the *enforceability* of the written contract.

7. *Contracts with an obvious or gross clerical (or typographic) error that clearly would not represent the agreement of the parties.* Parol evidence is admissible to correct an obvious typographic error. ■ **EXAMPLE 16.14** Davis agrees to lease office space from Stone Enterprises for $3,000 per month. The signed written lease provides for a monthly payment of $300 rather than the $3,000 agreed to by the parties. Because the error is obvious, Stone Enterprises will be allowed to admit parol evidence to correct the mistake. ■

In the following case, an appellate court considered whether the trial court should have admitted parol evidence regarding the terms of an apartment lease.

---

12. UCC 1–205, 2–202.

Frewil, LLC v. Price

Court of Appeals of South Carolina, 411 S.C. 525, 769 S.E.2d 250 (2015).

Background and Facts Madison Price and Carter Smith were planning to attend the College of Charleston in South Carolina. They contacted Frewil, LLC, about renting an apartment at the beginning of the fall semester. They asked if the apartment had a washer/dryer and dishwasher, and were told yes. The lease did not expressly state that the unit contained those appliances, but it provided that any overflow from a washing machine or dishwasher was the responsibility of the tenant and that the dishwasher had to be clean for a refund of the security deposit.

When Price and Smith arrived to move in, the apartment had no washer/dryer or dishwasher and no connections for them. The students found housing elsewhere. Frewil filed a suit in a South Carolina state court against Price and Smith, claiming breach of contract. The defendants sought to introduce parol evidence to challenge Frewil's claim. The court denied the request and issued a judgment in Frewil's favor. Price and Smith appealed.

In the Language of the Court

KONDUROS, J. [Judge]

 * * * *

 * * * If a writing, on its face, appears to express the whole agreement between the parties, parol evidence cannot be admitted to add another term thereto. However, *where a contract is silent as to a particular matter, and ambiguity thereby arises, parol evidence may be admitted to supply the deficiency and establish the true intent. For, generally, parol evidence is admissible to show the true meaning of an ambiguous written contract.* Such a contract is one capable of being understood in more ways than just one, or an agreement unclear in meaning because it expresses its purpose in an indefinite manner. When an agreement is ambiguous, the court may consider the circumstances surrounding its execution in determining the intent. Where the contract is susceptible of more than one interpretation, the ambiguity will be resolved against the party who prepared the contract. It would be virtually impossible for a contract to encompass all of the many possibilities which may be encountered by the parties. Indeed, neither law, nor equity,

Case 16.3 Continued

requires every term or condition to be set forth in a contract. If a situation is unaddressed in a contract, the court may look to the circumstances surrounding the bargain as an aid in determining the parties' intent. [Emphasis added.]

In this case, the [lower] court relied upon * * * the lease itself to conclude the girls had breached the lease as a matter of law. However, if a contract is subject to more than one interpretation, it is ambiguous and parol evidence is admissible. Frewil contends, and the [lower] court found, the lease unambiguously states the unit does not contain a washer/dryer or dishwasher. However, the lease states any overflow from washing machines or dishwashers is the responsibility of the tenant. Additionally, the Security Deposit Agreement * * * indicates the dishwasher must be clean in order for the tenant to receive a return of the security deposit. The lease does not explicitly indicate what appliances are or are not in the unit. Because the lease is ambiguous on this point, parol evidence was admissible. As these appliances are mentioned and Price and Smith allege they were told the washer/dryer and dishwasher were included, the [lower] court erred in concluding the lease * * * precluded any challenge to Frewil's breach of contract claim as a matter of law.

Decision and Remedy *A state intermediate appellate court reversed the judgment of the lower court. The court noted that, "the lease was ambiguous thereby permitting the introduction of parol evidence."*

Critical Thinking
- **Economic** *How does the parol evidence rule save time and money for the parties to a dispute and the court that hears it? Discuss.*

16–5b Integrated Contracts

In determining whether to allow parol evidence, courts consider whether the written contract is intended to be the complete and final statement of the terms of the agreement. If it is, the contract is referred to as an **integrated contract,** and extraneous evidence (evidence from outside the contract) is excluded.

■ **EXAMPLE 16.15** TKTS, Inc., offers to sell Gwen season tickets to the Dallas Cowboys football games in Cowboys Stadium. Prices and seat locations are indicated in diagrams in a brochure that accompanies the offer. Gwen responds, listing her seat preference. TKTS sends her the tickets, along with a different diagram showing seat locations. Also enclosed is a document that reads, "This is the entire agreement of the parties," which Gwen signs and returns. When Gwen goes to the first game, she discovers that her seat is not where she expected, based on the brochure. Under the parol evidence rule, however, the brochure is not part of the parties' agreement. The document that Gwen signed was identified as the parties' entire contract. Therefore, she cannot introduce in court any evidence of prior negotiations or agreements that contradict or vary the contract's terms. ■

A contract can be either completely or partially integrated. If it contains all of the terms of the parties' agreement, it is completely integrated. If it contains only some of the terms that the parties agreed on and not others, it is

partially integrated. If the contract is only partially integrated, evidence of consistent additional terms is admissible to supplement the written agreement.[13] Note that for both completely and partially integrated contracts, courts exclude any evidence that *contradicts* the writing. Parol evidence is allowed only to add to the terms of a partially integrated contract. Exhibit 16–4 illustrates the relationship between integrated contracts and the parol evidence rule.

16–6 The Statute of Frauds in the International Context

The Convention on Contracts for the International Sale of Goods (CISG) governs international sales contracts between citizens of countries that have ratified the convention (agreement). Article 11 of the CISG does not incorporate any Statute of Frauds provisions. Rather, it states that a "contract for sale need not be concluded in or evidenced by writing and is not subject to any other requirements as to form."

Article 11 accords with the legal customs of most nations, which no longer require contracts to meet certain

---

13. *Restatement (Second) of Contracts,* Section 216; and UCC 2–202.

EXHIBIT 16–4 The Parol Evidence Rule

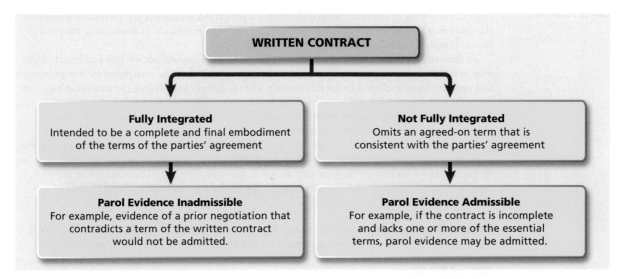

formal or writing requirements to be enforceable. Even England, the nation that created the original Statute of Frauds in 1677, has repealed all of it except the provisions relating to collateral promises and to transfers of interests in land. Many other countries that once had such statutes have also repealed all or parts of them. Some civil law countries, such as France, have never required certain types of contracts to be in writing.

Reviewing: The Writing Requirement in Our Digital World

Evelyn Vollmer orally agreed to loan Danny Lang $150,000 to make an investment in a local nightclub. The loan was to be repaid from the profits received from the investment. Their agreement was never memorialized in writing, however. Eighteen months later, Lang had paid only $15,000 on the loan from the profits from the business. Vollmer filed a lawsuit alleging breach of contract. Using the information presented in the chapter, answer the following questions.

1. Lang claimed that repayment of the loan would "almost certainly" take over a year and that his agreement with Vollmer was therefore unenforceable because it was not in writing. Is he correct? Explain.
2. Suppose that a week after Vollmer gave Lang the funds, she sent him an e-mail containing the terms of their loan agreement with her named typed at the bottom. Lang did not respond to the e-mail. Is this sufficient as a writing under the Statute of Frauds?
3. Assume that at trial the court finds that the contract falls within the Statute of Frauds. Further assume that the state in which the court sits recognizes every exception to the Statute of Frauds discussed in the chapter. What exception provides Vollmer with the best chance of enforcing the oral contract in this situation?
4. Suppose that at trial, Lang never raises the argument that the parties' agreement violates the Statute of Frauds, and the court rules in favor of Vollmer. Then Lang appeals and raises the Statute of Frauds for the first time. What exception can Vollmer now argue?

Debate This . . . *Many countries have eliminated the Statute of Frauds except for sales of real estate. The United States should do the same.*

Terms and Concepts

collateral promise 298	parol evidence rule 303	Statute of Frauds 295
integrated contract 305	prenuptial agreement 299	

Issue Spotters

1. GamesCo orders $800 worth of game pieces from Midstate Plastic, Inc. Midstate delivers, and GamesCo pays for $450 worth. GamesCo then says it wants no more pieces from Midstate. GamesCo and Midstate have never dealt with each other before and have nothing in writing. Can Midstate enforce a deal for the full $800? Explain your answer. (See *Contracts That Require a Writing.*)

2. Paula orally agrees to work with Next Corporation in New York City for two years. Paula moves her family and begins work. Three months later, Paula is fired for no stated cause. She sues for reinstatement and back pay. Next Corporation argues that there is no written contract between them. What will the court say? (See *Exceptions to the Writing Requirement.*)

- **Check your answers to the Issue Spotters against the answers provided in Appendix D at the end of this text.**

Business Scenarios

16–1. The One-Year Rule. On May 1, by telephone, Yu offers to hire Benson to perform personal services. On May 5, Benson returns Yu's call and accepts the offer. Discuss fully whether this contract falls under the Statute of Frauds in the following circumstances: (See *Contracts That Require a Writing.*)

(a) The contract calls for Benson to be employed for one year, with the right to begin performance immediately.

(b) The contract calls for Benson to be employed for nine months, with performance of services to begin on September 1.

(c) The contract calls for Benson to submit a written research report, with a deadline of two years for submission.

16–2. Collateral Promises. Mallory promises a local hardware store that she will pay for a lawn mower that her brother is purchasing on credit if the brother fails to pay the debt. Must this promise be in writing to be enforceable? Why or why not? (See *Contracts That Require a Writing.*)

Business Case Problems

16–3. The Parol Evidence Rule. Evangel Temple Assembly of God leased a facility from Wood Care Centers, Inc., to house evacuees who had lost their homes in Hurricane Katrina. One clause in the lease contract said that Evangel could terminate the lease at any time by giving Wood Care notice and paying 10 percent of the balance remaining on the lease. Another clause stated that if the facility was not given a property tax exemption (as a church), Evangel had the option to terminate the lease without making the 10 percent payment. Nine months later, the last of the evacuees left the facility, and Evangel notified Wood Care that it would end the lease. Wood Care demanded the 10 percent payment. Is parol evidence admissible to interpret this lease? Why or why not? [*Wood Care Centers, Inc. v. Evangel Temple Assembly of God of Wichita Falls,* 307 S.W.3d 816 (Tex.App.—Fort Worth 2010)] (See *The Parol Evidence Rule.*)

16–4. Sufficiency of the Writing. Newmark & Co. Real Estate, Inc., contacted 2615 East 17 Street Realty, LLC, to lease certain real property on behalf of a client. Newmark e-mailed the landlord a separate agreement for the payment of Newmark's commission. The landlord e-mailed it back with a separate demand to pay the commission in installments. Newmark revised the agreement and e-mailed a final copy to the landlord. Does the agreement qualify as a writing under the Statute of Frauds? Explain. [*Newmark & Co. Real Estate, Inc. v. 2615 East 17 Street Realty, LLC,* 80 A.D.3d 476, 914 N.Y.S.2d 162 (1 Dept. 2011)] (See *Sufficiency of the Writing.*)

16–5. Business Case Problem with Sample Answer— The Parol Evidence Rule. Rimma Vaks and her husband, Steven Mangano, executed a written contract with Denise Ryan and Ryan Auction Co. to auction their furnishings. The six-page contract provided a detailed summary of the parties' agreement. It addressed the items to be auctioned, how reserve prices would be determined, and the amount of Ryan's commission. When a dispute arose between the parties, Vaks and Mangano sued Ryan for breach of contract. Vaks and Mangano asserted that, before they executed the contract, Ryan made various oral representations that were inconsistent with the terms of their written agreement. Assuming that their written contract was valid, can Vaks and Mangano recover for breach of an oral contract? Why or why not? [*Vaks v. Ryan*, 2012 WL 194398 (Mass.App. 2012)] (See *The Parol Evidence Rule*.)

- For a sample answer to Problem 16–5, see Appendix E at the end of this text.

16–6. Promises Made in Consideration of Marriage.

After twenty-nine years of marriage, Robert and Mary Lou Tuttle were divorced. They admitted in court that before they were married, they had signed a prenuptial agreement. They agreed that the agreement had stated that each would keep his or her own property and anything derived from that property. Robert came into the marriage owning farmland, while Mary Lou owned no real estate. During the marriage, ten different parcels of land, totaling about six hundred acres, were acquired, and two corporations, Tuttle Grain, Inc., and Tuttle Farms, Inc., were formed. A copy of the prenuptial agreement could not be found. Can the court enforce the agreement without a writing? Why or why not? [*In re Marriage of Tuttle*, 2013 WL 164035 (Ill.App. 5 Dist. 2013)] (See *Contracts That Require a Writing*.)

16–7. Promises Made in Consideration of Marriage.

Before their marriage, Linda and Gerald Heiden executed a prenuptial agreement. The agreement provided that "no spouse shall have any right in the property of the other spouse, even in the event of the death of either party." The description of Gerald's separate property included a settlement from a personal injury suit. Twenty-four years later, Linda filed for divorce. The court ruled that the prenuptial agreement applied only in the event of death, not divorce, and entered a judgment that included a property division and spousal

support award. The ruling disparately favored Linda, whose monthly income with spousal support would be $4,467, leaving Gerald with only $1,116. Did the court interpret the Heidens' prenuptial agreement correctly? Discuss. [*Heiden v. Heiden*, 2015 WL 849006 (Mich.App. 2015)] (See *Contracts That Require a Writing*.)

16–8. A Question of Ethics—Exceptions to the Writing Requirement.

 Madeline Castellotti was the sole shareholder of Whole Pies, Inc., which owns John's Pizzeria in New York City. Her other assets included a 51 percent interest in a real estate partnership, a residence on Staten Island, and various bank accounts. When Madeline's son, Peter Castellotti, was going through a divorce, Madeline wanted to prevent Peter's then-wife Rea from benefiting from any of Madeline's assets. With this purpose in mind, she removed Peter from her will, leaving her daughter Lisa Free as the sole beneficiary. Lisa orally agreed to provide Peter with half of the income generated by the assets after their mother's death if his divorce was still pending and to transfer half of the assets after the divorce was final. In reliance on those promises, Peter agreed to pay the property taxes for the estate. Madeline died and Peter paid the taxes, but Lisa reneged on the deal. Peter filed a suit in a New York state court against his sister to recover. [Castellotti v. Free, 138 A.D.3d 198, 27 N.Y.S.3d 507 (1 Dept. 2016)] (See Exceptions to the Writing Requirement.)

(a) Should the court enforce the promise? On what legal theory?

(b) If the court enforces the promise, should Rea get a share of what Peter and his mother and sister were "hiding"? Discuss.

Legal Reasoning Group Activity

16–9. The Writing Requirement.

Jason Novell, doing business as Novell Associates, hired Barbara Meade to work for him. The parties orally agreed on the terms of employment, including payment of a share of the company's income to Meade, but they did not put anything in writing. Two years later, Meade quit. Novell then told Meade that she was entitled to $9,602—25 percent of the difference between the accounts receivable and the accounts payable as of Meade's last day of work. Meade disagreed and demanded more than $63,500—25 percent of the revenue from all invoices, less the cost of materials and outside processing, for each of the years that she had worked for Novell. Meade filed a lawsuit against Novell for breach of contract. (See *The Statute of Frauds*.)

(a) The first group should decide whether the parties had an enforceable contract.

(b) The second group should decide whether the parties' oral agreement falls within any exception to the Statute of Frauds.

(c) The third group should discuss how the lawsuit would be affected if Novell admitted that the parties had an oral contract under which Meade was entitled to 25 percent of the difference between accounts receivable and accounts payable as of the day Meade quit.

Third Party Rights

Once it has been determined that a valid and legally enforceable contract exists, attention can turn to the rights and duties of the parties to the contract. A contract is a private agreement between the parties who have entered into it, and traditionally these parties alone have rights and liabilities under the contract. This principle is referred to as **privity of contract.** A *third party*—one who is not a direct party to a particular contract—normally does not have rights under that contract.

There are exceptions to the rule of privity of contract. For instance, privity of contract is not required to recover damages under product liability laws. Hence, a person injured by a defective product can still recover damages even though she or he was not the buyer of the product. In this chapter, we look at two other exceptions. One exception allows a party to a contract to transfer the rights or duties arising from the contract to another person through an *assignment* (of rights) or a *delegation* (of duties). The other exception involves a *third party beneficiary contract*—a contract in which the parties to the contract intend that the contract benefit a third party.

17–1 Assignments and Delegations

In a bilateral contract, the two parties have corresponding rights and duties. One party has a *right* to require the other to perform some task, and the other has a *duty* to perform it. The transfer of contractual *rights* to a third party is known as an **assignment.** The transfer of contractual *duties* to a third party is known as a **delegation.** An assignment or a delegation occurs *after* the original contract was made.

17–1a Assignments

Assignments are important because they are used in many types of business financing. Lending institutions, such as banks, frequently assign their rights to receive payments under their loan contracts to other firms, which pay for those rights. ■ **EXAMPLE 17.1** Tia obtains a loan from a bank to finance an online business venture. She may later receive a notice from the bank stating that it has transferred (assigned) its rights to receive payments on the loan to another firm. When it is time to repay the loan, Tia must make the payments to that other firm. ■

Financial institutions that make *mortgage* loans (loans to enable prospective home buyers to purchase land or a home) often assign their rights to collect the mortgage payments to a third party, such as PNC Mortgage.

Following the assignment, the home buyers are notified that they must make future payments not to the bank that loaned them the funds but to the third party.

Billions of dollars change hands daily in the business world in the form of assignments of rights in contracts. If it were not possible to transfer contractual rights, many businesses could not continue to operate.

The Effect of an Assignment In an assignment, the party assigning the rights to a third party is known as the **assignor,**[1] and the party receiving the rights is the **assignee.**[2] Other traditional terms used to describe the parties in assignment relationships are **obligee** (the person to whom a duty, or obligation, is owed) and **obligor** (the person who is obligated to perform the duty).

Extinguishes the Rights of the Assignor. When rights under a contract are assigned unconditionally, the rights of the assignor are extinguished.[3] The third party (the assignee) has a right to demand performance from the other original party to the contract. The assignee takes only those rights that the assignor originally had, however. ■ **EXAMPLE 17.2** Brower is obligated by contract to pay Horton $1,000. Brower is the obligor because she

---

1. Pronounced uh-*sye*-nore.
2. Pronounced uh-*sye*-nee.
3. *Restatement (Second) of Contracts,* Section 317.

EXHIBIT 17–1   Assignment Relationships

In the assignment relationship illustrated here, Horton assigns his *rights* under a contract that he made with Brower to a third party, Kuhn. Horton thus becomes the *assignor* and Kuhn the *assignee* of the contractual rights. Brower, the *obligor,* now owes performance to Kuhn instead of Horton. Horton's original contractual rights are extinguished after assignment.

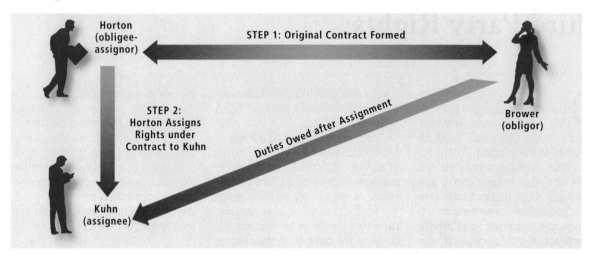

Horton
(obligee-
assignor)

STEP 1: Original Contract Formed

STEP 2:
Horton Assigns
Rights under
Contract to Kuhn

Duties Owed after Assignment

Brower
(obligor)

Kuhn
(assignee)

owes an obligation, or duty, to Horton. Horton is the obligee, the one to whom the obligation is owed. If Horton then assigns his right to receive the $1,000 to Kuhn, Horton is the assignor and Kuhn is the assignee. Kuhn now becomes the obligee because Brower owes Kuhn the $1,000. Here, a valid assignment of a debt exists. Kuhn (the assignee-obligee) is entitled to enforce payment

in court if Brower (the obligor) does not pay him the $1,000. (Horton is no longer entitled to enforce payment because the assignment extinguished his original contract rights.) ■ These concepts are illustrated in Exhibit 17–1.

In the following case, a lender assigned its rights to loan payments from a borrower. The court had to decide whether the borrower owed the payments to the assignee.

Case 17.1

Hosch v. Colonial Pacific Leasing Corp.

Court of Appeals of Georgia, 313 Ga.App. 873, 722 S.E.2d 778 (2012).

Background and Facts   Edward Hosch entered into four loan agreements with Citicapital Commercial Corporation to finance the purchase of heavy construction equipment. A few months later, Citicapital merged into Citicorp Leasing, Inc., which was then renamed GE Capital Commercial, Inc. One year later, GE Capital assigned the loans to Colonial Pacific Leasing Corporation. When Hosch defaulted on the loans, Colonial provided a notice of default and demanded payment. Hosch failed to repay the loans, so Colonial sued to collect the amount due. The trial court granted summary judgment to Colonial and entered final judgment against Hosch. On appeal, Hosch argued that there was insufficient evidence that the loans had been assigned to Colonial.

In the Language of the Court

McFADDEN, Judge.

* * * *

Hosch contends that the trial court erred in granting Colonial's motion for summary judgment because there is no evidence that the contracts were assigned to Colonial. However, the contention is refuted by the record, which includes affidavits of a GE litigation specialist, a written assignment and other documents establishing that Hosch's four loans were assigned to Colonial. Hosch has presented no contradictory evidence showing that the loans were not assigned to Colonial, and instead submitted his own affidavit stating that he had not been notified of any such assignment. However, the loan

Case 17.1 Continued

agreements expressly provide that the lender may transfer or assign any or all of its rights under the agreements without notice to or the consent of Hosch.

"A party may assign to another a contractual right to collect payment, including the right to sue to enforce the right. But an assignment must be in writing in order for the contractual right to be enforceable by the assignee." Because the record, as noted above, contains a written assignment of the loans to Colonial, as well as other evidence of the assignment, the trial court did not err in granting summary judgment to Colonial. [Emphasis added.]

Decision and Remedy *The Georgia appellate court found sufficient evidence that GE Capital had assigned the loans to Colonial. It therefore affirmed the trial court's judgment for Colonial.*

Critical Thinking

- **Legal Environment** *Do borrowers benefit from the fact that lenders may freely assign their rights under loan agreements? If so, how?*
- **What If the Facts Were Different?** *Suppose that Hosch had sold the equipment financed by the loans from Citicapital to a third party. Would Hosch still have been liable to Colonial Pacific? Why or why not?*

Assignee's Rights Are Subject to the Same Defenses. The assignee's rights are subject to the defenses that the obligor has against the assignor. In other words, the assignee obtains only those rights that the assignor originally had.

■ **EXAMPLE 17.3** Returning to *Example 17.2*, suppose Brower owes Horton the $1,000 under a contract in which Brower agreed to buy Horton's Surface Pro 4. When Brower decided to purchase the tablet, she relied on Horton's fraudulent misrepresentation that it had an Intel Core i7 processor. When Brower discovers that its processor is an Intel i3, she tells Horton that she is going to return the device to him and cancel the contract. Even though Horton has assigned his "right" to receive the $1,000 to Kuhn, Brower need not pay Kuhn the $1,000. Brower can raise the defense of Horton's fraudulent misrepresentation to avoid payment. ■

Form of the Assignment. In general, an assignment can take any form, oral or written. Naturally, it is more difficult to prove that an oral assignment occurred, so it is advisable to put all assignments in writing. Of course, assignments covered by the Statute of Frauds—such as an assignment of an interest in land—must be in writing to be enforceable. In addition, most states require contracts for the assignment of wages to be in writing.[4] There are other assignments that must be in writing as well.

Rights That Cannot Be Assigned As a general rule, all rights can be assigned. Exceptions are made, however, under certain circumstances. Some of these exceptions are listed here and described in more detail in the following subsections:

1. The assignment is prohibited by statute.
2. The contract is personal.
3. The assignment significantly changes the risk or duties of the obligor.
4. The contract prohibits assignment.

When a Statute Prohibits Assignment. When a statute expressly prohibits assignment of a particular right, that right cannot be assigned. ■ **EXAMPLE 17.4** Quincy is an employee of Specialty Travel, Inc. Specialty is an employer bound by workers' compensation statutes in its state, and thus Quincy is a covered employee. Quincy is injured on the job and begins to collect monthly workers' compensation checks. In need of a loan, Quincy borrows from Draper, assigning to Draper all of her future workers' compensation benefits. A state statute prohibits the assignment of *future* workers' compensation benefits, and thus such rights cannot be assigned. ■

When a Contract Is Personal in Nature. If a contract is for personal services, the rights under the contract normally cannot be assigned unless all that remains is a monetary payment.[5] ■ **EXAMPLE 17.5** Anton signs a contract to be a tutor for Marisa's children. Marisa then attempts to assign to Roberto (who also has children) her right to Anton's services. Roberto cannot enforce the contract against Anton. Roberto's children may be more difficult to tutor than Marisa's. Thus, if Marisa could assign her rights to Anton's services to Roberto, it would change the nature of Anton's obligation. Because personal services are unique to the person rendering them, rights to receive personal services are likewise unique and cannot be assigned. ■

---

4. See, for example, California Labor Code Section 300.

5. *Restatement (Second) of Contracts*, Sections 317 and 318.

Note that when legal actions involve personal rights, they are considered personal in nature and cannot be assigned. For instance, personal-injury tort claims generally are nonassignable as a matter of public policy. Thus, if Elizabeth is injured by Randy's defamation, she cannot assign to someone else her right to sue Randy for damages.

When an Assignment Will Significantly Change the Risk or Duties of the Obligor.

A right cannot be assigned if the assignment will significantly increase or alter the risks to or the duties of the obligor.[6] ■ **EXAMPLE 17.6** Larson owns a hotel. To insure it, he takes out a policy with Southeast Insurance. The policy insures against fire, theft, floods, and vandalism. Larson attempts to assign the insurance policy to Hewitt, who also owns a hotel.

The assignment is ineffective because it substantially alters Southeast Insurance's *duty of performance*. An insurance company evaluates the particular risk of a certain party and tailors its policy to fit that risk. If the policy is assigned to a third party, the insurance risk is materially altered because the insurance company may have no information on the third party. Therefore, the assignment will not operate to give Hewitt any rights against Southeast Insurance. ■

When the Contract Prohibits Assignment.

When a contract specifically stipulates that a right cannot be assigned, then *ordinarily* it cannot be assigned. Note that restraints on the power to assign operate only against the parties themselves. They do not prohibit an assignment by operation of law, such as an assignment pursuant to bankruptcy or death.

Whether such an *antiassignment clause* is effective depends, in part, on how it is phrased. A contract that states that *any* assignment is void effectively prohibits any assignment. ■ **EXAMPLE 17.7** Ramirez agrees to build a house for Carmen. Their contract states "This contract cannot be assigned by Carmen without Ramirez's consent. Any assignment without such consent renders the contract void." This antiassignment clause is effective, and Carmen cannot assign her rights without obtaining Ramirez's consent. ■

The general rule that a contract can prohibit assignment has several exceptions:

1. A contract cannot prevent an assignment of the right to receive funds. This exception exists to encourage the free flow of funds and credit in modern business settings.
2. The assignment of rights in real estate often cannot be prohibited because such a prohibition is contrary to public policy in most states. Prohibitions of this kind are called restraints against **alienation** (transfer of land ownership).
3. The assignment of *negotiable instruments* (such as checks and promissory notes) cannot be prohibited.
4. In a contract for the sale of goods, the right to receive damages for breach of contract or payment of an account owed may be assigned even though the sales contract prohibits such an assignment.[7]

The lease and purchase agreement in the following case contained an antiassignment clause. The court had to decide whether the clause was enforceable.

---

6. Section 2–210(2) of the Uniform Commercial Code (UCC).

7. UCC 2–210(2).

Case 17.2

Bass-Fineberg Leasing, Inc. v. Modern Auto Sales, Inc.

Court of Appeals of Ohio, Ninth District, Medina County, __ N.E.3d __, 2015-Ohio-46 (2015).

Background and Facts Bass-Fineberg Leasing, Inc., leased a tour bus to Modern Auto Sales, Inc., and Michael Cipriani. The lease included an option to buy the bus. The lease prohibited Modern Auto and Cipriani from assigning their rights without Bass-Fineberg's written consent. Later, Cipriani left the bus with Anthony Allie at BVIP Limo Services, Ltd., for repairs. Modern Auto and Cipriani did not pay for the repairs. At the same time, they defaulted on the lease payments to Bass-Fineberg.

While BVIP retained possession of the bus, Allie signed an agreement with Cipriani to buy it and to make an initial $5,000 payment to Bass-Fineberg. Bass-Fineberg filed an action in an Ohio state court against Modern Auto, Cipriani, BVIP, and Allie to regain possession of the bus. The court ordered the bus returned to Bass-Fineberg and the $5,000 payment refunded to Allie. All of the parties appealed.

In the Language of the Court

WHITMORE, Judge.

* * * *

* * * Bass-Fineberg argues that the purported contract between Cipriani and Allie was void because Cipriani could not assign his rights or obligations under the lease without the written consent of

Bass-Fineberg. * * * BVIP responds that if the contract was void, then the parties should be returned to their pre-contract status, including refunding its $5,000 payment. We agree with Bass-Fineberg that there was not a valid contract between Allie and Cipriani, but we agree with BVIP as to the effect of that invalidity, namely that it was entitled to have its $5,000 returned.

Ohio enforces anti-assignment clauses where there is clear contractual language prohibiting an assignment. Violations of a non-assignment provision in a contract render the resulting agreement null and void. [Emphasis added.]

* * * *

The lease between Bass-Fineberg and Modern Auto and Cipriani contained the following provision:

MODERN AUTO AND CIPRIANI ACKNOWLEDGE THAT MODERN AUTO AND CIPRIANI MAY NOT ASSIGN OR IN ANY WAY TRANSFER OR DISPOSE OF ALL OR ANY PART OF MODERN AUTO AND CIPRIANI'S RIGHTS OR OBLIGATIONS UNDER THIS LEASE * * * WITHOUT BASS-FINEBERG'S PRIOR WRITTEN CONSENT.

This clear contractual language prohibited Modern Auto and Cipriani from transferring their rights or obligations under the lease agreement unless Bass-Fineberg consented in writing.

The purported agreement between Cipriani and Allie attempted to transfer Cipriani's right to purchase the bus to Allie and some of Cipriani's payment obligations to Allie. [David] Libman, Bass-Fineberg's lease sales manager, did not sign the agreement between Allie and Cipriani. Nor did the parties introduce evidence of anyone else from Bass-Fineberg providing written consent to the attempted assignment.

As the lease agreement prohibited an assignment without Bass-Fineberg's consent, the agreement between Cipriani and Allie was void. If a contract is void, then an obligation under it never existed. In such circumstances, the one who made a payment is entitled to a refund.

Decision and Remedy *A state intermediate appellate court affirmed the lower court's order. The contract between Cipriani and Allie was void because Cipriani could not assign his rights under the lease without Bass-Fineberg's written consent. Because the contract was void, the parties were to be returned to their pre-contract status, which included a refund of the $5,000 payment.*

Critical Thinking
- **Economic** *The repairs to the bus cost $1,341.50. Who should pay this amount? Why?*

Notice of Assignment Once a valid assignment of rights has been made, the assignee should notify the obligor of the assignment. For instance, in *Example 17.2*, when Horton assigns to Kuhn his right to receive the $1,000 from Brower, Kuhn (the assignee) should notify Brower (the obligor) of the assignment.

Giving notice is not legally necessary to establish the validity of the assignment: an assignment is effective immediately, whether or not notice is given. Two major problems arise, however, when notice of the assignment is not given to the obligor.

Priority Issues. If the assignor assigns the same right to two different persons, the question arises as to which one has priority—that is, which one has the right to the performance by the obligor. The rule most often observed in the United States is that the first assignment in time is the first in right. Nevertheless, some states follow the English rule, which basically gives priority to the first assignee who gives notice.

■ **EXAMPLE 17.8** Jason owes Alexis $5,000 under a contract. Alexis first assigns the claim to Carmen, who does not give notice to Jason. Alexis then assigns it to Dorman, who notifies Jason. In most states, Carmen would have priority because the assignment to her was first in time. In some states, however, Dorman would have priority because he gave first notice. ■

Potential for Discharge by Performance to the Wrong Party. Until the obligor has notice of an assignment, the obligor can discharge his or her obligation by performance to the assignor (the obligee). Performance by the obligor to the assignor constitutes a discharge to the assignee. Once the obligor receives proper notice, however, only performance to the assignee can discharge the obligor's obligations.

■ **EXAMPLE 17.9** Recall that Alexis, the obligee in *Example 17.8*, assigned to Carmen her right to collect $5,000 from Jason, and Carmen did not give notice to Jason. Jason subsequently pays Alexis the $5,000.

Although the assignment was valid, Jason's payment to Alexis is a discharge of the debt. Carmen's failure to notify Jason of the assignment causes her to lose the right to collect the $5,000 from Jason. (Note that Carmen still has a claim against Alexis for the $5,000.) If Carmen had given Jason notice of the assignment, Jason's payment to Alexis would not have discharged the debt. ■

17–1b Delegations

Just as a party can transfer rights through an assignment, a party can also transfer duties. Duties are not assigned, however, they are *delegated.* The party delegating the duties is the **delegator,** and the party to whom the duties are delegated is the **delegatee.** Normally, a delegation of duties does not relieve the delegator of the obligation to perform in the event that the delegatee fails to do so.

No special form is required to create a valid delegation of duties. As long as the delegator expresses an intention to make the delegation, it is effective. The delegator need not even use the word *delegate.* Exhibit 17–2 illustrates delegation relationships.

Duties That Cannot Be Delegated As a general rule, any duty can be delegated. There are, however, some exceptions to this rule. Delegation is prohibited in the following circumstances:

1. When special trust has been placed in the obligor or when performance depends on the personal skill or talents of the obligor.
2. When performance by a third party will vary materially from that expected by the obligee.
3. When the contract expressly prohibits delegation.

When the Duties Are Personal in Nature. When special trust has been placed in the obligor or when performance depends on the personal skill or talents of the obligor, contractual duties cannot be delegated. ■ **EXAMPLE 17.10** O'Brien, who is impressed with Brodie's ability to perform veterinary surgery, contracts with Brodie to have her perform surgery on O'Brien's prize-winning stallion in July. Brodie later decides that she would rather spend the summer at the beach, so she delegates her duties under the contract to Lopez, who is also a competent veterinary surgeon. The delegation is not effective without O'Brien's consent, no matter how competent Lopez is, because the contract is for *personal* performance. ■

In contrast, nonpersonal duties may be delegated. Assume that in *Example 17.10,* Brodie has contracted with O'Brien to pick up and deliver a large horse trailer to O'Brien's property. Brodie delegates this duty to Lopez, who owns a towing business. This delegation is effective because the performance required is of a *routine* and *nonpersonal* nature.

EXHIBIT 17–2 Delegation Relationships

In the delegation relationship illustrated here, Brower delegates her *duties* under a contract that she made with Horton to a third party, Kuhn. Brower thus becomes the *delegator* and Kuhn the *delegatee* of the contractual duties. Kuhn now owes performance of the contractual duties to Horton. Note that a delegation of duties normally does not relieve the delegator (Brower) of liability if the delegatee (Kuhn) fails to perform the contractual duties.

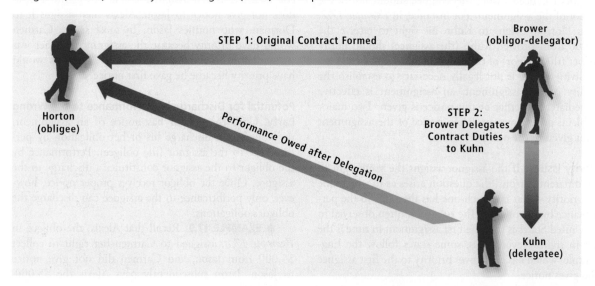

STEP 1: Original Contract Formed

Brower
(obligor-delegator)

Horton
(obligee)

Performance Owed after Delegation

STEP 2:
Brower Delegates
Contract Duties
to Kuhn

Kuhn
(delegatee)

When Performance by a Third Party Will Vary Materially from That Expected by the Obligee. When performance by a third party will vary materially from that expected by the obligee under the contract, contractual duties cannot be delegated. ■ **EXAMPLE 17.11** Jared, a wealthy investor, established the company Heaven Sent to provide grants of capital to struggling but potentially successful businesses. Jared contracted with Merilyn, whose judgment Jared trusted, to select the recipients of the grants. Later, Merilyn delegated this duty to Donald. Jared did not trust Donald's ability to select worthy recipients. This delegation is not effective because it materially alters Jared's expectations under the contract with Merilyn. ■

When the Contract Prohibits Delegation. When the contract expressly prohibits delegation by including an antidelegation clause, the duties cannot be delegated. ■ **EXAMPLE 17.12** Stark, Ltd., contracts with Belisario, a certified public accountant, to perform its annual audits for five years. The contract prohibits delegation. Belisario cannot delegate the duty to perform the audit to another accountant—not even an accountant at the same firm. ■

Effect of a Delegation If a delegation of duties is enforceable, the obligee must accept performance from the delegatee. The obligee can legally refuse performance from the delegatee only if the duty is one that cannot be delegated. ■ **EXAMPLE 17.13** Bryan has a duty to pick up and deliver metal fabrication equipment to Alicia's property. Bryan delegates his duty to Liam. Alicia (the obligee) must accept performance from Liam (the delegatee). ■

A valid delegation of duties does not relieve the delegator of obligations under the contract. Although there are exceptions, generally the obligee can sue both the delegatee and the delegator for nonperformance. Therefore, in *Example 17.13,* if Liam (the delegatee) fails to perform, Bryan (the delegator) is still liable to Alicia, and Alicia normally can sue Bryan, Liam, or both.

Concept Summary 17.1 outlines the basic principles of the laws governing assignments and delegations.

Concept Summary 17.1

Assignment and Delegations

Which Rights Can Be Assigned, and Which Duties Can Be Delegated?	All rights can be assigned *unless:* • A statute expressly prohibits assignment. • The contract is for personal services. • The assignment will materially alter the obligor's risk or duties. • The contract prohibits assignment. All duties can be delegated *unless:* • Performance depends on the obligor's personal skills or talents or special trust has been placed in the obligor. • Performance by a third party will materially vary from that expected by the obligee. • The contract prohibits delegation.
What If the Contract Prohibits Assignment or Delegation?	No rights can be assigned *except:* • Rights to receive funds. • Ownership rights in real estate. • Rights to negotiable instruments. • Rights to damages for breach of a sales contract or payments under a sales contract. No duties can be delegated.
What Is the Effect on the Original Party's Rights?	• On a valid assignment, effective immediately, the original party (assignor) no longer has any rights under the contract. • On a valid delegation, if the delegatee fails to perform, the original party (delegator) is liable to the obligee (who may also hold the delegatee liable).

17–1c Assignment of "All Rights"

When a contract provides for an "assignment of all rights," this wording may create both an assignment of rights and a delegation of duties.[8] Typically, this occurs when general words are used, such as "I assign the contract" or "I assign all my rights under the contract." A court normally will construe such words as implying both an assignment of rights and a delegation of any duties of performance. Thus, the assignor remains liable if the assignee fails to perform the contractual obligations.

17–2 Third Party Beneficiaries

Another exception to the doctrine of privity of contract arises when the contract is intended to benefit a third party. The original parties to a contract can agree that the contract performance should be rendered to or directly benefit a third person. When this happens, the third person becomes an *intended* **third party beneficiary** of the contract. As the **intended beneficiary** of the contract, the third party has legal rights and can sue the promisor directly for breach of the contract.

17–2a Who Is the Promisor?

Who, though, is the promisor? In a bilateral contract, both parties to the contract make promises that can be

enforced, so the court has to determine which party made the promise that benefits the third party. That person is the promisor. In effect, allowing a third party to sue the promisor directly circumvents the "middle person" (the promisee) and thus reduces the burden on the courts. Otherwise, the third party would sue the promisee, who would then sue the promisor.

■ **CASE IN POINT 17.14** The classic case that gave third party beneficiaries the right to bring a suit directly against a promisor was decided in 1859. The case involved three parties—Holly, Lawrence, and Fox. Holly had borrowed $300 from Lawrence. Shortly thereafter, Holly loaned $300 to Fox, who in return promised Holly that he would pay Holly's debt to Lawrence on the following day. When Lawrence failed to obtain the $300 from Fox, he sued Fox to recover the funds. The court had to decide whether Lawrence could sue Fox directly (rather than suing Holly). The court held that when "a promise [is] made for the benefit of another, he for whose benefit it is made may bring an action for its breach."[9] ■

In the following case, the third party beneficiary was a former front woman for a band. The promisor was the band's recording company and distributor. The promisee was a corporation formed by the band members to receive the band's royalties. The contract involved the payment of those royalties. The question before the court was whether the third party could sue for breach of contract when the promisee lacked the capacity to bring the suit.

---

8. *Restatement (Second) of Contracts*, Section 328; UCC 2–210(3), (4).

9. *Lawrence v. Fox*, 20 N.Y. 268 (1859).

Case Analysis 17.3

Bozzio v. EMI Group, Ltd.
United States Court of Appeals, Ninth Circuit, 811 F.3d 1144 (2016).

In the Language of the Court
CHRISTEN, Circuit Judge:
   * * * *

In 1980, Dale Bozzio * * * , Terry Bozzio, and Warren Cuccurullo founded the band Missing Persons. * * * As the band's front woman, [Dale] Bozzio personified the sound and the look of the new wave scene in 1980s Los Angeles.

Capitol Records signed the band and * * * the individual artists in 1982. Their agreement provided that the artists comprising Missing Persons would create master recordings that Capitol would sell and license. In return, Capitol promised to "pay royalties at rates ranging from 20% to 24% for sales in the United States and Canada,

and from 7% to 8% for sales in the rest of the world." The agreement also provided that the artists would receive 50% of Capitol's net royalties from licensing.

In 1983, Bozzio and the other band members formed Missing Persons, Inc., a California corporation, to serve as a loan-out company through which they would provide services to Capitol. A loan-out corporation is a legal fiction employed for the financial benefit of successful artists and entertainers. It is a duly organized corporation, typically wholly owned by an artist, the sole function of which is to "loan out" the services of the artist-owner to producers and other potential employers.

Capitol subsequently entered into a new contract, called the Loan-Out Agreement, with Missing Persons, Inc. The Loan-Out Agreement substituted Missing Persons, Inc. in place of the individual band members in the original * * * Agreement and required Capitol to pay all artist royalties to Missing Persons, Inc., not to the artists. It also stated that Missing Persons, Inc. was to receive all contractual benefits, and that it, not Capitol, was to pay the individual artists all required royalties and advances. As part of the Loan-Out Agreement, each band member executed an Artist Declaration * * * . Bozzio's

Case 17.3 Continued

declaration states that she "agrees to look solely to Missing Persons, Inc. for the payment of her fees and/or royalties * * *, and will not assert any claims in this regard against Capitol."

The music group disbanded in 1986, and, as of July 1, 1988, Missing Persons, Inc. was suspended under California Revenue and Taxation Code Section 23301 due to failure to pay [its] taxes. The parties do not dispute that Missing Persons, Inc. remains a suspended corporation.
* * * *

In 2012, Bozzio filed a * * * suit in [a federal district court in] the Northern District of California. The * * * complaint alleges breach of contract and other claims against EMI Group, Ltd., Capitol Records, LLC, [and others] (collectively, "Capitol"). Specifically, the complaint alleges that Capitol failed to "properly account for and pay its recording artists and music producers for income it has received, and continues to receive, from the licenses of its recorded music catalog for the sale of digital downloads, ringtones (or mastertones), and streaming music." It requests declaratory judgment, injunctive relief, restitution, and attorneys' fees.

Capitol moved to dismiss Bozzio's complaint * * *. Capitol primarily argued that Bozzio could not file suit because she expressly agreed in the Artist Declaration to "look solely to" the loan-out corporation for royalty payments and promised to "not assert any claim in this regard against Capitol." Bozzio countered that she was an intended third-party beneficiary of the Loan-Out Agreement with an individual right to sue that is separate from the corporation's. According to Bozzio, the Artist Declarations "only prohibit an artist from asserting a claim against EMI when there is a dispute among individual band members over the internal allocation and

distribution of royalties that have already been properly accounted for and paid by the record label."

* * * The district court granted Capitol's motion to dismiss. * * * The court * * * concluded that allowing Bozzio to sue as a third-party beneficiary of the recording contract would permit her to "use the corporate entity to contract, and gain the benefits of the corporate form, yet allow her to retain the right to sue as an individual, third party beneficiary even when the corporation could not, on account of its failure to comply with its corporate obligations * * *." Bozzio timely appealed [to the U.S. Court of Appeals for the Ninth Circuit].
* * * *

* * * On appeal, Bozzio argues that the suspended status of the contracting corporate party is irrelevant when the party bringing the action is a third-party beneficiary of the contract, and the district court's dismissal of the * * * complaint on that basis constitutes reversible error. We agree with Bozzio that the district court erred in holding that, even if Bozzio is a third-party beneficiary, she cannot bring an action while Missing Persons, Inc. is suspended.
* * * *

The parties have not cited, and we have not found, any California case holding that a third-party beneficiary cannot sue the promisor for breach of contract when the promisee is a suspended corporation.
* * * *

* * * *California courts do not consider the incapacity of the promisee to a contract to be an absolute bar to a lawsuit by a third-party beneficiary.* [Emphasis added.]
* * * *

When sitting in diversity jurisdiction, this court will follow a state supreme court's interpretation * * *. Where the

state's highest court has not decided an issue, this court looks for guidance to decisions by intermediate appellate courts of the state * * *. Here, the California Supreme Court has not decided whether a promisee corporation's suspended status precludes suit by a third-party beneficiary of the contract, but * * * the California Court of Appeal [has] suggested that a third-party beneficiary suit may go forward notwithstanding the promisee's incapacity to sue. Therefore, the district court erred in its determination that a third-party beneficiary cannot state a claim if the promisee is a suspended corporation.
* * * *

In light of the above, it was an error to grant the motion to dismiss on the ground that Missing Persons, Inc. was a suspended corporation.
* * * *

Capitol strenuously argues that by agreeing "not to assert any claims * * * against Capitol," Bozzio waived her right to sue as a third-party beneficiary. Bozzio counters that this "look solely to" clause was intended to prohibit an artist from asserting a claim against Capitol only "when there is a dispute among individual band members over the internal allocation and distribution of royalties that have already been properly accounted for and paid by the record label to the artists' musical group or loan-out corporation." Nothing in the record forecloses Bozzio's reading of this contract language.

We agree with Bozzio that whether she forfeited the ability to sue as a third-party beneficiary is a fact-bound inquiry ill-suited to resolution at the motion to dismiss stage. On remand, a record can be developed that will allow consideration of Bozzio's claim that she was an intended third-party beneficiary of the Agreement.
* * * *

REVERSED AND REMANDED.

Legal Reasoning Questions

1. What did the lower court rule with respect to the plaintiff's complaint in this case? Why?

2. Did the appellate court agree or disagree with the lower court's ruling? Why?

3. Which issues remain to be determined in this case? Which court will make those determinations initially? Why?

17–2b Types of Intended Beneficiaries

The law traditionally recognized two types of intended third party beneficiaries: creditor beneficiaries and donee beneficiaries.

Creditor Beneficiary One type of intended beneficiary is a *creditor beneficiary*. Like the plaintiff in *Case in Point 17.14,* a creditor beneficiary benefits from a contract in which one party (the promisor) promises another party (the promisee) to pay a debt that the promisee owes to a third party (the creditor beneficiary).

■ **CASE IN POINT 17.15** Autumn Allan owned a condominium unit in a Texas complex located directly beneath a condo unit owned by Aslan Koraev. Over the course of two years, Allan's unit suffered eight incidents of water and sewage incursion as a result of plumbing problems and misuse of appliances in Koraev's unit. Allan sued Koraev for breach of contract and won.

Koraev appealed, arguing that he had no contractual duty to Allan. The court found that Allan was an intended third party beneficiary of the contract between Koraev and the condominium owners' association. Because the governing documents stated that each owner had to comply strictly with their provisions, failure to comply created grounds for an action by the condominium association or by an aggrieved (wronged) owner. Here, Allan was clearly an aggrieved owner and could sue Koraev directly for his failure to perform his contract duties to the condominium association.[10] ■

Donee Beneficiary Another type of intended beneficiary is a *donee beneficiary*. When a contract is made for the express purpose of giving a *gift* to a third party, the third party (the donee beneficiary) can sue the promisor directly to enforce the promise.[11]

The most common donee beneficiary contract is a life insurance contract. ■ **EXAMPLE 17.16** Ang (the promisee) pays premiums to Standard Life, a life insurance company. Standard Life (the promisor) promises to pay a certain amount upon Ang's death to anyone Ang designates as a beneficiary. The designated beneficiary is a donee beneficiary under the life insurance policy and can enforce the promise made by the insurance company to pay her or him on Ang's death. ■

The Modern View Most third party beneficiaries do not fit neatly into either the creditor beneficiary or the donee beneficiary category. Thus, the modern view adopted by the *Restatement (Second) of Contracts* does not draw clear lines between the types of intended beneficiaries. Today, courts frequently distinguish only between *intended beneficiaries* (who can sue to enforce contracts made for their benefit) and *incidental beneficiaries* (who cannot sue, as will be discussed shortly).

17–2c When the Rights of an Intended Beneficiary Vest

An intended third party beneficiary cannot enforce a contract against the original parties until the rights of the third party have *vested,* which means the rights have taken effect and cannot be taken away. Until these rights have vested, the original parties to the contract—the promisor and the promisee—can modify or rescind the contract without the consent of the third party.

When do the rights of third parties vest? The majority of courts hold that the rights vest when any of the following occurs:

1. When the third party demonstrates express consent to the agreement, such as by sending a letter, a note, or an e-mail acknowledging awareness of, and consent to, a contract formed for her or his benefit.
2. When the third party materially alters his or her position in detrimental reliance on the contract. For instance, a person contracts to have a home built in reliance on the receipt of funds promised to him or her in a donee beneficiary contract.
3. When the conditions for vesting are satisfied. For instance, the rights of a beneficiary under a life insurance policy vest when the insured person dies.[12]

If the contract expressly reserves to the contracting parties the right to cancel, rescind, or modify the contract, the rights of the third party beneficiary are subject to any changes that result. If the original contract reserves the right to revoke the promise or change the beneficiary, the vesting of the third party's rights does not terminate that power.[13] In most life insurance contracts, for instance, the policyholder reserves the right to change the designated beneficiary.

17–2d Incidental Beneficiaries

Sometimes, a third person receives a benefit from a contract even though that person's benefit is not the reason the contract was made. Such a person is known as an **incidental beneficiary.** Because the benefit is *unintentional,*

---

10. *Allan v. Nersesova,* 307 S.W.3d 564 (Tx.App.—Dallas 2010).
11. This principle was first enunciated in *Seaver v. Ransom,* 224 N.Y. 233, 120 N.E. 639 (1918).

12. *Restatement (Second) of Contracts,* Section 311.
13. Defenses against third party beneficiaries are given in the *Restatement (Second) of Contracts,* Section 309.

an incidental beneficiary cannot sue to enforce the contract.

■ **CASE IN POINT 17.17** Spectators at the infamous boxing match in which Mike Tyson was disqualified for biting his opponent's ear sued Tyson and the fight's promoters for a refund on the basis of breach of contract. The spectators claimed that they were third party beneficiaries of the contract between Tyson and the fight's promoters. The court, however, held that the spectators could not sue because they were not in contractual privity with the defendants. Any benefits they received from the contract were incidental to the contract. According to the court, the spectators got what they paid for: "the right to view whatever event transpired."[14] ■

17–2e Intended versus Incidental Beneficiaries

In determining whether a third party beneficiary is an intended or an incidental beneficiary, the courts focus on intent, as expressed in the contract language and implied by the surrounding circumstances. Any beneficiary who is not deemed an intended beneficiary is considered incidental. Exhibit 17–3 illustrates the distinction between intended beneficiaries and incidental beneficiaries.

---

14. *Castillo v. Tyson*, 268 A.D.2d 336, 701 N.Y.S.2d 423 (Sup.Ct.App.Div. 2000).

Although no single test can embrace all possible situations, courts often apply the *reasonable person* test: Would a reasonable person in the position of the beneficiary believe that the promisee intended to confer on the beneficiary the right to enforce the contract? In addition, the presence of one or more of the following factors strongly indicates that the third party is an intended beneficiary to the contract:

1. Performance is rendered directly to the third party.
2. The third party has the right to control the details of performance.
3. The third party is expressly designated as a beneficiary in the contract.

■ **CASE IN POINT 17.18** New York City decided to build a state-of-the-art forensic biology (DNA testing) laboratory next to Bellevue Hospital in Manhattan. The project was designed to be a fifteen-story structure with a two-level basement. The city turned the project over to the Dormitory Authority of the State of New York (DASNY), which oversees public projects. DASNY contracted with Perkins Eastman Architects, P.C., to provide architectural services for the project. Perkins hired Samson Construction Company to excavate the site and lay the foundation. Unfortunately, Samson's excavation of the site caused adjacent structures, including a building, sidewalks, roadbeds, sewers, and water systems, to "settle," sustaining about $37 million in damage.

EXHIBIT 17–3 Third Party Beneficiaries

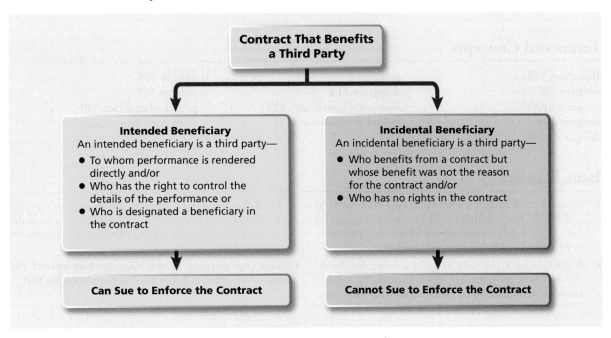

DASNY and the city filed a suit in a New York state court against Samson and Perkins, alleging breach of contract. The lower court dismissed the claim, finding that because the city was not named in the contract between Samson and Perkins, it was not a third party beneficiary. A state intermediate appellate court reversed. "The City raised an issue of fact whether it is an intended third party beneficiary of the contract. The contract expressly states that a City agency will operate the DNA laboratory, and the City retained control over various aspects of the project."[15] ■

---

15. *Dormitory Authority of the State of New York v. Samson Construction Co.*, 137 A.D.3d 433, 27 N.Y.S.3d 114 (1 Dept. 2016).

Reviewing: Third Party Rights

Myrtle Jackson owns several commercial buildings that she leases to businesses, one of which is a restaurant. The lease states that tenants are responsible for securing all necessary insurance policies but the landlord is obligated to keep the buildings in good repair. The owner of the restaurant, Joe McCall, tells his restaurant manager to purchase insurance, but the manager never does so. Jackson tells her son-in-law, Rob Dunn, to perform any necessary maintenance for the buildings. Dunn knows that the ceiling in the restaurant needs repair but fails to do anything about it.

One day a customer, Ian Faught, is dining in the restaurant when a chunk of the ceiling falls on his head and fractures his skull. Faught files suit against the restaurant and discovers that there is no insurance policy in effect. Faught then files a suit against Jackson. He argues that he is an intended third party beneficiary of the lease provision requiring the restaurant to carry insurance and thus can sue Jackson for failing to enforce that provision. Using the information presented in the chapter, answer the following questions.

1. Can Jackson delegate her duty to maintain the buildings to Dunn? Why or why not?
2. Who can be held liable for Dunn's failure to fix the ceiling, Jackson or Dunn? Why?
3. Was Faught an intended third party beneficiary of the lease between Jackson and McCall? Why or why not?
4. Suppose that Jackson tells Dan Stryker, a local builder to whom she owes $50,000, that he can collect the rents from the buildings' tenants until the debt is satisfied. Is this a valid assignment? Why or why not?

Debate This . . . *As a matter of public policy, personal-injury tort claims cannot be assigned. This public policy is wrong and should be changed.*

Terms and Concepts

alienation 312	delegation 309	obligee 309
assignee 309	delegator 314	obligor 309
assignment 309	incidental beneficiary 318	privity of contract 309
assignor 309	intended beneficiary 316	third party beneficiary 316
delegatee 314		

Issue Spotters

1. Brian owes Jeff $100. Ed tells Brian to give him the $100 and he will pay Jeff. Brian gives Ed the $100. Ed never pays Jeff. Can Jeff successfully sue Ed for the $100? Why or why not? (See *Assignments and Delegations*.)

2. Eagle Company contracts to build a house for Frank. The contract states that "any assignment of this contract renders the contract void." After Eagle builds the house, but before Frank pays, Eagle assigns its right to payment to Good Credit Company. Can Good Credit enforce the contract against Frank? Why or why not? (See *Assignments and Delegations*.)

• **Check your answers to the Issue Spotters against the answers provided in Appendix D at the end of this text.**

Business Scenarios

17–1. Assignment. Five years ago, Hensley purchased a house. At that time, being unable to pay the full purchase price, she borrowed funds from Thrift Savings and Loan, which in turn took a mortgage at 6.5 percent interest on the house. The mortgage contract did not prohibit the assignment of the mortgage. Then Hensley secured a new job in another city and sold the house to Sylvia. The purchase price included payment to Hensley of the value of her equity and the assumption of the mortgage debt still owed to Thrift. At the time the contract between Hensley and Sylvia was made, Thrift did not know about or consent to the sale. On the basis of these facts, if Sylvia defaults in making the mortgage payments to Thrift, what are Thrift's rights? Discuss. (See *Assignments and Delegations*.)

17–2. Assignment. Marsala, a college student, signs a one-year lease agreement that runs from September 1 to August 31. The lease agreement specifies that the lease cannot be assigned without the landlord's consent. In late May, Marsala decides not to go to summer school and assigns the balance of the lease (three months) to a close friend, Fred. The landlord objects to the assignment and denies Fred access to the apartment. Marsala claims that Fred is financially sound and should be allowed the full rights and privileges of an assignee. Discuss fully who is correct, the landlord or Marsala. (See *Assignments and Delegations*.)

17–3. Third Party Beneficiaries. Wilken owes Rivera $2,000. Howie promises Wilken that he will pay Rivera the $2,000 in return for Wilken's promise to give Howie's children guitar lessons. Is Rivera an intended beneficiary of the Howie-Wilken contract? Explain. (See *Third Party Beneficiaries*.)

17–4. Delegation. Inez has a specific set of plans to build a sailboat. The plans are detailed, and any boatbuilder can construct the boat. Inez secures bids, and the low bid is made by the Whale of a Boat Corp. Inez contracts with Whale to build the boat for $4,000. Whale then receives unexpected business from elsewhere. To meet the delivery date in the contract with Inez, Whale delegates its obligation to build the boat, without Inez's consent, to Quick Brothers, a reputable boatbuilder. When the boat is ready for delivery, Inez learns of the delegation and refuses to accept delivery, even though the boat is built to her specifications. Discuss fully whether Inez is obligated to accept and pay for the boat. Would your answer be any different if Inez had not had a specific set of plans but had instead contracted with Whale to design and build a sailboat for $4,000? Explain. (See *Assignments and Delegations*.)

Business Case Problems

17–5. Duties That Cannot Be Delegated. Bruce Albea Contracting, Inc., was the general contractor on a state highway project. Albea subcontracted the asphalt work to APAC-Southeast, Inc. Their contract prohibited any delegation without Albea's consent. In midproject, APAC delegated its duties to Matthews Contracting Co. Although Albea allowed Matthews to finish the work, Albea did not pay APAC for its work on the project. Albea argued that APAC had violated the antidelegation clause, rendering their contact void. Is Albea correct? Explain. [*Western Surety Co. v. APAC-Southeast, Inc.,* 302 Ga.App. 654, 691 S.E.2d 234 (2010)] (See *Assignments and Delegations*.)

17–6. Notice of Assignment. Arnold Kazery was the owner of a hotel leased to George Wilkinson. The lease included renewal options of ten years each. When Arnold transferred his interest in the property to his son, Sam, no one notified Wilkinson. For the next twenty years, Wilkinson paid the rent to Arnold and renewed the lease by notice to Arnold. When Wilkinson wrote to Arnold that he was exercising another option to renew, Sam filed a suit against him, claiming that the lease was void. Did Wilkinson give proper notice to renew? Discuss. [*Kazery v. Wilkinson,* 52 So.3d 1270 (Miss.App. 2011)] (See *Assignments and Delegations*.)

17–7. Business Case Problem with Sample Answer— Third Party Beneficiary. David and Sandra Dess contracted with Sirva Relocation, LLC, to assist in selling their home. In their contract, the Desses agreed to disclose all information about the property on which Sirva "and other prospective buyers may rely in deciding whether and on what terms to purchase the Property." The Kincaids contracted with Sirva to buy the house. After the closing, they discovered dampness in the walls, defective and rotten windows, mold, and other undisclosed problems. Can the Kincaids bring an action against the Desses for breach of their contract with Sirva? Why or why not? [*Kincaid v. Dess,* 298 P.3d 358 (2013)] (See *Third Party Beneficiaries*.)

• For a sample answer to Problem 17–7, go to Appendix E at the end of this text.

17–8. Third Party Beneficiaries. Randy Jones is an agent for Farmers Insurance Co. of Arizona. Through Jones, Robert and Marcia Murray obtained auto insurance with Farmers. On Jones's advice, the Murrays increased the policy's limits over the minimums required by the state of Arizona, except for uninsured/underinsured motorist coverage, for which Jones made no recommendation. Later, the Murrays' seventeen-year-old daughter, Jessyka, was in an accident that involved both an uninsured motorist and an underinsured motorist. She sustained a traumatic brain injury that permanently incapacitated her. Does Jessyka have standing to bring a claim against Jones and Farmers as a third party to her parents' contract for auto insurance? Explain. [*Lucas Contracting, Inc. v. Altisource Portfolio Solutions, Inc.,* __ N.E.2d __, 2016-Ohio-474 (Ohio App. 2016)] (See *Third Party Beneficiaries.*)

17–9. A Question of Ethics—Assignment and Delegation. *Premier Building & Development, Inc., entered into a list-*

ing agreement giving Sunset Gold Realty, LLC, the exclusive right to find a tenant for some commercial property. The terms of the listing agreement stated that it was binding on both parties and "their . . . assigns." Premier Building did not own the property at the time but had the option to purchase it. To secure financing for the

project, Premier Building established a new company called Cobblestone Associates. Premier Building then bought the property and conveyed it to Cobblestone the same day. Meanwhile, Sunset Gold found a tenant for the property, and Cobblestone became the landlord. Cobblestone acknowledged its obligation to pay Sunset Gold for finding a tenant, but it later refused to pay Sunset Gold's commission. Sunset Gold then sued Premier Building and Cobblestone for breach of the listing agreement. [Sunset Gold Realty, LLC v. Premier Building & Development, Inc., 133 Conn.App. 445, 36 A.3d 243 (2012)] (See Assignments and Delegations.)

(a) Is Premier Building relieved of its contractual duties if it assigned the contract to Cobblestone? Why or why not?

(b) Given that Sunset Gold performed its obligations under the listing agreement, did Cobblestone behave unethically in refusing to pay Sunset Gold's commission? Why or why not?

Legal Reasoning Group Activity

17–10. Assignment. The Smiths buy a house. They borrow 80 percent of the purchase price from the local ABC Savings and Loan. Before they make their first payment, ABC transfers the right to receive mortgage payments to Citibank. (See *Assignments and Delegations.*)

(a) The first group will outline what would happen if the Smiths continued to make all their payments to ABC Savings and Loan because ABC never notified them of the assignment.

(b) The second group will describe what would happen if the Smiths were notified by ABC of the assignment, but continued to make payments to ABC.

(c) A third group will determine what would happen if the Smiths failed to make any payments on the loan. Which financial institution would have the right to repossess their house?

CHAPTER 18

Performance and Discharge

The most common way to **discharge,** or terminate, contractual duties is by the **performance** of those duties. For instance, a buyer and seller enter into an agreement via e-mail for the sale of a 2018 Lexus RX for $44,000. This contract will be discharged by performance when the buyer pays $44,000 to the seller and the seller transfers possession of the Lexus to the buyer.

In a perfect world, every party who signed a contract would perform his or her duties completely and in a timely fashion, thereby discharging the contract. The real world is more complicated. Events often occur that affect our performance or our ability to perform contractual duties. In addition, the duty to perform under a contract is not always *absolute*. It may instead be *conditioned* on the occurrence or nonoccurrence of a certain event. The legal environment of business requires the identification of some point at which the parties can reasonably know that their duties have ended.

18–1 Conditions

In most contracts, promises of performance are not expressly conditioned or qualified. Instead, they are *absolute promises.* They must be performed, or the parties promising the acts will be in breach of contract. ■ **EXAMPLE 18.1** Paloma Enterprises contracts to sell a truckload of organic produce to Tran for $10,000. The parties' promises are unconditional: Paloma will deliver the produce to Tran, and Tran will pay $10,000 to Paloma. The payment does not have to be made if the produce is not delivered. ■

In some situations, however, performance is *conditioned.* A **condition** is a qualification in a contract based on a possible future event. The occurrence or nonoccurrence of the event will trigger the performance of a legal obligation or terminate an existing obligation under a contract.[1] If the condition is not satisfied, the obligations of the parties are discharged.

Three types of conditions can be present in contracts: conditions *precedent,* conditions *subsequent,* and *concurrent* conditions. Conditions can also be classified as *express* or *implied.*

18–1a Conditions Precedent

A condition that must be fulfilled before a party's performance can be required is called a **condition precedent.** The condition precedes the absolute duty to perform.

A contract to lease university housing, for instance, may be conditioned on the person's being a student at the university. ■ **CASE IN POINT 18.2** James Maciel leased an apartment in a university-owned housing facility for Regent University (RU) students in Virginia. The lease ran until the end of the fall semester. Maciel had an option to renew the lease semester by semester as long as he maintained his status as an RU student.

When Maciel told RU that he intended to withdraw, the university told him that he had to move out of the apartment by May 31, the final day of the semester. Maciel asked for two additional weeks, but the university denied the request. On June 1, RU changed the locks on the apartment. Maciel entered through a window and e-mailed the university that he planned to stay "for another one or two weeks." He was convicted of trespassing. He appealed, arguing that he had "legal authority" to occupy the apartment. The reviewing court affirmed his conviction. "Regent's deadline was consistent with the lease agreement, and Maciel's eligibility to reside in student housing was *conditioned* upon his status as a Regent student." In other words, being enrolled as a student in RU was a condition precedent to living in its student housing.[2] ■

---

1. The *Restatement (Second) of Contracts*, Section 224, defines a condition as "an event, not certain to occur, which must occur, unless its nonoccurrence is excused, before performance under a contract becomes due."

2. *Maciel v. Commonwealth,* 2011 WL 65942 (Va.App. 2011).

Life insurance contracts frequently specify that certain conditions, such as passing a physical examination, must be met before the insurance company will be obligated to perform under the contract. In addition, many contracts are conditioned on an independent appraisal of value. ■ **EXAMPLE 18.3** iMotors offers to buy Gabe's 1959 Thunderbird only if an appraiser estimates that it can be restored for less than a certain price. Therefore, the parties' obligations are conditional. If the condition is not satisfied—that is, if the appraiser deems the cost to be above that price—their obligations are discharged. ■

18–1b Conditions Subsequent

When a condition operates to terminate a party's absolute promise to perform, it is called a **condition subsequent.** The condition follows, or is subsequent to, the time at which the absolute duty to perform arose. If the condition occurs, the party's duty to perform is discharged. ■ **EXAMPLE 18.4** A law firm hires Julie Mendez, a recent law school graduate. Their contract provides that the firm's obligation to continue employing Mendez is discharged if Mendez fails to pass the bar exam by her second attempt. This is a condition subsequent because a failure to pass the exam—and thus to obtain a license to practice law—would discharge a duty (employment) that has already arisen. ■

Generally, conditions precedent are common, and conditions subsequent are rare. Indeed, the *Restatement (Second) of Contracts* does not use the terms *condition subsequent* and *condition precedent* but refers to both simply as conditions.[3]

18–1c Concurrent Conditions

When each party's performance is conditioned on the other party's performance or tender of performance (offer to perform), **concurrent conditions** are present. These conditions exist only when the contract expressly or impliedly calls for the parties to perform their respective duties *simultaneously.*

■ **EXAMPLE 18.5** If Janet Feibush promises to pay for goods when Hewlett-Packard delivers them, the parties' promises to perform are mutually dependent. Feibush's duty to pay for the goods does not become absolute until Hewlett-Packard either delivers or tenders the goods. Likewise, Hewlett-Packard's duty to deliver the goods does not become absolute until Feibush tenders or actually makes payment. Therefore, neither can recover from the other for breach without first tendering performance. ■

Exhibit 18–1 reviews the types of conditions.

---

3. *Restatement (Second) of Contracts,* Section 224.

EXHIBIT 18–1 Conditions of Performance

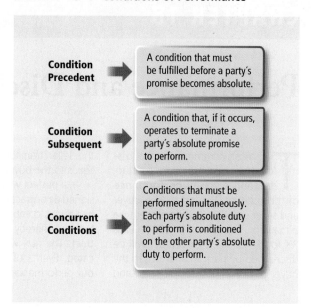

Condition Precedent	A condition that must be fulfilled before a party's promise becomes absolute.
Condition Subsequent	A condition that, if it occurs, operates to terminate a party's absolute promise to perform.
Concurrent Conditions	Conditions that must be performed simultaneously. Each party's absolute duty to perform is conditioned on the other party's absolute duty to perform.

18–1d Express and Implied Conditions

Conditions can also be classified as express or implied in fact. *Express conditions* are provided for by the parties' agreement. Although no particular words are necessary, express conditions are normally prefaced by the words *if, provided, after,* or *when.* For instance, most automobile insurance policies include what is known as a cooperation clause. This clause states that if the insured person is involved in an accident, he or she must cooperate with the insurance company in the defense of any claim or lawsuit.

Implied conditions are understood to be part of the agreement, but they are not found in the express language of the agreement. Courts may imply conditions from the purpose of the contract or from the intent of the parties. Conditions are often implied when they are inherent in the actual performance of the contract.

18–2 Discharge by Performance

The great majority of contracts, as noted earlier, are discharged by performance. The contract comes to an end when both parties fulfill their respective duties by performing the acts they have promised.

Performance can also be accomplished by *tender.* **Tender** is an unconditional offer to perform by a person who is ready, willing, and able to do so. Therefore, a seller who places goods at the disposal of a buyer has tendered delivery and can demand payment. A buyer who offers to pay for goods has tendered payment and can demand delivery of the goods.

Once performance has been tendered, the party making the tender has done everything possible to carry out the terms of the contract. If the other party then refuses to perform, the party making the tender can sue for breach of contract. There are two basic types of performance—*complete performance* and *substantial performance.*

18–2a Complete Performance

When a party performs exactly as agreed, there is no question as to whether the contract has been performed. When a party's performance is perfect, it is said to be complete. Normally, conditions expressly stated in a contract must fully occur in all respects for complete performance (strict performance) of the contract to take place. Any deviation breaches the contract and discharges the other party's obligation to perform.

Most construction contracts, for instance, require the builder to meet certain specifications. If the specifications are conditions, complete performance is required to avoid material breach (*material breach* will be discussed shortly). If the conditions are met, the other party to the contract must then fulfill her or his obligation to pay the builder.

If the parties to the contract did not expressly make the specifications a condition, however, and the builder fails to meet the specifications, performance is not complete. What effect does such a failure have on the other party's obligation to pay? The answer is part of the doctrine of *substantial performance.*

18–2b Substantial Performance

A party who in good faith performs substantially all of the terms of a contract can enforce the contract against the other party under the doctrine of substantial performance. The basic requirements for performance to qualify as substantial performance are as follows:

1. The party must have performed in good faith. Intentional failure to comply with the contract terms is a breach of the contract.
2. The performance must not vary greatly from the performance promised in the contract. An omission, variance, or defect in performance is considered minor if it can easily be remedied by compensation (monetary damages).
3. The performance must create substantially the same benefits as those promised in the contract.

Courts Must Decide Courts decide whether the performance was substantial on a case-by-case basis, examining all of the facts of the particular situation. ■ **CASE IN POINT 18.6** Eugene Pegg had been an electrician in North Dakota for thirty years and had brought a large customer, Sungold, with him through several employers. When an acquaintance, Kelly Kohn, started Kohn Electric, LLC, Pegg approached him to become partners.

Kohn and Pegg orally agreed that Pegg could become a partner in Kohn Electric if he contributed $10,000 in capital and the Sungold account. In return, Pegg was to receive 10 percent of the gross revenue generated by the Sungold account, among other things. Pegg paid $9,152.49 for a pickup truck titled in Kohn Electric's name and paid for tools and equipment for the business. Later, the relationship soured, and Pegg quit. Pegg sued in a state court to recover the proceeds due under the agreement. Kohn denied that they were partners, but he paid Pegg $9,152.49 for the truck.

The state court found that there was an oral partnership agreement and that Pegg had substantially performed by contributing the pickup and bringing in the Sungold account. Therefore, he was entitled to damages in an amount equal to 10 percent of the gross revenue generated from the Sungold account. The court's decision was affirmed on appeal.[4] ■

Effect on Duty to Perform If one party's performance is substantial, the other party's duty to perform remains absolute. In other words, the parties must continue performing under the contract. For instance, the party who substantially performed is entitled to payment. If performance is not substantial, there is a material breach (to be discussed shortly), and the nonbreaching party is excused from further performance.

Measure of Damages Because substantial performance is not perfect, the other party is entitled to damages to compensate for the failure to comply with the contract. The measure of the damages is the cost to bring the object of the contract into compliance with its terms, if that cost is reasonable under the circumstances.

What if the cost is unreasonable? Then the measure of damages is the difference in value between the performance rendered and the performance that would have been rendered if the contract had been performed completely.

The following case is a classic illustration that there is no exact formula for deciding when a contract has been substantially performed.

---

4. *Pegg v. Kohn*, 861 N.W.2d 764, 2015 ND 79 (2015).

Jacob & Youngs v. Kent

Court of Appeals of New York, 230 N.Y. 239, 129 N.E. 889 (1921).

Background and Facts The plaintiff, Jacob & Youngs, Inc., was a builder that had contracted with George Kent to construct a country residence for him. A specification in the building contract required that "all wrought-iron pipe must be well galvanized, lap welded pipe of the grade known as 'standard pipe' of Reading manufacture." Jacob & Youngs installed substantially similar pipe that was not of Reading manufacture. When Kent became aware of the difference, he ordered the builder to remove all of the plumbing and replace it with the Reading type. To do so would have required removing finished walls that encased the plumbing—an expensive and difficult task. The builder explained that the plumbing was of the same quality, appearance, value, and cost as Reading pipe. When Kent nevertheless refused to pay the $3,483.46 still owed for the work, Jacob & Youngs sued to compel payment. The trial court ruled in favor of Kent. The plaintiff appealed, and the appellate court reversed the trial court's decision. Kent then appealed to the Court of Appeals of New York, the state's highest court.

In the Language of the Court

CARDOZO, Justice.

* * * *

* * * The courts never say that one who makes a contract fills the measure of his duty by less than full performance. They do say, however, that *an omission, both trivial and innocent, will sometimes be atoned [compensated] for by allowance of the resulting damage, and will not always be the breach of a condition[.]* [Emphasis added.]

* * * Where the line is to be drawn between the important and the trivial cannot be settled by a formula. * * * *We must weigh the purpose to be served, the desire to be gratified, the excuse for deviation from the letter, [and] the cruelty of enforced adherence. Then only can we tell whether literal fulfillment is to be implied by law as a condition.* [Emphasis added.]

* * * We think the measure of the allowance is not the cost of replacement, which would be great, but the difference in value, which would be either nominal or nothing. * * * The owner is entitled to the money which will permit him to complete, unless the cost of completion is grossly and unfairly out of proportion to the good to be attained.

Decision and Remedy *New York's highest court affirmed the appellate court's decision, holding that Jacob & Youngs had substantially performed the contract.*

Impact of This Case on Today's Law *At the time of the Jacob & Youngs case, some courts did not apply the doctrine of substantial performance to disputes involving breaches of contract. This landmark decision contributed to a developing trend toward equity and fairness in those circumstances. Today, an unintentional and trivial deviation from the terms of a contract will not prevent its enforcement but will permit an adjustment in the value of its performance.*

Critical Thinking

- **Legal Environment** *The New York Court of Appeals found that Jacob & Youngs had substantially performed the contract. To what, if any, remedy was Kent entitled?*

18–2c Performance to the Satisfaction of Another

Contracts often state that completed work must personally satisfy one of the parties or a third person. The question then is whether this satisfaction becomes a condition precedent, requiring actual personal satisfaction or approval for discharge, or whether the performance need only satisfy a *reasonable person*.

When the Contract Is Personal When the subject matter of the contract is *personal*, the obligation is conditional, and performance must actually satisfy the party specified in the contract. For instance, contracts for portraits, works of art, and tailoring are considered personal because they involve matters of personal taste. Therefore, only the personal satisfaction of the party fulfills the condition. (An exception exists, of course, if a court finds that the party is expressing dissatisfaction simply to avoid payment or otherwise is not acting in good faith.)

Reasonable Person Standard Most other contracts need to be performed only to the satisfaction of a reasonable person unless they *expressly state otherwise*. When the subject matter of the contract is mechanical, courts are more likely to find that the performing party has performed satisfactorily if a reasonable person would be satisfied with what was done. ■ **EXAMPLE 18.7** Mason signs a contract with Jen to mount a new heat pump on a concrete platform to her satisfaction. Such a contract normally need only be performed to the satisfaction of a reasonable person. ■

When contracts require performance to the satisfaction of a third party with superior knowledge or training in the subject matter—such as a supervising engineer—the courts are divided. A majority of courts require the work to be satisfactory to a reasonable person, but some courts require the personal satisfaction of the third party designated in the contract. (Again, the personal judgment must be made honestly, or the condition will be excused.)

18–2d Material Breach of Contract

A **breach of contract** is the nonperformance of a contractual duty. The breach is *material* when performance is

not at least substantial.[5] As mentioned earlier, when there is a material breach, the nonbreaching party is excused from the performance of contractual duties. That party can also sue the breaching party for damages resulting from the breach.

■ **EXAMPLE 18.8** When country singer Garth Brooks's mother died, he donated $500,000 to a hospital in his hometown in Oklahoma to build a new women's health center named after his mother. After several years passed and the health center was not built, Brooks demanded a refund. The hospital refused, claiming that while it had promised to honor his mother in some way, it had not promised to build a women's health center. Brooks sued for breach of contract. A jury determined that the hospital's failure to build a women's health center and name it after Brooks's mother was a material breach of the contract. The jury awarded Brooks $1 million in damages. ■

Material versus Minor Breach If the breach is *minor* (not material), the nonbreaching party's duty to perform is not entirely excused, but it can sometimes be suspended until the breach has been remedied. Once the minor breach has been cured, the nonbreaching party must resume performance of the contractual obligations.

Both parties in the following case were arguably in breach of their contract. Which party's breach was material?

---

5. *Restatement (Second) of Contracts*, Section 241.

Kohel v. Bergen Auto Enterprises, L.L.C.

Superior Court of New Jersey, Appellate Division, 2013 WL 439970 (2013).

In the Language of the Court

PER CURIAM. [By the Whole Court]

* * * *

On May 24, 2010, plaintiffs Marc and Bree Kohel entered into a sales contract with defendant Bergen Auto Enterprises, L.L.C. d/b/a Wayne Mazda Inc. (Wayne Mazda), for the purchase of a used 2009 Mazda. Plaintiffs agreed to pay $26,430.22 for the Mazda and were credited $7,000 as a trade-in, for their 2005 Nissan Altima. As plaintiffs still owed $8,118.28 on the Nissan, Wayne Mazda assessed plaintiffs a net pay-off of

this amount and agreed to remit the balance due to satisfy the outstanding lien.

Plaintiffs took possession of the Mazda with temporary plates and left the Nissan with defendant. A few days later, a representative of defendant advised plaintiffs that the Nissan's vehicle identification tag (VIN tag) was missing. The representative claimed it was unable to sell the car and offered to rescind the transaction. Plaintiffs refused.

When the temporary plates on the Mazda expired on June 24, 2010, defendant refused to provide plaintiffs with

the permanent plates they had paid for. In addition, defendant refused to pay off plaintiffs' outstanding loan on the Nissan, as they had agreed. As a result, plaintiffs were required to continue to make monthly payments on both the Nissan and the Mazda.

On July 28, 2010, plaintiffs filed a complaint in [a New Jersey state court] against Wayne Mazda * * * . Plaintiffs alleged breach of contract.

* * * *

Case 18.2 Continues

Case 18.2 Continued

On February 2, 2012, the court rendered an oral decision finding that there was a breach of contract by Wayne Mazda * * * . On February 17, 2012, the court entered judgment in the amount of $5,405.17 in favor of plaintiffs against Wayne Mazda. [The defendant appealed to a state intermediate appellate court.]

* * * *

Defendant argues that plaintiffs' delivery of the Nissan without a VIN tag was, itself, a breach of the contract of sale and precludes a finding that defendant breached the contract. However, the trial court found that plaintiffs were not aware that the Nissan lacked a VIN tag when they offered it in trade. Moreover, defendant's representatives examined the car twice before accepting it in trade and did not notice the missing VIN until they took the car to an auction where they tried to sell it.

There is a material distinction in plaintiffs' conduct, which the court found unintentional, and defendant's refusal to release the permanent plates for which the plaintiffs had paid, an action the court concluded was done to maintain "leverage." [Emphasis added.]

* * * The evidence * * * indicated that * * * the problem with the missing VIN tag could be rectified. Marc Kohel applied and paid for a replacement VIN tag at Meadowlands [Nissan for $35.31]. While he initially made some calls to Meadowlands, he did not follow up in obtaining the VIN tag after the personnel at Wayne Mazda began refusing to take his calls.

* * * The court concluded that "Wayne Mazda didn't handle this as—as adroitly [skillfully] as they could * * * ." Kevin DiPiano, identified in the complaint as the owner and/or CEO of

Wayne Mazda, would not even take [the plaintiffs'] calls to discuss this matter. The court found:

> Mr. DiPiano could have been a better businessman, could have been a little bit more compassionate or at least responsive, you know? He was not. He acted like he didn't care. That obviously went a long way to infuriate the plaintiffs. I don't blame them for being infuriated.

* * * *

* * * Here, plaintiffs attempted to remedy the VIN tag issue but this resolution was frustrated by defendant's unreasonable conduct. We thus reject defendant's argument that plaintiffs' failure to obtain the replacement VIN tag amounted to a repudiation of the contract.

* * * *

Affirmed.

Legal Reasoning Questions

1. What is a material breach of contract? When a material breach occurs, what are the nonbreaching party's options?
2. What is a minor breach of contract? When a minor breach occurs, is the nonbreaching party excused from performance? Explain.
3. In this case, the defendant—Wayne Mazda—argued that the plaintiffs should not be granted relief for the defendant's breach. What were the defendant's main arguments in support of this position?

Underlying Policy Note that any breach entitles the nonbreaching party to sue for damages, but only a material breach discharges the nonbreaching party from the contract. The policy underlying these rules allows a contract to go forward when only minor problems occur but allows it to be terminated if major difficulties arise. Exhibit 18–2 reviews how performance can discharge a contract.

18–2e Anticipatory Repudiation

Before either party to a contract has a duty to perform, one of the parties may refuse to carry out his or her contractual obligations. This is called **anticipatory repudiation**[6] of the contract.

Repudiation Is a Material Breach When an anticipatory repudiation occurs, it is treated as a material

breach of the contract, and the nonbreaching party is permitted to bring an action for damages immediately. The nonbreaching party can file suit even though the scheduled time for performance under the contract may still be in the future. Until the nonbreaching party treats an early repudiation as a breach, however, the repudiating party can retract the anticipatory repudiation by proper notice and restore the parties to their original obligations.[7]

An anticipatory repudiation is treated as a present, material breach for two reasons. First, the nonbreaching party should not be required to remain ready and willing to perform when the other party has already repudiated the contract. Second, the nonbreaching party should have the opportunity to seek a similar contract elsewhere and may have a duty to do so to minimize his or her loss.[8]

---

6. *Restatement (Second) of Contracts*, Section 253; Section 2–610 of the Uniform Commercial Code (UCC).

7. See UCC 2–611.

8. The doctrine of anticipatory repudiation first arose in the landmark case of *Hochster v. De La Tour,* 2 Ellis and Blackburn Reports 678 (1853). An English court recognized the delay and expense inherent in a rule requiring a nonbreaching party to wait until the time of performance before suing on an anticipatory repudiation.

EXHIBIT 18–2 Discharge by Performance

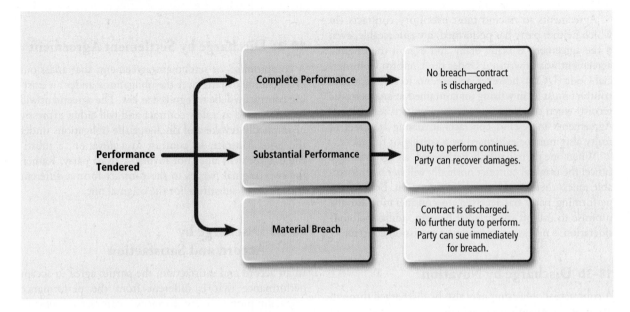

Anticipatory Repudiation and Market Prices

Quite often, anticipatory repudiation occurs when performance of the contract would be extremely unfavorable to one of the parties because of a sharp fluctuation in market prices.

■ **EXAMPLE 18.9** Mobile X enters into an e-contract to manufacture and sell 100,000 smartphones to Best Com, a global telecommunications company. Delivery is to be made two months from the date of the contract. One month later, three inventory suppliers raise their prices to Mobile X. Because of these higher prices, Mobile X stands to lose $500,000 if it sells the smartphones to Best Com at the contract price.

Mobile X immediately sends an e-mail to Best Com, stating that it cannot deliver the 100,000 smartphones at the contract price. Even though you may sympathize with Mobile X, its e-mail is an anticipatory repudiation of the contract. Best Com can treat the repudiation as a material breach and immediately pursue remedies, even though the contract delivery date is still a month away. ■

18-2f Time for Performance

If no time for performance is stated in a contract, a *reasonable time* is implied.[9] If a specific time is stated, the parties must usually perform by that time. Unless time is expressly stated to be vital, though, a delay in

performance will not destroy the performing party's right to payment.

When time is expressly stated to be "of the essence" or vital, the parties normally must perform within the stated time period because the time element becomes a condition. Even when the contract states that time is of the essence, however, a court may find that a party who fails to complain about the other party's delay has waived the breach of the time provision.

18-3 Discharge by Agreement

Any contract can be discharged by agreement of the parties. The agreement can be contained in the original contract, or the parties can form a new contract for the express purpose of discharging the original contract.

18-3a Discharge by Mutual Rescission

As mentioned in previous chapters, *rescission* is the process by which a contract is canceled or terminated and the parties are returned to the positions they occupied prior to forming it. For **mutual rescission** to take place, the parties must make another agreement that also satisfies the legal requirements for a contract. There must be an *offer,* an *acceptance,* and *consideration.* Ordinarily, if the parties agree to rescind the original contract, their promises not to perform the acts stipulated in the

---

9. See UCC 2–204.

original contract will be legal consideration for the second contract (the rescission).

Agreements to rescind most executory contracts (in which neither party has performed) are enforceable, even if the agreement is made orally and even if the original agreement was in writing. Under the Uniform Commercial Code (UCC), however, agreements to rescind a sales contract must be in writing (or contained in an electronic record) when the contract requires a written rescission.[10] Agreements to rescind contracts involving transfers of realty also must be evidenced by a writing or record.

When one party has fully performed, an agreement to cancel the original contract normally will *not* be enforceable unless there is additional consideration. Because the performing party has received no consideration for the promise to call off the original bargain, additional consideration is necessary to support a rescission contract.

18–3b Discharge by Novation

A contractual obligation may also be discharged through novation. A **novation** occurs when both of the parties to a contract agree to substitute a third party for one of the original parties. The requirements of a novation are as follows:

1. A previous valid obligation.
2. An agreement by all parties to a new contract.
3. The extinguishing of the old obligation (discharge of the prior party).
4. A new contract that is valid.

■ **EXAMPLE 18.10** Union Corporation contracts to sell its pharmaceutical division to British Pharmaceuticals, Ltd. Before the transfer is completed, Union, British Pharmaceuticals, and a third company, Otis Chemicals, execute a new agreement to transfer all of British Pharmaceuticals' rights and duties in the transaction to Otis Chemicals. As long as the new contract is supported by consideration, the novation will discharge the original contract (between Union and British Pharmaceuticals) and replace it with the new contract (between Union and Otis Chemicals). ■

A novation expressly or impliedly revokes and discharges a prior contract. The parties involved may expressly state in the new contract that the old contract is now discharged. If the parties do not expressly discharge the old contract, it will be impliedly discharged if the new contract's terms are inconsistent with the old contract's terms. It is this immediate discharge of the prior contract that distinguishes a novation from both an accord and satisfaction, discussed shortly, and an assignment of all rights.

18–3c Discharge by Settlement Agreement

A compromise, or settlement agreement, that arises out of a genuine dispute over the obligations under an existing contract will be recognized at law. The agreement will be substituted as a new contract and will either expressly or impliedly revoke and discharge the obligations under the prior contract. In contrast to a novation, a substituted agreement does not involve a third party. Rather, the two original parties to the contract form a different agreement to substitute for the original one.

18–3d Discharge by Accord and Satisfaction

In an accord and satisfaction, the parties agree to accept performance that is different from the performance originally promised. An *accord* is a contract to perform some act to satisfy an existing contractual duty that is not yet discharged.[11] A *satisfaction* is the performance of the accord agreement. An accord and its satisfaction discharge the original contractual obligation.

Once the accord has been made, the original obligation is merely suspended until the accord agreement is fully performed. If it is not performed, the obligee (the one to whom performance is owed) can file a lawsuit based on either the original obligation or the accord. ■ **EXAMPLE 18.11** Fahreed has a judgment against Ling for $8,000. Later, both parties agree that the judgment can be satisfied by Ling's transfer of his automobile to Fahreed. This agreement to accept the auto in lieu of $8,000 in cash is the accord. If Ling transfers the car to Fahreed, the accord is fully performed, and the debt is discharged. If Ling refuses to transfer the car, the accord is breached. Because the original obligation was merely suspended, Fahreed can sue Ling to enforce the original judgment for $8,000 in cash or bring an action for breach of the accord. ■

18–4 Discharge by Operation of Law

Under specified circumstances, contractual duties may be discharged by operation of law. These circumstances include material alteration of the contract, the running

---

10. UCC 2–209(2), (4).

11. *Restatement (Second) of Contracts*, Section 281.

of the statute of limitations, bankruptcy, and the impossibility or impracticability of performance.

18–4a Material Alteration of the Contract

To discourage parties from altering written contracts, the law allows an innocent party to be discharged when the other party has materially altered a written contract without consent. For instance, suppose that a party alters a material term of a contract, such as the stated quantity or price, without the knowledge or consent of the other party. In this situation, the party who was unaware of the alteration can treat the contract as discharged.

18–4b Statutes of Limitations

As mentioned earlier in this text, statutes of limitations restrict the period during which a party can sue on a particular cause of action. After the applicable limitations period has passed, a suit can no longer be brought. The limitations period for bringing suits for breach of oral contracts usually is two to three years, and for written contracts, four to five years. Parties generally have ten to twenty years to file for recovery of amounts awarded in judgments, depending on state law.

Lawsuits for breach of a contract for the sale of goods usually must be brought within four years after the cause of action has accrued.[12] A cause of action for a sales contract generally accrues when the breach occurs, even if the aggrieved party is not aware of the breach. A breach of warranty normally occurs when the seller delivers the goods to the buyer. By their original agreement, the parties can reduce this four-year period to not less than one year, but they cannot agree to extend it.

18–4c Bankruptcy

A proceeding in bankruptcy attempts to allocate the debtor's assets to the creditors in a fair and equitable fashion. Once the assets have been allocated, the debtor receives a **discharge in bankruptcy.** A discharge in bankruptcy ordinarily prevents the creditors from enforcing most of the debtor's contracts. Partial payment of a debt *after* discharge in bankruptcy will not revive the debt.

18–4d Impossibility of Performance

After a contract has been made, supervening events (such as a fire) may make performance impossible in an objective sense. This is known as **impossibility of performance** and can discharge a contract.[13] The doctrine of impossibility of performance applies only when the parties could not have reasonably foreseen, at the time the contract was formed, the event that rendered performance impossible. Performance may also become so difficult or costly due to some unforeseen event that a court will consider it commercially unfeasible, or impracticable, as will be discussed later in the chapter.

Objective impossibility ("It can't be done") must be distinguished from *subjective impossibility* ("I'm sorry, I simply can't do it"). An example of subjective impossibility occurs when a party cannot deliver goods on time because of freight car shortages or cannot make payment on time because the bank is closed. In effect, in each of these situations the party is saying, "It is impossible for *me* to perform," not "It is impossible for *anyone* to perform." Accordingly, such excuses do not discharge a contract, and the nonperforming party is normally held in breach of contract.

When Performance Is Impossible Three basic types of situations may qualify as grounds for the discharge of contractual obligations based on impossibility of performance:[14]

1. *When one of the parties to a personal contract dies or becomes incapacitated prior to performance.* ■ **EXAMPLE 18.12** Frederic, a famous dancer, contracts with Ethereal Dancing Guild to play a leading role in its new ballet. Before the ballet can be performed, Frederic becomes ill and dies. His personal performance was essential to the completion of the contract. Thus, his death discharges the contract and his estate's liability for his nonperformance. ■

2. *When the specific subject matter of the contract is destroyed.* ■ **EXAMPLE 18.13** A-1 Farm Equipment agrees to sell Gunther the green tractor on its lot and promises to have the tractor ready for Gunther to pick up on Saturday. On Friday night, however, a truck veers off the nearby highway and smashes into the tractor, destroying it beyond repair. Because the contract was for this specific tractor, A-1's performance is rendered impossible owing to the accident. ■

3. *When a change in law renders performance illegal.* ■ **EXAMPLE 18.14** Hopper contracts with Playlist, Inc., to create a Web site through which users can post and share movies, music, and other forms of digital entertainment. Hopper goes to work. Before the site is operational, however, Congress passes the No Online Piracy in Entertainment (NOPE) Act.

---

12. Section 2–725 of the UCC contains this four-year limitation period.

13. *Restatement (Second) of Contracts*, Section 261.
14. *Restatement (Second) of Contracts*, Sections 262–266; UCC 2–615.

The NOPE Act makes it illegal to operate a Web site on which copyrighted works are posted without the copyright owners' consent. In this situation, the contract is discharged by operation of law. The purpose of the contract has been rendered illegal, and contract performance is objectively impossible. ∎

The following case involved a financial institution participating in the federal Troubled Asset Relief Program (TARP). Could the institution assert TARP's prohibition on "golden parachute" payments as a defense to a breach of contract action brought by one of its former senior executive officers?

Case 18.3

Hampton Roads Bankshares, Inc. v. Harvard

Virginia Supreme Court, 291 Va. 42, 781 S.E.2d 172 (2016).

Background and Facts Scott Harvard was a senior executive officer of Hampton Roads Bankshares, Inc. (HRB), headquartered in Virginia Beach, Virginia. Harvard's employment contract included a "golden parachute"—a payment of approximately three times his average annual compensation if he quit.

In 2008, during the Great Recession, Congress enacted the Emergency Economic Stabilization Act (EESA) "to restore liquidity and stability to the financial system."[a] EESA included the Troubled Asset Relief Program (TARP), which allowed the government to buy "troubled assets" from financial institutions to promote market stability. TARP barred participating institutions from making golden parachute payments, defined as "any payment to a senior executive officer for departure from a company for any reason."

HRB participated in TARP. Later, Harvard quit the firm and filed a suit in a Virginia state court against HRB to obtain his golden parachute payment. The court ordered HRB to make the payment. HRB appealed to the Virginia Supreme Court.

In the Language of the Court
Opinion by Justice William C. *MIMS*.
* * * *

The defense of impossibility of performance is an established principle of contract law. In Virginia, *it is well settled that where impossibility is due to domestic law, to the death or illness of one who by the terms of the contract was to do an act requiring his personal performance, or to the fortuitous destruction or change in the character of something to which the contract related, or which by the terms of the contract was made a necessary means of performance, the promisor will be excused, unless he either expressly agreed in the contract to assume the risk of performance, whether possible or not, or the impossibility was due to his fault.* [Emphasis added.]

Harvard does not dispute that EESA directly bars HRB from making the severance payment to Harvard upon the termination of his employment, because the payment falls within the definition of a prohibited "golden parachute payment." Moreover, Harvard does not suggest that HRB expressly agreed in the contract to assume the risk of performance, whether possible or not. Nor could he; the * * * Employment Agreement clearly places the risk of * * * the law regulating golden parachute payments on Harvard.

On December 31, 2008, Harvard agreed [with HRB to amend] the Employment Agreement [to provide that it] "will be interpreted, administered and construed to, comply with EESA."

By its plain language, the amended Employment Agreement must be read to comply with EESA. Nothing therein exempts the agreement from * * * EESA * * * or places the risk of performance * * * on HRB.
* * * *

There is nothing in the record that would suggest HRB refused to make the golden parachute payment in bad faith. After Harvard terminated his employment, HRB sought guidance from [the U.S. Department of the] Treasury regarding its contractual obligation to make the disputed golden parachute payment, and whether it could perform that obligation in light of EESA. In response, Treasury provided informal guidance indicating that HRB could not make the payment and comply with EESA. Where, as here, the government has clearly expressed its intent to enforce the law, and the promisor cannot in

---
a. 12 U.S.C. Section 5201.

Case 18.3 Continued

good faith perform its contractual obligation without violating the law, the promisor is discharged from its obligation.

Decision and Remedy *The Virginia Supreme Court reversed the order of the lower court, which "erred when it ordered HRB to make the golden parachute payment despite the federal prohibition on such payments found in EESA." Under EESA, payment of the golden parachute would violate the law.*

Critical Thinking
- **Legal Environment** *What advantage does the discharge of a contractual obligation under the rule applied in this case offer to the contract's parties? Discuss.*
- **Ethical** *Did HRB violate any ethical duty by refusing to make Harvard's golden parachute payment? Explain.*

Temporary Impossibility An occurrence or event that makes performance temporarily impossible operates to suspend performance until the impossibility ceases.

Performance Normally Is Only Delayed. Once the temporary event ends, the parties ordinarily must perform the contract as originally planned. ■ **CASE IN POINT 18.15** Keefe Hurwitz contracted to sell his home in Louisiana to Wesley and Gwendolyn Payne for $241,500. Four days later, Hurricane Katrina made landfall and caused extensive damage to the house. The cost of repairs was estimated at $60,000. Hurwitz refused to pay for the repairs only to sell the property to the Paynes for the previously agreed-on price. The Paynes filed a lawsuit to enforce the contract. Hurwitz argued that Hurricane Katrina had made it impossible for him to perform and had discharged his duties under the contract. The court, however, ruled that Hurricane Katrina had caused only a temporary impossibility. Hurwitz was required to pay for the necessary repairs and to perform the contract as written. He could not obtain a higher purchase price to offset the cost of the repairs.[15] ■

Performance Can Be Discharged. Sometimes, the lapse of time and the change in circumstances surrounding the contract make it substantially more burdensome for the parties to perform the promised acts. In that situation, the contract is discharged. ■ **CASE IN POINT 18.16** In 1942, actor Gene Autry was drafted into the U.S. Army. Being drafted rendered his contract with a Hollywood movie company temporarily impossible to perform, and it was suspended until the end of World War II in 1945. When

Autry got out of the army, the purchasing power of the dollar had declined so much that performance of the contract would have been substantially burdensome to him. Therefore, the contract was discharged.[16] ■

It can be difficult to predict how a court will—or should—rule on whether performance is impossible in a particular situation, as discussed in this chapter's *Ethics Today* feature.

18–4e Commercial Impracticability

Courts may also excuse parties from their performance when it becomes much more difficult or expensive than the parties originally contemplated at the time the contract was formed. In one classic case, for example, a court held that a contract could be discharged because a party would otherwise have had to pay ten times more than the original estimate to excavate a certain amount of gravel.[17]

For someone to invoke the doctrine of **commercial impracticability** successfully, however, the anticipated performance must become *significantly* more difficult or costly.[18] In addition, the added burden of performing *must not have been foreseeable by the parties when the contract was made.*

18–4f Frustration of Purpose

Closely allied with the doctrine of commercial impracticability is the doctrine of **frustration of purpose.** In principle, a contract will be discharged if supervening

---

15. *Payne v. Hurwitz*, 978 So.2d 1000 (La.App. 1st Cir. 2008).

16. *Autry v. Republic Productions*, 30 Cal.2d 144, 180 P.2d 888 (1947).
17. *Mineral Park Land Co. v. Howard*, 172 Cal. 289, 156 P. 458 (1916).
18. *Restatement (Second) of Contracts*, Section 264.

ETHICS TODAY — When Is Impossibility of Performance a Valid Defense?

The doctrine of impossibility of performance is applied only when the parties could not have reasonably foreseen, at the time the contract was formed, the event or events that rendered performance impossible. In some cases, the courts may seem to go too far in holding that the parties should have foreseen certain events or conditions. Such a holding means that the parties cannot avoid their contractual obligations under the doctrine of impossibility of performance.

Actually, courts today are more likely to allow parties to raise this defense than courts in the past, which rarely excused parties from performance under the impossibility doctrine. Indeed, until the latter part of the nineteenth century, courts were reluctant to discharge a contract even when performance appeared to be impossible.

Generally, the courts must balance the freedom of parties to contract (and thereby assume the risks involved) against the injustice that may result when certain contractual obligations are enforced. If the courts allowed parties to raise impossibility of performance as a defense to contractual obligations more often, freedom of contract would suffer.

Critical Thinking *Why might those entering into contracts be worse off in the long run if the courts increasingly accepted impossibility of performance as a defense?*

circumstances make it impossible to attain the purpose both parties had in mind when they made the contract. As with commercial impracticability and impossibility, the supervening event must not have been reasonably foreseeable at the time the contract was formed.

There are some differences between these doctrines, however. Commercial impracticability usually involves an event that increases the cost or difficulty of performance. In contrast, frustration of purpose typically involves an event that decreases the value of what a party receives under the contract.[19]

See Exhibit 18–3 for a summary of the ways in which a contract can be discharged.

_____
19. See, for instance, *Direct Supply, Inc. v. Specialty Hospitals of America, LLC*, 935 F.Supp.2d 137 (D.C.Cir. 2013).

EXHIBIT 18–3 Contract Discharge

BY OPERATION OF LAW	BY PERFORMANCE	BY AGREEMENT
• Material alteration • Statutes of limitations • Bankruptcy • Impossibility or impracticability of performance • Frustration of purpose	• Complete • Substantial	• Mutual rescission • Novation • Settlement agreement • Accord and satisfaction

BY FAILURE OF A CONDITION	BY BREACH
If performance is conditional, duty to perform does not become absolute until that condition occurs.	• Material breach • Anticipatory repudiation

Reviewing: Performance and Discharge

Val's Foods signs a contract to buy 1,500 pounds of basil from Sun Farms, a small organic herb grower, as long as an independent organization inspects the crop and certifies that it contains no pesticide or herbicide residue. Val's has a contract with several restaurant chains to supply pesto and intends to use Sun Farms' basil in the pesto to fulfill these contracts. While Sun Farms is preparing to harvest the basil, an unexpected hailstorm destroys half the crop. Sun Farms attempts to purchase additional basil from other farms, but it is late in the season, and the price is twice the normal market price. Sun Farms is too small to absorb this cost and immediately notifies Val's that it will not fulfill the contract. Using the information presented in the chapter, answer the following questions.

1. Suppose that the basil does not pass the chemical-residue inspection. Which concept discussed in the chapter might allow Val's to refuse to perform the contract in this situation?
2. Under which legal theory or theories might Sun Farms claim that its obligation under the contract has been discharged by operation of law? Discuss fully.
3. Suppose that Sun Farms contacts every basil grower in the country and buys the last remaining chemical-free basil anywhere. Nevertheless, Sun Farms is able to ship only 1,475 pounds to Val's. Would this fulfill Sun Farms' obligations to Val's? Why or why not?
4. Now suppose that Sun Farms sells its operations to Happy Valley Farms. As a part of the sale, all three parties agree that Happy Valley will provide the basil as stated under the original contract. What is this type of agreement called?

Debate This . . .   *The doctrine of commercial impracticability should be abolished.*

Terms and Concepts

anticipatory repudiation 328	condition precedent 323	impossibility of performance 331
breach of contract 327	condition subsequent 324	mutual rescission 329
commercial impracticability 333	discharge 323	novation 330
concurrent conditions 324	discharge in bankruptcy 331	performance 323
condition 323	frustration of purpose 333	tender 324

Issue Spotters

1. Ready Foods contracts to buy two hundred carloads of frozen pizzas from Stealth Distributors. Before Ready or Stealth starts performing, can the parties call off the deal? What if Stealth has already shipped the pizzas? Explain your answers. (See *Discharge by Performance.*)
2. C&D Services contracts with Ace Concessions, Inc., to service Ace's vending machines. Later, C&D wants Dean Vending Services to assume the duties under a new contract. Ace consents. What type of agreement is this? Are Ace's obligations discharged? Why or why not? (See *Discharge by Agreement.*)

- Check your answers to the Issue Spotters against the answers provided in Appendix D at the end of this text.

Business Scenarios

18–1. Conditions of Performance. The Caplans contract with Faithful Construction, Inc., to build a house for them for $360,000. The specifications state "all plumbing bowls and fixtures . . . to be Crane brand." The Caplans leave on vacation, and during their absence, Faithful is unable to buy and install Crane plumbing fixtures. Instead, Faithful installs Kohler brand fixtures, an equivalent in the industry. On completion of the building contract, the Caplans inspect the work, discover the substitution, and refuse to accept the house, claiming Faithful has breached the conditions set forth in the specifications. Discuss fully the Caplans' claim. (See *Conditions.*)

18–2. Discharge by Agreement. Junior owes creditor Iba $1,000, which is due and payable on June 1. Junior has been in a car accident, has missed a great deal of work, and consequently will not have the funds on June 1. Junior's father, Fred, offers to pay Iba $1,100 in four equal installments if Iba will discharge Junior from any further liability on the debt. Iba accepts. Is this transaction a novation or an accord and satisfaction? Explain. (See *Discharge by Agreement.*)

18–3. Impossibility of Performance. In the following situations, certain events take place after the contracts are formed. Discuss which of these contracts are discharged because the events render the contracts impossible to perform. (See *Discharge by Operation of Law.*)

(a) Jimenez, a famous singer, contracts to perform in your nightclub. He dies prior to performance.

(b) Raglione contracts to sell you her land. Just before title is to be transferred, she dies.

(c) Oppenheim contracts to sell you one thousand bushels of apples from her orchard in the state of Washington. Because of a severe frost, she is unable to deliver the apples.

(d) Maxwell contracts to lease a service station for ten years. His principal income is from the sale of gasoline. Because of an oil embargo by foreign oil-producing nations, gasoline is rationed, cutting sharply into Maxwell's gasoline sales. He cannot make his lease payments.

Business Case Problems

18–4. Business Case Problem with Sample Answer— Material Breach. The Northeast Independent School District

in Bexar County, Texas, hired STR Constructors, Ltd., to renovate a middle school. STR subcontracted the tile work in the school's kitchen to Newman Tile, Inc. (NTI). The project had already fallen behind schedule. As a result, STR allowed other workers to walk over and damage the newly installed tile before it had cured, forcing NTI to constantly redo its work. Despite NTI's requests for payment, STR remitted only half the amount due under their contract. When the school district refused to accept the kitchen, including the tile work, STR told NTI to quickly make repairs. A week later, STR terminated their contract. Did STR breach the contract with NTI? Explain. [*STR Constructors, Ltd. v. Newman Tile, Inc.,* 395 S.W.3d 383 (Tex.App.—El Paso 2013)] (See *Discharge by Performance.*)

• **For a sample answer to Problem 18–4, go to Appendix E at the end of this text.**

18–5. Conditions of Performance. Russ Wyant owned Humble Ranch in Perkins County, South Dakota. Edward Humble, whose parents had previously owned the ranch, was Wyant's uncle. Humble held a two-year option to buy the ranch. The option included specific conditions. Once it was exercised, the parties had thirty days to enter into a purchase agreement, and the seller could become the buyer's lender by matching the terms of the proposed financing. After the option was exercised, the parties engaged in lengthy negotiations. Humble did not respond to Wyant's proposed purchase agreement nor advise him of available financing terms before the option expired, however. Six months later, Humble filed a suit against Wyant to enforce the option. Is Humble entitled to specific performance? Explain. [*Humble v. Wyant,* 843 N.W.2d 334 (S.Dak. 2014)] (See *Conditions.*)

18–6. Discharge by Operation of Law. Dr. Jake Lambert signed an employment agreement with Baptist Health Services, Inc., to provide cardiothoracic surgery services to Baptist Memorial Hospital–North Mississippi, Inc., in Oxford, Mississippi. Complaints about Lambert's behavior arose almost immediately. He was evaluated by a team of doctors and psychologists, who diagnosed him as suffering from obsessive-compulsive personality disorder and concluded that he was unfit to practice medicine. Based on this conclusion, the hospital suspended his staff privileges. Citing the suspension, Baptist Health Services claimed that Lambert had breached his employment contract. What is Lambert's best defense to this claim? Explain. [*Baptist Memorial Hospital–North Mississippi, Inc. v. Lambert,* 157 So.3d 109 (Miss.App. 2015)] (See *Discharge by Operation of Law.*)

18–7. Conditions. H&J Ditching & Excavating, Inc., was hired by JRSF, LLC, to perform excavating and grading work on Terra Firma, a residential construction project in West Knox County, Tennessee. Cornerstone Community Bank financed the project with a loan to JRSF. As the work progressed, H&J received payments totaling 90 percent of the price on its contract. JRSF then defaulted on the loan from Cornerstone, and Cornerstone foreclosed and took possession of the property. H&J filed a suit in a Tennessee state court against the bank to recover the final payment on its contract. The bank responded that H&J had not received its payment because it had failed to obtain an engineer's certificate of final completion, a condition under its contract with JRSF. H&J responded that it had completed all the work it had contracted to do. What type of contract condition does obtaining the engineer's certificate represent? Is H&J entitled to the final payment? Discuss. [*H&J Ditching & Excavating, Inc. v. Cornerstone Community Bank,* __ S.W.3d __, 2016 WL 675554 (Tenn.App. 2016)] (See *Conditions.*)

18–8. A Question of Ethics—Conditions. *King County, Washington, hired Frank Coluccio Construction Co. (FCCC) to act as general contractor for a public works project involving the construction of a small utility tunnel under the Duwamish Waterway. FCCC hired Donald B. Murphy Contractors, Inc. (DBM), as a subcontractor. DBM was responsible for constructing an access shaft at the eastern end of the tunnel. Problems arose during construction, including a "blow-in" of the access shaft that caused it to fill with water, soil, and debris. FCCC and DBM incurred substantial expenses from the repairs and delays. Under the project contract, King County was supposed to buy an insurance policy to "insure against physical loss or damage by perils included under an 'All-Risk' Builder's Risk policy." Any claim under this policy was to be filed through the insured. King County, which had general property damage insurance, did not obtain an all-risk builder's risk policy. For the losses attributable to the blow-in, FCCC and DBM submitted builder's risk claims, which the county denied. FCCC filed a suit in a Washington state court against King County, alleging, among other claims, breach of contract. [Frank Coluccio Construction Co. v. King County, 136 Wash.App. 751, 150 P.3d 1147 (Div. 1 2007)]* (See *Conditions.*)

(a) King County's property damage policy specifically excluded, at the county's request, coverage of tunnels. The county drafted its contract with FCCC to require the all-risk builder's risk policy and authorize itself to "sponsor" claims. When FCCC and DBM filed their claims, the county secretly colluded with its property damage insurer to deny payment. What do these facts indicate about the county's ethics and legal liability in this situation?

(b) Could DBM, as a third party to the contract between King County and FCCC, maintain an action on the contract against King County? Discuss.

(c) All-risk insurance is a promise to pay on the "fortuitous" (accidental) happening of a loss or damage from any cause except those that are specifically excluded. Payment usually is not made on a loss that, at the time the insurance was obtained, the claimant subjectively knew would occur. If a loss results from faulty workmanship on the part of a contractor, should the obligation to pay under an all-risk policy be discharged? Explain.

18–9. Special Case Analysis—Material Breach. Go to Case Analysis 18.2, *Kohel v. Bergen Auto Enterprises, L.L.C.* Read the excerpt, and answer the following questions.

(a) Issue: This case involved allegations of breach of contract involving which parties and for what actions?

(b) Rule of Law: What is the difference between a *material* breach and a *minor* breach of contract?

(c) Applying the Rule of Law: How did the court determine which party was in material breach of the contract in this case?

(d) Conclusion: Was the defendant liable for breach? Why or why not?

Legal Reasoning Group Activity

18–10. Anticipatory Repudiation. ABC Clothiers, Inc., has a contract with Taylor & Sons, a retailer, to deliver one thousand summer suits to Taylor's place of business on or before May 1. On April 1, Taylor receives a letter from ABC informing him that ABC will not be able to make the delivery as scheduled. Taylor is very upset, as he had planned a big ad campaign. (See *Discharge by Performance.*)

(a) The first group will discuss whether Taylor can immediately sue ABC for breach of contract (on April 2).

(b) Now suppose that Taylor's son, Tom, tells his father that they cannot file a lawsuit until ABC actually fails to deliver the suits on May 1. The second group will decide who is correct, Taylor senior or Tom.

(c) Assume that Taylor & Sons can either file immediately or wait until ABC fails to deliver the goods. The third group will evaluate which course of action is better, given the circumstances.

CHAPTER 19

Breach of Contract and Remedies

When one party breaches a contract, the other party—the nonbreaching party—can choose one or more of several remedies. (Does changing terms of service on a social networking site constitute a breach of contract? See this chapter's *Digital Update* feature for a look at this issue.) A *remedy* is the relief provided for an innocent party when the other party has breached the contract. It is the means employed to enforce a right or to redress an injury.

The most common remedies available to a nonbreaching party include *damages*, *rescission* and *restitution*, *specific performance*, and *reformation*. Courts distinguish between *remedies at law* and *remedies in equity*. The remedy at law normally is monetary damages. Usually, a court will not award equitable remedies—such as rescission and restitution, specific performance, and reformation—unless the remedy at law is inadequate.

19-1 Damages

A breach of contract entitles the nonbreaching party to sue for monetary damages. In contract law, damages compensate the nonbreaching party for the loss of the bargain (whereas tort law damages compensate for harm suffered as a result of another's wrongful act). Often, courts say that innocent parties are to be placed in the position they would have occupied had the contract been fully performed.[1]

Realize at the outset, though, that collecting damages through a court judgment requires litigation, which can be expensive and time consuming. Also keep in mind that court judgments are often difficult to enforce, particularly if the breaching party does not have sufficient assets to pay the damages awarded. For these reasons, most parties settle their lawsuits for damages (or other remedies) prior to trial.

19-1a Types of Damages

There are four broad categories of damages:

1. Compensatory (to cover direct losses and costs).
2. Consequential (to cover indirect and foreseeable losses).
3. Punitive (to punish and deter wrongdoing).
4. Nominal (to recognize wrongdoing when no monetary loss is shown).

Compensatory and punitive damages were discussed in the context of tort law. Here, we look at these types of damages, as well as consequential and nominal damages, in the context of contract law.

Compensatory Damages Damages that compensate the nonbreaching party for the *loss of the bargain* are known as *compensatory damages*. These damages compensate the injured party only for damages actually sustained and proved to have arisen directly from the loss of the bargain caused by the breach of contract. They simply replace what was lost because of the wrong or damage and, for this reason, are often said to "make the person whole."

■ **CASE IN POINT 19.1** Janet Murley was the vice president of marketing at Hallmark Cards, Inc., until Hallmark eliminated her position as part of a corporate restructuring. Murley and Hallmark entered into a separation agreement under which she agreed not to work in the greeting card industry for eighteen months and not to disclose or use any of Hallmark's confidential information. In exchange, Hallmark gave Murley a $735,000 severance payment.

---

1. *Restatement (Second) of Contracts*, Section 347.

When Do Changes in Social Media Terms of Service Constitute a Breach of Contract?

Hundreds of millions of individuals use some form of social media. To do so, they must agree to certain terms of service.

The Terms of Service Are a Contract

When you use social media or other services on the Internet or download an app for a mobile device, you normally have to indicate that you accept the terms of service associated with that service or app. Of course, users rarely, if ever, actually read those terms. They simply click on "accept" and start using the service. By clicking on "accept," however, those users are entering into a contract.

Instagram Changes Its Terms of Service

A few years ago, Instagram changed its terms of service to give it the right to transfer and otherwise use content placed on the site by users. The new terms appeared to allow Instagram to do this without compensating users. The terms also limited users' ability to bring class-action lawsuits against Instagram, limited the damages they could recover to $100, and required arbitration of any disputes.

Lucy Funes, an Instagram user in California, filed a class-action lawsuit against Instagram on behalf of herself and other users.[a] The suit claimed breach of contract and breach of the covenant of good faith and fair dealing that a contract implies. Instagram subsequently modified the language that appeared to give it the right to use photos without compensation. It retained other controversial terms, however, including the mandatory arbitration clause and a provision allowing it to place ads in conjunction with user content.

Instagram Seeks Dismissal of the Lawsuit

Funes contended that Instagram had breached their contract by changing its terms of service. Instagram argued that Funes could not claim breach of contract. The reason was that she—and other users—had been given thirty days' notice before the new terms of service took effect. Because Funes continued to use her account after that thirty-day period, Instagram maintained, in effect, she agreed to the new terms.

Instagram Changes Its Policies

Instagram continues to use its revised terms of service agreement. As mentioned, it abandoned some of its previous changes and denied any intention to sell user content. In the terms of service, Instagram states that it does "not claim ownership of any content user's post on or through the service."

Nonetheless, the terms state clearly that each user "hereby grants to Instagram a non-exclusive, fully paid and royalty-free, transferable, sublicensable, worldwide license to use content that the user posts." That means that Instagram can reassign the rights or relicense the work to any other party for free or for a fee. The user—anyone who posts on Instagram—need not be compensated or even given notice.

Critical Thinking *Within Instagram's current terms of service is the following statement: "we may not always identify paid services, sponsored content, or commercial communications as such." Is it ethical for Instagram to post advertisements without identifying them as advertisements? Discuss.*

a. *Funes v. Instagram, Inc.*, 3:12-CV06482-WHA (N.D.Cal. 2012). See also *Rodriguez v. Instagram, LLC*, 2013 WL 3732883 (N.D.Cal. 2013).

After eighteen months, Murley took a job with Recycled Paper Greetings (RPG) for $125,000 and disclosed confidential Hallmark information to RPG. Hallmark sued for breach of contract and won. The jury awarded $860,000 in damages (the $735,000 severance payment and $125,000 that Murley received from RPG). Murley appealed. The appellate court held that Hallmark was entitled only to the return of the $735,000 severance payment. Hallmark was not entitled to the other $125,000

because that additional award would have left Hallmark better off than if Murley had not breached the contract.[2] ■

There is a two-step process to determine whether a breach of contract has resulted in compensable damages. First, it must be established that there was a contract between the parties and a breach of that contract. Next, it must be proved that the breach caused damages. The following case concerned the second step of this process.

2. *Hallmark Cards, Inc. v. Murley*, 703 F.3d 456 (8th Cir. 2013).

Baird v. Owens Community College

Court of Appeals of Ohio, Tenth District, Franklin County, __ N.E.2d __, 2016-Ohio-537 (2016).

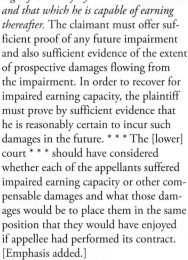

In the Language of the Court

BRUNNER, J. [Judge]

* * * *

[Carrianne Baird and the other sixty-one] plaintiffs-appellants * * * are former students in the registered nursing program of defendant-appellee, Owens Community College. The college lost its accreditation from the National League for Nursing Accreditation Commission ("NLNAC") in 2009.[a] The program remains approved by the Ohio Board of Nursing, which permits successful graduates to take the National Council Licensure Examination ("NCLEX") for their nursing license. Although the college received notice via a letter dated July 27, 2009 that the accreditation had been denied, it did not formally notify its students until it issued a letter on September 26, 2009, after classes for the fall semester already had begun. The appellants sued [in an Ohio state court] for breach of contract.

* * * The court [did not determine whether there was a contract between the college and the students or whether such a contract was breached by the loss of accreditation, but only] concluded that the loss of accreditation did not affect the students' ability to take the state licensing examination, and therefore that appellants suffered no actual damages from the alleged breach of contract. [The court issued a summary judgment in favor of the college.]

* * * *

On appeal from the summary judgment against them, appellants [contend that] the trial court erred when it granted the Motion for Summary Judgment of the Defendant-Appellee because the evidence creates a genuine issue of material fact as to whether Appellee's breach of the contract caused damages.

* * * *

a. In 2013, the NLNAC changed its name and is now known as the Accreditation Commission for Education in Nursing.

After the appellee lost its NLNAC accreditation graduates feared that they would face barriers to licensing, employment or further education in their field. Some programs, including The Ohio State University RN [registered nursing] to BSN [bachelor of science in nursing] option, would accept only nurses who received an associate's degree or diploma in nursing from an institution with NLNAC accreditation. In support of their allegations of damages, appellants submitted the * * * testimony of various "sample plaintiffs." * * * Carianne Baird stated that she could not attend the University of Toledo's RN to MSN [master of science in nursing] program without submitting a "portfolio" that would not have been required if appellee had maintained its accreditation. Other institutions would not accept her for continuing nursing education because her associate's degree is not from an NLNAC accredited institution.

Kelsey Darbyshire testified * * * that Lima Memorial Hospital required applicants to have graduated from an accredited nursing school. She indicated on her application that she did not graduate from an accredited program, and had no response. Miracle Huffman * * * applied to the U.S. Department of Veterans Affairs for psychiatric nurse practitioner positions and has received no response. She testified that the Veterans Affairs requires an NLNAC accredited degree, and she does not have it.

* * * *

* * * None of the appellants submitted sufficient evidence of economic damages based on their rejection from specific employment or a higher degree program. *However, a claimant's inability to demonstrate a specific denial of employment due to the program's loss of accreditation does not defeat damages on account of lost earning capacity * * *. The measure of damages for impairment of earning capacity is the difference between the amount*

which the plaintiff was capable of earning before his injury and that which he is capable of earning thereafter. The claimant must offer sufficient proof of any future impairment and also sufficient evidence of the extent of prospective damages flowing from the impairment. In order to recover for impaired earning capacity, the plaintiff must prove by sufficient evidence that he is reasonably certain to incur such damages in the future. * * * The [lower] court * * * should have considered whether each of the appellants suffered impaired earning capacity or other compensable damages and what those damages would be to place them in the same position that they would have enjoyed if appellee had performed its contract. [Emphasis added.]

Since there exists a genuine issue of material fact concerning damages, the [lower] court * * * must also determine, in addition to whether any appellant can prove diminished earning capacity, whether any appellant produced sufficient evidence that appellee breached its contract with her or him.

When a student enrolls in a college or university, pays his or her tuition and fees, and attends such school, the resulting relationship may reasonably be construed as being contractual in nature. The terms of such a contract may be found in the college or university catalog, handbook, and/or other guidelines supplied to the students.

On the first page of the registered nursing section of the course book appellee provided to students, appellee listed its NLNAC accreditation foremost, and according to appellants, providing an NLNAC accredited education was part and parcel of appellee's "deal" with each of them. By contrast, appellee urges that a text box in another part of the course book contains a disclaimer for changes in circumstance, stating that it "reserves the

Case 19.1 Continued

right to modify rules, policies, fees, program requirements, course scheduling and courses offered during any specific semester, and any other matter, without notice."

Appellee submits that summary judgment should be affirmed on the * * * basis that this language effectively excludes the loss of NLNAC accreditation from the contractual relationship

between it and its students. Without more evidence, or a more explicit disclaimer, we find that genuine issues remain to preclude summary judgment.

* * * *

* * * We remand this matter to the [lower] court * * * to ascertain as to each of the appellants whether the appellant has offered sufficient evidence to avoid

summary judgment on whether appellee has breached its contract to her or him in losing its NLNAC accreditation, and if such a breach is determined from the evidence, whether she or he has set forth sufficient evidence to create a material issue of fact in support of a claim for diminished earning capacity.

Legal Reasoning Questions

1. In this case, what was the basis for the students' suit?

2. What was the college's argument against the students' allegations?

3. In whose favor did the court rule? Why? What remains to be determined?

Standard Measure. The standard measure of compensatory damages is the difference between the value of the breaching party's promised performance under the contract and the value of her or his actual performance. This amount is reduced by any loss that the injured party has avoided.

■ **EXAMPLE 19.2** Randall contracts to perform certain services exclusively for Hernandez during the month of March for $4,000. Hernandez cancels the contract and is in breach. Randall is able to find another job during March but can earn only $3,000. He can sue Hernandez for breach and recover $1,000 as compensatory damages. Randall can also recover from Hernandez the amount that he spent to find the other job. ■ Expenses that are caused directly by a breach of contract—such as those incurred to obtain performance from another source—are known as **incidental damages.**

Note that the measure of compensatory damages often varies by type of contract. Certain types of contracts deserve special mention.

Sale of Goods. In a contract for the sale of goods, the usual measure of compensatory damages is an amount equal to the difference between the contract price and the market price.[3] ■ **EXAMPLE 19.3** Medik Laboratories contracts to buy ten model UTS network servers from Cal Industries for $4,000 each. Cal Industries, however, fails to deliver the ten servers to Medik. The market price of the servers at the time Medik learns of the breach is

$4,500. Therefore, Medik's measure of damages is $5,000 (10 × $500), plus any incidental damages (expenses) caused by the breach. ■

Sometimes, the buyer breaches when the seller has not yet produced the goods. In that situation, compensatory damages normally equal lost profits on the sale, not the difference between the contract price and the market price.

Sale of Land. Ordinarily, because each parcel of land is unique, the remedy for a seller's breach of a contract for a sale of real estate is specific performance. That is, the buyer is awarded the parcel of property for which she or he bargained. (*Specific performance* will be discussed more fully later in this chapter.) The majority of states follow this rule.

When the *buyer* is the party in breach, the measure of damages is typically the difference between the contract price and the market price of the land. The same measure is used when specific performance is not available (because the seller has sold the property to someone else, for example).

A minority of states apply a different rule when the seller breaches the contract and the breach is not deliberate (intentional).[4] These states limit the prospective buyer's damages to a refund of any down payment made plus any expenses incurred (such as fees for title searches, attorneys, and escrows). Thus, the minority rule

---

3. More specifically, the amount is the difference between the contract price and the market price at the time and place at which the goods were to be delivered or tendered. See Sections 2–708 and 2–713 of the Uniform Commercial Code (UCC).

4. "Deliberate" breaches include the seller's failure to convey (transfer title to) the land because the market price has gone up. "Nondeliberate" breaches include the seller's failure to convey the land because of a problem with the title. For instance, the discovery of an unknown easement that gives another party a right of use over the property would be a problem with the title.

effectively returns purchasers to the positions they occupied prior to the sale, rather than giving them the benefit of the bargain.

Construction Contracts. The measure of damages in a building or construction contract varies depending on which party breaches and when the breach occurs.

1. *Breach by owner.* The owner may breach at three different stages—before, during, or after performance. If the owner breaches *before performance has begun,* the contractor can recover only the profits that would have been made on the contract. (Profits equal the total contract price less the cost of materials and labor.) If the owner breaches *during performance,* the contractor can recover the profits plus the costs incurred in partially constructing the building. If the owner breaches *after the construction has been completed,* the contractor can recover the entire contract price, plus interest.

2. *Breach by contractor.* When the construction contractor breaches the contract—either by failing to begin construction or by stopping work partway through the project—the measure of damages is the cost of completion. The cost of completion includes reasonable compensation for any delay in performance. If the contractor finishes late, the measure of damages is the loss of use.

3. *Breach by both owner and contractor.* When the performance of both parties—the construction contractor and the owner—falls short of what their contract required, the courts attempt to strike a fair balance in awarding damages.

■ **CASE IN POINT 19.4** Jamison Well Drilling, Inc., contracted to drill a well for Ed Pfeifer for $4,130. Jamison drilled the well and installed a storage tank. The well did not comply with state health department requirements, however, and failed repeated tests for bacteria. The health department ordered the well to be abandoned and sealed. Pfeifer used the storage tank but paid Jamison nothing. Jamison filed a suit to recover. The court held that Jamison was entitled to $970 for the storage tank but was not entitled to the full contract price because the well was not usable.[5] ■

The rules concerning the measurement of damages in breached construction contracts are summarized in Exhibit 19–1.

Consequential Damages Foreseeable damages that result from a party's breach of contract are called **consequential damages,** or *special damages.* They differ from compensatory damages in that they are caused by special circumstances beyond the contract itself. They flow from

---

5. *Jamison Well Drilling, Inc. v. Pfeifer,* 2011 Ohio 521 (2011).

EXHIBIT 19–1   Measurement of Damages—Breach of Construction Contracts

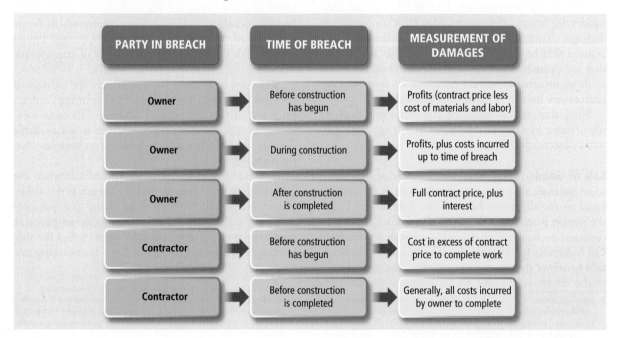

PARTY IN BREACH	TIME OF BREACH	MEASUREMENT OF DAMAGES
Owner	Before construction has begun	Profits (contract price less cost of materials and labor)
Owner	During construction	Profits, plus costs incurred up to time of breach
Owner	After construction is completed	Full contract price, plus interest
Contractor	Before construction has begun	Cost in excess of contract price to complete work
Contractor	Before construction is completed	Generally, all costs incurred by owner to complete

the consequences, or results, of a breach. When a seller fails to deliver goods, knowing that the buyer is planning to use or resell those goods immediately, a court may award consequential damages for the loss of profits from the planned resale.

■ **EXAMPLE 19.5** Marty contracts to buy a certain quantity of Quench, a specialty sports drink, from Nathan. Nathan knows that Marty has contracted with Ruthie to resell and ship the Quench within hours of its receipt. The beverage will then be sold to fans attending the Super Bowl. Nathan fails to deliver the Quench on time. Marty can recover the consequential damages—the loss of profits from the planned resale to Ruthie—caused by the nondelivery. (If Marty purchases Quench from another vender, he can also recover compensatory damages for any difference between the contract price and the market price.) ■

For the nonbreaching party to recover consequential damages, the breaching party must have known (or had reason to know) that special circumstances would cause the nonbreaching party to suffer an additional loss.[6]

Punitive Damages Punitive damages are very seldom awarded in lawsuits for breach of contract. Because punitive damages are designed to punish a wrongdoer and set an example to deter similar conduct in the future, they have no legitimate place in contract law. A contract is simply a civil relationship between the parties. The law may compensate one party for the loss of the bargain—no more and no less. When a person's actions cause both a breach of contract and a tort (such as fraud), however, punitive damages may be available.

Nominal Damages When no actual damage or financial loss results from a breach of contract and only a technical injury is involved, the court may award **nominal damages** to the innocent party. Awards of nominal damages are often small, such as one dollar, but they do establish that the defendant acted wrongfully. Most lawsuits for nominal damages are brought as a matter of principle under the theory that a breach has occurred and some damages must be imposed regardless of actual loss.

■ **EXAMPLE 19.6** Jackson contracts to buy potatoes from Stanley at fifty cents a pound. Stanley breaches the contract and does not deliver the potatoes. In the meantime, the price of potatoes has fallen. Jackson is able to buy them in the open market at half the price he con-

tracted for with Stanley. He is clearly better off because of Stanley's breach. Thus, because Jackson sustained only a technical injury and suffered no monetary loss, he is likely to be awarded only nominal damages if he brings a suit for breach of contract. ■

19–1b Mitigation of Damages

In most situations, when a breach of contract occurs, the innocent injured party is held to a duty to mitigate, or reduce, the damages that he or she suffers. Under this doctrine of **mitigation of damages,** the duty owed depends on the nature of the contract.

Rental Agreements Some states require a landlord to use reasonable means to find a new tenant if a tenant abandons the premises and fails to pay rent. If an acceptable tenant is found, the landlord is required to lease the premises to this tenant to mitigate the damages recoverable from the former tenant.

The former tenant is still liable for the difference between the amount of the rent under the original lease and the rent received from the new tenant. If the landlord has not taken reasonable steps to find a new tenant, a court will likely reduce any award made by the amount of rent the landlord could have received had he or she done so.

Employment Contracts In the majority of states, a person whose employment has been wrongfully terminated owes a duty to mitigate the damages that he or she suffered. In other words, a wrongfully terminated employee has a duty to take a similar job if one is available.

If the employee fails to mitigate, the damages awarded will be equivalent to the person's former salary less the income he or she would have received in a similar job obtained by reasonable means. The employer has the burden of proving that such a job existed and that the employee could have been hired. Normally, the employee is under no duty to take a job of a different type and rank.

19–1c Liquidated Damages versus Penalties

A **liquidated damages** provision in a contract specifies that a certain dollar amount is to be paid in the event of a *future* default or breach of contract. (*Liquidated* means determined, settled, or fixed.)

Liquidated damages differ from penalties. Like liquidated damages, a **penalty** specifies a certain amount

---

6. This rule was first enunciated in *Hadley v. Baxendale,* 156 Eng.Rep. 145 (1854).

to be paid in the event of a default or breach of contract. Unlike liquidated damages, it is designed to penalize the breaching party, not to make the innocent party whole.

Liquidated damages provisions usually are enforceable. In contrast, if a court finds that a provision calls for a penalty, the agreement as to the amount will not be enforced. Recovery will be limited to actual damages.

Enforceability To determine if a particular provision is for liquidated damages or for a penalty, a court must answer two questions:

1. When the contract was entered into, was it apparent that damages would be difficult to estimate in the event of a breach?
2. Was the amount set as damages a reasonable estimate and not excessive?[7]

If the answers to both questions are yes, the provision normally will be enforced. If either answer is no, the provision usually will not be enforced.

In the following *Spotlight Case,* the court had to decide whether a clause in a contract was an enforceable liquidated damages provision or an unenforceable penalty.

---

7. *Restatement (Second) of Contracts,* Section 356(1).

Spotlight on Liquidated Damages

Case 19.2 Kent State University v. Ford
Court of Appeals of Ohio, Eleventh District, Portage County, 26 N.E.3d 868, 2015-Ohio-41 (2015).

Background and Facts Gene Ford signed a five-year contract with Kent State University in Ohio to work as the head coach for the men's basketball team. The contract provided that if Ford quit before the end of the term, he would pay liquidated damages to the school. The amount was to equal his salary ($300,000) multiplied by the number of years remaining on the contract. Laing Kennedy, Kent State's athletic director, told Ford that the contract would be renegotiated within a few years. Four years before the contract expired, however, Ford left Kent State and began to coach for Bradley University at an annual salary of $700,000. Kent State filed a suit in an Ohio state court against Ford, alleging breach of contract. The court enforced the liquidated damages clause and awarded the university $1.2 million. Ford appealed, arguing that the liquidated damages clause in his employment contract was an unenforceable penalty.

In the Language of the Court
Diane V. GRENDELL, J. [Judge]

* * * *

* * * The parties agreed on an amount of damages, stated in clear terms in Ford's * * * employment contract. * * * *It is apparent that such damages were difficult, if not impossible, to determine.* * * * The departure of a university's head basketball coach may result in a decrease in ticket sales, impact the ability to successfully recruit players and community support for the team, and require a search for both a new coach and additional coaching staff. Many of these damages cannot be easily measured or proven. This is especially true given the nature of how such factors may change over the course of different coaches' tenures with a sports program or team. [Emphasis added.]

* * * *

* * * Kennedy's statements to Ford that the contract would be renegotiated within a few years made it clear that Kent State desired Ford to have long-term employment, which was necessary to establish the stability in the program that would benefit recruitment, retention of assistant coaching staff, and community participation and involvement. The breach of the contract impacted all of these areas.

* * * *

Regarding the alleged unreasonableness of the damages, * * * based on the record, we find that the damages were reasonable. * * * Finding a coach of a similar skill and experience level as Ford, which was gained based partially on the investment of Kent State in his development, would have an increased cost. This is evident from the fact that Ford was able to more than double his yearly salary when hired

Case 19.2 Continued

by Bradley University. The salary Ford earned at Bradley shows the loss of market value in coaching experienced by Kent State, $400,000 per year, for four years. Although this may not have been known at the time the contract was executed, it could have been anticipated, and was presumably why Kent State wanted to renegotiate the contract * * * . There was also an asserted decrease in ticket sales, costs associated with the trips for the coaching search, and additional potential sums that may be expended. * * * *

As discussed extensively above, there was justification for seeking liquidated damages to compensate for Kent State's losses, and, thus, there was a valid compensatory purpose for including the clause. * * * Given all of the circumstances and facts in this case, and the consideration of the factors above, we cannot find that the liquidated damages clause was a penalty. [Emphasis added.]

Decision and Remedy *A state intermediate appellate court affirmed the lower court's award. At the time Ford's contract was entered into, ascertaining the damages resulting from a breach was "difficult, if not impossible." The court found, "based on the record, . . . that the damages were reasonable." Thus, the clause was not a penalty—it had "a valid compensatory purpose."*

Critical Thinking

- **Cultural** *How does a college basketball team's record of wins and losses, and its ranking in its conference, support the court's decision in this case?*

Liquidated Damages Common in Certain Contracts Liquidated damages provisions are frequently used in construction contracts. For instance, a provision requiring a construction contractor to pay $300 for every day he or she is late in completing the project is a liquidated damages provision. Such provisions are also common in contracts for the sale of goods.[8] In addition, contracts with entertainers and professional athletes often include liquidated damages provisions.

■ **EXAMPLE 19.7** Johnny Chavis, formerly the defensive coordinator for the Louisiana State University (LSU) football team, had a liquidated damages provision in his employment contract with LSU. The clause stated that if he quit with less than eleven months remaining on his contract term, he would owe no damages. If he left with more than eleven months remaining, he would owe LSU $400,000 in liquidated damages. When Chavis and LSU could not agree on terms to renew their contract, which was set to expire at the end of 2015, Chavis gave his thirty-day notice. He then took a position at Texas A&M. Chavis gave notice on January 5, 2015, which meant his employment would officially end on February 4, with less than eleven months left on his contract term. LSU demanded that he pay the $400,000 damages, however, because he had allegedly started recruiting for Texas A&M before February 1. Chavis claimed that he owed LSU nothing, but the dispute has not yet been resolved. ■

19–2 Equitable Remedies

Sometimes, damages are an inadequate remedy for a breach of contract. In these situations, the nonbreaching party may ask the court for an equitable remedy. Equitable remedies include rescission and restitution, specific performance, and reformation.

19–2a Rescission and Restitution

Rescission is essentially an action to undo, or terminate, a contract—to return the contracting parties to the positions they occupied prior to the transaction.[9] When fraud, a mistake, duress, undue influence, misrepresentation, or lack of capacity to contract is present, unilateral rescission is available. Rescission may also be available by statute.[10] The failure of one party to perform entitles the other party to rescind the contract. The rescinding party must give prompt notice to the breaching party.

Restitution Generally, to rescind a contract, both parties must make **restitution** to each other by returning

---

8. Section 2–718(1) of the UCC specifically authorizes the use of liquidated damages provisions.

9. The rescission discussed here is unilateral rescission, in which only one party wants to undo the contract. In mutual rescission, both parties agree to undo the contract. Mutual rescission discharges the contract. Unilateral rescission generally is available as a remedy for breach of contract.

10. Many states have statutes allowing individuals who enter "home solicitation contracts" to rescind those contracts within three business days for any reason. See, for example, California Civil Code Section 1689.5.

goods, property, or funds previously conveyed.[11] If the property or goods can be returned, they must be. If the goods or property have been consumed, restitution must be made in an equivalent dollar amount.

Essentially, restitution involves the plaintiff's recapture of a benefit conferred on the defendant that has unjustly enriched her or him. ■ **EXAMPLE 19.8** Katie contracts with Mikhail to design a house for her. Katie pays Mikhail $9,000 and agrees to make two more payments of $9,000 (for a total of $27,000) as the design progresses. The next day, Mikhail calls Katie and tells her that he has taken a position with a large architectural firm in another state and cannot design the house. Katie decides to hire another architect that afternoon. Katie can obtain restitution of the $9,000. ■

---

11. *Restatement (Second) of Contracts*, Section 370.

Restitution Is Not Limited to Rescission Cases

Restitution may be appropriate when a contract is rescinded, but the right to restitution is not limited to rescission cases. Because an award of restitution basically returns something to its rightful owner, a party can seek restitution in actions for breach of contract, tort actions, and other types of actions.

Restitution can be obtained, for instance, when funds or property have been transferred by mistake or because of fraud or incapacity. Similarly, restitution may be available when there has been misconduct by a party in a confidential or other special relationship. Even in criminal cases, a court can order restitution of funds or property obtained through embezzlement, conversion, theft, or copyright infringement.

As mentioned, one of the bases that a court may use to order the rescission of a contract is fraud. That was the ground for the order of rescission in the following case.

Case 19.3

Clara Wonjung Lee, DDS, Ltd. v. Robles

Appellate Court of Illinois, First District, 2014 WL 976776 (2014).

Background and Facts   Clara Lee agreed to buy Rosalina Robles's dental practice and to lease her dental offices in Chicago, Illinois. The price was $267,000, with $133,500 allocated to goodwill—that is, the market value of the business's good reputation. After Lee took over the practice, *Chicago Magazine* and other local media revealed that Gary Kimmel, one of Robles's dentists, had illegally treated underage prostitutes in the practice's offices after hours. The media reported that Kimmel was under investigation by federal officials for this and other activities.

Lee filed a suit in an Illinois state court against Robles, seeking to rescind the contract. Lee alleged that Robles had deliberately withheld the information about Kimmel and that this information "adversely impacted the desirability and economic value of the practice." The court ruled in Lee's favor and awarded rescission and damages, which included the purchase price less Lee's unpaid rent and a portion of her income during her ownership of the practice. Robles appealed.

In the Language of the Court

Justice *LIU* delivered the judgment of the court:

* * * *

Section 6 of the Purchase Agreement required that Dr. Robles, as "seller, shall disclose to Dr. Lee, any material or significant information and/or charges that have occurred in the practice, (including but not limited to any pending litigation, actions, threatened actions by the Illinois State Board of Dental Examiners, or from any other governmental agency that materially alter the desirability or economic potential of the assets) up to the time of the date of transfer." *The question then was whether Dr. Robles had a duty to disclose the information she had about Dr. Kimmel's activities and the federal investigation to Dr. Lee.* Defendants offered no evidence to rebut the testimony of both Dr. Lee and [Bruce Lowery, a business appraiser], who indicated that such information would have been material to a reasonable dentist's decision to purchase the practice. Based on such evidence, we agree with the trial court's holding that information about Dr. Kimmel's activities and his association with the practice was material to Dr. Lee's decision to acquire the practice and to enter into the loan, and that Dr. Robles had a duty to disclose it to Dr. Lee under section 6 of the Purchase Agreement. [Emphasis added.]

Case 19.3 Continued

*** Defendants' actions were purposeful and not the result of any mistake or accident. Dr. Robles' nondisclosure was designed to prevent plaintiffs from gaining relevant information that may have caused them to not proceed with the sale transaction.

*** Here, the trial judge had the opportunity to assess the credibility of the witnesses and to weigh the evidence presented at trial. In doing so, he concluded that Dr. Robles had knowledge of the investigations involving Dr. Kimmel's illicit use of the dental practice and that she deliberately withheld the information from Dr. Lee. Despite evidence that she had been interviewed by the FBI and by *Chicago Magazine* about Dr. Kimmel's activities, Dr. Robles testified that she was unaware of the nature of such activities. The *** court characterized Dr. Robles' testimony as "incredible." We hold that no opposite conclusion is clearly evident from the record.

Accordingly, we find that the *** court's judgment was consistent with the manifest weight of the evidence presented at trial.

Decision and Remedy *A state intermediate court affirmed the lower court's award of rescission and damages. Robles's nondisclosure was "designed to prevent Lee from gaining relevant information" that "would have been material to a reasonable dentist's decision to purchase the practice."*

Critical Thinking

- **Legal Environment** *When rescission is awarded, what is the measure of recovery? What did the recovery include in this case?*

19–2b Specific Performance

The equitable remedy of **specific performance** calls for the performance of the act promised in the contract. This remedy is attractive to a nonbreaching party because it provides the exact bargain promised in the contract. It also avoids some of the problems inherent in a suit for damages, such as collecting a judgment and arranging another contract. In addition, the actual performance may be more valuable than the monetary damages.

Normally, however, specific performance will not be granted unless the party's legal remedy (monetary damages) is inadequate.[12] For this reason, contracts for the sale of goods rarely qualify for specific performance. The legal remedy—monetary damages—is ordinarily adequate in such situations because substantially identical goods can be bought or sold in the market. Only if the goods are unique will a court grant specific performance. For instance, paintings, sculptures, or rare books or coins are so unique that monetary damages will not enable a buyer to obtain substantially identical substitutes in the market.

Sale of Land A court may grant specific performance to a buyer in an action for a breach of contract involving the sale of land. In this situation, the legal remedy of monetary damages may not compensate the buyer adequately. After all, every parcel of land is unique: the same

land in the same location obviously cannot be obtained elsewhere. Only when specific performance is unavailable (such as when the seller has sold the property to someone else) will monetary damages be awarded instead.

A seller of land can also seek specific performance of the contract. ■ **CASE IN POINT 19.9** Developer Charles Ghidorzi formed Crabtree Ridge, LLC, for the sole purpose of purchasing twenty-three acres of vacant land from Cohan Lipp, LLC. Crabtree signed a contract agreeing to pay $3.1 million for the land, which would be developed and paid for in three phases. When an environmental survey showed that the land might contain some wetlands that could not be developed, Crabtree backed out of the deal. Lipp sued Crabtree for breach of contract, seeking specific performance. The court held that Lipp was entitled to specific performance of the land-sale contract.[13] ■

Contracts for Personal Services Contracts for personal services require one party to work personally for another party. Courts generally refuse to grant specific performance of personal-service contracts. One reason is that to order a party to perform personal services against his or her will amounts to a type of involuntary servitude.[14]

---

12. *Restatement (Second) of Contracts*, Section 359.

13. *Cohan Lipp, LLC v. Crabtree Ridge, LLC*, 358 Wis.2d 711, 856 N.W.2d 346 (2014).

14. Involuntary servitude, or slavery, is contrary to the public policy expressed in the Thirteenth Amendment to the U.S. Constitution. A court can, however, enter an order (injunction) prohibiting a person who breached a personal-service contract from engaging in similar contracts for a period of time in the future.

Moreover, the courts do not want to monitor contracts for personal services, which usually require the exercise of personal judgment or talent. ■ **EXAMPLE 19.10** Nicole contracts with a surgeon to perform surgery to remove a tumor on her brain. If he refuses, the court would not compel (nor would Nicole want) the surgeon to perform under those circumstances. A court cannot ensure meaningful performance in such a situation.[15] ■

19–2c Reformation

Reformation is an equitable remedy used when the parties have *imperfectly* expressed their agreement in writing. Reformation allows a court to rewrite the contract to reflect the parties' true intentions.

Exhibit 19–2 graphically summarizes the remedies, including reformation, that are available to the nonbreaching party.

Fraud or Mutual Mistake Is Present Courts order reformation most often when fraud or mutual mistake (for example, a clerical error) is present. Typically, a party seeks reformation so that some other remedy may then be pursued.

■ **EXAMPLE 19.11** If Carson contracts to buy a forklift from Yoshie but their contract mistakenly refers to a crane, a mutual mistake has occurred. Accordingly, a court can reform the contract so that it conforms to the parties' intentions and accurately refers to the forklift being sold. ■

---

15. Similarly, courts often refuse to order specific performance of construction contracts because courts are not set up to operate as construction supervisors or engineers.

Written Contract Incorrectly States the Parties' Oral Agreement A court will also reform a contract when two parties enter into a binding oral contract but later make an error when they attempt to put the terms into writing. Normally, a court will allow into evidence the correct terms of the oral contract, thereby reforming the written contract.

Covenants Not to Compete Courts also may reform contracts that contain a written covenant not to compete. Such covenants are often included in contracts for the sale of ongoing businesses and in employment contracts. The agreements restrict the area and time in which one party can directly compete with the other party.

A covenant not to compete may be for a valid and legitimate purpose, but may impose unreasonable area or time restraints. In such instances, some courts will reform the restraints by making them reasonable and will then enforce the entire contract as reformed. Other courts will throw out the entire restrictive covenant as illegal. Thus, when businesspersons create restrictive covenants, they must make sure that the restrictions imposed are reasonable.

■ **CASE IN POINT 19.12** Cardiac Study Center, Inc., a medical practice group, hired Dr. Robert Emerick. Later, Emerick became a shareholder of Cardiac and signed an agreement that included a covenant not to compete. The covenant stated that a physician who left the group promised not to practice competitively in the surrounding area for a period of five years.

After Cardiac began receiving complaints from patients and other physicians about Emerick, it terminated his employment. Emerick sued Cardiac, claiming

EXHIBIT 19–2 Remedies for Breach of Contract

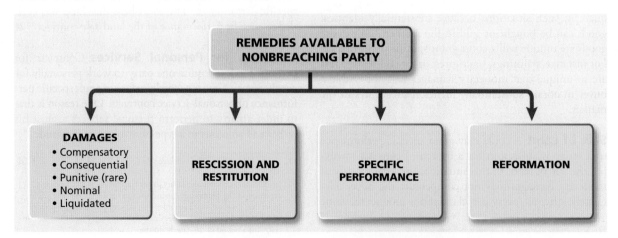

that the covenant not to compete that he had signed was unreasonable and should be declared illegal. Ultimately, a state appellate court held that the covenant was both reasonable and enforceable. Cardiac had a legitimate interest in protecting its existing client base and prohibiting Emerick from taking its clients.[16] ■

19–3 Recovery Based on Quasi Contract

In some situations, when no actual contract exists, a court may step in to prevent one party from being unjustly enriched at the expense of another party. Quasi contract is a legal theory under which an obligation is imposed in the absence of an agreement.

The legal obligation arises because the law considers that the party accepting the benefits has made an implied promise to pay for them. Generally, when one party has conferred a benefit on another party, justice requires that the party receiving the benefit pay the reasonable value for it. The party conferring the benefit can recover in *quantum meruit,*[17] which means "as much as he or she deserves."

19–3a When Quasi Contract Is Used

Quasi contract allows a court to act as if a contract exists when there is no actual contract or agreement between the parties. Therefore, if the parties have entered into a contract concerning the matter in controversy, a court normally will not impose a quasi contract. A court can also use this theory when the parties entered into a contract, but it is unenforceable for some reason.

Quasi-contractual recovery is often granted when one party has partially performed under a contract that is unenforceable. It provides an alternative to suing for damages and allows the party to recover the reasonable value of the partial performance. Depending on the case, the amount of the recovery may be measured either by the benefit received or by the detriment suffered.

■ **EXAMPLE 19.13** Ericson contracts to build two oil derricks for Petro Industries. The derricks are to be built over a period of three years, but the parties do not make a written contract. Thus, the writing requirement will bar enforcement of the contract.[18] After Ericson completes one derrick, Petro Industries informs him that it will not pay for the derrick. Ericson can sue Petro Industries under the theory of quasi contract. ■

19–3b The Requirements of Quasi Contract

To recover under the theory of quasi contract, the party seeking recovery must show the following:

1. The party has conferred a benefit on the other party.
2. The party conferred the benefit with the reasonable expectation of being paid.
3. The party did not act as a volunteer in conferring the benefit.
4. The party receiving the benefit would be unjustly enriched if allowed to retain the benefit without paying for it.

Applying these requirements to *Example 19.13*, Ericson can sue in quasi contract because all of the conditions for quasi-contractual recovery have been fulfilled. Ericson conferred a benefit on Petro Industries by building the oil derrick. Ericson built the derrick with the reasonable expectation of being paid. He was not intending to act as a volunteer. The derrick conferred an obvious benefit on Petro Industries. Petro Industries would be unjustly enriched if it was allowed to keep the derrick without paying Ericson for the work. Therefore, Ericson should be able to recover in *quantum meruit* the reasonable value of the oil derrick that was built, which is ordinarily equal to its fair market value.

Concept Summary 19.1 reviews all of the equitable remedies, including quasi contract, that may be available in the event that a contract is breached.

19–4 Waiver of Breach

Under certain circumstances, a nonbreaching party may be willing to accept a defective performance of the contract. This knowing relinquishment of a legal right (that is, the right to require satisfactory and full performance) is called a **waiver.**

19–4a Consequences of a Waiver of Breach

When a waiver of a breach of contract occurs, the party waiving the breach cannot take any later action on it. In effect, the waiver erases the past breach, and the contract continues as if the breach had never occurred. Of course, the waiver of breach of contract extends only to the matter waived and not to the whole contract.

---

16. *Emerick v. Cardiac Study Center, Inc.,* 166 Wash.App. 1039 (2012).
17. Pronounced *kwahn*-tuhm *mehr*-oo-wit.
18. Contracts that by their terms cannot be performed within one year must be in writing to be enforceable.

Concept Summary 19.1

Equitable Remedies

Rescission and Restitution	• *Rescission*—A remedy whereby a contract is canceled and the parties are restored to the original positions that they occupied prior to the transaction. • *Restitution*—When a contract is rescinded, both parties must make restitution to each other by returning the goods, property, or funds previously conveyed.
Specific Performance	• An equitable remedy calling for the performance of the act promised in the contract. • Only available when monetary damages would be inadequate and never available in personal-service contracts.
Reformation	• An equitable remedy allowing a contract to be reformed, or rewritten, to reflect the parties' true intentions. • Available when an agreement is imperfectly expressed in writing, such as when a mutual mistake has occurred.
Recovery Based on Quasi Contract	• An equitable theory under which a party who confers a benefit on another—with the reasonable expectation of being paid—can seek a court order for the fair market value of the benefit conferred.

19–4b Reasons for Waiving a Breach

Businesspersons often waive breaches of contract to obtain whatever benefit is still possible out of the contract. ■ **EXAMPLE 19.14** A seller, Purdue Resources, contracts with a buyer, Bladco Enterprises, to deliver ten thousand tons of coal on or before November 1. The contract calls for Bladco to pay by November 10 for coal delivered. Because of a coal miners' strike, coal is hard to find. Purdue breaches the contract by not tendering delivery until November 5. Bladco will likely choose to waive the seller's breach, accept delivery of the coal, and pay as contracted. ■

19–4c Waiver of Breach and Subsequent Breaches

Ordinarily, a waiver by a contracting party will not operate to waive subsequent, additional, or future breaches of contract. This is always true when the subsequent breaches are unrelated to the first breach. ■ **EXAMPLE 19.15** Ashton owns a multimillion-dollar apartment complex that is under construction. Ashton allows the contractor to complete a stage of construction late. By doing so, Ashton waives his right to sue for the delay. Ashton does not, however, waive the right to sue for failure to comply with engineering specifications on the same job. ■

Pattern-of-Conduct Exception A waiver can extend to subsequent defective performance if a reasonable person would conclude that similar defective performance in the future will be acceptable. Therefore, a *pattern of conduct* that waives a number of successive breaches will operate as a continued waiver. To change this result, the nonbreaching party should give notice to the breaching party that full performance will be required in the future.

Effect on the Contract The party who has rendered defective or less-than-full performance remains liable for the damages caused by the breach of contract. In effect, the waiver operates to keep the contract going. The waiver prevents the nonbreaching party from declaring the contract at an end or rescinding the contract. The contract continues, but the nonbreaching party can recover damages caused by the defective or less-than-full performance.

19–5 Contract Provisions Limiting Remedies

A contract may include provisions stating that no damages can be recovered for certain types of breaches or that damages will be limited to a maximum amount. A contract may also provide that the only remedy for breach is replacement, repair, or refund of the purchase price. Finally, a contract may provide that one party can seek injunctive relief if the other party breaches the contract. Provisions stating that no damages can be recovered are called *exculpatory clauses*. Provisions that affect the availability of certain remedies are called *limitation-of-liability clauses*.

19–5a The UCC Allows Sales Contracts to Limit Remedies

The Uniform Commercial Code (UCC) provides that in a contract for the sale of goods, remedies can be limited. We will examine the UCC provisions on limited remedies in a later chapter in the context of contracts for the sale or lease of goods.[19]

---

19. See UCC 2–719(1).

19–5b Enforceability of Limitation-of-Liability Clauses

Whether a limitation-of-liability clause in a contract will be enforced depends on the type of breach that is excused by the provision. Normally, a provision excluding liability for fraudulent or intentional injury will not be enforced. Likewise, a clause excluding liability for illegal acts, acts that are contrary to public policy, or violations of law will not be enforced. A clause that excludes liability for negligence may be enforced in some situations when the parties have roughly equal bargaining positions.

■ **CASE IN POINT 19.16** Engineering Consulting Services, Ltd. (ECS), contracted with RSN Properties, Inc., a real estate developer. ECS was to perform soil studies for $2,200 and render an opinion on the use of septic systems in a particular subdivision being developed. A clause in the contract limited ECS's liability to RSN to the value of the engineering services or the sum of $50,000, whichever was greater.

ECS concluded that most of the lots were suitable for septic systems, so RSN proceeded with the development. RSN constructed the roads and water lines to the subdivision in reliance on ECS's conclusions, which turned out to be incorrect. RSN sued ECS for breach of contract and argued that the limitation of liability was against public policy and unenforceable. The court, however, enforced the limitation-of-liability clause as "a reasonable allocation of risks in an arm's-length business transaction."[20] ■

---

20. *RSN Properties, Inc. v. Engineering Consulting Services, Ltd.*, 301 Ga.App. 52, 686 S.E.2d 853 (2009).

Reviewing: Breach of Contract and Remedies

Kyle Bruno enters a contract with X Entertainment to be a stuntman in a movie. Bruno is widely known as the best motorcycle stuntman in the business, and the movie to be produced, *Xtreme Riders,* has numerous scenes involving high-speed freestyle street-bike stunts. Filming is set to begin August 1 and end by December 1 so that the film can be released the following summer. Both parties to the contract have stipulated that the filming must end on time to capture the profits from the summer movie market. The contract states that Bruno will be paid 10 percent of the net proceeds from the movie for his stunts.

The contract also includes a liquidated damages provision, which specifies that if Bruno breaches the contract, he will owe X Entertainment $1 million. In addition, the contract includes a limitation-of-liability clause stating that if Bruno is injured during filming, X Entertainment's liability is limited to nominal damages. Using the information presented in the chapter, answer the following questions.

1. One day, while Bruno is preparing for a difficult stunt, he gets into an argument with the director and refuses to perform any stunts at all. Can X Entertainment seek specific performance of the contract? Why or why not?
2. Suppose that while performing a high-speed wheelie on a motorcycle, Bruno is injured by the intentionally reckless act of an X Entertainment employee. Will a court be likely to enforce the limitation-of-liability clause? Why or why not?

Continues

3. What factors would a court consider to determine whether the $1 million liquidated damages provision constitutes valid damages or is a penalty?

4. Suppose that there was no liquidated damages provision (or the court refused to enforce it) and X Entertainment breached the contract. The breach caused the release of the film to be delayed until after summer. Could Bruno seek consequential (special) damages for lost profits from the summer movie market in that situation? Explain.

Debate This . . . *Courts should always uphold limitation-of-liability clauses, whether or not the two parties to the contract had equal bargaining power.*

Terms and Concepts

consequential damages 342	nominal damages 343	restitution 345
incidental damages 341	penalty 343	specific performance 347
liquidated damages 343	*quantum meruit* 349	waiver 349
mitigation of damages 343	reformation 348	

Issue Spotters

1. Greg contracts to build a storage shed for Haney, who pays Greg in advance, but Greg completes only half the work. Haney pays Ipswich $500 to finish the shed. If Haney sues Greg, what will be the measure of recovery? (See *Damages.*)

2. Lyle contracts to sell his ranch to Marley, who is to take possession on June 1. Lyle delays the transfer until August 1.

Marley incurs expenses in providing for cattle that he bought for the ranch. When they made the contract, Lyle had no reason to know of the cattle. Is Lyle liable for Marley's expenses in providing for the cattle? Why or why not? (See *Damages.*)

• **Check your answers to the Issue Spotters against the answers provided in Appendix D at the end of this text.**

Business Scenarios

19–1. Liquidated Damages. Cohen contracts to sell his house and lot to Windsor for $100,000. The terms of the contract call for Windsor to pay 10 percent of the purchase price as a down payment. The terms further stipulate that if the buyer breaches the contract, Cohen will retain the deposit as liquidated damages. Windsor pays the deposit, but because her expected financing of the $90,000 balance falls through, she breaches the contract. Two weeks later, Cohen sells the house and lot to Ballard for $105,000. Windsor demands her $10,000 back, but Cohen refuses, claiming that Windsor's breach and the contract terms entitle him to keep the deposit. Discuss who is correct. (See *Damages.*)

19–2. Specific Performance. In which of the following situations would specific performance be an appropriate remedy? Discuss fully. (See *Equitable Remedies.*)

(a) Thompson contracts to sell her house and lot to Cousteau. Then, on finding another buyer willing to pay a higher purchase price, she refuses to deed the property to Cousteau.

(b) Amy contracts to sing and dance in Fred's nightclub for one month, beginning May 1. She then refuses to perform.

(c) Hoffman contracts to purchase a rare coin owned by Erikson, who is breaking up his coin collection. At the last minute, Erikson decides to keep his coin collection intact and refuses to deliver the coin to Hoffman.

(d) ABC Corp. has three shareholders: Panozzo, who owns 48 percent of the stock; Chang, who owns another 48 percent; and Ryan, who owns 4 percent. Ryan contracts to sell her 4 percent to Chang. Later, Ryan refuses to transfer the shares to Chang.

Business Case Problems

19–3. Liquidated Damages and Penalties. Planned Pethood Plus, Inc., is a veterinarian-owned clinic. It borrowed $389,000 from KeyBank at an interest rate of 9.3 percent per year for ten years. The loan had a "prepayment penalty" clause that clearly stated that if the loan was repaid early, a specific formula would be used to assess a lump-sum payment to extinguish the obligation. The sooner the loan was paid off, the higher the prepayment penalty. After a year, the veterinarians decided to pay off the loan. KeyBank invoked a prepayment penalty of $40,525.92, which was equal to 10.7 percent of the balance due. The veterinarians sued, contending that the prepayment requirement was unenforceable because it was a penalty. The bank countered that the amount was not a penalty but liquidated damages and that the sum was reasonable. The trial court agreed with the bank, and the veterinarians appealed. Was the loan's prepayment charge reasonable, and should it have been enforced? Why or why not? [*Planned Pethood Plus, Inc. v. KeyCorp, Inc.,* 228 P.3d 262 (Colo.App. 2010)] (See *Damages.*)

19–4. Measure of Damages. Before buying a house, Dean and Donna Testa hired Ground Systems, Inc. (GSI), to inspect the sewage and water disposal system. GSI reported a split system with a watertight septic tank, a wastewater tank, a distribution box, and a leach field. The Testas bought the house. Later, Dean saw that the system was not as GSI described—there was no distribution box or leach field, and there was only one tank, which was not watertight. The Testas arranged for the installation of a new system and sold the house. Assuming that GSI is liable for breach of contract, what is the measure of damages? [*Testa v. Ground Systems, Inc.,* 206 N.J. 330, 20 A.3d 435 (App.Div. 2011)] (See *Damages.*)

19–5. Business Case Problem with Sample Answer— Consequential Damages. After submitting the high bid at

a foreclosure sale, David Simard entered into a contract to purchase real property in Maryland for $192,000. Simard defaulted (failed to pay) on the contract. A state court ordered the property to be resold at Simard's expense, as required by state law. The property was then resold for $163,000, but the second purchaser also defaulted. The court then ordered a second resale, resulting in a final price of $130,000. Assuming that Simard is liable for consequential damages, what is the extent of his liability? Is he liable for losses and expenses related to the first resale? If so, is he also liable for losses and expenses related to the second resale? Why or why not? [*Burson v. Simard,* 35 A.3d 1154 (Md. 2012)] (See *Damages.*)

- **For a sample answer to Problem 19–5, go to Appendix E at the end of this text.**

19–6. Liquidated Damages. Cuesport Properties, LLC, sold a condominium in Anne Arundel County, Maryland, to Critical Developments, LLC. As part of the sale, Cuesport agreed to build a wall between Critical Developments' unit and an adjacent unit within thirty days of closing. If Cuesport failed to do so, it was to pay $126 per day until completion. This was an estimate of the amount of rent that Critical Developments would lose until the wall was finished and the unit could be rented. Actual damages were otherwise difficult to estimate at the time of the contract. The wall was built on time, but without a county permit, and it did not comply with the county building code. Critical Developments did

not modify the wall to comply with the code until 260 days after the date of the contract deadline for completion of the wall. Does Cuesport have to pay Critical Developments $126 for each of the 260 days? Explain. [*Cuesport Properties, LLC v. Critical Developments, LLC,* 209 Md.App. 607, 61 A.3d 91 (2013)] (See *Damages.*)

19–7. Limitation-of-Liability Clauses. Mia Eriksson was a seventeen-year-old competitor in horseback-riding events. Her riding coach was Kristi Nunnink. Eriksson signed an agreement that released Nunnink from all liability except for damages caused by Nunnink's "direct, willful and wanton negligence." During an event at Galway Downs in Temecula, California, Eriksson's horse struck a hurdle. She fell from the horse and the horse fell on her, causing her death. Her parents, Karan and Stan Eriksson, filed a suit in a California state court against Nunnink for wrongful death. Is the limitation-of-liability agreement that Eriksson signed likely to be enforced in her parents' case? If so, how will it affect their claim? Explain. [*Eriksson v. Nunnink,* 233 Cal.App.4th 708, 183 Cal.Rptr.3d 234 (4 Dist. 2015)] (See *Contract Provisions Limiting Remedies.*)

19–8. Damages. Robert Morris was a licensed insurance agent working for his father's independent insurance agency when he contacted Farmers Insurance Exchange in Alabama about becoming a Farmers agent. According to Farmers' company policy, Morris was an unsuitable candidate due to his relationship with his father's agency. But no Farmers representative told Morris of this policy, and none of the documents that he signed expressed it. Farmers trained Morris and appointed him its agent. About three years later, however, Farmers terminated the appointment for "a conflict of interest because his father was in the insurance business." Morris filed a suit in an Alabama state court against Farmers, claiming that he had been fraudulently induced to leave his father's agency to work for Farmers. If Morris was successful, what type of damages was he most likely awarded? What was the measure of damages? Discuss. [*Farmers Insurance Exchange v. Morris,* __ So.3d __, 2016 WL 661671 (Ala. 2016)] (See *Damages.*)

19–9. A Question of Ethics—Remedies. *On a weekday,*

Tamara Cohen, a real estate broker, showed a townhouse owned by Ray and Harriet Mayer to Jessica Seinfeld, the wife of comedian Jerry Seinfeld. On the weekend, when Cohen was unavailable because her religious beliefs prevented her from working, the Seinfelds revisited the townhouse on their own and agreed to buy it. The contract stated that the "buyers will pay buyer's real estate broker's fees." [Cohen v. Seinfeld, 15 Misc.3d 1118(A), 839 N.Y.S.2d 432 (Sup. 2007)] (See Equitable Remedies.)

(a) Is Cohen entitled to payment even though she was not available to show the townhouse to the Seinfelds on the weekend? Explain.

(b) What obligation do parties involved in business deals owe to each other with respect to their religious beliefs? How might the situation in this case have been avoided?

Legal Reasoning Group Activity

19–10. Breach and Remedies. Frances Morelli agreed to sell Judith Bucklin a house in Rhode Island for $177,000. The sale was supposed to be closed by September 1. The contract included a provision that "if Seller is unable to convey good, clear, insurable, and marketable title, Buyer shall have the option to: (a) accept such title as Seller is able to convey without reduction of the Purchase Price, or (b) cancel this Agreement and receive a return of all Deposits."

An examination of the public records revealed that the house did not have marketable title. Bucklin offered Morelli additional time to resolve the problem, and the closing did not occur as scheduled. Morelli decided that "the deal was over" and offered to return the deposit. Bucklin refused and, in mid-October, decided to exercise her option to accept the house without marketable title. She notified Morelli, who did not respond. She then filed a lawsuit against Morelli in a state court. (See *Damages.*)

(a) One group will discuss whether Morelli breached the contract and will decide in whose favor the court should rule.

(b) A second group will assume that Morelli did breach the contract and will determine what the appropriate remedy is in this situation.

Fantasy Sports—Legal Gambling?

A *fantasy sport* involves games in which the participants compile imaginary teams made up of real players in a professional sport. As in real sports, fantasy sports team owners draft, trade, and drop players. The teams are grouped into leagues and compete based on the statistical performance of the players in actual games.

Fantasy sports is a multibillion-dollar industry that includes more than three hundred companies, ranging from small start-ups to large corporations. For example, CBSSports.com, which offers fantasy sports games on its Web site, is a brand operated by CBS Interactive, a division of CBS Corporation. More than 50 million U.S. adults play fantasy sports.

One of the most important issues confronting the industry is whether participation in fantasy sports constitutes illegal gambling.

Do Fantasy Sports Constitute Gambling under State Law?

To *gamble* is to play a game of chance or bet on the outcome of an uncertain event in the hope of winning. State laws concerning the legality of gambling vary. Even in states where most forms of gambling are illegal, however, some activities that would otherwise fall within the definition of gambling are allowed.

Consideration, Reward, and Chance In most states, an activity constitutes gambling if it involves consideration, reward, and chance. Most courts construe *consideration* narrowly in this context, limiting it to money or valuable property exchanged for a chance to win a prize. Some courts apply the term more broadly to any form of legal detriment exchanged for a chance to win.

A *reward* is the prize for winning. Courts generally hold that the reward, or prize, must be something tangible, regardless of its value.[1]

Chance requires that an activity's outcome be determined unpredictably by factors outside a participant's control, not by judgment, practice, or skill. Most states deem an activity to involve chance if greater than 50 percent of the outcome is determined by outside factors.

Entry Fees, Prizes, and Skill In states that apply these three elements to determine whether an activity constitutes gambling, the lack of any one of them argues in favor of an activity's lawfulness. For example, fantasy sports leagues that offer free entry for participants lack the element of consideration. Games that do not include prizes lack the element of reward.

Other fantasy sports games are not so clearly legal. For example, a game that extends for less than a full professional sports season involves a greater degree of chance and is thus less likely to qualify as legal.[2] The shorter the time, the less opportunity a participant's skill has to offset such factors as a player's health, the decisions of a team manager or coach, and weather. There is also less time for participants to negotiate trades and manage their fantasy teams.

Continues

---

1. See, for example, *State of Arkansas v. 26 Gaming Machines*, 356 Ark. 47, 145 S.W.3d 368 (2004).
2. See *Three Kings Holdings, L.L.C. v. Six*, 45 Kan.App.2d 1043, 255 P.3d 1218 (2011).

Stricter Standards The standards are stricter in some states. For example, states that apply the contract definition of *consideration*—something of legally sufficient value—to fantasy sports games will not exempt a game simply because there is no entry fee.

Some states interpret the element of chance to involve *any* chance. In those states, all fantasy sports games violate gambling laws. Other states have indicated or expressly stated that the games are illegal.[3]

Does Federal Law Define Fantasy Sports as Gambling?

Most federal laws related to gambling were enacted to help states enforce their gambling laws. There are, however, at least two federal acts that may apply to fantasy sports.

"Wagering Schemes" The professional sports industry lobbied Congress to enact the Professional and Amateur Sports Protection Act (PAPSA)[4] in 1992. This act prohibits, with certain exceptions, the operation of a "wagering scheme" based on a game in which "professional or amateur athletes participate."

It is not likely that PAPSA would apply to fantasy sports generally—most professional sports leagues operate their own fantasy sports Web sites and endorse seasonal play. But the act could apply to *daily* fantasy sports games—games played over a brief period, such as a week or a single day, rather than an entire sports season. Their sponsors emphasize payouts and prizes, giving daily games the appearance of "wagering schemes."

Skill of the Participants The Unlawful Internet Gambling Enforcement Act (UIGEA) of 2006[5] prohibits persons "engaged in the business of betting" to "knowingly accept" funds "in connection with the participation of another person in unlawful Internet gambling." Under the act, "unlawful Internet gambling" is knowingly transmitting a bet, via the Internet, if the bet is otherwise illegal where it is "initiated, received, or . . . made." In other words, if a person places a bet in a state in which gambling is illegal, a business that accepts the bet violates the UIGEA, regardless of the business's location.[6]

The UIGEA exempts fantasy sports games in which, among other requirements, the "outcomes reflect the relative knowledge and skill of the participants and are determined predominantly by the performance of individuals . . . in multiple real-world sporting events." It is likely that *daily* fantasy sports games do not meet this requirement. Their short duration decreases the effect of a participant's skill and increases the effect of luck on the result.

Daily Fantasy Sports—Skill or Gamble?

DraftKings and FanDuel operate daily fantasy sports (DFS) Web sites. In the fall of 2015, the two companies saturated the media with advertising, emphasizing million-dollar payouts. Then, in early October, DraftKings employee Brian Haskell allegedly used inside information to beat more than 200,000 other participants and win $350,000 in a game on FanDuel's site. Draft-Kings denied the allegation. Both companies announced, "Nothing is more important . . . than the integrity of the games we offer to our customers."

---

3. These states include Arizona, Iowa, Louisiana, Montana, and Washington.

4. 28 U.S.C. Sections 3701–3704.

5. 31 U.S.C. Sections 5361–5367.

6. See *Interactive Media Entertainment and Gaming Association Inc. v. Attorney General of United States*, 580 F.3d 113 (3d Cir. 2009).

Before the end of the month, the Federal Bureau of Investigation and U.S. Department of Justice opened an investigation. ESPN announced that it would stop running segments sponsored by DraftKings. The National Collegiate Athletic Association (NCAA) barred DraftKings and FanDuel from advertising at NCAA championship events and prohibited student athletes from participating in DFS. The National Football League limited the amount of money its players could win from DFS.

Meanwhile, a dozen states began considering new fantasy sports legislation. The Nevada Gaming Control Board ruled that DFS should be considered gambling and banned DFS sites from operating in the state. New York Attorney General Eric Schneiderman, characterizing DFS as games of chance rather than skill, ordered DraftKings and FanDuel to stop accepting "wagers" from New York residents.

> Daily fantasy sports companies are engaged in illegal gambling . . . , causing the same kinds of social and economic harms as other forms of illegal gambling. . . . Daily fantasy sports is neither victimless nor harmless, and it is clear that DraftKings and FanDuel are the leaders of a massive, multi-billion-dollar scheme intended to evade the law and fleece sports fans across the country.[7]

Ethical Connection

DraftKings and FanDuel contend that they are not taking bets—that the games on their sites involve more skill than luck. They have a legal right to argue this point in a New York state court on a challenge to the order of the state's attorney general. And, in the best interest of their owners and customers, they may have an ethical duty to challenge the order.

In the meantime, do the two sites have an ethical duty to *comply* with the order? Or do they have an ethical obligation to *defy* the order to play to completion the games that New York residents started? The sites might thereby gain additional support for their argument to challenge the attorney general. Or their open defiance might undercut any sympathy a court might have for their situation. It is a judgment call—an ethical gamble—and the question for the sites might be, "Do you feel lucky?"

Ethics Question *Is gambling less ethical than trading in securities or funding a start-up? Why?*

Critical Thinking *What is the most significant factor in determining whether fantasy sports games constitute gambling? Explain.*

---

7. Press Release, New York State Office of the Attorney General, *A.G. Schneiderman Issues Cease-and-Desist Letters to FanDuel and DraftKings, Demanding That Companies Stop Accepting Illegal Wagers in New York State* (Nov. 11, 2015) (http://www.ag.ny.gov/press-release/ag-schneiderman-issues-cease-and-desist-letters-fanduel-and-draftkings-demanding).

Domestic and International Sales and Lease Contracts

CHAPTER 20

The Formation of Sales and Lease Contracts

When we turn to contracts for the sale and lease of goods, we move away from common law principles and into the area of statutory law. State statutory law governing sales and lease transactions is based on the Uniform Commercial Code (UCC), which has been adopted as law by all of the states.[1] Of all the

attempts to produce a uniform body of laws relating to commercial transactions in the United States, none has been as successful as the UCC.

The goal of the UCC is to simplify and to streamline commercial transactions. The UCC allows parties to form sales and lease contracts, including those entered into online, without observing the same degree of formality used in forming other types of contracts.

Today, businesses often engage in sales and lease transactions on a global scale. The United Nations Convention on Contracts for the International Sale of Goods (CISG) governs international sales contracts. The CISG is a model uniform law that applies only when a nation has adopted it, just as the UCC applies only to the extent that it has been adopted by a state.

---

1. Louisiana has not adopted Articles 2 and 2A, however.

20-1 The Uniform Commercial Code

In the early years of this nation, sales law varied from state to state, and this lack of uniformity complicated the formation of multistate sales contracts. The problems became especially troublesome in the late nineteenth century as multistate contracts became the norm. At that time, the National Conference of Commissioners on Uniform State Laws (NCCUSL) began drafting uniform laws relating to commercial transactions to address these problems.

In 1945, the NCCUSL began to work on the Uniform Commercial Code (UCC) to integrate various uniform acts into a single uniform law. The UCC was completed in 1949. Over the next several years, it was substantially accepted by almost every state in the nation.

20-1a Comprehensive Coverage of the UCC

The UCC is the single most comprehensive codification of the broad spectrum of laws involved in a total commercial transaction. The UCC views the entire "commercial transaction for the sale of and payment for goods" as a single legal occurrence having numerous facets. The

articles and sections of the UCC are periodically revised or supplemented to clarify certain aspects or to establish new rules as needed when the business environment changes.

You can gain an idea of the UCC's comprehensiveness by looking at the titles of the articles of the UCC in Appendix C. As you will note, Article 1, titled General Provisions, sets forth definitions and general principles applicable to commercial transactions. Article 1 thus provides the basic groundwork for the remaining articles, each of which focuses on a particular aspect of commercial transactions.

For instance, Article 1 sets forth an obligation to perform in "good faith" all contracts falling under the UCC [UCC 1–304]. Note, though, that many contracts do not fall under the UCC, because they do not involve commercial transactions.

■ **CASE IN POINT 20.1** Peter Amaya was a third-year medical student at Indiana University School of Medicine (IUSM) when three professors saw him cheating on an exam. He denied cheating and maintained that he was merely looking over at the clock on the wall. When he was dismissed from the school, Amaya filed suit in state court against the dean and IUSM, alleging breach of contract and breach of the duty of good faith.

The court granted IUSM's motion for summary judgment. Amaya appealed, but the reviewing court affirmed. Because a contract between a university and its students is not a sale of goods, the UCC's duty of good faith does not apply. The university's conclusion that Amaya failed to maintain acceptable professional standards was a "rational determination" arrived at after deliberation and after Amaya had numerous opportunities to be heard.[2] ■

20–1b A Single, Integrated Framework for Commercial Transactions

The UCC attempts to provide a consistent and integrated framework of rules to deal with all the phases *ordinarily arising* in a commercial sales transaction from start to finish. Consider the following events, all of which may occur during a single transaction:

1. *A contract for the sale or lease of goods is formed and executed.* Article 2 and Article 2A of the UCC provide rules governing all aspects of this transaction.
2. *The transaction may involve a payment—by check, electronic fund transfer, or other means.* Article 3 (on negotiable instruments), Article 4 (on bank deposits and collections), Article 4A (on fund transfers), and Article 5 (on letters of credit) cover this part of the transaction.
3. *The transaction may involve a bill of lading or a warehouse receipt that covers goods when they are shipped or stored.* Article 7 (on documents of title) deals with this subject.
4. *The transaction may involve a demand by the seller or lender for some form of security for the remaining balance owed.* Article 9 (on secured transactions) covers this part of the transaction.

20–2 The Scope of Articles 2 (Sales) and 2A (Leases)

Article 2 of the UCC sets forth the requirements for *sales contracts,* as well as the duties and obligations of the parties involved in the sales contract. Article 2A covers similar issues for *lease contracts.* Bear in mind, however, that the parties to sales or lease contracts are free to agree to terms different from those stated in the UCC.

20–2a Article 2—The Sale of Goods

Article 2 of the UCC (as adopted by state statutes) governs **sales contracts,** or contracts for the sale of goods.

---

2. *Amaya v. Brater,* 981 N.E.2d 1235 (Ind.App. 2013).

To facilitate commercial transactions, Article 2 modifies some of the common law contract requirements that were discussed in the previous chapters.

To the extent that it has not been modified by the UCC, however, the common law of contracts also applies to sales contracts. In other words, the common law requirements for a valid contract—agreement consideration, capacity, and legality—are also applicable to sales contracts.

In general, the rule is that whenever a conflict arises between a common law contract rule and the state statutory law based on the UCC, the UCC controls. Thus, when a UCC provision addresses a certain issue, the UCC rule governs. When the UCC is silent, the common law governs. The relationship between general contract law and the law governing sales of goods is illustrated in Exhibit 20–1.

In regard to Article 2, keep two points in mind.

1. Article 2 deals with the sale of *goods.* It does not deal with real property (real estate), services, or intangible property such as stocks and bonds. Thus, if the subject matter of a dispute is goods, the UCC governs. If it is real estate or services, the common law applies.
2. In some situations, the rules can vary depending on whether the buyer or the seller is a *merchant.*

We look now at how the UCC defines a *sale, goods,* and *merchant status.*

What Is a Sale? The UCC defines a **sale** as "the passing of title [evidence of ownership rights] from the seller to the buyer for a price" [UCC 2–106(1)]. The price may be payable in cash or in other goods or services. (For a discussion of whether states can impose taxes on online sales, see this chapter's *Digital Update* feature.)

What Are Goods? To be characterized as a *good,* an item of property must be *tangible,* and it must be *movable.* **Tangible property** has physical existence—it can be touched or seen. **Intangible property**—such as corporate stocks and bonds, patents and copyrights, and ordinary contract rights—has only conceptual existence and thus does not come under Article 2. A *movable* item can be carried from place to place. Hence, real estate is excluded from Article 2.

Goods Associated with Real Estate. Goods *associated* with real estate often do fall within the scope of Article 2, however [UCC 2–107]. For instance, a contract for the sale of minerals, oil, or gas is a contract for the sale of goods if *severance, or separation, is to be made by the seller.* Similarly, a contract for the sale of growing crops or

EXHIBIT 20–1 The Law Governing Contracts

This exhibit graphically illustrates the relationship between general contract law and statutory law (UCC Articles 2 and 2A) governing contracts for the sale and lease of goods. Sales contracts are not governed exclusively by Article 2 of the UCC but are also governed by general contract law whenever it is relevant and has not been modified by the UCC.

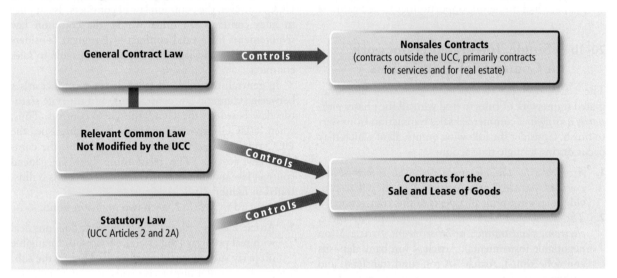

timber to be cut is a contract for the sale of goods *regardless of who severs them from the land.*

■ **CASE IN POINT 20.2** Perry Dan Cruse owned a business in Indiana that bought standing timber, cut it, and then resold it. Donald Freyberger had a contract with Cruse under which Cruse was to harvest 120 choice trees from Freyberger's land within six months. As payment, Freyberger would receive a percentage of the net proceeds from the sale of the cut timber. Cruse harvested and cut the trees but then filed for bankruptcy before the timber was sold. Freyberger filed a claim with the bankruptcy court, asserting that he had a "vendor's lien" on the timber because Cruse owed him $15,150 on the contract. (A lien would give Freyberger's claim priority over Cruse's other creditors.)

The bankruptcy court held that the timber was personal property (goods) under the UCC regardless of who cut it. Because no vendor's lien can arise on personal property under Indiana law, Freyberger's claim did not receive any special priority under bankruptcy law, and the debt could be discharged.[3] ■

Goods and Services Combined. When contracts involve a combination of goods and services, courts generally use the **predominant-factor test** to determine whether a contract is primarily for the sale of goods or the sale of

services.[4] If a court decides that a mixed contract is primarily a goods contract, *any* dispute, even a dispute over the services portion, will be decided under the UCC.

■ **CASE IN POINT 20.3** H & C Ag Services, LLC, entered into a contract with Ohio Fresh Eggs, LLC, that referred to "manure brokering services." H & C agreed to pay Ohio Fresh "service fees" for "all available tonnage per year of manure," which would then be resold to other parties. But the parties' contract did not specify the amount of manure. When Ohio Fresh did not carry out the contract, H & C sued for breach. A jury ruled that the primary purpose of the contract was for "manure brokering" (a service) rather than the "purchase of manure" (goods) and thus the UCC did not apply. The state trial court awarded H & C more than $2.5 million in damages. Ohio Fresh appealed.

The reviewing court held that the UCC governed the parties' contract under the predominant-factor test. The purpose of the contract was for the sale of goods—the manure—not the removal or resale of it. Despite the contract's use of the words *brokering* and *service fees,* H & C was clearly the buyer of manure from Ohio Fresh, who was the seller. Therefore, the UCC applied. Because the quantity term was left open, the parties had *not* agreed on

---

3. *In re Cruse,* 2013 WL 323275 (S.D. Indiana 2013).

4. UCC 2–314(1) does stipulate that serving food or drinks is a "sale of goods" for purposes of the implied warranty of merchantability, which will be discussed in the context of warranties. The UCC also specifies that selling unborn animals or rare coins qualifies as a "sale of goods."

DIGITAL UPDATE   Taxing Web Purchases

In 1992, the United States Supreme Court ruled that an individual state cannot compel an out-of-state business that lacks a substantial physical presence within that state to collect and remit state taxes.[a] Congress has the power to pass legislation requiring out-of-state corporations to collect and remit state sales taxes, but it has not yet done so. Thus, only online retailers that also have a physical presence within a state must collect state taxes on Web sales made to residents of that state. (State residents are supposed to self-report their purchases and pay use taxes to the state, which they rarely do.)

Redefining Physical Presence

A number of states have found a way to collect taxes on Internet sales made to state residents by out-of-state corporations—by redefining *physical presence*. New York started the trend in 2008 when it changed its tax laws in this manner. Now, an online retailer that pays any party within New York to solicit business for its products is considered to have a physical presence in the state and must collect state taxes. Since New York changed its law, around half of the states have made similar changes in an effort to increase their revenues by collecting sales tax from online retailers.

These new laws, often called the "Amazon tax" laws because they are largely aimed at Amazon.com, affect all online sellers, including Overstock.com and Drugstore.com. These laws especially affect retailers that pay affiliates to direct traffic to their Web sites. A federal appellate court in 2016 upheld the constitutionality of Colorado's so-called Amazon tax law, reasoning that the statute was necessary to avoid creating a tax shelter for online retailers.[b]

Local Governments Sue Online Travel Companies

Travelocity, Priceline.com, Hotels.com, and Orbitz.com are online travel companies (OTCs) that offer, among other things, hotel booking services. By 2018, more than twenty-five cities, including Atlanta, Charleston, Philadelphia, and San Antonio, had filed suits claiming that the OTCs owed taxes on hotel reservations that they had booked. All of the cities involved in the suits impose a hotel occupancy tax, which is essentially a sales tax.

Initially, some cities won their cases, but more recently, they have been losing in court.[c] As of 2018, courts in twenty-three states have concluded that the OTCs are not subject to hotel occupancy tax, and courts in six states have found the OTCs were liable for taxes. In Wyoming, for example, the state's highest court ruled that Travelocity, Priceline, Hotwire, Expedia, and Trip Network had to collect and remit sales tax.[d]

The Market Place Fairness Act

By the time you read this, online sales taxes may have become a reality for every online business that has annual revenues in excess of $1 million. For several years now, legislation called the Market Place Fairness Act has been introduced in the U.S. Senate. The act, if passed, would allow states to collect sales taxes from online retailers for in-state transactions.

A significant problem with such legislation is the complexity of collecting taxes for multiple jurisdictions. The current tax system involves 9,600 taxing jurisdictions. Even one zip code may cover multiple taxing entities, such as different cities and counties. Just consider that the Dallas–Fort Worth airport includes six separate taxing jurisdictions. Current software solutions for retailers that allow them to collect and remit sales taxes for different jurisdictions are extremely costly to install and operate. Overstock.com, for example, spent $1.3 million to add just one state to its sales tax collection system.

Critical Thinking *Some argue that if online retailers must pay sales taxes in jurisdictions in which they have no physical presence, they have no democratic way to fight high taxes in those places. Is this an instance of taxation without representation? Discuss.*

---

a. *Quill Corp. v. North Dakota*, 504 U.S. 298, 112 S.Ct. 1904, 119 L.Ed.2d 91 (1992).
b. *Direct Marketing Association v. Brohl*, 814 F.3d 1129 (10th Cir. 2016).
c. *Montana Dept. of Revenue v. Priceline.com, Inc.*, 380 Mont. 352, 354 P.3d 631 (2015); and *Travelscape, LLC v. South Carolina Dept. of Revenue*, 391 S.C. 89, 705 S.E.2d 28 (2011).
d. *Travelocity.com, LP v. Wyoming Dept. of Revenue*, 329 P.3d 131 (2014). Also see *Expedia, Inc. v. District of Columbia*, 120 A.3d 623 (D.C.App. 2015).

an essential term. This meant that the contract was not enforceable under the UCC (open terms are discussed later in this chapter). Therefore, the appellate court reversed the lower court's decision and held in favor of Ohio Fresh.[5] ■

Who Is a Merchant? Article 2 governs the sale of goods in general. It applies to sales transactions between all buyers and sellers. In a limited number of instances, though, the UCC presumes that special business standards ought to be imposed because of merchants' relatively high degree of commercial expertise.[6] Such standards do not apply to the casual or inexperienced seller or buyer (consumer).

Section 2–104 sets forth three ways in which merchant status can arise:

1. A merchant is a person who *deals in goods of the kind* involved in the sales contract. Thus, a retailer, a wholesaler, or a manufacturer is a merchant of the goods sold in his or her business. A merchant for one type of goods is not necessarily a merchant for another type. For instance, a sporting goods retailer is a merchant when selling tennis rackets but not when selling a used computer.
2. A merchant is a person who, by occupation, *holds himself or herself out as having knowledge and skill* unique to the practices or goods involved in the transaction. This broad definition may include banks or universities as merchants.
3. A person who *employs a merchant as a broker, agent, or other intermediary* has the status of merchant in that transaction. Hence, if an art collector hires a broker to purchase or sell art for her, the collector is considered a merchant in the transaction.

In summary, a person is a **merchant** when she or he, acting in a mercantile capacity, possesses or uses an expertise specifically related to the goods being sold. This basic distinction is not always clear-cut. For instance, state courts appear to be split on whether farmers should be considered merchants.

20–2b Article 2A—Leases

Leases of personal property (goods such as automobiles and industrial equipment) have become increasingly common. In this context, a lease is a transfer of the right to possess and use goods for a period of time in exchange for payment. Article 2A of the UCC was created to fill the need for uniform guidelines in this area.

Article 2A covers any transaction that creates a lease of goods or a sublease of goods [UCC 2A–102, 2A–103(1)(k)]. Article 2A is essentially a repetition of Article 2, except that it applies to leases of goods rather than sales of goods and thus varies to reflect differences between sales and lease transactions. (Note that Article 2A is not concerned with leases of real property, such as land or buildings.)

Definition of a Lease Agreement Article 2A defines a **lease agreement** as a lessor's and lessee's bargain with respect to the lease of goods, as found in their language and as implied by other circumstances [UCC 2A–103(1)(k)]. A **lessor** is one who transfers the right to the possession and use of goods under a lease [UCC 2A–103(1)(p)]. A **lessee** is one who acquires the right to the possession and use of goods under a lease [UCC 2A–103(1)(o)]. In other words, the lessee is the party who is leasing the goods from the lessor.

Article 2A applies to all types of leases of goods. Special rules apply to certain types of leases, however, including consumer leases and finance leases.

Consumer Leases A *consumer lease* involves three elements:

1. A lessor who regularly engages in the business of leasing or selling.
2. A lessee (except an organization) who leases the goods "primarily for a personal, family, or household purpose."
3. Total lease payments that are less than $25,000 [UCC 2A–103(1)(e)].

To ensure special protection for consumers, certain provisions of Article 2A apply only to consumer leases. For instance, one provision states that a consumer may recover attorneys' fees if a court determines that a term in a consumer lease contract is unconscionable [UCC 2A–108(4)(a)].

Finance Leases A *finance lease* involves a lessor, a lessee, and a supplier. The lessor buys or leases goods from the supplier and leases or subleases them to the lessee [UCC 2A–103(1)(g)]. Typically, in a finance lease, the lessor is simply financing the transaction. ■ **EXAMPLE 20.4** Marlin Corporation wants to lease a crane for use in its construction business. Marlin's bank agrees to purchase the equipment from Jenco, Inc., and lease the equipment to Marlin. In this situation, the bank is the lessor-financer, Marlin is the lessee, and Jenco is the supplier. ■

---

5. *H & C Ag Services, LLC v. Ohio Fresh Eggs, LLC,* 41 N.E.3d 915 (Ohio App. 2015).
6. The provisions that apply only to merchants deal principally with the Statute of Frauds, firm offers, confirmatory memoranda, warranties, and contract modification. These special rules reflect expedient business practices commonly known to merchants in the commercial setting. They will be discussed later in this chapter.

Article 2A, unlike ordinary contract law, makes the lessee's obligations under a finance lease irrevocable and independent from the financer's obligations [UCC 2A–407]. In other words, the lessee must perform and continue to make lease payments even if the leased equipment turns out to be defective. The lessee must look almost entirely to the supplier for any recovery.

■ **EXAMPLE 20.5** McKessen Company obtains surgical ophthalmic equipment from a manufacturer and leases it to Vasquez for use at his medical eye center. When the equipment turns out to be defective, Vasquez stops making the lease payments. McKessen sues. Because the lease clearly qualifies as a finance lease under Article 2A, a court will hold in favor of McKessen. Vasquez is obligated to make all payments due under the lease regardless of the condition or performance of the leased equipment. Vasquez can sue the manufacturer of the defective equipment, however. ■

20–3 The Formation of Sales and Lease Contracts

In regard to the formation of sales and lease contracts, the UCC modifies the common law in several ways. We look here at how Articles 2 and 2A of the UCC modify common law contract rules. Remember, though, that parties to sales and lease contracts are basically free to establish whatever terms they wish.

The UCC comes into play when the parties either fail to provide certain terms in their contract or wish to change the effect of the UCC's terms in the contract's application. The UCC makes this very clear by its repeated use of such phrases as "unless the parties otherwise agree" and "absent a contrary agreement by the parties."

20–3a Offer

In general contract law, the moment a definite offer is met by an unqualified acceptance, a binding contract is formed. In commercial sales transactions, the verbal exchanges, correspondence, and actions of the parties may not reveal exactly when a binding contractual obligation arises. The UCC states that an agreement sufficient to constitute a contract can exist even if the moment of its making is undetermined [UCC 2–204(2), 2A–204(2)].

Open Terms According to general contract law, an offer must be definite enough for the parties (and the courts) to ascertain its essential terms when it is accepted. In contrast, the UCC states that a sales or lease contract will not fail for indefiniteness even if one or more terms are left open as long as *both* of the following are true:

1. The parties intended to make a contract.
2. There is a reasonably certain basis for the court to grant an appropriate remedy [UCC 2–204(3), 2A–204(3)].

The UCC provides numerous *open-term* provisions (discussed next) that can be used to fill the gaps in a contract. Thus, if a dispute occurs, all that is necessary to prove the existence of a contract is an indication (such as a purchase order) that there is a contract. Missing terms can be proved by evidence, or a court can presume that the parties intended whatever is reasonable under the circumstances.

Keep in mind, though, that if too many terms are left open, a court may find that the parties did not intend to form a contract. Also, the *quantity* of goods involved usually must be expressly stated in the contract. If the quantity term is left open, the courts will have no basis for determining a remedy.

Open Price Term. If the parties have not agreed on a price, the court will determine a "reasonable price at the time for delivery" [UCC 2–305(1)]. If either the buyer or the seller is to determine the price, the price is to be decided in good faith [UCC 2–305(2)]. Under the UCC, *good faith* means honesty in fact and the observance of reasonable commercial standards of fair dealing in the trade [UCC 2–103(1)(b)]. The concepts of *good faith* and *commercial reasonableness* permeate the UCC.

Sometimes, the price fails to be set through the fault of one of the parties. In that situation, the other party can treat the contract as canceled or determine a reasonable price. ■ **EXAMPLE 20.6** Perez and Merrick enter into a contract for the sale of goods and agree that Perez will determine the price. Perez refuses to specify the price. Merrick can either treat the contract as canceled or set a reasonable price [UCC 2–305(3)]. ■

Open Payment Term. When the parties do not specify payment terms, payment is due at the time and place at which the buyer is to receive the goods [UCC 2–310(a)]. The buyer can tender payment using any commercially normal or acceptable means, such as a check or credit card. If the seller demands payment in cash, however, the buyer must be given a reasonable time to obtain it [UCC 2–511(2)].

■ **CASE IN POINT 20.7** H. Daya International Co. is a clothing manufacturer and wholesaler based in Hong

Kong. H. Daya sold and delivered nearly $2 million worth of goods to two companies owned by Salomon Murciano. The businesses' principal place of business was in New York City. The companies, Do Denim, LLC, and Reward Jean, made only partial payments on the amounts due. After receiving discount credits, Do Denim still owed $282,029, and Reward Jean owed $721,155. H. Daya filed suit in a federal district court in New York against both companies for breach of contract. The court found in favor of H. Daya and awarded damages for the amounts due under the contract, plus prejudgment interest.

Under a New York statute, prejudgment interest of 9 percent begins accruing from "the earliest ascertainable date the cause of action existed." Because the UCC specifies that payment is due at the time the buyer receives the goods, the court held that interest started accruing from the receipt of the final shipment. Therefore, Do Denim owed an additional $44,645 in interest, and Reward Jean owed $109,181 in interest to H. Daya.[7] ∎

Open Delivery Term. When no delivery terms are specified, the buyer normally takes delivery at the seller's place of business [UCC 2–308(a)]. If the seller has no place of business, the seller's residence is used. When goods are located in some other place and both parties know it, delivery is made there. If the time for shipment or delivery is not clearly specified in the sales contract, then the court will infer a "reasonable" time for performance [UCC 2–309(1)].

Duration of an Ongoing Contract. A single contract might specify successive performances but not indicate how long the parties are required to deal with each other. In this situation, either party may terminate the ongoing contractual relationship. Nevertheless, principles of good faith and sound commercial practice call for reasonable notification before termination so as to give the other party sufficient time to seek a substitute arrangement [UCC 2–309(2), (3)].

Options and Cooperation with Regard to Performance. When the contract contemplates shipment of the goods but does not specify the shipping arrangements, the *seller* has the right to make these arrangements. The seller must make the arrangements in good faith, using commercial reasonableness in the situation [UCC 2–311].

When a sales contract omits terms relating to the assortment of goods, the *buyer* can specify the assortment. ∎ **EXAMPLE 20.8** Petry Drugs agrees to purchase one thousand toothbrushes from Marconi's Dental Supply. The toothbrushes come in a variety of colors, but the contract does not specify color. Petry, the buyer, has the right to take six hundred blue toothbrushes and four hundred green ones if it wishes. Petry, however, must exercise good faith and commercial reasonableness in making the selection [UCC 2–311]. ∎

Open Quantity Terms Normally, as mentioned earlier, if the parties do not specify a quantity, no contract is formed. A court will have no basis for determining a remedy, because there is almost no way to determine objectively what is a reasonable quantity of goods for someone to buy. (In contrast, a court can objectively determine a reasonable price for particular goods by looking at the market for like goods.) The UCC recognizes two exceptions to this rule in requirements and output contracts [UCC 2–306(1)].

Requirements Contracts. Requirements contracts are common in the business world and normally are enforceable. In a **requirements contract,** the buyer agrees to purchase and the seller agrees to sell all or up to a stated amount of what the buyer requires.

∎ **EXAMPLE 20.9** Newport Cannery forms a contract with Victor Tu. The cannery agrees to purchase from Tu, and Tu agrees to sell to the cannery, all of the green beans that the cannery requires during the following summer. There is implicit consideration in this contract because the buyer (the cannery) gives up the right to buy goods (green beans) from any other seller. This forfeited right creates a legal *detriment*—that is, consideration. ∎

If, however, the buyer promises to purchase only if he or she *wishes* to do so, the promise is illusory (without consideration) and unenforceable by either party. Similarly, if the buyer reserves the right to buy the goods from someone other than the seller, the promise is unenforceable (illusory) as a requirements contract.

Output Contracts. In an **output contract,** the seller agrees to sell and the buyer agrees to buy all or up to a stated amount of what the seller produces. ∎ **EXAMPLE 20.10** Ruth Sewell has planted two acres of organic tomatoes. Bella Union, a local restaurant, agrees to buy all of the tomatoes that Sewell produces that year to use at the restaurant. Again, because the seller essentially forfeits the right to sell goods to another buyer, there is implicit consideration in an output contract. ∎

The UCC imposes a *good faith limitation* on requirements and output contracts. The quantity under such contracts is the amount of requirements or the amount of output that occurs during a *normal* production period.

---

7. *H. Daya Inter. Co. v. Do Denim*, 2012 WL 2524729 (S.D.N.Y. 2012).

The actual quantity purchased or sold cannot be unreasonably disproportionate to normal or comparable prior requirements or output [UCC 2–306(1)].

Merchant's Firm Offer Under regular contract principles, an offer can be revoked at any time before acceptance. The major common law exception is an *option contract*, in which the offeree pays consideration for the offeror's irrevocable promise to keep the offer open for a stated period. The UCC creates a second exception for *firm offers* made by a merchant concerning the sale or lease of goods (regardless of whether or not the offeree is a merchant).

When a Merchant's Firm Offer Arises. A **firm offer** arises when a merchant-offeror gives *assurances in a signed writing* that the offer will remain open. The merchant's firm offer is irrevocable without the necessity of consideration[8] for the stated period or, if no definite period is stated, a reasonable period (neither to exceed three months) [UCC 2–205, 2A–205].

■ **EXAMPLE 20.11** Osaka, a used-car dealer, e-mails a letter to Gomez on January 1, stating, "I have a used 2016 Toyota RAV4 on the lot that I'll sell you for $22,000 any time between now and January 31." This e-mail creates a firm offer, and Osaka will be liable for breach of contract if he sells the RAV4 to another person before January 31. ■

Requirements for a Firm Offer. To qualify as a firm offer, the offer must be:

1. *Written* (or electronically recorded, such as in an e-mail).
2. *Signed* by the offeror.[9]

When a firm offer is contained in a form contract prepared by the offeree, the offeror must also sign a separate assurance of the firm offer. The requirement of a separate signature ensures that the offeror will be made aware of the firm offer.

For instance, an offeree might respond to an initial offer by sending its own form contract containing a clause stating that the offer will remain open for three months. If the firm offer is buried amid copious language on the last page of the offeree's form contract, the offeror may inadvertently sign the contract without realizing that it contains a firm offer. This would defeat the purpose of

the rule—which is to give effect to a merchant's *deliberate* intent to be bound to a firm offer.

20–3b Acceptance

Acceptance of an offer to buy, sell, or lease goods generally may be made in any reasonable manner and by any reasonable means. The UCC permits acceptance of an offer to buy goods "either by a prompt *promise* to ship or by the prompt or current shipment of conforming or nonconforming goods" [UCC 2–206(1)(b)]. *Conforming goods* accord with the contract's terms, whereas *nonconforming goods* do not.

The prompt shipment of nonconforming goods constitutes both an acceptance, which creates a contract, and a breach of that contract. This rule does not apply if the seller **seasonably** (within a reasonable amount of time) notifies the buyer that the nonconforming shipment is offered only as an *accommodation,* or as a favor. The notice of accommodation must clearly indicate to the buyer that the shipment does not constitute an acceptance and that, therefore, no contract has been formed.

■ **EXAMPLE 20.12** McFarren Pharmacy orders five cases of Johnson & Johnson 3-by-5-inch gauze pads from H.T. Medical Supply, Inc. If H.T. ships five cases of Xeroform 3-by-5-inch gauze pads instead, the shipment acts as both an acceptance of McFarren's offer and a breach of the resulting contract. McFarren may sue H.T. for any appropriate damages. If, however, H.T. notifies McFarren that the Xeroform pads are being shipped *as an accommodation*—because H.T. has only Xeroform pads in stock—the shipment does not act as an acceptance. Instead, it constitutes a counteroffer, and a contract will be formed only if McFarren accepts the Xeroform gauze pads. ■

Communication of Acceptance Under the common law, because a unilateral offer invites acceptance by performance, the offeree need not notify the offeror of performance unless the offeror would not otherwise know about it. In other words, a unilateral offer can be accepted by beginning performance.

The UCC is more stringent than the common law in this regard because it requires notification. Under the UCC, if the offeror is not notified within a reasonable time that the offeree has accepted the contract by beginning performance, then the offeror can treat the offer as having lapsed before acceptance [UCC 2–206(2), 2A–206(2)].

Additional Terms Recall that under the common law, the mirror image rule requires that the terms of the

---

8. If the offeree pays consideration, then an option contract (not a merchant's firm offer) is formed.
9. *Signed* includes any symbol executed or adopted by a party with a present intention to authenticate a writing [UCC 1–201(37)]. A complete signature is not required.

acceptance exactly match those of the offer. ■ **EXAMPLE 20.13** Adderson e-mails an offer to sell twenty Samsung Galaxy tablet model S2 to Beale. If Beale accepts the offer but changes it to require model S4 tablets, then there is no contract if the mirror image rule applies. ■

To avoid such problems, the UCC dispenses with the mirror image rule. Under the UCC, a contract is formed if the offeree's response indicates a *definite* acceptance of the offer, *even if the acceptance includes terms additional to or different from those contained in the offer* [UCC 2–207(1)]. Whether the additional terms become part of the contract depends, in part, on whether the parties are nonmerchants or merchants.

Rules When One Party or Both Parties Are Nonmerchants. If one (or both) of the parties is a *nonmerchant*, the contract is formed according to the terms of the original offer. The contract does not include any of the additional terms in the acceptance [UCC 2–207(2)].

■ **CASE IN POINT 20.14** OfficeSupplyStore.com sells office supplies on the Web. Employees of the Kansas City School District in Missouri ordered $17,642.54 worth of office supplies—without the authority or approval of their employer—from the Web site. The invoices accompanying the goods contained a *forum-selection clause* that required all disputes to be resolved in California.

When the goods were not paid for, Office Supply filed suit in California. The Kansas City School District objected, arguing that the forum-selection clause was not binding. The court held that the forum-selection clause was not part of the parties' contract. The clause was an additional term included in the invoices delivered to a nonmerchant buyer (the school district) with the purchased goods. Therefore, the clause did not become part of the contract unless the buyer expressly agreed, which did not happen in this case.[10] ■

Rules When Both Parties Are Merchants. The UCC includes a special rule for merchants to avoid the "battle of the forms," which occurs when two merchants exchange separate standard forms containing different contract terms.

Under UCC 2–207(2), in contracts *between merchants,* the additional terms *automatically* become part of the contract *unless* one of the following conditions arises:

1. The original offer expressly limited acceptance to its terms.
2. The new or changed terms materially alter the contract.
3. The offeror objects to the new or changed terms within a reasonable period of time.

When determining whether an alteration is material, courts consider several factors. Generally, if the modification does not involve any unreasonable element of surprise or hardship for the offeror, a court will hold that the modification did not materially alter the contract. Courts also consider the parties' prior dealings. As shown in the following case, however, what constitutes a material alteration is frequently a question of fact that only a court can decide.

---

10. *OfficeSupplyStore.com v. Kansas City School Board*, 334S.W.3d 574 (Kan. 2011).

Case 20.1

C. Mahendra (N.Y.), LLC v. National Gold & Diamond Center, Inc.

New York Supreme Court, Appellate Division, First Department, 125 A.D.3d 454, 3 N.Y.S.3d 27 (2015).

Background and Facts C. Mahendra (N.Y.), LLC, is a New York wholesaler of loose diamonds. National Gold & Diamond Center, Inc., is a California seller of jewelry. Over a ten-year period, National placed orders, totaling millions of dollars, with Mahendra by phoning and negotiating the terms. Mahendra shipped diamonds "on memorandum" for National to examine. Mahendra then sent invoices for the diamonds that National chose to keep. Both the memoranda and the invoices stated, "You consent to the exclusive jurisdiction of the . . . courts situated in New York County."

When two orders totaling $64,000 went unpaid, Mahendra filed a suit in a New York state court against National, alleging breach of contract. National filed a motion to dismiss the complaint for lack of personal jurisdiction, contending that the forum-selection clause was not binding. The court granted the motion. Mahendra appealed.

Case 20.1 Continued

In the Language of the Court

SWEENY, P.J. [Presiding Judge], MOSKOWITZ, DEGRASSE, MANZANET-DANIELS, CLARK, JJ. [Judges]
* * * *

* * * Defendant argued the forum-selection clause in the * * * memorandums was not binding because its president never signed the memorandums' terms and conditions. Defendant thus maintained that it had not signed or agreed to the forum-selection clause, nor had it otherwise consented to being sued in New York. Likewise, defendant asserted that because it had negotiated for and ordered the diamonds from California and did not sign or agree to the forum-selection clause, the consent to jurisdiction contained in the memorandums would materially alter the parties' agreements in contravention of UCC 2–207(2)(b). Thus, defendant concluded, it was not bound by the unsigned provision on the back of the * * * memorandums.
* * * *

* * * The [lower] court found the forum-selection clause invalid, noting that defendant did not sign the invoices. The court further found that under UCC 2–207(2), forum-selection clauses are additional terms that materially alter a contract, and must be construed as mere proposals for additions to the contract. Thus, the court concluded, the forum-selection clause was non-binding absent an express agreement. Indeed, the court noted, the complaint did not allege that defendant affirmatively expressed consent, either orally or in writing, to the forum-selection clause when it retained the invoices.
* * * *

The [lower] court correctly found that defendant is not bound by the forum-selection clause on plaintiff's invoices. UCC 2–207 contemplates situations like the one here, where parties do business through an exchange of forms such as purchase orders and invoices. As the parties did here, *merchants frequently include terms in their forms that were not discussed with the other side. UCC 2–207(2) addresses that scenario, providing, "the additional terms are to be construed as proposals for addition to the contract. Between merchants such terms become part of the contract unless: * * * (b) they materially alter it."* [Emphasis added.]

Here, during telephone discussions, the parties negotiated the essential terms required for contract formation, and the invoices were merely confirmatory. Thus, the forum-selection clause is an additional term that materially altered the parties' oral contracts, and defendant did not give its consent to that additional term.

Decision and Remedy *A state intermediate appellate court agreed that "the forum-selection clause is an additional term that materially altered the parties' . . . contracts, and defendant did not give its consent to that additional term." But the court reversed the dismissal of Mahendra's complaint on the ground that National's phone calls with Mahendra were sufficient contacts to subject the defendant to personal jurisdiction in New York under the state's long-arm statute.*

Critical Thinking

- **Legal** *What is Mahendra's best argument that the forum-selection clause was, in fact, binding on National? Discuss.*

Prior Dealings between Merchants. In contracts between merchants, courts also consider the parties' prior dealings. ■ **CASE IN POINT 20.15** WPS, Inc., submitted a proposal to manufacture equipment for Expro Americas, LLC, and Surface Production Systems, Inc. (SPS). Expro and SPS then submitted two purchase orders. WPS accepted the first purchase order in part and the second order conditionally. Among other things, WPS's acceptance required that Expro and SPS give their "full release to proceed" and agree to "pay all valid costs associated with any order cancellation." The parties' negotiations continued, and Expro and SPS eventually submitted a third purchase order.

Although the third purchase order did not comply with all of WPS's requirements, it did give WPS permission to proceed. It also specified that Expro and SPS would pay all cancellation costs. With Expro and SPS's knowledge, WPS began working on that order. Expro and SPS later canceled the order and refused to pay the cancellation costs. When the dispute ended in court,

Expro and SPS claimed that the additional terms in WPS's acceptance had materially altered the contract and rendered it unenforceable. The court found in favor of WPS. Expro and SPS had given a release to proceed that authorized WPS to go forward with manufacturing the equipment. Because "the parties operated as if they had additional time to resolve the outstanding differences," the court reasoned that Expro and SPS were contractually obligated to pay the cancellation costs.[11] ■

Conditioned on Offeror's Assent. The offeree's response is not an acceptance if it contains additional or different terms and is expressly *conditioned* on the offeror's assent to those terms [UCC 2–207(1)]. This is true whether or not the parties are merchants.

■ **EXAMPLE 20.16** Philips offers to sell Hundert 650 pounds of turkey thighs at a specified price and with specified delivery terms. Hundert responds, "I accept your offer for 650 pounds of turkey thighs *on the condition that you agree to give me ninety days to pay for them.*" Hundert's response will be construed not as an acceptance but as a counteroffer, which Philips may or may not accept. ■

Additional Terms May Be Stricken. The UCC provides yet another option for dealing with conflicting terms in the parties' writings. Section 2–207(3) states that conduct by both parties that recognizes the existence of a contract is sufficient to establish a contract for sale. This is so even if the writings of the parties do not otherwise establish a contract. In this situation, "the terms of the particular contract will consist of those terms on which the writings of the parties agree, together with any supplementary terms incorporated under any other provisions of this Act." In a dispute over contract terms, this provision allows a court simply to strike from the contract those terms on which the parties do not agree.

■ **EXAMPLE 20.17** SMT Marketing orders goods over the phone from Brigg Sales, Inc., which ships the goods to SMT with an acknowledgment form confirming the order. SMT accepts and pays for the goods. The parties' writings do not establish a contract, but there is no question that a contract exists. If a dispute arises over the terms, such as the extent of any warranties, UCC 2–207(3) provides the governing rule. ■

As noted previously, the fact that a merchant's acceptance frequently contains terms that add to or even conflict with those of the offer is often referred to as the "battle of the forms." Although the UCC tries to eliminate this battle, the problem of differing contract terms

still arises in commercial settings, particularly when standard forms (for placing and confirming orders) are used.

20–3c Consideration

The common law rule that a contract requires consideration also applies to sales and lease contracts. Unlike the common law, however, the UCC does not require a contract modification to be supported by new consideration. The UCC states that an agreement modifying a contract for the sale or lease of goods "needs no consideration to be binding" [UCC 2–209(1), 2A–208(1)]. Of course, any contract modification must be made in good faith [UCC 1–304].

In some situations, an agreement to modify a sales or lease contract without consideration must be in writing to be enforceable. For instance, if the contract itself specifies that any changes to the contract must be in a signed writing, only those changes agreed to in a signed writing are enforceable.

Sometimes, when a consumer (nonmerchant) is buying goods from a merchant-seller, the merchant supplies a form that contains a prohibition against oral modification. In those situations, the consumer must sign a separate acknowledgment of the clause for it to be enforceable [UCC 2–209(2), 2A–208(2)]. Also, any modification that makes a sales contract come under Article 2's writing requirement (its Statute of Frauds, discussed next) usually requires a writing (or electronic record) to be enforceable.

See Concept Summary 20.1 for a review of the UCC's rules on offer, acceptance, and consideration.

20–3d The Statute of Frauds

The UCC contains Statute of Frauds provisions covering sales and lease contracts. Under these provisions, sales contracts for goods priced at $500 or more and lease contracts requiring total payments of $1,000 or more must be in writing to be enforceable [UCC 2–201(1), 2A–201(1)]. (These low threshold amounts may eventually be raised.)

Sufficiency of the Writing A writing, including an e-mail or other electronic record, will be sufficient to satisfy the UCC's Statute of Frauds as long as it:

1. Indicates that the parties intended to form a contract.
2. Is signed by the party (or agent of the party) against whom enforcement is sought. (Remember that a typed name can qualify as a signature on an electronic record.)

---

11. *WPS, Inc. v. Expro Americas, LLC,* 369 S.W.3d 384 (Tex.App. 2012).

Concept Summary 20.1

Offer, Acceptance, and Consideration under the UCC

Offer
- Not all terms have to be included for a contract to be formed.
- The price does not have to be included for a contract to be formed.
- Particulars of performance can be left open.
- An offer by a merchant in a signed writing with assurances that the offer will not be withdrawn is irrevocable without consideration (for up to three months).

Acceptance
- Acceptance may be made by any reasonable means of communication. It is effective when dispatched.
- An offer can be made by a promise to ship or by the shipment of conforming goods, or by prompt shipment of nonconforming goods unless accompanied by a notice of accommodation.
- Acceptance by performance requires notice within a reasonable time. Otherwise, the offer can be treated as lapsed.
- A definite expression of acceptance creates a contract even if the terms of the acceptance differ from those of the offer (unless acceptance is expressly conditioned on consent to the additional or different terms).

Consideration
- A *modification* of a contract for the sale or lease of goods does not require consideration as long as it is made in good faith.

The contract normally will not be enforceable beyond the quantity of goods shown in the writing, however. All other terms can be proved in court by oral testimony. For leases, the writing must reasonably identify and describe the goods leased and the lease term.

Special Rules for Contracts between Merchants The UCC provides a special rule for merchants in sales transactions (there is no corresponding rule that applies to leases under Article 2A). Merchants can satisfy the Statute of Frauds if, after the parties have agreed orally, one of the merchants sends a signed written confirmation to the other merchant within a reasonable time.

The communication must indicate the terms of the agreement, and the merchant receiving the confirmation must have reason to know of its contents. Unless the merchant who receives the confirmation gives written notice of objection to its contents within ten days after receipt, the writing is sufficient against the receiving merchant, even though she or he has not signed it [UCC 2–201(2)].

■ **EXAMPLE 20.18** Alfonso is a merchant-buyer in Cleveland. He contracts over the telephone to purchase $6,000 worth of spare aircraft parts from Goldstein, a merchant-seller in New York City. Two days later, Goldstein e-mails a signed confirmation detailing the terms of the oral contract, and Alfonso subsequently receives it. Alfonso does not notify Goldstein in writing that he objects to the contents of the confirmation within ten days of receipt. Therefore, Alfonso cannot raise the Statute of Frauds as a defense against the enforcement of the oral contract. ■

Exceptions The UCC defines three exceptions to the writing requirements of the Statute of Frauds. An oral contract for the sale of goods priced at $500 or more or the lease of goods involving total payments of $1,000 or more will be enforceable despite the absence of a writing in the circumstances described next [UCC 2–201(3), 2A–201(4)].

Specially Manufactured Goods. An oral contract for the sale or lease of custom-made goods will be enforceable if:

1. The goods are *specially manufactured* for a particular buyer or specially manufactured or obtained for a particular lessee.

2. The goods are *not suitable for resale or lease* to others in the ordinary course of the seller's or lessor's business.
3. The seller or lessor *has substantially started to manufacture* the goods or has made commitments for the manufacture or procurement of the goods.

In these situations, once the seller or lessor has taken action, the buyer or lessee cannot repudiate the agreement claiming the Statute of Frauds as a defense.

■ **EXAMPLE 20.19** Womach orders custom window treatments to use at a day spa business from Hunter Douglas for $6,000. The contract is oral. When Hunter Douglas manufactures the window coverings and tenders delivery to Womach, she refuses to pay for them, even though the job has been completed on time. Womach claims that she is not liable because the contract was oral. If the unique style, size, and color of the window treatments make it improbable that Hunter Douglas can find another buyer, Womach is liable to Hunter Douglas. ■

Admissions. An oral contract for the sale or lease of goods is enforceable if the party against whom enforcement is sought admits in pleadings, testimony, or other court proceedings that a sales or lease contract was made. In this situation, the contract will be enforceable even though it was oral, but enforceability will be limited to the quantity of goods admitted.

■ **CASE IN POINT 20.20** Gerald Lindgren, a farmer, agreed by phone to sell his crops to Glacial Plains Cooperative. The parties reached four oral agreements: two for the delivery of soybeans and two for the delivery of corn. Lindgren made the soybean deliveries and part of the first corn delivery, but he sold the rest of his corn to another dealer. Glacial Plains bought corn elsewhere, paying a higher price, and then sued Lindgren for breach of contract. In papers filed with the court, Lindgren acknowledged his oral agreements with Glacial Plains and admitted that he did not fully perform. The court applied the admissions exception and held that the four agreements were enforceable.[12] ■

Partial Performance. An oral contract for the sale or lease of goods is enforceable if payment has been made and accepted or goods have been received and accepted. This is the "partial performance" exception. The oral contract will be enforced at least to the extent that performance actually took place.

■ **EXAMPLE 20.21** Quality Meats buys food products and sells them to retail operations. Quality orally contracts with A1 Food Services, Inc., to ship three orders

---

12. *Glacial Plains Cooperative v. Lindgren*, 759 N.W.2d 661 (Min.App. 2009).

of beef to Choice Processing, for which A1 agrees to pay. Quality ships the goods to Choice and sends invoices to A1. A1 bills Choice for all three orders, but pays Quality only for the first two. Quality then files a suit against A1 to recover the cost of the third order.

A1 argues that because the parties did not have a written agreement, there was no enforceable contract. But a court could find that even though A1 had not signed a written contract or purchase order, it had partially performed the contract by paying for the first two shipments. A1's conduct is likely sufficient to prove the existence of a contract, and the court could require A1 to pay for the last shipment. ■

The exceptions just discussed and other ways in which sales law differs from general contract law are summarized in Exhibit 20–2.

20–3e Parol Evidence

Recall that parol evidence consists of evidence outside the contract, such as evidence of the parties' prior negotiations, prior agreements, or contemporaneous oral agreements. When a contract completely sets forth all the terms and conditions agreed to by the parties and is intended as a final statement of their agreement, it is considered fully *integrated*. The terms of a **fully integrated contract** cannot be contradicted by evidence of any prior agreements or contemporaneous oral agreements.

If, however, the writing contains some of the terms the parties agreed on but not others, then the contract is not fully integrated. When a court finds that a contract is *not fully integrated,* then the court may allow evidence of *consistent additional terms* to explain or supplement the terms in the contract. The court may also allow the parties to submit evidence of *course of dealing, usage of trade,* or *course of performance* [UCC 2–202, 2A–202].

Course of Dealing and Usage of Trade Under the UCC, the meaning of any agreement, evidenced by the language of the parties and their actions, must be interpreted in light of commercial practices and other surrounding circumstances. In interpreting a commercial agreement, a court will assume that the course of dealing between the parties and the general usage of trade were taken into account when the agreement was phrased.

Course of Dealing. A **course of dealing** is a sequence of actions and communications between the parties to a particular transaction that establishes a common basis for their understanding [UCC 1–303(b)]. A course of dealing is restricted to the sequence of conduct between the parties in their transactions prior to the agreement.

EXHIBIT 20–2   Major Differences between Contract Law and Sales Law

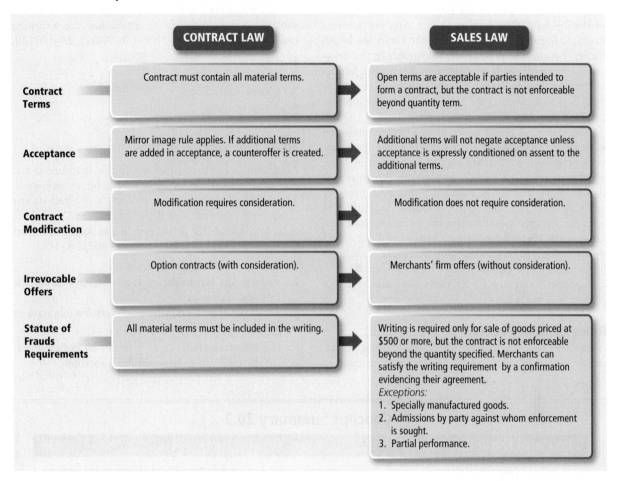

	CONTRACT LAW	SALES LAW
Contract Terms	Contract must contain all material terms.	Open terms are acceptable if parties intended to form a contract, but the contract is not enforceable beyond quantity term.
Acceptance	Mirror image rule applies. If additional terms are added in acceptance, a counteroffer is created.	Additional terms will not negate acceptance unless acceptance is expressly conditioned on assent to the additional terms.
Contract Modification	Modification requires consideration.	Modification does not require consideration.
Irrevocable Offers	Option contracts (with consideration).	Merchants' firm offers (without consideration).
Statute of Frauds Requirements	All material terms must be included in the writing.	Writing is required only for sale of goods priced at $500 or more, but the contract is not enforceable beyond the quantity specified. Merchants can satisfy the writing requirement by a confirmation evidencing their agreement. *Exceptions:* 1. Specially manufactured goods. 2. Admissions by party against whom enforcement is sought. 3. Partial performance.

Under the UCC, a course of dealing between the parties is relevant in ascertaining the meaning of the parties' agreement. It "may give particular meaning to specific terms of the agreement, and may supplement or qualify the terms of the agreement" [UCC 1–303(d)].

Usage of Trade. Some practices and methods of dealing are so regularly observed in a place, vocation, or trade that parties to contracts expect them to be observed in their transactions. Such a practice or method of dealing is known as a **usage of trade** [UCC 1–303(c)].

■ **EXAMPLE 20.22** Phat Khat Loans, Inc., hires Fleet Title Review Company to search the public records for prior claims on potential borrowers' assets. Fleet's invoice states, "Liability limited to amount of fee." In the title search industry, liability limits are common. After conducting many searches for Phat Khat, Fleet reports that there are no claims with respect to Main

Street Autos. Phat Khat lends $100,000 to Main, with payment guaranteed by Main's assets. When Main defaults on the loan, Phat Khat learns that another lender has priority to Main's assets under a previous claim. If Phat Khat sues Fleet for breach of contract, Fleet's liability will normally be limited to the amount of its fee. The statement in the invoice was part of the contract between Phat Khat and Fleet, according to the usage of trade in the industry and the parties' course of dealing. ■

Course of Performance The conduct that occurs under the terms of a particular agreement is called a **course of performance** [UCC 1–303(a)]. Presumably, the parties themselves know best what they meant by their words. Thus, the course of performance actually carried out under the parties' agreement is the best indication of what they meant [UCC 2–208(1), 2A–207(1)].

■ **EXAMPLE 20.23** Janson's Lumber Company contracts with Lopez to sell Lopez a specified number of two-by-fours. The lumber in fact does not measure exactly 2 inches by 4 inches but rather 1⅞ inches by 3¾ inches. Janson's agrees to deliver the lumber in five deliveries, and Lopez, without objection, accepts the lumber in the first three deliveries. On the fourth delivery, however, Lopez objects that the two-by-fours do not measure precisely 2 inches by 4 inches.

The course of performance in this transaction—that is, Lopez's acceptance of three deliveries without objection—is relevant in determining that here a "two-by-four" actually means a "1⅞-by-3¾." Janson's can also prove that two-by-fours need not be exactly 2 inches by 4 inches by applying usage of trade, course of dealing, or both. Janson's can, for example, show that in previous transactions, Lopez took 1⅞-inch-by-3¾-inch lumber without objection. In addition, Janson's can show that in the trade, two-by-fours are commonly 1⅞ inches by 3¾ inches. ■

Concept Summary 20.2 reviews the parol evidence rule.

Rules of Construction The UCC provides *rules of construction* for interpreting contracts. Express terms, course of performance, course of dealing, and usage of trade are to be construed to be consistent with each other whenever reasonable. When such a construction is unreasonable, however, the UCC establishes the following order of priority [UCC 1–303(e), 2–208(2), 2A–207(2)]:

1. Express terms.
2. Course of performance.
3. Course of dealing.
4. Usage of trade.

20-3f Unconscionability

An unconscionable contract is one that is so unfair and one sided that it would be unreasonable to enforce it. The UCC allows a court to evaluate a contract or any clause in a contract, and if the court deems it to have been unconscionable *at the time it was made,* the court can do any of the following [UCC 2–302, 2A–108]:

1. Refuse to enforce the contract.
2. Enforce the remainder of the contract without the unconscionable part.
3. Limit the application of the unconscionable term to avoid an unconscionable result.

The following classic case illustrates an early application of the UCC's unconscionability provisions.

Concept Summary 20.2

The Parol Evidence Rule

Definition	• Parol evidence is evidence outside the contract, such as the parties' prior negotiations, prior agreements, or oral agreements made at the time of the contract formation. • When the contract completely sets forth all the terms and conditions agreed to by the parties and is intended as the final statement of their agreement, it is considered fully integrated. • Under the parol evidence rule, the terms of a fully integrated contract cannot be contradicted by parol evidence.
When Parol Evidence Is Admissible	• If the writing (or record) contains some of the terms that the parties agreed to but not others, the contract is not fully integrated. A court may allow consistent additional terms to explain or supplement the terms stated in the contract. • If the contract terms are ambiguous, a court might allow the parties to submit parol evidence to explain their intentions. • If evidence of course of dealing, usage of trade, or course of performance is necessary to clarify the intentions of the parties to the contract.

Jones v. Star Credit Corp.

Supreme Court of New York, Nassau County, 59 Misc.2d 189, 298 N.Y.S.2d 264 (1969).

Background and Facts The Joneses agreed to purchase a freezer for $900 as the result of a sales-person's visit to their home. Tax and financing charges raised the total price to $1,234.80. Later, the Joneses, who had made payments totaling $619.88, brought a suit in a New York state court to have the purchase contract declared unconscionable under the UCC. At trial, the freezer was found to have a maximum retail value of approximately $300.

In the Language of the Court

Sol M. *WACHTLER*, Justice.

* * * *

* * * [Section 2–302 of the UCC] authorizes the court to find, as a matter of law, that a contract or a clause of a contract was "unconscionable at the time it was made," and upon so finding the court may refuse to enforce the contract, excise the objectionable clause or limit the application of the clause to avoid an unconscionable result.

* * * *

* * * The question which presents itself is whether or not, under the circumstances of this case, the sale of a freezer unit having a retail value of $300 for $900 ($1,439.69 including credit charges and $18 sales tax) is unconscionable as a matter of law.

Concededly, deciding [this case] is substantially easier than explaining it. No doubt, the mathematical disparity between $300, which presumably includes a reasonable profit margin, and $900, which is exorbitant on its face, carries the greatest weight. Credit charges alone exceed by more than $100 the retail value of the freezer. These alone may be sufficient to sustain the decision. Yet, a caveat [warning] is warranted lest we reduce the import of Section 2–302 solely to a mathematical ratio formula. It may, at times, be that; yet it may also be much more. The very limited financial resources of the purchaser, known to the sellers at the time of the sale, is entitled to weight in the balance. Indeed, the value disparity itself leads inevitably to the felt conclusion that knowing advantage was taken of the plaintiffs. In addition, *the meaningfulness of choice essential to the making of a contract can be negated by a gross inequality of bargaining power.* [Emphasis added.]

* * * *

* * * The defendant has already been amply compensated. In accordance with the statute, the application of the payment provision should be limited to amounts already paid by the plaintiffs and the contract be reformed and amended by changing the payments called for therein to equal the amount of payment actually so paid by the plaintiffs.

Decision and Remedy *The court held that the contract was not enforceable and reformed the contract so that no further payments were required.*

Impact of This Case on Today's Law *This early classic case illustrates the approach that many courts take today when deciding whether a sales contract is unconscionable—an approach that focuses on "excessive" price and unequal bargaining power. Most of the litigants who have used UCC 2–302 successfully could demonstrate both an absence of meaningful choice and contract terms that were unreasonably favorable to the other party.*

Critical Thinking

• **Social** *Why would the seller's knowledge of the buyers' limited resources support a finding of unconscionability?*

20–4 Contracts for the International Sale of Goods

International sales contracts between firms or individuals located in different countries may be governed by the 1980 United Nations Convention on Contracts for the International Sale of Goods (CISG). The CISG governs international contracts only if the countries of the parties to the contract have ratified the CISG and if the parties have not agreed that some other law will govern their contract.

As of 2018, the CISG had been adopted by eighty-four countries, including the United States, Canada, some Central and South American countries, China, most European nations, Japan, and Mexico. That means that the CISG is the uniform international sales law of countries that account for more than two-thirds of all global trade. (The appendix at the end of this chapter shows an actual international sales contract used by the Starbucks Coffee Company.)

Essentially, the CISG is to international sales contracts what Article 2 of the UCC is to domestic sales contracts. In domestic transactions, the UCC applies when the parties to a contract for a sale of goods have failed to specify in writing some important term, such as price or delivery. Similarly, whenever the parties to international transactions have failed to specify in writing the precise terms of a contract, the CISG will be applied.

Unlike the UCC, *the CISG does not apply to consumer sales.* Neither the UCC nor the CISG applies to contracts for services.

20–4a A Comparison of CISG and UCC Provisions

The provisions of the CISG, although similar for the most part to those of the UCC, differ from them in some respects. If the CISG and the UCC conflict, the CISG applies (because it is a treaty of the U.S. national government and therefore is supreme). We look here at some differences with respect to contract formation. CISG provisions relating to risk of loss, performance, remedies, and warranties will be discussed in other chapters as those topics are examined.

The Mirror Image Rule   Under the UCC, a definite expression of acceptance that contains additional terms can still result in the formation of a contract, unless the additional terms are conditioned on the assent of the offeror. In other words, as we have seen, the UCC does away with the mirror image rule in domestic sales contracts.

Article 19 of the CISG provides that a contract can be formed even though the acceptance contains additional terms, unless the additional terms materially alter the contract. Under the CISG, however, the definition of a "material alteration" includes almost any change in the terms. If an additional term relates to payment, quality, quantity, price, time and place of delivery, extent of one party's liability to the other, or the settlement of disputes, the CISG considers the added term a material alteration. In effect, then, the CISG requires that the terms of the acceptance mirror those of the offer.

Therefore, as a practical matter, businesspersons undertaking international sales transactions should not use the sale or purchase forms that they customarily use for transactions within the United States. Instead, they should draft specific forms to suit the needs of the particular transaction.

The court in the following case applied the CISG's mirror image rule to eighteen contracts for sales of frozen potatoes from a supplier in Canada to a company in Illinois.

Case Analysis 20.3

VLM Food Trading International, Inc. v. Illinois Trading Co.

United States Court of Appeals, Seventh Circuit, 811 F.3d 247 (2016).

In the Language of the Court
SYKES, Circuit Judge.

* * * *

This [is a] contract dispute between plaintiff VLM Food Trading International, Inc., a Canadian agricultural

supplier, and Illinois Trading Company, an Illinois produce reseller.

* * * *

* * * VLM sold frozen potatoes to Illinois Trading through nine separate transactions without incident. Illinois

Trading then encountered financial difficulty and failed to pay for the next nine shipments from VLM. The parties agree that each transaction occurred the same way. First,

Case 20.3 Continued

Illinois Trading sent a purchase order specifying the item, quantity, price, and place of delivery for the potatoes. Second, VLM responded with an e-mail confirming the terms of the sale. Third, VLM shipped the order and Illinois Trading accepted it. Finally, VLM followed up by mail with an invoice. Importantly for us, the trailing invoices included a provision purporting to make Illinois Trading liable for * * * attorney's fees if it breached the contracts.

When Illinois Trading stopped paying its invoices, VLM sued Illinois Trading [in a federal district court].

* * * The answer admitted that the defendant owed VLM the purchase price for the produce * * * but contested liability for attorney's fees.

* * * The judge applied the [United Nations Convention on Contracts for the International Sale of Goods] and held that the attorney's fees provision was *not* part of the contracts. [VLM appealed, challenging the court's analysis and application of the law to reach this conclusion.]

* * * *

The Convention's definition of the "loss" resulting from a breach of contract does not itself include attorney's fees. To succeed, VLM must show that its contracts with Illinois Trading expressly made Illinois Trading liable for VLM's attorney's fees in the event of a breach. To determine whether the fees provision was expressly accepted by Illinois Trading, we need to know when the terms of their agreement became binding. [Emphasis added.]

A contract is formed under the Convention when there is a valid offer and acceptance. An offer is valid if it is sufficiently definite and indicates the intention of the offeror to be bound in case of acceptance. An offer is sufficiently definite if it indicates the goods and expressly or implicitly fixes or makes provision for determining the quantity and price. Once a valid offer has been extended, the offeree can accept by words or conduct, but not by silence or inactivity. An acceptance becomes effective at the moment the indication of assent reaches the offeror. Acceptance

can also be demonstrated through the offeree's conduct, if allowed as a result of practices which the parties have established between themselves or of usage.

So far so good—these contract principles are familiar and very similar to those expressed in the UCC. But * * * the Convention departs dramatically from the UCC by using the common-law "mirror image" rule * * * to resolve "battles of the forms." Under the mirror-image rule, as expressed in Article 19(1) of the Convention, "a reply to an offer which purports to be an acceptance but contains additions, limitations or other modifications is a rejection of the offer and constitutes a counter-offer."

Each Illinois Trading purchase order met all the Convention's criteria for an offer; they included sufficiently definite terms, were directed to VLM specifically, and indicated that Illinois Trading intended to be bound by VLM's acceptance. Each of VLM's confirmation e-mails was, in turn, an effective acceptance of Illinois Trading's offer because each one confirmed and accepted the terms of the purchase order. As such, the contracts were formed when Illinois Trading received VLM's confirmation e-mails. The attorney's fees provision was *not* part of the agreement described in the purchase orders and the e-mail confirmations; that term first appeared in the trailing invoices that were mailed to Illinois Trading *after* VLM delivered the produce.

Under the Convention VLM had already bound itself to the contracts proposed by Illinois Trading when it confirmed Illinois Trading's purchase offer by e-mail. The attorney's fees provision therefore could not have been a counteroffer. Rather, * * * the attorney's fees * * * provision would be a proposed modification to the contracts. Under the mirror-image rule, a party does not have to object to a proposed modification in order to keep it from being incorporated; any term that is not "mirrored" in the offer and acceptance is excluded. Contracts can only be modified by agreement of the parties.

Illinois Trading never made any statements indicating its acceptance of the proposed attorney's fees modification. Indeed, the only possible activity that could have indicated Illinois Trading's acceptance of the proposed modification was its payment of the invoices. But that conduct is just as consistent with Illinois Trading's obligations under the original agreement as it is with any new acceptance. Furthermore, since VLM had already completely performed its duties under the original proposed agreement, it had no performance left to offer in consideration for any (gratuitous) agreement by Illinois Trading to assume liability for VLM's attorney's fees in the event of breach.

* * * *

VLM contends that despite the contract-formation analysis prescribed by the Convention, the parties subjectively intended the attorney's fees provision to apply. In VLM's view the Convention "commands" judges to consider extrinsic evidence to illuminate the parties' intent. This argument relies largely on Article 8(3), which reads: "In determining the intent of a party * * * due consideration is to be given to all relevant circumstances of the case including the negotiations, any practices which the parties have established between themselves, usages and any subsequent conduct of the parties." But the purpose of this intent test is to help courts interpret the statements and conduct of parties according to their intent where the other party knew * * * what that intent was. Although VLM's conduct, sending trailing invoices containing an attorney's fees provision, clearly indicates that *VLM* intended Illinois Trading to be liable for collection fees, there was never any indication of *mutual* intent at the time of contracting. Fee-shifting was never mentioned during any negotiations, and none of Illinois Trading's subsequent conduct indicates that it agreed to pay VLM's attorney's fees.

* * * *

VLM also points to Article 9(1), which says that "parties are bound to any

Case 20.3 Continues

Case 20.3 Continued

usage to which they have agreed and by any practices which they have established between themselves." This clause doesn't help for two reasons. First, there simply isn't any established "practice" between Illinois Trading and VLM regarding liability for attorney's fees. * * * Second, evidence of "usage" comes into play to clarify the meaning assigned to a contract term * * * . Here, no contract term is ambiguous and thus in need of clarification by evidence of usage. In other words, there's no disagreement about what the attorney's fees provision *means;* the only issue is whether it was part of the parties' agreement.

* * * *

Finally, the fact that some of Illinois Trading's contracts with other vendors included fee-shifting provisions is not relevant under the mirror-image rule, nor is the fact that Illinois Trading paid attorney's fees as part of its settlements with certain vendors. Nothing in the Convention indicates that common industry practices are automatically grafted onto contracts; rather, the content of each contract must be analyzed independently.

For all these reasons, the [district court] judge properly applied the Convention and held that the parties' contracts did not include the attorney's fees provision.

Legal Reasoning Questions

1. How did the CISG's rules regarding the formation of contracts affect the lower court's holding in this case?

2. Did the appellate court agree with the lower court's analysis and application of the CISG's rules? Why or why not?

3. What would have been the result if the court had applied the UCC instead of the CISG?

Irrevocable Offers UCC 2–205 provides that a merchant's firm offer is irrevocable, even without consideration, if the merchant gives assurances in a signed writing. In contrast, under the CISG, an offer can become irrevocable without a signed writing. Article 16(2) of the CISG provides that an offer will be irrevocable if:

1. The offeror states orally that the offer is irrevocable.

2. The offeree reasonably relies on the offer as being irrevocable.

In both of these situations, the offer will be irrevocable even without a writing and without consideration.

The Writing Requirement As discussed previously, the UCC has a Statute of Frauds provision. UCC 2–201 requires contracts for the sale of goods priced at $500 or more to be evidenced by a written or electronic record signed by the party against whom enforcement is sought. Article 11 of the CISG, however, states that a contract of sale "need not be concluded in or evidenced by writing and is not subject to any other requirements as to form. It may be proved by any means, including witnesses." Article 11 of the CISG accords with the legal customs of most nations, which no longer require contracts to meet certain formal or writing requirements to be enforceable.

Time of Contract Formation Under the common law of contracts and the UCC, an acceptance is effective on dispatch, so a contract is created when the acceptance is transmitted. Under the CISG, in contrast, a contract is created not at the time the acceptance is transmitted but only on its *receipt* by the offeror. (The offer becomes *irrevocable,* however, when the acceptance is sent.)

Article 18(2) states that an acceptance by return promise (a unilateral contract) "becomes effective at the moment the indication of assent reaches the offeror." Under Article 18(3), the offeree may also bind the offeror by performance even without giving any notice to the offeror. The acceptance becomes effective "at the moment the act is performed." Thus, it is the offeree's reliance, rather than the communication of acceptance to the offeror, that creates the contract.

20–4b Special Provisions in International Contracts

Language and legal differences among nations can create various problems for parties to international contracts when disputes arise. It is possible to avoid these problems by including in a contract special provisions relating to choice of language, choice of forum, choice of law, and the types of events that may excuse the parties from performance.

Choice-of-Language Clause A deal struck between a U.S. company and a company in another country frequently involves two languages. One party may not understand complex contractual terms that are written in the other party's language. Translating the terms poses its own problems, as typically many phrases are not readily translatable into another language.

To make sure that no disputes arise out of this language problem, an international sales contract should include a **choice-of-language clause.** This clause will designate the official language by which the contract will be interpreted in the event of disagreement. The clause might also specify that the agreement is to be translated into, say, Spanish, and that the translation is to be approved by both parties. If arbitration is anticipated, an additional clause must be added to indicate the official language that will be used at the arbitration proceeding.

Forum-Selection Clause

A **forum-selection clause** designates the forum (place, or court) in which any disputes that arise under the contract will be litigated. This clause should indicate the specific court that will have jurisdiction. The forum does not necessarily have to be within the geographic boundaries of either party's nation.

Including a forum-selection clause in an international contract is especially important because when several countries are involved, litigation may be sought in courts in different nations. There are no universally accepted rules regarding the jurisdiction of a particular court over subject matter or parties to a dispute, although the adoption of the 2005 Choice of Court Convention helped to resolve certain issues.

Under certain circumstances, a forum-selection clause will not be valid. Specifically, if the clause denies one party an effective remedy, or is the product of fraud or unconscionable conduct, the clause will not be enforced. Similarly, if the designated forum causes substantial inconvenience to one of the parties, or violates public policy, the clause may not be enforced.

Choice-of-Law Clause

A contractual provision designating the applicable law, called a **choice-of-law clause,** is typically included in every international contract. At common law (and in European civil law systems), parties are allowed to choose the law that will govern their contractual relationship.

There must normally be some connection between the chosen law and the contracting parties to show that the parties are not merely trying to avoid the laws of their own jurisdictions. ■ **EXAMPLE 20.24** A U.S. automaker contracts with a German company. The parties cannot choose the law of China to govern their agreement if neither the contract nor the parties have anything to do with China. The choice of Chinese law in that situation might reflect an attempt to avoid consumer, environmental, or employment laws that would otherwise apply to the transaction. ■

Under the UCC, parties may choose the law that will govern the contract as long as the choice is "reasonable." Article 6 of the CISG, however, imposes no limitation on the parties in their choice of what law will govern the contract. The 1986 Hague Convention on the Law Applicable to Contracts for the International Sale of Goods—often referred to as the Choice-of-Law Convention—allows unlimited autonomy in the choice of law. Whenever a choice of law is not specified in a contract, the Hague Convention indicates that the law of the country where the seller's place of business is located will govern.

Force Majeure Clause

Every contract, and particularly those involving international transactions, should have a ***force majeure* clause.** The French term *force majeure* means "impossible or irresistible force"—sometimes loosely defined as "an act of God." *Force majeure* clauses often stipulate that other events (in addition to acts of God) will excuse liability for nonperformance. Occurrences such as adverse governmental orders or regulations, embargoes, and extreme shortages of materials commonly excuse a party's nonperformance.

Note that some *force majeure* clauses require notice before a party's liability for nonperformance (or delay in performance) will be excused. ■ **CASE IN POINT 20.25** Bigge Power Constructors manufactures cranes and other heavy equipment. Bigge contracted to purchase castings from a supplier, Rexnord Industries, LLC, for $4.5 million. Bigge needed the castings for the manufacture of two large derricks that were to be used in building nuclear power plants. The parties' contract set forth a delivery schedule for the castings, which Rexnord failed to meet. Although Bigge accepted and used all of the castings Rexnord supplied, it withheld $1 million from the purchase price for costs it had incurred as a result of the supplier's delay.

Rexnord sued for breach, claiming that the delay was a *force majeure* event, which the contract defined as any event "beyond a party's reasonable control." The court held that Rexnord's delay was not excused because Rexnord had never given Bigge the required notice that events constituting a *force majeure* had occurred. Thus, Bigge was entitled to damages for Rexnord's untimely delivery of goods. (If the supplier had given the required notice, its delay normally would have been excused.)[13] ■

---

13. *Rexnord Industries, LLC v. Bigge Power Constructors,* 947 F.Supp.2d 951 (E.D. Wisconsin 2013).

Reviewing: The Formation of Sales and Lease Contracts

Guy Holcomb owns and operates Oasis Goodtime Emporium, an adult entertainment establishment. Holcomb wanted to create an adult Internet system for Oasis that would offer customers adult-theme videos and "live" chat room programs using performers at the club. On May 10, Holcomb signed a work order authorizing Thomas Consulting Group (TCG) "to deliver a working prototype of a customer chat system, demonstrating the integration of live video and chatting in a Web browser." In exchange for creating the prototype, Holcomb agreed to pay TCG $64,697. On May 20, Holcomb signed an additional work order in the amount of $12,943 for TCG to install a customized firewall system. The work orders stated that Holcomb would make monthly installment payments to TCG, and both parties expected the work would be finished by September.

Due to unforeseen problems largely attributable to system configuration and software incompatibility, the project required more time than anticipated. By the end of the summer, the Web site was still not ready, and Holcomb had fallen behind in his payments to TCG. TCG threatened to cease work and file a suit for breach of contract unless the bill was paid. Rather than make further payments, Holcomb wanted to abandon the Web site project. Using the information presented in the chapter, answer the following questions.

1. Would a court be likely to decide that the transaction between Holcomb and TCG was covered by the Uniform Commercial Code (UCC)? Why or why not?
2. Would a court be likely to consider Holcomb a merchant under the UCC? Why or why not?
3. Did the parties have a valid contract under the UCC? Were any terms left open in the contract? If so, which terms? How would a court deal with open terms?
4. Suppose that Holcomb and TCG meet in October in an attempt to resolve their problems. At that time, the parties reach an oral agreement that TCG will continue to work without demanding full payment of the past due amounts and Holcomb will pay TCG $5,000 per week. Assuming the contract falls under the UCC, is the oral agreement enforceable? Why or why not?

Debate This . . .   *The UCC should require the same degree of definiteness of terms, especially with respect to price and quantity, as contract law does.*

Terms and Concepts

choice-of-language clause 379	fully integrated contract 372	predominant-factor test 362
choice-of-law clause 379	intangible property 361	requirements contract 366
course of dealing 372	lease agreement 364	sale 361
course of performance 373	lessee 364	sales contract 361
firm offer 367	lessor 364	seasonably 367
force majeure clause 379	merchant 364	tangible property 361
forum-selection clause 379	output contract 366	usage of trade 373

Issue Spotters

1. E-Design, Inc., orders 150 computer desks. Fav-O-Rite Supplies, Inc., ships 150 printer stands. Is this an acceptance of the offer or a counteroffer? If it is an acceptance, is it a breach of the contract? Why or why not? What if Fav-O-Rite told E-Design it was sending the printer stands as "an accommodation"? (See *The Formation of Sales and Lease Contracts.*)

2. Truck Parts, Inc. (TPI), often sells supplies to United Fix-It Company (UFC), which services trucks. Over the phone, they negotiate for the sale of eighty-four sets of tires. TPI sends a letter to UFC detailing the terms and two weeks later ships the tires. Is there an enforceable contract between them? Why or why not? (See *The Formation of Sales and Lease Contracts.*)

• **Check your answers to the Issue Spotters against the answers provided in Appendix D at the end of this text.**

Business Scenarios

20–1. Merchant's Firm Offer. On May 1, Jennings, a car dealer, e-mails Wheeler and says, "I have a 1955 Thunderbird convertible in mint condition that I will sell you for $13,500 at any time before June 9. [Signed] Peter Jennings." By May 15, having heard nothing from Wheeler, Jennings sells the car to another. On May 29, Wheeler accepts Jennings's offer and tenders $13,500. When told Jennings has sold the car to another, Wheeler claims Jennings has breached their contract. Is Jennings in breach? Explain. (See *The Formation of Sales and Lease Contracts.*)

20–2. Additional Terms. Strike offers to sell Bailey one thousand shirts for a stated price. The offer declares that shipment will be made by Dependable truck line. Bailey replies, "I accept your offer for one thousand shirts at the price quoted. Delivery to be by Yellow Express truck line." Both Strike and Bailey are merchants. Three weeks later, Strike ships the shirts by Dependable truck line, and Bailey refuses to accept delivery. Strike sues for breach of contract. Bailey claims that there never was a contract because his reply, which included a modification of carriers, did not constitute an acceptance. Bailey further claims that even if there had been a contract, Strike would have been in breach because Strike shipped the shirts by Dependable, contrary to the contract terms. Discuss fully Bailey's claims. (See *The Formation of Sales and Lease Contracts.*)

Business Case Problems

20–3. Spotlight on Goods and Services—The Statute of Frauds. Fallsview Glatt Kosher Caterers ran a business that provided travel packages, including food, entertainment, and lectures on religious subjects, to customers during the Passover holiday at a New York resort. Willie Rosenfeld verbally agreed to pay Fallsview $24,050 for the Passover package for himself and his family. Rosenfeld did not appear at the resort and never paid the amount owed. Fallsview sued Rosenfeld for breach of contract. Rosenfeld claimed that the contract was unenforceable because it was not in writing and violated the UCC's Statute of Frauds. Is the contract valid? Explain. [*Fallsview Glatt Kosher Caterers, Inc. v. Rosenfeld,* 794 N.Y.S.2d 790 (N.Y.Super. 2005)] (See *The Formation of Sales and Lease Contracts.*)

20–4. Business Case Problem with Sample Answer—Additional Terms. B.S. International, Ltd. (BSI), makes costume jewelry. JMAM, LLC, is a wholesaler of costume jewelry. JMAM sent BSI a letter with the terms for orders, including the necessary procedure for obtaining credit for items that customers rejected. The letter stated, "By signing below, you agree to the terms." Steven Baracsi, BSI's owner, signed the letter and returned it. For six years, BSI made jewelry for JMAM, which resold it. Items rejected by customers were sent back to JMAM, but were never returned to BSI. BSI filed a suit against JMAM, claiming $41,294.21 for the unreturned items. BSI showed the court a copy of JMAM's terms. Across the bottom had been typed a "PS" requiring the return of rejected merchandise. Was this "PS" part of the contract? Discuss. [*B.S. International, Ltd. v. JMAM, LLC,* 13 A.3d 1057 (R.I. 2011)] (See *The Formation of Sales and Lease Contracts.*)

- For a sample answer to Problem 20–4, go to Appendix E at the end of this text.

20–5. Partial Performance and the Statute of Frauds. After a series of e-mails, Jorge Bonilla, the sole proprietor of a printing company in Uruguay, agreed to buy a used printer from Crystal Graphics Equipment, Inc., in New York. Crystal Graphics, through its agent, told Bonilla that the printing press was fully operational, contained all of its parts, and was in excellent condition except for some damage to one of the printing towers. Bonilla paid $95,000. Crystal Graphics sent him a signed, stamped invoice reflecting this payment. The invoice was dated six days after Bonilla's conversation with the agent.

When the printing press arrived, Bonilla discovered that it was missing parts and was damaged. Crystal Graphics sent replacement parts, but they did not work. Crystal Graphics was never able to make the printer operational. Bonilla sued, alleging breach of contract, breach of the implied covenant of good faith and fair dealing, breach of express warranty, and breach of implied warranty. Crystal Graphics claimed that the contract was not enforceable because it did not satisfy the Statute of Frauds. Can Crystal Graphics prevail on this basis? Why or why not? [*Bonilla v. Crystal Graphics Equipment, Inc.,* 2012 WL 360145 (S.D.Fla. 2012)] (See *The Formation of Sales and Lease Contracts.*)

20–6. The Statute of Frauds. Kendall Gardner agreed to buy from B&C Shavings a specially built shaving mill to produce wood shavings for poultry processors. B&C faxed an invoice to Gardner reflecting a purchase price of $86,200, with a 30 percent down payment and the "balance due before shipment." Gardner paid the down payment. B&C finished the mill and wrote Gardner a letter telling him to "pay the balance due or you will lose the down payment." By then, Gardner had lost his customers for the wood shavings, could not pay the balance due, and asked for the return of his down payment. Did these parties have an enforceable contract under the Statute of Frauds? Explain. [*Bowen v. Gardner,* 2013 Ark. App. 52, 425 S.W.3d 875 (2013)] (See *The Formation of Sales and Lease Contracts.*)

20–7. Goods and Services Combined. Allied Shelving and Equipment, Inc., sells and installs shelving systems. National Deli, LLC, contracted with Allied to provide and install a parallel rack system (a series of large shelves) in National's warehouse. Both parties were dissatisfied with the result. National filed a suit in a Florida state court against Allied, which filed a counterclaim. Each contended that the other had materially breached the contract. The court applied common law contract principles to rule in National's favor on both claims. Allied appealed, arguing that the court should have applied the UCC. When does a court apply common law principles to a contract that involves both goods and services? In this case, why might an appellate court rule that the UCC should be applied instead? Explain. [*Allied Shelving and Equipment, Inc. v. National Deli, LLC,* 40 Fla. L. Weekly D145, 154 So.3d 482 (Dist.App. 2015)] (See *The Scope of Articles 2 and 2A.*)

20–8. Acceptance. New England Precision Grinding, Inc. (NEPG), sells precision medical parts in Massachusetts. NEPG agreed to supply Kyphon, Inc., with stylets and nozzles. NEPG contracted with Simply Surgical, LLC, to obtain the parts from Iscon Surgicals, Ltd. The contract did not mention Kyphon or require Kyphon's acceptance of the parts. Before shipping, Iscon would certify that the parts conformed to NEPG's specifications. On receiving the parts, NEPG would certify that they conformed to Kyphon's specifications. On delivery, Kyphon would also inspect the parts. After about half a dozen transactions, NEPG's payments to Simply Surgical lagged, and the seller refused to make further deliveries. NEPG filed a suit in a Massachusetts state court against Simply Surgical, alleging breach of contract. NEPG claimed that Kyphon had rejected some of the parts, which gave NEPG the right not to pay for them. Do the UCC's rules with respect to acceptance support or undercut the parties' actions? Discuss. [*New England Precision Grinding, Inc. v. Simply Surgical, LLC,* 89 Mass.App.Ct.176, 46 N.E.3d 590 (2016)] (See *The Formation of Sales and Lease Contracts.*)

20–9. A Question of Ethics—Contract Terms. *Daniel* *Fox owned Fox & Lamberth Enterprises, Inc., a kitchen and bath remodeling business, in Dayton, Ohio. Fox leased a building from Carl and Bellulah Hussong. Craftsmen Home Improvement, Inc., also remodeled baths and kitchens. When Fox planned to close his business, Craftsmen expressed an interest in buying his showroom assets. Fox set a price of $50,000. Craftsmen's owners agreed and gave Fox a list of the desired items and "A Bill of Sale" that set the terms for payment. The parties did not discuss Fox's arrangement with the Hussongs, but Craftsmen expected to negotiate a new lease and extensively modified the premises, including removing some of the displays to its own showroom. When the Hussongs and Craftsmen could not agree on new terms, Craftsmen told Fox that the deal was off. [Fox & Lamberth Enterprises, Inc. v. Craftsmen Home Improvement, Inc., 2006-Ohio-1427 (2 Dist. 2006)] (See The Formation of Sales and Lease Contracts.)*

(a) In Fox's suit in an Ohio state court for breach of contract, Craftsmen raised the Statute of Frauds as a defense. What are the requirements of the Statute of Frauds? Did the deal between Fox and Craftsmen meet these requirements? Did it fall under one of the exceptions? Explain.

(b) Craftsmen also claimed that the predominant factor of its agreement with Fox was a lease for the Hussongs' building. What is the predominant-factor test? Does it apply here? In any event, is it fair to hold a party to a contract to buy a business's assets when the buyer cannot negotiate a favorable lease of the premises on which the assets are located? Discuss.

Legal Reasoning Group Activity

20–10. Parol Evidence. Mountain Stream Trout Co. agreed to buy "market size" trout from trout grower Lake Farms, LLC. Their five-year contract did not define *market size.* At the time, in the trade, *market size* referred to fish of one-pound live weight. After three years, Mountain Stream began taking fewer, smaller deliveries of larger fish, claiming that *market size* varied according to whatever its customers demanded and that its customers now demanded larger fish. Lake Farms filed a suit for breach of contract. (See *The Formation of Sales and Lease Contracts.*)

(a) The first group will decide whether parol evidence is admissible to explain the terms of this contract. Are there any exceptions that could apply?

(b) A second group will determine the impact of course of dealing and usage of trade on the interpretation of contract terms.

(c) A third group will discuss how parties to a commercial contract can avoid the possibility that a court will interpret the contract terms in accordance with trade usage.

OVERLAND COFFEE IMPORT CONTRACT
OF THE
GREEN COFFEE ASSOCIATION
OF
NEW YORK CITY, INC.*

Contract Seller's No.: __504617__
Buyer's No.: __P9264__
Date: __10/11/18__

1

2

SOLD BY: __XYZ Co.__
TO: __Starbucks__

3 QUANTITY: __Five Hundred__ (__500__) Tons of _____ (Bags) __Mexican__ _____ coffee
weighing about __152.117 lbs.__ per bag.

PACKAGING: Coffee must be packed in clean sound bags of uniform size made of sisal, henequen, jute, burlap, or similar
woven material, without inner lining or outer covering of any material properly sewn by hand and/or machine.
Bulk shipments are allowed if agreed by mutual consent of Buyer and Seller.

4

DESCRIPTION: __High grown Mexican Altura__

5

PRICE: At __Ten/$10.00 dollars__ _____ U.S. Currency, per __lb.__ net, (U.S. Funds)
Upon delivery in Bonded Public Warehouse at __Laredo, TX__
(City and State)

6 PAYMENT: __Cash against warehouse receipts__

Bill and tender to DATE when all import requirements and governmental regulations have been satisfied, and
coffee delivered or discharged (as per contract terms). Seller is obliged to give the Buyer two (2) calendar
days free time in Bonded Public Warehouse following but not including date of tender.

7 ARRIVAL: During __December__ via __truck__
(Period) (Method of Transportation)
from __Mexico__ for arrival at __Laredo, TX, USA__
(Country of Exportation) (Country of Importation)
Partial shipments permitted.

8 ADVICE OF
ARRIVAL: Advice of arrival with warehouse name and location, together with the quantity, description, marks and place of
entry, must be transmitted directly, or through Seller's Agent/Broker, to the Buyer or his Agent/ Broker. Advice
will be given as soon as known but not later than the fifth business day following arrival at the named warehouse.
Such advice may be given verbally with written confirmation to be sent the same day.

9 WEIGHTS: (1) DELIVERED WEIGHTS: Coffee covered by this contract is to be weighed at location named in tender.
Actual tare to be allowed.
(2) SHIPPING WEIGHTS: Coffee covered by this contract is sold on shipping weights. Any loss in
weight exceeding __1/2__ percent at location named in tender is for account of Seller at contract price.
(3) Coffee is to be weighed within fifteen (15) calendar days after tender. Weighing expenses, if any, for
account of __Seller__ (Seller or Buyer)

10 MARKINGS: Bags to be branded in English with the name of Country of Origin and otherwise to comply with laws
and regulations of the Country of Importation, in effect at the time of entry, governing marking of import
merchandise. Any expense incurred by failure to comply with these regulations to be borne by
Exporter/Seller.

11 RULINGS: The "Rulings on Coffee Contracts" of the Green Coffee Association of New York City, Inc., in effect on the
date this contract is made, is incorporated for all purposes as a part of this agreement, and together herewith,
constitute the entire contract. No variation or addition hereto shall be valid unless signed by the parties to
the contract.
Seller guarantees that the terms printed on the reverse hereof, which by reference are made a part hereof, are
identical with the terms as printed in By-Laws and Rules of the Green Coffee Association of New
York City, Inc., heretofore adopted.
Exceptions to this guarantee are:

ACCEPTED: COMMISSION TO BE PAID BY:
__XYZ Co.__ __Seller__
BY _____*DM*_____ Seller
Agent
__Starbucks__ Buyer
BY _____ __ABC Brokerage__
Agent Broker(s)

12

13 When this contract is executed by a person acting for another, such person hereby represents that he is
fully authorized to commit his principal.

(Continued)

1 This is a contract for a sale of coffee to be *imported* internationally. If the parties have their principal places of business located in different countries, the contract may be subject to the United Nations Convention on Contracts for the International Sale of Goods (CISG). If the parties' principal places of business are located in the United States, the contract may be subject to the Uniform Commercial Code (UCC).

2 Quantity is one of the most important terms to include in a contract. Without it, a court may not be able to enforce the contract.

3 Weight per unit (bag) can be exactly stated or approximately stated. If it is not so stated, usage of trade in international contracts determines standards of weight.

4 Packaging requirements can be conditions for acceptance and payment. Bulk shipments are not permitted without the consent of the buyer.

5 A description of the coffee and the "Markings" constitute express warranties. International contracts rely more heavily on descriptions and models or samples than do warranties in contracts for the domestic sales of goods.

6 Under the UCC, parties may enter into a valid contract even though the price is not set. Under the CISG, a contract must provide for an exact determination of the price.

7 The terms of payment may take one of two forms: credit or cash. Credit terms can be complicated. A cash term can be simple, and payment can be made by any means acceptable in the ordinary course of business (for example, a personal check or a letter of credit). If the seller insists on actual cash, the buyer must be given a reasonable time to get it.

8 *Tender* means the seller has placed goods that conform to the contract at the buyer's disposition. This contract requires that the coffee meet all import regulations and that it be ready for pickup by the buyer at a "Bonded Public Warehouse." (A bonded *warehouse* is a place in which goods can be stored without payment of taxes until the goods are removed.)

9 The delivery date is significant because, if it is not met, the buyer may hold the seller in breach of the contract. Under this contract, the seller is given a "period" within which to deliver the goods, instead of a specific day. The seller is also given some time to rectify goods that do not pass inspection (see the "Guarantee" clause on page two of the contract).

10 As part of a proper tender, the seller (or its agent) must inform the buyer (or its agent) when the goods have arrived at their destination.

11 In some contracts, delivered and shipping weights can be important. During shipping, some loss can be attributed to the type of goods (spoilage of fresh produce, for example) or to the transportation itself. A seller and buyer can agree on the extent to which either of them will bear such losses.

12 Documents are often incorporated in a contract by reference, because including them word for word can make a contract difficult to read. If the document is later revised, the entire contract might have to be reworked. Documents that are typically incorporated by reference include detailed payment and delivery terms, special provisions, and sets of rules, codes, and standards.

13 In international sales transactions, and for domestic deals involving certain products, brokers are used to form the contracts. When so used, the brokers are entitled to a commission.

An Example of a Contract for the International Sale of Coffee—Continued

TERMS AND CONDITIONS

ARBITRATION: (14) All controversies relating to, in connection with, or arising out of this contract, its modification, making or the authority or obligations of the signatories hereto, and whether involving the principals, agents, brokers, or others who actually subscribe hereto, shall be settled by arbitration in accordance with the "Rules of Arbitration" of the Green Coffee Association of New York City, Inc., as they exist at the time of the arbitration (including provisions as to payment of fees and expenses). Arbitration is the sole remedy hereunder, and it shall be held in accordance with the law of New York State, and judgment of any award may be entered in the courts of that State, or in any other court of competent jurisdiction. All notices or judicial service in reference to arbitration or enforcement shall be deemed given if transmitted as required by the aforesaid rules.

GUARANTEE: (15) (a) If all or any of the coffee is refused admission into the country of importation by reason of any violation of governmental laws or acts, which violation existed at the time the coffee arrived at Bonded Public Warehouse, seller is required, as to the amount not admitted and as soon as possible, to deliver replacement coffee in conformity to all terms and conditions of this contract, excepting only the Arrival terms, but not later than thirty (30) days after the date of the violation notice. Any payment made and expenses incurred for any coffee denied entry shall be refunded within ten (10) calendar days of denial of entry, and payment shall be made for the replacement delivery in accordance with the terms of this contract. Consequently, if Buyer removes the coffee from the Bonded Public Warehouse, Seller's responsibility as to such portion hereunder ceases.
(b) Contracts containing the overstamp "No Pass–No Sale" on the face of the contract shall be interpreted to mean: If any or all of the coffee is not admitted into the country of Importation in its original condition by reason of failure to meet requirements of the government's laws or Acts, the contract shall be deemed null and void as to that portion of the coffee which is not admitted in its original condition. Any payment made and expenses incurred for any coffee denied entry shall be refunded within ten (10) calendar days of denial of entry.

CONTINGENCY: This contract is not contingent upon any other contract.

CLAIMS: (16) Coffee shall be considered accepted as to quality unless within *fifteen* (15) calendar days after delivery at Bonded Public Warehouse or within *fifteen* (15) calendar days after all Government clearances have been received, whichever is later, either:
(a) Claims are settled by the parties hereto, or,
(b) Arbitration proceedings have been filed by one of the parties in accordance with the provisions hereof.
(c) If neither (a) nor (b) has been done in the stated period or if any portion of the coffee has been removed from the Bonded Public (17) Warehouse before representative sealed samples have been drawn by the Green Coffee Association of New York City, Inc., in accordance with its rules, Seller's responsibility for quality claims ceases for that portion so removed.
(d) Any question of quality submitted to arbitration shall be a matter of allowance only, unless otherwise provided in the contract.

DELIVERY: (18) (a) No more than three (3) chops may be tendered for each lot of 250 bags.
(b) Each chop of coffee tendered is to be uniform in grade and appearance. All expense necessary to make coffee uniform shall be for account of seller.
(c) Notice of arrival and/or sampling order constitutes a tender, and must be given not later than the fifth business day following arrival at Bonded Public Warehouse stated on the contract.

INSURANCE: Seller is responsible for any loss or damage, or both, until Delivery and Discharge of coffee at the Bonded Public Warehouse in the Country of Importation.

All Insurance Risks, costs and responsibility are for Seller's Account until Delivery and Discharge of coffee at the Bonded Public Warehouse in the Country of Importation.

Buyer's insurance responsibility begins from the day of importation or from the day of tender, whichever is later.

FREIGHT: (19) Seller to provide and pay for all transportation and related expenses to the Bonded Public Warehouse in the Country of Importation.

EXPORT DUTIES/TAXES: (20) Exporter is to pay all Export taxes, duties or other fees or charges, if any, levied because of exportation.

IMPORT DUTIES/TAXES: Any Duty or Tax whatsoever, imposed by the government or any authority of the Country of Importation, shall be borne by the Importer/Buyer.

INSOLVENCY OR FINANCIAL FAILURE OF BUYER OR SELLER: (21) If, at any time before the contract is fully executed, either party hereto shall meet with creditors because of inability generally to make payment of obligations when due, or shall suspend such payments, fail to meet his general trade obligations in the regular course of business, shall file a petition in bankruptcy or, for an arrangement, shall become insolvent, or commit an act of bankruptcy, then the other party may at his option, expressed in writing, declare the aforesaid to constitute a breach and default of this contract, and may, in addition to other remedies, decline to deliver further or make payment or may sell or purchase for the defaulter's account, and may collect damage for any injury or loss, or shall account for the profit, if any, occasioned by such sale or purchase.

This clause is subject to the provisions of (11 USC 365 (e) 1) if invoked.

BREACH OR DEFAULT OF CONTRACT: (22) In the event either party hereto fails to perform, or breaches or repudiates this agreement, the other party shall subject to the specific provisions of this contract be entitled to the remedies and relief provided for by the Uniform Commercial Code of the State of New York. The computation and ascertainment of damages, or the determination of any other dispute as to relief, shall be made by the arbitrators in accordance with the Arbitration Clause herein.

(23) Consequential damages shall not, however, be allowed.

(Continued)

An Example of a Contract for the International Sale of Coffee—Continued

14 Arbitration is the settling of a dispute by submitting it to a disinterested party (other than a court), which renders a decision. The procedures and costs can be provided for in an arbitration clause or incorporated through other documents. To enforce an award rendered in an arbitration, the winning party can "enter" (submit) the award in a court "of competent jurisdiction."

15 When goods are imported internationally, they must meet certain import requirements before being released to the buyer. Because of this, buyers frequently want a guaranty clause that covers the goods not admitted into the country. The clause may either require the seller to replace the goods within a stated time or allow the contract for those goods not admitted to be void.

16 In the "Claims" clause, the parties agree that the buyer has a certain time within which to reject the goods. The right to reject is a right by law and does not need to be stated in a contract. If the buyer does not exercise the right within the time specified in the contract, the goods will be considered accepted.

17 Many international contracts include definitions of terms so that the parties understand what they mean. Some terms are used in a particular industry in a specific way. Here, the word *chop* refers to a unit of like-grade coffee beans. The buyer has a right to inspect ("sample") the coffee. If the coffee does not conform to the contract, the seller must correct the nonconformity.

18 The "Delivery," "Insurance," and "Freight" clauses, with the "Arrival" clause on page one of the contract, indicate that this is a destination contract. The seller has the obligation to deliver the goods to the destination, not simply deliver them into the hands of a carrier. Under this contract, the destination is a "Bonded Public Warehouse" in a specific location. The seller bears the risk of loss until the goods are delivered at their destination. Typically, the seller will have bought insurance to cover the risk.

19 Delivery terms are commonly placed in all sales contracts. Such terms determine who pays freight and other costs and, in the absence of an agreement specifying otherwise, who bears the risk of loss. International contracts may use these delivery terms, or they may use INCOTERMS, which are published by the International Chamber of Commerce. For example, the INCOTERM DDP (delivered duty paid) requires the seller to arrange shipment, obtain and pay for import or export permits, and get the goods through customs to a named destination.

20 Exported and imported goods are subject to duties, taxes, and other charges imposed by the governments of the countries involved. International contracts spell out who is responsible for these charges.

21 This clause protects a party if the other party should become financially unable to fulfill the obligations under the contract. Thus, if the seller cannot afford to deliver, or the buyer cannot afford to pay, for the stated reasons, the other party can consider the contract breached. This right is subject to "11 USC 365(e)(1)," which refers to a specific provision of the U.S. Bankruptcy Code dealing with executory contracts.

22 In the "Breach or Default of Contract" clause, the parties agree that the remedies under this contract are the remedies (except for consequential damages) provided by the UCC, as in effect in the state of New York. The amount and "ascertainment" of damages, as well as other disputes about relief, are to be determined by arbitration.

23 Three clauses frequently included in international contracts are omitted here. There is no choice-of-language clause designating the official language to be used in interpreting the contract terms. There is no choice-of-forum clause designating the place in which disputes will be litigated, except for arbitration (law of New York State). Finally, there is no *force majeure* clause relieving the sellers or buyers from nonperformance due to events beyond their control.

CHAPTER 21

Title, Risk, and Insurable Interest

Before the creation of the Uniform Commercial Code (UCC), *title*—the right of ownership—was the central concept in sales law. Title controlled all issues of rights and remedies of the parties to a sales contract. There were numerous problems with this concept, however. Anything can happen between the time a contract is signed and the time the goods are transferred to the buyer's or lessee's possession. It was frequently difficult to determine when title actually passed from the seller to the buyer. It was also difficult to predict which party a court would decide had title at the time of a loss.

Because of such problems, the UCC has separated the question of title as much as possible from the question of the rights and obligations of buyers, sellers, and third parties.

In some situations, title is still relevant under the UCC, and the UCC has special rules for determining who has title. (These rules do not apply to leased goods, obviously, because title remains with the lessor, or owner, of the goods.) In most situations, however, the UCC has replaced the concept of title with three other concepts: identification, risk of loss, and insurable interest.

21–1 Identification

Before any interest in goods can pass from the seller or lessor to the buyer or lessee, the goods must be (1) in existence and (2) identified to the contract [UCC 2–105(2)]. **Identification** takes place when specific goods are designated as the subject matter of a sales or lease contract.

Title and risk of loss cannot pass to the buyer from the seller unless the goods are identified to the contract. (As mentioned, title to leased goods remains with the lessor.) Identification is significant because it gives the buyer or lessee the right to insure (or to have an insurable interest in) the goods and the right to recover from third parties who damage the goods.

The parties can agree in their contract on when identification will take place. (This type of agreement will not effectively pass title and risk of loss to the buyer on future goods, such as unborn cattle, however.) If the parties do not so specify, the UCC provisions discussed here determine when identification takes place [UCC 2–501(1), 2A–217].

21–1a Existing Goods

If the contract calls for the sale or lease of specific and determined goods that are already in existence, identification takes place at the time the contract is made. ■ **EXAMPLE 21.1** Litco Company contracts to lease a fleet of five cars designated by their vehicle identification numbers (VINs). Because the cars are identified by their VINs, identification has taken place, and Litco acquires an insurable interest in the cars at the time of contracting. ■

21–1b Future Goods

Any goods that are not in existence at the time of contracting are known as future goods. The following rules apply to identification of future goods:

1. If a sale or lease involves unborn animals to be born within twelve months after contracting, identification takes place when the animals are conceived.

2. If a sale involves crops that are to be harvested within twelve months (or the next harvest season occurring after contracting, whichever is longer), identification takes place when the crops are planted. Otherwise, identification takes place when the crops begin to grow.

3. In a sale or lease of any other future goods, identification occurs when the seller or lessor ships, marks, or otherwise designates the goods as those to which the contract refers. Future goods that fall into this category might include solar panels that are to be

designed and manufactured after a contract is signed for their purchase.[1]

21–1c Goods That Are Part of a Larger Mass

Goods that are part of a larger mass are identified when the goods are marked, shipped, or somehow designated by the seller or lessor as the particular goods to pass under the contract. ■ **EXAMPLE 21.2** Briggs orders 10,000 pairs of men's jeans from a lot that contains 90,000 articles of clothing for men, women, and children. Until the seller separates the 10,000 pairs of men's jeans from the other items, title and risk of loss remain with the seller. ■

A common exception to this rule involves fungible goods. **Fungible goods** are goods that are alike naturally, by agreement, or by trade usage. Typical examples include specific grades or types of wheat, petroleum, and

---

1. *In re Zhejiang Photovoltaic Co., Ltd.*, ___ Bankr. ___, 2015 WL 2260647 (D.N.J. 2015). For a case involving a boat, see *In re Carman*, 399 Bankr. 158 (D.Md. 2009).

cooking oil, which usually are stored in large containers. Owners of fungible goods typically hold title as *tenants in common* (owners with an undivided share of the whole), which facilitates further sales. A seller-owner can pass title and risk of loss to the buyer without actually separating the goods. The buyer replaces the seller as an owner in common [UCC 2–105(4)].

■ **EXAMPLE 21.3** Alvarez, Braudel, and Carpenter are farmers. They deposit, respectively, 5,000 bushels, 3,000 bushels, and 2,000 bushels of grain of the same grade and quality in a grain elevator. The three become owners in common, with Alvarez owning 50 percent of the 10,000 bushels, Braudel 30 percent, and Carpenter 20 percent. Alvarez contracts to sell her 5,000 bushels of grain to Treyton. Because the goods are fungible, she can pass title and risk of loss to Treyton without physically separating the 5,000 bushels. Treyton now becomes an owner in common with Braudel and Carpenter. ■

It is important to emphasize that what makes goods fungible is not simply that they are alike, but that they are of an *identical* grade or type. This distinction is illustrated by the facts in the following case.

Case Analysis 21.1

BMW Group, LLC v. Castle Oil Corp.

New York Supreme Court, Appellate Division, First Department, 139 A.D.3d 78, 29 N.Y.S.3d 253 (2016).

In the Language of the Court

SAXE, J. [Judge]

* * * *

* * * Plaintiffs allege that the * * * defendants provided their customers (plaintiffs) with inferior, adulterated heating oil, i.e. that the fuel oil that was delivered to them contained oils of lesser value mixed into the ordered grade of fuel oil, so that the delivered product did not meet the standards of the parties' contracts.

* * * *

* * * A sample of No. 4 fuel oil delivered by Castle [Oil Corporation] to a Manhattan [New York] building owned by plaintiff BMW Group LLC * * * did not conform to the specifications for No. 4 fuel oil [which BMW had ordered from Castle].

* * * *

* * * Mid Island L.P. and Carnegie Park Associates, L.P. own and manage residential and commercial buildings in the New York metropolitan area * * * .

They allege that they contracted with Hess [Corporation] for the purchase of No. 4 and No. 6 fuel oil * * * , but received a blend containing waste oil.

* * * *

[BMW and the other property owners filed a suit in a New York state court against Castle and Hess. Each defendant] moved to dismiss the complaint against it. The * * * court granted those motions * * * . It agreed with defendants that the complaints, while alleging that a blended fuel oil was delivered to plaintiffs, did not allege that any injury was caused to them by the use or the burning of this blended oil. [The plaintiffs appealed.]

* * * *

The issue is whether * * * plaintiffs' claims amount to merely "theoretical nonconformities" that do not justify a claim for breach of warranty or breach of contract.

* * * *

* * * *If the goods that are delivered do not conform to the goods contemplated by* *the sale contract, the purchaser has a cause of action under the Uniform Commercial Code.* [Emphasis added.]

An issue is raised as to whether plaintiffs successfully alleged that the delivered goods were nonconforming.

* * * The Administrative Code of the City of New York * * * defines "heating oil" as "oil refined for the purpose of use as a fuel for combustion in a heating system and that meets the specifications of the American Society for Testing and Materials * * * ." The applicable American Society of Testing and Materials (ASTM) specifications for fuel oil * * * establish detailed requirements for the different grades of oil, using such categories as minimum flash point temperature, viscosity, density, and maximum percentages of ash and sulfur.

Plaintiffs essentially allege that, consistent with the ASTM specifications, as well as common commercial usage,

Case 21.1 Continued

and pursuant to the UCC, customers purchasing goods described as No. 4 and No. 6 fuel oil are entitled to presume that they are receiving 100% fuel oil of the specified grade, and not a product consisting of a blend of No. 4 or No. 6 fuel oil with some other types of oil that do not meet the criteria of those ASTM specifications.

More specifically, plaintiffs in the Castle Oil matter allege that "Castle intentionally adulterates its fuel oil products by using other, cheaper oils (primarily used motor and lubricating oil) as filler, resulting in an inferior blended petroleum product." They explain that lubricating oil and fuel oil are different chemical substances, and that lubricating oils are designed with a higher boiling point than fuel oil and do not burn efficiently at temperatures typical in non-industrial heating systems. Additionally, because lubricating oils contain chemical additives not found in fuel oil, burning

them in heating systems such as those in plaintiffs' buildings will tend to produce more soot and particulate matter pollution, reducing the efficiency of the heating system and creating an increased risk of fire. They also assert that while regulations permit used lubricating oil to be re-refined and used as fuel in high-temperature industrial settings, the used lubricating oil purchased by Castle to blend with its fuel oil was never refined for use as fuel.

Plaintiffs in the Hess matter assert that * * * the Hess fuel oil [was mixed] with 15–25% "waste oil" as that term is defined in the Rules of the New York State Department of Environmental Conservation: "Used and/or reprocessed engine lubricating oil and/or any other used oil, including but not limited to, fuel oil, engine oil, gear oil, cutting oil, transmission fluid, hydraulic fluid, dielectric fluid, oil storage tank residue, animal oil and vegetable oil, which

has not subsequently been re-refined." They also assert that the waste oil contaminants impair the performance of the heating systems into which they are introduced, and that fuel oil adulterated with waste oil has a lower heat content than No. 4 and No. 6 fuel oil, so that they (the customers) needed to purchase more oil than they would have if they had received 100% fuel oil.
* * * *

* * * *Since we must infer from the complaint that plaintiffs received nonconforming oil deliveries of lesser value than those they contracted and paid for, causes of action for breach of contract and breach of warranty—including plaintiffs' damages—are stated in each action.* [Emphasis added.]
* * * *

Accordingly, the order of the [lower court] to dismiss the complaint, should be reversed, on the law, * * * and the motions denied.

Legal Reasoning Questions

1. What did the contracts between the plaintiffs and the defendants require the defendants to do? What goods did the contracts involve? What standards applied to the goods?
2. What was the plaintiffs' complaint? Why was this important?
3. What did the trial and appellate courts conclude with respect to the plaintiffs' allegations? Why?

21–2 When Title Passes

Once goods exist and are identified, the provisions of UCC 2–401 apply to the passage of title. In nearly all subsections of UCC 2–401, the words "unless otherwise explicitly agreed" appear. In other words, the buyer and the seller can reach an explicit agreement as to when title will pass.

Without an explicit agreement to the contrary, *title passes to the buyer at the time and the place the seller performs by delivering the goods* [UCC 2–401(2)]. For instance, if a person buys cattle at a livestock auction, title will pass to the buyer when the cattle are physically delivered to him or her (unless otherwise agreed). (In the future, the delivery of goods may sometimes be accomplished by drones, as discussed in this chapter's *Managerial Strategy* feature.)

■ **CASE IN POINT 21.4** Timothy Allen contracted with Indy Route 66 Cycles, Inc., to have a motorcycle custom

built for him. Indy built the motorcycle and issued a "Certificate of Origin." Later, federal law enforcement officers arrested Allen on drug charges and seized his property, including the Indy-made cycle, which officers found at the home of Allen's sister, Tena. The government alleged that the motorcycle was subject to forfeiture as the proceeds of drug trafficking. Indy filed a claim against the government, arguing that it owned the cycle because it still possessed the "Certificate of Origin." The court applied UCC Section 2–401(2) and ruled in favor of the government. Testimony by Indy's former vice president was "inconclusive" but implied that Indy had delivered the motorcycle to Allen. Indy had given up possession of the cycle to Allen, and this was sufficient to pass title, even though Indy had kept a "Certificate of Origin."[2] ■

---

2. *United States v. 2007 Custom Motorcycle,* 2011 WL 232331 (D.Ariz. 2011).

MANAGERIAL STRATEGY   Commercial Use of Drones

The commercial use of drones—small, pilotless aerial vehicles—has, until recently, been on hold in the United States. Possible commercial uses of drones are numerous—railroad track inspection, oil and gas pipeline review, real estate videos for use by brokers, discovery for land boundary disputes, and many others. In addition, businesses have begun making plans to use drones for delivery of goods. Amazon is developing Amazon Prime Air, a drone-based delivery service. Google Project Wing is another drone-based service that is under development.

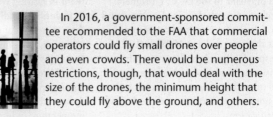

The Federal Aviation Administration Rules

The problem has been the Federal Aviation Administration (FAA). The FAA claims authority to regulate *all* unmanned aircraft systems (UASs). In 2012, Congress mandated the FAA "to establish a roadmap for getting UASs integrated into the national air space." Not until 2015, however, did the FAA issue its proposed rules on commercial drone use, and these rules still have not been finalized.[a]

The FAA's rules require operators to apply for a license to use drones commercially. Drone flights are limited to daylight hours, and drones will not be allowed to go above five hundred feet or faster than one hundred miles per hour. The proposed rules also require that licensed drone operators maintain a continuous visual line of sight with the drones during operation.

Since the rules were proposed, the FAA has received thousands of applications from small businesses seeking licenses to use UASs. It approves nearly fifty applications a week. Drones are widely used by the agricultural industry for general aerial surveying and by the real estate profession for general aerial photography. The lack of final regulations is delaying commercial drone delivery in the United States, however, although drone delivery service is widely available in Australia and China.

In 2016, a government-sponsored committee recommended to the FAA that commercial operators could fly small drones over people and even crowds. There would be numerous restrictions, though, that would deal with the size of the drones, the minimum height that they could fly above the ground, and others.

Court Actions

In the past, the FAA has attempted to fine other-than-recreational users of drones. One case involved Texas EquuSearch, a group that searches for missing persons. The organization requested an emergency injunction after receiving an e-mail from an FAA employee indicating that its drone use was illegal. The U.S. Court of Appeals for the District of Columbia Circuit refused to act on the suit. The court stated that the e-mail from the FAA did not have legal effect and therefore was not subject to judicial review.[b]

In a case involving an administrative hearing, the FAA assessed a civil penalty against Raphael Pirker for careless and reckless operation of an unmanned aircraft. Pirker flew a drone over the University of Virginia in 2011 while filming a video advertisement for the medical school. Pirker appealed to the National Transportation Safety Board Office of Administrative Law Judges. He prevailed in early 2014.[c]

Business Questions

1. What benefits can delivery by commercial drone provide to consumers?
2. Why might the United States be slow to adopt commercial drone delivery in comparison with some other nations?

---

a. The interim rule is Registration and Marking Requirements for Small Unmanned Aircraft, 70 Fed.Reg. 78594-01.

b. *Texas EquuSearch Mounted Search and Recovery Team, RP Search Services, Inc., v. Federal Aviation Administration,* 2014 WL 2860332 (C.A.D.C. 2014).

c. *Huerta v. Pirker,* Decisional Order of National Transportation Safety Board Office of Administrative Judges, 2014 WL 3388631 (N.T.S.B. March 6, 2014).

21–2a Shipment and Destination Contracts

Unless otherwise agreed, delivery arrangements can determine when title passes from the seller to the buyer. In a **shipment contract,** the seller is required or authorized to ship goods by carrier, such as a trucking company. The seller is required only to deliver the goods into the hands of the carrier, and title passes to the buyer at the time and place of shipment [UCC 2–401(2)(a)]. Generally, *all contracts are assumed to be shipment contracts if nothing to the contrary is stated in the contract.*

In a **destination contract,** the seller is required to deliver the goods to a particular destination, usually directly to the buyer, but sometimes to another party designated by the buyer. Title passes to the buyer when the goods are *tendered* at that destination [UCC 2–401(2)(b)].

Tender of delivery occurs when the seller places or holds conforming goods at the buyer's disposal (with any necessary notice), enabling the buyer to take possession [UCC 2–503(1)].

21–2b Delivery without Movement of the Goods

Sometimes, a sales contract does not call for the seller to ship or deliver the goods (such as when the buyer is to pick up the goods). In that situation, the passage of title depends on whether the seller must deliver a **document of title,** such as a bill of lading or a warehouse receipt, to the buyer. A *bill of lading*[3] is a receipt for goods that is signed by a carrier and serves as a contract for the transportation of the goods. A *warehouse receipt* is a receipt issued by a warehouser for goods stored in a warehouse.

When a Title Document Is Required When a title document is required, title passes to the buyer *when and where the document is delivered.* Thus, if the goods are stored in a warehouse, title passes to the buyer when the appropriate documents are delivered to the buyer. The goods never move. In fact, the buyer can choose to leave the goods at the same warehouse for a period of time, and the buyer's title to those goods will be unaffected.

When a Title Document Is Not Required When no document of title is required and the goods are identified to the contract, title passes at the time and place the sales contract is made. If the goods have not been identified, title does not pass until identification occurs.

■ **CASE IN POINT 21.5** Under a contract with Cheran Investments, LLC, Blasini, Inc., agreed to buy the business assets of the Attic Bar & Grill in Omaha, Nebraska. The contract required Blasini to make a down payment and monthly payments until the price was fully paid. Blasini obtained insurance on the property from Nautilus Insurance Co. Before the purchase price had been fully paid, a fire damaged the "personal property" (the business assets, such as furniture and equipment) in the Attic. The insurance company filed a suit to determine which party was entitled to the insurance proceeds for the damage. The court concluded that Blasini had "failed to consummate the purchase agreement" and declared Cheran the owner of the personal property. Blasini appealed.

A state intermediate appellate court reversed the lower court's ruling. The court based its reasoning on UCC Section 2–401. The goods in question had already been identified at the time of contracting, and no documents were to be delivered. Thus, title passed at the time and place of contracting. In other words, the sale of the Attic's assets passed title to the assets to Blasini, who became the owner.[4] ■

21–2c Sales or Leases by Nonowners

Problems occur when persons who acquire goods with imperfect titles attempt to sell or lease them. Sections 2–402 and 2–403 of the UCC deal with the rights of two parties who lay claim to the same goods sold with imperfect titles. Generally, a buyer acquires at least whatever title the seller has to the goods sold.

These same UCC sections also protect lessees. Obviously, a lessee does not acquire whatever title the lessor has to the goods. Rather, the lessee acquires a right to possess and use the goods—that is, a *leasehold interest.* A lessee acquires whatever leasehold interest the lessor has or has the power to transfer, subject to the lease contract [UCC 2A–303, 2A–304, 2A–305].

Void Title A buyer may unknowingly purchase goods from a seller who is not the owner of the goods. If the seller is a thief, the seller's title is *void*—legally, no title exists. Thus, the buyer acquires no title, and the real owner can reclaim the goods from the buyer. If the goods were leased instead, the same result would occur, because the lessor would have no leasehold interest to transfer.

■ **EXAMPLE 21.6** If Saki steals diamonds owned by Shannon, Saki has a *void title* to those diamonds. If Saki sells the diamonds to Valdez, Shannon can reclaim them from Valdez even though Valdez acted in good faith and honestly was not aware that the diamonds were stolen. (Valdez may file a tort claim against Saki under these circumstances, but here we are discussing only title to the goods.) ■ Article 2A contains similar provisions for leases.

Voidable Title A seller has a *voidable title* to goods in the following circumstances:

1. The goods were obtained by fraud.
2. The goods were paid for with a check that was later dishonored (returned for insufficient funds).

---

3. The term *bill of lading* has been used by international carriers for many years. It derives from *bill,* which historically referred to a schedule of costs for services, and the verb *to lade,* which means to load cargo onto a ship or other carrier.

4. *Nautilus Insurance Co. v. Cheran Investments, LLC,* 2014 WL 292809 (Neb.App. 2014).

3. The goods were purchased on credit when the seller was **insolvent.** Under the UCC, insolvency occurs when a person ceases to pay debts in the ordinary course of business, cannot pay debts as they become due, or is insolvent under federal bankruptcy law [UCC 1–201(23)].

Good Faith Purchasers. In contrast to a seller with void title, a seller with voidable title has the power to transfer good title to a good faith purchaser for value. A **good faith purchaser** is one who buys without knowledge of circumstances that would make an ordinary person inquire about the validity of the seller's title to the goods. One who purchases *for value* gives legally sufficient consideration (value) for the goods purchased. The original owner normally cannot recover goods from a good faith purchaser for value [UCC 2–403(1)].[5]

If the buyer is not a good faith purchaser for value, the actual owner can reclaim the goods from the buyer. (The owner can also reclaim the goods from the seller, if

the goods are still in the seller's possession.) Exhibit 21–1 illustrates these concepts.

Voidable Title and Leases. The same rules apply in situations involving leases. A lessor with voidable title has the power to transfer a valid leasehold interest to a good faith lessee for value. The real owner cannot recover the goods, except as permitted by the terms of the lease. The real owner can, however, receive all proceeds arising from the lease. The owner can also obtain a transfer of the rights that the lessor had under the lease, including the right to the return of the goods when the lease expires [UCC 2A–305(1)].

The Entrustment Rule Entrusting goods to a merchant *who deals in goods of that kind* gives the merchant the power to transfer all rights to *a buyer in the ordinary course of business* [UCC 2–403(2)]. This is known as the **entrustment rule.** Entrusting includes both turning over goods to the merchant and leaving purchased goods with the merchant for later delivery or pickup [UCC 2–403(3)]. Article 2A provides a similar rule for leased goods [UCC 2A–305(2)].

---

5. The real owner can sue the person who initially obtained voidable title to the goods.

EXHIBIT 21–1 Void and Voidable Titles

If goods are transferred from their owner to another by theft, the thief acquires no ownership rights. Because the thief's title is *void,* a later buyer can acquire no title, and the owner can recover the goods. If the transfer occurs by fraud, the transferee acquires a *voidable* title. A later good faith purchaser for value can acquire good title, and the original owner cannot recover the goods.

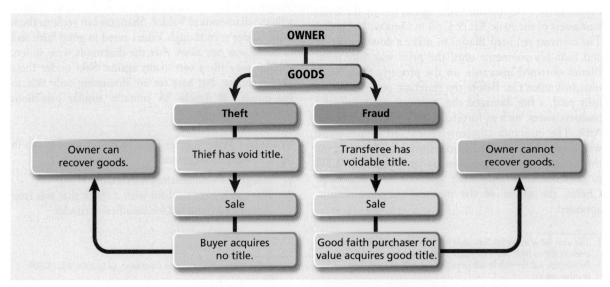

Under the UCC, a person is a **buyer in the ordinary course of business** if:

1. She or he buys goods in good faith (honestly).
2. The goods are purchased without knowledge that the sale violates the rights of another person in the goods.
3. The goods are purchased in the ordinary course from a merchant (other than a pawnbroker) in the business of selling goods of that kind.
4. The sale to that person comports with the usual or customary practices in the kind of business in which the seller is engaged [UCC 1–201(9)].

The entrustment rule basically allows innocent buyers to obtain legitimate title to goods purchased from merchants even if the merchants do not have good title. ■ **EXAMPLE 21.7** Jan leaves her watch with a jeweler to be repaired. The jeweler sells both new and used watches. The jeweler sells Jan's watch to Kim, a customer who is unaware that the jeweler has no right to sell it. Kim, as a good faith buyer, gets good title against Jan's claim of ownership.[6]

Kim, however, obtains only those rights held by the person entrusting the goods (Jan). Suppose that Jan had stolen the watch from Greg and left it with the jeweler to be repaired. In this situation, Kim would obtain good title against Jan, who entrusted the watch to the jeweler. But she would not obtain good title against Greg (the real owner), who neither entrusted the watch to Jan nor authorized Jan to entrust it. ■

A nonowner's sale of *Red Elvis,* an artwork by Andy Warhol, was at the center of the dispute over title in the following case.

---

6. Jan can sue the jeweler for the tort of conversion (or trespass to personal property) to obtain damages equivalent to the cash value of the watch.

Spotlight on Andy Warhol

Case 21.2 Lindholm v. Brant

Supreme Court of Connecticut, 283 Conn. 65, 925 A.2d 1048 (2007).

Background and Facts In 1987, Kerstin Lindholm of Greenwich, Connecticut, bought a silk-screen by Andy Warhol titled *Red Elvis* from Anders Malmberg, a Swedish art dealer, for $300,000. In 1998, Lindholm lent *Red Elvis* to the Guggenheim Museum in New York City for an exhibition to tour Europe.

Peter Brant, who was on the museum's board of trustees and also a Greenwich resident, believed that Lindholm was *Red Elvis*'s owner. He was told by Stellan Holm, a Swedish art dealer with whom he had dealt in the past, that Malmberg had bought the work, however. Holm also informed Brant that Malmberg would sell it for $2.9 million. Malmberg refused Brant's request to provide a copy of an invoice between Lindholm and himself on the ground that such documents normally and customarily are not disclosed in art deals.

To determine whether Malmberg had good title, Brant hired an attorney to search the Art Loss Register (an international database of stolen and missing artworks) and other sources. No problems were found, but Brant was cautioned that this provided only "minimal assurances." Brant's attorney drafted a formal contract, which conditioned payment on the delivery of *Red Elvis* to a warehouse in Denmark. The exchange took place in April 2000.[a] Later, Lindholm filed a suit in a Connecticut state court against Brant, alleging conversion, among other things. The court issued a judgment in Brant's favor. Lindholm appealed to the Connecticut Supreme Court.

In the Language of the Court

SULLIVAN, J. [Justice]

* * * *

* * * "A person buys goods in the ordinary course if the sale to the person comports with the usual or customary practices in the kind of business in which the seller is engaged or with the seller's own usual or

---

a. Unaware of this deal, Lindholm accepted a Japanese buyer's offer of $4.6 million for *Red Elvis.* The funds were wired to Malmberg, who kept them. Lindholm filed a criminal complaint against Malmberg in Sweden. In 2003, a Swedish court convicted Malmberg of "gross fraud embezzlement." The court awarded Lindholm $4.6 million and other relief.

Case 21.2 Continues

customary practices * * * " [according to Connecticut General Statutes Annotated Section 42a-1-201(9), Connecticut's version of UCC 1–201(9)]. *A person buys goods in good faith if there is "honesty in fact and the observance of reasonable commercial standards of fair dealing" in the conduct or transaction concerned* [under Section 42a-1-201(20)]. [Emphasis added.]

We are required, therefore, to determine whether the defendant followed the usual or customary practices and observed reasonable commercial standards of fair dealing in the art industry in his dealings with Malmberg. * * * The defendant presented expert testimony that the vast majority of art transactions, in which the buyer has no reason for concern about the seller's ability to convey good title, are "completed on a handshake and an exchange of an invoice." It is not customary for sophisticated buyers and sellers to obtain a signed invoice from the original seller to the dealer prior to a transaction, nor is it an ordinary or customary practice to request the underlying invoice or corroborating information as to a dealer's authority to convey title. Moreover, it is not customary to approach the owner of an artwork if the owner regularly worked with a particular art dealer because any inquiries about an art transaction customarily are presented to the art dealer rather than directly to the [owner]. *It is customary to rely upon representations made by respected dealers regarding their authority to sell works of art.* A dealer customarily is not required to present an invoice establishing when and from whom he bought the artwork or the conditions of the purchase. [Emphasis added.]

We are compelled to conclude, however, that the sale from Malmberg to the defendant was unlike the vast majority of art transactions. * * * Under such circumstances, a handshake and an exchange of invoice is not sufficient to confer status as a buyer in the ordinary course.

* * * *

* * * A merchant buyer has a heightened duty of inquiry when a reasonable merchant would have doubts or questions regarding the seller's authority to sell. * * * In the present case, the defendant had concerns about Malmberg's ability to convey good title to *Red Elvis* because he believed that Lindholm might have had a claim to the painting. The defendant also was concerned that Malmberg had not yet acquired title to the painting * * * .

Because of his concern that Lindholm might make a claim to *Red Elvis,* the defendant took the extraordinary step of hiring counsel to conduct an investigation and to negotiate a formal contract of sale on his behalf. * * * Such searches typically are not conducted during the course of a normal art transaction and, therefore, provided the defendant with at least some assurance that Lindholm had no claims to the painting.

Moreover, * * * both Malmberg and Holm had reputations as honest, reliable, and trustworthy art dealers. * * * The defendant had little reason to doubt Malmberg's claim that he was the owner of *Red Elvis,* and any doubts that he did have reasonably were allayed [reduced] by relying on Holm's assurances that Malmberg had bought the painting from the plaintiff * * * .

The defendant's concerns were further allayed when Malmberg delivered *Red Elvis* to a * * * warehouse in Denmark, the delivery location the parties had agreed to in the contract of sale. At the time of the sale, the painting was on loan to the Guggenheim, whose policy it was to release a painting on loan only to the true owner, or to someone the true owner had authorized to take possession. * * * We conclude that these steps were sufficient to conform to reasonable commercial standards for the sale of artwork under the circumstances and, therefore, that the defendant had status as a buyer in the ordinary course of business.

Decision and Remedy *The Connecticut Supreme Court affirmed the judgment of the lower court. The state supreme court concluded that "on the basis of all the circumstances surrounding this sale," Brant was a buyer in the ordinary course of business. He therefore took all rights to* Red Elvis *under UCC 2–403(2).*

Critical Thinking

- **Ethical** *How did the "usual and customary" methods of dealing in the art business help Malmberg deceive the other parties in this case? What additional steps might those parties have taken to protect themselves from such deceit?*
- **Global** *Considering the international locales in this case, why was Lindholm able to bring an action against Brant in Connecticut?*

21-3 Risk of Loss

At the various stages of a sale or lease transaction, the question may arise as to who bears the risk of loss. In other words, who suffers the financial loss if the goods are damaged, destroyed, or lost in transit? Under the UCC, risk of loss does not necessarily pass with title. When risk of loss passes from a seller or lessor to a buyer or lessee is generally determined by the contract between the parties.

Sometimes, the contract states expressly when the risk of loss passes. At other times, it does not, and a court must interpret the existing terms to determine whether the risk has passed. When no provision in the contract indicates when risk passes, the UCC provides special rules, based on delivery terms, to guide the courts.

Like risk of loss, the risk of liability that arises from the goods does not necessarily require the passage of title. And like risk of loss, when this risk passes from a seller to a buyer is generally determined by the contract between the parties, as in the following case.

Case 21.3

Person v. Bowman

Court of Appeals of Washington, 173 Wash.App. 1024 (2013).

Background and Facts Tammy Herring and Stacy Bowman signed an agreement titled "Bill of Sale—Purchase Agreement" involving a horse named Toby. The agreement defined Herring as the "buyer" and Stacy and Gregory Bowman, who owned Summit Stables in Puyallup, Washington, as the "seller." It required Herring to make monthly payments until she had paid $2,200 in total for Toby. It also required her to board Toby at Summit Stables until the balance was paid and to cover incidental costs, such as veterinary expenses. The Bowmans were to provide Toby's registration papers to Herring only when she had paid in full.

Diana Person was injured when she was thrown from a buggy drawn by Toby and driven by Herring's daughter, Alex. Person and her husband, Robert, filed a suit in a Washington state court against the Bowmans to recover for Person's injuries. The court ruled that liability rested not with the Bowmans, but with Herring. The court therefore ruled in the defendants' favor, and the Persons appealed.

In the Language of the Court
WORSWICK, C.J. [Chief Judge]
* * * *

The Persons argue that the trial court erred when it found that Herring owned Toby * * *. The Persons contend that Herring had not yet assumed ownership of Toby but, instead, was * * * leasing him, and, as a result, the Bowmans [are] liable.
* * * *

* * * The trial court ruled that the purchase agreement between the Bowmans and Herring established, as a matter of law, that Herring owned Toby and, as such, that liability rested solely with Alex Herring.
* * * *

Washington follows the objective manifestation theory of contract interpretation, under which courts try to ascertain the parties' intent by focusing on the objective manifestations of the agreement, rather than on the unexpressed subjective intent of the parties. [Emphasis added.]

* * * Looking at the contract * * * makes it clear that Herring owned Toby. The title of the agreement, the use of BUYER and SELLER, and the buyer's responsibility to board the horse and pay all incidental expenses all show ownership responsibility. While the contract requires keeping the horse at the stable, making timely payments, not removing the horse without permission, and it gives the seller the right to terminate the contract upon default, these provisions give the seller recourse should it have to recover the horse. In other words, these provisions act as the seller's security interest, protecting the seller until it no longer has a risk of loss.
* * * *

* * * Evidence presented to the trial court consisted of Herring's assertions that she did not own Toby at the time of the accident and did not believe she would own him until she paid the full contract price.

Case 21.3 Continues

Case 21.3 Continued

It consisted of Person's belief that Toby was a leased horse. And it consisted of statements [by] Stacy Bowman * * * using the word "lease," equating the situation as "a lease to own the horse," and acknowledging that she may have used the word "lease" in talking to Herring.

But none of these statements demonstrates that the parties intended to lease Toby. Each statement acknowledges that the Bowmans retained a security interest in Toby and that Herring would not own Toby free and clear or have the right to remove him from the stable until she made her final payment. *While Herring's subjective belief may have been that she did not own Toby and that this was a lease-like agreement, the parties' objective manifestations are consistent with this being a sale not a lease.* [Emphasis added.]

Decision and Remedy *A state intermediate appellate court affirmed the judgment in the Bowmans' favor. Herring (not the Bowmans) owned Toby at the time of the accident that resulted in Person's injuries.*

Critical Thinking
- **What If the Facts Were Different?** *If the agreement between Herring and the Bowmans had been a lease, would the result have been the same? Explain.*

21–3a Delivery with Movement of the Goods—Carrier Cases

When the contract involves movement of the goods via a common carrier but does not specify when risk of loss passes, the courts first look for specific delivery terms in the contract. The terms that have traditionally been used in contracts within the United States are listed and defined in Exhibit 21–2. *Unless the parties agree otherwise,* these terms will determine which party will pay the costs of delivering the goods and who will bear the risk of loss. If the contract does not include these terms, then the courts must decide whether the contract is a shipment or a destination contract.

EXHIBIT 21–2 Contract Terms—Definitions

The contract terms defined in this exhibit help to determine which party will bear the costs of delivery and when risk of loss will pass from the seller to the buyer.

F.O.B. (free on board)	Indicates that the selling price of goods includes transportation costs to the specific F.O.B. place named in the contract. The seller pays the expenses and carries the risk of loss to the F.O.B. place named [UCC 2–319(1)]. If the named place is the place from which the goods are shipped (for example, the seller's city or place of business), the contract is a shipment contract. If the named place is the place to which the goods are to be shipped (for example, the buyer's city or place of business), the contract is a destination contract.
F.A.S. (free alongside)	Requires that the seller, at his or her own expense and risk, deliver the goods alongside the carrier before risk passes to the buyer [UCC 2–319(2)]. An F.A.S. contract is essentially an F.O.B. contract for ships.
C.I.F. or C.&F. (cost, insurance, and freight or just cost and freight)	Requires, among other things, that the seller "put the goods in possession of a carrier" before risk passes to the buyer [UCC 2–320(2)]. (These are basically pricing terms, and the contracts remain shipment contracts, not destination contracts.)
Delivery ex-ship (delivery from the carrying vessel)	Means that risk of loss does not pass to the buyer until the goods are properly unloaded from the ship or other carrier [UCC 2–322].

Shipment Contracts In a shipment contract, the seller or lessor is required or authorized to ship goods by carrier, but is not required to deliver them to a particular destination. The risk of loss in a shipment contract passes to the buyer or lessee when the goods are delivered to the carrier [UCC 2–509(1)(a), 2A–219(2)(a)].

■ **EXAMPLE 21.8** Pitman, a seller in Texas, sells five hundred cases of grapefruit to a buyer in New York, F.O.B. Houston (free on board in Houston). This term means that the buyer pays the transportation charges from Houston—see Exhibit 21–2. The contract authorizes shipment by carrier. It does not require that the seller tender the grapefruit in New York. Risk passes to the buyer when conforming goods are properly placed in the possession of the carrier. If the goods are damaged in transit, the loss is the buyer's. (Actually, buyers have recourse against carriers, subject to certain limitations, and they usually insure the goods from the time the goods leave the seller.) ■

Destination Contracts In a destination contract, the risk of loss passes to the buyer or lessee when the goods are tendered to the buyer or lessee at the specified destination [UCC 2–509(1)(b), 2A–219(2)(b)]. In *Example 21.8*, if the contract had been a destination contract, F.O.B. New York, risk of loss during transit to New York would have been the seller's. Risk of loss would not have passed to the buyer until the carrier tendered the grapefruit to the buyer in New York.

Whether a contract is a shipment contract or a destination contract can have significant consequences for the parties. When an agreement is ambiguous as to whether it is a shipment or a destination contract, courts normally will presume that it is a shipment contract. Thus, the parties must use clear and explicit language to overcome this presumption and create a destination contract.

21–3b Delivery without Movement of the Goods

The UCC also addresses situations in which the contract does not require the goods to be shipped or moved. Frequently, the buyer or lessee is to pick up the goods from the seller or lessor, or the goods are to be held by a bailee. A **bailment** is a temporary delivery of personal property, without passage of title, into the care of another, called a *bailee*. Under the UCC, a bailee is a party who—by a bill of lading, warehouse receipt, or other document of title—acknowledges possession of goods and/or contracts to deliver them. For instance, a warehousing company or a trucking company may be a bailee.[7]

Goods Held by the Seller When the seller keeps the goods for pickup, a document of title usually is not used.

Nonmerchants. If the seller is not a merchant, the risk of loss to goods held by the seller passes to the buyer on *tender of delivery* [UCC 2–509(3)]. Thus, the seller bears the risk of loss until he or she makes the goods available to the buyer and notifies the buyer that the goods are ready to be picked up.

Merchants. If the seller is a merchant, risk of loss to goods held by the seller passes to the buyer when the buyer *actually takes physical possession of the goods* [UCC 2–509(3)]. In other words, the merchant bears the risk of loss between the time the contract is formed and the time the buyer picks up the goods.

■ **CASE IN POINT 21.9** Roger Adams bought a preassembled table saw from Sears Roebuck and Company. The saw weighed 288 pounds. When Adams went to the loading area to pick up the saw, a Sears employee used a hydraulic lift to elevate it to the height of Adams's pickup bed. Adams then pulled the saw onto the truck. Once the saw was loaded, the employee went back inside the store (and did not secure the saw).

Adams, who was standing in the bed of his truck, took a step and lost his balance. He grabbed the saw to steady himself. Both he and the saw fell off the truck, and he was injured. Adams sued Sears, alleging negligence, but the court granted summary judgment in favor of Sears. Sears was under no duty to help Adams secure the saw in the truck, so the employee had not been negligent. Once the truck was loaded, the risk of loss (or injury) passed to Adams under the UCC because he had taken physical possession of the goods.[8] ■

Leases. Except in a finance lease (in which the lessor acquires goods to supply the lessee), the lessor normally retains the risk of loss [UCC 2A–219]. If a lease contract provides that risk of loss is to pass to the lessee but does not specify when, then it depends on whether the lessor is a merchant. If the lessor is a merchant, the risk of loss passes to the lessee on the lessee's receipt of the goods. If the lessor is not a merchant, the risk passes to the lessee on tender of delivery (when goods are made available for pickup) [UCC 2A–219(2)(c)].

■ **EXAMPLE 21.10** Erikson Crane leases a helicopter from Jevis, Ltd., which is in the business of renting aircraft. While Erikson's pilot is on the way to Idaho to pick up the helicopter, the helicopter is damaged during an unexpected storm. In this situation, Jevis is a merchant-lessor,

---

7. The law requires bailees to take appropriate care of the bailed goods.

8. *Adams v. Sears Roebuck and Co.*, 2014 WL 670630 (D.Utah 2014).

so it bears the risk of loss to the leased helicopter until Erikson takes possession of the helicopter. ■

Goods Held by a Bailee When a bailee is holding goods that are to be delivered under a contract without being moved, the goods are usually represented by a document of title. The title document may be written on paper or evidenced by an electronic record.

Negotiability of Title Document. A document of title is either *negotiable* or *nonnegotiable,* depending on whether the transferee is a buyer or lessee and on how the title document is transferred. Negotiable and nonnegotiable documents may transfer different rights to the goods that the documents cover.

With a negotiable document of title, a party can transfer the rights by signing and delivering, or in some situations simply delivering, the document. The rights to the goods—free of any claims against the party that issued the document—pass with the document to the transferee. With a nonnegotiable document of title, the transferee obtains only the rights that the party transferring it had, subject to any prior claims.

When Risk of Loss Passes. When goods are held by a bailee, risk of loss passes to the buyer when one of the following occurs:

1. The buyer receives a negotiable document of title for the goods.
2. The bailee acknowledges the buyer's right to possess the goods.
3. The buyer receives a nonnegotiable document of title, *and* the buyer has had a *reasonable time* to present the document to the bailee and demand the goods. If the bailee refuses to honor the document, the risk of loss remains with the seller [UCC 2–503(4)(b), 2–509(2)].

With respect to leases, if goods held by a bailee are to be delivered without being moved, the risk of loss passes to the lessee on acknowledgment by the bailee of the lessee's right to possession of the goods [UCC 2A–219(2)(b)].

Concept Summary 21.1 reviews the rules for when title and risk of loss pass to the buyer or lessee when the seller or lessor is not required to ship or deliver the goods.

21–3c Conditional Sales

Buyers and sellers sometimes form sales contracts that are conditioned either on the buyer's approval of the goods or on the buyer's resale of the goods. The UCC states that (unless otherwise agreed) if the goods are for the buyer to use, the transaction is a *sale on approval.* If the goods are for the buyer to resell, the transaction is a *sale or return.*

Sale on Approval When a seller offers to sell goods to a buyer and permits the buyer to take the goods on a trial basis, a **sale on approval** is made. The goods are delivered primarily so that the prospective buyer can use the goods and be convinced of their appearance or performance. The term *sale* here is misleading, because only an *offer* to sell has been made, along with a bailment created by the buyer's possession.

Title and risk of loss (from causes beyond the buyer's control) remain with the seller until the buyer accepts (approves) the offer. Acceptance can be made expressly or by any act inconsistent with the trial purpose or the seller's ownership (such as reselling the goods). Thus, the buyer's decision not to return the goods within the trial period will be considered acceptance. If the buyer does not wish to accept, the buyer must notify the seller, and the return is made at the seller's expense and risk [UCC 2–327(1)]. Goods held on approval are not subject to the claims of the buyer's creditors until acceptance.

■ **EXAMPLE 21.11** Brad orders a Bowflex Tread-Climber online, and the manufacturer allows him to try it risk-free for thirty days. If Brad decides to keep the TreadClimber, then the sale is complete. If he returns it within thirty days, there will be no sale, and he will not be charged. If Brad files for bankruptcy within the thirty-day period and still has the TreadClimber in his possession, his creditors may not yet attach (seize) the TreadClimber, because he has not accepted it. ■

Sale or Return In a **sale or return,** in contrast, the sale is completed, but the buyer has an option to return the goods and undo the sale. Sale-or-return contracts often arise when a merchant purchases goods primarily for resale. The merchant has the right to return part or all of the goods in lieu of payment if the goods fail to be resold. Basically, a sale or return is a sale of goods in the present that may be undone at the buyer's option within a specified time period. ■ **EXAMPLE 21.12** Freedom Press, a publisher, delivers forty cases of a best-selling book to Powell's Books, a retailer. If Freedom Press agrees that Powell's can return any unsold copies of the books at the end of a year, the transaction is a sale or return. ■

Because the buyer receives possession at the time of the sale, title and risk of loss pass to the buyer and remain with the buyer unless the goods are returned within the time period specified. If the buyer decides to return the goods within this time period, the return is made at the buyer's risk and expense. Goods held under a sale-or-return contract are subject to the claims of the buyer's creditors while they are in the buyer's possession.

Concept Summary 21.1

Delivery without Movement of the Goods

Goods Not Represented by a Document of Title	• Title passes on the formation of the contract [UCC 2–401(3)(b)]. • Risk of loss passes to the buyer or lessee: (a) If the seller or lessor is a merchant, risk passes on the buyer's or lessee's *receipt* of the goods, or (b) If the seller or lessor is a nonmerchant, risk passes to the buyer or lessee on the seller's or lessor's *tender* of delivery of the goods [UCC 2–509(3), 2A–219(2)(c)]
Goods Represented by a Document of Title	• The buyer receives a negotiable document of title for the goods. • The bailee acknowledges the buyer's right to possess the goods. • The buyer receives a nonnegotiable document of title or a writing (record) directing the bailee to hand over the goods, and the buyer has had a reasonable time to present the document to the bailee and demand the goods [UCC 2–503(4)(b), 2–509(2)].
Leased Goods Held by a Bailee	• If leased goods held by a bailee are to be delivered without being moved, the risk of loss passes to the lessee on acknowledgment by the bailee of the lessee's right to possession of the goods [UCC 2A–219(2)(b)].

21–3d Risk of Loss When a Sales or Lease Contract Is Breached

When a sales or lease contract is breached, the transfer of risk operates differently depending on which party breaches. Generally, the party in breach bears the risk of loss.

When the Seller or Lessor Breaches If the goods are so nonconforming that the buyer has the right to reject them, the risk of loss does not pass to the buyer. ■ **EXAMPLE 21.13** May's Appliances orders stainless steel refrigerators from Whirlpool, F.O.B. Whirlpool's plant. Whirlpool ships white refrigerators instead. The white refrigerators (nonconforming goods) are damaged in transit. The risk of loss falls on Whirlpool. Had it shipped stainless steel refrigerators (conforming goods) instead, the risk would have fallen on May's [UCC 2–510(1)]. ■

With nonconforming goods, the risk of loss does not pass to the buyer until either:

1. The defects are *cured* (that is, the goods are repaired, replaced, or discounted in price by the seller).
2. The buyer accepts the goods in spite of their defects (thus waiving the right to reject).

When Acceptance Is Revoked. If a buyer accepts a shipment of goods and later discovers a defect, acceptance can be revoked. The revocation allows the buyer to pass the risk of loss back to the seller, at least to the extent that the buyer's insurance does not cover the loss [UCC 2–510(2)].

Leases. Article 2A provides a similar rule for leases. If the tender or delivery of goods is so nonconforming that the lessee has the right to reject them, the risk of loss remains with the lessor (or the supplier) until cure or acceptance [UCC 2A–220(1)(a)]. If the lessee accepts the goods and then rightfully revokes acceptance, the risk of loss passes back to the lessor to the extent that the lessee's insurance does not cover the loss [UCC 2A–220(1)(b)].

When the Buyer or Lessee Breaches The general rule is that when a buyer or lessee breaches a contract, the risk of loss *immediately shifts* to the buyer or lessee. This rule has three important limitations [UCC 2–510(3), 2A–220(2)]:

1. The seller or lessor must already have identified the contract goods.
2. The buyer or lessee bears the risk for only a *commercially reasonable* time after the seller or lessor has learned of the breach.
3. The buyer or lessee is liable only to the extent of any deficiency in the seller's or lessor's insurance coverage.

See Concept Summary 21.2 for a review of the rules on who bears the risk of loss when a contract is breached.

21–4 Insurable Interest

Parties to sales and lease contracts often obtain insurance coverage to protect against damage, loss, or destruction of goods. Any party purchasing insurance, however, must have a sufficient interest in the insured item to obtain a valid policy. Insurance laws—not the UCC—determine sufficiency. The UCC is helpful, though, because it contains certain rules regarding insurable interests in goods.

21–4a Insurable Interest of the Buyer or Lessee

A buyer or lessee has an **insurable interest** in *identified goods*. The moment the contract goods are identified by the seller or lessor, the buyer or lessee has a property interest in them. That interest allows the buyer or lessee to obtain the necessary insurance coverage for those goods even before the risk of loss has passed [UCC 2–501(1), 2A–218(1)].

Identification can be made at any time and in any manner agreed to by the parties. When the parties do not explicitly agree on identification in their contract, then the UCC provisions on identification discussed in this chapter apply.

Buyers obtain an insurable interest in crops at the time of identification. ■ **EXAMPLE 21.14** In March, a farmer sells a cotton crop that she hopes to harvest in October to her neighbor, Sue Ann. The contract does not specify when Sue Ann has an insurable interest. Sue Ann acquires an insurable interest in the crop when it is planted because the goods (the cotton crop) are identified to the sales contract at that time [UCC 2–501(1)(c)]. ■

21–4b Insurable Interest of the Seller or Lessor

A seller has an insurable interest in goods as long as he or she retains title to the goods. Even after title passes to a buyer, a seller who has a *security interest* (a right to secure payment) in the goods still has an insurable interest [UCC 2–501(2)]. Thus, both the buyer and the seller can have an insurable interest in identical goods at the same time. Of course, the buyer or seller must sustain an actual loss to have the right to recover from an insurance company.

In regard to leases, the lessor retains an insurable interest in leased goods unless the lessee exercises an option to buy. In that event, the risk of loss passes to the lessee [UCC 2A–218(3)].

Concept Summary 21.2

Risk of Loss When a Sales or Lease Contract Is Breached

When the Seller or Lessor Breaches the Contract	• If the seller or lessor breaches by tendering nonconforming goods that the buyer or lessee has a right to reject, the risk of loss does not pass to the buyer or lessee until the defects are cured or the buyer accepts the goods (thus waiving the right to reject) [UCC 2–510(1), 2A–220(1)].

When the Buyer or Lessee Breaches the Contract	• If the buyer or lessee breaches the contract, the risk of loss to identified goods immediately shifts to the buyer or lessee. Limitations to this rule are as follows [UCC 2–510(3), 2A–220(2)]:
	  • The seller or lessor must have already identified the contract goods.
	  • The buyer or lessee bears the risk for only a commercially reasonable time after the seller or lessor has learned of the breach.
	  • The buyer or lessee is liable only to the extent of any deficiency in the seller's or lessor's insurance coverage.

Reviewing: Title, Risk, and Insurable Interest

In December, Mendoza agreed to buy the broccoli grown on one hundred acres of Willow Glen's one-thousand-acre broccoli farm. The sales contract specified F.O.B. Willow Glen's field by Falcon Trucking. The broccoli was to be planted in February and harvested in March of the following year. Using the information presented in the chapter, answer the following questions.

1. At what point is a crop of broccoli identified to the contract under the Uniform Commercial Code? Why is identification significant?
2. When does title to the broccoli pass from Willow Glen to Mendoza under the contract terms? Why?
3. Suppose that while in transit, Falcon's truck overturns and spills the entire load. Who bears the loss, Mendoza or Willow Glen?
4. Suppose that instead of buying fresh broccoli, Mendoza contracted with Willow Glen to purchase one thousand cases of frozen broccoli from Willow Glen's processing plant. The highest grade of broccoli is packaged under the "FreshBest" label, and everything else is packaged under the "FamilyPac" label. Further suppose that although the contract specified that Mendoza was to receive FreshBest broccoli, Falcon Trucking delivered FamilyPac broccoli to Mendoza. If Mendoza refuses to accept the broccoli, who bears the loss?

Debate This . . . *The distinction between shipment and destination contracts for the purpose of deciding who will bear the risk of loss should be eliminated in favor of a rule that always requires the buyer to obtain insurance for the goods being shipped.*

Terms and Concepts

bailment 397
buyer in the ordinary course
  of business 393
destination contract 390
document of title 391

entrustment rule 392
fungible goods 388
good faith purchaser 392
identification 387
insolvent 392

insurable interest 400
sale on approval 398
sale or return 398
shipment contract 390

Issue Spotters

1. Adams Textiles in Kansas City sells certain fabric to Silk & Satin Stores in Oklahoma City. Adams packs the fabric and ships it by rail to Silk. While the fabric is in transit across Kansas, a tornado derails the train and shreds and scatters the fabric across miles of cornfields. What are the consequences if Silk bore the risk? If Adams bore the risk? (See *Insurable Interest.*)

2. Karlin takes her television set for repair to Orken, a merchant who sells new and used television sets. By accident, one of Orken's employees sells the set to Grady, an innocent purchaser-customer, who takes possession. Karlin wants her set back from Grady. If Karlin files a lawsuit, will she prevail? Why or why not? (See *When Title Passes.*)

• **Check your answers to the Issue Spotters against the answers provided in Appendix D at the end of this text.**

Business Scenarios

21–1. Risk of Loss. Mackey orders from Pride one thousand cases of Greenie brand peas from lot A at list price to be shipped F.O.B. Pride's city via Fast Freight Lines. Pride receives the order and immediately sends Mackey an acceptance of the order with a promise to ship promptly. Pride later separates the one thousand cases of Greenie peas and prints Mackey's name and address on each case. The peas are placed on Pride's dock, and Fast Freight is notified to pick up the shipment. The night before the pickup by Fast Freight, through no fault of Pride's, a fire destroys the one thousand cases of peas. Pride claims that title passed to Mackey at the time the contract was made and that risk of loss passed to Mackey when the goods were marked with Mackey's name and address. Discuss Pride's contentions. (See *Risk of Loss.*)

21–2. Risk of Loss. On May 1, Sikora goes into Carson's retail clothing store to purchase a suit. Sikora finds a suit he likes for $190 and buys it. The suit needs alterations. Sikora is to pick up the altered suit at Carson's store on May 10. Consider the following separate sets of circumstances. (See *Risk of Loss.*)

(a) One of Carson's major creditors obtains a judgment on the debt Carson owes. The creditor has the court issue a writ of execution to collect on that judgment all clothing in Carson's possession. (A writ of execution is a court order to seize a debtor's property to satisfy a debt.) Discuss Sikora's rights in the suit under these circumstances.

(b) On May 9, through no fault of Carson's, the store burns down, and all contents are a total loss. Between Carson and Sikora, who suffers the loss of the suit destroyed by the fire? Explain.

Business Case Problems

21–3. Delivery without Movement of the Goods. Aleris International, Inc., signed a contract to buy a John Deere loader from Holt Equipment Co. The agreement provided that "despite physical delivery of the equipment, title shall remain in the seller until" Aleris paid the full price. The next month, Aleris filed for bankruptcy. Holt filed a claim with the court to repossess the loader. Holt asserted that it was the owner. Who is entitled to the loader, and why? [*In re Aleris International, Ltd.,* 456 Bankr. 35 (D.Del. 2011)] (See *When Title Passes.*)

21–4. Goods Held by the Seller or Lessor. Douglas Singletary bought a manufactured home from Andy's Mobile Home and Land Sales. The contract stated that the buyer accepted the home "as is where is." Singletary paid the full price, and his crew began to ready the home to relocate it to his property. The night before the home was to be moved, however, it was destroyed by fire. Who suffered the loss? Explain. [*Singletary, III v. P&A Investments, Inc.,* 712 S.E.2d 681 (N.C.App. 2011)] (See *Risk of Loss.*)

21–5. Business Case Problem with Sample Answer— Passage of Title. Kenzie Godfrey, a college student major-ing in physics, was a passenger in a taxi when it collided with a car driven by Dawn Altieri. Altieri had originally leased the car from G.E. Capital Auto Lease, Inc. By the time of the accident, she had bought it, but she had not fully paid for it or completed the transfer-of-title paperwork. Godfrey suffered a brain injury and sought to recover damages from the owner of the car that Altieri was driving. Who had title to the car at the time of the accident? Explain. [*Godfrey v. G.E. Capital Auto Lease, Inc.,* 89 A.D.3d 471, 933 N.Y.S.2d 208 (1 Dept. 2011)] (See *When Title Passes.*)

- For a sample answer to Problem 21–5, go to Appendix E at the end of this text.

21–6. Risk of Loss. Ethicon, Inc., a pharmaceutical company, entered into an agreement with UPS Supply Chain Solutions, Inc., to transport pharmaceuticals. Under a contract with a UPS subsidiary, Worldwide Dedicated Services, Inc., (WDS), the drivers were provided by International Management Services Co. (IMSCO). During the transport of a shipment from Ethicon's facility in Texas to buyers "F.O.B. Tennessee," one of the trucks collided with a concrete barrier near Little Rock, Arkansas, and caught fire, damaging the goods. Who was liable for the loss? Why? [*Royal & Sun Alliance Insurance, PLC v. International Management Services Co.,* 703 F.3d 604 (2d Cir. 2013)] (See *Risk of Loss.*)

21–7. When Title Passes. James McCoolidge, a Nebraska resident, saw a used Honda Element for sale online. He contacted the seller, Daniel Oyvetsky, who offered to sell the vehicle for $7,500 on behalf of Car and Truck Center, LLC, a dealership in Nashville, Tennessee. McCoolidge paid the price and received the car and a certificate of title. Before he registered the certificate with the Nebraska Department of Motor Vehicles, he learned that the state of Tennessee had issued numerous certificates of title to the Element. Based on these documents, title could ultimately be traced to McCoolidge. But he chose to file a suit in a Nebraska state court against Oyvetsky, claiming that he had not received "clear" title. What does the UCC provide with respect to the passage of title under a sales contract? How does that rule impact McCoolidge's claim? Discuss. [*McCoolidge v. Oyvetsky,* 292 Neb. 955, 874 N.W.2d 892 (2016)] (See *When Title Passes.*)

21–8. A Question of Ethics—Void and Voidable Titles.
 *Kenneth West agreed to sell his car, a 1975 Corvette, to a man representing himself as Robert Wilson. In exchange for a cashier's check, West signed over the Corvette's title to Wilson and gave him the car. Ten days later, when West learned that the cashier's check was a forgery, he filed a stolen vehicle report with the police. The police could not immediately locate Wilson or the Corvette, however, and the case grew cold. Nearly two and a half years later, the police found the Corvette in the possession of Tammy Roberts, who also had the certificate of title. She said that she had bought the car from her brother, who had obtained it through an ad in a newspaper. West filed a suit in a Colorado state court against Roberts to reclaim the car. The court applied Colorado Revised Statutes Section 4-2-403 (Colorado's version of Section 2–403 of the Uniform Commercial Code) to determine the vehicle's rightful owner. [*West v. Roberts, 143 P.3d 1037 (Colo. 2006)*] (See *When Title Passes.*)*

(a) Under UCC 2–403, what title, if any, to the Corvette did "Wilson" acquire? What was the status of Roberts's title, if any? (Assume that she bought the car without knowledge of circumstances that would make a person of ordinary prudence inquire about the validity of the seller's title.) In whose favor should the court rule? Explain.

(b) If the original owner of a vehicle relinquishes it due to fraud, should he or she be allowed to recover the vehicle from a good faith purchaser? If not, which party or parties might the original owner sue for recovery? What is the ethical principle underlying your answer to these questions? Discuss.

21–9. Special Case Analysis—Goods That Are Part of a Larger Mass. Go to Case Analysis 21.1, *BMW Group, LLC v. Castle Oil Corp.* Read the excerpt and answer the following questions.

(a) Issue: What goods are at the center of this case? Why?

(b) Rule of Law: What does the Uniform Commercial Code provide with respect to causes of action for such goods?

(c) Applying the Rule of Law: How did the appellate court determine whether the plaintiffs' allegations were supported in this case?

(d) Conclusion: What did the trial and appellate courts rule with respect to the plaintiffs' claims, and what did the appellate court order as a result?

Legal Reasoning Group Activity

21–10. Shipment Contracts. Professional Products, Inc. (PPI), bought three pallets of computer wafers from Omneon Video Graphics. (A computer wafer is a thin, round slice of silicon from which microchips are made.) Omneon agreed to ship the wafers to the City University of New York "FOB Omneon's dock." Shipment was arranged through Haas Industries, Inc. The "conditions of carriage" on the back of the bill of lading stated that Haas's liability for lost goods was limited to fifty cents per pound. When the shipment arrived, it included only two pallets. (See *When Title Passes.*)

(a) The first group will determine who suffers the loss in this situation.

(b) The second group will discuss whether it is it fair for a carrier to limit its liability for lost goods.

CHAPTER 22

Performance and Breach
of Sales and Lease Contracts

The performance that is required of the parties under a sales or lease contract consists of the duties and obligations each party has under the terms of the contract. The basic obligation of the seller or lessor is to *transfer and deliver conforming goods.* The basic obligation of the buyer or lessee is to *accept and pay for conforming goods* in accordance with the contract [UCC 2–301, 2A–516(1)]. Overall performance of a sales or lease contract is controlled by the agreement between the parties. When the contract is unclear and disputes arise, the courts look to the UCC and impose standards of good faith and commercial reasonableness.

The obligations of good faith and commercial reasonableness underlie every sales and lease contract. The UCC's good faith provision, which can never be disclaimed, reads as follows: "Every contract or duty within this Act imposes an obligation of good faith in its performance or enforcement" [UCC 1–304]. *Good faith* means honesty in fact. For a merchant, it means honesty in fact and the observance of reasonable commercial standards of fair dealing in the trade [UCC 2–103(1)(b)]. In other words,

merchants are held to a higher standard of performance or duty than are nonmerchants.

Sometimes, circumstances make it difficult for a party to carry out the promised performance, leading to a breach of the contract. When a breach occurs, the aggrieved (wronged) party looks for remedies. Note that in contrast to the common law of contracts, remedies under the UCC are cumulative in nature—meaning that the aggrieved party is not limited to one exclusive remedy.

22-1 Obligations of the Seller or Lessor

The basic duty of the seller or lessor is to deliver the goods called for under the contract to the buyer or lessee. Goods that conform to the contract description in every way are called **conforming goods.** To fulfill the contract, the seller or lessor must either deliver or tender delivery of conforming goods to the buyer or lessee.

22-1a Tender of Delivery

Tender of delivery occurs when the seller or lessor makes conforming goods available and gives the buyer or lessee whatever notification is reasonably necessary to enable the buyer or lessee to take delivery [UCC 2–503(1), 2A–508(1)].

Tender must occur at a *reasonable hour* and in a *reasonable manner.* For example, a seller cannot call the buyer

at 2:00 A.M. and say, "The goods are ready. I'll give you twenty minutes to get them." Unless the parties have agreed otherwise, the goods must be tendered for delivery at a reasonable hour and kept available for a reasonable time to enable the buyer to take possession [UCC 2–503(1)(a)].

Normally, all goods called for by a contract must be tendered in a single delivery unless the parties have agreed on delivery in several lots or *installments* (discussed shortly) [UCC 2–307, 2–612, 2A–510]. ■ **EXAMPLE 22.1** An order for 1,000 Under Armour men's shirts cannot be delivered two shirts at a time. The parties may agree, however, that the shirts will be delivered in four orders of 250 each as they are produced (for summer, fall, winter, and spring inventory). Tender of delivery may then occur in this manner. ■

In the following case, the seller of a log-cabin kit gave the buyers two days' notice to arrange for their final payment on the contract and take delivery. Did this notice comply with UCC 2–503?

Garziano v. Louisiana Log Home Co.

United States Court of Appeals, Fifth Circuit, 569 Fed.Appx. 292 (2014).

Background and Facts Richard and Nancy Garziano contracted with Louisiana Log Home (LLH) Company for a log-cabin kit to be delivered to them in Pass Christian, Mississippi. The contract required three installment payments. The final payment, due at delivery, was to include the cost of transportation. Two days before delivery, LLH told the buyers that the final payment would be $7,686.43, plus the transportation cost of $2,625.60. The Garzianos replied that they thought they had paid off the balance for the cabin and that they expected the shipping costs to be lower. They refused to pay more, and LLH did not deliver the kit.

The Garzianos filed a claim in a federal district court against LLH, alleging that LLH had breached the contract by failing to inform them of the price of delivery in a timely manner. The court issued a judgment in LLH's favor and allowed the seller to keep the Garzianos' first two installment payments and the log-cabin kit without determining the actual amount of damages suffered. The Garzianos appealed.

In the Language of the Court

PER CURIAM [By the Whole Court]:
* * * *

The Garzianos * * * allege that LLH violated Section 75–2–503(1) of the Mississippi Code [Mississippi's version of UCC 2–503(1),] which imposes a duty to *"hold conforming goods at the buyer's disposition and give the buyer any notification reasonably necessary"* to enable the buyer to take delivery. * * * The Garzianos contend that LLH violated this statute and thereby breached the contract by failing to notify them of the amount of shipping charges until only two days before delivery, which constructively prohibited them from accepting delivery. * * * The argument seems to be that LLH's failure to inform the Garzianos of the price of delivery in a timely manner excused the Garzianos' later breach of the contract by refusing delivery. [Emphasis added.]

This argument fails.

The contracts in this case were simple and easily understood. They provided that "all costs of transportation shall be borne by the purchaser," that "shipping charges are paid directly to the trucking company at the time of delivery by cash or personal check," and specified an "F.O.B. [Free on Board] Factory Price." These contracts also made clear that the final price that would be paid, absent shipping costs, was $43,656.43. *Thus the explicit terms of the contract put the Garzianos on notice that they had both not paid off the balance on the log-home kit and that they were responsible for any shipping costs.* [Emphasis added.]
* * * *

* * * LLH was attempting to deliver the goods when the Garzianos breached by refusing to pay either the balance on the contract or the shipping charges—both of which they were obligated to pay under the contract. * * * There was no undisclosed, expiring window of time during which the Garzianos were required to claim the log cabin. * * * They were given reasonable notice of the date of delivery. * * * [On] July 17, * * * LLH advised the Garzianos that the package would be delivered on July 19 * * *. It was at this point that LLH informed the Garzianos that they still needed to make the third installment payment and pay $2,625 for the delivery fee. While the Garzianos may have been surprised at the size of the delivery fee, the notice provided to the Garzianos was not so deficient as to prevent them from effectively taking delivery so that their refusal to pay would be excused. The only obstacle to taking delivery was the Garzianos' refusal to pay for the goods and the shipping costs. As the [lower] court correctly held, LLH's "method of tender was in compliance with the terms of the contracts."

Decision and Remedy *The U.S. Court of Appeals for the Fifth Circuit affirmed the lower court's judgment. The Garzianos may have been surprised by the amount of the delivery fee, but the notice that LLH gave them was in compliance with the contract. The lower court had not determined the actual amount of LLH's damages, however. The court remanded the case to the lower court to make that finding and to remit to the Garzianos any funds paid that were in excess of LLH's actual damages.*

Critical Thinking

• **Legal Environment** *How might the parties have avoided the dispute in this case?*

22–1b Place of Delivery

The buyer and seller (or lessor and lessee) may agree that the goods will be delivered to a particular destination where the buyer or lessee will take possession. If the contract does not indicate where the goods will be delivered, then the place for delivery will be one of the following:

1. The *seller's place of business.*
2. The *seller's residence,* if the seller has no business location [UCC 2–308(a)].
3. The *location of the goods,* if both parties know at the time of contracting that the goods are located somewhere other than the seller's business [UCC 2–308(b)].

■ **EXAMPLE 22.2** Li Wan and Boyd both live in San Francisco. In San Francisco, Li Wan contracts to sell Boyd five used trucks, which both parties know are located in a Chicago warehouse. If nothing more is specified in the contract, the place of delivery for the trucks is Chicago. Li Wan may tender delivery by giving Boyd either a negotiable or a nonnegotiable document of title. Alternatively, Li Wan may obtain the bailee's (warehouser's) acknowledgment that Boyd is entitled to possession.[1] ■

22–1c Delivery via Carrier

In many instances, it is clear from the surrounding circumstances or delivery terms in the contract that the parties intended the goods to be moved by a carrier. In carrier contracts, the seller fulfills the obligation to deliver the goods through either a shipment contract or a destination contract.

Shipment Contracts Recall that a *shipment contract* requires or authorizes the seller to ship goods by a carrier, rather than to deliver them at a particular destination [UCC 2–319, 2–509(1)(a)]. Under a shipment contract, unless otherwise agreed, the seller must do the following:

1. Place the goods into the hands of the carrier.
2. Make a contract for their transportation that is reasonable according to the nature of the goods and their value. (For instance, certain types of goods need refrigeration in transit.)
3. Obtain and promptly deliver or tender to the buyer any documents necessary to enable the buyer to obtain possession of the goods from the carrier.

4. Promptly notify the buyer that shipment has been made [UCC 2–504].

If the seller does not make a reasonable contract for transportation or notify the buyer of the shipment, the buyer can reject the goods, but only if a *material loss* or a *significant delay* results. ■ **EXAMPLE 22.3** Zigi's Organic Fruits sells strawberries to Lozier under a shipment contract. If Zigi's does not arrange for refrigerated transportation and the berries spoil during transport, a material loss to Lozier will likely result. ■ Of course, the parties are free to make agreements that alter the UCC's rules and allow the buyer to reject goods for other reasons.

Destination Contracts In a *destination contract,* the seller agrees to deliver conforming goods to the buyer at a particular destination. The goods must be tendered at a reasonable hour and held at the buyer's disposal for a reasonable length of time. The seller must also give the buyer appropriate notice and any necessary documents to enable the buyer to obtain delivery from the carrier [UCC 2–503].

22–1d The Perfect Tender Rule

The seller or lessor has an obligation to ship or tender *conforming goods.* The buyer or lessee is then obligated to accept and pay for the goods according to the contract terms [UCC 2–507].

Under the common law, the seller was obligated to deliver goods that conformed with the terms of the contract in every detail (unless the doctrine of substantial performance applied). The UCC adopted the **perfect tender rule.** It states that if goods or tender of delivery fails *in any respect* to conform to the contract, the buyer or lessee may accept the goods, reject the entire shipment, or accept part and reject part [UCC 2–601, 2A–509].

The corollary to this rule is that if the goods conform in every respect, the buyer or lessee does not have a right to reject the goods. ■ **CASE IN POINT 22.4** U.S. Golf & Tennis Centers, Inc., agreed to buy 96,000 golf balls from Wilson Sporting Goods Company for a total price of $20,000. Wilson represented that U.S. Golf was receiving its lowest price ($5 per two-dozen unit).

Wilson shipped golf balls to U.S. Golf that conformed to the contract in quantity and quality, but it did not receive payment. U.S. Golf claimed that it had learned that Wilson had sold the product for $2 per unit to another buyer. U.S. Golf asked Wilson to reduce the contract price of the balls to $4 per unit. Wilson refused and filed a suit. The court ruled in favor of Wilson. Because it was undisputed that the shipment of golf balls conformed to the contract specifications, U.S. Golf

---

1. Unless the buyer objects, the seller may also tender delivery by instructing the bailee in a writing to release the goods to the buyer without the bailee's acknowledgment of the buyer's rights [UCC 2–503(4)]. Risk of loss, however, does not pass until the buyer has had a reasonable amount of time in which to present the document or the instructions.

was obligated to accept the goods and pay the agreed-on price.[2] ∎

22–1e Exceptions to the Perfect Tender Rule

Because of the rigidity of the perfect tender rule, several exceptions to the rule have been created, some of which we discuss here and outline in Exhibit 22–1.

Agreement of the Parties Exceptions to the perfect tender rule may be established by agreement. The parties may agree, for instance, that defective goods or parts will not be rejected if the seller or lessor is able to repair or replace them within a reasonable period of time. In this situation, the perfect tender rule does not apply.

---

2. *Wilson Sporting Goods Co. v. U.S. Golf and Tennis Centers, Inc.*, 2012 WL 601804 (Tenn.App. 2012).

Cure The UCC does not specifically define the term **cure,** but it refers to the right of the seller or lessor to repair, adjust, or replace defective or nonconforming goods [UCC 2–508, 2A–513].

The seller or lessor has a right to attempt to "cure" a defect when the following are true:

1. A delivery is rejected because the goods were nonconforming.
2. The time for performance has not yet expired.
3. The seller or lessor provides timely notice to the buyer or lessee of the intention to cure.
4. The cure can be made within the contract time for performance.

Reasonable Grounds. Even if the contract time for performance has expired, the seller or lessor can still cure if he or she had *reasonable grounds to believe that the nonconforming tender would be acceptable to the buyer or lessee* [UCC 2–508(2), 2A–513(2)].

EXHIBIT 22–1 The Perfect Tender Rule and Its Exceptions

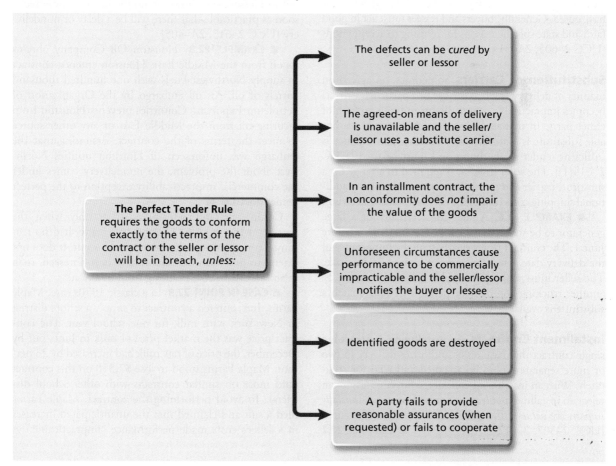

■ **EXAMPLE 22.5** In the past, Rio Electronics has frequently allowed Topps Company to substitute grey keyboards when the silver keyboards that Rio ordered were not in stock. Under a new contract for keyboards, Rio rejects a shipment of grey keyboards. In this situation, Topps had reasonable grounds to believe that Rio would accept the grey keyboards as a substitute. Therefore, normally Topps can cure within a reasonable time even if the conforming delivery will occur after the contract time for performance. ■

A seller or lessor will sometimes tender nonconforming goods with some type of price allowance (discount). A discounted price can serve as the "reasonable grounds" to believe that the buyer or lessee will accept the nonconforming tender.

Limits the Right to Reject Goods. The right to cure substantially restricts the right of the buyer or lessee to reject goods. To reject, the buyer or lessee must inform the seller or lessor of the particular defect. If the defect is not disclosed, the buyer or lessee cannot later assert the defect as a defense if the defect is one that the seller or lessor could have cured. Generally, buyers and lessees must act in good faith and state specific reasons for refusing to accept goods [UCC 2–605, 2A–514].

Substitution of Carriers Sometimes, an agreed-on manner of delivery (such as the use of a particular carrier) becomes impracticable or unavailable through no fault of either party. In that situation, if a commercially reasonable substitute is available, this substitute performance is sufficient tender to the buyer and must be used [UCC 2–614(1)]. The seller or lessor is required to arrange for a substitute carrier and normally is responsible for any additional shipping costs (unless the contract states otherwise).

■ **EXAMPLE 22.6** A sales contract calls for a large generator to be shipped by United Trucking on or before June 1. The contract terms clearly state the importance of the delivery date. The employees of United go on strike. The seller must make a reasonable substitute tender, by another trucking company or perhaps by rail, if such a substitute is available. ■

Installment Contracts An **installment contract** is a single contract that requires or authorizes delivery in two or more separate lots to be accepted and paid for separately. With an installment contract, a buyer or lessee can reject an installment *only if the nonconformity substantially impairs the value* of the installment and cannot be cured [UCC 2–307, 2–612(2), 2A–510(1)]. ■ **EXAMPLE 22.7**

A seller is to deliver fifteen freezers in lots of five each. In the first lot, four of the freezers have defective cooling units that cannot be repaired. The buyer in these circumstances can reject the entire lot. ■ If the buyer or lessee fails to notify the seller or lessor of the rejection, however, and subsequently accepts a nonconforming installment, the contract is reinstated [UCC 2–612(3), 2A–510(2)].

Unless the contract provides otherwise, the entire installment contract is breached only when one or more nonconforming installments *substantially* impair the value of the *whole contract*. The point to remember is that the UCC significantly alters the right of the buyer or lessee to reject the entire contract if the contract requires delivery to be made in several installments. The UCC strictly limits rejection to instances of *substantial* nonconformity.

Commercial Impracticability Occurrences unforeseen by either party when a contract was made may make performance commercially impracticable. When this occurs, the perfect tender rule no longer applies. The seller or lessor must, however, notify the buyer or lessee as soon as practicable that there will be a delay or nondelivery [UCC 2–615, 2A–405].

■ **EXAMPLE 22.8** Houston Oil Company obtains its oil from the Middle East. Houston enters a contract to supply Northwest Fuels with one hundred thousand barrels of oil. An oil embargo by the Organization of Petroleum Exporting Countries prevents Houston from securing oil from the Middle East or any other source to meet the terms of the contract. Assuming that the embargo was unforeseen, if Houston notifies Northwest about the problem, the nondelivery comes under the commercial impracticability exception to the perfect tender doctrine. ■

Commercial impracticability arises only when the parties, at the time the contract was made, had no reason to anticipate that the event would occur. It does not extend to problems that could have been foreseen, such as an increase in cost resulting from inflation.

■ **CASE IN POINT 22.9** In a classic 1970s case, Maple Farms, Inc., entered a contract to supply a school district in New York with milk for one school year. The contract price was the market price of milk in June, but by December, the price of raw milk had increased by 23 percent. Maple Farms stood to lose $7,350 on this contract (and more on similar contracts with other school districts). To avoid performing the contract, Maple Farms filed a suit and claimed that the unanticipated increases in a seller's costs made performance "impracticable." A

New York trial court disagreed. Because inflation and fluctuating prices could have been foreseen, they did not render performance of this contract impracticable. The court granted summary judgment in favor of the school district.[3] ▪

Commercial Impracticability and Partial Performance Sometimes, the unforeseen event only *partially* affects the capacity of the seller or lessor to perform. Therefore, the seller or lessor can *partially* fulfill the contract but cannot tender total performance. In this event, the seller or lessor is required to distribute any remaining goods or deliveries fairly and reasonably among the parties to whom it is contractually obligated [UCC 2–615(b), 2A–405(b)]. The buyer or lessee must receive notice of the allocation and has the right to accept or reject it [UCC 2–615(c), 2A–405(c)].

▪ **EXAMPLE 22.10** A Florida orange grower, Best Citrus, Inc., contracts to sell this season's crop to a number of customers, including Martin's grocery chain. Martin's contracts to purchase two thousand crates of oranges. Best Citrus has sprayed some of its orange groves with a chemical called Karmoxin. The U.S. Department of Agriculture discovers that Karmoxin poses a cancer risk and issues an order prohibiting the sale of products sprayed with the substance. Best Citrus picks all the oranges not sprayed with Karmoxin, but the quantity is insufficient to meet all the contracted-for deliveries.

In this situation, Best Citrus is required to allocate its production. It notifies Martin's that it cannot deliver the full quantity specified in the contract and indicates the amount it will be able to deliver. Martin's can either accept or reject the allocation, but Best Citrus has no further contractual liability. ▪

Destruction of Identified Goods Sometimes, an unexpected event, such as a fire, totally destroys goods through no fault of either party before risk passes to the buyer or lessee. In such a situation, *if the goods were identified at the time the contract was formed,* the parties are excused from performance [UCC 2–613, 2A–221]. If the goods are only partially destroyed, however, the buyer or lessee can inspect them and either treat the contract as void or accept the damaged goods with a reduction in the contract price.

▪ **EXAMPLE 22.11** Atlas Sporting Equipment agrees to lease to River Bicycles sixty bicycles of a particular

model that has been discontinued. No other bicycles of that model are available. River specifies that it needs the bicycles to rent to tourists. Before Atlas can deliver the bicycles, they are destroyed by a fire. In this situation, Atlas is not liable to River for failing to deliver the bicycles. Through no fault of either party, the goods were destroyed before the risk of loss passed to the lessee. The loss was total, so the contract is avoided. Clearly, Atlas has no obligation to tender the bicycles, and River has no obligation to make the lease payments for them. ▪

Assurance and Cooperation If one party has "reasonable grounds" to believe that the other party will not perform, the first party may *in writing* "demand adequate assurance of due performance" from the other party. Until such assurance is received, the first party may "suspend" further performance without liability. What constitutes "reasonable grounds" is determined by commercial standards. If the requested assurances are not forthcoming within a reasonable time (not to exceed thirty days), the failure to respond may be treated as a repudiation of the contract [UCC 2–609, 2A–401].

Sometimes, the performance of one party depends on the cooperation of the other. When cooperation is not forthcoming, the first party can either proceed to perform the contract in any reasonable manner or suspend performance without liability and hold the uncooperative party in breach [UCC 2–311(3)].

▪ **EXAMPLE 22.12** Aman is required by contract to deliver 1,200 LG washing machines to various locations in California on or before October 1. Friedman, the buyer, is to specify the locations for delivery. Aman repeatedly requests the delivery locations, but Friedman does not respond. The washing machines are ready for shipment on October 1, but Friedman still refuses to give Aman the delivery locations. If Aman does not ship on October 1, he cannot be held liable. Aman is excused for any resulting delay of performance because of Friedman's failure to cooperate. ▪

Concept Summary 22.1 reviews the obligations of the seller.

22–2 Obligations of the Buyer or Lessee

The main obligation of the buyer or lessee under a sales or lease contract is to pay for the goods tendered. Once the seller or lessor has adequately tendered delivery, the

---

3. *Maple Farms, Inc. v. City School District of Elmira,* 76 Misc.2d 1080, 352 N.Y.S.2d 784 (1974).

Concept Summary 22.1

Obligations of the Seller or Lessor

Tender of Delivery	• Tender of delivery occurs when the seller or lessor makes *conforming goods* available and gives the buyer or lessee whatever notification is reasonably necessary to enable the buyer or lessee to take delivery [UCC 2–503(1), 2A–508(1)]. • Unless the parties have agreed otherwise, the conforming goods must be tendered for delivery at a *reasonable hour* and in a *reasonable manner* [UCC 2–503(1)(a)].
The Perfect Tender Rule	Under the perfect tender doctrine, the seller or lessor must tender goods that conform exactly to the terms of the contract. Exceptions to this rule are as follows: • *Cure*—The right of the seller or lessor to *cure*—that is, repair, adjust, or replace—nonconforming goods within the contract time for performance [UCC 2–508, 2A–513]. • *Substitution of carriers*—If the agreed-on means of delivery becomes impracticable or unavailable, the seller must substitute an alternative carrier, if a reasonable one is available [UCC 2–614(1)]. • *Installment contracts*—Unless the contract provides otherwise, the entire installment contract is breached only when one or more nonconforming installments *substantially* impair the value of the *whole* contract [UCC 2–612(2), 2A–510(1)]. • *Commercial impracticability*—When performance becomes commercially impracticable owing to circumstances unforeseen when the contract was formed, the perfect tender rule no longer applies [UCC 2–615, 2A–405]. • *Destruction of identified goods*—When an unexpected event, such as a fire, totally destroys goods that were identified to the contract when it was formed, through no fault of either party, performance is excused [UCC 2–613, 2A–221]. • *Assurance and cooperation*—If a party has reasonable grounds to believe that the other party is not going to perform and demands assurances, the other party's failure to respond in a reasonable time may be treated as a repudiation (breach) and excuse further performance [UCC 2–609, 2A–401]. A party's failure to cooperate with the other party may also excuse the party from further performing [UCC 2–311(3)].

buyer or lessee is obligated to accept the goods and pay for them according to the terms of the contract. We discuss the obligations of the buyer or lessee under the UCC next, and they are outlined in Exhibit 22–2.

22–2a Payment

In the absence of any specific agreements, the buyer or lessee must make payment at the time and place the goods are *received* [UCC 2–310(a), 2A–516(1)]. When a sale is made on credit, the buyer is obligated to pay according to the specified credit terms (for example, 60, 90, or 120 days), not when the goods are received. The credit period usually begins on the *date of shipment* [UCC 2–310(d)]. Under a lease contract, a lessee must make the lease payment that was specified in the contract [UCC 2A–516(1)].

Payment can be made by any means agreed on between the parties—cash or any other method generally acceptable in the commercial world. If the seller demands

EXHIBIT 22-2 Obligations of the Buyer or Lessee

THE PAYMENT OF THE GOODS	THE RIGHT OF INSPECTION	THE ACCEPTANCE OF THE GOODS
• On tender of delivery by the seller or lessor, the buyer or lessee must pay for the goods at the time and place the goods are *received*, unless the sale is made on credit [UCC 2–310(a)]. • Payment can be made by any method generally acceptable in the commercial world, but the seller can demand cash [UCC 2–511].	• Unless otherwise agreed or in C.O.D. (collect on delivery) shipments, the buyer or lessee has an absolute right to inspect the goods before acceptance [UCC 2–513(1), 2A–515(1)].	• The buyer or lessee can manifest acceptance of delivered goods in words or by conduct, such as by failing to reject the goods after having had a reasonable opportunity to inspect them [UCC 2–606(1), 2A–515(1)]. • A buyer will be deemed to have accepted goods if he or she performs any act inconsistent with the seller's ownership [UCC 2–606(1)(c)].

cash, the seller must permit the buyer reasonable time to obtain it [UCC 2–511].

22–2b Right of Inspection

Unless the parties otherwise agree, or for C.O.D. (collect on delivery) transactions, the buyer or lessee has an absolute right to inspect the goods before making payment. This right allows the buyer or lessee to verify that the goods tendered or delivered conform to the contract. If the goods are not as ordered, the buyer or lessee has no duty to pay. *An opportunity for inspection is therefore a condition precedent to the right of the seller or lessor to enforce payment* [UCC 2–513(1), 2A–515(1)].

Inspection can take place at any reasonable place and time and in any reasonable manner. Generally, what is reasonable is determined by custom of the trade, past practices of the parties, and the like. The buyer bears the costs of inspecting the goods but can recover the costs from the seller if the goods do not conform and are rejected [UCC 2–513(2)].

■ **CASE IN POINT 22.13** Jessie Romero offered to deliver two trade-in vehicles to Scoggin-Dickey Chevrolet Buick, Inc., in exchange for a 2006 Silverado pickup. Scoggin-Dickey agreed. The parties negotiated a price, including a value for the trade-in vehicles, plus cash. Romero paid the cash and took the 2006 Silverado (but the dealer kept the title to it). Several weeks later, Romero delivered the two trade-in vehicles.

On inspecting the trade-in vehicles, Scoggin-Dickey found that they had little value. One of them did not even run. The dealer repossessed the Silverado. Romero sued for breach of contract, claiming that the dealer had no right to reject the trade-in vehicles after the contract was signed. The court held that the contract for the sale was not completed until Romero traded in the two vehicles. Scoggin-Dickey had a right to inspect them and did so within a reasonable time after they were delivered. The dealership was entitled to reject the trade-in vehicles and keep the 2006 Silverado, but it had to refund Romero's cash and return the trade-in vehicles.[4] ■

22–2c Acceptance

After having had a reasonable opportunity to inspect the goods, the buyer or lessee can demonstrate acceptance in any of the following ways:

1. The buyer or lessee indicates (by words or conduct) to the seller or lessor that the goods are conforming or that he or she will retain them in spite of their nonconformity [UCC 2–606(1)(a), 2A–515(1)(a)].
2. The buyer or lessee fails to reject the goods within a reasonable period of time [UCC 2–602(1), 2–606(1)(b), 2A–515(1)(b)].

---

4. *Romero v. Scoggin-Dickey Chevrolet Buick, Inc.*, 2010 WL 456910 (Tex. Civ.App.—Amarillo 2010).

3. In sales contracts, the buyer will be deemed to have accepted the goods if he or she performs any act inconsistent with the seller's ownership. For instance, any use or resale of the goods—except for the limited purpose of testing or inspecting the goods—generally constitutes an acceptance [UCC 2–606(1)(c)].

22–2d Partial Acceptance

If some of the goods delivered do not conform to the contract and the seller or lessor has failed to cure, the buyer or lessee can make a *partial* acceptance [UCC 2–601(c), 2A–509(1)]. The same is true if the nonconformity was not reasonably discoverable before acceptance. (In the latter situation, the buyer or lessee may be able to revoke the acceptance, as will be discussed later in this chapter.)

A buyer or lessee cannot accept less than a single commercial unit, however. The UCC defines a *commercial unit* as a unit of goods that, by commercial usage, is viewed as a "single whole" for purposes of sale. A commercial unit cannot be divided without materially impairing the character of the unit, its market value, or its use [UCC 2–105(6), 2A–103(1)(c)]. A commercial unit can be a single article (such as a machine), a set of articles (such as a suite of furniture), a quantity (such as a bale, a gross, or a carload), or any other unit treated in the trade as a single whole.

22–2e Anticipatory Repudiation

What if, before the time for contract performance, one party clearly communicates to the other the intention *not* to perform? Such an action is a breach of the contract by *anticipatory repudiation.*

Suspension of Performance Obligations When anticipatory repudiation occurs, the nonbreaching party has a choice of two responses:

1. Treat the repudiation as a final breach by pursuing a remedy.
2. Wait to see if the repudiating party will decide to honor the contract despite the avowed intention to renege [UCC 2–610, 2A–402].

In either situation, the nonbreaching party may suspend performance.

A Repudiation May Be Retracted The UCC permits the breaching party to "retract" his or her repudiation (subject to some limitations). This can be done by any method that clearly indicates the party's intent to perform. Once retraction is made, the rights of the repudiating party under the contract are reinstated. There can be no retraction, however, if since the time of the repudiation the other party has canceled or materially changed position or otherwise indicated that the repudiation is final [UCC 2–611, 2A–403].

■ **EXAMPLE 22.14** On April 1, Cora Lyn, who owns a small inn, purchases a suite of furniture from Tom Horton, proprietor of Horton's Furniture Warehouse. The contract states that "delivery must be made on or before May 1." On April 10, Horton informs Lyn that he cannot make delivery until May 10 and asks her to consent to the modified delivery date.

In this situation, Lyn has two options. She can either treat Horton's notice of late delivery as a final breach of contract and pursue a remedy or agree to the later delivery date. Suppose that Lyn does neither for two weeks. On April 24, Horton informs Lyn that he will be able to deliver the furniture by May 1 after all. In effect, Horton has retracted his repudiation, reinstating the rights and obligations of the parties under the original contract. Note that if Lyn had told Horton that she was canceling the contract after he repudiated, he would not have been able to retract his repudiation. ■

22–3 Remedies of the Seller or Lessor

Note that remedies for breach under the UCC are *cumulative* in nature—meaning that the aggrieved (wronged) party is not limited to one exclusive remedy. When the buyer or lessee is in breach, the remedies available to the seller or lessor depend on the circumstances existing at the time of the breach. The most pertinent considerations are which party has possession of the goods, whether the goods are in transit, and whether the buyer or lessee has rejected or accepted the goods.

22–3a When the Goods Are in the Possession of the Seller or Lessor

If the buyer or lessee breaches the contract *before the goods have been delivered,* the seller or lessor has the right to pursue the following remedies:

1. Cancel (rescind) the contract.
2. Withhold delivery of the goods.
3. Resell the goods and sue to recover damages.

4. Sue to recover the purchase price or lease payments due.
5. Sue to recover damages for the buyer's nonacceptance of goods.

The Right to Cancel the Contract If the buyer or lessee breaches the contract, the seller or lessor can choose to simply cancel the contract [UCC 2–703(f), 2A–523(1)(a)]. The seller or lessor must notify the buyer or lessee of the cancellation, and at that point all remaining obligations of the seller or lessor are discharged. The buyer or lessee is not discharged from all remaining obligations, however. She or he is in breach, and the seller or lessor can pursue remedies available under the UCC for breach.

The Right to Withhold Delivery In general, sellers and lessors can withhold delivery or discontinue performance of their obligations under sales or lease contracts when the buyers or lessees are in breach [UCC 2–703(a), 2A–523(1)(c)]. This is true whether a buyer or lessee has wrongfully rejected or revoked acceptance of contract goods (discussed later), failed to make a payment, or repudiated the contract. The seller or lessor can also refuse to deliver the goods to a buyer or lessee who is insolvent (unable to pay debts as they become due) unless the buyer or lessee pays in cash [UCC 2–702(1), 2A–525(1)].

The Right to Resell or Dispose of the Goods When a buyer or lessee breaches or repudiates the contract while the seller or lessor is in possession of the goods, the seller or lessor can resell or dispose of the goods. Any resale of the goods must be made in good faith and in a commercially reasonable manner. The seller must give the original buyer reasonable notice of the resale, unless the goods are perishable or will rapidly decline in value [UCC 2–706(2), (3)].

The seller can retain any profits made as a result of the sale and can hold the buyer or lessee liable for any loss [UCC 2–703(d), 2–706(1), 2A–523(1)(e), 2A–527(1)]. (Here, a loss is any deficiency between the resale price and the contract price.) In lease transactions, the lessor can lease the goods to another party and recover damages from the original lessee. Damages include any unpaid lease payments up to the time the new lease begins. The lessor can also recover any deficiency between the lease payments due under the original lease and those due under the new lease, along with incidental damages [UCC 2A–527(2)].

When the goods contracted for are *unfinished at the time of the breach*, the seller or lessor can do either of the following:

1. Cease manufacturing the goods and resell them for scrap or salvage value.
2. Complete the manufacture and resell or dispose of the goods, and hold the buyer or lessee liable for any deficiency.

In choosing between these two alternatives, the seller or lessor must exercise reasonable commercial judgment in order to mitigate the loss and obtain maximum value from the unfinished goods [UCC 2–704(2), 2A–524(2)].

The Right to Recover the Purchase Price or Lease Payments Due Under the UCC, an unpaid seller or lessor can bring an action to recover the purchase price or the payments due under the lease contract, plus incidental damages [UCC 2–709(1), 2A–529(1)]. If a seller or lessor is unable to resell or dispose of the goods and sues for the contract price or lease payments due, the goods must be held for the buyer or lessee. The seller or lessor can resell the goods at any time before collecting the judgment from the buyer or lessee. If the goods are resold, the net proceeds from the sale must be credited to the buyer or lessee because of the duty to mitigate damages.

■ **EXAMPLE 22.15** Cascade School contracts with Stickme.com to purchase ten thousand bumper stickers with the school's name and logo on them. Stickme tenders delivery of the stickers, but Cascade wrongfully refuses to accept them. In this situation, Stickme can bring an action for the purchase price. Stickme has delivered conforming goods, and Cascade has refused to accept or pay for the goods. Obviously, Stickme will not likely be able to resell the stickers, so this situation falls under UCC 2–709. Stickme is required to make the bumper stickers available for Cascade. In the unlikely event that it can find another buyer, it can sell the stickers at any time prior to collecting the judgment from Cascade. ■

The Right to Recover Damages for the Buyer's Nonacceptance If a buyer or lessee repudiates a contract or wrongfully refuses to accept the goods, a seller or lessor can bring an action to recover the damages sustained. Ordinarily, the amount of damages equals the difference between the contract price or lease payments and the market price or lease payments at the time and place of tender of the goods, plus incidental damages [UCC 2–708(1), 2A–528(1)].

When the ordinary measure of damages is inadequate to put the seller or lessor in as good a position as the buyer's or lessee's performance would have, the UCC provides an alternative. In that situation, the proper measure of damages is the lost profits of the seller or lessor, including a reasonable allowance for overhead and other expenses [UCC 2–708(2), 2A–528(2)].

22–3b When the Goods Are in Transit

When the seller or lessor has delivered the goods to a carrier or a bailee but the buyer or lessee has not yet received them, the goods are said to be *in transit.*

Effect of Insolvency and Breach If the seller or lessor learns that the buyer or lessee is insolvent, the seller or lessor can stop the delivery of the goods still in transit, regardless of the quantity of goods shipped. A different rule applies if the buyer or lessee is in breach but is not insolvent. In this situation, the seller or lessor can stop the goods in transit only if the quantity shipped is at least a carload, a truckload, a planeload, or a larger shipment [UCC 2–705(1), 2A–526(1)].

■ **EXAMPLE 22.16** Arturo Ortega orders a truckload of lumber from Timber Products, Inc., to be shipped to Ortega six weeks later. Ortega, who has not paid Timber Products for a past shipment, promises to pay the debt immediately and to pay for the current shipment as soon as it is received. After the lumber has been shipped, a bankruptcy court judge notifies Timber Products that Ortega has filed a petition in bankruptcy and listed Timber Products as one of his creditors. If the goods are still in transit, Timber Products can stop the carrier from delivering the lumber to Ortega. ■

Requirements for Stopping Delivery To stop delivery, the seller or lessor must *timely notify* the carrier or other bailee that the goods are to be returned or held for the seller or lessor. If the carrier has sufficient time to stop delivery, the goods must be held and delivered according to the instructions of the seller or lessor. The seller or lessor is liable to the carrier for any additional costs incurred [UCC 2–705(3), 2A–526(3)].

The seller or lessor has the right to stop delivery of the goods under UCC 2–705(2) and 2A–526(2) until the time when:

1. The buyer or lessee receives the goods.
2. The carrier or the bailee acknowledges the rights of the buyer or lessee in the goods (by reshipping or holding the goods for the buyer or lessee, for example).
3. A negotiable document of title covering the goods has been properly transferred to the buyer in a sales transaction, giving the buyer ownership rights in the goods [UCC 2–705(2)].

Once the seller or lessor reclaims the goods in transit, she or he can pursue the remedies allowed to sellers and lessors when the goods are in their possession.

22–3c When the Goods Are in the Possession of the Buyer or Lessee

When the buyer or lessee breaches the contract while the goods are in his or her possession, the seller or lessor can sue. The seller or lessor can recover the purchase price of the goods or the lease payments due, plus incidental damages [UCC 2–709(1), 2A–529(1)].

In some situations, a seller may also have a right to reclaim the goods from the buyer. For instance, in a sales contract, if the buyer has received the goods on credit and the seller discovers that the buyer is insolvent, the seller can demand the return of the goods [UCC 2–702(2)]. Ordinarily, the demand must be made within ten days of the buyer's receipt of the goods.[5] The seller's right to reclaim the goods is subject to the rights of a good faith purchaser or other subsequent buyer in the ordinary course of business who purchases the goods from the buyer before the seller reclaims them.

In regard to lease contracts, if the lessee is in default (fails to make payments that are due, for instance), the lessor may reclaim leased goods that are in the lessee's possession [UCC 2A–525(2)].

22–4 Remedies of the Buyer or Lessee

When the seller or lessor breaches the contract, the buyer or lessee has numerous remedies available under the UCC. Like the remedies available to sellers and lessors, the remedies available to buyers and lessees depend on the circumstances at the time of the breach. Relevant factors include whether the seller has refused to deliver conforming goods or has delivered nonconforming goods.

22–4a When the Seller or Lessor Refuses to Deliver the Goods

If the seller or lessor refuses to deliver the goods to the buyer or lessee, the basic remedies available to the buyer or lessee include the right to:

---

5. The seller can demand and reclaim the goods at any time if the buyer misrepresented his or her solvency in writing within three months prior to the delivery of the goods.

1. Cancel (rescind) the contract.
2. Obtain goods that have been paid for if the seller or lessor is insolvent.
3. Sue to obtain specific performance if the goods are unique or if damages are an inadequate remedy.
4. Buy other goods (obtain *cover*) and recover damages from the seller.
5. Sue to obtain identified goods held by a third party (*replevy* goods).
6. Sue to obtain damages.

The Right to Cancel the Contract When a seller or lessor fails to make proper delivery or repudiates the contract, the buyer or lessee can cancel, or rescind, the contract. The buyer or lessee is relieved of any further obligations under the contract but retains all rights to other remedies against the seller or lessor [UCC 2–711(1), 2A–508(1)(a)]. (The right to cancel the contract is also available to a buyer or lessee who has rightfully rejected goods or revoked acceptance, as will be discussed shortly.)

The Right to Obtain the Goods upon Insolvency If a buyer or lessee has partially or fully paid for goods that are in the possession of a seller or lessor who becomes insolvent, the buyer or lessee can obtain the goods. The seller or lessor must have become insolvent within ten days after receiving the first payment, and the goods must be identified to the contract. To exercise this right, the buyer or lessee must pay the seller or lessor any unpaid balance of the purchase price or lease payments [UCC 2–502, 2A–522].

The Right to Obtain Specific Performance A buyer or lessee can obtain specific performance if the goods are unique or the remedy at law (monetary damages) is inadequate [UCC 2–716(1), 2A–521(1)]. Ordinarily, an award of damages is sufficient to place a buyer or lessee in the position she or he would have occupied if the seller or lessor had fully performed.

When the contract is for the purchase of a particular work of art or a similarly unique item, however, damages may not be sufficient. Under these circumstances, equity requires that the seller or lessor perform exactly by delivering the particular goods identified to the contract (the remedy of specific performance).

■ **CASE IN POINT 22.17** Together, Doreen Houseman and Eric Dare bought a house and a pedigreed dog. When the couple separated, they agreed that Dare would keep the house (and pay Houseman for her interest in it) and that Houseman would keep the dog. Houseman

allowed Dare to take the dog for visits, but after one visit, Dare kept the dog. Houseman filed a lawsuit seeking specific performance of their agreement. The court found that because pets have special subjective value to their owners, a dog can be considered a unique good. Thus, an award of specific performance was appropriate.[6] ■

The Right of Cover In certain situations, buyers and lessees can protect themselves by obtaining **cover**—that is, by buying or leasing substitute goods for those that were due under the contract. This option is available when the seller or lessor repudiates the contract or fails to deliver the goods, or when a buyer or lessee has rightfully rejected goods or revoked acceptance. In purchasing or leasing substitute goods, the buyer or lessee must act in good faith and without unreasonable delay [UCC 2–712, 2A–518].

After obtaining substitute goods, the buyer or lessee can recover from the seller or lessor:

1. The difference between the cost of cover and the contract price (or lease payments).
2. Incidental damages that resulted from the breach.
3. *Consequential damages* to compensate for indirect losses (such as lost profits) resulting from the breach that were reasonably foreseeable at the time of contract formation. The amount of consequential damages is reduced by any amount the buyer or lessee saved as a result of the breach. (For instance, the buyer might obtain cover without having to pay delivery charges that were part of the original sales contract.)

Buyers and lessees are not required to cover, and failure to do so will not bar them from using any other remedies available under the UCC. A buyer or lessee who fails to cover, however, risks collecting a lower amount of consequential damages. A court may reduce the consequential damages by the amount of the loss that could have been avoided had the buyer or lessee purchased or leased substitute goods.

The Right to Replevy Goods Buyers and lessees also have the right to replevy goods. **Replevin**[7] is an action to recover identified goods in the hands of a party who is unlawfully withholding them. Under the UCC, a buyer or lessee can replevy goods identified to the contract if the seller or lessor has repudiated or breached the contract. To maintain an action to replevy goods, buyers and lessees must usually show that they were unable to cover for the

---

6. *Houseman v. Dare*, 405 N.J.Super. 538, 966 A.2d 24 (2009).
7. Pronounced ruh-*pleh*-vun, derived from the Old French word *plevir*, meaning "to pledge."

goods after making a reasonable effort [UCC 2–716(3), 2A–521(3)].

The Right to Recover Damages

If a seller or lessor repudiates the contract or fails to deliver the goods, the buyer or lessee can sue for damages. For the buyer, the measure of recovery is the difference between the contract price and the market price of the goods at the time the buyer *learned* of the breach. For the lessee, the measure is the difference between the lease payments and the lease payments that could be obtained for the goods at the time the lessee learned of the breach. The market price or market lease payments are determined at the place where the seller or lessor was supposed to deliver the goods. The buyer or lessee can also recover incidental and consequential damages less the expenses that were saved as a result of the breach [UCC 2–713, 2A–519].

■ **CASE IN POINT 22.18** Les Entreprises Jacques Defour & Fils, Inc., contracted to buy a thirty-thousand-gallon industrial tank from Dinsick Equipment Corporation for $70,000. Les Entreprises hired Xaak Transport, Inc., to pick up the tank, but when Xaak arrived at the pickup location, there was no tank. Les Entreprises paid Xaak $7,459 for its services and filed a suit against Dinsick.

The court awarded compensatory damages of $70,000 for the tank and incidental damages of $7,459 for the transport. To establish a breach of contract requires an enforceable contract, substantial performance by the nonbreaching party, a breach by the other party, and damages. In this case, Les Entreprises agreed to buy a tank and paid the price. Dinsick failed to tender or deliver the tank, or to refund the price. The shipping costs were a necessary part of performance, so this was a reasonable expense.[8] ■

22–4b When the Seller or Lessor Delivers Nonconforming Goods

When the seller or lessor delivers nonconforming goods, the buyer or lessee has several remedies available under the UCC.

The Right to Reject the Goods

If either the goods or their tender fails to conform to the contract in any respect, the buyer or lessee can reject all of the goods or any commercial unit of the goods [UCC 2–601, 2A–509]. On rejecting the goods, the buyer or lessee may obtain cover or cancel the contract, and may seek damages just as if the seller or lessor had refused to deliver the goods.

Timeliness and Reason for Rejection Are Required. The buyer or lessee must reject the goods within a reasonable amount of time after delivery or tender of delivery and must seasonably notify the seller or lessor [UCC 2–602(1), 2A–509(2)]. If the buyer or lessee fails to reject the goods within a reasonable amount of time, acceptance will be presumed.

When rejecting goods, the buyer or lessee must also designate defects that are ascertainable by reasonable inspection. Failure to do so precludes the buyer or lessee from using such defects to justify rejection or to establish breach if the seller or lessor could have cured the defects [UCC 2–605, 2A–514].

Duties of Merchant-Buyers and Lessees When Goods Are Rejected. Sometimes, a *merchant-buyer or lessee* rightfully rejects goods, and the seller or lessor has no agent or business at the place of rejection. In that situation, the merchant-buyer or lessee has a good faith obligation to follow any reasonable instructions received from the seller or lessor with respect to the goods [UCC 2–603, 2A–511]. The buyer or lessee is entitled to be reimbursed for the care and cost entailed in following the instructions. The same requirements apply if the buyer or lessee rightfully revokes her or his acceptance of the goods at some later time [UCC 2–608(3), 2A–517(5)]. (Revocation of acceptance will be discussed shortly.)

If no instructions are forthcoming and the goods are perishable or threaten to decline in value quickly, the buyer or lessee can resell the goods. The buyer or lessee must exercise good faith and can take appropriate reimbursement and a selling commission (not to exceed 10 percent of the gross proceeds) from the proceeds [UCC 2–603(1), (2); 2A–511(1)]. If the goods are not perishable, the buyer or lessee may store them for the seller or lessor or reship them to the seller or lessor [UCC 2–604, 2A–512].

Revocation of Acceptance

Acceptance of the goods precludes the buyer or lessee from exercising the right of rejection. It does not necessarily prevent the buyer or lessee from pursuing other remedies, however. In certain circumstances, a buyer or lessee is permitted to *revoke* his or her acceptance of the goods.

Revoking Acceptance of a Commercial Unit. Acceptance of a lot or a commercial unit can be revoked if the nonconformity *substantially* impairs the value of the lot or unit *and* if one of the following factors is present:

1. Acceptance was based on the reasonable assumption that the nonconformity would be cured, and it has not been cured within a reasonable period of time [UCC 2–608(1)(a), 2A–517(1)(a)].

---

8. *Les Entreprises Jacques Defour & Fils, Inc. v. Dinsick Equipment Corp.,* 2011 WL 307501 (N.D.Ill. 2011).

2. The failure of the buyer or lessee to discover the nonconformity was reasonably induced either by the difficulty of discovery before acceptance or by assurances made by the seller or lessor [UCC 2–608(1)(b), 2A–517(1)(b)].

■ **CASE IN POINT 22.19** Armadillo Distribution Enterprises, Inc., is a major distributor of musical instruments. Armadillo contracted with a Chinese corporation, Hai Yun Musical Instruments Manufacture Co., Ltd., to manufacture one thousand drum kits. Hai Yun had made drums for Armadillo in the past. Hai Yun furnished samples for Armadillo's approval prior to manufacturing the kits. After Armadillo inspected and approved the samples, Hai Yun delivered five shipping containers of drum kits, and Armadillo began distribution.

Armadillo soon started receiving numerous complaints from its retail outlet customers concerning product returns due to cosmetic and structural defects in the drum kits. Armadillo immediately inspected the remaining four shipment containers and discovered that a high percentage of the drum kits were defective and unfit for commercial distribution. Armadillo revoked its acceptance of the kits and filed a suit in federal court for breach of contract. The district court ruled that Hai Yun

had breached the contract by delivering nonconforming goods. The court awarded Armadillo nearly $90,000 in direct and incidental damages.[9] ■

Notice of Revocation. Revocation of acceptance is not effective until notice is given to the seller or lessor. Notice must occur within a reasonable time after the buyer or lessee either discovers or *should have discovered* the grounds for revocation. Additionally, revocation must occur before the goods have undergone any substantial change (such as spoilage) not caused by their own defects [UCC 2–608(2), 2A–517(4)]. Once acceptance is revoked, the buyer or lessee can pursue remedies, just as if the goods had been rejected.

To effectively revoke acceptance, a buyer must "relinquish dominion over the goods." This requires a buyer to return the goods or at least to stop using them, unless the use is necessary to avoid substantial hardship. At issue in the following case was whether the purchaser of lights for a commercial building sufficiently relinquished dominion over the goods to revoke acceptance.

---

9. *Armadillo Distribution Enterprises, Inc. v. Hai Yun Musical Instruments Manufacture Co. Ltd.*, ___ F.Supp.3d ___, 2015 WL 6750813 (M.D.Fla. 2015).

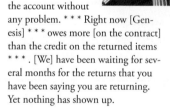

Case Analysis 22.2

Genesis Health Clubs, Inc. v. LED Solar & Light Co.
United States Court of Appeals, Tenth Circuit, __ F.3d __, 2016 WL 373699 (2016).

In the Language of the Court
HARRIS L. HARTZ, Circuit Judge.

* * * *

Genesis [Health Clubs, Inc.], based in Kansas, operates health clubs. LED Solar [& Light Company], based in Virginia, manufactures and sells LED lighting.

* * * LED Solar submitted a proposed contract "to furnish the replacement lamps for Genesis's building" for $82,271.50. LED Solar "warranted watt for watt exchange a minimum of 35% deduction in wattage consumption." * * * Genesis executed the contract later that month.

Soon after installation began, Genesis encountered problems with the lights. [Genesis] complained that "the defect rate on these lamps is * * * 73% * * *," "the LED tubes * * * are not consistent in color," [and there are] multiple light failures throughout Genesis's facility.

* * * [LED Solar] found "no fault with [the] lamps" and instructed [Genesis] to return problem lights for a refund.

* * * Genesis returned a shipment of lights, seeking a $3,777 refund.

* * * [A later e-mail to LED Solar explained] that Genesis would be "returning all of the lights" one shipment at a time in exchange for a refund, "allowing Genesis to phase out the faulty lamps."

But the return/refund process never got off the ground because of a dispute regarding whether Genesis had been properly credited for its [previous] shipment of lights * * * . On the same day as [the] email saying that Genesis would return the lights one shipment at a time, [LED Solar] responded by email, telling [Genesis]:

> * * * Everything you have shipped back that was not damaged in handling works fine. If you ship those

items back not damaged we will credit the account without any problem. * * * Right now [Genesis] * * * owes more [on the contract] than the credit on the returned items * * * . [We] have been waiting for several months for the returns that you have been saying you are returning. Yet nothing has shown up.

[Genesis] replied * * * :

> * * * You have not been prompt in your commitment to refund for returned items. * * * You have your money for the entire order that was pre-paid. * * * We are trying to replace the defective lights with the refund dollars for the product returned.

* * * [LED Solar] never paid Genesis the $3,777 and Genesis never returned any more lights.

Case 22.2 Continues

Case 22.2 Continued

* * * Genesis filed a * * * petition [in a Kansas state court] asserting claims of breach of * * * warranty. LED Solar removed the case to federal court based on diversity jurisdiction.

* * * *

* * * The court concluded that Genesis could not recover the purchase price because it failed to reject or revoke acceptance of the lights. [Genesis appealed.]

* * * *

Under the * * * Uniform Commercial Code, a buyer may cancel the contract and recover the purchase price by rightfully rejecting or justifiably revoking acceptance. *Rejection is available for goods that fail in any respect to conform to the contract, and it must be communicated to the seller within a reasonable time after the goods' delivery or tender. What constitutes a reasonable time depends on the nature, purpose, and circumstances of the action.* [Emphasis added.]

Even after the goods have been accepted, the buyer may revoke his acceptance of a lot or commercial unit whose nonconformity substantially impairs its value to him if he has accepted it * * * on the reasonable assumption that its nonconformity would be cured and it has not been seasonably cured. A buyer who revokes has

the same rights and duties with regard to the goods involved as if he had rejected them. Thus, revocation requires notification to the seller within a reasonable time after the buyer discovers or should have discovered the ground for it and before any substantial change in condition of the goods which is not caused by their own defects.

In the case of both remedies, the buyer's exercise of ownership or dominion over the goods may negate an attempt to cancel the contract and recover the purchase price. * * * *A buyer's act of dominion over the goods * * * is inconsistent with a claim by the buyer that acceptance has been revoked.* [Emphasis added.]

In the case before us, Genesis did not effectively reject or revoke acceptance of the lights because it never relinquished dominion over them. Despite allegedly agreeing with LED Solar to return all the lights in stages, it never returned any after reaching the agreement and continued to use them.

Genesis argues that without the $3,777 refund for an earlier (preagreement) shipment of lights to LED Solar, it was unable "to continue the return and replacement process. * * * [LED Solar] was aware that Genesis * * * would have to find and purchase new lights to

replace LED Solar's * * * bulbs prior to removing them all from the facility."

True, a buyer's continued use of the goods after the supposed revocation is not inconsistent with revocation if such use was necessary to avoid substantial hardship. But Genesis made no showing of substantial hardship. It offered no financial evidence that it could not afford to return any more lights without the $3,777 refund * * * . It cites no evidence that it attempted to resolve the impasse and reach some accommodation with LED Solar for future returns. It did not even produce evidence that LED Solar was incorrect in saying that the $3,777 had been credited toward what Genesis still owed. Nor does it explain why it could not afford to return lights that were not functioning. In short, no reasonable jury could find that Genesis reasonably continued using the lights after it informed LED Solar that it wanted to return them. Genesis had no excuse for using the bulbs until LED Solar accepted the * * * financial terms demanded by Genesis to govern the returns. There was no proper rejection or revocation of acceptance of the bulbs.

We conclude that summary judgment was properly entered on Genesis's claim for a refund of the purchase price.

Legal Reasoning Questions

1. According to the UCC, if delivered goods do not conform to a sales contract, how can the buyer revoke acceptance?

2. In this case, what was the dispute between the buyer and the seller? How did this dispute end in litigation?

3. On what key point did the lower and appellate courts agree? Why?

The Right to Recover Damages for Accepted Goods A buyer or lessee who has accepted nonconforming goods may also keep the goods and recover damages [UCC 2–714(1), 2A–519(3)]. To do so, the buyer or lessee must notify the seller or lessor of the breach within a reasonable time after the defect was or should have been discovered. Failure to give notice of the defects (breach) to the seller or lessor normally bars the buyer or lessee from pursuing any remedy [UCC 2–607(3), 2A–516(3)]. In addition, the parties to a sales or lease contract can insert into the contract a

provision requiring the buyer or lessee to give notice of any defects in the goods within a prescribed period.

When the goods delivered are not as promised, the measure of damages generally equals the difference between the value of the goods as accepted and their value if they had been delivered as warranted. An exception occurs if special circumstances show proximately caused damages of a different amount [UCC 2–714(2), 2A–519(4)]. The buyer or lessee is also entitled to incidental and consequential damages when appropriate

[UCC 2–714(3), 2A–519]. With proper notice to the seller or lessor, the buyer or lessee can also deduct all or any part of the damages from the price or lease payments still due under the contract [UCC 2–717, 2A–516(1)].

Is two years after a sale of goods a reasonable time period in which to discover a defect in those goods and notify the seller of a breach? That was the question in the following case.

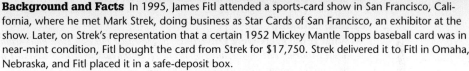

Spotlight on Baseball Cards

Case 22.3 Fitl v. Strek

Supreme Court of Nebraska, 269 Neb. 51, 690 N.W.2d 605 (2005).

Background and Facts In 1995, James Fitl attended a sports-card show in San Francisco, California, where he met Mark Strek, doing business as Star Cards of San Francisco, an exhibitor at the show. Later, on Strek's representation that a certain 1952 Mickey Mantle Topps baseball card was in near-mint condition, Fitl bought the card from Strek for $17,750. Strek delivered it to Fitl in Omaha, Nebraska, and Fitl placed it in a safe-deposit box.

In May 1997, Fitl sent the card to Professional Sports Authenticators (PSA), a sports-card grading service. PSA told Fitl that the card was ungradable because it had been discolored and doctored. Fitl complained to Strek, who replied that Fitl should have initiated a return of the card sooner. According to Strek, "a typical grace period for the unconditional return of a card [was within] 7 days to 1 month" of its receipt. In August, Fitl sent the card to ASA Accugrade, Inc. (ASA), another grading service, for a second opinion of the value. ASA also concluded that the card had been refinished and trimmed. Fitl filed a suit in a Nebraska state court against Strek, seeking damages. The court awarded Fitl $17,750, plus his court costs. Strek appealed to the Nebraska Supreme Court.

In the Language of the Court

WRIGHT, J. [Judge]

* * * *

Strek claims that the [trial] court erred in determining that notification of the defective condition of the baseball card 2 years after the date of purchase was timely pursuant to [UCC] 2–607(3)(a).

* * * The [trial] court found that Fitl had notified Strek within a reasonable time after discovery of the breach. Therefore, our review is whether the [trial] court's finding as to the reasonableness of the notice was clearly erroneous.

Section 2–607(3)(a) states: "Where a tender has been accepted * * * the buyer must within a reasonable time after he discovers or should have discovered any breach notify the seller of breach or be barred from any remedy." [Under UCC 1–204(2),] *"what is a reasonable time for taking any action depends on the nature, purpose and circumstances of such action."* [Emphasis added.]

The notice requirement set forth in Section 2–607(3)(a) serves three purposes.

* * * The most important one is to enable the seller to make efforts to cure the breach by making adjustments or replacements in order to minimize the buyer's damages and the seller's liability. A second policy is to provide the seller a reasonable opportunity to learn the facts so that he may adequately prepare for negotiation and defend himself in a suit. A third policy * * * is the same as the policy behind statutes of limitation: to provide a seller with a terminal point in time for liability.

* * * *A party is justified in relying upon a representation made to the party as a positive statement of fact when an investigation would be required to ascertain its falsity.* In order for Fitl to have determined that the baseball card had been altered, he would have been required to conduct an investigation. We find that he was not required to do so. Once Fitl learned that the baseball card had been altered, he gave notice to Strek. [Emphasis added.]

* * * One of the most important policies behind the notice requirement * * * is to allow the seller to cure the breach by making adjustments or replacements to minimize the buyer's damages and the seller's liability. However, even if Fitl had learned immediately upon taking possession of the baseball card that it was not authentic and had notified Strek at that time, there is no evidence that Strek could have made any adjustment or taken any action that would have minimized his liability. In its altered condition, the baseball card was worthless.

Case 22.3 Continues

Case 22.3 Continued

* * * Earlier notification would not have helped Strek prepare for negotiation or defend himself in a suit because the damage to Fitl could not be repaired. Thus, the policies behind the notice requirement, to allow the seller to correct a defect, to prepare for negotiation and litigation, and to protect against stale claims at a time beyond which an investigation can be completed, were not unfairly prejudiced by the lack of an earlier notice to Strek. Any problem Strek may have had with the party from whom he obtained the baseball card was a separate matter from his transaction with Fitl, and an investigation into the source of the altered card would not have minimized Fitl's damages.

Decision and Remedy   *The state supreme court affirmed the decision of the lower court. Under the circumstances, notice of a defect in the card two years after its purchase was reasonable. The buyer had reasonably relied on the seller's representation that the card was "authentic" (which it was not), and when the defects were discovered, the buyer had given timely notice.*

Critical Thinking

- **What If the Facts Were Different?**   *Suppose that Fitl and Strek had included in their deal a written clause requiring Fitl to give notice of any defect in the card within "7 days to 1 month" of its receipt. Would the result have been different? Why or why not?*
- **Legal Environment**   *What might a court award to a buyer who prevails in a dispute such as the one in this case?*

22–5 Additional Provisions Affecting Remedies

The parties to a sales or lease contract can vary their respective rights and obligations by contractual agreement. For instance, a seller and buyer can expressly provide for remedies in addition to those provided in the UCC. They can also specify remedies in lieu of those provided in the UCC (including liquidated damages clauses), or they can change the measure of damages. A seller can provide that the buyer's only remedy on the seller's breach will be repair or replacement of the item. Alternatively, the seller can limit the buyer's remedy to return of the goods and refund of the purchase price.

In sales and lease contracts, an agreed-on remedy is in addition to those provided in the UCC unless the parties expressly agree that the remedy is exclusive of all others [UCC 2–719(1), 2A–503(1),(2)].

22–5a Exclusive Remedies

If the parties state that a remedy is *exclusive,* then it is the sole remedy. ■ **EXAMPLE 22.20** Standard Tool Company agrees to sell a pipe-cutting machine to United Pipe & Tubing Corporation. The contract limits United's remedy exclusively to repair or replacement of any defective parts. Thus, repair or replacement of defective parts is the buyer's only remedy under this contract. ■

When circumstances cause an exclusive remedy to fail in its essential purpose, it is no longer exclusive, and the buyer or lessee may pursue other remedies available under the UCC [UCC 2–719(2), 2A–503(2)]. In *Example 22.20*, suppose that Standard Tool Company was unable to repair a defective part, and no replacement parts were available. In this situation, because the exclusive remedy failed in its essential purpose (to provide recovery), the buyer could pursue other remedies available under the UCC.

22–5b Consequential Damages

As discussed earlier, consequential damages are special damages that compensate for indirect losses (such as lost profits) resulting from a breach of contract that were reasonably foreseeable. Under the UCC, parties to a contract can limit or exclude consequential damages, provided the limitation is not unconscionable. When the buyer or lessee is a consumer, any limitation of consequential damages for personal injuries resulting from consumer goods is presumed to be unconscionable. The limitation of consequential damages is not necessarily unconscionable when the loss is commercial in nature—for instance, lost profits and property damage [UCC 2–719(3), 2A–503(3)].

22–5c Statute of Limitations

An action for breach of contract under the UCC must be commenced *within four years after the cause of action accrues* [UCC 2–725(1)]. This means that a buyer or lessee must file the lawsuit within four years after the breach occurs.[10] Thus, the buyer or lessee has four years from

---

10. For breach of warranty, the cause of action arises when the seller or lessor delivers the contracted goods [UCC 2–725(2), 2A–506(2)].

the delivery date to file a suit for breach of warranty. The parties can agree in their contract to reduce this period to not less than one year, but cannot extend it beyond four years [UCC 2–725(1), 2A–506(1)].

If a buyer or lessee has accepted nonconforming goods, that party has a reasonable time to notify the seller or lessor of the breach. Failure to provide notice will bar the buyer or lessee from pursuing any remedy [UCC 2–607(3)(a), 2A–516(3)].

22–6 Dealing with International Contracts

Buyers and sellers (or lessees and lessors) engaged in international business transactions may be separated by thousands of miles. Therefore, special precautions are often taken to ensure performance under international contracts. Sellers and lessors want to avoid delivering goods for which they might not be paid. Buyers and lessees desire the assurance that sellers and lessors will not be paid until there is evidence that the goods have been shipped. Thus, **letters of credit** frequently are used to facilitate international business transactions.

22–6a Letter-of-Credit Transactions

In a simple letter-of-credit transaction, the *issuer* (a bank or other financial institution) agrees to issue a letter of credit and to ascertain whether the *beneficiary* (seller or lessor) performs certain acts. In return, the *account party* (buyer or lessee) promises to reimburse the issuer for the amount paid to the beneficiary. The transaction may also involve an *advising bank* that transmits information and a *paying bank* that expedites payment under the letter of credit. See Exhibit 22–3 for an illustration of a letter-of-credit transaction.

EXHIBIT 22–3 A Letter-of-Credit Transaction

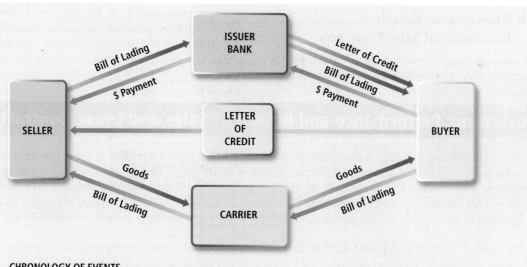

CHRONOLOGY OF EVENTS

1. Buyer contracts with issuer bank to issue a letter of credit. This sets forth the bank's obligation to pay on the letter of credit and buyer's obligation to pay the bank.

2. Letter of credit is sent to seller informing seller that on compliance with the terms of the letter of credit (such as presentment of necessary documents—in this example, a bill of lading), the bank will issue payment for the goods.

3. Seller delivers goods to carrier and receives a bill of lading.

4. Seller delivers the bill of lading to issuer bank and, if the document is proper, receives payment.

5. Issuer bank delivers the bill of lading to buyer.

6. Buyer delivers the bill of lading to carrier.

7. Carrier delivers the goods to buyer.

8. Buyer settles with issuer bank.

Payment under a Letter of Credit Under a letter of credit, the issuer is bound to pay the beneficiary (seller or lessor) when the beneficiary has complied with the terms and conditions of the letter of credit. The letter of credit assures the beneficiary of payment at the same time as it assures the account party (buyer or lessee) of performance. Typically, a letter of credit will require that the beneficiary deliver a *bill of lading* (the carrier's contract) to prove that shipment has been made.

The Value of a Letter of Credit The basic principle behind letters of credit is that payment is made against the documents presented by the beneficiary and not against the facts that the documents purport to reflect. Thus, in a letter-of-credit transaction, the issuer (bank) does not police the underlying contract. The letter of credit is independent of the underlying contract between the buyer and the seller. Eliminating the need for the bank (issuer) to inquire into whether actual contractual conditions have been satisfied greatly reduces the costs of letters of credit. Moreover, the use of a letter of credit protects both buyers and sellers.

22–6b Remedies for Breach of International Sales Contracts

The United Nations Convention on Contracts for the International Sale of Goods (CISG) provides international sellers and buyers with remedies very similar to those available under the UCC. Article 74 of the CISG provides for money damages, including foreseeable consequential damages, on a contract's breach. As under the UCC, the measure of damages normally is the difference between the contract price and the market price of the goods.

Under Article 49, the buyer is permitted to avoid obligations under the contract if the seller breaches the contract or fails to deliver the goods during the time specified in the contract or later agreed on by the parties. Similarly, under Article 64, the seller can avoid obligations under the contract if the buyer breaches the contract, fails to accept delivery of the goods, or fails to pay for the goods.

The CISG also allows for specific performance as a remedy under Article 28, which provides that "one party is entitled to require performance of any obligation by the other party." Nevertheless, a court may grant specific performance under Article 28 only if it would do so "under its own [national] law." As already discussed, U.S. courts normally grant specific performance only if no adequate remedy at law (monetary damages) is available and the goods are unique in nature. In other countries, such as Germany, however, specific performance is a commonly granted remedy for breach of contract.

Reviewing: Performance and Breach of Sales and Lease Contracts

GFI, Inc., a Hong Kong company, makes audio decoder chips, an essential component in the manufacture of smartphones. Egan Electronics contracts with GFI to buy 10,000 chips on an installment contract, with 2,500 chips to be shipped every three months, F.O.B. Hong Kong, via Air Express. At the time for the first delivery, GFI delivers only 2,400 chips. GFI explains, however, that although the shipment is 4 percent short, the chips are of a higher quality than those specified in the contract and are worth 5 percent more. Egan accepts the shipment and pays GFI the contract price.

At the time for the second shipment, GFI makes a shipment identical to the first. Egan again accepts and pays for the chips. At the time for the third shipment, GFI ships 2,400 of the same chips, but this time GFI sends them via Hong Kong Air instead of Air Express. While in transit, the chips are destroyed. When it is time for the fourth shipment, GFI again sends 2,400 chips, but this time Egan rejects the chips without explanation. Using the information presented in the chapter, answer the following questions.

1. Did GFI have a legitimate reason to expect that Egan would accept the fourth shipment? Why or why not?
2. Did the substitution of carriers in the third shipment constitute a breach of the contract by GFI? Explain.
3. Suppose that the silicon used for the chips becomes unavailable for a period of time. Consequently, GFI cannot manufacture enough chips to fulfill the contract but does ship as many as it can to Egan. Under what doctrine might a court release GFI from further performance of the contract?
4. Under the UCC, does Egan have a right to reject the fourth shipment? Why or why not?

Debate This . . .   *If a contract specifies a particular carrier, then the shipper must use that carrier or be in breach of the contract—no exceptions should ever be allowed.*

Terms and Concepts

conforming goods 404	installment contract 408	replevin 415
cover 415	letter of credit 421	tender of delivery 404
cure 407	perfect tender rule 406	

Issue Spotters

1. Country Fruit Stand orders eighty cases of peaches from Downey Farms. Without stating a reason, Downey delivers thirty cases instead of eighty and delivers at the wrong time. Does Country have the right to reject the shipment? Explain. (See *Obligations of the Seller or Lessor.*)

2. Brite Images agrees to sell Poster Planet five thousand posters of celebrities, to be delivered on May 1. On April 1, Brite repudiates the contract. Poster Planet informs Brite that it expects delivery. Can Poster Planet sue Brite without waiting until May 1? Why or why not? (See *Obligations of the Buyer or Lessee.*)

- **Check your answers to the Issue Spotters against the answers provided in Appendix D at the end of this text.**

Business Scenarios

22–1. Anticipatory Repudiation. Moore contracted in writing to sell her 2017 Hyundai Santa Fe to Hammer for $18,500. Moore agreed to deliver the car on Wednesday, and Hammer promised to pay the $18,500 on the following Friday. On Tuesday, Hammer informed Moore that he would not be buying the car after all. By Friday, Hammer had changed his mind again and tendered $18,500 to Moore. Moore, although she had not sold the car to another party, refused the tender and refused to deliver. Hammer claimed that Moore had breached their contract. Moore contended that Hammer's repudiation released her from her duty to perform under the contract. Who is correct, and why? (See *Obligations of the Buyer or Lessee.*)

22–2. Remedies of the Buyer or Lessee. Lehor collects antique cars. He contracts to purchase spare parts for a 1938 engine from Beem. These parts are not made anymore and are scarce. To obtain the contract with Beem, Lehor agrees to pay 50 percent of the purchase price in advance. Lehor sends the payment on May 1, and Beem receives it on May 2. On May 3, Beem, having found another buyer willing to pay substantially more for the parts, informs Lehor that he will not deliver as contracted. That same day, Lehor learns that Beem is insolvent. Discuss fully any possible remedies available to Lehor to enable him to take possession of these parts. (See *Remedies of the Buyer or Lessee.*)

Business Case Problems

22–3. Spotlight on Revocation of Acceptance—Remedies of the Buyer. L.V.R.V., Inc., sells recreational vehicles (RVs) in Las Vegas, Nevada, as Wheeler's Las Vegas RV. In September 1997, Wheeler's sold a Santara RV made by Coachmen Recreational Vehicle Co. to Arthur and Roswitha Waddell. The Waddells hoped to spend two or three years driving around the country, but almost immediately—and repeatedly—they experienced problems with the RV. Its entry door popped open. Its cooling and heating systems did not work properly. Its batteries did not maintain a charge. Most significantly, its engine overheated when ascending a moderate grade. The Waddells brought it to Wheeler's service department for repairs. Over the next year and a half, the RV spent more than seven months at Wheeler's. In March 1999, the Waddells filed a complaint in a Nevada state court against the dealer to revoke their acceptance of the RV. What are the requirements for a buyer's revocation of acceptance? Were the requirements met in this case? In whose favor should the court rule? Why? [*Waddell v. L.V.R.V., Inc.,* 122 Nev. 15, 125 P.3d 1160 (2006)] (See *Remedies of the Buyer or Lessee.*)

22–4. The Right to Recover Damages. Woodridge USA Properties, L.P., bought eighty-seven commercial truck trailers from Southeast Trailer Mart, Inc. (STM). Gerald McCarty, an independent sales agent who arranged the deal, showed Woodridge the documents of title. They did not indicate that Woodridge was the buyer. Woodridge asked McCarty to sell the trailers, and within three months they were sold, but McCarty did not give the proceeds to Woodridge. Woodridge—without mentioning the title documents—asked STM to refund the contract price. STM refused. Does Woodridge have a right to recover damages from STM? Explain. [*Woodridge USA Properties, L.P. v. Southeast Trailer Mart, Inc.,* 412 Fed.Appx. 218 (11th Cir. 2011)] (See *Remedies of the Buyer or Lessee.*)

22–5. Business Case Problem with Sample Answer—Nonconforming Goods. Padma Paper Mills, Ltd., converts waste paper into usable paper. In 2007, Padma entered into a contract with Universal Exports, Inc., under which Universal Exports certified that it would ship white envelope cuttings. Padma paid $131,000 for the paper. When the shipment arrived, however, Padma discovered that Universal Exports had sent multicolored paper plates and other brightly colored paper products. Padma accepted the goods but notified Universal Exports that they did not conform to the contract. Can Padma recover even though it accepted the goods knowing that they were nonconforming? If so, how? [*Padma Paper Mills, Ltd. v. Universal Exports, Inc.,* 34 Misc.3d 1236(A) (N.Y.Sup. 2012)] (See *Remedies of the Buyer or Lessee.*)

- For a sample answer for Problem 22–5, go to Appendix E at the end of this text.

22–6. The Right of Rejection. Erb Poultry, Inc., is a distributor of fresh poultry products in Lima, Ohio. CEME, LLC, does business as Bank Shots, a restaurant in Trotwood, Ohio. CEME ordered chicken wings and "dippers" from Erb, which were delivered and for which CEME issued a check in payment. A few days later, CEME stopped payment on the check. When contacted by Erb, CEME alleged that the products were beyond their freshness date, mangled, spoiled, and the wrong sizes. CEME did not provide any evidence to support the claims or arrange to return the products. Is CEME entitled to a full refund of the amount paid for the chicken? Explain. [*Erb Poultry, Inc. v. CEME, LLC,* 20 N.E.3d 1228 (Ohio App. 2 Dist. 2014)] (See *Remedies of the Buyer or Lessee.*)

22–7. Remedies for Breach. LO Ventures, LLC, doing business as Reefpoint Brewhouse in Racine, Wisconsin, contracted with Forman Awnings and Construction, LLC, for the fabrication and installation of an awning system over an outdoor seating area. After the system was complete, Reefpoint expressed concerns about the workmanship but did not give Forman a chance to make repairs. The brewhouse used the awning for two months and then had it removed so that siding on the building could be replaced. The parties disagreed about whether cracked and broken welds observed after the removal of the system were due to shoddy workmanship. Reefpoint paid only $400 on the contract price of $8,161. Can Reefpoint rescind the contract and obtain a return of its $400? Is Forman entitled to recover the difference between Reefpoint's payment and the contract price? Discuss. [*Forman Awnings and Construction, LLC v. LO Ventures, LLC,* 360 Wis.2d 492, 864 N.W.2d 121 (2015)] (See *Remedies of the Buyer or Lessee.*)

22–8. Remedies of the Buyer or Lessee. M. C. and Linda Morris own a home in Gulfport, Mississippi, that was extensively damaged in Hurricane Katrina. The Morrises contracted with Inside Outside, Inc. (IO), to rebuild their kitchen. When the new kitchen cabinets were delivered, some defects were apparent, and as installation progressed, others were revealed. IO ordered replacement parts to cure the defects. Before the parts arrived, however, the parties' relationship deteriorated, and IO offered to remove the cabinets and refund the price. The Morrises also asked to be repaid for the installation fee. IO refused but emphasized that it was willing to fulfill its contractual obligations. At this point, are the Morrises entitled to revoke their acceptance of the cabinets? Why or why not? [*Morris v. Inside Outside, Inc.,* 185 So.3d 413 (Miss.App. 2016)] (See *Remedies of the Buyer or Lessee.*)

22–9. A Question of Ethics—Revocation of Acceptance. *Scotwood Industries, Inc., sells calcium chloride flake for* *use in ice melt products. Between July and September 2004, Scotwood delivered thirty-seven shipments of flake to Frank Miller & Sons, Inc. After each delivery, Scotwood billed Miller, which paid thirty-five of the invoices and processed 30 to 50 percent of the flake. In August, Miller began complaining about the product's quality. Scotwood assured Miller that it would remedy the situation. Finally, in October, Miller told Scotwood, "This is totally unacceptable. We are willing to discuss Scotwood picking up the material." Miller claimed that the flake was substantially defective because it was chunked. Calcium chloride maintains its purity for up to five years, but if it is exposed to and absorbs moisture, it chunks and becomes unusable. Scotwood sued to collect payment on the unpaid invoices. In response, Miller filed a counterclaim in a federal district court for breach of contract, seeking to recover based on revocation of acceptance, among other things. [*Scotwood Industries, Inc. v. Frank Miller & Sons, Inc., 435 F.Supp.2d 1160 (D.Kan. 2006)]* (See *Remedies of the Buyer or Lessee.*)

(a) What is revocation of acceptance? How does a buyer effectively exercise this option? Do the facts in this case support this theory as a ground for Miller to recover damages? Why or why not?

(b) Is there an ethical basis for allowing a buyer to revoke acceptance of goods and recover damages? If so, is there an ethical limit to this right? Discuss.

Legal Reasoning Group Activity

22–10. Performance Obligations. Kodiak agrees to sell one thousand espresso machines to Lin to be delivered on May 1. Due to a strike during the last week of April, there is a temporary shortage of delivery vehicles. Kodiak can deliver the espresso makers two hundred at a time over a period of ten days, with the first delivery on May 1. (See *Obligations of the Buyer or Lessee.*)

(a) The first group will determine if Kodiak has the right to deliver the goods in five lots. What happens if Lin objects to delivery in lots?

(b) A second group will analyze whether the doctrine of commercial impracticability applies to this scenario and, if it does, what the result will be.

CHAPTER 23

Warranties

Most goods are covered by some type of warranty designed to protect buyers. In sales and lease law, a warranty is an assurance or guarantee by the seller or lessor about the quality and features of the goods being sold or leased.

The Uniform Commercial Code (UCC) has numerous rules governing product warranties as they occur in sales and lease contracts. Articles 2 (on sales) and 2A (on leases) designate several types of warranties that can arise in a sales or lease contract, including warranties of title, express warranties, and implied warranties. In addition, federal law imposes certain requirements on warranties.

Because a warranty imposes a duty on the seller or lessor, a breach of warranty is a breach of the seller's or lessor's promise. Assuming that the parties have not agreed to limit or modify the remedies available, if the seller or lessor breaches a warranty, the buyer or lessee can sue to recover damages. Under some circumstances, a breach of warranty can allow the buyer or lessee to rescind (cancel) the agreement.

23–1 Warranties of Title

Under the UCC, three types of title warranties—*good title, no liens,* and *no infringements*—can automatically arise in sales and lease contracts [UCC 2–312, 2A–211]. Normally, a seller or lessor can disclaim or modify these title warranties only by including *specific language* in the contract. For instance, sellers may assert that they are transferring only such rights, title, and interest as they have in the goods.

23–1a Good Title

In most sales, sellers warrant that they have good and valid title to the goods sold and that the transfer of the title is rightful [UCC 2–312(1)(a)]. If the buyer subsequently learns that the seller did not have valid title to the goods that were purchased, the buyer can sue the seller for breach of this warranty.

■ **EXAMPLE 23.1** Alexis steals two iPads from Camden and sells them to Emma, who does not know that they are stolen. If Camden discovers that Emma has the iPads, then he has the right to reclaim them from her. When Alexis sold Emma the iPads, Alexis *automatically* warranted to Emma that the title conveyed was valid and that its transfer was rightful. Because a thief has no title to stolen goods, Alexis breached the warranty of

title imposed by UCC 2–312(1)(a) and became liable to Emma for appropriate damages. ■

23–1b No Liens

A second warranty of title protects buyers and lessees who are *unaware* of any encumbrances against goods at the time the contract is made [UCC 2–312(1)(b), 2A–211(1)]. (Such encumbrances—that is, claims, charges, or liabilities—are usually called *liens.*[1])

This warranty protects buyers who, for instance, unknowingly purchase goods that are subject to a creditor's security interest. (A *security interest* in this context is an interest in the goods that secures payment or performance of an obligation.) If a creditor legally repossesses the goods from a buyer *who had no actual knowledge of the security interest,* the buyer can recover from the seller for breach of warranty. (In contrast, a buyer who has *actual knowledge of a security interest* has no recourse against a seller.)

■ **EXAMPLE 23.2** Henderson buys a used boat from Loring for cash. A month later, Barish proves that she has a valid security interest in the boat and that Loring, who has missed five payments, is in default. Barish then repossesses the boat from Henderson. Henderson demands his cash back from Loring. Under Section 2–312(1)(b),

---

1. Pronounced *leens.*

Henderson has legal grounds to recover from Loring. As a seller of goods, Loring warrants that the goods are delivered free from any security interest or other lien of which the buyer has no knowledge. ■

Article 2A affords similar protection for lessees. Section 2A–211(1) provides that during the term of the lease, no claim of any third party will interfere with the lessee's enjoyment of the leasehold interest.

23–1c No Infringements

A third type of warranty of title arises automatically when the seller or lessor is a merchant. A merchant-seller or lessor warrants that the buyer or lessee takes the goods *free of infringements* from any copyright, trademark, or patent claims of a third person[2] [UCC 2–312(3), 2A–211(2)].

Notice in Sales Contracts If the buyer is subsequently sued by a third party holding copyright, trademark, or patent rights in the goods, then this warranty is breached. The buyer *must notify the seller* of the litigation within a reasonable time to enable the seller to decide whether to defend the lawsuit. The seller then decides whether to defend the buyer and bear all expenses in the action.

If the seller agrees in a writing to defend and to pay the expenses, then the buyer must turn over control of the litigation to the seller. Otherwise, the buyer is barred from any remedy against the seller for liability established by the litigation [UCC 2–607(3)(b), 2–607(5)(b)]. Thus, if a buyer wins at trial but did not notify the seller of the litigation, the buyer cannot sue the seller to recover the expenses of the lawsuit.

Notice in Lease Contracts In situations that involve leases rather than sales, Article 2A provides for the same notice of infringement litigation [UCC 2A–516(3)(b), 2A–516(4)(b)]. After being notified of the lawsuit, the lessor (or supplier, in a finance lease) who agrees to pay all expenses can demand that the lessee turn over the control of the litigation. Failure to provide notice normally bars any subsequent remedy against the lessor for liability established by the litigation.

There is an exception for leases to individual consumers for personal, family, or household purposes. A consumer who fails to notify the lessor within a reasonable time does not lose his or her remedy against the lessor for whatever liability is established in the litigation [UCC 2A–516(3)(b)].

---

2. Recall that a *merchant* is defined in UCC 2–104(1) as a person who deals in goods of the kind involved in the sales contract or who, by occupation, presents himself or herself as having knowledge or skill peculiar to the goods involved in the transaction.

23–2 Express Warranties

A seller or lessor can create an **express warranty** by making representations concerning the quality, condition, description, or performance potential of the goods.

23–2a Statements That Create Express Warranties

Under UCC 2–313 and 2A–210, express warranties arise when a seller or lessor indicates any of the following:

1. That the goods conform to any *affirmation* (declaration that something is true) *of fact or promise* that the seller or lessor makes to the buyer or lessee about the goods. Such affirmations or promises are usually made during the bargaining process. ■ **EXAMPLE 23.3** D. J. Vladick, a salesperson at Home Depot, tells a customer, "These drill bits will easily penetrate stainless steel—and without dulling." Vladick's statement is an express warranty. ■

2. That the goods conform to any *description* of them. ■ **EXAMPLE 23.4** A label reads "Crate contains one Kawasaki Brute Force 750 4X4i EPS ATV," and a contract calls for the delivery of a "wool coat." Both statements create express warranties that the goods sold conform to the descriptions. ■

3. That the goods conform to any *sample or model* of the goods shown to the buyer or lessee. ■ **EXAMPLE 23.5** Melissa Faught orders a stainless steel 5500 Super Angel juicer for $1,100 after seeing a dealer demonstrate its use at a health fair. The Super Angel is shipped to her. When the juicer arrives, it is an older model, not the 5500 model. This is a breach of an express warranty because the dealer warranted that the juicer would be the same model used in the demonstration. ■

Express warranties can be found in a seller's or lessor's advertisement, brochure, or promotional materials, in addition to being made orally or in an express warranty provision in a sales or lease contract.

See Concept Summary 23.1 for a review of warranties of title and express warranties.

23–2b Basis of the Bargain

To create an express warranty, a seller or lessor does not have to use formal words, such as *warrant* or *guarantee*. It is only necessary that a reasonable buyer or lessee would regard the representation as being part of the basis of the bargain [UCC 2–313(2), 2A–210(2)].

The UCC does not explicitly define the phrase "basis of the bargain." Generally, it means that the buyer or

---

Concept Summary 23.1

Warranties of Title and Express Warranties

Warranties of Title	
	• *Good title*—A seller warrants that he or she has the right to pass good and rightful title to the goods [UCC 2–312(1)(a)].
	• *No liens*—A seller warrants that the goods sold are free of any encumbrances, such as claims, charges, or liabilities (usually called *liens*). A lessor warrants that the lessee will not be disturbed in her or his possession of the goods by the claims of a third party [UCC 2–312(1)(b), 2A–211(1)].
	• *No infringements*—A merchant-seller warrants that the goods are free of infringement claims (claims that a patent, trademark, or copyright has been infringed) by third parties. Lessors make similar warranties [UCC 2–312(3), 2A–211(2)].

Express Warranties	
	• Under UCC 2–313 and 2A–210, an express warranty arises when a seller or lessor indicates any of the following as part of the sale or bargain:
	• An affirmation of fact or promise.
	• A description of the goods.
	• A sample or model shown as conforming to the contract goods.
	• Under the Magnuson-Moss Warranty Act, an express written warranty covering consumer goods priced at more than $25, *if made*, must be labeled as either a full warranty or a limited warranty.

---

lessee must have relied on the representation at the time of entering into the agreement. Therefore, a court must determine in each case whether a representation was made at such a time and in such a way that it induced the buyer or lessee to enter into the contract.

23–2c Statements of Opinion and Value

Only statements of fact create express warranties. A seller or lessor who states an opinion about or recommends the goods thus does not create an express warranty [UCC 2–313(2), 2A–210(2)].

■ **CASE IN POINT 23.6** Kathleen Arthur underwent a surgical procedure for neck pain. Her surgeon implanted an Infuse Bone Graft device made by Medtronic, Inc. Although the device was not approved for this use, a sales representative for Medtronic allegedly had told the surgeon that the Infuse device could be appropriate for this surgery. The surgery did not resolve Arthur's neck pain, and she developed numbness in her arm and fingers. She filed a breach of warranty claim against Medtronic, alleging that the salesperson's statements created an express warranty. The court dismissed Arthur's case, however. The alleged statements of a sales representative on whether it was "appropriate" to use the Infuse device

in such a procedure were opinion and did not create an express warranty.[3] ■

Similarly, a seller or lessor who makes a statement about the value or worth of the goods does not create an express warranty. Thus, a statement such as "this is worth a fortune" or "anywhere else you'd pay $10,000 for it" usually does not create a warranty.

Opinions by Experts Ordinarily, statements of opinion do not create warranties. If the seller or lessor is an expert, however, and gives an opinion as an expert to a layperson, then a warranty may be created. ■ **EXAMPLE 23.7** Stephen is an art dealer and an expert in seventeenth-century paintings. If Stephen tells Lauren, a purchaser, that in his opinion a particular painting is by Rembrandt, Stephen has warranted the accuracy of his opinion. ■

Reasonable Reliance It is not always easy to determine whether a statement constitutes an express warranty or puffery ("seller's talk"). The reasonableness of the buyer's or lessee's reliance appears to be the controlling criterion in many cases. ■ **EXAMPLE 23.8** A salesperson's statements that a ladder will "never break" and will "last

---

3. *Arthur v. Medtronic, Inc.*, 123 F.Supp.3d 1145 (E.D.Mo. 2015).

a lifetime" are so clearly improbable that they do not create a warranty. No reasonable buyer would rely on such statements. ■

Additionally, the context in which a statement is made may be relevant in determining the reasonableness of a buyer's or lessee's reliance. For instance, a reasonable person is more likely to rely on a written statement made in an advertisement than on a statement made orally by a salesperson. ■ **CASE IN POINT 23.9** Lennox International, Inc., makes heating, ventilating, and air conditioning (HVAC) systems. T & M Solar and Air Conditioning, Inc., is a California corporation that contracts to install HVAC systems. T & M became interested in Lennox solar panel systems. Lennox advertised that the systems could run through the existing HVAC system, rather than through an electrical panel. This meant that the systems, unlike traditional solar panel systems, could be installed without modifying the electrical panels in a residence.

Lennox representatives repeatedly assured T & M that their systems would operate as advertised and would pass National Electric Code requirements. Lennox sent representatives to California to advertise the systems to potential clients of T & M. T & M ordered and paid for six Lennox systems for customers. The systems that Lennox supplied could not be operated or installed as promised, however, and T & M ultimately had to remove them from customers' homes at its own expense. T & M filed suit, alleging breach of an express warranty. The court found that T & M had ordered the Lennox systems precisely because they could operate through the HVAC system without modification of existing electrical panels. That was sufficient evidence of reasonable reliance to justify a trial.[4] ■

In the following case, the plaintiffs relied on the word *premium* and similar general terms in automobile advertisements as the basis for a claim against the automobile's manufacturer.

---

4. *T & M Solar and Air Conditioning, Inc. v. Lennox International, Inc.*, 83 F.Supp.3d 855 (N.D.Cal. 2015).

Spotlight on Nissan

Case 23.1 Hurst v. Nissan North America Inc.

Missouri Court of Appeals, Western District, __ S.W.3d __, 2016 WL 1128297 (2016).

Background and Facts Nissan North America, Inc., makes and sells Infiniti autos, including a sport utility vehicle called the FX. According to Nissan, its marketing brochures for the FX contain many statements that are meant to convey "an overall image of a very refined vehicle" and a promise of "premium automotive machinery."

Robert Hurst bought an Infiniti FX that, with other models made at the same time, developed dashboard bubbling. Hurst and other FX owners with bubbling dashboards filed a suit in a Missouri state court against the automaker under the Missouri Merchandising Practices Act (MMPA). The plaintiffs alleged that Nissan violated the MMPA by making representations in its brochures that were not in accord with the facts regarding the quality of the FX.

A jury issued a verdict in the plaintiffs' favor and awarded damages. Nissan filed a motion for a judgment notwithstanding the verdict, which the court denied. Nissan appealed, arguing that the alleged misrepresentations were not actionable statements of fact but puffery.

In the Language of the Court

JAMES EDWARD WELSH, Judge

* * * *

* * * The MMPA bars an "assertion that is not in accord with the facts," and deceptions in advertising that have a tendency "to create a false impression."

Many statements made in advertising, however, are not actionable statements of fact but are merely the puffing of wares, sales propaganda, or other expression of opinion. *A seller may puff his wares or express his opinion about the quality and value of his goods even to the point of exaggeration without incurring liability. Indeed, puffing of wares, sales propaganda, and other expressions of opinion are common, are permitted, and should be expected.* [Emphasis added.]

Puffing of wares and expressions of opinion are mutually exclusive from statements of fact. *A factual claim is a statement that (1) admits of being adjudged true or false in a way that (2) admits of empirical* *verification.* To be actionable, the statement must be a specific and measurable claim, capable of being proved false or of being reasonably interpreted as a statement of objective fact. Generally, opinions are not actionable. * * * If a statement is a specific, measurable claim or can be reasonably interpreted as being a factual claim, *i.e.,* one capable of verification, the statement is one of fact. Conversely, if the statement is not specific and measurable, and cannot be reasonably interpreted as providing a benchmark by which the veracity of the statement can be ascertained, the statement constitutes puffery. [Emphasis added.]

Thus, a pasta maker may declare that it is "America's Favorite Pasta" and Papa John's may proclaim "Better Ingredients. Better Pizza" without incurring liability. * * * Such statements are unquantifiable, not susceptible of exact knowledge, and are not capable of being proved false or of being reasonably interpreted as a statement of objective fact.

None of the statements that Hurst complains about are capable of being proved false or capable of being reasonably interpreted as a statement of objective fact. Statements that the FX was a "premium" vehicle with a "premium automotive experience," a "leader in style," a "luxury" car, a "superior product representing excellent value," and a vehicle of "uncompromising style and luxury" are classic examples of statements not susceptible of exact knowledge. They are very general statements and are not capable of being proved false or of being reasonably interpreted as a statement of objective fact. The advertising employed by Nissan was merely dealer's talk, trade talk, puffing of manufacturer's wares, and sales propaganda, and the statements used in the advertising were mere statements of opinion, promises, expectations, and estimates, which are not actionable.

Decision and Remedy *A state intermediate appellate court reversed the judgment of the lower court and remanded the case for the entry of a judgment in favor of Nissan. Hurst had not shown that Nissan made an actionable misrepresentation in its advertising for the FX. The statements Hurst relied on were not statements of fact but statements of opinion.*

Critical Thinking
- **Legal Environment** *The court in the* Nissan *case indicated that the word* premium *may be considered puffing when viewed in isolation. Is the term also puffing when considered in a broader context? Explain.*
- **What If the Facts Were Different?** *Suppose that the court in the* Nissan *case had held the defendant liable based on the statements in its marketing brochures. What impact would this holding likely have on the results in future cases? Discuss.*

23–3 Implied Warranties

An **implied warranty** is one that *the law derives* by inference from the nature of the transaction or the relative situations or circumstances of the parties. Under the UCC, merchants impliedly warrant that the goods they sell or lease are merchantable and, in certain circumstances, fit for a particular purpose. In addition, an implied warranty may arise from a course of dealing or usage of trade. These three types of implied warranties are illustrated in Exhibit 23–1 and examined in the following subsections.

23–3a Implied Warranty of Merchantability

Every sale or lease of goods made by a merchant who deals in goods of the kind sold or leased automatically gives rise to an **implied warranty of merchantability** [UCC 2–314, 2A–212]. Thus, a merchant who is in the business of selling ski equipment makes an implied warranty of merchantability every time he sells a pair of skis. A neighbor selling her skis at a garage sale does not (because she is not in the business of selling goods of this type).

Merchantable Goods To be *merchantable,* goods must be "reasonably fit for the ordinary purposes for which such goods are used." They must be of at least average, fair, or medium-grade quality. The quality must be comparable to quality that will pass without objection in the trade or market for goods of the same description. The warranty of merchantability may be breached even though the merchant did not know or could not have discovered that a product was defective (not merchantable).

To be merchantable, the goods must also be adequately packaged and labeled. In addition, they must

EXHIBIT 23–1 Types of Implied Warranties

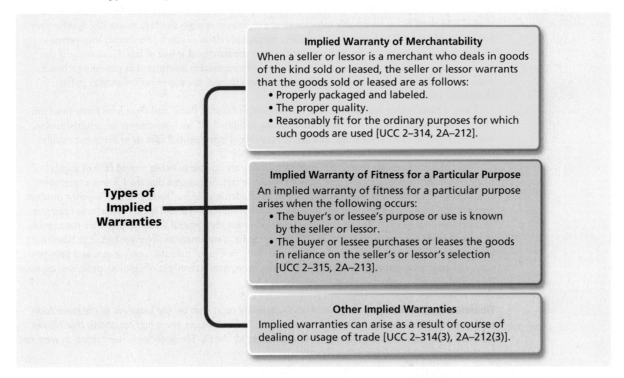

Types of Implied Warranties

Implied Warranty of Merchantability
When a seller or lessor is a merchant who deals in goods of the kind sold or leased, the seller or lessor warrants that the goods sold or leased are as follows:
• Properly packaged and labeled.
• The proper quality.
• Reasonably fit for the ordinary purposes for which such goods are used [UCC 2–314, 2A–212].

Implied Warranty of Fitness for a Particular Purpose
An implied warranty of fitness for a particular purpose arises when the following occurs:
• The buyer's or lessee's purpose or use is known by the seller or lessor.
• The buyer or lessee purchases or leases the goods in reliance on the seller's or lessor's selection [UCC 2–315, 2A–213].

Other Implied Warranties
Implied warranties can arise as a result of course of dealing or usage of trade [UCC 2–314(3), 2A–212(3)].

conform to the promises or affirmations of fact made on the container or label, if any. Of course, merchants are not absolute insurers against *all* accidents arising in connection with the goods. A bar of soap is not unmerchantable merely because a user could slip and fall by stepping on it.

The implied warranty of merchantability may be breached when the warrantor has unsuccessfully attempted to repair or replace defective parts. ■ **CASE IN POINT 23.10** Ilan Brand leased a new Hyundai Genesis from Allen Hyundai. The next day, when he was driving on an interstate highway, the sunroof began opening and closing, although Brand was not pushing the sunroof buttons. He immediately returned the vehicle to the Hyundai dealer. He was told it had a defective sunroof switch, which would be repaired within 24 hours. In spite of the dealer's assurances, however, the problem was not repaired. Ten days later, Brand—who still had not been able to pick up the vehicle—attempted to rescind the lease. Hyundai would not allow him to do so.

Brand then filed an action for breach of the implied warranty of merchantability in state court. The trial court dismissed the case, but the appellate court reversed. The reviewing court held that a reasonable jury could conclude that the opening and closing of the sunroof constituted a safety hazard and therefore breached the implied warranty of merchantability. The court remanded the case for a jury trial.[5] ■

Merchantable Food The serving of food or drink to be consumed on or off the premises is also treated as a sale of goods and subject to the implied warranty of merchantability [UCC 2–314(1)]. "Merchantable" food is food that is fit to eat.

Courts generally determine whether food is fit to eat on the basis of consumer expectations. Consumers should reasonably expect to find on occasion bones in fish fillets, cherry pits in cherry pie, a nutshell in a package of shelled nuts, and the like. Such substances are, after all, natural to the ingredients or the finished food product. In contrast, consumers would not reasonably expect to find an inchworm in a can of peas or a piece of glass in a soft drink.

In the following classic case, the court had to determine whether one should reasonably expect to find a fish bone in fish chowder.

---

5. *Brand v. Hyundai Motor America*, 226 Cal.App.4th 1538, 173 Cal.Rptr.3d 454 (4th Dist. 2014).

Webster v. Blue Ship Tea Room, Inc.

Supreme Judicial Court of Massachusetts, 347 Mass. 421 198 N.E.2d 309 (1964).

Background and Facts Blue Ship Tea Room, Inc., was located in Boston in an old building overlooking the ocean. Priscilla Webster, who had been born and raised in New England, went to the restaurant and ordered fish chowder. The chowder was milky in color. After three or four spoonfuls, she felt something lodged in her throat. As a result, she underwent two esophagoscopies (procedures in which an instrument is used to look into the throat). In the second esophagoscopy, a fish bone was found and removed. Webster filed a suit against the restaurant in a Massachusetts state court for breach of the implied warranty of merchantability. The jury rendered a verdict for Webster, and the restaurant appealed to the state's highest court.

In the Language of the Court

REARDON, Justice.

[The plaintiff] ordered a cup of fish chowder. Presently, there was set before her "a small bowl of fish chowder." * * * After 3 or 4 [spoonfuls] she was aware that something had lodged in her throat because she "couldn't swallow and couldn't clear her throat by gulping and she could feel it." This misadventure led to two esophagoscopies at the Massachusetts General Hospital, in the second of which, on April 27, 1959, a fish bone was found and removed. The sequence of events produced injury to the plaintiff which was not insubstantial.

We must decide whether a fish bone lurking in a fish chowder, about the ingredients of which there is no other complaint, constitutes a breach of implied warranty under applicable provisions of the Uniform Commercial Code * * * . As the judge put it in his charge [jury instruction], "Was the fish chowder fit to be eaten and wholesome? * * * Nobody is claiming that the fish itself wasn't wholesome. * * * But the bone of contention here—I don't mean that for a pun—but was this fish bone a foreign substance that made the fish chowder unwholesome or not fit to be eaten?"

* * * *

[We think that it] is not too much to say that a person sitting down in New England to consume a good New England fish chowder embarks on a gustatory [taste-related] adventure which may entail the removal of some fish bones from his bowl as he proceeds. We are not inclined to tamper with age-old recipes by any amendment reflecting the plaintiff's view of the effect of the Uniform Commercial Code upon them. We are aware of the heavy body of case law involving foreign substances in food, but we sense a strong distinction between them and those relative to unwholesomeness of the food itself, [for example,] tainted mackerel, and a fish bone in a fish chowder. * * * We consider that the joys of life in New England include the ready availability of fresh fish chowder. *We should be prepared to cope with the hazards of fish bones, the occasional presence of which in chowders is, it seems to us, to be anticipated, and which, in the light of a hallowed tradition, do not impair their fitness or merchantability.* [Emphasis added.]

Decision and Remedy *The Supreme Judicial Court of Massachusetts "sympathized with a plaintiff who has suffered a peculiarly New England injury" but entered a judgment for the defendant, Blue Ship Tea Room. A fish bone in fish chowder is not a breach of the implied warranty of merchantability.*

Impact of This Case on Today's Law *This classic case, phrased in memorable language, was an early application of the UCC's implied warranty of merchantability to food products. The case established the rule that consumers should expect to find, on occasion, elements of food products that are natural to the product (such as fish bones in fish chowder). Courts today still apply this rule.*

Critical Thinking

- **E-Commerce** *If Webster had made the chowder herself from a recipe that she had found on the Internet, could she have successfully brought an action against its author for a breach of the implied warranty of merchantability? Explain.*

23–3b Implied Warranty of Fitness for a Particular Purpose

The **implied warranty of fitness for a particular purpose** arises in the sale or lease of goods when a seller or lessor (merchant or nonmerchant) knows *both* of the following:

1. The particular purpose for which a buyer or lessee will use the goods.
2. That the buyer or lessee is relying on the skill and judgment of the seller or lessor to select suitable goods [UCC 2–315, 2A–213].

Particular versus Ordinary Purpose A "particular purpose" of the buyer or lessee differs from the "ordinary purpose for which goods are used" (merchantability). Goods can be merchantable but unfit for a particular purpose.

■ **EXAMPLE 23.11** Sheryl needs a gallon of paint to match the color of her living room walls—a light shade somewhere between coral and peach. She takes a sample to Sherwin-Williams and requests a gallon of paint of that color. Instead, the salesperson gives her a gallon of bright blue paint. Here, the salesperson has not breached any warranty of implied merchantability—the bright blue paint is of high quality and suitable for interior walls. The salesperson has breached an implied warranty of fitness for a particular purpose, though, because the paint is not the right color for Sheryl's purpose (to match her living room walls). ■

Knowledge and Reliance Requirements A seller or lessor need not have actual knowledge of the buyer's or lessee's particular purpose. It is sufficient if a seller or lessor "has reason to know" the purpose. For an implied warranty to be created, however, the buyer or lessee must have *relied* on the skill or judgment of the seller or lessor in selecting or furnishing suitable goods. Moreover, the seller or lessor must have reason to know that the buyer or lessee is relying on her or his judgment or skill.

■ **EXAMPLE 23.12** Carlos Fuentes tells Tyrone, a salesperson at GamerPC, that he is looking for a new PC, such as the Cyberpower Black Pearl or Velocity Raptor Signature Edition, to use for gaming. Fuentes's statement implies that he needs a PC with a video card that is capable of running fast-paced video games with detailed graphics. Tyrone recommends and sells to Carlos a computer that does not have a video card and is too slow to run such video games. By doing so, Tyrone has breached the implied warranty of fitness for a particular purpose. ■

23–3c Warranties Implied from Prior Dealings or Trade Custom

Implied warranties can also arise (or be excluded or modified) as a result of course of dealing or usage of trade [UCC 2–314(3), 2A–212(3)]. Without evidence to the contrary, when both parties to a sales or lease contract have knowledge of a well-recognized trade custom, the courts will infer that both parties intended for that custom to apply to their contract.

■ **EXAMPLE 23.13** Industry-wide custom is to lubricate a new car before it is delivered. If a dealer fails to lubricate a car, the dealer can be held liable to a buyer for damages resulting from the breach of an implied warranty. (This would also be negligence on the part of the dealer.) ■

23–3d Lemon Laws

Purchasers of defective automobiles—called "lemons"—may have remedies in addition to those offered by the UCC. All of the states and the District of Columbia have enacted *lemon laws*. Basically, state lemon laws provide remedies to consumers who buy automobiles that repeatedly fail to meet standards of quality and performance.

Although lemon laws vary by state, typically they apply to automobiles under warranty that are defective in a way that significantly affects the vehicle's value or use. Lemon laws do not necessarily cover used-car purchases (unless the car is covered by a manufacturer's extended warranty) or vehicles that are leased.[6]

Seller Has Had the Opportunity to Remedy Defect Generally, the car's owner must notify the dealer or manufacturer of the defect and give the dealer or manufacturer a number of opportunities to remedy it (usually four). If the seller fails to cure the problem despite a reasonable number of attempts (as specified by state law), the buyer may be entitled to a new car, replacement of defective parts, or return of all consideration paid. Buyers who prevail in a lemon-law dispute may also be entitled to reimbursement of their attorneys' fees.

Arbitration Often Required In many states, even after the dealer or manufacturer has failed to cure the defect, the owner cannot take the case directly to court.

---

6. Note that in some states, such as California, these laws may extend beyond automobile purchases and apply to other consumer goods.

Instead, the owner must submit the complaint to the arbitration program specified in the manufacturer's warranty.

Decisions by arbitration panels are binding on the manufacturer—that is, cannot be appealed by the manufacturer to the courts—but usually are not binding on the purchaser. Most major automobile companies operate their own arbitration panels. All arbitration boards must meet state and/or federal standards of impartiality, and some states have established mandatory government-sponsored arbitration programs for lemon-law disputes.

23–3e Magnuson-Moss Warranty Act

The Magnuson-Moss Warranty Act of 1975[7] was designed to prevent deception in warranties by making them easier to understand.

Applies Only to Consumer Transactions The Magnuson-Moss Warranty Act modifies UCC warranty rules to some extent when *consumer* transactions are involved. The UCC, however, remains the primary codification of warranty rules for commercial transactions.

Under the Magnuson-Moss Act, no seller is *required* to give a written warranty for consumer goods sold. If a seller chooses to make an express written warranty, however, and the cost of the consumer goods is more than $25, the warranty must be labeled as either "full" or "limited."

A *full warranty* requires free repair or replacement of any defective part. If the product cannot be repaired within a reasonable time, the consumer has the choice of a refund or a replacement without charge. A full warranty can be for an unlimited or a limited time period, such as a "full twelve-month warranty."

A *limited warranty* is one in which the buyer's recourse is limited in some fashion, such as to replacement of an item. The fact that only a limited warranty is being given must be conspicuously stated.

Requires Certain Disclosures The Magnuson-Moss Act further requires the warrantor to make certain disclosures fully and conspicuously in a single document in "readily understood language." The seller must disclose the name and address of the warrantor, specifically what is warranted, and the procedures for enforcing the warranty. The seller must also clarify that the buyer has legal rights and explain limitations on warranty relief.

---

7. 15 U.S.C. Sections 2301–2312.

23–4 Overlapping Warranties

Sometimes, two or more warranties are made in a single transaction. An implied warranty of merchantability, an implied warranty of fitness for a particular purpose, or both can exist in addition to an express warranty. ■ **EXAMPLE 23.14** A sales contract for a new car states that "this car engine is warranted to be free from defects for 36,000 miles or thirty-six months, whichever occurs first." This statement creates an express warranty against all defects, as well as an implied warranty that the car will be fit for normal use. ■

23–4a When the Warranties Are Consistent

The rule under the UCC is that express and implied warranties are construed as *cumulative* if they are consistent with one another [UCC 2–317, 2A–215]. In other words, courts interpret two or more warranties as being in agreement with each other unless this construction is unreasonable. If it is unreasonable for the two warranties to be consistent, then the court looks at the intention of the parties to determine which warranty is dominant.

23–4b Conflicting Warranties

If the warranties are *inconsistent,* the courts usually apply the following rules to interpret which warranty is most important:

1. *Express* warranties displace inconsistent *implied* warranties, except implied warranties of fitness for a particular purpose.
2. Samples take precedence over inconsistent general descriptions.
3. Exact or technical specifications displace inconsistent samples or general descriptions.

■ **EXAMPLE 23.15** Innova, Ltd., leases a high-speed server from Vernon Sources. The contract contains an express warranty concerning the speed of the CPU and the application programs that the server is capable of running. Innova does not realize that the speed expressly warranted in the contract is insufficient for its needs until it tries to run the software and the server slows to a crawl.

Because Innova made it clear that it was leasing the server to perform certain tasks, Innova files an action against Vernon for breach of the implied warranty of fitness for a particular purpose. In this situation, Innova normally will prevail. Although the express warranty on CPU speed takes precedence over the implied warranty of merchantability, it normally does not take precedence over an implied warranty of fitness for a particular purpose. ■

23-5 Warranty Disclaimers and Limitations on Liability

The UCC generally permits warranties to be disclaimed or limited by specific and unambiguous language, provided that this is done in a manner that protects the buyer or lessee from surprise. Because each type of warranty is created in a different way, the manner in which a seller or lessor can disclaim warranties varies with the type of warranty.

23-5a Express Warranties

A seller or lessor can disclaim all oral express warranties by including in the contract a written disclaimer. The disclaimer must be in language that is clear and conspicuous and must be called to a buyer's or lessee's attention [UCC 2–316(1), 2A–214(1)]. This allows the seller or lessor to avoid false allegations that oral warranties were made. It also ensures that only representations made by properly authorized individuals are included in the bargain.

Note that a buyer or lessee must be made aware of any warranty disclaimers or modifications *at the time the contract is formed.* In other words, the seller or lessor cannot modify any warranties or disclaimers made during the bargaining process without the consent of the buyer or lessee.

23-5b Implied Warranties

Normally, unless circumstances indicate otherwise, the implied warranties of merchantability and fitness are disclaimed by an expression such as "as is" or "with all faults." Both parties must be able to clearly understand from the language used that there are no implied warranties [UCC 2–316(3)(a), 2A–214(3)(a)]. (Note, however, that some states have passed consumer protection statutes that forbid "as is" sales or make it illegal to disclaim warranties of merchantability on consumer goods.)

■ **CASE IN POINT 23.16** Mandy Morningstar advertised a "lovely, eleven-year-old mare" with extensive jumping ability for sale. After examining the horse twice, Sue Hallett contracted to buy the horse. She signed a contract that described the horse as an eleven-year-old mare being sold "as is." Shortly after the purchase, a veterinarian determined that the horse was actually sixteen years old and in no condition for jumping. Hallett stopped payment, and Morningstar filed a lawsuit for breach of contract.

The court held that the statement in the contract describing the horse as eleven years old constituted an express warranty, which Morningstar had breached. The "as is" clause effectively disclaimed any implied warranties (of merchantability and fitness for a particular purpose, such as jumping). It did not, however, disclaim the express warranty concerning the horse's age.[8] ■

In the following case, the court explained the rationale behind the effect of an "as is" clause.

---

8. *Morningstar v. Hallett*, 858 A.2d 125 (Pa.Super.Ct. 2004).

Roberts v. Lanigan Auto Sales
Court of Appeals of Kentucky, 406 S.W.3d 882 (2013).

In the Language of the Court
VANMETER, Judge:
* * * *

* * * [Evan] Roberts purchased a used vehicle from Lanigan [Auto Sales] in September 2009. Roberts and Lanigan executed a purchase contract, which contained a clause stating the vehicle is "sold as is * * * without any guarantee express or implied." Following the purchase, Roberts independently obtained a report which indicated that the vehicle had previously been involved in an accident and

suffered damage to the undercarriage of the vehicle.

Roberts filed the underlying action [in a Kentucky state court] alleging that Lanigan * * * committed fraud by omitting, suppressing, and concealing the vehicle's prior damage and accident history in order to induce Roberts into purchasing the vehicle. Lanigan maintained it never represented that the vehicle had not been damaged or involved in a wreck and filed a * * * motion to dismiss the action for failure to state a claim upon

which relief can be granted. * * * The trial court * * * dismissed Roberts' action on the basis that the purchase contract, which contained the express term "sold as is," barred his action for fraud. This appeal followed.

On appeal, Roberts argues the trial court erred by dismissing his action because the "sold as is" clause in the purchase contract did not bar his action for fraud. We disagree.
* * * *

Case 23.3 Continued

[Kentucky Revised Statute] 355.2–316 [Kentucky's version of UCC 2–316] seeks to provide a structure for construing both oral representations and written disclaimers within an agreement for the sale of goods. To carry out that purpose, the statute provides that, "unless the circumstances indicate otherwise, all implied warranties are excluded by expressions like 'as is,' 'with all faults' or other language which in common understanding calls the buyer's attention to the exclusion of warranties."

* * * *An "as is" clause in a sales contract is understood to mean that the buyer takes the entire risk as to the quality of the goods involved. * * * A valid "as is" agreement prevents a buyer from holding a seller liable if the thing sold turns out to be worth less than the price paid, because it is impossible for the buyer's injury on account of this disparity to have been caused by the seller and the sole cause of the buyer's injury is the buyer himself or herself.* Thus, by agreeing to purchase something "as is," a buyer agrees to make his or her own appraisal of the bargain and to accept the risk that he or she may

be wrong, and the seller gives no assurances, express or implied, concerning the value or condition of the thing sold. [Emphasis added.]

In an action for fraud, a party must prove by clear and convincing evidence that (1) the seller made a material misrepresentation to the buyer, (2) which was false, (3) known by the seller to be false, (4) made with the intent to be relied upon, (5) was reasonably relied upon and (6) caused injury. Here, Roberts executed a written sales contract which stated the car was "sold as is" and acknowledging, "I hereby make this purchase knowingly without any guarantee expressed or implied by this dealer or his agent." * * * The effect of the "sold as is" clause is to shift the assumption of risk regarding the value or condition of the vehicle to Roberts despite any express or implied warranties that were made by Lanigan. Since the only claimed injury concerns the value or condition of the car sold, and because the sole cause of such an injury is the buyer himself, Roberts is unable to prove that the seller's representation caused the injury.

Furthermore, by agreeing to buy the vehicle "as is," Roberts agreed to make his own assessment of the condition of the vehicle in spite of Lanigan's representations. Thus, he cannot later claim that he reasonably relied on those representations when agreeing to purchase the vehicle.

This is not to say that an "as is" clause bars any claim of fraud; when circumstances indicate otherwise, express or implied warranties may not be disclaimed by a written contract. Different circumstances could support an action for fraud despite an "as is" clause when the injury results in consequential damages, [that is,] injury to a person or property as a result of a breach of warranty, rather than an injury as a result of decreased value of the goods. Our holding here merely follows the rationale that an "as is" clause transfers the risk to the buyer that the condition or value of the goods is not what the seller represents. In accordance with that rationale, the trial court did not err by dismissing Roberts' action.

The order of the [trial court] is affirmed.

Legal Reasoning Questions

1. What language in a sales contract excludes all implied warranties?

2. How does an "as is" clause in a sales contract affect the bargain between the buyer and the seller?

3. In this case, what did the court rule on the effect of the "as is" clause? Why?

Disclaimer of the Implied Warranty of Merchantability To specifically disclaim an implied warranty of merchantability, a seller or lessor must mention the word *merchantability*. The disclaimer need not be written, but if it is, the writing must be conspicuous [UCC 2–316(2), 2A–214(4)].

Under the UCC, a term or clause is conspicuous when it is written or displayed in such a way that a reasonable person would notice it. Conspicuous terms include words set in capital letters, in a larger font size, or in a different color so as to be set off from the surrounding text.

Disclaimer of the Implied Warranty of Fitness To disclaim an implied warranty of fitness for a particular

purpose, the disclaimer must be in a writing and must be conspicuous. The writing does not have to mention the word *fitness*. It is sufficient if, for instance, the disclaimer states, "There are no warranties that extend beyond the description on the face hereof."

23–5c Buyer's or Lessee's Examination or Refusal to Inspect

If a buyer or lessee examines the goods (or a sample or model) as fully as desired, there is no implied warranty with respect to defects that are found or that could be found on a reasonable examination [UCC 2–316(3)(b), 2A–214(2)(b)]. Also, if a buyer or lessee refuses to examine the goods on the seller's or lessor's request that he or she do so, there is no implied warranty with respect to reasonably evident defects.

■ **EXAMPLE 23.17** Janna buys a table at Gershwin's Home Store. No express warranties are made. Gershwin asks Janna to inspect the table before buying it, but she refuses. Had Janna inspected the table, she would have noticed that one of its legs was obviously cracked, which made it unstable. Janna takes the table home and sets a lamp on it. The table later collapses, and the lamp starts a fire that causes significant damage. Janna normally will not be able to hold Gershwin's liable for breach of the warranty of merchantability, because she refused to examine the table as Gershwin requested. Janna therefore assumed the risk that the table was defective. ■

23–5d Warranty Disclaimers and Unconscionability

The UCC sections dealing with warranty disclaimers do not refer specifically to unconscionability as a factor.

Ultimately, however, the courts will test warranty disclaimers with reference to the UCC's unconscionability standards [UCC 2–302, 2A–108]. Factors such as lack of bargaining position, "take-it-or-leave-it" choices, and a buyer's or lessee's failure to understand or know of a warranty disclaimer will be relevant to the issue of unconscionability.

23–5e Statutes of Limitations

A cause of action for breach of contract under the UCC must be commenced within four years after the breach occurs (unless the parties agree to a shorter period). An action for breach of warranty accrues when the seller or lessor *tenders* delivery, even if the buyer or lessee is unaware of the breach at that time [UCC 2–725(2), 2A–506(2)]. In addition, the nonbreaching party usually must notify the breaching party within a reasonable time after discovering the breach or be barred from pursuing any remedy [UCC 2–607(3)(a), 2A–516(3)].

Reviewing: Warranties

Shalene Kolchek bought a Great Lakes spa from Val Porter, a dealer who was selling spas at the state fair. Porter told Kolchek that Great Lakes spas were "top of the line" and "the Cadillac of spas." He also indicated that the spa she was buying was "fully warranted for three years." Kolchek signed an installment contract. Then, Porter handed her the manufacturer's paperwork and arranged for the spa to be delivered and installed for her. Three months later, Kolchek noticed that one corner of the spa was leaking onto her new deck and causing damage. She complained to Porter, but he did nothing about the problem. Kolchek's family continued to use the spa. Using the information presented in the chapter, answer the following questions.

1. Did Porter's statement that the spa was "top of the line" and "the Cadillac of spas" create any type of warranty? Why or why not?
2. If the paperwork provided to Kolchek after her purchase indicated that the spa had no warranty, would this be an effective disclaimer under the Uniform Commercial Code? Explain.
3. Can Kolchek sue Porter for breach of the implied warranty of merchantability because the spa leaked? Explain.
4. Suppose that one year later, Pacific Credit Union contacted Kolchek and claimed that it had a security interest in the spa. Would this be a breach of any of the title warranties discussed in the chapter? Explain.

Debate This . . . *No express warranties should be created by the oral statements made by salespersons about a product.*

Terms and Concepts

express warranty 426	implied warranty of fitness for a	implied warranty of
implied warranty 429	particular purpose 432	merchantability 429

Issue Spotters

1. General Construction Company (GCC) tells Industrial Supplies, Inc., that it needs an adhesive to do a particular job. Industrial provides a five-gallon bucket of a certain brand. When it does not perform to GCC's specifications, GCC sues Industrial, which claims, "We didn't expressly promise anything." What should GCC argue? (See *Implied Warranties*.)

2. Stella bought a cup of coffee at the Roasted Bean Drive-Thru. The coffee had been heated to 190 degrees and consequently had dissolved the inside of the cup. When Stella lifted the lid, the cup collapsed, spilling the contents on her lap. To recover for third-degree burns on her thighs, Stella filed a suit against the Roasted Bean. Can Stella recover for breach of the implied warranty of merchantability? Why or why not? (See *Implied Warranties*.)

• **Check your answers to the Issue Spotters against the answers provided in Appendix D at the end of this text.**

Business Scenarios

23–1. Implied Warranties. Moon, a farmer, needs to install a two-thousand-pound piece of equipment in his barn. This will require lifting the equipment thirty feet up into a hayloft. Moon goes to Davidson Hardware and tells Davidson that he needs some heavy-duty rope to be used on his farm. Davidson recommends a one-inch-thick nylon rope, and Moon purchases two hundred feet of it. Moon ties the rope around the piece of equipment; puts the rope through a pulley; and, with a tractor, lifts the equipment off the ground. Suddenly, the rope breaks. The equipment crashes to the ground and is severely damaged. Moon files a suit against Davidson for breach of the implied warranty of fitness for a particular purpose. Discuss how successful Moon will be in his suit. (See *Implied Warranties*.)

23–2. Warranty Disclaimers. Tandy purchased a washing machine from Marshall Appliances. The sales contract included a provision explicitly disclaiming all express or implied warranties, including the implied warranty of merchantability. The disclaimer was printed in the same size and color as the rest of the contract. The machine never functioned properly. Tandy sought a refund of the purchase price, claiming that Marshall had breached the implied warranty of merchantability. Can Tandy recover the purchase price, notwithstanding the warranty disclaimer in the contract? Explain. (See *Warranty Disclaimers and Limitations on Liability*.)

Business Case Problems

23–3. Express Warranties. Videotape is recorded magnetically. The magnetic particles that constitute the recorded image are bound to the tape's polyester base. The binder that holds the particles to the base breaks down over time. This breakdown, which is called *sticky shed syndrome,* causes the image to deteriorate. The Walt Disney Co. made many of its movies available on tape. Buena Vista Home Entertainment, Inc., sold the tapes, which it described as part of a "Gold Collection" or "Masterpiece Collection." The advertising included such statements as "Give Your Children the memories of a lifetime—Collect Each Timeless Masterpiece!" and "Available for a Limited Time Only!"

Charmaine Schreib and others who bought the tapes filed a suit in an Illinois state court against Disney and Buena Vista, alleging, among other things, breach of warranty. The plaintiffs claimed that the defendants' marketing promised the tapes would last for generations. In reality, the tapes were as subject to sticky shed syndrome as other tapes. Did the ads create an express warranty? In whose favor should the court rule on this issue? Explain. [*Schreib v. Walt Disney Co.,* 2006 WL 573008 (Ill.App. 1 Dist. 2006)] (See *Express Warranties*.)

23–4. Implied Warranties. Peter and Tanya Rothing operated Diamond R Stables near Belgrade, Montana, where they bred, trained, and sold horses. Arnold Kallestad owned a ranch in Gallatin County, Montana, where he grew hay and grain, and raised Red Angus cattle. For more than twenty years, Kallestad had sold between three hundred and one thousand tons of hay annually, sometimes advertising it for sale in the *Bozeman Daily Chronicle*. In 2001, the Rothings bought hay from Kallestad for $90 a ton. They received delivery on April 23. In less than two weeks, at least nine of the Rothings' horses exhibited symptoms of poisoning that was diagnosed as botulism. Before the outbreak was over, nineteen animals had died. Robert Whitlock, associate professor of medicine and the director of the Botulism Laboratory at the University of Pennsylvania, concluded that Kallestad's hay was the source. The Rothings filed a suit in a Montana state court against Kallestad, claiming, in part, breach of the implied warranty of merchantability. Kallestad asked the court to dismiss this claim on the ground that, if botulism had been present, it had been in no way foreseeable. Should the court grant this request? Why or why not? [*Rothing v.*

Kallestad, 337 Mont. 193, 159 P.3d 222 (2007)] (See *Implied Warranties.*)

23–5. Spotlight on Apple—Implied Warranties. Alan

Vitt purchased an iBook G4 laptop computer from Apple, Inc. Shortly after the one-year warranty expired, the laptop failed to work due to a weakness in the product manufacture. Vitt sued Apple, arguing that the laptop should have lasted "at least a couple of years," which Vitt believed was a reasonable consumer expectation for a laptop. Vitt claimed that Apple's descriptions of the laptop as "durable," "rugged," "reliable," and "high performance" were affirmative statements concerning the quality and performance of the laptop, which Apple did not meet. How should the court rule? Why? [*Vitt v. Apple Computer, Inc.,* 469 Fed.Appx. 605 (9th Cir. 2011)] (See *Implied Warranties.*)

23–6. Business Case Problem with Sample Answer— Implied Warranties. Bariven, S.A., agreed to buy 26,000

metric tons of powdered milk for $123.5 million from Absolute Trading Corp. to be delivered in shipments from China to Venezuela. After the first three shipments, China halted dairy exports due to the presence of melamine in some products. Absolute assured Bariven that its milk was safe, and when China resumed dairy exports, Absolute delivered sixteen more shipments. Tests of samples of the milk revealed that it contained dangerous levels of melamine. Did Absolute breach any implied warranties? Discuss. [*Absolute Trading Corp. v. Bariven S.A.,* 503 Fed.Appx. 694 (11th Cir. 2013)] (See *Implied Warranties.*)

• For a sample answer to Problem 23–6, go to Appendix E at the end of this text.

23–7. Express Warranties. Charity Bell bought a used Toyota Avalon from Awny Gobran of Gobran Auto Sales, Inc. The odometer showed that the car had been driven 147,000 miles. Bell asked whether it had been in any accidents. Gobran replied that it was in good condition. The parties signed a warranty disclaimer that the vehicle was sold "as is." Problems with the car arose the same day as the purchase. Gobran made a few ineffectual attempts to repair it before refusing to do more. Meanwhile, Bell obtained a vehicle history report from Carfax, which showed that the Avalon had been damaged in an accident and that its last reported odometer reading was 237,271. Was the "as is" disclaimer sufficient to put Bell on notice that the odometer reading could be false and that the car might have been in an accident? Can Gobran avoid any liability that might otherwise be imposed because Bell did not obtain the Carfax report until *after* she bought the car? Discuss. [*Gobran Auto Sales Inc. v. Bell,* 335 Ga.App. 873, 783 S.E.2d 389 (2016)] (See *Warranty Disclaimers and Limitations on Liability.*)

23–8. A Question of Ethics—Lemon Laws. *Randal Schwei-*

ger bought a 2008 Kia Spectra EX from Kia Motors America, Inc., for his stepdaughter, April Kirichkow. The cost was $17,231, plus sales tax, fees, and other items. April had trouble starting the car. The Kia dealership replaced various parts of the motor several times but was unable to fix the problem. Schweiger sought a refund under the state's lemon law. When they could not agree on the amount, Schweiger filed a suit in a Wisconsin state court against Kia. From a judgment in Schweiger's favor, Kia appealed. [Schweiger v. Kia Motors America, Inc., 347 Wis.2d 550, 830 N.W.2d 723 (2013)] (See *Implied Warranties.*)

(a) Kia offered a refund of $3,306.24. Should this offer bar Schweiger's claim for a refund? Why or why not?

(b) Schweiger claimed that Kia's offer did not include the $1,301 cost of a service contract. Kia argued that the "payoff to the lender" of $13,060.16, which Schweiger agreed was the correct amount, "would by definition refund the cost of the service contract." The court found "no logical basis" for this argument. Is it ethical for a party to argue a position for which there is no logical basis? Discuss.

Legal Reasoning Group Activity

23–9. Warranties. Milan purchased saffron extract, marketed as "America's Hottest New Way to a Flat Belly," online from Dr. Chen. The Web site stated that recently published studies showed a significant weight loss (more than 25 percent) for people who used pure saffron extract as a supplement *without diet and exercise.* Dr. Chen said that the saffron suppresses appetite by increasing levels of serotonin, which reduces emotional eating. Milan took the extract as directed without any resulting weight loss. (See *Express Warranties.*)

(a) The first group will determine whether Dr. Chen's Web site made any express warranty on the saffron extract or its effectiveness in causing weight loss.

(b) The second group will discuss whether the implied warranty of merchantability applies to the purchase of weight-loss supplements.

(c) The third group will decide if Dr. Chen's sale of saffron extract breached the implied warranty of fitness for a particular purpose.

CHAPTER 24

International and Space Law

Commerce has always crossed national borders. But technology has fueled dramatic growth in world trade and the emergence of a global business community. Exchanges of goods, services, and intellectual property on a global level are now routine. Therefore, students of business law and the legal environment should be familiar with the laws pertaining to international business transactions.

Laws affecting the international legal environment of business include both international law and national law. **International law** can be defined as a body of law—formed as a result of international customs, treaties, and organizations—that governs relations among or between nations. International law may be created when individual nations agree to comply with certain standards (such as by signing a treaty). It may also be created when industries or nations establish international standards for private transactions that cross national borders (such as a law that prohibits importation of genetically modified organisms).

National law is the law of a particular nation, such as Brazil, Germany, Japan, or the United States. In some ways, national laws that involve property rights, border searches, regulations, and taxes effectively become international law when they are applied at a nation's borders.

An emerging area of global importance is space law, which governs humans' activities in outer space. Space law also has both international and national components.

24-1 International Law

The major difference between international law and national law is that government authorities can enforce national law. What government, however, can enforce international law?

By definition, a *nation* is a sovereign entity—which means that there is no higher authority to which that nation must submit. If a nation violates an international law and persuasive tactics fail, other countries or international organizations have no recourse except to take coercive actions. Coercive actions might include economic sanctions, severance of diplomatic relations, boycotts, and, as a last resort, war against the violating nation.

■ **EXAMPLE 24.1** In 2014, Russia sent troops into the neighboring nation of Ukraine and supported an election that allowed Crimea (part of Ukraine) to secede from Ukraine. Because Russia's actions violated Ukraine's independent sovereignty, the United States and the European Union imposed economic sanctions on Russia. Nevertheless, Russia continued to support military action in Eastern Ukraine into 2017. ■

In essence, international law attempts to reconcile each country's need to be the final authority over its own affairs with the desire of nations to benefit economically from trade and harmonious relations with one another. Sovereign nations can, and do, voluntarily agree to be governed in certain respects by international law, usually for the purpose of facilitating international trade and commerce. As a result, a body of international law has evolved.

24-1a Sources of International Law

Basically, there are three sources of international law: international customs, treaties and international agreements, and international organizations. We look at each of these sources here.

International Customs One important source of international law consists of the international customs that have evolved among nations in their relations with one another. Article 38(1) of the Statute of the International Court of Justice refers to an international custom as "evidence of a general practice accepted as law." The legal principles and doctrines that you will read about shortly are rooted in international customs and traditions that have evolved over time in the international arena.

Treaties and International Agreements Treaties and other explicit agreements between or among foreign nations provide another important source of international law. A **treaty** is an agreement or contract between two or more nations that must be authorized and ratified by the supreme power of each nation. Under Article II, Section 2, of the U.S. Constitution, the president has the power "by and with the Advice and Consent of the Senate, to make Treaties, provided two-thirds of the Senators present concur."

A *bilateral* agreement, as the term implies, is an agreement formed by two nations to govern their commercial exchanges or other relations with one another. A *multilateral* agreement is formed by several nations. For instance, regional trade associations such as the Andean Community, the Association of Southeast Asian Nations, and the European Union are the result of multilateral trade agreements.

International Organizations The term **international organization** generally refers to an organization composed mainly of officials of member nations and usually established by treaty. The United States is a member of more than one hundred multilateral and bilateral organizations, including at least twenty through the United Nations.

Adopt Resolutions. International organizations adopt resolutions, declarations, and other types of standards that often require nations to behave in a particular manner. The General Assembly of the United Nations, for instance, has adopted numerous nonbinding resolutions and declarations that embody principles of international law. Disputes with respect to these resolutions and declarations may be brought before the International Court of Justice. That court, however, normally has authority to settle legal disputes only when nations voluntarily submit to its jurisdiction.

Create Uniform Rules. The United Nations Commission on International Trade Law has made considerable progress in establishing uniformity in international law as it relates to trade and commerce. One of the commission's most significant creations to date is the 1980 Convention on Contracts for the International Sale of Goods (CISG).

The CISG is similar to Article 2 of the Uniform Commercial Code in that it is designed to settle disputes between parties to sales contracts. It spells out the duties of international buyers and sellers that will apply if the parties have not agreed otherwise in their contracts. The CISG governs only sales contracts between trading partners in nations that have ratified the CISG.

24–1b Common Law and Civil Law Systems

Companies operating in foreign nations are subject to the laws of those nations. In addition, international disputes are often resolved through the court systems of individual nations. Therefore, businesspersons should understand that legal systems around the globe generally are divided into *common law* and *civil law* systems. Exhibit 24–1 lists some of the nations that use civil law systems and some that use common law systems.

Common Law Systems Recall that in a common law system, such as the United States, the courts independently develop the rules governing certain areas of law, such as torts and contracts. These common law rules apply to all areas not covered by statutory law. Although the common law doctrine of *stare decisis* obligates judges to follow precedential decisions in their jurisdictions, courts may modify or even overturn precedents when deemed necessary.

Civil Law Systems In contrast to common law countries, most European nations, as well as nations in Latin America, Africa, and Asia, base their legal systems on Roman civil law, or "code law." The term *civil law,* as used here, refers not to civil as opposed to criminal law but to *codified* law—an ordered grouping of legal principles enacted into law by a legislature or other governing body.

In a **civil law system,** the primary source of law is a statutory code. Courts interpret the code and apply the rules to individual cases, but courts may not depart from the code and develop their own laws. Judicial precedents are not binding, as they are in a common law system. In theory, the law code sets forth all of the principles needed for the legal system. Trial procedures also differ in civil law systems. Unlike judges in common law systems, judges in civil systems often actively question witnesses.

Islamic Legal Systems A third, less prevalent, legal system is common in Islamic countries, where the law is often influenced by *sharia,* the religious law of Islam. *Sharia* is a comprehensive code of principles that governs both the public and the private lives of persons of the Islamic faith. *Sharia* directs many aspects of day-to-day life, including politics, economics, banking, business law, contract law, and social issues.

EXHIBIT 24–1 The Legal Systems of Selected Nations

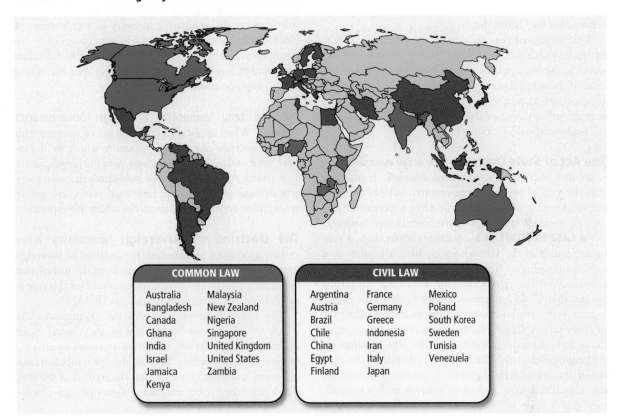

COMMON LAW		CIVIL LAW		
Australia	Malaysia	Argentina	France	Mexico
Bangladesh	New Zealand	Austria	Germany	Poland
Canada	Nigeria	Brazil	Greece	South Korea
Ghana	Singapore	Chile	Indonesia	Sweden
India	United Kingdom	China	Iran	Tunisia
Israel	United States	Egypt	Italy	Venezuela
Jamaica	Zambia	Finland	Japan	
Kenya				

Although *sharia* affects the legal codes of many Muslim countries, the extent of its impact, as well as its interpretation, vary widely. In some Middle Eastern nations, aspects of *sharia* have been codified and are enforced by national judicial systems.

24–1c International Principles and Doctrines

Over time, a number of legal principles and doctrines have evolved in the international context. These principles and doctrines are employed—to a greater or lesser extent—by the courts of various nations to resolve or reduce conflicts that involve a foreign element. The three important legal principles discussed next are based primarily on courtesy and respect, and are applied in the interests of maintaining harmonious relations among nations.

The Principle of Comity The principle of **comity** basically refers to legal reciprocity. One nation will defer and give effect to the executive, legislative, and judicial acts of another country, as long as the acts are consistent with the law and public policy of the accommodating nation. For instance, a U.S. court ordinarily will recognize and enforce a default judgment from an Australian court because the legal procedures in Australia are compatible with those in the United States. Nearly all nations recognize the validity of marriage decrees (at least those between a man and a woman) issued in another country.

■ **CASE IN POINT 24.2** Karen Goldberg's husband was killed in a terrorist bombing in Israel. She filed a lawsuit in a federal court in New York against UBS AG, a Switzerland-based global financial services company with many offices in the United States. Goldberg claimed that UBS was liable under the U.S. Anti-Terrorism Act for aiding and abetting in the murder of her husband. She argued that UBS was liable because it provided financial services to the international terrorist organizations responsible for his murder.

UBS requested that the case be transferred to a court in Israel, which would offer a remedy "substantially the same" as the one available in the United States. The court refused, however. Transferring the case would require an Israeli court to take evidence and judge the emotional damage suffered by Goldberg, "raising distinct concerns of comity and enforceability."[1] ■

The Act of State Doctrine

The **act of state doctrine** is another important international doctrine. It provides that the judicial branch of one country will not examine the validity of public acts committed by a recognized foreign government within that government's own territory.

■ **CASE IN POINT 24.3** Spectrum Stores, Inc., a gasoline retailer in the United States, filed a lawsuit in a U.S. court against Citgo Petroleum Corporation, which is owned by the government of Venezuela. Spectrum alleged that Citgo had conspired with other oil companies in Venezuela and Saudi Arabia to limit production of crude oil and thereby fix the prices of petroleum products sold in the United States. Because Citgo is owned by a foreign government, the U.S. court dismissed the case under the act of state doctrine. A government controls the natural resources, such as oil reserves, within its territory. A U.S. court will not rule on the validity of a foreign government's acts within its own territory.[2] ■

When a Foreign Government Takes Private Property. The act of state doctrine can have important consequences for individuals and firms doing business with, and investing in, other countries. This doctrine is frequently employed in cases involving expropriation or confiscation.

Expropriation occurs when a government seizes a privately owned business or privately owned goods for a proper public purpose and awards just compensation. When a government seizes private property for an illegal purpose and without just compensation, the taking is referred to as a **confiscation**. The line between these two forms of taking is sometimes blurred because of differing interpretations of what is illegal and what constitutes just compensation.

■ **EXAMPLE 24.4** Flaherty, Inc., a U.S. company, owns a mine in Brazil. The government of Brazil seizes the mine for public use and claims that the profits Flaherty has already realized from the mine constitute just compensation. Flaherty disagrees, but the act of state doctrine may prevent the company's recovery in a U.S. court. ■ Note that in a case alleging that a foreign government has wrongfully taken the plaintiff's property, the defendant government has the burden of proving that the taking was an expropriation, not a confiscation.

Doctrine May Immunize a Foreign Government's Actions. When applicable, both the act of state doctrine and the doctrine of *sovereign immunity,* which we discuss next, tend to shield foreign nations from the jurisdiction of U.S. courts. As a result, firms or individuals that own property overseas generally have little legal protection against government actions in the countries where they operate.

The Doctrine of Sovereign Immunity

When certain conditions are satisfied, the doctrine of **sovereign immunity** exempts foreign nations from the jurisdiction of the U.S. courts. In 1976, Congress codified this rule in the Foreign Sovereign Immunities Act (FSIA).[3]

The FSIA exclusively governs the circumstances in which an action may be brought in the United States against a foreign nation, including attempts to attach a foreign nation's property. Because the law is jurisdictional in nature, a plaintiff generally has the burden of showing that a defendant is not entitled to sovereign immunity.

When a Foreign State Will Not Be Immune. Section 1605 of the FSIA sets forth the major exceptions to the jurisdictional immunity of a foreign state. A foreign state is not immune from the jurisdiction of U.S. courts in the following situations:

1. When the foreign state has waived its immunity either explicitly or by implication.
2. When the foreign state has engaged in commercial activity within the United States or in commercial activity outside the United States that has "a direct effect in the United States."
3. When the foreign state has committed a tort in the United States or has violated certain international laws.
4. When a foreign state that has been designated "a state sponsor of terrorism" is sued under the FSIA for "personal injury or death that was caused by an act of torture" or a related act of terrorism.

The following case involved an action against a foreign state that had been held liable under the FSIA's exception from immunity for acts of terrorism.

---

1. *Goldberg v. UBS AG*, 690 F.Supp.2d 92 (E.D.N.Y. 2010). For another case on the financing of terrorism and the Anti-Terrorism Act, see *Linde v. Arab Bank, PLC*, 706 F.3d 92 (2d Cir. 2013).
2. *Spectrum Stores, Inc. v. Citgo Petroleum Corp.*, 632 F.3d 938 (5th Cir. 2011).

3. 28 U.S.C. Sections 1602–1611.

Bennett v. Islamic Republic of Iran

United States Court of Appeals, Ninth Circuit, __ F.3d __, 2016 WL 3257780 (2016).

In the Language of the Court

GRABER, Circuit Judge:

* * * *

Approximately 90 United States citizens (or the representatives of their estates) are attempting to collect on unsatisfied money judgments that they hold against the Islamic Republic of Iran for deaths and injuries suffered in terrorist attacks sponsored by Iran. The assets that are the subject of this * * * action are monies contractually owed to Bank Melli by Visa Inc. and Franklin Resources Inc. ("Franklin"). Bank Melli is an instrumentality of Iran [an entity controlled by Iran's government]. It asserts that Plaintiffs cannot execute on the assets because Bank Melli enjoys sovereign immunity under the Foreign Sovereign Immunities Act of 1976 ("FSIA").

* * * *

The FSIA establishes * * * that foreign states are immune from suit in United States courts. Congress enacted the statute to provide a comprehensive * * * set of legal standards governing claims of immunity in every civil action against a foreign state or its political subdivisions, agencies, or instrumentalities.

The FSIA includes many exceptions to its general rule of immunity. Relevant here, in 1996, Congress added a new exception, stripping a foreign state of its sovereign immunity when (1) the United States officially designates the foreign state a state sponsor of terrorism and (2) the foreign state is sued "for personal injury or death that was caused by an act of torture, extrajudicial killing, aircraft sabotage, hostage taking, or the provision of material support or resources for such an act."

Iran was designated a terrorist party [by the U.S. Department of State]. That designation means that Iran is not entitled to sovereign immunity for claims under [the FSIA].

* * * *

* * * In 2008, Congress * * * added [Section 1610(g)] to the FSIA, which provides in part that

the property of a foreign state against which a judgment is entered under [FSIA] Section 1605A and the property of an agency or instrumentality of such a state * * * is subject to attachment * * * and execution upon that judgment.

* * * *

[Maria Bennett was an American student at Hebrew University in Jerusalem when she was killed in a terrorist attack sponsored by Iran. Her parents, Michael and Linda Bennett,] obtained a judgment [against Iran in a federal district court] for damages of nearly $13 million for Iran's role in the [attack].

Bank Melli, Iran's largest financial institution, is wholly owned by the government of Iran. It is undisputed that Bank Melli qualifies as an instrumentality of Iran under the FSIA.

Visa and Franklin owe about $17.6 million to Bank Melli pursuant to a commercial relationship that involves the use of Visa credit cards in Iran. [The Bennetts] filed a complaint [in a federal district court] against Visa and Franklin, seeking to attach and execute against [the legal process of seizing property to ensure satisfaction of a debt] the * * * assets. Visa and Franklin responded by * * * naming as defendant Bank Melli * * * . Bank Melli * * * moved to dismiss the action.

* * * The district court denied the motion to dismiss. [Bank Melli appealed.]

* * * *

* * * Bank Melli argues that its assets cannot be attached or executed upon because the assets at issue in this case were not "used for a commercial activity in the United States," a requirement in FSIA Section 1610(a), and Bank Melli has not itself "engaged in commercial

activity in the United States," a requirement in Section 1610(b). We are not persuaded.

We hold that Section 1610(g) contains a freestanding provision for attaching and executing against assets of a foreign state or its agencies or instrumentalities. Section 1610(g) covers a different subject than Sections 1610(a) [and (b)]; by its express terms, it applies only to certain actions, specifically, judgments "entered under Section 1605A." In turn, *Section 1605A revokes sovereign immunity for damages claims against a foreign state for personal injury or death caused by "torture, extrajudicial killing, aircraft sabotage, hostage taking, or the provision of material support" for such an act.* By definition, such claims do not arise from commercial activity; they arise from acts of torture (and the like). Section 1610(g) requires only that a judgment under Section 1605A have been rendered against the foreign state; in that event, both the property of the foreign state and the property of an agency or instrumentality of that state are subject to attachment and execution. [Emphasis added.]

* * * *

* * * If Section 1610(g) is interpreted to require that, to be subject to attachment and execution, property must be used by the foreign state for a commercial activity, or that the instrumentality must be engaged in commercial activity in the United States, then we would have to read into Section 1610(g) a limitation that Congress did not insert. * * * Congress did not limit the type of property subject to attachment and execution under Section 1610(g) to property connected to commercial activity in the United States. The only requirement is that property be "the property of" the foreign state or its instrumentality.

Case 24.1 Continues

Case 24.1 Continued

* * * *

* * * It is quite clear that [in adding Section 1610(g) to the FSIA] Congress meant to expand successful plaintiffs' options for collecting judgments against state sponsors of terrorism.

* * * *

We hold [that] Section 1610(g) authorizes attachment and execution of the monies owed to Bank Melli. AFFIRMED.

Legal Reasoning Questions

1. Could Bank Melli have successfully argued that Section 1610(g) does not permit the attachment and execution of the assets sought by the Bennetts because those assets are owned by Visa and Franklin, not the bank?

2. Why did Congress create an exception from immunity under the FSIA for foreign state sponsors of terrorism?

3. The Treaty of Amity between the United States and Iran requires that the United States respect the legal status of Iranian companies and protect their property in accord with international law. The treaty also prohibits the U.S. government from discriminating against Iranian companies. Does this treaty conflict with Section 1610(g)? Discuss.

Application of the Act. When courts apply the FSIA, questions frequently arise as to whether an entity is a "foreign state" and what constitutes a "commercial activity." Under Section 1603 of the FSIA, a *foreign state* includes both a political subdivision of a foreign state and an instrumentality of a foreign state. An *instrumentality* includes any department or agency of any branch of a government.

Section 1603 broadly defines a *commercial activity* as a regular course of commercial conduct, a transaction, or an act that is carried out by a foreign state within the United States. Section 1603, however, does not describe the particulars of what constitutes a commercial activity.

Thus, the courts are left to decide whether a particular activity is governmental or commercial in nature.

See Exhibit 24–2 for a graphic illustration of the three principles of international law just discussed.

24–2 Doing Business Internationally

A U.S. domestic firm can engage in international business transactions in a number of ways. The simplest way

EXHIBIT 24–2 Examples of International Principles and Doctrines

THE PRINCIPLE OF COMITY	THE ACT OF STATE DOCTRINE	THE DOCTRINE OF SOVEREIGN IMMUNITY
Nations will defer to and give effect to the laws and judicial decrees of other nations when those laws are consistent with their own.	U.S. courts will avoid passing judgment on the validity of public acts committed by a recognized foreign government within its own territory.	Foreign nations are immune from U.S. jurisdiction under the Foreign Sovereign Immunities Act when certain circumstances are satisfied. Some major exceptions apply, however.
Example: A U.S. court will most likely uphold the validity of a contract created in England, because England's legal procedures are compatible with those in the United States.	*Example:* A U.S. gas company files a lawsuit against a Saudi Arabian petroleum company, claiming a price-fixing conspiracy. A U.S. court will dismiss the case under the act of state doctrine because Saudi Arabia controls its own natural resources.	*Example:* A German governmental agency engages in commercial activity in New York. If a party in New York files a lawsuit against the agency, the foreign state is not immune from U.S. jurisdiction.

is for U.S. firms to **export** their goods and services to foreign markets. Alternatively, a U.S. firm can establish foreign production facilities to be closer to the foreign market or markets in which its products are sold. The advantages may include lower labor costs, fewer government regulations, and lower taxes and trade barriers. A domestic firm can also obtain revenues by licensing its technology to an existing foreign company or by selling franchises to overseas entities. (In some situations,

domestic companies have profited by marketing goods, such as beer, as "imported," when it is not, as discussed in this chapter's *Ethics Today* feature.)

24–2a Exporting

Exporting can take two forms: direct exporting and indirect exporting. Companies that export indirectly can make use of agency relationships or distributorships.

ETHICS TODAY

Is It Ethical (and Legal) to Brew "Imported" Beer Brands Domestically?

Imported beer represents over a quarter of total beer purchases in the United States. While imported beer generally costs more than domestic beer, those who purchase and consume it believe that its superior taste justifies the higher price.

When Imported Beer Really Isn't Imported

The label on Beck's beer says: "German quality." But for a number of years, Beck's has been brewed in St. Louis, Missouri. The ads for Foster's feature Australian countryside scenes and Australian accents. Foster's is brewed in Fort Worth, Texas. Killian's Irish Red is not brewed in Ireland. It is brewed in Colorado. Kirin sells itself as Japanese, but it is not made in Asia. It is brewed in Virginia and Southern California. The Japanese beer Sapporo that is sold in the United States is actually brewed in Canada.

A Violation of Country-of-Origin Labeling

A number of lawsuits have been filed against the owners of imported beer brands brewed in the United States. Many of them have been class actions brought under state consumer protection laws involving country-of-origin labeling violations. One was filed against Anheuser-Busch Companies, LLC, for mislabeling the origin of its "imported" beers.[a] Attorneys for the plaintiffs argued that labels such as "brewed under the German Purity Law of 1516" and "originated in Bremen, German" were misleading, given that the beer was brewed in the United States. The defendants

argued that text on each bottle stated that the beer was a "Product of U.S.A." The case was ultimately settled out of court. Under the settlement, purchasers of Beck's beer could apply for up to $50 in refunds.

Other class action suits have been brought against other owners of imported beer brands. For example, a New York resident is suing Miller Brewing Company as part of a class action over the fact that its Foster's beer is not made in Australia. The brewing company argues that "it even employs an Australian brew master so that the beer taste is as true to its origin as possible."

Country-of-Origin Labeling Lawsuits Can Go Both Ways

Ironically, Anheuser-Busch is defending a class action lawsuit in California concerning a beer labeled as a product of the United States. The plaintiffs allege that the company has misled consumers by labeling Busch beer a U.S. product even though it is made with imported hops. This is a purported violation of the California Business and Professional Code. The code prohibits the use of an unqualified U.S.-origin claim when 100 percent of the product is not of U.S. origin.[b]

Critical Thinking *Imported beer is not the only product whose labeling may be misleading. For instance, although BMW is a German brand, most BMW X3s and X5s purchased in the United States are actually manufactured in South Carolina. Are there any legal or ethical issues involved?*

---

a. *Marty v. Anheuser-Busch Companies, LLC,* Case No. 1:13-cv-23656, U.S. District Court for the Southern District of Florida.

b. *Nixon v. Anheuser-Busch Companies, LLC,* Case No. CGC-15-544985, Superior Court of California for the County of San Francisco.

Direct versus Indirect Exporting In *direct exporting,* a U.S. company signs a sales contract with a foreign purchaser that provides for the conditions of shipment and payment for the goods.

If sufficient business develops in a foreign country, a U.S. company may establish a specialized marketing organization there by appointing a foreign agent or a foreign distributor. This is called *indirect exporting.*

Agency Relationships versus Distributorships
When a U.S. firm engaged in indirect exporting wishes to limit its involvement in an international market, it will typically establish an *agency relationship* with a foreign firm. The foreign firm then acts as the U.S. firm's agent and can enter contracts in the foreign location on behalf of the principal (the U.S. company).

When a foreign country represents a substantial market, a U.S. firm may wish to appoint a distributor located in that country. The U.S. firm and the distributor enter into a **distribution agreement.** This is a contract setting out the terms and conditions of the distributorship, such as price, currency of payment, guarantee of supply availability, and method of payment. Disputes concerning distribution agreements may involve jurisdictional or other issues, as well as contract law.

24–2b Manufacturing Abroad

An alternative to direct or indirect exporting is the establishment of foreign manufacturing facilities. Typically, U.S. firms establish manufacturing plants abroad when they believe that by doing so they will reduce costs. Costs for labor, shipping, and raw materials may be lower in foreign nations, which can enable the business to compete more effectively in foreign markets.

Foreign firms have done the same in the United States. Sony, Nissan, and other Japanese manufacturers, for instance, have established U.S. plants to avoid import duties that the U.S. Congress may impose on Japanese products entering this country.

There are several ways in which an American firm can manufacture in other countries. They include licensing and franchising, as well as investing in a wholly owned subsidiary or a joint venture.

Licensing A U.S. firm may license a foreign manufacturing company to use its copyrighted, patented, or trademarked intellectual property or trade secrets. Basically, licensing allows the foreign firm to use an established

brand name for a fee. A licensing agreement with a foreign-based firm is much the same as any other licensing agreement. Its terms require a payment of royalties on some basis—such as so many cents per unit produced or a certain percentage of profits from units sold in a particular geographic territory.

■ **EXAMPLE 24.5** The Coca-Cola Bottling Company licenses firms worldwide to use (and keep confidential) its secret formula for the syrup in its soft drink. In return, the company receives a percentage of the income earned from the sale of Coca-Cola by those firms. ■

The firm that receives the license can take advantage of an established reputation for quality. The firm that grants the license receives income from the foreign sales of its products and also establishes a global reputation. Once a firm's trademark is known worldwide, the demand for other products manufactured or sold by that firm may increase—obviously, an important consideration.

Franchising Franchising is a well-known form of licensing and is evident the world over. The owner of a trademark, trade name, or copyright (the franchisor) licenses another (the franchisee) to use the mark, name, or copyright, under certain conditions, in the selling of goods or services. Franchising allows the franchisor to maintain greater control over the business operation than is possible with most other licensing agreements. In return, the franchisee pays a fee, usually based on a monthly percentage of gross or net sales. Examples of international franchises include Holiday Inn and Hertz.

Subsidiaries Another way to expand into a foreign market is to establish a wholly owned subsidiary firm in a foreign country. In many European countries, a subsidiary would likely take the form of a *société anonyme* (S.A.), which is similar to a U.S. corporation. In German-speaking nations, it would be called an *Aktiengesellschaft* (A.G.). When a wholly owned subsidiary is established, the parent company remains in the United States. The parent maintains complete ownership of all of the facilities in the foreign country, as well as total authority and control over all phases of the operation.

Joint Ventures A U.S. firm can also expand into international markets through a *joint venture.* In a joint venture, the U.S. company owns only part of the operation. The rest is owned either by local owners in the foreign country or by another foreign entity. All of the firms involved in a joint venture share responsibilities, as well as profits and liabilities.

24–3 Regulation of Specific Business Activities

Doing business abroad can affect the economies, foreign policies, domestic politics, and other national interests of the countries involved. For this reason, nations impose laws to restrict or facilitate international business. Controls may also be imposed by international agreements.

24–3a Investment Protections

Firms that invest in foreign nations face the risk that the foreign government may expropriate the investment property. Expropriation, as mentioned earlier in this chapter, occurs when property is taken and the owner is paid just compensation for what is taken. This generally does not violate accepted principles of international law.

Confiscating property without compensation (or without adequate compensation), in contrast, normally violates international law. Few remedies are available for confiscation of property by a foreign government. Claims are often resolved by lump-sum settlements after negotiations between the United States and the taking nation.

Because the possibility of confiscation may deter potential investors, many countries guarantee compensation to foreign investors if their property is taken. A guaranty can be in the form of national constitutional or statutory laws or provisions in international treaties. As further protection for foreign investments, some countries provide insurance for their citizens' investments abroad.

24–3b Export Controls

Article I, Section 9, of the U.S. Constitution provides that "No Tax or Duty shall be laid on Articles exported from any State." Thus, Congress cannot impose any export taxes.

Congress can, however, use a variety of other devices to restrict or encourage exports, including the following:

1. *Export quotas.* Congress sets export **quotas,** or limits, on various items, such as grain being sold abroad.
2. *Restrictions on technology exports.* Under the Export Administration Act of 1979,[4] the flow of technologically advanced products and technical data can be restricted.
3. *Incentives and subsidies.* The United States (and other nations) also uses incentives and subsidies to

stimulate exports and thereby aid domestic businesses. ■ **EXAMPLE 24.6** The Export Trading Company Act[5] encouraged U.S. banks to invest in export trading companies, which are formed when exporting firms join together to export a line of goods. The Export-Import Bank of the United States provides financial assistance, primarily in the form of credit guaranties given to commercial bank, which in turn lend funds to U.S. exporting companies. ■

24–3c Import Controls

All nations have restrictions on imports, and the United States is no exception. Restrictions include strict prohibitions, quotas, and tariffs.

Prohibitions Under the Trading with the Enemy Act,[6] no goods may be imported from nations that have been designated enemies of the United States. Other laws prohibit the importation of illegal drugs, of agricultural products that pose dangers to domestic crops or animals, and of goods that infringe on U.S. patents. The International Trade Commission is the government agency that investigates allegations that imported goods infringe U.S. patents and imposes penalties if necessary.

Quotas and Tariffs Limits on the amounts of goods that can be imported are known as import quotas. At one time, the United States had legal quotas on the number of automobiles that could be imported from Japan. Today, Japan "voluntarily" restricts the number of automobiles exported to the United States.

Tariffs are taxes on imports. A tariff is usually a percentage of the value of the import, but it can be a flat rate per unit (such as per barrel of oil). Tariffs raise the prices of imported goods, causing some consumers to purchase domestically manufactured goods instead of imports.

Antidumping Duties The United States has laws specifically directed at what it sees as unfair international trade practices. **Dumping,** for example, is the sale of imported goods at "less than fair value." Foreign firms that engage in dumping in the United States hope to undersell U.S. businesses and obtain a larger share of the U.S. market. To prevent this, an extra tariff—known as an *antidumping duty*—may be assessed on the imports.

---

4. 50 U.S.C. Sections 2401–2420.

5. 15 U.S.C. Sections 4001, 4003.
6. 12 U.S.C. Section 95a.

Two U.S. government agencies are instrumental in imposing antidumping duties: the International Trade Commission (ITC) and the International Trade Administration (ITA). The ITC assesses the effects of dumping on domestic businesses and then makes recommendations to the president concerning temporary import restrictions. The ITA, which is part of the Department of Commerce, decides whether imports were sold at less than fair value.

Fair value is usually determined by the domestic price of the goods in the exporting country. The ITA's determination of fair value establishes the amount of the antidumping duties. These duties are set to equal the difference between the price charged in the United States and the price charged in the exporting country. A duty may be retroactive to cover past dumping.

24–3d Minimizing Trade Barriers

Restrictions on imports are also known as *trade barriers.* The elimination of trade barriers is sometimes seen as essential to the world's economic well-being. Various regional trade agreements and associations also help to minimize trade barriers between nations.

The World Trade Organization Most of the world's leading trading nations are members of the World Trade Organization (WTO), which was established in 1995. To minimize trade barriers among nations, each member country is required to grant **normal trade relations (NTR) status** to other member countries. This means that each member must treat other members at least as well as it treats the country that receives its most favorable treatment with regard to imports or exports.

The European Union (EU) The European Union (EU) arose out of the 1957 Treaty of Rome. The treaty created the Common Market, a free trade zone comprising the nations of Belgium, France, Italy, Luxembourg, the Netherlands, and West Germany. Today, the EU is a single integrated trading unit made up of twenty-seven European nations.

The EU has gone a long way toward creating a new body of law to govern all of the member nations. Its governing authorities issue regulations, or directives, that define EU law in various areas, such as environmental law, product liability, anticompetitive practices, and corporations. The directives normally are binding on all member countries. Nevertheless, some of the EU's efforts to create uniform laws have been confounded by nationalism.

The North American Free Trade Agreement (NAFTA) The North American Free Trade Agreement (NAFTA) created a regional trading unit consisting of Canada, Mexico, and the United States. The goal of NAFTA was to eliminate tariffs among these three nations on substantially all goods by reducing the tariffs incrementally over a period of time.

NAFTA gives the three countries a competitive advantage by retaining tariffs on goods imported from countries outside the NAFTA trading unit. Additionally, NAFTA provides for the elimination of barriers that traditionally have prevented the cross-border movement of services, such as financial and transportation services. NAFTA also attempts to eliminate citizenship requirements for the licensing of accountants, attorneys, physicians, and other professionals.

The Central America–Dominican Republic–United States Free Trade Agreement (CAFTA-DR) The Central America–Dominican Republic–United States Free Trade Agreement (CAFTA-DR) was formed by Costa Rica, the Dominican Republic, El Salvador, Guatemala, Honduras, Nicaragua, and the United States. Its purpose is to reduce trade tariffs and improve market access among all of the signatory nations. Legislatures from all seven countries have approved the CAFTA-DR, despite significant opposition in certain nations.

The Republic of Korea–United States Free Trade Agreement (KORUS FTA) The United States ratified its first free trade agreement with South Korea in 2011 called the Republic of Korea–United States Free Trade Agreement (KORUS FTA). Provisions in KORUS are aimed at eliminating 95 percent of each nation's tariffs on industrial and consumer exports from the other nation.

KORUS was the largest free trade agreement that the United States had entered into since NAFTA. It was expected to boost U.S. exports and benefit U.S. automakers, farmers, ranchers, and manufacturers by enabling them to compete in new markets. To date, however, exports have not increased as much as predicted.

The Trans-Pacific Partnership (TPP) The United States negotiated a 2015 trade agreement among twelve Pacific Rim countries called the Trans-Pacific Partnership

(TPP).[7] The agreement is aimed at increasing U.S. exports to China, Japan, and other Asian nations and eliminating or decreasing tariffs charged by those nations.

For instance, according to the United States Trade Office, 20 percent of U.S. farm income (roughly $150 billion) comes from agricultural exports, and one-third of those exports are to TPP countries. Yet, in the past, nations like Malaysia charged a 40 percent tariff on U.S. poultry. The TPP will eliminate almost all tariffs on U.S. farm products and textiles.

The TPP contains thirty chapters. Some of them are aimed at addressing new trade challenges, such as protecting intellectual property rights and setting rules on digital trade. Others contain provisions that protect workers, as well as the environment. Still others deal with expediting customs procedures and establishing dispute settlement procedures.

Other Free Trade Agreements Congress has also ratified free trade agreements with Colombia and Panama. The Colombian trade agreement includes a provision requiring an exchange of tax information, and the Panama bill incorporates assurances on labor rights.

24–4 International Dispute Resolution

International contracts frequently include arbitration clauses. By means of such clauses, the parties agree in advance to be bound by the decision of a specified third party in the event of a dispute.

24–4a The New York Convention

The United Nations Convention on the Recognition and Enforcement of Foreign Arbitral Awards (often referred to as the New York Convention) assists in the enforcement of arbitration clauses. (Specific treaties among nations may also include such provisions.) Basically, the convention requires courts in nations that have signed it to honor private agreements to arbitrate and recognize arbitration awards made in other con-

tracting states. The New York Convention has been implemented in nearly one hundred countries, including the United States.

Under the New York Convention, a court will compel the parties to arbitrate their dispute if all of the following are true:

1. There is a written (or recorded) agreement to arbitrate the matter.
2. The agreement provides for arbitration in a convention signatory nation.
3. The agreement arises out of a commercial legal relationship.
4. One party to the agreement is not a U.S. citizen. In other words, both parties cannot be U.S. citizens.

■ **CASE IN POINT 24.7** Juridica Investments, Ltd. (JIL), entered into a financing contract with S & T Oil Equipment & Machinery, Ltd., a U.S. company. The contract was signed and performed in Guernsey, which is a British Crown dependency in the English Channel. It included an arbitration clause. When a dispute arose between the parties, JIL initiated arbitration in Guernsey, and S & T filed a suit in a U.S. court. JIL filed a motion to dismiss in favor of arbitration, which the court granted. S & T appealed. A federal appellate court affirmed and compelled arbitration under the New York Convention.[8] ■

24–4b Effect of Choice-of-Law and Forum-Selection Clauses

If a sales contract does not include an arbitration clause, litigation may occur. When the contract contains forum-selection and choice-of-law clauses, the lawsuit will be heard by a court in the specified forum and decided according to that forum's law.

As you may recall, a *forum-selection clause* indicates what court, jurisdiction, or tribunal will decide any disputes arising under the contract. A *choice-of-law clause* designates the applicable law. Both are useful additions to international contracts.

In the following case, the court considered whether a party that had not signed a forum-selection clause was bound to it.

---

7. You can read this agreement on the United States Trade Representative's Web site at **ustr.gov/trade-agreements/free-trade-agreements/ trans-pacific-partnership/TPP-Full-Text.**

8. *S & T Oil Equipment & Machinery, Ltd. v. Juridica Investments, Ltd.,* 456 Fed.Appx. 481 (5th Cir. 2012).

Carlyle Investment Management, LLC v. Moonmouth Co. SA

United States Court of Appeals, Third Circuit, 779 F.3d 214 (2015).

Background and Facts Moonmouth Co. SA bought stock in Carlyle Capital Corp., Ltd. (CCC), an investment fund, under a subscription agreement. Moonmouth was incorporated in the British Virgin Islands, and CCC was incorporated in Guernsey, a dependency of the United Kingdom. Carlyle Investment Management, LLC, which owned CCC, signed the agreement on CCC's behalf. Plaza Management Overseas SA signed on Moonmouth's behalf. Plaza was Moonmouth's director, and both were owned by Louis Reijtenbagh.

The agreement provided that "the courts of the State of Delaware shall have exclusive jurisdiction over any action . . . with respect to this Subscription Agreement." Later, the global financial crisis depleted CCC's cash reserves, and CCC entered liquidation (the process of liquidating its assets). Plaza then threatened to hold CCC liable for all damages that Moonmouth had sustained in connection with its investment. Carlyle and its owners filed a suit in a Delaware state court against Plaza and its owner to enforce the forum-selection clause. Plaza sought to move the case to a federal district court. That court remanded the case to the state court. Plaza appealed.

In the Language of the Court

ROTH, Circuit Judge:

* * * *

Delaware courts have set forth a three-part test for determining whether a non-signatory to an agreement should be bound by its forum-selection clause: (1) is the forum-selection clause valid, (2) is the non-signatory a third-party beneficiary of the agreement or closely related to the agreement, and (3) does the claim at hand arise from the non-signatory's status related to the agreement?

For the first element, forum-selection clauses are presumed to be valid. *The clause is considered valid unless the challenging party clearly shows that enforcement would be unreasonable and unjust, or that the clause is invalid for such reasons as fraud or overreaching.* [Emphasis added.]

With respect to the second element, even if defendants are not parties to the agreement or third-party beneficiaries of it, they may be bound by the forum-selection clause if they are closely related to the agreement in such a way that it would be foreseeable that they would be bound. In determining whether a non-signatory is closely related to a contract, courts consider the non-signatory's ownership of the signatory, its involvement in the negotiations, the relationship between the two parties and whether the non-signatory received a direct benefit from the agreement.

* * * Plaza was Moonmouth's director and it executed the Subscription Agreement on Moonmouth's behalf. Plaza and Moonmouth are affiliated entities that are both owned and controlled by [Louis] Reijtenbagh. * * * Negotiations related to the Subscription Agreement were conducted by Moonmouth, Plaza, and Reijtenbagh. The Subscription Agreement states that the "source of funds" for Moonmouth's investment in CCC was Plaza's income. * * * Thus, * * * the three parties were closely related to the Subscription Agreement.

* * * *

The third issue we consider in determining whether the forum clause may be enforced is whether the claims against defendants arise from their status relating to the agreement.

* * * *

Here, Carlyle's claims stem from Moonmouth's initial investment in CCC. * * * The defendants would not have any claims * * * but for the original Subscription Agreement that contains the forum-selection clause. It is clear that the relationship between plaintiffs and defendants * * * stem from the Subscription Agreement. Thus, the claims are "with respect to" the Subscription Agreement.

Decision and Remedy *The U.S. Court of Appeals for the Third Circuit affirmed the lower court's remand of the case to state court. Plaza was not a signatory to the subscription agreement but was held bound by the forum-selection clause because the clause was valid. Plaza was "closely related to the agreement," and the claim arose from Plaza's status related to it.*

Critical Thinking

- **Legal Environment** *Would Plaza have been bound to the forum-selection clause if it had signed the subscription agreement as Moonmouth's director but had no other relation to the agreement? Discuss.*

24–5 U.S. Laws in a Global Context

The globalization of business raises questions about the extraterritorial application of a nation's laws—that is, the effect of the country's laws outside its boundaries. To what extent do U.S. domestic laws apply to other nations' businesses? To what extent do U.S. domestic laws apply to U.S. firms doing business abroad? Here, we discuss the extraterritorial application of certain U.S. laws, including antitrust laws, tort laws, and laws prohibiting employment discrimination.

24–5a U.S. Antitrust Laws

U.S. antitrust laws have a wide application. They may *subject* firms in foreign nations to their provisions, as well as *protect* foreign consumers and competitors from violations committed by U.S. citizens. Section 1 of the Sherman Act—the most important U.S. antitrust law—provides for the extraterritorial effect of the U.S. antitrust laws.

Any conspiracy that has a *substantial effect* on U.S. commerce is within the reach of the Sherman Act. The law applies even if the violation occurs outside the United States, and foreign governments as well as businesses can be sued for violations. Before U.S. courts will exercise jurisdiction and apply antitrust laws, however, it must be shown that the alleged violation had a substantial effect on U.S. commerce.

■ **EXAMPLE 24.8** An investigation by the U.S. government revealed that a Tokyo-based auto-parts supplier, Furukawa Electric Company, and its executives had conspired with competitors in an international price-fixing agreement. The agreement lasted more than ten years and resulted in automobile manufacturers' paying noncompetitive, higher prices for parts in cars sold to U.S. consumers. Because the conspiracy had a substantial effect on U.S. commerce, the United States had jurisdiction to prosecute the case. In 2011, Furukawa agreed to plead guilty and pay a $200 million fine. The Furukawa executives from Japan also agreed to serve up to eighteen months in a U.S. prison and to cooperate fully with the ongoing investigation. ■

24–5b International Tort Claims

The international application of tort liability is growing in significance and controversy. An increasing number of U.S. plaintiffs are suing foreign (or U.S.) entities for torts that these entities have allegedly committed overseas. Often, these cases involve human rights violations by foreign governments.

The Alien Tort Claims Act (ATCA)[9] allows even foreign citizens to bring civil suits in U.S. courts for injuries caused by violations of the law of nations or a treaty of the United States. Foreign plaintiffs have increasingly used this act to bring actions against companies operating in nations such as Colombia, Ecuador, Egypt, Guatemala, India, Indonesia, Nigeria, and Saudi Arabia.[10] Some of these cases have involved alleged environmental destruction. Others have involved human rights violations and oppressive government regimes.

In the following *Spotlight Case,* the United States Supreme Court considers the parameters of the ATCA. The question is whether the statute allows U.S. courts to exercise jurisdiction over a cause of action based on conduct that occurred outside the United States.

---

9. 28 U.S.C. Section 1350.
10. See, for example, *Kiobel v. Royal Dutch Petroleum Co.*, __ U.S. __, 133 S.Ct. 1659, 185 L.Ed. 671 (2013) on atrocities committed in Nigeria; and *Khulumani v. Barclay National Bank, Ltd.*, 504 F.3d 254 (2007) on South Africa's apartheid regime.

Spotlight on International Torts

Case 24.3 Daimler AG[a] v. Bauman

Supreme Court of the United States, __ U.S. __, 134 S.Ct. 746, 187 L.Ed.2d 624 (2014).

Background and Facts Barbara Bauman and twenty-one other residents of Argentina filed a suit in a federal district court in California against Daimler AG, a German company. They alleged that Mercedes-Benz (MB) Argentina, a subsidiary of Daimler, had collaborated with state security forces to kidnap, detain, torture, and kill certain MB Argentina workers. These workers included the plaintiffs and some of their relatives. Their claims were asserted under the Alien Tort Claims Act.

---

a. The initials *A.G.* stand for "Automotive Group."

Continues

Case 24.3 Continued   Personal jurisdiction was based on the California contacts of Mercedes-Benz USA (MBUSA), a Daimler subsidiary incorporated in Delaware with its principal place of business in New Jersey. MBUSA distributes Daimler-made vehicles to dealerships throughout the United States, including California. The district court dismissed the suit for lack of jurisdiction. The U.S. Court of Appeals for the Ninth Circuit reversed this ruling. Daimler appealed to the United States Supreme Court.

In the Language of the Court

Justice *GINSBURG* delivered the opinion of the Court.

* * * *

Even if we were to assume that MBUSA is at home in California, and further to assume MBUSA's contacts are imputable [attributable] to Daimler, there would still be no basis to subject Daimler to general jurisdiction in California, for Daimler's slim contacts with the State hardly render it at home there.

* * * Only a limited set of affiliations with a forum will render a defendant amenable to all-purpose jurisdiction there. For an individual, the paradigm forum [the typical forum] for the exercise of general jurisdiction is the individual's domicile; for a corporation, it is an equivalent place, one in which the corporation is fairly regarded as at home. *With respect to a corporation, the place of incorporation and principal place of business are paradigm * * * bases for general jurisdiction.* Those affiliations have the virtue of being unique—that is, each ordinarily indicates only one place—as well as easily ascertainable. These bases afford plaintiffs recourse to at least one clear and certain forum in which a corporate defendant may be sued on any and all claims. [Emphasis added.]

[This does not mean] that a corporation may be subject to general jurisdiction *only* in a forum where it is incorporated or has its principal place of business * * * . [But] plaintiffs would have us look beyond the exemplar bases identified [above] and approve the exercise of general jurisdiction in every State in which a corporation engages in a substantial, continuous, and systematic course of business. That formulation, we hold, is unacceptably grasping.

* * * The inquiry * * * is not whether a foreign corporation's in-forum contacts can be said to be in some sense continuous and systematic; it is whether that corporation's affiliations with the State are so continuous and systematic as to render it essentially at home in the forum State.

Here, neither Daimler nor MBUSA is incorporated in California, nor does either entity have its principal place of business there. If Daimler's California activities sufficed to allow adjudication of this Argentina-rooted case in California, the same global reach would presumably be available in every other State in which MBUSA's sales are sizable. Such exorbitant exercises of all-purpose jurisdiction would scarcely permit out-of-state defendants to structure their primary conduct with some minimum assurance as to where that conduct will and will not render them liable to suit.

It was therefore [an] error for the Ninth Circuit to conclude that Daimler, even with MBUSA's contacts attributed to it, was at home in California, and hence subject to suit there on claims by foreign plaintiffs having nothing to do with anything that occurred or had its principal impact in California.

Decision and Remedy *The United States Supreme Court reversed the decision of the lower court. A federal district court in California could not exercise jurisdiction over Daimler in this case, given the absence of any California connection to the atrocities, perpetrators, or victims described in the complaint.*

Critical Thinking
- **Legal Environment** *What are the consequences for Daimler of the decision in this case?*
- **Global** *If the Court had adopted the plaintiffs' argument, how might U.S. citizens have been affected?*

24–5c Antidiscrimination Laws

As you probably know, federal laws in the United States prohibit discrimination on the basis of race, color, national origin, religion, gender, age, and disability. These laws, as they affect employment relationships, generally apply extraterritorially.

Thus, U.S. employees working abroad for U.S. employers are protected under the Age Discrimination in

Employment Act. Similarly, the Americans with Disabilities Act, which requires employers to accommodate the needs of workers with disabilities, applies to U.S. nationals working abroad for U.S. firms.

In addition, the major U.S. law regulating employment discrimination—Title VII of the Civil Rights Act—applies extraterritorially to all U.S. employees working for U.S. employers abroad. Generally, U.S. employers must abide by U.S. discrimination laws unless to do so would violate the laws of the country where their workplaces are located. This "foreign laws exception" allows employers to avoid being subjected to conflicting laws.

24–6 Space Law

Space law consists of the international and national laws that govern activities in outer space. For the first fifty years of space exploration, national governments conducted most of those activities. Thus, space law was directed primarily at governments and government activities. In the last decade, private companies have been preparing to undertake some space-related activities and open outer space to the rest of us. Space law, accordingly, faces new challenges.

24–6a International Space Law

International space law consists of international treaties—primarily negotiated by the United Nations (U.N.)—and U.N. resolutions. These sources recognize fundamentally that activities conducted in outer space and the benefits derived from those activities should improve the welfare of all nations and all humanity.

The major space law treaties were concluded by the U.N. Committee on the Peaceful Uses of Outer Space (COPUS). COPUS also administers the treaties and advises the international community on space policy matters.

Exploration and Exploitation The foundation of international space law is the U.N. Treaty on Principles Governing the Activities of States in the Exploration and Use of Outer Space, including the Moon and Other Celestial Bodies.[11] This treaty—generally referred to as the Outer Space Treaty—established the framework for later international agreements and U.N. resolutions.

The Outer Space Treaty expresses general principles that have been expanded and applied in subsequent treaties. In Article I and Article II, outer space is declared to be free for the exploration and use of all nations. The moon, the planets, asteroids, and other celestial bodies are not subject to the appropriation of any single nation.[12] In addition, space objects are to be used exclusively for peaceful purposes. No weapons of mass destruction are permitted in outer space under Article IV.[13]

According to Article VI, each nation is responsible for its activities in outer space, whether they are conducted by the government or by a private entity. In fact, the activities of private entities require authorization and supervision by a government. Article VIII provides that each nation retains jurisdiction and control over its space objects and the personnel on them. Article VII imposes on each nation liability for damage caused by its space objects. Finally, Article IX requires that space exploration be conducted so as to avoid "harmful contamination."[14]

Astronauts and Space Objects The Outer Space Treaty was followed by several other agreements:

- The Agreement on the Rescue of Astronauts, the Return of Astronauts and the Return of Objects Launched into Outer Space (the Rescue Agreement).[15]
- The Convention on International Liability for Damage Caused by Space Objects (the Liability Convention).[16]
- The Convention on Registration of Objects Launched into Outer Space (the Registration Convention).[17]

The Rescue Agreement expands on Articles V and VIII of the Outer Space Treaty. It provides that each nation will undertake to rescue and assist astronauts in distress and return them to their "launching State." All nations are to assist in recovering space objects that return to earth outside the territory of the launching state.

The Liability Convention elaborates on Article VII of the Outer Space Treaty. This agreement provides that a launching state is absolutely liable for personal injury and property damage caused by its space objects on the surface of the earth or to aircraft in flight. Liability for injury or damage in space is subject to a determination of fault. The convention also prescribes procedures for the settlement of claims for damages.

---

11. 18 U.S.T. 2410, T.I.A.S. 6347, 610 U.N.T.S. 205.

12. After the treaty entered into force, the United States and Russia conducted joint space activities.
13. Establishing military bases, testing weapons, and conducting military maneuvers are prohibited.
14. Other articles promote further international cooperation in the exploration and use of space.
15. 19 U.S.T. 7570, T.I.A.S. 6599, 672 U.N.T.S. 119.
16. 24 U.S.T. 2389, T.I.A.S. 7762, 961 U.N.T.S. 187.
17. 28 U.S.T. 695, T.I.A.S. 8480, 1023 U.N.T.S. 15.

The Registration Convention provides for the mandatory registration of objects launched into outer space. Each launching state is to maintain a registry of the objects that it launches into space. The intent is to assist in the objects' identification.

Space Debris An estimated 600,000 objects made by humans are in orbit around the earth. Most of these objects are no longer under any party's control and are classified as *space debris*. In 2009, two orbiting satellites collided for the first time. Fragments generated by collisions are expected to be a significant source of space debris in the future. As noted previously, the Liability Convention sets out principles of liability to apply in instances of injury or damage in space.

The U.N. has endorsed guidelines to reduce space debris.[18] The guidelines, which reflect the current practices of a number of national and international organizations, apply to the planning, design, manufacture, and operational phases of spacecraft. Among other points, the guidelines suggest that systems should be designed not to release debris during normal operations. They also recognize that some objects no longer in operation should be removed from orbit if this can be accomplished in a controlled manner.

24–6b U.S. Space Law

In the United States, each government agency that operates or authorizes spacecraft is responsible for complying with U.S. law and international treaties. Federal law, state law, and more than half a century of common practices in space-related industries also affect government and private space activities.

Commercial Spaceflight The Federal Aviation Administration (FAA) regulates private spaceports and the launch and reentry of private spacecraft under the Commercial Space Launch Act.[19]

The FAA is working to establish licensing and safety criteria for private spacecraft. Some states, including

Florida, New Mexico, Texas, and Virginia, limit the liability of space tourism providers under state tort law. But state legislatures and, ultimately, courts will need to consider other issues in this context, including insurance requirements and the enforceability of liability waivers.

In 2015, Congress passed landmark legislation aimed at encouraging commercial spaceflight companies. The U.S. Commercial Space Launch Competitiveness Act[20] streamlines regulatory processes and promotes safety standards. In addition, the new law provides that if a U.S. citizen or company retrieves minerals or other resources from an asteroid or other space location, that person or company owns them.

Exports of Space Technology Currently, under U.S. regulations, all spacecraft are classified as "defense articles." The defense classification restricts the transfer of space technology and related information to any foreign person or nation under the U.S. Department of State's International Traffic in Arms Regulations.[21] This restriction makes it difficult for U.S. space companies to compete in global space markets.

Property Rights to Space Resources Article II of the Outer Space Treaty bans the national appropriation of territory in space. If the United States cannot appropriate territory in space, then it cannot give U.S. citizens title to property associated with this territory. Under U.S. law, the government must have sovereignty over territory before it can confer title to associated property to its citizens.

Article VIII, however, provides that a state party to the treaty retains jurisdiction over objects on its space registry that are launched into space. In addition, Article IX prohibits interference with space activities. In effect, these provisions confer the protections associated with property rights on private space activities.

The 2015 U.S. Commercial Space Launch Competitiveness Act changed the law somewhat by granting private citizens property rights over asteroid resources that they obtain from space. The act specifically recognizes that the United States is not attempting to assert sovereignty or exclusive right or jurisdiction over any celestial body.

---

18. Space Debris Mitigation Guidelines of the Committee on the Peaceful Uses of Outer Space, G.A. Res. 62/217, U.N. GAOR, 50th Sess., U.N.Doc. A/62/20 (Dec. 22, 2007).
19. 51 U.S.C. Sections 50901 *et seq.*

20. Pub. L. No. 114-90, 129 Stat. 704, November 25, 2015.
21. 22 C.F.R. Sections 120.1 *et seq.*

Reviewing: International and Space Law

Robco, Inc., was a Florida arms dealer. The armed forces of Honduras contracted to purchase weapons from Robco over a six-year period. After the government was replaced and a democracy installed, the Honduran government sought to reduce the size of its military, and its relationship with Robco deteriorated. Honduras refused to honor the contract and purchase the inventory of arms, which Robco could sell only at a much lower price. Robco filed a suit in a federal district court in the United States to recover damages for this breach of contract by the government of Honduras. Using the information presented in the chapter, answer the following questions.

1. Should the Foreign Sovereign Immunities Act (FSIA) preclude this lawsuit? Why or why not?
2. Does the act of state doctrine bar Robco from seeking to enforce the contract? Explain.
3. Suppose that prior to this lawsuit, the new government of Honduras had enacted a law making it illegal to purchase weapons from foreign arms dealers. What doctrine of deference might lead a U.S. court to dismiss Robco's case in that situation?
4. Now suppose that the U.S. court hears the case and awards damages to Robco. The government of Honduras, however, has no assets in the United States that can be used to satisfy the judgment. Under which doctrine might Robco be able to collect the damages by asking another nation's court to enforce the U.S. judgment?

Debate This . . .   *The U.S. federal courts are accepting too many lawsuits initiated by foreigners that concern matters not relevant to this country.*

Terms and Concepts

act of state doctrine 442
civil law system 440
comity 441
confiscation 442
distribution agreement 446
dumping 447
export 445

expropriation 442
international law 439
international organization 440
national law 439
normal trade relations
   (NTR) status 448

quota 447
sovereign immunity 442
space law 453
tariff 447
treaty 440

Issue Spotters

1. Café Rojo, Ltd., an Ecuadoran firm, agrees to sell coffee beans to Dark Roast Coffee Company, a U.S. firm. Dark Roast accepts the beans but refuses to pay. Café Rojo sues Dark Roast in an Ecuadoran court and is awarded damages, but Dark Roast's assets are in the United States. Under what circumstances would a U.S. court enforce the judgment of the Ecuadoran court? (See *International Law.*)
2. Gems International, Ltd., is a foreign firm that has a 12 percent share of the U.S. market for diamonds. To capture a larger share, Gems offers its products at a below-cost discount to U.S. buyers (and inflates the prices in its own country to make up the difference). How can this attempt to undersell U.S. businesses be defeated? (See *Regulation of Specific Business Activities.*)

• **Check your answers to the Issue Spotters against the answers provided in Appendix D at the end of this text.**

Business Scenarios

24–1. Doing Business Internationally. Macrotech, Inc., develops an innovative computer chip and obtains a patent on it. The firm markets the chip under the trademarked brand name "Flash." Macrotech wants to sell the chip to Nitron, Ltd., in Pacifica, a foreign country. Macrotech is concerned, however, that after an initial purchase, Nitron will duplicate the chip, pirate it, and sell the pirated version to computer manufacturers in Pacifica. To avoid this possibility, Macrotech could establish its own manufacturing facility in Pacifica, but it does not want to do this. How can Macrotech, without establishing a manufacturing facility in Pacifica, protect Flash from being pirated by Nitron? (See *Doing Business Internationally*.)

24–2. Dumping. The U.S. pineapple industry alleged that producers of canned pineapple from the Philippines were selling their canned pineapple in the United States for less than its fair market value (dumping). In addition to canned pineapple, the Philippine producers exported other products, such as pineapple juice and juice concentrate. These products used separate parts of the same fresh pineapple used for the canned pineapple. All these products shared raw material costs with the canned fruit, according to the producers' own financial records. To determine fair value and antidumping duties, the pineapple industry argued that a court should calculate the Philippine producers' cost of production and allocate a portion of the shared fruit costs to the canned fruit. The result

of this allocation showed that more than 90 percent of the canned fruit sales were below the cost of production. Is this a reasonable approach to determining the production costs and fair market value of canned pineapple in the United States? Why or why not? (See *Regulation of Specific Business Activities*.)

24–3. Sovereign Immunity. Taconic Plastics, Ltd., is a manufacturer incorporated in Ireland with its principal place of business in New York. Taconic enters into a contract with a German firm, Werner Voss Architects and Engineers, acting as an agent for the government of Saudi Arabia. The contract calls for Taconic to supply special material for tents designed to shelter religious pilgrims visiting holy sites in Saudi Arabia. Most of the material is made in, and shipped from, New York. The German company does not pay Taconic and files for bankruptcy. Taconic files a suit in a U.S. Court against the government of Saudi Arabia, seeking to collect $3 million. The defendant files a motion to dismiss the suit based on the doctrine of sovereign immunity. Under what circumstances does this doctrine apply? What are its exceptions? Should this suit be dismissed? Explain. (See *International Law*.)

Business Case Problems

24–4. Dumping. Nuclear power plants use low-enriched uranium (LEU) as a fuel. LEU consists of feed uranium enriched by energy to a certain assay—the percentage of the isotope necessary for a nuclear reaction. The amount of energy required is described by an industry standard as a "separative work unit" (SWU). A nuclear utility may buy LEU from an enricher, or the utility may provide an enricher with feed uranium and pay for the SWUs necessary to produce LEU. Under an SWU contract, the LEU returned to the utility may not be exactly the uranium the utility provided. This is because feed uranium is fungible and trades like a commodity (such as wheat or corn), and profitable enrichment requires the constant processing of undifferentiated stock. Foreign enrichers, including Eurodif, S.A., allegedly exported LEU to the United States and sold it for "less than fair value." Did this constitute dumping? Explain. If so, what could be done to prevent it? [*United States v. Eurodif, S.A.*, 555 U.S. 305, 129 S.Ct. 878, 172 L.Ed.2d 679 (2009)] (See *Regulation of Specific Business Activities*.)

24–5. Sovereign Immunity. In 1954, the government of Bolivia began expropriating land from Francisco Loza for public projects, including an international airport. The government directed the payment of compensation in exchange for at least some of his land. But the government never paid the full amount. Decades later, his heirs, Genoveva and Marcel Loza, who were both U.S. citizens, filed a suit in a federal district court in the United States against the government of Bolivia. The Lozas sought damages for the taking. Can the court exercise jurisdiction? Explain. [*Santivanez v. Estado Plurinacional de Bolivia*, 512 Fed.Appx. 887 (11th Cir. 2013)] (See *International Law*.)

24–6. Business Case Problem with Sample Answer— Import Controls. The Wind Tower Trade Coalition is an association of domestic manufacturers of utility-scale wind towers. The coalition filed a suit in the U.S. Court of International Trade against the U.S. Department of Commerce. It challenged the Commerce Department's decision to impose only *prospective* antidumping duties, rather than *retrospective* (retroactive) duties, on imports of utility-scale wind towers from China and Vietnam. The department had found that the domestic industry had not suffered any "material injury" or "threat of material injury" from such imports. It had further found that the industry would be protected by a prospective assessment. Can an antidumping duty be assessed retrospectively? If so, should it be assessed here? Discuss. [*Wind Tower Trade Coalition v. United States*, 741 F.3d 89 (Fed.Cir. 2014)] (See *Regulation of Specific Business Activities*.)

- **For a sample answer to Problem 24–6, go to Appendix E at the end of this text.**

24–7. The Principle of Comity. Holocaust survivors and the heirs of Holocaust victims filed a suit in a U.S. federal district court against the Hungarian national railway, the Hungarian national bank, and several private Hungarian banks. The plaintiffs alleged that the defendants had participated in expropriating the property of Hungarian Jews who were victims of the Holocaust. The claims arose from events in Hungary seventy years ago. The plaintiffs, however, had not exhausted remedies available through Hungarian courts. Indeed, they had not even attempted to seek remedies in Hungarian courts, and they did not provide a legally compelling reason for their failure to do so. The defendants asked the court to dismiss the suit. Does the principle of comity support the defendants' request? Explain. [*Fischer v. Magyar Államvasutak Zrt.,* 777 F.3d 847 (7th Cir. 2015)] (See *International Law.*)

24–8. International Law. For fifty years, the Soviet Union made and sold Stolichnaya vodka. At the time, VVO-SPI, a Soviet state enterprise, licensed the Stolichnaya trademark in the United States. When the Soviet Union collapsed, VVO–SPI was purportedly privatized and fell under the control of Spirits International B.V. (SPI). In 2000, a Russian court held that VVO-SPI had not been validly privatized under Russian law. Thus, ownership of the Stolichnaya mark remained with the Soviet Union's successor, the Russian Federation. The Russian Federation assigned the mark to Federal Treasury Enterprise Sojuzplodoimport, OAO (FTE). FTE then filed a suit in a U.S. federal district court against SPI, asserting unlawful misappropriation and commercial exploitation of the mark in violation of the Lanham Act. Is the validity of the assignment of the mark to FTE a question to be determined by the court? Why or why not? [*Federal Treasury Enterprise Sojuzplodoimport v. Spirits International B.V.,* 809 F.3d 737 (2d Cir. 2016)] (See *International Law.*)

24–9. A Question of Ethics—Terrorism. *On December 21, 1988, Pan Am Flight 103 exploded 31,000 feet in the air over Lockerbie, Scotland. All 259 passengers and crew on board and 11 people on the ground were killed. Among those killed was Roger Hurst, a U.S. citizen. An investigation determined that a portable radiocassette player packed in a brown Samsonite suitcase smuggled onto the plane was the source of the explosion. The explosive device was constructed with a digital timer specially made for, and bought by, Libya. Abdel Basset Ali Al-Megrahi was convicted by the Scottish High Court of Justiciary on criminal charges that he had planned and executed the bombing.*

*Al-Megrahi was a Libyan government official, an employee of the Libyan Arab Airline (LAA), and purportedly a member of the Jamahiriya Security Organization (JSO), the Libyan intelligence service. Members of the victims' families filed a suit in a U.S. district court against the JSO, the LAA, Al-Megrahi, and others. The plaintiffs claimed violations of U.S. federal law, including the Anti-Terrorism Act, and state law, including the intentional infliction of emotional distress. [*Hurst v. Socialist People's Libyan Arab Jamahiriya, 474 F.Supp.2d 19 (D.D.C. 2007)]* (See *International Law.*)

(a) Under what doctrine, codified in which federal statute, might the defendants claim to be immune from the jurisdiction of a U.S. court? Should this law include an exception for "state-sponsored terrorism"? Why or why not?

(b) The defendants agreed to pay $2.7 billion, or $10 million per victim, to settle all claims for "compensatory death damages." The families of eleven victims, including Hurst, were excluded from the settlement because they were "not wrongful death beneficiaries under applicable state law." These plaintiffs continued the suit. The defendants filed a motion to dismiss. Should the motion be granted on the ground that the settlement bars the plaintiffs' claims? Explain.

Legal Reasoning Group Activity

24–10. Globalization. Assume that you are manufacturing iPad accessories and that your business is becoming more successful. You are now considering expanding operations into another country. (See *Doing Business Internationally.*)

(a) One group will explore the costs and benefits of advertising on the Internet.

(b) Another group will consider whether to take in a partner from a foreign nation and will explain the benefits and risks of having a foreign partner.

(c) A third group will discuss what problems may arise if a business chooses to manufacture in a foreign location.

Success in Global Commerce

Businesses and individuals in all nations and under all legal systems agree on the principle that promises must be fulfilled. The concept was expressed at the time of the Roman Empire by the Latin phrase *pacta sunt servanda*—"agreements must be kept."[1] An ongoing international system of trade and commerce is possible only if this principle is recognized and applied.

Common Standards

Private enterprise and free markets thrive when there is a predictable and widely accepted legal environment supporting commercial transactions. This facilitates economic growth, which leads to higher living standards and new opportunities for further expansion.

The United Nations Commission on International Trade Law (UNCITRAL) is a legal arm of the United Nations that focuses on international trade law. UNCITRAL's business is to harmonize the rules on global commerce. To this end, UNCITRAL has issued conventions and model international laws. Conventions are designed to establish binding legal obligations. Model laws are recommendations for individual nations to adopt as part of their national law.

International Sales of Goods The United Nations Convention on Contracts for the International Sale of Goods (CISG) provides certainty in global commercial transactions between private businesses located in different countries.[2] As discussed in selected chapters throughout Unit Four, the CISG provides uniform rules for international sales of goods, just as the Uniform Commercial Code governs domestic sales contracts in the United States.[3] The CISG is complemented by the United Nations Convention on the Limitation Period in the International Sales of Goods. This convention specifies the period of time for a party to an international sales contract to file a claim based on the contract.[4]

E-Commerce The United Nations Convention on the Use of Electronic Communications in International Trade (ECC) provides that contracts entered into electronically are as valid and enforceable as contracts on paper.[5] The ECC applies to e-communication between businesses located in different countries, at least one of which has adopted the convention. This includes deals transacted on cell phones and other mobile devices.

The ECC promotes uniformity in commercial law by adapting some of the provisions of the CISG to e-commerce. In this and other ways, the ECC and other international conventions and model laws promote the reduction of judicial and legislative costs in the nations that apply them.[6]

---

1. *Black's Law Dictionary*, 10th ed. (2014).
2. April 11, 1980, U.N. Doc. A/CONF.9718, 19 I.L.M. 668, 52 Fed. Reg. 6262, 1489 U.N.T.S. 3, available at www.uncitral .org/pdf/english/principles/contracts/main.htm.
3. See *Dingxi Longhai Dairy, Ltd. v. Becwood Technology Group L.L.C.*, 635 F.3d 1106 (8th Cir. 2011).
4. June 14, 1974, 1511 U.N.T.S. 3, available at www.uncitral.org/pdf/english/texts/sales/ limit/limit_conv_E_Ebook.pdf.
5. November 23, 2005, U.N. Doc. A/RES/60/21, available at www.uncitral.org/pdf/english/texts/electcom/06-57452_Ebook .pdf
6. Other significant international conventions and model laws cover such issues as transport, finance, arbitration, secured transactions, and bankruptcy.

Cultural Variations

Individuals can differ in their understanding of what an agreement is and what it means to fulfill it. In the global marketplace, businesses located in different countries and influenced by different cultures can have different interpretations of the meaning and effect of their contracts. The consequences of these differences can be significant, as shown in the following examples.

The United States: Litigation In the United States, a business contract is generally regarded as important. We can see this in the details and definiteness of contract terms, the likelihood of a lawsuit if they are breached, and the reliability of the judicial system for their enforcement. A U.S. business contract typically sets out the exact scope of the agreement, states the parties' contractual rights and duties, and provides the basis for relief if it is breached.

The U.S. legal system considers a contract to be the expression of the agreement between the parties. If those parties cannot resolve a dispute over contract terms, it is acceptable to file an action in a court to reach a result. This does not always mean that the parties will stop doing business with each other. A dispute—even a breach—and its consequences often relate only to the deal under which it arises.

Japan: Reliance on Business Relations In Japan, a business contract is also generally regarded as important. A contract in Japan tends to contain more detail than a contract in the United States, and its primary purpose is to express the parties' contractual rights and duties. The Japanese court system supports the enforcement of a contract even if it is not signed. But legal actions over contracts are rarely filed. Japanese businesspersons rely on the strength of their business relations to resolve disputes, often through arbitration.

China: Loss of Business and Lack of Cooperation In China, a business contract is often more an expression of the framework of an agreement than an enforceable statement of it. A contract may outline all of the terms without the detail that often characterizes a Japanese business contract. The Chinese legal system will enforce a contract. But contract terms are considered to be subject to modification to accommodate any changes that either party needs to complete the deal.

If a suit is brought in a Chinese court to enforce a contract, the consequences may include the plaintiff's complete loss of the opposing party's business. Other participants in the same industry may also refuse to do business with the plaintiff in the future. And the suit may spell the end of any cooperative relationship that the plaintiff has had with government representatives.

Russia: Political or Economic Pressure A contract in Russia is considered to be a statement of the essentials of the underlying agreement, but a Russian businessperson may pay it little attention. Asserting the terms of a written document is not likely to bring a dispute to a satisfactory end.

Russian businesspersons do not often rely on the legal system to resolve contract disputes. Instead, they may attempt to negotiate or otherwise work out the issue amicably. If this fails, political or economic pressure may be brought to bear to enforce an agreement. Note, too, that a foreign party who takes a dispute to a Russian court is more likely to suffer an adverse judgment than his or her Russian counterpart.

Continues

Other Considerations

An increasing number of U.S. companies are not only buying goods and services from foreign producers and suppliers, but also making and selling products in other countries. Their goal is to obtain or provide the right product at the right price and the right time.

We have seen that these companies can expect to face cultural differences. In addition, they will likely encounter economic, proprietary, and political factors—fluctuating prices, loss of control of technology, and political turmoil, among others.

A company can take steps to minimize all of these effects. The specific goal for doing global business should be clear, and the company's chief decision maker should be committed to this goal. The company should conduct an ongoing review of which producer or supplier is the optimal source for a sought-after good or service or which market will result in the optimal return on a sale. Technology can be encrypted and security updated. Relying on multiple sources or markets, rather than only a few, can help the company avoid unsettling political events.

Ethical Connection

Most importantly, a participant in global commerce should be alert to cultural influences. The businessperson should consider these influences when entering into a contract, when deciding which terms to include, and when choosing a method to resolve a dispute.

When doing business overseas, the best course is to stay flexible to accommodate others' social and cultural practices. Anticipate that a party in another country may have contractual expectations that differ from those typical in the United States. To resolve a dispute, rely on the business relationship with a party instead of legal principles.

We began by quoting the ancient Roman adage *pacta sunt servanda*—"agreements must be kept." To succeed in global commerce, it may be advisable to follow advice that can be traced to the same era—"when in Rome, do as the Romans do."

Ethics Question *How does the type of "flexible" ethics proposed in this feature enhance the potential for success in global commerce?*

Critical Thinking *How do the CISG and other conventions promote international business?*

Negotiable Instruments

Negotiable Instruments

Most commercial transactions would be inconceivable without negotiable instruments. A **negotiable instrument** is a signed writing that contains an unconditional promise or order to pay an exact amount, either on demand or at a specific future time. Recall that writings include electronic records.

A negotiable instrument can function as a substitute for cash or as an extension of credit. The checks that you receive are negotiable instruments that act as substitutes for cash. The promissory note that you probably signed to obtain an educational loan is a negotiable instrument that functions as an extension of credit. Because negotiable instruments originally were paper documents, they are sometimes referred to as *commercial paper*.

For a negotiable instrument to operate *practically* as either a cash substitute or a credit device, it is essential that the instrument be *easily transferable without danger of being uncollectible*. This is a fundamental function of negotiable instruments.

The law governing negotiable instruments grew out of commercial necessity. In the medieval world, merchants developed their own set of rules, which eventually became known as the *Lex Mercatoria* (Law Merchant). The Law Merchant was later codified in England and is the forerunner of Article 3 of the Uniform Commercial Code (UCC). Article 3 imposes special requirements for the form and content of negotiable instruments. It also governs their negotiation, or transfer.

25-1 Types of Negotiable Instruments

UCC 3–104(b) defines an *instrument* as a "negotiable instrument."[1] For that reason, whenever the term *instrument* is used in this book, it refers to a negotiable instrument. As mentioned, negotiable instruments are also sometimes referred to as *commercial paper*.

The UCC specifies four types of negotiable instruments: *drafts, checks, notes,* and *certificates of deposit* (CDs). These instruments, which are summarized briefly in Exhibit 25–1, frequently are divided into two classifications: *orders to pay* (drafts and checks) and *promises to pay* (promissory notes and CDs). We will discuss both classifications in the following subsections.

Negotiable instruments may also be classified as either demand instruments or time instruments. A *demand instrument* is payable on demand—that is, it is payable immediately after it is issued and thereafter for a reasonable period of time.[2] **Issue** is "the first delivery of an instrument by the maker or drawer . . . for the purpose of giving rights on the instrument to any person" [UCC 3–105]. All checks are demand instruments because, by definition, they must be payable on demand. A *time instrument* is payable at a future date.

25-1a Drafts and Checks (Orders to Pay)

A **draft** is an unconditional written order that involves *three parties*. The party creating the draft (the **drawer**) orders another party (the **drawee**) to pay money, usually to a third party (the **payee**). The most common type of draft is a check, but drafts other than checks may be used in commercial transactions.

---

1. Note that all of the references to Article 3 of the UCC in this chapter are to the 1990 version of Article 3, which has been adopted by almost all of the states.

2. "A promise or order is 'payable on demand' if it (i) states that it is payable on demand or at sight, or otherwise indicates that it is payable at the will of the holder, or (ii) does not state any time of payment" [UCC 3–108(a)]. The UCC defines a *holder* as "the person in possession of a negotiable instrument that is payable either to bearer or to an identified person [who] is the person in possession" [UCC 1–201(21)(A)]. The term *bearer* will be defined later in this chapter.

EXHIBIT 25–1 Basic Types of Negotiable Instruments

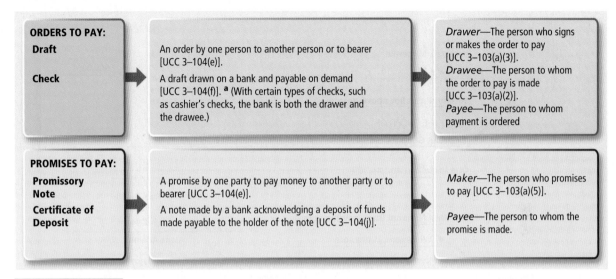

ORDERS TO PAY: **Draft** **Check**	An order by one person to another person or to bearer [UCC 3–104(e)]. A draft drawn on a bank and payable on demand [UCC 3–104(f)]. **a** (With certain types of checks, such as cashier's checks, the bank is both the drawer and the drawee.)	*Drawer*—The person who signs or makes the order to pay [UCC 3–103(a)(3)]. *Drawee*—The person to whom the order to pay is made [UCC 3–103(a)(2)]. *Payee*—The person to whom payment is ordered
PROMISES TO PAY: **Promissory Note** **Certificate of Deposit**	A promise by one party to pay money to another party or to bearer [UCC 3–104(e)]. A note made by a bank acknowledging a deposit of funds made payable to the holder of the note [UCC 3–104(j)].	*Maker*—The person who promises to pay [UCC 3–103(a)(5)]. *Payee*—The person to whom the promise is made.

a. Under UCC 4–105(1), banks include savings banks, savings and loan associations, credit unions, and trust companies (organizations that perform the fiduciary functions of trusts and agencies).

Time Drafts and Sight Drafts A *time draft* is payable at a definite future time. A *sight draft* (or demand draft) is payable on sight—that is, when it is presented to the drawee (usually a bank or financial institution) for payment. A sight draft may be payable on acceptance.

Acceptance is the drawee's written promise to pay the draft when it comes due. Usually, an instrument is accepted by writing the word *accepted* across its face, followed by the date of acceptance and the signature of the drawee. A draft can be both a time and a sight draft. Such a draft is payable at a stated time after sight. An example would be a draft that states that it is payable ninety days after sight.

Exhibit 25–2 shows a typical time draft. For the drawee to be obligated to honor the order, the drawee must be obligated to the drawer either by agreement or through a debtor-creditor relationship. ■ **EXAMPLE 25.1** On January 16, OurTown Real Estate orders $1,000 worth of office supplies from Eastman Supply Company, with payment due April 16. Also on January 16, OurTown sends Eastman a draft drawn on its account with the First National Bank of Whiteacre as payment. In this scenario, the drawer is OurTown, the drawee is OurTown's bank (First National Bank of Whiteacre), and the payee is Eastman Supply Company. First National Bank is obligated to honor the draft because of its account agreement with OurTown Real Estate. ■

Trade Acceptances A trade acceptance is a type of draft that is frequently used in the sale of goods. In a **trade acceptance,** the seller of the goods is both the drawer and the payee. The buyer to whom credit is extended is the drawee. Essentially, the draft orders the buyer to pay a specified amount to the seller, usually at a stated time in the future.

■ **EXAMPLE 25.2** Jackson Street Bistro buys its restaurant supplies from Osaka Industries. When Jackson requests supplies, Osaka creates a draft ordering Jackson to pay Osaka for the supplies within ninety days and sends it along with the supplies. When the supplies arrive, Jackson accepts the draft by signing its face and is then obligated to make the payment. This signed draft is a trade acceptance and can be sold to a third party if Osaka needs cash before the payment is due. (Osaka would sell the draft through the *commercial money market*—the market that businesses use for short-term borrowing.) ■

When a draft orders the buyer's bank to pay, it is called a **banker's acceptance.** Banker's acceptances are commonly used in international trade.

Checks As mentioned, the most commonly used type of draft is a **check.** Although fewer checks are written today and most transactions are electronic, checks are still more common than promissory notes or other types of negotiable instruments. (For a discussion of mobile payment

EXHIBIT 25–2 A Typical Time Draft

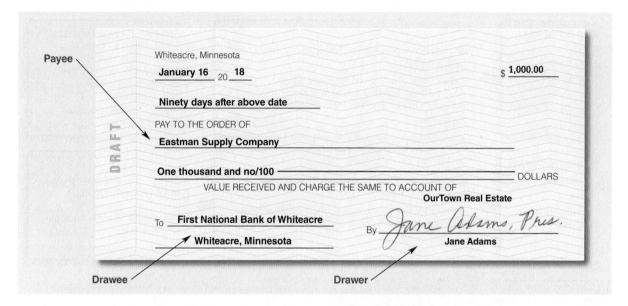

Payee → Whiteacre, Minnesota

January 16 __ 20 __ 18 ____ $ 1,000.00

Ninety days after above date

DRAFT

PAY TO THE ORDER OF

Eastman Supply Company

One thousand and no/100 ——————————————— DOLLARS

VALUE RECEIVED AND CHARGE THE SAME TO ACCOUNT OF

OurTown Real Estate

To   First National Bank of Whiteacre

Whiteacre, Minnesota

By *Jane Adams, Pres.*

Jane Adams

Drawee

Drawer

apps, which are increasingly popular as alternatives to checks, see this chapter's *Digital Update* feature.)

Checks are demand instruments because they are payable on demand. Most commonly, the writer of the check is the drawer, the bank on which the check is drawn is the drawee, and the person to whom the check is made payable is the payee. On certain types of checks, such as *cashier's checks,* the bank is both the drawer and the drawee. A cashier's check functions the same as cash because the bank has committed itself to paying the stated amount on demand.

25–1b Promissory Notes (Promises to Pay)

A **promissory note** is a written promise made by one person (the **maker** of the promise) to pay another (usually a payee) a specified sum. A promissory note, which is often referred to simply as a *note,* can be made payable at a definite time or on demand. It can name a specific payee or merely be payable to bearer (bearer instruments will be discussed later in this chapter).

■ **EXAMPLE 25.3** On April 30, Laurence and Margaret Roberts sign a writing unconditionally promising to pay "to the order of" the First National Bank of Whiteacre $3,000 (with 8 percent interest) on or before June 29. This writing is a promissory note. Laurence and Margaret Roberts are the note's co-makers, and the First National Bank of Whiteacre is the payee. ■ A typical promissory note is shown in Exhibit 25–3.

Promissory notes are commonly assigned (negotiated, or transferred) from one lender, or payee, to another. Assignment does not affect the maker's obligation to pay the note as promised. Promissory notes are also used in a variety of credit transactions. ■ **EXAMPLE 25.4** Nadine Fuller signs a promissory note to purchase an Ultra HD television. The note, which is payable in installments over a twelve-month period, is called an *installment note.* ■

A promissory note is not a debt—it is only the evidence of a debt. But does the loss of a note affect the rights of the owner? That was the question in the following case.

Case 25.1

Silicon Valley Bank v. Miracle Faith World Outreach, Inc.

Appellate Court of Connecticut, 140 Conn.App. 827, 60 A.3d 343 (2013).

Company Profile *Miracle Faith World Outreach, Inc., a religious corporation, was founded by Bobby and Christine Davis in 1964. The Miracle Faith World Outreach Church started with prayer meetings in Christine's mother's home in Stamford, Connecticut. As its numbers grew, the church expanded first into*

Case 25.1 Continued

the basement of a three-family house and later into churches in Springdale and Stamford before buying a new facility in Monroe. The twenty-acre property included a two-story church building and a fellowship hall totaling more than twenty thousand square feet.

Background and Facts Miracle Faith World Outreach borrowed $1,962,000 to buy the buildings and land in Monroe, signing a note payable to Silicon Valley Bank in Santa Clara, California. In the seventh year of the note's ten-year term, with more than $1,600,000 owing on the principal and almost $60,000 owing on unpaid interest, Miracle Faith defaulted. Silicon Valley filed an action in a Connecticut state court to foreclose. Eugene Wong, an associate at the bank, provided the court with only a copy of the note. Wong said that he had looked for the original at several of the bank's offices and at a third-party storage facility, but had been unable to find it. The court decided in the bank's favor, and Miracle Faith appealed. The church argued that "the court abused its discretion by determining that the plaintiff was the owner and holder of the note" even though the bank could produce only a copy.

In the Language of the Court
BEACH, J. [Judge]
* * * *

 *A bill or note is not a debt; it is only primary evidence of a debt; and where this is lost, impaired or destroyed bona fide, it may be supplied by secondary evidence * * *. The loss of a bill or note alters not the rights of the owner, but merely renders secondary evidence necessary and proper.* [Emphasis added.]

 The Uniform Commercial Code * * * addresses situations * * * where the instrument sought to be enforced is unavailable, by creating an exception to the general rule that one must hold an instrument in order to enforce its payment. General Statutes Section 42a–3–309(a) [Connecticut's version of UCC 3–309(a)] provides:

> "A person not in possession of an instrument is entitled to enforce the instrument if (i) the person was in possession of the instrument and entitled to enforce it when loss of possession occurred, (ii) the loss of possession was not the result of a transfer by the person or a lawful seizure, and (iii) the person cannot reasonably obtain possession of the instrument because the instrument was destroyed, its whereabouts cannot be determined, or it is in the wrongful possession of an unknown person or a person that cannot be found or is not amenable to service of process."

 Here, the court found that the plaintiff had sustained its burden of showing that the note was lost and that the copy it produced was authentic.

 The plaintiff established that it had entered into a transaction including a promissory note secured by a mortgage, a term loan agreement, and a mortgage with the defendant. Wong testified that ordinarily the original note would have been kept in the plaintiff's California headquarters. After a period of time, it would have been sent to a third-party storage facility. Wong testified that he checked "all the places where the note could possibly be," but he was unable to locate it. Although the original was lost, a copy of the note had been kept in the plaintiff's credit file for the subject loan. Although the defendant takes issue with the admission of the copy of the note, it does not claim that the copy was in any way inaccurate. The court, therefore, did not abuse its discretion in admitting a copy of the note.

Decision and Remedy *A state intermediate appellate court concluded that the lower court did not abuse its discretion in admitting a copy of the note and affirmed the judgment. A note is not a debt—it is only evidence of a debt—and its loss does not alter the rights of the owner. The bank showed that the note was lost and that the copy it produced was authentic.*

Critical Thinking
- **Legal Environment** *Wong testified that he had looked for the note at a third-party storage facility. If the note had been found there, would that mean that the note had been "transferred" to the facility, making the storage company the holder of the instrument? Explain.*
- **Technological** *If a note is the best primary evidence of the existence of a debt, what might be the best evidence of the amount of the debt and the interest calculation?*

EXHIBIT 25–3 A Typical Promissory Note

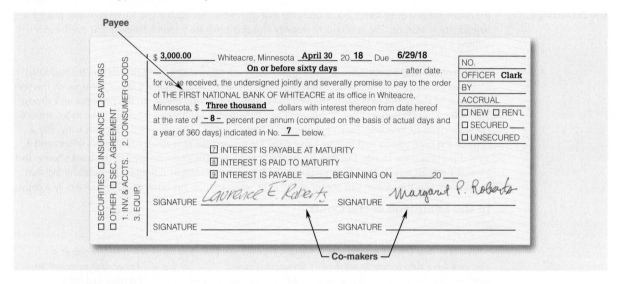

25–1c Certificates of Deposit (Promises to Pay)

A **certificate of deposit (CD)** is another type of note. A CD is issued when a party deposits funds with a bank and the bank promises to repay the funds, with interest, on a certain date [UCC 3–104(j)]. The bank is the maker of the note, and the depositor is the payee. ■ **EXAMPLE 25.5** On February 15, Sara Levin deposits $5,000 with the First National Bank of Whiteacre. The bank promises to repay the $5,000, plus 3.25 percent annual interest, on August 15. ■ Exhibit 25–4 shows an example of a small CD.

Because CDs are time deposits, the purchaser-payee typically is not allowed to withdraw the funds before the date of maturity (except in limited circumstances, such as disability or death). If a payee wants to access the funds before the maturity date, he or she can sell (negotiate) the CD to a third party. CDs in small denominations (for amounts up to $100,000) are often sold by savings and loan associations, savings banks, commercial banks, and credit unions.

25–2 Requirements for Negotiability

For an instrument to be negotiable, it must meet the following requirements:

1. Be in writing.
2. Be signed by the maker or the drawer.

3. Be an unconditional promise or order to pay.
4. State a fixed amount of money.
5. Be payable on demand or at a definite time.
6. Be payable to order or to bearer.

25–2a Written Form

Negotiable instruments must be in written form (but may be evidenced by electronic record) [UCC 3–103(a) (6), (9)].[3] Clearly, an oral promise can create the danger of fraud or make it difficult to determine liability.

1. The writing must be on material that lends itself to *permanence.* Promises carved in blocks of ice or inscribed in the sand or on other impermanent surfaces would not qualify as negotiable instruments. The UCC nevertheless gives considerable leeway as to what can be a negotiable instrument. ■ **EXAMPLE 25.6** Checks and notes have been written on napkins, menus, tablecloths, shirts, and a variety of other materials. Courts will enforce negotiable instruments written on these odd types of materials. ■
2. The writing must also have *portability.* Although the UCC does not explicitly state this requirement, if an instrument is not movable, it obviously cannot meet the requirement that it be freely transferable. ■ **EXAMPLE 25.7** Cullen writes on the side of

---

3. Under the Uniform Electronic Transactions Act (UETA), an electronic record may be sufficient to constitute a negotiable instrument (see UETA Section 16). A small number of states have also adopted amendments to Article 3 that explicitly authorize electronic negotiable instruments.

EXHIBIT 25–4 A Sample Certificate of Deposit

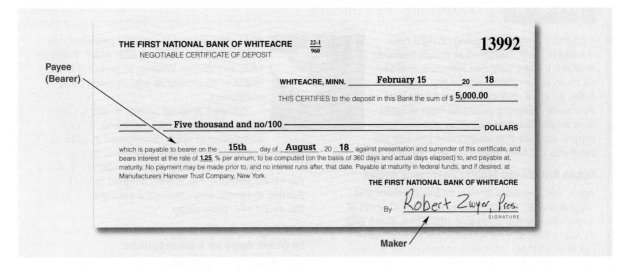

a cow, "I, Cullen, promise to pay $500 to the order of Merrill." Technically, this would meet the requirements of a negotiable instrument—except for portability. Because a cow cannot easily be transferred in the ordinary course of business, the "instrument" is nonnegotiable. ∎

25–2b Signatures

For an instrument to be negotiable, it must be signed by (1) the maker if it is a note or a certificate of deposit or (2) the drawer if it is a draft or a check [UCC 3–103(a)(3), (5)]. If a person signs an instrument as an authorized *agent* for the maker or drawer, the maker or drawer has effectively signed the instrument [UCC 3–402].

Signature Requirements The UCC is quite lenient with regard to what constitutes a signature. Nearly any symbol executed or adopted by a person with the intent to authenticate a written or electronic document can be a **signature** [UCC 1–201(37)]. A signature can be made by a device, such as a rubber stamp, or a thumbprint, and can consist of any name, including a trade or assumed name, or a word, mark, or symbol [UCC 3–401(b)]. If necessary, parol evidence (such as oral testimony) is admissible to identify the signer. When the signer is identified, the signature becomes effective.

Although there are almost no limitations on the manner in which a signature can be made, one should be careful about receiving an instrument that has been signed in an unusual way. Oddities on a negotiable instrument can open the door to disputes and lead to litigation. Furthermore, an unusual signature clearly will decrease the *marketability* of an instrument because it creates uncertainty.

Placement of the Signature The location of the signature on the document is unimportant, although the usual place is the lower right-hand corner. ∎ **EXAMPLE 25.8** A *handwritten* statement on the body of the instrument, such as "I, Kammie Orlik, promise to pay Janis Tan," is sufficient to act as a signature. ∎

25–2c Unconditional Promise or Order to Pay

The terms of the promise or order must be included in the writing on the face of a negotiable instrument. The terms must also be *unconditional*—that is, they cannot be conditioned on the occurrence or nonoccurrence of some other event or agreement [UCC 3–104(a)].

Promises For an instrument to be negotiable, it must contain an express promise or order to pay. ∎ **EXAMPLE 25.9** Kyra executes a promissory note that says "I promise to pay Alvarez $1,000 on demand for the purchase of these goods." These words satisfy the promise-to-pay requirement. ∎

A mere acknowledgment of the debt, such as an I.O.U. ("I owe you"), might logically *imply* a promise, but it is *not* sufficient under the UCC. This is because the UCC requires that a promise be an *affirmative* (express) undertaking [UCC 3–103(a)(9)]. In contrast, if such words as

DIGITAL UPDATE   Pay with Your Smartphone

A payment revolution is going on right now. Starting in 2009, customers at certain Starbucks locations in New York, San Francisco, and Seattle could use an iPhone app to pay for their lattes. By 2016, thousands of Starbucks locations were accepting payments from all types of smartphone-based operating systems. Some experts estimate that smartphone point-of-sale payments will total more than $61 billion in 2017.

Apple Enters the Mobile Payments Arena

Apple, Inc., provides its own mobile payment and "digital wallet" service, called Apple Pay. Owners of Apple iPhones and iPads sold after 2014, along with its Apple Watch, have access to the service. Apple Pay enables these devices to communicate wirelessly with special point-of-sale systems using near field communication (NFC) technology. A person using an iPhone holds it close to the point-of-sale terminal and authenticates the transaction by holding a fingerprint to the phone's Touch ID sensor. Customers' payment information is kept private from the retailer. The system generates a "dynamic security code" for each transaction.

Google and Samsung Provide Competition

Google created the Google Wallet wireless payment system even before Apple Pay was launched. Then, in 2015, Google and the mobile payments company Softcard contracted with AT&T, T-Mobile USA, and Verizon Wireless to preinstall Google Wallet in smartphones sold by those three companies.

Google's Android system is used on most Samsung smartphones. Samsung, a fierce competitor of Apple, announced in 2015 its purchase of LoopPay, a mobile payments startup. Also in 2015, Samsung created a direct competitor to Apple Pay called Samsung Pay. It was designed to work with existing magnetic-strip credit-card machines as well as the newer NFC technology.

Linking Digital Wallets to Other Apps on a Smartphone

The ultimate goal in this modern payment system world is a link from a digital wallet to another app within a single smartphone. For instance, Google allows its Google Wallet to link to its Google Offers, which is a discount-deal app. Mobile payment systems will eventually be tied to rewards programs and special offers at individual stores.

Critical Thinking *Does having a digital wallet in a smartphone entail more security risks than carrying a physical wallet? Explain.*

"to be paid on demand" or "due on demand" are added to an I.O.U., the need for an express promise is satisfied.

A certificate of deposit is exceptional in this respect because no express promise is required. The bank's acknowledgment of the deposit and the other terms of the instrument clearly indicate a promise by the bank to repay the sum of money [UCC 3–104(j)].

Orders An *order* is associated with three-party instruments, such as checks, drafts, and trade acceptances. An order directs a third party to pay the instrument as drawn. In the typical check, for instance, the word *pay* (to the order of a payee) is a command to the drawee bank to pay the check when presented, and thus it is an order.

A command, such as "pay," is mandatory in an order even if it is accompanied by courteous words, as in "Please pay" or "Kindly pay." Generally, the language used must indicate that a command, or order, is being given. Stating "I wish you would pay" does not fulfill this requirement.

An order may be addressed to one person or to more than one person, either jointly ("to A *and* B") or alternatively ("to A *or* B") [UCC 3–103(a)(6)].

Unconditionality of the Promise or Order Only *unconditional* promises or orders can be negotiable [UCC 3–104(a)]. A promise or order is conditional (and *not* negotiable) if it states *any* of the following:

1. An express condition to payment.
2. That the promise or order is subject to or governed by another writing.
3. That the rights or obligations with respect to the promise or order are stated in another writing.

A mere *reference* to another writing or record does not of itself make the promise or order conditional [UCC 3–106(a)]. For instance, including the phrase "as per contract" or "This debt arises from the sale of goods X and Y" does not render an instrument nonnegotiable. Similarly, a statement in the instrument that payment can be made only out of a particular fund or source (such as the proceeds of a particular crop) will not render the instrument nonnegotiable [UCC 3–106(b)(ii)].

■ **CASE IN POINT 25.10**   Sam and Odalis Groome entered into two contracts to buy a pair of alpacas from Alpacas of America, LLC (AOA). To finance the purchases, the buyers signed two notes, one for $18,750 and one for $20,250. Each note included a reference to a contract, a payment schedule, and a security agreement, which provided an interest in the alpacas to secure payment. Within a few months, the Groomes stopped making payments. When AOA sued to collect the unpaid amounts, the Groomes argued that the notes were nonnegotiable because they referred to and were governed by other writings (the contracts). Ultimately, a state appellate court ruled that the Groomes' notes did contain unconditional promises to pay and thus were negotiable.[4] ■

In contrast, if the payment is to be made from a fund that does not yet exist, or is conditioned on the occurrence of some future event, the instrument will be nonnegotiable. ■ **EXAMPLE 25.11**   Duffy's note promises to pay Sherman from the trust account that Duffy will establish when he receives the proceeds from his father's estate. This promise is conditional, and the note is nonnegotiable. ■

In the following case, the court considered the negotiability of a note that included a reference to a mortgage. The makers of the note argued that this reference rendered the note nonnegotiable.

---

4. *Alpacas of America, LLC v. Groome,* 179 Wash.App. 391, 317 P.3d 1103 (2014).

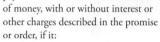

Case Analysis 25.2

OneWest Bank, FSB v. Nunez

District Court of Appeal of Florida, Fourth District, 41 Fla.L.Weekly. D540, __ So.3d __ (2016).

In the Language of the Court

WARNER, J. [Judge]

* * * *

* * * Jose and Jessica Nunez, and Felipa Delrio, executed [a] note to America's Wholesale Lender [Countrywide Home Loans, Inc.] together with a mortgage [to buy property in Hallandale, Florida]. The note and mortgage were assigned * * * to OneWest [Bank]. The [Nunezes and Delrio] defaulted, and OneWest filed a complaint [in a Florida state court] to foreclose on the mortgage [and collect on the note]. The [defendants] filed an answer * * *, including a claim that OneWest was not entitled to enforce the promissory note because it was not a negotiable instrument. They claimed that the note referred to and incorporated provisions of the mortgage, thus destroying its negotiability.

The promissory note in this case contains language that is standard in mortgage notes across the country. Specifically, Section 11 of the promissory note contains the following provision:

> In addition to the protections given to the Note Holder under this Note, a Mortgage * * * dated the same date as this Note, protects the Note Holder from possible losses that might result

if I do not keep the promises that I make in this Note. That * * * Instrument describes how and under what conditions I may be required to make immediate payment in full of all amounts I owe under this Note.

The promissory note then includes a provision from the mortgage relating to transfer of the property, including that the lender may require immediate payment of all sums secured by the mortgage if the borrower transfers the property without the lender's consent.

At the foreclosure trial, the court held that the note was not negotiable, and thus, OneWest * * * could not maintain the action on the note or the foreclosure action. The court entered an order * * * dismissing the complaint. [OneWest appealed.]

* * * *

* * * The trial court erred in concluding that the note in question was non-negotiable. Florida has adopted the Uniform Commercial Code, including its provision on negotiability and enforcement of negotiable instruments. Under Florida Statutes Section 673.1041(1) [Florida's version of UCC 3–104(a)] the term "negotiable instrument" means:

> An unconditional promise or order to pay a fixed amount of money, with or without interest or other charges described in the promise or order, if it:
>
> * * * *
>
> (c) Does not state any other undertaking or instruction by the person promising or ordering payment to do any act in addition to the payment of money.

Florida Statutes Section 673.1061 [UCC 3–106(a)] defines "unconditional" by stating those conditions that prevent it from being unconditional:

> (1) Except as provided in this section, for the purposes of [Florida Statutes] Section 673.1041(1), a promise or order is unconditional unless it states:
> (a) An express condition to payment;
> (b) That the promise or order is subject to or governed by another writing; or
> (c) That rights or obligations with respect to the promise or order are stated in another writing. A reference to another writing does not of itself make the promise or order conditional.
> (2) A promise or order is not made conditional:

Case 25.2 Continues

Case 25.2 Continued

(a) By a reference to another writing for a statement of rights with respect to collateral, prepayment, or acceleration.

The UCC comments to this section address the inclusion of language regarding collateral and acceleration, and confirm that the inclusion of such language does not make the note conditional:

Many notes issued in commercial transactions are secured by collateral, are subject to acceleration in the event of default, or are subject to prepayment, or acceleration does not prevent the note from being an instrument if the statement is in the note itself. * * * In some cases it may be convenient not to include a statement concerning collateral, prepayment, or acceleration in the note, but rather to refer to an accompanying loan agreement,

security agreement or mortgage for that statement. [Florida Statutes Section 673.1061(2)(a)] allows a reference to the appropriate writing for a statement of these rights. * * *

*Thus, the mention of the mortgage instrument as to the * * * rights of acceleration in the promissory note does not destroy the unconditional nature of the note.* [Emphasis added.]

Two cases from other jurisdictions have considered the exact language contained in the promissory note in this case and concluded that it did not render the note non-negotiable. In [the first case], the court relied on the UCC comment to the statutory provision to conclude that "the reference to the mortgage, in Section 11 of the note, with respect to rights of acceleration does not render the note nonnegotiable." * * * [The

second case] * * * dealt with nearly identical language, including the incorporation of the acceleration on transfer provisions of the mortgage in the note. The bankruptcy judge found that the provisions were conditions regarding acceleration, permissible under Section 3-106(b) of the UCC and not destroying negotiability. *We agree with the foregoing authority that Section 11 of the note refers to the mortgage for a statement of rights with respect to * * * acceleration and thus does not render the note nonnegotiable.* [Emphasis added.]
     * * * *

Because the court erred in dismissing the foreclosure proceeding based upon the non-negotiability of the promissory note, we reverse and remand for further proceedings.

Legal Reasoning Questions

1. The lower court concluded that the note was nonnegotiable and dismissed the bank's attempt to enforce it. Was this an error?
2. Suppose that the note in this case had stated, "The terms of the mortgage are by this reference made a part hereof." Would the result have been different?
3. How did the fact that "the promissory note in this case contains language that is standard in mortgage notes across the country" affect the court's reasoning?

25–2d A Fixed Amount of Money

Negotiable instruments must state with certainty a fixed amount of money to be paid at the time the instrument is payable [UCC 3–104(a)]. This requirement ensures that the value of the instrument can be determined with clarity and certainty.

Fixed Amount The term *fixed amount* (sometimes called *sum certain*) means that the amount must be ascertainable from the face of the instrument. Interest may be stated as a fixed or variable rate. A demand note payable with 10 percent interest meets the requirement of a fixed amount because its amount can be determined at the time it is payable [UCC 3–104(a)].

The rate of interest may also be determined with reference to information that is not contained in the instrument itself but is described by it, such as a formula or a source [UCC 3–112(b)]. For instance, an instrument that is payable at the *legal rate of interest* (a rate of interest

fixed by statute) is negotiable. Mortgage notes tied to a variable rate of interest (a rate that fluctuates as a result of market conditions) are also negotiable.

■ **CASE IN POINT 25.12** Alta Logistics, Inc., executed a promissory note to Bank of America (BOA) for the purpose of obtaining a revolving line of credit. The note stated the amount due as "the principal amount of One Hundred Twenty-Five Thousand 00/100 Dollars ($125,000.00) or so much as may be outstanding, together with interest on the unpaid outstanding principal balance of each advance." The note also indicated that the unpaid balance could be determined by indorsements on the note and BOA's internal records (including daily printouts).

Five years after the note came due, BOA filed an action against Alta to enforce the note. The court held that the note was not negotiable because it did not state a fixed amount on its face. This finding affected the statute of limitations for filing an action on the note. Since the note was not negotiable, UCC Article 3's six-year statute of limitations did not apply. The claim instead had to be treated as a breach of contract claim, which must be filed within four years. The court dismissed BOA's case because BOA did not file within this four-year statute of limitations period.[5] ∎

Payable in Money UCC 3–104(a) provides that a fixed amount is to be *payable in money*. The UCC defines money as "a medium of exchange authorized or adopted by a domestic or foreign government as a part of its currency" [UCC 1–201(24)]. Gold is not a medium of exchange adopted by the U.S. government, so a note made payable in gold is nonnegotiable. An instrument payable in the United States with a face amount stated in a foreign currency can be paid in the foreign money or in the equivalent in U.S. dollars [UCC 3–107].

25–2e Payable on Demand or at a Definite Time

A negotiable instrument must "be payable on demand or at a definite time" [UCC 3–104(a)(2)]. To determine the value of a negotiable instrument, it is necessary to know when the maker, drawee, or *acceptor* is required to pay. (An **acceptor** is a drawee who has accepted, or agreed to pay, an instrument when it is presented later for payment.) It is also necessary to know when the obligations of secondary parties, such as *indorsers*,[6] will arise.

Furthermore, it is necessary to know when an instrument is due in order to calculate when the statute of limitations may apply [UCC 3–118(a)]. Finally, with an interest-bearing instrument, it is necessary to know the exact interval during which the interest will accrue to determine the instrument's value at the present time.

Payable on Demand Instruments that are payable on demand include those that contain the words "Payable at sight" or "Payable upon presentment." **Presentment** occurs when a demand to either pay or accept an instrument is made by or on behalf of a person entitled to enforce the instrument [UCC 3–501]. In other words, presentment occurs when a person brings the instrument to the appropriate party for payment or acceptance.

The very nature of the instrument may indicate that it is payable on demand. For instance, a check, by definition, is payable on demand [UCC 3–104(f)]. If no time

for payment is specified and the person responsible for payment must pay on the instrument's presentment, the instrument is payable on demand [UCC 3–108(a)].

■ **CASE IN POINT 25.13** National City Bank gave Reger Development, LLC, a line of credit to finance potential development opportunities. Reger signed a promissory note requiring it to "pay this loan in full immediately upon Lender's demand." About a year later, the bank asked Reger to pay down the loan and stated that it would be reducing the amount of cash available through the line of credit. Reger sued, alleging that the bank had breached the terms of the note. The court ruled in the bank's favor. The promissory note was a demand instrument because it explicitly set forth the lender's right to demand payment at any time. Thus, National City had the right to collect payment from Reger at any time on demand.[7] ∎

Payable at a Definite Time If an instrument is not payable on demand, to be negotiable it must be payable at a definite time. An instrument is payable at a definite time if it states *any* of the following:

1. That it is payable on a specified date.
2. That it is payable within a definite period of time (such as thirty days) after being presented for payment.
3. That it is payable on a date or time readily ascertainable at the time the promise or order is issued [UCC 3–108(b)].

The maker or drawee is under no obligation to pay until the specified date.

When an instrument is payable by the maker or drawer *on or before* a stated date, it is clearly payable at a definite time. The maker or drawer has the *option* of paying before the stated maturity date, but the payee can still rely on payment being made by the maturity date. The option to pay early does not violate the definite-time requirement. ■ **EXAMPLE 25.14** Ari gives Ernesto an instrument dated May 1, 2017, that indicates on its face that it is payable *on or before* May 1, 2018. This instrument satisfies the definite-time requirement. ∎

In contrast, an instrument that is undated and made payable "one month after date" is clearly nonnegotiable. There is no way to determine the maturity date from the face of the instrument. Whether the time period is a month or a year, if the date is uncertain, the instrument is not payable at a definite time. ■ **EXAMPLE 25.15** An instrument states, "One year after the death of my grandfather, Jerome Adams, I promise to pay $5,000 to

---

5. *Bank of America, N.A. v. Alta Logistics, Inc.*, 2015 WL 505373 (Tex. App.—Dallas 2015).

6. We should note that because the UCC uses the spelling *indorse* (*indorsement*, and the like), rather than the more common spelling *endorse* (*endorsement*, and the like), we adopt the UCC's spelling here and in other chapters in this text.

7. *Reger Development, LLC v. National City Bank*, 592 F.3d 759 (7th Cir. 2010).

the order of Lucy Harmon. [Signed] Jacqueline Wells." It is nonnegotiable. The date that the instrument becomes payable is uncertain. ∎

Acceleration Clause An **acceleration clause** allows a payee or other holder of a time instrument to demand payment of the entire amount due, with interest, if a specified event occurs. (A **holder** is any person in possession of a negotiable instrument that is payable either to the bearer or to an identified person that is the person in possession [UCC 1–201(20)].)

∎ **EXAMPLE 25.16** Marta lends $1,000 to Ruth, who makes a negotiable note promising to pay $100 per month for eleven months. The note contains an acceleration provision. This provision permits Marta or any holder to immediately demand all the payments plus the interest owed to date if Ruth fails to pay an installment in any given month. Ruth fails to make the third payment. Marta accelerates the unpaid balance, and the note becomes due and payable in full. Ruth owes Marta the remaining principal plus any unpaid interest to that date. ∎

Instruments that include acceleration clauses are negotiable because the exact value of the instrument can be ascertained. In addition, the instrument will be payable on a specified date if the event allowing acceleration does not occur [UCC 3–108(b)(ii)]. Thus, the specified date is the outside limit used to determine the value of the instrument.

Extension Clause The reverse of an acceleration clause is an **extension clause,** which allows the date of maturity to be extended into the future [UCC 3–108(b)(iii), (iv)]. To keep the instrument negotiable, the interval of the extension must be specified if the right to extend the time of payment is given to the maker or the drawer of the instrument. If, however, the holder of the instrument can extend the time of payment, the extended maturity date need not be specified.

∎ **EXAMPLE 25.17** Alek executes a note that reads, "The maker has the right to postpone the time of payment of this note beyond its definite maturity date of January 1, 2018. This extension, however, shall be for no more than a reasonable time." A note with this language is not negotiable, because it does not satisfy the definite-time requirement. The right to extend is the maker's, and the maker has not indicated when the note will become due after the extension.

In contrast, suppose that Alek's note reads, "The holder of this note at the date of maturity, January 1, 2018, can extend the time of payment until the following June 1 or later, if the holder so wishes." This note is negotiable. The length of the extension does not have to

be specified, because the option to extend is solely that of the holder. After January 1, 2018, the note is, in effect, a demand instrument. ∎

25–2f Payable to Order or to Bearer

Because one of the functions of a negotiable instrument is to serve as a substitute for cash, freedom to transfer is essential. To ensure a proper transfer, the instrument must be "payable to order or to bearer" at the time it is issued or first comes into the possession of the holder [UCC 3–104(a)(1)]. An instrument is not negotiable unless it meets this requirement.

Order Instruments An **order instrument** is an instrument that is payable (1) "to the order of an identified person" or (2) "to an identified person or order" [UCC 3–109(b)]. An identified person is the person "to whom the instrument is initially payable" as determined by the intent of the maker or drawer [UCC 3–110(a)]. The identified person, in turn, may transfer the instrument to whomever he or she wishes.

Thus, the maker or drawer is agreeing to pay either the person specified on the instrument or whomever that person might designate. In this way, the instrument retains its transferability. ∎ **EXAMPLE 25.18** An instrument states, "Payable to the order of James Yung" or "Pay to James Yung or order." Clearly, the maker or drawer has indicated that payment will be made to Yung or to whomever Yung designates. The instrument is negotiable. ∎

Note that with order instruments, the person specified must be identified with *certainty,* because the transfer of an order instrument requires the indorsement, or signature, of the payee. An *indorsement* is a signature placed on an instrument, such as on the back of a check, generally for the purpose of transferring one's ownership rights in the instrument. An order instrument made "Payable to the order of my nicest cousin," for instance, is not negotiable, because it does not clearly specify the payee.

Bearer Instruments A **bearer instrument** is an instrument that does not designate a specific payee [UCC 3–109(a)]. The term **bearer** refers to a person in possession of an instrument that is payable to bearer or indorsed in blank (with a signature only) [UCC 1–201(5), 3–109(a), 3–109(c)]. This means that the maker or drawer agrees to pay anyone who presents the instrument for payment.

Any instrument containing terms such as the following is a bearer instrument:

1. "Payable to the order of bearer."
2. "Payable to Simon Reed or bearer."
3. "Payable to bearer."

4. "Pay cash."
5. "Pay to the order of cash."

■ **CASE IN POINT 25.19** Amine Nehme applied for credit at the Venetian Resort Hotel Casino in Las Vegas, Nevada, and was granted $500,000 in credit. He signed a gambling marker—that is, a promise to pay a gambling debt—for $500,000. Nehme quickly lost that amount gambling. The Venetian presented the marker for payment to Nehme's bank, Bank of America, which returned it for insufficient funds. The casino's owner, Las Vegas Sands, LLC, filed a suit against Nehme for failure to pay a negotiable instrument.

The court held that the marker fit the UCC's definitions of negotiable instrument and check. It was a means for payment of $500,000 from Bank of America to the order of the Venetian. It did not state a time for payment and thus was payable on demand. It was also unconditional—that is, it stated no promise by Nehme other than the promise to pay a fixed amount of money. Therefore, the marker was a negotiable instrument, and the Venetian was entitled to enforce it.[8] ■

Can Be Payable to Nonexistent Person. In addition, an instrument that "indicates that it is not payable to an identified person" is a bearer instrument [UCC 3–109(a)(3)]. Thus, an instrument that is "payable to X" can be negotiated as a bearer instrument, as though it were payable to cash. Similarly, an instrument that is "payable to Captain America" is negotiable as a bearer instrument because it is obvious that it is payable to a *nonexistent person*.

Cannot Be Payable to Nonexistent Organization. The UCC does not accept an instrument issued to a *nonexistent organization* as payable to bearer, however [UCC 3–109, Comment 2]. Therefore, an instrument "payable to the order of the Camrod Company," if no such company exists, would not be a bearer instrument or an order instrument. In fact, the instrument would not qualify as a negotiable instrument at all.

See Concept Summary 25.1 for a convenient review of the basic rules governing negotiability.

25–3 Factors That Do Not Affect Negotiability

Certain ambiguities or omissions will not affect the negotiability of an instrument. Article 3's rules for interpreting ambiguous terms include the following:

8. *Las Vegas Sands, LLC v. Nehme,* 632 F.3d 526 (9th Cir. 2011).

1. Unless the date of an instrument is necessary to determine a definite time for payment, the fact that an instrument is undated does not affect its negotiability. A typical example is an undated check, which is still negotiable. If a check is not dated, under the UCC its date is the date of its issue [UCC 3–113(b)]. The issue date is the date on which the drawer first delivers the check to another person to give that person rights in the check.

2. Antedating or postdating an instrument does not affect its negotiability [UCC 3–113(a)]. *Antedating* occurs when a party puts a date on an instrument that precedes the actual calendar date. *Postdating* occurs when a party puts a date on an instrument that is after the actual date. ■ **EXAMPLE 25.20** Crenshaw draws a check on his account at First Bank, payable to Sirah Imports. He postdates the check by fifteen days. Sirah Imports can immediately negotiate the check, and, unless Crenshaw tells First Bank otherwise, the bank can charge the amount of the check to Crenshaw's account [UCC 4–401(c)]. ■

3. Handwritten terms outweigh typewritten and printed terms (preprinted terms on forms, for example), and typewritten terms outweigh printed terms [UCC 3–114]. ■ **EXAMPLE 25.21** Most checks are preprinted "Pay to the order of" followed by a blank line, making them order instruments. In handwriting, Travis inserts in the blank "Anita Delgado or bearer." The handwritten terms will outweigh the printed form, and the check will be a bearer instrument. ■

4. Words outweigh figures unless the words are ambiguous [UCC 3–114]. This rule becomes important when the numerical amount and the written amount on a check differ. ■ **EXAMPLE 25.22** Reirson issues a check payable to Reliable Appliance Company. For the amount, she fills in the number "$100" but writes out the words "One thousand and 00/100" dollars. The check is payable in the amount of $1,000. ■

5. When an instrument simply states "with interest" and does not specify a particular interest rate, the interest rate is the *judgment rate of interest* [UCC 3–112(b)]. The judgment rate of interest refers to a rate of interest fixed by statute that applies to court judgments.

6. A check is negotiable even if there is a notation on it stating that it is "nonnegotiable" or "not governed by Article 3." Any other instrument, however, can be made nonnegotiable by the maker's or drawer's conspicuously noting on it that it is "nonnegotiable" or "not governed by Article 3" [UCC 3–104(d)].

In the following case, the court was asked to compare the words and figures in a promissory note to determine its amount.

Charles R. Tips Family Trust v. PB Commercial, LLC

Court of Appeals of Texas, Houston, First District, 459 S.W.3d 147 (2015).

Background and Facts The Charles R. Tips Family Trust signed a promissory note in favor of Patriot Bank to obtain a loan to buy a house in Harris County, Texas. The note identified the principal amount of the loan as "ONE MILLION SEVEN THOUSAND AND NO/100 ($1,700,000.00) DOLLARS." (Note the inconsistency between the spelled-out amount, $1,007,000, and the numerals, $1,700,000.). The family trust then made payments totaling only $595,586. PB Commercial, LLC (PBC), acquired the note, sold the residence for $874,125, and pursued litigation in a Texas state court against the borrower, alleging default.

The defendant, Charles R. Tips Family Trust, argued that the written words in an instrument control. Thus, the note had been satisfied in full by the amount of the payments plus the sale price of the house. In fact, the trust pointed out that PBC had collected a surplus of $189,111. The court entered a judgment in PBC's favor. The trust appealed, arguing one issue—that the amount of the loan must be determined from the printed words in the note and not the numerals.

In the Language of the Court

Michael *MASSENGALE,* Justice.

* * * *

* * * To recover on a promissory note on which the borrower has defaulted, PBC was required to prove that * * * a certain balance was due and owing on the note.

* * * *

* * * Under the Uniform Commercial Code, which governs negotiable instruments such as the Note, "if an instrument contains contradictory terms, * * * words prevail over numbers." * * * *This rule derives from the principle that writing words more likely represents the parties' true intentions than writing numbers.* [Emphasis added.]

* * * *

The Note * * * describes the original amount of the loan obligation as "ONE MILLION SEVEN THOUSAND AND NO/100 ($1,700,000.00) DOLLARS." The phrase "one million seven thousand and no/100 dollars" has a plain, unambiguous meaning, namely the sum of $1,007,000.00. Thus, the words and the numerals in the [Note] are in conflict, differing by $693,000.

* * * *

* * * It does not matter that the discrepancy between the words and numbers here is a large one. Neither [Texas Business & Commercial Code] Section 3.114 [Texas's version of UCC 3–114] nor Texas case law makes a distinction on the basis of the size of the obligation or the significance of the conflict in terms.

PBC argues that this case presents a unique circumstance in that the omission of a single word transforms "one million seven hundred thousand" into "one million seven thousand." If the former phrase were modified in any other way, according to PBC, we would be faced with either an ambiguous term or an unambiguous but absurd one. For example, PBC [proposes] a scenario in which a [clerk's] error rendered the phrase as "one seven hundred thousand," omitting the word "million." According to PBC, such an amount would be ambiguous, and the court would have to refer to the numerals and extrinsic [outside] evidence to resolve the ambiguity. But this hypothetical scenario has no bearing on this case because there is no ambiguity in the text here.

* * * *

Here, the words "one million seven thousand" control over the numerals "$1,700,000" to set the amount of the promissory note. [Emphasis added.]

Decision and Remedy *A state intermediate appellate court reversed the judgment of the lower court. Under the UCC, "if an instrument contains contradictory terms, . . . words prevail over numbers." In this case, the note's words and numerals were in conflict. Thus, the words "one million seven thousand" controlled over the numerals "$1,700,000" as the amount of the promissory note.*

Case 25.3 Continued   **Critical Thinking**

- **What If the Facts Were Different?** *Suppose that the note had described the amount of the loan as* *"ONE MILLION SEVEN HUNDRED THOUSAND AND NO/100 ($1,007,000.00) DOLLARS."* *What would have been the result?*

Concept Summary 25.1

Requirements for Negotiability

Must Be in Writing
- A writing can be on anything that is readily transferable and that has a degree of permanence.

Must Be Signed by the Maker or Drawer
- The signature can be anywhere on the face of the instrument.
- It can be in any form (such as a word, mark, or rubber stamp) that purports to be a signature and authenticates the writing.
- A signature may be made in a representative capacity.

Must Be a Definite Promise or Order
- A promise must be more than a mere acknowledgment of a debt.
- The words "I/We promise" or "Pay" meet this criterion.

Must Be Unconditional
- Payment cannot be expressly conditional on the occurrence of an event.
- Payment cannot be made subject to or governed by another agreement.

Must Be an Order or Promise to Pay a Fixed Amount
- An amount may be considered a fixed sum even if payable in installments, with a fixed or variable rate of interest, or at a foreign exchange rate.

Must Be Payable in Money
- Any medium of exchange recognized as the currency of a government is money.

Must Be Payable on Demand or at a Definite Time
- Any instrument that is payable on sight, presentment, or issue or that does not state any time for payment is a demand instrument.
- An instrument is still payable at a definite time, even if it is payable on or before a stated date or within a fixed period after sight or if the drawer or maker has the option to extend the time for a definite period.
- Acceleration clauses do not affect the negotiability of the instrument.

Must Be Payable to Order or to Bearer
- An order instrument must identify the payee with reasonable certainty.
- An instrument whose terms indicate payment to no particular person is payable to bearer.

Reviewing: Negotiable Instruments

Robert Durbin, a student, borrowed funds from a bank for his education and signed a promissory note for their repayment. The bank lent the funds under a federal program designed to assist students at postsecondary institutions. Under this program, repayment ordinarily begins nine to twelve months after the student borrower fails to carry at least one-half of the normal full-time course load at his or her school. The federal government guarantees that the note will be fully repaid. If the student defaults on the repayment, the lender presents the current balance—principal, interest, and costs—to the government. When the government pays the balance, it becomes the lender, and the borrower owes the government directly.

Durbin defaulted on his note, and the government paid the lender the balance due and took possession of the note. Durbin then refused to pay the government, claiming that the government was not the holder of the note. The government filed a suit in a federal district court against Durbin to collect the amount due. Using the information presented in the chapter, answer the following questions.

1. Using the categories discussed in the chapter, what type of negotiable instrument was the note that Durbin signed (an order to pay or a promise to pay)? Explain.
2. Suppose that the note did not state a specific interest rate but instead referred to a statute that established the maximum interest rate for government-guaranteed school loans. Would the note fail to meet the requirements for negotiability in that situation? Why or why not?
3. For the government to be a holder, which method must have been used to transfer the instrument from the bank to the government?
4. Suppose that, in court, Durbin argues that because the school closed down before he could finish his education, there was a failure of consideration. That is, he did not get something of value in exchange for his promise to pay. Assuming that the government is a holder of the promissory note, would this argument likely be successful against it? Why or why not?

Debate This . . .   *Congress should pass a law disallowing all negotiable instruments that are not written on paper.*

Terms and Concepts

acceleration clause 472
acceptance 463
acceptor 471
banker's acceptance 463
bearer 472
bearer instrument 472
certificate of deposit (CD) 466
check 463

draft 462
drawee 462
drawer 462
extension clause 472
holder 472
issue 462
maker 464

negotiable instrument 462
order instrument 472
payee 462
presentment 471
promissory note 464
signature 467
trade acceptance 463

Issue Spotters

1. Sasha owes $600 to Dale, who asks her to sign an instrument for the debt. Consider each of the following alternatives for the wording on that instrument:
   (a) "I.O.U. $600,"
   (b) "I promise to pay $600."
   (c) An instruction to Sasha's bank stating, "I wish you would pay $600 to Dale."
   Which of these phrases would prevent the instrument's negotiability? Why? (See *Requirements for Negotiability.*)

2. Marit worked for Town & Garden, a landscape design service owned by Donald. Marit signed a note payable to Donald to become a co-owner of Town & Garden. The note, which was undated, required installment payments, but Donald never asked for them. Is Marit's note a demand note? Explain. (See *Requirements for Negotiability.*)

• **Check your answers to the Issue Spotters against the answers provided in Appendix D at the end of this text.**

Business Scenarios

25–1. Negotiable Instruments. Sabrina Runyan writes the following note on a sheet of paper: "I, the undersigned, do hereby acknowledge that I owe Leo Woo one thousand dollars, with interest, payable out of the proceeds of the sale of my horse, Lightning, next month. Payment is to be made on or before six months from date." Discuss specifically why this is not a negotiable instrument. (See *Types of Negotiable Instruments.*)

25–2. Negotiability. Juan Sanchez writes the following note on the back of an envelope: "I, Juan Sanchez, promise to pay Kathy Martin or bearer $500 on demand." Is this a negotiable instrument? Discuss fully. (See *Requirements for Negotiability.*)

25–3. Promissory Notes. A college student, Austin Keynes, wished to purchase a new entertainment system from Friedman Electronics, Inc. Because Keynes did not have the cash to pay for the entertainment system, he offered to sign a note promising to pay $150 per month for the next six months. Friedman

Electronics, eager to sell the system to Keynes, agreed to accept the promissory note, which read, "I, Austin Keynes, promise to pay to Friedman Electronics or its order the sum of $150 per month for the next six months." The note was signed by Austin Keynes. A week later, Friedman Electronics, which was badly in need of cash, signed the back of the note and sold it to the First National Bank of Halston. Give the specific designation of each of the three parties on this note. (See *Types of Negotiable Instruments.*)

25–4. Bearer Instruments. Adam's checks are imprinted with the words "Pay to the order of" followed by a blank. Adam fills in an amount on one of the checks and signs it, but he does not write anything in the blank following the phrase "Pay to the order of." Adam gives this check to Beth. On another check, Adam writes in the blank "Carl or bearer." Which, if either, of these checks is a bearer instrument, and why? (See *Requirements for Negotiability.*)

Business Case Problems

25–5. Negotiability. Michael Scotto borrowed $2,970 from Cindy Vinueza. Both of their signatures appeared at the bottom of a note. The note stated, "I Michael Scotto owe Cindy Vinueza $2,970 (two thousand and nine-hundred & seventy dollars) & agree to pay her back in full. Signed on this 26th day of September 2009." More than a year later, Vinueza filed a suit against Scotto to recover on the note. Scotto admitted that he had borrowed the funds, but he contended—without proof—that he had paid Vinueza in full. Is this note negotiable? Which party is likely to prevail? Why? [*Vinueza v. Scotto,* 30 Misc.3d 1229, 924 N.Y.S.2d 312 (1 Dist. 2011)] (See *Requirements for Negotiability.*)

25–6. Business Case Problem with Sample Answer— Payable on Demand or at a Definite Time. Abby Novel signed a handwritten note that read, "Glen Gallwitz 1-8-2002 loaned me $5,000 at 6 percent interest a total of $10,000.00." The note did not state a time for repayment. Novel used the funds to manufacture and market a patented jewelry display design. More than seven years after Novel signed the note, Gallwitz filed a suit to recover the stated amount. Novel claimed that she did not have to pay because the note was not negotiable—it was incomplete. Is she correct? Explain. [*Gallwitz v. Novel,* 2011-Ohio-297 (5 Dist. 2011)] (See *Requirements for Negotiability.*)

- **For a sample answer to Problem 25–6, go to Appendix E at the end of this text.**

25–7. Bearer Instruments. Eligio Gaitan borrowed the funds to buy real property in Downers Grove, Illinois, and signed a note payable to Encore Credit Corp. Encore indorsed the note in blank. Later, when Gaitan defaulted on the payments, an action to foreclose on the property was filed in an Illinois state court by U.S. Bank, N.A. The note was in the bank's possession, but there was no evidence that the note had

been transferred or negotiated to the bank. Can U.S. Bank enforce payment of the note? Why or why not? [*U.S. Bank National Association v. Gaitan,* 2013 IL App (2d) 120105-U, 2013 WL 160378 (2013)] (See *Requirements for Negotiability.*)

25–8. Payable to Order or to Bearer. Thomas Caraccia signed a note and mortgage in favor of VirtualBank to obtain funds to buy property in Palm Beach Gardens, Florida. VirtualBank indorsed the note in blank, making it bearer paper, and transferred possession of the note to Bank of America. Bank of America transferred the note to U.S. Bank, which later gave the note back to Bank of America to collect Caraccia's payments on behalf of U.S. Bank. When Caraccia defaulted on the payments, U.S. Bank filed a suit in a Florida state court against him, seeking to enforce the note and foreclose on the property. Caraccia contended that because the note was indorsed in blank and was not in the physical possession of U.S. Bank, the bank could not enforce it. Could the bank successfully argue that although it did not *physically* possess the note, it *constructively* possessed (exercised legal control over) it? Explain. [*Caraccia v. U.S. Bank, National Association,* 41 Fla.L.Weekly. D476, 185 So.3d 1277 (Dist.Ct.App. 2016)] (See *Requirements for Negotiability.*)

25–9. A Question of Ethics—Promissory Notes. *In* *November 2000, Monay Jones signed a promissory note in favor of a mortgage company in the amount of $261,250. Jones used the deed to her home in Denver, Colorado, as collateral. Fifth Third Bank soon became the holder of the note. After Jones defaulted on a payment, in September 2001 she and the bank agreed to raise the note's balance to $280,231.23. She again defaulted. In November, the bank received a check from a third party as payment on Jones's note. It was the bank's policy to refuse personal checks in payoffs of large debts. The bank representative who worked on Jones's account noted receipt of the check in the bank's records and* *forwarded it to the "payoff department." A week later, the bank discovered that the check had been lost without having been posted to Jones's account or submitted for payment. The bank notified Jones, and both parties searched, without success, for a copy of the check or evidence of the identity of its maker, the drawee bank, or the amount. In late 2002, the bank filed a suit in a Colorado state court to foreclose on Jones's home. She insisted that the note had been paid in full by a cashier's check issued by an Arkansas bank at the request of her deceased aunt. [Fifth Third Bank v. Jones, 168 P.3d 1 (Colo.App. 2007)] (See Types of Negotiable Instruments.)*

(a) What evidence supports a finding that Jones gave the bank a check? Does it seem more likely that the check was a cashier's check or a personal check? Would it be fair for a court to find that the check had paid the note in full?

(b) Under UCC 3–310, if a cashier's check or other certified check "is taken for an obligation, the obligation is discharged." The bank argued that it had not "taken [Jones's check] for an obligation" because the bank's internal administrative actions were still pending when the check was lost. Would it be fair for the court to rule in the bank's favor based on this argument? Why or why not?

Legal Reasoning Group Activity

25–10. Requirements for Negotiability. Peter Gowin was an employee of a granite countertop business owned by Joann Stathis. In November 2015, Gowin signed a promissory note agreeing to pay $12,500 to become a co-owner of the business. The note was dated January 15, 2015—ten months before it was signed—and required Gowin to make installment payments starting in February 2015. Stathis told Gowin not to worry about the note and never requested any payments. Gowin continued to work at the business until 2017, when he quit, claiming that he owned half of the business. Stathis argued that Gowin was not a co-owner because he had never paid the $12,500 into the business. (See *Requirements for Negotiability.*)

(a) The first group will formulate an argument in favor of Stathis that Gowin did not own any interest in the business because he had not paid the $12,500.

(b) The second group will evaluate the strength of Gowin's argument. Gowin claimed that, because compliance with the stated dates was impossible, the note effectively did not state a date for its payment. It was thus a demand note under UCC 3–108(a). Gowin further argued that no demand for payment had been made. Therefore, his obligation to pay had not arisen, and the termination of his ownership interest in the granite business was improper.

CHAPTER 26

Transferability and Holder in Due Course

Once issued, a negotiable instrument can be transferred to others by *assignment* or by *negotiation*. Recall that an assignment is a transfer of rights under a contract. Under contract law principles, a transfer by assignment to an assignee gives the assignee only those rights that the assignor possessed. Any defenses that can be raised against an assignor can normally be raised against the assignee. This same rule applies when a negotiable instrument, such as a promissory note, is transferred by assignment to an assignee. The assignee receives only those rights in the instrument that the assignor had prior to the assignment.

In contrast, when an instrument is transferred by **negotiation,** the Uniform Commercial Code (UCC) provides that the transferee (the person to whom the instrument is transferred) becomes a *holder* [UCC 3–201(a)]. A holder receives, at the very least, the rights of the previous possessor [UCC 3–203(b), 3–305]. But unlike an assignment, a transfer by negotiation can make it possible for a holder to receive *more* rights in the instrument than the prior possessor had [UCC 3–305]. A holder who receives greater rights is known as a *holder in due course*.

26–1 Negotiation

As just described, negotiation is the transfer of an instrument in such form that the transferee becomes a holder. There are two methods of negotiating an instrument so that the receiver becomes a holder. The method used depends on whether the instrument is an *order instrument* or a *bearer instrument.*

26–1a Negotiating Order Instruments

An order instrument contains the name of a payee capable of indorsing, as in "Pay to the order of Jamie Fowler." If an instrument is an order instrument, it is negotiated by delivery with any necessary indorsements (discussed shortly). ■ **EXAMPLE 26.1** Welpac Corporation issues a payroll check "to the order of Elliot Goodseal." Goodseal takes the check to the bank, signs his name on the back (an indorsement), gives it to the teller (a delivery), and receives cash. Goodseal has negotiated the check to the bank [UCC 3–201(b)]. ■

Negotiating order instruments requires both delivery and indorsement. If Goodseal had taken the check to the bank and delivered it to the teller without signing it, the transfer would not qualify as a negotiation. In that situation, the transfer would be treated as an assignment, and the bank would become an assignee rather than a holder. In fact, whenever a transfer fails to qualify as a negotiation because it fails to meet one or more of the requirements of a negotiable instrument, it is treated as an assignment.

26–1b Negotiating Bearer Instruments

If an instrument is payable to bearer, it is negotiated by delivery—that is, by transfer into another person's possession. Indorsement is not necessary [UCC 3–201(b)]. The use of bearer instruments thus involves a greater risk of loss or theft than the use of order instruments.

■ **EXAMPLE 26.2** Alonzo Cruz writes a check payable to "cash," thus creating a bearer instrument. Cruz then hands the check to Blaine Parrington (a delivery). Parrington puts the check in his wallet, which is subsequently stolen. The thief now has possession of the check. At this point, the thief has no rights in the check. If the thief "delivers" the check to an innocent third person, however, negotiation will be complete. All rights to the check will pass *absolutely* to that third person, and Parrington will lose all right to recover the proceeds of the check from that person [UCC 3–306]. Of course, Parrington can recover his funds from the thief—if the thief can be found. ■

26-2 Indorsements

An indorsement is required whenever an order instrument is negotiated. An **indorsement** is a signature with or without additional words or statements. It is most often written on the back of the instrument itself. If there is no room on the instrument, the indorsement can be written on a separate piece of paper (called an *allonge*). That paper must be firmly affixed to the instrument, such as with staples. A paper firmly attached to a negotiable instrument is part of the instrument [UCC 3–204(a)].

A person who transfers a note or a draft by signing (indorsing) it and delivering it to another person is an **indorser.** The person to whom the check is indorsed and delivered is the **indorsee. ■ EXAMPLE 26.3** Luisa Perez receives a graduation check for $100. She can transfer the check to her mother (or to anyone) by signing it on the back. Luisa is an indorser. If Luisa indorses the check by writing "Pay to Avery Perez," Avery Perez is the indorsee. ■

There are four main categories of indorsements: blank, special, qualified, and restrictive. Note that a single indorsement may have characteristics of more than one category. In other words, these categories are not mutually exclusive.

26-2a Blank Indorsements

A **blank indorsement** does not specify a particular indorsee and can consist of a mere signature [UCC

EXHIBIT 26–1 A Blank Indorsement

Mark Deitsch

3–205(b)]. **■ EXAMPLE 26.4** A check payable "to the order of Mark Deitsch" can be indorsed in blank simply by writing Deitsch's signature on the back of the check. ■ Exhibit 26–1 shows a blank indorsement.

An order instrument indorsed in blank becomes a bearer instrument and can be negotiated by delivery alone [UCC 3–205(b)]. In other words, as will be discussed later, a blank indorsement converts an order instrument to a bearer instrument, which anybody can cash. **■ EXAMPLE 26.5** Rita Chou indorses in blank a check payable to her order and then loses it on the street. If Schaefer finds the check, he can sell it to Duncan for value without indorsing it. This constitutes a negotiation because Schaefer has made delivery of a bearer instrument (which was an order instrument until it was indorsed in blank). ■

Does an instrument that requires an indorsement for negotiation need to contain the written signature of an individual's name? That was the question in the following case.

Case 26.1

In re Bass

Supreme Court of North Carolina, 738 S.E.2d 173 (2013).

Background and Facts Tonya Bass signed a note with Mortgage Lenders Network USA, Inc., to borrow $139,988, repayable with interest in monthly installments of $810.75, to buy a house in Durham County, North Carolina. The note was transferred by stamped imprints to Emax Financial Group LLC, then to Residential Funding Corporation, and finally to U.S. Bank N.A. When Bass stopping paying on the note, U.S. Bank filed an action in a North Carolina state court to foreclose. The court issued an order permitting the foreclosure to proceed, and Bass appealed. She argued that the stamp transferring the note from Mortgage Lenders to Emax was invalid because it was not accompanied by a signature. A state intermediate appellate court issued a decision in Bass's favor based on the lack of a "proper indorsement." U.S. Bank appealed.

In the Language of the Court
MARTIN, Justice.
      * * * *

The UCC defines "signature" broadly, as "any symbol executed or adopted with present intention to adopt or accept a writing." The official comment explains that

Case 26.1 Continued

as the term "signed" is used in the Uniform Commercial Code, a complete signature is not necessary. The symbol may be printed, stamped or written; it may be by initials or by thumbprint. It may be on any part of the document and in appropriate cases may be found in a billhead or letterhead. No catalog of possible situations can be complete and the court must use common sense and commercial experience in passing upon these matters. The question always is whether the symbol was executed or adopted by the party with present intention to adopt or accept the writing.

Thus, the UCC does not limit a signature to a long-form writing of an individual person's name. Under this broad definition, the authenticating intent is sufficiently shown by the fact that the name of a party is written on the line which calls for the name of that party. Even if there might be some irregularities in the signature, the necessary intent can still be found based on the signature itself and other attendant circumstances. [Emphasis added.]

* * * [Bass] asserts the stamp by Mortgage Lenders does not qualify as an indorsement under [North Carolina General Statutes (N.C.G.S.)] Section 25–3–204(a) [North Carolina's version of UCC 3–204(a)]. She [contends] that an indorsement must include some representation of an individual signature to be valid.

The contested stamp indicates on its face an intent to transfer the debt from Mortgage Lenders to Emax:

Pay to the order of:
Emax Financial Group, LLC
without recourse
By: Mortgage Lenders Network USA, Inc.

In addition, the stamp appears on the page of the Note where other, uncontested indorsements were placed. We also observe that the original Note was indeed transferred in accordance with the stamp's clear intent. The stamp evidences that it was executed or adopted by the party with present intention to adopt or accept the writing. Under the broad definition of "signature" and the accompanying official comment, the stamp by Mortgage Lenders constitutes a signature.

* * * With no unambiguous evidence indicating the signature was made for any other purpose, the stamp was an indorsement that transferred the Note from Mortgage Lenders to Emax.

Decision and Remedy *The North Carolina Supreme Court reversed the decision of the lower court and held that U.S. Bank was the holder of the note. The indorsements on the note unambiguously indicated the intent of each creditor to transfer the note to a succeeding lender and finally to U.S. Bank.*

Critical Thinking
- **Legal Environment** *Even though forged or unauthorized signatures on negotiable instruments are uncommon, should U.S. Bank have had to prove that the indorsements on this note were valid and authorized? Why or why not?*
- **Economic** *How does the presumption that an indorsement is legitimate "without unambiguous evidence to the contrary" protect the transferability of a negotiable instrument?*

26–2b Special Indorsements

A **special indorsement** contains the signature of the indorser and identifies the person to whom the indorser intends to make the instrument payable—that is, it names the indorsee [UCC 3–205(a)]. ■ **EXAMPLE 26.6** Words such as "Pay to the order of Russell Clay" or "Pay to Russell Clay," followed by the signature of the indorser, are sufficient to identify the indorsee. ■ When an instrument is indorsed in this way, it is an order instrument.

To avoid the risk of loss from theft, a holder may convert a blank indorsement to a special indorsement by writing, above the signature of the indorser, words identifying the indorsee [UCC 3–205(c)]. This changes the bearer instrument back to an order instrument.

■ **EXAMPLE 26.7** A check is made payable to Hal Cohen. He signs his name on the back of the check—a blank indorsement—and negotiates the check by delivering it to William Hunter. Hunter is not able to cash the check immediately but wants to avoid any risk should he lose the check. He therefore writes "Pay to William Hunter" above Cohen's blank indorsement. In this manner, Hunter has converted Cohen's blank indorsement into a special indorsement. Further negotiation now requires William Hunter's indorsement, plus delivery. ■ Exhibit 26–2 shows a special indorsement.

In the following case, a note bore a series of special indorsements, ending in an assignment of the note to

EXHIBIT 26–2 A Special Indorsement

Pay to William Hunter
Hal Cohen

its holder at the time of the maker's default. The question was whether this indorsement and supporting evidence were sufficient to establish the holder's standing to enforce the note.

Case Analysis 26.2

AS Peleus, LLC v. Success, Inc.

Appellate Court of Connecticut, 162 Conn.App. 750, __ A.3d __ (2016).

In the Language of the Court

GRUENDEL, J. [Judge]

* * * *

This appeal concerns real property owned by the defendant [Success, Inc.] and known as 520 Success Avenue (property). That property is partially situated in Stratford and partially situated in Bridgeport [Connecticut]. * * * The defendant executed a promissory note (note) in favor of Greenpoint Mortgage Funding, Inc. (Greenpoint), in the principal amount of $525,000. The note was secured by two identical mortgage deeds on the property.

* * * When the defendant failed to make its * * * payments, the plaintiff [AS Peleus, LLC,] provided the defendant with written notice that it was in default of those obligations. The notice further stated that the plaintiff was "exercising its right under the loan documents to accelerate payment of the note" and therefore demanded "immediate payment and performance of all obligations under those documents * * *." The defendant failed to comply with that demand, and the plaintiff commenced the present foreclosure action in [a Connecticut state court against the defendant].

* * * The court * * * found that the plaintiff "has proven through documents and testimony that it is the owner and

holder of the note * * *." Accordingly, the court rendered a judgment of * * * foreclosure, and this appeal followed.

* * * *

The defendant claims that the court erroneously found that the plaintiff was the owner and holder of the note * * * in question.

* * * *

* * * *The holder of a note seeking to enforce the note through foreclosure must produce the note. The note must be endorsed so as to demonstrate that the foreclosing party is a holder, either by a specific endorsement to that party or by means of a blank endorsement to bearer* * * *. If the foreclosing party produces a note demonstrating that it is a valid holder of the note, the court is to presume that the foreclosing party is the rightful owner of the debt* * * *. The defending party may rebut the presumption that the holder is the rightful owner of the debt, but bears the burden to prove that the holder of the note is not the owner of the debt* * * *. The defending party does not carry its burden by merely identifying some documentary lacuna [gap] in the chain of title that might give rise to the possibility that a party other than the foreclosing party owns the debt* * * *. To rebut the presumption that the holder of a note endorsed specifically or to bearer is the rightful owner of the debt, the defending

party must prove that another party is the owner of the note and debt * * *. Without such proof, the foreclosing party may rest its standing to foreclose* * * on its status as the holder of the note. [Emphasis added.]

In the present case, the plaintiff introduced the original note into evidence at trial * * *. The note contains a series of allonges, under which ownership of the note was transferred by special endorsement to various entities. In the first allonge appended thereto, Greenpoint assigned the note to "Citigroup Global Markets Realty Corp." In the second such allonge, the note was assigned to "Waterfall Victoria Master Fund, Ltd." In the third allonge, the note was assigned to "Waterfall Victoria Depositor, LLC." In the fourth allonge, the note was assigned to "Waterfall Victoria Mortgage Trust 2011–SBC1." In the fifth allonge, the note was assigned to "Citibank, N.A., as Trustee for CMLTI Asset Trust." In the sixth and final allonge, the note was assigned to the plaintiff.

The record thus demonstrates that the plaintiff produced the original note, which bore a special endorsement to the plaintiff. In so doing, the plaintiff established its *prima facie* case against the defendant. The plaintiff also submitted into evidence the * * * default notice that it provided to the defendant. * * * The defendant introduced no evidence in response.

Furthermore, the plaintiff offered the testimony of Russell Schaub at trial. Schaub was the chief operating officer of Gregory Funding, LLC, the plaintiff's mortgage servicing company. * * * Schaub indicated that he was personally familiar with the books and records of

the plaintiff, which were maintained in the ordinary course of business by Gregory Funding, LLC. Schaub also testified that the plaintiff purchased the note from "an affiliate of Citigroup" * * * approximately six months prior to the commencement of this action. On that basis, Schaub testified that the plaintiff was the owner and holder of the note * * * at issue in this case.

* * * *

The record before us contains documentary and testimonial evidence that substantiates the court's finding that the plaintiff was the owner and holder of the note * * * in question. That finding, therefore, is not clearly erroneous.

* * * *

The judgment is affirmed.

Legal Reasoning Questions

1. What evidence did the plaintiff offer to establish standing to enforce the note? Was this sufficient proof? Explain.

2. What might have been the result if the assignments of the note had ended with the indorsement on the fifth allonge?

3. If the series of indorsements on the note had ended with a blank indorsement, would the lower court's holding have been in error?

26–2c Qualified Indorsements

Generally, an indorser, *merely by indorsing*, impliedly promises to pay the holder, or any subsequent indorser, the amount of the instrument in the event that the drawer or maker defaults on the payment [UCC 3–415(a)]. Usually, then, indorsements are *unqualified indorsements*. In other words, the indorser is guaranteeing payment of the instrument in addition to transferring title to it.

An indorser who does not wish to be liable on an instrument can use a **qualified indorsement** to disclaim this liability [UCC 3–415(b)]. The notation "without recourse" is commonly used to create a qualified indorsement.

■ **EXAMPLE 26.8** A check is made payable to the order of Sarah Jacobs. Sarah wants to negotiate the check to Allison Jong but does not want to assume liability for the check's payment. Sarah could create a qualified indorsement by indorsing the check as follows: "Pay to Allison Jong, without recourse, [signed] Sarah Jacobs" (see Exhibit 26–3). ■

The Effect of Qualified Indorsements Qualified indorsements are often used by persons acting in a representative capacity (agents). For instance, insurance agents sometimes receive checks payable to them that are really intended as payment to the insurance company. The agent is merely indorsing the payment through to the insurance company and should not be required to make good on a check if it is later dishonored.

EXHIBIT 26–3   A Qualified Indorsement

Pay to Allison Jong, without recourse
Sarah Jacobs

The "without recourse" indorsement relieves the agent from any liability on the check. If the instrument is dishonored, the holder cannot recover from the agent who indorsed "without recourse" unless the indorser breached one of the transfer warranties. (Transfer warranties, which relate to such matters as good title and authorized signature, will be discussed in a later chapter.)

Special versus Blank Qualified Indorsements
A qualified indorsement ("without recourse") can be accompanied by either a special indorsement or a blank indorsement. In either situation, the instrument still transfers title and can be further negotiated.

A special qualified indorsement includes the name of the indorsee as well as the words "without recourse," as shown in Exhibit 26–3. The special indorsement makes the instrument an order instrument, and it requires an indorsement, plus delivery, for negotiation.

A blank qualified indorsement ("without recourse, [signed] Jennie Cole") makes the instrument a bearer instrument, and only delivery is required for negotiation. ■ **CASE IN POINT 26.9** Thomas Brandt executed a promissory note with MortgageIT, Inc., to finance a home. Seven years later, Brandt still owed $132,000 on the note, and Green Tree Servicing, LLC, filed a suit to foreclose on the property. Brandt argued that MortgageIT had canceled the note because the note included an undated indorsement—"without recourse" to Wells Fargo Bank, NA—that had been crossed out and marked VOID. Another paper was attached to the note, however. It contained indorsements without recourse from MortgageIT to Countrywide Bank FSB, from Countrywide Bank FSB to Countrywide Home Loans, and from Countrywide Home Loans to blank. A state appellate court held that the note was payable to bearer. Because Green Tree Servicing was in possession of the note, it had title to, and was a holder of, the note. Therefore, the court ordered foreclosure on the property to pay Brandt's debt on the note to Green Tree.[1] ■

26–2d Restrictive Indorsements

A **restrictive indorsement** requires the indorsee to comply with certain instructions regarding the funds involved but does not prohibit further negotiation of the instrument [UCC 3–206(a)]. Although most indorsements are nonrestrictive, many forms of restrictive indorsements exist, including those discussed here.

Indorsements to Pay Only a Named Payee An indorsement such as "Pay to Julie Diaz only, [signed] Thomas Fasulo" does not destroy negotiability. Diaz can negotiate the paper to a holder just as if it had read "Pay to Julie Diaz, [signed] Thomas Fasulo" [UCC 3–206(a)]. If the holder gives value, this type of restrictive indorsement has the same legal effect as a special indorsement.

Conditional Indorsements When payment depends on the occurrence of some event specified in the indorsement, the instrument has a conditional indorsement [UCC 3–204(a)]. ■ **EXAMPLE 26.10** Keenan Barton indorses a check as follows: "Pay to Lars Johansen if he completes the renovation of my kitchen by June 1, 2019, [signed] Keenan Barton." Barton has created a conditional indorsement. ■

Article 3 states that an indorsement conditioning the right to receive payment "does not affect the right of the

indorsee to enforce the instrument" [UCC 3–206(b)]. A person paying or taking an instrument for value (*taking for value* will be discussed later in the chapter) can disregard the condition without liability.

The effect of a conditional indorsement, which appears on the back of an instrument, differs from the effect of conditional language that appears on the *face* (front) of an instrument. As noted, conditional indorsements need not prevent further negotiation. In contrast, an instrument with conditional language on its face is not negotiable, because it does not meet the requirement that a negotiable instrument must contain an unconditional promise to pay.

Indorsements for Deposit or Collection A common type of restrictive indorsement makes the indorsee (almost always a bank) a collecting agent of the indorser [UCC 3–206(c)]. In particular, the indorsements "For deposit only" and "For collection only" have the effect of locking the instrument into the bank collection process. Only a bank can acquire the rights of a holder following one of these indorsements until the item has been specially indorsed by a bank to a person who is not a bank [UCC 3–206(c), 4–201(b)]. Exhibit 26–4 illustrates this type of indorsement on a check payable and issued to Marcel Dumont.

Trust (Agency) Indorsements Indorsements to persons who are to hold or use the funds for the benefit of the indorser or a third party are called **trust indorsements** (also known as *agency indorsements*) [UCC 3–206(d), (e)]. ■ **EXAMPLE 26.11** Raj Gupta asks his accountant, Stephanie Malik, to pay some bills for him while he is out of the country. Gupta indorses his payroll check to Stephanie Malik "as agent for Raj Gupta." This trust (agency) indorsement obligates Malik to use the funds only for the benefit of Gupta. ■

EXHIBIT 26–4 "For Deposit Only" and "For Collection Only" Indorsements

For deposit only
Marcel Dumont

or

For collection only
Marcel Dumont

---

1. *Green Tree Servicing, LLC v. Brandt,* 2015 -Ohio- 4636, 2015 WL 6951589 (Ohio App. 2015).

The result of a trust indorsement is that legal rights in the instrument are transferred to the original indorsee. If the original indorsee pays or applies the proceeds consistently with the indorsement, the indorsee is a holder and can become a holder in due course (as described shortly). Sample trust (agency) indorsements are shown in Exhibit 26–5.

As noted, the original indorsee has a duty to use the funds only for the benefit of the indorser. This is a *fiduciary* duty—a duty mandated by a relationship involving trust and loyalty. The fiduciary restrictions on the instrument do not reach beyond the original indorsee, however [UCC 3–206(d), (e)]. Any subsequent purchaser can qualify as a holder in due course unless he or she has actual notice that the instrument was negotiated in breach of a fiduciary duty.

For a synopsis of the various indorsements and the consequences of using each type, see Concept Summary 26.1.

EXHIBIT 26–5 Trust (Agency) Indorsements

> Pay to Stephanie Malik as Agent for Raj Gupta
> Raj Gupta

or

> Pay to Ellen Cook in trust for Roger Callahan
> Roger Callahan

Concept Summary 26.1

Types of Indorsements and Their Effect

Blank Indorsements
- **Definition:** Indorser does not identify the person to whom the instrument is payable. This can merely consist of a signature, such as "Mary Bennett."
- **Effect:** Creates a bearer instrument, which can be negotiated by delivery alone.

Special Indorsements
- **Definition:** Indorser identifies the person to whom the instrument is payable, such as "Pay to the order of Roy Clark."
- **Effect:** Creates an order instrument. Negotiation requires indorsement and delivery.

Qualified Indorsements
- **Definition:** Indorser includes words indicating that he or she is not guaranteeing or assuming liability for payment, such as "Pay to Jack Leist without Recourse, Sarah Wu."
- **Effect:** Relieves indorser of any liability for payment of the instrument; frequently used by agents or others acting on behalf of another.

Restrictive Indorsements
- **Definition:** Indorser includes specific instructions regarding the funds involved or states a condition to the right of the indorsee to receive payment, such as "For Deposit (or Collection) Only."
- **Effect:** Only a bank can become a holder of instruments indorsed for deposit or collection. (In a trust indorsement, the agent has the rights of a holder but has a duty to use the funds consistent with the indorsement.)

How Indorsements Can Convert Order Instruments to Bearer Instruments and Vice Versa

Earlier, we saw that order instruments and bearer instruments are negotiated differently. The method used for negotiation depends on the character of the instrument *at the time the negotiation takes place*. Indorsement can convert an order instrument into a bearer instrument and vice versa.

As mentioned earlier, an instrument payable to the order of a named payee and indorsed in blank becomes a bearer instrument [UCC 3–205(b)]. ■ **EXAMPLE 26.12** A check is made payable to the order of Jessie Arnold. Arnold indorses it by signing her name on the back. The instrument, which is now a bearer instrument, can be negotiated by delivery without indorsement. Arnold can negotiate the check to whomever she wishes merely by delivery, and that person can negotiate by delivery without indorsement. If Arnold loses the check after she indorses it, anyone who finds the check can negotiate it further. ■

Similarly, a bearer instrument can be converted into an order instrument through indorsement. ■ **EXAMPLE 26.13** Jessie Arnold takes the check that she indorsed in blank (now a bearer instrument) and negotiates it, by delivery, to Jonas Tolling. Tolling indorses the check "Pay to Mark Hyatt, [signed] Jonas Tolling." By adding this special indorsement, Tolling has converted the check into an order instrument. The check can be further negotiated only by indorsement (by Mark Hyatt) and delivery [UCC 3–205(b)]. ■ Exhibit 26–6 illustrates how an indorsement can convert an order instrument into a bearer instrument and vice versa.

26–2e Miscellaneous Indorsement Problems

Of course, difficulties can arise with indorsements, such as when a party's name is misspelled or ambiguous. The UCC provides rules that attempt to resolve these issues.

Misspelled Names An indorsement should be identical to the name that appears on the instrument. A payee or indorsee whose name is misspelled can indorse with the misspelled name, the correct name, or both [UCC 3–204(d)]. ■ **EXAMPLE 26.14** Marley Ellison receives a check payable to the order of Mary Ellison. She can indorse the check either "Marley Ellison" or "Mary Ellison." ■ The usual practice is to indorse with the name as it appears on the instrument followed by the correct name.

Instruments Payable to Entities A negotiable instrument can be drawn payable to an entity such as an estate, a partnership, or an organization. In this situation, an authorized representative of the entity can negotiate the instrument. ■ **EXAMPLE 26.15** A check states "Pay to the order of the Red Cross." An authorized representative of the Red Cross can negotiate this check. ■

Similarly, negotiable paper can be payable to a public officer. For instance, checks reading "Pay to the order of the County Tax Collector" or "Pay to the order of Larry White, Receiver of Taxes" can be negotiated by whoever holds the office [UCC 3–110(c)].

EXHIBIT 26–6   Converting an Order Instrument to a Bearer Instrument and Vice Versa

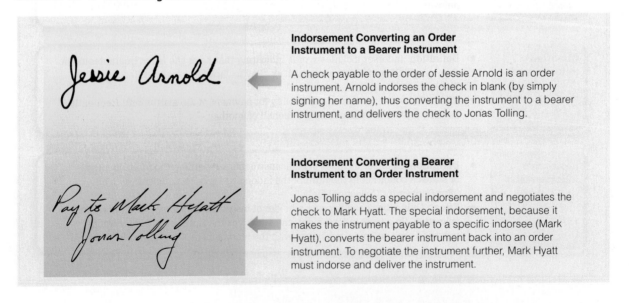

Indorsement Converting an Order Instrument to a Bearer Instrument

A check payable to the order of Jessie Arnold is an order instrument. Arnold indorses the check in blank (by simply signing her name), thus converting the instrument to a bearer instrument, and delivers the check to Jonas Tolling.

Indorsement Converting a Bearer Instrument to an Order Instrument

Jonas Tolling adds a special indorsement and negotiates the check to Mark Hyatt. The special indorsement, because it makes the instrument payable to a specific indorsee (Mark Hyatt), converts the bearer instrument back into an order instrument. To negotiate the instrument further, Mark Hyatt must indorse and deliver the instrument.

Alternative or Joint Payees An instrument payable to two or more persons *in the alternative* (for instance, "Pay to the order of Ying or Tuan") requires the indorsement of only one of the payees [UCC 3–110(d)]. If, however, an instrument is made payable to two or more persons *jointly* (for instance, "Pay to the order of Bridgette and Tony Van Horn"), all of the payees' indorsements are necessary for negotiation.

If the Instrument Is Ambiguous. What if an instrument payable to two or more persons does not clearly indicate whether it is payable in the alternative or payable jointly? In this situation, "the instrument is payable to the persons alternatively" [UCC 3–110(d)]. The same principles apply to special indorsements that identify more than one person to whom the indorser intends to make the instrument payable [UCC 3–205(a)].

■ **CASE IN POINT 26.16** Hyatt Corporation hired Skyscraper Building Maintenance, LLC, to perform maintenance. Skyscraper asked Hyatt to make checks for the services payable to Skyscraper and J&D Financial Corporation. Two of the checks issued by Hyatt were made payable to "J&D Financial Corp. Skyscraper Building Maint." Parties listed in this manner—without an "and" or "or" between them—are referred to as *stacked payees.* The checks were indorsed only by Skyscraper and negotiated by a bank.

J&D and Hyatt filed a lawsuit against the bank claiming that the checks were payable *jointly* and thus required indorsement by both payees. The bank argued that the checks were payable to J&D and Skyscraper *alternatively.* The court found that the bank was not liable. A check payable to stacked payees is ambiguous and thus payable *alternatively,* with indorsement by only one of the payees, under UCC 3–110(d).[2] ■

Suspension of the Drawer's Obligation. When a drawer gives one alternative or joint payee a check, the drawer's obligation on the check to other payees is suspended [UCC 3–310(b)(1)]. The payee who has possession of the check holds it for the benefit of all of the payees. In other words, the drawer has no obligation to make sure that the funds are allocated or distributed among the joint payees.

■ **CASE IN POINT 26.17** Vernon and Shirley Graves owned a building that they leased to John and Tamara Johnson to use for their towing business. The Johnsons insured the property and business through Westport Insurance Company. When a fire destroyed the building, Westport Insurance agreed to pay $98,000 in three payments, with the checks co-payable to Johnson's Towing

and Vernon Graves. Westport issued two checks, for $30,000 and $29,000, and delivered them to Graves. A third check was given to the Johnsons.

The Johnsons did not remit the funds from this third check to the Graveses, who subsequently filed a lawsuit against the Johnsons and Westport. The court dismissed the lawsuit, holding that the parties had agreed that the insurance company would issue the checks to joint payees and that Westport had complied with this agreement. Once Westport sent the checks to one of the joint payees, its obligation to the other joint payees was suspended until the check was either paid or dishonored.[3] ■

26–3 Holder in Due Course (HDC)

One of the most important distinctions in the law governing negotiable instruments is that between a holder and a *holder in due course* (HDC). Often, whether a holder is entitled to obtain payment will depend on whether she or he is an HDC.

26–3a Holder versus Holder in Due Course

When an instrument is transferred, an ordinary holder obtains only those rights that the transferor had in the instrument, as mentioned previously. In this respect, a holder has the same status as an assignee. Like an assignee, a holder normally is subject to the same defenses that could be asserted against the transferor.

In contrast, a **holder in due course (HDC)** takes an instrument *free* of most of the defenses and claims that could be asserted against the transferor. An HDC is a holder who meets certain acquisition requirements and therefore receives a higher level of protection from defenses and claims asserted by other parties.

■ **EXAMPLE 26.18** Shanna Morrison buys a BMW X3 SUV for her business from Heritage Motors in Irvine, California, signing a promissory note for $50,000 as part of the deal. Heritage negotiates the note to Apollo Financial Services, which promises to pay Heritage for it in six months. During the next two months, Morrison has significant problems with the SUV and sues Heritage for breach of contract. She also refuses to make further payments on the note.

Whether Apollo can hold Morrison liable on the note depends on whether it has met the requirements for HDC status. If Apollo has met these requirements and thus has HDC status, it is entitled to payment on the note. If

---

2. *Hyatt Corp. v. Palm Beach National Bank,* 840 So.2d 300 (Fla.App. 2003).

3. *Graves v. Johnson,* 862 N.E.2d 716 (Ind.App. 2007); see also *First Bank and Trust v. Scottsdale Insurance Company,* 2015 WL 7015419 (E.D.La. 2015).

Apollo has not met these requirements, it has the status of an ordinary holder, and Morrison's defense against payment to Heritage will also be effective against Apollo. ■

26–3b Requirements for HDC Status

The basic requirements for attaining HDC status are set forth in UCC 3–302. An HDC must be a holder of a negotiable instrument and must have taken the instrument (1) for value, (2) in good faith, and (3) without notice that it is defective. (An instrument is defective when, for instance, it is overdue, dishonored, irregular, or incomplete.) We now examine each of these requirements.

Taking for Value An HDC must have given value for the instrument [UCC 3–302(a)(2)(i), 3–303]. A person who receives an instrument as a gift or inherits it has *not* met the requirement of value. In these situations, the person normally becomes an ordinary holder and does not possess the rights of an HDC.

Under UCC 3–303(a), a holder takes an instrument for value if the holder has done any of the following:

1. Performed the promise for which the instrument was issued or transferred.
2. Acquired a security interest or other lien in the instrument, excluding a lien obtained by a judicial proceeding.
3. Taken the instrument in payment of, or as security for, a preexisting obligation (sometimes called an **antecedent claim**). ■ **EXAMPLE 26.19** Zon owes Dwyer $2,000 on a past-due account. Zon negotiates a $2,000 note signed by Gordon to Dwyer. If Dwyer accepts it to discharge the overdue account balance, Dwyer has given value for the instrument. ■

4. Given a negotiable instrument as payment. ■ **EXAMPLE 26.20** Justin issued a $5,000 negotiable promissory note to Paige. The note is due six months from the date issued. Paige needs cash and does not want to wait until the maturity date to collect. She negotiates the note to her friend Lexi, who pays $2,000 in cash and writes Paige a check—a negotiable instrument—for the balance of $3,000. Lexi has given full value for the note by paying $2,000 in cash and issuing Paige the check for $3,000. ■
5. Given an irrevocable commitment (such as a letter of credit) as payment.

Value Is Distinguishable from Consideration. The concept of *value* in the law of negotiable instruments is not the same as the concept of *consideration* in the law of contracts. Although a promise to give value in the future is valid consideration to support a contract, it does not constitute sufficient value to make the promisor an HDC. If a person promises to perform or give value in the future, that person is not an HDC.

A holder takes an instrument for value *only to the extent that the promise has been performed* [UCC 3–303(a)(1)]. Let's return to *Example 26.18*, in which Heritage Motors negotiates Shanna Morrison's promissory note to Apollo Financial Services in return for Apollo's promise to pay in six months. In this example, Apollo is not an HDC. At the time of Morrison's breach of contract lawsuit against Heritage, Apollo has not yet paid Heritage for the note. Thus, it did not take the note for value. If Apollo had paid Heritage for the note at the time of transfer (given value), it would be an HDC and could have held Morrison liable on the note. Exhibit 26–7 illustrates these concepts further.

EXHIBIT 26–7 Taking for Value

By exchanging defective goods (a defective BMW X3 SUV) for a promissory note, Heritage Motors breached its contract with Morrison. Morrison could assert this breach as a defense if Heritage presented the note to her for payment. Heritage exchanged the note for Apollo Financial Services' promise to pay in six months, however. Because Apollo did not take the note for value, it is not a holder in due course. Thus, Morrison can assert against Apollo the defense of Heritage's breach when Apollo submits the note to Morrison for payment. In contrast, if Apollo had taken the note for value, Morrison could not assert that defense and would be liable to pay the note.

(Photos from Shutterstock.com: Left, Yuri Areurs; center, Tupungato; right, wavebreakmedia)

Exceptions. In a few situations, the holder may pay for the instrument but not acquire HDC status. For instance, when the instrument is purchased at a judicial sale, such as a bankruptcy or creditor's sale, the holder will not be an HDC. Similarly, if the instrument is acquired as a result of taking over a trust or estate (as administrator), or as part of a corporate purchase of assets, the holder will have only the rights of an ordinary holder [UCC 3–302(c)].

Taking in Good Faith The second requirement for HDC status is that the holder must take the instrument in *good faith* [UCC 3–302(a)(2)(ii)]. This means that the holder must have acted honestly in the process of acquiring the instrument. UCC 3–103(a)(4) defines *good faith* as "honesty in fact and the observance of reasonable commercial standards of fair dealing" [UCC 3–103(a)(4)].

The good faith requirement applies only to the *holder.* It is immaterial whether the transferor acted in good faith. Thus, even a person who takes a negotiable instrument from a thief may become an HDC if the person acquired the instrument in good faith and had no reason to be suspicious of the transaction. The purchaser must honestly believe that the instrument was not defective, however. If a person purchases a $10,000 note for $300 from a stranger on a street corner, the issue of good faith can be raised. Both the suspicious circumstances and the grossly inadequate consideration (value) should make the purchaser suspicious.

In the following case, the court had to determine whether a check had been accepted in good faith.

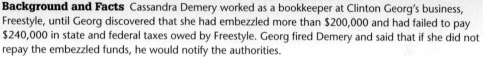

Spotlight on Holder in Due Course

Case 26.3 Georg v. Metro Fixtures Contractors, Inc.
Supreme Court of Colorado, 178 P.3d 1209 (2008).

Background and Facts Cassandra Demery worked as a bookkeeper at Clinton Georg's business, Freestyle, until Georg discovered that she had embezzled more than $200,000 and had failed to pay $240,000 in state and federal taxes owed by Freestyle. Georg fired Demery and said that if she did not repay the embezzled funds, he would notify the authorities.

Demery went to work as a bookkeeper for Metro Fixtures, a company owned by her parents. Without authorization, she wrote a check to Freestyle for $189,000 out of Metro's account and deposited it to Freestyle's checking account. She told Georg that the check was a loan to her from her family to enable her to repay him. Georg used the funds to pay his back taxes.

Two years later, Metro discovered Demery's theft and sued Georg and Freestyle for conversion because Demery had no authority to take the funds. The trial court held that Freestyle was a holder in due course (HDC) and granted summary judgment. Metro appealed. The appeals court reversed, holding that because Demery had deposited the check directly into Freestyle's account, Freestyle could not have been an HDC, as it never had actual possession of the check. Georg and Freestyle appealed.

In the Language of the Court
HOBBS, Justice.
* * * *

A check is a negotiable instrument. The holder in due course doctrine is designed to encourage the transfer and usage of checks and facilitate the flow of capital. *An entity may qualify as a holder in due course even if the instrument at issue may have passed through the hands of a thief.* A holder in due course must meet five conditions: (1) be a holder; (2) of a negotiable instrument who took it; (3) for value; (4) in good faith; (5) without notice of certain problems with the instrument. [Emphasis added.]

To be a holder one must meet two conditions * * * : (1) he or she must have possession (2) of an instrument drawn, issued, or indorsed to him or her. Possession is an element designed to prevent two or more claimants from qualifying as holders who could take free of the other party's claim of ownership. With rare exceptions, those claiming to be holders have physical ownership of the instrument in question.

An otherwise authorized signature on a negotiable instrument is not converted into an unauthorized forgery when an agent, authorized to sign negotiable instruments in his principal's name, abuses that authority by negotiating the instrument to a holder in due course for the agent's own personal benefit.

Case 26.3 Continues

Case 26.3 Continued

Section 4–201(a) [of Colorado's UCC statute] states that a collecting bank "is an agent or sub-agent of the owner of the item." Further, the statute states, "This provision applies regardless of the form of indorsement or lack of indorsement * * *." A check payable to a party and deposited in that party's account makes the party the "owner" of the check under the UCC. Further, the [well-known] treatise on the UCC speaks to a collecting bank as an agent for the owner's possession:

> Sometimes the one claiming to be a holder in due course will not have possession of the instrument at the time of the suit. When a collecting bank holds the check, the solution is simple for section 4-201 makes that bank the agent of the owner of the check. *Under traditional analysis, the agent's possession would be the owner's possession and thus the owner would have "possession."*

Thus, there are circumstances wherein requiring actual physical possession of the instrument would be problematic and constructive possession applies. *Nevertheless, a determination of constructive possession should occur only when delivery is clearly for an identifiable person under circumstances excluding any other party as a holder in due course.* [Emphasis added.]
* * * *

Colorado's UCC intends to promote reliability on issued instruments, not to undermine their efficacy by placing the burden on the person to whom it is issued to determine a check's validity. Metro's recourse is not against Freestyle, but rather against its agent employee for breaching her fiduciary duty to the company.

Having reviewed the holder in due course elements in light of the undisputed facts of the case, we determine that Freestyle was a holder with constructive possession of a negotiable instrument, which was given for value and taken in good faith without notice of a forgery or an unauthorized signature. Accordingly, we reverse the judgment of the court of appeals and remand with directions that the court of appeals return this case to the district court for entry of judgment in favor of Freestyle.

Decision and Remedy *The Colorado Supreme Court reinstated the verdict of the trial court and held that Freestyle had received the check in good faith, not knowing it involved theft. Demery was the wrong-doer in this case, and either Metro or Freestyle would have to absorb the loss. Because Freestyle had no reason to know of the theft and Metro did not take steps to prevent it, the loss should fall on Metro.*

Critical Thinking

- **What If the Facts Were Different?** *Suppose that Demery had gone to work for a company with which she had no relationship and had stolen funds from it to pay Georg. Would Georg then be the more innocent party? Why or why not?*
- **Ethical** *Georg knew that Demery had embezzled funds from Freestyle when she was an employee. Shouldn't he have been suspicious about the source of the funds that Demery was using to repay Freestyle? Why did the court conclude that Freestyle acted in good faith in accepting the check?*

Taking without Notice The final requirement for HDC status concerns notice of defects. A person cannot be an HDC if she or he knows or has reason to know that the instrument is defective in any one of the following ways [UCC 3–302(a)]:

1. It is overdue.
2. It has been dishonored.
3. It is part of a series in which at least one instrument has an uncured (uncorrected) default.
4. The instrument contains an unauthorized signature or has been altered.
5. There is a defense against the instrument or a claim to the instrument.

6. The instrument is so incomplete or irregular as to call into question its authenticity.

What Constitutes Notice? Under UCC 1–201(25), a person is considered to have notice in any of the following circumstances:

1. The person has actual knowledge of the defect.
2. The person has received a notice or notification about the defect (such as a letter from a bank identifying the serial numbers of stolen bearer instruments).
3. The person has reason to know that a defect exists, given all the facts and circumstances known at the time in question.

The holder must also have received the notice "at a time and in a manner that gives a reasonable opportunity to act on it" [UCC 3–302(f)]. A purchaser's knowledge of certain facts, such as insolvency proceedings against the maker or drawer of the instrument, does *not* constitute notice that the instrument is defective [UCC 3–302(b)].

Overdue Demand Instruments. What constitutes notice that an instrument is overdue depends on whether it is a demand instrument (payable on demand) or a time instrument (payable at a definite time).

A purchaser has notice that a *demand instrument* is overdue in two situations. One situation occurs when a person takes a demand instrument knowing that demand already has been made.

The other situation occurs when a person takes a demand instrument an unreasonable length of time after its date. For a check, a "reasonable time" is ninety days after the date of the check. For all other demand instruments, what will be considered a reasonable time depends on the circumstances [UCC 3–304(a)].

Overdue Time Instruments. Normally, a *time instrument* is overdue on the day after its due date. Anyone who takes a time instrument after the due date is on notice that it is overdue [UCC 3–304(b)].[4] Therefore, if a promissory note due on May 15 is purchased on May 16, the purchaser will be an ordinary holder, not an HDC.

If an instrument states that it is "Payable in thirty days," counting begins the day *after* the instrument is dated. For instance, a note dated December 1 that is payable in thirty days is due by midnight on December 31. If the payment date falls on a Sunday or holiday, the instrument is payable on the next business day.

A series of notes issued at the same time with successive maturity dates is overdue when any note in the series is overdue. This serves to notify prospective purchasers that they cannot qualify as HDCs [UCC 3–302(a)(2)(iii)].

If the principal is to be paid in installments, the default or nonpayment of any one installment will make the instrument overdue and provide notice to prospective purchasers of the default. The instrument will remain overdue until the default is cured [UCC 3–304(b)(1)].

An instrument does not become overdue if there is a default on a payment of interest only, however [UCC 3–304(c)]. For this reason, most installment notes

provide that any payment will be applied first to interest, and the remainder will then be applied to the principal. This serves as notice that any installment payment for less than the full amount results in a default on an installment payment toward the principal.

Dishonored Instruments. An instrument is *dishonored* when the party to whom the instrument is presented refuses to pay it. If a holder knows or has reason to know that an instrument has been dishonored, the holder is on notice and cannot claim HDC status [UCC 3–302(a)(2)]. Thus, a person who takes a check clearly stamped "insufficient funds" is put on notice. Conversely, if a person purchasing an instrument does not know and has no reason to know that it has been dishonored, the person is *not* put on notice. Therefore, that person can become an HDC.

■ **EXAMPLE 26.21** Lucinda Gonzalez holds a demand note dated September 1 on Apex, Inc., a local business firm. On September 17, she demands payment, and Apex refuses (that is, dishonors the instrument). On September 22, Gonzalez negotiates the note to Brenner, a purchaser who lives in another state. Brenner does not know, and has no reason to know, that the note has been dishonored. Because Brenner is *not* put on notice, Brenner can become an HDC. ■

Notice of Claims or Defenses. A holder cannot become an HDC if he or she has notice of any claim to the instrument or defense against it [UCC 3–302(a)(2)(v), (vi)]. A purchaser has notice if the claims or defenses are apparent on the instrument's face or if the purchaser had reason to know of them from facts surrounding the transaction.[5] For instance, a potential purchaser who knows that the maker of a note has breached the underlying contract with the payee cannot thereafter purchase the note as an HDC.

Knowledge of one defense precludes a holder from asserting HDC status in regard to all other defenses. ■ **EXAMPLE 26.22** James Wu, knowing that the note he has taken has a forged indorsement, presents it to the maker for payment. The maker refuses to pay on the ground of breach of the underlying contract. The maker can assert this defense against Wu even though Wu had no knowledge of the breach. Wu's knowledge

---

4. A time instrument also becomes overdue the day after an accelerated due date, unless the purchaser has no reason to know that the due date has been accelerated [UCC 3–302(a)(2)(iii), 3–304(b)(3)].

5. If an instrument contains a statement required by a statute or an administrative rule to the effect that the rights of a holder or transferee are subject to the claims or defenses that the issuer could assert against the original payee, the instrument is negotiable. There cannot be an HDC of the instrument, however. See UCC 3–106(d).

of the forgery prevents him from being an HDC in any circumstances. ∎

Incomplete Instruments. A purchaser cannot become an HDC of an instrument so incomplete on its face that an element of negotiability is lacking (for example, the amount is not filled in) [UCC 3–302(a)(1)]. Minor omissions (such as the omission of the date) are permissible because these do not call into question the validity of the instrument [UCC 3–113(b)].

Similarly, when a person accepts an instrument that has been completed without knowing that it was incomplete when issued, that person can take it as an HDC [UCC 3–115(b), 3–302(a)(1)]. Even if an instrument that is originally incomplete is later completed in an unauthorized manner, an HDC can still enforce the instrument as completed [UCC 3–407(c)].

∎ **EXAMPLE 26.23** Peyton asks Brittany to buy a textbook for him when she goes to the campus bookstore. Peyton writes a check payable to the campus store, leaves the amount blank, and tells Brittany to fill in the price of the textbook. The cost of the textbook is $85. If Brittany fills in the check for $150 before she gets to the bookstore, the bookstore cashier sees only a properly completed instrument. Therefore, because the bookstore had no notice that the check was incomplete when it was issued, the bookstore can take the check for $150 and become an HDC. ∎

Irregular Instruments. Any irregularity on the face of an instrument (such as an obvious forgery or alteration) that calls into question its validity or ownership will bar HDC status. In addition, any irregularity that creates an ambiguity as to the party to pay prevents a holder from becoming an HDC.

A difference between the handwriting used in the body of a check and that used in the signature will not by itself make an instrument irregular. Nor will antedating or postdating a check or stating the amount in digits but failing to write out the numbers. Visible evidence that a maker's or drawer's signature is forged, however, will disqualify a purchaser from HDC status.

Nevertheless, a good forgery of a signature or a careful alteration can go undetected by reasonable examination. In that situation, the purchaser can qualify as an HDC [UCC 3–302(a)(1)]. Losses that result from well-crafted forgeries usually fall on the party to whom the forger transferred the instrument (assuming, of course, that the forger cannot be found). Typically, this means the bank that accepts a check despite evidence on the check's face that it is irregular will bear the loss if the check later turns out to be forged.

26–4 Holder through an HDC

A person who does not qualify as an HDC but who derives his or her title through an HDC can acquire the rights and privileges of an HDC. This rule, which is sometimes called the **shelter principle,** is set out in UCC 3–203(b):

> Transfer of an instrument, whether or not the transfer is a negotiation, vests in the transferee any right of the transferor to enforce the instrument, including any right as a holder in due course, but the transferee cannot acquire rights of a holder in due course by a transfer, directly or indirectly, from a holder in due course if the transferee engaged in fraud or illegality affecting the instrument.

26–4a The Purpose of the Shelter Principle

The shelter principle extends the benefits of HDC status and is designed to aid the HDC in readily disposing of the instrument. Anyone, no matter how far removed from an HDC, who can ultimately trace her or his title back to an HDC comes within the shelter principle. The idea is based on the legal theory that the transferee of an instrument receives at least the rights that the transferor had. By extending the benefits of HDC status, the shelter principle promotes the marketability and free transferability of negotiable instruments.

26–4b Limitations on the Shelter Principle

There are some limitations on the shelter principle. If a holder participated in fraud or illegality affecting the instrument, that holder is not allowed to improve her or his status by repurchasing the instrument from a later HDC. Similarly, a holder who had notice of a claim or defense against an instrument cannot gain HDC status by later reacquiring the instrument from an HDC [UCC 3–203(b)].

∎ **EXAMPLE 26.24** Matthew and Carla collaborate to defraud Dina. Dina is induced to give Carla a negotiable note payable to Carla's order. Carla then specially indorses the note for value to Ling, an HDC. Matthew and Carla split the proceeds. Ling negotiates the note to Stuart, another HDC. Stuart then negotiates the note for value to Matthew. Matthew, even though he obtained the note through an HDC, is not a holder through an HDC because he participated in the original fraud and can never acquire HDC rights in this note. ∎

See Concept Summary 26.2 for a review of the requirements for HDC status.

Concept Summary 26.2

Requirements for HDC Status

Must Be a *Holder*	A *holder* is defined as a person in possession of an instrument "if the instrument is payable to bearer or, in the cases of an instrument payable to an identified person, if the identified person is in possession"[UCC 1–201(20)].
Must Take for *Value*	A holder gives *value* by performing the promise for which the instrument was issued or transferred; acquiring a security interest or other lien in the instrument; taking the instrument in payment of, or as security for, an antecedent debt; giving a negotiable instrument as payment; or giving an irrevocable commitment as payment [UCC 3–303].
Must Take in *Good Faith*	*Good faith* is defined for purposes of revised Article 3 as "honesty in fact and the observance of reasonable commercial standards of fair dealing" [UCC 3–103(a)(4)].
Must Take *without Notice*	A holder must not be *on notice* that the instrument is defective in any of the following ways: (1) The instrument is overdue, (2) the instrument has been dishonored, (3) there is an uncured default with respect to another instrument issued as part of the same series, (4) the instrument contains an unauthorized signature or has been altered, (5) there is a defense against the instrument or a claim to the instrument, and (6) the instrument is so irregular or incomplete as to call into question its authenticity [UCC 3–302, 3–304].
The Shelter Principle	A holder who cannot qualify as an HDC has the rights of an HDC if he or she derives title through an HDC [UCC 3–203(b)].

Reviewing: Transferability and Holder in Due Course

The Brown family owns several companies, including the J. H. Stevedoring Company and Penn Warehousing and Distribution, Inc. Many aspects of the companies' operations and management are intertwined. Dennis Bishop worked for J. H. and Penn for more than ten years until, by 2017, he had become the financial controller at J. H. His responsibilities included approving invoices for payment and reconciling the corporate checkbook. In December 2018, Bishop began stealing from Penn and J. H. by writing checks on the corporate accounts and using the funds for his own benefit (committing the crime of embezzlement). Several members of the Brown family signed the checks for Bishop without hesitation because he was a longtime, trusted employee. Over the next two years, Bishop embezzled $1,209,436. He used $670,632 to buy horses from the Fasig-Tipton Company and Fasig-Tipton Midlantic, Inc., with Penn and J. H. checks made payable to those firms. When Bishop's fraud was revealed, J. H. and Penn filed a suit in a federal district court against the Fasig-Tipton firms (the defendants) to recover the amounts of the checks made payable to them. Using the information presented in the chapter, answer the following questions.

Continues

1. What method was most likely used to negotiate the instruments described here?
2. Suppose that all of the checks issued to the defendants were made payable to "Fasig-Tipton Co., Fasig-Tipton Midlantic, Inc." Under the Uniform Commercial Code, were the instruments payable jointly or in the alternative? Why is this significant?
3. Do the defendants in this situation (the two Fasig-Tipton firms) meet the requirements of an HDC? Why or why not?
4. In whose favor should the court rule, and why?

Debate This . . . *We should eliminate the status of holder in due course for those who possess negotiable instruments.*

Terms and Concepts

antecedent claim 488	indorsement 480	restrictive indorsement 484
blank indorsement 480	indorser 480	shelter principle 492
holder in due course (HDC) 487	negotiation 479	special indorsement 481
indorsee 480	qualified indorsement 483	trust indorsement 484

Issue Spotters

1. Kurt receives from Nabil a check that is made out "Pay to the order of Kurt." Kurt turns it over and writes on the back, "Pay to Adam. [Signed] Kurt." What type of indorsement is this? What effect does this indorsement have on whether the check is considered an order instrument or a bearer instrument? Explain. (See *Negotiation.*)

2. Ben contracts with Amy to fix her roof. Amy writes Ben a check, but Ben never makes the repairs. Carl knows Ben breached the contract but cashes the check anyway. Can Carl become an HDC? Why or why not? (See *Holder in Due Course.*)

• **Check your answers to the Issue Spotters against the answers provided in Appendix D at the end of this text.**

Business Scenarios

26–1. Indorsements. A check drawn by Cullen for $500 is made payable to the order of Jordan and issued to Jordan. Jordan owes his landlord $500 in rent and transfers the check to his landlord with the following indorsement: "For rent paid, [signed] Jordan." Jordan's landlord has contracted to have Deborah do some landscaping on the property. When Deborah insists on immediate payment, the landlord transfers the check to Deborah without indorsement. Later, to pay for some palm trees purchased from Better-Garden Nursery, Deborah transfers the check with the following indorsement: "Pay to Better-Garden Nursery, without recourse, [signed] Deborah." Better-Garden Nursery sends the check to its bank indorsed "For deposit only, [signed] Better-Garden Nursery." (See *Indorsements.*)

(a) Classify each of these indorsements.

(b) Was the transfer from Jordan's landlord to Deborah, without indorsement, an assignment or a negotiation? Explain.

26–2. Holder in Due Course. Through negotiation, Emilio has received from dishonest payees two checks with the following histories:

(a) The drawer issued a check to the payee for $9. The payee cleverly altered the numeral amount on the check from $9 to $90 and the written word from "nine" to "ninety."

(b) The drawer issued a check to the payee without filling in the amount. The drawer authorized the payee to fill in the amount for no more than $90. The payee filled in the amount of $900.

Discuss whether Emilio, by giving value to the payees, can qualify as a holder in due course of these checks. (See *Holder in Due Course.*)

26–3. Negotiation. Bertram writes a check for $200 payable to "cash." He puts the check in his pocket and drives to the bank to cash the check. As he gets out of his car in the bank's parking lot, the check slips out of his pocket and falls to the pavement. Jerrod walks by moments later, picks up the check, and later that day delivers it to Amber, to whom he owes $200. Amber indorses the check "For deposit only, [signed] Amber Dowel" and deposits it into her checking account. In light of these circumstances, answer the following questions:

(a) Is the check a bearer instrument or an order instrument?

(b) Did Jerrod's delivery of the check to Amber constitute a valid negotiation? Why or why not?

(c) What type of indorsement did Amber make?

(d) Does Bertram have a right to recover the $200 from Amber? Explain. (See *Negotiation*.)

Business Case Problems

26–4. Transfer and Holder in Due Course. Germanie Fequiere executed and delivered a promissory note in the principal amount of $240,000 to BNC Mortgage. As security for the note, Fequiere executed and delivered a mortgage on real property. BNC indorsed the promissory note in blank. Later, Chase Home Finance, LLC, became the holder in due course of the note and holder of the mortgage. When Fequiere failed to make payments on the note, Chase sought to foreclose on the property. Fequiere asserted that Chase could not foreclose on the property because the mortgage on the property had not been properly transferred from BNC to Chase. Assuming that is true, does it mean that Chase, as holder of the negotiable note, cannot foreclose on the collateral (the property secured by the mortgage)? Explain your answer. [*Chase Home Finance, LLC v. Fequiere*, 119 Conn.App. 570, 989 A.2d 606 (2010)] (See *Holder in Due Course*.)

26–5. Business Case Problem with Sample Answer— Negotiation. Sandra Ford signed a note and a mortgage on

her home in Westwood, New Jersey, to borrow $403,750 from Argent Mortgage Co. Argent transferred the note and mortgage to Wells Fargo Bank, N.A., without indorsement. The following spring, Ford stopped making payments on the note. Wells Fargo filed a suit in a New Jersey state court against Ford to foreclose on the mortgage. Ford asserted that Argent had committed fraud in connection with the note by providing misleading information and charging excessive fees. Ford contended that Wells Fargo was subject to these defenses because the bank was not a holder in due course of the note. Was the transfer of the note from Argent to Wells Fargo a negotiation or an assignment? What difference does that make? If Argent indorsed the note to Wells Fargo now, would the bank's status change? Discuss. [*Wells Fargo Bank, N.A. v. Ford*, 418 N.J.Super. 592, 15 A.3d 327 (App.Div. 2011)] (See *Negotiation*.)

- **For a sample answer to Problem 26–5, go to Appendix E at the end of this text.**

26–6. Indorsements. Angela Brock borrowed $544,000 and signed a note payable to Amerifund Mortgage Services, LLC, to buy a house in Silver Spring, Maryland. The note was indorsed in blank and transferred several times "without recourse" before Brock fell behind on the payments. On behalf of Deutsche Bank National Trust Co., BAC Home Loans Servicing LP initiated foreclosure. Brock filed an action in a Maryland state court to block it, arguing that BAC could not foreclose because Deutsche Bank, not BAC, owned the note. Can BAC enforce the note? Explain. [*Deutsche Bank National Trust Co. v. Brock*, 430 Md. 714, 63 A.3d 40 (2013)] (See *Indorsements*.)

26–7. Transfer by Negotiation. Thao Thi Duong signed a note in the amount of $200,000 in favor of Country Home Loans, Inc., to obtain a loan to buy a house in Marrero, Louisiana. The note was indorsed "PAY TO THE ORDER OF [blank space] WITHOUT RECOURSE COUNTRY HOME LOANS, INC." Almost five years later, Duong defaulted on the payments. The Federal National Mortgage Association (Fannie Mae) had come into possession of the note. Fannie Mae wanted to foreclose on the house and sell it to recover the balance due. Duong argued that the words "to the order of [blank space]" in the indorsement made the note an incomplete order instrument and that Fannie Mae thus could not enforce it. What is Fannie Mae's best response to this argument? [*Federal National Mortgage Association v. Thao Thi Duong*, 167 So.3d 920 (La.App. 5 Cir. 2015)] (See *Negotiation*.)

26–8. Indorsements. Denise and Nick Purificato signed a note secured by real property in Florida. The note was transferred through several parties to Aurora Loan Services, LLC. The Purificatos defaulted on the payments. Aurora filed a suit in a Florida state court against them, seeking a judgment of foreclosure to recover the unpaid debt. While proceedings were pending, Nationstar Mortgage, LLC, succeeded Aurora and became the plaintiff in the suit. At trial, Nationstar provided a screen shot of the note and an allonge, which had been imaged as a single document before Aurora filed the complaint against the Purificatos. Nationstar also provided the original note and allonge, which ended in a blank indorsement. The allonge stated that it was "affixed and a permanent part of said note." Did this evidence establish that the allonge was sufficiently affixed to the note to prove Nationstar's status as the holder with the right to enforce it? Discuss. [*Purificato v. Nationstar Mortgage, LLC*, 41 Fla.L.Weekly. D104, 182 So.3d 821 (Dist.Ct.App. 4 Dist. 2016)] (See *Indorsements*.)

26–9. A Question of Ethics—Indorsements. *As an*

assistant comptroller for Interior Crafts, Inc., in Chicago, Illinois, Todd Leparski was authorized to receive checks from Interior's customers and deposit the checks into Interior's account. Over a period of five months, Leparski stole more than $500,000 from Interior by indorsing the checks "Interior Crafts—For Deposit Only" but then depositing some of them into his own account at Marquette Bank. Leparski used an automated teller machine owned by Pan American Bank to make the deposits into Marquette. Marquette alerted Interior, which was able to recover about $250,000 from Leparski. Interior also recovered $250,000 under its policy with American Insurance Co. To collect the rest of the missing funds, Interior filed a suit in an Illinois state court against Leparski *and the banks. The court ruled in favor of Interior, and Pan American appealed to a state intermediate appellate court. [Interior Crafts, Inc. v. Leparski, 366 Ill.App.3d 1148, 853 N.E.2d 1244, 304 Ill.Dec. 878 (3 Dist. 2006)]* (See *Indorsements.*)

(a) What type of indorsement is "Interior Crafts—For Deposit Only"? What is the obligation of a party that receives a check with this indorsement? Does the fact that Interior authorized Leparski to indorse its checks but not to deposit those checks into his own account absolve Pan American of liability? Explain.

(b) From an ethical perspective, how might a business firm such as Interior discourage an employee's thievery such as Leparski's acts in this case? Discuss.

Legal Reasoning Group Activity

26–10. Holder in Due Course. Celine issues a ninety-day negotiable promissory note payable to the order of Hayden. The amount of the note is left blank, pending a determination of the amount that Hayden will need to purchase a used car for Celine. Celine authorizes any amount not to exceed $2,000. Hayden, without authority, fills in the note in the amount of $5,000 and thirty days later sells the note to First National Bank of Oklahoma for $4,850. Hayden does not buy the car and leaves the state. First National Bank has no knowledge that the instrument was incomplete when issued or that Hayden had no authority to complete the instrument in the amount of $5,000. (See *Holder in Due Course.*)

(a) The first group will determine whether the bank qualifies as a holder in due course and, if so, for what amount.

(b) The second group will decide what would have happened if Hayden had sold the note to a stranger in a bar for $500. Would the stranger qualify as a holder in due course? Explain.

CHAPTER 27

Liability, Defenses, and Discharge

iability on a negotiable instrument can arise either from a person's signature on the instrument (*signature liability*) or from the warranties that are implied when the person presents the instrument for negotiation (*warranty liability*). A person who signs a negotiable instrument is potentially liable for payment of the amount stated on the instrument. Unlike signature liability, warranty liability does not require a signature and extends to both signers and nonsigners. A breach of warranty can occur when the instrument is transferred or presented for payment.

This chapter focuses on the liability *of the instrument itself or the warranties connected with the transfer or presentment of the instrument.* Suppose that Donna agrees to buy one thousand wearable fitness activity trackers from Luis and issues a check to Luis in payment. The liability discussed in this chapter does not relate directly to the contract (for instance, whether the fitness monitors are of proper quality or fit for their intended purpose). Instead, the chapter discusses the liability connected with the *check* (such as what recourse Luis will have if Donna's bank refuses to pay the check due to insufficient funds in her account).

27–1 Signature Liability

The key to liability on a negotiable instrument is a signature. The Uniform Commercial Code (UCC) broadly defines a signature to include any name, word, mark, or symbol that is executed or adopted by a person [UCC 1–201(37), 3–401(b)].

The general rule is that every party, except a qualified indorser,[1] who signs a negotiable instrument is either primarily or secondarily liable for payment of that instrument when it comes due. A person is *not* liable on an instrument unless he or she has signed it personally or through an authorized representative (agent) [UCC 3–401(a)].

27–1a Primary Liability

Primary liability is unconditional. A person who is primarily liable on a negotiable instrument is absolutely required to pay the instrument—unless, of course, he or she has a valid defense to payment. Liability is immediate when the instrument is signed or issued. No action by the holder of the instrument is required. Only *makers*

(who promise to pay) and *acceptors* (such as a bank that has agreed to pay an instrument when presented later) are primarily liable [UCC 3–412, 3–413].

Makers The maker of a promissory note unconditionally promises to pay the note according to its terms. It is the maker's promise to pay that renders the instrument negotiable. Even if the promissory note was incomplete at the time the maker signed it, the maker is still obligated to pay. The maker must pay it according to either its stated terms or terms that were agreed on and later filled in to complete the instrument [UCC 3–115, 3–407, 3–412].

■ **EXAMPLE 27.1** Tristan executes a preprinted promissory note to Sharon without filling in the due-date blank. If Sharon does not complete the form by adding the date, the note will be payable on demand. If Sharon subsequently writes in a due date that Tristan authorized, the note is payable on the stated due date. In either situation, Tristan (the maker) is obligated to pay the note. (Note that if Sharon fills in a date that Tristan did not authorize, Tristan can claim material alteration as a defense to payment.) ■

Acceptors An *acceptor* is a drawee that promises to pay an instrument when it is presented later for payment [UCC 3–409(a)]. ■ **EXAMPLE 27.2** Premier Electric,

---

1. A qualified indorser—one who indorses "without recourse"—undertakes no obligation to pay [UCC 3–415(b)]. A qualified indorser merely assumes warranty liability, which will be discussed later in this chapter.

LLC, brings a draft made payable to R&C Services to Banner Bank for acceptance. Banner Bank accepts the draft by stamping "accepted" on its face, signing it, and dating it. Banner Bank is now obligated to pay the draft when it is presented for payment. ■ The drawee's acceptance is a promise to pay that places the drawee in almost the same position as the maker of a promissory note [UCC 3–413]. Failure to pay an accepted draft when presented leads to primary signature liability for the drawee-acceptor.

27–1b Secondary Liability

Drawers and *indorsers* are secondarily liable. On a negotiable instrument, secondary liability is *contingent liability*. In other words, a drawer or an indorser will be liable *only if* the party that is primarily responsible for paying the instrument refuses to do so—that is, **dishonors** the instrument.

On drafts and checks, a drawer's secondary liability does not arise until the drawee fails to pay or to accept the instrument, whichever is required. With regard to promissory notes, an indorser's secondary liability does not arise until the maker, who is primarily liable, has defaulted on the instrument [UCC 3–412, 3–415].

Thus, dishonor of an instrument triggers the liability of parties who are secondarily liable on the instrument—that is, the drawer and *unqualified* indorsers. ■ **EXAMPLE 27.3** Nina Lee writes a check for $1,000 on her account at Western Bank payable to the order of Rick Carerra. Carerra indorses and delivers the check, for value, to Eric Deere. Deere deposits the check into his account at Universal Bank, but the bank returns the check to Deere marked "insufficient funds," thus dishonoring the check. The question for Deere is whether the drawer (Lee) or the drawee-indorser (Carerra) can be held liable on the check after the bank has dishonored it. The answer to the question depends on whether certain conditions for secondary liability (outlined next) have been satisfied. ■

Parties are secondarily liable on a negotiable instrument *only if* the following events occur:[2]

1. The instrument is properly and timely presented.
2. The instrument is dishonored.
3. Timely notice of dishonor is given to the secondarily liable party.[3]

---

2. An instrument can be drafted to include a waiver of the presentment and notice of dishonor requirements [UCC 3–504]. Presume, for simplicity's sake, that such waivers have *not* been incorporated into the instruments described in this chapter.

3. These requirements are necessary for a secondarily liable party to have *signature* liability on a negotiable instrument, but they are not necessary for a secondarily liable party to have *warranty* liability.

Presentment Recall that *presentment* occurs when a person presents an instrument either to the party liable on the instrument for payment or to a drawee for acceptance. The holder must present the instrument to the appropriate party, in a timely fashion, and give reasonable identification if requested [UCC 3–414(f), 3–415(e), 3–501].

Proper Presentment. Presentment can be made by any commercially reasonable means, including oral, written, or electronic communication [UCC 3–501(b)].

The party to whom the instrument must be presented depends on the type of instrument involved. A note or certificate of deposit (CD) must be presented to the maker for payment. A check is presented to the drawee (bank) for payment [UCC 3–501(a), 3–502(b)]. A draft is presented to the drawee for payment or acceptance.

■ **EXAMPLE 27.4** Urban Furnishings receives a draft that is payable thirty days from the date of issue. Urban can present the draft to the drawee, Elmore Credit Union, the next day for acceptance. Alternatively, Urban can wait thirty days and present the draft to Elmore for payment. ■

Timely Presentment. Timeliness is important for proper presentment [UCC 3–414(f), 3–415(e), 3–501(b)(4)]. Failure to present an instrument on time is a common reason for improper presentment and can discharge unqualified indorsers from secondary liability. The appropriate time for presentment is determined by the nature of the instrument, any usage of banking or trade, and the facts of the particular case.

If the instrument is payable on demand, the holder must present it for payment or acceptance within a reasonable time. If it is a promissory note, the holder must present it to the maker on the note's due date. The holder of a domestic check must present it for payment or collection within thirty days of its *date* to make the drawer secondarily liable. With respect to indorsers, the holder must present a check within thirty days after its indorsement to make the indorser secondarily liable [UCC 3–414(f), 3–415(e)].

The time for proper presentment for different types of instruments is shown in Exhibit 27–1.

Dishonor As mentioned, an instrument is dishonored when the required payment or acceptance is refused or cannot be obtained within the prescribed time. An instrument is also dishonored when the required presentment is excused (as it is, for instance, if the maker has died) and the instrument is not properly accepted or paid [UCC 3–502(e), 3–504].

EXHIBIT 27–1 Time for Proper Presentment

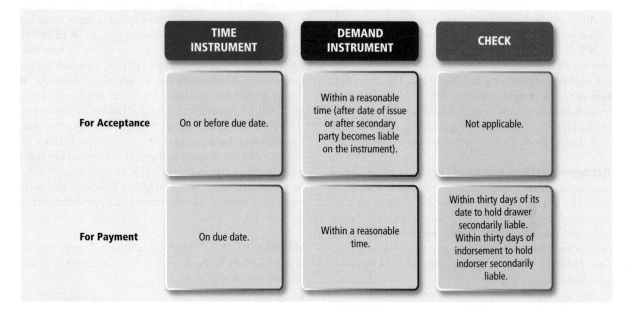

	TIME INSTRUMENT	**DEMAND INSTRUMENT**	**CHECK**
For Acceptance	On or before due date.	Within a reasonable time (after date of issue or after secondary party becomes liable on the instrument).	Not applicable.
For Payment	On due date.	Within a reasonable time.	Within thirty days of its date to hold drawer secondarily liable. Within thirty days of indorsement to hold indorser secondarily liable.

In the following situations, a delay in payment or a refusal to pay an instrument will *not dishonor* the instrument:

1. When presentment is made after an established cutoff hour (not earlier than 2:00 P.M.), a bank can postpone payment until the following business day without dishonoring the instrument [UCC 3–501(b)(4)].
2. When the holder refuses to exhibit the instrument, to give reasonable identification, or to sign a receipt for the payment on the instrument, a bank's refusal to pay does not dishonor the instrument [UCC 3–501(b)(2)].
3. When an instrument is returned because it lacks a proper indorsement, the instrument is not dishonored [UCC 3–501(b)(3)(i)].

Proper Notice Once an instrument has been dishonored, proper notice must be given to secondary parties (drawers and indorsers) for them to be held liable. ■ **EXAMPLE 27.5** Oman writes a check on his account at People's Bank payable to Leah. Leah indorses the check in blank and cashes it at Midwest Grocery, which transfers it to People's Bank for payment. If People's Bank refuses to pay it, Midwest must timely notify Leah to hold her liable. ■

Notice can be given in any reasonable manner, including an oral, written, or electronic communication, as well as a notice written or stamped on the instrument itself

[UCC 3–503(b)].[4] Any necessary notice must be given by a bank before its midnight deadline (midnight of the next banking day after receipt) [UCC 3–503(c)]. Any party other than a bank must give notice within thirty days following the day of dishonor (or the day on which the person learned of the dishonor) [UCC 3–503(c)].

27–1c Accommodation Parties

An **accommodation party** is one who signs an instrument for the purpose of lending his or her name as credit to another party on the instrument [UCC 3–419(a)]. Banks may require an accommodation party—a cosigner—to secure against nonpayment of a negotiable instrument. A parent who cosigns a promissory note with her or his son or daughter, for instance, is an accommodation party, and the child (the maker) is the accommodated party.

Accommodation Makers If the accommodation party signs on behalf of the *maker,* he or she is an *accommodation maker* and is primarily liable on the instrument. ■ **CASE IN POINT 27.6** Anis Algahmee co-signed a $10,000 promissory note enabling Louis Irizarry to obtain

---

4. Written notice is preferable because a secondary party may claim that an oral notice was never received. Also, to give proper notice of the dishonor of a foreign draft (a draft drawn in one country and payable in another), a formal notice called a *protest* is required [UCC 3–505(b)].

a student loan to attend Ohio State University. The terms of the note stated that both the borrower and the cosigner "individually and collectively" promised to pay the debt with 6.36 percent interest and a finance charge.

When Irizarry stopped making payments on the note, the National Collegiate Student Loan Trust filed a lawsuit against both Irizarry and Algahmee. The court held that under the terms of the note, Algahmee was primarily liable as an accommodation maker. Therefore, the court granted a summary judgment against Algahmee for balance due on the student loan (more than $17,000).[5] ■

Accommodation Indorsers If the accommodation party signs on behalf of a *payee or other holder* (usually to make the instrument more marketable), she or he is an *accommodation indorser.* As an indorser, she or he is secondarily liable. ■ **EXAMPLE 27.7** Frank Huston applies to Northeast Bank for a $20,000 loan to start a small business. Huston's lender (which has possession of the note) asks Susan Smith, who has invested in Huston's business, to sign the note. In this situation, Smith is an indorser and thus has secondary liability—that is, the lender must pursue Huston first before seeking payment from Smith. If Smith ends up paying the amount due on the note, she has a right to reimbursement from Huston (the accommodated party) [UCC 3–419(e)]. ■

27–1d Authorized Agents' Signatures

Agency law applies to negotiable instruments. Questions often arise as to the liability on an instrument signed by an agent. An **agent** is a person who agrees to represent or act for another, called the **principal.**

Agents can sign negotiable instruments, just as they can sign contracts, and thereby bind their principals [UCC 3–401(a)(ii), 3–402(a)]. Without such a rule, all corporate commercial business would stop, as every corporation can and must act through its agents. Certain requirements must be met, however, before the principal becomes liable on the instrument. A basic requirement to hold the principal liable on the instrument is that the agent must be *authorized* to sign the instrument on the principal's behalf.

Liability of the Principal Generally, an authorized agent binds a principal on an instrument if the agent *clearly names* the principal in the signature (in handwriting or by some mark or symbol). In this situation, the UCC presumes that the signature is authorized and

genuine [UCC 3–308(a)]. The agent can add his or her own name, but if the signature shows clearly that it is made on behalf of a specific principal, the agent is not liable on the instrument [UCC 3–402(b)(1)]. ■ **EXAMPLE 27.8** Either of the following signatures by Sandra Binney as agent for Bob Aronson will bind Aronson on the instrument: "Aronson, by Binney, agent" or "Aronson." ■

An agent who signs only his or her own name, however, will be personally liable to a holder in due course (HDC) who has no notice of his or her agency status. For ordinary holders, an agent can escape liability by proving that the original parties did not intend the agent to be liable on the instrument [UCC 3–402(a), (b)(2)].[6] In either situation, the principal is bound if the party entitled to enforce the instrument can prove the agency relationship.

Liability of the Agent An authorized agent may be held personally liable on a negotiable instrument in the following three situations.

1. When the agent signs his or her own name on the instrument with no indication of agency status, an HDC can hold the agent personally liable, as noted above.
2. When the agent signs in both the agent's name and the principal's name, but nothing on the instrument indicates the agency relationship, the agent may be liable.
3. When the agent indicates his or her agency status in signing a negotiable instrument but fails to name the principal (such as, "Sandra Binney, agent"), the agent may be liable [UCC 3–402(b)(2)].

Obviously, to protect against potential liability, an authorized agent should disclose on the instrument the identity of the principal and also indicate that the agent is signing in a representative capacity. Failure to do so can lead to personal liability.

■ **EXAMPLE 27.9** Hugh Carter, the president of International Supply, Inc., hires Greenscape Design to landscape International's office complex. Carter signs a promissory note as "Hugh Carter, International Supply, Inc." International does not make any payments on the note, so Greenscape files a suit against both Carter and International. Carter argues that he signed the note as an agent and therefore should not be personally liable for the debt. But a court in this situation will likely decide that Carter is personally liable because nothing on the note indicates that Carter was signing it as an agent for International. ■

Corporate officers often act as agents on behalf of their employers. Like a corporation, a limited liability

5. *National College Student Loan Trust 2004-1 v. Irizarry,* 2015 -Ohio- 1798 (Ohio App. 2015).

6. See UCC 3–402, Comment 1.

company (LLC) is a business entity that can protect its officers from personal liability for obligations entered into on the company's behalf. But an officer may be personally liable for an LLC's business debts if the officer personally guaranties payment. Whether that occurred in the following case was the question before the court.

Case Analysis 27.1

Envision Printing, LLC v. Evans

Court of Appeals of Georgia, __ Ga.App. __, __ S.E.2d __, 2016 WL 906335 (2016).

In the Language of the Court

MERCIER, Judge.

Envision Printing, LLC sued Bernie Evans [in a Georgia state court], alleging that he defaulted on a promissory note. Evans moved for summary judgment, asserting that he was not personally responsible for the debt because he had signed the promissory note solely in his capacity as an officer of a limited liability company. * * *

* * * The record shows that Evans was the CEO [chief executive officer] of Red Rhino Market Group, LLC ("Red Rhino"), that Red Rhino was a customer of Envision Printing, and that Red Rhino was in arrears on its account with Envision Printing. * * * Evans executed a promissory note (hereafter, the "note") in favor of Envision Printing. In pertinent part, the note states:

> FOR VALUE RECEIVED, the undersigned (hereinafter referred to as "Maker") promises to pay to the order of Envision Printing, LLC * * * .

The terms of the note are set out thereafter, and [a signature block follows. Beneath the words "Red Rhino Market Group, LLC" are] the signatures of Evans and one witness * * * . There are no other signatures on the note.

In moving for summary judgment, Evans pointed to the following evidence: the note contained no language indicating that Evans would be personally responsible for the debt; the note used the singular term "Maker" throughout, and the signature box was titled "Red Rhino Market Group, LLC," under which were spaces for several signatures; the only address listed in the note as the Maker's address was Red Rhino's

corporate address; Evans averred in an affidavit that he had signed the note solely in his capacity as CEO of Red Rhino; prior to signing the note, a Red Rhino employee sent an e-mail to Envision Printing stating that "Bernie [has] full authorization under the LLC documents to sign for Red Rhino Market Group;" an Envision Printing employee replied to that e-mail, also by e-mail, instructing the Red Rhino employee to "have Bernie sign it," and did not object to the "to sign for Red Rhino" statement; Envision Printing sent the note to Red Rhino's e-mail address for signatures; and a Red Rhino employee witnessed Evans's signing of the note.

In its response, Envision Printing argued that Evans was personally responsible for the debt. Envision Printing pointed to, among other things, the affidavit of * * * Envision Printing's president wherein the latter averred that Evans had "signed the Note personally, and Envision accepted the Note as a personal obligation of Bernie Evans and continued to do business with Red Rhino after receiving the Note." Envision Printing also asserted that Evans had signed the note without indicating thereon that he was doing so in a representative capacity.

In its order granting summary judgment to Evans, the trial court found that Evans had signed the promissory note solely in his representative capacity and was not personally liable. The court further found that Envision Printing knew that Evans had not signed in his personal capacity.

[Envision Printing appealed.] Envision Printing contends that the trial court erred by granting summary

judgment to Evans when he was personally liable under the note. We disagree.

Generally, a corporation's officers and the corporation are entirely separate and distinct entities. Contracts may be signed by one acting in a representative capacity, or a representative may make himself liable for the debt of the corporation; this Court examines the language of the contract to determine in what capacity the representative is bound. [Emphasis added.]

The construction of contracts involves three steps. At least initially, construction is a matter of law for the court. First, the trial court must decide whether the language is clear and unambiguous. If it is, no construction is required, and the court simply enforces the contract according to its clear terms. Next, if the contract is ambiguous in some respect, the court must apply the rules of contract construction to resolve the ambiguity. Finally, if the ambiguity remains after applying the rules of construction, the issue of what the ambiguous language means and what the parties intended must be resolved by a jury.

The cardinal rule of contract construction is to ascertain the intention of the parties. * * * In this case, looking at the whole contract, we conclude that there is ambiguity as to the capacity in which Evans signed, but, as discussed below, that ambiguity can be resolved by applying the rules of contract construction.

[Official Code of Georgia Annotated (OCGA)] Section 11–3–402(b)(2) [Georgia's version of UCC 3–402(b)(2)] prescribes the conditions under which an authorized representative's signature

Case 27.1 Continues

on a note may make the representative personally liable for the obligation. That statute provides, in pertinent part:

> *** if the form of the signature does not show unambiguously that the signature is made in a representative capacity or the represented person is not identified in the instrument, the representative is liable on the instrument to a holder in due course

that took the instrument without notice that the representative was not intended to be liable on the instrument.

In this case, the form of Evans's signature does not show unambiguously that he signed the instrument in a representative capacity. At the same time, the represented person (Red Rhino Market Group, LLC) is clearly identified in the instrument. Thus, under OCGA Section 11–3–402(b)(2), Evans is liable if Envision Printing took the note "without notice that [he] was not intended to be liable on the instrument." We conclude that Envision Printing had notice that Evans was not intended to be personally liable on the note.

* * * *

Judgment affirmed.

Legal Reasoning Questions

1. On Evans's motion for summary judgment, what evidence did the opposing parties emphasize? Based on this evidence, what did the court conclude?

2. How did the rules of contract construction apply in this case?

3. Suppose that the name Red Rhino Market Group, LLC, had not been included on the note. Would Evans have been personally liable for its payment? Discuss.

Checks Signed by Agents An important exception to the rules on agent liability is made for checks that are signed by agents. If an agent signs his or her own name on a *check that is payable from the account of the principal,* and the principal is identified on the check, the agent will not be personally liable on the check [UCC 3–402(c)]. ■ **EXAMPLE 27.10** Sandra Binney, who is *authorized* to draw checks on Aronson Company's account, signs a check that is preprinted with Aronson Company's name. The signature reads simply "Sandra Binney." In this situation, Binney will not be personally liable on the check. ■

27–1e Unauthorized Signatures

Unauthorized signatures arise in two situations:

1. When a person forges another person's name on a negotiable instrument.
2. When an agent who lacks the authority signs an instrument on behalf of a principal.

The General Rule The general rule is that an unauthorized signature is wholly inoperative and will not bind the person whose name is signed or forged. ■ **EXAMPLE 27.11** Parker finds Dolby's checkbook lying in the street, writes out a check to himself, and forges Dolby's signature. Banks normally have a duty to determine whether a person's signature on a check is forged. If a bank fails to determine that Dolby's signature is not genuine and cashes the check for Parker, the bank will generally be liable to Dolby for the amount. ■

The general rule also applies to agents' signatures. If an agent lacks the authority to sign the principal's name or has exceeded the authority given by the principal, the signature does not bind the principal but will bind the "unauthorized signer" [UCC 3–403(a)]. ■ **EXAMPLE 27.12** Maya Campbell is the principal, and Lena Shem is her agent. Shem, without authority, signs a promissory note as follows: "Maya Campbell, by Lena Shem, agent." Because Maya Campbell's "signature" is unauthorized, Campbell cannot be held liable, but Shem is liable to a holder of the note. This would be true even if Shem had signed the note "Maya Campbell," without indicating any agency relationship. In either situation, the unauthorized signer, Shem, is liable on the instrument. ■

Exceptions to the General Rule There are two exceptions to the general rule that an unauthorized signature will not bind the person whose name is signed:

1. *Ratification.* When the person whose name is signed *ratifies* (affirms) the signature, he or she will be bound [UCC 3–403(a)]. The parties involved need not be principal and agent for this section of the UCC to apply. For instance, a mother may ratify her daughter's forgery of the mother's signature so that the daughter will not be prosecuted for forgery.

A person can ratify an unauthorized signature either expressly (by affirming the signature) or impliedly (by other conduct, such as keeping any benefits received in the transaction or failing to repudiate the signature).

2. *Negligence.* When the negligence of the person whose name was forged substantially contributed to the forgery, a court may not allow the person to deny the effectiveness of an unauthorized signature [UCC 3–115, 3–406, 4–401(d)(2)].

■ **EXAMPLE 27.13** Roger writes and signs a check, leaves blank the amount and the name of the payee, and then sets the check in a place available to the public. Joan finds the check, fills it in, and cashes it. Roger, on the basis of his negligence, can be estopped (prevented) from denying liability for payment of the check. Whatever loss occurs may be allocated between the parties on the basis of *comparative negligence,* however [UCC 3–406(b)]. If Roger can demonstrate that the bank was negligent in paying the check, a court may require the bank to bear a portion of the loss. ■

When the Holder Is a Holder in Due Course A person who forges a check or signs an instrument without authorization can be held personally liable for payment by a holder in due course, or HDC [UCC 3–403(a)]. This is true even if the name of the person signing the instrument without authorization does not appear on the instrument.

■ **EXAMPLE 27.14** If Michel Vuillard signs "Paul Richman" without Richman's authorization, Vuillard is personally liable just as if he had signed his own name. Vuillard's liability is limited, however, to persons who in good faith pay the instrument or take it for value. A holder who knew the signature was unauthorized would not qualify as an HDC (because of the good faith requirement) and thus could not recover from Vuillard on the instrument. (The defenses that are effective against ordinary holders versus HDCs will be discussed later in this chapter.) ■

27–1f Special Rules for Unauthorized Indorsements

Generally, when an indorsement is forged or unauthorized, the burden of loss falls on the first party to take the instrument with the forged or unauthorized indorsement. The reason for this general rule is that the first party to take an instrument is in the best position to prevent the loss.

■ **EXAMPLE 27.15** Jen Nilson steals a check drawn on Universal Bank and payable to the order of Inga Leed. Nilson indorses the check "Inga Leed" and presents the check to Universal Bank for payment. The bank, without

asking Nilson for identification, pays the check, and Nilson disappears. In this situation, Leed will not be liable on the check. because her indorsement was forged. The bank will bear the loss, which it might have avoided if it had asked Nilson for identification. ■

This general rule has two important exceptions that cause the loss to fall on the maker or drawer. These exceptions arise when an indorsement is made by an *imposter* or by a *fictitious payee.*

Imposter Rule An **imposter** is one who, through deception, induces a maker or drawer to issue an instrument in the name of an impersonated payee. The imposter may carry out the deception by her or his personal appearance or by use of mail, Internet, telephone, or other communication.

Focus Is on the Maker's or Drawer's Intent. If the maker or drawer believes the imposter to be the named payee at the time of issue, the imposter's indorsement is not treated as unauthorized when the instrument is transferred to an innocent party. This is because the maker or drawer *intended* the imposter to receive the instrument.

In these situations, the unauthorized indorsement of a payee's name can be as effective as if the real payee had signed. The UCC's *imposter rule* provides that an imposter's indorsement will be effective—that is, not a forgery—insofar as the drawer or maker is concerned [UCC 3–404(a)].

Comparative Negligence Applies. The comparative negligence standard mentioned previously also applies to situations involving imposters [UCC 3–404(d)]. Thus, if a bank fails to exercise ordinary care in cashing a check made out to an imposter, the drawer may be able to recover a portion of the loss from the bank.

■ **EXAMPLE 27.16** Carol impersonates Donna and induces Edward to write a check payable to the order of Donna. Carol, continuing to impersonate Donna, negotiates the check to First National Bank as payment on her loan there. As the drawer of the check, Edward is liable for its amount to First National. If the bank failed to use due care when taking the check from Carol, however, Edward may be able to recover a portion of his loss from First National. ■

Fictitious Payees When a person causes an instrument to be issued to a payee who will have *no interest* in the instrument, the payee is referred to as a **fictitious payee.** A fictitious payee can be a person or firm that does not truly exist, or it may be an identifiable party that will not acquire any interest in the instrument.

Under the UCC's *fictitious payee rule,* the payee's indorsement is not treated as a forgery, and an innocent holder can hold the maker or drawer liable on the instrument [UCC 3–404(b), 3–405]. Basically, the loss falls on the maker or drawer of the instrument rather than on the third party that accepts it or on the bank that cashes it.

Fictitious payees most often arise in two situations:

1. When a dishonest employee deceives the employer into signing an instrument payable to a party with no right to receive payment on the instrument.
2. When a dishonest employee or agent has the authority to issue an instrument on behalf of the employer and issues a check to a party who has no interest in the instrument.

■ **CASE IN POINT 27.17** Braden Furniture Company gave its bookkeeper, Bonnie Manning, general authority to access the company's accounting program and create checks. Over the course of seven years, Manning created more than two hundred unauthorized checks, totaling $470,000, which she deposited in her own account at Union State Bank. Braden Furniture was not a customer of Union State Bank.

The majority of the checks did not identify a payee (the payee line on the check was left blank). Braden Furniture (the drawer) sued Union State Bank for the loss, claiming that the bank was negligent in accepting and paying the blank checks. The court, however, held that the fictitious payee rule applied. Therefore, under the UCC, the loss fell on Braden Furniture, not on Union State Bank.[7] ■

For a synopsis of the rules relating to signature liability, see Concept Summary 27.1.

27–2 Warranty Liability

In addition to signature liability, transferors make certain implied warranties regarding the instruments that they are negotiating. Warranty liability arises even when a transferor does not indorse (sign) the instrument [UCC 3–416, 3–417].

Warranty liability is particularly important when a holder cannot hold a party liable on her or his signature, such as when a person delivers a bearer instrument. *Unlike secondary signature liability, warranty liability is not*

subject to the conditions of proper presentment, dishonor, or notice of dishonor.

Warranties fall into two categories: those that arise from the *transfer* of a negotiable instrument and those that arise on *presentment.* Both transfer and presentment warranties attempt to shift liability back to the wrongdoer or to the person who dealt face to face with the wrongdoer and thus was in the best position to prevent the wrongdoing.

27–2a Transfer Warranties

A person who transfers an instrument *for consideration* makes the following five **transfer warranties** to all subsequent transferees and holders who take the instrument in good faith [UCC 3–416]:

1. The transferor is entitled to enforce the instrument.
2. All signatures are authentic and authorized.
3. The instrument has not been altered.
4. The instrument is not subject to a defense or claim of any party that can be asserted against the transferor.
5. The transferor has no knowledge of any bankruptcy proceedings against the maker, the acceptor, or the drawer of the instrument.[8]

Note that for transfer warranties to arise, an instrument *must be transferred for consideration.* ■ **EXAMPLE 27.18** Quality Products Corporation sells goods to Royal Retail Stores and receives in payment Royal Retail's promissory note. Quality then sells the note, for value, to Superior Finance Company. In this situation, the instrument has been transferred for consideration. ■

Parties to Whom Warranty Liability Extends
The manner of transfer and the type of negotiation that are used determine how far a transfer warranty will run and whom it will cover. Transfer of an order instrument by indorsement and delivery extends warranty liability to any subsequent holder who takes the instrument in good faith. The warranties of a person who, for consideration, transfers *without indorsement* (by delivery of a bearer instrument), however, will extend only to the immediate transferee [UCC 3–416(a)].

---

7. *Braden Furniture Co. v. Union State Bank*, 109 So.3d 625 (Ala. 2012).

8. A 2002 amendment to UCC 3–416(a) adds a sixth warranty. It involves "a remotely created consumer item," such as an electronic check, drawn on a customer's account, which is not created by the payor bank and does not contain the drawer's handwritten signature. This amendment has been adopted in only a few states. Under this amendment, a bank that accepts and pays the instrument warrants to the next bank in the collection chain that the consumer authorized the item in that amount.

Concept Summary 27.1

Signature Liability

Primary and Secondary Liability	• *Primary Liability*—Makers and acceptors are primarily liable [UCC 3–409, 3–412, 3–413]. • *Secondary Liability*—Drawers and indorsers are secondarily liable. Parties who are secondarily liable on an instrument promise to pay on that instrument only if the instrument is properly and timely presented, the instrument is dishonored, or timely notice of dishonor is given [UCC 3–414, 3–415, 3–501, 3–502, 3–503].
Accommodation Parties	• An *accommodation party* is one who signs an instrument for the purpose of lending his or her name as credit to another party on the instrument [UCC 3–419]. • Accommodation *makers* are primarily liable; accommodation *indorsers* are secondarily liable.
Agents' Signatures	• An *agent* is a person who agrees to represent or act for another, called the *principal*. Agents can sign negotiable instruments and thereby bind their principals. • Liability on the instrument depends on whether the agent is authorized and on whether the agent's representative capacity and the principal's identity are both indicated on the instrument [UCC 3–401, 3–402, 3–403]. • Agents need not indicate their representative capacity on *checks*—provided the checks clearly identify the principal and are drawn on the principal's account.

Unauthorized Signatures	• An unauthorized signature is wholly inoperative as the signature of the person whose name is signed *unless:*
	   1. The person whose name is signed ratifies (affirms) it or is precluded from denying it [UCC 3–115, 3–403, 3–406, 4–401].
	   2. The instrument has been negotiated to a holder in due course [UCC 3–403].

Special Rules for Unauthorized Indorsements	• An unauthorized indorsement will not bind the maker or drawer of the instrument except in the following circumstances:
	   1. When an imposter induces the maker or drawer of an instrument to issue it to the imposter *(imposter rule)* [UCC 3–404(a)].
	   2. When a person causes an instrument to be issued to a payee who will have *no interest* in the instrument *(fictitious payee rule)* [UCC 3–404(b), 3–405].

■ **EXAMPLE 27.19** Lyle forges Kim's name as a maker of a promissory note. The note is made payable to Lyle. Lyle indorses the note in blank, negotiates it for consideration to Bret, and then leaves the country. Bret, without indorsement, delivers the note for consideration to Fern. Fern, also without indorsement, delivers the note for consideration to Rick. On Rick's presentment of the note to Kim, the forgery is discovered. Rick can hold Fern (the immediate transferor) liable for breach of the warranty that all signatures are genuine. Rick cannot hold Bret liable, because Bret is not Rick's immediate transferor. Rather, Bret is a prior nonindorsing transferor.

Note that if Lyle had added a special indorsement ("Payable to Bret") instead of a blank indorsement, the instrument would have remained an order instrument. In that situation, Bret would have had to indorse the instrument to negotiate it to Fern, and his transfer warranties would extend to all subsequent holders, including Rick. This example shows the importance of the distinction between transfer by indorsement and delivery (of an order instrument) and transfer by delivery only, without indorsement (of a bearer instrument). ■

Concept Summary 27.2 illustrates the rules on transfer warranty liability.

Recovery for Breach of Warranty A holder who takes an instrument in good faith can sue for breach of

a warranty as soon as he or she has reason to know of the breach [UCC 3–416(d)]. The transferee or holder must notify the warrantor of the breach of warranty claim within thirty days of discovering the breach [UCC 3–416(c)]. Failure to give notice relieves the warrantor from liability for any loss caused by a delay.

The transferee or holder can recover damages for the breach in an amount equal to the loss suffered (but not more than the amount of the instrument). Damages can also include expenses and any loss of interest caused by the breach [UCC 3–416(b)].

These warranties cannot be disclaimed with regard to checks [UCC 3–416(c)]. In the check-collection process, banks rely on these warranties. For all other instruments, the immediate parties can agree to a disclaimer, and an indorser can disclaim by including in the indorsement such words as "without warranties."

27–2b Presentment Warranties

Any person who presents an instrument for payment or acceptance makes the following **presentment warranties** to any other person who in good faith pays or accepts the instrument [UCC 3–417(a), (d)]:

1. The person obtaining payment or acceptance is entitled to enforce the instrument or is authorized to

---

Concept Summary 27.2

Transfer Warranty Liability for Transferors Who Receive Consideration

TRANSFER WARRANTIES

1. The transferor is entitled to enforce the instrument.
2. All signatures are authentic and authorized.
3. The instrument has not been altered.
4. The instrument is not subject to a defense or claim of any party that can be asserted against the transferor.
5. The transferor has no knowledge of insolvency proceedings against the maker, acceptor, or drawer of the instrument.

Indorser who receives consideration obtains transfer warranties that extend *to any subsequent holder* who takes the instrument in good faith.

Nonindorser who receives consideration obtains the same transfer warranties, but they extend *only to the immediate transferee.*

obtain payment or acceptance on behalf of a person who is entitled to enforce the instrument. (This is, in effect, a warranty that there are no missing or unauthorized indorsements.)

2. The instrument has not been altered.
3. The person obtaining payment or acceptance has no knowledge that the signature of the drawer of the instrument is unauthorized.[9]

Protect the Transferee These warranties are referred to as *presentment warranties* because they protect the person to whom the instrument is presented. They often have the effect of shifting liability back to the party that was in the best position to prevent the wrongdoing.

Limitations The second and third warranties do not apply to makers, acceptors, and drawers. It is assumed that a drawer or a maker will recognize his or her own signature and that a maker or an acceptor will recognize whether an instrument has been materially altered.

Presentment warranties cannot be disclaimed with respect to checks. Also, a party claiming breach of warranty must notify the warrantor within thirty days after the claimant knows or has reason to know of the breach. If the claim is made after thirty days, the warrantor is not liable for any loss caused by the delay [UCC 3–417(e)].

---

9. As mentioned, 2002 amendments to Article 3 of the UCC provide additional protection for "a remotely created consumer item."

27–3 Defenses and Limitations

Certain defenses can bar collection from persons who would otherwise be liable on an instrument. There are two general categories of defenses—*universal defenses* and *personal defenses*—as shown in Exhibit 27–2.

27–3a Universal Defenses

Universal defenses (also called *real defenses*) are valid against *all* holders, including HDCs and holders through HDCs. Universal defenses include those listed next and described in the following subsections.

1. Forgery of a signature on the instrument.
2. Fraud in the execution.
3. Material alteration.
4. Discharge in bankruptcy.
5. Minority.
6. Illegality, mental incapacity, or extreme duress.

Forgery A forged signature will not bind the person whose name is used. Thus, when a person forges an instrument, the person whose name is forged has no liability to pay any holder or any HDC the value of the forged instrument. If the person whose name is forged ratifies (approves or validates) the signature, however, he or she may be liable. Similarly, a maker or drawer who is barred from denying a forgery (because it was made possible by

EXHIBIT 27–2 Defenses against Liability on Negotiable Instruments

UNIVERSAL (REAL) DEFENSES	PERSONAL (LIMITED) DEFENSES
Valid against all holders, including holders in due course	**Valid against ordinary holders but not against holders in due course**
1. Forgery. 2. Fraud in the execution. 3. Material alteration. 4. Discharge in bankruptcy. 5. Minority, if the contract is voidable. 6. Illegality, mental incapacity, or duress, if the contract is void under state law.	1. Breach of contract (including breach of contract warranties). 2. Lack or failure of consideration. 3. Fraud in the inducement (ordinary fraud). 4. Illegality, mental incapacity, or duress, if the contract is voidable. 5. Previous payment or cancellation of the instrument. 6. Unauthorized completion of an incomplete instrument and nondelivery of the instrument.

his or her negligence, for instance) may also be held liable [UCC 3–401(a), 3–403(a)].

Fraud in the Execution

If a person is deceived into signing a negotiable instrument by being told that it is something else, *fraud in the execution* (or inception) is committed against the signer [UCC 3–305(a)(1)(iii)]. ■ **EXAMPLE 27.20** Connor, a salesperson, asks Javier, a customer, to sign a paper. Connor says that it is a receipt for the delivery of goods that Javier is picking up from the store. In fact, it is a promissory note, but Javier is unfamiliar with the English language and does not realize this. In this situation, even if the note is negotiated to an HDC, Javier has a valid defense against payment. ■

This defense cannot be raised if a reasonable inquiry would have revealed the nature and terms of the instrument. Thus, the signer's age, experience, and intelligence are relevant because they frequently determine whether the signer should have understood the nature of the transaction before signing.

Material Alteration

An alteration is *material* if it changes the contract terms between two parties *in any way*. Examples include any unauthorized addition of words or numbers or other changes to complete an incomplete instrument that affect the obligation of a party to the instrument [UCC 3–407(a)]. Making any change in the amount, the date, or the rate of interest—even if the change is only one penny, one day, or 1 percent—is material.

It is not a material alteration, however, to correct the maker's address or to draw a red line across the instrument to indicate that an auditor has checked it. It is also not a material alteration to change the figures on a check so that they agree with the written amount. If the alteration is not material, any holder is entitled to enforce the instrument according to its original terms.

A Complete or Partial Defense. Material alteration is a *complete defense* against an ordinary holder but only a *partial defense* against an HDC. An ordinary holder can recover nothing on an instrument that has been materially altered [UCC 3–407(b)]. In contrast, when an original term has been altered, an HDC can enforce the instrument against the maker or drawer—but only according to the original terms [UCC 3–407(c)(i)]. For instance, if the amount payable has been altered, the HDC can enforce the instrument for the original amount but not the altered amount.

Note that if an alteration is readily apparent (such as a number changed on the face of a check), then obviously the holder has notice of some defect or defense. Thus, the holder cannot be an HDC (and therefore cannot enforce the instrument) [UCC 3–302(a)(1), (2)(iv)].

An HDC Can Enforce an Incomplete Instrument That Was Subsequently Altered. If an instrument was originally incomplete and was later completed in an unauthorized manner, alteration can no longer be claimed as a defense against an HDC [UCC 3–407(b), (c)]. The HDC can enforce the instrument as completed because a drawer or maker who issued an incomplete instrument normally will be held responsible for such an alteration. A drawer or maker could have avoided the alteration by the exercise of greater care in completing the instrument.

Discharge in Bankruptcy

Discharge in bankruptcy is an absolute defense on any instrument regardless of the status of the holder [UCC 3–305(a)(1)(iv)]. This defense exists because the purpose of bankruptcy is to settle finally all of the insolvent party's debts.

Minority

Minority, or infancy, is a universal defense only to the extent that state law recognizes it as a defense to a simple contract. Because state laws on minority vary, so do determinations of whether minority is a universal defense against an HDC [UCC 3–305(a)(1)(i)].

Illegality

Certain types of illegality constitute universal defenses, whereas others are personal defenses. If a statute provides that an illegal transaction is void, then the defense is universal—that is, absolute against both an ordinary holder and an HDC. If the law merely makes the instrument voidable, then the illegality is a personal defense against an ordinary holder, but not against an HDC [UCC 3–305(a)(1)(ii)].

Mental Incapacity

If a court has declared a person to be mentally incompetent, then any instrument issued by that person is void. The instrument is void *ab initio* (from the beginning) and unenforceable by any holder or HDC [UCC 3–305(a)(1)(ii)]. Mental incapacity in these circumstances is a universal defense. If a court has not declared a person to be mentally incompetent, then mental incapacity operates as a personal defense against ordinary holders but not against HDCs.

Extreme Duress

When a person signs and issues a negotiable instrument under extreme duress, the instrument is void and unenforceable by any holder or HDC [UCC 3–305(a)(1)(ii)]. An immediate threat of force or violence (for instance, at gunpoint) would qualify as extreme duress. (Ordinary duress is a defense against ordinary holders but not against HDCs.)

27–3b Personal Defenses

Personal defenses (sometimes called *limited defenses*) are used to avoid payment to an ordinary holder of a negotiable instrument. They are not a defense against an HDC or a holder through an HDC. Personal defenses include the following:

1. Breach of contract or breach of warranty.
2. Lack or failure of consideration.
3. Fraud in the inducement (ordinary fraud).
4. Illegality.
5. Mental incapacity.
6. Ordinary duress or undue influence rendering the contract voidable [UCC 3–305(a)(1)(ii)].
7. Previous payment or cancellation [UCC 3–601(b), 3–602(a), 3–603, 3–604].
8. Unauthorized completion of an incomplete instrument [UCC 3–115, 3–302, 3–407, 4–401(d)(2)].
9. Nondelivery of the instrument [UCC 1–201(14), 3–105(b), 3–305(a)(2)].

Breach of Contract or Breach of Warranty A breach of the underlying contract for which the negotiable instrument was issued is a personal defense. If a breach occurs, the maker of a note can refuse to pay it, or the drawer of a check can order his or her bank to stop payment on the check. Breach of warranty can also be claimed as a defense to liability on the instrument.

■ **EXAMPLE 27.21** Elias purchases two dozen pairs of athletic shoes from De Soto. The shoes are to be delivered in six weeks. Elias gives De Soto a promissory note for $1,000, which is the price of the shoes. The shoes arrive, but many of them are discolored, and the soles of several pairs are coming apart. Elias has a defense to liability on the note on the basis of breach of contract and breach of warranty. (A seller impliedly promises that the goods being sold are at least merchantable.)

If, however, the note is no longer in the hands of the payee-seller (De Soto) but is presented for payment by an HDC, the result is different. The maker-buyer (Elias) in that situation will not be able to plead breach of contract or warranty as a defense against liability on the note. ■

Lack or Failure of Consideration The absence of consideration (value) may be a successful defense in some instances [UCC 3–303(b), 3–305(a)(2)]. ■ **EXAMPLE 27.22** Tony gives Cleo, as a gift, a note that states, "I promise to pay you $100,000," and Cleo accepts the note. No consideration is given in return for Tony's promise, and a court will not enforce the promise. ■

Similarly, if delivery of goods becomes impossible, a party who has issued a draft or note under the contract has a defense for not paying it. Thus, in *Example 27.21,* if the shoes were lost in an accident and delivery became impossible, De Soto could not subsequently enforce Elias's promise to pay the $1,000 promissory note. (If the note was in the hands of an HDC, however, Elias's defense would not be available against the HDC.)

In the following case, a party asserted lack of consideration as a defense for not paying a promissory note.

Case Analysis 27.2

Mills v. Chauvin

Supreme Court of New York, Appellate Division, Third Department, 103 A.D.3d 1041, 962 N.Y.S.2d 412 (2013).

In the Language of the Court
PER CURIAM.

* * * *

Plaintiff, Gregory Mills, and defendant, Robert Chauvin, are two experienced attorneys who shared both a friendship and a professional/business relationship. Those longstanding relationships deteriorated and gave rise to this action.

* * * *

* * * The parties formed a partnership and took ownership of a commercial office building located on Crescent Road in the Town of Clifton Park, Saratoga County. * * * After Chauvin

decided, for a variety of reasons, that he no longer wished to maintain his ownership of the Crescent Road property, the parties agreed that Mills would purchase Chauvin's one-half interest in such property and they executed a purchase and sale agreement establishing a purchase price of $261,176.67 and a closing date.

* * * *

Chauvin was an investor in the Amelia Village [real estate development] project [in Virginia]. Over a course of time, Mills made multiple monetary payments to Chauvin—totaling $395,750—which Chauvin claims were investments in the project and Mills claims were loans.

Ultimately, Mills requested that Chauvin return the payments he had advanced. In connection therewith, Chauvin executed a promissory note * * * that obligated him to pay Mills $395,750. However, Chauvin later challenged the validity of the promissory note and claimed that Mills was not entitled to a return of his investments.

* * * *

Mills subsequently filed [a] complaint [in a New York state court against Chauvin] to recover the payments Mills had made with respect to the Amelia Village project, based upon claims of breach

Case 27.2 Continues

Case 27.2 Continued

of contract and unjust enrichment, respectively.

* * * *

The action proceeded to a nonjury trial * * * . At the conclusion thereof, Supreme Court [the trial court] found * * * that the promissory note was valid and enforceable and that Mills was entitled to recover pursuant to its terms. Chauvin now appeals from the judgment entered upon that decision.

* * * *

* * * Initially, we reject Chauvin's claim that Supreme Court erred in concluding that the * * * promissory note was enforceable. Chauvin does not dispute that Mills had previously paid him $395,750 in connection with the Amelia Village project, that he signed the promissory note promising to repay that amount to Mills, or that he tendered the note to Mills for the purpose of providing documentation to Mills' lending institution in support of Mills'

application for financing of the purchase of the Crescent Road property. Instead, Chauvin claims that the promissory note was not enforceable because it was not given to secure a debt and, therefore, lacked consideration.

In this regard, Mills testified that * * * the parties * * * agreed that Chauvin would repay Mills all of the money that Mills had contributed to the Amelia Village project and that the promissory note confirmed their agreement. On the other hand, Chauvin claims that the payments that Mills made to the Amelia Village project were investments that could not be returned when Mills withdrew from that project, and that the promissory note was not intended to be a promise of repayment.

* * * *

The record amply supports Supreme Court's finding that the consideration for the promissory note was the $395,750 that Mills had provided to

Chauvin in connection with the Amelia Village project and that the promissory note represented security for Chauvin's antecedent obligation to repay such funds. *The note itself—which was drafted by Chauvin, signed by him, notarized and transmitted to Mills clearly states that it was executed in return for a loan received by Chauvin and contained an unconditional promise or order to pay a sum certain in money. In addition, Mills took the note as a holder in due course.* Based upon our independent evaluation of the evidence and, giving due deference to the trial court's credibility determinations concerning witnesses, we conclude that Supreme Court's determination that Chauvin failed to establish a bona fide defense of lack of consideration is supported by the record. [Emphasis added.]

* * * *

ORDERED that the order and judgments are affirmed, with costs to plaintiff.

Legal Reasoning Questions

1. If the court had accepted Chauvin's claim that Mills's funds represented an investment, would the result in this case have been different? Explain.

2. Do the facts in this case support the court's conclusion that Mills took Chauvin's note as an HDC? Why or why not?

3. How did Mills's status as an HDC affect Chauvin's asserted defense?

Fraud in the Inducement (Ordinary Fraud) A person who issues a negotiable instrument based on false statements by the other party will be able to avoid payment on that instrument, unless the holder is an HDC. ■ **CASE IN POINT 27.23** New Houston Gold Exchange, Inc. (HGE), issued a $3,500 postdated check to Shelly McKee to buy a purportedly genuine Rolex watch. McKee indorsed the check and presented it to RR Maloan Investments, Inc., a check-cashing service. RR Maloan cashed the check. Meanwhile, HGE issued a stop-payment order on the check based on information that the watch was counterfeit. When RR Maloan presented the check to HGE's bank for payment, the bank refused to honor it. HGE claimed that RR Maloan was not a holder in due course because of McKee's fraud in selling an allegedly fake Rolex. RR Maloan filed a suit in a Texas state

court against HGE to recover the funds, asserting that it was an HDC entitled to collect on the check.

Ultimately, a state appellate court found that McKee's ostensible fraud toward HGE did not prevent RR Maloan from obtaining the status of an HDC. The check-cashing service took the check in good faith and for fair value, unaware of McKee's alleged fraud in inducing HGE to issue the check. Therefore, RR Maloan was entitled to payment on the check.[10] ■

Illegality As mentioned, if a statute provides that an illegal transaction is voidable, the defense is personal. For instance, some states make contracts in restraint of trade

---

10. *RR Maloan Investments, Inc. v. New HGE, Inc.,* 428 S.W.3d 355 (Tex. App.—Houston 2014).

voidable. Thus, an instrument given in payment of a contract to restrain trade in those states is voidable and operates as a personal defense.

Mental Incapacity If a maker or drawer issues a negotiable instrument while mentally incompetent but before a court has declared him or her to be so, the instrument is voidable. In this situation, mental incapacity serves as a personal defense.

27–3c Federal Limitations on the Rights of HDCs

The federal government limits the rights of HDCs in certain circumstances because of the harsh effects that the HDC rules can sometimes have on consumers. Under the HDC doctrine, a consumer who purchased a defective product (such as a defective automobile) would continue to be liable to HDCs even if the consumer returned the defective product to the retailer.

■ **EXAMPLE 27.24** To buy a used truck with a one-year warranty, Brian pays $5,000 down and signs a promissory note to the dealer for the remaining $15,000. The truck turns out to be defective, and Brian returns it to the dealer, but the dealer has already sold the note to an HDC. Under the HDC doctrine, Brian would remain liable to the HDC for $15,000 in this situation because his claim of breach of warranty is a personal defense, not a universal defense. ■

To protect consumers who purchase defective products, the Federal Trade Commission (FTC) adopted Rule 433, which effectively abolished the HDC doctrine in consumer transactions.[11]

FTC Rule 433 FTC Rule 433 severely limits the rights of HDCs that purchase instruments arising out of *consumer credit* transactions. The rule applies to consumers who purchase goods or services for personal, family, or household use using a consumer credit contract. The regulation prevents a consumer from being required to make payment for a defective product to a third party HDC who has acquired a promissory note that formed part of the consumer's contract with the dealer who sold the defective good.

Rule 433 requires the following provision to be included in boldface type in consumer credit contracts:

NOTICE

ANY HOLDER OF THIS CONSUMER CREDIT CONTRACT IS SUBJECT TO ALL CLAIMS AND DEFENSES WHICH THE DEBTOR COULD ASSERT AGAINST THE SELLER OF GOODS OR SERVICES OBTAINED PURSUANT HERETO OR WITH THE PROCEEDS HEREOF. RECOVERY HEREUNDER BY THE DEBTOR SHALL NOT EXCEED AMOUNTS PAID BY THE DEBTOR HEREUNDER.

Effect of the Rule When a negotiable instrument contains the required notice, a consumer can bring any defense that she or he has against the seller of a product against a subsequent holder as well. In essence, FTC Rule 433 places an HDC of the instrument in the position of a contract assignee.

The rule makes the buyer's duty to pay conditional on the seller's full performance of the contract. It also clearly reduces the degree of transferability of negotiable instruments resulting from consumer credit contracts. An instrument that contains this notice or a similar statement required by law remains negotiable, but there cannot be an HDC of such an instrument [UCC 3–106(d)].

There is a loophole, however. FTC Rule 433 does not prohibit third parties from purchasing notes or credit contracts that do *not* contain the required notice. If a third party purchases an instrument arising from a consumer credit transaction that lacks the notice, that third party normally is not subject to the buyer's defenses against the seller. Thus, some consumers remain unprotected by the FTC rule.[12]

27–4 Discharge

Discharge from liability on an instrument can come from payment, cancellation, or material alteration. Discharge can also occur if a party reacquires an instrument, if a holder impairs another party's right of recourse, or if a holder surrenders collateral without consent.

---

11. 16 C.F.R. Section 433.2. The rule was enacted in 1976 pursuant to the FTC's authority under the Federal Trade Commission Act, 15 U.S.C. Sections 41–58.

12. A 2002 amendment to UCC 3–305(e) closes this loophole, but only a minority of the states have adopted the amendment. The amendment makes a third party holder in possession of a note or other instrument that was supposed to include this notice subject to a buyer's defenses against a seller even if the instrument did not include the notice.

27–4a Discharge by Payment or Tender of Payment

All parties to a negotiable instrument will be discharged when the party primarily liable on it pays to a holder the full amount due [UCC 3–602, 3–603]. The liability of all parties is also discharged when the drawee of an unaccepted draft or check makes payment in good faith to the holder.

Payment by any other party (for instance, an indorser) discharges only the liability of that party and subsequent parties. The party making such a payment still has the right to recover on the instrument from any prior parties.[13]

Good Faith Required A party will not be discharged if that party knowingly (in bad faith) pays a holder who acquired the instrument by theft or who obtained the instrument from someone else who acquired it by theft [UCC 3–602(b)(2)]. An exception to this rule is made if the person has the rights of an HDC.

Tender of Payment Sometimes, a tender (offer) of payment is made to a person entitled to enforce the instrument, and the tender is refused. In that situation, the rights of indorsers and accommodation parties to seek reimbursement are impaired (impairment of the right of recourse is discussed shortly). Therefore, the indorsers and accommodation parties are discharged to the extent of the amount of the tender [UCC 3–603(b)].

■ **EXAMPLE 27.25** Megan Caldwell is entitled to enforce a $15,000 promissory note, which was indorsed by Bret Reznor and Jill Sanchez. Omni Ventures, LLC, tenders a $10,000 payment on the note, but Caldwell refuses. In this situation, Reznor's and Sanchez's liability on the note is discharged to the extent of the tender ($10,000). ■

When a tender of payment of the amount due on an instrument is made to a person entitled to enforce the instrument, the obligation to pay interest after the date of tender is discharged [UCC 3–603(c)].

27–4b Discharge by Cancellation or Surrender

Intentional cancellation of an instrument discharges the liability of all parties [UCC 3–604]. Destruction or mutilation of a negotiable instrument is considered cancellation only if it is done with the intention of eliminating obligation on the instrument [UCC 3–604(a)(i)]. Thus, if an instrument is destroyed or mutilated by accident, the instrument is not discharged, and the original terms can be established by parol evidence [UCC 3–309].

Any of the following acts—if done by the holder *with the intent to cancel* the obligation—will discharge liability:

1. Writing "Paid" across the face of an instrument.
2. Intentionally tearing up an instrument.
3. Crossing out a party's signature. Doing this will discharge that party's liability and the liability of subsequent indorsers who have already signed the instrument.
4. Surrendering the instrument (such as a promissory note) to the party to be discharged.

■ **CASE IN POINT 27.26** Edith Mark bought a Ford pickup and signed a loan contract and promissory note with Huntington National Bank to finance the purchase. She had made twenty of the sixty-six payments required on the loan when she received the original agreement, stamped "PAID," in the mail, along with the title certificate. Mark stopped making payments on the loan, and the bank filed a lawsuit. Mark argued that the note had been discharged by surrender, but the bank claimed that the documents had been returned to her due to an inadvertent clerical error. The court held that because the bank did not intend to discharge the note when it returned the documents to Mark, the surrender did not constitute a valid cancellation of the note.[14] ■

27–4c Discharge by Material Alteration

Materially altering an instrument may discharge the liability of all parties, as previously discussed [UCC 3–407(b)]. (An HDC may be able to enforce a materially altered instrument against its maker or drawer according to the instrument's *original* terms, however.)

27–4d Discharge by Reacquisition

The reacquisition of an instrument by a person who held it previously discharges all intervening indorsers against subsequent holders who do not qualify as HDCs [UCC 3–207]. Of course, the person reacquiring the instrument may be liable to subsequent holders if the instrument is dishonored.

---

13. Under a 2002 amendment to UCC 3–602(b), when a party entitled to enforce an instrument transfers it without giving notice to the parties obligated to pay it, and one of those parties pays the transferor, that payment is effective. For instance, Roberto borrows $5,000 from Consumer Finance Company on a note payable to the lender. Consumer Finance transfers the note to Delta Investment Corporation but continues to collect payments from Roberto. Under this amendment, those payments effectively discharge Roberto to the extent of their amount.

14. *Huntington National Bank v. Mark*, 2004 -Ohio- 3856 (Ohio App. 2004).

27–4e Discharge by Impairment of Recourse

Discharge can also occur when a party's right of recourse is impaired [UCC 3–605]. A *right of recourse* is a right to seek reimbursement. Ordinarily, when a holder collects the amount of an instrument from an indorser, the indorser has a right of recourse against prior indorsers, the maker or drawer, and accommodation parties.

If the holder has adversely affected the indorser's right to seek reimbursement from these other parties, however, the indorser is not liable on the instrument (to the extent that the indorser's right of recourse is impaired). This occurs when, for instance, the holder releases or agrees not to sue a party against whom the indorser has a right of recourse. It also occurs when a holder agrees to an extension of the instrument's due date or to some other material modification that results in an impairment of the indorser's right of recourse [UCC 3–605(c), (d)].[15]

---

15. The 2002 amendments to UCC 3–605 essentially apply the principles of suretyship and guaranty to circumstances involving the impairment of the right of recourse of "secondary obligors." These obligors include indorsers and accommodation parties. Amended UCC 3–605(a) differs from these principles, however, in that the release of a principal obligor by a person entitled to enforce a check grants a complete discharge to an indorser of the check without requiring proof of harm.

27–4f Discharge by Impairment of Collateral

Sometimes, a party to an instrument gives collateral as security that her or his performance will occur. When a holder "impairs the value" of that collateral without the consent of the parties who would benefit from it in the event of nonpayment, those parties are discharged to the extent of the impairment [UCC 3–605(e), (f)].

■ **EXAMPLE 27.27** Jerome and Myra sign a note as co-makers, putting up Jerome's property as collateral. The note is payable to Montessa. Montessa is required by law to file a *financing statement* with the state to put others on notice of her interest in Jerome's property. If Montessa fails to file the financing statement and Jerome goes through bankruptcy, the property may be sold to pay other debts. Jerome will be unable to pay anything on the note.

In other words, Montessa's failure to file the statement prevents her from taking possession of the collateral, selling it, and crediting the amount owed on the note. This impairs the value of the collateral to Myra, because the proceeds from the sale would have discharged her liability on the note. Myra, as co-maker, is discharged to the extent of this impairment. She is responsible only for any remaining indebtedness, not for the entire unpaid balance. ■

Reviewing: Liability, Defenses, and Discharge

Nancy Mahar was the office manager at Golden Years Nursing Home, Inc. She was given a signature stamp to issue checks to the nursing home's employees for up to $100 as advances on their pay. The checks were drawn on Golden Years' account at First National Bank. Over a seven-year period, Mahar wrote a number of checks to employees exclusively for the purpose of embezzling funds for herself. She forged the employees' indorsements on the checks, signed her name as a second indorser, and deposited the checks in her personal account at Star Bank. The employees whose names were on the checks never actually requested them. When the scheme was uncovered, Golden Years filed a suit against Mahar, Star Bank, and others to recover the funds. Using the information presented in the chapter, answer the following questions.

1. With regard to signature liability, which provision of the Uniform Commercial Code (UCC) discussed in this chapter applies to this scenario?
2. What is the rule set forth by that provision?
3. Under the UCC, which party, Golden Years or Star Bank, must bear the loss in this situation? Why?
4. Based on these facts, describe any transfer or presentment warranties that Mahar may have violated.

Debate This . . .   *Because signature stamps create so many opportunities for embezzlement, they should be banned.*

Terms and Concepts

accommodation party 499
agent 500
dishonor 498
fictitious payee 503

imposter 503
personal defense 509
presentment warranty 506
principal 500

transfer warranty 504
universal defense 507

Issue Spotters

1. Rye signs corporate checks for Suchin Corporation. Rye writes a check payable to U-All Company, even though Suchin does not owe U-All anything. Rye signs the check, forges U-All's indorsement, and cashes the check at Viceroy Bank, the drawee. Does Suchin have any recourse against the bank for the payment? Why or why not? (See *Signature Liability.*)

2. Skye asked Jim to buy a textbook for her at the campus bookstore. Skye wrote a check payable to the bookstore and left the amount blank for Jim to fill in the price of the book. The cost of the book was $100. Jim filled in the check for $200 before he got to the bookstore. The clerk at the bookstore took the check for $200 and gave Jim the book, plus $100 in cash. Was the bookstore a holder in due course on Skye's check? (See *Discharge.*)

• **Check your answers to the Issue Spotters against the answers provided in Appendix D at the end of this text.**

Business Scenarios

27–1. Material Alteration. Williams purchased a used car from Stein for $1,000. Williams paid for the car with a check (written in pencil) payable to Stein for $1,000. Stein, through careful erasures and alterations, changed the amount on the check to read $10,000 and negotiated the check to Boz. Boz took the check for value, in good faith, and without notice of the alteration. He thus met the Uniform Commercial Code's requirements for the status of a holder in due course. Can Williams successfully raise the universal (real) defense of material alteration to avoid payment on the check? Explain. (See *Defenses and Limitations.*)

27–2. Signature Liability. Waldo makes out a negotiable promissory note payable to the order of Grace. Grace indorses the note by writing on it "Without recourse, Grace" and transfers the note for value to Adam. Adam, in need of cash,

negotiates the note to Keith by indorsing it with the words "Pay to Keith, Adam." On the due date, Keith presents the note to Waldo for payment, only to learn that Waldo has filed for bankruptcy and will have all debts (including the note) discharged. Discuss fully whether Keith can hold Waldo, Grace, or Adam liable on the note. (See *Signature Liability.*)

27–3. Defenses. Niles sold Kennedy a small motorboat for $1,500, telling Kennedy that the boat was in excellent condition. Kennedy gave Niles a check for $1,500, which Niles indorsed and gave to Frazier for value. When Kennedy took the boat for a trial run, she discovered that the boat leaked, needed to be painted, and required a new motor. Kennedy stopped payment on her check, which had not yet been cashed. Niles had disappeared. Can Frazier recover from Kennedy as a holder in due course? Discuss. (See *Defenses and Limitations.*)

Business Case Problems

27–4. Business Case Problem with Sample Answer— Defenses. Thomas Klutz obtained a franchise from Kahala Franchise Corp. to operate a Samurai Sam's restaurant. Under their agreement, Klutz could transfer the franchise only if he obtained Kahala's approval and paid a transfer fee. Without telling Kahala, Klutz sold the restaurant to William Thorbecke. Thorbecke signed a note for the price. When Kahala learned of the deal, the franchisor told Thorbecke to stop using the Samurai Sam's name. Thorbecke stopped paying on the note, and Klutz filed a claim for the unpaid amount. In defense, Thorbecke asserted breach of contract and fraud. Are these defenses effective against Klutz? Explain. [*Kahala Franchise Corp. v. Hit*

Enterprises, LLC, 159 Wash.App. 1013 (Div. 2 2011)] (See *Defenses and Limitations.*)

• **For a sample answer to Problem 27–4, go to Appendix E at the end of this text.**

27–5. Defenses. Damion and Kiya Carmichael took out a loan from Ameriquest Mortgage Co. to refinance their mortgage. They signed a note to make monthly payments on the loan. Later, Deutsche Bank National Trust Co. acquired the note. The Carmichaels stopped making payments and filed for bankruptcy. Deutsche asked the court to foreclose on the mortgage. The Carmichaels asserted that they had been fraudulently induced to make the loan and sign the note. Was the bank free of this defense? Explain. *[In re Carmichael,* 443 Bankr. 698 (E.D.Pa. 2011)] (See *Defenses and Limitations.*)

27–6. Unauthorized Indorsements. Angela Brock borrowed $544,000 and signed a note payable to Amerifund Mortgage Services, LLC, to buy a house in Silver Spring, Maryland. The note was indorsed in blank and transferred several times "without recourse" before Brock fell behind on the payments. On behalf of Deutsche Bank National Trust Co., BAC Home Loans Servicing LP initiated foreclosure. Brock filed an action in a Maryland state court to block it, arguing that BAC could not foreclose because Deutsche Bank, not BAC, owned the note. Can BAC enforce the note? Explain. [*Deutsche Bank National Trust Co. v. Brock,* 63 A.3d 40 (Md. 2013)] (See *Signature Liability.*)

27–7. Signature Liability. Guillermo and Guadalupe Albarran and their sons, Ruben and Rolando, owned R. Cleaning Impact, Inc. (RCI). Neresh Kumar owned Amba II, Inc., a check-cashing business. The Albarrans cashed checks through Amba on a regular basis, often delivering a stack of employee paychecks to Amba for cashing. Later, the Albarrans' bank refused payment on some of the checks. Kumar learned that some of these items were payable to fictitious payees with fictitious addresses. Others had been filled out for amounts greater than real employees' pay. Meanwhile, RCI became insolvent and closed its account, and Guillermo and Guadalupe filed for bankruptcy. Amba was left with many unpaid checks. Among these parties, who can be held liable for the loss on the unpaid checks? Explain. *[Albarran v. Amba II, Inc.,* 2016 WL 688924 (2016)] (See *Signature Liability.*)

27–8. Special Case Analysis—Defenses. Go to Case Analysis Case 27.2, *Mills v. Chauvin.* Read the excerpt and answer the following questions.

(a) Issue: What document was at the center of the dispute in this case?

(b) Rule of Law: What are the elements of consideration? What are the requirements for attaining the status of a holder in due course (HDC)?

(c) Applying the Rule of Law: Did the document at the center of the dispute in this case satisfy the elements of consideration? Did the party in possession of the document take it as an HDC? Explain.

(d) Conclusion: Who did the court determine was liable? Why?

27–9. A Question of Ethics—Primary and Secondary Liability. *Clarence Morgan, Jr., owned Easy Way Automotive, a* *car dealership in D'Lo, Mississippi. Easy Way sold a truck to Loyd Barnard, who signed a note for the amount of the price payable to Trustmark National Bank in six months. Before the note came due, Barnard returned the truck to Easy Way, which sold it to another buyer. Using some of the proceeds from the second sale, Easy Way sent a check to Trustmark to pay Barnard's note. Meanwhile, Barnard obtained another truck from Easy Way, financed through another six-month note payable to Trustmark. After eight of these deals, some of which involved more than one truck, an Easy Way check to Trustmark was dishonored. In a suit in a Mississippi state court, Trustmark sought to recover the amounts of two of the notes from Barnard. Trustmark had not secured titles to two of the trucks covered by the notes, however, and this complicated Barnard's efforts to reclaim the vehicles from the later buyers. [*Trustmark National Bank v. Barnard, 930 So.2d 1281 (Miss.App. 2006)]* (See *Signature Liability.*)

(a) On what basis might Barnard be liable on the Trustmark notes? Would he be primarily or secondarily liable? Could this liability be discharged on the theory that Barnard's right of recourse had been impaired when Trustmark did not secure titles to the trucks covered by the notes? Explain.

(b) Easy Way's account had been subject to other recent overdrafts, and a week after the check to Trustmark was returned for insufficient funds, Morgan committed suicide. At the same time, Barnard was unable to obtain a mortgage because the unpaid notes affected his credit rating. How do the circumstances of this case underscore the importance of practicing business ethics?

Legal Reasoning Group Activity

27–10. Agents' Signatures. Robert Helmer and Percy Helmer, Jr., were authorized signatories on the corporate checking account of Event Marketing, Inc. The Helmers signed a check drawn on Event Marketing's account and issued to Rummel Technologies, Inc. (RTI), in the amount of $84,965. The check was signed on July 13, 2015, but dated August 14. When RTI presented the check for payment, it was dishonored due to insufficient funds. RTI filed a suit in a

Georgia state court against the Helmers to collect the amount of the check. (See *Signature Liability.*)

(a) The first group will determine whether an authorized signatory on a corporate account can be held personally liable for corporate checks returned for insufficient funds.

(b) The second group will decide if the Helmers were personally liable on Event Marketing's check in this situation.

CHAPTER 28

Banking in the Digital Age

Many people today use debit cards rather than checks for their retail transactions, and payments are increasingly being made via smartphones, tablets, and other mobile devices. Nonetheless, commercial checks remain an integral part of the U.S. economic system. In fact, checks are the most common type of negotiable instruments regulated by the Uniform Commercial Code (UCC).

Articles 3 and 4 of the UCC govern issues relating to checks. Article 3 sets forth the requirements for all negotiable instruments, including checks. Article 4 establishes a framework for deposit and checking agreements between a bank and its customers.

Article 4 also governs the relationships of banks with one another as they process checks for payment. A check therefore may fall within the scope of Article 3 and yet be subject to the provisions of Article 4 while in the course of collection. If a conflict arises between Articles 3 and 4, Article 4 controls [UCC 4–102(a)].

28-1 Checks

A **check** is a special type of draft that is drawn on a bank, ordering the bank to pay a fixed amount of money on demand [UCC 3–104(f)]. Article 4 defines a *bank* as "a person engaged in the business of banking, including a savings bank, savings and loan association, credit union or trust company" [UCC 4–105(1)]. If any other institution (such as a brokerage firm) handles a check for payment or for collection, then the check is not covered by Article 4.

A person who writes a check is called the *drawer*. The drawer is usually a depositor in the bank on which the check is drawn. The person to whom the check is payable is the *payee*. The bank or financial institution on which the check is drawn is the *drawee*. Thus, if Anne Tomas writes a check on her checking account to pay her college tuition, she is the drawer, her bank is the drawee, and her college is the payee.

Between the time a check is drawn and the time it reaches the drawee, the effectiveness of the check may be altered in some way. For instance, the account on which the check is drawn may no longer have sufficient funds to pay the check. To avoid such problems, a payee may insist on payment by an instrument that has already been accepted by the drawee, such as a cashier's check, a traveler's check, or a certified check.

28-1a Cashier's Checks

Checks are usually three-party instruments, but on some checks, the bank serves as both the drawer *and* the drawee. For instance, when a bank draws a check on itself, the check is called a **cashier's check** and is a negotiable instrument on issue (see Exhibit 28–1) [UCC 3–104(g)]. Normally, a cashier's check identifies a specific payee. In effect, with a cashier's check, the bank assumes responsibility for paying the check, thus making the check more readily acceptable as a substitute for cash.

■ **EXAMPLE 28.1** Blake needs to pay a moving company $8,000 for moving his household goods to his new home in another state. The moving company requests payment in the form of a cashier's check. Blake goes to a bank (he need not have an account at the bank) and purchases a cashier's check, payable to the moving company, in the amount of $8,000. Blake has to pay the bank the $8,000 for the check, plus a small service fee. He then gives the check to the moving company. ■

Cashier's checks are sometimes used in the business community as nearly the equivalent of cash. Except in very limited circumstances, the issuing bank *must* honor its cashier's checks when they are presented for payment. If a bank wrongfully dishonors a cashier's check, a holder can recover from the bank all expenses incurred, interest, and consequential damages [UCC 3–411].

■ **CASE IN POINT 28.2** James Berwick purchased a $250,000 cashier's check from Bank of Colorado that

EXHIBIT 28–1 A Cashier's Check

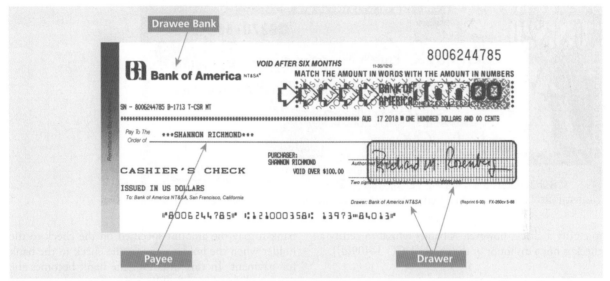

*The abbreviation *NT&SA* stands for National Trust and Savings Association. The Bank of America NT&SA is a subsidiary of Bank of America Corporation.

was made payable to Ron Bryant. Berwick instructed the bank to give the check to James Kalhorn, who was to deliver the check to Bryant. The next day, Bryant presented the cashier's check to a Las Vegas Sands casino, which called Bank of Colorado to verify that it had issued the cashier's check. Las Vegas Sands then deposited the check into its bank account. Before the cashier's check was returned to Bank of Colorado for payment, however, Berwick claimed that it was lost and requested the bank to stop payment on it. The bank refused to pay the cashier's check, and litigation followed. A court found that Bank of Colorado had improperly honored Berwick's stop-payment order and was liable for wrongfully refusing to pay the cashier's check.[1] ■

28–1b Traveler's Checks

A **traveler's check** is an instrument that is payable on demand, drawn on or payable at a financial institution (such as a bank), and designated as a traveler's check. The issuing institution is directly obligated to accept and pay its traveler's check according to the check's terms.

Traveler's checks are designed to be a safe substitute for cash when a person is on vacation or traveling. Each check is issued for a fixed amount, such as $20, $50, or $100. The purchaser is required to sign the check at the time it is purchased and again at the time it is used

[UCC 3–104(i)]. Instead of issuing traveler's checks, most major banks purchase and issue American Express traveler's checks for their customers (see Exhibit 28–2).

28–1c Certified Checks

A **certified check** is a check that has been *accepted* by the bank on which it is drawn [UCC 3–409(d)]. When a drawee bank *certifies* (accepts) a check, it immediately charges the drawer's account with the amount of the check and transfers those funds to its own certified-check account. In effect, the bank is agreeing in advance to accept that check when it is presented for payment and to make payment from those funds reserved in the certified-check account. Certification, then, is a promise that sufficient funds are on deposit and *have been set aside* to cover the check.

To certify a check, the bank writes or stamps the word *certified* on the face of the check and typically indicates the amount that it will pay.[2] Once a check is certified, the drawer and any prior indorsers are completely discharged from liability on the check [UCC 3–414(c), 3–415(d)]. Only the certifying bank is required to pay the instrument.

Either the drawer or the holder (payee) of a check can request certification. The drawee bank is not required

---

1. *Bank of Colorado v. Berwick,* 2011 WL 1135349 (D.Colo. 2011).

2. If the certification does not state an amount, and the amount is later increased and the instrument negotiated to a holder in due course (HDC), the certifying bank must pay the amount of the instrument when it was taken by the HDC [UCC 3–413(b)].

EXHIBIT 28–2 An American Express Traveler's Check

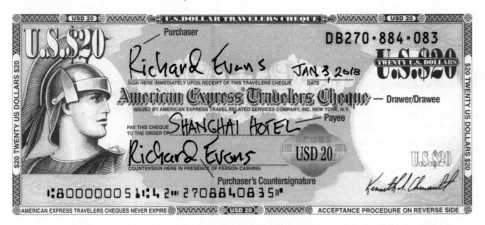

to certify a check, however. A bank's refusal to certify a check is not a dishonor of the check [UCC 3–409(d)].

28–2 The Bank-Customer Relationship

The bank-customer relationship begins when the customer opens a checking account and deposits funds. Essentially, three types of relationships arise at this time—creditor-debtor, agency, and contractual.

28–2a Creditor-Debtor Relationship

A creditor-debtor relationship is created between a customer and a bank when, for instance, the customer makes cash deposits into a checking account. When a customer makes a deposit, the customer becomes a creditor, and the bank a debtor, for the amount deposited.

28–2b Agency Relationship

An agency relationship also arises between the customer and the bank when the customer writes a check on his or her account. In effect, the customer is ordering the bank to pay the amount specified on the check to the holder when the holder presents the check to the bank for payment. In this situation, the bank becomes the customer's agent and is obligated to honor the customer's request.

Similarly, when the customer deposits a check into his or her account, the bank, as the customer's agent, is obligated to collect payment on the check from the bank on which the check was drawn. Thus, when checking account funds are transferred among different banks, each bank acts as the collection agent for its customers [UCC 4–201(a)].

28–2c Contractual Relationship

Whenever a bank-customer relationship is established, certain contractual rights and duties arise. The contractual rights and duties of the bank and the customer depend on the nature of the transaction. These rights and duties are discussed in detail in the sections that follow.

The following case arose when a company realized that the balance in its corporate bank account was depleted. In fact, service charges had resulted in a negative balance. Under the parties' account agreement, was the bank liable for the loss of the funds?

Case 28.1

Royal Arcanum Hospital Association of Kings County, Inc. v. Herrnkind

New York Supreme Court, Appellate Division, Second Department, 113 A.D.3d 672, 978 N.Y.S.2d 355 (2014).

Background and Facts The board of the Royal Arcanum Hospital Association of Kings County, Inc., passed a resolution to require that all corporate checks be signed by two of three officers. These officers were Frank Vassallo, Joseph Rugilio, and William Herrnkind. The three were also named as

Case 28.1 Continued

signatories on the firm's account with Capital One Bank, but the terms of the account did not include the two-signature requirement. After Vassallo and Rugilio died, Herrnkind opened a new account in the corporate name that expressly permitted checks to be drawn on it with only one signature. Only Herrnkind's name appeared on the signature card. The account statements were sent to Royal Arcanum "care of William Herrnkind."

Over the next four years, a series of transactions reduced the balance of the account from nearly $200,000 to zero. Royal Arcanum filed a suit in a New York state court against Herrnkind and Capital One to recover the funds. The court dismissed the complaint against the bank. Royal Arcanum appealed.

In the Language of the Court

Thomas A. *DICKERSON*, J.P. [Judge Presiding], Cheryl E. *CHAMBERS*, Sheri S. *ROMAN*, and Robert J. *MILLER*, JJ. [Judges]
* * * *

A bank and its depositor have the contractual relationship of debtor and creditor, with an implicit understanding that the bank will pay out a customer's funds only in accordance with its instructions. Contrary to the plaintiff's contention, in support of its motion, *the Bank established*, prima facie, *that [it] * * * did not agree to a two-signature requirement when the plaintiff opened the initial account * * *, or when it opened the subsequent account, and therefore that the [Bank] * * * did not breach any such requirement in allowing the withdrawals to be made in the absence of the approval of two officers.* Moreover, as the [lower] Court correctly concluded, insofar as the Bank's transactions with the plaintiff were concerned, the plaintiff conferred, at the least, apparent authority on Herrnkind to act on its behalf. The Bank established, *prima facie,* that it exercised due care and diligence under the circumstances, and that the circumstances surrounding the subject transactions were not such as would arouse the suspicion of its employees. In opposition to the Bank's *prima facie* showing of its entitlement to judgment as a matter of law, the plaintiff failed to raise a triable issue of fact. [Emphasis added.]
* * * *

Accordingly, the [lower] Court properly granted the Bank's motion for summary judgment dismissing the complaint insofar as asserted against it.

Decision and Remedy *The state intermediate appellate court affirmed the decision of the lower court to dismiss Royal Arcanum's complaint against Capital One. The bank was not liable for the payment of unauthorized withdrawals on the firm's corporate accounts because the terms never included a two-signature requirement for the transactions.*

Critical Thinking
- **Legal Environment** *What circumstances indicated that Herrnkind had Royal Arcanum's authority to act on its behalf?*

28–3 The Bank's Duty to Honor Checks

When a banking institution provides checking services, it agrees to honor the checks written by its customers, with the usual stipulation that sufficient funds must be available in the account. When a drawee bank *wrongfully* fails to honor a check, it is liable to its customer for damages resulting from its refusal to pay [UCC 4–402(b)]. The customer does not have to prove that the bank breached its contractual commitment or was negligent.

The customer's agreement with the bank includes a general obligation to keep sufficient funds on deposit to cover all checks written. The customer is liable to the payee or to the holder of a check in a civil suit if a check is dishonored for insufficient funds. If intent to defraud can be proved, the customer can also be subject to criminal prosecution for writing a bad check.

When the bank properly dishonors a check for insufficient funds, it has no liability to the customer. The bank may rightfully refuse payment on a customer's check in other circumstances as well. Next, we examine the rights and duties of both the bank and its customers in specific situations.

28–3a Overdrafts

When the bank receives an item properly payable from its customer's checking account but the account contains insufficient funds to cover the check, the bank has two options. It can either dishonor the item, or it can pay the item and charge the customer's account, thus creating an **overdraft** [UCC 4–401(a)]. The bank can subtract the difference (plus a service charge) from the customer's next deposit because the check carries with it an enforceable implied promise to reimburse the bank.

With a joint account, however, the bank cannot hold any joint-account owner liable for payment of the overdraft unless that customer signed the check or benefited from its proceeds [UCC 4–401(b)]. ■ **EXAMPLE 28.3** Aaron and Sarah are married and have a joint bank account. Aaron writes a check to pay the electric bill for their apartment. If the check results in an overdraft, both Aaron and Sarah will be liable, because both obviously benefited from having electricity in their apartment. ■

A bank can expressly agree with a customer to accept overdrafts through an "overdraft protection agreement." If such an agreement is formed, any failure of the bank to honor a check because it would create an overdraft breaches this agreement and is considered a wrongful dishonor [UCC 4–402(a), (b)].

If a bank posts items to a customer's account only once a day, several items of different amounts may accumulate before the posting. Depending on the order in which the items are posted, an overdraft may occur earlier or later in the sequence. If the bank charges its customer a separate fee for honoring each item after an overdraft occurs, the sequencing of items can significantly impact the amount of fees that the customer is charged. At the center of the following case was one bank's decision to switch its sequencing to post items of the highest amount first.

Case Analysis 28.2

Legg v. West Bank
Supreme Court of Iowa, 873 N.W.2d 763 (2016).

In the Language of the Court
ZAGER, Justice.
* * * *

West Bank is a state-chartered Iowa bank.

West Bank issues bank cards to its customers. Customers use their bank cards in one of two ways: automatic teller machine withdrawals (ATM withdrawals) or point of sale purchases (POS purchases). Customers may also make electronic payments using their West Bank accounts that are processed in the same way as ATM withdrawals and POS purchases. All three of these transactions are classified as "bank card transactions."
* * * *

If West Bank is called upon to pay a Bank Card transaction when there are insufficient funds in the account, the bank advances sufficient money to cover the amount by which the account is short, and assesses a non-sufficient funds (NSF) fee. Those advances are automatically deducted from the customer account and repaid to the bank the next time a deposit sufficient to cover the advances is made to the account.

* * * The NSF fee West Bank charged customers was originally $27.00. It was later raised to $30.00.

West Bank does not post customer account balances in real time. Rather, transactions are posted in a batch at the end of the day. Prior to July 1, 2006, West Bank posted bank card transactions with the lowest amount for each day's debits posted first and the highest amount posted last (low-to-high sequencing). After July 1, 2006, West Bank reversed its posting sequencing and posted bank card transactions with the highest amount posted first and the lowest amount posted last (high-to-low sequencing). Beginning October 1, 2010, West Bank changed its posting order back to low-to-high sequencing.
* * * *

[Darla and Jason Legg had a joint checking account with West Bank. Over a three-week period] the Leggs were charged [separate] NSF fees [for each of five transactions that resulted in overdrafts under West Bank's] new high-to-low sequencing.

* * * If the bank card transactions had been posted in the low-to-high sequence, the Leggs would have only been charged one NSF fee. [A few months later] the Leggs were charged four NSF fees for bank card transactions. The Leggs would have only been charged two NSF fees if

the transactions were posted low-to-high.
* * * *

The Leggs filed this action [in an Iowa state court against West Bank, claiming that West Bank breached its duty to act in good faith when it changed the sequencing order of bank card transactions to high-to-low. West Bank filed a motion for summary judgment.]
* * * *

* * * The * * * court denied West Bank's motion for summary judgment * * *. West Bank [appealed to this court.]
* * * *

When the Leggs opened their account with West Bank, they were provided with a [Deposit Account] Agreement that included the statement that West Bank "shall have an obligation to Depositor to exercise good faith and ordinary care in connection with each account." Before West Bank initiated the sequencing change, it consulted with an Iowa Bankers Association Compliance Officer. After this consultation, West Bank concluded in an internal memo that the previous practice of posting low-to-high created a business expectation with customers and it would be necessary to notify them of the change.

Case 28.2 Continued

Although West Bank's memo specifically discussed notifying its customers of the sequencing change with regard to bank card transactions, West Bank nonetheless made the change without notifying customers. [Emphasis added.]

The [lower] court, relying on the opinions of other courts that have heard similar issues, concluded that the plaintiffs could pursue their good-faith claim. One case the * * * court discussed addressed whether express contract terms were being carried out in good faith. In [another case,] the plaintiffs argued that the banks violated express contractual provisions to act in good faith by reordering postings to high-to-low sequencing. The court found that the plaintiffs

were not asking to vary the terms of the express contract. Rather, they were asking that the bank carry out its express agreement to exercise its discretion regarding the posting sequencing in good faith. The court cited to a number of cases where other courts held that when one party is given discretion to act under a contract, said discretion must be exercised in good faith.

Similarly, West Bank has discretion with regard to the sequencing order of bank card transactions in its agreements with the Leggs and its other customers. *The bank wrote the duty of good faith into its contract with customers.* The Leggs could reasonably argue that the change in sequencing of bank card transactions,

coupled with the lack of notification, violated the reasonable expectations of customers that the bank act in good faith when exercising its discretion to sequence transactions. [Emphasis added.]

* * * *

We conclude that the [lower] court [did not err] when it denied summary judgment to West Bank on * * * the [Leggs'] claim based on a potential breach of the express duty of good faith in the sequencing of postings of bank card transactions. The case is remanded for further proceedings consistent with this opinion.

Legal Reasoning Questions

1. After the initial sequencing change, West Bank provided its customers with a document titled "Miscellaneous Fees." A footnote in that document stated, "Checks written on your account will be paid in order daily with the largest check paid first and the smallest check paid last." Was this adequate notice to the customers of the change? Explain.

2. How did the decisions of other courts in similar cases affect the rulings of the courts in this case?

3. Suppose that West Bank's "Deposit Account Agreement" had not included "an obligation to Depositor to exercise good faith and ordinary care in connection with each account." Would the result have been different? Discuss.

28–3b Postdated Checks

A bank may charge a postdated check against a customer's account unless the customer notifies the bank, in a timely manner, not to pay the check until the stated date. (Indeed, banks typically ignore the dates on checks and treat them as demand instruments unless a customer has notified the bank that a check was postdated.) The notice of postdating must be given in time to allow the bank to act on the notice before committing itself to pay on the check. A bank that fails to act on the customer's notice and charges the account before the date on the postdated check may be liable for any damages the customer incurred [UCC 4–401(c)].

28–3c Stale Checks

Commercial banking practice regards a check that is presented for payment more than six months from its date as a **stale check.** A bank is not obligated to pay an uncertified check presented more than six months from its date [UCC 4–404]. When it receives a stale check for payment,

the bank has the option of paying or not paying the check. If a bank pays a stale check in good faith without consulting the customer, the bank has the right to charge the customer's account for the amount of the check.

28–3d Stop-Payment Orders

A **stop-payment order** is an order by a customer to her or his bank not to pay a certain check.[3] Only a customer (or a person authorized to draw on the account) can order the bank not to pay the check when it is presented for payment [UCC 4–403(a)].

A customer has no right to stop payment on a check that has already been certified (or accepted) by a bank, however. A person who wrongfully stops payment on a check will be liable to the payee for the amount of the check. In addition, the customer-drawer must have a *valid legal ground* for issuing a stop-payment order, or the holder can sue the customer-drawer for payment.

---

3. Note that the right to stop payment is not limited to checks. It extends to any item payable by any bank. See Official Comment 3 to UCC 4–403.

Reasonable Time and Manner The customer-drawer must issue the stop-payment order within a reasonable time and in a reasonable manner to permit the bank to act on it [UCC 4–403(a)].

Although a stop-payment order can be given orally over the phone, it is generally binding on the bank for only fourteen calendar days unless confirmed in writing.[4] (Recall that an electronic record, such as a stop-payment order submitted via the bank's Web site, is a writing.) A written stop-payment order is effective for six months, at which time it must be renewed in writing [UCC 4–403(b)].

Bank's Liability for Wrongful Payment If the bank pays the check in spite of a stop-payment order, the bank will be obligated to recredit the customer's account. In addition, if the bank's payment over a stop-payment order causes subsequent checks written on the drawer's account to "bounce," the bank will be liable for the resultant costs the drawer incurs. The bank is liable only for the amount of the actual loss suffered by the drawer because of the wrongful payment, however [UCC 4–403(c)].

■ **EXAMPLE 28.4** Mike Murano orders one hundred smartphones from Advanced Communications, Inc., at $100 each. Murano pays in advance with a check for $10,000. Later that day, Advanced Communications tells Murano that it will not deliver the smartphones as arranged. Murano immediately calls the bank and stops payment on the check. Two days later, in spite of this stop-payment order, the bank inadvertently honors Murano's check to Advanced Communications for the undelivered phones. The bank will be liable to Murano for the full $10,000.

The result would be different, however, if Advanced Communications had delivered and Murano had accepted ninety phones. Because Murano would have owed Advanced Communications $9,000 for the goods delivered, Murano's actual loss would be only $1,000. Consequently, the bank would be liable to Murano for only $1,000. ■

28–3e Incompetence or Death of a Customer

A customer's mental incompetence or death does not automatically revoke a bank's authority to accept, pay, or collect an item. Only after the bank is notified of the

---

4. Some states do not recognize oral stop-payment orders. The orders must be in writing.

customer's incompetence or death and has reasonable time to act on the notice will the bank's authority be ineffective [UCC 4–405]. Without this provision, banks would constantly be required to verify the continued competence and life of their drawers.

Thus, if a bank is unaware that the customer who wrote a check has been declared incompetent or has died, the bank can pay without incurring liability. Even when a bank knows of the death of its customer, for ten days after the *date of death* it can pay or certify checks drawn on or before the date of death. An exception is made if a person claiming an interest in the account of the deceased customer, such as an heir, orders the bank to stop payment.

28–3f Forged Drawers' Signatures

When a bank pays a check on which the drawer's signature is forged, generally the bank suffers the loss. A bank may be able to recover at least some of the loss from the customer, however, if the customer's negligence substantially contributed to the forgery. A bank may also obtain partial recovery from the forger of the check (if the forger can be found) or from the holder who presented the check for payment (if the holder knew that the signature was forged).

The General Rule A forged signature on a check has no legal effect as the signature of a customer-drawer [UCC 3–403(a)]. The general rule is that the bank must recredit the customer's account when it pays on a forged signature.

For this reason, banks require a signature card from each customer who opens a checking account. Signature cards allow a bank to verify whether the signatures on its customers' checks are genuine. Banks today normally verify signatures only on checks that exceed a certain threshold, such as $2,500 or some higher amount, because it would be too costly to verify every signature.

Note that a bank may contractually shift to the customer the risk of forged checks created electronically or by the use of nonmanual signatures. For instance, the contract might stipulate that the customer is solely responsible for maintaining security over any signature stamp.

Customer Negligence When a customer's negligence substantially contributes to a forgery, the bank normally will *not* be obligated to recredit the customer's account for the amount of the check [UCC 3–406(a)]. The customer's liability may be reduced, however, by the amount of the loss caused by negligence on the part of the bank [UCC 3–406(b)].

■ **CASE IN POINT 28.5** Kenneth Wulf worked for Auto-Owners Insurance Company for ten years. During that time, Wulf opened a checking account at Bank One in the name of "Auto-Owners, Kenneth B. Wulf." Over a period of eight years, he deposited $546,000 worth of checks that he had stolen from Auto-Owners and indorsed with a stamp that read "Auto-Owners Insurance Deposit Only." When the thefts were finally discovered, Auto-Owners sued Bank One for negligence.

The insurance company claimed that the bank should not have allowed Wulf to open an account in Auto-Owners' name without proof that he was authorized to do so. The court ruled in favor of the bank, though, finding that Bank One's conduct was not a significant factor in bringing about the loss. Instead, the negligence of Auto-Owners contributed substantially to its own losses. Therefore, the bank did not have to recredit the customer's account.[5] ■

Timely Examination of Bank Statements Required. Banks typically send or provide online monthly statements that detail the activity in their customers' checking accounts. The statements provide the customer with information (check number, amount, and date of payment) that allows them to reasonably identify each check that the bank has paid [UCC 4–406(a), (b)].

In the past, banks routinely included the canceled checks themselves (or copies of them) with the statement, but that practice is unusual today. If the bank does retain the canceled checks, it must keep the checks—or legible images of them—for seven years [UCC 4–406(b)].

The customer has a duty to promptly examine bank statements (and canceled checks or copies, if they are included) with reasonable care and to report any alterations or forged signatures [UCC 4–406(c)]. The customer is also obligated to report any alteration or apparent forgery in the signatures of indorsers. If the customer fails to fulfill her or his duty and the bank suffers a loss as a result, the customer will be liable for the loss [UCC 4–406(d)].

Consequences of Failure to Detect Forgeries. Sometimes, the same wrongdoer forges the customer's signature on a series of checks. To recover for all of the forged items, the customer must discover and report the first forged check to the bank within thirty calendar days of the receipt or availability of the bank statement [UCC 4–406(d)(2)]. Failure to notify the bank within this time period discharges the bank's liability for all forged checks that it pays prior to notification.

■ **CASE IN POINT 28.6** Denise Kaplan opened two bank accounts with JPMorgan Chase Bank (JPMC) in 2009. Her agreement with JPMC stated that she would review her monthly statements for accuracy and report any unauthorized transactions or discrepancies within thirty days. Later that same year, her husband, Joel Kaplan, submitted new signature cards that added his name to the accounts.

In 2012, Denise notified JPMC that she was not able to access her monthly bank statements, which were being sent to her husband's e-mail address. When JPMC provided the statements to her, she discovered that her husband had been making withdrawals from her accounts. Denise obtained a court order preventing Joel from further accessing the accounts. She claimed that the signature cards that gave him this access had been forged and that she had not consented to the addition of his name to the accounts.

Denise sued JPMC for accepting the allegedly forged signature cards from Joel, but the court ruled in favor of JPMC. Because Denise did not notify the bank until 2012 that she had not been receiving her monthly statements, she was well beyond the thirty-day time period for detecting and reporting forgeries. Therefore, the bank was not liable for any unauthorized transactions.[6] ■

Negligence and the Bank's Duty of Care. In one situation, a bank customer can escape liability, at least in part, for failing to notify the bank of forged or altered checks within the required thirty-day period. When the customer can prove that the bank was also negligent—that is, that the bank failed to exercise ordinary care—then the bank, too, will be liable. The loss will be allocated between the bank and the customer on the basis of comparative negligence [UCC 4–406(e)].

The UCC defines *ordinary care* as the "observance of reasonable commercial standards, prevailing in the area in which [a] person is located, with respect to the business

---

5. *Auto-Owners Insurance Co. v. Bank One*, 879 N.E.2d 1086 (Ind.Sup.Ct. 2008).

6. *Kaplan v. JPMorgan Chase Bank, N.A.*, 2015 WL 2358240 (N.D.Ill. 2015).

in which that person is engaged" [UCC 3–103(a)(7)]. As mentioned earlier, it is customary in the banking industry to examine signatures only on checks that exceed a certain amount. Thus, if a bank fails to examine a signature on a particular check, the bank has not necessarily breached its duty to exercise ordinary care.

One-Year Time Limit. Regardless of the degree of care exercised by the customer or the bank, the UCC places an absolute time limit on the liability of a bank for paying a check with a customer's forged signature. A customer who fails to report a forged signature within one year loses the legal right to have the bank recredit her or his account [UCC 4–406(f)]. The year runs from the date on which the statement was made available for inspection. The parties can agree in their contract to a lower time limit, but the UCC stipulates that the bank has no liability on forged instruments after one year.

Other Parties from Whom the Bank May Recover As noted, a forged signature on a check has no legal effect as the signature of a drawer. Instead, the person who forged the signature is liable [UCC 3–403(a)]. Therefore, when a bank pays a check on which the drawer's signature is forged, the bank has a right to recover from the party who forged the signature (if he or she can be found).

The bank may also have a right to recover from a party who transferred a check bearing a forged drawer's signature and received payment. This right is limited, however, in that the bank cannot recover from a person who took the check in good faith and for value. A bank also cannot recover from a person who in good faith changed position in reliance on the payment or acceptance [UCC 3–418(c)].

28–3g Checks Bearing Forged Indorsements

A bank that pays a customer's check bearing a forged indorsement must recredit the customer's account or be liable to the customer (drawer) for breach of contract. ■ **EXAMPLE 28.7** Cameron issues a $500 check "to the order of Sophia Alonzo." Margo steals the check, forges Alonzo's indorsement, and cashes the check. When the check reaches Cameron's bank, the bank pays it and debits Cameron's account.

In this situation, the bank must recredit Cameron's account for the $500 because it failed to carry out

Cameron's order to pay "to the order of Sophia Alonzo" [UCC 4–401(a)]. Cameron's bank can in turn recover—for breach of warranty—from the bank that cashed the check when Margo presented it [UCC 4–207(a)(2)]. ■

Eventually, *the loss usually falls on the first party to take the instrument bearing the forged indorsement* because a forged indorsement does not transfer title. Thus, whoever takes an instrument with a forged indorsement cannot become a holder.

The customer, in any event, has a duty to report forged indorsements promptly. The bank is relieved of liability if the customer fails to report the forged indorsements within three years of receiving the bank statement that contained the forged items [UCC 4–111].[7]

■ **CASE IN POINT 28.8** The Michigan Basic Property Insurance Association (MBP) banked with Fifth Third Bank. MBP issued a check from its account to Joyce Washington, Countrywide Home Loans, and T & C Federal Credit Union as co-payees. Washington indorsed the check by signing all three payees' names and deposited it into her own account. When the check reached Fifth Third Bank, it notified MBP of the payment through a daily account statement. MBP did not object, so Fifth Third debited the funds from MBP's account. After MBP received its monthly account statement showing the payment, it again did not object.

When MBP was forced to issue a second check to Countrywide, it sued Fifth Third Bank seeking to have its account recredited. Ultimately, a state appellate court found that Fifth Third Bank was not liable to MBP. Under the UCC, the check was not properly payable because it had two forged indorsements. Thus, the bank would normally be required to recredit the amount of the check. But in this case, the parties had agreed by contract that if the bank was not promptly notified of forgery, the loss would fall on the customer. Because MBP did not promptly notify the bank of the forgeries as required under its account agreement, MBP was liable for any forged indorsements.[8] ■

28–3h Altered Checks

The customer's instruction to the bank is to pay the exact amount on the face of the check to the holder. The bank has an implicit duty to examine checks before making final payments. If it fails to detect an alteration, it is liable

---

7. This is a general statute of limitations for all actions under Article 4. It provides that any lawsuit must be brought within three years of the time that the cause of action arises.

8. *Michigan Basic Property Insurance Association v. Washington*, 2012 WL 20573 (Mich.App. 2012).

to its customer for the loss because it did not pay as the customer ordered.

The bank's loss is the difference between the original amount of the check and the amount actually paid. ■ **EXAMPLE 28.9** Hailey Lyonne writes a check for $11 that is increased to $111. Lyonne's account will be charged $11 (the amount the customer ordered the bank to pay). The bank will normally be responsible for the remaining $100 [UCC 4–401(d)(1)]. ■

Customer Negligence As in a situation involving a forged drawer's signature, a customer's negligence can shift the loss when payment is made on an altered check (unless the bank was also negligent). For instance, a person may carelessly write a check and leave large gaps around the numbers and words where additional numbers and words can be inserted.

Similarly, a person who signs a check and leaves the dollar amount for someone else to fill in is barred from protesting when the bank unknowingly and in good faith pays whatever amount is shown [UCC 4–401(d)(2)]. Finally, if the bank can trace its loss on successive altered checks to the customer's failure to discover the initial alteration, then the bank can reduce its liability for reimbursing the customer's account [UCC 4–406].

In every situation involving a forged drawer's signature or an alteration, a bank must observe reasonable commercial standards of care in paying on a customer's checks [UCC 4–406(e)]. The customer's contributory negligence can be asserted only if the bank has exercised ordinary care.

Other Parties from Whom the Bank May Recover The bank is entitled to recover the amount of loss (including expenses) from the transferor who presented the check for payment. A transferor, by presenting a check for payment, warrants that the check has not been altered.

There are two exceptions to this rule. First, if the bank is also the drawer (as it is on a cashier's check), it cannot recover from the presenting party if the party is a holder in due course (HDC) acting in good faith [UCC 3–417(a)(2), 4–208(a)(2)]. The reason is that an instrument's drawer is in a better position than an HDC to know whether the instrument has been altered.

Second, an HDC who presents a certified check for payment in good faith does not warrant to the check's certifier that the check was unaltered before the HDC acquired it [UCC 3–417(a)(2), 4–208(a)(2)]. ■ **EXAMPLE 28.10** Alan, the drawer, draws a check for

$500 payable to Rachel, the payee. Rachel alters the amount to $5,000. National City Bank, the drawee, certifies the check for $5,000. Rachel negotiates the check to Jordan, an HDC. The drawee bank pays Jordan $5,000. On discovering the mistake, the bank cannot recover from Jordan the $4,500 paid by mistake, even though the bank was not in a superior position to detect the alteration. This result is in accord with the purpose of certification, which is to obtain the definite obligation of a bank to honor a definite instrument. ■

For a synopsis of the rules governing the honoring of checks, see Concept Summary 28.1.

28–4 The Bank's Duty to Accept Deposits

A bank has a duty to its customer to accept the customer's deposits of cash and checks. When checks are deposited, the bank must make the funds represented by those checks available within certain time frames. A bank also has a duty to collect payment on any checks payable or indorsed to its customer and deposited by the customer into his or her account. Cash deposits made in U.S. currency are received into the customer's account without being subject to further collection procedures.

28–4a Availability Schedule for Deposited Checks

The Expedited Funds Availability Act (EFAA)[9] and Regulation CC[10] (the regulation implementing the act) establish when funds from deposited checks must be made available to the customer. The rules are as follows:

1. Any local check (drawn on a bank in the same area) deposited must be available for withdrawal by check or as cash within one business day from the date of deposit.
2. For nonlocal checks, the funds must be available for withdrawal within not more than five business days.
3. Under the Check Clearing in the 21st Century Act[11] (Check 21), a bank must credit a customer's account as soon as the bank receives the funds.
4. For cash deposits, wire transfers, and government checks, funds must be available on the next business day.

---

9. 12 U.S.C. Sections 4001–4010.
10. 12 C.F.R. Sections 229.1–229.42.
11. 12 U.S.C. Sections 5001–5018.

Concept Summary 28.1

Basic Rules for Honoring Checks

Wrongful Dishonor	• The bank is liable to its customer for actual damages proved if it wrongfully dishonors a check due to its own mistake [UCC 4–402].
Overdraft	• The bank has a right to charge a customer's account for any item properly payable, even if the charge results in an overdraft [UCC 4–401].
Postdated Check	• The bank may charge a postdated check against a customer's account, unless the customer notifies the bank of the postdating in time to allow the bank to act on the notice before the bank commits itself to pay on the check [UCC 4–401].
Stale Check	• The bank is not obligated to pay an uncertified check presented more than six months after its date, but the bank may do so in good faith without liability [UCC 4–404].
Stop-Payment Order	• The customer (or a person authorized to draw on the account) must institute a stop-payment order in time for the bank to have a reasonable opportunity to act. • A customer has no right to stop payment on a check that has been certified or accepted by the bank, however, and can be held liable for stopping payment on any check without a valid legal ground [UCC 4–403].
Death or Incompetence of a Customer	• So long as the bank does not know of the death or incompetence of a customer, the bank can pay an item without liability. Even with knowledge of a customer's death, a bank can honor or certify checks (in the absence of a stop-payment order) for ten days after the date of the customer's death [UCC 4–405].
Forged Signature or Alteration	• The customer has a duty to examine account statements with reasonable care on receipt and to notify the bank promptly of any unauthorized signatures or alterations. • The customer's failure to report promptly an unauthorized signature or alteration will discharge the bank's liability—unless the bank failed to exercise reasonable care (and then the bank may be responsible for some portion of the loss). • The customer is prevented from holding the bank liable after one year for unauthorized customer signatures or alterations and after three years for unauthorized indorsements [UCC 4–406].

5. The first $100 of any deposit must be available for cash withdrawal on the opening of the *next business day* after deposit.

A different availability schedule applies to deposits made at *nonproprietary* automated teller machines (ATMs). These are ATMs that are not owned or operated by the bank receiving the deposits. Basically, a five-day hold is permitted on all deposits, including cash deposits, made at nonproprietary ATMs. Other exceptions also exist. For instance, a banking institution has eight days to make funds available in new accounts (those open less than thirty days).

A bank that places a longer hold on a deposited check than that specified by the rules must notify the customer. A credit union's failure to provide this notice to its customer was at the center of the following case.

Case 28.3

Shahin v. Delaware Federal Credit Union

United States Court of Appeals, Third Circuit, 602 Fed.Appx. 50 (2015).

Background and Facts Nina Shahin deposited a check in the amount of $2,500 into her check-ing account at the Delaware Federal Credit Union (DelOne). DelOne placed a two-business-day "local hold" on the check, pending verification. Concerned that the drawer's signature did not match the handwriting on the rest of the check, the bank placed it on a fifteen-day "nonverified" hold. Mean-while, a payment from Shahin's checking account to Bank of America was denied for insufficient funds (NSF), and DelOne transferred funds from her savings account to cover other payments. DelOne then imposed two $30 penalties for NSF, as well as transfer fees totaling $6.

Shahin filed a suit in a federal district court against DelOne, alleging that the credit union had failed to give her proper notice of the extended hold. The court issued a summary judgment in Shahin's favor. She was awarded the amount of the NSF and transfer fees, plus $1,000, the maximum amount of liability for a notice violation under Regulation CC. Shahin appealed, claiming that the amount of damages was insufficient.

In the Language of the Court

PER CURIAM [By the Whole Court].

* * * *

* * * *Proper notice of the extended hold [is] required under 12 C.F.R. Section 229.13 [of Regulation CC].* [Emphasis added.]

* * * *

Shahin claims on appeal that the District Court failed to award sufficient * * * damages. * * * Pursu-ant to 12 C.F.R. Section 229.21, a depository institution that fails to comply with the notice provision of Section 229.13 with respect to any person:

(a) * * * is liable to that person in an amount equal to the sum of—

(1) Any actual damage sustained by that person as a result of the failure;

(2) Such additional amount as the court may allow, except that—

(i) In the case of an individual action, liability under this paragraph shall not be less than $100 nor greater than $1,000 * * * .

* * * In her motion for summary judgment, Shahin asserted * * * that DelOne imposed $60 in NSF charges and $6.00 in transfer fees. The summary judgment record supported the District Court's finding that DelOne was liable to Shahin for the NSF and "overdraft" fees it imposed; those actual damages totaled $66.00. * * * Shahin failed to argue or provide evidence to support any other claim for actual damages.

DelOne was subject to liability to Shahin for penalties under Section 229.21(a)(2). * * * The amount of $1,000 was the maximum amount allowable under that provision.

Decision and Remedy *The U.S. Court of Appeals for the Third Circuit affirmed the lower court's judg-ment and its award to Shahin of the amount of DelOne's NSF and transfer fees, plus $1,000. The court denied Shahin's claim for further damages.*

Critical Thinking

- **Economic** *Is $1,000 an appropriate penalty for the failure of a depository institution to comply with Regulation CC's notice provision? Why or why not?*

28–4b Interest-Bearing Accounts

Under the Truth-in-Savings Act (TISA)[12] and Regula-tion DD,[13] the act's implementing regulation, banks must pay interest based on the full balance of a cus-tomer's interest-bearing account over the relevant period.

12. 12 U.S.C. Sections 4301–4313.
13. 12 C.F.R. Sections 230.1–230.9.

■ **EXAMPLE 28.11** Nigel has an interest-bearing check-ing account with First National Bank. Nigel keeps a $500 balance in the account for most of the month but with-draws all but $50 the day before the bank posts the inter-est. The bank cannot pay interest on only the $50. The interest must be adjusted to account for the entire month, including those days when Nigel's balance was higher. ■

Before opening a deposit account, new customers must be provided certain information, including the following:

1. The minimum balance required to open an account and to be paid interest.
2. The interest, stated in terms of the annual percentage yield on the account.
3. How interest is calculated.
4. Any fees, charges, and penalties and how they are calculated.

Also, a customer's monthly statement must disclose the interest earned on the account, any fees that were charged, how the fees were calculated, and the number of days that the statement covers.

28–4c The Traditional Collection Process

Usually, deposited checks involve parties who do business at different banks, but sometimes checks are written between customers of the same bank. Either situation brings into play the bank collection process as it operates under Article 4 of the UCC. The check-collection process described in the following subsections has been modified as the banking industry continues to implement Check 21, which will be discussed shortly.

Designations of Banks The first bank to receive a check for payment is the **depositary bank.**[14] For instance, when a person deposits a tax-refund check from the Internal Revenue Service into a personal checking account at the local bank, that bank is the depositary bank.

The bank on which a check is drawn (the drawee bank) is called the **payor bank.** Any bank except the payor bank that handles a check during some phase of the collection process is a **collecting bank.** Any bank except the payor bank or the depositary bank to which an item is transferred in the course of this collection process is called an **intermediary bank.**

During the collection process, any bank can take on one or more of the various roles of depositary, payor, collecting, or intermediary bank. ■ **EXAMPLE 28.12** Brooke, a buyer in New York, writes a check on her New York bank and sends it to David, a seller in San Francisco. David deposits the check in his San Francisco bank account. David's bank is both a *depositary bank* and a *collecting bank.* Brooke's bank in New York is the *payor bank.* As the check travels from San Francisco to New York, any *collecting bank* handling the item in the collection process (other than the ones acting as depositary bank and payor bank) is also called an *intermediary bank.* ■

Exhibit 28–3 illustrates how various banks function in the check-collection process.

Check Collection between Customers of the Same Bank An item that is payable by the depositary bank that receives it (which in this situation is also the payor bank) is called an "on-us item." Usually, a bank issues a "provisional credit" for on-us items within the same day. If the bank does not dishonor the check by the opening of the second banking day following its receipt, the check is considered paid [UCC 4–215(e)(2)].

Check Collection between Customers of Different Banks Once a depositary bank receives a check, it must arrange to present the check, either directly or through intermediary banks, to the appropriate payor bank. When the check reaches the payor bank, that bank is liable for the face amount of the check, unless the payor bank dishonors it [UCC 4–302].[15]

Each bank in the collection chain must pass the check on before midnight of the next banking day following its receipt [UCC 4–202(b)].[16] A "banking day" is any part of a day on which the bank is open to carry on substantially all of its banking functions. Thus, if only a bank's drive-through facilities are open, a check deposited on Saturday will not trigger a bank's midnight deadline until the following Monday.

The UCC permits what is called *deferred posting.* According to UCC 4–108, "a bank may fix an afternoon hour of 2:00 P.M. or later as a cutoff hour for the handling of money and items and the making of entries on its books." Any checks received after that hour "may be treated as being received at the opening of the next banking day." Thus, if a bank's "cutoff hour" is 3:00 P.M., a check received by a payor bank at 4:00 P.M. on Monday will be deferred for posting until Tuesday. In this situation, the payor bank's deadline will be midnight Wednesday.

How the Federal Reserve System Clears Checks The **Federal Reserve System** is a network of twelve district banks located around the country and headed by the Federal Reserve Board of Governors. Most

---

14. All definitions in this section are found in UCC 4–105. The terms *depositary* and *depository* have different meanings in the banking context. A depository bank is a *physical place* (a bank or other institution) in which deposits or funds are held or stored.

15. Most checks are cleared by a computerized process. If a bank fails to meet its midnight deadline because of an electrical outage or equipment malfunction, the bank is "excused" from liability if the bank has exercised "such diligence as the circumstances require" [UCC 4–109(d)].

16. A bank may take a "reasonably longer time" in certain circumstances, such as a power failure that disrupts the bank's computer system [UCC 4–202(b)].

EXHIBIT 28–3 The Check-Collection Process

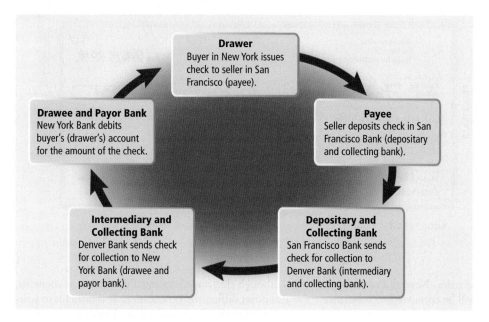

banks in the United States have Federal Reserve accounts. The Federal Reserve System acts as a **clearinghouse**—a place where banks exchange checks drawn on each other and settle daily balances.

■ **EXAMPLE 28.13** Tami Moy, who lives in Cleveland, Ohio, writes a check to Jeanne Sutton of Boston, Massachusetts. When Jeanne receives the check in the mail, she deposits it in her bank. Her bank then deposits the check in the Federal Reserve Bank of Boston, which transfers it to the Federal Reserve Bank of Cleveland. That Federal Reserve bank then sends the check to Moy's bank, which deducts the amount of the check from Moy's account. ■

Electronic Check Presentment In the past, most checks were processed manually. Today, most checks are processed electronically—a practice that has been facilitated by Check 21. Whereas manual check processing can take days, *electronic check presentment* can be done on the day of the deposit. Check information is encoded, transmitted electronically, and processed by other banks' computers. After encoding a check, a bank may retain it and present only its image or description for payment under an electronic presentment agreement [UCC 4–110].

A bank that encodes information for electronic presentment warrants to any subsequent bank or payor that the encoded information is correct [UCC 4–209]. Similarly, a bank that retains a check and presents its image or description for payment warrants that the image or description is accurate.

Regulation CC provides that a returned check must be encoded with the routing number of the depositary bank, the amount of the check, and other information. The regulation further states that a check must still be returned within the deadlines required by the UCC.

28–4d Check Clearing and the Check 21 Act

To streamline the costly and time-consuming traditional method of check collection, Congress enacted the Check Clearing in the 21st Century Act (Check 21). Check 21 changed the collection process by creating a new negotiable instrument called a **substitute check.** Although the act does not require banks to change their current check-collection practices, its creation of substitute checks facilitates the use of electronic check processing.

Substitute Checks A substitute check is a reproduction of the front and back of an original check that contains all of the same information required on checks for automated processing. A bank creates substitute checks from digital images of original checks (see Exhibit 28–4). It can then process the check information electronically or deliver substitute checks to banks that wish to continue receiving paper checks.

The original check can be destroyed after a substitute check is created, helping to prevent the check from being

EXHIBIT 28–4 A Sample Substitute Check

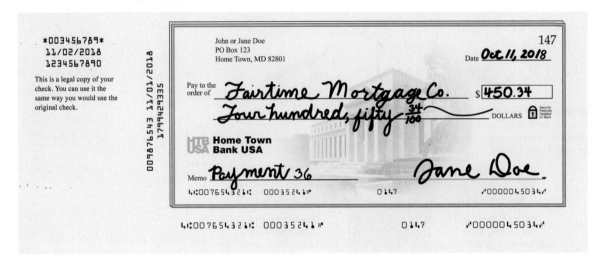

paid twice and reducing expenses. Nevertheless, at least for a while, not all checks will be converted to substitute checks.

Faster Access to Funds The Expedited Funds Availability Act requires the Federal Reserve Board to revise the availability schedule for funds from deposited checks to correspond to reductions in check-processing time. Therefore, as the speed of check processing increases under Check 21, the Federal Reserve Board will reduce the maximum time that a bank can hold funds from deposited checks before making them available to the depositor.

That means, of course, that account holders will have faster access to their deposited funds. It also means they will also have less *float time*—the time between when a check is written and when the amount is actually deducted from the account. Consequently, to avoid overdrafts, account holders need to make sure that funds are available to cover checks when they are written.

28–5 Electronic Fund Transfers

An **electronic fund transfer (EFT)** is a transfer of funds made through the use of an electronic terminal, smartphone, tablet, computer, or telephone. The law governing EFTs depends on the type of transfer involved. Consumer fund transfers are governed by the Electronic Fund Transfer Act (EFTA).[17] Commercial fund transfers are governed by Article 4A of the UCC.

---

17. 15 U.S.C. Sections 1693–1693r. The EFTA amended Title IX of the Consumer Credit Protection Act.

Although electronic banking offers numerous benefits, it also poses difficulties on occasion. It is difficult to issue stop-payment orders with electronic banking. Also, fewer records are available to prove or disprove that a transaction took place, and the possibilities for tampering with a person's private banking information have increased.

28–5a Types of EFT Systems

Most banks offer EFT services to their customers. The following are the most common types of EFT systems used by bank customers:

1. *Automated teller machines* (ATMs)—The machines are connected online to the bank's computers. A customer inserts a plastic card (called an ATM or debit card) issued by the bank and keys in a *personal identification number* (PIN) to access her or his accounts and conduct banking transactions.
2. *Point-of-sale systems*—Online terminals allow consumers to transfer funds to merchants to pay for purchases using a debit card.
3. *Direct deposits and withdrawals*—Customers can authorize the bank to allow another party, such as the government or an employer, to make direct deposits into their accounts. Similarly, a customer can ask the bank to make automatic payments to a third party at regular, recurrent intervals from the customer's funds (insurance premiums or loan payments, for instance).
4. *Online payment systems*—Most financial institutions permit their customers to access the institution's computer system via the Internet and direct a transfer of funds between accounts or pay a particular bill. Payments can be made on a one-time or a recurring basis.

28–5b Consumer Fund Transfers

The Electronic Fund Transfer Act (EFTA) provides a basic framework for the rights, liabilities, and responsibilities of users of EFT systems. The act gave the Federal Reserve Board authority to issue rules and regulations to help implement the act's provisions. The Federal Reserve Board's implemental regulation is called **Regulation E.**

The EFTA governs financial institutions that offer electronic transfers of funds involving customer accounts. The types of accounts covered include checking accounts, savings accounts, and any other asset accounts established for personal, family, or household purposes.

Disclosure Requirements The EFTA is essentially a disclosure law benefiting consumers. The act requires financial institutions to inform consumers of their rights and responsibilities, including those listed here, with respect to EFT systems.

1. The bank must provide a monthly statement for every month in which there is an electronic transfer of funds. The statement must show the amount and date of the transfer, the names of the retailers or other third parties involved, the location or identification of the terminal, and the fees.
2. If a customer's debit card is lost or stolen and used without her or his permission, the customer shall be required to pay no more than $50. The customer, however, must notify the bank of the loss or theft within two days of learning about it. Otherwise, the customer's liability increases to $500. The customer may be liable for more than $500 if she or he does not report the unauthorized use within sixty days after it appears on the customer's statement. (If a customer voluntarily gives her or his debit card to another, who then uses it improperly, the protections just mentioned do not apply.)
3. The customer must discover any error on the monthly statement within sixty days and notify the bank. The bank then has ten days to investigate and must report its conclusions to the customer in writing. If the bank takes longer than ten days, it must return the disputed amount to the customer's account until it finds the error. If there is no error, the customer is required to return the funds to the bank.
4. The bank must make receipts available for transactions made through computer terminals, but it is not obligated to do so for telephone transfers.

Violations and Damages EFT systems are vulnerable to fraud when someone uses another's card, code, or other means to make unauthorized transfers. Unauthorized access to an EFT system constitutes a federal felony, and those convicted may be fined up to $10,000 and sentenced to as long as ten years in prison. Banks must strictly comply with the terms of the EFTA and are liable for any failure to adhere to its provisions.

For a bank's violation of the EFTA, a consumer may recover both actual damages (including attorneys' fees and costs) and punitive damages of not less than $100 and not more than $1,000.[18] Failure to investigate an error in good faith makes the bank liable for treble damages (three times the amount of damages). Even when a customer has sustained no actual damage, the bank may be liable for legal costs and punitive damages if it fails to follow the proper procedures outlined by the EFTA for error resolution.

28–5c Commercial Fund Transfers

Funds are also transferred electronically "by wire" between commercial parties. In fact, the dollar volume of payments made by wire transfer is more than $1 trillion a day—an amount that far exceeds the dollar volume of payments made by other means. The two major wire payment systems are the Federal Reserve wire transfer network (Fedwire) and the New York Clearing House Interbank Payments Systems (CHIPS).

Commercial wire transfers are governed by Article 4A of the UCC, which has been adopted by most of the states. Article 4A uses the term *funds transfer* rather than *wire transfer* to describe the overall payment transaction.

■ **EXAMPLE 28.14** Jellux, Inc., owes $5 million to Perot Corporation. Instead of sending Perot a check or some other instrument that would enable Perot to obtain payment, Jellux instructs its bank, North Bank, to credit $5 million to Perot's account in South Bank. North Bank debits Jellux's North Bank account and wires $5 million to South Bank with instructions to credit $5 million to Perot's South Bank account. In more complex transactions, additional banks would be involved. ■

28–6 Online Banking and E-Money

Online banking is common in today's world. Within a few minutes, anybody with the proper software can access his or her account, transfer funds, write "checks," pay bills, monitor investments, and even buy and sell stocks.

Also commonplace is the use of **digital cash,** or **e-money,** which consists of funds stored on microchips in

---

18. In a class-action suit, a court can award up to $500,000 or 1 percent of the institution's net worth as punitive damages. 15 U.S.C. Section 1693m.

laptops, smartphones, tablets, and other devices. E-money replaces *physical* cash—coins and paper currency—with *virtual* cash in the form of electronic impulses.

All these developments are part of a general trend toward making payments electronically. Electronic payment systems are often replacing checks, as discussed in this chapter's *Digital Update* feature.

28–6a Online Banking

Most customers use three kinds of online banking services:

1. Consolidating bills and making payments.
2. Transferring funds among accounts.
3. Applying for loans and credit cards.

Withdrawing and depositing funds are two banking functions not yet widely available online. Nevertheless,

there are software applications (apps) that enable customers to make deposits into their accounts using electronic devices. For instance, JPMorgan Chase has an app that allows customers to deposit checks via their smartphones or tablets. The customer simply takes a photo of the check's front and back (showing proper indorsement) with a smartphone or tablet and then sends that image to the bank.

Mobile payment apps, such as Apple Pay, Android Pay, and Samsung Pay, are also popular. These apps allow people to use a smartphone, smart watch, or tablet to make purchases at a growing number of establishments. The person simply holds an iPhone or other device close to the point-of-sale terminal to authenticate the transaction. Customers' payment information is kept private while the system generates a "dynamic security code" for each transaction. Some experts estimate that smartphone point-of-sale payments will total more than $70 billion in 2018.

DIGITAL UPDATE — Electronic Payment Systems Are Reducing the Use of Checks

Most young people no longer use checks. Businesses, in contrast, use checks regularly. Indeed, businesses are still using checks for more than half of their transactions. Issuing checks is costly, though. A typical business spends $5 to $25 to issue a paper check. That same transaction, if done electronically, costs between $1 and $2. Nevertheless, U.S. businesses account for over two-thirds of the 22 billion checks written each year worldwide.

eBills on the Rise

In some areas of the world, such as within the European Union and parts of Latin America, businesses have been required to switch to digital invoices. That has not been the case in the United States.

Still, the use of electronic billing is on the rise in the United States. An electronic bill, or eBill, is simply an electronic version of a paper bill. eBills contain the same information as paper bills. The difference is that you can view and pay them online.

An increasing number of banks offer online banking services that enable customers to pay bills online. Such services include electronic bill payment and presentment (EBPP). One type of EBPP is offered directly by the company that provides goods or services to consumers. Another type allows consumers to pay multiple bills

electronically through their bank's online banking system.

Business-to-Business (B2B) Bill Paying and the Cloud

As U.S. businesses have grown more comfortable with cloud computing, they have also grown more comfortable with digital payments. The Association of Financial Professionals estimates that approximately 60 percent of today's businesses are very likely or somewhat likely to convert to electronic payments for their suppliers within the next few years. Whereas the use of checks for business-to-business payments was 80 percent of all transactions in 2004, it is estimated that by 2020, that figure will drop to 20 percent.

Several companies offer Internet-based payment systems for B2B bill paying. Typical companies of this kind charge a monthly subscription cost plus a small per-unit transaction fee. These companies carry out the payment process without any additional input from the companies requesting the transaction payments. A growing number of cloud-based companies, such as eBill.com and inHance Cloud, offer these services.

Critical Thinking *Are there additional risks in using electronic payment systems instead of checks?*

28–6b Stored-Value and Smart Cards

The simplest kind of e-money system uses *stored-value cards*. These are plastic cards embossed with magnetic strips containing magnetically encoded data. Frequently, a stored-value card can be used only to purchase specific goods and services offered by the card issuer. An example is a gift card that is redeemable only at a particular retail store or restaurant.

Smart cards are plastic cards containing microchips that can hold much more information than magnetic strips can. A smart card carries and processes security programming. This capability gives smart cards a technical advantage over stored-value cards. The microprocessors on smart cards can also authenticate the validity of transactions. Retailers can program electronic cash registers to confirm the authenticity of a smart card by examining a unique digital signature stored on its microchip. Common uses for smart cards are as credit cards and ATM cards.

Reviewing: Banking in the Digital Age

RPM Pizza, Inc., issued a check for $96,000 to Systems Marketing for an advertising campaign. A few days later, RPM decided not to go through with the deal and placed a written stop-payment order on the check. RPM and Systems had no further contact for many months. Three weeks after the stop-payment order expired, however, Toby Rierson, an employee at Systems, cashed the check. Bank One Cambridge, RPM's bank, paid the check with funds from RPM's account. The amount of the check was large, and the check was more than six months old (stale). The bank should therefore have verified the signature on the check according to standard banking procedures and the bank's own policies. Bank One did not do so, however. RPM filed a suit in a federal district court against Bank One to recover the amount of the check. Using the information presented in the chapter, answer the following questions.

1. How long is a written stop-payment order effective? What else could RPM have done to prevent this check from being cashed?
2. What would happen if it turned out that RPM did not have a legitimate reason for stopping payment on the check?
3. What are a bank's obligations with respect to stale checks? Should Bank One have contacted RPM before paying the check? Why or why not?
4. Assume that Rierson's indorsement on the check was a forgery. Would a court be likely to hold the bank liable for the amount of the check because it failed to verify the signature on the check? Why or why not?

Debate This . . .   *To reduce fraud, checks that utilize mechanical or electronic signature systems should not be honored.*

Terms and Concepts

cashier's check 516	electronic fund transfer (EFT) 530	Regulation E 531
certified check 517	e-money 531	smart card 533
check 516	Federal Reserve System 528	stale check 521
clearinghouse 529	intermediary bank 528	stop-payment order 521
collecting bank 528	overdraft 520	substitute check 529
depositary bank 528	payor bank 528	traveler's check 517
digital cash 531		

Issue Spotters

1. Lyn writes a check for $900 to Mac, who indorses the check in blank and transfers it to Nan. She presents the check to Omega Bank, the drawee bank, for payment. Omega does not honor the check. Is Lyn liable to Nan? Could Lyn be subject to criminal prosecution? Why or why not? (See *The Bank's Duty to Honor Checks*.)

2. Herb steals a check from Kay's checkbook, forges Kay's signature, and transfers the check to Will for value. Unaware that the signature is not Kay's, Will presents the check to First State Bank, the drawee. The bank cashes the check. Kay discovers the forgery and insists that the bank recredit her account. Can the bank refuse to recredit Kay's account? If not, can the bank recover the amount paid to Will? Why or why not? (See *The Bank's Duty to Honor Checks*.)

• **Check your answers to the Issue Spotters against the answers provided in Appendix D at the end of this text.**

Business Scenarios

28–1. Forged Signatures. Roy Supply, Inc., and R. M. R. Drywall, Inc., had checking accounts at Wells Fargo Bank. Both accounts required all checks to carry two signatures—that of Edward Roy and that of Twila June Moore, both of whom were executive officers of both companies. Between January 2015 and March 2016, the bank honored hundreds of checks on which Roy's signature was forged by Moore. On January 31, 2017, Roy and the two corporations notified the bank of the forgeries and then filed a suit in a California state court against the bank, alleging negligence. Who is liable for the amounts of the forged checks? Why? (See *The Bank's Duty to Honor Checks*.)

28–2. Customer Negligence. Gary goes grocery shopping and carelessly leaves his checkbook in his shopping cart. His checkbook, with two blank checks remaining, is stolen by Dolores. On May 5, Dolores forges Gary's name on a check for $100 and cashes the check at Gary's bank, Citizens Bank of Middletown. Gary has not reported the loss of his blank checks to his bank. On June 1, Gary receives his monthly bank statement from Citizens Bank. The statement shows the forged check, but Gary does not examine it. On June 20, Dolores forges Gary's last check for $1,000 and cashes it at Eastern City Bank, a bank with which she has previously done business. Citizens Bank honors the check. On July 1, Gary receives another bank statement, discovers both forgeries, and immediately notifies Citizens Bank. Dolores cannot be found. Gary claims that Citizens Bank must recredit his account for both checks, as his signature was forged. Discuss fully Gary's claim. (See *The Bank's Duty to Honor Checks*.)

Business Case Problems

28–3. Spotlight on Embezzlement—Forged Drawers' Signatures. In December 1999, Spacemakers of America, Inc., hired Jenny Triplett as a bookkeeper. Triplett was responsible for maintaining the company checkbook and reconciling it with the monthly statements from SunTrust Bank. She also handled invoices from vendors. Spacemakers' president, Dennis Rose, reviewed the invoices and signed the checks to pay them, but no other employee checked Triplett's work.

By the end of her first full month of employment, Triplett had forged six checks totaling more than $22,000, all payable to Triple M Entertainment, which was not a Spacemakers vendor. By October 2000, Triplett had forged fifty-nine more checks, totaling more than $475,000. A SunTrust employee became suspicious of an item that required sight inspection under the bank's fraud detection standards, which exceeded those of other banks in the area. Triplett was arrested. Spacemakers filed a suit in a Georgia state court against SunTrust. The bank filed a motion for summary judgment. On what basis could the bank avoid liability? In whose favor should the court rule, and why? [*Spacemakers of America, Inc. v. SunTrust Bank,* 271 Ga.App. 335, 609 S.E.2d 683 (2005)] (See *The Bank's Duty to Honor Checks*.)

28–4. Forged Drawers' Signatures. Debbie Brooks and Martha Tingstrom lived together. Tingstrom handled their finances. For five years, Brooks did not look at any statements concerning her accounts. When she finally reviewed the statements, she discovered that Tingstrom had taken $85,500 through Brooks's checking account with Transamerica Financial Advisors. Tingstrom had forged Brooks's name on six checks paid between one and two years earlier. Another year passed before Brooks filed a suit against Transamerica. Who is most likely to suffer the loss for the checks paid with Brooks's forged signature? Why? [*Brooks v. Transamerica Financial Advisors,* 57 So.3d 1153 (La.App. 2 Cir. 2011)] (See *The Bank's Duty to Honor Checks*.)

28–5. Business Case Problem with Sample Answer— Honoring Checks. Adley Abdulwahab (Wahab) opened an account on behalf of W Financial Group, LLC, with Wells Fargo Bank. Wahab was one of three authorized signers on the account. Five months later, Wahab withdrew $1,701,250 from W Financial's account to buy a cashier's check payable to Lubna Lateef. Wahab visited a different Wells Fargo branch and deposited the check into the account of CA Houston Investment Center, LLC. Wahab was the only authorized signer on this account. Lateef never received or indorsed the check. W Financial filed a suit to recover the amount. Applying the rules for payment on a forged indorsement, who is liable? Explain. [*Jones v. Wells Fargo Bank,* 666 F.3d 955 (5th Cir. 2012)] (See *The Bank's Duty to Honor Checks*.)

• **For a sample answer to Problem 28–5, go to Appendix E at the end of this text.**

28–6. Consumer Fund Transfers. Stephen Patterson held an account with Suntrust Bank in Alcoa, Tennessee. Juanita

Wehrman—with whom Patterson was briefly involved in a romantic relationship—stole his debit card. She used it for sixteen months (well beyond the length of their relationship) to make unauthorized purchases in excess of $30,000. When Patterson learned what was happening, he closed his account. The bank would reimburse Patterson only $677.46—the amount of unauthorized transactions that occurred within sixty days of the transmittal of the bank statement that revealed the first unauthorized transaction. Is the bank's refusal justifiable? Explain. [*Patterson v. Suntrust Bank,* 2013 WL 139315 (Tenn. App. 2013)] (See *Electronic Fund Transfers.*)

28–7. Forged Drawers' Signatures. Victor Nacim had a checking account at Compass Bank. The "Deposit Agreement" required him to report an unauthorized transaction within thirty days of his receipt of the statement on which it appeared to obtain a recredit. When Nacim moved to a new residence, he asked the bank to update the address on his account. Compass continued to mail his statements to his previous address, however, and Nacim did not receive them. In the meantime, Compass officer David Peterson made an unauthorized withdrawal of $34,000 from Nacim's account. A month later, Peterson told Nacim what he had done. The next month, Nacim asked the bank for a recredit. Compass refused on the ground that he had reported the withdrawal more than thirty days after the bank mailed the statement on which it appeared—a statement that Nacim never received. Is Nacim entitled to a recredit? Explain. [*Compass Bank v. Nacim,* 459 S.W.3d 95 (Tex.App.—El Paso 2015)] (See *The Bank's Duty to Honor Checks.*)

28–8. The Bank-Customer Relationship. Euro International Mortgage, Inc. (EIM), held two accounts—Account 9378 and Account 3998—at Bank of America. Ravi Kadiyala was an authorized signatory on Account 9378 but not on Account 3998. Through EIM, Kadiyala obtained a username and password to gain access to Account 3998, from which he transferred $200,000 to Account 9378. He then instructed the bank to issue cashier's checks against the new balance in Account 9378. Meanwhile, Mark Pupke, an authorized signatory on both accounts, learned what Kadiyala had done and told the bank to cancel the checks and reverse the transfer. Does the bank have a duty to honor either party's request? If so, whose? Why? [*Kadiyala v. Bank of America,* 630 Fed.Appx. 633 (7th Cir. 2016)] (See *The Bank-Customer Relationship.*)

28–9. A Question of Ethics—Death or Incompetence of a Customer. *New York resident Esther Braunstein worked as an usher at Lincoln Center, held an administrative position with Citibank, was a school crossing guard, and assisted disabled persons and others as a volunteer. Before her death, she drew a $5,000 check payable to each of two of her daughters, Sandra Braunstein and Carol Russo. The checks were drawn on a joint account held in the names of Esther and Sandra. Carol did not cash her check until five months after Esther's death. Sandra filed a suit in a New York state court against Carol to recover the funds. [Braunstein v. Russo, 988 N.Y.S.2d.521 (2 Dept. 2014)] (See The Bank's Duty to Honor Checks.)*

(a) Is one sister's attempt to recover funds given to another sister by their mother always unethical? Who is legally entitled to the funds? Discuss.

(b) If the check that Carol cashed five months after Esther's death had not been a gift from Esther, but instead had contained a forged drawer's signature, on whom could liability have been imposed? How might that circumstance have affected the ethics of the situation? Explain.

Legal Reasoning Group Activity

28–10. Bank's Duty to Honor Checks. On January 5, Brian drafts a check for $3,000 drawn on Southern Marine Bank and payable to his assistant, Shanta. Brian puts last year's date on the check by mistake. On January 7, before Shanta has had a chance to go to the bank, Brian is killed in an automobile accident. Southern Marine Bank is aware of Brian's death. On January 10, Shanta presents the check to the bank, and the bank honors the check by payment to Shanta. Later, Brian's widow, Joyce, claims that the bank acted wrongfully when it paid Shanta. Joyce points out that the bank knew of Brian's death and that the check was by date over one year old. As executor of Brian's estate and sole heir by his will, Joyce demands that Southern Marine Bank recredit Brian's estate for the check paid to Shanta. (See *The Bank's Duty to Honor Checks.*)

(a) The first group will determine whether the bank acted wrongfully by honoring Brian's check and paying Shanta.

(b) The second group will assess whether Joyce has a valid claim against Southern Marine Bank for the amount of the check paid to Shanta.

(c) A third group will assume that the check Brian drafted was on his business account rather than his personal account, and that he had two partners in the business. Would a business partner be in a better position to force Southern Marine Bank to recredit Brian's account than his widow? Why or why not?

Virtual Currency—Is It Safe?

Virtual currency is digital money. There are no coins or bills and no checks, notes, or other negotiable instruments in paper form. Virtual currency is "a medium of exchange that operates like a currency in some environments."[1] There are more than 150 branded virtual currencies. These include, most famously, bitcoin.

How Does Virtual Currency Work?

Virtual currency can be *mined,* or generated, with a computer. This is often how it is acquired. In the case of bitcoin, for example, a person can obtain twenty-five bitcoin by using a computer to solve a complex math puzzle.

Virtual currency is stored in a *digital wallet,* which may exist on a user's computer or a third party's server. Virtual currency in a digital wallet is identified by *public keys*—random sequences of sixty-four numbers and letters. The keys are kept on a public ledger known as a *block chain,* which is maintained over an international network of unidentified private computers. Accessing the currency requires corresponding sequences—*private keys*—which can be kept secret.

How Is Virtual Currency Used?

Virtual currency has legitimate uses. Transactions in virtual currency do not require banks or other financial institutions. Deals can be conducted anonymously and without transaction fees.

Payment for Goods and Services Some businesses, including Microsoft Corporation, accept virtual currency as payment for goods or services. Some small businesses like it because there are no credit card fees.

Virtual currency can be transferred using computers or mobile apps. Partly for this reason, international payments in virtual currency can be easy and cheap.

Investment Virtual currency can be bought through *virtual currency exchanges* online or with cash at dedicated kiosks, which look like automated teller machines (ATMs). The exchange rate fluctuates, which means that virtual currency can be bought and sold as investments.

Is Virtual Currency Risky?

Virtual currency is risky. Unlike real currency, virtual currency is not issued or backed by any government or bank, and so it does not have legal tender status. This means, for one thing, that no one is required to accept virtual currency in payment or to exchange it for real currency.

No Help Virtual currency is also generally unregulated. The lack of regulation becomes especially important if an exchange is holding others' virtual currencies when something goes wrong. The exchange will not be obligated to offer the currency owners the sort of help they might expect from a bank or a credit card company.

---

1. Financial Crimes Enforcement Network, U.S. Department of the Treasury, *FIN-2013-G001: Application of FinCEN's Regulations to Persons Administering, Exchanging, or Using Virtual Currencies* (March 18, 2013), *available at* www.fincen.gov/statutes_regs/guidance/pdf/FIN-2013-G001.pdf.

No Limits to Liability Unlike bank and credit union accounts, digital wallets are not insured by the Federal Deposit Insurance Corporation or the National Credit Union Share Insurance Fund. In the event of fraud or theft, there may be no limit to an owner's liability and no help in recovering stolen virtual currency.

No Way to Stop or Recover a Payment Even in the case of a mistake, there may be no recourse. For example, in the course of a transaction, the public and private key sequences must be entered perfectly, or virtual currency may be transferred to the wrong party. There may be no way to stop or recover a payment to the wrong party. And any third party, such as an exchange, facilitating the transfer can disclaim responsibility.

No Assurance of Trustworthiness Virtual currency exchanges are required to register with the Financial Crimes Enforcement Network (FinCEN), which is part of the U.S. Treasury Department, as money service businesses. In addition, some states require that exchanges must be licensed to operate in those states. A state's financial regulators can verify whether an exchange is licensed.

Registration does not mean that an exchange is trustworthy, however. Virtual currency lacks the safeguards that are associated with traditional financial institutions. And the anonymity of virtual currency makes it the medium of exchange of choice for persons and businesses engaging in illegal activities, including money laundering and terrorist financing.[2]

How Can the Risks Be Managed?

Risks in the use of virtual currency can be managed with a little effort and common sense.

Know and Verify A person buying virtual currency should know with whom he or she is dealing. The buyer should know how to contact the seller—a name, a phone number, and a location. The user of an exchange should verify that the exchange is registered with FinCEN.[3]

Research and Review A person considering an investment in virtual currency should research and review the potential investment thoroughly before its purchase. Information about potential fraud using virtual currency is available from the Securities and Exchange Commission.[4]

Understand the Costs Any person or business buying, selling, accepting payment in, or investing in virtual currency should understand the costs. This includes fees charged by an exchange. Also, the exchange rate for virtual currency can fluctuate widely in a single day. A change in the rate during a transaction can significantly affect the value of the virtual currency involved.

Be Aware of Contract Rights In any transaction involving virtual currency, each party should be aware of his or her contract rights and how to enforce them. Specific promises by an exchange

Continues

---

2. See Financial Action Task Force, *FATF Report: Virtual Currencies, Key Definitions and Potential AML/CFT Risks* (June 2014), *available at* http://www.fatf-gafi.org/publications/methodsandtrends/documents/virtual-currency-definitions-aml-cft-risk .html.

3. See FinCEN, *Money Services Businesses (MSB) Registrant Search Web Page*, www.fincen.gov/financial_institutions/msb/ msbstateselector.html.

4. See, for example, Securities and Exchange Commission, *Investor Alert: Ponzi Schemes Using Virtual Currencies* (July 2013), www.sec.gov/investor/alerts/ia_virtualcurrencies.pdf.

or other third party should also be taken into account. For instance, if there is a promise of reimbursement for an unauthorized transaction, is it in virtual currency or dollars? If there is insurance, what exactly is covered? And who gets the benefit of a positive fluctuation in the exchange rate during a transaction?

What Law Applies to Virtual Currency?

Federal registration and state licensing requirements apply to exchanges, as mentioned. The most comprehensive state rules for virtual currency are New York's regulations.[5] Other states have begun to look at how virtual currency and the businesses that use it interact with the states' money transmission and consumer protection rules.

In October 2015, the National Conference of Commissioners on Uniform State Laws issued a working draft for the Regulation of Virtual Currencies Act. Under this draft, "any person or entity that operates as a trusted intermediary in the performance of [virtual currency] services or offering of products to third parties, whether consumers or not, should be licensed." Besides licensing, the draft provides for consumer protection and for the deterrence and detection of money laundering and terrorism support.

Ethical Connection

The use of virtual currency can be ethical. Virtual currency can be safe to use, invest in, and trust others to hold. For that to happen, though, there must be informed awareness of the risks, and safeguards must be taken against hacking, fraud, and theft. In other words, with respect to virtual currency, as with other risky situations, the most ethical action you can take is to protect yourself.

Ethics Question *When is the use of virtual currency unethical? Why?*

Critical Thinking *What subjects are likely to be covered in the future regulation of virtual currency? Explain.*

---

5. See New York Department of State Department of Financial Services, *New York Codes, Rules, and Regulations Title 23, Department of Financial Services Chapter 1. Regulation of the Superintendent of Financial Services Part 200. Virtual Currencies* (January 2015), *available at* www.dfs.ny.gov/legal/regulations/adoptions/dfsp200t.pdf.

Creditors' Rights and Bankruptcy

CHAPTER 29

Creditors' Rights and Remedies

N ormally, creditors have no problem collecting the debts owed to them. When disputes arise over the amount owed, however, or when the debtor simply cannot or will not pay, what happens? What remedies are available to creditors when a debtor **defaults** (fails to pay as promised)? In this chapter, we focus on some basic laws that assist the debtor and creditor in resolving their dispute without resorting to bankruptcy.

The remedies we discuss in this chapter are available regardless of whether a creditor is secured or unsecured. *Secured creditors* are those whose loans are backed by *collateral,* which is specific property (such as a car or a house) pledged by a borrower to ensure repayment. The loans made by *unsecured creditors,* such as companies that provide credit cards, are not backed by collateral. Under Article 9 of the Uniform Commercial Code (UCC), certain remedies are available only to secured creditors.

29–1 Laws Assisting Creditors

Both the common law and statutory laws other than Article 9 of the UCC create various rights and remedies for creditors. Next, we discuss some of these rights and remedies, including liens, garnishment, and creditors' composition agreements.

29–1a Liens

A **lien** is an encumbrance on (claim against) property to satisfy a debt or protect a claim for the payment of a debt. Liens may arise under the common law (usually by possession of the property) or under statutory law. *Mechanic's liens* are statutory liens, whereas *artisan's liens* were recognized at common law. *Judicial liens* may be used by a creditor to collect on a debt before or after a judgment is entered by a court. Liens are a very important tool for creditors because they generally take priority over other claims against the same property.

Mechanic's Liens Sometimes, a person who has contracted for labor, services, or materials to be furnished for making improvements on real property does not immediately pay for the improvements. When that happens, the creditor can place a **mechanic's lien** on the property.

Real Property Secures the Debt. A mechanic's lien creates a special type of debtor-creditor relationship in which the real estate itself becomes security for the debt. ■ **EXAMPLE 29.1** Kirk contracts to paint Tanya's house for an agreed-on price to cover labor and materials. If Tanya refuses to pay or pays only a portion of the charges after the work is completed, a mechanic's lien against the property can be created. Kirk is then a lienholder, and the real property is encumbered (burdened) with the mechanic's lien for the amount owed. ■

If the property owner fails to pay the debt, the lienholder is technically entitled to foreclose on the real estate and sell it. (*Foreclosure* is the process by which a creditor legally takes a debtor's property to satisfy a debt.) The sale proceeds are then used to pay the debt and the costs of the legal proceedings. The surplus, if any, is paid to the former owner.

In the real world, however, small-amount mechanic's liens are rarely the basis of foreclosure. Rather, these liens simply remain on the books of the state until the house is sold. At closing (when the sale is finalized), the seller agrees to pay any mechanic's liens out of the proceeds of the sale before the seller receives any of the funds.

Governed by State Law. State law governs the procedures that must be followed to create a mechanic's (or other statutory) lien. Generally, the lienholder must file a written notice of lien within a specific time period (usually within 60 to 120 days) from the last date that material or labor was provided.

In the following case, the state mechanic's lien statute required the lien to be filed no more than 90 days after "the completion of the work." The contractor that filed the lien and the owner of the project against which the lien was filed disputed the meaning of the term "completion."

Case Analysis 29.1

Picerne Construction Corp. v. Villas

California Court of Appeal, Third District, 244 Cal.App.4th 1201, 199 Cal.Rptr.3d 257 (2016).

In the Language of the Court
MAURO, J. [Judge]

* * * *

Castellino [Villas, LLC] and Picerne [Construction Corporation] entered into an agreement in which Picerne would build an apartment complex called Castellino Villas at Laguna West (project or property) in the City of Elk Grove [California] (the City). The project consisted of 11 apartment buildings, separate garages, a clubhouse, and other facilities.

* * * *

The City issued certificates of occupancy for the 11 buildings within the project * * * after a city inspector conducted a final inspection of each building. The first certificates of occupancy were issued on May 3, 2006. The final certificate of occupancy was issued on July 25, 2006.

Picerne employees and subcontractors continued to perform work at the project after July 25, 2006.

* * * *

[John] Olsen [Castellino's representative for the project] signed a document titled "Owner's Acceptance of Site" for Castellino on September 8, 2006.

* * * *

Castellino began renting apartments at the property in October 2006.

Picerne recorded a claim of mechanic's lien on November 28, 2006.

Picerne filed a complaint [in a California state court] to foreclose its mechanic's lien on December 29, 2006.

* * * *

* * * The trial court * * * determined * * * Picerne is entitled to foreclose its lien.

* * * *

[On appeal to this court] Castellino * * * contends Picerne does not have a valid mechanic's lien because Picerne did not record a claim of mechanic's lien within 90 days after substantial completion of the project.

* * * *

*In order to have a valid mechanic's lien, a claimant must record a claim of lien within a prescribed period of time after completion of the work of improvement * * *. The failure of a claimant to timely record a claim of lien precludes the enforcement of a mechanic's lien.* [Emphasis added.]

[When Picerne filed its lien, mechanic's liens were governed by California Civil Code Section 3115, which] provided, "Each original contractor [a contractor who has a direct contractual relationship with the owner for the work], in order to enforce a lien, must record his claim of lien after he completes his contract and before the expiration of 90 days after the completion of the work of improvement." [According to Section 3116, the term "work of improvement" means the entire structure or scheme of improvement as a whole.]

* * * The [California State] Legislature defined the term completion as "actual completion of the work of improvement." In addition, * * * deemed to be equivalent to a completion [was] the acceptance by the owner or his agent of the work of improvement.

Substantial evidence supports the trial court's finding that the owner accepted the project as of September 8, 2006. * * * Picerne timely recorded its claim of mechanic's lien within 90 days after September 8, 2006.

* * * *

Castellino * * * nevertheless claims that the time for Picerne to record its claim of mechanic's lien began to run before September 8, 2006. [Castellino] asserts the phrase "completion of the work of improvement" in Section 3115 means substantial completion of the work of improvement, and the project was substantially completed by July 25, 2006, when the City issued the final certificate of occupancy.

There are cases construing the * * * mechanic's lien statute which interpreted "completion" as substantial completion.

* * * *

[But these cases were decided before the Legislature amended Section 3115 to define] completion of the work of improvement as actual completion of the work of improvement * * *. The Legislature did not define "completion of the work of improvement" as substantial completion. Courts have looked at whether the work at issue was required under the claimant's contract in determining whether a work of improvement was completed.

Castellino argues that interpreting the term "completion" * * * to mean substantial completion would be sound

Case 29.1 Continues

Case 29.1 Continued

public policy because it would ensure transparency, visibility, objectivity, and certainty in the relationship between the contractor and the owner in the filing of mechanic's liens. However, following the language of the statute by construing "completion" as "actual completion" does not create uncertainty when reference can be made to the parties' agreement and the labor and materials furnished. Moreover, * * * deemed equivalent to completion [is] acceptance of the work of improvement.

In addition, contrary to Castellino's argument, public policy supports the interpretation of completion as actual completion in this specific context. *The mechanic's lien statute is intended [primarily to benefit] persons who perform labor or furnish materials for works of improvement, and it is to be liberally construed for the protection of laborers and material suppliers, with doubts concerning the meaning of the statute generally resolved in favor of the lien claimant.* Interpreting completion as actual completion gives lien claimants the maximum amount of time

to assert their rights before such rights are cut off, whereas interpreting completion as substantial completion could cut off mechanic's lien rights much earlier. The interpretation espoused by Castellino would contravene the purpose of California's mechanic's lien law to protect the right to payment of those who have furnished labor or materials to works of improvement. Our construction of the term "completion" * * * effectuates the intent of the mechanic's lien law. [Emphasis added.]

Substantial evidence supports the trial court's findings that even though the City had issued certificates of occupancy for the 11 buildings within the project, roof and stairway work required under the general contract continued between July 25, 2006 and September 19, 2006. Elizar Ortiz [an installer employed by Picerne's stairway subcontractor] testified he worked 22½ hours on September 15, 18, and 19, 2006, installing grip tape on all of the stairs at the project. The general contract called for the installation of anti-slip grip tape

on all concrete stair treads. Ortiz's testimony established the work he performed on September 15, 18, and 19, 2006 was not corrective or repair work.

The president of Picerne's roofing subcontractor testified his company performed roofing work at the project after July 25, 2006. He said such work included straightening out some of the valleys in the roofs, installing nailers and hips on the roof ridges, and nailing trim. * * * The roof and stairway work performed after July 25, 2006, is not comparable to adding a few strokes of paint or turning a screw.

Picerne recorded a claim of mechanic's lien * * * within 90 days of the date Castellino accepted the project and when the stairway and roofing subcontractors performed work required under their contracts. Accordingly, the trial court did not err in concluding Picerne timely recorded its claim of mechanic's lien.

* * * *

* * * The judgment is affirmed.

Legal Reasoning Questions

1. How did the California legislature define the term "completion"? Was this definition clear? Discuss.

2. How did the owner of the project at the center of this case want the court to interpret "completion"? What arguments support this contention?

3. Ultimately, how did the court define "completion"? Why?

Artisan's Liens When a debtor fails to pay for labor and materials furnished for the repair or improvement of *personal* property, a creditor can recover payment through an **artisan's lien.** As mentioned, artisan's liens usually take priority over other creditors' claims to the same property.[1]

Lienholder Must Retain Possession. In contrast to a mechanic's lien, an artisan's lien is *possessory.* That is, the lienholder ordinarily must have retained possession of the property and have expressly or impliedly agreed to provide the services on a cash, not a credit, basis. The lien remains

in existence as long as the lienholder maintains possession, and the lien is terminated once possession is *voluntarily* surrendered, unless the surrender is only temporary.[2]

■ **CASE IN POINT 29.2** Carrollton Exempted Village School District (in Ohio) hired Clean Vehicle Solutions America, LLC (CVSA, based in New York) to convert ten school buses from diesel to compressed natural gas. The contract price was $660,000. The district paid a $400,000 deposit and agreed to pay installments of $26,000 to CVSA after the delivery of each converted bus. After the first two buses were delivered, the district

---

1. An artisan's lien has priority over a filed statutory lien (such as a title lien on an automobile or a lien filed under Article 9 of the UCC) and a bailee's lien (such as a storage lien).

2. Involuntary surrender of possession by a lienholder, such as when a police officer seizes goods from a lienholder, does not terminate the lien.

refused to continue the contract, claiming that the conversion made the two buses unsafe to drive.

Both parties filed breach of contract lawsuits. CVSA also asserted an artisan's lien over two other buses that it still had in its possession because it had started converting them to natural gas and spent $65,000 doing so. Regardless of the outcome in the parties' lawsuits, CVSA has an artisan's lien that gives it a priority claim to those two buses so long as they remain in its possession. The buses will act as security for the district's payment of at least the amount CVSA has spent converting them to natural gas.[3] ∎

Foreclosure on Personal Property. Modern statutes permit the holder of an artisan's lien to foreclose and sell the property subject to the lien to satisfy the debt. As with a mechanic's lien, the lienholder is required to give notice to the owner of the property before the foreclosure and sale. The sale proceeds are used to pay the debt and the costs of the legal proceedings, and the surplus, if any, is paid to the former owner.

Judicial Liens When a debt is past due, a creditor can bring a legal action against the debtor to collect the debt. If the action is successful, the court awards the creditor a judgment against the debtor (usually for the amount of the debt plus any interest and legal costs incurred). Frequently, however, the creditor is unable to collect the awarded amount.

To ensure that a judgment in the creditor's favor will be collectible, the creditor may request that certain property of the debtor be seized to satisfy the debt. (As will be discussed, under state or federal statutes, some kinds of property are exempt from attachment by creditors.) A court's order to seize the debtor's property is known as a *writ of attachment* if it is issued before a judgment. If the order is issued after a judgment, it is referred to as a *writ of execution.*

Writ of Attachment. In the context of judicial liens, **attachment** refers to a court-ordered seizure and taking into custody of property before a judgment is obtained on a past-due debt. (Attachment has a different meaning in the context of secured transactions.[4]) Because attachment is a *prejudgment* remedy, it occurs either at the time a lawsuit is filed or immediately afterward.

A creditor must comply with the specific state's statutory restrictions and requirements. The due process clause of the Fourteenth Amendment to the U.S. Constitution requires that the debtor be given notice and an opportunity to be heard. The creditor must have an enforceable right to payment of the debt under law and must follow certain procedures. Otherwise, the creditor can be liable for damages for wrongful attachment.

The typical procedure for attachment is as follows:

1. The creditor files with the court an *affidavit* (a written statement, made under oath). The affidavit states that the debtor has failed to pay and indicates the statutory grounds under which attachment is sought.
2. The creditor must post a bond to cover at least the court costs, the value of the property attached, and the value of the loss of use of that property suffered by the debtor.
3. When the court is satisfied that all the requirements have been met, it issues a **writ of attachment.** The writ directs the sheriff or other officer to seize the debtor's nonexempt property. If the creditor prevails at trial, the seized property can be sold to satisfy the judgment.

Writ of Execution. If a creditor wins a judgment against a debtor and the debtor will not or cannot pay the amount due, the creditor can request a **writ of execution** from the court. A writ of execution is an order that directs the sheriff to seize (levy) and sell any of the debtor's nonexempt real or personal property. The writ applies only to property that is within the court's geographic jurisdiction (usually the county in which the courthouse is located).

The proceeds of the sale are used to pay the judgment, accrued interest, and costs of the sale. Any excess is paid to the debtor. The debtor can pay the judgment and redeem the nonexempt property at any time before the sale takes place. (Because of exemption laws and bankruptcy laws, however, many judgments are practically uncollectible.)

29–1b Garnishment

An order for **garnishment** permits a creditor to collect a debt by seizing property of the debtor that is being held by a third party. As a result of a garnishment proceeding, for instance, the debtor's employer may be ordered by the court to turn over a portion of the debtor's wages to pay the debt. Many other types of property can be garnished as well, including funds in a bank account, tax refunds, pensions, and trust funds. It is only necessary that the property is not exempt from garnishment and is in the possession of a third party.

---

3. *Clean Vehicle Solutions America, LLC v. Carrollton Exempted Village School District Board of Education*, 2015 WL 5459852 (S.D.N.Y. 2015).
4. In secured transactions, *attachment* refers to the process through which a security interest becomes effective and enforceable against a debtor with respect to the debtor's collateral [UCC 9–203].

■ CASE IN POINT 29.3 When Edward G. Tinsley divorced Michelle Townsend, they entered into a marital settlement contract. They agreed to sell the marital home and split the proceeds evenly. But Tinsley refused to cooperate with the sale. A court therefore appointed a trustee to sell the house for them and ordered the sheriff to evict Tinsley. Tinsley then conveyed the house to a trust established in his name. Even after the sheriff evicted Tinsley from the house and changed the locks, Tinsley managed to move back in and change the locks again.

Tinsley was arrested for trespassing and charged with contempt of court (for disobeying court orders). In the meantime, Tinsley secretly sold the home for $150,000 and deposited the proceeds into a bank account held in the name of Edward G. Tinsley Living Trust at SunTrust Bank. After learning of the sale, the court-appointed trustee obtained a writ of garnishment on all of Tinsley's and his trust's bank accounts at SunTrust Bank. Despite numerous objections from Tinsley (and a trial and appeal), Sun Trust eventually complied with the garnishment order and sent all the funds to the trustee.[5] ■

Procedures Garnishment can be a prejudgment remedy, requiring a hearing before a court, but it is most often a postjudgment remedy. State law governs garnishment actions, so the specific procedures vary from state to state.

In some states, the judgment creditor needs to obtain only one order of garnishment, which will then apply continuously to the judgment debtor's wages until the entire debt is paid. In other states, the judgment creditor must go back to court for a separate order of garnishment for each pay period.

See this chapter's *Ethics Today* feature for a discussion of how creditors can obtain garnishment even when a debtor crosses state lines in an attempt to avoid paying the debt.

Laws Limiting the Amount of Wages Subject to Garnishment Both federal and state laws limit the amount that can be taken from a debtor's weekly take-home pay through garnishment proceedings.[6] Federal law provides a minimal framework to protect debtors from losing all their income to pay judgment debts.[7] State laws also provide dollar exemptions, and these amounts are often larger than those provided by federal law.

Under federal law, an employer cannot dismiss an employee because his or her wages are being garnished.

29–1c Creditors' Composition Agreements

Creditors may contract with the debtor for discharge of the debtor's liquidated debts (debts that are definite, or fixed, in amount) on payment of a sum less than that owed. These agreements are referred to as **creditors' composition agreements** (or *composition agreements*) and usually are held to be enforceable unless they are formed under duress.

29–2 Mortgages

When individuals purchase real property, they typically make a **down payment** in cash and borrow the remaining funds from a financial institution. The borrowed funds are secured by a **mortgage**—a written instrument that gives the creditor a lien on the debtor's real property as security for payment of a debt. The creditor is the *mortgagee,* and the debtor is the *mortgagor.*

29–2a Fixed-Rate versus Adjustable-Rate Mortgages

Lenders offer various types of mortgages to meet the needs of different borrowers, but a basic distinction is whether the interest rate is fixed or variable. A *fixed-rate mortgage* has a fixed, or unchanging, rate of interest, so the payments remain the same for the duration of the loan. Lenders determine the interest rate for a standard fixed-rate mortgage loan based on a variety of factors, including the borrower's credit history, credit score, income, and debts.

With an *adjustable-rate mortgage (ARM),* the rate of interest paid by the borrower changes periodically. Typically, the initial interest rate for an ARM is set at a relatively low fixed rate for a specified period, such as a year or three years. After that time, the interest rate adjusts annually or by some other period, such as biannually or monthly. The interest rate adjustment is calculated by adding a certain number of percentage points (called the margin) to an index rate (one of various government interest rates).

ARMs contractually shift the risk that the interest rate will change from the lender to the borrower. Borrowers will have lower initial payments if they are willing to assume the risk of interest rate increases.

---

5. *Tinsley v. SunTrust Bank*, 2016 WL 687545 (Md.App. 2016).
6. A few states (such as Texas) do not permit garnishment of wages by private parties except under a child-support order.
7. For instance, the federal Consumer Credit Protection Act, 15 U.S.C. Sections 1601–1693r, provides that a debtor can retain either 75 percent of his or her disposable earnings per week or an amount equivalent to thirty hours of work paid at federal minimum wage rates, whichever is greater.

ETHICS TODAY — Creditors' Rights When Debtors Move to Another State

Creditors have rights when debtors default. The former often go to court and win judgments against the latter. But what can creditors do when judgment debtors simply "pack up and leave"? That is to say, when debtors engage in the ethically suspect action of crossing state lines to avoid judgments, is there recourse for creditors?

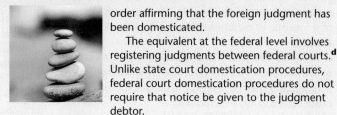

Full Faith and Credit

The Constitution of the United States provides that full faith and credit shall be given in each state to the public acts, records, and judicial proceedings of every other state.[a] Among other things, this means that judgments made in one state will be honored in other states. Fortunately for creditors, there is a long judicial history of the application of judgments to debtors who have moved to another state.[b]

The Uniform Enforcement of Foreign Judgments Act

Most states have adopted the Uniform Enforcement of Foreign Judgments Act.[c] The act allows judgments obtained in one jurisdiction (such as a state) to be "domesticated" (recognized and enforced) in a different jurisdiction (such as another state). One goal is to prevent judgment debtors from evading payment of their obligations by relocating to another state.

In most states, domestication of a foreign judgment can be accomplished rapidly. The judgment creditor files an authenticated copy of the judgment in the "foreign" state, along with an affidavit and a notice of foreign judgment. The notice of domestication action then is provided to the debtor. A local court enters an order affirming that the foreign judgment has been domesticated.

The equivalent at the federal level involves registering judgments between federal courts.[d] Unlike state court domestication procedures, federal court domestication procedures do not require that notice be given to the judgment debtor.

Time Is of the Essence

Once domestication of a foreign judgment has occurred, judgment creditors must record the domestication order with the proper authorities within the jurisdiction to put others on notice. Thus, if real property is involved, a title search will show the foreign judgment against the debtor who has an ownership interest in the real property.

All states have specific lifespans (statutes of limitations) for foreign judgments. Often, a judgment debtor will attempt to counter a foreign judgment by claiming that the lifespan of the foreign judgment had lapsed.[e] Domestications of foreign judgments can be renewed, however.

Garnishment Actions

When a judgment debtor moves to another state, one method of obtaining repayment for debts owed is through the process of garnishment. The benefit for the creditor in such cases is that judgment debtors are often surprised when their bank accounts are frozen or their regular salaries are reduced. Garnishments are typically served against a bank, which then has to freeze any accounts belonging the debtor.

Critical Thinking *Is it fair that property or wage garnishments may "surprise" a judgment debtor?*

a. U.S. Const., Art. IV, Section 1.
b. See, for example, *Aultman, Miller & Co. v. Mills*, 9 Wash. 68, 36 P.1046 (Wash. S. Ct. 1894).
c. Originally issued by the National Conference of Commissioners on Uniform State Laws (NCCUSL) in 1948. Revised in 1964.
d. 28 U.S.C. Section 1963.
e. See, for instance, *Independent Bank v. Pandy*, __ P.3d __, 2015 WL 188988 (Colo.App. 2015).

29–2b Mortgage Provisions

Because a mortgage involves a transfer of real property, it must be in writing to comply with the Statute of Frauds. Mortgages normally are lengthy and formal documents containing many provisions, including the following:

1. *The terms of the underlying loan.* These include the loan amount, the interest rate, the period of repayment, and other important financial terms, such as the margin and index rate for an ARM.

2. *A prepayment penalty clause.* A **prepayment penalty clause** requires the borrower to pay a penalty if the mortgage is repaid in full within a certain period. A prepayment penalty helps to protect the lender should the borrower refinance within a short time after obtaining a mortgage.

3. *Provisions relating to the maintenance of the property.* Because the mortgage conveys an interest in the property to the lender, the lender often requires the

borrower to maintain the property to protect the lender's investment.

4. *A statement obligating the borrower to maintain home-owner's insurance on the property.* **Homeowner's insurance** protects the lender's interest in the event of a loss due to certain hazards, such as fire or storm damage.

5. *A list of the non-loan financial obligations to be borne by the borrower.* For instance, the borrower typically is required to pay all property taxes, assessments, and other claims against the property.

6. *Creditor protections.* When creditors extend mortgages, they are advancing a significant amount of funds for a number of years. Consequently, creditors usually require debtors to obtain **mortgage insurance** if they do not make a down payment of at least 20 percent of the purchase price.

Creditors record the mortgage with the appropriate office in the county where the property is located, so that their interest in the property is officially on record.

29–2c Mortgage Foreclosure

If the homeowner *defaults,* or fails to make the mortgage payments, the lender has the right to foreclose on the mortgaged property. **Foreclosure** is the legal process by which the lender repossesses and auctions off the property that has secured the loan.

Foreclosure is expensive and time consuming. It generally benefits neither the borrowers, who lose their homes, nor the lenders, which face the prospect of losses on their loans. Therefore, both lenders and borrowers are motivated to avoid foreclosure proceedings if possible.

Ways to Avoid Foreclosure Possible methods of avoiding foreclosure include forbearance, workout agreements, and short sales (see Exhibit 29–1).

A **forbearance** is a postponement of part or all of the payments on a loan for a limited time. This option works well when the debtor can solve the problem by securing a new job, selling the property, or finding another acceptable solution.

EXHIBIT 29–1 **Methods of Avoiding Foreclosure**

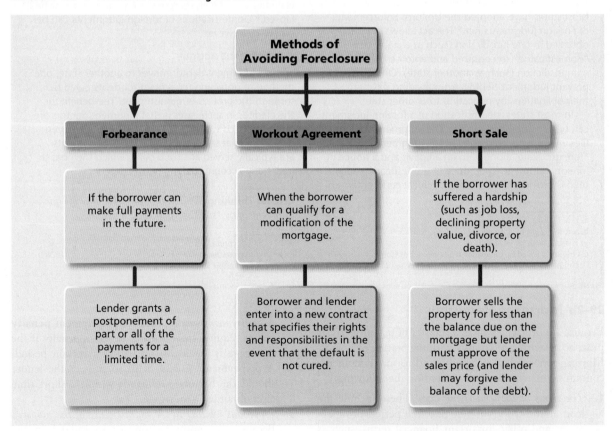

A **workout agreement** is a contract that describes the respective rights and responsibilities of the borrower and the lender as they try to resolve the default. Usually, the lender agrees to delay seeking foreclosure. In exchange, the borrower provides additional financial information that might be used to modify the mortgage.

A lender may sometimes agree to a **short sale,** which is a sale of the property for less than the balance due on the mortgage loan. Typically, the borrower has to show some hardship, such as the loss of a job, a decline in the value of the home, a divorce, or a death in the household. The lender often has approval rights in a short sale, so the sale process may take much longer than an ordinary real estate transaction.

Foreclosure Procedure If all efforts to find another solution fail, the lender will proceed to foreclosure. The lender must strictly comply with the state statute governing foreclosures. Many problems arose in the last ten years because lenders, facing a record number of foreclosures during the recent recession, had difficulty complying with the required statutory formalities.

To bring a foreclosure action, a bank must have standing to sue. In the following case, the court had to decide whether a bank could foreclose a mortgage even though the bank could not prove when it became the owner of the borrower's promissory note.

Spotlight on Foreclosures

Case 29.2 McLean v. JPMorgan Chase Bank, N.A.

District Court of Appeal of Florida, Fourth District, 79 So.3d 170 (2012).

Background and Facts On May 11, 2009, JPMorgan Chase Bank (Chase) filed a foreclosure action against Robert McLean. The complaint alleged that Chase was entitled to enforce the mortgage and promissory note on which McLean had defaulted. Nevertheless, the attached mortgage identified a different mortgagee and lender, and Chase claimed that the note had been "lost, stolen, or destroyed." When McLean filed a motion to dismiss, Chase produced a mortgage assignment dated May 14, 2009, which was three days after it had filed the lawsuit. Eventually, Chase also filed the original note. Although the indorsement to Chase was undated, Chase then filed a motion for summary judgment. The trial court granted Chase's motion even though the accompanying affidavit failed to show that Chase had owned the mortgage or note when it filed the complaint. McLean appealed.

In the Language of the Court

PER CURIAM [By the Whole Court].

* * * *

A crucial element in any mortgage foreclosure proceeding is that the party seeking foreclosure must demonstrate that it has standing to foreclose.

* * * *

* * * A party's standing is determined at the time the lawsuit was filed. Stated another way, *"the plaintiff's lack of standing at the inception of the case is not a defect that may be cured by the acquisition of standing after the case is filed." Thus, a party is not permitted to establish the right to maintain an action retroactively by acquiring standing to file a lawsuit after the fact.* [Emphasis added.]

* * * *

In the present case, as is common in recent foreclosure cases, Chase did not attach a copy of the original note to its complaint, but instead [filed a claim] to re-establish a lost note. Later, however, Chase filed * * * the original promissory note, which bore a special endorsement in favor of Chase. [Thus,] * * * it obtained standing to foreclose, at least at some point.

Nonetheless, the record evidence is insufficient to demonstrate that Chase had standing to foreclose *at the time the lawsuit was filed.* [Emphasis in original.] The mortgage was assigned to Chase three days after Chase filed the instant foreclosure complaint. While the original note contained an undated special endorsement in Chase's favor, the affidavit filed in support of summary judgment did not state when the endorsement was made to Chase. Furthermore, the affidavit, which was dated after the

Case 29.2 Continues

Case 29.2 Continued   lawsuit was filed, did not specifically state when Chase became the owner of the note, nor did the affidavit indicate that Chase was the owner of the note before suit was filed.

We therefore reverse the summary judgment and corresponding final judgment of foreclosure. On remand, in order for Chase to be entitled to summary judgment, it must show * * * that it was the holder of the note on the date the complaint was filed (that the note was endorsed to Chase on or before the date the lawsuit was filed). By contrast, if the evidence shows that the note was endorsed to Chase after the lawsuit was filed, then Chase had no standing at the time the complaint was filed, in which case the trial court should dismiss the instant lawsuit and Chase must file a new complaint.

Decision and Remedy   *The Florida appellate court held that Chase had not proved that it had standing to foreclose against McLean. The court therefore reversed the trial court's grant of summary judgment.*

Critical Thinking

- **Legal Environment**   *If Chase cannot prove that it owned the note at the time of its complaint, what will happen next? Will Chase prevail? Why or why not?*

Redemption Rights   Every state allows a defaulting borrower to redeem the property before the foreclosure sale by paying the full amount of the debt, plus any interest and costs that have accrued. This **equitable right of redemption** gives the defaulting buyer a chance to regain title and possession after default.

The *statutory right of redemption,* in contrast, entitles the borrower to repurchase property *after* a judicial foreclosure. In other words, in states that provide for statutory redemption, the homeowner has a right to buy the property back from a third party who bought it at a foreclosure sale. Generally, the borrower may exercise this right for up to one year from the time the house is sold at a foreclosure sale.[8] The borrower may retain possession of the property after the foreclosure sale until the statutory redemption period ends. If the borrower does not exercise the right of redemption, the new buyer receives title to and possession of the property.

Concept Summary 29.1 provides a synopsis of the remedies available to creditors.

29–3 Suretyship and Guaranty

When a third person promises to pay a debt owed by another in the event that the debtor does not pay, either a *suretyship* or a *guaranty* relationship is created. Exhibit 29–2 illustrates these relationships. The third person's creditworthiness becomes the security for the debt owed.

Suretyship and guaranty provide creditors with the right to seek payment from the third party if the primary debtor, or *principal,* defaults on her or his obligations. Normally a guaranty must be in writing to be enforceable under the Statute of Frauds, unless its main purpose is to benefit the guarantor. Traditionally, a suretyship agreement did not require a writing to be enforceable, and oral surety agreements were sufficient. Today, however, some states require a writing to enforce a suretyship.

At common law, there were significant differences in the liability of a surety and a guarantor. Today, however, the distinctions outlined here have been abolished in some states.

29–3a Suretyship

A contract of strict **suretyship** is a promise made by a third person to be responsible for the debtor's obligation. It is an express contract between the **surety** (the third party) and the creditor.

In the strictest sense, the surety is primarily liable for the debt of the principal. The creditor can demand payment from the surety from the moment the debt is due. The creditor need not exhaust all legal remedies against the principal debtor before holding the surety responsible for payment.

■ **EXAMPLE 29.4**   Roberto Delmar wants to borrow from the bank to buy a used car. Because Roberto is still in college, the bank will not lend him the funds without a cosigner. Roberto's father, José Delmar, who has dealt with the bank before, agrees to cosign the note, thereby becoming a surety who is jointly liable for payment of the debt. When José Delmar cosigns the note, he becomes primarily liable to the bank. On the note's due

---

8. Some states do not allow a borrower to waive the statutory right of redemption. This means that a buyer at auction must wait one year to obtain title to, and possession of, a foreclosed property.

Concept Summary 29.1

Remedies Available to Creditors

Liens
- *Mechanic's lien*—A lien placed on an owner's real estate for labor, services, or materials furnished for improvements made to the realty (real property).
- *Artisan's lien*—A lien placed on an owner's personal property for labor performed or value added to that property.
- *Judicial liens*—Including the following:
  a. Writ of attachment: A court-ordered seizure of property prior to a court's final determination of the creditor's rights to the property. Creditors must strictly comply with applicable state statutes to obtain a writ of attachment.
  b. Writ of execution: A court order directing the sheriff to seize (levy) and sell a debtor's nonexempt real or personal property to satisfy a court's judgment in the creditor's favor.

Garnishment
- A collection remedy that allows the creditor to attach a debtor's funds—such as wages owed or bank accounts—and property that are held by a third person.

Creditors' Composition Agreement
- A contract between a debtor and her or his creditors by which the debtor's debts are discharged by payment of a sum less than the amount that is actually owed.

Mortgage Foreclosure
- On the debtor's default, the entire mortgage debt is due and payable, allowing the creditor to foreclose on the realty by selling it to satisfy the debt.

EXHIBIT 29–2 Suretyship and Guaranty Parties

In a suretyship or guaranty arrangement, a third party promises to be responsible for a debtor's obligations. A third party who agrees to be responsible for the debt even if the primary debtor does not default is known as a *surety*. A third party who agrees to be *secondarily* responsible for the debt—that is, responsible only if the primary debtor defaults—is known as a *guarantor*. Normally, a promise of guaranty (a collateral, or secondary, promise) must be in writing to be enforceable.

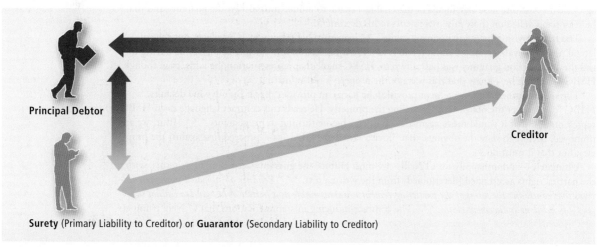

Principal Debtor

Creditor

Surety (Primary Liability to Creditor) or **Guarantor** (Secondary Liability to Creditor)

date, the bank can seek payment from either Roberto or José Delmar, or both jointly. ■

29–3b Guaranty

With a suretyship arrangement, the surety is *primarily* liable for the debtor's obligation. With a guaranty arrangement, the **guarantor**—the third person making the guaranty—is *secondarily* liable.

The guarantor can be required to pay the obligation *only after the principal debtor defaults,* and usually only after the creditor has made an attempt to collect from the debtor. The guaranty contract terms determine the extent and time of the guarantor's liability.

■ **EXAMPLE 29.5** BX Enterprises, a small corporation, needs to borrow funds to meet its payroll. BX's president is Dawson, a wealthy businessperson who owns 70 percent of the company. The bank is skeptical about the creditworthiness of BX and requires Dawson to sign an agreement making herself personally liable for payment if BX does not pay off the loan. As a guarantor of the loan, Dawson cannot be held liable until BX is in default. ■

The following case concerned a lender's attempt to recover on a loan guaranty.

Case 29.3

HSBC Realty Credit Corp. (USA) v. O'Neill

United States Court of Appeals, First Circuit, 745 F.3d 564 (2014).

Background and Facts To finance a development project in Delaware, Brandywine Partners, LLC, borrowed $15.9 million from HSBC Realty Credit Corp. (USA). As part of the deal, Brian O'Neill, principal for Brandywine, signed a guaranty that designated him the "primary obligor" for $8.1 million of the loan. Brandywine defaulted, and HSBC filed a suit in a federal district court against O'Neill to recover on the guaranty. O'Neill filed a counterclaim, alleging fraud.

O'Neill based his fraud claim on two provisions in the loan agreement. The first provision expressed the loan-to-value ratio. O'Neill alleged that this clause valued the property at $26.5 million and that HSBC knew this was not the property's real value. The second provision stated that if Brandywine defaulted, HSBC could recover its loan by selling the property. According to O'Neill, this clause represented that HSBC would try to recover by selling the property before trying to collect from the guaranty.

The court granted HSBC's motion to dismiss O'Neill's counterclaim and issued a judgment in HSBC's favor. O'Neill appealed, still arguing that HSBC had fraudulently induced him to sign the guaranty.

In the Language of the Court
THOMPSON, Circuit Judge.
* * * *

O'Neill loudly protests that his fraudulent-inducement claim should have been enough to defeat HSBC's dismissal efforts. His theory rises or falls on his belief that two provisions in the project-loan agreement constitute false statements of material fact made to induce him to sign the guaranty and that he reasonably relied on those false statements to his detriment.

The first provision he points to involves the * * * loan-to-value ratio, which he alleges put the collateral property's value at $26.5 million and is an HSBC representation that the chance of its having to call the $8.1 million guaranty was basically zero. HSBC made that representation, he adds, even though HSBC—and not he—knew that this was not the property's real value.

The second project-loan-agreement provision he harps on provides that if Brandywine defaults, HSBC "can recover the obligations" by selling the property. He reads this contract language as an HSBC representation that it would move against the property before turning to his guaranty * * * . [But] we are unmoved. Merely to state the obvious, that proviso says that HSBC "can" proceed first against the property, not that it must do so.

Ultimately—and unhappily for O'Neill—we must enforce the guaranty according to its terms, with the parties' rights ascertained [determined] from the written text. * * * *Reliance on supposed misrepresentations that contradict the terms of the parties' agreement is unreasonable as a matter of law and so cannot support a fraudulent-inducement claim.* * * * The contract-inducing misrepresentations that O'Neill trumpets

Case 29.3 Continued

are irreconcilably at odds with the guaranty's express terms. * * * O'Neill specifically warranted in the guaranty that he was familiar with the collateral property's value, that the property did not operate as an inducement for him to make the guaranty, and that HSBC said nothing to induce him to execute the guaranty—all of which destroys his fraudulent-inducement thesis centered on the project-loan agreement's loan-to-value-ratio provision. He also agreed with the guaranty's tagging him as the primary obligor and with its allowing HSBC to go after him first to recoup the debt—provisions that put the kibosh on [put an end to] his other suggestion that HSBC must first seek recourse against the property. [Emphasis added.]

* * * *

The net result of all this is that O'Neill's inducement-based arguments fail.

Decision and Remedy *The U.S. Court of Appeals for the First Circuit affirmed the lower court's judgment in favor of HSBC. The guaranty stated that O'Neill was familiar with the value of the property, that he was not relying on it as an inducement to sign the guaranty, and that HSBC made no representations to induce him to sign. The guaranty also provided that HSBC could enforce its rights against him without trying to recover on the property first.*

Critical Thinking

- **E-Commerce** *Do the principles applied to a written guaranty in this case also govern electronically recorded agreements and contracts entered into online? Why or why not?*
- **What If the Facts Were Different?** *Suppose that O'Neill had alleged a history of performance with HSBC that would have made his reliance on the complained-of representations reasonable. Could this have changed the result? Explain.*

29–3c Actions That Release the Surety and the Guarantor

Basically, the same actions will release either a surety or a guarantor from an obligation. For simplicity, this subsection and the following subsections will refer just to sureties, but remember that the same rules generally apply to guarantors.

1. *Material modification.* Making any material modification to the terms of the original contract without the surety's consent will discharge the surety's obligation. (The extent to which the surety is discharged depends on whether he or she was compensated and the amount of loss suffered from the modification. For instance, a father who receives no consideration for acting as a surety on his daughter's loan will be completely discharged if the loan contract is modified without his consent.)

2. *Surrender of property.* If a creditor surrenders the collateral to the debtor or impairs the collateral without the surety's consent, these acts can reduce the obligation of the surety. If the creditor's actions reduce the value of the property used as collateral, the surety is released to the extent of any loss suffered.

3. *Payment or tender of payment.* Naturally, any payment of the principal obligation by the debtor or by another person on the debtor's behalf will discharge the surety from the obligation. Even if the creditor refused to accept the payment when it was tendered, if the creditor knew about the suretyship, the obligation of the surety can be discharged.

29–3d Defenses of the Surety and the Guarantor

Generally, the surety or guarantor can also assert any of the defenses available to the principal debtor to avoid liability on the obligation to the creditor. A few exceptions do exist, however. They apply to both sureties and guarantors, but again, for simplicity, we refer just to sureties.

1. *Incapacity and bankruptcy.* Incapacity and bankruptcy are personal defenses, which can be asserted only by the person who is affected. Therefore, the surety cannot assert the principal debtor's incapacity or bankruptcy as a defense. (A surety may assert his or her own incapacity or bankruptcy as a defense, of course.)

2. *Statute of limitations.* The surety cannot assert the statute of limitations as a defense. (In contrast, the principal debtor can claim the statute of limitations as a defense to payment.)

3. *Fraud.* If the creditor fraudulently induced the person to act as a surety on the debt, the surety or guarantor can assert fraud as a defense. In most states, the creditor must inform the surety, before the formation of the suretyship contract, of material facts known by the creditor that would substantially increase the surety's risk. Failure to so inform may constitute fraud and render the suretyship obligation voidable.

29–3e Rights of the Surety and the Guarantor

When the surety or guarantor pays the debt owed to the creditor, he or she acquires certain rights, as discussed next. Again, for simplicity, the discussion refers just to sureties.

The Right of Subrogation The surety has the legal **right of subrogation.** Simply stated, this means that any right that the creditor had against the debtor now becomes the right of the surety. Included are creditor rights in bankruptcy, rights to collateral possessed by the creditor, and rights to judgments obtained by the creditor. In short, the surety now stands in the shoes of the creditor and may pursue any remedies that were available to the creditor against the debtor.

■ **CASE IN POINT 29.6** Guerrero Brothers, Inc. (GBI), contracted with the Public School System (PSS) to build a high school. Century Insurance Company (CIC) agreed to provide GBI with the required payment and performance bonds on the project. Thus, CIC acted as a surety of GBI's performance and promised to finish the project if GBI defaulted.

Four years after construction began, PSS canceled GBI's contract, and CIC fulfilled GBI's obligations by finishing construction of the school. Numerous disputes arose, and litigation ensued. Ultimately, PSS agreed to pay GBI $500,000 in contract funds. CIC then filed an action against GBI and PSS to recover the $867,000 it claimed PSS owed it for finishing the school. The court found that CIC, as a performing surety, was entitled to the remaining contract funds through the right of subrogation. It had performed GBI's obligations and therefore stepped into GBI's shoes and had the right to obtain payment from PSS.[9] ■

---

9. *Century Insurance Co. v. Guerrero Brothers, Inc.,* 2010 WL 997112 (N.Mariana Islands 2010).

The Right of Reimbursement The surety has a **right of reimbursement** from the debtor. Basically, the surety is entitled to receive from the debtor all outlays made on behalf of the suretyship arrangement. Such outlays can include expenses incurred as well as the actual amount of the debt paid to the creditor.

The Right of Contribution Two or more sureties are called **co-sureties.** When a co-surety pays more than her or his proportionate share on a debtor's default, she or he has a **right of contribution.** That means the co-surety is entitled to recover from the other co-sureties the amount paid above the surety's obligation. Generally, a co-surety's liability either is determined by agreement or, in the absence of agreement, is set at the maximum liability under the suretyship contract.

■ **EXAMPLE 29.7** Yasser and Itzhak, two co-sureties, are obligated under a suretyship contract to guarantee Jules's debt. Itzhak's maximum liability is $15,000, and Yasser's is $10,000. Jules owes $10,000 and is in default. Itzhak pays the creditor the entire $10,000.

In the absence of an agreement to the contrary, Itzhak can recover $4,000 from Yasser. The amount of the debt that Yasser agreed to cover ($10,000) is divided by the total amount that he and Itzhak together agreed to cover ($25,000). The result is multiplied by the amount of the default, yielding the amount that Yasser owes—($10,000 ÷ $25,000) × $10,000 = $4,000. ■

29–4 Protection for Debtors

The law protects debtors as well as creditors. Consumer protection statutes protect debtors' rights, for instance, and bankruptcy laws are designed specifically to assist debtors in need of help. In addition, in most states, certain types of real and personal property are exempt from execution or attachment. State exemption statutes usually include both real and personal property.

29–4a Exempted Real Property

Probably the most familiar exemption is the **homestead exemption.** The purpose of the homestead exemption is to ensure that the debtor will retain some form of shelter.

The General Rule Each state permits the debtor to retain the family home, either in its entirety or up to a specified dollar amount, free from the claims of unsecured creditors or trustees in bankruptcy. (Note that federal bankruptcy law places a cap on the amount that debtors filing bankruptcy can claim is exempt under their states' homestead exemption.)

■ **EXAMPLE 29.8** Vince Beere owes Chris Veltman $40,000. The debt is the subject of a lawsuit, and the court awards Veltman a judgment of $40,000 against Beere. Beere's homestead is valued at $50,000, and the homestead exemption is $25,000. There are no outstanding mortgages or other liens on his homestead. To satisfy the judgment debt, Beere's family home is sold at public auction for $45,000. The proceeds of the sale are distributed as follows:

1. Beere is given $25,000 as his homestead exemption.
2. Veltman is paid $20,000 toward the judgment debt, leaving a $20,000 deficiency judgment (that is, "leftover debt"). The deficiency judgment can be satisfied from any other nonexempt property (personal or real) that Beere may own, if permitted by state law. ■

Limitations In a few states, statutes allow the homestead exemption only if the judgment debtor has a family.

If a judgment debtor does not have a family, a creditor may be entitled to collect the full amount realized from the sale of the debtor's home. In addition, the homestead exemption interacts with other areas of law and can sometimes operate to cancel out a portion of a lien on a debtor's real property.

29–4b Exempted Personal Property

Personal property that is most often exempt from satisfaction of judgment debts includes the following:

1. Household furniture up to a specified dollar amount.
2. Clothing and certain personal possessions, such as family pictures or a Bible.
3. A vehicle (or vehicles) for transportation (at least up to a specified dollar amount).
4. Certain classified animals, usually livestock but including pets.
5. Equipment that the debtor uses in a business or trade, such as tools or professional instruments, up to a specified dollar amount.

Reviewing: Creditors' Rights and Remedies

Air Ruidoso, Ltd., operated a commuter airline and air charter service between Ruidoso, New Mexico, and airports in Albuquerque and El Paso. Executive Aviation Center, Inc., provided services for airlines at the Albuquerque International Airport. Air Ruidoso failed to pay more than $10,000 that it owed Executive Aviation on its account for fuel, oil, and oxygen. Executive Aviation then took possession of Air Ruidoso's plane, claiming that it had a lien on the plane. Using the information presented in the chapter, answer the following questions.

1. Can Executive Aviation establish an artisan's lien on the plane? Why or why not?
2. Suppose that Executive Aviation files a lawsuit in court against Air Ruidoso for the $10,000 past-due debt. What two methods discussed in this chapter would allow the court to order the seizure of Air Ruidoso's plane to satisfy the debt?
3. Suppose that Executive Aviation discovers that Air Ruidoso has sufficient assets in one of its bank accounts to pay the past-due amount. How might Executive Aviation attempt to obtain access to these funds?
4. Suppose that the contract between the companies provides that "if the airline becomes insolvent, Braden Fasco, the chief executive officer of Air Ruidoso, agrees to cover its outstanding debts." Is this a suretyship or a guaranty agreement?

> **Debate This** . . . *Because writs of attachment are a prejudgment remedy for nonpayment of a debt, they are unfair and should be abolished.*

Terms and Concepts

artisan's lien 542	creditors' composition	down payment 544
attachment 543	agreement 544	equitable right of redemption 548
co-surety 552	default 540	forbearance 546

Continues

Issue Spotters

1. Jorge contracts with Larry of Midwest Roofing to fix Jorge's roof. Jorge pays half of the contract price in advance. Larry and Midwest complete the job, but Jorge refuses to pay the rest of the price. What can Larry and Midwest do? (See *Laws Assisting Creditors.*)

2. Alyssa owes Don $5,000 and refuses to pay. Don obtains a garnishment order and serves it on Alyssa's employer. If the employer complies with the order and Alyssa stays on the job, is one order enough to garnish Alyssa's wages for each pay period until the debt is paid? Explain. (See *Laws Assisting Creditors.*)

• **Check your answers to the Issue Spotters against the answers provided in Appendix D at the end of this text.**

Business Scenarios

29–1. Liens. Kanahara is employed part-time by the Cross-Bar Packing Corp. and earns take-home pay of $400 per week. He is $2,000 in debt to the Holiday Department Store for goods purchased on credit over the past eight months. Most of this property is nonexempt and is now in Kanahara's apartment. Kanahara is in default on his payments to Holiday. Holiday learns that Kanahara has a girlfriend in another state and that he plans to give her most of this property for Christmas. Discuss what actions can be taken by Holiday to collect the debt owed by Kanahara. (See *Laws Assisting Creditors.*)

29–2. Liens. Nabil is the owner of a relatively old home valued at $105,000. The home's electrical system is failing, and the wiring needs to be replaced. Nabil contracts with Kandhari Electrical to replace the electrical system. Kandhari performs the repairs, and on June 1 submits a bill of $10,000 to Nabil. Because of financial difficulties, Nabil does not pay the bill. Nabil's only asset is his home, but his state's homestead exemption is $60,000. Discuss fully Kandhari's remedies in this situation. (See *Laws Assisting Creditors.*)

Business Case Problems

29–3. Foreclosure on Mortgages and Liens. LaSalle Bank loaned $8 million to Cypress Creek 1, LP, to build an apartment complex. The loan was secured by a mortgage. Cypress Creek hired contractors to provide concrete work, plumbing, carpentry, and other construction services. Cypress Creek later went bankrupt owing LaSalle $3 million. The contractors recorded mechanic's liens when they were not paid for their work. The property was sold to LaSalle at a sheriff's sale for $1.3 million. The contractors claimed that their mechanic's liens should be satisfied out of the $1.3 million before any funds were distributed to LaSalle for its mortgage. The trial court distributed the $1.3 million primarily to LaSalle, with only a small fraction going to the contractors. Do the liens come before the mortgage in priority of payment? Discuss. [*LaSalle Bank National Association v. Cypress Creek 1, LP,* 242 Ill.2d 231, 950 N.E.2d 1109 (2011)] (See *Mortgages.*)

29–4. Guaranty. Timothy Martinez, owner of Koenig & Vits, Inc. (K&V), guaranteed K&V's debt to Community Bank & Trust. The guaranty stated that the bank was not required to seek payment of the debt from any other source before enforcing the guaranty. K&V defaulted. Through a Wisconsin state court, the bank sought payment of $536,739.40, plus interest at the contract rate of 7.5 percent, from Martinez. Martinez argued that the bank could not enforce his guaranty while other funds were available to satisfy K&V's debt. For example, the debt might be paid out of the proceeds of a sale of corporate assets. Is this an effective defense to a guaranty? Why or why not? [*Community Bank & Trust v. Koenig & Vits, Inc.,* 346 Wis.2d 279 (Wis.App. 2013)] (See *Suretyship and Guaranty.*)

29–5. Business Case Problem with Sample Answer—Liens. Daniel and Katherine Balk asked Jirak Construction, LLC, to remodel their farmhouse in Lawler, Iowa. Jirak provided the Balks with an initial estimate of $45,975 for the cost. Over the course of the work, the Balks made significant changes to the plan. Jirak agreed to the changes and regularly advised the Balks about the increasing costs. In mid-project, Jirak provided an itemized breakdown at their request. The Balks paid Jirak $67,000, but refused to pay more. Jirak claimed that they still owed $55,000 in labor and materials. Jirak filed a suit in an Iowa state court against the Balks to collect. Which of the liens discussed in this chapter would be most effective to Jirak in its attempt to collect? How does that type of lien work? Is the court likely to enforce it in this case? Explain. [*Jirak Construction, LLC v. Balk,* 863 N.W.2d 35 (Iowa App. 2015)] (See *Laws Assisting Creditors.*)

- **For a sample answer to Problem 29–5, go to Appendix E at the end of this text.**

29–6. Laws Assisting Creditors. Grand Harbour Condominium Owners Association, Inc., obtained a judgment in an Ohio state court against Gene and Nancy Grogg for $45,458.86. To satisfy the judgment, Grand Harbour filed a notice of garnishment with the court, seeking funds held by the Groggs in various banks. The Groggs disputed Grand Harbour's right to garnish the funds. They claimed that the funds were exempt Social Security and pension proceeds, but they offered no proof of this claim. The banks responded by depositing $23,911.97 with the court. These funds were delivered to Grand Harbour. Later, the Groggs filed a petition for bankruptcy in a federal bankruptcy court. After they were granted a discharge, they filed a "motion to return funds to debtors" but provided no evidence that their debt to Grand Harbour had been included in the discharge. What is Grand Harbour's best argument in response to the Groggs' motion? [*Grand Harbour Condominium Owners Association, Inc. v. Grogg,* 2016-Ohio-1386, __ Ohio App.3d __, __ N.E.2d __ (2016)] (See *Laws Assisting Creditors.*)

29–7. A Question of Ethics: Guaranty. *73-75 Main Avenue, LLC, agreed to lease a portion of the commercial property at 73 Main Avenue, Norwalk, Connecticut, to PP Door Enterprise, Inc. Nan Zhang, as manager of PP Door, signed the lease agreement. The lessor required the principal officers of PP Door to execute personal guaranties. In addition, the principal officers agreed to provide the lessor with credit information. Apparently, both the lessor and the principals of PP Door signed the lease and guaranty agreements that were sent to PP Door's office. When PP Door failed to make monthly payments, 73-75 Main Avenue filed a suit against PP Door and its owner, Ping Ying Li. At trial, Li testified that she was the sole owner of PP Door but denied that Zhang was its manager. She also denied signing the guaranty agreement. She claimed that she had signed the credit authorization form because Zhang had told her he was too young to have good credit. Li claimed to have no knowledge of the lease agreement. She did admit, however, that she had paid the rent. She claimed that Zhang had been in a car accident and had asked her to help pay his bills, including the rent at 73 Main Avenue. Li further testified that she did not see the name PP Door on the storefront of the leased location. [73-75 Main Avenue, LLC v. PP Door Enterprise Inc., 120 Conn.App. 150, 991 A.2d 650 (2010)]* (See *Suretyship and Guaranty.*)

(a) Li argued that she was not liable on the lease agreement because Zhang was not authorized to bind her to the lease. Do the facts support Li? Why or why not?

(b) Li claimed that the guaranty for rent was not enforceable against her. Why might the court agree?

29–8. Special Case Analysis—Liens. Go to Case 29.1, *Picerne Construction Corp. v. Villas.* Read the excerpt and answer the following questions.

(a) Issue: What statutory term was the focus of the dispute in this case? Why?

(b) Rule of Law: Under the state statute that applied in this case, what must a party show to enforce a lien?

(c) Applying the Rule of Law: What proof supported the plaintiff's attempt to enforce its lien? What did the defendant argue in opposition?

(d) Conclusion: How did the court resolve the dispute between the creditor and debtor here? Who benefited from this decision?

Legal Reasoning Group Activity

29–9. Attachment. Brent Avery, on behalf of his law firm—The Law Office of Brent Avery—contracted with Marlin Broadcasting to air commercials on KRTV, a local radio station. Avery, who was the sole member of his firm, helped to create the commercials. The ads featured his voice, focused on his name and experience, and solicited direct contact with "defense attorney Brent Avery." When KRTV was not paid for the broadcasts, Marlin filed a lawsuit against Avery and his firm, alleging an outstanding balance of $35,250.

Pending the court's hearing of the suit, Marlin filed a request for a writ of attachment. Marlin offered in evidence the parties' contracts, the ads' transcripts, and KRTV's invoices. Avery contended that he could not be held personally liable for the cost of the ads. Marlin countered that the ads unjustly enriched Avery by conferring a personal benefit on him to Marlin's detriment. (See *Laws Assisting Creditors.*)

(a) The first group will explain the purpose of attachment.

(b) The second group will outline what a creditor must prove to obtain a writ of attachment.

(c) The third group will determine whether Marlin Broadcasting is entitled to attachment in this scenario.

CHAPTER 30

Secured Transactions

Whenever the payment of a debt is guaranteed, or *secured*, by personal property owned or held by the debtor, the transaction becomes known as a **secured transaction.** The concept of the secured transaction is as basic to modern business practice as the concept of credit. Logically, sellers and lenders do not want to risk nonpayment, so they usually will not sell goods or lend funds unless the promise of payment is somehow guaranteed. Indeed, business as we know it could not exist without laws permitting and governing secured transactions.

Article 9 of the Uniform Commercial Code (UCC) governs secured transactions in personal property. Personal property includes accounts, agricultural liens, and *chattel paper* (any documents or records evidencing a debt secured by personal property). It also includes commercial assignments of $1,000 or more, *fixtures* (certain property that is attached to land), instruments, and other types of intangible property, such as patents. Article 9 does not cover creditor-collection devices such as liens and mortgages on real property.

30–1 The Terminology of Secured Transactions

In every state, the UCC's terminology is now uniformly used in all documents that involve secured transactions. The following is a brief summary of the UCC's definitions of terms relating to secured transactions:

1. A **secured party** is any creditor who has a *security interest* in the debtor's *collateral*. This creditor can be a seller, a lender, a cosigner, or even a buyer of accounts or chattel paper [UCC 9–102(a)(72)].
2. A **debtor** is the party who *owes payment* or other performance of a secured obligation [UCC 9–102(a)(28)].
3. A **security interest** is the interest in the collateral (such as personal property, fixtures, or accounts) that *secures payment or performance* of an obligation [UCC 1–201(37)].
4. A **security agreement** is an *agreement* that creates or provides for a security interest [UCC 9–102(a)(73)].
5. **Collateral** is the *subject* of the *security interest* [UCC 9–102(a)(12)].
6. A **financing statement**—referred to as the UCC-1 form—is the *instrument normally filed to give public notice to third parties* of the secured party's security interest [UCC 9–102(a)(39)].

Together, these basic definitions form the concept under which a debtor-creditor relationship becomes a secured transaction relationship (see Exhibit 30–1).

30–2 Creation of a Security Interest

A creditor has two main concerns if the debtor defaults: (1) Can the debt be satisfied through the possession and (usually) sale of the collateral? (2) Will the creditor have priority over any other creditors or buyers who may have rights in the same collateral? These two concerns are met through the creation and perfection of a security interest. We begin by examining how a security interest is created.

30–2a Basic Requirements

To become a secured party, the creditor must obtain a security interest in the collateral of the debtor. Three requirements must be met for a creditor to have an enforceable security interest:

1. Unless the creditor has possession of the collateral, there must be a written or authenticated security agreement that clearly describes the collateral subject

EXHIBIT 30–1 Secured Transactions—Concept and Terminology

In a security agreement, a debtor and a creditor agree that the creditor will have a security interest in collateral in which the debtor has rights. In essence, the collateral secures the loan and ensures the creditor of payment should the debtor default.

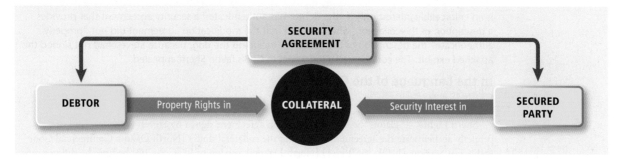

to the security interest. This agreement must be signed or authenticated by the debtor.

2. The secured party must give the debtor something of value.

3. The debtor must have rights in the collateral.

Once these requirements have been met, the creditor's rights are said to *attach* to the collateral. **Attachment** gives the creditor an enforceable security interest in the collateral [UCC 9–203].[1]

■ **EXAMPLE 30.1** To furnish his new office suite, Abdul applies for a credit card at an office supply store. The application contains a clause stating that the store will retain a security interest in the goods purchased with the card until the goods have been paid for in full. This application is considered a *written security agreement*, which is the first requirement for an enforceable security interest. The goods that Abdul buys with the card are the *something of value* from the secured party (the second requirement). Abdul's ownership interest in those goods is the *right* that he has in them (the third requirement). Thus, the requirements for an enforceable security

interest are met. When Abdul buys something with the card, the store's rights attach to the purchased goods. ■

30–2b Written or Authenticated Security Agreement

When the collateral is not in the possession of the secured party, the security agreement must be either written or authenticated. Here, **authenticate** means to sign or, on an electronic record, to adopt any symbol that verifies the intent to adopt or accept the record [UCC 9–102(a)(7)]. Authentication thus provides for electronic filing (the filing process will be discussed later). See this chapter's *Digital Update* feature for a discussion of a type of secured transaction that is performed online.

A security agreement must also contain a description of the collateral that reasonably identifies it. Generally, such phrases as "all the debtor's personal property" or "all the debtor's assets" would *not* constitute a sufficient description [UCC 9–108(c)].

If the debtor signs, or otherwise authenticates, a security agreement, does he or she also have to sign an attached list of the collateral to create a valid security interest? That was the question before the court in the following case.

---

1. The term *attachment* has a different meaning in secured transactions than in the context of judicial liens, where it refers to a court-ordered seizure of property.

Royal Jewelers, Inc. v. Light

Supreme Court of North Dakota, 2015 ND 44, 859 N.W.2d 921 (2015).

Background and Facts Steven Light bought a $55,050 wedding ring for his wife, Sherri Light, on credit from Royal Jewelers, Inc., a store in Fargo, North Dakota. The receipt granted Royal a security interest in the ring. Later, Royal assigned its interest to GRB Financial Corp. Steven and GRB signed a

Case 30.1 Continued

modification agreement changing the repayment terms. An attached exhibit listed the items pledged as security for the modification, including the ring. Steven did not separately sign the exhibit.

A year later, Steven died. Royal and GRB filed a suit in a North Dakota state court against Sherri, alleging that GRB had a valid security interest in the ring. Sherri cited UCC 9–203, under which there is an enforceable interest only if "the debtor has authenticated a security agreement that provides a description of the collateral." Sherri argued that the modification agreement did not "properly authenticate" the description of the collateral, including the ring, because Steven had not signed the attached exhibit. The court issued a judgment in GRB's favor. Sherri appealed.

In the Language of the Court

CROTHERS, Justice.

* * * *

Sherri Light * * * claims the * * * modification agreement signed by Steven Light * * * did not properly authenticate the agreement describing the collateral under [North Dakota Commercial Code (NDCC)] Section 41–09–13(2)(c)(1) [North Dakota's version of UCC 9–203] because he did not separately sign the exhibit identifying secured collateral, including the ring.

Section 41–09–13(2)(c)(1) provides:

2. * * * A security interest is enforceable against the debtor and third parties with respect to the collateral only if:

* * * *

c. One of the following conditions is met:

(1) The debtor has authenticated a security agreement that provides a description of the collateral * * *.

The plain language of that statute requires a debtor to authenticate a security agreement providing a description of the collateral. [Under NDCC Section 41–09–02(1)(g) [North Dakota's version of UCC 9–102(1)(g),] "authenticate" means "to sign" or "to execute or otherwise adopt a symbol, or encrypt or similarly process a record in whole or in part, with the present intent of the authenticating person to identify the person and adopt or accept a record." NDCC Section 41–09–08(2) [North Dakota's version of UCC 9–108(2)] says a description of collateral is sufficient if it reasonably identifies the collateral and may include a specific listing or any other method by which the collateral is objectively determinable.

* * * No authority [requires] a debtor to separately sign an exhibit attached to and referenced in a signed security agreement * * *. *A security agreement is not unenforceable merely because a description of collateral in an exhibit was attached to the security agreement * * *. Several documents may be considered together as a security agreement * * *.* [Emphasis added.]

Steven Light signed the * * * modification agreement which referenced an attached exhibit listing assets pledged as security for the note. * * * The attached exhibit listing the ring was part of the * * * agreement signed by Steven Light, and the [lower] court determined the modification agreement was properly executed by Steven Light. Evidence establishes Steven Light initially granted a valid security interest in the ring and the ring had not been fully paid for * * *. GRB Financial received an assignment of the security interest from Royal Jewelers * * *, and the court did not err in finding GRB Financial had a valid and enforceable security interest in the ring.

Decision and Remedy *The North Dakota Supreme Court affirmed the lower court's judgment. The court stated, "No authority [requires] a debtor to separately sign an exhibit attached to and referenced in a signed security agreement."*

Critical Thinking

- **Ethical** *Under the circumstances, is it ethical for GRB to enforce its security interest in the ring to recover the unpaid amount of the price? Discuss.*

30–2c Secured Party Must Give Value

The secured party must give something of value to the debtor. Under the UCC, value can include a binding commitment to extend credit and, in general, any consideration sufficient to support a simple contract [UCC 1–204]. Normally, the value given by a secured party involves a direct loan or a commitment to sell goods on credit.

DIGITAL UPDATE   Secured Transactions—Escrow Services Online

When you buy something online, you typically must use your credit card, make an electronic fund transfer, or send a check before the goods you bought are sent to you. If you are buying an expensive item, such as a car, you are not likely to send funds without being assured that you will receive the item in the condition promised. Enter the concept of escrow.

Escrow Accounts

Escrow accounts are commonly used in real estate transactions, but they are also useful for smaller transactions, particularly those done on the Internet. An escrow account involves three parties—the buyer, the seller, and a trusted third party that collects, holds, and disperses funds according to instructions from the buyer and seller.

Escrow services are provided by licensed and regulated escrow companies. For example, if you buy a car on the Internet, you and the seller will agree on an escrow company to which you send the funds. When you receive the car and are satisfied with it, the escrow company will release the funds to the seller. This is a type of secured transaction.

Escrow.com

One of the best-known online escrow firms is Escrow.com, which had processed more than $2.7 billion in secured transactions by 2017. All of its escrow services are offered via its Web site and provided independently by Internet Escrow Services, one of its operating subsidiaries. Escrow.com is particularly useful for transactions that involve an international buyer or seller. It has become the recommended transaction settlement service for AutoTrader, Resale Weekly, Cars.com, eBay Motors, and Flippa.com.

Critical Thinking *How could online escrow services reduce Internet fraud?*

30–2d Debtor Must Have Rights in the Collateral

The debtor must have rights in the collateral. That is, the debtor must have some ownership interest or right to obtain possession of that collateral. The debtor's rights can represent either a current or a future legal interest in the collateral. For instance, a retailer-debtor can give a secured party a security interest not only in existing inventory owned by the retailer but also in *future* inventory that the retailer will acquire. (A common misconception is that the debtor must have title to the collateral to have rights in it, but this is not a requirement.)

For a synopsis of the rules for creating a security interest, see Concept Summary 30.1.

30–3 Perfection of a Security Interest

Perfection is the legal process by which secured parties protect themselves against the claims of third parties who may wish to have their debts satisfied out of the same collateral. Whether a secured party's security interest is

---

Concept Summary 30.1

Creating a Security Interest

Requirements for Creating a Security Interest	1. Unless the creditor has possession of the collateral, there must be a written or authenticated security agreement signed or authenticated by the debtor that describes the collateral subject to the security interest. 2. The secured party must give value to the debtor. 3. The debtor must have rights in the collateral—that is, some ownership interest or right to obtain possession of the specified collateral.

perfected or unperfected can have serious consequences for the secured party.

What if a debtor has borrowed from two different creditors and used the same property as collateral for both loans? If the debtor defaults on both loans, which of the two creditors has first rights to the collateral? In this situation, the creditor with a perfected security interest will prevail.

Perfection usually is accomplished by filing a financing statement. In some circumstances, however, a security interest becomes perfected even though no financing statement is filed.

30-3a Perfection by Filing

The most common means of perfection is by filing a *financing statement* with the office of the appropriate government official. A financing statement gives public notice to third parties of the secured party's security interest. The security agreement itself can also be filed to perfect the security interest. The financing statement must provide the names of the debtor and the secured party, and it must indicate the collateral covered by the financing statement.

A uniform financing statement form (see Exhibit 30–2) is used in all states [UCC 9–521]. It must be filed in the appropriate office, together with payment of the correct

EXHIBIT 30–2 A Uniform Financing Statement Sample

UCC FINANCING STATEMENT

FOLLOW INSTRUCTIONS

A. NAME & PHONE OF CONTACT AT FILER (optional)

B. E-MAIL CONTACT AT FILER (optional)

C. SEND ACKNOWLEDGMENT TO: (Name and Address)

THE ABOVE SPACE IS FOR FILING OFFICE USE ONLY

1. DEBTOR'S NAME: Provide only one Debtor name (1a or 1b) (use exact, full name; do not omit, modify, or abbreviate any part of the Debtor's name); if any part of the Individual Debtor's name will not fit in line 1b, leave all of item 1 blank, check here ☐ and provide the Individual Debtor information in item 10 of the Financing Statement Addendum (Form UCC1Ad)

1a. ORGANIZATION'S NAME				
OR 1b. INDIVIDUAL'S SURNAME	FIRST PERSONAL NAME	ADDITIONAL NAME(S)/INITIAL(S)		SUFFIX
1c. MAILING ADDRESS	CITY	STATE	POSTAL CODE	COUNTRY

2. DEBTOR'S NAME: Provide only one Debtor name (2a or 2b) (use exact, full name; do not omit, modify, or abbreviate any part of the Debtor's name); if any part of the Individual Debtor's name will not fit in line 2b, leave all of item 2 blank, check her ☐ and provide the Individual Debtor information in item 10 of the Financing Statement Addendum (Form UCC1Ad)

2a. ORGANIZATION'S NAME				
OR 2b. INDIVIDUAL'S SURNAME	FIRST PERSONAL NAME	ADDITIONAL NAME(S)/INITIAL(S)		SUFFIX
2c. MAILING ADDRESS	CITY	STATE	POSTAL CODE	COUNTRY

3. SECURED PARTY'S NAME (or NAME of ASSIGNEE of ASSIGNOR SECURED PARTY): Provide only one Secured Party name (3a or 3b)

3a. ORGANIZATION'S NAME				
OR 3b. INDIVIDUAL'S SURNAME	FIRST PERSONAL NAME	ADDITIONAL NAME(S)/INITIAL(S)		SUFFIX
3c. MAILING ADDRESS	CITY	STATE	POSTAL CODE	COUNTRY

4. COLLATERAL: This financing statement covers the following collateral:

filing fee [UCC 9–516(a)]. The filing can be accomplished electronically [UCC 9–102(a)(18)]. Once completed, filings are indexed by the name of the debtor so that they can be located by subsequent searches. A financing statement may be filed even before a security agreement is made or a security interest attaches [UCC 9–502(d)].

The Debtor's Name The UCC requires that a financing statement be filed under the name of the debtor [UCC 9–502(a)(1)]. Slight variations in names normally will not be considered misleading if a search of the filing office's records, using a standard search engine routinely used by that office, would find the filings [UCC 9–506(c)].[2] If the debtor is identified by the correct name at the time the financing statement is filed, the secured party's interest retains its priority even if the debtor's name later changes.

Because most states use electronic filing systems, UCC 9–503 sets out detailed rules for determining when the debtor's name as it appears on a financing statement is sufficient.

1. *Corporations.* For corporations, which are organizations that have registered with the state, the debtor's name on the financing statement must be "the name of the debtor indicated on the public record of the debtor's jurisdiction of organization" [UCC 9–503(a)(1)].
2. *Trusts.* If the debtor is a trust or a trustee for property held in trust, the financing statement must disclose this information and provide the trust's name as specified in its official documents [UCC 9–503(a)(3)].
3. *Individuals and organizations.* For all others, the financing statement must disclose "the individual or organizational name of the debtor" [UCC 9–503(a)(4)(A)]. The word *organization* includes unincorporated associations, such as clubs and some churches, as well as joint ventures and general partnerships. If an organizational debtor does not have a group name, the names of the individuals in the group must be listed.
4. *Trade names.* Providing only the debtor's trade name (or a fictitious name) in a financing statement is *not* sufficient for perfection [UCC 9–503(c)]. Thus, the name Pete's Plumbing (if Pete's Plumbing is not a distinct legal entity) is not sufficient. The financing

---

2. If the name listed in the financing statement is so inaccurate that a search using the standard search engine will not find the debtor's name, the financing statement is deemed seriously misleading under UCC 9–506. See also UCC 9–507, which governs the effectiveness of financing statements found to be seriously misleading.

statement must also include the owner-debtor's actual name—Pete Hanson.

Changes in the Debtor's Name What if the debtor's name changes, and the financing statement becomes seriously misleading because of the name change? In this situation, the financing statement remains effective only for collateral the debtor acquired before or within four months after the name change. Unless an amendment to the financing statement is filed, the secured party's interest in goods that the debtor acquired after the four-month period is unperfected [UCC 9–507(b) and (c)].

A one-page uniform financing statement amendment form is available for filing name changes and for other purposes [UCC 9–521]. (See the discussion of amendments later in this chapter.)

Description of the Collateral Both the security agreement and the financing statement must describe the collateral in which the secured party has a security interest. (For land-related security interests, a legal description of the realty is also required [UCC 9–502(b)].)

The security agreement must describe the collateral because no security interest in goods can exist unless the parties agree on which goods are subject to the security interest. The financing statement must describe the collateral to provide public notice of the fact that certain goods of the debtor are subject to a security interest.

Sometimes, the descriptions in the two documents vary. The description in the security agreement must be more precise than the description in the financing statement. The UCC permits broad, general descriptions in the financing statement, such as "all assets" or "all personal property." Usually, if a financing statement accurately describes the agreement between the secured party and the debtor, the description is sufficient [UCC 9–504].

■ **EXAMPLE 30.2** A security agreement for a commercial loan to a manufacturer of automotive parts may list all of the manufacturer's equipment subject to the loan by serial number. The financing statement, in contrast, may simply state "all equipment owned or hereafter acquired." ■

Where to File In most states, a financing statement must be filed centrally in the appropriate state office in the state where the debtor is located. An exception occurs when the collateral consists of timber to be cut, fixtures, or items to be extracted—such as oil, coal, gas, and minerals [UCC 9–301(3) and (4), 9–502(b)]. In those circumstances, the financing statement is filed in the county where the collateral is located.

Note that the state in which a financing statement should be filed depends on the debtor's location, not the location of the collateral (with the exception of the collateral just mentioned) [UCC 9–301]. The debtor's location is determined as follows [UCC 9–307]:

1. For an *individual debtor,* it is the state of the debtor's principal residence.
2. For an organization registered with the state, such as a corporation, it is the state in which the organization is registered. Thus, if a debtor is incorporated in Delaware and has its chief executive office in New York, a secured party would file the financing statement in Delaware.
3. For *all other entities,* it is the state in which the business is located or, if the debtor has more than one office, the place from which the debtor manages its business operations and affairs.

Consequences of an Improper Filing Any improper filing renders the secured party's interest unperfected and reduces the secured party's claim to that of an unsecured creditor. For instance, if the debtor's name is incorrect or if the collateral is not sufficiently described on the financing statement, the filing may not be effective.

■ **EXAMPLE 30.3** Arthur Mendez Juarez, a strawberry farmer, leased farmland from Glendale Fruits, Inc., and borrowed funds from Glendale for payroll and production expenses. The sublease and other documents set out Juarez's full name, but Juarez generally went by the name "Mendez," and he signed the sublease "Arthur Mendez." To perfect its interests, Glendale filed financing statements that identified the debtor as "Arthur Mendez."

Some time later, Juarez contracted to sell strawberries to Frozun Fruits, LLC, which also advanced him funds secured by a financing statement. This statement identified the debtor as "Arthur Juarez." By the following year, Juarez was unable to pay his debts. He owed Glendale more than $200,000 and Frozun nearly $50,000. Both Glendale and Frozun filed suits against Juarez claiming to have priority under a perfected security interest.

In this situation, a properly filed financing statement would identify the debtor's true name (Arthur Juarez). Because a debtor name search for "Arthur Juarez" would not disclose a financing statement in the name of "Arthur Mendez," Glendale's financing statement was seriously misleading. Therefore, Frozun's security interest

would have priority because its financing statement was recorded properly. ■

30–3b Perfection without Filing

In two types of situations, security interests can be perfected without filing a financing statement. The first occurs when the collateral is transferred into the possession of the secured party. The second occurs when the security interest is one of a limited number under the UCC that can be perfected on attachment [UCC 9–309].

The phrase *perfected on attachment* means that these security interests are automatically perfected at the time of their creation, without a filing and without possession of the goods. Two of the most common security interests that are perfected on attachment are a *purchase-money security interest* in consumer goods (explained shortly) and an assignment of a beneficial interest in an estate of a deceased person [UCC 9–309(1), (13)].

Perfection by Possession In the past, one of the most frequently used means of obtaining financing under the common law was to pledge certain collateral as security for the debt. The collateral was then transferred into the creditor's possession. When the debt was paid, the collateral was returned to the debtor. Although the debtor usually entered into a written security agreement, oral security agreements were also enforceable as long as the secured party possessed the collateral.

The UCC retained the common law pledge and the principle that the security agreement need not be in writing if the collateral is transferred to the secured party [UCC 9–310, 9–312(b), 9–313]. ■ **EXAMPLE 30.4** Sheila needs cash to pay for a medical procedure. She obtains a loan for $4,000 from Trent. As security on the loan, she gives him a promissory note on which she is the payee. Even though the agreement to hold the note as collateral was oral, Trent has a perfected security interest. He does not need to file a financing statement, because he has possession of the note. No other creditor of Sheila's can attempt to recover the note from Trent in payment for other debts. ■

Certain items—such as stocks, bonds, negotiable instruments, and jewelry—are commonly transferred into the creditor's possession when they are used as collateral for loans. For most collateral, however, possession by the secured party is impractical because it would prevent the debtor from using or deriving income from the property to pay off the debt. ■ **EXAMPLE 30.5** Jeb, a farmer, takes out a loan to finance the purchase of a corn harvester and uses the equipment as collateral. Clearly, the purpose of the purchase would be defeated if Jeb transferred the collateral into the creditor's possession. ■

Perfection by Attachment—The Purchase-Money Security Interest in Consumer Goods

Under the UCC, fourteen types of security interests are perfected automatically at the time they are created [UCC 9–309]. The most common is the **purchase-money security interest (PMSI)** in *consumer goods* (items bought primarily for personal, family, or household purposes).

A PMSI in consumer goods is created when a seller or lender agrees to extend credit to a buyer for part or all of the purchase price of the goods in a sales transaction. The entity that extends the credit can be either the seller (a store, for instance) or a financial institution that lends the buyer the funds with which to purchase the goods [UCC 9–102(a)(2)].

Automatic Perfection. A PMSI in consumer goods is perfected automatically at the time of a credit sale—that is, at the time the PMSI is created. The seller in this situation does not need to do anything more to perfect her or his interest.

■ **EXAMPLE 30.6** Jami purchases a Whirlpool washer and dryer from West Coast Appliance for $2,500. Unable to pay the entire amount in cash, Jami signs a purchase agreement to pay $1,000 down and $100 per month until the balance, plus interest, is fully paid. West Coast Appliance is to retain a security interest in the appliances until full payment has been made. Because the security interest was created as part of the purchase agreement with a consumer, it is a PMSI, and West Coast Appliance's security interest is automatically perfected. ■

Exceptions to Automatic Perfection. There are two exceptions to the rule of automatic perfection for PMSIs:

1. Certain types of security interests that are subject to other federal or state laws may require additional steps to be perfected [UCC 9–311]. Many jurisdictions, for instance, have certificate-of-title statutes that establish perfection requirements for security interests in certain goods, including automobiles, trailers, boats, mobile homes, and farm tractors.

   ■ **EXAMPLE 30.7** Martin Sedek purchases a boat at a Florida dealership. Florida has a certificate-of-title

statute. Sedek obtains financing for his purchase through General Credit Corporation. General Credit Corporation will need to file a certificate of title with the appropriate state official to perfect the PMSI. ■

2. PMSIs in nonconsumer goods, such as a business's inventory or livestock, are not automatically perfected [UCC 9–324]. These types of PMSIs will be discussed later in this chapter in the context of priorities.

30–3c Perfection and the Classification of Collateral

Where or how to perfect a security interest sometimes depends on the classification or definition of the collateral. Collateral is generally divided into two classifications: *tangible collateral* (collateral that can be seen, felt, and touched) and *intangible collateral* (collateral that consists of or generates rights). Exhibit 30–3 summarizes various classifications of collateral and the methods of perfecting a security interest in collateral falling within each of those classifications.[3]

30–3d Effective Time Duration of Perfection

A financing statement is effective for five years from the date of filing [UCC 9–515]. If a **continuation statement** is filed *within six months prior to the expiration date,* the effectiveness of the original statement is continued for another five years. The continuation period starts with the expiration date of the first five-year period [UCC 9–515(d), (e)]. The effectiveness of the statement can be continued in the same manner indefinitely. Any attempt to file a continuation statement outside the six-month window will render the continuation ineffective, and the perfection will lapse at the end of the five-year period.

If a financing statement lapses, the security interest that had been perfected by the filing now becomes unperfected. A purchaser for value can take the property that was used as collateral as if the security interest had never been perfected [UCC 9–515(c)].

To review the ways of perfecting a security interest, see Concept Summary 30.2.

---

3. There are additional classifications, such as agricultural liens, commercial tort claims, and investment property. For definitions of these types of collateral, see UCC 9–102(a)(5), (a)(13), and (a)(49).

EXHIBIT 30–3 Selected Types of Collateral and Methods of Perfection

TANGIBLE COLLATERAL		METHOD OF PERFECTION
All things that are movable at the time the security interest attaches or that are attached to land, including timber and crops.		
Consumer Goods	Items bought primarily for personal, family, or household purposes, such as a home theatre system.	A purchase-money security interest (PMSI) in consumer goods is automatically perfected at the time it is created (except for certain vehicles that also must comply with certificate-of-title statutes). For other consumer goods, general rules of filing or possession apply.
Equipment	Goods bought for or used primarily in business (and not part of inventory or farm products)—for example, a delivery truck.	Filing or (rarely) possession by secured party.
Farm Products	Crops (including aquatic goods), livestock, or supplies produced in a farming operation —for example, ginned cotton, milk, eggs, and maple syrup.	Filing or (rarely) possession by secured party.
Inventory	Goods held by a person for sale or under a contract of service or lease; raw materials held for production and work in progress.	Filing or (rarely) possession by secured party.

INTANGIBLE COLLATERAL		METHOD OF PERFECTION
Nonphysical property that exists only in connection with something else.		
Chattel Paper	A writing or electronic record that evidences both a monetary obligation and a security interest in goods and software used in goods—for example, a security agreement.	Filing or possession or control by secured party.
Instruments	A negotiable instrument—such as a check, note, certificate of deposit, draft, or other writing—that evidences a right to the payment of money and is not a security agreement or lease, but rather a type that can ordinarily be transferred (after indorsement, if necessary) by delivery.	Normally, filing or possession. For the sale of promissory notes, perfection can be by attachment (automatically on the creation of the security interest).
Accounts	Any right to receive payment for property (real or personal), including intellectual licensed property, services, insurance policies, and certain other receivables.	Filing required except for certain assignments that can be perfected by attachment (automatically on the creation of the security interest).
Deposit Accounts	Any demand, time, savings, passbook, or similar account maintained with a bank.	Perfection by control, such as when the secured party is the bank in which the account is maintained or when the parties have agreed that the secured party can direct the disposition of funds in a particular account.

Concept Summary 30.2

Perfecting a Security Interest

Perfecting a Security Interest by Filing	The most common method of perfection is *by filing* a financing statement containing the names of the secured party and the debtor and indicating the collateral covered by the financing statement.
	• Communication of the financing statement to the appropriate filing office, together with the correct filing fee, constitutes a filing.
	• The financing statement must be filed under the name of the debtor. Fictitious (trade) names normally are not sufficient.

Perfecting a Security Interest without Filing	Two common methods to perfect a security interest *without filing* include the following:
	1. *By transfer of collateral*—The debtor can transfer possession of the collateral to the secured party. For example, a *pledge* is this type of transfer.
	2. *By attachment*—A limited number of security interests are perfected by attachment, such as a purchase-money security interest (PMSI) in consumer goods. If the secured party has a PMSI in consumer goods (for personal or household purposes, for example), the secured party's security interest is perfected automatically.

30–4 The Scope of a Security Interest

A security interest can cover property in which the debtor has either present or future ownership or possessory rights. Therefore, security agreements can cover the proceeds of the sale of collateral, after-acquired property, and future advances, as discussed next.

30–4a Proceeds

Proceeds are the cash or property received when collateral is sold or disposed of in some other way [UCC 9–102(a)(64)]. A security interest in the collateral gives the secured party a security interest in the proceeds acquired from the sale of that collateral.

■ **EXAMPLE 30.8** People's Bank has a perfected security interest in the inventory of a retail seller of heavy farm machinery. The retailer sells a tractor out of this inventory to Jacob Lamensdorf. Lamensdorf agrees, in a security agreement, to make monthly payments to the retailer for a period of twenty-four months. If the retailer goes into default on the loan from the bank, the bank is entitled to the remaining payments Lamensdorf owes to the retailer as proceeds. ■

A security interest in proceeds is automatically perfected at the same time as the secured party perfected its security interest in the original collateral. It remains perfected for twenty days after the debtor receives the proceeds from the sale of the collateral.

The parties can agree to extend the twenty-day automatic perfection period in the original security agreement [UCC 9–315(c), (d)]. Extensions are typically done when the collateral is the type that is likely to be sold, such as a retailer's inventory of tablets or smartphones. The UCC also permits a security interest in identifiable cash proceeds to remain perfected after twenty days [UCC 9–315(d)(2)].

The dispute in the following case focused on proceeds. The court was asked to decide whether the actions taken by the debtor and another creditor had stripped a secured creditor of its interest in certain proceeds.

Case 30.2

In re Tusa–Expo Holdings, Inc.

United States Court of Appeals, Fifth Circuit, 811 F.3d 786 (2016).

Background and Facts Tusa Office Solutions, Inc., a subsidiary of Tusa–Expo Holdings, Inc., was the largest retail dealer in new furniture made by Knoll, Inc. A customer ordered Knoll furniture from Tusa Office, which ordered it from Knoll and delivered it to the customer. The customer paid Tusa Office, which then paid Knoll. Knoll set a limit on the amount of the payments that could be outstanding before it would stop filling new orders. As part of the deal, Tusa Office granted Knoll a first-priority security interest in specified accounts receivable.

Meanwhile, Tusa Office obtained a loan from Textron Financial, Inc. Knoll and Textron agreed separately that Textron would have a first-priority security interest in all of Tusa Office's assets except Knoll's collateral.

The terms of the loan required Tusa Office to establish a bank account—called the lockbox—into which its customers made payments directly. Textron could withdraw funds from the lockbox and use them to increase the credit available to Tusa Office on its loan. Tusa Office used the increased credit to pay Knoll. By paying Knoll, Tusa Office kept its debt to Knoll below the furniture maker's limit, which enabled Tusa Office to fill new orders for its customers.

Ultimately, Tusa Office filed a bankruptcy petition in a federal bankruptcy court. Marilyn Garner, the bankruptcy trustee, sought to recapture some of the funds that Knoll had received through the lockbox.[a] To do this, Garner had to establish that Knoll had received more by these transfers than it would receive on Tusa Office's bankruptcy. The court issued a ruling against the trustee, who appealed.

In the Language of the Court

WIENER, Circuit Judge:

* * * *

* * * *A creditor who merely recovers its own collateral receives no more * * * than it would have received anyway.* [Emphasis added.]

The Trustee asserts that the transfers from Tusa Office to Knoll were not made from the proceeds of Knoll's collateral.

* * * *

The Trustee does not dispute that the payments Tusa Office's customers deposited into the lockbox were proceeds of Tusa Office's accounts receivable. She argues * * * that * * * Knoll's first-priority security interest in the payments was stripped by operation of [Texas Business and Commerce Code] Section 9.332(a) [Texas's version of UCC 9–332(a)]: "A transferee of money takes the money free of a security interest * * * ." Section 9.332(a) does not apply if such a transfer of money was made to the debtor. The Trustee therefore insists that Textron, not Tusa Office, was the transferee. In so doing, the Trustee contends that the lockbox was "owned * * * by Textron."

* * * *

* * * The Loan Agreement is clear. It specifies that * * * "Tusa Office shall have established a * * * lockbox * * * for its collections and the transfer thereof to Textron * * * ." The Loan Agreement also states that "Tusa Office shall have possession of Textron's Collateral."

Because Tusa Office, not Textron, owned the lockbox, Section 9.332(a) does not apply. Therefore, Knoll's first-priority security interest in the proceeds of Tusa Office's accounts receivable survived the deposit into the lockbox.

* * * *

The Trustee next contends that Section 9.332(b) [Texas's version of UCC 9–332(b)] stripped Knoll's first-priority security interest when they were transferred from the lockbox to Textron.

* * * *

---

a. A debtor files a petition in a federal bankruptcy court to liquidate its assets, pay its creditors with the proceeds, and obtain a discharge of any remaining debt. It is the job of the bankruptcy trustee to collect those assets and distribute them fairly among the debtor's creditors.

Case 30.2 Continued

The plain language of Section 9.332(b) states that a "transferee of funds from a deposit account takes the funds free of a security interest in the deposit account."

* * * *

The plain language of Section 9.332(b) is unambiguous. Knoll's first-priority security interest in the proceeds of Tusa Office's accounts receivable survived the transfer from the lockbox to Textron. Not only is this consistent with Section 9.332(b), but it is also consistent with the * * * Agreement between Knoll and Textron.

Decision and Remedy *The U.S. Court of Appeals for the Fifth Circuit affirmed the ruling of the lower court. The trustee could not recover the funds that were transferred to Knoll from Tusa Office through the lockbox because those funds were the proceeds of Knoll's own collateral.*

Critical Thinking
- **Legal Environment** *Why does UCC 9–332 permit transferees to take funds "free of a security interest"? How did this provision work to protect the parties in this case?*
- **Ethical** *Office Expo, Inc., a dealer in used furniture, was, like Tusa Office, a subsidiary of Tusa–Expo Holdings. Tusa Office operated profitably, but Office Expo did not. To bolster Office Expo, funds were transferred from Tusa Office to Office Expo on a regular basis, which caused problems for Tusa Office. Were these transfers unethical? Discuss.*

30–4b After-Acquired Property

After-acquired property is property that the debtor acquired after the execution of the security agreement. The security agreement may provide for a security interest in after-acquired property, such as a debtor's inventory [UCC 9–204(1)].

Generally, the debtor will purchase new inventory to replace the inventory sold. The secured party wants this newly acquired inventory to be subject to the original security interest. Thus, the after-acquired property clause continues the secured party's claim to any inventory acquired thereafter. (This is not to say that the original security interest will take priority over the rights of all other creditors with regard to this after-acquired inventory, as will be discussed later.)

■ **EXAMPLE 30.9** Amato buys factory equipment from Bronson on credit, giving as security an interest in all of her equipment—both what she is buying and what she already owns. The security agreement with Bronson contains an after-acquired property clause. Six months later, Amato pays cash to another seller of factory equipment for additional equipment. Six months after that, Amato goes out of business before she has paid off her debt to Bronson. Bronson has a security interest in all of Amato's equipment, even the equipment bought from the other seller. ■

30–4c Future Advances

Often, a debtor will arrange with a bank to have a *continuing line of credit* under which the debtor can borrow

funds intermittently. Advances against lines of credit can be subject to a properly perfected security interest in certain collateral.

The security agreement may provide that any future advances made against that line of credit are also subject to the security interest in the same collateral [UCC 9–204(c)]. Future advances need not be of the same type or otherwise related to the original advance to benefit from this type of **cross-collateralization.**[4] Cross-collateralization occurs when an asset that is not the subject of a loan is used to collateralize that loan.

■ **EXAMPLE 30.10** Stroh is the owner of a small manufacturing plant with equipment valued at $1 million. He has an immediate need for $40,000 of working capital. He obtains a loan from Midwestern Bank and signs a security agreement, putting up all of his equipment as security. The bank properly perfects its security interest. The security agreement provides that Stroh can borrow up to $500,000 in the future, using the same equipment as collateral for any future advances. Midwestern Bank does not have to execute a new security agreement and perfect a security interest each time an advance is made, up to a cumulative total of $500,000. For priority purposes, each advance is perfected as of the date of the *original* perfection. ■

30–4d The Floating-Lien Concept

A security agreement that provides for a security interest in proceeds, in after-acquired property, or in collateral subject

---
4. See Official Comment 5 to UCC 9–204.

to future advances by the secured party is often characterized as a **floating lien.** This type of security interest continues in the collateral or proceeds even if the collateral is sold, exchanged, or disposed of in some other way.

A Floating Lien in Inventory Floating liens commonly arise in the financing of inventories. A creditor is not interested in specific pieces of inventory, which are constantly changing, so the lien "floats" from one item to another as the inventory changes.

■ **EXAMPLE 30.11** Cascade Sports, Inc., an Oregon corporation, operates as a cross-country ski dealer. The company has a line of credit with Portland First Bank to finance its inventory of cross-country skis. Cascade and Portland First enter into a security agreement that provides for coverage of proceeds, after-acquired inventory, present inventory, and future advances. Portland First perfects its security interest in the inventory by filing centrally with the office of the secretary of state in Oregon. One day, Cascade sells a new pair of the latest cross-country skis and receives a used pair in trade. That same day, Cascade purchases two new pairs of cross-country skis from a local manufacturer for cash. Later that day, to meet its payroll, Cascade borrows $8,000 from Portland First Bank under the security agreement.

Portland First has a perfected security interest in the used pair of skis under the proceeds clause. It also has a perfected security interest in the two new pairs of skis purchased from the local manufacturer under the after-acquired property clause. The new amount of funds advanced to Cascade is secured on all of the above-mentioned collateral by the future-advances clause. All of this is accomplished under the original perfected security interest. The various items in the inventory have changed, but Portland First still has a perfected security interest in Cascade's inventory. Hence, it has a floating lien in the inventory. ■

A Floating Lien in a Shifting Stock of Goods
The concept of the floating lien can also apply to a shifting stock of goods. The lien can start with raw materials, follow them as they become finished goods and inventories, and continue as the goods are sold and are turned into accounts receivable, chattel paper, or cash.

30–5 Priorities

When more than one party claims an interest in the same collateral, which has priority? The UCC sets out detailed rules to answer this question. In many situations

the party who has a perfected security interest will have priority. There are, however, exceptions that give priority rights to another party, such as a buyer in the ordinary course of business.

30–5a General Rules of Priority

The basic rule is that when more than one security interest has been perfected in the same collateral, the first to be perfected (or filed) has priority over any perfected later. If only one of the conflicting security interests has been perfected, then that security interest has priority. If none of the security interests have been perfected, then the first security interest that attaches has priority.

The UCC's rules of priority can be summarized as follows:

1. *Perfected security interest versus unsecured creditors and unperfected security interests.* When two or more parties have claims to the same collateral, a perfected secured party's interest has priority over the interests of most other parties [UCC 9–322(a)(2)]. This includes priority to the proceeds from a sale of collateral resulting from a bankruptcy (giving the perfected secured party rights superior to those of the bankruptcy trustee).

2. *Conflicting perfected security interests.* When two or more secured parties have perfected security interests in the same collateral, generally the first to perfect (by filing or taking possession of the collateral) has priority [UCC 9–322(a)(1)].

3. *Conflicting unperfected security interests.* When two conflicting security interests are unperfected, the first to attach (be created) has priority [UCC 9–322(a)(3)]. This is sometimes called the "first-in-time" rule.

■ **EXAMPLE 30.12** Rick Morales and his wife and son own a dairy farm called Lost Creek Heifers (LCH) that has received multiple loans through Ag Services, Inc. Morales executes a promissory note and security agreement in favor of Ag Services. The note lists all of LCH's accounts, equipment, farm products, inventory, livestock, and proceeds as collateral. A year later, Morales and his wife separate, and he signs a separation agreement giving her some cash and land.

The following year, Morales buys out his son's interest in LCH by giving him a promissory note for $100,000. The note lists all of LCH's equipment, inventory, livestock, and proceeds as collateral. Morales also sells a herd of dairy cows for $500,000 and gives his former wife a check for $240,000. LCH files for bankruptcy shortly thereafter. A dispute arises over which party (Ag Services, Morales's son, or Morales's former wife) is entitled to the proceeds from the sale of the cows. In this situation, a court will likely find that because Ag Services' security interest in the proceeds was the first in time to *attach*, Ag Services has first priority to the proceeds. ■

30–5b Exceptions to the General Priority Rules

In some situations, on the debtor's default, the perfection of a security interest will not protect a secured party against certain other third parties having claims to the collateral. For instance, the UCC provides that in certain circumstances a PMSI, properly perfected,[5] will prevail over another security interest in after-acquired collateral, even though the other was perfected first.

Buyers in the Ordinary Course of Business A major exception to the priority rules exists for a buyer in the ordinary course of business. A *buyer in the ordinary course of business* is a person who, in good faith, buys goods from a party in the business of selling such goods [UCC 1–201(9)].

A buyer in the ordinary course takes the goods free from any security interest created by the seller *even if the security interest is perfected and the buyer knows of its existence* [UCC 9–320(a)]. In other words, a buyer in the ordinary course will have priority even if a previously perfected security interest exists as to the goods. The rationale for this rule is obvious. If buyers could not obtain the goods free and clear of any security interest the merchant had created, the free flow of goods in the marketplace would be hindered.

■ **EXAMPLE 30.13** Dubbs Auto grants a security interest in its inventory to Heartland Bank for a $300,000 line of credit. Heartland perfects its security interest by filing financing statements with the appropriate state offices. Dubbs uses $9,000 of its credit to buy two used trucks and delivers the certificates of title, which designate Dubbs as the owner, to Heartland.

Later, Dubbs sells one of the trucks to Samuel Murdoch and another to Michael Laxton. National City Bank finances both purchases. New certificates of title designate the buyers as the owners and Heartland as the "first lienholder," but Heartland receives none of the funds from the sales. If Heartland sues National City, claiming that its security interest in the vehicles takes priority, it

will lose. Because Murdoch and Laxton are buyers in the ordinary course of business, Heartland's security interest in the motor vehicles was extinguished when the vehicles were sold to them. ■

PMSI in Goods Other than Inventory and Livestock An important exception to the first-in-time rule involves a perfected PMSI in certain types of collateral, such as equipment, that is not inventory or livestock [UCC 9–324(a)]. (Remember that a PMSI that is *not* in consumer goods must still be perfected.) ■ **EXAMPLE 30.14** Piper Sandoval borrows funds from West Bank, signing a security agreement in which she puts up all of her present and after-acquired equipment as security. On May 1, West Bank perfects this security interest (which is not a PMSI). On July 1, Sandoval purchases a new piece of equipment from Zylex Company on credit, signing a security agreement. The delivery date for the new equipment is August 1.

Zylex thus has a PMSI in the new equipment (which is not part of its inventory), but the PMSI is not in consumer goods and thus is not automatically perfected. If Sandoval defaults on her payments to both West Bank and Zylex, which of them has priority with regard to the new piece of equipment? Generally, West Bank would have priority because its interest perfected first in time. In this situation, however, as long as Zylex perfected its PMSI in the new equipment within twenty days after Sandoval took possession on August 1, Zylex has priority. ■

PMSI in Inventory Another important exception to the first-in-time rule has to do with security interests in inventory. A perfected PMSI in inventory has priority over a conflicting security interest in the same inventory. To maintain this priority, the holder of the PMSI must notify the holder of the conflicting security interest on or before the time the debtor takes possession of the inventory [UCC 9–324(b)].

■ **EXAMPLE 30.15** On May 1, SNS Electronics borrows funds from Key Bank. SNS signs a security agreement that puts up all of its present inventory and any after-acquired inventory as collateral. Key Bank perfects its interest (not a PMSI) on that date. On June 10, SNS buys new inventory from Martin, Inc., a manufacturer, to use for its Fourth of July sale. SNS makes a down payment for the new inventory and signs a security agreement giving Martin a PMSI in the new inventory as collateral for the remaining debt. Martin delivers the inventory to SNS on June 28, but SNS's Fourth of July sale is a disaster, and most of its inventory remains unsold. In August, SNS defaults on its payments to both Key Bank and Martin.

---

5. Recall that, with some exceptions (such as motor vehicles), a PMSI in *consumer goods* is automatically perfected—no filing is necessary. A PMSI that is *not* in consumer goods must still be perfected, however.

Does Key Bank or Martin have priority with respect to the new inventory delivered to SNS on June 28? If Martin has not perfected its security interest by June 28, Key Bank's after-acquired collateral clause has priority because it was the first to be perfected (on May 1). If, however, Martin has perfected *and* gives proper notice of its security interest to Key Bank before SNS takes possession of the goods on June 28, Martin has priority. ■

Buyers of the Collateral The UCC recognizes that there are certain types of buyers whose interest in purchased goods could conflict with those of a perfected secured party on the debtor's default. These include buyers in the ordinary course of business (as discussed), as well as buyers of farm products, instruments, documents, or securities. The UCC sets down special rules of priority for these types of buyers.

Exhibit 30–4 describes the various rules regarding the priority of claims to a debtor's collateral.

30–6 Rights and Duties of Debtors and Creditors

The security agreement itself determines most of the rights and duties of the debtor and the secured party. The UCC, however, imposes some rights and duties that apply unless the security agreement states otherwise.

30–6a Information Requests

At the time of filing a financing statement, a secured party can also furnish a *copy* of the financing statement to the filing officer. The secured party can request that the officer note the file number, date, and hour of the original filing on the copy [UCC 9–523(a)]. The filing officer must send this copy to the person designated by the secured party or to the debtor, if the debtor makes the request.

The filing officer must also give information to a person who is contemplating obtaining a security interest from a prospective debtor [UCC 9–523(c), (d)]. If requested, the filing officer must issue a certificate (for a fee) that provides information on possible perfected financing statements with respect to the named debtor.

30–6b Release, Assignment, and Amendment

A secured party can release all or part of any collateral described in the financing statement, thereby terminating its security interest in that collateral. The release is recorded by filing a uniform amendment form [UCC 9–512, 9–521(b)].

A secured party can also assign all or part of the security interest to a third party (the assignee). The assignee becomes the secured party of record if the assignment is filed by use of a uniform amendment form [UCC 9–514, 9–521(a)].

If the debtor and the secured party agree, they can amend the information in the filed financing statement and can add or substitute new collateral. They do so by filing a uniform amendment form that indicates the file number of the initial financing statement [UCC 9–512(a)]. An amendment does not extend the time period of perfection. If new collateral is added, however, the perfection date (for priority purposes) for the new collateral begins on the date the amendment is filed [UCC 9–512(b), (c)].

30–6c Confirmation or Accounting Request by Debtor

The debtor may believe that the amount of the unpaid debt or the list of the collateral subject to the security interest is inaccurate. The debtor has the right to request a confirmation of the unpaid debt or list of collateral [UCC 9–210]. The debtor is entitled to one request without charge every six months.

The secured party must comply with the debtor's confirmation request by authenticating and sending to the debtor an accounting within fourteen days after the request is received. Otherwise, the secured party can be held liable for any loss suffered by the debtor, plus $500 [UCC 9–210, 9–625(f)].

30–6d Termination Statement

When the debtor has fully paid the debt, if the secured party perfected the security interest by filing, the debtor is entitled to have a termination statement filed. Such a statement demonstrates to the public that the filed perfected security interest has been terminated [UCC 9–513].

Whenever consumer goods are involved, the secured party *must* file a termination statement (or, alternatively,

EXHIBIT 30–4 Priority of Claims to a Debtor's Collateral

PARTIES	PRIORITY
Perfected Secured Party versus **Unsecured Parties and Creditors**	A perfected secured party's interest has priority over the interests of most other parties, including unsecured creditors, unperfected secured parties, subsequent lien creditors, trustees in bankruptcy, and buyers who do not purchase the collateral in the ordinary course of business.
Perfected Secured Party versus **Perfected Secured Party**	Between two perfected secured parties in the same collateral, the general rule is that the first in time of perfection is the first in right to the collateral [UCC 9–322(a)(1)].
Perfected Secured Party versus **Perfected PMSI**	A PMSI, even if second in time of perfection, has priority providing that the following conditions are met: 1. *Other collateral*—A PMSI has priority, providing it is perfected within twenty days after the debtor takes possession [UCC 9–324(a)]. 2. *Inventory*—A PMSI has priority if it is perfected and proper written or authenticated notice is given to the other security-interest holder on or before the time the debtor takes possession [UCC 9–324(b)]. 3. *Software*—Applies to a PMSI in software only if used in goods subject to a PMSI. If the goods are inventory, priority is determined the same as for inventory. If they are not, priority is determined as for goods other than inventory [UCC 9–103(c), 9–324(f)].

Perfected Secured Party versus **Purchaser of Debtor's Collateral**	1. *Buyer of goods in the ordinary course of the seller's business*—Buyer prevails over a secured party's security interest, even if perfected and even if the buyer knows of the security interest [UCC 9–320(a)].
	 2. *Buyer of consumer goods purchased outside the ordinary course of business*—Buyer prevails over a secured party's interest, even if perfected by attachment, providing the buyer purchased as follows:
	     a. For value.
	     b. Without actual knowledge of the security interest.
	     c. For use as a consumer good.
	     d. Prior to the secured party's perfection by filing [UCC 9–320(b)].
	 3. *Buyer of chattel paper*—Buyer prevails if the buyer:
	     a. Gave new value in making the purchase.
	     b. Took possession in the ordinary course of the buyer's business.
	     c. Took without knowledge of the security interest [UCC 9–330].
	 4. *Buyer of instruments, documents, or securities*—Buyer who is a holder in due course, a holder to whom negotiable documents have been duly negotiated, or a bona fide purchaser of securities has priority over a previously perfected security interest [UCC 9–330(d), 9–331(a)].
	 5. *Buyer of farm products*—Buyer from a farmer takes free and clear of perfected security interests unless, where permitted, a secured party files centrally an effective financing statement (EFS) or the buyer receives proper notice of the security interest before the sale.

Unperfected Secured Party versus **Unsecured Creditor**	An unperfected secured party prevails over unsecured creditors and creditors who have obtained judgments against the debtor but who have not begun the legal process to collect on those judgments [UCC 9–201(a)].

a release). The statement must be filed within one month of the final payment or within twenty days of receiving the debtor's authenticated demand, whichever is earlier [UCC 9–513(b)].

When the collateral is not consumer goods, the secured party is not required to file or to send a termination statement unless the debtor demands one [UCC 9–513(c)]. Whenever a secured party fails to file or send the termination statement as requested, the debtor can recover $500 plus any additional loss suffered [UCC 9–625(e)(4), (f)].

30–7 Default

Article 9 defines the rights, duties, and remedies of the secured party and of the debtor on the debtor's default. If the secured party fails to comply with his or her duties, the debtor is afforded particular rights and remedies under the UCC.

30–7a What Constitutes Default

What constitutes *default* is not always clear. In fact, Article 9 does not define the term. Instead, the UCC encourages the parties to include in their security agreements the standards under which their rights and duties will be measured [UCC 9–601, 9–603]. In so doing, parties can stipulate the conditions that will constitute a default. Often, these critical terms are shaped by creditors themselves in an attempt to provide the maximum protection possible.

The UCC does impose some requirements, however. The parties cannot agree to waive or alter certain UCC provisions, such as those involving the debtor's right to an accounting or disposition of collateral [UCC 9–602]. In addition, the terms may not run counter to the UCC's provisions regarding good faith and unconscionability.

Any breach of the terms of the security agreement can constitute default. Nevertheless, default occurs most commonly when the debtor fails to meet the scheduled payments that the parties have agreed on or when the debtor becomes bankrupt.

30–7b Basic Remedies

The rights and remedies of secured parties under Article 9 are *cumulative* [UCC 9–601(c)]. Therefore, if a creditor is unsuccessful in enforcing rights by one method, she

or he can pursue another method. Generally, a secured party's remedies can be divided into two basic categories: repossession and litigation.

Repossession of the Collateral—The Self-Help Remedy On the debtor's default, a secured party can take peaceful possession of the collateral covered by the security agreement without the use of the judicial process [UCC 9–609(b)]. This provision is referred to as the "self-help" provision of Article 9.

The UCC does not define what constitutes *peaceful possession.* The general rule is that the secured party must repossess the collateral without any breach of the peace (without trespassing or breaking and entering, for instance).

Judicial Remedies Alternatively, a secured party can relinquish the security interest and use any judicial remedy available, such as obtaining a judgment on the underlying debt, followed by execution and levy [UCC 9–601(a)]. **Execution** is the implementation of a court's decree or judgment. **Levy** is the legal process of obtaining of funds through the seizure and sale of nonexempt property, usually done after a writ of execution has been issued.

30–7c Disposition of Collateral

Once default has occurred and the secured party has obtained possession of the collateral, the secured party can:

1. Retain the collateral in full or partial satisfaction of the debt (subject to limitations, discussed next).
2. Sell, lease, license, or otherwise dispose of the collateral in any commercially reasonable manner and apply the proceeds toward satisfaction of the debt [UCC 9–602(7), 9–603, 9–610(a), 9–613, 9–620]. Any sale is always subject to procedures established by state law.

Retention of Collateral by the Secured Party Parties are sometimes better off if they do not sell the collateral. Therefore, the UCC generally allows secured parties to choose not to sell. A secured party may retain the collateral unless it consists of consumer goods and the debtor has paid 60 percent or more of the purchase price in a PMSI or debt in a non-PMSI [UCC 9–620(e)]. This general right to retain the collateral is subject to several limitations.

Notice Requirements. The secured party must notify the debtor of its proposal to retain the collateral. Notice is required unless the debtor has signed a statement renouncing or modifying her or his rights *after default* [UCC 9–620(a), 9–621].

If the collateral is consumer goods, the secured party does not need to give any other notice. In all other situations, the secured party must also send notice to any other secured party from whom the secured party has received notice of a claim of interest in the collateral. The secured party must also send notice to any *junior lienholder* who held a security interest (or statutory lien) in the collateral ten days before the debtor consented to the retention [UCC 9–621]. (A **junior lienholder** is a party holding a lien that is subordinate to one or more other liens on the same property.)

Objections. The debtor or other party notified of the retention has the right to object. If, within twenty days after the notice is sent, the secured party receives a written objection, the secured party must sell or otherwise dispose of the collateral. If no written objection is received, the secured party may retain the collateral in full or partial satisfaction of the debtor's obligation [UCC 9–620(a), 9–621].

Consumer Goods When the collateral is consumer goods and the debtor has paid 60 percent of the purchase price on a PMSI or loan amount, the secured party must sell or otherwise dispose of the repossessed collateral within ninety days [UCC 9–620(e), (f)]. Failure to comply opens the secured party to an action for conversion or other liability under UCC 9–625(b) and (c). A secured party will not be liable, however, if the consumer-debtor signed a written statement *after default* renouncing or modifying the right to demand the sale of the goods [UCC 9–624].

Disposition of Collateral by the Secured Party
A secured party who does not choose to retain the collateral or who is required to sell it must dispose of it in a *commercially reasonable* manner. The secured party must notify the debtor and other specified parties in writing ahead of time about the sale or disposition of the collateral. Notification is not required if the collateral is perishable, will decline rapidly in value, or is of a type customarily sold on a recognized market [UCC 9–611(b), (c)].[6]

Sale Can Be Public or Private. The UCC allows substantial flexibility with regard to disposition. The sale can be public or private. The collateral can be disposed of in its present condition or following any commercially reasonable preparation or processing [UCC 9–610(a)]. The secured party may purchase the collateral at a public sale, but normally not at a private sale [UCC 9–610(c)].

Must Be Commercially Reasonable. Every aspect of the disposition's method, manner, time, and place must be commercially reasonable [UCC 9–610(b)]. If the secured party does not dispose of the collateral in a commercially reasonable manner, the price paid for the collateral at the sale may be negatively affected. In that situation, a court can reduce the amount of any deficiency that the debtor owes to the secured party [UCC 9–626(a)(3)].

Although the purpose of requiring a commercially reasonable disposition is to obtain a satisfactory price, the courts look at many factors to determine reasonableness. ■ **CASE IN POINT 30.16** Shannon Hicklin bought a used Ford Explorer under an installment sales contract. When she fell three payments behind—still owing $5,741.65—Onyx Acceptance Corporation repossessed the car and sold it for $1,500 at a private auction. After deducting the costs of repossession and sale, there was a deficiency under the contract of $5,018.88. Onyx filed a suit to collect this amount from Hicklin.

Onyx claimed that the sale was commercially reasonable because the auction price ($1,500) was more than 50 percent of the estimated market value ($2,335). The court, however, found that the price alone was not enough to prove reasonableness. Onyx needed to show that every aspect of the sale was conducted in a commercially reasonable manner. Alternatively, under UCC 9–627(b)(3), Onyx could show that the sale conformed with the reasonable commercial practices among dealers in that type of property. Because Onyx did not do either, it could not collect any deficiency from Hicklin.[7] ■

In the following case, two defaulting debtors alleged that their creditor's sale of the debtors' shares of stock was commercially unreasonable. The debtors contended that a different type of sale or a different "inducement" might have attracted a higher price.

---

6. The debtor may waive the right to receive a notice of disposition, but only after default [UCC 9–624(a)].

7. *Hicklin v. Onyx Corp.,* 970 A.2d 244 (Del.Sup.Ct. 2009).

Smith v. Firstbank Corp.

Court of Appeals of Michigan, 2013 WL 951377 (2013).

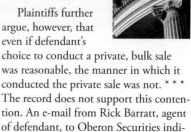

In the Language of the Court

PER CURIAM.

* * * *

The facts in this secured transactions case are not in dispute. Plaintiffs [Bradley Smith, on his own behalf and on behalf of the John J. Smith Revocable Living Trust] borrowed funds from [defendant Firstbank Corporation] in 2002; the notes to defendant were secured with pledges of Sparton Corporation stock as well as other collateral. Plaintiffs defaulted on these loans. Eventually, after many modifications and extensions, defendant took possession of the pledged shares of Sparton stock. Shortly thereafter, defendant sold the stock in two private transactions: on January 12, 2010, it sold 602,170 shares to a brokerage firm at $4.84 per share, and on February 19, 2010, it sold 450,000 shares to a brokerage firm at $5.05 per share. The parties agree that the closing price for Sparton stock on the New York Stock Exchange on both sale dates was $6.05 per share. Defendant then released the remaining collateral to plaintiffs and remitted to plaintiffs by cashier's check the excess funds collected in the private sales. The value of the collateral retained by plaintiffs was over five million dollars.

Plaintiffs filed suit [in a Michigan state court] against defendant, alleging that the sales violated defendant's contractual duties to plaintiffs because they were "commercially unreasonable" * * *. Defendant moved the trial court for summary disposition [judgment]. * * * The trial court issued an Opinion and Order granting defendant's motion * * *. This appeal followed.

* * * *

At issue in the instant case is the secured party's disposition of collateral after the debtors' default. Defendant, the secured party, was authorized by MCL [Michigan Compiled Laws] 440.9609 [Michigan's version of UCC 9–609] to

take possession of the collateral following plaintiffs' default. The parties agree that plaintiffs defaulted in the instant case, and that defendant was within its rights to take possession of the pledged shares.

MCL 440.9610 [Michigan's version of UCC 9–610] governs the disposition of collateral after default, and provides in relevant part: * * *

> Every aspect of a disposition of collateral, including the method, manner, time, place, and other terms, must be commercially reasonable.

Further, MCL 440.9627 [Michigan's version of UCC 9–627] provides guidance for determination of whether the disposition of collateral was commercially reasonable, and provides in relevant part: * * *

> The fact that a greater amount could have been obtained by a collection, enforcement, disposition, or acceptance at a different time or in a different method from that selected by the secured party is not of itself sufficient to preclude the secured party from establishing that the collection, enforcement, disposition, or acceptance was made in a commercially reasonable manner.

* * * *

* * * *The circumstances surrounding previous sales of Sparton stock on the public market, and concerns about what public sales would do to the share price, rendered defendant's choice to sell in private transactions reasonable.* * * * In 2008, Wachovia [Bank] sold approximately 400,000 shares of Sparton to satisfy plaintiff Smith's debts. The sale required 18 separate transactions over a two-month period; during that period the share price declined by almost 50 percent. * * * *It was not commercially unreasonable for defendant to seek a private sale to avoid this risk.* [Emphasis added.]

Plaintiffs further argue, however, that even if defendant's choice to conduct a private, bulk sale was reasonable, the manner in which it conducted the private sale was not. * * * The record does not support this contention. An e-mail from Rick Barratt, agent of defendant, to Oberon Securities indicated that, in addition to requesting that Oberon bring them a buyer, defendant * * * "directed [our investment banker] to bring similar type offers to us as well." In addition, defendant's Chief Executive Officer testified * * * that "discounts in large transactions, in thinly traded stocks, were common" and that he was advised by employees of Oberon Securities that selling a "block this large would require a discount of 15 to 20 percent."

The evidence thus does not support the contention that defendant did not seek multiple offers or seek to get the best price for the stock. Rather, the evidence shows that defendant * * * received one offer for Smith's stock, at a discount. Rather than risk public sales and a repeat of what happened in 2008, defendant made the sale. In fact, plaintiffs' contention that defendant did not attempt to garner the best sale price it could is contradicted by the fact that defendant was able to sell the second block of shares (the shares pledged by the trust) for 21 cents more per share, notwithstanding that the closing price for Sparton was exactly the same on the day of both the first and second sales.

* * * *

* * * Although plaintiffs speculate that public sales would have resulted in a higher price, or that the private buyer could have been induced to pay a higher price, speculation and conjecture are insufficient to allow an opposing party to survive a motion for summary disposition.

Affirmed.

Case 30.3 Continued

Legal Reasoning Questions

1. What type of property was at the center of the dispute in this case? How did that property become involved in the dispute?
2. On what ground did the plaintiffs argue that the bank should not have been granted a summary judgment?
3. Why does collateral have to be disposed of in a commercially reasonable manner? Is price alone enough to prove reasonableness? Why or why not?

Proceeds from Disposition Proceeds from the disposition of collateral after default on the underlying debt are distributed in the following order:

1. Reasonable expenses incurred by the secured party in repossessing, storing, and reselling the collateral.
2. Balance of the debt owed to the secured party.
3. Junior lienholders who have made written or authenticated demands.
4. Any surplus to the debtor, unless the collateral consists of accounts, payment intangibles, promissory notes, or chattel paper [UCC 9–608(a); 9–615(a), (e)].

Noncash Proceeds Sometimes, the secured party receives noncash proceeds from the disposition of collateral after default. Whenever that occurs, the secured party must make a value determination and apply this value in a commercially reasonable manner [UCC 9–608(a)(3), 9–615(c)].

Deficiency Judgment Often, after proper disposition of the collateral, the secured party still has not collected all that the debtor owes. Unless otherwise agreed, the debtor normally is liable for any deficiency, and the creditor can obtain a **deficiency judgment** from a court to collect the deficiency. Practically speaking, though, debtors who have defaulted on a loan rarely have the cash to pay any deficiency.

Note that if the underlying transaction is a sale of accounts, chattel paper, or promissory notes, the debtor is *not* liable for any deficiency. The debtor is also not entitled to any surplus from the disposition of these types of collateral, unless that right is granted by the security agreement [UCC 9–615(e)].

Redemption Rights The debtor or any other secured party can exercise the right of *redemption* of the collateral. Redemption may occur at any time before the secured party disposes of the collateral, enters into a contract for its disposition, or discharges the debtor's obligation by retaining the collateral. To redeem the collateral, the debtor or other secured party must tender the entire obligation that is owed, plus any reasonable expenses and attorneys' fees incurred by the secured party in retaking and maintaining the collateral [UCC 9–623].

Concept Summary 30.3 provides a review of the secured party's remedies on the debtor's default.

Concept Summary 30.3

Remedies of the Secured Party on the Debtor's Default

Repossession of the Collateral	The secured party may take possession (peacefully or by court order) of the collateral covered by the security agreement and then pursue one of two alternatives:
	1. *Retain the collateral*—unless the collateral is consumer goods and the debtor has paid 60 percent of the selling price on a PMSI or 60 percent of the debt on a non-PMSI. To retain the collateral, the secured party must—
	a. Give notice to the debtor if the debtor has not signed a statement renouncing or modifying his or her rights after default. With consumer goods, no other notice is necessary.
	b. Send notice to any other secured party who has given written or authenticated notice of a claim to the same collateral or who has filed a security interest or a statutory lien ten days before the debtor consented to the retention. If an objection is received within twenty days from the debtor or any other secured party given notice, the creditor must dispose of the collateral according to the requirements of UCC 9–602, 9–603, 9–610, and 9–613. Otherwise, the creditor may retain the collateral in full or partial satisfaction of the debt.
	2. *Dispose of the collateral*—in accordance with the requirements of UCC 9–602(7), 9–603, 9–610(a), and 9–613. To do so, the secured party must—
	a. Dispose of (sell, lease, or license) the goods in a commercially reasonable manner.
	b. Notify the debtor and (except in sales of consumer goods) other identified persons, including those who have given notice of claims to the collateral to be sold (unless the collateral is perishable or will decline rapidly in value).
	c. Apply the proceeds in the following order:
	i. Expenses incurred by the secured party in repossessing, storing, and reselling the collateral.
	ii. The balance of the debt owed to the secured party.
	iii. Junior lienholders who have made written or authenticated demands.
	iv. Surplus to the debtor (unless the collateral consists of accounts, payment intangibles, promissory notes, or chattel paper).
Judicial Remedies	The secured party may relinquish the security interest and proceed with any judicial remedy available, such as obtaining a judgment on the underlying debt, followed by execution and levy on the nonexempt assets of the debtor.

Reviewing: Secured Transactions

Paul Barton owned a small property-management company, doing business as Brighton Homes. In October, Barton went on a spending spree. First, he bought a Bose surround-sound system for his home from KDM Electronics. The next day, he purchased a Wilderness Systems kayak and roof rack from Outdoor Outfitters, and the day after that he bought a new Toyota 4-Runner financed through Bridgeport Auto. Two weeks later, Barton purchased six new iMac computers for his office, also from KDM Electronics. Barton bought each of these items under an installment sales contract. Six months later, Barton's property-management business was failing. He could not make the payments due on any of these purchases and thus defaulted on the loans. Using the information presented in the chapter, answer the following questions.

1. For which of Barton's purchases (the surround-sound system, the kayak, the 4-Runner, and the iMacs) would the creditor need to file a financing statement to perfect its security interest?
2. Suppose that Barton's contract for the office computers mentioned only the name *Brighton Homes*. What would be the consequences if KDM Electronics filed a financing statement that listed only Brighton Homes as the debtor's name?
3. Which of these purchases would qualify as a PMSI in consumer goods?
4. Suppose that after KDM Electronics repossesses the surround-sound system, it decides to keep the system rather than sell it. Can KDM do this under Article 9? Why or why not?

Debate This . . .   *A financing statement that does not have the debtor's exact name should still be effective because creditors should always be protected when debtors default.*

Terms and Concepts

after-acquired property 567	deficiency judgment 575	proceeds 565
attachment 557	execution 572	purchase-money security
authenticate 557	financing statement 556	interest (PMSI) 563
collateral 556	floating lien 568	secured party 556
continuation statement 563	junior lienholder 573	secured transaction 556
cross-collateralization 567	levy 572	security agreement 556
debtor 556	perfection 559	security interest 556

Issue Spotters

1. Nero needs $500 to buy textbooks and other supplies. Olivia agrees to loan Nero $500, accepting Nero's computer as collateral. They put their agreement in writing. How can Olivia let other creditors know of her interest in the computer? (See *Creation of a Security Interest*.)
2. Liberty Bank loans Michelle $5,000 to buy a car, which is used as collateral to secure the loan. After repaying less than 50 percent of the loan, Michelle defaults. Liberty could repossess and keep the car, but the bank does not want it. What are the alternatives? (See *Default*.)

• **Check your answers to the Issue Spotters against the answers provided in Appendix D at the end of this text.**

Business Scenarios

30–1. Priorities. Redford is a seller of electric generators. He purchases a large quantity of generators from a manufacturer, Mallon Corp., by making a down payment and signing an agreement to make the balance of payments over a period of time. The agreement gives Mallon Corp. a security interest in the generators and the proceeds. Mallon Corp. properly files a financing statement on its security interest. Redford receives the generators and immediately sells one of them to Garfield on an installment contract, with payment to be made in twelve equal installments. At the time of the sale, Garfield knows of Mallon's security interest. Two months later, Redford goes into default on his payments to Mallon. Discuss Mallon's rights against Garfield in this situation. (See *Priorities.*)

30–2. Perfection of a Security Interest. Marsh has a prize horse named Arabian Knight. Marsh is in need of working capital. She borrows $50,000 from Mendez, who takes possession of Arabian Knight as security for the loan. No written agreement is signed. Discuss whether, in the absence of a written agreement, Mendez has a security interest in Arabian Knight. If Mendez does have a security interest, is it a

perfected security interest? Explain. (See *Perfection of a Security Interest.*)

30–3. The Scope of a Security Interest. Edward owned a retail sporting goods shop. A new ski resort was being constructed in his area, and to take advantage of the potential business, Edward decided to expand his operations. He borrowed a large sum from his bank, which took a security interest in his present inventory and any after-acquired inventory as collateral for the loan. The bank properly perfected the security interest by filing a financing statement. Edward's business was profitable, so he doubled his inventory. A year later, just a few months after the ski resort had opened, an avalanche destroyed the ski slope and lodge. Edward's business consequently took a turn for the worse, and he defaulted on his debt to the bank. The bank then sought possession of his entire inventory, even though the inventory was now twice as large as it had been when the loan was made. Edward claimed that the bank had rights to only half of his inventory. Was Edward correct? Explain. (See *The Scope of a Security Interest.*)

Business Case Problems

30–4. Spotlight on Radio Shack—Priorities. In June

1995, Michael and Debra Boudreaux, doing business as D&J Enterprises, Inc., bought a retail electronics store operated under a franchise from Radio Shack. They borrowed from Cabool State Bank to pay for the business and signed loan documents and a financing statement, which identified them as "Debtors." Elsewhere on the financing statement, the bank identified "D&J Enterprises, Inc., Radio Shack, Dealer, Debra K. Boudreaux, Michael C. Boudreaux" as "Debtors." The statement covered, in part, the store inventory.

Before the end of the year, Michael and Debra changed the name of their business to Tri-B Enterprises, Inc. In January 1998, the store closed. The next month, Radio Shack terminated the franchise. Despite the lack of a security interest, Radio Shack took possession of the inventory, claiming that the couple and Tri-B owed the company $6,394.73. The bank filed a suit in a Missouri state court against Radio Shack, claiming a perfected security interest in the inventory with priority over Radio Shack's claim. Did the bank's security interest take priority over Radio Shack's claim? Why or why not? [*Cabool State Bank v. Radio Shack,* 65 S.W.3d 613 (Mo. App. 2002)] (See *Priorities.*)

30–5. Default. Primesouth Bank issued a loan to Okefenokee Aircraft, Inc. (OAI), to buy a plane. OAI executed a note in favor of Primesouth in the amount of $161,306.25 plus interest. The plane secured the note. When OAI defaulted, Primesouth repossessed the plane. Instead of disposing of the collateral and seeking a deficiency judgment, however, the bank retained possession of the plane and filed a suit in

a Georgia state court against OAI to enforce the note. OAI did not deny that it had defaulted on the note or dispute the amount due. Instead, OAI argued that Primesouth Bank was not acting in a commercially reasonable manner. According to OAI, the creditor must sell the collateral and apply the proceeds against the debt. What is a secured creditor's obligation in these circumstances? Can the creditor retain the collateral and seek a judgment for the amount of the underlying debt, or is a sale required? Discuss. [*Okefenokee Aircraft, Inc. v. Primesouth Bank,* 296 Ga.App. 782, 676 S.E.2d 394 (2009)] (See *Default.*)

30–6. Disposition of Collateral. PRA Aviation, LLC, borrowed $3 million from Center Capital Corp. to buy a Gates Learjet 55B. Center perfected a security interest in the plane. Later, PRA defaulted on the loan, and Center obtained possession of the jet. The market, design, and mechanical condition of similar aircraft were reviewed to estimate the jet's value at $1.45 million. The jet was marketed in trade publications, on the Internet, and by direct advertising to select customers for $1.595 million. There were three offers. Center sold the jet to the high bidder for $1.3 million. Was the sale commercially reasonable? Explain. [*Center Capital Corp. v. PRA Aviation, LLC,* 2011 WL 867516 (E.D.Pa. 2011)] (See *Default.*)

30–7. Business Case Problem with Sample Answer— Perfecting a Security Interest. Thomas Tille owned

M.A.T.T. Equipment Co. To operate the business, Tille borrowed funds from Union Bank. For each loan, Union filed a financing statement that included Tille's signature and address, the bank's address, and a description of the collateral. The first loan covered all of Tille's equipment, including "any after-acquired property." The second loan covered a truck crane "whether owned now or acquired later." The third loan covered a "Bobcat mini-excavator." Did these financing statements perfect Union's security interests? Explain. [*Union Bank Co. v. Heban*, 2012-Ohio-30 (Ohio App. 2012)] (See *Perfection of a Security Interest.*)

- **For a sample answer for Problem 30–7, go to Appendix E at the end of this text.**

30–8. Disposition of Collateral. With a loan of 1.4 million euros from Barclays Bank, PLC, Thomas Poynter bought a yacht. The loan agreement gave Barclays multiple stand-alone options on default. One option required the lender to give ten days' advance notice of a sale. A different option permitted the lender to avoid this requirement. When Poynter did not repay the loan, Barclays repossessed the yacht and notified Poynter that it would be sold—but did not specify a date, time, or place. Two months later, the yacht was sold. The sale price was less than Poynter owed, and Barclays filed a suit in a federal district court for the deficiency. Is Barclays entitled to collect even though it did not give Poynter ten days' advance notice of the sale? Explain. [*Barclays Bank PLC v. Poynter*, 710 F.3d 16 (1st Cir. 2013)] (See *Default.*)

30–9. Perfection of a Security Interest. G&K Farms, a North Dakota partnership, operated a farm in Texas. G&K was insured under the Supplemental Revenue Assistance Payments Program (SURE), through which the federal government provides financial assistance for crop losses caused by natural disasters. PHI Financial Services, Inc., loaned G&K $6.6 million. PHI filed a financing statement that described the collateral as the debtor's interest in "Government Payments." The document did not refer to the farm's crops. G&K defaulted on the loan. Later, G&K received a SURE payment for crop losses and transferred some of the funds to its law firm, Johnston Law Office, P.C., in payment for services. PHI brought an action against Johnston to recover those funds as partial payment on its loan to G&K. Johnston argued that PHI did not have a perfected security interest in the SURE payment because the financing statement did not identify the crops. Was the description of the collateral in the financing statement sufficient? Why or why not? [*PHI Financial Services, Inc. v. Johnston Law Office, P.C.*, 2016 ND 20, 874 N.W.2d 910 (2016)] (See *Perfection of a Security Interest.*)

30–10. A Question of Ethics—Priorities. Mark Denton 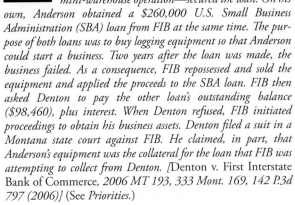 cosigned a $101,250 loan issued by the First Interstate Bank (FIB) in Missoula, Montana, to Denton's friend Eric Anderson. Denton's business assets—a mini-warehouse operation—secured the loan. On his own, Anderson obtained a $260,000 U.S. Small Business Administration (SBA) loan from FIB at the same time. The purpose of both loans was to buy logging equipment so that Anderson could start a business. Two years after the loan was made, the business failed. As a consequence, FIB repossessed and sold the equipment and applied the proceeds to the SBA loan. FIB then asked Denton to pay the other loan's outstanding balance ($98,460), plus interest. When Denton refused, FIB initiated proceedings to obtain his business assets. Denton filed a suit in a Montana state court against FIB. He claimed, in part, that Anderson's equipment was the collateral for the loan that FIB was attempting to collect from Denton. [*Denton v. First Interstate Bank of Commerce*, 2006 MT 193, 333 Mont. 169, 142 P.3d 797 (2006)] (See *Priorities.*)

(a) Denton's assets served as the security for Anderson's loan because Anderson had nothing to offer. When the loan was obtained, Dean Gillmore, FIB's loan officer, explained to them that if Anderson defaulted, the proceeds from the sale of the logging equipment would be applied to the SBA loan first. Under these circumstances, is it fair to hold Denton liable for the unpaid balance of Anderson's loan? Why or why not?

(b) Denton argued that the loan contract was unconscionable and constituted a "contract of adhesion." What makes a contract unconscionable? Did the transaction between the parties in this case qualify? What is a "contract of adhesion"? Was this deal unenforceable on that basis? Explain.

Legal Reasoning Group Activity

30–11. Security Interests. Nick Sabol, doing business in the recording industry as Sound Farm Productions, applied to Morton Community Bank for a $58,000 loan to expand his business. Besides the loan application, Sabol signed a promissory note that referred to the bank's rights in "any collateral." Sabol also signed a letter authorizing Morton Community Bank to execute, file, and record all financing statements, amendments, and other documents required by Article 9 to establish a security interest. Sabol did not sign any other documents, including the financing statement, which contained a description of the collateral. Two years later, without having repaid the loan, Sabol filed for bankruptcy. The bank claimed a security interest in Sabol's sound equipment. (See *Creation of a Security Interest.*)

(a) The first group will list all the requirements of an enforceable security interest and explain why each of these elements is necessary.

(b) The second group will determine if Morton Community Bank had a valid security interest.

(c) The third group will discuss whether a bank should be able to execute financing statements on a debtor's behalf without the debtor being present or signing them. Are there are any drawbacks to this practice? Explain.

CHAPTER 31

Bankruptcy Law

Many people in today's economy are struggling to pay their debts. Although in the old days, debtors were punished and sometimes even sent to prison for failing to pay what they owed, debtors today rarely go to jail. They have many other options, including *bankruptcy*—the last resort in resolving debtor-creditor problems.

The right to petition for bankruptcy relief under federal law is an essential aspect of our capitalistic society, in which we have great opportunities for financial success but may also encounter financial difficulties. Therefore, every businessperson should have some understanding of this topic.

31–1 The Bankruptcy Code

Bankruptcy relief is provided under federal law. Although state laws may play a role in bankruptcy proceedings, particularly state laws governing property, the governing law is based on federal legislation.

Article I, Section 8, of the U.S. Constitution gave Congress the power to establish "uniform laws on the subject of bankruptcies throughout the United States." Federal bankruptcy legislation was first enacted in 1898 and since then has undergone several modifications, most recently in the 2005 Bankruptcy Reform Act.[1] Federal bankruptcy laws (as amended) are called the Bankruptcy Code or, more simply, the Code.

31–1a Goals of Bankruptcy Law

Bankruptcy law in the United States has two main goals:

1. To protect a debtor by giving him or her a fresh start without creditors' claims.
2. To ensure equitable treatment of creditors who are competing for a debtor's assets.

Thus, the law attempts to balance the rights of the debtor and of the creditors.

Although the twin goals of bankruptcy remain the same, the balance between them shifted somewhat after the 2005 reform legislation. That law was enacted, in part, because of the growing concern that the law allowed

---

1. The full title of the act was the Bankruptcy Abuse Prevention and Consumer Protection Act, Pub. L. No. 109-8, 119 Stat. 23 (April 20, 2005).

too many debtors to avoid paying their debts. Thus, a major goal of the reforms was to require more consumers to pay as many of their debts as possible instead of having those debts fully extinguished in bankruptcy.

31–1b Bankruptcy Courts

Bankruptcy proceedings are held in federal bankruptcy courts, which are under the authority of U.S. district courts. Rulings from bankruptcy courts can be appealed to the district courts.

A bankruptcy court can conduct a jury trial if the appropriate district court has authorized it and the parties to the bankruptcy consent. Bankruptcy courts follow the Federal Rules of Bankruptcy Procedure rather than the Federal Rules of Civil Procedure. Bankruptcy court judges are appointed for terms of fourteen years.

31–1c Types of Bankruptcy Relief

The Bankruptcy Code is contained in Title 11 of the *United States Code* and has eight chapters. Chapters 1, 3, and 5 of the Code contain general definitional provisions, as well as provisions governing case administration, creditors, the debtor, and the estate. These three chapters normally apply to all kinds of bankruptcies.

Four chapters of the Code set forth the most important types of relief that debtors can seek:

1. Chapter 7 provides for **liquidation** proceedings (the selling of all nonexempt assets and the distribution of the proceeds to the debtor's creditors).

2. Chapter 11 governs reorganizations.

3. Chapter 12 (for family farmers and family fishermen) and 13 (for individuals) provide for the adjustment of debts by persons with regular incomes.[2]

Note that a debtor (except for a municipality) need not be insolvent[3] to file for bankruptcy relief under the Bankruptcy Code. Anyone obligated to a creditor can declare bankruptcy.

31–1d Special Requirements for Consumer-Debtors

A **consumer-debtor** is a debtor whose debts result primarily from the purchase of goods for personal, family, or household use. The Bankruptcy Code requires that the clerk of the court give all consumer-debtors written notice of the general purpose, benefits, and costs of each chapter under which they might proceed. In addition, the clerk must provide consumer-debtors with information on the types of services available from credit counseling agencies.

31–2 Liquidation Proceedings

Liquidation under Chapter 7 of the Bankruptcy Code is probably the most familiar type of bankruptcy proceeding and is often referred to as an *ordinary*, or *straight*, *bankruptcy*. Put simply, a debtor in a liquidation bankruptcy turns all assets over to a **bankruptcy trustee,** a person appointed by the court to manage the debtor's funds. The trustee sells the nonexempt assets and distributes the proceeds to creditors. With certain exceptions, the remaining debts are then **discharged** (extinguished), and the debtor is relieved of the obligation to pay the debts.

Any "person"—defined as including individuals, partnerships, and corporations[4]—may be a debtor in a liquidation proceeding. A husband and wife may file jointly

for bankruptcy under a single petition. Railroads, insurance companies, banks, savings and loan associations, investment companies licensed by the Small Business Administration, and credit unions *cannot* be debtors in a liquidation bankruptcy, however. Other chapters of the Bankruptcy Code or other federal or state statutes apply to them.

A straight bankruptcy can be commenced by the filing of either a voluntary or an involuntary **petition in bankruptcy**—the document that is filed with a bankruptcy court to initiate bankruptcy proceedings. If a debtor files the petition, the bankruptcy is voluntary. If one or more creditors file a petition to force the debtor into bankruptcy, the bankruptcy is involuntary. We discuss both voluntary and involuntary bankruptcy proceedings under Chapter 7 in the following subsections.

31–2a Voluntary Bankruptcy

To bring a voluntary petition in bankruptcy, the debtor files official forms designated for that purpose in the bankruptcy court. The law now requires that *before* debtors can file a petition, they must receive credit counseling from an approved nonprofit agency within the 180-day period preceding the date of filing. Debtors filing a Chapter 7 petition must include a certificate proving that they have received individual or group counseling from an approved agency within the last 180 days.

A consumer-debtor who is filing for liquidation bankruptcy must confirm the accuracy of the petition's contents. The debtor must also state in the petition, at the time of filing, that he or she understands the relief available under other chapters of the Code and has chosen to proceed under Chapter 7.

Attorneys representing the consumer-debtors must file an affidavit stating that they have informed the debtors of the relief available under each chapter of the Bankruptcy Code. In addition, the attorneys must reasonably attempt to verify the accuracy of the consumer-debtors' petitions and schedules (described next). Failure to do so is considered perjury.

Chapter 7 Schedules The voluntary petition must contain the following schedules:

1. A list of both secured and unsecured creditors, their addresses, and the amount of debt owed to each.

2. A statement of the financial affairs of the debtor.

3. A list of all property owned by the debtor, including property that the debtor claims is exempt.

4. A list of current income and expenses.

---

2. There are no Chapters 2, 4, 6, 8, or 10 in Title 11. Such "gaps" are not uncommon in the *United States Code*. They occur because chapter numbers (or other subdivisional unit numbers) are sometimes reserved for future use when a statute is enacted. (A gap may also appear if a law has been repealed.)

3. The inability to pay debts as they become due is known as *equitable* insolvency. *Balance sheet* insolvency, which exists when a debtor's liabilities exceed assets, is not the test. Thus, debtors whose cash-flow problems become severe may petition for bankruptcy voluntarily or be forced into involuntary bankruptcy even though their assets far exceed their liabilities.

4. The definition of *corporation* includes unincorporated companies and associations. It also covers labor unions.

5. A certificate of credit counseling (as mentioned previously).
6. Proof of payments received from employers within sixty days prior to the filing of the petition.
7. A statement of the amount of monthly income, itemized to show how the amount is calculated.
8. A copy of the debtor's federal income tax return for the most recent year ending immediately before the filing of the petition.

The official forms must be completed accurately, sworn to under oath, and signed by the debtor. To conceal assets or knowingly supply false information on these schedules is a crime under the bankruptcy laws.

With the exception of tax returns, failure to file the required schedules within forty-five days after the filing of the petition will result in an automatic dismissal of the petition. (An extension may be granted, however.) The debtor has up to seven days before the date of the first creditors' meeting to provide a copy of the most recent tax returns to the trustee.

Tax Returns during Bankruptcy In addition, a debtor may be required to file a tax return at the end of each tax year while the case is pending and to provide a copy to the court. This may be done at the request of the court or the **U.S. trustee**—a government official who performs administrative tasks that a bankruptcy judge would otherwise have to perform. Any *party in interest* (a party, such as a creditor, who has a valid interest in the outcome of the proceedings) may make this request as well. Debtors may also be required to file tax returns during Chapter 11 and 13 bankruptcies.

Substantial Abuse—Means Test In the past, a bankruptcy court could dismiss a Chapter 7 petition if the use of Chapter 7 would constitute a "substantial abuse" of bankruptcy law. Today, the law provides a *means test* to determine a debtor's eligibility for Chapter 7.

The purpose of the test is to keep upper-income people from abusing the bankruptcy process by filing for Chapter 7, as was thought to have happened in the past. The test forces more people to file for Chapter 13 bankruptcy rather than have their debts discharged under Chapter 7.

The Basic Formula. A debtor wishing to file for bankruptcy must complete the means test to determine whether she or he qualifies for Chapter 7. The debtor's average monthly income in recent months is compared with the median income in the geographic area in which the person lives. (The U.S. Trustee Program provides these data at its Web site.) If the debtor's income is below

the median income, the debtor usually is allowed to file for Chapter 7 bankruptcy, as there is no presumption of bankruptcy abuse.

Applying the Means Test to Future Disposable Income. If the debtor's income is above the median income, then further calculations must be made. The calculations are meant to determine whether the person will have sufficient disposable income in the future to repay at least some of his or her unsecured debts.

As a basis for the calculations, it is presumed that the debtor's recent monthly income will continue for the next sixty months. *Disposable income* is then calculated by subtracting living expenses and secured debt payments, such as mortgage payments, from monthly income.

Living expenses are amounts allowed under formulas used by the Internal Revenue Service (IRS). The IRS allowances include modest allocations for food, clothing, housing, utilities, transportation (including a car payment), health care, and other necessities. (The U.S. Trustee Program's Web site also provides these amounts.) The allowances do not include expenditures for items such as cell phones and cable television service.

Can the Debtor Afford to Pay Unsecured Debts? Once future disposable income has been estimated, that amount is used to determine whether the debtor will have income that could be applied to unsecured debts. The courts may also consider the debtor's bad faith or other circumstances indicating abuse.

■ **CASE IN POINT 31.1** Christopher Dean Ng and his wife filed for Chapter 7 bankruptcy, hoping primarily to discharge their mortgage debt of $464,830. At the time the petition was filed, Ng was forty-three years old and worked as an electronic technician. He earned a monthly salary of $7,439.47, as well as a military pension of $1,439.88 a month. His wife was not employed. From Ng's monthly salary, he made a voluntary contribution of $520 to an employer 401(k) plan and a $343 payment on a pension loan. In calculating his disposable income, Ng excluded these amounts.

The U.S. trustee filed a motion to dismiss Ng's petition due to substantial abuse, claiming that the retirement contributions should be disallowed. The court agreed and dismissed the Chapter 7 petition. The Ngs appealed, and the appellate court affirmed. Ng's retirement contributions were not reasonably necessary based on his age, his financial circumstances, and his testimony that he was not planning to retire for at least twenty years. The Ngs could afford to repay some of their debts before they made monthly contributions toward retirement.[5] ■

---

5. *In re Ng*, 422 Bankr. 118 (9th Cir. 2012).

Additional Grounds for Dismissal As already noted, a court can dismiss a debtor's voluntary petition for Chapter 7 relief for substantial abuse or for failure to provide the necessary documents within the specified time.

In addition, a court might dismiss a Chapter 7 in two other situations. First, if the debtor has been convicted of a violent crime or a drug-trafficking offense, the victim can file a motion to dismiss the voluntary petition.[6] Second, if the debtor fails to pay postpetition domestic-support obligations (which include child and spousal support), the court may dismiss the debtor's petition.

Order for Relief If the voluntary petition for bankruptcy is found to be proper, the filing of the petition will itself constitute an **order for relief.** (An order for relief is a court's grant of assistance to a petitioner.) Once a consumer-debtor's voluntary petition has been filed, the trustee and creditors must be given notice of the order for relief by mail not more than twenty days after entry of the order.

31–2b Involuntary Bankruptcy

An involuntary bankruptcy occurs when the debtor's creditors force the debtor into bankruptcy proceedings. An involuntary case cannot be filed against a charitable institution or a farmer (an individual or business that receives more than 50 percent of gross income from farming operations).

An involuntary petition should not be used as an everyday debt-collection device, and the Code provides penalties for the filing of frivolous petitions against debtors. If the court dismisses an involuntary petition, the petitioning creditors may be required to pay the costs and attorneys' fees incurred by the debtor in defending against the petition. If the petition was filed in bad faith, damages can be awarded for injury to the debtor's reputation. Punitive damages may also be awarded.

Requirements For an involuntary action to be filed, the following requirements must be met:

1. If the debtor has twelve or more creditors, three or more of these creditors having unsecured claims totaling at least $15,325 must join in the petition.
2. If a debtor has fewer than twelve creditors, one or more creditors having a claim totaling $15,325 or more may file.[7]

---

6. Note that the court may not dismiss a case on this ground if the debtor's bankruptcy is necessary to satisfy a claim for a domestic-support obligation.
7. 11 U.S.C. Section 303. The amounts stated in this chapter are in accordance with those computed on April 1, 2016.

Order for Relief If the debtor challenges the involuntary petition, a hearing will be held, and the bankruptcy court will enter an order for relief if it finds either of the following:

1. The debtor is not paying debts as they come due.
2. A general receiver, assignee, or custodian took possession of, or was appointed to take charge of, substantially all of the debtor's property within 120 days before the filing of the petition.

If the court grants an order for relief, the debtor will be required to supply the same information in the bankruptcy schedules as in a voluntary bankruptcy.

31–2c Automatic Stay

The moment a petition, either voluntary or involuntary, is filed, an **automatic stay,** or suspension, of all actions by creditors against the debtor or the debtor's property normally goes into effect. The automatic stay prohibits creditors from taking any act to collect, assess, or recover a claim against the debtor that arose before the filing of the petition. The stay normally continues until the bankruptcy proceeding is closed or dismissed. (In some circumstances, it is possible to petition the bankruptcy court for relief from the automatic stay, as will be discussed shortly.)

If a creditor *knowingly* violates the automatic stay (a willful violation), any injured party, including the debtor, is entitled to recover actual damages, costs, and attorneys' fees. Punitive damages may be awarded as well.

■ **CASE IN POINT 31.2** Stefanie Kuehn filed for bankruptcy. When she requested a transcript from the university at which she had obtained her master's degree, the university refused because she owed more than $6,000 in tuition. Kuehn complained to the court. The court ruled that the university had violated the automatic stay by refusing to provide a transcript because it was attempting to collect an unpaid tuition debt.[8] ■

The Adequate Protection Doctrine Underlying the Code's automatic-stay provision for a secured creditor is a concept known as *adequate protection.* The **adequate protection doctrine,** among other things, protects secured creditors from losing their security as a result of the automatic stay.

The bankruptcy court can provide adequate protection by requiring the debtor or trustee to make periodic cash payments or a one-time cash payment. The court can also require the debtor or trustee to provide additional collateral or replacement liens to the extent that

---

8. *In re Kuehn*, 563 F.3d 289 (7th Cir. 2009).

the stay may actually cause the value of the property to decrease.

Exceptions to the Automatic Stay The Code provides the following exceptions to the automatic stay:

1. Collection efforts can continue for domestic-support obligations. These obligations include any debt owed to or recoverable by a spouse, a former spouse, a child of the debtor, that child's parent or guardian, or a governmental unit.
2. Proceedings against the debtor related to divorce, child custody or visitation, domestic violence, and support enforcement are not stayed.
3. Investigations by a securities regulatory agency (such as an investigation into insider trading) can continue.
4. Certain statutory liens for property taxes are not stayed.

Requests for Relief from the Automatic Stay
A secured creditor or other party in interest can petition the bankruptcy court for relief from the automatic stay. If a creditor or other party requests relief from the stay, the stay will automatically terminate sixty days after the request, unless the court grants an extension[9] or the parties agree otherwise.

Secured Property The automatic stay on secured property terminates forty-five days after the creditors' meeting unless the debtor redeems or reaffirms certain debts. (Creditors' meetings and reaffirmation will be discussed later in this chapter.) In other words, the debtor cannot keep the secured property (such as a financed automobile), even if she or he continues to make payments on it, without reinstating the rights of the secured party to collect on the debt.

Bad Faith If the debtor had two or more bankruptcy petitions dismissed during the prior year, the Code presumes bad faith. In such a situation, the automatic stay does *not* go into effect until the court determines that the petition was filed in good faith.

In addition, the automatic stay on secured debts will terminate thirty days after the petition is filed if the debtor filed a bankruptcy petition that was dismissed within the prior year. Any party in interest can request that the court extend the stay by showing that the filing is in good faith.

31–2d Estate in Bankruptcy

On the commencement of a liquidation proceeding under Chapter 7, an *estate in bankruptcy* (sometimes called an *estate in property*) is created. The estate consists of all the debtor's interests in property currently held, wherever located. The estate in bankruptcy includes all of the following:

1. *Community property* (property jointly owned by married persons in certain states).
2. Property transferred in a transaction voidable by the trustee.
3. Proceeds and profits from the property of the estate.

Certain after-acquired property to which the debtor becomes entitled *within 180 days after filing* may also become part of the estate. Such after-acquired property includes gifts, inheritances, property settlements (from divorce), and life insurance death proceeds.

Generally, though, the filing of a bankruptcy petition fixes a dividing line. Property acquired prior to the filing of the petition becomes property of the estate, and property acquired after the filing of the petition, except as just noted, remains the debtor's.

31–2e The Bankruptcy Trustee

Promptly after the order for relief in the liquidation proceeding has been entered, a trustee is appointed. The basic duty of the trustee is to collect the debtor's available estate and reduce it to cash for distribution, preserving the interests of both the debtor and the unsecured creditors. The trustee is held accountable for administering the debtor's estate.

To enable the trustee to accomplish this duty, the Code gives the trustee certain powers, stated in both general and specific terms. These powers must be exercised within two years of the order for relief.

Duties for Means Testing The trustee is required to promptly review all materials filed by the debtor to determine if there is substantial abuse. Within ten days after the first meeting of the creditors (discussed shortly), the trustee must file a statement indicating whether the case is presumed to be an abuse under the means test. The trustee must provide a copy of this statement to all creditors within five days.

When there is a presumption of abuse, the trustee must either file a motion to dismiss the petition (or convert it to a Chapter 13 petition) or file a statement explaining why a motion would not be appropriate. If the debtor owes a domestic-support obligation (such as

---

9. The court might grant an extension, for example, on a motion by the trustee that the property is of value to the estate.

child support), the trustee must provide written notice of the bankruptcy to the claim holder (a former spouse, for instance).

The Trustee's Powers The trustee has the power to require persons holding the debtor's property at the time the petition is filed to deliver the property to the trustee.[10] To enable the trustee to implement this power, the Code provides that the trustee has rights *equivalent* to those of certain other parties, such as a creditor who has a judicial lien. This power of a trustee, which is equivalent to that of a lien creditor, is known as *strong-arm power*.

In addition, the trustee has specific *powers of avoidance*. They enable the trustee to set aside (avoid) a sale or other transfer of the debtor's property and take the property back for the debtor's estate. These powers apply to voidable rights available to the debtor, preferences, and fraudulent transfers by the debtor. Each power is discussed in more detail next. In addition, a trustee can avoid certain statutory liens (creditors' claims against the debtor's property).

The debtor shares most of the trustee's avoidance powers. Thus, if the trustee does not take action to enforce one of the rights just mentioned, the debtor in a liquidation bankruptcy can enforce that right.[11]

Voidable Rights A trustee steps into the shoes of the debtor. Thus, any reason that a debtor can use to obtain the return of her or his property can be used by the trustee as well. These grounds include fraud, duress, incapacity, and mutual mistake.

■ **EXAMPLE 31.3** Ben sells his boat to Tara. Tara gives Ben a check, knowing that she has insufficient funds in her bank account to cover the check. Tara has committed fraud. Ben has the right to avoid that transfer and recover the boat from Tara. If Ben files for bankruptcy relief under Chapter 7, the trustee can exercise the same right to recover the boat from Tara, and the boat becomes a part of the debtor's estate. ■

Preferences A debtor is not permitted to transfer property or to make a payment that favors—or gives a **preference** to—one creditor over others. The trustee is

allowed to recover payments made both voluntarily and involuntarily to one creditor in preference over another.

To have made a recoverable preferential payment, an *insolvent* debtor must have transferred property, for a *pre-existing* debt, within *ninety days* before the filing of the bankruptcy petition. The transfer must have given the creditor more than the creditor would have received as a result of the bankruptcy proceedings. The Code presumes that a debtor is insolvent during the ninety-day period before filing a petition.

If a **preferred creditor** (one who has received a preferential transfer) has sold the property to an innocent third party, the trustee cannot recover the property from the innocent party. The preferred creditor, however, generally can be held liable for the value of the property.

Preferences to Insiders. Sometimes, the creditor receiving the preference is an insider. An **insider** is an individual, partner, partnership, corporation, or officer or director of a corporation (or a relative of one of these) who has a close relationship with the debtor. In this situation, the avoidance power of the trustee extends to transfers made within *one year* before filing. (If the transfer was fraudulent, as will be discussed shortly, the trustee can avoid transfers made within *two years* before filing.) The trustee must, however, prove that the debtor was insolvent when the transfer occurred and that it was made to or for the benefit of an insider.

Transfers That Do Not Constitute Preferences. Not all transfers are preferences. Most courts generally assume that payment for services rendered *within fifteen days* before the payment is not a preference. If a creditor receives payment in the ordinary course of business from a debtor, such as payment of last month's cell phone bill, the bankruptcy trustee cannot recover the payment.

To be recoverable, a preference must be a transfer for an antecedent (preexisting) debt, such as a year-old landscaping bill. In addition, the Code permits a consumer-debtor to transfer any property to a creditor up to a total value of $6,225 without the transfer's constituting a preference. Payment of domestic-support debts does not constitute a preference.

Fraudulent Transfers The trustee may avoid fraudulent transfers or obligations if they (1) were made within two years prior to the filing of the petition or (2) were made with actual intent to hinder, delay, or defraud a creditor. ■ **EXAMPLE 31.4** Amy is planning to petition for bankruptcy, so she sells her gold jewelry, worth $10,000, to a friend for $500. The friend agrees that in

---

10. Usually, though, the trustee takes constructive, rather than actual, possession of the debtor's property. For instance, to obtain control of a debtor's business inventory, a trustee might change the locks on the doors to the business and hire a security guard.

11. Under a Chapter 11 bankruptcy, for which no trustee other than the debtor generally exists, the debtor has the same avoidance powers as a trustee under Chapter 7. Under Chapters 12 and 13, a trustee must be appointed.

the future he will "sell" the jewelry back to Amy for the same amount. This is a fraudulent transfer that the trustee can undo. ■

Transfers made for less than reasonably equivalent consideration are also vulnerable if the debtor thereby became insolvent or was left engaged in business with an unreasonably small amount of capital. When a fraudulent transfer is made outside the Code's two-year limit, creditors may seek alternative relief under state laws. Some state laws may allow creditors to recover transfers made up to three years before the filing of a petition.

31–2f Exemptions

As just described, the trustee takes control of the debtor's property in a Chapter 7 bankruptcy, but an individual debtor is entitled to exempt (exclude) certain property from the bankruptcy.

Federal Exemptions The Bankruptcy Code exempts the following property, up to a specified dollar amount that changes every three years:[12]

1. A portion of equity in the debtor's home (the homestead exemption).
2. Motor vehicles, up to a certain value (usually just one vehicle).
3. Reasonably necessary clothing, household goods and furnishings, and household appliances (the aggregate value not to exceed a certain amount).
4. Jewelry, up to a certain value.
5. Tools of the debtor's trade or profession, up to a certain value.
6. A portion of unpaid but earned wages.
7. Pensions.
8. Public benefits, including public assistance (welfare), Social Security, and unemployment compensation, accumulated in a bank account.
9. Damages awarded for personal injury up to a certain amount.

Property that is *not* exempt under federal law includes bank accounts, cash, family heirlooms, collections of stamps and coins, second cars, and vacation homes.

State Exemptions Individual states have the power to pass legislation precluding debtors from using the federal exemptions within the state. A majority of the states have done this. In those states, debtors may use only state,

not federal, exemptions. In the rest of the states, debtors may choose either the exemptions provided under state law or the federal exemptions.

Limitations on the Homestead Exemption The Bankruptcy Code limits the amount of equity that can be claimed under the homestead exemption. In general, if the debtor acquired the homestead within three and a half years preceding the date of filing, the maximum equity exempted is $155,675, even if state law would permit a higher amount.

In addition, the state homestead exemption is available only if the debtor has lived in a state for two years before filing the bankruptcy petition. Furthermore, a debtor who has violated securities laws, been convicted of a felony, or engaged in certain other intentional misconduct may not be permitted to claim the homestead exemption.

31–2g Creditors' Meeting

Within a reasonable time after the order for relief has been granted (not more than forty days), the trustee must call a meeting of the creditors listed in the schedules filed by the debtor. The bankruptcy judge does not attend this meeting. The debtor is required to attend (unless excused by the court) and to submit to examination under oath by the creditors and the trustee. At the meeting, the trustee ensures that the debtor is aware of the potential consequences of bankruptcy and of the possibility of filing under a different chapter of the Code.

31–2h Creditors' Claims

To be entitled to receive a portion of the debtor's estate, each creditor normally files a *proof of claim* with the bankruptcy court within ninety days of the creditors' meeting. A proof of claim is necessary if there is any dispute concerning the claim. The proof of claim lists the creditor's name and address, as well as the amount that the creditor asserts is owed to the creditor by the debtor.

When the debtor has no assets—called a "no-asset case"—creditors are notified of the debtor's petition for bankruptcy but are instructed not to file a claim. In no-asset cases, the unsecured creditors will receive no payment, and most, if not all, of these debts will be discharged.

31–2i Distribution of Property

The Code provides specific rules for the distribution of the debtor's property to secured and unsecured creditors.

---

12. The dollar amounts stated in the Bankruptcy Code are adjusted automatically every three years on April 1 based on changes in the Consumer Price Index. The adjusted amounts are rounded to the nearest $25.

If any amount remains after the priority classes of creditors have been satisfied, it is turned over to the debtor.

Distribution to Secured Creditors

The Code requires that consumer-debtors file a statement of intention with respect to secured collateral. They can choose to pay off the debt and redeem the collateral, claim it is exempt, reaffirm the debt and continue making payments, or surrender the property to the secured party.

If the collateral is surrendered to the secured party, the secured creditor can enforce the security interest. The secured party can either (1) accept the property in full satisfaction of the debt or (2) sell the collateral and use the proceeds to pay off the debt. Thus, the secured party has priority over unsecured parties as to the proceeds from the disposition of the collateral. Should the collateral be insufficient to cover the secured debt owed, the secured creditor becomes an unsecured creditor for the difference (deficiency).

There are limited exceptions to these rules. For instance, certain unsecured creditors can sometimes step into the shoes of secured tax creditors in Chapter 7 liquidation proceedings. In such situations, when the collateral securing the tax claims is sold, the unsecured creditors are paid first. This exception does not include holders of unsecured claims for administrative expenses incurred in Chapter 11 cases that are converted to Chapter 7 liquidations. In the following case, the plaintiff argued that it should.

Case 31.1

In re Anderson

United States Court of Appeals, Fourth Circuit, 811 F.3d 166 (2016).

Background and Facts Henry Anderson filed a voluntary petition in a federal bankruptcy court for relief under Chapter 11 of the Bankruptcy Code. The U.S. Department of the Treasury, through the Internal Revenue Service (IRS), filed a proof of claim against the bankruptcy estate for $997,551.80, of which $987,082.88 was secured by the debtor's property. Stubbs & Perdue, P.A., served as Anderson's counsel. During the proceedings, the court approved compensation of $200,000 to Stubbs for its services. These fees constituted an unsecured claim against the estate for administrative expenses. Later, Anderson's case was converted to a Chapter 7 liquidation. The trustee accumulated $702,630.25 for distribution to the estate's creditors—not enough to pay the claims of both the IRS and Stubbs. The trustee excluded Stubbs's claim. Stubbs objected. The court dismissed Stubbs's objection. A federal district court upheld the dismissal. Stubbs appealed, arguing that the IRS's claim should be subordinated to Stubbs's claim for fees.

In the Language of the Court

Pamela *HARRIS,* Circuit Judge:

* * * *

* * * Before any of the events at issue here, Section 724(b)(2) * * * provided all holders of administrative expense claims, like Stubbs, with the right to subordinate secured tax creditors in Chapter 7 liquidations. But that statutory scheme was criticized on the ground that it created perverse incentives, encouraging Chapter 11 debtors and their representatives to incur administrative expenses even where there was no real hope for a successful reorganization, to the detriment of secured tax creditors when Chapter 7 liquidation ultimately proved necessary.

* * * Congress responded with a fix * * * to limit the class of administrative expenses covered by Section 724(b)(2) * * *. *In order to provide greater protection for holders of tax liens * * *, unsecured Chapter 11 administrative expense claims would no longer take priority over secured tax claims in Chapter 7 liquidations.* [Emphasis added.]

* * * *

* * * The Bankruptcy Technical Corrections Act [BTCA] * * * clarified that Chapter 11 administrative expense claimants do not hold subordination rights under Section 724(b)(2).

* * * Eleven months later, the Debtor's bankruptcy case converted from Chapter 11 to Chapter 7, implicating Section 724(b)(2) for the first time.

* * * *

* * * *As a general rule, a court is to apply the law in effect at the time it renders its decision.* [Emphasis added.]

Case 31.1 Continues

Case 31.1 Continued   * * * *

Stubbs argues, however, that it would be unjust to apply the BTCA version of Section 724(b)(2) * * * to disallow payment on its unsecured claim for Chapter 11 fees. Prior to the BTCA, Stubbs contends, it was entitled to subordinate the IRS's secured claim.

The problem with Stubbs's argument is its premise: that Stubbs held subordination rights under Section 724(b)(2) before the BTCA was enacted * * * . Before the BTCA was enacted, Section 724(b)(2) had no application to the Debtor's case at all. It afforded Stubbs no entitlement to subordinate the IRS's secured tax claim for the threshold reason that it simply did not apply in the Chapter 11 proceedings that began in this case * * * and did not end until * * * eleven months *after* the BTCA's passage. The pre-BTCA version of Section 724(b)(2) that Stubbs invokes, in other words, never controlled this case.

Decision and Remedy *The U.S. Court of Appeals for the Fourth Circuit affirmed the dismissal of Stubbs's claim. Under Section 724(b)(2), "it is clear that Stubbs is not entitled to subordinate the IRS's secured tax claim in favor of its unsecured claim to Chapter 11 administrative expenses."*

Critical Thinking

- **Legal Environment** *Why, as a general rule, should a court apply the law that is in effect at the time the court renders its decision?*
- **What If the Facts Were Different?** *Suppose that Anderson had filed his initial bankruptcy petition under Chapter 7, not under Chapter 11. Would the result have been different? Discuss.*

Distribution to Unsecured Creditors Bankruptcy law establishes an order of priority for debts owed to *unsecured* creditors, and they are paid in the order of their priority. Claims for domestic-support obligations, such as child support and alimony, have the highest priority among unsecured creditors, so these claims must be paid first. Each class, or group, must be fully paid before the next class is entitled to any of the remaining proceeds.

If there are insufficient proceeds to fully pay all the creditors in a class, the proceeds are distributed *proportionately* to the creditors in that class. Classes lower in priority receive nothing. In almost all Chapter 7 bankruptcies, the funds will be insufficient to pay all creditors.

Exhibit 31–1 illustrates the collection and distribution of property in most voluntary bankruptcies. The exhibit includes a listing of the classes of unsecured creditors.

31–2j Discharge

From the debtor's point of view, the primary purpose of liquidation is to obtain a fresh start through a discharge of debts. A discharge voids, or sets aside, any judgment on a discharged debt and prevents any action to collect it. Certain debts, however, are not dischargeable in bankruptcy. Also, certain debtors may not qualify to have all debts discharged in bankruptcy. These situations are discussed next.

Exceptions to Discharge Claims that are not dischargeable in bankruptcy include the following:

1. Claims for back taxes accruing within two years prior to bankruptcy.
2. Claims for amounts borrowed by the debtor to pay federal taxes or any nondischargeable taxes.[13]
3. Claims against property or funds obtained by the debtor under false pretenses or by false representations.
4. Claims by creditors who were not notified of the bankruptcy. These claims did not appear on the schedules the debtor was required to file.
5. Claims based on fraud[14] or misuse of funds by the debtor while acting in a fiduciary capacity or claims involving the debtor's embezzlement or larceny.
6. Domestic-support obligations and property settlements as provided for in a separation agreement or divorce decree.
7. Claims for amounts due on a retirement account loan.
8. Claims based on willful or malicious conduct by the debtor toward another or the property of another. ■ **CASE IN POINT 31.5** Anthony Mickletz owned a pizza restaurant that employed John Carmello.

---

13. Taxes accruing within three years prior to bankruptcy are nondischargeable, including federal and state income taxes, employment taxes, taxes on gross receipts, property taxes, excise taxes, customs duties, and any other taxes for which the government claims the debtor is liable in some capacity. See 11 U.S.C. Sections 507(a)(8) and 523(a)(1).
14. Even if a debtor who is sued for fraud settles the lawsuit, the settlement agreement may not be discharged in bankruptcy because of the underlying fraud. See *Archer v. Warner*, 538 U.S. 314, 123 S.Ct. 1462, 155 L.Ed.2d 454 (2003); and *In re Sager*, ___ Bankr. ___, 2015 WL 1650654 (E.D. Pa. 2015).

EXHIBIT 31–1 Collection and Distribution of Property in Most Voluntary Bankruptcies

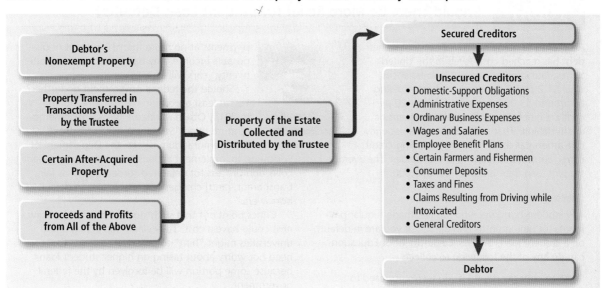

One night after Carmello had finished his shift, Mickletz called him back into the restaurant and accused him of stealing. An argument ensued, and Mickletz shoved Carmello, causing him to fall and injure his back. Because Mickletz did not provide workers' compensation coverage as required by law, the state prosecuted him criminally. He was ordered to pay more than $45,000 in restitution to Carmello for his injuries. Carmello also filed a civil suit against Mickletz, which the parties agreed to settle for $175,000. Later, Mickletz filed a petition for bankruptcy. Carmello argued that these debts were nondischargeable, and the court agreed. The exception from discharge includes any debts for willful (deliberate or intentional) injury, and Mickletz's actions were deliberate.[15] ■

9. Certain government fines and penalties.
10. Student loans, unless payment of the loans imposes an undue hardship on the debtor and the debtor's dependents. (For an example of what constitutes undue hardship, see *Case in Point 31.6,* which follows this list.)
11. Consumer debts of more than $650 for luxury goods or services owed to a single creditor incurred within ninety days of the order for relief.
12. Cash advances totaling more than $925 that are extensions of open-end consumer credit obtained by the debtor within seventy days of the order for relief.
13. Judgments against a debtor as a result of the debtor's operation of a motor vehicle while intoxicated.

14. Fees or assessments arising from property in a homeowners' association, as long as the debtor retained an interest in the property.
15. Taxes with respect to which the debtor failed to provide required or requested tax documents.

■ **CASE IN POINT 31.6** At the time he filed for Chapter 7 bankruptcy, Terence Wolfe had not been consistently employed for twenty years. He had been fired from numerous positions for behavioral issues and had difficulty finding and holding a job. Wolfe had been diagnosed with personality disorders and ultimately was granted disability status by the U.S. government. He was living on disability payments of $1,126 per month at the time he filed for Chapter 7 bankruptcy.

Among Wolfe's debts were more than $131,000 in student loan debts. Wolfe sought to have these debts discharged because repaying them would constitute undue hardship. The court agreed and granted a discharge. According to the court, although Wolfe is intelligent, "he has been unable, for more than two decades, to maintain full-time employment for any meaningful length of time. He is living at a minimal standard of living and it is unlikely that he will ever be able to repay these loans."[16] ■ See this chapter's *Ethics Today* feature for a discussion of whether the law should make it easier to obtain a discharge of student loan debts.

15. *In re Mickletz,* 544 Bankr. 804 (E.D. Pa. 2016).

16. *In re Wolfe,* 501 Bankr. 426, 24 Fla.L.WeeklyFed. B235 (M.D.Fla. 2011).

ETHICS TODAY

Should There Be More Relief for Student Loan Defaults?

According to many observers, student loan debt has reached crisis levels in the United States. Outstanding student loan balances total $1.2 *trillion* nationally and are growing by around $3,000 *per second*. About 20 percent are ninety or more days' delinquent or are in default. That is the highest delinquency rate among all forms of debt, including credit cards, automobile loans, and mortgages. The average student loan debt is more than $30,000.

Consequences of Default

Any student borrower who has not made regular payments for nine months is in default. If you are in default on a student loan, the U.S. Department of Education can do any of the following to collect:

1. Keep your tax refund if you were supposed to receive one.
2. Garnish your paycheck without obtaining a court judgment.
3. Take your federal benefits, such as Social Security retirement payments or disability payments.

In addition, in some states any professional license that you have can be revoked. The Department of Education can also bring a lawsuit against you. If it wins, it can collect the judgment from your bank accounts or place a lien on any real property that you own.

Caps on Interest Rates, Forgiveness, and Income-Based Plans

Recently, Congress attempted to ease the burden on student loan debtors by reducing the interest rates they can be charged. In addition, President Barack Obama signed an executive order putting into place an income-based repayment plan. This plan caps payments at no more than 10 percent of disposable income. Any balance not paid off after twenty years will be forgiven.

Should the federal government go further? Yes, at least according to President Obama. In 2015, Obama signed a presidential memorandum titled "Student Aid Bill of Rights." The memorandum directs the Department of Education to implement actions to ensure that the debt collection process for defaulted student loans "is fair, transparent, [and] charges reasonable fees to defaulted borrowers."

Critics point out that such student loan debt forgiveness could have a cost. They claim that colleges and universities might "hint" to potential students that they need not worry about taking on higher student loans because some portion will be forgiven by the federal government.

Political Impetus

Politicians are increasingly discussing student loan debt and the costs of higher education. Some are asking Congress to allow federal student loans to be discharged in most bankruptcy proceedings. Others advocate making college education free or at least reducing the costs charged to certain students. One plan calls for allowing students to refinance their loans at very low interest rates. Another proposal is to prohibit the federal government from profiting from student loan debt (the government brings in more than $41 billion a year from student loans).

Critical Thinking *Why does the Bankruptcy Code provide that student loans should not be dischargeable unless there is undue hardship? What argument can be made in favor of allowing student loans to be dischargeable?*

Today, however, the federal government guarantees many student loans (similar to the way the government backs certain mortgages). When student loans are guaranteed, the lenders are not affected by default in the same way and have no reason to refuse to finance education. This bolsters the argument that student loan debts should be dischargeable in the same way as other types of debts.

Objections to Discharge In addition to the exceptions to discharge previously discussed, a bankruptcy court may also deny discharge based on the debtor's *conduct*. Grounds for denial of discharge of the debtor include the following:

1. The debtor's concealment or destruction of property with the intent to hinder, delay, or defraud a creditor.
2. The debtor's fraudulent concealment or destruction of financial records.
3. The grant of a discharge to the debtor within eight years before the petition was filed.
4. The debtor's failure to complete the required consumer education course.
5. The debtor's involvement in proceedings in which the debtor could be found guilty of a felony. (Basically, a court may not discharge any debt until the completion of felony proceedings against the debtor.)

When a discharge is denied under any of these circumstances, the debtor's assets are still distributed to the creditors. After the bankruptcy proceeding, however, the debtor remains liable for the unpaid portion of all claims.

In addition, a discharge may be revoked (taken back) within one year if it is discovered that the debtor acted fraudulently or dishonestly during the bankruptcy proceeding. If that occurs, a creditor whose claim was not satisfied in the distribution of the debtor's property can proceed with his or her claim against the debtor.

Whether a bankruptcy court properly denied a discharge based on the debtors' conduct was the issue in the following case.

Case 31.2

In re Cummings

United States Court of Appeals, Ninth Circuit, 595 Fed.Appx. 707 (2015).

Background and Facts Clarence and Pamela Cummings filed a petition for a Chapter 7 bankruptcy in a federal bankruptcy court. After the debtors filed two amended versions of the required schedules, the trustee asked for additional time to investigate. The court granted the request. The debtors then filed a third amended schedule. In it, they disclosed for the first time the existence of First Beacon Management Company, a corporation that they planned to use as part of their postbankruptcy "fresh start."

The trustee claimed that the Cummingses' failure to disclose their interest in First Beacon was a "false oath relating to a material fact made knowingly and fraudulently" in violation of the Bankruptcy Code. The court agreed and denied the debtors a discharge. The Bankruptcy Appellate Panel (BAP) affirmed the court's decision. The Cummingses appealed.

In the Language of the Court

MEMORANDUM.

* * * *

Chapter 7 debtors Clarence Thomas Cummings and Pamela K. Cummings appeal the judgment of the Bankruptcy Appellate Panel ("BAP") affirming * * * the bankruptcy court's order denying discharge on the ground that the debtors made false oaths * * * . The bankruptcy court rejected the explanatory testimony of Mr. Cummings as "not credible" and "beyond not credible" and the BAP found that "there is ample evidence to support the bankruptcy court's findings.

* * * *

* * * Debtors claim that the bankruptcy court failed to consider other "voluminous independent and undisputed documentary evidence" introduced at trial that, they assert, "completely obliterated any suggestion of fraudulent intent."

* * * These materials do not advance debtors' claim of inadvertence [lack of intent] or otherwise suggest bankruptcy court error. To the contrary, *the documents corroborate the obviousness of debtors' fraud and the objective it advanced, [namely], to insulate First Beacon Management Co.,* * * * *the new corporate anchor of their post-petition fresh start, from the stigma of bankruptcy.* [Emphasis added.]

Debtors' eventual disclosure of their interest in First Beacon on their third amended Schedule * * * does not negate their initial fraud. To the contrary, the sequence of debtors' filings substantiates the presence of fraud: they elected, twice, to amend their Schedule * * * without adding First Beacon, and disclosed First Beacon only after the issuance of an order granting the Trustee additional time to investigate.

* * * *

The Trustee fully carried its burden of proving by a preponderance of the evidence * * * that under the circumstances, debtors' failure to disclose their interest in First Beacon as debtor property was a "false oath" relating to a material fact made knowingly and fraudulently.

Decision and Remedy *The U.S. Court of Appeals for the Ninth Circuit affirmed the ruling of the Bankruptcy Appellate Panel. The Cummingses' bankruptcy filings revealed the presence of fraud. Thus, their Chapter 7 petition for discharge of their debts was denied.*

Critical Thinking

• **Economic** *Why would a debtor risk the denial of a discharge to conceal assets? Discuss.*

31–2k Reaffirmation of Debt

An agreement to pay a debt dischargeable in bankruptcy is called a **reaffirmation agreement.** A debtor may wish to pay a debt—such as a debt owed to a family member, physician, bank, or some other creditor—even though the debt could be discharged in bankruptcy. Also, as noted previously, a debtor cannot retain secured property while continuing to pay without entering into a reaffirmation agreement.

Procedures To be enforceable, reaffirmation agreements must be made before the debtor is granted a discharge. The agreement must be signed and filed with the court. Court approval is required unless the debtor is represented by an attorney during the negotiation of the reaffirmation and submits the proper documents and certifications. Even when the debtor is represented by an attorney, court approval may be required if it appears that the reaffirmation will result in undue hardship to the debtor.

When court approval is required, a separate hearing will take place. The court will approve the reaffirmation only if it finds that the agreement will not result in undue hardship to the debtor and that the reaffirmation is consistent with the debtor's best interests.

Required Disclosures To discourage creditors from engaging in abusive reaffirmation practices, the law provides specific language for disclosures that must be given to debtors entering into reaffirmation agreements. Among other things, these disclosures explain that the debtor is not required to reaffirm any debt. They also inform the debtor that liens on secured property, such as mortgages and cars, will remain in effect even if the debt is not reaffirmed.

The reaffirmation agreement must disclose the amount of the debt reaffirmed, the rate of interest, the date payments begin, and the right to rescind. The disclosures also caution the debtor: "Only agree to reaffirm a debt if it is in your best interest. Be sure you can afford the payments you agree to make."

The original disclosure documents must be signed by the debtor, certified by the debtor's attorney, and filed with the court at the same time as the reaffirmation agreement. A reaffirmation agreement that is not accompanied by the original signed disclosures will not be effective.

■ **CASE IN POINT 31.7** Howard Lapides, who owned a seafood import business, signed a secured promissory note for $400,000 with Venture Bank for a revolving line-of-credit loan. Part of the collateral for that loan was a third mortgage on the Lapideses' home (two other banks held prior mortgages). Eventually, Howard and his wife filed for Chapter 7 bankruptcy protection, and their personal debts were discharged. Afterward, Venture Bank convinced the Lapideses to sign a reaffirmation agreement by telling them that it would refinance all three mortgages so that they could keep their house.

The Lapideses made twelve $3,500 payments to Venture Bank, but when the bank did not refinance the other mortgages, they stopped making payments. Venture Bank filed suit, but a court refused to enforce the reaffirmation agreement because it violated the Bankruptcy Code. The agreement had never been signed by Lapideses' attorney or filed with the bankruptcy court.[17] ■

31–3 Reorganizations

The type of bankruptcy proceeding most commonly used by corporate debtors is the Chapter 11 *reorganization*. In a reorganization, the creditors and the debtor formulate a plan under which the debtor pays a portion of the debts and is discharged of the remainder. The debtor is allowed to continue in business.

As noted, this type of bankruptcy generally involves a corporate reorganization. Nevertheless, any debtor (except a stockbroker or a commodities broker) who is eligible for Chapter 7 relief is eligible for relief under Chapter 11. Railroads are also eligible.

Congress has established a "fast-track" Chapter 11 procedure for small-business debtors whose liabilities do not exceed $2.49 million and who do not own or manage real estate. The fast track enables a debtor to avoid the appointment of a creditors' committee and also shortens the filing periods and relaxes certain other requirements. Because the process is shorter and simpler, it is less costly.

The same principles that govern the filing of a liquidation (Chapter 7) petition apply to reorganization (Chapter 11) proceedings. The case may be brought either voluntarily or involuntarily. The automatic-stay provision and its exceptions (such as substantial abuse), as well as the adequate protection doctrine, apply in reorganizations.

31–3a Workouts

In some instances, to avoid bankruptcy proceedings, creditors may prefer private, negotiated adjustments of creditor-debtor relations, also known as **workouts.** Often, these out-of-court workouts are much more

---

17. *Venture Bank v. Lapides,* 800 F.3d 442 (8th Cir. 2015).

flexible and thus more conducive to a speedy settlement. Speed is critical because delay is one of the most costly elements in any bankruptcy proceeding. Another advantage of workouts is that they avoid the various administrative costs of bankruptcy proceedings.

31–3b Best Interests of the Creditors

Once a Chapter 11 petition has been filed, a bankruptcy court can dismiss or suspend proceedings at any time if dismissal or suspension would better serve the interests of the creditors. Before taking such an action, the court must give notice and conduct a hearing. The Code also allows a court, after notice and a hearing, to dismiss a case under reorganization "for cause" when there is no reasonable likelihood of rehabilitation. Similarly, a court can dismiss when there is an inability to effect a plan or an unreasonable delay by the debtor that may harm the interests of creditors. A debtor whose petition is dismissed for these reasons can file a subsequent Chapter 11 petition in the future.[18]

31–3c Debtor in Possession

On entry of the order for relief, the debtor generally continues to operate the business as a **debtor in possession (DIP).** The court, however, may appoint a trustee (often referred to as a *receiver*) to operate the debtor's business. The court will choose this action if gross mismanagement of the business is shown or if appointing a trustee is in the best interests of the estate.

The DIP's role is similar to that of a trustee in a liquidation bankruptcy.[19] The DIP is entitled to avoid preferential payments made to creditors and fraudulent transfers of assets. The DIP can also exercise a trustee's strong-arm powers. The DIP has the power to decide whether to cancel or assume prepetition executory contracts (contracts that are not yet performed) or unexpired leases.

Cancellation of executory contracts or unexpired leases can be of substantial benefit to a Chapter 11 debtor. ■ **EXAMPLE 31.8** Five years ago, APT Corporation leased an office building for a twenty-year term. Now, APT can no longer pay the rent due under the lease and has filed for Chapter 11 reorganization. In this situation, the debtor in possession can cancel the lease, and APT will not be required to continue paying the substantial rent due for fifteen more years. ■

31–3d Creditors' Committees

As soon as practicable after the entry of the order for relief, a creditors' committee of unsecured creditors is appointed.[20] The business's suppliers may serve on the committee. The committee can consult with the trustee or the DIP concerning the administration of the case or the formulation of the plan. Additional creditors' committees may be appointed to represent special interest creditors.

Generally, no orders affecting the estate will be entered without the consent of the committee or after a hearing in which the judge is informed of the committee's position. As mentioned earlier, businesses with debts of less than $2.49 million that do not own or manage real estate can avoid creditors' committees. In these fast-track proceedings, orders can be entered without a committee's consent.

31–3e The Reorganization Plan

A reorganization plan to rehabilitate the debtor is a plan to conserve and administer the debtor's assets in the hope of an eventual return to successful operation and solvency. The plan must be fair and equitable and must do the following:

1. Designate classes of claims and interests.
2. Specify the treatment to be afforded to the classes of creditors. (The plan must provide the same treatment for all claims in a particular class.)
3. Provide an adequate means for the plan's execution. (Individual debtors are required to utilize postpetition assets as necessary to execute the plan.)
4. Provide for payment of tax claims over a five-year period.

The plan need not provide for full repayment to unsecured creditors. Instead, creditors receive a percentage of each dollar owed to them by the debtor.

Filing the Plan Only the debtor may file a plan within the first 120 days after the date of the order for relief. This period may be extended, but not beyond eighteen months from the date of the order for relief. If the debtor does not meet the 120-day deadline or obtain an extension, any party may propose a plan. If a small-business debtor chooses to avoid a creditors' committee, the time for the debtor's filing is 180 days.

Acceptance of the Plan Once the plan has been developed, it is submitted to each class of creditors for

---

18. See 11 U.S.C. Section 1112(b).
19. 11 U.S.C. Section 544(a).

20. If the debtor has filed a reorganization plan accepted by the creditors, the trustee may decide not to call a meeting of the creditors.

acceptance. For the plan to be adopted, each class must accept it. A class has accepted the plan when a majority of the creditors in the class, representing two-thirds of the amount of the total claim, vote to approve it. If the debtor fails to procure creditor consent of the plan within 180 days, any party may propose a plan.

Confirmation of the Plan Confirmation is conditioned on the debtor's certifying that all postpetition domestic-support obligations have been paid in full. In addition, even when all classes of creditors accept the plan, the court may refuse to confirm it if it is not "in the best interests of the creditors." For small-business debtors, if the plan meets the listed requirements, the court must confirm the plan within forty-five days (unless this period is extended).

The plan can be modified on the request of the debtor, the DIP, the trustee, the U.S. trustee, or a holder of an unsecured claim. If an unsecured creditor objects to the plan, specific rules apply to the value of property to be distributed under the plan. Tax claims must be paid over a five-year period.

Even if only one class of creditors has accepted the plan, the court may still confirm the plan under the Code's so-called **cram-down provision.** In other words, the court may confirm the plan over the objections of a class of creditors. Before the court can exercise the right of cram-down confirmation, it must be demonstrated that the plan does not discriminate unfairly against any creditors and is fair and equitable.

Discharge The plan is binding on confirmation. Nevertheless, the law provides that confirmation of a plan does not discharge an individual debtor. *For individual debtors, the plan must be completed before discharge will be granted,* unless the court orders otherwise. For all other debtors, the court may order discharge at any time after the plan is confirmed.

On discharge, the debtor is given a reorganization discharge from all claims not protected under the plan. This discharge does not apply to any claims that would be denied discharge under liquidation.

31–4 **Bankruptcy Relief under Chapter 12 and Chapter 13**

In addition to bankruptcy relief through liquidation and reorganization, the Code also provides for family-farmer and family-fisherman debt adjustments (Chapter 12) and

individuals' repayment plans (Chapter 13). The procedures for filing Chapter 12 and Chapter 13 plans are very similar. Because Chapter 13 plans are the more commonly used of the two types, we discuss Chapter 13 first.

31–4a **Individuals' Repayment Plans—Chapter 13**

Chapter 13 of the Bankruptcy Code provides for "Adjustment of Debts of an Individual with Regular Income." Individuals with regular income who owe fixed (liquidated) unsecured debts of less than $383,175 or fixed secured debts of less than $1,149,525 may take advantage of bankruptcy repayment plans. Partnerships and corporations are excluded.

Among those eligible are salaried employees and sole proprietors, as well as individuals who live on welfare, Social Security, fixed pensions, or investment income. Many small-business debtors have a choice of filing under either Chapter 11 or Chapter 13. Repayment plans offer some advantages because they are less expensive and less complicated than reorganization or liquidation proceedings.

Filing the Petition A Chapter 13 repayment plan case can be initiated only by the debtor's filing of a voluntary petition or by court conversion of a Chapter 7 petition. Recall that a court may convert a Chapter 7 petition because of a finding of substantial abuse under the means test. In addition, certain liquidation and reorganization cases may be converted to repayment plan cases with the consent of the debtor.[21]

A trustee, who will make payments under the plan, must be appointed. On the filing of a repayment plan petition, the automatic stay previously discussed takes effect. Although the stay applies to all or part of the debtor's consumer debt, it does not apply to any business debt incurred by the debtor or to any domestic-support obligations.

Good Faith Requirement The Bankruptcy Code imposes the requirement of good faith on a debtor at both the time of the filing of the petition and the time of the filing of the plan. The Code does not define good faith, but if the circumstances on the whole indicate bad faith, a court can dismiss a debtor's Chapter 13 petition.

---

21. A Chapter 13 repayment plan may be converted to a Chapter 7 liquidation at the request of the debtor or, under certain circumstances, by a creditor "for cause." A Chapter 13 case may be converted to a Chapter 11 case after a hearing.

In determining whether a Chapter 13 plan was proposed in good faith, should the bankruptcy court consider whether the debtor included his Social Security income in the amount of disposable income available for payment of unsecured creditors? That was the issue in the following case.

In re Welsh

United States Court of Appeals, Ninth Circuit, 711 F.3d 1120 (2013).

In the Language of the Court

RIPPLE, Senior Circuit Judge:

* * * *

[David and Sharon Welsh] filed a voluntary Chapter 13 petition [in a federal bankruptcy court]. Their required schedules revealed the following assets: a home in Missoula, Montana, valued at $400,000, encumbered by a secured claim of $330,593.66; a Ford F-250 valued at $10,000, encumbered by a secured claim of $18,959; a 2006 Subaru Outback valued at of $9,500, encumbered by a secured claim of $12,211; a 2005 Toyota Matrix valued at $2,200, encumbered by a secured claim of $1,996; a 2005 Airstream trailer valued at $23,000, encumbered by a secured claim of $39,000; and two 2007 Honda ATVs each valued at $2,700, encumbered by secured claims of $3,065 and $4,500. In addition to their secured debts, the schedules revealed unsecured claims totaling approximately $180,500, the largest of which were their daughter's student loan debt in the amount of $60,000 and a joint debt owed to Bank of America on a line of credit in the amount of $50,000.

Mrs. Welsh is employed as a nurse and reported on Schedule I a monthly income of $6,975.40. She also draws a pension of $1,100 per month. Mr. Welsh is retired, but listed a monthly income of $358.03 from wages, salary and commissions, as well as Social Security income in the amount of $1,165.

Because their income exceeds the median for the state of Montana, the debtors calculated their disposable income according to the means test. * * * They listed their current monthly income as $8,116.31; their current monthly income did not include Mr.

Welsh's Social Security income of $1,165 because Social Security income is excluded from the current monthly income calculation. After deducting future payments on secured claims, the debtors were left with a disposable income of $218.12 per month.

The Welshes proposed a plan that provided for payments of $125 per month to unsecured creditors for the first thirty months of the plan. After their vehicle loans were paid, the payments would increase to $500 per month for the last thirty months of the plan. The proposed plan would pay off approximately $14,700 of the debtors' $180,500 unsecured debt.

The [Bankruptcy] Trustee objected on the ground that the debtors had not proposed their plan in good faith * * * because [they failed] to commit one hundred percent of their disposable income to the plan.

* * * *

The bankruptcy court * * * rejected the Trustee's argument.

[On the Trustee's appeal] the [Bankruptcy Appellate Panel (BAP) for the Ninth Circuit] affirmed the bankruptcy court's judgment.

* * * *

In this appeal, the Trustee * * * maintains that, in determining whether the Welshes proposed their Chapter 13 plan in good faith, the bankruptcy court * * * should have considered Mr. Welsh's Social Security income.

* * * *

In 2005, Congress * * * enacted the Bankruptcy Abuse Prevention and Consumer Protection Act ("BAPCPA"). The good faith requirement * * * remained the same, but there were significant changes with respect to the calculation

of disposable income. Before the BAPCPA, bankruptcy judges had authority to determine a debtor's ability to pay based on the individual circumstances of each case and each debtor. Congress replaced this discretion with a detailed, mechanical means test, which requires debtors with above-median income to calculate their "disposable income" by subtracting specific expenses from "current monthly income," as defined by the Bankruptcy Code. For our purposes, several elements of this calculation are important. *The debtor begins with his "current monthly income," which, by definition, explicitly "excludes benefits received under the Social Security Act."* The debtor then subtracts living expenses based on the Internal Revenue Service's "Collection Financial Standards," a detailed series of averages for living expenses that the Service uses to calculate necessary expenditures for delinquent taxpayers. The debtor also subtracts his averaged payments to secured creditors due during the following sixty months. [Emphasis added.]

As is the case here, the manner in which the means test calculates "disposable income" may underestimate the amount of actual funds that a taxpayer has available to pay unsecured creditors. A debtor who receives Social Security income * * * does not have to account for that income when calculating "disposable income" according to the means test. * * * The result may be that * * * little "disposable income," as that figure is calculated, remains to pay unsecured creditors.

* * * *

Here, the Trustee does not contend, of course, that the calculation of

Case 31.3 Continued

disposable income should have incorporated Social Security income; the statutory language is clearly to the contrary. Instead, he concedes that disposable income was calculated correctly under the BAPCPA, but nevertheless maintains that the Welshes' failure to dedicate Mr. Welsh's Social Security income to the payment of unsecured creditors requires a conclusion that the plan was not proposed in good faith * * * . We cannot conclude, however, that a plan prepared completely in accordance with the very detailed calculations that Congress set forth is not proposed in good faith. To hold otherwise would be to allow the bankruptcy court to substitute its judgment of how much and what kind of income should be dedicated to the payment of unsecured creditors for the judgment of Congress. Such an approach would not only flout the express language of Congress, but also one of Congress's purposes in enacting the BAPCPA, namely to reduce the amount of discretion that bankruptcy courts previously had over the calculation of an above-median debtor's income and expenses.

* * * *

We conclude that Congress's adoption of the BAPCPA forecloses a court's consideration of a debtor's Social Security income * * * as part of the inquiry into good faith * * * . We therefore affirm the judgment of the BAP.

Legal Reasoning Questions

1. On what ground did the trustee contend that the debtors had not proposed their Chapter 13 plan in good faith?

2. How did the court rule with respect to the trustee's argument? Why?

3. In evaluating a debtor's petition, what factors should be part of a good faith analysis? Should consideration of the calculation of disposable income play a role? Why or why not?

The Repayment Plan A plan of rehabilitation by repayment must provide for the following:

1. The turning over to the trustee of such future earnings or income of the debtor as is necessary for execution of the plan.

2. Full payment through deferred cash payments of all claims entitled to priority, such as taxes.[22]

3. Identical treatment of all claims within a particular class. (The Code permits the debtor to list co-debtors, such as guarantors or sureties, as a separate class.)

The repayment plan may provide either for payment of all obligations in full or for payment of a lesser amount. The debtor must begin making payments under the proposed plan within thirty days after the plan has been filed and must continue to make "timely" payments.[23] If the debtor fails to make timely payments or to commence payments within the thirty-day period, the court can convert the case to a Chapter 7 bankruptcy or dismiss the petition.

Allowable Expenses. In putting together a repayment plan, a debtor must apply the means test to identify the amount of disposable income that will be available to repay creditors. The debtor is allowed to deduct certain expenses from monthly income to arrive at this amount, but only if they are appropriate.

■ **CASE IN POINT 31.9** Jason Ransom filed a Chapter 13 bankruptcy petition. Among his assets, he listed a Toyota Camry that he owned free of any debt. In his monthly expenses, he claimed a car-ownership deduction of $471 and a separate $388 deduction for costs to operate the car. He proposed a five-year plan that would repay about 25 percent of his unsecured debt.

FIA Card Services, N.A., an unsecured creditor, objected to the plan. FIA argued that Ransom was not entitled to the car-ownership allowance because he did not owe money on the car. Ultimately, the United States Supreme Court ruled in FIA's favor. A deduction is appropriate only if the debtor will incur that expense during the life of the Chapter 13 plan. A debtor who does not make loan or lease payments may not take a car-ownership deduction.[24] ■

Length of the Plan. The length of the payment plan can be three or five years, depending on the debtor's family income. If the family income is greater than the median family income in the relevant geographic area under the

---

22. As with a Chapter 11 reorganization plan, full repayment of all claims is not always required.

23. The bankruptcy trustee holds on to these payments until the court either confirms or denies the debtor's plan. If the court confirms the plan, the trustee distributes the funds to creditors as stated in the plan. If the court denies the debtor's plan, the trustee returns the funds, minus administrative expenses, to the debtor.

24. *Ransom v. FIA Card Services, N.A.,* 562 U.S. 61, 131 S.Ct. 716, 178 L.Ed.2d 603 (2011).

means test, the term of the proposed plan must be three years.[25] The term may not exceed five years.

Confirmation of the Plan. After the plan is filed, the court holds a confirmation hearing, at which interested parties (such as creditors) may object to the plan. The hearing must be held at least twenty days, but no more than forty-five days, after the meeting of the creditors. The debtor must have filed all prepetition tax returns and paid all postpetition domestic-support obligations before a court will confirm any plan.

The court will confirm a plan with respect to each claim of a secured creditor under any of the following circumstances:

1. If the secured creditors have accepted the plan.
2. If the plan provides that secured creditors retain their liens until there is payment in full or until the debtor receives a discharge.
3. If the debtor surrenders the property securing the claims to the creditors.

In addition, for a motor vehicle purchased within 910 days before the petition is filed, the plan must provide that a creditor with a purchase-money security interest (PMSI) retains its lien until the entire debt is paid. For PMSIs on other personal property, the payment plan must cover debts incurred within a one-year period preceding the filing.

Discharge After the debtor has completed all payments, the court grants a discharge of all debts provided for by the repayment plan. Generally, all debts are dischargeable except the following:

1. Allowed claims not provided for by the plan.
2. Certain long-term debts provided for by the plan.
3. Certain tax claims and payments on retirement accounts.
4. Claims for domestic-support obligations.
5. Debts related to injury or property damage caused while driving under the influence of alcohol or drugs.

An order granting discharge is final as to the debts listed in the repayment plan. ■ **CASE IN POINT 31.10** Francisco Espinosa filed a petition for an individual repayment plan under Chapter 13 of the Bankruptcy Code. His plan proposed to pay only the principal on his student loan and to discharge the interest. United Student Aid Funds, Inc. (the creditor), had notice of the plan and did not object. The court confirmed the plan without finding that payment of the student loan

interest would cause undue hardship (as required under the Code).

Years later, United filed a motion asking the bankruptcy court to rule that its order confirming the plan was void because it was in violation of the rules governing bankruptcy. The court denied United's petition and ordered the creditor to cease its collection efforts. The case ultimately reached the United States Supreme Court, which affirmed the lower court's holding that the student loan debt was discharged.[26] ■

31–4b Family Farmers and Fishermen—Chapter 12

Congress created Chapter 12 of the Bankruptcy Code to help relieve economic pressure on small farmers. In 2005, Congress extended this protection to family fishermen, modified its provisions somewhat, and made it a permanent chapter in the Bankruptcy Code. (Previously, the statutes authorizing Chapter 12 had to be periodically renewed by Congress.)

Concept Summary 31.1 compares bankruptcy procedures under Chapters 7, 11, 12, and 13.

Definitions For purposes of Chapter 12, a *family farmer* is one whose gross income is at least 50 percent farm dependent and whose debts are at least 50 percent farm related. The total debt for a family farmer must not exceed $4,031,575. A partnership or close corporation that is at least 50 percent owned by the farm family can also qualify as a family farmer.[27]

A *family fisherman* is one whose gross income is at least 50 percent dependent on commercial fishing operations[28] and whose debts are at least 80 percent related to commercial fishing. The total debt for a family fisherman must not exceed $1,868,200. As with family farmers, a partnership or close corporation can also qualify.

Filing the Petition The procedure for filing a family-farmer or family-fisherman bankruptcy plan is similar to the procedure for filing a repayment plan under Chapter 13. The debtor must file a plan not later than ninety days after the order for relief has been entered. The filing of the

---

25. See 11 U.S.C. Section 1322(d) for details on when the court will find that the Chapter 13 plan should extend to a five-year period.

26. *United Student Aid Funds, Inc. v. Espinosa*, 559 U.S. 260, 130 S.Ct. 1367, 176 L.Ed.2d 158 (2010).

27. Note that for a corporation or partnership to qualify under Chapter 12, at least 80 percent of the value of the firm's assets must consist of assets related to the farming operation.

28. Commercial fishing operations include catching, harvesting, or raising fish, shrimp, lobsters, urchins, seaweed, shellfish, or other aquatic species or products.

Concept Summary 31.1

Forms of Bankruptcy Relief Compared

FORM	CHAPTER 7	CHAPTER 11	CHAPTERS 12 AND 13
Purpose	Liquidation.	Reorganization.	Adjustment.
Who Can Petition	Debtor (voluntary) or creditors (involuntary).	Debtor (voluntary) or creditors (involuntary).	Debtor (voluntary) only.
Who Can Be a Debtor	Any "person" (including partnerships, corporations, and municipalities) except railroads, insurance companies, banks, savings and loan institutions, investment companies licensed by the Small Business Administration, and credit unions. Farmers and charitable institutions cannot be involuntarily petitioned. If the court finds the petition to be a substantial abuse of the use of Chapter 7, the debtor may be required to convert to a Chapter 13 repayment plan.	Any debtor eligible for Chapter 7 relief. Railroads are also eligible. Individuals have specific rules and limitations.	**Chapter 12**—Any family farmer (one whose gross income is at least 50 percent farm dependent and whose debts are at least 50 percent farm related) or family fisherman (one whose gross income is at least 50 percent dependent on commercial fishing operations and whose debts are at least 80 percent related to commercial fishing) or any partnership or close corporation at least 50 percent owned by a family farmer or fisherman, when total debt does not exceed a specified amount ($4,031,575 for farmers and $1,868,200 for fishermen). **Chapter 13**—Any individual (not partnerships or corporations) with regular income who owes fixed (liquidated) unsecured debts of less than $383,175 or fixed secured debts of less than $1,149,525.
Procedure Leading to Discharge	Nonexempt property is sold, and the proceeds are distributed (in order) to priority groups. Dischargeable debts are terminated.	Plan is submitted. If the plan is approved and followed, debts are discharged.	Plan is submitted and must be approved if the value of the property to be distributed equals the amount of the claims or if the debtor turns over disposable income for a three-year or five-year period. If the plan is followed, debts are discharged.
Advantages	On liquidation and distribution, most or all debts are discharged, and the debtor has an opportunity for a fresh start.	Debtor continues in business. Creditors can either accept the plan, or it can be "crammed down" on them. The plan allows for the reorganization and liquidation of debts over the plan period.	Debtor continues in business or possession of assets. If the plan is approved, most debts are discharged after the plan period.

petition acts as an automatic stay against creditors' and co-obligors' actions against the estate.

A farmer or fisherman who has already filed a reorganization or repayment plan may convert it to a Chapter 12 plan. The debtor may also convert a Chapter 12 plan to a liquidation plan.

Content and Confirmation of the Plan   The content of a plan under Chapter 12 is basically the same as that of a Chapter 13 repayment plan. Generally, the plan must be confirmed or denied within forty-five days of filing.

The plan must provide for payment of secured debts at the value of the collateral. If the secured debt exceeds the value of the collateral, the remaining debt is unsecured.

For unsecured debtors, the plan must be confirmed in either of the following circumstances: (1) the value of the property to be distributed under the plan equals the amount of the claim, or (2) the plan provides that all of the debtor's disposable income to be received in a three-year period (or longer, by court approval) will be applied to making payments. Disposable income is all income received less amounts needed to support the farmer or fisherman and his or her family and to continue the farming or commercial fishing operation. Completion of payments under the plan discharges all debts provided for by the plan.

Reviewing: Bankruptcy Law

Three months ago, Janet Hart's husband of twenty years died of cancer. Although he had medical insurance, he left Janet with outstanding medical bills of more than $50,000. Janet has two teenage daughters to support. She has worked at the local library for the past ten years, earning $1,500 per month. Since her husband's death, she has also received $1,500 in Social Security benefits and $1,100 in life insurance proceeds every month, for a total monthly income of $4,100. After making the mortgage payment of $1,500 and paying the amounts due on other debts, Janet has barely enough left to buy groceries for her family. She decides to file for Chapter 7 bankruptcy, hoping for a fresh start. Using the information presented in the chapter, answer the following questions.

1. What must Janet do *before* filing a petition for relief under Chapter 7?
2. How much time does Janet have after filing the bankruptcy petition to submit the required schedules? What happens if Janet does not meet the deadline?
3. Assume that Janet files a petition under Chapter 7. Further assume that the median family income in the geographic area in which Janet lives is $49,300. What steps would a court take to determine whether Janet's petition is presumed to be "substantial abuse" using the means test?
4. Suppose that the court determines that no *presumption* of substantial abuse applies in Janet's case. Nevertheless, the court finds that Janet does have the ability to pay at least a portion of the medical bills out of her disposable income. What would the court likely order in that situation?

Debate This . . .   *Rather than being allowed to file Chapter 7 bankruptcy petitions, individuals and couples should always be forced to make an effort to pay off their debts through Chapter 13.*

Terms and Concepts

adequate protection doctrine 583	discharge 581	preference 585
automatic stay 583	insider 585	preferred creditor 585
bankruptcy trustee 581	liquidation 580	reaffirmation agreement 592
consumer-debtor 581	order for relief 583	U.S. trustee 582
cram-down provision 594	petition in bankruptcy 581	workout 592
debtor in possession (DIP) 593		

Issue Spotters

1. After graduating from college, Tina works briefly as a salesperson before filing for bankruptcy. Tina's petition states that her only debts are student loans, taxes accruing within the last year, and a claim against her based on her misuse of customers' funds during her employment. Are these debts dischargeable in bankruptcy? Explain. (See *Liquidation Proceedings*.)

2. Ogden is a vice president of Plumbing Service, Inc. (PSI). On May 1, Ogden loans PSI $10,000. On June 1, the firm repays the loan. On July 1, PSI files for bankruptcy. Quentin is appointed trustee. Can Quentin recover the $10,000 paid to Ogden on June 1? Why or why not? (See *Liquidation Proceedings*.)

• Check your answers to the Issue Spotters against the answers provided in Appendix D at the end of this text.

Business Scenarios

31–1. Voluntary versus Involuntary Bankruptcy. Burke has been a rancher all her life, raising cattle and crops. Her ranch is valued at $500,000, almost all of which is exempt under state law. Burke has eight creditors and a total indebtedness of $70,000. Two of her largest creditors are Oman ($30,000 owed) and Sneed ($25,000 owed). The other six creditors have claims of less than $5,000 each. A drought has ruined all of Burke's crops and forced her to sell many of her cattle at a loss. She cannot pay off her creditors. (See *Liquidation Proceedings*.)

(a) Under the Bankruptcy Code, can Burke, with a $500,000 ranch, voluntarily petition herself into bankruptcy? Explain.

(b) Could either Oman or Sneed force Burke into involuntary bankruptcy? Explain.

31–2. Distribution of Property. Montoro petitioned himself into voluntary bankruptcy. There were three major claims against his estate. One was made by Carlton, a friend who held Montoro's negotiable promissory note for $2,500. Another was made by Elmer, Montoro's employee, who claimed that Montoro owed him three months' back wages of $4,500. The last major claim was made by the United Bank of the Rockies on an unsecured loan of $5,000. In addition, Dietrich, an accountant retained by the trustee, was owed $500, and property taxes of $1,000 were owed to Rock County. Montoro's nonexempt property was liquidated, with proceeds of $5,000. Discuss fully what amount each party will receive, and why. (See *Liquidation Proceedings*.)

Business Case Problems

31–3. Discharge in Bankruptcy. Caroline McAfee loaned $400,000 to Carter Oaks Crossing. Joseph Harman, president of Carter Oaks Crossing, signed a promissory note providing that the company would repay the amount with interest in installments beginning in 1999 and ending by 2006. Harman signed a personal guaranty for the note. Carter Oaks Crossing defaulted on the note, so McAfee sued Harman for payment under the guaranty. Harman moved for summary judgment on the ground that McAfee's claim against him had been discharged in his Chapter 7 bankruptcy case. The case had been filed after 1999 but before the default on the note. The guaranty was not listed among Harman's debts in the bankruptcy filing. Would the obligation under the guaranty have been discharged in bankruptcy, as Harman claimed? Why or why not? [*Harman v. McAfee,* 302 Ga.App. 698, 691 S.E.2d 586 (2010)] (See *Liquidation Proceedings*.)

31–4. Automatic Stay. Michelle Gholston leased a Chevy Impala from EZ Auto Van Rentals. In November 2011, Gholston filed for bankruptcy. Around November 21, the bankruptcy court notified EZ Auto of Gholston's bankruptcy and the imposition of an automatic stay. Nevertheless, because Gholston had fallen behind on her payments, EZ Auto repossessed the vehicle on November 28. Gholston's attorney then

reminded EZ Auto about the automatic stay, but the company failed to return the car. As a result of the car's repossession, Gholston suffered damages that included emotional distress, lost wages, attorneys' fees, and car rental expenses. Can Gholston recover from EZ Auto? Why or why not? [*In re Gholston,* 2012 WL 639288 (M.D.Fla. 2012)] (See *Liquidation Proceedings*.)

31–5. Business Case Problem with Sample Answer— Discharge in Bankruptcy. Like many students, Barbara Hann financed her education partially through loans. These loans included three federally insured Stafford Loans of $7,500 each ($22,500 in total). Hann believed that she had repaid the loans, but when she filed a Chapter 13 petition, Educational Credit Management Corp. (ECMC) filed an unsecured proof of claim based on the loans. Hann objected. At a hearing at which ECMC failed to appear, Hann submitted correspondence from the lender that indicated the loans had been paid. The court entered an order sustaining Hann's objection. Despite the order, can ECMC resume its effort to collect on Hann's loans? Explain. [*In re Hann,* 711 F.3d 235 (1st Cir. 2013)] (See *Liquidation Proceedings*.)

• For a sample answer to Problem 31–5, go to Appendix E at the end of this text.

31–6. Discharge. Michael and Dianne Shankle divorced. An Arkansas state court ordered Michael to pay Dianne alimony and child support, as well as half of the $184,000 in their investment accounts. Instead, Michael withdrew more than half of the investment funds and spent them. Over the next several years, the court repeatedly held Michael in contempt for failing to pay Dianne. Six years later, Michael filed for Chapter 7 bankruptcy, including in the petition's schedule the debt to Dianne of unpaid alimony, child support, and investment funds. Is Michael entitled to a discharge of this debt, or does it qualify as an exception? Explain. [*In re Shankle,* 554 Fed.Appx. 264 (5th Cir. 2014)] (See *Liquidation Proceedings.*)

31–7. Discharge under Chapter 13. James Thomas and Jennifer Clark married and had two children. They bought a home in Ironton, Ohio, with a loan secured by a mortgage. Later, they took out a second mortgage. On their divorce, the court gave Clark custody of the children and required Clark to pay the first mortgage. The divorce decree also required Thomas and Clark to make equal payments on the second mortgage and provided that Clark would receive all proceeds on the sale of the home. Thomas failed to make any payments, and Clark sold the home. At that point, she learned that Auto Now had a lien on the home because Thomas had not made payments on his car. Clark used all the sale proceeds to pay off the lien and the mortgages. When Thomas filed a petition for a Chapter 13 bankruptcy in a federal bankruptcy court, Clark filed a proof of claim for the mortgage and lien debts. Clark claimed that Thomas should not be able to discharge these debts because they were part of his domestic-support obligations. Are these debts dischargeable? Explain. [*In re Thomas,* 591 Fed.Appx. 443 (6th Cir. 2015)] (See *Bankruptcy Relief under Chapter 12 and Chapter 13.*)

31–8. Liquidation Proceedings. Jeffrey Krueger and Michael Torres, shareholders of Cru Energy, Inc., were embroiled in litigation in a Texas state court. Both claimed to act on Cru's behalf, and each charged the other with attempting to obtain control of Cru through fraud and other misconduct.

Temporarily prohibited from participating in Cru's business, Krueger formed Kru, a company with the same business plan and many of the same shareholders as Cru. Meanwhile, to delay the state court proceedings, Krueger filed a petition for a Chapter 7 liquidation in a federal bankruptcy court. He did not reveal his interest in Kru to the bankruptcy court. Ownership of Krueger's Cru shares passed to the bankruptcy trustee, but Krueger ignored this. He called a meeting of Cru's shareholders—except Torres—and voted those shares to remove Torres from the board and elect himself chairman, president, chief executive officer, and treasurer. The Cru board then dismissed all of Cru's claims against Krueger in his suit with Torres. Are there sufficient grounds for the bankruptcy court to dismiss Krueger's bankruptcy petition? Discuss. [*In re Krueger,* 812 F.3d 365 (5th Cir. 2016)] (See *Liquidation Proceedings.*)

31–9. A Question of Ethics—Discharge in Bankruptcy. Monica Sexton filed a petition for Chapter 13 reorganization. One of her creditors was Friedman's Jewelers. Her petition misclassified Friedman's claim as $800 of unsecured debt. Within days, Friedman's filed proof of a secured claim for $300 and an unsecured claim for $462. Eventually, Friedman's was sent payments of about $300 by check. None of the checks were cashed. By then, Friedman's had filed its own petition under Chapter 11, Bankruptcy Receivables Management (BRM) had bought Friedman's unpaid accounts, and the checks had not been forwarded. Sexton received a discharge on the completion of her plan. BRM was not notified. BRM wrote to Sexton's attorney to ask about the status of her case, but received no response. BRM demanded that Sexton surrender the collateral on its claim. Sexton asked the court to impose sanctions on BRM for violating the discharge order. [In re Sexton, *2011 WL 284180 (E.D.N.C. 2011)*] (See *Liquidation Proceedings.*)

(a) Was Sexton's debt to Friedman's dischargeable? Discuss.

(b) Should BRM be sanctioned for willfully violating the discharge order? Why or why not?

Legal Reasoning Group Activity

31–10. Discharge in Bankruptcy. Cathy Coleman took out loans to complete her college education. After graduation, Coleman was irregularly employed as a teacher before filing a petition in a federal bankruptcy court under Chapter 13. The court confirmed a five-year plan under which Coleman was required to commit all of her disposable income to paying the student loans. Less than a year later, when Coleman was laid off, she still owed more than $100,000 to Educational Credit Management Corp. Coleman asked the court to discharge the debt on the ground that it would be an undue hardship for her to pay it. (See *Liquidation Proceedings.*)

(a) The first group will determine when a debtor normally is entitled to a discharge under Chapter 13.

(b) The second group will discuss whether student loans are dischargeable and when "undue hardship" is a legitimate ground for an exception to the general rule.

(c) The third group will outline the goals of bankruptcy law and make an argument, based on these facts and principles, in support of Coleman's request.

Federal Student Loans—Default and Discharge

Ruby borrows $16,000 from the U.S. Department of Education (DOE) to help pay for her education at State University. To obtain the funds, she signs a note for the borrowed amount plus interest payable to DOE. She does not make payments on the loan when they come due.

Has Ruby defaulted on the loan? What will happen?

Federal Student Loan Programs

Federal government loans make up about 93 percent of the $1.2 trillion student loan market. Loans from private lenders make up the rest. It is important for borrowers to know which type of loan they owe. The collection methods available to private lenders are different from the methods available to federal lenders.

Federal student loan programs include the following.[1]

- *William D. Ford Federal Direct Loans*, which are made by the DOE.[2]
- *Federal Perkins Loans*, which are made by schools to students who demonstrate financial need.[3]
- *Federal Family Education Loans (FFEL)*, which were made by banks or other private lenders before July 1, 2010. The federal government guaranteed these loans. This program has been discontinued, but the outstanding amounts of any of the loans must still be paid.[4]

Default

A borrower is in default on a federal student loan if he or she fails to repay it according to the terms in the note. For most federal student loans, this occurs if a payment has not been made for more than 270 days (330 days for FFELs).[5]

Consequences of Default on a Federal Student Loan

If a borrower defaults on a federal student loan, the entire balance of the loan, including both principal and interest, can become due in a single payment.

Transfer of the Note to a Collection Agency Once default occurs, the holder of the note—which may be the DOE, the school that made the loan, a state agency, or a private nonprofit organization—can transfer the note to a collection agency to recover the unpaid debt.

Any additional costs to collect payment can then be added to the outstanding principal.[6] These expenses can be up to 18.5 percent of the defaulted amount of the principal and interest for Federal Direct Loans and FFELs, and more for Federal Perkins Loans.

---

1. Each program has eligibility requirements, interest rates, loan limits, and other stipulations that are subject to change. See U.S. Department of Education, *Loans* (Dec. 7, 2015) *available at* https://studentaid.ed.gov/sa/types/loans.
2. 20 U.S.C. Sections 1087a–1087j.
3. 20 U.S.C. Sections 1087aa–1087ii.
4. 20 U.S.C. Sections 1071–1087-4.
5. U.S. Department of Education, *Understanding Default* (Dec. 7, 2015) *available at* https://studentaid.ed.gov/sa/repay-loans/default.
6. *Marx v. General Revenue Corp.*, __ U.S. __, 133 S.Ct. 1166, 185 L.Ed.2d 242 (2013).

Treasury Offset   There are other actions that the holder of the note might take. The DOE has the authority to collect the amount of the loan. This can be done by withholding funds from the defaulted borrower's sources of income. For instance, the DOE can ask the Department of the Treasury to withhold a defaulted debtor's federal income tax refund and other payments of federal funds, including Social Security payments.[7] This is known as a *Treasury offset.*

Garnishment   The DOE or any other holder of the note can order the debtor's employer to withhold up to 15 percent of the debtor's disposable pay. No court order is necessary (unlike with a garnishment to recover the unpaid amount of a *private* student loan, which requires a court order). The withholding can continue until the debt is paid or otherwise taken out of default.[8] The DOE can arrange for a similar amount to be withheld from a federal employee's wages through the *federal salary offset program.*

Whether a debtor's employer is a private business or the federal government, the debtor has rights with regard to garnishment or offset. The debtor has a right to be notified of a proposed garnishment or offset, a right to object to it, and a right to a hearing on the objection.

Forgiveness, Cancellation, and Discharge

A federal student loan must be repaid. This is true even for borrowers who do not finish school, do not find a job related to their program of study, or are not satisfied with the education they received.

In certain circumstances, however, some or all of a loan may be forgiven, canceled, or discharged. For all federal student loans, these circumstances include the following.

- *Closed school*—A debtor may be entitled to a discharge if the school closes while the student is enrolled or within 120 days after he or she withdraws.
- *Total and permanent disability*—To prove total and permanent disability, the debtor must show that he or she is unable to engage in any substantial gainful activity due to a physical or mental impairment.
- *Death*—If a borrower dies, his or her federal student loan will be discharged.
- *Bankruptcy*—A loan may be discharged in bankruptcy if its repayment would cause undue hardship. Undue hardship requires that repaying the loan would prevent the debtor from maintaining a minimal standard of living, the situation would continue for a significant portion of the repayment period, and good faith efforts to repay the loan were made before the bankruptcy filing.

Federal Direct Loans and FFELs may be discharged or forgiven in the following additional circumstances.

- *False certification of student eligibility*—This can happen when a school falsely certifies a student's eligibility to benefit from its program. It can also happen when the student does not qualify for the occupation in which he or she paid to be educated (because of a health condition, for instance). Finally, it can result from forgery or identity theft.
- *Unauthorized payment*—A loan may be discharged if a school signed a student's name on the loan application or endorsed the loan check without the student's knowledge. An exception exists when the proceeds were paid to the student or applied against charges owed by the student to the school.

Continues

---

7. *Lockhart v. United States,* 548 U.S. 142, 126 S.Ct. 699, 163 L.Ed.2d 557 (2005).
8. *Sanon v. Department of Higher Education,* 453 Fed.Appx. 28 (2d Cir. 2011).

- *Unpaid refund*—An unpaid refund occurs when a student takes out a loan to attend a school and withdraws, but the school does not refund the appropriate amount to the DOE.
- *Full-time teacher*—A teacher who has been teaching full-time in a low-income school or educational service agency for five consecutive years may have some or all of a loan forgiven.

Some or all of a Federal Perkins Loan may be canceled for those who are employed in certain occupations. These include the following.

- Volunteers in the Peace Corps or VISTA.
- Military personnel (serving in areas of hostilities).
- Nurses and other medical technicians.
- Law enforcement and corrections officers.
- Workers for Head Start, and other child and family services.
- Professional providers of early intervention services for disabled persons.
- Teachers who have been teaching full-time in low-income schools or in certain subject areas.[9]

Finally, a Federal Direct Loan may be forgiven if the borrower is employed in a particular public service job and has made 120 payments on the loan.

Ethical Connection

Many of the ways to avoid paying a federal student loan without defaulting are ethical, and even laudable. For example, a loan may be forgiven for a debtor who is a teacher, a military serviceperson, a law enforcement officer, a nurse, or a child-care provider. Individuals who pursue these occupations are likely to have high ethical standards. Their contribution to the public good may exceed any amount that they borrowed to go to school. Ultimately, the public may accrue the greatest benefit from their service. Thus, it will be *us* who owe *them*—a debt of gratitude.

Ethics Question *In addition to the borrowers listed in this feature, who deserves to have their federal student loans forgiven? Why?*

Critical Thinking *What are the consequences in addition to those stated in this feature of failing to make timely payments on federal student loans? Discuss.*

---

9. For more information on these options, see U.S. Department of Education, *Forgiveness, Cancellation, and Discharge* (Dec. 7, 2015) *available at* https://studentaid.ed.gov/sa/repay-loans/forgiveness-cancellation.

Agency and Employment

CHAPTER 32

Agency Formation and Duties

One of the most common, important, and pervasive legal relationships is that of **agency.** In
an agency relationship involving two
parties, one of the parties, called the
agent, agrees to represent or act for
the other, called the *principal.* The
principal has the right to control the
agent's conduct in matters entrusted
to the agent.

Agency relationships are crucial in
the business world. By using agents,
a principal can conduct multiple

business operations at the same time
in different locations. Indeed, the only
way that certain business entities can
function is through their agents. For
instance, a corporate officer is an
agent who serves in a representative
capacity for the corporation. The officer has the authority to bind the corporation to a contract. Only through
its officers can corporations enter into
contracts.

Most employees are also considered to be agents of their employers.

Today, however, the United States is
experiencing a trend toward a so-
called *gig economy,* which centers
on short-term, independent workers
who are not employees. Companies
like Uber and Lyft (discussed in this
chapter's feature) provide evidence
of this trend. This type of on-demand
employment raises questions related
to agency, making agency an increasingly important topic for students of
business law and the legal environment to understand.

32–1 Agency Relationships

Section 1(1) of the *Restatement (Third) of Agency*[1] defines
agency as "the fiduciary relation [that] results from the
manifestation of consent by one person to another that
the other shall act in his [or her] behalf and subject to his
[or her] control, and consent by the other so to act." In
other words, in a principal-agent relationship, the parties
have agreed that the agent will act *on behalf and instead
of* the principal in negotiating and transacting business
with third parties.

The term **fiduciary** is at the heart of agency law. This
term can be used both as a noun and as an adjective.
When used as a noun, it refers to a person having a duty
created by his or her undertaking to act primarily for
another's benefit in matters connected with the undertaking. When used as an adjective, as in the phrase *fiduciary*

relationship, it means that the relationship involves trust
and confidence.

Agency relationships commonly exist between employers and employees. Agency relationships may sometimes
also exist between employers and independent contractors who are hired to perform special tasks or services.

32–1a Employer-Employee Relationships

Normally, all employees who deal with third parties are
deemed to be agents. A salesperson in a department store,
for instance, is an agent of the store's owner (the principal) and acts on the owner's behalf. Any sale of goods
made by the salesperson to a customer is binding on the
principal. Similarly, most representations of fact made by
the salesperson with respect to the goods sold are binding
on the principal.

Because employees who deal with third parties
generally are deemed to be agents of their employers, agency law and employment law overlap considerably. Agency relationships, however, can exist outside

---

1. The *Restatement (Third) of Agency* is an authoritative summary of the
   law of agency and is often referred to by judges in their decisions and
   opinions.

an employer-employee relationship, so agency law has a broader reach than employment law. Additionally, agency law is based on the common law, whereas much employment law is statutory law.

Employment laws (state and federal) apply only to the employer-employee relationship. Statutes governing Social Security, withholding taxes, workers' compensation, unemployment compensation, workplace safety, and employment discrimination apply only if an employer-employee relationship exists. *These laws do not apply to independent contractors.*

32–1b Employer–Independent Contractor Relationships

Independent contractors are not employees because, by definition, those who hire them have no control over the details of their work performance. Section 2 of the *Restatement (Third) of Agency* defines an **independent contractor** as follows:

> [An independent contractor is] a person who contracts with another to do something for him [or her] but who is not controlled by the other nor subject to the other's right to control with respect to his [or her] physical conduct in the performance of the undertaking. He [or she] may or may not be an agent.

Building contractors and subcontractors are independent contractors. A property owner who hires a contractor and subcontractors to complete a project does not control the details of the way they perform their work. Truck drivers who own their vehicles and hire out on a per-job basis are independent contractors, but truck drivers who drive company trucks on a regular basis usually are employees. See this chapter's *Ethics Today* feature for a discussion of disputes involving the classification of drivers working for Uber and Lyft.

The relationship between a principal and an independent contractor may or may not involve an agency relationship. To illustrate: A homeowner who hires a real estate broker to sell her house has contracted with an independent contractor (the broker). The homeowner has also established an agency relationship with the broker for the specific purpose of selling the property. Another example is an insurance agent, who is both an independent contractor and an agent of the insurance company for which he sells policies. (Note that an insurance *broker,* in contrast, normally is an agent of the person obtaining insurance and not of the insurance company.)

32–1c Determination of Employee Status

The courts are frequently asked to determine whether a particular worker is an employee or an independent contractor. How a court decides this issue can have a significant effect on the rights and liabilities of the parties. Employers are required to pay certain taxes, such as Social Security and unemployment taxes, for employees but not for independent contractors. Therefore, workers may benefit from obtaining employee status in some situations.

Criteria Used by the Courts In deciding whether a worker is categorized as an employee or an independent contractor, courts often consider the following questions:

1. *How much control does the employer exercise over the details of the work?* If the employer exercises considerable control over the details of the work and the day-to-day activities of the worker, this indicates employee status. This is perhaps the most important factor weighed by the courts in determining employee status.
2. *Is the worker engaged in an occupation or business distinct from that of the employer?* If so, this points to independent-contractor, not employee, status.
3. *Is the work usually done under the employer's direction or by a specialist without supervision?* If the work is usually done under the employer's direction, this indicates employee status.
4. *Does the employer supply the tools at the place of work?* If so, this indicates employee status.
5. *For how long is the person employed?* If the person is employed for a long period of time, this indicates employee status.
6. *What is the method of payment—by time period or at the completion of the job?* Payment by time period, such as once every two weeks or once a month, indicates employee status.
7. *What degree of skill is required of the worker?* If a great degree of skill is required, this may indicate that the person is an independent contractor hired for a specialized job and not an employee.

Whether a worker is an employee or an independent contractor can affect the employer's liability for the worker's actions. An employer normally is not responsible for the actions of an independent contractor. In the following case, the court had to determine the status of an auto service company and its tow truck driver who assaulted the passenger of a vehicle the company had been hired to tow.

Case **32.1**

Coker v. Pershad

Superior Court of New Jersey, Appellate Division, 2013 WL 1296271 (2013).

Background and Facts AAA North Jersey, Inc., contracted with Five Star Auto Service to perform towing and auto repair services for AAA. Terence Pershad, the driver of a tow truck for Five Star, responded to a call to AAA for assistance by the driver of a car involved in an accident in Hoboken, New Jersey. Pershad got into a fight with Nicholas Coker, a passenger in the car, and assaulted Coker with a knife.

Coker filed a suit in a New Jersey state court against Pershad, Five Star, and AAA. The court determined that Pershad was Five Star's employee and that Five Star was an independent contractor, not AAA's employee. Thus, AAA was "not responsible for the alleged negligence of its independent contractor, defendant Five Star, in hiring Mr. Pershad." Five Star entered into a settlement with Coker. Coker appealed the ruling in AAA's favor.

In the Language of the Court

PER CURIAM.
* * * *

   The important difference between an employee and an independent contractor is that one who hires an independent contractor has no right of control over the manner in which the work is to be done. [Emphasis added.]
* * * *

   * * * Plaintiff [Coker] argues AAA controlled the means and method of the work performed by Five Star. * * * Factors * * * [that] determine whether a principal maintains the right of control over an individual or a corporation claimed to be an independent contractor [include]:

   (a) the extent of control which, by the agreement, the master may exercise over the details of the work;
   (b) whether or not the one employed is engaged in a distinct occupation or business;
   (c) the kind of occupation, with reference to whether, in the locality, the work is usually done under the direction of the employer or by a specialist without supervision;
   (d) the skill required in the particular occupation;
   (e) whether the employer or the workman supplies the * * * tools * * * ;
   (f) the length of time for which the person is employed * * * .

   Applying these factors to the facts of this case, it is clear AAA did not control the manner and means of Five Star's work. The Agreement specifically stated Five Star was an independent contractor. Five Star purchased its own trucks and any other necessary equipment. AAA assigned jobs to Five Star and Five Star completed the work without any further supervision by AAA. Five Star chose the employees to send on towing calls and the trucks and equipment the employees would use.

   Five Star was also in business for itself and performed auto repair services for principals and customers other than AAA. Five Star hired and fired its own employees * * * .
* * * *

   Plaintiff also argues Five Star should be considered to be controlled by AAA because "providing towing and other roadside assistance is arguably the focus of the regular business of AAA." * * * [But] AAA is an automobile club that provides a wide variety of services to its members. It contracts with numerous service providers, such as gas stations, motels and other businesses, to provide these services. Thus, AAA is not solely in the towing business.

   * * * AAA had used Five Star to provide towing services for approximately eight years and there is nothing in the record to demonstrate it lacked the skill needed to provide these services.

Decision and Remedy *A state intermediate appellate court affirmed the lower court's ruling. AAA could not be held liable for the actions of Five Star, its independent contractor, because "AAA did not control the manner and means of Five Star's work."*

Critical Thinking

• **Legal** *Five Star's contract with AAA required Five Star to be available to provide service for AAA members. Does this support Coker's argument that Five Star was AAA's employee? Why or why not?*

Is It Fair to Classify Uber and Lyft Drivers as Independent Contractors?

The transportation-for-hire world has changed dramatically since Uber, Lyft, and other transportation-sharing companies came onto the scene. Uber started in San Francisco in 2009. Today, its services are available in one form or another in about 60 countries and more than 300 cities worldwide. Its main competitor, Lyft, was launched in 2012 and operates in more than 200 U.S. cities. The growth in transportation sharing has not been without its set-backs, though. Most of them involve laws that have prohibited Uber and Lyft from operating in certain cities, as well as lawsuits by drivers claiming that they were misclassified.

Classification of Workers

Workers in the United States generally fall into two categories: employees and independent contractors. Employment laws, including minimum wage and anti-discrimination statutes, cover employees. Such laws do not cover most independent contractors. Enter the digital age of on-demand workers who obtain job assignments via apps.

Workers for Lyft, Uber, and similar companies choose when and where they will perform their duties. They do not choose how much they will be paid, however. For them, employment is a take-it-or-leave-it proposition. They electronically accept the platform terms of the apps, or they obtain no work assignments.

Some critics of this contractual system argue that there should be a new category of workers with "dependent-contractor" status who receive some of the protections traditionally given only to employees. Certain aspects of current labor law would be attached to the relationships between dependent contractors and their employers.

Worker Misclassification Lawsuits

A number of former or current Uber and Lyft drivers have pursued legal remedies to change their job classification and to obtain better benefits. In California, for instance, two federal court judges allowed separate lawsuits to go before juries on the question of whether on-demand drivers should be considered employees rather than independent contractors.[a]

In a similar case, rather than go to court, Lyft settled a worker misclassification lawsuit for $12.25 million. The suit, which was settled in 2016, had been brought in 2013. The settlement did not achieve a reclassification of Lyft drivers as employees. Basically, Lyft agreed to change its terms of service to conform to California's independent contractor status regulations. For instance, the company can no longer deactivate drivers' accounts without reason and without warning the drivers. Drivers have to be given a fair hearing first. Even though the lawsuit and the agreement were California based, the new terms of service will apply to all Lyft's drivers nationwide.

Competitors Sue Uber

In many cities, competitors, especially taxi drivers, have sued Uber. These lawsuits have involved claims of unfair competition, lack of minimum wages, and unsafe vehicles. A taxi driver sued Uber in northern California, for instance, but a federal district court ruled in favor of Uber's request for summary judgment.[b]

Another suit was brought in Pennsylvania. In this one, Checker Cab of Philadelphia claimed that Uber was violating Pennsylvania's unfair competition law. Checker Cab sought a preliminary injunction to prevent Uber from taking away its customers. The federal district court refused to grant an injunction, however, because Checker Cab failed to show irreparable harm. That decision was upheld on appeal.[c]

Critical Thinking *What choices do disgruntled Uber and Lyft drivers have?*

a. *Cotter v. Lyft, Inc.*, 60 F.Supp.3d 1067 (N.D.Cal. 2015); *O'Connor v. Uber Technologies, Inc., et al.*, Case No. C-13-3826 EMC (N.D.Cal. 2015).
b. *Rosen v. Uber Technologies, Inc.*, __ F.Supp.3d __, 2016 WL 704078 (N.D.Cal. 2016).
c. *Checker Cab of Philadelphia v. Uber Technologies, Inc.*, __ Fed.Appx. __, 2016 WL 929310 (3d Cir. 2016).

Criteria Used by the IRS The Internal Revenue Service (IRS) has established its own criteria for determining whether a worker is an independent contractor or an employee. The most important factor is the degree of control the business exercises over the worker.

The IRS tends to closely scrutinize a firm's classification of its workers because, as mentioned, employers can avoid certain tax liabilities by hiring independent contractors instead of employees. Even when a firm has classified a worker as an independent contractor, the IRS may decide that the worker is actually an employee. If the IRS decides that an employee is misclassified, the employer will be responsible for paying any applicable Social Security, withholding, and unemployment taxes due for that employee.

Employee Status and "Works for Hire" Ordinarily, a person who creates a copyrighted work is the owner of it—unless it is a "work for hire." Under the Copyright Act, any copyrighted work created by an employee within the scope of her or his employment at the request of the employer is a "work for hire." The employer owns the copyright to the work.

In contrast, when an employer hires an independent contractor—such as a freelance artist, writer, or computer programmer—the independent contractor normally owns the copyright. An exception is made if the parties agree in writing that the work is a "work for hire" and the work falls into one of nine specific categories. The nine categories include audiovisual works, collective works (such as magazines), motion pictures, textbooks, tests, and translations.

■ **CASE IN POINT 32.1** As a freelance contractor, Brian Cooley created two sculptures of dinosaur eggs for the National Geographic Society for use in connection with an article in its magazine, *National Geographic*. Cooley spent hundreds of hours researching, designing, and constructing the sculptures. National Geographic hired Louis Psihoyos to photograph Cooley's sculptures for the article. Cooley and Psihoyos had separate contracts with National Geographic in which each transferred the copyrights in their works to National Geographic for a limited time.

The rights to the works were returned to the artists at different times after publication. Psihoyos then began licensing his photographs of Cooley's sculptures to third parties in return for royalties. He digitized the photographs and licensed them to various online stock photography companies, and they appeared in several books published by Penguin Group. Cooley sued Psihoyos for copyright infringement.

Psihoyos argued that he owned the photos and could license them however he saw fit, but a federal district court disagreed. The court found that Psihoyos did not have an unrestricted right to use and license the photos. When Psihoyos reproduced an image of a Cooley sculpture, he reproduced the sculpture, which infringed on Cooley's copyright. Therefore, the court granted a summary judgment to Cooley.[2] ■

---

2. *Cooley v. Penguin Group (USA), Inc.*, 31 F.Supp.3d 599 (S.D.N.Y. 2014).

32–2 Formation of the Agency Relationship

Agency relationships normally are consensual. They come about by voluntary consent and agreement between the parties. Normally, the agreement need not be in writing, and consideration is not required.

A person must have contractual capacity to be a principal.[3] The idea is that those who cannot legally enter into contracts directly should not be allowed to do so indirectly through an agent. Any person can be an agent, however, regardless of whether he or she has the capacity to contract (including minors).

An agency relationship can be created for any legal purpose. An agency relationship created for a purpose that is illegal or contrary to public policy is unenforceable. ■ **EXAMPLE 32.2** Archer (as principal) contracts with Burke (as agent) to sell illegal narcotics. The agency relationship is unenforceable because selling illegal narcotics is a felony and is contrary to public policy. If Burke sells the narcotics and keeps the profits, Archer cannot sue to enforce the agency agreement. ■

An agency relationship can arise in four ways: by agreement of the parties, by ratification, by estoppel, and by operation of law.

32–2a Agency by Agreement

Most agency relationships are based on an express or implied agreement that the agent will act for the principal and that the principal agrees to have the agent so act. An agency agreement can take the form of an express written contract or be created by an oral agreement. ■ **EXAMPLE 32.3** Reese asks Grace, a gardener, to contract with others for the care of his lawn on a regular basis. If Grace agrees, an agency relationship exists between Reese and Grace for the lawn care. ■

An agency agreement can also be implied by conduct. ■ **CASE IN POINT 32.4** Gilbert Bishop was admitted to a nursing home, Laurel Creek Health Care Center, suffering from various physical ailments. He was not able to use his hands well enough to write but was otherwise mentally competent. Bishop's sister offered to sign the admission papers for him, but it was Laurel Creek's

---

3. Note that some states allow a minor to be a principal. When a minor is permitted to be a principal, any resulting contracts will be voidable by the minor principal but *not* by the adult third party.

policy to have the patient's spouse sign the forms if the patient could not.

Bishop's sister then brought his wife, Anna, to the hospital to sign the paperwork, which included a mandatory arbitration clause. Later, when the family filed a lawsuit against Laurel Creek, the nursing home sought to enforce the arbitration clause. Ultimately, a Kentucky appellate court held that Bishop was bound by the contract and the arbitration clause his wife had signed. Bishop's conduct had indicated that he was giving his wife authority to act as his agent in signing the admission papers.[4] ∎

32–2b Agency by Ratification

On occasion, a person who is in fact not an agent (or who is an agent acting outside the scope of her or his authority) makes a contract on behalf of another (a principal). If the principal approves or affirms that contract by word or by action, an agency relationship is created by *ratification.* Ratification involves a question of intent, and intent can be expressed by either words or conduct.

32–2c Agency by Estoppel

Sometimes, a principal causes a third person to believe that another person is the principal's agent, and the third person acts to his or her detriment in reasonable reliance on that belief. When this occurs, the principal is "estopped to deny" (prevented from denying) the agency relationship. The principal's actions have created the *appearance* of an agency that does not in fact exist, creating an agency by estoppel.

The Third Party's Reliance Must Be Reasonable
The third person must prove that he or she *reasonably* believed that an agency relationship existed.[5] Facts and circumstances must show that an ordinary, prudent person familiar with business practice and custom would have been justified in concluding that the agent had authority.

Created by the Principal's Conduct
Note that the acts or declarations of a purported *agent* in and of themselves do not create an agency by estoppel. Rather, it is the deeds or statements of the *principal* that create an agency by estoppel. ∎ **CASE IN POINT 32.5** Francis Azur

---

4. *Laurel Creek Health Care Center v. Bishop,* 2010 WL 985299 (Ky.App. 2010).
5. These concepts also apply when a person who is, in fact, an agent undertakes an action that is beyond the scope of her or his authority.

was president and chief executive officer of ATM Corporation of America. Michelle Vanek was Azur's personal assistant. Among other duties, she reviewed his credit-card statements. For seven years, Vanek took unauthorized cash advances from Azur's credit-card account with Chase Bank. The charges appeared on at least sixty-five monthly statements.

When Azur discovered Vanek's fraud, he fired her and closed the account. He filed a suit against Chase, arguing that the bank should not have allowed Vanek to take cash advances. The court concluded that Azur (the principal) had given the bank reason to believe that Vanek (the agent) had authority. Therefore, Azur was estopped (prevented) from denying Vanek's authority.[6] ∎

32–2d Agency by Operation of Law

The courts may find an agency relationship in the absence of a formal agreement in other situations as well. This may occur in family relationships, such as when one spouse purchases certain basic necessaries and charges them to the other spouse's account. The courts often rule that a spouse is liable for payment for the necessaries because of either a social policy or a legal duty to supply necessaries to family members.

Agency by operation of law may also occur in emergency situations. If an agent cannot contact the principal and failure to act would cause the principal substantial loss, the agent may take steps beyond the scope of her or his authority. For instance, a railroad engineer may contract on behalf of his or her employer for medical care for an injured motorist hit by the train.

Concept Summary 32.1 reviews the various ways in which agency relationships are formed.

32–3 Duties of Agents and Principals

Once the principal-agent relationship has been created, both parties have duties that govern their conduct. As discussed previously, the principal-agent relationship is *fiduciary*—based on trust. In a fiduciary relationship, each party owes the other the duty to act with the utmost good faith. In this section, we examine the various duties of agents and principals.

---

6. *Azur v. Chase Bank, USA, N.A.,* 601 F.3d 212 (3d Cir. 2010).

Concept Summary 32.1

Formation of the Agency Relationship

By Agreement	• The agency relationship is formed through express consent (oral or written) or implied by conduct.
By Ratification	• The principal either by act or by agreement ratifies the conduct of a person who is not, in fact, an agent.
By Estoppel	• The principal causes a third person to believe that another person is the principal's agent, and the third person acts to his or her detriment in reasonable reliance on that belief.
By Operation of Law	• The agency relationship is based on a social or legal duty—such as the need to support family members. Or, it is formed in emergency situations when the agent is unable to contact the principal and failure to act outside the scope of the agent's authority would cause the principal substantial loss.

32–3a Agent's Duties to the Principal

Generally, the agent owes the principal five duties—performance, notification, loyalty, obedience, and accounting (see Exhibit 32–1).

Performance An implied condition in every agency contract is the agent's agreement to use reasonable diligence and skill in performing the work. When an agent fails to perform his or her duties, liability for breach of contract may result.

Standard of Care. The degree of skill or care required of an agent is usually that expected of a reasonable person under similar circumstances. Generally, this is interpreted to mean ordinary care. If an agent has represented herself or himself as possessing special skills, however, the agent is expected to exercise the degree of skill claimed. Failure to do so constitutes a breach of the agent's duty.

Gratuitous Agents. Not all agency relationships are based on contract. In some situations, an agent acts gratuitously—that is, without payment. A gratuitous agent cannot be liable for breach of contract because there is no contract. He or she is subject only to tort liability. Once a gratuitous agent has begun to act in an agency capacity, he or she has the duty to continue to perform in that

capacity. A gratuitous agent must perform in an acceptable manner and is subject to the same standards of care and duty to perform as other agents.

■ **EXAMPLE 32.6** Bower's friend Alcott is a real estate broker. Alcott offers to sell Bower's vacation home at no charge. If Alcott never attempts to sell the home, Bower has no legal cause of action to force her to do so. If Alcott does attempt to sell the home to Friedman, but then performs so negligently that the sale falls through, Bower can sue Alcott for negligence. ■

Notification An agent is required to notify the principal of all matters that come to her or his attention concerning the subject matter of the agency. This is the *duty of notification,* or the duty to inform.

■ **EXAMPLE 32.7** Perez, an artist, is about to negotiate a contract to sell a series of paintings to Barber's Art Gallery for $25,000. Perez's agent learns that Barber is insolvent and will be unable to pay for the paintings. The agent has a duty to inform Perez of Barber's insolvency because it is relevant to the subject matter of the agency, which is the sale of Perez's paintings. ■

Generally, the law assumes that the principal is aware of any information acquired by the agent that is relevant to the agency—regardless of whether the agent actually passes on this information to the principal. It is a basic tenet of agency law that notice to the agent is notice to the principal.

EXHIBIT 32–1 Duties of the Agent

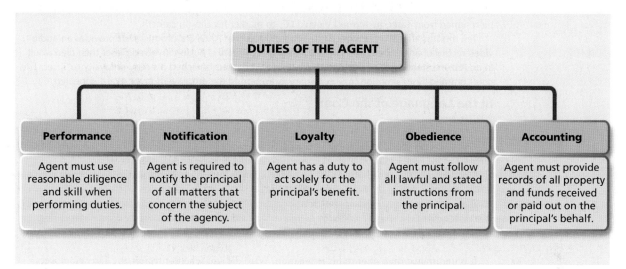

DUTIES OF THE AGENT

Performance	Notification	Loyalty	Obedience	Accounting
Agent must use reasonable diligence and skill when performing duties.	Agent is required to notify the principal of all matters that concern the subject of the agency.	Agent has a duty to act solely for the principal's benefit.	Agent must follow all lawful and stated instructions from the principal.	Agent must provide records of all property and funds received or paid out on the principal's behalf.

Loyalty Loyalty is one of the most fundamental duties in a fiduciary relationship. Basically, the agent has the duty to act *solely for the benefit of his or her principal* and not in the interest of the agent or a third party. For instance, an agent cannot represent two principals in the same transaction unless both know of the dual capacity and consent to it.

Maintain Confidentiality. The duty of loyalty also means that any information or knowledge acquired through the agency relationship is confidential. It is a breach of loyalty to disclose such information either during the agency relationship or after its termination. Typical examples of confidential information are trade secrets and customer lists compiled by the principal.

Actions Must Benefit the Principal. The agent's loyalty must be undivided. The agent's actions must be strictly for the benefit of the principal and must not result in any secret profit for the agent.

■ **EXAMPLE 32.8** Don contracts with Leo, a real estate agent, to negotiate the purchase of an office building. Leo discovers that the property owner will sell the building only as a package deal with another parcel. So Leo buys the two properties, intending to resell the building to Don. Leo has breached his fiduciary duty. As a real estate agent, Leo has a duty to communicate all offers to Don, his principal, and not to purchase the property secretly and then resell it to Don. Leo is required to act in Don's best interests and can become the purchaser in this situation only with Don's knowledge and approval. ■

In the following case, an employer alleged that a former employee had breached his duty of loyalty by planning a competing business while still working for the employer.

Spotlight on Taser International

Case 32.2 Taser International, Inc. v. Ward

Court of Appeals of Arizona, Division 1, 224 Ariz. 389, 231 P.3d 921 (2010).

Background and Facts Taser International, Inc., develops and makes electronic control devices, commonly called stun guns, as well as accessories for electronic control devices, including a personal video and audio recording device called the TASER CAM.

Steve Ward was Taser's vice president of marketing when he began to explore the possibility of developing and marketing devices of his own design, including a clip-on camera. Ward talked to

Case 32.2 Continues

Case 32.2 Continued

patent attorneys and a product development company and completed most of a business plan. After he resigned from Taser, he formed Vievu, LLC, to market his clip-on camera.

Ten months after Ward resigned, Taser announced the AXON, a product that provides an audio-video record of an incident from the visual perspective of the person involved. Taser then filed a suit in an Arizona state court against Ward, alleging that he had breached his duty of loyalty to Taser. The court granted Taser's motion for a summary judgment in the employer's favor. Ward appealed.

In the Language of the Court

PORTLEY, Judge.

* * * *

* * * An agent is under the duty to act with entire good faith and loyalty for the furtherance of the interests of his principal in all matters concerning or affecting the subject of his agency.

One aspect of this broad principle is that an employee is precluded from actively competing with his or her employer during the period of employment.

Although an employee may not compete prior to termination, the employee may take action during employment, not otherwise wrongful, to prepare for competition following termination of the agency relationship. Preparation cannot take the form of acts in direct competition with the employer's business. [Emphasis added.]

* * * *

It is undisputed that, prior to his resignation, Ward did not solicit or recruit any Taser employees, distributors, customers, or vendors; he did not buy, sell, or incorporate any business; he did not acquire office space or other general business services; he did not contact or enter into any agreements with suppliers or manufacturers for his proposed clip-on camera; and he did not sell any products. However, Ward did begin developing a business plan, counseled with several attorneys, explored and abandoned the concept of an eyeglass-mounted camera device, and engaged, to some extent, in the exploration and development of a clip-on camera device.

Ward argues that his pre-termination activities did not constitute active competition but were merely lawful preparation for a future business venture. Taser contends, however, that "this case is * * * about developing a rival design during employment, knowing full well TASER has sold such a device and continues to develop a second-generation product."

* * * *

* * * Assuming Taser was engaged in the research and development of a recording device during Ward's employment, assuming Ward knew or should have known of those efforts, and assuming Taser's device would compete with Ward's concept, substantial design and development efforts by Ward during his employment would constitute direct competition with the business activities of Taser and would violate his duty of loyalty. In the context of a business which engages in research, design, development, manufacture, and marketing of products, we cannot limit "competition" to just actual sales of competing products.

Decision and Remedy *A state intermediate appellate court agreed with Taser that an employee may not actively compete with his employer before his employment is terminated. But the parties disputed the extent of Ward's pre-termination efforts, creating a genuine issue of material fact that could not be resolved on a motion for summary judgment. The appellate court thus reversed the lower court's decision in Taser's favor and remanded the case for further proceedings.*

Critical Thinking

- **Legal Environment** *Did Ward breach any duties owed to his employer in addition to his alleged breach of the duty of loyalty? Discuss.*
- **What If the Facts Were Different?** *Suppose that Ward's pre-termination activities focused on a product that was not designed to compete with Taser's products. Would these efforts have breached the duty of loyalty? Why or why not?*

Obedience When acting on behalf of the principal, an agent has a duty to follow all lawful and clearly stated instructions of the principal. Any deviation from such instructions is a violation of this duty.

During emergency situations, however, when the principal cannot be consulted, the agent may deviate from the instructions without violating this duty. Whenever instructions are not clearly stated, the agent can fulfill the duty of obedience by acting in good faith and in a manner reasonable under the circumstances.

Accounting   Unless the agent and principal agree otherwise, the agent must keep and make available to the principal an account of all property and funds received and paid out on the principal's behalf. This includes gifts from third parties in connection with the agency. ■ **EXAMPLE 32.9**   Marla is a salesperson for Roadway Supplies. Knife River Construction gives Marla a new tablet as a gift for prompt deliveries of Roadway's paving materials. The tablet belongs to Roadway. ■

The agent has a duty to maintain a separate account for the principal's funds and must not intermingle these funds with the agent's personal funds. If a licensed professional (such as an attorney) violates this duty, he or she may be subject to disciplinary action by the licensing authority (such as the state bar association). Of course, the professional will also be liable to his or her client (the principal) for failure to account.

32–3b Principal's Duties to the Agent

The principal also has certain duties to the agent (as shown in Exhibit 32–2). These duties relate to compensation, reimbursement and indemnification, cooperation, and safe working conditions.

Compensation   In general, when a principal requests certain services from an agent, the agent reasonably expects payment. For instance, when an accountant or an attorney is asked to act as an agent, an agreement to compensate the agent for this service is implied. The principal therefore has a duty to pay the agent for services rendered.

Unless the agency relationship is gratuitous and the agent does not act in exchange for payment, the principal must pay the agreed-on value for the agent's services. If no amount has been expressly agreed on, then the principal owes the agent the customary compensation for such services. The principal also has a duty to pay that compensation in a timely manner.

■ **CASE IN POINT 32.10**   Keith Miller worked as a sales representative for Paul M. Wolff Company, a subcontractor specializing in concrete-finishing services. Sales representatives at Wolff are paid a 15 percent commission on projects that meet a 35 percent gross profit threshold. The commission is paid after the projects are completed. When Miller resigned, he asked for commissions on fourteen projects for which he had secured contracts but which had not yet been completed. Wolff refused, so Miller sued.

The court found that "an agent is entitled to receive commissions on sales that result from the agent's efforts," even after the employment or agency relationship ends. Miller had met the gross profit threshold on ten of the unfinished projects, and therefore, he was entitled to more than $21,000 in commissions.[7] ■

Reimbursement and Indemnification   Whenever an agent disburses funds at the request of the principal, the principal has a duty to reimburse the agent. The principal must also reimburse the agent (even a gratuitous

---

7. *Miller v. Paul M. Wolff Co.*, 178 Wash.App. 957, 316 P.3d 1113 (2014).

EXHIBIT 32–2 Duties of the Principal

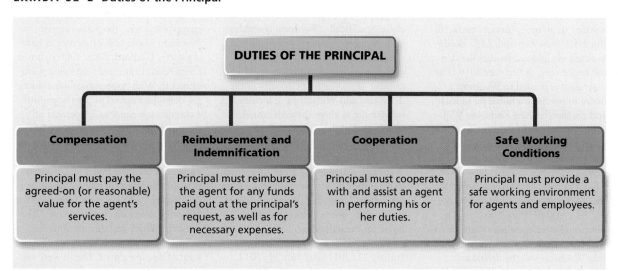

agent) for any necessary expenses incurred in the course of the reasonable performance of her or his agency duties. Agents cannot recover for expenses incurred as a result of their own misconduct or negligence, though.

Subject to the terms of the agency agreement, the principal has the duty to *indemnify* (compensate) an agent for liabilities incurred because of authorized and lawful acts and transactions. For instance, if the agent, on the principal's behalf, forms a contract with a third party, and the principal fails to perform the contract, the third party may sue the agent for damages. In this situation, the principal is obligated to compensate the agent for any costs incurred by the agent as a result of the principal's failure to perform the contract.

Additionally, the principal must indemnify the agent for the value of benefits that the agent confers on the principal. The amount of indemnification usually is specified in the agency contract. If it is not, the courts will look to the nature of the business and the type of loss to determine the amount. Note that this rule applies to acts by gratuitous agents as well.

Cooperation A principal has a duty to cooperate with the agent and to assist the agent in performing his or her duties. The principal must do nothing to prevent that performance.

For instance, when a principal grants an agent an exclusive territory, the principal creates an **exclusive agency,** in which the principal cannot compete with the agent or appoint or allow another agent to compete. If the principal does so, he or she violates the exclusive agency and is exposed to liability for the agent's lost profits.

■ **EXAMPLE 32.11** Penny (the principal) creates an exclusive agency by granting Andrew (the agent) a territory within which only Andrew may sell Penny's organic skin care products. If Penny starts to sell the products herself within Andrew's territory—or permits another agent to do so—Penny has failed to cooperate with the agent. Because she has violated the exclusive agency, Penny can be held liable for Andrew's lost sales or profits. ■

In the following case, a pair of potential homebuyers entered into an agreement with a realtor to act as the buyers' exclusive agent in locating and purchasing property. Later, the buyers executed an exclusive agency agreement with a different realtor. Neither agent knew about the other until the buyers found a home that they liked and bought it.

Case Analysis 32.3

NRT New England, LLC v. Jones
Appellate Court of Connecticut, 162 Conn.App. 840, 134 A.3d 632 (2016).

In the Language of the Court
HARPER, J. [Judge]
* * * *

The defendant [Christopher Jones] met Andrea Woolston, a licensed realtor working as an independent contractor [for NRT New England, LLC, doing business as Coldwell Banker Residential Brokerage], in October 2010. The defendant expressed to Woolston a desire to purchase a home for himself and his then fiancée, Katherine Wiltshire. One of the first things Woolston asked the defendant was whether he was represented by another agent. The defendant responded that he was not. After a number of conversations about the defendant's needs and wishes, the parties executed an exclusive right to represent buyer agreement (agreement), which established, among other things, that Woolston was the defendant's

exclusive agent for finding, negotiating, and purchasing property. Over the next several months, Woolston devoted a substantial amount of time searching for properties for the defendant to purchase. Specifically, Woolston researched available properties at six town halls in the communities in which the defendant was interested. She showcased a number of properties personally to the defendant and Wiltshire and introduced many more to them through e-mail. Woolston and the defendant had at least twenty appointments where they viewed multiple properties. Additionally, Woolston visited many properties alone to determine if they were suitable for the defendant. Altogether, Woolston spent hundreds of hours seeking a suitable home for the defendant.

The agreement was in effect from January 11, 2011 until July 11, 2011,

and set forth the geographical area that the defendant was interested in and the rate of compensation for the plaintiff's services. With respect to geographical area, the parties agreed that Woolston would seek properties in Killingworth, Guilford, Essex, Old Saybrook, Deep River, Lyme, and Old Lyme [Connecticut]. With respect to compensation, the defendant agreed to pay the plaintiff a commission equal to 2.5 percent of the purchase price of the property "if the [buyer] or any person or entity acting on the [buyer's] behalf purchases, options, exchanges, leases or trades any property, through the efforts of anyone, including the [buyer]." The agreement imposed the following duties on the defendant: "The [buyer] will not deal directly with any other broker, agent or licensee during the term of this agreement. The [buyer] will

Case 32.3 Continued

notify other brokers, agents or licensees at first contact that the [buyer] is being exclusively represented by [NRT]. The [buyer] will disclose to [NRT] any past and/or current contacts for any real property or with any other real estate broker or agent."

On May 10, 2011, the defendant informed Woolston via e-mail that he and Wiltshire purchased property at 300 Vineyard Point Road in Guilford for $1,375,000. The defendant learned of this property on May 4, 2011, from Mary Jane Burt, a realtor with H. Pearce Real Estate (H. Pearce), who previously had represented Wiltshire with the sale of her house in Hamden [Connecticut]. Woolston subsequently confronted the defendant and eventually learned that he and Wiltshire previously had executed an exclusive right to represent buyer agreement with Burt and H. Pearce. This agreement was in effect from August 1, 2010, until August 1, 2011, and contained a provision designating Burt as the exclusive agent for the defendant and Wiltshire. Thus, at the time the defendant purchased the property in Guilford, he was under contract for exclusive agency with both Woolston and Burt. The defendant never told Woolston or Burt that he had two agreements in effect at the same time. Woolston notified her superiors of what had transpired.

* * * [NRT] filed a * * * complaint [in a Connecticut state court] against the defendant [for] breach of contract * * * . After a trial * * * , the court * * * found that the plaintiff had proven * * * breach of contract * * * and damages. * * * The court awarded the plaintiff $34,375 in damages [which represented 2.5 percent of the purchase price for the Vineyard Point property] plus attorney's fees and costs. This appeal followed.

* * * *

The defendant * * * claims that the agreement was unenforceable. Specifically, he argues that the court improperly * * * found that it was inequitable to deny the plaintiff recovery.

* * * *

There is ample evidence in the record to support the court's conclusion that denying the plaintiff relief would be inequitable. Woolston testified, and the defendant himself conceded, that she rendered a significant amount of services to the defendant over several months. Specifically, Woolston researched properties at town halls for availability and encumbrances, contacted property owners, arranged personal visits, prepared and presented literature to the defendant on available properties, and attended appointments with the defendant and Wiltshire. Woolston spent hundreds of hours working for the defendant in total.

The defendant, on the other hand, accepted Woolston's services while under contract with another agent in violation of the agreement. Indeed, the defendant acknowledged that he was untruthful with Woolston at the beginning of their relationship when he told her that he was not represented by another agent. In fact, he was scheduling appointments and viewing properties with both Woolston and Burt at approximately the same time in May 2011. For example, the defendant e-mailed Woolston on May 2, 2011, thanking her for showing him a property. Approximately one week later, the defendant e-mailed Woolston to inform her that he viewed 300 Vineyard Point Road with Burt and had "put in an all cash bid that has been accepted."

The defendant nevertheless argues that it would not be inequitable to deny recovery to the plaintiff because Woolston performed no services in connection with his purchase of 300 Vineyard Point Road. We are not persuaded. *The defendant agreed to pay a commission "equal to 2.5% of the purchase price if the [buyer] or any person or entity acting on the [buyer's] behalf purchases * * * any property, through the efforts of anyone, including the [buyer], where an agreement to purchase the property was entered into during the term of this agreement."* However unjust this result may seem to the defendant in hindsight, we cannot say it is inequitable because it is precisely what he agreed to. [Emphasis added.]

* * * *

The judgment is affirmed.

Legal Reasoning Questions

1. What is the advantage to a principal of an exclusive agency agreement? What was the advantage to Jones of his agreement with Woolston? Discuss.

2. Why, in addition to damages, was the plaintiff awarded attorneys' fees and costs?

3. Jones's agreement with Woolston provided that on the purchase of the property, NRT "will, whenever feasible, seek compensation from the seller or the seller's agent." The court determined that it was not feasible. Why would it not be reasonable in this situation to ask the seller of the property to pay part of Woolston's commission?

Safe Working Conditions The common law requires the principal to provide safe working premises, equipment, and conditions for all agents and employees. The principal has a duty to inspect working areas and to warn agents and employees about any unsafe situations. When the agent is an employee, the employer's liability is frequently covered by state workers' compensation insurance. In addition, federal and state statutes often require the employer to meet certain safety standards.

32-4 Rights and Remedies of Agents and Principals

In general, for every duty of the principal, the agent has a corresponding right, and vice versa. When one party to the agency relationship violates his or her duty to the other party, the nonbreaching party is entitled to a remedy. The remedies available arise out of contract and tort law. These remedies include monetary damages, termination of the agency relationship, an injunction, and required accountings.

32-4a Agent's Rights and Remedies against the Principal

The agent has the right to be compensated, to be reimbursed and indemnified, and to have a safe working environment. An agent also has the right to perform agency duties without interference by the principal.

Tort and Contract Remedies   Remedies of the agent for breach of duty by the principal follow normal contract and tort remedies. ■ **EXAMPLE 32.12** Aaron Hart, a builder who has just constructed a new house, contracts with a real estate agent, Fran Boller, to sell the house. The contract calls for the agent to have an exclusive ninety-day listing and to receive 6 percent of the selling price when the home is sold. Boller holds several open houses and shows the home to a number of potential buyers.

One month before the ninety-day listing terminates, Hart agrees to sell the house to another buyer—not one to whom Boller has shown the house—after the ninety-day listing expires. Hart and the buyer agree that Hart will reduce the price of the house by 3 percent because he will sell it directly and thus will not have to pay Boller's commission. If Boller learns of Hart's actions, she can terminate the agency relationship and sue Hart for the 6 percent commission she should have earned on the sale of the house. ■

Demand for an Accounting   An agent can also withhold further performance and demand that the principal give an accounting. For instance, a sales agent may demand an accounting if the agent and principal disagree on the amount of commissions the agent should have received for sales made during a specific period.

No Right to Specific Performance   When the principal-agent relationship is not contractual, the agent has no right to specific performance. An agent can recover for past services and future damages but cannot force the principal to allow him or her to continue acting as an agent.

32-4b Principal's Rights and Remedies against the Agent

In general, a principal has contract remedies for an agent's breach of fiduciary duties. The principal also has tort remedies if the agent engages in misrepresentation, negligence, deceit, libel, slander, or trespass. In addition, any breach of a fiduciary duty by an agent may justify the principal's termination of the agency. The main actions available to the principal are constructive trust, avoidance, and indemnification.

Constructive Trust   Anything that an agent obtains by virtue of the employment or agency relationship belongs to the principal. An agent commits a breach of fiduciary duty if he or she secretly retains benefits or profits that, by right, belong to the principal. Therefore, the agent holds such property in a *constructive trust* (an equitable trust imposed for reasons of fairness) for the principal. ■ **EXAMPLE 32.13** Lee, a purchasing agent for Metcalf, receives cash rebates from a customer. If Lee keeps the rebates for himself, he violates his fiduciary duty to his principal, Metcalf. On finding out about the cash rebates, Metcalf can sue Lee and recover them. ■

Avoidance   When an agent breaches the agency agreement or agency duties under a contract, the principal has a right to avoid any contract entered into with the agent. This right of avoidance is at the election of the principal.

Indemnification   In certain situations, when a principal is sued by a third party for an agent's negligent conduct, the principal can sue the agent for indemnification—that is, for an equal amount of damages. The same holds true if the agent violates the principal's instructions.
■ **EXAMPLE 32.14** Parker (the principal) owns a used-car lot where Moore (the agent) works as a salesperson. Parker tells Moore to make no warranties for the used cars. Moore is eager to make a sale to Walters, a customer, and adds a 50,000-mile warranty for the car's engine. Parker may be liable to Walters for engine failure, but if Walters sues Parker, Parker normally can then sue Moore for indemnification for violating his instructions. ■

Sometimes, though, it is difficult to distinguish between instructions of the principal that limit an agent's authority and those that are merely advice. ■ **EXAMPLE 32.15** Gutierrez (the principal) owns an office supply company, and Logan (the agent) is the manager. Gutierrez tells Logan, "Don't purchase any more inventory this month." Gutierrez goes on vacation. A large order comes in from a local business, and the inventory on hand is insufficient to meet it. What is Logan to do? In this situation, Logan probably has the inherent authority to purchase more inventory despite Gutierrez's command. It is unlikely that Logan would be required to indemnify Gutierrez in the event that the local business subsequently canceled the order. ■

Reviewing: Agency Formation and Duties

James Blatt hired Marilyn Scott to sell insurance for the Massachusetts Mutual Life Insurance Company. Their contract stated, "Nothing in this contract shall be construed as creating the relationship of employer and employee." The contract was terminable at will by either party. Scott financed her own office and staff, was paid according to performance, had no taxes withheld from her checks, and could legally sell products of Massachusetts Mutual's competitors. Blatt learned that Scott was simultaneously selling insurance for Perpetual Life Insurance Corporation, one of Massachusetts Mutual's fiercest competitors. Blatt therefore withheld client contact information from Scott. Scott complained to Blatt that he was inhibiting her ability to sell insurance for Massachusetts Mutual. Blatt subsequently terminated their contract. Scott filed a suit in a New York state court against Blatt and Massachusetts Mutual. Scott claimed that she had lost sales for Massachusetts Mutual—and commissions—as a result of Blatt's withholding contact information from her. Using the information presented in the chapter, answer the following questions.

1. Who is the principal and who is the agent in this scenario? By which method was an agency relationship formed between Scott and Blatt?
2. What facts would the court consider most important in determining whether Scott was an employee or an independent contractor?
3. How would the court most likely rule on Scott's employee status? Why?
4. Which of the four duties that Blatt owed Scott in their agency relationship has probably been breached?

Debate This . . .   *All works created by independent contractors should be considered works for hire under copyright law.*

Terms and Concepts

agency 606   fiduciary 606   independent contractor 607
exclusive agency 616

Issue Spotters

1. Winona contracted with XtremeCast, a broadcast media firm, to cohost an Internet-streaming sports program. Winona and XtremeCast signed a new contract for each episode. In each contract, Winona agreed to work a certain number of days for a certain salary. During each broadcast, Winona was free to improvise her performance. She had no other obligation to work for XtremeCast. Was Winona an independent contractor? (See *Agency Relationships*.)

2. Dimka Corporation wants to build a new mall on a specific tract of land. Dimka contracts with Nadine to buy the property. There is a substantial difference between the price that Dimka is willing to pay and the price at which the owner is willing to sell. When Nadine learns of this, she wants to buy the land and sell it to Dimka herself. Can she do this? Discuss. (See *Duties of Agents and Principals*.)

• **Check your answers to the Issue Spotters against the answers provided in Appendix D at the end of this text.**

Business Scenarios

32–1. Agency Formation. Paul Gett is a well-known, wealthy financial expert living in the city of Torris. Adam Wade, Gett's friend, tells Timothy Brown that he is Gett's agent for the purchase of rare coins. Wade even shows Brown a local newspaper clipping mentioning Gett's interest in coin collecting. Brown, knowing of Wade's friendship with Gett, contracts with Wade to sell a rare coin valued at $25,000 to Gett. Wade takes the coin and disappears with it. On the payment due date, Brown seeks to collect from Gett, claiming that Wade's agency made Gett liable. Gett does not deny that Wade was a friend, but he claims that Wade was never his agent. Discuss fully whether an agency was in existence at the time the contract for the rare coin was made. (See *Formation of the Agency Relationship*.)

32–2. Duty of Loyalty. Peter hires Alice as an agent to sell a piece of property he owns. The price is to be at least $30,000. Alice discovers that the fair market value of Peter's property is actually at least $45,000 and could be higher because a shopping mall is going to be built nearby. Alice forms a real estate partnership with her cousin Carl. Then she prepares for Peter's signature a contract for the sale of the property to Carl for $32,000. Peter signs the contract. Just before closing and passage of title, Peter learns about the shopping mall and the increased fair market value of his property. Peter refuses to deed the property to Carl. Carl claims that Alice, as Peter's agent, solicited a price above that agreed on when the agency was created and that the contract is therefore binding and enforceable. Discuss fully whether Peter is bound to this contract. (See *Duties of Agents and Principals*.)

32–3. Employee versus Independent Contractor. Stephen Hemmerling was a driver for the Happy Cab Co. Hemmerling paid certain fixed expenses and followed various rules relating to the use of the cab, the hours that could be worked, and the solicitation of fares, among other things. Rates were set by the state. Happy Cab did not withhold taxes from Hemmerling's pay. While driving the cab, Hemmerling was injured in an accident and filed a claim for workers' compensation benefits in a state court. Such benefits are not available to independent contractors. On what basis might the court hold that Hemmerling was an employee? Explain. (See *Agency Relationships*.)

Business Case Problems

32–4. Agency by Ratification. Wesley Hall, an independent contractor managing property for Acree Investments, Ltd., lost control of a fire he had set to clear ten acres of Acree land. The runaway fire burned seventy-eight acres of Earl Barrs's property. Russell Acree, one of the owners of Acree Investments, had previously owned the ten acres, but he had put it into the company and was no longer the principal owner. Hall had worked for Russell Acree in the past and had told the state forestry department that he was burning the land for Acree. Barrs sued Russell Acree for the acts of his agent, Hall. In his suit, Barrs noted that Hall had been an employee of Russell Acree, Hall had talked about burning the land "for Acree," and Russell Acree had apologized to Barrs for the fire. Barrs also pointed out that Acree Investments had not been identified as the principal property owner until Barrs filed his lawsuit. Barrs argued that those facts were sufficient to create an agency by ratification to impose liability on Russell Acree. Was Barrs's agency by ratification claim valid? Why or why not? [*Barrs v. Acree,* 691 S.E.2d 575 (Ga.App. 2010)] (See *Formation of the Agency Relationship*.)

32–5. Employment Relationships. William Moore owned Moore Enterprises, a wholesale tire business. William's son, Jonathan, worked as a Moore Enterprises employee while he was in high school. Later, Jonathan started his own business, called Morecedes Tire. Morecedes regrooved tires and sold them to businesses, including Moore Enterprises. A decade after Jonathan started Morecedes, William offered him work with Moore Enterprises. On the first day, William told Jonathan to load certain tires on a trailer but did not tell him how to do it. Was Jonathan an independent contractor? Discuss. [*Moore v. Moore,* 152 Idaho 245, 269 P.3d 802 (2011)] (See *Agency Relationships*.)

32–6. Agent's Duties to Principal. William and Maxine Miller were shareholders of Claimsco International, Inc. They filed a suit against the other shareholders, Michael Harris and Kenneth Hoxie, and the accountant who worked for all of them—John Verchota. Among other things, the Millers alleged that Verchota had breached a duty that he owed them. They claimed that at Harris's instruction, Verchota had taken various actions that placed them at a disadvantage to the other shareholders. Verchota had allegedly adjusted Claimsco's books to maximize the Millers' financial liabilities, for instance, and had falsely reported distributions of income to them without actually transferring that income. Which duty are the Millers referring to? If the allegations can be proved, did Verchota breach this duty? Explain. [*Miller v. Harris,* 2013 IL App (2d) 120512, 985 N.E.2d 671 (2 Dist. 2013)] (See *Duties of Agents and Principals*.)

32–7. Business Case Problem with Sample Answer— Determining Employee Status. Nelson Ovalles worked as a cable installer for Cox Rhode Island Telecom, LLC, under an agreement with a third party, M&M Communications, Inc. The agreement stated that no employer-employee relationship existed between Cox and M&M's technicians, including Ovalles. Ovalles was required to designate his affiliation with Cox on his work van, clothing, and identification badge. Cox had minimal contact with him, however, and had limited power to control how he performed his duties. Cox supplied cable wire and similar items, but the equipment was delivered to M&M, not to Ovalles. On a workday, while Ovalles was fulfilling a work order, his van rear-ended a car driven by Barbara Cayer. Is Cox liable to Cayer? Explain. [*Cayer v. Cox*

Rhode Island Telecom, LLC, 85 A.3d 1140 (R.I. 2014)] (See *Agency Relationships.*)

• **For a sample answer to Problem 32–7, go to Appendix E at the end of this text.**

32–8. Agency Relationships. Standard Oil of Connecticut, Inc., sells home heating, cooling, and security systems. Standard schedules installation and service appointments with its customers and then contracts with installers and technicians to do the work. The company requires an installer or technician to complete a project by a certain time but to otherwise "exercise independent judgment and control in the execution of any work." The installers and technicians are licensed and certified by the state. Standard does not train them, provide instruction manuals, supervise them at customers' homes, or inspect their work. The installers and technicians use their own equipment and tools, and they can choose which days they work. Standard pays a set rate per project. According to criteria used by the courts, are these installers and technicians independent contractors or employees? Why? [*Standard Oil of Connecticut, Inc. v. Administrator, Unemployment Compensation Act,* 320 Conn. 611, __ A.3d __ (2016)] (See *Agency Relationships.*)

32–9. A Question of Ethics—Agency Formation and Duties. *Western Fire Truck, Inc., contracted with Emergency One, Inc. (EO), to be its exclusive dealer in Colorado and Wyoming through December 2003. James Costello, a Western salesperson, was authorized to order EO vehicles for his customers. Without informing Western, Costello e-mailed EO about Western's difficulties in obtaining cash to fund its operations. He asked about the viability of Western's contract and his possible employment with EO. On EO's request, and in disregard of Western's instructions, Costello sent some payments for EO vehicles directly to EO. In addition, Costello, with EO's help, sent a competing bid to a potential Western customer. EO's representative e-mailed Costello, "You have my permission to kick [Western's] ass." In April 2002, EO terminated its contract with Western. At about the same time, a Western manager discovered Costello's e-mails saying that he was dissatisfied with the company and fired Costello. Western filed a suit in a Colorado state court, alleging that Costello had breached his duty as an agent and that EO had aided and abetted the breach.* [*Western Fire Truck, Inc. v. Emergency One, Inc.,* 134 P.3d 570 (Colo.App. 2006)] (See *Formation of the Agency Relationship.*)

(a) Was there an agency relationship between Western and Costello? Western required monthly reports from its sales staff, but Costello did not report regularly. Does this indicate that Costello was not Western's agent? In determining whether an agency relationship exists, is the right to control or the fact of control more important? Explain.

(b) Did Costello owe Western a duty? If so, what was the duty? Did Costello breach it? If so, how?

(c) A Colorado state statute allows a court to award punitive damages in "circumstances of fraud, malice, or willful and wanton conduct." Did any of these circumstances exist in this case? Should punitive damages be assessed against either defendant? Why or why not?

Legal Reasoning Group Activity

32–10. Agent's Duties to Principal. John Warren wanted to buy a condominium in California. Hildegard Merrill was the agent for the seller. Because Warren's credit rating was poor, Merrill told him he needed a co-borrower to obtain a mortgage at a reasonable rate. Merrill said that her daughter Charmaine would "go on title" until the loan and sale were complete if Warren would pay her $10,000. Merrill also offered to defer her commission on the sale as a loan to Warren so that he could make a 20 percent down payment on the property. He agreed to both plans.

Merrill secured the mortgage in Charmaine's name alone by misrepresenting her daughter's address, business, and income. To close the sale, Merrill had Warren remove his name from the title to the property. In October, Warren moved into the condominium, repaid Merrill the amount of her deferred commission, and began paying the mortgage. Within a few months, Merrill had Warren evicted. Warren subsequently filed a suit against Merrill and Charmaine. (See *Duties of Agents and Principals.*)

(a) The first group will determine who among these parties was in an agency relationship.

(b) The second group will discuss the basic duty that an agent owes a principal and decide whether that duty was breached here.

CHAPTER 33

Agency Liability and Termination

We have already discussed how agency relationships are formed and the duties of the principal and agent in that relationship. This chapter deals with another important aspect of agency law—the liability of principals and agents to third parties.

We look first at the liability of principals for contracts formed by agents with third parties. Generally, the liability of the principal will depend on whether the agent was authorized to form the contract. The second part of the chapter deals with an agent's liability to third parties in contract and tort. It also discusses the principal's liability to third parties because of an agent's torts. The chapter concludes with a discussion of how agency relationships are terminated.

33–1 Scope of Agent's Authority

The liability of a principal to third parties with whom an agent contracts depends on whether the agent had the authority to enter into legally binding contracts on the principal's behalf. An agent's authority can be either *actual* (express or implied) or *apparent*. If an agent contracts outside the scope of his or her authority, the principal may still become liable by ratifying the contract.

33–1a Express Authority

Express authority is authority declared in clear, direct, and definite terms. Express authority can be given orally or in writing.

The Equal Dignity Rule In most states, the **equal dignity rule** requires that if the contract being executed is or must be in writing, then the agent's authority must also be in writing. (Recall that a writing includes an electronic record.) Failure to comply with the equal dignity rule can make a contract voidable *at the option of the principal.* The law regards the contract at that point as a mere offer. If the principal decides to accept the offer, the acceptance must be ratified, or affirmed, in writing.

■ **EXAMPLE 33.1** Paloma (the principal) orally asks Austin (the agent) to sell a ranch that Paloma owns. Austin finds a buyer and signs a sales contract on behalf of Paloma to sell the ranch. Because a contract for an interest in realty must be in writing, the equal dignity rule applies. The buyer cannot enforce the contract unless Paloma subsequently ratifies Austin's agency status *in a writing.* Once the sales contract is ratified, either party can enforce rights under the contract. ■

Modern business practice allows several exceptions to the equal dignity rule:

1. An executive officer of a corporation normally can conduct *ordinary* business transactions without obtaining written authority from the corporation.
2. When the agent acts in the presence of the principal, the rule does not apply.
3. When the agent's act of signing is merely a formality, then the agent does not need written authority to sign. ■ **EXAMPLE 33.2** Sandra Healy (the principal) negotiates a contract but is called out of town the day it is to be signed. If Healy orally authorizes Derek Santini to sign, the oral authorization is sufficient. ■

Power of Attorney Giving an agent a **power of attorney** confers express authority.[1] The power of attorney is a written document and is usually notarized. (A document is notarized when a **notary public**—a person authorized to attest to the authenticity of signatures—signs, dates, and imprints the document with her or his seal of authority.) Most states have statutory provisions for creating a power of attorney.

---

1. An agent who holds a power of attorney is called an *attorney-in-fact* for the principal. The holder does not have to be an attorney-at-law (and often is not).

A power of attorney can be *special* (permitting the agent to perform specified acts only), or it can be *general* (permitting the agent to transact all business for the principal). Because a general power of attorney (see Exhibit 33–1) grants extensive authority to the agent, it should be used with great caution and usually only in exceptional circumstances. Ordinarily, a power of attorney terminates on the incapacity or death of the person giving the power.[2]

---

[2]. A *durable* power of attorney, however, continues to be effective despite the principal's incapacity or death. An elderly person, for instance, might grant a durable power of attorney to provide for the handling of property and investments or specific health-care needs should he or she become incompetent.

EXHIBIT 33–1 A Sample General Power of Attorney

GENERAL POWER OF ATTORNEY

Know All Men by These Presents:
That I, _____ , hereinafter referred to as PRINCIPAL, in the County of _____
State of _____ , do(es) appoint _____ as my true and lawful attorney.

In principal's name, and for principal's use and benefit, said attorney is authorized hereby;

(1) To demand, sue for, collect, and receive all money, debts, accounts, legacies, bequests, interest, dividends, annuities, and demands as are now or shall hereafter become due, payable, or belonging to principal, and take all lawful means, for the recovery thereof and to compromise the same and give discharges for the same;

(2) To buy and sell land, make contracts of every kind relative to land, any interest therein or the possession thereof, and to take possession and exercise control over the use thereof;

(3) To buy, sell, mortgage, hypothecate, assign, transfer, and in any manner deal with goods, wares and merchandise, choses in action, certificates or shares of capital stock, and other property in possession or in action, and to make, do, and transact all and every kind of business of whatever nature;

(4) To execute, acknowledge, and deliver contracts of sale, escrow instructions, deeds, leases including leases for minerals and hydrocarbon substances and assignments of leases, covenants, agreements and assignments of agreements, mortgages and assignments of mortgages, conveyances in trust, to secure indebtedness or other obligations, and assign the beneficial interest thereunder, subordinations of liens or encumbrances, bills of lading, receipts, evidences of debt, releases, bonds, notes, bills, requests to reconvey deeds of trust, partial or full judgments, satisfactions of mortgages, and other debts, and other written instruments of whatever kind and nature, all upon such terms and conditions as said attorney shall approve.

GIVING AND GRANTING to said attorney full power and authority to do all and every act and thing whatsoever requisite and necessary to be done relative to any of the foregoing as fully to all intents and purposes as principal might or could do if personally present.

All that said attorney shall lawfully do or cause to be done under the authority of this power of attorney is expressly approved.

Dated: _____   /s/_____

State of_____ ⎫
County of_____ ⎬ SS.
On _____ , before me, the undersigned, a Notary Public in and for said
State, personally appeared _____

known to me to be the person _____ whose name _____ subscribed
to the within instrument and acknowledged that _____ _____ executed the same.
Witness my hand and official seal.   (Seal) _____
                                              Notary Public in and for said State.

33–1b Implied Authority

An agent has the **implied authority** to do what is reasonably necessary to carry out express authority and accomplish the objectives of the agency. Authority can also be implied by custom or inferred from the position the agent occupies.

■ **EXAMPLE 33.3**   Archer is employed by Packard Grocery to manage one of its stores. Packard has not expressly stated that Archer has authority to contract with third persons. Nevertheless, authority to manage a business implies authority to do what is reasonably required (as is customary or can be inferred from a manager's position) to operate the business. This includes forming contracts to hire employees, buying merchandise and equipment, and advertising the products sold in the store. ■

Note, however, that an agent's implied authority cannot contradict his or her express authority. Thus, if a principal has limited an agent's express authority, then the fact that the agent customarily would have such authority is irrelevant. ■ **EXAMPLE 33.4**   Juanita Alvarez is the owner of six Baja Tacos restaurants. Alvarez (the principal) strictly forbids the managers (agents) of her taco shops from entering into contracts to hire additional workers. Therefore, the fact that managers customarily would have authority to hire employees is immaterial. ■

33–1c Apparent Authority

Actual authority (express or implied) arises from what the principal makes clear *to the agent.* Apparent authority, in contrast, arises from what the principal causes a third party to believe. An agent has **apparent authority** when the principal, by either word or action, causes a *third party* reasonably to believe that the agent has authority to act, even though the agent has no express or implied authority.

A Pattern of Conduct   Apparent authority usually comes into existence through a principal's pattern of conduct over time. ■ **EXAMPLE 33.5**   Bailey is a traveling salesperson. She solicits orders for goods but does not carry them with her. She normally would not have the implied authority to collect payments from customers on behalf of the principal. Suppose that she does accept payments from Corgley Enterprises, however, and submits them to the principal's accounting department for processing. If the principal does nothing to stop Bailey from continuing this practice, a pattern develops over time, and the principal confers apparent authority on Bailey to accept payments from Corgley. ■

At issue in the following *Spotlight Case* was whether the manager of a horse breeding operation had the authority to bind the farm's owner in a contract guaranteeing breeding rights.

Spotlight on Apparent Authority of Managers

Case 33.1 Lundberg v. Church Farm, Inc.
Court of Appeals of Illinois, 502 N.E.2d 806, 151 Ill.App.3d (1986).

Background and Facts   Gilbert Church owned a horse breeding farm managed by Herb Bagley. Advertisements for the breeding rights to one of Church Farm's stallions, Imperial Guard, directed all inquiries to "Herb Bagley, Manager." Vern and Gail Lundberg bred Thoroughbred horses. The Lundbergs contacted Bagley and executed a preprinted contract giving them breeding rights to Imperial Guard "at Imperial Guard's location," subject to approval of the mares by Church. Bagley handwrote a statement on the contract that guaranteed the Lundbergs "six live foals in the first two years." He then signed it "Gilbert G. Church by H. Bagley."

The Lundbergs bred four mares, which resulted in one live foal. Church then moved Imperial Guard from Illinois to Oklahoma. The Lundbergs sued Church for breaching the contract by moving the horse. Church claimed that Bagley was not authorized to sign contracts for Church or to change or add terms, but only to present preprinted contracts to potential buyers. Church testified that although Bagley was his farm manager and the contact person for breeding rights, Bagley had never before modified the preprinted forms or signed Church's name on them. The jury found in favor of the Lundbergs and awarded $147,000 in damages. Church appealed.

In the Language of the Court
Justice *UNVERZAGT* delivered the opinion of the court.
  * * * *

  * * * *Defendant contends that plaintiffs have failed to establish that Bagley had apparent authority to negotiate and sign the Lundberg contract for Church Farm* * * *.

Case 33.1 Continued

*The party asserting an agency has the burden of proving its existence * * * but may do so by inference and circumstantial evidence. * * * Additionally, an agent may bind his principal by acts which the principal has not given him actual authority to perform, but which he appears authorized to perform. * * * An agent's apparent authority is that authority which "the principal knowingly permits the agent to assume or which he holds his agent out as possessing. It is the authority that a reasonably prudent man, exercising diligence and discretion, in view of the principal's conduct, would naturally suppose the agent to possess." [Emphasis added.]*

Plaintiffs produced evidence at trial that Gil Church approved the Imperial Guard advertisement listing Herb Bagley as Church Farm's manager, and directing all inquiries to him. Church also permitted Bagley to live on the farm and to handle its daily operations. Bagley was the only person available to visitors to the farm. Bagley answered Church Farm's phone calls, and there was a preprinted signature line for him on the breeding rights package.

The conclusion is inescapable that Gil Church affirmatively placed Bagley in a managerial position giving him complete control of Church Farm and its dealings with the public. We believe that this is just the sort of "holding out" of an agent by a principal that justifies a third person's reliance on the agent's authority.

We cannot accept defendant's contention that the Lundbergs were affirmatively obligated to seek out Church to ascertain the actual extent of Bagley's authority. Where an agent has apparent authority to act, the principal will be liable in spite of any undisclosed limitations the principal has placed on that authority.

Decision and Remedy *The state appellate court affirmed the lower court's judgment in favor of the Lundbergs for $147,000. Because Church allowed circumstances to lead the Lundbergs to believe Bagley had the authority to negotiate and sign the contract, Church was bound by Bagley's actions.*

Critical Thinking
- **Legal Environment** *The court held that Church had allowed the Lundbergs to believe that Bagley was his agent. What steps could Church have taken to protect himself against a finding of apparent authority?*
- **Ethical** *Does a principal have an ethical responsibility to inform an unaware third party that an apparent agent does not in fact have the authority to act on the principal's behalf? Explain.*

Apparent Authority and Estoppel A court can apply the doctrine of agency by estoppel when a principal has given a third party reason to believe that an agent has authority to act. If the third party honestly relies on the principal's representations to his or her detriment, the principal may be *estopped* (prevented) from denying that the agent had authority.

33–1d Emergency Powers

When an unforeseen emergency demands action by the agent to protect or preserve the property and rights of the principal, but the agent is unable to communicate with the principal, the agent has emergency power. ■ **EXAMPLE 33.6** Rob Fulsom is an engineer for Pacific Drilling Company. While Fulsom is acting within the scope of his employment, he is severely injured in an accident on an oil rig many miles from home. Acosta, the rig supervisor, directs Thompson, a physician, to give medical aid to Fulsom and to charge Pacific for the medical services.

Acosta, an agent, has no express or implied authority to bind the principal, Pacific Drilling, for Thompson's medical services. Because of the emergency situation, however, the law recognizes Acosta as having authority to act appropriately under the circumstances. ■

33–1e Ratification

Ratification occurs when the principal affirms, or accepts responsibility for, an agent's *unauthorized* act. When ratification occurs, the principal is bound to the agent's act, and the act is treated as if it had been authorized by the principal *from the outset*. Ratification can be either express or implied.

If the principal does not ratify the contract, the principal is not bound, and the third party's agreement with the agent is viewed as merely an unaccepted offer. Because the third party's agreement is an unaccepted offer, the third party can revoke it at any time, without liability, before the principal ratifies the contract. The agent, however, may be liable to the third party for misrepresenting her or his authority.

The requirements for ratification can be summarized as follows:

1. The agent must have acted on behalf of an identified principal who subsequently ratifies the action.
2. The principal must know all of the material facts involved in the transaction. If a principal ratifies a contract without knowing all of the facts, the principal can rescind (cancel) the contract.[3]
3. The principal must affirm the agent's act in its entirety.
4. The principal must have the legal capacity to authorize the transaction at the time the agent engages in the act and at the time the principal ratifies. The third party must also have the legal capacity to engage in the transaction.
5. The principal's affirmation (ratification) must occur before the third party withdraws from the transaction.

6. The principal must observe the same formalities when ratifying the act as would have been required to authorize it initially.

Concept Summary 33.1 summarizes the rules concerning an agent's authority to bind the principal and a third party.

33–2 Liability for Contracts

Liability for contracts formed by an agent depends on how the principal is classified and on whether the actions of the agent were authorized or unauthorized. Principals are classified as disclosed, partially disclosed, or undisclosed.[4]

1. A **disclosed principal** is a principal whose identity is known by the third party at the time the contract is made by the agent.

---

3. Note that if the third party has changed position in reliance on the apparent contract, the principal can still rescind the contract but must reimburse the third party for any costs.

4. *Restatement (Third) of Agency*, Section 1.04(2).

Concept Summary 33.1
Authority of an Agent to Bind the Principal and a Third Party

Express Authority	**Definition:** Authority expressly given by the principal to the agent.	**Effect:** Principal and third party are bound in contract.
Implied Authority	**Definition:** Authority implied (1) by custom, (2) from the position in which the principal has placed the agent, or (3) because such authority is necessary if the agent is to carry out expressly authorized duties and responsibilities.	**Effect:** Principal and third party are bound in contract.
Apparent Authority	**Definition:** Authority created when the conduct of the principal leads a third party to believe that the principal's agent has authority.	**Effect:** Principal and third party are bound in contract.
Unauthorized Acts	**Definition:** Acts committed by an agent that are outside the scope of his or her express, implied, or apparent authority.	**Effect:** Principal and third party are not bound in contract—*unless* the principal ratifies prior to the third party's withdrawal.

2. A **partially disclosed principal** is a principal whose identity is not known by the third party. Nevertheless, the third party knows that the agent is or *may* be acting for a principal at the time the contract is made. ■ **EXAMPLE 33.7** Eileen has contracted with a real estate agent to sell certain property. She wishes to keep her identity a secret, but the agent makes it clear to potential buyers of the property that he is acting in an agency capacity. In this situation, Eileen is a partially disclosed principal. ■

3. An **undisclosed principal** is a principal whose identity is totally unknown by the third party. In addition, the third party has no knowledge that the agent is acting in an agency capacity at the time the contract is made.

33–2a Authorized Acts

If an agent acts within the scope of her or his authority, normally the principal is obligated to perform the contract regardless of whether the principal was disclosed, partially disclosed, or undisclosed. Whether the *agent may also be held liable* under the contract, however, depends on the disclosed, partially disclosed, or undisclosed status of the principal.

Disclosed or Partially Disclosed Principal A disclosed or partially disclosed principal is liable to a third party for a contract made by the agent. If the principal is disclosed, the agent has no contractual liability for the nonperformance of the principal or the third party. If the principal is partially disclosed, in most states the agent is also treated as a party to the contract. Thus, the third party can hold the agent liable for contractual nonperformance.[5]

■ **CASE IN POINT 33.8** Stonhard, Inc., makes epoxy and urethane flooring and installs it in industrial and commercial buildings. Marvin Sussman contracted with Stonhard to install flooring at a Blue Ridge Farms food-manufacturing facility in Brooklyn, New York. Sussman did not disclose that he was acting as an agent for the facility's owner, Blue Ridge Foods, LLC, at the time of the contract.

When Stonhard was not paid for the flooring it installed, it filed a suit against the facility, its owner, and Sussman to recover damages for breach of contract. The lower court dismissed the complaint against Sussman personally, but on appeal a reviewing court reversed that decision. The contract had been signed by Sussman "of Blue Ridge Farms." That evidence indicated that

Sussman was acting as an agent for a partially disclosed principal, in that the agency relationship was known, but not the principal's identity. "As an agent for an undisclosed [or partially disclosed] principal, Sussman became personally liable under the contract."[6] ■

Undisclosed Principal When neither the fact of an agency relationship nor the identity of the principal is disclosed, the undisclosed principal is bound to perform just as if the principal had been fully disclosed at the time the contract was made.

■ **CASE IN POINT 33.9** Bobby Williams bought a car at Sherman Henderson's auto repair business in Louisiana for $3,000. Henderson (the agent) negotiated and made the sale for the car's owner, Joe Pike (the principal), whose name was not disclosed. Williams drove the car to Memphis, Tennessee, where his daughter was a student. Three days after the sale, the car's engine caught fire. Williams extinguished the blaze and contacted Henderson. The next day, the vehicle was stolen from a parking lot outside Williams's daughter's apartment.

Williams filed a suit in a Louisiana state court against Pike (the principal) and Henderson (the agent). The court awarded Williams $2,000, plus the costs of the suit, adding that if Williams had returned the car, it would have awarded him the entire price. A state appellate court affirmed. Both Pike and Henderson—the undisclosed principal and his agent—were liable to Williams.[7] ■

Indemnification. When a principal's identity is undisclosed and the agent is forced to pay the third party, the agent is entitled to be *indemnified* (compensated) by the principal. The principal had a duty to perform, even though his or her identity was undisclosed,[8] and failure to do so will make the principal ultimately liable.

Performance. Once the undisclosed principal's identity is revealed, the third party generally can elect to hold either the principal or the agent liable on the contract. Conversely, the undisclosed principal can require the third party to fulfill the contract, *unless* one of the following is true:

1. The undisclosed principal was expressly excluded as a party in the written contract.

---

5. *Restatement (Third) of Agency,* Section 6.02.

6. *Stonhard, Inc. v. Blue Ridge Farms, LLC,* 114 A.D.3d 757, 980 N.Y.S.2d 507 (2 Dept. 2014).
7. *Williams v. Pike,* 58 So.3d 525 (La.App. 2 Cir. 2011).
8. If the agent is a gratuitous agent, and the principal accepts the benefits of the agent's contract with a third party, then the principal will be liable to the agent on the theory of quasi contract.

2. The contract is a negotiable instrument signed by the agent with no indication of signing in a representative capacity.[9]

3. The performance of the agent is personal to the contract, thus allowing the third party to refuse the principal's performance.

33–2b Unauthorized Acts

If an agent has no authority but nevertheless contracts with a third party, the *principal* cannot be held liable on the contract. It does not matter whether the principal was disclosed, partially disclosed, or undisclosed. The *agent* is liable.

■ **EXAMPLE 33.10** Chu signs a contract for the purchase of a truck, purportedly acting as an agent under authority granted by Navarro. In fact, Navarro has not given Chu any such authority. Navarro refuses to pay for the truck, claiming that Chu had no authority to purchase it. The seller of the truck is entitled to hold Chu liable for payment. ■

Implied Warranty If the principal is disclosed or partially disclosed, and the agent contracts with a third party without authorization, the agent is liable to the third party. The agent's liability here is based on his or her breach of the *implied warranty of authority*, not on the breach of the contract itself.[10] An agent impliedly warrants that he or she has the authority to enter a contract on behalf of the principal.

■ **EXAMPLE 33.11** Pinnell, a reclusive artist, hires Auber to solicit offers for particular paintings from various galleries, but does not authorize her to enter into sales agreements. Olaf, a gallery owner, offers to buy two of Pinnell's paintings for an upcoming show. If Auber draws up a sales contract with Olaf, she impliedly warrants that she has the authority to enter into sales contracts on behalf of Pinnell. If Pinnell does not agree to ratify Auber's sales contract, Olaf cannot hold Pinnell liable, but he can hold Auber liable for breaching the implied warranty of authority. ■

Third Party's Knowledge Note that if the third party knows at the time the contract is made that the agent does not have authority, then the agent is not liable. Similarly, if the agent expresses to the third party *uncertainty* as to

the extent of her or his authority, the agent is not personally liable.

33–2c Actions by E-Agents

Although in the past standard agency principles applied only to *human* agents, today these same agency principles also apply to e-agents. An electronic agent, or **e-agent,** is a semiautonomous software program that is capable of executing specific tasks, such as searching through many databases and retrieving relevant information for the user.

The Uniform Electronic Transactions Act (UETA), which was discussed previously, sets forth provisions relating to the principal's liability for the actions of e-agents. According to Section 15 of the UETA, e-agents can enter into binding agreements on behalf of their principals—at least, in those states that have adopted the act. Thus, if consumers place an order over the Internet, and the company (principal) takes the order via an e-agent, the company cannot later claim that it did not receive the order.

The UETA also stipulates that if an e-agent does not provide an opportunity to prevent errors at the time of the transaction, the other party to the transaction can avoid the transaction. Therefore, if an e-agent fails to provide an on-screen confirmation of a purchase or sale, the other party can avoid the effect of any errors. ■ **EXAMPLE 33.12** Bigelow wants to purchase three copies of three different books (a total of nine items). The e-agent mistakenly records an order for thirty-three of a single book and does not provide an on-screen verification of the order. If thirty-three books are then sent to Bigelow, he can avoid the contract to purchase them. ■

33–3 Liability for Torts and Crimes

Obviously, any person, including an agent, is liable for his or her own torts and crimes. Whether a principal can also be held liable for an agent's torts and crimes depends on several factors, which we examine here. In some situations, a principal may be held liable not only for the torts of an agent but also for torts committed by an independent contractor.

33–3a Principal's Tortious Conduct

A principal who acts through an agent may be liable for harm resulting from the principal's own negligence or recklessness. Thus, a principal may be liable if he or she gives improper instructions, authorizes the use of improper materials or tools, or establishes improper rules that result in the agent's committing a tort.

---

9. Under the Uniform Commercial Code (UCC), only the agent is liable if the instrument neither names the principal nor shows that the agent signed in a representative capacity [UCC 3-402(b)(2)].

10. The agent is not liable on the contract because the agent was never intended personally to be a party to the contract.

■ **EXAMPLE 33.13** Parker knows that Audrey's driver's license has been suspended but nevertheless tells her to use the company truck to deliver some equipment to a customer. If someone is injured as a result, Parker will be liable for his own negligence in instructing Audrey to drive without a valid license. ■

33–3b Principal's Authorization of Agent's Tortious Conduct

Similarly, a principal who authorizes an agent to commit a tort may be liable to persons or property injured thereby, because the act is considered to be the principal's. ■ **EXAMPLE 33.14** Pedro directs his agent, Andy, to cut the corn on specific acreage, which neither of them has the right to do. The harvest is therefore a trespass (a tort), and Pedro is liable to the owner of the corn. ■

Note that an agent acting at the principal's direction can be liable, along with the principal, for committing the tortious act even if the agent was unaware that the act was wrong. Assume in *Example 33.14* that Andy, the agent, did not know that Pedro lacked the right to harvest the corn. Andy can nonetheless be held liable to the owner of the field for damages, along with Pedro, the principal.

33–3c Liability for Agent's Misrepresentation

A principal is exposed to tort liability whenever a third person sustains a loss due to the agent's misrepresentation. The principal's liability depends on whether the agent was actually or apparently authorized to make representations and whether the representations were made within the scope of the agency. The principal is always directly responsible for an agent's misrepresentation made within the scope of the agent's authority.

■ **EXAMPLE 33.15** Ainsley is a demonstrator for Pavlovich's products. Pavlovich sends Ainsley to a home show to demonstrate the products and to answer questions from consumers. Pavlovich has given Ainsley authority to make statements about the products. If Ainsley makes only true representations, all is fine. But if he makes false claims, Pavlovich will be liable for any injuries or damages sustained by third parties in reliance on Ainsley's false representations. ■

Apparent Implied Authority When a principal has placed an agent in a position of apparent authority—making it possible for the agent to defraud a third party—the principal may also be liable for the agent's fraudulent acts. For instance, partners in a partnership generally have the apparent implied authority to act as agents of the firm. Thus, if one of the partners commits a tort or a crime, the partnership itself—and often the other partners personally—can be held liable for the loss.

■ **EXAMPLE 33.16** Saulheim & Company is a securities brokerage firm that operates as a partnership and provides various financial services. The firm's managing partner, Dan Saulheim, is caught embezzling funds that clients have turned over to the firm for investment. After he is convicted, other partners in the firm claim that they are not liable for losses resulting from his illegal activities. In this situation, other partners may be liable if a court finds that Saulheim had apparent implied authority to act in the ordinary course of the partnership's business. Thus, the firm, as principal, is liable, and the personal assets of the individual partners, as agents, can be used to pay the firm's liability. ■

Innocent Misrepresentation Tort liability based on fraud requires proof that a material misstatement was made knowingly and with the intent to deceive. An agent's *innocent* misstatements in a contract or warranty transaction can also provide grounds for the third party's rescission of the contract and the award of damages. Justice dictates that when a principal knows that an agent is not accurately advised of facts but does not correct either the agent's or the third party's impressions, the principal is responsible. The point is that the principal is always directly responsible for an agent's misrepresentation made within the scope of authority.

33–3d Liability for Agent's Negligence

An agent is liable for his or her own torts. A principal may also be liable for harm an agent causes to a third party under the doctrine of ***respondeat superior***,[11] a Latin term meaning "let the master respond." Under the doctrine of *respondeat superior*, the principal-employer is liable for any harm caused to a third party by an agent-employee in the course or scope of employment. The doctrine imposes **vicarious liability,** or indirect liability, because the principal-employer is being held liable for torts committed by an agent-employee.

When an agent commits a negligent act in such a situation, *both* the agent and the principal are liable. ■ **EXAMPLE 33.17** Aegis hires SDI to provide landscaping services for its property. An herbicide sprayed by

---

11. Pronounced ree-*spahn*-dee-uht soo-*peer*-ee-your. The doctrine of *respondeat superior* applies not only to employer-employee relationships but also to other principal-agent relationships in which the principal has the right of control over the agent.

SDI employee David Hoggatt enters the Aegis building through the air-conditioning system and caused Catherine Warner, an Aegis employee, to suffer a heart attack. If Warner sues, both SDI (principal) and Hoggatt (agent) can be held liable for negligence. ■

The Doctrine of *Respondeat Superior*

The doctrine of *respondeat superior* is similar to the theory of strict liability in that liability is imposed regardless of fault. At early common law, a servant (employee) was viewed as the master's (employer's) property. The master was deemed to have absolute control over the servant's acts and was held strictly liable for them, no matter how carefully the master supervised the servant. Although employers today are not masters of their employees, control is still a central concept to liability. This chapter's *Global Insight* feature discusses whether nations that follow Islamic law recognize the doctrine of *respondeat superior.*

Underlying Rationale. The rationale for the doctrine of *respondeat superior* is based on the social duty that requires every person to manage his or her affairs so as not to injure another. This duty applies even when a person acts through an agent (controls the conduct of another).

Public Policy. Generally, public policy requires that an injured person be afforded effective relief, and a business enterprise is usually better able to provide that relief than is an individual employee. Employers normally carry liability insurance to cover any damages awarded as a result of such lawsuits. They are also able to spread the cost of risk over the entire business enterprise.

Application Today. The courts have applied the doctrine of *respondeat superior* for nearly two centuries. It continues to have practical implications in all situations involving principal-agent (employer-employee) relationships. Today, the small-town store with one clerk and the multinational corporation with thousands of employees are equally subject to the doctrine.

Determining the Scope of Employment

The key to determining whether a principal may be liable for the torts of an agent under the doctrine of *respondeat superior* is whether the torts are committed within the scope of the agency. Courts may consider the following factors in determining whether a particular act occurred within the course and scope of employment:

1. Whether the employee's act was authorized by the employer.
2. The time, place, and purpose of the act.
3. Whether the act was one commonly performed by employees on behalf of their employers.
4. The extent to which the employer's interest was advanced by the act.
5. The extent to which the private interests of the employee were involved.

GLOBAL INSIGHT — Islamic Law and *Respondeat Superior*

The doctrine of *respondeat superior* is well established in the legal systems of the United States and most Western countries. As you have already read, under this doctrine, employers can be held liable for the acts of their employees. The doctrine of *respondeat superior* is not universal, however. Most Middle Eastern countries, for example, do not follow this doctrine.

Codification of Islamic Law

Islamic law, as codified in the *sharia*, holds to a strict belief that responsibility for human actions lies with the individual and cannot be vicariously (indirectly) extended to others. This belief and other concepts of Islamic law are based on the writings of Muhammad, the seventh-century prophet whose revelations form the basis of the Islamic religion and, by extension, the

sharia. Muhammad's prophecies are documented in the Koran (Qur'an), which is the principal source of the *sharia.*

An Exception

Islamic law does allow for an employer to be responsible for an employee's actions when the actions result from a direct order given by the employer to the employee. This principle also applies to contractual obligations. Note that the master is responsible *only* if direct orders were given. Otherwise stated, unless an employee is obeying a direct order of the employer, liability for the employee's actions does not extend to the employer.

Critical Thinking *How would U.S. society be affected if employers could not be held vicariously liable for their employees' torts?*

6. Whether the employer furnished the means or instrumentality (such as a truck or a machine) by which an injury was inflicted.

7. Whether the employer had reason to know that the employee would perform the act in question and whether the employee had done it before.

8. Whether the act involved the commission of a serious crime.

In the following case, the court had to determine whether or not a dump truck operator was the employee of a concrete services contractor.

Asphalt & Concrete Services, Inc. v. Perry

Court of Special Appeals of Maryland, 221 Md.App. 235, 108 A.3d 558 (2015).

Background and Facts Asphalt & Concrete Services, Inc. (ACS), was working on a play pad at St. John Regional Catholic School in Frederick, Maryland. ACS project manager Blake Wood contacted William Johnson at Higher Power Trucking, LLC, to arrange for a dump truck to haul material from a quarry to the job site. One day, while Johnson was driving the dump truck between the job site and the quarry, the truck struck and injured Moran Perry, who was crossing an intersection.

To recover for his injuries, Perry filed a lawsuit in a Maryland state court against ACS. Perry alleged that Johnson's negligence in operating the dump truck was the proximate cause of his injuries and that Johnson was ACS's employee. ACS, however, claimed that Johnson was an independent contractor. A jury agreed with Perry and awarded him $529,500 in damages. The court issued a judgment in Perry's favor, and ACS appealed.

In the Language of the Court

GRAEFF, J. [Judge]

* * * *

* * * Pursuant to the doctrine of *respondeat superior,* an employer may be found liable for torts committed by its employee while acting in the scope of employment. ACS does not dispute this well-established rule, but it argues that the evidence showed that Mr. Johnson was not its employee.

* * * Maryland courts have traditionally considered five criteria in determining whether or not an employer/employee relationship exists between two parties. *These criteria, developed from the common law standard for determining the master/servant relationship, include (1) the power to select and hire the employee, (2) the payment of wages, (3) the power to discharge, (4) the power to control the employee's conduct, and (5) whether the work is part of the regular business of the employer.* [Emphasis added.]

Of the five factors, the factor of control stands out as the most important. * * * Whether the employer has the right to control and direct the employee in the performance of the work and in the manner in which the work is to be done is the decisive, or controlling, test.

* * * *

Here, * * * the evidence indicated as follows: (1) ACS called Mr. Johnson directly to reserve his trucking services; (2) Mr. Wood spoke only to Mr. Johnson when calling Higher Power; (3) ACS directed Mr. Johnson to go to the * * * quarry to pick up materials for the play pad project and gave him the time to be there for the pick-up; (4) Mr. Johnson was required to bring the materials directly to the job site after his truck was loaded, and if Mr. Johnson did not deliver the materials promptly, ACS had the right to dock his pay or to no longer employ him; (5) ACS paid Mr. Johnson on an hourly basis from the time he picked up his first load until ACS dismissed him from the job site; (6) after Mr. Johnson delivered his first load of materials, ACS directed him to return to the quarry to pick up and bring back additional materials; and (7) at the job site, Mr. Johnson was obligated to follow ACS's directions in terms of where to drop the materials, how much material to drop, and how many times he would need to return to the quarry. Based on that evidence, a jury could find that Mr. Johnson was subject to ACS's control, and ACS was liable for Mr. Johnson's negligence pursuant to the doctrine of *respondeat superior.*

Case 33.2 Continues

Decision and Remedy *The state intermediate appellate court affirmed the jury's finding with respect to Johnson's status as ACS's employee. The court disagreed, however, with the lower court's admission of certain evidence that may have influenced the jury's finding of proximate cause for Perry's injuries. As a result, the court reversed the judgment on this ground and remanded the case for a new trial.*

Critical Thinking
- **Economic** *Why did ACS contend that Johnson was not its employee? Discuss.*

The Distinction between a "Detour" and a "Frolic" A useful insight into the concept of "scope of employment" can be gained from Judge Baron Parke's classic distinction between a "detour" and a "frolic" in the case of *Joel v. Morison* (1834).[12] In this case, the English court held that if a servant merely took a detour from his master's business, the master will be responsible. If, however, the servant was on a "frolic of his own" and not in any way "on his master's business," the master will not be liable.

■ **EXAMPLE 33.18** While driving his employer's vehicle to call on a customer, Mandel decides to stop at a store—which is three blocks off his route—to take care of a personal matter. As Mandel approaches the store, he negligently runs into a parked vehicle owned by Chan. In this situation, because Mandel's detour from the employer's business is not substantial, he is still acting within the scope of employment, and the employer is liable.

But suppose instead that Mandel decides to pick up a few friends in another city for cocktails and in the process negligently runs his vehicle into Chan's. In this situation, the departure from the employer's business is substantial— Mandel is on a "frolic" of his own. Thus, the employer normally will not be liable to Chan for damages. ■

Employee Travel Time An employee going to and from work or to and from meals usually is considered to be outside the scope of employment. If travel is part of a person's position, however, as it is for a traveling salesperson, then travel time is normally considered within the scope of employment. For such an employee, the entire business trip, including the return trip home, is within the scope of employment unless there is a significant departure from the employer's business.

Notice of Dangerous Conditions The employer is charged with knowledge of any dangerous conditions discovered by an employee and pertinent to the employment situation.

---

12. 6 Car. & P. 501, 172 Eng.Rep. 1338 (1834).

■ **EXAMPLE 33.19** Brad, a maintenance employee in Martin's apartment building, notices a lead pipe protruding from the ground in the building's courtyard. Brad neglects either to fix the pipe or to inform Martin of the danger. John trips on the pipe and is injured. Martin is charged with knowledge of the dangerous condition regardless of whether Brad actually informed him. That knowledge is imputed to the employer by virtue of the employment relationship. ■

33–3e Liability for Agent's Intentional Torts

Most intentional torts that individuals commit have no relation to their employment, and their employers will not be held liable. Nevertheless, under the doctrine of *respondeat superior,* the employer can be liable for intentional torts that an employee commits within the course and scope of employment. For instance, a department store owner is liable when a security guard who is a store employee commits the tort of false imprisonment while acting within the scope of employment. Similarly, a nightclub owner is liable when a "bouncer" commits the tort of assault and battery while on the job.

In addition, an employer who knows or should know that an employee has a propensity for committing tortious acts is liable for the employee's acts even if they would not ordinarily be considered within the scope of employment. ■ **EXAMPLE 33.20** Chaz, the owner of the Comedy Club, hires Alec as a bouncer for the club even though he knows that Alec has a history of arrests for criminal assault and battery. In this situation, Chaz may be liable if Alec viciously attacks a customer in the parking lot after hours. ■

An employer is also liable for permitting an employee to engage in reckless actions that can injure others. ■ **EXAMPLE 33.21** The owner of Bates Trucking observes an employee smoking while filling containerized trucks with highly flammable liquids. Failure to stop the employee will cause the employer to be liable for any injuries that result if a truck explodes. ■ Needless to say, most employers purchase liability insurance to cover their potential liability for employee conduct in many situations.

Whether an agent's allegedly tortious conduct fell within the scope of the agent's employment, making the principal vicariously liable, was at the heart of the dispute in the following case.

Case Analysis 33.3

M.J. v. Wisan
Utah Supreme Court, 2016 UT 13, __ P.3d __ (2016).

In the Language of the Court
Associate Chief Justice *LEE* * * * :

* * * *

[The United Effort Plan Trust ("UEP Trust" or the "Trust") was formed in Utah by members of the Fundamentalist Church of Jesus Christ of Latter-Day Saints ("FLDS Church"). The Trust] members deeded their property to the UEP Trust to be managed by Church leaders. Church leaders, who were also trustees, then used this property to minister to the needs of the members.

* * * *

[At the time of the events leading up to this case,] the Trust was operated for the express purpose of furthering the doctrines of the FLDS Church, including the practice of * * * marriage involving underage girls.

* * * *

[Later, as a result of unrelated litigation, a state court reformed the Trust] by excising the purpose of advancing the religious doctrines and goals of the FLDS Church to the degree that any of these were illegal, including * * * sexual activity between adults and minors. [The court appointed Bruce Wisan to head the Trust.]

* * * *

[Later] M.J., a former member of the FLDS Church and beneficiary of the UEP Trust, [filed this suit in a Utah state court against Wisan, as head of the Trust, alleging that] when she was fourteen years old, she was forced to marry Allen Steed, her first cousin. The wedding was performed by Warren Jeffs, who at the time was acting president of both the FLDS Church and * * * the Trust. * * * M.J. claims that Steed repeatedly sexually assaulted and raped her

* * * . She requested a divorce from Steed on multiple occasions, but Jeffs refused to allow it. He also refused to let M.J. live * * * separately from her husband.

* * * She seeks to hold * * * the Trust vicariously liable for intentional infliction of emotional distress.

* * * M.J. * * * claims that Jeffs and other trustees were acting "in furtherance of the trust administration and within the scope of their authority," and thus contends that the Trust should be liable under the doctrine of *respondeat superior.*

* * * *

The Trust filed a series of motions for summary judgment. All of those motions were denied. The Trust then filed [this] petition for review.

* * * *

* * * Under [Utah Code Section 75–7–1010, Utah's version of Section 1010 of the Uniform Trust Code,] a trust is liable for the trustee's acts performed "in the course of administering the trust."

* * * The terms of the statute, in context, are quite clear. "In the course of" *is the traditional formulation of the standard for vicarious liability under the doctrine of* respondeat superior. *We accordingly interpret the Uniform Trust Act as incorporating the established standard of* respondeat superior *liability.* Thus, under [Section 75–7–1010] a trust is liable for the acts of a trustee when the trustee was acting within the scope of his responsibility as a trustee. [Emphasis added.]

* * * *

The difficult question for the law in this field has been to define the line between a course of conduct subject to the employer's control and an

independent course of conduct not connected to the principal. *An independent course of conduct is a matter so removed from the agent's duties that the law, in fairness, eliminates the principal's vicarious liability.* Such a course of conduct is one that represents a departure from, not an escalation of, conduct involved in performing assigned work or other conduct that an employer permits or controls. [Emphasis added.]

Our cases have identified three factors of relevance to this inquiry: (1) whether the agent's conduct is of the general kind the agent is employed to perform; (2) whether the agent is acting within the hours of the agent's work and the ordinary spatial boundaries of the employment; and (3) whether the agent's acts were motivated, at least in part, by the purpose of serving the principal's interest.

* * * In the case law of a number of states, spatial and time boundaries are no longer essential hallmarks of an agency relationship. Instead, the law now recognizes that agents may interact on an employer's behalf with third parties although the employee is neither situated on the employer's premises nor continuously or exclusively engaged in performing assigned work.

A number of courts have also questioned the viability of the requirement that an agent's acts be motivated in some part by an intention to serve the principal's purposes.

* * * In [some] jurisdictions, * * * courts avoid the use of motive or intention to determine whether an employee's tortious conduct falls within the scope of employment and adopt a different

Case 33.3 Continues

standard for identifying the tie between the tortfeasor's employment and the tort. One such standard is whether the tort is a generally foreseeable consequence of the enterprise undertaken by the employer or is incident to it—in other words, whether the agent's conduct is not so unusual or startling that it seems unfair to include the loss resulting from it in the employer's business costs, or whether the tort was engendered by the employment or an outgrowth of it. Another considers whether the employment furnished the specific impetus for a tort or increased the general risk that the tort would occur. These tests leave to the finder of fact the challenge of determining whether a tortfeasor's employment did more than create a happenstance opportunity to commit the tort.

* * * To resolve this case we need not choose * * * between the purpose or motive test * * * and the alternative formulations * * * because we find that the Trust's attempts to defeat its liability on summary judgment fail under any of the * * * formulations.

We do openly endorse one particular aspect of * * * the doctrine of *respondeat superior,* however. Specifically * * * we hold that an agent need not be acting within the hours of the employee's work and the ordinary spatial boundaries of the employment in order to be acting within the course of his employment. * * * We acknowledge that in today's business world much work is performed for an employer away from a defined work space and outside of a limited work shift. And we accordingly reject the Trust's attempt to escape liability on the ground that Jeffs's acts as a trustee were not performed while he was on the Trust's clock or at a work space designated for his work for the Trust. Instead we hold that the key question is whether Jeffs was acting within the scope of employment when performing work assigned by the employer or engaging in a course of conduct subject to the employer's control.

[The Trust argues] that settled case-law establishes "as a matter of law that the sexual misconduct of an employee is outside the scope of employment." Granted, there are many cases that so conclude * * * and some of those cases * * * turn principally on the ground that * * * an agent who commits a sexual assault * * * cannot be viewed as advancing, even in part, the purposes of his principal. Yet some of the cases in this field (particularly more recent ones) * * * adopt * * * a standard that turns not on motive or purpose but on foreseeability, or on whether the employee's acts were engendered by or an outgrowth of the employment, or the employment furnished the impetus for the tort.

* * * *

And we conclude that this is one of those cases. Given Jeffs's unique role as leader of the FLDS Church, and in light of the unusual, troubling function of * * * marriage involving young brides in the FLDS culture, we hold that a reasonable factfinder could conclude that Jeffs was acting within the scope of his role as a trustee in directing Steed to engage in sexual activity with M.J.

* * * *

* * * We affirm the denial of the Trust's motions for summary judgment on that basis.

Legal Reasoning Questions

1. Why do some courts apply a standard for imposing vicarious liability that does not rely on motive or purpose to determine whether an agent's tortious conduct falls within the scope of employment?

2. Why, in some states, are the boundaries of work time and space no longer essential factors in determining the scope of employment in an agency relationship?

3. Who does the result in this case benefit? Why?

33–3f Liability for Independent Contractor's Torts

Generally, an employer is not liable for physical harm caused to a third person by the negligent act of an independent contractor in the performance of the contract. This is because the employer does not have *the right to control* the details of an independent contractor's performance.

Courts make an exception to this rule when the contract involves unusually hazardous activities, such as blasting operations, the transportation of highly volatile chemicals, or the use of poisonous gases. In these situations, strict liability is imposed, and an employer cannot be shielded from liability merely by using an independent contractor.

33–3g Liability for Agent's Crimes

An agent is liable for his or her own crimes. A principal or employer normally is *not* liable for an agent's crime even if the crime was committed within the scope of authority or employment. An exception to this rule is made when the principal or employer participated in the crime by conspiracy or other action.

In addition, in some jurisdictions, a principal may be liable under specific statutes if an agent, in the course and scope of employment, violates certain regulations. For instance, a principal might be liable for an agent's violation of sanitation rules or regulations governing prices, weights, or the sale of liquor.

33–4 Termination of an Agency

Agency law is similar to contract law in that both an agency and a contract may be terminated by an act of the parties or by operation of law. Once the relationship between the principal and the agent has ended, the agent no longer has the right (*actual* authority) to bind the principal. For an agent's *apparent* authority to be terminated, though, third persons may also need to be notified that the agency has been terminated.

33–4a Termination by Act of the Parties

An agency may be terminated by certain acts of the parties, which are listed and described in Exhibit 33–2. Bases for termination by act of the parties include lapse of time, achievement of purpose, occurrence of a specific event, mutual agreement, and at the option of one party.

When an agency agreement specifies the time period during which the agency relationship will exist, the agency ends when that time period expires. If no definite time is stated, then the agency continues for a reasonable time and can be terminated at will by either party. What constitutes a reasonable time depends on the circumstances and the nature of the agency relationship.

The parties can, of course, mutually agree to end their agency relationship. In addition, as a general rule, either party can terminate the agency relationship without the agreement of the other. The act of termination is called *revocation* if done by the principal and *renunciation* if done by the agent. Note, however, that the terminating party may face liability if the termination is wrongful.

EXHIBIT 33–2 Termination by Act of the Parties

METHOD	RULES	ILLUSTRATION
1. Lapse of Time.	Agency terminates automatically at the end of the stated time.	Page lists her property for sale with Alex, a real estate agent, for six months. The agency ends in six months.
2. Purpose Achieved.	Agency terminates automatically on the completion of the purpose for which it was formed.	Calvin, a cattle rancher, hires Abe as his agent in the purchase of fifty breeding stock. The agency ends when the cattle have been purchased.
3. Occurrence of a Specific Event.	Agency normally terminates automatically on the event's occurrence.	Meredith appoints Allen to handle her business affairs while she is away. The agency terminates when Meredith returns.
4. Mutual Agreement.	Agency terminates when both parties consent to end the agency relationship.	Linda and Greg agree that Greg will no longer be her agent in procuring business equipment.
5. At the Option of One Party (*revocation*, if by principal; *renunciation*, if by agent).	Either party normally has a right to terminate the agency relationship. Wrongful termination can lead to liability for breach of contract.	When Patrick becomes ill, he informs Alice that he is revoking her authority to be his agent.

Wrongful Termination Although both parties have the *power* to terminate the agency, they may not always possess the *right* to do so. Wrongful termination can subject the canceling party to a lawsuit for breach of contract. ■ **EXAMPLE 33.22** Rawlins has a one-year employment contract with Munro to act as agent in return for $65,000. Munro has the *power* to discharge Rawlins before the contract period expires. But if he does so, he can be sued for breaching the contract, because he had no *right* to terminate the agency. ■

Even in an agency at will—in which either party may terminate at any time—the principal who wishes to terminate must give the agent *reasonable* notice. The notice must be at least sufficient to allow the agent to recoup his or her expenses and, in some situations, to make a normal profit.

Agency Coupled with an Interest A special rule applies to an *agency coupled with an interest*. In an **agency coupled with an interest,** the agent has some legal right to (an interest in) the property that is the subject of the agency. This type of agency is not an agency in the usual sense because it is created for the agent's benefit instead of for the principal's benefit.

■ **EXAMPLE 33.23** Sylvia owns Harper Hills, a vacation home. She needs some cash right away, so she enters into an agreement with Rob under which Rob will lend her $10,000. In return, she will grant Rob a one-half interest in Harper Hills and "the exclusive right to sell" it. The loan is to be repaid out of the sale's proceeds. Rob is Sylvia's agent, and their relationship is an agency coupled with an interest. The agency was created when the loan agreement was made for the purpose of securing the loan. Therefore, Rob's agency power is irrevocable. ■

An agency coupled with an interest should not be confused with a situation in which the agent merely derives proceeds or profits from the sale of the subject matter. Many agents are paid a commission for their services, but the agency relationship involved does not constitute an agency coupled with an interest. For instance, a real estate agent who merely receives a commission from the sale of real property does not have a beneficial interest in the property itself.

Notice of Termination When the parties terminate an agency, it is the principal's duty to inform any third parties who know of the existence of the agency that it has been terminated. No particular form is required for notice of termination to be effective. The principal can personally notify the agent, or the agent can learn of the termination through some other means.

Although an agent's actual authority ends when the agency is terminated, an agent's *apparent authority* continues until the third party receives notice (from any source) that such authority has been terminated. ■ **EXAMPLE 33.24** Manning bids on a shipment of steel, and Stone is hired as an agent to arrange transportation for the shipment. When Stone learns that Manning has lost the bid, Stone's authority to make the transportation arrangement terminates. ■

If the principal knows that a third party has dealt with the agent, the principal is expected to notify that person *directly*. For third parties who have heard about the agency but have not yet dealt with the agent, *constructive notice* is sufficient.[13] If the agent's authority is written, however, normally it must be revoked in writing (unless the written document contains an expiration date).

33–4b Termination by Operation of Law

Certain events terminate agency authority automatically because their occurrence makes it impossible for the agent to perform or improbable that the principal would continue to want performance. We look at these events here. Note that when an agency terminates by operation of law, there is no duty to notify third persons—unless the agent's authority is coupled with an interest.

1. *Death or insanity.* The general rule is that the death or insanity of either the principal or the agent automatically and immediately terminates an ordinary agency relationship.[14] Knowledge of the death or insanity is not required. ■ **EXAMPLE 33.25** Grey sends Bosley to Japan to purchase a rare book. Before Bosley makes the purchase, Grey dies. Bosley's agent status is terminated at the moment of Grey's death, even though Bosley does not know that Grey has died. ■ (Some states, however, have enacted statutes that change the common law rule to require an agent's knowledge of the principal's death before termination.)

---

13. With *constructive notice* of a fact, knowledge of the fact is imputed by law to a person if he or she could have discovered the fact through proper diligence. Constructive notice is often accomplished by publication in a newspaper.

14. An exception to this rule exists in the bank-customer relationship. A bank, as agent, can continue to exercise specific types of authority after the customer's death or insanity and can continue to pay checks drawn by the customer for ten days after death.

2. *Impossibility.* When the specific subject matter of an agency is destroyed or lost, the agency terminates. ■ **EXAMPLE 33.26** Pedro employs Vasquez to sell Pedro's house. Prior to any sale, the house is destroyed by fire. Vasquez's agency and authority to sell the house terminate. ■ Similarly, when it is impossible for the agent to perform the agency lawfully because of a change in the law, the agency terminates.

3. *Changed circumstances.* Sometimes, an event occurs that has such an unusual effect on the subject matter of the agency that the agent can reasonably infer that the principal will not want the agency to continue. In such situations, the agency terminates. ■ **EXAMPLE 33.27** Baird hires Joslen to sell a tract of land for $40,000. Subsequently, Joslen learns that there is oil under the land and that the land is therefore worth $1 million. The agency and Joslen's authority to sell the land for $40,000 are terminated. ■

4. *Bankruptcy.* If either the principal or the agent petitions for bankruptcy, the agency is *usually* terminated. In certain circumstances, such as when the agent's financial status is irrelevant to the purpose of the agency, the agency relationship may continue. Insolvency, as distinct from bankruptcy, does not necessarily terminate the relationship. (An *insolvent* person is one who cannot pay debts as they come due or whose liabilities exceed his or her assets.)

5. *War.* When the principal's country and the agent's country are at war with each other, the agency is terminated. In this situation, the agency is automatically suspended or terminated because there is no way to enforce the legal rights and obligations of the parties.

See Concept Summary 33.2 for a synopsis of the rules governing the termination of an agency by operation of law.

Concept Summary 33.2

Agency Termination by Operation of Law

Death or Insanity	Termination of the agency is automatic on the death or insanity of either the principal or the agent—except when the agency is coupled with an interest.
Impossibility	Agency termination occurs any time the agency cannot be performed because of an event beyond the parties' control, such as the destruction of the specific subject matter.
Changed Circumstances	When events are so unusual that it would be inequitable to allow the agency to exist, the agency will terminate.
Bankruptcy	Bankruptcy petition—but not mere insolvency—usually terminates the agency.
War between Countries	War between the principal's country and the agent's country automatically suspends or terminates agency because there is no way to enforce legal rights.

Reviewing: Agency Liability and Termination

Lynne Meyer, on her way to a business meeting and in a hurry, stopped at a Buy-Mart store for a new car charger for her smartphone. There was a long line at one of the checkout counters, but a cashier, Valerie Watts, opened another counter and began loading the cash drawer. Meyer told Watts that she was in a hurry and asked Watts to work faster. Instead, Watts slowed her pace. At this point, Meyer hit Watts. It is not clear whether Meyer hit Watts intentionally or, in an attempt to retrieve the car charger, hit her inadvertently.

In response, Watts grabbed Meyer by the hair and hit her repeatedly in the back of the head, while Meyer screamed for help. Management personnel separated the two women and questioned them about the incident. Watts was immediately fired for violating the store's no-fighting policy. Meyer subsequently sued Buy-Mart, alleging that the store was liable for the tort (assault and battery) committed by its employee. Using the information presented in the chapter, answer the following questions.

1. Under what doctrine discussed in this chapter might Buy-Mart be held liable for the tort committed by Watts?
2. What is the key factor in determining whether Buy-Mart is liable under this doctrine?
3. How is Buy-Mart's potential liability affected by whether Watts's behavior constituted an intentional tort or a tort of negligence?
4. Suppose that when Watts applied for the job at Buy-Mart, she disclosed in her application that she had previously been convicted of felony assault and battery. Nevertheless, Buy-Mart hired Watts as a cashier. How might this fact affect Buy-Mart's liability for Watts's actions?

Debate This . . . *The doctrine of* respondeat superior *should be modified to make agents solely liable for their tortious (wrongful) acts committed within the scope of employment.*

Terms and Concepts

agency coupled with an interest 636	express authority 622	ratification 625
apparent authority 624	implied authority 624	*respondeat superior* 629
disclosed principal 626	notary public 622	undisclosed principal 627
e-agent 628	partially disclosed principal 627	vicarious liability 629
equal dignity rule 622	power of attorney 622	

Issue Spotters

1. Davis contracts with Estee to buy a certain horse on her behalf. Estee asks Davis not to reveal her identity. Davis makes a deal with Farmland Stables, the owner of the horse, and makes a down payment. Estee does not pay the rest of the price. Farmland Stables sues Davis for breach of contract. Can Davis hold Estee liable for whatever damages he has to pay? Why or why not? (See *Liability for Contracts.*)

2. Vivian, owner of Wonder Goods Company, employs Xena as an administrative assistant. In Vivian's absence, and without authority, Xena represents herself as Vivian and signs a promissory note in Vivian's name. In what circumstance is Vivian liable on the note? (See *Liability for Contracts.*)

• **Check your answers to the Issue Spotters against the answers provided in Appendix D at the end of this text.**

Business Scenarios

33–1. Unauthorized Acts. Janell Arden is a purchasing agent–employee for the A&B Coal Supply partnership. Arden has authority to purchase the coal needed by A&B to satisfy the needs of its customers. While Arden is leaving a coal mine from which she has just purchased a large quantity of coal, her car breaks down. She walks into a small roadside grocery store for help. While there, she encounters Will Wilson, who owns 360 acres back in the mountains with all mineral rights. Wilson, in need of cash, offers to sell Arden the property for $1,500 per acre.

On inspection of the property, Arden forms the opinion that the subsurface contains valuable coal deposits. Arden contracts to purchase the property for A&B Coal Supply, signing the contract "A&B Coal Supply, Janell Arden, agent." The closing date is August 1. Arden takes the contract to the partnership. The managing partner is furious, as A&B is not in the property business. Later, just before closing, both Wilson and the partnership learn that the value of the land is at least $15,000 per acre. Discuss the rights of A&B and Wilson concerning the land contract. (See *Liability for Contracts.*)

33–2. Respondeat Superior. ABC Tire Corp. hires Arnez as a traveling salesperson and assigns him a geographic area and time schedule in which to solicit orders and service customers. Arnez is given a company car to use in covering the territory. One day, Arnez decides to take his personal car to cover part of his territory. It is 11:00 A.M., and Arnez has just finished calling on all customers in the city of Tarrytown. His next appointment is at 2:00 P.M. in the city of Austex, twenty miles down the road. Arnez starts out for Austex, but halfway there he decides to visit a former college roommate who runs a farm ten miles off the main highway. Arnez is enjoying his visit with his former roommate when he realizes that it is 1:45 P.M. and that he will be late for the appointment in Austex. Driving at a high speed down the country road to reach the main highway, Arnez crashes his car into a tractor, severely injuring Thomas, the driver of the tractor. Thomas claims that he can hold ABC Tire Corp. liable for his injuries. Discuss fully ABC's liability in this situation. (See *Liability for Torts and Crimes.*)

Business Case Problems

33–3. Liability Based on Apparent Authority. Summerall Electric Co. and other subcontractors were hired by National Church Services, Inc. (NCS), which was the general contractor on a construction project for the Church of God at Southaven. As work progressed, payments from NCS to the subcontractors were late and eventually stopped altogether. The church had paid NCS in full for the entire project beforehand, but apparently NCS had mismanaged the project. When payments from NCS stopped, the subcontractors filed mechanic's liens for the value of the work they had performed but for which they had not been paid. The subcontractors sued the church, contending that it was liable for the payments because NCS was its agent on the basis of either actual or apparent authority. Was NCS an agent for the church, thereby making the church liable to the subcontractors? Explain your reasoning. [*Summerall Electric Co. v. Church of God at Southaven,* 25 So.3d 1090 (Miss.App. 2010)] (See *Scope of Agent's Authority.*)

33–4. Disclosed Principal. To display desserts in restaurants, Mario Sclafani ordered refrigeration units from Felix Storch, Inc. Felix faxed a credit application to Sclafani. The application was faxed back with a signature that appeared to be Sclafani's. Felix delivered the units. When they were not paid for, Felix filed a suit against Sclafani to collect. Sclafani denied that he had seen the application or signed it. He testified that he referred all credit questions to "the girl in the office." Who was the principal? Who was the agent? Who is liable on the contract? Explain. [*Felix Storch, Inc. v. Martinucci Desserts USA, Inc.,* 30 Misc.3d 1217, 924 N.Y.S.2d 308 (Suffolk Co. 2011)] (See *Liability for Contracts.*)

33–5. Liability for Contracts. Thomas Huskin and his wife entered into a contract to have their home remodeled by House Medic Handyman Service. Todd Hall signed the contract as an authorized representative of House Medic. It turned out that House Medic was a fictitious name for Hall Hauling, Ltd. The contract did not indicate this, however, and Hall did not inform the Huskins about Hall Hauling. When a contract dispute later arose, the Huskins sued Todd Hall personally for breach of contract. Can Hall be held personally liable? Why or why not? [*Huskin v. Hall,* 2012 WL 553136 (Ohio Ct.App. 2012)] (See *Liability for Contracts.*)

33–6. Business Case Problem with Sample Answer— Agent's Authority. Basic Research, L.L.C., advertised its products on television networks owned by Rainbow Media Holdings, Inc., through an ad agency, Icebox Advertising, Inc. As Basic's agent, Icebox had the express authority to buy ads from Rainbow on Basic's behalf, but the authority was limited to buying ads with cash in advance. Despite this limit, Rainbow sold ads to Basic through Icebox on credit. Basic paid Icebox for the ads, but Icebox did not pass all of the payments on to Rainbow. Icebox filed for bankruptcy. Can Rainbow recoup the unpaid amounts from Basic? Explain. [*American Movie Classics v. Rainbow Media Holdings,* 508 Fed.Appx. 826 (10th Cir. 2013)] (See *Scope of Agent's Authority.*)

- **For a sample answer to Problem 33–6, go to Appendix E at the end of this text.**

33–7. Agent's Authority. Terry Holden's stepmother, Rosie, was diagnosed with amyotrophic lateral sclerosis (ALS), and Terry's wife, Susan, became Rosie's primary caregiver. Rosie executed a durable power of attorney appointing Susan as her agent. Susan opened a joint bank account with Rosie at Bank of America, depositing $9,643.62 of Rosie's funds. Susan used some of the money to pay for "household expenses to keep us going while we were taking care of her." Rosie died three months later. Terry's father, Charles, as executor of Rosie's estate, filed a petition in a Texas state court against Susan for an accounting. What general duty did Susan owe Rosie as her agent? What does an agent's duty of accounting require? Did Susan breach either of these duties? Explain.

[*Holden v. Holden,* 456 S.W.3d 642 (Tex.App.—Tyler 2015)] (See *Scope of Agent's Authority.*)

33–8. Scope of Agent's Authority. Kindred Nursing Centers East, LLC, owns and operates Whitesburg Gardens, a long-term care and rehabilitation facility, in Huntsville, Alabama. Lorene Jones was admitted to the facility following knee-replacement surgery. Jones's daughter, Yvonne Barbour, signed the admission forms required by Whitesburg Gardens as her mother's representative in her presence. Jones did not object. The forms included an "Alternative Dispute Resolution Agreement," which provided for binding arbitration in the event of a dispute between "the Resident" (Jones) and "the Facility" (Whitesburg Gardens). Six days later, Jones was transferred to a different facility. After recovering from the surgery, she filed a suit in an Alabama state court against Kindred, alleging substandard care on a claim of negligence. Can Jones be compelled to submit her claim to arbitration? Explain. [*Kindred Nursing Centers East, LLC v. Jones,* __ So.3d __, 2016 WL 762450 (Ala. 2016)] (See *Scope of Agent's Authority.*)

33–9. A Question of Ethics—Vicarious Liability. *Jamie* *Paliath worked as a real estate agent for Home Town Realty of Vandalia, LLC (the principal, a real estate broker). Torri Auer, a California resident, relied on Paliath's advice and assistance to buy three rental properties in Ohio. Before the sales, Paliath had represented that each property was worth approximately twice as much as what Auer would pay and that there was a waiting list of prospective tenants. Paliath also stated that all of the property needed work* and agreed to do the work for a specified price. Nearly a year later, substantial work was still needed, and only a few of the units had been rented. Auer sued Paliath and Home Town Realty for fraudulent misrepresentation. [*Auer v. Paliath, 140 Ohio St.3d 276, 17 N.E.3d 561, 2014-Ohio-3632 (2014)] (See *Liability for Torts and Crimes.*)

(a) Were Paliath's representations to Auer within the scope of her employment? Explain. Will the court hold the principal (Home Town Realty) liable for the misrepresentations of the agent (Paliath)?

(b) What is the ethical basis for imposing vicarious liability on a principal for an agent's tort?

33–10. Special Case Analysis—Liability for Torts and Crimes. Go to Case Analysis 33.3, *M.J. v. Wisan.* Read the excerpt and answer the following questions.

(a) **Issue:** What conduct was at the center of the dispute in this case? Who did the plaintiff allege was liable for this conduct? Which of these parties was the principal, and which was the agent?

(b) **Rule of Law:** What rule applied to determine the liability of the parties for the conduct in dispute?

(c) **Applying the Rule of Law:** What factors did the court indicate could be considered in deciding whether to impose liability in this case?

(d) **Conclusion:** How did the court rule on the question of vicarious liability?

Legal Reasoning Group Activity

33–11. Liability for Independent Contractor's Torts. Dean Brothers Corp. owns and operates a steel drum manufacturing plant. Lowell Wyden, the plant superintendent, hired Best Security Patrol, Inc. (BSP), a security company, to guard Dean property and "deter thieves and vandals." Some BSP security guards, as Wyden knew, carried firearms. Pete Sidell, a BSP security guard, was not certified as an armed guard but nevertheless came to work with his gun (in a briefcase).

While working at the Dean plant on October 31, Sidell fired his gun at Tyrone Gaines, in the belief that Gaines was an intruder. The bullet struck and killed Gaines. Gaines's mother filed a lawsuit claiming that her son's death was the result of BSP's negligence, for which Dean was responsible. (See *Liability for Torts and Crimes.*)

(a) The first group will determine what the plaintiff's best argument is to establish that Dean is responsible for BSP's actions.

(b) The second group will discuss Dean's best defense and formulate arguments to support it.

CHAPTER 34

Employment, Immigration, and Labor Law

Until the early 1900s, most employer-employee relationships were governed by the common law. Even today, under the common law *employment-at-will doctrine,* private employers have considerable freedom to hire and fire workers at will, regardless of the employees' performance.

Numerous statutes and administrative agency regulations now also govern the workplace. Thus, to a large extent, statutory law has displaced common law doctrines. In this chapter and the next, we look at the most significant laws regulating employment relationships.

This chapter discusses federal statutes that regulate various aspects of the workplace, including employee wages, hours, medical leave, safety, and pension and health plans. It also examines immigration law, a topic of special importance to employers in our diverse society. The chapter concludes with coverage of labor laws, which continue to have an impact on the employment environment.

34–1 Employment at Will

Employment relationships have traditionally been governed by the common law doctrine of **employment at will.** Under this doctrine, either party may terminate the employment relationship at any time and for any reason, unless doing so violates an employee's statutory or contractual rights.

Today, the majority of U.S. workers continue to have the legal status of "employees at will." In other words, this common law doctrine is still in widespread use, and only one state (Montana) does not apply it.

Nonetheless, federal and state statutes governing employment relationships prevent the doctrine from being applied in a number of circumstances. An employer may not fire an employee if doing so would violate a federal or state statute, such as a law prohibiting employment discrimination.

Note that the distinction made under agency law between employee status and independent-contractor status is important here. The employment laws that will be discussed apply only to the employer-employee relationship. They do not apply to independent contractors.

34–1a Common Law Exceptions to the Employment-at-Will Doctrine

As noted, statutory law has affected the application of the employment-at-will doctrine. In addition, the courts have carved out various exceptions to the doctrine based on contract theory, tort theory, and public policy.

Exceptions Based on Contract Theory Some courts have held that an *implied* employment contract exists between the employer and the employee. If the employee is fired outside the terms of the implied contract, he or she may succeed in an action for breach of contract even though no written employment contract exists.

■ **EXAMPLE 34.1** BDI Enterprises' employment manual and personnel bulletin both state that, as a matter of policy, workers will be dismissed only for good cause. Jing Chin is an employee at BDI. If Chin reasonably expects BDI to follow this policy, a court may find that there is an implied contract based on the terms stated in the manual and bulletin. ■ Generally, the key consideration in determining whether an employment manual creates an implied contractual obligation is the employee's reasonable expectations.

An employer's oral promises to employees regarding discharge policy may also be considered part of an implied contract. If the employer fires a worker in a manner contrary to what was promised, a court may hold that the employer has violated the implied contract and is liable for damages.

Exceptions Based on Tort Theory In some situations, the discharge of an employee may give rise to an action for wrongful discharge (discussed shortly) under tort theories. Abusive discharge procedures may result in a lawsuit for intentional infliction of emotional distress or defamation. In addition, some courts have permitted workers to sue their employers under the tort theory of fraud. Fraud might be alleged when an employer made false promises to a prospective employee.

■ **EXAMPLE 34.2** Goldfinch Consulting, Inc., induces Brianna to leave a lucrative job and move to another state by offering her "a long-term job with a thriving business." In fact, Goldfinch is not only having significant financial problems but is also planning a merger that will result in the elimination of the position offered to Brianna. If she takes the job in reliance on Goldfinch's representations and is fired shortly thereafter, Brianna may be able to bring an action against the employer for fraud. ■

Exceptions Based on Public Policy The most common exception to the employment-at-will doctrine is made on the basis that the employer's reason for firing the employee violates a fundamental public policy of the jurisdiction. Generally, the courts require that the public policy involved be expressed clearly in the statutory law governing the jurisdiction.

The public-policy exception may apply to an employee discharged for **whistleblowing**—that is, telling government authorities, upper-level managers, or the media that the employer is engaged in some unsafe or illegal activity. Normally, however, whistleblowers seek protection from retaliatory discharge under federal and state statutes, such as the Whistleblower Protection Act.[1]

■ **CASE IN POINT 34.3** Donald Waddell worked for the Boyce Thompson Institute for Plant Research. Waddell did not have an employment contract for a fixed term, and the institute's employee manual said that his job was "terminable at will." Soon after he was hired, the institute implemented a whistleblower policy designed to encourage "the highest standards of financial reporting and lawful and ethical behavior."

Waddell repeatedly told his supervisor, Sophia Darling, that she needed to file certain financial documents more promptly. Darling fired Waddell, telling him that he was disrespectful and insubordinate. Waddell then sued the institute, contending that he should not have been fired because he was acting under the company's whistleblowing policy.

A New York appellate court, however, found that Waddell could be fired. Waddell was employed at will. In addition, he was not protected under the whistle-blower policy, which had been implemented after his employment. Thus, he could not have detrimentally relied on the policy in accepting the job.[2] ■

34–1b Wrongful Discharge

Whenever an employer discharges an employee in violation of an employment contract or a statutory law protecting employees, the employee may bring an action for **wrongful discharge.** For instance, an employee who is terminated in retaliation for some protected activity, such as whistleblowing or participating in an employment-discrimination investigation, can sue for wrongful discharge.

Even if an employer's actions do not violate any provisions in an employment contract or statute, the employer may still be subject to liability. An employee can sue for wrongful discharge under a common law doctrine, such as a tort theory or agency. For instance, if while firing a female employee, an employer publicly discloses private facts about her sex life, that employee could sue for wrongful discharge based on an invasion of privacy.

34–2 Wages, Hours, and Layoffs

In the 1930s, Congress enacted several laws to regulate the wages and working hours of employees, including the following:

1. The Davis-Bacon Act[3] requires contractors and subcontractors working on federal government construction projects to pay "prevailing wages" to their employees.

2. The Walsh-Healey Act[4] applies to U.S. government contracts. It requires that a minimum wage, as well as overtime pay at 1.5 times regular pay rates, be paid to employees of manufacturers or suppliers entering into contracts with agencies of the federal government.

3. The Fair Labor Standards Act (FLSA)[5] extended wage-hour requirements to cover all employers engaged in interstate commerce or in producing goods for interstate commerce. Certain other types of businesses were included as well. The FLSA, as amended, provides the most comprehensive federal regulation of wages and hours today.

---

1. 5 U.S.C. Section 1201.
2. *Waddell v. Boyce Thompson Institute for Plant Research, Inc.*, 92 A.D.3d 1172, 940 N.Y.S.2d 331 (2012).
3. 40 U.S.C. Sections 276a–276a-5.
4. 41 U.S.C. Sections 35–45.
5. 29 U.S.C. Sections 201–260.

34–2a Child Labor

The FLSA prohibits oppressive child labor. Restrictions on child labor differ by age group.

Children under fourteen years of age are allowed to do only certain types of work. They can deliver newspapers, work for their parents, and be employed in entertainment and (with some exceptions) agriculture. Children aged fourteen and fifteen are allowed to work, but not in hazardous occupations. There are also restrictions on how many hours per day and per week children in these age groups can work.

Working times and hours are not restricted for persons between the ages of sixteen and eighteen, but they cannot be employed in hazardous jobs. None of these restrictions apply to those over the age of eighteen.

34–2b Minimum Wages

The FLSA provides that a **minimum wage** of $7.25 per hour must be paid to covered nonexempt employees. Most states also have minimum wages. More than half of the states have set their minimum wages above the federal minimum wage. When the state minimum wage is greater than the federal minimum wage, the employee is entitled to the higher wage.

■ **EXAMPLE 34.4** The Oakland Raiders paid $1.25 million in 2014 to settle wage claims made by the team's cheerleading squad (the Raiderettes) as a class action. The cheerleaders had complained that they were not being paid for hours that they spent attending other events and performing other tasks required of them by contract. After the time spent performing these other tasks was factored in, the cheerleaders were receiving wages that were well below California's minimum wage, persuading the Raiders to settle the dispute. ■

Are employees entitled to receive wages for all the time they spend at work, including times when they are taking a personal break? See this chapter's *Ethics Today* feature for a discussion of this issue.

34–2c Tipped Workers

When an employee receives tips while on the job, the FLSA gives employers a tip credit toward the minimum wage amount. The employer is required to pay only $2.13 an hour in direct wages—if that amount, plus the tips received, equals at least the federal minimum wage. If an employee's tips and direct wages do not equal the federal minimum wage, the employer must make up the difference. Note that some states have enacted laws to prevent employers from including tips in the minimum wage. In these states, tipped workers receive the regular minimum wage.

If employers pay at least the federal minimum wage, the FLSA allows them to take employee tips and make other arrangements for their distribution. ■ **CASE IN POINT 34.5** Misty Cumbie worked as a waitress at a café in Portland, Oregon, that was owned and operated by Woody Woo, Inc. Woody Woo paid its servers an hourly wage that was higher than the state's minimum wage, but the servers were required to contribute their tips to a "tip pool." Approximately one-third of the tip-pool funds went to the servers, and the rest was distributed to kitchen staff members, who otherwise rarely received tips for their services. When Cumbie filed a lawsuit against Woody Woo over her tips, the court held that the tip pool did not violate the FLSA.[6] ■

34–2d Overtime Provisions and Exemptions

Under the FLSA, any employee who works more than forty hours per week must be paid no less than 1.5 times her or his regular pay for all hours worked over forty. The FLSA overtime provisions apply only after an employee has worked more than forty hours per *week*. Therefore, employees who work ten hours a day, four days per week, are not entitled to overtime pay.

Certain employees are exempt from the FLSA's overtime provisions. These employees generally include executive, administrative, and professional employees, as well as outside salespersons and those who create computer code. Executive and administrative employees are those whose primary duty is management and who exercise discretion and independent judgment.

■ **CASE IN POINT 34.6** Patty Lee Smith was a pharmaceutical sales representative for Johnson and Johnson (J&J). She traveled to ten physicians' offices a day to promote the benefits of J&J's drug Concerta. Smith's work was unsupervised, she controlled her own schedule, and she received an annual salary of $66,000. When she filed a claim for overtime pay, the court held that she was an administrative employee and therefore exempt from the FLSA's overtime provisions.[7] ■

An employer can voluntarily pay overtime to ineligible employees but cannot waive or reduce the overtime requirements of the FLSA. In 2016, the Department of Labor updated its overtime regulations to allow millions more employees to receive overtime pay.[8]

---

6. *Cumbie v. Woody Woo, Inc.*, 596 F.3d 577 (9th Cir. 2010).
7. *Smith v. Johnson and Johnson*, 593 F.3d 280 (3d Cir. 2010).
8. 29 C.F.R. Part 541.

Is It Fair to Dock Employees' Pay for Bathroom Breaks?

For some employees, "punching a time clock" means accounting for *all* of the time that they are not working. These employees must "punch in" when they arrive and "punch out" when they leave for the day, of course, but they also must clock out when they take breaks. That includes bathroom breaks, coffee breaks, and smoking breaks.

What the Law Says

The Fair Labor Standards Act[a] does not require that an employer offer its employees personal breaks. If an employer does offer them, though, employees must be compensated during those breaks. Otherwise, the employer may effectively be in violation of federal minimum wage laws.

A Pennsylvania Publisher Faces Fines for Unpaid Bathroom Breaks

The issue of unpaid bathroom breaks came to the fore when the U.S. Department of Labor (DOL) filed a lawsuit against American Future Systems, Inc. (doing business as Progressive Business Publications). The DOL alleged that American Future Systems had created a compensation system in which none of its six thousand employees were compensated for bathroom breaks.[b]

The DOL argued that all workday breaks of twenty minutes or less are compensable time.[c] Because American Future Systems did not compensate its employees for such breaks, those employees were not properly credited for all compensable time. The result was that they had "been paid below the minimum wage established by the Fair Labor Standards Act (FLSA).[d]

U.S. district court judge L. Felipe Restrepo agreed, finding American Future Systems liable for unpaid wages under the FLSA, plus damages. The company will have to pay past and current employees almost $2 million, according to DOL estimates.

The Ethical Issue

Irrespective of the illegality of not paying for personal breaks, there is an ethical issue. Should workers have to face the choice of taking a bathroom break or getting paid? Adam Welsh, a senior trial attorney for the Department of Labor, argued that the answer was no. "I think it's the rare employer who doesn't allow its employees to go to the bathroom," Welsh said.

Critical Thinking *Consider a company whose employees include both smokers and nonsmokers. The smokers take numerous paid smoking breaks, while the nonsmokers do not. Is there an ethical issue here? Discuss.*

a. 29 U.S.C. Sections 201 *et seq.*
b. *U.S. Department of Labor v. American Future Systems, Inc.,* Memorandum, Case No. 12-6171 (E.D.Pa. 2015).
c. 29 C.F.R. Section 785.18.
d. 29 U.S.C. Section 206(a)(1)(c).

Whereas in the past, workers making more than $23,660 a year did not qualify for overtime pay, today, that threshold has been increased to $50,440 a year.

An employee's underreporting of hours worked can undercut his or her claim for overtime. But can an employee's underreporting *support* such a claim? That question was at the center of the following case.

Case 34.1

Bailey v. TitleMax of Georgia, Inc.

United States Court of Appeals, Eleventh Circuit, 776 F.3d 797 (2015).

Background and Facts Santonias Bailey was an employee of TitleMax of Georgia, Inc., in Jonesboro, Georgia. Bailey's supervisor told him that TitleMax did not pay overtime, so he regularly worked off the clock. For example, on some Saturdays, he would work from 8:30 A.M. to 5:30 P.M., but—as ordered by his supervisor—would log only seven hours despite having worked nine. His supervisor also

Case 34.1 Continued

edited Bailey's time records to report fewer hours than he actually worked by, for instance, subtracting a one-hour lunch break when there had been none.

Bailey resigned from TitleMax and filed a suit in a federal district court against the employer to recover for the unpaid overtime under the Fair Labor Standards Act (FLSA). TitleMax argued that Bailey was responsible for the unpaid time. According to TitleMax, he had never complained about his supervisor, and he had violated company policy with respect to keeping accurate time records. The court issued a judgment in the defendant's favor. Bailey appealed.

In the Language of the Court

MARTIN, Circuit Judge:

* * * *

* * * The goal of the FLSA is to counteract the inequality of bargaining power between employees and employers.

In the broadest sense, this principle * * * compels our holding here. If an employer knew or had reason to know that its employee underreported his hours, it cannot escape FLSA liability by asserting [a] defense based on that underreporting. To hold otherwise would allow an employer to wield its superior bargaining power to pressure or even compel its employees to underreport their work hours.

* * * *

If an employee has worked overtime without pay, he may bring a private FLSA action for damages. An unpaid-overtime claim has two elements: (1) an employee worked unpaid overtime, and (2) the employer knew or should have known of the overtime work. *Knowledge may be imputed [attributed] to the employer when its supervisors or management encourage artificially low reporting.* [Emphasis added.]

Mr. Bailey has shown both required elements. He worked overtime without pay. TitleMax knew or should have known he worked overtime, because Mr. Bailey's supervisor both encouraged artificially low reporting and squelched truthful timekeeping.

* * * *

* * * No one disputes that his supervisor knew he was working off the clock. *The supervisor's knowledge may be imputed to TitleMax, making it liable for the FLSA violation.* * * * TitleMax argues that * * * an employee [is] deprived of his FLSA claim because he underreported his time, even if knowledge of the underreporting is imputed to the employer. [Emphasis added.]

TitleMax has identified no case in which [any federal appellate court] approved the use of [this] defense as a total bar to an employee's FLSA claim when the employer knew the employee underreported his hours.

* * * The dearth [scarcity] of precedent supporting TitleMax's * * * argument is persuasive, if not conclusive, evidence that its argument is misguided.

Decision and Remedy *The U.S. Court of Appeals for the Eleventh Circuit reversed the judgment of the lower court and remanded the case for further proceedings. "Where, as here, an employer knew or had reason to know that its employee underreported his hours, it cannot invoke [a] defense based on that underreporting to bar the employee's FLSA claim."*

Critical Thinking

* **Legal Environment** *Congress enacted the FLSA in 1938. More than eight thousand FLSA suits are filed in federal district courts each year. How do these facts support the court's reasoning in this case?*

34–2e Layoffs

The Worker Adjustment and Retraining Notification (WARN) Act[9] applies to employers with at least one hundred full-time employees. The act requires these employers to provide sixty days' notice before implementing a mass layoff or closing a plant that employs more than fifty full-time workers. A mass layoff is a layoff of at least one-third of the full-time employees at a particular job site.

The WARN Act is intended to give workers advance notice so that they can start looking for new jobs while they are still employed. It is also intended to alert state

---

9. 29 U.S.C. Sections 2101 *et seq.*

agencies so that they can provide training and other resources for displaced workers. Employers thus must provide advance notice of the layoff both to the affected workers and to state and local government authorities. (An employer may notify the workers' union representative, if the workers are members of a labor union.) Even companies that anticipate filing for bankruptcy normally must provide notice under the WARN Act.

An employer that violates the WARN Act can be fined up to $500 for each day of the violation. Employees can recover back pay for each day of the violation (up to sixty days), plus reasonable attorneys' fees.

34–3 Family and Medical Leave

The Family and Medical Leave Act (FMLA)[10] allows employees to take time off work for family or medical reasons or in certain situations that arise from military service. A majority of the states have similar legislation. The FMLA does not supersede any state or local law that provides more generous protection.

34–3a Coverage and Application

The FMLA requires employers that have fifty or more employees to provide *unpaid* leave for specified reasons. (Some employers voluntarily offer paid family leave, but this is not a requirement of the FMLA.) The

FMLA expressly covers private and public (government) employees who have worked for their employers for at least a year.

An eligible employee may take up to *twelve weeks of leave* within a twelve-month period for any of the following reasons:

1. To care for a newborn baby within one year of birth.
2. To care for an adopted or foster child within one year of the time the child is placed with the employee.
3. To care for the employee's spouse, child, or parent who has a serious health condition.
4. If the employee suffers from a serious health condition and is unable to perform the essential functions of her or his job.
5. For any qualifying exigency (nonmedical emergency) arising out of the fact that the employee's spouse, son, daughter, or parent is a covered military member on active duty.[11] For instance, an employee can take leave to arrange for child care or to deal with financial or legal matters when a spouse is being deployed overseas.

In addition, an employee may take military caregiver leave to care for a family member with a serious injury or illness incurred as a result of military duty.[12] For military caregiver leave, the employee may take up to *twenty-six weeks* of leave within a twelve-month period.

In the following case, an employee asked for medical leave to care for her mother on a trip to Las Vegas, Nevada.

---

10. 29 U.S.C. Sections 2601, 2611–2619, 2651–2654.

11. 29 C.F.R. Section 825.126.
12. 29 C.F.R. Section 825.200.

Case 34.2

Ballard v. Chicago Park District

United States Court of Appeals, Seventh Circuit, 741 F.3d 838 (2014).

Background and Facts Beverly Ballard worked for the Chicago Park District. She lived with her mother, Sarah, who suffered from end-stage congestive heart failure. Beverly served as Sarah's primary caregiver with support from Horizon Hospice & Palliative Care. The hospice helped Sarah plan and secure funds for an end-of-life goal, a "family trip" to Las Vegas. To accompany Sarah as her caretaker, Beverly asked the Park District for unpaid time off under the Family Medical and Leave Act (FMLA). The employer refused, but Beverly and Sarah took the trip as planned.

Later, the Park District terminated Beverly for "unauthorized absences." She filed a suit in a federal district court against the employer. The court issued a decision in Beverly's favor. The Park District appealed, arguing that Beverly had been absent from work on a "recreational trip."

In the Language of the Court
FLAUM, Circuit Judge.
    * * * *

We begin with the text of the [FMLA]: an eligible employee is entitled to leave "in order to care for" a family member with a "serious health condition."

Case 34.2 Continued

* * * *

* * * *The FMLA's text does not restrict care to a particular place or geographic location.* For instance, it does not say that an employee is entitled to time off "to care *at home* for" a family member. *The only limitation it places on care is that the family member must have a serious health condition.* We are reluctant, without good reason, to read in another limitation that Congress has not provided. [Emphasis added.]

* * * *

Sarah's basic medical, hygienic, and nutritional needs did not change while she was in Las Vegas, and Beverly continued to assist her with those needs during the trip. In fact, * * * Beverly's presence proved quite important indeed when a fire at the hotel made it impossible to reach their room, requiring Beverly to find another source of insulin and pain medicine. Thus, at the very least, [Beverly] requested leave in order to provide physical care.

* * * *

* * * The Park District describes [Beverly's] travel as a "recreational trip" or a "non-medically related pleasure trip." It also raises the specter that employees will help themselves to unpaid FMLA leave in order to take personal vacations, simply by bringing seriously ill family members along. So perhaps what the Park District means to argue is that the real reason Beverly requested leave was in order to take a free pleasure trip, and not in order to care for her mother. * * * However, * * * an employer concerned about the risk that employees will abuse the FMLA's leave provisions may of course require that requests be certified by the family member's health care provider. And any worries about opportunistic leave-taking in this case should be tempered by the fact that this dispute arises out of the hospice and palliative care context.

If Beverly had sought leave to care for her mother in Chicago, her request would have fallen within the scope of the FMLA. So too if Sarah had lived in Las Vegas instead of with her daughter, and Beverly had requested leave to care for her mother there. Ultimately, other than a concern that our straightforward reading will "open the door to increased FMLA requests," the Park District gives us no reason to treat the current scenario any differently.

Decision and Remedy *The U.S. Court of Appeals for the Seventh Circuit affirmed the lower court's judgment. Under the FMLA, an eligible employee is entitled to take leave from work to care for a family member with a serious health condition. The care is not restricted to a particular place (such as "at home").*

Critical Thinking

- **What If the Facts Were Different?** *Suppose that Beverly had requested leave to make arrangements for a change in Sarah's care, such as a transfer to a nursing home. Is it likely that the result would have been different? Explain.*
- **Legal Environment** *Under the FMLA, an employee is eligible for leave when he or she is needed to care for a family member. Should "needed to care for" be interpreted to cover only ongoing physical care? Discuss.*

34–3b Benefits and Protections

When an employee takes FMLA leave, the employer must continue the worker's health-care coverage on the same terms as if the employee had continued to work. On returning from FMLA leave, most employees must be restored to their original position or to a comparable position (with nearly equivalent pay and benefits, for instance). An important exception allows the employer to avoid reinstating a *key employee*—defined as an employee whose pay falls within the top 10 percent of the firm's workforce.

34–3c Violations

An employer that violates the FMLA can be required to provide various remedies, including the following:

1. Damages to compensate the employee for lost wages and benefits, denied compensation, and actual monetary losses (such as the cost of providing care for a family member). Compensatory damages are available up to an amount equivalent to the employee's wages for twelve weeks.
2. Job reinstatement.
3. Promotion, if a promotion has been denied.

A successful plaintiff is also entitled to court costs and attorneys' fees. In addition, if the plaintiff shows that the employer acted in bad faith, the plaintiff can receive two times the amount of damages awarded by a judge or jury. Supervisors can also be held personally liable, as employers, for violations of the act.

Employers generally are required to notify employees when an absence will be counted against FMLA leave. If an employer fails to provide such notice, and that failure to notify causes harm to the employee, the employer can be sanctioned.[13]

34–4 Health, Safety, and Income Security

Under the common law, employees who were injured on the job had to file lawsuits against their employers to obtain recovery. Today, numerous state and federal statutes protect employees from the risk of accidental injury, death, or disease resulting from their employment. In addition, the government protects employees' income through Social Security, Medicare, unemployment insurance, and the regulation of pensions and health insurance plans.

34–4a The Occupational Safety and Health Act

At the federal level, the primary legislation protecting employees' health and safety is the Occupational Safety and Health Act,[14] which is administered by the Occupational Safety and Health Administration (OSHA). The act imposes on employers a general duty to keep the workplace safe.

To this end, OSHA has established specific safety standards that employers must follow, depending on the industry. For instance, OSHA regulations require the use of safety guards on certain mechanical equipment. It also sets maximum levels of exposure to substances in the workplace that may be harmful to workers' health.

Notices, Records, and Reports The act requires that employers post certain notices in the workplace, maintain specific records, and submit reports. Employers with eleven or more employees are required to keep occupational injury and illness records for each employee. Each record must be made available for inspection when requested by an OSHA compliance officer.

Whenever a work-related injury or disease occurs, employers must make reports directly to OSHA. If an employee dies or three or more employees are hospitalized because of a work-related incident, the employer must notify OSHA within eight hours. A company that fails to do so will be fined. Following the incident, a complete inspection of the premises is mandatory.

Inspections OSHA compliance officers may enter and inspect the facilities of any establishment covered by the Occupational Safety and Health Act. Employees may also file complaints of violations. Under the act, an employer cannot discharge an employee who files a complaint or who, in good faith, refuses to work in a high-risk area if bodily harm or death might result.

34–4b State Workers' Compensation Laws

State **workers' compensation laws** establish an administrative procedure for compensating workers injured on the job. Instead of suing, an injured worker files a claim with the state agency or board that administers local workers' compensation claims.

All states require employers to provide workers' compensation insurance, but the specific rules vary by state. Most states have a state fund that employers pay into for workers' compensation coverage. Usually, employers can purchase insurance from a private insurer as an alternative to paying into the state fund. Most states also allow certain employers to be *self-insured*—that is, employers that show an ability to pay claims do not need to buy insurance.

No state covers all employees under its workers' compensation statute. Typically, domestic workers, agricultural workers, temporary employees, and employees of common carriers (companies that provide transportation services to the public) are excluded. Minors are covered.

Requirements for Receiving Workers' Compensation In general, the only requirements to recover benefits under state workers' compensation laws are:

1. The existence of an employment relationship.
2. An *accidental* injury that *occurred on the job or in the course of employment,* regardless of fault. (An injury that occurs while an employee is commuting to or from work usually is not covered because it did not occur on the job or in the course of employment.)

---

13. This was the United States Supreme Court's holding in *Ragsdale v. Wolverine World Wide, Inc.*, 535 U.S. 81, 122 S.Ct. 1155, 152 L.Ed.2d 167 (2002).
14. 29 U.S.C. Sections 553, 651–678.

An injured employee must notify her or his employer promptly (usually within thirty days of the accident). Generally, an employee must also file a workers' compensation claim within a certain period (sixty days to two years) from the time the injury is first noticed, rather than from the time of the accident.

Workers' Compensation versus Litigation If an employee accepts workers' compensation benefits, he or she may not sue for injuries caused by the employer's negligence. By barring lawsuits for negligence, workers' compensation laws also prevent employers from avoiding liability by using defenses, such as contributory negligence or assumption of risk. A worker may sue an employer who *intentionally* injures the worker, however.

34–4c Income Security

Federal and state governments participate in insurance programs designed to protect employees and their families from the financial impact of retirement, disability, death, hospitalization, and unemployment. The key federal law on this subject is the Social Security Act.[15]

Social Security The Social Security Act provides for old-age (retirement), survivors', and disability insurance. The act is therefore often referred to as OASDI. Retired workers who are covered by Social Security receive monthly payments from the Social Security Administration, which administers the Social Security Act. Social Security benefits are fixed by statute but increase automatically with increases in the cost of living.

Medicare Medicare is a federal government health-insurance program administered by the Social Security Administration for people sixty-five years of age and older and for some under age sixty-five who are disabled. It originally had two parts, one pertaining to hospital costs and the other to nonhospital medical costs, such as visits to physicians' offices. It now offers additional coverage options and a prescription-drug plan. People who have Medicare hospital insurance can obtain additional federal medical insurance if they pay monthly premiums.

Tax Contributions Under the Federal Insurance Contributions Act (FICA),[16] both employers and employees contribute to Social Security and Medicare, although the contributions are determined differently. The employer withholds the employee's FICA contributions

from the employee's wages and ordinarily matches the contributions.

For Social Security, the basis for the contributions is the employee's annual wage base—the maximum amount of the employee's wages that is subject to the tax. As of 2016, the maximum amount subject to the tax was \$118,500, and the tax rate was 12.4 percent.

The Medicare tax rate is 2.9 percent. Unlike Social Security, Medicare has no cap on the amount of wages subject to the tax. So even if an employee's salary is well above the cap for Social Security, he or she will still owe Medicare tax on the total earned income.

For Social Security and Medicare together, typically the employer and the employee each pay 7.65 percent. This is equivalent to 6.2 percent (half of 12.4 percent) for Social Security plus 1.45 percent (half of 2.9 percent) for Medicare up to the maximum wage base. Any earned income above that threshold is taxed only for Medicare. Self-employed persons pay both the employer's and the employee's portions of the Social Security and Medicare taxes.

Under the Affordable Care Act, high-income earners are subject to an additional Medicare tax of 3.8 percent on most investment income. This additional tax applies to single wage earners making more than \$200,000 and married couples making more than \$250,000.

Private Retirement Plans The major federal statute that regulates employee retirement plans is the Employee Retirement Income Security Act (ERISA).[17] This act empowers a branch of the U.S. Department of Labor to enforce its provisions governing employers that have private pension funds for their employees. ERISA does *not* require an employer to establish a pension plan. When a plan exists, however, ERISA provides standards for its management.

ERISA created the Pension Benefit Guaranty Corporation (PBGC), an independent federal agency, to provide timely and uninterrupted payment of voluntary private pension benefits. The pension plans pay annual insurance premiums (at set rates adjusted for inflation) to the PBGC, which then pays benefits to participants in the event that a plan is unable to do so.

A key provision of ERISA concerns vesting. **Vesting** gives an employee a legal right to receive pension benefits when she or he stops working. Before ERISA was enacted, some employees who had worked for companies for many years received no pension benefits when their employment terminated because those benefits had not vested. Under ERISA, generally all employee contributions to pension plans vest immediately. Employee

---

15. 42 U.S.C. Sections 301–1397e.
16. 26 U.S.C. Sections 3101–3125.

17. 29 U.S.C. Sections 1001 *et seq.*

rights to employer contributions vest after five years of employment.

Unemployment Insurance The Federal Unemployment Tax Act (FUTA)[18] created a state-administered system that provides unemployment compensation to eligible individuals who have lost their jobs. The FUTA and state laws require employers that fall under the provisions of the act to pay unemployment taxes at regular intervals. The proceeds from these taxes are then paid out to qualified unemployed workers.

To be eligible for unemployment compensation, a worker must be willing and able to work. Workers who have been fired for misconduct or who have voluntarily left their jobs are not eligible for benefits. Normally, workers must be actively seeking employment to continue receiving benefits.

■ **EXAMPLE 34.7** Martha works for Baily Snowboards in Vermont. One day at work, Martha receives a text from her son saying that he has been taken to the hospital. Martha rushes to the hospital and does not return to work for several days. Bailey hires someone else for Martha's position, and Martha files for unemployment benefits. Martha's claim will be denied because she left her job voluntarily and made no effort to maintain contact with her employer. ■

COBRA The Consolidated Omnibus Budget Reconciliation Act (COBRA)[19] enables employees to continue, for a limited time, their health-care coverage after they are no longer eligible for group health-insurance plans. The workers—not the employers—pay the premiums for the continued coverage.

COBRA prohibits an employer from eliminating a worker's medical, vision, or dental insurance when the worker's employment is terminated or when a reduction in the worker's hours would affect coverage. Termination of employment may be voluntary or involuntary. Only workers fired for gross misconduct are excluded from protection. Employers, with some exceptions, must inform employees of COBRA's provisions before the termination or reduction of work hours.

A worker has sixty days (from the date that the group coverage would stop) to decide whether to continue with the employer's group insurance plan. If the worker chooses to continue coverage, the employer is obligated to keep the policy active for up to eighteen months (twenty-nine months if the worker is disabled). The coverage must be the same as that provided to the worker (and his or her family members) prior to the termination or reduction of work. An employer that does not comply with COBRA risks substantial penalties, including a tax of up to 10 percent of the annual cost of the group plan or $500,000, whichever is less.

Employer-Sponsored Group Health Plans The Health Insurance Portability and Accountability Act (HIPAA)[20] contains provisions that affect employer-sponsored group health plans. For instance, HIPAA restricts the manner in which employers collect, use, and disclose the health information of employees and their families. Employers must designate privacy officials, distribute privacy notices, and train employees to ensure that employees' health information is not disclosed to unauthorized parties.

Failure to comply with HIPAA regulations can result in civil penalties of up to $100 per person per violation (with a cap of $25,000 per year). Employers are also subject to criminal prosecution for certain types of HIPAA violations. An employer can face up to $250,000 in criminal fines and imprisonment for up to ten years if convicted.

Affordable Care Act The Affordable Care Act[21] (commonly referred to as Obamacare) requires most employers with fifty or more full-time employees to offer health-insurance benefits. Under the act, any business offering health benefits to its employees (even if not legally required to do so) may be eligible for tax credits of up to 35 percent to offset the costs.

An employer who fails to provide health benefits as required under the statute can be fined up to $2,000 for each employee after the first thirty people. (This is known as the 50/30 rule: employers with fifty employees must provide insurance, and those failing to do so will be fined for each employee after the first thirty.) An employer who offers a plan that costs an employee more than 9.5 percent of the employee's income may be assessed a penalty.

34–5 Employee Privacy Rights

Concerns about the privacy rights of employees have arisen as employers have purportedly used invasive tactics to monitor and screen workers. Perhaps the greatest privacy concern in employment today involves electronic monitoring of employees' activities.

---

18. 26 U.S.C. Sections 3301–3310.
19. 29 U.S.C. Sections 1161–1169.
20. 29 U.S.C. Sections 1181 *et seq.*
21. Pub. L. No. 111-148, 124 Stat. 119, March 23, 2010, codified in various sections of 42 U.S.C.

34–5a Electronic Monitoring

More than half of employers engage in some form of electronic monitoring of their employees. Many employers review employees' e-mail, as well as their social media posts and other Internet messages. Employers may also make video recordings of their employees at work, record their telephone conversations, and listen to their voice mail.

Employee Privacy Protection Employees of private (nongovernment) employers have some privacy protection under tort law and state constitutions. In addition, state and federal statutes may limit an employer's conduct in certain respects. For instance, the Electronic Communications Privacy Act prohibits employers from intercepting an employee's personal electronic communications unless they are made on devices and systems furnished by the employer.

Nonetheless, employers do have considerable leeway to monitor employees in the workplace. In addition, private employers generally are free to use filtering software to block access to certain Web sites, such as sites containing sexually explicit images. The First Amendment's protection of free speech prevents only *government employers* from restraining speech by blocking Web sites.

Reasonable Expectation of Privacy When determining whether an employer should be held liable for violating an employee's privacy rights, the courts generally weigh the employer's interests against the employee's reasonable expectation of privacy. Normally, if employees have been informed that their communications are being monitored, they cannot reasonably expect those interactions to be private. In addition, a court will typically hold that employees do not have a reasonable expectation of privacy when using a system (such as an e-mail system) provided by the employer.

If employees are *not* informed that certain communications are being monitored, the employer may be held liable for invading their privacy. Most employers that engage in electronic monitoring notify their employees about the monitoring. Nevertheless, a general policy may not sufficiently protect an employer monitoring forms of communications that the policy fails to mention. For instance, notifying employees that their e-mails and phone calls may be monitored does not necessarily protect an employer who monitors social media posts or text messages.

34–5b Other Types of Monitoring

In addition to monitoring their employees' online activities, employers also engage in other types of employee screening and monitoring. The practices discussed next have often been challenged as violations of employee privacy rights.

Lie-Detector Tests At one time, many employers required employees or job applicants to take polygraph examinations (lie-detector tests). Today, the Employee Polygraph Protection Act[22] generally prohibits employers from requiring employees or job applicants to take lie-detector tests or suggesting or requesting that they do so. The act also restricts employers' ability to use or ask about the results of any lie-detector test or to take any negative employment action based on the results.

Certain employers are exempt from these prohibitions. Federal, state, and local government employers, and certain security service firms, may conduct polygraph tests. In addition, companies that manufacture and distribute controlled substances may perform lie-detector tests. Other employers may use polygraph tests when investigating losses attributable to theft, including embezzlement and the theft of trade secrets.

Drug Testing In the interests of public safety and to reduce unnecessary costs, many employers, including the government, require their employees to submit to drug testing.

Public Employers. Government (public) employers are constrained in drug testing by the Fourth Amendment to the U.S. Constitution, which prohibits unreasonable searches and seizures. Drug testing of public employees is allowed by statute for transportation workers, however. Courts normally uphold drug testing of certain employees when drug use in a particular job may threaten public safety. Also, when there is a reasonable basis for suspecting public employees of drug use, courts often find that drug testing does not violate the Fourth Amendment.

Private Employers. The Fourth Amendment does not apply to drug testing conducted by private employers. Hence, the privacy rights and drug testing of private-sector employees are governed by state law. Many states have statutes that allow drug testing by private employers but restrict when and how the testing may be performed. A collective bargaining agreement (discussed later in this chapter) may also provide protection against drug testing (or may authorize drug testing in certain conditions).

The permissibility of testing a private employee for drugs often hinges on whether the employer's testing was reasonable. Random drug tests and even "zero-tolerance"

---

22. 29 U.S.C. Sections 2001 *et seq.*

policies (which deny a "second chance" to employees who test positive for drugs) have been held to be reasonable. It is also reasonable to require employees of private employers who are under contract with the federal government to undergo standard background investigations to disclose potential drug use.[23]

34–6 Immigration Law

The United States did not have any laws restricting immigration until the late nineteenth century. Immigration law has become increasingly important in recent years, however. An estimated 12 million undocumented immigrants now live in the United States, and many of them came to find jobs. Because U.S. employers face serious penalties if they hire undocumented workers, it is necessary for businesspersons to understand immigration laws. The most important laws affecting immigration in the context of employment are the Immigration Reform and Control Act (IRCA)[24] and the Immigration Act.[25]

34–6a The Immigration Reform and Control Act (IRCA)

When the IRCA was enacted in 1986, it provided amnesty to certain groups of aliens living illegally in the United States at the time. It also established a system that sanctions employers that hire immigrants who lack work authorization.

The IRCA makes it illegal to hire, recruit, or refer for a fee someone not authorized to work in this country. Through Immigration and Customs Enforcement officers, the federal government conducts random compliance audits and engages in enforcement actions against employers who hire undocumented workers.

I-9 Employment Verification To comply with IRCA requirements, an employer must perform **I-9 verifications** for new hires, including those hired as "contractors" or "day workers" if they work under the employer's direct supervision. Form I-9, Employment Eligibility Verification, which is available from U.S. Citizenship and Immigration Services,[26] must be completed *within three*

days of a worker's commencement of employment. The three-day period allows the employer to check the form's accuracy and to review and verify documents establishing the prospective worker's identity and eligibility for employment in the United States.

Documentation Requirements The employer must declare, under penalty of perjury, that an employee produced documents establishing his or her identity and legal employability. A U.S. passport establishing the person's citizenship is acceptable documentation. So is a document authorizing a foreign citizen to work in the United States, such as a permanent resident card or an *Alien Registration Receipt*.

Most legal actions alleging violations of I-9 rules are brought against employees who provide false information or documentation. If the employee enters false information on the I-9 form or presents false documentation, the employer can fire the worker, who then may be subject to deportation. Nevertheless, employers must be honest when verifying an employee's documentation. If an employer "should have known" that the worker was unauthorized, the employer has violated the rules.

Enforcement U.S. Immigration and Customs Enforcement (ICE) is the largest investigative arm of the U.S. Department of Homeland Security. ICE has a general inspection program that conducts random compliance audits. Other audits may occur if the agency receives a written complaint alleging that an employer has committed violations. Government inspections include a review of an employer's file of I-9 forms. The government does not need a subpoena or a warrant to conduct such an inspection.

If an investigation reveals a possible violation, ICE will bring an administrative action and issue a Notice of Intent to Fine, which sets out the charges against the employer. The employer has a right to a hearing on the enforcement action if it files a request within thirty days. This hearing is conducted before an administrative law judge, and the employer has a right to counsel and to discovery. The typical defense in such actions is good faith or substantial compliance with the documentation provisions.

Penalties An employer who violates the law by hiring an unauthorized worker is subject to substantial penalties. The employer can be fined up to $2,200 for each unauthorized employee for a first offense, $5,000 per employee for a second offense, and up to $11,000 for subsequent offenses. Employers who have engaged in a "pattern or

---

23. *See National Aeronautics and Space Administration v. Nelson,* 562 U.S. 134, 131 S.Ct. 746, 178 L.Ed.2d 667 (2011).
24. 29 U.S.C. Section 1802.
25. This act amended various provisions of the Immigration and Nationality Act of 1952, 8 U.S.C. Sections 1101 *et seq.*
26. U.S. Citizenship and Immigration Services is a federal agency that is part of the U.S. Department of Homeland Security.

practice of violations" are subject to criminal penalties, which include additional fines and imprisonment for up to ten years. A company can also be barred from future government contracts.

In determining the penalty, ICE considers the seriousness of the violation (such as intentional falsification of documents) and the employer's past compliance. ICE regulations also identify factors that will mitigate (lessen) or aggravate (increase) the penalty under certain circumstances. An employer that cooperates in the investigation, for instance, may receive a lesser penalty than an uncooperative employer.

34–6b The Immigration Act

Often, U.S. businesses find that they cannot hire enough domestic workers with specialized skills. For this reason, U.S. immigration laws have long made provisions for businesses to hire specially qualified foreign workers.

The Immigration Act of 1990 placed caps on the number of visas (entry permits) that can be issued to immigrants each year, including employment-based visas. Employment-based visas may be classified as permanent (immigrant) or temporary (nonimmigrant). Employers who wish to hire workers with either type of visa must comply with detailed government regulations.[27]

I-551 Alien Registration Receipts A company seeking to hire a noncitizen worker may do so if the worker is self-authorized. To be self-authorized, a worker must either be a lawful permanent resident or have a valid temporary Employment Authorization Document. A lawful permanent resident can prove his or her status to an employer by presenting an **I-551 Alien Registration Receipt,** known as a green card, or a properly stamped foreign passport.

Many immigrant workers are not already self-authorized, and an employer that wishes to hire them can attempt to obtain labor certification, or green cards, for them. A limited number of new green cards are issued each year. A green card can be obtained only for a person who is being hired for a permanent, full-time position. (A separate authorization system provides for the temporary entry and hiring of nonimmigrant visa workers.)

To gain authorization for hiring a foreign worker, an employer must show that no U.S. worker is qualified, willing, and able to take the job. The government has detailed regulations governing the advertising of positions as well as the certification process. Any U.S. applicants who meet the stated job qualifications must be interviewed for the position. The employer must also be able to show that the qualifications required for the job are a business necessity.

The H-1B Visa Program The most common and controversial visa program today is the H-1B visa system. To obtain an H1-B visa, the potential employee must be qualified in a "specialty occupation," meaning that the individual has highly specialized knowledge and has attained a bachelor's or higher degree or its equivalent. Individuals with H-1B visas can stay in the United States for three to six years and can work only for the sponsoring employer.

The recipients of these visas include numerous high-tech workers. A maximum of sixty-five thousand H-1B visas are set aside each year for new immigrants.[28] That limit is typically reached within the first few weeks of the year. Consequently, tech companies often complain that Congress needs to expand the number of H-1B visas available, to encourage the best and the brightest minds to work in the United States.

Critics of the H-1B visa program, however, believe that employers are sometimes using it to replace American workers with lower-paid foreign labor. For instance, Southern California Edison let go nearly five hundred workers from its information technology (IT) department in 2015. Shortly after that, allegations surfaced that the company had illegally replaced these employees with workers with H-1B visas, leading to a government investigation.

Labor Certification An employer who wishes to submit an H-1B application must first file a Labor Certification application on a form known as ETA 9035. The employer must agree to provide a wage level at least equal to the wages offered to other individuals with similar experience and qualifications. The employer must also show that the hiring will not adversely affect other workers similarly employed. The employer is required to inform U.S. workers of the intent to hire a foreign worker by posting the form. The U.S. Department of Labor reviews the applications and may reject them for omissions or inaccuracies.

H-2, O, L, and E Visas Other specialty temporary visas are available for other categories of employees. H-2 visas provide for workers performing agricultural labor of a seasonal nature. O visas provide entry for persons who

---

27. The most relevant regulations can be found at 20 C.F.R. Section 655 (for temporary employment) and 20 C.F.R. Section 656 (for permanent employment).

28. Immigration reform proposals generally raise this annual limit on H-1B visas to more than one hundred thousand.

have "extraordinary ability in the sciences, arts, education, business or athletics which has been demonstrated by sustained national or international acclaim." L visas allow a company's foreign managers or executives to work inside the United States. E visas permit the entry of certain foreign investors or entrepreneurs.

34–6c State Immigration Legislation

Until 2010, federal law exclusively governed immigration and the treatment of illegal immigrants. Then Arizona enacted a law that required Arizona law enforcement officials to identify and charge immigrants in Arizona who were there illegally, potentially leading to the immigrants' deportation. Among other things, that law required immigrants to carry their papers at all times and allowed police to check a person's immigration status during any law enforcement action.

Arizona's law was challenged in *Arizona v. United States,*[29] which reached the United States Supreme Court. The Court upheld the controversial "show-me-your-papers" provision, which requires police to check the immigration status of persons stopped for other violations. All other provisions of Arizona's law were struck down as unconstitutional violations of the supremacy clause.

The fact that the Supreme Court did not strike down all parts of Arizona's immigration law opened the door for other states to enact immigration legislation, and many states have done so. The Court's decision does set limits, however. Although states may require immigrants to show their papers if stopped by law enforcement for another reason, they may not make it a crime to fail to carry documentation. States also cannot authorize law enforcement to arrest anyone based solely on a reasonable suspicion that the person is in the country illegally.

34–7 Labor Unions

In the 1930s, in addition to wage and hour laws, Congress also enacted the first of several labor laws. These laws protect employees' rights to join labor unions, to bargain with management over the terms and conditions of employment, and to conduct strikes.

34–7a Federal Labor Laws

Federal labor laws governing union-employer relations have developed considerably since the first law was enacted in 1932. Initially, the laws were concerned with protecting the rights and interests of workers. Subsequent legislation placed some restraints on unions and granted rights to employers. We look here at four major federal statutes regulating union-employer relations.

Norris-LaGuardia Act Congress protected peaceful strikes, picketing, and boycotts in 1932 in the Norris-LaGuardia Act.[30] The statute restricted the power of federal courts to issue injunctions against unions engaged in peaceful strikes. In effect, this act declared a national policy permitting employees to organize.

National Labor Relations Act One of the foremost statutes regulating labor is the 1935 National Labor Relations Act (NLRA).[31] This act established the rights of employees to engage in collective bargaining and to strike.

Unfair Labor Practices. The NLRA specifically defined a number of employer practices as unfair to labor:

1. Interference with the efforts of employees to form, join, or assist labor organizations or to engage in concerted activities for their mutual aid or protection.
2. An employer's domination of a labor organization or contribution of financial or other support to it.
3. Discrimination in the hiring of or the awarding of tenure to employees for reason of union affiliation.
4. Discrimination against employees for filing charges under the act or giving testimony under the act.
5. Refusal to bargain collectively with the duly designated representative of the employees.

The National Labor Relations Board. The NLRA created the National Labor Relations Board (NLRB) to oversee union elections and to prevent employers from engaging in unfair and illegal union activities and unfair labor practices.

The NLRB has the authority to investigate employees' charges of unfair labor practices and to file complaints against employers in response to these charges. When violations are found, the NLRB may issue a **cease-and-desist order** compelling the employer to stop engaging in the unfair practices. Cease-and-desist orders can be enforced by a federal appellate court if necessary. After the NLRB rules on claims of unfair labor practices, its decision may be appealed to a federal court.

■ **CASE IN POINT 34.8** Roundy's, Inc., which operates a chain of stores in Wisconsin, became involved in a dispute with a local construction union. When union

---

29. ___ U.S. ___, 132 S.Ct. 2492, 183 L.Ed.2d 351 (2012).

30. 29 U.S.C. Sections 101–110, 113–115.
31. 20 U.S.C. Sections 151–169.

members started distributing "extremely unflattering" flyers outside the stores, Roundy's ejected them from the property. The NLRB filed a complaint against Roundy's for unfair labor practices. An administrative law judge ruled that Roundy's had violated the law by discriminating against the union, and a federal appellate court affirmed. It is an unfair labor practice for an employer to prohibit union members from distributing flyers outside a store when it allows nonunion members to do so.[32] ■

Good Faith Bargaining. Under the NLRA, employers and unions have a duty to bargain in good faith. Bargaining over certain subjects is mandatory, and a party's refusal to bargain over these subjects is an unfair labor practice that can be reported to the NLRB. For instance, bargaining is mandatory for subjects relating to wages or working hours.

Workers Protected by the NLRA. To be protected under the NLRA, an individual must be an employee or a job applicant. (If job applicants were not covered, the NLRA's ban on discrimination in regard to hiring would mean little.) Additionally, individuals who are hired by a union to organize a company (union organizers) are to be considered employees of the company for NLRA purposes.[33]

Even a temporary worker hired through an employment agency might qualify for protection under the NLRA. ■ **CASE IN POINT 34.9** Matthew Faush was an African American employee of Labor Ready, which provides temporary employees to businesses. Faush was assigned to a job stocking shelves at a Tuesday Morning store in Pennsylvania. After he was fired by Tuesday Morning, Faush filed a suit alleging discrimination. Tuesday Morning argued that Faush was not its employee. A federal court, however, found that the NLRA's protections may extend to temporary workers and that Faush was entitled to a trial.[34] ■

Labor-Management Relations Act The Labor-Management Relations Act (LMRA or Taft-Hartley Act) of 1947[35] was passed to prohibit certain unfair union practices. For instance, the act outlawed the **closed shop**—a firm that requires union membership as a condition of employment. The act preserved the legality of the union shop, however. A **union shop** does not require union membership as a prerequisite for employment but

can, and usually does, require that workers join the union after a specified time on the job.

The LMRA also prohibited unions from refusing to bargain with employers, engaging in certain types of picketing, and *featherbedding* (causing employers to hire more employees than necessary). In addition, the act allowed individual states to pass **right-to-work laws**—laws making it illegal for union membership to be required for *continued* employment in any establishment. Thus, union shops are technically illegal in the twenty-seven states that have right-to-work laws.

Labor-Management Reporting and Disclosure Act The Labor-Management Reporting and Disclosure Act (LMRDA)[36] established an employee bill of rights and reporting requirements for union activities. The act also outlawed **hot-cargo agreements,** in which employers voluntarily agree with unions not to handle, use, or deal in goods of other employers produced by nonunion employees.

The LMRDA strictly regulates unions' internal business procedures, including elections. For instance, it requires unions to hold regularly scheduled elections of officers using secret ballots. Former convicts are prohibited from holding union office. Moreover, union officials are accountable for union property and funds. Members have the right to attend and to participate in union meetings, to nominate officers, and to vote in most union proceedings.

34–7b Union Organization

Typically, the first step in organizing a union at a particular firm is to have the workers sign authorization cards. An **authorization card** usually states that the worker desires to have a certain union, such as the United Auto Workers, represent the workforce. If a majority of the workers sign authorization cards, the union organizers (unionizers) present the cards to the employer and ask for formal recognition of the union.

The employer is not required to recognize the union at this point in the process, but it may do so voluntarily on a showing of majority support. (Under pro-labor legislation proposed repeatedly, the employer would have to recognize the union as soon as a majority of the workers had signed authorization cards—without holding an election.)[37]

Union Elections If the employer refuses to voluntarily recognize the union—or if less than a majority of the workers sign authorization cards—the union organizers

32. *Roundy's, Inc. v. NLRB*, 647 F.3d 638 (7th Cir. 2012).
33. See the United States Supreme Court's landmark decision in *NLRB v. Town & Country Electric, Inc.*, 516 U.S. 85, 116 S.Ct. 450, 133 L.Ed.2d 371 (1995).
34. *Faush v. Tuesday Morning, Inc.*, 88 F.3d 208 (3d Cir. 2015).
35. 29 U.S.C. Sections 141 *et seq.*
36. 29 U.S.C. Sections 401 *et seq.*
37. The proposed legislation is the Employee Free Choice Act (or Card Check Bill).

can petition for an election. The organizers present the authorization cards to the NLRB with a petition to hold an election on unionization. For an election to be held, they must demonstrate that at least 30 percent of the workers to be represented support a union or an election.

Appropriate Bargaining Unit. Not every group of workers can form a single union. The proposed union must represent an *appropriate bargaining unit*. One key requirement is a *mutuality of interest* among all the workers to be represented by the union. Factors considered in determining whether there is a mutuality of interest include the similarity of the jobs of the workers to be unionized and their physical location.

New NLRB Rules Expedite Elections. New NLRB rules that took effect in 2015 significantly reduce the time between the filing of a petition and the ensuing election. As a result, the time before an election is held has changed from an average of thirty-eight days to as little as ten days after the filing. This change favors unions because it gives employers less time to respond to organizing campaigns, which unions often spend months preparing.

The NLRB now requires that a company hold a pre-election hearing within eight days after it receives a petition for an organizing election. On the day before the hearing, the company must also submit a "statement of position" laying out every argument it intends to make against the union. Any argument that the company does not include in its position paper can be excluded from evidence at the hearing. Once the hearing is held, an election can be scheduled right away.

Voting. If an election is held, the NLRB supervises the election and ensures secret voting and voter eligibility. If the proposed union receives majority support in a fair election, the NLRB certifies the union as the bargaining representative for the employees.

Union Election Campaigns Many disputes between labor and management arise during union election campaigns. Generally, the employer has control over unionizing activities that take place on company property and during working hours. Thus, the employer may limit the campaign activities of union supporters as long as it has a legitimate business reason for doing so. The employer may also reasonably limit when and where union solicitation may occur in the workplace, provided that the employer is not discriminating against the union. (Can union organizers use company e-mail during campaigns? See this chapter's *Managerial Strategy* feature for a discussion of this topic.)

■ **EXAMPLE 34.10** A union is seeking to organize clerks at a department store owned by Amanti Enterprises. Amanti can prohibit all union solicitation in areas of the store open to the public because the unionizing activities could interfere with the store's business. It can also restrict union-related activities to coffee breaks and lunch hours. If Amanti allows solicitation for charitable causes in the workplace, however, it may not prohibit union solicitation. ■

An employer may campaign among its workers against the union, but the NLRB carefully monitors and regulates the tactics used by management. If the employer issues threats ("If the union wins, you'll all be fired") or engages in other unfair labor practices, the NLRB may certify the union even though the union lost the election. Alternatively, the NLRB may ask a court to order a new election.

Whether an employer violated its employees' rights under the National Labor Relations Act during a union election campaign was at issue in the following case.

Case Analysis 34.3

Contemporary Cars, Inc. v. National Labor Relations Board
United States Court of Appeals, Seventh Circuit, 814 F.3d 859 (2016).

In the Language of the Court
HAMILTON, Circuit Judge.
* * * *

* * * Contemporary Cars, Inc., * * * sells and services cars in Maitland, Florida. Bob Berryhill, the dealership's general manager, is responsible for the dealership's overall operations. * * * AutoNation owns the dealership, as well as over 200 other dealerships throughout the United States.

This case focuses on the dealership's service department [which the dealership had previously split into three teams].

* * * The International Association of Machinists began a campaign * * * to organize the service technicians. * * * The technicians talked among themselves and held off-site meetings.
* * * *

* * * The union filed its representation petition. The [National Labor Relations Board] approved the proposed bargaining unit, and an election was scheduled.

In the weeks before the election, Berryhill and AutoNation vice president

Case 34.3 Continued

* * * Brian Davis held group [and individual] meetings [with the technicians]. * * * One week before the election, * * * Berryhill * * * announced that the dealership was working on fixing problems the technicians had and that he was replacing two team leaders, [Andre] Grobler and Oudit Manbahal, with new team leaders.

* * * Technician Anthony Roberts * * * was then playing a leading role in the union organizing. * * * About a week before the union election, the dealership laid off Roberts, though Roberts had a higher skill rating, more hours, and more seniority than many other technicians.

* * * *

* * * The technicians voted in favor of unionizing.

* * * After the election, the dealership challenged the certification of the union as the exclusive representative of a bargaining unit consisting of service technicians. * * * The [National Labor Relations] Board affirmed the certification.

* * * The Board * * * filed a complaint alleging that the dealership and AutoNation had violated * * * the National Labor Relations Act. * * * An administrative law judge found * * * that the dealership and AutoNation had indeed violated the Act by interfering with their employees' protected rights to engage in concerted activity and to organize a union [and] by firing Anthony Roberts due to anti-union animus [hostility]. [The judge ordered the dealership to cease its interference with its employees' rights and to reinstate Roberts. The judge also ordered AutoNation to post a notice at all of its dealerships that it was rescinding the no-solicitation rule.] The Board affirmed the * * * order.

The dealership and AutoNation petitioned [the U.S. Court of Appeals for Seventh Circuit] for judicial review. [The NLRB cross-petitioned for enforcement of the order.]

* * * *

The administrative law judge found, and the Board affirmed, that the dealership and AutoNation in a number of

instances acted unlawfully to frustrate their employees' protected rights to engage in concerted activity and to organize a union.

* * * *

* * * The dealership violated [the Act] in the run-up to the election by coercively creating an impression of surveillance of union activity, interrogating employees about union activity, and soliciting and promising to remedy employee grievances.

* * * *

[Team Leader] Grobler created a coercive impression of surveillance when he commented on technician Juan Cazorla's attendance of union meetings.

* * * Grobler asked [Cazorla] why he was in such a rush to leave work * * * , suggesting that Cazorla had "that meeting" to go to. Cazorla pretended not to know what Grobler was talking about, although he was in fact rushing to get to a union meeting. Again [on a different occasion] Grobler commented to Cazorla that he had "better rush" since he had a meeting * * * . It would have been reasonable for Cazorla to infer from Grobler's comments that his union activities were under management surveillance.

* * * *

* * * Berryhill coercively interrogated employees [when he] called them individually into his office and asked them about union activity. The dealership's service director was also present. * * * The setting of the meetings in Berryhill's office, Berryhill's and the director's positions of authority, and the fact that each technician was alone and outnumbered by managers all support the finding of coercion.

* * * *

* * * At the * * * meetings, Berryhill asked the technicians how the dealership could improve. * * * Berryhill [stated] that he was "working on" the problems and "in progress" on the solutions. * * * The * * * meetings also included inquiries about the union effort. * * * This was an effort to frustrate the union organizing drive by soliciting and at least implicitly promising to adjust grievances.

* * * *

* * * AutoNation vice president * * * Davis coercively interrogated a * * * technician, Tumeshwar Persaud * * * . Davis * * * asked him how he felt about the union election. * * * The question forced Persaud, who had not previously disclosed his union support, either to disclose his own union sympathies or to report on his perception of his fellow employees' union support.

* * * Davis held a meeting with employees at which he solicited employee complaints and, upon hearing that management had been unresponsive to employee complaints in the past, said that employees could call him or talk to him at any time. This meeting was part of a series of * * * meetings that management held in the run-up to the union election. * * * Davis was implicitly promising to remedy grievances with the goal of frustrating the union effort.

* * * *

* * * AutoNation * * * promulgated [publicized] an overly broad no-solicitation policy in the employee handbook used at all of its facilities. * * * AutoNation's policy prohibited any solicitation on AutoNation property at any time. * * * *The policy* * * * *amounted to an unfair labor practice because of the likelihood it would chill protected concerted activity.* [Emphasis added.]

* * * *

* * * The dealership's discharge of Anthony Roberts * * * a week before the election was motivated by anti-union animus.

* * * *

* * * Berryhill's identification of Roberts as a troublemaker and instigator of the organizational campaign established that anti-union animus was a substantial factor motivating Roberts's layoff. * * * The dealership's stated reason for firing Roberts—that he lacked sufficient electronic diagnostic skills—failed to establish that Roberts would have been laid off in the absence of anti-union animus. * * * Roberts was more productive and had a higher skill rating than many technicians who were retained.

Case 34.3 Continues

Case 34.3 Continued

* * * *

Substantial evidence and a reasonable basis in law support the Board's order and the administrative law judge's order to the extent affirmed by the Board. We DENY the dealership and AutoNation's petition for review and ENFORCE the Board's order in its entirety.

Legal Reasoning Questions

1. What might the dealership have asserted in defense to the charge that its actions violated its employees' rights?

2. After the election but before the union was certified, the dealership laid off four technicians and cut others' pay without bargaining with the union, claiming economic hard times. Did these steps constitute an unfair labor practice? Discuss.

3. What could the employer have done to avoid the charge in this case?

MANAGERIAL STRATEGY   Union Organizing Using a Company's E-Mail System

When union organizers start an organizing drive, there are certain restrictions on what they can do, particularly within the workplace. Both employers and employees must comply with Section 7 of the National Labor Relations Act (NLRA).

Protected Concerted Activities

Under Section 7, employees have certain rights to communicate among themselves. Section 7 states, "Employees shall have the right to self-organization, . . . and to engage in other concerted activities for the purpose of collective bargaining or other mutual aid or protection. . . ."

What about communication via e-mail? Can union organizers use a company-operated e-mail system for organizing purposes? Companies typically provide e-mail systems so that employees can communicate with outsiders and among themselves as part of their jobs. Generally, company policies have prohibited the use of company-owned and -operated e-mail systems for other than job-related communications. Starting in the early 2000s, some union organizers challenged this prohibition.

The NLRB's Perspective Evolves

The first major case concerning this issue was decided by the National Labor Relations Board (NLRB) in 2007.[a] The NLRB allowed an employer's written policy that prohibited the use of a company-provided e-mail system for non-job-related solicitations. This decision was affirmed in relevant part by a federal court two years later.[b]

In late 2014, the NLRB reversed its 2007 position. "We decide today that employee use of e-mail for statutorily protected communications on non-working time must presumptively be permitted by employers who have chosen to give employees access to their e-mail systems."[c] The NLRB argued that its 2007 decision had failed to adequately protect "employees' rights under the NLRA." The board also stated that it had a responsibility "to adapt the Act to the changing patterns of industrial life."

The new rules are clear. Once an organizing election is scheduled, a company must turn over all telephone numbers and home and e-mail addresses of the company's employees to union organizers within two days. The organizers can then communicate with employees via the company's e-mail system.

Business Questions

1. Employees meeting around the water cooler or coffee machine have always had the right to discuss work-related matters. Is an employer-provided e-mail system or social media outlet simply a digital water cooler? Why or why not?

2. If your company instituted a policy stating that employees should "think carefully about 'friending' co-workers," would that policy be lawful? Why or why not?

---

a. *Register Guard*, 351 NLRB 1110 (2007).
b. *Guard Publishing v. NLRB*, 571 F.3d 53 (D.C. Cir. 2009).

c. *Purple Communications, Inc. and Communication Workers of America, AFL-CIO*, Cases 21-CA-095151, 21-RC-091531, and 21-RC-091584, March 16, 2015.

34–7c Collective Bargaining

If the NLRB certifies the union, the union becomes the *exclusive bargaining representative* of the workers. The central legal right of a union is to engage in collective bargaining on the members' behalf. **Collective bargaining** is the process by which labor and management negotiate the terms and conditions of employment. Collective bargaining allows the representatives elected by union members to speak on behalf of the members at the bargaining table.

Terms and Conditions of Employment Wages, hours of work, and certain other conditions of employment may be discussed during collective bargaining sessions. For instance, subjects for negotiation may include workplace safety, employee discounts, health-care plans, pension funds, and apprentice and scholarship programs.

Good Faith Bargaining Once an employer and a union sit down at the conference table, they must negotiate in good faith and make a reasonable effort to come to an agreement. They are not obligated to reach an agreement. They must, however, approach the negotiations with the idea that an agreement is possible. Both parties may engage in hard bargaining, but the bargaining process itself must be geared to reaching a compromise—not avoiding a compromise.

Although good faith is a matter of subjective intent, a party's actions can be used to evaluate the party's good or bad faith. Excessive use of delaying tactics may be proof of bad faith, for instance, as is insistence on obviously unreasonable contract terms.

If an employer (or a union) refuses to bargain in good faith without justification, it has committed an unfair labor practice. Exhibit 34–1 illustrates some differences between good faith and bad faith bargaining.

34–7d Strikes

Even when labor and management have bargained in good faith, they may be unable to reach a final agreement. When extensive collective bargaining has been conducted and an impasse results, the union may call a strike against the employer to pressure it into making concessions.

In a **strike,** the unionized employees leave their jobs and refuse to work. The workers also typically picket the workplace, standing outside the facility with signs stating their complaints.

A strike is an extreme action. Striking workers lose their rights to be paid, and management loses production and may lose customers when orders cannot be filled. Labor law regulates the circumstances and conduct of strikes.

Most strikes take the form of "economic strikes," which are initiated because the union wants a better contract. ■ **EXAMPLE 34.11** Teachers in Eagle Point, Oregon, engage in an economic strike after contract

EXHIBIT 34–1 Good Faith versus Bad Faith in Collective Bargaining

GOOD FAITH BARGAINING	BAD FAITH BARGAINING
1. Negotiating with the belief that an agreement is possible	1. Excessive delaying tactics
2. Seriously considering the other side's positions	2. Insistence on unreasonable contract terms
3. Making reasonable proposals	3. Rejecting a proposal without offering a counterproposal
4. Being willing to compromise	4. Engaging in a campaign among workers to undermine the union
5. Sending bargainers who have the authority to enter into agreements for the company	5. Constantly shifting positions on disputed contract terms
	6. Sending bargainers who lack authority to commit the company to a contract

negotiations with the school district fail to bring an agreement on pay, working hours, and subcontracting jobs. The unionized teachers picket outside the school building. Classes are canceled for a few weeks until the district can find substitute teachers who will fill in during the strike. ■

The Right to Strike The right to strike is guaranteed by the NLRA, within limits. Strike activities, such as picketing, are protected by the free speech guarantee of the First Amendment to the U.S. Constitution. Persons who are not employees have a right to participate in picketing an employer. The NLRA also gives workers the right to refuse to cross a picket line of fellow workers engaged in a lawful strike. Employers are permitted to hire replacement workers to substitute for the striking workers.

Illegal Strikes In the following situations, the conduct of the strikers may cause the strikes to be illegal:

1. *Violent strikes.* The use of violence (including the threat of violence) against management employees or substitute workers is illegal.

2. *Massed picketing.* If the strikers form a barrier and deny management or other nonunion workers access to the plant, the strike is illegal.

3. *Sit-down strikes.* Strikes in which employees simply stay in the plant without working are illegal.

4. *No-strike clause.* A strike may be illegal if it contravenes a no-strike clause that was in the previous collective bargaining agreement between the employer and the union.

5. *Secondary boycotts.* A **secondary boycott** is an illegal strike that is directed against someone other than the strikers' employer, such as companies that sell materials to the employer. ■ **EXAMPLE 34.12** The unionized workers of SemiCo go out on strike. To increase their economic leverage, the workers picket the leading suppliers and customers of SemiCo in an attempt to hurt the company's business. SemiCo is considered the primary employer, and its suppliers and customers are considered secondary employers. Picketing of the suppliers or customers is a secondary boycott. ■

6. *Wildcat strikes.* A wildcat strike occurs when a small number of workers, perhaps dissatisfied with a union's representation, call their own strike. The union is the exclusive bargaining representative of a group of workers, and only the union can call a strike. Therefore, a wildcat strike, unauthorized by the certified union, is illegal.

After a Strike Ends In a typical strike, the employer has a right to hire permanent replacements during the strike. The employer need not terminate the replacement workers when the economic strikers seek to return to work. In other words, striking workers are not guaranteed the right to return to their jobs after the strike if satisfactory replacement workers have been found.

If the employer has not hired replacement workers to fill the strikers' positions, however, then the employer must rehire the economic strikers to fill any vacancies. Employers may not discriminate against former economic strikers, and those who are rehired retain their seniority rights.

34–7e Lockouts

Lockouts are the employer's counterpart to the workers' right to strike. A **lockout** occurs when the employer shuts down to prevent employees from working. Lockouts usually are used when the employer believes that a strike is imminent or the parties have reached a stalemate in collective bargaining.

■ **EXAMPLE 34.13** Owners of the teams in the National Football League (NFL) imposed a lockout on the NFL players' union in 2011 after negotiations on a new collective bargaining agreement broke down. The NFL owners had proposed to reduce players' salaries and extend the season by two games because of decreased profits due to the struggling economy. A settlement was reached before the start of the 2011 football season. The players accepted a somewhat smaller proportion of the revenue generated in exchange for better working conditions and more retirement benefits. The owners agreed to keep the same number of games per season.

The owners of the teams in the National Basketball Association (NBA) also locked out their players in 2011 after the two sides failed to reach a collective bargaining agreement. The dispute involved the division of revenue and a salary cap. During the lockout, the players could not access NBA facilities, trainers, or staff, and the owners could not trade, sign, or contract with players. The lockout lasted 161 days and resulted in the cancellation of all preseason games and several weeks of regular season games. ■

Some lockouts are illegal. An employer may not use a lockout as a tool to break the union and pressure employees into decertification, which occurs when union members vote to dissociate from the union. An employer must be able to show some economic justification for the lockout.

Reviewing: Employment, Immigration, and Labor Law

Rick Saldona began working as a traveling salesperson for Aimer Winery in 2008. Sales constituted 90 percent of Saldona's work time. Saldona worked an average of fifty hours per week but received no overtime pay. In June 2018, Saldona's new supervisor, Caesar Braxton, claimed that Saldona had been inflating his reported sales calls and required Saldona to submit to a polygraph test. Saldona reported Braxton to the U.S. Department of Labor, which prohibited Aimer from requiring Saldona to take a polygraph test for this purpose.

In August 2018, Saldona's wife, Venita, fell from a ladder and sustained a head injury while employed as a full-time agricultural harvester. Saldona presented Aimer's Human Resources Department with a letter from his wife's physician indicating that she would need daily care for several months, and Saldona took leave until December 2018. Aimer had sixty-three employees at that time. When Saldona returned to Aimer, he was informed that his position had been eliminated because his sales territory had been combined with an adjacent territory. Using the information presented in the chapter, answer the following questions.

1. Would Saldona have been legally entitled to receive overtime pay at a higher rate? Why or why not?
2. What is the maximum length of time Saldona would have been allowed to take leave to care for his injured spouse?
3. Under what circumstances would Aimer have been allowed to require an employee to take a polygraph test?
4. Would Aimer likely be able to avoid reinstating Saldona under the *key employee* exception? Why or why not?

Debate This . . .   *The U.S. labor market is highly competitive, so state and federal laws that require overtime pay are unnecessary and should be abolished.*

Terms and Concepts

authorization card 655
cease-and-desist order 654
closed shop 655
collective bargaining 659
employment at will 641
hot-cargo agreement 655
I-9 verification 652

I-551 Alien Registration
   Receipt 653
lockout 660
minimum wage 643
right-to-work law 655
secondary boycott 660

strike 659
union shop 655
vesting 649
whistleblowing 642
workers' compensation law 648
wrongful discharge 642

Issue Spotters

1. Erin, an employee of Fine Print Shop, is injured on the job. For Erin to obtain workers' compensation, must her injury have been caused by Fine Print's negligence? Does it matter whether the action causing the injury was intentional? Explain. (See *Health, Safety, and Income Security*.)

2. Onyx applies for work with Precision Design Company, which requires union membership as a condition of employment. She also applies for work with Quality

Engineering, Inc. That company does not require union membership as a condition of employment but requires employees to join a union after six months on the job. Are these conditions legal? Why or why not? (See *Labor Unions*.)

- **Check your answers to the Issue Spotters against the answers provided in Appendix D at the end of this text.**

Business Scenarios

34–1. Unfair Labor Practices. Consolidated Stores is undergoing a unionization campaign. Prior to the union election, management states that the union is unnecessary to protect workers. Management also provides bonuses and wage increases to the workers during this period. The employees reject the union. Union organizers protest that the wage increases during the election campaign unfairly prejudiced the vote. Should these wage increases be regarded as an unfair labor practice? Discuss. (See *Labor Unions.*)

34–2. Wrongful Discharge. Denton and Carlo were employed at an appliance plant. Their job required them to perform occasional maintenance work while standing on a wire mesh twenty feet above the plant floor. Other employees had fallen through the mesh, and one of them had been killed by the fall. When their supervisor told them to perform tasks that would likely involve walking on the mesh, Denton and Carlo refused because they feared they might suffer bodily injury or death. Because they refused to do the requested work, the two employees were fired from their jobs. Was their discharge wrongful? If so, under what federal employment law? To what federal agency or department should they turn for assistance? (See *Employment at Will.*)

Business Case Problems

34–3. Workers' Compensation. As a safety measure, Dynea USA, Inc., required an employee, Tony Fairbanks, to wear steel-toed boots. One of the boots caused a sore on Fairbanks's leg. The skin over the sore broke, and within a week, Fairbanks was hospitalized with a methicillin-resistant staphylococcus aureus (MRSA) infection. He filed a workers' compensation claim. Dynea argued that the MRSA bacteria that caused the infection had been on Fairbanks's skin before he came to work. What are the requirements to recover workers' compensation benefits? Does this claim qualify? Explain. [*Dynea USA, Inc. v. Fairbanks,* 241 Or.App. 311, 250 P.3d 389 (2011)] (See *Health, Safety, and Income Security.*)

34–4. Exceptions to the Employment-at-Will Doctrine. Li Li worked for Packard Bioscience, and Mark Schmeizl was her supervisor. In March 2000, Schmeizl told Li to call Packard's competitors, pretend to be a potential customer, and request "pricing information and literature." Li refused to perform the assignment. She told Schmeizl that she thought the work was illegal and recommended that he contact Packard's legal department. Although a lawyer recommended against the practice, Schmeizl insisted that Li perform the calls. Moreover, he later wrote negative performance reviews because she was unable to get the requested information when she called competitors and identified herself as a Packard employee. On June 1, 2000, Li was terminated on Schmeizl's recommendation. Can Li bring a claim for wrongful discharge? Why or why not? [*Li Li v. Canberra Industries,* 134 Conn.App. 448, 39 A.3d 789 (2012)] (See *Employment at Will.*)

34–5. Collective Bargaining. SDBC Holdings, Inc., acquired Stella D'oro Biscuit Co., a bakery in New York City. At the time, a collective bargaining agreement existed between Stella D'oro and Local 50, Bakery, Confectionary, Tobacco Workers and Grain Millers International Union. During negotiations to renew the agreement, Stella D'oro refused to give the union a copy of the company's financial statement. Stella D'oro did allow Local 50 to examine and take notes on the financial statement and offered the union an opportunity to make its own copy. Did Stella D'oro engage in an unfair labor practice? Discuss. [*SDBC Holdings, Inc. v. National Labor Relations Board,* 711 F.3d 281 (2d Cir. 2013)] (See *Labor Unions.*)

34–6. Business Case Problem with Sample Answer— Unemployment Compensation. Fior Ramirez worked as a housekeeper for Remington Lodging & Hospitality, a hotel in Atlantic Beach, Florida. After her father in the Dominican Republic suffered a stroke, she asked her employer for time off to be with him. Ramirez's manager, Katie Berkowski, refused the request. Two days later, Berkowski received a call from Ramirez to say that she was with her father. He died about a week later, and Ramirez returned to work, but Berkowski told her that she had abandoned her position. Ramirez applied for unemployment compensation. Under the applicable state statute, "an employee is disqualified from receiving benefits if he or she voluntarily left work without good cause." Does Ramirez qualify for benefits? Explain. [*Ramirez v. Reemployment Assistance Appeals Commission,* 39 Fla.L.Weekly D317, 135 So.3d 408 (1 Dist. 2014)] (See *Health, Safety, and Income Security.*)

- **For a sample answer to Problem 34–6, go to Appendix E at the end of this text.**

34–7. Labor Unions. Carol Garcia and Pedro Salgado were bus drivers for Latino Express, Inc., a transportation company. Garcia and Salgado began soliciting signatures from other drivers to certify the Teamsters Local Union No. 777 as the official representative of the employees. Latino Express fired Garcia and Salgado. The two drivers filed a claim with the National Labor Relations Board (NLRB), alleging that the employer had committed an unfair labor practice. Which employer practice defined by the National Labor Relations Act did the plaintiffs most likely charge Latino Express with committing? Is the employer's discharge of Garcia and Salgado likely to be construed as a legitimate act in opposition to union solicitation? If a violation is found, what can the NLRB do? Discuss. [*Ohr v. Latino Express, Inc.,* 776 F.3d 469 (7th Cir. 2015)] (See *Labor Unions.*)

34–8. Health, Safety, and Income Security. Jefferson Partners LP entered into a collective bargaining agreement (CBA) with the Amalgamated Transit Union. Under the CBA, drivers had to either join the union or pay a fair share—85 percent—of union dues, which were used to pay for administrative costs incurred by the union. An employee who refused to pay was subject to discharge. Jefferson hired Tiffany Thompson to work as a bus driver. When told of the CBA requirement, she said that she thought it was unfair. She asserted that it was illegal to compel her to join the union and that it would be illegal to discharge her for not complying. She refused either to join the union or to pay the dues. More than two years later, she was fired on the ground that her continued refusal constituted misconduct. Is Thompson eligible for unemployment compensation? Explain. [*Thompson v. Jefferson Partners LP,* 2016 WL 953038 (Minn.App. 2016)] (See *Health, Safety, and Income Security.*)

34–9. A Question of Ethics—Workers' Compensation Law.

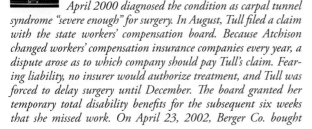 *In 1999, after working for Atchison Leather Products, Inc., for ten years, Beverly Tull began to complain of hand, wrist, and shoulder pain. Atchison recommended that she contact a certain physician, who in April 2000 diagnosed the condition as carpal tunnel syndrome "severe enough" for surgery. In August, Tull filed a claim with the state workers' compensation board. Because Atchison changed workers' compensation insurance companies every year, a dispute arose as to which company should pay Tull's claim. Fearing liability, no insurer would authorize treatment, and Tull was forced to delay surgery until December. The board granted her temporary total disability benefits for the subsequent six weeks that she missed work. On April 23, 2002, Berger Co. bought*

Atchison. The new employer adjusted Tull's work so that it was less demanding and stressful, but she continued to suffer pain. In July, a physician diagnosed her condition as permanent. The board granted her permanent partial disability benefits. By May 2005, bickering over the financial responsibility for Tull's claim involved five insurers—four of which had each covered Atchison for a single year and one of which covered Berger. [Tull v. Atchison Leather Products, Inc., 37 Kan.App.2d 87, 150 P.3d 316 *(2007)] (See Health, Safety, and Income Security.)*

(a) When an injured employee files a claim for workers' compensation, a proceeding is held to assess the injury and determine the amount of compensation. Should a dispute between insurers over the payment of the claim be resolved in the same proceeding? Why or why not?

(b) The board designated April 23, 2002, as the date of Tull's injury. What is the reason for determining the date of a worker's injury? Should the board in this case have selected this date or a different date? Why?

(c) How should the board assess liability for the payment of Tull's medical expenses and disability benefits? Would it be appropriate to impose joint and several liability on the insurers (holding each of them responsible for the full amount of damages)? Or should the individual liability of each of the insurers be determined? Explain.

Legal Reasoning Group Activity

34–10. Immigration. Nicole Tipton and Sadik Seferi owned and operated a restaurant in Iowa. Acting on a tip from the local police, agents of Immigration and Customs Enforcement executed search warrants at the restaurant and at an apartment where some restaurant workers lived. The agents discovered six undocumented aliens who worked at the restaurant and lived together. When the I-9 forms for the restaurant's employees were reviewed, none were found for the six aliens. They were paid in cash while other employees were

paid by check. Tipton and Seferi were charged with hiring and harboring undocumented aliens. (See *Immigration Law.*)

(a) The first group will develop an argument that Tipton and Seferi were guilty of hiring and harboring illegal aliens.

(b) The second group will assess whether Tipton and Seferi can assert a defense by claiming that they did not know that the workers were unauthorized aliens.

CHAPTER 35

Employment Discrimination

O ut of the 1960s civil rights movement to end racial and other forms of discrimination grew a body of law protecting employees against discrimination in the workplace. Legislation, judicial decisions, and administrative agency actions restrict employers from discriminating against workers on the basis of race, color, religion, national origin, gender, age, or disability. A class of persons defined by one or more of these criteria is known as a **protected class.**

Several federal statutes prohibit **employment discrimination** against members of protected classes. The most important is Title VII of the Civil Rights Act.[1] Title VII prohibits employment discrimination on the basis of race, color, religion, national origin, and gender. The Age Discrimination in Employment Act[2] and the Americans with Disabilities Act[3] pro-

---

1. 42 U.S.C. Sections 2000e–2000e-17.
2. 29 U.S.C. Sections 621–634.
3. 42 U.S.C. Sections 12102–12118.

hibit discrimination on the basis of age and disability, respectively. The protections afforded under these laws also extend to U.S. citizens who are working abroad for U.S. firms or for companies that are controlled by U.S. firms.

This chapter focuses on federal statutes, including the ones just mentioned. Many states have their own laws that protect employees against discrimination, however, and some provide more protection than federal laws do.

35–1 Title VII of the Civil Rights Act

Title VII of the Civil Rights Act prohibits job discrimination against employees, applicants, and union members on the basis of race, color, national origin, religion, and gender at any stage of employment. Title VII bans discrimination in the hiring process, discipline procedures, discharge, promotion, and benefits.

Title VII applies to employers with fifteen or more employees and labor unions with fifteen or more members. It also applies to labor unions that operate hiring halls (where members go regularly to be assigned jobs), employment agencies, and state and local governing units or agencies. The United States Supreme Court has ruled that an employer with fewer than fifteen employees is not automatically shielded from a lawsuit filed under Title VII.[4] In addition, the act prohibits discrimination in most federal government employment. When Title

VII applies to the employer, any employee—including an undocumented (alien) worker—can bring an action for employment discrimination.

35–1a The Equal Employment Opportunity Commission

The Equal Employment Opportunity Commission (EEOC) monitors compliance with Title VII. An employee alleging discrimination must file a claim with the EEOC before a lawsuit can be brought against the employer. The EEOC may investigate the dispute and attempt to obtain the parties' voluntary consent to an out-of-court settlement. If a voluntary agreement cannot be reached, the EEOC may file a suit against the employer on the employee's behalf.

■ **EXAMPLE 35.1** Jacqueline Cote met her wife, Diana Smithson, in Maine while they were both employees at Wal-Mart. They moved to Massachusetts and were married a few days after the state legalized same-sex marriage, and they continued working at a Wal-Mart there. Smithson eventually quit work to take care of Cote's elderly

---

4. *Arbaugh v. Y&H Corp.*, 546 U.S. 500, 126 S.Ct. 1235, 163 L.Ed.2d 1097 (2006).

mother. Cote tried to enroll her partner in Wal-Mart's health plan, but coverage was denied. Five years later, Smithson was diagnosed with cancer.

Cote filed a claim with the EEOC arguing that Wal-Mart had intentionally discriminated against her on the basis of sex. In 2014, the commission agreed that Cote "was treated differently and denied benefits because of her sex." The EEOC ordered Wal-Mart to work with Cote to help pay Smithson's medical bills. ■

The EEOC does not investigate every claim of employment discrimination. Generally, it takes only "priority cases," such as claims that affect many workers and those involving retaliatory discharge (firing an employee in retaliation for submitting a claim to the EEOC). If the EEOC decides not to investigate a claim, the EEOC issues a "right to sue" that allows the employee to bring his or her own lawsuit against the employer.

35–1b Limitations on Class Actions

In an important decision, the United States Supreme Court limited the rights of employees to bring discrimination claims against their employer as a group, or class. The decision did not affect the rights of individual employees to sue under Title VII, however.

■ **CASE IN POINT 35.2** A group of female employees sued Wal-Mart, the nation's largest private employer. The employees alleged that store managers who had discretion over pay and promotions were biased against women and disproportionately favored men. The employees wished to bring a class action—a lawsuit in which a small number of plaintiffs sue on behalf of a larger group. Lower courts ruled that the employees' class-action suit could proceed, and Wal-Mart appealed. The Supreme Court ruled in favor of Wal-Mart, effectively blocking the class action. The Court held that the women had failed to prove a company-wide policy of discrimination that had a common effect on all women included in the class. Therefore, they could not maintain a class action.[5] ■

35–1c Intentional and Unintentional Discrimination

Title VII of the Civil Rights Act prohibits both intentional and unintentional discrimination.

---

5. *Wal-Mart Stores, Inc. v. Dukes*, 564 U.S. 338, 131 S.Ct. 2541, 180 L.Ed.2d 374 (2011).

Intentional Discrimination Intentional discrimination by an employer against an employee is known as **disparate-treatment discrimination.** Because intent may sometimes be difficult to prove, courts have established certain procedures for resolving disparate-treatment cases.

Prima Facie **Case.** A plaintiff who sues on the basis of disparate-treatment discrimination must first make out a *prima facie* **case.** *Prima facie* is Latin for "at first sight" or "on its face." Legally, it refers to a fact that is presumed to be true unless contradicted by evidence.

To establish a *prima facie* case of disparate-treatment discrimination in hiring, a plaintiff must show all of the following:

1. The plaintiff is a member of a protected class.
2. The plaintiff applied and was qualified for the job in question.
3. The plaintiff was rejected by the employer.
4. The employer continued to seek applicants for the position or filled the position with a person not in a protected class.

A plaintiff who can meet these relatively easy requirements has made out a *prima facie* case of illegal discrimination in hiring and will win in the absence of a legally acceptable employer defense.

Sometimes, current and former employees make a claim of discrimination. When the plaintiff alleges that the employer fired or took some other adverse employment action against him or her, the same basic requirements apply. To establish a *prima facie* case, the plaintiff must show that he or she was fired or treated adversely for discriminatory reasons.

Burden-Shifting Procedure. Once the *prima facie* case is established, the burden then shifts to the employer-defendant, who must articulate a legal reason for not hiring the plaintiff. (Again, this also applies to firing and other adverse employment actions.) If the employer did not have a legal reason for taking the adverse employment action, the plaintiff wins.

If the employer can articulate a legitimate reason for the action, the burden shifts back to the plaintiff. To prevail, the plaintiff must then show that the employer's reason is a *pretext* (not the true reason) and that the employer's decision was actually motivated by discriminatory intent.

Unintentional Discrimination Employers often use interviews and tests to choose from among a large number of applicants for job openings. Minimum educational requirements are also common. Some employer practices, such as those involving educational requirements, may have an unintended discriminatory impact on a protected class.

Disparate-impact discrimination occurs when a protected group of people is adversely affected by an employer's practices, procedures, or tests, even though they do not appear to be discriminatory. In a disparate-impact discrimination case, the complaining party must first show that the employer's practices, procedures, or tests are effectively discriminatory. Once the plaintiff has made out a *prima facie* case, the burden of proof shifts to the employer to show that the practices or procedures in question were justified.

There are two ways of showing that an employer's practices, procedures, or tests are effectively discriminatory—that is, that disparate-impact discrimination exists.

Pool of Applicants. A plaintiff can prove a disparate impact by comparing the employer's workforce to the pool of qualified individuals available in the local labor market. The plaintiff must show that (1) as a result of educational or other job requirements or hiring procedures, (2) the percentage of nonwhites, women, or members of other protected classes in the employer's workforce (3) does not reflect the percentage of that group in the pool of qualified applicants. If the plaintiff can show a connection between the practice and the disparity, he or she has made out a *prima facie* case and need not provide evidence of discriminatory intent.

Rate of Hiring. A plaintiff can also prove disparate-impact discrimination by comparing the employer's *selection rates* of members and nonmembers of a protected class (nonwhites and whites, for instance, or women and men). When an educational or other job requirement or hiring procedure excludes members of a protected class from an employer's workforce at a substantially higher rate than nonmembers, discrimination occurs.

Under EEOC guidelines, a selection rate for a protected class that is less than four-fifths, or 80 percent, of the rate for the group with the highest rate of hiring generally is regarded as evidence of disparate impact. ■ **EXAMPLE 35.3** Shady Cove District Fire Department administers an exam to applicants for the position of firefighter. At the exam session, one hundred white applicants take the test, and fifty pass and are hired. At the same exam session, sixty minority applicants take the test, but only twelve pass and are hired. Because twelve is only 20 percent of sixty, the test will be considered discriminatory under the EEOC guidelines. ■

35–1d Discrimination Based on Race, Color, and National Origin

Title VII prohibits employers from discriminating against employees or job applicants on the basis of race, color, or national origin. Race is interpreted broadly to apply to the ancestry or ethnic characteristics of a group of persons, such as Native Americans. National origin refers to discrimination based on a person's birth in another country or his or her ancestry or culture, such as Hispanic.

If an employer's standards or policies for selecting or promoting employees have a discriminatory effect on employees or job applicants in these protected classes, then a presumption of illegal discrimination arises. To avoid liability, the employer must show that its standards or policies have a substantial, demonstrable relationship to realistic qualifications for the job in question.

■ **CASE IN POINT 35.4** Jiann Min Chang was an instructor at Alabama Agricultural and Mechanical University (AAMU). When AAMU terminated his employment, Chang filed a lawsuit claiming discrimination based on national origin. Chang established a *prima facie* case because he (1) was a member of a protected class, (2) was qualified for the job, (3) suffered an adverse employment action, and (4) was replaced by someone outside his protected class (a non-Asian instructor).

When the burden of proof shifted to the employer, however, AAMU showed that Chang had argued with a vice president and refused to comply with her instructions. The court ruled that the university had not renewed Chang's contract for a legitimate reason—insubordination—and therefore was not liable for unlawful discrimination.[6] ■

Reverse Discrimination Title VII also protects against *reverse discrimination*—that is, discrimination against members of a majority group, such as white males. ■ **EXAMPLE 35.5** An African American woman fires four white men from their management positions at a school district. The men file a lawsuit for reverse discrimination. They argue that the woman was trying to eliminate white males from the district administration in violation of Title VII. The woman claims that the terminations were part of a reorganization plan to cut costs.

If the judge (or jury, in a jury trial) agrees with the men that they were fired for racially discriminatory reasons, then they will be entitled to damages. If, however, the school district can show that the real reason for the terminations was a legitimate attempt to cut costs, then normally their case will be dismissed. ■

---

6. *Jiann Min Chang v. Alabama Agricultural and Mechanical University,* 355 Fed.Appx. 250 (11th Cir. 2009).

Potential Section 1981 Claims Victims of racial or ethnic discrimination may also have a cause of action under 42 U.S.C. Section 1981. This section, which was enacted in 1866 to protect the rights of freed slaves, prohibits discrimination on the basis of race or ethnicity in the formation or enforcement of contracts. Because employment is often a contractual relationship, Section 1981 can provide an alternative basis for a plaintiff's action and is potentially advantageous because there is no limit on the damages that can be awarded.

35–1e Discrimination Based on Religion

Title VII of the Civil Rights Act also prohibits government employers, private employers, and unions from discriminating against persons because of their religion. (This chapter's *Digital Update* feature discusses how employers who examine prospective employees' social media posts, including posts concerning religion, might engage in unlawful discrimination.)

Employers cannot treat their employees more or less favorably based on their religious beliefs or practices. They also cannot require employees to participate in any religious activity or forbid them from participating in one. ■ **EXAMPLE 35.6** Jason Sewell claims that his employer, a car dealership, fired him for not attending the weekly prayer meetings of dealership employees. If the dealership does require its employees to attend prayer gatherings and fired Sewell for not attending, he has a valid claim of religious discrimination. ■

Reasonable Accommodation An employer must "reasonably accommodate" the religious practices and sincerely held religious beliefs of its employees, unless to do so would cause undue hardship to the employer's business. An employee's religion might prohibit her or him from working on a certain day of the week, for instance, or at a certain type of job. Reasonable accommodation is required even if the belief is not based on the doctrines of a traditionally recognized religion, such as Christianity or Judaism, or of a denomination, such as Baptist.

Undue Hardship A reasonable attempt to accommodate does not necessarily require the employer to make every change an employee requests or to make a permanent change for an employee's benefit. An employer is not required to make an accommodation that would cause the employer undue hardship. ■ **CASE IN POINT 35.7** Miguel Sánchez-Rodríguez sold cell phones at kiosks in shopping malls for AT&T in Puerto Rico. After six years, Sánchez informed his

supervisors that he had become a Seventh Day Adventist and could no longer work on Saturdays for religious reasons. AT&T responded that his position required rotating Saturday shifts and that his inability to work on Saturdays would cause the company hardship.

As a reasonable accommodation, the company suggested that Sánchez swap schedules with others and offered him two alternative positions that would not require work on Saturdays. Sánchez was unable to find workers to swap shifts with him, however, and declined the other jobs because they would result in less income. He began missing work on Saturdays. After a time, AT&T indicated that it would discipline him for any additional Saturdays that he missed. Eventually, he was placed on active disciplinary status. Sánchez resigned and filed a religious discrimination lawsuit. The court found in favor of AT&T, and a federal appellate court affirmed. The company had made adequate efforts at accommodation by allowing Sánchez to swap shifts and offering him other positions that did not require work on Saturdays.[7] ■

35–1f Discrimination Based on Gender

Under Title VII and other federal acts, employers are forbidden from discriminating against employees on the basis of gender. Employers are prohibited from classifying or advertising jobs as male or female unless they can prove that the gender of the applicant is essential to the job. In addition, employers cannot have separate male and female seniority lists and cannot refuse to promote employees based on their gender.

Gender Must Be a Determining Factor Generally, to succeed in a suit for gender discrimination, a plaintiff must demonstrate that gender was a determining factor in the employer's decision to hire, fire, or promote him or her. Typically, this involves looking at all of the surrounding circumstances. ■ **CASE IN POINT 35.8** Wanda Collier worked for Turner Industries Group, LLC, in the maintenance department. She complained to her supervisor that Jack Daniell, the head of the department, treated her unfairly. Her supervisor told her that Daniell had a problem with her gender and was harder on women. The supervisor talked to Daniell about Collier's complaint but did not take any disciplinary action.

A month later, Daniell confronted Collier, pushing her up against a wall and berating her. After this incident, Collier filed a formal complaint and kept a male

---

7. *Sánchez-Rodríguez v. AT&T Mobility Puerto Rico, Inc.*, 673 F.3d 1 (1st Cir. 2012).

DIGITAL UPDATE — Hiring Discrimination Based on Social Media Posts

Human resource officers in most companies routinely check job candidates' social media posts when deciding whom to hire. Certainly, every young person is warned not to post photos that she or he might later regret having made available to potential employers. But a more serious issue involves standard reviewing of job candidates' social media information. Specifically, do employers discriminate based on such information?

An Experiment in Hiring Discrimination via Online Social Networks

Two researchers at Carnegie-Mellon University conducted an experiment to determine whether social media information posted by prospective employees influences employers' hiring decisions.[a] The researchers created false résumés and social media profiles. They submitted job applications on behalf of the fictional "candidates" to about four thousand U.S. employers. They then compared employers' responses to different groups—for example, to Muslim candidates versus Christian candidates.

The researchers found that candidates whose public profiles indicated that they were Muslim were less likely to be called for interviews than Christian applicants. The difference was particularly pronounced in parts of the country with more conservative residents. In those locations, Muslims received callbacks only 2 percent of the time, compared with 17 percent for Christian applicants. According to the authors of the study, "Hiring discrimination via online searches of candidates may not be widespread, but online disclosures of personal traits can significantly influence the hiring decisions of a self-selected set of employers."

Job Candidates' Perception of the Hiring Process

In another study, researchers at North Carolina State University looked at how job applicants view prospective employers' use of their social media profiles during the hiring process.[b] Job candidates appear to view the hiring process as unfair when they know that their social media profiles have been used in the selection process. This perception, according to the researchers, makes litigation more likely.

The EEOC Speaks Up

Since 2014, the Equal Employment Opportunity Commission (EEOC) has investigated how prospective employers can use social media to engage in discrimination in the hiring process. Given that the Society for Human Resource Management estimates that more than three-fourths of its members use social media in employment screening, the EEOC is interested in regulating this procedure.

Social media sites, examined closely, can provide information to a prospective employer on the applicant's race, color, national origin, disability, religion, and other protected characteristics. The EEOC has reminded employers that such information—whether it comes from social media postings or other sources—may not legally be used to make employment decisions on prohibited bases, such as race, gender, and religion.

Critical Thinking *Can you think of a way a company could use information from an applicant's social media posts without running the risk of being accused of hiring discrimination?*

b. J. W. Stoughton, L. F. Thompson, and A. W. Meade, "Examining Applicant Reactions to the Use of Social Networking Websites in Pre-Employment Screening," *Journal of Business and Psychology*, November 2013, DOI: 10.1007/s10869-013-9333-6.

a. A. Acquisti and C. N. Fong, "An Experiment in Hiring Discrimination via Online Social Networks," *Social Service Research Network*, October 26, 2014.

co-worker with her at all times. A month later, she was fired. She subsequently filed a lawsuit alleging gender discrimination. The court allowed Collier's claim to go to a jury because there was sufficient evidence that gender was a determining factor in Daniell's conduct.[8] ∎

8. *Collier v. Turner Industries Group, LLC,* 797 F.Supp.2d 1029 (D. Idaho 2011).

The Federal Bureau of Investigation (FBI) requires that its applicants meet certain physical fitness standards. For women, the standards include the ability to complete a minimum of fourteen push-ups. Men must be able to complete at least thirty. Whether this difference constitutes discrimination on the basis of gender was at issue in the following case.

Bauer v. Lynch

United States Court of Appeals, Fourth Circuit, 812 F.3d 340 (2016).

In the Language of the Court

KING, Circuit Judge.

* * * *

The FBI trains its Special Agent recruits at the FBI Academy in Quantico, Virginia. * * * All Trainees must pass a physical fitness test (the "PFT").

* * * The FBI requires every Special Agent recruit to pass the PFT twice: once to gain admission to the Academy, and a second time to graduate.

* * * *

* * * Trainees * * * need to satisfy the following standards * * * :

Event	Men	Women
Sit-ups	38	35
300-meter sprint	52.4s	64.9s
Push-ups	30	14
1.5-mile run	12m, 42s	13m, 5s

* * * *

After the attacks of September 11, 2001, * * * Jay Bauer resolved to contribute to the defense of our country by becoming a Special Agent in the FBI. [At the time,] he * * * served as an assistant professor at the University of Wisconsin–Milwaukee.

* * * Bauer took the PFT for the first time and failed. Although he achieved sixteen points on the test, Bauer completed only twenty-five push-ups * * *. The FBI allowed Bauer to retest [three months later] and he passed, that time completing thirty-two push-ups. With his fitness screening complete, the FBI invited Bauer to report to the Academy.

Bauer's time at the Academy largely showed great potential for a career as a Special Agent. He passed all academic tests, demonstrated proficiency in his firearms and defensive tactics training, and met all expectations for the practical applications and skills components of the Academy. Bauer's classmates also selected him as the class leader and spokesperson for the Academy

graduation. Unfortunately, Bauer faced a dilemma: he was unable to pass the PFT at Quantico.

During his twenty-two weeks at the Academy, Bauer took the PFT five times. On each occasion, he would have passed but for his failure to achieve the minimum standard for push-ups. Bauer's results, and his corresponding point scores for each event, were as follows:

Week	Sit-ups	300-meter sprint	Push-ups	1.5-mile run	Total Points
Week 1	40 (2)	42.6 sec. (8)	26 (0)	10:49 (4)	14
Week 7	47 (4)	43.4 sec. (7)	25 (0)	10:24 (5)	16
Week 14	50 (6)	43.7 sec. (7)	28 (0)	10:45 (4)	17
Week 18	51 (6)	43.8 sec. (7)	27 (0)	11:09 (4)	17
Week 22	49 (5)	44.1 sec. (6)	29 (0)	10:57 (4)	15

Following his final failure of the PFT, Bauer * * * was [allowed to] resign with the possibility of future employment with the FBI * * *. Bauer * * * immediately signed a resignation letter. Two weeks later, the FBI offered Bauer a position as an Intelligence Analyst in its Chicago Field Office. He accepted and has been employed in that position since.

* * * *

* * * Bauer filed this Title VII action in [a federal district court] against [Loretta Lynch,] the Attorney General. According to the claims in Bauer's complaint, the FBI's use of the gender-normed PFT standards contravened * * * Title VII * * * which prohibits sex discrimination by federal employers.

* * * *

In his summary judgment motion, Bauer maintained that the FBI's use of the gender-normed PFT standards was facially discriminatory [involving explicit categorization, such as by sex or race].

* * * *

* * * The district court agreed with Bauer, granting his motion for summary judgment.

* * * *

The Attorney General * * * filed a timely * * * appeal.

* * * *

Title VII requires that any "personnel actions affecting employees or applicants for employment" taken by federal employers "shall be made free from any discrimination based on * * * sex." * * * *A plaintiff is entitled to demonstrate discrimination by showing that the employer uses a facially discriminatory employment practice. [The Supreme Court has outlined] a "simple test" for identifying facial sex discrimination: such discrimination appears "where the evidence shows treatment of a person in a manner which but for that person's sex would be different."* [Emphasis added.]

* * * The district court applied [this] test and concluded that, because Bauer would have been held to a lower minimum number of push-ups had he been a woman, the gender-normed PFT standards constitute facial sex discrimination. The Attorney General maintains on appeal, however, that because the PFT assesses an overall level of physical fitness, and equally fit men and women possess innate physiological differences that lead to different performance outcomes, the PFT's gender-normed standards actually require the same level of fitness for all Trainees. In that way, the Attorney General contends, the PFT standards do not treat the sexes differently and therefore do not contravene Title VII.

* * * *

* * * The Attorney General * * * maintains that * * * some differential treatment of men and women based upon inherent physiological differences is not only lawful but also potentially required.

* * * *

Men and women simply are not physiologically the same for the purposes

Case 35.1 Continues

Case 35.1 Continued

of physical fitness programs. * * * Physical fitness standards suitable for men may not always be suitable for women, and accommodations addressing physiological differences between the sexes are not necessarily unlawful.

* * * The physiological differences between men and women impact their relative abilities to demonstrate the same levels of physical fitness. In other words, equally fit men and women demonstrate their fitness differently. Whether physical fitness standards discriminate based on sex, therefore, depends on whether they require men and women to demonstrate different levels of fitness.

Put succinctly, *an employer does not contravene Title VII when it utilizes physical fitness standards that distinguish between the sexes on the basis of their physiological differences but impose an equal burden of compliance on both men and women, requiring the same level of physical fitness of each.* Because the FBI purports to assess physical fitness by imposing the same burden on both men and women, this rule applies to Bauer's Title VII claims. Accordingly, the district court erred in failing to apply the rule in its disposition of Bauer's motion for summary judgment. [Emphasis added.]

* * * *

Pursuant to the foregoing, we vacate the judgment of the district court and remand for * * * further proceedings.

Legal Reasoning Questions

1. According to the reasoning of the court in the *Bauer* case, when do different employment standards for men and women satisfy Title VII's requirement of equality?

2. In what other circumstances might the rule in this case apply?

3. If Bauer had ultimately succeeded in his claim, what might the remedy have been? What else might have resulted?

Pregnancy Discrimination The Pregnancy Discrimination Act[9] expanded Title VII's definition of gender discrimination to include discrimination based on pregnancy. Women affected by pregnancy, childbirth, or related medical conditions must be treated the same as other persons not so affected but similar in ability to

work. For instance, an employer cannot discriminate against a pregnant woman by withholding benefits available to others under employee benefit programs.

In the following case, an employer accommodated many of its employees who had lifting restrictions due to disabilities. The employer refused to accommodate a pregnant employee with a similar restriction. Did this refusal constitute a violation of the Pregnancy Discrimination Act?

---
9. 42 U.S.C. Section 2000e(k).

Case 35.2

Young v. United Parcel Service, Inc.

Supreme Court of the United States, __ U.S. __, 135 S.Ct. 1338, 191 L.Ed.2d 279 (2015).

Background and Facts Peggy Young was a driver for United Parcel Service, Inc. (UPS). When she became pregnant, her doctor advised her not to lift more than twenty pounds. UPS required drivers to lift up to seventy pounds and told Young that she could not work under a lifting restriction. She filed a suit in a federal district court against UPS, claiming an unlawful refusal to accommodate her pregnancy-related lifting restriction. She alleged that UPS had multiple light-duty-for-injury categories to accommodate individuals whose non-pregnancy-related disabilities created work restrictions similar to hers.

UPS responded that, because Young did not fall into any of those categories, it had not discriminated against her. The court issued a summary judgment in UPS's favor. The U.S. Court of Appeals of the Fourth Circuit affirmed the judgment. Young appealed to the United States Supreme Court.

In the Language of the Court

Justice *BREYER* delivered the opinion of the Court.

* * * *

* * * A plaintiff alleging that the denial of an accommodation constituted disparate treatment under the Pregnancy Discrimination Act * * * may make out a *prima facie* case by showing that she belongs to

Case 35.2 Continued

the protected class, that she sought accommodation, that the employer did not accommodate her, and that the employer did accommodate others similar in their ability or inability to work.

The employer may then seek to justify its refusal to accommodate the plaintiff by relying on legitimate, non-discriminatory reasons for denying her accommodation. [Emphasis added.]

If the employer offers an apparently legitimate, nondiscriminatory reason for its actions, the plaintiff may in turn show that the employer's proffered reasons are in fact pretextual [contrived]. We believe that the plaintiff may reach a jury on this issue by providing sufficient evidence that the employer's policies impose a significant burden on pregnant workers, and that the employer's legitimate, nondiscriminatory reasons are not sufficiently strong to justify the burden, but rather—when considered along with the burden imposed—give rise to an inference of intentional discrimination.

The plaintiff can create a genuine issue of material fact as to whether a significant burden exists by providing evidence that the employer accommodates a large percentage of nonpregnant workers while failing to accommodate a large percentage of pregnant workers. Here, for example, if the facts are as Young says they are, she can show that UPS accommodates most nonpregnant employees with lifting limitations while categorically failing to accommodate pregnant employees with lifting limitations. Young might also add that the fact that UPS has multiple policies that accommodate nonpregnant employees with lifting restrictions suggests that its reasons for failing to accommodate pregnant employees with lifting restrictions are not sufficiently strong—to the point that a jury could find that its reasons for failing to accommodate pregnant employees give rise to an inference of intentional discrimination.

* * * *

* * * A party is entitled to summary judgment if there is no genuine dispute as to any material fact and the movant [that is, a person who applies to a court for a ruling in his or her favor] is entitled to judgment as a matter of law. * * * *Viewing the record in the light most favorable to Young, there is a genuine dispute as to whether UPS provided more favorable treatment to at least some employees whose situation cannot reasonably be distinguished from Young's.* [Emphasis added.]

Decision and Remedy *The United States Supreme Court vacated the judgment of the U.S. Court of Appeals for the Fourth Circuit and remanded the case for further proceedings. Young created a genuine dispute as to whether UPS had provided more favorable treatment to employees whose situation could not reasonably be distinguished from hers. On remand, the court must determine whether Young also created a genuine issue of material fact as to whether UPS's reasons for treating Young less favorably were a pretext.*

Critical Thinking
- **Legal Environment** *Could UPS have succeeded in this case if it had claimed simply that it would be more expensive or less convenient to include pregnant women among those whom it accommodates? Explain.*

Wage Discrimination The Equal Pay Act[10] requires equal pay for male and female employees working at the same establishment doing similar work. To determine whether the Equal Pay Act has been violated, a court looks to the primary duties of the two jobs—the job content rather than the job description controls. If a court finds that the wage differential is due to "any factor other than gender," such as a seniority or merit system, then it does not violate the Equal Pay Act.

The 2009 Lilly Ledbetter Fair Pay Act made discriminatory wages actionable under federal law regardless of when the discrimination began.[11] Previously, plaintiffs had to file a complaint within a limited time period. Today, if a plaintiff continues to work for the employer while receiving discriminatory wages, the time period for filing a complaint is practically unlimited.

Discrimination against Transgender Persons
In the past, most courts held that federal law (Title VII)

---

10. 29 U.S.C. Section 206(d).

11. Pub. L. No. 111-2, 123 Stat. 5 (January 5, 2009), amending 42 U.S.C. Section 2000e-5[e].

does not protect transgender persons from discrimination. The situation may be changing, however. A growing number of federal courts are interpreting Title VII's protections against gender discrimination to apply to transsexuals.

■ **CASE IN POINT 35.9** Dr. Deborah Fabian applied for a position as an on-call orthopedic surgeon at the Hospital of Central Connecticut. The hospital apparently declined to hire Fabian because she disclosed her identity as a transgender woman. Fabian sued the hospital alleging violations of Title VII of the Civil Rights Act and the Connecticut Fair Employment Practices Act (CFEPA).

The hospital filed a summary judgment motion, arguing that neither Title VII nor the Connecticut statute prohibits discrimination on the basis of transgender identity. The federal district court rejected this argument, however, finding that discrimination on the basis of transgender identity is discrimination on the basis of sex for Title VII purposes. Fabian was entitled to take her case to a jury and argue violations of Title VII and the CFEPA.[12] ■

35–1g Constructive Discharge

The majority of Title VII complaints involve unlawful discrimination in decisions to hire or fire employees. In some situations, however, employees who leave their jobs voluntarily can claim that they were "constructively discharged" by the employer. **Constructive discharge** occurs when the employer causes the employee's working conditions to be so intolerable that a reasonable person in the employee's position would feel compelled to quit.

When constructive discharge is claimed, the employee can pursue damages for loss of income, including back pay. These damages ordinarily are not available to an employee who left a job voluntarily.

Proving Constructive Discharge To prove constructive discharge, an employee must present objective proof of intolerable working conditions. The employee must also show that the employer knew or had reason to know about these conditions yet failed to correct them within a reasonable time period. In addition, courts generally require the employee to show causation—that the employer's unlawful discrimination caused the working conditions to be intolerable. Put in a different way, the employee's resignation must be a foreseeable result of the

employer's discriminatory action. Courts weigh the facts on a case-by-case basis.

Employee demotion is one of the most frequently cited reasons for a finding of constructive discharge, particularly when the employee was subjected to humiliation. ■ **EXAMPLE 35.10** Khalil's employer humiliates him by informing him in front of his co-workers that he is being demoted to an inferior position. Khalil's co-workers then continually insult him, harass him, and make derogatory remarks to him about his national origin (he is from Iran). The employer is aware of this discriminatory treatment but does nothing to remedy the situation, despite Khalil's repeated complaints. After several months, Khalil quits his job and files a Title VII claim. In this situation, Khalil will likely have sufficient evidence to maintain an action for constructive discharge in violation of Title VII. ■

Applies to All Title VII Discrimination Plaintiffs can use constructive discharge to establish any type of discrimination claim under Title VII, including race, color, national origin, religion, gender, and pregnancy. It is most commonly asserted in cases involving sexual harassment. Constructive discharge may also be used in cases involving discrimination based on age or disability (discussed later in this chapter).

35–1h Sexual Harassment

Title VII also protects employees against **sexual harassment** in the workplace. Sexual harassment can take two forms:

1. *Quid pro quo* harassment occurs when sexual favors are demanded in return for job opportunities, promotions, salary increases, or other benefits. *Quid pro quo* is a Latin phrase that is often translated as "something in exchange for something else."
2. *Hostile-environment* harassment occurs when a pattern of sexually offensive conduct runs throughout the workplace and the employer has not taken steps to prevent or discourage it. Such harassment exists when the workplace is permeated with discriminatory intimidation, ridicule, and insult, and this harassment is so severe or pervasive that it alters the conditions of employment.

A court considers a number of factors when determining whether the sexually offensive conduct was sufficiently severe or pervasive to create a hostile environment. As the following case shows, these factors include the nature and frequency of the conduct and whether it unreasonably interfered with the victim's work performance.

---

12. *Fabian v. Hospital of Central Connecticut,* ___ F.Supp.3d ___, 2016 WL 1089178 (D.Conn. 2016).

Roberts v. Mike's Trucking, Ltd.

Court of Appeals of Ohio, Twelfth District, 2014 -Ohio- 766, 9 N.E.3d 483 (2014).

Background and Facts Teresa Roberts worked for Mike's Trucking, Ltd., in Columbus, Ohio. Her supervisor was the company's owner, Mike Culbertson. According to Roberts, Culbertson called her his "sexretary" and constantly talked about his sex life. He often invited her to sit on "Big Daddy's" lap, rubbed against her, trapped her at the door and asked her for hugs or kisses, and inquired if she needed help in the restroom. Roberts asked him to stop this conduct, but he did not. She became less productive and began to suffer anxiety attacks and high blood pressure. Roberts filed a suit in an Ohio state court against Mike's, alleging a hostile work environment through sexual harassment in violation of Title VII. A jury decided in Roberts's favor, and Mike's appealed.

In the Language of the Court

HENDRICKSON, P.J. [Presiding Judge]

* * * *

* * * Conduct that is not severe or pervasive enough to create an objectively hostile or abusive work environment—an environment that a reasonable person would find hostile or abusive—is beyond Title VII's purview. Likewise, if the victim does not subjectively perceive the environment to be abusive, the conduct has not actually altered the conditions of the victim's employment, and there is no Title VII violation. Therefore, *the focus of this inquiry is: 1.) whether a reasonable person would find the environment objectively hostile; and 2.) whether the plaintiff subjectively found the conduct severe or pervasive.* [Emphasis added.]

* * * *

* * * Roberts' testimony was consistent with several witnesses affirming that Culbertson frequently engaged in a variety of conduct ranging from inappropriate discussions to groping women. The witnesses stated that Culbertson often discussed his sex life, asked Roberts and the women employees if they needed help in the bathroom * * * , referred to himself as "Big Daddy," asked Roberts and the women employees to sit in "Big Daddy's" lap, and asked them if they would give "Big Daddy" a hug.

The evidence established that the conduct occurred frequently. Roberts testified that throughout her employment, Culbertson's behavior became increasingly worse and that * * * he talked about sex hundreds of times, and attempted to corner her and hug and kiss her at least twice a week. [Former Mike's employees] testified that Culbertson talked about sex and asked the women if they needed help with the bathroom multiple times a week. The evidence also showed that the conduct became increasingly severe as Culbertson massaged Roberts [and] rubbed up against her * * * . Roberts testified that Culbertson's conduct was humiliating towards her as his remarks were in front of others and she often became "furious" with him. Other employees reported Roberts becoming angry towards Culbertson. Roberts also established that Culbertson's conduct unreasonably interfered with her work performance as she stated she did not want to go to work anymore, she became less productive, and she suffered anxiety attacks. Her fiancé testified that Roberts has lost confidence and that she is now prescribed anti-anxiety medication.

Consequently, there was sufficient and substantial evidence to support the jury's finding that a reasonable person would find Culbertson's conduct created a hostile environment and Roberts found the conduct to be sufficiently severe or pervasive to affect her employment.

Decision and Remedy *A state intermediate appellate court affirmed the lower court's judgment in Roberts's favor. During the trial, other Mike's employees and Roberts's fiancé testified to corroborate Roberts's account. The evidence sufficiently established that Culbertson's conduct was severe or pervasive enough to create a hostile work environment for Roberts.*

Critical Thinking

- **Ethical** *Was Culbertson's conduct at any point unethical? Discuss.*
- **Legal Environment** *Culbertson and some other witnesses testified that he did not engage in any sexually inappropriate behavior. Should an appellate court reverse a jury's decision simply due to contrary evidence? Why or why not?*

Harassment by Supervisors For an employer to be held liable for a supervisor's sexual harassment, the supervisor normally must have taken a *tangible employment action* against the employee. A **tangible employment action** is a significant change in employment status or benefits. Such an action occurs when an employee is fired, refused a promotion, demoted, or reassigned to a position with significantly different responsibilities, for instance. Only a supervisor, or another person acting with the authority of the employer, can cause this sort of harm. A constructive discharge also qualifies as a tangible employment action.

The United States Supreme Court issued several important rulings in cases alleging sexual harassment by supervisors that established what is known as the "*Ellerth/Faragher* affirmative defense."[13] The defense has two elements:

1. The employer must have taken reasonable care to prevent and promptly correct any sexually harassing behavior (by establishing effective harassment policies and complaint procedures, for instance).
2. The plaintiff-employee must have unreasonably failed to take advantage of preventive or corrective opportunities provided by the employer to avoid harm.

An employer that can prove both elements normally will not be liable for a supervisor's harassment.

Retaliation by Employers Employers sometimes retaliate against employees who complain about sexual harassment or other Title VII violations. Retaliation can take many forms. An employer might demote or fire the person, or otherwise change the terms, conditions, and benefits of employment.

Title VII prohibits retaliation, and employees can sue their employers when it occurs. In a *retaliation claim,* an individual asserts that she or he has suffered harm as a result of making a charge, testifying, or participating in a Title VII investigation or proceeding.

Requirements for Protection. To be protected under Title VII's retaliation provisions, the plaintiff must have opposed a practice prohibited by Title VII and suffered an adverse employment action as a result of that opposition. ■ **CASE IN POINT 35.11** Myrta Morales-Cruz had a tenure-track teaching position at the University of Puerto Rico School of Law. When her probationary period was almost over, Morales-Cruz asked the university's administrative committee to grant a one-year extension for her

tenure review. The dean recommended that the extension be granted but also called her "insecure," "immature," and "fragile." Another professor commented that had she shown "poor judgment" and exhibited "personality flaws."

After Morales-Cruz complained about these comments in writing to the chancellor, the dean recommended denying the one-year extension, and the administrative committee did just that. Morales-Cruz later filed a retaliation lawsuit. She claimed that the dean had retaliated against her for complaining to the chancellor about the "discriminatory" comments made in the course of her request for an extension.

The court held that Morales-Cruz had not provided a reasonable foundation for a retaliation action. Under Title VII, an employer may not retaliate against an employee because he or she has opposed a practice prohibited by Title VII. But the court found that Morales-Cruz did not allege any facts that could be construed as gender-based discrimination. Although the comments she complained about were hardly flattering, they were entirely gender-neutral. Thus, she was not engaging in protected conduct when she opposed the remarks.[14] ■

Protection May Extend to Others. The Supreme Court has ruled that Title VII's retaliation protection extended to an employee who spoke out about discrimination against another employee during an employer's internal investigation.[15] The Court has also held that Title VII protected an employee who was fired after his fiancée filed a gender discrimination claim against their employer.[16]

Harassment by Co-Workers and Others When the harassment of co-workers, rather than supervisors, creates a hostile working environment, an employee may still have a cause of action against the employer. Normally, though, the employer will be held liable only if it knew or should have known about the harassment and failed to take immediate remedial action.

Occasionally, a court may also hold an employer liable for harassment by *nonemployees* if the employer knew about the harassment and failed to take corrective action. ■ **EXAMPLE 35.12** Jordan, who owns and manages a Great Bites restaurant, knows that one of his regular customers, Dean, repeatedly harasses Kaylia, a waitress. If Jordan does nothing and permits the harassment to continue, he may be liable under Title VII even though Dean is not an employee of the restaurant. ■

---

13. *Burlington Industries, Inc. v. Ellerth,* 524 U.S. 742, 118 S.Ct. 2257, 141 L.Ed.2d 633 (1998); and *Faragher v. City of Boca Raton,* 524 U.S. 775, 118 S.Ct. 2275, 141 L.Ed.2d 662 (1998).

14. *Morales-Cruz v. University of Puerto Rico,* 676 F.3d 220 (1st Cir. 2012).
15. *Crawford v. Metropolitan Government of Nashville and Davidson County, Tennessee,* 555 U.S. 271, 129 S.Ct. 846, 172 L.Ed.2d 650 (2009).
16. See *Thompson v. North American Stainless, LP,* 562 U.S. 170, 131 S.Ct. 863, 178 L.Ed.2d 694 (2011).

Same-Gender Harassment In *Oncale v. Sundowner Offshore Services, Inc.,*[17] the United States Supreme Court held that Title VII protection extends to individuals who are sexually harassed by members of the same gender. Proving that the harassment in same-gender cases is "based on sex" can be difficult, though. It is easier to establish a case of same-gender harassment when the harasser is homosexual.

Sexual-Orientation Harassment Federal law (Title VII) does not prohibit discrimination or harassment based on a person's sexual orientation. Nonetheless, a growing number of states have enacted laws that prohibit sexual-orientation discrimination in private employment.[18] Some states, such as Oregon, explicitly prohibit discrimination based on a person's gender identity or expression. Many companies have also voluntarily established nondiscrimination policies that include sexual orientation.

35–1i Online Harassment

Employees' online activities can create a hostile working environment in many ways. Racial jokes, ethnic slurs, or other comments contained in e-mail, texts, blogs, or social media can lead to claims of hostile-environment harassment or other forms of discrimination. A worker who regularly sees sexually explicit images on a co-worker's computer screen may find the images offensive and claim that they create a hostile working environment. Nevertheless, employers may be able to avoid liability for online harassment by taking prompt remedial action.

35–1j Remedies under Title VII

Employer liability under Title VII can be extensive. If the plaintiff successfully proves that unlawful discrimination occurred, he or she may be awarded reinstatement, back pay, retroactive promotions, and damages.

Several limits apply to damages. Compensatory damages are available only in cases of intentional discrimination. Punitive damages may be recovered against a private employer only if the employer acted with malice or reckless indifference to an individual's rights. The total amount of compensatory and punitive damages that plaintiffs can recover from specific employers depends on the size of the employer. For instance, there is a $50,000 cap on damages from employers with one hundred or fewer employees.

35–2 Discrimination Based on Age

Age discrimination is potentially the most widespread form of discrimination because anyone—regardless of race, color, national origin, or gender—could be a victim at some point in life. The Age Discrimination in Employment Act[19] (ADEA), as amended, prohibits employment discrimination on the basis of age against individuals forty years of age or older. The act also prohibits mandatory retirement for nonmanagerial workers. In addition, the ADEA protects federal and private-sector employees from retaliation based on age-related complaints.[20]

For the act to apply, an employer must have twenty or more employees, and the employer's business activities must affect interstate commerce. The EEOC administers the ADEA, but the act also permits private causes of action against employers for age discrimination.

35–2a Procedures under the ADEA

The burden-shifting procedure under the ADEA differs from the procedure under Title VII. This difference resulted from a United States Supreme Court decision that dramatically changed the burden of proof in age discrimination cases.[21]

As explained earlier, if the plaintiff in a Title VII case can show that the employer was motivated, at least in part, by unlawful discrimination, the burden of proof shifts to the employer. Thus, in cases in which the employer has a "mixed motive" for discharging an employee, the employer has the burden of proving that its reason was legitimate.

Under the ADEA, in contrast, a plaintiff must show that the unlawful discrimination was not just *a* reason but *the* reason for the adverse employment action. In other words, the employee has the burden of establishing *but for* causation—that is, "but for" the employee's age, the action would not have been taken.

***Prima Facie* Age Discrimination** To establish a *prima facie* case of age discrimination, the plaintiff must show that she or he was the following:

1. A member of the protected age group.
2. Qualified for the position from which she or he was discharged.
3. Discharged because of age discrimination.

---

17. 523 U.S. 75, 118 S.Ct. 998, 140 L.Ed.2d 207 (1998).
18. See, for instance, 775 Illinois Compiled Statutes 5/1–103.

19. 29 U.S.C. Sections 621–634.
20. *Gomez-Perez v. Potter,* 553 U.S. 474, 128 S.Ct. 1931, 170 L.Ed.2d 887 (2008).
21. *Gross v. FBL Financial Services, Inc.,* 557 U.S. 167, 129 S.Ct. 2343, 174 L.Ed.2d 119 (2009).

Then the burden shifts to the employer to give a legitimate nondiscriminatory reason for the adverse action.

Pretext If the employer offers a legitimate reason for its action, then the plaintiff must show that the stated reason is only a pretext. The plaintiff is required to prove that the plaintiff's age was the real reason for the employer's decision.

■ **CASE IN POINT 35.13** Josephine Mora, a fund-raiser for Jackson Memorial Foundation, Inc., was sixty-two years old when the foundation's chief executive officer (CEO) fired her. Mora filed an age discrimination suit against the foundation. She asserted that when she was fired, the CEO told her, "I need someone younger I can pay less." A witness heard that statement and also heard the CEO say that Mora was "too old to be working here anyway." The CEO denied making these statements, and the foundation claimed that Mora had been terminated for poor job performance.

A district court granted a summary judgment in the foundation's favor, and Mora appealed. A federal appellate court reversed, concluding that the lower court's analysis of causation was incorrect. The court held that a reasonable juror could have accepted that the CEO had made discriminatory remarks and could have found that these remarks were sufficient evidence of a discriminatory motive. If so, that could show that Mora was fired because of her age. The court therefore remanded the case to the lower court for a trial.[22] ■

35–2b Replacing Older Workers with Younger Workers

Numerous age discrimination cases have been brought against employers who, to cut costs, replaced older, higher-salaried employees with younger, lower-salaried workers. In such situations, whether a firing is discriminatory or simply part of a rational business decision to prune the company's ranks is not always clear.

The plaintiff must prove that the discharge was motivated by age bias. The plaintiff need not prove that she or he was replaced by a person "outside the protected class" (under the age of forty). The replacement worker need only be younger than the plaintiff. Nevertheless, the greater the age gap, the more likely the plaintiff will succeed in showing age discrimination.

35–2c State Employees Not Covered by the ADEA

Generally, the states are immune from lawsuits brought by private individuals in federal court (unless a state consents to such a suit). This immunity stems from the United States Supreme Court's interpretation of the Eleventh Amendment.

State immunity under the Eleventh Amendment is not absolute. In some situations, such as when fundamental rights are at stake, Congress has the power to abrogate (abolish) state immunity to private suits through legislation. Such legislation must unequivocally show Congress's intent to subject states to private suits.[23]

Generally, though, the Court has found that state employers are immune from private suits brought by employees under the ADEA. State employers are also immune from suits brought under the Americans with Disabilities Act[24] and the Fair Labor Standards Act.[25] They are *not* immune from the requirements of the Family and Medical Leave Act.[26]

35–3 Discrimination Based on Disability

The Americans with Disabilities Act (ADA)[27] prohibits disability-based discrimination in all workplaces with fifteen or more workers. An exception is state government employers, who are generally immune under the Eleventh Amendment, as just mentioned. Basically, the ADA requires that employers "reasonably accommodate" the needs of persons with disabilities unless to do so would cause the employer to suffer an "undue hardship." The ADA Amendments Act[28] broadened the coverage of the ADA's protections, as discussed shortly.

35–3a Procedures under the ADA

To prevail on a claim under the ADA, a plaintiff must show that he or she (1) has a disability, (2) is otherwise qualified for the employment in question, and (3) was

---

22. *Mora v. Jackson Memorial Foundation, Inc.,* 597 F.3d 1201 (11th Cir. 2010).

23. *Tennessee v. Lane,* 541 U.S. 509, 124 S.Ct. 1978, 158 L.Ed.2d 820 (2004).
24. *Board of Trustees of the University of Alabama v. Garrett,* 531 U.S. 356, 121 S.Ct. 955, 148 L.Ed.2d 866 (2001).
25. *Alden v. Maine,* 527 U.S. 706, 119 S.Ct. 2240, 144 L.Ed.2d 636 (1999).
26. *Nevada Department of Human Resources v. Hibbs,* 538 U.S. 721, 123 S.Ct. 1972, 155 L.Ed.2d 953 (2003).
27. 42 U.S.C. Sections 12103–12118.
28. 42 U.S.C. Sections 12103 and 12205a.

excluded from the employment solely because of the disability. As in Title VII cases, the plaintiff must pursue the claim through the EEOC before filing an action in court for a violation of the ADA.

The EEOC may decide to investigate and perhaps sue the employer on behalf of the employee. The EEOC can bring a suit even if the employee previously signed an agreement with the employer to submit job-related disputes to arbitration.[29] If the EEOC decides not to sue, then the employee may do so.

Plaintiffs in lawsuits brought under the ADA may seek many of the same remedies that are available under Title VII. These include reinstatement, back pay, a limited amount of compensatory and punitive damages (for intentional discrimination), and certain other forms of relief. Repeat violators may be ordered to pay fines of up to $100,000.

35–3b What Is a Disability?

The ADA is broadly drafted to cover persons with physical or mental impairments that "substantially limit" their everyday activities. Specifically, the ADA defines a *disability* as including any of the following:

1. A physical or mental impairment that substantially limits one or more of the major life activities of the affected individual.
2. A record of having such an impairment.
3. Being regarded as having such an impairment.

Health conditions that have been considered disabilities under federal law include alcoholism, acquired immune deficiency syndrome (AIDS), blindness, cancer, cerebral palsy, diabetes, heart disease, muscular dystrophy, and paraplegia. Testing positive for the human immunodeficiency virus (HIV) has qualified as a disability, as has morbid obesity. (A morbidly obese person weighs twice the normal weight for his or her height.)

Association with Disabled Persons

A separate provision in the ADA prevents employers from taking adverse employment actions based on stereotypes or assumptions about individuals who associate with people who have disabilities.[30] An employer cannot, for instance, refuse to hire the parent of a child with a disability based on the assumption that the person will miss work too often or be unreliable.

■ **EXAMPLE 35.14** Joan, an employer, refuses to hire Edward, who has a daughter with a physical disability. She consciously bases her decision on the assumption that Edward will have to miss work frequently to care for his daughter. Edward can sue Joan for violating the ADA's provisions. ■

Mitigating Measures At one time, the courts focused on whether a person had a disability *after* the use of corrective devices or medication. Thus, a person with severe myopia (nearsightedness) whose eyesight could be corrected by wearing glasses did not qualify as having a disability. With the corrective lenses, the person's major life activities were not substantially impaired. Then Congress amended the ADA to strengthen its protections and prohibit employers from considering mitigating measures when determining if an individual has a disability.

Disability is now determined on a case-by-case basis. A condition may fit the definition of disability in one set of circumstances, but not in another. ■ **CASE IN POINT 35.15** Larry Rohr, a welding specialist for a power district in Arizona, was diagnosed with type 2 diabetes. To keep his condition under control, Rohr was required to follow a complex regimen of daily insulin injections and blood tests, as well as a strict diet. Therefore, his physician forbade him from taking work assignments that involved overnight, out-of-town travel, which were common in his job.

Because of these limitations, the power district asked him to transfer, apply for federal disability benefits, or take early retirement. Rohr sued for disability discrimination. The lower court granted summary judgment for the employer. Rohr appealed. A federal appellate court reversed. The court held that under the amended ADA, diabetes is a disability if it significantly restricts an individual's eating (a major life activity), as it did for Rohr. Therefore, Rohr was entitled to a trial on his discrimination claim.[31] ■

Disclosure of Confidential Medical Information

ADA provisions also require employers to keep their employees' medical information confidential.[32] An employee who discovers that an employer has disclosed his or her confidential medical information has a right to sue the employer—even if the employee was not technically disabled. The prohibition against disclosure also applies to other employees acting on behalf of the employer.

---

29. This was the Supreme Court's ruling in *EEOC v. Waffle House, Inc.,* 534 U.S. 279, 122 S.Ct. 754, 151 L.Ed.2d 755 (2002).
30. 42 U.S.C. Section 12112(b)(4).

31. *Rohr v. Salt River Project Agricultural Improvement and Power District,* 555 F.3d 850 (9th Cir. 2009).
32. 42 U.S.C. Sections 12112(d)(3)(B), (C), and 12112(d)(4)(C).

■ **CASE IN POINT 35.16** George Shoun was working at his job at Best Formed Plastics, Inc., when he fell and injured his shoulder. Another Best Formed employee, Jane Stewart, prepared an accident report for the incident and processed Shoun's workers' compensation claim. As a result of the injury, Shoun had to take several months off work and received workers' compensation.

Stewart posted on her Facebook page a statement about how Shoun's shoulder injury "kept him away from work for 11 months and now he is trying to sue us." Shoun sued Best Formed under the ADA for wrongfully disclosing confidential information about his medical condition to other people via Facebook. He claimed that the action resulted in loss of employment and impairment of his earning capacity. The court allowed Shoun's claim to go forward to trial.[33] ■

35–3c Reasonable Accommodation

The ADA does not require that employers accommodate the needs of job applicants or employees with disabilities who are not otherwise qualified for the work. If a job applicant or an employee with a disability, with reasonable accommodation, can perform essential job functions, however, the employer must make the accommodation.

Required modifications may include installing ramps for a wheelchair, establishing flexible working hours, creating or modifying job assignments, and designing or improving training materials and procedures. Generally, employers should give primary consideration to employees' preferences in deciding what accommodations should be made.

Undue Hardship Employers who do not accommodate the needs of persons with disabilities must demonstrate that the accommodations would cause *undue hardship* in terms of being significantly difficult or expensive for the employer. Usually, the courts decide whether an accommodation constitutes an undue hardship on a case-by-case basis.

■ **EXAMPLE 35.17** Bryan Lockhart, who uses a wheelchair, works for a cell phone company that provides parking for its employees. Lockhart informs his supervisor that the parking spaces are so narrow that he is unable to extend the ramp on his van that allows him to get in and out of the vehicle. Lockhart therefore requests that the company reasonably accommodate his needs by paying a monthly fee for him to use a larger parking space in an adjacent lot. In this situation, a court will likely find that

it is *not* an undue hardship for the employer to pay for additional parking for Lockhart. ■

Job Applications and Physical Exams Employers must modify their job-application and selection process so that those with disabilities can compete for jobs with those who do not have disabilities. For instance, a job announcement might be modified to allow applicants to respond by e-mail as well as by telephone, so that it does not discriminate against potential applicants with hearing impairments.

Employers are restricted in the kinds of questions they may ask on job-application forms and during pre-employment interviews. In addition, employers cannot require persons with disabilities to submit to preemployment physicals unless such exams are required of all other applicants. An employer can disqualify the applicant only if the medical problems discovered during a preemployment physical would make it impossible for the applicant to perform the job.

Health-Insurance Plans Workers with disabilities must be given equal access to any health insurance provided to other employees and cannot be excluded from coverage. An employer can put a limit, or cap, on health-care payments under its group health policy, but the cap must apply equally to all insured employees. Any group health-care plan that makes a disability-based distinction in its benefits violates the ADA (unless the employer can justify its actions under the business necessity defense, discussed shortly).

Substance Abusers Drug addiction is considered a disability under the ADA because it is a substantially limiting impairment. The act does not protect individuals who are actually using illegal drugs, however. Instead, the ADA protects only persons with *former* drug addictions—those who have completed or are now participating in a supervised drug-rehabilitation program. Individuals who have used drugs casually in the past also are not protected under the act. They are not considered addicts and therefore do not have a disability (addiction).

People suffering from alcoholism are also protected by the ADA. Employers cannot legally discriminate against employees simply because they suffer from alcoholism. Of course, employers can prohibit the use of alcohol in the workplace and require that employees not be under the influence of alcohol while working. Employers can also fire or refuse to hire a person who is an alcoholic if (1) the person poses a *substantial risk of harm* to himself or herself or to others, and (2) the risk cannot be reduced by reasonable accommodation.

---

33. *Shoun v. Best Formed Plastics, Inc.*, 28 F.Supp.3d 786 (N.D.Ind. 2014).

Exhibit 35–1 outlines the coverage of the employment discrimination laws discussed in this chapter.

35–4 Discrimination Based on Military Status

In 1994, Congress enacted the Uniformed Services Employment and Reemployment Rights Act (USERRA).[34] The USERRA protects civilian job rights and benefits for members of the military, former military personnel, and reservists. It also provides additional protections for veterans who are disabled. Most importantly, the USERRA prohibits discrimination against persons who have served in the military. In effect, it makes military service and status a protected class and gives members of this class a right to sue an employer for violations.

35–4a Broad Application and Provisions

The USERRA covers *all* employers, public and private, large and small. Even an employer with only one employee is subject to its provisions.[35] The act also applies to United States employers operating in foreign countries.

Under the USERRA, military plaintiffs can sue not only the employer but also individual employees who were acting in an official capacity for the employer. In other words, these employees—supervisors, for instance—can be held personally liable for violations. Additionally, there is no statute of limitations for bringing a lawsuit. The cause of action could have arisen ten weeks or ten years before the suit was filed.

The USERRA specifies that veterans can be terminated from their employment only "for cause." The employer is obligated to give employees a list of all the behaviors that would trigger a for-cause termination.

35–4b *Prima Facie* Case of Discrimination under the USERRA

To establish a *prima facie* case of discrimination (and retaliation) under the USERRA, the plaintiff must establish that the employer took an adverse employment action based in part on the employee's connection with the military. The connection to the military may be through the plaintiff's membership, service, or application for service, or it may be through providing testimony or statements concerning the military service of another.[36] If another similarly situated person who did not serve in the military or engage in a protected activity was treated more favorably than the plaintiff, the employer has violated the USERRA.

■ **CASE IN POINT 35.18** Baldo Bello, a staff sergeant with the United States Marine Corps Reserve, was employed by the Village of Skokie as a police officer. Police officers

---

34. Pub. L. No. 103-353, codified at 38 U.S.C. Sections 4301-4335.
35. 20 C.F.R. Section 1002.34(a).

36. 38 U.S.C. Section 4311(c).

EXHIBIT 35–1 Coverage of Employment Discrimination Laws

Title VII of the Civil Rights Act	Age Discrimination in Employment Act	Americans with Disabilities Act (as Amended)
Prohibits discrimination based on race, color, national origin, religion, gender (including wage discrimination), and pregnancy; prohibits sexual harassment.	Prohibits discrimination against persons over forty years of age.	Prohibits discrimination against persons with a mental or physical impairment that substantially limits a major life activity now or in the past, or who are regarded as having such an impairment, or who are associated with a disabled person.
Applies to employers with fifteen or more employees.	Applies to employers with twenty or more employees.	Applies to employers with fifteen or more employees.

in Skokie normally have nine regular days off (RDO) per month and eight sick days per year. Skokie officers who are in the reserve receive two weeks of paid leave for annual training each summer, but they do not receive pay for the required weekend military training. During his first four years as an officer at Skokie, Bello always requested RDOs to cover his weekend training drills.

After that, Bello started requesting military leave for the two to four days of drills per month, in addition to his nine RDO days. Skokie at first granted Bello military leave for monthly drills but later began to deny the requests. When Skokie officials told Bello that he needed to schedule his RDOs to cover his weekend military training, Bello filed suit in a federal district court alleging violations of the USERRA. Skokie filed a motion for summary judgment, which the court denied. The court found that Bello was meeting his employer's legitimate expectations. Bello was therefore entitled to a trial on the issue of whether Skokie had treated his leave requests less favorably than requests from other employees.[37] ∎

35–4c Plaintiffs May Be Entitled to Promotions

Under the USERRA, returning service members are to be reemployed in the jobs that they would have attained had they not been absent for military service. Reinstatement could affect their seniority, status, pay, and other rights and benefits (such as health and pension plans). In essence, this means that if a returning service member sues an employer for violations of the USERRA and is successful, she or he could receive not only damages and reinstatement but also a promotion.

35–5 Defenses to Employment Discrimination

The first line of defense for an employer charged with employment discrimination is to assert that the plaintiff has failed to meet his or her initial burden of proving that discrimination occurred. As noted, plaintiffs bringing age discrimination claims may find it difficult to meet this initial burden because they must prove that age discrimination was the reason for their employer's decision.

Once a plaintiff succeeds in proving that discrimination occurred, the burden shifts to the employer to justify the discriminatory practice. Possible justifications

include that the discrimination was the result of a business necessity, a bona fide occupational qualification, or a seniority system. In some situations, as noted earlier, an effective antiharassment policy and prompt remedial action when harassment occurs may shield employers from liability for sexual harassment under Title VII.

35–5a Business Necessity

An employer may defend against a claim of disparate-impact (unintentional) discrimination by asserting that a practice that has a discriminatory effect is a **business necessity**. ∎ **EXAMPLE 35.19** EarthFix, Inc., an international consulting agency, requires its applicants to be fluent in at least one foreign language. If this requirement is shown to have a discriminatory effect, EarthFix can defend it based on business necessity. That is, the company can argue that its workers must speak more than one language to perform their jobs at the required level of competence. If EarthFix can demonstrate a definite connection between foreign language fluency and job performance, it normally will succeed in this business necessity defense. ∎

35–5b Bona Fide Occupational Qualification

Another defense applies when discrimination against a protected class is essential to a job—that is, when a particular trait is a **bona fide occupational qualification (BFOQ).** Note that race, color, and national origin can never be BFOQs.

Generally, courts have restricted the BFOQ defense to situations in which the employee's gender or religion is essential to the job. For instance, a women's clothing store might legitimately hire only female sales attendants if part of an attendant's job involves assisting clients in the store's dressing rooms.

35–5c Seniority Systems

An employer with a history of discrimination may have no members of protected classes in upper-level positions. Nevertheless, the employer may have a defense against a discrimination suit if promotions or other job benefits have been distributed according to a fair *seniority system.* In a **seniority system,** workers with more years of service are promoted first or laid off last.

∎ **CASE IN POINT 35.20** Cathalene Johnson, an African American woman, was a senior service agent for Federal Express Corporation (FedEx) for more than seventeen

---

37. *Bello v. Village of Skokie,* ___ F.Supp.3d ___, 2015 WL 9582986 (N.D. Ill. 2015).

years. She resigned in 2014 and filed suit against FedEx for discrimination based on race and gender, as well as for violation of the Equal Pay Act. Johnson claimed that FedEx had paid a white male co-worker about two dollars more per hour than she had received for basically the same position. FedEx argued that the man had seniority. He had worked for FedEx for seven years longer, was the most senior employee at the station where Johnson worked, and had been a courier in addition to being a service agent. The court ruled that FedEx's seniority system was fair and provided a defense to Johnson's claims.[38] ■

35–5d After-Acquired Evidence of Employee Misconduct

In some situations, employers have attempted to avoid liability for employment discrimination on the basis of "after-acquired evidence" of an employee's misconduct. After-acquired evidence refers to evidence that the employer discovers after a lawsuit has been filed.

■ **EXAMPLE 35.21** Pratt Legal Services fires Lucy, who then sues Pratt for employment discrimination. During pretrial investigation, Pratt discovers that Lucy made material misrepresentations on her job application. Had Pratt known of these misrepresentations, it would have had grounds to fire Lucy. ■

After-acquired evidence of wrongdoing cannot shield an employer entirely from liability for employment discrimination. It may, however, be used to limit the amount of damages for which the employer is liable.

35–6 Affirmative Action

Federal statutes and regulations providing for equal opportunity in the workplace were designed to reduce or eliminate discriminatory practices with respect to hiring, retaining, and promoting employees. **Affirmative action** programs go a step further and attempt to "make up" for past patterns of discrimination by giving members of protected classes preferential treatment in hiring or promotion. During the 1960s, all federal and state government agencies, private companies that contracted to do business with the federal government, and institutions that received federal funding were required to implement affirmative action policies.

Title VII of the Civil Rights Act neither requires nor prohibits affirmative action. Thus, most private companies and organizations have not been required to implement affirmative action policies, though many have done so voluntarily. Affirmative action programs have been controversial, however, particularly when they have resulted in reverse discrimination against members of a majority group, such as white males.

35–6a Equal Protection Issues

Because of their inherently discriminatory nature, affirmative action programs may violate the equal protection clause of the Fourteenth Amendment to the U.S. Constitution. Any federal, state, or local government affirmative action program that uses racial or ethnic classifications as the basis for making decisions is subject to strict scrutiny (the highest standard to meet) by the courts.

Today, an affirmative action program normally is constitutional only if it attempts to remedy past discrimination and does not make use of quotas or preferences. Furthermore, once such a program has succeeded in the goal of remedying past discrimination, it must be changed or eliminated.

35–6b State Laws Prohibiting Affirmative Action Programs

Some states have enacted laws that prohibit affirmative action programs at public institutions (colleges, universities, and state agencies) within their borders. These states include California, Maryland, Michigan, New Hampshire, Oklahoma, Virginia, and Washington. The United States Supreme Court recognized that states have the power to enact such bans in 2014.

■ **CASE IN POINT 35.22** Michigan voters passed an initiative to amend the state's constitution to prohibit publicly funded colleges from granting preferential treatment to any group on the basis of race, sex, color, ethnicity, or national origin. The law also prohibited Michigan from considering race and gender in public hiring and contracting decisions.

A lawsuit was filed challenging the initiative as a violation of the equal protection clause in the U.S. Constitution. Although a federal appellate court held that the law violated the equal protection clause, the United States Supreme Court reversed. The Court ruled that a state has the inherent power to ban affirmative action within that state, but it did not rule on the constitutionality of any specific affirmative action program.[39] ■

---

38. *Johnson v. Federal Express Corp.*, 996 F.Supp.2d 302 (M.D.Pa. 2014).

39. *Schuette v. Coalition to Defend Affirmative Action, Integration and Immigrant Rights*, ___ U.S. ___, 134 S.Ct. 1623, 188 L.Ed.2d 613 (2014).

Reviewing: Employment Discrimination

Amaani Lyle, an African American woman, was hired by Warner Brothers Television Productions to be a scriptwriters' assistant for the writers of *Friends,* a popular adult-oriented television series. One of her essential job duties was to type detailed notes for the scriptwriters during brainstorming sessions in which they discussed jokes, dialogue, and story lines. The writers then combed through Lyle's notes after the meetings for script material. During these meetings, the three male scriptwriters told lewd and vulgar jokes and made sexually explicit comments and gestures. They often talked about their personal sexual experiences and fantasies, and some of these conversations were then used in episodes of *Friends.*

During the meetings, Lyle never complained that she found the writers' conduct offensive. After four months, Lyle was fired because she could not type fast enough to keep up with the writers' conversations during the meetings. She filed a suit against Warner Brothers, alleging sexual harassment and claiming that her termination was based on racial discrimination. Using the information presented in the chapter, answer the following questions.

1. Would Lyle's claim of racial discrimination be for intentional (disparate-treatment) or unintentional (disparate-impact) discrimination? Explain.
2. Can Lyle establish a *prima facie* case of racial discrimination? Why or why not?
3. When Lyle was hired, she was told that typing speed was extremely important to the position. At the time, she maintained that she could type eighty words per minute, so she was not given a typing test. It later turned out that Lyle could type only fifty words per minute. What impact might typing speed have on Lyle's lawsuit?
4. Lyle's sexual-harassment claim is based on the hostile working environment created by the writers' sexually offensive conduct at meetings that she was required to attend. The writers, however, argue that their behavior was essential to the "creative process" of writing for *Friends,* a show that routinely contained sexual innuendos and adult humor. Which defense discussed in the chapter might Warner Brothers assert using this argument?

Debate This . . .   *Members of minority groups and women have made enough economic progress in the last several decades that they no longer need special legislation to protect them.*

Terms and Concepts

affirmative action 681
bona fide occupational qualification
   (BFOQ) 680
business necessity 680
constructive discharge 672

disparate-impact
   discrimination 666
disparate-treatment
   discrimination 665
employment discrimination 664

prima facie case 665
protected class 664
seniority system 680
sexual harassment 672
tangible employment action 674

Issue Spotters

1. Ruth is a supervisor for a Subs & Suds restaurant. Tim is a Subs & Suds employee. The owner announces that some employees will be discharged. Ruth tells Tim that if he has sex with her, he can keep his job. Is this sexual harassment? Why or why not? (See *Title VII of the Civil Rights Act.*)

2. Koko, a person with a disability, applies for a job at Lively Sales Corporation for which she is well qualified, but she is rejected. Lively continues to seek applicants and eventually fills the position with a person who does not have a disability. Could Koko succeed in a suit against Lively for discrimination? Explain. (See *Discrimination Based on Disability.*)

• **Check your answers to the Issue Spotters against the answers provided in Appendix D at the end of this text.**

Business Scenarios

35–1. Title VII Violations. Discuss fully whether either of the following actions would constitute a violation of Title VII of the 1964 Civil Rights Act, as amended: (*See Title VII of the Civil Rights Act.*)

(a) Tennington, Inc., is a consulting firm with ten employees. These employees travel on consulting jobs in seven states. Tennington has an employment record of hiring only white males.

(b) Novo Films is making a movie about Africa and needs to employ approximately one hundred extras for this picture. To hire these extras, Novo advertises in all major newspapers in Southern California. The ad states that only African Americans need apply.

35–2. Religious Discrimination. Gina Gomez, a devout Roman Catholic, worked for Sam's Department Stores, Inc., in Phoenix, Arizona. Sam's considered Gomez a productive employee because her sales exceeded $200,000 per year. At the time, the store gave its managers the discretion to grant unpaid leave to employees but prohibited vacations or leave during the holiday season—October through December. Gomez felt that she had a "calling" to go on a "pilgrimage" in October to a location in Bosnia where some persons claimed to have had visions of the Virgin Mary. The Catholic Church had not designated the site an official pilgrimage site, the visions were not expected to be stronger in October, and tours were available at other times. The store managers denied Gomez's request for leave, but she had a nonrefundable ticket and left anyway. Sam's terminated her employment, and she could not find another job. Can Gomez establish a *prima facie* case of religious discrimination? Explain. (*See Title VII of the Civil Rights Act.*)

Business Case Problems

35–3. Spotlight on Dress Code Policies—Discrimination Based on Gender. Burlington Coat Factory Warehouse, Inc., had a dress code that required male salesclerks to wear business attire consisting of slacks, shirt, and a necktie. Female salesclerks, by contrast, were required to wear a smock so that customers could readily identify them. Karen O'Donnell and other female employees refused to wear smocks. Instead they reported to work in business attire and were suspended. After numerous suspensions, the female employees were fired for violating Burlington's dress code policy. All other conditions of employment, including salary, hours, and benefits, were the same for female and male employees. Was the dress code policy discriminatory? Why or why not? [*O'Donnell v. Burlington Coat Factory Warehouse, Inc.,* 656 F.Supp. 263 (S.D. Ohio 1987)] (*See Title VII of the Civil Rights Act.*)

35–4. Sexual Harassment by Co-Worker. Billie Bradford worked for the Kentucky Department of Community Based Services (DCBS). One of Bradford's co-workers, Lisa Stander, routinely engaged in extreme sexual behavior (such as touching herself and making crude comments) in Bradford's presence. Bradford and others regularly complained about Stander's conduct to their supervisor, Angie Taylor. Rather than resolve the problem, Taylor nonchalantly told Stander to stop, encouraged Bradford to talk to Stander, and suggested that Stander was just having fun. Assuming that Bradford was subjected to a hostile work environment, could DCBS be liable? Why or why not? [*Bradford v. Department of Community Based Services,* 2012 WL 360032 (E.D.Ky. 2012)] (*See Title VII of the Civil Rights Act.*)

35–5. Business Case Problem with Sample Answer—Age Discrimination. Beginning in 1986, Paul Rangel was a sales professional for the pharmaceutical company sanofi-aventis U.S. LLC (S-A). Rangel had satisfactory performance reviews until 2006, when S-A issued new "Expectations" guidelines that included sales call quotas and other standards that he failed to meet. After two years of negative performance reviews, Rangel—who was then more than forty years old—was terminated. The termination was part of a nationwide reduction in force of all sales professionals who had not met the "Expectations" guidelines, including younger workers. Did S-A engage in age discrimination? Discuss. [*Rangel v. sanofi aventis U.S. LLC,* 2013 WL 142040 (10th Cir. 2013)] (*See Discrimination Based on Age.*)

• **For a sample answer to Problem 35–5, go to Appendix E at the end of this text.**

35–6. Discrimination Based on Disability. Cynthia Horn worked for Knight Facilities Management–GM, Inc., in Detroit, Michigan, as a janitor. When Horn developed a sensitivity to cleaning products, her physician gave her a "no exposure to cleaning solutions" restriction. Knight discussed possible accommodations with Horn. She suggested that restrooms be eliminated from her cleaning route or that she be provided with a respirator. Knight explained that she would be exposed to cleaning solutions in any situation and concluded that there was no work available within her physician's restriction. Has Knight violated the Americans with Disabilities Act by failing to provide Horn with the requested accommodations? Explain. [*Horn v. Knight Facilities Management–GM, Inc.,* 556 Fed.Appx. 452 (6th Cir. 2014)] (*See Discrimination Based on Disability.*)

35–7. Sexual Harassment. Jamel Blanton was a male employee at a Pizza Hut restaurant operated by Newton Associates, Inc., in San Antonio, Texas. Blanton was subjected to sexual and racial harassment by the general manager, who was female. Newton had a clear, straightforward antidiscrimination policy and complaint procedure. The policy provided that in such a situation, an employee should complain to the harasser's supervisor. Blanton alerted a shift leader and an assistant manager about the harassment, but they were subordinate to the general manager and did not report the harassment to higher-level management. When Blanton finally complained to a manager with authority over the general manager, the employer investigated and fired the general manager within four days. Blanton filed a suit in a federal district court against Newton, seeking to impose liability on the employer for the general manager's actions. What is Newton's best defense? Discuss. [*Blanton v. Newton Associates, Inc.,* 593 Fed.Appx. 389 (5th Cir. 2015)] (See *Title VII of the Civil Rights Act.*)

35–8. Discrimination Based on Disability. Dennis Wallace was a deputy sheriff for Stanislaus County, California, when he injured his left knee. After surgery, he was subject to limits on prolonged standing, walking, and running. The county assigned him to work as a bailiff. The sergeants who supervised him rated his performance above average. Less than a year later, without consulting those supervisors, the county placed him on an unpaid leave of absence, under the mistaken belief that he could not safely perform the essential functions of the job. Wallace filed an action in a California state court against the county, alleging discrimination based on disability. Under state law, discriminatory intent is shown by evidence that an actual or perceived disability was a "substantial motivating factor or reason" for an employer's adverse employment action. An employee is not required to show that the action was motivated by animosity or ill will. Could Wallace likely prove the "substantial motivating factor or reason" element? Explain. [*Wallace v. County of Stanislaus,* 245 Cal.App.4th 109, 199 Cal.Rptr.3d 462 (5 Dist. 2016)] (See *Discrimination Based on Disability.*)

35–9. A Question of Ethics—Retaliation by Employers.

 Shane Dawson, a male homosexual, worked for Entek International. Some of Dawson's co-workers, including his supervisor, made derogatory comments about his sexual orientation. Dawson's work deteriorated. He filed a complaint with Entek's human resources department. Two days later, he was fired. State law made it unlawful for an employer to discriminate against an individual based on sexual orientation. [Dawson v. Entek International, *630 F.3d 928 (9th Cir. 2011)*] (See *Title VII of the Civil Rights Act.*)

(a) Could Dawson establish a claim for retaliation? Explain.

(b) Should homosexuals be a protected class under Title VII of the Civil Rights Act? Discuss the arguments for and against amending federal law to prohibit employment discrimination based on sexual orientation.

Legal Reasoning Group Activity

35–10. Racial Discrimination. Two African American plaintiffs sued the producers of the reality television series *The Bachelor* and *The Bachelorette* for racial discrimination. The plaintiffs claimed that the shows had never featured persons of color in the lead roles. The plaintiffs also alleged that the producers did not provide people of color who auditioned for the lead roles with the same opportunities to compete as white people who auditioned. (See *Title VII of the Civil Rights Act.*)

(a) The first group will assess whether the plaintiffs can establish a *prima facie* case of disparate-treatment discrimination.

(b) The second group will consider whether the plaintiffs can establish disparate-impact discrimination.

(c) The third group will assume that the plaintiffs established a *prima facie* case and that the burden has shifted to the employer to articulate a legal reason for not hiring the plaintiffs. What legitimate reasons might the employer assert for not hiring the plaintiffs in this situation? Should the law require television producers to hire persons of color for lead roles in reality television shows? Discuss.

Health Insurance and Small Business

Small businesses are the foundation of the U.S. economy. Increasing health-care costs and decreasing insurance coverage between 2000 and 2010 forced many small firms to stop offering health-care coverage to their employees.

Recent legislation put in place comprehensive health-insurance reforms intended to improve access, affordability, and quality in health care. An especially important law is the Patient Protection and Affordable Care Act (ACA) of 2010 (often referred to as Obamacare). The ACA sets forth responsibilities and benefits for businesses determined in part by the size of an employer's workforce.[1]

What Is a Small Business?

The ACA defines a *small business* as a firm with fewer than fifty full-time equivalent (FTE) employees. An FTE is an employee who works thirty or more hours per week. Two half-time employees count as one FTE.

This definition fits about 96 percent of all businesses (5.8 million out of 6 million firms). In fact, 90 percent of all U.S. firms have fewer than twenty FTEs.

What Responsibilities Does the ACA Impose on Small Businesses?

Large businesses—those with fifty or more FTEs—are required to offer health insurance to their employees or pay a penalty.[2] For a small business, there is no requirement to offer health insurance. For a small firm that chooses to do so, the ACA imposes minimum standards on health plans.

Summary of Benefits and Coverage All employers, including small businesses, are required to provide their employees with a "Summary of Benefits and Coverage" that includes an explanation of the costs. The summary should be in plain language. Employees can use this information to compare their employer's plan with private plans, which the employees may opt to buy instead. An employer is not required to contribute to the premium for an employee's private plan.

Waiting Period Employees who are eligible for employer-sponsored health insurance must not be made to wait more than ninety days for coverage.

Notice of Marketplace Coverage Options Small businesses that do not offer health insurance can provide their employees with a "Notice of Marketplace Coverage Options." The notice can inform employees about their options with respect to the health-insurance marketplace.

---

1. For the complete text of the ACA, see Pub. L. No. 111-148. Also significant are the health-care amendments of the Health Care and Education Reconciliation Act of 2010; see Pub. L. No. 111-152.
2. Before the ACA, more than 95 percent of these employers already offered health insurance to their employees.

Annual Returns All employers that provide self-insured health coverage are required to file annual information returns with the Internal Revenue Service for the individuals that are covered.[3]

What Benefits Does the ACA Offer Small Businesses?

The ACA provides benefits to small business by expanding insurance coverage options, reducing related costs, and giving employers and employees more control over their own health care.

Health-Insurance Marketplace A small business can buy health-insurance coverage for its employees through the ACA's Small Business Health Options Program (SHOP). Coverage can be offered to employees any time during the year.

The SHOP marketplace offers multiple plans from private insurance companies. An employer can choose which plans to make available to its employees, whether to cover the employees' dependents, how much of the premiums the employer will pay, and other options.[4]

Small Business Health-Care Tax Credit Employers with fewer than twenty-five FTEs, each of whom are paid an average annual wage of less than $50,000, may be eligible for a health-care tax credit. To be eligible, an employer must cover at least 50 percent of the cost of the premiums for its employees' health insurance and buy the coverage through SHOP. Dental and vision care coverage also qualifies. An employer does not need to offer coverage to part-time employees (those working fewer than thirty hours per week) or to employees' dependents to qualify for the credit.

The amount of the credit may be as much as 50 percent of an employer's contribution toward its employees' premium costs. The smaller the business, the higher the credit—the credit is highest for firms with fewer than ten employees paid an average of $25,000 or less. And eligible small businesses can claim a business expense deduction for the premiums in excess of the credit.[5]

Wellness Programs A wellness program requires individuals to meet a specific standard related to health, such as a lower blood cholesterol level, to obtain a reward. Employers that promote employee health through workplace wellness programs are eligible for a reward of up to 30 percent of the cost of health coverage. The reward for a program designed to prevent or reduce the use of tobacco can be as much as 50 percent. The cost of health coverage includes employer-paid premiums and benefits.

Rebates The ACA requires insurance companies to spend at least 80 percent of premiums on medical care, not administrative costs. Insurers who do not meet this goal must provide rebates to policyholders.[6] This includes employers that provide group health insurance for their employees.

3. 26 U.S.C. Section 6055.

4. See U.S. Department of Health and Human Services, *SHOP Marketplace How-To Guides, Fact Sheets, Tools, and Other Resources for Employers* (December 11, 2015), *available at* www.healthcare.gov/small-businesses/provide-shop-coverage/resources/.

5. See Internal Revenue Service, *Small Business Health Care Tax Credit and the SHOP Marketplace* (December 11, 2015), *available at* www.irs.gov/Affordable-Care-Act/Employers/Small-Business-Health-Care-Tax-Credit-and-the-SHOP-Marketplace.

6. See Internal Revenue Service, *Medical Loss Ration (MLR) FAQs* (December 11, 2015) at www.irs.gov/uac/Medical-Loss-Ratio-(MLR)-FAQs.

Standard Operating Rules The ACA accelerated the adoption of standard operating rules for health-insurance plan administration. Operating rules are the business rules and guidelines for health-insurance plans. The ACA requires one format and one set of codes for claims, remittance advice, service authorization, eligibility verification, and claims status inquiry.

Nondiscriminatory Pricing The ACA ended the discriminatory insurance industry practice of increasing premiums because an employee filed a claim or got older or because a business hired a woman. At one time, premiums could increase by up to 200 percent in these circumstances.

Ethical Connection

There has been considerable opposition to the ACA. For example, the mandate that large businesses offer health insurance to their employees or pay a penalty—called "the Obamacare effect"—has been much criticized. Detractors express concern that the mandate creates an incentive for large businesses to employ part-time workers instead of full-time employees. During the period preceding the start date of the ACA and the end of 2014, however, in the private sector the number of part-time jobs *decreased* and the number of full-time positions *increased*.

To date, there is controversial evidence that employers are reducing the hours of their employees to avoid the requirements of the ACA.[7] Many argue that the reduction in the percentage of Americans who could work but are choosing to remain out of the labor force is due to Obamacare. Why? Because good-paying full-time job opportunities have shrunk due to the higher employer cost of hiring.

Ethics Question *Are small businesses ethically obligated to offer their employees health insurance? Discuss.*

Critical Thinking *Should the mandate to offer employees health insurance be extended to include small businesses? Or should it be repealed altogether? Explain.*

---

7. Also, in separate legal challenges to the ACA, the United States Supreme Court has upheld key parts of the act. See *National Federation of Business v. Sebelius*, __ U.S. __, 132 S.Ct. 2566, 183 L.Ed.2d 450 (2012); and *King v. Burwell*, __ U.S. __, 135 S.Ct. 2480, 192 L.Ed.2d 483 (2015). The Court has held certain U.S. Department of Health and Human Services regulations issued under the act to be invalid, however. See *Burwell v. Hobby Lobby Stores, Inc.*, __ U.S. __, 134 S.Ct. 2751, 189 L.Ed.2d 675 (2014).

Business Organizations

BUSINESS LAW
CLARKSON · MILLER · CROSS

CHAPTER 36

Small Businesses and Franchises

A goal of many business students is to become an **entrepreneur,** one who initiates and assumes the financial risk of a new business enterprise and undertakes to provide or control its management. One of the first decisions an entrepreneur must make is which form of business organization will be most appropriate for the new endeavor.

In selecting an organizational form, the entrepreneur will consider a num-ber of factors. These include (1) ease of creation, (2) the liability of the own-ers, (3) tax considerations, and (4) the ability to raise capital. Keep these fac-tors in mind as you read this unit and learn about the various forms of busi-ness organization. Remember, too, in considering these business forms that the primary motive of an entrepreneur is to make profits.

Traditionally, entrepreneurs have used three major business forms—the sole proprietorship, the partnership, and the corporation. In this chapter, we examine sole proprietorships and also look at franchises. Although the franchise is not strictly speaking a business organizational form, it is widely used today by entrepreneurs.

36–1 General Considerations for Small Businesses

Most small businesses begin as sole proprietorships. Once the business is under way, the sole proprietorship form may become too limited. The owner and any additional investors may then want to establish a more formal orga-nization, such as a limited partnership (LP), a limited liability partnership (LLP), a limited liability company (LLC), or a corporation. These forms of business limit the owner's personal liability, or legal responsibility, for business debts and obligations. Each business form has its own advantages and disadvantages, but legal limited liability generally is necessary for those who wish to raise outside capital.

36–1a Requirements for All Business Forms

Any business, whatever its form, has to meet a vari-ety of legal requirements, which typically relate to the following:

1. Business name registration.
2. Occupational licensing.

3. State tax registration (for instance, to obtain permits for collecting and remitting sales taxes).
4. Health and environmental permits.
5. Zoning and building codes.
6. Import/export regulations.

If the business has employees, the owner must also comply with a host of laws governing the workplace.

36–1b Protecting Intellectual Property

Protecting rights in intellectual property is a central con-cern for many small businesses. For instance, software companies and app developers depend on their copy-rights and patents to protect their investments in the research and development required to create new pro-grams. Without copyright or patent protection, a com-petitor or a customer could simply copy the software or app.

Trademarks Choosing a trademark or service mark and making sure that it is protected under trademark law can be crucial to the success of a new business venture. Indeed, a factor to consider in choosing a name for a business entity is whether the business name will be used as a trademark. The general rule is that a trademark cannot be the same as another's mark or so similar that confusion might result.

For the most protection, trademarks should be registered with the U.S. Patent and Trademark Office (PTO). If the mark is federally registered, the owner may use the symbol ® with the mark. This well-known symbol puts others on notice of the registration and helps to prevent trademark infringement. An owner who has not registered can use the symbol ™. Registration with the PTO should be renewed five years after the initial registration and at ten-year intervals thereafter.

Trade Secrets Much of the value of a small business may lie in its trade secrets, such as information about product development, production processes and techniques, and customer lists. Preserving the secrecy of the information is necessary for legal protection.

As a practical matter, trade secrets must be divulged to key employees. Thus, any business runs the risk that those employees might disclose the secrets to competitors—or even set up competing businesses themselves.

To protect their trade secrets, companies may require employees who have access to trade secrets to agree in their employment contracts never to divulge those secrets. A small business may also choose to include a covenant not to compete in an employment contract. A noncompete clause will help to protect against the possibility that a key employee will go to work for a competitor or set up a competing business.

36–1c Obtaining Loans

Raising capital is critical to the growth of most small businesses. In the early days of a business, the sole proprietor may be able to contribute sufficient capital, but as the business becomes successful, more funds may be needed. The owner may want to raise capital from external sources to expand the business. One way to do this is to borrow funds.

Obtaining a bank loan is beneficial for small businesses because it allows the owner to retain full ownership and control of the business. Note, though, that the bank may place some restrictions on future business decisions as a condition of granting the loan. In addition, bank loans may not be available for some businesses. Banks are usually reluctant to lend significant sums to businesses that are not yet established. Even if a bank is willing to make

such a loan, the bank may require personal guaranty contracts from the owner, putting the owner's personal assets at risk.

Loans with desirable terms may be available from the U.S. Small Business Administration (SBA). One SBA program provides loans of up to $25,000 to businesspersons who are women, low-income individuals, or members of minority groups. Be aware that the SBA requires business owners to put some of their own funds at risk in the business. In addition, many states offer small-business grants to individuals starting a business.

36–2 Sole Proprietorships

In the earliest stages, as mentioned, a small business may operate as a **sole proprietorship,** which is the simplest form of business. In this form, the owner is the business. Thus, anyone who does business without creating a separate business organization has a sole proprietorship. The law considers all new, single-owner businesses to be sole proprietorships unless the owner affirmatively adopts some other form.

More than two-thirds of all U.S. businesses are sole proprietorships. Sole proprietors can own and manage any type of business from an informal, home-office or Web-based undertaking to a large restaurant or construction firm. About 99 percent of the sole proprietorships in the United States have revenues of less than $1 million per year.

36–2a Advantages of the Sole Proprietorship

A major advantage of the sole proprietorship is that the proprietor owns the entire business and receives all of the profits (because she or he assumes all of the risk). In addition, starting a sole proprietorship is easier and less costly than starting any other kind of business because few legal formalities are required. Generally, no documents need to be filed with the government to start a sole proprietorship.[1]

---

1. Although starting a sole proprietorship involves fewer legal formalities than other business organizational forms, even a small sole proprietorship may need to comply with zoning requirements, obtain a state business license, and the like.

Taxes A sole proprietor pays only personal income taxes (including Social Security and Medicare taxes) on the business's profits. The profits are reported as personal income on the proprietor's personal income tax return. In other words, the business itself need not file an income tax return. Sole proprietors are allowed to establish retirement accounts that are tax-exempt until the funds are withdrawn.

Like any form of business enterprise, a sole proprietorship can be liable for other taxes, such as those collected and applied to the disbursement of unemployment compensation. Whether liability for the unpaid unemployment compensation taxes of a sole proprietorship remains with the seller or must be assumed by the buyer was at issue in the following case.

Case Analysis 36.1

A. Gadley Enterprises, Inc. v. Department of Labor and Industry Office of Unemployment Compensation Tax Services

Commonwealth Court of Pennsylvania, __ A.3d __, 2016 WL 55591 (2016).

In the Language of the Court

SIMPSON, Judge.

* * * *

[Julianne Gresh (Predecessor)] operated [Romper Room Day Care (Romper Room)], a childcare center, as a sole proprietorship for 12 years. Predecessor owed the [Pennsylvania Department of Labor and Industry Office of Unemployment Compensation Tax Services (Department)] substantial unpaid UC [unemployment compensation] contributions, interest and penalties. She admitted liability and entered payment plans with the Department * * *. Pursuant to these payment plans, she made monthly payments in the minimal amount of $50. Predecessor was on the verge of losing her license to operate, and sought another entity to operate the location as a childcare facility.

[A. Gadley Enterprises, Inc. (Purchaser)] operated a childcare center, Young Environment Learning Center, in Erie, Pennsylvania. Purchaser decided to purchase assets from Predecessor in order to open a satellite location of Young Environmental Learning Center at the prior location of Romper Room. Purchaser and Predecessor executed an asset purchase agreement (Agreement).

Through the Agreement, Purchaser paid a total of $37,000 for Predecessor's tangible and intangible assets. This total was comprised of $10,000 for the use of the name "Romper Room," $10,790 for a covenant not to compete, and $17,210 for tangible assets listed on [an attached] Inventory List.

* * * The Inventory List did not include any of Predecessor's personal

assets other than those used in the operation of Romper Room.

* * * Four days *after* executing the Agreement, * * * Predecessor notified the Department of the sale.

* * * The Department issued Purchaser a Notice of Assessment (Notice) in the amount of $43,370.49 for UC contributions, interest and penalties owed by Predecessor. The Notice stated Purchaser was liable because it purchased 51% or more of Predecessor's assets.

In response, Purchaser filed a petition [with the Department] for reassessment.

* * * *

Based on the evidence presented at the hearing [held on the petition], the Department issued its decision and order denying the petition for reassessment.

* * * *

Purchaser then filed a petition to review to this Court.

* * * *

[43 Pennsylvania Statutes Section 788.3(a), part of the state's Unemployment Compensation Law] provides:

(a) Every employer * * *, who shall sell in bulk fifty-one percent or more of his assets, including but not limited to, any stock of goods, wares or merchandise of any kind, fixtures, machinery, equipment, building or real estate, shall give the department ten (10) days' notice of the sale prior to completion of the transfer * * *. The employer shall present to the purchaser of such property, a certificate * * * showing that all reports have been filed and contributions, interest and penalties paid to the date of the proposed transfer. The failure of the

purchaser to require such certificate shall render such purchaser liable to the department for the unpaid contributions, interest and penalties.

* * * *

There is no dispute that Purchaser did not obtain a clearance certificate reflecting Predecessor's payment of UC liability. There is also no dispute that Predecessor owed the Department for outstanding UC contributions, interest and penalties in the amount of $43,370.49 at the time of the sale.

* * * *

Purchaser argues substantial evidence does not support the Department's finding that it purchased more than 51% of the [Predecessor's] assets.

* * * *

The Agreement establishes that the Inventory List sets forth all business assets of Predecessor. Gresh confirmed the Inventory List was a complete list of assets used in the operation of her business.

The Inventory List reflects a total value of assets equaling $19,210. * * * The parties reduced the purchase price by $2,000 to account for the reduced value of the assets when Purchaser removed certain assets from the complete Inventory List. Purchaser acquired all the assets included in the Inventory List, other than those removed, for $17,210. The amount constitutes approximately 90% of the value of the complete list of assets ($19,210 × .9 = $17,289).

The Agreement, supplemented by corroborating [supporting] testimony,

Case 36.1 Continued

constitutes substantial evidence to support the Department's finding that the sale qualified as a bulk sale of more than 51% of Predecessor's assets.

* * * *

Purchaser also argues the Department erred in construing the term "assets" in the bulk sales provision to include only business assets when determining whether a sale met the 51% threshold. Purchaser asserts the provision does not differentiate between business and personal assets of an employer and there is no legal distinction when the employer is a sole proprietor.

* * * *

* * * The definition of "employer" [in the UC Law] includes a sole proprietor like Predecessor.

The word "assets" is not defined in the [UC] Law.

[In Section 788.3(a)] the term "assets" precedes a list of examples, followed by the phrase "including but not limited to."

* * * *

* * * The examples * * * indicate that the term "assets" refers to business assets. This conclusion is buttressed [reinforced] by the context of the statute as a whole, which pertains to employers operating businesses and paying employees as part of their business operations.

The factual circumstances surrounding the sale also indicate the term "assets" means "business assets." Here, the context is the sale of a business, in the childcare industry, to another business engaged in the same industry that intends to operate a childcare facility at the location of the former business. The Agreement reflects the intention of the parties that Purchaser would operate the childcare facility as a satellite location. [Emphasis added.]

* * * *

* * * The provision does not treat sole proprietors differently than other employers. The provision contains no exemption of liability for a purchaser when an employer operates as a sole proprietorship. Nor does it contain an exemption from liability when the former employer entered a repayment plan with the Department.

Moreover, Purchaser's interpretation does not consider *the purpose of the bulk sales provision. That purpose is to ensure an employer does not divest itself of assets without satisfying outstanding liabilities, either itself or by the purchaser.* This Court agrees with the Department that Gresh's repayment agreement in the minimal amount of $50 per month does not satisfy the UC liability. [Emphasis added.]

* * * *

In sum, the Department's construction of assets as business assets is reasonable and consistent with the context and purpose of [the] bulk sales provision. Purchaser's failure to obtain a clearance certificate rendered it liable for Predecessor's unpaid UC contributions, interest and penalties, regardless of Predecessor's repayment agreement. Therefore, this Court upholds the Department's interpretation of the bulk sales provision.

* * * *

* * * For the foregoing reasons, we affirm the Department.

Legal Reasoning Questions

1. As is clear from the law applied in this case, and the result, the liability of a business for unpaid taxes "follows the assets." Why?

2. What action can Gadley take now to avoid suffering the loss of the funds required to cover Gresh's unpaid taxes?

3. What action should a buyer take *before* purchasing the assets of a business to avoid liability for the seller's unpaid taxes?

Flexibility A sole proprietorship offers more flexibility than does a partnership or a corporation. The sole proprietor is free to make any decision she or he wishes concerning the business—including what kind of business to pursue, whom to hire, and when to take a vacation. The sole proprietor can sell or transfer all or part of the business to another party at any time without seeking approval from anyone else. In contrast, approval is typically required from partners in a partnership and from shareholders in a corporation.

36–2b Disadvantages of the Sole Proprietorship

The major disadvantage of the sole proprietorship is that the proprietor alone bears the burden of any losses or liabilities incurred by the business enterprise. In other words, the sole proprietor has unlimited liability for all obligations that arise in doing business. Any lawsuit against the business or its employees can lead to unlimited personal liability for the owner of a sole proprietorship.

■ **EXAMPLE 36.1** Aaron and Melissa Klein, owners of the Sweet Cakes by Melissa bakery, refused to bake a wedding cake for a same-sex couple's wedding. They claimed that their religious beliefs did not allow them to provide services for same-sex ceremonies. The Oregon State Bureau of Labor and Industries argued that their decision violated the law. In 2015, an administrative law judge ruled against the Kleins' motion to dismiss and ordered them to pay $135,000 in damages. As sole proprietors, the Kleins were personally responsible for paying the damages. ■

Personal Assets at Risk Creditors can pursue the owner's personal assets to satisfy any business debts. Although sole proprietors may obtain insurance to protect the business, liability can easily exceed policy limits. This unlimited liability is a major factor to be considered in choosing a business form.

■ **EXAMPLE 36.2** Sheila Fowler operates a golf shop near a world-class golf course as a sole proprietorship. One of Fowler's employees fails to secure a display of golf clubs. They fall on Dean Maheesh, a professional golfer, and seriously injure him. If Maheesh sues Fowler's shop and wins, Fowler's personal liability could easily exceed the limits of her insurance policy. Fowler could lose not only her business, but also her house, car, and any other personal assets that can be attached to pay the judgment. ■

Lack of Continuity and Limited Ability to Raise Capital The sole proprietorship also has the disadvantage of lacking continuity after the death of the proprietor. When the owner dies, so does the business—it is automatically dissolved.

Another disadvantage is that in raising capital, the proprietor is limited to his or her personal funds and any loans that he or she can obtain for the business. Lenders may be unwilling to make loans to sole proprietorships, particularly start-ups, because the sole proprietor risks unlimited personal liability and may not be able to pay. (See this chapter's *Digital Update* feature for a discussion of one court's refusal to discharge a loan made to a sole proprietor who had declared bankruptcy.)

DIGITAL UPDATE   A Sole Proprietorship, Facebook Poker, and Bankruptcy

One major downside of a sole proprietorship is that it is more difficult for a sole proprietor to obtain funding for start-up and expansion. Moreover, if funding is obtained through loans, the sole proprietor is exposed to personal liability.

Personal Liability Exposure for an Online Startup

A case in point went before the United States bankruptcy court in Massachusetts in 2015.[a] Michael Dewhurst, living in Raynham, Massachusetts, sometimes did computer work for Gerald Knappik. Dewhurst decided to start a new business venture—the commercial development of a Facebook poker–playing application. Dewhurst envisioned an application that would enable multiple individuals to play poker together over the Internet through Facebook. Dewhurst informed Knappik of his business plan and predicted that his Facebook poker application "was going to be something very big."

Knappik initially loaned $50,000 to Dewhurst for the project. The loan agreement stated, "The sole purpose of this loan agreement is to provide funds on a personal level for the startup of said business project, in conjunction with borrower's personal funds, not limited to startup costs, operating expenses, advertising costs."

That was the first of a series of personal loans that totaled $220,000.

Dewhurst had repaid only $9,000 on the total outstanding debt when he filed for bankruptcy. Ultimately, the bankruptcy court ascertained that at least $120,000 of the loans that were supposed to be used exclusively for the Facebook poker project had been used for other activities. Furthermore, Dewhurst kept "no contemporaneous records of his disbursements and uses of this cash, no cash journal, ledger, or disbursement slips of any kind."

The Lender Objects to a Bankruptcy Discharge of Monies Owed

During bankruptcy proceedings, Knappik requested that the bankruptcy court deny discharge of Dewhurst's debts to him. Upon review, the court stated that "Dewhurst's failure to keep and preserve adequate records makes it impossible to reconstruct an accurate and complete account of financial affairs and business transactions." The bankruptcy judge ultimately denied discharge of $120,000 of the debt owed to Knappik. Thus, a sole proprietor's failed attempt to create an online poker-playing application led to personal liability even after he had filed for bankruptcy.

Critical Thinking *Sole proprietorships, as well as other businesses, routinely seek funding for online projects. How can the individuals involved avoid personal liability?*

---

a. *In re Dewhurst*, 528 Bankr. 211 (D.Mass. 2015).

36–3 Franchises

Instead of setting up a sole proprietorship to market their own products or services, many entrepreneurs opt to purchase a franchise. A **franchise** is an arrangement in which the owner of intellectual property—such as a trademark, a trade name, or a copyright—licenses others to use it in the selling of goods or services. A **franchisee** (a purchaser of a franchise) is generally legally independent of the **franchisor** (the seller of the franchise). At the same time, the franchisee is economically dependent on the franchisor's integrated business system. In other words, a franchisee can operate as an independent businessperson but still obtain the advantages of a regional or national organization.

Today, franchising companies and their franchisees account for a significant portion of all retail sales in this country. Well-known franchises include McDonald's, 7-Eleven, and Holiday Inn. Franchising has also become a popular way for businesses to expand their operations internationally without violating the legal restrictions that many nations impose on foreign ownership of businesses.

36–3a Types of Franchises

Many different kinds of businesses sell franchises, and numerous types of franchises are available. Generally, though, franchises fall into one of three classifications: distributorships, chain-style business operations, and manufacturing arrangements.

Distributorship In a *distributorship,* a manufacturer (the franchisor) licenses a dealer (the franchisee) to sell its product. Often, a distributorship covers an exclusive territory. Automobile dealerships and beer distributorships are common examples.

■ **EXAMPLE 36.3** Black Bear Beer Company distributes its brands of beer through a network of authorized wholesale distributors, each with an assigned territory. Marik signs a distributorship contract for the area from Gainesville to Ocala, Florida. If the contract states that Marik is the exclusive distributor in that area, then no other franchisee may distribute Black Bear beer in that region. ■

Chain-Style Business Operation In a *chain-style business operation,* a franchise operates under a franchisor's trade name and is identified as a member of a select group of dealers that engage in the franchisor's business. The franchisee is generally required to follow standardized or prescribed methods of operation. Often, the franchisor insists that the franchisee maintain certain standards of performance.

In addition, the franchisee may be required to obtain materials and supplies exclusively from the franchisor. Chipotle Mexican Grill and most other fast-food chains are examples of this type of franchise. Chain-style franchises are also common in service-related businesses, including real estate brokerage firms, such as Century 21, and tax-preparing services, such as H&R Block, Inc.

Manufacturing Arrangement In a *manufacturing,* or *processing-plant, arrangement,* the franchisor transmits to the franchisee the essential ingredients or formula to make a particular product. The franchisee then markets the product either at wholesale or at retail in accordance with the franchisor's standards. Examples of this type of franchise include Pepsi-Cola and other soft-drink bottling companies.

36–3b Laws Governing Franchising

Because a franchise relationship is primarily a contractual relationship, it is governed by contract law. If the franchise exists primarily for the sale of products manufactured by the franchisor, the law governing sales contracts as expressed in Article 2 of the Uniform Commercial Code applies.

Additionally, the federal government and most states have enacted laws governing certain aspects of franchising. Generally, these laws are designed to protect prospective franchisees from dishonest franchisors and to prevent franchisors from terminating franchises without good cause.

Federal Regulation of Franchises The federal government regulates franchising through laws that apply to specific industries and through the Franchise Rule, created by the Federal Trade Commission (FTC).

Industry-Specific Standards. Congress has enacted laws that protect franchisees in certain industries, such as automobile dealerships and service stations. These laws protect the franchisee from unreasonable demands and bad faith terminations of the franchise by the franchisor.

An automobile manufacturer–franchisor cannot make unreasonable demands of dealer-franchisees or set unrealistically high sales quotas. If an automobile manufacturer–franchisor terminates a franchise because of a dealer-franchisee's failure to comply with unreasonable demands, the manufacturer may be liable for damages.[2]

---

2. Automobile Dealers' Franchise Act, also known as the Automobile Dealers' Day in Court Act, 15 U.S.C. Sections 1221 *et seq.*

Similarly, federal law prescribes the conditions under which a franchisor of service stations can terminate the franchise.[3] In addition, federal antitrust laws sometimes apply in specified circumstances to prohibit certain types of anticompetitive agreements.

The Franchise Rule. The FTC's Franchise Rule requires franchisors to disclose certain material facts that a prospective franchisee needs in order to make an informed decision concerning the purchase of a franchise.[4] Those who violate the Franchise Rule are subject to substantial civil penalties, and the FTC can sue on behalf of injured parties to recover damages.

The rule requires the franchisor to make numerous written disclosures to prospective franchisees (see Exhibit 36–1). All representations made to a prospective franchisee must have a reasonable basis. For instance, if a franchisor provides projected earnings figures, the franchisor must indicate whether the figures are based on actual data or hypothetical examples. If a franchisor makes sales or earnings projections based on actual data for a specific franchise location, the franchisor must disclose the number and percentage of its existing franchises that have achieved this result.

State Regulation of Franchising State legislation varies but often is aimed at protecting franchisees from unfair practices and bad faith terminations by franchisors.

State Disclosures. A number of states have laws similar to the federal rules that require franchisors to provide presale disclosures to prospective franchisees.[5] Many state laws also require that a disclosure document (known as the Franchise Disclosure Document, or FDD) be registered or filed with a state official. State laws may also require that a franchisor submit advertising aimed at prospective franchisees to the state for approval.

To protect franchisees, a state law might require the disclosure of information such as the actual costs of operation, recurring expenses, and profits earned, along with facts substantiating these figures. State deceptive trade

---

3. Petroleum Marketing Practices Act (PMPA), 15 U.S.C. Sections 2801 *et seq.*
4. 16 C.F.R. Section 436.1.

5. These states include California, Florida, Hawaii, Illinois, Indiana, Maryland, Michigan, Minnesota, New York, North Dakota, Oregon, Rhode Island, South Dakota, Texas, Utah, Virginia, Washington, and Wisconsin.

EXHIBIT 36–1   The FTC's Franchise Rule Requirements

REQUIREMENT	EXPLANATION
Written (or Electronic) Disclosures	The franchisor must make numerous disclosures, such as the range of goods and services included and the value and estimated profitability of the franchise. Disclosures can be delivered on paper or electronically. Prospective franchisees must be able to download or save any electronic disclosure documents.
Reasonable Basis for Any Representations	To prevent deception, all representations made to a prospective franchisee must have a reasonable basis at the time they are made.
Projected Earnings Figures	If a franchisor provides projected earnings figures, the franchisor must indicate whether the figures are based on actual data or hypothetical examples. The Franchise Rule does not require franchisors to provide potential earnings figures, however.
Actual Data	If a franchisor makes sales or earnings projections based on actual data for a specific franchise location, the franchisor must disclose the number and percentage of its existing franchises that have achieved this result.
Explanation of Terms	Franchisors are required to explain termination, cancellation, and renewal provisions of the franchise contract to potential franchisees before the agreement is signed.

practices acts may also apply and prohibit certain types of actions by franchisors.

May Require Good Cause to Terminate the Franchise. To prevent arbitrary or bad faith terminations, a state law may prohibit termination without "good cause" or require that certain procedures be followed in terminating a franchise. ■ **CASE IN POINT 36.4** FMS, Inc., entered into a franchise agreement with Samsung Construction Equipment North America to become an authorized dealership selling Samsung construction equipment. Samsung then sold its equipment business to Volvo Construction Equipment North America, Inc., which was to continue selling Samsung brand equipment.

Later, Volvo rebranded the construction equipment under its own name and canceled FMS's franchise. FMS sued, claiming that Volvo had terminated the franchise without "good cause" in violation of state law. Because Volvo was no longer manufacturing the Samsung brand equipment, the court found that Volvo had good cause to terminate FMS's franchise. If Volvo had continued making the Samsung equipment, though, it could not have terminated the franchise.[6] ■

36–3c The Franchise Contract

The franchise relationship is defined by the contract between the franchisor and the franchisee. The franchise contract specifies the terms and conditions of the franchise and spells out the rights and duties of the franchisor and the franchisee. If either party fails to perform its contractual duties, that party may be subject to a lawsuit for breach of contract. Furthermore, if a franchisee is induced to enter into a franchise contract by the franchisor's fraudulent misrepresentation, the franchisor may be liable for damages. Generally, statutes and the case law governing franchising tend to emphasize the importance of good faith and fair dealing in franchise relationships.

Because each type of franchise relationship has its own characteristics, franchise contracts tend to differ. Nonetheless, certain major issues typically are addressed in a franchise contract. We look at some of them next.

Payment for the Franchise The franchisee ordinarily pays an initial fee or lump-sum price for the franchise license (the privilege of being granted a franchise). This fee is separate from the various products that the franchisee purchases from or through the franchisor. The franchise agreement may also require the franchisee to pay a percentage of the franchisor's advertising costs and certain administrative expenses.

In some industries, the franchisor relies heavily on the initial sale of the franchise for realizing a profit. In other industries, the continued dealing between the parties brings profit to both. Generally, the franchisor receives a stated percentage of the annual (or monthly) sales or volume of business done by the franchisee.

Business Premises The franchise agreement may specify whether the premises for the business must be leased or purchased outright. Sometimes, a building must be constructed to meet the terms of the agreement. The agreement will specify whether the franchisor or the franchisee is responsible for supplying equipment and furnishings for the premises.

Location of the Franchise Typically, the franchisor determines the territory to be served. Some franchise contracts give the franchisee exclusive rights, or "territorial rights," to a certain geographic area. Other franchise contracts, while defining the territory allotted to a particular franchise, either specifically state that the franchise is nonexclusive or are silent on the issue of territorial rights.

Many franchise disputes arise over territorial rights, and the implied covenant of good faith and fair dealing often comes into play in this area of franchising. If the contract does not grant exclusive territorial rights to the franchisee and the franchisor allows a competing franchise to be established nearby, the franchisee may suffer significant lost profits. In this situation, a court may hold that the franchisor breached an implied covenant of good faith and fair dealing.

Business Organization The franchisor may require that the business use a particular organizational form and capital structure. The franchise agreement may also set out standards such as sales quotas and record-keeping requirements. Additionally, a franchisor may retain stringent control over the training of personnel involved in the operation and over administrative aspects of the business.

Quality Control by the Franchisor The day-to-day operation of the franchise business normally is left up to the franchisee. Nonetheless, the franchise agreement may specify that the franchisor will provide some degree of supervision and control so that it can protect the franchise's name and reputation.

Means of Control. When the franchise prepares a product, such as food, or provides a service, such as motel

---

6. *FMS, Inc. v. Volvo Construction Equipment North America, Inc.*, 557 F.3d 758 (7th Cir. 2009).

accommodations, the contract often states that the franchisor will establish certain standards for the facility. Typically, the contract will state that the franchisor is permitted to make periodic inspections to ensure that the standards are being maintained.

As a means of controlling quality, franchise agreements also typically limit the franchisee's ability to sell the franchise to another party. ■ **EXAMPLE 36.5** Mark Keller, Inc., an authorized Jaguar franchise, contracts to sell its dealership to Henrique Autos West. A Jaguar franchise generally cannot be sold without Jaguar Cars' permission. Prospective franchisees must meet Jaguar's customer satisfaction standards. If Henrique Autos fails to meet those standards, Jaguar can refuse to allow the sale and can terminate the franchise. ■

Degree of Control. As a general rule, the validity of a provision permitting the franchisor to establish and enforce certain quality standards is unquestioned. The franchisor has a legitimate interest in maintaining the quality of the product or service to protect its name and reputation.

If a franchisor exercises too much control over the operations of its franchisees, however, the franchisor risks potential liability. A franchisor may occasionally be held liable—under the doctrine of *respondeat superior*—for the tortious acts of the franchisees' employees.

■ **EXAMPLE 36.6** The National Labor Relations Board (NLRB) received 180 employee complaints that certain McDonald's restaurants had engaged in unfair labor practices. Employees alleged that the restaurants had fired or penalized workers for participating in protests over wages and working conditions. Investigators found that at least some of the complaints had merit. The NLRB ruled that McDonald's USA, LLC, could be held jointly liable along with several of its franchises for labor and wage violations. The NLRB reasoned that McDonald's exerts sufficient control over its franchises to be found liable for the franchisees' employment law violations. ■

Pricing Arrangements Franchises provide the franchisor with an outlet for the firm's goods and services. Depending on the nature of the business, the franchisor may require the franchisee to purchase certain supplies from the franchisor at an established price.[7] A franchisor cannot, however, set the prices at which the franchisee will resell the goods. Such price setting may be a violation of state or federal antitrust laws, or both. A franchisor can suggest retail prices but cannot mandate them.

36–4 Franchise Termination

The duration of the franchise is a matter to be determined between the parties. Sometimes, a franchise relationship starts with a short trial period, such as a year, so that the franchisee and the franchisor can determine whether they want to stay in business with one another. At other times, the duration of the franchise contract correlates with the term of the lease for the business premises, and both are renewable at the end of that period.

36–4a Grounds for Termination Set by Franchise Contract

Usually, the franchise agreement specifies that termination must be "for cause" and then defines the grounds for termination. Cause might include, for instance, the death or disability of the franchisee, insolvency of the franchisee, breach of the franchise agreement, or failure to meet specified sales quotas.

In the following case, franchise agreements provided that the franchisor could terminate a franchise for good cause.

---

7. Although a franchisor can require franchisees to purchase supplies from it, requiring a franchisee to purchase exclusively from the franchisor may violate federal antitrust laws.

Case 36.2

Century 21 Real Estate, LLC v. All Professional Realty, Inc.

United States Court of Appeals, Ninth Circuit, 600 Fed.Appx. 502 (2015).

Background and Facts Carol and Steve Wright owned All Professional Realty, Inc., and All Professional Hawaii Realty, Inc. The Wrights' companies signed four franchise agreements with Century 21 Real Estate, LLC, to operate offices in Sacramento and Folsom, California, and Honolulu, Hawaii, under the name "Century 21 All Professional." The agreements required All Professional to pay royalty and advertising fees. They also permitted Century 21 to terminate the agreements for good cause, including the franchisee's failure to operate at an approved location.

Case 36.2 Continued

All Professional signed a note for $75,000 payable to Century 21 and agreed to make annual payments on the note. Four years later, All Professional stopped remitting the fees and making payments on the note, and it closed the Folsom office. Century 21 terminated the franchise agreements. The Wrights and All Professional filed a suit against Century 21, alleging breach of contract. Century 21 filed a counterclaim for breach. A federal district court issued a summary judgment in the franchisor's favor. All Professional appealed.

In the Language of the Court
MEMORANDUM.
    * * * *

The district court did not err in granting summary judgment to Century 21 on the parties' cross-claims for breach of contract. *A * * * breach of contract claim requires a contract, breach of that contract, damages and that Century 21 performed its obligations under the contract.* [Emphasis added.]

The Wrights' companies breached the franchise agreements by not paying required fees, not paying principal due on the note and by abandoning the Folsom office.
    * * * *

* * * It is undisputed that Century 21 provided the Wrights' companies with access to the Century 21 system defined in the franchise agreements [as "policies, procedures, and techniques designed to enable offices to compete more effectively in the real estate sales market" and "common use and promotion of certain Marks, copyrights, trade secrets, centralized advertising programs, recruiting programs, referral programs and sales management training programs."] Moreover, the franchise agreements specifically stated that the success of the franchise depended on the Wrights' efforts and that Century 21 made no guarantee or warranty that the Wrights would be successful. The Wrights have not created a triable issue [one necessitating a trial] that Century 21 failed to perform on the contract and that any such failure excused payment on the note.

Century 21 did not breach the agreements by preventing the Wrights from curing their defaults. Although the Wrights now claim they have the funds to pay Century 21, they testified repeatedly before the district court that they did not have the financial ability to cure their defaults.

Century 21 did not terminate the franchise agreements in bad faith. * * * Century 21 had a legal right to terminate all four franchise agreements.

Decision and Remedy *The U.S. Court of Appeals for the Ninth Circuit affirmed the lower court's judgment in Century 21's favor. Century 21 did not breach the franchise agreements. All Professional did. The Wrights' nonpayment of the fees and the note, and the abandonment of one of the franchisee's offices, constituted a material breach of the contract. These actions provided Century 21 with legitimate grounds for termination of the franchise agreement.*

Critical Thinking
- **Economic** *What is the most likely reason that All Professional stopped paying the franchise fees and making note payments, in addition to closing one of its offices? Why is this an insufficient justification for breach of the franchisee's agreements with Century 21?*

Notice Requirements Most franchise contracts provide that notice of termination must be given. If no set time for termination is specified, then a reasonable time, with notice, is implied. A franchisee must be given reasonable time to wind up the business—that is, to do the accounting and return the copyright or trademark or any other property of the franchisor.

Opportunity to Cure a Breach A franchise agreement may allow the franchisee to attempt to cure an ordinary, curable breach within a certain time after notice so as to postpone, or even avoid, termination. Even when a contract contains a notice-and-cure provision, however, a franchisee's breach of the duty of honesty and fidelity may be enough to allow the franchisor to terminate the franchise.

■ **CASE IN POINT 36.7** Milind and Minaxi Upadhyaya entered into a franchise contract with 7-Eleven, Inc., to operate a store in Pennsylvania. The contract included a notice-and-cure provision. Under 7-Eleven's usual contract, franchisees lease the store and equipment, and receive a license to use 7-Eleven's trademarks and other intellectual property. 7-Eleven receives a percentage of the store's gross profit (net sales less the cost of goods sold).

A 7-Eleven manager noticed a high rate of certain questionable transactions at the Upadhyayas' store and began investigating. The investigation continued for nearly two years and revealed that the store had been misreporting its sales so as to conceal sales proceeds from 7-Eleven. Evidence indicated that nearly one-third of the store's sales transactions had not been properly recorded. 7-Eleven sent a "non-curable" notice of material breach and termination of the franchise to the Upadhyayas. The franchisees argued that they had not been given an opportunity to cure the breach. The court found there was sufficient evidence of fraud to warrant immediate termination without an opportunity to cure.[8] ■

36–4b Wrongful Termination

Because a franchisor's termination of a franchise often has adverse consequences for the franchisee, much franchise litigation involves claims of wrongful termination. Generally, the termination provisions of contracts are more favorable to the franchisor than to the franchisee. This means that the franchisee, who normally invests substantial time and financial resources in making the franchise operation successful, may receive little or nothing for the business on termination. The franchisor owns the trademark and hence the business.

It is in this area that statutory and case law become important. The federal and state laws discussed earlier

---

8. *7-Eleven, Inc. v. Upadhyaya*, 926 F.Supp.2d 614 (E.D.Penn. 2013).

attempt, among other things, to protect franchisees from the arbitrary or unfair termination of their franchises by the franchisors.

36–4c The Importance of Good Faith and Fair Dealing

Generally, both statutory law and case law emphasize the importance of good faith and fair dealing in terminating a franchise relationship. In determining whether a franchisor has acted in good faith when terminating a franchise agreement, the courts usually try to balance the rights of both parties.

■ **EXAMPLE 36.8** A car dealership enters into lending agreements, commonly known as floor plan financing, to enable it to buy new vehicles from General Motors Corporation (GM). At first, the dealership obtains floor plan financing from GM, but then it switches to Main Street Bank. Later, the bank declines to provide further financing, and the dealership is unable to obtain the financing from any other lender, including GM. The franchise contract gives GM a right to terminate a dealership for failure to maintain a line of credit. Therefore, GM can terminate the franchise because of the dealership's inability to obtain floor plan financing. ■

If a court perceives that a franchisor has arbitrarily or unfairly terminated a franchise, the franchisee will be provided with a remedy for wrongful termination. A court will be less likely to consider a termination wrongful if the franchisor's decision was made in the normal course of business and reasonable notice was given.

The importance of good faith and fair dealing in a franchise relationship is underscored by the consequences of the franchisor's acts in the following case.

Spotlight on Holiday Inns

Case 36.3 Holiday Inn Franchising, Inc. v. Hotel Associates, Inc.

Court of Appeals of Arkansas, 2011 Ark.App. 147, 382 S.W.3d 6 (2011).

Background and Facts Buddy House was in the construction business in Arkansas and Texas. For decades, he collaborated on projects with Holiday Inn Franchising, Inc. Their relationship was characterized by good faith—many projects were undertaken without written contracts. At Holiday Inn's request, House inspected a hotel in Wichita Falls, Texas, to estimate the cost of getting it into shape. Holiday Inn wanted House to renovate the hotel and operate it as a Holiday Inn. House estimated that recovering the cost of renovation would take him more than ten years, so he asked for a franchise term longer than Holiday Inn's usual ten years. Holiday Inn refused, but said that if the hotel was run "appropriately," the term would be extended at the end of ten years. House bought the hotel, renovated it, and operated it as Hotel Associates, Inc. (HAI), generating substantial profits. He refused offers to sell it for as much as $15 million.

Before the ten years had passed, Greg Aden, a Holiday Inn executive, developed a plan to license a different local hotel as a Holiday Inn instead of renewing House's franchise license. Aden stood to earn a commission from licensing the other hotel. No one informed House of Aden's plan. When the time came, HAI applied for an extension of its franchise, and Holiday Inn asked for major renovations. HAI spent $3 million to comply with this request. Holiday Inn did not renew HAI's license, however, but instead granted a franchise to the other hotel. HAI sold its hotel for $5 million and filed a suit in an Arkansas state court against Holiday Inn, asserting fraud. The court awarded HAI compensatory and punitive damages. Holiday Inn appealed.

In the Language of the Court

Raymond R. *ABRAMSON*, Judge.

* * * *

Generally, a mere failure to volunteer information does not constitute fraud. But *silence can amount to actionable fraud in some circumstances where the parties have a relation of trust or confidence, where there is inequality of condition and knowledge, or where there are other attendant circumstances.* [Emphasis added.]

In this case, substantial evidence supports the existence of a duty on Holiday Inn's part to disclose the Aden [plan] to HAI. Buddy House had a long-term relationship with Holiday Inn characterized by honesty, trust, and the free flow of pertinent information. He testified that [Holiday Inn's] assurances at the onset of licensure [the granting of the license] led him to believe that he would be relicensed after ten years if the hotel was operated appropriately. Yet, despite Holiday Inn's having provided such an assurance to House, it failed to apprise House of an internal business plan * * * that advocated licensure of another facility instead of the renewal of his license. *A duty of disclosure may exist where information is peculiarly within the knowledge of one party and is of such a nature that the other party is justified in assuming its nonexistence.* Given House's history with Holiday Inn and the assurance he received, we are convinced he was justified in assuming that no obstacles had arisen that jeopardized his relicensure. [Emphasis added.]

Holiday Inn asserts that it would have provided Buddy House with the Aden [plan] if he had asked for it. But, Holiday Inn cannot satisfactorily explain why House should have been charged with the responsibility of inquiring about a plan that he did not know existed. Moreover, several Holiday Inn personnel testified that Buddy House in fact should have been provided with the Aden plan. Aden himself stated that * * * House should have been given the plan. * * * In light of these circumstances, we see no ground for reversal on this aspect of HAI's cause of action for fraud.

Decision and Remedy   *The state intermediate appellate court affirmed the lower court's judgment and its award of compensatory damages. The appellate court increased the amount of punitive damages, however, citing Holiday Inn's "degree of reprehensibility."*

Critical Thinking

- **Legal Environment**   *Why should House and HAI have been advised of Holiday Inn's plan to grant a franchise to a different hotel in their territory?*
- **Economic**   *A jury awarded HAI $12 million in punitive damages. The court reduced this award to $1 million, but the appellate court reinstated the original award. What is the purpose of punitive damages? Did Holiday Inn's conduct warrant this award? Explain.*

Reviewing: Small Businesses and Franchises

Carlos Del Rey decided to open a Mexican fast-food restaurant and signed a franchise contract with a national chain called La Grande Enchilada. The contract required the franchisee to strictly follow the franchisor's operating manual and stated that failure to do so would be grounds for terminating the franchise contract. The manual set forth detailed operating procedures and safety standards, and provided that a La Grande Enchilada representative would inspect the restaurant monthly to ensure compliance.

Nine months after Del Rey began operating his restaurant, a spark from the grill ignited an oily towel in the kitchen. No one was injured, but by the time firefighters were able to put out the fire, the kitchen had sustained extensive damage. The cook told the fire department that the towel was "about two feet from the grill" when it caught fire. This was in compliance with the franchisor's manual that required towels be placed at least one foot from the grills. Nevertheless, the next day La Grande Enchilada notified Del Rey that his franchise would terminate in thirty days for failure to follow the prescribed safety procedures. Using the information presented in the chapter, answer the following questions.

1. What type of franchise was Del Rey's La Grande Enchilada restaurant?
2. If Del Rey operates the restaurant as a sole proprietorship, who bears the loss for the damaged kitchen? Explain.
3. Assume that Del Rey files a lawsuit against La Grande Enchilada, claiming that his franchise was wrongfully terminated. What is the main factor that a court would consider in determining whether the franchise was wrongfully terminated?
4. Would a court be likely to rule that La Grande Enchilada had good cause to terminate Del Rey's franchise in this situation? Why or why not?

Debate This . . . *All franchisors should be required by law to provide a comprehensive estimate of the profitability of a prospective franchise based on the experiences of their existing franchisees.*

Terms and Concepts

entrepreneur 690	franchisee 695	sole proprietorship 691
franchise 695	franchisor 695	

Issue Spotters

1. Frank plans to open a sporting goods store and to hire Gogi and Hap. Frank will invest only his own funds. He expects that he will not make a profit for at least eighteen months and will make only a small profit in the three years after that. He hopes to expand eventually. Would a sole proprietorship be an appropriate form for Frank's business? Why or why not? (See *Sole Proprietorships*.)

2. Anchor Bottling Company and U.S. Beverages, Inc. (USB), enter into a franchise agreement that states the franchise may be terminated at any time "for cause." Anchor fails to meet USB's specified sales quota. Does this constitute "cause" for termination? Why or why not? (See *Franchise Termination*.)

- Check your answers to the Issue Spotters against the answers provided in Appendix D at the end of this text.

Business Scenarios

36–1. Franchising. Maria, Pablo, and Vicky are recent college graduates who would like to go into business for themselves. They are considering purchasing a franchise. If they enter into a franchising arrangement, they would have the support of a large company that could answer any questions they might have. Also, a firm that has been in business for many years would be experienced in dealing with some of the problems that novice businesspersons might encounter. These and other attributes of franchises can lessen some of the risks of the marketplace. What other aspects of franchising—positive and negative—should Maria, Pablo, and Vicky consider before committing themselves to a particular franchise? (See *Franchises*.)

36–2. Control of a Franchise. National Foods, Inc., sells franchises to its fast-food restaurants, known as Chicky-D's. Under the franchise agreement, franchisees agree to hire and train employees strictly according to Chicky-D's standards. Chicky-D's regional supervisors are required to approve all job candidates before they are hired and all general policies

affecting those employees. Chicky-D's reserves the right to terminate a franchise for violating the franchisor's rules. In practice, however, Chicky-D's regional supervisors routinely approve new employees and individual franchisees' policies. After several incidents of racist comments and conduct by Tim, a recently hired assistant manager at a Chicky-D's, Sharon, a counterperson at the restaurant, resigns. Sharon files a suit in a federal district court against National. National files a motion for summary judgment, arguing that it is not liable for harassment by franchise employees. Will the court grant National's motion? Why or why not? (See *Franchises*.)

Business Case Problems

36–3. Spotlight on McDonald's—Franchise Termination.

J.C., Inc., had a franchise agreement with McDonald's Corp to operate McDonald's restaurants in Lancaster, Ohio. The agreement required J.C. to make monthly payments of certain percentages of gross sales to McDonald's. If any payment was more than thirty days late, McDonald's had the right to terminate the franchise. The agreement also stated that even if McDonald's accepted a late payment, that would not "constitute a waiver of any subsequent breach." McDonald's sometimes accepted J.C.'s late payments, but when J.C. defaulted on the payment for July 2010, McDonald's gave notice of thirty days to comply or surrender possession of the restaurants. J.C. missed the deadline. McDonald's demanded that J.C. vacate the restaurants, but J.C. refused. McDonald's alleged that J.C. had violated the franchise agreement. J.C. claimed that McDonald's had breached the implied covenant of good faith and fair dealing. Which party should prevail and why? [*McDonald's Corp. v. C.B. Management Co.,* 13 F.Supp.2d 705 (N.D.Ill. 1998)] (See *Franchise Termination*.)

36–4. Franchise Disclosure.
Peaberry Coffee, Inc., owned and operated about twenty company stores in the Denver area. The company began a franchise program and prepared a disclosure document as required by the Federal Trade Commission (FTC). Peaberry sold ten franchises, and each franchisee received a disclosure document. Later, when the franchises did not do well, the franchisees sued Peaberry, claiming that its FTC disclosure document had been fraudulent. Specifically, the franchisees claimed that Peaberry had not disclosed that most of the company stores were unprofitable and that its parent company had suffered significant financial losses over the years. In addition, the franchisees stated that Peaberry had included in the franchisees' information packets an article from the *Denver Business Journal* in which an executive had said that Peaberry was profitable. That statement had proved to be false. The FTC disclosure document had also contained an exculpatory clause that said the buyers should not rely on any material that was not in the franchise contract itself. Can a franchisor disclaim the relevance of the information it provides to franchisees? Why or why not? [*Colorado Coffee Bean, LLC v. Peaberry Coffee, Inc.,* 251 P.3d 9 (Colo.App. 2010)] (See *Franchises*.)

36–5. The Franchise Contract.
Kubota Tractor Corp. makes farm, industrial, and outdoor equipment. Its franchise contracts allow Kubota to enter into dealership agreements with "others at any location." Kejzar Motors, Inc., is a Kubota dealer in Nacogdoches and Jasper, Texas. These two Kejzar stores operate as one dealership with two locations. Kubota granted a dealership to Michael Hammer in Lufkin, Texas, which lies between Kejzar's two store locations. Kejzar filed a suit in a Texas state court against Kubota. Kejzar asked for an injunction to prevent Kubota from locating a dealership in the same market area. Kejzar argued that the new location would cause it to suffer a significant loss of profits. Which party in a franchise relationship typically determines the territory served by a franchisee? Which legal principles come into play in this area? How do these concepts most likely apply in this case? Discuss. [*Kejzar Motors, Inc. v. Kubota Tractor Corp.,* 334 S.W.3d 351 (Tex.App.—Tyler 2011)] (See *Franchises*.)

36–6. Business Case Problem with Sample Answer—Franchise Termination.

George Oshana and GTO Investments, Inc., operated a Mobil gas station franchise in Itasca, Illinois. In 2010, Oshana and GTO became involved in a rental dispute with Buchanan Energy, to which Mobil had assigned the lease for the gas station facility. In November 2011, Buchanan terminated the franchise because Oshana and GTO had failed to pay the rent. Oshana and GTO, however, alleged that they had been "ready, willing, and able to pay the rent" but that Buchanan had failed to accept their electronic fund transfer. Have Oshana and GTO stated a claim for wrongful termination of their franchise? Why or why not? [*Oshana v. Buchanan Energy,* 2012 WL 426921 (N.D.Ill. 2012)] (See *Franchise Termination*.)

• **For a sample answer to Problem 36–6, go to Appendix E at the end of this text.**

36–7. Quality Control.
JTH Tax, Inc., doing business as Liberty Tax Service, provides tax preparation and related loan services through company-owned and franchised stores. Liberty's agreement with its franchisees reserved the right to control their ads. In operations manuals, Liberty provided step-by-step instructions, directions, and limitations regarding the

franchisees' ads and retained the right to unilaterally modify the steps at any time. The California attorney general filed a suit in a California state court against Liberty, alleging that its franchisees had used misleading or deceptive ads regarding refund anticipation loans and e-refund checks. Can Liberty be held liable? Discuss. [*People v. JTH Tax, Inc.,* 212 Cal.App.4th 1219, 151 Cal.Rptr.3d 728 (1 Dist. 2013)] (See *Franchises.*)

36–8. Quality Control. The franchise agreement of Domino's Pizza, L.L.C., sets out operational standards, including safety requirements, for a franchisee to follow but provides that the franchisee is an independent contractor. Each franchisee is free to use its own means and methods. For example, Domino's does not know whether a franchisee's delivery drivers are complying with vehicle safety requirements. MAC Pizza Management, Inc., operates a Domino's franchise. A vehicle driven by Joshua Balka, a MAC delivery driver, hydroplaned due to a bald tire and wet pavement. It struck the vehicle of Devavaram and Ruth Christopher, killing Ruth and injuring Devavaram. Is Domino's liable for negligence? Explain. [*Domino's Pizza, L.L.C. v. Reddy,* 2015 WL 1247349 (Tex.App.—Beaumont 2015)] (See *Franchises.*)

36–9. Franchise Termination. Executive Home Care Franchising, LLC, sells in-home health-care franchises. Clint, Massare, and Greer Marshall entered into a franchise agreement with Executive Home Care. The agreement provided that the franchisees' failure to comply with the agreement's terms would likely cause irreparable harm to the franchisor, entitling it to an injunction. About two years later, the Marshalls gave up their franchise. They returned thirteen boxes of documents, stationery, operating manuals, marketing materials, and other items—everything in their possession that featured Executive Home Care trademarks. They quit operating out of the franchised location. They transferred the phone number back to the franchisor and informed their clients that they were no longer associated with Executive Home Care. They continued to engage in the home health-care business, however, under the

name "Well-Being Home Care Corp." Is Executive Home Care entitled to an injunction against the Marshalls and their new company? Discuss. [*Executive Home Care Franchising, LLC v. Marshall Health Corp.,* __ F.3d __, 2016 WL 703801 (3d Cir. 2016)] (See *Franchise Termination.*)

36–10. A Question of Ethics—Sole Proprietorship. *In* *August 2004, Ralph Vilardo contacted Travel Center, Inc., in Cincinnati, Ohio, to buy a trip to Florida in December for his family to celebrate his fiftieth wedding anniversary. Vilardo paid $6,900 to David Sheets, the sole proprietor of Travel Center. Vilardo also paid $195 to Sheets for a separate trip to Florida in February 2005. Sheets assured Vilardo that everything was set, but in fact no arrangements were made. Later, two unauthorized charges for travel services totaling $1,182.35 appeared on Vilardo's credit-card statement. Vilardo filed a suit in an Ohio state court against Sheets and his business, alleging, among other things, fraud and violations of the state consumer protection law. Vilardo served Sheets and Travel Center with copies of the complaint, the summons, a request for admissions, and other documents filed with the court, including a motion for summary judgment. Each of these filings asked for a response within a certain time period. Sheets responded once on his own behalf with a denial of all of Vilardo's claims. Travel Center did not respond. [*Vilardo v. Sheets, 2006 -Ohio- 3473 (12 Dist. 2006)] (See Sole Proprietorships.)*

(a) Almost four months after Vilardo filed his complaint, Sheets decided that he was unable to adequately represent himself and retained an attorney, who asked the court for more time. Should the court grant this request? Why or why not? Ultimately, what should the court rule?

(b) Sheets admitted that Travel Center, Inc., was a sole proprietorship. He also argued that liability might be imposed on his business but not on himself. How would you rule with respect to this argument? Why? Would there be anything unethical about allowing Sheets to avoid liability on this basis? Explain.

Legal Reasoning Group Activity

36–11. Franchise Termination. Walid Elkhatib, an Arab American, bought a Dunkin' Donuts franchise in Illinois. Ten years later, Dunkin' Donuts began offering breakfast sandwiches with bacon, ham, or sausage through its franchises. Elkhatib refused to sell these items at his store on the ground that his religion forbade the handling of pork. Elkhatib then opened a second franchise, at which he also refused to sell pork products.

The next year, at both locations, Elkhatib began selling meatless sandwiches. He also opened a third franchise. When he proposed to relocate this franchise, Dunkin' Donuts refused to approve the new location. The company also informed him that it would not renew any of his franchise

agreements because he did not carry the full sandwich line. Elkhatib filed a lawsuit against Dunkin' Donuts. (See *Franchise Termination.*)

(a) The first group will argue on behalf of Elkhatib that Dunkin' Donuts wrongfully terminated his franchises.

(b) The second group will take the side of Dunkin' Donuts and justify its decision to terminate the franchises.

(c) The third group will assess whether Dunkin' Donuts acted in good faith in its relationship with Elkhatib. Consider whether Dunkin' Donuts should be required to accommodate Elkhatib's religious beliefs and allow him not to serve pork in these three locations.

All Forms of Partnerships

Historically, two or more persons entering into business together have most commonly organized their business as a partnership or a corporation. A *partnership* arises from an agreement, express or implied, between two or more persons to carry on a business for a profit. Partners are co-owners of the business and have joint control over its operation and the right to share in its profits.

In this chapter, we examine several forms of partnership. These include ordinary partnerships, or *general partnerships,* and special forms of partnerships known as *limited partnerships* and *limited liability partnerships*.

Although general partnerships are less common today than in the past, the limited liability forms of partnership are quite prevalent. Accountants, attorneys, and architects frequently organize as limited liability partnerships. DLA Piper, the second-largest U.S. law firm, for instance, is structured as two limited liability partnerships—DLA Piper U.S., LLP, and DLA Piper International, LLP.

37-1 Basic Partnership Concepts

Partnerships are governed both by common law concepts—in particular, those relating to agency—and by statutory law. As in so many other areas of business law, the National Conference of Commissioners on Uniform State Laws has drafted uniform laws for partnerships, and these have been widely adopted by the states.

37-1a Agency Concepts and Partnership Law

When two or more persons agree to do business as partners, they enter into a special relationship with one another. To an extent, their relationship is similar to an agency relationship because each partner is deemed to be the agent of the other partners and of the partnership. Thus, agency concepts apply—specifically, the imputation of knowledge of, and responsibility for, acts carried out within the scope of the partnership relationship. In their relationships with one another, partners, like agents, are bound by fiduciary ties.

In one important way, however, partnership law differs from agency law. The partners in a partnership agree to commit funds or other assets, labor, and skills to the business with the understanding that profits and losses will be shared. Thus, each partner has an *ownership interest* in the firm. In a nonpartnership agency relationship, the agent usually does not have an ownership interest in the business and is not obligated to bear a portion of ordinary business losses.

37-1b The Uniform Partnership Act

The Uniform Partnership Act (UPA) governs the operation of partnerships *in the absence of express agreement* and has done much to reduce controversies in the law relating to partnerships. A majority of the states have enacted the most recent version of the UPA (introduced in 1997 and last amended in 2013).

37-1c Definition of a Partnership

The UPA defines a **partnership** as "an association of two or more persons to carry on as co-owners a business for profit" [UPA 101(6)]. Note that the UPA's definition of *person* includes corporations, so a corporation can be a partner in a partnership [UPA 101(10)]. The *intent* to associate is a key element of a partnership, and one cannot join a partnership unless all other partners consent [UPA 401(i)].

37-1d Essential Elements of a Partnership

Conflicts sometimes arise over whether a business enterprise is a legal partnership, especially when there is no formal, written partnership agreement. To determine whether a partnership exists, courts usually look for the following three essential elements, which are implicit in the UPA's definition:

1. A sharing of profits or losses.
2. A joint ownership of the business.
3. An equal right to be involved in the management of the business.

If the evidence in a particular case is insufficient to establish all three factors, the UPA provides a set of guidelines to be used.

The Sharing of Profits and Losses The sharing of both profits and losses from a business creates a presumption that a partnership exists. ■ **EXAMPLE 37.1** Syd and Drake start a business that sells fruit smoothies near a college campus. They open a joint bank account, from which they pay for supplies and expenses, and they share the proceeds (and losses) that the smoothie stand generates. If a conflict arises as to their business relationship, a court will assume that a partnership exists unless the parties prove otherwise. ■

A court will not presume that a partnership exists, however, if shared profits were received as payment of any of the following [UPA 202(c)(3)]:

1. A debt by installments or interest on a loan.
2. Wages of an employee or for the services of an independent contractor.
3. Rent to a landlord.
4. An annuity to a surviving spouse or representative of a deceased partner.
5. A sale of the **goodwill** (the valuable reputation of a business viewed as an intangible asset) of a business or property.

■ **EXAMPLE 37.2** A debtor, Mason Snopel, owes a creditor, Alice Burns, $5,000 on an unsecured debt. They agree that Mason will pay 10 percent of his monthly business profits to Alice until the loan with interest has been repaid. Although Mason and Alice are sharing profits from the business, they are not presumed to be partners. ■

Joint Property Ownership Joint ownership of property does not in and of itself create a partnership [UPA 202(c)(1) and (2)]. The parties' intentions are key. ■ **EXAMPLE 37.3** Chiang and Burke jointly own farmland and lease it to a farmer for a share of the profits from the farming operation in lieu of fixed rental payments. This arrangement normally would not make Chiang, Burke, and the farmer partners. ■

37-1e Entity versus Aggregate

At common law, a partnership was treated only as an aggregate of individuals and never as a separate legal entity. Thus, at common law a lawsuit could never be brought by or against the firm in its own name. Each individual partner had to sue or be sued.

Today, in contrast, a majority of the states follow the UPA and treat a partnership as an entity for most purposes. For instance, a partnership usually can sue or be sued, collect judgments, and have all accounting performed in the name of the partnership entity [UPA 201, 307(a)].

As an entity, a partnership may hold the title to real or personal property in its name rather than in the names of the individual partners. Additionally, federal procedural laws permit the partnership to be treated as an entity in suits in federal courts and bankruptcy proceedings.

37-1f Tax Treatment of Partnerships

Modern law does treat a partnership as an aggregate of the individual partners rather than a separate legal entity in one situation—for federal income tax purposes. The partnership is a pass-through entity and not a taxpaying entity. A **pass-through entity** is a business entity that has no tax liability. The entity's income is passed through to the owners, who pay income taxes on it.

Thus, the income or losses the partnership incurs are "passed through" the entity framework and attributed to the partners on their individual tax returns. The partnership itself pays no taxes and is responsible only for filing an **information return** with the Internal Revenue Service.

A partner's profit from the partnership (whether distributed or not) is taxed as individual income to the individual partner. Similarly, partners can deduct a share of the partnership's losses on their individual tax returns (in proportion to their partnership interests).

37-2 Formation and Operation

A partnership is a voluntary association of individuals. As such, it is formed by the agreement of the partners.

37–2a The Partnership Agreement

As a general rule, agreements to form a partnership can be *oral, written,* or *implied by conduct.* Some partnership agreements, however, such as one authorizing partners to transfer interests in real property, must be in writing to be legally enforceable.

A partnership agreement, also known as **articles of partnership,** can include almost any terms that the parties wish, unless they are illegal or contrary to public policy or statute [UPA 103]. The provisions commonly included in a partnership agreement are listed in Exhibit 37–1.

The rights and duties of partners are governed largely by the specific terms of their partnership agreement. In the absence of provisions to the contrary in the partnership agreement, the law imposes certain rights and duties, as discussed in the following subsections. The character and nature of the partnership business generally influence the application of these rights and duties.

37–2b Duration of the Partnership

The partnership agreement can specify the duration of the partnership by stating that it will continue until a designated date or until the completion of a particular project. This is called a *partnership for a term.* Generally, withdrawing from a partnership for a term prematurely (before the expiration date) constitutes a breach of the agreement, and the responsible partner can be held liable for any resulting losses [UPA 602(b)(2)]. If no fixed duration is specified, the partnership is a *partnership at will.* A partnership at will can be dissolved at any time without liability.

37–2c Partnership by Estoppel

When a third person has reasonably and detrimentally relied on the representation that a nonpartner was part of a partnership, a court may conclude that a **partnership by estoppel** exists.

EXHIBIT 37–1 Provisions Commonly Included in a Partnership Agreement

Basic Structure
- Name of the partnership and the names of the partners.
- Location of the business and the state law under which the partnership is organized.
- Purpose and duration of the partnership.

Capital Contributions
- Amount of capital that each partner is contributing.
- The agreed-on value of any real or personal property that is contributed instead of cash.
- How losses and gains on contributed capital will be allocated, and whether contributions will earn interest.

Sharing of Profits and Losses
- Percentage of the profits and losses of the business that each partner will receive.
- When distributions of profit will be made and how net profit will be calculated.

Management and Control
- How management responsibilities will be divided among the partners.
- Name(s) of the managing partner or partners, and whether other partners have voting rights.

Dissociation and Dissolution
- Events that will cause the dissociation of a partner or dissolve the firm, such as the retirement, death, or incapacity of any partner.
- How partnership property will be valued and apportioned on dissociation and dissolution.
- Whether an arbitrator will determine the value of partnership property on dissociation and dissolution and whether that determination will be binding.

Liability Imposed A partnership by estoppel may arise when a person who is not a partner holds himself or herself out as a partner and makes representations that third parties rely on. In this situation, a court may impose liability—but not partnership rights—on the alleged partner.

Nonpartner as Agent A partnership by estoppel may also be imposed when a partner represents, expressly or impliedly, that a nonpartner is a member of the firm. In this situation, the nonpartner may be regarded as an agent whose acts are binding on the partnership [UPA 308].

■ **CASE IN POINT 37.4** Jackson Paper Manufacturing Company made paper used by Stonewall Packaging, LLC. Jackson and Stonewall had officers and directors in common, and they shared employees, property, and equipment. In reliance on Jackson's business reputation, Best Cartage, Inc., agreed to provide transportation services for Stonewall and bought thirty-seven tractor-trailers to use in fulfilling the contract. Best provided the services until Stonewall terminated the agreement.

Best filed a suit for breach of contract against Stonewall and Jackson, seeking $500,678 in unpaid invoices and consequential damages of $1,315,336 for the tractor-trailers it had purchased. Best argued that Stonewall and Jackson had a partnership by estoppel. The court agreed, finding that "defendants combined labor, skills, and property to advance their alleged business partnership." Jackson had negotiated the agreement on Stonewall's behalf. Jackson also had bought real estate, equipment, and general supplies for Stonewall with no expectation that Stonewall would repay these expenditures. This was sufficient to prove a partnership by estoppel.[1] ■

37–2d Rights of Partners

The rights of partners in a partnership relate to the following areas: management, interest in the partnership, compensation, inspection of books, accounting, and property.

Management Rights In a general partnership, all partners have equal rights in managing the partnership [UPA 401(f)]. Unless the partners agree otherwise, each partner has one vote in management matters *regardless of the proportional size of his or her interest in the firm*. In a large partnership, partners often agree to delegate daily management responsibilities to a management committee made up of one or more of the partners.

The majority rule controls decisions on ordinary matters connected with partnership business, unless otherwise specified in the agreement. Decisions that significantly change the nature of the partnership or that are outside the ordinary course of the partnership business, however, require the *unanimous* consent of the partners [UPA 301(2), 401(i), 401(j)]. For instance, unanimous consent is likely required for a partnership to admit new partners, to amend the partnership agreement, or to enter a new line of business.

Interest in the Partnership Each partner is entitled to the proportion of business profits and losses that is specified in the partnership agreement. If the agreement does not apportion profits (indicate how the profits will be shared), the UPA provides that profits will be shared equally. If the agreement does not apportion losses, losses will be shared in the same ratio as profits [UPA 401(b)].

■ **EXAMPLE 37.5** The partnership agreement between Rick and Brett provides for capital contributions of $60,000 from Rick and $40,000 from Brett. If the agreement is silent as to how Rick and Brett will share profits or losses, they will share both profits and losses equally.

In contrast, if the agreement provides for profits to be shared in the same ratio as capital contributions, 60 percent of the profits will go to Rick, and 40 percent will go to Brett. Unless the agreement provides otherwise, losses will be shared in the same ratio as profits. ■

Compensation Devoting time, skill, and energy to partnership business is a partner's duty and generally is not a compensable service. Rather, as mentioned, a partner's income from the partnership takes the form of a distribution of profits according to the partner's share in the business.

Partners can, of course, agree otherwise. For instance, the managing partner of a law firm often receives a salary—in addition to her or his share of profits—for performing special administrative or managerial duties.

Inspection of the Books Partnership books and records must be kept accessible to all partners. Each partner has the right to receive full and complete information concerning the conduct of all aspects of partnership business [UPA 403]. Partners have a duty to provide the information to the firm, which has a duty to preserve it and to keep accurate records.

The partnership books must be kept at the firm's principal business office (unless the partners agree otherwise). Every partner is entitled to inspect all books and records on demand and can make copies of the materials. The

---

1. *Best Cartage, Inc. v. Stonewall Packaging, LLC*, 727 S.E.2d 291 (N.C.App. 2012).

personal representative of a deceased partner's estate has the same right of access to partnership books and records that the decedent would have had [UPA 403].

Accounting of Partnership Assets or Profits

An accounting of partnership assets or profits is required to determine the value of each partner's share in the partnership. An accounting can be performed voluntarily, or it can be compelled by court order. Under UPA 405(b), a partner has the right to bring an action for an accounting during the term of the partnership, as well as on the partnership's dissolution.

Property Rights Property acquired *by* a partnership is the property of the partnership and not of the partners individually [UPA 203]. Partnership property includes all property that was originally contributed to the partnership and anything later purchased by the partnership or in the partnership's name (except in rare circumstances) [UPA 204].

A partner may use or possess partnership property only on behalf of the partnership [UPA 401(g)]. A partner is *not* a co-owner of partnership property and has no right to sell, mortgage, or transfer partnership property to another [UPA 501].[2]

Because partnership property is owned by the partnership and not by the individual partners, the property cannot be used to satisfy the personal debts of individual partners. A partner's creditor, however, can petition a court for a **charging order** to attach the partner's *interest* in the partnership to satisfy the partner's obligation [UPA 502]. A partner's interest in the partnership includes her or his proportionate share of any profits that are distributed. A partner can also assign her or his right to receive a share of the partnership profits to another to satisfy a debt.

---

2. Under the previous version of the UPA, partners were *tenants in partnership*. This meant that every partner was a co-owner with all other partners of the partnership property. The current UPA does not recognize this concept.

37–2e Duties and Liabilities of Partners

The duties and liabilities of partners are derived from agency law. Each partner is an agent of every other partner and acts as both a principal and an agent in any business transaction within the scope of the partnership agreement.

Each partner is also a general agent of the partnership in carrying out the usual business of the firm "or business of the kind carried on by the partnership" [UPA 301(1)]. Thus, every act of a partner concerning partnership business and "business of the kind" and every contract signed in the partnership's name bind the firm.

Fiduciary Duties The fiduciary duties that a partner owes to the partnership and to the other partners are the duty of care and the duty of loyalty [UPA 404(a)]. Under the UPA, a partner's *duty of care* is limited to refraining from "grossly negligent or reckless conduct, intentional misconduct, or a knowing violation of law" [UPA 404(c)].[3] A partner is not liable to the partnership for simple negligence or honest errors in judgment in conducting partnership business.

The *duty of loyalty* requires a partner to account to the partnership for "any property, profit, or benefit" derived by the partner in the conduct of the partnership's business or from the use of its property. A partner must also refrain from competing with the partnership in business or dealing with the firm as an adverse party [UPA 404(b)].

The duty of loyalty can be breached by self-dealing, misusing partnership property, disclosing trade secrets, or usurping a partnership business opportunity. The following case is a classic example.

---

3. The previous version of the UPA touched only briefly on the duty of loyalty and left the details of the partners' fiduciary duties to be developed under the law of agency.

Classic Case 37.1

Meinhard v. Salmon

Court of Appeals of New York, 249 N.Y. 458, 164 N.E. 545 (1928).

Background and Facts Walter Salmon negotiated a twenty-year lease for the Hotel Bristol in New York City. To pay for the conversion of the building into shops and offices, Salmon entered into an agreement with Morton Meinhard to assume half of the cost. They agreed to share the profits and losses from the joint venture. (A *joint venture* is similar to a partnership but typically is created for a single project.) Salmon was to have the sole power to manage the building, however.

Less than four months before the end of the lease term, the building's owner, Elbridge Gerry, approached Salmon about a project to raze the converted structure, clear five adjacent lots, and

Case 37.1 Continues

Case 37.1 Continued

construct a single building across the whole property. Salmon agreed and signed a new lease in the name of his own business, Midpoint Realty Company, without telling Meinhard. When Meinhard learned of the deal, he filed a suit in a New York state court against Salmon. The court ruled in Meinhard's favor, and Salmon appealed.

In the Language of the Court

CARDOZO, C.J. [Chief Justice]

* * * *

Joint adventurers, like copartners, owe to one another, while the enterprise continues, the duty of the finest loyalty. Many forms of conduct permissible in a work-a-day world for those acting at arm's length are forbidden to those bound by fiduciary ties. * * * Not honesty alone, but the punctilio [strictness in observance of details] of an honor the most sensitive, is then the standard of behavior. As to this there has developed a tradition that is unbending and inveterate [entrenched]. Uncompromising rigidity has been the attitude of courts * * * when petitioned to undermine the rule of undivided loyalty.

* * * The trouble about [Salmon's] conduct is that he excluded his coadventurer from any chance to compete, from any chance to enjoy the opportunity for benefit.

* * * The very fact that Salmon was in control with exclusive powers of direction charged him the more obviously with the duty of disclosure, [because] only through disclosure could opportunity be equalized.

* * * Authority is, of course, abundant that one partner may not appropriate to his own use a renewal of a lease, though its term is to begin at the expiration of the partnership. The lease at hand with its many changes is not strictly a renewal. Even so, the standard of loyalty for those in trust relations is without the fixed divisions of a graduated scale. * * * *A man obtaining [an]* * * * *opportunity* * * * *by the position he occupies as a partner is bound by his obligation to his copartners in such dealings not to separate his interest from theirs, but, if he acquires any benefit, to communicate it to them. Certain it is also that there may be no abuse of special opportunities growing out of a special trust as manager or agent.* [Emphasis added.]

* * * Very likely [Salmon] assumed in all good faith that with the approaching end of the venture he might ignore his coadventurer and take the extension for himself. He had given to the enterprise time and labor as well as money. He had made it a success. Meinhard, who had given money, but neither time nor labor, had already been richly paid. * * * [But] Salmon had put himself in a position in which thought of self was to be renounced, however hard the abnegation [self-denial]. He was much more than a coadventurer. He was a managing coadventurer. For him and for those like him the rule of undivided loyalty is relentless and supreme.

Decision and Remedy *The Court of Appeals of New York held that Salmon had breached his fiduciary duty by failing to inform Meinhard of the business opportunity and secretly taking advantage of it himself. The court granted Meinhard an interest "measured by the value of half of the entire lease."*

Impact of This Case on Today's Law *This classic case involved a joint venture, not a partnership. At the time, a member of a joint venture had only the duty to refrain from actively subverting the rights of the other members. The decision in this case imposed the highest standard of loyalty on joint-venture members. The duty is now the same in both joint ventures and partnerships. Courts today frequently quote the eloquent language used in this opinion when describing the standard of loyalty that applies to partnerships.*

Critical Thinking

• **What If the Facts Were Different?** *Suppose that Salmon had disclosed Gerry's proposal to Meinhard, who had said that he was not interested. Would the result in this case have been different? Explain.*

Waiver of Fiduciary Duties A partner's fiduciary duties may not be waived or eliminated in the partnership agreement. In fulfilling them, each partner must act consistently with the obligation of good faith and fair dealing [UPA 103(b), 404(d)]. The agreement can specify acts that the partners agree will violate a fiduciary duty.

Note that a partner may pursue his or her own interests without automatically violating these duties [UPA 404(e)]. The key is whether the partner has disclosed the interest to the other partners. ■ **EXAMPLE 37.6** Jayne Trell, a partner at Jacoby & Meyers, owns a shopping mall. Trell may vote against a partnership proposal to open a competing mall, provided that she has fully disclosed her interest in the existing shopping mall to the other partners at the firm. ∎ A partner cannot make secret profits or put self-interest before his or her duty to the interest of the partnership, however.

Authority of Partners The UPA affirms general principles of agency law that pertain to a partner's authority to bind a partnership in contract. If a partner acts within the scope of her or his authority, the partnership is legally bound to honor the partner's commitments to third parties.

A partner may also subject the partnership to tort liability under agency principles. When a partner is carrying on partnership business with third parties in the usual way, apparent authority exists, and both the partner and the firm share liability. The partnership will not be liable, however, if the third parties *know* that the partner has no such authority.

Limitations on Authority. A partnership may limit a partner's capacity to act as the firm's agent or transfer property on its behalf by filing a "statement of partnership authority" in a designated state office [UPA 105, 303]. Such limits on a partner's authority normally are effective only with respect to third parties who are notified of the limitation. (An exception is made in real estate transactions when the statement of authority has been recorded with the appropriate state office.)

The Scope of Implied Powers. The agency concepts relating to apparent authority, actual authority, and ratification apply to partnerships. The extent of implied authority generally is broader for partners than for ordinary agents, however.

In an ordinary partnership, the partners can exercise all implied powers reasonably necessary and customary to carry on that particular business. Some customarily implied powers include the authority to make warranties on goods in the sales business and the power to enter into contracts consistent with the firm's regular course of business.

∎ **EXAMPLE 37.7** Jamie Schwab is a partner in a firm that operates a retail tire store. He regularly promises that "each tire will be warranted for normal wear for 40,000 miles." Because Schwab has authority to make warranties, the partnership is bound to honor the warranty. Schwab would not, however, have the authority to sell the partnership's office equipment or other property without the consent of all of the other partners. ∎

Liability of Partners One significant disadvantage associated with a traditional partnership is that the partners are *personally* liable for the debts of the partnership. In most states, the liability is essentially unlimited, because the acts of one partner in the ordinary course of business subject the other partners to personal liability [UPA 305]. Note that normally the partnership's assets must be exhausted before creditors can reach the partners' individual assets, however.

Joint Liability. Each partner in a partnership generally is jointly liable for the partnership's obligations. **Joint liability** means that a third party must sue all of the partners as a group, but each partner can be held liable for the full amount.[4] If, for instance, a third party sues one partner on a partnership contract, that partner has the right to demand that the other partners be sued with her or him. In fact, if the third party does not name all of the partners in the lawsuit, the assets of the partnership cannot be used to satisfy the judgment.

Joint and Several Liability. In the majority of the states, under UPA 306(a), partners are both jointly and severally (separately, or individually) liable for all partnership obligations. **Joint and several liability** means that a third party has the option of suing all of the partners together (jointly) or one or more of the partners separately (severally). All partners in a partnership can be held liable even if a particular partner did not participate in, know about, or ratify the conduct that gave rise to the lawsuit.

A judgment against one partner severally (separately) does not extinguish the others' liability. (Similarly, a release of one partner does not discharge the partners' several liability.) Those not sued in the first action normally may be sued subsequently, unless the court in the first action held that the partnership was in no way liable. If a plaintiff is successful in a suit against a partner or partners, he or she may collect on the judgment only against the assets of those partners named as defendants.

Indemnification. With joint and several liability, a partner who commits a tort can be required to indemnify (reimburse) the partnership for any damages it pays. Indemnification will typically be granted *unless* the tort was committed in the ordinary course of the partnership's business.

∎ **EXAMPLE 37.8** Nicole Martin, a partner at Patti's Café, is working in the café's kitchen one day when her young son suffers serious injuries to his hands from a dough press. Her son, through his father, files a negligence

---

4. Under the prior version of the UPA, partners were subject to joint liability on partnership debts and contracts, but not on partnership debts arising from torts.

lawsuit against the partnership. Even if the suit is successful and the partnership pays damages to Martin's son, the firm is not entitled to indemnification. Martin would not be required to indemnify the partnership because her negligence occurred in the ordinary course of the partnership's business (making food for customers). ■

Liability of Incoming Partners. A partner newly admitted to an existing partnership is not personally liable for any partnership obligations incurred *before* the person became a partner [UPA 306(b)]. In other words, the new partner's liability to existing creditors of the partnership is limited to her or his capital contribution to the firm.

■ **EXAMPLE 37.9** Smartclub, an existing partnership with four members, admits a new partner, Alex Jaff. He contributes $100,000 to the partnership. Smartclub has debts amounting to $600,000 at the time Jaff joins the firm. Although Jaff's capital contribution of $100,000 can be used to satisfy Smartclub's obligations, Jaff is not personally liable for partnership debts incurred before he became a partner. If, however, the partnership incurs additional debts after Jaff becomes a partner, he will be personally liable for those amounts, along with all the other partners. ■

37-3 Dissociation and Termination

Dissociation occurs when a partner ceases to be associated in the carrying on of the partnership business. Dissociation normally entitles the partner to have his or her interest purchased by the partnership. It also terminates the partner's actual authority to act for the partnership and to participate in running its business.

Once dissociation occurs, the partnership may continue to do business without the dissociated partner.[5] If the partners no longer wish to (or are unable to) continue the business, the partnership may be terminated (dissolved).

37-3a Events That Cause Dissociation

Under UPA 601, a partner can be dissociated from a partnership in any of the following ways:

1. By the partner's voluntarily giving notice of an "express will to withdraw." (When a partner gives

notice of intent to withdraw, the remaining partners must decide whether to continue the partnership business. If they decide not to continue, the voluntary dissociation of a partner will dissolve the firm [UPA 801(1)].)
2. By the occurrence of an event specified in the partnership agreement.
3. By a unanimous vote of the other partners under certain circumstances, such as when a partner transfers substantially all of her or his interest in the partnership.
4. By order of a court or arbitrator if the partner has engaged in wrongful conduct that affects the partnership business. The court can order dissociation if a partner breached the partnership agreement or violated a duty owed to the partnership or to the other partners. Dissociation may also be ordered if the partner engaged in conduct that makes it "not reasonably practicable to carry on the business in partnership with the partner" [UPA 601(5)].
5. By the partner's declaring bankruptcy, assigning his or her interest in the partnership for the benefit of creditors, or becoming physically or mentally incapacitated, or by the partner's death.

37-3b Wrongful Dissociation

A partner has the *power* to dissociate from a partnership at any time, but she or he may not have the *right* to do so. If the partner lacks the right to dissociate, then the dissociation is considered wrongful under the law [UPA 602]. When a partner's dissociation breaches a partnership agreement, for instance, it is wrongful.

■ **EXAMPLE 37.10** Jenkins & Whalen's partnership agreement states that it is a breach of the agreement for any partner to assign partnership property to a creditor without the consent of the other partners. If Kenzie, a partner, makes such an assignment, she has not only breached the agreement but has also wrongfully dissociated from the partnership. ■

A partner who wrongfully dissociates is liable to the partnership and to the other partners for damages caused by the dissociation. This liability is in addition to any other obligation of the partner to the partnership or to the other partners.

37-3c Effects of Dissociation

Dissociation (rightful or wrongful) terminates some of the rights of the dissociated partner and requires that the partnership purchase his or her interest. It also alters the liability of the parties to third parties.

---

5. Under the previous version of the UPA, when a partner withdrew from a partnership, the partnership was considered dissolved, and the business had to end. The new UPA dramatically changed the law governing partnership breakups by no longer requiring that a partnership end if one partner dissociates.

Rights and Duties On a partner's dissociation, his or her right to participate in the management and conduct of the partnership business terminates [UPA 603]. The partner's duty of loyalty also ends. A partner's duty of care continues only with respect to events that occurred before dissociation, unless the partner participates in winding up the partnership's business (discussed shortly).

■ **EXAMPLE 37.11** Debbie Pearson is a partner at the accounting firm Bubb & Flint. If she leaves the partnership, she can immediately compete with the firm for new clients. She must exercise care in completing ongoing client transactions that involved the partnership, however. She must also account to Bubb & Flint for any fees received from the old clients based on those transactions. ■

Buyouts After a partner's dissociation, his or her interest in the partnership must be purchased according to the rules in UPA 701. The **buyout price** is based on the amount that would have been distributed to the partner if the partnership had been wound up on the date of dissociation. Offset against the price are amounts owed by the partner to the partnership, including damages for wrongful dissociation.

Liability to Third Parties For two years after a partner dissociates from a continuing partnership, the partnership may be bound by the acts of the dissociated partner based on apparent authority [UPA 702]. In other words, if a third party reasonably believed at the time of a transaction that the dissociated partner was still a partner, the partnership may be liable. Similarly, a dissociated partner may be liable for partnership obligations entered into during the two-year period following dissociation [UPA 703].

To avoid this possible liability, a partnership should notify its creditors, customers, and clients of a partner's dissociation. In addition, either the partnership or the dissociated partner can file a statement of dissociation in the appropriate state office to limit the dissociated partner's authority to ninety days after the filing [UPA 704]. Filing this statement helps to minimize the firm's potential liability for the former partner and vice versa.

37–3d Partnership Termination

The same events that cause dissociation can result in the end of the partnership if the remaining partners no longer wish to (or are unable to) continue the partnership business. A partner's departure will not necessarily end the partnership, though. Generally, the partnership can continue if the remaining partners consent [UPA 801].

The termination of a partnership is referred to as **dissolution,** which essentially means the commencement of the winding up process. **Winding up** is the actual process of collecting, liquidating, and distributing the partnership assets.

Dissolution Dissolution of a partnership generally can be brought about by acts of the partners, by operation of law, or by judicial decree [UPA 801]. Any partnership (including one for a fixed term) can be dissolved by the partners' agreement. If the partnership agreement states that it will dissolve on a certain event, such as a partner's death or bankruptcy, then the occurrence of that event will dissolve the partnership. A partnership for a fixed term or a particular undertaking is dissolved by operation of law at the expiration of the term or on the completion of the undertaking.

■ **CASE IN POINT 37.12** Clyde Webster, James Theis, and Larry Thomas formed T&T Agri-Partners Company to own and farm 180 acres in Christian County, Illinois. Under the partnership agreement, the firm was to continue until January 31, 2010, unless it was dissolved. The death of any partner would dissolve the partnership.

Webster died in 2002, but Theis and Thomas did not liquidate T&T and distribute its assets. Webster's estate, through its personal representative, Joseph Webster, filed a complaint in state court seeking to dissolve the partnership. The court ordered the partnership to be dissolved, but Theis and Thomas did not dissolve it.

In 2011, after a trial, the court found that the partnership had expired by its own terms on January 31, 2010, and again ordered the partnership dissolved. Theis and Thomas appealed, but the reviewing court affirmed. A partnership business cannot continue after one partner dies when the partnership agreement specified that the death of one partner would terminate the business.[6] ■

Illegality or Impracticality. Any event that makes it unlawful for the partnership to continue its business will result in dissolution [UPA 801(4)]. Under the UPA, a court may order dissolution when it becomes obviously impractical for the firm to continue—for instance, if the business can only be operated at a loss [UPA 801(5)].

■ **CASE IN POINT 37.13** Members of the Russell family began operating Russell Realty Associates (RRA) as a partnership. Eddie Russell had decision-making authority over the partnership's business, which involved buying, holding, leasing, and selling investment properties. After several years, Eddie and his sister, Nina Russell,

---

6. *Estate of Webster v. Thomas,* 2013 IL App (5th) 120121-U, 2013 WL 164041 (2013).

started having disputes, and Nina began to routinely question Eddie's business decisions. Because of their disagreements, RRA experienced two years of delays before it could sell one piece of property. Although the firm continued to profit, Eddie filed a complaint seeking a judicial dissolution of the partnership, which the court granted. Nina appealed.

The Virginia Supreme Court affirmed the lower court's decision that Russell Realty must be judicially dissolved. The partners' relationship had deteriorated to the point where the partnership was unable to function effectively. As a result, the firm had incurred substantial and unnecessary added costs, which frustrated the partnership's economic purpose and made it impracticable to continue.[7] ■

Good Faith. Each partner must exercise good faith when dissolving a partnership. Some state statutes allow partners injured by another partner's bad faith to file a tort claim for wrongful dissolution of a partnership.

■ **CASE IN POINT 37.14** Attorneys Randall Jordan and Mary Helen Moses formed a two-member partnership. Although the partnership was for an indefinite term, Jordan ended the partnership three years later and asked the court for declarations concerning the partners' financial obligations. Moses, who had objected to ending the partnership, filed a claim against Jordan for wrongful dissolution and for appropriating $180,000 in fees that should have gone to the partnership.

Ultimately, the court held in favor of Moses. A claim for wrongful dissolution of a partnership may be based on the excluded partner's loss of "an existing, or continuing, business opportunity" or of income and material assets. Because Jordan had attempted to appropriate partnership assets through dissolution, Moses could sue for wrongful dissolution.[8] ■

Winding Up and Distribution of Assets After dissolution, the partnership continues for the limited purpose of winding up the business. The partners cannot create new obligations on behalf of the partnership. They have authority only to complete transactions begun but not finished at the time of dissolution and to wind up the business of the partnership [UPA 803, 804(1)].

Duties and Compensation. Winding up includes collecting and preserving partnership assets, discharging liabilities (paying debts), and accounting to each partner for

the value of his or her interest in the partnership. Partners continue to have fiduciary duties to one another and to the firm during this process.

UPA 401(h) provides that a partner is entitled to compensation for services in winding up partnership affairs above and apart from his or her share in the partnership profits. A partner may also receive reimbursement for expenses incurred in the process.

Creditors' Claims. Both creditors of the partnership and creditors of the individual partners can make claims on the partnership's assets. In general, partnership creditors share proportionately with the partners' individual creditors in the partners' assets, which include their interests in the partnership.

A partnership's assets are distributed according to the following priorities [UPA 807]:

1. Payment of debts, including those owed to partner and nonpartner creditors.
2. Return of capital contributions and distribution of profits to partners.[9]

If the partnership's liabilities are greater than its assets, the partners bear the losses in the same proportion in which they shared the profits unless they have agreed otherwise.

Partnership Buy-Sell Agreements Before entering into a partnership, partners may agree on how the assets will be valued and divided in the event that the partnership dissolves. Such an agreement may eliminate costly negotiations or litigation later.

The agreement may provide for one or more partners to buy out the other or others, should the situation warrant. This is called a **buy-sell agreement,** or simply a *buyout agreement.* Alternatively, the agreement may specify that one or more partners will determine the value of the interest being sold and that the other or others will decide whether to buy or sell.

Under UPA 701(a), if a partner's dissociation does not result in a dissolution of the partnership, a buyout of the partner's interest is mandatory. The UPA contains an extensive set of buyout rules that apply when the partners do not have a buyout agreement. Basically, a withdrawing partner receives the same amount through a buyout that he or she would receive if the business were winding up [UPA 701(b)].

---

7. *Russell Realty Associates v. Russell,* 724 S.E.2d 690 (Va.Sup.Ct. 2012).
8. *Jordan v. Moses,* 291 Ga. 39, 727 S.E.2d 469 (2012).

9. Under the previous version of the UPA, creditors of the partnership had priority over creditors of the individual partners. Also, in distributing partnership assets, third party creditors were paid before partner creditors, and capital contributions were returned before profits.

Which of two buyout provisions in five partnership agreements applied to the sale of one partner's interest was the dispute in the following case. Although this case involved limited liability partnerships (discussed shortly) rather than traditional partnerships, it illustrates how the courts interpret buyout provisions.

Case Analysis 37.2

Shamburger v. Shamburger

Court of Appeals of Arkansas, Division I, 2016 Ark.App. 57, 481 S.W.3d 448 (2016).

In the Language of the Court

Cliff *HOOFMAN*, Judge
* * * *

There are five LLPs [limited liability partnerships] at issue in this case: (1) CMH Management, LLP; (2) S.E. Management, LLP; (3) Bryant Hospitality, LLP; (4) Winners Circle Hospitality, LLP; and (5) SJS Management, LLP. At the time these LLPs were created, they were each composed of six partners, or three married couples: Sarah Jane and Robert Shamburger, Karyn Ann and Ricky Alan Johnson, and Thresa Kay and James Shamburger, Jr. Each partner had a 16.667% interest in each of the five LLPs.

The partners executed partnership agreements in connection with each LLP, as well as separate buy-sell agreements setting forth the required procedure through which partners could transfer their interests. The buy-sell agreements * * * contained similar language regarding the transfer of a partner's interest. As an example, the relevant provisions of the buy-sell agreement for Bryant Hospitality, LLP, are set forth below:

1. * * * The parties agree that the only manner in which any of the partners may transfer a partnership interest * * * shall be in the manner set forth herein:
(a) Any couple may give notice * * * of an intent to either buy the others' entire company interests or to sell their entire company interest. Such notice shall contain one price at which such transaction shall occur. The offeree couples, or any single partner, shall, for sixty (60) days, have the option to either buy the offerors' entire interests for such price, or to sell their entire interest for such price.

* * * *

(c) If neither option is timely accepted by both individuals of the offeree couples, the offer shall be deemed an offer to purchase only, and acceptance of such offer shall be presumed.

* * * *

3. In the event of the death or divorce of a partner, the purchase price of such partner's interest, and the spouse's interest, or the interest of both in the event of common disaster, shall be the higher of the figures achieved in paragraphs (a) and (b) below:
(a) The aggregate * * * revenue * * * for the preceding thirty-six months (or so long as the partnership has been in business, if less than that time), as reflected on the books of the partnership, multiplied by the partner's percentage ownership.
(b) The applicable percentage of partnership interest of the value of the real property * * * as determined by the average of two appraisals.

* * * *

Appellant [Thresa Kay Shamburger] and her husband, James, divorced. [Two and a half years later] Sarah Jane and Robert Shamburger mailed a letter to appellant and James, stating that their divorce proceeding had "adversely affected the operation of all the family partnerships" and that, "in an effort to avoid continued disagreements and acrimony harmful to the businesses we propose to purchase your collective interest in all the partnerships, for a total price of $400,000, or $200,000 to each of you." The letter further referred appellant and James to the buy-sell agreements associated with each partnership and stated that they had sixty days from their receipt of the letter to make their election.

Appellant received the letter * * * but did not respond. Instead, she filed a complaint [in an Arkansas state court] against appellees [all of the partnerships and the other partners], alleging that her divorce from James had triggered the terms of the buy-sell agreements dealing with a divorced party's interest and that appellees were attempting to bypass that provision by attempting to invoke the transfer provision set forth in Paragraph 1 of the agreements. * * * Appellant requested an order from the * * * court * * * determining that the attempted buy-sell arrangement by Sarah Jane and Robert Shamburger was in violation of the buy-sell agreements.

* * * *

Separate appellees Sarah Jane and Robert Shamburger filed a counterclaim against appellant, alleging that appellant had failed to respond to their purchase offer within the sixty-day period required by the buy-sell agreements and that the offer should therefore be deemed an offer to purchase her interest for $200,000. Robert and Sarah Jane requested that the * * * court order specific performance of the terms of the buy-sell agreements.

* * * *

* * * The court granted appellees' motion for summary judgment * * * . In addition, the court granted the relief for specific performance requested in the counterclaim * * * . Appellant timely appealed.

* * * *

* * * *Where two provisions of a contract conflict, the specific provision controls over*

Case 37.2 Continues

Case 37.2 Continued

a more general provision, as it is assumed that the specific provision expresses the parties' intent. [Emphasis added.]

* * * *

* * * We agree with appellant that the specific provision governing transfers in the event of a divorce or death of a partner controls over the more general provision found in Paragraph 1. Appellees argue that Sarah Jane and Robert Shamburger's offer to purchase appellant's and her ex-husband's interest was not necessarily due to the divorce. However, this argument is belied by Sarah Jane and Robert Shamburger's statements in their offer letter * * * . Appellees also contend that the death-or-divorce provision is not more specific than the provision in Paragraph 1, and they compare the length and detail of the two provisions at issue. As appellant responds, however, it is the fact that the death-or-divorce provision applies only under specific and limited circumstances that renders it controlling over the more general provision in Paragraph 1, not the specificity of the language used to describe each method of purchase.

* * * *

In addition to the rule of construction discussed above, * * * the use of the word "shall" in each buy-sell agreement's death-or-divorce provision further supports [appellant's] claim that application of this provision was mandatory under the circumstances in this case. * * * *"Shall" is defined as "has a duty to" or "is required to."* * * * *"Shall," when used in a contract provision, means that compliance with that provision is mandatory.* [Emphasis added.]

* * * The combination of the specific nature of the death-or-divorce provision and its use of mandatory language such as "shall," indicates that compliance with this particular provision was required under the circumstances in this case. Appellees also contend that interpreting the death-or-divorce provision as mandatory supersedes the procedure set forth in Paragraph 1 of the agreements and "neutralizes" that provision in violation of our rule of construction that we will not adopt an interpretation neutralizing a provision if the various clauses of a contract can be reconciled. We disagree

because interpreting the application of the death-or-divorce provision as mandatory in this case does not mean that the procedure set forth in Paragraph 1 of the agreements does not apply in all other situations that do not involve the death or divorce of a partner. Furthermore, as appellant argues, it is also possible to reconcile the two provisions in such a way that the general procedures set forth in Paragraph 1 apply, even in the event of a divorce or death of a partner, but the value of the partner's or couple's interest is determined pursuant to the formula set forth in the death-or-divorce provision.

Based on our rules of construction, we agree with appellant that the [lower] court erred in interpreting the buy-sell agreements in such a manner as to find that the death-or-divorce provisions did not apply to the offer to purchase appellant's interest in the LLPs. Accordingly, we reverse the * * * order granting summary judgment and remand for further proceedings.

Legal Reasoning Questions

1. Why would a partnership agreement contain one provision for a buyout on a partner's divorce or death and another for a partner's decision to quit the firm?

2. How did the court's interpretation of contract principles affect the result in this case?

3. The lower court awarded attorneys' fees to the defendants, who prevailed on their motion for summary judgment. By reversing the summary judgment, does the appellate court's decision also require a reversal of the award of attorneys' fees?

37–4 Limited Liability Partnerships

The **limited liability partnership (LLP)** is a hybrid form of business designed mostly for professionals who normally do business as partners in a partnership. Almost all of the states have enacted LLP statutes.

The major advantage of the LLP is that it allows a partnership to continue as a pass-through entity for tax purposes but limits the personal liability of the partners. The LLP is especially attractive for professional service firms and family businesses. All of the "Big Four" accounting firms—the four largest international accountancy and professional services firms—are organized as

LLPs, including Ernst & Young, LLP, and PricewaterhouseCoopers, LLP.

37–4a Formation of an LLP

LLPs must be formed and operated in compliance with state statutes, which may include provisions of the UPA. The appropriate form must be filed with a central state agency, usually the secretary of state's office, and the business's name must include either "Limited Liability Partnership" or "LLP" [UPA 1001, 1002]. An LLP must file an annual report with the state to remain qualified as an LLP in that state [UPA 1003].

In most states, it is relatively easy to convert a traditional partnership into an LLP because the firm's basic organizational structure remains the same. Additionally, all of the statutory and common law rules governing partnerships still apply, apart from those modified by the LLP statute. Normally, LLP statutes are simply amendments to a state's already existing partnership law.

37–4b Liability in an LLP

An LLP allows professionals, such as attorneys and accountants, to avoid personal liability for the malpractice of other partners. Of course, a partner in an LLP is still liable for her or his own wrongful acts, such as negligence. Also liable is the partner who supervised the individual who committed a wrongful act. (This generally is true for all types of partners and partnerships, not just LLPs.)

■ **EXAMPLE 37.15** Five lawyers operate a law firm as an LLP. One of the attorneys, Dan Kolcher, is sued for malpractice and loses. The firm's malpractice insurance is insufficient to pay the judgment. If the firm had been organized as a traditional (general) partnership, the personal assets of the other attorneys could be used to satisfy the obligation. Because the firm is organized as an LLP, however, no other partner at the firm can be held *personally* liable for Kolcher's malpractice, unless she or he acted as Kolcher's supervisor. In the absence of a supervisor, only Kolcher's personal assets can be used to satisfy the judgment. ■

Although LLP statutes vary from state to state, generally each state statute limits the liability of partners in some way. For instance, Delaware law protects each innocent partner from the "debts and obligations of the partnership arising from negligence, wrongful acts, or misconduct." The UPA more broadly exempts partners in an LLP from personal liability for any partnership obligation, "whether arising in contract, tort, or otherwise" [UPA 306(c)].

Liability outside the State of Formation When an LLP formed in one state wants to do business in another state, it may be required to file a statement of foreign qualification in the second state [UPA 1102]. Because state LLP statutes are not uniform, a question sometimes arises as to which law applies if the LLP statutes in the two states provide different liability protection. Most states apply the law of the state in which the LLP was formed, even when the firm does business in another state, which is also the rule under UPA 1101.

Sharing Liability among Partners When more than one partner in an LLP commits malpractice, there

is a question as to how liability should be shared. Is each partner jointly and severally liable for the entire result, as a general partner would be in most states?

Some states provide instead for proportionate liability—that is, for separate determinations of the negligence of the partners. ■ **EXAMPLE 37.16** Accountants Zach and Lyla are partners in an LLP, with Zach supervising Lyla. Lyla negligently fails to file a tax return for a client, Centaur Tools. Centaur files a suit against Zach and Lyla. Under a proportionate liability statute, Zach will be liable for no more than his portion of the responsibility for the missed tax deadline. In a state that does not allow for proportionate liability, Zach can be held liable for the entire loss. ■

37–4c Family Limited Liability Partnerships

A **family limited liability partnership (FLLP)** is a limited liability partnership in which the partners are related to each other—for example, as spouses, parents and children, siblings, or cousins. A person acting in a fiduciary capacity for persons so related can also be a partner. All of the partners must be natural persons or be acting in a fiduciary capacity for the benefit of natural persons.

Probably the most significant use of the FLLP form of business organization is in agriculture. Family-owned farms sometimes find this form to their benefit. The FLLP offers the same advantages as other LLPs with certain additional advantages. For instance, in Iowa, FLLPs are exempt from real estate transfer taxes when partnership real estate is transferred among partners.[10]

37–5 Limited Partnerships

We now look at a business organizational form that limits the liability of *some* of its owners—the **limited partnership (LP)**. Limited partnerships originated in medieval Europe and have been in existence in the United States since the early 1800s. Today, most states and the District of Columbia have adopted laws based on the Revised Uniform Limited Partnership Act (RULPA).

Limited partnerships differ from traditional (general) partnerships in several ways. Exhibit 37–2 compares the characteristics of general and limited partnerships.[11]

---

10. Iowa Statutes Section 428A.2.
11. Under the UPA, a general partnership can be converted into a limited partnership and vice versa [UPA 902, 903]. The UPA also provides for the merger of a general partnership with one or more general or limited partnerships [UPA 905].

EXHIBIT 37–2 A Comparison of General Partnerships and Limited Partnerships

	GENERAL PARTNERSHIP (UPA)	LIMITED PARTNERSHIP (RULPA)
Creation	By agreement of two or more persons to carry on a business as co-owners for profit.	By agreement of two or more persons to carry on a business as co-owners for profit. Must include one or more general partners and one or more limited partners. Filing of a certificate with the secretary of state is required.
Sharing of Profits and Losses	By agreement. In the absence of agreement, profits are shared equally by the partners, and losses are shared in the same ratio as profits.	Profits are shared as required in the certificate agreement, and losses are shared likewise, up to the amount of the limited partners' capital contributions. In the absence of a provision in the certificate agreement, profits and losses are shared on the basis of percentages of capital contributions.
Liability	Unlimited personal liability of all partners.	Unlimited personal liability of all general partners; limited partners liable only to the extent of their capital contributions.
Capital Contribution	No minimum or mandatory amount; set by agreement.	Set by agreement.
Management	By agreement. In the absence of agreement, all partners have an equal voice.	Only the general partner (or the general partners). Limited partners have no voice or else are subject to liability as general partners (but only if a third party has reason to believe that the limited partner is a general partner). A limited partner may act as an agent or employee of the partnership and vote on amending the certificate or on the sale or dissolution of the partnership.
Duration	Terminated by agreement of the partners, but can continue to do business even when a partner dissociates from the partnership.	Terminated by agreement in the certificate or by retirement, death, or mental incompetence of a general partner in the absence of the right of the other general partners to continue the partnership. Death of a limited partner does not terminate the partnership, unless he or she is the only remaining limited partner.
Distribution of Assets on Liquidation—Order of Priorities	1. Payment of debts, including those owed to partner and nonpartner creditors. 2. Return of capital contributions and distribution of profit to partners.	1. Outside creditors and partner creditors. 2. Partners and former partners entitled to distributions of partnership assets. 3. Unless otherwise agreed, return of capital contributions and distribution of profit to partners.

A limited partnership consists of at least one **general partner** and one or more **limited partners**. A general partner assumes management responsibility for the partnership and has full responsibility for the partnership and for all its debts. A limited partner contributes cash or other property and owns an interest in the firm but is not involved in management responsibilities. A limited partner is not personally liable for partnership debts beyond the amount of his or her investment. If a limited partner takes part in the management of the business, however, she or he may forfeit that limited liability.

In the following case, two firms—a corporation and a limited partnership—were involved in the construction of a residential development. One individual served as the president of the corporation and the sole general partner of the partnership. In addition, he took charge of the activities at the construction site. How did this individual's status affect his responsibility for those activities?

Case 37.3

DeWine v. Valley View Enterprises, Inc.

Court of Appeals of Ohio, Eleventh District, Trumbull County, 2015 –Ohio– 1222 (2015).

Background and Facts Valley View Enterprises, Inc., built Pine Lakes Golf Club and Estates in Trumbull County, Ohio, in two phases—Phase I and Phase II. Valley View Properties, Ltd., a limited partnership, cut out the roadways and constructed sewer, water, and storm-water lines with water inlets for the development. Joseph Ferrara was the owner and the president of Valley View Enterprises and the sole general partner of Valley View Properties. Ferrara failed to obtain the proper permits for the development work in a timely manner and failed to comply with their requirements once they had been obtained.

Michael DeWine, the state's attorney general, filed a lawsuit in an Ohio court against the Valley View entities and Ferrara, alleging violations of the state's water pollution control laws and seeking civil penalties. The court entered a judgment in the defendants' favor, holding with respect to Ferrara that "a corporate officer cannot be held liable merely by virtue of his status as a corporate officer." DeWine appealed.

In the Language of the Court

Timothy J. *CANNON*, P.J. [Presiding Judge]

* * * *

Here, the state sought civil penalties from three entities: the property owner and Phase II permit holder, Valley View Properties, Ltd.; the Phase I permit holder, Valley View Enterprises, Inc.; and the sole general partner of the property owner, Mr. Ferrara.

* * * The state alleges the trial court erred in its finding that "Valley View Properties is the only party against whom civil penalties can be assessed." The trial court also found Mr. Ferrara was not liable based on his "good faith" actions and Valley View Enterprises, Inc. was not liable because it had no relationship to Pine Lakes Estates; [and] the state failed to present evidence that Mr. Ferrara ordered activities that caused pollution.

* * * Although the trial court found that Valley View Enterprises, Inc. had no relationship to Pine Lake Estates, the evidence establishes that Valley View Enterprises, Inc. applied for and was granted the [Phase I] Permit and, as the permittee, was required to ensure compliance with the permit. The [Phase I] Permit explicitly states, "the permittee must comply with all conditions of this permit, any permit non-compliance constitutes a violation of [state law]." Additionally, * * * *the evidence demonstrates that Mr. Ferrara personally was in charge of the activities performed at the sites; authorized the construction activities at the sites; and failed to obtain necessary certifications and permits.* [Emphasis added.]

Moreover, the trial court's finding that "a corporate officer cannot be held liable merely by virtue of his status as a corporate officer" is erroneous and not supported by the evidence. Admittedly, Mr. Ferrara is the sole general partner of Valley View Properties, Ltd., an Ohio limited partnership. He is not, in relation to Valley View Properties, Ltd., a "corporate officer." Therefore, he is not, in the course of his conduct as the general partner of that limited partnership, entitled to the insulation from liability of a corporate officer.

Case 37.3 Continues

Decision and Remedy *A state intermediate appellate court reversed the lower court's judgment in favor of the defendants. With respect to Ferrara's status in relation to Valley View Properties, he was the general partner and therefore not "entitled to the insulation from liability of a corporate officer." On remand, the trial court was to determine the number of violations established by the state and to issue and apportion penalties among the liable parties.*

Critical Thinking

- **Legal Environment** *How are the penalties likely to be apportioned among the three defendants? Explain.*

37–5a Formation of an LP

In contrast to the private and informal agreement that usually suffices to form a general partnership, the formation of a limited partnership is a public and formal proceeding. The partners must strictly follow statutory requirements. Not only must a limited partnership have at least one general partner and one limited partner, but the partners must also sign a **certificate of limited partnership.**

The certificate of limited partnership must include certain information, including the name, mailing address, and capital contribution of each general and limited partner. The certificate must be filed with the designated state official—under the RULPA, the secretary of state. The certificate is usually open to public inspection.

37–5b Liabilities of Partners in an LP

General partners are personally liable to the partnership's creditors. Thus, at least one general partner is necessary in a limited partnership so that someone has personal liability. This policy can be circumvented in states that allow a corporation to be the general partner in a partnership. Because the corporation has limited liability by virtue of corporation statutes, if a corporation is the general partner, no one in the limited partnership has personal liability. (See this chapter's *Ethics Today* feature for a discussion of whether a general partner who is unaware of another general partner's wrongdoing should be held liable for it.)

The liability of a limited partner, as mentioned, is limited to the capital that she or he contributes or agrees to contribute to the partnership [RULPA 502]. Limited partners enjoy this limited liability only so long as they do not participate in management [RULPA 303].

A limited partner who participates in management will be just as liable as a general partner to any creditor who transacts business with the limited partnership.

Liability arises when the creditor believes, based on the limited partner's conduct, that the limited partner is a general partner [RULPA 303]. The extent to which a limited partner can engage in management before being exposed to liability is not always clear, however.

37–5c Rights and Duties in a Limited Partnership

With the exception of the right to participate in management, limited partners have essentially the same rights as general partners. Limited partners have a right of access to the partnership's books and to information regarding partnership business. On dissolution of the partnership, limited partners are entitled to a return of their contributions in accordance with the partnership certificate [RULPA 201(a)(10)]. They can also assign their interests subject to the certificate [RULPA 702, 704]. In addition, they can sue an outside party on behalf of the firm if the general partners with authority to do so have refused to file suit [RULPA 1001].

37–5d Dissociation and Dissolution

A general partner has the power to voluntarily dissociate, or withdraw, from a limited partnership unless the partnership agreement specifies otherwise. Under the RULPA, a limited partner can withdraw from the partnership by giving six months' notice, unless the partnership agreement specifies a term. In reality, though, most limited partnership agreements do specify a term, which eliminates the limited partner's right to withdraw. Also, some states have passed laws prohibiting the withdrawal of limited partners.

Events That Cause Dissociation In a limited partnership, a general partner's voluntary dissociation from the firm normally will lead to dissolution *unless* all partners

ETHICS TODAY

Should an Innocent General Partner Be Jointly Liable for Fraud?

When general partners in a limited partnership jointly engage in fraud, there is usually no question that they are jointly liable. But if one general partner engages in fraud and the other is unaware of the wrongdoing, is it fair to make the innocent partner share in the liability? Many states' limited partnership laws protect innocent general partners from suits for fraud brought by limited partners. The law is less clear, however, in some other situations.

A Developer's Misconduct

Robert Bisno and James Coxeter formed two limited partnerships to redevelop certain property in downtown Berkeley, California. Without Coxeter's knowledge, Bisno took almost $500,000 from one of the partnerships to buy a personal home. He also made material misrepresentations to potential investors.

One of those investors, George Miske—after purchasing an interest in the limited partnership—discovered the fraud and brought a lawsuit. Coxeter argued that he was an innocent general partner and should not

be liable to Miske for Bisno's tortious conduct. Coxeter also claimed that Miske was a limited partner, not an innocent third party, and that the state's limited partnership law protected Coxeter from liability to a limited partner.

A California Court Finds the Innocent Co-Developer Liable

The court disagreed with Coxeter, however. The fraud at issue had induced Miske to purchase the limited partnership interest. Therefore, the court reasoned, at the time the fraud was perpetrated by Bisno, Miske was an innocent third party. As a result, the court held that Coxeter—even though he was innocent of any wrongdoing—was jointly liable to Miske.[a]

Critical Thinking *Why might it be fair for the court to hold Coxeter liable for his partner's fraud?*

a. *Miske v. Bisno*, 204 Cal.App.4th 1249, 139 Cal.Rptr.3d 626 (2012). See also *In re Barlaam*, 2014 WL 3398381 (9th Cir. 2014).

---

agree to continue the business. Similarly, the bankruptcy, retirement, death, or mental incompetence of a general partner will cause the dissociation of that partner and the dissolution of the limited partnership unless the other members agree to continue the firm [RULPA 801].

Bankruptcy of a limited partner, however, does not dissolve the partnership unless it causes the bankruptcy of the firm. In addition, death or an assignment of the interest (right to receive distributions) of a limited partner does not dissolve a limited partnership [RULPA 702, 704, 705]. A limited partnership can be dissolved by court decree [RULPA 802].

Distribution of Assets On dissolution, creditors' claims, including those of partners who are creditors, take first priority. After that, partners and former partners receive unpaid distributions of partnership assets. Unless otherwise agreed, they are also entitled to a return of their contributions in the proportions in which they share in distributions [RULPA 804].

Valuation of Assets Disputes commonly arise about how the partnership's assets should be valued and distributed and whether the business should be sold. ■ **CASE IN POINT 37.17** Actor Kevin Costner was a limited partner

in Midnight Star Enterprises, LP, which runs a casino, bar, and restaurant in South Dakota. There were two other limited partners, Carla and Francis Caneva, who owned a small percentage of the partnership (3.25 units each) and received salaries for managing its operations. Another company owned by Costner, Midnight Star Enterprises, Limited (MSEL), was the general partner. Costner thus controlled a majority of the partnership (93.5 units).

When communications broke down between the partners, MSEL asked a court to dissolve the partnership. MSEL's accountant determined that the firm's fair market value was $3.1 million. The Canevas presented evidence that a competitor would buy the business for $6.2 million. The Canevas wanted the court to force Costner to either buy the business for that price within ten days or sell it on the open market to the highest bidder. Ultimately, the state's highest court held in favor of Costner. A partner cannot force the sale of a limited partnership when the other partners want to continue the business. The court also accepted the $3.1 million buyout price of MSEL's accountant and ordered Costner to pay the Canevas the value of their 6.5 partnership units.[12] ■

---

12. *In re Dissolution of Midnight Star Enterprises, LP*, 2006 SD 98, 724 N.W.2d 334 (S.D.Sup.Ct. 2006).

Buy-Sell Agreements As mentioned earlier, partners can agree ahead of time on how the partnership's assets will be valued and divided if the partnership dissolves. This is true for limited partnerships as well as for general partnerships. Buy-sell agreements can help the partners avoid disputes. Nonetheless, buy-sell agreements do not eliminate all potential for litigation, especially if the terms are subject to more than one interpretation.

■ **CASE IN POINT 37.18** Natural Pork Production II, LLP (NPP), an Iowa limited liability partnership, raises hogs. Under a partnership buy-sell agreement, NPP was obligated to buy a dissociating partner's interests but could defer the purchase if it would adversely affect the firm's capital or cash flow. After these "impairment circumstances" changed, NPP was to make the purchase within thirty days. Two of NPP's limited partners, Craton Capital, LP, and Kruse Investment Company, notified NPP of their dissociation. A wave of similar notices from other limited partners followed.

NPP declared an impairment circumstance and refused to buy out the limited partners. Craton and Kruse filed a suit asking a state court to order NPP to buy their units. NPP claimed that it was not required to buy out the limited partners because of the impairment circumstance. The court ruled in the plaintiffs' favor. The wording of the buyout provision stated the firm "shall" buy out the partners, which meant it was mandatory. The impairment circumstance only deferred the purchase, and thus NPP was required to buy out the limited partners.[13] ■

37–5e Limited Liability Limited Partnerships

A **limited liability limited partnership (LLLP)** is a type of limited partnership. An LLLP differs from a limited partnership in that a general partner in an LLLP has the same liability as a limited partner in a limited partnership. In other words, the liability of all partners is limited to the amount of their investments in the firm.

A few states provide expressly for LLLPs.[14] In states that do not provide for LLLPs but do allow for limited partnerships and limited liability partnerships, a limited partnership should probably still be able to register with the state as an LLLP.

---

13. *Craton Capital, LP v. Natural Pork Production II, LLP,* 797 N.W.2d 623 (Iowa App. 2011).
14. See, for example, Colorado Revised Statutes Annotated Section 7-62-109. Other states that provide for LLLPs include Delaware, Florida, Georgia, Kentucky, Maryland, Nevada, Texas, and Virginia.

Reviewing: All Forms of Partnerships

Grace Tarnavsky and her sons, Manny and Jason, bought a ranch known as the Cowboy Palace in March 2014, and the three verbally agreed to share the business for five years. Grace contributed 50 percent of the investment, and each son contributed 25 percent. Manny agreed to handle the livestock, and Jason agreed to handle the bookkeeping. The Tarnavskys took out joint loans and opened a joint bank account into which they deposited the ranch's proceeds and from which they made payments for property, cattle, equipment, and supplies.

In September 2017, Manny severely injured his back while baling hay and became permanently unable to handle livestock. Manny therefore hired additional laborers to tend the livestock, causing the Cowboy Palace to incur significant debt. In September 2018, Al's Feed Barn filed a lawsuit against Jason to collect $32,400 in unpaid debts. Using the information presented in the chapter, answer the following questions.

1. Was this relationship a partnership for a term or a partnership at will?
2. Did Manny have the authority to hire additional laborers to work at the ranch after his injury? Why or why not?
3. Under the current UPA, can Al's Feed Barn bring an action against Jason individually for the Cowboy Palace's debt? Why or why not?
4. Suppose that after his back injury in 2017, Manny sent his mother and brother a notice indicating his intent to withdraw from the partnership. Can he still be held liable for the debt to Al's Feed Barn? Why or why not?

Debate This . . .   *A partnership should automatically end when one partner dissociates from the firm.*

Terms and Concepts

articles of partnership 707
buyout price 713
buy-sell agreement 714
certificate of limited
  partnership 720
charging order 709
dissociation 712
dissolution 713
family limited liability partnership
  (FLLP) 717

general partner 719
goodwill 706
information return 706
joint and several liability 711
joint liability 711
limited liability limited partnership
  (LLLP) 722
limited liability partnership
  (LLP) 716
limited partner 719

limited partnership (LP) 717
partnership 705
partnership by estoppel 707
pass-through entity 706
winding up 713

Issue Spotters

1. Darnell and Eliana are partners in D&E Designs, an architectural firm. When Darnell dies, his widow claims that as
Darnell's heir, she is entitled to take his place as Eliana's
partner or to receive a share of the firm's assets. Is she right?
Why or why not? (See *Dissociation and Termination*.)

2. Finian and Gloria are partners in F&G Delivery Service. When business is slow, without Gloria's knowledge,

Finian leases the delivery vehicles as moving vans. Because
the vehicles would otherwise be sitting idle in a parking
lot, can Finian keep the income resulting from the leasing
of the delivery vehicles? Explain your answer. (See *Formation and Operation*.)

• **Check your answers to the Issue Spotters against the
answers provided in Appendix D at the end of this text.**

Business Scenarios

37–1. Partnership Formation. Daniel is the owner of a
chain of shoe stores. He hires Rubya to be the manager of a
new store, which is to open in Grand Rapids, Michigan. Daniel, by written contract, agrees to pay Rubya a monthly salary
and 20 percent of the profits. Without Daniel's knowledge,
Rubya represents himself to Classen as Daniel's partner and
shows Classen the agreement to share profits. Classen extends
credit to Rubya. Rubya defaults. Discuss whether Classen can
hold Daniel liable as a partner. (See *Formation and Operation*.)

37–2. Dissolution of a Limited Partnership. Dorinda,
Luis, and Elizabeth form a limited partnership. Dorinda is a
general partner, and Luis and Elizabeth are limited partners.
Consider the separate events below, and discuss fully whether
each event constitutes a dissolution of the limited partnership.
(See *Limited Partnerships*.)
(a) Luis assigns his partnership interest to Ashley.
(b) Elizabeth is petitioned into involuntary bankruptcy.
(c) Dorinda dies.

Business Case Problems

37–3. Fiduciary Duties of Partners. Karl Horvath, Hein
Rüsen, and Carl Thomas formed a partnership, HRT Enterprises, to buy a manufacturing plant. Rüsen and Thomas
leased the plant to their own company, Merkur Steel. Merkur
then sublet the premises to other companies owned by Rüsen
and Thomas. The rent that these companies paid to Merkur
was higher than the rent that Merkur paid to HRT. Rüsen and
Thomas did not tell Horvath about the subleases. Did Rüsen
and Thomas breach their fiduciary duties to HRT and Horvath? Discuss. [*Horvath v. HRT Enterprises*, 489 Mich.App.
992, 800 N.W.2d 595 (2011)] (See *Formation and Operation*.)

37–4. Partnership Formation. Patricia Garcia and Ber-
nardo Lucero were in a romantic relationship. While they
were seeing each other, Garcia and Lucero acquired an electronics service center, paying $30,000 apiece. Two years later,

they purchased an apartment complex. The property was
deeded to Lucero, but neither Garcia nor Lucero made a down
payment. The couple considered both properties to be owned
"50/50," and they agreed to share profits, losses, and management rights. When the couple's romantic relationship ended,
Garcia asked a court to declare that she had a partnership with
Lucero. In court, Lucero argued that the couple did not have
a written partnership agreement. Did they have a partnership?
Why or why not? [*Garcia v. Lucero*, 366 S.W.3d 275 (Tex.
App. 2012)] (See *Formation and Operation*.)

37–5. Winding Up. Dan and Lori Cole operated a Curves
franchise exercise facility in Angola, Indiana, as a partnership.
The firm leased commercial space from Flying Cat, LLC, for a
renewable three-year term and renewed the lease for a second
three-year term. But two years after the renewal, the Coles

divorced. By the end of the second term, Flying Cat was owed more than $21,000 on the lease. Without telling the landlord about the divorce, Lori signed another extension. More rent went unpaid. Flying Cat obtained a judgment in an Indiana state court against the partnership for almost $50,000. Can Dan be held liable? Why or why not? [*Curves for Women Angola v. Flying Cat, LLC,* 983 N.E.2d 629 (Ind.App. 2013)] (See *Dissociation and Termination.*)

37–6. Business Case Problem with Sample Answer— Partnerships. Karyl Paxton asked Christopher Sacco to

work with her interior design business, Pierce Paxton Collections, in New Orleans. At the time, they were in a romantic relationship. Sacco was involved in every aspect of the business—bookkeeping, marketing, and design—but was not paid a salary. He was reimbursed, however, for expenses charged to his personal credit card, which Paxton also used. Sacco took no profits from the firm, saying that he wanted to "grow the business" and "build sweat equity." When Paxton and Sacco's personal relationship soured, she fired him. Sacco objected, claiming that they were partners. Is Sacco entitled to 50 percent of the profits of Pierce Paxton Collections? Explain. [*Sacco v. Paxton,* 133 So.3d 213 (La.App. 2014)] (See *Formation and Operation.*)

- For a sample answer to Problem 37–6, go to Appendix E at the end of this text.

37–7. Formation. Leisa Reed and Randell Thurman lived together in Spring City, Tennessee. Randell and his father, Leroy, formed a cattle-raising operation and opened a bank account in the name of L&R Farm. Within a few years, Leroy quit the operation. Leisa and Randell each wrote a personal check for $5,000 to buy his cattle. Leisa picked up supplies, fed and administered medicine to cattle, collected hay, and participated in the bookkeeping for L&R. Later, checks drawn on her personal account for $12,000 to buy equipment and $35,000 to buy cattle were deposited into the L&R account. After several years, Leisa decided that she no longer wanted to associate with Randell, but they could not agree on a financial settlement. Was Leisa a partner in L&R? Is she entitled to half of the value of L&R's assets? Explain. [*Reed v. Thurman,* 2015 WL 1119449 (Tenn.App. 2015)] (See *Formation and Operation.*)

37–8. Formation and Operation. FS Partners is a general partnership whose partners are Jerry Stahlman, a professional engineer, and Fitz & Smith, Inc., a corporation in the business of excavating and paving. Timothy Smith signed the partnership agreement on Fitz & Smith's behalf and deals with FS matters on Fitz & Smith's behalf. Stahlman handles the payment of FS's bills, including its tax bills, and is the designated partner on FS's federal tax return. FS was formed to buy and develop twenty acres of unoccupied, wooded land in York County, Pennsylvania. The deed to the property lists the owner as "FS Partners, a general partnership." When the taxes on the real estate were not paid, the York County Tax Claim Bureau published notice that the property would be sold at a tax sale. The bureau also mailed a notice to FS's address of record and posted a notice on the land. Is this sufficient notice of the tax sale? Discuss. [*FS Partners v. York County Tax Claim Bureau,* 132 A.3d 577 (Pa. 2016)] (See *Formation and Operation.*)

37–9. A Question of Ethics—Wrongful Dissociation. *Elliot Willensky and Beverly Moran formed a partnership*

*to buy, renovate, and sell a house. Moran agreed to finance the effort, which was to cost no more than $60,000. Willensky agreed to oversee the work, which was to be done in six months. Willensky lived in the house during the renovation. As the project progressed, Willensky incurred excessive and unnecessary expenses, misappropriated funds for his personal use, did not pay bills on time, and did not keep Moran informed of the costs. More than a year later, the renovation was still not completed, and Willensky walked off the project. Moran completed the renovation, which ultimately cost $311,222, and sold the house. Moran then sued to dissolve the partnership and recover damages from Willensky for breach of contract and wrongful dissociation. [*Moran v. Willensky,* 339 S.W.3d 651 (Tenn.App.Ct. 2010)] (See* Dissociation and Termination.*)

(a) Moran alleged that Willensky had wrongfully dissociated from the partnership. When did this dissociation occur? Why was his dissociation wrongful?

(b) Which of Willensky's actions simply represent unethical behavior or bad management, and which constitute a breach of the agreement?

Legal Reasoning Group Activity

37–10. Liability of Partners. At least six months before the Summer Olympic Games in Atlanta, Georgia, Stafford Fontenot and four others agreed to sell Cajun food at the games and began making preparations. On May 19, the group (calling themselves "Prairie Cajun Seafood Catering of Louisiana") applied for a business license from the county health department. Later, Ted Norris sold a mobile kitchen to them for $40,000. They gave Norris an $8,000 check drawn on the "Prairie Cajun Seafood Catering of Louisiana" account and two promissory notes, one for $12,000 and the other for $20,000. The notes, which were dated June 12, listed only Fontenot "d/b/a Prairie Cajun Seafood" as the maker (*d/b/a* is an abbreviation for "doing business as").

On July 31, Fontenot and his friends signed a partnership agreement, which listed specific percentages of profits and losses. They drove the mobile kitchen to Atlanta, but business was "disastrous." When the notes were not paid, Norris filed a suit in a Louisiana state court against Fontenot, seeking payment. (See *Formation and Operation.*)

(a) The first group will discuss the elements of a partnership and determine whether a partnership exists among Fontenot and the others.

(b) The second group will determine who can be held liable on the notes and why.

CHAPTER 38

Limited Liability Companies and Special Business Forms

Our government allows entrepreneurs to choose from a variety of business organizational forms. In selecting among them, businesspersons are motivated to choose organizational forms that limit their liability. Limited liability may allow them to take more business risk, which is associated with the potential for higher profits.

A relatively new and increasingly common form of business organization is the *limited liability company (LLC)*. LLCs have become the organizational form of choice among many small businesses. Other special business forms include joint ventures, syndicates, joint stock companies, business trusts, and cooperatives.

38–1 The Limited Liability Company

A **limited liability company (LLC)** is a hybrid that combines the limited liability aspects of a corporation and the tax advantages of a partnership. The LLC has been available for only a few decades, but it has become the preferred structure for many small businesses.

LLCs are governed by state statutes, which vary from state to state. In an attempt to create more uniformity, the National Conference of Commissioners on Uniform State Laws issued the Uniform Limited Liability Company Act (ULLCA). Less than one-fifth of the states have adopted it, however. Thus, the law governing LLCs remains far from uniform.

Nevertheless, some provisions are common to most state statutes. We base our discussion of LLCs on these common elements.

38–1a The Nature of the LLC

LLCs share many characteristics with corporations. Like corporations, LLCs must be formed and operated in compliance with state law. Like the shareholders of a corporation, the owners of an LLC, who are called **members,** enjoy limited liability [ULLCA 303].[1]

Limited Liability of Members Members of LLCs are shielded from personal liability in most situations. In other words, the liability of members is normally limited to the amount of their investments.

An exception arises when a member has significantly contributed to the LLC's tortious conduct. ■ **CASE IN POINT 38.1** Randy Coley, the sole member and manager of East Coast Cablevision, LLC, installed cable television systems for many hotels and resorts. Coley established a DIRECTV Satellite Master Antenna Television (SMATV) account in the name of Massanutten Resort. The system provided programming to 168 timeshare units, as well as to the resort's bar, golf shop, lobbies, and waterpark. The bill for the resort's account was sent to (and paid by) East Coast Cablevision, which in turn billed the customers.

Over time, East Coast Cablevision began providing cable services to additional customers using the resort's SMATV account but did not pay DIRECTV for these other customers. Ultimately, another cable dealer affiliated with DIRECTV sued Coley for not paying for all of the DIRECTV programming transmissions that East Coast's customers had received. The court held that because Coley had played a direct role in the unauthorized transmissions, he could be held personally liable for them.[2] ■

When Liability May Be Imposed The members of an LLC, like the shareholders in a corporation, can lose their limited personal liability in certain circumstances. For instance, when an individual guarantees payment of

---

[1]. Members of an LLC can also bring derivative actions, which you will read about in regard to corporations, on behalf of the LLC [ULLCA 101]. As with a corporate shareholder's derivative suit, any damages recovered go to the LLC, not to the members personally.

[2]. *Sky Cable, LLC v. Coley,* ___ F.Supp.3d ___, 2013 WL 3517337 (W.D.Va. 2013).

a business loan to the LLC, that individual is personally liable for the business's obligation. In addition, if an LLC member fails to comply with certain formalities, such as by commingling personal and business funds, a court can impose personal liability.

Under various principles of corporate law, courts may hold the owners of a business liable for its debts. On rare occasions, for instance, courts ignore the corporate structure ("pierce the corporate veil") to expose the shareholders to personal liability when it is required to achieve justice.

Similarly, courts will sometimes pierce the veil of an LLC to hold its members personally liable. Note, however, that courts have reserved piercing the veil of an LLC for circumstances that are clearly extraordinary. There must normally be some flagrant disregard of the LLC formalities, as well as fraud or malfeasance on the part of the LLC member.

■ **CASE IN POINT 38.2** Tom and Shannon Brown purchased a new home in Hattiesburg, Mississippi, from Ray Richard and Nick Welch. Richard had hired Waldron Properties, LLC (WP), to build the home. Several years later, cracks began to develop in the walls of the Browns' home as a result of defects in the construction of the foundation. The Browns sued Murray Waldron, the sole member of WP, for breach of warranty under the state's New Home Warranty Act (NHWA). Because the required NHWA notice they had received when they bought the home was signed by Waldron personally, they claimed that Waldron was liable personally.

The trial court found that WP, not Waldron individually, was the builder of the Browns' home. The Browns appealed. They contended that even if WP was the builder, the court should pierce the veil of the LLC and hold Waldron personally liable. The state appellate court disagreed and affirmed the lower court's ruling. The Browns had not entered into a contract with either Waldron or WP. There was not sufficient evidence that Waldron had disregarded LLC formalities or had engaged in fraud or other misconduct to justify piercing the LLC's veil to hold him personally liable.[3] ■

Other Similarities to Corporations Another similarity between corporations and LLCs is that LLCs are legal entities apart from their owners. As a legal person, the LLC can sue or be sued, enter into contracts, and hold title to property [ULLCA 201]. The terminology used to describe LLCs formed in other states or nations is also similar to that used in corporate law. For instance, an LLC formed in one state but doing business in another state is referred to in the second state as a *foreign LLC.*

38–1b The Formation of the LLC

LLCs are creatures of statute and thus must follow state statutory requirements.

Articles of Organization To form an LLC, **articles of organization** must be filed with a central state agency—usually the secretary of state's office [ULLCA 202].[4] Typically, the articles must include the name of the business, its principal address, the name and address of a registered agent, the members' names, and how the LLC will be managed [ULLCA 203]. The business's name must include the words *Limited Liability Company* or the initials *LLC* [ULLCA 105(a)]. Although a majority of the states permit one-member LLCs, some states require at least two members.

Preformation Contracts Businesspersons sometimes enter into contracts on behalf of a business organization that is not yet formed. Persons who are forming a corporation, for instance, may enter into contracts during the process of incorporation but before the corporation becomes a legal entity. These contracts are referred to as *preincorporation contracts.* The individual promoters who sign the contracts are bound to their terms. Once the corporation is formed and adopts the preincorporation contracts (by means of a *novation,* which substitutes a new contract for the old contract), it can enforce the contract terms.

In dealing with the preorganization contracts of LLCs, courts may apply the well-established principles of corporate law relating to preincorporation contracts. That is to say, when the promoters of an LLC enter preformation contracts, the LLC, once formed, can adopt the contracts by a novation and then enforce them.

■ **CASE IN POINT 38.3** 607 South Park, LLC, entered into an agreement to sell a hotel to 607 Park View Associates, Ltd., which then assigned the rights to the purchase to another company, 02 Development, LLC. At the time, 02 Development did not yet exist—it was legally created several months later. 607 South Park subsequently refused to sell the hotel to 02 Development, and 02 Development sued for breach of the purchase agreement.

A California appellate court ruled that LLCs should be treated the same as corporations with respect to preorganization contracts. Although 02 Development did not exist when the agreement was executed, once it came into existence, it could enforce any preorganization contract made on its behalf.[5] ■

---

3. *Brown v. Waldron,* 186 So.3d 955 (Miss.App. 2016).

4. In addition to requiring articles of organization to be filed, a few states require that a notice of the intention to form an LLC be published in a local newspaper.

5. *02 Development, LLC v. 607 South Park, LLC,* 159 Cal.App.4th 609, 71 Cal.Rptr.3d 608 (2008). See also, *Davis Wine Co. v. Vina Y Bodega Estampa, S.A.,* 823 F.Supp.2d 1159 (D.Or. 2011).

38–1c Jurisdictional Requirements

As we have seen, LLCs and corporations share several characteristics, but a significant difference between these organizational forms involves federal jurisdictional requirements. Under the federal jurisdiction statute, a corporation is deemed to be a citizen of the state where it is incorporated and maintains its principal place of business. The statute does not mention the state citizenship of partnerships, LLCs, and other unincorporated associations. The courts, however, have tended to regard these entities as citizens of every state of which their members are citizens.

The state citizenship of an LLC may come into play when a party sues the LLC based on diversity of citizenship. Remember that when parties to a lawsuit are from different states and the amount in controversy exceeds $75,000, a federal court can exercise diversity jurisdiction. *Total* diversity of citizenship must exist, however.

■ **EXAMPLE 38.4** Jen Fong, a citizen of New York, wishes to bring a suit against Skycel, an LLC formed under the laws of Connecticut. One of Skycel's members also lives in New York. Fong will not be able to bring a suit against Skycel in federal court on the basis of diversity jurisdiction because the defendant LLC is also a citizen of New York. The same would be true if Fong was bringing a suit against multiple defendants and one of the defendants lived in New York. ■

38–1d Advantages of the LLC

The LLC offers many advantages to businesspersons, which is why this form of business organization has become increasingly popular.

Limited Liability A key advantage of the LLC is the limited liability of its members. The LLC as an entity can be held liable for any loss or injury caused by the wrongful acts or omissions of its members. As we have seen, however, members themselves generally are not personally liable.

In the following case, a consumer died as a result of using an allegedly defective product made and sold by an LLC. The consumer's children sought to hold the LLC's sole member and manager personally liable for the firm's actions.

Case 38.1

Hodge v. Strong Built International, LLC

Court of Appeal of Louisiana, Third Circuit, 159 So.3d 1159 (2015).

Background and Facts Donald Hodge was hunting in a deer stand when its straps—which held Hodge high up in a tree—failed. When the straps failed, Hodge and the deer stand fell to the ground, killing Hodge. Louisiana-based Strong Built International, LLC, was the maker and seller of the deer stand, and Ken Killen was Strong Built's sole member and manager.

Hodge's children, Donald and Rachel Hodge, filed a lawsuit in a Louisiana state court against Strong Built and Killen. They sought damages on a theory of product liability for the injury and death of their father caused by the allegedly defective deer stand. Killen filed a motion for summary judgment, asserting that he was not personally liable to the Hodges. The court granted the motion and issued a summary judgment in Killen's favor, dismissing the claims against him. The Hodges appealed.

In the Language of the Court

AMY, Judge.

* * * *

* * * An LLC member or manager's liability to third parties is delineated in [Louisiana Revised Statute (La.R.S.)] 12:1320, which states:

* * * *

* * * no member, manager, employee, or agent of a limited liability company is liable in such capacity for a debt, obligation, or liability of the limited liability company.

* * * *

* * * That protection is not unlimited. Pursuant to La.R.S. 12:1320(D), *a member or manager may be subjected to personal liability for claims involving * * * breach of a professional duty or other negligent or wrongful act.* [Emphasis added.]

* * * In an affidavit, Mr. Killen asserted that he is "not an engineer, nor a licensed professional in any profession in Louisiana or any other state." Mr. Killen also asserts that he:

Case 38.1 Continues

Case 38.1 Continued

was a participant in the creation of the deer stand which * * * Strong Built International, L.L.C. manufactured and sold, but he never personally dictated or participated in the design, selection of materials used in the manufacture, or the manufacture of, or the selection of any warnings to any deer stand for the use or consumption by any consumer beyond my input and work as a manager * * * and member of * * * Strong Built International, L.L.C.

The plaintiffs offered no evidence to contradict Mr. Killen's affidavit in this regard. Accordingly, we find no basis for Mr. Killen's personal liability under the "breach of professional duty" exception.

Neither do we find sufficient evidence in the record to create a genuine issue of material fact with regard to the "other negligent or wrongful act" exception.

* * * With regard to [this exception], the member (or manager) must have a duty of care to the plaintiff. * * * That duty must be "something more" than the duties arising out of the LLC's contract with the plaintiff.

* * * *

* * * Mr. Killen states in his affidavit that not only was he not personally responsible for the design and manufacture of the deer stands while involved with Strong Built International * * * but that any involvement that he may have had was in his capacity as a member and manager. *The plaintiffs have submitted nothing to show that Mr. Killen's actions are "something more" than his duties as a member/manager of the LLC.* [Emphasis added.]

Decision and Remedy *A state intermediate appellate court affirmed the judgment in Killen's favor. Under the applicable Louisiana state LLC statute, no member or manager of an LLC is liable in that capacity for the liability of the company. There are exceptions, but the Hodges failed to show that Killen's actions went beyond his duties as a member and manager of Strong Built.*

Critical Thinking
- **Economic** *Why does the law allow—and even encourage—limits to the liability of a business organization's owners and managers for the firm's actions? Discuss.*

Flexibility in Taxation Another advantage of the LLC is its flexibility in regard to taxation. An LLC that has *two or more members* can choose to be taxed as either a partnership or a corporation. A corporate entity normally must pay income taxes on its profits, and the shareholders must then pay personal income taxes on any of those profits that are distributed as dividends. An LLC that wants to distribute profits to its members almost always prefers to be taxed as a partnership to avoid the "double taxation" that is characteristic of the corporate entity.

Unless an LLC indicates that it wishes to be taxed as a corporation, the Internal Revenue Service (IRS) automatically taxes it as a partnership. This means that the LLC, as an entity, pays no taxes. Rather, as in a partnership, profits are "passed through" the LLC to the members, who then personally pay taxes on the profits. If an LLC's members want to reinvest profits in the business rather than distribute the profits to members, however, they may prefer to be taxed as a corporation. Corporate income tax rates may be lower than personal tax rates. Part of the attractiveness of the LLC is this flexibility with respect to taxation.

An LLC that has only *one member* cannot be taxed as a partnership. For federal income tax purposes, one-member LLCs are automatically taxed as sole proprietorships unless they indicate that they wish to be taxed as corporations. With respect to state taxes, most states follow the IRS rules.

Management and Foreign Investors Another advantage of the LLC for businesspersons is the flexibility it offers in terms of business operations and management, as will be discussed shortly. Foreign investors are allowed to become LLC members, so organizing as an LLC can enable a business to attract investors from other countries. (Many nations—including France, Germany, Japan and places in Latin America—have particular business forms that provide for limited liability much like an LLC.)

38–1e Disadvantages of the LLC

The main disadvantage of the LLC is that state LLC statutes are not uniform. Therefore, businesses that operate in more than one state may not receive consistent treatment in these states.

Generally, most states apply to a foreign LLC (an LLC formed in another state) the law of the state where the LLC was formed. Difficulties can arise, though, when one state's court must interpret and apply another state's laws.

38–2 LLC Management and Operation

The members of an LLC have considerable flexibility in managing and operating the business. Here, we discuss management options, fiduciary duties owed, and the operating agreement and general operating procedures of LLCs.

38–2a Management of an LLC

Basically, LLC members have two options for managing the firm, as shown in Exhibit 38–1. The firm can be either a "member-managed" LLC or a "manager-managed" LLC. Most state LLC statutes and the ULLCA

EXHIBIT 38–1 Management of an LLC

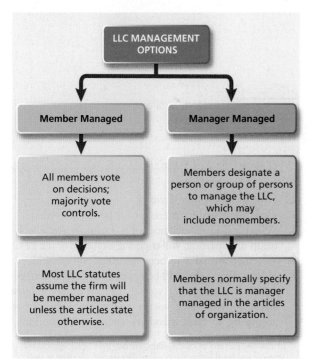

provide that unless the articles of organization specify otherwise, an LLC is assumed to be member managed [ULLCA 203(a)(6)].

In a *member-managed* LLC, all of the members participate in management, and decisions are made by majority vote [ULLCA 404(a)]. In a *manager-managed* LLC, the members designate a group of persons to manage the firm. The management group may consist of only members, both members and nonmembers, or only nonmembers.

However an LLC is managed, its managers need to be aware of the firm's potential liability under employment-discrimination laws. Those laws may sometimes extend to individuals who are not members of a protected class, as discussed in this chapter's *Managerial Strategy* feature.

38–2b Fiduciary Duties

Under the ULLCA, managers in a manager-managed LLC owe fiduciary duties (the duty of loyalty and the duty of care) to the LLC and its members [ULLCA 409(a), 409(h)]. (This same rule applies in corporate law—corporate directors and officers owe fiduciary duties to the corporation and its shareholders.) Because not all states have adopted the ULLCA, though, some state statutes provide that managers owe fiduciary duties only to the LLC and not to the LLC's members.

To whom the fiduciary duties are owed can affect the outcome of litigation. ■ **CASE IN POINT 38.5** Leslie Polk and his children, Yurii and Dusty Polk and Lezanne Proctor, formed Polk Plumbing, LLC, in Alabama. Dusty and Lezanne were managers of the LLC. Eventually, Yurii quit the firm. A year and a half later, Leslie "fired" Dusty and Lezanne and denied them access to the LLC's books and offices, but continued to operate the business.

Dusty and Lezanne filed a suit in an Alabama state court against Leslie, claiming breach of fiduciary duty. The trial court instructed the jury that it could not consider the plaintiffs' "firing" as part of their claim. Thus, although the jury found in their favor, it awarded only one dollar to each in damages. The plaintiffs appealed, and a state intermediate appellate court reversed and remanded the case for a new trial. Leslie did not have the authority under the terms of the LLC's operating agreement to fire two managers. The trial court had erred in not allowing the jury to consider the circumstances of Dusty and Lezanne's "firing" as part of their breach-of-fiduciary-duty claim.[6] ■

---

6. *Polk v. Polk,* 70 So.3d 363 (Ala.App. 2011).

Can a Person Who Is Not a Member of a Protected Class Sue for Discrimination?

Under federal law and the laws of most states, discrimination in employment based on race, color, religion, national origin, gender, age, or disability is prohibited. Persons who are members of these protected classes can sue if they are subjected to discrimination. But can a person subjected to discrimination bring a lawsuit if he is not a member of a protected class, even though managers and other employees believe that he is? This somewhat unusual situation occurred in New Jersey.

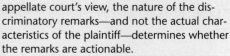

Courts in New Jersey

Myron Cowher worked at Carson & Roberts Site Construction & Engineering, Inc. For more than a year, at least two of his supervisors directed almost daily barrages of anti-Semitic remarks at him. They believed that he was Jewish, although his actual background was German-Irish and Lutheran.

Cowher brought a suit against the supervisors and the construction company, claiming a hostile work environment. The trial court, however, ruled that he did not have standing to sue under New Jersey law because he was not Jewish and, thus, was not a member of a protected class. Cowher appealed.

The appellate court disagreed with the trial court. The court ruled that if Cowher could prove that the discrimination "would not have occurred but for the perception that he was Jewish," his claim was covered by New Jersey's antidiscrimination law.[a] Thus, in the

appellate court's view, the nature of the discriminatory remarks—and not the actual characteristics of the plaintiff—determines whether the remarks are actionable.

Another New Jersey court followed the precedent set by the *Cowher* case to allow Shi-Juan Lin, a Chinese worker whose fiancé and child were black, to recover for racial discrimination. The employer created a hostile work environment by allowing Lin's supervisor to constantly use the "n" word at work. The employer knew that even though Lin was not black, she was hurt by the supervisor's remarks. Therefore, the court affirmed an administrative law judge's award of damages for pain and suffering, plus attorneys' fees.[b]

Business Questions

1. *Should a manager for an LLC respond to employee complaints of discrimination any differently than a manager at a corporation, a partnership, or a sole proprietorship? Why or why not?*

2. *How can a company, whether an LLC or some other business form, reduce the chances of discrimination lawsuits?*

a. *Cowher v. Carson & Roberts*, 425 N.J.Super. 285, 40 A.3d 1171 (2012). See also, *Sheridan v. Egg Harbor Township Board of Education*, 2015 WL 9694404 (N.J.Sup.Ct. 2016), involving a plaintiff who alleged discrimination based on obesity.

b. *Lin v. Dane Construction Co.*, 2014 WL 8131876 (N.J.Super.A.D. 2015).

38–2c The LLC Operating Agreement

The members of an LLC can decide how to operate the various aspects of the business by forming an **operating agreement** [ULLCA 103(a)]. In many states, an operating agreement is not required for an LLC to exist, and if there is one, it need not be in writing. Generally, though, LLC members should protect their interests by creating a written operating agreement.

Operating agreements typically contain provisions relating to the following areas:

1. Management and how future managers will be chosen or removed. (Although most LLC statutes are silent on this issue, the ULLCA provides that members

may choose and remove managers by majority vote [ULLCA 404(b)(3)].)

2. How profits will be divided.
3. How membership interests may be transferred.
4. Whether the dissociation of a member, such as by death or departure, will trigger dissolution of the LLC.
5. Whether formal members' meetings will be held.
6. How voting rights will be apportioned. (If the agreement does not cover voting, LLC statutes in most states provide that voting rights are apportioned according to each member's capital contributions.[7]

7. In contrast, partners in a partnership generally have equal rights in management and equal voting rights unless they specify otherwise in their partnership agreement.

EXHIBIT 38–2 Provisions Commonly Included in an LLC Operating Agreement

Management	Sets forth who will manage the LLC and how future managers will be chosen or removed. (The ULLCA provides that members may choose and remove managers by majority vote.)
Profits	Establishes how profits will be divided among members.
Membership	Specifies how membership interests may be transferred.
Dissociation and Dissolution	Clarifies which events cause the dissociation of a member—such as by death or retirement—and trigger the LLC's dissolution. Provides a method of calculating a buyout price for a member's dissociation.
Member Meetings	Determines whether or not formal members' meetings will be held.
Voting Rights	Details how voting rights will be apportioned, such as according to each member's capital contribution or by allowing one vote for each member.

Some states provide that, in the absence of an agreement to the contrary, each member has one vote.)

The provisions commonly included in operating agreements are also shown in Exhibit 38–2.

If a dispute arises and there is no agreement covering the topic under dispute, the state LLC statute will govern the outcome. For instance, most LLC statutes provide that if the members have not specified how profits will be divided, they will be divided equally among the members. When an issue is not covered by an operating agreement or by an LLC statute, the courts often apply principles of partnership law.

Of course, LLC members are bound by the operating agreement that they make, as the following case illustrates.

Case 38.2

Mekonen v. Zewdu

Court of Appeals of Washington, 179 Wash.App. 1042 (2014).

Background and Facts Green Cab Taxi and Disabled Service Association LLC ("Green Cab") is a taxi service company in King County, Washington. The operating agreement requires the members to pay weekly fees. Members who do not pay are in default and must return their taxi licenses to the company. In addition, a member in default cannot hold a seat on the board or withdraw from the company without the consent of all of the members.

Case 38.2 Continues

A disagreement arose among the members concerning the company's management, and several members, including Shumet Mekonen, withdrew from the company without the consent of the other members. Both sides continued to drive under the Green Cab name.

Mekonen's group filed a suit in a Washington state court against a group of members who had not withdrawn, including Dessie Zewdu. In part, the Mekonen group sought the right to operate as Green Cab. The court held that the plaintiffs could not represent themselves as Green Cab and ordered them to return their taxi licenses to the company. The plaintiffs appealed the order to return their licenses.

In the Language of the Court

LAU, J. [Judge]

* * * *

* * * The [lower] court found in defendants' favor regarding * * * the right of management and control over Green Cab. It found plaintiffs had no right to represent themselves as part of Green Cab's management or to operate under Green Cab's name.

* * * *

* * * Plaintiffs seek to retain the taxicab licenses affixed to the cars they own. According to Paragraph 6.4 of the LLC Operating Agreement, "the Company shall hold all rights to any taxi and other licenses and permits necessary to operate its vehicles." *The Plaintiffs have no right to use the taxicab licenses unless they are members of Green Cab LLC in good standing and are making any contributions toward the company's operating expenses that the board of directors deems necessary.* Plaintiffs admit that they withdrew their membership from Green Cab LLC and that they have paid no weekly fees since [their withdrawal]. As a result, the Plaintiffs have no legal right to retain the King County taxicab licenses currently in their possession. [Emphasis added.]

* * * The [lower] court deemed the members "defaulting members."

* * * *

* * * Plaintiffs admitted to default both in failing to make weekly payments and in withdrawing from the company in violation of article 5.6 of the operating agreement. That article states, "A Member may not withdraw as a Member prior to dissolution and commencement of winding up of the Company * * * without the written consent of all the other Members." The trial court imposed relief that was reasonably calculated to install defendants as the proper group to manage Green Cab and to preserve their interests in operating the company * * * . Given the relative interests of the parties and the LLC, the trial court acted well within its discretion to order plaintiffs to return their taxi licenses.

Decision and Remedy *A state intermediate appellate court upheld the lower court's order to the plaintiffs to return their taxi licenses to Green Cab. Under the provisions of the company's operating agreement, the plaintiffs, as "defaulting members," had no right to retain and use the licenses.*

Critical Thinking

- **What If the Facts Were Different?** *Suppose that Green Cab had maintained a company Web site on which it posted its operating agreement, conducted all internal company business, and offered a forum where members could vent their complaints. How might the result have been different? Why?*
- **Legal Environment** *During discovery, the plaintiffs were asked to answer requests for admission, but they did not respond. Does it seem likely that their failure to answer affected the outcome? Why or why not?*

38–3 Dissociation and Dissolution of an LLC

Recall that in a partnership, *dissociation* occurs when a partner ceases to be associated in the carrying on of the partnership business. The same concept applies to LLCs. And like a partner in a partnership, a member of an LLC has the *power* to dissociate at any time but may not have the *right* to dissociate.

Under the ULLCA, the events that trigger a member's dissociation from an LLC are similar to the events causing a partner to be dissociated under the Uniform Partnership Act (UPA). These include voluntary withdrawal, expulsion by other members, court order, incompetence, bankruptcy, and death. Generally, if a member dies or otherwise dissociates from an LLC, the other members may continue to carry on the LLC business unless the operating agreement provides otherwise.

38–3a Effects of Dissociation

When a member dissociates from an LLC, he or she loses the right to participate in management and the right to act as an agent for the LLC. The member's duty of loyalty to the LLC also terminates, and the duty of care continues only with respect to events that occurred before dissociation.

Generally, the dissociated member also has a right to have his or her interest in the LLC bought out by the other members. The LLC's operating agreement may contain provisions establishing a buyout price. If it does not, the member's interest is usually purchased at fair value. In states that have adopted the ULLCA, the LLC must purchase the interest at fair value within 120 days after the dissociation.

If the member's dissociation violates the LLC's operating agreement, it is considered legally wrongful, and the dissociated member can be held liable for damages caused by the dissociation. ■ **EXAMPLE 38.6** Chadwick and Barrow are members in an LLC. Chadwick manages the accounts, and Barrow, who has many connections in the community and is a skilled investor, brings in the business. If Barrow wrongfully dissociates from the LLC, the LLC's business will suffer, and Chadwick can hold Barrow liable for the loss of business resulting from her withdrawal. ■

38–3b Dissolution

Regardless of whether a member's dissociation was wrongful or rightful, normally the dissociated member has no right to force the LLC to dissolve. The remaining members can opt either to continue or to dissolve the business.

Members can also stipulate in their operating agreement that certain events will cause dissolution, or they can agree that they have the power to dissolve the LLC by vote. As with partnerships, a court can order an LLC to be dissolved in certain circumstances. For instance, a court might order dissolution when the members have engaged in illegal or oppressive conduct, or when it is no longer feasible to carry on the business.

■ **CASE IN POINT 38.7** Three men—Walter Perkins, Gary Fordham, and David Thompson—formed Venture Sales, LLC, to develop a subdivision in Petal, Mississippi. Each of them contributed land and funds, resulting in total holdings of 466 acres of land and about $158,000 in cash.

Perkins, who was working as an assistant coach for the Cleveland Browns, trusted Fordham and Thompson to develop the property. More than ten years later, however, they still had not done so, although they had formed two other LLCs and developed two other subdivisions in the area.

Fordham and Thompson claimed that they did not know when they could develop Venture's property and suggested selling it at a discounted price, but Perkins disagreed. Perkins then sought a judicial dissolution of Venture Sales. The court ordered the dissolution. Because Venture Sales was not meeting the economic purpose for which it was established (developing a subdivision), continuing the business was impracticable.[8] ■

A judge's exercise of discretion to order the dissolution of an LLC was disputed in the following case.

---

8. *Venture Sales, LLC v. Perkins*, 86 So.3d 910 (Miss.Sup. 2012).

Case Analysis 38.3

Reese v. Newman

District of Columbia Court of Appeals, 131 A.3d 880 (2016).

In the Language of the Court

KING, Senior Judge:

* * * Allison Reese and * * * Nicole Newman were co-owners of ANR Construction Management, LLC * * *. Following disputes over management of the company, Newman notified Reese in writing that she intended to * * * dissolve and wind-up the LLC. Reese did not want to dissolve the LLC but preferred that Newman simply be dissociated so that Reese could continue the business herself. Newman filed an action

for judicial dissolution in [a District of Columbia court against Reese]. Reese filed a counterclaim for Newman's dissociation * * *. Following a jury trial, the jury * * * found grounds for both judicial dissolution and forced dissociation of Newman; the court, thereafter, ordered judicial dissolution of the LLC. * * * Reese appeals.

* * * *

Reese argues that the trial court erred when it purported to use discretion in choosing between dissolution of the

LLC, as proposed by Newman, and forcing dissociation of Newman from the LLC, as proposed by Reese. Reese argues that the [District of Columbia (D.C.)] statute [governing dissociation from an LLC] does not allow for any discretion by the court, and that, in fact, the statute mandates that the court order dissociation of Newman based on the jury's findings.

In matters of statutory interpretation, we review the trial court's decision

Case 38.3 Continues

Case 38.3 Continued

de novo. Our analysis starts with the plain language of the statute, as the general rule of statutory interpretation is that the intent of the lawmaker is to be found in the language that he has used. To that end, *the words of the statute should be construed according to their ordinary sense and with the meaning commonly attributed to them.* [Emphasis added.]

Reese argues that the court was required to dissociate Newman from the LLC under [D.C. Code] Section 29–806.02(5) which reads:

> A person *shall* be dissociated as a member from a limited liability company when:
> * * * *
> (5) On application by the company, the person is expelled as a member by judicial order because the person has:
> (A) Engaged, or is engaging, in wrongful conduct that has adversely and materially affected, or will adversely and materially affect, the company's activities and affairs;
> (B) Willfully or persistently committed, or is willfully and persistently committing, a material breach of the operating agreement or the person's duties or obligations under Section 29–804.09; or
> (C) Engaged in, or is engaging, in conduct relating to the company's activities which makes it not reasonably practicable to carry on the activities with the person as a member.

Reese's interpretation of the statute is that, upon application to the court by a company, a judge shall dissociate a member of an LLC, when that member commits any one of the actions described in subsections (5)(A)-(C).

* * * While the introductory language of Section 29–806.02 does use the word "shall"—that command is in no way

directed at the trial judge. It reads, "a person shall be dissociated * * * when," and then goes on to recite fifteen separate circumstances describing different occasions when a person shall be dissociated from an LLC. That is to say, when one of the events described in subparagraphs (1) through (15) occurs, the member shall be dissociated. Subparagraph (5), however, is merely one instance for which a person shall be dissociated*;* that is, when and if a judge has ordered a member expelled because she finds that any conditions under (5)(A)-(C) have been established. In other words, the command in the introductory language is not directed at the trial judge, it is directed at all the circumstances set forth in subparagraphs (1) through (15) * * * . There is nothing in the language of Section 29–806.02(5) that strips a judge of her discretion because it does not require the judge to expel the member if any of the enumerated conditions are established. In short, Section 29–806.02(5) means: *when a judge has used her discretion to expel a member of an LLC by judicial order, under any of the enumerated circumstances in (5)(A)-(C), that member shall be dissociated.*

* * * Although Reese argues that the language of the "dissociation" section of the District's code should be read as forcing the hand of a trial judge who finds grounds for dissociation, Reese attempts to read the "dissolution" section differently.

Reese differentiates the sections by pointing to the dissolution section's express authorization to order a remedy other than dissolution in Section 29–807.01(b) which provides: "in a proceeding brought under subsection (a)(5) of this section, the * * * Court may order a remedy other than dissolution."

While we are satisfied that judicial dissolution of an LLC is discretionary under this statute, Reese's attempt to buttress [reinforce] her argument that Section 29–806.02(5) is compulsory by pointing to this express provision in the dissolution section and the absence of a similar express provision in the dissociation section is unavailing. First, * * * the only "shall" in the dissociation section is in the introductory language, and the same "shall" can be found in the same place, in the dissolution section: "a limited liability company is dissolved, and its activities and affairs *shall be wound up,* upon the occurrence of any of the following." If that language does not make the rest of the section mandatory in the dissolution section, and we are persuaded that it does not, it cannot be said that the "shall" in the introduction of the dissociation section does the opposite.

* * * *

In sum, we hold that Section 29–806.02(5) can only be interpreted to mean: when a judge finds that any of the events in (5)(A)-(C) have taken place, she may (*i.e.,* has discretion to) expel by judicial order a member of an LLC, and when a judge has done so the member shall be dissociated. *Moreover, when both grounds for dissociation of a member and dissolution of the LLC exist, the trial judge has discretion to choose either alternative.* [Emphasis added.]

Here, the jury * * * found that grounds were present for either outcome. The trial judge acknowledged that both options were on the table and then exercised her discretion in ordering that dissolution take place. We find no reason to disturb that order.

* * * *

Accordingly, the judgment in this appeal is therefore affirmed.

Legal Reasoning Questions

1. What dispute gave rise to the action filed in the court in this case? How did that dispute lead to the issue on appeal?

2. What is the role of an appellate court when reviewing the exercise of discretion by a trial court?

3. Newman alleged that after she delivered her notice to dissolve ANR, Reese locked her out of the LLC's bank accounts, blocked her access to the LLC's files and e-mail, and ended her salary and health benefits. Did any of the jury's findings support these allegations? Explain.

38–3c Winding Up

When an LLC is dissolved, any members who did not wrongfully dissociate may participate in the winding up process. To wind up the business, members must collect, liquidate, and distribute the LLC's assets.

Members may preserve the assets for a reasonable time to optimize their return, and they continue to have the authority to perform reasonable acts in conjunction with winding up. In other words, the LLC will be bound by the reasonable acts of its members during the winding up process.

Once all of the LLC's assets have been sold, the proceeds are distributed. Debts to creditors are paid first (including debts owed to members who are creditors of the LLC). The members' capital contributions are returned next, and any remaining amounts are then distributed to members in equal shares or according to their operating agreement.

38–4 Special Business Forms

Besides the business forms already discussed in this unit, several other forms can be used to organize a business. For the most part, these special business forms are hybrid organizations—that is, they combine features of other organizational forms, such as partnerships and corporations. These forms include joint ventures, syndicates, joint stock companies, business trusts, and cooperatives.

38–4a Joint Venture

In a **joint venture,** two or more persons or business entities combine their efforts or their property for a single transaction or project or a related series of transactions or projects. For instance, when several contractors combine their resources to build and sell houses in a single development, their relationship is a joint venture. Unless otherwise agreed, joint venturers share profits and losses equally and have an equal voice in controlling the project.

Joint ventures range in size from very small activities to multimillion-dollar joint actions carried out by some of the world's largest corporations. Large organizations often form joint ventures with other enterprises to produce new products or services. ■ **EXAMPLE 38.8** Intel Corporation and Micron Technology, Inc., formed a joint venture to manufacture NAND flash memory. NAND is a data-storage chip widely used in digital cameras, cell phones, and portable music players. ■

Similarities to Partnerships A joint venture resembles a partnership and is taxed like a partnership. For this reason, most courts apply the same principles to joint ventures as they apply to partnerships. Joint venturers owe each other the same fiduciary duties, including the duty of loyalty, that partners owe each other. Thus, if one of the venturers secretly buys land that was to be acquired by the joint venture, the other joint venturers may be awarded damages for the breach of loyalty.

Liability and Management Rights. A joint venturer can be held personally liable for the venture's debts (because joint venturers share losses as well as profits). Like partners, joint venturers have equal rights to manage the activities of the enterprise, but they can agree to give control of the operation to one of the members.

Authority to Enter Contracts. Joint venturers have authority as agents to enter into contracts that will bind the joint venture. ■ **CASE IN POINT 38.9** Murdo Cameron developed components for replicas of vintage P-51 Mustang planes. Cameron and Douglas Anderson agreed in writing to collaborate on the design and manufacture of two P-51s, one for each of them.

Without Cameron's knowledge, Anderson borrowed funds from SPW Associates, LLP, to finance the construction, using the first plane as security for the loan. After Anderson built one plane, he defaulted on the loan. SPW filed a lawsuit to obtain possession of the aircraft.

The court ruled that Anderson and Cameron had entered into a joint venture and that the plane was the venture's property. Under partnership law, partners have the power as agents to bind the partnership. Because this principle applies to joint ventures, Anderson had the authority to grant SPW a security interest in the plane, and SPW was entitled to take possession of the plane.[9] ■

Differences from Partnerships Joint ventures differ from partnerships in several important ways. A joint venture is typically created for a single project or series of transactions, whereas a partnership usually (though not always) involves an ongoing business. Also, unlike most partnerships, a joint venture normally terminates when the project or the transaction for which it was formed has been completed.

Because the activities of a joint venture are more limited than the business of a partnership, the members of a joint venture are presumed to have less power to bind their co-venturers. Thus, the members of a joint venture have less implied and apparent authority than the

---

9. *SPW Associates, LLP v. Anderson,* 2006 ND 159, 718 N.W.2d 580 (N.D.Sup.Ct. 2006).

partners in a partnership (each of whom is treated as an agent of the other partners). In *Case in Point 38.9,* for instance, if Anderson's loan agreement with SPW had not been directly related to the business of building vintage planes, the court might have concluded that Anderson lacked the authority to bind the joint venture.

38–4b Syndicate

In a **syndicate,** or *investment group,* several individuals or firms join together to finance a particular project. Syndicates can finance projects such as the construction of a shopping center or the purchase of a professional basketball franchise. The form of such groups varies considerably.

A syndicate may be organized as a corporation or as a general or limited partnership. In some situations, the members do not have a legally recognized business arrangement but merely purchase and own property jointly.

38–4c Joint Stock Company

A **joint stock company** is a true hybrid of a partnership and a corporation. It has many characteristics of a corporation in that (1) its ownership is represented by transferable shares of stock, (2) it is managed by directors and officers of the company or association, and (3) it can have a perpetual existence.

Most of its other features, however, are more characteristic of a partnership, and it generally is treated as a partnership. Like a partnership, a joint stock company is formed by agreement (not statute). Property usually is held in the names of the owners, who are called shareholders, and they have personal liability. In a joint stock company, however, shareholders are not considered to be agents of each other, as they would be in a true partnership.

38–4d Business Trust

A **business trust** is created by a written trust agreement that sets forth the interests of the beneficiaries and the obligations and powers of the trustees. Legal ownership and management of the trust's property stay with one or more of the trustees, and the profits are distributed to the beneficiaries.

A business trust resembles a corporation in many respects. Beneficiaries of the trust, for instance, are not personally responsible for the trust's debts or obligations. In fact, in a number of states, business trusts must pay corporate taxes.

38–4e Cooperative

A **cooperative** is an association that is organized to provide an economic service to its members (or shareholders). It may or may not be incorporated. Most cooperatives are organized under state statutes for cooperatives, general business corporations, or LLCs. Co-ops range in size from small, local cooperatives to national businesses such as Ace Hardware and Land O'Lakes, a well-known producer of dairy products.

The cooperative form of business is generally adopted by groups of individuals who wish to pool their resources to gain some advantage in the marketplace. *Consumer purchasing co-ops,* for instance, are formed to obtain lower prices through quantity discounts. *Seller marketing co-ops* are formed to control the market and thereby enable members to sell their goods at higher prices.

Incorporated Co-ops Generally, an incorporated cooperative distributes dividends, or profits, to its owners on the basis of their transactions with the cooperative rather than on the basis of the amount of capital they contributed. Members of incorporated cooperatives have limited liability, as do shareholders of corporations and members of LLCs.

Unincorporated Co-ops Cooperatives that are not incorporated are often treated like partnerships. The members have joint liability for the cooperative's acts.

See Concept Summary 38.1 for a review of the types of special business forms discussed in this chapter.

Concept Summary 38.1

Special Business Forms

Joint Venture
An organization created by two or more persons in contemplation of a limited activity or a single transaction; similar to a partnership in many respects.

Syndicate
An investment group that undertakes to finance a particular project; may be organized as a corporation or as a general or limited partnership.

Joint Stock Company
A business form similar to a corporation in some respects (transferable shares of stock, management by directors and officers, perpetual existence) but otherwise resembling a partnership.

Business Trust
A business form created by a written trust agreement that sets forth the interests of the beneficiaries and the obligations and powers of the trustee(s). A business trust is similar to a corporation in many respects. Beneficiaries are not personally liable for the debts or obligations of the business trust.

Cooperative
An association organized to provide an economic service, without profit, to its members. A cooperative can take the form of a corporation or a partnership.

Reviewing: Limited Liability Companies and Special Business Forms

The city of Papagos, Arizona, had a deteriorating bridge in need of repair on a prominent public roadway. The city posted notices seeking proposals for an artistic bridge design and reconstruction. Davidson Masonry, LLC, which was owned and managed by Carl Davidson and his wife, Marilyn Rowe, decided to submit a bid to create a decorative concrete structure that incorporated artistic metalwork. They contacted Shana Lafayette, a local sculptor who specialized in large-scale metal creations, to help them design the bridge. The city selected their bridge design and awarded them the contract for a commission of $184,000.

Davidson Masonry and Lafayette then entered into an agreement to work together on the bridge project. Davidson Masonry agreed to install and pay for concrete and structural work, and Lafayette agreed to install the metalwork at her expense. They agreed that overall profits would be split, with 25 percent going to Lafayette and 75 percent going to Davidson Masonry. Lafayette designed numerous metal sculptures of trout that were incorporated into colorful decorative concrete forms designed by Rowe. Davidson performed the structural engineering. The group worked together successfully until the completion of the project. Using the information presented in the chapter, answer the following questions.

1. Would Davidson Masonry automatically be taxed as a partnership or a corporation?
2. Is Davidson Masonry member managed or manager managed?

Continues

3. When Davidson Masonry and Lafayette entered an agreement to work together, what kind of special business form was created? Explain.

4. Suppose that during construction, Lafayette entered into an agreement to rent space in a warehouse that was close to the bridge so that she could work on her sculptures near the site where they would eventually be installed. She entered into the contract without the knowledge or consent of Davidson Masonry. In this situation, would a court be likely to hold that Davidson Masonry was bound by the contract that Lafayette entered? Why or why not?

Debate This . . . *Because LLCs are essentially just partnerships with limited liability for members, all partnership laws should apply.*

Terms and Concepts

articles of organization 726
business trust 736
cooperative 736
joint stock company 736

joint venture 735
limited liability company
  (LLC) 725

member 725
operating agreement 730
syndicate 736

Issue Spotters

1. Gabriel, Harris, and Ida are members of Jeweled Watches, LLC. What are their options with respect to the management of their firm? (See *LLC Management and Operation*.)

2. Greener Delivery Company and Hiway Trucking, Inc., form a business trust. Insta Equipment Company and Jiffy Supply Corporation form a joint stock company.

Kwik Mart, Inc., and Luscious Produce, Inc., form an incorporated cooperative. What do these forms of business organization have in common? (See *Special Business Forms*.)

• **Check your answers to the Issue Spotters against the answers provided in Appendix D at the end of this text.**

Business Scenarios

38–1. Limited Liability Companies. John, Lesa, and Tabir form a limited liability company. John contributes 60 percent of the capital, and Lesa and Tabir each contribute 20 percent. Nothing is decided about how profits will be divided. John assumes that he will be entitled to 60 percent of the profits, in accordance with his contribution. Lesa and Tabir, however, assume that the profits will be divided equally. A dispute over the profits arises, and ultimately a court has to decide the issue. What law will the court apply? In most states, what will result? How could this dispute have been avoided in the first place? Discuss fully. (See *The Limited Liability Company*.)

38–2. Special Business Forms. Bateson Corp. is considering entering into contracts with two organizations. One is a

joint stock company that distributes home products east of the Mississippi River. The other is a business trust formed by a number of sole proprietors who are sellers of home products on the West Coast. Both contracts will require Bateson to make large capital outlays in order to supply the businesses with restaurant equipment. In both business organizations, at least two shareholders or beneficiaries are personally wealthy, but the organizations themselves have limited financial resources. The owner-managers of Bateson are not familiar with either form of business organization. Because each form resembles a corporation, they are concerned about potential limits on liability in the event that either organization breaches the contract by failing to pay for the equipment. Discuss fully Bateson's concern. (See *Special Business Forms*.)

Business Case Problems

38–3. Joint Venture. Holiday Isle Resort & Marina, Inc., operated four restaurants, five bars, and various food kiosks at its resort in Islamorada, Florida. Holiday entered into a "joint-venture agreement" with Rip Tosun to operate a fifth

restaurant, called "Rip's—A Place for Ribs." The agreement gave Tosun authority over the employees and "full authority as to the conduct of the business." It also prohibited Tosun from competing with Rip's without Holiday's approval but did not prevent Holiday from competing. Later, Tosun sold half of his interest in Rip's to Thomas Hallock. Soon, Tosun and Holiday opened the Olde Florida Steakhouse next to Rip's. Holiday stopped serving breakfast at Rip's and diverted employees and equipment from Rip's to the steakhouse, which then started offering breakfast. Hallock filed a suit in a Florida state court against Holiday. Did Holiday breach the joint-venture agreement? Did it breach the duties that joint venturers owe each other? Explain. [*Hallock v. Holiday Isle Resort & Marina, Inc.,* 4 So.3d 17 (Fla.App. 3 Dist. 2009)] (See *Special Business Forms.*)

38–4. Limited Liability Companies. Coco Investments, LLC, and other investors participated in a condominium conversion project to be managed by Zamir Manager River Terrace, LLC. The participants entered into a new LLC agreement for the project. The investors subsequently complained that Zamir had failed to disclose its plans for dramatic changes involving higher-than-expected construction costs and delays. They also claimed that Zamir had failed to provide financial information and had restructured loans in a manner that allowed Zamir representatives to avoid personal liability. The investors sued Zamir on various grounds, including breach of contract and breach of fiduciary duty. Zamir moved for summary judgment. How should the court rule? Explain. [*Coco Investments, LLC v. Zamir Manager River Terrace, LLC,* 26 Misc.3d 1231 (N.Y.Sup. 2010)] (See *The Limited Liability Company.*)

38–5. LLC Dissolution. Walter Van Houten and John King formed 1545 Ocean Avenue, LLC, with each managing 50 percent of the business. Its purpose was to renovate an existing building and construct a new commercial building. Van Houten and King quarreled over many aspects of the work on the properties. King claimed that Van Houten paid the contractors too much for the work performed. As the projects neared completion, King demanded that the LLC be dissolved and that Van Houten agree to a buyout. Because the parties could not agree on a buyout, King sued for dissolution. The trial court enjoined (prevented) further work on the projects until the dispute was settled. As the ground for dissolution, King cited the fights over management decisions. There was no claim of fraud or frustration of purpose. The trial court ordered that the LLC be dissolved, and Van Houten appealed. Should either of the owners be forced to dissolve the LLC before the completion of its purpose—that is, before the building projects are finished? Explain. [*In re 1545 Ocean Avenue, LLC,* 893 N.Y.S.2d 590 (N.Y.A.D. 2 Dept. 2010)] (See *Dissociation and Dissolution of an LLC.*)

38–6. Business Case Problem with Sample Answer— LLC Operation. After Hurricane Katrina struck the Gulf Coast, James Williford, Patricia Mosser, Marquetta Smith, and Michael Floyd formed Bluewater Logistics, LLC, to bid on construction contracts. Under Mississippi law, every member of a member-managed LLC is entitled to participate in managing the business. The operating agreement provided for a "super majority" 75 percent vote to remove a member who

"has either committed a felony or under any other circumstances that would jeopardize the company status" as a contractor. After Bluewater had completed more than $5 million in contracts, Smith told Williford that she, Mosser, and Floyd were exercising their "super majority" vote to fire him. No reason was provided. Williford sued Bluewater and the other members. Did Smith, Mosser, and Floyd breach the state LLC statute, their fiduciary duties, or the Bluewater operating agreements? Discuss. [*Bluewater Logistics, LLC v. Williford,* 55 So.3d 148 (Miss. 2011)] (See *LLC Management and Operation.*)

• For a sample answer to Problem 38–6, go to Appendix E at the end of this text.

38–7. Jurisdictional Requirements. Fadal Machining Centers, LLC, and MAG Industrial Automation Centers, LLC, sued a New Jersey–based corporation, Mid-Atlantic CNC, Inc., in federal district court. Ten percent of MAG was owned by SP MAG Holdings, a Delaware LLC. SP MAG had six members, including a Delaware limited partnership called Silver Point Capital Fund and a Delaware LLC called SPCP Group III. In turn, Silver Point and SPCP Group had a common member, Robert O'Shea, who was a New Jersey citizen. Assuming that the amount in controversy exceeds $75,000, does the district court have diversity jurisdiction? Why or why not? [*Fadal Machining Centers, LLC v. Mid-Atlantic CNC, Inc.,* 2012 WL 8669 (9th Cir. 2012)] (See *The Limited Liability Company.*)

38–8. Jurisdictional Requirements. Siloam Springs Hotel, LLC, operates a Hampton Inn in Siloam Springs, Arkansas. Siloam bought insurance from Century Surety Co. to cover the hotel. When guests suffered injuries due to a leak of carbon monoxide from the heating element of an indoor swimming pool, Siloam filed a claim with Century. Century denied coverage, which Siloam disputed. Century asked a federal district court to resolve the dispute. In asserting that the federal court had jurisdiction, Century noted that the amount in controversy exceeded $75,000 and that the parties had complete diversity of citizenship. Century is "a corporation organized under the laws of Ohio, with its principal place of business in Michigan," and Siloam is "a corporation organized under the laws of Oklahoma, with its principal place of business in Arkansas." Can the court exercise diversity jurisdiction in this case? Discuss. [*Siloam Springs Hotel, L.L.C. v. Century Surety Co.,* 781 F.3d 1233 (10th Cir. 2015)] (See *The Limited Liability Company.*)

38–9. Special Business Forms. Randall and Peggy Norman operated a dairy farm in Pine River, Minnesota. About ten years after the operation was begun, the cows started to experience health issues. Over the next eighteen years, the herd suffered many serious health problems. Eventually, stray electrical voltage—which can use cow hooves as an unintended pathway, causing health issues—was detected. By then, milk production in the Normans' herd had declined from 27 percent above the state average to 20 percent below it. The Normans filed a suit in a Minnesota state court against Crow Wing

Cooperative Power & Light Company, a member-owned electrical cooperative that provided electricity to the Normans' farm. If Crow Wing is found to have acted negligently, can its members be held jointly liable for the cooperative's acts? Explain. [*Norman v. Crow Wing Co-operative Power & Light Co.,* __ N.W.2d __, 2016 WL 687472 (Minn.App. 2016)] (See *Special Business Forms.*)

38–10. A Question of Ethics—Limited Liability Companies.

 Blushing Brides, LLC, a publisher of wedding planning magazines in Columbus, Ohio, opened an account with Gray Printing Co. in July 2000. On behalf of Blushing Brides, Louis Zacks, the firm's member-manager, signed a credit agreement that identified the firm as the "purchaser" and required payment within thirty days. Despite the agreement, Blushing Brides typically took up to six months to pay the full amount for its orders. Gray printed and shipped 10,000 copies of a fall/winter 2001 issue for Blushing Brides but had not been paid when the firm ordered 15,000 copies of a spring/summer 2002 issue. Gray refused to print the new order without an assurance of payment. On May 22, Zacks signed a promissory note payable to Gray within thirty days for $14,778, plus interest at 6 percent per year. Gray printed the new order but by October had been paid only $7,500. Gray filed a suit in an Ohio state court against Blushing Brides and Zacks to collect the balance. [Gray Printing Co. v. Blushing Brides, LLC, 2006 WL 832587 (Ohio App. 2006)] (See *The Limited Liability Company.*)

(a) Under what circumstances is a member of an LLC liable for the firm's debts? In this case, is Zacks personally liable under the credit agreement for the unpaid amount on Blushing Brides' account? Did Zacks's promissory note affect the parties' liability on the account? Explain.

(b) Should a member of an LLC assume an ethical responsibility to meet the obligations of the firm? Discuss.

(c) Gray shipped only 10,000 copies of the spring/summer 2002 issue of Blushing Brides' magazine, waiting for the publisher to identify a destination for the other 5,000 copies. The magazine had a retail price of $4.50 per copy. Did Gray have a legal or ethical duty to "mitigate the damages" by attempting to sell or otherwise distribute these copies itself? Why or why not?

38–11. Special Case Analysis—LLC Dissolution.

Go to Case Analysis 38.3, *Reese v. Newman.* Read the excerpt and answer the following questions.

(a) Issue: Which party's choice between two alternatives was at the heart of the issue on the appeal of the *Reese* case?

(b) Rule of Law: What rules of interpretation did the appellate court use to construe the language of the statutes that created those alternatives?

(c) Applying the Rule of Law: How did the court construe the language of those statutes?

(d) Conclusion: How did the court's construction of that language lead to the result?

Legal Reasoning Group Activity

38–12. Fiduciary Duties in LLCs.

Newbury Properties Group owns, manages, and develops real property. Jerry Stoker and the Stoker Group, Inc. (the Stokers), also develop real property. Newbury entered into agreements with the Stokers concerning a large tract of property in Georgia. The parties formed Bellemare, LLC, to develop various parcels of the tract for residential purposes. The operating agreement of Bellemare indicated that "no Member shall be accountable to the LLC or to any other Member with respect to any other business or activity even if the business or activity competes with the LLC's business." Later, when the Newbury group

contracted with other parties to develop parcels within the tract in competition with Bellemare, LLC, the Stokers sued, alleging breach of fiduciary duty. (See *LLC Management and Operation.*)

(a) The first group will discuss and outline the fiduciary duties that the members of an LLC owe to each other.

(b) The second group will determine whether the terms of an operating agreement can alter these fiduciary duties.

(c) The last group will decide in whose favor the court should rule in this situation.

CHAPTER 39

Corporate Formation and Financing

The corporation is a creature of statute. A corporation is an artificial being, existing only in law and being neither tangible nor visible. Its existence generally depends on state law, although some corporations, especially public organizations, are created under federal law. Each state has its own body of corporate law, and these laws are not entirely uniform.

The Model Business Corporation Act (MBCA) is a codification of modern corporation law that has been influential in shaping state corporation statutes. Today, the majority of state statutes are guided by the most recent version of the MBCA, often referred to as the Revised Model Business Corporation Act (RMBCA).

Keep in mind, however, that there is considerable variation among the laws of states that have used the MBCA or the RMBCA as a basis for their statutes. In addition, several states do not follow either act. Consequently, individual state corporation laws should be relied on to determine corporate law rather than the MBCA or RMBCA.

39–1 The Nature and Classification of Corporations

A corporation is a legal entity created and recognized by state law. This business entity can have one or more owners (called shareholders), and it operates under a name distinct from the names of its owners. Both individuals and other businesses can be shareholders. The corporation substitutes itself for its shareholders when conducting corporate business and incurring liability. Its authority to act and the liability for its actions, however, are separate and apart from the shareholders who own it.

A corporation is recognized under U.S. law as a person—an artificial *legal person,* as opposed to a *natural person.* As a "person," it enjoys many of the same rights and privileges under state and federal law that U.S. citizens enjoy. For instance, corporations possess the same right of access to the courts as citizens and can sue or be sued. The constitutional guarantees of due process, free speech, and freedom from unreasonable searches and seizures also apply to corporations.

39–1a Corporate Personnel

In a corporation, the responsibility for the overall management of the firm is entrusted to a *board of directors,* whose members are elected by the shareholders. The board of directors makes the policy decisions and hires *corporate officers* and other employees to run the daily business operations.

When an individual purchases a share of stock in a corporation, that person becomes a shareholder and an owner of the corporation. Unlike the partners in a partnership, the body of shareholders can change constantly without affecting the continued existence of the corporation. A shareholder can sue the corporation, and the corporation can sue a shareholder. Additionally, under certain circumstances, a shareholder can sue on behalf of a corporation.

39–1b The Limited Liability of Shareholders

One of the key advantages of the corporate form is the limited liability of its owners. Normally, corporate shareholders are not personally liable for the obligations of the corporation beyond the extent of their investments.

In certain limited situations, however, a court can *pierce the corporate veil* and impose liability on shareholders for the corporation's obligations. Additionally, creditors often will not extend credit to small companies unless the shareholders assume personal liability, as guarantors, for corporate obligations.

39–1c Corporate Earnings and Taxation

When a corporation earns profits, it can either pass them on to shareholders in the form of **dividends** or retain them as profits. These **retained earnings,** if invested properly, will yield higher corporate profits in the future. In theory, higher profits will cause the price of the company's stock to rise. Individual shareholders can then reap the benefits in the capital gains they receive when they sell their stock.

Corporate Taxation Whether a corporation retains its profits or passes them on to the shareholders as dividends, those profits are subject to income taxation by various levels of government. Failure to pay taxes can lead to severe consequences. The state can suspend the organization's corporate status until the taxes are paid and can even dissolve the corporation for failing to pay taxes.

Another important aspect of corporate taxation is that corporate profits can be subject to double taxation. The company pays tax on its profits. Then, if the profits are passed on to the shareholders as dividends, the shareholders must also pay income tax on them. (This is true unless the dividends represent distributions of capital, which are returns of holders' investments in the stock of the company.) The corporation normally does not receive a tax deduction for dividends it distributes. This double-taxation feature is one of the major disadvantages of the corporate form.

Holding Companies Some U.S. corporations use holding companies to reduce or defer their U.S. income taxes. At its simplest, a **holding company** (sometimes referred to as a *parent company*) is a company whose business activity consists of holding shares in another company. Typically, the holding company is established in a low-tax or no-tax offshore jurisdiction, such as the Cayman Islands, Dubai, Hong Kong, Luxembourg, Monaco, or Panama.

Sometimes, a U.S. corporation sets up a holding company in a low-tax offshore environment and then transfers its cash, bonds, stocks, and other investments to the holding company. In general, any profits received by the holding company on these investments are taxed at the rate of the offshore jurisdiction where the company is registered. Once the profits are brought "onshore," though, they are taxed at the federal corporate income tax rate. Any payments received by the shareholders are also taxable at the full U.S. rates.

39–1d Criminal Acts

Under modern criminal law, a corporation may be held liable for the criminal acts of its agents and employees.

Although corporations cannot be imprisoned, they can be fined. (Of course, corporate directors and officers can be imprisoned, and many have been in recent years.) In addition, under sentencing guidelines for crimes committed by corporate employees (white-collar crimes), corporations can face fines amounting to hundreds of millions of dollars.

39–1e Tort Liability

A corporation is liable for the torts committed by its agents or officers within the course and scope of their employment. The doctrine of *respondeat superior* applies to corporations in the same way as it does to other agency relationships.

■ **CASE IN POINT 39.1** Mark Bloom was an officer and a director of MB Investment Partners, Inc. (MB), at the time that he formed North Hills, LP, a stock investment fund. Bloom and other MB employees used MB's offices and equipment to administer investments in North Hills.

Later, investors in North Hills requested a full redemption of their investments. By that time, however, most of the funds that had been invested were gone. North Hills had, in fact, been a Ponzi scheme that Bloom had used to finance his lavish personal lifestyle, taking at least $20 million from North Hills for his personal use.

Barry Belmont and other North Hills investors filed a suit in a federal district court against MB, alleging fraud. The court held that MB was liable for Bloom's fraud. MB appealed, and the appellate court affirmed. Tort liability can be attributed to a corporation for the acts of its agent that were committed within the scope of the agent's employment.[1] ■

Because corporations can be liable for their employees' fraud and other misconduct, companies need to be careful about whom they hire and how much they monitor or supervise their employees. Some companies are using special software designed to predict employee misconduct before it occurs, as discussed in this chapter's *Digital Update* feature.

39–1f Classification of Corporations

Corporations can be classified in several ways. The classification of a corporation normally depends on its location, purpose, and ownership characteristics, as described in the following subsections.

Domestic, Foreign, and Alien Corporations A corporation is referred to as a **domestic corporation** by its

---

1. *Belmont v. MB Investment Partners, Inc.,* 708 F.3d 470 (3d Cir. 2013).

DIGITAL UPDATE — Programs That Predict Employee Misconduct

Monitoring employees' e-mails and phone conversations at work is generally legal.[a] But what about using software to analyze employee behavior with the goal of predicting, rather than observing, wrongdoing? Now we are entering into the digital realm of *predictive analytics*.

Spy agencies around the world today use analytic software to predict who will engage in a terrorist act, where it will happen, and when. Software applied to data mining of employee behavior (usually just online) actually has been around for several years as well. For example, Amazon started using employee-monitoring programs to predict who might quit. But only recently have such programs been used to predict misconduct.

JPMorgan Chase Attempts to Reduce Its Legal Bills

JPMorgan, the world's largest private financial institution, also is perhaps the world's largest purchaser of legal services in that sector. Its legal bills have exceeded $36 billion since the financial crisis of 2008. The company's management found that employees had engaged in dubious mortgage bond sales and rigged foreign exchange and energy markets, among many other transgressions. The company hired an extra 2,500 compliance officers and spent almost $750 million on compliance operations during a recent three-year period.

Now JPMorgan is using new software to identify—in advance of any wrongdoing—"rogue" employees. The software analyzes a wide range of inputs on employees' behavior in an attempt to identify patterns that point to future misconduct. If successful, the program will certainly be copied by other financial institutions.

An Ethical Problem?

A former Federal Reserve Bank examiner, Mark Williams, has raised an important issue with respect to predictive analytics: "Policing intentions can be a slippery slope. Do people get a scarlet letter for something they have yet to do?" In other words, will employees be labeled as wrongdoers before they have actually done anything wrong?

Critical Thinking *Is thinking about committing a crime illegal?*

a. Electronic Communications Privacy Act, 18 U.S.C.A. Sec. 2511(2)(d).

---

home state (the state in which it incorporates). A corporation formed in one state but doing business in another is referred to in the second state as a **foreign corporation.** A corporation formed in another country (say, Mexico) but doing business in the United States is referred to in the United States as an **alien corporation.**

A corporation does not have an automatic right to do business in a state other than its state of incorporation. In some instances, it must obtain a *certificate of authority* in any state in which it plans to do business. Once the certificate has been issued, the corporation generally can exercise in that state all of the powers conferred on it by its home state. If a foreign corporation does business in a state without obtaining a certificate of authority, the state can impose substantial fines and sanctions on that corporation.

Note that most state statutes specify certain activities, such as soliciting orders via the Internet, that are not considered "doing business" within the state. For instance, a foreign corporation normally does not need a certificate of authority to sell goods or services via the Internet or by mail.

What constitutes doing business within a state? In the following case, the court answered that question.

Case 39.1

Drake Manufacturing Co. v. Polyflow, Inc.

Superior Court of Pennsylvania, 2015 PA Super 16, 109 A.3d 250 (2015).

Background and Facts Drake Manufacturing Company, a Delaware corporation, entered into a contract to sell certain products to Polyflow, Inc., headquartered in Pennsylvania. Drake promised to ship the goods from Drake's plant in Sheffield, Pennsylvania, to Polyflow's place of business in Oaks, Pennsylvania, as well as to addresses in California, Canada, and Holland.

Case 39.1 Continues

When Polyflow withheld payment of about $300,000 for some of the goods, Drake filed a breach of contract suit in a Pennsylvania state court against Polyflow seeking to collect the unpaid amount. But Drake had failed to obtain a certificate of authority to do business in Pennsylvania as a foreign corporation. Polyflow asserted that this failure to register with the state deprived Drake of the capacity to bring an action against Polyflow in the state's courts. The court issued a judgment in Drake's favor. Polyflow appealed.

In the Language of the Court
Opinion by *JENKINS*, J. [Judge]:
* * * *

[15 Pennsylvania Consolidated Statutes (Pa.C.S.)] Section 4121 provides: "A foreign business corporation, before doing business in this Commonwealth, shall procure a certificate of authority to do so from the Department of State."

* * * Typical conduct requiring a certificate of authority includes maintaining an office to conduct local intrastate business [and] entering into contracts relating to local business or sales.

A corporation is not "doing business" solely because it resorts to the courts of this Commonwealth to recover an indebtedness. [Emphasis added.]
* * * *

[15 Pa.C.S.] Section 4141(a) provides in relevant part that "a nonqualified foreign business corporation doing business in this Commonwealth * * * shall not be permitted to maintain any action or proceeding in any court of this Commonwealth until the corporation has obtained a certificate of authority."
* * * *

* * * The evidence demonstrates that Drake failed to submit a certificate of authority into evidence prior to the verdict in violation of 15 Pa.C.S. Section 4121. Therefore, the trial court should not have permitted Drake to prosecute its action.

The trial court contends that Drake is exempt from the certificate of authority requirement because it merely commenced suit in Pennsylvania to collect a debt * * * . Drake did much more, however, than file suit or attempt to collect a debt. Drake maintains an office in Pennsylvania to conduct local business, conduct which typically requires a certificate of authority. Drake also entered into a contract with Polyflow, and * * * shipped couplings and portable swaging machines to Polyflow's place of business in Pennsylvania * * * . In short, *Drake's conduct was * * * regular, systematic, and extensive, * * * thus constituting the transaction of business and requiring Drake to obtain a certificate of authority.* [Emphasis added.]

We also hold that Drake needed a certificate of authority to sue Polyflow in Pennsylvania for Polyflow's failure to pay for out-of-state shipments in California, Canada and Holland. A foreign corporation that "does business" in Pennsylvania * * * must obtain a certificate in order to prosecute a lawsuit in this Commonwealth, regardless of whether the lawsuit itself concerns in-state conduct or out-of-state conduct.

Decision and Remedy *A state intermediate appellate court reversed the judgment in Drake's favor. Under Pennsylvania state statutes, Drake was required to obtain a certificate of authority to do business in that state. Drake failed to do so. The court should not have allowed Drake to prosecute its action against Polyflow.*

Critical Thinking
- **Legal Environment** *Why would the appellate court permit Polyflow to get away with not paying for delivered and presumably merchantable goods?*

Public and Private Corporations A **public corporation** is a corporation formed by the government to meet some political or governmental purpose. Cities and towns that incorporate are common examples. In addition, many federal government organizations, such as the U.S. Postal Service, the Tennessee Valley Authority, and AMTRAK, are public corporations.

Note that a public corporation is not the same as a **publicly held corporation**. A publicly held corporation (often called a *public company*) is any corporation whose shares are publicly traded in a securities market, such as the New York Stock Exchange or the NASDAQ.

Private corporations, in contrast, are created either wholly or in part for private benefit—that is, for profit. Most corporations are private. Although they may serve a public purpose, as a public electric or gas utility does, they are owned by private persons rather than by a government.[2]

---

2. The United States Supreme Court first recognized the property rights of private corporations and clarified the distinction between public and private corporations in the landmark case *Trustees of Dartmouth College v. Woodward*, 17 U.S. (4 Wheaton) 518, 4 L.Ed. 629 (1819).

Nonprofit Corporations Corporations formed for purposes other than making a profit are called *nonprofit* or *not-for-profit* corporations. Private hospitals, educational institutions, charities, and religious organizations, for instance, are frequently organized as nonprofit corporations. The nonprofit corporation is a convenient form of organization that allows various groups to own property and to form contracts without exposing the individual members to personal liability.

In some circumstances, a nonprofit corporation and its members may also be immune from liability for a personal injury caused by its negligence. Whether those circumstances were present in the following case was the question before the court.

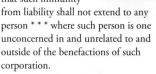

Case Analysis 39.2

Pantano v. Newark Museum

Superior Court of New Jersey, Appellate Division, __ A.3d __, 2016 WL 528771 (2016).

In the Language of the Court
PER CURIAM.
* * * *

* * * Plaintiff [Loredana Pantano] slipped and fell on icy steps at an entrance to the [Newark] Museum, suffering injuries to her back. At the time, plaintiff was employed as an immigration attorney by La Casa de Don Pedro (La Casa), a nonprofit organization located in Newark [New Jersey]. Upon arrival at her office that day, plaintiff was told by La Casa's Director of Personal Development to go to the Museum for an educational panel discussion being held as part of La Casa's fortieth anniversary celebration.

* * * The event was one of several organized to celebrate and commemorate the organization's history and role in the development of Newark. Staff members were not directly engaged in fundraising, but they were told to mingle with those attending the event, some of whom were contributors to La Casa. The Museum charged La Casa a fee for the use of the facility, specifically an auditorium to be used by the panel and those in attendance.

The Museum is a nonprofit association organized exclusively for charitable, artistic, scientific, educational, historical and cultural purposes * * * . It does, on occasion, rent its facilities to the public in order to generate income.

Plaintiff filed suit [in a New Jersey state court against the Museum] alleging the Museum was negligent in its maintenance of the premises. * * * The Museum moved for summary judgment, contending that plaintiff was a direct beneficiary of its charitable endeavors.
* * * *

* * * The judge granted the Museum's motion, and this appeal followed.

Plaintiff contends that she was not a beneficiary of the Museum's charitable purposes at the time of her fall because she was on the premises at the direction of her employer. We agree that pursuant to the [New Jersey Supreme] Court's holding in *Mayer v. Fairlawn Jewish Center*, 38 N.J. 549, 186 A.2d 274 (1962), plaintiff was not a direct recipient of the Museum's good works.
* * * *

In pertinent part, the [state Charitable Immunity Act (CIA)] provides:

No nonprofit corporation * * * shall * * * be liable to respond in damages to any person who shall suffer damage from the negligence * * * of such corporation * * * where such person is a beneficiary, to whatever degree, of the works of such nonprofit

corporation * * * ; provided, however, that such immunity from liability shall not extend to any person * * * where such person is one unconcerned in and unrelated to and outside of the benefactions of such corporation.

The CIA serves two primary purposes. *First, immunity preserves a charity's assets. Second, immunity recognizes that a beneficiary of the services of a charitable organization has entered into a relationship that exempts the benefactor from liability.* [Emphasis added.]

* * * The established test for determining whether a party is a beneficiary of the works of a charity has two prongs. The first is that the institution pleading the immunity, at the time in question, was engaged in the performance of the charitable objectives it was organized to advance. The second is that the injured party must have been a direct recipient of those good works.
* * * *

As to the first prong, * * * a qualifying organization does not lose its statutory immunity merely because it charges money for its services, unless it makes a profit or collects fees for services totally unrelated to its organizational pursuits. * * * Hosting an educational panel

Case 39.2 Continues

Case 39.2 Continued

discussion in the auditorium was entirely consistent with the Museum's charitable endeavors.

The second prong of the test * * * distinguishes between persons benefiting from the charity, and persons who contribute to the charity by virtue of their attendance or participation.

* * * *

In *Mayer*, * * * an employee of the Development Corporation for Israel was promoting the sale of bonds at a dinner on the premises of [Fairlawn Jewish Center, the defendant, when he sustained an injury].

* * * *

* * * He was there in fulfillment of his function and obligation as an employee to engage in the employer's work at the direction of the employer, and not for the purpose of receiving personally the philanthropy of the Center. Under the circumstances present he was a stranger to the charity and the [CIA did] not stand in the way of recovery.

* * * *

* * * *[Thus, under the CIA,] to be a beneficiary under the second prong, the injured party must be a direct recipient of the Museum's good works. Only those*

unconcerned in and unrelated to the benefactions of the organization are not beneficiaries. [Emphasis added.]

* * * *

As an intermediate appellate court, we are bound to follow and enforce the decisions of the Supreme Court. Under [*Mayer*], plaintiff, as an employee of La Casa who was ordered on the day of her fall to attend the panel discussion at the Museum, was not a direct beneficiary of the Museum's charitable endeavors.

We therefore reverse the order granting summary judgment to the Museum and remand the matter.

Legal Reasoning Questions

1. How do the purposes of the CIA support each other?

2. Can a person be a direct beneficiary of a nonprofit's good works even though the person is on the nonprofit's premises under the direction of a third party? Explain.

3. Suppose that the museum had not been hosting an educational panel in its auditorium but instead had rented the facility to an organization for a sales conference. Would the result have been different? Discuss.

Close Corporations Most corporate enterprises in the United States fall into the category of close corporations. A **close corporation** is one whose shares are held by relatively few persons, often members of a family. Close corporations are also referred to as *closely held, family,* or *privately held* corporations.

Usually, the members of the small group constituting the shareholders of a close corporation are personally known to each other. Because the number of shareholders is so small, there is no trading market for the shares. In practice, a close corporation is often operated like a partnership.

The statutes in many states allow close corporations to depart significantly from certain formalities required by traditional corporation law.[3] Under the RMBCA, close corporations have considerable flexibility in determining their operating rules [RMBCA 7.32]. If all of a corporation's shareholders agree in writing, the corporation can operate without directors and bylaws. In addition, the corporation can operate without annual or special shareholders' or directors' meetings, stock

certificates, or formal records of shareholders' or directors' decisions.[4]

Management of Close Corporations. Management of a close corporation resembles that of a sole proprietorship or a partnership, in that control is held by a single shareholder or a tightly knit group of shareholders. As a corporation, however, the firm must meet all specific legal requirements set forth in state statutes.

To prevent a majority shareholder from dominating the company, a close corporation may require that more than a simple majority of the directors approve any action taken by the board. In a larger corporation, such a requirement would typically apply only to extraordinary actions (such as selling all the corporate assets) and not to ordinary business decisions.

Transfer of Shares in Close Corporations. By definition, a close corporation has a small number of shareholders. Thus, the transfer of one shareholder's shares to someone else can cause serious management problems. The other

---

3. In some states, such as Maryland, a close corporation need not have a board of directors.

4. Shareholders cannot agree, however, to eliminate certain rights of shareholders, such as the right to inspect corporate records or the right to bring *derivative actions* (lawsuits on behalf of the corporation).

shareholders may find themselves required to share control with someone they do not know or like. ■ **EXAMPLE 39.2** Three siblings, Sherry, Karen, and Henry Johnson, are the only shareholders of Johnson's Car Wash, Inc. Henry wants to sell his shares, but Sherry and Karen do not want him to sell the shares to a third person unknown to them. ■

To avoid this situation, a close corporation can restrict the transferability of shares to outside persons. Shareholders can be required to offer their shares to the corporation or to the other shareholders before selling them to an outside purchaser. In fact, in a few states close corporations must transfer shares in this manner under state statutes.

One way the close corporation can effect restrictions on transferability is by spelling them out in a **shareholder agreement.** A shareholder agreement can also provide for proportional control when one of the original shareholders dies. The decedent's shares of stock in the corporation can be divided in such a way that the proportionate holdings of the survivors, and thus their proportionate control, will be maintained.

Misappropriation of Close Corporation Funds.
Sometimes, a majority shareholder in a close corporation takes advantage of his or her position and misappropriates company funds. In such situations, the normal remedy for the injured minority shareholders is to have their shares appraised and to be paid the fair market value for them. ■ **CASE IN POINT 39.3** John Murray, Stephen Hopkins, and Paul Ryan were officers, directors, employees, and majority shareholders of Olympic Adhesives, Inc. Merek Rubin was a minority shareholder. Murray, Hopkins, and Ryan were paid salaries. Twice a year, they paid themselves additional compensation—between 75 and 98 percent of Olympic's net profits, allocated according to their stock ownership. Rubin filed a suit against the majority shareholders, alleging that their compensation deprived him of his share of Olympic's profits.

The court explained that a salary should reasonably relate to a corporate officer's ability and the quantity and quality of his or her services. The court found that a reasonable amount of compensation would have been 10 percent of Olympic's average annual net sales. Therefore, the additional compensation the majority shareholders paid themselves—based on stock ownership and not on performance—was excessive. The court ordered the defendants to repay Olympic nearly $6 million to be distributed among its shareholders. On appeal, the reviewing court affirmed this decision.[5] ■

---

5. *Rubin v. Murray,* 79 Mass.App.Ct. 64, 943 N.E.2d 949 (2011).

S Corporations
A close corporation that meets the qualifying requirements specified in Subchapter S of the Internal Revenue Code can choose to operate as an **S corporation.** (A corporation will automatically be taxed under Subchapter C unless it elects S corporation status.) If a corporation has S corporation status, it can avoid the imposition of income taxes at the corporate level while retaining many of the advantages of a corporation, particularly limited liability.

Important Requirements.   Among the numerous requirements for S corporation status, the following are the most important:

1. The corporation must be a domestic corporation.
2. The corporation must not be a member of an affiliated group of corporations.
3. The shareholders must be individuals, estates, or certain trusts and tax-exempt organizations. Partnerships and nonqualifying trusts cannot be shareholders. Corporations can be shareholders under certain circumstances.
4. The corporation must have no more than one hundred shareholders.
5. The corporation must have only one class of stock, although it is not necessary that all shareholders have the same voting rights.
6. No shareholder of the corporation may be a nonresident alien.

Effect of S Election.   An S corporation is treated differently than a regular corporation for tax purposes. An S corporation is taxed like a partnership, so the corporate income passes through to the shareholders, who pay personal income tax on it. This treatment enables the S corporation to avoid the double taxation imposed on regular corporations.

In addition, the shareholders' tax brackets may be lower than the tax bracket that the corporation would have been in if the tax had been imposed at the corporate level. The resulting tax saving is particularly attractive when the corporation wants to accumulate earnings for some future business purpose. If the corporation has losses, the S election allows the shareholders to use the losses to offset other income.

In spite of these benefits, the S corporation has lost much of its appeal. The newer limited liability business forms (such as LLCs, LPs, and LLPs) offer similar tax advantages and greater flexibility.

Professional Corporations Professionals such as physicians, lawyers, dentists, and accountants can incorporate. A professional corporation is typically identified by the letters *P.C.* (professional corporation), *S.C.* (service corporation), or *P.A.* (professional association).

In general, the laws governing the formation and operation of professional corporations are similar to those governing ordinary business corporations. There are some differences in terms of liability, however, because the shareholder-owners are professionals who are held to a higher standard of conduct.

For liability purposes, some courts treat professional corporations somewhat like partnerships and hold each professional liable for malpractice committed within the scope of the business by others in the firm. A shareholder in a professional corporation generally cannot be held liable for torts committed by other professionals at the firm except those related to malpractice or breach of duty to clients.

Benefit Corporations A growing number of states have enacted legislation that creates a relatively new corporate form called a *benefit corporation*. A **benefit corporation** is a for-profit corporation that seeks to have a material positive impact on society and the environment. Benefit corporations differ from traditional corporations in the following ways:

1. *Purpose.* Although the corporation is designed to make a profit, its purpose is to benefit the public as a whole. (In contrast, the purpose of an ordinary business corporation is to provide long-term shareholder value.) The directors of a benefit corporation must, during the decision-making process, consider the impact of their decisions on society and the environment.
2. *Accountability.* Shareholders of a benefit corporation determine whether the company has achieved a material positive impact. Shareholders also have a right of private action, called a *benefit enforcement proceeding,* enabling them to sue the corporation if it fails to pursue or create public benefit.
3. *Transparency.* A benefit corporation must issue an annual benefit report on its overall social and environmental performance that uses a recognized third-party standard to assess its performance. The report must be delivered to the shareholders and posted on a public Web site.

See Concept Summary 39.1 for a review of the ways in which corporations are classified.

39–2 Corporate Formation and Powers

Many of today's largest companies started as sole proprietorships or partnerships. They converted to corporate entities as they grew because they needed to obtain additional capital by issuing shares of stock. Incorporating a business is much simpler today than it was twenty years ago, and many states allow businesses to incorporate via the Internet. Here, we examine the process by which a corporation comes into existence.

39–2a Promotional Activities

In the past, preliminary steps were taken to organize and promote a business prior to incorporating. Contracts were made with investors and others on behalf of the future corporation. Today, due to the relative ease of forming a corporation in most states, persons incorporating their business rarely, if ever, engage in preliminary promotional activities.

Nevertheless, businesspersons should understand that they are personally liable for any preincorporation contracts made with investors, accountants, or others on behalf of the future corporation. Personal liability continues until the newly formed corporation assumes liability for the preincorporation contracts through a novation.

39–2b Incorporation Procedures

Each state has its own set of incorporation procedures. Most often, they are listed on the secretary of state's Web site. Generally, however, all incorporators follow several basic steps, discussed next.

Select the State of Incorporation Because state corporate laws differ, individuals seeking to incorporate a business may look for the states that offer the most advantageous tax or other provisions. Many corporations, for instance, have chosen to incorporate in Delaware because it has historically had the least restrictive laws, along with provisions that favor corporate management. For reasons of convenience and cost, though, businesses often choose to incorporate in the state in which the corporation's business will primarily be conducted.

Secure the Corporate Name The choice of a corporate name is subject to state approval to ensure against duplication or deception. Most state statutes require a search to confirm that the chosen corporate name is available. A

Concept Summary 39.1

Classification of Corporations

Domestic, Foreign, and Alien Corporations	• A corporation is referred to as a *domestic corporation* in its home state (the state in which it incorporates). • A corporation is referred to as a *foreign corporation* by any state that is not its home state. • A corporation is referred to as an *alien corporation* if it originates in another country but does business in the United States.
Public and Private Corporations	• A *public corporation* is formed by a government (for instance, a city, town, or public project). • A *private corporation* is formed wholly or in part for private benefit (profit). Most corporations are private corporations.
Nonprofit Corporation	• A *nonprofit corporation* is formed without a profit-making purpose (for example, charitable, educational, and religious organizations and hospitals).
Close Corporation	• A *close corporation* is owned by a family or a relatively small number of individuals. Because the number of shareholders is small and the transfer of shares is usually restricted, the shares are not traded in a public securities market.
S Corporation	• An *S corporation* is a small domestic corporation (must have no more than one hundred shareholders) that, under Subchapter S of the Internal Revenue Code, is given special tax treatment. An S corporation allows shareholders to enjoy the limited legal liability of the corporate form but avoid its double-taxation feature. (Shareholders pay taxes on the income at personal income tax rates, and the S corporation is not taxed separately.)
Professional Corporation	• A *professional corporation* is formed by professionals—such as physicians or lawyers—to obtain the advantages of incorporation. A professional corporation functions like an ordinary corporation but is treated differently in terms of liability. Courts may treat the shareholders like partners with regard to malpractice liability.
Benefit Corporation	• A *benefit corporation* is designed for businesses that want to consider society and the environment in addition to profit. Shareholders have a right to sue the corporation in enforcement proceedings if it fails to benefit the public.

new corporation's name cannot be the same as, or deceptively similar to, the name of an existing corporation doing business within the state. All states require the corporation's name to include the word *Corporation (Corp.), Incorporated (Inc.), Company (Co.),* or *Limited (Ltd.).*[6]

---

6. Failure to use one of these terms to disclose corporate status may be grounds for holding an individual incorporator liable for corporate contracts under agency law.

Prepare the Articles of Incorporation The primary document needed to incorporate a business is the **articles of incorporation** (for a sample, see Exhibit 39–1). The articles include basic information about the corporation and serve as a primary source of authority for its future organization and business functions. The person or persons who execute (sign) the articles are the *incorporators.*

EXHIBIT 39–1 Sample Articles of Incorporation

ARTICLE I. The name of the corporation is _____ .

ARTICLE II. The period of its duration is _____ (may be a number of years or until a certain date).

ARTICLE III. The purpose (or purposes) for which the corporation is organized is (are) _____
_____
_____ .

ARTICLE IV. The aggregate number of shares that the corporation shall have the authority to issue is _____ with
the par value of _____ dollar(s) each (or without par value).

ARTICLE V. The corporation will not commence business until it has received for the issuance of its shares
consideration of the value of $1,000 (can be any sum not less than $1,000).

ARTICLE VI. The address of the corporation's registered office is _____
and the name of its registered agent at such address is _____
_____ .

ARTICLE VII. The number of initial directors is _____ , and the names and addresses of the directors are
_____
_____

ARTICLE VIII. The names and addresses of the incorporators are

_____	_____	_____
(Name)	(Address)	(Signature)
_____	_____	_____
(Name)	(Address)	(Signature)
_____	_____	_____
(Name)	(Address)	(Signature)

Sworn to on _____ by the above-named incorporators.
       (Date)

_____
                    Notary Public

(Notary Seal)

Articles of incorporation vary widely depending on the jurisdiction and the size and type of the corporation. Generally, though, the articles *must* include the following information [RMBCA 2.02]:

1. The name of the corporation.
2. The number of shares of stock the corporation is authorized to issue [RMBCA 2.02(a)]. (Large corporations often also state a par value for each share, such as $0.20 per share, and specify the various types or classes of stock authorized for issuance.)
3. The name and street address of the corporation's initial registered agent and registered office. The registered agent is the person who can receive legal documents (such as orders to appear in court) on behalf of the corporation. The registered office is usually the main corporate office.
4. The name and address of each incorporator.

In addition, the articles *may* set forth other information, such as the names and addresses of the initial members of the board of directors and the duration and purpose of the corporation. A corporation has perpetual existence unless the articles state otherwise. As to the corporation's purpose, a corporation can be formed for any lawful purpose, and the RMBCA does not require the articles to include a specific statement of purpose. Consequently, the articles often include only a general statement of purpose. By not mentioning specifics, the corporation avoids the need for future amendments to the corporate articles [RMBCA 2.02(b)(2)(i), 3.01]. Similarly, the articles do not provide much detail about the firm's operations, which are spelled out in the company's *bylaws* (discussed shortly).

File the Articles with the State Once the articles of incorporation have been prepared and signed, they are sent to the appropriate state official, usually the secretary of state, along with the required filing fee. In most states, the secretary of state then stamps the articles "Filed" and returns a copy of the articles to the incorporators. Once this occurs, the corporation officially exists.

39–2c First Organizational Meeting to Adopt Bylaws

After incorporation, the first organizational meeting must be held. If the articles of incorporation named the initial board of directors, then the directors, by majority vote, call the meeting. If the articles did not name the directors (as is typical), then the incorporators hold the meeting to elect the directors and complete any other business necessary.

Usually, the most important function of this meeting is the adoption of **bylaws,** which are the internal rules of management for the corporation. The bylaws cannot conflict with the state corporation statute or the articles of incorporation [RMBCA 2.06]. Under the RMBCA, the shareholders may amend or repeal the bylaws. The board of directors may also amend or repeal the bylaws, unless the articles of incorporation or provisions of the state corporation statute reserve this power to the shareholders [RMBCA 10.20].

The bylaws typically describe such matters as voting requirements for shareholders, the election of the board of directors, and the methods of replacing directors. Bylaws also frequently outline the manner and time of holding shareholders' and board meetings.

39–2d Improper Incorporation

The procedures for incorporation are very specific. If they are not followed precisely, others may be able to challenge the existence of the corporation. Errors in incorporation procedures can become important when, for instance, a third party who is attempting to enforce a contract or bring a suit for a tort injury learns of them.

De Jure Corporations If a corporation has substantially complied with all conditions precedent to incorporation, the corporation is said to have *de jure* (rightful and lawful) existence. In most states and under RMBCA 2.03(b), the secretary of state's filing of the articles of incorporation is conclusive proof that all mandatory statutory provisions have been met [RMBCA 2.03(b)].

Sometimes, the incorporators fail to comply with all statutory mandates. If the defect is minor, such as an incorrect address listed on the articles of incorporation, most courts will overlook the defect and find that a *de jure* corporation exists.

De Facto Corporations If the defect in formation is substantial, such as a corporation's failure to hold an organizational meeting to adopt bylaws, the outcome will vary depending on the jurisdiction. Some states, including Mississippi, New York, Ohio, and Oklahoma, recognize the common law doctrine of *de facto* corporation.[7] In those states, the courts will treat a corporation as a legal corporation despite a defect in its formation if the following three requirements are met:

1. A state statute exists under which the corporation can be validly incorporated.

---

7. See, for example, *In re Hausman,* 13 N.Y.3d 408, 921 N.E.2d 191, 893 N.Y.S.2d 499 (2009).

2. The parties have made a good faith attempt to comply with the statute.

3. The parties have already undertaken to do business as a corporation.

Many state courts, however, have interpreted their states' version of the RMBCA as abolishing the common law doctrine of *de facto* corporations. These states include Alaska, Arizona, Minnesota, New Mexico, Oregon, South Dakota, Tennessee, Utah, and Washington, as well as the District of Columbia. In those jurisdictions, if there is a substantial defect in complying with the incorporation statute, the corporation does not legally exist, and the incorporators are personally liable.

Corporation by Estoppel Sometimes, a business association holds itself out to others as being a corporation when it has made no attempt to incorporate. In those situations, the firm normally will be estopped (prevented) from denying corporate status in a lawsuit by a third party. The estoppel doctrine most commonly applies when a third party contracts with an entity that claims to be a corporation but has not filed articles of incorporation. It may also apply when a third party contracts with a person claiming to be an agent of a corporation that does not in fact exist.

When justice requires, courts in some states will treat an alleged corporation as if it were an actual corporation for the purpose of determining rights and liabilities in particular circumstances.[8] Recognition of corporate status does not extend beyond the resolution of the problem at hand.

■ **CASE IN POINT 39.4** W.P. Media, Inc., and Alabama MBA, Inc., agreed to form a wireless Internet services company. W.P. Media was to create a wireless network, and Alabama MBA was to contribute the capital. Hugh Brown signed the parties' contract on behalf of Alabama MBA as the chair of its board. At the time, however, Alabama MBA's articles of incorporation had not yet been filed. Brown filed the articles of incorporation the following year.

Later, Brown and Alabama MBA filed a suit alleging that W.P. Media had breached their contract by not building the wireless network. W.P. Media contended that Alabama MBA had not existed as a corporation when the agreement was signed and thus the agreement was void. The Supreme Court of Alabama held that because W.P.

Media had treated Alabama MBA as a corporation, W.P. Media was estopped from denying Alabama MBA's corporate existence.[9] ■

39–2e Corporate Powers

When a corporation is created, the express and implied powers necessary to achieve its purpose also come into existence.

Express Powers The express powers of a corporation are found in its articles of incorporation, in the law of the state of incorporation, and in the state and federal constitutions. Corporate bylaws and the resolutions of the corporation's board of directors also establish express powers.

The following order of priority is used if a conflict arises among the various documents involving a corporation:

1. The U.S. Constitution.
2. State constitutions.
3. State statutes.
4. The articles of incorporation.
5. Bylaws.
6. Resolutions of the board of directors.

It is important that the bylaws set forth the specific operating rules of the corporation. State corporation statutes frequently provide default rules that apply if the company's bylaws are silent on an issue.

On occasion, the U.S. government steps in to challenge what a corporation may consider one of its express powers. This chapter's *Global Insight* discusses a dispute between the government and Microsoft Corporation over a demand that the company provide the government with access to e-mail stored in servers on foreign soil.

Implied Powers When a corporation is created, it acquires certain implied powers. Barring express constitutional, statutory, or other prohibitions, the corporation has the implied power to perform all acts reasonably necessary to accomplish its corporate purposes. For this reason, a corporation has the implied power to borrow and lend funds within certain limits and to extend credit to parties with whom it has contracts.

Most often, the president or chief executive officer of the corporation signs the necessary documents on behalf of the corporation. Corporate officers such as these have the implied power to bind the corporation in matters directly connected with the *ordinary* business affairs of the enterprise.

---

8. Some states have expressly rejected the common law theory of corporation by estoppel, finding that it is inconsistent with their statutory law. Other states have abolished only the doctrines of *de facto* and *de jure* corporations. See, for example, *Stone v. Jetmar Properties, LLC*, 733 N.W.2d 480 (Minn.App. 2007).

9. *Brown v. W.P. Media, Inc.*, 17 So.3d 1167 (2009).

GLOBAL INSIGHT   Does Cloud Computing Have a Nationality?

Everyone has heard of "the cloud," and most people use it for the storage of their digital data—photos, e-mails, music, documents, and just about anything else. Not surprisingly, major global digital players like Apple, Amazon, Google, and Microsoft have spent billions to create "clouds" of servers all over the world. In the clouds are stored confidential, organized, and secure data. The revenues generated by the U.S. cloud computing industry exceed $100 billion a year. But is the long-term picture for such revenues in doubt?

Microsoft Battles and the Global Cloud Industry Waits

The U.S. government issued a warrant to Microsoft to produce e-mails related to a narcotics case from a Hotmail account. That account was hosted in a Microsoft cloud location in Ireland. Microsoft refused, but a magistrate judge in the Southern District of New York confirmed the government's right to the Ireland-located e-mails.[a] On appeal to a U.S. district court, Microsoft again lost.[b] Microsoft appealed to the United States Court of Appeals for the Second Circuit and won in 2016.[c]

a. *In re Warrant to Search a Certain E-Mail Account Controlled and Maintained by Microsoft Corp.*, 15 F.Supp.3d 466 (S.D.N.Y. 2014).
b. *In re Warrant to Search a Certain E-Mail Account Controlled and Maintained by Microsoft Corp.*, 2014 WL 4629624 (S.D.N.Y. 2014).
c. *In Matter of Warrant to Search a Certain E-Mail Account Controlled and Maintained by Microsoft Corp.*, ___ F.3d ___, 2016 WL 3770056 (2d Cir. 2016).

Microsoft maintained that "the power to embark on unilateral law enforcement incursions into a foreign sovereign country—directly or indirectly—has profound policy consequences. Worse still, it threatens the privacy of U.S. citizens." According to Microsoft's deputy general counsel, David Howard, "The U.S. government doesn't have the power to search a home in another country, nor should it have the power search the content of e-mails stored overseas."

A number of organizations—including the ACLU, Apple, eBay, and Fox News—apparently agreed with Microsoft. The federal appellate court was persuaded that the warrant could not be enforced against Microsoft extraterritorially.

Impact on the Industry

More was at stake in this case than the issues Microsoft identified. If Microsoft had lost, some industry experts predicted that U.S. technology companies would lose up to $35 billion a year from their cloud storage business. Foreign corporations and individuals would no longer trust U.S. companies to keep their data secret.

Critical Thinking *The law underlying the case against Microsoft is the Electronic Communications Privacy Act, which was enacted three years before the invention of the World Wide Web. Should that law still apply today? Why or why not?*

There is a limit to what a corporate officer can do, though. A corporate officer does not have the authority to bind the corporation to an action that will greatly affect the corporate purpose or undertaking, such as the sale of substantial corporate assets.

***Ultra Vires* Doctrine** The term *ultra vires* means "beyond the power." In corporate law, acts of a corporation that are beyond its express or implied powers are *ultra vires* acts. In the past, most cases dealing with *ultra vires* acts involved contracts made for unauthorized purposes. Now, because the articles of incorporation of most private corporations do not state a specific purpose, the *ultra vires* doctrine has declined in importance.

Today, cases that allege *ultra vires* acts usually involve nonprofit corporations or municipal (public) corporations. ■ **CASE IN POINT 39.5** Four men formed a nonprofit corporation to create the Armenian Genocide Museum

& Memorial (AGM&M). The bylaws appointed them as trustees (similar to corporate directors) for life. One of the trustees, Gerard L. Cafesjian, became the chair and president of AGM&M. Eventually, the relationship among the trustees deteriorated, and Cafesjian resigned.

The corporation then brought a suit claiming that Cafesjian had engaged in numerous *ultra vires* acts, self-dealing, and mismanagement. Although the bylaws required an 80 percent affirmative vote of the trustees to take action, Cafesjian had taken many actions without the board's approval. He had also entered into contracts for real estate transactions in which he had a personal interest. Because Cafesjian had taken actions that exceeded his authority and had failed to follow rules set forth in the bylaws, the court ruled that the corporation could go forward with its suit.[10] ■

---

10. *Armenian Assembly of America, Inc. v. Cafesjian*, 692 F.Supp.2d 20 (D.C. Cir. 2010).

Remedies for *Ultra Vires* Acts Under Section 3.04 of the RMBCA, shareholders can seek an injunction from a court to prevent (or stop) the corporation from engaging in *ultra vires* acts. The attorney general in the state of incorporation can also bring an action to obtain an injunction against the *ultra vires* transactions or to seek dissolution of the corporation. The corporation or its shareholders (on behalf of the corporation) can seek damages from the officers and directors who were responsible for the *ultra vires* acts.

39–3 Piercing the Corporate Veil

Occasionally, the owners use a corporate entity to perpetrate a fraud, circumvent the law, or in some other way accomplish an illegitimate objective. In these situations, the courts will ignore the corporate structure by **piercing the corporate veil** and exposing the shareholders to personal liability [RMBCA 2.04].

Generally, courts pierce the veil when the corporate privilege is abused for personal benefit or when the corporate business is treated so carelessly that it is indistinguishable from that of a controlling shareholder. When the facts show that great injustice would result from a shareholder's use of a corporation to avoid individual responsibility, a court will look behind the corporate structure to the individual shareholders.

39–3a Factors That Lead Courts to Pierce the Corporate Veil

The following are some of the factors that frequently cause the courts to pierce the corporate veil:

1. A party is tricked or misled into dealing with the corporation rather than the individual.
2. The corporation is set up never to make a profit or always to be insolvent. Alternatively, it is too thinly capitalized—that is, it has insufficient capital at the time it is formed to meet its prospective debts or potential liabilities.
3. The corporation is formed to evade an existing legal obligation.
4. Statutory corporate formalities, such as holding required corporation meetings, are not followed.
5. Personal and corporate interests are mixed together, or **commingled,** to such an extent that the corporation has no separate identity.

State corporation codes usually do not prohibit a shareholder from lending funds to her or his corporation. Courts will scrutinize such a transaction closely if the loan comes from an officer, director, or majority shareholder, however. Loans from persons who control the corporation must be made in good faith and for fair value.

In the following case, the court looked at various factors in deciding whether to pierce the corporate veil.

Dog House Investments, LLC v. Teal Properties, Inc.

Court of Appeals of Tennessee, 448 S.W.3d 905 (2014).

Background and Facts Dog House Investments, LLC, operated a dog "camp" in Nashville, Tennessee. Dog House leased the property from Teal Properties, Inc., which was owned by Jerry Teal, its sole shareholder. Under the lease, the landlord promised to repair damage from fire or other causes that rendered the property "untenantable" (unusable). Following a flood, Dog House notified Jerry that the property was untenantable. Jerry assured Dog House that the flood damage was covered by insurance but took no steps to restore the property. The parties then agreed that Dog House would undertake the repairs and be reimbursed by Teal Properties.

Dog House spent $39,000 to repair the damage and submitted invoices for reimbursement. Teal Properties recovered $40,000 from its insurance company but did not pay Dog House. Close to bankruptcy, Dog House filed a suit in a Tennessee state court against Teal Properties and Jerry. The court held Jerry personally liable for the repair costs. Jerry appealed.

In the Language of the Court

David R. *FARMER,* J. [Judge]
* * * *

It is well-settled that courts may pierce the corporate veil and attribute the actions of a corporation to its shareholders when appropriate. *A party seeking to pierce the corporate veil bears the burden of*

Case 39.3 Continued

demonstrating that the separate corporate entity is a sham or dummy or that disregarding the separate corporate entity is necessary to accomplish justice. [Emphasis added.] When determining whether piercing the corporate veil is appropriate, the court must consider whether the corporate entity has been used to work a fraud or injustice in contravention of public policy and also:

(1) whether there was a failure to collect paid-in capital; (2) whether the corporation was grossly undercapitalized; (3) the nonissuance of stock certificates; (4) the sole ownership of stock by one individual; (5) the use of the same office or business location; (6) the employment of the same employees or attorneys; (7) the use of the corporation as an instrumentality or business conduit for an individual or another corporation; (8) the diversion of corporate assets by or to a stockholder or other entity to the detriment of creditors, or the manipulation of assets and liabilities in another; (9) the use of the corporation as a subterfuge in illegal transactions; (10) the formation and use of the corporation to transfer to it the existing liability of another person or entity; and (11) the failure to maintain arms length relationships among related entities.

No single factor is conclusive and not every factor must exist to pierce the corporate veil. The question depends on the specific facts and circumstances of the case. The equities, however, must substantially favor the party requesting the court to disregard the corporate status. The presumption of the corporation's separate identity should be set aside only with great caution and not precipitately [hastily]. [Emphasis added.]

In this case, Mr. Teal denied personal liability but admitted * * * that he owned the property leased by Dog House in Nashville. The trial court found that Teal Properties owns no property, has no assets, and has no cash except that which is deposited by Mr. Jerry Teal when he has the opportunity to do so; that Teal Properties receives rents and immediately pays it out to pay Mr. Teal's financial obligations; that Mr. Teal is the sole stockholder of Teal Properties and owns the corporation; and that Teal Properties has no purpose other than to collect the rent on properties owned by Mr. Teal. The trial court also found that Mr. Teal does not receive a salary from Teal Properties but utilizes its assets, including the flood insurance proceeds at issue in this case, to pay Mr. Teal's personal expenses and his personal obligations. The trial court found that Mr. Teal did not maintain an arms-length relationship with the corporation, and that it was, in fact, his alter ego. Mr. Teal does not dispute these findings * * * , but asserts that "there is no proof that Teal Properties is a sham or dummy corporation * * * ." We discern no error on the part of the trial court and affirm on this issue.

Decision and Remedy *A state intermediate appellate court affirmed the lower court's decision. Teal Properties owned no property and had no assets. It received rent, but paid it immediately to Jerry Teal. "Mr. Teal did not maintain an arms-length relationship with the corporation, and . . . it was, in fact, his alter ego."*

Critical Thinking

- **Ethical** *The failure of Teal Properties and Jerry to reimburse the tenant, Dog House, for the repair costs placed Dog House in a dire financial situation. Does this consequence make the landlord's conduct unethical? Discuss.*
- **Legal Environment** *The trial court also concluded, and the appellate court affirmed, that Teal Properties had breached its contract with Dog House. What was the contract? How was it breached?*

39–3b A Potential Problem for Close Corporations

The potential for corporate assets to be used for personal benefit is especially great in a close corporation. In such a corporation, the separate status of the corporate entity and the shareholders (often family members) must be carefully preserved. Practices that invite trouble for a close corporation include the commingling of corporate and personal funds and the shareholders' continuous personal use of corporate property (for instance, vehicles).

Typically, courts are reluctant to hold shareholders in close corporations personally liable for corporate obligations unless there is some evidence of fraud or wrongdoing. ■ **CASE IN POINT 39.6** Pip, Jimmy, and Theodore Brennan are brothers and shareholders of Brennan's, Inc., which owns and operates New Orleans's famous Brennan's Restaurant. As a close corporation, Brennan's, Inc., did not hold formal corporate meetings with agendas and minutes, but it did maintain corporate books, hold corporate bank accounts, and file corporate tax returns.

The Brennan brothers retained attorney Edward Colbert to represent them in a family matter, and the attorney's bills were sent to the restaurant and paid from the corporate account. Later, when Brennan's, Inc., sued Colbert for malpractice, Colbert argued that the court should pierce the corporate veil because the Brennan brothers did not observe corporate formalities. The court refused to do so, however, because there was no evidence of fraud, malfeasance, or other wrongdoing by the Brennan brothers. There is no requirement for small, close corporations to operate with the formality usually expected of larger corporations.[11] ■

39–3c The Alter-Ego Theory

Sometimes, courts pierce the corporate veil under the theory that the corporation was not operated as a separate entity. Rather, it was just another side (the *alter ego*) of the individual or group that actually controlled the corporation. This is called the alter-ego theory.

The alter-ego theory is applied when a corporation is so dominated and controlled by an individual (or group) that the separate identities of the person (or group) and the corporation are no longer distinct. Courts use the alter-ego theory to avoid injustice or fraud that would result if wrongdoers were allowed to hide behind the protection of limited liability.

---

11. *Brennan's, Inc. v. Colbert*, 85 So.3d 787 (La.App.4th Cir. 2012).

■ **CASE IN POINT 39.7** Steiner Electric Company (Steiner) is an Illinois corporation that sells electrical products. Steiner sold goods to Delta Equipment Company and Sackett Systems, Inc., on credit. Both Delta and Sackett were owned and controlled by a single shareholder—Leonard J. Maniscalco. Steiner was not fully paid for the products it sold on credit to Delta and Sackett. Eventually, Steiner sued Delta and won a default judgment, but by that time, Delta had been dissolved. Steiner then asked a state court to pierce the corporate veil and hold Maniscalco liable for the debts of the two companies, claiming the companies were merely Maniscalco's alter egos.

The court agreed and held Maniscalco liable. Delta and Sackett were inadequately capitalized, transactions were not properly documented, funds were commingled, and corporate formalities were not observed. Maniscalco had consistently treated both companies in such a manner that they were, in practice, his alter egos.[12] ■

39–4 Corporate Financing

Part of the process of corporate formation involves financing. Corporations normally are financed by the issuance and sale of corporate securities. **Securities**—stocks and bonds—evidence an ownership interest in a corporation or a promise of repayment of debt by a corporation. The ways in which stocks and bonds differ are summarized in Exhibit 39–2.

---

12. *Steiner Electric Co. v. Maniscalco*, ___ N.E.3d ___, 2016 IL App (1st) 132023 (2016).

EXHIBIT 39–2 How Do Stocks and Bonds Differ?

STOCKS	BONDS
1. Stocks represent ownership.	1. Bonds represent debt.
2. Stocks (common) do not have a fixed dividend rate.	2. Interest on bonds must always be paid, whether or not any profit is earned.
3. Stockholders can elect the board of directors, which controls the corporation.	3. Bondholders usually have no voice in or control over management of the corporation.
4. Stocks do not have a maturity date. The corporation usually does not repay the stockholder.	4. Bonds have a maturity date, when the corporation is to repay the bondholder the face value of the bond.
5. All corporations issue or offer to sell stocks. This is the usual definition of a corporation.	5. Corporations do not necessarily issue bonds.
6. Stockholders have a claim against the property and income of the corporation after all creditors' claims have been met.	6. Bondholders have a claim against the property and income of the corporation that must be met before the claims of stockholders.

39–4a Bonds

Bonds are *debt securities*, which represent the borrowing of funds. Bonds are issued by business firms and by governments at all levels as evidence of funds they are borrowing from investors.

Bonds normally have a designated *maturity date*—the date when the principal, or face amount, of the bond is returned to the bondholder. Bondholders also receive fixed-dollar interest payments, usually semiannually, during the period of time prior to maturity. For that reason, they are sometimes referred to as *fixed-income securities*. Because debt financing represents a legal obligation of the corporation, various features and terms of a particular bond issue are specified in a lending agreement.

Of course, not all debt is in the form of bonds. For instance, some debt is in the form of accounts payable and notes payable, which typically are short-term debts. Bonds are simply a way for the corporation to split up its long-term debt so that it can be more easily marketed.

39–4b Stocks

Issuing stocks is another way for corporations to obtain financing [RMBCA 6.01]. **Stocks,** or *equity securities,* represent the purchase of ownership in the business firm. The two major types are *common stock* and *preferred stock.*

Common Stock The true ownership of a corporation is represented by **common stock.** Common stock provides an interest in the corporation with regard to (1) control, (2) earnings, and (3) net assets. A shareholder's interest is generally proportionate to the number of shares he or she owns out of the total number of shares issued. Any person who purchases common stock acquires voting rights—one vote per share held.

An issuing firm is not obligated to return a principal amount per share to each holder of its common stock, nor does the firm have to guarantee a dividend. Indeed, some corporations never pay dividends. Holders of common stock are investors who assume a *residual* position in the overall financial structure of a business. They benefit when the market price of the stock increases. In terms of receiving payment for their investments, they are last in line.

Preferred Stock **Preferred stock** is an equity security with *preferences.* Usually, this means that holders of preferred stock have priority over holders of common stock as to dividends and payment on dissolution of the corporation. The preferences must be stated in the articles of incorporation. Holders of preferred stock may or may not have the right to vote.

Like other equity securities, preferred shares have no fixed maturity date on which the firm must pay them off. Although firms occasionally buy back preferred stock, they are not legally obligated to do so.

Holders of preferred stock have assumed a more cautious position than holders of common stock. They have a stronger position than common shareholders with respect to dividends and claims on assets, but they will not share in the full prosperity of the firm if it grows successfully over time. Preferred stockholders do receive fixed dividends periodically, however, and they may benefit to some extent from changes in the market price of the shares.

Exhibit 39–3 offers a summary of the types of stocks issued by corporations.

39–4c Venture Capital and Private Equity Capital

Corporations traditionally obtain financing by issuing and selling securities (stocks and bonds) in the capital market. Many investors do not want to purchase stock in a business that lacks a track record, however, and banks generally are reluctant to extend loans to high-risk enterprises. Therefore, to obtain funds, many entrepreneurs seek alternative financing.

Venture Capital Start-up businesses and high-risk enterprises often obtain venture capital financing. **Venture capital** is capital provided to new businesses by professional, outside investors (*venture capitalists,* usually groups of wealthy investors and securities firms). Venture capital investments are high risk—the investors must be willing to lose all of their invested funds—but offer the potential for well-above-average returns in the future.

To obtain venture capital financing, the start-up business typically gives up a share of its ownership to the venture capitalists. In addition to funding, venture capitalists may provide managerial and technical expertise, and they nearly always are given some control over the new company's decisions. Many Internet-based companies, such as Google and Amazon, were initially financed by venture capital.

Private Equity Capital Private equity firms pool funds from wealthy investors and use this **private equity capital** to invest in existing corporations. Usually, a

EXHIBIT 39–3 Common and Preferred Stocks

COMMON STOCK	**PREFERRED STOCK**
Voting shares that represent ownership interest in a corporation. Common stock has the lowest priority with respect to payment of dividends and distribution of assets on the corporation's dissolution.	Stock that has priority over common stock shares as to payment of dividends and distribution of assets on dissolution. Dividend payments are usually a fixed percentage of the face value of the share. Preferred shares may or may not be voting shares.

CUMULATIVE PREFERRED STOCK	**PARTICIPATING PREFERRED STOCK**	**CONVERTIBLE PREFERRED STOCK**	**REDEEMABLE PREFERRED STOCK**
Preferred shares on which required dividends not paid in a given year must be paid in a subsequent year before any common-stock dividends can be paid.	Preferred shares entitling the owner to receive the preferred-stock dividend and additional dividends after the corporation has paid dividends on common stock.	Preferred shares that, under certain conditions, can be converted into a specified number of common shares either in the issuing corporation or, sometimes, in another corporation.	Preferred shares issued with the express condition that the issuing corporation has the right to repurchase the shares as specified. (Sometimes referred to as callable preferred stock.)

private equity firm buys an entire corporation and then reorganizes it. Sometimes, divisions of the purchased company are sold off to pay down debt.

Ultimately, the private equity firm may sell shares in the reorganized (and perhaps more profitable) company to the public in an *initial public offering (IPO)*. Then the private equity firm can make profits by selling its shares in the company to the public.

39–4d Crowdfunding

Start-up businesses can also attempt to obtain financing through *crowdfunding*. **Crowdfunding** is a cooperative activity in which people network and pool funds and other resources via the Internet to assist a cause or

invest in a venture. Sometimes, crowdfunding is used to raise funds for charitable purposes, such as disaster relief, but increasingly it is being used to finance budding entrepreneurs.

In 2016, new Securities and Exchange Commission (SEC) rules went into effect to allow companies to offer and sell securities through crowdfunding. The rules removed a decades-old ban on public solicitation for private investments, which means that companies can advertise investment opportunities to the general public. According to the SEC, the new rules are intended to help smaller companies raise capital while providing investors with additional protections. Companies are required to make specific disclosures and are limited to raising $1 million a year through crowdfunding.

Reviewing: Corporate Formation and Financing

William Sharp was the sole shareholder and manager of Chickasaw Club, Inc., an S corporation that operated a popular nightclub of the same name in Columbus, Georgia. Sharp maintained a corporate checking account but paid the club's employees, suppliers, and entertainers in cash out of the club's proceeds. Sharp owned the property on which the club was located. He rented it to the club but made mortgage payments out of the club's proceeds and often paid other personal expenses with Chickasaw corporate funds.

At 12:45 A.M. on July 31, eighteen-year-old Aubrey Lynn Pursley, who was already intoxicated, entered the Chickasaw Club. A city ordinance prohibited individuals under the age of twenty-one from entering nightclubs, but Chickasaw employees did not check Pursley's identification to verify her age. Pursley drank more alcohol at Chickasaw and was visibly intoxicated when she left the club at 3:00 A.M. with a beer in her hand. Shortly afterward, Pursley lost control of her car, struck a tree, and was killed. Joseph Dancause, Pursley's stepfather, filed a tort lawsuit in a Georgia state court against Chickasaw Club, Inc., and William Sharp, seeking damages. Using the information presented in the chapter, answer the following questions.

1. Under what theory might the court in this case make an exception to the limited liability of shareholders and hold Sharp personally liable for the damages? What factors would be relevant to the court's decision?
2. Suppose that Chickasaw's articles of incorporation failed to describe the corporation's purpose or management structure, as required by state law. Would the court be likely to rule that Sharp is personally liable to Dancause on that basis? Why or why not?
3. Suppose that the club extended credit to its regular patrons, although neither the articles of incorporation nor the corporate bylaws authorized this practice. Would the corporation likely have the power to engage in this activity? Explain.
4. How would the court classify the Chickasaw Club corporation—domestic or foreign, public or private? Why?

Debate This . . . *The sole shareholder of an S corporation should not be able to avoid liability for the torts of her or his employees.*

Terms and Concepts

alien corporation 743	dividends 742	publicly held corporation 745
articles of incorporation 750	domestic corporation 742	retained earnings 742
benefit corporation 748	foreign corporation 743	S corporation 747
bond 757	holding company 742	securities 756
bylaws 751	pierce the corporate veil 754	shareholder agreement 747
close corporation 746	preferred stock 757	stock 757
commingle 754	private equity capital 757	*ultra vires* 753
common stock 757	public corporation 744	venture capital 757
crowdfunding 758		

Issue Spotters

1. Northwest Brands, Inc., is a small business incorporated in Minnesota. Its one class of stock is owned by twelve members of a single family. Ordinarily, corporate income is taxed at the corporate and shareholder levels. Is there a way for Northwest Brands to avoid this double taxation? Explain your answer. (See *The Nature and Classification of Corporations*.)

2. The incorporators of Consumer Investments, Inc., want their new corporation to have the authority to transact nearly any conceivable type of business. Can they grant this authority to their firm? If so, how? If not, why not? (See *Piercing the Corporate Veil.*)

• **Check your answers to the Issue Spotters against the answers provided in Appendix D at the end of this text.**

Business Scenarios

39–1. Preincorporation. Cummings, Okawa, and Taft are recent college graduates who want to form a corporation to manufacture and sell digital tablets. Peterson tells them he will set in motion the formation of their corporation. First, Peterson makes a contract with Owens for the purchase of a piece of land for $20,000. Owens does not know of the prospective corporate formation at the time the contract is signed. Second, Peterson makes a contract with Babcock to build a small plant on the property being purchased. Babcock's contract is conditional on the corporation's formation. Peterson secures all necessary subscription agreements and capitalization, and he files the articles of incorporation. (See *Corporate Formation.*)

(a) Discuss whether the newly formed corporation, Peterson, or both are liable on the contracts with Owens and Babcock.

(b) Discuss whether the corporation is automatically liable to Babcock on formation.

39–2. *Ultra Vires* Doctrine. Oya Paka and two business associates formed a corporation called Paka Corp. for the purpose of selling computer services. Oya, who owned 50 percent of the corporate shares, served as the corporation's president. Oya wished to obtain a personal loan from her bank for $250,000, but the bank required the note to be cosigned by a third party. Oya cosigned the note in the name of the corporation. Later, Oya defaulted on the note, and the bank sued the corporation for payment. The corporation asserted, as a defense, that Oya had exceeded her authority when she cosigned the note on behalf of the corporation. Had she? Explain. (See *Corporate Formation and Powers.*)

Business Case Problems

39–3. Spotlight on Smart Inventions—Piercing the Corporate Veil. Thomas Persson and Jon Nokes founded

Smart Inventions, Inc., to market household consumer products. The success of their first product, the Smart Mop, continued with later products, which were sold through infomercials and other means. Persson and Nokes were the firm's officers and equal shareholders. Persson was responsible for product development, and Nokes was in charge of day-to-day operations. In time, they became dissatisfied with each other's efforts. Nokes represented the firm as financially "dying," "in a grim state, . . . worse than ever," and offered to buy all of Persson's shares for $1.6 million. Persson accepted.

On the day that they signed the agreement to transfer the shares, Smart Inventions began marketing a new product— the Tap Light. It was an instant success, generating millions of dollars in revenues. In negotiating with Persson, Nokes had intentionally kept the Tap Light a secret. Persson sued Smart Inventions, asserting fraud and other claims. Under what principle might Smart Inventions be liable for Nokes's fraud? Is Smart Inventions liable in this case? Explain. [*Persson v. Smart Inventions, Inc.,* 125 Cal.App.4th 1141, 23 Cal. Rptr.3d 335 (2 Dist. 2005)] (See *Piercing the Corporate Veil.*)

39–4. Piercing the Corporate Veil. Smith Services, Inc., a trucking business owned by Tony Smith, charged its fuel purchases to an account at Laker Express. When Smith Services was not paid on several contracts, it ceased doing business and was dissolved. Smith continued to provide trucking services, however, as a sole proprietor. Laker Express sought to

recover Smith Services' unpaid fuel charges, which amounted to about $35,000, from Smith. He argued that he was not personally liable for a corporate debt. Should the court pierce the corporate veil? Explain. [*Bear, Inc. v. Smith,* 303 S.W.3d 137 (Ky.App. 2010)] (See *Piercing the Corporate Veil.*)

39–5. Close Corporations. Mark Burnett and Kamran Pourgol were the only shareholders in a corporation that built and sold a house. When the buyers discovered that the house exceeded the amount of square footage allowed by the building permit, Pourgol agreed to renovate the house to conform to the permit. No work was done, however, and Burnett filed a suit against Pourgol. Burnett claimed that, without his knowledge, Pourgol had submitted incorrect plans to obtain the building permit, misrepresented the extent of the renovation, and failed to fix the house. Was Pourgol guilty of misconduct? If so, how might it have been avoided? Discuss. [*Burnett v. Pourgol,* 83 A.D.3d 756, 921 N.Y.S.2d 280 (2 Dept. 2011)] (See *Piercing the Corporate Veil.*)

39–6. Piercing the Corporate Veil. In 1997, Leon Greenblatt, Andrew Jahelka, and Richard Nichols incorporated Loop Corp. with only $1,000 of capital. Three years later, Banco Panamericano, Inc., which was run entirely by Greenblatt and owned by a Greenblatt family trust, extended a large line of credit to Loop. Loop's subsidiaries participated in the credit, giving $3 million to Loop while acquiring a security interest in Loop itself. Loop then opened an account with Wachovia Securities, LLC, to buy stock shares using credit provided by Wachovia. When the stock values plummeted, Loop owed Wachovia $1.89 million. Loop also defaulted on its loan from Banco, but Banco agreed to lend Loop millions of dollars more.

Rather than repay Wachovia with the influx of funds, Loop gave the funds to closely related entities and "compensated" Nichols and Jahelka without issuing any W-2 forms (forms reporting compensation to the Internal Revenue Service). Loop made loans to other related entities and shared office space, equipment, and telephone and fax numbers with related entities. Loop also moved employees among related entities, failed to file its tax returns on time (and sometimes did not file them at all), and failed to follow its own bylaws. In a lawsuit brought by Wachovia, can the court hold Greenblatt, Jahelka, and Nichols personally liable by piercing the corporate veil? Why or why not? [*Wachovia Securities, LLC v. Banco Panamericano, Inc.,* 674 F.3d 743 (9th Cir. 2012)] (See *Piercing the Corporate Veil.*)

39–7. Business Case Problem with Sample Answer— Piercing the Corporate Veil. Scott Snapp contracted with Castlebrook Builders, Inc., which was owned by Stephen Kappeler, to remodel a house. Kappeler estimated that the remodeling would cost around $500,000. Eventually, however, Snapp paid Kappeler more than $1.3 million. Snapp filed a suit in an Ohio state court against Castlebrook, alleging breach of contract and fraud, among other things. During the trial, it was revealed that Castlebrook had issued no shares of stock and that personal and corporate funds had been commingled. The minutes of the corporate meetings all looked exactly the same. In addition, Kappeler could not provide an accounting for the Snapp project. In particular, he could not explain evidence of double and triple billing nor demonstrate that the amount Snapp paid had actually been spent on the remodeling project. Are these sufficient grounds to pierce the corporate veil? Explain. [*Snapp v. Castlebrook Builders, Inc.,* 2014 -Ohio- 163, 7 N.E.3d 574 (2014)] (See *Corporate Formation and Powers.*)

- **For a sample answer to Problem 39–7, go to Appendix E at the end of this text.**

39–8. Torts. Jennifer Hoffman took her cell phone to a store owned by R&K Trading, Inc., for repairs. Later, Hoffman filed a suit in a New York state court against R&K, Verizon Wireless, Inc., and others. Hoffman sought to recover damages for a variety of torts, including infliction of emotional distress and negligent hiring and supervision. She alleged that an R&K employee, Keith Press, had examined her phone in a back room, accessed private photos of her stored on her phone, and disseminated the photos to the public. Hoffman testified that "after the incident, she learned from another R&K employee that personal information and pictures had been removed from the phones of other customers." Can R&K be held liable for the torts of its employees? Explain. [*Hoffman v. Verizon Wireless, Inc.,* 5 N.Y.S.3d 123, 125 A.D.3d 806 (2015)] (See *The Nature and Classification of Corporations.*)

39–9. A Question of Ethics—Piercing the Corporate Veil. *In New York City, 2406-12 Amsterdam Associates LLC brought an action in a New York state court against Alianza Dominicana and Alianza LLC to recover unpaid rent. The plaintiff asserted cause to pierce the corporate veil, alleging that Alianza Dominicana had made promises to pay its rent while discreetly forming Alianza LLC to avoid liability for it. According to 2406-12, Alianza LLC was 90 percent owned by Alianza Dominicana, had no employees, and had no function but to hold Alianza Dominicana's assets away from its creditors. The defendants filed a motion to dismiss the plaintiff's claim. [2406-12 Amsterdam Associates, LLC v. Alianza, LLC, 136 A.D.3d 512, 25 N.Y.S.2d 167 (1 Dept. 2016)] (See Piercing the Corporate Veil.)*

(a) Assuming that 2406-12's allegations are true, are there sufficient grounds to pierce Alianza LLC's corporate veil? Discuss.

(b) Suppose that the parties to this dispute were small, close corporations. How might that circumstance affect the result in this case?

Legal Reasoning Group Activity

39–10. Corporate versus LLC Form of Business. The limited liability company (LLC) may be the best organizational form for most businesses. For a significant number of firms, however, the corporate form or some other form of organization may be better. (See *The Nature and Classification of Corporations.*)

(a) The first group will outline several reasons why a firm might be better off as a corporation than as an LLC.

(b) The second group will discuss the differences between corporations and LLCs in terms of their management structures.

CHAPTER 40

Corporate Directors, Officers, and Shareholders

A corporation joins together the efforts and resources of a large number of individuals for the purpose of producing greater returns than those persons could have obtained individually. Corporate directors, officers, and shareholders all play different roles within the corporate entity.

Sometimes, actions that may benefit the corporation as a whole do not coincide with the separate interests of the individuals making up the corporation. In such situations, it is important to know the rights and duties of all participants in the corporate enterprise. This chapter focuses on these rights and duties and the ways in which conflicts among corporate participants are resolved.

40-1 Role of Directors and Officers

The board of directors is the ultimate authority in every corporation. Directors have responsibility for all policy-making decisions necessary to the management of all corporate affairs. Additionally, the directors must act as a body in carrying out routine corporate business. The board selects and removes the corporate officers, determines the capital structure of the corporation, and declares dividends. Each director has one vote, and customarily the majority rules. The general areas of responsibility of the board of directors are shown in Exhibit 40–1.

Directors are sometimes inappropriately characterized as *agents* because they act on behalf of the corporation. No *individual* director, however, can act as an agent to bind the corporation. As a group, directors collectively control the corporation in a way that no agent is able to control a principal. In addition, although directors occupy positions of trust and control over the corporation, they are not *trustees,* because they do not hold title to property for the use and benefit of others.

Few qualifications are required for directors. Only a handful of states impose minimum age and residency requirements. A director may be a shareholder, but that is not necessary (unless the articles of incorporation or bylaws require ownership interest).

40-1a Election of Directors

Subject to statutory limitations, the number of directors is set forth in the corporation's articles or bylaws.

Historically, the minimum number of directors has been three, but today many states permit fewer. Normally, the incorporators appoint the first board of directors at the time the corporation is created, or the directors are named in the articles of incorporation. The initial board serves until the first annual shareholders' meeting. Subsequent directors are elected by a majority vote of the shareholders.

A director usually serves for a term of one year—from annual meeting to annual meeting. Most state statutes permit longer and staggered terms. A common practice is to elect one-third of the board members each year for a three-year term. In this way, there is greater management continuity.

Removal of Directors A director can be removed *for cause*—that is, for failing to perform a required duty—either as specified in the articles or bylaws or by shareholder action. The board of directors may also have the power to remove a director for cause, subject to shareholder review. In most states, a director cannot be removed without cause unless the shareholders reserved the right to do so at the time of election.

Vacancies on the Board Vacancies occur on the board if a director dies or resigns or when a new position is created through amendment of the articles or bylaws. In these situations, either the shareholders or the board itself can fill the vacant position, depending on state law or on the provisions of the bylaws. Often, for instance, an election is held and shareholders vote to fill the vacancy.

EXHIBIT 40–1 Directors' Management Responsibilities

Authorize Major Corporate Policy Decisions

Examples:
- Oversee major contract negotiations and management-labor negotiations.

- Initiate negotiations on the sale or lease of corporate assets outside the regular course of business.

- Decide whether to pursue new product lines or business opportunities.

Make Executive-Level Personnel Decisions

Examples:
- Engage in selection of officers and determine their appropriate total compensation, which may include stock options.

- Supervise managerial employees and make decisions regarding their termination.

Make Financial Decisions

Examples:
- Make decisions regarding the issuance of authorized shares and bonds.

- Decide when to declare dividends to be paid to shareholders.

Note that even when an election is authorized, a court can invalidate the results if the directors have attempted to manipulate the election in order to reduce the shareholders' influence.

40–1b Compensation of Directors

In the past, corporate directors were rarely compensated. Today, directors are often paid at least nominal sums. In large corporations, they may receive more substantial compensation because of the time, work, effort, and especially risk involved.

Most states permit the corporate articles or bylaws to authorize compensation for directors. In fact, the Revised Model Business Corporation Act (RMBCA) states that unless the articles or bylaws provide otherwise, the board itself may set the directors' compensation [RMBCA 8.11]. Directors also receive indirect benefits, such as business contacts and prestige, and other rewards, such as stock options.

In many corporations, directors are also chief corporate officers (such as president or chief executive officer) and receive compensation in their managerial positions. A director who is also an officer of the corporation is referred to as an **inside director,** whereas a director who does not hold a management position is an **outside director.** Typically, a corporation's board of directors includes both inside and outside directors.

40–1c Board of Directors' Meetings

The board of directors conducts business by holding formal meetings with recorded minutes. The dates of regular meetings are usually established in the articles or bylaws or by board resolution, and ordinarily no further notice is required. Special meetings can be called as well, with notice sent to all directors.

Most states allow directors to participate in board of directors' meetings from remote locations. Directors can participate via telephone, Web conferencing, or Skype, provided that all the directors can simultaneously hear each other during the meeting [RMBCA 8.20].

Quorum of Directors Unless the articles of incorporation or bylaws specify a greater number, a majority of the board of directors normally constitutes a *quorum* [RMBCA 8.24]. (A **quorum** is the minimum number of members of a body of officials or other group that must be present for business to be validly transacted.) Some state statutes specifically allow corporations to set a quorum at less than a majority but not less than one-third of the directors.[1]

Voting Once a quorum is present, the directors transact business and vote on issues affecting the corporation.

---

1. See, for example, Delaware Code Annotated Title 8, Section 141(b); and New York Business Corporation Law Section 707.

Each director present at the meeting has one vote.[2] Ordinary matters generally require a simple majority vote, but certain extraordinary issues may require a greater-than-majority vote.

40–1d Committees of the Board of Directors

When a board of directors has a large number of members and must deal with myriad complex business issues, meetings can become unwieldy. Therefore, the boards of large, publicly held corporations typically create committees of directors and delegate certain tasks to these committees. By focusing on specific subjects, committees can increase the efficiency of the board.

Two common types of committees are the *executive committee* and the *audit committee.* An executive committee handles interim management decisions between board meetings. It is limited to dealing with ordinary business matters and does not have the power to declare dividends, amend the bylaws, or authorize the issuance of stock. The audit committee is responsible for the selection, compensation, and oversight of the independent public accountants that audit the firm's financial records. *The Sarbanes-Oxley Act requires all publicly held corporations to have an audit committee.*

40–1e Rights of Directors

A corporate director must have certain rights to function properly in that position, including the rights of participation, inspection, and indemnification.

Right to Participation The *right to participation* means that directors are entitled to participate in all board of directors' meetings and have a right to be notified of these meetings. Because the dates of regular board meetings are usually specified in the bylaws, no notice of these meetings is required. If special meetings are called, however, notice is required unless waived by the director [RMBCA 8.23].

Right of Inspection A director also has a *right of inspection,* which means that each director can access the corporation's books and records, facilities, and premises. Inspection rights are essential for directors to make informed decisions and to exercise the necessary supervision over corporate officers and employees. This right of inspection is almost absolute and cannot be restricted (by the articles, bylaws, or any act of the board of directors).

■ **CASE IN POINT 40.1** NavLink, Inc., a Delaware corporation, provides high-end data management for customers and governments in Saudi Arabia, Qatar, Lebanon, and the United Arab Emirates. NavLink's co-founders, George Chammas and Laurent Delifer, served on its board of directors.

Chammas and Delifer were concerned about the company's 2015 annual budget and three-year operating plan. Despite repeated requests, Chammas was never given the meeting minutes from several board meetings in 2015. Chammas and Delifer believed that the other directors were withholding information and holding secret "pre-board meetings" at which plans and decisions were being made without them. They filed suit in a Delaware state court seeking inspection rights.

The court ordered NavLink to provide the plaintiffs with board meeting minutes and with communications from NavLink's secretary regarding the minutes. The plaintiffs were also entitled to inspect corporate documents and communications concerning NavLink's 2015 budget and three-year plan.[3] ■

Right to Indemnification When a director becomes involved in litigation by virtue of her or his position, the director may have a *right to indemnification* (reimbursement) for the legal costs, fees, and damages incurred. Most states allow corporations to indemnify and purchase liability insurance for corporate directors [RMBCA 8.51].

40–1f Corporate Officers and Executives

Corporate officers and other executive employees are hired by the board of directors. At a minimum, most corporations have a president, one or more vice presidents, a secretary, and a treasurer. In most states, an individual can hold more than one office, such as president and secretary, and can be both an officer and a director of the corporation.

In addition to carrying out the duties articulated in the bylaws, corporate and managerial officers act as agents of the corporation. Therefore, the ordinary rules of agency normally apply to their employment.

Corporate officers and other high-level managers are employees of the company, so their rights are defined by employment contracts. Nevertheless, the board of directors normally can remove a corporate officer at any

---

2. Except in Louisiana, which allows a director to vote by proxy under certain circumstances.

3. *Chammas v. NavLink, Inc.,* 2016 WL 767714 (Del.Ch.Ct. 2016).

time with or without cause. If the directors remove an officer in violation of the terms of an employment contract, however, the corporation may be liable for breach of contract.

For a synopsis of the roles of directors and officers, see Concept Summary 40.1.

40–2 Duties and Liabilities of Directors and Officers

The duties of corporate directors and officers are similar because both groups are involved in decision making and

---

Concept Summary 40.1

Roles of Directors and Officers

Election of Directors	• The incorporators usually appoint the first board of directors. Thereafter, shareholders elect the directors. • Directors usually serve a one-year term, although the term can be longer. Few qualifications are required. • A director can be a shareholder but is not required to be. • Compensation usually is specified in the corporate articles or bylaws.
Board of Directors' Meetings	• The board of directors conducts business by holding formal meetings with recorded minutes. • The dates of regular meetings are usually established in the corporate articles or bylaws. • Special meetings can be called, with notice sent to all directors. • Usually, a quorum is a majority of the corporate directors. Once a quorum is present, each director has one vote, and the majority normally rules in ordinary matters.
Rights of Directors	• Directors' rights include the rights of participation, inspection, compensation, and indemnification.
Board of Directors' Committees	• Directors may appoint committees and delegate some of their responsibilities to the committees and to corporate officers and executives. For instance, directors commonly appoint an *executive committee*, which handles ordinary, interim management decisions between board of directors' meetings. • Directors may also appoint an *audit committee* to hire and supervise the independent public accountants who audit the corporation's financial records.
Role of Corporate Officers and Executives	• The board of directors normally hires the corporate officers and other executive employees. • In most states, a person can hold more than one office and can be both an officer and a director of a corporation. • The rights of corporate officers and executives are defined by employment contracts.

are in positions of control. Directors and officers are considered to be fiduciaries of the corporation because their relationship with the corporation and its shareholders is one of trust and confidence. As fiduciaries, directors and officers owe ethical—and legal—duties to the corporation and to the shareholders as a group. These fiduciary duties include the duty of care and the duty of loyalty.

40–2a Duty of Care

Directors and officers must exercise due care in performing their duties. The standard of *due care* has been variously described in judicial decisions and codified in many state corporation codes. Generally, it requires a director or officer to:

1. Act in good faith (honestly).
2. Exercise the care that an ordinarily prudent (careful) person would exercise in similar circumstances.
3. Do what she or he believes is in the best interests of the corporation [RMBCA 8.30(a), 8.42(a)].

If directors or officers fail to exercise due care and the corporation or its shareholders suffer harm as a result, the directors or officers can be held liable for negligence. (An exception is made if the *business judgment rule* applies, as will be discussed shortly.)

Duty to Make Informed Decisions Directors and officers are expected to be informed on corporate matters and to conduct a reasonable investigation of the situation before making a decision. They must, for instance, attend meetings and presentations, ask for information from those who have it, read reports, and review other written materials. In other words, directors and officers must investigate, study, and discuss matters and evaluate alternatives before making a decision. They cannot decide on the spur of the moment without adequate research.

Although directors and officers are expected to act in accordance with their own knowledge and training, they are also normally entitled to rely on information given to them by certain other persons. Under the laws of most states and Section 8.30(b) of the RMBCA, such persons include competent officers or employees, professionals such as attorneys and accountants, and committees of the board of directors. (The committee must be one on which the director does not serve, however.) The reliance must be in good faith to insulate a director from liability if the information later proves to be inaccurate or unreliable.

Duty to Exercise Reasonable Supervision Directors are also expected to exercise a reasonable amount of supervision when they delegate work to corporate officers and employees. ■ **EXAMPLE 40.2** Dana, a corporate bank director, fails to attend any board of directors' meetings for five years. In addition, Dana never inspects any of the corporate books or records and generally fails to supervise the activities of the bank president and the loan committee. Meanwhile, Brennan, the bank president, who is a corporate officer, makes various improper loans and permits large overdrafts. In this situation, Dana (the corporate director) can be held liable to the corporation for losses resulting from the unsupervised actions of the bank president and the loan committee. ■

Dissenting Directors Directors' votes at board of directors' meetings should be entered into the minutes. Sometimes, an individual director disagrees with the majority's vote (which becomes an act of the board of directors). Unless a dissent is entered in the minutes, the director is presumed to have assented. If the directors are later held liable for mismanagement as a result of a decision, dissenting directors are rarely held individually liable to the corporation. For this reason, a director who is absent from a given meeting sometimes registers a dissent with the secretary of the board regarding actions taken at the meeting.

40–2b The Business Judgment Rule

Directors and officers are expected to exercise due care and to use their best judgment in guiding corporate management, but they are not insurers of business success. Under the **business judgment rule,** a corporate director or officer will not be liable to the corporation or to its shareholders for honest mistakes of judgment and bad business decisions.

Courts give significant deference to the decisions of corporate directors and officers, and consider the reasonableness of a decision at the time it was made, without the benefit of hindsight. Thus, corporate decision makers are not subjected to second-guessing by shareholders or others in the corporation.

When the Rule Applies The business judgment rule will apply as long as the director or officer:

1. Took reasonable steps to become informed about the matter.
2. Had a rational basis for her or his decision.
3. Did not have a conflict between her or his personal interest and the interest of the corporation.

Whether these conditions were met formed the basis for the court's decision in the following case.

Oliveira v. Sugarman

Court of Special Appeals of Maryland, 226 Md.App. 524, 130 A.3d 1085 (2016).

Background and Facts   iStar, Inc., a Maryland corporation, promised to award shares of company stock to employees for their performance if the stock averaged a certain target price per share over a specific period. The stock price rose 300 percent, but the target was missed. The board changed the basis for an award from performance to service—an employee who had been with iStar for a certain period was entitled to an award. It then issued additional shares to pay the awards.

Albert and Lena Oliveira, iStar shareholders, demanded that the board rescind the awards. The Oliveiras alleged misconduct and demanded that the board file a suit on the company's behalf to seek damages or other relief. The board appointed Barry Ridings, an outside director, to investigate the allegation. Ridings recommended that the board refuse the demand. The board acted on his recommendation.

The Oliveiras filed a suit in a Maryland state court against Jay Sugarman, the board chairman, and the other directors, including Ridings, alleging a breach of fiduciary duty. The court dismissed the claim. The Oliveiras appealed.

In the Language of the Court

BURGER, J. [Judge]

* * * *

*Judicial review of a demand refusal is subject to the business judgment rule, and the court * * * limits its review to whether the board acted independently, in good faith, and within the realm of sound business judgment.* [Emphasis added.]

* * * *

* * * The Shareholders [the Oliveiras] assert that [Ridings's] investigation of the Shareholders' demand was rife with improper procedure. The Shareholders argue that * * * Ridings lacked sufficient corporate experience to make a proper recommendation to the Board and that Ridings was not sufficiently disinterested. Both contentions are baseless. Ridings has forty years of business experience, including service on the boards of several public companies, including the American Stock Exchange. Furthermore, Ridings hired highly respected and experienced legal counsel to assist him and conducted multiple interviews.

We further reject the Shareholders' contention that Ridings was interested or lacked independence. Ridings joined the Board after the challenged conduct and had no business, personal, social, or other relationships with any other member of the Board. Although Ridings's employer [Lazard Freres & Company, where Ridings was vice chairman of investment banking] performed banking services for iStar [for two years], Lazard has no ongoing business relationship with iStar. *Furthermore, allegations of mere personal friendship or a mere outside business relationship, standing alone, are insufficient to raise a reasonable doubt about a director's independence.* [Emphasis added.]

The Shareholders' contention that Ridings lacks independence because he is compensated for his service as a Director is similarly unfounded. The Shareholders further contend that Ridings lacks independence because he is a named defendant in this lawsuit. This assertion is contrary to established law. Accordingly, we reject the Shareholders' contentions that Ridings was interested or lacked independence.

* * * *

In conclusion, the Shareholders have failed to surmount the presumption of the business judgment rule. In failing to do so, they have failed to state a claim upon which relief may be granted.

Decision and Remedy   *A state intermediate appellate court affirmed the lower court's dismissal of the Oliveiras' claim. "The Shareholders' bald allegations of impropriety are plainly insufficient to overcome the presumption of the business judgment rule."*

Critical Thinking

- **Legal Environment**   *In a letter to the Oliveiras, the board explained that it saw "no upside—and much downside—to the action and lawsuit proposed in the Demand." What would the "downside" consist of?*
- **What If the Facts Were Different?**   *Only one member of the iStar board—Sugarman—received an award as an employee. The others who made the decision to change the award were, like Ridings, outside directors. Suppose that the opposite had been true. Would the result have been the same?*

Provides Broad Protections The business judgment rule provides broad protections to corporate decision makers. In fact, most courts will apply the rule unless there is evidence of bad faith, fraud, or a clear breach of fiduciary duties.

■ **CASE IN POINT 40.3** The board of directors of the Chugach Alaska Corporation (CAC) voted to remove Sheri Buretta as the chair and install Robert Henrichs. During his term, Henrichs acted without board approval, made decisions with only his supporters present, retaliated against directors who challenged his decisions, and ignored board rules for conducting meetings. He refused to comply with bylaws that required a special shareholders' meeting in response to a shareholder petition and personally mistreated directors, shareholders, and employees. After six months, the board voted to reinstall Buretta.

CAC filed a suit in an Alaska state court against Henrichs, alleging a breach of fiduciary duty. A jury found Henrichs liable, and the court barred him from serving on CAC's board for five years. The appellate court affirmed. Given the nature and seriousness of Henrichs's misconduct, the business judgment rule did not protect him.[4] ■

---

4. *Henrichs v. Chugach Alaska Corp.*, 250 P.3d 531 (Alaska Sup.Ct. 2011).

40–2c Duty of Loyalty

Loyalty can be defined as faithfulness to one's obligations and duties. In the corporate context, the duty of loyalty requires directors and officers to subordinate their personal interests to the welfare of the corporation. For instance, a director should not oppose a transaction that is in the corporation's best interest simply because pursuing it may cost the director his or her position. Directors cannot use corporate funds or confidential corporate information for personal advantage and must refrain from self-dealing.

Cases dealing with the duty of loyalty typically involve one or more of the following:

1. Competing with the corporation.
2. Usurping (taking personal advantage of) a corporate opportunity.
3. Pursuing an interest that conflicts with that of the corporation.
4. Using information that is not available to the public to make a profit trading securities (insider trading).
5. Authorizing a corporate transaction that is detrimental to minority shareholders.
6. Selling control over the corporation.

The following *Classic Case* illustrates the conflict that can arise between a corporate officer's personal interest and his or her duty of loyalty.

Classic Case 40.2

Guth v. Loft, Inc.
Supreme Court of Delaware, 23 Del.Ch. 255, 5 A.2d 503 (1939).

Background and Facts In 1930, Charles Guth became the president of Loft, Inc., a candy-and-restaurant chain. Guth and his family also owned Grace Company, which made syrups for soft drinks. Coca-Cola Company supplied Loft with cola syrup. Unhappy with what he felt was Coca-Cola's high price, Guth entered into an agreement with Roy Megargel to acquire the trademark and formula for Pepsi-Cola and form Pepsi-Cola Corporation. Neither Guth nor Megargel could finance the new venture, however, and Grace Company was insolvent.

Without the knowledge of Loft's board, Guth used Loft's capital, credit, facilities, and employees to further the Pepsi enterprise. At Guth's direction, a Loft employee made the concentrate for the syrup, which was sent to Grace to add sugar and water. Loft charged Grace for the concentrate but allowed forty months' credit. Grace charged Pepsi for the syrup but also granted substantial credit. Grace sold the syrup to Pepsi's customers, including Loft, which paid on delivery or within thirty days. Loft also paid for Pepsi's advertising. Finally, with profits declining as a result of switching from Coca-Cola, Loft filed a suit in a Delaware state court against Guth, Grace, and Pepsi, seeking their Pepsi stock and an accounting. The court entered a judgment in the plaintiff's favor. The defendants appealed to the Delaware Supreme Court.

In the Language of the Court
LAYTON, Chief Justice, delivering the opinion of the court:
    * * * *

Corporate officers and directors are not permitted to use their position of trust and confidence to further their private interests. * * * They stand in a fiduciary relation to the corporation and its stockholders.

Case 40.2 Continued

A public policy, existing through the years, and derived from a profound knowledge of human characteristics and motives, has established *a rule that demands of a corporate officer or director, peremptorily [not open for debate] and inexorably [unavoidably], the most scrupulous observance of his duty, not only affirmatively to protect the interests of the corporation committed to his charge, but also to refrain from doing anything that would work injury to the corporation* * * * . The rule that requires an undivided and unselfish loyalty to the corporation demands that there shall be no conflict between duty and self-interest. [Emphasis added.]

* * * *

* * * *If there is presented to a corporate officer or director a business opportunity which the corporation is financially able to undertake [that] is * * * in the line of the corporation's business and is of practical advantage to it * * * and, by embracing the opportunity, the self-interest of the officer or director will be brought into conflict with that of his corporation, the law will not permit him to seize the opportunity for himself.* * * * In such circumstances, * * * the corporation may elect to claim all of the benefits of the transaction for itself, and the law will impress a trust in favor of the corporation upon the property, interests and profits so acquired. [Emphasis added.]

* * * *

* * * The appellants contend that no conflict of interest between Guth and Loft resulted from his acquirement and exploitation of the Pepsi-Cola opportunity [and] that the acquisition did not place Guth in competition with Loft * * * . [In this case, however,] Guth was Loft, and Guth was Pepsi. He absolutely controlled Loft. His authority over Pepsi was supreme. As Pepsi, he created and controlled the supply of Pepsi-Cola syrup, and he determined the price and the terms. What he offered, as Pepsi, he had the power, as Loft, to accept. Upon any consideration of human characteristics and motives, he created a conflict between self-interest and duty. He made himself the judge in his own cause. * * * Moreover, a reasonable probability of injury to Loft resulted from the situation forced upon it. Guth was in the same position to impose his terms upon Loft as had been the Coca-Cola Company.

* * * The facts and circumstances demonstrate that Guth's appropriation of the Pepsi-Cola opportunity to himself placed him in a competitive position with Loft with respect to a commodity essential to it, thereby rendering his personal interests incompatible with the superior interests of his corporation; and this situation was accomplished, not openly and with his own resources, but secretly and with the money and facilities of the corporation which was committed to his protection.

Decision and Remedy   *The Delaware Supreme Court upheld the judgment of the lower court. The state supreme court was "convinced that the opportunity to acquire the Pepsi-Cola trademark and formula, goodwill and business belonged to [Loft], and that Guth, as its President, had no right to appropriate the opportunity to himself."*

Impact of This Case on Today's Law   *This early Delaware decision was one of the first to set forth a test for determining when a corporate officer or director has breached the duty of loyalty. The test has two basic parts: Was the opportunity reasonably related to the corporation's line of business, and was the corporation financially able to undertake the opportunity? The court also considered whether the corporation had an interest or expectancy in the opportunity. It recognized that when the corporation had "no interest or expectancy, the officer or director is entitled to treat the opportunity as his own."*

Critical Thinking

- **What If the Facts Were Different?**   *Suppose that Loft's board of directors had approved Pepsi-Cola's use of its personnel and equipment. Would the court's decision have been different? Discuss.*

40–2d Conflicts of Interest

Corporate directors often have many business affiliations, and a director may sit on the board of more than one corporation. Of course, directors are precluded from entering into or supporting businesses that operate in direct competition with corporations on whose boards they serve. Their fiduciary duty requires them to make a full disclosure of any potential conflicts of interest that might arise in any corporate transaction [RMBCA 8.60].

Sometimes, a corporation enters into a contract or engages in a transaction in which an officer or director has a personal interest. The director or officer must make a *full disclosure* of the nature of the conflicting interest and all facts pertinent to the transaction. He or she must also abstain from voting on the proposed transaction. When these rules are followed, the transaction can proceed. Otherwise, directors would be prevented from ever having financial dealings with the corporations they serve.

■ **EXAMPLE 40.4** Ballo Corporation needs office space. Stephanie Colson, one of its five directors, owns the building adjoining the corporation's headquarters. Colson can negotiate a lease for the space to Ballo if she fully discloses her conflicting interest and any facts known to her about the proposed transaction to Ballo and the other four directors. If the lease arrangement is fair and reasonable, Colson abstains from voting on

it, and the other members of the corporation's board of directors unanimously approve it, the contract is valid. ■

40–2e Liability of Directors and Officers

Directors and officers are exposed to liability on many fronts. They can be held liable for negligence in certain circumstances, as previously discussed. They may also be held liable for the crimes and torts committed by themselves or by corporate employees under their supervision. (See this chapter's *Global Insight* feature for a discussion of how the United States criminally prosecutes corporations and their managers for bribery.)

GLOBAL INSIGHT — Anti-Bribery Charges Take Their Toll on U.S. and Foreign Corporations

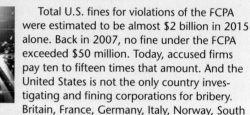

Hitachi, Ltd., was established in 1920 in Tokyo, Japan. Among other activities, it builds and operates electrical power systems throughout the world. Almost a hundred years after its founding, Hitachi agreed to a consent decree offered by the U.S. Securities and Exchange Commission (SEC).[a] (A consent decree is a means of resolving a dispute without going to trial or admitting guilt.) Part of that decree required Hitachi to pay a fine of $19 million for violating the Foreign Corrupt Practices Act (FCPA).[b]

Hitachi had admitted to creating a system to bribe South Africa's ruling political party to give Hitachi preference in awarding electrical power station contracts. The SEC claimed jurisdiction over Hitachi even though the company was no longer listed on the New York Stock Exchange (NYSE). While the bribery scheme was taking place, Hitachi was a company whose shares could be traded in the United States. The long arm of U.S. anti-bribery laws had struck again.

Anti-Bribery Lawsuits and Investigations Take Years

U.S.-owned and -based retailing giant Walmart was accused by the U.S. Department of Justice (DOJ) of bribing Mexican officials. By the time Walmart settles with the DOJ, it will have paid between $1 billion and $2 billion to forensic accountants and attorneys. Further, it will have to pay a fine. Finally, the company's managers will have spent thousands of hours conducting internal investigations.

Total U.S. fines for violations of the FCPA were estimated to be almost $2 billion in 2015 alone. Back in 2007, no fine under the FCPA exceeded $50 million. Today, accused firms pay ten to fifteen times that amount. And the United States is not the only country investigating and fining corporations for bribery. Britain, France, Germany, Italy, Norway, South Korea, and Switzerland assess bribery fines, as well.

The biggest bribery case during the decade 2000–2010 involved Siemens. That case took three years to resolve. Current cases, such as the one involving Walmart, could take up to ten years to resolve.

Costs Continue Even after a Settlement

In most anti-bribery settlements, the accused firms must also bear the cost of being overseen for a number of years by independent compliance monitors. In addition, firms that have been involved in bribery investigations often are excluded from bidding for new business in the countries in which they allegedly offered bribes. Some accused companies have also had to defend against shareholder lawsuits.

Not surprisingly, anti-bribery compliance departments within corporations have grown in size and therefore in cost. In Germany, Siemens has spent more than $3 billion on fines and costs since it was first accused of bribery in 2008. It now has a compliance department with about four hundred employees.

Critical Thinking *Why do you think officers and directors of accused companies accept consent decrees rather than contest accusations at trial?*

a. *Securities and Exchange Commission v. Hitachi, Ltd.*, 2015 WL 7566666 (D.D.C. 2015).

b. 15 U.S.C. Sections 78m(b)(2)(A) and (B).

Additionally, if shareholders perceive that the corporate directors are not acting in the best interests of the corporation, they may sue the directors on behalf of the corporation. (This is known as a *shareholder's derivative suit*, which will be discussed later in this chapter.) Directors and officers can also be held personally liable under a number of statutes, such as statutes enacted to protect consumers or the environment.

See Concept Summary 40.2 for a review of the duties and liabilities of directors and officers.

40–3 The Role of Shareholders

The acquisition of a share of stock makes a person an owner and a shareholder in a corporation. Shareholders thus own the corporation. Although they have no legal title to corporate property, such as buildings and equipment, they do have an equitable (ownership) interest in the firm.

As a general rule, shareholders have no responsibility for the daily management of the corporation, although they are ultimately responsible for choosing the board of directors, which does have such control. Ordinarily, corporate officers and other employees owe no direct duty to individual shareholders (unless some contract or special relationship exists between them in addition to the corporate relationship).

The duty of officers and directors is to act in the best interests of the corporation and its shareholder-owners *as a whole*. In turn, as you will read later in this chapter, controlling shareholders owe a fiduciary duty to minority shareholders.

40–3a Shareholders' Powers

Shareholders must approve fundamental changes affecting the corporation before the changes can be implemented. Hence, shareholder approval normally is required to amend the articles of incorporation or bylaws, to conduct a merger or dissolve the corporation, and

---

Concept Summary 40.2

Duties and Liabilities of Directors and Officers

Duties of Directors and Officers	1. *Duty of care*—Directors and officers are obligated to act in good faith, to use prudent business judgment in the conduct of corporate affairs, and to act in the corporation's best interests. If a director or officer fails to exercise this duty of care, he or she may be answerable to the corporation and to the shareholders for breaching the duty. The *business judgment rule* immunizes a director from liability for a corporate decision as long as it was within the power of the corporation and the authority of the director to make and was an informed, reasonable, and loyal decision. 2. *Duty of loyalty*—Directors and officers have a fiduciary duty to subordinate their own interests to those of the corporation in matters relating to the corporation. 3. *Conflicts of interest*—To fulfill their duty of loyalty, directors and officers must make a full disclosure of any potential conflicts between their personal interests and those of the corporation.
Liability of Directors and Officers	1. Corporate directors and officers are personally liable for their own torts and crimes (when not protected under the business judgment rule). Additionally, they may be held personally liable for the torts and crimes committed by corporate personnel under their direct supervision. 2. They may also be held personally liable for violating certain statutes, such as environmental and consumer protection laws, and can sometimes be sued by shareholders for mismanaging the corporation.

to sell all or substantially all of the corporation's assets. Some of these powers are subject to prior board approval. Shareholder approval may also be requested (though it is not required) for certain other actions, such as to approve an independent auditor.

Shareholders also have the power to vote to elect or remove members of the board of directors. As described earlier, the first board of directors is either named in the articles of incorporation or chosen by the incorporators to serve until the first shareholders' meeting. From that time on, selection and retention of directors are exclusively shareholder functions.

Directors usually serve their full terms. If the shareholders judge them unsatisfactory, they are simply not reelected. Shareholders have the inherent power, however, to remove a director from office *for cause* (breach of duty or misconduct) by a majority vote.[5] Some state statutes (and some articles of incorporation) permit removal of directors without cause by the vote of a majority of the shareholders entitled to vote.[6]

40–3b Shareholders' Meetings

Shareholders' meetings must occur at least annually. In addition, special meetings can be called to deal with urgent matters.

Notice of Meetings A corporation must notify its shareholders of the date, time, and place of an annual or special shareholders' meeting at least ten days, but not more than sixty days, before the meeting date [RMBCA 7.05].[7] (The date and time of the annual meeting can be specified in the bylaws.) Notice of a special meeting must include a statement of the purpose of the meeting, and business transacted at the meeting is limited to that purpose.

The RMBCA does not specify how the notice must be given. Most corporations do specify in their bylaws the acceptable methods of notifying shareholders about meetings. Also, some states' incorporation statutes outline the means of notice that a corporation can use in that jurisdiction. For instance, in Alaska, notice may be given in person, by mail, or by fax, e-mail, blog, or Web post—as long as the shareholder has agreed to that electronic method.[8]

Proxies It usually is not practical for owners of only a few shares of stock of publicly traded corporations to attend a shareholders' meeting. Therefore, the law allows stockholders to appoint another person as their agent to vote their shares at the meeting. The agent's formal authorization to vote the shares is called a **proxy** (from the Latin *procurare,* meaning "to manage or take care of"). Proxy materials are sent to all shareholders before shareholders' meetings.

Management often solicits proxies, but any person can solicit proxies to concentrate voting power. Proxies have been used by groups of shareholders as a device for taking over a corporation. Proxies normally are revocable (can be withdrawn), unless they are specifically designated as irrevocable and coupled with an interest. A proxy is coupled with an interest when, for instance, the person receiving the proxies from shareholders has agreed to buy their shares. Under RMBCA 7.22(c), proxies are valid for eleven months, unless the proxy agreement mandates a longer period.

Shareholder Proposals When shareholders want to change a company policy, they can put their ideas up for a shareholder vote. They do this by submitting a shareholder proposal to the board of directors and asking the board to include the proposal in the proxy materials that are sent to all shareholders before meetings.

Rules for Proxies and Shareholder Proposals The Securities and Exchange Commission (SEC) regulates the purchase and sale of securities. The SEC has special provisions relating to proxies and shareholder proposals. SEC Rule 14a-8 provides that all shareholders who own stock worth at least $1,000 are eligible to submit proposals for inclusion in corporate proxy materials. The corporation is required to include information on whatever proposals will be considered at the shareholders' meeting along with proxy materials. Only those proposals that relate to significant policy considerations, not ordinary business operations, must be included.

Under the SEC's e-proxy rules,[9] all public companies must post their proxy materials on the Internet and notify shareholders how to find that information. Although the law requires proxy materials to be posted online, public companies may also send the materials to shareholders

---

5. A director can often demand court review of removal for cause, however.
6. Most states allow *cumulative voting* for directors (described later in the chapter). If cumulative voting is authorized, a director may not be removed if the number of votes against removal would be sufficient to elect a director under cumulative voting. See, for instance, California Corporations Code Section 303A. See also Section 8.08(c) of the RMBCA.
7. The shareholder can waive the requirement of notice by signing a waiver form [RMBCA 7.06]. A shareholder who does not receive notice but who learns of the meeting and attends without protesting the lack of notice is said to have waived notice by such conduct.

8. Alaska Statutes Section 10.06.410 Notice of Shareholders' Meetings.
9. 17 C.F.R. Parts 240, 249, and 274.

by other means, including paper documents and DVDs sent by mail.

40-3c Shareholder Voting

Shareholders exercise ownership control through the power of their votes. Corporate business matters are presented in the form of *resolutions,* which shareholders vote to approve or disapprove. Each common shareholder normally is entitled to one vote per share.

The articles of incorporation can exclude or limit voting rights, particularly for certain classes of shares. For instance, owners of preferred shares are usually denied the right to vote [RMBCA 7.21]. If a state statute requires specific voting procedures, the corporation's articles or bylaws must be consistent with the statute.

Quorum Requirements   For shareholders to act during a meeting, a quorum must be present. Generally, a quorum exists when shareholders holding more than 50 percent of the outstanding shares are present. State laws often permit the articles of incorporation to set higher or lower quorum requirements, however. In some states,

obtaining the unanimous written consent of shareholders is a permissible alternative to holding a shareholders' meeting [RMBCA 7.25].

Once a quorum is present, voting can proceed. If a state statute requires specific voting procedures, the corporation's articles or bylaws must be consistent with the statute. A majority vote of the shares represented at the meeting usually is required to pass resolutions. At times, more than a simple majority vote is required, either by a state statute or by the corporate articles. Extraordinary corporate matters, such as a merger, consolidation, or dissolution of the corporation, require approval by a higher percentage of all corporate shares entitled to vote [RMBCA 7.27].

The corporation in the following case had eighty-four shares of voting common stock outstanding. The shareholder-appellee owned twenty shares, he and his estranged wife jointly held another sixteen shares, and three different individuals owned sixteen shares each. At a shareholders' meeting, the appellee was the only shareholder present in person. Another shareholder (not the appellee's wife) was present by proxy. Could the shares held jointly by the appellee and his wife be counted for purposes of a quorum?

Case Analysis 40.3

Case v. Sink & Rise, Inc.

Supreme Court of Wyoming, 2013 WY 19, 297 P.3d 762 (2013).

In the Language of the Court
HILL, Justice.

This case involves a dispute over corporate action during a shareholder meeting of Appellee Sink & Rise, Inc., (Sink & Rise) a Wyoming corporation. Appellee James Caleb Case (Cale Case) was the only shareholder present at the meeting. He concluded that a quorum existed and thus voted on and passed several resolutions. Cale Case also elected himself and another shareholder as the directors of the corporation, and replaced his estranged wife, Appellant Shirley Case, as the corporation's secretary.

Shirley Case took issue with her estranged husband's actions during the shareholder meeting and filed a complaint in [a Wyoming state] district court to set aside the corporate action that occurred at the shareholder meeting.
* * * The district court concluded that the resolutions were passed with requisite

authority and thus they were not set aside after trial. This appeal followed.
* * * *

* * * Shirley Case argues that because her estranged husband was not entitled to vote the jointly held shares, those same shares could not be counted for quorum purposes. She reasons that because she was absent from the meeting and because only shares "entitled to vote" are to be counted in establishing a quorum, the shares in question were essentially useless at the meeting.

* * * We find the answer in the Sink & Rise corporate documents, and within Wyoming law. First, we reiterate the [district court's] characterization of the stock as being owned by husband and wife with rights of survivorship. We agree with the district court's further classification of the stock as creating a presumption of tenancy by the entirety under Wyoming law. As tenants by the

entirety, each owns an undivided 100% interest in the 16 shares.

In an estate of the entirety, the husband and the wife during their joint lives each owns, not a part, or a separate or a separable interest, but the whole. [Emphasis added.]

To further help us in our consideration, we turn to the corporate documents.

* * * Sink & Rise's bylaws * * * define what constitutes a "quorum," and relate the corporation's rule on voting shares:

6. *Quorum.* A majority of the outstanding shares entitled to vote, represented in person or by proxy, shall constitute a quorum at a meeting of Shareholders. If a quorum is present, the affirmative vote of the majority of shares entitled to vote at the meeting shall be the act of the Shareholders. * * *

Case 40.3 Continues

7. *Voting of Shares.* * * * Each outstanding share is entitled to vote the number of shares owned by him/her on each matter submitted to a vote at a meeting of Shareholders. * * *

According to the bylaws, for the corporation to count shares in determining a quorum, the shares must be (1) entitled to vote, and (2) represented in person or by proxy. From our reading of the corporate documents, and because the joint stock was held by husband and wife as tenants by the entirety, we conclude that the shares held jointly by Cale Case

and Shirley Case were "entitled to vote" at the meeting. Cale Case represented the stock in person, as required by the bylaws. [Emphasis added.]

As the district court noted, and the parties agree here, the joint stock in question cannot be, and was not, voted without agreement between Cale Case and Shirley Case. * * * [But] the fact that Cale Case and Shirley Case must agree on how to vote the stock before it can actually be voted does not strip it of its voting privileges. Cale Case did not attempt to vote the stock at the meeting,

but instead considered it only for quorum purposes.

Sink & Rise's bylaws do not prevent stock owned by a husband and wife as tenants by the entirety * * * from being counted for purposes of a quorum if represented in person. The stock in question was represented in person by Cale Case at the * * * shareholder meeting, and it was properly counted to establish a quorum.

* * * *

We affirm the district court's decision.

Legal Reasoning Questions

1. How many shareholders were present at the shareholders' meeting that gave rise to the dispute in this case?

2. How did the court "characterize" and "classify" the shares of stock that Cale and Shirley Case held jointly?

3. According to the court, how many shares were represented at the shareholders' meeting? Was a quorum present? Explain.

Voting Lists The corporation prepares a voting list before each shareholders' meeting. Ordinarily, only persons whose names appear on the corporation's stockholder records as owners are entitled to vote.[10]

The voting list contains the name and address of each shareholder as shown on the corporate records on a given cutoff date, or *record date*. (Under RMBCA 7.07, the bylaws or board of directors may fix a record date that is as much as seventy days before the meeting.) The voting list also includes the number of voting shares held by each owner. The list is usually kept at the corporate headquarters and must be made available for shareholder inspection [RMBCA 7.20].

Cumulative Voting Most states permit, and many require, shareholders to elect directors by *cumulative voting*, a voting method designed to allow minority shareholders to be represented on the board of directors.[11]

Formula. With cumulative voting, each shareholder is entitled to a total number of votes equal to the number of

board members to be elected multiplied by the number of voting shares that the shareholder owns. The shareholder can cast all of these votes for one candidate or split them among several nominees for director. All candidates stand for election at the same time.

How Cumulative Voting Works. Cumulative voting can best be understood by example. ■ **EXAMPLE 40.5** A corporation has 10,000 shares issued and outstanding. The minority shareholders hold 3,000 shares, and the majority shareholders hold the other 7,000 shares. Three members of the board are to be elected. The majority shareholders' nominees are Alvarez, Beasley, and Caravel. The minority shareholders' nominee is Dovrik. Can Dovrik be elected to the board by the minority shareholders?

If cumulative voting is allowed, the answer is yes. The minority shareholders have 9,000 votes among them (the number of directors to be elected times the number of shares, or 3 × 3,000 = 9,000 votes). All of these votes can be cast to elect Dovrik. The majority shareholders have 21,000 votes (3 × 7,000 = 21,000 votes), but these votes must be distributed among their three nominees.

The principle of cumulative voting is that no matter how the majority shareholders cast their 21,000 votes, they will not be able to elect all three directors if the minority shareholders cast all of their 9,000 votes for Dovrik, as illustrated in Exhibit 40–2. ■ In contrast, when cumulative voting is not required, the entire board can be elected by a majority of shares.

---

10. When the legal owner of shares is deceased, bankrupt, mentally incompetent, or in some other way under a legal disability, his or her vote can be cast by a person designated by law to control and manage that owner's property.

11. See, for instance, California Corporations Code Section 708. Some states, such as Nebraska, require cumulative voting in their state constitutions. Under RMBCA 7.28, no cumulative voting rights exist unless the articles of incorporation so provide.

EXHIBIT 40–2 Results of Cumulative Voting

Ballot	Majority Shareholder Votes			Minority Shareholder Votes	Directors Elected
	Alvarez	*Beasley*	*Caravel*	*Dovrik*	
1	10,000	10,000	1,000	9,000	Alvarez, Beasley, Dovrik
2	9,001	9,000	2,999	9,000	Alvarez, Beasley, Dovrik
3	6,000	7,000	8,000	9,000	Beasley, Caravel, Dovrik

Other Voting Techniques Before a shareholders' meeting, a group of shareholders can agree in writing to vote their shares together in a specified manner. Such agreements, called *shareholder voting agreements,* usually are held to be valid and enforceable. A shareholder can also vote by proxy, as noted earlier.

Another technique is for shareholders to enter into a *voting trust.* A **voting trust** is an agreement (a trust contract) under which a shareholder assigns the right to vote his or her shares to a trustee, usually for a specified period of time. The trustee is then responsible for voting the shares on behalf of all the shareholders in the trust. The shareholder retains all rights of ownership (for instance, the right to receive dividend payments) except the power to vote the shares [RMBCA 7.30].

40–4 Rights of Shareholders

Shareholders possess numerous rights in addition to the right to vote their shares, and we examine several here.

40–4a Stock Certificates

In the past, corporations commonly issued **stock certificates** that evidenced ownership of a specified number of shares in the corporation. Only a few jurisdictions still require physical stock certificates, and shareholders there have the right to demand that the corporation issue certificates (or replace those that were lost or destroyed). Stock is intangible personal property, however, and the ownership right exists independently of the certificate itself.

In most states and under RMBCA 6.26, a board of directors may provide that shares of stock will be uncertificated, or "paperless"—that is, no actual, physical stock certificates will be issued. Notice of shareholders' meetings, dividends, and operational and financial reports are distributed according to the ownership lists recorded in the corporation's books.

40–4b Preemptive Rights

Sometimes, the articles of incorporation grant preemptive rights to shareholders [RMBCA 6.30]. With **preemptive rights,** a shareholder receives a preference over all other purchasers to subscribe to or purchase a prorated share of a new issue of stock. Generally, preemptive rights must be exercised within a specific time period (usually thirty days).

A shareholder who is given preemptive rights can purchase a percentage of the new shares being issued that is equal to the percentage of shares she or he already holds in the company. This allows each shareholder to maintain her or his proportionate control, voting power, and financial interest in the corporation. ■ **EXAMPLE 40.6** Katlin is a shareholder who owns 10 percent of a company. Because she also has preemptive rights, she can buy 10 percent of any new issue (to maintain her 10 percent position). Thus, if the corporation issues 1,000 more shares, Katlin can buy 100 of the new shares. ■

Preemptive rights are most important in close corporations because each shareholder owns a relatively small number of shares but controls a substantial interest in the corporation. Without preemptive rights, it would be possible for a shareholder to lose his or her proportionate control over the firm. Nevertheless, preemptive rights do not exist unless provided for in the articles of incorporation.

40–4c Stock Warrants

Stock warrants are rights given by a company to buy stock at a stated price by a specified date. Usually, when preemptive rights exist and a corporation is issuing additional shares, it gives its shareholders stock warrants. Warrants are often publicly traded on securities exchanges.

40–4d Dividends

As mentioned, a **dividend** is a distribution of corporate profits or income *ordered by the directors* and paid to the shareholders in proportion to their shares in the corporation. Dividends can be paid in cash, property, stock of the corporation that is paying the dividends, or stock of other corporations.[12]

State laws vary, but each state determines the general circumstances and legal requirements under which dividends are paid. State laws also control the sources of revenue to be used. All states allow dividends to be paid from the undistributed net profits earned by the corporation, for instance. A number of states allow dividends to be paid out of any surplus.

Illegal Dividends Dividends are illegal if they are improperly paid from an unauthorized account or if their payment causes the corporation to become insolvent. Generally, shareholders must return illegal dividends only if they knew that the dividends were illegal when the payment was received (or if the dividends were paid when the corporation was insolvent). Whenever dividends are illegal or improper, the board of directors can be held personally liable for the amount of the payment.

The Directors' Failure to Declare a Dividend When directors fail to declare a dividend, shareholders can ask a court to compel the directors to do so. To succeed, the shareholders must show that the directors have acted so unreasonably in withholding the dividend that their conduct is an abuse of their discretion.

Often, a corporation accumulates large cash reserves for a legitimate corporate purpose, such as expansion or research. The mere fact that the firm has sufficient earnings or surplus available to pay a dividend normally is not enough to compel the directors to declare a dividend. The courts are reluctant to interfere with corporate operations and will not compel directors to declare dividends unless abuse of discretion is clearly shown.

40–4e Inspection Rights

Shareholders in a corporation enjoy both common law and statutory inspection rights. The RMBCA provides that every shareholder is entitled to examine specified corporate records, including voting lists [RMBCA 7.20, 16.02]. The shareholder may inspect in person, or an attorney, accountant, or other authorized assistant can do so as the shareholder's agent. In some states, a shareholder must have held her or his shares for a minimum period of time immediately preceding the demand to inspect or must hold a certain percentage of outstanding shares.

Proper Purpose A shareholder has a right to inspect and copy corporate books and records only for a *proper purpose,* and the request to inspect must be made in advance. A shareholder who is denied the right of inspection can seek a court order to compel the inspection.

■ **CASE IN POINT 40.7** Trading Block Holdings, Inc., offers online brokerage services. On April 1, 2013, some shareholders of Trading Block, through an attorney, sent a letter asking to inspect specific items in the corporation's books and records. The letter indicated that the purpose was to determine the financial condition of the company, how it was being managed, and whether the company's financial practices were appropriate. It also stated that the shareholders wanted to know whether Trading Block's management had engaged in any self-dealing that had negatively impacted the company as a whole.

On April 30, Trading Block responded with a letter stating that the plaintiffs were on a "fishing expedition" and did not have a proper purpose for inspecting the corporate records. Eventually, the shareholders filed a motion to compel inspection in an Illinois state court. The trial court denied the plaintiffs' motion. On appeal, the reviewing court held that the plaintiffs' allegations of self-dealing by directors and officers constituted a proper purpose for their inspection request. The trial court's decision was reversed.[13] ■

Potential for Abuse The power of inspection is fraught with potential abuses, and the corporation is allowed to protect itself from them. For instance, a share-

---

12. On one occasion, a distillery declared and paid a dividend in bonded whiskey.

13. *Sunlitz Holding Co., W.L.L. v. Trading Block Holdings, Inc.,* 2014 IL App (1st) 133938, 17 N.E.3d 715, 384 Ill.Dec. 733 (4 Dist. 2014).

holder can properly be denied access to corporate records to prevent harassment or to protect trade secrets or other confidential corporate information.[14]

40–4f Transfer of Shares

Corporate stock represents an ownership right in intangible personal property. The law generally recognizes the owner's right to transfer stock to another person unless there are valid restrictions on its transferability, such as frequently occur with close corporation stock.

When shares are transferred, a new entry is made in the corporate stock book to indicate the new owner. Until the corporation is notified and the entry is complete, all rights—including voting rights, notice of shareholders' meetings, and the right to dividend distributions—remain with the current record owner.

40–4g The Shareholder's Derivative Suit

When the corporation is harmed by the actions of a third party, the directors can bring a lawsuit in the name of the corporation against that party. If the corporate directors fail to bring a lawsuit, shareholders can do so "derivatively" in what is known as a **shareholder's derivative suit.**

The right of shareholders to bring a derivative action is especially important when the wrong suffered by the corporation results from the actions of the corporate directors and officers. For obvious reasons, the directors and officers would probably be unwilling to take any action against themselves.

Written Demand Required Before shareholders can bring a derivative suit, they must submit a written demand to the corporation, asking the board of directors to take appropriate action [RMBCA 7.40]. The directors then have ninety days in which to act. Only if they refuse to do so can the derivative suit go forward. In addition, a court will dismiss a derivative suit if a majority of the directors or an independent panel determines in good faith that the lawsuit is not in the best interests of the corporation [RMBCA 7.44].

Any Damages Awarded Go to the Corporation When shareholders bring a derivative suit, they are not pursuing rights or benefits for themselves personally but are acting as guardians of the corporate entity. Therefore, if the suit is successful, any damages recovered normally

go into the corporation's treasury, not to the shareholders personally.[15]

40–5 Duties and Liabilities of Shareholders

One of the hallmarks of the corporate form of organization is that shareholders are not personally liable for the debts of the corporation. If the corporation fails, the shareholders can lose their investments, but that generally is the limit of their liability. As discussed previously, in certain instances, a court will pierce the corporate veil (disregard the corporate entity) and hold the shareholders individually liable. But these situations are the exception, not the rule.

A shareholder can also be personally liable in certain other rare instances. One relates to illegal dividends, which were mentioned previously. Another relates to *watered stock.* Finally, in certain instances, a majority shareholder who engages in oppressive conduct or attempts to exclude minority shareholders from receiving certain benefits can be held personally liable.

Concept Summary 40.3 reviews the role, rights, and liability of shareholders in a corporation.

40–5a Watered Stock

When a corporation issues shares for less than their fair market value, the shares are referred to as **watered stock.**[16] Usually, the shareholder who receives watered stock must pay the difference to the corporation (the shareholder is personally liable). In some states, the shareholder who receives watered stock may be liable to creditors of the corporation for unpaid corporate debts.

■ **EXAMPLE 40.8** During the formation of a corporation, Gomez, one of the incorporators, transfers his property, Sunset Beach, to the corporation for 10,000 shares of stock at a par value of $100 per share for a total price of $1 million. After the property is transferred and the shares are issued, Sunset Beach is carried on the corporate books at a value of $1 million.

On appraisal, it is discovered that the market value of the property at the time of transfer was only $500,000. The

---

14. See, for example, *United Technologies Corp. v. Treppel*, 109 A.3d 553 (Del.Ch. 2014).

15. The shareholders may be entitled to reimbursement for reasonable expenses of the derivative lawsuit, including attorneys' fees.

16. The phrase *watered stock* was originally used to describe cattle that were kept thirsty during a long drive and then were allowed to drink large quantities of water just before their sale. The increased weight of the watered stock allowed the seller to reap a higher profit.

Concept Summary 40.3

Role, Rights, and Liability of Shareholders

Shareholders' Powers	Shareholders' powers include approval of all fundamental changes affecting the corporation and election of the board of directors.
Shareholders' Meetings	Shareholders' meetings must occur at least annually, and special meetings can be called when necessary. Notice of the time and place of a meeting (and its purpose, if the meeting is specially called) must be sent to shareholders. A minimum number of shareholders (quorum) must be present to vote.
Shareholders' Rights	Shareholders have numerous rights, which may include the following: • Voting rights. • Preemptive rights (depending on the corporate articles). • The right to receive dividends (at the discretion of the directors). • The right to inspect the corporate records. • The right to transfer shares (this right may be restricted in close corporations). • The right to receive a share of corporate assets when the corporation is dissolved. • The right to sue on behalf of the corporation (bring a shareholder's derivative suit) when the directors fail to do so.
Shareholders' Liability	Shareholders may be liable for watered stock. In certain situations, majority shareholders may be regarded as having a fiduciary duty to minority shareholders and will be liable if that duty is breached.

shares issued to Gomez are therefore watered stock, and he is liable to the corporation for the difference between the value of the shares and the value of the property. ■

40–5b Duties of Majority Shareholders

In some instances, a majority shareholder is regarded as having a fiduciary duty to the corporation and to the minority shareholders. This duty arises when a single shareholder (or a few shareholders acting in concert) owns a sufficient number of shares to exercise *de facto* control over the corporation. In these situations, the majority shareholder owes a fiduciary duty to the minority shareholders.

When a majority shareholder breaches her or his fiduciary duty to a minority shareholder, the minority shareholder can sue for damages. A breach of fiduciary duties by those who control a close corporation normally constitutes what is known as *oppressive conduct*. A common example of a breach of fiduciary duty occurs when the majority shareholders "freeze out" the minority shareholders and exclude them from certain benefits of participating in the firm.

■ **EXAMPLE 40.9** Brodie, Jordan, and Barbara form a close corporation to operate a machine shop. Brodie and Jordan own 75 percent of the shares in the company, but all three are directors. After disagreements arise, Brodie asks the company to purchase his shares, but his requests are refused. A few years later, Brodie dies, and his wife, Ella, inherits his shares. Jordan and Barbara refuse to perform a valuation of the company, deny Ella access to corporate information, do not declare any dividends, and refuse to elect Ella as a director. In this situation, the majority shareholders have violated their fiduciary duty to Ella. ■

Reviewing: Corporate Directors, Officers, and Shareholders

David Brock was on the board of directors of Firm Body Fitness, Inc., which owned a string of fitness clubs in New Mexico. Brock owned 15 percent of the Firm Body stock and was also employed as a tanning technician at one of the fitness clubs. After the January financial report showed that Firm Body's tanning division was operating at a substantial net loss, the board of directors, led by Marty Levinson, discussed terminating the tanning operations. Brock successfully convinced a majority of the board that the tanning division was necessary to market the clubs' overall fitness package. By April, the tanning division's financial losses had risen. The board hired a business analyst, who conducted surveys and determined that the tanning operations did not significantly increase membership.

A shareholder, Diego Peñada, discovered that Brock owned stock in Sunglow, Inc., the company from which Firm Body purchased its tanning equipment. Peñada notified Levinson, who privately reprimanded Brock. Shortly thereafter, Brock and Mandy Vail, who owned 37 percent of the Firm Body stock and also held shares of Sunglow, voted to replace Levinson on the board of directors. Using the information presented in the chapter, answer the following questions.

1. What duties did Brock, as a director, owe to Firm Body?
2. Does the fact that Brock owned shares in Sunglow establish a conflict of interest? Why or why not?
3. Suppose that Firm Body brought an action against Brock claiming that he had breached the duty of loyalty by not disclosing his interest in Sunglow to the other directors. What theory might Brock use in his defense?
4. Now suppose that Firm Body did not bring an action against Brock. What type of lawsuit might Peñada be able to bring based on these facts?

Debate This . . . *Because most shareholders never bother to vote for directors, shareholders have no real control over corporations.*

Terms and Concepts

business judgment rule 766	preemptive rights 775	stock certificate 775
dividend 776	proxy 772	stock warrant 776
inside director 763	quorum 763	voting trust 775
outside director 763	shareholder's derivative suit 777	watered stock 777

Issue Spotters

1. Wonder Corporation has an opportunity to buy stock in XL, Inc. The directors decide that instead of Wonder buying the stock, the directors will buy it. Yvon, a Wonder shareholder, learns of the purchase and wants to sue the directors on Wonder's behalf. Can she do it? Explain. (See *Rights of Shareholders*.)

2. Nico is Omega Corporation's majority shareholder. He owns enough stock in Omega that if he were to sell it,

the sale would be a transfer of control of the firm. Discuss whether Nico owes a duty to Omega or the minority shareholders in selling his shares. (See *Duties and Liabilities of Shareholders*.)

- **Check your answers to the Issue Spotters against the answers provided in Appendix D at the end of this text.**

Business Scenarios

40–1. Conflicts of Interest. Oxy Corp. is negotiating with Wick Construction Co. for the renovation of Oxy's corporate headquarters. Wick, the owner of Wick Construction Co., is also one of the five members of Oxy's board of directors. The

contract terms are standard for this type of contract. Wick has previously informed two of the other directors of his interest in the construction company. Oxy's board approves the contract by a three-to-two vote, with Wick voting with the majority. Discuss whether this contract is binding on the corporation. (See *Duties and Liabilities of Directors and Officers.*)

40–2. Liability of Directors. AstroStar, Inc., has approximately five hundred shareholders. Its board of directors consists of three members—Eckhart, Dolan, and Macero. At a regular board meeting, the board selects Galiard as president of the corporation by a two-to-one vote, with Eckhart dissenting. The minutes of the meeting do not register Eckhart's dissenting vote. Later, an audit reveals that Galiard is a former convict and has embezzled $500,000 from the corporation that is not covered by insurance. Can the corporation hold directors Eckhart, Dolan, and Macero personally liable? Discuss. (See *Duties and Liabilities of Directors and Officers.*)

Business Case Problems

40–3. Fiduciary Duty of Officers. Designer Surfaces, Inc., supplied countertops to homeowners who shopped at stores such as Lowe's and Costco. The homeowners paid the store, which then contracted with Designer to fabricate and install the countertops. Designer bought materials from Arizona Tile, LLC, on an open account. Designer's only known corporate officers were Howard Berger and John McCarthy. Designer became insolvent and could not pay Arizona Tile for all the materials it had purchased, including materials for which Designer had already received payment from the retail stores. Arizona Tile sued Designer and won a default judgment, but the company had no funds. Arizona Tile then sued Berger and McCarthy personally for diverting company funds that Designer had received in trust for payment to Arizona Tile. Arizona Tile argued that the use of the funds for other purposes was a breach of fiduciary duty. Berger and McCarthy argued that corporate law imposed neither a fiduciary duty on corporate officers nor personal liability for breach of a duty to suppliers of materials. Which argument is more credible, and why? [*Arizona Tile, LLC v. Berger,* 223 Ariz. 491, 224 P.3d 988 (Ariz.App. 2010)] (See *Role of Directors and Officers.*)

40–4. Business Case Problem with Sample Answer— Rights of Shareholders. Stanka Woods was the sole member of Hair Ventures, LLC. Hair Ventures owned 3 million shares of stock in Biolustré, Inc. For several years, Woods and other Biolustré shareholders did not receive notice of shareholders' meetings or financial reports. On learning that Biolustré planned to issue more stock, Woods, through Hair Ventures, demanded to see Biolustré's books and records. Biolustré asserted that the request was not for a proper purpose. Does Woods have a right to inspect Biolustré's books and records? If so, what are the limits? Do any of those limits apply in this case? Explain. [*Biolustré Inc. v. Hair Ventures, LLC,* 2011 WL 540574 (Tex.App.—San Antonio 2011)] (See *Rights of Shareholders.*)

- **For a sample answer to Problem 40–4, go to Appendix E at the end of this text.**

40–5. Duty of Loyalty. Kids International Corp. produced children's wear for Walmart and other retailers. Gila Dweck was a Kids director and its chief executive officer. Because she felt that she was not paid enough, she started Success Apparel to compete with Kids. Success operated out of Kids' premises, used its employees, borrowed on its credit, took advantage of its business opportunities, and capitalized on its customer relationships. As an "administrative fee," Dweck paid Kids 1 percent of Success's total sales. Did Dweck breach any fiduciary duties? Explain. [*Dweck v. Nasser,* 2012 WL 3194069 (Del.Ch. 2012)] (See *Duties and Liabilities of Directors and Officers.*)

40–6. Duties of Majority Shareholders. Bill McCann was the president and chief executive officer of McCann Ranch & Livestock Co. He and his brother Ron each owned 36.7 percent of the stock. Ron had been removed from the board of directors on their father's death, however, and was not authorized to work for the firm. Their mother, Gertrude, owned the rest of the stock, which was to pass to Bill on her death. The corporation paid Gertrude's personal expenses in an amount that represented about 75 percent of the net corporate income. Bill received regular salary increases. The corporation did not issue a dividend. Was Ron the victim of a freeze-out? Discuss. [*McCann v. McCann,* 152 Idaho 809, 275 P.3d 824 (2012)] (See *Duties and Liabilities of Shareholders.*)

40–7. Business Judgment Rule. Country Contractors, Inc., contracted to provide excavation services for A Westside Storage of Indianapolis, Inc., but did not complete the job and later filed for bankruptcy. Stephen Songer and Jahn Songer were Country's sole shareholders. The Songers had not misused the corporate form to engage in fraud. The firm had not been undercapitalized, personal and corporate funds had not been commingled, and Country had kept accounting records and minutes of its annual board meetings. Are the Songers personally liable for Country's failure to complete its contract? Explain. [*Country Contractors, Inc. v. A Westside Storage of Indianapolis, Inc.,* 4 N.E.3d 677 (Ind.App. 2014)] (See *Duties and Liabilities of Directors and Officers.*)

40–8. Rights of Shareholders. FCR Realty, LLC, and Clifford B. Green & Sons, Inc., were co-owned by three brothers—Frederick, Clifford Jr., and Richard Green. Each brother was a shareholder of the corporation. Frederick was a controlling shareholder, as well as president. Each brother owned a one-third interest in the LLC. Clifford believed that Frederick had misused LLC and corporate funds to pay nonexistent debts and liabilities and had diverted LLC assets to the corporation. He also contended that Frederick had disbursed about $1.8 million in corporate funds to Frederick's own separate business. Clifford hired an attorney and filed an action on behalf of the two companies against Frederick for breach of fiduciary duty. Frederick argued that Clifford lacked the knowledge necessary to adequately represent the companies' interest because he did not understand financial statements. Can Clifford maintain the action against Frederick? If so, and if the suit is successful, who recovers the damages? Explain. [*FCR Realty, LLC v. Green,* __ Conn.Supp. __, __ Conn.L.Rptr. __, 2016 WL 571449 (Super. 2016)] (See *Rights of Shareholders.*)

40–9. A Question of Ethics—Duties of Directors and Officers.

 New Orleans Paddlewheels, Inc. (NOP), was a Louisiana corporation formed in 1982. James Smith, Sr., and Warren Reuther were its only shareholders, with each holding 50 percent of the stock. NOP was part of a sprawling enterprise of tourism and hospitality companies in New Orleans controlled by Smith and Reuther. The positions on the board of each company were split equally between the Smith and Reuther families.

At Smith's request, his son James Smith, Jr. (JES), became involved in the businesses. In 1999, NOP's board elected JES as president, to be in charge of day-to-day operations, and Reuther as chief executive officer (CEO), to be in charge of marketing and development. Over the next few years, animosity developed between Reuther and JES. In October 2001, JES terminated Reuther as CEO and denied him access to the offices and books of
NOP and the other companies, literally changing the locks on the doors. At the next meetings of the boards of NOP and the overall enterprise, deadlock ensued, with the directors voting along family lines on every issue.

Complaining that the meetings were a "waste of time," JES began to run the entire enterprise by taking advantage of an unequal balance of power on the companies' executive committees. In NOP's subsequent bankruptcy proceeding, Reuther filed a motion for the appointment of a trustee to formulate a plan for the firm's reorganization, alleging, among other things, misconduct by NOP's management. [In re New Orleans Paddlewheels, Inc., *350 Bankr. 667 (E.D.La. 2006)*] (See *Duties and Liabilities of Directors and Officers.*)

(a) Was Reuther legally entitled to have access to the books and records of NOP and the other companies? JES maintained, among other things, that NOP's books were "a mess." Was JES's denial of that access unethical? Why or why not?

(b) How would you describe JES's attempt to gain control of NOP and the other companies? Were his actions devious and self-serving in the pursuit of personal gain or legitimate and reasonable in the pursuit of a business goal? Discuss.

Legal Reasoning Group Activity

40–10. Shareholders' Duties.
Milena Weintraub and Larry Griffith were shareholders in Grand Casino, Inc., which operated a casino in South Dakota. Griffith owned 51 percent of the stock and Weintraub 49 percent. Weintraub managed the casino, which Griffith typically visited once a week. At the end of 2012, an accounting audit showed that the cash on hand was less than the amount posted in the casino's books. Later, more shortfalls were discovered. In October 2014, Griffith did a complete audit. Weintraub was unable to account for $200,500 in missing cash. Griffith then took all of the casino's most recent profits, including Weintraub's $90,447.20 share, and, without telling Weintraub, sold the casino for $400,000 and kept all of the proceeds. Weintraub filed a suit against

Griffith, asserting a breach of fiduciary duty. Griffith countered with evidence of Weintraub's misappropriation of corporate cash. (See *Duties and Liabilities of Shareholders.*)

(a) The first group will discuss the duties that these parties owed to each other and determine whether Weintraub or Griffith, or both, breached those duties.

(b) The second group will decide how this dispute should be resolved and who should pay what to whom to reconcile the finances.

(c) A third group will discuss whether Weintraub or Griffith violated any ethical duties to each other or to the corporation.

CHAPTER 41

Mergers and Takeovers

A corporation may grow simply by reinvesting retained earnings in more equipment or by hiring more employees. A corporation may also extend its operations by combining with another corporation through a merger, a consolidation, or a share exchange. In addition, a corporation may purchase the assets of, or a controlling interest in, another corporation.

This chapter examines each of these types of corporate expansion. We also discuss dissolution and winding up—the processes by which a corporation terminates its existence. The chapter concludes with a brief comparison of the major forms of business organization discussed in this text.

41–1 Merger, Consolidation, and Share Exchange

The terms *merger* and *consolidation* traditionally referred to two legally distinct proceedings, but some people today use the term *consolidation* to refer to all types of combinations. Whether a combination is a merger, a consolidation, or a share exchange, the rights and liabilities of shareholders, the corporation, and the corporation's creditors are the same. Note that the power to merge, consolidate, and exchange shares is conferred by statute, and thus state law establishes the specific procedures.

41–1a Merger

A **merger** involves the legal combination of two or more corporations. After a merger, only one of the corporations continues to exist. ■ **EXAMPLE 41.1** Corporation A and Corporation B decide to merge. They agree that A will absorb B. Therefore, after the merger, B ceases to exist as a separate entity, and A continues as the **surviving corporation.** ■ Exhibit 41–1 graphically illustrates this process.

One of the Firms Survives Continuing with *Example 41.1,* after the merger, Corporation A—the surviving corporation—is recognized as a single corporation, and B no longer exists as an entity. A's articles of incorporation are deemed amended to include any changes stated in the **articles of merger** (a document setting forth the terms and conditions of the merger). Corporation A will issue shares or pay some fair consideration to the shareholders of B.

It Inherits All Legal Rights and Obligations of the Other Firm After the merger, Corporation A possesses all of the rights, privileges, and powers of itself and B. It automatically acquires all of B's property and assets without the necessity of a formal transfer. In addition, it becomes liable for all of B's debts and obligations, and it inherits B's preexisting legal rights. Thus, if Corporation B had a right of action against a third party under tort or property law, Corporation A can bring a suit after the merger to recover B's damages.

41–1b Consolidation

In a **consolidation,** two or more corporations combine in such a way that each corporation ceases to exist and a new one emerges. ■ **EXAMPLE 41.2** Corporation A and

EXHIBIT 41–1 Merger

Corporation A and Corporation B decide to merge. They agree that A will absorb B, so after the merger, B no longer exists as a separate entity, and A continues as the surviving corporation.

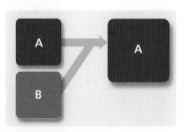

Corporation B consolidate to form an entirely new organization, Corporation C. In the process, A and B both terminate, and C comes into existence as a new entity. ■ Exhibit 41–2 graphically illustrates this process.

A New Corporation Is Formed The results of a consolidation are similar to those of a merger—only one company remains—but it is a completely new entity (the *consolidated corporation*). In terms of *Example 41.2,* Corporation C is recognized as a new corporation, while A and B cease to exist. C's *articles of consolidation* take the place of A's and B's original corporate articles and are thereafter regarded as C's corporate articles. As with a merger, the newly formed corporation will issue shares or pay some fair consideration to the shareholders of the disappearing corporations.

It Inherits All Rights and Liabilities of Both Predecessors Corporation C inherits all of the rights, privileges, and powers previously held by A and B. Title to any property and assets owned by A and B passes to C without a formal transfer. C assumes liability for all debts and obligations owed by A and B.

True consolidations have become less common among for-profit corporations because it is often advantageous for one of the combining firms to survive. In contrast, nonprofit corporations and associations may prefer consolidation because it suggests a new beginning in which neither of the two initial entities is dominant.

41–1c Share Exchange

In a **share exchange,** some or all of the shares of one corporation are exchanged for some or all of the shares of another corporation, but both corporations continue

to exist. Share exchanges are often used to create *holding companies* (companies that own part or all of other companies' outstanding stock).

If one corporation owns *all* of the shares of another corporation, it is referred to as the **parent corporation,** and the wholly owned company is the **subsidiary corporation.** ■ **EXAMPLE 41.3** United Continental Holdings, Inc. (UAL), is a large holding company that owns United Airlines. UAL is the parent corporation, and United Airlines is the subsidiary. ■

41–1d Merger, Consolidation, and Share Exchange Procedures

All states have statutes authorizing mergers, consolidations, and share exchanges for domestic (in-state) and foreign (out-of-state) corporations. The procedures vary somewhat among jurisdictions. In some states, for instance, a consolidation resulting in an entirely new corporation simply follows the same incorporation procedures as any new corporation, and other rules apply to other combinations.

The Revised Model Business Corporation Act (RMBCA) does set forth the following basic requirements for mergers and share exchanges [RMBCA 11.01–11.07]:

1. The board of directors of *each* corporation involved must approve the merger or share exchange plan.
2. The plan must specify any terms and conditions of the merger. It also must state how the value of the shares of each merging corporation will be determined and how they will be converted into shares or other securities, cash, property, or additional interests in another corporation.
3. The majority of the shareholders of *each* corporation must vote to approve the plan at a shareholders' meeting. If any class of stock is entitled to vote as a separate group, the majority of each separate voting group must approve the plan. Frequently, a corporation's articles of incorporation or bylaws require approval by more than a majority once a quorum is present. In addition, some state statutes require the approval of two-thirds of the outstanding shares of voting stock (not just the shareholders present at the meeting), and others require a four-fifths approval.
4. Once the plan is approved by the directors and the shareholders of each corporation, the surviving corporation files the plan (articles of merger, consolidation, or share exchange) with the appropriate official. Usually the plan is filed with the appropriate secretary of state.

EXHIBIT 41–2 Consolidation

Corporation A and Corporation B consolidate to form an entirely new organization, Corporation C. In the process, A and B terminate, and C comes into existence.

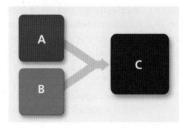

5. When state formalities are satisfied, the state issues a certificate of merger to the surviving corporation or a certificate of consolidation to the newly consolidated corporation.

In the following case, the attorneys for a group of shareholders argued that the shareholders had not been given enough information before they were asked to vote on a proposed merger.

In re Trulia, Inc. Stockholder Litigation

Court of Chancery of Delaware, 129 A.3d 884 (2016).

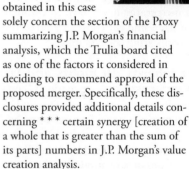

In the Language of the Court

BOUCHARD, C. [Chancellor]

This opinion concerns the proposed settlement of a stockholder class action challenging Zillow, Inc.'s acquisition of Trulia, Inc. in a stock-for-stock merger * * * . Shortly after the public announcement of the proposed transaction, four Trulia stockholders filed essentially identical complaints alleging that Trulia's directors had breached their fiduciary duties in approving the proposed merger * * * . Less than four months later, * * * the parties reached an agreement-in-principle to settle.

* * * Trulia agreed to supplement the proxy materials disseminated to its stockholders before they voted on the proposed transaction to include some additional information that theoretically would allow the stockholders to be better informed in exercising their [voting] rights. In exchange, plaintiffs dropped their motion to preliminarily enjoin the transaction and agreed to provide a release of claims on behalf of a proposed class of Trulia's stockholders.

Because a class action impacts the legal rights of absent class members, it is the responsibility of [this] Court * * * to exercise independent judgment to determine whether a proposed class settlement is fair and reasonable to the affected class members.

* * * *

I. BACKGROUND

* * * *

Defendant Trulia, Inc., a Delaware corporation, is an online provider of information on homes for purchase or for rent in the United States.

Defendant Zillow, Inc., a Washington corporation, is a real estate marketplace

that helps home buyers, sellers, landlords and others find and share information about homes. Defendant Zebra Holdco, Inc. ("Holdco"), now known as Zillow Group, Inc., is a Washington corporation that was formed to facilitate the merger at issue and is now the parent company of Zillow and Trulia.

* * * *

II. LEGAL ANALYSIS

* * * *

Under Delaware law, *when directors solicit stockholder action, they must disclose fully and fairly all material information within the board's control.* * * * *Information is material if there is a substantial likelihood that a reasonable shareholder would consider it important in deciding how to vote.* In other words, information is material if, from the perspective of a reasonable stockholder, there is a substantial likelihood that it significantly alters the total mix of information made available. [Emphasis added.]

Here, the * * * Proxy that Trulia and Zillow stockholders received in advance of their respective stockholders' meetings to consider whether to approve the proposed transaction ran 224 pages in length, excluding annexes. It contained extensive discussion concerning, among other things, the background of the mergers, each board's reasons for recommending approval of the proposed transaction, prospective financial information concerning the companies that had been reviewed by their respective boards and financial advisors, and explanations of the opinions of each company's financial advisor. In the case of Trulia, the opinion of J.P. Morgan [Securities LLC] was summarized in ten single-spaced pages.

The Supplemental Disclosures plaintiffs obtained in this case solely concern the section of the Proxy summarizing J.P. Morgan's financial analysis, which the Trulia board cited as one of the factors it considered in deciding to recommend approval of the proposed merger. Specifically, these disclosures provided additional details concerning * * * certain synergy [creation of a whole that is greater than the sum of its parts] numbers in J.P. Morgan's value creation analysis.

* * * Under Delaware law, when the board relies on the advice of a financial advisor in making a decision that requires stockholder action, those stockholders are entitled to receive in the proxy statement a fair summary of the substantive work performed by the investment bankers upon whose advice the recommendations of their board as to how to vote on a merger or tender rely.

A fair summary, however, is a *summary.* By definition, it need not contain all information underlying the financial advisor's opinion or contained in its report to the board. * * * *The summary does not need to provide sufficient data to allow the stockholders to perform their own independent valuation.* The essence of a fair summary is not a cornucopia [abundance] of financial data, but rather an accurate description of the advisor's methodology and key assumptions. * * * Disclosures that provide extraneous details do not contribute to a fair summary and do not add value for stockholders. [Emphasis added.]

* * * *

The Supplemental Disclosures provided some additional details in the

Case 41.1 Continued

sections of J.P. Morgan's analysis entitled "Value Creation Analysis—Intrinsic Value Approach" and "Value Creation Analysis—Market-Based Approach."

As supplemented, the disclosure concerning the Intrinsic Value Approach * * * added: * * *

> The present value of after-tax synergies was based on an estimate of $175.0 million in synergies * * * based on assumptions provided by Trulia's management.

Plaintiffs argue that the disclosure of the $175 million synergies figure * * * was important because it is substantially different from the $100 million in synergies that J.P. Morgan used in the Market-Based Approach * * * . There are three fundamental problems with this argument.

First, * * * plaintiffs question why J.P. Morgan used two different synergies figures in two different analyses * * * . [But] the Proxy accurately disclosed which synergies assumptions the financial advisor deemed appropriate to use in each analysis.

Second, the $175 million synergies figure that plaintiffs consider so important was not new information. It already was disclosed in the Proxy.

Third, * * * the Proxy indicates that the Market-Based Approach analysis was less important than the Intrinsic Value Approach analysis. Thus, the notion that the disclosure of the $175 million synergies figure used in one analysis * * * was significant because it was higher than the $100 million figure used in a second, different analysis is based on a false equivalence of the relative importance of the two analyses.

In sum, the disclosures in the original Proxy already provided a fair summary of J.P. Morgan's methodology and assumptions in its two "Value Creation" analyses. Inserting additional minutiae [details] underlying some of the assumptions could not reasonably have been expected to significantly alter the total mix of information and thus was not material. Indeed, * * * the supplemental information was not even helpful to stockholders.

* * * *

* * * As such, from the perspective of Trulia's stockholders, the "get" in the form of the Supplemental Disclosures does not provide adequate consideration to warrant the "give" of providing a release of claims to defendants and their affiliates * * * . Accordingly, * * * the proposed settlement is not fair or reasonable to Trulia's stockholders.

III. CONCLUSION

For the foregoing reasons, approval of the proposed settlement is DENIED.

Legal Reasoning Questions

1. The announcement of a proposed merger often triggers a shareholder action alleging that directors breached their fiduciary duty by agreeing to sell the corporation for an unfair price. When and how does such litigation benefit the shareholders?

2. In the *Trulia* case, the settlement, if approved, would not have yielded any genuine benefit for the shareholders. If the court had approved the settlement, however, who would have benefited?

3. When the parties to a dispute agree to a settlement, they share the same interest in obtaining the court's approval. What are the advantages and disadvantages of this situation?

41–1e Short-Form Mergers

RMBCA 11.04 provides a simplified procedure for the merger of a substantially owned subsidiary corporation into its parent corporation. Under these provisions, a **short-form merger**—also referred to as a *parent-subsidiary merger*—can be accomplished *without* the approval of the shareholders of either corporation.

The short-form merger can be used only when the parent corporation owns at least 90 percent of the outstanding shares of each class of stock of the subsidiary corporation. Once the board of directors of the parent corporation approves the plan, it is filed with the state, and copies are sent to each shareholder of record in the subsidiary corporation.

41–1f Shareholder Approval

As mentioned, except in a short-form merger, the shareholders of both corporations must approve a merger or other plan of consolidation. Shareholders invest in a corporation with the expectation that the board of directors will make decisions on *ordinary* business matters. For *extraordinary* matters, normally both the board of directors and the shareholders must approve the transaction.

Mergers and other combinations are extraordinary business matters, meaning that the board of directors must normally obtain the shareholders' approval and provide appraisal rights (discussed next). Amendments to the articles of incorporation and the dissolution of the corporation also generally require shareholder approval.

Sometimes, a transaction can be structured in such a way that shareholder approval is not required, but if the shareholders challenge the transaction, a court might require shareholder approval. For this reason, the board of directors may request shareholder approval even when it might not be legally required.

41–1g Appraisal Rights

What if a shareholder disapproves of a merger or a consolidation but is outvoted by the other shareholders? The law will not force a dissenting shareholder to become an unwilling shareholder in a corporation that is new or different from the one in which the shareholder originally invested.

Dissenting shareholders therefore have a statutory right to be paid the fair value of the shares they held on the date of the merger or consolidation. This right is referred to as the shareholder's **appraisal right.** The "fair value of the shares" normally is the value on the day prior to the date on which the vote was taken [RMBCA 13.21]. So long as the transaction does not involve fraud or other illegal conduct, appraisal rights are the exclusive remedy for a shareholder who is dissatisfied with the price received for the stock.

When Appraisal Rights Apply Appraisal rights normally extend to mergers, consolidations, share exchanges, and sales of substantially all of the corporate assets. Such rights can be particularly important in a short-form merger because the minority stockholders do not receive advance notice of the merger, the directors do not consider or approve it, and there is no vote. Appraisal rights are often the only recourse available to shareholders who object to short-form mergers.

Procedures Each state establishes the procedures for asserting appraisal rights in that jurisdiction. Shareholders may lose their appraisal rights if they do not adhere precisely to the procedures prescribed by statute. When they lose the right to an appraisal, dissenting shareholders must go along with the transaction despite their objections.

Concept Summary 41.1 reviews mergers, consolidations, and share exchanges.

41–2 Purchase of Assets

When a corporation acquires all or substantially all of the assets of another corporation by direct purchase, the *acquiring corporation* simply extends its ownership and control over more assets. Because no change in the legal entity occurs, the acquiring corporation usually does not need to obtain shareholder approval for the purchase.

In contrast, the corporation that is *selling* all of its assets is substantially changing its business position and perhaps its ability to carry out its corporate purposes. For that reason, the corporation whose assets are being sold must obtain approval from both its board of directors and its shareholders [RMBCA 12.02]. In most states and under RMBCA 13.02, dissenting shareholders of the selling corporation can demand appraisal rights.

Both the U.S. Department of Justice and the Federal Trade Commission have guidelines that significantly constrain and often prohibit mergers that could result from a purchase of assets. (These guidelines will be discussed in the materials covering federal antitrust laws.)

41–2a When Shareholder Approval May Be Required

Although shareholder approval is not typically required, it may be required in a few situations. If the acquiring corporation plans to pay for the assets with its stock but not enough authorized unissued shares are available, then the shareholders must approve the issuance of additional shares. Shareholder approval is also needed if the acquiring corporation's stock is traded on a national stock exchange and the corporation will be issuing a significant number of shares.

41–2b Successor Liability in Purchases of Assets

Generally, a corporation that purchases the assets of another corporation is *not automatically responsible for the liabilities of the selling corporation.* Exceptions are made in certain circumstances, however. In any of the following situations, the acquiring corporation will be held to have assumed *both* the assets and the liabilities of the selling corporation:

1. *Express or implicit agreement.* The purchasing corporation impliedly or expressly assumes the seller's liabilities.
2. *De facto merger.* The sale transaction amounts to a merger or consolidation of the two companies.
3. *Continuation.* The purchaser continues the seller's business and retains the same shareholders, directors, and officers.
4. *Fraud exception.* The sale is entered into fraudulently for the purpose of escaping liability.

Concept Summary 41.1

Merger, Consolidation, and Share Exchange

Merger	The legal combination of two or more corporations, with the result that the surviving corporation acquires all of the assets and obligations of the other corporation, which then ceases to exist.
Consolidation	The legal combination of two or more corporations, with the result that each corporation ceases to exist and a new one emerges. The new corporation assumes all of the assets and obligations of the former corporations.
Share Exchange	A form of business combination in which some or all of the shares of one corporation are exchanged for some or all of the shares of another corporation, but both firms continue to exist.
Procedure	Determined by state statutes. Basic requirements are the following: • The board of directors of each corporation involved must approve the plan of merger, consolidation, or share exchange. • The shareholders of each corporation must approve the merger or other consolidation plan at a shareholders' meeting. • Articles of merger or consolidation (the plan) must be filed, usually with the secretary of state. • The state issues a certificate of merger (or consolidation) to the surviving (or newly consolidated) corporation.
Short-Form Merger (Parent-Subsidiary Merger)	When the parent corporation owns at least 90 percent of the outstanding shares of each class of stock of the subsidiary corporation, shareholder approval is not required for the two firms to merge.
Appraisal Rights	Rights of dissenting shareholders (provided by state statute) to receive the fair value for their shares when a merger or consolidation takes place. If the shareholder and the corporation do not agree on the fair value, a court will determine it.

■ **CASE IN POINT 41.4** American Standard, Inc., sold its Kewanee Boiler division to OakFabco, Inc. The agreement stated that OakFabco would purchase Kewanee assets subject to Kewanee liabilities. "Kewanee liabilities" were defined as "all the debts, liabilities, obligations, and commitments (fixed or contingent) connected with or attributable to Kewanee existing and outstanding at the Closing Date."

Because the boilers manufactured by Kewanee had been insulated with asbestos, many tort claims arose in the years following the purchase of the business. Some of those claims were brought by plaintiffs who had suffered injuries after the closing of the transaction that were allegedly attributable to boilers manufactured and sold before the closing.

American Standard filed an action against OakFabco in New York, asking the court for a declaratory judgment on the issue of whether liabilities for such injuries were among the "Kewanee liabilities" that OakFabco had assumed. The court held that OakFabco had expressly assumed the liabilities of the selling corporation in the contract, including claims that arose after the closing date. A state appellate court affirmed that decision. According to the reviewing court, "nothing in the nature of the transaction suggested that the parties intended OakFabco, which got all the assets, to escape any of the related obligations."[1] ■

41–3 Purchase of Stock

An alternative to the purchase of another corporation's assets is the purchase of a substantial number of the voting shares of its stock. This enables the acquiring corporation to control the **target corporation** (the corporation being acquired). The process of acquiring control over a corporation in this way is commonly referred to as a corporate **takeover.**

41–3a Tender Offers

The acquiring corporation deals directly with the target company's shareholders in seeking to purchase the shares they hold. It does this by making a **tender offer** to buy shares of stock from all of the target company's shareholders in exchange for cash or stock. The tender offer can be conditioned on the receipt of a specified number of outstanding shares by a certain date.

To induce shareholders to accept the offer, the tender price offered generally is higher than the market price of the target's stock before the tender offer was announced. ■ **EXAMPLE 41.5** In a merger of two major pharmaceutical companies, Pfizer, Inc., paid $68 billion to acquire its rival, Wyeth. Wyeth shareholders received approximately $50.19 per share (part in cash and part in Pfizer stock), which amounted to a 15 percent premium over the market price of the stock. ■

41–3b Application of Securities Laws

Federal securities laws strictly control the terms, duration, and circumstances under which most tender offers are made. In addition, many states have passed antitakeover statutes.

Generally, the offering corporation does not need to notify the Securities and Exchange Commission (SEC) or the target corporation's management until after the tender offer is made. The offeror must then disclose to the SEC the source of the funds used in the offer, the purpose of the offer, and the acquiring corporation's plans for the firm if the takeover is successful.

41–3c Responses to Tender Offers

A firm may respond to a tender offer in numerous ways. If the target firm's board of directors views the tender offer as favorable, the board will recommend that the shareholders accept it. Frequently, though, the target corporation's management opposes the proposed takeover. This is referred to as a *hostile takeover.*

To resist a takeover, a target company may make a *self-tender,* in which it offers to acquire stock from its own shareholders and thereby retain corporate control. The target corporation may also engage in a media campaign to persuade its shareholders that the tender offer is not in their best interests. Another possible defense is for the target firm to issue additional stock, thereby increasing the number of shares that the acquiring corporation must purchase to gain control. Several other tactics to resist a takeover are described in Exhibit 41–3.

Concept Summary 41.2 reviews purchases of assets and purchases of stock.

41–3d Takeover Defenses and Directors' Fiduciary Duties

As mentioned, the board of directors of the target corporation often opposes the takeover. Clearly, board members have an interest in keeping their jobs and control, but they also have a fiduciary duty to the corporation and its shareholders to act in the best interests of the company.

In a hostile takeover attempt, sometimes directors' duties of care and loyalty collide with their self-interest. Then the shareholders, who would have received a premium for their shares as a result of the takeover, file lawsuits. Such lawsuits frequently allege that the directors breached their fiduciary duties in defending against the tender offer.

---

1. *American Standard, Inc. v. OakFabco, Inc.,* 14 N.Y.3d 399, 901 N.Y.S.2d 572 (2010).

EXHIBIT 41–3 The Terminology of Takeover De...

Term	Definition
Crown Jewel	When threatened with a takeover, management makes the company less attractive to the raider by selling the company's most valuable asset (the "crown jewel") to a third party.
Golden Parachute	When a takeover is successful, top management usually is changed. With this in mind, a company may establish special termination or retirement benefits that must be paid to top managers if they are "retired." In other words, a departing high-level manager's parachute will be "golden" when he or she is forced to "bail out" of the company.
Greenmail	To regain control, a target company may pay a higher-than-market price to repurchase all of the stock that the acquiring corporation bought. When a takeover is attempted through a gradual accumulation of target stock rather than a tender offer, the intent may be to induce the target company to buy back the shares at a premium price—a concept similar to blackmail.
Pac-Man	Named after the Atari video game, this is an aggressive defense in which the target corporation attempts its own takeover of the acquiring corporation.
Poison Pill	The target corporation issues to its stockholders rights to purchase additional shares at low prices when there is a takeover attempt. This makes the takeover undesirably or even prohibitively expensive for the acquiring corporation.
White Knight	The target corporation solicits a merger with a third party, which then makes a better (often simply a higher) tender offer to the target's shareholders. The third party that "rescues" the target is the "white knight."

Business Judgment Rule Courts apply the *business judgment rule* when analyzing whether the directors acted reasonably in resisting the takeover attempt. The directors must show that they had reasonable grounds to believe that the tender offer posed a danger to the corporation's policies and effectiveness.

In addition, the board's response must have been rational in relation to the threat posed. Basically, the defensive tactics used must have been reasonable, and the board of directors must have been trying to protect the corporation and its shareholders from a perceived danger. If the directors' actions were reasonable under the circumstances, then they are not liable for breaching their fiduciary duties.

An Example: The Poison Pill Defense One technique to avoid takeovers is the poison pill defense (described in Exhibit 41–3). With this defensive measure, a board gives shareholders the right to buy new, additional shares at low prices. The right is triggered when a party

acquires a certain proportion of the target corporation's stock—often between 15 and 20 percent. (This party, of course, does not have the right to purchase shares at a discount.) With more shares outstanding, the acquiring party's interest is diluted. The tactic is meant to make a takeover too expensive for the acquiring party.

■ **EXAMPLE 41.6** In 2012, Netflix, Inc., used the poison pill defense to effectively block a takeover attempt by billionaire investor Carl Icahn. Netflix gave its shareholders the right to acquire newly issued stock if any individual acquired more than 10 percent of the company. At the time, Icahn held 9.98 percent of the shares. If his interest had risen to 10 percent, new shares would have flooded the market, and his interest in the corporation would have been immediately diluted. Consequently, he was effectively prevented from buying more shares. ■

In the following case, shareholders claimed that the directors had breached their fiduciary duties in their use of a poison pill defense.

Concept Summary 41.2

Purchases of Assets and Purchases of Stock

Purchase of Assets	A purchase of assets occurs when one corporation acquires all or substantially all of the assets of another corporation.
	1. *Acquiring corporation*—The acquiring (purchasing) corporation is not required to obtain shareholder approval. The corporation is merely increasing its assets, and no fundamental business change occurs.
	2. *Acquired corporation*—The acquired (purchased) corporation is required to obtain the approval of both its directors and its shareholders for the sale of its assets because the sale will substantially change the corporation's business position.

Purchase of Stock	A purchase of stock occurs when one corporation acquires a substantial number of the voting shares of the stock of another (target) corporation.
	1. *Tender offer*—A public offer to all shareholders of the target corporation to purchase their stock at a price generally higher than the market price of the target stock prior to the announcement of the tender offer. Federal and state securities laws strictly control the terms, duration, and circumstances under which most tender offers are made.
	2. *Target responses*—The ways in which target corporations respond to takeover bids include self-tender (the target firm's offer to acquire its own shareholders' stock) and numerous other strategies (see Exhibit 41–3).

Case 41.2

Air Products and Chemicals, Inc. v. Airgas, Inc.

Court of Chancery of Delaware, 16 A.3d 48 (2011).

Background and Facts Air Products and Chemicals, Inc., which provides gases and chemicals for industrial uses, made a tender offer of $70 per share for all of the shares of Airgas, Inc. The Airgas board of directors, which had expressed the view that the company's stock was worth at least $78 per share, rejected the offer as "clearly inadequate." The board took defensive measures to block the bid, including a poison pill that would be triggered if any party acquired 15 percent of the Airgas stock. Air Products and some Airgas shareholders filed a suit in a Delaware state court against Airgas. The plaintiffs sought to compel the board to remove the poison pill and allow the Airgas shareholders to decide whether to accept Air Products' offer. The shareholders alleged that the board had breached its fiduciary duties.

In the Language of the Court

CHANDLER, Chancellor

* * * *

Now, having thoroughly read, reviewed, and reflected upon all of the evidence presented to me, and having carefully considered the arguments made by counsel, I conclude that the Airgas board * * * has not breached its fiduciary duties owed to the Airgas stockholders. I find that the board has acted in good faith and in the honest belief that the Air Products offer, at $70 per share, is inadequate.

*Inadequate price has become a form of substantive coercion * * *. That is, the idea that Airgas's stockholders will disbelieve the board's views on value * * * and so they may mistakenly tender into an inadequately*

Case 41.2 Continued

priced offer. Substantive coercion has been clearly recognized by [the Delaware] Supreme Court as a valid threat. [Emphasis added.]

* * * *

* * * *A board that has a good faith, reasonable basis to believe a bid is inadequate may block that bid using a poison pill, irrespective of stockholders' desire to accept it.* [Emphasis added.]

Here, * * * the Airgas board has demonstrated that it has a reasonable basis for sustaining its long-term corporate strategy—the Airgas board is independent, and has relied on the advice of three different outside independent financial advisors in concluding that Air Products' offer is inadequate. Air Products' own three nominees who were elected to the Airgas board have joined wholeheartedly in the Airgas board's determination, and when the Airgas board met to consider the $70 "best and final" offer, it was one of those Air Products Nominees who said, "We have to protect the pill." Indeed, one of Air Products' own directors conceded at trial that the Airgas board members had acted within their fiduciary duties in their desire to "hold out for the proper price," and that if an offer was made for Air Products that he considered to be unfair to the stockholders of Air Products * * * he would likewise use every legal mechanism available to hold out for the proper price as well. Under Delaware law, the Airgas directors have complied with their fiduciary duties.

Decision and Remedy *The court dismissed the shareholders' claims. The power to defeat an inadequate tender offer lies with the board of the target corporation. In this case, the Airgas board identified a valid threat—the allegedly inadequate price of Air Products' offer, coupled with the fact that a majority of Airgas's shareholders would likely accept it. The board responded reasonably and did not breach its fiduciary duties to shareholders.*

Critical Thinking

- **What If the Facts Were Different?** *Suppose that the Airgas board had opposed the takeover in order to perpetuate the directors' own corporate power, and not to preserve shareholder value. Would the result have been different? Explain.*
- **Social** *One reason for using a poison pill defense is to gain time for the shareholders of a target corporation to obtain the information they need to make an informed decision about a tender offer. How much time is enough?*

41–4 Termination

The termination of a corporation's existence has two phases—dissolution and winding up. **Dissolution** is the legal death of the artificial "person" of the corporation. Dissolution can be brought about by the following:

1. An act of the state.
2. An agreement of the shareholders and the board of directors.
3. The expiration of a time period stated in the certificate of incorporation.
4. A court order.

Winding up is the process by which corporate assets are *liquidated,* or converted into cash and distributed among creditors and shareholders according to specific rules of preference.[2]

---

2. Some prefer to call this phase *liquidation,* but we use the term *winding up* to mean all acts needed to bring the legal and financial affairs of the business to an end, including liquidating the assets and distributing them among creditors and shareholders. See RMBCA 14.05.

41–4a Voluntary Dissolution

Dissolution can be either voluntary or involuntary. State corporation statutes establish the procedures required for the voluntary dissolution of a corporation. Basically, there are two possible methods of voluntarily dissolving a corporation:

1. By the shareholders' unanimous vote to initiate dissolution proceedings (in some states).
2. By a proposal of the board of directors that is submitted to the shareholders at a shareholders' meeting.

Articles of Dissolution When a corporation is dissolved voluntarily, the corporation must file *articles of dissolution* with the state. The corporation must also establish a date (at least 120 days after the date of dissolution) by which all claims against the corporation must be received [RMBCA 14.06].

Notice to Creditors The corporation must notify its creditors of the dissolution. The creditors want to be notified so that they can file claims for payment. If a corporation's assets are liquidated without notice to a party who has a claim against the firm, shareholders of the former corporation can be held personally liable for the debt.

■ **CASE IN POINT 41.7** Richard and Kara Hartley were the sole shareholders of Hartley's Catering, Inc., a close corporation that operated Schlesinger's Deli Depot. Jennifer Esposito worked at the deli and was sexually harassed and physically assaulted by one of her co-workers. Esposito complained to Kara Hartley, who informed her husband, but the harassment continued and Esposito was fired.

Esposito sued Hartley's Catering (and the co-worker) for employment discrimination and won a $350,000 judgment. Soon afterwards, the Hartleys dissolved their close corporation, without notifying Esposito, and filed a petition for bankruptcy. The bankruptcy court found that because Hartley's Catering had not notified Esposito (a creditor) of the dissolution or bankruptcy, her claim against the corporation could not be discharged. Richard and Kara Hartley, as Hartley's shareholders, were held liable for paying the debt to Esposito.[3] ■

41–4b Involuntary Dissolution

Because corporations are creatures of statute, the state can also dissolve a corporation in certain circumstances. The secretary of state or the state attorney general can bring an action to dissolve a corporation that has failed to pay its annual taxes or submit required annual reports [RMBCA 14.20]. A state court can also dissolve a corporation for making fraudulent misrepresentations to the state during incorporation or for engaging in mismanagement [RMBCA 14.30].

In some circumstances, a shareholder or a group of shareholders may petition a court to have the corporation dissolved. The RMBCA permits any shareholder to initiate an action for dissolution in any of the following circumstances [RMBCA 14.30]:

1. The directors are deadlocked in the management of corporate affairs, and the shareholders are unable to break the deadlock. As a result, the corporation is suffering irreparable injury or is about to do so.
2. The acts of the directors or those in control of the corporation are illegal, oppressive, or fraudulent.
3. Corporate assets are being misapplied or wasted.
4. The shareholders are deadlocked in voting power and have failed, for a specified period (usually two annual meetings), to elect successors to directors whose terms have expired or would have expired with the election of successors.

■ **CASE IN POINT 41.8** Mt. Princeton Trout Club, Inc. (MPTC), was formed to own land in Colorado and to provide recreational benefits to its shareholders. The articles of incorporation prohibited MPTC from selling or leasing any of its property without the approval of a majority of the directors. Nevertheless, MPTC officers entered into leases and contracts to sell corporate property without even notifying the directors. When a shareholder petitioned for dissolution, the court dissolved MPTC based on a finding that its officers had engaged in illegal, oppressive, and fraudulent conduct.[4] ■

41–4c Winding Up

Winding up differs to some extent based on whether voluntary or involuntary dissolution has occurred. When dissolution takes place by voluntary action, the members of the board of directors act as trustees of the corporate assets. As trustees, they are responsible for winding up the affairs of the corporation for the benefit of corporate creditors and shareholders. This responsibility makes the board members personally liable for any breach of their fiduciary trustee duties.

When dissolution is involuntary—or if board members do not wish to act as trustees—the court will appoint a **receiver** to wind up corporate affairs and liquidate corporate assets. Courts may also appoint a receiver when shareholders or creditors can show that the board of directors should not be permitted to act as trustees of the corporate assets.

On dissolution, the liquidated assets are first used to pay creditors. Any remaining assets are distributed to shareholders according to their respective stock rights. Preferred stock has priority over common stock. Generally, the preferences are stated in the corporate articles.

41–5 Major Business Forms Compared

When deciding which form of business organization to choose, businesspersons normally consider several factors, including ease of creation, the liability of the owners, tax considerations, and the ability to raise capital. Each major form of business organization offers distinct advantages and disadvantages with respect to these and other factors.

Exhibit 41–4 summarizes the essential advantages and disadvantages of each of the forms of business organization discussed in this text.

---

3. *In re Hartley*, 479 Bankr. 635 (S.D.N.Y. 2012).

4. *Colt v. Mt. Princeton Trout Club, Inc.*, 78 P.3d 1115 (Colo.App. 2003).

EXHIBIT 41-4 Major Forms of Business Compared

	SOLE PROPRIETORSHIP	PARTNERSHIP	CORPORATION
Method of Creation	Created at will by owner.	Created by agreement of the parties.	Authorized by the state under the state's corporation law.
Legal Position	Not a separate entity; owner is the business.	A general partnership is a separate legal entity in most states.	Always a legal entity separate and distinct from its owners—a legal fiction for the purposes of owning property and being a party to litigation.
Liability	Unlimited liability.	Unlimited liability.	Limited liability of shareholders—shareholders are not liable for the debts of the corporation.
Duration	Determined by owner; automatically dissolved on owner's death.	Terminated by agreement of the partners, but can continue to do business even when a partner dissociates from the partnership.	Can have perpetual existence.
Transferability of Interest	Interest can be transferred, but individual's proprietorship then ends.	Although partnership interest can be assigned, assignee does not have full rights of a partner.	Shares of stock can be transferred.
Management	Completely at owner's discretion.	Each partner has a direct and equal voice in management unless expressly agreed otherwise in the partnership agreement.	Shareholders elect directors, who set policy and appoint officers.
Taxation	Owner pays personal taxes on business income.	Each partner pays pro rata share of income taxes on net profits, whether or not they are distributed.	Double taxation—corporation pays income tax on net profits, with no deduction for dividends, and shareholders pay income tax on disbursed dividends they receive.
Organizational Fees, Annual License Fees, and Annual Reports	None or minimal.	None or minimal.	All required.
Transaction of Business in Other States	Generally no limitation.	Generally no limitation.[a]	Normally must qualify to do business and obtain certificate of authority.

a. A few states have enacted statutes requiring that foreign partnerships qualify to do business there.

EXHIBIT 41–4 Major Forms of Business Compared *(Continued)*

	LIMITED PARTNERSHIP	LIMITED LIABILITY COMPANY	LIMITED LIABILITY PARTNERSHIP
Method of Creation	Created by agreement to carry on a business for profit. At least one party must be a general partner and the other(s) limited partner(s). Certificate of limited partnership is filed.	Created by an agreement of the member-owners of the company. Articles of organization are filed. Charter must be issued by the state.	Created by agreement of the partners. A statement of qualification for the limited liability partnership is filed.
Legal Position	Treated as a legal entity.	Treated as a legal entity.	Generally, treated same as a general partnership.
Liability	Unlimited liability of all general partners. Limited partners are liable only to the extent of capital contributions.	Member-owners' liability is limited to the amount of capital contributions or investments.	Varies, but under the Uniform Partnership Act, liability of a partner for acts committed by other partners is limited.
Duration	By agreement in certificate, or by termination of the last general partner (retirement, death, and the like) or last limited partner.	Unless a single-member LLC, can have perpetual existence (same as a corporation).	Remains in existence until cancellation or revocation.
Transferability of Interest	Interest can be assigned, but if assignee becomes a member with consent of other partners, certificate must be amended.	Member interests are freely transferable.	Interest can be assigned same as in a general partnership.
Management	General partners have equal voice or by agreement. Limited partners may not retain limited liability if they actively participate in management.	Member-owners can fully participate in management or can designate a group of persons to manage on behalf of the members.	Same as a general partnership.
Taxation	Generally taxed as a partnership.	LLC is not taxed, and members are taxed personally on profits "passed through" the LLC.	Same as a general partnership.
Organizational Fees, Annual License Fees, and Annual Reports	Organizational fee required; usually not others.	Organizational fee required. Others vary with states.	Fees are set by each state for filing statements of qualification, statements of foreign qualification, and annual reports.
Transaction of Business in Other States	Generally no limitations.	Generally no limitations, but may vary depending on state.	Must file a statement of foreign qualification before doing business in another state.

Reviewing: Mergers and Takeovers

Mario Bonsetti and Rico Sanchez incorporated Gnarly Vulcan Gear, Inc. (GVG), to manufacture windsurfing equipment. Bonsetti owned 60 percent and Sanchez owned 40 percent of the corporation's stock, and both men served on the board of directors. Hula Boards, Inc., owned solely by Mai Jin Li, made a public offer to buy GVG stock. Hula offered 30 percent more than the market price per share for the GVG stock, and Bonsetti and Sanchez each sold 20 percent of their stock to Hula. Jin Li became the third member of the GVG board of directors.

An irreconcilable dispute soon arose between Bonsetti and Sanchez over design modifications of their popular Baked Chameleon board. Sanchez and Jin Li voted to merge GVG with Hula Boards under the latter name, despite Bonsetti's dissent. GVG was dissolved, and production of the Baked Chameleon ceased. Using the information presented in the chapter, answer the following questions.

1. What rights does Bonsetti have (in most states) as a minority shareholder dissenting to the merger of GVG and Hula Boards?
2. Could the parties have used a short-form merger procedure in this situation? Why or why not?
3. What is the term used for Hula's offer to purchase GVG stock? By what method did Hula acquire control over GVG?
4. Suppose that after the merger, a person who was injured on a Baked Chameleon board sued Hula (the surviving corporation). Can Hula be held liable for an injury? Why or why not?

Debate This . . . *Corporate law should be altered to prohibit incumbent management from using most of the legal methods available for fighting takeovers.*

Terms and Concepts

appraisal right 786	parent corporation 783	surviving corporation 782
articles of merger 782	receiver 792	takeover 788
consolidation 782	share exchange 783	target corporation 788
dissolution 791	short-form merger 785	tender offer 788
merger 782	subsidiary corporation 783	

Issue Spotters

1. Macro Corporation and Micro Company combine, and a new organization, MM, Inc., takes their place. What is the term for this type of combination? What happens to the assets, property, and liabilities of Micro? (See *Merger, Consolidation, and Share Exchange.*)
2. Peppertree, Inc., hired Robert McClellan, a licensed contractor, to repair a condominium complex that was damaged in an earthquake. McClellan completes the work, but Peppertree fails to pay. McClellan is awarded $181,000 in an arbitration proceeding. Peppertree then forms another corporation and transfers all of its assets to the new corporation without notifying McClellan. Can McClellan hold Peppertree's shareholders personally liable for the debt? Why or why not? (See *Purchase of Assets.*)

- **Check your answers to the Issue Spotters against the answers provided in Appendix D at the end of this text.**

Business Scenarios

41–1. Corporate Merger. Alir owns 10,000 shares of Ajax Corp. Her shares represent a 10 percent ownership interest in Ajax. Zeta Corp. is interested in acquiring Ajax in a merger, and the board of directors of each corporation has approved the merger. The shareholders of Zeta have already approved the acquisition, and Ajax has called for a shareholders' meeting to approve the merger. Alir disapproves of the merger and does not want to accept Zeta shares for the Ajax shares she holds. The market price of Ajax shares is $20 per share the day before the shareholder vote and drops to $16 on the day the shareholders of Ajax approve the merger. Discuss Alir's rights in this matter, beginning with the notice of the proposed merger. (See *Merger, Consolidation, and Share Exchange.*)

41–2. Purchase of Assets. Paradise Pools, Inc. (PPI) entered into a contract with Vittorio, LLP, to build a pool as part of a hotel being developed by Takahashi Development. PPI built the pool, but Vittorio, the general contractor, defaulted on other parts of the project. Takahashi completed the construction. Litigation followed, and Takahashi was awarded $18,656 against PPI. Meanwhile, Paradise Corp. (PC) was incorporated with the same management as PPI, but different shareholders. PC acquired PPI's assets, without assuming its liabilities, and soon became known as "Paradise Pools and Spas." Takahashi sought to obtain a writ of garnishment against PC to enforce the judgment against PPI. Is PC liable for PPI's obligation to Takahashi? Why or why not? (See *Purchase of Assets.*)

41–3. Corporate Takeover. Alitech Corp. is a small midwestern business that owns a valuable patent. Alitech has approximately a thousand shareholders with 100,000 authorized and outstanding shares. Block Corp. would like to have the use of the patent, but Alitech refuses to give Block a license. Block has tried to acquire Alitech by purchasing Alitech's assets, but Alitech's board of directors has refused to approve the acquisition. Alitech's shares are selling for $5 per share. Discuss how Block Corp. might proceed to gain the control and use of Alitech's patent. (See *Purchase of Stock.*)

Business Case Problems

41–4. Successor Liability. In 2004, the Watergate Hotel in Washington, D.C., obtained a loan from PB Capital. At this time, hotel employees were represented by a labor union, and under a collective bargaining agreement, the hotel agreed to make contributions to an employees' pension fund run by the union. In 2007, the hotel was closed due to poor business, although the owner stated that the hotel would reopen in 2010. Despite this expectation, PB Capital—which was still owed $40 million by the hotel owner—instituted foreclosure proceedings. At the foreclosure sale, PB Capital bought the hotel and reopened it under new management and with a new workforce. The union sued PB Capital, contending that it should pay $637,855 owed by the previous owner into the employees' pension fund. Should PB Capital, as the hotel's new owner, have to incur the previous owner's obligation to pay into the pension fund under the theory of successor liability? Why or why not? [*Board of Trustees of Unite Here Local 25 v. MR Watergate, LLC,* 677 F.Supp.2d 229 (D.D.C. 2010)] (See *Purchase of Assets.*)

41–5. Business Case Problem with Sample Answer— Purchase of Assets. Grand Adventures Tour & Travel Publishing Corp. (GATT) provided travel services. Duane Boyd, a former GATT director, incorporated Interline Travel & Tour, Inc. At a public sale, Interline bought GATT's assets. Interline moved into GATT's office building, hired former GATT employees, and began to serve GATT's customers. A GATT creditor, Call Center Technologies, Inc., filed an action to collect the unpaid amount on a contract with GATT from Interline. Is Interline liable? Why or why not? [*Call Center Technologies, Inc. v. Grand Adventures Tour & Travel Publishing Corp.,* 635 F.3d 48 (2d Cir. 2011)] (See *Purchase of Assets.*)

• **For a sample answer to Problem 41–5, go to Appendix E at the end of this text.**

41–6. Purchase of Assets. Lockheed Martin Corporation owned an aluminum refinery in St. Croix, Virgin Islands, that produced hazardous waste. Lockheed sold the refinery to Glencore Ltd. Their contract provided that Glencore would indemnify Lockheed for "pre-closing" environmental conditions. Alcoa World Alumina LLC bought the refinery from Glencore. Their contract stated that the buyer assumed only certain liabilities, including those relating to two specific contracts. Glencore's contract with Lockheed was not on the list. A decade later, the government of the Virgin Islands brought actions against the current and former owners of the refinery to recover for the environmental damage. In a settlement, Lockheed agreed to pay for certain remediation costs. Lockheed then filed a suit against Glencore to recover costs related to the settlement. Does Alcoa have to indemnify Glencore for costs related to Lockheed's suit? Why or why not? [*Alcoa World Alumina LLC v. Glencore Ltd.,* __ Conn.Supp. __, __ Conn.L.Rptr. __, 2016 WL 521193 (Super. 2016)] (See *Purchase of Assets.*)

41–7. Special Case Analysis—Dissolution. Go to Case Analysis 41.1 *In re Trulia, Inc. Stockholder Litigation.* Read the excerpt and answer the following questions.

(a) **Issue:** On what basis did the plaintiffs in this case seek to enjoin the proposed merger?

(b) **Rule of Law:** What is the standard for the disclosure of information by corporate directors in connection with any shareholder action?

(c) **Applying the Rule of Law:** How did the disclosure standard apply to the reliance of the directors on the advice of a financial advisor in making a decision on a proposed merger?

(d) **Conclusion:** How did the court's conclusion with respect to the information provided to the shareholders relate to the court's decision concerning the parties' proposed settlement?

41–8. A Question of Ethics—Purchase of Stock. *Topps* *Co. makes baseball and other trading cards, including the Pokemon collection, and distributes Bazooka bubble gum and other confections. One of the company's founders was Joseph Shorin, who was the inspiration for "Bazooka Joe" (a character in the comic strip wrapped around each piece of gum). As of 2007, Arthur Shorin, Joseph's son, had worked for Topps for fifty years and had served as its board chair and chief executive officer since 1980. Shorin's son-in-law, Scott Silverstein, served as Topps's president and chief operating officer.*

When Topps's financial performance began to lag, the board considered selling the company. Michael Eisner (formerly head of Disney Studios) offered to pay $9.75 per share and to retain Topps's management in a merger with his company. Upper Deck Co., Topps's chief competitor in the sports-card business, offered $10.75 per share but did not offer to retain the managers. Topps
demanded that Upper Deck not reveal its bid publicly. Topps publicized the offer, however, and did not accurately represent Upper Deck's interest or its seriousness. Upper Deck asked Topps to allow it to tell its side of events and to make a tender offer to Topps's shareholders. Topps refused and scheduled a shareholder vote on the Eisner offer. Topps's shareholders filed a suit in a Delaware state court against their firm, asking the court to prevent the vote. [In re Topps Co. Shareholders Litigation, 926 A.2d 58 (Del. Ch. 2007)] (See Purchase of Stock.)

(a) The shareholders contended that Topps's conduct had "tainted the vote." What factors support this contention? How might these factors affect the vote?

(b) Why might Topps's board and management be opposed to either of the offers for the company? Is this opposition ethical? Should the court prevent the scheduled vote? Explain.

Legal Reasoning Group Activity

41–9. Mergers and Acquisitions. Angie Jolson is the chair of the board of directors of Artel, Inc., and Sam Douglas is the chair of the board of directors of Fox Express, Inc. Jolson and Douglas meet to consider the possibility of combining their corporations into a single corporate entity. They consider two alternative courses of action: Artel could acquire all of the stock and assets of Fox Express, or the corporations could combine to form a new corporation. Both Jolson and Douglas are concerned about the necessity of a formal transfer of property, liability for existing debts, and the need to amend the articles of incorporation. (See *Merger, Consolidation, and Share Exchange*.)

(a) The first group will identify the first proposed combination and outline its legal effect on the transfer of property, the liabilities of the combined corporations, and the need to amend the articles of incorporation.

(b) The second group will do the same for the second proposed combination. That is, it will identify the combination and describe its legal effect on the transfer of property, the liabilities of the combined corporations, and the need to amend the articles of incorporation.

CHAPTER 42

Investor Protection, Insider Trading, and Corporate Governance

After the stock market crash of October 29, 1929, and the ensuing economic depression, Congress enacted legislation to regulate securities markets. The result was the Securities Act of 1933[1] and the Securities Exchange Act of 1934.[2] Both acts were designed to provide investors with more information to help them make buying and selling decisions about securities and to prohibit

deceptive, unfair, and manipulative practices. **Securities** generally include any instruments evidencing corporate ownership (stock) or debt (bonds).

Today, the sale and transfer of securities are heavily regulated by federal and state statutes and by government agencies. The Securities and Exchange Commission (SEC) is the main independent regulatory agency that administers the 1933 and 1934 securities acts. The SEC also plays a key role in interpreting the provisions of these acts (and their amendments)

and in creating regulations governing the purchase and sale of securities. The agency continually updates regulations in response to legislation, such as the Dodd-Frank Wall Street Reform and Consumer Protection Act,[3] and particular challenges, such as climate change.[4]

3. Pub. L. No. 111-203, July 21, 2010, 124 Stat. 1376; codified at 12 U.S.C. Sections 5301 *et seq.*
4. The SEC now requires companies to make disclosures about the potential impacts of climate change on their future profitability. See 17 C.F.R. Parts 211, 231, and 241.

1. 15 U.S.C. Sections 77a-77aa.
2. 15 U.S.C. Sections 778a-78mm.

42-1 The Securities Act of 1933

The Securities Act of 1933 governs initial sales of stock by businesses. The act was designed to prohibit various forms of fraud and to stabilize the securities industry by requiring that investors receive financial and other significant information concerning the securities being offered for public sale. Basically, the purpose of this act is to require disclosure. The 1933 act provides that all securities transactions must be registered with the SEC unless they are specifically exempt from the registration requirements.

42-1a What Is a Security?

Section 2(1) of the Securities Act contains a broad definition of securities, which generally include the following:[5]

1. Instruments and interests commonly known as securities, such as preferred and common stocks, bonds, debentures, and stock warrants.
2. Interests commonly known as securities, such as stock options, puts, and calls, that involve the right

to purchase a security or a group of securities on a national security exchange.
3. Notes, instruments, or other evidence of indebtedness, including certificates of interest in a profit-sharing agreement and certificates of deposit.
4. Any fractional undivided interest in oil, gas, or other mineral rights.
5. Investment contracts, which include interests in limited partnerships and other investment schemes.

The *Howey* Test In interpreting the act, the United States Supreme Court has held that an **investment contract** is any transaction in which a person (1) invests (2) in a common enterprise (3) reasonably expecting profits (4) derived *primarily* or *substantially* from others' managerial or entrepreneurial efforts. Known as the *Howey* test, this definition continues to guide the determination of what types of contracts can be considered securities.[6]

■ **CASE IN POINT 42.1** James Nistler and his wife bought undeveloped land in Jackson County, Oregon, and created an LLC to develop it. The property, called Tennessee Acres, was divided into six lots. Nistler obtained investors for the development by telling them

5. 15 U.S.C. Section 77b(1). Amendments in 1982 added stock options.

6. *SEC v. W. J. Howey Co.*, 328 U.S. 293, 66 S.Ct. 1100, 90 L.Ed. 1244 (1946).

that they would earn 12 to 15 percent interest on their investment and be repaid in full within a specified time. The property was never developed, the investors were never paid, and a substantial part of the funds provided by investors were used to pay Nistler and his wife.

Nistler was convicted of securities fraud. He appealed, claiming that the investments at issue did not involve "securities," but a state appellate court affirmed his conviction. The court found that there had been a pooling of funds from a group of investors whose interests had been secured by the same land. The value of that land had been highly dependent on Nistler's use of the investors' funds to develop the land. In other words, the investors had engaged in a common enterprise from which they reasonably expected to profit, and that profit would be derived from the development efforts of Nistler.[7] ∎

Many Types of Securities For our purposes, it is convenient to think of securities in their most common form—stocks and bonds issued by corporations. Bear in mind, though, that securities can take many forms, including interests in whiskey, cosmetics, worms, beavers, boats, vacuum cleaners, muskrats, and cemetery lots. Almost any stake in the ownership or debt of a company can be considered a security. Investment contracts in condominiums, franchises, limited partnerships in real estate, and oil or gas or other mineral rights have qualified as securities.

42–1b Registration Statement

Section 5 of the Securities Act of 1933 broadly provides that if a security does not qualify for an exemption, that security must be *registered* before it is offered to the public. Issuing corporations must file a *registration statement* with the SEC and must provide all investors with a *prospectus.*

A **prospectus** is a disclosure document that describes the security being sold, the financial operations of the issuing corporation, and the investment or risk attaching to the security. The prospectus also serves as a selling tool for the issuing corporation. The SEC now allows an issuer to deliver its prospectus to investors electronically via the Internet.[8]

In principle, the registration statement and the prospectus supply sufficient information to enable unsophisticated investors to evaluate the financial risk involved.

Contents of the Registration Statement The registration statement must be written in plain English and fully describe the following:

1. The securities being offered for sale, including their relationship to the registrant's other securities.
2. The corporation's properties and business (including a financial statement certified by an independent public accounting firm).
3. The management of the corporation, including managerial compensation, stock options, pensions, and other benefits. (See this chapter's *Managerial Strategy* for a discussion of a new SEC rule that imposes additional requirements on the disclosure of management compensation.) Any interests of directors or officers in any material transactions with the corporation must also be disclosed.
4. How the corporation intends to use the proceeds of the sale.
5. Any pending lawsuits or special risk factors.

All companies, both domestic and foreign, must file their registration statements electronically so that they can be posted on the SEC's online EDGAR (Electronic Data Gathering, Analysis, and Retrieval) database. Investors can then access the statements via the Internet. The EDGAR database includes material on initial public offerings (IPOs), proxy statements (concerning voting authority), annual reports, registration statements, and other documents that have been filed with the SEC.

Registration Process The registration statement does not become effective until it has been reviewed and approved by the SEC (unless it is filed by a *well-known seasoned issuer,* as discussed shortly). The 1933 act restricts the types of activities that an issuer can engage in at each stage of the registration process. If an issuer violates these restrictions, investors can rescind their contracts to purchase the securities.

Prefiling Period. During the *prefiling period* (before the registration statement is filed), the issuer normally cannot sell or offer to sell the securities. Once the registration statement has been filed, a waiting period begins while the SEC reviews the registration statement for completeness.[9]

Waiting Period. During the waiting period, the securities can be offered for sale but cannot be sold by the issuing corporation. Only certain types of offers are allowed at this time. All issuers can distribute a *preliminary*

---

7. *State of Oregon v. Nistler,* 286 Or.App. 470, 342 P.3d 1035 (2015).
8. Basically, an electronic prospectus must meet the same requirements as a printed prospectus. The SEC rules address situations in which the graphics, images, or audio files in or accompanying a printed prospectus cannot be reproduced in an electronic form. 17 C.F.R. Section 232.304.

9. The waiting period must last at least twenty days but always extends much longer because the SEC inevitably requires numerous changes and additions to the registration statement.

MANAGERIAL STRATEGY

The SEC's New Pay-Ratio Disclosure Rule

After the financial meltdown of recent years, Congress passed the Dodd-Frank Wall Street Reform and Consumer Protection Act.[a]
One of the goals of the act was to improve accountability and transparency in the financial system. A brief section[b] in the lengthy bill requires a publicly held company to disclose the ratio of the total compensation of its chief executive officer (CEO) to the median compensation of its workers. For instance, if the annual pay of the median employee is $45,790 and the total compensation of the CEO is $12,260,000, then the pay ratio is 1 to 268. Otherwise stated, the CEO makes 268 times more than the median income for employees.

Five Years in the Making

For five years, the Securities and Exchange Commission (SEC) hesitated to adopt a disclosure rule as mandated by the Dodd-Frank act. The SEC received almost 300,000 comments and issued its own comments on the proposed rule.[c] The commissioners indicated that they were unsure what potential economic benefits, "if any," would be realized from making this information public. The SEC has estimated that the regulation will cause companies almost 550,000 annual paperwork hours, plus about $75 million per year to hire outside professionals.

a. Pub. L. No. 111-203, July 21, 2010, 124 Stat. 1376 (2010); codified at 12 U.S.C. Sections 5301 *et seq.*
b. *Ibid.*, Section 953(b).
c. 2013 WL 6503197 (2013, S.E.C. Release Nos. 33-9452 and 34-70443).

Dealing with the New Rule

The new rule is 1,800 words long, and managers initially may find it difficult to implement. Fortunately for them, the SEC realizes that it can only ask for "reasonable estimates" of the CEO-worker pay ratio.

The CEO's measured compensation includes salary, bonuses, stocks and options, incentive plans, and other compensation. In theory, calculating this amount is fairly straightforward.

Calculating the median income of the company's labor force is more difficult. Note that the median income is not the average income of employees. Rather, the rule requires the company to identify a "median" employee as the basis for comparison.

The rule does give companies flexibility in determining how to identify this median employee. Statistical sampling can be used, for instance. And the rule states, "Since identifying the median involves finding the employee in the middle, it may not be necessary to determine the exact compensation amounts for every employee paid more or less than that employee in the middle." The rule also permits companies to make the median employee determination only once every three years.

Business Questions

1. *Why might the new SEC pay-ratio disclosure rule cause certain businesses to eliminate low-wage workers?*
2. *How might the new SEC pay-ratio disclosure rule help shareholders?*

---

prospectus,[10] which contains most of the information that will be included in the final prospectus but often does not include a price.

Most issuers can use a *free-writing prospectus* during this period (although some inexperienced issuers will need to file a preliminary prospectus first).[11] A **free-writing prospectus** is any type of written, electronic, or graphic offer that describes the issuer or its securities and includes a legend indicating that the investor may obtain the prospectus at the SEC's Web site.

Posteffective Period. Once the SEC has reviewed and approved the registration statement and the waiting

period is over, the registration is effective, and the *posteffective period* begins. The issuer can now offer and sell the securities without restrictions.

If the company issued a preliminary or free-writing prospectus to investors, it must provide those investors with a final prospectus either before or at the time they purchase the securities. The issuer can make the final prospectus available to investors to download from a Web site if it notifies them of the appropriate Internet address.

42–1c Well-Known Seasoned Issuers

A *well-known seasoned issuer* (WKSI) is a firm that has issued at least $1 billion in securities in the last three years or has outstanding stock valued at $700 million or more in the hands of the public. WKSIs have greater flexibility than other issuers. They can file registration

---

10. A preliminary prospectus may also be called a *red herring prospectus.* The name comes from the legend printed in red across the prospectus stating that the registration has been filed but has not become effective.
11. See SEC Rules 164 and 433.

statements the day they announce a new offering and are not required to wait for SEC review and approval. They can also use a free-writing prospectus at any time, even during the prefiling period.

42–1d Exempt Securities and Transactions

Certain types of securities are exempt from the registration requirements of the Securities Act. These securities—which generally can also be resold without being registered—are summarized under the heading "Exempt Securities" in Exhibit 42–1.[12] The exhibit also lists and describes certain transactions that are exempt from registration requirements under various SEC regulations.

The transaction exemptions are important because they are very broad and can enable an issuer to avoid the high cost and complicated procedures associated with registration. Indeed, many sales occur without registration. Even when a transaction is exempt from the registration requirements, however, the offering is still subject to the antifraud provisions of the 1933 act (as well as those of the 1934 act, to be discussed later in this chapter).

Regulation A Offerings An exemption from registration is available for an issuer's security offerings that do not exceed $50 million during any twelve-month period.[13] Under Regulation A,[14] the issuer must file with the SEC a notice of the issue and an offering circular, which must also be provided to investors before the sale. Additional review requirements apply to issuers raising between $20 and $50 million. Overall, Regulation A provides a much less expensive process than the procedures associated with full registration.

Note that the cap for Regulation A was $5 million until 2015, when the SEC approved rule changes to make it easier for small and mid-sized businesses to raise capital. These changes were made in connection with the Jumpstart Our Business Startups, or JOBS, Act.[15] Expanding the issuers that qualify for exemption under Regulation A will likely decrease the significance of the other exemptions listed in Exhibit 42–1. In addition, the amended Regulation A—popularly known as Reg A+— has allowed for an increase in online crowdfunding.

Testing the Waters. Before preparing a Regulation A offering circular, companies are allowed to "test the waters" for potential interest. To *test the waters* means to determine potential interest without actually selling any securities or requiring any commitment from those who express interest. Small-business issuers can also use an integrated registration and reporting system that requires simpler forms than the full registration system.

Using the Internet. Some companies have sold their securities on the Internet using Regulation A. ■ **EXAMPLE 42.2** The Spring Street Brewing Company was the first company to sell securities via an online initial public offering (IPO). Spring Street raised about $1.6 million without incurring high expenses. ■ Online IPOs are particularly attractive to small companies and start-up ventures that may find it difficult to raise capital from institutional investors or through underwriters.

Small Offerings—Regulation D The SEC's Regulation D contains several exemptions from registration requirements (Rules 504, 505, and 506) for offers that either involve a small dollar amount or are made in a limited manner.

Rule 504. Rule 504 is the exemption used by most small businesses. It provides that noninvestment company offerings up to $1 million in any twelve-month period are exempt.[16] Noninvestment companies are firms that are not engaged primarily in the business of investing or trading in securities. (In contrast, an **investment company** is a firm that buys a large portfolio of securities and professionally manages it on behalf of many smaller shareholders/owners. A **mutual fund** is a well-known type of investment company.)

■ **EXAMPLE 42.3** Zeta Enterprises is a limited partnership that develops commercial property. Zeta intends to offer $600,000 of its limited partnership interests for sale between June 1 and next May 31. The buyers will become limited partners in Zeta. Because an interest in a limited partnership meets the definition of a security (discussed earlier), this offering would be subject to the registration and prospectus requirements of the Securities Act of 1933.

Under Rule 504, however, the sales of Zeta's interests are exempt from these requirements because Zeta is a noninvestment company making an offering of less than $1 million in a given twelve-month period. Therefore, Zeta can sell its interests without filing a registration statement with the SEC or issuing a prospectus to any investor. ■

---

12. 15 U.S.C. Section 77c.
13. 15 U.S.C. Section 77c(b).
14. 17 C.F.R. Sections 230.251–230.263.
15. Pub.L.No. 112-106 (June 19, 2012).

---

16. 17 C.F.R. Section 230.504. Small businesses in California may also be exempt under SEC Rule 1001. California's rule permits limited offerings of up to $5 million *per transaction*, if they satisfy certain conditions.

EXHIBIT 42–1   Exemptions for Securities Offerings under the 1933 Securities Act

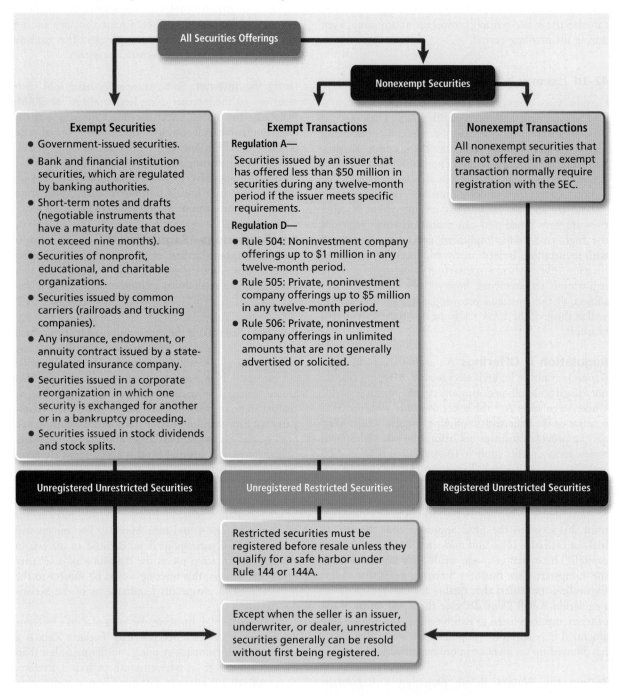

Rule 505. Another exemption is available under Rule 505 for private, noninvestment company offerings up to $5 million in any twelve-month period. The offer may be made to an unlimited number of *accredited investors* and up to thirty-five unaccredited investors.

Accredited investors include banks, insurance companies, investment companies, employee benefit plans, the issuer's executive officers and directors, and persons whose income or net worth exceeds a certain threshold.

The SEC must be notified of the sales, and precautions must be taken, because these *restricted securities* may be resold only by registration or in an exempt transaction. No general solicitation or advertising is allowed. The issuer must provide any unaccredited investors with disclosure documents, which generally are the same as those used in registered offerings.

Rule 506—Private Placement Exemption. Rule 506 exempts private, noninvestment company offerings in unlimited amounts that are not generally solicited or advertised. This exemption is often referred to as the *private placement exemption* because it exempts "transactions not involving any public offering."[17] There can be an unlimited number of accredited investors and up to thirty-five unaccredited investors. To qualify for the exemption, the issuer must believe that each unaccredited investor has sufficient knowledge or experience in financial matters to be capable of evaluating the investment's merits and risks.[18]

The private placement exemption is perhaps the most important exemption for firms that want to raise funds through the sale of securities without registering them. ■ **EXAMPLE 42.4** Citco Corporation needs to raise capital to expand its operations. Citco decides to make a private $10 million offering of its common stock directly to two hundred accredited investors and a group of thirty highly sophisticated, but unaccredited, investors. Citco provides all of these investors with a prospectus and material information about the firm, including its most recent financial statements.

As long as Citco notifies the SEC of the sale, this offering will likely qualify as an exempt transaction under Rule 506. The offering is nonpublic and not generally advertised. There are fewer than thirty-five unaccredited investors, and each of them possesses sufficient knowledge and experience to evaluate the risks involved. The issuer has provided all purchasers with the material information. Thus, Citco will likely *not* be required to comply with the registration requirements of the Securities Act of 1933. ■

Resales and Safe Harbor Rules Most securities can be resold without registration. The Securities Act provides exemptions for resales by most persons other than issuers or underwriters. The average investor who sells shares of stock need not file a registration statement with the SEC.

Resales of restricted securities acquired under Rule 505 or Rule 506, however, trigger the registration requirements *unless the party selling them complies with Rule 144 or Rule 144A*. These rules are sometimes referred to as safe harbors.

Rule 144. Rule 144 exempts restricted securities from registration on resale if all of the following conditions are met:

1. There is adequate current public information about the issuer. ("Adequate current public information" refers to the reports that certain companies are required to file under the 1934 Securities Exchange Act.)
2. The person selling the securities has owned them for at least six months if the issuer is subject to the reporting requirements of the 1934 act. If the issuer is not subject to the 1934 act's reporting requirements, the seller must have owned the securities for at least one year.
3. The securities are sold in certain limited amounts in unsolicited brokers' transactions.
4. The SEC is notified of the resale.[19]

Rule 144A. Securities that at the time of issue were not of the same class as securities listed on a national securities exchange or quoted in a U.S. automated interdealer quotation system may be resold under Rule 144A.[20] They may be sold only to a qualified institutional buyer (an institution, such as an insurance company or a bank, that owns and invests at least $100 million in securities). The seller must take reasonable steps to ensure that the buyer knows that the seller is relying on the exemption under Rule 144A.

42–1e Violations of the 1933 Act

It is a violation of the Securities Act to intentionally defraud investors by misrepresenting or omitting facts in a registration statement or prospectus. Liability may also be imposed on those who are negligent with respect to the preparation of these publications. Selling securities before the effective date of the registration statement or under an exemption for which the securities do not qualify also results in liability.

Can the omission of a material fact make a statement of opinion misleading to an ordinary investor? That was the question before the United States Supreme Court in the following case.

---

17. 15 U.S.C. Section 77d(2).
18. 17 C.F.R. Section 230.506.

19. 17 C.F.R. Section 230.144.
20. 17 C.F.R. Section 230.144A.

Omnicare, Inc. v. Laborers District Council Construction Industry Pension Fund

Supreme Court of the United States, __ U.S. __, 135 S.Ct. 1318, 191 L.Ed.2d 253 (2015).

Background and Facts Omnicare, Inc., a pharmacy services company, filed a registration state-ment in connection with a public offering. The statement expressed the company's opinion that it was in compliance with federal and state laws. Later, the federal government accused Omnicare of receiving kickbacks from pharmaceutical manufacturers. The Laborers District Council Construction Industry Pension Fund and others, which had bought the stock, filed a suit in a federal district court against Omnicare.

The plaintiffs alleged that Omnicare's legal-compliance opinion was "untrue" and that Omni-care had, in violation of the Securities Act, "omitted to state [material] facts necessary" to make that opinion not misleading. Omnicare argued that "no reasonable person, in any context, can understand a pure statement of opinion to convey anything more than the speaker's own mindset." The district court dismissed the pension funds' suit, but the U.S. Court of Appeals for the Sixth Circuit reversed the dismissal. Omnicare appealed to the United States Supreme Court.

In the Language of the Court

Justice *KAGAN* delivered the opinion of the Court.

＊ ＊ ＊ ＊

＊ ＊ ＊ Whether a statement is "misleading" depends on the perspective of a reasonable investor: The inquiry ＊ ＊ ＊ is objective.

＊ ＊ ＊ ＊

＊ ＊ ＊ A reasonable person understands, and takes into account, the difference ＊ ＊ ＊ between a state-ment of fact and one of opinion. She recognizes the import of words like "I think" or "I believe," and grasps that they convey some lack of certainty as to the statement's content.

But Omnicare takes its point too far, because a reasonable investor may, depending on the cir-cumstances, understand an opinion statement to convey facts about how the speaker has formed the opinion—or, otherwise put, about the speaker's basis for holding that view. And if the real facts are otherwise, but not provided, the opinion statement will mislead its audience. Consider an unadorned statement of opinion about legal compliance: "We believe our conduct is lawful." ＊ ＊ ＊ If the issuer made the statement in the face of its lawyers' contrary advice, or with knowledge that the Federal Government was taking the opposite view, the investor ＊ ＊ ＊ has cause to complain: He expects not just that the issuer believes the opinion (however irrationally), but that it fairly aligns with the information in the issuer's possession at the time. Thus, *if a registration statement omits material facts about the issuer's inquiry into or knowledge concerning a statement of opinion, and if those facts conflict with what a reasonable investor would take from the statement itself, then [the Securities Act] creates liability.* [Emphasis added.]

An opinion statement, however, is not necessarily misleading when an issuer knows, but fails to dis-close, some fact cutting the other way. ＊ ＊ ＊ A reasonable investor does not expect that *every* fact known to an issuer supports its opinion statement. [Emphasis in the original.]

Moreover, *whether an omission makes an expression of opinion misleading always depends on context.* Registration statements as a class are formal documents, filed with the SEC as a legal prerequisite for selling securities to the public. Investors do not, and are right not to, expect opinions contained in those statements to reflect baseless, off-the-cuff judgments, of the kind that an individual might communicate in daily life. At the same time, an investor reads each statement within such a document, whether of fact or opinion, in light of all its surrounding text, including hedges, disclaimers, and apparently conflicting information. And the investor takes into account the customs and practices of the relevant industry. ＊ ＊ ＊ The reasonable investor understands a statement of opinion in its full context, and [the Securities Act] creates liability only for the omission of material facts that cannot be squared with such a fair reading. [Emphasis added.]

Decision and Remedy *The United States Supreme Court concluded that "neither [lower court] consid-ered the Funds' omissions theory with the right standard in mind." The Court therefore vacated the decision*

Case 42.1 Continued *of the lower court and remanded the case "for a determination of whether the Funds have stated a viable omissions claim (or, if not, whether they should have a chance to replead)."*

Critical Thinking
- **Legal Environment** *Would a reasonable investor have cause to complain if an issuer, without having consulted a lawyer, states, "We believe our conduct is lawful"? Explain.*

Remedies Criminal violations are prosecuted by the U.S. Department of Justice. Violators may be fined up to $10,000, imprisoned for up to five years, or both.

The SEC is authorized to impose civil sanctions against those who willfully violate the 1933 act. It can request an injunction to prevent further sales of the securities involved or ask a court to grant other relief, such as ordering a violator to refund profits. Private parties who purchase securities and suffer harm as a result of false or omitted statements or other violations may bring a suit in a federal court to recover their losses and additional damages.

Defenses There are three basic defenses to charges of violations under the 1933 act. A defendant can avoid liability by proving any of the following:

1. The statement or omission was not material.
2. The plaintiff knew about the misrepresentation at the time the stock was purchased.
3. The defendant exercised *due diligence* in preparing or reviewing the registration and reasonably believed at the time that the statements were true. This important defense is available to an underwriter or subsequent seller but not to the issuer.

■ **CASE IN POINT 42.5** In preparation for an initial public offering (IPO), Blackstone Group, LP, filed a registration statement with the SEC. At the time, Blackstone's corporate private equity investments included FGIC Corporation (which insured investments in subprime mortgages) and Freescale Semiconductor, Inc. Before the IPO, FGIC's customers began to suffer large losses, and Freescale lost an exclusive contract to make wireless 3G chipsets for Motorola, Inc. (its largest customer). The losses suffered by these two companies would affect Blackstone. Nevertheless, Blackstone's registration statement did not mention the impact on its revenues of the investments in FGIC and Freescale.

Martin Litwin and others who had invested in Blackstone's IPO filed a suit in a federal district court against Blackstone and its officers, alleging material omissions from the statement. Blackstone argued as a defense that the omissions were not material, and the lower court dismissed the case. The plaintiffs appealed. A federal appellate court ruled that the alleged omissions were reasonably likely to be material, and remanded the case. The plaintiffs were entitled to the opportunity to prove at a trial that Blackstone had omitted material information that it was required to disclose.[21] ■

42–2 The Securities Exchange Act of 1934

The 1934 Securities Exchange Act provides for the regulation and registration of securities exchanges, brokers, dealers, and national securities associations, such as the National Association of Securities Dealers (NASD). Unlike the 1933 act, which is a one-time disclosure law, the 1934 act provides for continuous periodic disclosures by publicly held corporations to enable the SEC to regulate subsequent trading.

The Securities Exchange Act applies to companies that have assets in excess of $10 million and five hundred or more shareholders. These corporations are referred to as *Section 12 companies* because they are required to register their securities under Section 12 of the 1934 act. Section 12 companies are required to file reports with the SEC annually and quarterly, and sometimes even monthly if specified events occur (such as a merger).

The act also authorizes the SEC to engage in market surveillance to deter undesirable market practices such as fraud, market manipulation, and misrepresentation. In addition, the act provides for the SEC's regulation of proxy solicitations for voting.

42–2a Section 10(b), SEC Rule 10b-5, and Insider Trading

Section 10(b) is one of the more important sections of the Securities Exchange Act. This section prohibits the use of any manipulative or deceptive mechanism in violation of

21. *Litwin v. Blackstone Group, LP,* 634 F.3d 706 (2d Cir. 2011).

SEC rules and regulations. Among the rules that the SEC has promulgated pursuant to the 1934 act is **SEC Rule 10b-5,** which prohibits the commission of fraud in connection with the purchase or sale of any security.

SEC Rule 10b-5 applies to almost all cases concerning the trading of securities, whether on organized exchanges, in over-the-counter markets, or in private transactions. Generally, the rule covers just about any form of security. The securities need not be registered under the 1933 act for the 1934 act to apply.

Private parties can sue for securities fraud under Rule 10b-5. The basic elements of a securities fraud action are as follows:

1. A *material misrepresentation* (or omission) in connection with the purchase and sale of securities.
2. *Scienter* (a wrongful state of mind).
3. *Reliance* by the plaintiff on the material misrepresentation.
4. An *economic loss.*
5. *Causation,* meaning that there is a causal connection between the misrepresentation and the loss.

Insider Trading One of the major goals of Section 10(b) and SEC Rule 10b-5 is to prevent **insider trading,** which occurs when persons buy or sell securities on the basis of information that is not available to the public. Corporate directors, officers, and majority shareholders, among others, often have advance inside information that can affect the future market value of the corporate stock. Obviously, if they act on this information, their positions give them a trading advantage over the general public and other shareholders.

The 1934 act defines inside information. It also extends liability to those who take advantage of such information in their personal transactions when they know that the information is unavailable to those with whom they are dealing. Section 10(b) of the 1934 act

and SEC Rule 10b-5 apply to anyone who has access to or receives information of a nonpublic nature on which trading is based—not just to corporate "insiders."

Disclosure under SEC Rule 10b-5 Any material omission or misrepresentation of material facts in connection with the purchase or sale of a security may violate Section 10(b) of the 1934 act and SEC Rule 10b-5. The key to liability (which can be civil or criminal) is whether the information omitted or misrepresented is *material.*

The following are some examples of material facts calling for disclosure under SEC Rule 10b-5:

1. Fraudulent trading in the company stock by a broker-dealer.
2. A dividend change (whether up or down).
3. A contract for the sale of corporate assets.
4. A new discovery, a new process, or a new product.
5. A significant change in the firm's financial condition.
6. Potential litigation against the company.

Note that any one of these facts, by itself, is not automatically considered material. It will be regarded as a material fact only if it is significant enough that it would likely affect an investor's decision as to whether to purchase or sell the company's securities.

■ **EXAMPLE 42.6**   Zilotek, Inc., is the defendant in a class-action product liability suit that its attorney, Paula Frasier, believes the company will lose. Frasier has advised Zilotek's directors, officers, and accountants that the company will likely have to pay a substantial damages award. Zilotek plans to make a $5 million offering of newly issued stock before the date when the trial is expected to end. Zilotek's potential liability and the financial consequences to the firm are material facts that must be disclosed, because they are significant enough to affect an investor's decision to purchase the stock. ■

The case that follows is a *Classic Case* interpreting materiality under SEC Rule 10b-5.

Classic Case 42.2

SEC v. Texas Gulf Sulphur Co.

United States Court of Appeals, Second Circuit, 401 F.2d 833 (1968).

Background and Facts Texas Gulf Sulphur Company (TGS) conducted aerial geophysical surveys over more than 15,000 square miles of eastern Canada. The operations indicated concentrations of commercially exploitable minerals. At one site near Timmins, Ontario, TGS drilled a hole that appeared to yield a core with an exceedingly high mineral content. The company did not disclose the results of the core sample to the public.

After learning of the sample, TGS officers and employees made substantial purchases of TGS's stock or accepted stock options (rights to purchase stock). On April 11, 1964, an unauthorized report

Case 42.2 Continued

of the mineral find appeared in the newspapers. On the following day, TGS issued a press release that played down the discovery and stated that it was too early to tell whether the ore find would be significant.

Several months later, TGS announced that the strike was expected to yield at least 25 million tons of ore. Subsequently, the price of TGS stock rose substantially. The Securities and Exchange Commission (SEC) brought a suit against the officers and employees of TGS for violating SEC Rule 10b-5. The officers and employees argued that the information on which they had traded had not been material at the time of their trades because the mine had not then been commercially proved. The trial court held that most of the defendants had not violated SEC Rule 10b-5, and the SEC appealed.

In the Language of the Court

WATERMAN, Circuit Judge.

* * * *

* * * Whether facts are material within Rule 10b-5 when the facts relate to a particular event and are undisclosed by those persons who are knowledgeable thereof *will depend at any given time upon a balancing of both the indicated probability that the event will occur and the anticipated magnitude of the event in light of the totality of the company activity.* Here, * * * knowledge of the possibility, which surely was more than marginal, of the existence of a mine of the vast magnitude indicated by the remarkably rich drill core located rather close to the surface (suggesting mineability by the less expensive openpit method) within the confines of a large anomaly (suggesting an extensive region of mineralization) might well have affected the price of TGS stock and would certainly have been an important fact to a reasonable, if speculative, investor in deciding whether he should buy, sell, or hold. [Emphasis added.]

* * * *

* * * A major factor in determining whether the * * * discovery was a material fact is the importance attached to the drilling results by those who knew about it. * * * The timing by those who knew of it of their stock purchases * * *—purchases in some cases by individuals who had never before purchased * * * TGS stock—virtually compels the inference that the insiders were influenced by the drilling results.

Decision and Remedy   *The appellate court ruled in favor of the SEC. All of the trading by insiders who knew of the mineral find before its true extent had been publicly announced had violated SEC Rule 10b-5.*

Impact of This Case on Today's Law   *This landmark case affirmed the principle that the test of whether information is "material," for SEC Rule 10b-5 purposes, is whether it would affect the judgment of reasonable investors. The corporate insiders' purchases of stock and stock options indicated that they were influenced by the drilling results and that the information about the drilling results was material. The courts continue to cite this case when applying SEC Rule 10b-5 to cases of alleged insider trading.*

Critical Thinking

- **What If the Facts Were Different?**   *Suppose that further drilling had revealed that there was not enough ore at this site for it to be mined commercially. Would the defendants still have been liable for violating SEC Rule 10b-5? Why or why not?*

Outsiders and SEC Rule 10b-5   The traditional insider-trading case involves true insiders—corporate officers, directors, and majority shareholders who have access to (and trade on) inside information. Increasingly, however, liability under Section 10(b) of the 1934 act and SEC Rule 10b-5 has been extended to include certain "outsiders"—those who trade on inside information acquired indirectly. Two theories have been developed under which outsiders may be held liable for insider trading: the *tipper/tippee theory* and the *misappropriation theory.*

Tipper/Tippee Theory.   Anyone who acquires inside information as a result of a corporate insider's breach of his or her fiduciary duty can be liable under SEC Rule 10b-5. This liability extends to **tippees** (those who receive "tips" from insiders) and even *remote tippees* (tippees of tippees).

The key to liability under this theory is that the inside information must be obtained as a result of someone's breach of a fiduciary duty to the corporation whose shares are traded. The tippee is liable only if the following requirements are met:

1. There is a breach of a duty not to disclose inside information.
2. The disclosure is made in exchange for personal benefit.
3. The tippee knows (or should know) of this breach and benefits from it.

■ **EXAMPLE 42.7** Eric McPhail was a member of the same country club as an executive at American Superconductor. While they were golfing, the executive shared information with McPhail about the company's expected earnings, contracts, and other major developments, trusting that McPhail would keep the information confidential. Instead, McPhail tipped six of his other golfing buddies at the country club, and they all used the nonpublic information to their advantage in trading. In this situation, the executive breached his duty not to disclose the information, which McPhail knew. McPhail (the tippee) is liable under SEC Rule 10b-5, and so are his other golfing buddies (remote tippees). All traded on inside information to their benefit.[22] ■

Misappropriation Theory. Liability for insider trading may also be established under the misappropriation theory. This theory holds liable an individual who wrongfully obtains (misappropriates) inside information and trades on it for her or his personal gain. Basically, this individual has stolen information rightfully belonging to another.

The misappropriation theory has been controversial because it significantly extends the reach of SEC Rule 10b-5 to outsiders who ordinarily would *not* be deemed fiduciaries of the corporations in whose stock they trade. It is not always wrong to disclose material, nonpublic information about a company to a person who would not otherwise be privy to it. Nevertheless, a person who obtains the information and trades securities on it can be held liable.[23]

Insider Reporting and Trading—Section 16(b)

Section 16(b) of the 1934 act provides for the recapture by the corporation of all profits realized by an insider on a purchase and sale, or sale and purchase, of the corporation's stock within any six-month period.[24] It is irrelevant whether the insider actually uses inside information—all such **short-swing profits** must be returned to the corporation.

In the context of Section 16(b), insiders means officers, directors, and large stockholders of Section 12 corporations. (Large stockholders are those owning 10 percent of the class of equity securities registered under Section 12 of the 1934 act.) To discourage such insiders from using nonpublic information about their companies to their personal benefit in the stock market, the SEC requires them to file reports concerning their ownership and trading of the corporation's securities.

Section 16(b) applies not only to stock but also to warrants, options, and securities convertible into stock. In addition, the courts have fashioned complex rules for determining profits. Note, though, that the SEC exempts a number of transactions under Rule 16b-3.[25]

Exhibit 42–2 compares the effects of SEC Rule 10b-5 and Section 16(b). Because of the various ways in which insiders can incur liability under these provisions, corporate insiders should seek the advice of competent counsel before trading in the corporation's stock.

The Private Securities Litigation Reform Act

The disclosure requirements of SEC Rule 10b-5 had the unintended effect of deterring the disclosure of forward-looking information. To understand why, consider the following situation. ■ **EXAMPLE 42.8** XT Company announces that its projected earnings for a future time period will be a certain amount, but its forecast turns out to be wrong. The earnings are in fact much lower, and the price of XT's stock is affected negatively. The shareholders bring a class-action suit against XT, alleging that its directors violated SEC Rule 10b-5 by disclosing misleading financial information. ■

In an attempt to solve the problem and promote full disclosure, Congress passed the Private Securities Litigation Reform Act (PSLRA).[26] Among other things, the PSLRA provides a "safe harbor" for publicly held companies that make forward-looking statements, such as financial forecasts. Those who make such statements are protected against liability for securities fraud if they include "meaningful cautionary statements identifying important factors that could cause actual results to differ materially from those in the forward-looking statement."[27]

---

22. Three of the defendants in this case agreed to settle with the SEC and return the trading profits. See SEC press release 2014-134 "SEC Charges Group of Amateur Golfers in Insider Trading Ring."
23. See, for instance, *United States v. Gansman,* 657 F.3d 85 (2d Cir. 2011).
24. A person who expects the price of a particular stock to decline can realize profits by "selling short"—selling at a high price and repurchasing later at a lower price to cover the "short sale."
25. 17 C.F.R. Section 240.16b-3.
26. Pub.L.No. 104-67, 109 Stat. 737, codified in various sections of Title 15 of the *United States Code.*
27. 15 U.S.C. Sections 77z-2, 78u-5.

EXHIBIT 42–2 Comparison of Coverage, Application, and Liability under SEC Rule 10b-5 and Section 16(b)

AREA OF COMPARISON	SEC RULE 10b-5	SECTION 16(b)
What is the subject matter of the transaction?	Any security (does not have to be registered).	Any security (does not have to be registered).
What transactions are covered?	Purchase or sale.	Short-swing purchase and sale or short-swing sale and purchase.
Who is subject to liability?	Almost anyone with inside information under a duty to disclose—including officers, directors, controlling shareholders, and tippees.	Officers, directors, and certain shareholders who own 10 percent or more.
Is omission or misrepresentation necessary for liability?	Yes.	No.
Are there any exempt transactions?	No.	Yes, there are a number of exemptions.
Who may bring an action?	A person transacting with an insider, the SEC, or a purchaser or seller damaged by a wrongful act.	A corporation or a shareholder by derivative action.

The PSLRA also affected the level of detail required in securities fraud complaints. Plaintiffs must specify each misleading statement and say how it led them to a mistaken belief.

42–2b Regulation of Proxy Statements

Section 14(a) of the Securities Exchange Act regulates the solicitation of proxies from shareholders of Section 12 companies. The SEC regulates the content of proxy statements. Whoever solicits a proxy must fully and accurately disclose in the proxy statement all of the facts that are pertinent to the matter on which the shareholders are to vote. SEC Rule 14a-9 is similar to the antifraud provisions of SEC Rule 10b-5. Remedies for violations range from injunctions to prevent a vote from being taken to monetary damages.

42–2c Violations of the 1934 Act

As mentioned earlier, violations of Section 10(b) of the Securities Exchange Act and SEC Rule 10b-5, including insider trading, may lead to both criminal and civil liability.

***Scienter* Requirement** For either criminal or civil sanctions to be imposed, *scienter* must exist—that is, the violator must have had an intent to defraud or knowledge of his or her misconduct. *Scienter* can be proved by showing that the defendant made false statements or wrongfully failed to disclose material facts. In some situations, it can even be proved by showing that the defendant was consciously reckless as to the truth or falsity of his or her statements.

■ **CASE IN POINT 42.9** Alvin Gebhart and Jack Archer started a business venture purchasing mobile home parks (MHPs) from owners and converting them to resident ownership. They formed MHP Conversions, LP, to facilitate the conversion process and issue promissory notes that were sold to investors to raise funds for the purchases. Archer ran the MHP program, and Gebhart sold the promissory notes. Gebhart sold nearly $2.4 million in MHP promissory notes to clients, who bought the notes based on Gebhart's positive statements about the investment.

During the time Gebhart was selling the notes, however, he never actually looked into the finances of the MHP program. He relied entirely on information that Archer gave him, some of which was not true. When

Gebhart was later sued for securities fraud, a federal appellate court concluded that there was sufficient evidence of *scienter*. Gebhart knew that he had no knowledge of the financial affairs of MHP, and he had been consciously reckless as to the truth or falsity of his statements about investing in MHP.[28] ■

Complaint Must Raise an Inference of *Scienter*. In a complaint alleging a violation, the plaintiff must state facts giving rise to an inference of *scienter*. ■ **CASE IN POINT 42.10** Between May 4 and June 22, Boeing Company made announcements that its new plane called the Dreamliner, which had not yet flown, was on track for its first flight on June 30. Meanwhile, however, the plane failed important stress tests before and after redesign. On June 23, Boeing canceled the scheduled debut flight and warned of a delay in the delivery of the Dreamliner to the commercial airlines. Boeing's stock price dropped more than 10 percent.

A group of investors filed a suit against Boeing for securities fraud. They claimed that Boeing and its officers had known about the likely postponement of the first flight when they made public statements to the contrary. The plaintiffs argued that Boeing's "internal e-mails" would confirm this theory but did not identify the source of these messages. A federal court dismissed the suit, and that dismissal was affirmed on appeal. Allegations "merely implying unnamed confidential sources" was not sufficient to give rise to an inference of *scienter*. *Scienter* can also be established by showing a defendant's motive to commit fraud, but Boeing had nothing to gain by delaying the postponement of the first flight.[29] ■

Whether the plaintiff alleged sufficient facts to give rise to an inference of *scienter* was the question in the following case.

---

28. *Gebhart v. SEC*, 595 F.3d 1034 (9th Cir. 2010).

29. *City of Livonia Employees' Retirement System and Local 295/Local 851 v. Boeing Co.*, 711 F.3d 754 (7th Cir. 2013).

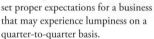

Case Analysis 42.3

Rand-Heart of New York, Inc. v. Dolan

United States Court of Appeals, Eighth Circuit, 812 F.3d 1172 (2016).

In the Language of the Court

BENTON, Circuit Judge.

* * * *

I.

[Dolan Company specializes in professional services and business information from its base in Minneapolis, Minnesota.] DiscoverReady—a subsidiary of Dolan Company—performed litigation support [discovery management and document review services, including technology services related to processing and hosting discovery data], working mostly for Bank of America. In May or June 2013, Bank of America met with James Dolan (Chief Executive Officer of Dolan Company) and other DiscoverReady representatives. Bank of America noted concerns about Dolan Company's finances * * * and indicated it would send no new work to DiscoverReady until the financial concerns were resolved. * * * Dolan reported what transpired at the meeting to Dolan Company's Board of Directors, which

proceeded to authorize DiscoverReady for sale. Bank of America stopped sending new work to DiscoverReady in June.

On August 1, Dolan Company released a Form 10-Q [for the second quarter], which stated:

> * * * To operate profitably on a continuous basis in the future, the Company must increase revenue and eliminate costs * * * . These challenges make it probable that the Company will be unable to comply with certain of its financial covenants.

Also on August 1, Dolan spoke with stock analysts. [Dolan made] the [following] statements during the conference:

> For 2013, we expect * * * Discover-Ready * * * to grow at double-digit rates over the prior year * * * . However, we must point out that we expect DiscoverReady's third quarter revenues to be below last year's all time record revenue quarter. We make this comment not to dampen enthusiasm

about our growth prospects for DiscoverReady, but to set proper expectations for a business that may experience lumpiness on a quarter-to-quarter basis.

Asked to elaborate about "lumpiness," Dolan stated:

> Well, it's hard to be very specific about the lumpiness now without getting into details we normally do not disclose. * * * These things do come and they come sometimes unexpectedly, sometimes quickly. So * * * we have to be cautious in how we describe things.

On November 12, 2013, Dolan * * * filed its Form 10-Q ending September 30. [Form 10-Q is a quarterly report required by the Securities and Exchange Commission.] The 10-Q reported that the decline in revenue "exceeded our expectations," largely due to "a reduction in new work from DiscoverReady's largest customer, a reduction that we identified

Case 42.3 Continued

towards the end of the quarter. We believe this reduction resulted from the customer's evaluation of the Company's overall financial condition." The closing price for Dolan Company stock fell to $2.08 on November 11, to $1.05 on November 12, to $0.90 on November 13.

On January 2, 2014, Dolan Company issued a final press release announcing the appointment of a Chief Restructuring Officer * * * . Share prices then fell by $0.14. In March, Dolan Company filed a Chapter 11 bankruptcy.

II.
    * * * *

Rand-Heart [of New York, Inc.] brought a class action suit [in a federal district court on behalf of purchasers of Dolan Company's securities between August 1, 2013, and January 2, 2014,] alleging Dolan made material misrepresentations and omissions about DiscoverReady's financial stability [in violation of Section 10(b) and Rule 10b–5]. The district court granted Dolan's motion to dismiss * * * . It found that Rand-Heart failed to allege *scienter*.

[Rand-Heart appealed the dismissal to the U.S. Court of Appeals for the Eighth Circuit.]

* * * *

A.

Rand-Heart argues the district court erred in finding inadequate allegations of *scienter*.
    * * * *

Rand-Heart maintains it adequately pled *scienter* by alleging that Dolan had been severely reckless. *Severe recklessness is defined as highly unreasonable omissions or misrepresentations involving an extreme departure from the standards of ordinary care, and presenting the danger of misleading buyers or sellers which is either known to the defendant or is so obvious that the defendant must have been aware of it.* [Emphasis added.]
    * * * *

Rand-Heart * * * argues that Dolan was reckless in failing to disclose that Bank of America had stopped sending new work to DiscoverReady in May or June 2013. Bank of America was DiscoverReady's biggest client, providing over 50% of DiscoverReady's work. In the second half of 2013, however, Bank of America work sharply declined. The complaint quoted DiscoverReady's Chief Operating Officer's acknowledgment: "We were, our work, our revenues

were dropping and our case origination had dropped, as I said earlier, to almost nothing from Bank of America." By May or June 2013, DiscoverReady had "completed a large document review project for Bank of America" immediately causing "great concerns." This decline prompted the Company's Board in June 2013 to "authorize the marketing of DiscoverReady for sale." Taking these allegations as true, DiscoverReady's financial instability caused by the decline in Bank of America work was, at the least, so obvious that Dolan must have been aware of it. The facts pled are sufficient to survive a motion to dismiss.

B.
    * * * *

The district court erred in dismissing the Section 10(b) and Rule 10b–5 claims for failure to state a claim.

III.
    * * * *

The district court's decision is * * * reversed * * * and remanded for proceedings consistent with this opinion.

Legal Reasoning Questions

1. *Scienter* can be established by showing a defendant's motive to commit fraud. In the context of the *Rand-Heart* case, what act might have established motive on Dolan's part?

2. When Bank of America met with Dolan to discuss his company's financial situation, it demanded that the company be restructured. Dolan did not disclose this fact in the Form 10-Q or in his conference with stock analysts. Was this omission misleading?

3. Suppose that Dolan had disclosed Bank of America's action with respect to DiscoverReady in the Form 10-Q and the conference. Would the result in this case have been different? Explain.

***Scienter* Not Required for Section 16(b) Violations** Violations of Section 16(b) include the sale by insiders of stock acquired less than six months before the sale (or, for a short sale, less than six months after the sale). (Recall that a short sale involves selling securities that one does not yet own.) These violations are subject to civil sanctions. Liability under Section 16(b) is strict liability. Neither *scienter* nor negligence is required.

Criminal Penalties For violations of Section 10(b) and Rule 10b-5, an individual may be fined up to $5 million, imprisoned for up to twenty years, or both. A partnership or a corporation may be fined up to $25 million. Under Section 807 of the Sarbanes-Oxley Act, for a *willful* violation of the 1934 act the violator can be imprisoned for up to twenty-five years (in addition to being subject to a fine).

For a defendant to be convicted in a criminal prosecution under the securities laws, there can be no reasonable doubt that the defendant knew he or she was acting wrongfully. In other words, a jury is not allowed merely to speculate that the defendant may have acted willfully.

■ **CASE IN POINT 42.11**   Douglas Newton was the president and sole director of Real American Brands, Inc. (RLAB). RLAB owned the Billy Martin's USA brand and operated a Billy Martin's retail boutique at the Trump Plaza in New York City. (Billy Martin's, a Western wear store, was co-founded by Billy Martin, the one-time manager of the New York Yankees.)

Newton agreed to pay kickbacks to Chris Russo, whom he believed to be the manager of a pension fund, to induce the fund to buy shares of RLAB stock. Newton later arranged for his friend Yan Skwara to pay similar kickbacks for the fund's purchase of stock in U.S. Farms, Inc. In reality, the pension fund was fictitious, and Newton and Skwara had been dealing with agents of the Federal Bureau of Investigation (FBI). Newton was charged with securities fraud and convicted by a jury (Skwara pled guilty). Newton appealed, but a federal appellate court upheld his conviction.

According to the court, the evidence established that in each transaction, the amount of the kickback was added to the price of the stock, which artificially increased the stock price. The evidence sufficiently proved that Newton had engaged in a scheme to defraud the supposed pension fund. His words and conduct, which were revealed on video at the trial, showed his intent to defraud the pension fund investors.[30] ■

Civil Sanctions   The SEC can also bring a civil action against anyone who purchases or sells a security while in possession of material nonpublic information in violation of the 1934 act or SEC rules.[31] The violation must occur through the use of a national securities exchange or a broker or dealer.[32] A court can assess a penalty amounting to as much as triple the profits gained or the loss avoided by the guilty party.[33]

The Insider Trading and Securities Fraud Enforcement Act enlarged the class of persons who may be subject to civil liability for insider trading. In addition, this act gave the SEC authority to offer monetary rewards to informants.[34]

Private parties may also sue violators of Section 10(b) and Rule 10b-5. A private party can obtain rescission (cancellation) of a contract to buy securities or damages to the extent of the violator's illegal profits. Those found liable have a right to seek contribution from those who share responsibility for the violations, including accountants, attorneys, and corporations. For violations of Section 16(b), a corporation can bring an action to recover the short-swing profits.

42–2d Securities Fraud Online and Ponzi Schemes

A problem facing the SEC today is how to enforce the antifraud provisions of the securities laws in the online environment. Internet-related forms of securities fraud include many types of investment scams. Spam, online newsletters and bulletin boards, chat rooms, blogs, social media, and tweets can all be used to spread false information and perpetrate fraud. For a relatively small cost, fraudsters can even build sophisticated Web pages to facilitate their investment scams.

Investment Newsletters   Hundreds of online investment newsletters provide information on stocks. Legitimate online newsletters can help investors gather valuable information, but some e-newsletters are used for fraud. The law allows companies to pay these newsletters to tout their securities. The newsletters are required to disclose who paid for the advertising, but many newsletters do not follow that law. Thus, an investor reading an online newsletter may believe that the information is unbiased, when in fact the fraudsters will directly profit by convincing investors to buy or sell particular stocks.

Ponzi Schemes   Although much securities fraud occurs online, schemes conducted primarily offline have not disappeared. In recent years, the SEC has filed an increasing number of enforcement actions against perpetrators of *Ponzi schemes*. (Ponzi schemes are fraudulent investment operations that pay returns to investors from new capital paid to the fraudsters rather than from a legitimate investment.) Such schemes sometimes target U.S. residents and convince them to invest in offshore companies or banks.

30. *United States v. Newton,* 559 Fed.Appx. 902 (11th Cir. 2014).
31. 15 U.S.C. Section 78u(d)(2)(A).
32. Transactions pursuant to a public offering by an issuer of securities are exempted.
33. 15 U.S.C. Section 78u(d)(2)(C).
34. 15 U.S.C. Section 78u-1.

42–3 State Securities Laws

Today, every state has its own corporate securities laws, or **blue sky laws,** that regulate the offer and sale of securities within its borders. (The phrase *blue sky laws* comes from a 1917 United States Supreme Court decision. The Court stated that the purpose of such laws was to prevent "speculative schemes which have no more basis than so many feet of 'blue sky.'")[35] Article 8 of the Uniform Commercial Code, which has been adopted by all of the states, also imposes various requirements relating to the purchase and sale of securities.

42–3a Requirements under State Securities Laws

State securities laws apply mainly to intrastate transactions (transactions within one state). Typically, state laws have disclosure requirements and antifraud provisions, many of which are patterned after Section 10(b) of the Securities Exchange Act of 1934 and SEC Rule 10b-5. State laws also provide for the registration of securities offered or issued for sale within the state and impose disclosure requirements.

■ **CASE IN POINT 42.12** Randall Fincke was the founder, director, and officer of Access Cardiosystems, Inc., a small start-up company that sold portable automated external heart defibrillators. Fincke prepared a business plan stating that Access's "patent counsel" had advised the firm that "its product does not infringe any patents." This statement was false—patent counsel never offered Access any opinion on the question of infringement.

Fincke gave this plan to potential investors, including Joseph Zimmel, who bought $1.5 million in Access shares. When the company later filed for Chapter 11 bankruptcy protection, Zimmel filed a complaint with the federal bankruptcy court, alleging that Fincke had violated the Massachusetts blue sky law. The court awarded Zimmel $1.5 million in damages, and the award was affirmed on appeal. Fincke had solicited investors "by means of" a false statement of material fact, in violation of the fraud provisions in the state's securities laws.[36] ■

Methods of registration, required disclosures, and exemptions from registration vary among states. Unless an exemption from registration is applicable, issuers must register or qualify their stock with the appropriate state official, often called a *corporations commissioner.* Additionally, most state securities laws regulate securities brokers and dealers.

42–3b Concurrent Regulation

Since the adoption of the 1933 and 1934 federal securities acts, the state and federal governments have regulated securities concurrently. Issuers must comply with both federal and state securities laws, and exemptions from federal law are not exemptions from state laws.

The dual federal and state system has not always worked well, particularly during the early 1990s, when the securities markets underwent considerable expansion. Today, many of the duplicate regulations have been eliminated, and the SEC has exclusive power to regulate most national securities activities.

The National Conference of Commissioners on Uniform State Laws has substantially revised the Uniform Securities Act to coordinate state and federal securities regulation and enforcement efforts. Nineteen states have adopted the most recent version of the Uniform Securities Act.[37]

42–4 Corporate Governance

Corporate governance can be narrowly defined as the relationship between a corporation and its shareholders. Some argue for a broader definition—that corporate governance specifies the rights and responsibilities among different participants in the corporation, such as the board of directors, managers, shareholders, and other stakeholders, and spells out the rules and procedures for making decisions on corporate affairs. Regardless of the way it is defined, effective corporate governance requires more than just compliance with laws and regulations.

Effective corporate governance is essential in large corporations because corporate ownership (by shareholders)

---

35. *Hall v. Geiger-Jones Co.,* 242 U.S. 539, 37 S.Ct. 217, 61 L.Ed. 480 (1917).
36. *In re Access Cardiosystems, Inc.,* 776 F.3d 60 (1st Cir. 2015).
37. At the time this book went to press, the Uniform Securities Act had been adopted in Georgia, Hawaii, Idaho, Indiana, Iowa, Kansas, Maine, Michigan, Minnesota, Mississippi, Missouri, New Hampshire, New Mexico, Oklahoma, South Carolina, South Dakota, Vermont, Wisconsin, and Wyoming, as well as in the U.S. Virgin Islands.

is separated from corporate control (by officers and managers). Under these circumstances, officers and managers may attempt to advance their own interests at the expense of the shareholders. The well-publicized corporate scandals in the early 2000s clearly illustrated how the misconduct of corporate managers can cause harm to companies and to society. Indeed, with the globalization of business, corporate governance has become even more important because a corporation's bad acts (or lack of control systems) can have far-reaching consequences.

42–4a Aligning the Interests of Officers and Shareholders

Some corporations have sought to align the financial interests of their officers with those of the company's shareholders by providing the officers with **stock options.** These options enable holders to purchase shares of the corporation's stock at a set price. When the market price rises above that level, the officers can sell their shares for a profit. Because a stock's market price generally increases as the corporation prospers, the options give the officers a financial stake in the corporation's well-being and supposedly encourage them to work hard for the benefit of the shareholders.

Problems with Stock Options Options have turned out to be an imperfect device for encouraging effective governance. Executives in some companies have been tempted to "cook" the company's books in order to keep share prices higher so that they can sell their stock for a profit. Executives in other corporations have experienced no losses when share prices dropped because their options were "repriced" so that they did not suffer from the price decline. Thus, although stock options theoretically can motivate officers to protect shareholder interests, stock option plans have sometimes become a way for officers to take advantage of shareholders.

Outside Directors With stock options generally failing to work as planned, there has been an outcry for more outside directors (those with no formal employment affiliation with the company). The theory is that independent directors will more closely monitor the actions of corporate officers. Hence, today we see more boards with outside directors. Note, though, that outside directors may not be truly independent of corporate officers. They may be friends or business associates of the leading officers.

42–4b Promoting Accountability

Effective corporate governance standards are designed to address problems such as those briefly discussed earlier and to motivate officers to make decisions that promote the financial interests of the company's shareholders. Generally, corporate governance entails corporate decision-making structures that monitor employees (particularly officers) to ensure that they are acting for the benefit of the shareholders. Thus, corporate governance involves, at a minimum:

1. The audited reporting of financial conditions at the corporation so that managers can be evaluated.
2. Legal protections for shareholders so that violators of the law who attempt to take advantage of shareholders can be punished for misbehavior and victims can recover damages for any associated losses.

Governance and Corporate Law State corporation statutes set up the legal framework for corporate governance. Under the corporate law of Delaware, where most major companies incorporate, all corporations must have certain structures of corporate governance in place. The most important structure, of course, is the board of directors, because the board makes the major decisions about the future of the corporation.

The Board of Directors Under corporate law, a corporation must have a board of directors elected by the shareholders. Directors are responsible for ensuring that the corporation's officers are operating wisely and in the exclusive interest of shareholders. Directors receive reports from the officers and give them managerial direction. In reality, though, corporate directors devote a relatively small amount of time to monitoring officers.

Ideally, shareholders would monitor the directors' supervision of the officers. In practice, however, it can be difficult for shareholders to monitor directors and hold them responsible for corporate failings. Although the directors can be sued if they fail to do their jobs effectively, directors are rarely held personally liable.

The Audit Committee. A crucial committee of the board of directors is the *audit committee,* which oversees the corporation's accounting and financial reporting processes, including both internal and outside auditors. Unless the committee members have sufficient expertise and are willing to spend the time to carefully examine the corporation's bookkeeping methods, however, the audit committee may be ineffective.

The audit committee also oversees the corporation's "internal controls." These controls, carried out largely by the company's internal auditing staff, are measures taken to ensure that reported results are accurate. For instance, internal controls help to determine whether a corporation's debts are collectible. If the debts are not collectible, it is up to the audit committee to make sure that the corporation's financial officers do not simply pretend that payment will eventually be made.

The Compensation Committee. Another important committee of the board of directors is the *compensation committee,* which determines the compensation of the company's officers. As part of this process, the committee must assess the officers' performance and attempt to design a compensation system that will align the officers' interests with those of the shareholders.

42–4c The Sarbanes-Oxley Act

In 2002, following a series of corporate scandals, Congress passed the Sarbanes-Oxley Act,[38] which addresses certain issues relating to corporate governance. Generally, the act attempts to increase corporate accountability by imposing strict disclosure requirements and harsh penalties for violations of securities laws. Among other things, the act requires chief corporate executives to take personal responsibility for the accuracy of financial statements and reports that are filed with the SEC.

Additionally, the act requires that certain financial and stock-transaction reports be filed with the SEC earlier than was required under the previous rules. The act also created a new entity, called the Public Company Accounting Oversight Board, to regulate and oversee public accounting firms. Other provisions of the act established private civil actions and expanded the SEC's remedies in administrative and civil actions.

Because of the importance of this act for corporate leaders and for those dealing with securities transactions, we highlight some of its key provisions relating to corporate accountability in Exhibit 42–3.

More Internal Controls and Accountability
The Sarbanes-Oxley Act introduced direct *federal* corporate governance requirements for publicly traded companies. The law addressed many of the corporate governance procedures just discussed and created new requirements

---

38. 15 U.S.C. Sections 7201 *et seq.*

in an attempt to make the system work more effectively. The requirements deal with independent monitoring of company officers by both the board of directors and auditors.

Sections 302 and 404 of the Sarbanes-Oxley Act require high-level managers (the most senior officers) to establish and maintain an effective system of internal controls. The system must include "disclosure controls and procedures" to ensure that company financial reports are accurate and timely and to document financial results prior to reporting.

Senior management must reassess the system's effectiveness annually. Some companies have had to take expensive steps to bring their internal controls up to the new federal standards. Hundreds of companies have reported that they identified and corrected shortcomings in their internal control systems as a result.

Exemptions for Smaller Companies
The act initially required all public companies to have an independent auditor file a report with the SEC on management's assessment of internal controls. Congress, however, enacted an exemption for smaller companies in 2010 in an effort to reduce compliance costs. Public companies with a market capitalization, or public float, of less than $75 million no longer need to have an auditor report on management's assessment of internal controls.

Certification and Monitoring Requirements
Section 906 of the Sarbanes-Oxley Act requires that chief executive officers and chief financial officers certify the accuracy of the information in the corporate financial statements. The statements must "fairly represent in all material respects, the financial conditions and results of operations of the issuer." This requirement makes the officers directly accountable for the accuracy of their financial reporting and precludes any "ignorance defense" if shortcomings are later discovered.

The act also includes requirements to improve directors' monitoring of officers' activities. All members of a publicly traded corporation's audit committee, which oversees the corporation's accounting and financial reporting processes, must be outside directors. The audit committee must have a written charter that sets out its duties and provides for performance appraisal. At least one "financial expert" must serve on the audit committee, which must hold executive meetings without company officers being present. In addition to reviewing the internal controls, the committee also monitors the actions of the outside auditor.

EXHIBIT 42–3 Some Key Provisions of the Sarbanes-Oxley Act Relating to Corporate Accountability

CERTIFICATION REQUIREMENTS

Under *Section 906* of the Sarbanes-Oxley Act, the chief executive officers (CEOs) and chief financial officers (CFOs) of most major companies listed on public stock exchanges must certify financial statements that are filed with the SEC. CEOs and CFOs have to certify that filed financial reports "fully comply" with SEC requirements and that all of the information reported "fairly represents in all material respects, the financial conditions and results of operations of the issuer."

Under *Section 302* of the act, CEOs and CFOs of reporting companies are required to certify that a signing officer reviewed each quarterly and annual filing with the SEC and that none contained untrue statements of material fact. Also, the signing officer or officers must certify that they have established an internal control system to identify all material information and that any deficiencies in the system were disclosed to the auditors.

INTERNAL CONTROLS

Financial Controls—*Section 404(a)* regulates all public companies are required to assess the effectiveness of their internal control over financial reporting. *Section 404(b)* requires independent auditors to report on management's assessment of internal controls, but certain companies are exempted.

Loans to Directors and Officers—*Section 402* prohibits any reporting company—as well as any private company that is filing an initial public offering—from making personal loans to directors and executive officers are exempted.

Protection for Whistleblowers—*Section 806* protects "whistleblowers"—employees who "blow the whistle" on securities violations by their employers—from being fired or in any way discriminated against by their employers.

Blackout Periods—*Section 306* prohibits certain types of securities transactions during "blackout periods"—periods during which the issuer's ability to purchase, sell, or otherwise transfer funds in individual account plans (such as pension funds) is suspended.

ENHANCED PENALTIES

- *Violations of Section 906 Certification Requirements*—A CEO or CFO who certifies a financial report or statement filed with the SEC knowing that the report or statement does not fulfill all of the requirements of *Section 906* will be subject to criminal penalties of up to $1 million in fines, ten years in prison, or both. *Willful* violators of the certification requirements may be subject to $5 million in fines, twenty years in prison, or both.

- *Violations of the Securities Exchange Act of 1934*—Penalties for securities fraud under the 1934 act were also increased. Individual violators may be fined up to $5 million, imprisoned for up to twenty years, or both. *Willful* violators may be imprisoned for up to twenty-five years in addition to being fined.

- *Destruction or Alteration of Documents*—Anyone who alters, destroys, or conceals documents or otherwise obstructs any official proceeding will be subject to fines, imprisonment for up to twenty years, or both.

- *Other Forms of White-Collar Crime*—The act stiffened the penalties for certain criminal violations, such as federal mail and wire fraud, and ordered the U.S. Sentencing Commission to revise the sentencing guidelines for white-collar crimes.

STATUTE OF LIMITATIONS FOR SECURITIES FRAUD

Section 804 provides that a private right of action for securities fraud may be brought no later than two years after the discovery of the violation or five years after the violation, whichever is earlier.

Reviewing: Investor Protection, Insider Trading, and Corporate Governance

Dale Emerson served as the chief financial officer for Reliant Electric Company, a distributor of electricity serving portions of Montana and North Dakota. Reliant was in the final stages of planning a takeover of Dakota Gasworks, Inc., a natural gas distributor that operated solely within North Dakota. Emerson went on a weekend fishing trip with his uncle, Ernest Wallace. Emerson mentioned to Wallace that he had been putting in a lot of extra hours at the office planning a takeover of Dakota Gasworks. When he returned from the fishing trip, Wallace purchased $20,000 worth of Reliant stock. Three weeks later, Reliant made a tender offer to Dakota Gasworks stockholders and purchased 57 percent of Dakota Gasworks stock. Over the next two weeks, the price of Reliant stock rose 72 percent before leveling out. Wallace then sold his Reliant stock for a gross profit of $14,400. Using the information presented in the chapter, answer the following questions.

1. Would registration with the SEC be required for Dakota Gasworks securities? Why or why not?
2. Did Emerson violate Section 10(b) of the Securities Exchange Act of 1934 and SEC Rule 10b-5? Why or why not?
3. What theory or theories might a court use to hold Wallace liable for insider trading?
4. Under the Sarbanes-Oxley Act, who would be required to certify the accuracy of the financial statements Reliant filed with the SEC?

Debate This . . .   *Insider trading should be legalized.*

Terms and Concepts

accredited investor 802	investment company 801	securities 798
blue sky laws 813	investment contract 798	short-swing profits 808
corporate governance 813	mutual fund 801	stock option 814
free-writing prospectus 800	prospectus 799	tippee 807
insider trading 806	SEC Rule 10b-5 806	

Issue Spotters

1. When a corporation wishes to issue certain securities, it must provide sufficient information for an unsophisticated investor to evaluate the financial risk involved. Specifically, the law imposes liability for making a false statement or omission that is "material." What sort of information would an investor consider material? (See *The Securities Exchange Act of 1934*.)

2. Lee is an officer of Magma Oil, Inc. Lee knows that a Magma geologist has just discovered a new deposit of oil. Can Lee take advantage of this information to buy and sell Magma stock? Why or why not? (See *The Securities Exchange Act of 1934*.)

• **Check your answers to the Issue Spotters against the answers provided in Appendix D at the end of this text.**

Business Scenarios

42–1. Registration Requirements. Estrada Hermanos, Inc., a corporation incorporated and doing business in Florida, decides to sell $1 million worth of its common stock to the public. The stock will be sold only within the state of Florida. José Estrada, the chair of the board, says the offering need not be registered with the Securities and Exchange Commission. His brother, Gustavo, disagrees. Who is right? Explain. (See *The Securities Act of 1933*.)

42–2. Registration Requirements. Huron Corp. has 300,000 common shares outstanding. The owners of these outstanding shares live in several different states. Huron has decided to split the 300,000 shares two for one. Will Huron Corp. have to file a registration statement and prospectus on the 300,000 new shares to be issued as a result of the split? Explain. (See *The Securities Act of 1933*.)

42–3. Insider Trading. David Gain was the chief executive officer (CEO) of Forest Media Corp., which became interested in acquiring RS Communications, Inc. To initiate negotiations, Gain met with RS's CEO, Gill Raz, on Friday,

July 12. Two days later, Gain phoned his brother Mark, who bought 3,800 shares of RS stock on the following Monday. Mark discussed the deal with their father, Jordan, who bought 20,000 RS shares on Thursday. On July 25, the day before the RS bid was due, Gain phoned his parents' home, and Mark bought another 3,200 RS shares. The same routine was followed over the next few days, with Gain periodically phoning Mark or Jordan, both of whom continued to buy RS shares.

Forest's bid was refused, but on August 5, RS announced its merger with another company. The price of RS stock rose 30 percent, increasing the value of Mark's and Jordan's shares by $664,024 and $412,875, respectively. Did Gain engage in insider trading? What is required to impose sanctions for this offense? Could a court hold Gain liable? Why or why not? (See *The Securities Exchange Act of 1934*.)

Business Case Problems

42–4. Business Case Problem with Sample Answer— Violations of the 1934 Act.

 Matrixx Initiatives, Inc., makes and sells over-the-counter pharmaceutical products. Its core brand is Zicam, which accounts for 70 percent of its sales. Matrixx received reports that some consumers had lost their sense of smell (a condition called anosmia) after using Zicam Cold Remedy. Four product liability suits were filed against Matrixx, seeking damages for anosmia. In public statements relating to revenues and product safety, however, Matrixx did not reveal this information.

James Siracusano and other Matrixx investors filed a suit in a federal district court against the company and its executives under Section 10(b) of the Securities Exchange Act of 1934 and SEC Rule 10b-5, claiming that the statements were misleading because they did not disclose information regarding the product liability suits. Matrixx argued that to be material, information must consist of a statistically significant number of adverse events that require disclosure. Because Siracusano's claim did not allege that Matrixx knew of a statistically significant number of adverse events, the company contended that the claim should be dismissed. What is the standard for materiality in this context? Should Siracusano's claim be dismissed? Explain. [*Matrixx Initiatives, Inc. v. Siracusano,* 563 U.S. 27, 131 S.Ct. 1309, 179 L.Ed.2d 398 (2011)] (See *The Securities Exchange Act of 1934*.)

- For a sample answer to Problem 42–4, go to Appendix E at the end of this text.

42–5. Disclosure under SEC Rule 10b-5.

Dodona I, LLC, invested $4 million in two securities offerings from Goldman, Sachs & Co. The investments were in collateralized debt obligations (CDOs). Their value depended on residential mortgage-backed securities (RMBS), whose value in turn depended on the performance of subprime residential mortgages.

Before marketing the CDOs, Goldman had noticed several "red flags" relating to investments in the subprime market, in which it had invested heavily. To limit its risk, Goldman began betting against subprime mortgages, RMBS, and CDOs, including the CDOs it had sold to Dodona. In other words, Goldman made investments based on the assumption that subprime mortgages and the securities instruments built upon them would decrease in value. In an internal e-mail, one Goldman official commented that the company had managed to "make some lemonade from some big old lemons." Nevertheless, Goldman's marketing materials provided only boilerplate statements about the risks of investing in the securities.

The CDOs were later downgraded to junk status, and Dodona suffered a major loss while Goldman profited. Assuming that Goldman did not affirmatively misrepresent any facts about the CDOs, can Dodona still recover under SEC Rule 10b-5? If so, how? [*Dodona I, LLC v. Goldman, Sachs & Co.,* 847 F.Supp.2d 624 (S.D.N.Y. 2012)] (See *The Securities Exchange Act of 1934*.)

42–6. Violations of the 1933 Act.

Three shareholders of iStorage sought to sell their stock through World Trade Financial Corp. The shares were *restricted securities*—that is, securities acquired in an unregistered, private sale. Restricted securities typically bear a "restrictive" legend clearly stating that they cannot be resold in the public marketplace. This legend had been wrongly removed from the iStorage shares, however. Information about the company that was publicly available included the fact that, despite a ten-year life, it had no operating history or earnings. In addition, it had net losses of about $200,000, and its stock was thinly traded. Without investigating the company or the status of its stock, World Trade sold more than 2.3 million shares to the public on behalf of the three customers. Did World Trade violate the Securities Act of 1933? Discuss. [*World Trade Financial Corp. v. Securities and Exchange Commission,* 739 F.3d 1243 (9th Cir. 2014)] (See *The Securities Act of 1933*.)

42–7. Securities Act of 1933.

Big Apple Consulting USA, Inc., provided small publicly traded companies with a variety of services, including marketing, business planning, and Web site development and maintenance. CyberKey Corp. sold customizable USB drives. CyberKey falsely informed Big Apple that CyberKey had been awarded a $25 million contract with the Department of Homeland Security. Big Apple used this information in aggressively promoting CyberKey's stock and was compensated for the effort in the form of CyberKey shares. When the Securities and Exchange Commission (SEC) began to investigate, Big Apple sold its shares for $7.8 million. The SEC filed an action in a federal district court against Big Apple, alleging a violation of the Securities Act of 1933. Can liability be imposed on a seller for a false statement that was made by someone else? Explain. [*U.S. Securities and Exchange*

Commission v. Big Apple Consulting USA, Inc., 783 F.3d 786 (11th Cir. 2015)] (See *The Securities Act of 1933*.)

42–8. The Securities Exchange Act of 1934. Dilean Reyes-Rivera was the president of Global Reach Trading (GRT), a corporation registered in Puerto Rico. His brother Jeffrey was the firm's accountant. Along with GRT sales agents and other promoters, the brothers solicited funds from individuals by promising to invest the funds in low-risk, short-term, high-yield securities. The investors were guaranteed a rate of return of up to 20 percent. Through this arrangement, more than 230 persons provided the brothers with about $22 million. This money was not actually invested. Instead, the funds received from later investors were used to pay "returns" to earlier investors. The Reyes-Riveras spent $4.6 million of the proceeds to buy luxury vehicles, houses, furniture, jewelry, and trips for themselves. What is this type of scheme called? What are the potential consequences? Discuss. [*United States v. Reyes-Rivera*, 812 F.3d 79 (1st Cir. 2016)] (See *The Securities Exchange Act of 1934*.)

42–9. A Question of Ethics—Violations of the 1934 Act. *Melvin Lyttle told John Montana and Paul Knight about a "Trading Program" that purportedly would buy and sell securities. Lyttle said the securities deals were fully insured, as well as monitored and controlled by the Federal Reserve. Without checking the details or even verifying whether the Program existed, Montana and Knight, with Lyttle's help, began to sell interests in the Program to investors. For a minimum investment of $1 million, the investors were* promised extraordinary rates of return—from 10 percent to as much as 100 percent per week—without risk. They were told, among other things, that the Program would "utilize banks that can ensure full bank integrity of The Transaction whose undertaking[s] are in complete harmony with international banking rules and protocol and who guarantee maximum security of a Funder's Capital Placement Amount." Nothing was required but the investors' funds and their silence—the Program was to be kept secret. Over a four-month period in 1999, Montana raised approximately $23 million from twenty-two investors. The promised gains did not accrue, however. Instead, Montana, Lyttle, and Knight depleted investors' funds in high-risk trades or spent the funds on themselves. [SEC v. Montana, *464 F.Supp.2d 772 (S.D.Ind. 2006)*] (See *The Securities Exchange Act of 1934*.)*

(a) The Securities and Exchange Commission (SEC) filed a suit in a federal district court against Montana and the others, seeking an injunction, civil penalties, and refund of profits with interest. The SEC alleged, among other things, violations of Section 10(b) of the Securities Exchange Act of 1934 and SEC Rule 10b-5. What is required to establish such violations? Describe how and why the facts in this case meet, or fail to meet, these requirements.

(b) It is often remarked, "There's a sucker born every minute!" Does that phrase describe the Program's investors? Ultimately, about half of the investors recouped the amount they invested. Should the others be considered at least partly responsible for their own losses? Why or why not?

Legal Reasoning Group Activity

42–10. Violations of Securities Laws. Karel Svoboda, a credit officer for Rogue Bank, evaluated and approved his employer's extensions of credit to clients. These responsibilities gave Svoboda access to nonpublic information about the clients' earnings, performance, acquisitions, and business plans from confidential memos, e-mail, and other sources. Svoboda devised a scheme with Alena Robles, an independent accountant, to use this information to trade securities. Pursuant to their scheme, Robles traded in the securities of more than twenty different companies and profited by more than $2 million. Svoboda also executed trades for his own profit of more than $800,000, despite their agreement that Robles would do all of the trading. Aware that their scheme violated Rogue Bank's policy, they attempted to conduct their trades in such a way as to avoid suspicion. When the bank questioned Svoboda about his actions, he lied, refused to cooperate, and was fired. (See *The Securities Exchange Act of 1934*.)

(a) The first group will determine whether Svoboda or Robles committed any crimes.

(b) The second group will decide whether Svoboda or Robles is subject to civil liability. If so, who could file a suit, and on what ground? What are the possible sanctions?

(c) A third group will identify any defenses that Svoboda or Robles could raise and determine their likelihood of success.

Business Start-Ups Online

Hundreds of thousands of new businesses open each year in the United States. A large percentage of them fail within the first five years. But those that succeed more than offset the losses—the survivors are responsible for the creation of most new jobs.

Today, many new businesses—following in the footsteps of Facebook, Inc., Google, Inc., Twitter, Inc., and others—start online. Going into business online can be a good way to reach a wider market and experience higher sales. Generally, the steps for setting up an online business are the same as those for starting a brick-and-mortar operation. But there are added legal considerations.

Starting an Online Business

Starting a business requires taking certain preliminary steps—for example, finding a product niche, researching potential markets, and formulating a business plan. Actually setting up the business involves additional steps. As noted, these steps are similar for all new businesses, but here we focus on online startups.

Create a Legal Entity and Obtain a License Creating a legal entity, such as a corporation or a limited liability company, under which to do business online can insulate the owners from personal liability. It may also give the business a greater appearance of solidity. Considerations for starting a business as a corporation, a limited liability company, or another form of organization were discussed earlier in this unit.

In any business situation, federal and state licenses and permits must be obtained if required. A license or permit is often needed to engage in an activity supervised and regulated by a federal or state administrative agency. For instance, sales of alcoholic beverages require a permit from the U.S. Treasury Department's Alcohol and Tobacco Tax and Trade Bureau.

Select and Register a Domain Name A domain name is the address of an online business. Once a name is selected, the registration process is simple. The Internet Corporation for Assigned Names and Numbers (ICANN), a nonprofit corporation, is responsible for coordinating the maintenance and procedures of several databases related to the namespaces of the Internet. Among other things, ICANN oversees the distribution of domain names.[1]

Choose a Web Host and Design a Site The Web host of an online business stores all the pages of the business's Web site and makes them available on the Internet. The Web host should be reliable, secure, and suitable for the business. Some Web hosts will perform site development and maintenance, as well as search engine registration.

The design of a site should comply with intellectual property laws. For instance, any trademark used on a site should not infringe on another's mark. Images used as part of the design should not infringe on others' copyrights.

---

1. A directory of registrars is available at https://www.internic.net.

Managing an Online Business

Managing any business requires complying with federal, state, and local laws. When transacting business online in global markets, there are also international regulations to follow.

Comply with Advertising Rules Advertising online is subject to many of the same laws as advertising offline. Goods and services must be described truthfully, disclosures must be clear and conspicuous, and customers must understand what they are paying for. If customers must click on a link to get the information, the link must be obvious. The purpose is to provide a marketplace in which businesses can compete free of deceptive and unfair practices.

Among the regulations that apply to advertising is the Federal Trade Commission's Mail, Internet, or Telephone Order Merchandise rule, which governs representations with respect to shipping.[2] Generally, a business must ship ordered merchandise within thirty days, unless a customer agrees otherwise, or promptly refund the price of the unshipped goods.

Protect Users' Privacy Businesses typically collect and retain their customers' account numbers and other personal information. Keeping this data private can protect against liability for wrongful disclosure or misuse. An online business is subject to federal and state privacy laws that cover offline businesses. And wherever a firm does business, it must comply with the location's data protection laws—many foreign countries have privacy laws that apply to online businesses.

Offer Payment Options Online businesses generally accept credit or debit cards for payment. International sales can be increased by offering a variety of payment options, especially options that match customers' local business practices. In many European countries, for example, consumers often pay online merchants by wire transfer.

Another option is a service such as PayPal that processes payments between businesses and their customers and forwards the funds to the appropriate party. Some services specialize in processing payments from international customers. Of course, there is always some risk, but in general these services guarantee the payments.

Collect State and Local Taxes Federal, state, and local tax laws apply to online businesses. A tax permit must be obtained from the appropriate government agency when this is required. State and local sales taxes must be collected from customers in a state in which an online business has a *nexus*, or physical presence—a store, an office, or a warehouse, for instance.[3]

Follow International Guidelines An online business can make sales to, and engage in other transactions with, businesses and individuals in every continent on the globe. Even the smallest firm has the potential to reach more than a billion customers online.

The Organization for Economic Cooperation and Development, of which the United States is a member, issued a set of guidelines for doing business in international markets online. The principles expressed in the guidelines make up a voluntary code of conduct that encourages an online business to do the following:

- Use fair marketing practices.
- Offer accurate, clear information about the business's goods and services.

---

2. 16 C.F.R. Chapter I, Subchapter D, Part 435.
3. *Quill v. North Dakota*, 504 U.S. 298, 112 S.Ct. 1904, 119 L.Ed.2d 91 (1992).

- Disclose full information about the terms and costs of a transaction.
- Provide a secure method for online payment.
- Protect consumer privacy.[4]

Comply with International Trade Laws Doing business online in global markets requires compliance with international trade laws, including shipping and tariff and tax regulations. Customers should be informed that tariffs and taxes can significantly increase the final prices of goods and services.[5]

The United States imposes additional requirements on businesses that export products. All goods are subject to the regulations that cover economic and trade sanctions against foreign countries, companies, and individuals. Nearly every commercial transaction with any sanctioned party is prohibited.

Goods with both commercial and military applications are known as *dual-use products*. These items must be licensed by the U.S. Department of Commerce under its Export Administrative Regulations.[6] The International Traffic in Arms Regulations control sales of defense-related goods. Under these regulations, items on the U.S. Munitions List must be licensed for export.[7]

Ethical Connection

Dealing in good faith can be more important in doing business online than in a brick-and-mortar location because Internet customers are more reliant on a business's reputation. For an online business, this involves more than minimal compliance with the relevant laws of the targeted market.

In some industries, the law imposes a repair, replace, or refund policy on merchants for some types of defects in delivered goods. In any industry, to build and maintain a customer base requires an effective customer service program. This program should go beyond what is legally required. How customer complaints are resolved is important to building trust and confidence.

Ethics Question *To attain success in global commerce, an online business should design its Web site with what in mind?*

Critical Thinking *Between 2 and 4 percent of online orders involve fraud. What can an online business do to avoid being the victim?*

---

4. A checklist of practices that follow these guidelines is in Federal Trade Commission, *Electronic Commerce: Selling Internationally A Guide for Businesses available at* https://www.ftc.gov/tips-advice/business-center/guidance/electronic-commerce-selling-internationally-guide-businesses.

5. Information on conducting business online, particularly in international markets, is provided by a number of federal agencies through BusinessUSA.gov, *Conducting Business Online, available at* business.usa.gov/export/a-guide-to-exporting-basics/conducting-business-online.

6. 15 C.F.R. Subtitle B, Chapter VII, Subchapter C.

7. 22 C.F.R. Chapter I, Subchapter M.

Government Regulation

CHAPTER 43

Administrative Agencies

Government agencies established to administer the law have a great impact on the day-to-day operations of businesses. In its early years, the United States had a simple, nonindustrial economy with little regulation. As the economy has grown and become more complex, the size of government has also increased, and so has the number, size, and power of administrative agencies.

In some instances, new agencies have been created in response to a crisis. In the wake of the financial crisis that led to the latest economic recession, for instance, Congress enacted the Dodd-Frank Wall Street Reform and Consumer Protection Act. Among other things, this statute created the Financial Stability Oversight Council to identify and respond to emerging risks in the financial system. It also created the Consumer

Financial Protection Bureau (CFPB) to protect consumers from alleged abusive practices by financial institutions, mortgage lenders, and credit-card companies.

As the number of agencies has multiplied, so have the rules, orders, and decisions that they issue. Today, there are rules covering almost every aspect of a business's operations. These regulations make up the body of *administrative law.*

43–1 The Practical Significance of Administrative Law

Whereas statutory law is created by legislatures, administrative law is created by administrative agencies. When Congress—or a state legislature—enacts legislation, it typically adopts a rather general statute and leaves its implementation to an **administrative agency.** The agency then creates the detailed rules and regulations necessary to carry out the statute. The administrative agency, with its specialized personnel, has the time, resources, and expertise to make the detailed decisions required for regulation.

43–1a Administrative Agencies Exist at All Levels of Government

Administrative agencies are spread throughout the government. At the federal level, the Securities and Exchange Commission regulates a firm's capital structure and financing, as well as its financial reporting. The National Labor Relations Board oversees relations between a firm and any unions with which it may deal. The Equal Employment Opportunity Commission also regulates employer-employee relationships. The Environmental Protection Agency and the Occupational

Safety and Health Administration affect the way a firm manufactures its products, and the Federal Trade Commission influences the way it markets those products.

There are administrative agencies at the state and local levels as well. Commonly, a state agency (such as a state pollution-control agency) is created as a parallel to a federal agency (such as the Environmental Protection Agency). Just as federal statutes take precedence over conflicting state statutes, so do federal agency regulations take precedence over conflicting state regulations. Because the rules of state and local agencies vary widely, we focus here exclusively on federal administrative law.

43–1b Agencies Provide a Comprehensive Regulatory Scheme

Often, administrative agencies at various levels of government work together and share the responsibility of creating and enforcing particular regulations. ■ **EXAMPLE 43.1** When Congress enacted the Clean Air Act, it provided only general directions for the prevention of air pollution. The specific pollution-control requirements imposed on businesses are almost entirely the product of decisions made by the Environmental Protection Agency (EPA). Moreover, the EPA works with parallel environmental agencies at the state level to analyze existing data and determine the appropriate pollution-control standards. ■

Legislation and regulations have significant benefits—in the example of the Clean Air Act, a cleaner environment than existed in decades past. At the same time, these benefits entail considerable costs for business. The EPA has estimated the costs of compliance with the Clean Air Act at many tens of billions of dollars yearly. Although the agency has calculated that the overall benefits of its regulations often exceed their costs, the burden on business is substantial. Business therefore has a strong incentive to try to influence the regulatory environment through lobbying.

43–2 Agency Creation and Powers

Congress creates federal administrative agencies. By delegating some of its authority to make and implement laws, Congress can indirectly monitor a particular area in which it has passed legislation. Delegation enables Congress to avoid becoming bogged down in the details relating to enforcement—details that are often best left to specialists.

To create an administrative agency, Congress passes **enabling legislation,** which specifies the name, purposes, functions, and powers of the agency being created. Federal administrative agencies can exercise only those powers that Congress has delegated to them in enabling legislation. Through similar enabling acts, state legislatures create state administrative agencies.

An agency's enabling statute defines its legal authority. An agency cannot regulate beyond the powers granted by the statute, and it may be required to take some regulatory action by the terms of that statute. When regulated groups oppose a rule adopted by an agency, they often bring a lawsuit arguing that the rule was not authorized by the enabling statute and is therefore void. Conversely, a group may file a suit claiming that an agency has illegally *failed* to pursue regulation required by the enabling statute.

43–2a Enabling Legislation—An Example

Congress created the Federal Trade Commission (FTC) in the Federal Trade Commission Act.[1] The act prohibits unfair methods of competition and deceptive trade practices. It also describes the procedures that the FTC must follow to charge persons or organizations with violations of the act, and it provides for judicial review of agency orders. The act grants the FTC the power to do the following:

---
1. 15 U.S.C. Sections 41–58.

1. Create "rules and regulations for the purpose of carrying out the Act."
2. Conduct investigations of business practices.
3. Obtain reports from interstate corporations concerning their business practices.
4. Investigate possible violations of federal antitrust statutes. (The FTC shares this task with the Antitrust Division of the U.S. Department of Justice.)
5. Publish findings of its investigations.
6. Recommend new legislation.
7. Hold trial-like hearings to resolve certain trade disputes that involve FTC regulations or federal antitrust laws.

The commission that heads the FTC is composed of five members. The president, with the advice and consent of the Senate, appoints each of the FTC commissioners for a term of seven years. The president also designates one of the commissioners to be the chair.

43–2b Types of Agencies

There are two basic types of administrative agencies: executive agencies and independent regulatory agencies. Federal *executive agencies* include the cabinet departments of the executive branch, which assist the president in carrying out executive functions, and the subagencies within the cabinet departments. The Occupational Safety and Health Administration, for instance, is a subagency within the U.S. Department of Labor.

Executive agencies usually have a single administrator, director, or secretary who is appointed by the president to oversee the agency and can be removed by the president at any time. Exhibit 43–1 lists the cabinet departments and some of their most important subagencies.

Independent regulatory agencies, such as the Federal Trade Commission and the Securities and Exchange Commission (SEC), are outside the federal executive departments (those headed by a cabinet secretary). The president's power is less pronounced in regard to independent agencies, whose officers serve for fixed terms and cannot be removed without just cause. See Exhibit 43–2 for a list of selected independent regulatory agencies and their principal functions.

43–2c Agency Powers and the Constitution

Administrative agencies occupy an unusual niche in the U.S. governmental structure, because they exercise powers that normally are divided among the three branches of government. Agencies' powers include functions

EXHIBIT 43–1 Executive Departments and Important Subagencies

DEPARTMENT	SELECTED SUBAGENCIES
State	Passport Office; Bureau of Diplomatic Security; Foreign Service; Bureau of Intelligence and Research
Treasury	Internal Revenue Service; U.S. Mint
Interior	U.S. Fish and Wildlife Service; National Park Service; Bureau of Indian Affairs; Bureau of Land Management
Justice[a]	Federal Bureau of Investigation; Drug Enforcement Administration; Bureau of Prisons; U.S. Marshals Service
Agriculture	Soil Conservation Service; Agricultural Research Service; Food Safety and Inspection Service
Commerce[b]	Bureau of the Census; Bureau of Economic Analysis; U.S. Patent and Trademark Office; National Oceanic and Atmospheric Administration
Labor[b]	Occupational Safety and Health Administration; Bureau of Labor Statistics; Employment Standards Administration; Office of Labor-Management Standards
Defense[c]	National Security Agency; Joint Chiefs of Staff; Departments of the Air Force, Navy, Army
Housing and Urban Development	Government National Mortgage Association; Office of Fair Housing and Equal Opportunity
Transportation	Federal Aviation Administration; Federal Highway Administration; National Highway Traffic Safety Administration
Energy	Office of Civilian Radioactive Waste Management; Office of Nuclear Energy; Energy Information Administration
Health and Human Services[d]	Food and Drug Administration; Centers for Medicare and Medicaid Services; Centers for Disease Control and Prevention; National Institutes of Health
Education[d]	Office of Elementary and Secondary Education; Office of Postsecondary Education; Office of Vocational and Adult Education
Veterans Affairs	Veterans Health Administration; Veterans Benefits Administration; National Cemetery Administration
Homeland Security	U.S. Citizenship and Immigration Services; Directorate of Border and Transportation Services; U.S. Coast Guard; Federal Emergency Management Agency

a. Formed from the Office of the Attorney General.
b. Formed from the Department of Commerce and Labor.
c. Formed from the Department of War and the Department of the Navy.
d. Formed from the Department of Health, Education, and Welfare.

associated with the legislature *(rulemaking),* the executive branch *(enforcement),* and the courts *(adjudication).*

The constitutional principle of *checks and balances* allows each branch of government to act as a check on the actions of the other two branches. Furthermore, the U.S. Constitution authorizes only the legislative branch to create laws. Yet administrative agencies, to which the Constitution does not specifically refer, can make **legislative rules,** or *substantive rules,* that are as legally binding as laws that Congress passes.

Administrative agencies also issue **interpretive rules,** which simply declare policy and do not affect legal rights or obligations. ■ **EXAMPLE 43.2** The Equal Employment Opportunity Commission periodically issues interpretive rules indicating how it plans to interpret the provisions of certain statutes, such as the Americans with

EXHIBIT 43–2 Selected Independent Regulatory Agencies

NAME OF AGENCY	PRINCIPAL DUTIES
Federal Reserve System (the Fed) Board of Governors	Determines policy with respect to interest rates, credit availability, and the money supply (including various "bailouts" in the financial sector).
Federal Trade Commission (FTC)	Prevents businesses from engaging in unfair trade practices; stops the formation of monopolies in the business sector.
Securities and Exchange Commission (SEC)	Regulates the nation's stock exchanges, in which shares of stock are bought and sold; enforces the securities laws.
Federal Communications Commission (FCC)	Regulates communications by telegraph, cable, telephone, radio, satellite, Internet, and television.
National Labor Relations Board (NLRB)	Protects employees' rights to join unions and bargain collectively with employers; attempts to prevent unfair labor practices by both employers and unions.
Equal Employment Opportunity Commission (EEOC)	Works to eliminate discrimination in employment based on religion, gender, race, color, disability, national origin, or age; investigates claims of discrimination.
Environmental Protection Agency (EPA)	Undertakes programs aimed at reducing air and water pollution; works with state and local agencies to help fight environmental hazards.
Nuclear Regulatory Commission (NRC)	Ensures that electricity-generating nuclear reactors in the United States are built and operated safely; regularly inspects operations of such reactors.

Disabilities Act. These informal rules provide enforcement guidelines for agency officials. ■

The Delegation Doctrine Courts generally hold that Article I of the U.S. Constitution is the basis for all administrative law. Section 1 of that article grants all legislative powers to Congress and requires Congress to oversee the implementation of all laws. Article I, Section 8, gives Congress the power to make all laws necessary for executing its specified powers. Under what is known as the **delegation doctrine,** courts interpret these passages as granting Congress the power to establish administrative agencies and delegate to them the power to create rules for implementing those laws.

The three branches of government exercise certain controls over agency powers and functions, as discussed next, but in many ways administrative agencies function independently. For this reason, administrative agencies, which constitute the **bureaucracy,** are sometimes referred to as the fourth branch of the U.S. government.

Executive Controls The executive branch of government exercises control over agencies both through the president's power to appoint federal officers and through the president's veto power. The president may veto enabling legislation passed by Congress or congressional attempts to modify an existing agency's authority.

Legislative Controls Congress exercises authority over agency powers through legislation. Congress gives power to an agency through enabling legislation and can take power away—or even abolish an agency altogether—through subsequent legislation. Legislative authority is required to fund an agency, and enabling legislation usually sets certain time and monetary limits on the funding of particular programs. Congress can always revise these limits.

In addition to its power to create and fund agencies, Congress has the authority to investigate the implementation of its laws and the agencies that it has created. Congress also has the power to "freeze" the enforcement of most federal regulations before the regulations take effect. (Another legislative check on agency actions is the Administrative Procedure Act, discussed shortly.)

The question that a court faces when confronted with an agency's interpretation of a statute it administers is always whether the agency has acted within its statutory authority. At issue in the following case was an agency's authority under a statute enacted in the nineteenth century.

Loving v. Internal Revenue Service

United States Court of Appeals, District of Columbia Circuit, 742 F.3d 1013 (2014).

Background and Facts The Internal Revenue Service (IRS) is a subagency of the U.S. Department of the Treasury. Responding to concerns about the performance of some paid tax-return preparers, the IRS issued a new rule. The rule required paid preparers to pass an initial certification exam, pay annual fees, and complete at least fifteen hours of continuing education courses each year. As authority for the rule, the IRS relied on a statute enacted in 1884 and recodified in 1982. The statute authorizes the agency to "regulate the practice of representatives of persons before the Department of the Treasury." Three independent preparers filed a suit in a federal district court against the IRS, contending that the rule exceeded the agency's authority. The court ruled in the plaintiffs' favor. The IRS appealed.

In the Language of the Court

KAVANAUGH, Circuit Judge.

* * * *

In our view, at least six considerations foreclose the IRS's interpretation of the statute.

First is the meaning of the key statutory term "representatives." * * * The term "representative" is traditionally and commonly defined as an agent with authority to bind others, a description that does not fit tax-return preparers.

Put simply, *tax-return preparers are not agents. They do not possess legal authority to act on the taxpayer's behalf. They cannot legally bind the taxpayer by acting on the taxpayer's behalf.* [Emphasis added.]

* * * *

Second is the meaning of the phrase "practice * * * before the Department of the Treasury."

* * * To "practice before" a court or agency ordinarily refers to practice during an investigation, adversarial hearing, or other adjudicative proceeding.

That is quite different from the process of filing a tax return. * * * *Tax-return preparers do not practice before the IRS when they simply assist in the preparation of someone else's tax return.* [Emphasis added.]

* * * *

Third is the history of [the statute]. The language [in the original statute included the phrase] "agents, attorneys, or other persons representing claimants."

That original language plainly would not encompass tax-return preparers. * * * When Congress re-codified the statute in 1982, Congress simplified the phrase * * * to the current "representatives of persons." But * * * Congress made clear in the statute itself that * * * the 1982 Act was designed "to revise, codify, and enact" the amended provisions "without substantive change."

* * * *

Fourth is the broader statutory framework.

* * * *

* * * [By enacting other statutes specific to tax-return preparers,] multiple Congresses have acted as if [the statute at the center of this case] did not extend so broadly as to cover tax-return preparers. * * * The meaning of one statute may be affected by other Acts, particularly where Congress has spoken * * * more specifically to the topic at hand. So it is here.

Fifth is the nature and scope of the authority being claimed by the IRS.

If we were to accept the IRS's interpretation of [the statute,] the IRS would be empowered for the first time to regulate hundreds of thousands of individuals in the multi-billion dollar tax-preparation industry. Yet nothing in the statute's text or the legislative record contemplates that vast expansion of the IRS's authority.

Sixth is the IRS's past approach to this statute. Until [now] the IRS never interpreted the statute to give it authority to regulate tax-return preparers.

* * * In light of the text, history, structure, and context of the statute, it becomes apparent that the IRS never before adopted its current interpretation for a reason: It is incorrect.

Case 43.1 Continued

Decision and Remedy *The U.S. Court of Appeals for the District of Columbia Circuit affirmed the lower court's ruling. Under the IRS's interpretation of the statute, the agency "would be empowered for the first time to regulate hundreds of thousands of individuals in the multi-billion dollar tax-preparation industry." Nothing in the statute's text, history, structure, or context "contemplates that vast expansion of the IRS's authority."*

Critical Thinking
- **Legal Environment** *As a policy matter, some observers might argue that the IRS should be allowed to regulate tax-return preparers more strictly. Under the reasoning of the court, who has the authority to give effect to such a policy, and how would it be accomplished?*

Judicial Controls The judicial branch exercises control over agency powers through the courts' review of agency actions. As you will read shortly, the Administrative Procedure Act provides for judicial review of most agency decisions. Agency actions are not automatically subject to judicial review, however. The party seeking court review must first exhaust all administrative remedies under what is called the **exhaustion doctrine.** In other words, the complaining party normally must have exhausted all available administrative remedies before seeking court review.[2]

■ **EXAMPLE 43.3** The Federal Trade Commission (FTC) claims that Sysco Industries used deceptive advertising and orders it to run new ads correcting the misstatements. Sysco contends that its ads were not deceptive. Under the exhaustion doctrine, Sysco must go through the entire FTC process before it can bring a suit against the FTC in court to challenge the order. ■

43–2d The Administrative Procedure Act

Sometimes, Congress specifies certain procedural requirements in an agency's enabling legislation. In the absence of any directives from Congress concerning a particular agency procedure, the Administrative Procedure Act (APA)[3] applies.

The Arbitrary and Capricious Test One of Congress's goals in enacting the APA was to provide for more judicial control over administrative agencies. To that end, the APA provides that courts should "hold unlawful and set aside" agency actions found to be "arbitrary, capricious, an abuse of discretion, or otherwise not in accordance with law."[4] Under this standard, parties can

challenge regulations as contrary to law or as so irrational that they are arbitrary and capricious.

There is no precise definition of what makes a rule arbitrary and capricious, but the standard includes factors such as whether the agency has done any of the following:

1. Failed to provide a rational explanation for its decision.
2. Changed its prior policy without justification.
3. Considered legally inappropriate factors.
4. Entirely failed to consider a relevant factor.
5. Rendered a decision plainly contrary to the evidence.

See this chapter's *Digital Update* feature for a discussion of administrative rules for broadband operators that have been challenged as arbitrary and capricious.

Fair Notice The APA also includes many requirements concerning the notice that regulatory agencies must give to those affected by its regulations. For instance, an agency may change the way it applies a certain regulatory principle. Before the change can be carried out, the agency must give fair notice of what conduct will be expected in the future.

■ **CASE IN POINT 43.4** The 1934 Communications Act established a system of limited-term broadcast licenses subject to various conditions. One condition was the indecency ban, which prohibited the uttering of "any obscene, indecent, or profane language by means of radio communication." For nearly thirty years, the Federal Communications Commission (FCC) invoked this ban only when the offensive language had been repeated, or "dwelled on," in the broadcast. It was not applied to "fleeting expletives" (offensive words used only briefly).

Then the FCC changed its policy, declaring that an offensive term, such as the F-word, was actionably indecent even if it was used only once. In 2006, the FCC applied this new rule to two Fox Television broadcasts, each of which

2. The plaintiff must also have *standing to sue* the agency.
3. 5 U.S.C. Sections 551–706.
4. 5 U.S.C. Section 706(2)(A).

DIGITAL UPDATE   Imposing a 1930s Regulatory Law on Broadband Operators

Since the advent of the Internet, it has remained largely unregulated. President Bill Clinton (1993–2001) said clearly and often that the Internet should remain lightly regulated, at most. During the Obama administration, however, pressure from the president himself applied to the Federal Communications Commission (FCC) started to change that thinking.

Communications Act of 1934.[c] Normally, a common carrier is a business that transports items from one place to another, such as a trucking company. Under the 1934 act, this definition was widened to include telephone companies. Under the new FCC rules, the Internet would fall under the act as well. The new rules are still under discussion, and legal challenges have been filed.

An Unsuccessful Attempt to Impose Regulation on Internet Service Providers

In 2010, under the authority of the Telecommunications Act of 1996,[a] the FCC attempted to regulate Internet service providers (ISPs) by enacting the "Open Internet Order." Under this order, the FCC would have required broadband ISPs to transfer data files equally, without consideration of the size or source of the files—so-called net neutrality. The policy prohibited providers from transmitting certain content at slower speeds or higher costs than other types of content. Challenged in court, the order was overturned.[b]

The Advent of "Obamanet"

In early 2015, the FCC commissioners voted to regulate ISPs as "common carriers" under Title II of the

What the New FCC Rules Mean

Here is a summary of the new rules:
- No Internet service provider can prevent a user from accessing "legal content, applications, services, or non-harmful devices" on the Internet. The goal to is prevent censorship and discrimination.
- No Internet service provider can deliberately reduce the speed of data from particular sites or applications.
- No Internet service provider can charge content providers more to provide them with faster service.

Critical Thinking *Some observers predict that numerous lawsuits will be filed against the FCC. Why would this be likely?*

a. 47 U.S.C. Sections 1302(a), (b).
b. *Verizon v. Federal Communications Commission,* 740 F.3d 623 (D.C. Cir. 2014).

c. 47 U.S.C. Sections 201 *et seq.*

---

contained a single use of the F-word. The broadcasts had aired before the FCC's change in policy. The FCC ruled that these two broadcasts were indecent, and Fox appealed the ruling. Ultimately, the case reached the United States Supreme Court, and the Court determined that the FCC's order should be set aside. Because the FCC did not provide fair notice prior to the broadcasts in question that fleeting expletives could constitute actionable indecency, the standards were unconstitutionally vague.[5] ∎

43–3 The Administrative Process

All federal agencies must follow specific procedural requirements as they go about fulfilling their three basic

functions: rulemaking, enforcement, and adjudication. These three functions make up what is known as the **administrative process.** As mentioned, the APA imposes requirements that all federal agencies must follow in the absence of contrary provisions in the enabling legislation. This act is an integral part of the administrative process.

43–3a Rulemaking

The major function of an administrative agency is **rulemaking**—the formulation of new regulations, or rules. The APA defines a *rule* as "an agency statement of general or particular applicability and future effect designed to implement, interpret, or prescribe law and policy."[6]

Regulations are sometimes said to be *legislative* because, like statutes, they have a binding effect. Thus, violators of agency rules may be punished. Because

5. *Federal Communications Commission v. Fox Television Stations, Inc.,* __ U.S. __, 132 S.Ct. 2307, 183 L.Ed.2d 234 (2012).

6. 5 U.S.C. Section 551(4).

agency rules have such significant legal force, the APA established procedures for agencies to follow in creating rules.

Many rules must be adopted using the APA's **notice-and-comment rulemaking,** which involves three basic steps:

1. Notice of the proposed rulemaking.
2. A comment period.
3. The final rule.

The APA recognizes some limited exceptions to its procedural requirements, but they are seldom invoked. ■ **EXAMPLE 43.5** The Occupational Safety and Health Act authorized the Occupational Safety and Health Administration (OSHA) to develop and issue rules governing safety in the workplace. When OSHA wants to formulate rules regarding safety in the steel industry, it has to follow the specific procedures outlined by the APA. ■

The impetus for rulemaking may come from various sources, including Congress and the agency itself. In addition, private parties may petition an agency to begin a rulemaking (or repeal a rule). For instance, environmental groups have petitioned for stricter air-pollution controls to combat emissions that may contribute to climate change.

Notice of the Proposed Rulemaking When a federal agency decides to create a new rule, the agency publishes a notice of the proposed rulemaking proceedings in the *Federal Register*. The *Federal Register* is a daily publication of the executive branch that prints government orders, rules, and regulations.

The agency's notice states where and when the proceedings will be held, the agency's legal authority for making the rule (usually its enabling legislation), and the terms or subject matter of the rule. The agency must also make available to the public certain other information, such as the key scientific data underlying the proposal. The proposed rule is often reported by the news media and published in the trade journals of the industries that will be affected.

Comment Period Following the publication of the notice of the proposed rulemaking proceedings, the agency must allow ample time for persons to comment in writing on the proposed rule. The purpose of this comment period is to give interested parties the opportunity to express their views on the proposed rule in an effort to influence agency policy. The comments can be made in writing or, if a hearing is held, orally. All comments become a public record that others can examine.

■ **EXAMPLE 43.6** Brown Trucking learns that the U.S. Department of Transportation is considering a new regulation that will have a negative impact on its ability to do business and on its profits. A notice of the rulemaking is published in the *Federal Register*. Later, a public hearing is held so that proponents and opponents can offer evidence and question witnesses. At this hearing, Brown's owner orally expresses his opinion about the pending rule. ■

The agency need not respond to all comments, but it must respond to any significant comments that bear directly on the proposed rule. The agency responds by either modifying its final rule or explaining, in a statement accompanying the final rule, why it did not make any changes. In some circumstances, particularly when less formal procedures are used, an agency may accept comments after the comment period is closed.

The Final Rule After the agency reviews the comments, it drafts the final rule and publishes it in the *Federal Register*. A final rule must contain a "concise general statement of . . . basis and purpose" that describes the reasoning behind the rule.[7] The final rule can include modifications based on the public comments. If substantial changes are made, however, a new proposal and a new opportunity for comment are required.

The final rule is later compiled along with the rules and regulations of other federal administrative agencies in the *Code of Federal Regulations*. Final rules have binding legal effect unless the courts later overturn them.

Failure to Follow Rulemaking Procedures If an agency fails to follow proper rulemaking procedures, the resulting rule may not be binding. ■ **EXAMPLE 43.7** Members of the Hemp Industries Association (HIA) manufacture and sell food products made from hemp seed and oil. These products may contain trace amounts of THC, a component of marijuana. Without following formal rulemaking procedures, the Drug Enforcement Administration (DEA) publishes rules that effectively ban the possession and sale of HIA's food products, treating them as controlled substances. A court will most likely overturn the rules because the DEA did not follow formal rulemaking procedures. ■

Informal Agency Actions Rather than take the time to conduct notice-and-comment rulemaking, agencies have increasingly been using more informal methods of policymaking, such as issuing interpretive rules and guidance documents. As mentioned earlier, unlike

---

7. 5 U.S.C. Section 555(c).

legislative rules, interpretive rules simply declare policy and do not affect legal rights or obligations. Guidance documents advise the public on the agencies' legal and policy positions.

Informal agency actions are exempt from the APA's requirements because they do not establish legal rights. A party cannot be directly prosecuted for violating an interpretive rule or a guidance document. Nevertheless, an informal action can be important because it warns regulated entities that the agency may engage in formal rulemaking if they ignore its informal policymaking.

43–3b Enforcement

Although rulemaking is the most prominent agency activity, rule enforcement is also critical. Often, an agency enforces its own rules. After a final rule is issued, agencies conduct investigations to monitor compliance with the rule or the terms of the enabling statute.

An agency investigation of this kind might begin when the agency receives a report of a possible violation. In addition, many agency rules require compliance reporting from regulated entities, and such a report may trigger an enforcement investigation.

Inspections and Tests   In conducting investigations, many agencies gather information through on-site inspections. Sometimes, inspecting an office, a factory, or some other business facility is the only way to obtain the evidence needed to prove a regulatory violation. At other times, an inspection or test is used in place of a formal hearing to show the need to correct or prevent an undesirable condition.

Administrative inspections and tests cover a wide range of activities, including safety inspections of underground coal mines, safety tests of commercial equipment and automobiles, and environmental monitoring of factory emissions. An agency may also ask a firm or individual to submit certain documents or records to the agency for examination.

Normally, business firms comply with agency requests to inspect facilities or business records because it is in any firm's interest to maintain a good relationship with regulatory bodies. In some instances, however, such as when a firm thinks an agency's request is unreasonable and disruptive, the firm may refuse to comply with the request. In such situations, an agency may resort to the use of a subpoena or a search warrant.

Subpoenas   There are two basic types of subpoenas. The subpoena *ad testificandum*[8] ("to testify") is an ordinary subpoena. It is a writ, or order, compelling a witness to appear at an agency hearing. The subpoena *duces tecum*[9] ("bring it with you") compels an individual or organization to hand over books, papers, records, or documents to the agency. An administrative agency may use either type of subpoena to obtain testimony or documents.

There are limits on what an agency can demand. To determine whether an agency is abusing its discretion in pursuing information as part of an investigation, a court may consider such factors as the following:

1. *The purpose of the investigation.* An investigation must have a legitimate purpose. Harassment is an example of an improper purpose. An agency may not issue an administrative subpoena to inspect business records if the motive is to harass or pressure the business into settling an unrelated matter.
2. *The relevance of the information being sought.* Information is relevant if it reveals that the law is being violated or if it assures the agency that the law is not being violated.
3. *The specificity of the demand for testimony or documents.* A subpoena must, for instance, adequately describe the material being sought.
4. *The burden of the demand on the party from whom the information is sought.* For instance, the cost to the company of copying requested documents or providing digital information may become burdensome. (Note that a business generally is protected from revealing information such as trade secrets.)

Search Warrants   The Fourth Amendment protects against unreasonable searches and seizures by requiring that in most instances a physical search for evidence must be conducted under the authority of a search warrant. An agency's search warrant is an order directing law enforcement officials to search a specific place for a specific item and seize it for the agency. It was once thought that administrative inspections were exempt from the warrant requirement, but the United States Supreme Court has held that the requirement does apply to the administrative process.[10]

Nevertheless, agencies can conduct warrantless searches in several situations. Warrants are not required to conduct searches in highly regulated industries. Firms that sell firearms or liquor, for instance, are automatically subject to inspections without warrants. Sometimes, a statute permits warrantless searches of certain types of hazardous operations, such as coal mines. Also, a warrantless inspection in an emergency situation is normally considered reasonable.

---

8. Pronounced ad tes-te-fe-*kan*-dum.

9. Pronounced *doo*-suhs *tee*-kum.
10. *Marshall v. Barlow's, Inc.,* 436 U.S. 307, 98 S.Ct. 1816, 56 L.Ed.2d 305 (1978).

43–3c Adjudication

After conducting an investigation of a suspected rule violation, an agency may initiate an administrative action against an individual or organization. Most administrative actions are resolved through negotiated settlements at their initial stages. Sometimes, though, an action ends in formal **adjudication**—the resolution of the dispute through a hearing conducted by the agency.

Negotiated Settlements Depending on the agency, negotiations may involve a simple conversation or a series of informal conferences. Whatever form the negotiations take, their purpose is to rectify the problem to the agency's satisfaction and eliminate the need for additional proceedings.

Settlement is an appealing option to firms for two reasons: to avoid appearing uncooperative and to avoid the expense involved in formal adjudication proceedings and in possible later appeals. Settlement is also an attractive option for agencies. To conserve their resources and avoid formal actions, administrative agencies devote a great deal of effort to giving advice and negotiating solutions to problems.

Formal Complaints If a settlement cannot be reached, the agency may issue a formal complaint against the suspected violator. ■ **EXAMPLE 43.8** The Environmental Protection Agency (EPA) finds that Acme Manufacturing, Inc., is polluting groundwater in violation of federal pollution laws. The EPA issues a complaint against Acme in an effort to bring the plant into compliance with federal regulations. This complaint is a public document, and a press release may accompany it. Acme will respond by filing an answer to the EPA's allegations. If Acme and the EPA cannot agree on a settlement, the case will be adjudicated. ■

The Hearing Agency adjudication may involve a trial-like arbitration procedure before an **administrative law judge (ALJ).** The Administrative Procedure Act (APA) requires that before the hearing takes place, the agency must issue a notice that includes the facts and law on which the complaint is based, the legal authority for the hearing, and its time and place. The administrative agency adjudication process is described next and illustrated graphically in Exhibit 43–3.

The Role of the Administrative Law Judge An ALJ presides over the hearing and has the power to administer oaths, take testimony, rule on questions of evidence, and make determinations of fact. Technically, the ALJ, who works for the agency prosecuting the case, is not an

EXHIBIT 43–3 The Formal Administrative Agency Adjudication Process

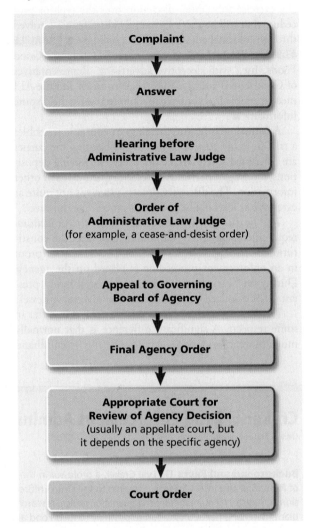

independent judge. Nevertheless, the law requires an ALJ to be unbiased.

Certain safeguards prevent bias on the part of the ALJ and promote fairness in the proceedings. For instance, the APA requires that the ALJ be separate from an agency's investigative and prosecutorial staff. The APA also prohibits *ex parte* (private) communications between the ALJ and any party to an agency proceeding, including the agency and the company involved. Finally, provisions of the APA protect the ALJ from agency disciplinary actions unless the agency can show good cause for such an action.

Hearing Procedures Hearing procedures vary widely from agency to agency. Administrative agencies generally exercise substantial discretion over the type of procedure that will be used. Frequently, disputes are resolved through informal adjudication proceedings. ■ **EXAMPLE 43.9** The Federal Trade Commission (FTC) charges Good Foods, Inc., with deceptive advertising. Representatives of Good Foods and the FTC, their counsel, and the ALJ meet at a table in a conference room to resolve the dispute informally. ■

A formal adjudicatory hearing, in contrast, resembles a trial in many respects. Prior to the hearing, the parties are permitted to undertake discovery—involving depositions, interrogatories, and requests for documents or other information. The discovery process usually is not quite as extensive as it would be in a court proceeding, however.

The hearing itself must comply with the procedural requirements of the APA and must also meet the constitutional standards of due process. The burden of proof in an enforcement proceeding is placed on the agency. During the hearing, the parties may give testimony, present other evidence, and cross-examine adverse witnesses.

Trials and administrative agency hearings do differ in some respects. A significant difference is that normally much more information, including hearsay (secondhand information), can be introduced as evidence during an administrative hearing.

Agency Orders Following a hearing, the ALJ renders an **initial order,** or decision, on the case. Either party can appeal the ALJ's decision to the board or commission that governs the agency. If displeased with the result, the party can appeal that decision to a federal appellate court.
■ **EXAMPLE 43.10** The EPA issues a complaint against Acme Manufacturing, Inc., for polluting groundwater. The complaint results in a hearing before an ALJ, who rules in the EPA's favor. If Acme is dissatisfied with the decision, it can appeal to the EPA commission and then to a federal appellate court. ■

If no party appeals the case, the ALJ's decision becomes the **final order** of the agency. The ALJ's decision also becomes final if a party appeals and the commission and the court decline to review the case. If a party appeals and the case is reviewed, the final order comes from the commission's decision or (if that decision is appealed) the decision of the reviewing court.

In the following case, a federal appeals court reviewed the Drug Enforcement Administration's denial of a university professor's application to register to cultivate marijuana.

Case 43.2

Craker v. Drug Enforcement Administration

United States Court of Appeals, First Circuit, 714 F.3d 17 (2013).

Background and Facts Dr. Lyle Craker, a professor in the University of Massachusetts's Department of Plant, Soil and Insect Sciences, applied to the Drug Enforcement Administration (DEA) for permission to register to manufacture marijuana for clinical research. He stated that "a second source of plant material is needed to facilitate privately funded Food and Drug Administration (FDA)-approved research into medical uses of marijuana, ensuring a choice of sources and an adequate supply of quality, research-grade marijuana for medicinal applications."

An administrative law judge recommended that Craker's application be granted, but a DEA deputy administrator issued an order denying his application. Under the DEA's interpretation, the Controlled Substances Act (CSA) requires an applicant to prove both that effective controls against diversion of the marijuana for unapproved purposes are in place and that its supply and the competition to supply it are inadequate. The administrator determined that the professor had not proved that effective controls against the marijuana's diversion were in place or that supply and competition were inadequate. Craker petitioned the U.S. Court of Appeals for the First Circuit to review the order.

In the Language of the Court
HOWARD, Circuit Judge.
   * * *

Since 1968, the National Center for Natural Products Research ("NCNPR") at the University of Mississippi has held the necessary registration and a government contract to grow marijuana for research purposes. The contract is administered by the National Institute on Drug Abuse ("NIDA"), a component of the National Institutes of Health ("NIH"), which, in turn, is a component of the [U.S.]

Case 43.2 Continued

Department of Health and Human Services ("HHS"). The contract is opened for competitive bidding every five years. The NCNPR is the only entity registered by the DEA to manufacture marijuana.

* * * *

Dr. Craker's argument with respect to competition is essentially that there cannot be "adequately competitive conditions" when there is only one manufacturer of marijuana.

The Administrator * * * observed that NIDA had provided marijuana manufactured by the University of Mississippi either at cost or free to researchers, and that Dr. Craker had made no showing of how he could provide it for less * * * . Additionally, the Administrator noted that Dr. Craker is free to bid on the contract when it comes up for renewal.

We see nothing improper in the Administrator's approach. The [CSA's] term "adequately competitive conditions" is not necessarily as narrow as the petitioner suggests. * * * That the current regime may not be the most competitive situation possible does not render it "inadequate." [Emphasis added.]

* * * *

In finding that Dr. Craker failed to demonstrate that the current supply of marijuana was not adequate and uninterrupted, the Administrator observed that there were over 1,000 kilograms of marijuana in NIDA possession, an amount which far exceeds present research demands and "any foreseeable" future demand. Dr. Craker does not dispute this finding, or that the current amount is more than ninety times the amount he proposes to supply. Instead, he argues that the adequacy of supply must not be measured against NIDA-approved research, but by whether the supply is adequate to supply projects approved by the FDA. But even if we were to accept his premise—which we don't—Dr. Craker fails to demonstrate that the supply is inadequate for those needs, either. He merely states that certain projects were rejected as "not bona-fide" by NIDA, a claim which does not address the adequacy of supply. The fact that Dr. Craker disagrees with the method by which marijuana research is approved does not undermine the substantial evidence that supports the Administrator's conclusion.

Decision and Remedy *The U.S. Court of Appeals for the First Circuit denied Craker's petition to review the agency's order "because the Administrator's interpretation of the CSA is permissible and her findings are reasonable and supported by the evidence."*

Critical Thinking

- **Economic** *Why should a court wait to review an agency's order until the order has gone through the entire procedural process and can be considered final?*
- **Legal Environment** *Under what standard does a court defer to an agency's interpretation of a statute? Did the court in this case appear to have applied that standard to the DEA's interpretation of the Controlled Substances Act? Discuss.*

43–4 Judicial Deference to Agency Decisions

When asked to review agency decisions, courts historically granted deference to the agency's judgment. In other words, the courts tended to accept the agency's judgment, often citing the agency's great expertise in the subject area of the regulation. This deference seems especially appropriate when applied to an agency's analysis of factual questions, but should it also extend to an agency's interpretation of its own legal authority? In *Chevron U.S.A., Inc. v. Natural Resources Defense Council, Inc.*,[11] the United States Supreme Court held that it should.

11. 467 U.S. 837, 104 S.Ct. 2778, 81 L.Ed.2d 694 (1984).

By so ruling, the Court created a standard of broadened deference to agencies on questions of legal interpretation.

43–4a The Holding of the *Chevron* Case

At issue in the *Chevron* case was whether the courts should defer to an agency's interpretation of a statute giving it authority to act. The Environmental Protection Agency (EPA) had interpreted the phrase "stationary source" in the Clean Air Act as referring to an entire manufacturing plant, and not to each facility within a plant. The agency's interpretation enabled it to adopt the so-called bubble policy, which allowed companies to offset increases in emissions in part of a plant with decreases elsewhere in the plant. This interpretation reduced pollution-control compliance costs to manufacturers. An environmental group challenged the legality of the EPA's interpretation.

The Supreme Court held that the courts should defer to an agency's interpretation of law as well as fact. The Court found that the agency's interpretation of the statute was reasonable. The Court's decision in the *Chevron* case created a new standard for courts to use when reviewing agency interpretations of law. This standard involves the following two questions:

1. Did Congress directly address the issue in dispute in the statute? If so, the statutory language prevails.
2. If the statute is silent or ambiguous, is the agency's interpretation "reasonable"? If it is, a court should uphold the agency's interpretation even if the court would have interpreted the law differently.

43–4b When Courts Will Give *Chevron* Deference to Agency Interpretation

The notion that courts should defer to agencies on matters of law was controversial. Under the holding of the *Chevron* case, when the meaning of a particular statute's language is unclear and an agency interprets it, the court must follow the agency's interpretation as long as it is reasonable. This led to considerable discussion and litigation to test the boundaries of the *Chevron* holding.

For instance, are courts required to give deference to all agency interpretations or only to those that result from adjudication or formal rulemaking procedures? The United States Supreme Court has held that in order for agency interpretations to be assured *Chevron* deference, they must meet the formal legal standards for notice-and-comment

rulemaking. Nevertheless, there are still gray areas, and many agency interpretations are challenged in court.

■ **CASE IN POINT 43.11** The Federal Insurance Contributions Act (FICA) requires employees and employers to pay Social Security taxes on all wages. The FICA excludes wages paid for any service to a school "performed by a student who is enrolled and regularly attending classes." The Mayo Foundation for Medical Education and Research offers educational residency programs to physicians who seek instruction in a chosen specialty. In addition to receiving instruction, the physicians are paid to spend fifty to eighty hours a week caring for patients. The U.S. Treasury Department issued a rule providing that anyone who works forty or more hours per week is an employee, not a student. The Mayo Foundation asserted that the rule did not apply to its residents.

The United States Supreme Court upheld the rule. Congress gave the Treasury Department the authority to make rules to enforce the Internal Revenue Code. The employee rule was issued after notice-and-comment procedures, and it was based on a reasonable determination that imposing Social Security taxes on medical residents would further the purpose of the statute. The physicians were "the kind of workers that Congress intended to both contribute to and benefit from the Social Security system."[12] ■

The following case involves a federal agency's role in determining whether alien pilots may be certified to operate large, U.S.-registered aircraft.

---

12. *Mayo Foundation for Medical Education and Research v. United States,* 562 U.S. 44, 131 S.Ct. 704, 178 L.Ed.2d 588 (2011).

Case Analysis 43.3

Olivares v. Transportation Security Administration

United States Court of Appeals, District of Columbia Circuit, 819 F.3d 454 (2016).

In the Language of the Court

EDWARDS, Senior Circuit Judge:
* * * *

I. BACKGROUND

In the aftermath of the tragic terrorist attacks on September 11, 2001, Congress created the Transportation Security Administration [TSA] to shore up our nation's civil aviation security. [TSA is part of the U.S.] Department of Homeland Security under the direction of the Secretary of Homeland Security.

* * * No pilot may serve in any capacity as an airman with respect to a civil aircraft * * * without an airman certificate from FAA [Federal Aviation Administration]. For large aircraft, pilots must obtain additional certification known as a Type Rating. [Under the Aviation and Transportation Security Act of 2001,] aliens who seek training and certification to operate large, U.S.-registered aircraft must first secure clearance by TSA. If TSA determines that an alien applicant presents a risk to aviation or national

security, then that applicant is ineligible to receive the training necessary to secure a large aircraft Type Rating from FAA.

* * * *

[Alberto Olivares (Petitioner), a citizen of Venezuela,] received [an] opportunity to pilot a large, U.S.-registered aircraft. * * * Petitioner applied to attend an FAA-certified flight school in France, and TSA conducted a background investigation.

Case 43.3 Continued

* * * *

* * * TSA concluded that Petitioner was a "Threat to Transportation/National Security" [and] sent an email to Petitioner denying his application.

* * * Petitioner filed his petition for review with this court. * * * Andrea Vara executed a sworn declaration explaining TSA's grounds for denying Petitioner's application for training. Ms. Vara is employed by [TSA] as the Alien Flight Student Program Manager. She has been responsible for managing TSA's Alien Flight Student Program, which conducts security threat assessments on individuals who are not U.S. citizens or nationals who seek flight instruction or recurrent training from FAA-certified flight training providers.

The Vara Declaration makes it clear that Ms. Vara was the Government official who made the determination that Petitioner's application should be denied * * * . The Vara Declaration states:

> * * * Petitioner submitted Training Request # 565192, seeking to train at FlightSafety International—Paris Learning Center.
>
> * * * Petitioner was subject to an investigation, which revealed the following. In 2007, Petitioner pled guilty to conspiracy to possess with intent to distribute controlled substances and the U.S. District Court for the Northern District of Illinois sentenced him to eighty (80) months imprisonment. Petitioner's conviction made him inadmissible to the United States and led to the revocation of his FAA Airman's Certificate. Petitioner was deported to his home country of Venezuela in March 2010.
>
> A public news article published after Petitioner was deported provided a U.S. address for Petitioner. Further, records indicated that Petitioner was a suspected international trafficker in firearms. There was evidence that Petitioner had previously been involved in the export of weapons and U.S. currency to Venezuela by private aircraft, was the second pilot of an aircraft from which several weapons and $500,000 was seized by local

authorities in Aruba, and that one of his associates was arrested in Aruba for smuggling firearms.

> This information, viewed as a whole, demonstrated Petitioner's willingness to consistently disregard the law and to use an aircraft for criminal activity, in opposition to U.S. security interests. The information also raised concerns that Petitioner may use his flight training to advance the interests of a criminal enterprise, which could include an enterprise that seeks to do harm to the United States.
>
> Based on all the foregoing information, I concluded Petitioner posed a threat to aviation and national security and * * * denied his training request.

* * * *

II. ANALYSIS
A. THE COURT'S JURISDICTION
* * * An action taken by TSA on behalf of the Secretary of Homeland Security is clearly subject to review.

* * * *

B. STANDARD OF REVIEW
Pursuant to the Administrative Procedure Act, we must uphold TSA's decisions unless they are arbitrary, capricious, an abuse of discretion, or otherwise not in accordance with law.

What is important here is that, because Congress has entrusted TSA with broad authority over civil aviation security, it is TSA's job—not * * * ours—to strike a balance between convenience and security. Therefore, *in cases of this sort, we must defer to TSA actions that reasonably interpret and enforce the safety and security obligations of the agency. * * * Courts do not second-guess expert agency judgments on potential risks to national security. Rather, we defer to the informed judgment of agency officials whose obligation it is to assess risks to national security.* [Emphasis added.]

* * * *

D. PETITIONER'S * * * CLAIM
* * * *

* * * Petitioner argues that TSA should not have used his suspected firearms trafficking or his Massachusetts

address to support its decision. [TSA had discovered that, even though Olivares had been deported with no right to return to the United States, he maintained a local address in Massachusetts.] Petitioner claims that the Massachusetts address actually belongs to his brother, and Petitioner insists that he has never illegally entered the United States. Petitioner also points out that the firearms incident occurred nearly two decades ago and that he was merely suspected of being involved. In light of the limited standard of review that controls the disposition of this case, these arguments are not persuasive. It was rational for TSA to find it suspicious and thus consider information indicating that a deported individual appeared to maintain a current U.S. address and had been suspected of involvement in firearms trafficking. The agency's weighing of this information, along with the information regarding Petitioner's known criminal history, was not inconsistent with reasoned decision making.

Given TSA's broad authority to assess potential risks to aviation and national security, the agency's clear and reasonable explanation offered in the Vara Declaration, and the limited standard of review [under the holding in the *Chevron* case], we are in no position to second-guess TSA's judgment in denying Petitioner's application. In assessing risks to national security, conclusions must often be based on informed judgment rather than concrete evidence, and that reality affects what we may reasonably insist on from the Government. When it comes to collecting evidence and drawing factual inferences in this area, the lack of competence on the part of the courts is marked, and respect for the Government's conclusions is appropriate. Where no factual certainties exist or where facts alone do not provide the answer * * * we require only that the agency so state and go on to identify the considerations it found persuasive.

It is self-evident that TSA's action against Petitioner was related to the agency's goals of improving the safety of air

Case 43.3 Continues

Case 43.3 Continued

travel. TSA was not required to show that Petitioner would engage in activities designed to compromise aviation or national security. Rather, the agency was merely required to give a reasonable

explanation as to why it believed that Petitioner presented a risk to aviation or national security. The Vara Declaration satisfies this legal obligation. [Emphasis added.]

III. CONCLUSION

    For the reasons set forth above, the petition for review is denied.

Legal Reasoning Questions

1. What impact did the Vara Declaration have on the court's ruling in this case?

2. Is a court's evaluation of an agency's assessment of a risk to national security different from a review of other agency determinations? Explain.

3. Should the agency at the center of this case have revealed the reasons for its decision before Olivares filed a suit challenging it? Explain.

43–5 Public Accountability

As a result of growing public concern over the powers exercised by administrative agencies, Congress passed several laws to make agencies more accountable through public scrutiny. Here, we discuss the most significant of these laws.

43–5a Freedom of Information Act

The Freedom of Information Act (FOIA)[13] requires the federal government to disclose certain records to any person or entity on written request, even if no reason is given for the request. All federal government agencies must make their records available electronically on the Internet and in other electronic formats.

    The FOIA exempts certain types of records, such as those pertaining to national security and those containing information that is confidential or personal. ■ **EXAMPLE 43.12** Juanita, a reporter from an online health magazine, makes an FOIA request to the Centers for Disease Control and Prevention for a list of people who have contracted a highly contagious virus. The Centers for Disease Control and Prevention will not have to comply, because the requested information is confidential and personal. ■

    For other records, a request that complies with the FOIA procedures need only contain a reasonable description of the information sought. An agency's failure to comply with an FOIA request can be challenged in a federal district court. The media, industry trade associations, public-interest groups, and even companies seeking

information about competitors rely on these FOIA provisions to obtain information from government agencies.

43–5b Government in the Sunshine Act

The Government in the Sunshine Act,[14] or open meeting law, requires that "every portion of every meeting of an agency" be open to "public observation." The act also requires that the public be provided with adequate advance notice of scheduled meetings and agendas.

    Like the FOIA, the Sunshine Act contains certain exceptions. Closed meetings are permitted in the following situations:

1. The subject of the meeting concerns accusing any person of a crime.

2. Open meetings would frustrate implementation of future agency actions.

3. The subject of the meeting involves matters relating to future litigation or rulemaking.

Courts interpret these exceptions to allow open access whenever possible.

43–5c Regulatory Flexibility Act

Concern over the effects of regulation on the efficiency of businesses, particularly smaller ones, led Congress to pass the Regulatory Flexibility Act[15] in 1980. Under this act, whenever a new regulation will have a "significant impact upon a substantial number of small entities," the

---

13. 5 U.S.C. Section 552.

14. 5 U.S.C. Section 552b.

15. 5 U.S.C. Sections 601–612.

agency must conduct a regulatory flexibility analysis. The analysis must measure the cost that the rule would impose on small businesses and consider less burdensome alternatives. The act also contains provisions to alert small businesses about forthcoming regulations. The act relieved small businesses of some record-keeping burdens, especially with regard to hazardous waste management.

43–5d Small Business Regulatory Enforcement Fairness Act

The Small Business Regulatory Enforcement Fairness Act[16] includes various provisions intended to ease the regulatory burden on small businesses:

16. 5 U.S.C. Sections 801 *et seq.*

1. Federal agencies must prepare guides that explain in plain English how small businesses can comply with federal regulations.
2. Congress may review new federal regulations for at least sixty days before they take effect, giving opponents of the rules time to present their arguments.
3. The courts may enforce the Regulatory Flexibility Act. This provision helps to ensure that federal agencies will consider ways to reduce the economic impact of new regulations on small businesses.
4. The Office of the National Ombudsman at the Small Business Administration was set up to receive comments from small businesses about their dealings with federal agencies. Based on these comments, Regional Small Business Fairness Boards rate the agencies and publicize their findings.

Reviewing: Administrative Agencies

Assume that the Securities and Exchange Commission (SEC) has a rule that it will enforce statutory provisions prohibiting insider trading only when the insiders make monetary profits for themselves. Then the SEC makes a new rule, declaring that it will now bring enforcement actions against individuals for insider trading even if the individuals did not personally profit from the transactions. In making the new rule, the SEC does not conduct a rulemaking procedure but simply announces its decision. A stockbrokerage firm objects that the new rule was unlawfully developed without opportunity for public comment. The brokerage firm challenges the rule in an action that ultimately is reviewed by a federal appellate court. Using the information presented in the chapter, answer the following questions.

1. Is the SEC an executive agency or an independent regulatory agency? Does it matter to the outcome of this dispute? Explain.
2. Suppose that the SEC asserts that it has always had the statutory authority to pursue persons for insider trading regardless of whether they personally profited from the transactions. This is the only argument the SEC makes to justify changing its enforcement rules. Would a court be likely to find that the SEC's action was arbitrary and capricious under the Administrative Procedure Act (APA)? Why or why not?
3. Would a court be likely to give *Chevron* deference to the SEC's interpretation of the law on insider trading? Why or why not?
4. Now assume that a court finds that the new rule is merely "interpretive." What effect would this determination have on whether the SEC had to follow the APA's rulemaking procedures?

Debate This . . . *Because an administrative law judge (ALJ) acts as both judge and jury, there should always be at least three ALJs in each administrative hearing.*

Terms and Concepts

adjudication 833	delegation doctrine 827	interpretive rule 826
administrative agency 824	enabling legislation 825	legislative rule 826
administrative law judge (ALJ) 833	exhaustion doctrine 829	notice-and-comment
administrative process 830	final order 834	rulemaking 831
bureaucracy 827	initial order 834	rulemaking 830

Issue Spotters

1. The U.S. Department of Transportation (DOT) sometimes hears an appeal from a party whose contract with the DOT has been canceled. An administrative law judge (ALJ) who works for the DOT hears this appeal. What safeguards promote the ALJ's fairness? (See *The Administrative Process.*)

2. Techplate Corporation learns that a federal administrative agency is considering a rule that will have a negative impact on the firm's ability to do business. Does the firm have any opportunity to express its opinion about the pending rule? Explain. (See *The Administrative Process.*)

- **Check your answers to the Issue Spotters against the answers provided in Appendix D at the end of this text.**

Business Scenarios

43–1. Rulemaking and Adjudication Powers. For decades, the Federal Trade Commission (FTC) resolved fair trade and advertising disputes through individual adjudications. In the 1960s, the FTC began promulgating rules that defined fair and unfair trade practices. In cases involving violations of these rules, the due process rights of participants were more limited and did not include cross-examination. Although anyone charged with violating a rule would receive a full adjudication, the legitimacy of the rule itself could not be challenged in the adjudication. Furthermore, a party charged with violating a rule was almost certain to lose the adjudication. Affected parties complained to a court, arguing that their rights before the FTC were unduly limited by the new rules. What would the court examine to determine whether to uphold the new rules? (See *The Administrative Process.*)

43–2. Informal Rulemaking. Assume that the Food and Drug Administration (FDA), using proper procedures, adopts a rule describing its future investigations. This new rule covers all future circumstances in which the FDA wants to regulate food additives. Under the new rule, the FDA is not to regulate food additives without giving food companies an opportunity to cross-examine witnesses. Later, the FDA wants to regulate methylisocyanate, a food additive. The FDA undertakes an informal rulemaking procedure, without cross-examination, and regulates methylisocyanate. Producers protest, saying that the FDA promised them the opportunity for cross-examination. The FDA responds that the Administrative Procedure Act does not require such cross-examination and that it is free to withdraw the promise made in its new rule. If the producers challenge the FDA in court, on what basis would the court rule in their favor? Explain. (See *The Administrative Process.*)

Business Case Problems

43–3. Rulemaking. The Investment Company Act prohibits a mutual fund from engaging in certain transactions when there may be a conflict of interest between the manager of the fund and its shareholders. Under rules issued by the Securities and Exchange Commission (SEC), however, a fund that meets certain conditions may engage in an otherwise prohibited transaction. In June 2004, the SEC added two new conditions. A year later, the SEC reconsidered the new conditions in terms of the costs that they would impose on the funds. Within eight days, and without asking for public input, the SEC readopted the conditions. The Chamber of Commerce of the United States asked a federal appellate court to review the new rules. The Chamber argued that in readopting the rules, the SEC relied on materials not in the "rulemaking record" without providing an opportunity for public comment. The SEC countered that the information was otherwise "publicly available." In adopting a rule, should an agency consider information that is not part of the rulemaking record? Why or why not? [*Chamber of Commerce of the United States v. Securities and Exchange Commission*, 443 F.3d 890 (D.C.Cir. 2006)] (See *The Administrative Process.*)

43–4. Business Case Problem with Sample Answer—Agency Powers. A well-documented rise in global temperatures has coincided with a significant increase in the concentration of carbon dioxide in the atmosphere. Many scientists believe that the two trends are related, because when carbon dioxide is released into the atmosphere, it produces a greenhouse effect, trapping solar heat. Under the Clean Air Act (CAA), the Environmental Protection Agency (EPA) is authorized to regulate "any" air pollutants "emitted into . . . the ambient air" that in its "judgment cause, or contribute to, air pollution."

A group of private organizations asked the EPA to regulate carbon dioxide and other "greenhouse gas" emissions from new motor vehicles. The EPA refused, stating, among other things, that Congress last amended the CAA in 1990 without authorizing new, binding auto emissions limits. Nineteen states, including Massachusetts, asked a district court to review the EPA's denial. Did the EPA have the authority to regulate greenhouse gas emissions from new motor vehicles? If so, was its stated reason for refusing to do so consistent with that authority? Discuss. [*Massachusetts v. Environmental*

Protection Agency, 549 U.S. 497, 127 S.Ct. 1438, 167 L.Ed.2d 248 (2007)] (See *Agency Creation and Powers.*)

- **For a sample answer to Problem 43–4, go to Appendix E at the end of this text.**

43–5. Judicial Deference. After Dave Conley died of lung cancer, his widow filed for benefits under the Black Lung Benefits Act. To qualify for benefits under the act, she had to show that exposure to coal dust was a substantial contributing factor to her husband's death. Conley had been a coal miner, but he had also been a longtime smoker. At the benefits hearing, a physician testified that coal dust was a substantial factor in Conley's death. No evidence was presented to support this conclusion, however. The administrative law judge awarded benefits. On appeal, should a court defer to this decision? Discuss. [*Conley v. National Mines Corp.,* 595 F.3d 297 (6th Cir. 2010)] (See *Judicial Deference to Agency Decisions.*)

43–6. Arbitrary and Capricious Test. Michael Manin, an airline pilot, was twice convicted of disorderly conduct, a minor misdemeanor. To renew his flight certification with the National Transportation Safety Board (NTSB), Manin filed an application that asked him about his criminal history. He did not disclose his two convictions. When these came to light more than ten years later, Manin argued that he had not known that he was required to report convictions for minor misdemeanors. The NTSB's policy was to consider an applicant's understanding of what information a question sought before determining whether an answer was false. But without explanation, the agency departed from this policy, refused to consider Manin's argument, and revoked his certification. Was this action arbitrary or capricious? Explain. [*Manin v. National Transportation Safety Board,* 627 F.3d 1239 (D.C.Cir. 2011)] (See *Agency Creation and Powers.*)

43–7. Adjudication. Mechanics replaced a brake assembly on the landing gear of a CRJ–700 plane operated by GoJet Airlines, LLC. The mechanics installed gear pins to lock the assembly in place during the repair but failed to remove one of the pins after they had finished. On the plane's next flight, a warning light alerted the pilots that the landing gear would not retract after takeoff. There was a potential for danger, but the pilots flew the CRJ–700 safely back to the departure airport. No one was injured, and no property was damaged. The Federal Aviation Administration (FAA) cited GoJet for violating FAA regulations by "carelessly or recklessly operating an unairworthy airplane." GoJet objected to the citation. To which court can GoJet appeal for review? On what ground might that court decline to review the case? [*GoJet Airlines, LLC v. F.A.A.,* 743 F.3d 1168 (8th Cir. 2014)] (See *The Administrative Process.*)

43–8. Judicial Deference to Agency Decisions. Knox Creek Coal Corporation operates coal mines in West Virginia. The U.S. Department of Labor charged Knox's Tiller No. 1 Mine with "significant and substantial" (S&S) violations of the Federal Mine Safety and Health Act. According to the charges, inadequately sealed enclosures of electrical equipment in the mine created the potential for an explosion. The Mine Act designates a violation as S&S when it "*could* significantly and substantially contribute to the cause and effect of a coal or other mine safety or health hazard." Challenging the S&S determination, Knox filed a suit against the secretary of labor. The secretary argued that "could" means "merely possible"—if there is a violation, the existence of a hazard is assumed. This position was consistent with agency and judicial precedent and the Mine Act's history and purpose. Knox argued that "could" requires proof of the likelihood of a hazard. When does a court defer to an agency's interpretation of law? Do those circumstances exist in this case? Discuss. [*Knox Creek Coal Corp v. Secretary of Labor,* 811 F.3d 148 (4th Cir. 2016)] (See *Judicial Deference to Agency Decisions.*)

43–9. A Question of Ethics—Rulemaking. *To ensure highway safety and protect driver health, Congress charged federal agencies with regulating the hours of service of commercial motor vehicle operators. Between 1940 and 2003, the regulations that applied to long-haul truck drivers were mostly unchanged. (Long-haul drivers are those who operate beyond a 150-mile radius of their base.) In 2003, the Federal Motor Carrier Safety Administration (FMCSA) revised the regulations significantly, increasing the number of daily and weekly hours that drivers could work. The agency had not considered the impact of the changes on the health of the drivers, however, and the revisions were overturned.*

The FMCSA then issued a notice that it would reconsider the revisions and opened them up for public comment. The agency analyzed the costs to the industry and the crash risks due to driver fatigue under different options. It concluded that the safety benefits of not increasing the hours were less than the economic costs. In 2005, the agency issued a rule that was nearly identical to the 2003 version. Public Citizen, Inc., and others, including the Owner-Operator Independent Drivers Association, asked the U.S. Court of Appeals for the District of Columbia Circuit to review the 2005 rule as it applied to long-haul drivers. [Owner-Operator Independent Drivers Association, Inc. v. Federal Motor Carrier Safety Administration, *494 F.3d 188 (D.C.Cir. 2007)*] (See *The Administrative Process.*)

(a) The FMCSA's cost-benefit analysis included new methods that were not disclosed to the public in time for comments. Was this unethical? Should the agency have disclosed the new methodology sooner? Why or why not?

(b) The FMCSA created a graph to show the risk of a crash as a function of the time a driver spent on the job. The graph plotted the first twelve hours of a day individually, but the rest of the time was depicted with an aggregate figure at the seventeenth hour. This made the risk at those hours appear to be lower. Is it unethical for an agency to manipulate data? Explain.

Legal Reasoning Group Activity

43–10. Investigation. Maureen Droge was a flight attendant for United Air Lines, Inc. (UAL). After being assigned to work in Paris, France, she became pregnant. Because UAL does not allow its flight attendants to fly during their third trimester of pregnancy, Droge was placed on involuntary leave. She applied for temporary disability benefits through the French social security system. Her request was denied because UAL does not contribute to the French system on behalf of its U.S.-based flight attendants. Droge filed a charge of discrimination with the U.S. Equal Employment Opportunity Commission (EEOC), alleging that UAL had discriminated against her and other Americans. The EEOC issued a subpoena, asking UAL to detail all benefits received by all UAL employees living outside the United States. UAL refused to provide the information on the ground that it was irrelevant and compliance would be unduly burdensome. The EEOC filed a suit in a federal district court against UAL. (See *The Administrative Process.*)

(a) The first group will decide whether the court should enforce the subpoena and explain why.

(b) The second group will discuss whether the EEOC should be able to force a U.S. company operating overseas to provide the same disability benefits to employees located there as it does to employees in the United States. Should UAL be required to contribute to the French social security system for employees who reside in France?

CHAPTER 44

Consumer Law

All statutes, agency rules, and common law judicial decisions that serve to protect the interests of consumers are classified as **consumer law.** Traditionally, in disputes involving consumers, it was assumed that the freedom to contract carried with it the obligation to live by the deal made. Over time, this attitude has changed considerably.

Today, countless federal and state laws attempt to protect consumers

from unfair trade practices, unsafe products, discriminatory or unreasonable credit requirements, and other problems related to consumer transactions. Nearly every agency and department of the federal government has an office of consumer affairs, and most states have one or more such offices to help consumers. Also, typically the attorney general's office assists consumers at the state level.

In recent years, there has been a renewed interest in attempting to protect consumers in their dealings with credit-card companies, financial institutions, and insurance companies. Congress has enacted new credit-card regulations and financial reforms to regulate the nation's largest banks. It has also enacted health-care reforms and revised food safety laws.

44–1 Advertising, Marketing, and Sales

Numerous federal laws have been passed to define the duties of sellers and the rights of consumers. Exhibit 44–1 shows many of the areas of consumer law that are regulated by federal statutes. We begin our discussion of this legislation by examining some of the laws and regulations relating to advertising, marketing, and sales. Although we focus on federal law, realize that state consumer protection laws in these and other areas often provide more sweeping and significant protections than do federal laws.

44–1a Deceptive Advertising

One of the most important federal consumer protection laws is the Federal Trade Commission Act.[1] The act created the Federal Trade Commission (FTC) to carry out the broadly stated goal of preventing unfair and deceptive trade practices, including deceptive advertising.

Generally, **deceptive advertising** occurs if a reasonable consumer would be misled by the advertising claim. Vague generalities and obvious exaggerations are permissible. These claims are known as *puffery*. When a claim

takes on the appearance of authenticity, however, it may create problems.

Claims That Appear to Be Based on Factual Evidence Advertising that *appears* to be based on factual evidence but, in fact, is not reasonably supported by evidence will be deemed deceptive. ■ **CASE IN POINT 44.1** MedLab, Inc., advertised that its weight-loss supplement ("The New Skinny Pill") would cause users to lose substantial amounts of weight rapidly. The ads claimed that "clinical studies prove" that people who take the pill lose "as much as 15 to 18 pounds per week and as much as 50 percent of all excess weight in just 14 days, without dieting or exercising." The FTC sued MedLab for deceptive advertising.

An expert hired by the FTC to evaluate the claim testified that to lose this much weight, "a 200-pound individual would need to run between 57 and 68 miles every day"—the equivalent of more than two marathons per day. The court concluded that the advertisement was false and misleading, granted the FTC a summary judgment, and issued a permanent injunction to stop MedLab from running the ads.[2] ■

The following case involved an advertising claim based on limited scientific evidence.

---

1. 15 U.S.C. Sections 41–58.

2. *Federal Trade Commission v. MedLab, Inc,* 615 F.Supp.2d 1068 (N.D.Cal. 2009).

EXHIBIT 44–1 Selected Areas of Consumer Law Regulated by Statutes

Labeling and Packaging

Example—The Fair Packaging and Labeling Act

Advertising

Example—The Federal Trade Commission Act

Sales

Example—The FTC Mail-Order Rule

CONSUMER LAW

Food and Drugs

Example—The Federal Food, Drug, and Cosmetic Act

Credit Protection

Example—The Consumer Credit Protection Act

Product Safety

Example—The Consumer Product Safety Act

Case 44.1

POM Wonderful, LLC v. Federal Trade Commission

United States Court of Appeals, District of Columbia Circuit, 777 F.3d 478 (2015).

Background and Facts POM Wonderful, LLC, makes and sells pomegranate-based products. In ads, POM touted medical studies claiming to show that daily consumption of its products could treat, prevent, or reduce the risk of heart disease, prostate cancer, and erectile dysfunction. These ads mischaracterized the scientific evidence.

The Federal Trade Commission (FTC) charged POM with, and held POM liable for, making false, misleading, and unsubstantiated representations in violation of the FTC Act. POM was barred from running future ads asserting that its products treat or prevent any disease unless "randomized, controlled, human clinical trials" (RCTs, for "randomized controlled trials") demonstrated statistically significant results. POM petitioned the U.S. Court of Appeals for the District of Columbia Circuit to review this injunctive order.

In the Language of the Court

SRINIVASAN, Circuit Judge:

  * * * *

  * * * POM's ads * * * convey the net impression that clinical studies or trials show that a causal relation has been established between the consumption of the challenged POM products and its efficacy to treat, prevent or reduce the risk of the serious diseases in question. The Commission found that experts in the relevant fields would require RCTs * * * to establish such a causal relationship.

The Commission examined each of the studies invoked by petitioners in their ads, concluding that the referenced studies fail to qualify as RCTs of the kind that could afford adequate substantiation. Petitioners' claims therefore were deceptive.

* * * *

* * * The Commission's finding is supported by substantial record evidence. That evidence includes written reports and testimony from medical researchers stating that experts in the fields of cardiology and urology require randomized, double-blinded, placebo-controlled clinical trials to substantiate any claim that a product treats, prevents, or reduces the risk of disease.

The Commission drew on that expert testimony to explain why the attributes of well-designed RCTs are necessary to substantiate petitioners' claims. A control group, for example, allows investigators to distinguish between real effects from the intervention, and other changes, including those due to the mere act of being treated (placebo effect) and the passage of time. Random assignment of a study's subjects to treatment and control groups increases the likelihood that the treatment and control groups are similar in relevant characteristics, so that any difference in the outcome between the two groups can be attributed to the treatment. And when a study is double-blinded ([that is,] when neither the study participants nor the investigators know which patients are in the treatment group and which patients are in the control group), it is less likely that participants or investigators will consciously or unconsciously take actions potentially biasing the results.

* * * *

* * * The need for RCTs is driven by the claims petitioners have chosen to make. * * * *An advertiser* * * *may assert a health-related claim backed by medical evidence falling short of an RCT if it includes an effective disclaimer disclosing the limitations of the supporting research.* Petitioners did not do so. [Emphasis added.]

Decision and Remedy *The U.S. Court of Appeals for the District of Columbia Circuit enforced the FTC's order with respect to POM's ads. The court pointed out that "An advertiser who makes express representations about the level of support for a particular claim must possess the level of proof claimed in the ad and must convey that information to consumers in a non-misleading way."*

Critical Thinking

- **Ethical** *POM claimed that it is unethical to require RCTs to substantiate disease-related claims about food products. It argued that, for instance, "doctors cannot . . . ethically deprive a control group of patients of all Vitamin C for a decade to determine whether Vitamin C helps prevent cancer." Is this a valid argument? Why or why not?*

Claims Based on Half-Truths Some advertisements contain "half-truths," meaning that the presented information is true but incomplete and may therefore lead consumers to a false conclusion. ■ **EXAMPLE 44.2** The maker of Campbell's soups advertised that "most" Campbell's soups are low in fat and cholesterol and thus helpful in fighting heart disease. What the ad did not say was that many Campbell's soups are high in sodium and that high-sodium diets may increase the risk of heart disease. Hence, the FTC ruled that Campbell's claims were deceptive. ■ In addition, advertising that contains an endorsement by a celebrity may be deemed deceptive if the celebrity does not actually use the product.

Bait-and-Switch Advertising The FTC has issued rules that govern specific advertising techniques. One of the most important rules is contained in the FTC's "Guides Against Bait Advertising."[3]

Some retailers systematically advertise merchandise at low prices to get customers into their stores. But when the customers arrive, they find that the merchandise is not in stock. Salespersons then encourage them to purchase more expensive items instead. This practice, known as **bait-and-switch advertising,** is a form of deceptive advertising. The low price is the "bait" to lure the consumer into the store. The salesperson is instructed to "switch" the consumer to a different, more expensive item.

Under the FTC guidelines, bait-and-switch advertising occurs if the seller does any of the following:

1. Refuses to show the advertised item.
2. Fails to have a reasonable quantity of the item in stock.
3. Fails to promise to deliver the advertised item within a reasonable time.
4. Discourages employees from selling the advertised item.

---

3. 16 C.F.R. Part 238.

Online Deceptive Advertising Deceptive advertising occurs in the online environment as well as offline. The FTC actively monitors online advertising. It has identified hundreds of Web sites that have made false or deceptive claims for products and services ranging from medical treatments to exercise equipment and weight-loss aids.

The FTC has issued guidelines to help online businesses comply with existing laws prohibiting deceptive advertising. These guidelines include the following requirements:

1. All ads—both online and offline—must be truthful and not misleading.
2. The claims made in an ad must be substantiated—that is, advertisers must have evidence to back up their claims.
3. Ads cannot be unfair, which the FTC defines as "likely to cause substantial consumer injury that consumers could not reasonably avoid and that is not outweighed by the benefit to consumers or competition."
4. Ads must disclose relevant limitations and qualifying information concerning the claims advertisers are making.
5. Required disclosures must be "clear and conspicuous." For instance, because consumers may not read an entire Web page, an online disclosure should be placed as close as possible to the claim being qualified. Generally, hyperlinks to a disclosure are recommended only for lengthy disclosures. If hyperlinks are used, they should be obvious and should be placed as close as possible to the relevant information it qualifies.

The FTC creates additional guidelines as needed to respond to new issues that arise with online advertising. One new issue involves so-called native ads, which are discussed in this chapter's *Digital Update* feature.

Federal Trade Commission Actions The FTC receives complaints from many sources, including competitors of alleged violators, consumers, trade associations, Better Business Bureaus, and government organizations and officials. When the agency receives numerous and widespread complaints about a particular problem, it will investigate.

Formal Complaint. If the FTC concludes that a given advertisement is unfair or deceptive, it drafts a formal complaint, which is sent to the alleged offender. The company may agree to settle the complaint without further proceedings. If not, the FTC can conduct a hearing in which the company can present its defense.

FTC Orders and Remedies. If the FTC succeeds in proving that an advertisement is unfair or deceptive, it usually issues a **cease-and-desist order** requiring the company to stop the challenged advertising. In some circumstances, it may also impose a sanction known as **counteradvertising.** This requires the company to advertise anew—in print, on the Internet, on radio, and on television—to inform the public about the earlier misinformation. The FTC sometimes institutes a **multiple product order,** which requires a firm to stop false advertising for all of its products, not just the product involved in the original action.

Damages When Consumers Are Injured. When a company's deceptive ad involves wrongful charges to consumers, the FTC may seek other remedies, including damages. ■ **CASE IN POINT 44.3** The FTC sued Bronson Partners, LLC, for deceptively advertising two products—Chinese Diet Tea and Bio-Slim Patch. Bronson's ads claimed that the diet tea "eliminates 91 percent of absorbed sugars," "prevents 83 percent of fat absorption," and "doubles your metabolic rate to burn calories fast." The Bio-Slim Patch ads promised "lasting weight loss" and claimed that "ugly fatty tissue will disappear at a spectacular rate" as product users wear the patch while carrying on their normal lifestyle.

Eventually, Bronson conceded that it had engaged in deceptive advertising, and the FTC sought damages. The court awarded the FTC $1,942,325, which was the amount of Bronson's revenues from the two products.[4] ■

Restitution Possible. When a company's deceptive ad leads to wrongful payments by consumers, the FTC may seek other remedies, including restitution. ■ **CASE IN POINT 44.4** Verity International, Ltd., billed phone-line subscribers who accessed certain online pornography sites at the rate for international calls to Madagascar. When consumers complained about the charges, Verity told them that the charges were valid and had to be paid, or the consumers would face further collection actions. A federal appellate court held that this representation of "uncontestability" was deceptive and a violation of the FTC act. The court ordered Verity to pay nearly $18 million in restitution to consumers.[5] ■

---

4. *Federal Trade Commission v. Bronson Partners, LLC,* 664 F.3d 359 (2d Cir. 2011).
5. *Federal Trade Commission v. Verity International, Ltd.,* 443 F.3d 48 (2d Cir. 2006).

DIGITAL UPDATE   Regulating "Native" Ads on the Internet

Sponsored content on the Internet—content that someone pays to put there—is everywhere. One particular type of sponsored content is the "native" ad. Here, *native* describes advertisements that follow the natural form and function of the user experience into which they are placed. Thus, such an ad matches the rest of a Web page's content, including the visual design, as if it were "native" to the page.

Native Ad Integration on Desktops and Mobile Devices

Perhaps the most obvious native ads are in search engine results. When you type "native ads" in a Google search box, you will find that the first several "hits" listed in the search results are actually sponsored ads. Yet they have the look and feel of the rest of the search results.

Additionally, native ads are often placed within stories in online publications. Suppose, for instance, that you are reading a story on new fashions on your smartphone. You will likely see a native ad that looks as if it is part of the story but that is actually sponsored and perhaps written by a clothing company.

Some native ads are delivered via "recommendation widgets." Usually, the widgets are integrated into a page but do not mimic the appearance of the page. Rather, they direct you to a different Web page—perhaps telling you that "you might like" that site. Clicking the widget takes you to the site.

Native ads have become increasingly popular because desktop, smartphone, and tablet users have figured out how to block traditional online ads. Moreover, native ads are less intrusive than traditional online

ads—important because of the increasing number of consumers who most often access small screens, such as those on smartphones.

The Federal Trade Commission Takes Action

In response to the growth in native advertising, the Federal Trade Commission (FTC) has issued guidelines.[a] The FTC starts out with the basic question "[A]s native advertising evolves, are consumers able to differentiate advertising from other content?" In its guidance document,[b] the FTC suggests the following:

- Disclosures should be placed where consumers will notice them.
- Disclosures should be placed not after the native ad, but before or above it.
- Disclosures should remain with native ads if the ads are republished.
- Once consumers arrive on a click- or tap-into page where the complete native ad appears, disclosures should be placed as close as possible to where consumers will look first.
- Disclosures should stand out and should be understandable.

Critical Thinking *What is the equivalent of native advertising in commercially released movies?*

a. Federal Trade Commission, *Native Advertising: A Guide to Business*, December 2015.
b. Federal Trade Commission, *.com Disclosures: How to Make Effective Disclosures in Digital Advertising*, March 2013, available at www.ftc.gov/tips-advice/business-center/guidance/com-disclosures-how-make-effective-disclosures-digital.

False Advertising Claims under the Lanham Act The Lanham Act[6] protects trademarks, as discussed elsewhere. The act also covers false advertising claims. To state a successful claim for false advertising under this act, a business must establish each of the following elements:

1. An injury to a commercial interest in reputation or sales.

6. 15 U.S.C. Sections 1051–1128.

2. Direct causation of the injury by false or deceptive advertising.
3. A loss of business from buyers who were deceived by the advertising.

The dispute between the parties in the following case focused initially on a mimicked microchip. When the case reached the United States Supreme Court, the question was whether Static Control Components, Inc., could sue Lexmark International, Inc., for false advertising under the Lanham Act.

Case 44.2

Lexmark International, Inc.
v. Static Control Components, Inc.

Supreme Court of the United States, __ U.S. __, 134 S.Ct. 1377, 188 L.Ed.2d 392 (2014).

Background and Facts Lexmark International, Inc., sells the only style of toner cartridges that work with the company's laser printers. Other businesses—known as remanufacturers—acquire and refurbish used Lexmark cartridges to sell in competition with the cartridges sold by Lexmark. To deter remanufacturing, Lexmark introduced a program that gave customers a 20 percent discount on new toner cartridges if they agreed to return the empty cartridges to Lexmark. Static Control Components, Inc., makes and sells components for the remanufactured cartridges, including microchips that mimic the chips in Lexmark's cartridges.

Lexmark released ads that claimed Static Control's microchips illegally infringed Lexmark's patents. Lexmark then filed a suit in a federal district court against Static Control, alleging violations of intellectual property law. Static Control counterclaimed, alleging that Lexmark had engaged in false advertising in violation of the Lanham Act. The court dismissed the counterclaim. It held that Static Control lacked standing to bring that claim. On Static Control's appeal, the U.S. Court of Appeals for the Sixth Circuit reversed the dismissal. Lexmark appealed to the United States Supreme Court.

In the Language of the Court

Justice *SCALIA* delivered the opinion of the Court.

* * * *

First, * * * a statutory cause of action extends only to plaintiffs whose interests fall within the zone of interests protected by the law invoked.

* * * *

* * * To come within the zone of interests in a suit for false advertising under [the Lanham Act,] a plaintiff must allege an injury to a commercial interest in reputation or sales.

* * * *

Second, * * * a statutory cause of action is limited to plaintiffs whose injuries are proximately caused by violations of the statute.

* * * *

* * * A plaintiff suing under [the Lanham Act] ordinarily must show economic or reputational injury flowing directly from the deception wrought by the defendant's advertising; and that occurs when deception of consumers causes them to withhold trade from the plaintiff.

* * * *

Applying those principles to Static Control's false-advertising claim, we conclude that Static Control comes within the class of plaintiffs whom Congress authorized to sue under [the Lanham Act].

To begin, Static Control's alleged injuries—lost sales and damage to its business reputation—are injuries to precisely the sorts of commercial interests the Act protects. *Static Control is suing not as a deceived consumer, but [in the words of the statute] as a "person engaged in * * * commerce within the control of Congress" whose position in the marketplace has been damaged by Lexmark's false advertising.* There is no doubt that it is within the zone of interests protected by the statute. [Emphasis added.]

Static Control also sufficiently alleged that its injuries were proximately caused by Lexmark's misrepresentations.

First, Static Control alleged that Lexmark disparaged its business and products by asserting that Static Control's business was illegal. *When a defendant harms a plaintiff's reputation by casting aspersions [abuse] on its business, the plaintiff's injury flows directly from the audience's belief in the disparaging statements.* [Emphasis added.]

* * * *

The District Court emphasized that Lexmark and Static Control are not direct competitors [since Static Control is not itself a remanufacturer]. But when a party claims reputational injury from disparagement, competition is not required for proximate cause; and that is true even if the defendant's aim was to harm its immediate competitors, and the plaintiff merely suffered collateral damage.

Case 44.2 Continued

In addition, Static Control adequately alleged proximate causation by alleging that it designed, manufactured, and sold microchips that both (1) were necessary for, and (2) had no other use than, refurbishing Lexmark toner cartridges. It follows from that allegation that any false advertising that reduced the remanufacturers' business necessarily injured Static Control as well.

Decision and Remedy *The United States Supreme Court affirmed the lower court's ruling. Static Control had adequately pleaded the elements of a cause of action under the Lanham Act for false advertising. The Court's decision clarified that businesses do not need to be direct competitors to bring an action for false advertising under the act.*

Critical Thinking
- **What If the Facts Were Different?** *Suppose that Lexmark had issued a retraction of its advertising claims before this case reached the Supreme Court. Would the outcome have been different? Discuss.*
- **Legal Environment** *Under the Court's ruling in this case, is Static Control now entitled to relief? Explain your answer.*

44–1b Marketing

In addition to regulating advertising practices, Congress has passed several laws to protect consumers against other marketing practices.

Telephone Solicitation The Telephone Consumer Protection Act (TCPA)[7] prohibits telephone solicitation using an automatic telephone dialing system or a prerecorded voice. In addition, most states have statutes regulating telephone solicitation. The TCPA also makes it illegal to transmit ads via fax without first obtaining the recipient's permission. (Most states also have laws regulating telephone solicitation.)

The Federal Communications Commission (FCC) enforces the TCPA. The FCC imposes substantial fines ($11,000 each day) on companies that violate the junk fax provisions of the act.[8] The TCPA also gives consumers a right to sue for either $500 for each violation of the act or for the actual monetary losses resulting from a violation, whichever is greater. If a court finds that a defendant willfully or knowingly violated the act, the court has the discretion to treble (triple) the amount of damages awarded.

Fraudulent Telemarketing The Telemarketing and Consumer Fraud and Abuse Prevention Act[9] directed the FTC to establish rules governing telemarketing and to bring actions against fraudulent telemarketers.

The FTC's Telemarketing Sales Rule (TSR)[10] requires a telemarketer to identify the seller's name, describe the product being sold, and disclose all material facts related to the sale (such as the total cost). The TSR makes it illegal for telemarketers to misrepresent information or facts about their goods or services. A telemarketer must also remove a consumer's name from its list of potential contacts if the customer so requests.

An amendment to the TSR established the national Do Not Call Registry. Telemarketers must refrain from calling those consumers who have placed their names on the list. Significantly, the TSR applies to any offer made to consumers in the United States—even if the offer comes from a foreign firm. Thus, the TSR helps to protect consumers from illegal cross-border telemarketing operations.

44–1c Sales

A number of statutes protect consumers by requiring the disclosure of certain terms in sales transactions and providing rules governing unsolicited merchandise. The FTC has regulatory authority in this area, as do some other federal agencies.

Many states and the FTC have **"cooling-off" laws** that permit the buyers of goods sold door to door to cancel their contracts within three business days. The FTC rule also requires that consumers be notified in Spanish of this right if the oral negotiations for the sale were in that language.

The contracts that fall under these cancellation rules include trade show sales contracts, contracts for home

---

7. 47 U.S.C. Sections 227 *et seq.*
8. See, for instance, *Imhoff Investment, LLC v. Alfoccinio, Inc.,* 792 F.3d 627 (6th Cir. 2015).
9. 15 U.S.C. 6101–6108.
10. 16 C.F.R. Sections 310.1–310.8.

equity loans, Internet purchase contracts, and home (door-to-door) sales contracts. In addition, certain states have passed laws allowing consumers to cancel contracts for dating services, gym memberships, and weight loss programs.

The FTC Mail or Telephone Order Merchandise Rule[11] protects consumers who purchase goods via mail, Internet, phone, or fax. Merchants are required to ship orders within the time promised in their advertisements and to notify consumers when orders cannot be shipped on time. If the seller does not give an estimated shipping time, it must ship within thirty days. Merchants must also issue a refund within a specified period of time when a consumer cancels an order.

44–2 Labeling and Packaging Laws

A number of federal and state laws deal specifically with the information given on labels and packages. In general, labels must be accurate, and they must use words that are easily understood by the ordinary consumer. In some instances, labels must specify the raw materials used in the product, such as the percentage of cotton, nylon, or other fiber used in a garment. In other instances, the product must carry a warning, such as those required on cigarette packages and advertising.[12]

44–2a Automobile Fuel Economy Labels

The Energy Policy and Conservation Act (EPCA)[13] requires automakers to attach an information label to every new car. The label must include the Environmental Protection Agency's fuel economy estimate for the vehicle. ■ **CASE IN POINT 44.5** Gaetano Paduano bought a new Honda Civic Hybrid in California. The information label on the car included the fuel economy estimate from the Environmental Protection Agency (EPA). Honda's sales brochure added, "Just drive the Hybrid like you would a conventional car and save on fuel bills."

When Paduano discovered that the car's fuel economy was less than half of the EPA's estimate, he sued Honda for deceptive advertising under a California law. The automaker claimed that the federal law (the EPCA) preempted the state's deceptive advertising law. The court held in Paduano's favor, finding that the federal statute did not preempt a claim for deceptive advertising made under state law.[14] ■

44–2b Food Labeling

Because the quality and safety of food are so important to consumers, several statutes deal specifically with food labeling. The Fair Packaging and Labeling Act requires that food product labels identify (1) the product, (2) the net quantity of the contents (and, if the number of servings is stated, the size of a serving), (3) the manufacturer, and (4) the packager or distributor. The act includes additional requirements concerning descriptions on packages, savings claims, components of nonfood products, and standards for the partial filling of packages.

Nutritional Content of Food Products Food products must bear labels detailing the nutritional content, including the number of calories and the amounts of various nutrients that the food contains. The Nutrition Labeling and Education Act[15] requires food labels to provide standard nutrition facts and regulates the use of such terms as *fresh* and *low fat*.

The U.S. Food and Drug Administration (FDA) and the U.S. Department of Agriculture (USDA) are the primary agencies that issue regulations on food labeling. These rules are published in the *Federal Register* and updated annually.

Caloric Content of Restaurant Foods The health-care reforms enacted in 2010 (the Affordable Care Act, or Obamacare) included provisions aimed at combating the problem of obesity in the United States. All restaurant chains with twenty or more locations are now required to post the caloric content of the foods on their menus so that customers will know how many calories the foods contain.[16] Foods offered through vending machines must also be labeled so that their caloric content is visible to would-be purchasers.

In addition, restaurants must post guidelines on the number of calories that an average person requires daily so that customers can determine what portion of a day's calories a particular food will provide. The hope is that consumers, armed with this information, will consider the number of calories when they make their food choices. The federal law on menu labeling supersedes all previous state and local laws in this area.

---

11. 16 C.F.R. Sections 435.1–435.2.
12. 15 U.S.C. Sections 1331–1341.
13. 49 U.S.C. Section 32908(b)(1).

14. *Paduano v. American Honda Motor Co.*, 169 Cal.App.4th 1453, 88 Cal. Rptr.3d 90 (2009).
15. 21 U.S.C. Section 343.1.
16. See Section 4205 of the Patient Protection and Affordable Care Act, Pub. L. No. 111-148, 124 Stat. 119 (March 23, 2010).

44–3 Protection of Health and Safety

Although labeling and packaging laws promote consumer health and safety, there is a significant distinction between regulating the information dispensed about a product and regulating the actual content of the product. The classic example is tobacco products. Producers of tobacco products must use labels that warn consumers about the health hazards associated with their use, but the sale of tobacco products has not been subjected to significant restrictions. We now examine various laws that regulate the actual products made available to consumers.

44–3a The Federal Food, Drug, and Cosmetic Act

The most important federal legislation regulating food and drugs is the Federal Food, Drug, and Cosmetic Act (FDCA).[17] The act protects consumers against adulterated (contaminated) and misbranded foods and drugs. The FDCA establishes food standards, specifies safe levels of potentially hazardous food additives, and provides classifications of foods and food advertising. Most of these statutory requirements are monitored and enforced by the Food and Drug Administration (FDA).

Interestingly, the European Union and a number of other countries, such as Canada, have banned some foods that the FDA assumes to be safe. These foods include brominated vegetable oil (a common ingredient in sports drinks, such as Gatorade) and Olestra/Olean (a cholesterol-free fat substitute found in certain potato chips). Food products containing such substances may not be sold in the European Union. Similarly, certain food colorings found in processed foods in the United States (in M&Ms and Kraft macaroni and cheese, for instance) are not allowed in foods in some other countries.

Tainted Foods In the last twenty years or so, many people in the United States have contracted food poisoning from eating foods that were contaminated, often with salmonella or *E. coli* bacteria. ■ **EXAMPLE 44.6** During 2015 and 2016, hundreds of people across the United States were sickened by eating tainted food at the popular restaurant chain Chipotle Mexican Grill. Causes of illness in these outbreaks included *E-coli* and salmonella, as well as the highly contagious norovirus. ■

In response to the problem of food contamination, Congress enacted the Food Safety Modernization Act (FSMA)[18] to provide greater government control over the U.S. food safety system. The act gives the FDA authority to directly recall any food products that it suspects are tainted, rather than relying on the producers to recall items.

The FSMA requires anyone who manufactures, processes, packs, distributes, receives, holds, or imports food products to pay a fee and register with the U.S. Department of Health and Human Services. (There are some exceptions for small farmers.) Owners and operators of such facilities are required to analyze and identify food safety hazards, implement preventive controls, monitor effectiveness, and take corrective actions. The FSMA places additional restrictions on importers of food and requires them to verify that imported foods meet U.S. safety standards.

Drugs and Medical Devices The FDA is also responsible under the FDCA for ensuring that drugs are safe and effective before they are marketed to the public. Because the FDA must ensure the safety of new medications, there is always a delay before drugs are available to the public, and this sometimes leads to controversy.

■ **CASE IN POINT 44.7** A group of citizens petitioned the FDA to allow everyone access to "Plan B"—the morning-after birth control pill—without a prescription. The FDA denied the petition and continued to require women under the age of seventeen to obtain a prescription. The group appealed to a federal district court, claiming that the prescription requirement can delay access to the pill. The pill should be taken as soon as possible after sexual intercourse, preferably within twenty-four hours. The court ruled in favor of the plaintiffs and ordered the FDA to make the morning-after pill available to people of any age without a prescription.[19] ■

44–3b The Consumer Product Safety Act

The Consumer Product Safety Act[20] created a comprehensive regulatory scheme over consumer safety matters and established the Consumer Product Safety Commission (CPSC).

The CPSC's Authority The CPSC conducts research on the safety of individual consumer products and maintains a clearinghouse on the risks associated with various products. The Consumer Product Safety Act authorizes the CPSC to do the following:

---

17. 21 U.S.C. Sections 301–393.
18. Pub. L. No. 111-353, 124 Stat. 3885 (January 4, 2011). This statute affected numerous parts of Title 21 of the U.S.C.
19. *Tummino v. Hamburg*, 936 F.Supp.2d 162 (E.D.N.Y. 2013).
20. 15 U.S.C. Sections 2051–2083.

1. Set safety standards for consumer products.
2. Ban the manufacture and sale of any product that the commission believes poses an "unreasonable risk" to consumers. (Products banned by the CPSC have included various types of fireworks, cribs, and toys, as well as many products containing asbestos or vinyl chloride.)
3. Remove from the market any products it believes to be imminently hazardous. The CPSC frequently works in conjunction with manufacturers to conduct voluntary recalls of defective products from stores. ■ **EXAMPLE 44.8** In cooperation with the CPSC, the Scandinavian company IKEA recalled three million baby bed canopies and thirty million wall-mounted children's lamps because they posed a strangulation risk to children. ■
4. Require manufacturers to report on any products already sold or intended for sale if the products have proved to be hazardous.
5. Administer other product-safety legislation, including the Child Protection and Toy Safety Act[21] and the Federal Hazardous Substances Act.[22]

Notification Requirements The Consumer Product Safety Act requires the distributors of consumer products to notify the CPSC immediately if they receive information that a product "contains a defect which . . . creates a substantial risk to the public" or "an unreasonable risk of serious injury or death."

■ **EXAMPLE 44.9** A company that sells juicers receives twenty-three letters from customers complaining that during operation the juicer suddenly exploded, sending pieces of glass and razor-sharp metal across the room. The company must immediately notify the CPSC because the alleged defect creates a substantial risk to the public. ■

44–3c Health-Care Reforms

The health-care reforms enacted in 2010 gave Americans new rights and benefits with regard to health care.[23] The legislation also prohibited certain insurance company practices.

Expanded Coverage for Children and Seniors The reforms enabled more children to obtain health-insurance coverage and allowed young adults (under age twenty-six) to remain on their parents' health insurance policies. The legislation also ended lifetime limits and most annual limits on care, and gave insured persons access to recommended preventive services (such as cancer screening and vaccinations) without cost. People can no longer be denied insurance because of preexisting conditions. Medicare recipients now receive a 50 percent discount on name-brand drugs, and the reforms will eliminate a gap in Medicare's prescription drug coverage by 2020.

Controlling Costs of Health Insurance In an attempt to control the rising costs of health insurance, certain restrictions were placed on insurance companies. Insurance companies must spend at least 85 percent of all premium dollars collected from large employers (80 percent of the premiums collected from individuals and small employers) on benefits and quality improvement. If insurance companies do not meet these goals, they must provide rebates to consumers. Additionally, states can require insurance companies to justify any premium increases to be eligible to participate in the new health-insurance exchanges. In spite of the legislation, health insurance costs have continued to increase.

44–4 Credit Protection

Credit protection is one of the more important aspects of consumer protection legislation. Nearly 80 percent of U.S. consumers have credit cards, and most carry a balance on these cards—a total of about $2.5 trillion of debt nationwide. The Consumer Financial Protection Bureau (CFPB) is the agency that oversees the credit practices of banks, mortgage lenders, and credit-card companies.[24]

44–4a The Truth-in-Lending Act

A key statute regulating the credit and credit-card industries is the Truth-in-Lending Act (TILA), the name commonly given to Title I of the Consumer Credit Protection Act, as amended.[25] The TILA is basically a *disclosure law*. It is administered by the Federal Reserve Board and requires sellers and lenders to disclose credit terms and loan terms so that individuals can shop around for the best financing arrangements.

21. 15 U.S.C. Section 1262(e).
22. 15 U.S.C. Sections 1261–1273.
23. Patient Protection and Affordable Health Care Act of 2010, Pub. L. No.111-148, 124 Stat. 119 (March 23, 2010); and the Health Care and Education Reconciliation Act of 2010, Pub. L. No. 111-152, 124 Stat. 1029 (March 30, 2010).
24. Title 10 of the Restoring American Financial Stability Act of 2010, S.B. 3217, April 15, 2010.
25. 15 U.S.C. Sections 1601–1693r.

Application TILA requirements apply only to those who, in the ordinary course of business, lend funds, sell on credit, or arrange for the extension of credit. Thus, sales or loans made between two consumers do not come under the protection of the act. Additionally, this law protects only debtors who are natural persons (as opposed to the artificial "person" of a corporation). It does not extend to other legal entities.

Disclosure Requirements The TILA's disclosure requirements are contained in **Regulation Z,** issued by the Federal Reserve Board of Governors. If the contracting parties are subject to the TILA, the requirements of Regulation Z apply to any transaction involving an installment sales contract that calls for payment to be made in more than four installments. Transactions subject to Regulation Z typically include installment loans, retail and installment sales, car loans, home-improvement loans, and certain real estate loans if the amount of financing is less than $25,000.

Under the provisions of the TILA, all of the terms of a credit instrument must be clearly and conspicuously disclosed. A lender must disclose the annual percentage rate (APR), finance charge, amount financed, and total payments (the sum of the amount loaned, plus any fees, finance charges, and interest). If a creditor fails to follow the *exact* procedures required by the TILA, the creditor risks contract rescission (cancellation) under the act.

Equal Credit Opportunity Congress enacted the Equal Credit Opportunity Act (ECOA)[26] as an amendment to the TILA. The ECOA prohibits the denial of credit solely on the basis of race, religion, national origin, color, gender, marital status, or age. The act also prohibits credit discrimination on the basis of whether an individual receives certain forms of income, such as public-assistance benefits.

Under the ECOA, a creditor may not require a cosigner on a credit instrument if the applicant qualifies under the creditor's standards of creditworthiness for the amount and terms of the credit request. ■ **CASE IN POINT 44.10** T.R. Hughes, Inc., and Summit Pointe, LLC, obtained financing from Frontenac Bank to construct two real estate developments near St. Louis, Missouri. The bank also required the builder, Thomas R. Hughes, and his wife, Carolyn Hughes, to sign personal guaranty agreements for the loans.

When the borrowers failed to make the loan payments, the bank sued the two companies and Thomas and Carolyn Hughes personally, and foreclosed on the properties. Carolyn claimed that the personal guaranty contracts that she signed were obtained in violation of the ECOA. The court held that because the applicant, Thomas R. Hughes, was creditworthy, the personal guarantys of Carolyn Hughes were obtained in violation of the ECOA and therefore unenforceable.[27] ■

Credit-Card Rules The TILA also contains provisions regarding credit cards. One provision limits the liability of a cardholder to $50 per card for unauthorized charges made before the creditor is notified that the card has been lost. If a consumer receives an *unsolicited* credit card in the mail that is later stolen, the company that issued the card cannot charge the consumer for any unauthorized charges.

Another provision requires credit-card companies to disclose the balance computation method that is used to determine the outstanding balance and to state when finance charges begin to accrue. Other provisions set forth procedures for resolving billing disputes with the credit-card company. These procedures are used if, for instance, a cardholder thinks that an error has occurred in billing or wishes to withhold payment for a faulty product purchased by credit card.

Amendments to Credit-Card Rules Amendments to the TILA's credit-card rules added the following protections:

1. A company may not retroactively increase the interest rates on existing card balances unless the account is sixty days delinquent.
2. A company must provide forty-five days' advance notice to consumers before changing its credit-card terms.
3. Monthly bills must be sent to cardholders twenty-one days before the due date.
4. The interest rate charged on a customer's credit-card balance may not be increased except in specific situations, such as when a promotional rate ends.
5. A company may not charge over-limit fees except in specified situations.
6. When the customer has balances at different interest rates, payments in excess of the minimum amount due must be applied first to the balance with the highest rate. (For instance, a higher interest rate is commonly charged for cash advances.)
7. A company may not compute finance charges based on the previous billing cycle (a practice known as double-cycle billing). This practice hurts consumers because they are charged interest for the previous cycle even if they have paid the bill in full.

---

26. 15 U.S.C. Sections 1691–1691f.

27. *Frontenac Bank v. T.R. Hughes, Inc.,* 404 S.W.3d 272 (Mo.App. 2012).

44–4b The Fair Credit Reporting Act

The Fair Credit Reporting Act (FCRA)[28] protects consumers against inaccurate credit reporting and requires that lenders and other creditors report correct, relevant, and up-to-date information. The act provides that con-

28. 15 U.S.C. Sections 1681–1681t.

sumer credit reporting agencies may issue credit reports to users only for specified purposes. Legitimate purposes include the extension of credit, the issuance of insurance policies, and responding to the consumer's request.

Whether an Internet service provider had a legitimate purpose to pull a customer's credit report was at issue in the following case.

Case Analysis 44.3

Santangelo v. Comcast Corporation

United States District Court, Northern District of Illinois, Eastern Division, __ F.Supp.3d __, 2016 WL 464223 (2016).

In the Language of the Court
John Z. *LEE*, United States District Judge
* * * *

I. Factual and Procedural Background

[Keith Santangelo filed a complaint in a federal district court against Comcast Corporation, alleging a violation of the Fair Credit Reporting Act (FCRA).] Santangelo alleges * * * that he contacted Comcast through the company's online customer service "Chat" function * * * and requested Internet service for his new apartment. During the chat session, a Comcast representative asked Santangelo for permission to run a credit inquiry. Santangelo asked if any option was available to avoid the credit inquiry. The Comcast representative told him that the company would forgo the inquiry if he paid a $50 deposit.

The option to pay a $50 deposit in order to avoid a credit inquiry was an explicit part of Comcast's official Risk Management Policy * * *. The policy also required a $50 deposit from any prospective customer who agreed to a credit inquiry but whose credit score proved to be unsatisfactory. According to Santangelo, the deposit policy "reflects Comcast's calculated business decision and belief that the collection of a $50 deposit is sufficient to cover the risk presented by a person with bad credit and is sufficient to cover the risk presented by a person who refuses a credit pull."

Santangelo opted to pay the $50 deposit in lieu of a credit inquiry. * * * Nevertheless, Comcast, without Santangelo's authorization, pulled his credit

report * * *. This credit inquiry depleted [lowered] Santangelo's credit score.
* * * *

* * * Comcast now moves to dismiss the * * * complaint.

II. Analysis
* * * *

*FCRA prohibits the obtaining of a "consumer report," commonly known as a credit report, except for purposes authorized by that statute. The statute lists specific permissible purposes, such as * * * any * * * "legitimate business need * * * in connection with a business transaction that is initiated by the consumer."* These limitations are intended to produce a balance between consumer privacy and the needs of a modern, credit-driven economy. [Emphasis added.]

Santangelo contends that Comcast did not have a permissible purpose for obtaining his credit report after he paid the $50 deposit in exchange for the company's promise not to check his credit. If he is correct and the company's violation was willful, he would be entitled to recover attorney's fees and either actual damages or statutory damages between $100 and $1,000. If the company's violation was merely negligent, Santangelo would be permitted to recover only attorney's fees and actual damages.
1. Standing

Comcast first argues that Santangelo lacks standing to bring his FCRA claim. To establish standing * * * a plaintiff must show * * * the injury is fairly traceable to the challenged action of the defendant.

According to Comcast, Santangelo has not alleged an injury-in-fact that is fairly traceable to the FCRA violation he claims. Santangelo responds that he has sustained three injuries-in-fact: the loss of the $50 he paid as a deposit, the violation of his legal right not to have his credit report pulled without a permissible purpose, and the resulting depletion of his credit score.
* * * *

* * * It was the very fact that Comcast received the $50 from Santangelo before it performed the credit check that made it illegal. * * * And once Comcast checked Santangelo's credit, it should have refunded the deposit immediately, rather than keeping it. Comcast's receipt and withholding of the $50, therefore, is inextricable [inseparable] from the FCRA violation and can be said to be fairly traceable to the FCRA violation. * * * Even if the $50.00 deposit were fully refundable, Santangelo still has standing based on the lost time-value of the money.

* * * Santangelo also has sufficiently alleged an injury-in-fact by alleging that Comcast obtained his credit report without a permissible purpose in violation of the FCRA.

*Because the FCRA grants consumers a legally protected interest in limiting access to their credit reports and provides redress for violations, * * * Santangelo's allegations about Comcast's interference with that legally protected interest are sufficient*

Case 44.3 Continued

to establish * * * *standing.* [Emphasis added.]

* * * Santangelo also alleges that the FCRA violation in this case depleted his credit score. In response, Comcast contends that a reduced credit score, without resulting damages, does not constitute an injury.

* * * The Court agrees with Santangelo that a depleted credit score is sufficient to constitute an injury * * * . Credit scores are of great importance in our economy, and a depleted credit score could affect a consumer in numerous ways, inflicting harm that often may be difficult to prove or quantify. Congress has the power to discourage the needless depletion of consumers' credit scores even when the depleted score cannot be neatly tied to a financial harm.

2. Sufficiency of Santangelo's allegations

Comcast next argues that Santangelo's allegations do not state an FCRA claim.

* * * *

In his * * * complaint, Santangelo * * * alleges that Comcast's deposit policies demonstrate its lack of a legitimate need to run credit checks with respect

to consumers who paid a $50 deposit. According to the * * * complaint, Comcast's established policy is to forgo a credit check in exchange for a $50 deposit. The company also has a policy of accepting a $50 deposit from consumers who opt for a credit check but prove to have poor credit. Santangelo compares this situation to that of a car dealer who accepts a cash payment for the full purchase price of a car. * * * The car dealer * * * does not have a legitimate need to obtain the purchaser's credit report. Similarly, a landlord does not have a legitimate need to obtain a tenant's credit report if the tenant is entitled to a lease renewal without regard to creditworthiness.

In response, Comcast * * * argues that it had a legitimate business need to establish Santangelo's creditworthiness despite his deposit because—unlike in the car dealer example—his $50 deposit would cover less than two months of service in a long-term contract. * * * [Santangelo] contends that, under company policy, his creditworthiness was irrelevant to Comcast's determination of his eligibility for service once the deposit

was collected, much like the tenants in [the landlord example].

* * * *

* * * Comcast's mere violation of its alleged agreement not to pull Santangelo's credit report does not support an FCRA claim. But the possibility that the company itself believed that its customers' creditworthiness was irrelevant if they paid a deposit is enough.

Comcast's final argument for dismissing Santangelo's FCRA claim is that he neither explicitly alleges that the company's actions were willful, which is necessary to trigger statutory damages, nor identifies any actual damages that he could recover if Comcast acted only negligently. Although [Santangelo] does not use the word willful in his complaint, he alleges that the company obtained his credit report despite that it "knew that it did not have a legitimate business need." This allegation implies recklessness at the very least, and reckless conduct qualifies as willful conduct under the FCRA.

* * * *

III. Conclusion

* * * The Court denies Comcast's motion to dismiss.

Legal Reasoning Questions

1. Comcast argued that it had refunded Santangelo's $50, plus interest in the amount of $10, four months after pulling his credit report. Does this argument undercut the plaintiff's claim to have standing? Why or why not?

2. What might discovery reveal that would affect the outcome in this case? Explain.

3. What damages might Santangelo be able to prove based on the depletion of his credit score?

Consumer Notification and Inaccurate Information Any time a consumer is denied credit or insurance on the basis of her or his credit report, the consumer must be notified of that fact. The notice must include the name and address of the credit-reporting agency that issued the report. The same notice must be sent to consumers who are charged more than others ordinarily would be for credit or insurance because of their credit reports.

Under the FCRA, consumers may request the source of any information used by the credit agency, as well as the identity of anyone who has received an agency's report.

Consumers are also permitted to access the information about them contained in a credit reporting agency's files.

If a consumer discovers that an agency's files contain inaccurate information, he or she should report the problem to the agency. On the consumer's written (or electronic) request, the agency must conduct a systematic examination of its records. Any unverifiable or erroneous information must be deleted within a reasonable period of time.

Remedies for Violations A credit reporting agency that fails to comply with the act is liable for actual damages, plus additional damages not to exceed $1,000 and attorneys' fees.[29] Creditors and other companies that use information from credit reporting agencies may also be liable for violations of the FCRA. The United States Supreme Court has held that an insurance company's failure to notify new customers that they were paying higher insurance rates as a result of their credit scores was a *willful* violation of the FCRA.[30]

■ **CASE IN POINT 44.11** Branch Banking & Trust Company of Virginia (BB&T) gave Rex Saunders an auto loan but failed to give him a payment coupon book and refused his attempts to make payments on the loan. In fact, BB&T told him that it had not extended a loan to him. Eventually, BB&T discovered its mistake and demanded full payment, plus interest and penalties.

When payment was not immediately forthcoming, BB&T declared that Saunders was in default. It then repossessed the car and forwarded adverse credit information about Saunders to credit reporting agencies, without noting that Saunders disputed the information. Saunders filed a lawsuit alleging violations of the FCRA and was awarded $80,000 in punitive damages. An appellate court found that the damages award was reasonable, given BB&T's willful violation.[31] ■

44–4c The Fair and Accurate Credit Transactions Act

Congress passed the Fair and Accurate Credit Transactions (FACT) Act in an effort to combat identity theft.[32] The act established a national fraud alert system. Consumers who suspect that they have been or may be victimized by identity theft can place an alert on their credit files. When a consumer establishes that identify theft has occurred, the credit reporting agency must stop reporting allegedly fraudulent account information.

The act also requires the major credit reporting agencies to provide consumers with free copies of their own credit reports every twelve months. Another provision requires account numbers on credit-card receipts to be truncated (shortened). Merchants, employees, or others who may have access to the receipts can no longer obtain the consumers' names and full credit-card numbers. Financial institutions must work with the FTC to identify

"red flag" indicators of identity theft and to develop rules for the disposal of sensitive credit information.

44–4d The Fair Debt Collection Practices Act

The Fair Debt Collection Practices Act (FDCPA)[33] attempts to curb perceived abuses by collection agencies. The act applies only to specialized debt-collection agencies and attorneys who regularly attempt to collect debts on behalf of someone else, usually for a percentage of the amount owed. Creditors attempting to collect debts are not covered by the act unless, by misrepresenting themselves, they cause debtors to believe they are collection agencies.

Requirements of the Act Under the FDCPA, a collection agency may not do any of the following:

1. Contact the debtor at the debtor's place of employment if the debtor's employer objects.
2. Contact the debtor at inconvenient or unusual times (such as three o'clock in the morning), or at any time if the debtor is being represented by an attorney.
3. Contact third parties other than the debtor's parents, spouse, or financial adviser about payment of a debt unless a court authorizes such action.
4. Harass or intimidate the debtor (by using abusive language or threatening violence, for instance) or make false or misleading statements (such as posing as a police officer).
5. Communicate with the debtor at any time after receiving notice that the debtor is refusing to pay the debt, except to advise the debtor of further action to be taken by the collection agency.

The FDCPA also requires a collection agency to include a **validation notice** when it initially contacts a debtor for payment of a debt or within five days of that initial contact. The notice must state that the debtor has thirty days in which to dispute the debt and to request a written verification of the debt from the collection agency.

Enforcement of the Act The Federal Trade Commission is primarily responsible for enforcing the FDCPA. A debt collector who fails to comply with the act is liable for actual damages, plus additional damages not to exceed $1,000 and attorneys' fees.

---

29. 15 U.S.C. Section 1681n.
30. *Safeco Insurance. Co. of America v. Burr,* 551 U.S. 47, 127 S.Ct. 2201, 167 L.Ed.2d 1045 (2007).
31. *Saunders v. Branch Banking & Trust Co. of Virginia,* 526 F.3d 142 (4th Cir. 2008).
32. Pub. L. No. 108-159, 117 Stat. 1952.

---

33. 15 U.S.C. Section 1692.

Debt collectors who violate the act are exempt from liability if they can show that the violation was not intentional and resulted from a bona fide error. Furthermore, the error must have occurred in spite of procedures the company had already put in place to avoid such errors. The "bona fide error" defense typically has been applied to mistakes of fact or clerical errors. A few courts have gone further and allowed the good faith error defense in other circumstances.[34]

34. See, for instance, *Zortman v. J.C. Christensen & Associates, Inc.*, 2012 WL 1563918 (D.Minn. 2012); see also *Mbaku v. Bank of America, N.A.*, 2013 WL 425981 (D.Colo. 2013).

Reviewing: Consumer Law

Leota Sage saw a local motorcycle dealer's newspaper advertisement offering a MetroRider EZ electric scooter for $1,699. When she went to the dealership, however, she learned that the EZ model had been sold out. The salesperson told Sage that he still had the higher-end MetroRider FX model in stock for $2,199 and would sell her one for $1,999. Sage was disappointed but decided to purchase the FX model.

When Sage said that she wished to purchase the scooter on credit, she was directed to the dealer's credit department. As she filled out the credit forms, the clerk told Sage, who is an Asian American, that she would need a cosigner to obtain a loan. Sage could not understand why she would need a cosigner and asked to speak to the store manager. The manager apologized, told her that the clerk was mistaken, and said that he would "speak to" the clerk. The manager completed Sage's credit application, and Sage then rode the scooter home. Seven months later, Sage received a letter from the manufacturer informing her that a flaw had been discovered in the scooter's braking system and that the model had been recalled. Using the information presented in the chapter, answer the following questions.

1. Did the dealer engage in deceptive advertising? Why or why not?
2. Suppose that Sage had ordered the scooter through the dealer's Web site but the dealer was unable to deliver it by the date promised. What would the FTC have required the merchant to do in that situation?
3. Assuming that the clerk required a cosigner based on Sage's race or gender, what act prohibits such credit discrimination?
4. What organization has the authority to ban the sale of scooters based on safety concerns?

Debate This . . .   *Laws against bait-and-switch advertising should be abolished because no consumer is ever forced to buy anything.*

Terms and Concepts

bait-and-switch advertising 845	"cooling-off" laws 849	multiple product order 846
cease-and-desist order 846	counteradvertising 846	Regulation Z 853
consumer law 843	deceptive advertising 843	validation notice 856

Issue Spotters

1. United Pharmaceuticals, Inc., believes that it has developed a new drug that will be effective in the treatment of patients with AIDS. The drug has had only limited testing, but United wants to make the drug widely available as soon as possible. To market the drug, what must United prove to the U.S. Food and Drug Administration? (See *Protection of Health and Safety.*)

2. Gert buys a notebook computer from EZ Electronics. She pays for it with her credit card. When the computer proves defective, she asks EZ to repair or replace it, but EZ refuses. What can Gert do? (See *Credit Protection.*)

- **Check your answers to the Issue Spotters against the answers provided in Appendix D at the end of this text.**

Business Scenarios

44–1. Unsolicited Merchandise. Andrew, a resident of California, received an advertising circular in the U.S. mail announcing a new line of regional cookbooks distributed by the Every-Kind Cookbook Co. Andrew didn't want any books and threw the circular away. Two days later, Andrew received in the mail an introductory cookbook entitled *Lower Mongolian Regional Cookbook*, as announced in the circular, on a "trial basis" from Every-Kind. Andrew was not interested but did not go to the trouble to return the cookbook. Every-Kind demanded payment of $20.95 for the *Lower Mongolian Regional Cookbook*. Discuss whether Andrew can be required to pay for the book. (See *Advertising, Marketing, and Sales*.)

44–2. Credit-Card Rules. Maria Ochoa receives two new credit cards on May 1. She has solicited one of them from Midtown Department Store, and the other arrives unsolicited from High-Flying Airlines. During the month of May, Ochoa makes numerous credit-card purchases from Midtown Department Store, but she does not use the High-Flying Airlines card. On May 31, a burglar breaks into Ochoa's home and steals both credit cards, along with other items. Ochoa notifies the Midtown Department Store of the theft on June 2, but she fails to notify High-Flying Airlines. Using the Midtown credit card, the burglar makes a $500 purchase on June 1 and a $200 purchase on June 3. The burglar then charges a vacation flight on the High-Flying Airlines card for $1,000 on June 5. Ochoa receives the bills for these charges and refuses to pay them. Discuss Ochoa's liability for the charges. (See *Credit Protection*.)

Business Case Problems

44–3. Spotlight on McDonald's—Food Labeling.

McDonald's Corp.'s Happy Meal® meal selection consists of an entrée, a small order of french fries, a small drink, and a toy. In the early 1990s, McDonald's began to aim its Happy Meal marketing at children aged one to three. In 1995, McDonald's began making nutritional information for its food products available in documents known as "McDonald's Nutrition Facts." Each document lists the food items that the restaurant serves and provides a nutritional breakdown, but the Happy Meal is not included.

Marc Cohen filed a suit against McDonald's in an Illinois state court. Among other things, Cohen alleged that McDonald's had violated a state law prohibiting consumer fraud and deceptive business practices by failing to adhere to the Nutrition Labeling and Education Act (NLEA). The NLEA sets out different requirements for products specifically intended for children under the age of four—for instance, the products' labels cannot declare the percent of daily value of nutritional components. Does it make sense to have different requirements for children of this age? Why or why not? Should a state court impose such regulations? Explain. [*Cohen v. McDonald's Corp.*, 347 Ill.App.3d 627, 808 N.E.2d 1, 283 Ill.Dec. 451 (1 Dist. 2004)] (See *Labeling and Packaging Laws*.)

44–4. Deceptive Advertising. Brian Cleary and Rita Burke filed a suit against cigarette maker Philip Morris USA, Inc., seeking class-action status for a claim of deceptive advertising. Cleary and Burke claimed that "light" cigarettes, such as Marlboro Lights, were advertised as safer than regular cigarettes, even though the health effects are the same. They contended that the tobacco companies concealed the true nature of light cigarettes. Philip Morris correctly claimed that it was authorized by the government to advertise cigarettes, including light cigarettes. Assuming that is true, should the plaintiffs still be able to bring a deceptive advertising claim against the tobacco company? Why or why not? [*Cleary v. Philip Morris USA, Inc.*, 683 F.Supp.2d 730 (N.D.Ill. 2010)] (See *Advertising, Marketing, and Sales*.)

44–5. Business Case Problem with Sample Answer— Fair Debt-Collection Practices. Bank of America hired

Atlantic Resource Management, LLC, to collect a debt from Michael E. Engler. Atlantic called Engler's employer and asked his supervisor about the company's policy concerning the execution of warrants. The caller then told the supervisor that, to stop process of the warrant, Engler needed to call Atlantic about "Case Number 37291 NY0969" during the first three hours of his next shift. When Engler's supervisor told him about the call, Engler feared that he might be arrested, and he experienced discomfort, embarrassment, and emotional distress at work. Can Engler recover under the Fair Debt Collection Practices Act? Why or why not? [*Engler v. Atlantic Resource Management, LLC*, 2012 WL 464728 (W.D.N.Y. 2012)] (See *Credit Protection*.)

• **For a sample answer to Problem 44–5, go to Appendix E at the end of this text.**

44–6. Deceptive Advertising. Innovative Marketing, Inc. (IMI), sold "scareware"—computer security software. IMI's Internet ads redirected consumers to sites where they were told that a scan of their computers had detected dangerous files— viruses, spyware, and "illegal" pornography. In fact, no scans were conducted. Kristy Ross, an IMI cofounder and vice president, reviewed and edited the ads, and was aware of the many complaints that consumers had made about them. An individual can be held liable under the Federal Trade Commission Act's prohibition of deceptive practices if the person (1) participated directly in the deceptive practices or had the authority to control them and (2) had or should have had knowledge of them. Were IMI's ads deceptive? If so, can Ross be held liable?

Explain. [*Federal Trade Commission v. Ross*, 743 F.3d 886 (4th Cir. 2014)] (See *Advertising, Marketing, and Sales*.)

44–7. A Question of Ethics—Fair Debt-Collection Practices. *Barry Sussman graduated from law school, but also served* *time in prison for attempting to collect debts by posing as an FBI agent. He theorized that if a debt-collection business collected only debts that it owned as a result of buying checks written on accounts with insufficient funds (NSF checks), it would not be subject to the Fair Debt Collection Practices Act (FDCPA). Sussman formed Check Investors, Inc., to act on his theory. Check Investors bought more than 2.2 million NSF checks, with an estimated face value of about $348 million, for pennies on the dollar. Check Investors added a fee of $125 or $130 (more than the legal limit in most states) to the face amount of each check and aggressively pursued its drawer to collect. The firm's employees were told to accuse drawers of being criminals and to threaten them with arrest and prosecution. The threats were false. Check Investors never took steps to* initiate a prosecution. *The employees contacted the drawers' family members and used "saturation phoning"—phoning a drawer numerous times in a short period. They used abusive language, referring to drawers as "deadbeats," "retards," "thieves," and "idiots." Between January 2000 and January 2003, Check Investors netted more than $10.2 million from its efforts.* [*Federal Trade Commission v. Check Investors, Inc., 502 F.3d 159 (3d Cir. 2007)*] (See *Credit Protection*.)

(a) The Federal Trade Commission filed a suit in a federal district court against Check Investors and others, alleging, in part, violations of the FDCPA. Was Check Investors a "debt collector," collecting "debts," within the meaning of the FDCPA? If so, did its methods violate the FDCPA? Were its practices unethical? What might Check Investors argue in its defense? Discuss.

(b) Are "deadbeats" the primary beneficiaries of laws such as the FDCPA? If not, how would you characterize debtors who default on their obligations?

Legal Reasoning Group Activity

44–8. Consumer Protections. Many states have enacted laws that go even further than federal law to protect consumers. These laws vary tremendously from state to state. (See *Advertising, Marketing, and Sales*.)

(a) The first group will decide whether having different laws is fair to sellers who may be prohibited from engaging in a practice in one state that is legal in another.

(b) The second group will consider how these different laws might affect a business.

(c) A third group will determine whether it is fair that residents of one state have more protection than residents of another.

CHAPTER 45

Environmental Protection

Concern over the degradation of the environment has increased over time in response to the environmental effects of population growth, urbanization, and industrialization. Environmental protection is not without a price, however. For many businesses, the costs of complying with environmental regulations are high, and for some they may seem too high. A constant tension exists between the desire to increase profits and productivity and the need to protect the environment.

To a great extent, environmental law consists of statutes passed by federal, state, or local governments and regulations issued by administrative agencies. Before examining statutory and regulatory environmental laws, however, we look at the remedies against environmental pollution that are available under the common law.

45–1 Common Law Actions

Common law remedies against environmental pollution originated centuries ago in England. Those responsible for operations that created dirt, smoke, noxious odors, noise, or toxic substances were sometimes held liable under common law theories of nuisance or negligence. Today, individuals who have suffered a harm from pollution continue to rely on the common law to obtain damages and injunctions against business polluters.

45–1a Nuisance

Under the common law doctrine of **nuisance,** persons may be held liable if they use their property in a manner that unreasonably interferes with others' rights to use or enjoy their own property. Courts typically balance the harm caused by the pollution against the costs of stopping it.

Courts have often denied injunctive relief on the ground that the hardships that would be imposed on the polluter and on the community are greater than the hardships suffered by the plaintiff. ■ **EXAMPLE 45.1** Hewitt's factory causes neighboring landowners to suffer from smoke, soot, and vibrations. But if the factory is the core of the local economy, a court may leave it in operation and award monetary damages to the injured parties. Damages can include compensation for any decline in the value of their property caused by Hewitt's operation. ■

To obtain relief from pollution under the nuisance doctrine, a property owner may have to identify a distinct harm separate from that affecting the general public. This harm is referred to as a "private" nuisance. Under the common law, individuals were denied standing (access to the courts) unless they suffered a harm distinct from that suffered by the public at large. Some states still require this. A public authority (such as a state's attorney general), however, can sue to stop a "public" nuisance.

45–1b Negligence and Strict Liability

An injured party may sue a business polluter in tort under negligence and strict liability theories. A negligence action is based on a business's alleged failure to use reasonable care toward a party whose injury was foreseeable and was caused by the lack of reasonable care. For instance, employees might sue an employer whose failure to use proper pollution controls has contaminated the air, causing the employees to suffer respiratory illnesses. Lawsuits for personal injuries caused by exposure to a toxic substance, such as asbestos, radiation, or hazardous waste, have given rise to a growing body of tort law known as **toxic torts.**

Businesses that engage in ultrahazardous activities—such as the transportation of radioactive materials—are strictly liable for any injuries the activities cause. In a strict liability action, the injured party does not have to prove that the business failed to exercise reasonable care.

45–2 Federal, State, and Local Regulations

All levels of government in the United States regulate some aspect of the environment. In this section, we look at some of the ways in which the federal, state, and local governments control business activities and land use in the interests of environmental preservation and protection.

45–2a State and Local Regulations

In addition to the federal regulations to be discussed shortly, many states have enacted laws to protect the environment. State laws may restrict a business's discharge of chemicals into the air or water or regulate its disposal of toxic wastes. States may also regulate the disposal or recycling of other wastes, including glass, metal, plastic containers, and paper. Additionally, states may restrict emissions from motor vehicles.

City, county, and other local governments also regulate some aspects of the environment. For instance, local zoning laws may be designed to inhibit or regulate the growth of cities and suburbs. In the interest of safeguarding the environment, such laws may prohibit certain land uses. Even when zoning laws permit a business's proposed development plan, the plan may have to be altered to lessen the development's environmental impact. In addition, cities and counties may impose rules regulating methods of waste removal, the appearance of buildings, the maximum noise level, and other aspects of the local environment.

State and local regulatory agencies also play a significant role in implementing federal environmental legislation. Typically, the federal government relies on state and local governments to enforce federal environmental statutes and regulations, such as those regulating air quality.

45–2b Federal Regulations

Congress has passed a number of statutes to control the impact of human activities on the environment. Exhibit 45–1 lists and summarizes the major federal environmental statutes discussed in this chapter. Most of these statutes are designed to address pollution in the air, water, or land. Some specifically regulate toxic chemicals, including pesticides, herbicides, and hazardous wastes.

Environmental Regulatory Agencies The primary federal agency regulating environmental law is the Environmental Protection Agency (EPA). Other federal agencies with authority to regulate specific environmental matters include the Department of the Interior, the Department of Defense, the Department of Labor, the Food and Drug Administration, and the Nuclear Regulatory Commission. In addition, as mentioned, state and local agencies play an important role in enforcing federal environmental legislation.

Most federal environmental laws provide that citizens can sue to enforce environmental regulations if government agencies fail to do so. Similarly, citizens can sue to limit enforcement actions if agencies go too far in their actions. Typically, a threshold hurdle in such suits is meeting the requirements for standing to sue.

In the following case, an animal advocacy organization brought a suit to stop the "taking" (killing or capture) of migratory birds at New York City's John F. Kennedy International Airport (JFK). Birds had been involved in several near-catastrophes at JFK. A collision between herring gulls and a passenger jet, for instance, had caused the jet's engine to explode and the aircraft to catch fire.

To reduce the risks, the Port Authority of New York and New Jersey—which operates JFK—obtained a permit from the U.S. Fish and Wildlife Service (FWS) to "take" certain birds that threatened to interfere with aircraft at JFK. The advocacy organization, Friends of Animals, challenged the issuance of this permit.

Case Analysis 45.1

Friends of Animals v. Clay

United States Court of Appeals, Second Circuit, 811 F.3d 94 (2016).

In the Language of the Court

José A. *CABRANES*, Circuit Judge.

  * * * *

BACKGROUND

The taking of migratory birds is governed by the Migratory Bird Treaty Act ("MBTA"). The MBTA, which implements a series of treaties as federal law, prohibits the taking of any bird protected by those treaties unless and except as permitted by regulations promulgated [declared] under the statute. * * * One such regulation is 50 C.F.R. [Code of Federal Regulations] Section 21.41. Under Section 21.41, FWS may issue "depredation permits" that authorize the taking (or possession or transport) of migratory birds that are causing injury to certain human interests.

Case 45.1 Continues

Case 45.1 Continued

* * * *

[Friends of Animals (FOA) filed a suit in a federal district court against William Clay, Deputy Administrator in the U.S. Department of Agriculture and others, including the U.S. Fish and Wildlife Service (FWS), challenging the issuance of the permit. The court issued a summary judgment in favor of the defendants. FOA appealed to the U.S. Court of Appeals for the Second Circuit.]

The permit * * * identifies eighteen species of migratory birds that have, in the past, compromised public safety at JFK, and authorizes the Port Authority to take a quota of birds of each species.

In addition to setting out these species-specific quotas, the challenged permit contains an "emergency-take" provision. This provision empowers the Port Authority, "in emergency situations only," to take any migratory bird (except bald eagles, golden eagles, or endangered or threatened species) that poses a "direct threat to human safety"—defined as a "threat of serious bodily injury or a risk to human life"—even if it is of a species not listed on the permit. FWS rarely includes an emergency take provision in its migratory bird permits, but—mindful of the grave risks that arise when birds congregate near aircraft—it makes an exception for airports.

DISCUSSION

FOA directs its challenge at the * * * permit's emergency-take provision. According to FOA, Section 21.41 does not authorize FWS to issue a permit that allows the emergency take of a migratory bird irrespective of its species. Instead, FOA argues, permit applicants like the Port Authority must provide species-specific information to FWS, and FWS may authorize the taking of only those species specifically listed on the permit.

Contending that FWS's alleged failure to abide by the requirements of Section 21.41 has resulted in the Port Authority's unlawful taking of a number of migratory birds, * * * FOA asks us to invalidate the operative permit as the product of agency action that was arbitrary, capricious, an abuse of discretion, or otherwise not in accordance with law.

* * * *

FWS's authority to issue depredation permits under Section 21.41 is limited in certain respects by subsections (c) and (d) of that provision. Subsection (d) provides, for instance, that a permit's duration is limited to one year. Subsection (c) sets forth conditions common to all permits, such as the prohibition of certain hunting practices and mandatory steps for disposing of birds that have been killed; it also states that depredation permits are subject to the general conditions set forth in 50 C.F.R. Part 13. Various provisions in Part 13, in turn, further hem in the agency's permitting authority. *But among the express limitations on FWS's discretion imposed by Section 21.41(c)–(d) and Part 13, we find nothing to indicate that FWS may not issue a permit that contains an emergency-take provision. Accordingly, unless some other feature of the regulatory regime counsels otherwise, we must conclude that FWS has authority to issue permits of the type challenged here.* [Emphasis added.]

FOA argues that this other feature is found in Section 21.41(b). This provision states that an application for a depredation permit must [identify] * * * "the particular species of migratory birds committing [an] injury." According to FOA, that regulation, when read in connection with Section 21.41(c)(1)—which provides that "permittees may not kill migratory birds unless specifically authorized on the permit"—makes

clear that a depredation permit may not authorize the taking of bird species not listed on the permit's face.

We disagree. Section 21.41(b) by its terms governs the conduct of applicants, not FWS, and specifies what information must be included in the permit application, not the permit itself. Indeed, the provision is styled as a direct address to applicants, to whom it gives point-by-point instructions for seeking a permit. FOA identifies no particular reason why we should read this subsection, contrary to its plain language, as a limit on FWS's authority to issue permits rather than as a means to ensure that applicants provide FWS with information germane to the permitting determination. Section 21.41(b) is a hopelessly slender reed on which to rest the argument that FWS is powerless to authorize the Port Authority to take migratory birds that threaten air safety.

Nor does the language of Section 21.41(c)(1) alter this conclusion. True, this subsection provides that permittees must "not kill migratory birds unless specifically authorized on the permit." But this is in no way inconsistent with the * * * permit's emergency-take provision. *The permit authorizes the Port Authority, in emergency situations, to "take * * * any migratory birds * * * when the migratory birds * * * are posing a direct threat to human safety."* The permit thus specifically authorizes the taking of migratory birds if certain conditions are met—and one method of taking a bird is killing it. [Emphasis added.]

* * * *

CONCLUSION

In sum, we hold that FWS did not run afoul of Section 21.41 in issuing to the Port Authority the * * * depredation permit. The * * * order of the District Court is accordingly AFFIRMED.

Legal Reasoning Questions

1. In what circumstance might the Port Authority—or anyone else—take a migratory bird without a permit and *not* be sanctioned?

2. Under the plaintiff's suggested reading of the regulation at issue in this case, what difficult choice would the Port Authority face?

3. Why is the taking of birds, or any wildlife, protected by treaty and federal law? What should be the limit to this protection?

EXHIBIT 45–1 Major Federal Environmental Statutes

POPULAR NAME	PURPOSE	STATUTE REFERENCE
Rivers and Harbors Appropriations Act	To prohibit ships and manufacturers from discharging and depositing refuse in navigable waterways.	33 U.S.C. Sections 401–418.
Federal Insecticide, Fungicide, and Rodenticide Act	To control the use of pesticides and herbicides.	7 U.S.C. Sections 136–136y.
Federal Water Pollution Control Act	To eliminate the discharge of pollutants from major sources into navigable waters.	33 U.S.C. Sections 1251–1387.
Clean Air Act	To control air pollution from mobile and stationary sources.	42 U.S.C. Sections 7401–7671q.
National Environmental Policy Act	To limit environmental harm from federal government activities.	42 U.S.C. Sections 4321–4370d.
Ocean Dumping Act	To prohibit the dumping of radiological, chemical, and biological warfare agents and high-level radioactive waste into the ocean.	16 U.S.C. Sections 1401–1445.
Endangered Species Act	To protect species that are threatened with extinction.	16 U.S.C. Sections 1531–1544.
Safe Drinking Water Act	To regulate pollutants in public drinking water systems.	42 U.S.C. Sections 300f–300j-25.
Toxic Substances Control Act	To regulate toxic chemicals and chemical compounds.	15 U.S.C. Sections 2601–2692.
Comprehensive Environmental Response, Compensation, and Liability Act	To regulate the clean-up of hazardous waste–disposal sites.	42 U.S.C. Sections 9601–9675.
Small Business Liability Relief and Brownfields Revitalization Act	To allow developers who comply with state voluntary clean-up programs to avoid federal liability for the properties that they decontaminate and develop.	42 U.S.C. Section 9628.

Environmental Impact Statements All agencies of the federal government must take environmental factors into consideration when making significant decisions. The National Environmental Policy Act[1] requires that an **environmental impact statement (EIS)** be prepared for every major federal action that significantly affects the quality of the environment. (See Exhibit 45–2.) An EIS must analyze the following:

1. The impact that the action will have on the environment.
2. Any adverse effects on the environment and alternative actions that might be taken.
3. Any irreversible effects the action might generate.

An action qualifies as "major" if it involves a substantial commitment of resources (monetary or otherwise). An action is "federal" if a federal agency has the power to control it. ■ **EXAMPLE 45.2** Development of a ski resort by a private developer on federal land may require an EIS. Construction or operation of a nuclear plant, which requires a federal permit, necessitates an EIS, as does creation of a dam as part of a federal project. ■

If an agency decides that an EIS is unnecessary, it must issue a statement supporting this conclusion. Private individuals, consumer interest groups, businesses, and others who believe that a federal agency's activities threaten the environment often use EISs as a means to challenge those activities.

---

1. 42 U.S.C. Sections 4321–4370d.

EXHIBIT 45–2 Environmental Impact Statements

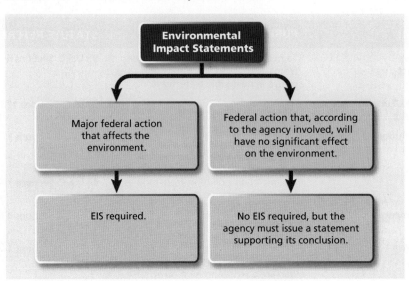

45-3 Air Pollution

Federal involvement with air pollution goes back to the 1950s and 1960s, when Congress authorized funds for air-pollution research and enacted the Clean Air Act.[2] The Clean Air Act provides the basis for issuing regulations to control multistate air pollution. It covers both mobile sources (such as automobiles and other vehicles) and stationary sources (such as electric utilities and industrial plants) of pollution.

45-3a Mobile Sources

Regulations governing air pollution from automobiles and other mobile sources specify pollution standards and establish time schedules for meeting the standards. The EPA periodically updates the pollution standards in light of new developments and data, usually reducing the amount of emissions allowed.

Reducing Emissions The Obama administration set a long-term goal of reducing emissions, including those from cars and sport utility vehicles, by 80 percent by 2050. The administration also ordered the EPA to develop national standards regulating fuel economy and

emissions for medium- and heavy-duty trucks starting with 2014 models.

Authority to Regulate Greenhouse Gases A growing concern among many scientists and others around the world is that greenhouse gases, such as carbon dioxide (CO_2), contribute to climate change. The Clean Air Act, as amended, however, does not specifically mention CO_2 emissions. Therefore, the EPA did not regulate CO_2 emissions from motor vehicles until 2009, after the Supreme Court ruled that it had the authority to do so.

■ **CASE IN POINT 45.3** Environmental groups and several states, including Massachusetts, sued the EPA in an effort to force the agency to regulate CO_2 emissions from motor vehicles. The case eventually reached the United States Supreme Court. The EPA argued that the plaintiffs lacked standing because global climate change has widespread effects, so the individual plaintiffs could not show particularized harm. Furthermore, the agency claimed that it did not have authority under the Clean Air Act to address global climate change and regulate CO_2.

The Court, however, ruled that Massachusetts had standing because its coastline, including state-owned lands, faced an imminent threat from rising sea levels purportedly caused by climate change. The Court also held that the Clean Air Act's broad definition of "air pollutant" gives the EPA authority to regulate CO_2. The Clean Air Act requires the EPA to regulate any air

---

2. 42 U.S.C. Sections 7401–7671q.

pollutants that might "endanger public health or welfare." Accordingly, the Court ordered the EPA to determine whether CO_2 was a pollutant that endangered public health.[3] ■

The EPA later concluded that greenhouse gases, including CO_2 emissions, *do* constitute a public danger. In fact, in 2015, the EPA started regulating greenhouse gas emissions from airplanes.

Controlling Climate Change In 2016, a federal district court in Oregon allowed an unprecedented lawsuit to go forward against the U.S. government for doing too little to control climate change. ■ **CASE IN POINT 45.4** A group of young people (aged eight to nineteen) filed a suit against the federal government, as well as the fossil fuel industry. The plaintiffs argued that the government has known for years that CO_2 pollution causes climate change and threatens catastrophic consequences. By failing to address the causes of this pollution, they claimed, the government has violated their constitutional rights.

The court found that the plaintiffs had alleged particular, concrete harms to young people and future generations sufficient to give them standing to pursue their claims in court. Of course, this ruling means only that the plaintiffs have met their threshold burden of establishing standing. The court simply denied the government's motion to dismiss—it did not decide the merits of the case or grant relief to the plaintiffs. Those issues have yet to be resolved.[4] ■

45–3b Stationary Sources

The Clean Air Act also authorizes the EPA to establish air-quality standards for stationary sources (such as manufacturing plants). But the act recognizes that the primary responsibility for implementing these standards rests with state and local governments. The standards are aimed at controlling hazardous air pollutants—those likely to cause death or a serious, irreversible, or incapacitating condition, such as cancer or neurological or reproductive damage.

The EPA sets primary and secondary levels of ambient standards—that is, maximum permissible levels of certain pollutants—and the states formulate plans to achieve those standards. Different standards apply depending on whether the sources of pollution are located in clean areas or polluted areas and whether they are existing sources or major new sources.

Hazardous Air Pollutants The Clean Air Act requires the EPA to list all hazardous air pollutants (HAPs) on a prioritized schedule. In all, nearly two hundred substances—including asbestos, benzene, beryllium, cadmium, mercury, and vinyl chloride—have been classified as hazardous. They are emitted from stationary sources by a variety of business activities, including smelting (melting ore to produce metal), dry cleaning, house painting, and commercial baking.

Maximum Achievable Control Technology Instead of establishing specific emissions standards for each hazardous air pollutant, the Clean Air Act requires major *new* sources[5] to use pollution-control equipment that represents the *maximum achievable control technology,* or MACT, to reduce emissions. The EPA issues guidelines as to what equipment meets this standard.[6]

45–3c Violations of the Clean Air Act

For violations of emission limits under the Clean Air Act, the EPA can assess civil penalties of up to $25,000 per day. Additional fines of up to $5,000 per day can be assessed for other violations, such as failure to maintain the required records. To penalize those who find it more cost-effective to violate the act than to comply with it, the EPA is authorized to impose a penalty equal to the violator's economic benefits from noncompliance. Persons who provide information about violators may be paid up to $10,000. Private citizens can also sue violators.

Those who knowingly violate the act, including corporate officers, may be subject to criminal penalties. For instance, knowingly making false statements or failing to report violations may be punishable by fines of up to $1 million and imprisonment for up to two years.

In the following case, the phrase "knowingly violate" was at the center of the dispute in an individual's appeal of his conviction for Clean Air Act violations.

---

3. *Massachusetts v. Environmental Protection Agency,* 549 U.S. 497, 127 S.Ct. 1438, 167 L.Ed.2d 248 (2007).
4. *Juliana v. United States,* ___ F.Supp.3d ___, 2016 WL 1442435 (D.Or. 2016).

5. The term *major new sources* includes existing sources modified by a change in a method of operation that increases emissions.
6. The EPA has also issued rules to regulate hazardous air pollutants emitted by landfills. See 40 C.F.R. Sections 60.750–60.759.

Case 45.2

United States v. O'Malley

United States Court of Appeals, Seventh Circuit, 739 F.3d 1001 (2014).

Background and Facts Duane O'Malley owned and operated Origin Fire Protection. Michael Pinski hired Origin to remove and dispose of 2,200 feet of insulation from a building Pinski owned in Kankakee, Illinois. The insulation contained asbestos, which Pinski, O'Malley, and O'Malley's employees recognized. O'Malley did not have a license to remove asbestos, and none of his employees were trained in complying with federal asbestos regulations. Nevertheless, Origin removed the debris and disposed of it at various sites, including a vacant lot where it spilled onto the soil, resulting in clean-up costs of nearly $50,000.

In a federal district court, a jury convicted O'Malley of removing, transporting, and dumping asbestos in violation of the Clean Air Act. The court sentenced him to 120 months of imprisonment, three years of supervised release, a fine of $15,000, and $47,085.70 in restitution to the Environmental Protection Agency (EPA). O'Malley appealed.

In the Language of the Court

TINDER, Circuit Judge.
* * * *

On appeal to this court, O'Malley * * * claims that because the [EPA's regulations] define "asbestos-containing material" as only six types of regulated asbestos, the government was required to prove that O'Malley knew that the asbestos in the building was one of the six forms of regulated asbestos. He asserts that the government did not present evidence to demonstrate O'Malley's knowledge of the type of asbestos in the building.
* * * *

O'Malley is correct that not all forms of asbestos are subject to regulation. The Clean Air Act [under Section 7412] authorizes the regulation of hazardous air pollutants, one of which is asbestos. "Because asbestos is not typically emitted through a conveyance designed and constructed to emit or capture it, such as a pipe or smokestack, but rather escapes from more diffuse sources such as open construction or demolition sites, EPA adopted a work-practice standard for the handling of asbestos in building demolition and renovation." * * * The work practice standard promulgated for the handling of asbestos applies only to the six types of "regulated asbestos-containing material (RACM)," [which includes "friable asbestos material"]. "Friable asbestos material" is defined as "any material containing more than 1 percent asbestos * * * that, when dry, can be crumbled, pulverized, or reduced to powder by hand pressure." Thus, there is no question that the material in [this case]—which was both friable and contained asbestos at concentrations ranging from four percent to forty-eight percent—was indeed "regulated asbestos-containing material."
* * * *

The Clean Air Act makes it a crime for any person to "knowingly violate any * * * *requirement or prohibition of* * * * *Section 7412,* * * * *including a requirement of any rule" promulgated under Section 7412.* * * * The district court instructed the jury on the knowledge elements as follows: "The government must prove * * * the defendant knew that asbestos-containing material was in the building." [Emphasis added.]

O'Malley argues that the knowledge element instruction should have required the government to prove that the defendant knew that regulated asbestos-containing material, not simply asbestos-containing material, was in the building. But this cannot be correct. * * * The phrase "knowingly violates" does not "carv[e] out an exception to the general rule that ignorance of the law is no excuse." The *mens rea* [criminal intent] required by the phrase is one that is higher than strict liability * * * . But it is certainly much lower than specific intent, especially when, as here, "dangerous * * * materials are involved," because "the probability of regulation is so great that anyone who is aware that he is in possession of them or dealing with them must be presumed to be aware of the regulation." The very fact that O'Malley was knowingly working with asbestos-containing material met the *mens rea* requirement.

Case 45.2 Continued

Decision and Remedy *The U.S. Court of Appeals for the Seventh Circuit affirmed the lower court's judgment. The appellate court disagreed with O'Malley's claim that the government was required to prove he knew the asbestos was one of the six types of regulated asbestos. "The very fact that O'Malley was knowingly working with asbestos-containing material met the* mens rea *requirement."*

Critical Thinking
- **What If the Facts Were Different?** *Suppose that O'Malley had been licensed to remove the asbestos. Would the result have been different? Why or why not?*

45–4 Water Pollution

Water pollution stems mostly from industrial, municipal, and agricultural sources. Pollutants entering streams, lakes, and oceans include organic wastes, heated water, sediments from soil runoff, nutrients (including fertilizers and human and animal wastes), and toxic chemicals and other hazardous substances.

Federal regulations governing water pollution can be traced back to the 1899 Rivers and Harbors Appropriations Act.[7] These regulations prohibited ships and manufacturers from discharging or depositing refuse in navigable waterways without a permit.[8] In 1948, Congress passed the Federal Water Pollution Control Act (FWPCA),[9] but its regulatory system and enforcement powers proved to be inadequate.

45–4a The Clean Water Act

In 1972, Congress passed amendments to the FWPCA, and the amended act became known as the Clean Water Act (CWA). The CWA established the following goals: (1) make waters safe for swimming, (2) protect fish and wildlife, and (3) eliminate the discharge of pollutants into the water. The CWA also set specific schedules, which were later extended by amendment and by the Water Quality Act.[10] Under these schedules, the EPA limits the discharge of various types of pollutants based on the technology available for controlling them.

Permit System for Point-Source Emissions The CWA established a permit system for regulating discharges from "point sources" of pollution, which include industrial, municipal (such as sewage pipes and treatment plants), and agricultural facilities.[11] Under this system, called the National Pollutant Discharge Elimination System (NPDES), any point source emitting pollutants into water must have a permit. Pollution not from point sources, such as runoff from small farms, is not subject to much regulation.

NPDES permits can be issued by the EPA and authorized state agencies and Indian tribes. The permits may be issued only if the discharge will not violate water-quality standards, and they must be reissued every five years. Although initially the NPDES system focused mainly on industrial wastewater, it was later expanded to cover stormwater discharges.

In practice, the NPDES system under the CWA includes the following elements:

1. National effluent (pollution) standards set by the EPA for each industry.
2. Water-quality standards set by the states under EPA supervision.
3. A discharge permit program that sets water-quality standards to limit pollution.
4. Special provisions for toxic chemicals and for oil spills.
5. Construction grants and loans from the federal government for publicly owned treatment works, primarily sewage treatment plants.

Standards for Equipment Regulations generally specify that the *best available control technology,* or BACT, be installed. The EPA issues guidelines as to what equipment meets this standard. Essentially, the guidelines require the most effective pollution-control equipment available.

New sources must install BACT equipment before beginning operations. Existing sources are subject to

---

7. 33 U.S.C. Sections 401–418.
8. The term *navigable waters* is interpreted today as including *intra*state lakes and streams used by interstate travelers and industries, as well as coastal and freshwater wetlands.
9. 33 U.S.C. Sections 1251–1387.
10. This act amended 33 U.S.C. Section 1251.

11. 33 U.S.C. Section 1342.

EXHIBIT 45–3 Pollution-Control Equipment Standards under the Clean Air Act and the Clean Water Act

THE CLEAN AIR ACT	THE CLEAN WATER ACT
• Major sources of pollution must use pollution-control equipment that represents the *maximum achievable control technology*, or MACT, to reduce emissions.	• New sources of pollution must install the *best available control technology*, or BACT, before beginning operations. • Existing sources must immediately install equipment that utilizes the *best practical control technology*, or BPCT, and meet a timetable for installing BACT equipment.

timetables for the installation of BACT equipment and must immediately install equipment that utilizes the *best practical control technology,* or BPCT. The EPA also issues guidelines as to what equipment meets this standard.

Exhibit 45–3 graphically illustrates the pollution-control equipment standards required under the Clean Air Act and the Clean Water Act.

The EPA must take into account many factors when issuing and updating its rules. Some provisions of the CWA instruct the EPA to weigh the cost of the technology required relative to the benefits achieved. The provision that covers power plants, however, neither requires nor prohibits a cost-benefit analysis. The question in the following case was whether the EPA could base its decision on such an analysis.

Case 45.3

Entergy Corp. v. Riverkeeper, Inc.

Supreme Court of the United States, 556 U.S. 208, 129 S.Ct. 1498, 173 L.Ed.2d 369 (2009).

Background and Facts As part of its implementation of the Clean Water Act, the Environmental Protection Agency (EPA) developed two sets of rules that apply to the cooling systems of power plants. Phase I rules require new power plants to restrict their inflow of water "to a level commensurate with that which can be attained by a closed-cycle recirculating cooling water system." Phase II rules apply "national performance standards" to more than five hundred existing plants but do not require closed-cycle systems.

The EPA had found that converting these existing facilities to closed-cycle operations would cost $3.5 billion per year. The facilities would then produce less power while burning the same amount of coal. Moreover, other technologies can attain nearly the same results as closed-cycle systems. Phase II rules also allow a variance from the national performance standards if a facility's cost of compliance "would be significantly greater than the benefits."

Environmental organizations, including Riverkeeper, Inc., challenged the Phase II regulations, arguing that existing plants should be required to convert to closed-cycle systems. The U.S. Court of Appeals for the Second Circuit issued a ruling in the plaintiffs' favor. Power-generating companies, including Entergy Corporation, appealed to the United States Supreme Court.

In the Language of the Court

Justice *SCALIA* delivered the opinion of the Court.
* * * *

In setting the Phase II national performance standards and providing for site-specific cost-benefit variances, the EPA relied on its view that [the] "best technology available" standard permits consideration of the technology's costs and of the relationship between those costs and the environmental benefits produced.

* * * The "best" technology—that which is "most advantageous"—may well be the one that produces the most of some good, here a reduction in adverse environmental impact. But "best technology" may also describe the technology that most efficiently produces some good. *In common parlance one could*

Case 45.3 Continued

certainly use the phrase "best technology" to refer to that which produces a good at the lowest per-unit cost, even if it produces a lesser quantity of that good than other available technologies. [Emphasis added.]

* * * This latter reading is [not] precluded by the statute's use of the phrase "for minimizing adverse environmental impact." *Minimizing* * * * *is a term that admits of degree and is not necessarily used to refer exclusively to the "greatest possible reduction."* [Emphasis added.]

Other provisions in the Clean Water Act also suggest the agency's interpretation. When Congress wished to mandate the greatest feasible reduction in water pollution, it did so in plain language: The provision governing the discharge of toxic pollutants into the Nation's waters requires the EPA to set "effluent limitations which shall require the elimination of discharges of all pollutants * * * ." The less ambitious goal of "minimizing adverse environmental impact" suggests, we think, that the agency retains some discretion to determine the extent of reduction that is warranted under the circumstances. That determination could plausibly involve a consideration of the benefits derived from reductions and the costs of achieving them.

* * * [Under other Clean Water Act provisions that impose standards on sources of pollution,] the EPA is instructed to consider, among other factors, "the total cost of application of technology in relation to the * * * benefits to be achieved."

* * * *

This * * * comparison of * * * statutory factors * * * leads us to the conclusion that it was well within the bounds of reasonable interpretation for the EPA to conclude that cost-benefit analysis is not categorically forbidden.

* * * *

While not conclusive, it surely tends to show that the EPA's current practice is a reasonable and hence legitimate exercise of its discretion to weigh benefits against costs that the agency has been proceeding in essentially this fashion for over 30 years.

Decision and Remedy *The United States Supreme Court concluded that the EPA had permissibly relied on a cost-benefit analysis to set national performance standards and to allow for variances from those standards. The Court reversed the lower court's judgment and remanded the case.*

Critical Thinking

- **Ethical** *In this case, aquatic organisms were most directly at risk. Is it acceptable to apply cost-benefit analyses to situations in which the lives of people are directly affected? Explain.*
- **Global** *In analyzing the costs and benefits of an action that affects the environment, should a line be drawn at a nation's borders? Why or why not?*

Wetlands The CWA prohibits the filling or dredging of **wetlands** unless a permit is obtained from the Army Corps of Engineers. The EPA defines *wetlands* as "those areas that are inundated or saturated by surface or ground water at a frequency and duration sufficient to support . . . vegetation typically adapted for life in saturated soil conditions." Wetlands are thought to be vital to the ecosystem because they filter streams and rivers and provide habitat for wildlife.

■ **CASE IN POINT 45.5** To build a home in Idaho, Michael and Chantell Sackett filled part of their residential lot with dirt and rock. A few months later, they received a compliance order from the EPA that required them to restore their property immediately or face fines of $75,000 a day. The EPA order claimed that, because their property was near a major lake, the Sacketts had polluted wetlands in violation of the Clean Water Act.

The Sacketts requested a hearing with the EPA, but it was denied. They then sued the EPA in federal district court, asserting, among other things, that the compliance order was "arbitrary and capricious" under the Administrative Procedure Act. The district court held that it could not review the EPA's compliance order because it was not a final agency action. An appellate court affirmed, but the United States Supreme Court reversed. The Court held that the Sacketts could challenge the EPA's compliance order in federal court. The government could not force them to comply with the EPA order without providing an opportunity for judicial review.[12] ■

---

12. *Sackett v. Environmental Protection Agency,* ___ U.S. ___, 132 S.Ct. 1367, 182 L.Ed.2d 367 (2012).

Violations of the Clean Water Act   Because point-source water pollution control is based on a permit system, the permits are the key to enforcement. States have primary responsibility for enforcing the permit system, subject to EPA monitoring.

Discharging emissions into navigable waters without a permit, or in violation of pollution limits under a permit, violates the CWA. Violators are subject to a variety of civil and criminal penalties. Depending on the violation, civil penalties range from $10,000 to $25,000 per day, but not more than $25,000 per violation. Lying about a violation is more serious than admitting the truth about improper discharges.

Criminal penalties apply only if a violation was intentional. Criminal penalties range from a fine of $2,500 per day and imprisonment for up to one year to a fine of $1 million and fifteen years' imprisonment. Injunctive relief and damages can also be imposed. The polluting party can be required to clean up the pollution or pay for the cost of doing so.

45–4b Drinking Water

The Safe Drinking Water Act[13] requires the EPA to set maximum levels for pollutants in public water systems. The operators of public water systems must come as close as possible to meeting the EPA's standards by using the best available technology that is economically and technologically feasible.

Under the act, each supplier of drinking water is required to send an annual statement describing the source of its water to every household it supplies. The statement must also disclose the level of any contaminants in the water and any possible health concerns associated with the contaminants.

■ **EXAMPLE 45.6** In 2014, Flint, Michigan, changed its source of drinking water from the Detroit water system to the Flint River. Detroit's water had been treated to prevent lead from leaching from aging lead pipes into the water. Flint River water was not treated, which allowed lead to leach into the water from the pipes. Flint's drinking water became contaminated with lead—a serious public health hazard. By the time Flint sent out the required EPA notices, thousands of children had been exposed to drinking water with high lead levels. Several civil lawsuits have been filed against government officials as a result of the incident, and three individuals face criminal prosecution. The city will end up paying millions to fix the problem. ■

---

13. 42 U.S.C. Sections 300f to 300j-25.

45–4c Ocean Dumping

The Marine Protection, Research, and Sanctuaries Act[14] (popularly known as the Ocean Dumping Act) regulates the transportation and dumping of pollutants into ocean waters. It prohibits the ocean dumping of any radiological, chemical, and biological warfare agents and high-level radioactive waste.

The act also established a permit program for transporting and dumping other materials, and designated certain areas as marine sanctuaries. Each violation of any provision or permit requirement in the Ocean Dumping Act may result in a civil penalty of up to $50,000. A knowing violation is a criminal offense that may result in a $50,000 fine, imprisonment for not more than a year, or both. A court may also grant an injunction to prevent an imminent or continuing violation.

45–4d Oil Pollution

When more than 10 million gallons of oil leaked into Alaska's Prince William Sound from the *Exxon Valdez* supertanker in 1989, Congress responded by passing the Oil Pollution Act.[15] (At that time, the *Exxon Valdez* disaster was the worst oil spill in U.S. history, but the British Petroleum oil spill in the Gulf of Mexico in 2010 surpassed it.)

Under the Oil Pollution Act, any oil facility, oil shipper, vessel owner, or vessel operator that discharges oil into navigable waters or onto an adjoining shore may be liable for clean-up costs and damages. The polluter can also be ordered to pay for damage to natural resources, private property, and the local economy, including the increased cost of providing public services.

45–5 Toxic Chemicals and Hazardous Waste

Originally, most environmental clean-up efforts were directed toward reducing smog and making water safe for fishing and swimming. Today, control of toxic chemicals and hazardous waste has become increasingly important. If not properly disposed of, these substances may seriously endanger human health and the environment—for instance, by contaminating public drinking water.

---

14. 16 U.S.C. Sections 1401–1445.
15. 33 U.S.C. Sections 2701–2761.

45–5a Pesticides and Herbicides

The Federal Insecticide, Fungicide, and Rodenticide Act (FIFRA)[16] regulates the use of pesticides and herbicides. These substances must be (1) registered before they can be sold, (2) certified and used only for approved applications, and (3) used in limited quantities when applied to food crops.

EPA Actions The EPA can cancel or suspend registration of substances that it has identified as harmful and can inspect the factories where the chemicals are made. A substance is deemed harmful if human exposure to the substance, including exposure through eating food, results in a risk of one in a million (or higher) of developing cancer.[17]

Violations and Penalties It is a violation of FIFRA to sell a pesticide or herbicide that is either unregistered or has had its registration canceled or suspended. It is also a violation to sell a pesticide or herbicide with a false or misleading label. For instance, it is an offense to sell a substance that has a chemical strength that is different from the concentration described on the label. It is also a violation to destroy or deface any labeling required under the act.

Penalties for commercial dealers include imprisonment for up to one year and a fine of up to $25,000 (producers can be fined up to $50,000). Farmers and other private users of pesticides or herbicides who violate the act are subject to a $1,000 fine and incarceration for up to thirty days.

Note that a state can also regulate the sale and use of federally registered pesticides. ■ **CASE IN POINT 45.7** The EPA conditionally registered Strongarm, a weed-killing pesticide made by Dow Agrosciences, LLC. Dow sold Strongarm to Texas peanut farmers. When the farmers applied it, Strongarm damaged their crops and failed to control the growth of weeds. The farmers sued Dow for violations of Texas law, but the lower courts ruled that FIFRA preempted their claims. The farmers appealed to the United States Supreme Court. The Court held that under a specific provision of FIFRA, a state can regulate the sale and use of federally registered pesticides so long as the regulation does not permit anything that FIFRA prohibits.[18] ■

45–5b Toxic Substances

The Toxic Substances Control Act[19] regulates chemicals and chemical compounds that are known to be toxic, such as asbestos and polychlorinated biphenyls (PCBs). The act also controls the introduction of new chemical compounds by requiring investigation of any possible harmful effects from these substances.

Under the act, the EPA can require that manufacturers, processors, and other entities planning to use chemicals first determine their effects on human health and the environment. The EPA can regulate substances that could pose an imminent hazard or an unreasonable risk of injury to health or the environment. The EPA can also require special labeling, limit the use of a substance, set production quotas, or prohibit the use of a substance altogether.

45–5c The Resource Conservation and Recovery Act

The Resource Conservation and Recovery Act (RCRA)[20] was Congress's response to growing concerns about the effects of hazardous waste materials on the environment. The RCRA required the EPA to determine which forms of solid waste should be considered hazardous and to establish regulations to monitor and control hazardous waste disposal.

Among other things, the act requires all producers of hazardous waste materials to label and package properly any hazardous waste to be transported. Amendments to the RCRA decrease the use of land containment in the disposal of hazardous waste and require smaller generators of hazardous waste to comply with the act.

Under the RCRA, a company may be assessed a civil penalty of up to $25,000 for each violation.[21] The penalty is based on the seriousness of the violation, the probability of harm, and the extent to which the violation deviates from RCRA requirements. Criminal penalties include fines of up to $50,000 for each day of violation, imprisonment for up to two years (in most instances), or both. Criminal fines and the time of imprisonment can be doubled for certain repeat offenders.

45–5d Superfund

The Comprehensive Environmental Response, Compensation, and Liability Act (CERCLA),[22] commonly known

---

16. 7 U.S.C. Sections 136–136y.
17. 21 U.S.C. Section 346a.
18. *Bates v. Dow Agrosciences, LLC*, 544 U.S. 431, 125 S.Ct. 1788, 161 L.Ed.2d 687 (2005).

19. 15 U.S.C. Sections 2601–2692.
20. 42 U.S.C. Sections 6901–6986.
21. 42 U.S.C. Section 6928(a).
22. 42 U.S.C. Sections 9601–9675.

as Superfund, regulates the clean-up of disposal sites in which hazardous waste is leaking into the environment. CERCLA, as amended, has four primary elements:

1. It established an information-gathering and analysis system that enables the government to identify chemical dump sites and determine the appropriate action.
2. It authorized the EPA to respond to emergencies and to arrange for the clean-up of a leaking site directly if the persons responsible fail to clean up the site.
3. It created a Hazardous Substance Response Trust Fund (also called *Superfund*) to pay for the clean-up of hazardous sites using funds obtained through taxes on certain businesses.
4. It allowed the government to recover the cost of clean-up from persons who were (even remotely) responsible for hazardous substance releases.

Potentially Responsible Parties Superfund provides that when a release or a potential release of hazardous chemicals from a site occurs, the following persons may be held responsible for cleaning up the site:

1. The person who generated the wastes disposed of at the site.
2. The person who transported the waste to the site.
3. The person who owned or operated the site at the time of the disposal.
4. The current owner or operator.

A person falling within one of these categories is referred to as a **potentially responsible party (PRP).** If the PRPs do not clean up the site, the EPA can clean up the site and recover the clean-up costs from the PRPs.

Strict Liability of PRPs. Superfund imposes strict liability on PRPs, and that liability cannot be avoided through transfer of ownership. Thus, selling a site where hazardous wastes were disposed of does not relieve the seller of liability, and the buyer also becomes liable for the clean-up.

Liability also extends to businesses that merge with or buy corporations that have violated CERCLA. A parent corporation is not automatically liable for the violations of its subsidiary. It can be held liable, however, if the subsidiary was merely a shell company or if the parent corporation participated in or controlled the facility.[23]

Joint and Several Liability of PRPs. Liability under Superfund is usually joint and several. In other words, a PRP who generated *only a fraction of the hazardous waste* disposed of at a site may nevertheless be liable for *all* of

the clean-up costs. CERCLA authorizes a party who has incurred clean-up costs to bring a "contribution action" against any other person who is liable or potentially liable for a percentage of the costs.

Minimizing Liability One way for a business to minimize its potential liability under Superfund is to conduct environmental compliance audits of its own operations regularly. That is, the business can investigate its own operations and property to determine whether any environmental hazards exist.

The EPA encourages companies to conduct self-audits and promptly detect, disclose, and correct wrongdoing. Companies that do so are subject to lighter penalties for violations of environmental laws. (Fines may be reduced as much as 75 percent.)

In addition, under EPA guidelines, the EPA will waive all fines if a small company corrects environmental violations within 180 days after being notified of the violations (or 360 days if pollution-prevention techniques are involved). The policy does not apply to criminal violations of environmental laws, though, or to violations that pose a significant threat to public health, safety, or the environment.

Defenses There are a few defenses to liability under CERCLA. The most important is the *innocent landowner defense*.[24] This defense may protect a landowner who acquired the property after it was used for hazardous waste disposal.

The landowner claiming the innocent landowner defense must not have had a contractual or employment relationship with the person (or other entity) who owned the land when the contamination occurred. Because land is often transferred by contract, it would seem that this defense would not normally be available. However, a landowner who can show that he or she had no knowledge of the hazardous waste disposal at the time of purchase can still assert the defense.

To succeed, the landowner must show that at the time the property was acquired, she or he had no reason to know that it had been used for hazardous waste disposal. The landowner must also show that at the time of the purchase, she or he undertook "all appropriate inquiries." That is, he or she investigated the previous ownership and uses of the property to determine whether there was reason for concern about hazardous substances. In effect, then, this defense protects only property owners who took precautions and investigated the possibility of environmental hazards before buying the property.

---

23. The landmark case establishing the liability of a parent corporation under CERCLA is *United States v. Bestfoods*, 524 U.S. 51, 118 S.Ct. 1876, 141 L.Ed.2d 43 (1998).

24. 42 U.S.C. Section 9601(35)(B).

Reviewing: Environmental Protection

Residents of Lake Caliopa, Minnesota, began noticing an unusually high number of lung ailments among the local population. Several concerned citizens pooled their resources and commissioned a study to compare the frequency of these health conditions in Lake Caliopa with national averages. The study concluded that residents of Lake Caliopa experienced four to seven times the rate of frequency of asthma, bronchitis, and emphysema as the population nationwide.

During the study period, citizens began expressing concerns about the large volume of smog emitted by the Cotton Design apparel manufacturing plant on the outskirts of town. The plant had a production facility two miles east of town beside the Tawakoni River and employed seventy full-time workers. Just downstream on the Tawakoni River, the city of Lake Caliopa operated a public water works facility, which supplied all city residents with water.

The Minnesota Pollution Control Agency required Cotton Design to install new equipment to control air and water pollution. Later, citizens sued Cotton Design for various respiratory ailments allegedly caused or compounded by smog from Cotton Design's factory. Using the information presented in the chapter, answer the following questions.

1. Under the common law, what would each plaintiff be required to identify in order to be given relief by the court?
2. What standard for limiting emissions into the air does Cotton Design's pollution-control equipment have to meet?
3. If Cotton Design's emissions violated the Clean Air Act, how much can the EPA assess in fines per day?
4. What information must the city send to every household that it supplies with water?

Debate This . . .   *The courts should reject all cases in which the wetlands in question do not consist of actual bodies of water that exist during the entire year.*

Terms and Concepts

environmental impact statement (EIS) 863	potentially responsible party (PRP) 872	wetlands 869
nuisance 860	toxic tort 860	

Issue Spotters

1. Resource Refining Company's plant emits smoke and fumes. Resource's operation includes a short railway system, and trucks enter and exit the grounds continuously. Constant vibrations from the trains and trucks rattle nearby residential neighborhoods. The residents sue Resource. Are there any reasons why the court might refuse to issue an injunction against Resource's operation? Explain. (See *Common Law Actions*.)

2. ChemCorp generates hazardous wastes from its operations. Disposal Trucking Company transports those wastes to Eliminators, Inc., which owns a site for hazardous waste disposal. Eliminators sells the property on which the disposal site is located to Fluid Properties, Inc. If the Environmental Protection Agency cleans up the site, from whom can it recover the cost? (See *Toxic Chemicals and Hazardous Waste*.)

• **Check your answers to the Issue Spotters against the answers provided in Appendix D at the end of this text.**

Business Scenarios

45–1. The Clean Water Act. Fruitade, Inc., is a processor of a soft drink called Freshen Up. Fruitade uses returnable bottles, which it cleans with a special acid to allow for further beverage processing. The acid is diluted with water and then allowed to pass into a navigable stream. Fruitade crushes its broken bottles and throws the crushed glass into the stream. Discuss fully any environmental laws that Fruitade has violated. (See *Water Pollution*.)

45–2. Environmental Protection. Moonbay is a home-building corporation that primarily develops retirement communities. Farmtex owns a number of feedlots in Sunny Valley. Moonbay purchases 20,000 acres of farmland in the same area and begins building and selling homes on this acreage. In the meantime, Farmtex continues to expand its feedlot business, and eventually only 500 feet separate the two operations.

Because of the odor and flies from the feedlots, Moonbay finds it difficult to sell the homes in its development. Moonbay wants to enjoin (prevent) Farmtex from operating its feedlot in the vicinity of the retirement home development. Under what common law theory would Moonbay file this action? Has Farmtex violated any federal environmental laws? Discuss. (See *Common Law Actions*.)

Business Case Problems

45–3. Spotlight on the Grand Canyon—Environmental Impact Statement. The U.S. National Park Service

(NPS) manages the Grand Canyon National Park in Arizona under a management plan that is subject to periodic review. In 2006, after nine years of background work and the completion of a comprehensive environmental impact statement, the NPS issued a new management plan for the park. The plan allowed for the continued use of rafts on the Colorado River, which runs through the Grand Canyon. The number of rafts was limited, however. Several environmental groups criticized the plan because they felt that it still allowed too many rafts on the river. The groups asked a federal appellate court to overturn the plan, claiming that it violated the wilderness status of the national park. When can a federal court overturn a determination by an agency such as the NPS? Explain. [*River Runners for Wilderness v. Martin*, 593 F.3d 1064 (9th Cir. 2010)] (See *Federal, State, and Local Regulations*.)

45–4. Superfund. A by-product of phosphate fertilizer production is pyrite waste, which contains arsenic and lead. From 1884 to 1906, seven phosphate fertilizer plants operated on a forty-three-acre site in Charleston, South Carolina. Planters Fertilizer & Phosphate Co. bought the site in 1906 and continued to make fertilizer. In 1966, Planters sold the site to Columbia Nitrogen Corp. (CNC), which also operated the fertilizer plants. In 1985, CNC sold the site to James Holcombe and J. Henry Fair. Holcombe and Fair subdivided and sold the site to Allwaste Tank Cleaning Inc., Robin Hood Container Express, the city of Charleston, and Ashley II of Charleston, Inc. Ashley spent almost $200,000 cleaning up the contaminated soil. Who can be held liable for the cost? Why? [*PCS Nitrogen Inc. v. Ashley II of Charleston LLC*, 714 F.3d 161 (4th Cir. 2013)] (See *Toxic Chemicals and Hazardous Waste*.)

45–5. Business Case Problem with Sample Answer—Environmental Impact Statements. The U.S. Forest Ser-

vice (USFS) proposed a travel management plan (TMP) for the Beartooth Ranger District in the Pryor and Absaroka Mountains in the Custer National Forest of southern Montana. The TMP would convert unauthorized user-created routes within the wilderness to routes authorized for motor vehicle use. It would also permit off-road "dispersed vehicle camping" within 300 feet of the routes, with some seasonal restrictions. The TMP would ban cross-country motorized travel outside the designated routes. Is an environmental impact statement required before

the USFS implements the TMP? If so, what aspects of the environment should the USFS consider in preparing it? Discuss. [*Pryors Coalition v. Weldon*, 551 Fed.Appx. 426 (9th Cir. 2014)] (See *Federal, State, and Local Regulations*.)

- **For a sample answer to Problem 45–5, go to Appendix E at the end of this text.**

45–6. The Clean Water Act. ICG Hazard, LLC, operates the Thunder Ridge surface coal mine in Leslie County, Kentucky, under a National Pollutant Discharge Elimination System permit issued by the Kentucky Division of Water (KDOW). As part of the operation, ICG discharges selenium into the surrounding water. Selenium is a naturally occurring element that endangers aquatic life once it reaches a certain concentration. KDOW knew when it issued the permit that mines in the area could produce selenium but did not specify discharge limits for the element in ICG's permit. Instead, the agency imposed a one-time monitoring requirement, which ICG met. Does ICG's discharge of selenium violate the Clean Water Act? Explain. [*Sierra Club v. ICG Hazard, LLC*, 781 F.3d 281 (6th Cir. 2015)] (See *Water Pollution*.)

45–7. Special Case Analysis—Environmental Regulatory Agencies. Go to Case Analysis 45.1, *Friends of Animals v. Clay*. Read the excerpt and answer the following questions.

(a) Issue: What regulation was at issue in this case? What activity does it regulate?

(b) Rule of Law: What rule of statutory interpretation did the court apply to construe this regulation?

(c) Applying the Rule of Law: How did the plaintiff want the regulation to be interpreted? What was the court's response?

(d) Conclusion: What were the results of the court's interpretation of the regulation?

45–8. A Question of Ethics—Clean Air Act. *In the Clean Air Act, Congress allowed California, which has particular problems with clean air, to adopt its own standard for emissions from cars and trucks. California's standard is subject to the approval of the Environmental Protection Agency (EPA) based on certain criteria. Congress also allowed other states to adopt California's standard after the EPA's approval.*

In 2004, in an effort to address climate change, the California Air Resources Board amended the state's standard to attain "the maximum feasible and cost-effective reduction of GHG [greenhouse gas] emissions from motor vehicles." The regulation, which applies to new passenger vehicles and light-duty trucks for 2009 and later, imposes decreasing limits on emissions of carbon dioxide through 2016. While EPA approval was pending, Vermont and other states adopted similar standards.

Green Mountain Chrysler Plymouth Dodge Jeep and other auto dealers, automakers, and associations of automakers filed a suit in a federal district court against George Crombie (then the secretary of the Vermont Agency of Natural Resources) and others, seeking relief from the state regulations. [Green Mountain Chrysler Plymouth Dodge Jeep v. Crombie, 508 F.Supp.2d 295 (D.Vt. 2007)] (See *Air Pollution.*)

(a) Under the Environmental Policy and Conservation Act (EPCA) of 1975, the National Highway Traffic Safety Administration sets fuel economy standards for new cars. The plaintiffs argued, among other things, that the EPCA, which prohibits states from adopting separate fuel economy standards, preempts Vermont's GHG regulation. Do the GHG rules equate to the fuel economy standards? Discuss.

(b) Do Vermont's rules tread on the efforts of the federal government to address climate change internationally? Who should regulate GHG emissions? The federal government? The state governments? Both? Neither? Why?

(c) The plaintiffs claimed that they would go bankrupt if they were forced to adhere to the state's GHG standards. Should they be granted relief on this basis? Does history support their claim? Explain.

Legal Reasoning Group Activity

45–9. Clean-Up Costs. It has been estimated that for every dollar spent cleaning up hazardous waste sites, administrative agencies spend seven dollars in overhead. (See *Toxic Chemicals and Hazardous Waste.*)

(a) The first group will list and explain possible ways to trim these administrative costs.

(b) The second group will evaluate whether the laws pertaining to hazardous waste clean-up can or should be changed to reduce the costs to government.

CHAPTER 46

Antitrust Law

After the Civil War (1861–1865), the American public became increasingly concerned about declining competition in the marketplace. Large corporate enterprises were attempting to reduce or eliminate competition by legally tying themselves together in *business trusts*.

The most famous trust was the Standard Oil trust of the late 1800s. Participants in the trust transferred their stock to a trustee. The trustee then fixed prices, controlled production, and established exclusive geographic markets for all of the oil companies that were members of the trust. Some observers began to argue that the trust wielded so much economic power that corporations outside the trust could not compete effectively.

Eventually, legislators at both the state and the federal level began to enact laws to rein in the trusts. Hence, the laws regulating economic competition in the United States today are referred to as **antitrust laws.** At the national level, antitrust legislation began when Congress passed the Interstate Commerce Act[1] in 1887, followed by the Sherman Antitrust Act[2] in 1890. In 1914, Congress passed the Clayton Act[3] and the Federal Trade Commission Act.[4] We examine these major federal antitrust statutes in this chapter.

The purpose of antitrust legislation was—and still is—to foster competition. Behind these laws lies our society's belief that competition leads to lower prices, better products, a wider selection of goods, and more product information.

---

1. 49 U.S.C. Sections 501–526

2. 15 U.S.C. Sections 1–7.
3. 15 U.S.C. Sections 12–27.
4. 15 U.S.C. Sections 41–58a.

46–1 The Sherman Antitrust Act

The author of the Sherman Antitrust Act, Senator John Sherman, was the brother of the famed Civil War general William Tecumseh Sherman. He was also a recognized financial authority. He had been concerned for years about what he saw as diminishing competition within U.S. industry and the emergence of monopolies. He told Congress that the Sherman Act "does not announce a new principle of law, but applies old and well-recognized principles of the common law."[5]

Indeed, today's antitrust laws are the direct descendants of common law actions intended to limit **restraints of trade** (agreements between or among firms that have the effect of reducing competition in the marketplace). Such actions date to the fifteenth century in England. The common law was not always consistent, however, and had not been effective in curbing the trusts. That is why Sherman proposed the Sherman Antitrust Act, often simply called the Sherman Act.

---

5. 21 *Congressional Record* 2456 (1890).

46–1a Major Provisions of the Sherman Act

Sections 1 and 2 contain the main provisions of the Sherman Act:

1. Every contract, combination in the form of trust or otherwise, or conspiracy, in restraint of trade or commerce among the several States, or with foreign nations, is hereby declared to be illegal [and is a felony punishable by fine and/or imprisonment].

2. Every person who shall monopolize, or attempt to monopolize, or combine or conspire with any other person or persons, to monopolize any part of the trade or commerce among the several States, or with foreign nations, shall be deemed guilty of a felony [and is similarly punishable].

46–1b Differences between Section 1 and Section 2

The two sections of the Sherman Act are quite different. Section 1 requires two or more persons, because a person cannot contract, combine, or conspire alone. Thus, the essence of the illegal activity is *the act of joining together*. Section 2, though, can apply either to one person or to two or more persons because it refers to "every person." Thus, unilateral conduct can result in a violation of Section 2.

It follows that the cases brought to the courts under Section 1 of the Sherman Act differ from those brought under Section 2. Section 1 cases are often concerned with whether an agreement (written or oral) leads to a restraint of trade. Section 2 cases deal with the structure of a monopoly that exists in the marketplace.

The term **monopoly** generally is used to describe a market in which there is a single seller or a very limited number of sellers. Whereas Section 1 focuses on agreements that are restrictive—that is, agreements that have a wrongful purpose—Section 2 looks at the so-called misuse of **monopoly power** in the marketplace. Monopoly power exists when a firm has an extreme amount of **market power**—the ability to affect the market price of its product.

Both Section 1 and Section 2 seek to curtail market practices that result in undesired monopoly pricing and output behavior. For a case to be brought under Section 2, however, the "threshold" or "necessary" amount of monopoly power must already exist. We illustrate the different requirements for violating these two sections of the Sherman Act in Exhibit 46–1.

46–1c Jurisdictional Requirements

The Sherman Act applies only to restraints that have a significant impact on interstate commerce. Courts have generally held that any activity that substantially affects interstate commerce falls within the scope of the Sherman Act. As will be discussed later in this chapter, the Sherman Act also extends to U.S. nationals abroad who are engaged in activities that affect U.S. foreign commerce.

Federal courts have exclusive jurisdiction over antitrust cases brought under the Sherman Act. State laws regulate local restraints on competition, and state courts decide claims brought under those laws.

46–2 Section 1 of the Sherman Act

The underlying assumption of Section 1 of the Sherman Act is that society's welfare is harmed if rival firms are permitted to join in an agreement that consolidates their market power or otherwise restrains competition. The types of trade restraints that Section 1 of the Sherman Act prohibits generally fall into two broad categories: *horizontal restraints* and *vertical restraints,* both of which will be discussed shortly. First, though, we look at the rules that the courts may apply when assessing the anticompetitive impact of alleged restraints of trade.

46–2a *Per Se* Violations versus the Rule of Reason

Some restraints are so substantially anticompetitive that they are deemed ***per se* violations**—illegal *per se* (inherently)—under Section 1. Other agreements, however, even though they result in enhanced market power, do not *unreasonably* restrain trade and are therefore lawful. Using the **rule of reason,** the courts analyze anticompetitive agreements that allegedly violate Section 1 of the Sherman Act to determine whether they actually constitute reasonable restraints of trade.

Rationale for the Rule of Reason The need for a rule-of-reason analysis of some agreements in restraint of trade is obvious. If the rule of reason had not been

EXHIBIT 46–1 Required Elements of a Sherman Act Violation

SECTION 1 VIOLATION REQUIREMENTS	SECTION 2 VIOLATION REQUIREMENTS
1. An agreement between two or more parties that 2. Unreasonably restrains competition and 3. Affects interstate commerce.	1. The possession of monopoly power in the relevant market, and 2. The willful acquisition or maintenance of that power as distinguished from its growth or development as a consequence of a superior product, business acumen, or historic accident.

developed, almost any business agreement could conceivably be held to violate the Sherman Act. United States Supreme Court Justice Louis Brandeis effectively phrased this sentiment in *Chicago Board of Trade v. United States,* a case decided in 1918:

> Every agreement concerning trade, every regulation of trade, restrains. To bind, to restrain, is of their very essence. The true test of legality is whether the restraint imposed is such as merely regulates and perhaps thereby promotes competition or whether it is such as may suppress or even destroy competition.[6]

Factors That Courts Consider When analyzing an alleged Section 1 violation under the rule of reason, a court will consider the following factors:

1. The purpose of the agreement.
2. The parties' ability to implement the agreement to achieve that purpose.
3. The effect or potential effect of the agreement on competition.
4. Whether the parties could have relied on less restrictive means to achieve their purpose.

■ **CASE IN POINT 46.1** A group of consumers sued NBC Universal, the Walt Disney Company, and other broadcasters, as well as cable and satellite distributors. The consumers claimed that the bundling together of high-demand and low-demand television channels in cable and satellite programming packages violates the Sherman Act. Bundling forces consumers to pay for channels they do not watch to have access to channels they watch regularly.

The consumers argued that the defendants, through their control of high-demand programming, exercised market power that made it impossible for any distributor to offer unbundled programs. A federal appellate court ruled in favor of the defendants and dismissed the case. The court reasoned that the Sherman Act applies to actions that diminish competition and that the bundling of channels does not injure competition.[7] ■

46–2b Horizontal Restraints

The term **horizontal restraint** is encountered frequently in antitrust law. A horizontal restraint is any agreement that in some way restrains competition between rival firms competing in the same market. Horizontal restraints may include price-fixing, group boycotts, market divisions, and trade associations.

Price Fixing Any **price-fixing agreement**—an agreement among competitors to fix prices—constitutes a *per se* violation of Section 1. The agreement on price need not be explicit. As long as it restricts output or artificially fixes price, it violates the law.

The Reason Behind the Agreement Is Not a Defense. A price-fixing agreement is always a violation of Section 1, even if there are good reasons behind it. ■ **CASE IN POINT 46.2** In a classic price-fixing case, independent oil producers in Texas and Louisiana were caught between falling demand due to the Great Depression of the 1930s and increasing supply from newly discovered oil fields. A group of the major refining companies agreed to buy "distress" gasoline (excess supplies) from the independents so as to dispose of it in an "orderly manner." Although there was no explicit agreement as to price, it was clear that the purpose of the agreement was to limit the supply of gasoline on the market and thereby raise prices.

There may have been good reasons for the agreement. Nonetheless, the United States Supreme Court recognized the potentially adverse effects that such an agreement could have on open and free competition. The Court held that the reasonableness of a price-fixing agreement is never a defense. Any agreement that restricts output or artificially fixes price is a *per se* violation of Section 1.[8] ■

Price-Fixing Cartels Today. Price-fixing cartels (groups) are still commonplace in today's business world, particularly among global companies. The U.S. government actively pursues companies that it suspects of being involved in price-fixing cartels. International price-fixing cartels have been alleged in numerous industries, including air freight, auto parts, computer monitors, digital commerce, and drug manufacturers.

■ **CASE IN POINT 46.3** After Amazon.com released the Kindle e-book reader, it began selling e-book downloads at $9.99 (lower than the actual cost) and made up the difference by selling more Kindles. When the iPad entered the e-book scene, Apple and some book publishers agreed to use Apple's "agency" model, which Apple was already using for games and apps. The agency model allowed the book publishers to set their own prices while Apple kept 30 percent as a commission.

The U.S. government sued Apple and the publishers for price fixing. Because the publishers involved in the arrangement chose prices that were relatively similar, the government argued that price fixing was evident

---

6. 246 U.S. 231, 38 S.Ct. 242, 62 L.Ed. 683 (1918).
7. *Brantley v. NBC Universal, Inc.,* 675 F.3d 1192 (9th Cir. 2012).

8. *United States v. Socony-Vacuum Oil Co.,* 310 U.S. 150, 60 S.Ct. 811, 84 L.Ed. 1129 (1940).

and "would not have occurred without the conspiracy among the defendants." Ultimately, a federal appellate court held that Apple's agreement with publishers to raise e-book prices was a *per se* illegal price-fixing conspiracy. As a result, Apple was ordered to pay $400 million to consumers and $50 million in attorneys' fees.[9] ■

Group Boycotts A **group boycott** is an agreement by two or more sellers to refuse to deal with (that is, to boycott) a particular person or firm. Because they involve concerted action, group boycotts have been held to constitute *per se* violations of Section 1 of the Sherman Act.

To prove a violation of Section 1, the plaintiff must demonstrate that the boycott or joint refusal to deal was undertaken with the intention of eliminating competition or preventing entry into a given market. Although most boycotts are illegal, a few, such as group boycotts against a supplier for political reasons, may be protected under the First Amendment right to freedom of expression.

Horizontal Market Division It is a *per se* violation of Section 1 of the Sherman Act for competitors to divide up territories or customers. ■ **EXAMPLE 46.4** Axm Electronics Basics, Halprin Servo Supplies, and Aicarus Prime Electronics compete against each other in the states of Kansas, Nebraska, and Oklahoma. The three firms agree that Axm will sell products only in Kansas, Halprin will sell only in Nebraska, and Aicarus will sell only in Oklahoma.

This concerted action violates Section 1 of the Sherman Act. It reduces marketing costs and allows all three firms (assuming there is no other competition) to raise the price of the goods sold in their respective states. The same violation would take place if the three firms divided up their customers by class rather than region. They might agree that Axm would sell only to institutional purchasers (such as governments and schools) in all three states, Halprin only to wholesalers, and Aicarus only to retailers. The result would be the same. ■

Trade Associations Businesses in the same general industry or profession frequently organize trade associations to pursue common interests. A trade association may engage in various joint activities, such as exchanging information, representing the members' business interests before governmental bodies, and conducting advertising campaigns. Trade associations also frequently are involved in setting regulatory standards to govern the industry or profession.

Generally, the rule of reason is applied to many of these horizontal actions. If a court finds that a trade association practice or agreement that restrains trade is sufficiently beneficial both to the association and to the public, it may deem the restraint reasonable.

In *concentrated industries,* however, trade associations can be, and have been, used as a means to facilitate anticompetitive actions, such as fixing prices or allocating markets. A **concentrated industry** is one in which either a single firm or a small number of firms control a large percentage of market sales. When trade association agreements have substantially anticompetitive effects, a court will consider them to be in violation of Section 1 of the Sherman Act.

Joint Ventures Joint ventures undertaken by competitors are also subject to antitrust laws. If a joint venture does not involve price fixing or market divisions, the agreement will be analyzed under the rule of reason. Whether the joint undertaking violates Section 1 will then depend on the factors stated earlier in this chapter. A court will look at the venture's purpose, the potential benefits relative to the likely harms, and whether there are less restrictive alternatives for achieving the same goals.

46–2c Vertical Restraints

A **vertical restraint** of trade results from an agreement between firms at different levels in the manufacturing and distribution process. In contrast to horizontal relationships, which occur at the same level of operation, vertical relationships encompass the entire chain of production.

The chain of production normally includes the purchase of inventory, basic manufacturing, distribution to wholesalers, and eventual sale of a product at the retail level. For some products, these distinct phases are carried on by different firms. In other instances, a single firm carries out two or more of the separate functional phases. Such enterprises are said to be **vertically integrated firms.**

Even though firms operating at different functional levels are not in direct competition with one another, they are in competition with other firms. Thus, agreements between firms standing in a vertical relationship may affect competition. Some vertical restraints are *per se* violations of Section 1. Others are judged under the rule of reason.

Territorial or Customer Restrictions In arranging for the distribution of its products, a manufacturing firm often wishes to insulate dealers from direct

---

9. *United States v. Apple, Inc.,* 791 F.3d 290 (2d Cir. 2015). Apple had previously agreed to settle the case for these amounts if its appeal was unsuccessful.

competition with other dealers selling its products. To do so, the manufacturer may institute territorial restrictions or attempt to prohibit wholesalers or retailers from reselling the products to certain classes of buyers, such as competing retailers.

May Have Legitimate Purpose. A firm may have legitimate reasons for imposing territorial or customer restrictions. For instance, an electronics manufacturer may wish to prevent a dealer from reducing costs and undercutting rivals by offering its products without promotion or customer service. In this situation, the cost-cutting dealer reaps the benefits (sales of the product) paid for by other dealers who undertake promotion and arrange for customer service. By not providing customer service (and relying on a nearby dealer to provide these services), the cost-cutting dealer may also harm the manufacturer's reputation.

Judged under the Rule of Reason. Territorial and customer restrictions were once considered *per se* violations of Section 1.[10] In 1977, the United States Supreme Court held that they should be judged under the rule of reason. ■ **CASE IN POINT 46.5** The Supreme Court case involved GTE Sylvania, Inc., a manufacturer of television sets. Sylvania limited the number of retail franchises that it granted in any given geographic area. It also required each franchisee to sell only Sylvania products from the location at which it was franchised. Sylvania retained sole discretion to increase the number of retailers in an area.

When Sylvania decided to open a new franchise, it terminated the franchise of Continental T.V., Inc., an existing franchisee in that area that would have been in competition with the new franchise. Continental filed a lawsuit claiming that Sylvania's vertically restrictive franchise system violated Section 1 of the Sherman Act. The United States Supreme Court found that "vertical restrictions promote interbrand competition by allowing the manufacturer to achieve certain efficiencies in the distribution of his products." Therefore, Sylvania's vertical system, which was not price restrictive, did not constitute a *per se* violation of Section 1 of the Sherman Act.[11] ■

The decision in the *Continental* case marked a definite shift from rigid characterization of territorial and customer restrictions to a more flexible, economic analysis

of these vertical restraints under the rule of reason. This rule is still applied in most vertical restraint cases.

Resale Price Maintenance Agreements An agreement between a manufacturer and a distributor or retailer in which the manufacturer specifies what the retail prices of its products must be is known as a **resale price maintenance agreement.** Such agreements were once considered to be *per se* violations of Section 1 of the Sherman Act.

Today, however, both *maximum* resale price maintenance agreements and *minimum* resale price maintenance agreements are judged under the rule of reason.[12] The setting of a maximum price that retailers and distributors can charge for a manufacturer's products may sometimes increase competition and benefit consumers.

46–3 Section 2 of the Sherman Act

Section 1 of the Sherman Act proscribes certain concerted, or joint, activities that restrain trade. In contrast, Section 2 condemns "every person who shall monopolize, or attempt to monopolize." Thus, two distinct types of behavior are subject to sanction under Section 2: *monopolization* and *attempts to monopolize.*

One tactic that may be involved in either offense is predatory pricing. **Predatory pricing** occurs when one firm (the predator) attempts to drive its competitors from the market by selling its product at prices substantially *below* the normal costs of production. Once the competitors are eliminated, the predator presumably will raise its prices far above their competitive levels to recapture its losses and earn higher profits.

46–3a Monopolization

The United States Supreme Court has defined **monopolization** as involving the following two elements:

1. The possession of monopoly power in the relevant market.
2. "The willful acquisition or maintenance of the power as distinguished from growth or development as a

---

10. See *United States v. Arnold, Schwinn & Co.*, 388 U.S. 365, 87 S.Ct. 1856, 18 L.Ed.2d 1249 (1967).
11. *Continental T.V., Inc. v. GTE Sylvania, Inc.*, 433 U.S. 36, 97 S.Ct. 2549, 53 L.Ed.2d 568 (1977).

12. The United States Supreme Court ruled that maximum resale price agreements should be judged under the rule of reason in *State Oil Co. v. Khan*, 522 U.S. 3, 118 S.Ct. 275, 139 L.Ed.2d 199 (1997). In *Leegin Creative Leather Products, Inc. v. PSKS, Inc.*, 551 U.S. 877, 127 S.Ct. 2705, 168 L.Ed.2d 623 (2007), the Supreme Court found that the rule of reason also applies to minimum resale price agreements.

consequence of a superior product, business acumen, or historic accident."[13]

To establish a violation of Section 2, a plaintiff must prove both of these elements—monopoly power and an *intent* to monopolize.

Defining Monopoly Power The Sherman Act does not define *monopoly*. In economic theory, monopoly refers to control of a specific market by a single entity. It is well established in antitrust law, however, that a firm may be a monopolist even though it is not the sole seller in a market.

Additionally, size alone does not determine whether a firm is a monopoly. ■ **EXAMPLE 46.6** A "mom and pop" grocery located in the isolated town of Happy Camp, Idaho, is a monopolist if it is the only grocery serving that particular market. Size in relation to the market is what matters, because monopoly involves the power to affect prices. ■

Proving Monopoly Power Monopoly power can be proved by direct evidence that the firm used its power to control prices and restrict output.[14] Usually, though, there is not enough evidence to show that the firm intentionally controlled prices, so the plaintiff has to offer indirect, or circumstantial, evidence of monopoly power.

To prove monopoly power indirectly, the plaintiff must show that the firm has a dominant share of the relevant market and that there are significant barriers for new competitors entering that market. ■ **CASE IN POINT 46.7** DuPont manufactures and sells para-aramid fiber, a synthetic fiber used to make body armor, fiber-optic cables, and tires, among other things. Although several companies around the world manufacture this fiber, only three sell in the U.S. market—DuPont (based in the United States), Teijin (based in the Netherlands), and Kolon Industries, Inc. (based in Korea). DuPont is the industry leader, and at times has produced 60 percent of all para-aramid fibers purchased in the United States.

After DuPont brought suit against Kolon for theft and misappropriation of trade secrets, Kolon counterclaimed that DuPont had illegally monopolized and attempted to monopolize the U.S. para-aramid market in violation of Section 2. Kolon claimed that, to deter competition, DuPont had illegally used multiyear supply agreements for all of its high-volume para-aramid customers. A

federal appellate court, however, found that there was insufficient proof that DuPont had possessed monopoly power in the U.S. market during the relevant time period (between 2006 and 2009). Additionally, the court concluded that Kolon had not shown that the supply agreements foreclosed competition. Therefore, the court held in favor of DuPont on the antitrust claims.[15] ■

Relevant Market Before a court can determine whether a firm has a dominant market share, it must define the relevant market. The relevant market consists of two elements: (1) a relevant product market and (2) a relevant geographic market.

Relevant Product Market. The relevant product market includes all products that have identical attributes (all brands of tea, for instance), as well as products that are reasonably interchangeable with them. Products are considered reasonably interchangeable if consumers treat them as acceptable substitutes. For instance, tea and coffee are reasonably interchangeable, so they may be included in the same relevant product market.

Establishing the relevant product market is often the key issue in monopolization cases because the way the market is defined may determine whether a firm has monopoly power. When the product market is defined narrowly, the degree of a firm's market power appears greater.

■ **EXAMPLE 46.8** White Whale Apps acquires Springleaf Apps, its main competitor in nationwide Android-based mobile phone apps. White Whale maintains that the relevant product market consists of all online retailers of mobile phone apps. The Federal Trade Commission (FTC), however, argues that the relevant product market consists of retailers that sell only apps for Android mobile phones. Under the FTC's narrower definition, White Whale can be seen to have a dominant share of the relevant product market. Thus, the FTC can take appropriate actions against White Whale. ■

In the following case, the FTC alleged that the leading U.S. producer of domestic ductile iron pipe fittings sought to maintain monopoly power in violation of antitrust law. The FTC filed this action under Section 5 of the Federal Trade Commission Act. Section 5, like Section 2 of the Sherman Act, requires proof of both the possession of monopoly power in the relevant market and the willful acquisition or maintenance of that power.

---

13. *United States v. Grinnell Corp.*, 384 U.S. 563, 86 S.Ct. 1698, 16 L.Ed.2d 778 (1966).
14. See, for example, *Broadcom Corp. v. Qualcomm, Inc.*, 501 F.3d 297 (3d Cir. 2007).
15. *Kolon Industries, Inc. v. E.I. DuPont de Nemours & Co.*, 748 F.3d 160 (4th Cir. 2014).

McWane, Inc. v. Federal Trade Commission

United States Court of Appeals, Eleventh Circuit, 783 F.3d 814 (2015).

In the Language of the Court

MARCUS, Circuit Judge:

* * * *

* * * Pipe fittings join together pipes and help direct the flow of pressurized water in pipeline systems. They are sold primarily to municipal water authorities and their contractors. Although there are several thousand unique configurations of fittings (different shapes, sizes, coatings, etc.), approximately 80% of the demand is for about 100 commonly used fittings.

Fittings are commodity products produced to American Water Works Association ("AWWA") standards, and any fitting that meets AWWA specifications is interchangeable, regardless of the country of origin.

* * * Certain municipal, state, and federal laws require [government] waterworks projects to use domestic-only fittings. Domestic fittings sold for use in projects with domestic-only specifications command higher prices than imported fittings.

* * * *

* * * In late 2009, McWane [Inc., headquartered in Birmingham, Alabama,] was the only supplier of domestic fittings.

* * * Looking to take advantage of the increased demand for domestic fittings prompted by [the passage of the American Recovery and Reinvestment Act of 2009 (ARRA), which provided a large infusion of money for waterworks projects that required domestic pipe fittings, Star Pipe Products] decided to enter the market for domestic [fittings].

In response to Star's forthcoming entry into the * * * market, McWane implemented its "Full Support Program" in order "to protect its domestic brands and market position." * * * McWane informed customers that if they did not "fully support McWane branded

products for their domestic fitting and accessory requirements," they "may forgo participation in any unpaid rebates they had accrued for domestic fittings and accessories or shipment of their domestic fitting and accessory orders of McWane products for up to 12 weeks."

* * * *

* * * The FTC issued a * * * complaint charging * * * that McWane's * * * Full Support Program constituted unlawful maintenance of a monopoly over the domestic fittings market.

* * * *

* * * The Commission found that the relevant market was the supply of domestically manufactured fittings for use in domestic-only waterworks projects, because imported fittings are not a substitute for domestic fittings for such projects. The Commission noted that this conclusion was bolstered by the higher prices charged for domestic fittings used in domestic-only projects. The Commission also found that McWane had monopoly power in that market, with 90–95% market share * * * and [that there were] substantial barriers to entry in the form of major capital outlays required to produce domestic fittings.

The Commission [also found] that McWane's Full Support Program * * * foreclosed Star's access to distributors for domestic fittings and harmed competition, thereby contributing significantly to the maintenance of McWane's monopoly power in the market. It noted that * * * the country's two largest waterworks distributors (with a combined 60% market share), prohibited their branches from purchasing domestic fittings from Star after the Full Support Program was announced * * * . Unable to attract [customers], Star was prevented from generating the revenue needed to acquire its own foundry, a

more efficient means of producing domestic fittings; thus, its growth into a rival that could challenge McWane's monopoly power was artificially stunted.

Moreover, the Commission found that * * * McWane's * * * conduct had an impact on price: after the Full Support Program was implemented, McWane raised domestic fittings prices and increased its gross profits despite flat production costs, and it did so across states, regardless of whether Star had entered the market as a competitor.

* * * *

[The Commission issued an order directing McWane to stop requiring exclusivity from its customers.] McWane filed a timely petition in this Court seeking review of the Commissioner's order.

* * * *

* * * *Given the identification of persistent price differences between domestic fittings and imported fittings, the distinct customers, and the lack of reasonable substitutes in this case, there was sufficient evidence to support the Commission's market definition.* [Emphasis added.]

* * * *

* * * The evidence of McWane's overwhelming market share (90%), the large capital outlays required to enter the domestic fittings market, and McWane's undeniable continued power over domestic fittings prices amount to sufficient evidence that a reasonable mind might accept as adequate to support the Commission's conclusion [that McWane possessed monopoly power in the relevant market].

* * * *

* * * We agree that [McWane's] conduct amounts to a violation of Section 5 of the Federal Trade Commission Act.

Accordingly, we AFFIRM.

Case 46.1 Continued

Legal Reasoning Questions

1. How did McWane's Full Support Program harm competition? Explain.

2. What did the Federal Trade Commission conclude? What "factual and economic" evidence supported this conclusion?

3. Instead of imposing an exclusivity policy, what action might McWane have taken to benefit its customers and compete with Star?

Relevant Geographic Market. The second component of the relevant market is the geographic extent of the market in which the firm and its competitors sell the product or services. For products that are sold nationwide, the geographic boundaries of the market can encompass the entire United States.

If transportation costs are significant or a producer and its competitors sell in only a limited area (one in which customers have no access to other sources of the product), then the geographic market is limited to that area. A national firm may thus compete in several distinct areas and have monopoly power in one geographic area but not in another.

Generally, the geographic market is that section of the country within which a firm can increase its price a bit without attracting new sellers or losing many customers to alternative suppliers outside that area. Of course, the Internet is changing perceptions of the size and limits of a geographic market. It may become difficult to perceive any geographic market as local, except for products that are not easily transported, such as concrete.

The Intent Requirement Monopoly power, in and of itself, does not constitute the offense of monopolization under Section 2 of the Sherman Act. The offense also requires an *intent* to monopolize.

A dominant market share may be the result of good business judgment or the development of a superior product. It may simply be the result of a historical accident. In these situations, the acquisition of monopoly power is not an antitrust violation. Indeed, it would be contrary to society's interest to condemn every firm that acquired a position of power because it was well managed and efficient and marketed a product desired by consumers.

If a firm possesses market power as a result of carrying out some purposeful act to acquire or maintain that power through anticompetitive means, then it is in violation of

Section 2. In most monopolization cases, intent may be inferred from evidence that the firm had monopoly power and engaged in anticompetitive behavior.

Unilateral Refusals to Deal As discussed previously, joint refusals to deal (group boycotts) are subject to close scrutiny under Section 1 of the Sherman Act. A single manufacturer acting unilaterally, though, normally is free to deal, or not to deal, with whomever it wishes.[16]

Nevertheless, in some instances, a unilateral refusal to deal will violate Section 2 of the Sherman Act. These instances occur only if (1) the firm refusing to deal has—or is likely to acquire—monopoly power and (2) the refusal is likely to have an anticompetitive effect on a particular market.

■ **EXAMPLE 46.9**   Clark Industries owns three of the four major downhill ski areas in Blue Hills, Idaho. Clark refuses to continue participating in a jointly offered six-day "all Blue Hills" lift ticket. Clark's refusal to cooperate with its smaller competitor is a violation of Section 2 of the Sherman Act. Because Clark owns three-fourths of the local ski areas, it has monopoly power. Thus, its unilateral refusal to deal has an anticompetitive effect on the market. ■

46–3b Attempts to Monopolize

Section 2 also prohibits **attempted monopolization** of a market, which requires proof of the following three elements:

1. Anticompetitive conduct.

2. The specific intent to exclude competitors and garner monopoly power.

---

16. For a classic case in this area, see *United States v. Colgate & Co.*, 250 U.S. 300, 39 S.Ct. 465, 63 L.Ed. 992 (1919). See also *Pacific Bell Telephone Co. v. Linkline Communications, Inc.*, 555 U.S. 438, 129 S.Ct. 1109, 172 L.Ed.2d 836 (2009).

3. A "dangerous" probability of success in achieving monopoly power. The probability cannot be dangerous unless the alleged offender possesses some degree of market power. Only serious threats of monopolization are condemned as violations.

As mentioned earlier, predatory pricing is a form of anticompetitive conduct that, in theory, could be used by firms that are attempting to monopolize. Related to predatory pricing is *predatory bidding*. This practice involves the acquisition and use of *monopsony power,*

which is market power on the *buy* side of a market. Predatory bidding occurs when a buyer bids up the price of an input too high for its competitors to pay, causing them to leave the market. The predatory bidder then attempts to drive down input prices to reap above-competitive profits and recoup any losses it suffered in bidding up the input prices.

The question in the following *Spotlight Case* was whether a claim of predatory bidding was sufficiently similar to a claim of predatory pricing that the same antitrust test should apply to both.

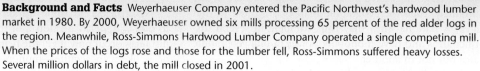

Spotlight on Weyerhaeuser

Case 46.2 Weyerhaeuser Co. v. Ross-Simmons Hardwood Lumber Co.
Supreme Court of the United States, 549 U.S. 312, 127 S.Ct. 1069, 166 L.Ed.2d 911 (2007).

Background and Facts Weyerhaeuser Company entered the Pacific Northwest's hardwood lumber market in 1980. By 2000, Weyerhaeuser owned six mills processing 65 percent of the red alder logs in the region. Meanwhile, Ross-Simmons Hardwood Lumber Company operated a single competing mill. When the prices of the logs rose and those for the lumber fell, Ross-Simmons suffered heavy losses. Several million dollars in debt, the mill closed in 2001.

Ross-Simmons filed a suit in a federal district court against Weyerhaeuser, alleging attempted monopolization under Section 2 of the Sherman Act. Ross-Simmons claimed that Weyerhaeuser used its dominant position in the market to bid up the prices of logs and prevent its competitors from being profitable. Weyerhaeuser argued that the antitrust test for predatory pricing applies to a claim of predatory bidding and that Ross-Simmons had not met this standard. The district court ruled in favor of the plaintiff, the U.S. Court of Appeals for the Ninth Circuit affirmed, and Weyerhaeuser appealed to the United States Supreme Court.

In the Language of the Court
Justice *THOMAS* delivered the opinion of the Court.
* * * *

Predatory-pricing and predatory-bidding claims are analytically similar. This similarity results from the close theoretical connection between monopoly and monopsony. The kinship between monopoly and monopsony suggests that similar legal standards should apply to claims of monopolization and to claims of monopsonization.

* * * Both claims involve the deliberate use of unilateral pricing measures for anticompetitive purposes. And both claims logically require firms to incur short-term losses on the chance that they might reap supracompetitive [above-competitive] profits in the future.
* * * *

* * * *"Predatory pricing schemes are rarely tried, and even more rarely successful." Predatory pricing requires a firm to suffer certain losses in the short term on the chance of reaping supracompetitive profits in the future. A rational business will rarely make this sacrifice.* The same reasoning applies to predatory bidding. [Emphasis added.]
* * * *

* * * A failed predatory-pricing scheme may benefit consumers. * * * Failed predatory-bidding schemes can also * * * benefit consumers.

In addition, predatory bidding presents less of a direct threat of consumer harm than predatory pricing. A predatory-pricing scheme ultimately achieves success by charging higher prices to consumers. By

Case 46.2 Continued

contrast, a predatory-bidding scheme could succeed with little or no effect on consumer prices because a predatory bidder does not necessarily rely on raising prices in the output market to recoup its losses.

* * * *

* * * [Thus,] our two-pronged [predatory pricing] test should apply to predatory-bidding claims.

* * * A plaintiff must prove that the alleged predatory bidding led to below-cost pricing of the predator's outputs. That is, the predator's bidding on the buy side must have caused the cost of the relevant output to rise above the revenues generated in the sale of those outputs. * * * Given the multitude of procompetitive ends served by higher bidding for inputs, the risk of chilling procompetitive behavior with too lax a liability standard is * * * serious * * *. Consequently, only higher bidding that leads to below-cost pricing in the relevant output market will suffice as a basis for liability for predatory bidding.

A predatory-bidding plaintiff also must prove that the defendant has a dangerous probability of recouping the losses incurred in bidding up input prices through the exercise of monopsony power. Absent proof of likely recoupment, a strategy of predatory bidding makes no economic sense because it would involve short-term losses with no likelihood of offsetting long-term gains.

Ross-Simmons has conceded that it has not satisfied [this] standard. Therefore, its predatory-bidding theory of liability cannot support the jury's verdict.

Decision and Remedy *The United States Supreme Court held that the antitrust test that applies to claims of predatory pricing also applies to claims of predatory bidding. Because Ross-Simmons conceded that it had not met this standard, the Court vacated the lower court's judgment and remanded the case.*

Critical Thinking
- **Social** *Do predatory-bidding schemes ever benefit consumers? Explain your answer.*
- **Economic** *Why does a plaintiff alleging predatory bidding have to prove that the defendant's "bidding on the buy side caused the cost of the relevant output to rise above the revenues generated in the sale of those outputs"?*

46-4 The Clayton Act

Congress enacted the Clayton Act to strengthen federal antitrust laws. The act was aimed at specific anticompetitive or monopolistic practices that the Sherman Act did not cover. The substantive provisions of the act—set out in Sections 2, 3, 7, and 8—deal with four distinct forms of business behavior, which are declared illegal but not criminal. For each provision, the act states that the behavior is *illegal only if it tends to substantially lessen competition or to create monopoly power.*

46-4a Section 2—Price Discrimination

Section 2 of the Clayton Act prohibits **price discrimination,** which occurs when a seller charges different prices to competing buyers for identical goods or services. Congress strengthened this section by amending it with the passage of the Robinson-Patman Act in 1936. As amended, Section 2 prohibits price discrimination that cannot be justified by differences in production costs, transportation costs, or cost differences due to other reasons. In short, a seller cannot charge one buyer a lower price than it charges that buyer's competitor.

Requirements To violate Section 2, the seller must be engaged in interstate commerce, the goods must be of like grade and quality, and the goods must have been sold to two or more purchasers. In addition, the effect of the price discrimination must be to substantially lessen competition, tend to create a monopoly, or otherwise injure competition. Without proof of an actual injury resulting from the price discrimination, the plaintiff cannot recover damages.

Note that price discrimination claims can arise from discounts, offsets, rebates, or allowances given to one buyer over another. Moreover, giving favorable credit terms, delivery, or freight charges to some buyers, but not others, can also lead to allegations of price discrimination. For instance, when a seller offers goods to different customers at the same price but includes free delivery for certain buyers, it may violate Section 2 in some circumstances.

Defenses There are several statutory defenses to liability for price discrimination.

1. *Cost justification.* If the seller can justify the price reduction by demonstrating that a particular buyer's purchases saved the seller costs in producing and selling the goods, the seller will not be liable for price discrimination.
2. *Meeting a competitor's prices.* If the seller charged the lower price in a good faith attempt to meet an equally low price of a competitor, the seller will not be liable for price discrimination. ■ **EXAMPLE 46.10** Rogue, Inc., is a retail dealer of Mercury Marine outboard motors in Shady Cove, Oregon. Mercury Marine also sells its motors to other dealers in the Shady Cove area. When Rogue discovers that Mercury is selling its outboard motors at a substantial discount to Rogue's largest competitor, it files a price discrimination lawsuit. Mercury Marine can defend itself by showing that the discounts given to Rogue's competitor were made in good faith to meet the low price charged by another manufacturer of marine motors. ■
3. *Changing market conditions.* A seller may lower its price on an item in response to changing conditions affecting the market for or the marketability of the goods concerned. Sellers are allowed to readjust their prices to meet the realities of the market without liability for price discrimination. Thus, if an advance in technology makes a particular product less marketable than it was previously, a seller can lower the product's price.

46–4b Section 3—Exclusionary Practices

Under Section 3 of the Clayton Act, sellers or lessors cannot condition the sale or lease of goods on the buyer's or lessee's promise not to use or deal in the goods of the seller's competitor. In effect, this section prohibits two types of vertical agreements involving exclusionary practices— exclusive-dealing contracts and tying arrangements.

Exclusive-Dealing Contracts A contract under which a seller forbids a buyer to purchase products from the seller's competitors is called an **exclusive-dealing contract.** A seller is prohibited from making an exclusive-dealing contract under Section 3 if the effect of the contract is "to substantially lessen competition or tend to create a monopoly."

In the past, courts were more inclined to find that exclusive-dealing contracts substantially lessened competition. ■ **CASE IN POINT 46.11** In one classic case, Standard Oil Company, the largest gasoline seller in the nation in the late 1940s, made exclusive-dealing contracts with independent stations in seven western states.

The contracts involved 16 percent of all retail outlets, whose sales were approximately 7 percent of all retail sales in that market. The United States Supreme Court ruled that the market was substantially concentrated because the seven largest gasoline suppliers all used exclusive-dealing contracts with their independent retailers and together controlled 65 percent of the market.

Looking at market conditions after the arrangements were instituted, the Court found that market shares were extremely stable and that entry into the market was apparently restricted. Thus, the Court held that the Clayton Act had been violated because competition was "foreclosed in a substantial share" of the relevant market.[17] ■ Note that since the Supreme Court's 1949 decision, a number of subsequent decisions have called the holding in this case into doubt.[18]

Today, it is clear that to violate antitrust law, an exclusive-dealing agreement (or a tying arrangement, discussed next) must qualitatively and substantially harm competition. To prevail, a plaintiff must present affirmative evidence that the performance of the agreement will foreclose competition and harm consumers.

Tying Arrangements When a seller conditions the sale of a product (the tying product) on the buyer's agreement to purchase another product (the tied product) produced or distributed by the same seller, a **tying arrangement** results. The legality of a tying arrangement (or *tie-in sales agreement*) depends on several factors, such as the purpose of the agreement. Courts also focus on the agreement's likely effect on competition in the relevant markets (the market for the tying product and the market for the tied product).

Section 3 of the Clayton Act has been held to apply only to commodities, not to services. Tying arrangements, however, can also be considered agreements that restrain trade in violation of Section 1 of the Sherman Act. Thus, cases involving tying arrangements of services have been brought under Section 1 of the Sherman Act. Although earlier cases condemned tying arrangements as illegal *per se,* courts now evaluate tying agreements under the rule of reason.[19]

---

17. *Standard Oil Co. of California v. United States*, 337 U.S. 293, 69 S.Ct. 1051, 93 L.Ed. 1371 (1949).
18. See, for example, *Illinois Tool Works, Inc. v. Independent Ink, Inc.*, 547 U.S. 28, 126 S.Ct. 1281, 164 L.Ed.2d 26 (2006); and *Stop & Shop Supermarket Co. v. Blue Cross & Blue Shield of Rhode Island*, 373 F.3d 57 (1st Cir. 2004).
19. *Illinois Tool Works, Inc. v. Independent Ink, Inc.*, 547 U.S. 28, 126 S.Ct. 1281, 164 L.Ed.2d 26 (2006). This decision was the first time the Supreme Court recognized that tying arrangements can have legitimate business justifications.

■ **CASE IN POINT 46.12** James Batson bought a nonrefundable ticket from Live Nation Entertainment, Inc., to attend a rock concert at the Charter One Pavilion in Chicago. The front of the ticket noted that the price included a nine-dollar parking fee. Batson did not have a car to park, however. In fact, he had walked to the concert venue and had bought the ticket just before the performance.

Frustrated at being charged for parking that he did not need, Batson filed a suit in a federal district court against Live Nation. He argued that the bundled parking fee was unfair because consumers were forced to pay it or forego the concert. He asserted that this was a tying arrangement in violation of Section 1 of the Sherman Act. The court dismissed the suit, and a federal appellate court affirmed. The court was unable to identify a product market in which Live Nation had sufficient power to force consumers who wanted to attend a concert (the tying product) to buy "useless parking rights" (the tied product). While such bundles may be annoying, there was no evidence that Live Nation's parking tie-in restrained competition for parking in Chicago.[20] ■

46–4c Section 7—Mergers

Under Section 7 of the Clayton Act, a person or business organization cannot hold stock or assets in more than one business when "the effect . . . may be to substantially lessen competition." Section 7 is the statutory authority for preventing mergers or acquisitions that could result in monopoly power or a substantial lessening of competition in the marketplace. Section 7 applies to both horizontal and vertical mergers, as discussed in the following subsections.

A crucial consideration in most merger cases is **market concentration.** Determining market concentration involves allocating percentage market shares among the various companies in the relevant market. When a small number of companies share a large part of the market, the market is concentrated. ■ **EXAMPLE 46.13** If the four largest grocery stores in Chicago account for 80 percent of all retail food sales, the market is concentrated in those four firms. If one of these stores absorbs the assets and liabilities of another, so that the other ceases to exist, the result is a merger that further concentrates the market and possibly diminishes competition. ■

Competition is not necessarily diminished solely as a result of market concentration, however. Courts will consider other factors in determining if a merger violates

Section 7. One factor of particular importance is whether the merger will make it more difficult for *potential* competitors to enter the relevant market.

Horizontal Mergers Mergers between firms that compete with each other in the same market are called **horizontal mergers.** If a horizontal merger creates an entity with a significant market share, the merger may be considered illegal because it increases market concentration. The Federal Trade Commission (FTC) and the U.S. Department of Justice (DOJ) have established guidelines for determining which mergers will be challenged.[21]

When analyzing the legality of a horizontal merger, the courts consider three additional factors. The first factor is the overall concentration of the relevant market. The second is the relevant market's history of tending toward concentration. The final factor is whether the merger is apparently designed to establish market power or restrict competition.

Vertical Mergers A **vertical merger** occurs when a company at one stage of production acquires a company at a higher or lower stage of production. An example of a vertical merger is a company merging with one of its suppliers or retailers.

Whether a vertical merger will be deemed illegal generally depends on several factors, such as whether the merger creates a single firm that controls an undue percentage share of the relevant market. The courts also analyze the concentration of firms in the market, barriers to entry into the market, and the apparent intent of the merging parties. If a merger does not prevent competitors of either of the merging firms from competing in a segment of the market, the merger will not be condemned as foreclosing competition and thus is legal.

46–4d Section 8— Interlocking Directorates

Section 8 of the Clayton Act deals with *interlocking directorates*—that is, the practice whereby individuals serve as directors on the boards of two or more competing companies simultaneously. Specifically, no person may be a director for two or more competing corporations at the same time if either of the corporations has capital, surplus, or undivided profits aggregating more than $31,841,000

---

20. *Batson v. Live Nation Entertainment, Inc.,* 746 F.3d 827 (7th Cir. 2014).

21. These guidelines include a formula for assessing the degree of concentration in the relevant market called the *Herfindahl-Hirschman Index* (HHI), which is available at **www.justice.gov/atr/public/guidelines/hmg-2010.html.**

or competitive sales of $3,184,100 or more. The Federal Trade Commission adjusts these threshold amounts each year. (The amounts given here are those announced by the commission in 2016.)

46–5 Enforcement and Exemptions

The federal agencies that enforce the federal antitrust laws are the U.S. Department of Justice (DOJ) and the Federal Trade Commission (FTC), which was established by the Federal Trade Commission Act. Section 5 of that act condemns all forms of anticompetitive behavior that are not covered under other federal antitrust laws.

46–5a Agency Actions

Only the DOJ can prosecute violations of the Sherman Act, which can be either criminal or civil offenses. Violations of the Clayton Act are not crimes, but the act can be enforced by either the DOJ or the FTC through civil proceedings.

The DOJ or the FTC may ask the courts to impose various remedies, including **divestiture** (making a company give up one or more of its operations) and dissolution. A meatpacking firm, for instance, might be forced to divest itself of control or ownership of butcher shops.

The FTC has sole authority to enforce violations of Section 5 of the Federal Trade Commission Act. FTC actions are effected through administrative orders, but if a firm violates an FTC order, the FTC can seek court sanctions for the violation.

46–5b Private Actions

A private party who has been injured as a result of a violation of the Sherman Act or the Clayton Act can sue for **treble damages** (three times the actual damages suffered) and attorneys' fees. In some instances, private parties may also seek injunctive relief to prevent antitrust violations. A party wishing to sue under the Sherman Act must prove that:

1. The antitrust violation either caused or was a substantial factor in causing the injury that was suffered.
2. The unlawful actions of the accused party affected business activities of the plaintiff that were protected by the antitrust laws.

Additionally, the United States Supreme Court has held that to pursue antitrust lawsuits, private parties must present some evidence suggesting that an illegal agreement was made.[22]

A private party can bring an action under Section 2 of the Sherman Act based on the attempted enforcement of a fraudulently obtained patent. This is called a *Walker Process* claim.[23] To prevail, the plaintiff must first show that the defendant obtained the patent by fraud on the U.S. Patent and Trademark Office and enforced the patent with knowledge of the fraud. The plaintiff must then establish all the other elements of a Sherman Act monopolization claim—anticompetitive conduct, an intent to monopolize, and a dangerous probability of achieving monopoly power.

In the following case, a respiratory filter maker was accused of patent infringement. The maker sought a declaratory judgment of non-infringement, asserting a *Walker Process* claim. One of the primary issues was whether attorney fees were an appropriate basis for damages.

---

22. *Bell Atlantic Corp. v. Twombly*, 550 U.S. 544, 127 S.Ct. 1955, 167 L.Ed.2d 929 (2007).
23. The name of the claim comes from the title of the case in which the claim originated—*Walker Process Equipment v. Food Machine and Chemical Corp.*, 382 U.S. 172, 86 S.Ct. 347, 15 L.Ed.2d 247 (1965).

Case 46.3

TransWeb, LLC v. 3M Innovative Properties Co.
United States Court of Appeals, Federal Circuit, 812 F.3d 1295 (2016).

Background and Facts TransWeb, LLC, makes respirator filters made of nonwoven fibrous material to be worn by workers at contaminated worksites. At a filtration industry exposition, TransWeb's founder, Kumar Ogale, handed out samples of TransWeb's filter material. At the time, 3M Innovative Products Company was experimenting with filter materials. At the expo, 3M employees obtained the TransWeb samples.

Case 46.3 Continued

More than a year later, 3M obtained patents for its filter products and filed a suit against TransWeb, claiming infringement. 3M asserted that it had not received the TransWeb samples until after its patent application had been filed. The suit was dismissed.

TransWeb then filed a suit in a federal district court, seeking a declaratory judgment of non-infringement and asserting a *Walker Process* claim. A jury found that 3M had obtained its patents through fraud, that its assertion of the patents against TransWeb violated antitrust law, and that Trans-Web was entitled to attorney fees as damages. TransWeb had incurred $7.7 million defending against 3M's infringement suit. The court trebled this to $23 million. 3M appealed.

In the Language of the Court
HUGHES, Circuit Judge.
* * * *

3M argues that the district court erred in awarding the $23 million of attorney-fees damages, because TransWeb failed to show any link between those attorney fees and an impact on competition. 3M argues that those attorney fees had no effect on competition because they did not force TransWeb out of the market or otherwise affect prices in the market.
* * * *

3M's argument focuses on the fact that the harmful effect on competition proven by TransWeb at trial never actually came about. TransWeb proved at trial that increased prices for fluorinated filter * * * respirators would have resulted had 3M succeeded in its suit.
* * * *

* * * 3M's unlawful act was * * * aimed at reducing competition and would have done so had the suit been successful. 3M's unlawful act was the bringing of suit based on a patent known to be fraudulently obtained. What made this act unlawful under the antitrust laws was its attempt to gain a monopoly based on this fraudulently obtained patent. TransWeb's attorney fees flow directly from this unlawful aspect of 3M's act. * * * The attorney fees are precisely the type of loss that the claimed violations would be likely to cause.
* * * *

* * * *It is the abuse of the legal process by the antitrust-defendant that makes the attorney fees incurred by the antitrust-plaintiff during that legal process a relevant antitrust injury.* [Emphasis added.]

No assertion of a patent known to be fraudulently obtained can be a proper use of legal process. No successful outcome of that litigation, regardless of how much the patentee subjectively desires it, would save that suit from being improper due to its tainted origin.

* * * The antitrust laws exist to protect competition. If we were to hold that TransWeb can seek antitrust damages only [by] forfeiture of competition, but not [by] defending the anticompetitive suit, then we would be incentivizing the former over the latter. * * * This is not in accord with the purpose of those very same antitrust laws.

Furthermore, it furthers the purpose of the antitrust laws to encourage TransWeb to bring its antitrust suit * * * instead of waiting to be excluded from the market * * * . If TransWeb proceeds only after being excluded from the market * * * , then the [injury] will no longer be borne by TransWeb alone, but rather would be shared by all consumers in the relevant markets.

Decision and Remedy *The U.S. Court of Appeals for the Federal Circuit affirmed the lower court's judgment and award of trebled attorney fees. "TransWeb's attorney fees appropriately flow from the unlawful aspect of 3M's antitrust violation and thus are an antitrust injury that can properly serve as the basis for antitrust damages."*

Critical Thinking
- **Legal Environment** *How would TransWeb's injury have been "shared by all consumers in the relevant markets" if TransWeb had not sued until after it had been driven out of those markets by 3M's actions?*
- **Ethical** *What does 3M's conduct suggest about its corporate ethics?*

46–5c Exemptions from Antitrust Laws

There are many legislative and constitutional limitations on antitrust enforcement. Most of the statutory and judicially created exemptions to the antitrust laws apply only in certain areas (see Exhibit 46–2). One of the most significant exemptions covers joint efforts by businesspersons to obtain legislative, judicial, or executive action. Under this exemption, for example, DVD producers can jointly lobby Congress to change the copyright laws without being held liable for attempting to restrain trade. Another exemption covers professional baseball teams.

46–6 U.S. Antitrust Laws in the Global Context

U.S. antitrust laws have a broad application. Not only may persons in foreign nations be subject to their provisions, but the laws may also be applied to protect foreign consumers and competitors from violations committed by U.S. business firms. Consequently, *foreign persons,* a term that by definition includes foreign governments, may sue under U.S. antitrust laws in U.S. courts.

46–6a The Extraterritorial Application of U.S. Antitrust Laws

Section 1 of the Sherman Act provides for the extraterritorial effect of the U.S. antitrust laws. Any conspiracy that has a *substantial effect* on U.S. commerce is within the reach of the Sherman Act. The violation may even occur outside the United States, and foreign governments as well as individuals can be sued for violation of U.S. antitrust laws.

Before U.S. courts will exercise jurisdiction and apply antitrust laws, it must be shown that the alleged violation had a substantial effect on U.S. commerce. U.S. jurisdiction is automatically invoked, however, when a *per se* violation occurs.

If a domestic firm, for instance, joins a foreign cartel to control the production, price, or distribution of goods, and this cartel has a *substantial effect* on U.S. commerce, a *per se* violation may arise. Hence, both the domestic firm and the foreign cartel could be sued for violation of the U.S. antitrust laws.

Likewise, if a foreign firm doing business in the United States enters into a price-fixing or other anticompetitive agreement to control a portion of U.S. markets, a *per se* violation may exist. ■ **CASE IN POINT 46.14** Carrier Corporation is a U.S. firm that manufactures air-conditioning and refrigeration (ACR) equipment. To make these products, Carrier uses ACR copper tubing it buys from Outokumpu Oyj, a Finnish company. Carrier is one of the world's largest purchasers of ACR copper tubing.

After the Commission of the European Communities found that Outokumpu had conspired with other companies to fix ACR tubing prices in Europe, Carrier filed a suit in a U.S. court. Carrier alleged that the cartel had also conspired to fix prices in the United States by agreeing that only Outokumpu would sell ACR tubing in the U.S. market. The district court dismissed the case for lack of jurisdiction, but a federal appellate court reversed. The reviewing court found that the alleged anticompetitive conspiracy had a substantial effect on U.S. commerce. Therefore, the U.S. courts had jurisdiction over the Finnish defendant.[24] ■

46–6b The Application of Foreign Antitrust Laws

Large U.S. companies increasingly must be concerned about the application of foreign antitrust laws. The European Union (EU), in particular, has stepped up its enforcement actions against antitrust violators.

European Union Enforcement The EU's laws promoting competition are stricter in many respects than those of the United States and define more conduct as anticompetitive. The EU actively pursues antitrust violators, especially individual companies and cartels that allegedly engage in monopolistic conduct. EU investigations of possible antitrust violations often take years. See this chapter's *Digital Update* feature for a discussion of how the EU is pursuing Google, Inc., for antitrust violations.

Increased Enforcement in Asia and Latin America Many other nations also have laws that promote competition and prohibit trade restraints. Japanese antitrust laws forbid unfair trade practices, monopolization, and restrictions that unreasonably restrain trade. China's antitrust rules restrict monopolization and price fixing (except that the Chinese government can set prices on exported goods). Indonesia, Malaysia, South Korea, and Vietnam all have statutes protecting competition.

---

24. *Carrier Corp. v. Outokumpu Oyj,* 673 F.3d 430 (6th Cir. 2012).

EXHIBIT 46–2 Exemptions to Antitrust Enforcement

EXEMPTION	SOURCE AND SCOPE
Labor	The Clayton Act—Permits unions to organize and bargain without violating antitrust laws and specifies that strikes and other labor activities normally do not violate any federal law.
Agricultural Associations	The Clayton Act and the Capper-Volstead Act—Allow agricultural cooperatives to set prices.
Fisheries	The Fisheries Cooperative Marketing Act—Allows the fishing industry to set prices.
Insurance Companies	The McCarran-Ferguson Act—Exempts the insurance business in states in which the industry is regulated.
Exporters	The Webb-Pomerene Act—Allows U.S. exporters to engage in cooperative activity to compete with similar foreign associations. The Export Trading Company Act—Permits the U.S. Department of Justice to exempt certain exporters.
Professional Baseball	The United States Supreme Court—Has held that professional baseball is exempt because it is not "interstate commerce."[a]
Oil Marketing	The Interstate Oil Compact—Allows states to set quotas on oil to be marketed in interstate commerce.
Defense Activities	The Defense Production Act—Allows the president to approve, and thereby exempt, certain activities to further the military defense of the United States.
Small Businesses' Cooperative Research	The Small Business Administration Act—Allows small firms to undertake cooperative research.
State Actions	The United States Supreme Court—Has held that actions by a state are exempt if the state clearly articulates and actively supervises the policy behind its action.[b]
Regulated Industries	Federal Agencies—Industries (such as airlines) are exempt when a federal administrative agency (such as the Federal Aviation Administration) has primary regulatory authority.
Businesspersons' Joint Efforts to Seek Government Action	The United States Supreme Court—Cooperative efforts by businesspersons to obtain legislative, judicial, or executive action are exempt unless it is clear that an effort is "objectively baseless" and is an attempt to make anticompetitive use of government processes.[c]

a. *Federal Baseball Club of Baltimore, Inc. v. National League of Professional Baseball Clubs,* 259 U.S. 200, 42 S.Ct. 465, 66 L.Ed. 898 (1922). See *City of San Jose v. Office of the Commissioner of Baseball,* 776 F.3d 686 (9th Cir. 2015).
b. See *Parker v. Brown,* 317 U.S. 341, 63 S.Ct. 307, 87 L.Ed. 315 (1943).
c. *Eastern Railroad Presidents Conference v. Noerr Motor Freight, Inc.,* 365 U.S. 127, 81 S.Ct. 523, 5 L.Ed.2d 464 (1961); and *United Mine Workers of America v. Pennington,* 381 U.S. 657, 89 S.Ct. 1585, 14 L.Ed.2d 626 (1965). These two cases established the exception often referred to as the *Noerr-Pennington* doctrine.

Argentina, Brazil, Chile, Peru, and several other Latin American countries have adopted modern antitrust laws as well.

Most of the antitrust laws apply extraterritorially, as U.S. antitrust laws do. This means that a U.S. company may be subject to another nation's antitrust laws if the company's conduct has a substantial effect on that nation's commerce. For instance, in 2015, China fined the U.S. chipmaker Qualcomm, Inc., $975 million for violating antitrust laws. China has also targeted Microsoft, Inc., in its antitrust investigations and has searched Microsoft's company servers in China for evidence of violations.

DIGITAL UPDATE · Google Faces an Antitrust Complaint from the European Union

"Just google it." Google's search engine is so dominant that the company name has become a verb synonymous with conducting an Internet search. According to the European Commissioner for Competition, Margrethe Vestager, Google has become too dominant, at least with respect to comparison shopping and product search. For that reason, the European Union (EU) has formally charged Google with an antitrust violation. The charges relate specifically to Google operations in the EU.

The EU's Antitrust Objections

According to the EU, Google is abusing a dominant position—a breach of EU antitrust rules. The EU has alleged that Google promotes its own comparison shopping service at the expense of competitors. It does this by "positioning and prominently displaying its comparison shopping service in its general search result pages, irrespective of its merits." As a result, "users do not necessarily see the most relevant results in response to queries—to the detriment of consumers and rival comparison shopping services." Presumably, this conduct started in 2008.

What the EU Wants Google to Do and Google's Response

Now that the EU has established its complaint against Google, here is what it wants Google to do: change the way it displays search results in the EU. When Google shows comparison shopping services in response to a user's query, the search results should show the most relevant services first.

In response to both the complaint and the suggested remedy, Google offered a 130-page rebuttal. It contends that it cannot change its core software. It also claims that the results in its search algorithms are based on relevance. In addition, Google contends that it has actually boosted traffic to its Web competitors. Therein lies the major argument against the EU's antitrust complaint. Search engines have proliferated on the Web, suggesting that Google's success has not eliminated competition.

The Compartmentalization of Search on the Web

More and more frequently, Internet users do not engage in general searches. Rather, they know exactly where to go to obtain product information. When they want information on movies, for instance, they go to the Internet Movie Data Base (IMDB) rather than Google. When they want information on music, they go to iTunes. When they want to search for the cheapest airfares, they go to Kayak or similar sites. When they want to find the best rates on hotels, they go to sites such as hotels.com. And when they are interested in buying a product, they frequently go to Amazon or eBay. Amazon, in particular, has fine-tuned its ability to generate advertising revenues through its Amazon-sponsored links.

And, of course, social media must be considered. More people are on social media sites than ever before, particularly on their mobile devices. Users spend four times more time on Facebook than they do on Google. These users often "crowdsource"—that is, look for answers from Facebook friends rather than search on Google. Facebook is also becoming increasingly competitive with Google in the services it offers, including mobile payments and the Facebook Messenger instant messaging service.

Whether the European Antitrust Commission accepts Google's arguments will determine Google's fate. Will it pay billions of dollars in fines and be forced to make significant changes in how it does business? That probably will not be decided any time soon. Experts estimate that the case could go on for years.

Critical Thinking *Which companies in Europe do you think may have pressured the European Union to lodge its antitrust complaint against Google?*

Reviewing: Antitrust Law

The Internet Corporation for Assigned Names and Numbers (ICANN) is a nonprofit entity that organizes Internet domain names. It is governed by a board of directors elected by various groups with commercial interests in the Internet. One of ICANN's functions is to authorize an entity to serve as a registry for certain "Top Level Domains" (TLDs). ICANN and VeriSign entered into an agreement that authorized VeriSign to serve as a registry for the ".com" TLD and provide registry services in accordance with ICANN's specifications. VeriSign complained that ICANN was restricting the services that it could make available as a registrar, blocking new services, imposing unnecessary conditions on those services, and setting the prices at which the services were offered. VeriSign claimed that ICANN's control of the registry services for domain names violated Section 1 of the Sherman Act. Using the information presented in the chapter, answer the following questions.

1. Should ICANN's actions be judged under the rule of reason or be deemed *per se* violations of Section 1 of the Sherman Act? Why?
2. Should ICANN's actions be viewed as a horizontal or a vertical restraint of trade? Why?
3. Does it matter that ICANN's directors are chosen by groups with a commercial interest in the Internet? Explain.
4. If the dispute is judged under the rule of reason, what might be ICANN's defense for having a standardized set of registry services that must be used?

Debate This . . .   *The Internet and the rise of e-commerce have rendered our current antitrust concepts and laws obsolete.*

Terms and Concepts

antitrust law 876
attempted monopolization 883
concentrated industry 879
divestiture 888
exclusive-dealing contract 886
group boycott 879
horizontal merger 887
horizontal restraint 878
market concentration 887
market power 877

monopolization 880
monopoly 877
monopoly power 877
per se violation 877
predatory pricing 880
price discrimination 885
price-fixing agreement 878
resale price maintenance
    agreement 880

restraint of trade 876
rule of reason 877
treble damages 888
tying arrangement 886
vertical merger 887
vertical restraint 879
vertically integrated firm 879

Issue Spotters

1. Under what circumstances would Pop's Market, a small store in a small, isolated town, be considered a monopolist? If Pop's is a monopolist, is it in violation of Section 2 of the Sherman Act? Why or why not? (See *Section 2 of the Sherman Act.*)
2. Maple Corporation conditions the sale of its syrup on the buyer's agreement to buy Maple's pancake mix. What factors would a court consider to decide whether this arrangement violates the Clayton Act? (See *The Clayton Act.*)

• **Check your answers to the Issue Spotters against the answers provided in Appendix D at the end of this text.**

Business Scenarios

46–1. Group Boycott. Jorge's Appliance Corp. was a new retail seller of appliances in Sunrise City. Because of its innovative sales techniques and financing, Jorge's attracted many customers. As a result, the appliance department of No-Glow Department Store, a large chain store with a great deal of buying power, lost a substantial number of sales. No-Glow told a number of appliance manufacturers from whom it made large-volume purchases that if they continued to sell to Jorge's, No-Glow would stop buying from them. The manufacturers immediately stopped selling appliances to Jorge's. Jorge's filed a suit against No-Glow and the manufacturers, claiming that their actions constituted an antitrust violation. No-Glow and the manufacturers were able to prove that Jorge's was a small retailer with a small market share. They claimed that because the relevant market was not substantially affected, they were not guilty of restraint of trade. Discuss fully whether there was an antitrust violation. (See *Section 1 of the Sherman Act*.)

46–2. Antitrust Laws. Allitron, Inc., and Donovan, Ltd., are interstate competitors selling similar appliances, principally in the states of Illinois, Indiana, Kentucky, and Ohio. Allitron and Donovan agree that Allitron will no longer sell in Indiana and Ohio and that Donovan will no longer sell in Illinois and Kentucky. Have Allitron and Donovan violated any antitrust laws? If so, which law? Explain. (See *Section 1 of The Sherman Act*.)

Business Case Problems

46–3. Section 2 of the Sherman Act. While Deer Valley Resort Co. (DVRC) was developing its ski resort in the Wasatch Mountains near Park City, Utah, it sold parcels of land in the resort village to third parties. Each sales contract reserved the right of approval over the conduct of certain businesses on the property, including ski rentals. For fifteen years, DVRC permitted Christy Sports, LLC, to rent skis in competition with DVRC's ski rental outlet. Then DVRC opened a new midmountain ski rental outlet and revoked Christy's permission to rent skis. This meant that most skiers who flew into Salt Lake City and shuttled to Deer Valley had few choices. They could carry their ski equipment with them on their flights, take a shuttle into Park City and look for cheaper ski rentals there, or rent from DVRC. Christy filed a suit in a federal district court against DVRC. Was DVRC's action an attempt to monopolize in violation of Section 2 of the Sherman Act? Why or why not? [*Christy Sports, LLC v. Deer Valley Resort Co.*, 555 F.3d 1188 (10th Cir. 2009)] (See *Section 2 of the Sherman Act*.)

46–4. Price Fixing. Together, EMI, Sony BMG Music Entertainment, Universal Music Group Recordings, Inc., and Warner Music Group Corp. produced, licensed, and distributed 80 percent of the digital music sold in the United States. The companies formed MusicNet to sell music to online services that sold the songs to consumers. MusicNet required all of the services to sell the songs at the same price and subject to the same restrictions. Digitization of music became cheaper, but MusicNet did not change its prices. Did MusicNet violate the antitrust laws? Explain. [*Starr v. Sony BMG Music Entertainment*, 592 F.3d 314 (2d Cir. 2010)] (See *Section 1 of the Sherman Act*.)

46–5. Business Case Problem with Sample Answer— Price Discrimination. Dayton Superior Corp. sells its products in interstate commerce to several companies, including Spa Steel Products, Inc. The purchasers often compete directly with each other for customers. From 2005 to 2007, one of Spa Steel's customers purchased Dayton Superior's products from two of Spa Steel's competitors. According to the customer, Spa Steel's prices were always 10 to 15 percent higher for the same products. As a result, Spa Steel lost sales to at least that customer and perhaps others. Spa Steel wants to sue Dayton Superior for price discrimination. Which requirements for such a claim under Section 2 of the Clayton Act does Spa Steel satisfy? What additional facts will it need to prove? [*Dayton Superior Corp. v. Spa Steel Products, Inc.*, 2012 WL 113663 (N.D.N.Y. 2012)] (See *The Clayton Act*.)

• **For a sample answer to Problem 46–5, go to Appendix E at the end of this text.**

46–6. Section 1 of the Sherman Act. The National Collegiate Athletic Association (NCAA) and the National Federation of State High School Associations (NFHS) set a new standard for non-wood baseball bats. Their goal was to ensure that aluminum and composite bats performed like wood bats in order to enhance player safety and reduce technology-driven home runs and other big hits. Marucci Sports, LLC, makes non-wood bats. Under the new standard, four of Marucci's eleven products were decertified for use in high school and collegiate games. Marucci filed suit against the NCAA and the NFHS under Section 1 of the Sherman Act. At trial, Marucci's evidence focused on injury to its own business. Did the NCAA and NFHS's standard restrain trade in violation of the Sherman Act? Explain. [*Marucci Sports, L.L.C. v. National Collegiate Athletic Association*, 751 F.3d 368 (5th Cir. 2014)] (See *Section 1 of the Sherman Act*.)

46–7. Mergers. St. Luke's Health Systems, Ltd., operated an emergency clinic in Nampa, Idaho. Saltzer Medical Group, P.A., had thirty-four physicians practicing at its offices in Nampa. Saint Alphonsus Medical Center operated the only hospital in Nampa. St. Luke's acquired Saltzer's assets and entered into a five-year professional service agreement with the Saltzer physicians. This affiliation resulted in a combined share of two-thirds of the Nampa adult primary care provider market. Together, the two entities could impose a significant increase in the prices charged to patients and insurers, and correspondence between the parties indicated that they would. Saint Alphonsus filed a suit against St. Luke's to block the merger. Did this affiliation violate antitrust law? Explain. [*Saint Alphonsus Medical Center-Nampa, Inc. v. St. Luke's Health System, Ltd.*, 778 F.3d 775 (9th Cir. 2015)] (See *The Clayton Act.*)

46–8. Section 1 of the Sherman Act. Manitou North America, Inc., makes and distributes telehandlers (forklifts with extendable telescopic booms) to dealers throughout the United States. Manitou agreed to make McCormick International, LLC, its exclusive dealer in the state of Michigan. Later, Manitou entered into an agreement with Gehl Company, which also makes and sells telehandlers. The companies agreed to allocate territories within Michigan among certain dealers for each manufacturer, limiting the dealers' selection of competitive products to certain models. Under this agreement, McCormick was precluded from buying or selling Gehl telehandlers. What type of trade restraint did the agreement between Manitou and Gehl represent? Is this a violation of antitrust law? If so, who was injured, and how were they injured? Explain. [*Manitou North America, Inc. v. McCormick International, LLC*, __ N.W.2d __, 2016 WL 439354 (2016)] (See *Section 1 of the Sherman Act.*)

46–9. A Question of Ethics—Section 1 of the Sherman **Act.** *In the 1990s, DuCoa, L.P., made choline chloride, a B-complex vitamin essential for the growth and development of animals. DuCoa, Bioproducts, Inc., and Chinook Group, Ltd., each had*

one-third of the U.S. market for choline chloride. To stabilize the market and keep the price of the vitamin higher than it would otherwise have been, the companies took action. They agreed to fix the price and allocate market share by deciding which of them would offer the lowest price to each customer. At times, however, the companies disregarded the agreement.

*During an increase in competitive activity in August 1997, Daniel Rose became president of DuCoa. The next month, a subordinate advised him of the conspiracy. By February 1998, Rose had begun to implement a strategy to persuade DuCoa's competitors to rejoin the conspiracy. By April, the three companies had reallocated their market shares and increased their prices. In June, the U.S. Department of Justice began to investigate allegations of price fixing in the vitamin market. Ultimately, a federal district court convicted Rose of conspiracy to violate Section 1 of the Sherman Act. [*United States v. Rose*, 449 F.3d 627 (5th Cir. 2006)] (See *Section 1 of the Sherman Act.*)

(a) The court "enhanced" Rose's sentence to thirty months' imprisonment, one year of supervised release, and a $20,000 fine. Among other things, the court based this enhancement on Rose's role as "a manager or supervisor" in the conspiracy. Rose appealed the enhancement to the U.S. Court of Appeals for the Fifth Circuit. Was it fair to increase Rose's sentence on this ground? Why or why not?

(b) Was Rose's participation in the conspiracy unethical? If so, how might Rose have behaved ethically instead? If not, could any of the participants' conduct be considered unethical? Explain.

Legal Reasoning Group Activity

46–10. Antitrust Violations. Residents of the city of Madison, Wisconsin, became concerned about overconsumption of liquor near the campus of the University of Wisconsin (UW). The city initiated a new policy, imposing conditions on area bars to discourage reduced-price "specials" that were believed to encourage high-volume and dangerous drinking. Later, the city began to draft an ordinance to ban all drink specials. Bar owners responded by announcing that they had "voluntarily" agreed to discontinue drink specials on Friday and Saturday nights after 8:00 P.M. The city put its ordinance on hold. Several UW students filed a lawsuit against the local

bar owners' association, alleging violations of antitrust law. (See *Section 1 of the Sherman Act.*)

(a) The first group will identify the grounds on which the plaintiffs might base their claim for relief and formulate an argument on behalf of the plaintiffs.

(b) The second group will determine whether the defendants are exempt from the antitrust laws.

(c) The third group will decide how the court should rule in this dispute and provide reasons for the ruling.

CHAPTER 47

Professional Liability and Accountability

Professionals, such as accountants, attorneys, physicians, and architects, are increasingly faced with the threat of liability. In part, this is because the public has become more aware that professionals are required to deliver competent services and adhere to certain standards of performance within their professions.

The failure of several major companies and leading public accounting firms in the past twenty years has focused attention on the importance of abiding by professional accounting standards. Numerous corporations and former corporations have been accused of engaging in accounting fraud. These include American International Group (AIG, the world's largest insurance company), HealthSouth, Goldman Sachs, Lehman Brothers, Tyco International, and India-based Satyam Computer Services, to name a few. These companies may have reported fictitious revenues, concealed liabilities or debts, or artificially inflated their assets.

Considering the many potential sources of legal liability that they face, accountants, attorneys, and other professionals should be very aware of their legal obligations. In this chapter, we look at the potential liability of professionals under both the common law and statutory law. We conclude the chapter with a brief examination of the relationships of professionals, particularly accountants and attorneys, with their clients.

47-1 Potential Liability to Clients

Under the common law, professionals may be liable to clients for breach of contract, negligence, or fraud.

47-1a Liability for Breach of Contract

Accountants and other professionals face liability under the common law for any breach of contract. A professional owes a duty to her or his client to honor the terms of their contract and to perform the contract within the stated time period. If the professional fails to perform as agreed in the contract, then she or he has breached the contract, and the client has the right to seek to recover damages from the professional.

Damages can include expenses incurred by the client to hire another professional to provide the contracted-for services and any other reasonable and foreseeable losses that arise from the professional's breach. For instance, if the client had to pay liquidated damages or penalties for failing to meet deadlines, the court may order the professional to pay an equivalent amount in damages to the client.

47-1b Liability for Negligence

Accountants and other professionals may also be held liable under the common law for negligence in the performance of their services. Recall that to establish negligence, the plaintiff must prove four elements: duty, breach, causation, and damages.

Negligence cases against professionals often focus on the standard of care exercised by the professionals. All professionals are subject to the standards of conduct and the ethical codes established by their profession, by state statutes, and by judicial decisions. They are also governed by the contracts they enter into with their clients.

In performing their contracts, professionals must exercise the established standards of care, knowledge, and judgment generally accepted by members of their professional group. How do those standards apply when an attorney stores confidential client information and other data on the cloud? See this chapter's *Ethics Today* feature for a discussion of this issue.

Accountant's Duty of Care Accountants play a major role in a business's financial system. Accountants

What Are an Attorney's Responsibilities for Protecting Data Stored in the Cloud?

To achieve both cost savings and better security, more and more attorneys are storing their data, including confidential client information, on the cloud. Sometimes, professionals assume that once their data have migrated to the cloud, they no longer have to be concerned with keeping the information secure. But cloud computing is simply the virtualization of the computing process. In other words, the professional is still ultimately responsible for the information.

Rules of Professional Conduct and Stored Information

Attorneys' obligations for their clients' information are spelled out in the American Bar Association's Model Rules of Professional Conduct, which serve as the basis for the ethics rules for attorneys adopted by most states. Comment 17 to Model Rule 1.6 states, "The lawyer must take reasonable precautions to prevent the [client's] information from coming into the hands of unintended recipients." Thus, lawyers have an ethical duty to safeguard confidential client information. It makes no difference whether the information is stored as documents in a filing cabinet or as electromagnetic impulses on a server that might be located anywhere. (Note that Rule 1.6 does not require an attorney to guarantee that a breach of confidentiality will never occur.)

Certainly, it is harder to maintain control over information stored on the cloud. Although the attorney "owns" the data, he or she probably does not even know the location of the computer where the information is stored. Furthermore, a provider of cloud computing services may move data from one server to another. Attorneys should be aware of jurisdictional issues and make sure that their cloud computing provider is complying with data protection regulations and privacy notification requirements wherever the provider's servers are located.

Litigation Issues

The problems presented by e-discovery become even more complex when information is stored in the cloud. Not only will adequate data maps have to be readily available during discovery and subsequent litigation, but the attorney will have to ascertain who will have access to sensitive information.

Attorneys must be particularly careful to avoid spoliation, or the negligent altering or destruction of evidence relevant to the litigation. Preserving information in the cloud can be more difficult if the data are spread across multiple physical storage sites. Sometimes, attorneys can be required to isolate the relevant data within their cloud computing provider's cloud resources.

Critical Thinking *To what extent must attorneys reveal to their clients where confidential data are stored?*

have the expertise and experience necessary to establish and maintain accurate financial records, and to design, control, and audit record-keeping systems. They also prepare reliable statements reflecting an individual's or a business's financial status, give tax advice, and prepare tax returns.

Generally, an accountant is expected to possess the skills that an ordinarily prudent accountant would have and to exercise the degree of care that an ordinarily prudent accountant would exercise. The level of skill expected of accountants and the degree of care that they should exercise in performing their services are reflected in the standards discussed next.

GAAP and GAAS. When performing their services, accountants must comply with **generally accepted accounting principles (GAAP)** and **generally accepted auditing standards (GAAS).** The Financial Accounting Standards Board (FASB, usually pronounced "faz-bee") determines what accounting conventions, rules, and procedures constitute GAAP at a given point in time. Similarly, the American Institute of Certified Public Accountants established GAAS to identify the professional qualities and the judgment that an auditor should exercise in auditing financial records.

A violation of GAAP and GAAS is considered *prima facie* evidence of negligence on the part of the accountant. Compliance with GAAP and GAAS, however, does not *necessarily* relieve an accountant from potential legal liability. An accountant may be held to a higher standard of conduct established by state statutes or by judicial decisions.

Global Accounting Rules. Although the United States has used the GAAP standards for many years, they are being replaced by global accounting rules. The Securities and Exchange Commission (SEC) now requires U.S. companies to use global accounting rules for all financial reports filed with the SEC. These rules, known as **International Financial Reporting Standards (IFRS),** are established by the London-based International Accounting Standards Board.

The SEC decided to replace GAAP with IFRS for several reasons. GAAP are rule based, whereas IFRS focus more on general principles. As a result, GAAP are very detailed and fill nearly 25,000 pages. IFRS are simpler, more straightforward, and shorter, filling only 2,500 pages. Consequently, companies should find it less difficult to comply with IFRS.

Another benefit is that investors will find it easier to make cross-country comparisons between the financial statements of, say, a technology company in Silicon Valley and one in Japan. Furthermore, having uniform accounting rules that apply to all nations makes sense in a global economy. The members of the European Union and more than one hundred other nations—including nearly all of the trading partners of the United States—use IFRS.

Discovering Improprieties. An accountant is not required to discover every impropriety, **defalcation**[1] (embezzlement), or fraud in a client's books. If, however, an impropriety goes undiscovered because of the accountant's negligence or failure to perform a duty, the accountant will be liable for any resulting losses suffered by the client. Therefore, an accountant who uncovers suspicious financial transactions and fails to investigate the matter fully or to inform the client of the discovery can be held liable to the client for the resulting loss.

Audits. One of the more important tasks that an accountant may perform for a business is an audit. An *audit* is a systematic inspection, by analyses and tests, of a business's financial records. An accountant qualified to perform audits is often called an **auditor.** After performing an audit, the auditor issues an opinion letter stating whether, in his or her opinion, the financial statements fairly present the business's financial position.

The purpose of an audit is to provide the auditor with evidence to support an opinion on the reliability of the business's financial statements. A normal audit is not intended to uncover fraud or other misconduct.

Nevertheless, an accountant may be liable for failing to detect misconduct if a normal audit would have revealed it. Also, if the auditor agreed to examine the records for evidence of fraud or other obvious misconduct and then failed to detect it, he or she may be liable.

Qualified Opinions and Disclaimers. In issuing an opinion letter, an auditor may *qualify* the opinion or include a *disclaimer.* In a qualified opinion, the auditor approves the financial statements overall but identifies one or two issues that are still in question. In a disclaimer, the auditor basically states that she or he does not have sufficient information to issue an opinion. A qualified opinion or a disclaimer must be specific and identify the reason for the qualification or disclaimer.

■ **EXAMPLE 47.1** Richard Zehr performs an audit of Lacey Corporation's financial statements. In the opinion letter, Zehr qualifies his opinion by stating that there is uncertainty about how a lawsuit against the firm will be resolved. In this situation, Zehr will not be liable if the outcome of the suit is unfavorable for the firm. Zehr could still be liable, however, if he failed to discover other problems that an audit in compliance with GAAS and IFRS would have revealed. ■

Unaudited Financial Statements. Sometimes, accountants are hired to prepare unaudited financial statements. (A financial statement is considered unaudited if incomplete auditing procedures have been used in its preparation or if insufficient procedures have been used to justify an opinion.) Lesser standards of care are typically required in this situation.

Nevertheless, accountants may be liable for omissions from unaudited statements. Accountants may be subject to liability for failing, in accordance with standard accounting procedures, to designate a balance sheet as "unaudited." An accountant will also be held liable for failure to disclose to a client facts or circumstances suggesting that misstatements have been made or that fraud has been committed.

Defenses to Negligence. If an accountant is found guilty of negligence, the client can collect damages for losses that arose from the accountant's negligence. An accountant facing a negligence claim, however, has several possible defenses, including the following:

1. The accountant was not negligent.
2. If the accountant was negligent, this negligence was not the proximate cause of the client's losses.
3. The client was also negligent (depending on whether the state applies contributory negligence or comparative negligence).

---

1. This term, pronounced deh-ful-*kay*-shun, is derived from the Latin *de* ("off") and *falx* ("sickle"—a tool for cutting grain or tall grass). In law, the term refers to the act of a defaulter or of an embezzler. As used here, it means embezzlement.

■ **EXAMPLE 47.2** Coopers & Peterson, LLP, provide accounting services for Bandon Steel Mills, Inc. (BSM). Coopers advises BSM to report a certain transaction as a $12.3 million gain on its financial statements. Later, BSM plans to make a public offering of its stock. The SEC reviews its financial statements and determines that the accounting treatment of the transaction has to be corrected before the sale.

Because of the delay, the public offering does not occur as planned on May 2, when BSM's stock is selling for $16 per share. It takes place instead on June 13, when, due to unrelated factors, the price has fallen to $13.50. If BSM files a lawsuit against Coopers claiming that the negligent accounting resulted in the stock's being sold at a lower price, BSM is unlikely to prevail. Although the accountant's negligence may have delayed the stock offering, the negligence was not the proximate cause of the decline in the stock price. Coopers would not be liable for damages based on the price decline. ■

Attorney's Duty of Care The conduct of attorneys is governed by rules established by each state and by the American Bar Association's Model Rules of Professional Conduct. All attorneys owe a duty to provide competent and diligent representation. Attorneys are required to be familiar with well-settled principles of law applicable to a case and to find relevant law that can be discovered through a reasonable amount of research. They must also investigate and discover facts that could materially affect clients' legal rights.

Normally, an attorney's performance is expected to be that of a reasonably competent general practitioner of ordinary skill, experience, and capacity. Often, an attorney holds himself or herself out as having expertise in a particular area of law (such as intellectual property). In this instance, the attorney is held to a higher standard of care in that area of law than attorneys without such knowledge.

Misconduct. Typically, state rules of professional conduct for attorneys provide that committing a criminal act that reflects adversely on the attorney's "honesty or trustworthiness, or fitness as a lawyer" is professional misconduct. The rules often further provide that a lawyer should not engage in conduct involving "dishonesty, fraud, deceit, or misrepresentation." Under these rules, state authorities can discipline attorneys for many types of misconduct.

Note, though, that states do not frequently discipline attorneys if their misconduct does not reflect on their honesty and trustworthiness. ■ **CASE IN POINT 47.3** Daniel Johns, a Wisconsin attorney, was the driver in a one-vehicle drunk driving accident in which his brother

was killed. He pleaded guilty to homicide by use of a vehicle while driving with a blood alcohol level over the legal limit. Johns served 120 days in jail and was released on five years' probation. The court terminated his probation early because of his good behavior, and he went back to practicing law.

The state's office of lawyer regulation (OLR) then initiated disciplinary proceedings seeking to suspend Johns's license to practice for sixty days for professional misconduct. The court, however, explained that the "commission of a criminal act by a Wisconsin licensed lawyer does not, *per se,* constitute professional misconduct." The OLR had not proved that Johns's crime reflected adversely on his honesty, trustworthiness, or fitness as a lawyer in other respects. In fact, except for this one tragic event, Johns had led an exemplary life without a hint of professional misconduct. The court therefore dismissed the disciplinary complaint.[2] ■

Liability for Malpractice. When an attorney fails to exercise reasonable care and professional judgment, she or he breaches the duty of care and can be held liable for *malpractice* (professional negligence). In malpractice cases—as in all cases involving allegations of negligence—the plaintiff must prove that the attorney's breach of the duty of care actually caused the plaintiff to suffer some injury.

■ **CASE IN POINT 47.4** The law firm of Husch Blackwell Sanders, LLP, represented Brian Nail in a dispute with his former employer over stock options. When Nail left the company, he acquired options to purchase his former employer's stock within eighteen months. But then the former employer merged with another company, and the stock was "locked up" for twelve months after the merger. The value of the stock declined significantly during this period. Husch Blackwell eventually negotiated a settlement that extended Nail's option period. When Nail attempted to exercise his options under the settlement agreement, however, complications arose that prevented him from immediately obtaining the stock.

Nail sued Husch Blackwell in a Missouri state court for malpractice, alleging that the firm had negligently drafted the settlement agreement and negligently delayed advising him to exercise the options. Nail sought to recover damages equal to the difference between the highest value of the stock during the lock-up period and his cost to acquire the stock. The trial court granted a summary judgment in favor of the law firm, and the Missouri Supreme Court affirmed. Nail had failed to prove that Husch Blackwell's alleged negligence was the proximate

---

2. *In re Disciplinary Proceedings against Johns,* 2014 WI 32, 353 Wis.2d 746, 847 N.W.2d 179 (2014).

cause of his damages. The decline in the stock price was unrelated to the law firm's alleged misconduct.[3] ∎

47–1c Liability for Fraud

Fraud, or misrepresentation, involves the following elements:

1. A misrepresentation of a material fact.
2. An intent to deceive.
3. Justifiable reliance by the innocent party on the misrepresentation.

In addition, to obtain damages, the innocent party must have been injured. Both actual and constructive fraud are potential sources of legal liability for an accountant or other professional.

Actual Fraud A professional may be held liable for *actual* fraud when (1) he or she intentionally misstates a material fact to mislead a client and (2) the client is injured as a result of justifiably relying on the misstated fact. A material fact is one that a reasonable person would consider important in deciding whether to act.

Among other penalties, an accountant guilty of fraudulent conduct may suffer penalties imposed by a state board of accountancy. ∎ **CASE IN POINT 47.5** Michael Walsh, a certified public accountant (CPA), impersonated his brother-in-law, Stephen Teiper, on the phone to obtain financial information from Teiper's insurance company. Teiper wrote a letter reporting Walsh's conduct to the Nebraska Board of Public Accountancy. After a hearing, the board reprimanded Walsh, placed him on probation for three months, and ordered him to attend four hours of ethics training. He also had to pay the costs of the hearing. The Nebraska Supreme Court affirmed the board's decision on appeal.[4] ∎

Constructive Fraud A professional may sometimes be held liable for **constructive fraud** whether or not he or she acted with fraudulent intent. Constructive fraud may be found when a professional is grossly negligent in performing his or her duties. ∎ **EXAMPLE 47.6** Paula, an accountant, is conducting an audit of ComCo, Inc. Paula accepts the explanations of Ron, a ComCo officer, regarding certain financial irregularities, despite evidence that contradicts those explanations and indicates that the irregularities may be illegal. Paula's conduct could be characterized as an intentional failure to perform a duty

in reckless disregard of the consequences of such failure. This would constitute gross negligence and could be held to be constructive fraud. ∎

47–2 Potential Liability to Third Parties

Traditionally, a professional owed a duty only to those with whom she or he had a direct contractual relationship—that is, those with whom she or he was in *privity of contract.* A professional's duty was only to her or his client. Violations of statutes, fraud, and other intentional or reckless acts of wrongdoing were the only exceptions to this general rule.

Today, this situation has changed, perhaps most noticeably with respect to accountants who conduct audits (auditors). Numerous third parties—including investors, shareholders, creditors, corporate managers and directors, and regulatory agencies—rely on the opinions of auditors when making decisions. In view of this extensive reliance, many courts have all but abandoned the privity requirement in regard to accountants' liability to third parties.

In this discussion, we focus primarily on the potential liability of auditors to third parties. Understanding an auditor's common law liability to third parties is critical. Often, when a business fails, its independent auditor may be one of the few defendants still *solvent*—that is, able to pay expenses and debts. The majority of courts now hold that auditors can be held liable to third parties for negligence, but the standard for the imposition of this liability varies.

47–2a The *Ultramares* Rule

The traditional rule regarding an accountant's liability to third parties based on privity of contract was enunciated by Chief Judge Benjamin Cardozo in 1931. ∎ **CASE IN POINT 47.7** Fred Stern & Company had hired the public accounting firm of Touche, Niven & Company to review Stern's financial records and prepare a balance sheet for the year ending December 31, 1923.[5] Touche prepared the balance sheet and supplied Stern with thirty-two certified copies. According to the certified balance sheet, Stern had a net worth (assets less liabilities) of $1,070,715.26.

---

3. *Nail v. Husch Blackwell Sanders, LLP,* 436 S.W.3d 556 (2014).
4. *Walsh v. State,* 276 Neb. 1034, 759 N.W.2d 100 (2009).

5. Banks, creditors, stockholders, purchasers, and sellers often rely on balance sheets when making decisions related to a company's business.

In reality, however, Stern's liabilities exceeded its assets—the company's records had been falsified by insiders at Stern to reflect a positive net worth. In reliance on the certified balance sheets, Ultramares Corporation loaned substantial amounts to Stern. After Stern was declared bankrupt, Ultramares brought an action against Touche for negligence in an attempt to recover damages.

The New York Court of Appeals (that state's highest court) refused to impose liability on Touche. The court concluded that Touche's accountants owed a duty of care only to those persons for whose "primary benefit" the statements were intended. In this case, the statements were intended only for the primary benefit of Stern. The court held that in the absence of privity or a relationship "so close as to approach that of privity," a party could not recover from an accountant.[6] ■

The Requirement of Privity The requirement of privity has since been referred to as the *Ultramares* rule, or the New York rule. It continues to be used in some states. ■ **CASE IN POINT 47.8** Toro Company supplied equipment and credit to Summit Power Equipment Distributors and required Summit to submit audited reports indicating its financial condition. Accountants at Krouse, Kern & Company prepared the reports, which allegedly contained mistakes and omissions regarding Summit's financial condition.

Toro extended large amounts of credit to Summit in reliance on the audited reports. When Summit was unable to repay these amounts, Toro brought a negligence action against Krouse and proved that the accountants knew the reports would be used by Summit to induce Toro to extend credit. Nevertheless, under the *Ultramares* rule, the court refused to hold the accounting firm liable because the firm was not in privity with Toro.[7] ■

Modification to Allow "Near Privity" The *Ultramares* rule was restated and somewhat modified in a 1985 New York case, *Credit Alliance Corp. v. Arthur Andersen & Co.*[8] In that case, the court held that if a third party has a sufficiently close relationship or *nexus* (connection) with an accountant, then the *Ultramares* privity requirement may be satisfied without the establishment of an accountant-client relationship. The rule enunciated in the *Credit Alliance* case is often referred to as the "near privity"

rule. Only a minority of states have adopted this rule of accountants' liability to third parties.

47–2b The *Restatement* Rule

The *Ultramares* rule has been severely criticized. Much of the work performed by auditors is intended for use by persons who are not parties to the contract. Critics of the *Ultramares* rule assert that auditors should owe a duty to these third parties. As support for this position has grown, there has been an erosion of the *Ultramares* rule, and accountants may now be liable to third parties in some situations.

The majority of courts have adopted the position taken by the *Restatement (Third) of Torts*. This rule states that accountants are subject to liability for negligence not only to their clients but also to foreseen, or known, users of their reports or financial statements. Under the *Restatement (Third) of Torts*, an accountant's liability extends to:

1. Persons for whose benefit and guidance the accountant intends to supply the information or knows that the recipient intends to supply it.
2. Persons whom the accountant intends the information to influence or knows that the recipient so intends.

■ **EXAMPLE 47.9** Steve, an accountant, prepares a financial statement for Tech Software, Inc., a client, knowing that Tech will submit that statement when it applies for a loan from First National Bank. If the statement includes negligent misstatements or omissions, the bank may hold Steve liable, because he knew that the bank would rely on his work when deciding whether to make the loan. ■

47–2c The "Reasonably Foreseeable Users" Rule

A small minority of courts hold accountants liable to any users whose reliance on an accountant's statements or reports was *reasonably foreseeable*. This standard has been criticized as extending liability too far and exposing accountants to massive liability.

The majority of courts have concluded that the *Restatement's* approach is more reasonable because it allows accountants to control their exposure to liability. Liability is "fixed by the accountants' particular knowledge at the moment the audit is published," not by the foreseeability of the harm that might occur to a third party after the report is released.

Exhibit 47–1 summarizes the three different views of accountants' liability to third parties.

---

6. *Ultramares Corp. v. Touche*, 255 N.Y. 170, 174 N.E. 441 (1931).
7. *Toro Co. v. Krouse, Kern & Co.*, 827 F.2d 155 (7th Cir. 1987). See also *Citibank, F.S.B. v. McGladrey & Pullen, LLP*, 2007 WL 7134666 (Ill. 2007).
8. 65 N.Y.2d 536, 483 N.E.2d 110 (1985). A "relationship sufficiently intimate to be equated with privity" is enough for a third party to sue another's accountant for negligence.

EXHIBIT 47–1 Three Basic Rules of an Accountant's Liability to Third Parties

RULE	DESCRIPTION	APPLICATION
The *Ultramares* Rule	Liability will be imposed only if the accountant is in privity, or near privity, with the third party.	A minority of courts apply this rule.
The *Restatement* Rule	Liability will be imposed only if the third party's reliance is foreseen, or known, or if the third party is among a class of foreseen, or known, users.	The majority of courts have adopted this rule.
The "Reasonably Foreseeable Users" Rule	Liability will be imposed only if the third party's use was reasonably foreseeable.	A small minority of courts use this rule.

47–2d Liability of Attorneys to Third Parties

Like accountants, attorneys may be held liable under the common law to third parties who rely on legal opinions to their detriment. Generally, an attorney is not liable to a nonclient unless the attorney has committed fraud (or malicious conduct). The liability principles stated in the *Restatement (Third) of Torts,* however, may apply to attorneys as well as to accountants.

Should an attorney's duty of care extend to third party beneficiaries whose rights were harmed by the attorney's malpractice? That question was at issue in the following case.

Case Analysis 47.1

Perez[a] v. Stern

Nebraska Supreme Court, 279 Neb. 187, 777 N.W.2d 545 (2010).

In the Language of the Court

GERRARD, J. [Justice]

* * * *

[Reyna] Guido is the mother of two minor children. [Domingo] Martinez, the children's father, died after he was run over by a car on July 8, 2001. Martinez was the victim of a hit-and-run accident.

Guido, as personal representative of Martinez's estate, retained [Sandra] Stern to file a wrongful death lawsuit. On July 8, 2003, Stern filed a wrongful death complaint in the district court. But Stern admits that she never perfected service of the complaint, and because the complaint was not served within six months of filing, the case was dismissed by operation of law.

---

a. Estaban Perez was one of the minor children of Domingo Martinez, the man killed in the accident.

* * * On February 6, 2007, Guido filed these legal malpractice claims against Stern on behalf of herself, the children, and the estate. Guido alleged that the wrongful death claim expired as a result of Stern's failure to timely perfect service of the complaint. Stern moved for summary judgment on the ground that the malpractice claims were barred by the two-year statute of limitations for professional negligence. Before the court ruled on the motion, Guido voluntarily dismissed her individual claim, but maintained claims as personal representative of the estate and next friend of the children.

The district court found that the malpractice claims accrued on May 7, 2004, when the wrongful death claim was dismissed. The court found that the estate's claim against Stern was time barred. In response to Guido's argument that the children's minority tolled

[suspended] the statute of limitations with respect to them, the court found that because the children could not have brought the underlying wrongful death claim in their own names, the statute of limitations for the legal malpractice claims was not tolled by reason of the children's minority. The court granted summary judgment in favor of Stern and dismissed the complaint.

* * * *

Guido [appealed, claiming] that the district court erred in granting Stern's motion for summary judgment on her affirmative defense of the statute of limitations and, specifically, determining that the children had no independent standing to sue Stern and that Stern owed no independent duty to the minor children to protect their rights and interests.

Case 47.1 Continued

We note that neither Guido's assignments of error nor the argument in her appellate brief challenges the district court's dismissal of Guido's claims as an individual and as personal representative of Martinez's estate. Therefore, those aspects of the court's judgment will be affirmed.

* * * *

The issue in this case is whether Stern owed an independent duty to the children, as Martinez's next of kin, to timely prosecute the underlying wrongful death claim.

* * * *

In Nebraska, *a lawyer owes a duty to his or her client to use reasonable care and skill in the discharge of his or her duties, but ordinarily this duty does not extend to third parties, absent facts establishing a duty to them.* [Emphasis added.]

But that does not end our analysis. * * * We have never said that privity [of

contract] is an absolute requirement of a legal malpractice claim. Instead, we have said that a lawyer's duty to use reasonable care and skill in the discharge of his or her duties *ordinarily* does not extend to third parties, *absent facts establishing a duty to them.* On the facts of this case, we conclude, as have other courts to have addressed this issue in the context of a wrongful death action, that the facts establish an independent legal duty from Stern to Martinez's statutory beneficiaries. [Emphasis in the original]

* * * Courts have repeatedly emphasized that *the starting point for analyzing an attorney's duty to a third party is determining whether the third party was a direct and intended beneficiary of the attorney's services.* [Emphasis added.]

* * * *

In this case, we conclude that Stern owed a duty to the children, as direct and intended beneficiaries of

her services, to competently represent their interests. To hold otherwise would deny legal recourse to the children for whose benefit Stern was hired in the first place.

* * * Stern owed a legal duty to Martinez's minor children to exercise reasonable care in representing their interests. Therefore, they have standing to sue Stern for neglecting that duty, and their claims against Stern were tolled by their minority. The district court erred in concluding that their claims were time barred. We affirm the court's dismissal of Guido's individual claim and its determination that the estate's claim against Stern was time barred. But with respect to the children, this cause is reversed and remanded for further proceedings to fully adjudicate Guido's claims on behalf of the children * * * .

Affirmed in part, and in part reversed and remanded for further proceedings.

Legal Reasoning Questions

1. If the children had suffered no harm as a result of the attorney's malpractice, would the outcome of this case have been different? Why or why not?

2. Why did the court affirm the dismissal of Guido's individual claim but not the claims that she had brought on behalf of the children?

3. If one of the children had not been a minor at the time of the father's death, the court would have dismissed that child's claims against Stern, even though the child was an intended beneficiary. Is it fair for the law to treat minors differently from other children with regard to a statute of limitations? Why or why not?

Concept Summary 47.1 reviews the common law rules under which accountants, attorneys, and other professionals may be held liable.

the 1934 act, or (3) that has filed a registration statement that has not yet become effective under the Securities Act of 1933.

47-3 The Sarbanes-Oxley Act

The Sarbanes-Oxley Act imposes a number of strict requirements on both domestic and foreign public accounting firms. These requirements apply to firms that provide auditing services to companies ("issuers") whose securities are sold to public investors. The act defines the term *issuer* as a company (1) that has securities registered under Section 12 of the Securities Exchange Act of 1934, (2) that is required to file reports under Section 15(d) of

47-3a The Public Company Accounting Oversight Board

The Sarbanes-Oxley Act increased government oversight of public accounting practices by creating the Public Company Accounting Oversight Board, which reports to the Securities and Exchange Commission. The board oversees the audit of public companies that are subject to securities laws. The goal is to protect public investors and to ensure that public accounting firms comply with the provisions of the act. The act defines *public accounting*

Concept Summary 47.1

Common Law Liability of Accountants and Other Professionals

Liability to Clients	
	• *Breach of contract*—A professional who fails to perform according to his or her contractual obligations can be held liable for breach of contract and resulting damages.
	• *Negligence*—An accountant, attorney, or other professional, in performing her or his duties, must use the care, knowledge, and judgment generally used by professionals in the same or similar circumstances. Failure to do so is negligence. An accountant's violation of generally accepted accounting principles and generally accepted auditing standards is *prima facie* evidence of negligence.
	• *Fraud*—Intentionally misrepresenting a material fact to a client, when the client relies on the misrepresentation, is actual fraud. Gross negligence in performance of duties is constructive fraud.

Liability to Third Parties	
	• *Liability of accountants*—An accountant may be liable for negligence to any third person the accountant knows or should have known will benefit from the accountant's work. The standard for imposing this liability varies, but generally courts follow the *Ultramares* rule, the *Restatement* rule, or the "Reasonably Foreseeable Users" rule.
	• *Liability of attorneys*—An attorney generally is not liable to a nonclient unless the attorney committed fraud or other malicious conduct. In some situations, an attorney may be liable to persons whose reliance is foreseen or known.

firms as firms "engaged in the practice of public accounting or preparing or issuing audit reports." Smaller companies—those with less than $75 million in publicly held shares—no longer need to file an auditor's report on management's assessment of internal controls under Section 404(b). The key provisions relating to the duties of the oversight board and the requirements relating to public accounting firms are summarized in Exhibit 47–2.

47–3b Requirements for Maintaining Working Papers

In performing an audit for a client, an accountant accumulates various **working papers**—the documents used and developed during the audit. These include notes, computations, memoranda, copies, and other papers that make up the work product of an accountant's services to a client.

Under the common law, which in this instance has been codified in a number of states, working papers remain the accountant's property. It is important for accountants to retain such records in the event that they need to defend against lawsuits for negligence or other actions in which their competence is challenged. The client also has a right to access an accountant's working papers because they reflect the client's financial situation. On a client's request, an accountant must return any of the client's records or journals to the client, and failure to do so may result in liability.

The Sarbanes-Oxley Act initially provided that accountants must maintain working papers relating to an audit or review for five years from the end of the fiscal period in which the audit or review was concluded. The period was subsequently increased to seven years. A knowing violation of this requirement will subject the accountant to a fine, imprisonment for up to ten years, or both.

EXHIBIT 47–2 Key Provisions of the Sarbanes-Oxley Act Relating to Public Accounting Firms

AUDITOR INDEPENDENCE

To help ensure that auditors remain independent of the firms that they audit, Title II of the Sarbanes-Oxley Act does the following:

1. Makes it unlawful for Registered Public Accounting Firms (RPAFs) to perform both audit and nonaudit services for the same company at the same time. Nonaudit services include the following:

   • Bookkeeping or other services related to the accounting records or financial statements of the audit client.
   • Financial information systems design and implementation.
   • Appraisal or valuation services.
   • Fairness opinions.
   • Management functions.
   • Broker or dealer, investment adviser, or investment banking services.

2. Requires preapproval for most auditing services from the issuer's (the corporation's) audit committee.

3. Requires audit partner rotation by prohibiting RPAFs from providing audit services to an issuer if either the lead audit partner or the audit partner

responsible for reviewing the audit has provided such services to that corporation in each of the prior five years.

4. Requires RPAFs to make timely reports to the audit committees of the corporations. The report must indicate all critical accounting policies and practices to be used; all alternative treatments of financial information within generally accepted accounting principles that have been discussed with the corporation's management officials, the ramifications of the use of such alternative treatments, and the treatment preferred by the auditor; and other material written communications between the auditor and the corporation's management.

5. Makes it unlawful for an RPAF to provide auditing services to an issuer if the corporation's chief executive officer, chief financial officer, chief accounting officer, or controller was previously employed by the auditor and participated in any capacity in the audit of the corporation during the one-year period preceding the date when the audit began.

DOCUMENT DESTRUCTION

The Sarbanes-Oxley Act provides that anyone who destroys, alters, or falsifies records with the intent to obstruct or influence a federal investigation or in relation to bankruptcy proceedings can be criminally prosecuted and sentenced to a fine, imprisonment for up to twenty years, or both.

DOCUMENT RETENTION

The Sarbanes-Oxley Act also requires accountants who audit or review publicly traded companies to retain all working papers related to the audit or review for a period of five years (now amended to seven years). Violators can be sentenced to a fine, imprisonment for up to ten years, or both.

47–4 Potential Liability of Accountants under Securities Laws

Both civil and criminal liability may be imposed on accountants under the Securities Act of 1933, the Securities Exchange Act of 1934, and the Private Securities Litigation Reform Act of 1995.[9]

47–4a Liability under the Securities Act of 1933

The Securities Act of 1933 requires registration statements to be filed with the Securities and Exchange Commission (SEC) prior to an offering of securities.[10] Accountants frequently prepare and certify the issuer's financial statements that are included in the registration statement.

---

9. Civil and criminal liability may also be imposed on accountants and other professionals under other statutes, including the Racketeer Influenced and Corrupt Organizations Act (RICO).

10. Many securities and transactions are expressly exempted from the 1933 act.

Liability under Section 11 Section 11 of the Securities Act imposes civil liability on accountants for misstatements and omissions of material facts in registration statements. Accountants may be held liable if a financial statement they prepared for inclusion "contained an untrue statement of a material fact or omitted to state a material fact required to be stated therein or necessary to make the statements therein not misleading."[11]

An accountant may be liable to anyone who acquires a security covered by the registration statement. A purchaser of a security need only demonstrate that she or he has suffered a loss on the security. Proof of reliance on the materially false statement or misleading omission ordinarily is not required. Nor is there a requirement of privity between the accountant and the security purchaser.

The Due Diligence Standard. Section 11 imposes a duty on accountants to use **due diligence** in preparing financial statements included in the filed registration statements. Once a purchaser has proved a loss on a security, the accountant has the burden of showing that he or she exercised due diligence.

To prove due diligence, the accountant must demonstrate that she or he followed generally accepted standards and did not commit negligence or fraud. The accountant must show that he or she:

1. Conducted a reasonable investigation.
2. Had reasonable grounds to believe and did believe, at the time the registration statement became effective, that the statements therein were true and that there was no omission of a material fact that would be misleading.[12]

In particular, the due diligence standard places a burden on accountants to verify information furnished by a corporation's officers and directors. Merely asking questions is not always sufficient to satisfy the requirement of due diligence. Accountants may be held liable, for instance, for failing to detect danger signals in documents furnished by corporate officers that required further investigation.

Other Defenses to Liability. Besides proving that he or she has acted with due diligence, an accountant may raise the following defenses to Section 11 liability:

1. There were no misstatements or omissions.
2. The misstatements or omissions were not of material facts.

3. The misstatements or omissions had no causal connection to the plaintiff's loss.
4. The plaintiff-purchaser invested in the securities knowing of the misstatements or omissions.

Liability under Section 12(2) Section 12(2) of the 1933 Securities Act imposes civil liability for fraud in relation to offerings or sales of securities.[13] Liability arises when the offeror or seller makes an oral statement to an investor or provides a written prospectus[14] that includes an untrue statement or omits a material fact. Accountants may be liable under Section 12(2) if they participated in preparing materials in which the false misrepresentation or omission was made.

Those who purchase securities and suffer harm as a result of a false or omitted statement, or some other violation, may bring a suit in a federal court to recover their losses and other damages. The U.S. Department of Justice brings criminal actions against those who commit willful violations.

The penalties include fines up to $10,000, imprisonment up to five years, or both. The SEC is authorized to seek an injunction against a willful violator to prevent further violations. The SEC can also ask a court to grant other relief, such as an order to a violator to refund profits derived from an illegal transaction.

47–4b Liability under the Securities Exchange Act of 1934

Under Sections 18 and 10(b) of the 1934 Securities Exchange Act and SEC Rule 10b-5, an accountant may be found liable for fraud. A plaintiff has a substantially heavier burden of proof under the 1934 act than under the 1933 act because an accountant does not have to prove due diligence to escape liability under the 1934 act. The 1934 act relieves an accountant from liability if the accountant acted in "good faith."

Liability under Section 18 Section 18 of the 1934 act imposes civil liability on an accountant who makes or causes to be made in any application, report, or document a statement that at the time and in light of the circumstances was false or misleading with respect to any material fact.[15]

Section 18 liability is narrow in that it applies only to applications, reports, documents, and registration

---

11. 15 U.S.C. Section 77k(a).
12. 15 U.S.C. Section 77k(b)(3).

13. 15 U.S.C. Section 77*l*.
14. A *prospectus* contains financial disclosures about the corporation for the benefit of potential investors.
15. 15 U.S.C. Section 78r(a).

statements filed with the SEC. In addition, it applies only to sellers and purchasers. Under Section 18, a seller or purchaser must prove one of the following:

1. The false or misleading statement affected the price of the security.
2. The purchaser or seller relied on the false or misleading statement in making the purchase or sale and was not aware of the inaccuracy of the statement.

Sellers and purchasers must bring a cause of action "within one year after the discovery of the facts constituting the cause of action and within three years after such cause of action accrued."[16] A court has the discretion to assess reasonable costs, including attorneys' fees, against accountants who violate Section 18.

Good Faith Defense. An accountant will not be liable for violating Section 18 if he or she acted in good faith in preparing the financial statement. To demonstrate good faith, an accountant must show that he or she had no knowledge that the financial statement was false or misleading. Also, the accountant must have had no intent to deceive, manipulate, defraud, or seek unfair advantage over another party.

Other Defenses. In addition to the good faith defense, accountants can escape liability by proving that the buyer or seller of the security in question knew that the financial statement was false and misleading. Note, too, that "mere" negligence in preparing a financial statement does not lead to liability under the 1934 act. This differs from the 1933 act, under which an accountant is liable for all negligent acts.

Liability under Section 10(b) and SEC Rule 10b-5 Accountants additionally face potential legal liability under the antifraud provisions contained in the Securities Exchange Act and SEC Rule 10b-5. The scope

of these antifraud provisions is very broad and allows private parties to bring civil actions against violators.

Prohibited Conduct. Section 10(b) makes it unlawful for any person, including an accountant, to use, in connection with the purchase or sale of any security, any manipulative or deceptive device or plan that is counter to SEC rules and regulations.[17] Rule 10b-5 further makes it unlawful for any person, by use of any means or instrumentality of interstate commerce, to do the following:

1. Employ any device, scheme, or strategy to defraud.
2. Make any untrue statement of a material fact or omit to state a material fact necessary to make the statements made, in light of the circumstances, not misleading.
3. Engage in any act, practice, or course of business that operates or would operate as a fraud or deceit on any person, in connection with the purchase or sale of any security.[18]

Extent of Liability. Accountants may be held liable only to sellers or purchasers of securities under Section 10(b) and Rule 10b-5. Privity is not necessary for a recovery. An accountant may be liable not only for fraudulent misstatements of material facts in written material filed with the SEC, but also for any fraudulent oral statements or omissions made in connection with the purchase or sale of any security.

For a plaintiff to succeed in recovering damages under these antifraud provisions, he or she must prove intent *(scienter)* to commit the fraudulent or deceptive act. Ordinary negligence is not enough.

Do accountants have a duty to correct misstatements that they discover in *previous* financial statements if they know that potential investors are relying on those statements? That was the question in the following case.

---

16. 15 U.S.C. Section 17r(c).

17. 15 U.S.C. Section 78j(b).
18. 17 C.F.R. Section 240.10b-5.

Spotlight on Accountant's Duty to Correct Mistakes

Case 47.2 Overton v. Todman & Co., CPAs
United States Court of Appeals, Second Circuit, 478 F.3d 479 (2007).

Background and Facts From 1999 through 2002, Todman & Company, CPAs, P.C., audited the financial statements of Direct Brokerage, Inc. (DBI), a broker-dealer in New York registered with the Securities and Exchange Commission (SEC). Each year, Todman issued an unqualified opinion that DBI's financial statements were accurate. DBI filed its statements and Todman's opinions with the SEC.

Case 47.2 Continues

Despite the certifications of accuracy, Todman made significant errors that concealed DBI's largest liability—its payroll taxes—in the 1999 and 2000 audits. The errors came to light in 2003 when the New York State Division of Taxation subpoenaed DBI's payroll records. It became clear that the company had not filed or paid its payroll taxes for 1999 and 2000. This put DBI in a precarious financial position, owing the state more than $3 million in unpaid taxes, interest, and penalties.

To meet its needs, DBI sought outside investors, including David Overton, who relied on DBI's statements and Todman's opinion for 2002 to invest in DBI. When DBI collapsed under the weight of its liabilities in 2004, Overton and others filed a suit in a federal district court against Todman. Among other things, the plaintiffs asserted fraud under Section 10(b) and Rule 10b-5. The court dismissed the complaint. The plaintiffs appealed to the U.S. Court of Appeals for the Second Circuit.

In the Language of the Court

STRAUB, Circuit Judge.

* * * *

A fundamental principle of securities law is that before an individual becomes liable for his silence, he must have an underlying duty to speak. [Emphasis added.]

* * * *

* * * The Supreme Court [has] held that [Section] 10(b) does not authorize aiding and abetting liability. In order to be liable under [Section] 10(b), the Court held, an actor must himself "mak[e] * * * a material misstatement (or omission) or * * * commit * * * a manipulative act." The rationale underpinning this holding was that (1) by its terms, [Section] 10(b) requires the making of a statement or omission and (2) without such a statement or omission, the "critical" element of reliance would be absent.

Although the Court did not specifically discuss an auditor's duty to correct, it made clear that * * * secondary actors such as accountants may incur primary liability based on their omissions * * * .

* * * For many years we have recognized the existence of an accountant's duty to correct its certified opinions, but never squarely held that such a duty exists for the purposes of primary liability under [Section] 10(b) of the 1934 Act and Rule 10b-5. Presented with an opportunity to do so, we now so hold. *Specifically, we hold that an accountant violates the "duty to correct" and becomes primarily liable under [Section] 10(b) and Rule 10b-5 when it (1) makes a statement in its certified opinion that is false or misleading when made; (2) subsequently learns or was reckless in not learning that the earlier statement was false or misleading; (3) knows or should know that potential investors are relying on the opinion and financial statements; yet (4) fails to take reasonable steps to correct or withdraw its opinion and/or the financial statements; and (5) all the other requirements for liability are satisfied.* [Emphasis added.]

* * * *

In light of the above principles, we conclude that the District Court erred in dismissing the complaint. Plaintiffs pled that Todman's certified opinion and DBI's 2002 financial statements were misleading at the time they were issued, especially with respect to DBI's payroll tax liability; Todman * * * subsequently learned that its certified opinion was false; Todman also knew that DBI was soliciting outside investors based in part on its 2002 certified financial statements and Todman's accompanying opinion; and that despite this knowledge, Todman took no action to correct or withdraw its opinion and/or DBI's financial statements. These allegations adequately state a claim of primary accountant liability under [Section] 10(b) and Rule 10b-5.

Decision and Remedy *The U.S. Court of Appeals for the Second Circuit held that an accountant is liable in these circumstances under Section 10(b) and Rule 10b-5. The court vacated the lower court's dismissal and remanded the case.*

Critical Thinking

- **What If the Facts Were Different?** *If Todman had conducted an audit for DBI but had not issued a certified opinion about DBI's financial statements, would the result in this case have been the same? Explain.*
- **Legal Environment** *Did Overton have a valid reason to sue DBI's auditors? Why or why not?*

47–4c The Private Securities Litigation Reform Act of 1995

The Private Securities Litigation Reform Act made some changes to the potential liability of accountants and other professionals in securities fraud cases. Among other things, the act imposed a statutory obligation on accountants. An auditor must use adequate procedures in an audit to detect any illegal acts of the company being audited. If something illegal is detected, the auditor must disclose it to the company's board of directors, the audit committee, or the SEC, depending on the circumstances.[19]

Proportionate Liability The act provides that, in most situations, a party is liable only for the proportion of damages for which he or she is responsible.[20] In other words, the parties are subject to proportionate liability rather than joint and several liability. An accountant who participates in, but is unaware of, illegal conduct may not be liable for the entire amount of the loss caused by the illegality.

■ **EXAMPLE 47.10** Nina Chavez, an accountant, helped the president and owner of Midstate Trucking Company draft financial statements that misrepresented Midstate's financial condition. If Nina was not actually aware of the fraud, she can still be held liable, but the amount of her liability could be less than the entire loss. ■

Aiding and Abetting The act also made it a crime to aid and abet a violation of the 1934 Securities Exchange Act. Aiding and abetting might include knowingly participating or assisting in some improper activity or keeping quiet about it. If an accountant knowingly aids and abets a primary violator, the SEC can seek an injunction or monetary damages.

■ **EXAMPLE 47.11** Smith & Jones, an accounting firm, performs an audit for Belco Sales Company that is so inadequate as to constitute gross negligence. Belco uses the financial statements provided by Smith & Jones as part of a scheme to defraud investors. When the scheme is uncovered, the SEC can bring an action against Smith & Jones for aiding and abetting. The firm knew or should have known that its audited statements contained material misrepresentations on which investors were likely to rely. ■

47–4d Potential Criminal Liability of Accountants

An accountant may be found criminally liable for violations of securities laws and tax laws. In addition, most states make it a crime to (1) knowingly certify false reports, (2) falsify, alter, or destroy books of account, and (3) obtain property or credit through the use of false financial statements.

Criminal Violations of Securities Laws Accountants may be subject to criminal penalties for *willful* violations of the 1933 Securities Act and the 1934 Securities Exchange Act. If convicted, they face imprisonment for up to five years and/or a fine of up to $10,000 under the 1933 act and imprisonment for up to ten years and a fine of $100,000 under the 1934 act.

Under the Sarbanes-Oxley Act, if an accountant's false or misleading certified audit statement is used in a securities filing, the accountant may be held criminally liable. The accountant may be fined up to $5 million, imprisoned for up to twenty years, or both.

Criminal Violations of Tax Laws The Internal Revenue Code makes it a felony to aid or assist in the preparation of a false tax return. Violations are punishable by a fine of $100,000 ($500,000 for a corporation's return) and imprisonment for up to three years.[21] This provision applies to anyone who prepares tax returns for others for compensation, not just to accountants.[22]

A penalty of $250 per tax return is levied on tax preparers for negligent understatement of the client's tax liability. For willful understatement of tax liability or reckless or intentional disregard of rules or regulations, a penalty of $1,000 is imposed.[23]

A tax preparer may also be subject to penalties for failing to furnish the taxpayer with a copy of the return, failing to sign the return, or failing to furnish the appropriate tax identification numbers.[24] In addition, those who prepare tax returns for others may be fined $1,000 per document for aiding and abetting another's understatement of tax liability (the penalty is increased to $10,000 for corporate returns).[25] The tax preparer's liability is limited to one penalty per taxpayer per tax year.

Concept Summary 47.2 outlines the potential statutory liability of accountants and other professionals.

19. 15 U.S.C. Section 78j-1.
20. 15 U.S.C. Section 78u-4(g).
21. 26 U.S.C. Section 7206(2).
22. 26 U.S.C. Section 7701(a)(36).
23. 26 U.S.C. Section 6694.
24. 26 U.S.C. Section 6695.
25. 26 U.S.C. Section 6701.

Concept Summary 47.2

Statutory Law Liability of Accountants and Other Professionals

Sarbanes-Oxley Act	• See Exhibit 47–2 for key the provisions of the act.
Securities Act of 1933, Sections 11 and 12(2)	• Under Section 11 of the 1933 Securities Act, an accountant who makes a false statement or omits a material fact in audited financial statements required for registration of securities under the law may be liable to anyone who acquires securities covered by the registration statement. • The accountant's defense is basically the use of due diligence and the reasonable belief that the work was complete and correct. The burden of proof is on the accountant. • Willful violations of this act may be subject to criminal penalties. • Section 12(2) of the 1933 act imposes civil liability for fraud on anyone who makes an untrue statement or omits a material fact when offering or selling a security to any purchaser of the security.
Securities Exchange Act of 1934, Sections 10(b) and 18	• Under Sections 10(b) and 18 of the 1934 Securities Exchange Act, accountants are held liable for false and misleading applications, reports, and documents required under the act. • The burden is on the plaintiff, and the accountant has numerous defenses, including good faith and lack of knowledge that what was submitted was false. • Willful violations of this act may be subject to criminal penalties.
Internal Revenue Code	• Aiding or assisting in the preparation of a false tax return is a felony. Aiding and abetting an individual's understatement of tax liability is a separate crime. • Tax preparers who negligently or willfully understate a client's tax liability or who recklessly or intentionally disregard Internal Revenue Code rules or regulations are subject to penalties. • Tax preparers who fail to provide a taxpayer with a copy of the return, fail to sign the return, or fail to furnish the appropriate tax identification numbers may also be subject to penalties.

47-5 Confidentiality and Privilege

Professionals are restrained by the ethical tenets of their professions to keep all communications with their clients confidential.

47-5a Attorney-Client Relationships

The confidentiality of attorney-client communications is protected by law, which confers a *privilege* on such communications. This privilege exists because of the client's need to fully disclose the facts of his or her case to the attorney.

To encourage frankness, confidential attorney-client communications relating to representation are normally held in strictest confidence and protected by law. The attorney and her or his employees may not discuss the client's case with anyone—even under court order—without the client's permission. The client holds the privilege, and only the client may waive it—by disclosing privileged information to someone outside the privilege, for example.

Note, however, that the SEC has implemented rules requiring attorneys who become aware that a client has violated securities laws to report the violation to the SEC. Reporting a client's misconduct could be a breach of the attorney-client privilege, so these rules have created a potential conflict for some attorneys.

Once an attorney-client relationship arises, all communications between the parties are privileged. The question in the following case was whether communications between an attorney and an individual *before* that individual was informed that the attorney was *not* his counsel were privileged.

Case 47.3

Commonwealth of Pennsylvania v. Schultz
Superior Court of Pennsylvania, 133 A.3d 294 (2016).

Background and Facts An investigation into allegations of sexual misconduct involving minors and Jerry Sandusky, former defensive coordinator for the Pennsylvania State University football team, led a grand jury to subpoena Gary Schultz. Schultz, a retired vice president of the university, had overseen the campus police at the time of the alleged events.

Before testifying, Schultz met with Cynthia Baldwin, counsel for Penn State. He told her that he did not have any documents relating to the two incidents, believing this disclosure to be in the strictest confidence between attorney and client. Baldwin, however, saw her role as counsel only for Penn State, representing Schultz as an agent of the university, not personally. She did not explain this to him, and she appeared with him during his testimony.

Later, a file was found in Schultz's office containing notes pertaining to the two incidents. When Baldwin was called to testify, she revealed what he had told her at their meeting. On the basis of this testimony, the grand jury charged Schultz with the crimes of perjury, obstruction of justice, and conspiracy. Before a trial was held on these charges, Schultz filed a motion to preclude Baldwin's testimony and quash (suppress) the charges, arguing that her testimony violated the attorney-client privilege. The court denied the motion. Schulz appealed.

In the Language of the Court
Opinion by *BOWES*, J. [Judge]
* * * *

Communications between a putative [assumed] client and corporate counsel are generally privileged prior to counsel informing the individual of the distinction between representing the individual as an agent of the corporation and representing the person in his or her personal capacity. [Emphasis added.]

When corporate counsel clarifies the potential inherent conflict of interest in representing the corporation and an individual and explains that the attorney may divulge the communications between that person and the attorney because they do not represent the individual, the individual may then make a knowing, intelligent, and voluntary decision whether to continue communicating with corporate counsel.
* * * *

* * * Where an attorney purports to offer only limited representation before and at a grand jury proceeding, * * * a putative client must be made expressly aware of that fact.

As Schultz consulted with Ms. Baldwin for purposes of preparing for his grand jury testimony * * *, and reasonably believed she represented him, and Ms. Baldwin neglected to adequately explain the distinction between personal representation and agency representation * * *, we conclude that all the communications between Schultz and Ms. Baldwin were protected by the attorney-client privilege.

* * * Accordingly, we preclude Ms. Baldwin from testifying in future proceedings regarding privileged communications between her and Schultz, absent a waiver by Schultz.
* * * *

* * * Schultz * * * was not aware that Ms. Baldwin was not appearing with him [during his grand jury testimony] in order to protect his interests and therefore unable to provide advice concerning whether he should answer potentially incriminating questions or invoke his right against self-incrimination. Since Schultz was constructively without counsel during his grand jury testimony, and he did not provide

Case 47.3 Continues

Case 47.3 Continued

informed consent as to limited representation, * * * his right against self-incrimination was not protected by Ms. Baldwin's agency representation, and the appropriate remedy is to quash the perjury charge.
    * * * *

[Finally] since the obstruction of justice and related conspiracy charges in this matter relied extensively on a presentment from an investigating grand jury privy to impermissible privileged communications, we quash the counts of obstruction of justice and the related conspiracy charge.

Decision and Remedy *A state intermediate appellate court reversed the order of the lower court regarding Schultz's pretrial motion. Baldwin was precluded from testifying about Schultz's privileged communications with her, and the charges of perjury, obstruction of justice, and conspiracy against Schultz were quashed.*

Critical Thinking
- **Legal Environment** *How does the result in this case further the purpose of the attorney-client privilege?*
- **What If the Facts Were Different?** *Suppose that a hearing had been held on the question of the attorney-client privilege* before *Baldwin testified. Would the result have been different?*

47–5b Accountant-Client Relationships

In a few states, accountant-client communications are privileged by state statute. In these states, accountant-client communications may not be revealed even in court or in court-sanctioned proceedings without the client's permission.

The majority of states, however, abide by the common law, which provides that, if a court so orders, an accountant must disclose information about his or her client to the court. Physicians and other professionals may similarly be compelled to disclose in court information given to them in confidence by patients or clients.

Communications between professionals and their clients—other than those between an attorney and her or his client—are not privileged under federal law. *In cases involving federal law, state-provided rights to confidentiality of accountant-client communications are not recognized.* Thus, in those cases, in response to a court order, an accountant must provide the information sought.

Reviewing: Professional Liability and Accountability

Superior Wholesale Corporation planned to purchase Regal Furniture, Inc., and wished to determine Regal's net worth. Superior hired Lynette Shuebke, of the accounting firm Shuebke Delgado, to review an audit that had been prepared by Norman Chase, the accountant for Regal. Shuebke advised Superior that Chase had performed a high-quality audit and that Regal's inventory on the audit dates was stated accurately on the general ledger. As a result of these representations, Superior went forward with its purchase of Regal.

After the purchase, Superior discovered that the audit by Chase had been materially inaccurate and misleading, primarily because the inventory had been grossly overstated on the balance sheet. Later, a former Regal employee who had begun working for Superior exposed an e-mail exchange between Chase and former Regal chief executive officer Buddy Gantry. The exchange revealed that Chase had cooperated in overstating the inventory and understating Regal's tax liability. Using the information presented in the chapter, answer the following questions.

1. If Shuebke's review was conducted in good faith and conformed to generally accepted accounting principles, can Superior hold Shuebke Delgado liable for negligently failing to detect material omissions in Chase's audit? Why or why not?
2. According to the rule adopted by the majority of courts to determine accountants' liability to third parties, could Chase be liable to Superior? Explain.
3. Generally, what requirements must be met before Superior can recover damages under Section 10(b) of the 1934 Securities Exchange Act and SEC Rule 10b-5? Can Superior meet these requirements? Why or why not?

4. Suppose that a court determined that Chase had aided Regal in willfully understating its tax liability. What is the maximum penalty that could be imposed on Chase?

Debate This . . .   *Only the largest publicly held companies should be subject to the Sarbanes-Oxley Act.*

Terms and Concepts

auditor 898	generally accepted accounting	International Financial Reporting
constructive fraud 900	principles (GAAP) 897	Standards (IFRS) 898
defalcation 898	generally accepted auditing	working papers 904
due diligence 906	standards (GAAS) 897	

Issue Spotters

1. Dave, an accountant, prepares a financial statement for Excel Company, a client, knowing that Excel will use the statement to obtain a loan from First National Bank. Dave makes negligent omissions in the statement that result in a loss to the bank. Can the bank successfully sue Dave? Why or why not? (See *Potential Liability to Third Parties.*)

2. Nora, an accountant, prepares a financial statement as part of a registration statement that Omega, Inc., files with the Securities and Exchange Commission before making a public offering of securities. The statement contains a misstatement of material fact that is not attributable to Nora's fraud or negligence. Pat relies on the misstatement, buys some of the securities, and suffers a loss. Can Nora be held liable to Pat? Explain. (See *Potential Liability of Accountants under Securities Laws.*)

• **Check your answers to the Issue Spotters against the answers provided in Appendix D at the end of this text.**

Business Scenarios

47–1. The *Ultramares* Rule. Larkin, Inc., retains Howard Patterson to manage its books and prepare its financial statements. Patterson, a certified public accountant, lives in Indiana and practices there. After twenty years, Patterson has become a bit bored with generally accepted accounting principles (GAAP) and has adopted more creative accounting methods. Now, though, Patterson has a problem, as he is being sued by Molly Tucker, one of Larkin's creditors. Tucker alleges that Patterson either knew or should have known that Larkin's financial statements would be distributed to various individuals. Furthermore, she asserts that these financial statements were negligently prepared and seriously inaccurate. What are the consequences of Patterson's failure to follow GAAP? Under the traditional *Ultramares* rule, can Tucker recover damages from Patterson? Explain. (See *Potential Liability to Third Parties.*)

47–2. The *Restatement* Rule. The accounting firm of Goldman, Walters, Johnson & Co. prepared financial statements for Lucy's Fashions, Inc. After reviewing the various financial statements, Happydays State Bank agreed to loan Lucy's Fashions $35,000 for expansion. When Lucy's Fashions declared bankruptcy under Chapter 11 six months later, Happydays State Bank promptly filed an action against Goldman, Walters, Johnson & Co., alleging negligent preparation of financial statements. Assuming that the court has abandoned the *Ultramares* approach, what is the result? What are the policy reasons for holding accountants liable to third parties with whom they are not in privity? (See *Potential Liability to Third Parties.*)

47–3. Accountant's Liability under Rule 10b-5. In early 2014, Bennett, Inc., offered a substantial number of new common shares to the public. Harvey Helms had a long-standing interest in Bennett because his grandfather had once been president of the company. On receiving a prospectus prepared and distributed by Bennett, Helms was dismayed by the pessimism it embodied. Helms decided to delay purchasing stock in the company. Later, Helms asserted that the prospectus prepared by the accountants was overly pessimistic and contained materially misleading statements. Discuss fully how successful Helms would be in bringing a cause of action under Rule 10b-5 against the accountants of Bennett, Inc. (See *Potential Liability of Accountants under Securities Laws.*)

Business Case Problems

47–4. Accountant's Liability for Audit. A West Virginia bank ran its asset value from $100 million to $1 billion over seven years by aggressively marketing subprime loans. The Office of the Comptroller of the Currency, a federal regulator, audited the bank and discovered that the books had been falsified for several years and that the bank was insolvent. The Comptroller closed the bank and brought criminal charges against its managers.

The Comptroller fined Grant Thornton, the bank's accounting firm, $300,000 for recklessly failing to meet generally accepted auditing standards during the years it audited the bank. The Comptroller claimed Thornton violated federal law by "participating in . . . unsafe and unsound banking practice." Thornton appealed, contending that it was not involved in bank operations to that extent based on its audit function. What would be the key to determining if the accounting firm could be held liable for that violation of federal law? [*Grant Thornton, LLP v. Office of the Comptroller of the Currency,* 514 F.3d 1328 (D.C. Cir. 2008)] (See *Potential Liability to Clients.*)

47–5. Professional's Liability. Soon after Teresa DeYoung's husband died, her mother-in-law also died, leaving an inheritance of more than $400,000 for DeYoung's children. DeYoung hired John Ruggerio, an attorney, to ensure that her children would receive it. Ruggerio advised her to invest the funds in his real estate business. She declined. A few months later, $300,000 of the inheritance was sent to Ruggerio. Without telling DeYoung, he deposited the $300,000 in his account and began to use the funds in his real estate business. Nine months later, $109,000 of the inheritance was sent to Ruggerio. He paid this to DeYoung. She asked about the remaining amount. Ruggerio lied to hide his theft. Unable to access these funds, DeYoung's children changed their college plans to attend less expensive institutions. Nearly three years later, DeYoung learned the truth. Can she bring a suit against Ruggerio? If so, on what ground? If not, why not? Did Ruggerio violate any standard of professional ethics? Discuss. [*DeYoung v. Ruggerio,* 185 Vt. 267, 971 A.2d 627 (2009)] (See *Potential Liability to Clients.*)

47–6. Professional Malpractice. Jeffery Guerrero hired James McDonald, a certified public accountant, to represent him and his business in an appeal to the Internal Revenue Service. The appeal was about audits that showed Guerrero owed more taxes. When the appeal failed, McDonald helped Guerrero prepare materials for an appeal to the Tax Court, which was also unsuccessful. Guerrero then sued McDonald for professional negligence in the preparation of his evidence for the court. Guerrero claimed that McDonald had failed to adequately prepare witnesses and to present all the arguments that could have been made on his behalf so that he could have won the case. Guerrero contended that McDonald was liable for all of the additional taxes he was required to pay. Is Guerrero's claim likely to result in liability on McDonald's part? What factors would the court consider? [*Guerrero v. McDonald,* 302 Ga.App. 164, 690 S.E.2d 486 (2010)] (See *Potential Liability to Clients.*)

47–7. Business Case Problem with Sample Answer—Potential Liability to Third Parties. In 2006, twenty-seven entities became limited partners in two hedge funds that had invested with Bernard Madoff and his investment firm. The partners' investment adviser gave them various investment information, including a memorandum indicating that an independent certified public accountant, KPMG, LLP, had audited the hedge funds' annual reports. Since 2004, KPMG had also prepared annual reports addressed to the funds' "Partners." Each report stated that KPMG had investigated the funds' financial statements, had followed generally accepted auditing principles, and had concluded that the statements fairly summarized the funds' financial conditions. Moreover, KPMG used the information from its audits to prepare individual tax statements for each fund partner.

In 2008, Madoff was charged with securities fraud for running a massive Ponzi scheme. In a 2009 report, the Securities and Exchange Commission identified numerous "red flags" that should have been discovered by investment advisers and auditors. Unfortunately, the auditors did not find them, and the hedge funds' partners lost millions of dollars. Is KPMG potentially liable to the funds' partners under the *Restatement (Third) of Torts*? Why or why not? [*Askenazy v. Tremont Group Holdings, Inc.,* 2012 WL 440675 (Mass.Super. 2012)] (See *Potential Liability to Third Parties.*)

- **For a sample answer to Problem 47–7, go to Appendix E at the end of this text.**

47–8. Attorney's Duty of Care. Luis and Maria Rojas contracted to buy a house in Westchester County, New York, from Andrew and Karen Paine. The house was on property designated as "Lot No. 8" on a subdivision map filed in the county clerk's office. The Paines had acquired the property in two parts by the transfer of two separate deeds. At the closing, they delivered a deed stating that it covered "the same property." In fact, however, the legal description attached to the deed covered only the portion of Lot No. 8 described in one of the two previous deeds. Attorney Paul Herrick represented the Rojases in the deal with the Paines. When the Rojases sought to sell the property two years later, the title search revealed that they owned only part of Lot No. 8, and the buyer refused to go through with the sale. Is Herrick liable for malpractice? Explain. [*Rojas v. Paine,* 125 A.D.3d 745, 4 N.Y.S.3d 223 (2 Dept. 2015)] (See *Potential Liability to Clients.*)

47–9. A Question of Ethics—Liability for Negligence.

Portland Shellfish Co. processes live shellfish in Maine. As one of the firm's two owners, Frank Wetmore held 300 voting and 150 nonvoting shares of the stock. Donna Holden held the other 300 voting shares. Donna's husband, Jeff, managed the company's daily operations, including production, procurement, and sales. The board of directors consisted of Frank and Jeff. In 2001, disagreements

arose over the company's management. The Holdens invoked the "Shareholders' Agreement," which provided that "[i]n the event of a deadlock, the directors shall hire an accountant at [Macdonald, Page, Schatz, Fletcher & Co., LLC] to determine the value of the outstanding shares. . . . [E]ach shareholder shall have the right to buy out the other shareholder(s)' interest."

Macdonald Page estimated the stock's "fair market value" at $1.09 million. Donna offered to buy Frank's shares at a price equal to his proportionate share. Frank countered by offering $1.25 million for Donna's shares. Donna rejected Frank's offer and insisted that he sell his shares to her or she would sue. In the face of this threat, Frank sold his shares to Donna for $750,705. Believing the stock to be worth more than twice Macdonald Page's estimate, Frank filed a suit in a federal district court against the accounting firm. [Wetmore v. Macdonald, Page, Schatz, Fletcher & Co., LLC, 476 F.3d 1 (1st Cir. 2007)] (See *Potential Liability to Clients*.)

(a) Frank claimed that in valuing the stock, the accounting firm had disregarded "commonly accepted and reliable methods of valuation in favor of less reliable methods." He alleged negligence, among other things. Macdonald Page filed a motion to dismiss the complaint. What are the elements that establish negligence? Which is the most critical element in this case?

(b) Macdonald Page evaluated the company's stock by identifying its "fair market value," defined as "the price at which the property would change hands between a willing buyer and a willing seller, neither being under a compulsion to buy or sell and both having reasonable knowledge of relevant facts." The firm knew that the shareholders would use its estimate to determine the price that one would pay to the other. Under these circumstances, was Frank's injury foreseeable? Discuss.

(c) What factor might have influenced Frank to sell his shares to Donna even though he thought that Macdonald Page's "fair market value" figure was less than half of what it should have been? Does this factor represent an unfair, or unethical, advantage? Explain.

Legal Reasoning Group Activity

47–10. Attorney-Client Privilege. Napster, Inc., offered a service that allowed its users to browse digital music files on other users' computers and download selections for free. Music industry principals sued Napster for copyright infringement, and the court ordered Napster to remove from its service files that were identified as infringing. When Napster failed to comply, it was shut down.

A few months later, Bertelsmann, a German corporation, loaned Napster $85 million to fund its anticipated transition to a licensed digital music distribution system. The terms allowed Napster to spend the loan on "general, administrative and overhead expenses." In an e-mail, Napster's chief executive officer referred to a "side deal" under which Napster could use up to $10 million of the loan to pay litigation expenses. Napster failed to launch the new system before declaring bankruptcy. The plaintiffs filed a suit against Bertelsmann, alleging that its loan had prolonged Napster's infringement. The plaintiffs asked the court to order the disclosure of all attorney-client communications related to the loan. (See *Confidentiality and Privilege*.)

(a) The first group will identify the principle that Bertelsmann could assert to protect these communications and outline the purpose of this protection.

(b) The second group will decide whether this principle should protect a client who consults an attorney for advice that will help the client commit fraud.

(c) A third group will determine whether the court should grant the plaintiffs' request.

Climate Change

Our planet's average temperature has risen by 1.5 degrees Fahrenheit over the last hundred years. It is predicted that it will rise another 0.5 to 4.5 degrees over the next century. These seemingly small increases in the average temperature can result in significant change to our climate.

What Are the Causes?

Over the last century, our atmosphere experienced a large increase in carbon dioxide and other *greenhouse gases (GHGs)*. GHGs act like a blanket around our planet, absorbing radiation from the surface, trapping it as heat in the atmosphere, and reflecting it back to the surface.

This process, known as the *greenhouse effect*, is necessary to support life. The recent increase in GHGs, however, may be changing our climate. Deforestation, industrial processes, and agricultural practices emit these gases, but the majority of GHGs come from burning fossil fuels to produce energy.[1]

What Are the Effects?

The warmer it gets, the greater the risk for more change to the climate. Ultimately, the climate that we are used to may no longer be a guide for what to expect in the future.

Changes in Weather Rising global temperatures have sometimes coincided with changes in weather. Some locations have seen altered rainfall, resulting in heavier rains and more floods, or more frequent and intense heat waves and droughts. The rising temperatures may also be making our planet's oceans warmer and more acidic. Some glaciers and ice caps are melting, which may cause sea levels to rise.

Impacts on Society The warmer temperatures and changes in weather can affect society in many ways. Agricultural yields, human health, and the supply of energy are affected. More severe weather can lead to higher food and energy prices and increasing insurance costs. (Note, though, that higher average temperatures could lead to more agricultural output and hence lower food prices.) Of course, any impact in one area of human activity can have widespread and unforeseen effects throughout society.

What Can We Do about It?

The effects of climate change may be lessened by choices that reduce GHGs. About half of the states have set statewide GHG emission goals.[2] In the areas of transportation and power generation, two of the options for reducing emissions are the use of low-emission fuels and increased energy efficiency.

Reduce Emissions at the Pump and the Plant Motor vehicles and transportation fuels are sources for nearly a third of U.S. GHG emissions. To reduce these emissions, the federal

---

1. Fossil fuel-burning power plants are the largest single source of U.S. GHG emissions—33 percent.
2. California established the first statewide goals in 2006 in the Global Warming Solutions Act.

government and the states impose emission standards on cars and trucks, and encourage the use of fuel-efficient vehicles and alternative fuels.

The federal Environmental Protection Agency (EPA) and National Highway Transportation Safety Administration have established standards for GHG emissions and fuel economy for new light-duty cars and trucks through the model year 2025.[3] The standards are projected to save about 4 billion barrels of oil and avoid 2 billion metric tons of GHG emissions per year.

Some states have set low-emission fuel standards. More than a dozen states have set renewable fuel standards to encourage the use of low-emission fuels. Incentives to use alternative fuels include tax exemptions, tax credits, and grants.

To reduce GHG emissions from coal- and gas-fired power plants, the EPA issued the Clean Power Plan (CPP).[4] It is projected that, when the CPP is fully in place in 2030, carbon pollution from the power sector will be 32 percent below 2005 levels. Emissions of sulfur dioxide from power plants will be 90 percent lower than 2005 levels, and emissions of nitrogen oxides will be 72 percent lower.

About two-thirds of the states will require power companies to generate a certain percentage or amount of power from renewable energy sources by a specific date, which varies by state. These targets aim to reduce emissions and to improve air quality, diversify energy sources, and create jobs in the renewable energy industry.

Become More Energy Efficient More than half of the states have set standards requiring power companies to save specified amounts of energy. To attain these goals, the utilities must adopt more efficient technology in their operations and encourage their customers to become more energy efficient.

About half of the states dedicate funds to the support of renewable energy projects. More than a dozen of these states formed the Clean Energy States Alliance to coordinate their investments.

Nearly all states permit utility customers to sell electricity back to the grid. In most states, utilities offer their customers the opportunity to have a portion of their power provided from renewable sources.

Many states participate in regional climate initiatives. For example, nine states in the northeastern United States formed the Regional Greenhouse Gas Initiative to implement a market-based program to reduce GHG emissions from power plants. The initiative sets an emissions budget, or cap, for each member state. Credits that exceed the actual emissions can be sold. The proceeds are generally invested in energy-efficient renewable energy programs.

Adapt to the Changes The EPA's State and Local Climate and Energy Program provides technical assistance, analytical tools, and outreach support on climate change issues to state, local, and tribal governments.[5] The program directs resource managers to set priorities and to design and implement climate and energy policies tailored to the particular circumstances of their locations.

Part of the process is to assess an area's vulnerability to the effects of climate change and to consider approaches for adapting to the effects. For example, a coastal estuary that is subject to

---

3. 40 C.F.R. Parts 85, 86, and 600, and 49 C.F.R. Parts 523, 531, 533, 600 *et al.* The United States Supreme Court has made clear that the Environmental Protection Agency can regulate GHGs under the Clean Air Act. See *Massachusetts v. E.P.A.*, 549 U.S. 497, 127 S.Ct. 1438, 167 L.Ed.2d 248 (2007).
4. 40 C.F.R. Part 60. This act is being challenged in court.
5. See Environmental Protection Agency, *State and Local Climate and Energy Program* (December 28, 2015) available at http://www3.epa.gov/statelocalclimate/index.html.

Continues

salt-water inundation as a consequence of rising sea levels might benefit from a coastal restoration project.

The U.S. Interagency Climate Change Adaptation Task Force coordinates the efforts for adaptation across government agencies.[6] The task force recommends actions that the federal government can take to respond to the needs of states and local communities. The top priority is to enhance the resilience of natural resources to absorb the impacts of climate change.

Agree to More Limits on Emissions The European Union and 195 nations, including the United States, participated in the 2015 United Nations Climate Change Conference in Paris, France. The parties negotiated the Paris Agreement to encourage the reduction of GHG emissions.[7] The agreement sets a goal of limiting the global temperature increase to less than 2 degrees Celsius. The parties agreed to make "nationally determined contributions" (NDCs) to this goal and to pursue domestic measures designed to achieve the NDCs.[8] None of these agreements are binding, however, and therefore rely on voluntary actions by governments throughout the world.

Ethical Connection

Have all these efforts had an effect? It seems that they have. The transition to clean energy is happening faster than anticipated, and GHG emissions and air pollution have decreased somewhat.

Furthermore, climate change could have some positive effects. For example, the goals to lessen the impact and adapt to the changes create economic opportunities. There are new markets for alternative sources of power and sales of GHG emission credits, for instance. Climate change also represents a political opportunity to improve air quality and develop domestic sources of clean energy.

A business that takes advantage of these opportunities is not acting unethically. Such a business is, in fact, acting in the best interest of all of us.

Ethics Question *Is it ethical to continue to use fossil fuels? Explain.*

Critical Thinking *What are the advantages of fossil fuels? What are the disadvantages? Discuss.*

---

6. Executive Order, *Preparing the United States for the Impacts of Climate Change* (November 11, 2013) available at https://www.whitehouse.gov/the-press-office/2013/11/01/executive-order-preparing-united-states-impacts-climate-change.

7. United Nations Framework Convention on Climate Change, Conference of the Parties, *Adoption of the Paris Agreement. Proposal by the President*, FCCC/CP/2015/L.9/Rev. 1 (December 12, 2015) available at http://unfccc.int/resource/docs/2015/cop21/eng/l09r01.pdf.

8. There are, however, no binding emission targets or financial commitments. And the agreement itself will not become binding until fifty-five of the participants who produce more than 55 percent of global GHGs have ratified it.

Property and Its Protection

CHAPTER 48

Personal Property and Bailments

Property consists of the legally protected rights and interests a person has in anything with an ascertainable value that is subject to ownership. For instance, virtual property has become quite valuable in today's world, as you will read later in this chapter. Property would have little value, however, if the law did not define the rights of owners to use, sell, dispose of, and control their property and prevent others from trespassing on it.

In the United States, a substantial body of law protects the rights of property owners, but that protection is not absolute. Property owners may have to prove that their ownership rights in a particular item of property are superior to the claims of others. In addition, through its police powers, the government can impose regulations and taxes on property, and can take or seize private property under certain circumstances.

In this chapter, we examine the differences between personal and real property and look at the methods of acquiring ownership of personal property. We also consider issues relating to mislaid, lost, and abandoned personal property. In the remainder of the chapter, we discuss bailment relationships. A *bailment* is created when personal property is temporarily delivered into the care of another without a transfer of title, such as when a person takes an item of clothing to the dry cleaners. The fact that there is no passage of title and no intent to transfer title is what distinguishes a bailment from a sale or a gift.

48–1 Personal Property versus Real Property

Property is divided into real property and personal property. **Real property** (sometimes called *realty* or *real estate*) means the land and everything permanently attached to it, including structures and anything permanently attached to the structures. Everything else is **personal property** (sometimes referred to as *personalty* or **chattel**). In essence, real property is immovable, whereas personal property is capable of being moved.

Personal property can be tangible or intangible. *Tangible* personal property, such as a flat-screen TV, heavy construction equipment, or a car, has physical substance.

Intangible personal property represents some set of rights and interests, but it has no physical existence. Stocks and bonds, patents, trademarks, and copyrights—as well as digital and virtual property—are examples of intangible personal property.

Both personal property and real property can be owned by an individual person or by some other entity. When two or more persons own real or personal property together, concurrent ownership exists. (The different types of joint or concurrent ownership will be discussed in the chapter on real property.)

In the following case, a concurrent owner of a copyright to an unpublished autobiography contended that she was entitled to an accounting for the use of the work to create a successful theatrical production.

Case 48.1

Corbello v. DeVito

United States Court of Appeals, Ninth Circuit, 777 F.3d 1058 (2015).

Background and Facts Rex Woodward contracted with Thomas DeVito, one of the original members of The Four Seasons rock band, to ghostwrite DeVito's autobiography. Before it was published, Woodward died, and his interest in the manuscript's copyright passed to his widow, Donna Corbello. Later, DeVito agreed to grant former bandmates Frankie Valli and Bob Gaudio the right to use "aspects of his life related to The Four Seasons, including . . . his creative contributions, biographies, events in

Case 48.1 Continued his life, name and likeness (the Materials)" to develop a musical about The Four Seasons. The result was a Broadway hit called *Jersey Boys*.

Actors and others involved in the show attributed their inspiration, in part, to DeVito's unpublished autobiography. Corbello filed a suit in a federal district court against DeVito and his bandmates for an accounting of the profits earned from this use of the work. The court issued a judgment in the defendants' favor. Corbello appealed.

In the Language of the Court

O'SCANNLAIN, Circuit Judge:
* * * *

A co-owner of a copyright must account to other co-owners for any profits he earns from * * * use of the copyright.
* * * *

Pursuant to [DeVito's agreement with former Four Seasons band members Frankie Valli and Bob Gaudio,] DeVito "granted to Valli and Gaudio the exclusive right to use and incorporate the Materials in one or more theatrical productions, and any and all ancillary and subsidiary exploitations thereof." As defined in the Agreement, "Materials" includes * * * DeVito's "biographies."
* * * *

In the context of the * * * Agreement, the term "biographies" is not ambiguous [confusing or uncertain]. [Under] standard dictionary definitions * * * a "biography" is a "history of a person's life" * * * that is "usually written" * * *. As an account of DeVito's life that has been reduced to writing, [Woodward's] Work, on its face, qualifies under these straightforward definitions as a "biography."
* * * *

* * * DeVito granted Valli and Gaudio the "exclusive right to use" his "biographies," unambiguously including [Woodward's] Work, to create a play. Such play constitutes a "derivative work," the right to create which resides in each copyright holder of the underlying work and may be transferred by that holder to a third party. Thus, in granting this exclusive right to create, * * * the * * * Agreement constitutes a transfer of ownership of DeVito's derivative-work right in the Work to Valli and Gaudio.
* * * *

* * * *A joint-owner cannot transfer more than he himself holds; thus, [a transfer] from one joint-owner to a third party cannot bind the other joint-owners or limit their rights in the copyright without their consent.* In other words, the third party's right is "exclusive" as to the [transferring] co-owner, but not as to the other co-owners. [Emphasis added.]
* * * *

* * * Because the Agreement unambiguously transfers DeVito's derivative-work right to Valli and Gaudio, and copyright co-owners must account to one another for any profits earned by exploiting that copyright, the district court erred in rejecting Corbello's claim for [an] accounting.

Decision and Remedy *The U.S. Court of Appeals for the Ninth Circuit reversed the lower court's judgment. Woodward's work qualified as a biography, the use of which DeVito granted to Valli and Gaudio to develop the Broadway play* Jersey Boys. *This grant constituted a transfer of DeVito's right in the work. As Woodward's widow and thus as a concurrent owner of the work's copyright, Corbello was entitled to an accounting of the profits from the play.*

Critical Thinking

• **Legal Environment** *Under what circumstances would Corbello* not *be entitled to an accounting? Why?*

48–1a Why Is the Distinction Important?

How property is taxed and what is required to transfer or acquire the property is determined by whether the property is classified as real or personal property.

Taxation The two types of property are usually subject to different types of taxes. Generally, each state assesses property taxes on real property. Typically, the tax rate is based on the market value of the real property and the services provided by the city, state, and county in which the property is located. For instance, higher taxes may be imposed on real property located within the city limits to pay for schools, roads, and libraries.

Businesses also often pay taxes on the personal property they own, use, or lease, including office or farm equipment and supplies. Individuals may pay sales tax when purchasing personal property, but generally they are not required to pay annual taxes on personal property that is not used for business.

Acquisition Another reason for distinguishing between real and personal property has to do with the way the property is acquired or transferred. Personal property can be transferred with a minimum of formality. In contrast, real property transfers generally involve a written sales contract and a *deed* that is recorded with the state.

Similarly, establishing ownership rights is simpler for personal property than for real property. ■ **EXAMPLE 48.1** If Mia gives Shawn an iPad Air as a gift, Shawn does not need to have any paperwork evidencing title, as he would if she had given him real property. (The ways to acquire ownership of personal property will be discussed shortly.) ■

48–1b Conversion of Real Property to Personal Property

Sometimes, real property can be turned into personal property by detaching it from the land. For instance, the trees, bushes, and plants growing on land are considered part of the real property (with the exception of crops that must be planted every year). If the property is sold, all the vegetation growing on the land normally is transferred to the new owner of the real property.

Once the items are severed (removed) from the land, however, they become personal property. If the trees are cut from the land, the timber is personal property. If apples, grapes, or raspberries are picked from trees or vines growing on real property, they become personal property. Similarly, if land contains minerals (including oil) or other natural resources (such as marble), the resources are part of the real property. But once removed, they become personal property.

Conversely, personal property may be converted into real property by permanently attaching it to the real property. When personal property is affixed to real property in a permanent way, as when tile is installed in a house, it is known as a *fixture*. (Fixtures will be discussed in the context of real property.)

48–2 Acquiring Ownership of Personal Property

The most common way of acquiring personal property is by purchasing it. (Today, even virtual property is often purchased, as discussed in this chapter's *Digital Update*

DIGITAL UPDATE   The Exploding World of Digital Property

Jon Jacobs took out a real mortgage on his real house so that he could pay $100,000 in real dollars for a virtual asteroid near the virtual Planet Calypso in the virtual world Entropia Universe. A few years later, he sold Club Neverdie, the virtual space resort he had constructed on the virtual asteroid, for more than $600,000. At the time, Jacobs was making $200,000 per year from players' purchases of virtual goods at the resort.

If the prospect of paying real funds for virtual property seems disconcerting, remember that property does not have to be tangible. Property consists of a bundle of rights in anything that has an ascertainable value and is subject to ownership—a definition that encompasses virtual property, including all the intangible objects used in virtual worlds like Entropia Universe and Second Life.

Digital Goods Have Value, Too

Digital goods include virtual goods, but more important, they include digital books, music libraries, and movie downloads, as well as domain names and expensively created Web sites. This digital property has real value. Some digital music libraries, for example, cost thousands of dollars.

Who Keeps the Digital Goods?

The growing value of digital goods raises some legal questions. For instance, what are the respective rights of the creator/owner of a virtual-world Web site and the players at that site? And what happens when a husband and wife decide to divorce after they have purchased virtual real estate or digital goods with real-world dollars? The couple—or a court—will have to figure out a way to divide the goods. Property and divorce laws will have to adapt to take into account this changing world.

Critical Thinking *How might a couple who enjoys purchasing digital goods together avoid property division issues in the event of a divorce?*

feature.) Another way in which personal property is often acquired is by will or inheritance. Here, we look at additional ways in which ownership of personal property can be acquired, including acquisition by possession, production, gift, accession, and confusion.

48–2a Possession

Sometimes, a person can become the owner of personal property merely by possessing it. For instance, one way to acquire ownership through possession is the capture of wild animals. Wild animals belong to no one in their natural state, and the first person to take possession of a wild animal normally owns it. A hunter who kills a deer, for instance, has assumed ownership of it (unless he or she acted in violation of the law). Those who find lost or abandoned property can also acquire ownership rights through mere possession of the property, as will be discussed later in this chapter.

48–2b Production

Production—the fruits of labor—is another means of acquiring ownership of personal property. For instance, writers, inventors, manufacturers, and others who produce personal property may thereby acquire title to it. (In some situations, though, as when a researcher is hired to invent a new product or technique, the researcher may not own what is produced.)

48–2c Gift

A **gift** is a fairly common means of acquiring or transferring ownership of property. A gift is essentially a *voluntary* transfer of property ownership for which no consideration is given. The presence of consideration is what distinguishes a contractual obligation to transfer ownership of property from a gift.

For a gift to be effective, the following three elements are required:

1. Donative intent on the part of the *donor* (the one giving the gift).
2. Delivery.
3. Acceptance by the *donee* (the one receiving the gift).

Until these three requirements are met, no effective gift has been made. ■ **EXAMPLE 48.2** Gary's Aunt Celia tells him that she is going to give him a new Mercedes-Benz for his next birthday. Aunt Celia has simply made a promise to make a gift. There is no gift until the Mercedes-Benz is delivered and accepted. ■

Donative Intent When a gift is challenged in court, the court will determine whether donative intent exists by looking at the language of the donor and the surrounding circumstances. A court may look at the relationship between the parties and the size of the gift in relation to the donor's other assets. When a person has given away a large portion of her or his assets, the court will scrutinize the transaction closely. The court will analyze the donor's mental capacity and look for indications of fraud or duress.

■ **CASE IN POINT 48.3** Over a period of three months, Jean Knowles Goodman, who was eighty-five years old, gave Steven Atwood several checks that totaled $56,100. Atwood was a veterinarian who had cared for Goodman's dogs for nearly twenty years, and he and Goodman had become friends. Shortly after writing the last check, Goodman was hospitalized and diagnosed with dementia (loss of brain function) and alcohol dependency.

The guardian who was appointed to represent Goodman filed a lawsuit to invalidate the gifts, claiming that Goodman had lacked mental capacity and donative intent. At trial, a psychiatrist who had examined Goodman testified on behalf of Atwood that while Goodman lacked the capacity to care for herself, she would have understood that she was giving away her funds. Therefore, the court concluded that Goodman had donative intent to make the gifts to Atwood.[1] ■

Delivery The gift must be delivered to the donee. Delivery may be accomplished by means of a third person who is the agent of either the donor or the donee. Naturally, no delivery is necessary if the gift is already in the hands of the donee (provided there is donative intent and acceptance). Delivery is obvious in most cases, but some objects cannot be relinquished physically. Then the question of delivery depends on the surrounding circumstances.

Constructive Delivery. When the object itself cannot be physically delivered, a symbolic, or constructive, delivery will be sufficient. **Constructive delivery** confers the right to take possession (rather than actual possession) of the object in question. It is a general term for all of those acts that the law holds to be equivalent to acts of real delivery.

■ **EXAMPLE 48.4** Teresa wants to make a gift of rare coins that she has stored in a safe-deposit box at her bank. Teresa certainly cannot deliver the box itself to the donee, and she does not want to take the coins out of the bank. In this situation, she can simply deliver the key to the box to the donee and authorize the donee's access to the box and its contents. This constitutes symbolic, or constructive, delivery of the contents of the box. ■

Constructive delivery is always necessary for gifts of intangible personal property—such as stocks, bonds,

---

1. *Goodman v. Atwood*, 78 Mass.App.Ct. 655, 940 N.E.2d 514 (2011).

insurance policies, and contracts. What will be delivered are documents that represent rights and are not, in themselves, the true property.

Relinquishing Dominion and Control. An effective delivery also requires that the donor give up complete control and **dominion** (power, ownership rights) over the subject matter of the gift. The outcome of disputes often turns on whether control has actually been relinquished. The Internal Revenue Service carefully examines transactions between relatives, especially when one has given income-producing property to another who is in a lower marginal tax bracket. Unless complete control over the property has been relinquished, the "donor"—not the family member who received the "gift"—will have to pay taxes on the income from that property.

In the following *Classic Case*, the court focused on the requirement that a donor must relinquish complete control and dominion over property before a gift can be effectively delivered.

Classic Case 48.2

In re Estate of Piper

Missouri Court of Appeals, 676 S.W.2d 897 (1984).

Background and Facts Gladys Piper died intestate (without a will). At the time of her death, she owned miscellaneous personal property worth $5,150 and had in her purse $206.75 in cash and two diamond rings. Wanda Brown, Piper's niece, took the contents of her purse, allegedly to preserve the items for the estate. Clara Kauffman, a friend of Gladys Piper, filed a claim against the estate for $4,800. For several years before Piper's death, Kauffman had taken Piper to the doctor, beauty salon, and grocery store. She had also written Piper's checks to pay her bills and helped her care for her home.

Kauffman maintained that Piper had promised to pay her for these services and that Piper had given her the diamond rings as a gift. The trial court denied Kauffman's request for payment of $4,800 on the basis that the services had been voluntary. Kauffman then filed a petition for delivery of personal property (the rings), which was granted by the trial court. The defendants—Piper's heirs and the administrator of Piper's estate—appealed.

In the Language of the Court

GREENE, Judge.

* * * *

While no particular form is necessary to effect a delivery, and while the delivery may be actual, constructive, or symbolical, there must be some evidence to support a delivery theory. What we have here, at best, * * * was an intention on the part of Gladys, at some future time, to make a gift of the rings to Clara. Such an intention, no matter how clearly expressed, which has not been carried into effect, confers no ownership rights in the property in the intended donee. *Language written or spoken, expressing an intention to give, does not constitute a gift, unless the intention is executed by a complete and unconditional delivery of the subject matter, or delivery of a proper written instrument evidencing the gift.* There is no evidence in this case to prove delivery, and, for such reason, the trial court's judgment is erroneous. [Emphasis added.]

Decision and Remedy *The judgment of the trial court was reversed. No effective gift of the rings had been made, because Piper had never delivered the rings to Kauffman.*

Impact of This Case on Today's Law *This classic case clearly illustrates the delivery requirement for making a gift. Assuming that Piper did, indeed, intend for Kauffman to have the rings, it was unfortunate that Kauffman had no right to receive them after Piper's death. Yet the alternative might lead to even more unfairness. The policy behind the delivery requirement is to protect alleged donors and their heirs from fraudulent claims based solely on parol evidence. If not for this policy, an alleged donee could easily claim that a gift had been made when, in fact, it had not.*

Case 48.2 Continued

Critical Thinking

- **What If the Facts Were Different?** *Suppose that Piper had told Kauffman that she was giving the rings to Kauffman but wished to keep them in her possession for a few more days. Would this have affected the court's decision in this case? Explain.*

Acceptance The final requirement of a valid gift is acceptance by the donee. This rarely presents any problems, because most donees readily accept their gifts. The courts generally assume acceptance unless the circumstances indicate otherwise.

Gifts *Inter Vivos* and Gifts *Causa Mortis* A gift made during the donor's lifetime is called a **gift *inter vivos.*** A gift made in contemplation of imminent death is a **gift *causa mortis*** (a so-called *deathbed gift*). To be effective, a gift *causa mortis* must meet the three requirements of intent, delivery, and acceptance.

In addition, a gift *causa mortis* does not become absolute until the donor dies from the contemplated illness or event, and it is automatically revoked if the donor survives.[2] ■ **EXAMPLE 48.5** Yang, who is about to undergo surgery to remove a cancerous tumor, delivers an envelope to Chao, a close business associate. The envelope contains a letter saying, "I want to give you $1 million in U.S. government bonds in the event of my death from this operation." Chao redeems (cashes in) the bonds. The surgeon performs the operation and removes the tumor. Yang recovers fully from the operation, but the day after he leaves the hospital, he is killed when his home is struck by a tornado.

If the administrator of Yang's estate tries to recover the $1 million, she will normally succeed. The gift *causa mortis* to Chao is automatically revoked if Yang survives the operation. The *specific event* that was contemplated in making the gift was death from a particular operation. Because Yang's death was not the result of this event, the gift is revoked, and the $1 million passes to Yang's estate. ■

A gift *causa mortis* may also be revoked if the prospective donee dies before the donor. Therefore, even if Yang in *Example 48.5* had died during the operation, the gift would have been revoked if Chao had died a few minutes earlier. In that event, the $1 million would have passed to Yang's estate, and not to Chao's heirs. ■

48–2d Accession

Accession means "something added." Accession occurs when someone adds value to an item of personal property by the use of either labor or materials.

Generally, there is no dispute about who owns the property after accession occurs, especially when the accession is accomplished with the owner's consent. ■ **EXAMPLE 48.6** Hays buys all the materials necessary to customize his Corvette. He hires Zach, a customizing specialist, to come his house to perform the work. Hays pays Zach for the value of the labor, obviously retaining title to the property. ■

If an improvement is made wrongfully—without the permission of the owner—the owner retains title to the property and normally does not have to pay for the improvement. This is true even if the accession increased the value of the property substantially. ■ **EXAMPLE 48.7** Colton steals a truck and puts expensive new tires on it. If the rightful owner later recovers the truck, the owner obviously will not be required to compensate Colton, a thief, for the value of the new tires. ■

48–2e Confusion

Confusion is the commingling (mixing together) of goods to such an extent that one person's personal property cannot be distinguished from another's. Confusion frequently occurs with *fungible goods,* such as grain or oil, which consist of identical units.[3]

If confusion occurs as a result of agreement, an honest mistake, or the act of some third party, the owners share ownership in the commingled goods in proportion to the amount each contributed. ■ **EXAMPLE 48.8** Five farmers in a small Iowa community enter into a cooperative arrangement. Each fall, the farmers harvest the same amount of number 2–grade yellow corn and store it in silos that are held by the cooperative. Each farmer thus owns one-fifth of the total corn in the silos. If a fire burns down one of the silos, each farmer will bear one-fifth of the loss. ■ If goods are confused due to an intentional

---

2. For a classic case on the requirement that the donor must die from the contemplated peril, see *Brind v. International Trust Co.*, 66 Colo. 60, 179 P. 148 (1919).

3. See Section 1–201(17) of the Uniform Commercial Code (UCC).

wrongful act, then the innocent party ordinarily acquires title to the whole.

Concept Summary 48.1 reviews various ways in which personal property can be acquired.

48–3 Mislaid, Lost, and Abandoned Property

As already noted, one of the methods of acquiring ownership of property is to possess it. Simply finding something and holding onto it, however, does not *necessarily* give the finder any legal rights in the property. Different rules apply, depending on whether the property was mislaid, lost, or abandoned.

48–3a Mislaid Property

Property that has been voluntarily placed somewhere by the owner and then inadvertently forgotten is **mislaid property.** A person who finds mislaid property does not obtain title to the goods. Instead, the owner of the place where the property was mislaid becomes the caretaker

---

Concept Summary 48.1

Acquisition of Personal Property

By Purchase or by Will	The most common means of acquiring ownership in personal property is by purchasing it. Another way in which personal property is often acquired is by will or inheritance.
Possession	Ownership may be acquired by possession if no other person has ownership title, such as capturing wild animals or finding abandoned property.
Production	Any product or item produced by an individual (with minor exceptions) becomes the property of that individual.
Gift	An effective gift is made when the following three requirements are met: • There is evidence of *intent* to make a gift of the property in question. • The gift is *delivered* (physically or constructively) to the donee or the donee's agent. • The gift is *accepted* by the donee.
Accession	When value is added to personal property by use of labor or materials, the owner of the original property generally retains title to the property and benefits from the added value.
Confusion	If confusion occurs as a result of agreement, an honest mistake, or the act of some third party, the owners share ownership in the commingled goods in proportion to the amount each contributed. If goods are confused due to an intentional wrongful act, the innocent party ordinarily acquires title to the whole.

of the property, because it is highly likely that the true owner will return.[4]

■ **EXAMPLE 48.9** Maya goes to a movie theater. While paying for popcorn at the concessions stand, she sets her smartphone on the counter and then leaves it there. The smartphone is mislaid property, and the theater owner is entrusted with the duty of reasonable care for it. ■

48–3b Lost Property

Property that is *involuntarily* left is **lost property.** A finder of lost property can claim title to the property against the whole world—*except the true owner.*[5] If the true owner is identified and demands that the lost property be returned, the finder must return it. In contrast, if a third party attempts to take possession of the lost property, the finder will have a better title than the third party.

■ **EXAMPLE 48.10** Kayla works in a large library at night. As she crosses the courtyard on her way home, she finds a gold bracelet set with what seem to be precious stones. She takes the bracelet to a jeweler to have it appraised. While pretending to weigh the bracelet, the jeweler's employee removes several of the stones. If Kayla brings an action to recover the stones from the jeweler, she normally will win, because she found lost property and holds title against everyone *except the true owner.* ■

Conversion of Lost Property When a finder of lost property knows the true owner and fails to return the property to that person, the finder is guilty of the tort of *conversion.* In *Example 48.10,* if Kayla knows that the gold bracelet she found belongs to Geneva and does not return the bracelet, Kayla is guilty of conversion. Many states require the finder to make a reasonably diligent search to locate the true owner of lost property.

Estray Statutes Many states have **estray statutes,** which encourage and facilitate the return of property to its true owner and reward the finder for honesty if the property remains unclaimed. These laws provide an incentive for finders to report their discoveries by enabling them, at the end of a specified time, to acquire legal title to the found property.

Generally, the item must be lost property, not merely mislaid property, for estray statutes to apply. Estray statutes usually require the finder or the county clerk to advertise the property in an attempt to help the owner recover what has been lost.

■ **CASE IN POINT 48.11** Drug smugglers often enter the United States illegally from Canada via a frozen river that flows through Van Buren, Maine. When two railroad employees in Van Buren found a duffel bag that contained $165,580 in cash, they reported their find to U.S. Customs agents, who took custody of it. A drug-sniffing dog gave a positive alert on the bag for the scent of drugs. The federal government filed a lawsuit claiming title to the property under criminal forfeiture laws (because the property was involved in illegal drug transactions).

The two employees argued that they were entitled to the $165,580 under Maine's estray statute. That statute required finders to (1) provide written notice to the town clerk within seven days after finding the property, (2) post a public notice, and (3) advertise in the town's newspaper. Because the employees had not fulfilled these requirements, the court ruled that they had not acquired title to the property. Thus, the U.S. government had a right to seize the cash.[6] ■

48–3c Abandoned Property

Property that has been *discarded* by the true owner, who has *no intention* of reclaiming title to it, is **abandoned property.** Someone who finds abandoned property acquires title to it, and that title is good against the whole world, *including the original owner.* If a person finds abandoned property while trespassing on another's property, however, the trespasser will not acquire title.

The owner of lost property who eventually gives up any further attempt to find it is frequently held to have abandoned the property. ■ **EXAMPLE 48.12** While Alekis is hiking in the redwoods, her expensive watch falls off. She retraces her route and searches for the watch but cannot find it. She finally gives up her search and returns home some five hundred miles away. When Frye later finds the watch, he acquires title to it that is good even against Alekis. By completely giving up her search, Alekis abandoned the watch just as effectively as if she had intentionally discarded it. ■

Exhibit 48–1 summarizes the distinctions among these types of property.

---

4. The finder of mislaid property is an *involuntary bailee* (as will be discussed later in this chapter).
5. For a landmark English case establishing finders' rights in property, see *Armory v. Delamirie,* 93 Eng.Rep. 664 (K.B. [King's Bench] 1722).
6. *United States v. One Hundred Sixty-Five Thousand Five Hundred Eighty Dollars ($165,580) in U.S. Currency,* 502 F.Supp.2d 114 (D.Me. 2007).

EXHIBIT 48–1 Mislaid, Lost, and Abandoned Property

TYPE OF PROPERTY	DESCRIPTION
Mislaid Property	Property that is placed somewhere voluntarily by the owner and then inadvertently forgotten. A finder of mislaid property will not acquire title to the goods, and the owner of the place where the property was mislaid becomes a caretaker of the mislaid property.
Lost Property	Property that is involuntarily left by the owner. A finder of lost property can claim title to the property against the whole world except the true owner.
Abandoned Property	Property that has been discarded by the true owner, who has no intention of reclaiming title to the property in the future. A finder of abandoned property can claim title to it against the whole world, including the original owner.

48–4 Bailments

Many routine personal and business transactions involve bailments. A **bailment** is formed by the delivery of personal property, without transfer of title, by one person (called a **bailor**) to another (called a **bailee**). What distinguishes a bailment from a sale or a gift is that possession is transferred without passage of title or intent to transfer title.

Bailment agreements usually are made for a particular purpose—for example, to loan, lease, store, repair, or transport the property. On completion of the purpose, the bailee is obligated to return the bailed property in the same or better condition to the bailor or a third person or to dispose of it as directed.

Although bailments typically arise by agreement, not all of the elements of a contract must necessarily be present for a bailment to be created. ■ **EXAMPLE 48.13** If Amy lends her bicycle to a friend, a bailment is created, but not by contract, because there is no consideration. Note, though, that many commercial bailments, such as the delivery of clothing to the cleaners for dry cleaning, are based on contract. ■

48–4a Elements of a Bailment

Not all transactions involving the delivery of property from one person to another create a bailment. For such a transfer to become a bailment, the following three elements must be present:

1. Personal property.
2. Delivery of possession (without title).
3. Agreement that the property will be returned to the bailor or otherwise disposed of according to its owner's directions.

Personal Property Requirement Only personal property, not real property or persons, can be the subject of a bailment. ■ **EXAMPLE 48.14** When you check your bags at the airport, a bailment of your luggage is created because it is personal property. When you board the plane as a passenger, no bailment is created. ■

Bailments commonly involve *tangible* items—jewelry, cattle, automobiles, and the like. Nevertheless, *intangible* personal property, such as promissory notes and shares of stock, may also be bailed.

Delivery of Possession *Delivery of possession* means transfer of possession of the property to the bailee. For delivery to occur, the bailee must be given *exclusive possession and control* over the property, and the bailee must *knowingly* accept the property.[7] In other words, the bailee must *intend* to exercise control over it.

If either delivery of possession or knowing acceptance is lacking, there is no bailment relationship. ■ **EXAMPLE 48.15** Delacroix goes to a five-star restaurant and checks her coat. She forgets that there is a $20,000 diamond necklace in the coat pocket. In accepting the coat, the bailee does not *knowingly* also accept the necklace. Thus, a bailment of the coat exists—because the restaurant has exclusive possession and control over the coat and knowingly accepted it—but not a bailment of the necklace. ■

Physical versus Constructive Delivery. Either *physical* or *constructive delivery* will result in the bailee's exclusive possession of and control over the property. As discussed earlier (in the context of gifts), constructive delivery is a substitute, or symbolic, delivery. What is delivered to the bailee is not the actual property bailed (such as a car) but something so related to the property (such as the car keys) that the requirement of delivery is satisfied.

---

7. This rule applies to *voluntary bailments*, not to *involuntary bailments*.

Involuntary Bailments. In certain situations, a court will find that a bailment exists despite the apparent lack of the requisite elements of control and knowledge. One situation in which this occurs is when the bailee acquires the property accidentally or by mistake—as in finding someone else's lost or mislaid property. A bailment is created even though the bailor did not voluntarily deliver the property to the bailee. Such bailments are referred to as *constructive* or *involuntary* bailments.

■ **EXAMPLE 48.16** Several corporate managers attend a meeting at the law firm of Jacobs & Matheson. One of the corporate officers, Kyle Gustafson, inadvertently leaves his briefcase behind at the conclusion of the meeting. In this situation, a court could find that an involuntary bailment was created even though Gustafson did not voluntarily deliver the briefcase and the law firm did not intentionally accept it. If an involuntary bailment exists, the firm is responsible for taking care of the briefcase and returning it to Gustafson. ■

48–4b The Bailment Agreement

A bailment agreement can be express or implied. Although a written contract is not required for bailments for less than one year, it is a good idea to have one, especially when valuable property is involved.

The bailment agreement expressly or impliedly provides for the return of the bailed property to the bailor or to a third person, or for disposal of the property by the bailee. It is assumed that the bailee will return the identical goods originally given by the bailor. In certain types of bailments, though, such as bailments of fungible goods,[8] the property returned need only be equivalent property.

■ **EXAMPLE 48.17** A bailment is created when Holman stores his grain (fungible goods) in Joe's Warehouse. At the end of the storage period, however, the warehouse is not obligated to return to Holman exactly the same grain that he stored. As long as the warehouse returns grain of the same *type, grade,* and *quantity,* the warehouse—the bailee—has performed its obligation. ■

48–5 Ordinary Bailments

Bailments are either *ordinary* or *special (extraordinary).* There are three types of ordinary bailments. They are distinguished according to *which party receives a benefit*

from the bailment. This factor will dictate the rights and liabilities of the parties. In addition, the courts may use it to determine the standard of care required of the bailee in possession of the personal property.

The three types of ordinary bailments are listed below and described in the following subsections:

1. Bailment for the sole benefit of the bailor.
2. Bailment for the sole benefit of the bailee.
3. Bailment for the mutual benefit of the bailee and the bailor.

48–5a Bailment for the Sole Benefit of the Bailor

A bailment for the sole benefit of the bailor is a type of *gratuitous bailment*—meaning that it involves no consideration. The bailment is for the convenience and benefit of the bailor. Basically, the bailee is caring for the bailor's property as a favor. Therefore, the bailee owes only a slight duty of care and will be liable only if she or he is grossly negligent in caring for the property.

■ **EXAMPLE 48.18** Allen asks Sumi to store his car in her garage while he is away. If Sumi agrees to do so, then a gratuitous bailment is created, because the bailment is for the sole benefit of the bailor (Allen). If the car is damaged while in Sumi's garage, Sumi will not be responsible for the damage unless it was caused by her gross negligence. ■

48–5b Bailment for the Sole Benefit of the Bailee

When one person lends an item to another person (the bailee) solely for that person's convenience and benefit, a bailment for the sole benefit of the bailee is created. Because the bailee is borrowing the item for her or his own benefit, the bailee owes a duty to exercise the utmost care and will be liable for even slight negligence.

■ **EXAMPLE 48.19** Jeremy asks to borrow Sumi's boat so that he can take his girlfriend sailing over the weekend. The bailment of the boat is for Jeremy's (the bailee's) sole benefit. If Jeremy fails to pay attention and runs the boat aground, damaging its hull, he is liable for the costs of repairing the boat. ■

48–5c Mutual-Benefit Bailments

The most common kind of bailment is for the mutual benefit of the bailee and the bailor, and involves some form of compensation for storing items or holding

---

8. As mentioned earlier, *fungible goods* are goods that consist of identical particles, such as wheat. Fungible goods are defined in UCC 1–201(17).

property. It is a contractual bailment and is often referred to as a *bailment for hire* or a *commercial bailment.*

In a commercial bailment, the bailee must exercise ordinary care, which is the care that a reasonably prudent person would use under the circumstances. If the bailee fails to exercise reasonable care, he or she will be liable for ordinary negligence.

■ **EXAMPLE 48.20** Allen leaves his car at Midas for an oil change. Because Midas will be paid to change Allen's oil, this is a mutual-benefit bailment. If Midas fails to put the correct amount of oil back into Allen's car and the engine is damaged as a result, Midas will be liable for failure to have exercised reasonable care. ■

48–5d Rights of the Bailee

Certain rights are implicit in the bailment agreement. Generally, the bailee has the right to take possession of the property and to utilize it for accomplishing the purpose of the bailment. The bailee also has a right to receive compensation (unless the bailment is intended to be gratuitous). In addition, the bailee may have the right to limit her or his liability for the bailed goods. These rights of the bailee are present (with some limitations) in varying degrees in all bailment transactions.

Right of Possession A hallmark of the bailment agreement is that the bailee acquires the *right to control and possess the property temporarily.* The duration of a bailment depends on the terms of the agreement. If the agreement specifies its duration, then the bailment continues for that time period, and an earlier termination by the bailor is a breach of contract. If no duration is stated, the bailment ends when either the bailor or the bailee requests its termination and the bailed property is returned to the bailor.

A bailee's right of possession, even though temporary, permits the bailee to recover damages from any third parties for damage or loss to the property. ■ **EXAMPLE 48.21** No-Spot Dry Cleaners sends all suede leather garments to Cleanall Company for special processing. If Cleanall loses or damages any leather goods, No-Spot has the right to recover from Cleanall. ■ If the bailed property is stolen, the bailee has a legal right to regain possession of it.

Right to Use Bailed Property In some bailments, a bailee may have a right to use the bailed property. When no express provision is made, the extent of use depends on how necessary it is for the goods to be at the bailee's disposal for the ordinary purpose of the bailment to be carried out.

■ **EXAMPLE 48.22** If Lauren borrows a car to drive a friend to the airport, she, as the bailee, will obviously be expected to use the car. In contrast, if Devin drives his own car to the airport and places it in long-term storage nearby, the storage company, as the bailee, will not be expected to use the car. The ordinary purpose of a storage bailment does not include use of the property. The bailee will, however, be expected to use or move the car if necessary in an emergency (such as a hurricane or flood) to protect it from harm. ■

Right of Compensation Except in a gratuitous bailment, a bailee has a right to be compensated as provided for in the bailment agreement. The bailee also has the right to be reimbursed for costs incurred and services rendered in keeping the bailed property (even in a gratuitous bailment).

To enforce the right of compensation, the bailee has a right to place a *possessory lien* on the specific bailed property until she or he has been fully compensated. Such a lien is sometimes referred to as a **bailee's lien,** or artisan's lien. If the bailor refuses to pay or cannot pay, in most states the bailee is entitled to foreclose on the lien and sell the property to recover the amount owed.

■ **EXAMPLE 48.23** Liam leaves his car at Dusty's Automotive for repairs. Dusty's informs Liam that the car needs a new transmission, and Liam authorizes Dusty's to perform the work. When Liam returns to pick up the car, he refuses to pay the amount due for the transmission work. Dusty's has a right to keep the car and place a lien on it until Liam pays for the repairs. If Liam continues to refuse to pay, Dusty's can follow the state's statutory process for foreclosing on the lien and selling the car to recover what is owed. ■

Right to Limit Liability In ordinary bailments, bailees have the right to limit their liability provided that both of the following are true:

1. *The limitations are called to the attention of the bailor.* It is essential that the bailor be informed of the limitation in some way. ■ **EXAMPLE 48.24** A sign in Nikolai's garage states that Nikolai will not be responsible "for loss due to theft, fire, or vandalism." Whether the sign will constitute notice will depend on the size of the sign, its location, and any other circumstances affecting the likelihood that customers will see it. ■

2. *The limitations are not against public policy.* Courts consider certain types of disclaimers of liability to be against public policy and therefore illegal, whether or not the bailor is aware of them. As previously discussed, the courts carefully scrutinize *exculpatory*

clauses, which limit a person's liability for her or his own wrongful acts. In bailments, especially mutual-benefit bailments, exculpatory clauses are often held to be illegal. ■ **EXAMPLE 48.25** A receipt from a parking garage expressly disclaims liability for any damage to parked cars, regardless of the cause. Because the bailee (the garage) has attempted to exclude liability for the bailee's own negligence, the clause will likely be deemed unenforceable because it is against public policy. ■

48–5e Duties of the Bailee

The bailee's duties are based on a mixture of tort law and contract law, and include the following two basic responsibilities:

1. To take appropriate care of the property.
2. To surrender the property to the bailor or dispose of it in accordance with the bailor's instructions at the end of the bailment.

The Duty of Care The bailee must exercise reasonable care in preserving the bailed property. What constitutes reasonable care in a bailment situation normally depends on the nature and specific circumstances of the bailment.

As already mentioned, the courts determine the appropriate standard of care on the basis of the type of bailment involved. In a bailment for the sole benefit of the bailor, the bailee need exercise only a slight degree of care, whereas in a bailment for the sole benefit of the bailee, the bailee must exercise great care.

Exhibit 48–2 illustrates the degree of care required of bailees in bailment relationships. Determining whether a bailee exercised an appropriate degree of care is usually a question of fact for the jury or for the judge (in a non-jury trial). A bailee's failure to exercise appropriate care in handling the bailor's property results in tort liability.

■ **CASE IN POINT 48.26** Bridge Tower Dental contracted with Meridian Computer Center to develop a computer system for its dental practice. Bridge Tower paid a computer consultant, Al Colson, to install the system and to provide maintenance and support. When Colson noticed that one of the server's two hard drives had stopped working, he informed Bridge Tower and took the server to Meridian Computer to be repaired. Meridian's owner, Jason Patten, agreed to replace the failing hard drive under the warranty. In attempting to copy data from the mirrored hard drive, however, Patten accidentally erased all the data, which he had not backed up. As a result, Bridge Tower lost all of its patients' records and contact information.

Bridge Tower sued Meridian for negligence. The Supreme Court of Idaho ruled in favor of Bridge Tower. Colson had entrusted Meridian with a server containing a failing hard drive (which was to be replaced) and a fully functional mirrored hard drive containing data. Meridian had a duty to protect and safeguard this bailed property in order to return it in the same condition it was in when delivered. Patten mistakenly erased the data on the mirrored hard drive, which constituted negligence.[9] ■

Duty to Return Bailed Property At the end of the bailment, the bailee normally must hand over the original property to either the bailor or someone the bailor designates, or must otherwise dispose of it as directed.[10] Failure to give up possession at the time the bailment ends is a breach of contract and could result in a tort lawsuit for conversion or negligence.

■ **CASE IN POINT 48.27** SANY America, Inc., loaned a crane to Turner Brothers, LLC, a construction contractor, for demonstration purposes. SANY wanted to sell the crane to Turner and continued to allow Turner to use it during their negotiations, but the parties never came to an agreement on a price. After the negotiations ended, SANY asked Turner for the crane's location to arrange retrieval. Before SANY retrieved the crane from Turner,

---

9. *Bridge Tower Dental, P.A. v. Meridian Computer Center, Inc.,* 272 P.3d 541 (Idaho Sup.Ct. 2012).
10. As mentioned earlier, if the bailment involves fungible goods, such as grain, then the bailee is not required to return exactly the same goods to the bailor. Instead, the bailee must return goods of the same type, grade, and quantity.

EXHIBIT 48–2 Degree of Care Required of a Bailee

Bailment for the Sole Benefit of the Bailor	Mutual-Benefit Bailment	Bailment for the Sole Benefit of the Bailee
	DEGREE OF CARE →	
SLIGHT	REASONABLE	GREAT

however, it was severely damaged while being operated at Turner's construction site.

Turner removed the inoperable crane from the site at its own expense and then notified SANY that it expected compensation for the transportation expenses. In addition, Turner refused to return the crane to SANY and began billing SANY for daily storage costs. SANY sued for conversion, and Turner counterclaimed. A federal district court held that the parties' transaction was a bailment. Because Turner had wrongfully retained the crane after SANY demanded its return, SANY was entitled to summary judgment for conversion.[11] ∎

A bailee may be liable for conversion or misdelivery if the goods are given to the wrong person. Hence, a bailee should verify that any person other than the bailor to whom the goods are given is authorized to take possession.

Lost or Damaged Property If the bailed property has been lost or is returned damaged, a court will presume that the bailee was negligent. The bailee's obligation is excused, however, if the property was destroyed, lost, or stolen through no fault of the bailee (or claimed by a third party with a superior claim). In other words, the bailee can rebut the presumption of negligence by showing that he or she exercised due care.

∎ **CASE IN POINT 48.28** Hornbeck Offshore Service engaged R&R Marine, Inc., to repair the ship *Erie*

Servic*e* at R&R's shipyard on Lake Sabine in Port Arthur, Texas. While repairs were being made, a tropical storm warning was issued for Port Arthur. R&R's personnel left the shipyard without securing or preparing the *Erie Service* for the storm. During the night, rain and water from Lake Sabine swamped the vessel. R&R's insurer, National Liability & Fire Insurance Company, asked a federal district court to declare that it was not required to pay the salvage cost. Hornbeck filed a counterclaim with the court alleging that R&R had been negligent. The lower court issued a decision in Hornbeck's favor, and R&R appealed.

A federal appellate court affirmed the lower court's ruling. The ship had been delivered to R&R afloat, R&R had full custody of the vessel, and it sank while in R&R's care. This gave rise to a presumption of negligence. The severity of the weather conditions in Port Arthur had been foreseeable, and R&R showed no evidence that it had exercised ordinary care. The court held that R&R—not the insurer—was liable for the salvage cost because R&R had been negligent in failing to protect the ship from damage from the storm.[12] ∎

In the following case, the court had to determine whether a constructive bailment existed over the personal property of tenants who were evicted. If so, was the landlord-bailor negligent for removing the tenants' personal property and leaving it outside?

---

11. *SANY America, Inc. v. Turner Brothers, LLC,* ___ F.Supp.3d ___, 2016 WL 1452341 (D.Mass. 2016).

12. *National Liability & Fire Insurance Co. v. R&R Marine, Inc.,* 756 F.3d 825 (5th Cir. 2014).

Case Analysis 48.3

Zissu v. IH2 Property Illinois, L.P.

United States District Court, Northern District of Illinois, Eastern Division, ___ F.Supp.3d ___, 2016 WL 212937 (2016).

In the Language of the Court
John Z. *LEE,* United States District Judge

Plaintiffs Pavel Zissu and Aise Zissu bring suit [in this federal district court] against the owner of the property where they resided, IH2 Property Illinois, L.P. The Zissus claim that after a Cook County [Illinois] Sheriff turned over possession of the premises to IH2 pursuant to an eviction order, the company removed all of their personal property from the premises and put it outside. In their complaint, the Zissus assert [that the company's actions

constituted] negligence [and a constructive] bailment.

FACTUAL BACKGROUND
* * * The Zissus resided at a property in the City of Chicago owned by IH2. * * * [An Illinois state court judge] issued an order for possession, allowing IH2 to evict the Zissus. The order was executed by a Cook County Sheriff.

Once IH2 was given possession of the premises, its agents took all of the Zissus' personal property that was in the apartment and placed it outside on the curb. The property, which included

jewelry, furniture, and personal documents, was then either stolen or damaged.

LEGAL STANDARD
A motion [to dismiss under the Federal Rules of Procedure] challenges the sufficiency of the complaint.

*A complaint * * * must * * * allege sufficient factual matter, accepted as true, to state a claim to relief that is plausible on its face. For a claim to have facial plausibility, a plaintiff must plead factual content that allows the court to draw the reasonable*

Case 48.3 Continued

inference that the defendant is liable for the misconduct alleged. [Emphasis added.]

ANALYSIS

This is a diversity suit. As such, we apply state substantive law and federal procedural law. Both parties cite Illinois law in their briefing, so the Court will apply Illinois law.

I. Negligence

The Zissus allege that IH2 negligently removed their personal property from the premises following the eviction, causing much of it to be damaged or stolen. * * * In its motion to dismiss, IH2 argues that the Zissus cannot state a claim for negligence because IH2, as the landlord, did not owe a duty to protect personal property left on the premises following the eviction.

* * * *

Because [the statutes of Illinois are silent on this issue and] the Illinois Supreme Court has not addressed this issue, this Court must attempt to divine [guess] how the [Illinois] Supreme Court would rule. In fact, only two courts have addressed the question of a landlord's duty under Illinois law. [In] *Centagon, Inc. v. Board of Directors of 1212 Lake Shore Drive Condominium Association*, __ F.Supp.2d __, 2001 WL 1491523 (N.D.Ill. 2001), a condo association had obtained a judgment granting exclusive possession of a unit that had belonged to the plaintiff. The sheriff's office executed the eviction and * * * removed the personal property onto the curb and sidewalk.

* * * The court held that the facts in that case were insufficient to impose an affirmative duty upon defendants to care for any personal property left in the Unit after eviction. The mere fact that the

representatives of the condo association had been present and had observed the eviction and removal of the property was not enough to establish a duty of care.

* * * An Illinois appellate court applied a similar analytical framework in *Dargis v. Paradise Park, Inc.*, 354 Ill. App.3d 171, 819 N.E.2d 1220 (2004). There, the court concluded that, while a landlord has no duty in such situations as a general matter, an exception is created when the landlord chooses to care for the property. * * * This decision is helpful because state appellate court decisions, although not binding, constitute persuasive authority.

In the end, the Court agrees with the reasoning in these cases and finds that the Illinois Supreme Court would hold that, although a landlord does not have a general duty under common law to care for the personal property of a former tenant after a proper and legal eviction, a duty of care does arise when a landlord acts as an actual or constructive bailee with respect to the tenant's property. [If] the complaint states a claim for bailment as further discussed below, the Court finds that Plaintiffs have sufficiently alleged the existence of a duty and a breach of that duty to survive a motion to dismiss as to their negligence claim.

II. Bailment

* * * The Zissus allege that a constructive (or implied) bailment was created when IH2 took control over the personal property that had been left behind. In its motion to dismiss, IH2 argues that the Zissus have failed to state a claim because IH2 never took possession of the personal property.

A bailment occurs when goods, or other personal property, are delivered to another,

who under contract either express or implied has agreed to accept delivery and deal with the property in a particular way. To recover under a bailment theory, the plaintiff must allege: (1) an express or implied agreement to create a bailment, (2) delivery of the property, (3) the bailee's acceptance of the property, and (4) the bailee's failure to return the property or the bailee's delivery of the property in a damaged condition. [Emphasis added.]

An implied bailment—also called a constructive bailment—may be found where the property of one person is voluntarily received by another for some purpose other than that of obtaining ownership. The implied bailment may be deduced from the circumstances surrounding the transaction, including the benefits received by the parties, their intentions, the kind of property involved, and the opportunities of each to exercise control over the property.

The Zissus contend that, by actively removing the property from the premises and putting it on the street, IH2 assumed control over the property. Unlike in *Centagon*, in which the defendants had watched the sheriff take out the property, IH2 itself took possession of the property and put it outside.

* * * It was IH2's alleged actions after the sheriff had turned over possession of the premises to IH2 that gave rise to the bailment relationship. * * * The allegations are sufficient [to establish this claim] at the pleading stage.

* * * *

CONCLUSION

For the reasons stated herein, the Court denies IH2's motion to dismiss.

Legal Reasoning Questions

1. How did related cases addressing the issue of a landlord's duty under Illinois law affect the court's reasoning in this case?

2. Besides negligence, are there other tort claims that the Zissus might have successfully alleged in their complaint? Discuss.

3. Suppose that instead of putting the Zissus' personal property outside, IH2 had taken it to a storage facility. Would the result have been different?

48–5f Duties of the Bailor

The duties of a bailor are essentially the same as the rights of a bailee. A bailor has a duty to compensate the bailee, as discussed earlier. A bailor also has an all-encompassing duty to provide the bailee with goods that are free from known defects that could cause injury to the bailee.

Bailor's Duty to Reveal Defects The bailor's duty to reveal defects to the bailee translates into two rules:

1. In a *mutual-benefit bailment,* the bailor must notify the bailee of all known defects and any hidden defects that the bailor knows of or could have discovered with reasonable diligence and proper inspection.
2. In a *bailment for the sole benefit of the bailee,* the bailor must notify the bailee of any known defects.

The bailor's duty to reveal defects is based on a negligence theory of tort law. A bailor who fails to give the appropriate notice is liable to the bailee and to any other person who might reasonably be expected to come into contact with the defective article.

■ **EXAMPLE 48.29** Rentco (the bailor) rents a tractor to Hal Iverson. Unknown to Rentco (but *discoverable* by reasonable inspection), the brake mechanism on the tractor is defective at the time the bailment is made. Iverson uses the defective tractor without knowledge of the brake problem and is injured along with two other field workers when the tractor rolls out of control. In this situation, Rentco is liable for the injuries sustained by Iverson and the other workers because it negligently failed to discover the defect and notify Iverson. ■

Warranty Liability for Defective Goods A bailor can also incur warranty liability under contract law for injuries resulting from the bailment of defective articles. Property that is leased from a bailor must be *fit for the intended purpose of the bailment.* The bailor's knowledge of or ability to discover any defects is immaterial.

Warranties of fitness arise by law in sales contracts, and courts have held that these warranties apply to bailments "for hire." Article 2A of the Uniform Commercial Code (UCC) extends the implied warranties of merchantability and fitness for a particular purpose to bailments that include rights to use the bailed goods.[13]

---

13. UCC 2A–212, 2A–213.

48–6 Special Types of Bailments

A business is likely to engage in some special types of bailment transactions. These include bailments in which the bailee's duty of care is *extraordinary* and the bailee's liability for loss or damage to the property is absolute. Such situations usually involve common carriers and hotel operators. Warehouse companies have the same duty of care as ordinary bailees, but like carriers, they are subject to extensive federal and state laws, including Article 7 of the UCC.

48–6a Common Carriers

Common carriers are publicly licensed to provide transportation services to the general public. They are legally bound to carry all passengers or freight as long as there is enough space, the fee is paid, and there are no reasonable grounds to refuse service. Common carriers differ from private carriers, which operate transportation facilities for only a select clientele. A private carrier is not required to provide service to every person or company making a request.

Strict Liability Applies The delivery of goods to a common carrier creates a bailment relationship between the shipper (bailor) and the common carrier (bailee). Unlike ordinary bailees, the common carrier is held to a standard of care based on *strict liability,* rather than reasonable care, in protecting the bailed personal property. This means that the common carrier is absolutely liable, regardless of care, for all loss or damage to goods except when damage was caused by a natural disaster or war.

Limitations on Liability Common carriers cannot contract away their liability for damaged goods. Subject to government regulations, however, they are permitted to limit their dollar liability to an amount stated on the shipment contract or rate filing. Carriers may also limit the value of property that they will transport.

■ **CASE IN POINT 48.30** Treiber & Straub, Inc., a jewelry store, used UPS to ship a diamond ring worth $105,000. The owner of the jewelry store arranged for the shipment on UPS's Web site, which required him to click on two on-screen boxes to agree to "My UPS Terms and Conditions." In these terms, UPS and its insurer limited their liability and the amount of insurance coverage on packages to $50,000, and refused to ship items worth more than $50,000. Both UPS and its insurer disclaimed liability *entirely* for such items. Nevertheless, the store owner purchased $50,000 in insurance for the package.

When the ring was lost, the jewelry store filed suit against UPS to recover $50,000 under the insurance policy. The court held that UPS's disclaimer of liability was enforceable. It also found that the jewelry store had breached the contract by indicating that the shipment was worth less than $50,000 when the ring was worth much more.[14] ■

48–6b Warehouse Companies

Warehousing is the business of providing storage of property for compensation. Like ordinary bailees, warehouse companies are liable for loss or damage to property resulting from *negligence*. But because a warehouse company is a professional bailee, it is expected to exercise a high degree of care to protect and preserve the goods.

Limitations on Liability A warehouse company can limit the dollar amount of its liability. Under the UCC, however, it must give the bailor the option of paying a higher storage rate for an increase in the liability limit.[15]

Warehouse Receipts Unlike ordinary bailees, a warehouse company can issue *documents of title*—in particular, *warehouse receipts*.[16] A warehouse receipt describes the bailed property and the terms of the bailment contract. It can be negotiable or nonnegotiable, depending on how it is written. It is negotiable if its terms provide that the warehouse company will deliver the goods "to the bearer" of the receipt or "to the order of" a person named on the receipt.[17]

---

14. *Treiber & Straub, Inc. v. United Parcel Service, Inc.*, 474 F.3d 379 (7th Cir. 2007).

15. UCC 7–204(1), (2).

16. A *document of title* is defined in UCC 1–201(15) as any "document which in the regular course of business or financing is treated as adequately evidencing that the person in possession of it is entitled to receive, hold, and dispose of the document and the goods it covers." A *warehouse receipt* is a document of title issued by a person engaged for hire in the business of storing goods.

17. UCC 7–104.

The warehouse receipt represents the goods (that is, it indicates title) and hence has value and utility in financing commercial transactions. ■ **EXAMPLE 48.31** Ossip delivers 6,500 cases of canned corn to Chaney, the owner of a warehouse. Chaney issues a negotiable warehouse receipt payable "to bearer" and gives it to Ossip. Ossip sells and delivers the warehouse receipt to Better Foods, Inc. Better Foods is now the owner of the corn and can obtain the cases by simply presenting the warehouse receipt to Chaney. ■

48–6c Hotel Operators

At common law, hotel owners were strictly liable for the loss of any cash or property that guests brought into their rooms. Today, state statutes continue to apply strict liability to hotel operators for any loss or damage to their guests' personal property. In many states, however, hotel operators can avoid strict liability for loss of guests' cash and valuables by:

1. Providing a safe in which to keep guests' valuables.
2. Notifying guests that a safe is available.

In addition, statutes often limit the liability of innkeepers with regard to articles that are not kept in the safe and may limit the availability of damages in the absence of negligence. Most statutes require that the hotel post these limitations on the doors of the rooms or otherwise notify guests.

■ **EXAMPLE 48.32** A guest at Crown Place hotel is traveling with jewelry valued at $1 million. She puts the jewelry in the safe in her room, but someone comes into the room and removes the jewelry from the safe without the use of force. The woman sues the hotel, which claims that it is not liable under the state statute. If Crown Place did not comply with statutory requirements that it post the legal limitations in the guest rooms, however, it will not be protected from liability. Crown Place will be strictly liable for the loss of the woman's jewelry. ■

Concept Summary 48.2 reviews the rights and duties of bailees and bailors.

Concept Summary 48.2

Rights and Duties of the Bailee and the Bailor

Rights of a Bailee (Duties of a Bailor)	• The right of possession allows a bailee to sue any third parties who damage, lose, or convert the bailed property. • The right to use the property to the extent it is necessary to carry out the purpose of the bailment. • The right to be compensated or reimbursed for keeping bailed property. In the event of nonpayment, the bailee has a right to place a possessory (bailee's) lien on the bailed property. • The right to limit liability. An ordinary bailee can limit the types of risk, monetary amount, or both, provided proper notice is given and the limitation is not against public policy. In special bailments, limitations on liability for negligence usually are not allowed, but limitations on the monetary amount of loss are permitted.
Duties of a Bailee (Rights of a Bailor)	• A bailee must exercise appropriate care over property entrusted to her or him. What constitutes appropriate care normally depends on the nature and circumstances of the bailment. A common carrier (special bailee) is held to a standard of care based on strict liability except when damage was caused by a natural disaster or war. • Bailed goods in a bailee's possession must be returned to the bailor or be disposed of according to the bailor's directions. Failure to return the property gives rise to a presumption of negligence.

Reviewing: Personal Property and Bailments

Vanessa Denai purchased forty acres of land in rural Louisiana. On the property were a 1,600-square-foot house and a metal barn. Denai later met Lance Finney, who had been seeking a small plot of rural property to rent. After several meetings, Denai invited Finney to live on a corner of her property in exchange for Finney's assistance in cutting wood and tending the property. Denai agreed to store Finney's sailboat in her barn.

With Denai's consent, Finney constructed a concrete and oak foundation on Denai's property. Finney then purchased a 190-square-foot dome from Dome Baja for $3,395. The dome was shipped by Doty Express, a transportation company licensed to serve the public. When it arrived, Finney installed the dome frame and fabric exterior so that the dome was detachable from the foundation. A year after Finney installed the dome, Denai wrote Finney a note stating, "I've decided to give you four acres of land surrounding your dome as drawn on this map." This gift violated no local land-use restrictions. Using the information presented in the chapter, answer the following questions.

1. Is the dome real property or personal property? Explain.
2. Is Denai's gift of land to Finney a testamentary gift, a gift *causa mortis*, or a gift *inter vivos*?
3. What type of bailment relationship was created when Denai agreed to store Finney's boat? What degree of care was Denai required to exercise in storing the boat?
4. What standard of care applied to the shipment of the dome by Doty Express?

Debate This . . .   *Common carriers should not be able to limit their liability.*

Terms and Concepts

abandoned property 927	confusion 925	lost property 927
accession 925	constructive delivery 923	mislaid property 926
bailee 928	dominion 924	personal property 920
bailee's lien 930	estray statute 927	property 920
bailment 928	gift 923	real property 920
bailor 928	gift *causa mortis* 925	
chattel 920	gift *inter vivos* 925	

Issue Spotters

1. Quintana Corporation sends important documents to Regal Nursery, Inc., via Speedy Messenger Service. While the documents are in Speedy's care, a third party causes an accident to Speedy's delivery vehicle that results in the loss of the documents. Does Speedy have a right to recover from the third party for the loss of the documents? Why or why not? (See *Ordinary Bailments*.)

2. Rosa de la Mar Corporation ships a load of goods via Southeast Delivery Company. The load of goods is lost in a hurricane in Florida. Who suffers the loss? Explain your answer. (See *Special Types of Bailments*.)

• **Check your answers to the Issue Spotters against the answers provided in Appendix D at the end of this text.**

Business Scenarios

48–1. Duties of the Bailee. Atka owns a valuable speedboat. She is going on vacation and asks her neighbor, Regina, to store the boat in one stall of Regina's double garage. Regina consents, and the boat is moved into the garage. Regina, in need of some grocery items for dinner, drives to the store. She leaves the garage door open, as is her custom. While she is at the store, the speedboat is stolen. What standard of care is required in this situation? Has Regina breached that duty? (See *Ordinary Bailments*.)

48–2. Duties of the Bailee. Orlando borrows a gasoline-driven lawn edger from his neighbor, Max. Max has not used the lawn edger for two years. Orlando has never owned a lawn edger and is not familiar with its use. Max previously used this edger often, and if he had made a reasonable inspection, he would have discovered that the blade was loose. Orlando is injured when the blade becomes detached while he is edging his yard. (See *Ordinary Bailments*.)

(a) Can Orlando hold Max liable for his injuries? Why or why not?

(b) Would your answer be different if Orlando had rented the edger from Max and paid a fee? Explain.

Business Case Problems

48–3. Gifts. John Wasniewski opened a brokerage account with Quick and Reilly, Inc., in his son James's name. Twelve years later, when the balance was $52,085, the account was closed, and the funds were transferred to a joint account in the names of John and James's brother. James did not learn of the existence of the account in his name until the transfer, when he received a tax form for the account's final year. He filed a suit in a Connecticut state court against Quick and Reilly, alleging breach of contract and seeking to recover the account's principal and interest. What are the elements of a valid gift? Did John's opening of the account with Quick and Reilly constitute a gift to James? What is the likely result in this case, and why? [*Wasniewski v. Quick and Reilly, Inc.,* 292 Conn. 98, 971 A.2d 8 (2009)] (See *Acquiring Ownership of Personal Property*.)

48–4. Business Case Problem with Sample Answer— Bailment Obligation. Bob Moreland left his plane at Don Gray's aircraft repair shop to be painted. When Moreland picked up the airplane, he was disappointed in the quality of the work and pointed out numerous defects. Moreland refused to pay Gray and flew the plane to another shop to have the work redone. Gray sued to collect, contending that Moreland had no right to take the plane to another shop without giving Gray a chance to fix any defects. Gray further argued that by taking the plane, Moreland had accepted Gray's work. Moreland counterclaimed for his expenses. Which party should be awarded damages, and why? [*Gray v. Moreland,* 2010 Ark. App. 207, 374 S.W.3d 178 (2010)] (See *Bailments*.)

• For a sample answer to Problem 48–4, go to Appendix E at the end of this text.

48–5. Gifts. Jennifer Koerner adopted a dog—called the Stig—from the Anti-Cruelty Society in Chicago, Illinois, for $95. Koerner wrote a poem and presented it to Kent Nielsen, her live-in boyfriend. In the poem, she expressed her intent to give the Stig to him as a gift. While Koerner and Nielsen lived together, they were both involved in the Stig's day-to-day care. They ended their relationship a year later, and Nielsen agreed to leave their shared residence. Can Nielsen take the Stig with him, or is Koerner the Stig's rightful owner? Explain. [*Koerner v. Nielsen*, 8 N.E.3d 161 (Ill.App. 1 Dist. 2014)] (See *Acquiring Ownership of Personal Property.*)

48–6. Lost Property. Sara Simon misplaced her Galaxy cell phone in Manhattan, Kansas. Days later, Shawn Vargo contacted her, claiming to have bought the phone from someone else. He promised to mail it to Simon if she would wire $100 to him through a third party, Mark Lawrence. When Simon spoke to Lawrence about the wire transfer, she referred to the phone as hers and asked, "Are you going to send my phone to me?" Simon paid, but she did not get the phone. Instead, Lawrence took it to a Best Buy store and traded it in for credit. Charged with the theft of lost property, Lawrence claimed that he did not know Simon was the owner of the phone. Was Simon's phone lost, mislaid, or abandoned? What is the finder's responsibility with respect to this type of property? Can Lawrence successfully argue that he did not know the phone was Simon's? Explain. [*State of Kansas v. Lawrence*, 347 P.3d 240 (Kan.App. 2015)] (See *Mislaid, Lost, and Abandoned Property.*)

48–7. Bailments. Christie's Fine Art Storage Services Inc. (CFASS) is in the business of storing fine works of art at its warehouse in Brooklyn, New York. The warehouse is next to the East River in a flood zone. Boyd Sullivan owns works of art by Alberto Vargas, including *Beauty and the Beast* and *Miss Universe*. Sullivan contracted to store the works at CFASS's facility under an agreement that limited the warehouser's liability for damage to the goods to $200,000. A few

months later, as Hurricane Sandy approached, CFASS was warned, along with the other businesses in the flood zone, of the potential for damage from the storm. CFASS e-mailed its clients that extra precautions were being taken. Despite this assurance, Sullivan's works were left exposed on a ground floor and sustained severe damage in the storm. Who is most likely to suffer the loss? Why? [*Sullivan v. Christie's Fine Art Storage Services, Inc.*, __ Misc.3d __, 2016 Slip Op. __, 2016 WL 427615 (Sup. N.Y. County, Trial Order No. 160733/2014 2016)] (See *Bailments.*)

48–8. A Question of Ethics—Gifts. Jason Crippen and Catharyn Campbell of Knoxville, Tennessee, were involved in a romantic relationship for many months. Their relationship culminated in an engagement on December 25, 2005, when Crippen placed an engagement ring on Campbell's finger and simultaneously proposed marriage. Campbell accepted the proposal, and the parties were engaged to be married. The engagement did not last, however. The parties broke up, their romantic relationship ended, and neither had any intent to marry the other. Crippen asked Campbell to return the ring. She refused. Crippen filed a suit in a Tennessee state court against Campbell to recover the ring. Both parties filed motions for summary judgment. The court ruled in Campbell's favor. Crippen appealed to a state intermediate appellate court. [*Crippen v. Campbell*, 2007 WL 2768076 (Tenn. App. 2007)] (See *Acquiring Ownership of Personal Property.*)

(a) Under what reasoning could the court affirm the award of the ring to Campbell? On what basis could the court reverse the judgment and order Campbell to return the ring? (Hint: Is an engagement ring a completed gift immediately on its delivery?) Which principle do you support, and why?

(b) Should the court determine who was responsible for breaking off the engagement before awarding ownership of the ring? Why or why not?

(c) If, instead of Crippen, one of his creditors had sought the ring in satisfaction of one of his debts, how should the court have ruled? Why?

Legal Reasoning Group Activity

48–9. Bailments. On learning that Sébastien planned to travel abroad, Roslyn asked him to deliver $25,000 in cash to her family in Mexico. During a customs inspection at the border, Sébastien told the customs inspector that he carried less than $10,000. The officer discovered the actual amount of cash that Sébastien was carrying, seized it, and arrested Sébastien. Roslyn asked the government to return what she claimed were her funds, arguing that the arrangement with Sébastien

was a bailment and that she still held title to the cash. (See *Bailments.*)

(a) The first group will argue that Roslyn is entitled to the cash.

(b) The second group will take the position of the government and develop an argument that Roslyn's agreement with Sébastien does not qualify as a bailment.

CHAPTER 49

Real Property and Landlord-Tenant Law

From the earliest times, property has provided a means for survival. Primitive peoples lived off the fruits of the land, eating the vegetation and wildlife. Later, as the wildlife was domesticated and the vegetation cultivated, property provided pastures and farmland. Throughout history, property has continued to be an indicator of family wealth and social position. In the Western world, the protection of an individual's right to his or her property has become one of our most important rights.

In this chapter, we look at the nature of real property and the ways in which it can be owned. We examine the legal requirements involved in the transfer of real property. We even consider, in this chapter's *Spotlight Case,* whether the buyer of a haunted house can rescind the sale.

Realize that real property rights are never absolute. There is a higher right—that of the government to take, for compensation, private land for public use. Later in the chapter, we discuss this right, as well as other restrictions on the ownership or use of property, including zoning laws. We conclude the chapter with a discussion of landlord-tenant relationships.

49–1 The Nature of Real Property

Real property (or realty) consists of land and everything permanently attached to it, including structures and other fixtures. Real property encompasses airspace and subsurface rights, as well as rights to plants and vegetation. In essence, real property is immovable.

49–1a Land and Structures

Land includes the soil on the surface of the earth and the natural products or artificial structures that are attached to it. Land further includes all the waters contained on or under its surface and much, but not necessarily all, of the airspace above it. The exterior boundaries of land extend down to the center of the earth and up to the farthest reaches of the atmosphere (subject to certain qualifications).

49–1b Airspace and Subsurface Rights

The owner of real property has rights to both the airspace above the land and the soil and minerals underneath it. Any limitations on either airspace rights or subsurface rights, called *encumbrances,* normally must be indicated on the document that transfers title at the time of purchase. The ways in which ownership rights in real property can be limited will be examined later in this chapter.

Airspace Rights Disputes concerning airspace rights may involve the right of commercial and private planes to fly over property and the right of individuals and governments to seed clouds and produce artificial rain. Flights over private land normally do not violate property rights unless the flights are so low and so frequent that they directly interfere with the owner's enjoyment and use of the land. Leaning walls or projecting eave spouts or roofs may also violate the airspace rights of an adjoining property owner.

Subsurface Rights In many states, ownership of land can be separated from ownership of its subsurface. In other words, the owner of the surface may sell subsurface rights to another person. When ownership is separated into surface and subsurface rights, each owner can pass title to what she or he owns without the consent of the other owner.

Subsurface rights can be extremely valuable, as these rights include the ownership of minerals, oil, or natural gas. But a subsurface owner's rights would be of little value if he or she could not use the surface to exercise those rights. Hence, a subsurface owner has a right (called a *profit,* discussed later in this chapter) to go onto the surface of the land to, for instance, find and remove minerals.

Of course, conflicts can arise between the surface owner's use of the property and the subsurface owner's need to extract minerals, oil, or natural gas. In that situation, one party's interest may become subservient (secondary) to the other party's interest either by statute or by case law. If the owners of the subsurface rights excavate, they are absolutely (strictly) liable if their excavation causes the surface to collapse. Many states have statutes that also make the excavators liable for any damage to structures on the land. Typically, these statutes set out precise requirements for excavations of various depths.

49–1c Plant Life and Vegetation

Plant life, both natural and cultivated, is also considered to be real property. In many instances, the natural vegetation, such as trees, adds greatly to the value of realty. When a parcel of land is sold and the land has growing crops on it, the sale includes the crops, unless otherwise specified in the sales contract. When crops are sold by themselves, however, they are considered to be personal property, or goods. Consequently, the sale of crops is a sale of goods and is governed by the Uniform Commercial Code (UCC) rather than by real property law.

49–1d Fixtures

Certain personal property can become so closely associated with the real property to which it is attached that the law views it as real property. Such property is known as a **fixture**—an item affixed to realty, meaning that it is attached to the real property in a permanent way. The item may be embedded in the land or permanently attached to the property or to another fixture on the property by means of cement, plaster, bolts, nails, or screws. An item, such as a statue, may even sit on the land without being attached, as long as the owner *intends* it to be a fixture.

Fixtures are included in the sale of land unless the sales contract specifies otherwise. The issue of whether an item is a fixture (and thus real estate) or not a fixture (and thus personal property) often arises with respect to land sales, real property taxation, insurance coverage, and divorces. How the issue is resolved can have important consequences for the parties involved.

Typical Fixtures Some items can only be attached to property permanently—such as tile floors, cabinets, and carpeting. Because such items are attached permanently, it is assumed that the owner intended them to be fixtures. Also, when an item of property is custom-made for installation on real property, as storm windows are, the item usually is classified as a fixture.

In addition, an item that is firmly attached to the land and integral to its use may be deemed a fixture. For instance, a mobile home or a complex irrigation system bolted to a cement slab on a farm can be a fixture. The courts assume that owners, in making such installations, intend the objects to become part of their real property.

The Role of Intent Generally, when the courts need to determine whether a certain item is a fixture, they examine the intention of the party who placed the object on the real property. When the intent of that party is in dispute, the courts will usually deem that the item is a fixture if either or both of the following are true:

- The property attached cannot be removed without causing substantial damage to the remaining realty.
- The property attached is so adapted to the rest of the realty as to have become a part of it.

■ **CASE IN POINT 49.1** Terminal 5, a facility owned by the Port of Seattle (Port), was used in loading and unloading the shipping containers used to transport goods by ship. APL Limited entered into a long-term lease with the Port for use of Terminal 5 and for use of Port-owned container cranes. Terminal 5 was substantially rebuilt, and steel cranes were constructed and installed. The cranes were 100 feet apart, 198 feet tall, and 85 feet wide, and were mounted on rails embedded in concrete. They were hard-wired to a dedicated high-voltage electrical system built specifically for Terminal 5 and were attached to the power substation by cables.

APL later filed a lawsuit against the state of Washington for a refund of sales tax it had paid on the lease of the cranes. The state argued that the cranes were personal property and, as such, subject to sales tax. The trial court ruled in favor of the state, but a Washington appellate court reversed. The reviewing court found that the trial court had not sufficiently taken the Port's intent into account in determining that the cranes were personal property, not fixtures. "When the owner and the person that [attaches property to realty] are one and the same, a rebuttable presumption arises that the owner's intention was for the [property] to become part of the realty." The reviewing court remanded the case so the lower court could examine evidence of the Port's intent.[1] ■

---

1. *APL Limited v. Washington State Department of Revenue,* 154 Wash.App. 1020 (2010).

Trade Fixtures Are Personal Property Trade fixtures are an exception to the rule that fixtures are a part of the real property to which they are attached. A **trade fixture** is personal property that is installed for a commercial purpose *by a tenant* (one who rents real property from the owner, or landlord).

Trade fixtures remain the property of the tenant unless removal would irreparably damage the building or realty. A walk-in cooler, for instance, purchased and installed by a tenant who uses the premises for a restaurant, is a trade fixture. The tenant can remove the cooler from the premises when the lease terminates but ordinarily must repair any damage that the removal causes or compensate the landlord for the damage.

49–2 Ownership and Other Interests in Real Property

Ownership of property is an abstract concept that cannot exist independently of the legal system. No one can actually possess, or *hold*, a piece of land, the air above it, the earth below it, and all the water contained on it. One can only possess *rights* in real property.

Numerous rights are involved in real property ownership, which is why property ownership is often viewed as a bundle of rights. One who possesses the entire bundle of rights is said to hold the property in *fee simple*, which is the most complete form of ownership. When only some of the rights in the bundle are transferred to another person, the effect is to limit the ownership rights of both the transferor of the rights and the recipient.

Ownership interests in real property have traditionally been referred to as *estates in land*, which include fee simple estates, life estates, and leasehold estates. We examine these types of estates in this section, and we also discuss several forms of concurrent ownership of property. Finally, we describe certain interests in real property that is owned by others.

49–2a Ownership in Fee Simple

In a **fee simple absolute**, the owner has the greatest aggregation of rights, privileges, and power possible. The owner can give the property away or dispose of the property by *deed* or by *will*. When there is no will, the fee simple passes to the owner's legal heirs on her or his death. A fee simple absolute is potentially infinite in duration and is assigned forever to a person and her or his heirs without limitation or condition.[2] The owner has the rights of *exclusive* possession and use of the property.

The rights that accompany a fee simple absolute include the right to use the land for whatever purpose the owner sees fit. Of course, other laws, including applicable zoning, noise, and environmental laws, may limit the owner's ability to use the property in certain ways. A person who uses his or her property in a manner that unreasonably interferes with others' right to use or enjoy their own property can be liable for the tort of *nuisance*.

■ **CASE IN POINT 49.2** Nancy and James Biglane owned and lived in a building next door to the Under the Hill Saloon, a popular bar that featured live music. During the summer, the Saloon, which had no air-conditioning, opened its windows and doors, and live music echoed up and down the street. The Biglanes installed extra insulation, thicker windows, and air-conditioning units in their building. Nevertheless, the noise from the Saloon kept the Biglanes awake at night. Eventually, they sued the owners of the Saloon for nuisance. The court held that the noise from the bar unreasonably interfered with the Biglanes' right to enjoy their property and prohibited the Saloon from opening its windows and doors while playing music.[3] ■

49–2b Life Estates

A **life estate** is an estate that lasts for the life of some specified individual. A **conveyance,** or transfer of real property, "to A for his life" creates a life estate.[4] The life tenant's ownership rights cease to exist on the life tenant's death.

The life tenant has the right to use the land, provided that he or she commits no **waste** (injury to the land). In other words, the life tenant cannot use the land in a manner that would adversely affect its value. The life tenant can use the land to harvest crops or, if mines and oil wells are already on the land, can extract minerals and oil from it, but the life tenant cannot establish new wells or mines. The life tenant can also create liens, *easements* (discussed shortly), and leases, but none can extend beyond the life

---

2. In another type of estate, the *fee simple defeasible*, ownership in fee simple automatically terminates if a stated event occurs. For instance, property might be conveyed (transferred) to a school only as long as it is used for school purposes. In addition, the fee simple may be subject to a *condition subsequent*. This means that if a stated event occurs, the prior owner of the property can bring an action to regain possession of the property.
3. *Biglane v. Under the Hill Corp.*, 949 So.2d 9 (Miss.Sup. 2007).
4. A less common type of life estate is created by the conveyance "to A for the life of B." This is known as an estate *pur autre vie*—that is, an estate for the duration of the life of another.

of the tenant. In addition, with few exceptions, the life tenant has an exclusive right to possession during his or her lifetime.

Along with these rights, the life tenant also has some duties—to keep the property in repair and to pay property taxes. In short, the owner of the life estate has the

same rights as a fee simple owner except that she or he must maintain the value of the property during her or his tenancy.

In the following case, the life tenant refused to pay the taxes and the premiums for the insurance on the property. Was this waste?

Case 49.1

Main Omni Realty Corp. v. Matus

New York Supreme Court, Appellate Division, Second Department, 124 A.D.3d 604, 1 N.Y.S.3d 319 (2015).

Background and Facts Craig Matus held a life estate in certain residential real property in Huntington, New York. On the termination of the life estate, title to the property was to transfer to Main Omni Realty Corporation, a wholly owned subsidiary of New York Community Bank. For a dozen years, Matus refused to pay premiums for insurance on the property. He also refused to pay the property taxes, resulting in tax liens.

To preserve its interest in the property, Main Omni paid the premiums and the liens, which avoided a foreclosure and sale of the property. Main Omni then filed a suit in a New York state court against Matus, seeking to recover the amount of the premiums and taxes on the ground of unjust enrichment. In addition, it sought to extinguish (end) the life estate on the ground of waste based on Matus's refusal to pay the taxes. The court denied Main Omni's motion for summary judgment. Main Omni appealed.

In the Language of the Court

Ruth C. *BALKIN*, J.P. [Judge Presiding], L. Priscilla *HALL*, Leonard B. *AUSTIN*, and Betsey *BARROS*, JJ. [Judges].
* * * *

The essential inquiry in any action for unjust enrichment or restitution is whether it is against equity and good conscience to permit the defendant to retain what is sought to be recovered. *A plaintiff must show that (1) the other party was enriched, (2) at the plaintiff's expense, and (3) that it is against equity and good conscience to permit the other party to retain what is sought to be recovered.* [Emphasis added.]

The plaintiffs established their *prima facie* entitlement to judgment as a matter of law on their first cause of action, which alleged unjust enrichment and sought restitution, and their second cause of action, which alleged waste and sought to extinguish the defendant's life estate. As life tenant, the defendant was obligated to pay the property taxes and * * * insurance on the subject property, and the intentional failure to do so constitutes waste. It is undisputed that the defendant intentionally failed to pay the property taxes and * * * insurance on the subject property, and he has clearly expressed his intention not to do so in the future. Under these circumstances, the remainder interest in the subject property is in constant danger of forfeiture in a tax lien sale, unless the plaintiffs continue paying the property taxes and * * * insurance premiums the defendant is otherwise obligated to pay. The plaintiffs therefore demonstrated, *prima facie,* that the defendant was unjustly enriched by the plaintiffs' payment of these expenses for the defendant, and that equity warrants extinguishing his life estate in the subject property.

Decision and Remedy *A state intermediate appellate court reversed the lower court's denial of Main Omni's motion and ordered a summary judgment in the plaintiff's favor. Because Matus continued to refuse to pay the taxes on the property, the court ended his life estate.*

Critical Thinking

- **Economic** *Why would the owner of a life estate refuse to pay the taxes and insurance premiums on the property of the estate? Should any reason for this refusal have influenced the court's decision in this case?*

49–2c Concurrent Ownership

Persons who share ownership rights simultaneously in particular property (including real property and personal property) are said to have **concurrent ownership.** There are two principal types of concurrent ownership: *tenancy in common* and *joint tenancy.* Concurrent ownership rights can also be held in a *tenancy by the entirety* or as *community property,* but these types of concurrent ownership are less common.

Tenancy in Common   The term **tenancy in common** refers to a form of co-ownership in which each of two or more persons owns an undivided interest in the property. The interest is undivided because each tenant shares rights in the whole property. On the death of a tenant in common, that tenant's interest in the property passes to her or his heirs.

■ **EXAMPLE 49.3**   Four friends purchase a condominium unit in Hawaii together as tenants in common. This means that each of them has a one-fourth ownership interest in the whole. If one of the four owners dies a year after the purchase, his ownership interest passes to his heirs (his wife and children, for example) rather than to the other tenants in common. ■

Unless the co-tenants have agreed otherwise, a tenant in common can transfer her or his interest in the property to another without the consent of the remaining co-owners. In most states, it is presumed that a co-tenancy is a tenancy in common unless there is specific language indicating the intent to establish a joint tenancy.

Joint Tenancy   In a **joint tenancy,** each of two or more persons owns an undivided interest in the property, but a deceased joint tenant's interest passes to the surviving joint tenant or tenants.

Right of Survivorship.   The right of a surviving joint tenant to inherit a deceased joint tenant's ownership interest—referred to as a *right of survivorship*—distinguishes a joint tenancy from a tenancy in common. ■ **EXAMPLE 49.4** Jerrold and Eva are married and purchase a house as joint tenants. The title to the house clearly expresses the intent to create a joint tenancy because it refers to Jerrold and Eva as "joint tenants with right of survivorship." Jerrold has three children from a prior marriage. If Jerrold dies, his interest in the house automatically passes to Eva rather than to his children from the prior marriage. ■

Termination of a Joint Tenancy.   A joint tenant can transfer her or his rights by sale or gift to another without the consent of the other joint tenants. Doing so terminates the joint tenancy, however. The person who purchases the property or receives it as a gift becomes a tenant in common, not a joint tenant. ■ **EXAMPLE 49.5** Three brothers, Brody, Saul, and Jacob, own a parcel of land as joint tenants. Brody is experiencing financial difficulties and sells his interest in the real property to Beth. The sale terminates the joint tenancy, and now Beth, Saul, and Jacob hold the property as tenants in common. ■

A joint tenant's interest can also be levied against (seized by court order) to satisfy the tenant's judgment creditors. If this occurs, the joint tenancy terminates, and the remaining owners hold the property as tenants in common. (Judgment creditors can also seize the interests of tenants in a tenancy in common.)

Tenancy by the Entirety   A less common form of shared ownership of real property by married persons is a **tenancy by the entirety.** It differs from a joint tenancy in that neither spouse may separately transfer his or her interest during his or her lifetime unless the other spouse consents. In some states in which statutes give the wife the right to convey her property, this form of concurrent ownership has effectively been abolished. A divorce, either spouse's death, or mutual agreement will terminate a tenancy by the entirety.

Community Property   A limited number of states[5] allow married couples to own property as **community property.** If property is held as community property, each spouse technically owns an undivided one-half interest in the property. This type of ownership applies to most property acquired by the husband or the wife during the course of the marriage. It generally does *not* apply to property acquired prior to the marriage or to property acquired by gift or inheritance as separate property during the marriage. After a divorce, community property is divided equally in some states and according to the discretion of the court in other states.

49–2d Leasehold Estates

A **leasehold estate** is created when a real property owner or lessor (landlord) agrees to convey the right to possess and use the property to a lessee (tenant) for a certain period of time. The tenant's right to possession is

---

5. These states include Alaska, Arizona, California, Idaho, Louisiana, Nevada, New Mexico, Texas, Washington, and Wisconsin. Puerto Rico allows property to be owned as community property as well.

temporary, which is what distinguishes a tenant from a purchaser, who acquires title to the property.

In every leasehold estate, the tenant has a *qualified* right to exclusive possession. It is qualified because the landlord has a right to enter onto the premises to ensure that no waste is being committed. In addition, the tenant can use the land—for instance, by harvesting crops—but cannot injure it by such activities as cutting down timber to sell or extracting oil.

Fixed-Term Tenancy A **fixed-term tenancy,** also called a *tenancy for years,* is created by an express contract stating that the property is leased for a specified period of time, such as a month, a year, or a period of years. Signing a one-year lease to occupy an apartment, for instance, creates a fixed-term tenancy. Note that the term need not be specified by date and can be conditioned on the occurrence of an event, such as leasing a cabin for the summer or an apartment during Mardi Gras.

At the end of the period specified in the lease, the lease ends (without notice), and possession of the property returns to the lessor. If the tenant dies during the period of the lease, the lease interest passes to the tenant's heirs as personal property. Often, leases include renewal or extension provisions.

Periodic Tenancy A **periodic tenancy** is created by a lease that does not specify a term but does specify that rent is to be paid at certain intervals, such as weekly, monthly, or yearly. The tenancy is automatically renewed for another rental period unless properly terminated. ■ **EXAMPLE 49.6** Jewel, LLC, enters into a lease with Capital Properties. The lease states, "Rent is due on the tenth day of every month." This provision creates a periodic tenancy from month to month. ■ A periodic tenancy sometimes arises after a fixed-term tenancy ends when the landlord allows the tenant to retain possession and continue paying monthly or weekly rent.

Under the common law, to terminate a periodic tenancy, the landlord or tenant must give at least one period's notice to the other party. If the tenancy is month to month, for instance, one month's notice must be given prior to the last month's rent payment. Today, however, state statutes often require a different period of notice before the termination of a tenancy.

Tenancy at Will With a **tenancy at will,** either party can terminate the tenancy without notice. This type of tenancy can arise if a landlord rents property to a tenant "for as long as both agree" or allows a person to live on the premises without paying rent. Tenancy at will is rare today

because most state statutes require a landlord to provide some period of notice to terminate a tenancy. States may also require a landowner to have sufficient cause (a legitimate reason) to end a residential tenancy.

Tenancy at Sufferance The mere possession of land without right is called a **tenancy at sufferance.** A tenancy at sufferance is not a true tenancy because it is created when a tenant *wrongfully* retains possession of property. Whenever a tenancy for years or a periodic tenancy ends and the tenant continues to retain possession of the premises without the owner's permission, a tenancy at sufferance is created.

49–2e Nonpossessory Interests

In contrast to the types of property interests just described, some interests in land do not include any rights to possess the property. These interests are therefore known as **nonpossessory interests.** They include *easements, profits,* and *licenses.*

An **easement** is the right of a person to make limited use of another person's real property without taking anything from the property. The right to walk across another's property, for example, is an easement. In contrast, a **profit** is the right to go onto land owned by another and take away some part of the land itself or some product of the land. ■ **EXAMPLE 49.7** Shawn owns real property known as the Dunes. Shawn gives Carmen the right to go there and remove all of the sand and gravel that she needs for her cement business. Carmen has a profit. ■

Easements and profits can be classified as either *appurtenant* or *in gross.* Because easements and profits are similar and the same rules apply to both, we discuss them together.

Easement or Profit Appurtenant An easement (or profit) *appurtenant* arises when the owner of one piece of land has a right to go onto (or remove something from) an adjacent piece of land owned by another. The land that is benefited by the easement is called the *dominant estate,* and the land that is burdened is called the *servient estate.*

Because easements appurtenant are intended to *benefit the land,* they run (are conveyed) with the land when it is transferred. ■ **EXAMPLE 49.8** Owen has a right to drive his car across Green's land, which is adjacent to Owen's property. This right-of-way over Green's property is an easement appurtenant to Owen's land. If Owen sells his land, the easement runs with the land to benefit the new owner. ■

Easement or Profit in Gross In an easement or profit *in gross,* the right to use or take things from another's land is given to one who does not own an adjacent tract of land. These easements are intended to *benefit a particular person or business,* not a particular piece of land, and cannot be transferred.

■ **EXAMPLE 49.9** Avery owns a parcel of land with a marble quarry. Avery conveys to Classic Stone Corporation the right to come onto her land and remove up to five hundred pounds of marble per day. Classic Stone owns a profit in gross and cannot transfer this right to another. ■ Similarly, when a utility company is granted an easement to run its power lines across another's property, it obtains an easement in gross.

Creation of an Easement or Profit Most easements and profits are created by an express grant in a contract, deed, or will. This allows the parties to include terms defining the extent and length of time of use. In some situations, however, an easement or profit can be created without an express agreement.

An easement or profit may arise by **implication** when the circumstances surrounding the division of a parcel of property imply its creation. ■ **EXAMPLE 49.10** Barrow divides a parcel of land that has only one well for drinking water. If Barrow conveys the half without a well to Dean, a profit by implication arises because Dean needs drinking water. ■

An easement may also be created by **necessity.** An easement by necessity does not require division of property for its existence. A person who rents an apartment, for instance, has an easement by necessity in the private road leading up to it.

An easement arises by **prescription** when one person exercises an easement, such as a right-of-way, on another person's land without the landowner's consent. The use must be apparent and continue for the length of time required by the applicable statute of limitations. (In much the same way, title to property may be obtained by adverse possession, as will be discussed later in this chapter.)

■ **CASE IN POINT 49.11** Junior and Wilma Thompson sold twenty-one of their fifty acres of land in Missouri to Walnut Bowls, Inc. The deed expressly reserved an easement to the Thompsons' remaining twenty-nine acres, but it did not fix a precise location for the easement. James and Linda Baker subsequently bought the remaining acreage of the Thompsons' land.

Many years later—on learning of the easement to the Bakers' property—a potential buyer of Walnut Bowls' property refused to go through with the sale. Walnut

Bowls then put steel cables across its driveway entrances, installed a lock and chain on an access gate, and bolted a "No Trespassing" sign facing the Bakers' property. The Bakers filed a suit in a Missouri state court to determine the location of the easement. Citing the lack of an express location, the court held that there was no easement.

The Bakers appealed, and a state intermediate appellate court reversed that decision. The reviewing court held that an easement existed and instructed the trial court to determine its location. An easement can be created by deed even though its specific location is not identified. The location can later be fixed by agreement between the parties or inferred from use. If the easement is not identified in either of these ways, a court must determine the location.[6] ■

Termination of an Easement or Profit An easement or profit can be terminated or extinguished in several ways. The simplest way is to deed it back to the owner of the land that is burdened by it. Similarly, if the owner of an easement or profit acquires the property burdened by it, then it is merged into the property.

Another way to terminate an easement or profit is to abandon it and provide evidence of the intent to relinquish the right to use it. Mere nonuse will not extinguish an easement or profit, however, *unless the nonuse is accompanied by an overt act showing the intent to abandon.* An overt act might be, for instance, installing and using a different access road to one's property and discontinuing using an easement across the neighboring property. In any case, a court must be convinced that there was an intent to abandon the easement or profit.

License In the context of real property, a **license** is the revocable right of a person to come onto another person's land. It is a personal privilege that arises from the consent of the owner of the land and can be revoked by the owner. A ticket to attend a movie at a theater or a concert is an example of a license.

In essence, a license grants a person the authority to enter the land of another and perform a specified act or series of acts without obtaining any permanent interest in the land. When a person with a license exceeds the authority granted and undertakes some action on the property that is not permitted, the property owner can sue that person for the tort of trespass.

■ **CASE IN POINT 49.12** A Catholic church granted Prince Realty Management, LLC, a three-month license to use a three-foot strip of its property adjacent to

---

6. *Baker v. Walnut Bowls, Inc.,* 423 S.W.3d 293 (Mo.App. 2014).

Prince's property. The license authorized Prince to "put up plywood panels," creating a temporary fence to protect Prince's property during the construction of a new building. During the license's term, Prince installed steel piles and beams on the licensed property. When Prince ignored the church's demands that these structures be removed, the church sued Prince for trespass. The court concluded that the license allowed only temporary structures and that Prince had exceeded its authority by installing steel piles and beams. Therefore, the church was entitled to damages.[7] ■

Exhibit 49–1 illustrates the various interests in real property discussed in this chapter.

49–3 Transfer of Ownership

Ownership interests in real property are frequently transferred by sale, and the terms of the transfer are specified in a real estate sales contract. When real property is sold, the type of interest being transferred and the conditions of the transfer normally are set forth in a *deed* executed by the person who is conveying the property. Real property ownership can also be transferred by gift, by will or inheritance, by adverse possession, or by eminent domain.

---

7. *Roman Catholic Church of Our Lady of Sorrows v. Prince Realty Management, LLC,* 47 A.D.3d 909, 850 N.Y.S.2d 569 (2008).

49–3a Real Estate Sales Contracts

In some ways, a sale of real estate is similar to a sale of goods because it involves a transfer of ownership, often with specific warranties. A sale of real estate, however, is a more complicated transaction that involves certain formalities that are not required in a sale of goods. In part because of these complications, real estate brokers or agents who are licensed by the state assist the buyers and sellers during the sales transaction.

Usually, after substantial negotiation (offers, counteroffers, and responses), the parties enter into a detailed contract setting forth their agreement. A contract for a sale of land includes such terms as the purchase price, the type of deed the buyer will receive, the condition of the premises, and any items that will be included.

Unless the buyer pays cash for the property, the buyer must obtain financing through a mortgage loan. Real estate sales contracts are often contingent on the buyer's ability to obtain financing at or below a specified rate of interest. The contract may also be contingent on certain events, such as the completion of a land survey or the property's passing one or more inspections. Normally, the buyer is responsible for having the premises inspected for physical or mechanical defects and for insect infestation.

Closing Date and Escrow   The contract usually fixes a date for performance, or **closing,** that frequently is four to twelve weeks after the contract is signed. On this day,

---

EXHIBIT 49–1   **Interests in Real Property**

TYPE OF INTEREST	DESCRIPTION

Ownership Interests	1. *Fee simple*—The most complete form of ownership.
	2. *Life estate*—An estate that lasts for the life of a specified individual.
	3. *Concurrent ownership*—When two or more persons hold title to property together, concurrent ownership exists.
	    a. Tenancy in common
	    b. Joint tenancy
	    c. Tenancy by the entirety
	    d. Community property

Leasehold Estates	1. Fixed-term tenancy (tenancy for years) 2. Periodic tenancy 3. Tenancy at will 4. Tenancy at sufferance
Nonpossessory Interests	1. Easements 2. Profits 3. Licenses

the seller conveys the property to the buyer by delivering the deed to the buyer in exchange for payment of the purchase price.

Deposits toward the purchase price normally are held in a special account, called an **escrow account,** until all of the conditions of sale have been met. Once the closing takes place, the funds in the escrow account are transferred to the seller.

Marketable Title The title to a particular parcel of property is especially important to the buyer. A grantor (seller) is obligated to transfer **marketable title,** or good title, to the grantee (buyer). Marketable title means that the grantor's ownership is free from encumbrances (except those disclosed by the grantor) and free of defects.

If the buyer signs a purchase contract and then discovers that the seller does not have a marketable title, the buyer can withdraw from the contract. ■ **EXAMPLE 49.13** Chan enters into an agreement to buy Fortuna Ranch from Hal. Chan then discovers that Hal has given Pearl an option to purchase the ranch and the option has not expired. In this situation, the title is not marketable, because Pearl could exercise the option and Hal would be compelled to sell the ranch to her. Therefore, Chan can withdraw from the contract to buy the property. ■

The most common way of ensuring title is through **title insurance,** which insures the buyer against loss from defects in title to real property. When financing the purchase of real property, almost all lenders require title insurance to protect their interests in the collateral for the loan.

Implied Warranties in the Sale of New Homes
The common law rule of *caveat emptor* ("let the buyer beware") held that the seller of a home made no warranty as to its soundness or fitness (unless the contract or deed stated otherwise). Today, however, most states imply a warranty—the **implied warranty of habitability**—in the sale of new homes.

Under this warranty, the seller of a new house warrants that it will be fit for human habitation even if the deed or contract of sale does not include such a warranty. Essentially, the seller is warranting that the house is in reasonable working order and is of reasonably sound construction. The seller can be liable if the home is defective. In some states, the warranty protects not only the first purchaser but any subsequent purchaser as well.

Seller's Duty to Disclose Hidden Defects In most jurisdictions, courts impose on sellers a duty to disclose any known defect that materially affects the value of the property and that the buyer could not reasonably discover. Failure to disclose such a defect gives the buyer a right to rescind the contract and to sue for damages based on fraud or misrepresentation.

There is normally a limit to the time within which the buyer can bring a suit against the seller based on the defect. Time limits run from either the date of the sale or the day that the buyer discovered (or should have discovered) the defect. ■ **EXAMPLE 49.14** Ian Newson partially renovates a house in Louisiana and sells it to Jerry and Tabitha Moreland for $87,000. Two months after the Morelands move in, they discover rotten wood behind the tile in the bathroom and experience problems with the plumbing. The state statute specifies that the Morelands have one year from the date of the sale or the discovery of the defect to file a lawsuit. Therefore, the Morelands must file suit within twelve months of discovering the defects (which would be fourteen months from the date of the sale). ■

In the following *Spotlight Case,* the court had to decide whether the buyer of a house had the right to rescind the sales contract because he was not told that the house was allegedly haunted.

Spotlight on Sales of Haunted Houses

Case 49.2 Stambovsky v. Ackley
Supreme Court, Appellate Division, New York, 572 N.Y.S.2d 672, 169 A.D.2d 254 (1991).

Background and Facts Jeffrey Stambovsky signed a contract to buy Helen Ackley's home in Nyack, New York. After the contract was signed, Stambovsky discovered that the house was widely reputed to be haunted. The Ackley family claimed to have seen poltergeists on numerous occasions over the prior nine years. The Ackleys had been interviewed and quoted in both a national publication (*Reader's Digest*) and the local newspaper. The house was described as "a riverfront Victorian (with ghost)" when it was part of a walking tour of Nyack, New York. When Stambovsky discovered the house's reputation, he sued to rescind the contract and recover his down payment. He alleged that Ackley and

Case 49.2 Continues

her real estate agent made material misrepresentations when they failed to disclose Ackley's belief that the home was haunted. Ackley argued that, under the doctrine of *caveat emptor,* she was under no duty to disclose to the buyer the home's haunted reputation. The trial court dismissed Stambovsky's case. Stambovsky appealed.

In the Language of the Court

Justice *RUBIN* delivered the opinion of the court.

* * * *

While I agree with [the trial court] that the real estate broker, as agent for the seller, is under no duty to disclose to a potential buyer the phantasmal reputation of the premises and that, in his pursuit of a legal remedy for fraudulent misrepresentation against the seller, plaintiff hasn't a ghost of a chance, I am nevertheless moved by the spirit of equity to allow the buyer to seek rescission of the contract of sale and recovery of his down payment. New York law fails to recognize any remedy for damages incurred as a result of the seller's mere silence, applying instead the strict rule of *caveat emptor.* Therefore, the theoretical basis for granting relief, even under the extraordinary facts of this case, is elusive if not ephemeral [short-lived].

* * * *

The doctrine of caveat emptor *requires that a buyer act prudently to assess the fitness and value of his purchase and operates to bar the purchaser who fails to exercise due care from seeking the equitable remedy of rescission.* * * * Applying the strict rule of *caveat emptor* to a contract involving a house possessed by poltergeists conjures up visions of a psychic or medium routinely accompanying the structural engineer and Terminix man on an inspection of every home subject to a contract of sale. It portends [warns] that the prudent attorney will establish an escrow account lest the subject of the transaction come back to haunt him and his client—or pray that his malpractice insurance coverage extends to supernatural disasters. In the interest of avoiding such untenable consequences, the notion that a haunting is a condition which can and should be ascertained upon reasonable inspection of the premises is a hobgoblin which should be exorcised from the body of legal precedent and laid quietly to rest. [Emphasis added.]

* * * *

In the case at bar [under consideration], defendant seller deliberately fostered the public belief that her home was possessed. Having undertaken to inform the public at large, to whom she has no legal relationship, about the supernatural occurrences on her property, she may be said to owe no less a duty to her contract vendee. It has been remarked that the occasional modern cases, which permit a seller to take unfair advantage of a buyer's ignorance so long as he is not actively misled are "singularly unappetizing." Where, as here, the seller not only takes unfair advantage of the buyer's ignorance but has created and perpetuated a condition about which he is unlikely to even inquire, enforcement of the contract (in whole or in part) is offensive to the court's sense of equity. Application of the remedy of rescission, within the bounds of the narrow exception to the doctrine of *caveat emptor* set forth herein, is entirely appropriate to relieve the unwitting purchaser from the consequences of a most unnatural bargain.

Decision and Remedy *The New York appellate court found that the doctrine of* caveat emptor *did not apply in this case. The court allowed Stambovsky to rescind the purchase contract and recover the down payment.*

Critical Thinking

- **Ethical** *In not disclosing the house's reputation to Stambovsky, was Ackley's behavior unethical? If so, was it unethical because she knew something he did not, or was it unethical because of the nature of the information she omitted? What if Ackley had failed to mention that the roof leaked or that the well was dry—conditions that a buyer would normally investigate? Explain your answer.*
- **Legal Environment** *Why did the court decide that applying the strict rule of* caveat emptor *was inappropriate in this case? How would applying this doctrine increase costs for the purchaser?*

49–3b Deeds

Possession and title to land are passed from person to person by means of a **deed**—the instrument used to transfer real property. Deeds must meet certain requirements, but unlike a contract, a deed does not have to be supported by legally sufficient consideration. Gifts of real property are common, and they require deeds even though there is no consideration for the gift.

To be valid, a deed must include the following:

1. The names of the grantor (the giver or seller) and the grantee (the donee or buyer).
2. Words evidencing the intent to convey (for instance, "I hereby bargain, sell, grant, or give"). No specific words are necessary. If the deed does not specify the type of estate being transferred, it presumptively transfers the property in fee simple absolute.
3. A legally sufficient description of the land. The description must include enough detail to distinguish the property being conveyed from every other parcel of land. The property can be identified by reference to an official survey or recorded plat map, or each boundary can be described by metes and bounds. **Metes and bounds** is a system of measuring boundary lines by the distance between two points, often using physical features of the local geography. A property description might say, for instance, "beginning at the southwesterly intersection of Court and Main Streets, then West 40 feet to the fence, then South 100 feet, then Northeast approximately 120 feet back to the beginning."
4. The grantor's (and usually his or her spouse's) signature.
5. Delivery of the deed.

Different types of deeds provide different degrees of protection against defects of title, as discussed next.

Warranty Deeds A **warranty deed** contains the greatest number of warranties and thus provides the most extensive protection against defects of title. In most states, special language is required to create a general warranty deed. Warranty deeds commonly include the following covenants:

1. A covenant that the grantor has the title to, and the power to convey, the property.
2. A covenant of quiet enjoyment (a warranty that the buyer will not be disturbed in her or his possession of the land).
3. A covenant that transfer of the property is made without knowledge of adverse claims of third parties.

Generally, the warranty deed makes the grantor liable for all defects of title during the time that the property was held by the grantor and previous titleholders. ■ **EXAMPLE 49.15** Sanchez sells a two-acre lot and office building by warranty deed to Fast Tech, LLC. Subsequently, Amy shows that she has better title than Sanchez had and evicts Fast Tech. Here, Fast Tech can sue Sanchez for breaching the covenant of quiet enjoyment. Fast Tech can recover the purchase price of the land, plus any other damages incurred as a result. ■

Special Warranty Deed A **special warranty deed**, or *limited warranty deed,* in contrast, warrants only that the grantor or seller held good title during his or her ownership of the property. In other words, the seller does not guarantee that there are no adverse claims by third parties against any previous owners of the property.

If the special warranty deed discloses all liens or other encumbrances, the seller will not be liable to the buyer if a third person subsequently interferes with the buyer's ownership. If the third person's claim arises out of, or is related to, some act of the seller, however, the seller will be liable to the buyer for damages.

Quitclaim Deed A **quitclaim deed** offers the least protection against defects in the title. Basically, a quitclaim deed conveys to the grantee whatever interest the grantor had. If the grantor had no interest, then the grantee receives no interest. (Naturally, if the grantor had a defective title or no title at all, a conveyance by warranty deed or special warranty deed would not cure the defect. Such a deed, however, would give the buyer a cause of action to sue the seller.)

Quitclaim deeds are often used when the seller, or grantor, is uncertain as to the extent of his or her rights in the property. They may also be used to release a party's interest in a particular parcel of property. This may be necessary, for instance, in divorce settlements or business dissolutions when the grantors are dividing up their interests in real property.

Grant Deed With a **grant deed,** the grantor simply states, "I grant the property to you" or "I convey, or bargain and sell, the property to you." By state statute, grant deeds carry with them an implied warranty that the grantor owns the property and has not previously transferred it to someone else or encumbered it, except as set out in the deed.

49–3c Recording Statutes

Once the seller delivers the deed to the buyer (at closing), legal title to the property is conveyed. Nevertheless, the buyer should promptly record the deed with the state records office. Every state has a **recording statute,** which allows deeds to be recorded in the public record for a fee. Deeds generally are recorded in the county in which the property is located. Many state statutes require that the grantor sign the deed in the presence of two witnesses before it can be recorded.

Recording a deed gives notice to the public that a certain person is now the owner of a particular parcel of real estate. By putting everyone on notice as to the true owner, recording a deed prevents the previous owners from fraudulently conveying the land to other purchasers.

49–3d Adverse Possession

A person who wrongfully possesses the real property of another (by occupying or using the property) may eventually acquire title to it through adverse possession. **Adverse possession** is a means of obtaining title to land without delivery of a deed and without the consent of—or payment to—the true owner. Thus, adverse possession is a method of *involuntarily* transferring title to the property from the true owner to the adverse possessor.

Essentially, when one person possesses the real property of another for a certain statutory period of time, that person acquires title to the land. The statutory period varies from three to thirty years, depending on the state, with ten years being most common.

Requirements for Adverse Possession For property to be held adversely, four elements must be satisfied:

1. *Possession must be actual and exclusive.* The possessor must physically occupy the property. This requirement is clearly met if the possessor lives on the property, but it may also be met if the possessor builds fences, erects structures, plants crops, or even grazes animals on the land.

2. *The possession must be open, visible, and notorious, not secret or clandestine.* The possessor must occupy the land for all the world to see. This requirement ensures that the true owner is on notice that someone is possessing the owner's property wrongfully.

3. *Possession must be continuous and peaceable for the required period of time.* This requirement means that the possessor must not be interrupted in the occupancy by the true owner or by the courts. Continuous does not mean constant. It simply means that the possessor has continuously occupied the property in some fashion for the statutory time. Peaceable means that no force was used to possess the land.

4. *Possession must be hostile and adverse.* In other words, the possessor cannot be living on the property with the owner's permission and must claim the property as against the whole world.

■ **CASE IN POINT 49.16** Charles Scarborough and Mildred Rollins were adjoining landowners, sharing one common boundary. Based on Rollins's survey of the property, Rollins believed that she owned a portion of a gravel road located to the south of the apartment buildings she owned. In contrast, Scarborough believed that the gravel road was located totally on his property and that he owned some property north of the gravel road toward Rollins's apartment buildings.

Scarborough filed a complaint seeking a court order stating that he had title to the property and was its sole owner. The court, however, ruled that Rollins owned a portion of the gravel road by adverse possession. She had used it openly for more than thirty-five years, it was generally thought to be part of her apartment complex, and she had paid taxes on it.[8] ■

The following case raises the question of whether a landowner next to a rail line can acquire a portion of the right-of-way by adverse possession.

---

8. *Scarborough v. Rollins,* 44 So.3d 381 (Miss.App. 2010).

Case Analysis 49.3

Montgomery County v. Bhatt

Court of Appeals of Maryland, 446 Md. 79, 130 A.3d 424 (2016).

In the Language of the Court

Glenn T. *HARRELL,* Jr., J. [Judge]

Driving that train, high on cocaine,
Casey Jones you better watch your speed.
Trouble ahead, trouble behind,

And you know that notion just crossed my mind.

—The Grateful Dead, *Casey Jones,* on Workingman's Dead (Warner Bros. Records 1970).

Although the record of the present case does not reflect a comparable level of drama as captured by the refrain of "Casey Jones,"

Case 49.3 Continued

it hints at plenty of potential trouble, both ahead and behind, for a pair of public works projects (one in place and the other incipient [in development]) cherished by the government and some citizens of Montgomery County.

The Capital Crescent Trail is a well-known hiker/biker route that runs between Georgetown in the District of Columbia and Silver Spring, Maryland. Its path was used formerly as the Georgetown Branch of the Baltimore & Ohio (B&O) Railroad. After the trains stopped running in 1985, the property was transferred in 1988 to the government of Montgomery County, Maryland, via a quitclaim deed for a consideration of $10 million. It is planned that the Maryland portion of the former rail line (and current interim hiker/biker trail) will become the proposed Purple Line, a commuter light rail project.

BACKGROUND

* * * Ajay Bhatt owns 3313 Coquelin Terrace (a subdivided, single-family residential lot—"Lot 8"—improved by a dwelling) in Chevy Chase, Montgomery County, Maryland. He purchased this property in 2006 from his aunt, who owned the property since at least the 1970s. The lot abuts the Georgetown Branch of the B&O Railroad/Capital Crescent Trail. In 1890, the right-of-way that was the rail line (and is today the hiker/biker trail) was conveyed in a fee-simple deed from George Dunlop, grantor, to the Metropolitan Southern Railroad Company ("the Railroad"), grantee.

The right-of-way was obtained by the County * * * from the Railroad pursuant to the federal Rails-to-Trails Act. [Federal regulations] allow the County to preserve the land as a hiker/biker trail until the County chooses whether and when to restore a form of rail service within the right-of-way.

On 18 October 2013, Montgomery County issued to Bhatt a civil citation asserting a violation of Section 49-10(b) of the Montgomery County Code, which prohibits a property owner from

erecting or placing "any structure, fence, post, rock, or other object in a public right-of-way." The * * * claimed violation was the placement and maintenance by Bhatt's predecessors-in-interest of Lot 8 of a fence and shed within the former rail line (and current hiker/biker trail) right-of-way, without a permit. * * * The District Court of Maryland, sitting in Montgomery County, * * * found Bhatt guilty * * * and ordered him to remove the fence and shed encroaching upon the County's right-of-way.

The appeal was heard *de novo* by the [Maryland] Circuit Court. [When a court hears a case *de novo*, it decides the issues without reference to the legal conclusions or assumptions made by the previous court.]

* * * *

Bhatt's defense to the charged violation of Section 49–10(b) was that he owned the encroached-upon land by adverse possession.

Bhatt argued that, because the fence had been located beyond the property line of Lot 8 since at least 1963, the Railroad was obliged to take action to remove it prior to the maturation of the twenty-year period for adverse possession.

* * * The Circuit Court vacated the District Court's judgment and dismissed the violation citation. * * * The Circuit Court concluded ultimately that Bhatt had a creditable claim for adverse possession.

The County petitioned this Court for a writ of *certiorari*. * * * We granted the Petition.

* * * *

DISCUSSION

I. Contentions

* * * The County contends * * * that, because this Court has considered previously a railroad line to be analogous to a public highway for most purposes, the land in question is not subject to an adverse possession claim.

* * * Bhatt rejects the public highway-railroad line analogy because the land was in private, not public, use during its operation as a rail line.

II. Analysis

a. Railroads as Public Highways

A railroad is in many essential respects a public highway, and the rules of law applicable to one are generally applicable to the other. Railroads are owned frequently by private corporations, but this has never been considered a matter of any importance * * * because the function performed is that of the State. Railroad companies operate as a public use and are not viewed strictly as private corporations since they are publicly regulated common carriers. *Essentially, a railroad is a highway dedicated to the public use.* [Emphasis added.]

* * * *

b. May a public highway (or any portion of its right-of-way, no matter the type of real property interest by which it is held) be possessed adversely by an abutting private citizen?

* * * *Nothing is more solidly established than the rule that title to property held by a municipal corporation in its governmental capacity, for a public use, cannot be acquired by adverse possession.* [Emphasis added.]

* * * *

* * * Because time does not run against the state, or the public, * * * public highways are not subject to a claim for adverse possession, except in the limited circumstances of a clear abandonment by the State. By parity [equivalence] of reasoning applied to the present case, railway lines [are] also not * * * subject to a claim for adverse possession, without evidence of clear abandonment or a clear shift away from public use.

c. Use of the right-of-way

* * * We do not find in this record, however, that there is any evidence of abandonment by the rail line operator (or Montgomery County) or that the right-of-way was taken out of public use such that a claim for adverse possession could ripen within this right-of-way.

* * * *

The 1890 Dunlop Deed shows that the purchase made by the Railroad was

Case 49.3 Continues

Case 49.3 Continued

from a private landowner. There was no evidence adduced [offered] by Bhatt supporting a conclusion that the right-of-way was abandoned and was not being used by the public, even during the period from 1985 when the freight service ended and 1988 when the property was conveyed to the County and became a hiker/biker trail as an interim public use.

* * * *

Because no evidence was presented by Bhatt to show that the current use of the right-of-way by Montgomery County is unreasonable or that the Railroad or the County abandoned the right-of-way, no claim for adverse possession will lie. Accordingly, we shall reverse the judgment of the Circuit Court. Bhatt's fence and shed encroached upon the right-of-way in violation of Montgomery

County Code Section 49–10(b). The District Court got it right.

JUDGMENT OF THE CIRCUIT COURT FOR MONTGOMERY COUNTY REVERSED. CASE REMANDED TO THAT COURT WITH INSTRUCTIONS TO AFFIRM THE JUDGMENT OF THE DISTRICT COURT OF MARYLAND, SITTING IN MONTGOMERY COUNTY.

Legal Reasoning Questions

1. Bhatt claimed to have met all of the requirements to acquire a strip of public land through adverse possession. Which element did the court find had *not* been met? Why?

2. What is the "potential trouble, both ahead and behind, for a pair of public works projects" hinted at in this case? In whose favor is that "trouble" likely to be resolved?

3. Should a private party, by encroaching on a public right-of-way, be able to acquire title adverse to the public rights? Discuss.

Purpose of the Doctrine There are a number of public-policy reasons for the adverse possession doctrine. These include society's interest in resolving boundary disputes, in determining title when title to property is in question, and in assuring that real property remains in the stream of commerce. More fundamentally, the doctrine punishes owners who do not take action when they see adverse possession and rewards possessors for putting land to productive use.

49–4 Limitations on the Rights of Property Owners

No ownership rights in real property can ever really be absolute—that is, an owner of real property cannot always do whatever she or he wishes on or with the property. Nuisance and environmental laws, for instance, restrict certain types of activities. Property ownership is also conditional on the payment of property taxes. Zoning laws and building permits frequently restrict the use of realty. In addition, if a property owner fails to pay debts, the property may be seized to satisfy judgment creditors. In short, the rights of every property owner are subject to certain conditions and limitations.

49–4a Eminent Domain

Even ownership in fee simple absolute is limited by a superior ownership. Just as the king was the ultimate

landowner in medieval England, today the government has an ultimate ownership right in all land in the United States. This right, known as **eminent domain,** is sometimes referred to as the *condemnation power* of government to take land for public use. It gives the government the right to acquire possession of real property in the manner directed by the U.S. Constitution and the laws of the state whenever the public interest requires it.

The power of eminent domain generally is invoked through **condemnation** proceedings. ■ **EXAMPLE 49.17** When a new public highway is to be built, the government decides where to build it and how much land to condemn. After the government determines that a particular parcel of land is necessary for the highway, it will first offer to buy the property. If the owner refuses the offer, the government brings a judicial (*condemnation*) proceeding to obtain title to the land. ■

Condemnation proceedings usually involve two distinct phases. The first seeks to establish the government's right to take the property, and the second determines the fair value of the property.

The Taking When the government takes land owned by a private party for public use, it is referred to as a **taking.** Under the *takings clause* of the Fifth Amendment to the U.S. Constitution, the government may take private property for public use, but it must pay "just compensation" to the owner. State constitutions contain similar provisions. In the first phase of condemnation proceedings, the government must prove that it needs to acquire privately owned property for a public use.

■ **EXAMPLE 49.18** Franklin County, Iowa, engages Bosque Systems to build a liquefied natural gas pipeline that crosses the property of more than two hundred landowners. Some property owners consent to this use and accept the Bosque's offer of compensation. Others refuse the offer. A court will likely deem the pipeline to be a public use. Therefore, the government can exert its eminent domain power to "take" the land, provided that it pays just compensation to the property owners. ■

The Compensation The U.S. Constitution and state constitutions require that the government pay just compensation to the landowner when invoking its condemnation power. Just compensation means fair value. In the second phase of the condemnation proceeding, the court determines the fair value of the land, which usually is approximately equal to its market value.

Property may be taken by the government only for public use, not for private benefit. But can eminent domain be used to promote private development when the development is deemed to be in the public interest? See this chapter's *Ethics Today* for a discussion of this issue.

49–4b Inverse Condemnation

Typically, a government agency exercises the power of eminent domain in the manner just discussed. **Inverse condemnation,** in contrast, occurs when a government simply takes private property from a landowner without paying any compensation, thereby forcing the landowner to sue the government for compensation.

The taking can be physical, as when a government agency uses or occupies the land, or it may be constructive, as when an agency regulation results in loss of property value. The United States Supreme Court has held that even temporary flooding of land by the government may result in liability under the takings clause.[9]

■ **CASE IN POINT 49.19** In Walton County, Florida, water flows through a ditch from Oyster Lake to the Gulf of Mexico. When Hurricane Opal caused the water to rise in Oyster Lake, Walton County reconfigured the drainage to divert the overflow onto the nearby property of William and Patricia Hemby. The flow was eventually

---

9. *Arkansas Game and Fish Commission v. United States,* ___ U.S. ___, 133 S.Ct. 511, 184 L.Ed.2d 417 (2012).

ETHICS TODAY

Should Eminent Domain Be Used to Promote Private Development?

Issues of fairness often arise when the government takes private property for public use. One issue is whether it is fair for a government to take property by eminent domain and then convey it to private developers.

For instance, suppose a city government decides that it is in the public interest to have a larger parking lot for a local, privately owned sports stadium. Or suppose it decides that its citizens would benefit from having a manufacturing plant locate in the city to create more jobs. The government may condemn certain tracts of existing housing or business property and then convey the land to the privately owned stadium or manufacturing plant.

Such actions may bring in private developers and businesses that provide jobs and increase tax revenues, thus revitalizing communities. But is the land really being taken for "public use," as required by the Fifth Amendment to the U.S. Constitution?

The Supreme Court's Ruling

In 2005, the United States Supreme Court ruled that the power of eminent domain may be used to further economic development.[a] At the same time, the Court recognized that individual states have the right to pass laws that prohibit takings for economic development.

The States' Responses

Since then, the vast majority of the states have passed laws to curb the government's ability to take private property and subsequently give it to private developers. Nevertheless, loopholes in some state legislation still allow takings for redevelopment of slum areas. Thus, the debate over whether (and when) it is fair for the government to take citizens' property for economic development continues.

Critical Thinking *At what point might the predicted benefits of a new private commercial endeavor outweigh the constitutional requirement of a taking only for public use?*

---

a. *Kelo v. City of New London, Connecticut,* 545 U.S. 469, 125 S.Ct. 2655, 162 L.Ed.2d 439 (2005).

restored to pre-hurricane conditions, but during a later emergency, water was diverted onto the Hembys' property again. This diversion was not restored.

The Hembys filed a suit against the county. After their deaths, their daughter Cozette Drake pursued the claim. The court found that by allowing the water diversion to remain on Drake's property long after the emergency had passed, the county had engaged in a permanent or continuous physical invasion. This invasion rendered Drake's property useless and deprived her of its beneficial enjoyment. Drake was therefore entitled to receive compensation from the county.[10] ■

49–4c Restrictive Covenants

A private restriction on the use of land is known as a **restrictive covenant.** If the restriction is binding on the party who initially purchases the property and on subsequent purchasers as well, it is said to "run with the land." A covenant running with the land must be in writing (usually it is in the deed), and subsequent purchasers must have reason to know about it.

■ **EXAMPLE 49.20** In the course of developing a fifty-lot suburban subdivision, Levitt records a declaration of restrictions effectively limiting construction on each lot to one single-family house. Each lot's deed includes a reference to the declaration with a provision that the purchaser and her or his successors are bound to those restrictions. Thus, each purchaser assumes ownership with notice of the restrictions. If an owner attempts to build a duplex (or any noncompliant structure) on a lot, the other owners may obtain a court order to prevent the construction.

Alternatively, Levitt might simply have included the restrictions on the subdivision's map, filed the map in the appropriate public office, and included a reference to the map in each deed. Under these circumstances, each owner would still have been held to have constructive notice of the restrictions. ■

49–5 Zoning and Government Regulations

The rules and regulations that collectively manage the development and use of land are known as **zoning laws.** Zoning laws were first used in the United States to segregate slaughterhouses, distilleries, kilns, and other businesses that might pose a nuisance to nearby residences.

The growth of modern urban areas led to an increased need to organize uses of land. Today, zoning laws enable municipalities to control the speed and type of development within their borders by creating different zones and regulating the use of property allowed in each zone.

The United States Supreme Court has held that zoning is a constitutional exercise of a government's police powers.[11] Therefore, as long as zoning ordinances are rationally related to the health, safety, or welfare of the community, a municipal government has broad discretion to carry out zoning as it sees fit.

49–5a Purpose and Scope of Zoning Laws

The purpose of zoning laws is to manage the land within a community in a way that encourages sustainable and organized development while controlling growth in a manner that serves the interests of the community. One of the basic elements of zoning is the classification of land by permissible use, but zoning extends to other aspects of land use as well.

Permissible Uses of Land Municipalities generally divide their available land into districts according to the land's present and potential future uses. Typically, land is classified into the following types of permissible uses:

1. *Residential.* In areas dedicated for **residential use,** landowners can construct buildings for human habitation.

2. *Commercial.* Land assigned for business activities is designated as being for **commercial use,** sometimes called business use. An area with a number of retail stores, offices, supermarkets, and hotels might be designated as a commercial or business district. Land used for entertainment purposes, such as movie theaters and sports stadiums, also falls into this category, as does land used for government activities.

3. *Industrial.* Areas designated for **industrial use** typically encompass light and heavy manufacturing, shipping, and heavy transportation. For instance, undeveloped land with easy access to highways and railroads might be classified as suitable for future use by industry. Although industrial uses can be profitable for a city seeking to raise tax revenue, such uses can also result in noise, smoke, or vibrations that interfere with others' enjoyment of their property. Consequently, areas zoned for industrial use generally are kept as far as possible from residential districts and some commercial districts.

---

10. *Drake v. Walton County,* 6 So.3d 717 (Fla.App. 2009).

11. *Village of Euclid v. Ambler Realty Co.,* 272 U.S. 365, 47 S.Ct. 114, 71 L.Ed. 303 (1926).

4. *Conservation districts.* Some municipalities also establish certain areas that are dedicated to carrying out local soil and water conservation efforts. For instance, wetlands might be designated as a conservation district.

A city's residential, commercial, and industrial districts may be divided, in turn, into subdistricts. For instance, zoning ordinances may regulate the type, density, size, and approved uses of structures within a given district. Thus, a residential district may be divided into low-density (single-family homes with large lots), high-density (single- and multiple-family homes with small lots), and planned-unit (condominiums or apartments) subdistricts.

Other Zoning Restrictions Zoning rules extend to much more than the permissible use of land. In residential districts, for instance, an ordinance may require a house or garage to be set back a specific number of feet from a neighbor's property line.

In commercial districts, zoning rules may attempt to maintain a certain visual aesthetic. Therefore, businesses may be required to construct buildings of a certain height and width so that they conform to the style of other commercial buildings in the area.

Businesses may also be required to provide parking for patrons or take other measures to manage traffic. Sometimes, municipalities limit construction of new businesses to prevent traffic congestion.

Zoning laws may even attempt to regulate the public morals of the community. For instance, cities commonly impose severe restrictions on the location and operation of adult businesses and medical (or recreational) marijuana dispensaries.

49–5b Exceptions to Zoning Laws

Zoning restrictions are not absolute. It is impossible for zoning laws to account for every contingency. The purpose of zoning is to control development, not to prevent it altogether or to limit the government's ability to adapt to changing circumstances or unforeseen needs. Hence, legal processes have been developed to allow for exceptions to zoning laws, such as *variances* and *special-use permits.*

Variances A property owner who wants to use his or her land in a manner not permitted by zoning rules can request a **variance,** which allows an exception to the rules. The property owner making the request must demonstrate that the requested variance:

1. Is necessary for reasonable development.
2. Is the least intrusive solution to the problem.
3. Will not alter the essential character of the neighborhood.

Hardship Situations. Property owners normally request variances in *hardship situations*—that is, when complying with the zoning rules would be too difficult or costly due to existing property conditions. ■ **EXAMPLE 49.21** Lin, a homeowner, wants to replace her single-car garage with a two-car garage. If she does so, however, the garage will be closer to her neighbor's property than is permitted by the zoning rules. In this situation, she may ask for a variance. She can claim that the configuration of her property would make it difficult and costly to comply with the zoning code, so compliance would create a hardship for her. ■

Similarly, a church might request a variance from height restrictions in order to erect a new steeple. Or a furniture store might ask for a variance from *footprint* limitations so that it can expand its showroom. (A building's footprint is the area of ground that it covers.)

Note that the hardship may not be self-created. In other words, a person who buys property with zoning restrictions in effect cannot usually then argue that he or she needs a variance in order to use the property as intended.

Public Hearing. In almost all instances, before a variance is granted, there must be a public hearing with adequate notice to neighbors who may object to the exception. After the public hearing, a hearing examiner appointed by the municipality (or the local zoning board or commission) determines whether to grant the exception. When a variance is granted, it applies only to the specific parcel of land for which it was requested and does not create a regulation-free zone.

Special-Use Permits Sometimes, zoning laws permit a certain use only if the property owner complies with specific requirements to ensure that the proposed use does not harm the immediate neighborhood. In such instances, the zoning board can issue **special-use permits,** also called conditional-use permits.

■ **EXAMPLE 49.22** An area is designated as a residential district, but small businesses are permitted to operate there so long as they do not affect the characteristics of the neighborhood. A bank asks the zoning board for a special-use permit to open a branch in the area. At the public hearing, the bank demonstrates that the branch will be housed in a building that conforms to the style of other structures in the area. The bank also shows that adequate parking will be available and that landscaping will shield the parking lot from public view. Unless there are strong objections from the branch's prospective neighbors, the board will likely grant the permit. ■

Special Incentives In addition to granting exceptions to zoning regulations, municipalities may also wish to encourage certain kinds of development. To do so, they offer incentives, often in the form of lower tax rates or tax credits. For instance, to attract new businesses that will provide jobs and increase the tax base, a city may offer lower property tax rates for a period of years. Similarly, homeowners may receive tax credits for historic preservation if they renovate and maintain older homes.

49–6 Landlord-Tenant Relationships

A landlord-tenant relationship is established by a lease contract. A **lease** contract arises when a property owner (landlord) agrees to give another party (the tenant) the exclusive right to possess the property for a limited time. In most states, statutes require leases for terms exceeding one year to be in writing. The lease should describe the property and indicate the length of the term, the amount of the rent, and how and when it is to be paid.

State or local law often dictates permissible lease terms. For instance, a statute or ordinance might prohibit the leasing of a structure that is in a certain physical condition or is not in compliance with local building codes. As in other areas of law, the National Conference of Commissioners on Uniform State Laws has issued a model act to create more uniformity in the law governing landlord-tenant relations. Twenty-one states have adopted variations of the Uniform Residential Landlord and Tenant Act (URLTA).

49–6a Rights and Duties

The rights and duties of landlords and tenants generally pertain to four broad areas of concern—the possession, use, maintenance, and, of course, rent of leased property.

Possession A landlord is obligated to give a tenant possession of the property that the tenant has agreed to lease. After obtaining possession, the tenant retains the property exclusively until the lease expires, unless the lease states otherwise.

Quiet Enjoyment. The covenant of quiet enjoyment mentioned previously also applies to leased premises. Under this covenant, the landlord promises that during the lease term, neither the landlord nor anyone having a superior title to the property will disturb the tenant's use and enjoyment of the property. This covenant forms the essence of the landlord-tenant relationship, and if it is breached, the tenant can terminate the lease and sue for damages.

Eviction. If the landlord deprives the tenant of possession of the leased property or interferes with the tenant's use or enjoyment of it, an **eviction** occurs. An eviction occurs, for instance, when the landlord changes the lock and refuses to give the tenant a new key.

A **constructive eviction** occurs when the landlord wrongfully performs or fails to perform any of the duties the lease requires, thereby making the tenant's further use and enjoyment of the property exceedingly difficult or impossible. Examples of constructive eviction include a landlord's failure to provide heat in the winter, light, or other essential utilities.

Use of the Premises The tenant normally may make any use of the leased property, provided the use is legal and does not injure the landlord's interest. The parties are free to limit by agreement the uses to which the property may be put. A tenant is not entitled to create a nuisance by substantially interfering with others' quiet enjoyment of their property rights.

Maintenance of the Premises The tenant is responsible for any damage to the premises that he or she causes, intentionally or negligently. The landlord can hold the tenant liable for the cost of returning the property to the physical condition it was in at the lease's inception. The tenant usually is not responsible for ordinary wear and tear, and the property's consequent depreciation in value.

In some jurisdictions, landlords of residential property are required by statute to maintain the premises in good repair. Landlords must also comply with applicable state statutes and city ordinances regarding maintenance and repair of commercial buildings.

In addition, the implied warranty of habitability discussed earlier may apply to *residential* leases. The warranty requires a landlord who leases residential property to ensure that the premises are habitable—that is, safe and suitable to live in. Also, the landlord must make repairs to maintain the premises in that condition for the lease's duration. Generally, this warranty applies to major, or *substantial*, physical defects that the landlord knows or should know about and has had a reasonable time to repair. A large hole in the roof, for instance, would be a substantial defect.

■ **EXAMPLE 49.23** Carol and Ken Galprin own a house within the city limits of Redmond. A city regulation states that a residence must be connected to the city sewer system before anyone, including tenants, can live in the residence. The Galprins' house is not connected to the city system. Thus, it is not legally habitable, and they cannot lease it to tenants. ■

Rent *Rent* is the tenant's payment to the landlord for the tenant's occupancy or use of the landlord's real property. Usually, the tenant must pay the rent even if she or he refuses to occupy the property or moves out for unjustified reasons while the lease is in force.

Under the common law, if the leased premises were destroyed by fire or flood, the tenant still had to pay rent. Today, however, if an apartment building burns down, most states' laws do not require tenants to continue to pay rent.

In some situations, such as when a landlord breaches the implied warranty of habitability, a tenant may be allowed to withhold rent as a remedy. When rent withholding is authorized under a statute, the tenant must usually put the amount withheld into an *escrow account.* The funds are held in the name of the tenant and are returned to the tenant if the landlord fails to make the premises habitable.

49–6b Transferring Rights to Leased Property

Either the landlord or the tenant may wish to transfer her or his rights to the leased property during the term of the lease. If the landlord sells the leased property, the tenant becomes the tenant of the new owner. The new owner may collect subsequent rent but must abide by the terms of the existing lease.

Assignment The tenant's transfer of his or her entire interest in the leased property to a third person is an *assignment of the lease.* Many leases require that an assignment have the landlord's written consent. The landlord can nullify (avoid) an assignment made without the required consent. State statutes may specify that the landlord may not unreasonably withhold consent, however. Also, a landlord who knowingly accepts rent from the assignee may be held to have waived the consent requirement.

When an assignment is valid, the assignee acquires all of the tenant's rights under the lease. An assignment, however,

does not release the original tenant (assignor) from the obligation to pay rent if the assignee defaults. Also, if the assignee exercises an option under the original lease to extend the term, the original tenant remains liable for the rent during the extension, unless the landlord agrees otherwise.

Sublease The tenant's transfer of all or part of the premises for a period shorter than the lease term is a **sublease.** The same restrictions that apply to an assignment of the tenant's interest in leased property apply to a sublease. If the landlord's consent is required, a sublease without such permission is ineffective. Also, like an assignment, a sublease does not release the tenant from her or his obligations under the lease.

■ **EXAMPLE 49.24** Derek, a student, leases an apartment for a two-year period. Although Derek had planned on attending summer school, he decides to accept a job offer in Europe for the summer months instead. Derek therefore obtains his landlord's consent to sublease the apartment to Ava. Ava is bound by the same terms of the lease as Derek, and the landlord can hold Derek liable if Ava violates the lease terms. ■

49–6c Termination of the Lease

Usually, a lease terminates when its term ends. The tenant surrenders the property to the landlord, who retakes possession. If the lease states the time it will end, the landlord is not required to give the tenant notice. The lease terminates automatically.

A lease can also be terminated in several other ways. If the tenant purchases the leased property from the landlord during the term of the lease, for instance, the lease will be terminated. The parties may also agree to end a tenancy before it would otherwise terminate. Finally, the tenant may *abandon* the premises—move out completely with no intention of returning before the lease term expires.

At common law, a tenant who abandoned leased property was still obligated to pay the rent for the full term of the lease. The landlord could let the property stand vacant and charge the tenant for the remainder of the term. This is still the rule in some states. In most states today, however, the landlord has a duty to *mitigate* his or her damages—that is, to make a reasonable attempt to lease the property to another party. Consequently, the tenant's liability for unpaid rent is restricted to the period of time that the landlord would reasonably need to lease the property to another tenant. Damages may also be allowed for the landlord's costs in leasing the property again.

Reviewing: Real Property and Landlord-Tenant Law

Vern Shoepke purchased a two-story home from Walter and Eliza Bruster in the town of Roche, Maine. The warranty deed did not specify what covenants would be included in the conveyance. The property was adjacent to a public park that included a popular Frisbee golf course. (Frisbee golf is a sport similar to golf but using Frisbees.) Wayakichi Creek ran along the north end of the park and along Shoepke's property. The deed allowed Roche citizens the right to walk across a five-foot-wide section of the lot beside Wayakichi Creek as part of a two-mile public trail system. Teenagers regularly threw Frisbee golf discs from the walking path behind Shoepke's property over his yard to the adjacent park. Shoepke habitually shouted and cursed at the teenagers, demanding that they not throw objects over his yard. Two months after moving into his Roche home, Shoepke leased the second floor to Lauren Slater for nine months. After three months of tenancy, Slater sublet the second floor to a local artist, Javier Indalecio. (The lease agreement did not specify that Shoepke's consent would be required to sublease the second floor.) Over the remaining six months, Indalecio's use of oil paints damaged the carpeting in Shoepke's home. Using the information presented in the chapter, answer the following questions.

1. What is the term for the right of Roche citizens to walk across Shoepke's land on the trail?
2. What covenants would most courts infer were included in the warranty deed that was used in the property transfer from the Brusters to Shoepke?
3. Suppose that Shoepke wants to file a trespass lawsuit against some teenagers who continually throw Frisbees over his land. Shoepke discovers, however, that when the city put in the Frisbee golf course, the neighborhood homeowners signed an agreement that limited their right to complain about errant Frisbees. What is this type of promise or agreement called in real property law?
4. Can Shoepke hold Slater financially responsible for the damage to the carpeting caused by Indalecio? Why or why not?

Debate This . . . *Under no circumstances should a local government be able to condemn property in order to sell it later to real estate developers for private use.*

Terms and Concepts

adverse possession 950	implication 945	recording statute 950
closing 946	implied warranty of habitability 947	residential use 954
commercial use 954	industrial use 954	restrictive covenant 954
community property 943	inverse condemnation 953	special-use permit 955
concurrent ownership 943	joint tenancy 943	special warranty deed 949
condemnation 952	lease 956	sublease 957
constructive eviction 956	leasehold estate 943	taking 952
conveyance 941	license 945	tenancy at sufferance 944
deed 949	life estate 941	tenancy at will 944
easement 944	marketable title 947	tenancy by the entirety 943
eminent domain 952	metes and bounds 949	tenancy in common 943
escrow account 947	necessity 945	title insurance 947
eviction 956	nonpossessory interest 944	trade fixture 941
fee simple absolute 941	periodic tenancy 944	variance 955
fixed-term tenancy 944	prescription 945	warranty deed 949
fixture 940	profit 944	waste 941
grant deed 949	quitclaim deed 949	zoning laws 954

Issue Spotters

1. Bernie sells his house to Consuela under a warranty deed. Later, Delmira appears, holding a better title to the house than Consuela has. Delmira wants to have Consuela evicted from the property. What can Consuela do? (See *Transfer of Ownership.*)

2. Grey owns a commercial building in fee simple. Grey transfers temporary possession of the building to Haven Corporation. Can Haven transfer possession for even less time to Idyll Company? Explain. (See *Ownership and Other Interests in Real Property.*)

• Check your answers to the Issue Spotters against the answers provided in Appendix D at the end of this text.

Business Scenarios

49–1. Property Ownership. Madison owned a tract of land, but he was not sure that he had full title to the property. When Rafael expressed an interest in buying the land, Madison sold it to Rafael and executed a quitclaim deed. Rafael properly recorded the deed immediately. Several months later, Madison learned that he had had full title to the tract of land. He then sold the land to Linda by warranty deed. Linda knew of the earlier purchase by Rafael but took the deed anyway and later sued to have Rafael evicted from the land. Linda claimed that because she had a warranty deed, her title to the land was better than that conferred by Rafael's quitclaim deed. Will Linda succeed in claiming title to the land? Explain. (See *Transfer of Ownership.*)

49–2. Eviction. James owns a three-story building. He leases the ground floor to Juan's Mexican restaurant. The lease is to run for a five-year period and contains an express covenant of quiet enjoyment. One year later, James leases the top two stories to the Upbeat Club, a dance club for teens. The club's hours run from 5:00 P.M. to 11:00 P.M. The noise from the Upbeat Club is so loud that it is driving customers away from Juan's restaurant. Juan has notified James of the interference and has called the police on a number of occasions. James refuses to talk to the owners of the Upbeat Club or to do anything to remedy the situation. Juan abandons the premises. James files a suit for breach of the lease agreement and for the rental payments still due under the lease. Juan claims that he was constructively evicted and files a countersuit for damages. Discuss who will be held liable. (See *Landlord-Tenant Relationships.*)

Business Case Problems

49–3. Commercial Lease Terms. Gi Hwa Park entered into a lease with Landmark HHH, LLC, for retail space in the Plaza at Landmark, a shopping center in Virginia. The lease required the landlord to keep the roof "in good repair" and the tenant to obtain insurance on her inventory and absolve the landlord from any losses to the extent of the insurance proceeds. Park opened a store—The Four Seasons—in the space, specializing in imported men's suits and accessories. Within a month and continuing for nearly eight years, water intermittently leaked through the roof, causing damage. Landmark eventually had a new roof installed, but water continued to leak into The Four Seasons. On a night of record rainfall, the store suffered substantial water damage, and Park was forced to close. On what basis might Park seek to recover from Landmark? What might Landmark assert in response? Which party's argument is more likely to succeed, and why? [*Landmark HHH, LLC v. Gi Hwa Park,* 277 Va. 50, 671 S.E.2d 143 (2009)] (See *Landlord-Tenant Relationships.*)

49–4. Business Case Problem with Sample Answer— Adverse Possession. The McKeag family operated a marina on their lakefront property in Bolton, New York. For more than forty years, the McKeags used a section of property belonging to their neighbors, the Finleys, as a beach for the marina's customers. The McKeags also stored a large float on the beach during the winter months, built their own retaining wall, and planted bushes and flowers there. The McKeags prevented others from using the property, including the Finleys. Nevertheless, the families always had a friendly relationship, and one of the Finleys gave the McKeags permission to continue using the beach in 1992. He also reminded them of his ownership several times, to which they said nothing. The McKeags also asked for permission to mow grass on the property and once apologized for leaving a jet ski there. Can the McKeags establish adverse possession over the statutory period of ten years? Why or why not? [*McKeag v. Finley,* 939 N.Y.S.2d 644 (N.Y.App.Div. 2012)] (See *Transfer of Ownership.*)

• For a sample answer to Problem 49–4, go to Appendix E at the end of this text.

49–5. Rent. Flawlace, LLC, leased unfinished commercial real estate in Las Vegas, Nevada, from Francis Lin to operate a beauty salon. The lease required Flawlace to obtain a "certificate of occupancy" from the city to commence business. This required the installation of a fire protection system. The lease did not allocate responsibility for the installation to either party. Lin voluntarily undertook to install the system. After a month of delays, Flawlace moved out. Three months later, the installation was complete, and Lin leased the premises to a new tenant. Did Flawlace owe rent for the three months between the time that it moved out and the time that the new tenant moved in? Explain. [*Tri-Lin Holdings, LLC v. Flawlace, LLC,* 2014 WL 1101577 (Nev.Sup.Ct. 2014)] (See *Landlord-Tenant Relationships.*)

49–6. Landlord-Tenant Relationships. Bhanmattie Kumar was walking on a sidewalk in Flushing, New York, when she tripped over a chipped portion of the sidewalk and fell. The defective sidewalk was in front of a Pretty Girl store—one of a chain of apparel stores headquartered in Brooklyn—on premises leased from PI Associates, LLC. Kumar filed a claim in a New York state court against PI, seeking to recover damages for her injuries. PI filed a cross-claim against Pretty Girl. On what basis would the court impose liability on PI? In what situation would Pretty Girl be the liable party? Is there any circumstance in which Kumar could be at least partially responsible for her injury? Discuss. [*Bhanmattie Rajkumar Kumar v. PI Associates, LLC,* 125 A.D.3d 609, 3 N.Y.S.3d 372 (2 Dept. 2015)] (See *Landlord-Tenant Relationships.*)

49–7. Ownership and Other Interests in Real Property. Arthur and Diana Ebanks owned three properties in the Cayman Islands in joint tenancy. With respect to joint tenancies, Cayman law is the same as U.S. law. When the Ebanks divorced, the decree did not change the tenancy in which the properties were held. On the same day as the divorce filing, Arthur executed a will providing that "any property in my name and that of another as joint tenants . . . will pass to the survivor, and I instruct my Personal Representative to make no claim thereto." Four years later, Arthur died. His brother Curtis, the personal representative of his estate, asserted that Arthur's interest in the Cayman properties was part of the estate. Diana said that the sole interest in the properties was

hers. Who do the Cayman properties belong to? Why? [*Ebanks v. Ebanks,* 41 Fla. L. Weekly D291, __ So.3d __ (2 Dist. 2016)] (See *Ownership and Other Interests in Real Property.*)

49–8. Special Case Analysis—Adverse Possession. Go to Case Analysis 49.3, *Montgomery County v. Bhatt.* Read the excerpt, and answer the following questions.

(a) Issue: What conflict, and between which parties, did this case highlight?

(b) Rule of Law: On which specific requirement of what rule of law did the outcome in this case depend?

(c) Applying the Rule of Law: What exception to the applied rule of law might have resulted in a decision in the plaintiff's favor? Why did that exception not apply in this case?

(d) Conclusion: In light of the rule of law applied in this case, what was the judgment?

49–9. A Question of Ethics—Adverse Possession.
 Alana Mansell built a garage on her property that encroached on the property of her neighbor, Betty Hunter, by fourteen feet. Hunter knew of the encroachment and informally agreed to it, but she did not transfer ownership of the property to Mansell. A survey twenty-eight years later confirmed the encroachment, and Hunter sought the removal of the garage. Mansell asked a court to declare that she was the owner of the property by adverse possession. [Hunter v. Mansell, *240 P.3d 469 (Colo.App. 2010)]* (See *Transfer of Ownership.*)

(a) Did Mansell obtain title by adverse possession? Would the open occupation of the property for nearly thirty years be in Mansell's favor? Why or why not?

(b) Was Mansell's conduct in any way unethical? Discuss.

Legal Reasoning Group Activity

49–10. Adverse Possession. The Wallen family owned a cabin on Lummi Island in the state of Washington. A driveway ran from the cabin across their property to South Nugent Road. Floyd Massey bought the adjacent lot and built a cabin on it in 1980. To gain access to his property, Massey used a bulldozer to extend the driveway, without the Wallens' permission but also without their objection. In 2005, the Wallens sold their property to Wright Fish Company. Massey continued to use and maintain the driveway without permission or objection. In 2011, Massey sold his property to Robert Drake. Drake and his employees continued to use and maintain the driveway without permission or objection, although Drake knew it was located largely on Wright's property. In 2013, Wright sold its lot to Robert Smersh. The next year, Smersh told Drake to stop using the driveway. Drake filed a suit against Smersh, claiming an easement by prescription

(which is created by meeting the same requirements as adverse possession). (See *Transfer of Ownership.*)

(a) The first group will decide whether Drake's use of the driveway meets all of the requirements for adverse possession (easement by prescription).

(b) The second group will determine how the court should rule in this case and why. Does it matter that Drake knew the driveway was located largely on Wright's (and then Smersh's) property? Should it matter? Why or why not?

(c) A third group will evaluate the underlying policy and fairness of adverse possession laws. Should the law reward persons who take possession of someone else's land for their own use? Does it make sense to punish owners who allow someone else to use their land without complaint? Explain.

CHAPTER 50

Insurance

Protecting against loss is a foremost concern of all property owners. No one can predict whether an accident or a fire will occur, so individuals and businesses typically protect their personal and financial interests by obtaining insurance.

Insurance is a contract in which the insurance company (the insurer) promises to pay or otherwise compensate another (either the insured or the beneficiary) for a particular loss.

Insurance may provide for compensation in the event of (1) the injury or death of the insured or another, (2) damage to the insured's property, or (3) other types of losses, such as those resulting from lawsuits. Basically, insurance is an arrangement for *transferring and allocating risk.* In general, **risk** can be described as a prediction concerning potential loss based on known and unknown factors.

Risk management normally involves the transfer of certain risks from the individual to the insurance company by a contractual agreement. We examine the insurance contract and its provisions in this chapter. First, however, we look at some basic insurance terminology and concepts.

50–1 Insurance Terminology and Concepts

Like other legal areas, insurance has its own special concepts and terminology. An insurance contract is called a **policy.** The consideration paid to the insurer is called a **premium,** and the insurance company is sometimes called an **underwriter.** The parties to an insurance policy are the *insurer* (the insurance company) and the *insured* (the person covered by its provisions).

Insurance contracts usually are obtained through an *agent,* who normally works for the insurance company, or through a *broker,* who is ordinarily an *independent contractor.* When a broker deals with an applicant for insurance, the broker is, in effect, the applicant's agent (and not an agent of the insurance company).

In contrast, an insurance agent is an agent of the insurance company, not an agent of the applicant. Thus, the agent owes fiduciary duties to the insurer (the insurance company), but not to the person who is applying for insurance. As a general rule, the insurance company is bound by the acts of its agents when they act within the scope of the agency relationship. In most situations, state law determines the status of all parties writing or obtaining insurance.

50–1a Classifications of Insurance

Insurance is classified according to the nature of the risk involved. Fire insurance, casualty insurance, life insurance, and title insurance apply to different types of risk and protect different persons and interests. This is reasonable because the types of losses that are expected and the types that are foreseeable or unforeseeable vary with the nature of the activity. Exhibit 50–1 provides a list of common insurance classifications.

50–1b Insurable Interest

A person must have an **insurable interest** in something in order to insure it. Without an insurable interest, there is no enforceable contract, and a transaction to purchase insurance coverage would have to be treated as a wager. The existence of an insurable interest is a primary concern in determining liability under an insurance policy.

Life Insurance In regard to life insurance, a person must have a reasonable expectation of benefit from the continued life of another to have an insurable interest in that person's life. The insurable interest must exist *at the time the policy is obtained.*

EXHIBIT 50–1 Selected Insurance Classifications

TYPE OF INSURANCE	COVERAGE
Accident	Covers expenses, losses, and suffering incurred by the insured because of accidents causing physical injury and any consequent disability; sometimes includes a specified payment to heirs of the insured if death results from an accident.
All-Risk	Covers all losses that the insured may incur except those that are specifically excluded. Typical exclusions are losses due to war, pollution, earthquakes, and floods.
Automobile	May cover damage to automobiles resulting from specified hazards or occurrences (such as fire, vandalism, theft, or collision); normally provides protection against liability for personal injuries and property damage resulting from the operation of the vehicle.
Casualty	Protects against losses incurred by the insured as a result of being held liable for personal injuries or property damage sustained by others.
Disability	Replaces a portion of the insured's monthly income from employment in the event that illness or injury causes a short- or long-term disability. Some states require employers to provide short-term disability insurance. Benefits typically last a set period of time, such as six months for short-term coverage or five years for long-term coverage.
Fire	Covers losses to the insured caused by fire.
Floater	Covers movable property, as long as the property is within the territorial boundaries specified in the contract.
Homeowners'	Protects homeowners against some or all risks of loss to their residences and the residences' contents or liability arising from the use of the property.
Key-Person	Protects a business in the event of the death or disability of a key employee.
Liability	Protects against liability imposed on the insured as a result of injuries to the person or property of another.
Life	Covers the death of the policyholder. On the death of the insured, the insurer pays the amount specified in the policy to the insured's beneficiary.
Major Medical	Protects the insured against major hospital, medical, or surgical expenses.
Malpractice	A form of liability insurance that protects professionals (physicians, lawyers, and others) against malpractice claims brought against them by their patients or clients.
Term Life	Provides life insurance for a specified period of time (term) with no cash surrender value. It usually is renewable.

Life Insurance on Family Members. Close family relationships give a person an insurable interest in the life of another. For instance, a husband can take out an insurance policy on his wife and vice versa, or parents can take out life insurance policies on their children. A policy that a person takes out on his or her spouse remains valid even if they divorce, unless a specific provision in the policy calls for its termination on divorce.

Key-Person Life Insurance. *Key-person insurance* is insurance obtained by an organization on the life of a person who is important to that organization. Because the organization expects to experience financial gain from the continuation of the key person's life or financial loss from the key person's death, the organization has an insurable interest.

Typically, a small company will insure the lives of its important employees. Similarly, a corporation has an insurable interest in the life of a key executive (such as a talented CEO) whose death would result in financial loss to the company. If a firm insures a key person's life and that person leaves the firm and subsequently dies, the firm can collect on the insurance policy, provided that it has continued to pay the premiums.

Property Insurance For property insurance, an insurable interest exists when the insured derives a monetary benefit from the preservation and continued existence of the property. The insurable interest must exist at the time the loss occurs but need not exist when the policy is purchased.

■ **CASE IN POINT 50.1** ABM Industries, Inc., operated the heating, ventilation, and air-conditioning systems at the World Trade Center (WTC) in New York City in 2001. ABM also maintained all of the WTC's common areas. At the time, ABM employed more than eight hundred workers at the WTC. Zurich American Insurance Company insured ABM against losses resulting from "business interruption" caused by direct physical loss or

damage "to property owned, controlled, used, leased or intended for use" by ABM.

After the terrorist attacks on September 11, ABM filed a claim to recover for the loss of all income derived from its WTC operations. Zurich argued that the recovery should be limited to the income lost as a result of the destruction of ABM's office and storage space and supplies. A federal appellate court, however, ruled that ABM was entitled to compensation for the loss of all of its WTC operations. The court reasoned that the "policy's scope expressly includes real or personal property that the insured 'used,' 'controlled,' or 'intended for use.'" Because ABM's income depended on "the common areas and leased premises in the WTC complex," it had an insurable interest in that property at the time of the loss.[1] ■

In the following case, the plaintiff sought to retain his insurable interest in a home he no longer owned.

---

1. *Zurich American Insurance Co. v. ABM Industries, Inc.*, 397 F.3d 158 (2d Cir. 2005).

Breeden v. Buchanan

Court of Appeals of Mississippi, 164 So.3d 1057 (2015).

Background and Facts Donald Breeden and Willie Buchanan were married in Marion County, Mississippi. They lived in a home in Sandy Hook. Nationwide Property & Casualty Insurance Company insured the home under a policy bought by Breeden that named him as the insured. The policy provided that the spouse of the named insured was covered as an insured. After eight years of marriage, Breeden and Buchanan divorced. Breeden transferred his interest in the home to Buchanan as part of the couple's property settlement.

Less than a year later, a fire completely destroyed the home. An insurance claim was filed with Nationwide. Nationwide paid Buchanan. Breeden then filed a suit in a Mississippi state court against Buchanan and Nationwide. The plaintiff asserted claims for breach of contract and bad faith, and sought to recover the proceeds under the policy. The court dismissed the suit. Breeden appealed.

In the Language of the Court

GRIFFIS, P.J. [Presiding Judge], for the Court:

* * * *

Breeden's claims for breach of contract [and] bad-faith denial of insurance benefits * * * are based on the insurance policy. The [lower] court ruled that Breeden had no "insurable interest" in the Nationwide policy and had no right to the proceeds of the policy. Specifically, the * * * court ruled:

> The court finds that the pleadings reflect no insurable interest in Breeden in and to the policy or to the proceeds, as Breeden transferred and conveyed his right, title, and interest in and to the insured property to his former spouse, Buchanan, as part and parcel of their divorce proceeding and property settlement agreement, this transfer and conveyance having transpired several months before the occurrence of the loss, which is the subject matter of Breeden's complaint.
>
> Finding that Breeden had no insurable interest in and to the property—and thus no entitlement to any of the insurance proceeds—it follows that Nationwide did not breach the insurance contract by failing to pay Breeden any insurance proceeds from the loss, nor did it act in bad faith.

Case 50.1 Continues

* * * *

Breeden argues that the [lower] court was in error to determine that he had no insurable interest in the home. The home, which was Breeden's and Buchanan's marital residence, was insured under a Nationwide homeowners' insurance policy. The policy was effective from May 27, 2010, to May 27, 2011. The policy insured the home and its contents. At the beginning of the policy period, May 27, 2010, both Breeden and Buchanan had an insurable interest in the home because they were married and lived together in the home. The policy provided that the spouse of the named insured who resides at the same premises is covered as an insured. Based on the allegations of the complaint, the documents attached to the complaint, and Nationwide's motion [to dismiss], the * * * judge determined that Breeden did not have an insurable interest in the home at the time of the fire loss.

The fire loss occurred in April 2011. *At that time, Breeden did not have an insurable interest in the home. * * * The factual allegations of the complaint indicated that he did not have any ownership interest in the home at the time of the loss.* [Emphasis added.]

* * * *

Based on the complaint and the accompanying documents, there was simply nothing further that Nationwide owed under the insurance policy.

Decision and Remedy *A state intermediate appellate court affirmed the lower court's dismissal of Breeden's suit. Buchanan, not Breeden, was entitled to the proceeds of the insurance claim filed with Nationwide. At the time of the fire, the insurable interest in the property existed solely with Buchanan.*

Critical Thinking
• **Economic** *Why is an insurable interest required for the enforcement of an insurance contract?*

50–2 The Insurance Contract

An insurance contract is governed by the general principles of contract law, although the insurance industry is heavily regulated by each state.[2] Thus, for the insurance contract to be binding, consideration (in the form of a premium) must be given. In addition, the parties forming the contract must have the required contractual capacity to do so.

50–2a Application for Insurance

Customarily, a party offers to purchase insurance by submitting an application to the insurance company. The company can either accept or reject the offer. Sometimes, the insurance company's acceptance is conditional—on the results of a life insurance applicant's medical examination, for instance.

The filled-in application form is usually attached to the policy and made a part of the insurance contract. Thus, an insurance applicant is bound by any false statements that appear in the application (subject to certain exceptions). Insurance companies evaluate their risk

based on the information included in the application. Therefore, an applicant's misstatements or misrepresentations can void a policy, especially if the insurance company can show that it would not have extended insurance if it had known the facts.

50–2b Effective Date

The effective date of an insurance contract—that is, the date on which the insurance coverage begins—is important. Any loss sustained before the effective date will not be covered by the policy.

In some situations, the insurance applicant is not protected until a formal written policy is issued. In other situations, the applicant is protected between the time an application is received and the time the insurance company either accepts or rejects it. In these situations, a *binder* may be written.

Binder Recall that a broker is an agent of the applicant, not an agent of the insurance company. Therefore, if a person hires a broker to obtain insurance, and the broker fails to procure a policy, the applicant normally is not insured.

In contrast, a person who is obtaining insurance from an insurance company's agent is usually protected from

2. The states were given authority to regulate the insurance industry by the McCarran-Ferguson Act of 1945, 15 U.S.C. Sections 1011–1015.

the moment the application is made, provided that some form of premium has been paid. Usually, the agent will write a memorandum, or **binder,** indicating that a policy is pending and stating its essential terms. The binder provides temporary coverage until a formal policy is accepted or denied.

Life Insurance Parties may agree that a life insurance policy will be binding at the time the insured pays the first premium. The policy may, however, be expressly contingent on the applicant's passing a physical examination. If the applicant pays the premium and passes the examination, then the policy coverage is continuously in effect. If the applicant pays the premium but dies before having the physical examination, the policy may still be effective. In order to collect, the applicant's estate normally must show that the applicant would have passed the examination had he or she not died.

50-2c Provisions and Clauses

Some of the important provisions and clauses contained in insurance contracts are discussed in the following subsections and listed in Exhibit 50–2.

Provisions Mandated by Statute If a statute mandates that a certain provision be included in insurance contracts, a court will interpret the insurance policy as containing that provision. If a statute requires that any limitations on coverage be stated in the contract, a court will not allow an insurer to avoid liability by relying on an unexpressed restriction.

Incontestability Clauses Statutes commonly require that a policy for life or health insurance include an **incontestability clause**. Such a clause provides that after the policy has been in force for a specified length of time—often two or three years—the insurer cannot contest statements made in the application.

Once a policy becomes incontestable, the insurer cannot later avoid a claim on the basis of, for instance, fraud on the part of the insured, unless the clause provides an exception for that circumstance. The clause does not prevent an insurer from asserting other defenses to a claim, such as the nonpayment of premiums, failure to file proof of death, or lack of an insurable interest.

Coinsurance Clauses Often, when taking out fire insurance policies, property owners insure their property

EXHIBIT 50–2 Insurance Contract Provisions and Clauses

TYPE OF CLAUSE	DEFINITION
Antilapse Clause	An antilapse clause provides that a life insurance policy will not automatically lapse if no payment is made on the date due. Ordinarily, under such a provision, the insured has a *grace period* of thirty or thirty-one days within which to pay an overdue premium before the policy is canceled.
Appraisal Clause	Insurance policies frequently provide that if the parties cannot agree on the amount of a loss covered under the policy or the value of the property lost, an appraisal, or estimate, by an impartial and qualified third party can be demanded.
Arbitration Clause	Many insurance policies include clauses that call for arbitration of any disputes that arise between the insurer and the insured concerning the settlement of claims.
Coinsurance Clause	Many property insurance policies include a coinsurance clause that applies in the event of a partial loss and determines what percentage of the value of the property must be insured for an owner to be fully reimbursed for a loss. If the owner insures the property up to a specified percentage (typically 80 percent) of its value, she or he will recover any loss up to the face amount of the policy.
Incontestability Clause	An incontestability clause provides that after a policy has been in force for a specified length of time—usually two or three years—the insurer cannot contest statements made in the application.
Multiple Insurance Clause	Many insurance policies include a clause providing that if the insured has multiple insurance policies that cover the same property and the amount of coverage exceeds the loss, the loss will be shared proportionally by the insurance companies.

for less than full value because most fires do not result in a total loss. To encourage owners to insure their property for an amount as close to full value as possible, fire insurance policies generally include a coinsurance clause.

Typically, a **coinsurance clause** provides that if the owner insures the property up to a specified percentage—usually 80 percent—of its value, she or he will recover any loss up to the face amount of the policy. If the insurance is for less than the specified percentage, the owner is responsible for a proportionate share of the loss. In effect, the owner becomes a coinsurer.

Coinsurance applies only in instances of partial loss. The amount of the recovery is calculated by using the following formula:

$$\text{Loss} \times \left(\frac{\text{Amount of Insurance Coverage}}{\text{Coinsurance Percentage} \times \text{Property Value}} \right) = \text{Amount of Recovery}$$

■ **EXAMPLE 50.2** Madison, who owns property valued at $200,000, takes out a policy in the amount of $100,000. If Madison then suffers a loss of $80,000, her recovery will be $50,000. Madison will be responsible for (coinsure) the balance of the loss, or $30,000, which is the amount of loss ($80,000) minus the amount of recovery ($50,000).

$$\$80,000 \times \left(\frac{\$100,000}{0.8 \times \$200,000} \right) = \$50,000$$

Suppose that, instead, Madison had taken out a policy in the amount of 80 percent of the value of the property, or $160,000. Then, according to the same formula, she would have recovered the full amount of the loss (the face amount of the policy). ■

Appraisal and Arbitration Clauses Most fire insurance policies provide that if the parties cannot agree on the amount of a loss covered under the policy or on the value of the property lost, an *appraisal* can be demanded. An appraisal is an estimate of the property's value determined by a suitably qualified individual who has no interest in the property. Typically, two appraisers are used, with one appointed by each party. A third party, or umpire, may be called on to resolve differences. Other types of insurance policies also contain provisions for appraisal and arbitration when the insured and insurer disagree on the value of a loss.

Multiple Insurance Coverage Sometimes, an insured has *multiple insurance coverage*—that is, policies with several companies covering the same insurable interest. If the amount of coverage exceeds the loss, the insured can collect from each insurer only the company's proportionate share of the liability relative to the total amount of insurance.

Many fire insurance policies include a pro rata clause, which requires that all carriers proportionately share in any loss. ■ **EXAMPLE 50.3** Green insured $50,000 worth of property with two companies. Each policy had a liability limit of $40,000. If the property is totally destroyed, Green can collect only $25,000 from each insurer. ■

Antilapse Clauses A life insurance policy may provide, or a statute may require a policy to provide, that it will not automatically lapse if no payment is made on the date due. Ordinarily, under an **antilapse provision,** the insured has a *grace period* of thirty or thirty-one days within which to pay an overdue premium.

If the insured fails to pay a premium altogether, there are alternatives to cancellation:

1. The insurer may be required to extend the insurance for a period of time.
2. The insurer may issue a policy with less coverage to reflect the amount of the payments made.
3. The insurer may pay to the insured the policy's **cash surrender value**—the amount the insurer has agreed to pay on the policy's cancellation before the insured's death. (This value depends on the type of policy. It also depends on the period that the policy has already run, the amount of the premium, the insured's age and life expectancy, and amounts to be repaid on any outstanding loans taken out against the policy.)

When the insurance contract states that the insurer cannot cancel the policy, these alternatives are important.

50–2d Interpreting Provisions of an Insurance Contract

The courts recognize that most people do not have the special training necessary to understand the intricate terminology used in insurance policies. Therefore, when disputes arise, the courts will interpret the words used in an insurance contract according to their ordinary meanings in light of the nature of the coverage involved.

When there is an ambiguity in the policy, the provision generally is interpreted *against the insurance company.* Also, when it is unclear whether an insurance contract actually exists because the written policy has not been delivered, the uncertainty normally is resolved against the insurance company. The court presumes that the policy is in effect unless the company can show otherwise. Similarly, an insurer must make sure that the insured is adequately notified of any change in coverage under an existing policy.

Disputes over insurance often focus on the application of exclusions in the policy. ■ **CASE IN POINT 50.4** Alberto and Karelli Mila were insured under a liability policy that contained a list of twelve exclusions. "Exclusion k" stated that coverage did not apply to "bodily injury arising out of sexual molestation, corporal punishment or physical or mental abuse." Verushka Valero, on behalf of her child, filed a suit against the Milas, charging them with negligent supervision of a perpetrator who sexually molested Valero's child.

The Milas filed a claim with their insurer to provide a defense against the charges. The insurer refused and sought a court order declaring that it had no obligation under the policy to provide such a defense. The court ruled in favor of the insurer, and the decision was affirmed on appeal. The language in the Milas' policy excluding coverage for "bodily injury arising out of sexual molestation" was clear and unambiguous. The exclusion applied to preclude coverage.[3] ■

50–2e Cancellation

The insured can cancel a policy at any time, and the insurer can cancel under certain circumstances. When an insurance company can cancel its insurance contract, the policy or a state statute usually requires that the insurer give advance written notice of the cancellation. The same requirement applies when only part of a policy is canceled. Any premium paid in advance and not yet earned may be refundable on the policy's cancellation. The insured may also be entitled to a life insurance policy's cash surrender value.

The insurer may cancel an insurance policy for various reasons, depending on the type of insurance. For example:

1. Automobile insurance can be canceled for nonpayment of premiums or suspension of the insured's driver's license.
2. Property insurance can be canceled for nonpayment of premiums or for other reasons, including the insured's fraud or misrepresentation, gross negligence, or conviction for a crime that increases the risk assumed by the insurer.

3. Life and health policies can be canceled because of false statements made by the insured in the application, but the cancellation must take place before the effective date of an incontestability clause.

An insurer cannot cancel—or refuse to renew—a policy for discriminatory reasons or other reasons that violate public policy. Also, an insurer cannot cancel a policy because the insured has appeared as a witness in a case brought against the company.

50–2f Duties and Obligations of the Parties

Both parties to an insurance contract are responsible for the obligations they assume under the contract. In addition, both the insured and the insurer have an implied duty to act in good faith.

Duties of the Insured Good faith requires the party who is applying for insurance to reveal everything necessary for the insurer to evaluate the risk of issuing the policy. In other words, the applicant must disclose all facts that an insurer would consider in determining whether to charge a higher premium or to refuse to issue a policy altogether. Many insurance companies require that an applicant give the company permission to access other information, such as private medical records and credit ratings, for the purpose of evaluating risk.

Once the insurance policy is issued, the insured has three basic duties under the contract:

1. To pay the premiums as stated in the contract.
2. To notify the insurer within a reasonable time if an event occurs that gives rise to a claim.
3. To cooperate with the insurer during any investigation or litigation.

Duties of the Insurer Once the insurer has accepted the risk, and some event occurs that gives rise to a claim, the insurer has a *duty to investigate* to determine the facts. When a policy provides insurance against third party claims, the insurer is obligated to make reasonable efforts to settle any such claim.

If a settlement cannot be reached, then regardless of the claim's merit, the insurer has a *duty to defend* any suit against the insured. Usually, a policy provides that in this situation the insured must *cooperate* in the defense and attend hearings and trials if necessary.

The insurer also owes a *duty to pay* any legitimate claims up to the face amount of the policy. An insurer has a duty to provide or pay an attorney to defend its insured when a complaint alleges facts that could, if

---

3. *Valero v. Florida Insurance Guaranty Association, Inc.,* 59 So.3d 1166 (Fla. App. 2011).

proved, impose liability on the insured within the policy's coverage.

■ **CASE IN POINT 50.5** Dentist Robert Woo installed implants for one of his employees, Tina Alberts, whose family raised potbellied pigs. As a joke, while Alberts was anesthetized, Woo installed a set of "flippers" (temporary partial bridges) shaped like boar tusks and took photos. A month later, Woo's staff showed the photos to Alberts at a party. Alberts refused to return to work. She filed a suit against Woo for battery.

Woo's insurance company refused to defend him in the suit, and he ended up paying Alberts $250,000 to settle her claim. Woo then sued the insurance company and won. The court held that the insurance company had a duty to defend Woo under the professional liability provision of his policy because Woo's practical joke took place during a routine dental procedure.[4] ■

Bad Faith Actions Although insurance law generally follows contract law, most states now recognize a "bad faith" tort action against insurers. Thus, if an insurer in bad faith denies coverage of a claim, the insured may sue. If successful, the insured can recover an amount exceeding the policy's coverage limits and may also recover punitive damages. Some courts have held insurers liable for a bad faith refusal to settle claims for reasonable amounts within the policy limits.

50–2g Defenses against Payment

An insurance company can raise any of the defenses that would be valid in an ordinary action on a contract, as well as the following defenses:

1. *Fraud or misrepresentation.* If the insurance company can show that the policy was procured through fraud or misrepresentation, it may have a valid defense for not paying on a claim. (The insurance company may also have the right to disaffirm or rescind the insurance contract.)
2. *Lack of insurable interest.* An absolute defense exists if the insurer can show that the insured lacked an insurable interest—thus rendering the policy void from the beginning.
3. *Illegal actions of the insured.* Improper actions, such as those that are against public policy or that are otherwise illegal, can also give the insurance company a defense against the payment of a claim or allow it to rescind the contract.

---

4. *Woo v. Fireman's Fund Insurance Co.,* 161 Wash.2d 43, 164 P.3d 454 (2007).

In some situations, the insurance company may be prevented, or estopped, from asserting defenses that normally are available. For instance, an insurance company ordinarily cannot escape payment on the death of an insured on the ground that the person's age was stated incorrectly on the application. Also, incontestability clauses prevent the insurer from asserting certain defenses.

50–3 Types of Insurance

There are four general types of insurance coverage: life insurance, fire and homeowners' insurance, automobile insurance, and business liability insurance. We now examine briefly the coverage available under each of these types of insurance.

50–3a Life Insurance

There are five basic types of life insurance:

1. **Whole life** provides protection with an accumulated cash surrender value that can be used as collateral for a loan. The insured pays premiums during his or her entire lifetime, and the beneficiary receives a fixed payment on the death of the insured. (It is also sometimes referred to as straight life, ordinary life, or cash-value insurance.)
2. **Limited-payment life** is a type of policy under which premiums are paid for a stated number of years. After that time, the policy is paid up and fully effective during the insured's lifetime. For instance, a policy might call for twenty payments. Naturally, premiums are higher than for whole life. Like whole life, this insurance also has a cash surrender value.
3. **Term insurance** is a type of policy for which premiums are paid for a specified term. Payment on the policy is due only if death occurs within the term period. Premiums are lower than for whole life or limited-payment life, and there usually is no cash surrender value. Frequently, this type of insurance can be converted to another type of life insurance.
4. **Endowment insurance** involves fixed premium payments that are made for a definite term. At the end of the term, a fixed amount is paid to the insured or, if the insured dies during the specified term, to a beneficiary. Endowment insurance has a rapidly increasing cash surrender value, but premiums are high because a payment must be made at the end of the term even if the insured is still living.

5. Universal life combines aspects of both term insurance and whole life insurance. From every payment, usually called a "contribution," the issuing life insurance company makes two deductions. The first is a charge for term insurance protection. The second is for company expenses and profit. The funds that remain after these deductions earn interest for the policyholder at a rate determined by the company. The interest-earning amount is called the policy's *cash value,* but that term does not mean the same thing as it does for a traditional whole life insurance policy. With a universal life policy, the cash value grows at a variable interest rate rather than at a predetermined rate.

The rights and liabilities of the parties to life insurance contracts are basically dependent on the specific contract. A few features deserve special attention.

Insurer's Liability The life insurance contract determines not only the extent of the insurer's liability but also, generally, whether the insurer is liable on the death of the insured. Many life insurance contracts exclude liability for death caused by suicide, and some contain other exclusions, such as liability for death caused by military action during war. In the absence of contractual exclusion, most courts today construe any cause of death to be one of the insurer's risks.

Adjustment Due to Misstatement of Age The insurance policy constitutes the agreement between the parties. As noted earlier, the application for insurance is part of the policy and is usually attached to the policy. When the insured misstates his or her age on the application, an error is introduced, particularly as to the amount of premiums paid. As mentioned, misstatement of age is not a material error sufficient to allow the insurer to void the policy. Instead, on discovery of the error, the insurer will adjust the premium payments and/or benefits accordingly.

Assignment Most life insurance policies allow the insured to change beneficiaries. When this is permitted, in the absence of any prohibition or notice requirement, the insured can assign the rights to the policy without the consent of the insurer or the beneficiary. The insured may, for instance, wish to assign the rights to the policy as security for a loan.

If the beneficiary's right is *vested*—that is, has become absolute, entitling the beneficiary to payment of the proceeds—the policy cannot be assigned without the beneficiary's consent. For the most part, life insurance contracts permit assignment and require notice only to the insurer to be effective.

Creditors' Rights Unless insurance proceeds are exempt under state law, the insured's interest in life insurance is an asset that is subject to the rights of judgment creditors. These creditors generally can reach all of the following:

1. Insurance proceeds payable to the insured's estate.
2. Insurance proceeds payable to anyone if the payment of premiums constituted a fraud on creditors.
3. Insurance proceeds payable to a named beneficiary unless the beneficiary's rights have vested.

Creditors, however, cannot compel the insured to make available the cash surrender value of the policy or to change the named beneficiary to that of the creditor. Almost all states exempt at least a part of the proceeds of life insurance from creditors' claims.

Termination Although the insured can cancel and terminate the policy, the insurer generally cannot do so. Therefore, termination usually takes place only if one of the following occurs:

1. Default in premium payments, which causes the policy to lapse.
2. Death and payment of benefits.
3. Expiration of the term of the policy.
4. Cancellation by the insured.

50–3b Fire and Homeowners' Insurance

There are basically two types of insurance policies for a home: standard fire insurance policies and homeowners' policies.

Standard Fire Insurance Policies The standard fire insurance policy protects the homeowner against fire and lightning, as well as damage from smoke and water caused by the fire or the fire department. Most fire insurance policies are classified according to the type of property covered and the extent of the issuer's liability. Exhibit 50–3 lists typical fire insurance policies.

Liability. The insurer's liability is determined from the terms of the policy. Most policies limit recovery to losses resulting from *hostile* fires—basically, those that break out or begin in places where no fire was intended to burn. A *friendly* fire—one burning in a place where it was intended to burn—is often not covered. Therefore, smoke from a fireplace is not covered, but smoke from a fire caused by a defective electrical outlet is covered. Sometimes, owners add "extended coverage" to the fire policy to cover losses from "friendly" fires.

EXHIBIT 50–3 Typical Fire Insurance Policies

TYPE OF POLICY	COVERAGE
Blanket	Covers a class of property rather than specific property, because the property is expected to shift or vary in nature. A policy covering the inventory of a business is an example.
Floater	Usually supplements a specific policy. It is intended to cover property that may change in either location or quantity. For instance, if a painting is to be exhibited during the year at numerous locations throughout the state, a floater policy would be desirable.
Open	A policy that does not state an agreed-on value for the property. The policy usually provides for a maximum liability of the insurer, but payment for loss is restricted to the fair market value of the property at the time of loss or to the insurer's limit, whichever is less.
Specific	Covers a specific item of property at a specific location. An example is a particular painting located in a residence or a piece of machinery located in a factory or business.
Valued	A policy that, by agreement, places a specific value on the subject to be insured to cover the eventuality of its total loss.

If the policy is a *valued* policy (see Exhibit 50–3) and the subject matter is completely destroyed, the insurer is liable for the amount specified in the policy. If it is an *open* policy, then the extent of the actual loss must be determined. The insurer is liable only for the amount of the loss or for the maximum amount specified in the policy, whichever is less. For partial losses, actual loss must always be determined, and the insurer's liability is limited to that amount. Most insurance policies permit the insurer either to restore or replace the property destroyed or to pay for the loss.

Proof of Loss. As a condition for recovery, fire insurance policies require the insured to file a proof of loss with the insurer within a specified period or immediately (within a reasonable time). Failure to comply *could* allow the insurance carrier to avoid liability. Courts vary somewhat on the enforcement of such clauses.

Occupancy Clause. Most standard policies include clauses that require that the premises be occupied at the time of the loss. If the premises are vacant or unoccupied for a given period and the insurer has not consented to the vacancy, then coverage is suspended until the premises are reoccupied. Persons going on extended vacations should check their policies regarding this point.

In the following case, the court had to consider how long a house must be left vacant before it can be considered "unoccupied." The court also addressed the question of whether the risk of hazard is always greater when a home is unoccupied.

Case Analysis 50.2

Estate of Luster v. Allstate Insurance Co.

United States Court of Appeals, Seventh Circuit, 598 F.3d 903 (2010).

In the Language of the Court
POSNER, Circuit Judge.
* * * *

This diversity suit for breach of an insurance contract was dismissed on summary judgment * * * , and the plaintiff's [Estate of Luster's] appeal presents issues of both contract interpretation and Indiana insurance law.

[Wavie] Luster was a widow living alone in her house in Merrillville, Indiana. She had a homeowner's insurance policy from Allstate [Insurance Company]. In October 2001, when she was eighty-three, she was injured in a fall, and after being released from the hospital moved into an extended-care facility. She executed a power of attorney to her lawyer, Rick Gikas, who is the representative of her estate in this litigation. She never returned home and died in April 2006, some four and a half years after her fall. Gikas had notified Allstate of his power of attorney and had directed the company to bill the insurance premiums to his law

Case 50.2 Continued

office. No one lived in the house after she left it.

Three months after her death—her house still unoccupied—a fire caused extensive damage. Gikas submitted a claim on behalf of the estate. An investigation indicated that the fire may well have been started by burglars, but the plaintiff denies this and the district judge made no finding.

In the course of the investigation Allstate discovered that the house had been unoccupied for four and a half years before Mrs. Luster's death and denied the claim, precipitating this suit. Allstate continued billing Gikas for premiums, however, and he continued paying them until October 2008, more than two years after the fire, when Allstate—which claims not to have known that the policy was still in force until its lawyers read the estate's summary-judgment brief that month—purported to cancel the policy retroactively to November 2001, and returned the premiums for the subsequent period to the estate.

The appeal requires us to consider [certain] provisions of the insurance policy: [The policy required the insured to notify Allstate of any change in occupancy of the premises and excluded coverage for property loss caused by "any substantial change or increase in hazard" or by "vandalism or malicious mischief" if the insured's dwelling was unoccupied for more than thirty consecutive days immediately prior to the vandalism or malicious mischief.]

* * * *

Gikas argues that * * * the house was *not* unoccupied, because right up until her death Luster expressed the intention of returning to live there when her health permitted.

*Regardless of the owner's intentions, * * * four and a half years of continuous absence of human occupation constitutes a change in occupancy.* [Emphasis added.]

The duty-to-notify provision entitled Allstate to cancel the policy in the event the house became unoccupied.

Although the policy expressly authorizes the insurer to cancel it for a violation of any of its terms, it also requires the insurer to give thirty days' notice of intention to cancel, and Allstate failed to do that after discovering in the wake of the fire that the house had been unoccupied for years. *The requirement of notice of intent to cancel is important; it gives the insured an opportunity to prevent a lapse of coverage, by taking steps to reinstate the policy or obtain a substitute policy from another insurer. Retroactive termination is inconsistent with the requirement of advance notice.* [Emphasis added.]

* * * *

The district judge ruled that leaving the house unoccupied constituted a "substantial change or increase in hazard" within the meaning [of the policy]. The judge seems to have thought that to leave a house unoccupied for however short a time causes an "increase in hazard" as a matter of law. Allstate takes the more moderate position that any gap in occupation of more than thirty days increases hazard as a matter of law.

Neither position is correct. Houses are rarely occupied continuously. A homeowner might take a thirty-one-day trip; Allstate implies that if a fire occurred during that period the insured would be uncovered. That is not the law.

Allstate's argument thus implies that if you have a second home the homeowner's policy on your primary residence is illusory; you're away a lot

and so coverage lapses. That's nonsense. And even if the house is unoccupied in the relevant sense—the sense that triggers the duty to notify the insurance company of a change in occupancy—it doesn't follow that you have created a "substantial * * * increase in hazard." Maybe you fitted the house with an array of locks and alarms and hired a security company to check on the house daily and so made the house more secure than when you were living there—an especially plausible inference if you happen to be an elderly person who might if in residence damage it inadvertently by leaving appliances on or failing to remove combustibles [flammable items] like cans containing paint or oil-soaked rags or to attend to defects in the electrical wiring of the house. *There is no rule that moving out of a house per se [in itself] increases the hazards against which the insurance company has insured you.* [Emphasis added.]

* * * *

There may well have been vandalism, by burglars, and if so it occurred more than thirty days after the house became unoccupied, whenever precisely occupancy ceased—sometime during the four and a half years between Luster's fall and her death. But we do not know whether the vandalism caused the loss—there is no judicial finding that the fire that was the immediate cause of the loss was the result of vandalism. To decide whether it was will require an evidentiary hearing, as will Allstate's alternative ground that nonoccupancy substantially increased the risk of loss.

* * * *

REVERSED AND REMANDED.

Legal Reasoning Questions

1. Why did the court conclude that an unoccupied house did not necessarily create a substantial increase in hazard?

2. Why did the court hold that Allstate's cancellation of the policy, retroactive to November 2001 (when Luster moved to an extended-care facility), was ineffective?

3. Was Luster's intent to return to her home when her health permitted sufficient to constitute occupancy? Why or why not?

Assignment. Before a loss has occurred, a fire insurance policy is not assignable without the consent of the insurer. The theory is that the fire insurance policy is a personal contract between the insured and the insurer. The non-assignability of a policy is extremely important when a house is purchased. It means that the purchaser must procure his or her own insurance. If the purchaser wishes to assume the seller's remaining period of insurance coverage, the insurer's consent is essential.

■ **EXAMPLE 50.6** Kiana is selling her home and lot to Jayden. Kiana has a one-year fire policy with Ajax Insurance Company, with six months of coverage remaining at the date on which the sale is to close. Kiana agrees to assign the balance of her policy, but Ajax has not given its consent. One day after passage of the deed, a fire totally destroys the house. Can Jayden recover from Ajax?

The answer is no. The policy is actually voided on the closing of the transaction and the deeding of the property. The reason the policy is voided is that Kiana no longer has an insurable interest at the time of loss, and Jayden has no rights in a nonassignable policy. ■

Homeowners' Policies A homeowners' policy provides protection against a number of risks under a single policy, allowing the policyholder to avoid the cost of buying each protection separately. There are two basic types of homeowners' coverage: property coverage and liability coverage.

Property Coverage. *Property coverage* includes the house, garage, and other private buildings on the policyholder's lot. It also includes the personal possessions and property of the policyholder at home, at work, or while traveling. If the policyholder is forced to live away from home because of a fire or some other covered peril, the policy covers additional living expenses.

Perils insured under property coverage often include fire, lightning, wind, hail, vandalism, and theft (of personal property). Standard homeowners' insurance typically does not cover flood damage. In the absence of a specific provision, such items of personal property as motor vehicles, farm equipment, airplanes, and boats normally are not included under property coverage. Coverage for other property, such as jewelry and securities, usually is limited to a specified dollar amount.

Liability Coverage. *Liability coverage* under a homeowners' policy is for personal liability in the event that someone is injured on the insured's property because of an unsafe condition on the property. It also applies when the insured damages someone else's property or injures someone else (unless the injury involves an automobile, as noted below). In addition, it applies when the policyholder is negligent.

Similar to liability coverage is coverage for the medical payments of others who are injured on the policyholder's property and for the property of others that is damaged by a member of the policyholder's family.

Liability coverage normally does not apply to a liability that arises from business or professional activities or from the operation of a motor vehicle, which are subjects for separate policies. Also excluded is liability arising from intentional misconduct.

Renters' Policies. Renters also take out insurance policies to protect against losses to personal property. Renters' insurance covers personal possessions against various perils and includes coverage for additional living expenses and liability.

50–3c Automobile Insurance

There are two basic kinds of automobile insurance: liability insurance and collision and comprehensive insurance.

Liability Insurance Automobile liability insurance covers liability for bodily injury and property damage. Liability limits are usually described by a series of three numbers, such as 100/300/50. This means that, for one accident, the policy will pay a maximum of $100,000 for bodily injury to one person, a maximum of $300,000 for bodily injury to more than one person, and a maximum of $50,000 for property damage. Many insurance companies offer liability coverage in amounts up to $500,000 and sometimes higher.

Individuals who are dissatisfied with the maximum liability limits offered by regular automobile insurance coverage can purchase separate coverage under an *umbrella policy.* Umbrella limits sometimes go as high as $10 million. Umbrella policies also cover personal liability in excess of the liability limits of a homeowners' policy.

Collision and Comprehensive Insurance Collision insurance covers damage to the insured's car in any type of collision. Usually, it is not advisable to purchase full collision coverage (otherwise known as *zero deductible*). The price per year is relatively high because it is likely that some small repair jobs will be required each year. Most people prefer to take out policies with a deductible of $250, $500, or $1,000, which cost substantially less than zero-deductible coverage.

Comprehensive insurance covers loss, damage, and destruction due to fire, hurricane, hail, vandalism, and theft. It can be obtained separately from collision insurance.

Other Automobile Insurance Other types of automobile insurance coverage include the following:

1. *Uninsured motorist coverage.* Uninsured motorist coverage insures the driver and passengers against injury caused by any driver without insurance or by a hit-and-run driver. Some states require that it be included in all auto insurance policies sold.
2. *Accidental death benefits.* Sometimes referred to as *double indemnity,* accidental death benefits provide for a payment of twice the policy's face amount if the policyholder dies in an accident. This coverage generally costs very little, but it may not be necessary if the insured has a sufficient amount of life insurance.
3. *Medical payment coverage.* Medical payment coverage provided by an auto insurance policy pays hospital and other medical bills and sometimes funeral expenses. This type of insurance protects all the passengers in the insured's car when the insured is driving.
4. *Other-driver coverage.* An **omnibus clause,** or *other-driver clause,* protects the vehicle owner who has taken out the insurance and anyone who drives the vehicle with the owner's permission. This coverage may be held to extend to a third party who drives the vehicle with the permission of the person to whom the owner gave permission.

50–3d Business Liability Insurance

A business may be vulnerable to all sorts of risks. A key employee may die or become disabled, a customer may be injured when using a manufacturer's product, or a professional may overlook some important detail and be liable for malpractice. If a key employee (such as the company president) dies, the firm may have some protection under a key-person insurance policy, discussed earlier. In the other circumstances, other types of insurance may apply.

General Liability Comprehensive general liability insurance can encompass as many risks as the insurer agrees to cover. It can protect a business from liability for injuries arising from on-premises events held after work hours, such as company social functions. It can protect bars and liquor stores, which in many jurisdictions are liable when a buyer of liquor becomes intoxicated as a result of the sale and injures a third party. General liability insurance can protect a business not only from liability for physical injuries, but also from liability for the loss of financial support suffered by a family because of the injuries.

Product Liability Manufacturers and retailers may be subject to liability for injuries resulting from the products they sell, and product liability insurance can be written to match specific products' risks. Coverage can be procured under a comprehensive general liability policy or under a separate policy. The coverage may include payment for expenses incurred to recall and replace a product that has proved to be defective.

Professional Malpractice Attorneys, physicians, architects, engineers, and other professionals often become the targets of negligence suits. Professionals purchase malpractice insurance to protect themselves against such claims. The large judgments in some malpractice suits have contributed to a significant increase in malpractice insurance premiums.

Workers' Compensation Workers' compensation insurance covers payments to employees who are injured in accidents arising out of and in the course of employment (that is, on the job). State statutes govern workers' compensation.

Reviewing: Insurance

Provident Insurance, Inc., issued an insurance policy to a company providing an employee, Steve Matlin, with disability insurance. Soon thereafter, Matlin was diagnosed with "panic disorder and phobia of returning to work." He lost his job and sought disability coverage. Provident denied coverage, doubting the diagnosis of disability. Matlin and his employer sued Provident.

During pretrial discovery, the insurer learned that Matlin had stated on the policy application that he had never been treated for any "emotional, mental, nervous, urinary, or digestive disorder" or any kind of heart disease. In fact, before Matlin filled out the application, he had visited a physician for chest pains and general anxiety, and the physician had prescribed an antidepressant and recommended that Matlin stop smoking. Using the information presented in the chapter, answer the following questions.

Continues

1. Did Matlin commit a misrepresentation on his policy application? Explain.
2. If there was any ambiguity on the application, should it be resolved in favor of the insured or the insurer? Why?
3. Assuming that the policy is valid, does Matlin's situation fall within the terms of the disability policy? Why or why not?
4. If Matlin is covered by the policy but is also disqualified by his misrepresentation on the application for coverage, might the insurer still be liable for bad faith denial of coverage? Explain.

Debate This . . .   *Whenever an insurance company can prove that the applicant committed fraud during the application process, it should not have to pay on the policy.*

Terms and Concepts

antilapse provision 966	insurable interest 961	risk 961
binder 965	insurance 961	risk management 961
cash surrender value 966	limited-payment life 968	term insurance 968
coinsurance clause 966	omnibus clause 973	underwriter 961
endowment insurance 968	policy 961	universal life 969
incontestability clause 965	premium 961	whole life 968

Issue Spotters

1. Neal applies to Farm Insurance Company for a life insurance policy. On the application, Neal understates his age. Neal obtains the policy, but for a lower premium than he would have had to pay had he disclosed his actual age. The policy includes an incontestability clause. Six years later, Neal dies. Can the insurer refuse payment? Why or why not? (See *The Insurance Contract.*)

2. Al is divorced and owns a house. Al has no reasonable expectation of benefit from the life of Bea, his former spouse, but applies for insurance on her life anyway. Al obtains a fire insurance policy on the house and then sells the house. Al continues to pay the premiums on both the life insurance policy and the fire insurance policy. Ten years later, Bea dies and the house is destroyed by fire. Can Al obtain payment for these events? Explain your answers. (See *Insurance Terminology and Concepts.*)

• **Check your answers to the Issue Spotters against the answers provided in Appendix D at the end of this text.**

Business Scenarios

50–1. Insurable Interest. Adia owns a house and has an elderly third cousin living with her. Adia decides she needs fire insurance on the house and a life insurance policy on her third cousin to cover funeral and other expenses that will result from her cousin's death. Adia takes out a fire insurance policy from Ajax Insurance Co. and a $10,000 life insurance policy from Beta Insurance Co. on her third cousin. Six months later, Adia sells the house to John and transfers title to him. Adia and her cousin move into an apartment. With two months remaining on the Ajax policy, a fire totally destroys the house. At the same time, Adia's third cousin dies. Both insurance companies say that they have no liability under the insurance contracts because Adia did not have an insurable interest, and they return the premiums. Discuss the companies' claims. (See *Insurance Terminology and Concepts.*)

50–2. Insurer's Defenses. Patrick contracts with an Ajax Insurance Co. agent for a $50,000 ordinary life insurance policy. The application form is filled in to show Patrick's age as thirty-two. In addition, the application form asks whether Patrick has ever had any heart ailments or problems. Patrick answers no, forgetting that as a young child he was diagnosed as having a slight heart murmur. A policy is issued. Three years later, Patrick becomes seriously ill and dies. A review of the policy discloses that Patrick was actually thirty-three at the time of the application and the issuance of the policy and that he erred in answering the question about a history of heart ailments. Discuss whether Ajax can void the policy and escape liability on Patrick's death. (See *The Insurance Contract.*)

50–3. Assignment. Sapata has an ordinary life insurance policy on her life and a fire insurance policy on her house.

Both policies have been in force for a number of years. Sapata's life insurance names her son, Rory, as beneficiary. Sapata has specifically removed her right to change beneficiaries, and the life insurance policy is silent on the right of assignment. Sapata is going on a one-year European vacation and borrows money from Leonard to finance the trip. Leonard takes an assignment of the life insurance policy as security for the loan, as the policy has accumulated a substantial cash surrender value. Sapata also rents out her house to Leonard and assigns her fire insurance policy to him. Discuss fully whether Sapata's assignment of these policies is valid. (See *Types of Insurance*.)

Business Case Problems

50–4. Interpreting Provisions. Richard Vanderbrook's home in New Orleans, Louisiana, was insured through Unitrin Preferred Insurance Co. His policy excluded coverage for "flood, surface water, waves, tidal water, overflow of a body of water, or spray from any of these, whether or not driven by wind." The policy did not define the term *flood*. In 2005, Hurricane Katrina struck along the coast of the Gulf of Mexico, devastating portions of Louisiana. In New Orleans, some of the most significant damage occurred when the levees along three canals ruptured, and water submerged about 80 percent of the city, including Vanderbrook's home. He filed a claim for the loss, but Unitrin refused to pay.

Vanderbrook and others whose policies contained similar exclusions asked a federal district court to order their insurers to pay. They contended that their losses were due to the negligent design, construction, and maintenance of the levees. They argued that the policies did not clearly exclude coverage for an inundation of water induced by negligence. On what does a decision in this case hinge? What reasoning supports a ruling in the plaintiffs' favor? In the defendants' favor? [*In re Katrina Canal Breaches Litigation*, 495 F.3d 191 (5th Cir. 2007)] (See *The Insurance Contract*.)

50–5. Duty to Cooperate. James Bubenik, a dentist, had two patients die while under sedation within six months. Bubenik had medical malpractice insurance with Medical Protective Co. (MPC). The families of both patients sued Bubenik for malpractice. A clause in Bubenik's policy stated that the "Insured shall at all times fully cooperate with the Company in any claim hereunder and shall attend and assist in the preparation and trial of any such claim." During the litigation, however, Bubenik refused to submit to depositions, answer interrogatories, or testify at trial, invoking the privilege against self-incrimination. He also refused to communicate with MPC and instead agreed to assist the patients in obtaining payment. MPC filed suit. Under these circumstances, did MPC have a legal or ethical duty to defend against the claim? Could MPC refuse to pay it? Explain. [*Medical Protective Co. v. Bubenik*, 594 F.3d 1047 (8th Cir. 2010)] (See *The Insurance Contract*.)

50–6. Bad Faith Actions. Leo and Mary Deters owned Deters Tower Service, Inc., in Iowa. Deters Tower serviced television and radio towers and antennas in a multistate area. The firm obtained a commercial general liability policy issued by USF Insurance Co. to provide coverage for its officers, including Leo. One afternoon, Leo and two Deters Tower employees were working on a TV tower in Council Bluffs when they fell from the tower to their deaths. The workers' families filed a negligence suit against Leo's estate. USF refused to defend the Deters estate against the suit and pay any resulting claim but did not provide a reason for its refusal. Is USF liable to the Deters estate for this refusal? If so, on what basis might the Deters estate recover, and how much? [*Deters v. USF Insurance Co.*, 797 N.W.2d 621 (Iowa App. 2011)] (See *The Insurance Contract*.)

50–7. Business Case Problem with Sample Answer— Insurance Provisions and Clauses. Darling's Rent-a-Car carried property insurance on its cars under a policy issued by Philadelphia Indemnity Insurance Co. The policy listed Darling's as the "insured." Darling's rented a car to Joshuah Farrington. In the rental contract, Farrington agreed to be responsible for any damage to the car and declined the optional insurance. Later, Farrington collided with a moose. Philadelphia paid Darling's for the damage to the car and sought to collect this amount from Farrington. Farrington argued that he was an "insured" under Darling's policy. How should "insured" be interpreted in this case? Why? [*Philadelphia Indemnity Insurance Co. v. Farrington*, 37 A.3d 305 (Me. 2012)] (See *The Insurance Contract*.)

- **For a sample answer to Problem 50–7, go to Appendix E at the end of this text.**

50–8. Types of Insurance. American National Property and Casualty Co. issued an insurance policy to Robert Houston, insuring certain residential property and its contents against fire and other hazards. Twenty months later, Houston issued a quitclaim deed to the property to John and Judy Sykes, reserving a life estate for himself. The American policy was renewed continuously by John, even after Houston died. When a fire substantially damaged the property, John filed a claim with the insurer on behalf of Houston, whom John said was out of town and unavailable. On learning that Houston had died, American refused to pay, claiming that it had no liability. Who will suffer the loss under these circumstances? Why? How might this loss have been avoided? Explain. [*American National Property and Casualty Co. v. Sykes*, __ F.Supp.3d __, 2016 WL 390069 (S.D.Miss., E.Div. 2016)] (See *Types of Insurance*.)

50–9. A Question of Ethics—Insurance Coverage.

Paul and Julie Leonard's two-story home in Pascagoula, Mississippi, is only twelve feet above sea level and fewer than two hundred yards from the Gulf of Mexico. In 1989, the Leonards bought a homeowners' insurance policy from Jay Fletcher, an agent for Nationwide Mutual Insurance Co. The policy covered any damage caused by wind. It excluded all damage caused by water, including flooding. With each annual renewal, Nationwide reminded the Leonards that their policy did not cover flood damage, but that such coverage was available. The policy also contained an anti-concurrent-causation (ACC) clause that excluded coverage for damage caused by the synergistic action of a covered peril such as wind and an excluded peril such as water. In August 2005, Hurricane Katrina battered Pascagoula with torrential rain and sustained winds in excess of one hundred miles per hour. Wind damage to the Leonards' home was modest, but the storm drove ashore a seventeen-foot storm surge that flooded the ground floor. When Nationwide refused to pay for the damage to the ground floor, the Leonards filed a suit in a federal district court against the insurer. [Leonard v. Nationwide Mutual Insurance Co., 499 F.3d 419 (5th Cir. 2007)] (See *The Insurance Contract.*)

(a) Nationwide argued that the storm surge was a concurrently caused peril—a wall of water pushed ashore by hurricane winds. Thus, according to Nationwide, its damage was excluded under the ACC clause. How would you rule on this point? Should a court "enlarge" an insurer's policy obligations? Why or why not?

(b) When the Leonards bought their policy in 1989, Fletcher told them that all hurricane damage was covered. Ten years later, Fletcher told Paul Leonard that they did not need additional flood coverage. Did these statements materially misrepresent or alter the policy? Were they unethical? Discuss.

Legal Reasoning Group Activity

50–10. Insurance Coverage. PAJ, Inc., a jewelry company, had a commercial general liability (CGL) policy from Hanover Insurance Co. The policy required PAJ to notify Hanover of any claim or suit against PAJ "as soon as practicable." Yurman Designs sued PAJ for copyright infringement because of the design of a particular jewelry line. Because PAJ did not realize that the CGL policy had a clause that covered infringement claims, it did not notify Hanover of the suit until four to six months after litigation began. Hanover contended that the policy did not apply to this incident because the late notification had violated its terms. PAJ sued Hanover, seeking a declaration that it was obligated to defend and indemnify PAJ. (See *The Insurance Contract.*)

(a) The first group will decide whether Hanover had an obligation to provide PAJ with legal assistance.

(b) The second group will determine the effect that PAJ's late notice to the insurance company had on its ability to provide assistance and mount a defense. Should the court require the insurance company to indemnify PAJ in this situation? Why or why not?

CHAPTER 51

Wills and Trusts

As the adage says, "You can't take it with you." After you die, all of the real and personal property that you own will be transferred to others. A person can direct the passage of his or her property after death by *will,* subject to certain limitations imposed by the state.

Alternatively, a person can transfer property through a *trust.* When a trust is created, the owner (who may be called the *grantor* or the *settlor*) of the property transfers legal title to a trustee. The trustee has a duty imposed by law to hold the property for the use or benefit of another (the beneficiary).

Wills and trusts are two basic devices used in the process of **estate planning**—determining in advance how one's property and obligations should be transferred on death. Estate planning may also involve transferring property through life insurance and joint-tenancy arrangements, as well as executing powers of attorney and living wills.

51–1 Wills

A **will** is the final declaration of how a person desires to have her or his property disposed of after death. It is a formal instrument that must follow exactly the requirements of state law to be effective.

A will can serve other purposes besides the distribution of property. It can appoint a guardian for minor children or incapacitated adults. It can also appoint a personal representative to settle the affairs of the deceased.

Exhibit 51–1 presents excerpts from the will of Michael Jackson, the "King of Pop," who died from cardiac arrest at the age of fifty. Jackson held a substantial amount of tangible and intangible property, including the publishing rights to most of The Beatles' music catalogue. Jackson's will also appointed his mother, Katherine Jackson, as the guardian of his three minor children.

51–1a Terminology of Wills

A person who makes a will is known as a **testator** (from the Latin *testari,* "to make a will"). A will is referred to as a *testamentary disposition* of property, and one who dies after having made a valid will is said to have died **testate.** The court responsible for administering any legal problems surrounding a will is called a *probate court.* When a person dies, a personal representative administers the estate and settles all of the decedent's (deceased person's) affairs.

An **executor** is a personal representative named in a will, whereas an **administrator** is a personal representative appointed by the court for a decedent who dies without a will. The court will also appoint a representative if the will does not name an executor or if the named person lacks the capacity to serve as an executor.

A person who dies without having created a valid will is said to have died **intestate.** In this situation, state **intestacy laws** (sometimes referred to as *laws of descent*) prescribe the distribution of the property among heirs or next of kin. If no heirs or kin can be found, the property will **escheat**[1] (title will be transferred to the state).

A gift of real estate by will is generally called a **devise,** and a gift of personal property by will is called a **bequest,** or **legacy.** The recipient of a gift by will is a **devisee** or a **legatee,** depending on whether the gift was a devise or a legacy.

51–1b Laws Governing Wills

To **probate** a will means to establish its validity and to carry the administration of the estate through a court process. Probate laws vary from state to state. The National

---

1. Pronounced is-*cheet.*

EXHIBIT 51-1 Excerpts from Michael Jackson's Will

I, MICHAEL JOSEPH JACKSON, a resident of the State of California, declare this to be my last Will, and do hereby revoke all former wills and codicils made by me.

I. I declare that I am not married. My marriage to DEBORAH JEAN ROWE JACKSON has been dissolved. I have three children now living, PRINCE MICHAEL JACKSON, JR., PARIS MICHAEL KATHERINE JACKSON and PRINCE MICHAEL JOSEPH JACKSON, II. I have no other children, living or deceased.

II. It is my intention by this Will to dispose of all property which I am entitled to dispose of by will. I specifically refrain from exercising all powers of appointment that I may possess at the time of my death.

III. I give my entire estate to the Trustee or Trustees then acting under that certain Amended and Restated Declaration of Trust executed on March 22, 2002 by me as Trustee and Trustor which is called the MICHAEL JACKSON FAMILY TRUST, giving effect to any amendments thereto made prior to my death. All such assets shall be held, managed and distributed as a part of said Trust according to its terms and not as a separate testamentary trust.

If for any reason this gift is not operative or is invalid, or if the aforesaid Trust fails or has been revoked, I give my residuary estate to the Trustee or Trustees named to act in the MICHAEL JACKSON FAMILY TRUST, as Amended and Restated on March 22, 2002, and I direct said Trustee or Trustees to divide, administer, hold and distribute the trust estate pursuant to the provisions of said Trust * * * .
* * * *

IV. I direct that all federal estate taxes and state inheritance or succession taxes payable upon or resulting from or by reason of my death (herein "Death Taxes") attributable to property which is part of the trust estate of the MICHAEL JACKSON FAMILY TRUST, including property which passes to said trust

from my probate estate shall be paid by the Trustee of said trust in accordance with its terms. Death Taxes attributable to property passing outside this Will, other than property constituting the trust estate of the trust mentioned in the preceding sentence, shall be charged against the taker of said property.

V. I appoint JOHN BRANCA, JOHN McCLAIN and BARRY SIEGEL as co-Executors of this Will. In the event of any of their deaths, resignations, inability, failure or refusal to serve or continue to serve as a co-Executor, the other shall serve and no replacement need be named. The co-Executors serving at any time after my death may name one or more replacements to serve in the event that none of the three named individuals is willing or able to serve at any time.

The term "my executors" as used in this Will shall include any duly acting personal representative or representatives of my estate. No individual acting as such need post a bond.

I hereby give to my Executors, full power and authority at any time or times to sell, lease, mortgage, pledge, exchange or otherwise dispose of the property, whether real or personal comprising my estate, upon such terms as my Executors shall deem best, to continue any business enterprises, to purchase assets from my estate, to continue in force and pay any insurance policy * * * .

VI. Except as otherwise provided in this Will or in the Trust referred to in Article III hereof, I have intentionally omitted to provide for my heirs. I have intentionally omitted to provide for my former wife, DEBORAH JEAN ROWE JACKSON.
* * * *

VIII. If any of my children are minors at the time of my death, I nominate my mother, KATHERINE JACKSON as guardian of the persons and estates of such minor children. If KATHERINE JACKSON fails to survive me, or is unable or unwilling to act as guardian, I nominate DIANA ROSS as guardian of the persons and estates of such minor children.
* * * *

Conference of Commissioners on Uniform State Laws issued the Uniform Probate Code (UPC) to promote more uniformity among the states. The UPC codifies general principles and procedures for the resolution of conflicts in settling estates. The UPC also relaxes some of the requirements for a valid will contained in earlier state laws.

Almost half of the states have enacted some part of the UPC and incorporated it into their own probate codes. Nonetheless, succession and inheritance laws still vary

widely among the states, and one should always check the particular laws of the state involved.[2]

51-1c Types of Gifts

Gifts by will can be specific, general, or residuary. If a decedent's assets are not sufficient to cover all the gifts identified in the will, an abatement is necessary.

---

2. For example, California law differs substantially from the UPC.

Specific and General Devises or Bequests A *specific* devise or bequest (legacy) describes particular property (such as "Eastwood Estate" or "my gold pocket watch") that can be distinguished from all the rest of the testator's property.

A *general* devise or bequest (legacy) does not single out any particular item of property to be transferred by will. For instance, "I devise all my lands" is a general devise. A general bequest may specify the property's value in monetary terms (such as "two diamonds worth $10,000") or simply state a dollar amount (such as "$30,000 to my nephew, Carleton").

Residuary Clause Sometimes, a will provides that any assets remaining after the estate's debts have been paid and specific gifts have been made are to be distributed in a specific way through a *residuary clause.* Residuary clauses are often used when the exact amount to be distributed cannot be determined until all of the other gifts and payouts have been made. If the testator has not indicated what party or parties should receive the residuary of the estate, the residuary passes according to state laws of intestacy.

■ **CASE IN POINT 51.1** Katherine Hagan executed a will in 1994 that left the residuary of her estate to various organizations, such as the Humane Society. In 2001, Hagan inherited $830,000 from a relative. At this time, Hagan did not have the mental capacity to revise or modify her will. When she died in 2005, her residuary estate was worth $1.48 million.

Hagan's relatives, including Janice Benjamin, tried to invalidate the will's provisions regarding the residuary estate so that the funds would pass to them by intestacy laws. The court, however, found that Hagan's intent controlled. She had not intended to give any portion of her estate to her relatives. Because the will specifically stated that the residuary estate should be distributed to the charities, the court enforced these provisions (and Hagan's relatives received nothing).[3] ■

Abatement If the assets of an estate are insufficient to pay in full all general bequests provided for in the will, an *abatement* takes place. An abatement means that the legatees receive reduced benefits. ■ **EXAMPLE 51.2** Julie's will leaves $15,000 to each of her children, Tamara and Lynn. On Julie's death, only $10,000 is available to honor these bequests. By abatement, each child will receive $5,000. ■ If bequests are more complicated, abatement may be

more complex. The testator's intent, as expressed in the will, controls.

Lapsed Legacies If a legatee dies before the death of the testator or before the legacy is payable, a *lapsed legacy* results. At common law, the legacy failed. Today, the legacy may not lapse if the legatee is in a certain blood relationship to the testator (such as a child, grandchild, brother, or sister) and has left a child or other surviving descendant.

51–1d Requirements for a Valid Will

A will must comply with statutory formalities designed to ensure that the testator understood his or her actions at the time the will was made. These formalities are intended to help prevent fraud. Unless they are followed, the will is declared void, and the decedent's property is distributed according to the laws of intestacy of that state.

Although the required formalities vary among jurisdictions, most states have certain basic requirements for executing a will. Most states require proof of (1) the testator's capacity, (2) testamentary intent, (3) a written document, (4) the testator's signature, and (5) the signatures of persons who witnessed the testator's signing of the will.

Testamentary Capacity and Intent For a will to be valid, the testator must have testamentary capacity— that is, the testator must be of legal age and sound mind *at the time the will is made.* The minimum legal age for executing a will in most states and under the UPC is eighteen years [UPC 2–501]. Thus, the will of a twenty-one-year-old decedent written when the person was sixteen is invalid if, under state law, the legal age for executing a will is eighteen.

The concept of "being of sound mind" refers to the testator's ability to formulate and to comprehend a personal plan for the disposition of property. Persons who have been declared incompetent in a legal proceeding do not meet the sound mind requirement.

■ **CASE IN POINT 51.3** Marjorie Sirgo, a Louisiana resident, executed a will in which she left her estate equally to her children, Susie and Rene. Soon after, Marjorie—suffering from Parkinson's disease—began living at a nursing home. She stayed there until August 2005, when she was evacuated due to Hurricane Katrina. Three months later, while Marjorie was a resident of Poplar Springs Nursing Center, Susie took her to execute another will. This will left Marjorie's entire estate to Susie. Marjorie died, and Susie filed a petition in a

---

3. *Benjamin v. JPMorgan Chase Bank, N.A.*, 305 S.W.3d 446 (Ky.App. 2010).

Louisiana state court to probate her mother's second will. Rene objected, claiming their mother had lacked testamentary capacity when she had executed the second will. The court declared the second will void and ordered the probate of Marjorie's first will. Susie appealed.

A state intermediate appellate court affirmed the order of the lower court. Nurses' notes in Marjorie's medical records at Poplar Springs indicated that she suffered from cognitive impairment and lacked the ability to make even small decisions. In the same month in which she executed the second will, it was noted that Marjorie suffered from "short-term and long-term memory problems." For instance, she was unable to recall the current season or the location of her room.[4] ■

Related to the requirement of capacity is the concept of intent. A valid will is one that represents the maker's intention to transfer and distribute her or his property. Generally, a testator must:

1. Know the nature of the act (intend to make a will).
2. Comprehend and remember the people to whom the testator would naturally leave his or her estate (such as family members and friends).
3. Know the nature and extent of her or his property.
4. Understand the distribution of assets called for by the will.

Undue Influence. When it can be shown that the decedent's plan of distribution was the result of fraud or undue influence, the will is declared invalid. A court may sometimes infer undue influence when the named beneficiary was in a position to influence the making of the will. A presumption of undue influence might arise, for instance, if the testator ignored blood relatives and named as a beneficiary a nonrelative who was in constant close contact with the testator.

■ **CASE IN POINT 51.4** Belton Johnson, whose family owned the famous King Ranch in Texas, was married three times. He had three children from his first marriage and eight grandchildren. While married to his second wife, he executed a will that provided for her during her lifetime and left the remainder of his estate in a trust for his children and grandchildren. When his second wife died, he changed the will to give $1 million to each grandchild and the remainder to five charities. His children were provided for in a separate trust. While married to his third wife, Laura, he executed a will that left $1 million to each grandchild and the rest to Laura. Later, another will left his entire estate in trust to Laura for her life and then to a foundation that she controlled.

After Johnson's death, a dispute arose over the validity of the latest will.

The court concluded that Johnson's last will was invalid due to Laura's undue influence. Johnson was an admitted alcoholic with permanent cognitive defects and memory problems that would have caused him to be more susceptible to undue influence. Evidence suggested that Laura had exerted substantial control over many aspects of Johnson's life. Other evidence established that Johnson wanted to provide for his descendants, as well as for the charities named in the earlier will.[5] ■

Disinheritance. Although a testator must be able to remember the persons who would naturally be heirs to the estate, there is no requirement that testators give their estates to the natural heirs. A testator may decide to disinherit, or leave nothing to, an individual for various reasons. Most states have laws that attempt to prevent accidental disinheritance, however. There are also laws that protect minor children from the loss of the family residence. Therefore, the testator's intent to disinherit needs to be clear.

■ **CASE IN POINT 51.5** In 1975, William Melton executed a will that, among other things, stated that his daughter, Vicki Palm, was to receive nothing. In 1979, he added a handwritten note to the will, saying that his friend, Alberta Kelleher, was to receive a small portion of his estate.

In 1995, Melton sent a signed, handwritten letter to Kelleher. The letter said that Melton wanted to put "something in writing" leaving Kelleher his "entire estate." Melton also said, "I *do not* want my brother Larry J. Melton or Vicki Palm or any of my other relatives to have one penny of my estate."

When Melton died in 2008, Kelleher had already passed away, and Melton's daughter, Vicki Palm, was his only natural heir. The state of Nevada argued that it should receive everything because Palm had been disinherited. Nevertheless, the trial court applied the state's intestacy laws and distributed the entire estate to Palm. The state appealed. The Nevada Supreme Court reversed the judgment of the lower court. It held that the disinheritance clause was clear and enforceable and that Melton's estate should therefore go to the state of Nevada.[6] ■

Writing Requirements Generally, a will must be in writing. The writing itself can be informal as long as it substantially complies with the statutory requirements. In some states, a will can be handwritten in crayon or ink.

---

4. *In re Succession of Sirgo*, 164 So.3d 832 (La. 2014).

5. *In re Estate of Johnson*, 340 S.W.3d 769 (Tex.App.—San Antonio 2011).
6. *In re Estate of Melton*, 272 P.3d 668 (Nev.Sup.Ct. 2012).

It can be written on a sheet or scrap of paper, on a paper bag, or on a piece of cloth. A will that is completely in the handwriting of the testator is called a **holographic will** (sometimes referred to as an *olographic will*).

A **nuncupative will** is an oral will made before witnesses. Oral wills are not permitted in most states. Where authorized by statute, such wills are generally valid only if made during the last illness of the testator and are therefore sometimes referred to as *deathbed wills.* Normally, only personal property can be transferred by a nuncupative will. Statutes may also permit members of the military to make nuncupative wills when on active duty.

Signature Requirements A fundamental requirement is that the testator's signature must appear on the will, generally at the end. Each jurisdiction dictates by statute and court decision what constitutes a signature. Initials, an X or other mark, and words such as "Mom" have all been upheld as valid when it was shown that the testators *intended* them to be signatures.

Witness Requirements A will usually must be *attested* (sworn to) by two, and sometimes three, witnesses. The number of witnesses, their qualifications, and the manner in which the witnessing must be done are generally set out in a statute. A witness may be required to be disinterested—that is, not a beneficiary under the will. The UPC, however, allows even interested witnesses to attest to a will [UPC 2–505]. There are no age requirements for witnesses, but they must be mentally competent.

The purpose of the witnesses is to verify that the testator actually executed (signed) the will and had the requisite intent and capacity at the time. A witness need not read the contents of the will. Usually, the testator and all witnesses sign in the sight or the presence of one another. The UPC does not require all parties to sign in one another's presence, however, and deems it sufficient if the testator acknowledges her or his signature to the witnesses [UPC 2–502].

51–1e Revocation of Wills

The testator can revoke a will at any time during her or his life, either by a physical act, such as tearing up the will, or by a subsequent writing. Wills can also be revoked by operation of law. Revocation can be partial or complete, and it must follow certain strict formalities.

Revocation by a Physical Act A testator can revoke a will by *intentionally* burning, tearing, canceling, obliterating, or otherwise destroying it.[7] A testator can also revoke a will by intentionally having someone else destroy it in the testator's presence and at the testator's direction. Note that when a state statute prescribes the specific methods for revoking a will by a physical act, only those methods can be used to revoke the will.

In some states, a testator can partially revoke a will by the physical act of crossing out some provisions in the will. The portions that are crossed out are dropped, and the remaining portions are valid. In no circumstances, however, can a provision be crossed out and an additional or substitute provision written in its place. Such altered provisions require that the will be reexecuted (signed again) and reattested (rewitnessed).

In the following case, the court had to decide whether the testator had intended to revoke part or all of her will by making certain changes to it after it was executed.

---

7. The destruction cannot be inadvertent. The testator must have intent to revoke the will.

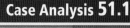

Case Analysis 51.1

Peterson v. Harrell

Supreme Court of Georgia, 690 S.E.2d 151 (2010).

In the Language of the Court
THOMPSON, Justice.

Testator Marion E. Peterson died in 2008. She was survived by her two siblings [brother and sister], Arvin Peterson and Carolyn Peterson Basner (caveators[a]).

---

a. In the context of wills, a *caveator* is one who files a *caveat* attacking the validity of an alleged will.

After testator's death, Vasta Lucas, testator's longtime companion and executor of testator's estate, filed a petition to probate testator's will in solemn form. Lucas died during the pendency of this appeal [while the appeal was pending], and appellee Richard Harrell was appointed as successor executor and trustee for the estate. Caveators filed a

caveat to the petition to probate, alleging the will was not properly executed or had been revoked due to obliterations. The trial court admitted the will to probate and caveators appealed.

OCGA [the Official Code of Georgia Annotated] Section 53-4-20(b) of the

Case 51.1 Continues

Case 51.1 Continued

Revised Probate Code of 1998 provides that "a will shall be attested and subscribed in the presence of the testator by two or more competent witnesses." The record evidence in this case establishes that testator executed a will on June 9, 1976. The will was witnessed by two subscribing witnesses, only one of whom was living at the time of trial. Having been provided a copy of testator's will, the surviving witness testified to its due execution by deposition testimony presented at trial and via written interrogatories filed with the court. Caveators presented no evidence challenging either the validity of the signatures on the will or testator's capacity at the time the will was executed. Accordingly, the evidence supports the trial court's finding that the will was duly executed.

The will contained a bequest to Lucas in the form of a trust and provided that upon Lucas's death the trustee shall distribute any remaining assets to four beneficiaries, including caveators. Some time after the will was executed, testator struck through with an ink pen the names of all successor beneficiaries of the trust estate, as well as language in the will nominating Richard Harrell as successor executor and trustee. None of the strike-throughs were witnessed or attested to. Near the end of the will, testator wrote, "My executrix is Julie Peterson." Caveators contend these alterations constitute material cancellations that effect a revocation of the will.

To effect a revocation of a will by obliteration, caveators must show that testator made material obliterations to her will or directed another to do so and that testator intended for this act to revoke the will. *Joint operation of act and intention is necessary to revoke a will. The intent to revoke the will in its entirety shall be presumed from the obliteration or cancellation of a material portion of the will, but such presumption may be overcome by a preponderance of the evidence.* [Emphasis added.]

Even assuming, arguendo [for the sake of argument], that the alterations to testator's will constituted a material cancellation within the meaning of OCGA Section 53-4-44, we find no error in the trial court's conclusion that testator did not intend to revoke her entire will. The record supports the trial court's findings that caveators had no knowledge of the circumstances surrounding what they allege to be the revocation of the will, that testator never discussed revoking her will with caveators, and that caveators were not present when testator made the alterations to the will. Caveators presented no evidence of testator's intent other than the alterations themselves, and they satisfied their initial burden only by proving that testator made alterations to the will.

The record also shows, however, that the will was found in good condition on testator's desk among her personal papers. It bore the signatures of both testator and her subscribing witnesses and set out a primary bequest to Lucas which remained intact. Handwritten alterations crossing out the names of the successor beneficiaries with a single line were initialed by testator and she added language to the will indicating her desire to substitute Julie Peterson as her executrix. As found by the trial court, this evidence clearly indicates testator's intent to cancel only certain provisions of the will, not an intent to revoke the will in its entirety as required for revocation under OCGA Section 53-4-44.

* * * *

Judgment affirmed.

Legal Reasoning Questions

1. Why would the caveators argue that the entire will should be revoked? How would the will's revocation benefit them?

2. What could the testator have done differently to clarify her intentions in her will?

3. How might the availability of a secure online repository for a person's will affect a challenge to the will?

Revocation by a Subsequent Writing A will may also be wholly or partially revoked by a **codicil,** a written instrument separate from the will that amends or revokes provisions in the will. A codicil eliminates the necessity of redrafting an entire will merely to add to it or amend it. A codicil can also be used to revoke an entire will. The codicil must be executed with the same formalities required for a will, and it must refer expressly to the will. In effect, it updates a will because the will is "incorporated by reference" into the codicil.

A new will (second will) can be executed that may or may not revoke the first or a prior will, depending on the language used. To revoke a prior will, the second will must use language specifically revoking other wills, such as, "This will hereby revokes all prior wills." If the second will is otherwise valid and properly executed, it will revoke all prior wills. If the express *declaration of revocation* is missing, then both wills are read together. If there are any discrepancies between the wills, the second will controls.

Revocation by Operation of Law Revocation by operation of law occurs when marriage, divorce, annulment, or the birth of a child takes place after a will has been executed.

Marriage and Divorce. In most states, when a testator marries after executing a will and the will does not provide for the new spouse, the new spouse can still receive a share of the testator's estate. On the testator's death, the surviving spouse can receive the amount he or she would have taken had the testator died intestate (intestacy laws will be discussed shortly). The rest of the estate passes under the will [UPC 2–301, 2–508].

If, however, the new spouse is otherwise provided for in the will (or by transfer of property outside the will), he or she will not be given an intestate amount. Also, if the parties had a valid *prenuptial agreement*, its provisions dictate what the surviving spouse receives.

Divorce does not necessarily revoke the entire will. Rather, a divorce or an annulment occurring after a will has been executed revokes those dispositions of property made under the will to the former spouse [UPC 2–508].

Children. If a child is born after a will has been executed, that child may be entitled to a portion of the estate. Most state laws allow a child of the deceased to receive some portion of a parent's estate even if no provision is made in the parent's will. This is true *unless it is clear from the will's terms that the testator intended to disinherit the child* (see *Case in Point 51.5,* presented earlier). Under the UPC, the rule is the same.

51–1f Rights under a Will

The law imposes certain limitations on the way a person can dispose of property in a will. For instance, a married person who makes a will generally cannot avoid leaving a certain portion of the estate to the surviving spouse unless there is a valid prenuptial agreement. In most states, this is called an *elective share* or a *forced share,* and it is often one-third of the estate or an amount equal to a spouse's share under intestacy laws.

Beneficiaries under a will have rights as well. A beneficiary can renounce (disclaim) his or her share of the property given under a will. Further, a surviving spouse can renounce the amount given under a will and elect to take the forced share when the forced share is larger than the amount of the gift. State statutes provide the methods by which a surviving spouse accomplishes renunciation. The purpose of these statutes is to allow the spouse to obtain whichever distribution would be more advantageous. The UPC gives the surviving spouse an elective right to take a percentage of the total estate determined by the length of time that the spouse and the decedent were married to each other [UPC 2–201].

51–1g Probate Procedures

Recall that probate is the court process by which a will is proved valid or invalid. As mentioned, probate laws vary from state to state. Typically, the procedures used to probate a will depend on the size of the decedent's estate.

Informal Probate For smaller estates, most state statutes provide for the distribution of assets without formal probate proceedings. Faster and less expensive methods are then used. Property can be transferred by *affidavit* (a written statement taken in the presence of a person who has authority to affirm it). Problems or questions can be handled during an administrative hearing. Some states allow title to cars, savings and checking accounts, and certain other property to be transferred simply by filling out forms.

A majority of states also provide for *family settlement agreements,* which are private agreements among the beneficiaries. Once a will is admitted to probate, the family members can agree among themselves on how to distribute the decedent's assets. Although a family settlement agreement speeds the settlement process, a court order is still needed to protect the estate from future creditors and to clear title to the assets involved.

Formal Probate For larger estates, formal probate proceedings normally are undertaken, and the probate court supervises every aspect of the process. Additionally, in some situations—such as when a guardian for minor children must be appointed—more formal probate procedures cannot be avoided.

Formal probate proceedings may take several months or several years to complete, depending on the size and complexity of the estate and whether the will is contested. When the will is contested, or someone objects to the actions of the personal representative, the duration of probate is extended. As a result, a sizable portion of the decedent's assets (as much as 10 percent) may go to pay the fees charged by attorneys and personal representatives, as well as court costs.

51–1h Property Transfers outside the Probate Process

Often, people can avoid the cost of probate by employing various **will substitutes.** Examples include *living trusts* (discussed later in this chapter), life insurance policies, and individual retirement accounts (IRAs) with named beneficiaries.

One way to transfer property outside the probate process is to make gifts to one's children or others while one is still living. Another way is to own property in a joint tenancy. As previously discussed, in a joint tenancy, when one joint tenant dies, the other joint tenant or tenants automatically inherit the deceased tenant's share of the property. This is true even if the deceased tenant has provided otherwise in her or his will. Not all alternatives to formal probate administration are suitable to every estate, however.

See Concept Summary 51.1 for a review of basic information about wills.

Concept Summary 51.1

Wills

Terminology

- *Intestate*—Describes one who dies without a valid will.
- *Testator*—A person who makes a will.
- *Personal representative*—A person appointed in a will or by a court to settle the affairs of a decedent. A personal representative named in the will is an *executor*. A personal representative appointed by the court for an intestate decedent is an *administrator*.
- *Devise*—A gift of real estate by will, whether general or specific. The recipient of a devise is a *devisee*.
- *Bequest or legacy*—A gift of personal property by will, which can be general or specific. The recipient of a bequest (legacy) is a *legatee*.

Requirements for a Valid Will

- The testator must have *testamentary capacity*—that is, be of legal age and sound mind at the time the will is made.
- A will must be in writing (except for nuncupative wills).
- A will must be signed by the testator, and usually several people must witness the signing, depending on the state statute.

Revocation of Wills

- *By a physical act*—Intentionally tearing up, canceling, obliterating, or deliberately destroying part or all of a will revokes it.
- *By subsequent writing*—
    1. Codicil—A formal, separate document that amends or revokes an existing will.
    2. Second will or new will—A new, properly executed will expressly revoking the existing will.
- *By operation of law*—
    1. Marriage—Generally revokes a will written before the marriage to the extent of providing for the spouse.
    2. Divorce or annulment—Revokes dispositions of property made to the former spouse under a will made before the divorce or annulment.
    3. Subsequently born child—It is inferred that the child is entitled to receive the portion of the estate granted under intestacy distribution laws.

Probate Procedures

- To *probate* a will means to establish its validity and to carry out the administration of the estate through a court process. Probate laws vary from state to state. Probate procedures may be informal or formal, depending on the size of the estate and other factors, such as whether a guardian for minor children must be appointed.

51–2 Intestacy Laws

Each state regulates by statute how property will be distributed when a person dies intestate (without a valid will). Intestacy laws attempt to carry out the likely intent and wishes of the decedent.

These laws assume that deceased persons would have intended that their natural heirs (spouses, children, grandchildren, or other family members) inherit their property. Therefore, intestacy statutes set out rules and priorities under which these heirs inherit the property. If no heirs exist, the state will assume ownership of the property.

The rules of descent vary widely from state to state. It is thus important to refer to the exact language of the applicable state statutes when addressing any problem of intestacy distribution.

51–2a Surviving Spouse and Children

Usually, state statutes provide that first the debts of the decedent must be satisfied out of the estate. Then the remaining assets pass to the surviving spouse and to the children. A surviving spouse usually receives only a share of the estate—typically, one-half if there is also a surviving child and one-third if there are two or more children.[8] Only if no children or grandchildren survive the decedent will a surviving spouse receive the entire estate.

■ **EXAMPLE 51.6**   Adrian dies intestate and is survived by his wife, Betty, and his children, Duane and Tara. Allen's property passes according to intestacy laws. After his outstanding debts are paid, Betty will receive the family home (either in fee simple or as a life estate) and ordinarily a one-third to one-half interest in all other property. The remaining real and personal property will pass to Duane and Tara in equal portions. ■

Under most state intestacy laws and under the UPC, in-laws do not share in an estate. Thus, if a child dies before his or her parents, the child's spouse will not receive an inheritance on the parents' death. In *Example 51.6*, if Duane died before his father (Adrian), Duane's widow would not inherit his share of Adrian's estate.

51–2b When There Is No Surviving Spouse or Child

When there is no surviving spouse or child, the order of inheritance is generally grandchildren, then parents

of the decedent. These relatives usually are called *lineal* relatives.

If there are no lineal heirs, then *collateral heirs*—brothers and sisters, nieces and nephews, and aunts and uncles of the decedent—are the next groups that share. If there are no survivors in any of these groups, most statutes provide for the property to be distributed among the next of kin of the collateral heirs.

51–2c Stepchildren, Adopted Children, and Illegitimate Children

Under intestacy laws, stepchildren are not considered kin. Legally adopted children, however, are recognized as lawful heirs of their adoptive parents. (This is also true of children who are in the process of being adopted at the time of a prospective parent's death.)

Statutes vary from state to state in regard to the inheritance rights of illegitimate children (children born out of wedlock). Although illegitimate children have inheritance rights in most states, their rights are not necessarily identical to those of legitimate children.

In some states, an illegitimate child has the right to inherit only from the mother and her relatives, unless the father's paternity has been established by a legal proceeding. In the majority of states, however, a child born of any union that has the characteristics of a formal marriage relationship (such as unmarried parents who cohabit) is considered to be legitimate.

Under the revised UPC, a child is generally considered the child of the natural (biological) parents, regardless of their marital status. The child cannot inherit from a natural parent, however, unless that natural parent has openly treated the child as his (or hers) and has not refused to support the child [UPC 2–114].

51–2d Grandchildren

Usually, a decedent's will provides for how the estate will be distributed to descendants of deceased children (grandchildren whose parents have died). If a will does not include such a provision—or if a person dies intestate—the question arises as to what share the grandchildren of the decedent will receive. Each state uses one of two methods of distributing the assets of intestate decedents—*per stirpes* or *per capita*.

Per Stirpes Distribution   Under the ***per stirpes***[9] method, within a class or group of distributees (such as

---

8. UPC 2–102(2) provides a formula for computing a surviving spouse's share that is contingent on the number of surviving children and parents. For instance, if the decedent has no surviving children and one surviving parent, the surviving spouse takes the first $200,000, plus three-fourths of any balance of the intestate estate.

9. *Per stirpes* is a Latin term meaning "by the roots" or "by stock." When used in estate law, it means proportionally divided between beneficiaries according to each beneficiary's deceased ancestor's share.

grandchildren), the children of a descendant take the share that their deceased parent *would have been* entitled to inherit. Thus, a grandchild with no siblings inherits all of his or her parent's share, while grandchildren with siblings divide their parent's share.

■ **EXAMPLE 51.7** Michael, a widower, has two children, Scott and Jillian. Scott has two children (Becky and Holly), and Jillian has one child (Paul). Scott and Jillian die before their father. When Michael dies, if his estate is distributed *per stirpes,* Becky and Holly each receive one-fourth of the estate (dividing Scott's one-half share). Paul receives one-half of the estate (taking Jillian's one-half share). Exhibit 51–2 illustrates the *per stirpes* method of distribution. ■

Per Capita Distribution An estate may also be distributed on a **per capita**[10] basis, which means that each person in a class or group takes an equal share of the estate. ■ **EXAMPLE 51.8** If Michael's estate is distributed *per capita,* Becky, Holly, and Paul will each receive a one-third share. Exhibit 51–3 illustrates the *per capita* method of distribution. ■

51–3 Trusts

A **trust** is any arrangement by which property is transferred from one person to a trustee to be administered for the transferor's or another party's benefit. It can also

---

10. *Per capita* is a Latin term meaning "per person" or "for each head." When used in estate law, it means divided equally among beneficiaries within a class.

be defined as a right of property (real or personal) held by one party for the benefit of another. A trust can be created to become effective during a person's lifetime or after a person's death. Trusts may be established for any purpose that is not illegal or against public policy, and they may be express or implied.

The essential elements of a trust are as follows:

1. A designated beneficiary (except in charitable trusts, discussed shortly).
2. A designated trustee.
3. A fund sufficiently identified to enable title to pass to the trustee.
4. Actual delivery by the *settlor* or *grantor* (the person creating the trust) to the trustee with the intention of passing title.

51–3a Express Trusts

An express trust is created or declared in explicit terms, usually in writing. There are numerous types of express trusts, each with its own special characteristics.

Living Trusts A **living trust**—or *inter vivos* trust (*inter vivos* is Latin for "between or among the living")—is a trust created by a grantor during her or his lifetime. Living trusts have become a popular estate-planning option because at the grantor's death, assets held in a living trust can pass to the heirs without going through probate.

Note, however, that living trusts do not necessarily shelter assets from estate taxes. The grantor may also have to pay income taxes on trust earnings, depending on whether the trust is revocable or irrevocable.

EXHIBIT 51–2 *Per Stirpes* Distribution

Under this method of distribution, an heir takes the share that his or her deceased parent would have been entitled to inherit had the parent lived. This may mean that a class of distributees—the grandchildren in this example—will not inherit in equal portions. Note that Becky and Holly receive only one-fourth of Michael's estate while Paul inherits one-half.

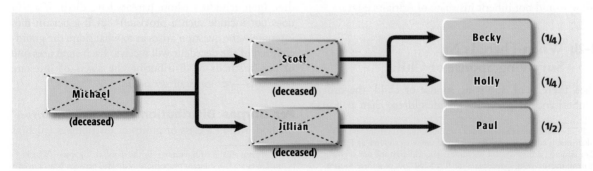

EXHIBIT 51–3 *Per Capita* Distribution

Under this method of distribution, all heirs in a certain class—in this example, the grandchildren—inherit equally. Note that Becky and Holly in this situation each inherit one-third, as does Paul.

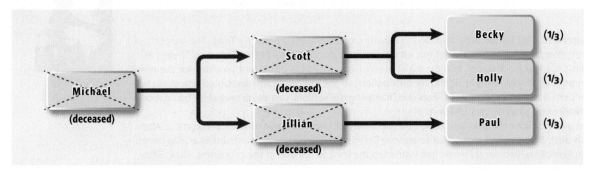

Revocable Living Trusts. In a revocable living trust, which is the most common type, the grantor retains control over the trust property during her or his lifetime. The grantor deeds the property to the trustee but retains the power to amend, alter, or revoke the trust during her or his lifetime.

The grantor may also serve as a trustee or co-trustee and can arrange to receive income earned by the trust assets during her or his lifetime. Because the grantor is in control of the funds, she or he is required to pay income taxes on the trust earnings. Unless the trust is revoked, the principal of the trust is transferred to the trust beneficiary on the grantor's death.

■ **EXAMPLE 51.9** James Cortez owns and operates a large farm. After his wife dies, James contacts his attorney to create a living trust for the benefit of his three children, Alicia, Emma, and Jacob. His attorney prepares the documents creating the trust. James executes a deed conveying the farm to the trust and transfers the farm's bank accounts into the name of the trust.

The trust designates James as the trustee and names his son Jacob as the *successor trustee,* who will take over the management of the trust when James dies or becomes incapacitated. Each of the children and James (as *income beneficiaries*) will receive an income from the trust while James is alive. When James dies, the farm will pass to them without having to go through probate. By holding the property in a revocable living trust, James retains control over the farm during his life (and can make changes to the trust at any time). This trust arrangement is illustrated in Exhibit 51–4. ■

The following case involved a revocable living trust that included the phrase "death of each." The resolution of the dispute turned on whether, in the context, "each" meant "either" or "both."

EXHIBIT 51–4 A Revocable Living Trust Arrangement

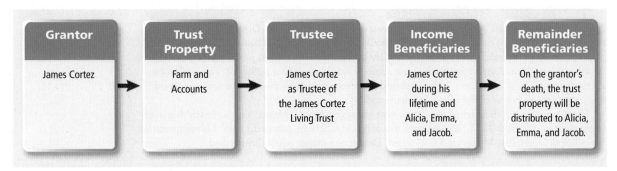

Dowdy v. Dowdy

District Court of Appeal of Florida, Second District, 41 Fla. L. Weekly D85, 182 So.3d 807 (2016).

Background and Facts Betty and Dennis Dowdy created the Dowdy Family Trust. The property of the trust comprised of two parcels of real estate. The trust document identified Betty and Dennis as the settlors, the initial trustees, and the initial beneficiaries. The trust document provided for the revocation or amendment of the trust and for distributions to the settlors. It also appointed one of each settlor's children as co-successor trustees and, following the settlors' deaths, provided for liquidation and distribution to all of their children.

Dennis had three children, and Betty had two—they did not have any children in common. After Dennis died, Betty amended the trust to remove Dennis's children as successor trustees and as beneficiaries. Previously, Betty and Dennis had instructed the trust to sell one of the properties. Now, Betty sold the remaining trust property.

Dennis's son Michael, who was named as a co-successor trustee in the trust document, learned of the sale and filed a petition in a Florida state court against Betty. Michael maintained that Betty's amendment was invalid because it had been executed after Dennis's death. He argued that when Dennis died, the trust became irrevocable and he succeeded Dennis as co-trustee. The court ordered Betty to deposit the proceeds of the sale with the court pending its construction of the trust. Betty appealed.

In the Language of the Court

NORTHCUTT, Judge.

* * * *

* * * Article IV of the original trust document provided as follows:

> During the Settlors' lifetime, the Trustees, in the Trustees' sole discretion, may pay, invade, or apply the income or corpus [trust property], or so much as they may choose, to or for the benefit, support and maintenance of the initial primary beneficiaries * * * .

Thus, if Betty was the only trustee following the death of her husband, she had sole and unfettered authority to sell the trust property for her own benefit.

Michael claims to be a successor co-trustee under article III of the original trust:

> * * * In the event of the death of each of the Initial Trustees, * * * the Settlors nominate and appoint Settlors' son and stepson, Michael R. Dowdy * * * , and Settlors' daughter and stepdaughter, Deborah Ann Andrews [Betty's daughter], as Co-Successor Trustees.

In Michael's view, the phrase "death of each" meant the death of *either* initial trustee. Therefore, he asserts that he became a co-trustee with Betty upon his father's death.

* * * Our view [is] that the succession of trustees occurred only upon the death of *both* initial trustees. This view is confirmed by the use of the same phraseology elsewhere in the original trust document.

Article V provides:

> After the death of each of the Settlors, the Co-Successor Trustees are directed to liquidate the Trust Estate and immediately pay and distribute the Trust Estate to the children and stepchildren of the Settlors * * * .

Clearly, in this instance the phrase "death of each" must mean the death of both. Otherwise, the article's direction to liquidate the trust estate and immediately distribute it to the settlors' children would nullify article IV's grant of authority to invade the income or corpus of the trust for the benefit of the initial primary beneficiaries "or the survivor." Indeed, upon the death of one settlor it would altogether nullify the survivor's status as beneficiary. This, of course, would be an absurd interpretation in complete contravention [contradiction] of a central purpose of the trust. [Emphasis added.]

There is nothing in the original trust document to suggest that the phrase "death of each" has a different meaning in article III. To the contrary, that article is otherwise consistent with this interpretation. We conclude, then, that Michael did not succeed Dennis as a trustee when Dennis died.

Case 51.2 Continued

Decision and Remedy *The state intermediate appellate court reversed the order of the lower court. Under the appellate court's interpretation of the terms of the trust, "at all times . . . , Betty has been the sole trustee and beneficiary of the trust . . . . As such, she had sole authority and discretion to sell the remaining trust property for her own benefit." The court concluded that Michael's petition had no likelihood of success.*

Critical Thinking
- **Legal Environment** *According to Michael's view of the phrase "death of each," how many co-trustees would have succeeded Dennis on his death? Explain.*
- **What If the Facts Were Different?** *Suppose that the Dowdy Family Trust had provided for a specific child to become co-trustee on the death of his or her parent—Deborah to succeed Betty, for example. How would the result have been different?*

Irrevocable Living Trusts. In an irrevocable living trust, the grantor permanently gives up control over the property to the trustee. The grantor executes a trust deed, and legal title to the trust property passes to the named trustee. The trustee has a duty to administer the property as directed by the grantor for the benefit and in the interest of the beneficiaries.

The trustee must preserve the trust property and make it productive. If required by the terms of the trust agreement, the trustee must pay income to the beneficiaries in accordance with the terms of the trust. Because the grantor has, in effect, given over the property for the benefit of the beneficiaries, he or she is no longer responsible for paying income taxes on the trust earnings.

Testamentary Trusts A **testamentary trust** is created by will and comes into existence on the grantor's death. Although a testamentary trust has a trustee who maintains legal title to the trust property, the trustee's actions are subject to judicial approval. The trustee can be named in the will or appointed by the court (if not named in the will). The legal responsibilities of the trustee are the same as in a living trust.

If a court finds that the will setting up a testamentary trust is invalid, then the trust will also be invalid. The property that was to be in the trust will then pass according to intestacy laws, not according to the terms of the trust.

If the court finds that a condition of the trust is invalid because it is illegal or against public policy, the court will invalidate that condition only and enforce the trust without it. ■ **EXAMPLE 51.10** Linzy Herman's will creates a testamentary trust. A condition of Herman's trust states, "to my son, if he never gets married." Because the condition is against public policy, the court will read the terms of the trust as not including the invalid restraint on marriage. ■

Charitable Trusts A **charitable trust** is an express trust designed for the benefit of a segment of the public or the public in general. It differs from other types of trusts in that the identities of the beneficiaries are uncertain and it can be established to last indefinitely. Usually, to be deemed a charitable trust, a trust must be created for charitable, educational, religious, or scientific purposes.

Spendthrift Trusts A **spendthrift trust** is created to provide for the maintenance of a beneficiary by preventing him or her from being careless with the bestowed funds. Unlike the beneficiaries of other trusts, the beneficiary in a spendthrift trust is not permitted to transfer or assign his or her rights to the trust's principal or future payments from the trust.

Essentially, the beneficiary can draw only a certain portion of the total amount to which he or she is entitled at any one time. The majority of states allow spendthrift trust provisions that prohibit creditors from attaching such trusts, with a few exceptions, such as for payment of a beneficiary's domestic-support obligations.

Totten Trusts A **Totten trust**[11] is created when a grantor deposits funds into an account in her or his own name with instructions that in the event of the grantor's death, whatever is in that account should go to a specific beneficiary. This type of trust is revocable at will until the depositor dies or completes the gift in her or his lifetime (by delivering the funds to the intended beneficiary, for instance). The beneficiary has no access to the funds until the depositor's death, when the beneficiary obtains property rights to the balance on hand.

---

11. This type of trust derives its unusual name from *In the Matter of Totten*, 179 N.Y. 112, 71 N.E. 748 (1904).

51–3b Implied Trusts

Sometimes, a trust will be imposed (implied) by law, even in the absence of an express trust. Implied trusts include constructive trusts and resulting trusts.

Constructive Trusts A **constructive trust** is imposed by a court in the interests of fairness and justice. In a constructive trust, the owner of the property is declared to be a trustee for the parties who are, in equity, actually entitled to the benefits that flow from the trust.

Courts often impose constructive trusts when someone who is in a confidential or fiduciary relationship with another person, such as a guardian to a ward, has breached a duty to that person. A court may also impose a constructive trust when someone wrongfully holds legal title to property. This may occur when the property was obtained through fraud or in breach of a legal duty, for instance.

■ **CASE IN POINT 51.11** Stella Jankowski added her niece Genevieve Viarengo as a joint owner on bank accounts and other financial assets valued at $500,000. Jankowski also executed a will that divided her estate equally among her ten nieces, nephews, and cousins. The will named Viarengo and Richard Golebiewski as coexecutors. She did not tell the attorney who drafted the will about the jointly held accounts.

When Jankowski died, Viarengo emptied Jankowski's safe and removed her financial records. Viarengo also claimed that the funds in the accounts were hers. Jankowski's other relatives filed a suit and asked the court to impose a constructive trust. The court found that Viarengo had committed fraud in obtaining the assets that she had held jointly with Jankowski and would be unjustly enriched if she were allowed to retain them. Therefore, the court imposed a constructive trust.[12] ■

Resulting Trusts A **resulting trust** arises from the conduct of the parties. Here, the trust results, or is created, when circumstances raise an inference that the party holding legal title to the property does so for the benefit of another. The trust will result unless the inference is refuted.

■ **EXAMPLE 51.12** Gabriela Fuentes wants to put one acre of land she owns on the market for sale. Because she is going out of the country for two years and will not be available to deed the property to a buyer during that period, she conveys the property to her good friend Raul Cruz. Cruz can then attempt to sell the property while Fuentes is gone.

The transaction in which Fuentes conveys the property to Cruz is intended to be neither a sale nor a gift. Consequently, Cruz will hold the property in a resulting trust for the benefit of Fuentes. When Fuentes returns, Cruz will be required either to deed the property back to her or, if the property has been sold, to turn over the proceeds (held in trust) to her. ■

Concept Summary 51.2 provides a synopsis of basic information about trusts.

51–3c The Trustee

The trustee is the person holding the trust property. Anyone legally capable of holding title to, and dealing in, property can be a trustee. If a trust fails to name a trustee, or if a named trustee cannot or will not serve, the trust does not fail. An appropriate court can appoint a trustee.

Trustee's Duties A trustee must act with honesty, good faith, and prudence in administering the trust and must exercise a high degree of loyalty toward the trust beneficiary. The general standard of care is the degree of care a prudent person would exercise in his or her own personal affairs.[13] The duty of loyalty requires that the trustee act in the exclusive interest of the beneficiary.

A trustee's specific duties include the following:

1. Maintain clear and accurate accounts of the trust's administration.
2. Furnish complete and correct information to the beneficiary.
3. Keep trust assets separate from her or his own assets.
4. Pay to an income beneficiary the net income of the trust assets at reasonable intervals.
5. Limit the risk of loss from investments by reasonable diversification and dispose of assets that do not represent prudent investments. (Prudent investment choices might include federal, state, or municipal bonds and some corporate bonds and stocks.)

Trustee's Powers When a grantor creates a trust, he or she may set forth the trustee's powers and performance. State law governs in the absence of specific terms in the trust, and the states often restrict the trustee's investment of trust funds.

Typically, statutes confine trustees to investments in conservative debt securities such as government, utility, and railroad bonds and certain real estate loans.

---

12. *Garrigus v. Viarengo*, 112 Conn.App. 655, 963 A.2d 1065 (2009).

13. Revised Uniform Principal and Income Act, Section 2(a)(3); and *Restatement (Third) of Trusts (Prudent Investor Rule)*, Section 227. This rule is in force in a majority of the states by statute and a small number of states under common law.

Concept Summary 51.2

Trusts

Definition and Essential Elements	• A *trust* is any arrangement by which property is transferred from one person to a trustee to be administered for another's benefit. • The essential elements of a trust are a designated beneficiary, a designated trustee, a fund sufficiently identified to enable title to pass to the trustee, and actual delivery to the trustee with the intention of passing title.
Types of Trusts	• *Living* (inter vivos) *trust*—A trust executed by a grantor during his or her lifetime. A living trust may be revocable or irrevocable. • *Testamentary trust*—A trust created by will and coming into existence on the death of the grantor. • *Charitable trust*—A trust designed for the benefit of a segment of the public or the public in general. • *Spendthrift trust*—A trust created to provide for the maintenance of a beneficiary by allowing her or him to receive only a certain portion of the total amount at any one time. • *Totten trust*—A trust created when one person deposits funds in his or her own name with instructions that the funds should go to a beneficiary on the depositor's death.

Implied Trusts	• *Implied trusts*, which are imposed by law in the interests of fairness and justice, include the following:
	    1. *Constructive trust*—Arises by operation of law when a transaction occurs in which the person who takes title to property is, in equity, not entitled to enjoy the benefits from it.
	    2. *Resulting trust*—Arises from the conduct of the parties when an *apparent intention* to create a trust is present.

Frequently, though, a grantor gives a trustee discretionary investment power. In that circumstance, any statute may be considered only advisory, with the trustee's decisions subject in most states to the prudent person rule.

Of course, a trustee is responsible for carrying out the purposes of the trust. If the trustee fails to comply with the terms of the trust or the controlling statute, he or she is personally liable for any loss.

Allocations between Principal and Income

Often, a grantor will provide one beneficiary with a life estate and another beneficiary with the remainder interest in the trust. A farmer, for instance, may create a testamentary trust providing that the farm's income be paid to the surviving spouse and that, on the surviving spouse's death, the farm be given to their children. In this situation, the surviving spouse has a *life estate* in the farm's income, and the children have a *remainder interest* in the farm (the principal).

When a trust is set up in this manner, questions may arise as to how the receipts and expenses for the farm's management and the trust's administration should be allocated between income and principal. When a trust instrument does not provide instructions, a trustee must refer to applicable state law.

The general rule is that ordinary receipts and expenses are chargeable to the income beneficiary, whereas extraordinary receipts and expenses are allocated to the principal beneficiaries.[14] The receipt of rent from trust realty would be ordinary, as would the expense of paying the property's taxes. The cost of long-term improvements and proceeds from the property's sale, however, would be extraordinary.

51–3d Trust Termination

The terms of a trust should expressly state the event on which the grantor wishes it to terminate—for instance, the beneficiary's or the trustee's death. If the trust instrument does not provide for termination on the beneficiary's death, the beneficiary's death will not end the trust. Similarly, without an express provision, a trust will not terminate on the trustee's death.

Typically, a trust instrument specifies a termination date. For instance, a trust created to educate the grantor's child may provide that the trust ends when the beneficiary reaches the age of twenty-five. If the trust's purpose is fulfilled before that date, a court may order the trust's termination. If no date is specified, a trust will terminate when its purpose has been fulfilled. Of course, if a trust's purpose becomes impossible or illegal, the trust will terminate.

51–4 Other Estate-Planning Issues

Estate planning involves making difficult decisions about the future, such as who will inherit the family home and other assets and who will take care of minor children. Estate planning also involves preparing in advance for other contingencies, such as illness and incapacity. For instance, what happens if you become incapacitated and cannot make your own decisions? Who will take care of your finances and other affairs? Do you want to be kept alive by artificial means, and whom do you trust to make decisions about your health care in the event that you cannot? Powers of attorney and living wills are frequently executed in conjunction with a will or trust to help resolve these matters.

51–4a Power of Attorney

A power of attorney is often used in business situations to give a person (an agent) authority to act on another's behalf. The powers usually are limited to a specific context, such as negotiating a deal with a buyer or entering into various contracts necessary to achieve a particular objective. Powers of attorney are also commonly used in estate planning.

Durable Power of Attorney One method of providing for future disability is to use a durable power of attorney. A **durable power of attorney** authorizes an individual to act on behalf of another when he or she becomes incapacitated. It can be drafted to take effect immediately or only after a physician certifies that the person is incapacitated. The person to whom the power is given can then write checks, collect insurance proceeds, and otherwise manage the incapacitated person's affairs, including health care.

Adult children may seek a durable power of attorney from their aging parents, particularly if the parents are becoming mentally incapacitated by Alzheimer's disease or some other condition. A husband and wife may give each other a power of attorney to make decisions in the event that one of them is hospitalized and unable to express her or his wishes. A person who is undergoing an operation may sign a durable power of attorney to a loved one who can take over his or her affairs in the event of incapacity.

If you become incapacitated without having executed a durable power of attorney, a court may need to appoint a conservator to handle your financial affairs. Although a spouse may have the ability to write checks on joint accounts, her or his power is often significantly limited. In most situations, it is better to have named a person you wish to handle your affairs in the event that you cannot.

Health-Care Power of Attorney A **health-care power of attorney** designates a person who will have the power to choose what type of and how much medical treatment a person who is unable to make such decisions will receive. The importance of appointing a person to make health-care decisions has grown as medical technology enables physicians and hospitals to keep people alive for ever-increasing periods of time.

■ **EXAMPLE 51.13** Terri Schiavo, a Florida woman, was kept alive in a vegetative state from 1990 to 2005. It took more than twenty court hearings for her husband to convince the court that he had a right to ask physicians to remove her feeding tube and let her die. If Schiavo had given her husband a health-care power of attorney, he would have had the right to make the decision to remove the feeding tube without going to court. ■

51–4b Living Will

A living will is not a will in the usual sense—that is, it does not appoint an estate representative, dispose of property, or establish a trust. Rather, a **living will** is an

---

14. Revised Uniform Principal and Income Act, Sections 3, 6, 8, and 13; and *Restatement (Third) of Trusts, (Prudent Investor Rule)*, Section 233.

advance health directive that allows a person to control what medical treatment may be used after a serious accident or illness. Through a living will, a person can indicate whether he or she wants certain lifesaving procedures to be undertaken in situations in which the treatment will not result in a reasonable quality of life.

Most states have enacted statutes permitting living wills, and it is important that the requirements of state law be followed exactly in creating such wills. Typically, state statutes require physicians to abide by the terms of living wills, and living wills are often included with a patient's medical records.

Reviewing: Wills and Trusts

In June 2016, Bernard Ramish set up a $48,000 trust fund through West Plains Credit Union to provide tuition for his nephew, Nathan Covacek, to attend Tri-State Polytechnic Institute. The trust was established under Ramish's control and went into effect that August. In December, Ramish suffered a brain aneurysm that caused frequent, severe headaches with no other symptoms. Shortly thereafter, Ramish met with an attorney to formalize in writing that he wanted no artificial life-support systems to be used should he suffer a serious illness. He also designated his cousin, Lizzie Johansen, to make decisions on his behalf should he become incapacitated.

In August 2017, Ramish developed heatstroke on the golf course at La Prima Country Club. After recuperating at the clubhouse, Ramish quickly wrote his will on the back of a wine list. It stated, "My last will and testament: Upon my death, I give all of my personal property to my friend Steve Eshom and my home to Lizzie Johansen." He signed the will at the bottom in the presence of five men in the La Prima clubhouse, and all five men signed as witnesses.

A week later, Ramish suffered a second aneurysm and died in his sleep. He was survived by his mother (Dorris Ramish), his nephew (Nathan Covacek), his son-in-law (Bruce Lupin), and his granddaughter (Tori Lupin). Using the information presented in the chapter, answer the following questions.

1. What type of trust did Ramish create for the benefit of Covacek? Was it revocable or irrevocable?
2. Does Ramish's testament on the back of the wine list meet the requirements for a valid will? Why or why not?
3. What would the order of inheritance have been if Ramish had died intestate?
4. Was Johansen granted a durable power of attorney or a health-care power of attorney for Ramish? Had Ramish created a living will? Explain.

Debate This . . .   *Any changes to existing, fully witnessed wills should also have to be witnessed.*

Terms and Concepts

Issue Spotters

1. Sheila makes a will leaving her property in equal thirds to Toby and Umeko, her children, and Velda, her niece. Two years later, Sheila is adjudged mentally incompetent, and that same year, she dies. Can Toby and Umeko have Sheila's will revoked on the ground that she did not have the capacity to make a will? Why or why not? (See *Wills.*)

2. Rafael dies without having made a will. He is survived by many relatives—a spouse, biological children, adopted children, sisters, brothers, uncles, aunts, cousins, nephews, and nieces. What determines who inherits what? (See *Intestacy Laws.*)

• **Check your answers to the Issue Spotters against the answers provided in Appendix D at the end of this text.**

Business Scenarios

51–1. Wills and Intestacy Laws. Benjamin is a widower who has two married children, Edward and Patricia. Patricia has two children, Perry and Paul. Edward has no children. Benjamin dies, and his typewritten will leaves all of his property equally to his children, Edward and Patricia, and provides that should a child predecease him, the grandchildren are to take *per stirpes*. The will was witnessed by Patricia and by Benjamin's lawyer, and it was signed by Benjamin in their presence. Patricia has predeceased Benjamin. Edward claims the will is invalid. (See *Intestacy Laws.*)

(a) Discuss whether the will is valid.

(b) Discuss the distribution of Benjamin's estate if the will is invalid.

(c) Discuss the distribution of Benjamin's estate if the will is valid.

51–2. Specific Bequests. Gary Mendel drew up a will in which he left his favorite car, a 1966 red Ferrari, to his daughter, Roberta. A year prior to his death, Mendel sold the 1966 Ferrari and purchased a 1969 Ferrari. Discuss whether Roberta will inherit the 1969 Ferrari under the terms of her father's will. (See *Wills.*)

51–3. Revocation of Wills. While single, James made out a will naming his mother, Carol, as sole beneficiary. Later, James married Lisa. (See *Wills.*)

(a) If James died while married to Lisa without changing his will, would the estate go to his mother, Carol? Explain.

(b) Assume that James made out a new will on his marriage to Lisa, leaving his entire estate to Lisa. Later, he divorced Lisa and married Mandis, but he did not change his will. Discuss the rights of Lisa and Mandis to James's estate after his death.

(c) Assume that James divorced Lisa, married Mandis, and changed his will, leaving his estate to Mandis. Later, a daughter, Claire, was born. James died without having included Claire in his will. Discuss fully whether Claire has any rights in the estate.

Business Case Problems

51–4. Intestacy Laws. A Florida statute provides that the right of election of a surviving spouse can be waived by written agreement: "A waiver of 'all rights,' or equivalent language, in the property or estate of a present or prospective spouse . . . is a waiver of all rights to elective share." The day before Mary Ann Taylor married Louis Taylor in Florida, they entered into a prenuptial agreement. The agreement stated that all property belonging to each spouse would "forever remain his or her personal estate, . . . forever free of claim by the other." The parties would retain "full rights and authority" over their property as they would have "if not married." After Louis died without a will, his only child, Joshua Taylor, filed a petition in a Florida state court for a determination of the beneficiaries of Louis's estate. How much of the estate can Mary Ann elect to receive? Explain. [*Taylor v. Taylor,* 1 So.3d 348 (Fla.App. 1 Dist. 2009)] (See *Intestacy Laws.*)

51–5. Wills. Elnora Maxey became the guardian of Sean Hall after his parents died. In 1996, Maxey died, and her will left the two houses in her estate to Hall. Julia Jordan became Hall's new guardian, and when she died, her husband, John Jordan, became Hall's guardian. In 1998, when Hall was eighteen years old, he died intestate, and Jordan was appointed as the administrator of Hall's estate. The two houses had remained in Maxey's estate, but Jordan paid the mortgage and tax payments on the houses for Hall's estate because Hall had inherited the houses. Anthony Cooper, a relative of Maxey, petitioned the probate court to be appointed executor of Maxey's estate, stating that there was now no heir. The court granted the request. Jordan was not aware of the proceedings. Cooper then sold both houses for the incredibly low price of $20,000 each to Quan Smith, without informing Jordan. The houses were then resold to JSD Properties, LLC, for a total of $190,000. Learning of the sale, Jordan sued, contending that Cooper had breached his fiduciary duty and had lied to the court, as Maxey's will had clearly left the houses to Hall. Does Jordan have the right to demand that JSD return the property? What factors would be considered in making this decision? [*Witcher v. JSD Properties, LLC,* 286 Ga. 717, 690 S.E.2d 855 (2010)] (See *Wills.*)

51–6. Business Case Problem with Sample Answer—Undue Influence. Susie Walker executed a will that left her entire estate to her grandson. When her grandson died, Susie executed a new will that named her great-grandson as her sole beneficiary and specifically disinherited her son, Tommy. At the time, Tommy's ex-wife was living with Susie. After Susie died, Tommy filed a suit, claiming that her will was the product of undue influence on the part of his ex-wife. Several witnesses testified that Susie had been mentally competent when she executed her will. Does undue influence appear likely based on these facts? Why or why not? [*In re Estate of Walker*, 80 A.D.3d 865, 164 L.Ed.2d 480 (3 Dept. 2011)] (See *Wills.*)

- **For a sample answer to Problem 51–6, go to Appendix E at the end of this text.**

51–7. Requirements of a Will. Sherman Hemsley was a well-known actor from the 1970s. Most notably, he played George Jefferson on the television shows *All in the Family* and *The Jeffersons*. He was born to Arsena Chisolm and William Thornton. Thornton was married to another woman, and Hemsley never had a relationship with his father or his father's side of the family. Hemsley never married and had no children. He lived with Flora Bernal, his business manager. Diagnosed with cancer, Hemsley executed a will naming Bernal the sole beneficiary of his estate. At the signing, Hemsley indicated that he knew he was executing his will and that he had deliberately chosen Bernal, but he did not discuss his relatives or the nature of his property with his attorney or the witnesses. After his death, the Thorntons challenged the will. Was Hemsley of sound mind? Discuss. [*In re Estate of Hemsley*, 460 S.W.3d 629 (Tex.App.—El Paso 2014)] (See *Wills.*)

51–8. Wills. Andrew Walker executed a will giving a certain parcel of real estate in fee simple to his three children from a previous marriage, Mark Walker, Michelle Peters, and Andrea Knox. The will granted a "life use" in the property to Walker's current spouse, Nora Walker. A year later, Andrew, who suffered from asbestosis, was discharged from a hospital to spend his last days at home. He told Nora that he wished to execute a new will to change the disposition of the property to devise half of it to her. Nora recorded his wish and took her notes to the office of attorney Frederick Meagher to have the document drafted. Meagher did not see Nora's notes and did not talk to Walker..When Walker signed the document, he did not declare that it was his will, as required by state law, and no one from Meagher's office was present at the signing. Is the document a valid will? Explain. [*In re Estate of Walker*, 124 A.D.3d 970, 2 N.Y.S.3d 628 (3 Dept. 2015)] (See *Wills.*)

51–9. A Question of Ethics—Wills. 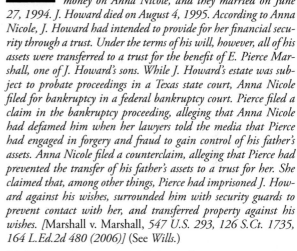 *Vickie Lynn Smith, an actress and model also known as Anna Nicole Smith, met J. Howard Marshall II in 1991. During their courtship, J. Howard lavished gifts and large sums of money on Anna Nicole, and they married on June 27, 1994. J. Howard died on August 4, 1995. According to Anna Nicole, J. Howard had intended to provide for her financial security through a trust. Under the terms of his will, however, all of his assets were transferred to a trust for the benefit of E. Pierce Marshall, one of J. Howard's sons. While J. Howard's estate was subject to probate proceedings in a Texas state court, Anna Nicole filed for bankruptcy in a federal bankruptcy court. Pierce filed a claim in the bankruptcy proceeding, alleging that Anna Nicole had defamed him when her lawyers told the media that Pierce had engaged in forgery and fraud to gain control of his father's assets. Anna Nicole filed a counterclaim, alleging that Pierce had prevented the transfer of his father's assets to a trust for her. She claimed that, among other things, Pierce had imprisoned J. Howard against his wishes, surrounded him with security guards to prevent contact with her, and transferred property against his wishes. [Marshall v. Marshall, 547 U.S. 293, 126 S.Ct. 1735, 164 L.Ed.2d 480 (2006)] (See Wills.)*

(a) What is the purpose underlying the requirements for a valid will? Which of these requirements might be at issue in this case? How should it apply here? Why?

(b) State courts generally have jurisdiction over the probate of a will and the administration of an estate. Does the Texas state court thus have the sole authority to adjudicate all of the claims in this case? Why or why not?

(c) How should Pierce's claim against Anna Nicole and her counterclaim be resolved?

(d) Anna Nicole executed her will in 2001. The beneficiary—Daniel, her son, who was not J. Howard's child—died in 2006, shortly after Anna Nicole gave birth to a daughter, Dannielynn. In 2007, before executing a new will, Anna Nicole died. What happens if a will's beneficiary dies before the testator? What happens if a child is born after a will is executed?

Legal Reasoning Group Activity

51–10. Intestacy Laws. Three and a half years after Lauren and Warren Woodward were married, they were informed that Warren had leukemia. At the time, the couple had no children, and physicians told the Woodwards that the leukemia treatment might leave Warren sterile. The couple arranged for Warren's sperm to be collected and placed in a sperm bank for later use.

Two years after Warren died, Lauren gave birth to twin girls who had been conceived through artificial insemination using his sperm. The following year, Lauren applied for Social Security survivor benefits for the two children. Her application was rejected on the ground that she had not established that the twins were the husband's children within the meaning of the Social Security Act. Woodward then filed a paternity action in Massachusetts, and the probate court determined that Warren Woodward was the twins' father. She then filed an action in court to determine the inheritance rights of the twins. (See *Intestacy Laws.*)

(a) The first group will outline how a court should decide the inheritance rights of children conceived from the sperm of a deceased individual and his surviving spouse.

(b) The second group will decide if children conceived after a parent's death (by means of artificial insemination or *in vitro* fertilization) still inherit under intestate succession laws, and will explain why or why not.

(c) The third group will consider the inheritance rights of a child who was conceived by means of artificial insemination, *in vitro* fertilization, or a surrogate. Should they be different from the rights of a child conceived in the traditional manner? Assuming the biological parent is not part of the child's life, should the child still be able to inherit from the biological parent? Why or why not?

Business Planning for Divorce

Larry starts Auto Masters, an auto repair service. Through Larry's efforts, Auto Masters becomes successful. At the same time, however, Larry's marriage to Rachel falls apart. Unfortunately, Larry has not taken steps to make sure that his business will not break up along with his marriage.

The court orders a settlement that takes into consideration the value of all of the couple's assets, including the business. To pay the settlement, Larry is forced to sell Auto Masters for cash at a lower price than would otherwise have been possible.

As this example illustrates, planning for divorce is an important part of a business plan for the owners of the business.

Separate and Marital Property

A divorce formally dissolves a legal marriage. Following a divorce, if the spouses have not otherwise divided their property between them, a court can do it. For this purpose, there are two different types of property—separate and marital.

Separate Property Any property that only one spouse owns is *separate property*. This includes property owned by only one spouse before the marriage, as well as inheritances and gifts received by only one spouse during the marriage. Separate property commingled with marital assets may lose its separate status. In addition, in many states, *an increase in value* in separate property during a marriage may be considered a marital asset.[1]

Marital Property Any other property that the spouses acquired individually or jointly during the marriage is *marital property*. This can include professional licenses, such as an attorney's license, as well as shares of stock, interests in limited partnerships, and closely held businesses.

Dividing the Property In a few states—community property jurisdictions—spouses are held to be equal owners of the marital property.[2] Those assets are allocated in equal shares.

Most states provide instead for an equitable division of assets. An *equitable division* is an allocation consistent with fairness and justice, which may not call for equal shares. A court will consider a number of factors, including at least the following:

- The parties' respective contributions to the accumulation of marital property.
- The parties' respective liabilities.
- Whether only one spouse will receive income-producing property.
- The parties' respective earning capacity and employability.
- The value of each party's separate property.
- The tax consequences.[3]

1. See, for example, *St. Marie v. Roy*, 29 So.3d 708 (La.App. 3d Cir. 2010).
2. There are nine community property states—Arizona, California, Idaho, Louisiana, Nevada, New Mexico, Texas, Washington, and Wisconsin.
3. The Uniform Marriage and Divorce Act (UMDA), which has been adopted in eight states, lists these and other factors, including "the age, health, station, occupation, . . . and needs of each of the parties" [UMDA Section 307].

Continues

Is a Business Separate or Marital Property?

A business begun during marriage with joint funds is marital property. A business started before marriage or financed with separate funds during marriage is most likely separate property.

A business may be considered entirely or partially marital property, depending on the spouses' respective contributions to the business during the marriage. The contributions may be financial or operational.

Suppose, for instance, that Rita starts App Solutions, a software coding and development firm, with her own funds before marrying Hector. During the marriage, Hector markets the firm's services and contributes joint funds to its operation. The business grows and appreciates in value. If the spouses divorce, normally the business will be considered marital property.

Determining Value

To sell a business or to buy out one spouse's interest requires determining the value of the business and of each spouse's interest in it. This calculation usually requires the services of an accredited or certified professional business appraiser. The appraiser reviews the business's financial statements, tax returns, and other relevant data, and determines the value according to the appropriate method.[4]

Protecting Assets

A business owner can protect business assets from the claims of a spouse without concealing those assets or otherwise committing fraud. One way to obtain this protection is to avoid involving the spouse (or prospective spouse) in the business. If he or she does not contribute to the business, it is not likely to be construed as marital property. Other steps include prenuptial agreements, postnuptial agreements, and an agreement among the owners of the business to adhere to certain conditions.

Prenuptial Agreements As defined earlier, a *prenuptial agreement* is an agreement made before marriage that defines each party's ownership rights in the other's property. A court will normally enforce a prenuptial agreement in the following circumstances.

- Each future spouse was represented by an attorney.
- The agreement is in writing.
- Each party signed the agreement voluntarily.
- The assets covered by the agreement were fully disclosed.

If a business is subject to both parties' interests, the agreement should provide a projected split of the assets and a process or a method for determining the value. It should also identify how and when payment is to be made.

---

4. These methods include the *market approach*, which bases value on the price of a similar, recently sold business; the *income approach*, which converts expected profit or cash flow into current value; and the *asset approach*, which bases value on assets and liabilities.

Postnuptial Agreements A *postnuptial agreement* is an agreement made *after* marriage that defines each spouse's rights in the other spouse's property. Like a prenuptial agreement, a postnuptial agreement must involve each party's attorney, be in writing, be signed voluntarily, and be preceded by full disclosure. Unlike prenuptial agreements, postnuptial agreements are not recognized in all states. Even in states where these agreements are recognized, they may be more difficult to enforce than prenuptial agreements.[5]

Business Agreements For some types of businesses that could be subject to a spousal claim, an agreement among the owners can protect the owners' interests. This can be true whether the owners are partners, corporate shareholders, or members of limited liability companies.

Such an agreement can require an unmarried owner to provide the firm with a prenuptial agreement before marriage, including a waiver by the owner's prospective spouse of any future interest in the business. The agreement can also restrict the transfer of an owner's interest without the consent of the other owners. The other owners can be given the right to buy the interest to keep control of the enterprise. The method of valuation and means of payment should be included as well.

If both spouses are part of the firm, the agreement should provide that only persons actively involved in the business are entitled to own an interest in it. The agreement should add that if either spouse leaves the firm, his or her interest must be sold to the spouse who is still active. And it should be stipulated that in the event of a divorce, one spouse must quit (and agree not to compete, according to certain reasonable terms).

Ethical Connection

There is room for debate over the ethics of executing a plan to protect assets that might otherwise be considered the property of another. This is particularly true in the context of a marriage and a divorce.

Of course, everyone who creates a corporation, a partnership, or a limited liability company is taking a step to protect the business's assets from creditors and others. Most do not consider such actions unethical. Similarly, there is nothing unethical about asking a business's co-owner or a future spouse to consent to the terms of the agreements suggested here.

But it is not ethical to form a business organization to keep property out of the hands of an owner's spouse who might deserve better treatment. Perhaps it is the timing and the purpose of a plan that finally determine whether it should be considered ethical.

Ethics Question *With respect to the division of property on divorce, should the conduct of the spouses during the marriage be a factor? Why or why not?*

Critical Thinking *How might a spouse or ex-spouse overcome the business asset protection devices and techniques discussed in this feature? Explain.*

---

5. See, for example, *Bedrick v. Bedrick*, 17 A.3d 17, 300 Conn. 691 (2011).

How to Brief Cases and Analyze Case Problems

How to Brief Cases

To fully understand the law with respect to business, you need to be able to read and understand court decisions. To make this task easier, you can use a method of case analysis that is called *briefing*. There is a fairly standard procedure that you can follow when you "brief" any court case. You must first read the case opinion carefully. When you feel you understand the case, you can prepare a brief of it.

Although the format of the brief may vary, typically it will present the essentials of the case under headings such as the following:

1. **Citation.** Give the full citation for the case, including the name of the case, the date it was decided, and the court that decided it.
2. **Facts.** Briefly indicate (a) the reasons for the lawsuit; (b) the identity and arguments of the plaintiff(s) and defendant(s), respectively; and (c) the lower court's decision—if appropriate.
3. **Issue.** Concisely phrase, in the form of a question, the essential issue before the court. (If more than one issue is involved, you may have two—or even more—questions here.)
4. **Decision.** Indicate here—with a "yes" or "no," if possible—the court's answer to the question (or questions) in the *Issue* section above.
5. **Reason.** Summarize as briefly as possible the reasons given by the court for its decision (or decisions) and the case or statutory law relied on by the court in arriving at its decision.

An Example of a Briefed Sample Court Case

As an example of the format used in briefing cases, we present here a briefed version of the sample court case that was presented in Chapter 1 in Exhibit 1–6.

ROSA AND RAYMOND PARKS INSTITUTE FOR SELF DEVELOPMENT v. TARGET CORPORATION

United States Court of Appeals, Eleventh Circuit, 812 F.3d 824 (2016).

FACTS In December 1955, on a bus in Montgomery, Alabama, Rosa Parks refused to give up her seat to a white man in violation of the city's segregation law. This "courageous act" sparked the modern civil rights movement. Parks's role in "the most significant social movement in the history of the United States" has been chronicled in books and movies, and featured on mementoes, some of which are offered for sale by Target Corp. The Rosa and Raymond Parks Institute for Self Development is a Michigan firm that owns Parks's name and likeness. The Institute filed a suit in a federal district court against Target, alleging misappropriation in violation of the Institute's right of publicity. The court dismissed the complaint. The Institute appealed to the U.S. Court of Appeals for the Eleventh Circuit.

ISSUE Are Target's sales of books, movies, and other items that depict or discuss Rosa Parks and the modern civil rights movement protected by Michigan's common-law qualified privilege?

DECISION Yes. The U.S. Court of Appeals for the Eleventh Circuit affirmed the lower court's decision to dismiss the Institute's complaint. The items offered for sale by Target that feature or discuss Rosa Parks and her role in history are protected by Michigan's qualified privilege protecting matters of public interest.

REASON Michigan's common-law right of publicity prohibits the commercial use of a person's name or likeness without his or her consent. But this privacy right has limits. It "must yield to the qualified privilege to communicate on matters of public interest." The court recognized that "Rosa Parks is a figure of great historical significance and the civil rights movement a matter of legitimate and important public interest." The items identified by the Institute and sold by Target are "*bona fide* works" discussing Parks and her role in the modern civil rights movement. The items "communicate information, express opinions, recite grievances, and protest claimed abuses on behalf of a movement whose existence and objectives continue to be of the highest public interest and concern." Therefore, they fall within Michigan's qualified privilege.

A Review of the Briefed Sample Court Case

Here, we provide a review of the briefed case to indicate the kind of information that is contained in each section.

CITATION The name of the case is *Rosa and Raymond Parks Institute for Self Development v. Target Corporation.* The Rosa and Raymond Parks Institute for Self Development is the plaintiff. Target is the defendant. The U.S. Court of Appeals for the Eleventh Circuit decided this case in 2016. The citation states that this case can be found in Volume 812 of the *Federal Reporter, Third Series,* on page 824.

FACTS The *Facts* section identifies the plaintiff and the defendant. It also describes the events leading up to this suit and the allegations made by the plaintiff in the suit. Because this case is a decision of one of the U.S. courts of appeals, the lower court's ruling, the party appealing, and sometimes the appellant's contention on appeal are included here.

ISSUE The *Issue* section presents the central issue (or issues) decided by the court. In this case, the court considers whether the sales of books and other items that depict or discuss Rosa Parks and the modern civil rights movement are protected by Michigan's common-law qualified privilege.

DECISION The *Decision* section includes the court's decision on the issues before it. The decision reflects the opinion of the judge or justice hearing the case. In this case, the court decided that the items offered for sale focusing on or featuring Rosa Parks and her role in history fall within Michigan's qualified privilege, which protects depictions and discussions of matters of public interest. Decisions by appellate courts are frequently phrased in reference to the lower court's decision. That is, the appellate court may "affirm" the lower court's ruling or "reverse" it. A case may also be remanded, or sent back to the lower court, for further proceedings.

REASON The *Reason* section includes references to the relevant laws and legal principles that the court applied in coming to the conclusion arrived at in the case. The relevant law here includes Michigan's common-law qualified privilege protecting the use of others' names and likenesses in depictions and discussions of matters in the pubic interest. This section also explains the court's application of the law to the facts in this case.

Analyzing Case Problems

In addition to learning how to brief cases, students also find it helpful to know how to analyze case problems. Part of the study of business law and the legal environment usually involves analyzing case problems, such as those included in this text at the end of each chapter.

For each case problem in this book, we provide the relevant background and facts of the lawsuit and the issue before the court. When you are assigned one of these problems, your job will be to determine how the court should decide the issue, and why. In other words, you will need to engage in legal analysis and reasoning. Here, we offer some suggestions on how to make this task less daunting. We begin by presenting a SAMPLE PROBLEM:

> While Janet Lawson, a famous pianist, was shopping in Quality Market, she slipped and fell on a wet floor in one of the aisles. The floor had recently been mopped by one of the store's employees, but there were no signs warning customers that the floor in that area was wet. As a result of the fall, Lawson injured her right arm and was unable to perform piano concerts for the next six months. Had she been able to perform the scheduled concerts, she would have earned approximately $60,000 over that period of time. Lawson sued Quality Market for this amount, plus another $10,000 in medical expenses. She claimed that the store's failure to warn customers of the wet floor constituted negligence and therefore the market was liable for her injuries. Will the court agree with Lawson? Discuss.

Understand the Facts

This may sound obvious, but before you can analyze or apply the relevant law to a specific set of facts, you must clearly understand those facts. In other words, you should read through the case problem carefully—more than once, if necessary—to make sure you understand the identity of the plaintiff(s) and defendant(s) in the case and the progression of events that led to the lawsuit.

In the sample case problem just given, the identity of the parties is fairly obvious. Janet Lawson is the one bringing the suit; therefore, she is the plaintiff. Quality Market, against whom she is bringing the suit, is the defendant. Some of the case problems you may work on have multiple plaintiffs or defendants. Often, it is helpful to use abbreviations for the parties. To indicate a reference to a plaintiff, for example, the *pi* symbol—π—is often used, and a defendant is denoted by a *delta*—Δ—a triangle.

The events leading to the lawsuit are also fairly straightforward. Lawson slipped and fell on a wet floor, and she contends that Quality Market should be liable for her injuries because it was negligent in not posting a sign warning customers of the wet floor.

When you are working on case problems, realize that the facts should be accepted as they are given. For example, in our sample problem, it should be accepted that the floor was wet and that there was no sign. In other words, avoid making conjectures, such as "Maybe the floor wasn't too wet," or "Maybe an employee was getting a sign to put up," or "Maybe someone stole the sign." Questioning the facts as they are presented only adds confusion to your analysis.

Legal Analysis and Reasoning

Once you understand the facts given in the case problem, you can begin to analyze the case. The IRAC method is a helpful tool to use in the legal analysis and reasoning process. IRAC is an acronym for Issue, Rule, Application, Conclusion. Applying this method to our sample problem would involve the following steps:

1. First, you need to decide what legal **issue** is involved in the case. In our sample case, the basic issue is whether Quality Market's

failure to warn customers of the wet floor constituted negligence. As discussed in the text, negligence is a *tort*—a civil wrong. In a tort lawsuit, the plaintiff seeks to be compensated for another's wrongful act. A defendant will be deemed negligent if he or she breached a duty of care owed to the plaintiff and the breach of that duty caused the plaintiff to suffer harm.

2. Once you have identified the issue, the next step is to determine what **rule of law** applies to the issue. To make this determination, you will want to review carefully the text of the chapter in which the relevant rule of law for the problem appears. Our sample case problem involves the tort of negligence. The applicable rule of law is the tort law principle that business owners owe a duty to exercise reasonable care to protect their customers ("business invitees"). Reasonable care, in this context, includes either removing—or warning customers of—*foreseeable* risks about which the owner *knew* or *should have known*. Business owners need not warn customers of "open and obvious" risks, however. If a business owner breaches this duty of care (fails to exercise the appropriate degree of care toward customers), and the breach of duty causes a customer to be injured, the business owner will be liable to the customer for the customer's injuries.

3. The next—and usually the most difficult—step in analyzing case problems is the **application** of the relevant rule of law to the specific facts of the case you are studying. In the sample problem, applying the tort law principle just discussed presents few difficulties. An employee of the store had mopped the floor in the aisle where Lawson slipped and fell, but no sign was present indicating that the floor was wet. That a customer might fall on a wet floor is clearly a foreseeable risk. Therefore, the failure to warn customers about the wet floor was a breach of the duty of care owed by the business owner to the store's customers.

4. Once you have completed Step 3 in the IRAC method, you should be ready to draw your **conclusion.** In our sample problem, Quality Market is liable to Lawson for her injuries, because the market's breach of its duty of care caused Lawson's injuries.

The fact patterns in the business scenarios and case problems presented in this text are not always as simple as those presented in our sample problem. Often, for example, a case has more than one plaintiff or defendant. A case may also involve more than one issue and have more than one applicable rule of law. Furthermore, in some case problems the facts may indicate that the general rule of law should not apply.

For example, suppose that a store employee advised Lawson not to walk on the floor in the aisle because it was wet, but Lawson decided to walk on it anyway. This fact could alter the outcome of the case because the store could then raise the defense of assumption of risk. Nonetheless, a careful review of the chapter text should always provide you with the knowledge you need to analyze the problem thoroughly and arrive at accurate conclusions.

APPENDIX B

The Constitution of the United States

Preamble

We the People of the United States, in Order to form a more perfect Union, establish Justice, insure domestic Tranquility, provide for the common defence, promote the general Welfare, and secure the Blessings of Liberty to ourselves and our Posterity, do ordain and establish this Constitution for the United States of America.

Article I

Section 1. All legislative Powers herein granted shall be vested in a Congress of the United States, which shall consist of a Senate and House of Representatives.

Section 2. The House of Representatives shall be composed of Members chosen every second Year by the People of the several States, and the Electors in each State shall have the Qualifications requisite for Electors of the most numerous Branch of the State Legislature.

No Person shall be a Representative who shall not have attained to the Age of twenty five Years, and been seven Years a Citizen of the United States, and who shall not, when elected, be an Inhabitant of that State in which he shall be chosen.

Representatives and direct Taxes shall be apportioned among the several States which may be included within this Union, according to their respective Numbers, which shall be determined by adding to the whole Number of free Persons, including those bound to Service for a Term of Years, and excluding Indians not taxed, three fifths of all other Persons. The actual Enumeration shall be made within three Years after the first Meeting of the Congress of the United States, and within every subsequent Term of ten Years, in such Manner as they shall by Law direct. The Number of Representatives shall not exceed one for every thirty Thousand, but each State shall have at Least one Representative; and until such enumeration shall be made, the State of New Hampshire shall be entitled to chuse three, Massachusetts eight, Rhode Island and Providence Plantations one, Connecticut five, New York six, New Jersey four, Pennsylvania eight, Delaware one, Maryland six, Virginia ten, North Carolina five, South Carolina five, and Georgia three.

When vacancies happen in the Representation from any State, the Executive Authority thereof shall issue Writs of Election to fill such Vacancies.

The House of Representatives shall chuse their Speaker and other Officers; and shall have the sole Power of Impeachment.

Section 3. The Senate of the United States shall be composed of two Senators from each State, chosen by the Legislature thereof, for six Years; and each Senator shall have one Vote.

Immediately after they shall be assembled in Consequence of the first Election, they shall be divided as equally as may be into three Classes. The Seats of the Senators of the first Class shall be vacated at the Expiration of the second Year, of the second Class at the Expiration of the fourth Year, and of the third Class at the Expiration of the sixth Year, so that one third may be chosen every second Year; and if Vacancies happen by Resignation, or otherwise, during the Recess of the Legislature of any State, the Executive thereof may make temporary Appointments until the next Meeting of the Legislature, which shall then fill such Vacancies.

No Person shall be a Senator who shall not have attained to the Age of thirty Years, and been nine Years a Citizen of the United States, and who shall not, when elected, be an Inhabitant of that State for which he shall be chosen.

The Vice President of the United States shall be President of the Senate, but shall have no Vote, unless they be equally divided.

The Senate shall chuse their other Officers, and also a President pro tempore, in the Absence of the Vice President, or when he shall exercise the Office of President of the United States.

The Senate shall have the sole Power to try all Impeachments. When sitting for that Purpose, they shall be on Oath or Affirmation. When the President of the United States is tried, the Chief Justice shall preside: And no Person shall be convicted without the Concurrence of two thirds of the Members present.

Judgment in Cases of Impeachment shall not extend further than to removal from Office, and disqualification to hold and enjoy any Office of honor, Trust, or Profit under the United States: but the Party convicted shall nevertheless be liable and subject to Indictment, Trial, Judgment, and Punishment, according to Law.

Section 4. The Times, Places and Manner of holding Elections for Senators and Representatives, shall be prescribed in each State by the Legislature thereof; but the Congress may at any time by Law make or alter such Regulations, except as to the Places of chusing Senators.

The Congress shall assemble at least once in every Year, and such Meeting shall be on the first Monday in December, unless they shall by Law appoint a different Day.

Section 5. Each House shall be the Judge of the Elections, Returns, and Qualifications of its own Members, and a Majority of each shall constitute a Quorum to do Business; but a smaller Number may adjourn from day to day, and may be authorized to compel the Attendance of absent Members, in such Manner, and under such Penalties as each House may provide.

Each House may determine the Rules of its Proceedings, punish its Members for disorderly Behavior, and, with the Concurrence of two thirds, expel a Member.

Each House shall keep a Journal of its Proceedings, and from time to time publish the same, excepting such Parts as may in their Judgment require Secrecy; and the Yeas and Nays of the

Members of either House on any question shall, at the Desire of one fifth of those Present, be entered on the Journal.

Neither House, during the Session of Congress, shall, without the Consent of the other, adjourn for more than three days, nor to any other Place than that in which the two Houses shall be sitting.

Section 6. The Senators and Representatives shall receive a Compensation for their Services, to be ascertained by Law, and paid out of the Treasury of the United States. They shall in all Cases, except Treason, Felony and Breach of the Peace, be privileged from Arrest during their Attendance at the Session of their respective Houses, and in going to and returning from the same; and for any Speech or Debate in either House, they shall not be questioned in any other Place.

No Senator or Representative shall, during the Time for which he was elected, be appointed to any civil Office under the Authority of the United States, which shall have been created, or the Emoluments whereof shall have been increased during such time; and no Person holding any Office under the United States, shall be a Member of either House during his Continuance in Office.

Section 7. All Bills for raising Revenue shall originate in the House of Representatives; but the Senate may propose or concur with Amendments as on other Bills.

Every Bill which shall have passed the House of Representatives and the Senate, shall, before it become a Law, be presented to the President of the United States; If he approve he shall sign it, but if not he shall return it, with his Objections to the House in which it shall have originated, who shall enter the Objections at large on their Journal, and proceed to reconsider it. If after such Reconsideration two thirds of that House shall agree to pass the Bill, it shall be sent together with the Objections, to the other House, by which it shall likewise be reconsidered, and if approved by two thirds of that House, it shall become a Law. But in all such Cases the Votes of both Houses shall be determined by Yeas and Nays, and the Names of the Persons voting for and against the Bill shall be entered on the Journal of each House respectively. If any Bill shall not be returned by the President within ten Days (Sundays excepted) after it shall have been presented to him, the Same shall be a Law, in like Manner as if he had signed it, unless the Congress by their Adjournment prevent its Return in which Case it shall not be a Law.

Every Order, Resolution, or Vote, to which the Concurrence of the Senate and House of Representatives may be necessary (except on a question of Adjournment) shall be presented to the President of the United States; and before the Same shall take Effect, shall be approved by him, or being disapproved by him, shall be repassed by two thirds of the Senate and House of Representatives, according to the Rules and Limitations prescribed in the Case of a Bill.

Section 8. The Congress shall have Power To lay and collect Taxes, Duties, Imposts and Excises, to pay the Debts and provide for the common Defence and general Welfare of the United States; but all Duties, Imposts and Excises shall be uniform throughout the United States;

To borrow Money on the credit of the United States;

To regulate Commerce with foreign Nations, and among the several States, and with the Indian Tribes;

To establish an uniform Rule of Naturalization, and uniform Laws on the subject of Bankruptcies throughout the United States;

To coin Money, regulate the Value thereof, and of foreign Coin, and fix the Standard of Weights and Measures;

To provide for the Punishment of counterfeiting the Securities and current Coin of the United States;

To establish Post Offices and post Roads;

To promote the Progress of Science and useful Arts, by securing for limited Times to Authors and Inventors the exclusive Right to their respective Writings and Discoveries;

To constitute Tribunals inferior to the supreme Court;

To define and punish Piracies and Felonies committed on the high Seas, and Offenses against the Law of Nations;

To declare War, grant Letters of Marque and Reprisal, and make Rules concerning Captures on Land and Water;

To raise and support Armies, but no Appropriation of Money to that Use shall be for a longer Term than two Years;

To provide and maintain a Navy;

To make Rules for the Government and Regulation of the land and naval Forces;

To provide for calling forth the Militia to execute the Laws of the Union, suppress Insurrections and repel Invasions;

To provide for organizing, arming, and disciplining, the Militia, and for governing such Part of them as may be employed in the Service of the United States, reserving to the States respectively, the Appointment of the Officers, and the Authority of training the Militia according to the discipline prescribed by Congress;

To exercise exclusive Legislation in all Cases whatsoever, over such District (not exceeding ten Miles square) as may, by Cession of particular States, and the Acceptance of Congress, become the Seat of the Government of the United States, and to exercise like Authority over all Places purchased by the Consent of the Legislature of the State in which the Same shall be, for the Erection of Forts, Magazines, Arsenals, dock-Yards, and other needful Buildings;—And

To make all Laws which shall be necessary and proper for carrying into Execution the foregoing Powers, and all other Powers vested by this Constitution in the Government of the United States, or in any Department or Officer thereof.

Section 9. The Migration or Importation of such Persons as any of the States now existing shall think proper to admit, shall not be prohibited by the Congress prior to the Year one thousand eight hundred and eight, but a Tax or duty may be imposed on such Importation, not exceeding ten dollars for each Person.

The privilege of the Writ of Habeas Corpus shall not be suspended, unless when in Cases of Rebellion or Invasion the public Safety may require it.

No Bill of Attainder or ex post facto Law shall be passed.

No Capitation, or other direct, Tax shall be laid, unless in Proportion to the Census or Enumeration herein before directed to be taken.

No Tax or Duty shall be laid on Articles exported from any State.

No Preference shall be given by any Regulation of Commerce or Revenue to the Ports of one State over those of another: nor shall Vessels bound to, or from, one State be obliged to enter, clear, or pay Duties in another.

No Money shall be drawn from the Treasury, but in Consequence of Appropriations made by Law; and a regular Statement and Account of the Receipts and Expenditures of all public Money shall be published from time to time.

No Title of Nobility shall be granted by the United States: And no Person holding any Office of Profit or Trust under them, shall, without the Consent of the Congress, accept of any present, Emolument, Office, or Title, of any kind whatever, from any King, Prince, or foreign State.

Section 10. No State shall enter into any Treaty, Alliance, or Confederation; grant Letters of Marque and Reprisal; coin Money; emit Bills of Credit; make any Thing but gold and silver Coin a Tender in Payment of Debts; pass any Bill of Attainder, ex post facto Law, or Law impairing the Obligation of Contracts, or grant any Title of Nobility.

No State shall, without the Consent of the Congress, lay any Imposts or Duties on Imports or Exports, except what may be absolutely necessary for executing its inspection Laws: and the net Produce of all Duties and Imposts, laid by any State on Imports or Exports, shall be for the Use of the Treasury of the United States; and all such Laws shall be subject to the Revision and Controul of the Congress.

No State shall, without the Consent of Congress, lay any Duty of Tonnage, keep Troops, or Ships of War in time of Peace, enter into any Agreement or Compact with another State, or with a foreign Power, or engage in War, unless actually invaded, or in such imminent Danger as will not admit of delay.

Article II

Section 1. The executive Power shall be vested in a President of the United States of America. He shall hold his Office during the Term of four Years, and, together with the Vice President, chosen for the same Term, be elected, as follows:

Each State shall appoint, in such Manner as the Legislature thereof may direct, a Number of Electors, equal to the whole Number of Senators and Representatives to which the State may be entitled in the Congress; but no Senator or Representative, or Person holding an Office of Trust or Profit under the United States, shall be appointed an Elector.

The Electors shall meet in their respective States, and vote by Ballot for two Persons, of whom one at least shall not be an Inhabitant of the same State with themselves. And they shall make a List of all the Persons voted for, and of the Number of Votes for each; which List they shall sign and certify, and transmit sealed to the Seat of the Government of the United States, directed to the President of the Senate. The President of the Senate shall, in the Presence of the Senate and House of Representatives, open all the Certificates, and the Votes shall then be counted. The Person having the greatest Number of Votes shall

be the President, if such Number be a Majority of the whole Number of Electors appointed; and if there be more than one who have such Majority, and have an equal Number of Votes, then the House of Representatives shall immediately chuse by Ballot one of them for President; and if no Person have a Majority, then from the five highest on the List the said House shall in like Manner chuse the President. But in chusing the President, the Votes shall be taken by States, the Representation from each State having one Vote; A quorum for this Purpose shall consist of a Member or Members from two thirds of the States, and a Majority of all the States shall be necessary to a Choice. In every Case, after the Choice of the President, the Person having the greater Number of Votes of the Electors shall be the Vice President. But if there should remain two or more who have equal Votes, the Senate shall chuse from them by Ballot the Vice President.

The Congress may determine the Time of chusing the Electors, and the Day on which they shall give their Votes; which Day shall be the same throughout the United States.

No person except a natural born Citizen, or a Citizen of the United States, at the time of the Adoption of this Constitution, shall be eligible to the Office of President; neither shall any Person be eligible to that Office who shall not have attained to the Age of thirty five Years, and been fourteen Years a Resident within the United States.

In Case of the Removal of the President from Office, or of his Death, Resignation or Inability to discharge the Powers and Duties of the said Office, the same shall devolve on the Vice President, and the Congress may by Law provide for the Case of Removal, Death, Resignation or Inability, both of the President and Vice President, declaring what Officer shall then act as President, and such Officer shall act accordingly, until the Disability be removed, or a President shall be elected.

The President shall, at stated Times, receive for his Services, a Compensation, which shall neither be increased nor diminished during the Period for which he shall have been elected, and he shall not receive within that Period any other Emolument from the United States, or any of them.

Before he enter on the Execution of his Office, he shall take the following Oath or Affirmation: "I do solemnly swear (or affirm) that I will faithfully execute the Office of President of the United States, and will to the best of my Ability, preserve, protect and defend the Constitution of the United States."

Section 2. The President shall be Commander in Chief of the Army and Navy of the United States, and of the Militia of the several States, when called into the actual Service of the United States; he may require the Opinion, in writing, of the principal Officer in each of the executive Departments, upon any Subject relating to the Duties of their respective Offices, and he shall have Power to grant Reprieves and Pardons for Offenses against the United States, except in Cases of Impeachment.

He shall have Power, by and with the Advice and Consent of the Senate to make Treaties, provided two thirds of the Senators present concur; and he shall nominate, and by and with the Advice and Consent of the Senate, shall appoint Ambassadors, other public Ministers and Consuls, Judges of the supreme

Court, and all other Officers of the United States, whose Appointments are not herein otherwise provided for, and which shall be established by Law; but the Congress may by Law vest the Appointment of such inferior Officers, as they think proper, in the President alone, in the Courts of Law, or in the Heads of Departments.

The President shall have Power to fill up all Vacancies that may happen during the Recess of the Senate, by granting Commissions which shall expire at the End of their next Session.

Section 3. He shall from time to time give to the Congress Information of the State of the Union, and recommend to their Consideration such Measures as he shall judge necessary and expedient; he may, on extraordinary Occasions, convene both Houses, or either of them, and in Case of Disagreement between them, with Respect to the Time of Adjournment, he may adjourn them to such Time as he shall think proper; he shall receive Ambassadors and other public Ministers; he shall take Care that the Laws be faithfully executed, and shall Commission all the Officers of the United States.

Section 4. The President, Vice President and all civil Officers of the United States, shall be removed from Office on Impeachment for, and Conviction of, Treason, Bribery, or other high Crimes and Misdemeanors.

Article III

Section 1. The judicial Power of the United States, shall be vested in one supreme Court, and in such inferior Courts as the Congress may from time to time ordain and establish. The Judges, both of the supreme and inferior Courts, shall hold their Offices during good Behaviour, and shall, at stated Times, receive for their Services a Compensation, which shall not be diminished during their Continuance in Office.

Section 2. The judicial Power shall extend to all Cases, in Law and Equity, arising under this Constitution, the Laws of the United States, and Treaties made, or which shall be made, under their Authority;—to all Cases affecting Ambassadors, other public Ministers and Consuls;—to all Cases of admiralty and maritime Jurisdiction;—to Controversies to which the United States shall be a Party;—to Controversies between two or more States;—between a State and Citizens of another State;—between Citizens of different States;—between Citizens of the same State claiming Lands under Grants of different States, and between a State, or the Citizens thereof, and foreign States, Citizens or Subjects.

In all Cases affecting Ambassadors, other public Ministers and Consuls, and those in which a State shall be a Party, the supreme Court shall have original Jurisdiction. In all the other Cases before mentioned, the supreme Court shall have appellate Jurisdiction, both as to Law and Fact, with such Exceptions, and under such Regulations as the Congress shall make.

The Trial of all Crimes, except in Cases of Impeachment, shall be by Jury; and such Trial shall be held in the State where the said Crimes shall have been committed; but when not committed within any State, the Trial shall be at such Place or Places as the Congress may by Law have directed.

Section 3. Treason against the United States, shall consist only in levying War against them, or, in adhering to their Enemies, giving them Aid and Comfort. No Person shall be convicted of Treason unless on the Testimony of two Witnesses to the same overt Act, or on Confession in open Court.

The Congress shall have Power to declare the Punishment of Treason, but no Attainder of Treason shall work Corruption of Blood, or Forfeiture except during the Life of the Person attainted.

Article IV

Section 1. Full Faith and Credit shall be given in each State to the public Acts, Records, and judicial Proceedings of every other State. And the Congress may by general Laws prescribe the Manner in which such Acts, Records and Proceedings shall be proved, and the Effect thereof.

Section 2. The Citizens of each State shall be entitled to all Privileges and Immunities of Citizens in the several States.

A Person charged in any State with Treason, Felony, or other Crime, who shall flee from Justice, and be found in another State, shall on Demand of the executive Authority of the State from which he fled, be delivered up, to be removed to the State having Jurisdiction of the Crime.

No Person held to Service or Labour in one State, under the Laws thereof, escaping into another, shall, in Consequence of any Law or Regulation therein, be discharged from such Service or Labour, but shall be delivered up on Claim of the Party to whom such Service or Labour may be due.

Section 3. New States may be admitted by the Congress into this Union; but no new State shall be formed or erected within the Jurisdiction of any other State; nor any State be formed by the Junction of two or more States, or Parts of States, without the Consent of the Legislatures of the States concerned as well as of the Congress.

The Congress shall have Power to dispose of and make all needful Rules and Regulations respecting the Territory or other Property belonging to the United States; and nothing in this Constitution shall be so construed as to Prejudice any Claims of the United States, or of any particular State.

Section 4. The United States shall guarantee to every State in this Union a Republican Form of Government, and shall protect each of them against Invasion; and on Application of the Legislature, or of the Executive (when the Legislature cannot be convened) against domestic Violence.

Article V

The Congress, whenever two thirds of both Houses shall deem it necessary, shall propose Amendments to this Constitution, or, on the Application of the Legislatures of two thirds of the several States, shall call a Convention for proposing Amendments, which, in either Case, shall be valid to all Intents and Purposes, as part of this Constitution, when ratified by the Legislatures of three fourths of the several States, or by Conventions in three fourths thereof, as the one or the other Mode of Ratification may be proposed by the Congress; Provided that no

Amendment which may be made prior to the Year One thousand eight hundred and eight shall in any Manner affect the first and fourth Clauses in the Ninth Section of the first Article; and that no State, without its Consent, shall be deprived of its equal Suffrage in the Senate.

Article VI

All Debts contracted and Engagements entered into, before the Adoption of this Constitution shall be as valid against the United States under this Constitution, as under the Confederation.

This Constitution, and the Laws of the United States which shall be made in Pursuance thereof; and all Treaties made, or which shall be made, under the Authority of the United States, shall be the supreme Law of the Land; and the Judges in every State shall be bound thereby, any Thing in the Constitution or Laws of any State to the Contrary notwithstanding.

The Senators and Representatives before mentioned, and the Members of the several State Legislatures, and all executive and judicial Officers, both of the United States and of the several States, shall be bound by Oath or Affirmation, to support this Constitution; but no religious Test shall ever be required as a Qualification to any Office or public Trust under the United States.

Article VII

The Ratification of the Conventions of nine States shall be sufficient for the Establishment of this Constitution between the States so ratifying the Same.

Amendment I [1791]

Congress shall make no law respecting an establishment of religion, or prohibiting the free exercise thereof; or abridging the freedom of speech, or of the press; or the right of the people peaceably to assembly, and to petition the Government for a redress of grievances.

Amendment II [1791]

A well regulated Militia, being necessary to the security of a free State, the right of the people to keep and bear Arms, shall not be infringed.

Amendment III [1791]

No Soldier shall, in time of peace be quartered in any house, without the consent of the Owner, nor in time of war, but in a manner to be prescribed by law.

Amendment IV [1791]

The right of the people to be secure in their persons, houses, papers, and effects, against unreasonable searches and seizures, shall not be violated, and no Warrants shall issue, but upon probable cause, supported by Oath or affirmation, and particularly describing the place to be searched, and the persons or things to be seized.

Amendment V [1791]

No person shall be held to answer for a capital, or otherwise infamous crime, unless on a presentment or indictment of a Grand Jury, except in cases arising in the land or naval forces, or in the Militia, when in actual service in time of War or public danger; nor shall any person be subject for the same offence to be twice put in jeopardy of life or limb; nor shall be compelled in any criminal case to be a witness against himself, nor be deprived of life, liberty, or property, without due process of law; nor shall private property be taken for public use, without just compensation.

Amendment VI [1791]

In all criminal prosecutions, the accused shall enjoy the right to a speedy and public trial, by an impartial jury of the State and district wherein the crime shall have been committed, which district shall have been previously ascertained by law, and to be informed of the nature and cause of the accusation; to be confronted with the witnesses against him; to have compulsory process for obtaining witnesses in his favor, and to have the Assistance of Counsel for his defence.

Amendment VII [1791]

In Suits at common law, where the value in controversy shall exceed twenty dollars, the right of trial by jury shall be preserved, and no fact tried by jury, shall be otherwise re-examined in any Court of the United States, than according to the rules of the common law.

Amendment VIII [1791]

Excessive bail shall not be required, nor excessive fines imposed, nor cruel and unusual punishments inflicted.

Amendment IX [1791]

The enumeration in the Constitution, of certain rights, shall not be construed to deny or disparage others retained by the people.

Amendment X [1791]

The powers not delegated to the United States by the Constitution, nor prohibited by it to the States, are reserved to the States respectively, or to the people.

Amendment XI [1795]

The Judicial power of the United States shall not be construed to extend to any suit in law or equity, commenced or prosecuted against one of the United States by Citizens of another State, or by Citizens or Subjects of any Foreign State.

Amendment XII [1804]

The Electors shall meet in their respective states, and vote by ballot for President and Vice-President, one of whom, at least, shall not be an inhabitant of the same state with themselves; they shall name in their ballots the person voted for as

President, and in distinct ballots the person voted for as Vice-President, and they shall make distinct lists of all persons voted for as President, and of all persons voted for as Vice-President, and of the number of votes for each, which lists they shall sign and certify, and transmit sealed to the seat of the government of the United States, directed to the President of the Senate;—The President of the Senate shall, in the presence of the Senate and House of Representatives, open all the certificates and the votes shall then be counted;—The person having the greatest number of votes for President, shall be the President, if such number be a majority of the whole number of Electors appointed; and if no person have such majority, then from the persons having the highest numbers not exceeding three on the list of those voted for as President, the House of Representatives shall choose immediately, by ballot, the President. But in choosing the President, the votes shall be taken by states, the representation from each state having one vote; a quorum for this purpose shall consist of a member or members from two-thirds of the states, and a majority of all states shall be necessary to a choice. And if the House of Representatives shall not choose a President whenever the right of choice shall devolve upon them, before the fourth day of March next following, then the Vice-President shall act as President, as in the case of the death or other constitutional disability of the President.—The person having the greatest number of votes as Vice-President, shall be the Vice-President, if such number be a majority of the whole number of Electors appointed, and if no person have a majority, then from the two highest numbers on the list, the Senate shall choose the Vice-President; a quorum for the purpose shall consist of two-thirds of the whole number of Senators, and a majority of the whole number shall be necessary to a choice. But no person constitutionally ineligible to the office of President shall be eligible to that of Vice-President of the United States.

Amendment XIII [1865]

Section 1. Neither slavery nor involuntary servitude, except as a punishment for crime whereof the party shall have been duly convicted, shall exist within the United States, or any place subject to their jurisdiction.

Section 2. Congress shall have power to enforce this article by appropriate legislation.

Amendment XIV [1868]

Section 1. All persons born or naturalized in the United States, and subject to the jurisdiction thereof, are citizens of the United States and of the State wherein they reside. No State shall make or enforce any law which shall abridge the privileges or immunities of citizens of the United States; nor shall any State deprive any person of life, liberty, or property, without due process of law; nor deny to any person within its jurisdiction the equal protection of the laws.

Section 2. Representatives shall be apportioned among the several States according to their respective numbers, counting the whole number of persons in each State, excluding Indians not taxed. But when the right to vote at any election for the choice of electors for President and Vice President of the United States, Representatives in Congress, the Executive and Judicial officers of a State, or the members of the Legislature thereof, is denied to any of the male inhabitants of such State, being twenty-one years of age, and citizens of the United States, or in any way abridged, except for participation in rebellion, or other crime, the basis of representation therein shall be reduced in the proportion which the number of such male citizens shall bear to the whole number of male citizens twenty-one years of age in such State.

Section 3. No person shall be a Senator or Representative in Congress, or elector of President and Vice President, or hold any office, civil or military, under the United States, or under any State, who having previously taken an oath, as a member of Congress, or as an officer of the United States, or as a member of any State legislature, or as an executive or judicial officer of any State, to support the Constitution of the United States, shall have engaged in insurrection or rebellion against the same, or given aid or comfort to the enemies thereof. But Congress may by a vote of two-thirds of each House, remove such disability.

Section 4. The validity of the public debt of the United States, authorized by law, including debts incurred for payment of pensions and bounties for services in suppressing insurrection or rebellion, shall not be questioned. But neither the United States nor any State shall assume or pay any debt or obligation incurred in aid of insurrection or rebellion against the United States, or any claim for the loss or emancipation of any slave; but all such debts, obligations and claims shall be held illegal and void.

Section 5. The Congress shall have power to enforce, by appropriate legislation, the provisions of this article.

Amendment XV [1870]

Section 1. The right of citizens of the United States to vote shall not be denied or abridged by the United States or by any State on account of race, color, or previous condition of servitude.

Section 2. The Congress shall have power to enforce this article by appropriate legislation.

Amendment XVI [1913]

The Congress shall have power to lay and collect taxes on incomes, from whatever source derived, without apportionment among the several States, and without regard to any census or enumeration.

Amendment XVII [1913]

Section 1. The Senate of the United States shall be composed of two Senators from each State, elected by the people thereof, for six years; and each Senator shall have one vote. The electors in each State shall have the qualifications requisite for electors of the most numerous branch of the State legislatures.

Section 2. When vacancies happen in the representation of any State in the Senate, the executive authority of such State shall issue writs of election to fill such vacancies: *Provided*, That the legislature of any State may empower the executive thereof to make temporary appointments until the people fill the vacancies by election as the legislature may direct.

Section 3. This amendment shall not be so construed as to affect the election or term of any Senator chosen before it becomes valid as part of the Constitution.

Amendment XVIII [1919]

Section 1. After one year from the ratification of this article the manufacture, sale, or transportation of intoxicating liquors within, the importation thereof into, or the exportation thereof from the United States and all territory subject to the jurisdiction thereof for beverage purposes is hereby prohibited.

Section 2. The Congress and the several States shall have concurrent power to enforce this article by appropriate legislation.

Section 3. This article shall be inoperative unless it shall have been ratified as an amendment to the Constitution by the legislatures of the several States, as provided in the Constitution, within seven years from the date of the submission hereof to the States by the Congress.

Amendment XIX [1920]

Section 1. The right of citizens of the United States to vote shall not be denied or abridged by the United States or by any State on account of sex.

Section 2. Congress shall have power to enforce this article by appropriate legislation.

Amendment XX [1933]

Section 1. The terms of the President and Vice President shall end at noon on the 20th day of January, and the terms of Senators and Representatives at noon on the 3d day of January, of the years in which such terms would have ended if this article had not been ratified; and the terms of their successors shall then begin.

Section 2. The Congress shall assemble at least once in every year, and such meeting shall begin at noon on the 3d day of January, unless they shall by law appoint a different day.

Section 3. If, at the time fixed for the beginning of the term of the President, the President elect shall have died, the Vice President elect shall become President. If the President shall not have been chosen before the time fixed for the beginning of his term, or if the President elect shall have failed to qualify, then the Vice President elect shall act as President until a President shall have qualified; and the Congress may by law provide for the case wherein neither a President elect nor a Vice President elect shall have qualified, declaring who shall then act as President, or the manner in which one who is to act shall be selected, and such person shall act accordingly until a President or Vice President shall have qualified.

Section 4. The Congress may by law provide for the case of the death of any of the persons from whom the House of Representatives may choose a President whenever the right of choice shall have devolved upon them, and for the case of the death of any of the persons from whom the Senate may choose a Vice President whenever the right of choice shall have devolved upon them.

Section 5. Sections 1 and 2 shall take effect on the 15th day of October following the ratification of this article.

Section 6. This article shall be inoperative unless it shall have been ratified as an amendment to the Constitution by the legislatures of three-fourths of the several States within seven years from the date of its submission.

Amendment XXI [1933]

Section 1. The eighteenth article of amendment to the Constitution of the United States is hereby repealed.

Section 2. The transportation or importation into any State, Territory, or possession of the United States for delivery or use therein of intoxicating liquors, in violation of the laws thereof, is hereby prohibited.

Section 3. This article shall be inoperative unless it shall have been ratified as an amendment to the Constitution by conventions in the several States, as provided in the Constitution, within seven years from the date of the submission hereof to the States by the Congress.

Amendment XXII [1951]

Section 1. No person shall be elected to the office of the President more than twice, and no person who has held the office of President, or acted as President, for more than two years of a term to which some other person was elected President shall be elected to the office of President more than once. But this Article shall not apply to any person holding the office of President when this Article was proposed by the Congress, and shall not prevent any person who may be holding the office of President, or acting as President, during the term within which this Article becomes operative from holding the office of President or acting as President during the remainder of such term.

Section 2. This article shall be inoperative unless it shall have been ratified as an amendment to the Constitution by the legislatures of three-fourths of the several States within seven years from the date of its submission to the States by the Congress.

Amendment XXIII [1961]

Section 1. The District constituting the seat of Government of the United States shall appoint in such manner as the Congress may direct:

A number of electors of President and Vice President equal to the whole number of Senators and Representatives in Congress to which the District would be entitled if it were a State, but in no event more than the least populous state; they shall be in addition to those appointed by the states, but they shall be considered, for the purposes of the election of President and Vice President, to be electors appointed by a state; and they shall meet in the District and perform such duties as provided by the twelfth article of amendment.

Section 2. The Congress shall have power to enforce this article by appropriate legislation.

Amendment XXIV [1964]

Section 1. The right of citizens of the United States to vote in any primary or other election for President or Vice President, for electors for President or Vice President, or for Senator or Representative in Congress, shall not be denied or abridged by the United States, or any State by reason of failure to pay any poll tax or other tax.

Section 2. The Congress shall have power to enforce this article by appropriate legislation.

Amendment XXV [1967]

Section 1. In case of the removal of the President from office or of his death or resignation, the Vice President shall become President.

Section 2. Whenever there is a vacancy in the office of the Vice President, the President shall nominate a Vice President who shall take office upon confirmation by a majority vote of both Houses of Congress.

Section 3. Whenever the President transmits to the President pro tempore of the Senate and the Speaker of the House of Representatives his written declaration that he is unable to discharge the powers and duties of his office, and until he transmits to them a written declaration to the contrary, such powers and duties shall be discharged by the Vice President as Acting President.

Section 4. Whenever the Vice President and a majority of either the principal officers of the executive departments or of such other body as Congress may by law provide, transmit to the President pro tempore of the Senate and the Speaker of the House of Representatives their written declaration that the President is unable to discharge the powers and duties of his office, the Vice President shall immediately assume the powers and duties of the office as Acting President.

Thereafter, when the President transmits to the President pro tempore of the Senate and the Speaker of the House of Representatives his written declaration that no inability exists, he shall resume the powers and duties of his office unless the Vice President and a majority of either the principal officers of the executive department or of such other body as Congress may by law provide, transmit within four days to the President pro tempore of the Senate and the Speaker of the House of Representatives their written declaration that the President is unable to discharge the powers and duties of his office. Thereupon Congress shall decide the issue, assembling within forty-eight hours for that purpose if not in session. If the Congress, within twenty-one days after receipt of the latter written declaration, or, if Congress is not in session, within twenty-one days after Congress is required to assemble, determines by two-thirds vote of both Houses that the President is unable to discharge the powers and duties of his office, the Vice President shall continue to discharge the same as Acting President; otherwise, the President shall resume the powers and duties of his office.

Amendment XXVI [1971]

Section 1. The right of citizens of the United States, who are eighteen years of age or older, to vote shall not be denied or abridged by the United States or by any State on account of age.

Section 2. The Congress shall have power to enforce this article by appropriate legislation.

Amendment XXVII [1992]

No law, varying the compensation for the services of the Senators and Representatives, shall take effect, until an election of Representatives shall have intervened.

APPENDIX C
The Uniform Commercial Code

(Adopted in fifty-two jurisdictions—all fifty States, although Louisiana has adopted only Articles 1, 3, 4, 7, 8, and 9; the District of Columbia; and the Virgin Islands.)

The Code consists of the following articles:

Article
1. General Provisions
2. Sales
2A. Leases
3. Negotiable Instruments
4. Bank Deposits and Collections
4A. Funds Transfers
5. Letters of Credit
6. Repealer of U.C.C.—Article 6: Bulk Transfers and [Revised] Article 6: Bulk Sales
7. Warehouse Receipts, Bills of Lading and Other Documents of Title
8. Investment Securities
9. Secured Transactions

ARTICLE 1: GENERAL PROVISIONS

Part 1—General Provisions

§ 1–101. Short Titles.
(a) This [Act] may be cited as Uniform Commercial Code.
(b) This article may be cited as Uniform Commercial Code—Uniform Provisions.

§ 1–102. Scope of Article.
This article applies to a transaction to the extent that it is governed by another article of [the Uniform Commercial Code].

§ 1–103. Construction of [Uniform Commercial Code] to Promote Its Purpose and Policies; Applicability of Supplemental Principles of Law.
(a) [The Uniform Commercial Code] must be liberally construed and applied to promote its underlying purposes and policies, which are:
    (1) to simplify, clarify, and modernize the law govern-ing commercial transactions;
    (2) to permit the continued expansion of commercial practices through custom, usage, and agreement of the parties; and
    (3) to make uniform the law among the various jurisdictions.
(b) Unless displaced by the particular provisions of [the Uniform Commercial Code], the principles of law and equity, including the law merchant and the law relative to capacity to contract, principal and agent, estoppel, fraud, misrepresentation, duress, coercion, mistake, bankruptcy, and other validating or invalidating cause, supplement its provisions.

§ 1–104. Construction Against Implicit Repeal.
This Act being a general act intended as a unified coverage of its subject matter, no part of it shall be deemed to be impliedly repealed by subsequent legislation if such construction can reasonably be avoided.

§ 1–105. Severability.
If any provision or clause of [the Uniform Commercial Code] or its application to any person or circumstance is held invalid, the invalidity does not affect other provisions or applications of [the Uniform Commercial Code] which can be given effect without the invalid provision or application, and to this end the provisions of [the Uniform Commercial Code] are severable.

§ 1–106. Use of Singular and Plural; Gender.
In [the Uniform Commercial Code], unless the statutory context otherwise requires:
(1) words in the singular number include the plural, and those in the plural include the singular; and
(2) words of any gender also refer to any other gender.

§ 1–107. Section Captions.
Section captions are part of [the Uniform Commercial Code].

§ 1–108. Relation to Electronic Signatures in Global and National Commerce Act.
This article modifies, limits, and supersedes the Federal Electronic Signatures in Global and National Commerce Act, 15 U.S.C. Sections 7001 *et seq.,* except that nothing in this article modifies, limits, or supersedes Section 7001(c) of that act or authorizes electronic delivery of any of the notices described in Section 7003(b) of that Act.

Part 2—General Definitions and Principles of Interpretation

§ 1–201. General Definitions.
Subject to additional definitions contained in the subsequent Articles of this Act which are applicable to specific Articles or Parts thereof, and unless the context otherwise requires, in this Act:
(1) "Action", in the sense of a judicial proceeding, includes recoupment, counterclaim, set-off, suit in equity, and any other proceedings in which rights are determined.
(2) "Aggrieved party" means a party entitled to resort to a remedy.
(3) "Agreement", as distinguished from "contract", means the bargain of the parties in fact, as found in their language or by implication from other circumstances, including course of performance, course of dealing, or usage of trade as provided in Section 1–303.
(4) "Bank" means a person engaged in the business of banking and includes a savings bank, savings and loan association, credit union, and trust company.
(5) "Bearer" means a person in control of a negotiable electronic document of title or a person in possession of a negotiable instrument.

negotiable tangible document of title, or certificated security that is payable to bearer or indorsed in blank.

(6) "Bill of lading" means a document of title evidencing the receipt of goods for shipment issued by a person engaged in the business of directly or indirectly transporting or forwarding goods. The term does not include a warehouse receipt.

(7) "Branch" includes a separately incorporated foreign branch of a bank.

(8) "Burden of establishing" a fact means the burden of persuading the trier of fact that the existence of the fact is more probable than its nonexistence.

(9) "Buyer in ordinary course of business" means a person that buys goods in good faith, without knowledge that the sale violates the rights of another person in the goods, and in the ordinary course from a person, other than a pawnbroker, in the business of selling goods of that kind. A person buys goods in the ordinary course if the sale to the person comports with the usual or customary practices in the kind of business in which the seller is engaged or with the seller's own usual or customary practices. A person that sells oil, gas, or other minerals at the wellhead or minehead is a person in the business of selling goods of that kind. A buyer in ordinary course of business may buy for cash, by exchange of other property, or on secured or unsecured credit, and may acquire goods or documents of title under a pre-existing contract for sale. Only a buyer that takes possession of the goods or has a right to recover the goods from the seller under Article 2 may be a buyer in ordinary course of business. A person that acquires goods in a transfer in bulk or as security for or in total or partial satisfaction of a money debt is not a buyer in ordinary course of business.

(10) "Conspicuous", with reference to a term, means so written, displayed, or presented that a reasonable person against which it is to operate ought to have noticed it. Whether a term is "conspicuous" or not is a decision for the court. Conspicuous terms include the following:

(A) a heading in capitals equal to or greater in size than the surrounding text, or in contrasting type, font, or color to the surrounding text of the same or lesser size; and

(B) language in the body of a record or display in larger type than the surrounding text, or in contrasting type, font, or color to the surrounding text of the same size, or set off from surrounding text of the same size by symbols or other marks that call attention to the language.

(11) "Consumer" means an individual who enters into a transaction primarily for personal, family, or household purposes.

(12) "Contract", as distinguished from "agreement", means the total legal obligation that results from the parties' agreement as determined by [the Uniform Commercial Code] as supplemented by any other laws.

(13) "Creditor" includes a general creditor, a secured creditor, a lien creditor and any representative of creditors, including an assignee for the benefit of creditors, a trustee in bankruptcy, a receiver in equity and an executor or administrator of an insolvent debtor's or assignor's estate.

(14) "Defendant" includes a person in the position of defendant in a counterclaim, cross-action, or third-party claim.

(15) "Delivery" with respect to an electronic document of title means voluntary transfer of control and with respect to an instrument, a tangible document of title, or chattel paper means voluntary transfer of possession.

(16) "Document of title" means a record (i) that in regular course of business or financing is treated as adequately evidencing that the person in possession or control of the record is entitled to receive, control, hold, and dispose of the record and the goods the record covers and (ii) that purports to be issued by or addressed to a bailee and to cover goods in the bailee's possession which are either identified or are fungible portions of an identified mass. The term includes a bill of lading, transport document, dock warrant, dock receipt, warehouse receipt, and order for delivery of goods. An electronic document of title means a document of title evidenced by a record consisting of information stored in an electronic medium. A tangible document of title means a document of title evidenced by a record consisting of information that is inscribed on a tangible medium.

(17) "Fault" means a default, breach, or wrongful act or omission.

(18) "Fungible goods" means:

(A) goods of which any unit, by nature or usage of trade, is the equivalent of any other like unit; or

(B) goods that by agreement are treated as equivalent.

(19) "Genuine" means free of forgery or counterfeiting.

(20) "Good faith," except as otherwise provided in Article 5, means honesty in fact and the observance of reasonable commercial standards of fair dealing.

(21) "Holder" means:

(A) the person in possession of a negotiable instrument that is payable either to bearer or to an identified person that is the person in possession;

(B) the person in possession of a negotiable tangible document of title if the goods are deliverable either to bearer or to the order of the person in possession; or

(C) the person in control of a negotiable electronic document of title.

(22) "Insolvency proceeding" includes an assignment for the benefit of creditors or other proceeding intended to liquidate or rehabilitate the estate of the person involved.

(23) "Insolvent" means:

(A) having generally ceased to pay debts in the ordinary course of business other than as a result of bona fide dispute;

(B) being unable to pay debts as they become due; or

(C) being insolvent within the meaning of federal bankruptcy law.

(24) "Money" means a medium of exchange currently authorized or adopted by a domestic or foreign government. The term includes a monetary unit of account established by an intergovernmental organization or by agreement between two or more countries.

(25) "Organization" means a person other than an individual.

(26) "Party", as distinguished from "third party", means a person that has engaged in a transaction or made an agreement subject to [the Uniform Commercial Code].

(27) "Person" means an individual, corporation, business trust, estate, trust, partnership, limited liability company, association, joint venture, government, governmental subdivision, agency, or instrumentality, public corporation, or any other legal or commercial entity.

(28) "Present value" means the amount as of a date certain of one or more sums payable in the future, discounted to the date certain by use of either an interest rate specified by the parties if that rate is not manifestly unreasonable at the time the transaction is entered into or, if an interest rate is not so specified, a commercially reasonable rate that takes into account the facts and circumstances at the time the transaction is entered into.

(29) "Purchase" means taking by sale, lease, discount, negotiation, mortgage, pledge, lien, security interest, issue or reissue, gift, or any other voluntary transaction creating an interest in property.

(30) "Purchaser" means a person that takes by purchase.

(31) "Record" means information that is inscribed on a tangible medium or that is stored in an electronic or other medium and is retrievable in perceivable form.

(32) "Remedy" means any remedial right to which an aggrieved party is entitled with or without resort to a tribunal.

(33) "Representative" means a person empowered to act for another, including an agent, an officer of a corporation or association, and a trustee, executor, or administrator of an estate.

(34) "Right" includes remedy.

(35) "Security interest" means an interest in personal property or fixtures which secures payment or performance of an obligation. "Security interest" includes any interest of a consignor and a buyer of accounts, chattel paper, a payment intangible, or a promissory note in a transaction that is subject to Article 9. "Security interest" does not include the special property interest of a buyer of goods on identification of those goods to a contract for sale under Section 2–401, but a buyer may also acquire a "security interest" by complying with Article 9. Except as otherwise provided in Section 2–505, the right of a seller or lessor of goods under Article 2 or 2A to retain or acquire possession of the goods is not a "security interest", but a seller or lessor may also acquire a "security interest" by complying with Article 9. The retention or reservation of title by a seller of goods notwithstanding shipment or delivery to the buyer under Section 2–401 is limited in effect to a reservation of a "security interest." Whether a transaction in the form of a lease creates a "security interest" is determined pursuant to Section 1–203.

(36) "Send" in connection with a writing, record, or notice means:

    (A) to deposit in the mail or deliver for transmission by any other usual means of communication with postage or cost of transmission provided for and properly addressed and, in the case of an instrument, to an address specified thereon or otherwise agreed, or if there be none to any address reasonable under the circumstances; or

    (B) in any other way to cause to be received any record or notice within the time it would have arrived if properly sent.

(37) "Signed" includes using any symbol executed or adopted with present intention to adopt or accept a writing.

(38) "State" means a State of the United States, the District of Columbia, Puerto Rico, the United States Virgin Islands, or any territory or insular possession subject to the jurisdiction of the United States.

(39) "Surety" includes a guarantor or other secondary obligor.

(40) "Term" means a portion of an agreement that relates to a particular matter.

(41) "Unauthorized signature" means a signature made without actual, implied, or apparent authority. The term includes a forgery.

(42) "Warehouse receipt" means a document of title issued by a person engaged in the business of storing goods for hire.

(43) "Writing" includes printing, typewriting, or any other intentional reduction to tangible form. "Written" has a corresponding meaning. As amended in 2003.

§ 1–202. Notice; Knowledge.

(a) Subject to subsection (f), a person has "notice" of a fact if the person:

    (1) has actual knowledge of it;

    (2) has received a notice or notification of it; or

    (3) from all the facts and circumstances known to the person at the time in question, has reason to know that it exists.

(b) "Knowledge" means actual knowledge. "Knows" has a corresponding meaning.

(c) "Discover", "learn", or words of similar import refer to knowledge rather than to reason to know.

(d) A person "notifies" or "gives" a notice or notification to another person by taking such steps as may be reasonably required to inform the other person in ordinary course, whether or not the other person actually comes to know of it.

(e) Subject to subsection (f), a person "receives" a notice or notification when:

    (1) it comes to that person's attention; or

    (2) it is duly delivered in a form reasonable under the circumstances at the place of business through which the contract was made or at another location held out by that person as the place for receipt of such communications.

(f) Notice, knowledge, or a notice or notification received by an organization is effective for a particular transaction from the time it is brought to the attention of the individual conducting that transaction and, in any event, from the time it would have been brought to the individual's attention if the organization had exercised due diligence. An organization exercises due diligence if it maintains reasonable routines for communicating significant information to the person conducting the transaction and there is reasonable compliance with the routines. Due diligence does not require an individual acting for the organization to communicate information unless the communication is part of the individual's regular duties or the individual has reason to know of the transaction and that the transaction would be materially affected by the information.

§ 1–203. Lease Distinguished from Security Interest.

(a) Whether a transaction in the form of a lease creates a lease or security interest is determined by the facts of each case.

(b) A transaction in the form of a lease creates a security interest if the consideration that the lessee is to pay the lessor for the right to possession and use of the goods is an obligation for the term of the lease and is not subject to termination by the lessee, and:

    (1) the original term of the lease is equal to or greater than the remaining economic life of the goods;

    (2) the lessee is bound to renew the lease for the remaining economic life of the goods or is bound to become the owner of the goods;

    (3) the lessee has an option to renew the lease for the remaining economic life of the goods for no additional consideration or for nominal additional consideration upon compliance with the lease agreement; or

    (4) the lessee has an option to become the owner of the goods for no additional consideration or for nominal additional consideration upon compliance with the lease agreement.

(c) A transaction in the form of a lease does not create a security interest merely because:

    (1) the present value of the consideration the lessee is obligated to pay the lessor for the right to possession and use of the goods is substantially equal to or is greater than the fair market value of the goods at the time the lease is entered into;

    (2) the lessee assumes risk of loss of the goods;

(3) the lessee agrees to pay, with respect to the goods, taxes, insurance, filing, recording, or registration fees, or service or maintenance costs;

(4) the lessee has an option to renew the lease or to become the owner of the goods;

(5) the lessee has an option to renew the lease for a fixed rent that is equal to or greater than the reasonably predictable fair market rent for the use of the goods for the term of the renewal at the time the option is to be performed; or

(6) the lessee has an option to become the owner of the goods for a fixed price that is equal to or greater than the reasonably predictable fair market value of the goods at the time the option is to be performed.

(d) Additional consideration is nominal if it is less than the lessee's reasonably predictable cost of performing under the lease agreement if the option is not exercised. Additional consideration is not nominal if:

(1) when the option to renew the lease is granted to the lessee, the rent is stated to be the fair market rent for the use of the goods for the term of the renewal determined at the time the option is to be performed; or

(2) when the option to become the owner of the goods is granted to the lessee, the price is stated to be the fair market value of the goods determined at the time the option is to be performed.

(e) The "remaining economic life of the goods" and "reasonably predictable" fair market rent, fair market value, or cost of performing under the lease agreement must be determined with reference to the facts and circumstances at the time the transaction is entered into.

§ 1–204. Value.

Except as otherwise provided in Articles 3, 4, [and] 5, [and 6], a person gives value for rights if the person acquires them:

(1) in return for a binding commitment to extend credit or for the extension of immediately available credit, whether or not drawn upon and whether or not a charge-back is provided for in the event of difficulties in collection;

(2) as security for, or in total or partial satisfaction of, a preexisting claim;

(3) by accepting delivery under a preexisting contract for purchase; or

(4) in return for any consideration sufficient to support a simple contract.

§ 1–205. Reasonable Time; Seasonableness.

(a) Whether a time for taking an action required by [the Uniform Commercial Code] is reasonable depends on the nature, purpose, and circumstances of the action.

(b) An action is taken seasonably if it is taken at or within the time agreed or, if no time is agreed, at or within a reasonable time.

§ 1–206. Presumptions.

Whenever [the Uniform Commercial Code] creates a "presumption" with respect to a fact, or provides that a fact is "presumed," the trier of fact must find the existence of the fact unless and until evidence is introduced that supports a finding of its nonexistence.

Part 3—Territorial Applicability and General Rules

§ 1–301. Territorial Applicability; Parties' Power to Choose Applicable Law.

(a) In this section:

(1) "Domestic transaction" means a transaction other than an international transaction.

(2) "International transaction" means a transaction that bears a reasonable relation to a country other than the United States.

(b) This section applies to a transaction to the extent that it is governed by another article of the [Uniform Commercial Code].

(c) Except as otherwise provided in this section:

(1) an agreement by parties to a domestic transaction that any or all of their rights and obligations are to be determined by the law of this State or of another State is effective, whether or not the transaction bears a relation to the State designated; and

(2) an agreement by parties to an international transaction that any or all of their rights and obligations are to be determined by the law of this State or of another State or country is effective, whether or not the transaction bears a relation to the State or country designated.

(d) In the absence of an agreement effective under subsection (c), and except as provided in subsections (e) and (g), the rights and obligations of the parties are determined by the law that would be selected by application of this State's conflict of laws principles.

(e) If one of the parties to a transaction is a consumer, the following rules apply:

(1) An agreement referred to in subsection (c) is not effective unless the transaction bears a reasonable relation to the State or country designated.

(2) Application of the law of the State or country determined pursuant to subsection (c) or (d) may not deprive the consumer of the protection of any rule of law governing a matter within the scope of this section, which both is protective of consumers and may not be varied by agreement: (A) of the State or country in which the consumer principally resides, unless subparagraph (B) applies; or (B) if the transaction is a sale of goods, of the State or country in which the consumer both makes the contract and take delivery of those goods, if such State or country is not the State or country in which the consumer principally resides.

(f) An agreement otherwise effective under subsection (c) is not effective to the extent that application of the law of the State or country designated would be contrary to a fundamental policy of the State or country whose law would govern in the absence of agreement under subsection (d).

(g) To the extent that [the Uniform Commercial Code] governs a transaction, if one of the following provisions of [the Uniform Commercial Code] specifies the applicable law, that provision governs and a contrary agreement is effective only to the extent permitted by the law so specified: (1) Section 2–402; (2) Sections 2A–105 and 2A–106; (3) Section 4–102; (4) Section 4A–507; (5) Section 5–116; [(6) Section 6–103;] (7) Section 8–110; (8) Sections 9–301 through 9–307.

§ 1–302. Variation by Agreement.

(a) Except as otherwise provided in subsection (b) or elsewhere in [the Uniform Commercial Code], the effect of provisions of [the Uniform Commercial Code] may be varied by agreement.

(b) The obligations of good faith, diligence, reasonableness, and care prescribed by [the Uniform Commercial Code] may not be disclaimed by agreement. The parties, by agreement, may determine the standards by which the performance of those obligations is to be measured if those standards are not manifestly unreasonable.

Whenever [the Uniform Commercial Code] requires an action to be taken within a reasonable time, a time that is not manifestly unreasonable may be fixed by agreement.

(c) The presence in certain provisions of [the Uniform Commercial Code] of the phrase "unless otherwise agreed", or words of similar import, does not imply that the effect of other provisions may not be varied by agreement under this section.

§ 1–303. Course of Performance, Course of Dealing, and Usage of Trade.

(a) A "course of performance" is a sequence of conduct between the parties to a particular transaction that exists if:

    (1) the agreement of the parties with respect to the transaction involves repeated occasions for performance by a party; and

    (2) the other party, with knowledge of the nature of the performance and opportunity for objection to it, accepts the performance or acquiesces in it without objection.

(b) A "course of dealing" is a sequence of conduct concerning previous transactions between the parties to a particular transaction that is fairly to be regarded as establishing a common basis of understanding for interpreting their expressions and other conduct.

(c) A "usage of trade" is any practice or method of dealing having such regularity of observance in a place, vocation, or trade as to justify an expectation that it will be observed with respect to the transaction in question. The existence and scope of such a usage must be proved as facts. If it is established that such a usage is embodied in a trade code or similar record, the interpretation of the record is a question of law.

(d) A course of performance or course of dealing between the parties or usage of trade in the vocation or trade in which they are engaged or of which they are or should be aware is relevant in ascertaining the meaning of the parties' agreement, may give particular meaning to specific terms of the agreement, and may supplement or qualify the terms of the agreement. A usage of trade applicable in the place in which part of the performance under the agreement is to occur may be so utilized as to that part of the performance.

(e) Except as otherwise provided in subsection (f), the express terms of an agreement and any applicable course of performance, course of dealing, or usage of trade must be construed whenever reasonable as consistent with each other. If such a construction is unreasonable:

    (1) express terms prevail over course of performance, course of dealing, and usage of trade;

    (2) course of performance prevails over course of dealing and usage of trade; and

    (3) course of dealing prevails over usage of trade.

(f) Subject to Section 2–209 and Section 2A–208, a course of performance is relevant to show a waiver or modification of any term inconsistent with the course of performance.

(g) Evidence of a relevant usage of trade offered by one party is not admissible unless that party has given the other party notice that the court finds sufficient to prevent unfair surprise to the other party.

§ 1–304. Obligation of Good Faith.

Every contract or duty within [the Uniform Commercial Code] imposes an obligation of good faith in its performance and enforcement.

§ 1–305. Remedies to be Liberally Administered.

(a) The remedies provided by [the Uniform Commercial Code] must be liberally administered to the end that the aggrieved party may be put in as good a position as if the other party had fully performed but neither consequential or special damages nor penal damages may be had except as specifically provided in [the Uniform Commercial Code] or by other rule of law.

(b) Any right or obligation declared by [the Uniform Commercial Code] is enforceable by action unless the provision declaring it specifies a different and limited effect.

§ 1–306. Waiver or Renunciation of Claim or Right After Breach.

A claim or right arising out of an alleged breach may be discharged in whole or in part without consideration by agreement of the aggrieved party in an authenticated record.

§ 1–307. *Prima Facie* Evidence by Third-Party Documents.

A document in due form purporting to be a bill of lading, policy or certificate of insurance, official weigher's or inspector's certificate, consular invoice, or any other document authorized or required by the contract to be issued by a third party is *prima facie* evidence of its own authenticity and genuineness and of the facts stated in the document by the third party.

§ 1–308. Performance or Acceptance Under Reservation of Rights.

(a) A party that with explicit reservation of rights performs or promises performance or assents to performance in a manner demanded or offered by the other party does not thereby prejudice the rights reserved. Such words as "without prejudice," "under protest," or the like are sufficient.

(b) Subsection (a) does not apply to an accord and satisfaction.

§ 1–309. Option to Accelerate at Will.

A term providing that one party or that party's successor in interest may accelerate payment or performance or require collateral or additional collateral "at will" or when the party "deems itself insecure," or words of similar import, means that the party has power to do so only if that party in good faith believes that the prospect of payment or performance is impaired. The burden of establishing lack of good faith is on the party against which the power has been exercised.

§ 1–310. Subordinated Obligations.

An obligation may be issued as subordinated to performance of another obligation of the person obligated, or a creditor may subordinate its right to performance of an obligation by agreement with either the person obligated or another creditor of the person obligated. Subordination does not create a security interest as against either the common debtor or a subordinated creditor.

ARTICLE 2: SALES

Part 1—Short Title, General Construction and Subject Matter

§ 2–101. Short Title.

This Article shall be known and may be cited as Uniform Commercial Code—Sales.

§ 2–102. Scope; Certain Security and Other Transactions Excluded From This Article.

Unless the context otherwise requires, this Article applies to transactions in goods; it does not apply to any transaction which although in the form of an unconditional contract to sell or present sale is intended to operate only as a security transaction nor does this Article impair or repeal any statute regulating sales to consumers, farmers or other specified classes of buyers.

§ 2–103. Definitions and Index of Definitions.

(1) In this Article unless the context otherwise requires

(a) "Buyer" means a person who buys or contracts to buy goods.

(b) "Good faith" in the case of a merchant means honesty in fact and the observance of reasonable commercial standards of fair dealing in the trade.

(c) "Receipt" of goods means taking physical possession of them.

(d) "Seller" means a person who sells or contracts to sell goods.

(2) Other definitions applying to this Article or to specified Parts thereof, and the sections in which they appear are:

"Acceptance". Section 2–606.
"Banker's credit". Section 2–325.
"Between merchants". Section 2–104.
"Cancellation". Section 2–106(4).
"Commercial unit". Section 2–105.
"Confirmed credit". Section 2–325.
"Conforming to contract". Section 2–106.
"Contract for sale". Section 2–106.
"Cover". Section 2–712.
"Entrusting". Section 2–403.
"Financing agency". Section 2–104.
"Future goods". Section 2–105.
"Goods". Section 2–105.
"Identification". Section 2–501.
"Installment contract". Section 2–612.
"Letter of Credit". Section 2–325.
"Lot". Section 2–105.
"Merchant". Section 2–104.
"Overseas". Section 2–323.
"Person in position of seller". Section 2–707.
"Present sale". Section 2–106.
"Sale". Section 2–106.
"Sale on approval". Section 2–326.
"Sale or return". Section 2–326.
"Termination". Section 2–106.

(3) The following definitions in other Articles apply to this Article:

"Check". Section 3–104.
"Consignee". Section 7–102.
"Consignor". Section 7–102.
"Consumer goods". Section 9–109.
"Dishonor". Section 3–507.
"Draft". Section 3–104.

(4) In addition Article 1 contains general definitions and principles of construction and interpretation applicable throughout this Article.

As amended in 1994 and 1999.

§ 2–104. Definitions: "Merchant"; "Between Merchants"; "Financing Agency".

(1) "Merchant" means a person who deals in goods of the kind or otherwise by his occupation holds himself out as having knowledge or skill peculiar to the practices or goods involved in the transaction or to whom such knowledge or skill may be attributed by his employment of an agent or broker or other intermediary who by his occupation holds himself out as having such knowledge or skill.

(2) "Financing agency" means a bank, finance company or other person who in the ordinary course of business makes advances against goods or documents of title or who by arrangement with either the seller or the buyer intervenes in ordinary course to make or collect payment due or claimed under the contract for sale, as by purchasing or paying the seller's draft or making advances against it or by merely taking it for collection whether or not documents of title accompany the draft. "Financing agency" includes also a bank or other person who similarly intervenes between persons who are in the position of seller and buyer in respect to the goods (Section 2–707).

(3) "Between merchants" means in any transaction with respect to which both parties are chargeable with the knowledge or skill of merchants.

§ 2–105. Definitions: Transferability; "Goods"; "Future" Goods; "Lot"; "Commercial Unit".

(1) "Goods" means all things (including specially manufactured goods) which are movable at the time of identification to the contract for sale other than the money in which the price is to be paid, investment securities (Article 8) and things in action. "Goods" also includes the unborn young of animals and growing crops and other identified things attached to realty as described in the section on goods to be severed from realty (Section 2–107).

(2) Goods must be both existing and identified before any interest in them can pass. Goods which are not both existing and identified are "future" goods. A purported present sale of future goods or of any interest therein operates as a contract to sell.

(3) There may be a sale of a part interest in existing identified goods.

(4) An undivided share in an identified bulk of fungible goods is sufficiently identified to be sold although the quantity of the bulk is not determined. Any agreed proportion of such a bulk or any quantity thereof agreed upon by number, weight or other measure may to the extent of the seller's interest in the bulk be sold to the buyer who then becomes an owner in common.

(5) "Lot" means a parcel or a single article which is the subject matter of a separate sale or delivery, whether or not it is sufficient to perform the contract.

(6) "Commercial unit" means such a unit of goods as by commercial usage is a single whole for purposes of sale and division of which materially impairs its character or value on the market or in use. A commercial unit may be a single article (as a machine) or a set of articles (as a suite of furniture or an assortment of sizes) or a quantity (as a bale, gross, or carload) or any other unit treated in use or in the relevant market as a single whole.

§ 2–106. Definitions: "Contract"; "Agreement"; "Contract for Sale"; "Sale"; "Present Sale"; "Conforming to Contract"; "Termination"; "Cancellation".

(1) In this Article unless the context otherwise requires "contract" and "agreement" are limited to those relating to the present or future sale of goods. "Contract for sale" includes both a present sale of goods and a contract to sell goods at a future time. A "sale" consists in the passing of title from the seller to the buyer for a price (Section 2–401). A "present sale" means a sale which is accomplished by the making of the contract.

(2) Goods or conduct including any part of a performance are "conforming" or conform to the contract when they are in accordance with the obligations under the contract.

(3) "Termination" occurs when either party pursuant to a power created by agreement or law puts an end to the contract otherwise than for its breach. On "termination" all obligations which are still executory on both sides are discharged but any right based on prior breach or performance survives.

(4) "Cancellation" occurs when either party puts an end to the contract for breach by the other and its effect is the same as that of "termination" except that the cancelling party also retains any remedy for breach of the whole contract or any unperformed balance.

§ 2–107. Goods to Be Severed From Realty: Recording.

(1) A contract for the sale of minerals or the like (including oil and gas) or a structure or its materials to be removed from realty is a contract for the sale of goods within this Article if they are to be severed by the seller but until severance a purported present sale thereof which is not effective as a transfer of an interest in land is effective only as a contract to sell.

(2) A contract for the sale apart from the land of growing crops or other things attached to realty and capable of severance without material harm thereto but not described in subsection (1) or of timber to be cut is a contract for the sale of goods within this Article whether the subject matter is to be severed by the buyer or by the seller even though it forms part of the realty at the time of contracting, and the parties can by identification effect a present sale before severance.

(3) The provisions of this section are subject to any third party rights provided by the law relating to realty records, and the contract for sale may be executed and recorded as a document transferring an interest in land and shall then constitute notice to third parties of the buyer's rights under the contract for sale.

As amended in 1972.

Part 2—Form, Formation and Readjustment of Contract

§ 2–201. Formal Requirements; Statute of Frauds.

(1) Except as otherwise provided in this section a contract for the sale of goods for the price of $500 or more is not enforceable by way of action or defense unless there is some writing sufficient to indicate that a contract for sale has been made between the parties and signed by the party against whom enforcement is sought or by his authorized agent or broker. A writing is not insufficient because it omits or incorrectly states a term agreed upon but the contract is not enforceable under this paragraph beyond the quantity of goods shown in such writing.

(2) Between merchants if within a reasonable time a writing in confirmation of the contract and sufficient against the sender is received and the party receiving it has reason to know its contents, its satisfies the requirements of subsection (1) against such party unless written notice of objection to its contents is given within ten days after it is received.

(3) A contract which does not satisfy the requirements of subsection (1) but which is valid in other respects is enforceable

    (a) if the goods are to be specially manufactured for the buyer and are not suitable for sale to others in the ordinary course of the seller's business and the seller, before notice of repudiation is received and under circumstances which reasonably indicate that the goods are for the buyer, has made either a substantial beginning of their manufacture or commitments for their procurement; or

    (b) if the party against whom enforcement is sought admits in his pleading, testimony or otherwise in court that a contract for sale was made, but the contract is not enforceable under this provision beyond the quantity of goods admitted; or

    (c) with respect to goods for which payment has been made and accepted or which have been received and accepted (Sec. 2–606).

§ 2–202. Final Written Expression: Parol or Extrinsic Evidence.

Terms with respect to which the confirmatory memoranda of the parties agree or which are otherwise set forth in a writing intended by the parties as a final expression of their agreement with respect to such terms as are included therein may not be contradicted by evidence of any prior agreement or of a contemporaneous oral agreement but may be explained or supplemented

    (a) by course of dealing or usage of trade (Section 1–205) or by course of performance (Section 2–208); and

    (b) by evidence of consistent additional terms unless the court finds the writing to have been intended also as a complete and exclusive statement of the terms of the agreement.

§ 2–203. Seals Inoperative.

The affixing of a seal to a writing evidencing a contract for sale or an offer to buy or sell goods does not constitute the writing a sealed instrument and the law with respect to sealed instruments does not apply to such a contract or offer.

§ 2–204. Formation in General.

(1) A contract for sale of goods may be made in any manner sufficient to show agreement, including conduct by both parties which recognizes the existence of such a contract.

(2) An agreement sufficient to constitute a contract for sale may be found even though the moment of its making is undetermined.

(3) Even though one or more terms are left open a contract for sale does not fail for indefiniteness if the parties have intended to make a contract and there is a reasonably certain basis for giving an appropriate remedy.

§ 2–205. Firm Offers.

An offer by a merchant to buy or sell goods in a signed writing which by its terms gives assurance that it will be held open is not revocable, for lack of consideration, during the time stated or if no time is stated for a reasonable time, but in no event may such period of irrevocability exceed three months; but any such term of assurance on a form supplied by the offeree must be separately signed by the offeror.

§ 2–206. Offer and Acceptance in Formation of Contract.

(1) Unless other unambiguously indicated by the language or circumstances

    (a) an offer to make a contract shall be construed as inviting acceptance in any manner and by any medium reasonable in the circumstances;

    (b) an order or other offer to buy goods for prompt or current shipment shall be construed as inviting acceptance either by a prompt promise to ship or by the prompt or current shipment of conforming or nonconforming goods, but such a shipment of non-conforming goods does not constitute an acceptance if the seller seasonably notifies the buyer that the shipment is offered only as an accommodation to the buyer.

(2) Where the beginning of a requested performance is a reasonable mode of acceptance an offeror who is not notified of acceptance within a reasonable time may treat the offer as having lapsed before acceptance.

§ 2–207. Additional Terms in Acceptance or Confirmation.

(1) A definite and seasonable expression of acceptance or a written confirmation which is sent within a reasonable time operates as an acceptance even though it states terms additional to or different from those offered or agreed upon, unless acceptance is expressly made conditional on assent to the additional or different terms.

(2) The additional terms are to be construed as proposals for addition to the contract. Between merchants such terms become part of the contract unless:

    (a) the offer expressly limits acceptance to the terms of the offer;

    (b) they materially alter it; or

    (c) notification of objection to them has already been given or is given within a reasonable time after notice of them is received.

(3) Conduct by both parties which recognizes the existence of a contract is sufficient to establish a contract for sale although the writings of the parties do not otherwise establish a contract. In such case the terms of the particular contract consist of those terms on which the writings of the parties agree, together with any supplementary terms incorporated under any other provisions of this Act.

§ 2–208. Course of Performance or Practical Construction.

(1) Where the contract for sale involves repeated occasions for performance by either party with knowledge of the nature of the performance and opportunity for objection to it by the other, any course of performance accepted or acquiesced in without objection shall be relevant to determine the meaning of the agreement.

(2) The express terms of the agreement and any such course of performance, as well as any course of dealing and usage of trade, shall be construed whenever reasonable as consistent with each other; but when such construction is unreasonable, express terms shall control course of performance and course of performance shall control both course of dealing and usage of trade (Section 1–205).

(3) Subject to the provisions of the next section on modification and waiver, such course of performance shall be relevant to show a waiver or modification of any term inconsistent with such course of performance.

§ 2–209. Modification, Rescission and Waiver.

(1) An agreement modifying a contract within this Article needs no consideration to be binding.

(2) A signed agreement which excludes modification or rescission except by a signed writing cannot be otherwise modified or rescinded, but except as between merchants such a requirement on a form supplied by the merchant must be separately signed by the other party.

(3) The requirements of the statute of frauds section of this Article (Section 2–201) must be satisfied if the contract as modified is within its provisions.

(4) Although an attempt at modification or rescission does not satisfy the requirements of subsection (2) or (3) it can operate as a waiver.

(5) A party who has made a waiver affecting an executory portion of the contract may retract the waiver by reasonable notification received by the other party that strict performance will be required of any term waived, unless the retraction would be unjust in view of a material change of position in reliance on the waiver.

§ 2–210. Delegation of Performance; Assignment of Rights.

(1) A party may perform his duty through a delegate unless otherwise agreed or unless the other party has a substantial interest in having his original promisor perform or control the acts required by the contract. No delegation of performance relieves the party delegating of any duty to perform or any liability for breach.

(2) Except as otherwise provided in Section 9–406, unless otherwise agreed, all rights of either seller or buyer can be assigned except where the assignment would materially change the duty of the other party, or increase materially the burden or risk imposed on him by his contract, or impair materially his chance of obtaining return performance. A right to damages for breach of the whole contract or a right arising out of the assignor's due performance of his entire obligation can be assigned despite agreement otherwise.

(3) The creation, attachment, perfection, or enforcement of a security interest in the seller's interest under a contract is not a transfer that materially changes the duty of or increases materially the burden or risk imposed on the buyer or impairs materially the buyer's chance of obtaining return performance within the purview of subsection (2) unless, and then only to the extent that, enforcement actually results in a delegation of material performance of the seller. Even in that event, the creation, attachment, perfection, and enforcement of the security interest remain effective, but (i) the seller is liable to the buyer for damages caused by the delegation to the extent that the damages could not reasonably by prevented by the buyer, and (ii) a court having jurisdiction may grant other appropriate relief, including cancellation of the contract for sale or an injunction against enforcement of the security interest or consummation of the enforcement.

(4) Unless the circumstances indicate the contrary a prohibition of assignment of "the contract" is to be construed as barring only the delegation to the assignee of the assignor's performance.

(5) An assignment of "the contract" or of "all my rights under the contract" or an assignment in similar general terms is an assignment of rights and unless the language or the circumstances (as in an assignment for security) indicate the contrary, it is a delegation of performance of the duties of the assignor and its acceptance by the assignee constitutes a promise by him to perform those duties. This promise is enforceable by either the assignor or the other party to the original contract.

(6) The other party may treat any assignment which delegates performance as creating reasonable grounds for insecurity and may without prejudice to his rights against the assignor demand assurances from the assignee (Section 2–609).

As amended in 1999.

Part 3—General Obligation and Construction of Contract

§ 2–301. General Obligations of Parties.

The obligation of the seller is to transfer and deliver and that of the buyer is to accept and pay in accordance with the contract.

§ 2–302. Unconscionable Contract or Clause.

(1) If the court as a matter of law finds the contract or any clause of the contract to have been unconscionable at the time it was made the court may refuse to enforce the contract, or it may enforce the remainder of the contract without the unconscionable clause, or it may so limit the application of any unconscionable clause as to avoid any unconscionable result.

(2) When it is claimed or appears to the court that the contract or any clause thereof may be unconscionable the parties shall be afforded a reasonable opportunity to present evidence as to its commercial setting, purpose and effect to aid the court in making the determination.

§ 2–303. Allocations or Division of Risks.

Where this Article allocates a risk or a burden as between the parties "unless otherwise agreed", the agreement may not only shift the allocation but may also divide the risk or burden.

§ 2–304. Price Payable in Money, Goods, Realty, or Otherwise.

(1) The price can be made payable in money or otherwise. If it is payable in whole or in part in goods each party is a seller of the goods which he is to transfer.

(2) Even though all or part of the price is payable in an interest in realty the transfer of the goods and the seller's obligations with reference to them are subject to this Article, but not the transfer of the interest in realty or the transferor's obligations in connection therewith.

§ 2–305. Open Price Term.

(1) The parties if they so intend can conclude a contract for sale even though the price is not settled. In such a case the price is a reasonable price at the time for delivery if

(a) nothing is said as to price; or

(b) the price is left to be agreed by the parties and they fail to agree; or

(c) the price is to be fixed in terms of some agreed market or other standard as set or recorded by a third person or agency and it is not so set or recorded.

(2) A price to be fixed by the seller or by the buyer means a price for him to fix in good faith.

(3) When a price left to be fixed otherwise than by agreement of the parties fails to be fixed through fault of one party the other may at his option treat the contract as cancelled or himself fix a reasonable price.

(4) Where, however, the parties intend not to be bound unless the price be fixed or agreed and it is not fixed or agreed there is no contract. In such a case the buyer must return any goods already received or if unable so to do must pay their reasonable value at the time of delivery and the seller must return any portion of the price paid on account.

§ 2–306. Output, Requirements and Exclusive Dealings.

(1) A term which measures the quantity by the output of the seller or the requirements of the buyer means such actual output or requirements as may occur in good faith, except that no quantity unreasonably disproportionate to any stated estimate or in the absence of a stated estimate to any normal or otherwise comparable prior output or requirements may be tendered or demanded.

(2) A lawful agreement by either the seller or the buyer for exclusive dealing in the kind of goods concerned imposes unless otherwise agreed an obligation by the seller to use best efforts to supply the goods and by the buyer to use best efforts to promote their sale.

§ 2–307. Delivery in Single Lot or Several Lots.

Unless otherwise agreed all goods called for by a contract for sale must be tendered in a single delivery and payment is due only on such tender but where the circumstances give either party the right to make or demand delivery in lots the price if it can be apportioned may be demanded for each lot.

§ 2–308. Absence of Specified Place for Delivery.

Unless otherwise agreed

(a) the place for delivery of goods is the seller's place of business or if he has none his residence; but

(b) in a contract for sale of identified goods which to the knowledge of the parties at the time of contracting are in some other place, that place is the place for their delivery; and

(c) documents of title may be delivered through customary banking channels.

§ 2–309. Absence of Specific Time Provisions; Notice of Termination.

(1) The time for shipment or delivery or any other action under a contract if not provided in this Article or agreed upon shall be a reasonable time.

(2) Where the contract provides for successive performances but is indefinite in duration it is valid for a reasonable time but unless otherwise agreed may be terminated at any time by either party.

(3) Termination of a contract by one party except on the happening of an agreed event requires that reasonable notification be received by the other party and an agreement dispensing with notification is invalid if its operation would be unconscionable.

§ 2–310. Open Time for Payment or Running of Credit; Authority to Ship Under Reservation.

Unless otherwise agreed

(a) payment is due at the time and place at which the buyer is to receive the goods even though the place of shipment is the place of delivery; and

(b) if the seller is authorized to send the goods he may ship them under reservation, and may tender the documents of title, but the buyer may inspect the goods after their arrival before payment is due unless such inspection is inconsistent with the terms of the contract (Section 2–513); and

(c) if delivery is authorized and made by way of documents of title otherwise than by subsection (b) then payment is due at the time and place at which the buyer is to receive the documents regardless of where the goods are to be received; and

(d) where the seller is required or authorized to ship the goods on credit the credit period runs from the time of shipment but post-dating the invoice or delaying its dispatch will correspondingly delay the starting of the credit period.

§ 2–311. Options and Cooperation Respecting Performance.

(1) An agreement for sale which is otherwise sufficiently definite (subsection (3) of Section 2–204) to be a contract is not made invalid by the fact that it leaves particulars of performance to be specified by one of the parties. Any such specification must be made in good faith and within limits set by commercial reasonableness.

(2) Unless otherwise agreed specifications relating to assortment of the goods are at the buyer's option and except as otherwise provided in subsections (1)(c) and (3) of Section 2–319 specifications or arrangements relating to shipment are at the seller's option.

(3) Where such specification would materially affect the other party's performance but is not seasonably made or where one party's cooperation is necessary to the agreed performance of the other but is not seasonably forthcoming, the other party in addition to all other remedies

(a) is excused for any resulting delay in his own performance; and

(b) may also either proceed to perform in any reasonable manner or after the time for a material part of his own performance treat the failure to specify or to cooperate as a breach by failure to deliver or accept the goods.

§ 2–312. Warranty of Title and Against Infringement; Buyer's Obligation Against Infringement.

(1) Subject to subsection (2) there is in a contract for sale a warranty by the seller that

(a) the title conveyed shall be good, and its transfer rightful; and

(b) the goods shall be delivered free from any security interest or other lien or encumbrance of which the buyer at the time of contracting has no knowledge.

(2) A warranty under subsection (1) will be excluded or modified only by specific language or by circumstances which give the buyer reason to know that the person selling does not claim title in himself or that he is purporting to sell only such right or title as he or a third person may have.

(3) Unless otherwise agreed a seller who is a merchant regularly dealing in goods of the kind warrants that the goods shall be delivered free of the rightful claim of any third person by way of infringement or the like but a buyer who furnishes specifications to the seller must hold the seller harmless against any such claim which arises out of compliance with the specifications.

§ 2–313. Express Warranties by Affirmation, Promise, Description, Sample.

(1) Express warranties by the seller are created as follows:

(a) Any affirmation of fact or promise made by the seller to the buyer which relates to the goods and becomes part of the basis of the bargain creates an express warranty that the goods shall conform to the affirmation or promise.

(b) Any description of the goods which is made part of the basis of the bargain creates an express warranty that the goods shall conform to the description.

(c) Any sample or model which is made part of the basis of the bargain creates an express warranty that the whole of the goods shall conform to the sample or model.

(2) It is not necessary to the creation of an express warranty that the seller use formal words such as "warrant" or "guarantee" or that he have a specific intention to make a warranty, but an affirmation merely of the value of the goods or a statement purporting to be merely the seller's opinion or commendation of the goods does not create a warranty.

§ 2–314. Implied Warranty: Merchantability; Usage of Trade.

(1) Unless excluded or modified (Section 2–316), a warranty that the goods shall be merchantable is implied in a contract for their sale if the seller is a merchant with respect to goods of that kind. Under this section the serving for value of food or drink to be consumed either on the premises or elsewhere is a sale.

(2) Goods to be merchantable must be at least such as

(a) pass without objection in the trade under the contract description; and

(b) in the case of fungible goods, are of fair average quality within the description; and

(c) are fit for the ordinary purposes for which such goods are used; and

(d) run, within the variations permitted by the agreement, of even kind, quality and quantity within each unit and among all units involved; and

(e) are adequately contained, packaged, and labeled as the agreement may require; and

(f) conform to the promises or affirmations of fact made on the container or label if any.

(3) Unless excluded or modified (Section 2–316) other implied warranties may arise from course of dealing or usage of trade.

§ 2–315. Implied Warranty: Fitness for Particular Purpose.

Where the seller at the time of contracting has reason to know any particular purpose for which the goods are required and that the buyer is relying on the seller's skill or judgment to select or furnish suitable goods, there is unless excluded or modified under the next section an implied warranty that the goods shall be fit for such purpose.

§ 2–316. Exclusion or Modification of Warranties.

(1) Words or conduct relevant to the creation of an express warranty and words or conduct tending to negate or limit warranty shall be construed wherever reasonable as consistent with each other; but subject to the provisions of this Article on parol or extrinsic evidence (Section 2–202) negation or limitation is inoperative to the extent that such construction is unreasonable.

(2) Subject to subsection (3), to exclude or modify the implied warranty of merchantability or any part of it the language must mention merchantability and in case of a writing must be conspicuous, and to exclude or modify any implied warranty of fitness the exclusion must be by a writing and conspicuous. Language to exclude all implied warranties of fitness is sufficient if it states, for example, that "There are no warranties which extend beyond the description on the face hereof."

(3) Notwithstanding subsection (2)

(a) unless the circumstances indicate otherwise, all implied warranties are excluded by expressions like "as is", "with all faults" or other language which in common understanding calls the buyer's attention to the exclusion of warranties and makes plain that there is no implied warranty; and

(b) when the buyer before entering into the contract has examined the goods or the sample or model as fully as he desired or has refused to examine the goods there is no implied warranty with regard to defects which an examination ought in the circumstances to have revealed to him; and

(c) an implied warranty can also be excluded or modified by course of dealing or course of performance or usage of trade.

(4) Remedies for breach of warranty can be limited in accordance with the provisions of this Article on liquidation or limitation of damages and on contractual modification of remedy (Sections 2–718 and 2–719).

§ 2–317. Cumulation and Conflict of Warranties Express or Implied.

Warranties whether express or implied shall be construed as consistent with each other and as cumulative, but if such construction is unreasonable the intention of the parties shall determine which warranty is dominant. In ascertaining that intention the following rules apply:

(a) Exact or technical specifications displace an inconsistent sample or model or general language of description.

(b) A sample from an existing bulk displaces inconsistent general language of description.

(c) Express warranties displace inconsistent implied warranties other than an implied warranty of fitness for a particular purpose.

§ 2–318. Third Party Beneficiaries of Warranties Express or Implied.

Note: If this Act is introduced in the Congress of the United States this section should be omitted. (States to select one alternative.)

Alternative A

A seller's warranty whether express or implied extends to any natural person who is in the family or household of his buyer or who is a guest in his home if it is reasonable to expect that such person may use, consume or be affected by the goods and who is injured in person by breach of the warranty. A seller may not exclude or limit the operation of this section.

Alternative B

A seller's warranty whether express or implied extends to any natural person who may reasonably be expected to use, consume or be affected by the goods and who is injured in person by breach of the warranty. A seller may not exclude or limit the operation of this section.

Alternative C

A seller's warranty whether express or implied extends to any person who may reasonably be expected to use, consume or be affected by the goods and who is injured by breach of the warranty. A seller may not exclude or limit the operation of this section with respect to injury to the person of an individual to whom the warranty extends. As amended 1966.

§ 2–319. F.O.B. and F.A.S. Terms.

(1) Unless otherwise agreed the term F.O.B. (which means "free on board") at a named place, even though used only in connection with the stated price, is a delivery term under which

(a) when the term is F.O.B. the place of shipment, the seller must at that place ship the goods in the manner provided in this Article (Section 2–504) and bear the expense and risk of putting them into the possession of the carrier; or

(b) when the term is F.O.B. the place of destination, the seller must at his own expense and risk transport the goods to that place and there tender delivery of them in the manner provided in this Article (Section 2–503);

(c) when under either (a) or (b) the term is also F.O.B. vessel, car or other vehicle, the seller must in addition at his own expense and risk load the goods on board. If the term is F.O.B. vessel the buyer must name the vessel and in an appropriate case the seller must comply with the provisions of this Article on the form of bill of lading (Section 2–323).

(2) Unless otherwise agreed the term F.A.S. vessel (which means "free alongside") at a named port, even though used only in connection with the stated price, is a delivery term under which the seller must

(a) at his own expense and risk deliver the goods alongside the vessel in the manner usual in that port or on a dock designated and provided by the buyer; and

(b) obtain and tender a receipt for the goods in exchange for which the carrier is under a duty to issue a bill of lading.

(3) Unless otherwise agreed in any case falling within subsection (1)(a) or (c) or subsection (2) the buyer must seasonably give any needed instructions for making delivery, including when the term is F.A.S. or F.O.B. the loading berth of the vessel and in an appropriate case its name and sailing date. The seller may treat the failure of needed instructions as a failure of cooperation under this Article (Section 2–311). He may also at his option move the goods in any reasonable manner preparatory to delivery or shipment.

(4) Under the term F.O.B. vessel or F.A.S. unless otherwise agreed the buyer must make payment against tender of the required documents and the seller may not tender nor the buyer demand delivery of the goods in substitution for the documents.

§ 2–320. C.I.F. and C. & F. Terms.

(1) The term C.I.F. means that the price includes in a lump sum the cost of the goods and the insurance and freight to the named destination. The term C. & F. or C.F. means that the price so includes cost and freight to the named destination.

(2) Unless otherwise agreed and even though used only in connection with the stated price and destination, the term C.I.F. destination or its equivalent requires the seller at his own expense and risk to

(a) put the goods into the possession of a carrier at the port for shipment and obtain a negotiable bill or bills of lading covering the entire transportation to the named destination; and

(b) load the goods and obtain a receipt from the carrier (which may be contained in the bill of lading) showing that the freight has been paid or provided for; and

(c) obtain a policy or certificate of insurance, including any war risk insurance, of a kind and on terms then current at the port of shipment in the usual amount, in the currency of the contract, shown to cover the same goods covered by the bill of lading and providing for payment of loss to the order of the buyer or for the account of whom it may concern; but the seller may add to the price the amount of the premium for any such war risk insurance; and

(d) prepare an invoice of the goods and procure any other documents required to effect shipment or to comply with the contract; and

(e) forward and tender with commercial promptness all the documents in due form and with any indorsement necessary to perfect the buyer's rights.

(3) Unless otherwise agreed the term C. & F. or its equivalent has the same effect and imposes upon the seller the same obligations and risks as a C.I.F. term except the obligation as to insurance.

(4) Under the term C.I.F. or C. & F. unless otherwise agreed the buyer must make payment against tender of the required documents and the seller may not tender nor the buyer demand delivery of the goods in substitution for the documents.

§ 2–321. C.I.F. or C. & F.: "Net Landed Weights"; "Payment on Arrival"; Warranty of Condition on Arrival.

Under a contract containing a term C.I.F. or C. & F.

(1) Where the price is based on or is to be adjusted according to "net landed weights", "delivered weights", "out turn" quantity or quality or the like, unless otherwise agreed the seller must reasonably estimate the price. The payment due on tender of the documents called for by the contract is the amount so estimated, but after final adjustment of the price a settlement must be made with commercial promptness.

(2) An agreement described in subsection (1) or any warranty of quality or condition of the goods on arrival places upon the seller the risk of ordinary deterioration, shrinkage and the like in transportation but has no effect on the place or time of identification to the contract for sale or delivery or on the passing of the risk of loss.

(3) Unless otherwise agreed where the contract provides for payment on or after arrival of the goods the seller must before payment allow such preliminary inspection as is feasible; but if the goods are lost delivery of the documents and payment are due when the goods should have arrived.

§ 2–322. Delivery "Ex-Ship".

(1) Unless otherwise agreed a term for delivery of goods "ex-ship" (which means from the carrying vessel) or in equivalent language is not restricted to a particular ship and requires delivery from a ship which has reached a place at the named port of destination where goods of the kind are usually discharged.

(2) Under such a term unless otherwise agreed

  (a) the seller must discharge all liens arising out of the carriage and furnish the buyer with a direction which puts the carrier under a duty to deliver the goods; and

  (b) the risk of loss does not pass to the buyer until the goods leave the ship's tackle or are otherwise properly unloaded.

§ 2–323. Form of Bill of Lading Required in Overseas Shipment; "Overseas".

(1) Where the contract contemplates overseas shipment and contains a term C.I.F. or C. & F. or F.O.B. vessel, the seller unless otherwise agreed must obtain a negotiable bill of lading stating that the goods have been loaded on board or, in the case of a term C.I.F. or C. & F., received for shipment.

(2) Where in a case within subsection (1) a bill of lading has been issued in a set of parts, unless otherwise agreed if the documents are not to be sent from abroad the buyer may demand tender of the full set; otherwise only one part of the bill of lading need be tendered. Even if the agreement expressly requires a full set

  (a) due tender of a single part is acceptable within the provisions of this Article on cure of improper delivery (subsection (1) of Section 2–508); and

  (b) even though the full set is demanded, if the documents are sent from abroad the person tendering an incomplete set may nevertheless require payment upon furnishing an indemnity which the buyer in good faith deems adequate.

(3) A shipment by water or by air or a contract contemplating such shipment is "overseas" insofar as by usage of trade or agreement it is subject to the commercial, financing or shipping practices characteristic of international deep water commerce.

§ 2–324. "No Arrival, No Sale" Term.

Under a term "no arrival, no sale" or terms of like meaning, unless otherwise agreed,

  (a) the seller must properly ship conforming goods and if they arrive by any means he must tender them on arrival but he assumes no obligation that the goods will arrive unless he has caused the non-arrival; and

  (b) where without fault of the seller the goods are in part lost or have so deteriorated as no longer to conform to the contract or arrive after the contract time, the buyer may proceed as if there had been casualty to identified goods (Section 2–613).

§ 2–325. "Letter of Credit" Term; "Confirmed Credit".

(1) Failure of the buyer seasonably to furnish an agreed letter of credit is a breach of the contract for sale.

(2) The delivery to seller of a proper letter of credit suspends the buyer's obligation to pay. If the letter of credit is dishonored, the seller may on seasonable notification to the buyer require payment directly from him.

(3) Unless otherwise agreed the term "letter of credit" or "banker's credit" in a contract for sale means an irrevocable credit issued by a financing agency of good repute and, where the shipment is overseas, of good international repute. The term "confirmed credit" means that the credit must also carry the direct obligation of such an agency which does business in the seller's financial market.

§ 2–326. Sale on Approval and Sale or Return; Rights of Creditors.

(1) Unless otherwise agreed, if delivered goods may be returned by the buyer even though they conform to the contract, the transaction is

  (a) a "sale on approval" if the goods are delivered primarily for use, and

  (b) a "sale or return" if the goods are delivered primarily for resale.

(2) Goods held on approval are not subject to the claims of the buyer's creditors until acceptance; goods held on sale or return are subject to such claims while in the buyer's possession.

(3) Any "or return" term of a contract for sale is to be treated as a separate contract for sale within the statute of frauds section of this Article (Section 2–201) and as contradicting the sale aspect of the contract within the provisions of this Article on parol or extrinsic evidence (Section 2–202).

As amended in 1999.

§ 2–327. Special Incidents of Sale on Approval and Sale or Return.

(1) Under a sale on approval unless otherwise agreed

  (a) although the goods are identified to the contract the risk of loss and the title do not pass to the buyer until acceptance; and

  (b) use of the goods consistent with the purpose of trial is not acceptance but failure seasonably to notify the seller of election to return the goods is acceptance, and if the goods conform to the contract acceptance of any part is acceptance of the whole; and

  (c) after due notification of election to return, the return is at the seller's risk and expense but a merchant buyer must follow any reasonable instructions.

(2) Under a sale or return unless otherwise agreed

  (a) the option to return extends to the whole or any commercial unit of the goods while in substantially their original condition, but must be exercised seasonably; and

  (b) the return is at the buyer's risk and expense.

§ 2–328. Sale by Auction.

(1) In a sale by auction if goods are put up in lots each lot is the subject of a separate sale.

(2) A sale by auction is complete when the auctioneer so announces by the fall of the hammer or in other customary manner. Where a bid is made while the hammer is falling in acceptance of a prior bid the auctioneer may in his discretion reopen the bidding or declare the goods sold under the bid on which the hammer was falling.

(3) Such a sale is with reserve unless the goods are in explicit terms put up without reserve. In an auction with reserve the auctioneer may withdraw the goods at any time until he announces completion of the sale. In an auction without reserve, after the auctioneer calls for bids on an article or lot, that article or lot cannot be withdrawn unless no bid is made within a reasonable time. In either case a bidder may retract his bid until the auctioneer's announcement of completion of the sale, but a bidder's retraction does not revive any previous bid.

(4) If the auctioneer knowingly receives a bid on the seller's behalf or the seller makes or procures such as bid, and notice has not been given that liberty for such bidding is reserved, the buyer may at his option avoid the sale or take the goods at the price of the last good faith bid prior to the completion of the sale. This subsection shall not apply to any bid at a forced sale.

Part 4—Title, Creditors and Good Faith Purchasers

§ 2–401. Passing of Title; Reservation for Security; Limited Application of This Section.

Each provision of this Article with regard to the rights, obligations and remedies of the seller, the buyer, purchasers or other third parties applies irrespective of title to the goods except where the provision refers to such title. Insofar as situations are not covered by the other provisions of this Article and matters concerning title became material the following rules apply:

(1) Title to goods cannot pass under a contract for sale prior to their identification to the contract (Section 2–501), and unless otherwise explicitly agreed the buyer acquires by their identification a special property as limited by this Act. Any retention or reservation by the seller of the title (property) in goods shipped or delivered to the buyer is limited in effect to a reservation of a security interest. Subject to these provisions and to the provisions of the Article on Secured Transactions (Article 9), title to goods passes from the seller to the buyer in any manner and on any conditions explicitly agreed on by the parties.

(2) Unless otherwise explicitly agreed title passes to the buyer at the time and place at which the seller completes his performance with reference to the physical delivery of the goods, despite any reservation of a security interest and even though a document of title is to be delivered at a different time or place; and in particular and despite any reservation of a security interest by the bill of lading

    (a) if the contract requires or authorizes the seller to send the goods to the buyer but does not require him to deliver them at destination, title passes to the buyer at the time and place of shipment; but

    (b) if the contract requires delivery at destination, title passes on tender there.

(3) Unless otherwise explicitly agreed where delivery is to be made without moving the goods,

    (a) if the seller is to deliver a document of title, title passes at the time when and the place where he delivers such documents; or

    (b) if the goods are at the time of contracting already identified and no documents are to be delivered, title passes at the time and place of contracting.

(4) A rejection or other refusal by the buyer to receive or retain the goods, whether or not justified, or a justified revocation of acceptance revests title to the goods in the seller. Such revesting occurs by operation of law and is not a "sale".

§ 2–402. Rights of Seller's Creditors Against Sold Goods.

(1) Except as provided in subsections (2) and (3), rights of unsecured creditors of the seller with respect to goods which have been identified to a contract for sale are subject to the buyer's rights to recover the goods under this Article (Sections 2–502 and 2–716).

(2) A creditor of the seller may treat a sale or an identification of goods to a contract for sale as void if as against him a retention of possession by the seller is fraudulent under any rule of law of the state where the goods are situated, except that retention of possession in good faith and current course of trade by a merchant-seller for a commercially reasonable time after a sale or identification is not fraudulent.

(3) Nothing in this Article shall be deemed to impair the rights of creditors of the seller

    (a) under the provisions of the Article on Secured Transactions (Article 9); or

    (b) where identification to the contract or delivery is made not in current course of trade but in satisfaction of or as security for a pre-existing claim for money, security or the like and is made under circumstances which under any rule of law of the state where the goods are situated would apart from this Article constitute the transaction a fraudulent transfer or voidable preference.

§ 2–403. Power to Transfer; Good Faith Purchase of Goods; "Entrusting".

(1) A purchaser of goods acquires all title which his transferor had or had power to transfer except that a purchaser of a limited interest acquires rights only to the extent of the interest purchased. A person with voidable title has power to transfer a good title to a good faith purchaser for value. When goods have been delivered under a transaction of purchase the purchaser has such power even though

    (a) the transferor was deceived as to the identity of the purchaser, or

    (b) the delivery was in exchange for a check which is later dishonored, or

    (c) it was agreed that the transaction was to be a "cash sale", or

    (d) the delivery was procured through fraud punishable as larcenous under the criminal law.

(2) Any entrusting of possession of goods to a merchant who deals in goods of that kind gives him power to transfer all rights of the entruster to a buyer in ordinary course of business.

(3) "Entrusting" includes any delivery and any acquiescence in retention of possession regardless of any condition expressed between the parties to the delivery or acquiescence and regardless of whether the procurement of the entrusting or the possessor's disposition of the goods have been such as to be larcenous under the criminal law.

(4) The rights of other purchasers of goods and of lien creditors are governed by the Articles on Secured Transactions (Article 9), Bulk Transfers (Article 6) and Documents of Title (Article 7).

As amended in 1988.

Part 5—Performance

§ 2–501. Insurable Interest in Goods; Manner of Identification of Goods.

(1) The buyer obtains a special property and an insurable interest in goods by identification of existing goods as goods to which the contract refers even though the goods so identified are non-conforming and he has an option to return or reject them. Such identification can be made at any time and in any manner explicitly agreed to by the parties. In the absence of explicit agreement identification occurs

    (a) when the contract is made if it is for the sale of goods already existing and identified;

    (b) if the contract is for the sale of future goods other than those described in paragraph (c), when goods are shipped, marked or otherwise designated by the seller as goods to which the contract refers;

    (c) when the crops are planted or otherwise become growing crops or the young are conceived if the contract is for the sale of unborn young to be born within twelve months after contracting or for the sale of crops to be harvested within twelve months or the next normal harvest season after contracting whichever is longer.

(2) The seller retains an insurable interest in goods so long as title to or any security interest in the goods remains in him and where the identification is by the seller alone he may until default or insolvency or notification to the buyer that the identification is final substitute other goods for those identified.

(3) Nothing in this section impairs any insurable interest recognized under any other statute or rule of law.

§ 2–502. Buyer's Right to Goods on Seller's Insolvency.

(1) Subject to subsections (2) and (3) and even though the goods have not been shipped a buyer who has paid a part or all of the price of goods in which he has a special property under the provisions of the immediately preceding section may on making and keeping good a tender of any unpaid portion of their price recover them from the seller if:

    (a) in the case of goods bought for personal, family, or household purposes, the seller repudiates or fails to deliver as required by the contract; or

    (b) in all cases, the seller becomes insolvent within ten days after receipt of the first installment on their price.

(2) The buyer's right to recover the goods under subsection (1)(a) vests upon acquisition of a special property, even if the seller had not then repudiated or failed to deliver.

(3) If the identification creating his special property has been made by the buyer he acquires the right to recover the goods only if they conform to the contract for sale.

As amended in 1999.

§ 2–503. Manner of Seller's Tender of Delivery.

(1) Tender of delivery requires that the seller put and hold conforming goods at the buyer's disposition and give the buyer any notification reasonably necessary to enable him to take delivery. The manner, time and place for tender are determined by the agreement and this Article, and in particular

    (a) tender must be at a reasonable hour, and if it is of goods they must be kept available for the period reasonably necessary to enable the buyer to take possession; but

    (b) unless otherwise agreed the buyer must furnish facilities reasonably suited to the receipt of the goods.

(2) Where the case is within the next section respecting shipment tender requires that the seller comply with its provisions.

(3) Where the seller is required to deliver at a particular destination tender requires that he comply with subsection (1) and also in any appropriate case tender documents as described in subsections (4) and (5) of this section.

(4) Where goods are in the possession of a bailee and are to be delivered without being moved

    (a) tender requires that the seller either tender a negotiable document of title covering such goods or procure acknowledgment by the bailee of the buyer's right to possession of the goods; but

    (b) tender to the buyer of a non-negotiable document of title or of a written direction to the bailee to deliver is sufficient tender unless the buyer seasonably objects, and receipt by the bailee of notification of the buyer's rights fixes those rights as against the bailee and all third persons; but risk of loss of the goods and of any failure by the bailee to honor the non-negotiable document of title or to obey the direction remains on the seller until the buyer has had a reasonable time to present the document or direction, and a refusal by the bailee to honor the document or to obey the direction defeats the tender.

(5) Where the contract requires the seller to deliver documents

    (a) he must tender all such documents in correct form, except as provided in this Article with respect to bills of lading in a set (subsection (2) of Section 2–323); and

    (b) tender through customary banking channels is sufficient and dishonor of a draft accompanying the documents constitutes non-acceptance or rejection.

§ 2–504. Shipment by Seller.

Where the seller is required or authorized to send the goods to the buyer and the contract does not require him to deliver them at a particular destination, then unless otherwise agreed he must

    (a) put the goods in the possession of such a carrier and make such a contract for their transportation as may be reasonable having regard to the nature of the goods and other circumstances of the case; and

    (b) obtain and promptly deliver or tender in due form any document necessary to enable the buyer to obtain possession of the goods or otherwise required by the agreement or by usage of trade; and

    (c) promptly notify the buyer of the shipment.

Failure to notify the buyer under paragraph (c) or to make a proper contract under paragraph (a) is a ground for rejection only if material delay or loss ensues.

§ 2–505. Seller's Shipment under Reservation.

(1) Where the seller has identified goods to the contract by or before shipment:

    (a) his procurement of a negotiable bill of lading to his own order or otherwise reserves in him a security interest in the goods. His procurement of the bill to the order of a financing agency or of the buyer indicates in addition only the seller's expectation of transferring that interest to the person named.

    (b) a non-negotiable bill of lading to himself or his nominee reserves possession of the goods as security but except in a case of conditional delivery (subsection (2) of Section 2–507) a non-negotiable bill of lading naming the buyer as consignee reserves no security interest even though the seller retains possession of the bill of lading.

(2) When shipment by the seller with reservation of a security interest is in violation of the contract for sale it constitutes an improper contract for transportation within the preceding section but impairs neither the rights given to the buyer by shipment and identification of the goods to the contract nor the seller's powers as a holder of a negotiable document.

§ 2–506. Rights of Financing Agency.

(1) A financing agency by paying or purchasing for value a draft which relates to a shipment of goods acquires to the extent of the payment or purchase and in addition to its own rights under the draft and any document of title securing it any rights of the shipper in the goods including the right to stop delivery and the shipper's right to have the draft honored by the buyer.

(2) The right to reimbursement of a financing agency which has in good faith honored or purchased the draft under commitment to or authority from the buyer is not impaired by subsequent discovery of defects with reference to any relevant document which was apparently regular on its face.

§ 2–507. Effect of Seller's Tender; Delivery on Condition.

(1) Tender of delivery is a condition to the buyer's duty to accept the goods and, unless otherwise agreed, to his duty to pay for them. Tender entitles the seller to acceptance of the goods and to payment according to the contract.

(2) Where payment is due and demanded on the delivery to the buyer of goods or documents of title, his right as against the seller to retain or dispose of them is conditional upon his making the payment due.

§ 2–508. Cure by Seller of Improper Tender or Delivery; Replacement.

(1) Where any tender or delivery by the seller is rejected because non-conforming and the time for performance has not yet expired, the seller may seasonably notify the buyer of his intention to cure and may then within the contract time make a conforming delivery.

(2) Where the buyer rejects a non-conforming tender which the seller had reasonable grounds to believe would be acceptable with or without money allowance the seller may if he seasonably notifies the buyer have a further reasonable time to substitute a conforming tender.

§ 2–509. Risk of Loss in the Absence of Breach.

(1) Where the contract requires or authorizes the seller to ship the goods by carrier

(a) if it does not require him to deliver them at a particular destination, the risk of loss passes to the buyer when the goods are duly delivered to the carrier even though the shipment is under reservation (Section 2–505); but

(b) if it does require him to deliver them at a particular destination and the goods are there duly tendered while in the possession of the carrier, the risk of loss passes to the buyer when the goods are there duly so tendered as to enable the buyer to take delivery.

(2) Where the goods are held by a bailee to be delivered without being moved, the risk of loss passes to the buyer

(a) on his receipt of a negotiable document of title covering the goods; or

(b) on acknowledgment by the bailee of the buyer's right to possession of the goods; or

(c) after his receipt of a non-negotiable document of title or other written direction to deliver, as provided in subsection (4)(b) of Section 2–503.

(3) In any case not within subsection (1) or (2), the risk of loss passes to the buyer on his receipt of the goods if the seller is a merchant; otherwise the risk passes to the buyer on tender of delivery.

(4) The provisions of this section are subject to contrary agreement of the parties and to the provisions of this Article on sale on approval (Section 2–327) and on effect of breach on risk of loss (Section 2–510).

§ 2–510. Effect of Breach on Risk of Loss.

(1) Where a tender or delivery of goods so fails to conform to the contract as to give a right of rejection the risk of their loss remains on the seller until cure or acceptance.

(2) Where the buyer rightfully revokes acceptance he may to the extent of any deficiency in his effective insurance coverage treat the risk of loss as having rested on the seller from the beginning.

(3) Where the buyer as to conforming goods already identified to the contract for sale repudiates or is otherwise in breach before risk of their loss has passed to him, the seller may to the extent of any deficiency in his effective insurance coverage treat the risk of loss as resting on the buyer for a commercially reasonable time.

§ 2–511. Tender of Payment by Buyer; Payment by Check.

(1) Unless otherwise agreed tender of payment is a condition to the seller's duty to tender and complete any delivery.

(2) Tender of payment is sufficient when made by any means or in any manner current in the ordinary course of business unless the seller demands payment in legal tender and gives any extension of time reasonably necessary to procure it.

(3) Subject to the provisions of this Act on the effect of an instrument on an obligation (Section 3–310), payment by check is conditional and is defeated as between the parties by dishonor of the check on due presentment.
As amended in 1994.

§ 2–512. Payment by Buyer Before Inspection.

(1) Where the contract requires payment before inspection non-conformity of the goods does not excuse the buyer from so making payment unless

(a) the non-conformity appears without inspection; or

(b) despite tender of the required documents the circumstances would justify injunction against honor under this Act (Section 5–109(b)).

(2) Payment pursuant to subsection (1) does not constitute an acceptance of goods or impair the buyer's right to inspect or any of his remedies.
As amended in 1995.

§ 2–513. Buyer's Right to Inspection of Goods.

(1) Unless otherwise agreed and subject to subsection (3), where goods are tendered or delivered or identified to the contract for sale, the buyer has a right before payment or acceptance to inspect them at any reasonable place and time and in any reasonable manner. When the seller is required or authorized to send the goods to the buyer, the inspection may be after their arrival.

(2) Expenses of inspection must be borne by the buyer but may be recovered from the seller if the goods do not conform and are rejected.

(3) Unless otherwise agreed and subject to the provisions of this Article on C.I.F. contracts (subsection (3) of Section 2–321), the buyer is not entitled to inspect the goods before payment of the price when the contract provides

> **(a)** for delivery "C.O.D." or on other like terms; or
>
> **(b)** for payment against documents of title, except where such payment is due only after the goods are to become available for inspection.

(4) A place or method of inspection fixed by the parties is presumed to be exclusive but unless otherwise expressly agreed it does not postpone identification or shift the place for delivery or for passing the risk of loss. If compliance becomes impossible, inspection shall be as provided in this section unless the place or method fixed was clearly intended as an indispensable condition failure of which avoids the contract.

§ 2–514. When Documents Deliverable on Acceptance; When on Payment.

Unless otherwise agreed documents against which a draft is drawn are to be delivered to the drawee on acceptance of the draft if it is payable more than three days after presentment; otherwise, only on payment.

§ 2–515. Preserving Evidence of Goods in Dispute.

In furtherance of the adjustment of any claim or dispute

> **(a)** either party on reasonable notification to the other and for the purpose of ascertaining the facts and preserving evidence has the right to inspect, test and sample the goods including such of them as may be in the possession or control of the other; and
>
> **(b)** the parties may agree to a third party inspection or survey to determine the conformity or condition of the goods and may agree that the findings shall be binding upon them in any subsequent litigation or adjustment.

Part 6—Breach, Repudiation and Excuse

§ 2–601. Buyer's Rights on Improper Delivery.

Subject to the provisions of this Article on breach in installment contracts (Section 2–612) and unless otherwise agreed under the sections on contractual limitations of remedy (Sections 2–718 and 2–719), if the goods or the tender of delivery fail in any respect to conform to the contract, the buyer may

> **(a)** reject the whole; or
>
> **(b)** accept the whole; or
>
> **(c)** accept any commercial unit or units and reject the rest.

§ 2–602. Manner and Effect of Rightful Rejection.

(1) Rejection of goods must be within a reasonable time after their delivery or tender. It is ineffective unless the buyer seasonably notifies the seller.

(2) Subject to the provisions of the two following sections on rejected goods (Sections 2–603 and 2–604),

> **(a)** after rejection any exercise of ownership by the buyer with respect to any commercial unit is wrongful as against the seller; and

> **(b)** if the buyer has before rejection taken physical possession of goods in which he does not have a security interest under the provisions of this Article (subsection (3) of Section 2–711), he is under a duty after rejection to hold them with reasonable care at the seller's disposition for a time sufficient to permit the seller to remove them; but
>
> **(c)** the buyer has no further obligations with regard to goods rightfully rejected.

(3) The seller's rights with respect to goods wrongfully rejected are governed by the provisions of this Article on Seller's remedies in general (Section 2–703).

§ 2–603. Merchant Buyer's Duties as to Rightfully Rejected Goods.

(1) Subject to any security interest in the buyer (subsection (3) of Section 2–711), when the seller has no agent or place of business at the market of rejection a merchant buyer is under a duty after rejection of goods in his possession or control to follow any reasonable instructions received from the seller with respect to the goods and in the absence of such instructions to make reasonable efforts to sell them for the seller's account if they are perishable or threaten to decline in value speedily. Instructions are not reasonable if on demand indemnity for expenses is not forthcoming.

(2) When the buyer sells goods under subsection (1), he is entitled to reimbursement from the seller or out of the proceeds for reasonable expenses of caring for and selling them, and if the expenses include no selling commission then to such commission as is usual in the trade or if there is none to a reasonable sum not exceeding ten per cent on the gross proceeds.

(3) In complying with this section the buyer is held only to good faith and good faith conduct hereunder is neither acceptance nor conversion nor the basis of an action for damages.

§ 2–604. Buyer's Options as to Salvage of Rightfully Rejected Goods.

Subject to the provisions of the immediately preceding section on perishables if the seller gives no instructions within a reasonable time after notification of rejection the buyer may store the rejected goods for the seller's account or reship them to him or resell them for the seller's account with reimbursement as provided in the preceding section. Such action is not acceptance or conversion.

§ 2–605. Waiver of Buyer's Objections by Failure to Particularize.

(1) The buyer's failure to state in connection with rejection a particular defect which is ascertainable by reasonable inspection precludes him from relying on the unstated defect to justify rejection or to establish breach

> **(a)** where the seller could have cured it if stated seasonably; or
>
> **(b)** between merchants when the seller has after rejection made a request in writing for a full and final written statement of all defects on which the buyer proposes to rely.

(2) Payment against documents made without reservation of rights precludes recovery of the payment for defects apparent on the face of the documents.

§ 2–606. What Constitutes Acceptance of Goods.

(1) Acceptance of goods occurs when the buyer

(a) after a reasonable opportunity to inspect the goods signifies to the seller that the goods are conforming or that he will take or retain them in spite of their nonconformity; or

(b) fails to make an effective rejection (subsection (1) of Section 2–602), but such acceptance does not occur until the buyer has had a reasonable opportunity to inspect them; or

(c) does any act inconsistent with the seller's ownership; but if such act is wrongful as against the seller it is an acceptance only if ratified by him.

(2) Acceptance of a part of any commercial unit is acceptance of that entire unit.

§ 2–607. Effect of Acceptance; Notice of Breach; Burden of Establishing Breach After Acceptance; Notice of Claim or Litigation to Person Answerable Over.

(1) The buyer must pay at the contract rate for any goods accepted.

(2) Acceptance of goods by the buyer precludes rejection of the goods accepted and if made with knowledge of a non-conformity cannot be revoked because of it unless the acceptance was on the reasonable assumption that the non-conformity would be seasonably cured but acceptance does not of itself impair any other remedy provided by this Article for non-conformity.

(3) Where a tender has been accepted

(a) the buyer must within a reasonable time after he discovers or should have discovered any breach notify the seller of breach or be barred from any remedy; and

(b) if the claim is one for infringement or the like (subsection (3) of Section 2–312) and the buyer is sued as a result of such a breach he must so notify the seller within a reasonable time after he receives notice of the litigation or be barred from any remedy over for liability established by the litigation.

(4) The burden is on the buyer to establish any breach with respect to the goods accepted.

(5) Where the buyer is sued for breach of a warranty or other obligation for which his seller is answerable over

(a) he may give his seller written notice of the litigation. If the notice states that the seller may come in and defend and that if the seller does not do so he will be bound in any action against him by his buyer by any determination of fact common to the two litigations, then unless the seller after seasonable receipt of the notice does come in and defend he is so bound.

(b) if the claim is one for infringement or the like (subsection (3) of Section 2–312) the original seller may demand in writing that his buyer turn over to him control of the litigation including settlement or else be barred from any remedy over and if he also agrees to bear all expense and to satisfy any adverse judgment, then unless the buyer after seasonable receipt of the demand does turn over control the buyer is so barred.

(6) The provisions of subsections (3), (4) and (5) apply to any obligation of a buyer to hold the seller harmless against infringement or the like (subsection (3) of Section 2–312).

§ 2–608. Revocation of Acceptance in Whole or in Part.

(1) The buyer may revoke his acceptance of a lot or commercial unit whose non-conformity substantially impairs its value to him if he has accepted it

(a) on the reasonable assumption that its nonconformity would be cured and it has not been seasonably cured; or

(b) without discovery of such non-conformity if his acceptance was reasonably induced either by the difficulty of discovery before acceptance or by the seller's assurances.

(2) Revocation of acceptance must occur within a reasonable time after the buyer discovers or should have discovered the ground for it and before any substantial change in condition of the goods which is not caused by their own defects. It is not effective until the buyer notifies the seller of it.

(3) A buyer who so revokes has the same rights and duties with regard to the goods involved as if he had rejected them.

§ 2–609. Right to Adequate Assurance of Performance.

(1) A contract for sale imposes an obligation on each party that the other's expectation of receiving due performance will not be impaired. When reasonable grounds for insecurity arise with respect to the performance of either party the other may in writing demand adequate assurance of due performance and until he receives such assurance may if commercially reasonable suspend any performance for which he has not already received the agreed return.

(2) Between merchants the reasonableness of grounds for insecurity and the adequacy of any assurance offered shall be determined according to commercial standards.

(3) Acceptance of any improper delivery or payment does not prejudice the party's right to demand adequate assurance of future performance.

(4) After receipt of a justified demand failure to provide within a reasonable time not exceeding thirty days such assurance of due performance as is adequate under the circumstances of the particular case is a repudiation of the contract.

§ 2–610. Anticipatory Repudiation.

When either party repudiates the contract with respect to a performance not yet due the loss of which will substantially impair the value of the contract to the other, the aggrieved party may

(a) for a commercially reasonable time await performance by the repudiating party; or

(b) resort to any remedy for breach (Section 2–703 or Section 2–711), even though he has notified the repudiating party that he would await the latter's performance and has urged retraction; and

(c) in either case suspend his own performance or proceed in accordance with the provisions of this Article on the seller's right to identify goods to the contract notwithstanding breach or to salvage unfinished goods (Section 2–704).

§ 2–611. Retraction of Anticipatory Repudiation.

(1) Until the repudiating party's next performance is due he can retract his repudiation unless the aggrieved party has since the repudiation cancelled or materially changed his position or otherwise indicated that he considers the repudiation final.

(2) Retraction may be by any method which clearly indicates to the aggrieved party that the repudiating party intends to perform, but must include any assurance justifiably demanded under the provisions of this Article (Section 2–609).

(3) Retraction reinstates the repudiating party's rights under the contract with due excuse and allowance to the aggrieved party for any delay occasioned by the repudiation.

§ 2–612. "Installment Contract"; Breach.

(1) An "installment contract" is one which requires or authorizes the delivery of goods in separate lots to be separately accepted, even though the contract contains a clause "each delivery is a separate contract" or its equivalent.

(2) The buyer may reject any installment which is non-conforming if the non-conformity substantially impairs the value of that installment and cannot be cured or if the non-conformity is a defect in the required documents; but if the non-conformity does not fall within subsection (3) and the seller gives adequate assurance of its cure the buyer must accept that installment.

(3) Whenever non-conformity or default with respect to one or more installments substantially impairs the value of the whole contract there is a breach of the whole. But the aggrieved party reinstates the contract if he accepts a non-conforming installment without seasonably notifying of cancellation or if he brings an action with respect only to past installments or demands performance as to future installments.

§ 2–613. Casualty to Identified Goods.

Where the contract requires for its performance goods identified when the contract is made, and the goods suffer casualty without fault of either party before the risk of loss passes to the buyer, or in a proper case under a "no arrival, no sale" term (Section 2–324) then

    (a) if the loss is total the contract is avoided; and

    (b) if the loss is partial or the goods have so deteriorated as no longer to conform to the contract the buyer may nevertheless demand inspection and at his option either treat the contract as voided or accept the goods with due allowance from the contract price for the deterioration or the deficiency in quantity but without further right against the seller.

§ 2–614. Substituted Performance.

(1) Where without fault of either party the agreed berthing, loading, or unloading facilities fail or an agreed type of carrier becomes unavailable or the agreed manner of delivery otherwise becomes commercially impracticable but a commercially reasonable substitute is available, such substitute performance must be tendered and accepted.

(2) If the agreed means or manner of payment fails because of domestic or foreign governmental regulation, the seller may withhold or stop delivery unless the buyer provides a means or manner of payment which is commercially a substantial equivalent. If delivery has already been taken, payment by the means or in the manner provided by the regulation discharges the buyer's obligation unless the regulation is discriminatory, oppressive or predatory.

§ 2–615. Excuse by Failure of Presupposed Conditions.

Except so far as a seller may have assumed a greater obligation and subject to the preceding section on substituted performance:

    (a) Delay in delivery or non-delivery in whole or in part by a seller who complies with paragraphs (b) and (c) is not a breach of his duty under a contract for sale if performance as agreed has been made impracticable by the occurrence of a contingency the nonoccurrence of which was a basic assumption on which the contract was made or by compliance in good faith with any applicable foreign or domestic governmental regulation or order whether or not it later proves to be invalid.

    (b) Where the causes mentioned in paragraph (a) affect only a part of the seller's capacity to perform, he must allocate production and deliveries among his customers but may at his option include regular customers not then under contract as well as his own requirements for further manufacture. He may so allocate in any manner which is fair and reasonable.

    (c) The seller must notify the buyer seasonably that there will be delay or non-delivery and, when allocation is required under paragraph (b), of the estimated quota thus made available for the buyer.

§ 2–616. Procedure on Notice Claiming Excuse.

(1) Where the buyer receives notification of a material or indefinite delay or an allocation justified under the preceding section he may by written notification to the seller as to any delivery concerned, and where the prospective deficiency substantially impairs the value of the whole contract under the provisions of this Article relating to breach of installment contracts (Section 2–612), then also as to the whole,

    (a) terminate and thereby discharge any unexecuted portion of the contract; or

    (b) modify the contract by agreeing to take his available quota in substitution.

(2) If after receipt of such notification from the seller the buyer fails so to modify the contract within a reasonable time not exceeding thirty days the contract lapses with respect to any deliveries affected.

(3) The provisions of this section may not be negated by agreement except in so far as the seller has assumed a greater obligation under the preceding section.

Part 7—Remedies

§ 2–701. Remedies for Breach of Collateral Contracts Not Impaired.

Remedies for breach of any obligation or promise collateral or ancillary to a contract for sale are not impaired by the provisions of this Article.

§ 2–702. Seller's Remedies on Discovery of Buyer's Insolvency.

(1) Where the seller discovers the buyer to be insolvent he may refuse delivery except for cash including payment for all goods theretofore delivered under the contract, and stop delivery under this Article (Section 2–705).

(2) Where the seller discovers that the buyer has received goods on credit while insolvent he may reclaim the goods upon demand made within ten days after the receipt, but if misrepresentation of solvency has been made to the particular seller in writing within three months before delivery the ten day limitation does not apply. Except as provided in this subsection the seller may not base a right to reclaim goods on the buyer's fraudulent or innocent misrepresentation of solvency or of intent to pay.

(3) The seller's right to reclaim under subsection (2) is subject to the rights of a buyer in ordinary course or other good faith purchaser under this Article (Section 2–403). Successful reclamation of goods excludes all other remedies with respect to them.

§ 2–703. Seller's Remedies in General.

Where the buyer wrongfully rejects or revokes acceptance of goods or fails to make a payment due on or before delivery or repudiates with respect to a part or the whole, then with respect to any goods directly affected and, if the breach is of the whole contract (Section 2–612), then also with respect to the whole undelivered balance, the aggrieved seller may

(a) withhold delivery of such goods;

(b) stop delivery by any bailee as hereafter provided (Section 2–705);

(c) proceed under the next section respecting goods still unidentified to the contract;

(d) resell and recover damages as hereafter provided (Section 2–706);

(e) recover damages for non-acceptance (Section 2–708) or in a proper case the price (Section 2–709);

(f) cancel.

§ 2–704. Seller's Right to Identify Goods to the Contract Notwithstanding Breach or to Salvage Unfinished Goods.

(1) An aggrieved seller under the preceding section may

    (a) identify to the contract conforming goods not already identified if at the time he learned of the breach they are in his possession or control;

    (b) treat as the subject of resale goods which have demonstrably been intended for the particular contract even though those goods are unfinished.

(2) Where the goods are unfinished an aggrieved seller may in the exercise of reasonable commercial judgment for the purposes of avoiding loss and of effective realization either complete the manufacture and wholly identify the goods to the contract or cease manufacture and resell for scrap or salvage value or proceed in any other reasonable manner.

§ 2–705. Seller's Stoppage of Delivery in Transit or Otherwise.

(1) The seller may stop delivery of goods in the possession of a carrier or other bailee when he discovers the buyer to be insolvent (Section 2–702) and may stop delivery of carload, truckload, planeload or larger shipments of express or freight when the buyer repudiates or fails to make a payment due before delivery or if for any other reason the seller has a right to withhold or reclaim the goods.

(2) As against such buyer the seller may stop delivery until

    (a) receipt of the goods by the buyer; or

    (b) acknowledgment to the buyer by any bailee of the goods except a carrier that the bailee holds the goods for the buyer; or

    (c) such acknowledgment to the buyer by a carrier by reshipment or as warehouseman; or

    (d) negotiation to the buyer of any negotiable document of title covering the goods.

(3) (a) To stop delivery the seller must so notify as to enable the bailee by reasonable diligence to prevent delivery of the goods.

    (b) After such notification the bailee must hold and deliver the goods according to the directions of the seller but the seller is liable to the bailee for any ensuing charges or damages.

    (c) If a negotiable document of title has been issued for goods the bailee is not obliged to obey a notification to stop until surrender of the document.

    (d) A carrier who has issued a non-negotiable bill of lading is not obliged to obey a notification to stop received from a person other than the consignor.

§ 2–706. Seller's Resale Including Contract for Resale.

(1) Under the conditions stated in Section 2–703 on seller's remedies, the seller may resell the goods concerned or the undelivered balance thereof. Where the resale is made in good faith and in a commercially reasonable manner the seller may recover the difference between the resale price and the contract price together with any incidental damages allowed under the provisions of this Article (Section 2–710), but less expenses saved in consequence of the buyer's breach.

(2) Except as otherwise provided in subsection (3) or unless otherwise agreed resale may be at public or private sale including sale by way of one or more contracts to sell or of identification to an existing contract of the seller. Sale may be as a unit or in parcels and at any time and place and on any terms but every aspect of the sale including the method, manner, time, place and terms must be commercially reasonable. The resale must be reasonably identified as referring to the broken contract, but it is not necessary that the goods be in existence or that any or all of them have been identified to the contract before the breach.

(3) Where the resale is at private sale the seller must give the buyer reasonable notification of his intention to resell.

(4) Where the resale is at public sale

    (a) only identified goods can be sold except where there is a recognized market for a public sale of futures in goods of the kind; and

    (b) it must be made at a usual place or market for public sale if one is reasonably available and except in the case of goods which are perishable or threaten to decline in value speedily the seller must give the buyer reasonable notice of the time and place of the resale; and

    (c) if the goods are not to be within the view of those attending the sale the notification of sale must state the place where the goods are located and provide for their reasonable inspection by prospective bidders; and

    (d) the seller may buy.

(5) A purchaser who buys in good faith at a resale takes the goods free of any rights of the original buyer even though the seller fails to comply with one or more of the requirements of this section.

(6) The seller is not accountable to the buyer for any profit made on any resale. A person in the position of a seller (Section 2–707) or a buyer who has rightfully rejected or justifiably revoked acceptance must account for any excess over the amount of his security interest, as hereinafter defined (subsection (3) of Section 2–711).

§ 2–707. "Person in the Position of a Seller".

(1) A "person in the position of a seller" includes as against a principal an agent who has paid or become responsible for the price of goods on behalf of his principal or anyone who otherwise holds a security interest or other right in goods similar to that of a seller.

(2) A person in the position of a seller may as provided in this Article withhold or stop delivery (Section 2–705) and resell (Section 2–706) and recover incidental damages (Section 2–710).

§ 2–708. Seller's Damages for Non-Acceptance or Repudiation.

(1) Subject to subsection (2) and to the provisions of this Article with respect to proof of market price (Section 2–723), the measure of damages for non-acceptance or repudiation by the buyer is the difference between the market price at the time and place for tender and the unpaid contract price together with any incidental damages provided in this Article (Section 2–710), but less expenses saved in consequence of the buyer's breach.

(2) If the measure of damages provided in subsection (1) is inadequate to put the seller in as good a position as performance would have done then the measure of damages is the profit (including reasonable overhead) which the seller would have made from full performance by the buyer, together with any incidental damages provided in this Article (Section 2–710), due allowance for costs reasonably incurred and due credit for payments or proceeds of resale.

§ 2–709. Action for the Price.

(1) When the buyer fails to pay the price as it becomes due the seller may recover, together with any incidental damages under the next section, the price

    (a) of goods accepted or of conforming goods lost or damaged within a commercially reasonable time after risk of their loss has passed to the buyer; and

    (b) of goods identified to the contract if the seller is unable after reasonable effort to resell them at a reasonable price or the circumstances reasonably indicate that such effort will be unavailing.

(2) Where the seller sues for the price he must hold for the buyer any goods which have been identified to the contract and are still in his control except that if resale becomes possible he may resell them at any time prior to the collection of the judgment. The net proceeds of any such resale must be credited to the buyer and payment of the judgment entitles him to any goods not resold.

(3) After the buyer has wrongfully rejected or revoked acceptance of the goods or has failed to make a payment due or has repudiated (Section 2–610), a seller who is held not entitled to the price under this section shall nevertheless be awarded damages for non-acceptance under the preceding section.

§ 2–710. Seller's Incidental Damages.

Incidental damages to an aggrieved seller include any commercially reasonable charges, expenses or commissions incurred in stopping delivery, in the transportation, care and custody of goods after the buyer's breach, in connection with return or resale of the goods or otherwise resulting from the breach.

§ 2–711. Buyer's Remedies in General; Buyer's Security Interest in Rejected Goods.

(1) Where the seller fails to make delivery or repudiates or the buyer rightfully rejects or justifiably revokes acceptance then with respect to any goods involved, and with respect to the whole if the breach goes to the whole contract (Section 2–612), the buyer may cancel and whether or not he has done so may in addition to recovering so much of the price as has been paid

    (a) "cover" and have damages under the next section as to all the goods affected whether or not they have been identified to the contract; or

    (b) recover damages for non-delivery as pro-vided in this Article (Section 2–713).

(2) Where the seller fails to deliver or repudiates the buyer may also

    (a) if the goods have been identified recover them as provided in this Article (Section 2–502); or

    (b) in a proper case obtain specific performance or replevy the goods as provided in this Article (Section 2–716).

(3) On rightful rejection or justifiable revocation of acceptance a buyer has a security interest in goods in his possession or control

for any payments made on their price and any expenses reasonably incurred in their inspection, receipt, transportation, care and custody and may hold such goods and resell them in like manner as an aggrieved seller (Section 2–706).

§ 2–712. "Cover"; Buyer's Procurement of Substitute Goods.

(1) After a breach within the preceding section the buyer may "cover" by making in good faith and without unreasonable delay any reasonable purchase of or contract to purchase goods in substitution for those due from the seller.

(2) The buyer may recover from the seller as damages the difference between the cost of cover and the contract price together with any incidental or consequential damages as hereinafter defined (Section 2–715), but less expenses saved in consequence of the seller's breach.

(3) Failure of the buyer to effect cover within this section does not bar him from any other remedy.

§ 2–713. Buyer's Damages for Non-Delivery or Repudiation.

(1) Subject to the provisions of this Article with respect to proof of market price (Section 2–723), the measure of damages for non-delivery or repudiation by the seller is the difference between the market price at the time when the buyer learned of the breach and the contract price together with any incidental and consequential damages provided in this Article (Section 2–715), but less expenses saved in consequence of the seller's breach.

(2) Market price is to be determined as of the place for tender or, in cases of rejection after arrival or revocation of acceptance, as of the place of arrival.

§ 2–714. Buyer's Damages for Breach in Regard to Accepted Goods.

(1) Where the buyer has accepted goods and given notification (subsection (3) of Section 2–607) he may recover as damages for any non-conformity of tender the loss resulting in the ordinary course of events from the seller's breach as determined in any manner which is reasonable.

(2) The measure of damages for breach of warranty is the difference at the time and place of acceptance between the value of the goods accepted and the value they would have had if they had been as warranted, unless special circumstances show proximate damages of a different amount.

(3) In a proper case any incidental and consequential damages under the next section may also be recovered.

§ 2–715. Buyer's Incidental and Consequential Damages.

(1) Incidental damages resulting from the seller's breach include expenses reasonably incurred in inspection, receipt, transportation and care and custody of goods rightfully rejected, any commercially reasonable charges, expenses or commissions in connection with effecting cover and any other reasonable expense incident to the delay or other breach.

(2) Consequential damages resulting from the seller's breach include

    (a) any loss resulting from general or particular requirements and needs of which the seller at the time of contracting had reason to know and which could not reasonably be prevented by cover or otherwise; and

(b) injury to person or property proximately resulting from any breach of warranty.

§ 2–716. Buyer's Right to Specific Performance or Replevin.

(1) Specific performance may be decreed where the goods are unique or in other proper circumstances.

(2) The decree for specific performance may include such terms and conditions as to payment of the price, damages, or other relief as the court may deem just.

(3) The buyer has a right of replevin for goods identified to the contract if after reasonable effort he is unable to effect cover for such goods or the circumstances reasonably indicate that such effort will be unavailing or if the goods have been shipped under reservation and satisfaction of the security interest in them has been made or tendered. In the case of goods bought for personal, family, or household purposes, the buyer's right of replevin vests upon acquisition of a special property, even if the seller had not then repudiated or failed to deliver.

As amended in 1999.

§ 2–717. Deduction of Damages From the Price.

The buyer on notifying the seller of his intention to do so may deduct all or any part of the damages resulting from any breach of the contract from any part of the price still due under the same contract.

§ 2–718. Liquidation or Limitation of Damages; Deposits.

(1) Damages for breach by either party may be liquidated in the agreement but only at an amount which is reasonable in the light of the anticipated or actual harm caused by the breach, the difficulties of proof of loss, and the inconvenience or nonfeasibility of otherwise obtaining an adequate remedy. A term fixing unreasonably large liquidated damages is void as a penalty.

(2) Where the seller justifiably withholds delivery of goods because of the buyer's breach, the buyer is entitled to restitution of any amount by which the sum of his payments exceeds

   (a) the amount to which the seller is entitled by virtue of terms liquidating the seller's damages in accordance with subsection (1), or

   (b) in the absence of such terms, twenty per cent of the value of the total performance for which the buyer is obligated under the contract or $500, whichever is smaller.

(3) The buyer's right to restitution under subsection (2) is subject to offset to the extent that the seller establishes

   (a) a right to recover damages under the provisions of this Article other than subsection (1), and

   (b) the amount or value of any benefits received by the buyer directly or indirectly by reason of the contract.

(4) Where a seller has received payment in goods their reasonable value or the proceeds of their resale shall be treated as payments for the purposes of subsection (2); but if the seller has notice of the buyer's breach before reselling goods received in part performance, his resale is subject to the conditions laid down in this Article on resale by an aggrieved seller (Section 2–706).

§ 2–719. Contractual Modification or Limitation of Remedy.

(1) Subject to the provisions of subsections (2) and (3) of this section and of the preceding section on liquidation and limitation of damages,

   (a) the agreement may provide for remedies in addition to or in substitution for those provided in this Article and may limit or alter the measure of damages recoverable under this Article, as by limiting the buyer's remedies to return of the goods and repayment of the price or to repair and replacement of nonconforming goods or parts; and

   (b) resort to a remedy as provided is optional unless the remedy is expressly agreed to be exclusive, in which case it is the sole remedy.

(2) Where circumstances cause an exclusive or limited remedy to fail of its essential purpose, remedy may be had as provided in this Act.

(3) Consequential damages may be limited or excluded unless the limitation or exclusion is unconscionable. Limitation of consequential damages for injury to the person in the case of consumer goods is *prima facie* unconscionable but limitation of damages where the loss is commercial is not.

§ 2–720. Effect of "Cancellation" or "Rescission" on Claims for Antecedent Breach.

Unless the contrary intention clearly appears, expressions of "cancellation" or "rescission" of the contract or the like shall not be construed as a renunciation or discharge of any claim in damages for an antecedent breach.

§ 2–721. Remedies for Fraud.

Remedies for material misrepresentation or fraud include all remedies available under this Article for non-fraudulent breach. Neither rescission or a claim for rescission of the contract for sale nor rejection or return of the goods shall bar or be deemed inconsistent with a claim for damages or other remedy.

§ 2–722. Who Can Sue Third Parties for Injury to Goods.

Where a third party so deals with goods which have been identified to a contract for sale as to cause actionable injury to a party to that contract

(a) a right of action against the third party is in either party to the contract for sale who has title to or a security interest or a special property or an insurable interest in the goods; and if the goods have been destroyed or converted a right of action is also in the party who either bore the risk of loss under the contract for sale or has since the injury assumed that risk as against the other;

(b) if at the time of the injury the party plaintiff did not bear the risk of loss as against the other party to the contract for sale and there is no arrangement between them for disposition of the recovery, his suit or settlement is, subject to his own interest, as a fiduciary for the other party to the contract;

(c) either party may with the consent of the other sue for the benefit of whom it may concern.

§ 2–723. Proof of Market Price: Time and Place.

(1) If an action based on anticipatory repudiation comes to trial before the time for performance with respect to some or all of the goods, any damages based on market price (Section 2–708 or Section 2–713) shall be determined according to the price of such goods prevailing at the time when the aggrieved party learned of the repudiation.

(2) If evidence of a price prevailing at the times or places described in this Article is not readily available the price prevailing within any reasonable time before or after the time described or at any other place which in commercial judgment or under usage of trade would serve as a reasonable substitute for the one described may be used, making any proper allowance for the cost of transporting the goods to or from such other place.

(3) Evidence of a relevant price prevailing at a time or place other than the one described in this Article offered by one party is not admissible unless and until he has given the other party such notice as the court finds sufficient to prevent unfair surprise.

§ 2–724. Admissibility of Market Quotations.

Whenever the prevailing price or value of any goods regularly bought and sold in any established commodity market is in issue, reports in official publications or trade journals or in newspapers or periodicals of general circulation published as the reports of such market shall be admissible in evidence. The circumstances of the preparation of such a report may be shown to affect its weight but not its admissibility.

§ 2–725. Statute of Limitations in Contracts for Sale.

(1) An action for breach of any contract for sale must be commenced within four years after the cause of action has accrued. By the original agreement the parties may reduce the period of limitation to not less than one year but may not extend it.

(2) A cause of action accrues when the breach occurs, regardless of the aggrieved party's lack of knowledge of the breach. A breach of warranty occurs when tender of delivery is made, except that where a warranty explicitly extends to future performance of the goods and discovery of the breach must await the time of such performance the cause of action accrues when the breach is or should have been discovered.

(3) Where an action commenced within the time limited by subsection (1) is so terminated as to leave available a remedy by another action for the same breach such other action may be commenced after the expiration of the time limited and within six months after the termination of the first action unless the termination resulted from voluntary discontinuance or from dismissal for failure or neglect to prosecute.

(4) This section does not alter the law on tolling of the statute of limitations nor does it apply to causes of action which have accrued before this Act becomes effective.

ARTICLE 2A: LEASES

Part 1—General Provisions

§ 2A–101. Short Title.

This Article shall be known and may be cited as the Uniform Commercial Code—Leases.

§ 2A–102. Scope.

This Article applies to any transaction, regardless of form, that creates a lease.

§ 2A–103. Definitions and Index of Definitions.

(1) In this Article unless the context otherwise requires:

(a) "Buyer in ordinary course of business" means a person who in good faith and without knowledge that the sale to him [or her] is in violation of the ownership rights or security interest or leasehold interest of a third party in the goods buys in ordinary course from a person in the business of selling goods of that kind but does not include a pawnbroker. "Buying" may be for cash or by exchange of other property or on secured or unsecured credit and includes receiving goods or documents of

title under a pre-existing contract for sale but does not include a transfer in bulk or as security for or in total or partial satisfaction of a money debt.

(b) "Cancellation" occurs when either party puts an end to the lease contract for default by the other party.

(c) "Commercial unit" means such a unit of goods as by commercial usage is a single whole for purposes of lease and division of which materially impairs its character or value on the market or in use. A commercial unit may be a single article, as a machine, or a set of articles, as a suite of furniture or a line of machinery, or a quantity, as a gross or carload, or any other unit treated in use or in the relevant market as a single whole.

(d) "Conforming" goods or performance under a lease contract means goods or performance that are in accordance with the obligations under the lease contract.

(e) "Consumer lease" means a lease that a lessor regularly engaged in the business of leasing or selling makes to a lessee who is an individual and who takes under the lease primarily for a personal, family, or household purpose [, if the total payments to be made under the lease contract, excluding payments for options to renew or buy, do not exceed $_____].

(f) "Fault" means wrongful act, omission, breach, or default.

(g) "Finance lease" means a lease with respect to which:

(i) the lessor does not select, manufacture or supply the goods;

(ii) the lessor acquires the goods or the right to possession and use of the goods in connection with the lease; and

(iii) one of the following occurs:

(A) the lessee receives a copy of the contract by which the lessor acquired the goods or the right to possession and use of the goods before signing the lease contract;

(B) the lessee's approval of the contract by which the lessor acquired the goods or the right to possession and use of the goods is a condition to effectiveness of the lease contract;

(C) the lessee, before signing the lease contract, receives an accurate and complete statement designating the promises and warranties, and any disclaimers of warranties, limitations or modifications of remedies, or liquidated damages, including those of a third party, such as the manufacturer of the goods, provided to the lessor by the person supplying the goods in connection with or as part of the contract by which the lessor acquired the goods or the right to possession and use of the goods; or

(D) if the lease is not a consumer lease, the lessor, before the lessee signs the lease contract, informs the lessee in writing (a) of the identity of the person supplying the goods to the lessor, unless the lessee has selected that person and directed the lessor to acquire the goods or the right to possession and use of the goods from that person, (b) that the lessee is entitled under this Article to any promises and warranties, including those of any third party, provided to the lessor by the person supplying the goods in connection with or as part of the contract by which the lessor acquired the goods or the right to possession and use of the goods, and (c) that the lessee may communicate with the person supplying the goods to the lessor and receive an accurate and complete statement of those promises and warranties, including any disclaimers and limitations of them or of remedies.

(h) "Goods" means all things that are movable at the time of identification to the lease contract, or are fixtures (Section 2A–309), but the term does not include money, documents, instruments, accounts, chattel paper, general intangibles, or minerals or the like, including oil and gas, before extraction. The term also includes the unborn young of animals.

(i) "Installment lease contract" means a lease contract that authorizes or requires the delivery of goods in separate lots to be separately accepted, even though the lease contract contains a clause "each delivery is a separate lease" or its equivalent.

(j) "Lease" means a transfer of the right to possession and use of goods for a term in return for consideration, but a sale, including a sale on approval or a sale or return, or retention or creation of a security interest is not a lease. Unless the context clearly indicates otherwise, the term includes a sublease.

(k) "Lease agreement" means the bargain, with respect to the lease, of the lessor and the lessee in fact as found in their language or by implication from other circumstances including course of dealing or usage of trade or course of performance as provided in this Article. Unless the context clearly indicates otherwise, the term includes a sublease agreement.

(l) "Lease contract" means the total legal obligation that results from the lease agreement as affected by this Article and any other applicable rules of law. Unless the context clearly indicates otherwise, the term includes a sublease contract.

(m) "Leasehold interest" means the interest of the lessor or the lessee under a lease contract.

(n) "Lessee" means a person who acquires the right to possession and use of goods under a lease. Unless the context clearly indicates otherwise, the term includes a sublessee.

(o) "Lessee in ordinary course of business" means a person who in good faith and without knowledge that the lease to him [or her] is in violation of the ownership rights or security interest or leasehold interest of a third party in the goods, leases in ordinary course from a person in the business of selling or leasing goods of that kind but does not include a pawnbroker. "Leasing" may be for cash or by exchange of other property or on secured or unsecured credit and includes receiving goods or documents of title under a pre-existing lease contract but does not include a transfer in bulk or as security for or in total or partial satisfaction of a money debt.

(p) "Lessor" means a person who transfers the right to possession and use of goods under a lease. Unless the context clearly indicates otherwise, the term includes a sublessor.

(q) "Lessor's residual interest" means the lessor's interest in the goods after expiration, termination, or cancellation of the lease contract.

(r) "Lien" means a charge against or interest in goods to secure payment of a debt or performance of an obligation, but the term does not include a security interest.

(s) "Lot" means a parcel or a single article that is the subject matter of a separate lease or delivery, whether or not it is sufficient to perform the lease contract.

(t) "Merchant lessee" means a lessee that is a merchant with respect to goods of the kind subject to the lease.

(u) "Present value" means the amount as of a date certain of one or more sums payable in the future, discounted to the date certain. The discount is determined by the interest rate specified by the parties if the rate was not manifestly unreasonable at the time the transaction

was entered into; otherwise, the discount is determined by a commercially reasonable rate that takes into account the facts and circumstances of each case at the time the transaction was entered into.

(v) "Purchase" includes taking by sale, lease, mortgage, security interest, pledge, gift, or any other voluntary transaction creating an interest in goods.

(w) "Sublease" means a lease of goods the right to possession and use of which was acquired by the lessor as a lessee under an existing lease.

(x) "Supplier" means a person from whom a lessor buys or leases goods to be leased under a finance lease.

(y) "Supply contract" means a contract under which a lessor buys or leases goods to be leased.

(z) "Termination" occurs when either party pursuant to a power created by agreement or law puts an end to the lease contract otherwise than for default.

(2) Other definitions applying to this Article and the sections in which they appear are:

"Accessions". Section 2A–310(1).
"Construction mortgage". Section 2A–309(1)(d).
"Encumbrance". Section 2A–309(1)(e).
"Fixtures". Section 2A–309(1)(a).
"Fixture filing". Section 2A–309(1)(b).
"Purchase money lease". Section 2A–309(1)(c).

(3) The following definitions in other Articles apply to this Article:

"Accounts". Section 9–106.
"Between merchants". Section 2–104(3).
"Buyer". Section 2–103(1)(a).
"Chattel paper". Section 9–105(1)(b).
"Consumer goods". Section 9–109(1).
"Document". Section 9–105(1)(f).
"Entrusting". Section 2–403(3).
"General intangibles". Section 9–106.
"Good faith". Section 2–103(1)(b).
"Instrument". Section 9–105(1)(i).
"Merchant". Section 2–104(1).
"Mortgage". Section 9–105(1)(j).
"Pursuant to commitment". Section 9–105(1)(k).
"Receipt". Section 2–103(1)(c).
"Sale". Section 2–106(1).
"Sale on approval". Section 2–326.
"Sale or return". Section 2–326.
"Seller". Section 2–103(1)(d).

(4) In addition Article 1 contains general definitions and principles of construction and interpretation applicable throughout this Article. As amended in 1990 and 1999.

§ 2A–104. Leases Subject to Other Law.

(1) A lease, although subject to this Article, is also subject to any applicable:

    (a) certificate of title statute of this State: (list any certificate of title statutes covering automobiles, trailers, mobile homes, boats, farm tractors, and the like);

    (b) certificate of title statute of another jurisdiction (Section 2A–105); or

    (c) consumer protection statute of this State, or final consumer protection decision of a court of this State existing on the effective date of this Article.

(2) In case of conflict between this Article, other than Sections 2A–105, 2A–304(3), and 2A–305(3), and a statute or decision referred to in subsection (1), the statute or decision controls.

(3) Failure to comply with an applicable law has only the effect specified therein.

As amended in 1990.

§ 2A–105. Territorial Application of Article to Goods Covered by Certificate of Title.

Subject to the provisions of Sections 2A–304(3) and 2A–305(3), with respect to goods covered by a certificate of title issued under a statute of this State or of another jurisdiction, compliance and the effect of compliance or noncompliance with a certificate of title statute are governed by the law (including the conflict of laws rules) of the jurisdiction issuing the certificate until the earlier of (a) surrender of the certificate, or (b) four months after the goods are removed from that jurisdiction and thereafter until a new certificate of title is issued by another jurisdiction.

§ 2A–106. Limitation on Power of Parties to Consumer Lease to Choose Applicable Law and Judicial Forum.

(1) If the law chosen by the parties to a consumer lease is that of a jurisdiction other than a jurisdiction in which the lessee resides at the time the lease agreement becomes enforceable or within 30 days thereafter or in which the goods are to be used, the choice is not enforceable.

(2) If the judicial forum chosen by the parties to a consumer lease is a forum that would not otherwise have jurisdiction over the lessee, the choice is not enforceable.

§ 2A–107. Waiver or Renunciation of Claim or Right After Default.

Any claim or right arising out of an alleged default or breach of warranty may be discharged in whole or in part without consideration by a written waiver or renunciation signed and delivered by the aggrieved party.

§ 2A–108. Unconscionability.

(1) If the court as a matter of law finds a lease contract or any clause of a lease contract to have been unconscionable at the time it was made the court may refuse to enforce the lease contract, or it may enforce the remainder of the lease contract without the unconscionable clause, or it may so limit the application of any unconscionable clause as to avoid any unconscionable result.

(2) With respect to a consumer lease, if the court as a matter of law finds that a lease contract or any clause of a lease contract has been induced by unconscionable conduct or that unconscionable conduct has occurred in the collection of a claim arising from a lease contract, the court may grant appropriate relief.

(3) Before making a finding of unconscionability under subsection (1) or (2), the court, on its own motion or that of a party, shall afford the parties a reasonable opportunity to present evidence as to the setting, purpose, and effect of the lease contract or clause thereof, or of the conduct.

(4) In an action in which the lessee claims unconscionability with respect to a consumer lease:

  (a) If the court finds unconscionability under subsection (1) or (2), the court shall award reasonable attorney's fees to the lessee.

  (b) If the court does not find unconscionability and the lessee claiming unconscionability has brought or maintained an action he [or she] knew to be groundless, the court shall award reasonable attorney's fees to the party against whom the claim is made.

  (c) In determining attorney's fees, the amount of the recovery on behalf of the claimant under subsections (1) and (2) is not controlling.

§ 2A–109. Option to Accelerate at Will.

(1) A term providing that one party or his [or her] successor in interest may accelerate payment or performance or require collateral or additional collateral "at will" or "when he [or she] deems himself [or herself] insecure" or in words of similar import must be construed to mean that he [or she] has power to do so only if he [or she] in good faith believes that the prospect of payment or performance is impaired.

(2) With respect to a consumer lease, the burden of establishing good faith under subsection (1) is on the party who exercised the power; otherwise the burden of establishing lack of good faith is on the party against whom the power has been exercised.

Part 2—Formation and Construction of Lease Contract

§ 2A–201. Statute of Frauds.

(1) A lease contract is not enforceable by way of action or defense unless:

  (a) the total payments to be made under the lease contract, excluding payments for options to renew or buy, are less than $1,000; or

  (b) there is a writing, signed by the party against whom enforcement is sought or by that party's authorized agent, sufficient to indicate that a lease contract has been made between the parties and to describe the goods leased and the lease term.

(2) Any description of leased goods or of the lease term is sufficient and satisfies subsection (1)(b), whether or not it is specific, if it reasonably identifies what is described.

(3) A writing is not insufficient because it omits or incorrectly states a term agreed upon, but the lease contract is not enforceable under subsection (1)(b) beyond the lease term and the quantity of goods shown in the writing.

(4) A lease contract that does not satisfy the requirements of subsection (1), but which is valid in other respects, is enforceable:

  (a) if the goods are to be specially manufactured or obtained for the lessee and are not suitable for lease or sale to others in the ordinary course of the lessor's business, and the lessor, before notice of repudiation is received and under circumstances that reasonably indicate that the goods are for the lessee, has made either a substantial beginning of their manufacture or commitments for their procurement;

  (b) if the party against whom enforcement is sought admits in that party's pleading, testimony or otherwise in court that a lease contract was made, but the lease contract is not enforceable under this provision beyond the quantity of goods admitted; or

  (c) with respect to goods that have been received and accepted by the lessee.

(5) The lease term under a lease contract referred to in subsection (4) is:

  (a) if there is a writing signed by the party against whom enforcement is sought or by that party's authorized agent specifying the lease term, the term so specified;

(b) if the party against whom enforcement is sought admits in that party's pleading, testimony, or otherwise in court a lease term, the term so admitted; or

(c) a reasonable lease term.

§ 2A–202. Final Written Expression: Parol or Extrinsic Evidence.

Terms with respect to which the confirmatory memoranda of the parties agree or which are otherwise set forth in a writing intended by the parties as a final expression of their agreement with respect to such terms as are included therein may not be contradicted by evidence of any prior agreement or of a contemporaneous oral agreement but may be explained or supplemented:

(a) by course of dealing or usage of trade or by course of performance; and

(b) by evidence of consistent additional terms unless the court finds the writing to have been intended also as a complete and exclusive statement of the terms of the agreement.

§ 2A–203. Seals Inoperative.

The affixing of a seal to a writing evidencing a lease contract or an offer to enter into a lease contract does not render the writing a sealed instrument and the law with respect to sealed instruments does not apply to the lease contract or offer.

§ 2A–204. Formation in General.

(1) A lease contract may be made in any manner sufficient to show agreement, including conduct by both parties which recognizes the existence of a lease contract.

(2) An agreement sufficient to constitute a lease contract may be found although the moment of its making is undetermined.

(3) Although one or more terms are left open, a lease contract does not fail for indefiniteness if the parties have intended to make a lease contract and there is a reasonably certain basis for giving an appropriate remedy.

§ 2A–205. Firm Offers.

An offer by a merchant to lease goods to or from another person in a signed writing that by its terms gives assurance it will be held open is not revocable, for lack of consideration, during the time stated or, if no time is stated, for a reasonable time, but in no event may the period of irrevocability exceed 3 months. Any such term of assurance on a form supplied by the offeree must be separately signed by the offeror.

§ 2A–206. Offer and Acceptance in Formation of Lease Contract.

(1) Unless otherwise unambiguously indicated by the language or circumstances, an offer to make a lease contract must be construed as inviting acceptance in any manner and by any medium reasonable in the circumstances.

(2) If the beginning of a requested performance is a reasonable mode of acceptance, an offeror who is not notified of acceptance within a reasonable time may treat the offer as having lapsed before acceptance.

§ 2A–207. Course of Performance or Practical Construction.

(1) If a lease contract involves repeated occasions for performance by either party with knowledge of the nature of the performance and opportunity for objection to it by the other, any course of performance accepted or acquiesced in without objection is relevant to determine the meaning of the lease agreement.

(2) The express terms of a lease agreement and any course of performance, as well as any course of dealing and usage of trade, must be construed whenever reasonable as consistent with each other; but if that construction is unreasonable, express terms control course of performance, course of performance controls both course of dealing and usage of trade, and course of dealing controls usage of trade.

(3) Subject to the provisions of Section 2A–208 on modification and waiver, course of performance is relevant to show a waiver or modification of any term inconsistent with the course of performance.

§ 2A–208. Modification, Rescission and Waiver.

(1) An agreement modifying a lease contract needs no consideration to be binding.

(2) A signed lease agreement that excludes modification or rescission except by a signed writing may not be otherwise modified or rescinded, but, except as between merchants, such a requirement on a form supplied by a merchant must be separately signed by the other party.

(3) Although an attempt at modification or rescission does not satisfy the requirements of subsection (2), it may operate as a waiver.

(4) A party who has made a waiver affecting an executory portion of a lease contract may retract the waiver by reasonable notification received by the other party that strict performance will be required of any term waived, unless the retraction would be unjust in view of a material change of position in reliance on the waiver.

§ 2A–209. Lessee under Finance Lease as Beneficiary of Supply Contract.

(1) The benefit of the supplier's promises to the lessor under the supply contract and of all warranties, whether express or implied, including those of any third party provided in connection with or as part of the supply contract, extends to the lessee to the extent of the lessee's leasehold interest under a finance lease related to the supply contract, but is subject to the terms warranty and of the supply contract and all defenses or claims arising therefrom.

(2) The extension of the benefit of supplier's promises and of warranties to the lessee (Section 2A–209(1)) does not: (i) modify the rights and obligations of the parties to the supply contract, whether arising therefrom or otherwise, or (ii) impose any duty or liability under the supply contract on the lessee.

(3) Any modification or rescission of the supply contract by the supplier and the lessor is effective between the supplier and the lessee unless, before the modification or rescission, the supplier has received notice that the lessee has entered into a finance lease related to the supply contract. If the modification or rescission is effective between the supplier and the lessee, the lessor is deemed to have assumed, in addition to the obligations of the lessor to the lessee under the lease contract, promises of the supplier to the lessor and warranties that were so modified or rescinded as they existed and were available to the lessee before modification or rescission.

(4) In addition to the extension of the benefit of the supplier's promises and of warranties to the lessee under subsection (1), the lessee retains all rights that the lessee may have against the supplier which arise from an agreement between the lessee and the supplier or under other law.

As amended in 1990.

§ 2A–210. Express Warranties.

(1) Express warranties by the lessor are created as follows:

(a) Any affirmation of fact or promise made by the lessor to the lessee which relates to the goods and becomes part of the basis of the bargain creates an express warranty that the goods will conform to the affirmation or promise.

(b) Any description of the goods which is made part of the basis of the bargain creates an express warranty that the goods will conform to the description.

(c) Any sample or model that is made part of the basis of the bargain creates an express warranty that the whole of the goods will conform to the sample or model.

(2) It is not necessary to the creation of an express warranty that the lessor use formal words, such as "warrant" or "guarantee," or that the lessor have a specific intention to make a warranty, but an affirmation merely of the value of the goods or a statement purporting to be merely the lessor's opinion or commendation of the goods does not create a warranty.

§ 2A–211. Warranties Against Interference and Against Infringement; Lessee's Obligation Against Infringement.

(1) There is in a lease contract a warranty that for the lease term no person holds a claim to or interest in the goods that arose from an act or omission of the lessor, other than a claim by way of infringement or the like, which will interfere with the lessee's enjoyment of its leasehold interest.

(2) Except in a finance lease there is in a lease contract by a lessor who is a merchant regularly dealing in goods of the kind a warranty that the goods are delivered free of the rightful claim of any person by way of infringement or the like.

(3) A lessee who furnishes specifications to a lessor or a supplier shall hold the lessor and the supplier harmless against any claim by way of infringement or the like that arises out of compliance with the specifications.

§ 2A–212. Implied Warranty of Merchantability.

(1) Except in a finance lease, a warranty that the goods will be merchantable is implied in a lease contract if the lessor is a merchant with respect to goods of that kind.

(2) Goods to be merchantable must be at least such as

(a) pass without objection in the trade under the description in the lease agreement;

(b) in the case of fungible goods, are of fair average quality within the description;

(c) are fit for the ordinary purposes for which goods of that type are used;

(d) run, within the variation permitted by the lease agreement, of even kind, quality, and quantity within each unit and among all units involved;

(e) are adequately contained, packaged, and labeled as the lease agreement may require; and

(f) conform to any promises or affirmations of fact made on the container or label.

(3) Other implied warranties may arise from course of dealing or usage of trade.

§ 2A–213. Implied Warranty of Fitness for Particular Purpose.

Except in a finance of lease, if the lessor at the time the lease contract is made has reason to know of any particular purpose for which the goods are required and that the lessee is relying on the lessor's skill or judgment to select or furnish suitable goods, there is in the lease contract an implied warranty that the goods will be fit for that purpose.

§ 2A–214. Exclusion or Modification of Warranties.

(1) Words or conduct relevant to the creation of an express warranty and words or conduct tending to negate or limit a warranty must be construed wherever reasonable as consistent with each other; but, subject to the provisions of Section 2A–202 on parol or extrinsic evidence, negation or limitation is inoperative to the extent that the construction is unreasonable.

(2) Subject to subsection (3), to exclude or modify the implied warranty of merchantability or any part of it the language must mention "merchantability", be by a writing, and be conspicuous. Subject to subsection (3), to exclude or modify any implied warranty of fitness the exclusion must be by a writing and be conspicuous. Language to exclude all implied warranties of fitness is sufficient if it is in writing, is conspicuous and states, for example, "There is no warranty that the goods will be fit for a particular purpose".

(3) Notwithstanding subsection (2), but subject to subsection (4),

(a) unless the circumstances indicate otherwise, all implied warranties are excluded by expressions like "as is" or "with all faults" or by other language that in common understanding calls the lessee's attention to the exclusion of warranties and makes plain that there is no implied warranty, if in writing and conspicuous;

(b) if the lessee before entering into the lease contract has examined the goods or the sample or model as fully as desired or has refused to examine the goods, there is no implied warranty with regard to defects that an examination ought in the circumstances to have revealed; and

(c) an implied warranty may also be excluded or modified by course of dealing, course of performance, or usage of trade.

(4) To exclude or modify a warranty against interference or against infringement (Section 2A–211) or any part of it, the language must be specific, be by a writing, and be conspicuous, unless the circumstances, including course of performance, course of dealing, or usage of trade, give the lessee reason to know that the goods are being leased subject to a claim or interest of any person.

§ 2A–215. Cumulation and Conflict of Warranties Express or Implied.

Warranties, whether express or implied, must be construed as consistent with each other and as cumulative, but if that construction is unreasonable, the intention of the parties determines which warranty is dominant. In ascertaining that intention the following rules apply:

(a) Exact or technical specifications displace an inconsistent sample or model or general language of description.

(b) A sample from an existing bulk displaces inconsistent general language of description.

(c) Express warranties displace inconsistent implied warranties other than an implied warranty of fitness for a particular purpose.

§ 2A–216. Third-Party Beneficiaries of Express and Implied Warranties.

Alternative A

A warranty to or for the benefit of a lessee under this Article, whether express or implied, extends to any natural person who is in the family or household of the lessee or who is a guest in the lessee's home if it is reasonable to expect that such person may use, consume, or be affected by the goods and who is injured in person by breach of the warranty. This section does not displace principles of law and equity that extend a warranty to or for the benefit of a lessee to other persons. The operation of this section may not be excluded, modified, or limited, but an exclusion, modification, or limitation of the warranty, including any with respect to rights and remedies, effective against the lessee is also effective against any beneficiary designated under this section.

Alternative B

A warranty to or for the benefit of a lessee under this Article, whether express or implied, extends to any natural person who may reasonably be expected to use, consume, or be affected by the goods and who is injured in person by breach of the warranty. This section does not displace principles of law and equity that extend a warranty to or for the benefit of a lessee to other persons. The operation of this section may not be excluded, modified, or limited, but an exclusion, modification, or limitation of the warranty, including any with respect to rights and remedies, effective against the lessee is also effective against the beneficiary designated under this section.

Alternative C

A warranty to or for the benefit of a lessee under this Article, whether express or implied, extends to any person who may reasonably be expected to use, consume, or be affected by the goods and who is injured by breach of the warranty. The operation of this section may not be excluded, modified, or limited with respect to injury to the person of an individual to whom the warranty extends, but an exclusion, modification, or limitation of the warranty, including any with respect to rights and remedies, effective against the lessee is also effective against the beneficiary designated under this section.

§ 2A–217. Identification.

Identification of goods as goods to which a lease contract refers may be made at any time and in any manner explicitly agreed to by the parties. In the absence of explicit agreement, identification occurs:

(a) when the lease contract is made if the lease contract is for a lease of goods that are existing and identified;

(b) when the goods are shipped, marked, or otherwise designated by the lessor as goods to which the lease contract refers, if the lease contract is for a lease of goods that are not existing and identified; or

(c) when the young are conceived, if the lease contract is for a lease of unborn young of animals.

§ 2A–218. Insurance and Proceeds.

(1) A lessee obtains an insurable interest when existing goods are identified to the lease contract even though the goods identified are nonconforming and the lessee has an option to reject them.

(2) If a lessee has an insurable interest only by reason of the lessor's identification of the goods, the lessor, until default or insolvency or notification to the lessee that identification is final, may substitute other goods for those identified.

(3) Notwithstanding a lessee's insurable interest under subsections (1) and (2), the lessor retains an insurable interest until an option to buy has been exercised by the lessee and risk of loss has passed to the lessee.

(4) Nothing in this section impairs any insurable interest recognized under any other statute or rule of law.

(5) The parties by agreement may determine that one or more parties have an obligation to obtain and pay for insurance covering the goods and by agreement may determine the beneficiary of the proceeds of the insurance.

§ 2A–219. Risk of Loss.

(1) Except in the case of a finance lease, risk of loss is retained by the lessor and does not pass to the lessee. In the case of a finance lease, risk of loss passes to the lessee.

(2) Subject to the provisions of this Article on the effect of default on risk of loss (Section 2A–220), if risk of loss is to pass to the lessee and the time of passage is not stated, the following rules apply:

(a) If the lease contract requires or authorizes the goods to be shipped by carrier

(i) and it does not require delivery at a particular destination, the risk of loss passes to the lessee when the goods are duly delivered to the carrier; but

(ii) if it does require delivery at a particular destination and the goods are there duly tendered while in the possession of the carrier, the risk of loss passes to the lessee when the goods are there duly so tendered as to enable the lessee to take delivery.

(b) If the goods are held by a bailee to be delivered without being moved, the risk of loss passes to the lessee on acknowledgment by the bailee of the lessee's right to possession of the goods.

(c) In any case not within subsection (a) or (b), the risk of loss passes to the lessee on the lessee's receipt of the goods if the lessor, or, in the case of a finance lease, the supplier, is a merchant; otherwise the risk passes to the lessee on tender of delivery.

§ 2A–220. Effect of Default on Risk of Loss.

(1) Where risk of loss is to pass to the lessee and the time of passage is not stated:

(a) If a tender or delivery of goods so fails to conform to the lease contract as to give a right of rejection, the risk of their loss remains with the lessor, or, in the case of a finance lease, the supplier, until cure or acceptance.

(b) If the lessee rightfully revokes acceptance, he [or she], to the extent of any deficiency in his [or her] effective insurance coverage, may treat the risk of loss as having remained with the lessor from the beginning.

(2) Whether or not risk of loss is to pass to the lessee, if the lessee as to conforming goods already identified to a lease contract repudiates or is otherwise in default under the lease contract, the lessor, or, in the case of a finance lease, the supplier, to the extent of any deficiency in his [or her] effective insurance coverage may treat the risk of loss as resting on the lessee for a commercially reasonable time.

§ 2A–221. Casualty to Identified Goods.

If a lease contract requires goods identified when the lease contract is made, and the goods suffer casualty without fault of the lessee, the lessor or the supplier before delivery, or the goods suffer casualty before risk of loss passes to the lessee pursuant to the lease agreement or Section 2A–219, then:

(a) if the loss is total, the lease contract is avoided; and

(b) if the loss is partial or the goods have so deteriorated as to no longer conform to the lease contract, the lessee may nevertheless demand inspection and at his [or her] option either treat the lease contract as avoided or, except in a finance lease that is not a consumer lease, accept the goods with due allowance from the rent payable for the balance of the lease term for the deterioration or the deficiency in quantity but without further right against the lessor.

Part 3—Effect of Lease Contract

§ 2A–301. Enforceability of Lease Contract.
Except as otherwise provided in this Article, a lease contract is effective and enforceable according to its terms between the parties, against purchasers of the goods and against creditors of the parties.

§ 2A–302. Title to and Possession of Goods.
Except as otherwise provided in this Article, each provision of this Article applies whether the lessor or a third party has title to the goods, and whether the lessor, the lessee, or a third party has possession of the goods, notwithstanding any statute or rule of law that possession or the absence of possession is fraudulent.

§ 2A–303. Alienability of Party's Interest Under Lease Contract or of Lessor's Residual Interest in Goods; Delegation of Performance; Transfer of Rights.
(1) As used in this section, "creation of a security interest" includes the sale of a lease contract that is subject to Article 9, Secured Transactions, by reason of Section 9–109(a)(3).
(2) Except as provided in subsections (3) and Section 9–407, a provision in a lease agreement which (i) prohibits the voluntary or involuntary transfer, including a transfer by sale, sublease, creation or enforcement of a security interest, or attachment, levy, or other judicial process, of an interest of a party under the lease contract or of the lessor's residual interest in the goods, or (ii) makes such a transfer an event of default, gives rise to the rights and remedies provided in subsection (4), but a transfer that is prohibited or is an event of default under the lease agreement is otherwise effective.
(3) A provision in a lease agreement which (i) prohibits a transfer of a right to damages for default with respect to the whole lease contract or of a right to payment arising out of the transferor's due performance of the transferor's entire obligation, or (ii) makes such a transfer an event of default, is not enforceable, and such a transfer is not a transfer that materially impairs the prospect of obtaining return performance by, materially changes the duty of, or materially increases the burden or risk imposed on, the other party to the lease contract within the purview of subsection (4).
(4) Subject to subsection (3) and Section 9–407:
　　(a) if a transfer is made which is made an event of default under a lease agreement, the party to the lease contract not making the transfer, unless that party waives the default or otherwise agrees, has the rights and remedies described in Section 2A–501(2);
　　(b) if paragraph (a) is not applicable and if a transfer is made that (i) is prohibited under a lease agreement or (ii) materially impairs the prospect of obtaining return performance by, materially changes the duty of, or materially increases the burden or risk imposed on, the other party to the lease contract, unless the party not making the transfer agrees at any time to the transfer in the lease contract or otherwise, then, except as limited by contract, (i) the transferor is liable to the party not making the transfer for damages caused by the transfer to the extent that the damages could not reasonably be prevented by the party not making the transfer and (ii) a court having jurisdiction may grant other appropriate relief, including cancellation of the lease contract or an injunction against the transfer.
(5) A transfer of "the lease" or of "all my rights under the lease", or a transfer in similar general terms, is a transfer of rights and, unless the language or the circumstances, as in a transfer for security, indicate the contrary, the transfer is a delegation of duties by the transferor to the transferee. Acceptance by the transferee constitutes a promise by the transferee to perform those duties. The promise is enforceable by either the transferor or the other party to the lease contract.
(6) Unless otherwise agreed by the lessor and the lessee, a delegation of performance does not relieve the transferor as against the other party of any duty to perform or of any liability for default.
(7) In a consumer lease, to prohibit the transfer of an interest of a party under the lease contract or to make a transfer an event of default, the language must be specific, by a writing, and conspicuous.
As amended in 1990 and 1999.

§ 2A–304. Subsequent Lease of Goods by Lessor.
(1) Subject to Section 2A–303, a subsequent lessee from a lessor of goods under an existing lease contract obtains, to the extent of the leasehold interest transferred, the leasehold interest in the goods that the lessor had or had power to transfer, and except as provided in subsection (2) and Section 2A–527(4), takes subject to the existing lease contract. A lessor with voidable title has power to transfer a good leasehold interest to a good faith subsequent lessee for value, but only to the extent set forth in the preceding sentence. If goods have been delivered under a transaction of purchase the lessor has that power even though:
　　(a) the lessor's transferor was deceived as to the identity of the lessor;
　　(b) the delivery was in exchange for a check which is later dishonored;
　　(c) it was agreed that the transaction was to be a "cash sale"; or
　　(d) the delivery was procured through fraud punishable as larcenous under the criminal law.
(2) A subsequent lessee in the ordinary course of business from a lessor who is a merchant dealing in goods of that kind to whom the goods were entrusted by the existing lessee of that lessor before the interest of the subsequent lessee became enforceable against that lessor obtains, to the extent of the leasehold interest transferred, all of that lessor's and the existing lessee's rights to the goods, and takes free of the existing lease contract.
(3) A subsequent lessee from the lessor of goods that are subject to an existing lease contract and are covered by a certificate of title issued under a statute of this State or of another jurisdiction takes no greater rights than those provided both by this section and by the certificate of title statute.
As amended in 1990.

§ 2A–305. Sale or Sublease of Goods by Lessee.
(1) Subject to the provisions of Section 2A–303, a buyer or sublessee from the lessee of goods under an existing lease contract obtains, to the extent of the interest transferred, the leasehold interest in the goods that the lessee had or had power to transfer, and except as provided in subsection (2) and Section 2A–511(4), takes subject to the existing lease contract. A lessee with a voidable leasehold interest has power to transfer a good leasehold interest to a good faith buyer for value or a good faith sublessee for value, but only to the

extent set forth in the preceding sentence. When goods have been delivered under a transaction of lease the lessee has that power even though:

(a) the lessor was deceived as to the identity of the lessee;

(b) the delivery was in exchange for a check which is later dishonored; or

(c) the delivery was procured through fraud punishable as larcenous under the criminal law.

(2) A buyer in the ordinary course of business or a sublessee in the ordinary course of business from a lessee who is a merchant dealing in goods of that kind to whom the goods were entrusted by the lessor obtains, to the extent of the interest transferred, all of the lessor's and lessee's rights to the goods, and takes free of the existing lease contract.

(3) A buyer or sublessee from the lessee of goods that are subject to an existing lease contract and are covered by a certificate of title issued under a statute of this State or of another jurisdiction takes no greater rights than those provided both by this section and by the certificate of title statute.

§ 2A–306. Priority of Certain Liens Arising by Operation of Law.

If a person in the ordinary course of his [or her] business furnishes services or materials with respect to goods subject to a lease contract, a lien upon those goods in the possession of that person given by statute or rule of law for those materials or services takes priority over any interest of the lessor or lessee under the lease contract or this Article unless the lien is created by statute and the statute provides otherwise or unless the lien is created by rule of law and the rule of law provides otherwise.

§ 2A–307. Priority of Liens Arising by Attachment or Levy on, Security Interests in, and Other Claims to Goods.

(1) Except as otherwise provided in Section 2A–306, a creditor of a lessee takes subject to the lease contract.

(2) Except as otherwise provided in subsection (3) and in Sections 2A–306 and 2A–308, a creditor of a lessor takes subject to the lease contract unless the creditor holds a lien that attached to the goods before the lease contract became enforceable.

(3) Except as otherwise provided in Sections 9–317, 9–321, and 9–323, a lessee takes a leasehold interest subject to a security interest held by a creditor of the lessor.

As amended in 1990 and 1999.

§ 2A–308. Special Rights of Creditors.

(1) A creditor of a lessor in possession of goods subject to a lease contract may treat the lease contract as void if as against the creditor retention of possession by the lessor is fraudulent under any statute or rule of law, but retention of possession in good faith and current course of trade by the lessor for a commercially reasonable time after the lease contract becomes enforceable is not fraudulent.

(2) Nothing in this Article impairs the rights of creditors of a lessor if the lease contract (a) becomes enforceable, not in current course of trade but in satisfaction of or as security for a pre-existing claim for money, security, or the like, and (b) is made under circumstances which under any statute or rule of law apart from this Article would constitute the transaction a fraudulent transfer or voidable preference.

(3) A creditor of a seller may treat a sale or an identification of goods to a contract for sale as void if as against the creditor retention of possession by the seller is fraudulent under any statute or rule of law, but retention of possession of the goods pursuant to a lease contract entered into by the seller as lessee and the buyer as lessor in connection with the sale or identification of the goods is not fraudulent if the buyer bought for value and in good faith.

§ 2A–309. Lessor's and Lessee's Rights When Goods Become Fixtures.

(1) In this section:

(a) goods are "fixtures" when they become so related to particular real estate that an interest in them arises under real estate law;

(b) a "fixture filing" is the filing, in the office where a mortgage on the real estate would be filed or recorded, of a financing statement covering goods that are or are to become fixtures and conforming to the requirements of Section 9–502(a) and (b);

(c) a lease is a "purchase money lease" unless the lessee has possession or use of the goods or the right to possession or use of the goods before the lease agreement is enforceable;

(d) a mortgage is a "construction mortgage" to the extent it secures an obligation incurred for the construction of an improvement on land including the acquisition cost of the land, if the recorded writing so indicates; and

(e) "encumbrance" includes real estate mortgages and other liens on real estate and all other rights in real estate that are not ownership interests.

(2) Under this Article a lease may be of goods that are fixtures or may continue in goods that become fixtures, but no lease exists under this Article of ordinary building materials incorporated into an improvement on land.

(3) This Article does not prevent creation of a lease of fixtures pursuant to real estate law.

(4) The perfected interest of a lessor of fixtures has priority over a conflicting interest of an encumbrancer or owner of the real estate if:

(a) the lease is a purchase money lease, the conflicting interest of the encumbrancer or owner arises before the goods become fixtures, the interest of the lessor is perfected by a fixture filing before the goods become fixtures or within ten days thereafter, and the lessee has an interest of record in the real estate or is in possession of the real estate; or

(b) the interest of the lessor is perfected by a fixture filing before the interest of the encumbrancer or owner is of record, the lessor's interest has priority over any conflicting interest of a predecessor in title of the encumbrancer or owner, and the lessee has an interest of record in the real estate or is in possession of the real estate.

(5) The interest of a lessor of fixtures, whether or not perfected, has priority over the conflicting interest of an encumbrancer or owner of the real estate if:

(a) the fixtures are readily removable factory or office machines, readily removable equipment that is not primarily used or leased for use in the operation of the real estate, or readily removable replacements of domestic appliances that are goods subject to a consumer lease, and before the goods become fixtures the lease contract is enforceable; or

(b) the conflicting interest is a lien on the real estate obtained by legal or equitable proceedings after the lease contract is enforceable; or

(c) the encumbrancer or owner has consented in writing to the lease or has disclaimed an interest in the goods as fixtures; or

(d) the lessee has a right to remove the goods as against the encumbrancer or owner. If the lessee's right to remove terminates, the priority of the interest of the lessor continues for a reasonable time.

(6) Notwithstanding paragraph (4)(a) but otherwise subject to subsections (4) and (5), the interest of a lessor of fixtures, including the lessor's residual interest, is subordinate to the conflicting interest of an encumbrancer of the real estate under a construction mortgage recorded before the goods become fixtures if the goods become fixtures before the completion of the construction. To the extent given to refinance a construction mortgage, the conflicting interest of an encumbrancer of the real estate under a mortgage has this priority to the same extent as the encumbrancer of the real estate under the construction mortgage.

(7) In cases not within the preceding subsections, priority between the interest of a lessor of fixtures, including the lessor's residual interest, and the conflicting interest of an encumbrancer or owner of the real estate who is not the lessee is determined by the priority rules governing conflicting interests in real estate.

(8) If the interest of a lessor of fixtures, including the lessor's residual interest, has priority over all conflicting interests of all owners and encumbrancers of the real estate, the lessor or the lessee may (i) on default, expiration, termination, or cancellation of the lease agreement but subject to the agreement and this Article, or (ii) if necessary to enforce other rights and remedies of the lessor or lessee under this Article, remove the goods from the real estate, free and clear of all conflicting interests of all owners and encumbrancers of the real estate, but the lessor or lessee must reimburse any encumbrancer or owner of the real estate who is not the lessee and who has not otherwise agreed for the cost of repair of any physical injury, but not for any diminution in value of the real estate caused by the absence of the goods removed or by any necessity of replacing them. A person entitled to reimbursement may refuse permission to remove until the party seeking removal gives adequate security for the performance of this obligation.

(9) Even though the lease agreement does not create a security interest, the interest of a lessor of fixtures, including the lessor's residual interest, is perfected by filing a financing statement as a fixture filing for leased goods that are or are to become fixtures in accordance with the relevant provisions of the Article on Secured Transactions (Article 9).

As amended in 1990 and 1999.

§ 2A–310. Lessor's and Lessee's Rights When Goods Become Accessions.

(1) Goods are "accessions" when they are installed in or affixed to other goods.

(2) The interest of a lessor or a lessee under a lease contract entered into before the goods became accessions is superior to all interests in the whole except as stated in subsection (4).

(3) The interest of a lessor or a lessee under a lease contract entered into at the time or after the goods became accessions is superior to all subsequently acquired interests in the whole except as stated in subsection (4) but is subordinate to interests in the whole existing at the time the lease contract was made unless the holders of such interests in the whole have in writing consented to the lease or disclaimed an interest in the goods as part of the whole.

(4) The interest of a lessor or a lessee under a lease contract described in subsection (2) or (3) is subordinate to the interest of

(a) a buyer in the ordinary course of business or a lessee in the ordinary course of business of any interest in the whole acquired after the goods became accessions; or

(b) a creditor with a security interest in the whole perfected before the lease contract was made to the extent that the creditor makes subsequent advances without knowledge of the lease contract.

(5) When under subsections (2) or (3) and (4) a lessor or a lessee of accessions holds an interest that is superior to all interests in the whole, the lessor or the lessee may (a) on default, expiration, termination, or cancellation of the lease contract by the other party but subject to the provisions of the lease contract and this Article, or (b) if necessary to enforce his [or her] other rights and remedies under this Article, remove the goods from the whole, free and clear of all interests in the whole, but he [or she] must reimburse any holder of an interest in the whole who is not the lessee and who has not otherwise agreed for the cost of repair of any physical injury but not for any diminution in value of the whole caused by the absence of the goods removed or by any necessity for replacing them. A person entitled to reimbursement may refuse permission to remove until the party seeking removal gives adequate security for the performance of this obligation.

§ 2A–311. Priority Subject to Subordination.

Nothing in this Article prevents subordination by agreement by any person entitled to priority.

As added in 1990.

Part 4—Performance of Lease Contract: Repudiated, Substituted and Excused

§ 2A–401. Insecurity: Adequate Assurance of Performance.

(1) A lease contract imposes an obligation on each party that the other's expectation of receiving due performance will not be impaired.

(2) If reasonable grounds for insecurity arise with respect to the performance of either party, the insecure party may demand in writing adequate assurance of due performance. Until the insecure party receives that assurance, if commercially reasonable the insecure party may suspend any performance for which he [or she] has not already received the agreed return.

(3) A repudiation of the lease contract occurs if assurance of due performance adequate under the circumstances of the particular case is not provided to the insecure party within a reasonable time, not to exceed 30 days after receipt of a demand by the other party.

(4) Between merchants, the reasonableness of grounds for insecurity and the adequacy of any assurance offered must be determined according to commercial standards.

(5) Acceptance of any nonconforming delivery or payment does not prejudice the aggrieved party's right to demand adequate assurance of future performance.

§ 2A–402. Anticipatory Repudiation.

If either party repudiates a lease contract with respect to a performance not yet due under the lease contract, the loss of which performance will substantially impair the value of the lease contract to the other, the aggrieved party may:

(a) for a commercially reasonable time, await retraction of repudiation and performance by the repudiating party;

(b) make demand pursuant to Section 2A–401 and await assurance of future performance adequate under the circumstances of the particular case; or

(c) resort to any right or remedy upon default under the lease contract or this Article, even though the aggrieved party has notified the repudiating party that the aggrieved party would await the repudiating party's performance and assurance and has urged retraction. In addition, whether or not the aggrieved party is pursuing one of the foregoing remedies, the aggrieved party may suspend performance or, if the aggrieved party is the lessor, proceed in accordance with the provisions of this Article on the lessor's right to identify goods to the lease contract notwithstanding default or to salvage unfinished goods (Section 2A–524).

§ 2A–403. Retraction of Anticipatory Repudiation.

(1) Until the repudiating party's next performance is due, the repudiating party can retract the repudiation unless, since the repudiation, the aggrieved party has cancelled the lease contract or materially changed the aggrieved party's position or otherwise indicated that the aggrieved party considers the repudiation final.

(2) Retraction may be by any method that clearly indicates to the aggrieved party that the repudiating party intends to perform under the lease contract and includes any assurance demanded under Section 2A–401.

(3) Retraction reinstates a repudiating party's rights under a lease contract with due excuse and allowance to the aggrieved party for any delay occasioned by the repudiation.

§ 2A–404. Substituted Performance.

(1) If without fault of the lessee, the lessor and the supplier, the agreed berthing, loading, or unloading facilities fail or the agreed type of carrier becomes unavailable or the agreed manner of delivery otherwise becomes commercially impracticable, but a commercially reasonable substitute is available, the substitute performance must be tendered and accepted.

(2) If the agreed means or manner of payment fails because of domestic or foreign governmental regulation:

　(a) the lessor may withhold or stop delivery or cause the supplier to withhold or stop delivery unless the lessee provides a means or manner of payment that is commercially a substantial equivalent; and

　(b) if delivery has already been taken, payment by the means or in the manner provided by the regulation discharges the lessee's obligation unless the regulation is discriminatory, oppressive, or predatory.

§ 2A–405. Excused Performance.

Subject to Section 2A–404 on substituted performance, the following rules apply:

(a) Delay in delivery or nondelivery in whole or in part by a lessor or a supplier who complies with paragraphs (b) and (c) is not a default under the lease contract if performance as agreed has been made impracticable by the occurrence of a contingency the nonoccurrence of which was a basic assumption on which the lease contract was made or by compliance in good faith with any applicable foreign or domestic governmental regulation or order, whether or not the regulation or order later proves to be invalid.

(b) If the causes mentioned in paragraph (a) affect only part of the lessor's or the supplier's capacity to perform, he [or she] shall allocate production and deliveries among his [or her] customers but at his [or her] option may include regular customers not then under contract

for sale or lease as well as his [or her] own requirements for further manufacture. He [or she] may so allocate in any manner that is fair and reasonable.

(c) The lessor seasonably shall notify the lessee and in the case of a finance lease the supplier seasonably shall notify the lessor and the lessee, if known, that there will be delay or nondelivery and, if allocation is required under paragraph (b), of the estimated quota thus made available for the lessee.

§ 2A–406. Procedure on Excused Performance.

(1) If the lessee receives notification of a material or indefinite delay or an allocation justified under Section 2A–405, the lessee may by written notification to the lessor as to any goods involved, and with respect to all of the goods if under an installment lease contract the value of the whole lease contract is substantially impaired (Section 2A–510):

　(a) terminate the lease contract (Section 2A–505(2)); or

　(b) except in a finance lease that is not a consumer lease, modify the lease contract by accepting the available quota in substitution, with due allowance from the rent payable for the balance of the lease term for the deficiency but without further right against the lessor.

(2) If, after receipt of a notification from the lessor under Section 2A–405, the lessee fails so to modify the lease agreement within a reasonable time not exceeding 30 days, the lease contract lapses with respect to any deliveries affected.

§ 2A–407. Irrevocable Promises: Finance Leases.

(1) In the case of a finance lease that is not a consumer lease the lessee's promises under the lease contract become irrevocable and independent upon the lessee's acceptance of the goods.

(2) A promise that has become irrevocable and independent under subsection (1):

　(a) is effective and enforceable between the parties, and by or against third parties including assignees of the parties, and

　(b) is not subject to cancellation, termination, modification, repudiation, excuse, or substitution without the consent of the party to whom the promise runs.

(3) This section does not affect the validity under any other law of a covenant in any lease contract making the lessee's promises irrevocable and independent upon the lessee's acceptance of the goods. As amended in 1990.

Part 5—Default

A. In General

§ 2A–501. Default: Procedure.

(1) Whether the lessor or the lessee is in default under a lease contract is determined by the lease agreement and this Article.

(2) If the lessor or the lessee is in default under the lease contract, the party seeking enforcement has rights and remedies as provided in this Article and, except as limited by this Article, as provided in the lease agreement.

(3) If the lessor or the lessee is in default under the lease contract, the party seeking enforcement may reduce the party's claim to judgment, or otherwise enforce the lease contract by self-help or any available judicial procedure or nonjudicial procedure, including administrative proceeding, arbitration, or the like, in accordance with this Article.

(4) Except as otherwise provided in Section 1–106(1) or this Article or the lease agreement, the rights and remedies referred to in subsections (2) and (3) are cumulative.

(5) If the lease agreement covers both real property and goods, the party seeking enforcement may proceed under this Part as to the goods, or under other applicable law as to both the real property and the goods in accordance with that party's rights and remedies in respect of the real property, in which case this Part does not apply. As amended in 1990.

§ 2A–502. Notice After Default.

Except as otherwise provided in this Article or the lease agreement, the lessor or lessee in default under the lease contract is not entitled to notice of default or notice of enforcement from the other party to the lease agreement.

§ 2A–503. Modification or Impairment of Rights and Remedies.

(1) Except as otherwise provided in this Article, the lease agreement may include rights and remedies for default in addition to or in substitution for those provided in this Article and may limit or alter the measure of damages recoverable under this Article.

(2) Resort to a remedy provided under this Article or in the lease agreement is optional unless the remedy is expressly agreed to be exclusive. If circumstances cause an exclusive or limited remedy to fail of its essential purpose, or provision for an exclusive remedy is unconscionable, remedy may be had as provided in this Article.

(3) Consequential damages may be liquidated under Section 2A–504, or may otherwise be limited, altered, or excluded unless the limitation, alteration, or exclusion is unconscionable. Limitation, alteration, or exclusion of consequential damages for injury to the person in the case of consumer goods is *prima facie* unconscionable but limitation, alteration, or exclusion of damages where the loss is commercial is not *prima facie* unconscionable.

(4) Rights and remedies on default by the lessor or the lessee with respect to any obligation or promise collateral or ancillary to the lease contract are not impaired by this Article. As amended in 1990.

§ 2A–504. Liquidation of Damages.

(1) Damages payable by either party for default, or any other act or omission, including indemnity for loss or diminution of anticipated tax benefits or loss or damage to lessor's residual interest, may be liquidated in the lease agreement but only at an amount or by a formula that is reasonable in light of the then anticipated harm caused by the default or other act or omission.

(2) If the lease agreement provides for liquidation of damages, and such provision does not comply with subsection (1), or such provision is an exclusive or limited remedy that circumstances cause to fail of its essential purpose, remedy may be had as provided in this Article.

(3) If the lessor justifiably withholds or stops delivery of goods because of the lessee's default or insolvency (Section 2A–525 or 2A–526), the lessee is entitled to restitution of any amount by which the sum of his [or her] payments exceeds:

    (a) the amount to which the lessor is entitled by virtue of terms liquidating the lessor's damages in accordance with subsection (1); or

    (b) in the absence of those terms, 20 percent of the then present value of the total rent the lessee was obligated to pay for the balance of the lease term, or, in the case of a consumer lease, the lesser of such amount or $500.

(4) A lessee's right to restitution under subsection (3) is subject to offset to the extent the lessor establishes:

    (a) a right to recover damages under the provisions of this Article other than subsection (1); and

    (b) the amount or value of any benefits received by the lessee directly or indirectly by reason of the lease contract.

§ 2A–505. Cancellation and Termination and Effect of Cancellation, Termination, Rescission, or Fraud on Rights and Remedies.

(1) On cancellation of the lease contract, all obligations that are still executory on both sides are discharged, but any right based on prior default or performance survives, and the cancelling party also retains any remedy for default of the whole lease contract or any unperformed balance.

(2) On termination of the lease contract, all obligations that are still executory on both sides are discharged but any right based on prior default or performance survives.

(3) Unless the contrary intention clearly appears, expressions of "cancellation," "rescission," or the like of the lease contract may not be construed as a renunciation or discharge of any claim in damages for an antecedent default.

(4) Rights and remedies for material misrepresentation or fraud include all rights and remedies available under this Article for default.

(5) Neither rescission nor a claim for rescission of the lease contract nor rejection or return of the goods may bar or be deemed inconsistent with a claim for damages or other right or remedy.

§ 2A–506. Statute of Limitations.

(1) An action for default under a lease contract, including breach of warranty or indemnity, must be commenced within 4 years after the cause of action accrued. By the original lease contract the parties may reduce the period of limitation to not less than one year.

(2) A cause of action for default accrues when the act or omission on which the default or breach of warranty is based is or should have been discovered by the aggrieved party, or when the default occurs, whichever is later. A cause of action for indemnity accrues when the act or omission on which the claim for indemnity is based is or should have been discovered by the indemnified party, whichever is later.

(3) If an action commenced within the time limited by subsection (1) is so terminated as to leave available a remedy by another action for the same default or breach of warranty or indemnity, the other action may be commenced after the expiration of the time limited and within 6 months after the termination of the first action unless the termination resulted from voluntary discontinuance or from dismissal for failure or neglect to prosecute.

(4) This section does not alter the law on tolling of the statute of limitations nor does it apply to causes of action that have accrued before this Article becomes effective.

§ 2A–507. Proof of Market Rent: Time and Place.

(1) Damages based on market rent (Section 2A–519 or 2A–528) are determined according to the rent for the use of the goods concerned for a lease term identical to the remaining lease term of the original lease agreement and prevailing at the times specified in Sections 2A–519 and 2A–528.

(2) If evidence of rent for the use of the goods concerned for a lease term identical to the remaining lease term of the original lease agreement and prevailing at the times or places described in this Article is not readily available, the rent prevailing within any reasonable time before or after the time described or at any other place or for a different lease term which in commercial judgment or under usage of trade would serve as a reasonable substitute for the one described may be used, making any proper allowance for the difference, including the cost of transporting the goods to or from the other place.

(3) Evidence of a relevant rent prevailing at a time or place or for a lease term other than the one described in this Article offered by one party is not admissible unless and until he [or she] has given the other party notice the court finds sufficient to prevent unfair surprise.

(4) If the prevailing rent or value of any goods regularly leased in any established market is in issue, reports in official publications or trade journals or in newspapers or periodicals of general circulation published as the reports of that market are admissible in evidence. The circumstances of the preparation of the report may be shown to affect its weight but not its admissibility.

As amended in 1990.

B. Default by Lessor

§ 2A–508. Lessee's Remedies.

(1) If a lessor fails to deliver the goods in conformity to the lease contract (Section 2A–509) or repudiates the lease contract (Section 2A–402), or a lessee rightfully rejects the goods (Section 2A–509) or justifiably revokes acceptance of the goods (Section 2A–517), then with respect to any goods involved, and with respect to all of the goods if under an installment lease contract the value of the whole lease contract is substantially impaired (Section 2A–510), the lessor is in default under the lease contract and the lessee may:

    (a) cancel the lease contract (Section 2A–505(1));

    (b) recover so much of the rent and security as has been paid and is just under the circumstances;

    (c) cover and recover damages as to all goods affected whether or not they have been identified to the lease contract (Sections 2A–518 and 2A–520), or recover damages for nondelivery (Sections 2A–519 and 2A–520);

    (d) exercise any other rights or pursue any other remedies provided in the lease contract.

(2) If a lessor fails to deliver the goods in conformity to the lease contract or repudiates the lease contract, the lessee may also:

    (a) if the goods have been identified, recover them (Section 2A–522); or

    (b) in a proper case, obtain specific performance or replevy the goods (Section 2A–521).

(3) If a lessor is otherwise in default under a lease contract, the lessee may exercise the rights and pursue the remedies provided in the lease contract, which may include a right to cancel the lease, and in Section 2A–519(3).

(4) If a lessor has breached a warranty, whether express or implied, the lessee may recover damages (Section 2A–519(4)).

(5) On rightful rejection or justifiable revocation of acceptance, a lessee has a security interest in goods in the lessee's possession or control for any rent and security that has been paid and any expenses reasonably incurred in their inspection, receipt, transportation, and care and custody and may hold those goods and dispose of them in good faith and in a commercially reasonable manner, subject to Section 2A–527(5).

(6) Subject to the provisions of Section 2A–407, a lessee, on notifying the lessor of the lessee's intention to do so, may deduct all or any part of the damages resulting from any default under the lease contract from any part of the rent still due under the same lease contract. As amended in 1990.

§ 2A–509. Lessee's Rights on Improper Delivery; Rightful Rejection.

(1) Subject to the provisions of Section 2A–510 on default in installment lease contracts, if the goods or the tender or delivery fail in any respect to conform to the lease contract, the lessee may reject or accept the goods or accept any commercial unit or units and reject the rest of the goods.

(2) Rejection of goods is ineffective unless it is within a reasonable time after tender or delivery of the goods and the lessee seasonably notifies the lessor.

§ 2A–510. Installment Lease Contracts: Rejection and Default.

(1) Under an installment lease contract a lessee may reject any delivery that is nonconforming if the nonconformity substantially impairs the value of that delivery and cannot be cured or the nonconformity is a defect in the required documents; but if the nonconformity does not fall within subsection (2) and the lessor or the supplier gives adequate assurance of its cure, the lessee must accept that delivery.

(2) Whenever nonconformity or default with respect to one or more deliveries substantially impairs the value of the installment lease contract as a whole there is a default with respect to the whole. But, the aggrieved party reinstates the installment lease contract as a whole if the aggrieved party accepts a nonconforming delivery without seasonably notifying of cancellation or brings an action with respect only to past deliveries or demands performance as to future deliveries.

§ 2A–511. Merchant Lessee's Duties as to Rightfully Rejected Goods.

(1) Subject to any security interest of a lessee (Section 2A–508(5)), if a lessor or a supplier has no agent or place of business at the market of rejection, a merchant lessee, after rejection of goods in his [or her] possession or control, shall follow any reasonable instructions received from the lessor or the supplier with respect to the goods. In the absence of those instructions, a merchant lessee shall make reasonable efforts to sell, lease, or otherwise dispose of the goods for the lessor's account if they threaten to decline in value speedily. Instructions are not reasonable if on demand indemnity for expenses is not forthcoming.

(2) If a merchant lessee (subsection (1)) or any other lessee (Section 2A–512) disposes of goods, he [or she] is entitled to reimbursement either from the lessor or the supplier or out of the proceeds for reasonable expenses of caring for and disposing of the goods and, if the expenses include no disposition commission, to such commission as is usual in the trade, or if there is none, to a reasonable sum not exceeding 10 percent of the gross proceeds.

(3) In complying with this section or Section 2A–512, the lessee is held only to good faith. Good faith conduct hereunder is neither acceptance or conversion nor the basis of an action for damages.

(4) A purchaser who purchases in good faith from a lessee pursuant to this section or Section 2A–512 takes the goods free of any rights of the lessor and the supplier even though the lessee fails to comply with one or more of the requirements of this Article.

§ 2A–512. Lessee's Duties as to Rightfully Rejected Goods.

(1) Except as otherwise provided with respect to goods that threaten to decline in value speedily (Section 2A–511) and subject to any security interest of a lessee (Section 2A–508(5)):

(a) the lessee, after rejection of goods in the lessee's possession, shall hold them with reasonable care at the lessor's or the supplier's disposition for a reasonable time after the lessee's seasonable notification of rejection;

(b) if the lessor or the supplier gives no instructions within a reasonable time after notification of rejection, the lessee may store the rejected goods for the lessor's or the supplier's account or ship them to the lessor or the supplier or dispose of them for the lessor's or the supplier's account with reimbursement in the manner provided in Section 2A–511; but

(c) the lessee has no further obligations with regard to goods rightfully rejected.

(2) Action by the lessee pursuant to subsection (1) is not acceptance or conversion.

§ 2A–513. Cure by Lessor of Improper Tender or Delivery; Replacement.

(1) If any tender or delivery by the lessor or the supplier is rejected because nonconforming and the time for performance has not yet expired, the lessor or the supplier may seasonally notify the lessee of the lessor's or the supplier's intention to cure and may then make a conforming delivery within the time provided in the lease contract.

(2) If the lessee rejects a nonconforming tender that the lessor or the supplier had reasonable grounds to believe would be acceptable with or without money allowance, the lessor or the supplier may have a further reasonable time to substitute a conforming tender if he [or she] seasonally notifies the lessee.

§ 2A–514. Waiver of Lessee's Objections.

(1) In rejecting goods, a lessee's failure to state a particular defect that is ascertainable by reasonable inspection precludes the lessee from relying on the defect to justify rejection or to establish default:

(a) if, stated seasonably, the lessor or the supplier could have cured it (Section 2A–513); or

(b) between merchants if the lessor or the supplier after rejection has made a request in writing for a full and final written statement of all defects on which the lessee proposes to rely.

(2) A lessee's failure to reserve rights when paying rent or other consideration against documents precludes recovery of the payment for defects apparent on the face of the documents.

§ 2A–515. Acceptance of Goods.

(1) Acceptance of goods occurs after the lessee has had a reasonable opportunity to inspect the goods and

(a) the lessee signifies or acts with respect to the goods in a manner that signifies to the lessor or the supplier that the goods are conforming or that the lessee will take or retain them in spite of their nonconformity; or

(b) the lessee fails to make an effective rejection of the goods (Section 2A–509(2)).

(2) Acceptance of a part of any commercial unit is acceptance of that entire unit.

§ 2A–516. Effect of Acceptance of Goods; Notice of Default; Burden of Establishing Default after Acceptance; Notice of Claim or Litigation to Person Answerable Over.

(1) A lessee must pay rent for any goods accepted in accordance with the lease contract, with due allowance for goods rightfully rejected or not delivered.

(2) A lessee's acceptance of goods precludes rejection of the goods accepted. In the case of a finance lease, if made with knowledge of a nonconformity, acceptance cannot be revoked because of it. In any other case, if made with knowledge of a nonconformity, acceptance cannot be revoked because of it unless the acceptance was on the reasonable assumption that the nonconformity would be seasonably cured. Acceptance does not of itself impair any other remedy provided by this Article or the lease agreement for nonconformity.

(3) If a tender has been accepted:

(a) within a reasonable time after the lessee discovers or should have discovered any default, the lessee shall notify the lessor and the supplier, if any, or be barred from any remedy against the party notified;

(b) except in the case of a consumer lease, within a reasonable time after the lessee receives notice of litigation for infringement or the like (Section 2A–211) the lessee shall notify the lessor or be barred from any remedy over for liability established by the litigation; and

(c) the burden is on the lessee to establish any default.

(4) If a lessee is sued for breach of a warranty or other obligation for which a lessor or a supplier is answerable over the following apply:

(a) The lessee may give the lessor or the supplier, or both, written notice of the litigation. If the notice states that the person notified may come in and defend and that if the person notified does not do so that person will be bound in any action against that person by the lessee by any determination of fact common to the two litigations, then unless the person notified after seasonable receipt of the notice does come in and defend that person is so bound.

(b) The lessor or the supplier may demand in writing that the lessee turn over control of the litigation including settlement if the claim is one for infringement or the like (Section 2A–211) or else be barred from any remedy over. If the demand states that the lessor or the supplier agrees to bear all expense and to satisfy any adverse judgment, then unless the lessee after seasonable receipt of the demand does turn over control the lessee is so barred.

(5) Subsections (3) and (4) apply to any obligation of a lessee to hold the lessor or the supplier harmless against infringement or the like (Section 2A–211).

As amended in 1990.

§ 2A–517. Revocation of Acceptance of Goods.

(1) A lessee may revoke acceptance of a lot or commercial unit whose nonconformity substantially impairs its value to the lessee if the lessee has accepted it:

(a) except in the case of a finance lease, on the reasonable assumption that its nonconformity would be cured and it has not been seasonably cured; or

(b) without discovery of the nonconformity if the lessee's acceptance was reasonably induced either by the lessor's assurances or, except in the case of a finance lease, by the difficulty of discovery before acceptance.

(2) Except in the case of a finance lease that is not a consumer lease, a lessee may revoke acceptance of a lot or commercial unit if the lessor defaults under the lease contract and the default substantially impairs the value of that lot or commercial unit to the lessee.

(3) If the lease agreement so provides, the lessee may revoke acceptance of a lot or commercial unit because of other defaults by the lessor.

(4) Revocation of acceptance must occur within a reasonable time after the lessee discovers or should have discovered the ground for it and before any substantial change in condition of the goods which is not caused by the nonconformity. Revocation is not effective until the lessee notifies the lessor.

(5) A lessee who so revokes has the same rights and duties with regard to the goods involved as if the lessee had rejected them.
As amended in 1990.

§ 2A–518. Cover; Substitute Goods.

(1) After a default by a lessor under the lease contract of the type described in Section 2A–508(1), or, if agreed, after other default by the lessor, the lessee may cover by making any purchase or lease of or contract to purchase or lease goods in substitution for those due from the lessor.

(2) Except as otherwise provided with respect to damages liquidated in the lease agreement (Section 2A–504) or otherwise determined pursuant to agreement of the parties (Sections 1–102(3) and 2A–503), if a lessee's cover is by lease agreement substantially similar to the original lease agreement and the new lease agreement is made in good faith and in a commercially reasonable manner, the lessee may recover from the lessor as damages (i) the present value, as of the date of the commencement of the term of the new lease agreement, of the rent under the new lease agreement applicable to that period of the new lease term which is comparable to the then remaining term of the original lease agreement minus the present value as of the same date of the total rent for the then remaining lease term of the original lease agreement, and (ii) any incidental or consequential damages, less expenses saved in consequence of the lessor's default.

(3) If a lessee's cover is by lease agreement that for any reason does not qualify for treatment under subsection (2), or is by purchase or otherwise, the lessee may recover from the lessor as if the lessee had elected not to cover and Section 2A–519 governs.
As amended in 1990.

§ 2A–519. Lessee's Damages for Non-Delivery, Repudiation, Default, and Breach of Warranty in Regard to Accepted Goods.

(1) Except as otherwise provided with respect to damages liquidated in the lease agreement (Section 2A–504) or otherwise determined pursuant to agreement of the parties (Sections 1–102(3) and 2A–503), if a lessee elects not to cover or a lessee elects to cover and the cover is by lease agreement that for any reason does not qualify for treatment under Section 2A–518(2), or is by purchase or otherwise, the measure of damages for non-delivery or repudiation by the lessor or for rejection or revocation of acceptance by the lessee is the present value, as of the date of the default, of the then market rent minus the present value as of the same date of the original

rent, computed for the remaining lease term of the original lease agreement, together with incidental and consequential damages, less expenses saved in consequence of the lessor's default.

(2) Market rent is to be determined as of the place for tender or, in cases of rejection after arrival or revocation of acceptance, as of the place of arrival.

(3) Except as otherwise agreed, if the lessee has accepted goods and given notification (Section 2A–516(3)), the measure of damages for non-conforming tender or delivery or other default by a lessor is the loss resulting in the ordinary course of events from the lessor's default as determined in any manner that is reasonable together with incidental and consequential damages, less expenses saved in consequence of the lessor's default.

(4) Except as otherwise agreed, the measure of damages for breach of warranty is the present value at the time and place of acceptance of the difference between the value of the use of the goods accepted and the value if they had been as warranted for the lease term, unless special circumstances show proximate damages of a different amount, together with incidental and consequential damages, less expenses saved in consequence of the lessor's default or breach of warranty.
As amended in 1990.

§ 2A–520. Lessee's Incidental and Consequential Damages.

(1) Incidental damages resulting from a lessor's default include expenses reasonably incurred in inspection, receipt, transportation, and care and custody of goods rightfully rejected or goods the acceptance of which is justifiably revoked, any commercially reasonable charges, expenses or commissions in connection with effecting cover, and any other reasonable expense incident to the default.

(2) Consequential damages resulting from a lessor's default include:

    (a) any loss resulting from general or particular requirements and needs of which the lessor at the time of contracting had reason to know and which could not reasonably be prevented by cover or otherwise; and

    (b) injury to person or property proximately resulting from any breach of warranty.

§ 2A–521. Lessee's Right to Specific Performance or Replevin.

(1) Specific performance may be decreed if the goods are unique or in other proper circumstances.

(2) A decree for specific performance may include any terms and conditions as to payment of the rent, damages, or other relief that the court deems just.

(3) A lessee has a right of replevin, detinue, sequestration, claim and delivery, or the like for goods identified to the lease contract if after reasonable effort the lessee is unable to effect cover for those goods or the circumstances reasonably indicate that the effort will be unavailing.

§ 2A–522. Lessee's Right to Goods on Lessor's Insolvency.

(1) Subject to subsection (2) and even though the goods have not been shipped, a lessee who has paid a part or all of the rent and security for goods identified to a lease contract (Section 2A–217) on making and keeping good a tender of any unpaid portion of the rent and security due under the lease contract may recover the goods identified from the lessor if the lessor becomes insolvent within 10 days after receipt of the first installment of rent and security.

(2) A lessee acquires the right to recover goods identified to a lease contract only if they conform to the lease contract.

C. Default by Lessee

§ 2A–523. **Lessor's Remedies.**

(1) If a lessee wrongfully rejects or revokes acceptance of goods or fails to make a payment when due or repudiates with respect to a part or the whole, then, with respect to any goods involved, and with respect to all of the goods if under an installment lease contract the value of the whole lease contract is substantially impaired (Section 2A–510), the lessee is in default under the lease contract and the lessor may:

    (a) cancel the lease contract (Section 2A–505(1));

    (b) proceed respecting goods not identified to the lease contract (Section 2A–524);

    (c) withhold delivery of the goods and take possession of goods previously delivered (Section 2A–525);

    (d) stop delivery of the goods by any bailee (Section 2A–526);

    (e) dispose of the goods and recover damages (Section 2A–527), or retain the goods and recover damages (Section 2A–528), or in a proper case recover rent (Section 2A–529)

    (f) exercise any other rights or pursue any other remedies provided in the lease contract.

(2) If a lessor does not fully exercise a right or obtain a remedy to which the lessor is entitled under subsection (1), the lessor may recover the loss resulting in the ordinary course of events from the lessee's default as determined in any reasonable manner, together with incidental damages, less expenses saved in consequence of the lessee's default.

(3) If a lessee is otherwise in default under a lease contract, the lessor may exercise the rights and pursue the remedies provided in the lease contract, which may include a right to cancel the lease. In addition, unless otherwise provided in the lease contract:

    (a) if the default substantially impairs the value of the lease contract to the lessor, the lessor may exercise the rights and pursue the remedies provided in subsections (1) or (2); or

    (b) if the default does not substantially impair the value of the lease contract to the lessor, the lessor may recover as provided in subsection (2).

As amended in 1990.

§ 2A–524. **Lessor's Right to Identify Goods to Lease Contract.**

(1) After default by the lessee under the lease contract of the type described in Section 2A–523(1) or 2A–523(3)(a) or, if agreed, after other default by the lessee, the lessor may:

    (a) identify to the lease contract conforming goods not already identified if at the time the lessor learned of the default they were in the lessor's or the supplier's possession or control; and

    (b) dispose of goods (Section 2A–527(1)) that demonstrably have been intended for the particular lease contract even though those goods are unfinished.

(2) If the goods are unfinished, in the exercise of reasonable commercial judgment for the purposes of avoiding loss and of effective realization, an aggrieved lessor or the supplier may either complete manufacture and wholly identify the goods to the lease contract or cease manufacture and lease, sell, or otherwise dispose of the goods for scrap or salvage value or proceed in any other reasonable manner.

As amended in 1990.

§ 2A–525. **Lessor's Right to Possession of Goods.**

(1) If a lessor discovers the lessee to be insolvent, the lessor may refuse to deliver the goods.

(2) After a default by the lessee under the lease contract of the type described in Section 2A–523(1) or 2A–523(3)(a) or, if agreed, after other default by the lessee, the lessor has the right to take possession of the goods. If the lease contract so provides, the lessor may require the lessee to assemble the goods and make them available to the lessor at a place to be designated by the lessor which is reasonably convenient to both parties. Without removal, the lessor may render unusable any goods employed in trade or business, and may dispose of goods on the lessee's premises (Section 2A–527).

(3) The lessor may proceed under subsection (2) without judicial process if that can be done without breach of the peace or the lessor may proceed by action.

As amended in 1990.

§ 2A–526. **Lessor's Stoppage of Delivery in Transit or Otherwise.**

(1) A lessor may stop delivery of goods in the possession of a carrier or other bailee if the lessor discovers the lessee to be insolvent and may stop delivery of carload, truckload, planeload, or larger shipments of express or freight if the lessee repudiates or fails to make a payment due before delivery, whether for rent, security or otherwise under the lease contract, or for any other reason the lessor has a right to withhold or take possession of the goods.

(2) In pursuing its remedies under subsection (1), the lessor may stop delivery until

    (a) receipt of the goods by the lessee;

    (b) acknowledgment to the lessee by any bailee of the goods, except a carrier, that the bailee holds the goods for the lessee; or

    (c) such an acknowledgment to the lessee by a carrier via reshipment or as warehouseman.

(3) (a) To stop delivery, a lessor shall so notify as to enable the bailee by reasonable diligence to prevent delivery of the goods.

    (b) After notification, the bailee shall hold and deliver the goods according to the directions of the lessor, but the lessor is liable to the bailee for any ensuing charges or damages.

    (c) A carrier who has issued a nonnegotiable bill of lading is not obliged to obey a notification to stop received from a person other than the consignor.

§ 2A–527. **Lessor's Rights to Dispose of Goods.**

(1) After a default by a lessee under the lease contract of the type described in Section 2A–523(1) or 2A–523(3)(a) or after the lessor refuses to deliver or takes possession of goods (Section 2A–525 or 2A–526), or, if agreed, after other default by a lessee, the lessor may dispose of the goods concerned or the undelivered balance thereof by lease, sale, or otherwise.

(2) Except as otherwise provided with respect to damages liquidated in the lease agreement (Section 2A–504) or otherwise determined pursuant to agreement of the parties (Sections 1–102(3) and 2A–503), if the disposition is by lease agreement substantially similar to the original lease agreement and the new lease agreement is made in good faith and in a commercially reasonable manner, the lessor may recover from the lessee as damages (i) accrued and unpaid rent as of the date of the commencement of the term of the new lease agreement, (ii) the present value, as of the same date, of the total rent for the then remaining lease term of the original lease agreement minus the present value, as of the same date, of the rent under the new lease agreement applicable to that period of the new lease term which is comparable to the then remaining term of the original lease agreement, and (iii) any incidental damages allowed under Section 2A–530, less expenses saved in consequence of the lessee's default.

(3) If the lessor's disposition is by lease agreement that for any reason does not qualify for treatment under subsection (2), or is by sale or otherwise, the lessor may recover from the lessee as if the lessor had elected not to dispose of the goods and Section 2A–528 governs.

(4) A subsequent buyer or lessee who buys or leases from the lessor in good faith for value as a result of a disposition under this section takes the goods free of the original lease contract and any rights of the original lessee even though the lessor fails to comply with one or more of the requirements of this Article.

(5) The lessor is not accountable to the lessee for any profit made on any disposition. A lessee who has rightfully rejected or justifiably revoked acceptance shall account to the lessor for any excess over the amount of the lessee's security interest (Section 2A–508(5)).
As amended in 1990.

§ 2A–528. Lessor's Damages for Non-acceptance, Failure to Pay, Repudiation, or Other Default.

(1) Except as otherwise provided with respect to damages liquidated in the lease agreement (Section 2A–504) or otherwise determined pursuant to agreement of the parties (Section 1–102(3) and 2A–503), if a lessor elects to retain the goods or a lessor elects to dispose of the goods and the disposition is by lease agreement that for any reason does not qualify for treatment under Section 2A–527(2), or is by sale or otherwise, the lessor may recover from the lessee as damages for a default of the type described in Section 2A–523(1) or 2A–523(3)(a), or if agreed, for other default of the lessee, (i) accrued and unpaid rent as of the date of the default if the lessee has never taken possession of the goods, or, if the lessee has taken possession of the goods, as of the date the lessor repossesses the goods or an earlier date on which the lessee makes a tender of the goods to the lessor, (ii) the present value as of the date determined under clause (i) of the total rent for the then remaining lease term of the original lease agreement minus the present value as of the same date of the market rent as the place where the goods are located computed for the same lease term, and (iii) any incidental damages allowed under Section 2A–530, less expenses saved in consequence of the lessee's default.

(2) If the measure of damages provided in subsection (1) is inadequate to put a lessor in as good a position as performance would have, the measure of damages is the present value of the profit, including reasonable overhead, the lessor would have made from full performance by the lessee, together with any incidental damages allowed under Section 2A–530, due allowance for costs reasonably incurred and due credit for payments or proceeds of disposition.
As amended in 1990.

§ 2A–529. Lessor's Action for the Rent.

(1) After default by the lessee under the lease contract of the type described in Section 2A–523(1) or 2A–523(3)(a) or, if agreed, after other default by the lessee, if the lessor complies with subsection (2), the lessor may recover from the lessee as damages:

    (a) for goods accepted by the lessee and not repossessed by or tendered to the lessor, and for conforming goods lost or damaged within a commercially reasonable time after risk of loss

passes to the lessee (Section 2A–219), (i) accrued and unpaid rent as of the date of entry of judgment in favor of the lessor (ii) the present value as of the same date of the rent for the then remaining lease term of the lease agreement, and (iii) any incidental damages allowed under Section 2A–530, less expenses saved in consequence of the lessee's default; and

    (b) for goods identified to the lease contract if the lessor is unable after reasonable effort to dispose of them at a reasonable price or the circumstances reasonably indicate that effort will be unavailing, (i) accrued and unpaid rent as of the date of entry of judgment in favor of the lessor, (ii) the present value as of the same date of the rent for the then remaining lease term of the lease agreement, and (iii) any incidental damages allowed under Section 2A–530, less expenses saved in consequence of the lessee's default.

(2) Except as provided in subsection (3), the lessor shall hold for the lessee for the remaining lease term of the lease agreement any goods that have been identified to the lease contract and are in the lessor's control.

(3) The lessor may dispose of the goods at any time before collection of the judgment for damages obtained pursuant to subsection (1). If the disposition is before the end of the remaining lease term of the lease agreement, the lessor's recovery against the lessee for damages is governed by Section 2A–527 or Section 2A–528, and the lessor will cause an appropriate credit to be provided against a judgment for damages to the extent that the amount of the judgment exceeds the recovery available pursuant to Section 2A–527 or 2A–528.

(4) Payment of the judgment for damages obtained pursuant to subsection (1) entitles the lessee to the use and possession of the goods not then disposed of for the remaining lease term of and in accordance with the lease agreement.

(5) After default by the lessee under the lease contract of the type described in Section 2A–523(1) or Section 2A–523(3)(a) or, if agreed, after other default by the lessee, a lessor who is held not entitled to rent under this section must nevertheless be awarded damages for non-acceptance under Sections 2A–527 and 2A–528.
As amended in 1990.

§ 2A–530. Lessor's Incidental Damages.

Incidental damages to an aggrieved lessor include any commercially reasonable charges, expenses, or commissions incurred in stopping delivery, in the transportation, care and custody of goods after the lessee's default, in connection with return or disposition of the goods, or otherwise resulting from the default.

§ 2A–531. Standing to Sue Third Parties for Injury to Goods.

(1) If a third party so deals with goods that have been identified to a lease contract as to cause actionable injury to a party to the lease contract (a) the lessor has a right of action against the third party, and (b) the lessee also has a right of action against the third party if the lessee:

    (i) has a security interest in the goods;

    (ii) has an insurable interest in the goods; or

    (iii) bears the risk of loss under the lease contract or has since the injury assumed that risk as against the lessor and the goods have been converted or destroyed.

(2) If at the time of the injury the party plaintiff did not bear the risk of loss as against the other party to the lease contract and there is no arrangement between them for disposition of the recovery, his [or her] suit or settlement, subject to his [or her] own interest, is as a fiduciary for the other party to the lease contract.

(3) Either party with the consent of the other may sue for the benefit of whom it may concern.

§ 2A–532. Lessor's Rights to Residual Interest.
In addition to any other recovery permitted by this Article or other law, the lessor may recover from the lessee an amount that will fully compensate the lessor for any loss of or damage to the lessor's residual interest in the goods caused by the default of the lessee.
As added in 1990.

REVISED ARTICLE 3: NEGOTIABLE INSTRUMENTS

Part 1—General Provisions and Definitions

§ 3–101. Short Title.
This Article may be cited as Uniform Commercial Code–Negotiable Instruments.

§ 3–102. Subject Matter.
(a) This Article applies to negotiable instruments. It does not apply to money, to payment orders governed by Article 4A, or to securities governed by Article 8.
(b) If there is conflict between this Article and Article 4 or 9, Articles 4 and 9 govern.
(c) Regulations of the Board of Governors of the Federal Reserve System and operating circulars of the Federal Reserve Banks supersede any inconsistent provision of this Article to the extent of the inconsistency.

§ 3–103. Definitions.
(a) In this Article:
  (1) "Acceptor" means a drawee who has accepted a draft.
  (2) "Drawee" means a person ordered in a draft to make payment.
  (3) "Drawer" means a person who signs or is identified in a draft as a person ordering payment.
  (4) "Good faith" means honesty in fact and the observance of reasonable commercial standards of fair dealing.
  (5) "Maker" means a person who signs or is identified in a note as a person undertaking to pay.
  (6) "Order" means a written instruction to pay money signed by the person giving the instruction. The instruction may be addressed to any person, including the person giving the instruction, or to one or more persons jointly or in the alternative but not in succession. An authorization to pay is not an order unless the person authorized to pay is also instructed to pay.
  (7) "Ordinary care" in the case of a person engaged in business means observance of reasonable commercial standards, prevailing in the area in which the person is located, with respect to the business in which the person is engaged. In the case of a bank that takes an instrument for processing for collection or payment by automated means, reasonable commercial standards do not require the bank to examine the instrument if the failure to examine does not violate the bank's prescribed procedures and the bank's procedures do not vary unreasonably from general banking usage not disapproved by this Article or Article 4.
  (8) "Party" means a party to an instrument.
  (9) "Promise" means a written undertaking to pay money signed by the person undertaking to pay. An acknowledgment of an obligation by the obligor is not a promise unless the obligor also undertakes to pay the obligation.
  (10) "Prove" with respect to a fact means to meet the burden of establishing the fact (Section 1–201(8)).
  (11) "Remitter" means a person who purchases an instrument from its issuer if the instrument is payable to an identified person other than the purchaser.
(b) [Other definitions' section references deleted.]
(c) [Other definitions' section references deleted.]
(d) In addition, Article 1 contains general definitions and principles of construction and interpretation applicable throughout this Article.

§ 3–104. Negotiable Instrument.
(a) Except as provided in subsections (c) and (d), "negotiable instrument" means an unconditional promise or order to pay a fixed amount of money, with or without interest or other charges described in the promise or order, if it:
  (1) is payable to bearer or to order at the time it is issued or first comes into possession of a holder;
  (2) is payable on demand or at a definite time; and
  (3) does not state any other undertaking or instruction by the person promising or ordering payment to do any act in addition to the payment of money, but the promise or order may contain (i) an undertaking or power to give, maintain, or protect collateral to secure payment, (ii) an authorization or power to the holder to confess judgment or realize on or dispose of collateral, or (iii) a waiver of the benefit of any law intended for the advantage or protection of an obligor.
(b) "Instrument" means a negotiable instrument.
(c) An order that meets all of the requirements of subsection (a), except paragraph (1), and otherwise falls within the definition of "check" in subsection (f) is a negotiable instrument and a check.
(d) A promise or order other than a check is not an instrument if, at the time it is issued or first comes into possession of a holder, it contains a conspicuous statement, however expressed, to the effect that the promise or order is not negotiable or is not an instrument governed by this Article.
(e) An instrument is a "note" if it is a promise and is a "draft" if it is an order. If an instrument falls within the definition of both "note" and "draft," a person entitled to enforce the instrument may treat it as either.
(f) "Check" means (i) a draft, other than a documentary draft, payable on demand and drawn on a bank or (ii) a cashier's check or teller's check. An instrument may be a check even though it is described on its face by another term, such as "money order."
(g) "Cashier's check" means a draft with respect to which the drawer and drawee are the same bank or branches of the same bank.
(h) "Teller's check" means a draft drawn by a bank (i) on another bank, or (ii) payable at or through a bank.
(i) "Traveler's check" means an instrument that (i) is payable on demand, (ii) is drawn on or payable at or through a bank, (iii) is designated by the term "traveler's check" or by a substantially similar term, and (iv) requires, as a condition to payment, a countersignature by a person whose specimen signature appears on the instrument.
(j) "Certificate of deposit" means an instrument containing an acknowledgment by a bank that a sum of money has been received by the bank and a promise by the bank to repay the sum of money. A certificate of deposit is a note of the bank.

§ 3–105. Issue of Instrument.

(a) "Issue" means the first delivery of an instrument by the maker or drawer, whether to a holder or nonholder, for the purpose of giving rights on the instrument to any person.

(b) An unissued instrument, or an unissued incomplete instrument that is completed, is binding on the maker or drawer, but nonissuance is a defense. An instrument that is conditionally issued or is issued for a special purpose is binding on the maker or drawer, but failure of the condition or special purpose to be fulfilled is a defense.

(c) "Issuer" applies to issued and unissued instruments and means a maker or drawer of an instrument.

§ 3–106. Unconditional Promise or Order.

(a) Except as provided in this section, for the purposes of Section 3–104(a), a promise or order is unconditional unless it states (i) an express condition to payment, (ii) that the promise or order is subject to or governed by another writing, or (iii) that rights or obligations with respect to the promise or order are stated in another writing. A reference to another writing does not of itself make the promise or order conditional.

(b) A promise or order is not made conditional (i) by a reference to another writing for a statement of rights with respect to collateral, prepayment, or acceleration, or (ii) because payment is limited to resort to a particular fund or source.

(c) If a promise or order requires, as a condition to payment, a countersignature by a person whose specimen signature appears on the promise or order, the condition does not make the promise or order conditional for the purposes of Section 3–104(a). If the person whose specimen signature appears on an instrument fails to countersign the instrument, the failure to countersign is a defense to the obligation of the issuer, but the failure does not prevent a transferee of the instrument from becoming a holder of the instrument.

(d) If a promise or order at the time it is issued or first comes into possession of a holder contains a statement, required by applicable statutory or administrative law, to the effect that the rights of a holder or transferee are subject to claims or defenses that the issuer could assert against the original payee, the promise or order is not thereby made conditional for the purposes of Section 3–104(a); but if the promise or order is an instrument, there cannot be a holder in due course of the instrument.

§ 3–107. Instrument Payable in Foreign Money.

Unless the instrument otherwise provides, an instrument that states the amount payable in foreign money may be paid in the foreign money or in an equivalent amount in dollars calculated by using the current bank-offered spot rate at the place of payment for the purchase of dollars on the day on which the instrument is paid.

§ 3–108. Payable on Demand or at Definite Time.

(a) A promise or order is "payable on demand" if it (i) states that it is payable on demand or at sight, or otherwise indicates that it is payable at the will of the holder, or (ii) does not state any time of payment.

(b) A promise or order is "payable at a definite time" if it is payable on elapse of a definite period of time after sight or acceptance or at a fixed date or dates or at a time or times readily ascertainable at the time the promise or order is issued, subject to rights of (i) prepayment, (ii) acceleration, (iii) extension at the option of the holder, or (iv) extension to a further definite time at the option of the maker or acceptor or automatically upon or after a specified act or event.

(c) If an instrument, payable at a fixed date, is also payable upon demand made before the fixed date, the instrument is payable on demand until the fixed date and, if demand for payment is not made before that date, becomes payable at a definite time on the fixed date.

§ 3–109. Payable to Bearer or to Order.

(a) A promise or order is payable to bearer if it:

(1) states that it is payable to bearer or to the order of bearer or otherwise indicates that the person in possession of the promise or order is entitled to payment;

(2) does not state a payee; or

(3) states that it is payable to or to the order of cash or otherwise indicates that it is not payable to an identified person.

(b) A promise or order that is not payable to bearer is payable to order if it is payable (i) to the order of an identified person or (ii) to an identified person or order. A promise or order that is payable to order is payable to the identified person.

(c) An instrument payable to bearer may become payable to an identified person if it is specially indorsed pursuant to Section 3–205(a). An instrument payable to an identified person may become payable to bearer if it is indorsed in blank pursuant to Section 3–205(b).

§ 3–110. Identification of Person to Whom Instrument Is Payable.

(a) The person to whom an instrument is initially payable is determined by the intent of the person, whether or not authorized, signing as, or in the name or behalf of, the issuer of the instrument. The instrument is payable to the person intended by the signer even if that person is identified in the instrument by a name or other identification that is not that of the intended person. If more than one person signs in the name or behalf of the issuer of an instrument and all the signers do not intend the same person as payee, the instrument is payable to any person intended by one or more of the signers.

(b) If the signature of the issuer of an instrument is made by automated means, such as a check-writing machine, the payee of the instrument is determined by the intent of the person who supplied the name or identification of the payee, whether or not authorized to do so.

(c) A person to whom an instrument is payable may be identified in any way, including by name, identifying number, office, or account number. For the purpose of determining the holder of an instrument, the following rules apply:

(1) If an instrument is payable to an account and the account is identified only by number, the instrument is payable to the person to whom the account is payable. If an instrument is payable to an account identified by number and by the name of a person, the instrument is payable to the named person, whether or not that person is the owner of the account identified by number.

(2) If an instrument is payable to:

(i) a trust, an estate, or a person described as trustee or representative of a trust or estate, the instrument is payable to the trustee, the representative, or a successor of either, whether or not the beneficiary or estate is also named;

(ii) a person described as agent or similar representative of a named or identified person, the instrument is payable to the represented person, the representative, or a successor of the representative;

(iii) a fund or organization that is not a legal entity, the instrument is payable to a representative of the members of the fund or organization; or

(iv) an office or to a person described as holding an office, the instrument is payable to the named person, the incumbent of the office, or a successor to the incumbent.

(d) If an instrument is payable to two or more persons alternatively, it is payable to any of them and may be negotiated, discharged, or enforced by any or all of them in possession of the instrument. If an instrument is payable to two or more persons not alternatively, it is payable to all of them and may be negotiated, discharged, or enforced only by all of them. If an instrument payable to two or more persons is ambiguous as to whether it is payable to the persons alternatively, the instrument is payable to the persons alternatively.

§ 3–111. Place of Payment.

Except as otherwise provided for items in Article 4, an instrument is payable at the place of payment stated in the instrument. If no place of payment is stated, an instrument is payable at the address of the drawee or maker stated in the instrument. If no address is stated, the place of payment is the place of business of the drawee or maker. If a drawee or maker has more than one place of business, the place of payment is any place of business of the drawee or maker chosen by the person entitled to enforce the instrument. If the drawee or maker has no place of business, the place of payment is the residence of the drawee or maker.

§ 3–112. Interest.

(a) Unless otherwise provided in the instrument, (i) an instrument is not payable with interest, and (ii) interest on an interest-bearing instrument is payable from the date of the instrument.

(b) Interest may be stated in an instrument as a fixed or variable amount of money or it may be expressed as a fixed or variable rate or rates. The amount or rate of interest may be stated or described in the instrument in any manner and may require reference to information not contained in the instrument. If an instrument provides for interest, but the amount of interest payable cannot be ascertained from the description, interest is payable at the judgment rate in effect at the place of payment of the instrument and at the time interest first accrues.

§ 3–113. Date of Instrument.

(a) An instrument may be antedated or postdated. The date stated determines the time of payment if the instrument is payable at a fixed period after date. Except as provided in Section 4–401(c), an instrument payable on demand is not payable before the date of the instrument.

(b) If an instrument is undated, its date is the date of its issue or, in the case of an unissued instrument, the date it first comes into possession of a holder.

§ 3–114. Contradictory Terms of Instrument.

If an instrument contains contradictory terms, typewritten terms prevail over printed terms, handwritten terms prevail over both, and words prevail over numbers.

§ 3–115. Incomplete Instrument.

(a) "Incomplete instrument" means a signed writing, whether or not issued by the signer, the contents of which show at the time of signing that it is incomplete but that the signer intended it to be completed by the addition of words or numbers.

(b) Subject to subsection (c), if an incomplete instrument is an instrument under Section 3–104, it may be enforced according to its terms if it is not completed, or according to its terms as augmented by completion. If an incomplete instrument is not an instrument under Section 3–104, but, after completion, the requirements of Section 3–104 are met, the instrument may be enforced according to its terms as augmented by completion.

(c) If words or numbers are added to an incomplete instrument without authority of the signer, there is an alteration of the incomplete instrument under Section 3–407.

(d) The burden of establishing that words or numbers were added to an incomplete instrument without authority of the signer is on the person asserting the lack of authority.

§ 3–116. Joint and Several Liability; Contribution.

(a) Except as otherwise provided in the instrument, two or more persons who have the same liability on an instrument as makers, drawers, acceptors, indorsers who indorse as joint payees, or anomalous indorsers are jointly and severally liable in the capacity in which they sign.

(b) Except as provided in Section 3–419(e) or by agreement of the affected parties, a party having joint and several liability who pays the instrument is entitled to receive from any party having the same joint and several liability contribution in accordance with applicable law.

(c) Discharge of one party having joint and several liability by a person entitled to enforce the instrument does not affect the right under subsection (b) of a party having the same joint and several liability to receive contribution from the party discharged.

§ 3–117. Other Agreements Affecting Instrument.

Subject to applicable law regarding exclusion of proof of contemporaneous or previous agreements, the obligation of a party to an instrument to pay the instrument may be modified, supplemented, or nullified by a separate agreement of the obligor and a person entitled to enforce the instrument, if the instrument is issued or the obligation is incurred in reliance on the agreement or as part of the same transaction giving rise to the agreement. To the extent an obligation is modified, supplemented, or nullified by an agreement under this section, the agreement is a defense to the obligation.

§ 3–118. Statute of Limitations.

(a) Except as provided in subsection (e), an action to enforce the obligation of a party to pay a note payable at a definite time must be commenced within six years after the due date or dates stated in the note or, if a due date is accelerated, within six years after the accelerated due date.

(b) Except as provided in subsection (d) or (e), if demand for payment is made to the maker of a note payable on demand, an action to enforce the obligation of a party to pay the note must be commenced within six years after the demand. If no demand for payment is made to the maker, an action to enforce the note is barred if neither principal nor interest on the note has been paid for a continuous period of 10 years.

(c) Except as provided in subsection (d), an action to enforce the obligation of a party to an unaccepted draft to pay the draft must be commenced within three years after dishonor of the draft or 10 years after the date of the draft, whichever period expires first.

(d) An action to enforce the obligation of the acceptor of a certified check or the issuer of a teller's check, cashier's check, or traveler's check must be commenced within three years after demand for payment is made to the acceptor or issuer, as the case may be.

(e) An action to enforce the obligation of a party to a certificate of deposit to pay the instrument must be commenced within six years after demand for payment is made to the maker, but if the instrument states a due date and the maker is not required to pay before that date, the six-year period begins when a demand for payment is in effect and the due date has passed.

(f) An action to enforce the obligation of a party to pay an accepted draft, other than a certified check, must be commenced (i) within six years after the due date or dates stated in the draft or acceptance if the obligation of the acceptor is payable at a definite time, or (ii) within six years after the date of the acceptance if the obligation of the acceptor is payable on demand.

(g) Unless governed by other law regarding claims for indemnity or contribution, an action (i) for conversion of an instrument, for money had and received, or like action based on conversion, (ii) for breach of warranty, or (iii) to enforce an obligation, duty, or right arising under this Article and not governed by this section must be commenced within three years after the [cause of action] accrues.

§ 3–119. Notice of Right to Defend Action.

In an action for breach of an obligation for which a third person is answerable over pursuant to this Article or Article 4, the defendant may give the third person written notice of the litigation, and the person notified may then give similar notice to any other person who is answerable over. If the notice states (i) that the person notified may come in and defend and (ii) that failure to do so will bind the person notified in an action later brought by the person giving the notice as to any determination of fact common to the two litigations, the person notified is so bound unless after seasonable receipt of the notice the person notified does come in and defend.

Part 2—Negotiation, Transfer, and Indorsement

§ 3–201. Negotiation.

(a) "Negotiation" means a transfer of possession, whether voluntary or involuntary, of an instrument by a person other than the issuer to a person who thereby becomes its holder.

(b) Except for negotiation by a remitter, if an instrument is payable to an identified person, negotiation requires transfer of possession of the instrument and its indorsement by the holder. If an instrument is payable to bearer, it may be negotiated by transfer of possession alone.

§ 3–202. Negotiation Subject to Rescission.

(a) Negotiation is effective even if obtained (i) from an infant, a corporation exceeding its powers, or a person without capacity, (ii) by fraud, duress, or mistake, or (iii) in breach of duty or as part of an illegal transaction.

(b) To the extent permitted by other law, negotiation may be rescinded or may be subject to other remedies, but those remedies may not be asserted against a subsequent holder in due course or a person paying the instrument in good faith and without knowledge of facts that are a basis for rescission or other remedy.

§ 3–203. Transfer of Instrument; Rights Acquired by Transfer.

(a) An instrument is transferred when it is delivered by a person other than its issuer for the purpose of giving to the person receiving delivery the right to enforce the instrument.

(b) Transfer of an instrument, whether or not the transfer is a negotiation, vests in the transferee any right of the transferor to enforce the instrument, including any right as a holder in due course, but the transferee cannot acquire rights of a holder in due course by a transfer, directly or indirectly, from a holder in due course if the transferee engaged in fraud or illegality affecting the instrument.

(c) Unless otherwise agreed, if an instrument is transferred for value and the transferee does not become a holder because of lack of indorsement by the transferor, the transferee has a specifically enforceable right to the unqualified indorsement of the transferor, but negotiation of the instrument does not occur until the indorsement is made.

(d) If a transferor purports to transfer less than the entire instrument, negotiation of the instrument does not occur. The transferee obtains no rights under this Article and has only the rights of a partial assignee.

§ 3–204. Indorsement.

(a) "Indorsement" means a signature, other than that of a signer as maker, drawer, or acceptor, that alone or accompanied by other words is made on an instrument for the purpose of (i) negotiating the instrument, (ii) restricting payment of the instrument, or (iii) incurring indorser's liability on the instrument, but regardless of the intent of the signer, a signature and its accompanying words is an indorsement unless the accompanying words, terms of the instrument, place of the signature, or other circumstances unambiguously indicate that the signature was made for a purpose other than indorsement. For the purpose of determining whether a signature is made on an instrument, a paper affixed to the instrument is a part of the instrument.

(b) "Indorser" means a person who makes an indorsement.

(c) For the purpose of determining whether the transferee of an instrument is a holder, an indorsement that transfers a security interest in the instrument is effective as an unqualified indorsement of the instrument.

(d) If an instrument is payable to a holder under a name that is not the name of the holder, indorsement may be made by the holder in the name stated in the instrument or in the holder's name or both, but signature in both names may be required by a person paying or taking the instrument for value or collection.

§ 3–205. Special Indorsement; Blank Indorsement; Anomalous Indorsement.

(a) If an indorsement is made by the holder of an instrument, whether payable to an identified person or payable to bearer, and the indorsement identifies a person to whom it makes the instrument payable, it is a "special indorsement." When specially indorsed, an instrument becomes payable to the identified person and may be negotiated only by the indorsement of that person. The principles stated in Section 3–110 apply to special indorsements

(b) If an indorsement is made by the holder of an instrument and it is not a special indorsement, it is a "blank indorsement." When indorsed in blank, an instrument becomes payable to bearer and may be negotiated by transfer of possession alone until specially indorsed.

(c) The holder may convert a blank indorsement that consists only of a signature into a special indorsement by writing, above the signature of the indorser, words identifying the person to whom the instrument is made payable.

(d) "Anomalous indorsement" means an indorsement made by a person who is not the holder of the instrument. An anomalous indorsement does not affect the manner in which the instrument may be negotiated.

§ 3–206. Restrictive Indorsement.

(a) An indorsement limiting payment to a particular person or otherwise prohibiting further transfer or negotiation of the instrument is not effective to prevent further transfer or negotiation of the instrument.

(b) An indorsement stating a condition to the right of the indorsee to receive payment does not affect the right of the indorsee to enforce the instrument. A person paying the instrument or taking it for value or collection may disregard the condition, and the rights and liabilities of that person are not affected by whether the condition has been fulfilled.

(c) If an instrument bears an indorsement (i) described in Section 4–201(b), or (ii) in blank or to a particular bank using the words "for deposit," "for collection," or other words indicating a purpose of having the instrument collected by a bank for the indorser or for a particular account, the following rules apply:

(1) A person, other than a bank, who purchases the instrument when so indorsed converts the instrument unless the amount paid for the instrument is received by the indorser or applied consistently with the indorsement.

(2) A depositary bank that purchases the instrument or takes it for collection when so indorsed converts the instrument unless the amount paid by the bank with respect to the instrument is received by the indorser or applied consistently with the indorsement.

(3) A payor bank that is also the depositary bank or that takes the instrument for immediate payment over the counter from a person other than a collecting bank converts the instrument unless the proceeds of the instrument are received by the indorser or applied consistently with the indorsement.

(4) Except as otherwise provided in paragraph (3), a payor bank or intermediary bank may disregard the indorsement and is not liable if the proceeds of the instrument are not received by the indorser or applied consistently with the indorsement.

(d) Except for an indorsement covered by subsection (c), if an instrument bears an indorsement using words to the effect that payment is to be made to the indorsee as agent, trustee, or other fiduciary for the benefit of the indorser or another person, the following rules apply:

(1) Unless there is notice of breach of fiduciary duty as provided in Section 3–307, a person who purchases the instrument from the indorsee or takes the instrument from the indorsee for collection or payment may pay the proceeds of payment or the value given for the instrument to the indorsee without regard to whether the indorsee violates a fiduciary duty to the indorser.

(2) A subsequent transferee of the instrument or person who pays the instrument is neither given notice nor otherwise affected by the restriction in the indorsement unless the transferee or payor knows that the fiduciary dealt with the instrument or its proceeds in breach of fiduciary duty.

(e) The presence on an instrument of an indorsement to which this section applies does not prevent a purchaser of the instrument from becoming a holder in due course of the instrument unless the purchaser is a converter under subsection (c) or has notice or knowledge of breach of fiduciary duty as stated in subsection (d).

(f) In an action to enforce the obligation of a party to pay the instrument, the obligor has a defense if payment would violate an indorsement to which this section applies and the payment is not permitted by this section.

§ 3–207. Reacquisition.

Reacquisition of an instrument occurs if it is transferred to a former holder, by negotiation or otherwise. A former holder who reacquires the instrument may cancel indorsements made after the reacquirer first became a holder of the instrument. If the cancellation causes the instrument to be payable to the reacquirer or to bearer, the reacquirer may negotiate the instrument. An indorser whose indorsement is canceled is discharged, and the discharge is effective against any subsequent holder.

Part 3—Enforcement of Instruments

§ 3–301. Person Entitled to Enforce Instrument.

"Person entitled to enforce" an instrument means (i) the holder of the instrument, (ii) a nonholder in possession of the instrument who has the rights of a holder, or (iii) a person not in possession of the instrument who is entitled to enforce the instrument pursuant to Section 3–309 or 3–418(d). A person may be a person entitled to enforce the instrument even though the person is not the owner of the instrument or is in wrongful possession of the instrument.

§ 3–302. Holder in Due Course.

(a) Subject to subsection (c) and Section 3–106(d), "holder in due course" means the holder of an instrument if:

(1) the instrument when issued or negotiated to the holder does not bear such apparent evidence of forgery or alteration or is not otherwise so irregular or incomplete as to call into question its authenticity; and

(2) the holder took the instrument (i) for value, (ii) in good faith, (iii) without notice that the instrument is overdue or has been dishonored or that there is an uncured default with respect to payment of another instrument issued as part of the same series, (iv) without notice that the instrument contains an unauthorized signature or has been altered, (v) without notice of any claim to the instrument described in Section 3–306, and (vi) without notice that any party has a defense or claim in recoupment described in Section 3–305(a).

(b) Notice of discharge of a party, other than discharge in an insolvency proceeding, is not notice of a defense under subsection (a), but discharge is effective against a person who became a holder in due course with notice of the discharge. Public filing or recording of a document does not of itself constitute notice of a defense, claim in recoupment, or claim to the instrument.

(c) Except to the extent a transferor or predecessor in interest has rights as a holder in due course, a person does not acquire rights of a holder in due course of an instrument taken (i) by legal process or by purchase in an execution, bankruptcy, or creditor's sale or similar proceeding, (ii) by purchase as part of a bulk transaction not in ordinary course of business of the transferor, or (iii) as the successor in interest to an estate or other organization.

(d) If, under Section 3–303(a)(1), the promise of performance that is the consideration for an instrument has been partially performed, the holder may assert rights as a holder in due course of the instrument only to the fraction of the amount payable under the instrument equal to the value of the partial performance divided by the value of the promised performance.

(e) If (i) the person entitled to enforce an instrument has only a security interest in the instrument and (ii) the person obliged to pay the instrument has a defense, claim in recoupment, or claim to the instrument that may be asserted against the person who granted the security interest, the person entitled to enforce the instrument may assert rights as a holder in due course only to an amount payable under the instrument which, at the time of enforcement of the instrument, does not exceed the amount of the unpaid obligation secured.

(f) To be effective, notice must be received at a time and in a manner that gives a reasonable opportunity to act on it.

(g) This section is subject to any law limiting status as a holder in due course in particular classes of transactions.

§ 3–303. Value and Consideration.

(a) An instrument is issued or transferred for value if:

(1) the instrument is issued or transferred for a promise of performance, to the extent the promise has been performed;

(2) the transferee acquires a security interest or other lien in the instrument other than a lien obtained by judicial proceeding;

(3) the instrument is issued or transferred as payment of, or as security for, an antecedent claim against any person, whether or not the claim is due;

(4) the instrument is issued or transferred in exchange for a negotiable instrument; or

(5) the instrument is issued or transferred in exchange for the incurring of an irrevocable obligation to a third party by the person taking the instrument.

(b) "Consideration" means any consideration sufficient to support a simple contract. The drawer or maker of an instrument has a defense if the instrument is issued without consideration. If an instrument is issued for a promise of performance, the issuer has a defense to the extent performance of the promise is due and the promise has not been performed. If an instrument is issued for value as stated in subsection (a), the instrument is also issued for consideration.

§ 3–304. Overdue Instrument.

(a) An instrument payable on demand becomes overdue at the earliest of the following times:

(1) on the day after the day demand for payment is duly made;

(2) if the instrument is a check, 90 days after its date; or

(3) if the instrument is not a check, when the instrument has been outstanding for a period of time after its date which is unreasonably long under the circumstances of the particular case in light of the nature of the instrument and usage of the trade.

(b) With respect to an instrument payable at a definite time the following rules apply:

(1) If the principal is payable in installments and a due date has not been accelerated, the instrument becomes overdue upon default under the instrument for nonpayment of an installment, and the instrument remains overdue until the default is cured.

(2) If the principal is not payable in installments and the due date has not been accelerated, the instrument becomes overdue on the day after the due date.

(3) If a due date with respect to principal has been accelerated, the instrument becomes overdue on the day after the accelerated due date.

(c) Unless the due date of principal has been accelerated, an instrument does not become overdue if there is default in payment of interest but no default in payment of principal.

§ 3–305. Defenses and Claims in Recoupment.

(a) Except as stated in subsection (b), the right to enforce the obligation of a party to pay an instrument is subject to the following:

(1) a defense of the obligor based on (i) infancy of the obligor to the extent it is a defense to a simple contract, (ii) duress, lack of legal capacity, or illegality of the transaction which, under other law, nullifies the obligation of the obligor, (iii) fraud that induced the obligor to sign the instrument with neither knowledge nor reasonable opportunity to learn of its character or its essential terms, or (iv) discharge of the obligor in insolvency proceedings;

(2) a defense of the obligor stated in another section of this Article or a defense of the obligor that would be available if the person entitled to enforce the instrument were enforcing a right to payment under a simple contract; and

(3) a claim in recoupment of the obligor against the original payee of the instrument if the claim arose from the transaction that gave rise to the instrument; but the claim of the obligor may be asserted against a transferee of the instrument only to reduce the amount owing on the instrument at the time the action is brought.

(b) The right of a holder in due course to enforce the obligation of a party to pay the instrument is subject to defenses of the obligor stated in subsection (a)(1), but is not subject to defenses of the obligor stated in subsection (a)(2) or claims in recoupment stated in subsection (a)(3) against a person other than the holder.

(c) Except as stated in subsection (d), in an action to enforce the obligation of a party to pay the instrument, the obligor may not assert against the person entitled to enforce the instrument a defense, claim in recoupment, or claim to the instrument (Section 3–306) of another person, but the other person's claim to the instrument may be asserted by the obligor if the other person is joined in the action and personally asserts the claim against the person entitled to enforce the instrument. An obligor is not obliged to pay the instrument if the person seeking enforcement of the instrument does not have rights of a holder in due course and the obligor proves that the instrument is a lost or stolen instrument.

(d) In an action to enforce the obligation of an accommodation party to pay an instrument, the accommodation party may assert against the person entitled to enforce the instrument any defense or claim in recoupment under subsection (a) that the accommodated party could assert against the person entitled to enforce the instrument, except the defenses of discharge in insolvency proceedings, infancy, and lack of legal capacity.

§ 3–306. Claims to an Instrument.

A person taking an instrument, other than a person having rights of a holder in due course, is subject to a claim of a property or possessory right in the instrument or its proceeds, including a claim to rescind a negotiation and to recover the instrument or its proceeds. A person having rights of a holder in due course takes free of the claim to the instrument.

§ 3–307. Notice of Breach of Fiduciary Duty.

(a) In this section:

(1) "Fiduciary" means an agent, trustee, partner, corporate officer or director, or other representative owing a fiduciary duty with respect to an instrument.

(2) "Represented person" means the principal, beneficiary, partnership, corporation, or other person to whom the duty stated in paragraph (1) is owed.

(b) If (i) an instrument is taken from a fiduciary for payment or collection or for value, (ii) the taker has knowledge of the fiduciary status of the fiduciary, and (iii) the represented person makes a claim to the instrument or its proceeds on the basis that the transaction of the fiduciary is a breach of fiduciary duty, the following rules apply:

(1) Notice of breach of fiduciary duty by the fiduciary is notice of the claim of the represented person.

(2) In the case of an instrument payable to the represented person or the fiduciary as such, the taker has notice of the breach of fiduciary duty if the instrument is (i) taken in payment of or as security for a debt known by the taker to be the personal debt of the fiduciary, (ii) taken in a transaction known by the taker to be for the personal benefit of the fiduciary, or (iii) deposited to an account other than an account of the fiduciary, as such, or an account of the represented person.

(3) If an instrument is issued by the represented person or the fiduciary as such, and made payable to the fiduciary personally, the taker does not have notice of the breach of fiduciary duty unless the taker knows of the breach of fiduciary duty.

(4) If an instrument is issued by the represented person or the fiduciary as such, to the taker as payee, the taker has notice of the breach of fiduciary duty if the instrument is (i) taken in payment of or as security for a debt known by the taker to be the personal debt of the fiduciary, (ii) taken in a transaction known by the taker to be for the personal benefit of the fiduciary, or (iii) deposited to an account other than an account of the fiduciary, as such, or an account of the represented person.

§ 3–308. Proof of Signatures and Status as Holder in Due Course.

(a) In an action with respect to an instrument, the authenticity of, and authority to make, each signature on the instrument is admitted unless specifically denied in the pleadings. If the validity of a signature is denied in the pleadings, the burden of establishing validity is on the person claiming validity, but the signature is presumed to be authentic and authorized unless the action is to enforce the liability of the purported signer and the signer is dead or incompetent at the time of trial of the issue of validity of the signature. If an action to enforce the instrument is brought against a person as the undisclosed principal of a person who signed the instrument as a party to the instrument, the plaintiff has the burden of establishing that the defendant is liable on the instrument as a represented person under Section 3–402(a).

(b) If the validity of signatures is admitted or proved and there is compliance with subsection (a), a plaintiff producing the instrument is entitled to payment if the plaintiff proves entitlement to enforce the instrument under Section 3–301, unless the defendant proves a defense or claim in recoupment. If a defense or claim in recoupment is proved, the right to payment of the plaintiff is subject to the defense or claim, except to the extent the plaintiff proves that the plaintiff has rights of a holder in due course which are not subject to the defense or claim.

§ 3–309. Enforcement of Lost, Destroyed, or Stolen Instrument.

(a) A person not in possession of an instrument is entitled to enforce the instrument if (i) the person was in possession of the instrument and entitled to enforce it when loss of possession occurred, (ii) the loss of possession was not the result of a transfer by the person or a lawful seizure, and (iii) the person cannot reasonably obtain possession of the instrument because the instrument was destroyed, its whereabouts cannot be determined, or it is in the wrongful possession of an unknown person or a person that cannot be found or is not amenable to service of process.

(b) A person seeking enforcement of an instrument under subsection (a) must prove the terms of the instrument and the person's right to enforce the instrument. If that proof is made, Section 3–308 applies to the case as if the person seeking enforcement had produced the instrument. The court may not enter judgment in favor of the person seeking enforcement unless it finds that the person required to pay the instrument is adequately protected against loss that might occur by reason of a claim by another person to enforce the instrument. Adequate protection may be provided by any reasonable means.

§ 3–310. Effect of Instrument on Obligation for Which Taken.

(a) Unless otherwise agreed, if a certified check, cashier's check, or teller's check is taken for an obligation, the obligation is discharged to the same extent discharge would result if an amount of money equal to the amount of the instrument were taken in payment of the obligation. Discharge of the obligation does not affect any liability that the obligor may have as an indorser of the instrument.

(b) Unless otherwise agreed and except as provided in subsection (a), if a note or an uncertified check is taken for an obligation, the obligation is suspended to the same extent the obligation would be discharged if an amount of money equal to the amount of the instrument were taken, and the following rules apply:

(1) In the case of an uncertified check, suspension of the obligation continues until dishonor of the check or until it is paid or certified. Payment or certification of the check results in discharge of the obligation to the extent of the amount of the check.

(2) In the case of a note, suspension of the obligation continues until dishonor of the note or until it is paid. Payment of the note results in discharge of the obligation to the extent of the payment.

(3) Except as provided in paragraph (4), if the check or note is dishonored and the obligee of the obligation for which the instrument was taken is the person entitled to enforce the instrument, the obligee may enforce either the instrument or the obligation. In the case of an instrument of a third person which is negotiated to the obligee by the obligor, discharge of the obligor on the instrument also discharges the obligation.

(4) If the person entitled to enforce the instrument taken for an obligation is a person other than the obligee, the obligee may not enforce the obligation to the extent the obligation is suspended. If the obligee is the person entitled to enforce the instrument but no longer has possession of it because it was lost, stolen, or destroyed, the obligation may not be enforced to the extent of the amount payable on the instrument, and to that extent the obligee's rights against the obligor are limited to enforcement of the instrument.

(c) If an instrument other than one described in subsection (a) or (b) is taken for an obligation, the effect is (i) that stated in subsection (a) if the instrument is one on which a bank is liable as maker or acceptor, or (ii) that stated in subsection (b) in any other case.

§ 3–311. Accord and Satisfaction by Use of Instrument.

(a) If a person against whom a claim is asserted proves that (i) that person in good faith tendered an instrument to the claimant as full satisfaction of the claim, (ii) the amount of the claim was unliquidated or subject to a bona fide dispute, and (iii) the claimant obtained payment of the instrument, the following subsections apply.

(b) Unless subsection (c) applies, the claim is discharged if the person against whom the claim is asserted proves that the instrument or an accompanying written communication contained a conspicuous statement to the effect that the instrument was tendered as full satisfaction of the claim.

(c) Subject to subsection (d), a claim is not discharged under subsection (b) if either of the following applies:

(1) The claimant, if an organization, proves that (i) within a reasonable time before the tender, the claimant sent a conspicuous statement to the person against whom the claim is asserted that communications concerning disputed debts, including an instrument tendered as full satisfaction of a debt, are to be sent to a designated person, office, or place, and (ii) the instrument or accompanying communication was not received by that designated person, office, or place.

(2) The claimant, whether or not an organization, proves that within 90 days after payment of the instrument, the claimant tendered repayment of the amount of the instrument to the person against whom the claim is asserted. This paragraph does not apply if the claimant is an organization that sent a statement complying with paragraph (1)(i).

(d) A claim is discharged if the person against whom the claim is asserted proves that within a reasonable time before collection of the instrument was initiated, the claimant, or an agent of the claimant having direct responsibility with respect to the disputed obligation, knew that the instrument was tendered in full satisfaction of the claim.

§ 3–312. Lost, Destroyed, or Stolen Cashier's Check, Teller's Check, or Certified Check.*

(a) In this section:

(1) "Check" means a cashier's check, teller's check, or certified check.

(2) "Claimant" means a person who claims the right to receive the amount of a cashier's check, teller's check, or certified check that was lost, destroyed, or stolen.

(3) "Declaration of loss" means a written statement, made under penalty of perjury, to the effect that (i) the declarer lost possession of a check, (ii) the declarer is the drawer or payee of the check, in the case of a certified check, or the remitter or payee of the check, in the case of a cashier's check or teller's check, (iii) the loss of possession was not the result of a transfer by the declarer or a lawful seizure, and (iv) the declarer cannot reasonably obtain possession of the check because the check was destroyed, its whereabouts cannot be determined, or it is in the wrongful possession of an unknown person or a person that cannot be found or is not amenable to service of process.

(4) "Obligated bank" means the issuer of a cashier's check or teller's check or the acceptor of a certified check.

(b) A claimant may assert a claim to the amount of a check by a communication to the obligated bank describing the check with reasonable certainty and requesting payment of the amount of the check, if (i) the claimant is the drawer or payee of a certified check or the remitter or payee of a cashier's check or teller's check, (ii) the communication contains or is accompanied by a declaration of loss of the claimant with respect to the check, (iii) the communication is received at a time and in a manner affording the bank a reasonable time to act on it before the check is paid, and (iv) the claimant provides reasonable identification if requested by the obligated bank. Delivery of a declaration of loss is a warranty of the truth of the statements made in the declaration. If a claim is asserted in compliance with this subsection, the following rules apply:

(1) The claim becomes enforceable at the later of (i) the time the claim is asserted, or (ii) the 90th day following the date of the check, in the case of a cashier's check or teller's check, or the 90th day following the date of the acceptance, in the case of a certified check.

(2) Until the claim becomes enforceable, it has no legal effect and the obligated bank may pay the check or, in the case of a teller's check, may permit the drawee to pay the check. Payment to a person entitled to enforce the check discharges all liability of the obligated bank with respect to the check.

(3) If the claim becomes enforceable before the check is presented for payment, the obligated bank is not obliged to pay the check.

(4) When the claim becomes enforceable, the obligated bank becomes obliged to pay the amount of the check to the claimant if payment of the check has not been made to a person entitled to enforce the check. Subject to Section 4–302(a)(1), payment to the claimant discharges all liability of the obligated bank with respect to the check.

(c) If the obligated bank pays the amount of a check to a claimant under subsection (b)(4) and the check is presented for payment by a person having rights of a holder in due course, the claimant is obliged to (i) refund the payment to the obligated bank if the check is paid, or (ii) pay the amount of the check to the person having rights of a holder in due course if the check is dishonored.

(d) If a claimant has the right to assert a claim under subsection (b) and is also a person entitled to enforce a cashier's check, teller's check, or certified check which is lost, destroyed, or stolen, the claimant may assert rights with respect to the check either under this section or Section 3–309.

Added in 1991.

Part 4—Liability of Parties

§ 3–401. Signature.

(a) A person is not liable on an instrument unless (i) the person signed the instrument, or (ii) the person is represented by an agent or representative who signed the instrument and the signature is binding on the represented person under Section 3–402.

(b) A signature may be made (i) manually or by means of a device or machine, and (ii) by the use of any name, including a trade or assumed name, or by a word, mark, or symbol executed or adopted by a person with present intention to authenticate a writing.

§ 3–402. Signature by Representative.

(a) If a person acting, or purporting to act, as a representative signs an instrument by signing either the name of the represented person or the name of the signer, the represented person is bound by the signature to the same extent the represented person would be bound if the signature were on a simple contract. If the represented person is bound, the signature of the representative is the "authorized signature of the represented person" and the represented person is liable on the instrument, whether or not identified in the instrument.

(b) If a representative signs the name of the representative to an instrument and the signature is an authorized signature of the represented person, the following rules apply:

(1) If the form of the signature shows unambiguously that the signature is made on behalf of the represented person who is identified in the instrument, the representative is not liable on the instrument.

(2) Subject to subsection (c), if (i) the form of the signature does not show unambiguously that the signature is made in a representative capacity or (ii) the represented person is not identified in the instrument, the representative is liable on the instrument to a holder in due course that took the instrument without notice that the representative was not intended to be liable on the instrument. With respect to any other person, the representative is liable on the instrument unless the representative proves that the original parties did not intend the representative to be liable on the instrument.

(c) If a representative signs the name of the representative as drawer of a check without indication of the representative status and the check is payable from an account of the represented person who is identified on the check, the signer is not liable on the check if the signature is an authorized signature of the represented person.

§ 3–403. Unauthorized Signature.

(a) Unless otherwise provided in this Article or Article 4, an unauthorized signature is ineffective except as the signature of the unauthorized signer in favor of a person who in good faith pays the instrument or takes it for value. An unauthorized signature may be ratified for all purposes of this Article.

(b) If the signature of more than one person is required to constitute the authorized signature of an organization, the signature of the organization is unauthorized if one of the required signatures is lacking.

(c) The civil or criminal liability of a person who makes an unauthorized signature is not affected by any provision of this Article which makes the unauthorized signature effective for the purposes of this Article.

§ 3–404. Impostors; Fictitious Payees.

(a) If an impostor, by use of the mails or otherwise, induces the issuer of an instrument to issue the instrument to the impostor, or to a person acting in concert with the impostor, by impersonating the payee of the instrument or a person authorized to act for the payee, an indorsement of the instrument by any person in the name of the payee is effective as the indorsement of the payee in favor of a person who, in good faith, pays the instrument or takes it for value or for collection.

(b) If (i) a person whose intent determines to whom an instrument is payable (Section 3–110(a) or (b)) does not intend the person identified as payee to have any interest in the instrument, or (ii) the person identified as payee of an instrument is a fictitious person, the following rules apply until the instrument is negotiated by special indorsement:

(1) Any person in possession of the instrument is its holder.

(2) An indorsement by any person in the name of the payee stated in the instrument is effective as the indorsement of the payee in favor of a person who, in good faith, pays the instrument or takes it for value or for collection.

(c) Under subsection (a) or (b), an indorsement is made in the name of a payee if (i) it is made in a name substantially similar to that of the payee or (ii) the instrument, whether or not indorsed, is deposited in a depositary bank to an account in a name substantially similar to that of the payee.

(d) With respect to an instrument to which subsection (a) or (b) applies, if a person paying the instrument or taking it for value or for collection fails to exercise ordinary care in paying or taking the instrument and that failure substantially contributes to loss resulting from payment of the instrument, the person bearing the loss may recover from the person failing to exercise ordinary care to the extent the failure to exercise ordinary care contributed to the loss.

§ 3–405. Employer's Responsibility for Fraudulent Indorsement by Employee.

(a) In this section:

(1) "Employee" includes an independent contractor and employee of an independent contractor retained by the employer.

(2) "Fraudulent indorsement" means (i) in the case of an instrument payable to the employer, a forged indorsement purporting to be that of the employer, or (ii) in the case of an instrument with respect to which the employer is the issuer, a forged indorsement purporting to be that of the person identified as payee.

(3) "Responsibility" with respect to instruments means authority (i) to sign or indorse instruments on behalf of the employer, (ii) to process instruments received by the employer for bookkeeping purposes, for deposit to an account, or for other disposition, (iii) to prepare or process instruments for issue in the name of the employer, (iv) to supply information determining the names or addresses of payees of instruments to be issued in the name of the employer, (v) to control the disposition of instruments to be issued in the name of the employer, or (vi) to act otherwise with respect to instruments in a responsible capacity. "Responsibility" does not include authority that merely allows an employee to have access to instruments or blank or incomplete instrument forms that are being stored or transported or are part of incoming or outgoing mail, or similar access.

(b) For the purpose of determining the rights and liabilities of a person who, in good faith, pays an instrument or takes it for value or for collection, if an employer entrusted an employee with responsibility with respect to the instrument and the employee or a person acting in concert with the employee makes a fraudulent indorsement of the instrument, the indorsement is effective as the indorsement of the person to whom the instrument is payable if it is made in the name of that person. If the person paying the instrument or taking it for value or for collection fails to exercise ordinary care in paying or taking the instrument and that failure substantially contributes to loss resulting from the fraud, the person bearing the loss may recover from the person failing to exercise ordinary care to the extent the failure to exercise ordinary care contributed to the loss.

(c) Under subsection (b), an indorsement is made in the name of the person to whom an instrument is payable if (i) it is made in a name substantially similar to the name of that person or (ii) the instrument, whether or not indorsed, is deposited in a depositary bank to an account in a name substantially similar to the name of that person.

§ 3–406. Negligence Contributing to Forged Signature or Alteration of Instrument.

(a) A person whose failure to exercise ordinary care substantially contributes to an alteration of an instrument or to the making of a forged signature on an instrument is precluded from asserting the alteration or the forgery against a person who, in good faith, pays the instrument or takes it for value or for collection.

(b) Under subsection (a), if the person asserting the preclusion fails to exercise ordinary care in paying or taking the instrument and that failure substantially contributes to loss, the loss is allocated between the person precluded and the person asserting the preclusion according to the extent to which the failure of each to exercise ordinary care contributed to the loss.

(c) Under subsection (a), the burden of proving failure to exercise ordinary care is on the person asserting the preclusion. Under subsection (b), the burden of proving failure to exercise ordinary care is on the person precluded.

§ 3–407. Alteration.

(a) "Alteration" means (i) an unauthorized change in an instrument that purports to modify in any respect the obligation of a party, or (ii) an unauthorized addition of words or numbers or other change to an incomplete instrument relating to the obligation of a party.

(b) Except as provided in subsection (c), an alteration fraudulently made discharges a party whose obligation is affected by the alteration unless that party assents or is precluded from asserting the alteration. No other alteration discharges a party, and the instrument may be enforced according to its original terms.

(c) A payor bank or drawee paying a fraudulently altered instrument or a person taking it for value, in good faith and without notice of the alteration, may enforce rights with respect to the instrument (i) according to its original terms, or (ii) in the case of an incomplete instrument altered by unauthorized completion, according to its terms as completed.

§ 3–408. Drawee Not Liable on Unaccepted Draft.

A check or other draft does not of itself operate as an assignment of funds in the hands of the drawee available for its payment, and the drawee is not liable on the instrument until the drawee accepts it.

§ 3–409. Acceptance of Draft; Certified Check.

(a) "Acceptance" means the drawee's signed agreement to pay a draft as presented. It must be written on the draft and may consist of the drawee's signature alone. Acceptance may be made at any time and becomes effective when notification pursuant to instructions is given or the accepted draft is delivered for the purpose of giving rights on the acceptance to any person.

(b) A draft may be accepted although it has not been signed by the drawer, is otherwise incomplete, is overdue, or has been dishonored.

(c) If a draft is payable at a fixed period after sight and the acceptor fails to date the acceptance, the holder may complete the acceptance by supplying a date in good faith.

(d) "Certified check" means a check accepted by the bank on which it is drawn. Acceptance may be made as stated in subsection (a) or by a writing on the check which indicates that the check is certified. The drawee of a check has no obligation to certify the check, and refusal to certify is not dishonor of the check.

§ 3–410. Acceptance Varying Draft.

(a) If the terms of a drawee's acceptance vary from the terms of the draft as presented, the holder may refuse the acceptance and treat the draft as dishonored. In that case, the drawee may cancel the acceptance.

(b) The terms of a draft are not varied by an acceptance to pay at a particular bank or place in the United States, unless the acceptance states that the draft is to be paid only at that bank or place.

(c) If the holder assents to an acceptance varying the terms of a draft, the obligation of each drawer and indorser that does not expressly assent to the acceptance is discharged.

§ 3–411. Refusal to Pay Cashier's Checks, Teller's Checks, and Certified Checks.

(a) In this section, "obligated bank" means the acceptor of a certified check or the issuer of a cashier's check or teller's check bought from the issuer.

(b) If the obligated bank wrongfully (i) refuses to pay a cashier's check or certified check, (ii) stops payment of a teller's check, or (iii) refuses to pay a dishonored teller's check, the person asserting the right to enforce the check is entitled to compensation for expenses and loss of interest resulting from the nonpayment and may recover consequential damages if the obligated bank refuses to pay after receiving notice of particular circumstances giving rise to the damages.

(c) Expenses or consequential damages under subsection (b) are not recoverable if the refusal of the obligated bank to pay occurs because (i) the bank suspends payments, (ii) the obligated bank asserts a claim or defense of the bank that it has reasonable grounds to believe is available against the person entitled to enforce the instrument, (iii) the obligated bank has a reasonable doubt whether the person demanding payment is the person entitled to enforce the instrument, or (iv) payment is prohibited by law.

§ 3–412. Obligation of Issuer of Note or Cashier's Check.

The issuer of a note or cashier's check or other draft drawn on the drawer is obliged to pay the instrument (i) according to its terms at the time it was issued or, if not issued, at the time it first came into possession of a holder, or (ii) if the issuer signed an incomplete instrument, according to its terms when completed, to the extent stated in Sections 3–115 and 3–407. The obligation is owed to a person entitled to enforce the instrument or to an indorser who paid the instrument under Section 3–415.

§ 3–413. Obligation of Acceptor.

(a) The acceptor of a draft is obliged to pay the draft (i) according to its terms at the time it was accepted, even though the acceptance states that the draft is payable "as originally drawn" or equivalent terms, (ii) if the acceptance varies the terms of the draft, according to the terms of the draft as varied, or (iii) if the acceptance is of a draft that is an incomplete instrument, according to its terms when completed, to the extent stated in Sections 3–115 and 3–407. The obligation is owed to a person entitled to enforce the draft or to the drawer or an indorser who paid the draft under Section 3–414 or 3–415.

(b) If the certification of a check or other acceptance of a draft states the amount certified or accepted, the obligation of the acceptor is that amount. If (i) the certification or acceptance does not state an amount, (ii) the amount of the instrument is subsequently raised, and (iii) the instrument is then negotiated to a holder in due course, the obligation of the acceptor is the amount of the instrument at the time it was taken by the holder in due course.

§ 3–414.   Obligation of Drawer.

(a) This section does not apply to cashier's checks or other drafts drawn on the drawer.

(b) If an unaccepted draft is dishonored, the drawer is obliged to pay the draft (i) according to its terms at the time it was issued or, if not issued, at the time it first came into possession of a holder, or (ii) if the drawer signed an incomplete instrument, according to its terms when completed, to the extent stated in Sections 3–115 and 3–407. The obligation is owed to a person entitled to enforce the draft or to an indorser who paid the draft under Section 3–415.

(c) If a draft is accepted by a bank, the drawer is discharged, regardless of when or by whom acceptance was obtained.

(d) If a draft is accepted and the acceptor is not a bank, the obligation of the drawer to pay the draft if the draft is dishonored by the acceptor is the same as the obligation of an indorser under Section 3–415(a) and (c).

(e) If a draft states that it is drawn "without recourse" or otherwise disclaims liability of the drawer to pay the draft, the drawer is not liable under subsection (b) to pay the draft if the draft is not a check. A disclaimer of the liability stated in subsection (b) is not effective if the draft is a check.

(f) If (i) a check is not presented for payment or given to a depositary bank for collection within 30 days after its date, (ii) the drawee suspends payments after expiration of the 30-day period without paying the check, and (iii) because of the suspension of payments, the drawer is deprived of funds maintained with the drawee to cover payment of the check, the drawer to the extent deprived of funds may discharge its obligation to pay the check by assigning to the person entitled to enforce the check the rights of the drawer against the drawee with respect to the funds.

§ 3–415.   Obligation of Indorser.

(a) Subject to subsections (b), (c), and (d) and to Section 3–419(d), if an instrument is dishonored, an indorser is obliged to pay the amount due on the instrument (i) according to the terms of the instrument at the time it was indorsed, or (ii) if the indorser indorsed an incomplete instrument, according to its terms when completed, to the extent stated in Sections 3–115 and 3–407. The obligation of the indorser is owed to a person entitled to enforce the instrument or to a subsequent indorser who paid the instrument under this section.

(b) If an indorsement states that it is made "without recourse" or otherwise disclaims liability of the indorser, the indorser is not liable under subsection (a) to pay the instrument.

(c) If notice of dishonor of an instrument is required by Section 3–503 and notice of dishonor complying with that section is not given to an indorser, the liability of the indorser under subsection (a) is discharged.

(d) If a draft is accepted by a bank after an indorsement is made, the liability of the indorser under subsection (a) is discharged.

(e) If an indorser of a check is liable under subsection (a) and the check is not presented for payment, or given to a depositary bank for collection, within 30 days after the day the indorsement was made, the liability of the indorser under subsection (a) is discharged.
As amended in 1993.

§ 3–416.   Transfer Warranties.

(a) A person who transfers an instrument for consideration warrants to the transferee and, if the transfer is by indorsement, to any subsequent transferee that:

(1) the warrantor is a person entitled to enforce the instrument;

(2) all signatures on the instrument are authentic and authorized;

(3) the instrument has not been altered;

(4) the instrument is not subject to a defense or claim in recoupment of any party which can be asserted against the warrantor; and

(5) the warrantor has no knowledge of any insolvency proceeding commenced with respect to the maker or acceptor or, in the case of an unaccepted draft, the drawer.

(b) A person to whom the warranties under subsection (a) are made and who took the instrument in good faith may recover from the warrantor as damages for breach of warranty an amount equal to the loss suffered as a result of the breach, but not more than the amount of the instrument plus expenses and loss of interest incurred as a result of the breach.

(c) The warranties stated in subsection (a) cannot be disclaimed with respect to checks. Unless notice of a claim for breach of warranty is given to the warrantor within 30 days after the claimant has reason to know of the breach and the identity of the warrantor, the liability of the warrantor under subsection (b) is discharged to the extent of any loss caused by the delay in giving notice of the claim.

(d) A [cause of action] for breach of warranty under this section accrues when the claimant has reason to know of the breach.

§ 3–417.   Presentment Warranties.

(a) If an unaccepted draft is presented to the drawee for payment or acceptance and the drawee pays or accepts the draft, (i) the person obtaining payment or acceptance, at the time of presentment, and (ii) a previous transferor of the draft, at the time of transfer, warrant to the drawee making payment or accepting the draft in good faith that:

(1) the warrantor is, or was, at the time the warrantor transferred the draft, a person entitled to enforce the draft or authorized to obtain payment or acceptance of the draft on behalf of a person entitled to enforce the draft;

(2) the draft has not been altered; and

(3) the warrantor has no knowledge that the signature of the drawer of the draft is unauthorized.

(b) A drawee making payment may recover from any warrantor damages for breach of warranty equal to the amount paid by the drawee less the amount the drawee received or is entitled to receive from the drawer because of the payment. In addition, the drawee is entitled to compensation for expenses and loss of interest resulting from the breach. The right of the drawee to recover damages under this subsection is not affected by any failure of the drawee to exercise ordinary care in making payment. If the drawee accepts the draft, breach of warranty is a defense to the obligation of the acceptor. If the acceptor makes payment with respect to the draft, the acceptor is entitled to recover from any warrantor for breach of warranty the amounts stated in this subsection.

(c) If a drawee asserts a claim for breach of warranty under subsection (a) based on an unauthorized indorsement of the draft or an alteration of the draft, the warrantor may defend by proving that the indorsement is effective under Section 3–404 or 3–405 or the drawer is precluded under Section 3–406 or 4–406 from asserting against the drawee the unauthorized indorsement or alteration.

(d) If (i) a dishonored draft is presented for payment to the drawer or an indorser or (ii) any other instrument is presented for payment to a party obliged to pay the instrument, and (iii) payment is received, the following rules apply:

(1) The person obtaining payment and a prior transferor of the instrument warrant to the person making payment in good faith that the warrantor is, or was, at the time the warrantor transferred the instrument, a person entitled to enforce the instrument or authorized to obtain payment on behalf of a person entitled to enforce the instrument.

(2) The person making payment may recover from any warrantor for breach of warranty an amount equal to the amount paid plus expenses and loss of interest resulting from the breach.

(e) The warranties stated in subsections (a) and (d) cannot be disclaimed with respect to checks. Unless notice of a claim for breach of warranty is given to the warrantor within 30 days after the claimant has reason to know of the breach and the identity of the warrantor, the liability of the warrantor under subsection (b) or (d) is discharged to the extent of any loss caused by the delay in giving notice of the claim.

(f) A [cause of action] for breach of warranty under this section accrues when the claimant has reason to know of the breach.

§ 3–418. Payment or Acceptance by Mistake.

(a) Except as provided in subsection (c), if the drawee of a draft pays or accepts the draft and the drawee acted on the mistaken belief that (i) payment of the draft had not been stopped pursuant to Section 4–403 or (ii) the signature of the drawer of the draft was authorized, the drawee may recover the amount of the draft from the person to whom or for whose benefit payment was made or, in the case of acceptance, may revoke the acceptance. Rights of the drawee under this subsection are not affected by failure of the drawee to exercise ordinary care in paying or accepting the draft.

(b) Except as provided in subsection (c), if an instrument has been paid or accepted by mistake and the case is not covered by subsection (a), the person paying or accepting may, to the extent permitted by the law governing mistake and restitution, (i) recover the payment from the person to whom or for whose benefit payment was made or (ii) in the case of acceptance, may revoke the acceptance.

(c) The remedies provided by subsection (a) or (b) may not be asserted against a person who took the instrument in good faith and for value or who in good faith changed position in reliance on the payment or acceptance. This subsection does not limit remedies provided by Section 3–417 or 4–407.

(d) Notwithstanding Section 4–215, if an instrument is paid or accepted by mistake and the payor or acceptor recovers payment or revokes acceptance under subsection (a) or (b), the instrument is deemed not to have been paid or accepted and is treated as dishonored, and the person from whom payment is recovered has rights as a person entitled to enforce the dishonored instrument.

§ 3–419. Instruments Signed for Accommodation.

(a) If an instrument is issued for value given for the benefit of a party to the instrument ("accommodated party") and another party to the instrument ("accommodation party") signs the instrument for the purpose of incurring liability on the instrument without being a direct beneficiary of the value given for the instrument, the instrument is signed by the accommodation party "for accommodation."

(b) An accommodation party may sign the instrument as maker, drawer, acceptor, or indorser and, subject to subsection (d), is obliged to pay the instrument in the capacity in which the accommodation party signs. The obligation of an accommodation party may be enforced notwithstanding any statute of frauds and whether or not the accommodation party receives consideration for the accommodation.

(c) A person signing an instrument is presumed to be an accommodation party and there is notice that the instrument is signed for accommodation if the signature is an anomalous indorsement or is accompanied by words indicating that the signer is acting as surety or guarantor with respect to the obligation of another party to the instrument. Except as provided in Section 3–605, the obligation of an accommodation party to pay the instrument is not affected by the fact that the person enforcing the obligation had notice when the instrument was taken by that person that the accommodation party signed the instrument for accommodation.

(d) If the signature of a party to an instrument is accompanied by words indicating unambiguously that the party is guaranteeing collection rather than payment of the obligation of another party to the instrument, the signer is obliged to pay the amount due on the instrument to a person entitled to enforce the instrument only if (i) execution of judgment against the other party has been returned unsatisfied, (ii) the other party is insolvent or in an insolvency proceeding, (iii) the other party cannot be served with process, or (iv) it is otherwise apparent that payment cannot be obtained from the other party.

(e) An accommodation party who pays the instrument is entitled to reimbursement from the accommodated party and is entitled to enforce the instrument against the accommodated party. An accommodated party who pays the instrument has no right of recourse against, and is not entitled to contribution from, an accommodation party.

§ 3–420. Conversion of Instrument.

(a) The law applicable to conversion of personal property applies to instruments. An instrument is also converted if it is taken by transfer, other than a negotiation, from a person not entitled to enforce the instrument or a bank makes or obtains payment with respect to the instrument for a person not entitled to enforce the instrument or receive payment. An action for conversion of an instrument may not be brought by (i) the issuer or acceptor of the instrument or (ii) a payee or indorsee who did not receive delivery of the instrument either directly or through delivery to an agent or a co-payee.

(b) In an action under subsection (a), the measure of liability is presumed to be the amount payable on the instrument, but recovery may not exceed the amount of the plaintiff's interest in the instrument.

(c) A representative, other than a depositary bank, who has in good faith dealt with an instrument or its proceeds on behalf of one who was not the person entitled to enforce the instrument is not liable in conversion to that person beyond the amount of any proceeds that it has not paid out.

Part 5—Dishonor

§ 3–501. Presentment.

(a) "Presentment" means a demand made by or on behalf of a person entitled to enforce an instrument (i) to pay the instrument made to the drawee or a party obliged to pay the instrument or, in the case of a note or accepted draft payable at a bank, to the bank, or (ii) to accept a draft made to the drawee.

(b) The following rules are subject to Article 4, agreement of the parties, and clearing-house rules and the like:

(1) Presentment may be made at the place of payment of the instrument and must be made at the place of payment if the instrument is payable at a bank in the United States; may be made by any commercially reasonable means, including an oral, written, or electronic communication; is effective when the demand for payment or acceptance is received by the person to whom presentment is made; and is effective if made to any one of two or more makers, acceptors, drawees, or other payors.

(2) Upon demand of the person to whom presentment is made, the person making presentment must (i) exhibit the instrument, (ii) give reasonable identification and, if presentment is made on behalf of another person, reasonable evidence of authority to do so, and (. . .) sign a receipt on the instrument for any payment made or surrender the instrument if full payment is made.

(3) Without dishonoring the instrument, the party to whom presentment is made may (i) return the instrument for lack of a necessary indorsement, or (ii) refuse payment or acceptance for failure of the presentment to comply with the terms of the instrument, an agreement of the parties, or other applicable law or rule.

(4) The party to whom presentment is made may treat presentment as occurring on the next business day after the day of presentment if the party to whom presentment is made has established a cut-off hour not earlier than 2 p.m. for the receipt and processing of instruments presented for payment or acceptance and presentment is made after the cut-off hour.

§ 3–502. Dishonor.

(a) Dishonor of a note is governed by the following rules:

(1) If the note is payable on demand, the note is dishonored if presentment is duly made to the maker and the note is not paid on the day of presentment.

(2) If the note is not payable on demand and is payable at or through a bank or the terms of the note require presentment, the note is dishonored if presentment is duly made and the note is not paid on the day it becomes payable or the day of presentment, whichever is later.

(3) If the note is not payable on demand and paragraph (2) does not apply, the note is dishonored if it is not paid on the day it becomes payable.

(b) Dishonor of an unaccepted draft other than a documentary draft is governed by the following rules:

(1) If a check is duly presented for payment to the payor bank otherwise than for immediate payment over the counter, the check is dishonored if the payor bank makes timely return of the check or sends timely notice of dishonor or nonpayment under Section 4–301 or 4–302, or becomes accountable for the amount of the check under Section 4–302.

(2) If a draft is payable on demand and paragraph (1) does not apply, the draft is dishonored if presentment for payment is duly made to the drawee and the draft is not paid on the day of presentment.

(3) If a draft is payable on a date stated in the draft, the draft is dishonored if (i) presentment for payment is duly made to the drawee and payment is not made on the day the draft becomes payable or the day of presentment, whichever is later, or (ii) presentment for acceptance is duly made before the day the draft becomes payable and the draft is not accepted on the day of presentment.

(4) If a draft is payable on elapse of a period of time after sight or acceptance, the draft is dishonored if presentment for acceptance is duly made and the draft is not accepted on the day of presentment.

(c) Dishonor of an unaccepted documentary draft occurs according to the rules stated in subsection (b)(2), (3), and (4), except that payment or acceptance may be delayed without dishonor until no later than the close of the third business day of the drawee following the day on which payment or acceptance is required by those paragraphs.

(d) Dishonor of an accepted draft is governed by the following rules:

(1) If the draft is payable on demand, the draft is dishonored if presentment for payment is duly made to the acceptor and the draft is not paid on the day of presentment.

(2) If the draft is not payable on demand, the draft is dishonored if presentment for payment is duly made to the acceptor and payment is not made on the day it becomes payable or the day of presentment, whichever is later.

(e) In any case in which presentment is otherwise required for dishonor under this section and presentment is excused under Section 3–504, dishonor occurs without presentment if the instrument is not duly accepted or paid.

(f) If a draft is dishonored because timely acceptance of the draft was not made and the person entitled to demand acceptance consents to a late acceptance, from the time of acceptance the draft is treated as never having been dishonored.

§ 3–503. Notice of Dishonor.

(a) The obligation of an indorser stated in Section 3–415(a) and the obligation of a drawer stated in Section 3–414(d) may not be enforced unless (i) the indorser or drawer is given notice of dishonor of the instrument complying with this section or (ii) notice of dishonor is excused under Section 3–504(b).

(b) Notice of dishonor may be given by any person; may be given by any commercially reasonable means, including an oral, written, or electronic communication; and is sufficient if it reasonably identifies the instrument and indicates that the instrument has been dishonored or has not been paid or accepted. Return of an instrument given to a bank for collection is sufficient notice of dishonor.

(c) Subject to Section 3–504(c), with respect to an instrument taken for collection by a collecting bank, notice of dishonor must be given (i) by the bank before midnight of the next banking day following the banking day on which the bank receives notice of dishonor of the instrument, or (ii) by any other person within 30 days following the day on which the person receives notice of dishonor. With respect to any other instrument, notice of dishonor must be given within 30 days following the day on which dishonor occurs.

§ 3–504. Excused Presentment and Notice of Dishonor.

(a) Presentment for payment or acceptance of an instrument is excused if (i) the person entitled to present the instrument cannot with reasonable diligence make presentment, (ii) the maker or acceptor has repudiated an obligation to pay the instrument or is dead or in insolvency proceedings, (iii) by the terms of the instrument presentment is not necessary to enforce the obligation of indorsers or the drawer, (iv) the drawer or indorser whose obligation is being enforced has waived presentment or otherwise has no reason to expect or right to require that the instrument be paid or accepted, or (v) the drawer instructed the drawee not to pay or accept the draft or the drawee was not obligated to the drawer to pay the draft.

(b) Notice of dishonor is excused if (i) by the terms of the instrument notice of dishonor is not necessary to enforce the obligation of a party to pay the instrument, or (ii) the party whose obligation is being enforced waived notice of dishonor. A waiver of presentment is also a waiver of notice of dishonor.

(c) Delay in giving notice of dishonor is excused if the delay was caused by circumstances beyond the control of the person giving the notice and the person giving the notice exercised reasonable diligence after the cause of the delay ceased to operate.

§ 3–505. Evidence of Dishonor.

(a) The following are admissible as evidence and create a presumption of dishonor and of any notice of dishonor stated:

(1) a document regular in form as provided in subsection (b) which purports to be a protest;

(2) a purported stamp or writing of the drawee, payor bank, or presenting bank on or accompanying the instrument stating that acceptance or payment has been refused unless reasons for the refusal are stated and the reasons are not consistent with dishonor;

(3) a book or record of the drawee, payor bank, or collecting bank, kept in the usual course of business which shows dishonor, even if there is no evidence of who made the entry.

(b) A protest is a certificate of dishonor made by a United States consul or vice consul, or a notary public or other person authorized to administer oaths by the law of the place where dishonor occurs. It may be made upon information satisfactory to that person. The protest must identify the instrument and certify either that presentment has been made or, if not made, the reason why it was not made, and that the instrument has been dishonored by nonacceptance or nonpayment. The protest may also certify that notice of dishonor has been given to some or all parties.

Part 6—Discharge and Payment

§ 3–601. Discharge and Effect of Discharge.

(a) The obligation of a party to pay the instrument is discharged as stated in this Article or by an act or agreement with the party which would discharge an obligation to pay money under a simple contract.

(b) Discharge of the obligation of a party is not effective against a person acquiring rights of a holder in due course of the instrument without notice of the discharge.

§ 3–602. Payment.

(a) Subject to subsection (b), an instrument is paid to the extent payment is made (i) by or on behalf of a party obliged to pay the instrument, and (ii) to a person entitled to enforce the instrument. To the extent of the payment, the obligation of the party obliged to pay the instrument is discharged even though payment is made with knowledge of a claim to the instrument under Section 3–306 by another person.

(b) The obligation of a party to pay the instrument is not discharged under subsection (a) if:

(1) a claim to the instrument under Section 3–306 is enforceable against the party receiving payment and (i) payment is made with knowledge by the payor that payment is prohibited by injunction or similar process of a court of competent jurisdiction, or (ii) in the case of an instrument other than a cashier's check, teller's check, or certified check, the party making payment accepted, from the person having a claim to the instrument, indemnity against loss resulting from refusal to pay the person entitled to enforce the instrument; or

(2) the person making payment knows that the instrument is a stolen instrument and pays a person it knows is in wrongful possession of the instrument.

§ 3–603. Tender of Payment.

(a) If tender of payment of an obligation to pay an instrument is made to a person entitled to enforce the instrument, the effect of tender is governed by principles of law applicable to tender of payment under a simple contract.

(b) If tender of payment of an obligation to pay an instrument is made to a person entitled to enforce the instrument and the tender is refused, there is discharge, to the extent of the amount of the tender, of the obligation of an indorser or accommodation party having a right of recourse with respect to the obligation to which the tender relates.

(c) If tender of payment of an amount due on an instrument is made to a person entitled to enforce the instrument, the obligation of the obligor to pay interest after the due date on the amount tendered is discharged. If presentment is required with respect to an instrument and the obligor is able and ready to pay on the due date at every place of payment stated in the instrument, the obligor is deemed to have made tender of payment on the due date to the person entitled to enforce the instrument.

§ 3–604. Discharge by Cancellation or Renunciation.

(a) A person entitled to enforce an instrument, with or without consideration, may discharge the obligation of a party to pay the instrument (i) by an intentional voluntary act, such as surrender of the instrument to the party, destruction, mutilation, or cancellation of the instrument, cancellation or striking out of the party's signature, or the addition of words to the instrument indicating discharge, or (ii) by agreeing not to sue or otherwise renouncing rights against the party by a signed writing.

(b) Cancellation or striking out of an indorsement pursuant to subsection (a) does not affect the status and rights of a party derived from the indorsement.

§ 3–605. Discharge of Indorsers and Accommodation Parties.

(a) In this section, the term "indorser" includes a drawer having the obligation described in Section 3–414(d).

(b) Discharge, under Section 3–604, of the obligation of a party to pay an instrument does not discharge the obligation of an indorser or accommodation party having a right of recourse against the discharged party.

(c) If a person entitled to enforce an instrument agrees, with or without consideration, to an extension of the due date of the obligation of a party to pay the instrument, the extension discharges an indorser or accommodation party having a right of recourse against the party whose obligation is extended to the extent the indorser or accommodation party proves that the extension caused loss to the indorser or accommodation party with respect to the right of recourse.

(d) If a person entitled to enforce an instrument agrees, with or without consideration, to a material modification of the obligation of a party other than an extension of the due date, the modification discharges the obligation of an indorser or accommodation party having a right of recourse against the person whose obligation is modified to the extent the modification causes loss to the indorser or accommodation party with respect to the right of recourse. The loss suffered by the indorser or accommodation party as a result of the modification is equal to the amount of the right of recourse unless the person enforcing the instrument proves that no loss was caused by the modification or that the loss caused by the modification was an amount less than the amount of the right of recourse.

(e) If the obligation of a party to pay an instrument is secured by an interest in collateral and a person entitled to enforce the instrument impairs the value of the interest in collateral, the obligation of an indorser or accommodation party having a right of recourse against the obligor is discharged to the extent of the impairment. The value of an interest in collateral is impaired to the extent (i) the value of the interest is reduced to an amount less than the amount of the right of recourse of the party asserting discharge, or (ii) the reduction in value of the interest causes an increase in the amount by which the amount of the right of recourse exceeds the value of the interest. The burden of proving impairment is on the party asserting discharge.

(f) If the obligation of a party is secured by an interest in collateral not provided by an accommodation party and a person entitled to enforce the instrument impairs the value of the interest in collateral, the obligation of any party who is jointly and severally liable with respect to the secured obligation is discharged to the extent the impairment causes the party asserting discharge to pay more than that party would have been obliged to pay, taking into account rights of contribution, if impairment had not occurred. If the party asserting discharge is an accommodation party not entitled to discharge under subsection (e), the party is deemed to have a right to contribution based on joint and several liability rather than a right to reimbursement. The burden of proving impairment is on the party asserting discharge.

(g) Under subsection (e) or (f), impairing value of an interest in collateral includes (i) failure to obtain or maintain perfection or recordation of the interest in collateral, (ii) release of collateral without substitution of collateral of equal value, (iii) failure to perform a duty to preserve the value of collateral owed, under Article 9 or other law, to a debtor or surety or other person secondarily liable, or (iv) failure to comply with applicable law in disposing of collateral.

(h) An accommodation party is not discharged under subsection (c), (d), or (e) unless the person entitled to enforce the instrument knows of the accommodation or has notice under Section 3–419(c) that the instrument was signed for accommodation.

(i) A party is not discharged under this section if (i) the party asserting discharge consents to the event or conduct that is the basis of the discharge, or (ii) the instrument or a separate agreement of the party provides for waiver of discharge under this section either specifically or by general language indicating that parties waive defenses based on suretyship or impairment of collateral.

ADDENDUM TO REVISED ARTICLE 3
Notes to Legislative Counsel
1. If revised Article 3 is adopted in your state, the reference in Section 2–511 to Section 3–802 should be changed to Section 3–310.
2. If revised Article 3 is adopted in your state and the Uniform Fiduciaries Act is also in effect in your state, you may want to consider amending Uniform Fiduciaries Act § 9 to conform to Section 3–307(b)(2)(iii) and (4)(iii). See Official Comment 3 to Section 3–307.

REVISED ARTICLE 4: BANK DEPOSITS AND COLLECTIONS

Part 1—General Provisions and Definitions

§ 4–101. Short Title.
This Article may be cited as Uniform Commercial Code—Bank Deposits and Collections.
As amended in 1990.

§ 4–102. Applicability.
(a) To the extent that items within this Article are also within Articles 3 and 8, they are subject to those Articles. If there is conflict, this Article governs Article 3, but Article 8 governs this Article.
(b) The liability of a bank for action or non-action with respect to an item handled by it for purposes of presentment, payment, or collection is governed by the law of the place where the bank is located. In the case of action or non-action by or at a branch or separate office of a bank, its liability is governed by the law of the place where the branch or separate office is located.

§ 4–103. Variation by Agreement; Measure of Damages; Action Constituting Ordinary Care.
(a) The effect of the provisions of this Article may be varied by agreement, but the parties to the agreement cannot disclaim a bank's responsibility for its lack of good faith or failure to exercise ordinary care or limit the measure of damages for the lack or failure. However, the parties may determine by agreement the standards by which the bank's responsibility is to be measured if those standards are not manifestly unreasonable.
(b) Federal Reserve regulations and operating circulars, clearing-house rules, and the like have the effect of agreements under subsection (a), whether or not specifically assented to by all parties interested in items handled.
(c) Action or non-action approved by this Article or pursuant to Federal Reserve regulations or operating circulars is the exercise of ordinary care and, in the absence of special instructions, action or non-action consistent with clearing-house rules and the like or with a general banking usage not disapproved by this Article, is *prima facie* the exercise of ordinary care.
(d) The specification or approval of certain procedures by this Article is not disapproval of other procedures that may be reasonable under the circumstances.
(e) The measure of damages for failure to exercise ordinary care in handling an item is the amount of the item reduced by an amount that could not have been realized by the exercise of ordinary care. If there is also bad faith it includes any other damages the party suffered as a proximate consequence.
As amended in 1990.

§ 4–104. Definitions and Index of Definitions.
(a) In this Article, unless the context otherwise requires:
   (1) "Account" means any deposit or credit account with a bank, including a demand, time, savings, passbook, share draft, or like account, other than an account evidenced by a certificate of deposit;
   (2) "Afternoon" means the period of a day between noon and midnight;
   (3) "Banking day" means the part of a day on which a bank is open to the public for carrying on substantially all of its banking functions;
   (4) "Clearing house" means an association of banks or other payors regularly clearing items;
   (5) "Customer" means a person having an account with a bank or for whom a bank has agreed to collect items, including a bank that maintains an account at another bank;
   (6) "Documentary draft" means a draft to be presented for acceptance or payment if specified documents, certificated securities (Section 8–102) or instructions for uncertificated securities (Section 8–102), or other certificates, statements, or

the like are to be received by the drawee or other payor before acceptance or payment of the draft;

(7) "Draft" means a draft as defined in Section 3–104 or an item, other than an instrument, that is an order;

(8) "Drawee" means a person ordered in a draft to make payment;

(9) "Item" means an instrument or a promise or order to pay money handled by a bank for collection or payment. The term does not include a payment order governed by Article 4A or a credit or debit card slip;

(10) "Midnight deadline" with respect to a bank is midnight on its next banking day following the banking day on which it receives the relevant item or notice or from which the time for taking action commences to run, whichever is later;

(11) "Settle" means to pay in cash, by clearing-house settlement, in a charge or credit or by remittance, or otherwise as agreed. A settlement may be either provisional or final;

(12) "Suspends payments" with respect to a bank means that it has been closed by order of the supervisory authorities, that a public officer has been appointed to take it over, or that it ceases or refuses to make payments in the ordinary course of business.

(b) [Other definitions' section references deleted.]

(c) [Other definitions' section references deleted.]

(d) In addition, Article 1 contains general definitions and principles of construction and interpretation applicable throughout this Article.

§ 4–105.   "Bank"; "Depositary Bank"; "Payor Bank"; "Intermediary Bank"; "Collecting Bank"; "Presenting Bank".

In this Article:

(1) "Bank" means a person engaged in the business of banking, including a savings bank, savings and loan association, credit union, or trust company;

(2) "Depositary bank" means the first bank to take an item even though it is also the payor bank, unless the item is presented for immediate payment over the counter;

(3) "Payor bank" means a bank that is the drawee of a draft;

(4) "Intermediary bank" means a bank to which an item is transferred in course of collection except the depositary or payor bank;

(5) "Collecting bank" means a bank handling an item for collection except the payor bank;

(6) "Presenting bank" means a bank presenting an item except a payor bank.

§ 4–106.   Payable Through or Payable at Bank: Collecting Bank.

(a) If an item states that it is "payable through" a bank identified in the item, (i) the item designates the bank as a collecting bank and does not by itself authorize the bank to pay the item, and (ii) the item may be presented for payment only by or through the bank.

Alternative A

(b) If an item states that it is "payable at" a bank identified in the item, the item is equivalent to a draft drawn on the bank.

Alternative B

(b) If an item states that it is "payable at" a bank identified in the item, (i) the item designates the bank as a collecting bank and does not by itself authorize the bank to pay the item, and (ii) the item may be presented for payment only by or through the bank.

(c) If a draft names a nonbank drawee and it is unclear whether a bank named in the draft is a co-drawee or a collecting bank, the bank is a collecting bank.

As added in 1990.

§ 4–107.   Separate Office of Bank.

A branch or separate office of a bank is a separate bank for the purpose of computing the time within which and determining the place at or to which action may be taken or notices or orders shall be given under this Article and under Article 3.

As amended in 1962 and 1990.

§ 4–108.   Time of Receipt of Items.

(a) For the purpose of allowing time to process items, prove balances, and make the necessary entries on its books to determine its position for the day, a bank may fix an afternoon hour of 2 p.m. or later as a cutoff hour for the handling of money and items and the making of entries on its books.

(b) An item or deposit of money received on any day after a cutoff hour so fixed or after the close of the banking day may be treated as being received at the opening of the next banking day.

As amended in 1990.

§ 4–109.   Delays.

(a) Unless otherwise instructed, a collecting bank in a good faith effort to secure payment of a specific item drawn on a payor other than a bank, and with or without the approval of any person involved, may waive, modify, or extend time limits imposed or permitted by this [act] for a period not exceeding two additional banking days without discharge of drawers or indorsers or liability to its transferor or a prior party.

(b) Delay by a collecting bank or payor bank beyond time limits prescribed or permitted by this [act] or by instructions is excused if (i) the delay is caused by interruption of communication or computer facilities, suspension of payments by another bank, war, emergency conditions, failure of equipment, or other circumstances beyond the control of the bank, and (ii) the bank exercises such diligence as the circumstances require.

§ 4–110.   Electronic Presentment.

(a) "Agreement for electronic presentment" means an agreement, clearing-house rule, or Federal Reserve regulation or operating circular, providing that presentment of an item may be made by transmission of an image of an item or information describing the item ("presentment notice") rather than delivery of the item itself. The agreement may provide for procedures governing retention, presentment, payment, dishonor, and other matters concerning items subject to the agreement.

(b) Presentment of an item pursuant to an agreement for presentment is made when the presentment notice is received.

(c) If presentment is made by presentment notice, a reference to "item" or "check" in this Article means the presentment notice unless the context otherwise indicates.

As added in 1990.

§ 4–111.   Statute of Limitations.

An action to enforce an obligation, duty, or right arising under this Article must be commenced within three years after the [cause of action] accrues.

As added in 1990.

Part 2—Collection of Items: Depositary and Collecting Banks

§ 4–201. Status of Collecting Bank as Agent and Provisional Status of Credits; Applicability of Article; Item Indorsed "Pay Any Bank".

(a) Unless a contrary intent clearly appears and before the time that a settlement given by a collecting bank for an item is or becomes final, the bank, with respect to an item, is an agent or sub-agent of the owner of the item and any settlement given for the item is provisional. This provision applies regardless of the form of indorsement or lack of indorsement and even though credit given for the item is subject to immediate withdrawal as of right or is in fact withdrawn; but the continuance of ownership of an item by its owner and any rights of the owner to proceeds of the item are subject to rights of a collecting bank, such as those resulting from outstanding advances on the item and rights of recoupment or setoff. If an item is handled by banks for purposes of presentment, payment, collection, or return, the relevant provisions of this Article apply even though action of the parties clearly establishes that a particular bank has purchased the item and is the owner of it.

(b) After an item has been indorsed with the words "pay any bank" or the like, only a bank may acquire the rights of a holder until the item has been:
  (1) returned to the customer initiating collection; or
  (2) specially indorsed by a bank to a person who is not a bank.
As amended in 1990.

§ 4–202. Responsibility for Collection or Return; When Action Timely.

(a) A collecting bank must exercise ordinary care in:
  (1) presenting an item or sending it for presentment;
  (2) sending notice of dishonor or nonpayment or returning an item other than a documentary draft to the bank's transferor after learning that the item has not been paid or accepted, as the case may be;
  (3) settling for an item when the bank receives final settlement; and
  (4) notifying its transferor of any loss or delay in transit within a reasonable time after discovery thereof.

(b) A collecting bank exercises ordinary care under subsection (a) by taking proper action before its midnight deadline following receipt of an item, notice, or settlement. Taking proper action within a reasonably longer time may constitute the exercise of ordinary care, but the bank has the burden of establishing timeliness.

(c) Subject to subsection (a)(1), a bank is not liable for the insolvency, neglect, misconduct, mistake, or default of another bank or person or for loss or destruction of an item in the possession of others or in transit.
As amended in 1990.

§ 4–203. Effect of Instructions.

Subject to Article 3 concerning conversion of instruments (Section 3–420) and restrictive indorsements (Section 3–206), only a collecting bank's transferor can give instructions that affect the bank or constitute notice to it, and a collecting bank is not liable to prior parties for any action taken pursuant to the instructions or in accordance with any agreement with its transferor.

§ 4–204. Methods of Sending and Presenting; Sending Directly to Payor Bank.

(a) A collecting bank shall send items by a reasonably prompt method, taking into consideration relevant instructions, the nature of the item, the number of those items on hand, the cost of collection involved, and the method generally used by it or others to present those items.

(b) A collecting bank may send:
  (1) an item directly to the payor bank;
  (2) an item to a nonbank payor if authorized by its transferor; and
  (3) an item other than documentary drafts to a nonbank payor, if authorized by Federal Reserve regulation or operating circular, clearing-house rule, or the like.

(c) Presentment may be made by a presenting bank at a place where the payor bank or other payor has requested that presentment be made.
As amended in 1990.

§ 4–205. Depositary Bank Holder of Unindorsed Item.

If a customer delivers an item to a depositary bank for collection:
(1) the depositary bank becomes a holder of the item at the time it receives the item for collection if the customer at the time of delivery was a holder of the item, whether or not the customer indorses the item, and, if the bank satisfies the other requirements of Section 3–302, it is a holder in due course; and
(2) the depositary bank warrants to collecting banks, the payor bank or other payor, and the drawer that the amount of the item was paid to the customer or deposited to the customer's account.
As amended in 1990.

§ 4–206. Transfer Between Banks.

Any agreed method that identifies the transferor bank is sufficient for the item's further transfer to another bank.
As amended in 1990.

§ 4–207. Transfer Warranties.

(a) A customer or collecting bank that transfers an item and receives a settlement or other consideration warrants to the transferee and to any subsequent collecting bank that:
  (1) the warrantor is a person entitled to enforce the item;
  (2) all signatures on the item are authentic andauthorized;
  (3) the item has not been altered;
  (4) the item is not subject to a defense or claim in recoupment (Section 3–305(a)) of any party that can be asserted against the warrantor; and
  (5) the warrantor has no knowledge of any insolvency proceeding commenced with respect to the maker or acceptor or, in the case of an unaccepted draft, the drawer.

(b) If an item is dishonored, a customer or collecting bank transferring the item and receiving settlement or other consideration is obliged to pay the amount due on the item (i) according to the terms of the item at the time it was transferred, or (ii) if the transfer was of an incomplete item, according to its terms when completed as stated in Sections 3–115 and 3–407. The obligation of a transferor is owed to the transferee and to any subsequent collecting bank that takes the item in good faith. A transferor cannot disclaim its obligation under this subsection by an indorsement stating that it is made "without recourse" or otherwise disclaiming liability.

(c) A person to whom the warranties under subsection (a) are made and who took the item in good faith may recover from the warrantor as damages for breach of warranty an amount equal to the loss suffered as a result of the breach, but not more than the amount of the item plus expenses and loss of interest incurred as a result of the breach.

(d) The warranties stated in subsection (a) cannot be disclaimed with respect to checks. Unless notice of a claim for breach of warranty is given to the warrantor within 30 days after the claimant has reason to know of the breach and the identity of the warrantor, the warrantor is discharged to the extent of any loss caused by the delay in giving notice of the claim.

(e) A cause of action for breach of warranty under this section accrues when the claimant has reason to know of the breach.
As amended in 1990.

§ 4–208. Presentment Warranties.

(a) If an unaccepted draft is presented to the drawee for payment or acceptance and the drawee pays or accepts the draft, (i) the person obtaining payment or acceptance, at the time of presentment, and (ii) a previous transferor of the draft, at the time of transfer, warrant to the drawee that pays or accepts the draft in good faith that:

> **(1)** the warrantor is, or was, at the time the warrantor transferred the draft, a person entitled to enforce the draft or authorized to obtain payment or acceptance of the draft on behalf of a person entitled to enforce the draft;
> **(2)** the draft has not been altered; and
> **(3)** the warrantor has no knowledge that the signature of the purported drawer of the draft is unauthorized.

(b) A drawee making payment may recover from a warrantor damages for breach of warranty equal to the amount paid by the drawee less the amount the drawee received or is entitled to receive from the drawer because of the payment. In addition, the drawee is entitled to compensation for expenses and loss of interest resulting from the breach. The right of the drawee to recover damages under this subsection is not affected by any failure of the drawee to exercise ordinary care in making payment. If the drawee accepts the draft (i) breach of warranty is a defense to the obligation of the acceptor, and (ii) if the acceptor makes payment with respect to the draft, the acceptor is entitled to recover from a warrantor for breach of warranty the amounts stated in this subsection.

(c) If a drawee asserts a claim for breach of warranty under subsection (a) based on an unauthorized indorsement of the draft or an alteration of the draft, the warrantor may defend by proving that the indorsement is effective under Section 3–404 or 3–405 or the drawer is precluded under Section 3–406 or 4–406 from asserting against the drawee the unauthorized indorsement or alteration.

(d) If (i) a dishonored draft is presented for payment to the drawer or an indorser or (ii) any other item is presented for payment to a party obliged to pay the item, and the item is paid, the person obtaining payment and a prior transferor of the item warrant to the person making payment in good faith that the warrantor is, or was, at the time the warrantor transferred the item, a person entitled to enforce the item or authorized to obtain payment on behalf of a person entitled to enforce the item. The person making payment may recover from any warrantor for breach of warranty an amount equal to the amount paid plus expenses and loss of interest resulting from the breach.

(e) The warranties stated in subsections (a) and (d) cannot be disclaimed with respect to checks. Unless notice of a claim for breach of warranty is given to the warrantor within 30 days after the claimant has reason to know of the breach and the identity of the warrantor, the warrantor is discharged to the extent of any loss caused by the delay in giving notice of the claim.

(f) A cause of action for breach of warranty under this section accrues when the claimant has reason to know of the breach.
As amended in 1990.

§ 4–209. Encoding and Retention Warranties.

(a) A person who encodes information on or with respect to an item after issue warrants to any subsequent collecting bank and to the payor bank or other payor that the information is correctly encoded. If the customer of a depositary bank encodes, that bank also makes the warranty.

(b) A person who undertakes to retain an item pursuant to an agreement for electronic presentment warrants to any subsequent collecting bank and to the payor bank or other payor that retention and presentment of the item comply with the agreement. If a customer of a depositary bank undertakes to retain an item, that bank also makes this warranty.

(c) A person to whom warranties are made under this section and who took the item in good faith may recover from the warrantor as damages for breach of warranty an amount equal to the loss suffered as a result of the breach, plus expenses and loss of interest incurred as a result of the breach.
As added in 1990.

§ 4–210. Security Interest of Collecting Bank in Items, Accompanying Documents and Proceeds.

(a) A collecting bank has a security interest in an item and any accompanying documents or the proceeds of either:

> **(1)** in case of an item deposited in an account, to the extent to which credit given for the item has been withdrawn or applied;
> **(2)** in case of an item for which it has given credit available for withdrawal as of right, to the extent of the credit given, whether or not the credit is drawn upon or there is a right of charge-back; or
> **(3)** if it makes an advance on or against the item.

(b) If credit given for several items received at one time or pursuant to a single agreement is withdrawn or applied in part, the security interest remains upon all the items, any accompanying documents or the proceeds of either. For the purpose of this section, credits first given are first withdrawn.

(c) Receipt by a collecting bank of a final settlement for an item is a realization on its security interest in the item, accompanying documents, and proceeds. So long as the bank does not receive final settlement for the item or give up possession of the item or accompanying documents for purposes other than collection, the security interest continues to that extent and is subject to Article 9, but:

> **(1)** no security agreement is necessary to make the security interest enforceable (Section 9–203(1)(a));
> **(2)** no filing is required to perfect the security interest; and
> **(3)** the security interest has priority over conflicting perfected security interests in the item, accompanying documents, or proceeds.

As amended in 1990 and 1999.

§ 4–211. When Bank Gives Value for Purposes of Holder in Due Course.

For purposes of determining its status as a holder in due course, a bank has given value to the extent it has a security interest in an

item, if the bank otherwise complies with the requirements of Section 3–302 on what constitutes a holder in due course.
As amended in 1990.

§ 4–212. Presentment by Notice of Item Not Payable by, Through, or at Bank; Liability of Drawer or Indorser.

(a) Unless otherwise instructed, a collecting bank may present an item not payable by, through, or at a bank by sending to the party to accept or pay a written notice that the bank holds the item for acceptance or payment. The notice must be sent in time to be received on or before the day when presentment is due and the bank must meet any requirement of the party to accept or pay under Section 3–501 by the close of the bank's next banking day after it knows of the requirement.

(b) If presentment is made by notice and payment, acceptance, or request for compliance with a requirement under Section 3–501 is not received by the close of business on the day after maturity or, in the case of demand items, by the close of business on the third banking day after notice was sent, the presenting bank may treat the item as dishonored and charge any drawer or indorser by sending it notice of the facts.
As amended in 1990.

§ 4–213. Medium and Time of Settlement by Bank.

(a) With respect to settlement by a bank, the medium and time of settlement may be prescribed by Federal Reserve regulations or circulars, clearing-house rules, and the like, or agreement. In the absence of such prescription:

    (1) the medium of settlement is cash or credit to an account in a Federal Reserve bank of or specified by the person to receive settlement; and

    (2) the time of settlement is:

        (i) with respect to tender of settlement by cash, a cashier's check, or teller's check, when the cash or check is sent or delivered;

        (ii) with respect to tender of settlement by credit in an account in a Federal Reserve Bank, when the credit is made;

        (iii) with respect to tender of settlement by a credit or debit to an account in a bank, when the credit or debit is made or, in the case of tender of settlement by authority to charge an account, when the authority is sent or delivered; or

        (iv) with respect to tender of settlement by a funds transfer, when payment is made pursuant to Section 4A–406(a) to the person receiving settlement.

(b) If the tender of settlement is not by a medium authorized by subsection (a) or the time of settlement is not fixed by subsection (a), no settlement occurs until the tender of settlement is accepted by the person receiving settlement.

(c) If settlement for an item is made by cashier's check or teller's check and the person receiving settlement, before its midnight deadline:

    (1) presents or forwards the check for collection, settlement is final when the check is finally paid; or

    (2) fails to present or forward the check for collection, settlement is final at the midnight deadline of the person receiving settlement.

(d) If settlement for an item is made by giving authority to charge the account of the bank giving settlement in the bank receiving settlement, settlement is final when the charge is made by the bank receiving settlement if there are funds available in the account for the amount of the item.
As amended in 1990.

§ 4–214. Right of Charge-Back or Refund; Liability of Collecting Bank: Return of Item.

(a) If a collecting bank has made provisional settlement with its customer for an item and fails by reason of dishonor, suspension of payments by a bank, or otherwise to receive settlement for the item which is or becomes final, the bank may revoke the settlement given by it, charge back the amount of any credit given for the item to its customer's account, or obtain refund from its customer, whether or not it is able to return the item, if by its midnight deadline or within a longer reasonable time after it learns the facts it returns the item or sends notification of the facts. If the return or notice is delayed beyond the bank's midnight deadline or a longer reasonable time after it learns the facts, the bank may revoke the settlement, charge back the credit, or obtain refund from its customer, but it is liable for any loss resulting from the delay. These rights to revoke, charge back, and obtain refund terminate if and when a settlement for the item received by the bank is or becomes final.

(b) A collecting bank returns an item when it is sent or delivered to the bank's customer or transferor or pursuant to its instructions.

(c) A depositary bank that is also the payor may charge back the amount of an item to its customer's account or obtain refund in accordance with the section governing return of an item received by a payor bank for credit on its books (Section 4–301).

(d) The right to charge back is not affected by:

    (1) previous use of a credit given for the item; or

    (2) failure by any bank to exercise ordinary care with respect to the item, but a bank so failing remains liable.

(e) A failure to charge back or claim refund does not affect other rights of the bank against the customer or any other party.

(f) If credit is given in dollars as the equivalent of the value of an item payable in foreign money, the dollar amount of any charge-back or refund must be calculated on the basis of the bank-offered spot rate for the foreign money prevailing on the day when the person entitled to the charge-back or refund learns that it will not receive payment in ordinary course.
As amended in 1990.

§ 4–215. Final Payment of Item by Payor Bank; When Provisional Debits and Credits Become Final; When Certain Credits Become Available for Withdrawal.

(a) An item is finally paid by a payor bank when the bank has first done any of the following:

    (1) paid the item in cash;

    (2) settled for the item without having a right to revoke the settlement under statute, clearing-house rule, or agreement; or

    (3) made a provisional settlement for the item and failed to revoke the settlement in the time and manner permitted by statute, clearing-house rule, or agreement.

(b) If provisional settlement for an item does not become final, the item is not finally paid.

(c) If provisional settlement for an item between the presenting and payor banks is made through a clearing house or by debits or credits in an account between them, then to the extent that provisional debits or credits for the item are entered in accounts between the presenting and payor banks or between the presenting and successive prior collecting banks seriatim, they become final upon final payment of the item by the payor bank.

(d) If a collecting bank receives a settlement for an item which is or becomes final, the bank is accountable to its customer for the amount of the item and any provisional credit given for the item in an account with its customer becomes final.

(e) Subject to (i) applicable law stating a time for availability of funds and (ii) any right of the bank to apply the credit to an obligation of the customer, credit given by a bank for an item in a customer's account becomes available for withdrawal as of right:

   (1) if the bank has received a provisional settlement for the item, when the settlement becomes final and the bank has had a reasonable time to receive return of the item and the item has not been received within that time;

   (2) if the bank is both the depositary bank and the payor bank, and the item is finally paid, at the opening of the bank's second banking day following receipt of the item.

(f) Subject to applicable law stating a time for availability of funds and any right of a bank to apply a deposit to an obligation of the depositor, a deposit of money becomes available for withdrawal as of right at the opening of the bank's next banking day after receipt of the deposit.

As amended in 1990.

§ 4–216. **Insolvency and Preference.**

(a) If an item is in or comes into the possession of a payor or collecting bank that suspends payment and the item has not been finally paid, the item must be returned by the receiver, trustee, or agent in charge of the closed bank to the presenting bank or the closed bank's customer.

(b) If a payor bank finally pays an item and suspends payments without making a settlement for the item with its customer or the presenting bank which settlement is or becomes final, the owner of the item has a preferred claim against the payor bank.

(c) If a payor bank gives or a collecting bank gives or receives a provisional settlement for an item and thereafter suspends payments, the suspension does not prevent or interfere with the settlement's becoming final if the finality occurs automatically upon the lapse of certain time or the happening of certain events.

(d) If a collecting bank receives from subsequent parties settlement for an item, which settlement is or becomes final and the bank suspends payments without making a settlement for the item with its customer which settlement is or becomes final, the owner of the item has a preferred claim against the collecting bank.

As amended in 1990.

Part 3—Collection of Items: Payor Banks

§ 4–301. **Deferred Posting; Recovery of Payment by Return of Items; Time of Dishonor; Return of Items by Payor Bank.**

(a) If a payor bank settles for a demand item other than a documentary draft presented otherwise than for immediate payment over the counter before midnight of the banking day of receipt, the payor bank may revoke the settlement and recover the settlement if, before it has made final payment and before its midnight deadline, it

   (1) returns the item; or

   (2) sends written notice of dishonor or non-payment if the item is unavailable for return.

(b) If a demand item is received by a payor bank for credit on its books, it may return the item or send notice of dishonor and may revoke any credit given or recover the amount thereof withdrawn by its customer, if it acts within the time limit and in the manner specified in subsection (a).

(c) Unless previous notice of dishonor has been sent, an item is dishonored at the time when for purposes of dishonor it is returned or notice sent in accordance with this section.

(d) An item is returned:

   (1) as to an item presented through a clearing house, when it is delivered to the presenting or last collecting bank or to the clearing house or is sent or delivered in accordance with clearing-house rules; or (2) in all other cases, when it is sent or delivered to the bank's customer or transferor or pursuant to instructions.

As amended in 1990.

§ 4–302. **Payor Bank's Responsibility for Late Return of Item.**

(a) If an item is presented to and received by a payor bank, the bank is accountable for the amount of:

   (1) a demand item, other than a documentary draft, whether properly payable or not, if the bank, in any case in which it is not also the depositary bank, retains the item beyond midnight of the banking day of receipt without settling for it or, whether or not it is also the depositary bank, does not pay or return the item or send notice of dishonor until after its midnight deadline; or

   (2) any other properly payable item unless, within the time allowed for acceptance or payment of that item, the bank either accepts or pays the item or returns it and accompanying documents.

(b) The liability of a payor bank to pay an item pursuant to subsection (a) is subject to defenses based on breach of a presentment warranty (Section 4–208) or proof that the person seeking enforcement of the liability presented or transferred the item for the purpose of defrauding the payor bank.

As amended in 1990.

§ 4–303. **When Items Subject to Notice, Stop-Payment Order, Legal Process, or Setoff; Order in Which Items May Be Charged or Certified.**

(a) Any knowledge, notice, or stop-payment order received by, legal process served upon, or setoff exercised by a payor bank comes too late to terminate, suspend, or modify the bank's right or duty to pay an item or to charge its customer's account for the item if the knowledge, notice, stop-payment order, or legal process is received or served and a reasonable time for the bank to act thereon expires or the setoff is exercised after the earliest of the following:

   (1) the bank accepts or certifies the item;

   (2) the bank pays the item in cash;

   (3) the bank settles for the item without having a right to revoke the settlement under statute, clearing-house rule, or agreement;

   (4) the bank becomes accountable for the amount of the item under Section 4–302 dealing with the payor bank's responsibility for late return of items; or

   (5) with respect to checks, a cutoff hour no earlier than one hour after the opening of the next banking day after the banking day on which the bank received the check and no later than the close of that next banking day or, if no cutoff hour is fixed, the close of the next banking day after the banking day on which the bank received the check.

(b) Subject to subsection (a), items may be accepted, paid, certified, or charged to the indicated account of its customer in any order.

As amended in 1990.

Part 4—Relationship Between Payor Bank and Its Customer

§ 4–401. When Bank May Charge Customer's Account.

(a) A bank may charge against the account of a customer an item that is properly payable from the account even though the charge creates an overdraft. An item is properly payable if it is authorized by the customer and is in accordance with any agreement between the customer and bank.

(b) A customer is not liable for the amount of an overdraft if the customer neither signed the item nor benefited from the proceeds of the item.

(c) A bank may charge against the account of a customer a check that is otherwise properly payable from the account, even though payment was made before the date of the check, unless the customer has given notice to the bank of the postdating describing the check with reasonable certainty. The notice is effective for the period stated in Section 4–403(b) for stop-payment orders, and must be received at such time and in such manner as to afford the bank a reasonable opportunity to act on it before the bank takes any action with respect to the check described in Section 4–303. If a bank charges against the account of a customer a check before the date stated in the notice of postdating, the bank is liable for damages for the loss resulting from its act. The loss may include damages for dishonor of subsequent items under Section 4–402.

(d) A bank that in good faith makes payment to a holder may charge the indicated account of its customer according to:

> **(1)** the original terms of the altered item; or
>
> **(2)** the terms of the completed item, even though the bank knows the item has been completed unless the bank has notice that the completion was improper.

As amended in 1990.

§ 4–402. Bank's Liability to Customer for Wrongful Dishonor; Time of Determining Insufficiency of Account.

(a) Except as otherwise provided in this Article, a payor bank wrongfully dishonors an item if it dishonors an item that is properly payable, but a bank may dishonor an item that would create an overdraft unless it has agreed to pay the overdraft.

(b) A payor bank is liable to its customer for damages proximately caused by the wrongful dishonor of an item. Liability is limited to actual damages proved and may include damages for an arrest or prosecution of the customer or other consequential damages. Whether any consequential damages are proximately caused by the wrongful dishonor is a question of fact to be determined in each case.

(c) A payor bank's determination of the customer's account balance on which a decision to dishonor for insufficiency of available funds is based may be made at any time between the time the item is received by the payor bank and the time that the payor bank returns the item or gives notice in lieu of return, and no more than one determination need be made. If, at the election of the payor bank, a subsequent balance determination is made for the purpose of reevaluating the bank's decision to dishonor the item, the account balance at that time is determinative of whether a dishonor for insufficiency of available funds is wrongful.

As amended in 1990.

§ 4–403. Customer's Right to Stop Payment; Burden of Proof of Loss.

(a) A customer or any person authorized to draw on the account if there is more than one person may stop payment of any item drawn on the customer's account or close the account by an order to the bank describing the item or account with reasonable certainty received at a time and in a manner that affords the bank a reasonable opportunity to act on it before any action by the bank with respect to the item described in Section 4–303. If the signature of more than one person is required to draw on an account, any of these persons may stop payment or close the account.

(b) A stop-payment order is effective for six months, but it lapses after 14 calendar days if the original order was oral and was not confirmed in writing within that period. A stop-payment order may be renewed for additional six-month periods by a writing given to the bank within a period during which the stop-payment order is effective.

(c) The burden of establishing the fact and amount of loss resulting from the payment of an item contrary to a stop-payment order or order to close an account is on the customer. The loss from payment of an item contrary to a stop-payment order may include damages for dishonor of subsequent items under Section 4–402.

As amended in 1990.

§ 4–404. Bank Not Obliged to Pay Check More Than Six Months Old.

A bank is under no obligation to a customer having a checking account to pay a check, other than a certified check, which is presented more than six months after its date, but it may charge its customer's account for a payment made thereafter in good faith.

§ 4–405. Death or Incompetence of Customer.

(a) A payor or collecting bank's authority to accept, pay, or collect an item or to account for proceeds of its collection, if otherwise effective, is not rendered ineffective by incompetence of a customer of either bank existing at the time the item is issued or its collection is undertaken if the bank does not know of an adjudication of incompetence. Neither death nor incompetence of a customer revokes the authority to accept, pay, collect, or account until the bank knows of the fact of death or of an adjudication of incompetence and has reasonable opportunity to act on it.

(b) Even with knowledge, a bank may for 10 days after the date of death pay or certify checks drawn on or before the date unless ordered to stop payment by a person claiming an interest in the account.

As amended in 1990.

§ 4–406. Customer's Duty to Discover and Report Unauthorized Signature or Alteration.

(a) A bank that sends or makes available to a customer a statement of account showing payment of items for the account shall either return or make available to the customer the items paid or provide information in the statement of account sufficient to allow the customer reasonably to identify the items paid. The statement of account provides sufficient information if the item is described by item number, amount, and date of payment.

(b) If the items are not returned to the customer, the person retaining the items shall either retain the items or, if the items are destroyed, maintain the capacity to furnish legible copies of the items until the expiration of seven years after receipt of the items. A customer may request an item from the bank that paid the item, and that bank must provide in a reasonable time either the item or, if the item has been destroyed or is not otherwise obtainable, a legible copy of the item.

(c) If a bank sends or makes available a statement of account or items pursuant to subsection (a), the customer must exercise reasonable promptness in examining the statement or the items to determine whether any payment was not authorized because of an alteration of an item or because a purported signature by or on behalf of the customer was not authorized. If, based on the statement or items provided, the customer should reasonably have discovered the unauthorized payment, the customer must promptly notify the bank of the relevant facts.

(d) If the bank proves that the customer failed, with respect to an item, to comply with the duties imposed on the customer by subsection (c), the customer is precluded from asserting against the bank:

> **(1)** the customer's unauthorized signature or any alteration on the item, if the bank also proves that it suffered a loss by reason of the failure; and
>
> **(2)** the customer's unauthorized signature or alteration by the same wrongdoer on any other item paid in good faith by the bank if the payment was made before the bank received notice from the customer of the unauthorized signature or alteration and after the customer had been afforded a reasonable period of time, not exceeding 30 days, in which to examine the item or statement of account and notify the bank.

(e) If subsection (d) applies and the customer proves that the bank failed to exercise ordinary care in paying the item and that the failure substantially contributed to loss, the loss is allocated between the customer precluded and the bank asserting the preclusion according to the extent to which the failure of the customer to comply with subsection (c) and the failure of the bank to exercise ordinary care contributed to the loss. If the customer proves that the bank did not pay the item in good faith, the preclusion under subsection (d) does not apply.

(f) Without regard to care or lack of care of either the customer or the bank, a customer who does not within one year after the statement or items are made available to the customer (subsection (a)) discover and report the customer's unauthorized signature on or any alteration on the item is precluded from asserting against the bank the unauthorized signature or alteration. If there is a preclusion under this subsection, the payor bank may not recover for breach or warranty under Section 4–208 with respect to the unauthorized signature or alteration to which the preclusion applies.

As amended in 1990.

§ 4–407. Payor Bank's Right to Subrogation on Improper Payment.

If a payor has paid an item over the order of the drawer or maker to stop payment, or after an account has been closed, or otherwise under circumstances giving a basis for objection by the drawer or maker, to prevent unjust enrichment and only to the extent necessary to prevent loss to the bank by reason of its payment of the item, the payor bank is subrogated to the rights

> **(1)** of any holder in due course on the item against the drawer or maker;
>
> **(2)** of the payee or any other holder of the item against the drawer or maker either on the item or under the transaction out of which the item arose; and

> **(3)** of the drawer or maker against the payee or any other holder of the item with respect to the transaction out of which the item arose.

As amended in 1990.

Part 5—Collection of Documentary Drafts

§ 4–501. Handling of Documentary Drafts; Duty to Send for Presentment and to Notify Customer of Dishonor.

A bank that takes a documentary draft for collection shall present or send the draft and accompanying documents for presentment and, upon learning that the draft has not been paid or accepted in due course, shall seasonably notify its customer of the fact even though it may have discounted or bought the draft or extended credit available for withdrawal as of right.

As amended in 1990.

§ 4–502. Presentment of "On Arrival" Drafts.

If a draft or the relevant instructions require presentment "on arrival", "when goods arrive" or the like, the collecting bank need not present until in its judgment a reasonable time for arrival of the goods has expired. Refusal to pay or accept because the goods have not arrived is not dishonor; the bank must notify its transferor of the refusal but need not present the draft again until it is instructed to do so or learns of the arrival of the goods.

§ 4–503. Responsibility of Presenting Bank for Documents and Goods; Report of Reasons for Dishonor; Referee in Case of Need.

Unless otherwise instructed and except as provided in Article 5, a bank presenting a documentary draft:

> **(1)** must deliver the documents to the drawee on acceptance of the draft if it is payable more than three days after presentment, otherwise, only on payment; and
>
> **(2)** upon dishonor, either in the case of presentment for acceptance or presentment for payment, may seek and follow instructions from any referee in case of need designated in the draft or, if the presenting bank does not choose to utilize the referee's services, it must use diligence and good faith to ascertain the reason for dishonor, must notify its transferor of the dishonor and of the results of its effort to ascertain the reasons therefor, and must request instructions.

However, the presenting bank is under no obligation with respect to goods represented by the documents except to follow any reasonable instructions seasonably received; it has a right to reimbursement for any expense incurred in following instructions and to prepayment of or indemnity for those expenses.

As amended in 1990.

§ 4–504. Privilege of Presenting Bank to Deal With Goods; Security Interest for Expenses.

(a) A presenting bank that, following the dishonor of a documentary draft, has seasonably requested instructions but does not receive them within a reasonable time may store, sell, or otherwise deal with the goods in any reasonable manner.

(b) For its reasonable expenses incurred by action under subsection (a) the presenting bank has a lien upon the goods or their proceeds, which may be foreclosed in the same manner as an unpaid seller's lien.

As amended in 1990.

ARTICLE 4A: FUNDS TRANSFERS

Part 1—Subject Matter and Definitions

§ 4A–101. Short Title.
This Article may be cited as Uniform Commercial Code—Funds Transfers.

§ 4A–102. Subject Matter.
Except as otherwise provided in Section 4A–108, this Article applies to funds transfers defined in Section 4A–104.

§ 4A–103. Payment Order–Definitions.
(a) In this Article:
  (1) "Payment order" means an instruction of a sender to a receiving bank, transmitted orally, electronically, or in writing, to pay, or to cause another bank to pay, a fixed or determinable amount of money to a beneficiary if:
    (i) the instruction does not state a condition to payment to the beneficiary other than time of payment,
    (ii) the receiving bank is to be reimbursed by debiting an account of, or otherwise receiving payment from, the sender, and
    (iii) the instruction is transmitted by the sender directly to the receiving bank or to an agent, funds-transfer system, or communication system for transmittal to the receiving bank.
  (2) "Beneficiary" means the person to be paid by the beneficiary's bank.
  (3) "Beneficiary's bank" means the bank identified in a payment order in which an account of the beneficiary is to be credited pursuant to the order or which otherwise is to make payment to the beneficiary if the order does not provide for payment to an account.
  (4) "Receiving bank" means the bank to which the sender's instruction is addressed.
  (5) "Sender" means the person giving the instruction to the receiving bank.
(b) If an instruction complying with subsection (a)(1) is to make more than one payment to a beneficiary, the instruction is a separate payment order with respect to each payment.
(c) A payment order is issued when it is sent to the receiving bank.

§ 4A–104. Funds Transfer–Definitions.
In this Article:
(a) "Funds transfer" means the series of transactions, beginning with the originator's payment order, made for the purpose of making payment to the beneficiary of the order. The term includes any payment order issued by the originator's bank or an intermediary bank intended to carry out the originator's payment order. A funds transfer is completed by acceptance by the beneficiary's bank of a payment order for the benefit of the beneficiary of the originator's payment order.
(b) "Intermediary bank" means a receiving bank other than the originator's bank or the beneficiary's bank.
(c) "Originator" means the sender of the first payment order in a funds transfer.
(d) "Originator's bank" means (i) the receiving bank to which the payment order of the originator is issued if the originator is not a bank, or (ii) the originator if the originator is a bank.

§ 4A–105. Other Definitions.
(a) In this Article:
  (1) "Authorized account" means a deposit account of a customer in a bank designated by the customer as a source of payment of payment orders issued by the customer to the bank. If a customer does not so designate an account, any account of the customer is an authorized account if payment of a payment order from that account is not inconsistent with a restriction on the use of that account.
  (2) "Bank" means a person engaged in the business of banking and includes a savings bank, savings and loan association, credit union, and trust company. A branch or separate office of a bank is a separate bank for purposes of this Article.
  (3) "Customer" means a person, including a bank, having an account with a bank or from whom a bank has agreed to receive payment orders.
  (4) "Funds-transfer business day" of a receiving bank means the part of a day during which the receiving bank is open for the receipt, processing, and transmittal of payment orders and cancellations and amendments of payment orders.
  (5) "Funds-transfer system" means a wire transfer network, automated clearing house, or other communication system of a clearing house or other association of banks through which a payment order by a bank may be transmitted to the bank to which the order is addressed.
  (6) "Good faith" means honesty in fact and the observance of reasonable commercial standards of fair dealing.
  (7) "Prove" with respect to a fact means to meet the burden of establishing the fact (Section 1–201(8)).
(b) Other definitions applying to this Article and the sections in which they appear are:

"Acceptance"	Section 4A–209
"Beneficiary"	Section 4A–103
"Beneficiary's bank"	Section 4A–103
"Executed"	Section 4A–301
"Execution date"	Section 4A–301
"Funds transfer"	Section 4A–104
"Funds-transfer system rule"	Section 4A–501
"Intermediary bank"	Section 4A–104
"Originator"	Section 4A–104
"Originator's bank"	Section 4A–104
"Payment by beneficiary's bank to beneficiary"	Section 4A–405
"Payment by originator to beneficiary"	Section 4A–406
"Payment by sender to receiving bank"	Section 4A–403
"Payment date"	Section 4A–401
"Payment order"	Section 4A–103
"Receiving bank"	Section 4A–103
"Security procedure"	Section 4A–201
"Sender"	Section 4A–103

(c) The following definitions in Article 4 apply to this Article:

"Clearing house"	Section 4–104
"Item"	Section 4–104
"Suspends payments"	Section 4–104

(d) In addition, Article 1 contains general definitions and principles of construction and interpretation applicable throughout this Article.

§ 4A–106. Time Payment Order Is Received.

(a) The time of receipt of a payment order or communication cancelling or amending a payment order is determined by the rules applicable to receipt of a notice stated in Section 1–201(27). A receiving bank may fix a cut-off time or times on a funds-transfer business day for the receipt and processing of payment orders and communications cancelling or amending payment orders. Different cut-off times may apply to payment orders, cancellations, or amendments, or to different categories of payment orders, cancellations, or amendments. A cut-off time may apply to senders generally or different cut-off times may apply to different senders or categories of payment orders. If a payment order or communication cancelling or amending a payment order is received after the close of a funds-transfer business day or after the appropriate cut-off time on a funds-transfer business day, the receiving bank may treat the payment order or communication as received at the opening of the next funds-transfer business day.

(b) If this Article refers to an execution date or payment date or states a day on which a receiving bank is required to take action, and the date or day does not fall on a funds-transfer business day, the next day that is a funds-transfer business day is treated as the date or day stated, unless the contrary is stated in this Article.

§ 4A–107. Federal Reserve Regulations and Operating Circulars.

Regulations of the Board of Governors of the Federal Reserve System and operating circulars of the Federal Reserve Banks supersede any inconsistent provision of this Article to the extent of the inconsistency.

§ 4A–108. Exclusion of Consumer Transactions Governed by Federal Law.

This Article does not apply to a funds transfer any part of which is governed by the Electronic Fund Transfer Act of 1978 (Title XX, Public Law 95–630, 92 Stat. 3728, 15 U.S.C. § 1693 *et seq.*) as amended from time to time.

Part 2—Issue and Acceptance of Payment Order

§ 4A–201. Security Procedure.

"Security procedure" means a procedure established by agreement of a customer and a receiving bank for the purpose of (i) verifying that a payment order or communication amending or cancelling a payment order is that of the customer, or (ii) detecting error in the transmission or the content of the payment order or communication. A security procedure may require the use of algorithms or other codes, identifying words or numbers, encryption, callback procedures, or similar security devices. Comparison of a signature on a payment order or communication with an authorized specimen signature of the customer is not by itself a security procedure.

§ 4A–202. Authorized and Verified Payment Orders.

(a) A payment order received by the receiving bank is the authorized order of the person identified as sender if that person authorized the order or is otherwise bound by it under the law of agency.

(b) If a bank and its customer have agreed that the authenticity of payment orders issued to the bank in the name of the customer as sender will be verified pursuant to a security procedure, a payment order received by the receiving bank is effective as the order of the customer, whether or not authorized, if (i) the security procedure is a

commercially reasonable method of providing security against unauthorized payment orders, and (ii) the bank proves that it accepted the payment order in good faith and in compliance with the security procedure and any written agreement or instruction of the customer restricting acceptance of payment orders issued in the name of the customer. The bank is not required to follow an instruction that violates a written agreement with the customer or notice of which is not received at a time and in a manner affording the bank a reasonable opportunity to act on it before the payment order is accepted.

(c) Commercial reasonableness of a security procedure is a question of law to be determined by considering the wishes of the customer expressed to the bank, the circumstances of the customer known to the bank, including the size, type, and frequency of payment orders normally issued by the customer to the bank, alternative security procedures offered to the customer, and security procedures in general use by customers and receiving banks similarly situated. A security procedure is deemed to be commercially reasonable if (i) the security procedure was chosen by the customer after the bank offered, and the customer refused, a security procedure that was commercially reasonable for that customer, and (ii) the customer expressly agreed in writing to be bound by any payment order, whether or not authorized, issued in its name and accepted by the bank in compliance with the security procedure chosen by the customer.

(d) The term "sender" in this Article includes the customer in whose name a payment order is issued if the order is the authorized order of the customer under subsection (a), or it is effective as the order of the customer under subsection (b).

(e) This section applies to amendments and cancellations of payment orders to the same extent it applies to payment orders.

(f) Except as provided in this section and in Section 4A–203(a)(1), rights and obligations arising under this section or Section 4A–203 may not be varied by agreement.

§ 4A–203. Unenforceability of Certain Verified Payment Orders.

(a) If an accepted payment order is not, under Section 4A–202(a), an authorized order of a customer identified as sender, but is effective as an order of the customer pursuant to Section 4A–202(b), the following rules apply:

> **(1)** By express written agreement, the receiving bank may limit the extent to which it is entitled to enforce or retain payment of the payment order.

> **(2)** The receiving bank is not entitled to enforce or retain payment of the payment order if the customer proves that the order was not caused, directly or indirectly, by a person (i) entrusted at any time with duties to act for the customer with respect to payment orders or the security procedure, or (ii) who obtained access to transmitting facilities of the customer or who obtained, from a source controlled by the customer and without authority of the receiving bank, information facilitating breach of the security procedure, regardless of how the information was obtained or whether the customer was at fault. Information includes any access device, computer software, or the like.

(b) This section applies to amendments of payment orders to the same extent it applies to payment orders.

§ 4A–204. Refund of Payment and Duty of Customer to Report with Respect to Unauthorized Payment Order.

(a) If a receiving bank accepts a payment order issued in the name of its customer as sender which is (i) not authorized and not effective as the order of the customer under Section 4A–202, or (ii) not enforceable, in whole or in part, against the customer under Section 4A–203, the bank shall refund any payment of the payment order received from the customer to the extent the bank is not entitled to enforce payment and shall pay interest on the refundable amount calculated from the date the bank received payment to the date of the refund. However, the customer is not entitled to interest from the bank on the amount to be refunded if the customer fails to exercise ordinary care to determine that the order was not authorized by the customer and to notify the bank of the relevant facts within a reasonable time not exceeding 90 days after the date the customer received notification from the bank that the order was accepted or that the customer's account was debited with respect to the order. The bank is not entitled to any recovery from the customer on account of a failure by the customer to give notification as stated in this section.

(b) Reasonable time under subsection (a) may be fixed by agreement as stated in Section 1–204(1), but the obligation of a receiving bank to refund payment as stated in subsection (a) may not otherwise be varied by agreement.

§ 4A–205. Erroneous Payment Orders.

(a) If an accepted payment order was transmitted pursuant to a security procedure for the detection of error and the payment order (i) erroneously instructed payment to a beneficiary not intended by the sender, (ii) erroneously instructed payment in an amount greater than the amount intended by the sender, or (iii) was an erroneously transmitted duplicate of a payment order previously sent by the sender, the following rules apply:

(1) If the sender proves that the sender or a person acting on behalf of the sender pursuant to Section 4A–206 complied with the security procedure and that the error would have been detected if the receiving bank had also complied, the sender is not obliged to pay the order to the extent stated in paragraphs (2) and (3).

(2) If the funds transfer is completed on the basis of an erroneous payment order described in clause (i) or (iii) of subsection (a), the sender is not obliged to pay the order and the receiving bank is entitled to recover from the beneficiary any amount paid to the beneficiary to the extent allowed by the law governing mistake and restitution.

(3) If the funds transfer is completed on the basis of a payment order described in clause (ii) of subsection (a), the sender is not obliged to pay the order to the extent the amount received by the beneficiary is greater than the amount intended by the sender. In that case, the receiving bank is entitled to recover from the beneficiary the excess amount received to the extent allowed by the law governing mistake and restitution.

(b) If (i) the sender of an erroneous payment order described in subsection (a) is not obliged to pay all or part of the order, and (ii) the sender receives notification from the receiving bank that the order was accepted by the bank or that the sender's account was debited with respect to the order, the sender has a duty to exercise ordinary care, on the basis of information available to the sender, to discover the error with respect to the order and to advise the bank of the relevant facts within a reasonable time, not exceeding 90 days, after the bank's notification was received by the sender. If the bank proves that the sender failed to perform that duty, the sender is liable to the bank for the loss the bank proves it incurred as a result of the failure, but the liability of the sender may not exceed the amount of the sender's order.

(c) This section applies to amendments to payment orders to the same extent it applies to payment orders.

§ 4A–206. Transmission of Payment Order through Funds-Transfer or Other Communication System.

(a) If a payment order addressed to a receiving bank is transmitted to a funds-transfer system or other third party communication system for transmittal to the bank, the system is deemed to be an agent of the sender for the purpose of transmitting the payment order to the bank. If there is a discrepancy between the terms of the payment order transmitted to the system and the terms of the payment order transmitted by the system to the bank, the terms of the payment order of the sender are those transmitted by the system. This section does not apply to a funds-transfer system of the Federal Reserve Banks.

(b) This section applies to cancellations and amendments to payment orders to the same extent it applies to payment orders.

§ 4A–207. Misdescription of Beneficiary.

(a) Subject to subsection (b), if, in a payment order received by the beneficiary's bank, the name, bank account number, or other identification of the beneficiary refers to a nonexistent or unidentifiable person or account, no person has rights as a beneficiary of the order and acceptance of the order cannot occur.

(b) If a payment order received by the beneficiary's bank identifies the beneficiary both by name and by an identifying or bank account number and the name and number identify different persons, the following rules apply:

(1) Except as otherwise provided in subsection (c), if the beneficiary's bank does not know that the name and number refer to different persons, it may rely on the number as the proper identification of the beneficiary of the order. The beneficiary's bank need not determine whether the name and number refer to the same person.

(2) If the beneficiary's bank pays the person identified by name or knows that the name and number identify different persons, no person has rights as beneficiary except the person paid by the beneficiary's bank if that person was entitled to receive payment from the originator of the funds transfer. If no person has rights as beneficiary, acceptance of the order cannot occur.

(c) If (i) a payment order described in subsection (b) is accepted, (ii) the originator's payment order described the beneficiary inconsistently by name and number, and (iii) the beneficiary's bank pays the person identified by number as permitted by subsection (b)(1), the following rules apply:

(1) If the originator is a bank, the originator is obliged to pay its order.

(2) If the originator is not a bank and proves that the person identified by number was not entitled to receive payment from the originator, the originator is not obliged to pay its order unless the originator's bank proves that the originator, before acceptance of the originator's order, had notice that payment of a payment order issued by the originator might be made by the beneficiary's bank on the basis of an identifying or bank account number even if it identifies a person different from the named beneficiary. Proof of notice may be made by any admissible evidence. The originator's bank satisfies the burden of proof if it proves that the originator, before the payment order was accepted, signed a writing stating the information to which the notice relates.

(d) In a case governed by subsection (b)(1), if the beneficiary's bank rightfully pays the person identified by number and that person was not entitled to receive payment from the originator, the amount paid may be recovered from that person to the extent allowed by the law governing mistake and restitution as follows:

(1) If the originator is obliged to pay its payment order as stated in subsection (c), the originator has the right to recover.

(2) If the originator is not a bank and is not obliged to pay its payment order, the originator's bank has the right to recover.

§ 4A–208. Misdescription of Intermediary Bank or Beneficiary's Bank.

(a) This subsection applies to a payment order identifying an intermediary bank or the beneficiary's bank only by an identifying number.

(1) The receiving bank may rely on the number as the proper identification of the intermediary or beneficiary's bank and need not determine whether the number identifies a bank.

(2) The sender is obliged to compensate the receiving bank for any loss and expenses incurred by the receiving bank as a result of its reliance on the number in executing or attempting to execute the order.

(b) This subsection applies to a payment order identifying an intermediary bank or the beneficiary's bank both by name and an identifying number if the name and number identify different persons.

(1) If the sender is a bank, the receiving bank may rely on the number as the proper identification of the intermediary or beneficiary's bank if the receiving bank, when it executes the sender's order, does not know that the name and number identify different persons. The receiving bank need not determine whether the name and number refer to the same person or whether the number refers to a bank. The sender is obliged to compensate the receiving bank for any loss and expenses incurred by the receiving bank as a result of its reliance on the number in executing or attempting to execute the order.

(2) If the sender is not a bank and the receiving bank proves that the sender, before the payment order was accepted, had notice that the receiving bank might rely on the number as the proper identification of the intermediary or beneficiary's bank even if it identifies a person different from the bank identified by name, the rights and obligations of the sender and the receiving bank are governed by subsection (b)(1), as though the sender were a bank. Proof of notice may be made by any admissible evidence. The receiving bank satisfies the burden of proof if it proves that the sender, before the payment order was accepted, signed a writing stating the information to which the notice relates.

(3) Regardless of whether the sender is a bank, the receiving bank may rely on the name as the proper identification of the intermediary or beneficiary's bank if the receiving bank, at the time it executes the sender's order, does not know that the name and number identify different persons. The receiving bank need not determine whether the name and number refer to the same person.

(4) If the receiving bank knows that the name and number identify different persons, reliance on either the name or the number in executing the sender's payment order is a breach of the obligation stated in Section 4A–302(a)(1).

§ 4A–209. Acceptance of Payment Order.

(a) Subject to subsection (d), a receiving bank other than the beneficiary's bank accepts a payment order when it executes the order.

(b) Subject to subsections (c) and (d), a beneficiary's bank accepts a payment order at the earliest of the following times:

(1) When the bank (i) pays the beneficiary as stated in Section 4A–405(a) or 4A–405(b), or (ii) notifies the beneficiary of receipt of the order or that the account of the beneficiary has been credited with respect to the order unless the notice indicates that the bank is rejecting the order or that funds with respect to the order may not be withdrawn or used until receipt of payment from the sender of the order;

(2) When the bank receives payment of the entire amount of the sender's order pursuant to Section 4A–403(a)(1) or 4A–403(a)(2); or

(3) The opening of the next funds-transfer business day of the bank following the payment date of the order if, at that time, the amount of the sender's order is fully covered by a withdrawable credit balance in an authorized account of the sender or the bank has otherwise received full payment from the sender, unless the order was rejected before that time or is rejected within (i) one hour after that time, or (ii) one hour after the opening of the next business day of the bank following the payment date if that time is later. If notice of rejection is received by the sender after the payment date and the authorized account of the sender does not bear interest, the bank is obliged to pay interest to the sender on the amount of the order for the number of days elapsing after the payment date to the day the sender receives notice or learns that the order was not accepted, counting that day as an elapsed day. If the withdrawable credit balance during that period falls below the amount of the order, the amount of interest payable is reduced accordingly.

(c) Acceptance of a payment order cannot occur before the order is received by the receiving bank. Acceptance does not occur under subsection (b)(2) or (b)(3) if the beneficiary of the payment order does not have an account with the receiving bank, the account has been closed, or the receiving bank is not permitted by law to receive credits for the beneficiary's account.

(d) A payment order issued to the originator's bank cannot be accepted until the payment date if the bank is the beneficiary's bank, or the execution date if the bank is not the beneficiary's bank. If the originator's bank executes the originator's payment order before the execution date or pays the beneficiary of the originator's payment order before the payment date and the payment order is subsequently cancelled pursuant to Section 4A–211(b), the bank may recover from the beneficiary any payment received to the extent allowed by the law governing mistake and restitution.

§ 4A–210. Rejection of Payment Order.

(a) A payment order is rejected by the receiving bank by a notice of rejection transmitted to the sender orally, electronically, or in writing. A notice of rejection need not use any particular words and is sufficient if it indicates that the receiving bank is rejecting the order or will not execute or pay the order. Rejection is effective when the notice is given if transmission is by a means that is reasonable in the circumstances. If notice of rejection is given by a means that is not reasonable, rejection is effective when the notice is received. If an agreement of the sender and receiving bank establishes the means to be used to reject a payment order, (i) any means complying with the agreement is reasonable and (ii) any means not complying is not reasonable unless no significant delay in receipt of the notice resulted from the use of the noncomplying means.

(b) This subsection applies if a receiving bank other than the beneficiary's bank fails to execute a payment order despite the existence on the execution date of a withdrawable credit balance in an authorized account of the sender sufficient to cover the order. If the sender does not receive notice of rejection of the order on the execution date and the authorized account of the sender does not bear interest, the bank is obliged to pay interest to the sender on the amount of the order for the number of days elapsing after the execution date to the earlier of the day the order is cancelled pursuant to Section 4A–211(d) or the day the sender receives notice or learns that the order was not executed, counting the final day of the period as an elapsed day. If the withdrawable credit balance during that period falls below the amount of the order, the amount of interest is reduced accordingly.

(c) If a receiving bank suspends payments, all unaccepted payment orders issued to it are are deemed rejected at the time the bank suspends payments.

(d) Acceptance of a payment order precludes a later rejection of the order. Rejection of a payment order precludes a later acceptance of the order.

§ 4A–211. Cancellation and Amendment of Payment Order.

(a) A communication of the sender of a payment order cancelling or amending the order may be transmitted to the receiving bank orally, electronically, or in writing. If a security procedure is in effect between the sender and the receiving bank, the communication is not effective to cancel or amend the order unless the communication is verified pursuant to the security procedure or the bank agrees to the cancellation or amendment.

(b) Subject to subsection (a), a communication by the sender cancelling or amending a payment order is effective to cancel or amend the order if notice of the communication is received at a time and in a manner affording the receiving bank a reasonable opportunity to act on the communication before the bank accepts the payment order.

(c) After a payment order has been accepted, cancellation or amendment of the order is not effective unless the receiving bank agrees or a funds-transfer system rule allows cancellation or amendment without agreement of the bank.

   (1) With respect to a payment order accepted by a receiving bank other than the beneficiary's bank, cancellation or amendment is not effective unless a conforming cancellation or amendment of the payment order issued by the receiving bank is also made.

   (2) With respect to a payment order accepted by the beneficiary's bank, cancellation or amendment is not effective unless the order was issued in execution of an unauthorized payment order, or because of a mistake by a sender in the funds transfer which resulted in the issuance of a payment order (i) that is a duplicate of a payment order previously issued by the sender, (ii) that orders payment to a beneficiary not entitled to receive payment from the originator, or (iii) that orders payment in an amount greater than the amount the beneficiary was entitled to receive from the originator. If the payment order is cancelled or amended, the beneficiary's bank is entitled to recover from the beneficiary any amount paid to the beneficiary to the extent allowed by the law governing mistake and restitution.

(d) An unaccepted payment order is cancelled by operation of law at the close of the fifth funds-transfer business day of the receiving bank after the execution date or payment date of the order.

(e) A cancelled payment order cannot be accepted. If an accepted payment order is cancelled, the acceptance is nullified and no person has any right or obligation based on the acceptance. Amendment of a payment order is deemed to be cancellation of the original order at the time of amendment and issue of a new payment order in the amended form at the same time.

(f) Unless otherwise provided in an agreement of the parties or in a funds-transfer system rule, if the receiving bank, after accepting a payment order, agrees to cancellation or amendment of the order by the sender or is bound by a funds-transfer system rule allowing cancellation or amendment without the bank's agreement, the sender, whether or not cancellation or amendment is effective, is liable to the bank for any loss and expenses, including reasonable attorney's fees, incurred by the bank as a result of the cancellation or amendment or attempted cancellation or amendment.

(g) A payment order is not revoked by the death or legal incapacity of the sender unless the receiving bank knows of the death or of an adjudication of incapacity by a court of competent jurisdiction and has reasonable opportunity to act before acceptance of the order.

(h) A funds-transfer system rule is not effective to the extent it conflicts with subsection (c)(2).

§ 4A–212. Liability and Duty of Receiving Bank Regarding Unaccepted Payment Order.

If a receiving bank fails to accept a payment order that it is obliged by express agreement to accept, the bank is liable for breach of the agreement to the extent provided in the agreement or in this Article, but does not otherwise have any duty to accept a payment order or, before acceptance, to take any action, or refrain from taking action, with respect to the order except as provided in this Article or by express agreement. Liability based on acceptance arises only when acceptance occurs as stated in Section 4A–209, and liability is limited to that provided in this Article. A receiving bank is not the agent of the sender or beneficiary of the payment order it accepts, or of any other party to the funds transfer, and the bank owes no duty to any party to the funds transfer except as provided in this Article or by express agreement.

Part 3—Execution of Sender's Payment Order by Receiving Bank

§ 4A–301. Execution and Execution Date.

(a) A payment order is "executed" by the receiving bank when it issues a payment order intended to carry out the payment order received by the bank. A payment order received by the beneficiary's bank can be accepted but cannot be executed.

(b) "Execution date" of a payment order means the day on which the receiving bank may properly issue a payment order in execution of the sender's order. The execution date may be determined by instruction of the sender but cannot be earlier than the day the order is received and, unless otherwise determined, is the day the order is received. If the sender's instruction states a payment date, the execution date is the payment date or an earlier date on which execution is reasonably necessary to allow payment to the beneficiary on the payment date.

§ 4A–302. Obligations of Receiving Bank in Execution of Payment Order.

(a) Except as provided in subsections (b) through (d), if the receiving bank accepts a payment order pursuant to Section 4A–209(a), the bank has the following obligations in executing the order:

(1) The receiving bank is obliged to issue, on the execution date, a payment order complying with the sender's order and to follow the sender's instructions concerning (i) any intermediary bank or funds-transfer system to be used in carrying out the funds transfer, or (ii) the means by which payment orders are to be transmitted in the funds transfer. If the originator's bank issues a payment order to an intermediary bank, the originator's bank is obliged to instruct the intermediary bank according to the instruction of the originator. An intermediary bank in the funds transfer is similarly bound by an instruction given to it by the sender of the payment order it accepts.

(2) If the sender's instruction states that the funds transfer is to be carried out telephonically or by wire transfer or otherwise indicates that the funds transfer is to be carried out by the most expeditious means, the receiving bank is obliged to transmit its payment order by the most expeditious available means, and to instruct any intermediary bank accordingly. If a sender's instruction states a payment date, the receiving bank is obliged to transmit its payment order at a time and by means reasonably necessary to allow payment to the beneficiary on the payment date or as soon thereafter as is feasible.

(b) Unless otherwise instructed, a receiving bank executing a payment order may (i) use any funds-transfer system if use of that system is reasonable in the circumstances, and (ii) issue a payment order to the beneficiary's bank or to an intermediary bank through which a payment order conforming to the sender's order can expeditiously be issued to the beneficiary's bank if the receiving bank exercises ordinary care in the selection of the intermediary bank. A receiving bank is not required to follow an instruction of the sender designating a funds-transfer system to be used in carrying out the funds transfer if the receiving bank, in good faith, determines that it is not feasible to follow the instruction or that following the instruction would unduly delay completion of the funds transfer.

(c) Unless subsection (a)(2) applies or the receiving bank is otherwise instructed, the bank may execute a payment order by transmitting its payment order by first class mail or by any means reasonable in the circumstances. If the receiving bank is instructed to execute the sender's order by transmitting its payment order by a particular means, the receiving bank may issue its payment order by the means stated or by any means as expeditious as the means stated.

(d) Unless instructed by the sender, (i) the receiving bank may not obtain payment of its charges for services and expenses in connection with the execution of the sender's order by issuing a payment order in an amount equal to the amount of the sender's order less the amount of the charges, and (ii) may not instruct a subsequent receiving bank to obtain payment of its charges in the same manner.

§ 4A–303. Erroneous Execution of Payment Order.

(a) A receiving bank that (i) executes the payment order of the sender by issuing a payment order in an amount greater than the amount of the sender's order, or (ii) issues a payment order in execution of the sender's order and then issues a duplicate order, is entitled to payment of the amount of the sender's order under Section 4A–402(c) if that subsection is otherwise satisfied. The bank is entitled to recover from the beneficiary of the erroneous order the excess payment received to the extent allowed by the law governing mistake and restitution.

(b) A receiving bank that executes the payment order of the sender by issuing a payment order in an amount less than the amount of the sender's order is entitled to payment of the amount of the sender's order under Section 4A–402(c) if (i) that subsection is otherwise satisfied and (ii) the bank corrects its mistake by issuing an additional payment order for the benefit of the beneficiary of the sender's order. If the error is not corrected, the issuer of the erroneous order is entitled to receive or retain payment from the sender of the order it accepted only to the extent of the amount of the erroneous order. This subsection does not apply if the receiving bank executes the sender's payment order by issuing a payment order in an amount less than the amount of the sender's order for the purpose of obtaining payment of its charges for services and expenses pursuant to instruction of the sender.

(c) If a receiving bank executes the payment order of the sender by issuing a payment order to a beneficiary different from the beneficiary of the sender's order and the funds transfer is completed on the basis of that error, the sender of the payment order that was erroneously executed and all previous senders in the funds transfer are not obliged to pay the payment orders they issued. The issuer of the erroneous order is entitled to recover from the beneficiary of the order the payment received to the extent allowed by the law governing mistake and restitution.

§ 4A–304. Duty of Sender to Report Erroneously Executed Payment Order.

If the sender of a payment order that is erroneously executed as stated in Section 4A–303 receives notification from the receiving bank that the order was executed or that the sender's account was debited with respect to the order, the sender has a duty to exercise ordinary care to determine, on the basis of information available to the sender, that the order was erroneously executed and to notify the bank of the relevant facts within a reasonable time not exceeding 90 days after the notification from the bank was received by the sender. If the sender fails to perform that duty, the bank is not obliged to pay interest on any amount refundable to the sender under Section 4A–402(d) for the period before the bank learns of the execution error. The bank is not entitled to any recovery from the sender on account of a failure by the sender to perform the duty stated in this section.

§ 4A–305. Liability for Late or Improper Execution or Failure to Execute Payment Order.

(a) If a funds transfer is completed but execution of a payment order by the receiving bank in breach of Section 4A–302 results in delay in payment to the beneficiary, the bank is obliged to pay interest to either the originator or the beneficiary of the funds transfer for the period of delay caused by the improper execution. Except as provided in subsection (c), additional damages are not recoverable.

(b) If execution of a payment order by a receiving bank in breach of Section 4A–302 results in (i) noncompletion of the funds transfer, (ii) failure to use an intermediary bank designated by the originator, or (iii) issuance of a payment order that does not comply with the terms of the payment order of the originator, the bank is liable to the originator for its expenses in the funds transfer and for incidental expenses and interest losses, to the extent not covered by subsection (a), resulting from the improper execution. Except as provided in subsection (c), additional damages are not recoverable.

(c) In addition to the amounts payable under subsections (a) and (b), damages, including consequential damages, are recoverable to the extent provided in an express written agreement of the receiving bank.

(d) If a receiving bank fails to execute a payment order it was obliged by express agreement to execute, the receiving bank is liable to the sender for its expenses in the transaction and for incidental expenses and interest losses resulting from the failure to execute. Additional damages, including consequential damages, are recoverable to the extent provided in an express written agreement of the receiving bank, but are not otherwise recoverable.

(e) Reasonable attorney's fees are recoverable if demand for compensation under subsection (a) or (b) is made and refused before an action is brought on the claim. If a claim is made for breach of an agreement under subsection (d) and the agreement does not provide for damages, reasonable attorney's fees are recoverable if demand for compensation under subsection (d) is made and refused before an action is brought on the claim.

(f) Except as stated in this section, the liability of a receiving bank under subsections (a) and (b) may not be varied by agreement.

Part 4—Payment

§ 4A–401. Payment Date.

"Payment date" of a payment order means the day on which the amount of the order is payable to the beneficiary by the beneficiary's bank. The payment date may be determined by instruction of the sender but cannot be earlier than the day the order is received by the beneficiary's bank and, unless otherwise determined, is the day the order is received by the beneficiary's bank.

§ 4A–402. Obligation of Sender to Pay Receiving Bank.

(a) This section is subject to Sections 4A–205 and 4A–207.

(b) With respect to a payment order issued to the beneficiary's bank, acceptance of the order by the bank obliges the sender to pay the bank the amount of the order, but payment is not due until the payment date of the order.

(c) This subsection is subject to subsection (e) and to Section 4A–303. With respect to a payment order issued to a receiving bank other than the beneficiary's bank, acceptance of the order by the receiving bank obliges the sender to pay the bank the amount of the sender's order. Payment by the sender is not due until the execution date of the sender's order. The obligation of that sender to pay its payment order is excused if the funds transfer is not completed by acceptance by the beneficiary's bank of a payment order instructing payment to the beneficiary of that sender's payment order.

(d) If the sender of a payment order pays the order and was not obliged to pay all or part of the amount paid, the bank receiving payment is obliged to refund payment to the extent the sender was not obliged to pay. Except as provided in Sections 4A–204 and 4A–304, interest is payable on the refundable amount from the date of payment.

(e) If a funds transfer is not completed as stated in subsection (c) and an intermediary bank is obliged to refund payment as stated in subsection (d) but is unable to do so because not permitted by applicable law or because the bank suspends payments, a sender in the funds transfer that executed a payment order in compliance with an instruction, as stated in Section 4A–302(a)(1), to route the funds transfer through that intermediary bank is entitled to receive or retain payment from the sender of the payment order that it accepted. The first sender in the funds transfer that issued an instruction requiring routing through that intermediary bank is subrogated to the right of the bank that paid the intermediary bank to refund as stated in subsection (d).

(f) The right of the sender of a payment order to be excused from the obligation to pay the order as stated in subsection (c) or to receive refund under subsection (d) may not be varied by agreement.

§ 4A–403. Payment by Sender to Receiving Bank.

(a) Payment of the sender's obligation under Section 4A–402 to pay the receiving bank occurs as follows:

(1) If the sender is a bank, payment occurs when the receiving bank receives final settlement of the obligation through a Federal Reserve Bank or through a funds-transfer system.

(2) If the sender is a bank and the sender (i) credited an account of the receiving bank with the sender, or (ii) caused an account of the receiving bank in another bank to be credited, payment occurs when the credit is withdrawn or, if not withdrawn, at midnight of the day on which the credit is withdrawable and the receiving bank learns of that fact.

(3) If the receiving bank debits an account of the sender with the receiving bank, payment occurs when the debit is made to the extent the debit is covered by a withdrawable credit balance in the account.

(b) If the sender and receiving bank are members of a funds-transfer system that nets obligations multilaterally among participants, the receiving bank receives final settlement when settlement is complete in accordance with the rules of the system. The obligation of the sender to pay the amount of a payment order transmitted through the funds-transfer system may be satisfied, to the extent permitted by the rules of the system, by setting off and applying against the sender's obligation the right of the sender to receive payment from the receiving bank of the amount of any other payment order transmitted to the sender by the receiving bank through the funds-transfer system. The aggregate balance of obligations owed by each sender to each receiving bank in the funds-transfer system may be satisfied, to the extent permitted by the rules of the system, by setting off and applying against that balance the aggregate balance of obligations owed to the sender by other members of the system. The aggregate balance is determined after the right of setoff stated in the second sentence of this subsection has been exercised.

(c) If two banks transmit payment orders to each other under an agreement that settlement of the obligations of each bank to the other under Section 4A–402 will be made at the end of the day or other period, the total amount owed with respect to all orders transmitted by one bank shall be set off against the total amount owed with respect to all orders transmitted by the other bank. To the extent of the setoff, each bank has made payment to the other.

(d) In a case not covered by subsection (a), the time when payment of the sender's obligation under Section 4A–402(b) or 4A–402(c) occurs is governed by applicable principles of law that determine when an obligation is satisfied.

§ 4A–404. Obligation of Beneficiary's Bank to Pay and Give Notice to Beneficiary.

(a) Subject to Sections 4A–211(e), 4A–405(d), and 4A–405(e), if a beneficiary's bank accepts a payment order, the bank is obliged to pay the amount of the order to the beneficiary of the order. Payment is due on the payment date of the order, but if acceptance occurs on the payment date after the close of the funds-transfer business day of the bank, payment is due on the next funds-transfer business day. If the bank refuses to pay after demand by the beneficiary and receipt of notice of particular circumstances that will give rise to consequential damages as a result of nonpayment, the beneficiary may recover damages resulting from the refusal to pay to the extent the bank had notice of the damages, unless the bank proves that it did not pay because of a reasonable doubt concerning the right of the beneficiary to payment.

(b) If a payment order accepted by the beneficiary's bank instructs payment to an account of the beneficiary, the bank is obliged to notify the beneficiary of receipt of the order before midnight of the next funds-transfer business day following the payment date. If the payment order does not instruct payment to an account of the beneficiary, the bank is required to notify the beneficiary only if notice is required by the order. Notice may be given by first class mail or any other means reasonable in the circumstances. If the bank fails to give the required notice, the bank is obliged to pay interest to the beneficiary on the amount of the payment order from the day notice should have been given until the day the beneficiary learned of receipt of the payment order by the bank. No other damages are recoverable. Reasonable attorney's fees are also recoverable if demand for interest is made and refused before an action is brought on the claim.

(c) The right of a beneficiary to receive payment and damages as stated in subsection (a) may not be varied by agreement or a funds-transfer system rule. The right of a beneficiary to be notified as stated in subsection (b) may be varied by agreement of the beneficiary or by a funds-transfer system rule if the beneficiary is notified of the rule before initiation of the funds transfer.

§ 4A–405. Payment by Beneficiary's Bank to Beneficiary.

(a) If the beneficiary's bank credits an account of the beneficiary of a payment order, payment of the bank's obligation under Section 4A–404(a) occurs when and to the extent (i) the beneficiary is notified of the right to withdraw the credit, (ii) the bank lawfully applies the credit to a debt of the beneficiary, or (iii) funds with respect to the order are otherwise made available to the beneficiary by the bank.

(b) If the beneficiary's bank does not credit an account of the beneficiary of a payment order, the time when payment of the bank's obligation under Section 4A–404(a) occurs is governed by principles of law that determine when an obligation is satisfied.

(c) Except as stated in subsections (d) and (e), if the beneficiary's bank pays the beneficiary of a payment order under a condition to payment or agreement of the beneficiary giving the bank the right to recover payment from the beneficiary if the bank does not receive payment of the order, the condition to payment or agreement is not enforceable.

(d) A funds-transfer system rule may provide that payments made to beneficiaries of funds transfers made through the system are provisional until receipt of payment by the beneficiary's bank of the payment order it accepted. A beneficiary's bank that makes a payment that is provisional under the rule is entitled to refund from the beneficiary if (i) the rule requires that both the beneficiary and the originator be given notice of the provisional nature of the payment before the funds transfer is initiated, (ii) the beneficiary, the beneficiary's bank, and the originator's bank agreed to be bound by the rule, and (iii) the beneficiary's bank did not receive payment of

the payment order that it accepted. If the beneficiary is obliged to refund payment to the beneficiary's bank, acceptance of the payment order by the beneficiary's bank is nullified and no payment by the originator of the funds transfer to the beneficiary occurs under Section 4A–406.

(e) This subsection applies to a funds transfer that includes a payment order transmitted over a funds-transfer system that (i) nets obligations multilaterally among participants, and (ii) has in effect a loss-sharing agreement among participants for the purpose of providing funds necessary to complete settlement of the obligations of one or more participants that do not meet their settlement obligations. If the beneficiary's bank in the funds transfer accepts a payment order and the system fails to complete settlement pursuant to its rules with respect to any payment order in the funds transfer, (i) the acceptance by the beneficiary's bank is nullified and no person has any right or obligation based on the acceptance, (ii) the beneficiary's bank is entitled to recover payment from the beneficiary, (iii) no payment by the originator to the beneficiary occurs under Section 4A–406, and (iv) subject to Section 4A–402(e), each sender in the funds transfer is excused from its obligation to pay its payment order under Section 4A–402(c) because the funds transfer has not been completed.

§ 4A–406. Payment by Originator to Beneficiary; Discharge of Underlying Obligation.

(a) Subject to Sections 4A–211(e), 4A–405(d), and 4A–405(e), the originator of a funds transfer pays the beneficiary of the originator's payment order (i) at the time a payment order for the benefit of the beneficiary is accepted by the beneficiary's bank in the funds transfer and (ii) in an amount equal to the amount of the order accepted by the beneficiary's bank, but not more than the amount of the originator's order.

(b) If payment under subsection (a) is made to satisfy an obligation, the obligation is discharged to the same extent discharge would result from payment to the beneficiary of the same amount in money, unless (i) the payment under subsection (a) was made by a means prohibited by the contract of the beneficiary with respect to the obligation, (ii) the beneficiary, within a reasonable time after receiving notice of receipt of the order by the beneficiary's bank, notified the originator of the beneficiary's refusal of the payment, (iii) funds with respect to the order were not withdrawn by the beneficiary or applied to a debt of the beneficiary, and (iv) the beneficiary would suffer a loss that could reasonably have been avoided if payment had been made by a means complying with the contract. If payment by the originator does not result in discharge under this section, the originator is subrogated to the rights of the beneficiary to receive payment from the beneficiary's bank under Section 4A–404(a).

(c) For the purpose of determining whether discharge of an obligation occurs under subsection (b), if the beneficiary's bank accepts a payment order in an amount equal to the amount of the originator's payment order less charges of one or more receiving banks in the funds transfer, payment to the beneficiary is deemed to be in the amount of the originator's order unless upon demand by the beneficiary the originator does not pay the beneficiary the amount of the deducted charges.

(d) Rights of the originator or of the beneficiary of a funds transfer under this section may be varied only by agreement of the originator and the beneficiary.

Part 5—Miscellaneous Provisions

§ 4A–501. Variation by Agreement and Effect of Funds-Transfer System Rule.

(a) Except as otherwise provided in this Article, the rights and obligations of a party to a funds transfer may be varied by agreement of the affected party.

(b) "Funds-transfer system rule" means a rule of an association of banks (i) governing transmission of payment orders by means of a funds-transfer system of the association or rights and obligations with respect to those orders, or (ii) to the extent the rule governs rights and obligations between banks that are parties to a funds transfer in which a Federal Reserve Bank, acting as an intermediary bank, sends a payment order to the beneficiary's bank. Except as otherwise provided in this Article, a funds-transfer system rule governing rights and obligations between participating banks using the system may be effective even if the rule conflicts with this Article and indirectly affects another party to the funds transfer who does not consent to the rule. A funds-transfer system rule may also govern rights and obligations of parties other than participating banks using the system to the extent stated in Sections 4A–404(c), 4A–405(d), and 4A–507(c).

§ 4A–502. Creditor Process Served on Receiving Bank; Setoff by Beneficiary's Bank.

(a) As used in this section, "creditor process" means levy, attachment, garnishment, notice of lien, sequestration, or similar process issued by or on behalf of a creditor or other claimant with respect to an account.

(b) This subsection applies to creditor process with respect to an authorized account of the sender of a payment order if the creditor process is served on the receiving bank. For the purpose of determining rights with respect to the creditor process, if the receiving bank accepts the payment order the balance in the authorized account is deemed to be reduced by the amount of the payment order to the extent the bank did not otherwise receive payment of the order, unless the creditor process is served at a time and in a manner affording the bank a reasonable opportunity to act on it before the bank accepts the payment order.

(c) If a beneficiary's bank has received a payment order for payment to the beneficiary's account in the bank, the following rules apply:

(1) The bank may credit the beneficiary's account. The amount credited may be set off against an obligation owed by the beneficiary to the bank or may be applied to satisfy creditor process served on the bank with respect to the account.

(2) The bank may credit the beneficiary's account and allow withdrawal of the amount credited unless creditor process with respect to the account is served at a time and in a manner affording the bank a reasonable opportunity to act to prevent withdrawal.

(3) If creditor process with respect to the beneficiary's account has been served and the bank has had a reasonable opportunity to act on it, the bank may not reject the payment order except for a reason unrelated to the service of process.

(d) Creditor process with respect to a payment by the originator to the beneficiary pursuant to a funds transfer may be served only on the beneficiary's bank with respect to the debt owed by that bank to the beneficiary. Any other bank served with the creditor process is not obliged to act with respect to the process.

§ 4A–503. Injunction or Restraining Order with Respect to Funds Transfer.

For proper cause and in compliance with applicable law, a court may restrain (i) a person from issuing a payment order to initiate a funds transfer, (ii) an originator's bank from executing the payment order of the originator, or (iii) the beneficiary's bank from releasing funds to the beneficiary or the beneficiary from withdrawing the funds. A court may not otherwise restrain a person from issuing a payment order, paying or receiving payment of a payment order, or otherwise acting with respect to a funds transfer.

§ 4A–504. Order in Which Items and Payment Orders May Be Charged to Account; Order of Withdrawals from Account.

(a) If a receiving bank has received more than one payment order of the sender or one or more payment orders and other items that are payable from the sender's account, the bank may charge the sender's account with respect to the various orders and items in any sequence.

(b) In determining whether a credit to an account has been withdrawn by the holder of the account or applied to a debt of the holder of the account, credits first made to the account are first withdrawn or applied.

§ 4A–505. Preclusion of Objection to Debit of Customer's Account.

If a receiving bank has received payment from its customer with respect to a payment order issued in the name of the customer as sender and accepted by the bank, and the customer received notification reasonably identifying the order, the customer is precluded from asserting that the bank is not entitled to retain the payment unless the customer notifies the bank of the customer's objection to the payment within one year after the notification was received by the customer.

§ 4A–506. Rate of Interest.

(a) If, under this Article, a receiving bank is obliged to pay interest with respect to a payment order issued to the bank, the amount payable may be determined (i) by agreement of the sender and receiving bank, or (ii) by a funds-transfer system rule if the payment order is transmitted through a funds-transfer system.

(b) If the amount of interest is not determined by an agreement or rule as stated in subsection (a), the amount is calculated by multiplying the applicable Federal Funds rate by the amount on which interest is payable, and then multiplying the product by the number of days for which interest is payable. The applicable Federal Funds rate is the average of the Federal Funds rates published by the Federal Reserve Bank of New York for each of the days for which interest is payable divided by 360. The Federal Funds rate for any day on which a published rate is not available is the same as the published rate for the next preceding day for which there is a published rate. If a receiving bank that accepted a payment order is required to refund payment to the sender of the order because the funds transfer was not completed, but the failure to complete was not due to any fault by the bank, the interest payable is reduced by a percentage equal to the reserve requirement on deposits of the receiving bank.

§ 4A–507. Choice of Law.

(a) The following rules apply unless the affected parties otherwise agree or subsection (c) applies:

(1) The rights and obligations between the sender of a payment order and the receiving bank are governed by the law of the jurisdiction in which the receiving bank is located.

(2) The rights and obligations between the beneficiary's bank and the beneficiary are governed by the law of the jurisdiction in which the beneficiary's bank is located.

(3) The issue of when payment is made pursuant to a funds transfer by the originator to the beneficiary is governed by the law of the jurisdiction in which the beneficiary's bank is located.

(b) If the parties described in each paragraph of subsection (a) have made an agreement selecting the law of a particular jurisdiction to govern rights and obligations between each other, the law of that jurisdiction governs those rights and obligations, whether or not the payment order or the funds transfer bears a reasonable relation to that jurisdiction.

(c) A funds-transfer system rule may select the law of a particular jurisdiction to govern (i) rights and obligations between participating banks with respect to payment orders transmitted or processed through the system, or (ii) the rights and obligations of some or all parties to a funds transfer any part of which is carried out by means of the system. A choice of law made pursuant to clause (i) is binding on participating banks. A choice of law made pursuant to clause (ii) is binding on the originator, other sender, or a receiving bank having notice that the funds-transfer system might be used in the funds transfer and of the choice of law by the system when the originator, other sender, or receiving bank issued or accepted a payment order. The beneficiary of a funds transfer is bound by the choice of law if, when the funds transfer is initiated, the beneficiary has notice that the funds-transfer system might be used in the funds transfer and of the choice of law by the system. The law of a jurisdiction selected pursuant to this subsection may govern, whether or not that law bears a reasonable relation to the matter in issue.

(d) In the event of inconsistency between an agreement under subsection (b) and a choice-of-law rule under subsection (c), the agreement under subsection (b) prevails.

(e) If a funds transfer is made by use of more than one funds-transfer system and there is inconsistency between choice-of-law rules of the systems, the matter in issue is governed by the law of the selected jurisdiction that has the most significant relationship to the matter in issue.

REVISED ARTICLE 5: LETTERS OF CREDIT

§ 5–101 Short Title.

This article may be cited as Uniform Commercial Code—Letters of Credit.

§ 5–102. Definitions.

(a) In this article:

(1) "Adviser" means a person who, at the request of the issuer, a confirmer, or another adviser, notifies or requests another adviser to notify the beneficiary that a letter of credit has been issued, confirmed, or amended.

(2) "Applicant" means a person at whose request or for whose account a letter of credit is issued. The term includes a person who requests an issuer to issue a letter of credit on behalf of another if the person making the request undertakes an obligation to reimburse the issuer.

(3) "Beneficiary" means a person who under the terms of a letter of credit is entitled to have its complying presentation honored. The term includes a person to whom drawing rights have been transferred under a transferable letter of credit.

(4) "Confirmer" means a nominated person who undertakes, at the request or with the consent of the issuer, to honor a presentation under a letter of credit issued by another.

(5) "Dishonor" of a letter of credit means failure timely to honor or to take an interim action, such as acceptance of a draft, that may be required by the letter of credit.

(6) "Document" means a draft or other demand, document of title, investment security, certificate, invoice, or other record, statement, or representation of fact, law, right, or opinion (i) which is presented in a written or other medium permitted by the letter of credit or, unless prohibited by the letter of credit, by the standard practice referred to in Section 5–108(e) and (ii) which is capable of being examined for compliance with the terms and conditions of the letter of credit. A document may not be oral.

(7) "Good faith" means honesty in fact in the conduct or transaction concerned.

(8) "Honor" of a letter of credit means performance of the issuer's undertaking in the letter of credit to pay or deliver an item of value. Unless the letter of credit otherwise provides, "honor" occurs

   (i) upon payment,

   (ii) if the letter of credit provides for acceptance, upon acceptance of a draft and, at maturity, its payment, or

   (iii) if the letter of credit provides for incurring a deferred obligation, upon incurring the obligation and, at maturity, its performance.

(9) "Issuer" means a bank or other person that issues a letter of credit, but does not include an individual who makes an engagement for personal, family, or household purposes.

(10) "Letter of credit" means a definite undertaking that satisfies the requirements of Section 5–104 by an issuer to a beneficiary at the request or for the account of an applicant or, in the case of a financial institution, to itself or for its own account, to honor a documentary presentation by payment or delivery of an item of value.

(11) "Nominated person" means a person whom the issuer (i) designates or authorizes to pay, accept, negotiate, or otherwise give value under a letter of credit and (ii) undertakes by agreement or custom and practice to reimburse.

(12) "Presentation" means delivery of a document to an issuer or nominated person for honor or giving of value under a letter of credit.

(13) "Presenter" means a person making a presentation as or on behalf of a beneficiary or nominated person.

(14) "Record" means information that is inscribed on a tangible medium, or that is stored in an electronic or other medium and is retrievable in perceivable form.

(15) "Successor of a beneficiary" means a person who succeeds to substantially all of the rights of a beneficiary by operation of law, including a corporation with or into which the beneficiary has been merged or consolidated, an administrator, executor, personal representative, trustee in bankruptcy, debtor in possession, liquidator, and receiver.

(b) Definitions in other Articles applying to this article and the sections in which they appear are:

"Accept" or "Acceptance" Section 3–409

"Value" Sections 3–303, 4–211

(c) Article 1 contains certain additional general definitions and principles of construction and interpretation applicable throughout this article.

§ 5–103. Scope.

(a) This article applies to letters of credit and to certain rights and obligations arising out of transactions involving letters of credit.

(b) The statement of a rule in this article does not by itself require, imply, or negate application of the same or a different rule to a situation not provided for, or to a person not specified, in this article.

(c) With the exception of this subsection, subsections (a) and (d), Sections 5–102(a)(9) and (10), 5–106(d), and 5–114(d), and except to the extent prohibited in Sections 1–102(3) and 5–117(d), the effect of this article may be varied by agreement or by a provision stated or incorporated by reference in an undertaking. A term in an agreement or undertaking generally excusing liability or generally limiting remedies for failure to perform obligations is not sufficient to vary obligations prescribed by this article.

(d) Rights and obligations of an issuer to a beneficiary or a nominated person under a letter of credit are independent of the existence, performance, or nonperformance of a contract or arrangement out of which the letter of credit arises or which underlies it, including contracts or arrangements between the issuer and the applicant and between the applicant and the beneficiary.

§ 5–104. Formal Requirements.

A letter of credit, confirmation, advice, transfer, amendment, or cancellation may be issued in any form that is a record and is authenticated (i) by a signature or (ii) in accordance with the agreement of the parties or the standard practice referred to in Section 5–108(e).

§ 5–105. Consideration.

Consideration is not required to issue, amend, transfer, or cancel a letter of credit, advice, or confirmation.

§ 5–106. Issuance, Amendment, Cancellation, and Duration.

(a) A letter of credit is issued and becomes enforceable according to its terms against the issuer when the issuer sends or otherwise transmits it to the person requested to advise or to the beneficiary. A letter of credit is revocable only if it so provides.

(b) After a letter of credit is issued, rights and obligations of a beneficiary, applicant, confirmer, and issuer are not affected by an amendment or cancellation to which that person has not consented except to the extent the letter of credit provides that it is revocable or that the issuer may amend or cancel the letter of credit without that consent.

(c) If there is no stated expiration date or other provision that determines its duration, a letter of credit expires one year after its stated date of issuance or, if none is stated, after the date on which it is issued.

(d) A letter of credit that states that it is perpetual expires five years after its stated date of issuance, or if none is stated, after the date on which it is issued.

§ 5–107. Confirmer, Nominated Person, and Adviser.

(a) A confirmer is directly obligated on a letter of credit and has the rights and obligations of an issuer to the extent of its confirmation. The confirmer also has rights against and obligations to the issuer as if the issuer were an applicant and the confirmer had issued the letter of credit at the request and for the account of the issuer.

(b) A nominated person who is not a confirmer is not obligated to honor or otherwise give value for a presentation.

(c) A person requested to advise may decline to act as an adviser. An adviser that is not a confirmer is not obligated to honor or give value for a presentation. An adviser undertakes to the issuer and to the beneficiary accurately to advise the terms of the letter of credit, confirmation, amendment, or advice received by that person and undertakes to the beneficiary to check the apparent authenticity of the request to advise. Even if the advice is inaccurate, the letter of credit, confirmation, or amendment is enforceable as issued.

(d) A person who notifies a transferee beneficiary of the terms of a letter of credit, confirmation, amendment, or advice has the rights and obligations of an adviser under subsection (c). The terms in the notice to the transferee beneficiary may differ from the terms in any notice to the transferor beneficiary to the extent permitted by the letter of credit, confirmation, amendment, or advice received by the person who so notifies.

§ 5–108. Issuer's Rights and Obligations.

(a) Except as otherwise provided in Section 5–109, an issuer shall honor a presentation that, as determined by the standard practice referred to in subsection (e), appears on its face strictly to comply with the terms and conditions of the letter of credit. Except as otherwise provided in Section 5–113 and unless otherwise agreed with the applicant, an issuer shall dishonor a presentation that does not appear so to comply.

(b) An issuer has a reasonable time after presentation, but not beyond the end of the seventh business day of the issuer after the day of its receipt of documents:

(1) to honor,

(2) if the letter of credit provides for honor to be completed more than seven business days after presentation, to accept a draft or incur a deferred obligation, or

(3) to give notice to the presenter of discrepancies in the presentation.

(c) Except as otherwise provided in subsection (d), an issuer is precluded from asserting as a basis for dishonor any discrepancy if timely notice is not given, or any discrepancy not stated in the notice if timely notice is given.

(d) Failure to give the notice specified in subsection (b) or to mention fraud, forgery, or expiration in the notice does not preclude the issuer from asserting as a basis for dishonor fraud or forgery as described in Section 5–109(a) or expiration of the letter of credit before presentation.

(e) An issuer shall observe standard practice of financial institutions that regularly issue letters of credit. Determination of the issuer's observance of the standard practice is a matter of interpretation for the court. The court shall offer the parties a reasonable opportunity to present evidence of the standard practice.

(f) An issuer is not responsible for:

(1) the performance or nonperformance of the underlying contract, arrangement, or transaction,

(2) an act or omission of others, or

(3) observance or knowledge of the usage of a particular trade other than the standard practice referred to in subsection (e).

(g) If an undertaking constituting a letter of credit under Section 5–102(a)(10) contains nondocumentary conditions, an issuer shall disregard the nondocumentary conditions and treat them as if they were not stated.

(h) An issuer that has dishonored a presentation shall return the documents or hold them at the disposal of, and send advice to that effect to, the presenter.

(i) An issuer that has honored a presentation as permitted or required by this article:

(1) is entitled to be reimbursed by the applicant in immediately available funds not later than the date of its payment of funds;

(2) takes the documents free of claims of the beneficiary or presenter;

(3) is precluded from asserting a right of recourse on a draft under Sections 3–414 and 3–415;

(4) except as otherwise provided in Sections 5–110 and 5–117, is precluded from restitution of money paid or other value given by mistake to the extent the mistake concerns discrepancies in the documents or tender which are apparent on the face of the presentation; and

(5) is discharged to the extent of its performance under the letter of credit unless the issuer honored a presentation in which a required signature of a beneficiary was forged.

§ 5–109. Fraud and Forgery.

(a) If a presentation is made that appears on its face strictly to comply with the terms and conditions of the letter of credit, but a required document is forged or materially fraudulent, or honor of the presentation would facilitate a material fraud by the beneficiary on the issuer or applicant:

(1) the issuer shall honor the presentation, if honor is demanded by (i) a nominated person who has given value in good faith and without notice of forgery or material fraud, (ii) a confirmer who has honored its confirmation in good faith, (iii) a holder in due course of a draft drawn under the letter of credit which was taken after acceptance by the issuer or nominated person, or (iv) an assignee of the issuer's or nominated person's deferred obligation that was taken for value and without notice of forgery or material fraud after the obligation was incurred by the issuer or nominated person; and

(2) the issuer, acting in good faith, may honor or dishonor the presentation in any other case.

(b) If an applicant claims that a required document is forged or materially fraudulent or that honor of the presentation would facilitate a material fraud by the beneficiary on the issuer or applicant, a court of competent jurisdiction may temporarily or permanently enjoin the issuer from honoring a presentation or grant similar relief against the issuer or other persons only if the court finds that:

(1) the relief is not prohibited under the law applicable to an accepted draft or deferred obligation incurred by the issuer;

(2) a beneficiary, issuer, or nominated person who may be adversely affected is adequately protected against loss that it may suffer because the relief is granted;

(3) all of the conditions to entitle a person to the relief under the law of this State have been met; and

(4) on the basis of the information submitted to the court, the applicant is more likely than not to succeed under its claim of forgery or material fraud and the person demanding honor does not qualify for protection under subsection (a)(1).

§ 5–110. Warranties.

(a) If its presentation is honored, the beneficiary warrants:

(1) to the issuer, any other person to whom presentation is made, and the applicant that there is no fraud or forgery of the kind described in Section 5–109(a); and

(2) to the applicant that the drawing does not violate any agreement between the applicant and beneficiary or any other agreement intended by them to be augmented by the letter of credit.

(b) The warranties in subsection (a) are in addition to warranties arising under Article 3, 4, 7, and 8 because of the presentation or transfer of documents covered by any of those articles.

§ 5–111. Remedies.

(a) If an issuer wrongfully dishonors or repudiates its obligation to pay money under a letter of credit before presentation, the beneficiary, successor, or nominated person presenting on its own behalf may recover from the issuer the amount that is the subject of the dishonor or repudiation. If the issuer's obligation under the letter of credit is not for the payment of money, the claimant may obtain specific performance or, at the claimant's election, recover an amount equal to the value of performance from the issuer. In either case, the claimant may also recover incidental but not consequential damages. The claimant is not obligated to take action to avoid damages that might be due from the issuer under this subsection. If, although not obligated to do so, the claimant avoids damages, the claimant's recovery from the issuer must be reduced by the amount of damages avoided. The issuer has the burden of proving the amount of damages avoided. In the case of repudiation the claimant need not present any document.

(b) If an issuer wrongfully dishonors a draft or demand presented under a letter of credit or honors a draft or demand in breach of its obligation to the applicant, the applicant may recover damages resulting from the breach, including incidental but not consequential damages, less any amount saved as a result of the breach.

(c) If an adviser or nominated person other than a confirmer breaches an obligation under this article or an issuer breaches an obligation not covered in subsection (a) or (b), a person to whom the obligation is owed may recover damages resulting from the breach, including incidental but not consequential damages, less any amount saved as a result of the breach. To the extent of the confirmation, a confirmer has the liability of an issuer specified in this subsection and subsections (a) and (b).

(d) An issuer, nominated person, or adviser who is found liable under subsection (a), (b), or (c) shall pay interest on the amount owed thereunder from the date of wrongful dishonor or other appropriate date.

(e) Reasonable attorney's fees and other expenses of litigation must be awarded to the prevailing party in an action in which a remedy is sought under this article.

(f) Damages that would otherwise be payable by a party for breach of an obligation under this article may be liquidated by agreement or undertaking, but only in an amount or by a formula that is reasonable in light of the harm anticipated.

§ 5–112. Transfer of Letter of Credit.

(a) Except as otherwise provided in Section 5–113, unless a letter of credit provides that it is transferable, the right of a beneficiary to draw or otherwise demand performance under a letter of credit may not be transferred.

(b) Even if a letter of credit provides that it is transferable, the issuer may refuse to recognize or carry out a transfer if:

(1) the transfer would violate applicable law; or

(2) the transferor or transferee has failed to comply with any requirement stated in the letter of credit or any other requirement relating to transfer imposed by the issuer which is within the standard practice referred to in Section 5–108(e) or is otherwise reasonable under the circumstances.

§ 5–113. Transfer by Operation of Law.

(a) A successor of a beneficiary may consent to amendments, sign and present documents, and receive payment or other items of value in the name of the beneficiary without disclosing its status as a successor.

(b) A successor of a beneficiary may consent to amendments, sign and present documents, and receive payment or other items of value in its own name as the disclosed successor of the beneficiary. Except as otherwise provided in subsection (e), an issuer shall recognize a disclosed successor of a beneficiary as beneficiary in full substitution for its predecessor upon compliance with the requirements for recognition by the issuer of a transfer of drawing rights by operation of law under the standard practice referred to in Section 5–108(e) or, in the absence of such a practice, compliance with other reasonable procedures sufficient to protect the issuer.

(c) An issuer is not obliged to determine whether a purported successor is a successor of a beneficiary or whether the signature of a purported successor is genuine or authorized.

(d) Honor of a purported successor's apparently complying presentation under subsection (a) or (b) has the consequences specified in Section 5–108(i) even if the purported successor is not the successor of a beneficiary. Documents signed in the name of the beneficiary or of a disclosed successor by a person who is neither the beneficiary nor the successor of the beneficiary are forged documents for the purposes of Section 5–109.

(e) An issuer whose rights of reimbursement are not covered by subsection (d) or substantially similar law and any confirmer or nominated person may decline to recognize a presentation under subsection (b).

(f) A beneficiary whose name is changed after the issuance of a letter of credit has the same rights and obligations as a successor of a beneficiary under this section.

§ 5–114. Assignment of Proceeds.

(a) In this section, "proceeds of a letter of credit" means the cash, check, accepted draft, or other item of value paid or delivered upon honor or giving of value by the issuer or any nominated person under the letter of credit. The term does not include a beneficiary's drawing rights or documents presented by the beneficiary.

(b) A beneficiary may assign its right to part or all of the proceeds of a letter of credit. The beneficiary may do so before presentation as a present assignment of its right to receive proceeds contingent upon its compliance with the terms and conditions of the letter of credit.

(c) An issuer or nominated person need not recognize an assignment of proceeds of a letter of credit until it consents to the assignment.

(d) An issuer or nominated person has no obligation to give or withhold its consent to an assignment of proceeds of a letter of credit, but consent may not be unreasonably withheld if the assignee possesses

and exhibits the letter of credit and presentation of the letter of credit is a condition to honor.

(e) Rights of a transferee beneficiary or nominated person are independent of the beneficiary's assignment of the proceeds of a letter of credit and are superior to the assignee's right to the proceeds.

(f) Neither the rights recognized by this section between an assignee and an issuer, transferee beneficiary, or nominated person nor the issuer's or nominated person's payment of proceeds to an assignee or a third person affect the rights between the assignee and any person other than the issuer, transferee beneficiary, or nominated person. The mode of creating and perfecting a security interest in or granting an assignment of a beneficiary's rights to proceeds is governed by Article 9 or other law. Against persons other than the issuer, transferee beneficiary, or nominated person, the rights and obligations arising upon the creation of a security interest or other assignment of a beneficiary's right to proceeds and its perfection are governed by Article 9 or other law.

§ 5–115. Statute of Limitations.

An action to enforce a right or obligation arising under this article must be commenced within one year after the expiration date of the relevant letter of credit or one year after the [claim for relief] [cause of action] accrues, whichever occurs later. A [claim for relief] [cause of action] accrues when the breach occurs, regardless of the aggrieved party's lack of knowledge of the breach.

§ 5–116. Choice of Law and Forum.

(a) The liability of an issuer, nominated person, or adviser for action or omission is governed by the law of the jurisdiction chosen by an agreement in the form of a record signed or otherwise authenticated by the affected parties in the manner provided in Section 5–104 or by a provision in the person's letter of credit, confirmation, or other undertaking. The jurisdiction whose law is chosen need not bear any relation to the transaction.

(b) Unless subsection (a) applies, the liability of an issuer, nominated person, or adviser for action or omission is governed by the law of the jurisdiction in which the person is located. The person is considered to be located at the address indicated in the person's undertaking. If more than one address is indicated, the person is considered to be located at the address from which the person's undertaking was issued. For the purpose of jurisdiction, choice of law, and recognition of interbranch letters of credit, but not enforcement of a judgment, all branches of a bank are considered separate juridical entities and a bank is considered to be located at the place where its relevant branch is considered to be located under this subsection.

(c) Except as otherwise provided in this subsection, the liability of an issuer, nominated person, or adviser is governed by any rules of custom or practice, such as the Uniform Customs and Practice for Documentary Credits, to which the letter of credit, confirmation, or other undertaking is expressly made subject. If (i) this article would govern the liability of an issuer, nominated person, or adviser under subsection (a) or (b), (ii) the relevant undertaking incorporates rules of custom or practice, and (iii) there is conflict between this article and those rules as applied to that undertaking, those rules govern except to the extent of any conflict with the nonvariable provisions specified in Section 5–103(c).

(d) If there is conflict between this article and Article 3, 4, 4A, or 9, this article governs.

(e) The forum for settling disputes arising out of an undertaking within this article may be chosen in the manner and with the binding effect that governing law may be chosen in accordance with subsection (a).

§ 5–117. Subrogation of Issuer, Applicant, and Nominated Person.

(a) An issuer that honors a beneficiary's presentation is subrogated to the rights of the beneficiary to the same extent as if the issuer were a secondary obligor of the underlying obligation owed to the beneficiary and of the applicant to the same extent as if the issuer were the secondary obligor of the underlying obligation owed to the applicant.

(b) An applicant that reimburses an issuer is subrogated to the rights of the issuer against any beneficiary, presenter, or nominated person to the same extent as if the applicant were the secondary obligor of the obligations owed to the issuer and has the rights of subrogation of the issuer to the rights of the beneficiary stated in subsection (a).

(c) A nominated person who pays or gives value against a draft or demand presented under a letter of credit is subrogated to the rights of:

> **(1)** the issuer against the applicant to the same extent as if the nominated person were a secondary obligor of the obligation owed to the issuer by the applicant;
>
> **(2)** the beneficiary to the same extent as if the nominated person were a secondary obligor of the underlying obligation owed to the beneficiary; and
>
> **(3)** the applicant to same extent as if the nominated person were a secondary obligor of the underlying obligation owed to the applicant.

(d) Notwithstanding any agreement or term to the contrary, the rights of subrogation stated in subsections (a) and (b) do not arise until the issuer honors the letter of credit or otherwise pays and the rights in subsection (c) do not arise until the nominated person pays or otherwise gives value. Until then, the issuer, nominated person, and the applicant do not derive under this section present or prospective rights forming the basis of a claim, defense, or excuse.

§ 5–118. Security Interest of Issuer or Nominated Person.

(a) An issuer or nominated person has a security interest in a document presented under a letter of credit to the extent that the issuer or nominated person honors or gives value for the presentation.

(b) So long as and to the extent that an issuer or nominated person has not been reimbursed or has not otherwise recovered the value given with respect to a security interest in a document under subsection (a), the security interest continues and is subject to Article 9, but:

> **(1)** a security agreement is not necessary to make the security interest enforceable under Section 9–203(b)(3);
>
> **(2)** if the document is presented in a medium other than a written or other tangible medium, the security interest is perfected; and
>
> **(3)** if the document is presented in a written or other tangible medium and is not a certificated security, chattel paper, a document of title, an instrument, or a letter of credit, the security interest is perfected and has priority over a conflicting security interest in the document so long as the debtor does not have possession of the document.

As added in 1999.

Transition Provisions

§ [ ]. Effective Date.
This [Act] shall become effective on _____, 20__.

§ [ ]. Repeal.
This [Act] [repeals] [amends] [insert citation to existing Article 5].

§ [ ]. Applicability.
This [Act] applies to a letter of credit that is issued on or after the effective date of this [Act]. This [Act] does not apply to a transaction, event, obligation, or duty arising out of or associated with a letter of credit that was issued before the effective date of this [Act].

§ [ ]. Savings Clause.
A transaction arising out of or associated with a letter of credit that was issued before the effective date of this [Act] and the rights, obligations, and interests flowing from that transaction are governed by any statute or other law amended or repealed by this [Act] as if repeal or amendment had not occurred and may be terminated, completed, consummated, or enforced under that statute or other law.

REPEALER OF U.C.C.—ARTICLE 6: BULK TRANSFERS AND [REVISED] ARTICLE 6: BULK SALES

(States to Select One Alternative)

Alternative A

§ 1. Repeal
Article 6 and Section 9–111 of the Uniform Commercial Code are hereby repealed, effective _____.

§ 2. Amendment
Section 1–105(2) of the Uniform Commercial Code is hereby amended to read as follows:

(2) Where one of the following provisions of this Act specifies the applicable law, that provision governs and a contrary agreement is effective only to the extent permitted by the law (including the conflict of laws rules) so specified:

Rights of creditors against sold goods. Section 2–402.

Applicability of the Article on Leases. Section 2A–105 and 2A-106.

Applicability of the Article on Bank Deposits and Collections. Section 4–102.

Applicability of the Article on Investment Securities. Section 8–106.

Perfection provisions of the Article on Secured Transactions. Section 9–103.

§ 3. Amendment.
Section 2–403(4) of the Uniform Commercial Code is hereby amended to read as follows:

(4) The rights of other purchasers of goods and of lien creditors are governed by the Articles on Secured Transactions (Article 9) and Documents of Title (Article 7).

§ 4. Savings Clause.
Rights and obligations that arose under Article 6 and Section 9–111 of the Uniform Commercial Code before their repeal remain valid and may be enforced as though those statutes had not been repealed.]

Alternative B

§ 6–101. Short Title.

This Article shall be known and may be cited as Uniform Commercial Code—Bulk Sales.

§ 6–102. Definitions and Index of Definitions.

(1) In this Article, unless the context otherwise requires:

(a) "Assets" means the inventory that is the subject of a bulk sale and any tangible and intangible personal property used or held for use primarily in, or arising from, the seller's business and sold in connection with that inventory, but the term does not include:

(i) fixtures (Section 9–102(a)(41)) other than readily removable factory and office machines;

(ii) the lessee's interest in a lease of real property; or

(iii) property to the extent it is generally exempt from creditor process under nonbankruptcy law.

(b) "Auctioneer" means a person whom the seller engages to direct, conduct, control, or be responsible for a sale by auction.

(c) "Bulk sale" means:

(i) in the case of a sale by auction or a sale or series of sales conducted by a liquidator on the seller's behalf, a sale or series of sales not in the ordinary course of the seller's business of more than half of the seller's inventory, as measured by value on the date of the bulk-sale agreement, if on that date the auctioneer or liquidator has notice, or after reasonable inquiry would have had notice, that the seller will not continue to operate the same or a similar kind of business after the sale or series of sales; and

(ii) in all other cases, a sale not in the ordinary course of the seller's business of more than half the seller's inventory, as measured by value on the date of the bulk-sale agreement, if on that date the buyer has notice, or after reasonable inquiry would have had notice, that the seller will not continue to operate the same or a similar kind of business after the sale.

(d) "Claim" means a right to payment from the seller, whether or not the right is reduced to judgment, liquidated, fixed, matured, disputed, secured, legal, or equitable. The term includes costs of collection and attorney's fees only to the extent that the laws of this state permit the holder of the claim to recover them in an action against the obligor.

(e) "Claimant" means a person holding a claim incurred in the seller's business other than:

(i) an unsecured and unmatured claim for employment compensation and benefits, including commissions and vacation, severance, and sick-leave pay;

(ii) a claim for injury to an individual or to property, or for breach of warranty, unless:

(A) a right of action for the claim has accrued;

(B) the claim has been asserted against the seller; and

(C) the seller knows the identity of the person asserting the claim and the basis upon which the person has asserted it; and

(States to Select One Alternative)

Alternative A

[**(iii)** a claim for taxes owing to a governmental unit.]

Alternative B

[**(iii)** a claim for taxes owing to a governmental unit, if:

(A) a statute governing the enforcement of the claim permits or requires notice of the bulk sale to be given to the governmental unit in a manner other than by compliance with the requirements of this Article; and

(B) notice is given in accordance with the statute.]

(f) "Creditor" means a claimant or other person holding a claim.

(g)(i) "Date of the bulk sale" means:

(A) if the sale is by auction or is conducted by a liquidator on the seller's behalf, the date on which more than ten percent of the net proceeds is paid to or for the benefit of the seller; and

(B) in all other cases, the later of the date on which:

(I) more than ten percent of the net contract price is paid to or for the benefit of the seller; or

(II) more than ten percent of the assets, as measured by value, are transferred to the buyer.

(ii) For purposes of this subsection:

(A) delivery of a negotiable instrument (Section 3–104(1)) to or for the benefit of the seller in exchange for assets constitutes payment of the contract price pro tanto;

(B) to the extent that the contract price is deposited in an escrow, the contract price is paid to or for the benefit of the seller when the seller acquires the unconditional right to receive the deposit or when the deposit is delivered to the seller or for the benefit of the seller, whichever is earlier; and

(C) an asset is transferred when a person holding an unsecured claim can no longer obtain through judicial proceedings rights to the asset that are superior to those of the buyer arising as a result of the bulk sale. A person holding an unsecured claim can obtain those superior rights to a tangible asset at least until the buyer has an unconditional right, under the bulk-sale agreement, to possess the asset, and a person holding an unsecured claim can obtain those superior rights to an intangible asset at least until the buyer has an unconditional right, under the bulk-sale agreement, to use the asset.

(h) "Date of the bulk-sale agreement" means:

(i) in the case of a sale by auction or conducted by a liquidator (subsection (c)(i)), the date on which the seller engages the auctioneer or liquidator; and

(ii) in all other cases, the date on which a bulk-sale agreement becomes enforceable between the buyer and the seller.

(i) "Debt" means liability on a claim.

(j) "Liquidator" means a person who is regularly engaged in the business of disposing of assets for businesses contemplating liquidation or dissolution.

(k) "Net contract price" means the new consideration the buyer is obligated to pay for the assets less:

(i) the amount of any proceeds of the sale of an asset, to the extent the proceeds are applied in partial or total satisfaction of a debt secured by the asset; and

(ii) the amount of any debt to the extent it is secured by a security interest or lien that is enforceable against the asset before and after it has been sold to a buyer. If a debt is secured by an asset and other property of the seller, the amount of the debt secured by a security interest or lien that is enforceable against the asset is determined by multiplying the debt by a fraction, the numerator of which is the value of the new consideration for the asset on the date of the bulk sale and the denominator of which is the value of all property securing the debt on the date of the bulk sale.

(l) "Net proceeds" means the new consideration received for assets sold at a sale by auction or a sale conducted by a liquidator on the seller's behalf less:

(i) commissions and reasonable expenses of the sale;

(ii) the amount of any proceeds of the sale of an asset, to the extent the proceeds are applied in partial or total satisfaction of a debt secured by the asset; and

(iii) the amount of any debt to the extent it is secured by a security interest or lien that is enforceable against the asset before and after it has been sold to a buyer. If a debt is secured by an asset and other property of the seller, the amount of the debt secured by a security interest or lien that is enforceable against the asset is determined by multiplying the debt by a fraction, the numerator of which is the value of the new consideration for the asset on the date of the bulk sale and the denominator of which is the value of all property securing the debt on the date of the bulk sale.

(m) A sale is "in the ordinary course of the seller's business" if the sale comports with usual or customary practices in the kind of business in which the seller is engaged or with the seller's own usual or customary practices.

(n) "United States" includes its territories and possessions and the Commonwealth of Puerto Rico.

(o) "Value" means fair market value.

(p) "Verified" means signed and sworn to or affirmed.

(2) The following definitions in other Articles apply to this Article:

(a) "Buyer."	Section 2–103(1)(a).
(b) "Equipment."	Section 9–102(a)(33).
(c) "Inventory."	Section 9–102(a)(48).
(d) "Sale."	Section 2–106(1).
(e) "Seller."	Section 2–103(1)(d).

(3) In addition, Article 1 contains general definitions and principles of construction and interpretation applicable throughout this Article.

As amended in 1999.

§ 6–103. Applicability of Article.

(1) Except as otherwise provided in subsection (3), this Article applies to a bulk sale if:

(a) the seller's principal business is the sale of inventory from stock; and

(b) on the date of the bulk-sale agreement the seller is located in this state or, if the seller is located in a jurisdiction that is not a part of the United States, the seller's major executive office in the United States is in this state.

(2) A seller is deemed to be located at his [or her] place of business. If a seller has more than one place of business, the seller is deemed located at his [or her] chief executive office.

(3) This Article does not apply to:

(a) a transfer made to secure payment or performance of an obligation;

(b) a transfer of collateral to a secured party pursuant to Section 9–503;

(c) a disposition of collateral pursuant to Section 9–610;

(d) retention of collateral pursuant to Section 9–620;

(e) a sale of an asset encumbered by a security interest or lien if (i) all the proceeds of the sale are applied in partial or total satisfaction of the debt secured by the security interest or lien or (ii) the security interest or lien is enforceable against the asset after it has been sold to the buyer and the net contract price is zero;

(f) a general assignment for the benefit of creditors or to a subsequent transfer by the assignee;

(g) a sale by an executor, administrator, receiver, trustee in bankruptcy, or any public officer under judicial process;

(h) a sale made in the course of judicial or administrative proceedings for the dissolution or reorganization of an organization;

(i) a sale to a buyer whose principal place of business is in the United States and who:

(i) not earlier than 21 days before the date of the bulk sale, (A) obtains from the seller a verified and dated list of claimants of whom the seller has notice three days before the seller sends or delivers the list to the buyer or (B) conducts a reasonable inquiry to discover the claimants;

(ii) assumes in full the debts owed to claimants of whom the buyer has knowledge on the date the buyer receives the list of claimants from the seller or on the date the buyer completes the reasonable inquiry, as the case may be;

(iii) is not insolvent after the assumption; and

(iv) gives written notice of the assumption not later than 30 days after the date of the bulk sale by sending or delivering a notice to the claimants identified in subparagraph (ii) or by filing a notice in the office of the [Secretary of State];

(j) a sale to a buyer whose principal place of business is in the United States and who:

(i) assumes in full the debts that were incurred in the seller's business before the date of the bulk sale;

(ii) is not insolvent after the assumption; and

(iii) gives written notice of the assumption not later than 30 days after the date of the bulk sale by sending or delivering a notice to each creditor whose debt is assumed or by filing a notice in the office of the [Secretary of State];

(k) a sale to a new organization that is organized to take over and continue the business of the seller and that has its principal place of business in the United States if:

(i) the buyer assumes in full the debts that were incurred in the seller's business before the date of the bulk sale;

(ii) the seller receives nothing from the sale except an interest in the new organization that is subordinate to the claims against the organization arising from the assumption; and

(iii) the buyer gives written notice of the assumption not later than 30 days after the date of the bulk sale by sending or delivering a notice to each creditor whose debt is assumed or by filing a notice in the office of the [Secretary of State];

(l) a sale of assets having:

(i) a value, net of liens and security interests, of less than $10,000. If a debt is secured by assets and other property of the seller, the net value of the assets is determined by subtracting from their value an amount equal to the product of the debt multiplied by a fraction, the numerator of which is the value of the assets on the date of the bulk sale and the denominator of which is the value of all property securing the debt on the date of the bulk sale; or

(ii) a value of more than $25,000,000 on the date of the bulk-sale agreement; or

(m) a sale required by, and made pursuant to, statute.

(4) The notice under subsection (3)(i)(iv) must state:(i) that a sale that may constitute a bulk sale has been or will be made; (ii) the date or prospective date of the bulk sale; (iii) the individual, partnership, or corporate names and the addresses of the seller and buyer; (iv) the address to which inquiries about the sale may be made, if different from the seller's address; and (v) that the buyer has assumed or will assume in full the debts owed to claimants of whom the buyer has knowledge on the date the buyer receives the list of claimants from the seller or completes a reasonable inquiry to discover the claimants.

(5) The notice under subsections (3)(j)(iii) and (3)(k)(iii) must state: (i) that a sale that may constitute a bulk sale has been or will be made; (ii) the date or prospective date of the bulk sale; (iii) the individual, partnership, or corporate names and the addresses of the seller and buyer; (iv) the address to which inquiries about the sale may be made, if different from the seller's address; and (v) that the buyer has assumed or will assume the debts that were incurred in the seller's business before the date of the bulk sale.

(6) For purposes of subsection (3)(l), the value of assets is presumed to be equal to the price the buyer agrees to pay for the assets. However, in a sale by auction or a sale conducted by a liquidator on the seller's behalf, the value of assets is presumed to be the amount the auctioneer or liquidator reasonably estimates the assets will bring at auction or upon liquidation.

As amended in 1999.

§ 6–104. Obligations of Buyer.

(1) In a bulk sale as defined in Section 6–102(1)(c)(ii) the buyer shall:

(a) obtain from the seller a list of all business names and addresses used by the seller within three years before the date the list is sent or delivered to the buyer;

(b) unless excused under subsection (2), obtain from the seller a verified and dated list of claimants of whom the seller has notice three days before the seller sends or delivers the list to the buyer and including, to the extent known by the seller, the address of and the amount claimed by each claimant;

(c) obtain from the seller or prepare a schedule of distribution (Section 6–106(1));

(d) give notice of the bulk sale in accordance with Section 6–105;

(e) unless excused under Section 6–106(4), distribute the net contract price in accordance with the undertakings of the buyer in the schedule of distribution; and

(f) unless excused under subsection (2), make available the list of claimants (subsection (1)(b)) by:

(i) promptly sending or delivering a copy of the list without charge to any claimant whose written request is received by the buyer no later than six months after the date of the bulk sale;

(ii) permitting any claimant to inspect and copy the list at any reasonable hour upon request received by the buyer no later than six months after the date of the bulk sale; or

(iii) filing a copy of the list in the office of the [Secretary of State] no later than the time for giving a notice of the bulk sale (Section 6–105(5)). A list filed in accordance with this subparagraph must state the individual, partnership, or corporate name and a mailing address of the seller.

(2) A buyer who gives notice in accordance with Section 6–105(2) is excused from complying with the requirements of subsections (1)(b) and (1)(f).

§ 6–105. Notice to Claimants.

(1) Except as otherwise provided in subsection (2), to comply with Section 6–104(1)(d) the buyer shall send or deliver a written notice of the bulk sale to each claimant on the list of claimants (Section 6–104(1)(b)) and to any other claimant of which the buyer has knowledge at the time the notice of the bulk sale is sent or delivered.

(2) A buyer may comply with Section 6–104(1)(d) by filing a written notice of the bulk sale in the office of the [Secretary of State] if:

(a) on the date of the bulk-sale agreement the seller has 200 or more claimants, exclusive of claimants holding secured or matured claims for employment compensation and benefits, including commissions and vacation, severance, and sick-leave pay; or

(b) the buyer has received a verified statement from the seller stating that, as of the date of the bulk-sale agreement, the number of claimants, exclusive of claimants holding secured or matured claims for employment compensation and benefits, including commissions and vacation, severance, and sick-leave pay, is 200 or more.

(3) The written notice of the bulk sale must be accompanied by a copy of the schedule of distribution (Section 6–106(1)) and state at least:

(a) that the seller and buyer have entered into an agreement for a sale that may constitute a bulk sale under the laws of the State of _____ ;

(b) the date of the agreement;

(c) the date on or after which more than ten percent of the assets were or will be transferred;

(d) the date on or after which more than ten percent of the net contract price was or will be paid, if the date is not stated in the schedule of distribution;

(e) the name and a mailing address of the seller;

(f) any other business name and address listed by the seller pursuant to Section 6–104(1)(a);

(g) the name of the buyer and an address of the buyer from which information concerning the sale can be obtained;

(h) a statement indicating the type of assets or describing the assets item by item;

(i) the manner in which the buyer will make available the list of claimants (Section 6–104(1)(f)), if applicable; and

(j) if the sale is in total or partial satisfaction of an antecedent debt owed by the seller, the amount of the debt to be satisfied and the name of the person to whom it is owed.

(4) For purposes of subsections (3)(e) and (3)(g), the name of a person is the person's individual, partnership, or corporate name.

(5) The buyer shall give notice of the bulk sale not less than 45 days before the date of the bulk sale and, if the buyer gives notice in accordance with subsection (1), not more than 30 days after obtaining the list of claimants.

(6) A written notice substantially complying with the requirements of subsection (3) is effective even though it contains minor errors that are not seriously misleading.

(7) A form substantially as follows is sufficient to comply with subsection (3):

Notice of Sale

(1) _____, whose address is _____, is described in this notice as the "seller."

(2) _____, whose address is _____, is described in this notice as the "buyer."

(3) The seller has disclosed to the buyer that within the past three years the seller has used other business names, operated at other addresses, or both, as follows: _____ _____ .

(4) The seller and the buyer have entered into an agreement dated _____, for a sale that may constitute a bulk sale under the laws of the state of _____.

(5) The date on or after which more than ten percent of the assets that are the subject of the sale were or will be transferred is _____, and [if not stated in the schedule of distribution] the date on or after which more than ten percent of the net contract price was or will be paid is _____ .

(6) The following assets are the subject of the sale: _____ .

(7) [If applicable] The buyer will make available to claimants of the seller a list of the seller's claimants in the following manner: _____ .

(8) [If applicable] The sale is to satisfy $ _____ of an antecedent debt owed by the seller to _____ .

(9) A copy of the schedule of distribution of the net contract price accompanies this notice.

[End of Notice]

§ 6–106. Schedule of Distribution.

(1) The seller and buyer shall agree on how the net contract price is to be distributed and set forth their agreement in a written schedule of distribution.

(2) The schedule of distribution may provide for distribution to any person at any time, including distribution of the entire net contract price to the seller.

(3) The buyer's undertakings in the schedule of distribution run only to the seller. However, a buyer who fails to distribute the net contract price in accordance with the buyer's undertakings in the schedule of distribution is liable to a creditor only as provided in Section 6–107(1).

(4) If the buyer undertakes in the schedule of distribution to distribute any part of the net contract price to a person other than the seller, and, after the buyer has given notice in accordance with Section 6–105, some or all of the anticipated net contract price is or becomes unavailable for distribution as a consequence of the buyer's or seller's having complied with an order of court, legal process, statute, or rule of law, the buyer is excused from any obligation arising under this Article or under any contract with the seller to distribute the net contract price in accordance with the buyer's undertakings in the schedule if the buyer:

(a) distributes the net contract price remaining available in accordance with any priorities for payment stated in the schedule of distribution and, to the extent that the price is insufficient to pay all the debts having a given priority, distributes the price pro rata among those debts shown in the schedule as having the same priority;

(b) distributes the net contract price remaining available in accordance with an order of court;

(c) commences a proceeding for interpleader in a court of competent jurisdiction and is discharged from the proceeding; or

(d) reaches a new agreement with the seller for the distribution of the net contract price remaining available, sets forth the new agreement in an amended schedule of distribution, gives notice of the amended schedule, and distributes the net contract price remaining available in accordance with the buyer's undertakings in the amended schedule.

(5) The notice under subsection (4)(d) must identify the buyer and the seller, state the filing number, if any, of the original notice, set forth the amended schedule, and be given in accordance with subsection (1) or (2) of Section 6–105, whichever is applicable, at least 14 days before the buyer distributes any part of the net contract price remaining available.

(6) If the seller undertakes in the schedule of distribution to distribute any part of the net contract price, and, after the buyer has given notice in accordance with Section 6–105, some or all of the anticipated net contract price is or becomes unavailable for distribution as a consequence of the buyer's or seller's having complied with an order of court, legal process, statute, or rule of law, the seller and any person in control of the seller are excused from any obligation arising under this Article or under any agreement with the buyer to distribute the net contract price in accordance with the seller's undertakings in the schedule if the seller:

(a) distributes the net contract price remaining available in accordance with any priorities for payment stated in the schedule of distribution and, to the extent that the price is insufficient to pay all the debts having a given priority, distributes the price pro rata among those debts shown in the schedule as having the same priority;

(b) distributes the net contract price remaining available in accordance with an order of court;

(c) commences a proceeding for interpleader in a court of competent jurisdiction and is discharged from the proceeding; or

(d) prepares a written amended schedule of distribution of the net contract price remaining available for distribution, gives notice of the amended schedule, and distributes the net contract price remaining available in accordance with the amended schedule.

(7) The notice under subsection (6)(d) must identify the buyer and the seller, state the filing number, if any, of the original notice, set forth the amended schedule, and be given in accordance with subsection (1) or (2) of Section 6–105, whichever is applicable, at least 14 days before the seller distributes any part of the net contract price remaining available.

§ 6–107. Liability for Noncompliance.

(1) Except as provided in subsection (3), and subject to the limitation in subsection (4):

(a) a buyer who fails to comply with the requirements of Section 6–104(1)(e) with respect to a creditor is liable to the creditor for damages in the amount of the claim, reduced by any amount that the creditor would not have realized if the buyer had complied; and

(b) a buyer who fails to comply with the requirements of any other subsection of Section 6–104 with respect to a claimant is liable to the claimant for damages in the amount of the claim, reduced by any amount that the claimant would not have realized if the buyer had complied.

(2) In an action under subsection (1), the creditor has the burden of establishing the validity and amount of the claim, and the buyer has the burden of establishing the amount that the creditor would not have realized if the buyer had complied.

(3) A buyer who:

(a) made a good faith and commercially reasonable effort to comply with the requirements of Section 6–104(1) or to exclude the sale from the application of this Article under Section 6–103(3); or

(b) on or after the date of the bulk-sale agreement, but before the date of the bulk sale, held a good faith and commercially reasonable belief that this Article does not apply to the particular sale is not liable to creditors for failure to comply with the requirements of Section 6–104. The buyer has the burden of establishing the good faith and commercial reasonableness of the effort or belief.

(4) In a single bulk sale the cumulative liability of the buyer for failure to comply with the requirements of Section 6–104(1) may not exceed an amount equal to:

(a) if the assets consist only of inventory and equipment, twice the net contract price, less the amount of any part of the net contract price paid to or applied for the benefit of the seller or a creditor; or

(b) if the assets include property other than inventory and equipment, twice the net value of the inventory and equipment less the amount of the portion of any part of the net contract price paid to or applied for the benefit of the seller or a creditor which is allocable to the inventory and equipment.

(5) For the purposes of subsection (4)(b), the "net value" of an asset is the value of the asset less (i) the amount of any proceeds of the sale of an asset, to the extent the proceeds are applied in partial or total satisfaction of a debt secured by the asset and (ii) the amount of any debt to the extent it is secured by a security interest or lien that is enforceable against the asset before and after it has been sold to a buyer. If a debt is secured by an asset and other property of the seller, the amount of the debt secured by a security interest or lien that is enforceable against the asset is determined by multiplying the debt by a fraction, the numerator of which is the value of the asset on the date of the bulk sale and the denominator of which is the value of all property securing the debt on the date of the bulk sale. The portion of a part of the net contract price paid to or applied for the benefit of the seller or a creditor that is "allocable to the inventory and equipment" is the portion that bears the same ratio to that part of the net contract price as the net value of the inventory and equipment bears to the net value of all of the assets.

(6) A payment made by the buyer to a person to whom the buyer is, or believes he [or she] is, liable under subsection (1) reduces pro tanto the buyer's cumulative liability under subsection (4).

(7) No action may be brought under subsection (1)(b) by or on behalf of a claimant whose claim is unliquidated or contingent.

(8) A buyer's failure to comply with the requirements of Section 6–104(1) does not (i) impair the buyer's rights in or title to the assets, (ii) render the sale ineffective, void, or voidable, (iii) entitle a creditor to more than a single satisfaction of his [or her] claim, or (iv) create liability other than as provided in this Article.

(9) Payment of the buyer's liability under subsection (1) discharges pro tanto the seller's debt to the creditor.

(10) Unless otherwise agreed, a buyer has an immediate right of reimbursement from the seller for any amount paid to a creditor in partial or total satisfaction of the buyer's liability under subsection (1).

(11) If the seller is an organization, a person who is in direct or indirect control of the seller, and who knowingly, intentionally, and without legal justification fails, or causes the seller to fail, to distribute the net contract price in accordance with the schedule of distribution is liable to any creditor to whom the seller undertook to make payment under the schedule for damages caused by the failure.

§ 6–108. Bulk Sales by Auction; Bulk Sales Conducted by Liquidator.

(1) Sections 6–104, 6–105, 6–106, and 6–107 apply to a bulk sale by auction and a bulk sale conducted by a liquidator on the seller's behalf with the following modifications:

(a) "buyer" refers to auctioneer or liquidator, as the case may be;

(b) "net contract price" refers to net proceeds of the auction or net proceeds of the sale, as the case may be;

(c) the written notice required under Section 6–105(3) must be accompanied by a copy of the schedule of distribution (Section 6–106(1)) and state at least:

(i) that the seller and the auctioneer or liquidator have entered into an agreement for auction or liquidation services that may constitute an agreement to make a bulk sale under the laws of the State of _____ ;

(ii) the date of the agreement;

(iii) the date on or after which the auction began or will begin or the date on or after which the liquidator began or will begin to sell assets on the seller's behalf;

(iv) the date on or after which more than ten percent of the net proceeds of the sale were or will be paid, if the date is not stated in the schedule of distribution;

(v) the name and a mailing address of the seller;

(vi) any other business name and address listed by the seller pursuant to Section 6–104(1)(a);

(vii) the name of the auctioneer or liquidator and an address of the auctioneer or liquidator from which information concerning the sale can be obtained;

(viii) a statement indicating the type of assets or describing the assets item by item;

(ix) the manner in which the auctioneer or liquidator will make available the list of claimants (Section 6–104(1)(f)), if applicable; and

(x) if the sale is in total or partial satisfaction of an antecedent debt owed by the seller, the amount of the debt to be satisfied and the name of the person to whom it is owed; and

(d) in a single bulk sale the cumulative liability of the auctioneer or liquidator for failure to comply with the requirements of this section may not exceed the amount of the net proceeds of the sale allocable to inventory and equipment sold less the amount of the portion of any part of the net proceeds paid to or applied for the benefit of a creditor which is allocable to the inventory and equipment.

(2) A payment made by the auctioneer or liquidator to a person to whom the auctioneer or liquidator is, or believes he [or she] is, liable under this section reduces pro tanto the auctioneer's or liquidator's cumulative liability under subsection (1)(d).

(3) A form substantially as follows is sufficient to comply with subsection (1)(c):

Notice of Sale

(1) _____, whose address is _____, is described in this notice as the "seller."

(2) _____, whose address is _____ , is described in this notice as the "auctioneer" or "liquidator."

(3) The seller has disclosed to the auctioneer or liquidator that within the past three years the seller has used other business names, operated at other addresses, or both, as follows: _____ .

(4) The seller and the auctioneer or liquidator have entered into an agreement dated _____ for auction or liquidation services that may constitute an agreement to make a bulk sale under the laws of the State of _____ .

(5) The date on or after which the auction began or will begin or the date on or after which the liquidator began or will begin to sell assets on the seller's behalf is _____, and [if not stated in the schedule of distribution] the date on or after which more than ten percent of the net proceeds of the sale were or will be paid is _____ .

(6) The following assets are the subject of the sale: _____ .

(7) [If applicable] The auctioneer or liquidator will make available to claimants of the seller a list of the seller's claimants in the following manner: _____ .

(8) [If applicable] The sale is to satisfy $ _____ of an antecedent debt owed by the seller to _____ .

(9) A copy of the schedule of distribution of the net proceeds accompanies this notice.

[End of Notice]

(4) A person who buys at a bulk sale by auction or conducted by a liquidator need not comply with the requirements of Section 6–104(1) and is not liable for the failure of an auctioneer or liquidator to comply with the requirements of this section.

§ 6–109. What Constitutes Filing; Duties of Filing Officer; Information from Filing Officer.

(1) Presentation of a notice or list of claimants for filing and tender of the filing fee or acceptance of the notice or list by the filing officer constitutes filing under this Article.

(2) The filing officer shall:

(a) mark each notice or list with a file number and with the date and hour of filing;

(b) hold the notice or list or a copy for public inspection;

(c) index the notice or list according to each name given for the seller and for the buyer; and

(d) note in the index the file number and the addresses of the seller and buyer given in the notice or list.

(3) If the person filing a notice or list furnishes the filing officer with a copy, the filing officer upon request shall note upon the copy the file number and date and hour of the filing of the original and send or deliver the copy to the person.

(4) The fee for filing and indexing and for stamping a copy furnished by the person filing to show the date and place of filing is $ _____ for the first page and $ _____ for each additional page. The fee for indexing each name beyond the first two is $ _____ .

(5) Upon request of any person, the filing officer shall issue a certificate showing whether any notice or list with respect to a particular seller or buyer is on file on the date and hour stated in the certificate. If a notice or list is on file, the certificate must give the date and hour of filing of each notice or list and the name and address of each seller, buyer, auctioneer, or liquidator. The fee for the certificate is $ _____ if the request for the certificate is in the standard form prescribed by the [Secretary of State] and otherwise is $ _____ . Upon request of any person, the filing officer shall furnish a copy of any filed notice or list for a fee of $ _____ .

(6) The filing officer shall keep each notice or list for two years after it is filed.

§ 6–110. Limitation of Actions.

(1) Except as provided in subsection (2), an action under this Article against a buyer, auctioneer, or liquidator must be commenced within one year after the date of the bulk sale.

(2) If the buyer, auctioneer, or liquidator conceals the fact that the sale has occurred, the limitation is tolled and an action under this Article may be commenced within the earlier of (i) one year after the person bringing the action discovers that the sale has occurred or (ii) one year after the person bringing the action should have discovered that the sale has occurred, but no later than two years after the date of the bulk sale. Complete noncompliance with the requirements of this Article does not of itself constitute concealment.

(3) An action under Section 6–107(11) must be commenced within one year after the alleged violation occurs.

Conforming Amendment to Section 2–403

States adopting Alternative B should amend Section 2–403(4) of the Uniform Commercial Code to read as follows:

(4) The rights of other purchasers of goods and of lien creditors are governed by the Articles on Secured Transactions (Article 9), Bulk Sales (Article 6) and Documents of Title (Article 7).

ARTICLE 7: WAREHOUSE RECEIPTS, BILLS OF LADING AND OTHER DOCUMENTS OF TITLE

Part 1—General

§ 7–101. Short Title.

This Article shall be known and may be cited as Uniform Commercial Code–Documents of Title.

§ 7–102. Definitions and Index of Definitions.

(1) In this Article, unless the context otherwise requires:

(a) "Bailee" means the person who by a warehouse receipt, bill of lading or other document of title acknowledges possession of goods and contracts to deliver them.

(b) "Consignee" means the person named in a bill to whom or to whose order the bill promises delivery.

(c) "Consignor" means the person named in a bill as the person from whom the goods have been received for shipment.

(d) "Delivery order" means a written order to deliver goods directed to a warehouseman, carrier or other person who in the ordinary course of business issues warehouse receipts or bills of lading.

(e) "Document" means document of title as defined in the general definitions in Article 1 (Section 1–201).

(f) "Goods" means all things which are treated as movable for the purposes of a contract of storage or transportation.

(g) "Issuer" means a bailee who issues a document except that in relation to an unaccepted delivery order it means the person who orders the possessor of goods to deliver. Issuer includes any person for whom an agent or employee purports to act in issuing a document if the agent or employee has real or apparent authority to issue documents, notwithstanding that the issuer received no goods or that the goods were misdescribed or that in any other respect the agent or employee violated his instructions.

(h) "Warehouseman" is a person engaged in the business of storing goods for hire.

(2) Other definitions applying to this Article or to specified Parts thereof, and the sections in which they appear are:

"Duly negotiate". Section 7–501.

"Person entitled under the document". Section 7–403(4).

(3) Definitions in other Articles applying to this Article and the sections in which they appear are:

"Contract for sale". Section 2–106.

"Overseas". Section 2–323.

"Receipt" of goods. Section 2–103.

(4) In addition Article 1 contains general definitions and principles of construction and interpretation applicable throughout this Article.

§ 7–103. Relation of Article to Treaty, Statute, Tariff, Classification or Regulation.

To the extent that any treaty or statute of the United States, regulatory statute of this State or tariff, classification or regulation filed or issued pursuant thereto is applicable, the provisions of this Article are subject thereto.

§ 7–104. Negotiable and Non-Negotiable Warehouse Receipt, Bill of Lading or Other Document of Title.

(1) A warehouse receipt, bill of lading or other document of title is negotiable

    (a) if by its terms the goods are to be delivered to bearer or to the order of a named person; or

    (b) where recognized in overseas trade, if it runs to a named person or assigns.

(2) Any other document is nonnegotiable. A bill of lading in which it is stated that the goods are consigned to a named person is not made negotiable by a provision that the goods are to be delivered only against a written order signed by the same or another named person.

§ 7–105. Construction Against Negative Implication.

The omission from either Part 2 or Part 3 of this Article of a provision corresponding to a provision made in the other Part does not imply that a corresponding rule of law is not applicable.

Part 2—Warehouse Receipts: Special Provisions

§ 7–201. Who May Issue a Warehouse Receipt; Storage Under Government Bond.

(1) A warehouse receipt may be issued by any warehouseman.

(2) Where goods including distilled spirits and agricultural commodities are stored under a statute requiring a bond against withdrawal or a license for the issuance of receipts in the nature of warehouse receipts, a receipt issued for the goods has like effect as a warehouse receipt even though issued by a person who is the owner of the goods and is not a warehouseman.

§ 7–202. Form of Warehouse Receipt; Essential Terms; Optional Terms.

(1) A warehouse receipt need not be in any particular form.

(2) Unless a warehouse receipt embodies within its written or printed terms each of the following, the warehouseman is liable for damages caused by the omission to a person injured thereby:

    (a) the location of the warehouse where the goods are stored;

    (b) the date of issue of the receipt;

    (c) the consecutive number of the receipt;

    (d) a statement whether the goods received will be delivered to the bearer, to a specified person, or to a specified person or his order;

    (e) the rate of storage and handling charges, except that where goods are stored under a field warehousing arrangement a statement of that fact is sufficient on a non-negotiable receipt;

    (f) a description of the goods or of the packages containing them;

    (g) the signature of the warehouseman, which may be made by his authorized agent;

    (h) if the receipt is issued for goods of which the warehouseman is owner, either solely or jointly or in common with others, the fact of such ownership; and

    (i) a statement of the amount of advances made and of liabilities incurred for which the warehouseman claims a lien or security interest (Section 7–209). If the precise amount of such advances made or of such liabilities incurred is, at the time of the issue of the receipt, unknown to the warehouseman or to his agent who issues it, a statement of the fact that advances have been made or liabilities incurred and the purpose thereof is sufficient.

(3) A warehouseman may insert in his receipt any other terms which are not contrary to the provisions of this Act and do not impair his obligation of delivery (Section 7–403) or his duty of care (Section 7–204). Any contrary provisions shall be ineffective.

§ 7–203. Liability for Non-Receipt or Misdescription.

A party to or purchaser for value in good faith of a document of title other than a bill of lading relying in either case upon the description therein of the goods may recover from the issuer damages caused by the nonreceipt or misdescription of the goods, except to the extent that the document conspicuously indicates that the issuer does not know whether any part or all of the goods in fact were received or conform to the description, as where the description is in terms of marks or labels or kind, quantity or condition, or the receipt or description is qualified by "contents, condition and quality unknown", "said to contain" or the like, if such indication be true, or the party or purchaser otherwise has notice.

§ 7–204. Duty of Care; Contractual Limitation of Warehouseman's Liability.

(1) A warehouseman is liable for damages for loss of or injury to the goods caused by his failure to exercise such care in regard to them as a reasonably careful man would exercise under like circumstances but unless otherwise agreed he is not liable for damages which could not have been avoided by the exercise of such care.

(2) Damages may be limited by a term in the warehouse receipt or storage agreement limiting the amount of liability in case of loss or damage, and setting forth a specific liability per article or item, or value per unit of weight, beyond which the warehouseman shall not be liable; provided, however, that such liability may on written request of the bailor at the time of signing such storage agreement or within a reasonable time after receipt of the warehouse receipt be increased on part or all of the goods thereunder, in which event increased rates may be charged based on such increased valuation, but that no such increase shall be permitted contrary to a lawful limitation of liability contained in the warehouseman's tariff, if any. No such limitation is effective with respect to the warehouseman's liability for conversion to his own use.

(3) Reasonable provisions as to the time and manner of presenting claims and instituting actions based on the bailment may be included in the warehouse receipt or tariff.

(4) This section does not impair or repeal . . .

Note: *Insert in subsection (4) a reference to any statute which imposes a higher responsibility upon the warehouseman or invalidates contractual limitations which would be permissible under this Article.*

§ 7–205. Title Under Warehouse Receipt Defeated in Certain Cases.

A buyer in the ordinary course of business of fungible goods sold and delivered by a warehouseman who is also in the business of buying and selling such goods takes free of any claim under a warehouse receipt even though it has been duly negotiated.

§ 7–206. Termination of Storage at Warehouseman's Option.

(1) A warehouseman may on notifying the person on whose account the goods are held and any other person known to claim an interest in the goods require payment of any charges and removal of the goods from the warehouse at the termination of the period of storage fixed by the document, or, if no period is fixed, within a stated period not less than thirty days after the notification. If the goods are not removed before the date specified in the notification, the warehouseman may sell them in accordance with the provisions of the section on enforcement of a warehouseman's lien (Section 7–210).

(2) If a warehouseman in good faith believes that the goods are about to deteriorate or decline in value to less than the amount of his lien within the time prescribed in subsection (1) for notification, advertisement and sale, the warehouseman may specify in the notification any reasonable shorter time for removal of the goods and in case the goods are not removed, may sell them at public sale held not less than one week after a single advertisement or posting.

(3) If as a result of a quality or condition of the goods of which the warehouseman had no notice at the time of deposit the goods are a hazard to other property or to the warehouse or to persons, the warehouseman may sell the goods at public or private sale without advertisement on reasonable notification to all persons known to claim an interest in the goods. If the warehouseman after a reasonable effort is unable to sell the goods he may dispose of them in any lawful manner and shall incur no liability by reason of such disposition.

(4) The warehouseman must deliver the goods to any person entitled to them under this Article upon due demand made at any time prior to sale or other disposition under this section.

(5) The warehouseman may satisfy his lien from the proceeds of any sale or disposition under this section but must hold the balance for delivery on the demand of any person to whom he would have been bound to deliver the goods.

§ 7–207. Goods Must Be Kept Separate; Fungible Goods.

(1) Unless the warehouse receipt otherwise provides, a warehouseman must keep separate the goods covered by each receipt so as to permit at all times identification and delivery of those goods except that different lots of fungible goods may be commingled.

(2) Fungible goods so commingled are owned in common by the persons entitled thereto and the warehouseman is severally liable to each owner for that owner's share. Where because of overissue a mass of fungible goods is insufficient to meet all the receipts which the warehouseman has issued against it, the persons entitled include all holders to whom overissued receipts have been duly negotiated.

§ 7–208. Altered Warehouse Receipts.

Where a blank in a negotiable warehouse receipt has been filled in without authority, a purchaser for value and without notice of the want of authority may treat the insertion as authorized. Any other unauthorized alteration leaves any receipt enforceable against the issuer according to its original tenor.

§ 7–209. Lien of Warehouseman.

(1) A warehouseman has a lien against the bailor on the goods covered by a warehouse receipt or on the proceeds thereof in his possession for charges for storage or transportation (including demurrage and terminal charges), insurance, labor, or charges present or future in relation to the goods, and for expenses necessary for preservation of the goods or reasonably incurred in their sale pursuant to law. If the person on whose account the goods are held is liable for like charges or expenses in relation to other goods whenever deposited and it is stated in the receipt that a lien is claimed for charges and expenses in relation to other goods, the warehouseman also has a lien against him for such charges and expenses whether or not the other goods have been delivered by the warehouseman. But against a person to whom a negotiable warehouse receipt is duly negotiated a warehouseman's lien is limited to charges in an amount or at a rate specified on the receipt or if no charges are so specified then to a reasonable charge for storage of the goods covered by the receipt subsequent to the date of the receipt.

(2) The warehouseman may also reserve a security interest against the bailor for a maximum amount specified on the receipt for charges other than those specified in subsection (1), such as for money advanced and interest. Such a security interest is governed by the Article on Secured Transactions (Article 9).

(3)(a) A warehouseman's lien for charges and expenses under subsection (1) or a security interest under subsection (2) is also effective against any person who so entrusted the bailor with possession of the goods that a pledge of them by him to a good faith purchaser for value would have been valid but is not effective against a person as to whom the document confers no right in the goods covered by it under Section 7–503.

(b) A warehouseman's lien on household goods for charges and expenses in relation to the goods under subsection (1) is also effective against all persons if the depositor was the legal possessor of the goods at the time of deposit. "Household goods" means furniture, furnishings and personal effects used by the depositor in a dwelling.

(4) A warehouseman loses his lien on any goods which he voluntarily delivers or which he unjustifiably refuses to deliver.

§ 7–210. Enforcement of Warehouseman's Lien.

(1) Except as provided in subsection (2), a warehouseman's lien may be enforced by public or private sale of the goods in bloc or in parcels, at any time or place and on any terms which are commercially reasonable, after notifying all persons known to claim an interest in the goods. Such notification must include a statement of the amount due, the nature of the proposed sale and the time and place of any public sale. The fact that a better price could have been obtained by a sale at a different time or in a different method from that selected by the warehouseman is not of itself sufficient to establish that the sale was not made in a commercially reasonable manner. If the warehouseman either sells the goods in the usual manner in any recognized market therefor, or if he sells at the price current in such market at the time of his sale, or if he has otherwise sold in conformity with commercially reasonable practices among dealers in the type of goods sold, he has sold in a commercially reasonable manner. A sale of more goods than apparently necessary to be offered to ensure satisfaction of the obligation is not commercially reasonable except in cases covered by the preceding sentence.

(2) A warehouseman's lien on goods other than goods stored by a merchant in the course of his business may be enforced only as follows:

(a) All persons known to claim an interest in the goods must be notified.

(b) The notification must be delivered in person or sent by registered or certified letter to the last known address of any person to be notified.

(c) The notification must include an itemized statement of the claim, a description of the goods subject to the lien, a demand for payment within a specified time not less than ten days after receipt of the notification, and a conspicuous statement that unless the claim is paid within the time the goods will be advertised for sale and sold by auction at a specified time and place.

(d) The sale must conform to the terms of the notification.

(e) The sale must be held at the nearest suitable place to that where the goods are held or stored.

(f) After the expiration of the time given in the notification, an advertisement of the sale must be published once a week for two weeks consecutively in a newspaper of general circulation where the sale is to be held. The advertisement must include a description of the goods, the name of the person on whose account they are being held, and the time and place of the sale. The sale must take place at least fifteen days after the first publication. If there is no newspaper of general circulation where the sale is to be held, the advertisement must be posted at least ten days before the sale in not less than six conspicuous places in the neighborhood of the proposed sale.

(3) Before any sale pursuant to this section any person claiming a right in the goods may pay the amount necessary to satisfy the lien and the reasonable expenses incurred under this section. In that event the goods must not be sold, but must be retained by the warehouseman subject to the terms of the receipt and this Article.

(4) The warehouseman may buy at any public sale pursuant to this section.

(5) A purchaser in good faith of goods sold to enforce a warehouseman's lien takes the goods free of any rights of persons against whom the lien was valid, despite noncompliance by the warehouseman with the requirements of this section.

(6) The warehouseman may satisfy his lien from the proceeds of any sale pursuant to this section but must hold the balance, if any, for delivery on demand to any person to whom he would have been bound to deliver the goods.

(7) The rights provided by this section shall be in addition to all other rights allowed by law to a creditor against his debtor.

(8) Where a lien is on goods stored by a merchant in the course of his business the lien may be enforced in accordance with either subsection (1) or (2).

(9) The warehouseman is liable for damages caused by failure to comply with the requirements for sale under this section and in case of willful violation is liable for conversion.
As amended in 1962.

Part 3—Bills of Lading: Special Provisions

§ 7–301. Liability for Non-Receipt or Misdescription; "Said to Contain"; "Shipper's Load and Count"; Improper Handling.

(1) A consignee of a non-negotiable bill who has given value in good faith or a holder to whom a negotiable bill has been duly negotiated relying in either case upon the description therein of the goods, or upon the date therein shown, may recover from the issuer damages caused by the misdating of the bill or the nonreceipt or misdescription of the goods, except to the extent that the document indicates that the issuer does not know whether any part of all of the goods in fact were received or conform to the description, as where the description is in terms of marks or labels or kind, quantity, or condition or the receipt or description is qualified by "contents or condition of contents of packages unknown", "said to contain", "shipper's weight, load and count" or the like, if such indication be true.

(2) When goods are loaded by an issuer who is a common carrier, the issuer must count the packages of goods if package freight and ascertain the kind and quantity if bulk freight. In such cases "shipper's weight, load and count" or other words indicating that the description was made by the shipper are ineffective except as to freight concealed by packages.

(3) When bulk freight is loaded by a shipper who makes available to the issuer adequate facilities for weighing such freight, an issuer who is a common carrier must ascertain the kind and quantity within a reasonable time after receiving the written request of the shipper to do so. In such cases "shipper's weight" or other words of like purport are ineffective.

(4) The issuer may by inserting in the bill the words "shipper's weight, load and count" or other words of like purport indicate that the goods were loaded by the shipper; and if such statement be true the issuer shall not be liable for damages caused by the improper loading. But their omission does not imply liability for such damages.

(5) The shipper shall be deemed to have guaranteed to the issuer the accuracy at the time of shipment of the description, marks, labels, number, kind, quantity, condition and weight, as furnished by him; and the shipper shall indemnify the issuer against damage caused by inaccuracies in such particulars. The right of the issuer to such indemnity shall in no way limit his responsibility and liability under the contract of carriage to any person other than the shipper.

§ 7–302. Through Bills of Lading and Similar Documents.

(1) The issuer of a through bill of lading or other document embodying an undertaking to be performed in part by persons acting as its agents or by connecting carriers is liable to anyone entitled to recover on the document for any breach by such other persons or by a connecting carrier of its obligation under the document but to the extent that the bill covers an undertaking to be performed overseas or in territory not contiguous to the continental United States or an undertaking including matters other than transportation this liability may be varied by agreement of the parties.

(2) Where goods covered by a through bill of lading or other document embodying an undertaking to be performed in part by persons other than the issuer are received by any such person, he is subject with respect to his own performance while the goods are in his possession to the obligation of the issuer. His obligation is discharged by delivery of the goods to another such person pursuant to the document, and does not include liability for breach by any other such persons or by the issuer.

(3) The issuer of such through bill of lading or other document shall be entitled to recover from the connecting carrier or such other person in possession of the goods when the breach of the obligation under the document occurred, the amount it may be required to pay to anyone entitled to recover on the document therefor, as may be evidenced by any receipt, judgment, or transcript thereof, and the amount of any expense reasonably incurred by it in defending any action brought by anyone entitled to recover on the document therefor.

§ 7–303. Diversion; Reconsignment; Change of Instructions.

(1) Unless the bill of lading otherwise provides, the carrier may deliver the goods to a person or destination other than that stated in the bill or may otherwise dispose of the goods on instructions from

    (a) the holder of a negotiable bill; or

    (b) the consignor on a non-negotiable bill not-withstanding contrary instructions from the consignee; or

    (c) the consignee on a non-negotiable bill in the absence of contrary instructions from the consignor, if the goods have arrived at the billed destination or if the consignee is in possession of the bill; or

    (d) the consignee on a non-negotiable bill if he is entitled as against the consignor to dispose of them.

(2) Unless such instructions are noted on a negotiable bill of lading, a person to whom the bill is duly negotiated can hold the bailee according to the original terms.

§ 7–304. Bills of Lading in a Set.

(1) Except where customary in overseas transportation, a bill of lading must not be issued in a set of parts. The issuer is liable for damages caused by violation of this subsection.

(2) Where a bill of lading is lawfully drawn in a set of parts, each of which is numbered and expressed to be valid only if the goods have not been delivered against any other part, the whole of the parts constitute one bill.

(3) Where a bill of lading is lawfully issued in a set of parts and different parts are negotiated to different persons, the title of the holder to whom the first due negotiation is made prevails as to both the document and the goods even though any later holder may have received the goods from the carrier in good faith and discharged the carrier's obligation by surrender of his part.

(4) Any person who negotiates or transfers a single part of a bill of lading drawn in a set is liable to holders of that part as if it were the whole set.

(5) The bailee is obliged to deliver in accordance with Part 4 of this Article against the first presented part of a bill of lading lawfully drawn in a set. Such delivery discharges the bailee's obligation on the whole bill.

§ 7–305. Destination Bills.

(1) Instead of issuing a bill of lading to the consignor at the place of shipment a carrier may at the request of the consignor procure the bill to be issued at destination or at any other place designated in the request.

(2) Upon request of anyone entitled as against the carrier to control the goods while in transit and on surrender of any outstanding bill of lading or other receipt covering such goods, the issuer may procure a substitute bill to be issued at any place designated in the request.

§ 7–306. Altered Bills of Lading.

An unauthorized alteration or filling in of a blank in a bill of lading leaves the bill enforceable according to its original tenor.

§ 7–307. Lien of Carrier.

(1) A carrier has a lien on the goods covered by a bill of lading for charges subsequent to the date of its receipt of the goods for storage or transportation (including demurrage and terminal charges) and for expenses necessary for preservation of the goods incident to their transportation or reasonably incurred in their sale pursuant to law. But against a purchaser for value of a negotiable bill of lading a carrier's lien is limited to charges stated in the bill or the applicable tariffs, or if no charges are stated then to a reasonable charge.

(2) A lien for charges and expenses under subsection (1) on goods which the carrier was required by law to receive for transportation is effective against the consignor or any person entitled to the goods unless the carrier had notice that the consignor lacked authority to subject the goods to such charges and expenses. Any other lien under subsection (1) is effective against the consignor and any person who permitted the bailor to have control or possession of the goods unless the carrier had notice that the bailor lacked such authority.

(3) A carrier loses his lien on any goods which he voluntarily delivers or which he unjustifiably refuses to deliver.

§ 7–308. Enforcement of Carrier's Lien.

(1) A carrier's lien may be enforced by public or private sale of the goods, in bloc or in parcels, at any time or place and on any terms which are commercially reasonable, after notifying all persons known to claim an interest in the goods. Such notification must include a statement of the amount due, the nature of the proposed sale and the time and place of any public sale. The fact that a better price could have been obtained by a sale at a different time or in a different method from that selected by the carrier is not of itself sufficient to establish that the sale was not made in a commercially reasonable manner. If the carrier either sells the goods in the usual manner in any recognized market therefor or if he sells at the price current in such market at the time of his sale or if he has otherwise sold in conformity with commercially reasonable practices among dealers in the type of goods sold he has sold in a commercially reasonable manner. A sale of more goods than apparently necessary to be offered to ensure satisfaction of the obligation is not commercially reasonable except in cases covered by the preceding sentence.

(2) Before any sale pursuant to this section any person claiming a right in the goods may pay the amount necessary to satisfy the lien and the reasonable expenses incurred under this section. In that event the goods must not be sold, but must be retained by the carrier subject to the terms of the bill and this Article.

(3) The carrier may buy at any public sale pursuant to this section.

(4) A purchaser in good faith of goods sold to enforce a carrier's lien takes the goods free of any rights of persons against whom the lien was valid, despite noncompliance by the carrier with the requirements of this section.

(5) The carrier may satisfy his lien from the proceeds of any sale pursuant to this section but must hold the balance, if any, for delivery on demand to any person to whom he would have been bound to deliver the goods.

(6) The rights provided by this section shall be in addition to all other rights allowed by law to a creditor against his debtor.

(7) A carrier's lien may be enforced in accordance with either subsection (1) or the procedure set forth in subsection (2) of Section 7–210.

(8) The carrier is liable for damages caused by failure to comply with the requirements for sale under this section and in case of willful violation is liable for conversion.

§ 7–309. Duty of Care; Contractual Limitation of Carrier's Liability.

(1) A carrier who issues a bill of lading whether negotiable or non-negotiable must exercise the degree of care in relation to the goods which a reasonably careful man would exercise under like circumstances. This subsection does not repeal or change any law or rule of law which imposes liability upon a common carrier for damages not caused by its negligence.

(2) Damages may be limited by a provision that the carrier's liability shall not exceed a value stated in the document if the carrier's rates are dependent upon value and the consignor by the carrier's tariff is afforded an opportunity to declare a higher value or a value as lawfully provided in the tariff, or where no tariff is filed he is otherwise advised of such opportunity; but no such limitation is effective with respect to the carrier's liability for conversion to its own use.

(3) Reasonable provisions as to the time and manner of presenting claims and instituting actions based on the shipment may be included in a bill of lading or tariff.

Part 4—Warehouse Receipts and Bills of Lading: General Obligations

§ 7–401. Irregularities in Issue of Receipt or Bill or Conduct of Issuer.

The obligations imposed by this Article on an issuer apply to a document of title regardless of the fact that

(a) the document may not comply with the requirements of this Article or of any other law or regulation regarding its issue, form or content; or

(b) the issuer may have violated laws regulating the conduct of his business; or

(c) the goods covered by the document were owned by the bailee at the time the document was issued; or

(d) the person issuing the document does not come within the definition of warehouseman if it purports to be a warehouse receipt.

§ 7–402. Duplicate Receipt or Bill; Overissue.

Neither a duplicate nor any other document of title purporting to cover goods already represented by an outstanding document of the same issuer confers any right in the goods, except as provided in the case of bills in a set, overissue of documents for fungible goods and substitutes for lost, stolen or destroyed documents. But the issuer is liable for damages caused by his overissue or failure to identify a duplicate document as such by conspicuous notation on its face.

§ 7–403. Obligation of Warehouseman or Carrier to Deliver; Excuse.

(1) The bailee must deliver the goods to a person entitled under the document who complies with subsections (2) and (3), unless and to the extent that the bailee establishes any of the following:

(a) delivery of the goods to a person whose receipt was rightful as against the claimant;

(b) damage to or delay, loss or destruction of the goods for which the bailee is not liable [, but the burden of establishing negligence in such cases is on the person entitled under the document];

Note: *The brackets in (1)(b) indicate that State enactments may differ on this point without serious damage to the principle of uniformity.*

(c) previous sale or other disposition of the goods in lawful enforcement of a lien or on warehouseman's lawful termination of storage;

(d) the exercise by a seller of his right to stop delivery pursuant to the provisions of the Article on Sales (Section 2–705);

(e) a diversion, reconsignment or other disposition pursuant to the provisions of this Article (Section 7–303) or tariff regulating such right;

(f) release, satisfaction or any other fact affording a personal defense against the claimant;

(g) any other lawful excuse.

(2) A person claiming goods covered by a document of title must satisfy the bailee's lien where the bailee so requests or where the bailee is prohibited by law from delivering the goods until the charges are paid.

(3) Unless the person claiming is one against whom the document confers no right under Sec. 7–503(1), he must surrender for cancellation or notation of partial deliveries any outstanding negotiable document covering the goods, and the bailee must cancel the document or conspicuously note the partial delivery thereon or be liable to any person to whom the document is duly negotiated.

(4) "Person entitled under the document" means holder in the case of a negotiable document, or the person to whom delivery is to be made by the terms of or pursuant to written instructions under a non-negotiable document.

§ 7–404. No Liability for Good Faith Delivery Pursuant to Receipt or Bill.

A bailee who in good faith including observance of reasonable commercial standards has received goods and delivered or otherwise disposed of them according to the terms of the document of title or pursuant to this Article is not liable therefor. This rule applies even though the person from whom he received the goods had no authority to procure the document or to dispose of the goods and even though the person to whom he delivered the goods had no authority to receive them.

Part 5—Warehouse Receipts and Bills of Lading: Negotiation and Transfer

§ 7–501. Form of Negotiation and Requirements of "Due Negotiation".

(1) A negotiable document of title running to the order of a named person is negotiated by his indorsement and delivery. After his indorsement in blank or to bearer any person can negotiate it by delivery alone.

(2) **(a)** A negotiable document of title is also negotiated by delivery alone when by its original terms it runs to bearer.

(b) When a document running to the order of a named person is delivered to him the effect is the same as if the document had been negotiated.

(3) Negotiation of a negotiable document of title after it has been indorsed to a specified person requires indorsement by the special indorsee as well as delivery.

(4) A negotiable document of title is "duly negotiated" when it is negotiated in the manner stated in this section to a holder who purchases it in good faith without notice of any defense against or claim to it on the part of any person and for value, unless it is established that the negotiation is not in the regular course of business or financing or involves receiving the document in settlement or payment of a money obligation.

(5) Indorsement of a nonnegotiable document neither makes it negotiable nor adds to the transferee's rights.

(6) The naming in a negotiable bill of a person to be notified of the arrival of the goods does not limit the negotiability of the bill nor constitute notice to a purchaser thereof of any interest of such person in the goods.

§ 7–502. Rights Acquired by Due Negotiation.

(1) Subject to the following section and to the provisions of Section 7–205 on fungible goods, a holder to whom a negotiable document of title has been duly negotiated acquires thereby:

    (a) title to the document;

    (b) title to the goods;

    (c) all rights accruing under the law of agency or estoppel, including rights to goods delivered to the bailee after the document was issued; and

    (d) the direct obligation of the issuer to hold or deliver the goods according to the terms of the document free of any defense or claim by him except those arising under the terms of the document or under this Article. In the case of a delivery order the bailee's obligation accrues only upon acceptance and the obligation acquired by the holder is that the issuer and any indorser will procure the acceptance of the bailee.

(2) Subject to the following section, title and rights so acquired are not defeated by any stoppage of the goods represented by the document or by surrender of such goods by the bailee, and are not impaired even though the negotiation or any prior negotiation constituted a breach of duty or even though any person has been deprived of possession of the document by misrepresentation, fraud, accident, mistake, duress, loss, theft or conversion, or even though a previous sale or other transfer of the goods or document has been made to a third person.

§ 7–503. Document of Title to Goods Defeated in Certain Cases.

(1) A document of title confers no right in goods against a person who before issuance of the document had a legal interest or a perfected security interest in them and who neither

    (a) delivered or entrusted them or any document of title covering them to the bailor or his nominee with actual or apparent authority to ship, store or sell or with power to obtain delivery under this Article (Section 7–403) or with power of disposition under this Act (Sections 2–403 and 9–307) or other statute or rule of law; nor

    (b) acquiesced in the procurement by the bailor or his nominee of any document of title.

(2) Title to goods based upon an unaccepted delivery order is subject to the rights of anyone to whom a negotiable warehouse receipt or bill of lading covering the goods has been duly negotiated. Such a title may be defeated under the next section to the same extent as the rights of the issuer or a transferee from the issuer.

(3) Title to goods based upon a bill of lading issued to a freight forwarder is subject to the rights of anyone to whom a bill issued by the freight forwarder is duly negotiated; but delivery by the carrier in accordance with Part 4 of this Article pursuant to its own bill of lading discharges the carrier's obligation to deliver.

As amended in 1999.

§ 7–504. Rights Acquired in the Absence of Due Negotiation; Effect of Diversion; Seller's Stoppage of Delivery.

(1) A transferee of a document, whether negotiable or nonnegotiable, to whom the document has been delivered but not duly negotiated, acquires the title and rights which his transferor had or had actual authority to convey.

(2) In the case of a nonnegotiable document, until but not after the bailee receives notification of the transfer, the rights of the transferee may be defeated

    (a) by those creditors of the transferor who could treat the sale as void under Section 2–402; or

    (b) by a buyer from the transferor in ordinary course of business if the bailee has delivered the goods to the buyer or received notification of his rights; or

    (c) as against the bailee by good faith dealings of the bailee with the transferor.

(3) A diversion or other change of shipping instructions by the consignor in a nonnegotiable bill of lading which causes the bailee not to deliver to the consignee defeats the consignee's title to the goods if they have been delivered to a buyer in ordinary course of business and in any event defeats the consignee's rights against the bailee.

(4) Delivery pursuant to a nonnegotiable document may be stopped by a seller under Section 2–705, and subject to the requirement of due notification there provided. A bailee honoring the seller's instructions is entitled to be indemnified by the seller against any resulting loss or expense.

§ 7–505. Indorser Not a Guarantor for Other Parties.

The indorsement of a document of title issued by a bailee does not make the indorser liable for any default by the bailee or by previous indorsers.

§ 7–506. Delivery Without Indorsement: Right to Compel Indorsement.

The transferee of a negotiable document of title has a specifically enforceable right to have his transferor supply any necessary indorsement but the transfer becomes a negotiation only as of the time the indorsement is supplied.

§ 7–507. Warranties on Negotiation or Transfer of Receipt or Bill.

Where a person negotiates or transfers a document of title for value otherwise than as a mere intermediary under the next following section, then unless otherwise agreed he warrants to his immediate purchaser only in addition to any warranty made in selling the goods

(a) that the document is genuine; and

(b) that he has no knowledge of any fact which would impair its validity or worth; and

(c) that his negotiation or transfer is rightful and fully effective with respect to the title to the document and the goods it represents.

§ 7–508. Warranties of Collecting Bank as to Documents.

A collecting bank or other intermediary known to be entrusted with documents on behalf of another or with collection of a draft or other claim against delivery of documents warrants by such delivery of the documents only its own good faith and authority. This rule applies even though the intermediary has purchased or made advances against the claim or draft to be collected.

§ 7–509. Receipt or Bill: When Adequate Compliance With Commercial Contract.

The question whether a document is adequate to fulfill the obligations of a contract for sale or the conditions of a credit is governed by the Articles on Sales (Article 2) and on Letters of Credit (Article 5).

Part 6—Warehouse Receipts and Bills of Lading: Miscellaneous Provisions

§ 7–601. Lost and Missing Documents.

(1) If a document has been lost, stolen or destroyed, a court may order delivery of the goods or issuance of a substitute document and the bailee may without liability to any person comply with such order. If the document was negotiable the claimant must post security approved by the court to indemnify any person who may suffer loss as a result of non-surrender of the document. If the document was not negotiable, such security may be required at the discretion of the court. The court may also in its discretion order payment of the bailee's reasonable costs and counsel fees.

(2) A bailee who without court order delivers goods to a person claiming under a missing negotiable document is liable to any person injured thereby, and if the delivery is not in good faith becomes liable for conversion. Delivery in good faith is not conversion if made in accordance with a filed classification or tariff or, where no classification or tariff is filed, if the claimant posts security with the bailee in an amount at least double the value of the goods at the time of posting to indemnify any person injured by the delivery who files a notice of claim within one year after the delivery.

§ 7–602. Attachment of Goods Covered by a Negotiable Document.

Except where the document was originally issued upon delivery of the goods by a person who had no power to dispose of them, no lien attaches by virtue of any judicial process to goods in the possession of a bailee for which a negotiable document of title is outstanding unless the document be first surrendered to the bailee or its negotiation enjoined, and the bailee shall not be compelled to deliver the goods pursuant to process until the document is surrendered to him or impounded by the court. One who purchases the document for value without notice of the process or injunction takes free of the lien imposed by judicial process.

§ 7–603. Conflicting Claims; Interpleader.

If more than one person claims title or possession of the goods, the bailee is excused from delivery until he has had a reasonable time to ascertain the validity of the adverse claims or to bring an action to compel all claimants to interplead and may compel such interpleader, either in defending an action for nondelivery of the goods, or by original action, whichever is appropriate.

REVISED ARTICLE 8: INVESTMENT SECURITIES

Part 1—Short Title and General Matters

§ 8–101. Short Title.

This Article may be cited as Uniform Commercial Code—Investment Securities.

§ 8–102. Definitions.

(a) In this Article:

(1) "Adverse claim" means a claim that a claimant has a property interest in a financial asset and that it is a violation of the rights of the claimant for another person to hold, transfer, or deal with the financial asset.

(2) "Bearer form," as applied to a certificated security, means a form in which the security is payable to the bearer of the security certificate according to its terms but not by reason of an indorsement.

(3) "Broker" means a person defined as a broker or dealer under the federal securities laws, but without excluding a bank acting in that capacity.

(4) "Certificated security" means a security that is represented by a certificate.

(5) "Clearing corporation" means:

(i) a person that is registered as a "clearing agency" under the federal securities laws;

(ii) a federal reserve bank; or

(iii) any other person that provides clearance or settlement services with respect to financial assets that would require it to register as a clearing agency under the federal securities laws but for an exclusion or exemption from the registration requirement, if its activities as a clearing corporation, including promulgation of rules, are subject to regulation by a federal or state governmental authority.

(6) "Communicate" means to:

(i) send a signed writing; or

(ii) transmit information by any mechanism agreed upon by the persons transmitting and receiving the information.

(7) "Entitlement holder" means a person identified in the records of a securities intermediary as the person having a security entitlement against the securities intermediary. If a person acquires a security entitlement by virtue of Section 8–501(b)(2) or (3), that person is the entitlement holder.

(8) "Entitlement order" means a notification communicated to a securities intermediary directing transfer or redemption of a financial asset to which the entitlement holder has a security entitlement.

(9) "Financial asset," except as otherwise provided in Section 8–103, means:

(i) a security;

(ii) an obligation of a person or a share, participation, or other interest in a person or in property or an enterprise of a person, which is, or is of a type, dealt in or traded on financial markets, or which is recognized in any area in which it is issued or dealt in as a medium for investment; or

(iii) any property that is held by a securities intermediary for another person in a securities account if the securities intermediary has expressly agreed with the other person that the property is to be treated as a financial asset under this Article. As context requires, the term means either the interest itself or the means by which a person's claim to it is evidenced, including a certificated or uncertificated security, a security certificate, or a security entitlement.

(10) "Good faith," for purposes of the obligation of good faith in the performance or enforcement of contracts or duties within this Article, means honesty in fact and the observance of reasonable commercial standards of fair dealing.

(11) "Indorsement" means a signature that alone or accompanied by other words is made on a security certificate in registered form or on a separate document for the purpose of assigning, transferring, or redeeming the security or granting a power to assign, transfer, or redeem it.

(12) "Instruction" means a notification communi-cated to the issuer of an uncertificated security which directs that the transfer of the security be registered or that the security be redeemed.

(13) "Registered form," as applied to a certificated security, means a form in which:

(i) the security certificate specifies a person entitled to the security; and

(ii) a transfer of the security may be registered upon books maintained for that purpose by or on behalf of the issuer, or the security certificate so states.

(14) "Securities intermediary" means:

(i) a clearing corporation; or

(ii) a person, including a bank or broker, that in the ordinary course of its business maintains securities accounts for others and is acting in that capacity.

(15) "Security," except as otherwise provided in Section 8–103, means an obligation of an issuer or a share, participation, or other interest in an issuer or in property or an enterprise of an issuer:

(i) which is represented by a security certificate in bearer or registered form, or the transfer of which may be registered upon books maintained for that purpose by or on behalf of the issuer;

(ii) which is one of a class or series or by its terms is divisible into a class or series of shares, participations, interests, or obligations; and

(iii) which:

(A) is, or is of a type, dealt in or traded on securities exchanges or securities markets; or

(B) is a medium for investment and by its terms expressly provides that it is a security governed by this Article.

(16) "Security certificate" means a certificate representing a security.

(17) "Security entitlement" means the rights and property interest of an entitlement holder with respect to a financial asset specified in Part 5.

(18) "Uncertificated security" means a security that is not represented by a certificate.

(b) Other definitions applying to this Article and the sections in which they appear are:

Appropriate person	Section 8–107
Control	Section 8–106
Delivery	Section 8–301
Investment company security	Section 8–103
Issuer	Section 8–201
Overissue	Section 8–210
Protected purchaser	Section 8–303
Securities account	Section 8–501

(c) In addition, Article 1 contains general definitions and principles of construction and interpretation applicable throughout this Article.

(d) The characterization of a person, business, or transaction for purposes of this Article does not determine the characterization of the person, business, or transaction for purposes of any other law, regulation, or rule.

§ 8–103. Rules for Determining Whether Certain Obligations and Interests Are Securities or Financial Assets.

(a) A share or similar equity interest issued by a corporation, business trust, joint stock company, or similar entity is a security.

(b) An "investment company security" is a security. "Investment company security" means a share or similar equity interest issued by an entity that is registered as an investment company under the federal investment company laws, an interest in a unit investment trust that is so registered, or a face-amount certificate issued by a face-amount certificate company that is so registered. Investment company security does not include an insurance policy or endowment policy or annuity contract issued by an insurance company.

(c) An interest in a partnership or limited liability company is not a security unless it is dealt in or traded on securities exchanges or in securities markets, its terms expressly provide that it is a security governed by this Article, or it is an investment company security. However, an interest in a partnership or limited liability company is a financial asset if it is held in a securities account.

(d) A writing that is a security certificate is governed by this Article and not by Article 3, even though it also meets the requirements of that Article. However, a negotiable instrument governed by Article 3 is a financial asset if it is held in a securities account.

(e) An option or similar obligation issued by a clearing corporation to its participants is not a security, but is a financial asset.

(f) A commodity contract, as defined in Section 9–102(a)(15), is not a security or a financial asset.

As amended in 1999.

§ 8–104. Acquisition of Security or Financial Asset or Interest Therein.

(a) A person acquires a security or an interest therein, under this Article, if:

(1) the person is a purchaser to whom a security is delivered pursuant to Section 8–301; or

(2) the person acquires a security entitlement to the security pursuant to Section 8–501.

(b) A person acquires a financial asset, other than a security, or an interest therein, under this Article, if the person acquires a security entitlement to the financial asset.

(c) A person who acquires a security entitlement to a security or other financial asset has the rights specified in Part 5, but is a purchaser of any security, security entitlement, or other financial asset held by the securities intermediary only to the extent provided in Section 8–503.

(d) Unless the context shows that a different meaning is intended, a person who is required by other law, regulation, rule, or agreement to transfer, deliver, present, surrender, exchange, or otherwise put in the possession of another person a security or financial asset satisfies that requirement by causing the other person to acquire an interest in the security or financial asset pursuant to subsection (a) or (b).

§ 8–105. Notice of Adverse Claim.

(a) A person has notice of an adverse claim if:

(1) the person knows of the adverse claim;

(2) the person is aware of facts sufficient to indicate that there is a significant probability that the adverse claim exists and deliberately avoids information that would establish the existence of the adverse claim; or

(3) the person has a duty, imposed by statute or regulation, to investigate whether an adverse claim exists, and the investigation so required would establish the existence of the adverse claim.

(b) Having knowledge that a financial asset or interest therein is or has been transferred by a representative imposes no duty of inquiry into the rightfulness of a transaction and is not notice of an adverse claim. However, a person who knows that a representative has transferred a financial asset or interest therein in a transaction that is, or whose proceeds are being used, for the individual benefit of the representative or otherwise in breach of duty has notice of an adverse claim.

(c) An act or event that creates a right to immediate performance of the principal obligation represented by a security certificate or sets a date on or after which the certificate is to be presented or surrendered for redemption or exchange does not itself constitute notice of an adverse claim except in the case of a transfer more than:

(1) one year after a date set for presentment or surrender for redemption or exchange; or

(2) six months after a date set for payment of money against presentation or surrender of the certificate, if money was available for payment on that date.

(d) A purchaser of a certificated security has notice of an adverse claim if the security certificate:

(1) whether in bearer or registered form, has been indorsed "for collection" or "for surrender" or for some other purpose not involving transfer; or

(2) is in bearer form and has on it an unambiguous statement that it is the property of a person other than the transferor, but the mere writing of a name on the certificate is not such a statement.

(e) Filing of a financing statement under Article 9 is not notice of an adverse claim to a financial asset.

§ 8–106. Control.

(a) A purchaser has "control" of a certificated security in bearer form if the certificated security is delivered to the purchaser.

(b) A purchaser has "control" of a certificated security in registered form if the certificated security is delivered to the purchaser, and:

(1) the certificate is indorsed to the purchaser or in blank by an effective indorsement; or

(2) the certificate is registered in the name of the purchaser, upon original issue or registration of transfer by the issuer.

(c) A purchaser has "control" of an uncertificated secu-rity if:

(1) the uncertificated security is delivered to the purchaser; or

(2) the issuer has agreed that it will comply with instructions originated by the purchaser without further consent by the registered owner.

(d) A purchaser has "control" of a security entitlement if:

(1) the purchaser becomes the entitlement holder;

(2) the securities intermediary has agreed that it will comply with entitlement orders originated by the purchaser without further consent by the entitlement holder; or

(3) another person has control of the security entitlement on behalf of the purchaser or, having previously acquired control of the security entitlement, acknowledges that it has control on behalf of the purchaser.

(e) If an interest in a security entitlement is granted by the entitlement holder to the entitlement holder's own securities intermediary, the securities intermediary has control.

(f) A purchaser who has satisfied the requirements of subsection (c) or (d) has control, even if the registered owner in the case of subsection (c) or the entitlement holder in the case of subsection (d) retains the right to make substitutions for the uncertificated security or security entitlement, to originate instructions or entitlement orders to the issuer or securities intermediary, or otherwise to deal with the uncertificated security or security entitlement.

(g) An issuer or a securities intermediary may not enter into an agreement of the kind described in subsection (c)(2) or (d)(2) without the consent of the registered owner or entitlement holder, but an issuer or a securities intermediary is not required to enter into such an agreement even though the registered owner or entitlement holder so directs. An issuer or securities intermediary that has entered into such an agreement is not required to confirm the existence of the agreement to another party unless requested to do so by the registered owner or entitlement holder. As amended in 1999.

§ 8–107. Whether Indorsement, Instruction, or Entitlement Order Is Effective.

(a) "Appropriate person" means:

(1) with respect to an indorsement, the person specified by a security certificate or by an effective special indorsement to be entitled to the security;

(2) with respect to an instruction, the registered owner of an uncertificated security;

(3) with respect to an entitlement order, the entitlement holder;

(4) if the person designated in paragraph (1), (2), or (3) is deceased, the designated person's successor taking under other law or the designated person's personal representative acting for the estate of the decedent; or

(5) if the person designated in paragraph (1), (2), or (3) lacks capacity, the designated person's guardian, conservator, or other similar representative who has power under other law to transfer the security or financial asset.

(b) An indorsement, instruction, or entitlement order is effective if:

(1) it is made by the appropriate person;

(2) it is made by a person who has power under the law of agency to transfer the security or financial asset on behalf of the appropriate person, including, in the case of an instruction or entitlement order, a person who has control under Section 8–106(c)(2) or (d)(2); or

(3) the appropriate person has ratified it or is otherwise precluded from asserting its ineffectiveness.

(c) An indorsement, instruction, or entitlement order made by a representative is effective even if:

(1) the representative has failed to comply with a controlling instrument or with the law of the State having jurisdiction of the representative relationship, including any law requiring the representative to obtain court approval of the transaction; or

(2) the representative's action in making the indorsement, instruction, or entitlement order or using the proceeds of the transaction is otherwise a breach of duty.

(d) If a security is registered in the name of or specially indorsed to a person described as a representative, or if a securities account is maintained in the name of a person described as a representative, an indorsement, instruction, or entitlement order made by the person is effective even though the person is no longer serving in the described capacity.

(e) Effectiveness of an indorsement, instruction, or entitlement order is determined as of the date the indorsement, instruction, or entitlement order is made, and an indorsement, instruction, or entitlement order does not become ineffective by reason of any later change of circumstances.

§ 8–108. Warranties in Direct Holding.

(a) A person who transfers a certificated security to a purchaser for value warrants to the purchaser, and an indorser, if the transfer is by indorsement, warrants to any subsequent purchaser, that:

(1) the certificate is genuine and has not been materially altered;

(2) the transferor or indorser does not know of any fact that might impair the validity of the security;

(3) there is no adverse claim to the security;

(4) the transfer does not violate any restriction on transfer;

(5) if the transfer is by indorsement, the indorsement is made by an appropriate person, or if the indorsement is by an agent, the agent has actual authority to act on behalf of the appropriate person; and

(6) the transfer is otherwise effective and rightful.

(b) A person who originates an instruction for registration of transfer of an uncertificated security to a purchaser for value warrants to the purchaser that:

(1) the instruction is made by an appropriate person, or if the instruction is by an agent, the agent has actual authority to act on behalf of the appropriate person;

(2) the security is valid;

(3) there is no adverse claim to the security; and

(4) at the time the instruction is presented to the issuer:

(i) the purchaser will be entitled to the registration of transfer;

(ii) the transfer will be registered by the issuer free from all liens, security interests, restrictions, and claims other than those specified in the instruction;

(iii) the transfer will not violate any restriction on transfer; and

(iv) the requested transfer will otherwise be effective and rightful.

(c) A person who transfers an uncertificated security to a purchaser for value and does not originate an instruction in connection with the transfer warrants that:

(1) the uncertificated security is valid;

(2) there is no adverse claim to the security;

(3) the transfer does not violate any restriction on transfer; and

(4) the transfer is otherwise effective and rightful.

(d) A person who indorses a security certificate warrants to the issuer that:

(1) there is no adverse claim to the security; and

(2) the indorsement is effective.

(e) A person who originates an instruction for registration of transfer of an uncertificated security warrants to the issuer that:

(1) the instruction is effective; and

(2) at the time the instruction is presented to the issuer the purchaser will be entitled to the registration of transfer.

(f) A person who presents a certificated security for registration of transfer or for payment or exchange warrants to the issuer that the person is entitled to the registration, payment, or exchange, but a purchaser for value and without notice of adverse claims to whom transfer is registered warrants only that the person has no knowledge of any unauthorized signature in a necessary indorsement.

(g) If a person acts as agent of another in delivering a certificated security to a purchaser, the identity of the principal was known to the person to whom the certificate was delivered, and the certificate delivered by the agent was received by the agent from the principal or received by the agent from another person at the direction of the principal, the person delivering the security certificate warrants only that the delivering person has authority to act for the principal and does not know of any adverse claim to the certificated security.

(h) A secured party who redelivers a security certificate received, or after payment and on order of the debtor delivers the security certificate to another person, makes only the warranties of an agent under subsection (g).

(i) Except as otherwise provided in subsection (g), a broker acting for a customer makes to the issuer and a purchaser the warranties provided in subsections (a) through (f). A broker that delivers a security certificate to its customer, or causes its customer to be registered as the owner of an uncertificated security, makes to the customer the warranties provided in subsection (a) or (b), and has the rights and privileges of a purchaser under this section. The warranties of and in favor of the broker acting as an agent are in addition to applicable warranties given by and in favor of the customer.

§ 8–109. Warranties in Indirect Holding.

(a) A person who originates an entitlement order to a securities intermediary warrants to the securities intermediary that:

(1) the entitlement order is made by an appropriate person, or if the entitlement order is by an agent, the agent has actual authority to act on behalf of the appropriate person; and

(2) there is no adverse claim to the security entitlement.

(b) A person who delivers a security certificate to a securities intermediary for credit to a securities account or originates an instruction with respect to an uncertificated security directing that the uncertificated security be credited to a securities account makes to the securities intermediary the warranties specified in Section 8–108(a) or (b).

(c) If a securities intermediary delivers a security certificate to its entitlement holder or causes its entitlement holder to be registered as the owner of an uncertificated security, the securities intermediary makes to the entitlement holder the warranties specified in Section 8–108(a) or (b).

§ 8–110. Applicability; Choice of Law.

(a) The local law of the issuer's jurisdiction, as specified in subsection (d), governs:

(1) the validity of a security;

(2) the rights and duties of the issuer with respect to registration of transfer;

(3) the effectiveness of registration of transfer by the issuer;

(4) whether the issuer owes any duties to an adverse claimant to a security; and

(5) whether an adverse claim can be asserted against a person to whom transfer of a certificated or uncertificated security is registered or a person who obtains control of an uncertificated security.

(b) The local law of the securities intermediary's jurisdiction, as specified in subsection (e), governs:

(1) acquisition of a security entitlement from the securities intermediary;

(2) the rights and duties of the securities intermediary and entitlement holder arising out of a security entitlement;

(3) whether the securities intermediary owes any duties to an adverse claimant to a security entitlement; and

(4) whether an adverse claim can be asserted against a person who acquires a security entitlement from the securities intermediary or a person who purchases a security entitlement or interest therein from an entitlement holder.

(c) The local law of the jurisdiction in which a security certificate is located at the time of delivery governs whether an adverse claim can be asserted against a person to whom the security certificate is delivered.

(d) "Issuer's jurisdiction" means the jurisdiction under which the issuer of the security is organized or, if permitted by the law of that jurisdiction, the law of another jurisdiction specified by the issuer. An issuer organized under the law of this State may specify the law of another jurisdiction as the law governing the matters specified in subsection (a)(2) through (5).

(e) The following rules determine a "securities intermediary's jurisdiction" for purposes of this section:

(1) If an agreement between the securities intermediary and its entitlement holder specifies that it is governed by the law of a particular jurisdiction, that jurisdiction is the securities intermediary's jurisdiction.

(2) If an agreement between the securities intermediary and its entitlement holder does not specify the governing law as provided in paragraph (1), but expressly specifies that the securities account is maintained at an office in a particular jurisdiction, that jurisdiction is the securities intermediary's jurisdiction.

(3) If neither paragraph (1) nor paragraph (2) applies and an agreement between the securities intermediary and its entitlement holder governing the securities account expressly provides that the securities account is maintained at an office in a particular jurisdiction, that jurisdiction is the securities intermediary's jurisdiction.

(4) If none of the preceding paragraph applies, the securities intermediary's jurisdiction is the jurisdiction in which the office identified in an account statement as the office serving the entitlement holder's account is located.

(5) If none of the preceding paragraphs applies, the securities intermediary's jurisdiction is the jurisdiction in which the chief executive office of the securities intermediary is located.

(f) A securities intermediary's jurisdiction is not determined by the physical location of certificates representing financial assets, or by the jurisdiction in which is organized the issuer of the financial asset with respect to which an entitlement holder has a security entitlement, or by the location of facilities for data processing or other record keeping concerning the account.

As amended in 1999.

§ 8–111. Clearing Corporation Rules.

A rule adopted by a clearing corporation governing rights and obligations among the clearing corporation and its participants in the clearing corporation is effective even if the rule conflicts with this [Act] and affects another party who does not consent to the rule.

§ 8–112. Creditor's Legal Process.

(a) The interest of a debtor in a certificated security may be reached by a creditor only by actual seizure of the security certificate by the officer making the attachment or levy, except as otherwise provided in subsection (d). However, a certificated security for which the certificate has been surrendered to the issuer may be reached by a creditor by legal process upon the issuer.

(b) The interest of a debtor in an uncertificated security may be reached by a creditor only by legal process upon the issuer at its chief executive office in the United States, except as otherwise provided in subsection (d).

(c) The interest of a debtor in a security entitlement may be reached by a creditor only by legal process upon the securities intermediary with whom the debtor's securities account is maintained, except as otherwise provided in subsection (d).

(d) The interest of a debtor in a certificated security for which the certificate is in the possession of a secured party, or in an uncertificated security registered in the name of a secured party, or a security entitlement maintained in the name of a secured party, may be reached by a creditor by legal process upon the secured party.

(e) A creditor whose debtor is the owner of a certificated security, uncertificated security, or security entitlement is entitled to aid from a court of competent jurisdiction, by injunction or otherwise, in reaching the certificated security, uncertificated security, or security entitlement or in satisfying the claim by means allowed at law or in equity in regard to property that cannot readily be reached by other legal process.

§ 8–113. Statute of Frauds Inapplicable.

A contract or modification of a contract for the sale or purchase of a security is enforceable whether or not there is a writing signed or record authenticated by a party against whom enforcement is sought, even if the contract or modification is not capable of performance within one year of its making.

§ 8–114. Evidentiary Rules Concerning Certificated Securities.

The following rules apply in an action on a certificated security against the issuer:

(1) Unless specifically denied in the pleadings, each signature on a security certificate or in a necessary indorsement is admitted.

(2) If the effectiveness of a signature is put in issue, the burden of establishing effectiveness is on the party claiming under the signature, but the signature is presumed to be genuine or authorized.

(3) If signatures on a security certificate are admitted or established, production of the certificate entitles a holder to recover on it unless the defendant establishes a defense or a defect going to the validity of the security.

(4) If it is shown that a defense or defect exists, the plaintiff has the burden of establishing that the plaintiff or some person under whom the plaintiff claims is a person against whom the defense or defect cannot be asserted.

§ 8–115. Securities Intermediary and Others Not Liable to Adverse Claimant.

A securities intermediary that has transferred a financial asset pursuant to an effective entitlement order, or a broker or other agent or bailee that has dealt with a financial asset at the direction of its customer or principal, is not liable to a person having an adverse claim to the financial asset, unless the securities intermediary, or broker or other agent or bailee:

(1) took the action after it had been served with an injunction, restraining order, or other legal process enjoining it from doing so, issued by a court of competent jurisdiction, and had a reasonable opportunity to act on the injunction, restraining order, or other legal process; or

(2) acted in collusion with the wrongdoer in violating the rights of the adverse claimant; or

(3) in the case of a security certificate that has been stolen, acted with notice of the adverse claim.

§ 8–116. Securities Intermediary as Purchaser for Value.

A securities intermediary that receives a financial asset and establishes a security entitlement to the financial asset in favor of an entitlement holder is a purchaser for value of the financial asset. A securities intermediary that acquires a security entitlement to a financial asset from another securities intermediary acquires the security entitlement for value if the securities intermediary acquiring the security entitlement establishes a security entitlement to the financial asset in favor of an entitlement holder.

Part 2—Issue and Issuer

§ 8–201. Issuer.

(a) With respect to an obligation on or a defense to a security, an "issuer" includes a person that:

(1) places or authorizes the placing of its name on a security certificate, other than as authenticating trustee, registrar, transfer agent, or the like, to evidence a share, participation, or other interest in its property or in an enterprise, or to evidence its duty to perform an obligation represented by the certificate;

(2) creates a share, participation, or other interest in its property or in an enterprise, or undertakes an obligation, that is an uncertificated security;

(3) directly or indirectly creates a fractional interest in its rights or property, if the fractional interest is represented by a security certificate; or

(4) becomes responsible for, or in place of, another person described as an issuer in this section.

(b) With respect to an obligation on or defense to a security, a guarantor is an issuer to the extent of its guaranty, whether or not its obligation is noted on a security certificate.

(c) With respect to a registration of a transfer, issuer means a person on whose behalf transfer books are maintained.

§ 8–202. Issuer's Responsibility and Defenses; Notice of Defect or Defense.

(a) Even against a purchaser for value and without notice, the terms of a certificated security include terms stated on the certificate and terms made part of the security by reference on the certificate to another instrument, indenture, or document or to a constitution, statute, ordinance, rule, regulation, order, or the like, to the extent the terms referred to do not conflict with terms stated on the certificate. A reference under this subsection does not of itself charge a purchaser for value with notice of a defect going to the validity of the security, even if the certificate expressly states that a person accepting it admits notice. The terms of an uncertificated security include those stated in any instrument, indenture, or document or in a constitution, statute, ordinance, rule, regulation, order, or the like, pursuant to which the security is issued.

(b) The following rules apply if an issuer asserts that a security is not valid:

(1) A security other than one issued by a government or governmental subdivision, agency, or instrumentality, even though issued with a defect going to its validity, is valid in the hands of a purchaser for value and without notice of the particular defect unless the defect involves a violation of a constitutional provision. In that case, the security is valid in the hands of a purchaser for value and without notice of the defect, other than one who takes by original issue.

(2) Paragraph (1) applies to an issuer that is a government or governmental subdivision, agency, or instrumentality only if there has been substantial compliance with the legal requirements governing the issue or the issuer has received a substantial consideration for the issue as a whole or for the particular security and a stated purpose of the issue is one for which the issuer has power to borrow money or issue the security.

(c) Except as otherwise provided in Section 8–205, lack of genuineness of a certificated security is a complete defense, even against a purchaser for value and without notice.

(d) All other defenses of the issuer of a security, including nondelivery and conditional delivery of a certificated security, are ineffective against a purchaser for value who has taken the certificated security without notice of the particular defense.

(e) This section does not affect the right of a party to cancel a contract for a security "when, as and if issued" or "when distributed" in the event of a material change in the character of the security that is the subject of the contract or in the plan or arrangement pursuant to which the security is to be issued or distributed.

(f) If a security is held by a securities intermediary against whom an entitlement holder has a security entitlement with respect to the security, the issuer may not assert any defense that the issuer could not assert if the entitlement holder held the security directly.

§ 8–203. Staleness as Notice of Defect or Defense.

After an act or event, other than a call that has been revoked, creating a right to immediate performance of the principal obligation represented by a certificated security or setting a date on or after which the security is to be presented or surrendered for redemption or exchange, a purchaser is charged with notice of any defect in its issue or defense of the issuer, if the act or event:

(1) requires the payment of money, the delivery of a certificated security, the registration of transfer of an uncertificated security, or any of them on presentation or surrender of the security certificate, the money or security is available on the date set for payment or exchange, and the purchaser takes the security more than one year after that date; or

(2) is not covered by paragraph (1) and the purchaser takes the security more than two years after the date set for surrender or presentation or the date on which performance became due.

§ 8–204. Effect of Issuer's Restriction on Transfer.

A restriction on transfer of a security imposed by the issuer, even if otherwise lawful, is ineffective against a person without knowledge of the restriction unless:

   (1) the security is certificated and the restriction is noted conspicuously on the security certificate; or

   (2) the security is uncertificated and the registered owner has been notified of the restriction.

§ 8–205. Effect of Unauthorized Signature on Security Certificate.

An unauthorized signature placed on a security certificate before or in the course of issue is ineffective, but the signature is effective in favor of a purchaser for value of the certificated security if the purchaser is without notice of the lack of authority and the signing has been done by:

   (1) an authenticating trustee, registrar, transfer agent, or other person entrusted by the issuer with the signing of the security certificate or of similar security certificates, or the immediate preparation for signing of any of them; or

   (2) an employee of the issuer, or of any of the persons listed in paragraph (1), entrusted with responsible handling of the security certificate.

§ 8–206. Completion of Alteration of Security Certificate.

(a) If a security certificate contains the signatures necessary to its issue or transfer but is incomplete in any other respect:

   (1) any person may complete it by filling in the blanks as authorized; and

   (2) even if the blanks are incorrectly filled in, the security certificate as completed is enforceable by a purchaser who took it for value and without notice of the incorrectness.

(b) A complete security certificate that has been improperly altered, even if fraudulently, remains enforceable, but only according to its original terms.

§ 8–207. Rights and Duties of Issuer with Respect to Registered Owners.

(a) Before due presentment for registration of transfer of a certificated security in registered form or of an instruction requesting registration of transfer of an uncertificated security, the issuer or indenture trustee may treat the registered owner as the person exclusively entitled to vote, receive notifications, and otherwise exercise all the rights and powers of an owner.

(b) This Article does not affect the liability of the registered owner of a security for a call, assessment, or the like.

§ 8–208. Effect of Signature of Authenticating Trustee, Registrar, or Transfer Agent.

(a) A person signing a security certificate as authenticating trustee, registrar, transfer agent, or the like, warrants to a purchaser for value of the certificated security, if the purchaser is without notice of a particular defect, that:

   (1) the certificate is genuine;

   (2) the person's own participation in the issue of the security is within the person's capacity and within the scope of the authority received by the person from the issuer; and

   (3) the person has reasonable grounds to believe that the certificated security is in the form and within the amount the issuer is authorized to issue.

(b) Unless otherwise agreed, a person signing under subsection (a) does not assume responsibility for the validity of the security in other respects.

§ 8–209. Issuer's Lien.

A lien in favor of an issuer upon a certificated security is valid against a purchaser only if the right of the issuer to the lien is noted conspicuously on the security certificate.

§ 8–210. Overissue.

(a) In this section, "overissue" means the issue of securities in excess of the amount the issuer has corporate power to issue, but an overissue does not occur if appropriate action has cured the overissue.

(b) Except as otherwise provided in subsections (c) and (d), the provisions of this Article which validate a security or compel its issue or reissue do not apply to the extent that validation, issue, or reissue would result in overissue.

(c) If an identical security not constituting an overissue is reasonably available for purchase, a person entitled to issue or validation may compel the issuer to purchase the security and deliver it if certificated or register its transfer if uncertificated, against surrender of any security certificate the person holds.

(d) If a security is not reasonably available for purchase, a person entitled to issue or validation may recover from the issuer the price the person or the last purchaser for value paid for it with interest from the date of the person's demand.

Part 3—Transfer of Certificated and Uncertificated Securities

§ 8–301. Delivery.

(a) Delivery of a certificated security to a purchaser occurs when:

   (1) the purchaser acquires possession of the security certificate;

   (2) another person, other than a securities intermediary, either acquires possession of the security certificate on behalf of the purchaser or, having previously acquired possession of the certificate, acknowledges that it holds for the purchaser; or

   (3) a securities intermediary acting on behalf of the purchaser acquires possession of the security certificate, only if the certificate is in registered form and is (i) registered in the name of the purchaser, (ii) payable to the order of the purchaser, or (iii) specially indorsed to the purchaser by an effective indorsement and has not been indorsed to the securities intermediary or in blank.

(b) Delivery of an uncertificated security to a purchaser occurs when:

   (1) the issuer registers the purchaser as the registered owner, upon original issue or registration of transfer; or

   (2) another person, other than a securities intermediary, either becomes the registered owner of the uncertificated security on behalf of the purchaser or, having previously become the registered owner, acknowledges that it holds for the purchaser.

As amended in 1999.

§ 8–302. Rights of Purchaser.

(a) Except as otherwise provided in subsections (b) and (c), upon delivery of a certificated or uncertificated security to a purchaser, the purchaser acquires all rights in the security that the transferor had or had power to transfer.

(b) A purchaser of a limited interest acquires rights only to the extent of the interest purchased.

(c) A purchaser of a certificated security who as a previous holder had notice of an adverse claim does not improve its position by taking from a protected purchaser.

As amended in 1999.

§ 8–303. Protected Purchaser.

(a) "Protected purchaser" means a purchaser of a certificated or uncertificated security, or of an interest therein, who:

(1) gives value;

(2) does not have notice of any adverse claim to the security; and

(3) obtains control of the certificated or uncertificated security.

(b) In addition to acquiring the rights of a purchaser, a protected purchaser also acquires its interest in the security free of any adverse claim.

§ 8–304. Indorsement.

(a) An indorsement may be in blank or special. An indorsement in blank includes an indorsement to bearer. A special indorsement specifies to whom a security is to be transferred or who has power to transfer it. A holder may convert a blank indorsement to a special indorsement.

(b) An indorsement purporting to be only of part of a security certificate representing units intended by the issuer to be separately transferable is effective to the extent of the indorsement.

(c) An indorsement, whether special or in blank, does not constitute a transfer until delivery of the certificate on which it appears or, if the indorsement is on a separate document, until delivery of both the document and the certificate.

(d) If a security certificate in registered form has been delivered to a purchaser without a necessary indorsement, the purchaser may become a protected purchaser only when the indorsement is supplied. However, against a transferor, a transfer is complete upon delivery and the purchaser has a specifically enforceable right to have any necessary indorsement supplied.

(e) An indorsement of a security certificate in bearer form may give notice of an adverse claim to the certificate, but it does not otherwise affect a right to registration that the holder possesses.

(f) Unless otherwise agreed, a person making an indorsement assumes only the obligations provided in Section 8–108 and not an obligation that the security will be honored by the issuer.

§ 8–305. Instruction.

(a) If an instruction has been originated by an appropriate person but is incomplete in any other respect, any person may complete it as authorized and the issuer may rely on it as completed, even though it has been completed incorrectly.

(b) Unless otherwise agreed, a person initiating an instruction assumes only the obligations imposed by Section 8–108 and not an obligation that the security will be honored by the issuer.

§ 8–306. Effect of Guaranteeing Signature, Indorsement, or Instruction.

(a) A person who guarantees a signature of an indorser of a security certificate warrants that at the time of signing:

(1) the signature was genuine;

(2) the signer was an appropriate person to indorse, or if the signature is by an agent, the agent had actual authority to act on behalf of the appropriate person; and

(3) the signer had legal capacity to sign.

(b) A person who guarantees a signature of the originator of an instruction warrants that at the time of signing:

(1) the signature was genuine;

(2) the signer was an appropriate person to originate the instruction, or if the signature is by an agent, the agent had actual authority to act on behalf of the appropriate person, if the person specified in the instruction as the registered owner was, in fact, the registered owner, as to which fact the signature guarantor does not make a warranty; and

(3) the signer had legal capacity to sign.

(c) A person who specially guarantees the signature of an originator of an instruction makes the warranties of a signature guarantor under subsection (b) and also warrants that at the time the instruction is presented to the issuer:

(1) the person specified in the instruction as the registered owner of the uncertificated security will be the registered owner; and

(2) the transfer of the uncertificated security requested in the instruction will be registered by the issuer free from all liens, security interests, restrictions, and claims other than those specified in the instruction.

(d) A guarantor under subsections (a) and (b) or a special guarantor under subsection (c) does not otherwise warrant the rightfulness of the transfer.

(e) A person who guarantees an indorsement of a security certificate makes the warranties of a signature guarantor under subsection (a) and also warrants the rightfulness of the transfer in all respects.

(f) A person who guarantees an instruction requesting the transfer of an uncertificated security makes the warranties of a special signature guarantor under subsection (c) and also warrants the rightfulness of the transfer in all respects.

(g) An issuer may not require a special guaranty of signature, a guaranty of indorsement, or a guaranty of instruction as a condition to registration of transfer.

(h) The warranties under this section are made to a person taking or dealing with the security in reliance on the guaranty, and the guarantor is liable to the person for loss resulting from their breach. An indorser or originator of an instruction whose signature, indorsement, or instruction has been guaranteed is liable to a guarantor for any loss suffered by the guarantor as a result of breach of the warranties of the guarantor.

§ 8–307. Purchaser's Right to Requisites for Registration of Transfer.

Unless otherwise agreed, the transferor of a security on due demand shall supply the purchaser with proof of authority to transfer or with any other requisite necessary to obtain registration of the transfer of the security, but if the transfer is not for value, a transferor need not comply unless the purchaser pays the necessary expenses. If the transferor fails within a reasonable time to comply with the demand, the purchaser may reject or rescind the transfer.

Part 4—Registration

§ 8–401. Duty of Issuer to Register Transfer.

(a) If a certificated security in registered form is presented to an issuer with a request to register transfer or an instruction is presented to an issuer with a request to register transfer of an uncertificated security, the issuer shall register the transfer as requested if:

(1) under the terms of the security the person seeking registration of transfer is eligible to have the security registered in its name;

(2) the indorsement or instruction is made by the appropriate person or by an agent who has actual authority to act on behalf of the appropriate person;

(3) reasonable assurance is given that the indorsement or instruction is genuine and authorized (Section 8–402);

(4) any applicable law relating to the collection of taxes has been complied with;

(5) the transfer does not violate any restriction on transfer imposed by the issuer in accordance with Section 8–204;

(6) a demand that the issuer not register transfer has not become effective under Section 8–403, or the issuer has complied with Section 8–403(b) but no legal process or indemnity bond is obtained as provided in Section 8–403(d); and

(7) the transfer is in fact rightful or is to a protected purchaser.

(b) If an issuer is under a duty to register a transfer of a security, the issuer is liable to a person presenting a certificated security or an instruction for registration or to the person's principal for loss resulting from unreasonable delay in registration or failure or refusal to register the transfer.

§ 8–402. Assurance That Indorsement or Instruction Is Effective.

(a) An issuer may require the following assurance that each necessary indorsement or each instruction is genuine and authorized:

(1) in all cases, a guaranty of the signature of the person making an indorsement or originating an instruction including, in the case of an instruction, reasonable assurance of identity;

(2) if the indorsement is made or the instruction is originated by an agent, appropriate assurance of actual authority to sign;

(3) if the indorsement is made or the instruction is originated by a fiduciary pursuant to Section 8–107(a)(4) or (a)(5), appropriate evidence of appointment or incumbency;

(4) if there is more than one fiduciary, reasonable assurance that all who are required to sign have done so; and

(5) if the indorsement is made or the instruction is originated by a person not covered by another provision of this subsection, assurance appropriate to the case corresponding as nearly as may be to the provisions of this subsection.

(b) An issuer may elect to require reasonable assurance beyond that specified in this section.

(c) In this section:

(1) "Guaranty of the signature" means a guaranty signed by or on behalf of a person reasonably believed by the issuer to be responsible. An issuer may adopt standards with respect to responsibility if they are not manifestly unreasonable.

(2) "Appropriate evidence of appointment or incumbency" means:

(i) in the case of a fiduciary appointed or qualified by a court, a certificate issued by or under the direction or supervision of the court or an officer thereof and dated within 60 days before the date of presentation for transfer; or

(ii) in any other case, a copy of a document showing the appointment or a certificate issued by or on behalf of a person reasonably believed by an issuer to be responsible or, in the absence of that document or certificate, other evidence the issuer reasonably considers appropriate.

§ 8–403. Demand That Issuer Not Register Transfer.

(a) A person who is an appropriate person to make an indorsement or originate an instruction may demand that the issuer not register transfer of a security by communicating to the issuer a notification that identifies the registered owner and the issue of which the security is a part and provides an address for communications directed to the person making the demand. The demand is effective only if it is received by the issuer at a time and in a manner affording the issuer reasonable opportunity to act on it.

(b) If a certificated security in registered form is presented to an issuer with a request to register transfer or an instruction is presented to an issuer with a request to register transfer of an uncertificated security after a demand that the issuer not register transfer has become effective, the issuer shall promptly communicate to (i) the person who initiated the demand at the address provided in the demand and (ii) the person who presented the security for registration of transfer or initiated the instruction requesting registration of transfer a notification stating that:

(1) the certificated security has been presented for registration of transfer or the instruction for registration of transfer of the uncertificated security has been received;

(2) a demand that the issuer not register transfer had previously been received; and

(3) the issuer will withhold registration of transfer for a period of time stated in the notification in order to provide the person who initiated the demand an opportunity to obtain legal process or an indemnity bond.

(c) The period described in subsection (b)(3) may not exceed 30 days after the date of communication of the notification. A shorter period may be specified by the issuer if it is not manifestly unreasonable.

(d) An issuer is not liable to a person who initiated a demand that the issuer not register transfer for any loss the person suffers as a result of registration of a transfer pursuant to an effective indorsement or instruction if the person who initiated the demand does not, within the time stated in the issuer's communication, either:

(1) obtain an appropriate restraining order, injunction, or other process from a court of competent jurisdiction enjoining the issuer from registering the transfer; or

(2) file with the issuer an indemnity bond, sufficient in the issuer's judgment to protect the issuer and any transfer agent, registrar, or other agent of the issuer involved from any loss it or they may suffer by refusing to register the transfer.

(e) This section does not relieve an issuer from liability for registering transfer pursuant to an indorsement or instruction that was not effective.

§ 8–404. Wrongful Registration.

(a) Except as otherwise provided in Section 8–406, an issuer is liable for wrongful registration of transfer if the issuer has registered a transfer of a security to a person not entitled to it, and the transfer was registered:

(1) pursuant to an ineffective indorsement or instruction;

(2) after a demand that the issuer not register transfer became effective under Section 8–403(a) and the issuer did not comply with Section 8–403(b);

(3) after the issuer had been served with an injunction, restraining order, or other legal process enjoining it from registering the transfer, issued by a court of competent jurisdiction, and the issuer had a reasonable opportunity to act on the injunction, restraining order, or other legal process; or

(4) by an issuer acting in collusion with the wrongdoer.

(b) An issuer that is liable for wrongful registration of transfer under subsection (a) on demand shall provide the person entitled to the security with a like certificated or uncertificated security, and any payments or distributions that the person did not receive as a result of the wrongful registration. If an overissue would result, the issuer's liability to provide the person with a like security is governed by Section 8–210.

(c) Except as otherwise provided in subsection (a) or in a law relating to the collection of taxes, an issuer is not liable to an owner or other person suffering loss as a result of the registration of a transfer of a security if registration was made pursuant to an effective indorsement or instruction.

§ 8–405. Replacement of Lost, Destroyed, or Wrongfully Taken Security Certificate.

(a) If an owner of a certificated security, whether in registered or bearer form, claims that the certificate has been lost, destroyed, or wrongfully taken, the issuer shall issue a new certificate if the owner:

(1) so requests before the issuer has notice that the certificate has been acquired by a protected purchaser;

(2) files with the issuer a sufficient indemnity bond; and

(3) satisfies other reasonable requirements imposed by the issuer.

(b) If, after the issue of a new security certificate, a protected purchaser of the original certificate presents it for registration of transfer, the issuer shall register the transfer unless an overissue would result. In that case, the issuer's liability is governed by Section 8–210. In addition to any rights on the indemnity bond, an issuer may recover the new certificate from a person to whom it was issued or any person taking under that person, except a protected purchaser.

§ 8–406. Obligation to Notify Issuer of Lost, Destroyed, or Wrongfully Taken Security Certificate.

If a security certificate has been lost, apparently destroyed, or wrongfully taken, and the owner fails to notify the issuer of that fact within a reasonable time after the owner has notice of it and the issuer registers a transfer of the security before receiving notification, the owner may not assert against the issuer a claim for registering the transfer under Section 8–404 or a claim to a new security certificate under Section 8–405.

§ 8–407. Authenticating Trustee, Transfer Agent, and Registrar.

A person acting as authenticating trustee, transfer agent, registrar, or other agent for an issuer in the registration of a transfer of its securities, in the issue of new security certificates or uncertificated securities, or in the cancellation of surrendered security certificates has the same obligation to the holder or owner of a certificated or uncertificated security with regard to the particular functions performed as the issuer has in regard to those functions.

Part 5 Security Entitlements

§ 8–501. Securities Account; Acquisition of Security Entitlement from Securities Intermediary.

(a) "Securities account" means an account to which a financial asset is or may be credited in accordance with an agreement under which the person maintaining the account undertakes to treat the person for whom the account is maintained as entitled to exercise the rights that comprise the financial asset.

(b) Except as otherwise provided in subsections (d) and (e), a person acquires a security entitlement if a securities intermediary:

(1) indicates by book entry that a financial asset has been credited to the person's securities account;

(2) receives a financial asset from the person or acquires a financial asset for the person and, in either case, accepts it for credit to the person's securities account; or

(3) becomes obligated under other law, regulation, or rule to credit a financial asset to the person's securities account.

(c) If a condition of subsection (b) has been met, a person has a security entitlement even though the securities intermediary does not itself hold the financial asset.

(d) If a securities intermediary holds a financial asset for another person, and the financial asset is registered in the name of, payable to the order of, or specially indorsed to the other person, and has not been indorsed to the securities intermediary or in blank, the other person is treated as holding the financial asset directly rather than as having a security entitlement with respect to the financial asset.

(e) Issuance of a security is not establishment of a security entitlement.

§ 8–502. Assertion of Adverse Claim against Entitlement Holder.

An action based on an adverse claim to a financial asset, whether framed in conversion, replevin, constructive trust, equitable lien, or other theory, may not be asserted against a person who acquires a security entitlement under Section 8–501 for value and without notice of the adverse claim.

§ 8–503. Property Interest of Entitlement Holder in Financial Asset Held by Securities Intermediary.

(a) To the extent necessary for a securities intermediary to satisfy all security entitlements with respect to a particular financial asset, all interests in that financial asset held by the securities intermediary are held by the securities intermediary for the entitlement holders, are not property of the securities intermediary, and are not subject to claims of creditors of the securities intermediary, except as otherwise provided in Section 8–511.

(b) An entitlement holder's property interest with respect to a particular financial asset under subsection (a) is a pro rata property interest in all interests in that financial asset held by the securities intermediary, without regard to the time the entitlement holder acquired the security entitlement or the time the securities intermediary acquired the interest in that financial asset.

(c) An entitlement holder's property interest with respect to a particular financial asset under subsection (a) may be enforced against the securities intermediary only by exercise of the entitlement holder's rights under Sections 8–505 through 8–508.

(d) An entitlement holder's property interest with respect to a particular financial asset under subsection (a) may be enforced against a purchaser of the financial asset or interest therein only if:

(1) insolvency proceedings have been initiated by or against the securities intermediary;

(2) the securities intermediary does not have sufficient interests in the financial asset to satisfy the security entitlements of all of its entitlement holders to that financial asset;

(3) the securities intermediary violated its obligations under Section 8–504 by transferring the financial asset or interest therein to the purchaser; and

(4) the purchaser is not protected under sub-section (e).

The trustee or other liquidator, acting on behalf of all entitlement holders having security entitlements with respect to a particular financial asset, may recover the financial asset, or interest therein, from the purchaser. If the trustee or other liquidator elects not to pursue that right, an entitlement holder whose security entitlement remains unsatisfied has the right to recover its interest in the financial asset from the purchaser.

(e) An action based on the entitlement holder's property interest with respect to a particular financial asset under subsection (a), whether framed in conversion, replevin, constructive trust, equitable lien, or other theory, may not be asserted against any purchaser of a financial asset or interest therein who gives value, obtains control, and does not act in collusion with the securities intermediary in violating the securities intermediary's obligations under Section 8–504.

§ 8–504. Duty of Securities Intermediary to Maintain Financial Asset.

(a) A securities intermediary shall promptly obtain and thereafter maintain a financial asset in a quantity corresponding to the aggregate of all security entitlements it has established in favor of its entitlement holders with respect to that financial asset. The securities intermediary may maintain those financial assets directly or through one or more other securities intermediaries.

(b) Except to the extent otherwise agreed by its entitlement holder, a securities intermediary may not grant any security interests in a financial asset it is obligated to maintain pursuant to subsection (a).

(c) A securities intermediary satisfies the duty in subsection (a) if:

(1) the securities intermediary acts with respect to the duty as agreed upon by the entitlement holder and the securities intermediary; or

(2) in the absence of agreement, the securities intermediary exercises due care in accordance with reasonable commercial standards to obtain and maintain the financial asset.

(d) This section does not apply to a clearing corporation that is itself the obligor of an option or similar obligation to which its entitlement holders have security entitlements.

§ 8–505. Duty of Securities Intermediary with Respect to Payments and Distributions.

(a) A securities intermediary shall take action to obtain a payment or distribution made by the issuer of a financial asset. A securities intermediary satisfies the duty if:

(1) the securities intermediary acts with respect to the duty as agreed upon by the entitlement holder and the securities intermediary; or

(2) in the absence of agreement, the securities intermediary exercises due care in accordance with reasonable commercial standards to attempt to obtain the payment or distribution.

(b) A securities intermediary is obligated to its entitlement holder for a payment or distribution made by the issuer of a financial asset if the payment or distribution is received by the securities intermediary.

§ 8–506. Duty of Securities Intermediary to Exercise Rights as Directed by Entitlement Holder.

A securities intermediary shall exercise rights with respect to a financial asset if directed to do so by an entitlement holder. A securities intermediary satisfies the duty if:

(1) the securities intermediary acts with respect to the duty as agreed upon by the entitlement holder and the securities intermediary; or

(2) in the absence of agreement, the securities intermediary either places the entitlement holder in a position to exercise the rights directly or exercises due care in accordance with reasonable commercial standards to follow the direction of the entitlement holder.

§ 8–507. Duty of Securities Intermediary to Comply with Entitlement Order.

(a) A securities intermediary shall comply with an entitlement order if the entitlement order is originated by the appropriate person, the securities intermediary has had reasonable opportunity to assure itself that the entitlement order is genuine and authorized, and the securities intermediary has had reasonable opportunity to comply with the entitlement order. A securities intermediary satisfies the duty if:

(1) the securities intermediary acts with respect to the duty as agreed upon by the entitlement holder and the securities intermediary; or

(2) in the absence of agreement, the securities intermediary exercises due care in accordance with reasonable commercial standards to comply with the entitlement order.

(b) If a securities intermediary transfers a financial asset pursuant to an ineffective entitlement order, the securities intermediary shall reestablish a security entitlement in favor of the person entitled to it, and pay or credit any payments or distributions that the person did not receive as a result of the wrongful transfer. If the securities intermediary does not reestablish a security entitlement, the securities intermediary is liable to the entitlement holder for damages.

§ 8–508. Duty of Securities Intermediary to Change Entitlement Holder's Position to Other Form of Security Holding.

A securities intermediary shall act at the direction of an entitlement holder to change a security entitlement into another available form of holding for which the entitlement holder is eligible, or to cause the financial asset to be transferred to a securities account of the entitlement holder with another securities intermediary. A securities intermediary satisfies the duty if:

(1) the securities intermediary acts as agreed upon by the entitlement holder and the securities intermediary; or

(2) in the absence of agreement, the securities intermediary exercises due care in accordance with reasonable commercial standards to follow the direction of the entitlement holder.

§ 8–509. Specification of Duties of Securities Intermediary by Other Statute or Regulation; Manner of Performance of Duties of Securities Intermediary and Exercise of Rights of Entitlement Holder.

(a) If the substance of a duty imposed upon a securities intermediary by Sections 8–504 through 8–508 is the subject of other statute, regulation, or rule, compliance with that statute, regulation, or rule satisfies the duty.

(b) To the extent that specific standards for the performance of the duties of a securities intermediary or the exercise of the rights of an entitlement holder are not specified by other statute, regulation, or rule or by agreement between the securities intermediary and entitlement holder, the securities intermediary shall perform its duties and the entitlement holder shall exercise its rights in a commercially reasonable manner.

(c) The obligation of a securities intermediary to perform the duties imposed by Sections 8–504 through 8–508 is subject to:

> **(1)** rights of the securities intermediary arising out of a security interest under a security agreement with the entitlement holder or otherwise; and

> **(2)** rights of the securities intermediary under other law, regulation, rule, or agreement to withhold performance of its duties as a result of unfulfilled obligations of the entitlement holder to the securities intermediary.

(d) Sections 8–504 through 8–508 do not require a securities intermediary to take any action that is prohibited by other statute, regulation, or rule.

§ 8–510. Rights of Purchaser of Security Entitlement from Entitlement Holder.

(a) An action based on an adverse claim to a financial asset or security entitlement, whether framed in conversion, replevin, constructive trust, equitable lien, or other theory, may not be asserted against a person who purchases a security entitlement, or an interest therein, from an entitlement holder if the purchaser gives value, does not have notice of the adverse claim, and obtains control.

(b) If an adverse claim could not have been asserted against an entitlement holder under Section 8–502, the adverse claim cannot be asserted against a person who purchases a security entitlement, or an interest therein, from the entitlement holder.

(c) In a case not covered by the priority rules in Article 9, a purchaser for value of a security entitlement, or an interest therein, who obtains control has priority over a purchaser of a security entitlement, or an interest therein, who does not obtain control. Except as otherwise provided in subsection (d), purchasers who have control rank according to priority in time of:

> **(1)** the purchaser's becoming the person for whom the securities account, in which the security entitlement is carried, is maintained, if the purchaser obtained control under Section 8–106(d)(1);

> **(2)** the securities intermediary's agreement to comply with the purchaser's entitlement orders with respect to security entitlements carried or to be carried in the securities account in which the security entitlement is carried, if the purchaser obtained control under Section 8–106(d)(2); or

> **(3)** if the purchaser obtained control through another person under Section 8–106(d)(3), the time on which priority would be based under this subsection if the other person were the secured party.

(d) A securities intermediary as purchaser has priority over a conflicting purchaser who has control unless otherwise agreed by the securities intermediary.
As amended in 1999.

§ 8–511. Priority among Security Interests and Entitlement Holders.

(a) Except as otherwise provided in subsections (b) and (c), if a securities intermediary does not have sufficient interests in a particular financial asset to satisfy both its obligations to entitlement holders who have security entitlements to that financial asset and its obligation to a creditor of the securities intermediary who has a security interest in that financial asset, the claims of entitlement holders, other than the creditor, have priority over the claim of the creditor.

(b) A claim of a creditor of a securities intermediary who has a security interest in a financial asset held by a securities intermediary has priority over claims of the securities intermediary's entitlement holders who have security entitlements with respect to that financial asset if the creditor has control over the financial asset.

(c) If a clearing corporation does not have sufficient financial assets to satisfy both its obligations to entitlement holders who have security entitlements with respect to a financial asset and its obligation to a creditor of the clearing corporation who has a security interest in that financial asset, the claim of the creditor has priority over the claims of entitlement holders.

Part 6—Transition Provisions for Revised Article 8

§ 8–601. Effective Date.
This [Act] takes effect . . . .

§ 8–602. Repeals.
This [Act] repeals . . . .

§ 8–603. Savings Clause.

(a) This [Act] does not affect an action or proceeding commenced before this [Act] takes effect.

(b) If a security interest in a security is perfected at the date this [Act] takes effect, and the action by which the security interest was perfected would suffice to perfect a security interest under this [Act], no further action is required to continue perfection. If a security interest in a security is perfected at the date this [Act] takes effect but the action by which the security interest was perfected would not suffice to perfect a security interest under this [Act], the security interest remains perfected for a period of four months after the effective date and continues perfected thereafter if appropriate action to perfect under this [Act] is taken within that period. If a security interest is perfected at the date this [Act] takes effect and the security interest can be perfected by filing under this [Act], a financing statement signed by the secured party instead of the debtor may be filed within that period to continue perfection or thereafter to perfect.

REVISED ARTICLE 9: SECURED TRANSACTIONS

Part 1—General Provisions

[Subpart 1. Short Title, Definitions, and General Concepts]

§ 9–101. Short Title.
This article may be cited as Uniform Commercial Code—Secured Transactions.

§ 9–102. Definitions and Index of Definitions.

(a) In this article:

> **(1)** "Accession" means goods that are physically united with other goods in such a manner that the identity of the original goods is not lost.

> **(2)** "Account", except as used in "account for", means a right to payment of a monetary obligation, whether or not earned by performance, (i) for property that has been or is to be sold,

leased, licensed, assigned, or otherwise disposed of, (ii) for services rendered or to be rendered, (iii) for a policy of insurance issued or to be issued, (iv) for a secondary obligation incurred or to be incurred, (v) for energy provided or to be pro-vided, (vi) for the use or hire of a vessel under a charter or other contract, (vii) arising out of the use of a credit or charge card or information contained on or for use with the card, or (viii) as winnings in a lottery or other game of chance operated or sponsored by a State, governmental unit of a State, or person licensed or authorized to operate the game by a State or governmental unit of a State. The term includes health-care insurance receivables. The term does not include (i) rights to payment evidenced by chattel paper or an instrument, (ii) commercial tort claims, (iii) deposit accounts, (iv) investment property, (v) letter-of-credit rights or letters of credit, or (vi) rights to payment for money or funds advanced or sold, other than rights arising out of the use of a credit or charge card or information contained on or for use with the card.

(3) "Account debtor" means a person obligated on an account, chattel paper, or general intangible. The term does not include persons obligated to pay a negotiable instrument, even if the instrument constitutes part of chattel paper.

(4) "Accounting", except as used in "accounting for", means a record:

   (A) authenticated by a secured party;

   (B) indicating the aggregate unpaid secured obligations as of a date not more than 35 days earlier or 35 days later than the date of the record; and

   (C) identifying the components of the obligations in reasonable detail.

(5) "Agricultural lien" means an interest, other than a security interest, in farm products:

   (A) which secures payment or performance of an obligation for:

      (i) goods or services furnished in connection with a debtor's farming operation; or

      (ii) rent on real property leased by a debtor in connection with its farming operation;

   (B) which is created by statute in favor of a person that:

      (i) in the ordinary course of its business furnished goods or services to a debtor in connection with a debtor's farming operation; or

      (ii) leased real property to a debtor in connection with the debtor's farming operation; and

   (C) whose effectiveness does not depend on the person's possession of the personal property.

(6) "As-extracted collateral" means:

   (A) oil, gas, or other minerals that are subject to a security interest that:

      (i) is created by a debtor having an interest in the minerals before extraction; and

      (ii) attaches to the minerals as extracted; or

   (B) accounts arising out of the sale at the wellhead or minehead of oil, gas, or other minerals in which the debtor had an interest before extraction.

(7) "Authenticate" means:

   (A) to sign; or

   (B) to execute or otherwise adopt a symbol, or encrypt or similarly process a record in whole or in part, with the present intent of the authenticating person to identify the person and adopt or accept a record.

(8) "Bank" means an organization that is engaged in the business of banking. The term includes savings banks, savings and loan associations, credit unions, and trust companies.

(9) "Cash proceeds" means proceeds that are money, checks, deposit accounts, or the like.

(10) "Certificate of title" means a certificate of title with respect to which a statute provides for the security interest in question to be indicated on the certificate as a condition or result of the security interest's obtaining priority over the rights of a lien creditor with respect to the collateral.

(11) "Chattel paper" means a record or records that evidence both a monetary obligation and a security interest in specific goods, a security interest in specific goods and software used in the goods, a security interest in specific goods and license of software used in the goods, a lease of specific goods, or a lease of specific goods and license of software used in the goods. In this paragraph, "monetary obligation" means a monetary obligation secured by the goods or owed under a lease of the goods and includes a monetary obligation with respect to software used in the goods. The term does not include (i) charters or other contracts involving the use or hire of a vessel or (ii) records that evidence a right to payment arising out of the use of a credit or charge card or information contained on or for use with the card. If a transaction is evidenced by records that include an instrument or series of instruments, the group of records taken together constitutes chattel paper.

(12) "Collateral" means the property subject to a security interest or agricultural lien. The term includes:

   (A) proceeds to which a security interest attaches;

   (B) accounts, chattel paper, payment intangibles, and promissory notes that have been sold; and

   (C) goods that are the subject of a consignment.

(13) "Commercial tort claim" means a claim arising in tort with respect to which:

   (A) the claimant is an organization; or

   (B) the claimant is an individual and the claim:

      (i) arose in the course of the claimant's business or profession; and

      (ii) does not include damages arising out of personal injury to or the death of an individual.

(14) "Commodity account" means an account maintained by a commodity intermediary in which a commodity contract is carried for a commodity customer.

(15) "Commodity contract" means a commodity futures contract, an option on a commodity futures contract, a commodity option, or another contract if the contract or option is:

   (A) traded on or subject to the rules of a board of trade that has been designated as a contract market for such a contract pursuant to federal commodities laws; or

   (B) traded on a foreign commodity board of trade, exchange, or market, and is carried on the books of a commodity intermediary for a commodity customer.

(16) "Commodity customer" means a person for which a commodity intermediary carries a commodity contract on its books.

(17) "Commodity intermediary" means a person that:

   (A) is registered as a futures commission merchant under federal commodities law; or

(B) in the ordinary course of its business provides clearance or settlement services for a board of trade that has been designated as a contract market pursuant to federal commodities law.

(18) "Communicate" means:

(A) to send a written or other tangible record;

(B) to transmit a record by any means agreed upon by the persons sending and receiving the record; or

(C) in the case of transmission of a record to or by a filing office, to transmit a record by any means prescribed by filing-office rule.

(19) "Consignee" means a merchant to which goods are delivered in a consignment.

(20) "Consignment" means a transaction, regardless of its form, in which a person delivers goods to a merchant for the purpose of sale and:

(A) the merchant:

(i) deals in goods of that kind under a name other than the name of the person making delivery;

(ii) is not an auctioneer; and

(iii) is not generally known by its creditors to be substantially engaged in selling the goods of others;

(B) with respect to each delivery, the aggregate value of the goods is $1,000 or more at the time of delivery;

(C) the goods are not consumer goods immediately before delivery; and

(D) the transaction does not create a security interest that secures an obligation.

(21) "Consignor" means a person that delivers goods to a consignee in a consignment.

(22) "Consumer debtor" means a debtor in a consumer transaction.

(23) "Consumer goods" means goods that are used or bought for use primarily for personal, family, or household purposes.

(24) "Consumer-goods transaction" means a consumer transaction in which:

(A) an individual incurs an obligation primarily for personal, family, or household purposes; and

(B) a security interest in consumer goods secures the obligation.

(25) "Consumer obligor" means an obligor who is an individual and who incurred the obligation as part of a transaction entered into primarily for personal, family, or household purposes.

(26) "Consumer transaction" means a transaction in which (i) an individual incurs an obligation primarily for personal, family, or household purposes, (ii) a security interest secures the obligation, and (iii) the collateral is held or acquired primarily for personal, family, or household purposes. The term includes consumer-goods transactions.

(27) "Continuation statement" means an amendment of a financing statement which:

(A) identifies, by its file number, the initial financing statement to which it relates; and

(B) indicates that it is a continuation statement for, or that it is filed to continue the effectiveness of, the identified financing statement.

(28) "Debtor" means:

(A) a person having an interest, other than a security interest or other lien, in the collateral, whether or not the person is an obligor;

(B) a seller of accounts, chattel paper, payment intangibles, or promissory notes; or

(C) a consignee.

(29) "Deposit account" means a demand, time, savings, passbook, or similar account maintained with a bank. The term does not include investment property or accounts evidenced by an instrument.

(30) "Document" means a document of title or a receipt of the type described in Section 7–201(2).

(31) "Electronic chattel paper" means chattel paper evidenced by a record or records consisting of information stored in an electronic medium.

(32) "Encumbrance" means a right, other than an ownership interest, in real property. The term includes mortgages and other liens on real property.

(33) "Equipment" means goods other than inventory, farm products, or consumer goods.

(34) "Farm products" means goods, other than standing timber, with respect to which the debtor is engaged in a farming operation and which are:

(A) crops grown, growing, or to be grown, including:

(i) crops produced on trees, vines, and bushes; and

(ii) aquatic goods produced in aquacultural operations;

(B) livestock, born or unborn, including aquatic goods produced in aquacultural operations;

(C) supplies used or produced in a farming operation; or

(D) products of crops or livestock in their unmanufactured states.

(35) "Farming operation" means raising, cultivating, propagating, fattening, grazing, or any other farming, livestock, or aquacultural operation.

(36) "File number" means the number assigned to an initial financing statement pursuant to Section 9–519(a).

(37) "Filing office" means an office designated in Section 9–501 as the place to file a financing statement.

(38) "Filing-office rule" means a rule adopted pursuant to Section 9–526.

(39) "Financing statement" means a record or records composed of an initial financing statement and any filed record relating to the initial financing statement.

(40) "Fixture filing" means the filing of a financing statement covering goods that are or are to become fixtures and satisfying Section 9–502(a) and (b). The term includes the filing of a financing statement covering goods of a transmitting utility which are or are to become fixtures.

(41) "Fixtures" means goods that have become so related to particular real property that an interest in them arises under real property law.

(42) "General intangible" means any personal property, including things in action, other than accounts, chattel paper, commercial tort claims, deposit accounts, documents, goods, instruments, investment property, letter-of-credit rights, letters of credit, money, and oil, gas, or other minerals before extraction. The term includes payment intangibles and software.

(43) "Good faith" means honesty in fact and the observance of reasonable commercial standards of fair dealing.

(44) "Goods" means all things that are movable when a security interest attaches. The term includes (i) fixtures, (ii) standing timber that is to be cut and removed under a conveyance or contract for sale, (iii) the unborn young of animals, (iv) crops grown, growing, or to be grown, even if the crops are produced on trees, vines, or bushes, and (v) manufactured homes. The term also includes a computer program embedded in goods and any supporting information provided in connection with a transaction relating to the program if (i) the program is associated with the goods in such a manner that it customarily is considered part of the goods, or (ii) by becoming the owner of the goods, a person acquires a right to use the program in connection with the goods. The term does not include a computer program embedded in goods that consist solely of the medium in which the program is embedded. The term also does not include accounts, chattel paper, commercial tort claims, deposit accounts, documents, general intangibles, instruments, investment property, letter-of-credit rights, letters of credit, money, or oil, gas, or other minerals before extraction.

(45) "Governmental unit" means a subdivision, agency, department, county, parish, municipality, or other unit of the government of the United States, a State, or a foreign country. The term includes an organization having a separate corporate existence if the organization is eligible to issue debt on which interest is exempt from income taxation under the laws of the United States.

(46) "Health-care-insurance receivable" means an interest in or claim under a policy of insurance which is a right to payment of a monetary obligation for health-care goods or services provided.

(47) "Instrument" means a negotiable instrument or any other writing that evidences a right to the payment of a monetary obligation, is not itself a security agreement or lease, and is of a type that in ordinary course of business is transferred by delivery with any necessary indorsement or assignment. The term does not include (i) investment property, (ii) letters of credit, or (iii) writings that evidence a right to payment arising out of the use of a credit or charge card or information contained on or for use with the card.

(48) "Inventory" means goods, other than farm products, which:

(A) are leased by a person as lessor;

(B) are held by a person for sale or lease or to be furnished under a contract of service;

(C) are furnished by a person under a contract of service; or

(D) consist of raw materials, work in process, or materials used or consumed in a business.

(49) "Investment property" means a security, whether certificated or uncertificated, security entitlement, securities account, commodity contract, or commodity account.

(50) "Jurisdiction of organization", with respect to a registered organization, means the jurisdiction under whose law the organization is organized.

(51) "Letter-of-credit right" means a right to payment or performance under a letter of credit, whether or not the beneficiary has demanded or is at the time entitled to demand payment or performance. The term does not include the right of a beneficiary to demand payment or performance under a letter of credit.

(52) "Lien creditor" means:

(A) a creditor that has acquired a lien on the property involved by attachment, levy, or the like;

(B) an assignee for benefit of creditors from the time of assignment;

(C) a trustee in bankruptcy from the date of the filing of the petition; or

(D) a receiver in equity from the time of appointment.

(53) "Manufactured home" means a structure, transportable in one or more sections, which, in the traveling mode, is eight body feet or more in width or 40 body feet or more in length, or, when erected on site, is 320 or more square feet, and which is built on a permanent chassis and designed to be used as a dwelling with or without a permanent foundation when connected to the required utilities, and includes the plumbing, heating, air-conditioning, and electrical systems contained therein. The term includes any structure that meets all of the requirements of this paragraph except the size requirements and with respect to which the manufacturer voluntarily files a certification required by the United States Secretary of Housing and Urban Development and complies with the standards established under Title 42 of the United States Code.

(54) "Manufactured-home transaction" means a secured transaction:

(A) that creates a purchase-money security interest in a manufactured home, other than a manufactured home held as inventory; or

(B) in which a manufactured home, other than a manufactured home held as inventory, is the primary collateral.

(55) "Mortgage" means a consensual interest in real property, including fixtures, which secures payment or performance of an obligation.

(56) "New debtor" means a person that becomes bound as debtor under Section 9–203(d) by a security agreement previously entered into by another person.

(57) "New value" means (i) money, (ii) money's worth in property, services, or new credit, or (iii) release by a transferee of an interest in property previously transferred to the transferee. The term does not include an obligation substituted for another obligation.

(58) "Noncash proceeds" means proceeds other than cash proceeds.

(59) "Obligor" means a person that, with respect to an obligation secured by a security interest in or an agricultural lien on the collateral, (i) owes payment or other performance of the obligation, (ii) has provided property other than the collateral to secure payment or other performance of the obligation, or (iii) is otherwise accountable in whole or in part for payment or other performance of the obligation. The term does not include issuers or nominated persons under a letter of credit.

(60) "Original debtor", except as used in Section 9–310(c), means a person that, as debtor, entered into a security agreement to which a new debtor has become bound under Section 9–203(d).

(61) "Payment intangible" means a general intangible under which the account debtor's principal obligation is a monetary obligation.

(62) "Person related to", with respect to an individual, means:

(A) the spouse of the individual;

(B) a brother, brother-in-law, sister, or sister-in-law of the individual;

(C) an ancestor or lineal descendant of the individual or the individual's spouse; or

(D) any other relative, by blood or marriage, of the individual or the individual's spouse who shares the same home with the individual.

(63) "Person related to", with respect to an organization, means:

(A) a person directly or indirectly controlling, controlled by, or under common control with the organization;

(B) an officer or director of, or a person performing similar functions with respect to, the organization;

(C) an officer or director of, or a person performing similar functions with respect to, a person described in subparagraph (A);

(D) the spouse of an individual described in subparagraph (A), (B), or (C); or

(E) an individual who is related by blood or marriage to an individual described in subparagraph (A), (B), (C), or (D) and shares the same home with the individual.

(64) "Proceeds", except as used in Section 9–609(b), means the following property:

(A) whatever is acquired upon the sale, lease, license, exchange, or other disposition of collateral;

(B) whatever is collected on, or distributed on account of, collateral;

(C) rights arising out of collateral;

(D) to the extent of the value of collateral, claims arising out of the loss, nonconformity, or interference with the use of, defects or infringement of rights in, or damage to, the collateral; or

(E) to the extent of the value of collateral and to the extent payable to the debtor or the secured party, insurance payable by reason of the loss or nonconformity of, defects or infringement of rights in, or damage to, the collateral.

(65) "Promissory note" means an instrument that evidences a promise to pay a monetary obligation, does not evidence an order to pay, and does not contain an acknowledgment by a bank that the bank has received for deposit a sum of money or funds.

(66) "Proposal" means a record authenticated by a secured party which includes the terms on which the secured party is willing to accept collateral in full or partial satisfaction of the obligation it secures pursuant to Sections 9–620, 9–621, and 9–622.

(67) "Public-finance transaction" means a secured transaction in connection with which:

(A) debt securities are issued;

(B) all or a portion of the securities issued have an initial stated maturity of at least 20 years; and

(C) the debtor, obligor, secured party, account debtor or other person obligated on collateral, assignor or assignee of a secured obligation, or assignor or assignee of a security interest is a State or a governmental unit of a State.

(68) "Pursuant to commitment", with respect to an advance made or other value given by a secured party, means pursuant to the secured party's obligation, whether or not a subsequent event of default or other event not within the secured party's control has relieved or may relieve the secured party from its obligation.

(69) "Record", except as used in "for record", "of record", "record or legal title", and "record owner", means information that is inscribed on a tangible medium or which is stored in an electronic or other medium and is retrievable in perceivable form.

(70) "Registered organization" means an organization organized solely under the law of a single State or the United States and as to which the State or the United States must maintain a public record showing the organization to have been organized.

(71) "Secondary obligor" means an obligor to the extent that:

(A) the obligor's obligation is secondary; or

(B) the obligor has a right of recourse with respect to an obligation secured by collateral against the debtor, another obligor, or property of either.

(72) "Secured party" means:

(A) a person in whose favor a security interest is created or provided for under a security agreement, whether or not any obligation to be secured is outstanding;

(B) a person that holds an agricultural lien;

(C) a consignor;

(D) a person to which accounts, chattel paper, payment intangibles, or promissory notes have been sold;

(E) a trustee, indenture trustee, agent, collateral agent, or other representative in whose favor a security interest or agricultural lien is created or provided for; or

(F) a person that holds a security interest arising under Section 2–401, 2–505, 2–711(3), 2A–508(5), 4–210, or 5–118.

(73) "Security agreement" means an agreement that creates or provides for a security interest.

(74) "Send", in connection with a record or notification, means:

(A) to deposit in the mail, deliver for transmission, or transmit by any other usual means of communication, with postage or cost of transmission provided for, addressed to any address reasonable under the circumstances; or

(B) to cause the record or notification to be received within the time that it would have been received if properly sent under subparagraph (A).

(75) "Software" means a computer program and any supporting information provided in connection with a transaction relating to the program. The term does not include a computer program that is included in the definition of goods.

(76) "State" means a State of the United States, the District of Columbia, Puerto Rico, the United States Virgin Islands, or any territory or insular possession subject to the jurisdiction of the United States.

(77) "Supporting obligation" means a letter-of-credit right or secondary obligation that supports the payment or performance of an account, chattel paper, a document, a general intangible, an instrument, or investment property.

(78) "Tangible chattel paper" means chattel paper evidenced by a record or records consisting of information that is inscribed on a tangible medium.

(79) "Termination statement" means an amendment of a financing statement which:

(A) identifies, by its file number, the initial financing statement to which it relates; and

(B) indicates either that it is a termination statement or that the identified financing statement is no longer effective.

(80) "Transmitting utility" means a person primarily engaged in the business of:

(A) operating a railroad, subway, street railway, or trolley bus;

(B) transmitting communications electrically, electromagnetically, or by light;

(C) transmitting goods by pipeline or sewer; or

(D) transmitting or producing and transmitting electricity, steam, gas, or water.

(b) The following definitions in other articles apply to this article:

"Applicant."	Section 5–102
"Beneficiary."	Section 5–102
"Broker."	Section 8–102
"Certificated security."	Section 8–102
"Check."	Section 3–104
"Clearing corporation."	Section 8–102
"Contract for sale."	Section 2–106
"Customer."	Section 4–104
"Entitlement holder."	Section 8–102
"Financial asset."	Section 8–102
"Holder in due course."	Section 3–302
"Issuer" (with respect to a letter of credit or letter-of-credit right).	Section 5–102
"Issuer" (with respect to a security).	Section 8–201
"Lease."	Section 2A–103
"Lease agreement."	Section 2A–103
"Lease contract."	Section 2A–103
"Leasehold interest."	Section 2A–103
"Lessee."	Section 2A–103
"Lessee in ordinary course of business."	Section 2A–103
"Lessor."	Section 2A–103
"Lessor's residual interest."	Section 2A–103
"Letter of credit."	Section 5–102
"Merchant."	Section 2–104
"Negotiable instrument."	Section 3–104
"Nominated person."	Section 5–102
"Note."	Section 3–104
"Proceeds of a letter of credit."	Section 5–114
"Prove."	Section 3–103
"Sale."	Section 2–106
"Securities account."	Section 8–501
"Securities intermediary."	Section 8–102
"Security."	Section 8–102
"Security certificate."	Section 8–102
"Security entitlement."	Section 8–102
"Uncertificated security."	Section 8–102

(c) Article 1 contains general definitions and principles of construction and interpretation applicable throughout this article.

Amended in 1999 and 2000.

§ 9–103. Purchase-Money Security Interest; Application of Payments; Burden of Establishing.

(a) In this section:

(1) "purchase-money collateral" means goods or software that secures a purchase-money obligation incurred with respect to that collateral; and

(2) "purchase-money obligation" means an obligation of an obligor incurred as all or part of the price of the collateral or for value given to enable the debtor to acquire rights in or the use of the collateral if the value is in fact so used.

(b) A security interest in goods is a purchase-money security interest:

(1) to the extent that the goods are purchase-money collateral with respect to that security interest;

(2) if the security interest is in inventory that is or was purchase-money collateral, also to the extent that the security interest secures a purchase-money obligation incurred with respect to other inventory in which the secured party holds or held a purchase-money security interest; and

(3) also to the extent that the security interest secures a purchase-money obligation incurred with respect to software in which the secured party holds or held a purchase-money security interest.

(c) A security interest in software is a purchase-money security interest to the extent that the security interest also secures a purchase-money obligation incurred with respect to goods in which the secured party holds or held a purchase-money security interest if:

(1) the debtor acquired its interest in the software in an integrated transaction in which it acquired an interest in the goods; and

(2) the debtor acquired its interest in the software for the principal purpose of using the software in the goods.

(d) The security interest of a consignor in goods that are the subject of a consignment is a purchase-money security interest in inventory.

(e) In a transaction other than a consumer-goods transaction, if the extent to which a security interest is a purchase-money security interest depends on the application of a payment to a particular obligation, the payment must be applied:

(1) in accordance with any reasonable method of application to which the parties agree;

(2) in the absence of the parties' agreement to a reasonable method, in accordance with any intention of the obligor manifested at or before the time of payment; or

(3) in the absence of an agreement to a reasonable method and a timely manifestation of the obligor's intention, in the following order:

(A) to obligations that are not secured; and

(B) if more than one obligation is secured, to obligations secured by purchase-money security interests in the order in which those obligations were incurred.

(f) In a transaction other than a consumer-goods transaction, a purchase-money security interest does not lose its status as such, even if:

(1) the purchase-money collateral also secures an obligation that is not a purchase-money obligation;

(2) collateral that is not purchase-money collateral also secures the purchase-money obligation; or

(3) the purchase-money obligation has been renewed, refinanced, consolidated, or restructured.

(g) In a transaction other than a consumer-goods transaction, a secured party claiming a purchase-money security interest has the burden of establishing the extent to which the security interest is a purchase-money security interest.

(h) The limitation of the rules in subsections (e), (f), and (g) to transactions other than consumer-goods transactions is intended to leave to the court the determination of the proper rules in consumer-goods transactions. The court may not infer from that limitation the nature of the proper rule in consumer-goods transactions and may continue to apply established approaches.

§ 9–104. Control of Deposit Account.

(a) A secured party has control of a deposit account if:

(1) the secured party is the bank with which the deposit account is maintained;

(2) the debtor, secured party, and bank have agreed in an authenticated record that the bank will comply with instructions originated by the secured party directing disposition of the funds in the deposit account without further consent by the debtor; or

(3) the secured party becomes the bank's customer with respect to the deposit account.

(b) A secured party that has satisfied subsection (a) has control, even if the debtor retains the right to direct the disposition of funds from the deposit account.

§ 9–105. Control of Electronic Chattel Paper.

A secured party has control of electronic chattel paper if the record or records comprising the chattel paper are created, stored, and assigned in such a manner that:

(1) a single authoritative copy of the record or records exists which is unique, identifiable and, except as otherwise provided in paragraphs (4), (5), and (6), unalterable;

(2) the authoritative copy identifies the secured party as the assignee of the record or records;

(3) the authoritative copy is communicated to and maintained by the secured party or its designated custodian;

(4) copies or revisions that add or change an identified assignee of the authoritative copy can be made only with the participation of the secured party;

(5) each copy of the authoritative copy and any copy of a copy is readily identifiable as a copy that is not the authoritative copy; and

(6) any revision of the authoritative copy is readily identifiable as an authorized or unauthorized revision.

§ 9–106. Control of Investment Property.

(a) A person has control of a certificated security, uncertificated security, or security entitlement as provided in Section 8–106.

(b) A secured party has control of a commodity contract if:

(1) the secured party is the commodity intermediary with which the commodity contract is carried; or

(2) the commodity customer, secured party, and commodity intermediary have agreed that the commodity intermediary will apply any value distributed on account of the commodity contract as directed by the secured party without further consent by the commodity customer.

(c) A secured party having control of all security entitlements or commodity contracts carried in a securities account or commodity account has control over the securities account or commodity account.

§ 9–107. Control of Letter-of-Credit Right.

A secured party has control of a letter-of-credit right to the extent of any right to payment or performance by the issuer or any nominated person if the issuer or nominated person has consented to an assignment of proceeds of the letter of credit under Section 5–114(c) or otherwise applicable law or practice.

§ 9–108. Sufficiency of Description.

(a) Except as otherwise provided in subsections (c), (d), and (e), a description of personal or real property is sufficient, whether or not it is specific, if it reasonably identifies what is described.

(b) Except as otherwise provided in subsection (d), a description of collateral reasonably identifies the collateral if it identifies the collateral by:

(1) specific listing;

(2) category;

(3) except as otherwise provided in subsection (e), a type of collateral defined in [the Uniform Commercial Code];

(4) quantity;

(5) computational or allocational formula or procedure; or

(6) except as otherwise provided in subsection (c), any other method, if the identity of the collateral is objectively determinable.

(c) A description of collateral as "all the debtor's assets" or "all the debtor's personal property" or using words of similar import does not reasonably identify the collateral.

(d) Except as otherwise provided in subsection (e), a description of a security entitlement, securities account, or commodity account is sufficient if it describes:

(1) the collateral by those terms or as investment property; or

(2) the underlying financial asset or commodity contract.

(e) A description only by type of collateral defined in [the Uniform Commercial Code] is an insufficient description of:

(1) a commercial tort claim; or

(2) in a consumer transaction, consumer goods, a security entitlement, a securities account, or a commodity account.

[Subpart 2. Applicability of Article]

§ 9–109. Scope.

(a) Except as otherwise provided in subsections (c) and (d), this article applies to:

(1) a transaction, regardless of its form, that creates a security interest in personal property or fixtures by contract;

(2) an agricultural lien;

(3) a sale of accounts, chattel paper, payment intangibles, or promissory notes;

(4) a consignment;

(5) a security interest arising under Section 2–401, 2–505, 2–711(3), or 2A–508(5), as provided in Section 9–110; and

(6) a security interest arising under Section 4–210 or 5–118.

(b) The application of this article to a security interest in a secured obligation is not affected by the fact that the obligation is itself secured by a transaction or interest to which this article does not apply.

(c) This article does not apply to the extent that:

(1) a statute, regulation, or treaty of the United States preempts this article;

(2) another statute of this State expressly governs the creation, perfection, priority, or enforcement of a security interest created by this State or a governmental unit of this State;

(3) a statute of another State, a foreign country, or a governmental unit of another State or a foreign country, other than a statute generally applicable to security interests, expressly governs creation, perfection, priority, or enforcement of a security interest created by the State, country, or governmental unit; or

(4) the rights of a transferee beneficiary or nominated person under a letter of credit are independent and superior under Section 5–114.

(d) This article does not apply to:

(1) a landlord's lien, other than an agricultural lien;

(2) a lien, other than an agricultural lien, given by statute or other rule of law for services or materials, but Section 9–333 applies with respect to priority of the lien;

(3) an assignment of a claim for wages, salary, or other compensation of an employee;

(4) a sale of accounts, chattel paper, payment intangibles, or promissory notes as part of a sale of the business out of which they arose;

(5) an assignment of accounts, chattel paper, payment intangibles, or promissory notes which is for the purpose of collection only;

(6) an assignment of a right to payment under a contract to an assignee that is also obligated to perform under the contract;

(7) an assignment of a single account, payment intangible, or promissory note to an assignee in full or partial satisfaction of a preexisting indebtedness;

(8) a transfer of an interest in or an assignment of a claim under a policy of insurance, other than an assignment by or to a health-care provider of a health-care-insurance receivable and any subsequent assignment of the right to payment, but Sections 9–315 and 9–322 apply with respect to proceeds and priorities in proceeds;

(9) an assignment of a right represented by a judgment, other than a judgment taken on a right to payment that was collateral;

(10) a right of recoupment or set-off, but:

(A) Section 9–340 applies with respect to the effectiveness of rights of recoupment or set-off against deposit accounts; and

(B) Section 9–404 applies with respect to defenses or claims of an account debtor;

(11) the creation or transfer of an interest in or lien on real property, including a lease or rents thereunder, except to the extent that provision is made for:

(A) liens on real property in Sections 9–203 and 9–308;

(B) fixtures in Section 9–334;

(C) fixture filings in Sections 9–501, 9–502, 9–512, 9–516, and 9–519; and

(D) security agreements covering personal and real property in Section 9–604;

(12) an assignment of a claim arising in tort, other than a commercial tort claim, but Sections 9–315 and 9–322 apply with respect to proceeds and priorities in proceeds; or

(13) an assignment of a deposit account in a consumer transaction, but Sections 9–315 and 9–322 apply with respect to proceeds and priorities in proceeds.

§ 9–110. Security Interests Arising under Article 2 or 2A.
A security interest arising under Section 2–401, 2–505, 2–711(3), or 2A–508(5) is subject to this article. However, until the debtor obtains possession of the goods:

(1) the security interest is enforceable, even if Section 9–203(b)(3) has not been satisfied;

(2) filing is not required to perfect the security interest;

(3) the rights of the secured party after default by the debtor are governed by Article 2 or 2A; and

(4) the security interest has priority over a conflicting security interest created by the debtor.

Part 2—Effectiveness of Security Agreement; Attachment of Security Interest; Rights of Parties to Security Agreement

[Subpart 1. Effectiveness and Attachment]

§ 9–201. General Effectiveness of Security Agreement.
(a) Except as otherwise provided in [the Uniform Commercial Code], a security agreement is effective according to its terms between the parties, against purchasers of the collateral, and against creditors.

(b) A transaction subject to this article is subject to any applicable rule of law which establishes a different rule for consumers and [insert reference to (i) any other statute or regulation that regulates the rates, charges, agreements, and practices for loans, credit sales, or other extensions of credit and (ii) any consumer-protection statute or regulation].

(c) In case of conflict between this article and a rule of law, statute, or regulation described in subsection (b), the rule of law, statute, or regulation controls. Failure to comply with a statute or regulation described in subsection (b) has only the effect the statute or regulation specifies.

(d) This article does not:

(1) validate any rate, charge, agreement, or practice that violates a rule of law, statute, or regulation described in subsection (b); or

(2) extend the application of the rule of law, statute, or regulation to a transaction not otherwise subject to it.

§ 9–202. Title to Collateral Immaterial.
Except as otherwise provided with respect to consignments or sales of accounts, chattel paper, payment intangibles, or promissory notes, the provisions of this article with regard to rights and obligations apply whether title to collateral is in the secured party or the debtor.

§ 9–203. Attachment and Enforceability of Security Interest; Proceeds; Supporting Obligations; Formal Requisites.
(a) A security interest attaches to collateral when it becomes enforceable against the debtor with respect to the collateral, unless an agreement expressly postpones the time of attachment.

(b) Except as otherwise provided in subsections (c) through (i), a security interest is enforceable against the debtor and third parties with respect to the collateral only if:

(1) value has been given;

(2) the debtor has rights in the collateral or the power to transfer rights in the collateral to a secured party; and

(3) one of the following conditions is met:

(A) the debtor has authenticated a security agreement that provides a description of the collateral and, if the security interest covers timber to be cut, a description of the land concerned;

(B) the collateral is not a certificated security and is in the possession of the secured party under Section 9–313 pursuant to the debtor's security agreement;

(C) the collateral is a certified security in registered form and the security certificate has been delivered to the secured party under Section 8–301 pursuant to the debtor's security agreement; or

(D) the collateral is deposit accounts, electronic chattel paper, investment property, or letter-of-credit rights, and the secured party has control under Section 9–104, 9–105, 9–106, or 9–107 pursuant to the debtor's security agreement.

(c) Subsection (b) is subject to Section 4–210 on the security interest of a collecting bank, Section 5–118 on the security interest of a letter-of-credit issuer or nominated person, Section 9–110 on a security interest arising under Article 2 or 2A, and Section 9–206 on security interests in investment property.

(d) A person becomes bound as debtor by a security agreement entered into by another person if, by operation of law other than this article or by contract:

(1) the security agreement becomes effective to create a security interest in the person's property; or

(2) the person becomes generally obligated for the obligations of the other person, including the obligation secured under the security agreement, and acquires or succeeds to all or substantially all of the assets of the other person.

(e) If a new debtor becomes bound as debtor by a security agreement entered into by another person:

(1) the agreement satisfies subsection (b)(3) with respect to existing or after-acquired property of the new debtor to the extent the property is described in the agreement; and

(2) another agreement is not necessary to make a security interest in the property enforceable.

(f) The attachment of a security interest in collateral gives the secured party the rights to proceeds provided by Section 9–315 and is also attachment of a security interest in a supporting obligation for the collateral.

(g) The attachment of a security interest in a right to payment or performance secured by a security interest or other lien on personal or real property is also attachment of a security interest in the security interest, mortgage, or other lien.

(h) The attachment of a security interest in a securities account is also attachment of a security interest in the security entitlements carried in the securities account.

(i) The attachment of a security interest in a commodity account is also attachment of a security interest in the commodity contracts carried in the commodity account.

§ 9–204. After-Acquired Property; Future Advances.

(a) Except as otherwise provided in subsection (b), a security agreement may create or provide for a security interest in after-acquired collateral.

(b) A security interest does not attach under a term constituting an after-acquired property clause to:

(1) consumer goods, other than an accession when given as additional security, unless the debtor acquires rights in them within 10 days after the secured party gives value; or

(2) a commercial tort claim.

(c) A security agreement may provide that collateral secures, or that accounts, chattel paper, payment intangibles, or promissory notes are sold in connection with, future advances or other value, whether or not the advances or value are given pursuant to commitment.

§ 9–205. Use or Disposition of Collateral Permissible.

(a) A security interest is not invalid or fraudulent against creditors solely because:

(1) the debtor has the right or ability to:

(A) use, commingle, or dispose of all or part of the collateral, including returned or repossessed goods;

(B) collect, compromise, enforce, or otherwise deal with collateral;

(C) accept the return of collateral or make repossessions; or

(D) use, commingle, or dispose of proceeds; or

(2) the secured party fails to require the debtor to account for proceeds or replace collateral.

(b) This section does not relax the requirements of possession if attachment, perfection, or enforcement of a security interest depends upon possession of the collateral by the secured party.

§ 9–206. Security Interest Arising in Purchase or Delivery of Financial Asset.

(a) A security interest in favor of a securities intermediary attaches to a person's security entitlement if:

(1) the person buys a financial asset through the securities intermediary in a transaction in which the person is obligated to pay the purchase price to the securities intermediary at the time of the purchase; and

(2) the securities intermediary credits the financial asset to the buyer's securities account before the buyer pays the securities intermediary.

(b) The security interest described in subsection (a) secures the person's obligation to pay for the financial asset.

(c) A security interest in favor of a person that delivers a certificated security or other financial asset represented by a writing attaches to the security or other financial asset if:

(1) the security or other financial asset:

(A) in the ordinary course of business is transferred by delivery with any necessary indorsement or assignment; and

(B) is delivered under an agreement between persons in the business of dealing with such securities or financial assets; and

(2) the agreement calls for delivery against payment.

(d) The security interest described in subsection (c) secures the obligation to make payment for the delivery.

[Subpart 2. Rights and Duties]

§ 9–207. Rights and Duties of Secured Party Having Possession or Control of Collateral.

(a) Except as otherwise provided in subsection (d), a secured party shall use reasonable care in the custody and preservation of collateral in the secured party's possession. In the case of chattel paper or an instrument, reasonable care includes taking necessary steps to preserve rights against prior parties unless otherwise agreed.

(b) Except as otherwise provided in subsection (d), if a secured party has possession of collateral:

(1) reasonable expenses, including the cost of insurance and payment of taxes or other charges, incurred in the custody, preservation, use, or operation of the collateral are chargeable to the debtor and are secured by the collateral;

(2) the risk of accidental loss or damage is on the debtor to the extent of a deficiency in any effective insurance coverage;

(3) the secured party shall keep the collateral identifiable, but fungible collateral may be commingled; and

(4) the secured party may use or operate the collateral:

   (A) for the purpose of preserving the collateral or its value;

   (B) as permitted by an order of a court having competent jurisdiction; or

   (C) except in the case of consumer goods, in the manner and to the extent agreed by the debtor.

(c) Except as otherwise provided in subsection (d), a secured party having possession of collateral or control of collateral under Section 9–104, 9–105, 9–106, or 9–107:

   (1) may hold as additional security any proceeds, except money or funds, received from the collateral;

   (2) shall apply money or funds received from the collateral to reduce the secured obligation, unless remitted to the debtor; and

   (3) may create a security interest in the collateral.

(d) If the secured party is a buyer of accounts, chattel paper, payment intangibles, or promissory notes or a consignor:

   (1) subsection (a) does not apply unless the secured party is entitled under an agreement:

      (A) to charge back uncollected collateral; or

      (B) otherwise to full or limited recourse against the debtor or a secondary obligor based on the nonpayment or other default of an account debtor or other obligor on the collateral; and

   (2) subsections (b) and (c) do not apply.

§ 9–208. Additional Duties of Secured Party Having Control of Collateral.

(a) This section applies to cases in which there is no outstanding secured obligation and the secured party is not committed to make advances, incur obligations, or otherwise give value.

(b) Within 10 days after receiving an authenticated demand by the debtor:

   (1) a secured party having control of a deposit account under Section 9–104(a)(2) shall send to the bank with which the deposit account is maintained an authenticated statement that releases the bank from any further obligation to comply with instructions originated by the secured party;

   (2) a secured party having control of a deposit account under Section 9–104(a)(3) shall:

      (A) pay the debtor the balance on deposit in the deposit account; or

      (B) transfer the balance on deposit into a deposit account in the debtor's name;

   (3) a secured party, other than a buyer, having control of electronic chattel paper under Section 9–105 shall:

      (A) communicate the authoritative copy of the electronic chattel paper to the debtor or its designated custodian;

      (B) if the debtor designates a custodian that is the designated custodian with which the authoritative copy of the electronic chattel paper is maintained for the secured party, communicate to the custodian an authenticated record releasing the designated custodian from any further obligation to comply with instructions originated by the secured party and instructing the custodian to comply with instructions originated by the debtor; and

      (C) take appropriate action to enable the debtor or its designated custodian to make copies of or revisions to the authoritative copy which add or change an identified assignee of the authoritative copy without the consent of the secured party;

   (4) a secured party having control of investment property under Section 8–106(d)(2) or 9–106(b) shall send to the securities intermediary or commodity intermediary with which the security entitlement or commodity contract is maintained an authenticated record that releases the securities intermediary or commodity intermediary from any further obligation to comply with entitlement orders or directions originated by the secured party; and

   (5) a secured party having control of a letter-of-credit right under Section 9–107 shall send to each person having an unfulfilled obligation to pay or deliver proceeds of the letter of credit to the secured party an authenticated release from any further obligation to pay or deliver proceeds of the letter of credit to the secured party.

§ 9–209. Duties of Secured Party If Account Debtor Has Been Notified of Assignment.

(a) Except as otherwise provided in subsection (c), this section applies if:

   (1) there is no outstanding secured obligation; and

   (2) the secured party is not committed to make advances, incur obligations, or otherwise give value.

(b) Within 10 days after receiving an authenticated demand by the debtor, a secured party shall send to an account debtor that has received notification of an assignment to the secured party as assignee under Section 9–406(a) an authenticated record that releases the account debtor from any further obligation to the secured party.

(c) This section does not apply to an assignment constituting the sale of an account, chattel paper, or payment intangible.

§ 9–210. Request for Accounting; Request Regarding List of Collateral or Statement of Account.

(a) In this section:

   (1) "Request" means a record of a type described in paragraph (2), (3), or (4).

   (2) "Request for an accounting" means a record authenticated by a debtor requesting that the recipient provide an accounting of the unpaid obligations secured by collateral and reasonably identifying the transaction or relationship that is the subject of the request.

   (3) "Request regarding a list of collateral" means a record authenticated by a debtor requesting that the recipient approve or correct a list of what the debtor believes to be the collateral securing an obligation and reasonably identifying the transaction or relationship that is the subject of the request.

   (4) "Request regarding a statement of account" means a record authenticated by a debtor requesting that the recipient approve or correct a statement indicating what the debtor believes to be the aggregate amount of unpaid obligations secured by collateral as of a specified date and reasonably identifying the transaction or relationship that is the subject of the request.

(b) Subject to subsections (c), (d), (e), and (f), a secured party, other than a buyer of accounts, chattel paper, payment intangibles, or promissory notes or a consignor, shall comply with a request within 14 days after receipt:

(1) in the case of a request for an accounting, by authenticating and sending to the debtor an accounting; and

(2) in the case of a request regarding a list of collateral or a request regarding a statement of account, by authenticating and sending to the debtor an approval or correction.

(c) A secured party that claims a security interest in all of a particular type of collateral owned by the debtor may comply with a request regarding a list of collateral by sending to the debtor an authenticated record including a statement to that effect within 14 days after receipt.

(d) A person that receives a request regarding a list of collateral, claims no interest in the collateral when it receives the request, and claimed an interest in the collateral at an earlier time shall comply with the request within 14 days after receipt by sending to the debtor an authenticated record:

(1) disclaiming any interest in the collateral; and

(2) if known to the recipient, providing the name and mailing address of any assignee of or successor to the recipient's interest in the collateral.

(e) A person that receives a request for an accounting or a request regarding a statement of account, claims no interest in the obligations when it receives the request, and claimed an interest in the obligations at an earlier time shall comply with the request within 14 days after receipt by sending to the debtor an authenticated record:

(1) disclaiming any interest in the obligations; and

(2) if known to the recipient, providing the name and mailing address of any assignee of or successor to the recipient's interest in the obligations.

(f) A debtor is entitled without charge to one response to a request under this section during any six-month period. The secured party may require payment of a charge not exceeding $25 for each additional response.

As amended in 1999.

Part 3—Perfection and Priority

[Subpart 1. Law Governing Perfection and Priority]

§ 9–301. Law Governing Perfection and Priority of Security Interests.

Except as otherwise provided in Sections 9–303 through 9–306, the following rules determine the law governing perfection, the effect of perfection or nonperfection, and the priority of a security interest in collateral:

(1) Except as otherwise provided in this section, while a debtor is located in a jurisdiction, the local law of that jurisdiction governs perfection, the effect of perfection or nonperfection, and the priority of a security interest in collateral.

(2) While collateral is located in a jurisdiction, the local law of that jurisdiction governs perfection, the effect of perfection or nonperfection, and the priority of a possessory security interest in that collateral.

(3) Except as otherwise provided in paragraph (4), while negotiable documents, goods, instruments, money, or tangible chattel paper is located in a jurisdiction, the local law of that jurisdiction governs:

(A) perfection of a security interest in the goods by filing a fixture filing;

(B) perfection of a security interest in timber to be cut; and

(C) the effect of perfection or nonperfection and the priority of a nonpossessory security interest in the collateral.

(4) The local law of the jurisdiction in which the wellhead or minehead is located governs perfection, the effect of perfection or nonperfection, and the priority of a security interest in as-extracted collateral.

§ 9–302. Law Governing Perfection and Priority of Agricultural Liens.

While farm products are located in a jurisdiction, the local law of that jurisdiction governs perfection, the effect of perfection or nonperfection, and the priority of an agricultural lien on the farm products.

§ 9–303. Law Governing Perfection and Priority of Security Interests in Goods Covered by a Certificate of Title.

(a) This section applies to goods covered by a certificate of title, even if there is no other relationship between the jurisdiction under whose certificate of title the goods are covered and the goods or the debtor.

(b) Goods become covered by a certificate of title when a valid application for the certificate of title and the applicable fee are delivered to the appropriate authority. Goods cease to be covered by a certificate of title at the earlier of the time the certificate of title ceases to be effective under the law of the issuing jurisdiction or the time the goods become covered subsequently by a certificate of title issued by another jurisdiction.

(c) The local law of the jurisdiction under whose certificate of title the goods are covered governs perfection, the effect of perfection or nonperfection, and the priority of a security interest in goods covered by a certificate of title from the time the goods become covered by the certificate of title until the goods cease to be covered by the certificate of title.

§ 9–304. Law Governing Perfection and Priority of Security Interests in Deposit Accounts.

(a) The local law of a bank's jurisdiction governs perfection, the effect of perfection or nonperfection, and the priority of a security interest in a deposit account maintained with that bank.

(b) The following rules determine a bank's jurisdiction for purposes of this part:

(1) If an agreement between the bank and the debtor governing the deposit account expressly provides that a particular jurisdiction is the bank's jurisdiction for purposes of this part, this article, or [the Uniform Commercial Code], that jurisdiction is the bank's jurisdiction.

(2) If paragraph (1) does not apply and an agreement between the bank and its customer governing the deposit account expressly provides that the agreement is governed by the law of a particular jurisdiction, that jurisdiction is the bank's jurisdiction.

(3) If neither paragraph (1) nor paragraph (2) applies and an agreement between the bank and its customer governing the deposit account expressly provides that the deposit account is maintained at an office in a particular jurisdiction, that jurisdiction is the bank's jurisdiction.

(4) If none of the preceding paragraphs applies, the bank's jurisdiction is the jurisdiction in which the office identified in an account statement as the office serving the customer's account is located.

(5) If none of the preceding paragraphs applies, the bank's jurisdiction is the jurisdiction in which the chief executive office of the bank is located.

§ 9–305. Law Governing Perfection and Priority of Security Interests in Investment Property.

(a) Except as otherwise provided in subsection (c), the following rules apply:

(1) While a security certificate is located in a jurisdiction, the local law of that jurisdiction governs perfection, the effect of perfection or nonperfection, and the priority of a security interest in the certificated security represented thereby.

(2) The local law of the issuer's jurisdiction as specified in Section 8–110(d) governs perfection, the effect of perfection or nonperfection, and the priority of a security interest in an uncertificated security.

(3) The local law of the securities intermediary's jurisdiction as specified in Section 8–110(e) governs perfection, the effect of perfection or nonperfection, and the priority of a security interest in a security entitlement or securities account.

(4) The local law of the commodity intermediary's jurisdiction governs perfection, the effect of perfection or nonperfection, and the priority of a security interest in a commodity contract or commodity account.

(b) The following rules determine a commodity intermediary's jurisdiction for purposes of this part:

(1) If an agreement between the commodity intermediary and commodity customer governing the commodity account expressly provides that a particular jurisdiction is the commodity intermediary's jurisdiction for purposes of this part, this article, or [the Uniform Commercial Code], that jurisdiction is the commodity intermediary's jurisdiction.

(2) If paragraph (1) does not apply and an agreement between the commodity intermediary and commodity customer governing the commodity account expressly provides that the agreement is governed by the law of a particular jurisdiction, that jurisdiction is the commodity intermediary's jurisdiction.

(3) If neither paragraph (1) nor paragraph (2) applies and an agreement between the commodity intermediary and commodity customer governing the commodity account expressly provides that the commodity account is maintained at an office in a particular jurisdiction, that jurisdiction is the commodity intermediary's jurisdiction.

(4) If none of the preceding paragraphs applies, the commodity intermediary's jurisdiction is the jurisdiction in which the office identified in an account statement as the office serving the commodity customer's account is located.

(5) If none of the preceding paragraphs applies, the commodity intermediary's jurisdiction is the jurisdiction in which the chief executive office of the commodity intermediary is located.

(c) The local law of the jurisdiction in which the debtor is located governs:

(1) perfection of a security interest in investment property by filing;

(2) automatic perfection of a security interest in investment property created by a broker or securities intermediary; and

(3) automatic perfection of a security interest in a commodity contract or commodity account created by a commodity intermediary.

§ 9–306. Law Governing Perfection and Priority of Security Interests in Letter-of-Credit Rights.

(a) Subject to subsection (c), the local law of the issuer's jurisdiction or a nominated person's jurisdiction governs perfection, the effect of perfection or nonperfection, and the priority of a security interest in a letter-of-credit right if the issuer's jurisdiction or nominated person's jurisdiction is a State.

(b) For purposes of this part, an issuer's jurisdiction or nominated person's jurisdiction is the jurisdiction whose law governs the liability of the issuer or nominated person with respect to the letter-of-credit right as provided in Section 5–116.

(c) This section does not apply to a security interest that is perfected only under Section 9–308(d).

§ 9–307. Location of Debtor.

(a) In this section, "place of business" means a place where a debtor conducts its affairs.

(b) Except as otherwise provided in this section, the following rules determine a debtor's location:

(1) A debtor who is an individual is located at the individual's principal residence.

(2) A debtor that is an organization and has only one place of business is located at its place of business.

(3) A debtor that is an organization and has more than one place of business is located at its chief executive office.

(c) Subsection (b) applies only if a debtor's residence, place of business, or chief executive office, as applicable, is located in a jurisdiction whose law generally requires information concerning the existence of a nonpossessory security interest to be made generally available in a filing, recording, or registration system as a condition or result of the security interest's obtaining priority over the rights of a lien creditor with respect to the collateral. If subsection (b) does not apply, the debtor is located in the District of Columbia.

(d) A person that ceases to exist, have a residence, or have a place of business continues to be located in the jurisdiction specified by subsections (b) and (c).

(e) A registered organization that is organized under the law of a State is located in that State.

(f) Except as otherwise provided in subsection (i), a registered organization that is organized under the law of the United States and a branch or agency of a bank that is not organized under the law of the United States or a State are located:

(1) in the State that the law of the United States designates, if the law designates a State of location;

(2) in the State that the registered organization, branch, or agency designates, if the law of the United States authorizes the registered organization, branch, or agency to designate its State of location; or

(3) in the District of Columbia, if neither paragraph (1) nor paragraph (2) applies.

(g) A registered organization continues to be located in the jurisdiction specified by subsection (e) or (f) notwithstanding:

(1) the suspension, revocation, forfeiture, or lapse of the registered organization's status as such in its jurisdiction of organization; or

(2) the dissolution, winding up, or cancellation of the existence of the registered organization.

(h) The United States is located in the District of Columbia.

(i) A branch or agency of a bank that is not organized under the law of the United States or a State is located in the State in which the branch or agency is licensed, if all branches and agencies of the bank are licensed in only one State.

(j) A foreign air carrier under the Federal Aviation Act of 1958, as amended, is located at the designated office of the agent upon which service of process may be made on behalf of the carrier.

(k) This section applies only for purposes of this part.

[Subpart 2. Perfection]

§ 9–308. When Security Interest or Agricultural Lien Is Perfected; Continuity of Perfection.

(a) Except as otherwise provided in this section and Section 9–309, a security interest is perfected if it has attached and all of the applicable requirements for perfection in Sections 9–310 through 9–316 have been satisfied. A security interest is perfected when it attaches if the applicable requirements are satisfied before the security interest attaches.

(b) An agricultural lien is perfected if it has become effective and all of the applicable requirements for perfection in Section 9–310 have been satisfied. An agricultural lien is perfected when it becomes effective if the applicable requirements are satisfied before the agricultural lien becomes effective.

(c) A security interest or agricultural lien is perfected continuously if it is originally perfected by one method under this article and is later perfected by another method under this article, without an intermediate period when it was unperfected.

(d) Perfection of a security interest in collateral also perfects a security interest in a supporting obligation for the collateral.

(e) Perfection of a security interest in a right to payment or performance also perfects a security interest in a security interest, mortgage, or other lien on personal or real property securing the right.

(f) Perfection of a security interest in a securities account also perfects a security interest in the security entitlements carried in the securities account.

(g) Perfection of a security interest in a commodity account also perfects a security interest in the commodity contracts carried in the commodity account.

Legislative Note: *Any statute conflicting with subsection (e) must be made expressly subject to that subsection.*

§ 9–309. Security Interest Perfected upon Attachment.

The following security interests are perfected when they attach:

(1) a purchase-money security interest in consumer goods, except as otherwise provided in Section 9–311(b) with respect to consumer goods that are subject to a statute or treaty described in Section 9–311(a);

(2) an assignment of accounts or payment intangibles which does not by itself or in conjunction with other assignments to the same assignee transfer a significant part of the assignor's outstanding accounts or payment intangibles;

(3) a sale of a payment intangible;

(4) a sale of a promissory note;

(5) a security interest created by the assignment of a health-care-insurance receivable to the provider of the health-care goods or services;

(6) a security interest arising under Section 2–401, 2–505, 2–711(3), or 2A–508(5), until the debtor obtains possession of the collateral;

(7) a security interest of a collecting bank arising under Section 4–210;

(8) a security interest of an issuer or nominated person arising under Section 5–118;

(9) a security interest arising in the delivery of a financial asset under Section 9–206(c);

(10) a security interest in investment property created by a broker or securities intermediary;

(11) a security interest in a commodity contract or a commodity account created by a commodity intermediary;

(12) an assignment for the benefit of all creditors of the transferor and subsequent transfers by the assignee thereunder; and

(13) a security interest created by an assignment of a beneficial interest in a decedent's estate; and

(14) a sale by an individual of an account that is a right to payment of winnings in a lottery or other game of chance.

§ 9–310. When Filing Required to Perfect Security Interest or Agricultural Lien; Security Interests and Agricultural Liens to Which Filing Provisions Do Not Apply.

(a) Except as otherwise provided in subsection (b) and Section 9–312(b), a financing statement must be filed to perfect all security interests and agricultural liens.

(b) The filing of a financing statement is not necessary to perfect a security interest:

(1) that is perfected under Section 9–308(d), (e), (f), or (g);

(2) that is perfected under Section 9–309 when it attaches;

(3) in property subject to a statute, regulation, or treaty described in Section 9–311(a);

(4) in goods in possession of a bailee which is perfected under Section 9–312(d)(1) or (2);

(5) in certificated securities, documents, goods, or instruments which is perfected without filing or possession under Section 9–312(e), (f), or (g);

(6) in collateral in the secured party's possession under Section 9–313;

(7) in a certificated security which is perfected by delivery of the security certificate to the secured party under Section 9–313;

(8) in deposit accounts, electronic chattel paper, investment property, or letter-of-credit rights which is perfected by control under Section 9–314;

(9) in proceeds which is perfected under Section 9–315; or

(10) that is perfected under Section 9–316.

(c) If a secured party assigns a perfected security interest or agricultural lien, a filing under this article is not required to continue the perfected status of the security interest against creditors of and transferees from the original debtor.

§ 9–311. Perfection of Security Interests in Property Subject to Certain Statutes, Regulations, and Treaties.

(a) Except as otherwise provided in subsection (d), the filing of a financing statement is not necessary or effective to perfect a security interest in property subject to:

(1) a statute, regulation, or treaty of the United States whose requirements for a security interest's obtaining priority over the rights of a lien creditor with respect to the property preempt Section 9–310(a);

(2) [list any certificate-of-title statute covering automobiles, trailers, mobile homes, boats, farm tractors, or the like, which provides for a security interest to be indicated on the certificate as a condition or result of perfection, and any non-Uniform Commercial Code central filing statute]; or

(3) a certificate-of-title statute of another jurisdiction which provides for a security interest to be indicated on the certificate as a condition or result of the security interest's obtaining priority over the rights of a lien creditor with respect to the property.

(b) Compliance with the requirements of a statute, regulation, or treaty described in subsection (a) for obtaining priority over the rights of a lien creditor is equivalent to the filing of a financing statement under this article. Except as otherwise provided in subsection (d) and Sections 9–313 and 9–316(d) and (e) for goods covered by a certificate of title, a security interest in property subject to a statute, regulation, or treaty described in subsection (a) may be perfected only by compliance with those requirements, and a security interest so perfected remains perfected notwithstanding a change in the use or transfer of possession of the collateral.

(c) Except as otherwise provided in subsection (d) and Section 9–316(d) and (e), duration and renewal of perfection of a security interest perfected by compliance with the requirements prescribed by a statute, regulation, or treaty described in subsection (a) are governed by the statute, regulation, or treaty. In other respects, the security interest is subject to this article.

(d) During any period in which collateral subject to a statute specified in subsection (a)(2) is inventory held for sale or lease by a person or leased by that person as lessor and that person is in the business of selling goods of that kind, this section does not apply to a security interest in that collateral created by that person.

Legislative Note: *This Article contemplates that perfection of a security interest in goods covered by a certificate of title occurs upon receipt by appropriate State officials of a properly tendered application for a certificate of title on which the security interest is to be indicated, without a relation back to an earlier time. States whose certificate-of-title statutes provide for perfection at a different time or contain a relation-back provision should amend the statutes accordingly.*

§ 9–312. Perfection of Security Interests in Chattel Paper, Deposit Accounts, Documents, Goods Covered by Documents, Instruments, Investment Property, Letter-of-Credit Rights, and Money; Perfection by Permissive Filing; Temporary Perfection without Filing or Transfer of Possession.

(a) A security interest in chattel paper, negotiable documents, instruments, or investment property may be perfected by filing.

(b) Except as otherwise provided in Section 9–315(c) and (d) for proceeds:

> **(1)** a security interest in a deposit account may be perfected only by control under Section 9–314;
>
> **(2)** and except as otherwise provided in Section 9–308(d), a security interest in a letter-of-credit right may be perfected only by control under Section 9–314; and
>
> **(3)** a security interest in money may be perfected only by the secured party's taking possession under Section 9–313.

(c) While goods are in the possession of a bailee that has issued a negotiable document covering the goods:

> **(1)** a security interest in the goods may be perfected by perfecting a security interest in the document; and
>
> **(2)** a security interest perfected in the document has priority over any security interest that becomes perfected in the goods by another method during that time.

(d) While goods are in the possession of a bailee that has issued a nonnegotiable document covering the goods, a security interest in the goods may be perfected by:

> **(1)** issuance of a document in the name of the secured party;
>
> **(2)** the bailee's receipt of notification of the secured party's interest; or
>
> **(3)** filing as to the goods.

(e) A security interest in certificated securities, negotiable documents, or instruments is perfected without filing or the taking of possession for a period of 20 days from the time it attaches to the extent that it arises for new value given under an authenticated security agreement.

(f) A perfected security interest in a negotiable document or goods in possession of a bailee, other than one that has issued a negotiable document for the goods, remains perfected for 20 days without filing if the secured party makes available to the debtor the goods or documents representing the goods for the purpose of:

> **(1)** ultimate sale or exchange; or
>
> **(2)** loading, unloading, storing, shipping, transshipping, manufacturing, processing, or otherwise dealing with them in a manner preliminary to their sale or exchange.

(g) A perfected security interest in a certificated security or instrument remains perfected for 20 days without filing if the secured party delivers the security certificate or instrument to the debtor for the purpose of:

> **(1)** ultimate sale or exchange; or
>
> **(2)** presentation, collection, enforcement, renewal, or registration of transfer.

(h) After the 20-day period specified in subsection (e), (f), or (g) expires, perfection depends upon compliance with this article.

§ 9–313. When Possession by or Delivery to Secured Party Perfects Security Interest without Filing.

(a) Except as otherwise provided in subsection (b), a secured party may perfect a security interest in negotiable documents, goods, instruments, money, or tangible chattel paper by taking possession of the collateral. A secured party may perfect a security interest in certificated securities by taking delivery of the certificated securities under Section 8–301.

(b) With respect to goods covered by a certificate of title issued by this State, a secured party may perfect a security interest in the goods by taking possession of the goods only in the circumstances described in Section 9–316(d).

(c) With respect to collateral other than certificated securities and goods covered by a document, a secured party takes possession of collateral in the possession of a person other than the debtor, the secured party, or a lessee of the collateral from the debtor in the ordinary course of the debtor's business, when:

> **(1)** the person in possession authenticates a record acknowledging that it holds possession of the collateral for the secured party's benefit; or
>
> **(2)** the person takes possession of the collateral after having authenticated a record acknowledging that it will hold possession of collateral for the secured party's benefit.

(d) If perfection of a security interest depends upon possession of the collateral by a secured party, perfection occurs no earlier than the time the secured party takes possession and continues only while the secured party retains possession.

(e) A security interest in a certificated security in registered form is perfected by delivery when delivery of the certificated security occurs under Section 8–301 and remains perfected by delivery until the debtor obtains possession of the security certificate.

(f) A person in possession of collateral is not required to acknowledge that it holds possession for a secured party's benefit.

(g) If a person acknowledges that it holds possession for the secured party's benefit:

    (1) the acknowledgment is effective under subsection (c) or Section 8–301(a), even if the acknowledgment violates the rights of a debtor; and

    (2) unless the person otherwise agrees or law other than this article otherwise provides, the person does not owe any duty to the secured party and is not required to confirm the acknowledgment to another person.

(h) A secured party having possession of collateral does not relinquish possession by delivering the collateral to a person other than the debtor or a lessee of the collateral from the debtor in the ordinary course of the debtor's business if the person was instructed before the delivery or is instructed contemporaneously with the delivery:

    (1) to hold possession of the collateral for the secured party's benefit; or

    (2) to redeliver the collateral to the secured party.

(i) A secured party does not relinquish possession, even if a delivery under subsection (h) violates the rights of a debtor. A person to which collateral is delivered under subsection (h) does not owe any duty to the secured party and is not required to confirm the delivery to another person unless the person otherwise agrees or law other than this article otherwise provides.

§ 9–314. Perfection by Control.

(a) A security interest in investment property, deposit accounts, letter-of-credit rights, or electronic chattel paper may be perfected by control of the collateral under Section 9–104, 9–105, 9–106, or 9–107.

(b) A security interest in deposit accounts, electronic chattel paper, or letter-of-credit rights is perfected by control under Section 9–104, 9–105, or 9–107 when the secured party obtains control and remains perfected by control only while the secured party retains control.

(c) A security interest in investment property is perfected by control under Section 9–106 from the time the secured party obtains control and remains perfected by control until:

    (1) the secured party does not have control; and

    (2) one of the following occurs:

        (A) if the collateral is a certificated security, the debtor has or acquires possession of the security certificate;

        (B) if the collateral is an uncertificated security, the issuer has registered or registers the debtor as the registered owner; or

        (C) if the collateral is a security entitlement, the debtor is or becomes the entitlement holder.

§ 9–315. Secured Party's Rights on Disposition of Collateral and in Proceeds.

(a) Except as otherwise provided in this article and in Section 2–403(2):

    (1) a security interest or agricultural lien continues in collateral notwithstanding sale, lease, license, exchange, or other disposition thereof unless the secured party authorized the disposition free of the security interest or agricultural lien; and

    (2) a security interest attaches to any identifiable proceeds of collateral.

(b) Proceeds that are commingled with other property are identifiable proceeds:

    (1) if the proceeds are goods, to the extent provided by Section 9–336; and

    (2) if the proceeds are not goods, to the extent that the secured party identifies the proceeds by a method of tracing, including application of equitable principles, that is permitted under law other than this article with respect to commingled property of the type involved.

(c) A security interest in proceeds is a perfected security interest if the security interest in the original collateral was perfected.

(d) A perfected security interest in proceeds becomes unperfected on the 21st day after the security interest attaches to the proceeds unless:

    (1) the following conditions are satisfied:

        (A) a filed financing statement covers the original collateral;

        (B) the proceeds are collateral in which a security interest may be perfected by filing in the office in which the financing statement has been filed; and

        (C) the proceeds are not acquired with cash proceeds;

    (2) the proceeds are identifiable cash proceeds; or

    (3) the security interest in the proceeds is perfected other than under subsection (c) when the security interest attaches to the proceeds or within 20 days thereafter.

(e) If a filed financing statement covers the original collateral, a security interest in proceeds which remains perfected under subsection (d)(1) becomes unperfected at the later of:

    (1) when the effectiveness of the filed financing statement lapses under Section 9–515 or is terminated under Section 9–513; or

    (2) the 21st day after the security interest attaches to the proceeds.

§ 9–316. Continued Perfection of Security Interest Following Change in Governing Law.

(a) A security interest perfected pursuant to the law of the jurisdiction designated in Section 9–301(1) or 9–305(c) remains perfected until the earliest of:

    (1) the time perfection would have ceased under the law of that jurisdiction;

    (2) the expiration of four months after a change of the debtor's location to another jurisdiction; or

    (3) the expiration of one year after a transfer of collateral to a person that thereby becomes a debtor and is located in another jurisdiction.

(b) If a security interest described in subsection (a) becomes perfected under the law of the other jurisdiction before the earliest time or event described in that subsection, it remains perfected thereafter. If the security interest does not become perfected under the law of the other jurisdiction before the earliest time or event, it becomes unperfected and is deemed never to have been perfected as against a purchaser of the collateral for value.

(c) A possessory security interest in collateral, other than goods covered by a certificate of title and as-extracted collateral consisting of goods, remains continuously perfected if:

(1) the collateral is located in one jurisdiction and subject to a security interest perfected under the law of that jurisdiction;

(2) thereafter the collateral is brought into another jurisdiction; and

(3) upon entry into the other jurisdiction, the security interest is perfected under the law of the other jurisdiction.

(d) Except as otherwise provided in subsection (e), a security interest in goods covered by a certificate of title which is perfected by any method under the law of another jurisdiction when the goods become covered by a certificate of title from this State remains perfected until the security interest would have become unperfected under the law of the other jurisdiction had the goods not become so covered.

(e) A security interest described in subsection (d) becomes unperfected as against a purchaser of the goods for value and is deemed never to have been perfected as against a purchaser of the goods for value if the applicable requirements for perfection under Section 9–311(b) or 9–313 are not satisfied before the earlier of:

(1) the time the security interest would have become unperfected under the law of the other jurisdiction had the goods not become covered by a certificate of title from this State; or

(2) the expiration of four months after the goods had become so covered.

(f) A security interest in deposit accounts, letter-of-credit rights, or investment property which is perfected under the law of the bank's jurisdiction, the issuer's jurisdiction, a nominated person's jurisdiction, the securities intermediary's jurisdiction, or the commodity intermediary's jurisdiction, as applicable, remains perfected until the earlier of:

(1) the time the security interest would have become unperfected under the law of that jurisdiction; or

(2) the expiration of four months after a change of the applicable jurisdiction to another jurisdiction.

(g) If a security interest described in subsection (f) becomes perfected under the law of the other jurisdiction before the earlier of the time or the end of the period described in that subsection, it remains perfected thereafter. If the security interest does not become perfected under the law of the other jurisdiction before the earlier of that time or the end of that period, it becomes unperfected and is deemed never to have been perfected as against a purchaser of the collateral for value.

[**Subpart 3. Priority**]

§ 9–317. Interests That Take Priority over or Take Free of Security Interest or Agricultural Lien.

(a) A security interest or agricultural lien is subordinate to the rights of:

(1) a person entitled to priority under Section 9–322; and

(2) except as otherwise provided in subsection (e), a person that becomes a lien creditor before the earlier of the time:

(A) the security interest or agricultural lien is perfected; or

(B) one of the conditions specified in Section 9–203(b)(3) is met and a financing statement covering the collateral is filed.

(b) Except as otherwise provided in subsection (e), a buyer, other than a secured party, of tangible chattel paper, documents, goods, instruments, or a security certificate takes free of a security interest or agricultural lien if the buyer gives value and receives delivery of the collateral without knowledge of the security interest or agricultural lien and before it is perfected.

(c) Except as otherwise provided in subsection (e), a lessee of goods takes free of a security interest or agricultural lien if the lessee gives value and receives delivery of the collateral without knowledge of the security interest or agricultural lien and before it is perfected.

(d) A licensee of a general intangible or a buyer, other than a secured party, of accounts, electronic chattel paper, general intangibles, or investment property other than a certificated security takes free of a security interest if the licensee or buyer gives value without knowledge of the security interest and before it is perfected.

(e) Except as otherwise provided in Sections 9–320 and 9–321, if a person files a financing statement with respect to a purchase-money security interest before or within 20 days after the debtor receives delivery of the collateral, the security interest takes priority over the rights of a buyer, lessee, or lien creditor which arise between the time the security interest attaches and the time of filing.

As amended in 2000.

§ 9–318. No Interest Retained in Right to Payment That Is Sold; Rights and Title of Seller of Account or Chattel Paper with Respect to Creditors and Purchasers.

(a) A debtor that has sold an account, chattel paper, payment intangible, or promissory note does not retain a legal or equitable interest in the collateral sold.

(b) For purposes of determining the rights of creditors of, and purchasers for value of an account or chattel paper from, a debtor that has sold an account or chattel paper, while the buyer's security interest is unperfected, the debtor is deemed to have rights and title to the account or chattel paper identical to those the debtor sold.

§ 9–319. Rights and Title of Consignee with Respect to Creditors and Purchasers.

(a) Except as otherwise provided in subsection (b), for purposes of determining the rights of creditors of, and purchasers for value of goods from, a consignee, while the goods are in the possession of the consignee, the consignee is deemed to have rights and title to the goods identical to those the consignor had or had power to transfer.

(b) For purposes of determining the rights of a creditor of a consignee, law other than this article determines the rights and title of a consignee while goods are in the consignee's possession if, under this part, a perfected security interest held by the consignor would have priority over the rights of the creditor.

§ 9–320. Buyer of Goods.

(a) Except as otherwise provided in subsection (e), a buyer in ordinary course of business, other than a person buying farm products from a person engaged in farming operations, takes free of a security interest created by the buyer's seller, even if the security interest is perfected and the buyer knows of its existence.

(b) Except as otherwise provided in subsection (e), a buyer of goods from a person who used or bought the goods for use primarily for personal, family, or household purposes takes free of a security interest, even if perfected, if the buyer buys:

(1) without knowledge of the security interest;

(2) for value;

(3) primarily for the buyer's personal, family, or household purposes; and

(4) before the filing of a financing statement covering the goods.

(c) To the extent that it affects the priority of a security interest over a buyer of goods under subsection (b), the period of effectiveness of a filing made in the jurisdiction in which the seller is located is governed by Section 9–316(a) and (b).

(d) A buyer in ordinary course of business buying oil, gas, or other minerals at the wellhead or minehead or after extraction takes free of an interest arising out of an encumbrance.

(e) Subsections (a) and (b) do not affect a security interest in goods in the possession of the secured party under Section 9–313.

§ 9–321. Licensee of General Intangible and Lessee of Goods in Ordinary Course of Business.

(a) In this section, "licensee in ordinary course of business" means a person that becomes a licensee of a general intangible in good faith, without knowledge that the license violates the rights of another person in the general intangible, and in the ordinary course from a person in the business of licensing general intangibles of that kind. A person becomes a licensee in the ordinary course if the license to the person comports with the usual or customary practices in the kind of business in which the licensor is engaged or with the licensor's own usual or customary practices.

(b) A licensee in ordinary course of business takes its rights under a nonexclusive license free of a security interest in the general intangible created by the licensor, even if the security interest is perfected and the licensee knows of its existence.

(c) A lessee in ordinary course of business takes its leasehold interest free of a security interest in the goods created by the lessor, even if the security interest is perfected and the lessee knows of its existence.

§ 9–322. Priorities among Conflicting Security Interests in and Agricultural Liens on Same Collateral.

(a) Except as otherwise provided in this section, priority among conflicting security interests and agricultural liens in the same collateral is determined according to the following rules:

(1) Conflicting perfected security interests and agricultural liens rank according to priority in time of filing or perfection. Priority dates from the earlier of the time a filing covering the collateral is first made or the security interest or agricultural lien is first perfected, if there is no period thereafter when there is neither filing nor perfection.

(2) A perfected security interest or agricultural lien has priority over a conflicting unperfected security interest or agricultural lien.

(3) The first security interest or agricultural lien to attach or become effective has priority if conflicting security interests and agricultural liens are unperfected.

(b) For the purposes of subsection (a)(1):

(1) the time of filing or perfection as to a security interest in collateral is also the time of filing or perfection as to a security interest in proceeds; and

(2) the time of filing or perfection as to a security interest in collateral supported by a supporting obligation is also the time of filing or perfection as to a security interest in the supporting obligation.

(c) Except as otherwise provided in subsection (f), a security interest in collateral which qualifies for priority over a conflicting security interest under Section 9–327, 9–328, 9–329, 9–330, or 9–331 also has priority over a conflicting security interest in:

(1) any supporting obligation for the collateral; and

(2) proceeds of the collateral if:

(A) the security interest in proceeds is perfected;

(B) the proceeds are cash proceeds or of the same type as the collateral; and

(C) in the case of proceeds that are proceeds of proceeds, all intervening proceeds are cash proceeds, proceeds of the same type as the collateral, or an account relating to the collateral.

(d) Subject to subsection (e) and except as otherwise provided in subsection (f), if a security interest in chattel paper, deposit accounts, negotiable documents, instruments, investment property, or letter-of-credit rights is perfected by a method other than filing, conflicting perfected security interests in proceeds of the collateral rank according to priority in time of filing.

(e) Subsection (d) applies only if the proceeds of the collateral are not cash proceeds, chattel paper, negotiable documents, instruments, investment property, or letter-of-credit rights.

(f) Subsections (a) through (e) are subject to:

(1) subsection (g) and the other provisions of this part;

(2) Section 4–210 with respect to a security interest of a collecting bank;

(3) Section 5–118 with respect to a security interest of an issuer or nominated person; and

(4) Section 9–110 with respect to a security interest arising under Article 2 or 2A.

(g) A perfected agricultural lien on collateral has priority over a conflicting security interest in or agricultural lien on the same collateral if the statute creating the agricultural lien so provides.

§ 9–323. Future Advances.

(a) Except as otherwise provided in subsection (c), for purposes of determining the priority of a perfected security interest under Section 9–322(a)(1), perfection of the security interest dates from the time an advance is made to the extent that the security interest secures an advance that:

(1) is made while the security interest is perfected only:

(A) under Section 9–309 when it attaches; or

(B) temporarily under Section 9–312(e), (f), or (g); and

(2) is not made pursuant to a commitment entered into before or while the security interest is perfected by a method other than under Section 9–309 or 9–312(e), (f), or (g).

(b) Except as otherwise provided in subsection (c), a security interest is subordinate to the rights of a person that becomes a lien creditor to the extent that the security interest secures an advance made more than 45 days after the person becomes a lien creditor unless the advance is made:

(1) without knowledge of the lien; or

(2) pursuant to a commitment entered into without knowledge of the lien.

(c) Subsections (a) and (b) do not apply to a security interest held by a secured party that is a buyer of accounts, chattel paper, payment intangibles, or promissory notes or a consignor.

(d) Except as otherwise provided in subsection (e), a buyer of goods other than a buyer in ordinary course of business takes free of a security interest to the extent that it secures advances made after the earlier of:

(1) the time the secured party acquires knowledge of the buyer's purchase; or

(2) 45 days after the purchase.

(e) Subsection (d) does not apply if the advance is made pursuant to a commitment entered into without knowledge of the buyer's purchase and before the expiration of the 45-day period.

(f) Except as otherwise provided in subsection (g), a lessee of goods, other than a lessee in ordinary course of business, takes the leasehold interest free of a security interest to the extent that it secures advances made after the earlier of:

    (1) the time the secured party acquires knowledge of the lease; or

    (2) 45 days after the lease contract becomes enforceable.

(g) Subsection (f) does not apply if the advance is made pursuant to a commitment entered into without knowledge of the lease and before the expiration of the 45-day period.

As amended in 1999.

§ 9–324. Priority of Purchase-Money Security Interests.

(a) Except as otherwise provided in subsection (g), a perfected purchase-money security interest in goods other than inventory or livestock has priority over a conflicting security interest in the same goods, and, except as otherwise provided in Section 9–327, a perfected security interest in its identifiable proceeds also has priority, if the purchase-money security interest is perfected when the debtor receives possession of the collateral or within 20 days thereafter.

(b) Subject to subsection (c) and except as otherwise provided in subsection (g), a perfected purchase-money security interest in inventory has priority over a conflicting security interest in the same inventory, has priority over a conflicting security interest in chattel paper or an instrument constituting proceeds of the inventory and in proceeds of the chattel paper, if so provided in Section 9–330, and, except as otherwise provided in Section 9–327, also has priority in identifiable cash proceeds of the inventory to the extent the identifiable cash proceeds are received on or before the delivery of the inventory to a buyer, if:

    (1) the purchase-money security interest is perfected when the debtor receives possession of the inventory;

    (2) the purchase-money secured party sends an authenticated notification to the holder of the conflicting security interest;

    (3) the holder of the conflicting security interest receives the notification within five years before the debtor receives possession of the inventory; and

    (4) the notification states that the person sending the notification has or expects to acquire a purchase-money security interest in inventory of the debtor and describes the inventory.

(c) Subsections (b)(2) through (4) apply only if the holder of the conflicting security interest had filed a financing statement covering the same types of inventory:

    (1) if the purchase-money security interest is perfected by filing, before the date of the filing; or

    (2) if the purchase-money security interest is temporarily perfected without filing or possession under Section 9–312(f), before the beginning of the 20-day period thereunder.

(d) Subject to subsection (e) and except as otherwise provided in subsection (g), a perfected purchase-money security interest in livestock that are farm products has priority over a conflicting security interest in the same livestock, and, except as otherwise provided in Section 9–327, a perfected security interest in their identifiable proceeds and identifiable products in their unmanufactured states also has priority, if:

    (1) the purchase-money security interest is perfected when the debtor receives possession of the livestock;

    (2) the purchase-money secured party sends an authenticated notification to the holder of the conflicting security interest;

    (3) the holder of the conflicting security interest receives the notification within six months before the debtor receives possession of the livestock; and

    (4) the notification states that the person sending the notification has or expects to acquire a purchase-money security interest in livestock of the debtor and describes the livestock.

(e) Subsections (d)(2) through (4) apply only if the holder of the conflicting security interest had filed a financing statement covering the same types of livestock:

    (1) if the purchase-money security interest is perfected by filing, before the date of the filing; or

    (2) if the purchase-money security interest is temporarily perfected without filing or possession under Section 9–312(f), before the beginning of the 20-day period thereunder.

(f) Except as otherwise provided in subsection (g), a perfected purchase-money security interest in software has priority over a conflicting security interest in the same collateral, and, except as otherwise provided in Section 9–327, a perfected security interest in its identifiable proceeds also has priority, to the extent that the purchase-money security interest in the goods in which the software was acquired for use has priority in the goods and proceeds of the goods under this section.

(g) If more than one security interest qualifies for priority in the same collateral under subsection (a), (b), (d), or (f):

    (1) a security interest securing an obligation incurred as all or part of the price of the collateral has priority over a security interest securing an obligation incurred for value given to enable the debtor to acquire rights in or the use of collateral; and

    (2) in all other cases, Section 9–322(a) applies to the qualifying security interests.

§ 9–325. Priority of Security Interests in Transferred Collateral.

(a) Except as otherwise provided in subsection (b), a security interest created by a debtor is subordinate to a security interest in the same collateral created by another person if:

    (1) the debtor acquired the collateral subject to the security interest created by the other person;

    (2) the security interest created by the other person was perfected when the debtor acquired the collateral; and

    (3) there is no period thereafter when the security interest is unperfected.

(b) Subsection (a) subordinates a security interest only if the security interest:

    (1) otherwise would have priority solely under Section 9–322(a) or 9–324; or

    (2) arose solely under Section 2–711(3) or 2A–508(5).

§ 9–326. Priority of Security Interests Created by New Debtor.

(a) Subject to subsection (b), a security interest created by a new debtor which is perfected by a filed financing statement that is effective solely under Section 9–508 in collateral in which a new debtor has or acquires rights is subordinate to a security interest in the same collateral which is perfected other than by a filed financing statement that is effective solely under Section 9–508.

(b) The other provisions of this part determine the priority among conflicting security interests in the same collateral perfected by filed financing statements that are effective solely under Section 9–508. However, if the security agreements to which a new debtor became bound as debtor were not entered into by the same original debtor, the conflicting security interests rank according to priority in time of the new debtor's having become bound.

§ 9–327. Priority of Security Interests in Deposit Account.

The following rules govern priority among conflicting security interests in the same deposit account:

(1) A security interest held by a secured party having control of the deposit account under Section 9–104 has priority over a conflicting security interest held by a secured party that does not have control.

(2) Except as otherwise provided in paragraphs (3) and (4), security interests perfected by control under Section 9–314 rank according to priority in time of obtaining control.

(3) Except as otherwise provided in paragraph (4), a security interest held by the bank with which the deposit account is maintained has priority over a conflicting security interest held by another secured party.

(4) A security interest perfected by control under Section 9–104(a)(3) has priority over a security interest held by the bank with which the deposit account is maintained.

§ 9–328. Priority of Security Interests in Investment Property.

The following rules govern priority among conflicting security interests in the same investment property:

(1) A security interest held by a secured party having control of investment property under Section 9–106 has priority over a security interest held by a secured party that does not have control of the investment property.

(2) Except as otherwise provided in paragraphs (3) and (4), conflicting security interests held by secured parties each of which has control under Section 9–106 rank according to priority in time of:

(A) if the collateral is a security, obtaining control;

(B) if the collateral is a security entitlement carried in a securities account and:

(i) if the secured party obtained control under Section 8–106(d)(1), the secured party's becoming the person for which the securities account is maintained;

(ii) if the secured party obtained control under Section 8–106(d)(2), the securities intermediary's agreement to comply with the secured party's entitlement orders with respect to security entitlements carried or to be carried in the securities account; or

(iii) if the secured party obtained control through another person under Section 8–106(d)(3), the time on which priority would be based under this paragraph if the other person were the secured party; or

(C) if the collateral is a commodity contract carried with a commodity intermediary, the satisfaction of the requirement for control specified in Section 9–106(b)(2) with respect to commodity contracts carried or to be carried with the commodity intermediary.

(3) A security interest held by a securities intermediary in a security entitlement or a securities account maintained with the securities intermediary has priority over a conflicting security interest held by another secured party.

(4) A security interest held by a commodity intermediary in a commodity contract or a commodity account maintained with the commodity intermediary has priority over a conflicting security interest held by another secured party.

(5) A security interest in a certificated security in registered form which is perfected by taking delivery under Section 9–313(a) and not by control under Section 9–314 has priority over a conflicting security interest perfected by a method other than control.

(6) Conflicting security interests created by a broker, securities intermediary, or commodity intermediary which are perfected without control under Section 9–106 rank equally.

(7) In all other cases, priority among conflicting security interests in investment property is governed by Sections 9–322 and 9–323.

§ 9–329. Priority of Security Interests in Letter-of-Credit Right.

The following rules govern priority among conflicting security interests in the same letter-of-credit right:

(1) A security interest held by a secured party having control of the letter-of-credit right under Section 9–107 has priority to the extent of its control over a conflicting security interest held by a secured party that does not have control.

(2) Security interests perfected by control under Section 9–314 rank according to priority in time of obtaining control.

§ 9–330. Priority of Purchaser of Chattel Paper or Instrument.

(a) A purchaser of chattel paper has priority over a security interest in the chattel paper which is claimed merely as proceeds of inventory subject to a security interest if:

(1) in good faith and in the ordinary course of the purchaser's business, the purchaser gives new value and takes possession of the chattel paper or obtains control of the chattel paper under Section 9–105; and

(2) the chattel paper does not indicate that it has been assigned to an identified assignee other than the purchaser.

(b) A purchaser of chattel paper has priority over a security interest in the chattel paper which is claimed other than merely as proceeds of inventory subject to a security interest if the purchaser gives new value and takes possession of the chattel paper or obtains control of the chattel paper under Section 9–105 in good faith, in the ordinary course of the purchaser's business, and without knowledge that the purchase violates the rights of the secured party.

(c) Except as otherwise provided in Section 9–327, a purchaser having priority in chattel paper under subsection (a) or (b) also has priority in proceeds of the chattel paper to the extent that:

(1) Section 9–322 provides for priority in the proceeds; or

(2) the proceeds consist of the specific goods covered by the chattel paper or cash proceeds of the specific goods, even if the purchaser's security interest in the proceeds is unperfected.

(d) Except as otherwise provided in Section 9–331(a), a purchaser of an instrument has priority over a security interest in the instrument perfected by a method other than possession if the purchaser gives value and takes possession of the instrument in good faith and without knowledge that the purchase violates the rights of the secured party.

(e) For purposes of subsections (a) and (b), the holder of a purchase-money security interest in inventory gives new value for chattel paper constituting proceeds of the inventory.

(f) For purposes of subsections (b) and (d), if chattel paper or an instrument indicates that it has been assigned to an identified secured party other than the purchaser, a purchaser of the chattel paper or instrument has knowledge that the purchase violates the rights of the secured party.

§ 9–331. Priority of Rights of Purchasers of Instruments, Documents, and Securities under Other Articles; Priority of Interests in Financial Assets and Security Entitlements under Article 8.

(a) This article does not limit the rights of a holder in due course of a negotiable instrument, a holder to which a negotiable document of title has been duly negotiated, or a protected purchaser of a security. These holders or purchasers take priority over an earlier security interest, even if perfected, to the extent provided in Articles 3, 7, and 8.

(b) This article does not limit the rights of or impose liability on a person to the extent that the person is protected against the assertion of a claim under Article 8.

(c) Filing under this article does not constitute notice of a claim or defense to the holders, or purchasers, or persons described in subsections (a) and (b).

§ 9–332. Transfer of Money; Transfer of Funds from Deposit Account.

(a) A transferee of money takes the money free of a security interest unless the transferee acts in collusion with the debtor in violating the rights of the secured party.

(b) A transferee of funds from a deposit account takes the funds free of a security interest in the deposit account unless the transferee acts in collusion with the debtor in violating the rights of the secured party.

§ 9–333. Priority of Certain Liens Arising by Operation of Law.

(a) In this section, "possessory lien" means an interest, other than a security interest or an agricultural lien:

   (1) which secures payment or performance of an obligation for services or materials furnished with respect to goods by a person in the ordinary course of the person's business;

   (2) which is created by statute or rule of law in favor of the person; and

   (3) whose effectiveness depends on the person's possession of the goods.

(b) A possessory lien on goods has priority over a security interest in the goods unless the lien is created by a statute that expressly provides otherwise.

§ 9–334. Priority of Security Interests in Fixtures and Crops.

(a) A security interest under this article may be created in goods that are fixtures or may continue in goods that become fixtures. A security interest does not exist under this article in ordinary building materials incorporated into an improvement on land.

(b) This article does not prevent creation of an encumbrance upon fixtures under real property law.

(c) In cases not governed by subsections (d) through (h), a security interest in fixtures is subordinate to a conflicting interest of an encumbrancer or owner of the related real property other than the debtor.

(d) Except as otherwise provided in subsection (h), a perfected security interest in fixtures has priority over a conflicting interest of an encumbrancer or owner of the real property if the debtor has an interest of record in or is in possession of the real property and:

   (1) the security interest is a purchase-money security interest;

   (2) the interest of the encumbrancer or owner arises before the goods become fixtures; and

   (3) the security interest is perfected by a fixture filing before the goods become fixtures or within 20 days thereafter.

(e) A perfected security interest in fixtures has priority over a conflicting interest of an encumbrancer or owner of the real property if:

   (1) the debtor has an interest of record in the real property or is in possession of the real property and the security interest:

      (A) is perfected by a fixture filing before the interest of the encumbrancer or owner is of record; and

      (B) has priority over any conflicting interest of a predecessor in title of the encumbrancer or owner;

   (2) before the goods become fixtures, the security interest is perfected by any method permitted by this article and the fixtures are readily removable:

      (A) factory or office machines;

      (B) equipment that is not primarily used or leased for use in the operation of the real property; or

      (C) replacements of domestic appliances that are consumer goods;

   (3) the conflicting interest is a lien on the real property obtained by legal or equitable proceedings after the security interest was perfected by any method permitted by this article; or

   (4) the security interest is:

      (A) created in a manufactured home in a manufactured-home transaction; and

      (B) perfected pursuant to a statute described in Section 9–311(a)(2).

(f) A security interest in fixtures, whether or not perfected, has priority over a conflicting interest of an encumbrancer or owner of the real property if:

   (1) the encumbrancer or owner has, in an authenticated record, consented to the security interest or disclaimed an interest in the goods as fixtures; or

   (2) the debtor has a right to remove the goods as against the encumbrancer or owner.

(g) The priority of the security interest under paragraph (f)(2) continues for a reasonable time if the debtor's right to remove the goods as against the encumbrancer or owner terminates.

(h) A mortgage is a construction mortgage to the extent that it secures an obligation incurred for the construction of an improvement on land, including the acquisition cost of the land, if a recorded record of the mortgage so indicates. Except as otherwise provided in subsections (e) and (f), a security interest in fixtures is subordinate to a construction mortgage if a record of the mortgage is recorded before the goods become fixtures and the goods become fixtures before the completion of the construction. A mortgage has this priority to the same extent as a construction mortgage to the extent that it is given to refinance a construction mortgage.

(i) A perfected security interest in crops growing on real property has priority over a conflicting interest of an encumbrancer or owner of the real property if the debtor has an interest of record in or is in possession of the real property.

(j) Subsection (i) prevails over any inconsistent provisions of the following statutes:

[List here any statutes containing provisions inconsistent with subsection (i).]

Legislative Note: *States that amend statutes to remove provisions inconsistent with subsection (i) need not enact subsection (j).*

§ 9–335. Accessions.

(a) A security interest may be created in an accession and continues in collateral that becomes an accession.

(b) If a security interest is perfected when the collateral becomes an accession, the security interest remains perfected in the collateral.

(c) Except as otherwise provided in subsection (d), the other provisions of this part determine the priority of a security interest in an accession.

(d) A security interest in an accession is subordinate to a security interest in the whole which is perfected by compliance with the requirements of a certificate-of-title statute under Section 9–311(b).

(e) After default, subject to Part 6, a secured party may remove an accession from other goods if the security interest in the accession has priority over the claims of every person having an interest in the whole.

(f) A secured party that removes an accession from other goods under subsection (e) shall promptly reimburse any holder of a security interest or other lien on, or owner of, the whole or of the other goods, other than the debtor, for the cost of repair of any physical injury to the whole or the other goods. The secured party need not reimburse the holder or owner for any diminution in value of the whole or the other goods caused by the absence of the accession removed or by any necessity for replacing it. A person entitled to reimbursement may refuse permission to remove until the secured party gives adequate assurance for the performance of the obligation to reimburse.

§ 9–336. Commingled Goods.

(a) In this section, "commingled goods" means goods that are physically united with other goods in such a manner that their identity is lost in a product or mass.

(b) A security interest does not exist in commingled goods as such. However, a security interest may attach to a product or mass that results when goods become commingled goods.

(c) If collateral becomes commingled goods, a security interest attaches to the product or mass.

(d) If a security interest in collateral is perfected before the collateral becomes commingled goods, the security interest that attaches to the product or mass under subsection (c) is perfected.

(e) Except as otherwise provided in subsection (f), the other provisions of this part determine the priority of a security interest that attaches to the product or mass under subsection (c).

(f) If more than one security interest attaches to the product or mass under subsection (c), the following rules determine priority:

(1) A security interest that is perfected under subsection (d) has priority over a security interest that is unperfected at the time the collateral becomes commingled goods.

(2) If more than one security interest is perfected under subsection (d), the security interests rank equally in proportion to the value of the collateral at the time it became commingled goods.

§ 9–337. Priority of Security Interests in Goods Covered by Certificate of Title.

If, while a security interest in goods is perfected by any method under the law of another jurisdiction, this State issues a certificate of title that does not show that the goods are subject to the security interest or contain a statement that they may be subject to security interests not shown on the certificate:

(1) a buyer of the goods, other than a person in the business of selling goods of that kind, takes free of the security interest if the buyer gives value and receives delivery of the goods after issuance of the certificate and without knowledge of the security interest; and

(2) the security interest is subordinate to a conflicting security interest in the goods that attaches, and is perfected under Section 9–311(b), after issuance of the certificate and without the conflicting secured party's knowledge of the security interest.

§ 9–338. Priority of Security Interest or Agricultural Lien Perfected by Filed Financing Statement Providing Certain Incorrect Information.

If a security interest or agricultural lien is perfected by a filed financing statement providing information described in Section 9–516(b)(5) which is incorrect at the time the financing statement is filed:

(1) the security interest or agricultural lien is subordinate to a conflicting perfected security interest in the collateral to the extent that the holder of the conflicting security interest gives value in reasonable reliance upon the incorrect information; and

(2) a purchaser, other than a secured party, of the collateral takes free of the security interest or agricultural lien to the extent that, in reasonable reliance upon the incorrect information, the purchaser gives value and, in the case of chattel paper, documents, goods, instruments, or a security certificate, receives delivery of the collateral.

§ 9–339. Priority Subject to Subordination.

This article does not preclude subordination by agreement by a person entitled to priority.

[Subpart 4. Rights of Bank]

§ 9–340. Effectiveness of Right of Recoupment or Set-Off against Deposit Account.

(a) Except as otherwise provided in subsection (c), a bank with which a deposit account is maintained may exercise any right of recoupment or set-off against a secured party that holds a security interest in the deposit account.

(b) Except as otherwise provided in subsection (c), the application of this article to a security interest in a deposit account does not affect a right of recoupment or set-off of the secured party as to a deposit account maintained with the secured party.

(c) The exercise by a bank of a set-off against a deposit account is ineffective against a secured party that holds a security interest in the deposit account which is perfected by control under Section 9–104(a)(3), if the set-off is based on a claim against the debtor.

§ 9–341. Bank's Rights and Duties with Respect to Deposit Account.

Except as otherwise provided in Section 9–340(c), and unless the bank otherwise agrees in an authenticated record, a bank's rights and duties with respect to a deposit account maintained with the bank are not terminated, suspended, or modified by:

(1) the creation, attachment, or perfection of a security interest in the deposit account;

(2) the bank's knowledge of the security interest; or

(3) the bank's receipt of instructions from the secured party.

§ 9–342. Bank's Right to Refuse to Enter into or Disclose Existence of Control Agreement.

This article does not require a bank to enter into an agreement of the kind described in Section 9–104(a)(2), even if its customer so requests or directs. A bank that has entered into such an agreement is not required to confirm the existence of the agreement to another person unless requested to do so by its customer.

Part 4—Rights of Third Parties

§ 9–401. Alienability of Debtor's Rights.

(a) Except as otherwise provided in subsection (b) and Sections 9–406, 9–407, 9–408, and 9–409, whether a debtor's rights in collateral may be voluntarily or involuntarily transferred is governed by law other than this article.

(b) An agreement between the debtor and secured party which prohibits a transfer of the debtor's rights in collateral or makes the transfer a default does not prevent the transfer from taking effect.

§ 9–402. Secured Party Not Obligated on Contract of Debtor or in Tort.

The existence of a security interest, agricultural lien, or authority given to a debtor to dispose of or use collateral, without more, does not subject a secured party to liability in contract or tort for the debtor's acts or omissions.

§ 9–403. Agreement Not to Assert Defenses against Assignee.

(a) In this section, "value" has the meaning provided in Section 3–303(a).

(b) Except as otherwise provided in this section, an agreement between an account debtor and an assignor not to assert against an assignee any claim or defense that the account debtor may have against the assignor is enforceable by an assignee that takes an assignment:

    (1) for value;

    (2) in good faith;

    (3) without notice of a claim of a property or possessory right to the property assigned; and

    (4) without notice of a defense or claim in recoupment of the type that may be asserted against a person entitled to enforce a negotiable instrument under Section 3–305(a).

(c) Subsection (b) does not apply to defenses of a type that may be asserted against a holder in due course of a negotiable instrument under Section 3–305(b).

(d) In a consumer transaction, if a record evidences the account debtor's obligation, law other than this article requires that the record include a statement to the effect that the rights of an assignee are subject to claims or defenses that the account debtor could assert against the original obligee, and the record does not include such a statement:

    (1) the record has the same effect as if the record included such a statement; and

    (2) the account debtor may assert against an assignee those claims and defenses that would have been available if the record included such a statement.

(e) This section is subject to law other than this article which establishes a different rule for an account debtor who is an individual and who incurred the obligation primarily for personal, family, or household purposes.

(f) Except as otherwise provided in subsection (d), this section does not displace law other than this article which gives effect to an agreement by an account debtor not to assert a claim or defense against an assignee.

§ 9–404. Rights Acquired by Assignee; Claims and Defenses against Assignee.

(a) Unless an account debtor has made an enforceable agreement not to assert defenses or claims, and subject to subsections (b) through (e), the rights of an assignee are subject to:

    (1) all terms of the agreement between the account debtor and assignor and any defense or claim in recoupment arising from the transaction that gave rise to the contract; and

    (2) any other defense or claim of the account debtor against the assignor which accrues before the account debtor receives a notification of the assignment authenticated by the assignor or the assignee.

(b) Subject to subsection (c) and except as otherwise provided in subsection (d), the claim of an account debtor against an assignor may be asserted against an assignee under subsection (a) only to reduce the amount the account debtor owes.

(c) This section is subject to law other than this article which establishes a different rule for an account debtor who is an individual and who incurred the obligation primarily for personal, family, or household purposes.

(d) In a consumer transaction, if a record evidences the account debtor's obligation, law other than this article requires that the record include a statement to the effect that the account debtor's recovery against an assignee with respect to claims and defenses against the assignor may not exceed amounts paid by the account debtor under the record, and the record does not include such a statement, the extent to which a claim of an account debtor against the assignor may be asserted against an assignee is determined as if the record included such a statement.

(e) This section does not apply to an assignment of a health-care-insurance receivable.

§ 9–405. Modification of Assigned Contract.

(a) A modification of or substitution for an assigned contract is effective against an assignee if made in good faith. The assignee acquires corresponding rights under the modified or substituted contract. The assignment may provide that the modification or substitution is a breach of contract by the assignor. This subsection is subject to subsections (b) through (d).

(b) Subsection (a) applies to the extent that:

    (1) the right to payment or a part thereof under an assigned contract has not been fully earned by performance; or

    (2) the right to payment or a part thereof has been fully earned by performance and the account debtor has not received notification of the assignment under Section 9–406(a).

(c) This section is subject to law other than this article which establishes a different rule for an account debtor who is an individual and who incurred the obligation primarily for personal, family, or household purposes.

(d) This section does not apply to an assignment of a health-care-insurance receivable.

§ 9–406. Discharge of Account Debtor; Notification of Assignment; Identification and Proof of Assignment; Restrictions on Assignment of Accounts, Chattel Paper, Payment Intangibles, and Promissory Notes Ineffective.

(a) Subject to subsections (b) through (i), an account debtor on an account, chattel paper, or a payment intangible may discharge its obligation by paying the assignor until, but not after, the account debtor receives a notification, authenticated by the assignor or the assignee, that the amount due or to become due has been assigned and that payment is to be made to the assignee. After receipt of the notification, the account debtor may discharge its obligation by paying the assignee and may not discharge the obligation by paying the assignor.

(b) Subject to subsection (h), notification is ineffective under subsection (a):

(1) if it does not reasonably identify the rights assigned;

(2) to the extent that an agreement between an account debtor and a seller of a payment intangible limits the account debtor's duty to pay a person other than the seller and the limitation is effective under law other than this article; or

(3) at the option of an account debtor, if the notification notifies the account debtor to make less than the full amount of any installment or other periodic payment to the assignee, even if:

(A) only a portion of the account, chattel paper, or payment intangible has been assigned to that assignee;

(B) a portion has been assigned to another assignee; or

(C) the account debtor knows that the assignment to that assignee is limited.

(c) Subject to subsection (h), if requested by the account debtor, an assignee shall seasonably furnish reasonable proof that the assignment has been made. Unless the assignee complies, the account debtor may discharge its obligation by paying the assignor, even if the account debtor has received a notification under subsection (a).

(d) Except as otherwise provided in subsection (e) and Sections 2A–303 and 9–407, and subject to subsection (h), a term in an agreement between an account debtor and an assignor or in a promissory note is ineffective to the extent that it:

(1) prohibits, restricts, or requires the consent of the account debtor or person obligated on the promissory note to the assignment or transfer of, or the creation, attachment, perfection, or enforcement of a security interest in, the account, chattel paper, payment intangible, or promissory note; or

(2) provides that the assignment or transfer or the creation, attachment, perfection, or enforcement of the security interest may give rise to a default, breach, right of recoupment, claim, defense, termination, right of termination, or remedy under the account, chattel paper, payment intangible, or promissory note.

(e) Subsection (d) does not apply to the sale of a payment intangible or promissory note.

(f) Except as otherwise provided in Sections 2A–303 and 9–407 and subject to subsections (h) and (i), a rule of law, statute, or regulation that prohibits, restricts, or requires the consent of a government, governmental body or official, or account debtor to the assignment or transfer of, or creation of a security interest in, an account or chattel paper is ineffective to the extent that the rule of law, statute, or regulation:

(1) prohibits, restricts, or requires the consent of the government, governmental body or official, or account debtor to the assignment or transfer of, or the creation, attachment, perfection, or enforcement of a security interest in the account or chattel paper; or

(2) provides that the assignment or transfer or the creation, attachment, perfection, or enforcement of the security interest may give rise to a default, breach, right of recoupment, claim,

defense, termination, right of termination, or remedy under the account or chattel paper.

(g) Subject to subsection (h), an account debtor may not waive or vary its option under subsection (b)(3).

(h) This section is subject to law other than this article which establishes a different rule for an account debtor who is an individual and who incurred the obligation primarily for personal, family, or household purposes.

(i) This section does not apply to an assignment of a health-care-insurance receivable.

(j) This section prevails over any inconsistent provisions of the following statutes, rules, and regulations:

[List here any statutes, rules, and regulations containing provisions inconsistent with this section.]

Legislative Note: *States that amend statutes, rules, and regulations to remove provisions inconsistent with this section need not enact subsection (j).*

As amended in 1999 and 2000.

§ 9–407. Restrictions on Creation or Enforcement of Security Interest in Leasehold Interest or in Lessor's Residual Interest.

(a) Except as otherwise provided in subsection (b), a term in a lease agreement is ineffective to the extent that it:

(1) prohibits, restricts, or requires the consent of a party to the lease to the assignment or transfer of, or the creation, attachment, perfection, or enforcement of a security interest in an interest of a party under the lease contract or in the lessor's residual interest in the goods; or

(2) provides that the assignment or transfer or the creation, attachment, perfection, or enforcement of the security interest may give rise to a default, breach, right of recoupment, claim, defense, termination, right of termination, or remedy under the lease.

(b) Except as otherwise provided in Section 2A–303(7), a term described in subsection (a)(2) is effective to the extent that there is:

(1) a transfer by the lessee of the lessee's right of possession or use of the goods in violation of the term; or

(2) a delegation of a material performance of either party to the lease contract in violation of the term.

(c) The creation, attachment, perfection, or enforcement of a security interest in the lessor's interest under the lease contract or the lessor's residual interest in the goods is not a transfer that materially impairs the lessee's prospect of obtaining return performance or materially changes the duty of or materially increases the burden or risk imposed on the lessee within the purview of Section 2A–303(4) unless, and then only to the extent that, enforcement actually results in a delegation of material performance of the lessor.

As amended in 1999.

§ 9–408. Restrictions on Assignment of Promissory Notes, Health-Care-Insurance Receivables, and Certain General Intangibles Ineffective.

(a) Except as otherwise provided in subsection (b), a term in a promissory note or in an agreement between an account debtor and a debtor which relates to a health-care-insurance receivable or a general intangible, including a contract, permit, license, or franchise, and which term prohibits, restricts, or requires the consent of the person obligated on the promissory note or the account debtor to, the assignment or transfer of, or creation, attachment, or perfection of a security interest in, the promissory note, health-care-insurance receivable, or general intangible, is ineffective to the extent that the term:

(1) would impair the creation, attachment, or perfection of a security interest; or

(2) provides that the assignment or transfer or the creation, attachment, or perfection of the security interest may give rise to a default, breach, right of recoupment, claim, defense, termination, right of termination, or remedy under the promissory note, health-care-insurance receivable, or general intangible.

(b) Subsection (a) applies to a security interest in a payment intangible or promissory note only if the security interest arises out of a sale of the payment intangible or promissory note.

(c) A rule of law, statute, or regulation that prohibits, restricts, or requires the consent of a government, governmental body or official, person obligated on a promissory note, or account debtor to the assignment or transfer of, or creation of a security interest in, a promissory note, health-care-insurance receivable, or general intangible, including a contract, permit, license, or franchise between an account debtor and a debtor, is ineffective to the extent that the rule of law, statute, or regulation:

(1) would impair the creation, attachment, or perfection of a security interest; or

(2) provides that the assignment or transfer or the creation, attachment, or perfection of the security interest may give rise to a default, breach, right of recoupment, claim, defense, termination, right of termination, or remedy under the promissory note, health-care-insurance receivable, or general intangible.

(d) To the extent that a term in a promissory note or in an agreement between an account debtor and a debtor which relates to a health-care-insurance receivable or general intangible or a rule of law, statute, or regulation described in subsection (c) would be effective under law other than this article but is ineffective under subsection (a) or (c), the creation, attachment, or perfection of a security interest in the promissory note, health-care-insurance receivable, or general intangible:

(1) is not enforceable against the person obligated on the promissory note or the account debtor;

(2) does not impose a duty or obligation on the person obligated on the promissory note or the account debtor;

(3) does not require the person obligated on the promissory note or the account debtor to recognize the security interest, pay or render performance to the secured party, or accept payment or performance from the secured party;

(4) does not entitle the secured party to use or assign the debtor's rights under the promissory note, health-care-insurance receivable, or general intangible, including any related information or materials furnished to the debtor in the transaction giving rise to the promissory note, health-care-insurance receivable, or general intangible;

(5) does not entitle the secured party to use, assign, possess, or have access to any trade secrets or confidential information of the person obligated on the promissory note or the account debtor; and

(6) does not entitle the secured party to enforce the security interest in the promissory note, health-care-insurance receivable, or general intangible.

(e) This section prevails over any inconsistent provisions of the following statutes, rules, and regulations:

[List here any statutes, rules, and regulations containing provisions inconsistent with this section.]

Legislative Note: *States that amend statutes, rules, and regulations to remove provisions inconsistent with this section need not enact subsection (e).* As amended in 1999.

§ 9–409. Restrictions on Assignment of Letter-of-Credit Rights Ineffective.

(a) A term in a letter of credit or a rule of law, statute, regulation, custom, or practice applicable to the letter of credit which prohibits, restricts, or requires the consent of an applicant, issuer, or nominated person to a beneficiary's assignment of or creation of a security interest in a letter-of-credit right is ineffective to the extent that the term or rule of law, statute, regulation, custom, or practice:

(1) would impair the creation, attachment, or perfection of a security interest in the letter-of-credit right; or

(2) provides that the assignment or the creation, attachment, or perfection of the security interest may give rise to a default, breach, right of recoupment, claim, defense, termination, right of termination, or remedy under the letter-of-credit right.

(b) To the extent that a term in a letter of credit is ineffective under subsection (a) but would be effective under law other than this article or a custom or practice applicable to the letter of credit, to the transfer of a right to draw or otherwise demand performance under the letter of credit, or to the assignment of a right to proceeds of the letter of credit, the creation, attachment, or perfection of a security interest in the letter-of-credit right:

(1) is not enforceable against the applicant, issuer, nominated person, or transferee beneficiary;

(2) imposes no duties or obligations on the applicant, issuer, nominated person, or transferee beneficiary; and

(3) does not require the applicant, issuer, nominated person, or transferee beneficiary to recognize the security interest, pay or render performance to the secured party, or accept payment or other performance from the secured party.

As amended in 1999.

Part 5—Filing

[Subpart 1. Filing Office; Contents and Effectiveness of Financing Statement]

§ 9–501. Filing Office.

(a) Except as otherwise provided in subsection (b), if the local law of this State governs perfection of a security interest or agricultural lien, the office in which to file a financing statement to perfect the security interest or agricultural lien is:

(1) the office designated for the filing or recording of a record of a mortgage on the related real property, if:

(A) the collateral is as-extracted collateral or timber to be cut; or

(B) the financing statement is filed as a fixture filing and the collateral is goods that are or are to become fixtures; or

(2) the office of [ ] [or any office duly authorized by [ ]], in all other cases, including a case in which the collateral is goods that are or are to become fixtures and the financing statement is not filed as a fixture filing.

(b) The office in which to file a financing statement to perfect a security interest in collateral, including fixtures, of a transmitting utility is the office of [ ]. The financing statement also constitutes a fixture filing as to the collateral indicated in the financing statement which is or is to become fixtures.

Legislative Note: *The State should designate the filing office where the brackets appear. The filing office may be that of a governmental official (e.g., the Secretary of State) or a private party that maintains the State's filing system.*

§ 9–502.   Contents of Financing Statement; Record of Mortgage as Financing Statement; Time of Filing Financing Statement.

(a) Subject to subsection (b), a financing statement is sufficient only if it:

(1) provides the name of the debtor;

(2) provides the name of the secured party or a representative of the secured party; and

(3) indicates the collateral covered by the financing statement.

(b) Except as otherwise provided in Section 9–501(b), to be sufficient, a financing statement that covers as-extracted collateral or timber to be cut, or which is filed as a fixture filing and covers goods that are or are to become fixtures, must satisfy subsection (a) and also:

> **(1)** indicate that it covers this type of collateral;
>
> **(2)** indicate that it is to be filed [for record] in the real property records;
>
> **(3)** provide a description of the real property to which the collateral is related [sufficient to give constructive notice of a mortgage under the law of this State if the description were contained in a record of the mortgage of the real property]; and
>
> **(4)** if the debtor does not have an interest of record in the real property, provide the name of a record owner.

(c) A record of a mortgage is effective, from the date of recording, as a financing statement filed as a fixture filing or as a financing statement covering as-extracted collateral or timber to be cut only if:

> **(1)** the record indicates the goods or accounts that it covers;
>
> **(2)** the goods are or are to become fixtures related to the real property described in the record or the collateral is related to the real property described in the record and is as-extracted collateral or timber to be cut;
>
> **(3)** the record satisfies the requirements for a financing statement in this section other than an indication that it is to be filed in the real property records; and
>
> **(4)** the record is [duly] recorded.

(d) A financing statement may be filed before a security agreement is made or a security interest otherwise attaches.

Legislative Note: *Language in brackets is optional. Where the State has any special recording system for real property other than the usual grantor-grantee index (as, for instance, a tract system or a title registration or Torrens system) local adaptations of subsection (b) and Section 9–519(d) and (e) may be necessary. See, e.g., Mass. Gen. Laws Chapter 106, Section 9–410.*

§ 9–503.   Name of Debtor and Secured Party.

(a) A financing statement sufficiently provides the name of the debtor:

> **(1)** if the debtor is a registered organization, only if the financing statement provides the name of the debtor indicated on the

public record of the debtor's jurisdiction of organization which shows the debtor to have been organized;

(2) if the debtor is a decedent's estate, only if the financing statement provides the name of the decedent and indicates that the debtor is an estate;

(3) if the debtor is a trust or a trustee acting with respect to property held in trust, only if the financing statement:

> **(A)** provides the name specified for the trust in its organic documents or, if no name is specified, provides the name of the settlor and additional information sufficient to distinguish the debtor from other trusts having one or more of the same settlors; and
>
> **(B)** indicates, in the debtor's name or otherwise, that the debtor is a trust or is a trustee acting with respect to property held in trust; and

(4) in other cases:

> **(A)** if the debtor has a name, only if it provides the individual or organizational name of the debtor; and
>
> **(B)** if the debtor does not have a name, only if it provides the names of the partners, members, associates, or other persons comprising the debtor.

> **(b)** A financing statement that provides the name of the debtor in accordance with subsection (a) is not rendered ineffective by the absence of:

(1) a trade name or other name of the debtor; or

(2) unless required under subsection (a)(4)(B), names of partners, members, associates, or other persons comprising the debtor.

(c) A financing statement that provides only the debtor's trade name does not sufficiently provide the name of the debtor.

(d) Failure to indicate the representative capacity of a secured party or representative of a secured party does not affect the sufficiency of a financing statement.

(e) A financing statement may provide the name of more than one debtor and the name of more than one secured party.

§ 9–504.   Indication of Collateral.

A financing statement sufficiently indicates the collateral that it covers if the financing statement provides:

> **(1)** a description of the collateral pursuant to Section 9–108; or
>
> **(2)** an indication that the financing statement covers all assets or all personal property.

As amended in 1999.

§ 9–505.   Filing and Compliance with Other Statutes and Treaties for Consignments, Leases, Other Bailments, and Other Transactions.

(a) A consignor, lessor, or other bailor of goods, a licensor, or a buyer of a payment intangible or promissory note may file a financing statement, or may comply with a statute or treaty described in Section 9–311(a), using the terms "consignor", "consignee", "lessor", "lessee", "bailor", "bailee", "licensor", "licensee", "owner", "registered owner", "buyer", "seller", or words of similar import, instead of the terms "secured party" and "debtor".

(b) This part applies to the filing of a financing statement under subsection (a) and, as appropriate, to compliance that is equivalent to filing a financing statement under Section 9–311(b), but the filing or compliance is not of itself a factor in determining whether the collateral secures an obligation. If it is determined for another reason that the collateral secures an obligation, a security interest held by the consignor, lessor, bailor, licensor, owner, or buyer which attaches to the collateral is perfected by the filing or compliance.

§ 9–506. Effect of Errors or Omissions.

(a) A financing statement substantially satisfying the requirements of this part is effective, even if it has minor errors or omissions, unless the errors or omissions make the financing statement seriously misleading.

(b) Except as otherwise provided in subsection (c), a financing statement that fails sufficiently to provide the name of the debtor in accordance with Section 9–503(a) is seriously misleading.

(c) If a search of the records of the filing office under the debtor's correct name, using the filing office's standard search logic, if any, would disclose a financing statement that fails sufficiently to provide the name of the debtor in accordance with Section 9–503(a), the name provided does not make the financing statement seriously misleading.

(d) For purposes of Section 9–508(b), the "debtor's correct name" in subsection (c) means the correct name of the new debtor.

§ 9–507. Effect of Certain Events on Effectiveness of Financing Statement.

(a) A filed financing statement remains effective with respect to collateral that is sold, exchanged, leased, licensed, or otherwise disposed of and in which a security interest or agricultural lien continues, even if the secured party knows of or consents to the disposition.

(b) Except as otherwise provided in subsection (c) and Section 9–508, a financing statement is not rendered ineffective if, after the financing statement is filed, the information provided in the financing statement becomes seriously misleading under Section 9–506.

(c) If a debtor so changes its name that a filed financing statement becomes seriously misleading under Section 9–506:

(1) the financing statement is effective to perfect a security interest in collateral acquired by the debtor before, or within four months after, the change; and

(2) the financing statement is not effective to perfect a security interest in collateral acquired by the debtor more than four months after the change, unless an amendment to the financing statement which renders the financing statement not seriously misleading is filed within four months after the change.

§ 9–508. Effectiveness of Financing Statement If New Debtor Becomes Bound by Security Agreement.

(a) Except as otherwise provided in this section, a filed financing statement naming an original debtor is effective to perfect a security interest in collateral in which a new debtor has or acquires rights to the extent that the financing statement would have been effective had the original debtor acquired rights in the collateral.

(b) If the difference between the name of the original debtor and that of the new debtor causes a filed financing statement that is effective under subsection (a) to be seriously misleading under Section 9–506:

(1) the financing statement is effective to perfect a security interest in collateral acquired by the new debtor before, and within four months after, the new debtor becomes bound under Section 9B–203(d); and

(2) the financing statement is not effective to perfect a security interest in collateral acquired by the new debtor more than four months after the new debtor becomes bound under Section 9–203(d) unless an initial financing statement providing the name of the new debtor is filed before the expiration of that time.

(c) This section does not apply to collateral as to which a filed financing statement remains effective against the new debtor under Section 9–507(a).

§ 9–509. Persons Entitled to File a Record.

(a) A person may file an initial financing statement, amendment that adds collateral covered by a financing statement, or amendment that adds a debtor to a financing statement only if:

(1) the debtor authorizes the filing in an authenticated record or pursuant to subsection (b) or (c); or

(2) the person holds an agricultural lien that has become effective at the time of filing and the financing statement covers only collateral in which the person holds an agricultural lien.

(b) By authenticating or becoming bound as debtor by a security agreement, a debtor or new debtor authorizes the filing of an initial financing statement, and an amendment, covering:

(1) the collateral described in the security agreement; and

(2) property that becomes collateral under Section 9–315(a)(2), whether or not the security agreement expressly covers proceeds.

(c) By acquiring collateral in which a security interest or agricultural lien continues under Section 9–315(a)(1), a debtor authorizes the filing of an initial financing statement, and an amendment, covering the collateral and property that becomes collateral under Section 9–315(a)(2).

(d) A person may file an amendment other than an amendment that adds collateral covered by a financing statement or an amendment that adds a debtor to a financing statement only if:

(1) the secured party of record authorizes the filing; or

(2) the amendment is a termination statement for a financing statement as to which the secured party of record has failed to file or send a termination statement as required by Section 9–513(a) or (c), the debtor authorizes the filing, and the termination statement indicates that the debtor authorized it to be filed.

(e) If there is more than one secured party of record for a financing statement, each secured party of record may authorize the filing of an amendment under subsection (d).

As amended in 2000.

§ 9–510. Effectiveness of Filed Record.

(a) A filed record is effective only to the extent that it was filed by a person that may file it under Section 9–509.

(b) A record authorized by one secured party of record does not affect the financing statement with respect to another secured party of record.

(c) A continuation statement that is not filed within the six-month period prescribed by Section 9–515(d) is ineffective.

§ 9–511. Secured Party of Record.

(a) A secured party of record with respect to a financing statement is a person whose name is provided as the name of the secured party or a representative of the secured party in an initial financing statement that has been filed. If an initial financing statement is filed under Section 9–514(a), the assignee named in the initial financing statement is the secured party of record with respect to the financing statement.

(b) If an amendment of a financing statement which provides the name of a person as a secured party or a representative of a secured party is filed, the person named in the amendment is a secured party of record. If an amendment is filed under Section 9–514(b), the assignee named in the amendment is a secured party of record.

(c) A person remains a secured party of record until the filing of an amendment of the financing statement which deletes the person.

§ 9–512. Amendment of Financing Statement.

[Alternative A]

(a) Subject to Section 9–509, a person may add or delete collateral covered by, continue or terminate the effectiveness of, or, subject to subsection (e), otherwise amend the information provided in, a financing statement by filing an amendment that:

(1) identifies, by its file number, the initial financing statement to which the amendment relates; and

(2) if the amendment relates to an initial financing statement filed [or recorded] in a filing office described in Section 9–501(a)(1), provides the information specified in Section 9–502(b).

[Alternative B]

(a) Subject to Section 9–509, a person may add or delete collateral covered by, continue or terminate the effectiveness of, or, subject to subsection (e), otherwise amend the information provided in, a financing statement by filing an amendment that:

(1) identifies, by its file number, the initial financing statement to which the amendment relates; and

(2) if the amendment relates to an initial financing statement filed [or recorded] in a filing office described in Section 9–501(a)(1), provides the date [and time] that the initial financing statement was filed [or recorded] and the information specified in Section 9–502(b).

[End of Alternatives]

(b) Except as otherwise provided in Section 9–515, the filing of an amendment does not extend the period of effectiveness of the financing statement.

(c) A financing statement that is amended by an amendment that adds collateral is effective as to the added collateral only from the date of the filing of the amendment.

(d) A financing statement that is amended by an amendment that adds a debtor is effective as to the added debtor only from the date of the filing of the amendment.

(e) An amendment is ineffective to the extent it:

(1) purports to delete all debtors and fails to provide the name of a debtor to be covered by the financing statement; or

(2) purports to delete all secured parties of record and fails to provide the name of a new secured party of record.

Legislative Note: *States whose real-estate filing offices require additional information in amendments and cannot search their records by both the name of the debtor and the file number should enact Alternative B to Sections 9–512(a), 9–518(b), 9–519(f), and 9–522(a).*

§ 9–513. Termination Statement.

(a) A secured party shall cause the secured party of record for a financing statement to file a termination statement for the financing statement if the financing statement covers consumer goods and:

(1) there is no obligation secured by the collateral covered by the financing statement and no commitment to make an advance, incur an obligation, or otherwise give value; or

(2) the debtor did not authorize the filing of the initial financing statement.

(b) To comply with subsection (a), a secured party shall cause the secured party of record to file the termination statement:

(1) within one month after there is no obligation secured by the collateral covered by the financing statement and no commitment to make an advance, incur an obligation, or otherwise give value; or

(2) if earlier, within 20 days after the secured party receives an authenticated demand from a debtor.

(c) In cases not governed by subsection (a), within 20 days after a secured party receives an authenticated demand from a debtor, the secured party shall cause the secured party of record for a financing statement to send to the debtor a termination statement for the financing statement or file the termination statement in the filing office if:

(1) except in the case of a financing statement covering accounts or chattel paper that has been sold or goods that are the subject of a consignment, there is no obligation secured by the collateral covered by the financing statement and no commitment to make an advance, incur an obligation, or otherwise give value;

(2) the financing statement covers accounts or chattel paper that has been sold but as to which the account debtor or other person obligated has discharged its obligation;

(3) the financing statement covers goods that were the subject of a consignment to the debtor but are not in the debtor's possession; or

(4) the debtor did not authorize the filing of the initial financing statement.

(d) Except as otherwise provided in Section 9–510, upon the filing of a termination statement with the filing office, the financing statement to which the termination statement relates ceases to be effective. Except as otherwise provided in Section 9–510, for purposes of Sections 9–519(g), 9–522(a), and 9–523(c), the filing with the filing office of a termination statement relating to a financing statement that indicates that the debtor is a transmitting utility also causes the effectiveness of the financing statement to lapse.

As amended in 2000.

§ 9–514. Assignment of Powers
of Secured Party of Record.

(a) Except as otherwise provided in subsection (c), an initial financing statement may reflect an assignment of all of the secured party's power to authorize an amendment to the financing statement by providing the name and mailing address of the assignee as the name and address of the secured party.

(b) Except as otherwise provided in subsection (c), a secured party of record may assign of record all or part of its power to authorize an amendment to a financing statement by filing in the filing office an amendment of the financing statement which:

(1) identifies, by its file number, the initial financing statement to which it relates;

(2) provides the name of the assignor; and

(3) provides the name and mailing address of the assignee.

(c) An assignment of record of a security interest in a fixture covered by a record of a mortgage which is effective as a financing statement filed as a fixture filing under Section 9–502(c) may be made only by an assignment of record of the mortgage in the manner provided by law of this State other than [the Uniform Commercial Code].

§ 9–515. Duration and Effectiveness of Financing Statement; Effect of Lapsed Financing Statement.

(a) Except as otherwise provided in subsections (b), (e), (f), and (g), a filed financing statement is effective for a period of five years after the date of filing.

(b) Except as otherwise provided in subsections (e), (f), and (g), an initial financing statement filed in connection with a public-finance transaction or manufactured-home transaction is effective for a period of 30 years after the date of filing if it indicates that it is filed in connection with a public-finance transaction or manufactured-home transaction.

(c) The effectiveness of a filed financing statement lapses on the expiration of the period of its effectiveness unless before the lapse a continuation statement is filed pursuant to subsection (d). Upon lapse, a financing statement ceases to be effective and any security interest or agricultural lien that was perfected by the financing statement becomes unperfected, unless the security interest is perfected otherwise. If the security interest or agricultural lien becomes unperfected upon lapse, it is deemed never to have been perfected as against a purchaser of the collateral for value.

(d) A continuation statement may be filed only within six months before the expiration of the five-year period specified in subsection (a) or the 30-year period specified in subsection (b), whichever is applicable.

(e) Except as otherwise provided in Section 9–510, upon timely filing of a continuation statement, the effectiveness of the initial financing statement continues for a period of five years commencing on the day on which the financing statement would have become ineffective in the absence of the filing. Upon the expiration of the five-year period, the financing statement lapses in the same manner as provided in subsection (c), unless, before the lapse, another continuation statement is filed pursuant to subsection (d). Succeeding continuation statements may be filed in the same manner to continue the effectiveness of the initial financing statement.

(f) If a debtor is a transmitting utility and a filed financing statement so indicates, the financing statement is effective until a termination statement is filed.

(g) A record of a mortgage that is effective as a financing statement filed as a fixture filing under Section 9–502(c) remains effective as a financing statement filed as a fixture filing until the mortgage is released or satisfied of record or its effectiveness otherwise terminates as to the real property.

§ 9–516. What Constitutes Filing; Effectiveness of Filing.

(a) Except as otherwise provided in subsection (b), communication of a record to a filing office and tender of the filing fee or acceptance of the record by the filing office constitutes filing.

(b) Filing does not occur with respect to a record that a filing office refuses to accept because:

(1) the record is not communicated by a method or medium of communication authorized by the filing office;

(2) an amount equal to or greater than the applicable filing fee is not tendered;

(3) the filing office is unable to index the record because:

(A) in the case of an initial financing statement, the record does not provide a name for the debtor;

(B) in the case of an amendment or correction statement, the record:

(i) does not identify the initial financing statement as required by Section 9–512 or 9–518, as applicable; or

(ii) identifies an initial financing statement whose effectiveness has lapsed under Section 9–515;

(C) in the case of an initial financing statement that provides the name of a debtor identified as an individual or an amendment that provides a name of a debtor identified as an individual which was not previously provided in the financing statement to which the record relates, the record does not identify the debtor's last name; or

(D) in the case of a record filed [or recorded] in the filing office described in Section 9–501(a)(1), the record does not provide a sufficient description of the real property to which it relates;

(4) in the case of an initial financing statement or an amendment that adds a secured party of record, the record does not provide a name and mailing address for the secured party of record;

(5) in the case of an initial financing statement or an amendment that provides a name of a debtor which was not previously provided in the financing statement to which the amendment relates, the record does not:

(A) provide a mailing address for the debtor;

(B) indicate whether the debtor is an individual or an organization; or

(C) if the financing statement indicates that the debtor is an organization, provide:

(i) a type of organization for the debtor;

(ii) a jurisdiction of organization for the debtor; or

(iii) an organizational identification number for the debtor or indicate that the debtor has none;

(6) in the case of an assignment reflected in an initial financing statement under Section 9–514(a) or an amendment filed under Section 9–514(b), the record does not provide a name and mailing address for the assignee; or

(7) in the case of a continuation statement, the record is not filed within the six-month period prescribed by Section 9–515(d).

(c) For purposes of subsection (b):

(1) a record does not provide information if the filing office is unable to read or decipher the information; and

(2) a record that does not indicate that it is an amendment or identify an initial financing statement to which it relates, as required by Section 9–512, 9–514, or 9–518, is an initial financing statement.

(d) A record that is communicated to the filing office with tender of the filing fee, but which the filing office refuses to accept for a reason other than one set forth in subsection (b), is effective as a filed record except as against a purchaser of the collateral which gives value in reasonable reliance upon the absence of the record from the files.

§ 9–517. Effect of Indexing Errors.

The failure of the filing office to index a record correctly does not affect the effectiveness of the filed record.

§ 9–518. Claim Concerning Inaccurate or Wrongfully Filed Record.

(a) A person may file in the filing office a correction statement with respect to a record indexed there under the person's name if the person believes that the record is inaccurate or was wrongfully filed.

[Alternative A]

(b) A correction statement must:

(1) identify the record to which it relates by the file number assigned to the initial financing statement to which the record relates;

(2) indicate that it is a correction statement; and

(3) provide the basis for the person's belief that the record is inaccurate and indicate the manner in which the person believes the record should be amended to cure any inaccuracy or provide the basis for the person's belief that the record was wrongfully filed.

[Alternative B]

(b) A correction statement must:

(1) identify the record to which it relates by:

(A) the file number assigned to the initial financing statement to which the record relates; and

(B) if the correction statement relates to a record filed [or recorded] in a filing office described in Section 9–501(a)(1), the date [and time] that the initial financing statement was filed [or recorded] and the information specified in Section 9–502(b);

(2) indicate that it is a correction statement; and

(3) provide the basis for the person's belief that the record is inaccurate and indicate the manner in which the person believes the record should be amended to cure any inaccuracy or provide the basis for the person's belief that the record was wrongfully filed.

[End of Alternatives]

(c) The filing of a correction statement does not affect the effectiveness of an initial financing statement or other filed record.

Legislative Note: *States whose real-estate filing offices require additional information in amendments and cannot search their records by both the name of the debtor and the file number should enact Alternative B to Sections 9–512(a), 9–518(b), 9–519(f), and 9–522(a).*

[Subpart 2. Duties and Operation of Filing Office]

§ 9–519. Numbering, Maintaining, and Indexing Records; Communicating Information Provided in Records.

(a) For each record filed in a filing office, the filing office shall:

(1) assign a unique number to the filed record;

(2) create a record that bears the number assigned to the filed record and the date and time of filing;

(3) maintain the filed record for public inspection; and

(4) index the filed record in accordance with subsections (c), (d), and (e).

(b) A file number [assigned after January 1, 2002,] must include a digit that:

(1) is mathematically derived from or related to the other digits of the file number; and

(2) aids the filing office in determining whether a number communicated as the file number includes a single-digit or transpositional error.

(c) Except as otherwise provided in subsections (d) and (e), the filing office shall:

(1) index an initial financing statement according to the name of the debtor and index all filed records relating to the initial financing statement in a manner that associates with one another an initial financing statement and all filed records relating to the initial financing statement; and

(2) index a record that provides a name of a debtor which was not previously provided in the financing statement to which the record relates also according to the name that was not previously provided.

(d) If a financing statement is filed as a fixture filing or covers as-extracted collateral or timber to be cut, [it must be filed for record and] the filing office shall index it:

(1) under the names of the debtor and of each owner of record shown on the financing statement as if they were the mortgagors under a mortgage of the real property described; and

(2) to the extent that the law of this State provides for indexing of records of mortgages under the name of the mortgagee, under the name of the secured party as if the secured party were the mortgagee thereunder, or, if indexing is by description, as if the financing statement were a record of a mortgage of the real property described.

(e) If a financing statement is filed as a fixture filing or covers as-extracted collateral or timber to be cut, the filing office shall index an assignment filed under Section 9–514(a) or an amendment filed under Section 9–514(b):

(1) under the name of the assignor as grantor; and

(2) to the extent that the law of this State provides for indexing a record of the assignment of a mortgage under the name of the assignee, under the name of the assignee.

[Alternative A]

(f) The filing office shall maintain a capability:

(1) to retrieve a record by the name of the debtor and by the file number assigned to the initial financing statement to which the record relates; and

(2) to associate and retrieve with one another an initial financing statement and each filed record relating to the initial financing statement.

[Alternative B]

(f) The filing office shall maintain a capability:

(1) to retrieve a record by the name of the debtor and:

(A) if the filing office is described in Section 9–501(a)(1), by the file number assigned to the initial financing statement to which the record relates and the date [and time] that the record was filed [or recorded]; or

(B) if the filing office is described in Section 9–501(a)(2), by the file number assigned to the initial financing statement to which the record relates; and

(2) to associate and retrieve with one another an initial financing statement and each filed record relating to the initial financing statement.

[End of Alternatives]

(g) The filing office may not remove a debtor's name from the index until one year after the effectiveness of a financing statement naming the debtor lapses under Section 9–515 with respect to all secured parties of record.

(h) The filing office shall perform the acts required by subsections (a) through (e) at the time and in the manner prescribed by filing-office rule, but not later than two business days after the filing office receives the record in question.

[(i) Subsection[s] [(b)] [and] [(h)] do[es] not apply to a filing office described in Section 9–501(a)(1).]

Legislative Notes:

1. States whose filing offices currently assign file numbers that include a verification number, commonly known as a "check digit," or can implement this requirement before the effective date of this Article should omit the bracketed language in subsection (b).

2. In States in which writings will not appear in the real property records and indices unless actually recorded the bracketed language in subsection (d) should be used.

3. States whose real-estate filing offices require additional information in amendments and cannot search their records by both the name of the debtor and the file number should enact Alternative B to Sections 9–512(a), 9–518(b), 9–519(f), and 9–522(a).

4. A State that elects not to require real-estate filing offices to comply with either or both of subsections (b) and (h) may adopt an applicable variation of subsection (i) and add "Except as otherwise provided in subsection (i)," to the appropriate subsection or subsections.

§ 9–520. Acceptance and Refusal to Accept Record.

(a) A filing office shall refuse to accept a record for filing for a reason set forth in Section 9–516(b) and may refuse to accept a record for filing only for a reason set forth in Section 9–516(b).

(b) If a filing office refuses to accept a record for filing, it shall communicate to the person that presented the record the fact of and reason for the refusal and the date and time the record would have been filed had the filing office accepted it. The communication must be made at the time and in the manner prescribed by filing-office rule but [, in the case of a filing office described in Section 9–501(a)(2),] in no event more than two business days after the filing office receives the record.

(c) A filed financing statement satisfying Section 9–502(a) and (b) is effective, even if the filing office is required to refuse to accept it for filing under subsection (a). However, Section 9–338 applies to a filed financing statement providing information described in Section 9–516(b)(5) which is incorrect at the time the financing statement is filed.

(d) If a record communicated to a filing office provides information that relates to more than one debtor, this part applies as to each debtor separately.

Legislative Note: *A State that elects not to require real-property filing offices to comply with subsection (b) should include the bracketed language.*

§ 9–521. Uniform Form of Written Financing Statement and Amendment.

(a) A filing office that accepts written records may not refuse to accept a written initial financing statement in the following form and format except for a reason set forth in Section 9–516(b):

[NATIONAL UCC FINANCING STATEMENT (FORM UCC1) (REV. 7/29/98)]

[NATIONAL UCC FINANCING STATEMENT ADDENDUM (FORM UCC1Ad)(REV. 07/29/98)]

(b) A filing office that accepts written records may not refuse to accept a written record in the following form and format except for a reason set forth in Section 9–516(b):

[NATIONAL UCC FINANCING STATEMENT AMENDMENT (FORM UCC3)(REV. 07/29/98)]

[NATIONAL UCC FINANCING STATEMENT AMENDMENT ADDENDUM (FORM UCC3Ad)(REV. 07/29/98)]

§ 9–522. Maintenance and Destruction of Records.

[Alternative A]

(a) The filing office shall maintain a record of the information provided in a filed financing statement for at least one year after the effectiveness of the financing statement has lapsed under Section 9–515 with respect to all secured parties of record. The record must be retrievable by using the name of the debtor and by using the file number assigned to the initial financing statement to which the record relates.

[Alternative B]

(a) The filing office shall maintain a record of the information provided in a filed financing statement for at least one year after the effectiveness of the financing statement has lapsed under Section 9–515 with respect to all secured parties of record. The record must be retrievable by using the name of the debtor and:

> **(1)** if the record was filed [or recorded] in the filing office described in Section 9–501(a)(1), by using the file number assigned to the initial financing statement to which the record relates and the date [and time] that the record was filed [or recorded]; or

> **(2)** if the record was filed in the filing office described in Section 9–501(a)(2), by using the file number assigned to the initial financing statement to which the record relates.

[End of Alternatives]

(b) Except to the extent that a statute governing disposition of public records provides otherwise, the filing office immediately may destroy any written record evidencing a financing statement. However, if the filing office destroys a written record, it shall maintain another record of the financing statement which complies with subsection (a).

Legislative Note: *States whose real-estate filing offices require additional information in amendments and cannot search their records by both the name of the debtor and the file number should enact Alternative B to Sections 9–512(a), 9–518(b), 9–519(f), and 9–522(a).*

§ 9–523. Information from Filing Office; Sale or License of Records.

(a) If a person that files a written record requests an acknowledgment of the filing, the filing office shall send to the person an image of the record showing the number assigned to the record pursuant to Section 9–519(a)(1) and the date and time of the filing of the record. However, if the person furnishes a copy of the record to the filing office, the filing office may instead:

> **(1)** note upon the copy the number assigned to the record pursuant to Section 9–519(a)(1) and the date and time of the filing of the record; and

> **(2)** send the copy to the person.

(b) If a person files a record other than a written record, the filing office shall communicate to the person an acknowledgment that provides:

> **(1)** the information in the record;

> **(2)** the number assigned to the record pursuant to Section 9–519(a)(1); and

> **(3)** the date and time of the filing of the record.

(c) The filing office shall communicate or otherwise make available in a record the following information to any person that requests it:

> **(1)** whether there is on file on a date and time specified by the filing office, but not a date earlier than three business days before the filing office receives the request, any financing statement that:
>
>> **(A)** designates a particular debtor [or, if the request so states, designates a particular debtor at the address specified in the request];
>>
>> **(B)** has not lapsed under Section 9–515 with respect to all secured parties of record; and
>>
>> **(C)** if the request so states, has lapsed under Section 9–515 and a record of which is maintained by the filing office under Section 9–522(a);
>
> **(2)** the date and time of filing of each financing statement; and
>
> **(3)** the information provided in each financing statement.

(d) In complying with its duty under subsection (c), the filing office may communicate information in any medium. However, if requested, the filing office shall communicate information by issuing [its written certificate] [a record that can be admitted into evidence in the courts of this State without extrinsic evidence of its authenticity].

(e) The filing office shall perform the acts required by subsections (a) through (d) at the time and in the manner prescribed by filing-office rule, but not later than two business days after the filing office receives the request.

(f) At least weekly, the [insert appropriate official or governmental agency] [filing office] shall offer to sell or license to the public on a nonexclusive basis, in bulk, copies of all records filed in it under this part, in every medium from time to time available to the filing office.

Legislative Notes:

1. States whose filing office does not offer the additional service of responding to search requests limited to a particular address should omit the bracketed language in subsection (c)(1)(A).

2. A State that elects not to require real-estate filing offices to comply with either or both of subsections (e) and (f) should specify in the appropriate subsection(s) only the filing office described in Section 9–501(a) (2).

§ 9–524. Delay by Filing Office.

Delay by the filing office beyond a time limit prescribed by this part is excused if:

(1) the delay is caused by interruption of communication or computer facilities, war, emergency conditions, failure of equipment, or other circumstances beyond control of the filing office; and

(2) the filing office exercises reasonable diligence under the circumstances.

§ 9–525. Fees.

(a) Except as otherwise provided in subsection (e), the fee for filing and indexing a record under this part, other than an initial financing statement of the kind described in subsection (b), is [the amount specified in subsection (c), if applicable, plus]:

> **(1)** $[X] if the record is communicated in writing and consists of one or two pages;
>
> **(2)** $[2X] if the record is communicated in writing and consists of more than two pages; and
>
> **(3)** $[1/2X] if the record is communicated by another medium authorized by filing-office rule.

(b) Except as otherwise provided in subsection (e), the fee for filing and indexing an initial financing statement of the following kind is [the amount specified in subsection (c), if applicable, plus]:

> **(1)** $_____ if the financing statement indicates that it is filed in connection with a public-finance transaction;
>
> **(2)** $_____ if the financing statement indicates that it is filed in connection with a manufactured-home transaction.

[**Alternative A**]

(c) The number of names required to be indexed does not affect the amount of the fee in subsections (a) and (b).

[**Alternative B**]

(c) Except as otherwise provided in subsection (e), if a record is communicated in writing, the fee for each name more than two required to be indexed is $_____.

[**End of Alternatives**]

(d) The fee for responding to a request for information from the filing office, including for [issuing a certificate showing] [communicating] whether there is on file any financing statement naming a particular debtor, is:

> **(1)** $_____ if the request is communicated in writing; and
>
> **(2)** $_____ if the request is communicated by another medium authorized by filing-office rule.

(e) This section does not require a fee with respect to a record of a mortgage which is effective as a financing statement filed as a fixture filing or as a financing statement covering as-extracted collateral or timber to be cut under Section 9–502(c). However, the recording and satisfaction fees that otherwise would be applicable to the record of the mortgage apply.

Legislative Notes:

1. To preserve uniformity, a State that places the provisions of this section together with statutes setting fees for other services should do so without modification.

2. A State should enact subsection (c), Alternative A, and omit the bracketed language in subsections (a) and (b) unless its indexing system entails a substantial additional cost when indexing additional names.
As amended in 2000.

§ 9–526. Filing-Office Rules.

(a) The [insert appropriate governmental official or agency] shall adopt and publish rules to implement this article. The filing-office rules must be[:

> **(1)**] consistent with this article[; and
>
> **(2)** adopted and published in accordance with the [insert any applicable state administrative procedure act]].

(b) To keep the filing-office rules and practices of the filing office in harmony with the rules and practices of filing offices in other jurisdictions that enact substantially this part, and to keep the technology used by the filing office compatible with the technology used by filing offices in other jurisdictions that enact substantially this part, the [insert appropriate governmental official or agency], so far as is consistent with the purposes, policies, and provisions of this article, in adopting, amending, and repealing filing-office rules, shall:

> **(1)** consult with filing offices in other jurisdictions that enact substantially this part; and
>
> **(2)** consult the most recent version of the Model Rules promulgated by the International Association of Corporate Administrators or any successor organization; and

(3) take into consideration the rules and practices of, and the technology used by, filing offices in other jurisdictions that enact substantially this part.

§ 9–527. Duty to Report.

The [insert appropriate governmental official or agency] shall report [annually on or before _____] to the [Governor and Legislature] on the operation of the filing office. The report must contain a statement of the extent to which:

(1) the filing-office rules are not in harmony with the rules of filing offices in other jurisdictions that enact substantially this part and the reasons for these variations; and

(2) the filing-office rules are not in harmony with the most recent version of the Model Rules promulgated by the International Association of Corporate Administrators, or any successor organization, and the reasons for these variations.

Part 6—Default

[Subpart 1. Default and Enforcement of Security Interest]

§ 9–601. Rights after Default; Judicial Enforcement; Consignor or Buyer of Accounts, Chattel Paper, Payment Intangibles, or Promissory Notes.

(a) After default, a secured party has the rights provided in this part and, except as otherwise provided in Section 9–602, those provided by agreement of the parties. A secured party:

(1) may reduce a claim to judgment, foreclose, or otherwise enforce the claim, security interest, or agricultural lien by any available judicial procedure; and

(2) if the collateral is documents, may proceed either as to the documents or as to the goods they cover.

(b) A secured party in possession of collateral or control of collateral under Section 9–104, 9–105, 9–106, or 9–107 has the rights and duties provided in Section 9–207.

(c) The rights under subsections (a) and (b) are cumulative and may be exercised simultaneously.

(d) Except as otherwise provided in subsection (g) and Section 9–605, after default, a debtor and an obligor have the rights provided in this part and by agreement of the parties.

(e) If a secured party has reduced its claim to judgment, the lien of any levy that may be made upon the collateral by virtue of an execution based upon the judgment relates back to the earliest of:

(1) the date of perfection of the security interest or agricultural lien in the collateral;

(2) the date of filing a financing statement covering the collateral; or

(3) any date specified in a statute under which the agricultural lien was created.

(f) A sale pursuant to an execution is a foreclosure of the security interest or agricultural lien by judicial procedure within the meaning of this section. A secured party may purchase at the sale and thereafter hold the collateral free of any other requirements of this article.

(g) Except as otherwise provided in Section 9–607(c), this part imposes no duties upon a secured party that is a consignor or is a buyer of accounts, chattel paper, payment intangibles, or promissory notes.

§ 9–602. Waiver and Variance of Rights and Duties.

Except as otherwise provided in Section 9–624, to the extent that they give rights to a debtor or obligor and impose duties on a secured party, the debtor or obligor may not waive or vary the rules stated in the following listed sections:

(1) Section 9–207(b)(4)(C), which deals with use and operation of the collateral by the secured party;

(2) Section 9–210, which deals with requests for an accounting and requests concerning a list of collateral and statement of account;

(3) Section 9–607(c), which deals with collection and enforcement of collateral;

(4) Sections 9–608(a) and 9–615(c) to the extent that they deal with application or payment of noncash proceeds of collection, enforcement, or disposition;

(5) Sections 9–608(a) and 9–615(d) to the extent that they require accounting for or payment of surplus proceeds of collateral;

(6) Section 9–609 to the extent that it imposes upon a secured party that takes possession of collateral without judicial process the duty to do so without breach of the peace;

(7) Sections 9–610(b), 9–611, 9–613, and 9–614, which deal with disposition of collateral;

(8) Section 9–615(f), which deals with calculation of a deficiency or surplus when a disposition is made to the secured party, a person related to the secured party, or a secondary obligor;

(9) Section 9–616, which deals with explanation of the calculation of a surplus or deficiency;

(10) Sections 9–620, 9–621, and 9–622, which deal with acceptance of collateral in satisfaction of obligation;

(11) Section 9–623, which deals with redemption of collateral;

(12) Section 9–624, which deals with permissible waivers; and

(13) Sections 9–625 and 9–626, which deal with the secured party's liability for failure to comply with this article.

§ 9–603. Agreement on Standards Concerning Rights and Duties.

(a) The parties may determine by agreement the standards measuring the fulfillment of the rights of a debtor or obligor and the duties of a secured party under a rule stated in Section 9–602 if the standards are not manifestly unreasonable.

(b) Subsection (a) does not apply to the duty under Section 9–609 to refrain from breaching the peace.

§ 9–604. Procedure If Security Agreement Covers Real Property or Fixtures.

(a) If a security agreement covers both personal and real property, a secured party may proceed:

(1) under this part as to the personal property without prejudicing any rights with respect to the real property; or

(2) as to both the personal property and the real property in accordance with the rights with respect to the real property, in which case the other provisions of this part do not apply.

(b) Subject to subsection (c), if a security agreement covers goods that are or become fixtures, a secured party may proceed:

(1) under this part; or

(2) in accordance with the rights with respect to real property, in which case the other provisions of this part do not apply.

(c) Subject to the other provisions of this part, if a secured party holding a security interest in fixtures has priority over all owners and encumbrancers of the real property, the secured party, after default, may remove the collateral from the real property.

(d) A secured party that removes collateral shall promptly reimburse any encumbrancer or owner of the real property, other than the debtor, for the cost of repair of any physical injury caused by the removal. The secured party need not reimburse the encumbrancer or owner for any diminution in value of the real property caused by the absence of the goods removed or by any necessity of replacing them. A person entitled to reimbursement may refuse permission to remove until the secured party gives adequate assurance for the performance of the obligation to reimburse.

§ 9–605. Unknown Debtor or Secondary Obligor.

A secured party does not owe a duty based on its status as secured party:

(1) to a person that is a debtor or obligor, unless the secured party knows:

(A) that the person is a debtor or obligor;

(B) the identity of the person; and

(C) how to communicate with the person; or

(2) to a secured party or lienholder that has filed a financing statement against a person, unless the secured party knows:

(A) that the person is a debtor; and

(B) the identity of the person.

§ 9–606. Time of Default for Agricultural Lien.

For purposes of this part, a default occurs in connection with an agricultural lien at the time the secured party becomes entitled to enforce the lien in accordance with the statute under which it was created.

§ 9–607. Collection and Enforcement by Secured Party.

(a) If so agreed, and in any event after default, a secured party:

(1) may notify an account debtor or other person obligated on collateral to make payment or otherwise render performance to or for the benefit of the secured party;

(2) may take any proceeds to which the secured party is entitled under Section 9–315;

(3) may enforce the obligations of an account debtor or other person obligated on collateral and exercise the rights of the debtor with respect to the obligation of the account debtor or other person obligated on collateral to make payment or otherwise render performance to the debtor, and with respect to any property that secures the obligations of the account debtor or other person obligated on the collateral;

(4) if it holds a security interest in a deposit account perfected by control under Section 9–104(a)(1), may apply the balance of the deposit account to the obligation secured by the deposit account; and

(5) if it holds a security interest in a deposit account perfected by control under Section 9–104(a)(2) or (3), may instruct the bank to pay the balance of the deposit account to or for the benefit of the secured party.

(b) If necessary to enable a secured party to exercise under subsection (a)(3) the right of a debtor to enforce a mortgage nonjudicially, the secured party may record in the office in which a record of the mortgage is recorded:

(1) a copy of the security agreement that creates or provides for a security interest in the obligation secured by the mortgage; and

(2) the secured party's sworn affidavit in recordable form stating that:

(A) a default has occurred; and

(B) the secured party is entitled to enforce the mortgage nonjudicially.

(c) A secured party shall proceed in a commercially reasonable manner if the secured party:

(1) undertakes to collect from or enforce an obligation of an account debtor or other person obligated on collateral; and

(2) is entitled to charge back uncollected collateral or otherwise to full or limited recourse against the debtor or a secondary obligor.

(d) A secured party may deduct from the collections made pursuant to subsection (c) reasonable expenses of collection and enforcement, including reasonable attorney's fees and legal expenses incurred by the secured party.

(e) This section does not determine whether an account debtor, bank, or other person obligated on collateral owes a duty to a secured party. As amended in 2000.

§ 9–608. Application of Proceeds of Collection or Enforcement; Liability for Deficiency and Right to Surplus.

(a) If a security interest or agricultural lien secures payment or performance of an obligation, the following rules apply:

(1) A secured party shall apply or pay over for application the cash proceeds of collection or enforcement under Section 9–607 in the following order to:

(A) the reasonable expenses of collection and enforcement and, to the extent provided for by agreement and not prohibited by law, reasonable attorney's fees and legal expenses incurred by the secured party;

(B) the satisfaction of obligations secured by the security interest or agricultural lien under which the collection or enforcement is made; and

(C) the satisfaction of obligations secured by any subordinate security interest in or other lien on the collateral subject to the security interest or agricultural lien under which the collection or enforcement is made if the secured party receives an authenticated demand for proceeds before distribution of the proceeds is completed.

(2) If requested by a secured party, a holder of a subordinate security interest or other lien shall furnish reasonable proof of the interest or lien within a reasonable time. Unless the holder complies, the secured party need not comply with the holder's demand under paragraph (1)(C).

(3) A secured party need not apply or pay over for application noncash proceeds of collection and enforcement under Section 9–607 unless the failure to do so would be commercially unreasonable. A secured party that applies or pays over for application noncash proceeds shall do so in a commercially reasonable manner.

(4) A secured party shall account to and pay a debtor for any surplus, and the obligor is liable for any deficiency.

(b) If the underlying transaction is a sale of accounts, chattel paper, payment intangibles, or promissory notes, the debtor is not entitled to any surplus, and the obligor is not liable for any deficiency. As amended in 2000.

§ 9–609. Secured Party's Right to Take Possession after Default.

(a) After default, a secured party:

(1) may take possession of the collateral; and

(2) without removal, may render equipment unusable and dispose of collateral on a debtor's premises under Section 9–610.

(b) A secured party may proceed under subsection (a):

(1) pursuant to judicial process; or

(2) without judicial process, if it proceeds without breach of the peace.

(c) If so agreed, and in any event after default, a secured party may require the debtor to assemble the collateral and make it available to the secured party at a place to be designated by the secured party which is reasonably convenient to both parties.

§ 9–610. Disposition of Collateral after Default.

(a) After default, a secured party may sell, lease, license, or otherwise dispose of any or all of the collateral in its present condition or following any commercially reasonable preparation or processing.

(b) Every aspect of a disposition of collateral, including the method, manner, time, place, and other terms, must be commercially reasonable. If commercially reasonable, a secured party may dispose of collateral by public or private proceedings, by one or more contracts, as a unit or in parcels, and at any time and place and on any terms.

(c) A secured party may purchase collateral:

(1) at a public disposition; or

(2) at a private disposition only if the collateral is of a kind that is customarily sold on a recognized market or the subject of widely distributed standard price quotations.

(d) A contract for sale, lease, license, or other disposition includes the warranties relating to title, possession, quiet enjoyment, and the like which by operation of law accompany a voluntary disposition of property of the kind subject to the contract.

(e) A secured party may disclaim or modify warranties under subsection (d):

(1) in a manner that would be effective to disclaim or modify the warranties in a voluntary disposition of property of the kind subject to the contract of disposition; or

(2) by communicating to the purchaser a record evidencing the contract for disposition and including an express disclaimer or modification of the warranties.

(f) A record is sufficient to disclaim warranties under subsection (e) if it indicates "There is no warranty relating to title, possession, quiet enjoyment, or the like in this disposition" or uses words of similar import.

§ 9–611. Notification before Disposition of Collateral.

(a) In this section, "notification date" means the earlier of the date on which:

(1) a secured party sends to the debtor and any secondary obligor an authenticated notification of disposition; or

(2) the debtor and any secondary obligor waive the right to notification.

(b) Except as otherwise provided in subsection (d), a secured party that disposes of collateral under Section 9–610 shall send to the persons specified in subsection (c) a reasonable authenticated notification of disposition.

(c) To comply with subsection (b), the secured party shall send an authenticated notification of disposition to:

(1) the debtor;

(2) any secondary obligor; and

(3) if the collateral is other than consumer goods:

(A) any other person from which the secured party has received, before the notification date, an authenticated notification of a claim of an interest in the collateral;

(B) any other secured party or lienholder that, 10 days before the notification date, held a security interest in or other lien on the collateral perfected by the filing of a financing statement that:

(i) identified the collateral;

(ii) was indexed under the debtor's name as of that date; and

(iii) was filed in the office in which to file a financing statement against the debtor covering the collateral as of that date; and

(C) any other secured party that, 10 days before the notification date, held a security interest in the collateral perfected by compliance with a statute, regulation, or treaty described in Section 9–311(a).

(d) Subsection (b) does not apply if the collateral is perishable or threatens to decline speedily in value or is of a type customarily sold on a recognized market.

(e) A secured party complies with the requirement for notification prescribed by subsection (c)(3)(B) if:

(1) not later than 20 days or earlier than 30 days before the notification date, the secured party requests, in a commercially reasonable manner, information concerning financing statements indexed under the debtor's name in the office indicated in subsection (c)(3)(B); and

(2) before the notification date, the secured party:

(A) did not receive a response to the request for information; or

(B) received a response to the request for information and sent an authenticated notification of disposition to each secured party or other lienholder named in that response whose financing statement covered the collateral.

§ 9–612. Timeliness of Notification
before Disposition of Collateral.

(a) Except as otherwise provided in subsection (b), whether a notification is sent within a reasonable time is a question of fact.

(b) In a transaction other than a consumer transaction, a notification of disposition sent after default and 10 days or more before the earliest time of disposition set forth in the notification is sent within a reasonable time before the disposition.

§ 9–613. Contents and Form of Notification
before Disposition of Collateral: General.

Except in a consumer-goods transaction, the following rules apply:

(1) The contents of a notification of disposition are sufficient if the notification:

(A) describes the debtor and the secured party;

(B) describes the collateral that is the subject of the intended disposition;

(C) states the method of intended disposition;

(D) states that the debtor is entitled to an accounting of the unpaid indebtedness and states the charge, if any, for an accounting; and

(E) states the time and place of a public disposition or the time after which any other disposition is to be made.

(2) Whether the contents of a notification that lacks any of the information specified in paragraph (1) are nevertheless sufficient is a question of fact.

(3) The contents of a notification providing substantially the information specified in paragraph (1) are sufficient, even if the notification includes:

    (A) information not specified by that paragraph; or

    (B) minor errors that are not seriously misleading.

(4) A particular phrasing of the notification is not required.

(5) The following form of notification and the form appearing in Section 9–614(3), when completed, each provides sufficient information:

NOTIFICATION OF DISPOSITION OF COLLATERAL

To: *[Name of debtor, obligor, or other person to which the notification is sent]*

From: *[Name, address, and telephone number of secured party]*

Name of Debtor(s): *[Include only if debtor(s) are not an addressee]*

[For a public disposition:]

We will sell [or lease or license, as applicable] the [*describe collateral*] [to the highest qualified bidder] in public as follows:

Day and Date: _____

Time: _____

Place: _____

[For a private disposition:]

We will sell [or lease or license, as *applicable*] the [*describe collateral*] privately sometime after [*day and date*].

You are entitled to an accounting of the unpaid indebtedness secured by the property that we intend to sell [or lease or license, as applicable] [for a charge of $_____]. You may request an accounting by calling us at [telephone number].

[End of Form]

As amended in 2000.

§ 9–614. Contents and Form of Notification before Disposition of Collateral: Consumer-Goods Transaction.

In a consumer-goods transaction, the following rules apply:

(1) A notification of disposition must provide the following information:

    (A) the information specified in Section 9–613(1);

    (B) a description of any liability for a deficiency of the person to which the notification is sent;

    (C) a telephone number from which the amount that must be paid to the secured party to redeem the collateral under Section 9–623 is available; and

    (D) a telephone number or mailing address from which additional information concerning the disposition and the obligation secured is available.

(2) A particular phrasing of the notification is not required.

(3) The following form of notification, when completed, provides sufficient information:

[Name and address of secured party]

[Date]

NOTICE OF OUR PLAN TO SELL PROPERTY

[Name and address of any obligor who is also a debtor]

Subject: *[Identification of Transaction]*

We have your [describe collateral], because you broke promises in our agreement.

[For a public disposition:]

We will sell [describe collateral] at public sale. A sale could include a lease or license. The sale will be held as follows:

Date: _____

Time: _____

Place: _____

If you need more information about the sale call us at [*telephone number*] [or write us at [*secured party's address*]].

We are sending this notice to the following other people who have an interest in [describe collateral] or who owe money under your agreement:

[Names of all other debtors and obligors, if any]

[End of Form]

(4) A notification in the form of paragraph (3) is sufficient, even if additional information appears at the end of the form.

(5) A notification in the form of paragraph (3) is sufficient, even if it includes errors in information not required by paragraph (1), unless the error is misleading with respect to rights arising under this article.

(6) If a notification under this section is not in the form of paragraph (3), law other than this article determines the effect of including information not required by paragraph (1).

§ 9–615. Application of Proceeds of Disposition; Liability for Deficiency and Right to Surplus.

(a) A secured party shall apply or pay over for application the cash proceeds of disposition under Section 9–610 in the following order to:

    (1) the reasonable expenses of retaking, holding, preparing for disposition, processing, and disposing, and, to the extent provided for by agreement and not prohibited by law, reasonable attorney's fees and legal expenses incurred by the secured party;

    (2) the satisfaction of obligations secured by the security interest or agricultural lien under which the disposition is made;

    (3) the satisfaction of obligations secured by any subordinate security interest in or other subordinate lien on the collateral if:

        (A) the secured party receives from the holder of the subordinate security interest or other lien an authenticated demand for proceeds before distribution of the proceeds is completed; and

        (B) in a case in which a consignor has an interest in the collateral, the subordinate security interest or other lien is senior to the interest of the consignor; and

    (4) a secured party that is a consignor of the collateral if the secured party receives from the consignor an authenticated demand for proceeds before distribution of the proceeds is completed.

(b) If requested by a secured party, a holder of a subordinate security interest or other lien shall furnish reasonable proof of the interest or lien within a reasonable time. Unless the holder does so, the secured party need not comply with the holder's demand under subsection (a)(3).

(c) A secured party need not apply or pay over for application non-cash proceeds of disposition under Section 9–610 unless the failure to do so would be commercially unreasonable. A secured party that applies or pays over for application noncash proceeds shall do so in a commercially reasonable manner.

(d) If the security interest under which a disposition is made secures payment or performance of an obligation, after making the payments and applications required by subsection (a) and permitted by subsection (c):

(1) unless subsection (a)(4) requires the secured party to apply or pay over cash proceeds to a consignor, the secured party shall account to and pay a debtor for any surplus; and

(2) the obligor is liable for any deficiency.

(e) If the underlying transaction is a sale of accounts, chattel paper, payment intangibles, or promissory notes:

(1) the debtor is not entitled to any surplus; and

(2) the obligor is not liable for any deficiency.

(f) The surplus or deficiency following a disposition is calculated based on the amount of proceeds that would have been realized in a disposition complying with this part to a transferee other than the secured party, a person related to the secured party, or a secondary obligor if:

(1) the transferee in the disposition is the secured party, a person related to the secured party, or a secondary obligor; and

(2) the amount of proceeds of the disposition is significantly below the range of proceeds that a complying disposition to a person other than the secured party, a person related to the secured party, or a secondary obligor would have brought.

(g) A secured party that receives cash proceeds of a disposition in good faith and without knowledge that the receipt violates the rights of the holder of a security interest or other lien that is not subordinate to the security interest or agricultural lien under which the disposition is made:

(1) takes the cash proceeds free of the security interest or other lien;

(2) is not obligated to apply the proceeds of the disposition to the satisfaction of obligations secured by the security interest or other lien; and

(3) is not obligated to account to or pay the holder of the security interest or other lien for any surplus.

As amended in 2000.

§ 9–616. **Explanation of Calculation of Surplus or Deficiency.**

(a) In this section:

(1) "Explanation" means a writing that:

(A) states the amount of the surplus or deficiency;

(B) provides an explanation in accordance with subsection (c) of how the secured party calculated the surplus or deficiency;

(C) states, if applicable, that future debits, credits, charges, including additional credit service charges or interest, rebates, and expenses may affect the amount of the surplus or deficiency; and

(D) provides a telephone number or mailing address from which additional information concerning the transaction is available.

(2) "Request" means a record:

(A) authenticated by a debtor or consumer obligor;

(B) requesting that the recipient provide an explanation; and

(C) sent after disposition of the collateral under Section 9–610.

(b) In a consumer-goods transaction in which the debtor is entitled to a surplus or a consumer obligor is liable for a deficiency under Section 9–615, the secured party shall:

(1) send an explanation to the debtor or consumer obligor, as applicable, after the disposition and:

(A) before or when the secured party accounts to the debtor and pays any surplus or first makes written demand

on the consumer obligor after the disposition for payment of the deficiency; and

(B) within 14 days after receipt of a request; or

(2) in the case of a consumer obligor who is liable for a deficiency, within 14 days after receipt of a request, send to the consumer obligor a record waiving the secured party's right to a deficiency.

(c) To comply with subsection (a)(1)(B), a writing must provide the following information in the following order:

(1) the aggregate amount of obligations secured by the security interest under which the disposition was made, and, if the amount reflects a rebate of unearned interest or credit service charge, an indication of that fact, calculated as of a specified date:

(A) if the secured party takes or receives possession of the collateral after default, not more than 35 days before the secured party takes or receives possession; or

(B) if the secured party takes or receives possession of the collateral before default or does not take possession of the collateral, not more than 35 days before the disposition;

(2) the amount of proceeds of the disposition;

(3) the aggregate amount of the obligations after deducting the amount of proceeds;

(4) the amount, in the aggregate or by type, and types of expenses, including expenses of retaking, holding, preparing for disposition, processing, and disposing of the collateral, and attorney's fees secured by the collateral which are known to the secured party and relate to the current disposition;

(5) the amount, in the aggregate or by type, and types of credits, including rebates of interest or credit service charges, to which the obligor is known to be entitled and which are not reflected in the amount in paragraph (1); and

(6) the amount of the surplus or deficiency.

(d) A particular phrasing of the explanation is not required. An explanation complying substantially with the requirements of subsection (a) is sufficient, even if it includes minor errors that are not seriously misleading.

(e) A debtor or consumer obligor is entitled without charge to one response to a request under this section during any six-month period in which the secured party did not send to the debtor or consumer obligor an explanation pursuant to subsection (b)(1). The secured party may require payment of a charge not exceeding $25 for each additional response.

§ 9–617. **Rights of Transferee of Collateral.**

(a) A secured party's disposition of collateral after default:

(1) transfers to a transferee for value all of the debtor's rights in the collateral;

(2) discharges the security interest under which the disposition is made; and

(3) discharges any subordinate security interest or other subordinate lien [other than liens created under [cite acts or statutes providing for liens, if any, that are not to be discharged]].

(b) A transferee that acts in good faith takes free of the rights and interests described in subsection (a), even if the secured party fails to comply with this article or the requirements of any judicial proceeding.

(c) If a transferee does not take free of the rights and interests described in subsection (a), the transferee takes the collateral subject to:

(1) the debtor's rights in the collateral;

(2) the security interest or agricultural lien under which the disposition is made; and

(3) any other security interest or other lien.

§ 9–618. Rights and Duties of Certain Secondary Obligors.

(a) A secondary obligor acquires the rights and becomes obligated to perform the duties of the secured party after the secondary obligor:

(1) receives an assignment of a secured obligation from the secured party;

(2) receives a transfer of collateral from the secured party and agrees to accept the rights and assume the duties of the secured party; or

(3) is subrogated to the rights of a secured party with respect to collateral.

(b) An assignment, transfer, or subrogation described in subsection (a):

(1) is not a disposition of collateral under Section 9–610; and

(2) relieves the secured party of further duties under this article.

§ 9–619. Transfer of Record or Legal Title.

(a) In this section, "transfer statement" means a record authenticated by a secured party stating:

(1) that the debtor has defaulted in connection with an obligation secured by specified collateral;

(2) that the secured party has exercised its post-default remedies with respect to the collateral;

(3) that, by reason of the exercise, a transferee has acquired the rights of the debtor in the collateral; and

(4) the name and mailing address of the secured party, debtor, and transferee.

(b) A transfer statement entitles the transferee to the transfer of record of all rights of the debtor in the collateral specified in the statement in any official filing, recording, registration, or certificate-of-title system covering the collateral. If a transfer statement is presented with the applicable fee and request form to the official or office responsible for maintaining the system, the official or office shall:

(1) accept the transfer statement;

(2) promptly amend its records to reflect the transfer; and

(3) if applicable, issue a new appropriate certificate of title in the name of the transferee.

(c) A transfer of the record or legal title to collateral to a secured party under subsection (b) or otherwise is not of itself a disposition of collateral under this article and does not of itself relieve the secured party of its duties under this article.

§ 9–620. Acceptance of Collateral in Full or Partial Satisfaction of Obligation; Compulsory Disposition of Collateral.

(a) Except as otherwise provided in subsection (g), a secured party may accept collateral in full or partial satisfaction of the obligation it secures only if:

(1) the debtor consents to the acceptance under subsection (c);

(2) the secured party does not receive, within the time set forth in subsection (d), a notification of objection to the proposal authenticated by:

(A) a person to which the secured party was required to send a proposal under Section 9–621; or

(B) any other person, other than the debtor, holding an interest in the collateral subordinate to the security interest that is the subject of the proposal;

(3) if the collateral is consumer goods, the collateral is not in the possession of the debtor when the debtor consents to the acceptance; and

(4) subsection (e) does not require the secured party to dispose of the collateral or the debtor waives the requirement pursuant to Section 9–624.

(b) A purported or apparent acceptance of collateral under this section is ineffective unless:

(1) the secured party consents to the acceptance in an authenticated record or sends a proposal to the debtor; and

(2) the conditions of subsection (a) are met.

(c) For purposes of this section:

(1) a debtor consents to an acceptance of collateral in partial satisfaction of the obligation it secures only if the debtor agrees to the terms of the acceptance in a record authenticated after default; and

(2) a debtor consents to an acceptance of collateral in full satisfaction of the obligation it secures only if the debtor agrees to the terms of the acceptance in a record authenticated after default or the secured party:

(A) sends to the debtor after default a proposal that is unconditional or subject only to a condition that collateral not in the possession of the secured party be preserved or maintained;

(B) in the proposal, proposes to accept collateral in full satisfaction of the obligation it secures; and

(C) does not receive a notification of objection authenticated by the debtor within 20 days after the proposal is sent.

(d) To be effective under subsection (a)(2), a notification of objection must be received by the secured party:

(1) in the case of a person to which the proposal was sent pursuant to Section 9–621, within 20 days after notification was sent to that person; and

(2) in other cases:

(A) within 20 days after the last notification was sent pursuant to Section 9–621; or

(B) if a notification was not sent, before the debtor consents to the acceptance under subsection (c).

(e) A secured party that has taken possession of collateral shall dispose of the collateral pursuant to Section 9–610 within the time specified in subsection (f) if:

(1) 60 percent of the cash price has been paid in the case of a purchase-money security interest in consumer goods; or

(2) 60 percent of the principal amount of the obligation secured has been paid in the case of a non-purchase-money security interest in consumer goods.

(f) To comply with subsection (e), the secured party shall dispose of the collateral:

(1) within 90 days after taking possession; or

(2) within any longer period to which the debtor and all secondary obligors have agreed in an agreement to that effect entered into and authenticated after default.

(g) In a consumer transaction, a secured party may not accept collateral in partial satisfaction of the obligation it secures.

§ 9–621. Notification of Proposal to Accept Collateral.

(a) A secured party that desires to accept collateral in full or partial satisfaction of the obligation it secures shall send its proposal to:

(1) any person from which the secured party has received, before the debtor consented to the acceptance, an authenticated notification of a claim of an interest in the collateral;

(2) any other secured party or lienholder that, 10 days before the debtor consented to the acceptance, held a security interest in or other lien on the collateral perfected by the filing of a financing statement that:

(A) identified the collateral;

(B) was indexed under the debtor's name as of that date; and

(C) was filed in the office or offices in which to file a financing statement against the debtor covering the collateral as of that date; and

(3) any other secured party that, 10 days before the debtor consented to the acceptance, held a security interest in the collateral perfected by compliance with a statute, regulation, or treaty described in Section 9–311(a).

(b) A secured party that desires to accept collateral in partial satisfaction of the obligation it secures shall send its proposal to any secondary obligor in addition to the persons described in subsection (a).

§ 9–622. Effect of Acceptance of Collateral.

(a) A secured party's acceptance of collateral in full or partial satisfaction of the obligation it secures:

(1) discharges the obligation to the extent consented to by the debtor;

(2) transfers to the secured party all of a debtor's rights in the collateral;

(3) discharges the security interest or agricultural lien that is the subject of the debtor's consent and any subordinate security interest or other subordinate lien; and

(4) terminates any other subordinate interest.

(b) A subordinate interest is discharged or terminated under subsection (a), even if the secured party fails to comply with this article.

§ 9–623. Right to Redeem Collateral.

(a) A debtor, any secondary obligor, or any other secured party or lienholder may redeem collateral.

(b) To redeem collateral, a person shall tender:

(1) fulfillment of all obligations secured by the collateral; and

(2) the reasonable expenses and attorney's fees described in Section 9–615(a)(1).

(c) A redemption may occur at any time before a secured party:

(1) has collected collateral under Section 9–607;

(2) has disposed of collateral or entered into a contract for its disposition under Section 9–610; or

(3) has accepted collateral in full or partial satisfaction of the obligation it secures under Section 9–622.

§ 9–624. Waiver.

(a) A debtor or secondary obligor may waive the right to notification of disposition of collateral under Section 9–611 only by an agreement to that effect entered into and authenticated after default.

(b) A debtor may waive the right to require disposition of collateral under Section 9–620(e) only by an agreement to that effect entered into and authenticated after default.

(c) Except in a consumer-goods transaction, a debtor or secondary obligor may waive the right to redeem collateral under Section 9–623 only by an agreement to that effect entered into and authenticated after default.

[**Subpart 2. Noncompliance with Article**]

§ 9–625. Remedies for Secured Party's Failure to Comply with Article.

(a) If it is established that a secured party is not proceeding in accordance with this article, a court may order or restrain collection, enforcement, or disposition of collateral on appropriate terms and conditions.

(b) Subject to subsections (c), (d), and (f), a person is liable for damages in the amount of any loss caused by a failure to comply with this article. Loss caused by a failure to comply may include loss resulting from the debtor's inability to obtain, or increased costs of, alternative financing.

(c) Except as otherwise provided in Section 9–628:

(1) a person that, at the time of the failure, was a debtor, was an obligor, or held a security interest in or other lien on the collateral may recover damages under subsection (b) for its loss; and

(2) if the collateral is consumer goods, a person that was a debtor or a secondary obligor at the time a secured party failed to comply with this part may recover for that failure in any event an amount not less than the credit service charge plus 10 percent of the principal amount of the obligation or the time-price differential plus 10 percent of the cash price.

(d) A debtor whose deficiency is eliminated under Section 9–626 may recover damages for the loss of any surplus. However, a debtor or secondary obligor whose deficiency is eliminated or reduced under Section 9–626 may not otherwise recover under subsection (b) for noncompliance with the provisions of this part relating to collection, enforcement, disposition, or acceptance.

(e) In addition to any damages recoverable under subsection (b), the debtor, consumer obligor, or person named as a debtor in a filed record, as applicable, may recover $500 in each case from a person that:

(1) fails to comply with Section 9–208;

(2) fails to comply with Section 9–209;

(3) files a record that the person is not entitled to file under Section 9–509(a);

(4) fails to cause the secured party of record to file or send a termination statement as required by Section 9–513(a) or (c);

(5) fails to comply with Section 9–616(b)(1) and whose failure is part of a pattern, or consistent with a practice, of noncompliance; or

(6) fails to comply with Section 9–616(b)(2).

(f) A debtor or consumer obligor may recover damages under subsection (b) and, in addition, $500 in each case from a person that, without reasonable cause, fails to comply with a request under Section 9–210. A recipient of a request under Section 9–210 which never claimed an interest in the collateral or obligations that are the subject of a request under that section has a reasonable excuse for failure to comply with the request within the meaning of this subsection.

(g) If a secured party fails to comply with a request regarding a list of collateral or a statement of account under Section 9–210, the secured party may claim a security interest only as shown in the list or statement included in the request as against a person that is reasonably misled by the failure.
As amended in 2000.

§ 9–626. Action in Which Deficiency or Surplus Is in Issue.

(a) In an action arising from a transaction, other than a consumer transaction, in which the amount of a deficiency or surplus is in issue, the following rules apply:

(1) A secured party need not prove compliance with the provisions of this part relating to collection, enforcement, disposition, or acceptance unless the debtor or a secondary obligor places the secured party's compliance in issue.

(2) If the secured party's compliance is placed in issue, the secured party has the burden of establishing that the collection, enforcement, disposition, or acceptance was conducted in accordance with this part.

(3) Except as otherwise provided in Section 9–628, if a secured party fails to prove that the collection, enforcement, disposition, or acceptance was conducted in accordance with the provisions of this part relating to collection, enforcement, disposition, or acceptance, the liability of a debtor or a secondary obligor for a deficiency is limited to an amount by which the sum of the secured obligation, expenses, and attorney's fees exceeds the greater of:

(A) the proceeds of the collection, enforcement, disposition, or acceptance; or

(B) the amount of proceeds that would have been realized had the noncomplying secured party proceeded in accordance with the provisions of this part relating to collection, enforcement, disposition, or acceptance.

(4) For purposes of paragraph (3)(B), the amount of proceeds that would have been realized is equal to the sum of the secured obligation, expenses, and attorney's fees unless the secured party proves that the amount is less than that sum.

(5) If a deficiency or surplus is calculated under Section 9–615(f), the debtor or obligor has the burden of establishing that the amount of proceeds of the disposition is significantly below the range of prices that a complying disposition to a person other than the secured party, a person related to the secured party, or a secondary obligor would have brought.

(b) The limitation of the rules in subsection (a) to transactions other than consumer transactions is intended to leave to the court the determination of the proper rules in consumer transactions. The court may not infer from that limitation the nature of the proper rule in consumer transactions and may continue to apply established approaches.

§ 9–627. Determination of Whether Conduct Was Commercially Reasonable.

(a) The fact that a greater amount could have been obtained by a collection, enforcement, disposition, or acceptance at a different time or in a different method from that selected by the secured party is not of itself sufficient to preclude the secured party from establishing that the collection, enforcement, disposition, or acceptance was made in a commercially reasonable manner.

(b) A disposition of collateral is made in a commercially reasonable manner if the disposition is made:

(1) in the usual manner on any recognized market;

(2) at the price current in any recognized market at the time of the disposition; or

(3) otherwise in conformity with reasonable commercial practices among dealers in the type of property that was the subject of the disposition.

(c) A collection, enforcement, disposition, or acceptance is commercially reasonable if it has been approved:

(1) in a judicial proceeding;

(2) by a bona fide creditors' committee;

(3) by a representative of creditors; or

(4) by an assignee for the benefit of creditors.

(d) Approval under subsection (c) need not be obtained, and lack of approval does not mean that the collection, enforcement, disposition, or acceptance is not commercially reasonable.

§ 9–628. Nonliability and Limitation on Liability of Secured Party; Liability of Secondary Obligor.

(a) Unless a secured party knows that a person is a debtor or obligor, knows the identity of the person, and knows how to communicate with the person:

(1) the secured party is not liable to the person, or to a secured party or lienholder that has filed a financing statement against the person, for failure to comply with this article; and

(2) the secured party's failure to comply with this article does not affect the liability of the person for a deficiency.

(b) A secured party is not liable because of its status as secured party:

(1) to a person that is a debtor or obligor, unless the secured party knows:

(A) that the person is a debtor or obligor;

(B) the identity of the person; and

(C) how to communicate with the person; or

(2) to a secured party or lienholder that has filed a financing statement against a person, unless the secured party knows:

(A) that the person is a debtor; and

(B) the identity of the person.

(c) A secured party is not liable to any person, and a person's liability for a deficiency is not affected, because of any act or omission arising out of the secured party's reasonable belief that a transaction is not a consumer-goods transaction or a consumer transaction or that goods are not consumer goods, if the secured party's belief is based on its reasonable reliance on:

(1) a debtor's representation concerning the purpose for which collateral was to be used, acquired, or held; or

(2) an obligor's representation concerning the purpose for which a secured obligation was incurred.

(d) A secured party is not liable to any person under Section 9–625(c)(2) for its failure to comply with Section 9–616.

(e) A secured party is not liable under Section 9–625(c)(2) more than once with respect to any one secured obligation.

Part 7—Transition

§ 9–701. Effective Date.
This [Act] takes effect on July 1, 2001.

§ 9–702. Savings Clause.

(a) Except as otherwise provided in this part, this [Act] applies to a transaction or lien within its scope, even if the transaction or lien was entered into or created before this [Act] takes effect.

(b) Except as otherwise provided in subsection (c) and Sections 9–703 through 9–709:

(1) transactions and liens that were not governed by [former Article 9], were validly entered into or created before this [Act] takes effect, and would be subject to this [Act] if they had been entered into or created after this [Act] takes effect, and the rights, duties, and interests flowing from those transactions and liens remain valid after this [Act] takes effect; and

(2) the transactions and liens may be terminated, completed, consummated, and enforced as required or permitted by this [Act] or by the law that otherwise would apply if this [Act] had not taken effect.

(c) This [Act] does not affect an action, case, or proceeding commenced before this [Act] takes effect.

As amended in 2000.

§ 9–703. Security Interest Perfected before Effective Date.

(a) A security interest that is enforceable immediately before this [Act] takes effect and would have priority over the rights of a person that becomes a lien creditor at that time is a perfected security interest under this [Act] if, when this [Act] takes effect, the applicable requirements for enforceability and perfection under this [Act] are satisfied without further action.

(b) Except as otherwise provided in Section 9–705, if, immediately before this [Act] takes effect, a security interest is enforceable and would have priority over the rights of a person that becomes a lien creditor at that time, but the applicable requirements for enforceability or perfection under this [Act] are not satisfied when this [Act] takes effect, the security interest:

(1) is a perfected security interest for one year after this [Act] takes effect;

(2) remains enforceable thereafter only if the security interest becomes enforceable under Section 9–203 before the year expires; and

(3) remains perfected thereafter only if the applicable requirements for perfection under this [Act] are satisfied before the year expires.

§ 9–704. Security Interest Unperfected before Effective Date.

A security interest that is enforceable immediately before this [Act] takes effect but which would be subordinate to the rights of a person that becomes a lien creditor at that time:

(1) remains an enforceable security interest for one year after this [Act] takes effect;

(2) remains enforceable thereafter if the security interest becomes enforceable under Section 9–203 when this [Act] takes effect or within one year thereafter; and

(3) becomes perfected:

(A) without further action, when this [Act] takes effect if the applicable requirements for perfection under this [Act] are satisfied before or at that time; or

(B) when the applicable requirements for perfection are satisfied if the requirements are satisfied after that time.

§ 9–705. Effectiveness of Action Taken before Effective Date.

(a) If action, other than the filing of a financing statement, is taken before this [Act] takes effect and the action would have resulted in priority of a security interest over the rights of a person that becomes a lien creditor had the security interest become enforceable before this [Act] takes effect, the action is effective to perfect a security interest that attaches under this [Act] within one year after this [Act] takes effect. An attached security interest becomes unperfected one year after this [Act] takes effect unless the security interest becomes a perfected security interest under this [Act] before the expiration of that period.

(b) The filing of a financing statement before this [Act] takes effect is effective to perfect a security interest to the extent the filing would satisfy the applicable requirements for perfection under this [Act].

(c) This [Act] does not render ineffective an effective financing statement that, before this [Act] takes effect, is filed and satisfies the applicable requirements for perfection under the law of the jurisdiction governing perfection as provided in [former Section 9–103]. However, except as otherwise provided in subsections (d) and (e) and Section 9–706, the financing statement ceases to be effective at the earlier of:

(1) the time the financing statement would have ceased to be effective under the law of the jurisdiction in which it is filed; or

(2) June 30, 2006.

(d) The filing of a continuation statement after this [Act] takes effect does not continue the effectiveness of the financing statement filed before this [Act] takes effect. However, upon the timely filing of a continuation statement after this [Act] takes effect and in accordance with the law of the jurisdiction governing perfection as provided in Part 3, the effectiveness of a financing statement filed in the same office in that jurisdiction before this [Act] takes effect continues for the period provided by the law of that jurisdiction.

(e) Subsection (c)(2) applies to a financing statement that, before this [Act] takes effect, is filed against a transmitting utility and satisfies the applicable requirements for perfection under the law of the jurisdiction governing perfection as provided in [former Section 9–103] only to the extent that Part 3 provides that the law of a jurisdiction other than the jurisdiction in which the financing statement is filed governs perfection of a security interest in collateral covered by the financing statement.

(f) A financing statement that includes a financing statement filed before this [Act] takes effect and a continuation statement filed after this [Act] takes effect is effective only to the extent that it satisfies the requirements of Part 5 for an initial financing statement.

§ 9–706. When Initial Financing Statement Suffices to Continue Effectiveness of Financing Statement.

(a) The filing of an initial financing statement in the office specified in Section 9–501 continues the effectiveness of a financing statement filed before this [Act] takes effect if:

(1) the filing of an initial financing statement in that office would be effective to perfect a security interest under this [Act];

(2) the pre-effective-date financing statement was filed in an office in another State or another office in this State; and

(3) the initial financing statement satisfies subsection (c).

(b) The filing of an initial financing statement under subsection (a) continues the effectiveness of the pre-effective-date financing statement:

(1) if the initial financing statement is filed before this [Act] takes effect, for the period provided in [former Section 9–403] with respect to a financing statement; and

(2) if the initial financing statement is filed after this [Act] takes effect, for the period provided in Section 9–515 with respect to an initial financing statement.

(c) To be effective for purposes of subsection (a), an initial financing statement must:

(1) satisfy the requirements of Part 5 for an initial financing statement;

(2) identify the pre-effective-date financing statement by indicating the office in which the financing statement was filed and providing the dates of filing and file numbers, if any, of the financing statement and of the most recent continuation statement filed with respect to the financing statement; and

(3) indicate that the pre-effective-date financing statement remains effective.

§ 9–707. Amendment of Pre-Effective-Date Financing Statement.

(a) In this section, "Pre-effective-date financing statement" means a financing statement filed before this [Act] takes effect.

(b) After this [Act] takes effect, a person may add or delete collateral covered by, continue or terminate the effectiveness of, or otherwise amend the information provided in, a pre-effective-date financing statement only in accordance with the law of the jurisdiction governing perfection as provided in Part 3. However, the effectiveness of a pre-effective-date financing statement also may be terminated in accordance with the law of the jurisdiction in which the financing statement is filed.

(c) Except as otherwise provided in subsection (d), if the law of this State governs perfection of a security interest, the information in a pre-effective-date financing statement may be amended after this [Act] takes effect only if:

(1) the pre-effective-date financing statement and an amendment are filed in the office specified in Section 9–501;

(2) an amendment is filed in the office specified in Section 9–501 concurrently with, or after the filing in that office of, an initial financing statement that satisfies Section 9–706(c); or

(3) an initial financing statement that provides the information as amended and satisfies Section 9–706(c) is filed in the office specified in Section 9–501.

(d) If the law of this State governs perfection of a security interest, the effectiveness of a pre-effective-date financing statement may be continued only under Section 9–705(d) and (f) or 9–706.

(e) Whether or not the law of this State governs perfection of a security interest, the effectiveness of a pre-effective-date financing statement filed in this State may be terminated after this [Act] takes effect by filing a termination statement in the office in which the pre-effective-date financing statement is filed, unless an initial financing statement that satisfies Section 9–706(c) has been filed in the office specified by the law of the jurisdiction governing perfection as provided in Part 3 as the office in which to file a financing statement. As amended in 2000.

§ 9–708. Persons Entitled to File Initial Financing Statement or Continuation Statement.

A person may file an initial financing statement or a continuation statement under this part if:

(1) the secured party of record authorizes the filing; and

(2) the filing is necessary under this part:

(A) to continue the effectiveness of a financing statement filed before this [Act] takes effect; or

(B) to perfect or continue the perfection of a security interest.

As amended in 2000.

§ 9–709. Priority.

(a) This [Act] determines the priority of conflicting claims to collateral. However, if the relative priorities of the claims were established before this [Act] takes effect, [former Article 9] determines priority.

(b) For purposes of Section 9–322(a), the priority of a security interest that becomes enforceable under Section 9–203 of this [Act] dates from the time this [Act] takes effect if the security interest is perfected under this [Act] by the filing of a financing statement before this [Act] takes effect which would not have been effective to perfect the security interest under [former Article 9]. This subsection does not apply to conflicting security interests each of which is perfected by the filing of such a financing statement. As amended in 2000.

APPENDIX D

Answers to the *Issue Spotters*

CHAPTER 1

1. *Under what circumstances might a judge rely on case law to determine the intent and purpose of a statute?* Case law includes courts' interpretations of statutes, as well as constitutional provisions and administrative rules. Statutes often codify common law rules. For these reasons, a judge might rely on the common law as a guide to the intent and purpose of a statute.

2. *Assuming that these convicted war criminals had not disobeyed any law of their country and had merely been following their government's orders, what law had they violated? Explain.* At the time of the Nuremberg trials, "crimes against humanity" were new international crimes. The laws criminalized such acts as murder, extermination, enslavement, deportation, and other inhumane acts committed against any civilian population. These international laws derived their legitimacy from "natural law."

Natural law, which is the oldest and one of the most significant schools of jurisprudence, holds that governments and legal systems should reflect the moral and ethical ideals that are inherent in human nature. Because natural law is universal and discoverable by reason, its adherents believe that all other law is derived from natural law. Natural law therefore supersedes laws created by humans (national, or "positive," law), and in a conflict between the two, national or positive law loses its legitimacy.

The Nuremberg defendants asserted that they had been acting in accordance with German law. The judges dismissed these claims, reasoning that the defendants' acts were commonly regarded as crimes and that the accused must have known that the acts would be considered criminal. The judges clearly believed the tenets of natural law and expected that the defendants, too, should have been able to realize that their acts ran afoul of it. The fact that the "positivist law" of Germany at the time required them to commit these acts is irrelevant. Under natural law theory, the international court was justified in finding the defendants guilty of crimes against humanity.

CHAPTER 2

1. *Does the court in Sue's state have jurisdiction over Tipton? What factors will the court consider in determining jurisdiction?* Yes, the court in Sue's state has jurisdiction over Tipton on the basis of the company's minimum contacts with the state.

Courts look at the following factors in determining whether minimum contacts exist: the quantity of the contacts, the nature and quality of the contacts, the source and connection of the cause of action to the contacts, the interest of the forum state, and the convenience of the parties. Attempting to exercise jurisdiction without sufficient minimum contacts would violate the

due process clause. Generally, courts have found that jurisdiction is proper when there is substantial business conducted online (with contracts, sales, and so on). Even when there is only some interactivity through a Web site, courts have sometimes held that jurisdiction is proper. Jurisdiction is not proper when there is merely passive advertising.

Here, all of these factors suggest that the defendant had sufficient minimum contacts with the state to justify the exercise of jurisdiction over the defendant. Two especially important factors were that the plaintiff sold the security system to a resident of the state and that litigating in the defendant's state would be relatively inconvenient for the plaintiff.

2. *If the dispute is not resolved, or if either party disagrees with the decision of the mediator or arbitrator, will a court hear the case? Explain.* Yes, if the dispute is not resolved, or if either party disagrees with the decision of the mediator or arbitrator, a court will hear the case. It is required that the dispute be submitted to mediation or arbitration, but this outcome is not binding.

CHAPTER 3

1. *Tom can call his first witness. What else might he do?* Tom could file a motion for a directed verdict. This motion asks the judge to direct a verdict for Tom on the ground that Sue presented no evidence that would justify granting Sue relief. The judge grants the motion if there is insufficient evidence to raise an issue of fact.

2. *Who can appeal to a higher court?* Either a plaintiff or a defendant, or both, can appeal a judgment to a higher court. An appellate court can affirm, reverse, or remand a case, or take any of these actions in combination. To appeal successfully, it is best to appeal on the basis of an error of law, because appellate courts do not usually reverse on findings of fact.

CHAPTER 4

1. *Can a state, in the interest of energy conservation, ban all advertising by power utilities if conservation could be accomplished by less restrictive means? Why or why not?* No. Even if commercial speech is neither related to illegal activities nor misleading, it may be restricted if a state has a substantial interest that cannot be achieved by less restrictive means. In this case, the interest in energy conservation is substantial, but it could be achieved by less restrictive means. That would be the utilities' defense against the enforcement of this state law.

2. *Is this a violation of equal protection if the only reason for the tax is to protect the local firms from out-of-state competition? Explain.* Yes. The tax would limit the liberty of some persons (out-of-state businesses), so it is subject to a review under the equal protection clause. Protecting local businesses from out-of-state competition is not a legitimate government objective. Thus, such a tax would violate the equal protection clause.

CHAPTER 5

1. *Does this raise an ethical conflict between Acme's employees? Between Acme and its employees? Between Acme and its shareholders? Explain your answers.* When a corporation decides to respond to what it sees as a moral obligation to correct for past discrimination by adjusting pay differences among its employees, an ethical conflict is raised between the firm and its employees and between the firm and its shareholders. This dilemma arises directly out of the effect such a decision has on the firm's profits. If satisfying this obligation increases profitability, then the dilemma is easily resolved in favor of "doing the right thing."

2. *Does Delta have an ethical duty to remove this product from the market, even if the injuries result only from misuse? Why or why not?* Maybe. On the one hand, it is not the company's "fault" when a product is misused. Also, keeping the product on the market is not a violation of the law, and stopping sales would hurt profits. On the other hand, suspending sales could reduce suffering and could stop potential negative publicity.

CHAPTER 6

1. *Can Lou recover from Jana? Why or why not?* Probably. To recover on the basis of negligence, the injured party as a plaintiff must show that the truck's owner owed the plaintiff a duty of care, that the owner breached that duty, that the plaintiff was injured, and that the breach caused the injury.

In this situation, the owner's actions breached the duty of reasonable care. The billboard falling on the plaintiff was the direct cause of the injury, not the plaintiff's own negligence. Thus, liability turns on whether the plaintiff can connect the breach of duty to the injury. This involves the test of proximate cause—the question of foreseeability. The consequences to the injured party must have been a foreseeable result of the owner's carelessness.

2. *What might the firm successfully claim in defense?* The company might defend against this electrician's claim by asserting that the electrician should have known of the risk and, therefore, the company had no duty to warn. According to the problem, the danger is common knowledge in the electrician's field and should have been apparent to this electrician, given his years of training and experience. In other words, the company most likely had no need to warn the electrician of the risk.

The firm could also raise comparative negligence. Both parties' negligence, if any, could be weighed and the liability distributed proportionately. The defendant could also assert assumption of risk, claiming that the electrician voluntarily entered into a dangerous situation, knowing the risk involved.

CHAPTER 7

1. *Is Superior Vehicles liable? Explain your answer.* Yes. The manufacturer is liable for the injuries to the user of the product. A manufacturer is liable for its failure to exercise due care to any person who sustains an injury proximately caused by a negligently made (defective) product.

2. *What defense might Bensing assert to avoid liability under state law?* Bensing can assert the defense of preemption. An injured party may not be able to sue the manufacturer of defective products that are subject to comprehensive federal regulatory schemes. If the federal government has a comprehensive regulatory scheme (such as it does with medical devices and vaccines), then it is assumed that the rules were designed to ensure a product's safety, and the federal rules will preempt any state regulations. Therefore, Bensing could not be held liable under state law if it complied with the federal drug-labeling requirements.

CHAPTER 8

1. *Has Roslyn violated any of the intellectual property rights discussed in this chapter? Explain.* Yes, Roslyn has committed theft of trade secrets. Lists of suppliers and customers cannot be patented, copyrighted, or trademarked, but the information they contain is protected against appropriation by others as trade secrets. And most likely, Roslyn signed a contract agreeing not to use this information outside her employment by Organic. But even without this contract, Organic could make a convincing case against its ex-employee for a theft of trade secrets.

2. *Is this patent infringement? If so, how might Global save the cost of suing World for infringement and at the same time profit from World's sales?* This is patent infringement. A software maker in this situation might best protect its product, save litigation costs, and profit from its patent by the use of a license. In the context of this problem, a license would grant permission to sell a patented item. (A license can be limited to certain purposes and to the licensee only.)

CHAPTER 9

1. *Has Karl done anything wrong? Explain.* Karl may have committed trademark infringement. A site that appropriates the key words of other sites with more frequent hits will appear in the same search engine results as the more popular sites. But using another's trademark as a key word without the owner's permission normally constitutes trademark infringement. Of course, some uses of another's trademark as a meta tag may be permissible if the use is reasonably necessary and does not suggest that the owner authorized or sponsored the use.

2. *Can Eagle Corporation stop this use of eagle? If so, what must the company show? Explain.* Yes. This may be an instance of trademark dilution. Dilution occurs when a trademark is used, without permission, in a way that diminishes the distinctive quality of the mark. Dilution does not require proof that consumers are likely to be confused by the use of the unauthorized mark. The products involved do not have to be similar. Dilution does require, however, that a mark be famous when the dilution occurs.

CHAPTER 10

1. *With respect to the gas station, has she committed a crime? If so, what is it?* Yes. With respect to the gas station, she has obtained goods by false pretenses. She might also be charged with larceny and forgery, and most states have special statutes covering illegal use of credit cards.

2. *Has Ben committed a crime? If so, what is it?* Yes. The Counterfeit Access Device and Computer Fraud and Abuse Act provides that a person who accesses a computer online, without permission, to obtain classified data—such as consumer credit files in a credit agency's database—is subject to criminal prosecution. The crime has two elements: accessing the computer without permission and taking data. It is a felony if done for private financial gain. Penalties include fines and imprisonment for up to twenty years. The victim of the theft can also bring a civil suit against the criminal to obtain damages and other relief.

CHAPTER 11

1. *Can Ed recover? Why or why not?* No. This contract, although not fully executed, is for an illegal purpose and therefore is void. A void contract gives rise to no legal obligation on the part of any party. A contract that is void is no contract. There is nothing to enforce.

2. *Can Alison recover from Jerry the amount that she paid? Why or why not?* Yes, because a person who is unjustly enriched at the expense of another can be required to account for the benefit under the theory of quasi contract. The parties here did not have a contract, but the law will impose one to avoid the unjust enrichment.

CHAPTER 12

1. *Do Fidelity and Ron have a contract? Why or why not?* No. Revocation of an offer may be implied by conduct inconsistent with the offer. When the corporation hired someone else, and the offeree learned of the hiring, the offer was revoked. The acceptance was too late.

2. *Under the Uniform Electronic Transactions Act, what determines the effect of the electronic documents evidencing the parties' deal? Is a party's "signature" necessary? Explain.* First, it might be noted that the UETA does not apply unless the parties to a contract agree to use e-commerce in their transaction. In this deal, of course, the parties used e-commerce. The UETA removes barriers to e-commerce by giving the same legal effect to e-records and e-signatures as to paper documents and signatures. The UETA does not include rules for those transactions, however.

CHAPTER 13

1. *Is the new contract binding? Explain.* Yes. The original contract was executory. The parties rescinded it and agreed to a new contract. If Sharyn had broken the contract to accept a contract with another employer, she might have been held liable for damages for the breach.

2. *Is Fred's promise binding? Explain.* Yes. Under the doctrine of detrimental reliance, or promissory estoppel, the promisee is entitled to payment of $5,000 from the promisor on graduation. There was a promise, on which the promisee relied, the reliance was substantial and definite (the promisee went to college for the full term, incurring considerable expenses, and will likely graduate), and it would only be fair to enforce the promise.

CHAPTER 14

1. *Can Kenwood enforce the lease against Joan? Why or why not?* No. Joan is a minor and may disaffirm this contract. Because the apartment was a necessary, however, she remains liable for the reasonable value of her occupancy of the apartment.

2. *If the cause of an accident is found to be the airline's negligence, can it use the clause as a defense to liability? Why or why not?* No. Generally, an exculpatory clause (a clause attempting to absolve parties of negligence or other wrongs) is not enforced if the party seeking its enforcement is involved in a business that is important to the public as a matter of practical necessity, such as an airline. Because of the essential nature of such services, this party has an advantage in bargaining strength and could insist that anyone contracting for its services agree not to hold it liable.

CHAPTER 15

1. *Can she rescind the deal? Why or why not?* Yes. Rescission may be granted on the basis of fraudulent misrepresentation. The elements of fraudulent misrepresentation include intent to deceive, or *scienter*. *Scienter* exists if a party makes a statement recklessly, without regard to whether it is true or false, or if a party says or implies that a statement is made on some basis such as personal knowledge or personal investigation when it is not.

2. *Can Elle be held liable to GCC? Why or why not?* Yes. The accountant may be liable on the ground of negligent misrepresentation. A misrepresentation is negligent if a person fails to exercise reasonable care in disclosing material facts or does not use the skill and competence required by his or her business or profession.

CHAPTER 16

1. *Can Midstate enforce a deal for the full $800? Explain your answer.* No. Under the UCC, a contract for a sale of goods priced at $500 or more must be in writing to be enforceable. In this case, the contract is not enforceable beyond the quantity already delivered and paid for.

2. *Next Corporation argues that there is no written contract between them. What will the court say?* The court might conclude that under the doctrine of promissory estoppel, the employer is estopped from claiming the lack of a written contract as a defense. The oral contract may be enforced because the employer made a promise on which the employee justifiably relied in moving to New York, the reliance was foreseeable, and injustice can be avoided only by enforcing the promise. If the court strictly enforces the Statute of Frauds, however, the employee may be without a remedy.

CHAPTER 17

1. *Can Jeff successfully sue Ed for the $100? Why or why not?* Yes. When one person makes a promise with the intention of benefiting a third person, the third person can sue to enforce it. This is a third party beneficiary contract. The third party in this problem is an intended beneficiary.

2. *Can Good Credit enforce the contract against Frank? Why or why not?* Yes. Generally, if a contract clearly states that a right is not assignable, no assignment will be effective, but there are exceptions. Assignment of the right to receive monetary payment cannot be prohibited.

CHAPTER 18

1. *Before Ready or Stealth starts performing, can the parties call off the deal? What if Stealth has already shipped the pizzas? Explain your answers.* Contracts that are executory on both sides—contracts on which neither party has performed—can be rescinded solely by agreement. Contracts that are executed on one side—contracts on which one party has performed—can be rescinded only if the party who has performed receives consideration for the promise to call off the deal.

2. *What type of agreement is this? Are Ace's obligations discharged? Why or why not?* This is a novation because it substitutes a new party for an original party, by agreement of all the parties. The requirements are a previous valid obligation, an agreement of all the parties to a new contract, extinguishment of the old obligation, and a new, valid contract. Ace's obligations are discharged.

CHAPTER 19

1. *If Haney sues Greg, what will be the measure of recovery?* A nonbreaching party is entitled to his or her benefit of the bargain under the contract. Here, the innocent party is entitled to be put in the position she would have been in if the contract had been fully performed. The measure of the benefit is the cost to complete the work ($500). These are compensatory damages.

2. *Is Lyle liable for Marley's expenses in providing for the cattle? Why or why not?* No. To recover damages that flow from the consequences of a breach but that are caused by circumstances beyond the contract (consequential damages), the breaching party must know, or have reason to know, that special

circumstances will cause the nonbreaching party to suffer the additional loss. That was not the circumstance in this problem.

CHAPTER 20

1. *Is this an acceptance of the offer or a counteroffer? If it is an acceptance, is it a breach of the contract? Why or why not? What if Fav-O-Rite told E-Design it was sending the printer stands as "an accommodation"?* A shipment of nonconforming goods constitutes an acceptance of the offer and a breach, unless the seller seasonably notifies the buyer that the nonconforming shipment does not constitute an acceptance and is offered only as an accommodation. Thus, since there was no notification here, the shipment was both an acceptance and a breach. If, however, Fav-O-Rite had notified E-Design that it was sending the printer stands as an accommodation, the shipment would not constitute an acceptance, and Fav-O-Rite would not be in breach.

2. *Is there an enforceable contract between them? Why or why not?* Yes. In a transaction between merchants, the requirement of a writing is satisfied if one of them sends to the other a signed written confirmation that indicates the terms of the agreement, and the merchant receiving it has reason to know of its contents. If the merchant who receives the confirmation does not object in writing within ten days after receipt, the writing will be enforceable against him or her even though he or she has not signed anything.

CHAPTER 21

1. *What are the consequences if Silk bore the risk? If Adams bore the risk?* Buyers and sellers can have an insurable interest in identical goods at the same time. If the buyer (Silk & Satin) bore the risk, it must pay and seek reimbursement from its insurance company. If the seller (Adams Textiles) bore the risk, it must seek reimbursement from its insurance company and may still have an obligation to deliver the identified goods (the fabric) to Silk & Satin.

2. *If Karlin files a lawsuit, will she prevail? Why or why not?* When a person "entrusts" goods to a merchant (a person who deals in goods of that kind), the merchant has the power to transfer a good title to any purchaser who acquires the goods in the *ordinary course of business*. Karlin entrusted her set to merchant Orken. Orken deals in goods of that kind. Therefore, Orken could pass good title to the set to a customer (Grady) who purchased the goods in the ordinary course of business. Consequently, Karlin cannot get the set back from Grady. (But the merchant is liable to the true owner, Karlin, for the equivalent value of the set.)

CHAPTER 22

1. *Does Country have the right to reject the shipment? Explain.* Yes. A seller is obligated to deliver goods in conformity with a contract in every detail. This is the perfect tender rule. The exception of the seller's right to cure does not apply here, because the seller delivered too little too late to take advantage of this exception.

2. Can Poster Planet sue Brite without waiting until May 1? Why or why not? Yes. When anticipatory repudiation occurs, a buyer (or lessee) can resort to any remedy for breach even if the buyer tells the seller (the repudiating party in this problem) that the buyer will wait for the seller's performance.

CHAPTER 23

1. When it does not perform to GCC's specifications, GCC sues Industrial, which claims, "We didn't expressly promise anything." What should GCC argue? The buyer should argue that the seller breached an implied warranty of fitness for a particular purpose. An implied warranty of fitness for a particular purpose arises when a seller knows a particular purpose for which a buyer will use goods and that the buyer is relying on the seller's skill and judgment to select suitable goods.

2. Can Stella recover for breach of the implied warranty of merchantability? Why or why not? Yes, Stella can recover from Roasted Bean for breach of the implied warranty of merchantability. An implied warranty of merchantability arises in every sale of goods sold by a merchant who deals in goods of the kind. Goods that are merchantable are fit for the ordinary purposes for which such goods are used. A sale of food or drink is a sale of goods. Merchantable food is food that is fit to eat or drink on the basis of consumer expectations. A consumer should reasonably expect hot coffee to be hot, but not to be so scalding that it causes third-degree burns.

CHAPTER 24

1. Under what circumstances would a U.S. court enforce the judgment of the Ecuadoran court? Under the principle of comity, a U.S. court would defer and give effect to foreign laws and judicial decrees that are consistent with U.S. law and public policy.

2. How can this attempt to undersell U.S. businesses be defeated? The practice described in this problem is known as dumping, which is regarded as an unfair international trade practice. Dumping is the sale of imported goods at "less than fair value." Based on the price of those goods in the exporting country, an extra tariff—known as an antidumping duty—can be imposed on the imports.

CHAPTER 25

1. Which of these phrases would prevent the instrument's negotiability? A statement that "I.O.U." money (or anything else) or an instruction to a bank stating, "I wish you would pay," would render any instrument nonnegotiable. To be negotiable, an instrument must contain an express promise to pay. An I.O.U. is only an acknowledgment of indebtedness. An order stating, "I wish you would pay," is not sufficiently precise.

2. Is Marit's note a demand note? Explain. Yes. Instruments that are payable on demand may state "Payable on demand." The nature of an instrument may indicate that it is payable on demand. If no time for payment is specified, then the instrument is also payable on demand. Here, the note required installments but did not state a date for their payment. That Donald did not make a demand for payment did not affect this characteristic of the note.

CHAPTER 26

1. What type of indorsement is this? What effect does this indorsement have on whether the check is considered an order instrument or a bearer instrument? Explain. This is a special indorsement, which names the indorsee (Kurt). No special words are needed. A special indorsement makes an instrument order paper. Thus, further negotiation requires Kurt's indorsement.

2. Can Carl become an HDC? Why or why not? No. One of the requirements for HDC status is that the holder must have performed the promise for which the instrument was issued. A holder takes the instrument for value only to the extent that the promise has been performed. Because Ben did not perform his promise to repair Amy's roof, he is not an HDC. Thus, Carl—who took the instrument from Ben—cannot trace his title back to an HDC, so he is not be protected as an HDC under the shelter principle.

CHAPTER 27

1. Does Suchin have any recourse against the bank for the payment? Why or why not? No. When a drawer's employee provides the drawer with the name of a fictitious payee (a payee whom the drawer does not actually intend to have any interest in an instrument), a forgery of the payee's name is effective to pass good title to subsequent transferees.

2. Was the bookstore a holder in due course on Skye's check? Yes. One of the requirements for HDC status is a lack of notice that an instrument is defective. A party will not attain this status if he or she knows, or has reason to know, that an incomplete instrument was later completed in an unauthorized manner. Notice of a defective instrument is given when a holder has reason to know that a defect exists, given all of the facts known at the time. Here, the bookstore did not have notice that Skye's check was incomplete when it was issued. The bookstore saw only a properly completed instrument.

CHAPTER 28

1. Is Lyn liable to Nan? Could Lyn be subject to criminal prosecution? Why or why not? Yes, to both questions. In a civil suit, a drawer (Lyn) is liable to a payee (Nan) or to a holder of a check that is not honored. If intent to defraud can be proved, the drawer (Lyn) can also be subject to criminal prosecution for writing a bad check.

2. Can the bank refuse to recredit Kay's account? If not, can the bank recover the amount paid to Will? Why or why not?

The general rule is that the bank must recredit a customer's account when it pays on a forged signature. The bank has no right to recover from a holder who, without knowledge, cashes a check bearing a forged drawer's signature. Thus, the bank in this problem can collect from neither its customer nor the party who cashed the check. The bank's recourse is to look for the thief.

CHAPTER 29

1. What can Larry and Midwest do? Each of the parties can place a mechanic's lien on the debtor's property. If the debtor does not pay what is owed, the property can be sold to satisfy the debt. The only requirements are that the lien be filed within a specific time from the time of the work, depending on the state statute, and that notice of the foreclosure and sale be given to the debtor in advance.

2. If the employer complies with the order and Alyssa stays on the job, is one order enough to garnish all of Alyssa's wages for each pay period until the debt is paid? Explain. No. In some states, a creditor must go back to court for a separate order of garnishment for each pay period. Also, federal and state laws limit the amount of money that can be garnished from a debtor's pay.

CHAPTER 30

1. How can Olivia let other creditors know of her interest in the computer? A creditor can put other creditors on notice by perfecting its interest: by filing a financing statement in the appropriate public office, or by taking possession of the collateral until the debtor repays the loan.

2. Liberty could repossess and keep the car, but the bank does not want it. What are the alternatives? When collateral is consumer goods with a PMSI, and the debtor has paid less than 60 percent of the debt or the purchase price, the creditor can dispose of the collateral in a commercially reasonable manner, which generally requires notice to the debtor of the place, time, and manner of sale. A debtor can waive the right to notice, but only after default. Before the disposal, a debtor can redeem the collateral by tendering performance of all of the obligations secured by it and by paying the creditor's reasonable expenses in retaking and maintaining it.

CHAPTER 31

1. Are these debts dischargeable in bankruptcy? Explain. No. Besides the claims listed in this problem, the debts that cannot be discharged in bankruptcy include amounts borrowed to pay back taxes, goods obtained by fraud, debts that were not listed in the petition, domestic support obligations, certain cash advances, and others.

2. Can Quentin recover the $10,000 paid to Ogden on June 1? Why or why not? Yes. A debtor's payment to a creditor made for a preexisting debt, within ninety days (one year in the case of an insider or fraud) of a bankruptcy filing, can be recovered if it gives a creditor more than he or she would have received in the

bankruptcy proceedings. A trustee can recover this preference using his or her specific avoidance powers.

CHAPTER 32

1. Was Winona an independent contractor? Yes. An independent contractor is a person who contracts with another—the principal—to do something but who is neither controlled by the other nor subject to the other's right to control with respect to the performance. Independent contractors are not employees, because those who hire them have no control over the details of their performance.

2. When Nadine learns of this, she wants to buy the land and sell it to Dimka herself. Can she do this? Discuss. No. Nadine, as an agent, is prohibited from taking advantage of the agency relationship to obtain property that the principal (Dimka Corporation) wants to purchase. This is the duty of loyalty that arises with every agency relationship.

CHAPTER 33

1. Can Davis hold Estee liable for whatever damages he has to pay? Why or why not? Yes. A principal has a duty to indemnify an agent for liabilities incurred because of authorized and lawful acts and transactions and for losses suffered because of the principal's failure to perform his or her duties.

2. In what circumstance is Vivian liable on the note? When a person enters into a contract on another's behalf without the authority to do so, the other may be liable on the contract if he or she approves or affirms that contract. In other words, the employer-principal would be liable for the note in this problem on ratifying it. Whether the employer-principal ratifies the note or not, the unauthorized agent is most likely also liable for it.

CHAPTER 34

1. For Erin to obtain workers' compensation, must her injury have been caused by Fine Print's negligence? Does it matter whether the action causing the injury was intentional? Explain. Workers' compensation laws establish a procedure for compensating workers who are injured on the job. Instead of suing to collect benefits, an injured worker notifies the employer of an injury and files a claim with the appropriate state agency.

The right to recover is normally determined without regard to negligence or fault, but intentionally inflicted injuries are not covered. Unlike the potential for recovery in a lawsuit based on negligence or fault, recovery under a workers' compensation statute is limited to the specific amount designated in the statute for the employee's injury.

2. Are these conditions legal? Why or why not? No. A closed shop (a company that requires union membership as a condition of employment) is illegal. A union shop (a company that does not require union membership as a condition of employment but requires workers to join the union after a certain time on the job) is illegal in a state with a right-to-work law, which makes it illegal to require union membership for continued employment.

CHAPTER 35

1. *Is this sexual harassment? Why or why not?* Yes. One type of sexual harassment occurs when a request for sexual favors is a condition of employment, and the person making the request is a supervisor or acts with the authority of the employer. A tangible employment action, such as continued employment, may also lead to the employer's liability for the supervisor's conduct. That the injured employee is a male and the supervisor a female, instead of the other way around, would not affect the outcome. Same-gender harassment is also actionable.

2. *Could Koko succeed in a suit against Lively for discrimination? Explain.* Yes, if she can show that Lively failed to hire her solely because of her disability. The other elements for a discrimination suit based on a disability are that the plaintiff (1) has a disability and (2) is otherwise qualified for the job. Both of these elements appear to be satisfied in this problem.

CHAPTER 36

1. *Would a sole proprietorship be an appropriate form for Frank's business? Why or why not?* Yes. When a business is relatively small and is not diversified, employs relatively few people, has modest profits, and is not likely to expand significantly or require extensive financing in the immediate future, the most appropriate form for doing business may be a sole proprietorship.

2. *Does this constitute "cause" for termination? Why or why not?* Yes. Failing to meet a specified sales quota can constitute a breach of a franchise agreement. If the franchisor is acting in good faith, "cause" may also include the death or disability of the franchisee, the insolvency of the franchisee, and a breach of another term of the franchise agreement.

CHAPTER 37

1. *When Darnell dies, his widow claims that as Darnell's heir, she is entitled to take his place as Eliana's partner or to receive a share of the firm's assets. Is she right? Why or why not?* No. A widow (or widower) has no right to take a dead partner's place. A partner's death causes dissociation, after which the partnership must purchase the dissociated partner's partnership interest. Therefore, the surviving partners must pay the decedent's estate (for his widow) the value of the deceased partner's interest in the partnership.

2. *Because the vehicles would otherwise be sitting idle in a parking lot, can Finian keep the income that results from leasing the delivery vehicles? Explain your answer.* No. Under the partners' fiduciary duty, a partner must account to the partnership for any personal profits or benefits derived without the consent of all the partners in connection with the use of any partnership property. Here, the leasing partner may not keep the money.

CHAPTER 38

1. *What are their options with respect to the management of their firm?* The members of a limited liability company (LLC) may designate a group to run their firm, in which situation the firm would be considered a manager-managed LLC. The group may include only members, only nonmembers, or members and nonmembers. If, instead, all members participate in management, the firm would be a member-managed LLC. In fact, unless the members agree otherwise, all members are considered to participate in the management of the firm.

2. *What do these forms of business organization have in common?* Although there are differences, all of these forms of business organizations resemble corporations. A joint stock company, for example, features ownership by shares of stock, is managed by directors and officers, and has perpetual existence. A business trust, like a corporation, distributes profits to persons who are not personally responsible for the debts of the organization. Management of a business trust is in the hands of trustees, just as the management of a corporation is in the hands of directors and officers. An incorporated cooperative, which is subject to state laws covering nonprofit corporations, distributes profits to its owners.

CHAPTER 39

1. *Is there a way for Northwest Brands to avoid this double taxation? Explain your answer.* Yes. Small businesses that meet certain requirements can qualify as S corporations, created specifically to permit small businesses to avoid double taxation. The six requirements of an S corporation are (1) the firm must be a domestic corporation, (2) the firm must not be a member of an affiliated group of corporations, (3) the firm must have less than a certain number of shareholders, (4) the shareholders must be individuals, estates, or qualified trusts (or corporations in some cases), (5) there can be only one class of stock, and (6) no shareholder can be a nonresident alien.

2. *Can they grant this authority to their firm? If so, how? If not, why not?* Broad authority to conduct business can be granted in a corporation's articles of incorporation. For example, the term "any lawful purpose" is often used. This can be important because acts of a corporation that are beyond the authority given to it in its articles or charter (or state statutes) are considered illegal, *ultra vires* acts.

CHAPTER 40

1. *Yvon, a Wonder shareholder, learns of the purchase and wants to sue the directors on Wonder's behalf. Can she do it? Explain.* Yes. A shareholder can bring a derivative suit on behalf of a corporation, if some wrong is done to the corporation. Normally, any damages recovered go into the corporate treasury.

2. *Discuss whether Nico owes a duty to Omega or the minority shareholders in selling his shares.* Yes. A single shareholder—or a few shareholders acting together—who owns enough stock to exercise *de facto* control over a corporation owes the corporation and minority shareholders a fiduciary duty when transferring those shares.

CHAPTER 41

1. *What is the term for this type of combination? What happens to the assets, property, and liabilities of Micro?* This combination is a consolidation (a new entity takes the place of the consolidating, disappearing firms). In a merger, in contrast, one of the merging entities continues to exist. In this consolidation, the new corporation, MM, Inc., inherits all of Micro's assets, property, and liabilities.

2. *Can McClellan hold Peppertree's shareholders personally liable for the debt? Why or why not?* Maybe. If a corporation organizes another corporation with practically the same shareholders and directors and transfers all the assets but does not pay all the first corporation's debts, a court can hold the new corporation liable. Here, the new corporation continued to carry on the same business as Peppertree with all of Peppertree's assets, so it would be fair for a court to hold the new corporation liable for Peppertree's obligations.

CHAPTER 42

1. *What sort of information would an investor consider material?* The average investor is not concerned with minor inaccuracies but with facts that if disclosed would tend to deter him or her from buying the securities. This would include facts that have an important bearing on the condition of the issuer and its business—liabilities, loans to officers and directors, customer delinquencies, and pending lawsuits.

2. *Can Lee take advantage of this information to buy and sell Magma stock? Why or why not?* No. The Securities Exchange Act of 1934 extends liability to officers and directors in their personal transactions for taking advantage of inside information when they know it is unavailable to the persons with whom they are dealing.

CHAPTER 43

1. *What safeguards promote the ALJ's fairness?* Under the Administrative Procedure Act (APA), the administrative law judge (ALJ) must be separate from the agency's investigative and prosecutorial staff. *Ex parte* communications between the ALJ and a party to a proceeding are prohibited. Under the APA, an ALJ is exempt from agency discipline except on a showing of good cause.

2. *Does the firm have any opportunity to express its opinion about the pending rule? Explain.* Yes. Administrative rulemaking starts with the publication of a notice of the rulemaking in the *Federal Register*. A public hearing is held at which proponents and opponents can offer evidence and question witnesses. After the hearing, the agency considers what was presented at the hearing and drafts the final rule.

CHAPTER 44

1. *To market the drug, what must United prove to the U.S. Food and Drug Administration?* Under an extensive set of procedures established by the U.S. Food and Drug Administration, which administers the federal Food, Drug, and Cosmetic Act, drugs must be shown to be effective as well as safe before they may be marketed to the public. In general, manufacturers are responsible for ensuring that the drugs they offer for sale are free of any substances that could injure consumers.

2. *What can Gert do?* Under the Truth-in-Lending Act, a buyer who wishes to withhold payment for a faulty product purchased with a credit card must follow specific procedures to settle the dispute. The credit card issuer then must intervene and attempt to settle the dispute.

CHAPTER 45

1. *Are there any reasons that the court might refuse to issue an injunction against Resource's operation? Explain.* Yes. On the ground that the hardships that would be imposed on the polluter and on the community are greater than the hardships suffered by the residents, the court might deny an injunction. If the plant is the core of the local economy, for instance, the residents may be awarded only damages.

2. *If the Environmental Protection Agency cleans up the site, from whom can it recover the cost?* The Comprehensive Environmental Response, Compensation, and Liability Act of 1980 regulates the clean-up of hazardous waste disposal sites. Any potentially responsible party can be charged with the entire cost of cleaning up a site. Potentially responsible parties include the person that generated the waste (ChemCorp) the person that transported the waste to the site (Disposal), the person that owned or operated the site at the time of the disposal (Eliminators), and the current owner or operator of the site (Fluid). A party held responsible for the entire cost may be able to recoup some of it in a lawsuit against other potentially responsible parties.

CHAPTER 46

1. *Under what circumstances would Pop's Market, a small store in a small, isolated town, be considered a monopolist? If Pop's is a monopolist, is it in violation of Section 2 of the Sherman Act? Why or why not?* Size alone does not determine whether a firm is a monopoly—size in relation to the market is what matters. A small store in a small, isolated town is a monopolist if it is the only store serving that market. Monopoly involves the power to affect prices and output. If a firm has sufficient market power to control prices and exclude competition, that firm has monopoly power. Monopoly power in itself is not a violation of Section 2 of the Sherman Act. The offense also requires that the defendant intended to acquire or maintain that power through anticompetitive means.

2. *What factors would a court consider to decide whether this arrangement violates the Clayton Act?* This agreement is a tying arrangement. The legality of a tying arrangement depends on the purpose of the agreement, the agreement's likely effect on competition in the relevant markets (the market for the tying product and the market for the tied product), and other factors. Tying arrangements for commodities are subject to Section 3 of the Clayton Act. Tying arrangements for services can be agreements in restraint of trade in violation of Section 1 of the Sherman Act.

CHAPTER 47

1. *Can the bank successfully sue Dave? Why or why not?* Yes. In these circumstances, when the accountant knows that the bank will use the statement, the bank is a foreseeable user. A foreseeable user is a third party within the class of parties to whom an accountant may be liable for negligence.

2. *Can Nora be held liable to Pat? Explain.* No. In the circumstances described, the accountant will not be held liable to a purchaser of the securities. Although an accountant may be liable under securities laws for including untrue statements or omitting material facts from financial statements, due diligence is a defense to liability.

Due diligence requires an accountant to conduct a reasonable investigation and have reason to believe that the financial statements were true at the time. The facts say that the misstatement of material fact in Omega's financial statement was not attributable to any fraud or negligence on Nora's part. Therefore, Nora can show that she used due diligence and will not be held liable to Pat.

CHAPTER 48

1. *Does Speedy have a right to recover from the third party for the loss of the documents? Why or why not?* Yes. A bailee's right of possession, even though temporary, permits the bailee to recover damages from any third persons for damage or loss to the property.

2. *Who suffers the loss? Explain your answer.* Rosa de la Mar Corporation, the shipper, suffers the loss. A common carrier is liable for damage caused by the willful acts of third persons or by an accident. Other losses must be borne by the shipper (or the recipient, depending on the terms of their contract). This shipment was lost due to an act of God.

CHAPTER 49

1. *Delmira wants to have Consuela evicted from the property. What can Consuela do?* This is a breach of the warranty deed's covenant of quiet enjoyment. The buyer can sue the seller and recover the purchase price of the house, plus any damages.

2. *Can Haven transfer possession for even less time to Idyll Company? Explain.* Yes. An owner of a fee simple has the most rights possible—he or she can give the property away, sell it, transfer it by will, use it for almost any purpose, possess it to the exclusion of all the world, or as in this case, transfer possession for any period of time. The party to whom possession is transferred can also transfer his or her interest (usually only with the owner's permission) for any lesser period of time.

CHAPTER 50

1. *Can the insurer refuse payment? Why or why not?* No. An incorrect statement as to the age of an insured is a misrepresentation. Under an incontestability clause, however, after a policy has been in force for a certain time (usually two or three years), the insurer cannot cancel the policy or avoid a claim on the basis of statements made in the application.

2. *Can Al obtain payment for these events? Explain your answers.* No. To obtain insurance, one must have a sufficiently substantial interest in whatever is to be insured. One has an insurable interest in property if one would suffer a pecuniary loss from its destruction. This interest must exist *when the loss occurs.*

To obtain insurance on another's life, one must have a reasonable expectation of benefit from the continued life of the other. The benefit may be founded on a relationship, but "ex-spouse" alone is not such a relationship. An interest in someone's life must exist *when the policy is obtained.*

CHAPTER 51

1. *Can Toby and Umeko have Sheila's will revoked on the ground that she did not have the capacity to make a will? Why or why not?* No. To have testamentary capacity, a testator must be of legal age and sound mind *at the time the will is made.* Generally, the testator must (1) know the nature of the act, (2) comprehend and remember the "natural objects of his or her bounty," (3) know the nature and extent of her or his property, and (4) understand the distribution of assets called for by the will. In this situation, Sheila had testamentary capacity at the time she made the will. The fact that she was ruled mentally incompetent two years after making the will does not provide sufficient grounds to revoke it.

2. *What determines who inherits what?* The estate will pass according to the state's intestacy laws. Intestacy laws set out how property is distributed when a person dies without a will. Their purpose is to carry out the likely intent of the decedent. The laws determine which of the deceased's natural heirs (including the surviving spouse, lineal descendants, parents, and collateral heirs) inherit his or her property.

Sample Answers for *Business Case Problems with Sample Answer*

Problem 1–5. *Reading Citations.* The court's opinion in this case—*Equal Employment Opportunity Commission v. Autozone, Inc.,* 809 F.3d 916 (7th Cir. 2016)—can be found in Volume 809 of *Federal Reporter, Third Series* on page 916. The U.S. Court of Appeals for the Seventh Circuit issued this opinion in 2016.

Problem 2–7. *Corporate Contacts.* No, the defendants' motion to dismiss the suit for lack of personal jurisdiction should not be granted. A corporation normally is subject to jurisdiction in a state in which it is doing business. A court applies the minimum-contacts test to determine whether it can exercise jurisdiction over an out-of-state corporation. This requirement is met if the corporation sells its products within the state or places its goods in the "stream of commerce" with the intent that the goods be sold in the state.

In this problem, the state of Washington filed a suit in a Washington state court against LG Electronics, Inc., and nineteen other foreign companies that participated in the global market for cathode ray tube (CRT) products. The state alleged a conspiracy to raise prices and set production levels in the market for CRTs in violation of a state consumer protection statute. The defendants filed a motion to dismiss the suit for lack of personal jurisdiction. These goods were sold for many years in high volume in the United States, including the state of Washington. In other words, the corporations purposefully established minimum contacts in the state of Washington. This is a sufficient basis for a Washington state court to assert personal jurisdiction over the defendants.

In the actual case on which this problem is based, the court dismissed the suit for lack of personal jurisdiction. On appeal, a state intermediate appellate court reversed on the reasoning stated above.

Problem 3–7. *Discovery.* Yes. The items that were deleted from a Facebook page can be recovered. Normally, a party must hire an expert to recover material in an electronic format, and this can be time consuming and expensive.

Electronic evidence, or e-evidence, consists of all computer-generated or electronically recorded information, such as posts on Facebook and other social media sites. The effect that e-evidence can have in a case depends on its relevance and what it reveals. In the facts presented in this problem, Isaiah should be sanctioned—he should be required to cover Allied's cost to hire the recovery expert and attorney's fees to confront the misconduct. In a jury trial, the court might also instruct the jury to presume that any missing items are harmful to Isaiah's case. If all of the material is retrieved and presented at the trial, any

prejudice to Allied's case might thereby be mitigated. If not, the court might go so far as to order a new trial.

In the actual case on which this problem is based, Allied hired an expert, who determined that Isaiah had in fact removed some photos and other items from his Facebook page. After the expert testified about the missing material, Isaiah provided Allied with all of it, including the photos that he had deleted. Allied sought a retrial, but the court instead reduced the amount of Isaiah's damages by the amount that it cost Allied to address his "misconduct."

Problem 4–4. *The Dormant Commerce Clause.* The court ruled that, like a state, Puerto Rico generally may not enact policies that discriminate against out-of-state commerce. The law requiring companies that sell cement in Puerto Rico to place certain labels on their products is clearly an attempt to regulate the cement market. The law imposed labeling regulations that affect transactions between the citizens of Puerto Rico and private companies. State laws that on their face discriminate against foreign commerce are almost always invalid, and this Puerto Rican law is such a law. The discriminatory labeling requirement placed sellers of cement manufactured outside Puerto Rico at a competitive disadvantage. This law therefore contravenes the dormant commerce clause.

Problem 5–3. *Online Privacy.* Facebook created a program that makes decisions for users. Using duty-based ethics, many believe that privacy is an extremely important right that should be fiercely protected. Accordingly, any program that has a default of giving out information is unethical. Facebook should create the program as an opt-in program. In addition, under the Kantian categorical imperative, if every company created opt-out programs that disclosed potentially personal information, the concept of privacy may be reduced to a theoretical concept only. One could argue that this reduction or elimination of privacy would not make the world a better place. From a utilitarian or outcome-based approach, the benefits of an opt-out program might be in ease of creation and start up, as well as ease of recruiting partner programs. The detriment is the elimination of choice on the part of users to disclose information about themselves. An opt-in program maintains that user control but may be harder to start, as it requires more marketing up front in order to convince users to opt in.

Problem 6–5. *Negligence.* Negligence requires proof that (1) the defendant owed a duty of care to the plaintiff, (2) the defendant breached that duty, (3) the defendant's breach caused the plaintiff's injury, and (4) the plaintiff suffered a legally recognizable injury. With respect to the duty of care, a business owner has a duty to use reasonable care to protect business invitees. This duty includes an obligation to discover and correct or warn of unreasonably dangerous conditions that the owner of the premises should reasonably foresee might endanger an invitee. Some risks are so obvious that an owner need not warn of them. But even if a risk is obvious, a business owner may not be excused from the duty to protect its customers from foreseeable harm.

Because Lucario was the Weatherford's business invitee, the hotel owed her a duty of reasonable care to make its premises safe for her use. The balcony ran nearly the entire width of the window in Lucario's room. She could have reasonably believed that the window was a means of access to the balcony. The window/balcony configuration was dangerous, however, because the window opened wide enough for an adult to climb out, but the twelve-inch gap between one side of the window and the balcony was unprotected. This unprotected gap opened to a drop of more than three stories to a concrete surface below.

Should the hotel have anticipated the potential harm to a guest who opened the window in Room 59 and attempted to access the balcony? The hotel encouraged guests to "step out onto the balcony" to smoke. The dangerous condition of the window/balcony configuration could have been remedied at a minimal cost. These circumstances could be perceived as creating an "unreasonably dangerous" condition. And it could be concluded that the hotel created or knew of the condition and failed to take reasonable steps to warn of it or correct it. Of course, the Weatherford might argue that the window/ balcony configuration was so obvious that the hotel was not liable for Lucario's fall.

In the actual case on which this problem is based, the court concluded that the Weatherford did not breach its duty of care to Lucario. On McMurtry's appeal, a state intermediate appellate court held that this conclusion was in error, vacated the lower court's judgment in favor of the hotel on this issue, and remanded the case.

Problem 7–6. *Product Liability.* Here, the accident was caused by Jett's inattention, not by the texting device in the cab of his truck. In a product liability case based on a design defect, the plaintiff has to prove that the product was defective at the time it left the hands of the seller or lessor. The plaintiff must also show that this defective condition made it "unreasonably dangerous" to the user or consumer. If the product was delivered in a safe condition and subsequent mishandling made it harmful to the user, the seller or lessor normally is not liable. To successfully assert a design defect, a plaintiff has to show that a reasonable alternative design was available and that the defendant failed to use it.

The plaintiffs could contend that the defendant manufacturer of the texting device owed them a duty of care because injuries to vehicle drivers and passengers, and others on the roads, were reasonably foreseeable due to the product's design, which (1) required the driver to divert his eyes from the road to view an incoming text from the dispatcher, and (2) permitted the

receipt of texts while the vehicle was moving. But manufacturers are not required to design a product incapable of distracting a driver. The duty owed by a manufacturer to the user or consumer of a product does not require guarding against hazards that are commonly known or obvious or protecting against injuries that result from a user's careless conduct. That is what happened here.

In the actual case on which this problem is based, the court reached the same conclusion, based on the reasoning stated above, and an intermediate appellate court affirmed the judgment.

Problem 8–6. *Patents.* One ground on which the denial of the patent application in this problem could be reversed on appeal is that the design of Raymond Gianelli's "Rowing Machine" is *not obvious* in light of the design of the "Chest Press Apparatus for Exercising Regions of the Upper Body."

To obtain a patent, an applicant must demonstrate to the satisfaction of the U.S. Patent and Trademark Office (PTO) that the invention, discovery, process, or design is novel, useful, and not obvious in light of current technology. In this problem, the PTO denied Gianelli's application for a patent for his "Rowing Machine"—an exercise machine on which a user *pulls* on handles to perform a rowing motion against a selected resistance to strengthen the back muscles. The PTO considered the device obvious in light of a patented "Chest Press Apparatus for Exercising Regions of the Upper Body"—a chest press exercise machine on which a user *pushes* on handles to overcome a selected resistance. But it can be easily argued that it is *not* obvious to modify a machine with handles designed to be *pushed* into one with handles designed to be *pulled*. In fact, anyone who has used exercise machines knows that a way to cause injury is to use a machine in a manner not intended by the manufacturer.

In the actual case on which this problem is based, the U.S. Court of Appeals for the Federal Circuit reversed the PTO's denial of Gianelli's application for a patent, based on the reasoning stated above.

Problem 9–3. *Privacy.* No, Rolfe did not have a privacy interest in the information obtained by the subpoenas issued to Midcontinent Communications. The right to privacy is guaranteed by at least one interpretation of the U.S. Constitution's Bill of Rights and by some state constitutions. A person must have a reasonable expectation of privacy, though, to maintain a suit or to assert a successful defense for an invasion of privacy. People clearly have a reasonable expectation of privacy when they enter their personal banking or credit card information online. They also have a reasonable expectation that online companies will follow their own privacy policies. But people do not have a reasonable expectation of privacy in statements made on Twitter and other data that they publicly disseminate. In other words, there is no violation of a subscriber's right to privacy when a third-party Internet provider receives a subpoena and discloses the subscriber's information.

Here, Rolfe supplied his e-mail address and other personal information, including his Internet protocol address, to

Midcontinent. In other words, Rolfe publicly disseminated this information. Law enforcement officers obtained this information from Midcontinent through the subpoenas issued by the South Dakota state court. Rolfe provided his information to Midcontinent—he had no legitimate expectation of privacy in that information.

In the actual case on which this problem is based, Rolfe was charged with, and convicted of, possessing, manufacturing, and distributing child pornography, as well as other crimes. As part of the proceedings, the court found that Rolfe had no expectation of privacy in the information that he made available to Midcontinent. On appeal, the South Dakota Supreme Court upheld the conviction.

Problem 10–4. *Criminal Liability.* Yes, Green exhibited the required mental state to establish criminal liability. A wrongful mental state (*mens rea*) is one of the elements typically required to establish criminal liability. The required mental state, or intent, is indicated in an applicable statute or law. For example, for murder, the required mental state is the intent to take another's life. A court can also find that the required mental state is present when a defendant's acts are reckless or criminally negligent. A defendant is criminally reckless if he or she consciously disregards a substantial and unjustifiable risk.

In this problem, Green was clearly aware of the danger to which he was exposing people on the street below. Although he did not indicate that he specifically intended to harm anyone, the risk of death created by his conduct was obvious. He must have known what was likely to happen if a bottle or plate thrown from the height of twenty-six stories hit a pedestrian or the windshield of an occupied motor vehicle on the street below. Despite his claim that he was intoxicated, he was sufficiently aware to stop throwing things from the balcony when he saw police in the area, and he later recalled what he had done and what had happened.

In the actual case on which this problem is based, after a jury trial, Green was convicted of reckless endangerment. On appeal, a state intermediate appellate court affirmed the conviction, based in part on the reasoning stated above.

Problem 11–4. *Quasi Contract.* Gutkowski does not have a valid claim for payment, nor should he recover on the basis of a quasi contract. Quasi contracts are imposed by courts on parties in the interest of fairness and justice. Usually, a quasi contract is imposed to avoid the unjust enrichment of one party at the expense of another. Gutkowski was compensated as a consultant. For him to establish a claim that he is due more compensation based on unjust enrichment, he must have proof. As it is, he has only his claim that there were discussions about his being a part owner of YES. Discussions and negotiations are not a basis for recovery on a quasi contract. In the actual case on which this problem is based, the court dismissed Gutkowski's claim for payment.

Problem 12–4. *Online Acceptances.* No. A shrink-wrap agreement is an agreement whose terms are expressed inside the box in which the goods are packaged. The party who opens the box may be informed that he or she agrees to the terms by keeping whatever is in the box. In many cases, the courts have enforced the terms of shrink-wrap agreements just as they enforce the terms of other contracts. But not all of the terms presented in shrink-wrap agreements have been enforced by the courts. One important consideration is whether the buyer had adequate notice of the terms.

A click-on agreement is formed when a buyer, completing a transaction on a computer, is required to indicate his or her assent to be bound by the terms of an offer by clicking on a button that says, for example, "I agree." In Reasonover's situation, no such agreement was formed with respect to Clearwire's "Terms of Service" (TOS). The e-mail did not give adequate notice of the TOS. It did not contain a direct link to the terms—accessing them required clicks on further links through the firm's homepage. The written, shrink-wrap materials accompanying the modem did not provide adequate notice of the TOS. There was only a reference to Clearwire's Web site in small print at the bottom of one page. Similarly, Reasonover's access to an "I accept terms" box did not establish notice of the terms. She did not click on the box but quit the page. Even if any of these references was sufficient notice, Reasonover kept the modem only because Clearwire told her that she could not return it.

In the actual case on which this problem is based, the court refused to compel arbitration on the basis of the clause in Clearwire's TOS.

Problem 13–7. *Consideration.* Citynet's employee incentive plan was an offer for a unilateral contract. A Citynet employee who stayed on the job when he or she was under no obligation to do so could be considered to have accepted Citynet's offer and to have provided sufficient consideration to make the offer a binding and enforceable promise. Consideration has two elements—it must consist of something of legal value and must provide the basis for the bargain between the parties. A unilateral contract involves a promise in return for performance. The promisor becomes bound to the contract when the promisee performs—or, in many cases, begins to perform—the act. Both the promise and the performance have legal value.

Here, Citynet set up an employee incentive plan "to attract and retain experienced individuals." The plan provided that a participant who left Citynet's employ could "cash out" his or her entire vested balance. When Ray Toney terminated his employment and asked to redeem his vested balance, however, Citynet refused. But Toney had long stayed on the job when he did not have to. This was sufficient consideration to make Citynet's offer under the incentive plan a binding and enforceable contract with Toney.

In the actual case on which this problem is based, a West Virginia state court issued a judgment in Toney's favor. The West Virginia Supreme Court of Appeals affirmed, on the reasoning and principles stated above.

Problem 14–3. *Unconscionable Contracts or Clauses.* In this case, the agreement that restricted the buyer's options for resolution of a dispute to arbitration and limited the amount of damages was both procedurally and substantively unconscionable. Procedural unconscionability concerns the manner in which the parties enter into a contract. Substantive unconscionability can occur when a contract leaves one party to the agreement without a remedy for the nonperformance of the other.

Here, GeoEx told customers that the arbitration terms in its release form were nonnegotiable and that climbers would encounter the same requirements with any other travel company. This amounted to procedural unconscionability, underscoring the customers' lack of bargaining power. The imbalance resulted in oppressive terms, with no real negotiation and an absence of meaningful choice. Furthermore, the restriction on forum (San Francisco) and the limitation on damages (the cost of the trip)—with no limitation on GeoEx's damages—amounted to substantive unconscionability. In the actual case on which this problem is based, the court ruled that the agreement was unconscionable.

Problem 15–7. *Fraudulent Misrepresentation.* Yes, the facts in this problem evidence fraud. There are three elements to fraud: (1) the misrepresentation of a material fact, (2) an intent to deceive, and (3) an innocent party's justifiable reliance on the misrepresentation. To collect damages, the innocent party must suffer an injury.

Here, Pervis represented to Pauley that no further commission would be paid by Osbrink. This representation was false—despite Pervis's statement to the contrary, Osbrink continued to send payments to Pervis. Pervis knew the representation was false, as shown by the fact that she made it more than once during the time that she was continuing to receive payments from Osbrink. Each time Pauley asked about commissions, Pervis replied that she was not receiving any. Pauley's reliance on her business associate's statements was justified and reasonable. And for the purpose of recovering damages, Pauley suffered an injury in the amount of her share of the commissions that Pervis received as a result of the fraud.

In the actual case on which this problem is based, Pauley filed a suit in a Georgia state court against Pervis, who filed for bankruptcy in a federal bankruptcy court to stay the state action. The federal court held Pervis liable on the ground of fraud for the amount of the commissions that were not paid to Pauley and denied Pervis a discharge of the debt.

Problem 16–5. *The Parol Evidence Rule.* Vaks and Mangano may not recover for breach of an oral contract. Under the parol evidence rule, if there is a written contract representing the complete and final statement of the parties' agreement, a party may not introduce any evidence of past agreements. Here, the written agreement was an integrated contract because the parties intended it to be a complete and final statement of the terms of their agreement. Vaks and Mangano therefore may not introduce evidence of any inconsistent oral representations made before the contract was executed.

Problem 17–7. *Third Party Beneficiary.* Yes, the Kincaids can bring an action against the Desses for breach of their contract with Sirva. A third person becomes an intended third party beneficiary of a contract when the original parties to the contract expressly agree that the performance should be rendered to or directly benefit a third person. As the intended beneficiary of a contract, a third party has legal rights and can sue the promisor directly for breach of the contract.

Here, the Desses agreed in their contract with Sirva to disclose all information about their property. They further agreed that Sirva and "other prospective buyers" could rely on the Desses' disclosure in deciding "whether and on what terms to purchase the Property." The Kincaids were not direct parties to the contract between Sirva and the Desses, but the Kincaids were "other prospective buyers." Thus, the language of the contract indicated that the Kincaids were intended by Sirva and the Desses to be third party beneficiaries of it. As intended beneficiaries of the contract, the Kincaids could sue the Desses directly for its breach.

In the actual case on which this problem is based, the Kincaids filed a suit in a Kansas state court against the Desses. From a judgment in the Desses' favor (for lack of privity), the Kincaids appealed. A state intermediate appellate court reversed on the basis of the reasoning stated above and remanded the case for trial.

Problem 18–4. *Material Breach.* Yes, STR breached the contract with NTI. A breach of contract is the nonperformance of a contractual duty. A breach is *material* when performance is not at least substantial. On a material breach, the nonbreaching party is excused from performance. If a breach is *minor*, the non-breaching party's duty to perform can sometimes be suspended until the breach has been remedied, but the duty to perform is not entirely excused. Once a minor breach has been cured, the nonbreaching party must resume performance. Any breach—material or minor—entitles the nonbreaching party to sue for damages.

In this problem, NTI had to redo its work constantly because STR permitted its employees and the employees of other subcontractors to walk over and damage the newly installed tile. Furthermore, despite NTI's requests for payment, STR remitted only half the amount due under their contract. Thus, NTI was deprived of at least half of the money it was owed under the contract. And STR terminated the contract, apparently wrongfully and without cause—the tile work would have been completed satisfactorily if STR had not allowed other workers to trample on the newly installed tile before it had cured.

In the actual case on which this problem is based, when STR refused to pay NTI and then terminated their contract, the subcontractor filed a suit in a Texas state court to recover. From a jury verdict in NTI's favor, STR appealed. A state intermediate appellate court affirmed. "The evidence presented was legally sufficient for the jury to conclude that STR materially breached the contract."

Problem 19–5. *Consequential Damages.* Simard is liable only for the losses and expenses related to the first resale. Simard could reasonably have anticipated that his breach would require another sale and that the sales price might be less than what he had agreed to pay. Therefore, he should be liable for the difference between his sales price and the first resale price ($29,000), plus any expenses arising from the first resale. Simard is not liable, however, for any expenses and losses related to the second resale. After all, Simard did not cause the second purchaser's default, and he could not reasonably have foreseen that default as a probable result of his breach.

Problem 20–4. *Additional Terms.* No. Under the common law, variations in terms between the offer and the offeree's acceptance violate the mirror image rule, which requires that the terms of an acceptance exactly mirror the terms of the offer. The UCC dispenses with this rule. Under the UCC, a contract is formed if the offeree makes a definite expression of acceptance even though the terms of the acceptance modify or add to the terms of the offer. When both parties to the contract are merchants, the additional terms become part of their contract unless (1) the original offer expressly required acceptance of its terms, (2) the new or changed terms materially alter the contract, or (3) the offeror rejects the new or changed terms within a reasonable time.

In this problem, the UCC applies because the transactions involve sales of goods. The original offer stated, "By signing below, you agree to the terms." This statement could be construed to expressly require acceptance of the terms to make the offer a binding contract (Exception 1 above). The contract stated that JMAM was to receive credit for any rejected merchandise. Nothing indicated that the merchandise would be returned to BSI. Baracsi, BSI's owner (the offeree), signed JMAM's (the offeror's) letter in the appropriate location. This indicated BSI's agreement to the terms. Thus, BSI made a definite expression of acceptance. The practice of the parties—for six years rejected items were not returned—further supports the conclusion that their contract did not contemplate the return of those items. The "PS" could be interpreted as materially altering the contract (Exception 2 above).

In the actual case on which this problem is based, the court dismissed BSI's complaint.

Problem 21–5. *Passage of Title.* Altieri held title to the car that she was driving at the time of the accident in which Godfrey was injured. Once goods exist and are identified, title can be determined. Under the UCC, any explicit understanding between the buyer and the seller determines when title passes. If there is no such agreement, title passes to the buyer at the time and place that the seller physically delivers the goods. In lease contracts, title to the goods is retained by the lessor-owner of the goods. The UCC's provisions relating to passage to title do not apply to leased goods.

Here, Altieri originally leased the car from G.E. Capital Auto Lease, Inc., but by the time of the accident she had bought it. Even though she had not fully paid for the car or completed the transfer-of-title paperwork, she owned it. Title to the car passed to Altieri when she bought it and took delivery of it. Thus, Altieri, not G.E., was the owner of the car at the time of the accident. In the actual case on which this problem is based,

the court concluded that G.E. was not the owner of the vehicle when Godfrey was injured.

Problem 22–5. *Nonconforming Goods.* Padma notified Universal Exports about its breach, so Padma has two ways to recover even though it accepted the goods. Padma's first option is to argue that it revoked its acceptance, giving it the right to reject the goods. To revoke acceptance, Padma would have to show that (1) the nonconformity substantially impaired the value of the shipment, (2) it predicated its acceptance on a reasonable assumption that Universal Exports would cure the nonconformity, and (3) Universal Exports did not cure the nonconformity within a reasonable time. Padma's second option is to keep the goods and recover for the damages caused by Universal Exports' breach. Under this option, Padma could recover at least the difference between the value of the goods as promised and their value as accepted.

Problem 23–6. *Implied Warranties.* Yes, Absolute breached the implied warranties of merchantability and fitness for a particular purpose. Under the UCC, merchants impliedly warrant that the goods they sell or lease are merchantable and, in certain circumstances, fit for a particular purpose. To be merchantable, goods must be "reasonably fit for the ordinary purposes for which such goods are used." They must be at least average, fair, or medium-grade quality—quality that will pass without objection in the trade or market for the goods. For example, merchantable food is food that is fit to eat. To be fit for a particular purpose, the seller must know (or have reason to know) the purpose for which the buyer will use the goods and that the buyer is relying on the judgment of the seller to select suitable goods.

In this problem, Bariven agreed to buy 26,000 metric tons of powdered milk for $123.5 million from Absolute Trading Corp. to be delivered in shipments from China to Venezuela. Absolute assured Bariven that its milk was safe, but tests of samples of the milk revealed that it contained dangerous levels of melamine. This is not quality that will pass without objection in the market for the goods. Nor is milk contaminated with melamine "reasonably fit for the ordinary purposes for which such goods are used." The value of the milk as food was impaired because it was potentially lethal and thus not fit to be consumed. Absolute had reason to know the purpose for which Bariven bought the milk and that the buyer was relying on Absolute to select safe milk. In view of the potential hazards and liabilities of the contaminated milk, Absolute was in breach of the implied warranties of merchantability and fitness for a particular purpose.

In the actual case on which this problem is based, Bariven revoked its acceptance of the first nineteen shipments of the milk and canceled the twentieth. From a decision against Absolute in its suit against Bariven, the seller appealed. The U.S. Court of Appeals for the Eleventh Circuit affirmed. Bariven's revocation was not invalid because "the value of the milk was impaired."

Problem 24–6. *Import Controls.* Yes, an antidumping duty can be assessed retrospectively (retroactively). But it does not seem likely that such a duty should be assessed here.

In this problem, the Wind Tower Trade Coalition (an association of domestic manufacturers of utility-scale wind towers) filed a suit in the U.S. Court of International Trade against the U.S. Department of Commerce, challenging its decision to impose only *prospective* antidumping duties on imports of utility-scale wind towers from China and Vietnam. The Commerce Department had found that the domestic industry had not suffered any "material injury" or "threat of material injury," and that it would be protected by a prospective assessment. Without a previously cognizable injury—and given the fact that any retrospective duties collected would not be payable to the members of the domestic industry in any event—it does not seem likely that retroactive duties should be imposed.

In the actual case on which this problem is based, the court denied the plaintiff's request for an injunction. On appeal, the U.S. Court of Appeals for the Federal Circuit affirmed the denial, holding that the lower court acted within its discretion in determining that retrospective duties were not appropriate.

Problem 25–6. *Payable on Demand or at a Definite Time.* No. Novel is not correct. The instrument is a note, and Novel is bound to pay it. For an instrument to be negotiable under UCC 3–104, it must meet the following requirements: (1) be in writing, (2) be signed by the maker or the drawer, (3) be an unconditional promise or order to pay, (4) state a fixed amount of money, (5) be payable on demand or at a definite time, and (6) be payable to order or to bearer unless it is a check. When no time for payment is stated on an instrument, the instrument is payable on demand.

Applying these principles to the facts in this problem, all of the requirements to establish the instrument as negotiable are met: (1) the instrument is in writing; (2) it is signed by Novel; (3) there are no conditions or promises other than the unconditional promise to pay; (4) the instrument states a fixed amount—$10,000; (5) the instrument does not include a definite repayment date, which means that it is payable on demand; and (6) the instrument is payable to Gallwitz. In the actual case on which this problem is based, the court ruled in favor of Gallwitz for payment of the note.

Problem 26–5. *Negotiation.* A negotiable instrument can be transferred by assignment or by negotiation. An assignment is a transfer of rights by contract. A transfer by assignment to an assignee gives the assignee only those rights that the assignor possessed. Any defenses that can be raised against the assignor can be raised against the assignee. When an instrument is transferred by negotiation, the transferee becomes a holder. A holder receives at least the rights of the previous possessor. Unlike an assignment, a transfer by negotiation can make it possible for the holder to receive more rights in the instrument than the prior possessor had. A holder who receives greater rights is a holder in due course (HDC) and takes the instrument free of any claims to it and defenses against its payment. Negotiating order instruments requires delivery and indorsement. If a party to whom a negotiable note is made payable signs it and delivers it to a bank, the transfer is a negotiation, and the bank becomes a holder. If

the party does not sign the note, however, the transfer is treated as an assignment, and the bank becomes an assignee instead of a holder.

In this problem, Argent was the payee of the note and its holder. Argent transferred the note to Wells Fargo without an indorsement. Thus, the transfer was not a negotiation but an assignment. Wells Fargo did not then become a holder of the note but an assignee. As an assignee, the bank acquired only those rights that the lender possessed before the assignment. And any defenses—including fraud in connection with the note—that Ford could assert against the lender could also be asserted by the borrower against the bank. If Argent indorsed the note to Wells Fargo after the defendant's response to the complaint, the bank could become a holder of the note, but it could not become an HDC. One of the requirements for HDC status is that a holder must take an instrument without notice of defenses against payment. The bank could not do this, because it would now be aware of the borrower's defenses.

In the actual case on which this problem is based, the court issued a judgment in Wells Fargo's favor, and Ford appealed. A state intermediate appellate court reversed the judgment and remanded the case for trial, finding that the bank had failed to prove that it was a holder, an assignee, or even a transferee of the note.

Problem 27–4. *Defenses.* When an instrument is transferred by negotiation, the transferee becomes a holder. A holder can become an HDC if the holder takes the instrument for value, in good faith, and without notice of any defects. An HDC takes an instrument free of most defenses against payment that could be asserted against the transferor. Defenses against payment fall into two categories. Universal defenses are good against all holders, including HDCs. Personal defenses are used to avoid payment to an ordinary holder, but not an HDC. Personal defenses include breach of contract, ordinary fraud, and any other defenses that can be asserted to avoid payment on a contract. Between the maker and the payee, a promissory note is a contract to pay money. Defenses that may be asserted by the maker against payment on a note include the personal defenses.

In this problem, Klutz does not qualify as an HDC. Thorbecke signed a note as the maker for most of the price for the purchase of the restaurant. Klutz may have taken Thorbecke's note for value—at least to the extent that he performed the part of the contract for the sale of the restaurant—but he did not take it in good faith or without notice. He misrepresented his authority to sell the franchise. In other words, under the facts as presented, Klutz appears to have committed fraud in the inducement and to have breached the contract of sale. Thorbecke appears to have reasonably relied on the misrepresentation and to be entitled to damages as a result. Thorbecke may also be justified in asserting these defenses against payment on the note.

In the actual case on which this problem is based, the court issued a decision in Thorbecke's favor to allow the suit to go to trial to determine whether Klutz misrepresented his authority to transfer the franchise, whether Thorbecke reasonably relied on the misrepresentation, the extent of any damages, and the amount due on the note.

Problem 28–5. *Honoring Checks.* A bank that pays a customer's check bearing a forged indorsement must recredit the customer's account or be liable to the customer-drawer for breach of contract. The bank must recredit the account because it failed to carry out the drawer's order to pay to the order of the named party. Eventually, the loss falls on the first party to take the instrument bearing the forged indorsement because a forged indorsement does not transfer title. Thus, whoever takes an instrument with a forged indorsement cannot become a holder.

Under these rules, Wells Fargo is liable to W Financial for the amount of the check. The bank had an obligation to ensure that the check was properly indorsed. The bank did not pay the check to the order of Lateef, the named payee, but accepted the check for deposit into the account of CA Houston without Lateef's indorsement. The bank did not obtain title to the instrument and could not become a holder, nor was it entitled to enforce the instrument on behalf of any other party who was entitled to enforce it. In the actual case on which this problem is based, the court held the bank liable to pay the amount of the check to W Financial.

Problem 29–5. *Liens.* Among the liens discussed in this chapter, a mechanic's lien would likely be most effective to Jirak in its attempt to collect the unpaid cost of its work for the Balks. A creditor can place a mechanic's lien on the real property of a debtor who has contracted for improvements to the property and has not paid the price. When a creditor obtains a mechanic's lien, the debtor's real estate becomes security for the debt. If the debtor does not pay, the creditor can foreclose on the property and sell it to collect the amount due.

In this problem, the Balks contracted with Jirak for the remodel of their farmhouse. Due to the Balks' changes to the project during the course of the work, the costs exceeded the amount of Jirak's original estimate. Although Jirak regularly advised the Balks about the increasing costs and provided an itemized breakdown at their request, they refused to pay the price. The use of a mechanic's lien is likely the best way for Jirak to collect the unpaid amount.

In the actual case on which this problem is based, Jirak filed a suit in an Iowa state court against the Balks to foreclose on their property by way of a mechanic's lien and collect the unpaid amount. The court entered a judgment in Jirak's favor and enforced the lien. A state intermediate appellate court affirmed the judgment.

Problem 30–7. *Perfecting a Security Interest.* Yes, these financing statements were sufficient to perfect the bank's security interests in Tille's equipment. In most situations, perfection is accomplished by filing a financing statement with the appropriate official. To effectively perfect a security interest, a financing statement must contain (1) the debtor's signature, (2) the debtor's and creditor's addresses, and (3) a description of the collateral by type or item.

In this case, all of Union's financing statements were sufficient to perfect security interests. Each of them provided the name and address of the debtor (Tille), the name and address of the secured party (Union Bank), and a description of the collateral covered by the financing statement—for one loan, all of Tille's equipment, including after-acquired property; for another, the truck crane; and for the third, a Bobcat mini-excavator. These descriptions were clearly sufficient to put a prospective creditor on notice that the collateral was the subject of a security interest.

In the actual case on which this problem is based, the court concluded that all of the statements created perfected security interests.

Problem 31–5. *Discharge in Bankruptcy.* No, ECMC cannot now resume its effort to collect on Hann's loans. After the debtor has completed all payments, the court grants a discharge of all debts provided for by the repayment plan. All debts generally are dischargeable, especially those for which the court either declared that there was no obligation or disallowed on the ground that the underlying debt was satisfied.

In this problem, Hann financed her education partially through loans. When she filed a Chapter 13 petition, Educational Credit Management Corp. (ECMC) filed an unsecured proof of claim based on the loans. Hann believed that she had repaid the loans in full and objected. The court held a hearing at which ECMC failed to appear, and Hann submitted correspondence from the lender indicating the loans had been paid. The court then entered an order sustaining Hann's objection to ECMC's claim, in effect declaring that there was no obligation and the underlying debt was satisfied. By later attempting to renew efforts to collect on the loans, ECMC would violate the court's order.

In the actual case on which this problem is based, ECMC resumed collection efforts after the bankruptcy. Hann reopened her case and filed a complaint against ECMC, alleging that it had violated the order sustaining her objection. The court ruled in Hann's favor and sanctioned ECMC for attempting to collect on the debt. On ECMC's appeal, the U.S. Court of Appeals for the First Circuit affirmed.

Problem 32–7. *Determining Employee Status.* No, Cox is not liable to Cayer for any injuries or damage that she sustained in the accident with Ovalles. Generally, an employer is not liable for physical harm caused to a third person by the negligent act of an independent contractor in the performance of a contract. This is because the employer does not have the right to control the details of the performance. In determining whether a worker has the status of an independent contractor, how much control the employer can exercise over the details of the work is the most important factor weighed by the courts.

In this problem, Ovalles worked as a cable installer for Cox under an agreement with M&M. The agreement disavowed any employer-employee relationship between Cox and M&M's installers. Ovalles was required to designate his affiliation with Cox on his van, clothing, and an ID badge. But Cox had minimal contact with Ovalles and limited power to control the manner in which he performed his work. Cox supplied cable wire and other equipment, but these items were delivered to M&M, not Ovalles. These facts indicate that Ovalles was an independent contractor, not an employee. Thus, Cox was not liable to Cayer for the harm caused to her by Ovalles when his van rear-ended Cayer's car.

In the actual case on which this problem is based, the court issued a judgment in Cox's favor. The Rhode Island Supreme Court affirmed, applying the principles stated above to arrive at the same conclusion.

Problem 33–6. *Agent's Authority.* No, Rainbow cannot recoup the unpaid amounts from Basic. Express authority is authority declared in clear, direct, and definite terms. Express authority can be given orally or in writing. In most states, if the contract being executed is or must be in writing, then the agent's authority must also be in writing. Otherwise, the contract may be avoided (or ratified) by the principal. If it is ratified, the ratification must be in writing. An agent has the implied authority to do what is reasonably necessary to carry out express authority. For example, authority to manage a business implies authority to do what is reasonably required to operate the business. But an agent's implied authority cannot contradict his or her express authority. Thus, if a principal has limited an agent's express authority, then the fact that the agent customarily would have such authority is irrelevant.

In this problem, Basic Research advertised its products on television networks owned by Rainbow Media Holdings through an ad agency, Icebox Advertising. Basic paid Icebox for the ads, but Icebox did not make all of the payments to Rainbow. Icebox filed for bankruptcy. Rainbow cannot recover what it was owed from Basic. As Basic's agent, Icebox had the express authority to buy ads from Rainbow on Basic's behalf, but that authority was limited to purchasing ads with cash in advance. Thus, Icebox did not have the authority—express or implied—to buy ads on Basic's credit. And Basic did not ratify the contracts that represented purchases on credit.

In the actual case on which this problem is based, on Basic's appeal from a judgment in Rainbow's favor, the U.S. Court of Appeals for the Tenth Circuit reversed that judgment and ruled in Basic's favor.

Problem 34–6. *Unemployment Compensation.* Yes, Ramirez qualifies for unemployment compensation. Generally, to be eligible for unemployment compensation, a worker must be willing and able to work. Workers who have been fired for misconduct or who have voluntarily left their jobs are not eligible for benefits. In the facts of this problem, the applicable state statute disqualifies an employee from receiving benefits if he or she voluntarily leaves work without "good cause."

The issue is whether Ramirez left her job for "good cause." When her father in the Dominican Republic had a stroke, she asked her employer for time off to be with him. Her employer refused the request. But Ramirez left to be with her father and called to inform her employer. It seems likely that this family emergency would constitute "good cause," and Ramirez's call and return to work after her father's death indicated that she did not disregard her employer's interests.

In the actual case on which this problem is based, the state of Florida denied Ramirez unemployment compensation. On Ramirez's appeal, a state intermediate appellate court reversed, on the reasoning stated above.

Problem 35–5. *Age Discrimination.* No, sanofi-aventis U.S. LLC (S-A) does not appear to have engaged in age discrimination. The Age Discrimination in Employment Act (ADEA) prohibits employment discrimination on the basis of age against individuals forty years of age or older. For the act to apply, an employer must have twenty or more employees, and the employer's business activities must affect interstate commerce. To establish a *prima facie* case, a plaintiff must show that he or she was (1) a member of the protected age group, (2) qualified for the position from which he or she was discharged, and (3) discharged because of age discrimination. If the employer offers a legitimate reason for its action, the plaintiff must show that the stated reason is only a pretext.

In this problem, Rangel was over forty years old. But he also had negative sales performance reviews for more than two years before he was terminated as part of S-A's nationwide reduction in force of all sales professionals who had not met the "Expectations" guidelines, including younger workers. The facts do not indicate that a person younger than Rangel replaced him or that S-A intended to discriminate against him on the basis of age. Based on these facts, Rangel could not establish a *prima facie* case of age discrimination on the part of S-A.

In the actual case on which this problem is based, in Rangel's suit against S-A alleging age discrimination, a federal district court issued a judgment in S-A's favor. On Rangel's appeal, the U.S. Court of Appeals for the Tenth Circuit affirmed, according to the reasoning stated above.

Problem 36–6. *Franchise Termination.* Oshana and GTO have stated a claim for wrongful termination of their franchise. A franchisor must act in good faith when terminating a franchise agreement. If the termination is arbitrary or unfair, a franchisee may have a claim for wrongful termination. In this case, Oshana and GTO have alleged that Buchanan acted in bad faith. Their failure to pay rent would ordinarily be a valid basis for termination, but not if it was entirely precipitated by Buchanan. Thus, Oshana and GTO may recover if they can prove that their allegations are true.

Problem 37–6. *Partnerships.* Yes, Sacco is entitled to 50 percent of the profits of Pierce Paxton Collections. The requirements for establishing a partnership are (1) a sharing of profits and losses, (2) a joint ownership of the business, and (3) an equal right to be involved in the management of the business.

The effort and time that Sacco expended in the business constituted a sharing of losses, and his proprietary interest in the assets of the partnership consisted of his share of the profits, which he had expressly left in the business to "grow the company" and "build sweat equity" for the future. He was involved in every aspect of the business. Although he was not paid a salary, he was reimbursed for business expenses charged to his personal credit card, which Paxton also used. These facts arguably meet the requirements for establishing a partnership.

In the actual case on which this problem is based, Sacco filed a suit in a Louisiana state court against Paxton, and the court awarded Sacco 50 percent of the profits. A state intermediate appellate court affirmed, based generally on the reasoning stated above.

Problem 38–6. *LLC Operation.* Part of the attractiveness of an LLC as a form of business enterprise is its flexibility. The members can decide how to operate the business through an operating agreement. For example, the agreement can set forth procedures for choosing or removing members or managers.

Here, the Bluewater operating agreement provided for a "super majority" vote to remove a member under circumstances that would jeopardize the firm's contractor status. Thus, one Bluewater member could not unilaterally "fire" another member without providing a reason. In fact, a majority of the members could not terminate the other's interest in the firm without providing a reason. Moreover, the only acceptable reason would be a circumstance that undercut the firm's status as a contractor.

The flexibility of the LLC business form relates to its framework, not to its members' capacity to violate its operating agreement. In the actual case on which this problem is based, Smith attempted to "fire" Williford without providing a reason. In Williford's suit, the court issued a judgment in his favor.

Problem 39–7. *Piercing the Corporate Veil.* Yes, there are sufficient grounds in the facts of this problem to support piercing the corporate veil and holding Kappeler personally liable to Snapp. First, in a case in which a plaintiff seeks to pierce a corporate veil, there must be a fraud or other injustice to be remedied. In that situation, the factors that a court will consider in determining whether to pierce the corporate veil include (1) a party is tricked or misled into dealing with the corporation rather than the individual, (2) the corporation has insufficient capital to meet its prospective debts or other potential liabilities, (3) corporate formalities, such as holding required corporate meetings, are not followed, and (4) personal and corporate interests are commingled.

In this problem, the amount that Snapp ultimately paid the builder exceeded the original estimate by nearly $1 million—and the project was still unfinished. Kappeler could not provide an accounting for the Snapp project—he could not explain double and triple charges nor whether the amount that Snapp paid had actually been spent on the project. These facts support a conclusion of fraud. And they also indicate that Kappeler may have tricked or misled Snapp into dealing with the corporation rather than with Kappeler as an individual. Castlebrook had issued no shares of stock, which indicates insufficient capitalization. The minutes of the corporate meetings "all looked exactly the same," indicating that in fact the required corporate meetings had not been held. And Kappeler had commingled personal and corporate funds.

In the actual case on which this problem is based, in Snapp's suit against the builder, the court pierced the corporate veil and held Kappeler personally liable. A state intermediate appellate court affirmed.

Problem 40–4. *Rights of Shareholders.* Yes. Woods has a right to inspect Biolustré's books and records. Every shareholder is entitled to examine corporate records. A shareholder can inspect the books in person or through an agent such as an attorney, accountant, or other authorized assistant.

The right of inspection is limited to the inspection and copying of corporate books and records for a proper purpose. This is because the power of inspection is fraught with potential for abuse—for example, it can involve the disclosure of trade secrets and other confidential information. Thus, a corporation is allowed to protect itself. Here, Woods, through Hair Ventures, has the right to inspect Biolustré's books and records. She has a proper purpose for the inspection—to obtain information about Biolustré's financial situation. She, along with other shareholders, had not received notice of shareholders' meetings or corporate financial reports for years, or notice of Biolustré's plan to issue additional stock. Hair Ventures had a substantial investment in the company. In the actual case on which this problem is based, the court ordered Biolustré to produce its books and records for Hair Ventures' inspection.

Problem 41–5. *Purchase of Assets.* Yes. Interline is most likely liable for the unpaid amount on the GATT contract with Call Center. An acquiring corporation will be held to have assumed the liabilities of the selling corporation in the following situations:

1. The purchasing corporation expressly or impliedly assumes the seller's liabilities.
2. The sale transaction is in effect a merger or consolidation of the two companies.
3. The purchaser continues the seller's business and retains the same personnel (shareholders, directors, and officers).
4. The sale is entered into fraudulently for the purpose of escaping liability.

In this problem, Interline acquired GATT's assets at a public sale. There is no indication that Interline agreed to assume GATT's liabilities, there was no merger or other combination of the two companies, and it does not appear that the sale was fraudulently entered into to escape liability.

Thus, the focus is on the third item listed above—whether Interline was liable for GATT's debts because it continued GATT's business with the same personnel. Boyd was not a GATT employee, but he was a former GATT director. Other members of Interline's staff were former GATT employees. GATT and Interline operated out of the same office building. Both companies were in the business of providing travel services to many of the same customers. These factors indicate that Interline is responsible for GATT's liabilities, including its debt to Call Center. In the actual case on which this problem is based, the court focused on the same principles discussed here to issue a judgment in Call Center's favor.

Problem 42–4. *Violations of the 1934 Act.* An omission or misrepresentation of a material fact in connection with the purchase or sale of a security may violate Section 10(b) of the Securities Exchange Act of 1934 and SEC Rule 10b-5. The key question is whether the omitted or misrepresented information is material. A fact, by itself, is not automatically material. A fact will be regarded as material only if it is significant enough that it would likely affect an investor's decision as to whether to buy or sell the company's securities. For example, a company's potential liability in a product liability suit and the financial consequences to the firm are material facts that must be disclosed because they are significant enough to affect an investor's decision as to whether to buy stock in the company.

In this case, the plaintiffs' claim should not be dismissed. To prevail on their claim that the defendants made material omissions in violation of Section 10(b) and SEC Rule 10b-5, the plaintiffs must prove that the omission was material. Their complaint alleged the omission of information linking Zicam and anosmia (a loss of the sense of smell) and plausibly suggested that reasonable investors would have viewed this information as material. Zicam products account for 70 percent of Matrixx's sales. Matrixx received reports of consumers who suffered anosmia after using Zicam Cold Remedy.

In public statements discussing revenues and product safety, Matrixx did not disclose this information. But the information was significant enough to likely affect a consumer's decision to use the product, and this would affect revenue and ultimately the commercial viability of the product. The information was therefore significant enough to likely affect an investor's decision whether to buy or sell Matrixx's stock, and this would affect the stock price. Thus, the plaintiffs' allegations were sufficient. Contrary to the defendants' assertion, statistical sampling is not required to show materiality—reasonable investors could view reports of adverse events as material even if the reports did not provide statistically significant evidence.

Problem 43–4. *Agency Powers.* The United States Supreme Court held that greenhouse gases fit within the Clean Air Act's (CAA's) definition of "air pollutant." Thus, the Environmental Protection Agency (EPA) has the authority under that statute to regulate the emission of such gases from new motor vehicles. According to the Court, the definition, which includes "any" air pollutant, embraces all airborne compounds "of whatever stripe." The EPA's focus on Congress's 1990 amendments (or their lack) indicates nothing about the original intent behind the statute (and its amendments before 1990). Nothing in the statute suggests that Congress meant to curtail the agency's power to treat greenhouse gases as air pollutants. In other words, the agency has a preexisting mandate to regulate "any air pollutant" that may endanger the public welfare.

The EPA also argued that, even if it had the authority to regulate greenhouse gases, the agency would not exercise that authority because any regulation would conflict with other administration priorities. The Court acknowledged that the CAA conditions EPA action on the agency's formation of a "judgment," but explained that judgment must relate to whether a pollutant "cause[s], or contribute[s] to, air pollution which may reasonably be anticipated to endanger public health or welfare." Thus, the EPA can avoid issuing regulations only if the agency determines that greenhouse gases do not contribute to climate change (or if the agency reasonably explains why it cannot or will not determine whether they do). The EPA's refusal

to regulate was thus "arbitrary, capricious, or otherwise not in accordance with law," The Court remanded the case for the EPA to "ground its reasons for action or inaction in the statute."

Problem 44–5. *Fair Debt-Collection Practices.* Engler may recover under the Fair Debt Collection Practices Act (FDCPA). Atlantic is subject to the FDCPA because it is a debt-collection agency and was attempting to collect a debt on behalf of Bank of America. Atlantic used offensive tactics to collect from Engler. After all, Atlantic gave Engler's employer the false impression that Engler was a criminal, had a pending case, and was about to be arrested. Finally, Engler suffered harm because he experienced discomfort, embarrassment, and distress as a result of Atlantic's abusive conduct. Engler may recover actual damages, statutory damages, and attorneys' fees from Atlantic.

Problem 45–5. *Environmental Impact Statements.* Yes, an environmental impact statement (EIS) is required before the U.S. Forest Service (USFS) implements its proposed travel management plan (TMP). An EIS must be prepared for every major federal action that significantly affects the quality of the environment. An action is "major" if it involves a substantial commitment of resources. An action is "federal" if a federal agency has the power to control it. An EIS must analyze (1) the impact on the environment that the action will have, (2) any adverse effects on the environment and alternative actions that might be taken, and (3) irreversible effects that the action might generate.

Here, the resources committed to the implementation of the USFS's TMP could include the resources within the wilderness and the time and effort dedicated by the agency. The wilderness resources would include the soil, the vegetation, the wildlife, the wildlife habitat, any threatened or endangered species, and other natural assets impacted by the TMP. The agency's resources would include its funds and its staff—to design, map, maintain, and enforce the TMP. These resources seem substantial. Of course, the implementation of the TMP is federal because the USFS has the power to control it.

As for the aspects of the environment that the agency might consider in preparing the EIS, some of the important factors are listed above—the soil, vegetation, wildlife, wildlife habitat, and threatened or endangered species. Other aspects of the environment impacted by the TMP might include cultural resources, historical resources, wilderness suitability, and other authorized uses of the wilderness. There is a potential for impact by every route that is designed to be part of the system, as well as the "dispersed vehicle camping" to be permitted on the terrain.

In the actual case on which this problem is based, the USFS considered all of the factors listed above. The agency then issued an EIS and a decision implementing the TMP. On a challenge to the EIS, a federal district court issued a judgment in the USFS's favor. The U.S. Court of Appeals for the Ninth Circuit affirmed. "The Forest Service took the requisite hard look at the environmental impacts."

Problem 46–5. *Price Discrimination.* Spa Steel satisfies most of the requirements for a price discrimination claim under

Section 2 of the Clayton Act. Dayton Superior is engaged in interstate commerce, and it sells goods of like grade and quality to at least three purchasers. Moreover, Spa Steel can show that, because it sells Dayton Superior's products at a higher price, it lost business and thus suffered an injury. To recover, however, Spa Steel will also need to prove that Dayton Superior charged Spa Steel's competitors a lower price for the same product. Spa Steel cannot recover if its prices were higher for reasons related to its own business, such as having higher overhead expenses or seeking a larger profit.

Problem 47–7. *Potential Liability to Third Parties.* KPMG is potentially liable to the hedge funds' partners under the *Restatement (Second) of Torts.* Under Section 552 of the *Restatement,* an auditor owes a duty to "persons for whose benefit and guidance the accountant intends to supply . . . information." In this case, KPMG prepared annual reports on the hedge funds and addressed them to the funds' "Partners." Additionally, KPMG knew who the partners were because it prepared individual tax forms for them each year. Thus, KPMG's annual reports were for the partners' benefit and guidance. The partners relied on the reports, including their representations that they complied with generally accepted accounting principles. As a result, they lost millions of dollars, which exposes KPMG to possible liability under Section 552.

Problem 48–4. *Bailment Obligation.* Moreland should be awarded damages, and Gray should take nothing. The bailee must exercise reasonable care in preserving the bailed property. What constitutes reasonable care in a bailment situation normally depends on the nature and specific circumstances of the bailment. If the bailed property has been lost or is returned damaged, a court will presume that the bailee was negligent.

In the circumstances of this problem, when the bailor (Moreland, the owner of the aircraft) entrusted the plane to the bailee's (Gray's) repair shop for painting, the work was not properly performed. This violated the bailee's duty to exercise reasonable care and breached the bailment contract. Because the plane was returned damaged, this may also constitute negligence. In the event of a breach, the bailor may sue for damages. The measure of damages is the difference between the value of the bailed property in its present condition and what it would have been worth if the work had been properly performed.

Thus, Gray is liable to Moreland for failing to properly paint the plane. In the actual case on which this problem is based, the court upheld a jury award to Moreland of damages and attorneys' fees.

Problem 49–4. *Adverse Possession.* The McKeags satisfied the first three requirements for adverse possession:

1. Their possession was actual and exclusive because they used the beach and prevented others from doing so, including the Finleys.
2. Their possession was open, visible, and notorious because they made improvements to the beach and regularly kept their belongings there.

3. Their possession was continuous and peaceable for the required ten years. They possessed the property for more than four decades, and they even kept a large float there during the winter months.

Nevertheless, the McKeags' possession was *not* hostile and adverse, which is the fourth requirement. The Finleys had substantial evidence that they gave the McKeags permission to use the beach. Rather than reject the Finleys' permission as unnecessary, the McKeags sometimes said nothing and other times seemingly affirmed that the property belonged to the Finleys. Thus, because the McKeags did not satisfy all four requirements, they cannot establish adverse possession.

Problem 50–7. *Insurance Provisions and Clauses.* Farrington should not be included as an insured within the meaning of the property insurance policy between Darling's and Philadelphia. The existence of an insurable interest is a primary concern when determining liability under an insurance policy. In the case of personal property, an insurable interest exists when the insured derives a pecuniary benefit from the preservation and continued existence of the property. One has an insurable interest in property when one would sustain a financial loss from its destruction. As for an insurance policy's language, courts interpret the words according to their ordinary meanings and in light of the nature of the coverage involved.

Darling's is entitled to recover the value of the loss to covered vehicles by virtue of its ownership of those vehicles and the fact that it is the owner that suffers the loss when one of its vehicles is damaged. In other words, under the Philadelphia policy, Darling's had an insurable interest in the car when Farrington smashed into the moose. Farrington might have had an insurable interest as well when he agreed to be responsible for any damage to the car, but he declined the insurance coverage offered in the rental contract.

In the actual case on which this problem is based, in Philadelphia's suit against Farrington, the court entered a judgment in the insurer's favor.

Problem 51–6. *Undue Influence.* No, undue influence does not appear to have occurred in this problem. To invalidate a will on the basis of undue influence, a plaintiff must show that the decedent's plan of distribution was the result of improper pressure brought by another person. Undue influence may be inferred if the testator ignores blood relatives and names as a beneficiary a nonrelative who is in constant close contact and in a position to influence the making of the will.

In this problem, although Tommy's ex-wife lived with Susie and was thus in a position to influence Susie's will, she was not a beneficiary under it, so there is no inference of undue influence. Moreover, neither of the wills that Walker executed left any property to her son, so there was no indication that she had been influenced to change her mind regarding the distribution of her estate. Additionally, she expressly disinherited her son, and several witnesses testified that she was mentally competent at the time she made the will.

In the actual case on which this problem is based, the court presumed that the will was valid.

Glossary

A

abandoned property Property that has been discarded by the owner, who has no intention of reclaiming it.

acceleration clause (1) A clause in an installment contract that provides for all future payments to become due immediately on the failure to tender timely payments or on the occurrence of a specified event. (2) A clause in a mortgage loan contract that makes the entire loan balance become due if the borrower misses or is late making monthly mortgage payments.

acceptance (1) In contract law, the offeree's notification to the offeror that the offeree agrees to be bound by the terms of the offeror's proposal. (2) In negotiable instruments law, the drawee's signed agreement to pay a draft when presented.

acceptor The person (the drawee) who accepts a draft and who agrees to be primarily responsible for its payment.

accession The addition of value to personal property by the use of labor or materials.

accommodation party A person who signs an instrument for the purpose of lending his or her name as credit to another party on the instrument.

accord and satisfaction An agreement for payment (or other performance) between two parties, one of whom has a right of action against the other. After the payment has been accepted or other performance has been made, the "accord and satisfaction" is complete, and the obligation is discharged.

accredited investor In the context of securities offerings, sophisticated investors, such as banks, insurance companies, investment companies, the issuer's executive officers and directors, and persons whose income or net worth exceeds certain limits.

act of state doctrine A doctrine that provides that the judicial branch of one country will not examine the validity of public acts committed by a recognized foreign government within its own territory.

actionable Capable of serving as the basis of a lawsuit.

actual malice A condition that exists when a person makes a statement with either knowledge of its falsity or reckless disregard for the truth. In a defamation suit, a statement made about a public figure normally must be made with actual malice for liability to be incurred.

actus reus (pronounced *ak*-tus *ray-uhs*) A guilty (prohibited) act. The commission of a prohibited act and the intent to commit a crime are the two essential elements required for criminal liability.

adequate protection doctrine In bankruptcy law, a doctrine that protects secured creditors from losing their security as a result of an automatic stay. In certain circumstances, the bankruptcy court may provide adequate protection by requiring the debtor or trustee to pay the creditor or provide additional guaranties to protect the creditor against the losses suffered by the creditor as a result of the stay.

adhesion contract A "standard-form" contract, such as that between a large retailer and a consumer, in which the stronger party dictates the terms.

adjudication The process of resolving a dispute by presenting evidence and arguments before a neutral third party decision maker in a court or an administrative law proceeding.

administrative agency A federal or state government agency created by the legislature to perform a specific function, such as to make and enforce rules pertaining to the environment.

administrative law The body of law created by administrative agencies in order to carry out their duties and responsibilities.

administrative law judge (ALJ) One who presides over an administrative agency hearing and has the power to administer oaths, take testimony, rule on questions of evidence, and make determinations of fact.

administrative process The procedure used by administrative agencies in fulfilling their three basic functions: rulemaking, enforcement, and adjudication.

administrator One who is appointed by a court to administer an estate if the decedent died without a valid will or if the executor named in the will cannot serve.

adverse possession The acquisition of title to real property through open occupation, without the consent of the owner, for a period of time specified by a state statute. The occupation must be actual, exclusive, open, continuous, and in opposition to all others, including the owner.

affidavit A written voluntary statement of facts, confirmed by the oath or affirmation of the party making it and made before a person having the authority to administer the oath or affirmation.

affirmative action Job-hiring policies that give special consideration to members of protected classes in an effort to overcome present effects of past discrimination.

affirmative defense A response to a plaintiff's claim that does not deny the plaintiff's facts but attacks the plaintiff's legal right to bring an action. An example is the running of the statute of limitations.

after-acquired property Property of the debtor that is acquired after the execution of a security agreement.

age of majority The age at which an individual is considered legally capable of conducting himself or herself responsibly. A person of this age is entitled to the full rights of citizenship, including the right to vote. In contract law, the age at which one is no longer an infant and can no longer disaffirm a contract.

agency A relationship between two parties in which one party (the agent) agrees to represent or act for the other (the principal).

agency coupled with an interest An agency, created for the benefit of the agent, in which the agent has some legal right (interest) in the property that is the subject of the agency.

agent A person who agrees to represent or act for another, called the principal.

agreement A meeting of two or more minds in regard to the terms of a contract; usually broken down into two events—an offer by one party to form a contract, and an acceptance of the offer by the person to whom the offer is made.

alien corporation A corporation formed in another country but doing business in the United States.

alienation In real property law, the voluntary transfer of property from one person to another (as opposed to a transfer by operation of law).

allege To state, recite, assert, or charge.

alternative dispute resolution (ADR) The resolution of disputes in ways other than those involved in the traditional judicial process. Negotiation, mediation, and arbitration are forms of ADR.

answer Procedurally, a defendant's response to the plaintiff's complaint.

antecedent claim A preexisting claim. In negotiable instruments law, taking an instrument in satisfaction of an antecedent claim is taking the instrument for value.

anticipatory repudiation An assertion or action by a party indicating that he or she will not perform an obligation that he or she is contractually obligated to perform at a future time.

antilapse provision A clause in an insurance contract that gives the insured a grace period (usually thirty days) within which to pay an overdue premium.

antitrust law Laws protecting commerce from unlawful restraints and anticompetitive practices.

apparent authority Authority that is only apparent, not real. An agent's apparent authority arises when the principal causes a third party to believe that the agent has authority, even though she or he does not.

appellant The party who takes an appeal from one court to another.

appellee The party against whom an appeal is taken—that is, the party who opposes setting aside or reversing the judgment.

appraisal right The right of a dissenting shareholder, if he or she objects to an extraordinary transaction of the corporation (such as a merger or consolidation), to have his or her shares appraised and to be paid the fair value of the shares by the corporation.

arbitration The settling of a dispute by submitting it to a disinterested third party (other than a court), who renders a decision. The decision may or may not be legally binding.

arbitration clause A clause in a contract that provides that, in the event of a dispute, the parties will submit the dispute to arbitration rather than litigate the dispute in court.

arson The malicious burning of another's dwelling. Some statutes have expanded arson to include any real property, regardless of ownership, and the destruction of property by other means—for example, by explosion.

articles of incorporation The document that is filed with the appropriate state official, usually the secretary of state, when a business is incorporated and that contains basic information about the corporation.

articles of merger A document, filed with the secretary of state, that sets forth the terms and conditions of a merger.

articles of partnership A written agreement that sets forth each partner's rights and obligations with respect to the partnership.

artisan's lien A possessory lien given to a person who has made improvements and added value to another person's personal property as security for payment for services performed.

assault Any word or action intended to make another person fearful of immediate physical harm; a reasonably believable threat.

assignee The person to whom contract rights are assigned.

assignment The act of transferring to another all or part of one's rights arising under a contract.

assignor The person who assigns contract rights.

assumption of risk A defense against negligence that can be used when the plaintiff was aware of a danger and voluntarily assumed the risk of injury from that danger.

attachment (1) In the context of secured transactions, the process by which a security interest in the property of another becomes enforceable. (2) In the context of judicial liens, a court-ordered seizure and taking into custody of property prior to the securing of a judgment for a past-due debt.

attempted monopolization An action by a firm that involves anticompetitive conduct, the intent to gain monopoly power, and a "dangerous probability" of success in achieving monopoly power.

auditor An accountant qualified to perform audits (systematic inspections) of a business's financial records.

authenticate To sign or, on an electronic record, to adopt any symbol that verifies the intent to adopt or accept the record.

authorization card A card signed by an employee that gives a union permission to act on his or her behalf in negotiations with management.

automatic stay In bankruptcy proceedings, the suspension of almost all litigation and other action by creditors against the debtor or the debtor's property. The stay is effective the moment the debtor files a petition in bankruptcy.

award In the context of litigation, the amount of money awarded to a plaintiff in a civil lawsuit as damages. In the context of arbitration, the arbitrator's decision.

B

bailee One to whom goods are entrusted by a bailor.

bailee's lien A possessory (artisan's) lien that a bailee entitled to compensation can place on the bailed property to ensure that he or she will be paid for the services provided.

bailment A situation in which the personal property of one person (a bailor) is entrusted to another (a bailee), who is obligated to return the bailed property to the bailor or dispose of it as directed.

bailor One who entrusts goods to a bailee.

bait-and-switch advertising Advertising a product at an attractive price and then telling the consumer that the advertised product is not available or is of poor quality and encouraging her or him to purchase a more expensive item.

banker's acceptance A banker's acceptance is a promised future payment, or time draft, which is accepted and guaranteed by a bank and drawn on a deposit at the bank. The banker's acceptance specifies the amount of money, the date, and the person to which the payment is due, and is commonly used in international trade.

bankruptcy court A federal court of limited jurisdiction that handles only bankruptcy proceedings.

bankruptcy trustee A person appointed by the court to manage the debtor's funds in a bankruptcy proceeding.

battery The unprivileged, intentional touching of another.

bearer A person in the possession of an instrument payable to bearer or indorsed in blank.

bearer instrument Any instrument that is not payable to a specific person, including instruments payable to the bearer or to "cash."

benefit corporation A type of for-profit corporation, available by statute in a number of states, that seeks to have a material positive impact on society and the environment.

bequest A gift of personal property by will (from the verb *to bequeath*).

beyond a reasonable doubt The standard used to determine the guilt or innocence of a person criminally charged. To be guilty of a crime, one must be proved guilty "beyond and to the exclusion of every reasonable doubt." A reasonable doubt is one that would cause a prudent person to hesitate before acting in matters important to him or her.

bilateral contract A type of contract that arises when a promise is given in exchange for a promise.

bilateral mistake A mistake that occurs when both parties to a contract are mistaken about the same material fact.

Bill of Rights The first ten amendments to the U.S. Constitution.

binder A written, temporary insurance policy.

binding authority Any source of law that a court must follow when deciding a case.

blank indorsement An indorsement that specifies no particular indorsee and can consist of a mere signature. An order instrument that is indorsed in blank becomes a bearer instrument.

blue sky laws State laws that regulate the offer and sale of securities.

bona fide occupational qualification (BFOQ) An identifiable characteristic reasonably necessary to the normal operation of a particular business. Such characteristics can include gender, national origin, and religion, but not race.

bond A security that evidences a corporate (or government) debt.

botnet Short for robot network—a group of computers that run an application controlled and manipulated only by the software source. Usually, the term is reserved for computers that have been infected by malicious robot software.

breach To violate a law, by an act or an omission, or to break a legal obligation that one owes to another person or to society.

breach of contract The failure, without legal excuse, of a promisor to perform the obligations of a contract.

brief A formal legal document submitted by the attorney for the appellant—or the appellee (in answer to the appellant's brief)—to an appellate court when a case is appealed. The appellant's brief outlines the facts and issues of the case, the judge's rulings or jury's findings that should be reversed or modified, the applicable law, and the arguments on the client's behalf.

browse-wrap terms Terms and conditions of use that are presented to an Internet user at the time a product, such as software, is downloaded but that need not be agreed to before the product is installed or used.

bureaucracy A large organization that is structured hierarchically to carry out specific functions.

burglary The unlawful entry into a building with the intent to commit a felony. Some state statutes have expanded burglary to include the intent to commit any crime.

business ethics Ethics in a business context; a consensus of what constitutes right or wrong behavior in the world of business and the application of moral principles to situations that arise in a business setting.

business invitees Those people, such as customers or clients, who are invited onto business premises by the owner of those premises for business purposes.

business judgment rule A rule under which courts will not hold corporate officers and directors liable for honest mistakes of judgment and bad business decisions that were made in good faith.

business necessity A defense to an allegation of employment discrimination in which the employer demonstrates that an employment practice that discriminates against members of a protected class is related to job performance.

business trust A form of business organization, created by a written trust agreement, that resembles a corporation. Legal ownership and management of the trust's property stay with the trustees, and the profits are distributed to the beneficiaries, who have limited liability.

buy-sell agreement In the context of partnerships, an express agreement made at the time of partnership formation for one or more of the partners to buy out the other or others should the situation warrant.

buyer in the ordinary course of business A buyer who, in good faith and without knowledge that the sale violates the ownership rights or security interest of a third party in the goods, purchases goods in the ordinary course of business from a person in the business of selling goods of that kind.

buyout price The amount payable to a partner on his or her dissociation from a partnership, based on the amount distributable to that partner if the firm were wound up on that date, and offset by any damages for wrongful dissociation.

bylaws The internal rules of management adopted by a corporation at its first organizational meeting.

C

case law The rules of law announced in court decisions. Case law interprets statutes, regulations, constitutional provisions, and other case law.

case on point A previous case involving factual circumstances and issues that are similar to those in the case before the court.

cash surrender value The amount that the insurer has agreed to pay to the insured if a life insurance policy is canceled before the insured's death.

cashier's check A check drawn by a bank on itself.

categorical imperative A concept developed by the philosopher Immanuel Kant as an ethical guideline for behavior. In deciding whether an action is right or wrong, or desirable or undesirable, a person should evaluate the action in terms of what would happen if everybody else in the same situation, or category, acted the same way.

causation in fact An act or omission without ("but for") which an event would not have occurred.

cease-and-desist order An administrative or judicial order prohibiting a person or business firm from conducting activities that an agency or court has deemed illegal.

certificate of deposit (CD) A note of a bank in which the bank acknowledges a receipt of money from a party and promises to repay the money, with interest, to the party on a specified date.

certificate of limited partnership The document that must be filed with a designated state official to form a limited partnership.

certification mark A mark used by one or more persons, other than the owner, to certify the region, materials, mode of manufacture, quality, or accuracy of the owner's goods or services. Examples of certification marks include the "Good Housekeeping Seal of Approval" and "UL Tested."

certified check A check that has been accepted by the bank on which it is drawn. Essentially, the bank, by certifying (accepting) the check, promises to pay the check at the time the check is presented.

charging order In partnership law, an order granted by a court to a judgment creditor that entitles the creditor to attach a partner's interest in the partnership.

charitable trust A trust in which the property held by the trustee must be used for a charitable purpose, such as the advancement of health, education, or religion.

chattel Personal property.

check A draft drawn by a drawer ordering the drawee bank or financial institution to pay a certain amount of money to the holder on demand.

check A special type of draft that is drawn on a bank, ordering the bank to pay a fixed amount of money on demand.

checks and balances The system by which each of the three branches of the national government (executive, legislative, and judicial) exercises checks on the powers of the other branches.

choice-of-language clause A clause in a contract designating the official language by which the contract will be interpreted in the event of a future disagreement over the contract's terms.

choice-of-law clause A clause in a contract designating the law (such as the law of a particular state or nation) that will govern the contract.

citation A reference to a publication in which a legal authority—such as a statute or a court decision—or other source can be found.

civil law The branch of law dealing with the definition and enforcement of all private or public rights, as opposed to criminal matters.

civil law system A system of law derived from that of the Roman Empire and based on a code rather than case law; the predominant system of law in the nations of continental Europe and the nations that were once their colonies. In the United States, Louisiana is the only state that has a civil law system.

clearinghouse A system or place where banks exchange checks and drafts drawn on each other and settle daily balances.

click-on agreement An agreement that arises when a buyer, engaging in a transaction on a computer, indicates his or her assent to be bound by the terms of an offer by clicking on a button that says, for example, "I agree"; sometimes referred to as a *click-on license* or a *click-wrap agreement.*

close corporation A corporation whose shareholders are limited to a small group of persons, often family members.

closed shop A firm that requires union membership on the part of its workers as a condition of employment.

closing The final step in the sale of real estate, in which ownership is transferred to the buyer in exchange for payment of the purchase price.

closing argument An argument made at a trial after the plaintiff and defendant have rested their cases. Closing arguments are made prior to the jury charges.

cloud computing The delivery to users of on-demand services from third-party servers over a network.

co-surety A joint surety; one who assumes liability jointly with another surety for the payment of an obligation.

codicil A written supplement or modification to a will. A codicil must be executed with the same formalities as a will.

coinsurance clause A clause in an insurance contract that encourages property owners to insure their property for an amount as close to full value as possible. If the owner insures the property up to a specified percentage—usually 80

percent—of its value, she or he will recover any loss up to the face amount of the policy.

collateral Under Article 9 of the Uniform Commercial Code, the property subject to a security interest.

collateral promise A secondary promise that is ancillary (subsidiary) to a principal transaction or primary contractual relationship, such as a promise made by one person to pay the debts of another if the latter fails to perform. A collateral promise normally must be in writing to be enforceable.

collecting bank Any bank handling an item for collection, except the payor bank.

collective bargaining The process by which labor and management negotiate the terms and conditions of employment, including working hours and workplace conditions.

collective mark A mark used by members of a cooperative, association, or other organization to certify the region, materials, mode of manufacture, quality, or accuracy of the specific goods or services. Examples of collective marks include the labor union marks found on tags of certain products and the credits of movies, which indicate the various associations and organizations that participated in the making of the movies.

comity A deference by which one nation gives effect to the laws and judicial decrees of another nation.

commerce clause The provision in Article I, Section 8, of the U.S. Constitution that gives Congress the power to regulate interstate commerce.

commercial impracticability A doctrine under which a seller may be excused from performing a contract when (1) a contingency occurs, (2) the contingency's occurrence makes performance impracticable, and (3) the nonoccurrence of the contingency was a basic assumption on which the contract was made.

commercial use Use of land for business activities only; sometimes called *business use.*

commingle To put funds or goods together into one mass so that they are mixed to such a degree that they no longer have separate identities.

common law The body of law developed from custom or judicial decisions in English and U.S. courts, not attributable to a legislature.

common stock A security that evidences ownership in a corporation. A share of common stock gives the owner a proportionate interest in the corporation with regard to control, earnings, and net assets. Common stock is lowest in priority with respect to payment of dividends and distribution of the corporation's assets on dissolution.

community property A form of concurrent property ownership in which each spouse owns an undivided one-half interest in property acquired during the marriage.

comparative negligence A theory in tort law under which the liability for injuries resulting from negligent acts is shared by all parties who were negligent (including the injured party) on the basis of each person's proportionate negligence.

compelling government interest A test of constitutionality that requires the government to have compelling reasons for passing any law that restricts fundamental rights, such as free speech, or distinguishes between people based on a suspect trait.

compensatory damages A money award equivalent to the actual value of injuries or damages sustained by the aggrieved party.

complaint The pleading made by a plaintiff alleging wrongdoing on the part of the defendant; the document that, when filed with a court, initiates a lawsuit.

computer crime Any violation of criminal law that involves knowledge of computer technology for its perpetration, investigation, or prosecution.

concentrated industry An industry in which a single firm or a small number of firms control a large percentage of market sales.

concurrent conditions Conditions in a contract that must occur or be performed at the same time; they are mutually dependent. No obligations arise until these conditions are simultaneously performed.

concurrent jurisdiction Jurisdiction that exists when two different courts have the power to hear a case. For example, some cases can be heard in either a federal or a state court.

concurrent ownership Joint ownership.

concurring opinion A court opinion by one or more judges or justices who agree with the majority but want to make or emphasize a point that was not made or emphasized in the majority's opinion.

condemnation The judicial procedure by which the government exercises its power of eminent domain. It generally involves two phases: a taking and a determination of fair value.

condition A possible future event, the occurrence or nonoccurrence of which will trigger the performance of a legal obligation or terminate an existing obligation under a contract.

condition precedent A condition in a contract that must be met before a party's promise becomes absolute.

condition subsequent A condition in a contract that operates to terminate a party's absolute promise to perform.

confiscation A government's taking of privately owned business or personal property without a proper public purpose or an award of just compensation.

conforming goods Goods that conform to contract specifications.

confusion The mixing together of goods belonging to two or more owners to such an extent that the separately owned goods cannot be identified.

consequential damages Special damages that compensate for a loss that is not direct or immediate (for example, lost profits). The special damages must have been reasonably foreseeable at the time the breach or injury occurred in order for the plaintiff to collect them.

consideration Generally, the value given in return for a promise or a performance. The consideration, which must be present to make the contract legally binding, must be something of legally sufficient value and must be bargained for.

consolidation A contractual and statutory process in which two or more corporations join to become a completely new corporation.

constitutional law Law that is based on the U.S. Constitution and the constitutions of the various states.

constructive delivery A symbolic delivery of property that cannot be physically delivered.

constructive discharge A termination of employment brought about by making the employee's working conditions so intolerable that the employee reasonably feels compelled to leave.

constructive eviction A form of eviction that occurs when a landlord fails to perform adequately any of the duties required by the lease, thereby making the tenant's further use and enjoyment of the property exceedingly difficult or impossible.

constructive fraud Conduct that is treated as fraud under the law even when there is no proof of intent to defraud, usually because of the existence of a special relationship or fiduciary duty.

constructive trust An equitable trust that is imposed in the interests of fairness and justice when someone wrongfully holds legal title to property.

consumer-debtor One whose debts result primarily from the purchase of goods for personal, family, or household use.

consumer law The body of statutes, agency rules, and judicial decisions protecting consumers of goods and services from dangerous manufacturing techniques, mislabeling, unfair credit practices, deceptive advertising, and other such practices.

continuation statement A statement that, if filed within six months prior to the expiration date of the original financing statement, continues the perfection of the original security interest for another five years. The perfection of a security interest can be continued in the same manner indefinitely.

contract An agreement that can be enforced in court; formed by two or more parties, each of whom agrees to perform or to refrain from performing some act now or in the future.

contractual capacity The legal ability to enter into contracts; the threshold mental capacity required by law for a party who enters into a contract to be bound by that contract.

contributory negligence A theory in tort law under which a complaining party's own negligence contributed to or caused his or her injuries. Contributory negligence is an absolute bar to recovery in a minority of jurisdictions.

conversion The wrongful taking, using, or retaining possession of personal property that belongs to another.

conveyance The transfer of title to real property from one person to another by deed or other document.

cookie A small file sent from a Web site and stored in a user's Web browser to track the user's Web browsing activities.

"cooling-off" laws Laws that allow buyers of goods sold in certain transactions to cancel their contracts within three business days.

cooperative An association, which may or may not be incorporated, that is organized to provide an economic service to its members. Unincorporated cooperatives are often treated like partnerships for tax and other legal purposes.

copyright The exclusive right of authors to publish, print, or sell an intellectual production for a statutory period of time. A copyright has the same monopolistic nature as a patent or trademark, but it differs in that it applies exclusively to works of art, literature, and other works of authorship, including computer programs.

corporate governance A set of policies specifying the rights and responsibilities of the various participants in a corporation and spelling out the rules and procedures for making corporate decisions.

corporate social responsibility The concept that corporations can and should act ethically, and be accountable to society for their actions.

cost-benefit analysis A decision-making technique that involves weighing the costs of a given action against the benefits of the action.

counteradvertising New advertising that is undertaken to correct earlier false claims that were made about a product.

counterclaim A claim made by a defendant in a civil lawsuit that in effect sues the plaintiff.

counteroffer An offeree's response to an offer in which the offeree rejects the original offer and at the same time makes a new offer.

course of dealing Prior conduct between parties to a contract that establishes a common basis for their understanding.

course of performance The conduct that occurs under the terms of a particular agreement. Such conduct indicates what the parties to an agreement intended it to mean.

court of equity A court that decides controversies and administers justice according to the rules, principles, and precedents of equity.

court of law A court in which the only remedies that could be granted were things of value, such as money damages. In the early English king's courts, courts of law were distinct from courts of equity.

covenant not to compete A contractual promise to refrain from competing with another party for a certain period of time and within a certain geographic area. Although covenants not to compete restrain trade, they are commonly found in partnership agreements, business sale agreements, and employment contracts. If they are ancillary to such agreements, covenants not to compete will normally be enforced by the courts unless the time period or geographic area is deemed unreasonable.

covenant not to sue An agreement to substitute a contractual obligation for some other type of legal action based on a valid claim.

cover A buyer's or lessee's purchase on the open market of goods to substitute for those promised but never delivered by the seller or lessor. Under the Uniform Commercial Code, if the cost of cover exceeds the cost of the contract goods, the buyer or lessee can recover the difference, plus incidental and consequential damages.

cram-down provision A provision of the Bankruptcy Code that allows a court to confirm a debtor's Chapter 11 reorganization plan even though only one class of creditors has accepted it.

creditors' composition agreement An agreement formed between a debtor and his or her creditors in which the creditors agree to accept a lesser sum than that owed by the debtor in full satisfaction of the debt.

crime A wrong against society proclaimed in a statute and punishable by society through fines and/or imprisonment— or, in some cases, death.

criminal law The branch of law that defines and punishes wrongful actions committed against the public.

cross-collateralization The use of an asset that is not the subject of a loan to collateralize that loan.

cross-examination The questioning of an opposing witness during a trial.

crowdfunding A cooperative activity in which people network and pool funds and other resources via the Internet to assist a cause (such as disaster relief) or invest in a business venture (such as a startup).

cure Under the Uniform Commercial Code, the right of a party who tenders nonconforming performance to correct his or her performance within the contract period.

cyber crime A crime that occurs online, in the virtual community of the Internet, as opposed to the physical world.

cyber fraud Fraud that involves the online theft of credit-card information, banking details, and other information for criminal use.

cyber tort A tort committed via the Internet.

cyberlaw An informal term used to refer to all laws governing electronic communications and transactions, particularly those conducted via the Internet.

cybersquatting Registering a domain name that is the same as, or confusingly similar to, the trademark of another and then offering to sell that domain name back to the trademark owner.

D

damages A monetary award sought as a remedy for a breach of contract or a tortious act.

debtor Under Article 9 of the Uniform Commercial Code, any party who owes payment or performance of a secured obligation, whether or not the party actually owns or has rights in the collateral.

debtor in possession (DIP) In Chapter 11 bankruptcy proceedings, a debtor who is allowed to continue in possession of the estate in property (the business) and to continue business operations.

deceptive advertising Advertising that misleads consumers, either by making unjustified claims about a product's performance or by omitting a material fact concerning the product's composition or performance.

deed A document by which title to real property is passed.

defalcation Embezzlement or misappropriation of funds.

defamation Any published or publicly spoken false statement that causes injury to another's good name, reputation, or character.

default Failure to pay a debt when it is due.

default judgment A judgment entered by a court against a defendant who has failed to appear in court to answer or defend against the plaintiff's claim.

defendant One against whom a lawsuit is brought, or the accused person in a criminal proceeding.

defense Reasons that a defendant offers in an action or suit as to why the plaintiff should not obtain what he or she is seeking.

deficiency judgment A judgment against a debtor for the amount of a debt remaining unpaid after collateral has been repossessed and sold.

delegatee One to whom contract duties are delegated by another, called the delegator.

delegation The transfer of a contractual duty to a third party. The party delegating the duty (the delegator) to the third party (the delegatee) is still obliged to perform on the contract should the delegatee fail to perform.

delegation doctrine A doctrine based on Article I, Section 8, of the U.S. Constitution, which has been construed to allow Congress to delegate some of its power to make and implement laws to administrative agencies. The delegation is considered to be proper as long as Congress sets standards outlining the scope of the agency's authority.

delegator One who delegates his or her duties under a contract to another, called the delegatee.

depositary bank The first bank to receive a check for payment.

deposition The testimony of a party to a lawsuit or of a witness taken under oath before a trial.

destination contract A contract in which the seller is required to ship the goods by carrier and deliver them at a particular destination. The seller assumes liability for any losses or damage to the goods until they are tendered at the destination specified in the contract.

devise A gift of real property by will, or the act of giving real property by will.

devisee One designated in a will to receive a gift of real property.

digital cash Funds contained on computer software, in the form of secure programs stored on microchips and other computer devices.

dilution With respect to trademarks, a doctrine under which distinctive or famous trademarks are protected from certain unauthorized uses of the marks regardless of a showing of competition or a likelihood of confusion. Congress created a federal cause of action for dilution in 1995 with the passage of the Federal Trademark Dilution Act.

direct examination The examination of a witness by the attorney who calls the witness to the stand at trial to testify on behalf of the attorney's client.

disaffirmance The legal avoidance, or setting aside, of a contractual obligation.

discharge (1) The termination of an obligation, such as occurs when the parties to a contract have fully performed their contractual obligations. (2) The termination of a bankruptcy debtor's obligation to pay debts.

discharge in bankruptcy The release of a debtor from all debts that are provable, except those specifically excepted from discharge by statute.

disclosed principal A principal whose identity is known to a third party at the time the agent makes a contract with the third party.

discovery A phase in the litigation process during which the opposing parties may obtain information from each other and from third parties prior to trial.

dishonor To refuse to accept or pay a draft or a promissory note when it is properly presented. An instrument is dishonored when presentment is properly made and acceptance or payment is refused or cannot be obtained within the prescribed time.

disparagement of property An economically injurious false statement made about another's product or property. A general term for torts that are more specifically referred to as *slander of quality* or *slander of title*.

disparate-impact discrimination Discrimination that results from certain employer practices or procedures that, although not discriminatory on their face, have a discriminatory effect.

disparate-treatment discrimination A form of employment discrimination that results when an employer intentionally discriminates against employees who are members of protected classes.

dissenting opinion A court opinion that presents the views of one or more judges or justices who disagree with the majority's decision.

dissociation The severance of the relationship between a partner and a partnership.

dissolution The formal disbanding of a partnership, corporation, or other business entity. For instance, partnerships can be dissolved by acts of the partners, by operation of law, or by judicial decree.

distributed network A network that can be used by persons located (distributed) around the country or the globe to share computer files.

distribution agreement A contract between a seller and a distributor of the seller's products setting out the terms and conditions of the distributorship.

diversity of citizenship Under Article III, Section 2, of the Constitution, a basis for federal court jurisdiction over a lawsuit between (1) citizens of different states, (2) a foreign country and citizens of a state or of different states, or (3) citizens of a state and citizens or subjects of a foreign country. The amount in controversy must be more than $75,000 before a federal court can take jurisdiction in such cases.

divestiture A company's sale of one or more of its divisions' operating functions under court order as part of the enforcement of the antitrust laws.

dividend A distribution of corporate profits to the corporation's shareholders in proportion to the number of shares held.

document of title A writing exchanged in the regular course of business that evidences the right to possession of goods (for example, a bill of lading or a warehouse receipt).

domain name The series of letters and symbols used to identify a site operator on the Internet; an Internet "address."

domestic corporation In a given state, a corporation that is organized under the law of that state.

dominion Ownership rights in property, including the right to possess and control the property.

double jeopardy A situation occurring when a person is tried twice for the same criminal offense; prohibited by the Fifth Amendment to the Constitution.

down payment The part of the purchase price of real property that is paid in cash up front, reducing the amount of the loan or mortgage.

draft Any instrument (such as a check) drawn on a drawee (such as a bank) that orders the drawee to pay a certain sum of money, usually to a third party (the payee), on demand or at a definite future time.

dram shop act A state statute that imposes liability on the owners of bars and taverns, as well as those who serve alcoholic drinks to the public, for injuries resulting from accidents caused by intoxicated persons when the sellers or servers of alcoholic drinks contributed to the intoxication.

drawee The party that is ordered to pay a draft or check. With a check, a financial institution is always the drawee.

drawer The party that initiates a draft (writes a check, for example), thereby ordering the drawee to pay.

due diligence A required standard of care that certain professionals, such as accountants, must meet to avoid liability for securities violations.

due process clause The provisions of the Fifth and Fourteenth Amendments to the U.S. Constitution that guarantee that no person shall be deprived of life, liberty, or property without due process of law. Similar clauses are found in most state constitutions.

dumping The selling of goods in a foreign country at a price below the price charged for the same goods in the domestic market.

durable power of attorney A document that authorizes a person to act on behalf of another person—write checks, collect insurance proceeds, and otherwise manage the disabled person's affairs, including health care—when that person becomes incapacitated.

duress   Unlawful pressure brought to bear on a person, causing the person to perform an act that he or she would not otherwise perform (or refrain from doing something the person would otherwise have done).

duty of care   The duty of all persons, as established by tort law, to exercise a reasonable amount of care in their dealings with others. Failure to exercise due care, which is normally determined by the "reasonable person standard," constitutes the tort of negligence.

duty-based ethics   An ethical philosophy rooted in the idea that every person has certain duties to others, including both humans and the planet. Those duties may be derived from religious principles or from other philosophical reasoning.

E

e-agent   A semiautonomous computer program that is capable of executing specific tasks.

e-contract   A contract that is entered into in cyberspace and is evidenced only by electronic impulses (such as those that make up a computer's memory), rather than, for example, a typewritten form.

e-evidence   A type of evidence that consists of computer-generated or electronically recorded information, including e-mail, voice mail, spreadsheets, word-processing documents, and other data.

e-money   Prepaid funds recorded on a computer or a card (such as a *smart card*).

e-signature   As defined by the Uniform Electronic Transactions Act, "an electronic sound, symbol, or process attached to or logically associated with a record and executed or adopted by a person with the intent to sign the record."

early neutral case evaluation   A form of alternative dispute resolution in which a neutral third party evaluates the strengths and weakness of the disputing parties' positions. The evaluator's opinion forms the basis for negotiating a settlement.

easement   A nonpossessory right, established by express or implied agreement, to make limited use of another's property without removing anything from the property.

electronic fund transfer (EFT)   A transfer of funds through the use of an electronic terminal, a telephone, a computer, or magnetic tape.

emancipation   In regard to minors, the act of being freed from parental control; occurs when a child's parent or legal guardian relinquishes the legal right to exercise control over the child. Normally, a minor who leaves home to support himself or herself is considered emancipated.

embezzlement   The fraudulent appropriation of money or other property by a person to whom the money or property has been entrusted.

eminent domain   The power of a government to take land from private citizens for public use on the payment of just compensation.

employment at will   A common law doctrine under which either party may terminate an employment relationship at any time for any reason, unless a contract specifies otherwise.

employment discrimination   Unequal treatment of employees or job applicants on the basis of race, color, national origin, religion, gender, age, or disability; prohibited by federal statutes.

enabling legislation   A statute enacted by Congress that authorizes the creation of an administrative agency and specifies the name, composition, purpose, and powers of the agency being created.

endowment insurance   A type of life insurance in which the policyholder pays fixed premiums for a definite term, after which a fixed amount is paid to the policyholder or, if the policyholder has died, to a beneficiary.

entrapment   In criminal law, a defense in which the defendant claims that he or she was induced by a public official—usually an undercover agent or police officer—to commit a crime that he or she would otherwise not have committed.

entrepreneur   One who initiates and assumes the financial risk of a new business enterprise and undertakes to provide or control its management.

entrustment rule   A rule under which entrusting goods to a merchant who deals in goods of that kind gives the merchant the power to transfer all rights to a buyer in the ordinary course of business.

environmental impact statement (EIS)   A formal analysis required for any major federal action that will significantly affect the quality of the environment to determine the action's impact and explore alternatives.

equal dignity rule   A rule requiring that an agent's authority be in writing if the contract to be made on behalf of the principal must be in writing.

equal protection clause   The provision in the Fourteenth Amendment to the U.S. Constitution that guarantees that no state will "deny to any person within its jurisdiction the equal protection of the laws." This clause mandates that state governments treat similarly situated individuals in a similar manner.

equitable maxims   General propositions or principles of law that have to do with fairness (equity).

equitable right of redemption   The right of a defaulting borrower to redeem property before a foreclosure sale by paying the full amount of the debt, plus any interest and costs that have accrued.

escheat   The transfer of property to the state when the owner of the property dies without heirs.

escrow account An account generally held in the name of the depositor and escrow agent. The funds in the account are paid to a third person on fulfillment of the escrow condition.

establishment clause The provision in the First Amendment to the U.S. Constitution that prohibits Congress from creating any law "respecting an establishment of religion."

estate planning Planning in advance how one's property and obligations should be transferred on one's death. Wills and trusts are two basic devices used in estate planning.

estopped Barred, impeded, or precluded.

estray statute A statute defining finders' rights in property when the true owners are unknown.

ethical reasoning A reasoning process in which an individual links his or her moral convictions or ethical standards to the particular situation at hand.

ethics Moral principles and values applied to social behavior.

eviction A landlord's act of depriving a tenant of possession of the leased premises.

exclusionary rule In criminal procedure, a rule under which any evidence that is obtained in violation of the accused's constitutional rights guaranteed by the Fourth, Fifth, and Sixth Amendments, as well as any evidence derived from illegally obtained evidence, will not be admissible in court.

exclusive agency An agency in which a principal grants an agent an exclusive territory and does not allow another agent to compete in that territory.

exclusive-dealing contract An agreement under which a seller forbids a buyer to purchase products from the seller's competitors.

exclusive jurisdiction Jurisdiction that exists when a case can be heard only in a particular court or type of court, such as a federal court or a state court.

exculpatory clause A clause that releases a contractual party from liability in the event of monetary or physical injury, no matter who is at fault.

executed contract A contract that has been completely performed by both parties.

execution An action to carry into effect the directions in a court decree or judgment.

executive agency An administrative agency within the executive branch of government. At the federal level, executive agencies are those within the cabinet departments.

executor A person appointed by a testator in a will to administer the testator's estate.

executory contract A contract that has not yet been fully performed.

exhaustion doctrine In administrative law, the principle that a complaining party normally must have exhausted all available administrative remedies before seeking judicial review.

export To sell products to buyers located in other countries.

express authority Authority expressly given by one party to another. In agency law, an agent has express authority to act for a principal if both parties agree, orally or in writing, that an agency relationship exists in which the agent has the power (authority) to act in the place of, and on behalf of, the principal.

express contract A contract in which the terms of the agreement are fully and explicitly stated in words, oral or written.

express warranty A seller's or lessor's oral or written promise, ancillary to an underlying sales or lease agreement, as to the quality, description, or performance of the goods being sold or leased.

expropriation The seizure by a government of privately owned business or personal property for a proper public purpose and with just compensation.

extension clause A clause in a time instrument that allows the instrument's date of maturity to be extended into the future.

extrinsic evidence Evidence that relates to a contract but is not contained within the document itself, including the testimony of the parties, the testimony of witnesses, and additional agreements and communications. A court may consider extrinsic evidence only when a contract term is ambiguous and the evidence does not contradict the express terms of the contract.

F

family limited liability partnership (FLLP) A limited liability partnership (LLP) in which the majority of the partners are members of a family.

federal form of government A system of government in which the states form a union and the sovereign power is divided between a central government and the member states.

federal question A question that pertains to the U.S. Constitution, acts of Congress, or treaties. A federal question provides a basis for federal jurisdiction.

Federal Reserve System A network of twelve central banks, located throughout the United States and headed by the Federal Reserve Board of Governors. Most banks in the United States have Federal Reserve accounts.

Federal Rules of Civil Procedure (FRCP) The rules controlling procedural matters in civil trials brought before the federal district courts.

fee simple absolute An ownership interest in land in which the owner has the greatest possible aggregation of rights, privileges, and power. The owner can use, possess, or dispose of the property as he or she chooses during his or her lifetime. On death, the interest in the property passes to the owner's heirs.

felony A crime—such as arson, murder, rape, or robbery—that carries the most severe sanctions, usually ranging from one year in a state or federal prison to the forfeiture of one's life.

fictitious payee A payee on a negotiable instrument whom the maker or drawer does not intend to have an interest in the instrument. Indorsements by fictitious payees are not treated as unauthorized under Article 3 of the Uniform Commercial Code.

fiduciary As a noun, a person having a duty created by his or her undertaking to act primarily for another's benefit in matters connected with the undertaking; as an adjective, a relationship founded on trust and confidence.

filtering software A computer program that screens incoming data according to rules built into the software and blocks access to Web sites with content not consistent with these rules.

final order The final decision of an administrative agency on an issue. If no appeal is taken, or if the case is not reviewed or considered anew by the agency commission, the administrative law judge's initial order becomes the final order of the agency.

financing statement A document prepared by a secured creditor and filed with the appropriate government official to give notice to the public that the creditor claims an interest in collateral belonging to the debtor named in the statement. The financing statement must contain the names and addresses of both the debtor and the creditor, and describe the collateral by type or item.

firm offer An offer (by a merchant) that is irrevocable without consideration for a period of time (not longer than three months). A firm offer by a merchant must be in writing and must be signed by the offeror.

fixed-term tenancy A type of tenancy under which property is leased for a specified period of time, such as a month, a year, or a period of years; also called a *tenancy for years*.

fixture An item of personal property that has become so closely associated with real property that it is legally regarded as part of that real property.

floating lien A security interest in proceeds, after-acquired property, or property purchased under a line of credit (or all three); a security interest in collateral that is retained even when the collateral changes in character, classification, or location.

forbearance The act of refraining from exercising a legal right; an agreement between a lender and a borrower in which the lender agrees to temporarily cease requiring mortgage payments, to delay foreclosure, or to accept smaller payments than previously scheduled.

force majeure (pronounced mah-*zhure*) **clause** A provision in a contract stipulating that certain unforeseen events—such as war, political upheavals, acts of God, and the like—will excuse a party from liability for nonperformance of contractual obligations.

foreclosure A proceeding in which a mortgagee either takes title to or forces the sale of the mortgagor's property in satisfaction of a debt.

foreign corporation In a given state, a corporation that does business in that state but is not incorporated there.

forgery The fraudulent making or altering of any writing in a way that changes the legal rights and liabilities of another.

formal contract A contract that by law requires a specific form, such as being executed under seal, to be valid.

forum-selection clause A provision in a contract designating the court, jurisdiction, or tribunal that will decide any disputes arising under the contract.

franchise Any arrangement in which the owner of a trademark, trade name, or copyright licenses another to use that trademark, trade name, or copyright in the selling of goods or services.

franchisee One receiving a license to use another's (the franchisor's) trademark, trade name, or copyright in the sale of goods and services.

franchisor One licensing another (the franchisee) to use the owner's trademark, trade name, or copyright in the selling of goods or services.

fraudulent misrepresentation (fraud) Any misrepresentation, either by misstatement or omission of a material fact, knowingly made with the intention of deceiving another and on which a reasonable person would and does rely to his or her detriment.

free exercise clause The provision in the First Amendment to the U.S. Constitution that prohibits Congress from making any law "prohibiting the free exercise" of religion.

free-writing prospectus A written, electronic, or graphic communication associated with the offer to sell a security and used during the waiting period to supplement other information about the security.

frustration of purpose A court-created doctrine under which a party to a contract will be relieved of his or her duty to perform when the objective purpose for performance no longer exists (due to reasons beyond that party's control).

full faith and credit clause A clause in Article IV, Section 1, of the U.S. Constitution that provides that "Full Faith and Credit shall be given in each State to the public Acts, Records, and Judicial Proceedings of every other State." The clause ensures that rights established under deeds, wills, contracts, and the like in one state will be honored by the other states and that any judicial decision with respect to such property rights will be honored and enforced in all states.

fully integrated contract A contract that completely sets forth all the terms and conditions agreed to by the parties and is intended as a final statement of their agreement.

fungible goods Goods that are alike by physical nature, by agreement, or by trade usage. Examples are wheat, oil, and wine that are identical in type and quality.

G

garnishment A legal process used by a creditor to collect a debt by seizing property of the debtor (such as wages) that is being held by a third party (such as the debtor's employer).

general damages In a tort case, an amount awarded to compensate individuals for the nonmonetary aspects of the harm suffered, such as pain and suffering; not available to companies.

general partner In a limited partnership, a partner who assumes responsibility for the management of the partnership and has full liability for all partnership debts.

generally accepted accounting principles (GAAP) The conventions, rules, and procedures developed by the Financial Accounting Standards Board to define accepted accounting practices at a particular time.

generally accepted auditing standards (GAAS) Standards established by the American Institute of Certified Public Accountants to define the professional qualities and judgment that should be exercised by an auditor in performing an audit.

gift A voluntary transfer of property made without consideration, past or present.

gift *causa mortis* A gift made in contemplation of imminent death. The gift is revoked if the donor does not die as contemplated.

gift *inter vivos* A gift made during one's lifetime and not in contemplation of imminent death, in contrast to a gift *causa mortis*.

good faith purchaser A purchaser who buys without notice of any circumstance that would put a person of ordinary prudence on inquiry as to whether the seller has valid title to the goods being sold.

Good Samaritan statute A state statute that provides that persons who rescue or provide emergency services to others in peril—unless they do so recklessly, thus causing further harm—cannot be sued for negligence.

goodwill In the business context, the valuable reputation of a business viewed as an intangible asset.

grand jury A group of citizens called to decide, after hearing the state's evidence, whether a reasonable basis (probable cause) exists for believing that a crime has been committed and whether a trial ought to be held.

grant deed A deed that simply states that property is being conveyed from the grantor to another. Under statute, a grant deed may impliedly warrant that the grantor has at least not conveyed the property's title to someone else.

group boycott An agreement by two or more sellers to refuse to deal with a particular person or firm.

guarantor A person who agrees to satisfy the debt of another (the debtor) only after the principal debtor defaults. A guarantor's liability is thus secondary.

H

hacker A person who uses one computer to break into another.

health-care power of attorney A document that designates a person who will have the power to choose what type of and how much medical treatment a person who is unable to make such a choice will receive.

hearsay An oral or written statement made out of court that is later offered in court by a witness (not the person who made the statement) to prove the truth of the matter asserted in the statement. Hearsay is generally inadmissible as evidence.

historical school A school of legal thought that looks to the past to determine what the principles of contemporary law should be.

holder Any person in the possession of an instrument drawn, issued, or indorsed to him or her, to his or her order, to bearer, or in blank.

holder in due course (HDC) A holder who acquires a negotiable instrument for value; in good faith; and without notice that the instrument is overdue, that it has been dishonored, that any person has a defense against it or a claim to it, or that the instrument contains unauthorized signatures, alterations, or is so irregular or incomplete as to call into question its authenticity.

holding company A company whose business activity is holding shares in another company.

holographic will A will written entirely in the testator's handwriting.

homeowner's insurance A form of property insurance that protects the home of the insured person and its contents against losses.

homestead exemption A law permitting a debtor to retain the family home, either in its entirety or up to a specified dollar amount, free from the claims of unsecured creditors or trustees in bankruptcy.

horizontal merger A merger between two firms that are competing in the same market.

horizontal restraint Any agreement that restrains competition between rival firms competing in the same market.

hot-cargo agreement An illegal agreement in which employers voluntarily agree with unions not to handle, use, or deal in the non-union-produced goods of other employers.

I

I-551 Alien Registration Receipt A document known as a "green card" that shows that a foreign-born individual can legally work in the United States.

I-9 verification The process of verifying the employment eligibility and identity of a new immigrant worker. It must be completed within three days after the worker commences employment.

identification In a sale of goods, the express designation of the specific goods provided for in the contract.

identity theft The act of stealing another's identifying information—such as a name, date of birth, or Social Security number—and using that information to access the victim's financial resources.

impeach To challenge the credibility of a person's testimony or attempt to discredit a party or witness.

implication A way of creating an easement or profit in real property when it is reasonable to imply its existence from the circumstances surrounding the division of the property.

implied authority Authority that is created not by an explicit oral or written agreement but by implication. In agency law, implied authority (of the agent) can be conferred by custom, inferred from the position the agent occupies, or implied by virtue of being reasonably necessary to carry out express authority.

implied contract A contract formed in whole or in part from the conduct of the parties (as opposed to an express contract).

implied warranty A warranty that the law derives by implication or inference from the nature of the transaction or the relative situation or circumstances of the parties.

implied warranty of fitness for a particular purpose A warranty that goods sold or leased are fit for a particular purpose. The warranty arises when any seller or lessor knows the particular purpose for which a buyer or lessee will use the goods and knows that the buyer or lessee is relying on the skill and judgment of the seller or lessor to select suitable goods.

implied warranty of habitability An implied promise by a seller of a new house that the house is fit for human habitation. Also, the implied promise by a landlord that rented residential premises are habitable.

implied warranty of merchantability A warranty that goods being sold or leased are reasonably fit for the ordinary purpose for which they are sold or leased, are properly packaged and labeled, and are of fair quality. The warranty automatically arises in every sale or lease of goods made by a merchant who deals in goods of the kind sold or leased.

impossibility of performance A doctrine under which a party to a contract is relieved of his or her duty to perform when performance becomes impossible or totally impracticable (through no fault of either party).

imposter One who, by use of the mail, telephone, or personal appearance, induces a maker or drawer to issue an instrument in the name of an impersonated payee. Indorsements by imposters are not treated as unauthorized under Article 3 of the Uniform Commercial Code.

***in personam* jurisdiction** Court jurisdiction over the "person" involved in a legal action; personal jurisdiction.

***in rem* jurisdiction** Court jurisdiction over a defendant's property.

incidental beneficiary A third party who incidentally benefits from a contract but whose benefit was not the reason the contract was formed. An incidental beneficiary has no rights in a contract and cannot sue to have the contract enforced.

incidental damages Damages that compensate for expenses directly incurred because of a breach of contract, such as those incurred to obtain performance from another source.

incontestability clause A clause in a policy for life or health insurance stating that after the policy has been in force for a specified length of time (usually two or three years), the insurer cannot contest statements made in the policyholder's application.

independent contractor One who works for, and receives payment from, an employer but whose working conditions and methods are not controlled by the employer. An independent contractor is not an employee but may be an agent.

independent regulatory agency An administrative agency that is not considered part of the government's executive branch and is not subject to the authority of the president. Independent agency officials cannot be removed without cause.

indictment (pronounced in-*dyte*-ment) A charge by a grand jury that a reasonable basis (probable cause) exists for believing that a crime has been committed and that a trial should be held.

indorsee A person to whom a negotiable instrument is transferred by indorsement.

indorsement A signature placed on an instrument for the purpose of transferring ownership rights in the instrument.

indorser A person who transfers an instrument by signing (indorsing) it and delivering it to another person.

industrial use Land use for light or heavy manufacturing, shipping, or heavy transportation.

informal contract A contract that does not require a specified form or formality in order to be valid.

information A formal accusation or complaint (without an indictment) issued in certain types of actions (usually criminal actions involving lesser crimes) by a law officer, such as a magistrate.

information return A tax return submitted by a partnership that reports the business's income and losses. The partnership itself does not pay taxes on the income, but each partner's share of the profit (whether distributed or not) is taxed as individual income to that partner.

initial order In the context of administrative law, an agency's disposition in a matter other than a rulemaking. An administrative law judge's initial order becomes final unless it is appealed.

innocent misrepresentation A false statement of fact or an act made in good faith that deceives and causes harm or injury to another.

inside director A person on a corporation's board of directors who is also an officer of the corporation.

insider (1) A corporate director or officer, or other employee or agent, with access to confidential information and a duty not to disclose that information in violation of insider-trading laws. (2) In bankruptcy proceedings, an individual, partner, partnership, corporation, or officer or director of a corporation (or a relative of one of these) who has a close relationship with the debtor.

insider trading The purchase or sale of securities on the basis of information that has not been made available to the public.

insolvent Under the Uniform Commercial Code, a term describing a person who ceases to pay "his debts in the ordinary course of business or cannot pay his debts as they become due or is insolvent within the meaning of federal bankruptcy law" [UCC 1–201(23)].

installment contract Under the Uniform Commercial Code, a contract that requires or authorizes delivery in two or more separate lots to be accepted and paid for separately.

insurable interest (1) A property interest in goods being sold or leased that is sufficiently substantial to permit a party to insure against damage to the goods. (2) An interest either in a person's life or well-being that is sufficiently substantial that insuring against injury to (or the death of) the person does not amount to a mere wagering (betting) contract.

insurance A contract by which the insurer promises to reimburse the insured or a beneficiary in the event that the insured is injured, dies, or sustains damage to property as a result of particular, stated contingencies.

intangible property Property that is incapable of being apprehended by the senses (such as by sight or touch). Intellectual property is an example of intangible property.

integrated contract A written contract that constitutes the final expression of the parties' agreement. If a contract is integrated, evidence extraneous to the contract that contradicts or alters the meaning of the contract in any way is inadmissible.

intellectual property Property resulting from intellectual, creative processes. Patents, trademarks, and copyrights are examples of intellectual property.

intended beneficiary A third party for whose benefit a contract is formed; an intended beneficiary can sue the promisor if such a contract is breached.

intentional tort A wrongful act knowingly committed.

intermediary bank Any bank to which an item is transferred in the course of collection, except the depositary or payor bank.

International Financial Reporting Standards (IFRS) A set of global accounting standards that are being phased in by companies in the United States.

international law The law that governs relations among nations. International customs and treaties are generally considered to be two of the most important sources of international law.

international organization In international law, a term that generally refers to an organization composed mainly of nations and usually established by treaty. The United States is a member of more than one hundred multilateral and bilateral organizations, including at least twenty through the United Nations.

Internet service provider (ISP) A business or organization that offers users access to the Internet and related services.

interpretive rule A nonbinding rule or policy statement issued by an administrative agency that explains how it interprets and intends to apply the statutes it enforces.

interrogatories A series of written questions for which written answers are prepared and then signed under oath by a party to a lawsuit, usually with the assistance of the party's attorney.

intestacy laws State statutes that specify how property will be distributed when a person dies intestate (without a valid will).

intestate As a noun, one who has died without having created a valid will. As an adjective, the state of having died without a will.

inverse condemnation The taking of private property by the government without payment of just compensation as required by the U.S. Constitution. The owner must sue the government to recover just compensation.

investment company A company that acts on the behalf of many smaller shareholders-owners by buying a large portfolio of securities and professionally managing that portfolio.

investment contract In securities law, a transaction in which a person invests in a common enterprise reasonably expecting profits that are derived primarily from the efforts of others.

issue In negotiable instruments law, the first transfer, or delivery, of an instrument to a holder.

J

joint and several liability In partnership law, a doctrine under which a plaintiff may sue, and collect a judgment from, all of the partners together (jointly) or one or more of the partners separately (severally, or individually). A partner can be held liable even if she or he did not participate in, ratify, or know about the conduct that gave rise to the lawsuit.

joint liability In partnership law, the partners' shared liability for partnership obligations and debts. A third party must sue all of the partners as a group, but each partner can be held liable for the full amount.

joint stock company A hybrid form of business organization that combines characteristics of a corporation and a partnership. Usually, a joint stock company is regarded as a partnership for tax and other legal purposes.

joint tenancy Joint ownership of property by two or more co-owners in which each co-owner owns an undivided portion of the property. On the death of one of the joint tenants, his or her interest automatically passes to the surviving joint tenant(s).

joint venture A joint undertaking by two or more persons or business entities to combine their efforts or their property for a single transaction or project, or for a related series of transactions or projects. A joint venture is generally treated like a partnership for tax and other legal purposes.

judicial review The process by which courts decide on the constitutionality of legislative enactments and actions of the executive branch.

junior lienholder A person or business that holds a lien that is subordinate to one or more other liens on the same property.

jurisdiction The authority of a court to hear a case and decide a specific action.

jurisprudence The science or philosophy of law.

L

laches The equitable doctrine that bars a party's right to legal action if the party has neglected for an unreasonable length of time to act on his or her rights.

larceny The wrongful taking and carrying away of another person's personal property with the intent to permanently deprive the owner of the property. Some states classify larceny as either grand or petit, depending on the property's value.

latent defect A defect that is not obvious or cannot readily be ascertained.

law A body of enforceable rules governing relationships among individuals and between individuals and their society.

lease Under Article 2A of the UCC, a transfer of the right to possess and use goods for a period of time in exchange for payment. In the context of real property, an agreement by which a property owner (landlord) agrees to give another party (the tenant) the exclusive right to possess the property for a limited time.

lease agreement In regard to the lease of goods, an agreement in which one person (the lessor) agrees to transfer the right to the possession and use of property to another person (the lessee) in exchange for rental payments.

leasehold estate An interest in real property that gives a tenant a qualified right to possess and/or use the property for a limited time under a lease.

legacy A gift of personal property under a will.

legal positivism A school of legal thought centered on the assumption that there is no law higher than the laws created by a national government. Laws must be obeyed, even if they are unjust, to prevent anarchy.

legal realism A school of legal thought that holds that the law is only one factor to be considered when deciding cases and that social and economic circumstances should also be taken into account.

legal reasoning The process of reasoning by which a judge harmonizes his or her opinion with the judicial decisions in previous cases.

legatee One designated in a will to receive a gift of personal property.

legislative rule An administrative agency rule that carries the same weight as a congressionally enacted statute.

lessee A person who pays for the use or possession of another's property.

lessor A property owner who allows others to use his or her property in exchange for the payment of rent.

letter of credit A written instrument, usually issued by a bank on behalf of a customer or other party, in which the issuer promises to honor drafts or other demands for payment by third parties in accordance with the terms of the instrument.

levy The obtaining of money by legal process through the seizure and sale of property, usually done after a writ of execution has been issued.

liability The state of being legally responsible (liable) for something, such as a debt or obligation.

libel Defamation in writing or in some other form (such as in a digital recording) having the quality of permanence.

license In the context of intellectual property, a contract permitting the use of a trademark, copyright, patent, or trade secret of certain purposes. In the context of real property, a revocable right or privilege of a person to come on another person's land.

licensee One who receives a license to use, or enter onto, another's property.

lien (pronounced *leen*) A claim against specific property to satisfy a debt.

life estate An interest in land that exists only for the duration of the life of a specified individual, usually the holder of the estate.

limited liability company (LLC) A hybrid form of business enterprise that offers the limited liability of a corporation and the tax advantages of a partnership.

limited liability limited partnership (LLLP) A type of limited partnership in which the liability of the general partner is the same as the liability of the limited partners—that is, the liability of all partners is limited to the amount of their investments in the firm.

limited liability partnership (LLP) A hybrid form of business organization that is used mainly by professionals who normally do business in a partnership. An LLP is a pass-through entity for tax purposes, but a partner's personal liability for the malpractice of other partners is limited.

limited partner In a limited partnership, a partner who contributes capital to the partnership but has no right to participate in its management and has no liability for partnership debts beyond the amount of her or his investment.

limited partnership (LP) A partnership consisting of one or more general partners and one or more limited partners.

limited-payment life A type of life insurance for which premiums are payable for a definite period, after which the policy is fully paid.

liquidated damages An amount, stipulated in the contract, that the parties to a contract believe to be a reasonable estimation of the damages that will occur in the event of a breach.

liquidated debt A debt that is due and certain in amount.

liquidation The sale of the nonexempt assets of a debtor and the distribution of the funds received to creditors.

litigation The process of resolving a dispute through the court system.

living trust A trust created by the grantor (settlor) and effective during his or her lifetime.

living will A document that allows a person to control the methods of medical treatment that may be used after a serious accident or illness.

lockout An action in which an employer shuts down to prevent employees from working, typically because it cannot reach a collective bargaining agreement with the employees' union.

long arm statute A state statute that permits a state to obtain personal jurisdiction over nonresident defendants. A defendant must have "minimum contacts" with that state for the statute to apply.

lost property Property that the owner has involuntarily parted with and then cannot find or recover.

M

mailbox rule A rule providing that an acceptance of an offer becomes effective on dispatch.

majority opinion A court opinion that represents the views of the majority (more than half) of the judges or justices deciding the case.

maker One who promises to pay a certain sum to the holder of a promissory note or certificate of deposit (CD).

malpractice Professional misconduct or the failure to exercise the requisite degree of skill as a professional. Negligence—the failure to exercise due care—on the part of a professional, such as a physician or an attorney, is commonly referred to as malpractice.

malware Malicious software programs designed to disrupt or harm a computer, network, smartphone, or other device.

market concentration The degree to which a small number of firms control a large percentage of a relevant market.

market power The power of a firm to control the market price of its product. A monopoly has the greatest degree of market power.

market-share liability A theory under which liability is shared among all firms that manufactured and distributed a particular product during a certain period of time. This theory of liability is used only when the specific source of the harmful product is unidentifiable.

marketable title Title to real estate that is reasonably free from encumbrances, defects in the chain of title, and other matters that affect title, such as adverse possession.

mechanic's lien A statutory lien on the real property of another, created to ensure payment for work performed and materials furnished in the repair or improvement of real property, such as a building.

mediation A method of settling disputes outside of court by using the services of a neutral third party, called a mediator. The mediator acts as a communicating agent between the parties and suggests ways in which the parties can resolve their dispute.

member A person who has an ownership interest in a limited liability company.

mens rea (pronounced *mehns ray*-uh) Criminal intent. The commission of a prohibited act and the intent to commit a crime are the two essential elements required for criminal liability.

merchant A person who is engaged in the purchase and sale of goods. Under the Uniform Commercial Code, a person who deals in goods of the kind involved in the sales contract; for further definitions, see UCC 2–104.

merger A contractual and statutory process in which one corporation (the surviving corporation) acquires all of the assets and liabilities of another corporation.

meta tag Word inserted into a Web site's key-words field to increase the site's appearance in search engine results.

metadata Data that are automatically recorded by electronic devices on their hard drives and that provide information about who created a file and when, and who accessed, modified, or transmitted it. Metadata can be described as "data about data."

metes and bounds A way of describing the boundary lines of land according to the distance between two points, often using physical features of the local geography.

mini-trial A private proceeding in which each party to a dispute argues its position before the other side. A neutral third party may be present and act as an adviser if the parties fail to reach an agreement.

minimum wage The lowest wage, either by government regulation or by union contract, that an employer may pay an hourly worker.

mirror image rule A common law rule that requires, for a valid contractual agreement, that the terms of the offeree's acceptance adhere exactly to the terms of the offeror's offer.

misdemeanor A lesser crime than a felony, punishable by a fine or imprisonment for up to one year in other than a state or federal penitentiary.

mislaid property Property that the owner has voluntarily parted with and then has inadvertently forgotten.

mitigation of damages A rule requiring a plaintiff to have done whatever was reasonable to minimize the damages caused by the defendant.

money laundering Falsely reporting income that has been obtained through criminal activity as income obtained through a legitimate business enterprise—in effect, "laundering" the "dirty money."

monopolization The possession of monopoly power in the relevant market and the willful acquisition or maintenance of that power, as distinguished from growth or development as a consequence of a superior product, business acumen, or historic accident.

monopoly A market in which there is a single seller or a very limited number of sellers.

monopoly power The ability of a monopoly to dictate what takes place in a given market.

moral minimum The minimum degree of ethical behavior expected of a business firm, which is usually defined as compliance with the law.

mortgage A written instrument that gives a creditor (the mortgagee) an interest in, or lien on, the debtor's (mortgagor's) real property as security for a debt. If the debt is not paid, the property can be sold by the creditor and the proceeds used to pay the debt.

mortgage insurance Insurance that compensates a lender for losses due to a borrower's default on a mortgage loan.

motion A procedural request or application presented by an attorney to the court on behalf of a client.

motion for a directed verdict In a state court, a party's request that the judge enter a judgment in her or his favor before the case is submitted to a jury because the other party has not presented sufficient evidence to support the claim. The federal courts refer to this request as a *motion for judgment as a matter of law.*

motion for a judgment as a matter of law In a federal court, a party's request that the judge enter a judgment in her or his favor before the case is submitted to a jury because the other party has not presented sufficient evidence to support the claim. The state courts refer to this request as a *motion for a directed verdict.*

motion for a new trial A motion asserting that the trial was so fundamentally flawed (because of error, newly discovered evidence, prejudice, or other reason) that a new trial is necessary to prevent a miscarriage of justice.

motion for judgment *n.o.v.* A motion requesting the court to grant judgment in favor of the party making the motion on the ground that the jury verdict against him or her was unreasonable and erroneous.

motion for judgment on the pleadings A motion by either party to a lawsuit at the close of the pleadings requesting the court to decide the issue solely on the pleadings without proceeding to trial. The motion will be granted only if no facts are in dispute.

motion for summary judgment A motion requesting the court to enter a judgment without proceeding to trial. The motion can be based on evidence outside the pleadings and will be granted only if no facts are in dispute.

motion to dismiss A pleading in which a defendant asserts that the plaintiff's claim fails to state a cause of action (that is, has no basis in law) or that there are other grounds on which a suit should be dismissed.

multiple product order An order requiring a firm that has engaged in deceptive advertising to cease and desist from false advertising in regard to all the firm's products.

mutual fund A specific type of investment company that continually buys or sells to investors shares of ownership in a portfolio.

mutual rescission An agreement between the parties to cancel their contract, releasing the parties from further obligations under the contract. The object of the agreement is to restore the parties to the positions they would have occupied had no contract ever been formed.

N

national law Law that pertains to a particular nation (as opposed to international law).

natural law The oldest school of legal thought, based on the belief that the legal system should reflect universal ("higher") moral and ethical principles that are inherent in human nature.

necessaries Necessities required for life, such as food, shelter, clothing, and medical attention; may include whatever is believed to be necessary to maintain a person's standard of living or financial and social status.

necessity In criminal law, a defense against liability. Under Section 3.02 of the Model Penal Code, this defense is justifiable if "the harm or evil sought to be avoided" by a given action "is greater than that sought to be prevented by the law defining the offense charged." In real property law, a way of creating an easement when one party must have the easement in order to have access to his or her property.

negligence The failure to exercise the standard of care that a reasonable person would exercise in similar circumstances.

negligent misrepresentation Any manifestation through words or conduct that amounts to an untrue statement of fact made in circumstances in which a reasonable and prudent person would not have done that which led to the misrepresentation. A representation made with an honest belief in its truth may still be negligent due to (1) a lack of reasonable care in ascertaining the facts, (2) the manner of expression, or (3) the absence of the skill or competence required by a particular business or profession.

negotiable instrument A signed writing that contains an unconditional promise or order to pay an exact sum of money, on demand or at an exact future time, to a specific person or order, or to bearer.

negotiation In regard to dispute settlement, a process in which parties attempt to settle their dispute without going to court, with or without attorneys to represent them. In regard

to negotiable instruments, the transfer of an instrument in such a way that the transferee (the person to whom the instrument is transferred) becomes a holder.

nominal damages A small monetary award (often one dollar) granted to a plaintiff when no actual damage was suffered or when the plaintiff is unable to show such loss with sufficient certainty.

nonpossessory interest In the context of real property, an interest that involves the right to use land but not the right to possess it.

normal trade relations (NTR) status A status granted through an international treaty by which each member nation must treat other members at least as well as it treats the country that receives its most favorable treatment. This status was formerly known as most-favored-nation status.

notary public A public official authorized to attest to the authenticity of signatures.

notice-and-comment rulemaking An administrative rulemaking procedure that involves the publication of a notice of a proposed rulemaking in the *Federal Register,* a comment period for interested parties to express their views on the proposed rule, and the publication of the agency's final rule in the *Federal Register.*

novation The substitution, by agreement, of a new contract for an old one, with the rights under the old one being terminated. Typically, there is a substitution of a new person who is responsible for the contract and the removal of an original party's rights and duties under the contract.

nuisance A common law doctrine under which persons may be held liable for using their property in a manner that unreasonably interferes with others' rights to use or enjoy their own property.

nuncupative will An oral will (often called a *deathbed will*) made before witnesses. Usually, such wills are limited to transfers of personal property.

O

objective theory of contracts A theory under which the intent to form a contract will be judged by outward, objective facts as interpreted by a reasonable person, rather than by the party's own secret, subjective intentions. Objective facts might include what a party said when entering into the contract, how a party acted or appeared, and the circumstances surrounding the transaction.

obligee One to whom an obligation is owed.

obligor One who owes an obligation to another.

offer A promise or commitment to perform or refrain from performing some specified act in the future.

offeree A person to whom an offer is made.

offeror A person who makes an offer.

omnibus clause A provision in an automobile insurance policy that protects the vehicle owner who has taken out the policy and anyone who drives the vehicle with the owner's permission.

online dispute resolution (ODR) The resolution of disputes with the assistance of organizations that offer dispute-resolution services via the Internet.

opening statement A statement made to the jury at the beginning of a trial by a party's attorney, prior to the presentation of evidence. The attorney briefly outlines the evidence that will be offered and the legal theory that will be pursued.

operating agreement An agreement in which the members of a limited liability company set forth the details of how the business will be managed and operated.

opinion A statement by a court expressing the reasons for its decision in a case.

option contract A contract under which the offeror cannot revoke his or her offer for a stipulated time period and the offeree can accept or reject the offer at any time during this period. The offeree must give consideration for the option to be enforceable.

order for relief A court's grant of assistance to a complainant. In bankruptcy proceedings, the order relieves the debtor of the immediate obligation to pay the debts listed in the bankruptcy petition.

order instrument A negotiable instrument that is payable "to the order of an identified person" or "to an identified person or order."

ordinance A law passed by a local governing unit, such as a city or a county.

outcome-based ethics An ethical philosophy that focuses on the impacts of a decision on society or on key stakeholders.

output contract An agreement in which a seller agrees to sell and a buyer agrees to buy all or up to a stated amount of what the seller produces.

outside director A person on a corporation's board of directors who does not hold a management position at the corporation.

overdraft A check written on a checking account in which there are insufficient funds to cover the amount of the check.

P

parent corporation A corporation that owns all of the shares of another corporation (known as its subsidiary).

parol evidence rule A substantive rule of contracts under which a court will not receive into evidence the parties' prior negotiations, prior agreements, or contemporaneous oral agreements if that evidence contradicts or varies the terms of the parties' written contract.

partially disclosed principal A principal whose identity is unknown by a third party, but the third party knows that the agent is or may be acting for a principal at the time the agent and the third party form a contract.

partnering agreement An agreement between a seller and a buyer who frequently do business with each other on the terms and conditions that will apply to all subsequently formed electronic contracts.

partnership An agreement by two or more persons to carry on, as co-owners, a business for profit.

partnership by estoppel A partnership imposed by a court when nonpartners have held themselves out to be partners, or have allowed themselves to be held out as partners, and others have detrimentally relied on their misrepresentations.

pass-through entity A business entity that has no tax liability. The entity's income is passed through to the owners, and they pay taxes on the income.

past consideration Something given or some act done in the past, which cannot ordinarily be consideration for a later bargain.

patent A government grant that gives an inventor the exclusive right or privilege to make, use, or sell his or her invention for a limited time period.

payee A person to whom an instrument is made payable.

payor bank The bank on which a check is drawn (the drawee bank).

peer-to-peer (P2P) networking The sharing of resources (such as files, hard drives, and processing styles) among multiple computers without the requirement of a central network server.

penalty A sum inserted into a contract not as a measure of compensation for its breach but rather as punishment for a default. The agreement as to the amount will not be enforced, and recovery will be limited to actual damages.

per capita A method of distributing an intestate's estate so that each heir in a certain class (such as grandchildren) receives an equal share.

per curiam **opinion** By the whole court; a court opinion written by the court as a whole instead of being authored by a judge or justice.

per se **violation** A restraint of trade that is so anticompetitive that it is deemed inherently *(per se)* illegal.

per stirpes A method of distributing an intestate's estate so that each heir in a certain class (such as grandchildren) takes the share to which her or his deceased ancestor (such as a mother or father) would have been entitled.

perfect tender rule A common law rule under which a seller was required to deliver to the buyer goods that conformed perfectly to the requirements stipulated in the sales contract. A tender of nonconforming goods would automatically constitute a breach of contract. Under the Uniform Commercial Code, the rule has been greatly modified.

perfection The legal process by which secured parties protect themselves against the claims of third parties who may wish to have their debts satisfied out of the same collateral; usually accomplished by the filing of a financing statement with the appropriate government official.

performance In contract law, the fulfillment of one's duties arising under a contract with another; the normal way of discharging one's contractual obligations.

periodic tenancy A lease interest in land for an indefinite period involving payment of rent at fixed intervals, such as week to week, month to month, or year to year.

personal defense A defense that can be used to avoid payment to an ordinary holder of a negotiable instrument but not a holder in due course (HDC) or a holder with the rights of an HDC. Personal defenses are also called *limited defenses*.

personal property Property that is movable; any property that is not real property.

persuasive authority Any legal authority or source of law that a court may look to for guidance but need not follow when making its decision.

petition in bankruptcy The document that is filed with a bankruptcy court to initiate bankruptcy proceedings.

petitioner In equity practice, a party that initiates a lawsuit.

petty offense In criminal law, the least serious kind of criminal offense, such as a traffic or building-code violation.

phishing Online fraud in which criminals pretend to be legitimate companies by using e-mails or malicious Web sites that trick individuals and companies into providing useful information, such as bank account numbers, Social Security numbers, and credit-card numbers.

piercing the corporate veil The action of a court to disregard the corporate entity and hold the shareholders personally liable for corporate debts and obligations.

plaintiff A party that initiates a lawsuit.

plea bargaining The process by which a criminal defendant and the prosecutor in a criminal case work out a mutually satisfactory disposition of the case, subject to court approval; usually involves the defendant's pleading guilty to a lesser offense in return for a lighter sentence.

pleadings Formal statements made by the plaintiff and the defendant in a lawsuit that detail the facts, allegations, and defenses involved in the litigation; the complaint and answer are part of the pleadings.

pledge A common law security device (retained in Article 9 of the Uniform Commercial Code) in which personal property is turned over to a creditor as security for the payment of a debt and retained by the creditor until the debt is paid.

plurality opinion A court opinion that is joined by the largest number of the judges or justices hearing the case, but fewer than half of the total number.

police powers Powers possessed by states as part of their inherent sovereignty. These powers may be exercised to protect or promote the public order, health, safety, morals, and general welfare.

policy In insurance law, the contract between the insurer and the insured.

potentially responsible party (PRP) A party liable for the costs of cleaning up a hazardous waste disposal site under the Comprehensive Environmental Response, Compensation, and Liability Act.

power of attorney Authorization for another to act as one's agent or attorney either in specified circumstances (special) or in all situations (general).

precedent A court decision that furnishes an example or authority for deciding subsequent cases involving identical or similar facts.

predatory pricing The pricing of a product below cost with the intent to drive competitors out of the market.

predominant-factor test A test courts use to determine whether a contract is primarily for the sale of goods or for the sale of services.

preemption A doctrine under which certain federal laws preempt, or take precedence over, conflicting state or local laws.

preemptive rights The right of a shareholder in a corporation to have the first opportunity to purchase a new issue of that corporation's stock in proportion to the amount of stock already owned by the shareholder.

preference In bankruptcy proceedings, a property transfer or payment made by the debtor that favors one creditor over others.

preferred creditor In the context of bankruptcy, a creditor who has received a preferential transfer from a debtor.

preferred stock A security that entitles the holder to payment of fixed dividends and that has priority over common stock in the distribution of assets on the corporation's dissolution.

premium In insurance law, the price paid by the insured for insurance protection for a specified period of time.

prenuptial agreement An agreement made before marriage that defines each partner's ownership rights in the other partner's property. Prenuptial agreements must be in writing to be enforceable.

prepayment penalty clause A provision in a mortgage loan contract that requires the borrower to pay a penalty if the mortgage is repaid in full within a certain period.

prescription A way of creating an easement or profit in real property by openly using the property, without the owner's consent, for the required period of time (similar to adverse possession).

presentment The act of presenting an instrument to the party liable on the instrument to collect payment; the act of presenting an instrument to a drawee for acceptance.

presentment warranty Implied warranty made by any person who presents an instrument for payment or acceptance that (1) he or she is entitled to enforce the instrument or authorized to obtain payment or acceptance on behalf of a person who is entitled, (2) the instrument has not been altered, and (3) he or she has no knowledge that the signature of the drawer is unauthorized.

pretrial conference A conference, scheduled before the trial begins, between the judge and the attorneys litigating the suit. The parties may settle the dispute, clarify the issues, schedule discovery, and so on during the conference.

pretrial motion A written or oral application to a court for a ruling or order, made before trial.

price discrimination A seller's act of charging competing buyers different prices for identical products or services.

price-fixing agreement An agreement between competitors to fix the prices of products or services at a certain level.

prima facie case A case in which the plaintiff has produced sufficient evidence of his or her claim that the case will be decided for the plaintiff unless the defendant produces evidence to rebut it.

principal In agency law, a person who agrees to have another, called the agent, act on his or her behalf.

principle of rights The principle that human beings have certain fundamental rights (to life, freedom, and the pursuit of happiness, for example). A key factor in determining whether a business decision is ethical under this theory is how that decision affects the rights of others, such as employees, consumers, suppliers, and the community.

private equity Capital funds invested by a private equity firm in an existing corporation, usually to purchase and reorganize it.

privilege In tort law, the ability to act contrary to another person's right without that person's having legal redress for such acts. Privilege may be raised as a defense to defamation.

privileges and immunities clause Article IV, Section 2, of the U.S. Constitution requires states not to discriminate against one another's citizens. A resident of one state cannot be treated as an alien when in another state; he or she may not be denied such privileges and immunities as legal protection, access to courts, travel rights, and property rights.

privity of contract The relationship that exists between the promisor and the promisee of a contract.

probable cause Reasonable grounds for believing that a search should be conducted or that a person should be arrested.

probate The process of proving and validating a will, and settling all matters pertaining to an estate.

probate court A state court of limited jurisdiction that conducts proceedings relating to the settlement of a deceased person's estate.

procedural law Law that establishes the methods of enforcing the rights established by substantive law.

proceeds Under Article 9 of the Uniform Commercial Code, whatever is received when collateral is sold or otherwise disposed of.

product liability The legal liability of manufacturers, sellers, and lessors of goods to consumers, users, and bystanders for injuries or damages that are caused by the goods.

product misuse A defense against product liability that may be raised when the plaintiff used a product in a manner not intended by the manufacturer. If the misuse is reasonably foreseeable, the seller will not escape liability unless measures were taken to guard against the harm that could result from the misuse.

profit In the context of real property, the right to enter onto another's property and remove something of value from that property.

promise A person's assurance that he or she will or will not do something.

promisee A person to whom a promise is made.

promisor A person who makes a promise.

promissory estoppel A doctrine that applies when a promisor makes a clear and definite promise on which the promisee justifiably relies. Such a promise is binding if justice will be better served by the enforcement of the promise.

promissory note A written promise made by one person (the maker) to pay a fixed sum of money to another person (the payee or a subsequent holder) on demand or on a specified date.

property Legally protected rights and interests in anything with an ascertainable value that is subject to ownership.

prospectus A written document required by securities laws when a security is being sold. The prospectus describes the security, the financial operations of the issuing corporation, and the risk attaching to the security.

protected class A group of persons protected by specific laws because of the group's defining characteristics, including race, color, religion, national origin, gender, age, and disability.

proximate cause Legal cause; exists when the connection between an act and an injury is strong enough to justify imposing liability.

proxy Authorization to represent a corporate shareholder to serve as his or her agent and vote his or her shares in a certain manner.

public corporation A corporation owned by a federal, state, or municipal government—not to be confused with a publicly held corporation.

public figure An individual in the public limelight. Public figures include government officials and politicians, movie stars, well-known businesspersons, and generally anybody who becomes known to the public because of his or her position or activities.

publicly held corporation A corporation whose shares are publicly traded in securities markets, such as the New York Stock Exchange or the NASDAQ.

puffery A salesperson's exaggerated claims concerning the quality of goods offered for sale. Such claims involve opinions rather than facts and are not considered to be legally binding promises or warranties.

punitive damages Money damages that may be awarded to a plaintiff to punish the defendant and deter future similar conduct.

purchase-money security interest (PMSI) A security interest that arises when a seller or lender extends credit for part or all of the purchase price of goods purchased by a buyer.

Q

qualified indorsement An indorsement on a negotiable instrument in which the indorser disclaims any contract liability on the instrument; the notation "without recourse" is commonly used to create a qualified indorsement.

quantum meruit A Latin phrase, meaning "as much as he deserves," that describes the extent of compensation owed under a quasi contract.

quasi contract A fictional contract imposed on parties by a court in the interests of fairness and justice; usually, quasi contracts are imposed to avoid the unjust enrichment of one party at the expense of another.

question of fact In a lawsuit, an issue involving a factual dispute. A question of fact can be decided by a judge or a jury.

question of law In a lawsuit, an issue involving the application or interpretation of a law. Only a judge, and not a jury, can decide a question of law.

quitclaim deed A deed that conveys only whatever interest the grantor had in the property and therefore offers the least amount of protection against defects of title.

quorum The number of members of a decision-making body that must be present before business may be transacted.

quota A quota is a government-imposed trade restriction that limits the number, or sometimes the value, of goods and services that can be imported or exported during a particular time period.

R

ratification The act of accepting and giving legal force to an obligation that previously was not enforceable.

reaffirmation agreement An agreement between a debtor and a creditor in which the debtor voluntarily agrees to pay a debt dischargeable in bankruptcy.

real property Land and everything attached to it, such as trees and buildings.

reasonable person standard The standard of behavior expected of a hypothetical "reasonable person." The standard against which negligence is measured and that must be observed to avoid liability for negligence.

rebuttal The refutation of evidence introduced by an adverse party's attorney.

receiver In a corporate dissolution, a court-appointed person who winds up corporate affairs and liquidates corporate assets.

record According to the Uniform Electronic Transactions Act, information that is either inscribed on a tangible medium or stored in an electronic or other medium, and that is retrievable.

recording statute A statute that allow deeds, mortgages, and other real property transactions to be recorded so as to provide notice to future purchasers or creditors of an existing claim on the property.

reformation A court-ordered correction of a written contract so that it reflects the true intentions of the parties.

Regulation E A set of rules issued by the Federal Reserve System's Board of Governors under the authority of the Electronic Fund Transfer Act to protect users of electronic fund transfer systems.

Regulation Z A set of rules issued by the Federal Reserve Board of Governors to implement the provisions of the Truth-in-Lending Act.

rejoinder The defendant's answer to the plaintiff's rebuttal.

release A contract in which one party forfeits the right to pursue a legal claim against the other party.

relevant evidence Evidence tending to make a fact at issue in the case more or less probable than it would be without the evidence. Only relevant evidence is admissible in court.

remedy The relief given to an innocent party to enforce a right or compensate for the violation of a right.

remedy at law A remedy available in a court of law. Money damages are awarded as a remedy at law.

remedy in equity A remedy allowed by courts in situations where remedies at law are not appropriate. Remedies in equity include injunction, specific performance, rescission and restitution, and reformation.

replevin (pronounced rih-*pleh*-vin) An action to recover specific goods in the hands of a party who is wrongfully withholding them from the other party.

reporter A publication in which court cases are published, or reported.

requirements contract An agreement in which a buyer agrees to purchase and the seller agrees to sell all or up to a stated amount of what the buyer needs or requires.

resale price maintenance agreement An agreement between a manufacturer and a retailer in which the manufacturer specifies what the retail prices of its products must be.

rescission (pronounced rih-*sih*-zhen) A remedy whereby a contract is canceled and the parties are returned to the positions they occupied before the contract was made; may be effected through the mutual consent of the parties, by their conduct, or by court decree.

residential use Use of land for construction of buildings for human habitation only.

respondeat superior A doctrine under which a principal-employer is liable for any harm caused to a third party by an agent-employee in the course or scope of employment.

respondent In equity practice, the party who answers a complaint or other proceeding.

restitution An equitable remedy under which a person is restored to his or her original position prior to loss or injury, or placed in the position he or she would have been in had the breach not occurred.

restraint of trade Any contract or combination that tends to eliminate or reduce competition, effect a monopoly, artificially maintain prices, or otherwise hamper the course of trade and commerce as it would be carried on if left to the control of natural economic forces.

restrictive covenant A private restriction on the use of land. If its benefit or obligation passes with the land's ownership, it is said to "run with the land."

restrictive indorsement Any indorsement on a negotiable instrument that requires the indorsee to comply with certain instructions regarding the funds involved. A restrictive indorsement does not prohibit the further negotiation of the instrument.

resulting trust An implied trust that arises when one party holds the legal title to another's property only for that other's benefit.

retained earnings The portion of a corporation's profits that has not been paid out as dividends to shareholders.

revocation In contract law, the withdrawal of an offer by an offeror. Unless an offer is irrevocable, it can be revoked at any time prior to acceptance without liability.

right of contribution The right of a co-surety who pays more than his or her proportionate share on a debtor's default to recover the excess paid from other co-sureties.

right of reimbursement The legal right of a person to be restored, repaid, or indemnified for costs, expenses, or losses incurred or expended on behalf of another.

right of subrogation The right of a person to stand in the place of (be substituted for) another, giving the substituted party the same legal rights that the original party had.

right-to-work law A state law providing that employees may not be required to join a union as a condition of retaining employment.

risk A prediction concerning potential loss based on known and unknown factors.

risk management In the context of insurance, the transfer of certain risks from the insured to the insurance company by contractual agreement.

robbery The act of forcefully and unlawfully taking personal property of any value from another; force or intimidation is usually necessary for an act of theft to be considered a robbery.

rule of four A rule of the United States Supreme Court under which the Court will not issue a writ of *certiorari* unless at least four justices agree to do so.

rule of reason A test used to determine whether an anticompetitive agreement constitutes a reasonable restraint on trade. Courts consider such factors as the purpose of the agreement, its effect on competition, and whether less restrictive means could have been used.

rulemaking The process by which an administrative agency formally adopts a new regulation or amends an old one.

rules of evidence Rules governing the admissibility of evidence in trial courts.

S

S corporation A close business corporation that has most of the attributes of a corporation, including limited liability, but qualifies under the Internal Revenue Code to be taxed as a partnership.

sale The passing of title (evidence of ownership rights) from a seller to a buyer for a price.

sale on approval A type of conditional sale in which the buyer may take the goods on a trial basis. The sale becomes absolute only when the buyer approves of (or is satisfied with) the goods being sold.

sale or return A type of conditional sale in which title and possession pass from the seller to the buyer; however, the buyer retains the option to return the goods during a specified period, even though the goods conform to the contract.

sales contract A contract for the sale of goods under which the ownership of goods is transferred from a seller to a buyer for a price.

scienter (pronounced sy-*en*-ter) Knowledge by the misrepresenting party that material facts have been falsely represented or omitted with an intent to deceive.

search warrant An order granted by a public authority, such as a judge, that authorizes law enforcement personnel to search particular premises or property.

seasonably Within a specified time period. If no period is specified, within a reasonable time.

SEC Rule 10b-5 A rule of the Securities and Exchange Commission that prohibits the commission of fraud in connection with the purchase or sale of any security.

secondary boycott A union's refusal to work for, purchase from, or handle the products of a secondary employer, with whom the union has no dispute, for the purpose of forcing that employer to stop doing business with the primary employer, with whom the union has a labor dispute.

secured party A lender, seller, or any other person in whose favor there is a security interest, including a person to whom accounts or chattel paper has been sold.

secured transaction Any transaction in which the payment of a debt is guaranteed, or secured, by personal property owned by the debtor or in which the debtor has a legal interest.

securities Generally, stocks, bonds, or other items that represent an ownership interest in a corporation or a promise of repayment of debt by a corporation.

security agreement An agreement that creates or provides for a security interest between the debtor and a secured party.

security interest Any interest "in personal property or fixtures which secures payment or performance of an obligation" [UCC 1–201(37)].

self-defense The legally recognized privilege to protect one's self or property against injury by another. The privilege of self-defense protects only acts that are reasonably necessary to protect one's self or property.

self-incrimination Giving testimony in a trial or other legal proceeding that could expose the person testifying to criminal prosecution.

seniority system A system in which those who have worked longest for an employer are first in line for promotions, salary increases, and other benefits, and are last to be laid off if the workforce must be reduced.

service mark A mark used in the sale or the advertising of services, such as to distinguish the services of one person from the services of others. Titles, character names, and other distinctive features of radio and television programs may be registered as service marks.

service of process The delivery of the complaint and summons to a defendant.

sexual harassment The demanding of sexual favors in return for job promotions or other benefits, or language or conduct that is so sexually offensive that it creates a hostile working environment.

share exchange A process in which some or all of the shares of one corporation are exchanged for some or all of the shares of another corporation, and both corporations continue to exist.

shareholder agreement An agreement between shareholders that restricts the transferability of shares, often entered into for the purpose of maintaining proportionate control of a close corporation.

shareholder's derivative suit A suit brought by a shareholder to enforce a corporate cause of action against a third person.

shelter principle The principle that the holder of a negotiable instrument who cannot qualify as a holder in due course (HDC), but who derives his or her title through an HDC, acquires the rights of an HDC.

shipment contract A contract in which the seller is required to ship the goods by carrier. The buyer assumes liability for any losses or damage to the goods after they are delivered to the carrier. Generally, a contract is assumed to be a shipment contract if nothing to the contrary is stated in the contract.

short-form merger A merger between a subsidiary corporation and a parent corporation that owns at least 90 percent of the outstanding shares of each class of stock issued by the subsidiary corporation.

short sale A sale of real property for an amount that is less than the balance owed on the mortgage loan, usually due to financial hardship.

short-swing profits Profits earned by a purchase and sale, or sale and purchase, of the same security within a six-month period.

shrink-wrap agreement An agreement whose terms are expressed in a document located inside a box in which goods (usually software) are packaged; sometimes called a *shrink-wrap license.*

signature Under the Uniform Commercial Code, "any symbol executed or adopted by a party with a present intention to authenticate a writing."

slander Defamation in oral form.

slander of quality The publication of false information about another's product, alleging that it is not what its seller claims.

slander of title The publication of a statement that denies or casts doubt on another's legal ownership of any property causing financial loss to that property's owner; also called *trade libel.*

small claims court Special courts in which parties may litigate small claims (usually, claims involving $2,500 or less). Attorneys are not required in small claims courts and in many states are not allowed to represent the parties.

smart card Prepaid funds recorded on a microprocessor chip embedded on a card; one type of *e-money.*

social media Forms of communication through which users create and share information, ideas, messages, and other content via the Internet.

sociological school A school of legal thought that views the law as a tool for promoting justice in society.

sole proprietorship The simplest form of business organization, in which the owner is the business. The owner reports business income on his or her personal income tax return and is legally responsible for all debts and obligations incurred by the business.

sovereign immunity A doctrine that immunizes foreign nations from the jurisdiction of U.S. courts when certain conditions are satisfied.

sovereignty The quality of having independent authority over a geographic area. For instance, state governments have the authority to regulate affairs within their borders.

space law Law consisting of the international and national laws that govern activities in outer space.

spam Bulk, unsolicited (junk) e-mail.

special damages In a tort case, an amount awarded to compensate the plaintiff for quantifiable monetary losses, such as medical expenses, property damage, and lost wages and benefits (now and in the future).

special indorsement An indorsement on an instrument that indicates the specific person to whom the indorser intends to make the instrument payable—that is, it names the indorsee.

special-use permit A permit granted by local zoning authorities that allows for a specific exemption to zoning regulations for a particular piece of land.

special warranty deed A deed that warrants only that the grantor held good title during his or her ownership of the property and does not warrant that there were no defects of title when the property was held by previous owners.

specific performance An equitable remedy requiring the breaching party to perform as promised under the contract; usually granted only when money damages would be an inadequate remedy and the subject matter of the contract is unique (for example, real property).

spendthrift trust A trust created to protect the beneficiary from spending all the funds to which she or he is entitled. Only a certain portion of the total amount is given to the beneficiary at any one time, and most states prohibit creditors from attaching assets of the trust.

stakeholders Groups, other than the company's shareholders, that are affected by corporate decisions. Stakeholders include employees, customers, creditors, suppliers, and the community in which the corporation operates.

stale check A check, other than a certified check, that is presented for payment more than six months after its date.

standing to sue The requirement that an individual must have a sufficient stake in a controversy before he or she can bring a lawsuit. The plaintiff must demonstrate that he or she has been either injured or threatened with injury.

stare decisis A common law doctrine under which judges are obligated to follow the precedents established in prior decisions.

Statute of Frauds A state statute under which certain types of contracts must be in writing to be enforceable.

statute of limitations A federal or state statute setting the maximum time period during which a certain action can be brought or certain rights enforced.

statute of repose Basically, a statute of limitations that is not dependent on the happening of a cause of action. Statutes of repose generally begin to run at an earlier date and run for a longer period of time than statutes of limitations.

statutory law The body of law enacted by legislative bodies (as opposed to constitutional law, administrative law, or case law).

stock An ownership (equity) interest in a corporation, measured in units of shares.

stock certificate A certificate issued by a corporation evidencing the ownership of a specified number of shares in the corporation.

stock option A right to buy a given number of shares of stock at a set price, usually within a specified time period.

stock warrant A certificate that grants the owner the option to buy a given number of shares of stock, usually within a set time period.

stop-payment order An order by a bank customer to his or her bank not to pay or certify a certain check.

strict liability Liability regardless of fault. In tort law, strict liability may be imposed on defendants in cases involving abnormally dangerous activities, dangerous animals, or defective products.

strike An action undertaken by unionized workers when collective bargaining fails. The workers leave their jobs, refuse to work, and (typically) picket the employer's workplace.

sublease A tenant's transfer of all or part of the leased premises to a third person for a period shorter than the lease term.

subsidiary corporation A corporation wholly owned by another corporation (the parent corporation).

substantive law Law that defines, describes, regulates, and creates legal rights and obligations.

substitute check A negotiable instrument that is a paper reproduction of the front and back of an original check and contains all of the same information required on checks for automated processing.

summary jury trial A method of settling disputes in which a trial is held, but the jury's verdict is not binding. The verdict acts only as a guide to both sides in reaching an agreement during the mandatory negotiations that immediately follow the summary jury trial.

summons A document informing a defendant that a legal action has been commenced against him or her and that the defendant must appear in court on a certain date to answer the plaintiff's complaint. The document is delivered by a sheriff or any other person so authorized.

superseding cause An intervening force or event that breaks the connection between a wrongful act and an injury to another; in negligence law, a defense to liability.

supremacy clause The provision in Article VI of the U.S. Constitution that provides that the Constitution, laws, and treaties of the United States are "the supreme Law of the Land." Under this clause, state and local laws that directly conflict with federal law will be rendered invalid.

surety A person, such as a cosigner on a note, who agrees to be primarily responsible for the debt of another.

suretyship An express contract in which a third party to a debtor-creditor relationship (the surety) promises to be primarily responsible for the debtor's obligation.

surviving corporation The remaining, or continuing, corporation following a merger.

symbolic speech Nonverbal conduct that expresses opinions or thoughts about a subject. Symbolic speech is protected under the First Amendment's guarantee of freedom of speech.

syndicate A group of individuals or firms that join together to finance a project; also called an *investment group*.

T

takeover The acquisition of control over a corporation through the purchase of a substantial number of the voting shares of the corporation.

taking The government's taking of private property for public use through the power of eminent domain.

tangible employment action A significant change in employment status or benefits, such as occurs when an employee is fired, refused a promotion, or reassigned to a lesser position.

tangible property Property that has physical existence and can be distinguished by the senses of touch, sight, and so on. A car is tangible property.

target corporation The corporation to be acquired in a corporate takeover; a corporation to whose shareholders a tender offer is submitted.

tariff A tax on imported goods.

tenancy at sufferance A tenancy that arises when a tenant wrongfully continues to occupy leased property after the lease has terminated.

tenancy at will A type of tenancy that either the landlord or the tenant can terminate without notice.

tenancy by the entirety Joint ownership of property by a married couple in which neither spouse can transfer his or her interest in the property without the consent of the other.

tenancy in common Joint ownership of property in which each party owns an undivided interest that passes to his or her heirs at death.

tender An unconditional offer to perform an obligation by a person who is ready, willing, and able to do so.

tender of delivery Under the Uniform Commercial Code, a seller's or lessor's act of placing conforming goods at the disposal of the buyer or lessee and giving the buyer or lessee whatever notification is reasonably necessary to enable the buyer or lessee to take delivery.

tender offer An offer to purchase made by one company directly to the shareholders of another (target) company; often referred to as a "takeover bid."

term insurance A type of life insurance policy for which premiums are paid for a specified term and payment is made by the insurer only if the insured dies within the term period.

testamentary trust A trust that is created by will and therefore does not take effect until the death of the testator.

testate Having left a will at death.

testator One who makes and executes a will.

third party beneficiary One for whose benefit a promise is made in a contract but who is not a party to the contract.

tippee A person who receives inside information.

title insurance Insurance commonly purchased by a purchaser of real property to protect against loss in the event that the title to the property is not free from liens or superior ownership claims.

tolling Temporary suspension of the running of a prescribed period (such as a statute of limitations). For instance, a statute of limitations may be tolled until the party suffering an injury has discovered it or should have discovered it.

tort A civil wrong not arising from a breach of contract. A breach of a legal duty that proximately causes harm or injury to another.

tortfeasor One who commits a tort.

Totten trust A trust created when a person deposits funds in his or her own name for a specific beneficiary, who will receive the funds on the depositor's death. The trust is revocable at will until the depositor dies or completes the gift.

toxic tort A civil wrong arising from exposure to a toxic substance, such as asbestos, radiation, or hazardous waste.

trade acceptance A draft that is drawn by a seller of goods ordering the buyer to pay a specified sum of money to the seller, usually at a stated time in the future. The buyer accepts the draft by signing the face of the draft, thus creating an enforceable obligation to pay the draft when it comes due. On a trade acceptance, the seller is both the drawer and the payee.

trade dress The image and overall appearance of a product—for example, the distinctive decor, menu, layout, and style of service of a particular restaurant. Basically, trade dress is subject to the same protection as trademarks.

trade fixture The personal property of a commercial tenant that has been installed or affixed to real property for a business purpose. When the lease ends, the tenant can remove the fixture but must repair any damage to the real property caused by the fixture's removal.

trade libel The publication of false information about another's product, alleging that it is not what its seller claims; also referred to as *slander of quality.*

trade name A term that is used to indicate part or all of a business's name and that is directly related to the business's reputation and goodwill. Trade names are protected under the common law (and under trademark law, if the name is the same as the firm's trademark).

trade secret Information or a process that gives a business an advantage over competitors who do not know the information or process.

trademark A distinctive mark, motto, device, or implement that a manufacturer stamps, prints, or otherwise affixes to the goods it produces so that they may be identified on the market and their origins made known. Once a trademark is established (under the common law or through registration), the owner is entitled to its exclusive use.

transfer warranty Implied warranty made by any person who transfers an instrument for consideration to subsequent transferees and holders who take the instrument in good faith that (1) the transferor is entitled to enforce the instrument, (2) all signatures are authentic and authorized, (3) the instrument has not been altered, (4) the instrument is not subject to a defense or claim of any party that can be asserted against the transferor, and (5) the transferor has no knowledge of any insolvency proceedings against the maker, the acceptor, or the drawer of the instrument.

transferred intent A legal principle under which a person who intends to harm one individual, but unintentionally harms a different individual, can be liable to the second victim for an intentional tort.

traveler's check A check that is payable on demand, drawn on or payable through a bank, and designated as a traveler's check.

treaty An agreement formed between two or more independent nations.

treble damages Damages that, by statute, are three times the amount of actual damages suffered.

trespass to land The entry onto, above, or below the surface of land owned by another without the owner's permission or legal authorization.

trespass to personal property The unlawful taking or harming of another's personal property; interference with another's right to the exclusive possession of his or her personal property.

triple bottom line The idea that investors and others should consider not only corporate profits, but also the corporation's impact on people and on the planet in assessing the firm. (The bottom line is people, planet, and profits.)

trust An arrangement in which title to property is held by one person (a trustee) for the benefit of another (a beneficiary).

trust indorsement An indorsement for the benefit of the indorser or a third person; also known as an *agency indorsement*. The indorsement results in legal title vesting in the original indorsee.

tying arrangement A seller's act of conditioning the sale of a product or service on the buyer's agreement to purchase another product or service from the seller.

typosquatting A form of cybersquatting that relies on mistakes, such as typographical errors, made by Internet users when inputting information into a Web browser.

U

U.S. trustee A government official who performs certain administrative tasks that a bankruptcy judge would otherwise have to perform.

***ultra vires* acts** Acts of a corporation that are beyond its express and implied powers to undertake (the Latin phrase means "beyond the powers").

unconscionable (pronounced un-*kon*-shun-uh-bul) **contract or clause** A contract or clause that is void on the basis of public policy because one party, as a result of his or her disproportionate bargaining power, is forced to accept terms that are unfairly burdensome and that unfairly benefit the dominating party.

underwriter In insurance law, the insurer, or the one assuming a risk in return for the payment of a premium.

undisclosed principal A principal whose identity is unknown by a third party, and that person has no knowledge that the agent is acting for a principal at the time the agent and the third party form a contract.

undue influence Persuasion that is less than actual force but more than advice and that induces a person to act according to the will or purposes of the dominating party.

unenforceable contract A valid contract rendered unenforceable by some statute or law.

uniform law A model law created by the National Conference of Commissioners on Uniform State Laws and/or the American Law Institute for the states to consider adopting. If the state adopts the law, it becomes statutory law in that state. Each state has the option of adopting or rejecting all or part of a uniform law.

unilateral contract A contract that results when an offer can be accepted only by the offeree's performance.

unilateral mistake A mistake that occurs when one party to a contract is mistaken as to a material fact.

union shop A firm that requires all workers, once employed, to become union members within a specified period of time as a condition of their continued employment.

universal defense A defense that is valid against all holders of a negotiable instrument, including holders in due course (HDCs) and holders with the rights of HDCs. Universal defenses are also called *real defenses*.

universal life A type of insurance that combines some aspects of term insurance with some aspects of whole life insurance.

unliquidated debt A debt that is uncertain in amount.

unreasonably dangerous product In product liability, a product that is defective to the point of threatening a consumer's health and safety. A product will be considered unreasonably dangerous if it is dangerous beyond the expectation of the ordinary consumer or if a less dangerous alternative was economically feasible for the manufacturer, but the manufacturer failed to produce it.

usage of trade Any practice or method of dealing having such regularity of observance in a place, vocation, or trade as to justify an expectation that it will be observed with respect to the transaction in question.

usury Charging an illegal rate of interest.

utilitarianism An approach to ethical reasoning in which ethically correct behavior is related to an evaluation of the consequences of a given action on those who will be affected by it. In utilitarian reasoning, a "good" decision is one that results in the greatest good for the greatest number of people affected by the decision.

V

valid contract A contract that results when the elements necessary for contract formation (agreement, consideration, contractual capacity, and legality) are present.

validation notice An initial notice to a debtor from a collection agency informing the debtor that he or she has thirty days to challenge the debt and request verification.

variance An exception from zoning rules granted to a property owner by local zoning authorities.

venture capital Financing provided by professional, outside investors—that is, *venture capitalists,* usually groups of wealthy investors and securities firms—to new business ventures.

venue (pronounced *ven*-yoo) The geographical district in which an action is tried and from which the jury is selected.

verdict A formal decision made by a jury.

vertical merger The acquisition by a company at one stage of production of a company at a higher or lower stage of production (as when a company merges with one of its suppliers or retailers).

vertical restraint A restraint of trade created by an agreement between firms at different levels in the manufacturing and distribution process.

vertically integrated firm A firm that carries out two or more functional phases (manufacturing, distribution, and retailing, for example) of the chain of production.

vesting The creation of an absolute or unconditional right or power.

vicarious liability Indirect liability imposed on a supervisory party (such as an employer) for the actions of a subordinate (such as an employee) because of the relationship between the two parties.

virus A type of malware that is transmitted between computers and attempts to do deliberate damage to systems and data.

void contract A contract having no legal force or binding effect.

voidable contract A contract that may be legally avoided (canceled) at the option of one of the parties.

voir dire A French phrase meaning, literally, "to see, to speak" that refers to the jury-selection process. In *voir dire,* the attorneys question prospective jurors to determine whether they are biased or have any connection with a party to the action or with a prospective witness.

voluntary consent Knowing and voluntary agreement to the terms of a contract. If voluntary consent is lacking, the contract will be voidable.

voting trust An agreement (trust contract) under which legal title to shares of corporate stock is transferred to a trustee who is authorized by the shareholders to vote the shares on their behalf.

W

waiver An intentional, knowing relinquishment of a legal right.

warranty deed A deed in which the grantor promises that she or he has title to the property conveyed in the deed, that there are no undisclosed encumbrances on the property, and that the grantee will enjoy quiet possession of the property; provides the greatest amount of protection for the grantee.

waste The use of real property in a manner that damages or destroys its value.

watered stock Shares of stock issued by a corporation for which the corporation receives, as payment, less than the fair market value of the shares.

wetlands Areas of land designated by government agencies as protected areas that support wildlife and that therefore cannot be filled in or dredged by private parties.

whistleblowing An employee's disclosure to government authorities, upper-level managers, or the media that the employer is engaged in unsafe or illegal activities.

white-collar crime Nonviolent crime committed by individuals or corporations to obtain a personal or business advantage.

whole life A type of life insurance in which the insured pays a level premium for his or her entire life and in which there is a constantly accumulating cash value that can be withdrawn or borrowed against by the borrower; sometimes referred to as *straight life insurance.*

will An instrument made by a testator directing what is to be done with her or his property after death.

will substitutes Various instruments, such as living trusts and life insurance plans, that may be used to avoid the formal probate process.

winding up The second of two stages in the termination of a partnership or corporation, in which the firm's assets are collected, liquidated, and distributed, and liabilities are discharged.

workers' compensation law A state statute establishing an administrative procedure for compensating workers for injuries that arise out of, or in the course of, their employment, regardless of fault. Instead of suing the employer, an injured worker files a claim with the state agency or board that administers local workers' compensation claims.

working papers The documents used and developed by an accountant during an audit, such as notes, computations, and memoranda.

workout agreement A formal contract between a debtor and his or her creditors in which the parties agree to negotiate a payment plan for the amount due on the loan instead of proceeding to foreclosure.

worm A type of malware that is designed to copy itself from one computer to another without human interaction. A worm can copy itself automatically and can replicate in great volume and with great speed.

writ of attachment A court's order, prior to a trial to collect a debt, directing the sheriff or other officer to seize nonexempt property of the debtor. If the creditor prevails at trial, the seized property can be sold to satisfy the judgment.

writ of *certiorari* (pronounced sur-shee-uh-*rah*-ree) A writ from a higher court asking the lower court for the record of a case.

writ of execution A court's order, after a judgment has been entered against the debtor, directing the sheriff to seize (levy) and sell any of the debtor's nonexempt real or personal property. The proceeds of the sale are used to pay off the judgment, accrued interest, and costs of the sale. Any surplus is paid to the debtor.

wrongful discharge An employer's termination of an employee's employment in violation of the law or an employment contract.

Z

zoning laws Rules and regulations that collectively manage the development and use of land.

Table of Cases

Following is a list of all the cases mentioned in this text, including those within the footnotes, features, and case problems. Any case that was an excerpted case for a chapter is given special emphasis by having its title **boldfaced.**

Index